THE
ALL ENGLAND
LAW REPORTS

1978
Volume 2

Consulting editor
R N G HARRISON BA
of Lincoln's Inn,
Barrister

Acting editor
WENDY SHOCKETT
of Gray's Inn,
Barrister

London
BUTTERWORTHS

ENGLAND: BUTTERWORTH & CO. (PUBLISHERS) LTD.
LONDON: 88 Kingsway, London WC2 6AB
AUSTRALIA: BUTTERWORTHS PTY. LTD.
SYDNEY: 271–273 Lane Cove Road, North Ryde, NSW 2113
Also at Melbourne, Brisbane, Adelaide and Perth
CANADA: BUTTERWORTH & CO. (CANADA) LTD.
TORONTO: 2265 Midland Avenue, Scarborough, MIP 4SI
NEW ZEALAND: BUTTERWORTHS OF NEW ZEALAND LTD.
WELLINGTON: 33–35 Cumberland Place, Wellington
SOUTH AFRICA: BUTTERWORTH & CO. (SOUTH AFRICA) (PTY.) LTD.
DURBAN: 152–154 Gale Street, Durban
USA: BUTTERWORTH & CO. (PUBLISHERS) INC.
BOSTON: 10 Tower Office Park, Woburn, Mass. 01801

©
Butterworth & Co (Publishers) Ltd
1978
Reprinted 1982

ISBN 0 406 85121 2

Printed in Great Britain by Thomson Litho Ltd, East Kilbride, Scotland

House of Lords

The Lord High Chancellor: Lord Elwyn-Jones

Lords of Appeal in Ordinary

Lord Wilberforce
Lord Diplock
Viscount Dilhorne
Lord Salmon
Lord Edmund-Davies

Lord Fraser of Tullybelton
Lord Russell of Killowen
Lord Keith of Kinkel
Lord Scarman

Court of Appeal

The Lord High Chancellor

The Lord Chief Justice of England: Lord Widgery

The Master of The Rolls: Lord Denning

The President of the Family Division: Sir George Gillespie Baker

Lords Justices of Appeal

Sir John Megaw
Sir Denys Burton Buckley
Sir Edward Blanshard Stamp
Sir John Frederick Eustace Stephenson
Sir Alan Stewart Orr
Sir Eustace Wentworth Roskill
Sir Frederick Horace Lawton
Sir Roger Fray Greenwood Ormrod
Sir Patrick Reginald Evelyn Browne

Sir Geoffrey Dawson Lane
Sir Reginald William Goff
Sir Nigel Cyprian Bridge
Sir Sebag Shaw
Sir George Stanley Waller
Sir James Roualeyn Hovell-Thurlow
　　Cumming-Bruce
Sir Edward Walter Eveleigh

Chancery Division

The Lord High Chancellor

The Vice-Chancellor: Sir Robert Edgar Megarry

Sir John Patrick Graham
Sir Peter Harry Batson Woodroffe Foster
Sir John Norman Keates Whitford
Sir John Anson Brightman
Sir Ernest Irvine Goulding
Sir Sydney William Templeman

Sir Raymond Henry Walton
Sir Peter Raymond Oliver
Sir Michael John Fox
Sir Christopher John Slade
Sir Nicolas Christopher Henry Browne-Wilkinson

Queen's Bench Division

The Lord Chief Justice of England

Sir Aubrey Melford Steed Stevenson
Sir Gerald Alfred Thesiger
Sir Basil Nield
   (retired 7th May 1978)
Sir Alan Abraham Mocatta
Sir John Thompson
Sir Helenus Patrick Joseph Milmo
Sir Joseph Donaldson Cantley
Sir Hugh Eames Park
Sir Stephen Chapman
Sir John Ramsay Willis
Sir Graham Russell Swanwick
Sir Patrick McCarthy O'Connor
Sir John Francis Donaldson
Sir Samuel Burgess Ridgway Cooke
   (died 12th April 1978)
Sir Bernard Caulfield
Sir Hilary Gwynne Talbot
Sir William Lloyd Mars-Jones
Sir Ralph Kilner Brown
Sir Philip Wien
Sir Peter Henry Rowley Bristow
Sir Hugh Harry Valentine Forbes
Sir Desmond James Conrad Ackner
Sir William Hugh Griffiths
Sir Robert Hugh Mais
Sir Neil Lawson

Sir David Powell Croom-Johnson
Sir Tasker Watkins VC
Sir John Raymond Phillips
Sir Leslie Kenneth Edward Boreham
Sir John Douglas May
Sir Michael Robert Emanuel Kerr
Sir Alfred William Michael Davies
Sir John Dexter Stocker
Sir Kenneth George Illtyd Jones
Sir Haydn Tudor Evans
   (transferred from Family Division,
   6th June 1978)
Sir Peter Richard Pain
Sir Kenneth Graham Jupp
Sir Robert Lionel Archibald Goff
Sir Stephen Brown
Sir Gordon Slynn
Sir Roger Jocelyn Parker
Sir Ralph Brian Gibson
Sir Derek Hodgson
Sir Anthony John Leslie Lloyd
Sir Frederick Maurice Drake
Sir Brian Thomas Neill
Sir Roderick Philip Smith
   (appointed 10th June 1978)
Sir Michael John Mustill
   (appointed 19th June 1978)

Family Division

The President of the Family Division

Sir Reginald Withers Payne
Sir John Brinsmead Latey
Dame Elizabeth Kathleen Lane
Sir Henry Vivian Brandon
Sir Robin Horace Walford Dunn
Sir Alfred Kenneth Hollings
Sir John Lewis Arnold
Sir Charles Trevor Reeve
Sir Haydn Tudor Evans
   (transferred to Queen's Bench Division,
   6th June 1978)

Sir Francis Brookes Purchas
Dame Rose Heilbron
Sir Brian Drex Bush
Sir Alfred John Balcombe
Sir John Kember Wood
Sir James Peter Comyn
Sir Ronald Gough Waterhouse
Sir John Gervase Kensington Sheldon
Sir Thomas Michael Eastham
   (appointed 8th May 1978)

CITATION

These reports are cited thus:

[1978] 2 All ER

REFERENCES

These reports contain references, which follow after the headnotes, to the following major works of legal reference described in the manner indicated below.

Halsbury's Laws of England

The reference 35 Halsbury's Laws (3rd Edn) 366, para 524, refers to paragraph 524 on page 366 of volume 35 of the third edition, and the reference 2 Halsbury's Laws (4th Edn) para 1535 refers to paragraph 1535 on page 708 of volume 2 of the fourth edition of Halsbury's Laws of England.

Halsbury's Statutes of England

The reference 5 Halsbury's Statutes (3rd Edn) 302 refers to page 302 of volume 5 of the third edition of Halsbury's Statutes of England.

English and Empire Digest

References are to the replacement volumes (including reissue volumes) of the Digest, and to the continuation volumes of the replacement volumes.

The reference 44 Digest (Repl) 144, 1240, refers to case number 1240 on page 144 of Digest Replacement Volume 44.

The reference Digest (Cont Vol B) 287, 7540b, refers to case number 7540b on page 287 of Digest Continuation Volume B.

The reference 28(1) Digest (Reissue) 167, 507, refers to case number 507 on page 167 of Digest Replacement Volume 28(1) Reissue.

Halsbury's Statutory Instruments

The reference 12 Halsbury's Statutory Instruments (Third Reissue) 125, refers to page 125 of the third reissue of volume 12 of Halsbury's Statutory Instruments; references to subsequent reissues are similar.

CORRIGENDA

[1978] 2 All ER

p 205. **R v Hull Prison Board of Visitors.** Line *j*3: the following line was inadvertently omitted from the foot of page 205, 'in the air, whether for days or for weeks. The same goes for the kind of disciplinary'.

p 214. **Moriarty v McCarthy.** Counsel for the plaintiff: read '*John Wilmers QC* and *Jonathan Playford*' instead of as printed. Counsel for the defendant: read '*Michael Wright QC* and *Graeme Hamilton*' instead of as printed.

p 314. **Laundon v Hartlepool Borough Council.** Lines *h*3 and *h*4: the following line was inadvertently omitted, 'dwelling throughout the qualifying period, which included the ten days, so disentitling'. The missing line should follow immediately after line *h*3 which ends with the word 'private'.

p 393. **R H Willis and Son (a firm) v British Car Auctions Ltd.** Line *c*4: read 'claiming £275 being the outstanding hire-purchase instalments on the car. The auctioneers contended' instead of as printed.

p 520. **Warnford Investments Ltd v Duckworth.** Line *d*1: delete comma at end of line, so that it reads 'the original lessee ceases'. Page 522, line *g*6: for 'prove the liquidation' read 'prove in the liquidation'. Page 526, lines *d*3, and *d*4: for 'a person who as principal, undertook towards the lessor, the obligations' read 'a person who, as principal, undertook towards the lessor the obligations'.

Cases reported in volume 2

Re Caines (deceased)
Knapman v Servian and another

CHANCERY DIVISION
MEGARRY V-C
12th, 31st OCTOBER 1977

Pleading – Striking out – No reasonable cause of action – Originating summons – Evidence inadmissable on an application to strike out – Affidavit in support of originating summons – Affidavit constituting evidence and not pleading – Originating summons containing nothing to show no reasonable cause of action – Defendants relying for purpose of application on contents of plaintiff's affidavit in support of originating summons – Whether affidavit constituting 'evidence on an application' to strike out – Whether court entitled to have regard to affidavit in determining application – RSC Ord 18, r 19(1)(a)(2)(3).

By an originating summons the plaintiff brought an action against the executors of a will. In the summons the plaintiff alleged that he was a beneficiary under the will and claimed an order for the administration of the real and personal estate of the testator with all necessary and proper accounts, directions and enquiries. The plaintiff swore an affidavit in support of the summons which disclosed that the testator had died leaving a will and two codicils. By the will the testator had devised 'my freehold dwellinghouse' to his trustees on trust for sale and to hold the proceeds of sale and the net rents and profits until sale in trust to pay the income to his wife for her life and after her death, as to capital and income, in trust for the plaintiff. It emerged however that the house was not his sole property but belonged to him and his wife. Accordingly, by the second codicil the testator gave 'all my share and interest in the net proceeds of sale and the net rents and profits until sale' of the house on the trust declared in the will as to the house. The testator was survived by his wife by a little over four months. Just before her death the plaintiff's solicitors made enquiries about the nature of the testator's interest in the house, in particular whether he was a joint tenant with his wife or a tenant in common. The answer was that he had been a joint tenant but had signed a notice of severance. There was however doubt whether the joint tenancy had been effectively severed because it appeared that the testator's solicitors had not served the notice of severance on his wife. By his summons the plaintiff sought in effect to compel the executors to bring proceedings against the testator's solicitors for their failure to avoid the depletion of the testator's estate by serving the notice of severance in time. By a procedure summons taken out under RSC Ord 18, r 19(1)(a)[a], the executors sought an order dismissing the proceedings

---

[a] Rule 19 provides:
'(1) The Court may at any stage of the proceedings order to be struck out or amended any pleading or the indorsement of any writ in the action, or anything in any pleading or in the indorsement, on the ground that—(a) it discloses no reasonable cause of action or defence, as the case may be; or (b) it is scandalous, frivolous or vexatious; or (c) it may prejudice, embarrass or delay the fair trial of the action; or (d) it is otherwise an abuse of the process of the court; and may order the action to be stayed or dismissed or judgment to be entered accordingly, as the case may be.
'(2) No evidence shall be admissible on an application under paragraph (1)(a).
'(3) This rule shall, so far as applicable, apply to an originating summons and a petition as if the summons or petition, as the case may be, were a pleading.'

on the ground that the plaintiff had no locus standi to bring them and that they did not disclose any cause of action. At the hearing of the procedure summons the *a* plaintiff's affidavit was before the master. The application was adjourned to a judge before whom the plaintiff, by way of a preliminary objection, contended (i) that the affidavit constituted evidence; (ii) that, in accordance with RSC Ord 18, r 19(2), the judge could not look at the affidavit; and (iii) in consequence it was impossible to say that the originating summons disclosed no cause of action.

b

Held – (i) The plaintiff's preliminary objection failed for the following reasons—

    (a) The words 'so far as applicable' in r 19(3) were to be read as permitting and requiring some degree of flexibility in applying to originating summonses a rule that was drafted for writs and pleadings (see p 4 *c d*, post).

    (b) The prohibition in r 19(2) was expressed as being that evidence was inadmissible 'on' an application under r 19(1)(*a*), i e as prohibiting evidence to support or rebut an *c* application, but was not to be construed as enabling a party to object to an affidavit that had already been put in for the purpose of supporting an originating summons, for such an affidavit was not truly evidence 'on' the application but evidence which antedated the application and had been put in for a different purpose. Rule 19(2) could not therefore be construed as amounting to an absolute prohibition against looking at the affidavit in such cases (see p 4 *e f* and p 5 *d e*, post). *d*

    (c) Under Chancery procedure the hearing before the judge was properly to be regarded as a continuation of the proceedings begun before the master and not as separate proceedings or even as a separate stage in the same proceedings. Since the plaintiff had made no objection to the use of the affidavit before the master, but had argued his case on the basis of that affidavit, it was too late for him to object to its use in what was merely part of the same proceedings in the same court (see p 4 *j* to p 5 *a* *e* and *d* to *g*, post); dicta of Kindersley V-C in *Leeds v Lewis* (1857) 3 Jur NS at 1290 and in *Re Mitchell* (1863) 33 LJCh at 187, 188 and *Lloyd's Bank v Princess Royal Colliery Co* (1900) 82 LT 559 applied.

    (ii) There did not appear to be any basis for the plaintiff's contention that the terms of the second codicil would carry to him any damages that the executors might recover against the solicitors for negligence, for a bequest of 'all my share and interest *f* in the net proceeds of sale' could not be construed as including any damages which the testator was entitled to recover against his solicitors for negligence in failing to ensure that he did have some share and interest in the proceeds of the sale of the house. However, with regard to the issue of severance, it could not be said that it was clear that the plaintiff's case was wholly untenable. The executors' summons therefore failed and would be dismissed (see p 6 *h j* and p 7 *a* to *h*, post). *g*

Notes

For the power to strike out a pleading on the ground that it discloses no reasonable cause of action, see 30 Halsbury's Laws (3rd Edn) 37, 38, para 76, and for cases on the subject, see 50 Digest (Repl) 60-72, *491-563*.

h

Cases referred to in judgment

Leeds v Lewis (1857) 3 Jur NS 1290, 51 Digest (Repl) 627, *2392*.
Lloyd's Bank v Princess Royal Colliery Co (1900) 82 LT 559, 16 Digest (Repl) 206, *954*.
Mitchell, Re (1863) 33 LJCh 187.
Robertson v Fleming (1861) 4 Macq 167, HL, 43 Digest (Repl) 116, *1053*.
Wenlock v Moloney [1965] 2 All ER 871, [1965] 1 WLR 1238, CA, 50 Digest (Repl) 62, *502*. *j*

Cases also cited

Clowes v Hilliard (1876) 4 Ch D 413.
Esso Petroleum Co Ltd v Mardon [1976] 2 All ER 5, [1976] QB 801, CA.

a   *Hubbuck & Sons Ltd v Wilkinson, Heywood & Clark Ltd* [1899] 1 QB 86, [1895-9] All ER Rep 244, CA.
Parsons, Re, Stockley v Parsons (1890) 45 Ch D 51.
Randell, Re, Hood v Randell (1887) 56 LT 8, CA.
Republic of Peru v Peruvian Guano Co (1887) 36 Ch D 489, [1886-90] All ER Rep 368.

Procedure summons

b   By an originating summons dated 25th October 1976 the plaintiff, Eric David Knapman, brought an action against the defendants, (1) Cecil Servian and (2) Frank Kenneth Liddiard Hives, the executors of the will and two codicils dated respectively 10th December 1974, 8th May 1975 and 23rd June 1975 of Harry Edward Ingram Caines deceased ('the testator'), by which he sought an order for the administration of the real and personal estate of the testator with all necessary and proper accounts, direc-
c   tions and inquiries. By a summons dated 21st January 1977 the defendants applied for an order that the plaintiff's action be dismissed on the ground that he had no locus standi to bring the proceedings and that they disclosed no cause of action. The facts are set out in the judgment.

Jonathan Playford for the defendants.
d   *Robert M K Gray* for the plaintiff.

Cur adv vult

31st October. **MEGARRY V-C** delivered the following judgment: This pro-
e   cedure summons raises some interesting questions. The summons, which was taken out by the defendants, seeks the dismissal of the proceedings on the ground that the plaintiff has no locus standi to bring them, and that they disclose no cause of action. The proceedings were commenced by an originating summons in which the plaintiff states that he is a beneficiary under the will of Harry Edward Ingram Caines deceased, whom I shall call 'the testator'; and the relief sought is an order for the administration
f   of the real and personal estate of the testator, with all necessary and proper accounts, directions and inquiries. It was common ground between counsel for the defendants and counsel for the plaintiff that the procedure summons was taken out under para (a) of RSC Ord 18, r 19(1), relating to pleadings or indorsements of a writ that disclose no reasonable cause of action, and not under paras (b), (c) or (d) of that rule, relating to them being scandalous, frivolous or vexatious, or prejudicing, embarrassing or delaying the trial, or being otherwise an abuse of the process of the court. Rule 19(2)
g   provides that 'no evidence shall be admissible on an application under paragraph (1)(a)', and r 19(3) provides that 'this rule shall, so far as applicable, apply to an originating summons and a petition as if the summons or petition . . . were a pleading'.
    That brings me to the first point, raised in a preliminary objection by counsel for the plaintiff. He says that in hearing the procedure summons I must look at the
h   originating summons, and the originating summons alone, for the purpose of deciding whether it discloses any reasonable cause of action, and that I must not look at the affidavit sworn by the plaintiff in support of the originating summons. Of course, unlike a statement of claim in an action begun by writ, most originating summonses are remarkably uninformative documents. They usually ask a series of questions, or state the various forms of relief sought, but most of them disclose little or nothing
j   of what the case is about or what the plaintiff's contentions are. In this case, the originating summons simply asserts that the plaintiff is a beneficiary under the will of the testator, and claims an order for the administration of the testator's estate with ancillary relief, and nothing more. Most of the material that in an action by writ is provided by the statement of claim is, under an originating summons, normally provided by the affidavit in support of the originating summons. But that affidavit.

said counsel for the plaintiff, constitutes evidence, and so is something that, in obedience to RSC Ord 18, r 19(2), I must not look at. Accordingly, it is impossible for the *a* defendants to show that the originating summons discloses no cause of action.

Let me say at the outset that I think that the operation of RSC Ord 18, r 19, in the case of originating summonses is something that the rules committee might with advantage consider. If counsel for the plaintiff's submission is sound, then the application of the rule to originating summonses is likely in most cases to be nugatory. Of course, if under RSC Ord 28, r 8, an order had been made for the affidavits in the *b* case to stand as pleadings, then the difficulty would disappear. But that is not the case here. The question is thus whether r 19(1)(*a*) is inapplicable to the usual reticent form of originating summons, and applies only to those that are more forthcoming.

I can see no grounds on which it could be said that, in making r 19(1) apply to originating summonses, r 19(3) intended to leave most originating summonses outside the practical operation of the rule, and to include only the minority within it. There *c* seem to me to be three considerations which point to r 19(1) being given its full scope in relation to an originating summons such as the one that is before me. First, there are the words 'so far as applicable' in r 19(3). If instead the words had been 'with any necessary modifications', then they would, of course, have given greater support to the contention that r 19(1) applies generally to originating summonses. But I think that even the phrase 'so far as applicable' can be read as permitting and requiring *d* some degree of flexibility in applying to originating summonses a rule that was drafted for writs and pleadings.

Second, the prohibition in r 19(2) is expressed as being that evidence is to be inadmissible 'on' an application under r 19(1)(*a*). In other words, when an application is made under r 19(1)(*a*), the applicant cannot put in evidence to support his application, and the respondent cannot put in evidence to rebut that application. An application *e* under the rule is not to be made into a preliminary hearing. But that ought not to enable a party to object to an affidavit that has already been put in for the purpose of supporting the originating summons; for such an affidavit is not truly evidence 'on' the application, but evidence which antedates the application and has been put in for a different purpose. In short, on an application under r 19(1)(*a*) you must take the proceedings as you find them, though evidence to support or repel the application *f* cannot be added. Views of this kind were, I understand, initially held by counsel for the plaintiff, though on reflection after the hearing before the master he resiled from them. I regard it as being important that the purpose to be discerned in the Rules of the Supreme Court should not be stultified by an over-literal approach to their language.

Third, in this case there is an additional factor, based on what I may call the unity *g* of proceedings in the Chancery Division. When this procedure summons came before the master, he told counsel that he had read the affidavit which the plaintiff had sworn in support of the originating summons. That affidavit was accordingly not formally read to him, but the argument on both sides proceeded on the footing that the affidavit was duly before the master; and no objection to it was made. What counsel for the plaintiff did object to was a further affidavit that counsel for the *h* defendants sought to use; and before me counsel for the defendants disclaimed any reliance on that affidavit, which I have not seen. Accordingly, the present position is that counsel for the plaintiff is objecting to the admissibility of the plaintiff's own affidavit which, without objection, formed the basis of the argument before the master. He contends that although the proceedings before me are not an appeal from the master but merely an adjournment, the proceedings have now reached a new stage, *j* and so it is open to him to object to what he had not objected to before.

The answer to that (or an answer) lies, I think, in what I have called the unity of proceedings in the Chancery Division. When proceedings are adjourned from the master to the judge, this produces no separate proceedings, nor even a separate stage in the proceedings; it is merely a continuation of the proceedings begun before

a the master. In Chancery theory, an adjournment from the master to the judge is no
more a break in the proceedings than is an adjournment of a hearing before the judge
from one day to the next. That seems to me to be well settled in principle; but if
authority be needed, see *Leeds v Lewis*[1] and *Re Mitchell*[2]. As Kindersley V-C[3] pointed
out in the former case, speaking in days when the present-day masters were called
chief clerks, the hearing by the judge 'is merely a continuation of the hearing begun
before the chief clerk'. As he said in the latter case[4], the right of the litigant is 'not to
b have a matter adjourned into Court, but to have it brought before the Judge'; and
'Ordinarily the proceedings in Court are part of the proceedings in chambers'. Further,
an order in fact made by a master is nevertheless treated as being an order of the
judge: *Lloyd's Bank v Princess Royal Colliery Co*[5]. I do not think that the fact that
an order of the master no longer bears the name of the judge (see the amended
version of RSC Ord 32, r 14(3)) can have altered the point of principle. I should add
c that although these authorities were not cited in argument, I put the point to counsel
for the plaintiff, and his answers did not persuade me. *Wenlock v Moloney*[6], which
he cited, was an appeal from the Queen's Bench Division where the facts and issues
were very different.

The question, then, is whether, on the footing that what I am hearing is merely a
continuation of the hearing before the master, it is now open to the plaintiff to seek
d to exclude his own affidavit which, up to this point, has been used without objection.
I would answer No to that question. I do not consider that r 19(2) amounts to an
absolute prohibition against looking at the plaintiff's affidavit in a case such as this.
I think that the rule is directed against the admission of evidence which seeks to
support or disprove the contention that no reasonable cause of action is disclosed, and
not against an affidavit which is intended to disclose the cause of action. It is one thing
e for r 19(2) to prevent applications under r 19(1)(*a*) from becoming a preliminary trial
of disputed issues, and very much another thing to prevent the court from finding
out what the cause of action is.

Furthermore, as the plaintiff made no objection to the use of the affidavit before
the master but argued the case on the basis of that affidavit, I think that it is now too
late for him to object to its use in what is merely part of the same proceedings in the
f same court. Master and judge, together or separately, are each merely parts of the
same division of the same court. In civil proceedings, of course, a party entitled to
object to the admission of evidence may, by failing to object to it in time, allow the
admission of what he might have had excluded. No doubt the court itself could,
under r 19(2), exclude evidence, despite the failure of any of the parties to object to it;
and in most cases no doubt the court would do this. But I think that the court must
g have some discretion in the matter, and there are some cases in which it would be
wrong for the court to exclude the evidence. If ever there was such a case, this is that
case.

I may add that even if, contrary to my view, the hearing before the judge on
adjournment from the master does constitute a separate stage in the proceedings in
the High Court, I very much doubt whether what has been used before the master,
whether or not it was treated as being evidence, can, when the case is before the judge,
h be excluded on the ground that it is inadmissible evidence. What is in is in, and stays
in. But primarily I rest my decision on the proceedings before master and judge
being all one, as well as on the construction of r 19(2), (3). At the conclusion of the
argument on the matter I held that counsel for the plaintiff's preliminary objection
failed, and I said that I would give my reasons later. This I have now done.

j ───
1   (1857) 3 Jur NS 1290
2   (1863) 33 LJCh 187
3   3 Jur NS 1290
4   33 LJCh 187 at 187, 188
5   (1900) 82 LT 559
6   [1965] 2 All ER 871, [1965] 1 WLR 1238

Once the plaintiff's affidavit is read, it becomes possible to say what the case is about. The testator died on 30th June 1975, leaving a will dated 10th December 1974 and two codicils. The will appointed the two defendants to be the testator's executors and trustees, and they duly proved the will and the codicils. By the will, the testator devised 'my freehold dwellinghouse' to his trustees on trust for sale, and to hold the proceeds of sale and the net rents and profits until sale in trust to pay the net income to his wife for her life, and after her death, as to capital and income, in trust for the plaintiff. By his second codicil, the testator gave 'all my share and interest in the net proceeds of sale and the net rents and profits until sale' of the house on the trust declared in the will as to the house. This codicil was necessary because it appears to have emerged that the house was not the testator's sole property but belonged to him and his wife, so that he was beneficially entitled not to the house but only to an interest under a trust for sale of the house.

The testator was survived by his widow for a little over four months; she died on 5th November 1975. Not long before her death, the plaintiff's solicitors had made enquiries of the defendants' solicitors about the exact nature of the testator's interest in the house. In particular, they enquired whether he had been a joint tenant (presumably with his wife), and whether, if this was the case, any severance of the joint tenancy had taken place. This enquiry elicited the information that the testator had been a joint tenant with his wife and that he had signed a notice of severance, but that as he was in hospital suffering from cancer (from which he died a week later), and his wife was a mental patient, the notice had not been served on her. If, of course, the joint tenancy had not been severed before the testator died, his interest passed by survivorship to his wife. The gift to the plaintiff was thus adeemed, and so failed.

On those facts, one possible line of action for the plaintiff to consider was to sue the testator's solicitors for damages in respect of their failure to serve the notice of severance in time. The obvious difficulty in this is that the solicitors could say that although they owed the testator a duty of care, they owed none to the plaintiff, who was not their client, and so they could not be guilty of a breach of any duty of care owed to the plaintiff. The position, indeed, is a variant of the familiar story of the legatee whose complaint is that a legacy to him has failed because of some negligence in the solicitor in preparing the will, and that he is left without remedy. _Robertson v Fleming_[1], a decision of the House of Lords in a Scottish appeal, is a leading case on this branch of the law. In other jurisdictions, means have been found of providing the disappointed legatee with a remedy[2]; but, so far as I know, these have not yet found a place in English law. I shall say no more about this point, as it is not before me. I mention it, however, as it explains at least part of the course taken by the plaintiff in this case.

I turn, then, to the proceedings brought by the plaintiff. As I have said, these consist of an originating summons which asks for an order for the administration of the estate of the testator, with all necessary and proper accounts, directions and enquiries. By doing this, the plaintiff seeks to compel the executors to bring proceedings for negligence against the testator's solicitors for their failure to swell the estate of the testator (or prevent its reduction) by serving the notice of severance in due time. But, says counsel for the defendants, if this is done all that will happen is that any damages recovered will fall into residue, and as the plaintiff admittedly has no interest in residue, he has nothing which entitles him to require such proceedings to be brought. On that footing, the originating summons should be dismissed because the plaintiff has no locus standi.

If that were all, counsel for the defendants would have a very strong case. But it is not all. The proposed action for negligence is necessarily founded on the proposition that at the moment of his death the testator was a joint tenant of the house. If instead

---

1   (1861) 4 Macq 167
2   See, for example, (1965) 81 LQR 478

he was a tenant in common, then, of course, the plaintiff appears plainly to be bene-
a ficially entitled to the testator's half-share in the proceeds of sale of the house; and
on that footing there is prima facie no claim for negligence against the solicitors.
Accordingly, a crucial question is whether or not the testator was a joint tenant when
he died. Counsel for the plaintiff contends that there are two routes whereby he may
succeed in establishing that in equity the testator was a tenant in common. First, there
is the conveyance to the testator and his wife, which I have not seen. There may, said
b counsel for the plaintiff, be some arguable question that on its true construction the
conveyance created not a joint tenancy, as the defendants assert, but a tenancy in
common. At this stage this is plainly no more than a possibility; but it ought not to
be dismissed out of hand. Second, there is the point that was raised by the plaintiff's
solicitors at an early stage of the correspondence. This is that the solicitors for the
testator may also have been solicitors for his wife, with sufficient authority to receive
c any notice of severance on her behalf. If this is the case, then the delivery of the
notice by the testator to the solicitors may have amounted to service of the notice
on his wife, thereby effecting a severance before the testator died.

In addition to these contentions, counsel for the plaintiff staked his claim on another
point. If the testator had died a joint tenant, then it was not beyond argument, he
said, that the terms of the second codicil would carry to the plaintiff any damages
d that the defendants might recover against the solicitors for negligence. Counsel for
the plaintiff never succeeded in making me see why this was not a hopeless contention.
I cannot see how a bequest of 'all my share and interest in the net proceeds of sale'
of a house could include any damages which the testator was entitled to recover
against solicitors for their negligence in failing to ensure that he did have some share
and interest in the proceeds of sale of the house. (In saying that, I naturally do not
e express any view, one way or the other, on whether there has been any negligence
by the solicitors.) A gift of something seems to me incapable of constituting a gift of
damages to which the donor is entitled for losing that something. The damages are
not the thing given but compensation for its loss. However, I suppose that it is not
beyond possibility that with more ample argument counsel for the plaintiff's ingenuity
will be able to get even this contention on to its legs.
f   The issue on severance is quite different. I certainly cannot say that it is clear
beyond doubt that the plaintiff's claim is wholly untenable on the face of it. There
are obvious difficulties in the path of the plaintiff, and opinions may well differ on
his prospects of success; but to say that his chances of succeeding seem at present to be
small is not to say that his case is unarguable. I certainly cannot say that it is clear
that the plaintiff has no locus standi and has disclosed no cause of action. In the end, I
g think that counsel for the defendants was constrained to accept that this was so. The
plaintiff's contentions certainly seem to have developed considerably since the case
was before the master. In those circumstances, it seems to me that the defendants'
summons seeking the dismissal of the proceedings must fail and be dismissed.

That is all that is formally before me; but as the estate is not large, and a full
administration order is plainly not what the plaintiff really wants, I shall invite
h counsel to assist me in considering whether I can give directions which will save costs
and assist in securing the determination of the real issues.

Application dismissed.

Solicitors: *Waterhouse & Co*, agents for *Hart Brown & Co*, Guildford (for the plaintiff);
j *Davies Arnold & Cooper* (for the defendant).

Hazel Hartman Barrister.

R v Anderson

a

COURT OF APPEAL, CRIMINAL DIVISION
ORMROD LJ, THOMPSON AND JUPP JJ
14th, 15th NOVEMBER 1977

Criminal law – Bankruptcy order – Financial limit on jurisdiction to make order – Aggregate *b*
of loss or damage from offences of which accused convicted and other relevant offences –
Offences which the court takes into consideration in determining sentence – Prosecution
proceeding on sample counts – List of outstanding offences of similar nature submitted to
defendant – Defendant convicted on sample counts – Outstanding offences with defendant's
consent taken into consideration in passing sentence – Whether offences taken into consideration
'other relevant offences' – Whether court entitled to take account of loss or damage from out- *c*
standing offences in determining aggregate of loss or damage – Powers of Criminal Courts Act
1973, s 39(1)(2).

Criminal Law – Bankruptcy order – Form of order – Requirement that amount of loss or
damage resulting from each offence be specified – Prosecution proceeding on sample counts –
Whether sufficient to list other offences with dates and amount of loss or damage in schedule to *d*
order – Powers of Criminal Courts Act 1973, s 39(3)(a).

The appellant was charged and convicted on 13 counts on an indictment which involved offences of obtaining money by deception from his employers to the value of
£7,112. A schedule to the indictment set out 20 similar offences involving some
£19,600 but they were not proceeded with by the Crown. They were however taken *e*
into consideration by the trial judge when sentencing the appellant to a term of imprisonment. The judge also made a criminal bankruptcy order against the appellant
under s 39(1)ᵃ of the Powers of Criminal Courts Act 1973. On appeal against the
making of the order, it was contended by the appellant that the trial judge had no
jurisdiction to make it since the offences charged on the indictment did not involve
loss or damage exceeding £15,000 as required by s 39(1)(b). *f*

Held – The expression 'offences which the court takes into consideration in determining . . . sentence' in s 39(2)ᵇ of the 1973 Act meant offences for which the sentence
had been passed, which included offences which the accused had asked to be taken into
consideration on the passing of sentence or offences which had not been proceeded
with on indictment because the accused had been tried and found guilty on sample *g*
counts only. Notwithstanding that the loss or damage resulting from the counts on
which the appellant had been specifically found guilty amounted to only £7,112, the
judge had acted within his jurisdiction in taking into consideration when making the
order both the offences on which the appellant had been found guilty and the similar
offences which had not been proceeded with, the aggregate of the loss or damage
resulting from which exceeded £15,000. The appeal would therefore be dismissed *h*
(see p 11 g to j, p 12 b and p 14 b c, post).
　　Per Curiam. In drawing up a criminal bankruptcy order when the prosecution has
proceeded on sample counts it is sufficient compliance with the requirement of
s 39(3)(a)ᶜ that the order 'specify the amount of the loss or damage appearing to the
court to have resulted from the offence or, if more than one, each of the offences' to
set out in separate schedules to the order (1) the specific offences which appeared as *j*
counts in the indictment on which the appellant was convicted and (2) a detailed list

---

a　Section 39(1), so far as material, is set out at p 10 *d*, post
b　Section 39(2), so far as material, is set out at p 10 *e*, post
c　Section 39(3) is set out at p 12 *d e*, post

a of the dates of the offences and the amount of damage or loss suffered from which the
sample counts were taken (see p 13 g h and p 14 a to c, post).

Notes

For criminal bankruptcy orders, see 11 Halsbury's Laws (4th Edn) para 803.

For the Powers of Criminal Courts Act 1973, s 39, see 43 Halsbury's Statutes (3rd
Edn) 334.

b

Case referred to in judgment

R v Huchison [1972] 1 All ER 936, [1972] 1 WLR 398, 136 JP 304, 56 Cr App Rep 307, CA,
14(2) Digest (Reissue) 679, 5611.

Cases also cited

c R v Batchelor (1952) 36 Cr App Rep 64, CA.

R v Jackson (Alan Victor) [1974] 2 All ER 211, [1974] QB 517, CA.

R v Thomas [1949] 2 All ER 662, [1950] 1 KB 26, CA.

Appeal

On 25th October 1976 at the Central Criminal Court before his Honour Judge Neil
d McKinnon QC the appellant, Keith Anthony Anderson, was convicted of one offence
of procuring the execution of a valuable security by deception (count 1), seven offences
of obtaining property by deception (counts 2, 3, 4, 6, 7, 9 and 11), four offences of
causing the transfer of property by a forged instrument (counts 5, 8, 10 and 12) and one
offence of attempting to obtain property by deception (count 13). He was sentenced
to six years' imprisonment on each count to run concurrently. In addition a criminal
e bankruptcy order was made under s 39(1) of the Powers of Criminal Courts Act 1973
in the sum of £26,754·61 in respect of damage flowing from the offences committed
on the indictment. The appellant was also ordered to pay £168 towards the legal aid
costs of his defence. He appealed against conviction with leave of the single judge and
applied for leave to appeal against sentence. On 14th November 1977 the court
dismissed the appeal against conviction but granted the application for leave to appeal
f against sentence, treated it as the hearing of the appeal and varied the sentence to four
years' imprisonment concurrent. At the hearing the appellant alleged that the trial
judge had no jurisdiction to make the criminal bankruptcy order. The appeal was
adjourned for counsel for the Director of Public Prosecutions to be instructed as
amicus curiae to assist the court regarding the order.

g Kenneth Bagnall QC and John Foy for the appellant.
Ann Goddard for the Crown.
Philip Mott for the Director of Public Prosecutions as amicus curiae.

ORMROD LJ delivered the following judgment of the court: In addition to the
h sentence of imprisonment, with which this court dealt yesterday, in this case, the
judge below, after some considerable discussion with counsel, decided to make a
criminal bankruptcy order under what is now s 39 of the Powers of Criminal Courts
Act 1973. That was a course which, at the time, counsel for the appellant agreed with
in preference to a compensation order being made. The trial judge then went in
considerable detail into the background of criminal bankruptcy orders, and was at
j great pains to make sure that the criminal bankruptcy order which he intended to
make should be factually right.

It was accepted in the course of that discussion that the total amount involved in
this case, and I use that phrase deliberately, was of the order of £29,000, although in
fact it was subsequently reduced to a figure of about £26,000, for reasons which do
not matter so far as this judgment is concerned, and the court proceeded on that

footing. Difficulties then arose when it came to drawing the actual order. Two
outstanding difficulties have been brought to the attention of this court. The first one,
which is the important one, goes directly to the jurisdiction to make a criminal bankruptcy order, and in those circumstances, in spite of the fact that there is an express
statutory provision which precludes a right of appeal against criminal bankruptcy
orders, it is plain that where the suggestion is that the order is a nullity, this court
can adjudicate on that matter as has been held in relation to other similar problems.
So no question arises as to this court's jurisdiction to deal with the problem.

The problem which has arisen is that the aggregate sum involved in the actual
counts in the indictment in this case does not amount to the minimum figure fixed
by s 39(1) of the 1973 Act. That is the figure of £15,000. The total of the items or
counts which were specifically charged, and of which the appellant was specifically
found guilty, amounts to £7,112 and therefore is less than £15,000. So, the first
question here is: had the court below jurisdiction, in the sense of power, to make a
criminal bankruptcy order? That takes us to s 39(1), which is the jurisdiction section
and which reads as follows:

'Where a person is convicted of an offence before the Crown Court and it
appears to the court that—(a) as a result of the offence, or of that offence taken
together with any other relevant offence or offences, loss or damage (not attributable to personal injury) has been suffered by one or more persons whose
identity is known to the court; and (b) the amount, or aggregate amount, of the
loss or damage exceeds £15,000; the court may, in addition to dealing with the
offender in any other way . . . make a criminal bankruptcy order against him in
respect of the offence or, as the case may be, that offence and the other relevant
offence or offences.'

In s 39(2) 'other relevant offence or offences' is defined as meaning—

'an offence or offences of which the person in question is convicted in the same
proceedings or which the court takes into consideration in determining his
sentence.'

The crux of the matter, therefore, lies in the meaning to be given to the words, 'or
which the court takes into consideration in determining his sentence'. There are two
points of view which have been argued most helpfully by all three counsel in this
case, and we are indebted to them all for the assistance they have given on what is
undoubtedly a difficult point.

Before saying anything about the construction of that phrase in this section, it is
wise to bear in mind the particular nature of this section and those immediately
following it which deal with criminal bankruptcy orders, for this reason: that this
section and the earlier one, s 35, dealing with compensation are really attempts to
bridge a gap which has always existed, and has never been bridged before, between
the criminal law, or criminal code if one uses a more general phrase, and the civil
code. These two sections are clearly designed by Parliament to make it easier and
cheaper and more practicable in certain cases to bring into the criminal procedure an
element of civil remedy, or alternatively to bring some part of the criminal law into
the civil procedure. So far as s 39 is concerned, it creates this new concept of a criminal
bankruptcy order, and what Parliament has in effect done, as we understand it, is to
create a new kind of act of bankruptcy. So, when this section has to be construed, it
would not be right, in our view, to construe it strictly as if it were a criminal statute
with the various traditional methods and restrictions on construction of such a statute.
We are construing here what is essentially a bridging section, designed primarily to
simplify procedure.

With that in mind one comes to consider the phrase, 'the offences which the court
takes into consideration'. It has been pointed out, quite rightly, that this phrase is

first to be found, as far as researches go, in the Criminal Justice Act 1972, and it was
a that Act which introduced for the first time criminal bankruptcy orders, and also
introduced the concept of compensation orders, and at the same time significantly
extended the powers of the court in relation to restitution orders under s 28 of the
Theft Act 1968. In all those three contexts the Criminal Justice Act 1972 uses this same
phrase in ss 6 and 7, and in the compensation section (s 1) also. The question is: does
that phrase mean offences taken into consideration in the technical procedural sense
b in which it is so often used, or has it got a wider significance?

There are arguments both ways on this, but if this phrase is read literally as it
stands in the Act, it means what it says, simply offences which the court has taken into
consideration in determining the sentence. There is no doubt whatever that in this
case the court below, in pronouncing a sentence of six years' imprisonment, which was
yesterday reduced to four, unquestionably and indeed expressly took into account the
c fact that the total sum involved in the dishonesty was of the order of £26,000, far in
excess of the total of the specific charges which had been proved. Is that right, or is
that wrong? Well, the first observation to be made is that the whole idea of taking into
consideration other offences is a matter of practice and not of statute. That is made
perfectly clear by Archbold[1] and by various decisions of this court in cases to which it
is not necessary to refer. For various good practical reasons the courts have worked
d out a procedure to be followed in most of these cases: the procedure of making out a
list of specific charges outstanding and submitting the list to the accused person, and
asking him or her whether or not he or she wishes the other offences to be taken into
consideration. From the point of view of the accused it has the advantage of clearing
up his record and getting rid of a lot of outstanding offences which might otherwise
bring him before the court again. It saves the court's time in hearing separate cases
e involving the other offences, and it is obviously a highly advantageous system. It has
been necessary to introduce a fairly formal procedure in relation to it to avoid the
consequent confusion which might arise if a fairly strict procedure has not been
followed, but in the view of this court there is no compelling reason to read that
procedure into the various sections of what was originally in the 1972 Act, and is now
in s 39 of the Powers of Criminal Courts Act 1973.
f That being so, what are the limitations on this phrase? The practical limitations are
not very difficult to define. They are what the Act says they are, the offences taken
into consideration in determining the sentence. Counsel for the appellant has pointed
out that in certain cases such as, for example, deciding to pass an extended sentence,
the court takes into account not previous offences but previous convictions. The
court here is only concerned with two possible circumstances, as we see it, and indeed
g as counsel for the Director of Public Prosecutions has put it to us. We are concerned
with the ordinary situation where a list of other offences is submitted to the accused
or the defendant and he admits his guilt of all of those offences or some of them, and
they are then cleared up by including them in the sentence passed. That is one
situation. The other situation, which arises in relation to fraud cases of all kinds, is
that for convience's sake the prosecution elect to proceed on what are called sample
h offences. Police enquiries have revealed, very often, a whole series of offences, in some
cases all committed against the same person, the same victim; in other cases, of
course, the offences will be committed against many different people. In those cases
it is a matter of practical convenience, for everybody, to select certain sample charges
or counts and proceed only on them, it being understood by the prosecution and the
defence that there are many other similar offences which could have been charged,
j but have not in fact been specifically charged. The trial proceeds on that basis, and
sentence is in due course passed on that basis.

If there is any doubt about it, there is, in the view of this court, ample opportunity
for the defendant represented by counsel to make clear at an early stage whether or

---

1 Criminal Pleading, Evidence and Practice (39th Edn, 1976), para 637

not the other offences not included in the indictment are in some way or other to be differentiated from those which have been included in the indictment. Here, as I said, there was no question but that all the other offences, which added up to the sum of £29,000 odd, were of almost precisely similar nature to the ones in the indictment.

The conclusion which this court has come to on the construction of s 39 of the 1973 Act is that the phrase 'offences which the court takes into consideration' must be construed as meaning exactly what it says: the offences for which the sentence is passed. In this case that is the aggregate sum of £29,000 or £26,000, whichever it may be. That deals with the question of jurisdiction. The court below, therefore, was quite right in thinking that it had the jurisdiction to make a criminal bankruptcy order.

The only other problem which has arisen, and which has given us a considerable amount of thought, arises under s 39(3). This does not go to jurisdiction at all, but to the actual drawing up of the criminal bankruptcy order, and also to its evidential effect, and it is right that we should say something about it. Section 39(3) provides:

> 'A criminal bankruptcy order shall specify—(a) the amount of the loss or damage appearing to the court to have resulted from the offence or, if more than one, each of the offences; (b) the person or persons appearing to the court to have suffered that loss or damage; (c) the amount of that loss or damage which it appears to the court that that person, or each of those persons, has suffered; and (d) the date which is to be the relevant date for the purpose of the exercise by the High Court of its powers under paragraph 10 of Schedule 2 to this Act in relation to dispositions made by the offender, being the date which appears to the court to be the earliest date on which the offence or, if more than one, the earliest of the offences, was committed.'

Reference has now to be made to Sch 2, which contains all the mechanism involved in this new concept. Turning to Sch 2, para 1 of Part 1 says:

> 'Subject to the provisions of this Schedule, where a criminal bankruptcy order is made against any person he shall be treated as a debtor who has committed an act of bankruptcy on the date on which the order is made.'

That is the provision which was referred to earlier as being an additional act of bankruptcy, a new type of act of bankruptcy created by this Act. Then, under para 2 of Sch 2:

> 'A person specified in a criminal bankruptcy order as having suffered loss or damage of any amount shall be treated for the purpose of any ensuing proceedings pursuant to—(a) ... or (b) ... as a creditor for debt of that amount provable in the bankruptcy ...'

That brings him into line with the ordinary creditor.

Then we go on to Part II of Sch 2. Under Part II, the next important paragraph is para 6. Paragraph 6 reads:

> 'For the purposes of section 5(2) and (3) of the [Bankruptcy Act 1914] (matters to be proved before receiving order is made) the act of bankruptcy which a person is treated by this Schedule as having committed and any criminal bankruptcy debt shall be treated as conclusively proved by the production of a copy of the criminal bankruptcy order in question ...'

So that for the limited purposes of leading to the making of the receiving order, the terms of the order as specified in sub-s (3) of s 39 are to be taken as conclusively proving the matters set out in the order, but it is only for the purpose of leading to a receiving order that the contents of the criminal bankruptcy order are to be taken

as proof, because when one looks at para 9 of Sch 2 to the 1973 Act, which deals in
a substance with proof of debt or debts in the bankruptcy, it is then perfectly plain
that the criminal bankruptcy order is no more than prima facie evidence of the
existence of the debts specified in the criminal bankruptcy order. Under that paragraph it is open to either the creditor or the criminal debtor to dispute the amount
of the alleged debt, either by saying the criminal bankruptcy order understates the
amount of the debt or alternatively overstates it. So it is no more than prima facie
b evidence.

Counsel for the appellant rightly drew our attention to para 9(3) which reads:

'Nothing in sub-paragraph (1) above shall be construed as entitling any person
to contend that the offence or offences specified in a criminal bankruptcy order
were not committed by the person against whom the order was made.'

c The effect of that sub-paragraph seems to be that, insofar as it is a question of whether
the offences were committed by the person in question, the criminal bankruptcy
order is conclusive; it is not, of course, equivalent to a conviction, it is simply
conclusive evidence that he or she committed the offences referred to.

Paragraph 10 also contains an important provision in relation to dispositions of
property, because under that paragraph, the relevant date for the purposes of setting
d aside dispositions of property goes back to the date which has to be specified in the
criminal bankruptcy order, and that brings in s 39(3)(*d*). Under that paragraph, the
court making the criminal bankruptcy order is required to specify the date which
appears to it to be the earliest date on which the first offence was committed. So it
dates the period in respect of subsequent dispositions right back to the date of the first
offence. It follows that it is very important for the criminal court making a criminal
e bankruptcy order to be explicit in specifying the date of the first offence in question.

The difficulty in applying s 39(3) arises principally in relation to the first of the
requirements of the order, that the order shall specify the amount of the loss or
damage appearing to the court to have resulted from the offence, or, if more than
one, 'the offences'. It is not immediately obvious why it was considered to be necessary
to require the court to allocate the loss or damage to each individual offence, but the
f fact is that the order is mandatory in form and must be complied with. Paragraphs
(*b*), (*c*) and (*d*) are all perfectly comprehensible, para (*b*) identifying the persons who
are in effect adjudged to be creditors and para (*c*) indicating the total amount which
each of those creditors has lost. But para (*a*) goes beyond that: it requires the court, in
the bankruptcy order, to allocate the loss to each offence, if more than one. There is no
doubt that this may cause considerable difficulty when it comes to drawing criminal
g bankruptcy orders.

In the present case the difficulty has been got round by the Central Criminal Court
office. When I say 'got round' I do not mean to criticise them, but they have resolved
this problem, and they have dealt with it by specifying in Sch A the specific offences
which appeared as counts in the indictment on which the appellant was convicted,
and in Sch B they have set a detailed list showing dates of offences and amount of
h damage or loss suffered in a schedule running to two and a half sheets. That is based,
of course, on the enquiries and investigations that were made by the police, and in
fact it represents a list of all the invoices which were affected by the same criminal
deception as those on which the accused was convicted. What happened at the trial
was that the Crown in opening stated the total amount of damage or loss suffered in
this case by the appellant's employers, and produced all the relevant invoices and
j made them exhibits, and produced either a schedule in the same form as Sch B or
something very similar, and the trial proceeded on the footing that all these offences
were of the same character and nature as the offences actually charged in the indictment, and the whole matter proceeded in the usual way in this type of case. In other
words this is a case of system, and what the Crown was doing was to say that the
appellant had been engaged in a systematic fraud over a period of some considerable

time, involving a very large sum of money, and they proved that by selecting their six or so specific counts.

In the view of this court the method of dealing with the drawing of this order is a satisfactory one. The Powers of Criminal Courts Act 1973 makes it plain that in practice, where a court is contemplating making a criminal bankruptcy order, it will be very important for the judge making the order to ensure that in due time the order can be drawn up in accordance with the provisions of s 39, and that will or may involve having available some such schedule as was produced in this case. We need say no more about it.

It also follows from what we have said that it is of great importance to fix accurately the date of the first offence for the purposes of the criminal bankruptcy order. That being the position this court has come to the conclusion that the trial judge was entitled to make the order for the reasons we have given, and that the form of the order drawn up in the office at the Central Criminal Court itself was also right and in accordance with the provisions of the Act. Therefore we need say no more than that the criminal bankruptcy order stands.

We would like to say once more how grateful we are to counsel for all the assistance we have been given. We have not referred specifically to the three cases we were referred to, simply because we do not think they really take the matter any further. The only case which perhaps we should have mentioned in passing, is R v Huchison[1]. We only refer to that case, because in the course of the judgment of this court given by Phillimore LJ[2] express reference is made to what he called 'sample counts', simply to draw attention to the fact that that form of prosecution is a well recognised one in appropriate cases. For those reasons the criminal bankruptcy order must stand.

Order accordingly. Leave to appeal to the House of Lords refused.

25th November. The court certified, under s 33 of the Criminal Appeal Act 1968, that the following point of law of general public importance was involved in the case: what is the true construction in s 39(1) of the Powers of Criminal Courts Act 1973 of the words 'offence or offences which the court takes into consideration in determining his sentence' so as to found the jurisdiction of the Crown Court to make a criminal bankruptcy order?

19th January 1978. The Appeal Committee of the House of Lords granted leave to appeal.

Solicitors: *Registrar of Criminal Appeals; Solicitor, Metropolitan Police; Director of Public Prosecutions.*

N P Metcalfe Esq Barrister.

---

1   [1972] 1 All ER 936, [1972] 1 WLR 398
2   [1972] 1 All ER 936 at 937, [1972] 1 WLR 398 at 400

Clarks of Hove Ltd v Bakers' Union

a

EMPLOYMENT APPEAL TRIBUNAL
KILNER BROWN J, MR M L CLEMENT-JONES AND MR S C MARLEY
30th MAY 1977

b
Redundancy – Employer's duty to consult appropriate trade union – Special circumstances rendering it not reasonably practicable to comply with duty – Insolvency – Company deciding to cease trading because of insolvency – Dismissal of employees as redundant in consequence – No consultation with trade union representatives before decision made to cease trading – Company hoping to continue trading up to last minute – Whether circumstances of insolvency may amount to 'special circumstances' which render it not reasonably practicable for the employer to comply with the requirement to consult union representatives – Employment
c *Protection Act 1975, s 99(8).*

The employers were a company which manufactured and sold confectionery. In 1976 they were in financial difficulties but, up to the day before they ceased trading, they were hoping that they could carry on by one means or another. In the event they were unable to do so, and ceased trading, making their workforce of 380 people
d redundant. No consultation took place with the employees' union about the possibility of redundancies before the decision was made to cease trading. In consequence, once the decision had been made, the employers failed to comply with s 99(3)^a of the Employment Protection Act 1975 by consulting the union about the redundancies at least 90 days before the first of the dismissals took effect. The union complained to an industrial tribunal under s 101(1)^b of the 1975 Act. The tribunal held that the com-
e plaint was well founded and made a protective award of 49 days' remuneration. The employers appealed, contending that their sudden insolvency was a special circumstance which made it impracticable for them to comply with the requirement of s 99(3) to consult the union, and that therefore they were protected by s 99(8)^c of the 1975 Act.

f **Held** – Insolvency by itself was not a 'special circumstance' relieving an employer from the duty to consult the appropriate trade union but the situation in which the insolvency occurred might be a 'special circumstance'. The questions to be considered in deciding whether that was the case included whether it might have been avoided, and whether it was practicable or sensible for the employer to decide 90 days in advance to consult a trade union on whether or not insolvency was likely. Since the
g tribunal had failed to consider whether the circumstances of the insolvency amounted to 'special circumstances', within s 99(8), the appeal would be allowed, and the case remitted to the tribunal so that the point could be determined (see p 18 *e f* and *h* to p 19 *g*, post).

Notes
h For an employer's duty to consult trade union on redundancies, see 16 Halsbury's Laws (4th Edn) para 654: 1.

---

a Section 99(3), so far as material, provides: 'The consultation required by this section shall begin at the earliest opportunity, and shall in any event begin—(*a*) where the employer is proposing to dismiss as redundant 100 or more employees at one establishment within
j a period of 90 days or less, at least 90 days before the first of those dismissals takes effect . . .'
b Section 101(1) provides: 'An appropriate trade union may present a complaint to an industrial tribunal on the ground that an employer has dismissed as redundant or is proposing to dismiss as redundant one or more employees and has not complied with any of the requirements of section 99 above.'
c Section 99(8), so far as material, is set out at p 18 *c*, post

For the Employment Protection Act 1975, ss 99, 101, see 45 Halsbury's Statutes (3rd Edn) 2412, 2415.

Case referred to in judgment

National Union of Dyers, Bleachers and Textile Workers v Job Beaumont & Son Ltd (28th October 1976) unreported, Leeds industrial tribunal.

Appeal

This was an appeal by Clarks of Hove Ltd ('the employers') against the decision of an industrial tribunal (chairman G I A D Draper Esq) sitting at Brighton on 14th January 1977 which upheld a complaint made by the Bakers' Union ('the union'), on behalf of its members who were employed by the employers, under s 101(1) of the Employment Protection Act 1975. The facts are set out in judgment of the appeal tribunal.

Anthony Grabiner for the employers.
Q Barry, solicitor, for the union.

KILNER BROWN J delivered the following judgment of the appeal tribunal: This is an appeal against the unanimous decision of a industrial tribunal held at Brighton on 14th January 1977. On that occasion the tribunal decided that 'the complaint made under s 101(1) of the Employment Protection Act 1975 is well-founded and succeeds' accordingly. Further to that, in their discretion, they decided that it was a proper case in which there should be a protective award amounting to a total period of 49 days' remuneration. It was a reserved decision of the industrial tribunal, and we would wish to say how very appreciative we are of the very great care with which this industrial tribunal went into this matter and the admirable way in which with detail they set out the arguments and recited the facts. Consequently it is all the more unfortunate that we are unanimously of the opinion that in one respect the industrial tribunal have not given appropriate consideration to a section of the 1975 Act (to which reference will be made in detail) and to the application of the facts.

The problem of a practical nature which arises in this case is whether or not on the facts as found and as set out in their reasons it would be proper for us to assume that we should, in the circumstances, make a decision along the lines contended for by Mr Barry for the union, who were the applicants before the industrial tribunal. Had we been unanimous it would have been a clear case in which we should not have shirked our responsibility and should ourselves have substituted a decision if we felt the evidence was clear. However, we are quite open about this, we are not unanimous. In an important case like this where we do not find unanimity it is much better for the industrial tribunal which took so much trouble in this case, to reconsider their decision along the lines of the guidance which we propose to give. The reappraisal requires an assessment of the witnesses which we are not able to embark on.

This was a case of a workforce, varying in assessment between 368 and 380. The reason why a variation exists is due to the fact that, of a total of 380, there were 368 apparently who were qualified to join the union but had not in fact done so. As soon as they realised that the union, on behalf of a very small minority, were taking steps to see what could be done, they promptly joined the union. This was very sensible of them even though it was at the eleventh hour and fifty-ninth minute.

The employers were a company which had carried on business for many years and lately got into grave difficulties. They were confectioners, they had many shops, and the position was reached in the autumn of 1976 when the writing was on the wall as far as any reasonable management was concerned. However, it is important to bear in mind that this industrial tribunal, having heard the witnesses, having gone into it with very great care, produced a finding of fact, at the end of the reasons, to

this effect: 'We consider that in this case the [employers] were hoping, albeit unrealis-
a   tically, up to the last moment that they could carry on trading.' That paragraph then
goes on to fault the employers for their failure to consult with the appropriate trade
union. The tribunal then considered the nature of the protective award.

It is necessary to remind ourselves just what this part of the 1975 Act lays down.
Section 99(1) reads as follows:

b   'An employer proposing to dismiss as redundant an employee of a description
in respect of which an independent trade union is recognised by him shall consult
representatives of that trade union about the dismissal in accordance with the
following provisions of this section.'

Pausing there for a moment, this group of sections is headed 'Procedure for handling
redundancies'. It is quite plain that it envisages the situation in which an employer is
c   contemplating making a group, whether small or large, in excess of ten of the workforce redundant. As one of our number with many years' experience in the trade
union movement is the first to recognise, it is a fact of life that where there is a keen
trade union, and where there are keen members of the trade union, a good number of
people will come in for any benefits resulting from action taken by the key ones and
those who 'carry the torch', if one may use that expression.

d   Section 99(3) says that consultation with the representatives of the trade union 'shall
begin at the earliest opportunity', and that where there is a workforce which is about
to be dismissed in excess of 100 employees the period of consultation has to be at least
90 days before the first of the dismissals takes effect. One of the extraordinary features
of this section in its approach is this: it means quite plainly that as soon as there is in
the mind of the employer a sufficient decision that he is proposing to dismiss 100 or
e   more employees on the grounds of redundancy, that even if he consults with the
trade union the very next day, once his mind is that sufficiently clear, and after a
month there is no more money and the business is closed down, he has still theoretically broken the terms of this section. As Mr Barry for the union says, one hopes that
broadly speaking a sensible trade union would not make a complaint, which it has
power to do, that consultation did not continue for 90 days; but we can envisage a
f   situation in which a trade union may well take the view that it is nonetheless going
to take the employers to court. Indeed there was recently in this tribunal a case in
which the local representative of the trade union adopted that very attitude. He
regarded this as a section with penal consequences, the penal consequences arising, of
course, out of the ability to make a protective award, where the fault of the employer
is one of the matters which an industrial tribunal has to bear in mind and consider.

g   So there is no doubt about it at all in this case, because the employers frankly
admitted that in October 1976, although this section had been in force for some two
or three months by then, they had never heard of this requirement in the 1975 Act.
They did not realise that the law said that they had to consult with the appropriate
trade union. So there was no answer to the first part of this section. They did propose
to dismiss as redundant more than 100. They proposed to dismiss the whole work-
h   force. But right up to Sunday afternoon, 24th October, as was stated in the industrial
tribunal's reasons, they were still hoping that they could carry on trading. They tried
all sorts of people. They tried the bank, they tried to sell off shops, they tried to
raise money all over the place and they still had on the Saturday a final hope that
somebody who had been involved in the previous transactions might want to take
them over and 'bail them out', if one may lapse into the vernacular for a moment.
j   But by midday Sunday the last of these proposals had turned out to be of no further
use. So they said, 'Well, there is no money. We can't borrow money anywhere.
We'll just have to stop trading.' One reason why they had to stop trading is, of course,
being a company of limited liability, they had to bear in mind the provisions of
s 332 of the Companies Act 1948. We think that the industrial tribunal missed the
point of this section, which was referred to in the course of this hearing. It may

well be that it does not make it an offence until the winding-up is in process. Nevertheless anyone who knows anything about what might happen during the winding-up process would be very foolish indeed if he went on trading when there was no money in the kitty. All he is doing is building up the debt to the creditors which sooner or later a receiver has to meet. So that is the one area where in our view this industrial tribunal failed to give proper weight to one of the factors which must have operated in the mind of the employers.

The reason why the receiver who has now taken over this company in liquidation is most anxious that this decision should be tested is that there is what is called, in other circumstances, in these various statutes, an 'escape' clause. The escape clause is to be found in s 99(8) of the 1975 Act which reads as follows:

'If in any case there are special circumstances which render it not reasonably practicable for the employer to comply with any of the requirements of subsections (3), (5) or (7) above, the employer shall take all such steps . . . as are reasonably practicable in those circumstances.'

This case turns in the end on what is the meaning of 'special circumstances'. The word 'special' has acquired a significance in various statutes. One turns, simply for the sake of analysis and by way of analogy, to the use of the term 'special' in breaches of the Road Traffic Acts involving disqualification for holding a driver's licence. In that area it has been laid down that 'special' reasons have to be special to the facts of the case. In that area various categories of persons have been, and still are, excluded from relying on the exclusion granted to a person who is in breach of the law and is rightly to be disqualified, by a claim that the class of person or type of function gives rise to a special reason. Regrettably, in our view, and in this respect all three of us are unanimous, the approach of the industrial tribunal to the interpretation was far too generalised. The reason for that, we think, is to be found in their reliance on the decision of a Leeds industrial tribunal in *National Union of Dyers, Bleachers and Textile Workers v Job Beaumont & Son Ltd (in liquidation)*[1]. Broadly speaking what that case said, and broadly speaking what the industrial tribunal in this case said, was that insolvency on its own is not a special circumstance. Of course it is not. Nobody ever suggested that it was. What was said in the *National Union of Dyers* case, apparently, and seems to have been said in this case also, is that employers who are in the process of going into liquidation should not avoid the implications of the 1975 Act. In broad general terms, by way of generalisation, insolvency is normally something which is forseeable. It is perfectly obvious in a number of cases that an employer can be faulted, if he ultimately goes bankrupt and does not say to the appropriate trade union, 'The writing is on the wall. We may have to close down. We have got to start consulting and see what we can do about redundancies.' Or, as Mr Barry for the union has put it one might have a sensible employer and a sensible trade union official getting together to see if it was necessary to close down the business altogether, if it was possible to reorganise, and matters of that kind. Unfortunately this is precisely where, in our unanimous judgment, this industrial tribunal fell into error. They did not, in our view, apply the fact of insolvency to the special circumstances of this case. The special circumstances of this case were that maybe the employers were too optimistic, maybe they were unrealistic, but at least, as the industrial tribunal found, they were genuinely hoping right up to the last minute, Sunday midday, 24th October, that they could carry on trading.

Now it is urged, and urged most strongly, by counsel for the employers that you could hardly have a clearer case where there are special circumstances. On the other hand, we are not unanimous in saying that any reasonable tribunal applying its mind to the facts of this case, applying a sensible application of the words 'special circumstances', would necessarily have come to the same view or necessarily have come to a

_____
1 (28th October 1976) unreported

different view. All that is left in this case, in our view, is for a reassessment of whether
a or not these employers, through the receiver, have established that this was a case in
which the insolvency was not inevitable, that the insolvency might have been avoided,
and that it was not, therefore, reasonably practicable or even sensible for these
employers to have decided 90 days in advance that they would have to consult a trade
union as to whether or not insolvency was likely.

Consequently, and this may be really the only important point of principle in this
b case, it seems to us that this industrial tribunal, and, by implication, the Leeds industrial tribunal in *National Union of Dyers, Bleachers and Textile Workers v Job Beaumont &*
Son Ltd (in liquidation)[1], approached this question of the escape clause far too widely and
did not do justice to the situation where an employer might very well be hanging on
quite sensibly and quite properly and quite reasonably, and therefore in those circumstances has proved and established, as he has to do, that there are special circumstances
c in the case.

Accordingly, for the reasons we have given, we then turn to the other aspect to
which some reference has been made, namely is there to be spelled out from all the
facts of this case a clear-cut answer? In our view it is not possible. On the one hand, one
has the finding specifically stated that the employers were hoping up to the last
minute that they could carry on trading. On the other hand, one has in the same
d paragraph an observation, not a finding of fact, that 'ordinary prudent businessmen
should have foreseen the impending financial disaster well before it occurred'. Those
findings are in relation to whether or not there should be a protective award. None of
them, regrettably, is set out or analysed in the context of the interpretation and
meaning of the term 'special circumstances'. Consequently, although it may be that
in the end it will be a waste of time, and although it may be that it is going to cause a
e lot of extra trouble, it seems to all three of us that this is one of those cases in which,
within that very limited area, the industrial tribunal should think again. Applying
their minds to the guidance which we have given (that they must not make such
a blanket approach to 'special circumstances' in the context of insolvency as they
have done), we are confident that this industrial tribunal will be able quite shortly
and very simply, within that very small area of further investigation, to make a
f decision one way or the other whether or not the employers have satisfied a reasonable
tribunal that there were special circumstances in this particular case which enabled
them to avoid the consequences of the failure to consult with a representative of
the appropriate trade union. Within that area, and that area alone, we allow the
appeal and refer the case back for further investigation.

There is also another question which will have to be reconsidered, in our view, and
g that is the question of the amount of days as a protective award. We have not investigated this; we have not expressed a view one way or the other. Mr Barry for the
union obviously contends that it is right and reasonable; counsel for the employers has
said that it is too much in any event. Once this case has been re-opened along the lines
we have indicated, we think that the industrial tribunal might also consider at the same
time whether the period of 49 days' protective award is not excessive in the
h circumstances of this case.

Appeal allowed. Case remitted to the industrial tribunal for further consideration.

Solicitors: *Wilde, Sapte & Co* (for the employers); *Donne, Mileham & Haddock*, Brighton
(for the union).

j
Salim H J Merali Esq   Barrister.

---

1 (28th October 1976) unreported

Saggers v British Railways Board

EMPLOYMENT APPEAL TRIBUNAL
ARNOLD J, MRS D EWING AND MR J D HUGHES
12TH MAY 1977

Unfair dismissal – Determination whether dismissal fair or unfair – Dismissal for refusing to join trade union in accordance with union membership agreement – Refusal to join on grounds of religious belief – Personal religious belief – Personal belief as opposed to belief of religious sect to which employee belongs – Sect not proscribing trade union membership – Employee's conscience based on religious convictions not permitting him to join union – Whether employee's refusal to join union based 'on grounds of religious belief' – Trade Union and Labour Relations Act 1974, Sch 1, para 6(5) (as amended by the Trade Union and Labour Relations (Amendment) Act 1976, ss 1(e), 3(5)).

Unfair dismissal – Determination whether dismissal fair or unfair – Dismissal for refusing to join trade union in accordance with union membership agreement – Refusal to join on ground of religious belief – Conscientious objection based on moral belief – Whether conscientious objection based on moral belief justifying refusal to join union – Trade Union and Labour Relations Act 1974, Sch 1, para 6(5) (as amended by the Trade Union and Labour Relations (Amendment) Act 1976, ss 1(e), 3(5)).

In about 1938 the employee joined a trade union. Some time before 1958 he became a member of a religious sect known as Jehovah's Witnesses. The sect permitted membership of a trade union. In 1958 he left the union because of a dispute over his union dues. When the Trade Union and Labour Relations Act 1974 came into operation it became likely that the union and the employers would enter into a closed shop agreement. The employee therefore wrote to the employers, in October 1975, stating that he wished to be excused from joining a union because, by reason of his Christian convictions, his conscience did not permit him to join any union. The employers set up a panel to determine whether his employment should be terminated for refusal to join the union. Before the panel the employee confirmed that his religion did not proscribe union membership. He also stated that but for the dispute with the union in 1958 he might still have been a member of it. The panel refused to grant him exemption from joining the union on the ground of religious belief and he was dismissed from his employment. The employee applied to an industrial tribunal for compensation for unfair dismissal. The tribunal, while accepting that the employee's objection to joining a union was genuine and sincere, dismissed the application because they were not satisfied that his objection was grounded on 'religious belief', within para 6(5)[a] of Sch 1 to the 1974 Act, which they held to mean the beliefs of the religious body to which the employee belonged and not his personal religious beliefs. The employee appealed.

Held – (i) Under para 6(5) of Sch 1 to the 1974 Act, only conscientious objections to joining a union which were based on religious belief, and not conscientious objections

---

a   Paragraph 6(5), as amended, provides: 'Dismissal of an employee by an employer shall be regarded as fair for the purposes of this Schedule if—(a) it is the practice, in accordance with a union membership agreement, for employees for the time being of the same class as the dismissed employee to belong to a specified independent trade union, or to one of a number of specified independent trade unions; and (b) the reason for the dismissal was that the employee was not a member of the specified union or one of the specified unions, or had refused or proposed to refuse to become or remain a member of that union or one of those unions; unless the employee genuinely objects on grounds of religious belief to being a member of any trade union whatsoever, in which case the dismissal shall be regarded as unfair.'

based on moral belief, could render dismissal for refusing to join a union unfair (see
a p 23 *b* to *f*, post); dictum of Lord Thomson in *Hynds v Spillers French Baking Ltd* (1974)
9 ITR at 265 not followed.

(ii) To determine what was the employee's religious belief for the purpose of para
6(5) of Sch 1 to the 1974 Act, the tribunal were entitled to consider not only the
beliefs of the sect or denomination to which he belonged but also his personal religious
beliefs. Where the two differed and the tribunal were satisfied that the employee's
b personal religious beliefs were genuine, they were entitled to accept those beliefs as
his religious belief. Since the tribunal had not made a specific finding whether the
employee's refusal to join any union was grounded in his personal religious beliefs, as
opposed to the beliefs of Jehovah's Witnesses, the case would be remitted to an
industrial tribunal and the appeal allowed accordingly (see p 23 *j* to p 24 *b* and p 26
a b and *g*, post).

c

Notes
For dismissal pursuant to a closed shop agreement, see 16 Halsbury's Laws (4th Edn)
paras 626, 627.

For the Trade Union and Labour Relations Act 1974, Sch 1, para 6, see 44 Halsbury's
Statutes (3rd Edn) 1789.

d

Cases referred to in judgment
Hynds v Spillers French Baking Ltd (1974) 9 ITR 261, NIRC.
Newell v Gillingham Corpn [1941] 1 All ER 552, 165 LT 184, 39 LGR 191, 31 Digest
(Repl) 323, 2432.

e **Appeal**
This was an appeal by the employee, Mr L J Saggers, against the majority decision
of an industrial tribunal (chairman E G Lawrence Esq) sitting in London on 13th
September 1976 dismissing his claim for compensation on the ground that he had
been unfairly dismissed by his employers, British Railways Board ('the railways
board'), for refusing to join a trade union. The ground of appeal was that the tribunal
f had erred in finding that his objection to joining a union was not grounded on 'religious
belief', within para 6(5) of Sch 1 to the Trade Union and Labour Relations Act 1974,
because they had wrongly interpreted 'religious belief' as referring to the religious
beliefs of the organisation, congregation or other religious body to which the claimant
belonged, and not to his personal religious beliefs. The facts are set out in the
judgment of the appeal tribunal.

g

Rodger Bell for Mr Saggers.
F Marr-Johnson for the railways board.

ARNOLD J delivered the following judgment of the appeal tribunal: This is an
appeal by Mr Saggers from a decision of an industrial tribunal held at London on 13th
h September 1976. By that decision the tribunal rejected Mr Sagger's claim for compensation for unfair dismissal against his former employees, the British Railways
Board, the respondents to this appeal. The claim of unfair dismissal was a claim which
arose under para 6(5) of Sch 1 to the Trade Union and Labour Relations Act 1974,
as amended by the Trade Union and Labour Relations (Amendment) Act 1976, and
was based on the proposition that Mr Saggers had been dismissed from that employ-
j ment in relation to which it was, as indeed it was, the practice in accordance with a
union membership agreement for all the employees to belong to a specified independent trade union, the National Union of Railwaymen, and that, as indeed was the case,
the reason for his dismissal was that he was not a member of that union or had refused
to become a member of that union. The controversial aspect was the third proposition
that had to be fulfilled in order to bring the matter within the unfair dismissal

category under that paragraph, namely that Mr Saggers genuinely objected on grounds of religious belief to being a member of any trade union whatever. It is about that last matter that the controversy exists.

The matter really falls to be argued in two rather sharply distinct areas. One is how one should approach as a matter of the proper construction of para 6(5) of Sch 1 to the 1974 Act the task of finding out on which side of the line the particular case falls. The other is, having done one's best to come to a conclusion on that matter, to apply it to the facts of the case as found by the tribunal to see whether it can be said on which side of the line Mr Sagger's case falls or whether, if it cannot be so discerned, the matter will have to be reconsidered.

There are a number of matters arising on construction. The first arises not so much on the language of this particular paragraph, but on that language taken in comparison with the predecessor provision in the Industrial Relations Act 1971. The 1971 Act contained the corresponding provisions in s 9. It is not necessary to read the whole of that section. The corresponding phrase appears in s 9(1)(b) which relates to a worker who objects on grounds of conscience to being a member of a trade union. That was translated, when this provision of the 1971 Act, in common with many other provisions relating to dismissal, was re-enacted in Sch 1 to the 1974 Act, from the language of s 9 to the differing language of para 6(5) of Sch 1 and in particular, for grounds of conscience one finds grounds of religious belief. The tribunal said in its decision that it attached importance to that fact, and that view certainly contributed to the tribunal's conclusion.

There is much to be said for the view that, at any rate in very many cases, perhaps the overwhelming majority of cases, there will not in fact be any distinction between conscience as a factor forbidding or grounding an objection to belonging to a trade union or indeed doing anything else, and religious belief providing that ground. Indeed, in a case as long ago as 1941, *Newell v Gillingham Corpn*[1], a case concerning the word 'conscientious' as used in the phrase 'conscientious objector', Atkinson J, referring to the problem which he had to consider, whether the plaintiff in that case was a conscientious objector or not, said[2]:

'... it is perfectly plain that the plaintiff was not a conscientious objector in the true sense. He was a political conscientious objector. A true conscientious objector which is what Parliament had in mind, is one who on religious grounds thinks it wrong to kill and to resist force by force. He thinks that that is the teaching of Christ ...'

That seems to suggest two things: first of all, that in a proper context one can have someone who is not a religious conscientious objector nevertheless described as a conscientious objector, in that case, a political conscientious objector; but secondly, that in the ordinary way, if one is to describe someone as a conscientious objector, one would expect to find a religious basis for his objection.

In 1974, in *Hynds v Spillers French Baking Ltd*[3], which came before the National Industrial Relations Court where it was heard by Lord Thomson and two other members of the court, in the judgment in that case, which was a judgment in which the expression 'grounds of conscience' as used in s 9 in the passage which I have quoted from the 1971 Act was under consideration, the court said[4]:

'In our opinion "grounds of conscience" necessarily points to and involves a belief or conviction based on religion in the broadest sense as contrasted with personal feeling, however strongly held, or intellectual creed.'

1 [1941] 1 All ER 552
2 [1941] 1 All ER 552 at 553, 554
3 (1974) 9 ITR 262
4 9 ITR 262 at 265

Of course, if that is right, if it necessarily points to and involves a religious belief or
a religious conviction, and as between those two we see no distinction, the change of
language from 'grounds of conscience' to the phrase used in the 1974 Act would not be
of significance, because every ground of conscience would equate to a ground of
religious belief and it could hardly be suggested that there would be some ground
of religious belief which validly founded an objection which did not constitute itself
a ground of conscience. But with the greatest respect to the tribunal which decided
b *Hynds v Spillers French Baking Ltd*[1] we find it impossible to go the whole way with
that dictum. We can conceive, rare though they may be, that there may well be cases
in which conscience directs or forbids a certain course of action, be it joining a trade
union or anything else, having been brought to that point of conviction by moral or
ethical considerations which do not possess a religious content. An obvious example
might be provided by a consideration of an acknowledged atheist who is nevertheless
c a man of strong moral principle, whose mind is possessed by a conviction that it would
be ethically wrong to do such-and-such an act; and it seems to us that it could fairly
be said that to do that act would be against his conscience. Yet there is, by definition,
no religious motivation or causation involved in that conclusion or the formulation
of that conviction. One can conceive, perhaps more probably, of a man who whilst a
religious man in that he is a convinced believer in religious dogma or creed or idio-
d syncratic religious convictions forms a moral objection to a particular course of action
for reasons other than those which inform his religious life. If that is the right view,
then there is significance in a general way in the change of language as between the
1971 Act and the 1974 Act in that it would not be any objection based on grounds of
conscience which after the substitution of the 1974 Act would justify the refusal,
but only such objections based on grounds of conscience as could be discerned to be
e based also on religious grounds. There would, to put it another way, be some conscientious objections which did not qualify. That would be a matter of importance
in a case in which at the material time there was some reason to suppose that considerations other than religious considerations operated on the mind of the claimant,
the refuser, so as to cause him to refuse to join the union or to insist on leaving the
union. It would not be an important distinction in a case in which the only moral
f factors which informed his conscience could be religious factors. That would be a
matter for evidence in each case. That is the first point of construction which has been
ventilated, and that is our conclusion on that point.

The next matter for consideration has been this. In many cases, one might perhaps
go so far as to say in almost all cases, a man's religious belief is identifiable with the
accepted belief within a religious organisation to which he adheres. It therefore
g follows that in almost every case, in order to determine what is the religious belief
of the subject of the enquiry, it will be sufficient to enquire what is the body of religious
belief which is accepted within the denomination or sect to which he belongs. The
question is whether that is always and necessarily so. That question falls to be
answered by a consideration of the language which is used in para 6(5) of Sch 1 to the
1974 Act in the context of what common sense tells one are the available possibilities.
h The language which is used is this: 'the employee genuinely objects on grounds of
religious belief.' The objection which has to be taken into consideration quite simply
must be the objection of the employee. Then one has to consider on what that objection is grounded, that is religious belief. The word 'belief', first of all, seems to us to
suggest that which is believed by the person whose belief is under consideration; and
for that reason it seems to us that the word more naturally describes the content of
j intellectual acceptance by the person under consideration than an established body of
creed or dogma appertaining to himself as well as a number of other persons. In
almost every case, no doubt, the two are identical. In many cases it will not be easily
credible that a faithful adherent to a particular organisation has developed a body of

---

1 (1974) 9 ITR 262

belief which can truly and accurately be described as religious and which differs from
that generally accepted within that body. But it seems to us that if, perhaps in the   *a*
exceptional case, the tribunal, having considered the evidence of what the body
generally believes, and having considered the evidence of what the employee claims
to believe, is convinced that in spite of differences between the two the employee's
claim is truly and genuinely justified as being that which the tribunal is convinced
that he does really and truly believe, then there is no conceptual impossibility about
accepting that that is indeed his religious belief. But, of course, it cannot be sufficiently   *b*
stressed that these are practical matters to be decided by practical men. A very strong
pointer, no doubt, to the question what his religious belief really and truly extends to
will in almost every case be assisted with insight by establishing what is the body of
belief commonly held by the sect or denomination to which he belongs.

We have dealt with this matter rather widely on a general consideration because,
very reasonably, the railways board, who are parties to this appeal, have stressed   *c*
that their personnel representatives working with the corresponding union representatives have as a practical matter to decide these questions without, perhaps,
the refinements with which they are liable to be invested when debated before a
tribunal; and therefore it would be of immense assistance to them, if there could be
evolved some rule of thumb to make consideration of the matter easier than it might
otherwise be. They have suggested, understandably, that that simplification would be   *d*
achieved if their review of the matter could be confined to an examination of the
accepted creed of the body to which the employee belongs, so that they would have
to do no more than consider whether the rejection of trade union membership was
an integral part of that creed or not. We are sympathetic to the idea that that would
make their consideration of the matter simpler and more certain; but we cannot
find that that is a satisfactory procedure on the language of para 6(5) of Sch 1 to the   *e*
1974 Act.

From those general considerations we proceed to an examination of the details of
this appeal. What happened here was this, that in about 1938, fairly early in the very
long service which Mr Saggers had on the railway, he joined the National Union of
Railwaymen and he remained a member of that union for 20 years. In 1958, by which
time he had for some time already been a member of the denomination, if that is   *f*
the right word to use, to which he now belongs (that of the Watch Tower Society,
otherwise Jehovah's Witnesses), he fell out with the union over matters which had
nothing whatever to do with ethical, moral or religious considerations; it was all
about how much his arrears of subscription were when he was transferred from one
branch to another. And he left the union for those reasons. Later on, after he had
been away from the union for quite a time, in the run-up it is fair to say, to the enact-   *g*
ment of the 1971 Act the question of a closed shop was being agitated; it is unnecessary
to go into any greater detail than that. In January 1971, Mr Saggers had an interview
with the branch secretary of the union in the relevant area. He was accompanied by
Mr Lindars who was a personnel officer of the railways board, and at the end of a
discussion in which it was made plain that Mr Saggers had no intention of becoming
a member of any trade union, he was instructed by Mr Lindars, on behalf of his   *h*
employers, either to join the recognised trade union or to apply for exemption. And
he did apply for exemption by letter of 25th January 1971 in which he said, shortly
put, that he was so busy promoting the Christian faith, that was in the context of
membership of the Watch Tower Society, that he had no time to devote to other
matters and that that was why he was unwilling to join the union; and he wished to
claim exemption from joining it on that account. That was an indication of a refusal or   *j*
unwillingness to join the union with religious connections; but it is not claimed, and
could not be claimed, that that was an objection on the grounds of religious belief.
Thus stood the matter in 1971.

Then there came into operation the 1974 Act which for various reasons, which it is
not necessary to describe, made the proceeding of the union and railways board to a

closed shop situation more likely and more immediate. In that context the matter
a of Mr Sagger's continuing non-membership of the union came up again. On 14th
October 1975 Mr Saggers wrote to the area signal manager at Brighton, Mr Tubb,
obviously referring to what had happened in 1971, saying he thought the matter to be
settled on the basis, in effect, that he would pay the equivalent of his dues to a charitable
organisation, and ending up with these words: 'With my Christian convictions as
they are, my conscience does not permit my joining any union or political organisa-
b tion.' That created a problem which could only be solved by a conclusion as to
whether he could be persuaded to change his mind, or should be dismissed. The
matter was reported through the usual channels within the railways board and
in due course an internal body was set up, referred to as a 'panel', consisting of
representatives of the railways board and the relevant unions, to consider what the
position really and truly was with regard to Mr Saggers. That body sat on 18th
c March 1976. Five days before that, on 13th March, Mr Saggers again wrote about
the matter. He said this, in exactly the same terms as the previous letter, so far
as material: 'I therefore wish to be excused from joining. My Christian convictions
as they are, my conscience does not permit my joining any union or political organisation.' On 18th March the body sat and Mr Saggers appeared before it to explain the
position. A note is before the tribunal recorded by Mr Baldock, a manpower officer
d from regional headquarters of the railways board, in terms which are not challenged as
being an accurate record of what passed. This is what Mr Baldock wrote down:

> 'Mr. Saggers is a member of Jehovah's Witnesses. He confirmed: (a) his religion
> does not proscribe trade union membership and he thought some Jehovah's
> Witnesses were also trade union members; (b) but for a mix-up some years back
> which resulted in loss of trade union membership [that was 1958] he might still
> *e* be a trade union member today.'

The formal minute of that meeting, which is also in evidence, confirms those two
items.
    The conclusion which was reached by that panel was that exemption from joining
an appropriate trade union could not be granted in respect of Mr Saggers and accor-
f dingly he had to be dismissed. And dismissed he was, with effect from some date in
the following August, but his last participation in the events which led up to his
dismissal was his attitude as displayed on 18th March when he appeared before the
panel.
    Before the tribunal which heard this matter on 13th September 1976, Mr Saggers
agreed in cross-examination that he had made those points to which we have referred
g on 18th March. He was pressed as a result of that admission with the inconsistency
between the attitude thus displayed, that he might well still be a member of his
union, and his objections as now voiced. He said that he felt now, at the date of the
hearing, that he would have come out of the union five years ago, which seems to
suggest that the way it was being put then was that some time about 1971 he would
have found himself compelled by his conscience to resign from the union, had he
h still been a member, had the 1958 business not caused his membership to cease, which
seems to suggest that it was about that time that he was put into his adoption of an
attitude of conscience inconsistent with union membership.
    All those matters in the 1938 to 1958 history, the 1958 departure from the union, the
letter of 1971, the two letters of 1975 and 1976, the hearing before the panel in March
1976, and the cross-examination of Mr Saggers before the industrial tribunal, were in
j the minds of the members of the tribunal when they made their decision. In that
decision there is no specific conclusion as to whether or not Mr Saggers's objection
was really grounded on religious belief. The form which the decision took was this,
that the majority of the membership of the tribunal apparently reached the conclusion that religious belief had to be an identifiable belief shared by the employee
whose refusal was under consideration and by the other persons with whom he was

religiously associated. The dissenting member took the view that religious belief was personal to the man concerned and did not refer to the religious belief of the *a* organisation. We have indicated our acceptance of that dissenting view of the law. But because that was the way in which the matter was decided, there is no specific finding whether or not Mr Saggers's idiosyncratic conclusion of conscience was or was not one which was grounded in an idiosyncratic religious belief. We are invited on behalf of Mr Saggers, on the one hand, to say that there is enough material in the findings of the industrial tribunal to enable us to say on those findings that had they *b* taken the view of the law which we have taken they would be bound to have said, 'Yes, this refusal of Mr Saggers was grounded on religious belief'. We are urged on behalf of the railways board to say that, looking at the matter in general in relation to the findings, in relation to the primary material which the tribunal had before it, we could safely adopt the opposite conclusion and say that this was a case in which the industrial tribunal must have said that they were not satisfied that the objection was *c* grounded on religious belief. We have little difficulty in rejecting the latter course. In the course of their findings, after mentioning the content of the letter of October 1975, 'With my Christian convictions as they are, my conscience does not permit my joining any union', the tribunal proceeded thus:

> 'There were obviously discussions and the usual procedures were gone through *d* [between October and March] regarding Mr Saggers but Mr Saggers maintained his position and may we add here that we accept without question the genuineness and sincerity of the attitude adopted by Mr Saggers.'

That included an expression of attitude that his Christian convictions being what they were, his conscience did not permit him to join any union. It seems impossible in the face of that fact to say that, whatever exactly they meant by that passage, and *e* it is not very clear what they did mean, there is sufficient material to say with confidence that they would not have accepted the view that his objection was grounded on religious belief. On the other hand, we think that, given the varying attitude demonstrated by the history which we have recounted and given that the tribunal's acceptance of the genuineness and sincerity of Mr Saggers's attitude was not pin-pointed in relation to any particular expression of that attitude and did not proceed from any *f* examination in the context of that statement of what are to some extent inconsistencies in the history, we equally do not feel that we can with confidence ourselves supply the conclusion which is not arrived at by the industrial tribunal that this is a case in which Mr Saggers had demonstrated the accuracy of the proposition that his objections were grounded on religious belief. There is therefore, as we think, no alternative, unattractive as this is, to sending the matter back for a new conclusion by *g* the industrial tribunal on the basis of the guidance on the law which we have done our best to lay down.

Consideration has been given, with the parties, to whether the matter should be heard further by the same or by a differently constituted industrial tribunal. The parties were neither of them disposed to object to the same tribunal hearing it; indeed, great advantages were discerned on both sides in that respect. On the other *h* hand, because of the difficulties which this tribunal knows stand in the way of reconstituting an industrial tribunal, we include in our decision no direction that it shall be heard by the same tribunal.

Appeal allowed. Case remitted to an industrial tribunal.

j

Solicitors: *George D Ide & Co*, Chichester (for Mr Saggers); *Solicitor, British Railways Board*.

Salim H J Merali Esq Barrister.

a

Re O (a minor) (wardship: adopted child)

COURT OF APPEAL, CIVIL DIVISION
STAMP AND ORMROD LJJ
17th, 20th JUNE 1977

b
Ward of court – Care and control – Factors to be considered – Adopted child – Application to counter effect of adoption order – Dismissal of application in limine – Welfare of child first and paramount consideration – Circumstances justifying investigation by court – Application by child's natural mother – Mother and father having consented to adoption – Adoption of child by man – Intention that mother should continue to care for child after adoption – Mother living with adoptive father and caring for child – Adoptive father subsequently preventing mother from having contact with child – Mother starting wardship proceedings and seeking
c *care and control – Whether proceedings should be dismissed in limine.*

A child was born in 1964 to elderly parents who lived in poor financial circumstances in Ireland. The father was a good deal older than the mother and a chronic alcoholic. In 1969 O'B, a wealthy man, started taking an interest in the child and wanted to adopt him, but it was not then legally possible. In 1973, with the consent of both parents, O'B was appointed legal guardian. He brought the child to England and set up house
d with the child's mother, who eventually obtained a legal separation from the father. On 31st July 1974 an adoption order was made in favour of O'B with the consent of both parents. The child, the mother and O'B continued to live together in England. The mother and O'B were joint tenants of the house in which they lived but there was no sexual relationship between them. In February 1976 the mother went to Switzerland for treatment for back trouble. O'B suggested that she was also suffering from
e a mental disorder. When she returned in the summer of 1976, she telephoned the child and then received a letter from O'B saying that if she attempted to contact him an injunction would be sought against her. In September she issued an originating summons making the child a ward of court. At the hearing in March 1977 O'B and the Official Solicitor as guardian ad litem contended that the summons should be dismissed in limine without a hearing. The judge[a] dismissed the application, holding
f that, once made, an adoption order was final and the mother had failed to show that the case was an exceptional one which justified continuance of the wardship proceedings despite the adoption. The mother appealed.

Held – The question whether the wardship was to continue so that the case could be fully investigated or the proceedings dismissed in limine was to be determined entirely on the basis of what was in the best interests of the child. In the circum-
g stances there was an overwhelming case for investigating the matter further since the case was wholly exceptional in many respects, and in particular in the fact that it was plain on the evidence that it had been the intention of O'B and the mother that, after the adoption, she should continue to care for the child as if she were still the legal mother. The appeal would therefore be allowed (see p 30 *j*, p 31 *a* to *h* and p 32 *j*,
h post).
J v C [1969] 1 All ER 788 and *Re L (minors)* [1974] 1 All ER 913 applied.
Decision of Latey J [1978] 1 All ER 145 reversed.

Notes
For the court's jurisdiction over wards of court, see 21 Halsbury's Laws (3rd Edn) 216-217, paras 478, 479, and for cases on the subject, see 28(2) Digest (Reissue) 911-916,
j 2220-2248.
For the effect of an adoption order on rights of natural parents, see 21 Halsbury's Laws (3rd Edn) 238, para 514.

---

a [1978] 1 All ER 145

Cases referred to in judgments

Dunhill, Re (1967) 111 Sol Jo 113.

J v C [1969] 1 All ER 788, [1970] AC 668, [1969] 2 WLR 540, HL, 28(2) Digest (Reissue) 800, 1230.

L (minors), Re [1974] 1 All ER 913, [1974] 1 WLR 250, CA, Digest (Cont Vol D) 520, 1237a.

Appeal

On 31st July 1974 an adoption order was made in favour of the adoptive father, the child's mother and father having given their consent. On 22nd September 1976 the child's mother issued a wardship summons asking that the child should be removed from the care of the adoptive father and committed to her care and control. On 31st March 1977 Latey J[1] dismissed the summons. The wife appealed. The facts are set out in the judgment of Ormrod LJ.

Alan Ward for the mother.
Francis Gilbert for the adoptive father.
Donald Ratee QC for the Official Solicitor as the child's guardian ad litem.

ORMROD LJ delivered the first judgment at the invitation of Stamp LJ. This case had been described as unprecedented; in my judgment correctly. Equally it should not, I think, ever be cited as a precedent for anything. It is an extraordinary situation and one which is gravely disturbing. It is an appeal from an order made by Latey J[1] on 31st March 1977 by which he dismissed the mother's application that the child should remain a ward of court and that directions should be given in relation to his welfare. That in itself is a strange and unusual order, but the circumstances of this case, as I have already mentioned, are unprecedented.

I shall state the facts very shortly indeed. The father and mother of this child were married in 1950 and they had three children, two daughters who are now grown up, and this boy, who was born on 4th June 1964 and is now therefore 13. The father was a good deal older than the mother and they were in fact, on any view, elderly parents; he was very much the Benjamin of the family. It is said that the father, who is now dead, was ill and was a chronic alcoholic. They lived in Ireland apparently in conditions of considerable financial difficulty, the details of which do not matter.

In 1969 Mr O'B appeared on the scene, in circumstances about which we do not know very much, and showed a keen interest in this child. The father and mother in Ireland, after some time, discussed the possibility of Mr O'B adopting this little boy as he then was. By Irish law two parents, both living, apparently are not able to consent to the adoption of their child by anybody else, so adoption could not be pursued in Ireland. They eventually entered into some document which purported to appoint Mr O'B as the legal guardian of the child, and as such he took the child abroad for an extended holiday. Mr O'B apparently is a man of considerable financial means. The boy was said to be ill and very unhappy at his school. That was in 1973.

In May 1973 Mr O'B, with this boy, came to England, or set up house in England, the mother coming with them. Eventually she obtained a legal separation from her husband in Ireland, and on 31st July 1974 an adoption order was made by the High Court (in fact by Latey J as it turned out purely by chance) in favour of Mr O'B, the mother and the father both consenting to this adoption.

The extraordinary feature of this case is that the mother was at all times in contact with the boy, and in fact for most of the time living with the boy and Mr O'B, although there was no sort of sexual relationship between the two adults. They continued after the adoption order to live together in Devonshire. In fact the mother and Mr O'B

---

1   [1978] 1 All ER 145, [1977] 3 WLR 725

were joint tenants of the house in which they lived in Devon. That continued until
a February 1976 when the mother developed sciatica or a severe slipped disc or something of that kind and went to stay with a cousin of hers in Switzerland. I propose
to say nothing about the details of this. I think it would be quite undesirable to do so,
but it is sufficient to say this; that once she had gone to Switzerland, where she had
received some treatment, there were suggestions that she was also suffering from
some kind of mental upset at that time. Whether she was or not will be one of the
b issues in this case if it is ever heard. Certainly Mr O'B was making out that she was
suffering from some form of mental disorder. She eventually was treated by an
osteopath in Switzerland for her back, as far as one knows unsuccessfully, and she
came back to this country some time last summer. She was operated on and so far
as we know her back is now all right. But she has never succeeded in seeing the child
again. In fact after making one or two telephone calls to the child she received a
c letter from Mr O'B's solicitors saying that he would apply for an injunction against
her if she did not cease attempting to contact the child. It was in those circumstances
that on 22nd September 1976 she issued her originating summons making the child
a ward of court.

The wardship summons came on for hearing before Latey J on 22nd, 23rd and 31st
March 1977. At that hearing counsel for the adoptive father, Mr O'B, and the Official
d Solicitor as guardian ad litem, both submitted that the summons should be dismissed
in limine without a full hearing of the evidence, written and oral. The mother, of
course, argued that this was a case where there should be a full hearing and investigation. It could not be disputed that the court had jurisdiction to entertain the summons, notwithstanding the fact that Mr O'B was the adoptive parent and that the
mother had ceased to have, in law, the rights of a mother. Counsel for the mother,
e who appeared for her there as he has appeared for her here, contended that at the
very least she had a status in the wardship proceedings similar to the well meaning
stranger. In my view, in the context of this particular case, she had a great deal more
than that. But it was argued on behalf of Mr O'B, and I think by the Official Solicitor
also, that it would be very dangerous if the court were to entertain wardship proceedings following an adoption order; I quote from Latey J's judgment in open
f court[1]:

> 'Where an adoption order has been made, transferring to the adoptive parent
> all the rights and duties of parenthood and at the same time depriving the
> natural parent of all those rights and duties, it is an improper exercise of the
> court's discretion to continue the wardship application to a full investigation
> unless exceptional circumstances exist. For the natural mother it is contended
g that where minors are concerned the wardship jurisdiction prevails over all
> others. It is conceded that the court, while having that jurisdiction, has also a
> discretion to discontinue the wardship at any stage. In exercising the discretion
> whether or not to continue the wardship the court must regard the interest or
> welfare of the ward as the paramount consideration. This means that, with very
h rare exceptions, the court must hear the application in full as, if it does not, it
> deprives itself of the best opportunity of finding out what is the best for the
> ward.'

In support of the case for Mr O'B and for the guardian ad litem both counsel relied
on *Re Dunhill*[2] and the practice direction by Cross J.[3] That case establishes, and there
is no dispute about it, that in proper cases the court has power to determine a ward-
j ship application and dismiss it in limine.

The point that was argued on behalf of Mr O'B and the guardian ad litem was that

---

1 [1978] 1 All ER 145 at 147, 148, [1977] 3 WLR 725 at 728
2 (1967) 111 Sol Jo 113
3 [1967] 1 All ER 828, [1967] 1 WLR 623

where an adoption order has been made, an attempt by a natural parent to reassert parental rights through the medium of ward of court proceedings would be totally *a* inconsistent with the basis of adoption established by statute, namely that an adoption order once made is final, subject only to appeal out of time, and that to permit the use by a natural parent of wardship proceedings would enable a natural parent to undermine, and perhaps even reverse, the effect of an adoption order.

Counsel for the mother not unnaturally relied on the terms of s 1 of the Guardianship of Minors Act 1971 (which is merely repeating what has been in the successive *b* Guardianship of Infants Acts) which provides:

'Where in any proceedings before any court ... the custody or upbringing of a minor ... is in question, the court, in deciding that question, shall regard the welfare of the minor as the first and paramount consideration.'

The learned judge, in the event, accepted the submissions that were made on *c* behalf of Mr O'B and the guardian ad litem. The learned judge then went on to say this[1]:

'All this, to my mind, is readily reconcilable. Parliament has said that the adoption order is final with the sole reservation that wardship is available for use in the exceptional case where there are compelling reasons for its use. In simple *d* terms, people must recognise that an adoption order, once made, is in the vast majority of cases the end of the matter and it is in the interests of children that it should be. But there will be some rare cases where the courts should still be able to intervene.'

That in substance, I think, was the effect of that part of the learned judge's judgment that he gave in open court. He went on to elaborate it a little later on in his judgment *e* by saying this[2]:

'The proper approach I believe to be this. When there has been an adoption order and when a natural parent seeks to counter its effect by invoking the wardship jurisdiction, that parent must show that there is a strong prima facie case for an exceptional course to be taken before the court should embark on a *f* full enquiry with all that that entails in anxiety and distress, not to say expense, and encouragement to other parents who for one reason or another regret having given their consent or having had their consent dispensed with.'

Then he asked himself: 'Has the mother showed a strong prima facie case ...?' To that I will come back in a moment.

Speaking for myself, I agree with the learned judge's view, and indeed it is conceded, *g* that the wardship jurisdiction is not excluded altogether by the effect of an adoption order. I would however hesitate to put it on the footing that the judge did, using the word 'exceptional circumstances', for this reason alone: 'exceptional' is one of those words which means what people want it to mean and it does not help very much. The approach which I would personally favour is the approach which Buckley LJ *h* adopted in Re L (minors)[3] the case in which he reviewed all the existing authorities relating to kidnapping cases, and concluded in the light of Lord MacDermott's judgment in J v C[4] (which in my judgment remains the locus classicus for this type of case), that the question had to be resolved entirely on the basis of where the best interests of the child lay; and just as in some kidnapping cases it is possible for the court to know that the interests of the child require that the wardship should not be *j*

1   [1978] 1 All ER 145 at 149, [1977] 3 WLR 725 at 729
2   [1978] 1 All ER 145 at 151, [1977] 3 WLR 725 at 731
3   [1974] 1 All ER 913, [1974] 1 WLR 250
4   [1969] 1 All ER 788, [1970] AC 668

pursued any further than the making of an order returning the child to the jurisdiction
a of the court from which it has been taken, so in an application by a natural parent
against an adoptive parent the test should be whether or not it is in the best interests
of the child that the wardship should be carried through to its conclusion after a full
investigation, or whether on the facts as they are put before the court on both sides
and by the guardian ad litem the court can see that it is not in the interests of the child
to pursue the wardship proceedings further. Such would of course be the position
b in the ordinary normal adoption situation where the natural parent or parents have
parted with the child and have not seen the child at all and the adoptive parents (in
the plural) have assumed the parental role so far as the child is concerned. It is quite
obvious that if there was such a case and the natural parent brought such a case under
wardship proceedings, such a parent would have to make out an extremely strong
prima facie case to justify the matter proceeding further. But in this particular
c case, using whichever test is appropriate, whether Latey J's test of it being an exceptional
situation or the other one I personally favour, there appears to me to be an
absolutely overwhelming case for investigation. It is a wholly exceptional case on the
facts. It is wholly exceptional in many respects but there is only one of those exceptional
respects which I need refer to. That is this. It is plain on the evidence that was
before the learned judge in the court below (and the evidence in this respect comes
d from Mr O'B, the adoptive father, and it is confirmed by reference to the Official
Solicitor's report on the adoption proceedings) that it was the intention of Mr O'B
and the mother that she should remain de facto caring for this child as if she still
were the legal mother. That alone would take this case into the exceptional category,
and it would also take the case into the class in which the court must investigate the
mother's allegations in full. She may have ceased in law to be the mother by reason
e of the adoption, but in human terms her relationship with the child was entirely
unaffected by the adoption order. What happened was that the natural father was
replaced by Mr O'B. In fact to all intents and purposes this is exactly analogous to an
adoption by a natural parent and second spouse, which was a very familiar situation
until fairly recently.

So in those circumstances it is a matter of some surprise to me that it was suggested
f that this was not a proper case for investigation by the court in wardship proceedings.
The mother in this case has no alternative remedy if the arrangement which she had
clearly entered into with Mr O'B, expressly or by implication, is in some way interfered
with subsequent to the adoption order.

So in my judgment on the facts of this particular case this case should be treated
as if Mr O'B was the child's natural father and the mother the child's natural mother,
g and it should be dealt with accordingly; and nice legal points about adoptive parents
and natural parents abandoning their parental rights should be treated, since we are
dealing with the welfare of a child, as irrelevant. On the facts of this case there is,
in my judgment, an overwhelming case for enquiry. I say no more about the facts
except to say this. Speaking for myself the case fills me with anxiety. I hope that no
adoption in such circumstances ever takes place again. It is a most dangerous situation
h and the result seems to have been, from the point of view of the child, enough to
justify the expression 'very grave anxiety'. Just how grave the anxiety is can be seen
from certain facts which emerged in this court this morning; namely that since
Latey J's order, Mr O'B has taken this child abroad to a destination which is unknown
to his instructing solicitors or counsel, and we have now no idea where this child is,
what is happening to him or anything else. It is true that Mr O'B is not in contempt
j of court because Latey J dismissed the wardship summons. Had he not dismissed the
wardship summons of course Mr O'B would have been in contempt. He will now be
in contempt because this court will reverse the judge's order and direct that the
wardship shall continue and a full and proper investigation be carried out as soon as
possible in the circumstances. The fact that Mr O'B has removed this child from the
country in these circumstances and while this appeal was pending is enough in itself

to justify the most rigorous enquiries in the interests of the child. Moreover, so far as the evidence goes, and there is nothing to contradict it on Mr O'B's side, there is nothing to suggest that the child is at school or has been at school or has been receiving any education except from him, if he has been receiving any education at all, since 1975. It is a situation which is almost unbelievable. In those circumstances in my judgment the appeal must be allowed, the wardship must continue and the matter must be heard as soon as possible by another judge of the Family Division. In the meanwhile this court in the circumstances as they are should give certain directions.

The first direction the court gives is that Mr O'B be directed and informed either by the press or personally through his solicitors, if they can communicate with him, that the child is to be brought back into the jurisdiction within seven days from today. The second matter is this. In the view of this court the judge hearing this wardship summons will certainly require to see, as we have done, the adoption file, and I say no more about that except that it makes it abundantly clear that the continued presence of the mother in this child's life was undoubtedly one of the factors operating in the mind of the judge when he made the adoption order. That file should be available to the judge when he hears the case. We think, although we do not order, that the mother should file a full medical report dealing with both her physical and mental health, and in relation to that I would suggest that any doctor who is called on to make a report should be provided with the whole of the file in this case to read, and his attention might be specifically directed, among other things, to the local doctor's letter dealing with his prescription of anti-depressant drugs to the mother. And of course he ought to see Dr Newton's report and Dr Prince's report on the child. We also think that arrangements should be made, if it is possible to make them, for the child to be examined by an independent psychiatrist as soon as possible. Prima facie that would be at Mr O'B's expense. Such an independent psychiatrist would most conveniently, I think, be found by asking the President of the Royal College of Psychiatrists to nominate someone for the purpose, because it seems to me absolutely essential that the court has before it a totally independent assessment of this boy's present state, and as to his educational position (he is alleged to be dyslexic, and one of the matters in which the court might be interested is finding out whether he is in fact dyslexic or whether he is just backward). Be that as it may those are the steps which must be taken as soon as possible in this case.

I would therefore allow the appeal and make that order accordingly.

STAMP LJ. I agree. In view of the course which we propose to adopt it is undesirable that I should add more than a few words to what Ormrod LJ has said. I would only say this. In the first place just as a natural father may not always be the best person to have the care and control of his child, so the same applies in the case of an adoptive father. Secondly I accept that one should not allow the wardship procedure to be invoked at the suit of a 'stranger' (and I say in parenthesis that I put that word in inverted commas without defining it) whether on an application made for the purpose of removing the care of a child from a natural or adoptive parent unless it be shown that there is good enough ground for invoking the jurisdiction in the interests of the child. Thirdly, like Ormrod LJ, I would emphasise that the adoption in the instant case was made on the footing that the mother was going to live under the same roof as Mr O'B and care for the adopted child.

I agree with the order suggested by Ormrod LJ.

Appeal allowed.

Solicitors: *Ward Bowie* (for the mother); *Hill & Coxe*, Exeter (for the adoptive father); *Treasury Solicitor.*

A S Virdi Esq Barrister.

a

R (B M) v R (D N) (child: surname)

COURT OF APPEAL, CIVIL DIVISION
STAMP AND ORMROD LJJ
30TH JUNE, 1ST JULY 1977

b   *Divorce – Custody – Change of surname – Relevance – Mother having custody of three of four children of family – Custody of fourth child subsequently given to mother – Mother adopting surname of man with whom she was living – Children known in neighbourhood by his name – Father appealing against order giving custody of fourth child to mother – Whether change of surname relevant – Matrimonial Causes (Amendment) Rules 1974 (SI 1974 No 2168), r 92(8).*

c   *Court of Appeal – Practice – Documents to be lodged by appellant – Duty of solicitor to lodge documents relevant only to issue on appeal – RSC Ord 59, r 9(1).*

The father and mother were married and had four children, two girls and two boys. In July 1974 the mother left the father and the children and went to live with W, a
d   soldier. She was unable to take the children with her as she could not obtain accommodation for them. The father found a house for himself and the children and was joined there by Mrs G and her young son. In 1976, shortly before the mother obtained a decree of divorce, the father handed over the children to her, as Mrs G was expecting a baby and felt unable to look after them as well as her own child during her pregnancy. C, the younger boy, was disturbed by the change and was returned to the
e   father. The mother was given custody of the three other children and the father was given custody of C. The army authorities gave the mother and W married quarters in an army camp. She applied for custody of C, who was then aged 6½. The judge, after hearing the witnesses and reading the welfare officers' reports, found, inter alia, that the father and Mrs G were bringing up C quite adequately and that he was happy with them; that the accommodation they provided was not as good as that
f   proposed by the mother; that the mother was more aware of the intellectual and emotional needs of the children than Mrs G was, and was firmer with them; that the three children living with the mother were happy and that she was making every effort to help them readjust; that W was extremely fond of the children and would make it clear to them that he was not their real father and ensure that they remembered that their real father was alive and very fond of them; that the relationship between the mother and W was stronger than that between the father and Mrs G;
g   and that C enjoyed visiting his mother and W and the other children and could be very happy living with them. The judge concluded that, although the short-term result of removing C from the custody of the father might be traumatic, it would be better in the long run for C to live with his own brother and sisters as otherwise he might, in the future, resent having received different treatment from them by being
h   brought up in a different family. The judge accordingly ordered that custody of C be given to the mother. The father appealed, contending, inter alia, that the order should be set aside as the judge's finding that W would always be ready to remind them of their real father was contradicted by the fact, of which the judge might not have been aware, that the three other children were known in the army camp by W's name.

j   **Held** – The fact that the three other children were known by W's name rather than their father's had no significance as regards the characters of W and the mother. It was merely more convenient that they should be known by W's name in the camp in which they were being brought up where he was the head of the family. On the evidence the judge had taken into account all that could properly be said in support

of the father's claim and there were no grounds for interfering with his decision.
It followed that the appeal would be dismissed (see p 37 *e f* and p 38 *d e* and *j*, post).   *a*

Per Ormrod LJ. It may be that r 92(8)*ᵃ* of the Matrimonial Causes (Amendment)
Rules 1974 about changing names has been drawn in a wider sense than the draftsman
intended. It was directed to preventing parents with custody or care and control
orders changing children's names by deed poll or by some other formal means,
and was not intended to cause difficulty to school authorities or to embarrass children
who do not wish to be known by a surname other than their mother's (see p 39 *a* to *c*, post).   *b*

Per Stamp LJ. It is the duty of a solicitor preparing a case for an appeal to comply
with RSC Ord 59, r 9(1)(i), by ensuring that documents lodged by the appellant
are relevant to issues on the appeal (see p 39 *e*, post).

Notes

As to the exercise of the court's discretion in making a custody order, see 13 Halsbury's   *c*
Laws (4th Edn) para 809, and for cases on custody, see 27(2) Digest (Reissue) 669-673,
5073-5103.

Appeal

On 11th June 1975 the wife ('the mother') petitioned for a divorce on the ground that
the marriage had irretrievably broken down in that the husband ('the father') had   *d*
behaved in such a way that she could not reasonably be expected to live with him.
On 14th April 1976 she was granted a decree nisi in the Barnet County Court by his
Honour Judge Eric Stockdale, who ordered that the four children of the family should
not be removed from her care and control until further order. On 30th June that
order was varied by his Honour Judge Lonsdale who ordered that the three eldest
children of the family should remain in her custody with reasonable access to the   *e*
father, and that the custody of the fourth child, C, should be given to the father,
with reasonable access to the mother. The decree nisi was made absolute on 23rd
July. On 11th February 1977 a custody order was made by Judge Lonsdale in similar
terms to that of 30th June 1976. The mother, wishing to obtain custody of C as
well, appealed against it. On 4th May 1977 the Court of Appeal (Lawton and Bridge
LJJ) ordered the matter to be transferred to the High Court in London for hearing   *f*
by a High Court judge and that the application for custody of C be heard de novo.
On 16th June Bush J ordered that the custody of C should be given to the mother.
On 23rd June the father appealed and applied ex parte for a stay of execution of
the order of 16th June pending the appeal. The application was refused by the
Court of Appeal (Stamp and Ormrod LJJ). The facts are set out in the judgment of
Stamp LJ.   *g*

Michael Evans QC and *Roger Garfield* for the father.
Anthony Temple for the mother.

STAMP LJ. This is, in my view, a hopeless appeal, in which counsel has said all
that could possibly be said on behalf of the father's claim. The appeal is an appeal   *h*
from an order of Bush J made on 16th June 1977, whereby the custody of the child C,
who was born on 12th December 1970 and is the youngest of four children of the
parties to the marriage between the father and mother, was committed to his mother.
His age is 6½.

It is convenient, I think, to state at the outset that the other three children were
at the time of the hearing before the learned judge and had been for some time in   *j*

---

a Rule 92(8) provides: 'Unless otherwise directed, any order giving a parent custody or care
and control of a child shall provide that no step (other than the institution of proceedings
in any court) be taken by that parent which would result in the child being known by a new
surname before he or she attains the age of 18 years or, being a female, marries below that
age, except with the leave of a judge or the consent in writing of the other parent.'

the custody of the mother under an order of the court made on 14th April 1976,
a an order made immediately after the granting of the decree nisi in the case.

The father, who was then married, met the mother in 1963. They commenced
living together in 1965 after the mother had become pregnant. In March 1965 the
child A was born, she is now 12; in July 1966 the child A was born, he is now ten; and
on 16th December 1967 the mother and father married, the father's marriage having
in the meantime been dissolved. On 24th April 1969 a girl M was born, now aged
b eight, and then along came C on 12th December 1970.

The learned judge in the court below found that by March 1974 the marriage had
broken down. While the father was a serving soldier in Northern Ireland with his
unit, the mother committed adultery with another serving soldier, Sergeant W,
and she is now living with Sergeant W, at the present moment I think in Bovington
Camp. Having discovered the adultery, the father was not pleased and beat her up
c on more than one occasion, to the extent that she suffered personal injuries.

There is, as I understand it, some disagreement as to the details of the subsequent
events, which do not, I think, matter much, but the findings of the judge were these.
On 8th July 1974 the mother left the matrimonial home, which was the married
quarters at Mill Hill, and the children were divided, the two eldest went to the father's
sister and the two youngest to the grandparents in South Wales. The mother agreed
d to the children going to the relatives, but she thought all the children were going to
the grandparents in Wales and would not, therefore, be split up. However, that was
not possible. The mother was unable to provide accommodation herself for the
children, because she was setting up with Sergeant W and could not obtain married
quarters at that time. She could not continue to live with the father, and was under
pressure to leave the married quarters where she had been.

e The father was most anxious to get the children together, so the judge found, and
he bought himself out of the army, and in October 1974 was living in a council house
at Maerdy in Glamorgan with all four children. His sister lived nearby and assisted
with the care of the children, particularly when the father was at work. Then in July
they moved to another council house in the Rhondda and they were joined by a
Mrs C G, and she had a young child. Then there was a further move in April 1976,
f when the father moved to another address in the Rhondda.

The judge found that for a period of almost two years the mother, who was living
in a bedsitter in Farnham with Sergeant W, saw the children only twice, namely once
in 1974 and once in 1975. I understand on each occasion it was about Christmas time.
The learned judge found that although the mother might have kept away from the
children because she feared violence, he did not think that that would have of itself
g deterred her from seeing the children, and he found that what she really feared was
a continuation of rows in front of the children, and also, the judge thought, a feeling
of helplessness at not being able to offer the children a home herself discouraged her
from visiting them.

On 11th June 1975 the mother presented a petition for divorce based on unreasonable conduct. The father filed an answer and sought a decree on the ground of
h adultery, but eventually the wife's petition went undefended on 14th April 1976,
when she was granted a decree nisi on the ground of the father's conduct. At the
same time, immediately thereafter, I suppose, his Honour Judge Eric Stockdale decided
that all four children should remain in the care and control of the mother, and he
directed a welfare officer's report. The reason that was made was because, so the
learned judge found, about a week earlier on 8th April the father had arrived at
j short notice at Farnham, where the mother was in a flat with Sergeant W, in order
to deliver to the wife all the children. The reason for this was that Mrs G was pregnant
of a child (subsequently born in July 1976) and simply could not face the prospect of
coping with the four children as well as her own young child while she was pregnant.
The three elder children remained with the mother thereafter and have remained
with her down to this day. C, the boy with whom we are concerned, on the other

hand, was disturbed, and he was returned to South Wales to his father and lived with and still was living with his father and Mrs G at the time the matter came before *a* Bush J. The army authorities had at some time granted the mother and Sergeant W married quarters, and the three elder children are, as the judge found, and I quote his words, 'living with their mother and Mr W in delightful surroundings at Boving-ton Camp in Dorset'.

Each party before the learned judge criticised the other's care of the children. The judge was, however, satisfied that from C's point of view both parents and their *b* co-habitees cared for the children in their case as well as could be expected. There was an allegation that the father had been violent against Mrs G in the presence of C, but the judge, while expressing the view that there was an element of violence in the father's make-up, found that that particular allegation was not established, and, more important, he found that the element of violence in the father's character did not have the effect of making the children afraid of him or unhappy; and the judge *c* quoted, as I would do, a passage in the welfare officer's report, dated 30th November 1976, in which Mr Rees (Mr Rees being the welfare officer) said:

'I have been able to speak to [C] both on his own for a short time and for a larger period in the company of Mrs G, who he [that is to say, the boy] referred to as his mother. Conversation seemed to be quite spontaneous and there were no indications of his having been rehearsed. [C] impressed as being a well adjusted *d* child despite the unsettled period that he has experienced and he presented as being bright and alert and having a cheerful personality. Observation of the interaction between Mrs G and [C] suggested that there is a great deal of warmth in their relationship and to date [C] seems unaffected by the birth of his step-brother. Indeed he talked quite proudly of the baby and it is not felt that [C] has been significantly deprived of attention by the arrival of [the new baby]. *e* Although [C] indicated that he would like to see his brother and sisters again, his feelings at this stage seem to be dominated by the bond with his father. He talked with great affection of the occasions he sits on his father's knee and of how he wants to grow up to be a soldier like his father. It is realised that [C] is not yet 6 years of age and thus is hardly in a position to make rational judgments. Nonetheless he appears to be generally quite contented in the present situation *f* and the impression gained is that an enforced separation from his father at this stage could well prove to be unsettling for him, at least in the short term, although he has shown such resilience in the past that it is difficult to predict whether such a course of action would have any long-term effect upon him.'

As the judge remarked, that was not a picture of a child who was unhappy with his *g* father.

The judge found that the accommodation provided by the father was not as good as that proposed by the mother, but was adequate. He pointed out that C does not remember any home except the Rhonnda Valley. The judge found that the father was genuinely fond of his children, that he was a strong personality, that Mrs G, who was aged about 22, was not a strong personality, but the judge was satisfied from the *h* physical point of view she had brought and was bringing up C quite adequately.

The judge thought, as far as discipline was concerned, that Mrs G was not as firm as the mother and that this resulted in C appearing to be unruly when he stayed with his mother. He found that the child of Mrs G and C were apparently very close, and what was said by the father was that C really looked on the two children of Mrs G as his brothers. On the other hand, remarked the judge, the three children with the *j* mother missed C and looked forward to their meetings during access, and C also looks forward to the meetings. He found that the mother (who was in her early thirties) was a forceful, strong-minded personality, 'tigrish in the defence of her young' were the words he used, and this is important; he took the view that the mother was more aware of the intellectual and emotional needs of the children than was

Mrs G. He pointed out that she had impressed such social workers as had dealings
a with her. He quoted in particular a report by Mr Whitfield (another welfare officer),
in the course of which it was said:

> '[The mother] has established such a good relationship with the children in a
> short time [that is, the three children who stayed with Mrs R after April] that
> I feel it must have a good and secure foundation prior to the separation. The
> three children with her are clearly happy and progressing well, and I have been
b impressed by the thoughtful care and effort—as well as the energy—she has
> directed towards helping them readjust.'

That again seems to me to be an important finding.

The judge found regarding Sergeant W that he was extremely fond of the R children,
had made financial sacrifices to assist in their upbringing as far as he could, was a very
c solid type, I quote the words of the judge, 'and very slow to anger'. The judge was
satisfied that Sergeant W would always be ready to remind the children that he was
not their real father, but their real father was alive and well and very fond of them.
The judge thought he would make it a point of honour to ensure that any of the
children that were with him continued to remember and respect the father.

I think it is convenient to mention that the point was made by counsel for the
d father in the course of his submissions in this court that the judge might not have
been aware at that point or had it present to his mind at that point in his judgment
that the three elder children, now in the camp where they are, are known officially
by the surname of W, and it was suggested that this rather tended to counter the
judge's findings that Sergeant W would always be ready to remind the children that
he was not their real father, and a good deal of play was made by counsel for the
e father regarding this change in the way the children are known in the camp. I am
bound to say I do not think that the fact that the three elder children are known as W
now in Bovington Camp really signifies anything as regards the characters of Sergeant
W and the mother. I think that too much attention is paid to these matters of names
of children, the names by which they are known, on some occasions at least, and it
must be most convenient that they should be known as W in the camp in which they
f are being brought up where Sergeant W is the head of the family.

The judge went on to say that he found the relationship between the mother and
Sergeant W was very strong indeed, and he regarded it as a stronger relationship
than that between the father and Mrs G, and was satisfied that C could be very
happy living with his mother and Sergeant W and his brother and sisters. Taking a
long-term view, of course, that is a very important finding. On the other hand, the
g judge recognised that in the short-term, as one must, the change over would be
very traumatic indeed. As the mother recognised, there was a risk, said the judge,
that C would have psychological problems similar to those experienced by the brother
A at one time when he left his mother. The temptation, said the judge, to leave C
where he is at present and apparently happy is very strong, and one looks also,
before making a final decision, at the last report of the welfare officer, the report of
h Miss Nowell, made on 13th June 1977. 'It is really', said the learned judge, 'with her
assessment of C that I am most concerned.' She said:

> '[C] I first saw in his father's home. He was immediately friendly and talkative.
> At this time he had recently had a day out with his mother, his brother and
> sisters . . . At this time [C] was expecting to go to Dorset with his father the fol-
j lowing day and was looking forward to seeing A and the girls once again. He
> was aware that his mother was anxious for him to live in Dorset and he told me
> firmly that he did not wish to leave his present home, Mrs G and his two "little
> brothers" [C] appeared to be very much at home in these surroundings and ran
> in and out of the house playing happily during my visit. When on the second
> occasion I saw [C] at his mother's home, he again appeared to be at ease and was

friendly and talkative. [The mother] maintained there had been no indication
of upset when he first came to her and, apart from somewhat unruly behaviour, *a*
had fitted in happily with the family. He had at this time asked his mother
whether he need return to Wales and indicated that he wished to stay with her.
On this occasion I spoke with [C] on his own. Although he talked quite happily
about arrangements for his future, it was very apparent that he was not really
fully appreciative of the situation and had very mixed views regarding what
might happen to him in the future. At one moment he was talking quite happily *b*
of going to school with [M] and of what he would do when he lived in Dorset,
but the next moment he was indicating that he did not wish to leave his father.'

There is a report from the headmistress at the school in the Rhonnda, who described
C as always being clean and tidy and well kept, a happy and contented little boy and
an able pupil who progressed well.

c

Then the learned judge came to answer the vital question whether to leave things as
they are where the boy is being brought up well and is apparently happy or whether
there should be a change because of the importance of children of one family being
brought up together. He pointed out that in the short-term the answer would be to
leave him where he is, but the judge, looking at the long-term, which it is necessary
to look at, came to the conclusion that in years to come, if C was brought up separately *d*
from his brother and sisters, he would resent the different treatment that he would
of necessity receive by being brought up in a different family.

Having heard the witnesses and read a number of welfare officers' reports, the
judge came down on the side of his mother. In doing so it appears to me that, in
the course of his very careful judgment, and a judgment which was far from un-
sympathetic to the father, he has taken into account all that could properly be said *e*
in support of the father's claim. I find it quite impossible to say that he, who had all
the advantages which we have not got, came to a wrong conclusion; in fact, I think it
was probably the right conclusion. One could certainly not be satisfied that it was a
wrong conclusion.

I perhaps might add this, that following the judge's order, the judge having ordered
C to be handed over on 23rd June, the matter came before this court on an application *f*
for a stay of the order, which was refused. On the following day a senior probation
officer of the Dorset County Council visited the mother's home and saw C, who
seemed quite content and to be playing with his toys most of the time the probation
officer was in the house. The probation officer, in a letter to Miss Nowell written on
28th June, remarked that on that occasion he tended to be boisterous and rather
excitable, but 'I would not say that he showed any sign of disturbance. He appears *g*
to be quite content to be in the company of his mother.' Then the probation officer
went on to say (as I said, this letter was written on 28th June):

> 'He commenced at Bovington First School yesterday and I telephoned the
> headmaster of that school, Mr Davies, today. The headmaster then asked [C's]
> form teacher for a report on [C's] behaviour, without telling him the reason for
> this. The form teacher reported back as follows: "[C] has settled down very *h*
> well and is responsive. His reading ability appears to be good and he is well
> adjusted for his age. No signs of disturbance in the classroom".'

That is somewhat reassuring, I think, of course, suggesting perhaps that the judge's
fears as to the immediate effect of the transfer may have been exaggerated, but, as I
have said, I find it quite impossible to accept that the judge came to the wrong *j*
conclusion, and I would dismiss the appeal.

ORMROD LJ. I have come to exactly the same conclusion and do not wish to add
anything at all to what Stamp LJ has said, except this. There has been in this case a
great deal of litigation and there may be some danger that litigation will become

chronic in this family, and I am very anxious to discourage it, if I can. Counsel for
a the father drew attention in the course of his submissions to this name problem,
and that, of course, is now a pregnant problem, or could be. All I want to say about
it is this: it may be, I say no more than that, that r 92(8) of the Matrimonial Causes
(Amendment) Rules 1974[1], the new rule about changing names, has been drawn in a
wider sense than the draftsman intended. I remember that at the time it was directed
to preventing parents with custody or care and control orders changing children's
b names by deed poll or by some other formal means, but, unfortunately, it now seems
to be causing a great deal of trouble and difficulty to school authorities and to children,
and the very last thing that any rule of this court is intended to do is to embarrass
children. It should not be beyond our capacity as adults to cope with the problem
of dealing with children who naturally do not want to be picked out and distinguished
by their friends and known by a surname other than their mother's, if they are thinking
c about it at all. It is very embarrassing for school authorities and indeed to the court
if efforts have to be made to stop a little girl signing her name 'W' when it really is 'R'.
We are in danger of losing our sense of proportion. All one can say in this particular
case is that one can understand the situation, which is not at all unusual, and I just
hope that no one is going to make a point about this name business, in other words,
to treat it as a symbol of something which it is not. There is nothing in this case that
d suggests that the mother or Sergeant W want to make a takeover bid for this family
from the father and turn these children into their own children, nothing at all.
Therefore, I hope that it can be treated as counsel in his exchanges with the learned
judge below observed, 'This is a peripheral matter.' I would endorse that strongly.

e **STAMP LJ.** I have to add a postscript to my judgment and I hope this will be
reported. It is the duty of solicitors preparing cases for an appeal to consult, if they
do not know them, the provisions of RSC Ord 59. RSC Ord 59, r 9(1) and the notes
relative to that rule in the Supreme Court Practice[2] appear to have been wholly
ignored in preparing documents relevant to the issues on this appeal. We have before
us three bundles containing respectively 80, 55 and 144 pages. Most, perhaps all, of the
f 80 page bundle, headed 'Pleadings, Orders and Welfare Officers Reports' might, I
suppose, have been required for the purposes of this appeal, and I have no quarrel
with that bundle having been prepared for the purposes of the appeal. The other two
bundles appear to me not to be 'relevant', and I am quoting the word in RSC Ord 59,
r 9(1)(i), to the issues on this appeal, and in directing legal aid taxation on both sides,
this court also orders that the attention of the taxing master be directed to the remarks
g which I have made.

Appeal dismissed.

Solicitors: *Theodore Goddard & Co*, agents for *Morgan, Bruce & Nicholas*, Porth, Rhondda
Valley (for the father); *Gregory Rowcliffe & Co*, agents for *Humphries, Kirk & Miller*,
h Wareham, Dorset (for the mother).

A S Virdi Esq   Barrister.

---

1   SI 1974 No 2168
2   Supreme Court Practice 1976, vol 1, pp 862-864, paras 59/9/1-4

Murray (Inspector of Taxes) v Goodhews   *a*

COURT OF APPEAL, CIVIL DIVISION
BUCKLEY, EVELEIGH LJJ AND SIR JOHN PENNYCUICK
21st, 22nd, 23rd NOVEMBER 1977

b

Income tax – Profits – Trading receipts – Voluntary payment – Motive of payer in making payment – Relevance – Unsolicited payment to trader – Motive of payer to acknowledge long and friendly relationship with trader and to maintain goodwill and image in industry – Trading relationship between payer and trader continuing but payment not linked to future relationship – No disclosure by payer of basis on which payment calculated – No bargaining or negotiation between parties over amount – Taxpayer holding public houses on tied tenancies from payer – Termination of tied tenancies by payer – Ex gratia payments made to taxpayer in consequence of termination – Whether payments chargeable to tax as profits arising or accruing from taxpayer's trade.

c

The taxpayer company ('Goodhews') was the tenant of a number of tied public houses owned by another company ('Watney'). In 1968 Watney decided to terminate   *d*
13 tenancy agreements with Goodhews over a period of two years as from January 1969. Although there was no provision in any of the tenancy agreements that Watney should give more than three months' notice of termination in respect of any of the relevant tenancies, they nevertheless chose to make voluntary payments, amounting to £81,651, to Goodhews during the accounting periods ending on 31st March 1970 and 31st March 1971. Goodhews was assessed to corporation tax on the basis *e*
that the payments represented compensation for loss of profits arising from the loss of the tenancies and accordingly were profits or gains arising from its trade. On appeal, the Special Commissioners found (a) that when the representative of Watney had visited Goodhews to explain the change of policy he had mentioned that there would be an ex gratia payment, but had said nothing about the amount or basis of calculation; (b) that there had been no bargaining or negotiation about *f*
the amount of the payments; (c) that Watney had made the payments to acknowledge a long and friendly association with Goodhews and to maintain its name, goodwill and image in the brewing industry; (d) that the payments were not linked with any future trading relationship between the parties; and (e) that they had been computed by reference to the rateable values of the relevant public houses and had no connection with the profits which any of those houses had earned. On *g*
the basis of their findings, the commissioners held that the payments were not chargeable to tax as trading receipts and on appeal their decision was affirmed by Walton J. The Crown appealed, contending that the payments were trading receipts in the hands of Goodhews since, although not made in pursuance of any legal obligation, they constituted compensation made in recognition of the injury suffered by Goodhews in consequence of the interruption of their trade.   *h*

Held – Every case of a voluntary payment had to be considered on its own facts to ascertain the nature of the receipt in the recipient's hands, for it was the character of the receipt that was significant; the motive of the payer was only significant so far as it bore, if at all, on that character. On the findings of fact made by the commissioners, in particular the findings that there had been no disclosure by Watney to *j*
Goodhews of the way in which the payments had been calculated, that there had been no subsequent negotiation about the payments, that the amount of the payment had had no connection with the profits earned by Goodhews, and that the calculation had not been linked with any future trading relationship between the parties, the commissioners had been fully justified in finding that the sums paid to Goodhews

were not trading receipts. Accordingly the appeal would be dismissed (see p 42
a *f g*, p 46 *c* to *h*, p 47 *b* and *g* to p 48 *a d* to *h* and p 49 *a* to *c*, post).

    Chibbett (Inspector of Taxes) v Joseph Robinson & Sons [1924] All ER Rep 684, *Walker (Inspector of Taxes) v Carnaby, Harrower, Barham & Pykett* [1970] 1 All ER 502 and *Simpson (Inspector of Taxes) v John Reynolds & Co (Insurances) Ltd* [1975] 2 All ER 88 applied.

    Ensign Shipping Co Ltd v Inland Revenue Comrs (1928) 12 Tax Cas 1169, *Australia*
b *(Commonwealth) Comr of Taxation v Squatting Investment Co Ltd* [1954] 1 All ER 349, *Severne (Inspector of Taxes) v Dadswell* [1954] 3 All ER 243, *Inland Revenue Comrs v Falkirk Ice Rink Ltd* [1975] STC 434 and *McGowan (Inspector of Taxes) v Brown and Cousins* [1977] 3 All ER 844 distinguished.

    Decision of Walton J [1976] 2 All ER 296 affirmed.

Notes
c For trade receipts, see 20 Halsbury's Laws (3rd Edn) 149-158, paras 262-276, and for cases on the subject, see 28(1) Digest (Reissue) 23-57, 85-226.

Cases referred to in judgments
Australia (Commonwealth) Comr of Taxation v Squatting Investment Co Ltd [1954] 1 All ER 349, [1954] AC 182, [1954] 2 WLR 186, 33 ATC 38, [1954] TR 37, PC, 28(1) Digest
d (Reissue) 58, *57.
Chibbett (Inspector of Taxes) v Joseph Robinson & Sons [1924] All ER Rep 684, 9 Tax Cas 48, 132 LT 26, 28(1) Digest (Reissue) 32, *124.*
Ensign Shipping Co Ltd v Inland Revenue Comrs (1928) 12 Tax Cas 1169, 139 LT 111, 17 Asp MLC 472, CA, 28(1) Digest (Reissue) 590, *2186.*
Inland Revenue Comrs v Falkirk Ice Rink Ltd [1975] STC 434, 54 ATC 266, [1975] TR 223,
e CS, Digest (Cont Vol D) 482, *1135Bb.*
McGowan (Inspector of Taxes) v Brown and Cousins (trading as Stuart Edwards) [1977] 3 All ER 844, [1977] 1 WLR 1403, [1977] STC 342.
Severne (Inspector of Taxes) v Dadswell [1954] 3 All ER 243, [1954] 1 WLR 1204, 35 Tax Cas 649, 33 ATC 366, [1954] TR 319, 47 R & IT 584, 28(1) Digest (Reissue) 38, *158.*
Simpson (Inspector of Taxes) v John Reynolds & Co (Insurances) Ltd [1975] 2 All ER 88,
f [1975] 1 WLR 617, [1975] STC 271, 49 Tax Cas 693, [1975] TR 33, [1975] 1 Lloyd's Rep 512, CA, Digest (Cont Vol D) 441, *201a.*
Walker (Inspector of Taxes) v Carnaby, Harrower, Barham & Pykett [1970] 1 All ER 502, [1970] 1 WLR 276, 46 Tax Cas 561, 48 ATC 439, [1969] TR 435, 28(1) Digest (Reissue) 49, *201.*
Watney Mann Ltd v Langley [1963] 3 All ER 976, [1966] 1 QB 457, [1964] 2 WLR 858,
g 128 JP 97, 62 LGR 432, [1964] RVR 22, Digest (Cont Vol A) 1297, *1235a.*

Cases also cited
Bush, Beach & Gent Ltd v Road [1939] 3 All ER 302, [1939] 2 KB 524, 22 Tax Cas 519.
Edwards (Inspector of Taxes) v Bairstow [1955] 3 All ER 48, [1956] AC 14, 36 Tax Cas 207, HL.
Inland Revenue Comrs v Fleming & Co (Machinery) Ltd 1952 SC 120, 33 Tax Cas 57.
h
Appeal
The taxpayer company, Goodhews, carried on the trade of running licensed catering establishments, which consisted mainly of public houses with restaurants attached. Most of those establishments were held by Goodhews on tied tenancy agreements from another company, Watney Coombe Reid & Co Ltd
j ('Watney'). For a great many years Watney and Goodhews had enjoyed a good relationship. In 1968 Watney decided, having regard to the increased values of its freehold properties and the need to achieve a better return on capital, to take back 13 tenancies over a period of two years commencing from January 1969. During the accounting periods ended 31st March 1970 and 31st March 1971, Goodhews received from Watney ex gratia payments totalling £35,823 and £45,828 respectively in

connection with the loss of those tenancies. Goodhews was assessed to corporation tax on the basis that the payments represented compensation for loss of profits arising *a* from the loss of tenancies and accordingly were annual profits or gains arising from Goodhews' trade. Goodhews appealed to the Special Commissioners who found (a) that Watney had decided to make the payments to acknowledge a long and friendly association with Goodhews and to maintain its own name, goodwill and image in the brewing industry; (b) that the payments were not linked with any future trading relationship between Watney and Goodhews; and (c) that they were computed by *b* reference to the rateable values of the tied public houses taken back and had no connection with the profits earned by any of those houses. Accordingly they allowed Goodhews' appeal, holding that the payments in the hands of Goodhews were capital receipts. Immediately after the determination of the appeal the Crown declared its dissatisfaction therewith as being erroneous in point of law and on 9th November 1973 required the commissioners to state a case for the opinion of the High Court. On *c* 20th February Walton J[1] dismissed the appeal. The Crown appealed to the Court of Appeal.

John Vinelott QC and Michael Hart for the Crown.
Michael Nolan QC and Philip Lawton for Goodhews.

d

BUCKLEY LJ. This is an appeal from a decision of Walton J[1] of 20th February 1976, when he dismissed an appeal from a decision of the Special Commissioners, who had held that certain sums paid by Watney Coombe Reid & Co Ltd (whom I shall call 'Watney') to the taxpayer company (whom I shall call 'Goodhews') amounting to *e* £35,823 in the year 1970 and £45,828 in the year 1971 were not trading receipts to be taken into account in the computation of Goodhews' profits from its trade, chargeable to corporation tax. The decision below is reported[1] and the case stated is set out in full in the report. All the relevant facts are there to be found and I shall not repeat them.

I would, however, draw attention to the following findings of fact, which seem to me to be crucial. First, in para 5(5) of the case, the commissioners find as a fact *f* that when Watney's representative visited the Goodhews' board of directors to explain Watney's change of policy, he mentioned that there would be an ex gratia payment, but said nothing about the amount or basis of calculation. Secondly, in para 5(10) the commissioners find as a fact that apart from the letters referred to in that paragraph and set out elsewhere in the case, there was no correspondence between the two companies, nor was there any bargaining or negotiation. Thirdly, *g* in para 5(11), the commissioners find as a fact that the amounts of the payments had no connection with the profits earned or barrellage taken by any house; nor was it (which I take to mean the calculation of those amounts) linked with future trading relations between Watney and Goodhews.

The question which has to be determined, I think, is whether the sums in issue fall within the description of annual profits or gains arising or accruing to Goodhews *h* from their trade (Income and Corporation Taxes Act 1970, s 108, para 1(a)(ii)); or, to put it more precisely in relation to the present case, whether they are receipts which should be taken into account in ascertaining the profits or gains of Goodhews' trade for the two years of receipt.

The leases of public houses which Watney determined were terminated by notices in the ordinary course and Goodhews had no legal basis for claiming any compensa- *j* tion. There is one possible exception to that, but it is of comparatively small extent and it is not necessary for me to go into that question. The payments made by

---

1 [1976] 2 All ER 296, [1976] STC 128

Watney were entirely voluntary. This feature, however, provides no conclusive
a answer to the question whether they should be regarded for the relevant purpose
as arising or accruing from Goodhews' trade so as to be proper to be brought into
account in ascertaining the profits or gains of that trade.

In *Australia (Commonwealth) Comr of Taxation v Squatting Investment Co Ltd*[1], the
taxpayers carried on business as growers of wool. In the relevant years the Australian
government bought compulsorily the whole of their production. The taxpayers
b received the whole price to which they were entitled under the relevant regulations.
The Australian government made a substantial profit, and under a statute provision
was made for the disposal of this profit rateably amongst all the wool growers whose
sales to the government had contributed to it. The taxpayers received £22,851 and,
being still in business as wool growers, were charged with income tax in respect of
this sum. The advice of the Privy Council[2] proceeded on the basis that the payment
c was a voluntary one, though it fulfilled a well-founded hope or expectation on the
part of the suppliers.

Their Lordships reached the conclusion that the payment must be regarded as an
additional payment voluntarily made to the respondent for wool supplied for
appraisement; or, if compulsory acquisition can properly be described as a sale, a
voluntary addition made by the Commonwealth for the purchase price of the wool.
d They went on to say[3]:

> 'The respondents were in business as wool suppliers at all material times,
> and the payment was made to them, not because of any personal qualities,
> but because they, among others, supplied participating wool. They supplied
> the wool in the course of their trade and this further payment was made to them
> because they supplied it. In the present case, the respondents were still trading
e > when the payment was made. It was in their hands a trade receipt of an income
> nature.'

In *Severne (Inspector of Taxes) v Dadswell*[4] the taxpayer was a miller who had ceased
to trade in 1929, but in 1941, wishing to start milling again, he obtained a licence
to do so from the Ministry of Food, who controlled the flour industry at that time.
f As a licensed miller he was entitled to receive rebates based on the flour that he milled,
but as he had not been a miller at the outbreak of war he was not entitled to remuneration under the agreement made between the British Millers' Mutual Pool Ltd and the
Ministry, by which millers in the pool were entitled to a rebate for a loss suffered
under the system of rebates. The taxpayer was required to furnish accounts on lines
similar to the accounts furnished by millers who were in the pool, and he was told
g by the Ministry that the basis on which he would be remunerated for his production
of flour was under consideration and that he would be informed in due course what
the decision was. Before any decision was reached he ceased to carry on business in
September 1945. His accountant was required to furnish accounts in respect of his
business in order that his remuneration, so called, could be determined; and in 1949,
four years after he had ceased to carry on business, he received £3,289 from the
h Ministry as 'remuneration'. It was held that when the taxpayer discontinued to
trade in 1945, the payment for the work which he had done had not been finally
settled, and that the payment of £3,289 for that work, although it was gratuitous
and not made in pursuance of any legal claim, enabled his accounts for the relevant
year to be reopened so as to let in that sum which was held to be analagous to a
trading debt at the amount actually received. It was therefore held that the sum of
j

---

1   [1954] 1 All ER 349, [1954] AC 182
2   [1954] 1 All ER 349 at 360, [1954] AC 182 at 212, per Lord Morton
3   [1954] 1 All ER 349 at 361, [1954] AC 182 at 214
4   [1954] 3 All ER 243, [1954] 1 WLR 1204, 35 Tax Cas 649

£3,289 should be included in his profits for the relevant year, or years, and that he
was taxable accordingly. In both those cases the receipts in question were voluntary *a*
awards received after the event for a transaction, or transactions, carried out in the
course of the taxpayer's trade.

Counsel for the Crown contends that by analagous reasoning the payments in
the present case, which were, he says, made in recognition of the injury suffered by
Goodhews in consequence of what he described as an unfair interruption of their
trade, should be regarded in the same light in which compensation for the loss of the *b*
tenancies would be regarded if such compensation had been legally recoverable. If
the word 'unfair' is considered to be too censorious, I suppose one could substitute
'harsh'.

Counsel for the Crown referred to *Ensign Shipping Co Ltd v Inland Revenue Comrs*[1]
which related to a payment of compensation which may have been ex gratia, although
this is not clear, for two colliers having been detained in port for some days by govern- *c*
ment order while engaged in transporting coal. This compensation was held to
have been properly assessed as a trading receipt for excess profits duty purposes,
on the basis that the compensation was in lieu of what the ships would have earned
if not detained; that is to say, it was compensation for loss of profits. Just so, says
counsel for the Crown, the sums paid in the present case should be treated as compensation for the loss of the profitable use of the houses of which they lost their *d*
tenancies.

We were also referred to *Chibbett (Inspector of Taxes) v Joseph Robinson & Sons*[2]
where a substantial benefit in money's worth which was given voluntarily to a firm
of ship managers in the liquidation of a steamship company by whom they were
employed, was held not to be taxable to income tax and excess profit duty, on the
basis that it was in truth a testimonial for work the ship managers had done for the *e*
company in the past. In that case the Crown had argued that the benefit was not
compensation for loss of office, but a windfall received because of the taxpayer's
position as managers of the company's ships.

In *Walker (Inspector of Taxes) v Carnaby, Harrower, Barham & Pykett*[3] a firm of accountants who had acted as auditors for six companies and were not reappointed, received
an unsolicited and voluntary solatium for their loss of office in the form of a cheque *f*
for a sum equivalent to a year's audit fees. Pennycuick J said[4]:

> 'It seems to me that a gift of that kind made by a former client cannot reason-
> ably be treated as a receipt of a business which consists in rendering professional
> services. The subject-matter of the assessments under Cases I and II is the full
> amount of the profits or gains of the trade or profession. Those profits have to be *g*
> computed, it is well established, on ordinary commercial principles. It does
> not seem to me that ordinary commercial principles require the bringing into
> account of this sort of voluntary payment, not made as the consideration for
> any services rendered by the firm, but by way of recognition of past services or
> by way of consolation for the termination of a contract. It is difficult to amplify
> the point any further. I fully appreciate that the taxpayer firm would not *h*
> have received this payment if they had not previously rendered professional
> services to the companies. Again, I fully appreciate that the payment was made
> to them as a firm and not because the companies had a particular affection for
> any member of the firm personally.'

The payments were therefore treated as having been gifts not made as a considera- *j*
tion for services rendered, and on that footing were held not to be chargeable to tax.

---

1   (1928) 12 Tax Cas 1169
2   (1924) 9 Tax Cas 48, [1924] All ER Rep 684
3   [1970] 1 All ER 502, [1970] 1 WLR 276, 46 Tax Cas 561
4   [1970] 1 All ER 502 at 511, [1970] 1 WLR 276 at 287, 46 Tax Cas 561 at 573

Simpson (Inspector of Taxes) v John Reynolds & Co (Insurances) Ltd[1] is another case
a of a voluntary payment, made in that case by a client to an insurance broker on the
cesser of that relationship. Russell LJ considered the case in relation to five features[2].
Those were features of the facts of that particular case. They cannot be treated as
criteria for the decision of other cases. Russell LJ said[3]:

b
'For the Crown it was contended that the fact that a payment is made without
legal obligation does not per se elude the fiscal grasp. This is true. Gifts made or
promised during the relevant connection may well be caught. It was also pointed
out that the fact that payments are made after the connection has ceased does
not per se elude the fiscal grasp. This also is true: for it may be part of the connection that such payments after its determination are to be expected. But this
does not in my view lead to the suggested conclusion that when both of those
c circumstances are present—that is to say, where the gift is wholly voluntary and
made unexpectedly after the business connection has come to an end—the payment is within the statutory language.'

He reached the conclusion that the payment could not be held to come within the
charge to tax under Sch D. Stamp LJ said[4]:

d
'It is not in question that the series of payments, of which this payment of
£1,000 was one, was made and promised voluntarily. The payments were promised to be made by the former customer after the relationship of customer and
broker had terminated. They were not made to satisfy any legal liability, real
or imagined, to which the customer was or believed itself to be subject. The
payments were not made by way of additional reward for any particular service
rendered by the brokers or for their services generally. They were not made
e pursuant to the terms of a trading contract or as compensation for the breach
of any such contract. The brokers were not entitled to, and indeed did not
expect to receive them. Then, out of the blue came the promise, unenforceable
as it was, to make them. By the time they were promised to be made, the
trading relationship was, as I have said, terminated. The payments were voluntary payments, and I find wholly satisfactory the description of them as made
f by way of recognition of past services or by way of consolation for the rupture of
a business relationship: a rupture which no doubt the client company were sad
to see. It is no doubt a convenient way of describing them to say that they came
to the taxpayer "by virtue of its trade" because the taxpayer would never have
got them had it not for many years carried on the trade and performed valuable
services to the donor. But the words "by virtue of the trade" are not in the section
g and it is in my judgment inappropriate to describe the payments as arising from
the trade.'

Inland Revenue Comrs v Falkirk Ice Rink Ltd[5] and *McGowan (Inspector of Taxes) v Brown
and Cousins*[6] may be said to fall on the other side of the line. In the former the taxpayer was a proprietor of an ice rink which was used for skating and curling. A curling
h club rented rooms from the taxpayer in the same building, where social facilities
were available for the members of the club. They used the rink for curling, as did
other members of the public. The members of the club made a voluntary payment of
£1,500 to the taxpayer to assist the taxpayer in improving the curling facilities
provided on the rink. This was held to be a taxable receipt.

---

j 1   [1975] 2 All ER 88, [1975] 1 WLR 617, [1975] STC 271
   2   [1975] 2 All ER 88 at 90, [1975] 1 WLR 617 at 619, [1975] STC 271 at 273
   3   [1975] 2 All ER 88 at 91, [1975] 1 WLR 617 at 619, 620, [1975] STC 271 at 274
   4   [1975] 2 All ER 88 at 91, 92, [1975] 1 WLR 617 at 620, 621, [1975] STC 271 at 274, 275
   5   [1975] STC 434
   6   [1977] 3 All ER 844, [1977] 1 WLR 1403, [1977] STC 342

In *McGowan (Inspector of Taxes) v Brown and Cousins*[1] the owner of a building estate, who was unwilling to employ the taxpayers, a firm of estate agents who had acted *a* for the owner's predecessor in the purchase of the estate, to act as agents on sales of the developed lots, voluntarily paid them £2,500 as compensation for loss of the opportunity to secure this profitable business. It was held on the facts that the payment was made in recognition of the fact that the taxpayers had acted for inadequate remuneration on the purchase of the estate in a reasonable expectation that they would get the profitable business of which they were disappointed. On *b* this basis the receipt of the £2,500 was treated as being in the nature of delayed remuneration for the work they had done on the purchase and so was held to be taxable.

In my opinion a perusal of these authorities leads to the conclusion that every case of a voluntary payment, and we are only concerned with cases of that kind in the present appeal, must be considered on its own facts to ascertain the nature of *c* the receipt in the recipient's hands. All relevant circumstances must be taken into account. These may include the purpose for which the payer makes the payment, or the terms, if any, on which it is made, as for example in the *Falkirk* case[2], where the payment was made for the purpose of its being applied in the recipient's business in the future; or it may be made by way of voluntarily supplementing the price paid for goods or services provided by the taxpayer in the course of his trade or business in *d* the past, as in *Australia (Commonwealth) Comr of Taxation v Squatting Investment Co Ltd*[3] and *Severne v Dadswell*[4] and *McGowan v Brown and Cousins*[1]; or the payment may be merely in the nature of a testimonial or a solatium which, although it recognises the value of past services, is not paid specifically in respect of any of those services, or of expected future services, by the taxpayer to the payer, as in the case of *Chibbett v Joseph Robinson & Sons*[5], *Walker v Carnaby, Harrower, Barham & Pykett*[6] and *Simpson* *e* *v John Reynolds & Co (Insurances) Ltd*[7]. I stress that it is the character of the receipt in the recipient's hands that is significant; the motive of the payer is only significant so far as it bears, if at all, on that character.

Counsel for the Crown has emphasised that a business relationship continued, and still continues, between Watney and Goodhews in relation to other public houses than those of which the tenancies were determined. He has contended that the pay- *f* ments were made, inter alia, to maintain goodwill between the two companies. I do not think that the finding of fact in para 5(11) of the case stated goes so far as this. The commissioners found that the payments were made to maintain Watney's own name, goodwill and image in the trade and that the calculation of them was not linked with any future trading relations between Watney and Goodhews. The commissioners also found in the same paragraph that the amounts paid were not connected *g* with the profits earned or beer sold through any house, which contradicts any suggestion which might be made that the payments were in the nature of compensation for lost profits, or at the very least tends to do so.

It seems to me that on the findings of fact made by the commissioners, and particularly those to which I specifically drew attention at the beginning of this judgment, the commissioners were fully justified in holding, as in effect I think they did, that *h* the sums now in question were not receipts of Goodhews arising or accruing from Goodhews' trade or business, and on that ground I would dismiss this appeal.

---

1   [1977] 3 All ER 844, [1977] 1 WLR 1403, [1977] STC 342   *j*
2   [1975] STC 434
3   [1954] 1 All ER 349, [1954] AC 182
4   [1954] 3 All ER 243, [1954] 1 WLR 1204, 35 Tax Cas 649
5   (1924) 9 Tax Cas 48, [1924] All ER Rep 684
6   [1970] 1 All ER 502, [1970] 1 WLR 276, 46 Tax Cas 561
7   [1975] 2 All ER 88, [1975] 1 WLR 617, [1975] STC 271

a Counsel for the Crown presented his argument to the court in two parts, the first being concerned with the question whether the payments accrued or arose from Goodhews trade, and the second being whether, if so, the payments were of a capital or income nature. In view of the conclusion that I have reached on the first of those two questions, it is not necessary for me to express any opinion on the second, and I do not do so.

For these reasons I would dismiss this appeal.

b

EVELEIGH LJ. I agree. This appeal really involves a simple, although not easy, question of fact. I am tempted to recall, I hope not irreverently, the many decisions in workmen's compensation cases on the words 'arising out of and on the course of the employment', which produce answers falling either side of a very fine line.

c In this case, on the basis of the commissioners' finding, this was not a payment for any commercial consideration or return, past or future, insofar as the taxpayer's business was concerned. Counsel for the Crown has in effect challenged the findings of the commissioners to which Buckley LJ has just referred; in the forefront of his challenge was the fact that the claim was based on a rateable value, and counsel for the Crown has pointed out that in the case of a tied house the profits are an important

d factor in arriving at rateable value. He referred us to *Watney Mann Ltd v Langley*[1], and in particular to the observations of Thompson J[2].

For my part I regarded that aspect of the case as a powerful factor from the point of view of the Crown; I do regard it as a powerful consideration in deciding this matter, but there is nothing to show that the commissioners did not have regard to it. There was in this case no legal claim that Goodhews had for loss of profits, and there have

e been a number of cases where the sum paid has been arrived at by reference to earnings of the taxpayer in the past without that fact leading inevitably to the conclusion that the sum received was a profit or gain arising or accruing from any trade. (One such example is *Simpson v John Reynolds & Co (Insurances) Ltd*[3].) A person intending to give another a present may well go through various mental processes in arriving at the amount that it is appropriate to give, and he may regard an amount equivalent

f to a previously earned annual salary as an appropriate figure which would not be regarded as ungenerous. On the other hand such a payment may very strongly point to the conclusion that it was given as compensation.

But it is all a question of fact, and I agree that the commissioners were entitled to find the facts that they did find here, and on that basis the conclusion to which they arrived, although not very clearly stated, was, I am sure, the one that Buckley LJ

g has said. It was justified by the facts that they found.

I agree that this appeal should be dismissed.

SIR JOHN PENNYCUICK. I agree. There is no question here of a personal gift in the sense of a gift made by the donor out of regard or compassion for the donee

h as an individual. The payments were made by one trader to another in the course of trade, no less in the case of Goodhews than in the case of Watneys. The question is whether, in the hands of Goodhews, the payment ought properly to be brought into account as a receipt in the computation of the profit arising from its trade. Subject to any overriding statutory provisions the profit of a trade must be computed in accordance with the ordinary principles of commercial accountancy.

j The answer to a question of this kind in any given case of a voluntary payment to a trader must depend on all the circumstances of the particular case. Counsel for the Crown

---

1   [1963] 3 All ER 967, [1966] 1 QB 457
2   [1963] 3 All ER 967 at 970, [1966] 1 QB 457 at 463
3   [1975] 2 All ER 88, [1975] 1 WLR 617, [1975] STC 271

accepted that this is so. It is impossible to lay down any precise guidelines, and one should not attempt to do so. One broad consideration which has been acted on in a *a* line of cases of the highest authority is whether the payments can fairly be related to some antecedent transaction in the course of trade; for example, a transaction in respect of which the payer is content to regard the recipient as having been inadequately rewarded for goods sold or services rendered. In such a case the receipt, albeit voluntary, is equated to a payment made in consideration of such goods or services pursuant to a contractual provision.

b

The point was neatly made by Templeman J in a recent case, *McGowan (Inspector of Taxes) v Brown and Cousins*[1], where he said:

'As a result of all the authorities it seems to me that the broad line of distinction, so far as taxability on this kind of voluntary gift is concerned, is a distinction which takes its origin in the question of whether the payment is attributable to specific work carried out by the recipient. If work is carried out, *c* then the payment, although voluntary, is made because payment has been earned.'

In the present case the payments are not related to any specific transaction; they represent compensation for the loss of a long established and valuable trading connection. I do not myself see how a gratuitous receipt of this character could properly *d* be brought into a trading account made up on the ordinary principles of commercial accountancy. There is no commercial outgoing of a revenue character, even in the widest or most indirect sense, in return for which it could be said that payment was received by Goodhews.

The Special Commissioners had, as appears from the case stated, accountancy evidence before them, but they made no finding on the principles of commercial *e* accountancy. All that is mentioned in the case stated is that the sums in question were credited to Goodhews' capital reserve in its account because, in the view of Goodhews' auditors, those sums bore no relationship to Goodhews' normal trading and were not paid by Watney in discharge of any liability other than a possible statutory right to compensation in respect of one public house.

Counsel for the Crown accepted that there is no universal rule under which a trader *f* is bound to bring a voluntary payment into account. Unless I misunderstood him, he did, however, advance a general principle in these terms: the determining factor is the payer's reason for making the payment; if that was a commercial reason, the payment is taxable in the hands of the recipient. With all respect, I do not think that that is a correct formulation of principle. The basic principle in the present connection is that one looks at the character of the receipt from the point of view of *g* the recipient. In so doing, as has often been pointed out, one must take into account the motive of the payer in making the payment, but it is an inversion of the basic principle to treat the motive of the payer as the conclusive factor in the character of the receipt in the hands of the recipient.

A significant factor in the present case is certainly that Goodhews not merely continued to trade, but retained part of its trading connection with Watney; but I *h* do not think this factor is of itself sufficient to turn a gratuitous payment by way of compensation for loss of a greater part of this trading connection into a receipt properly to be taken into account in the calculation of the profit arising from Goodhews' trade. I do not find it useful to investigate the question which would have arisen if the payment had been made for valuable consideration. The answer to that question would depend on the particular circumstances in which, and the terms on which, *j* the payment was made, and the question is academic for the purposes of the present appeal.

---

1 [1977] 3 All ER 844 at 850, [1977] 1 WLR 1403 at 1407, [1977] STC 342 at 348

a In my judgment the commissioners reached a legitimate conclusion on the facts found or admitted before them, and I see no ground on which the court could interfere with that conclusion. I would myself go further, and say that I am not persuaded that the commissioners could have legitimately reached any other conclusion on those facts. The question here is simply whether or not these voluntary payments should be treated as receipts in the computation of the profit arising from the trade of Goodhews. If the answer to that question is in the negative then Goodhews, being

b a limited company, is bound to bring the payments into account somewhere, and has properly brought them into account as a capital reserve. The common question whether a receipt for commercial consideration should be treated as of a revenue or of a capital nature does not arise here.

I would add that my decision is not based on the view that the leasehold interests in the various houses comprised in the determined leases may have represented

c capital assets, albeit of very small value, in the hands of Goodhews.

I too would dismiss this appeal.

Appeal dismissed; leave to appeal to House of Lords refused.

Solicitors: *Solicitor of Inland Revenue*; *Crossman, Block & Keith* (for Goodhews).

d

J H Fazan Esq Barrister

Re Gerald Cooper Chemicals Ltd

e CHANCERY DIVISION
TEMPLEMAN J
2nd, 3rd, 22nd NOVEMBER 1977

Company – Winding-up – Fraudulent trading – Carrying on business with intent to defraud creditors – Whether single transaction capable of amounting to 'carrying on business with
f *intent to defraud creditors' – Companies Act 1948, s 332(1).*

Company – Winding-up – Fraudulent trading – Parties to the carrying on of the company's business – Loan made by third party to company to finance production of indigo – Company accepting advance payment from customer for supply of indigo – Company not carrying out order but repaying third party's loan with money advanced – Company insolvent –
g *Whether third party knowingly party to company carrying on business with intent to defraud creditors – Companies Act 1948, s 332(1).*

In March 1976 the respondents, J Ltd and its two directors, G and H, agreed to provide £150,000 to enable C Ltd, a company controlled by C, to purchase and install
h plant at a factory for the production of indigo. In return C Ltd agreed to pay J Ltd £150,000 by 30th June 1976 and to pay a further £1.35 million to it by 26th March 1977. C Ltd expected to obtain that money out of profits from the sale of indigo. The respondents' £150,000 proved insufficient to finance the production of indigo. By the end of July 1976 C Ltd was insolvent. C, on C Ltd's behalf, solicited an order for indigo from the applicants, H Ltd, on advance payment terms. On 19th August he obtained from them an order for 5,000 kilos of indigo to be delivered
j during September. On 20th August H Ltd paid the purchase price amounting to £125,698.32. On the same day C Ltd paid £110,000 to J Ltd in part discharge of its debt of £150,000 which should have been paid by 30th June. C Ltd went into liquidation. H Ltd applied for a declaration, under s 332(1)[a] of the Companies Act

---

a Section 332(1), so far as material, is set out at p 51 c d, post

1948, that the respondents were personally responsible for C Ltd's debts on the ground that they had knowingly been parties to fraudulent trading. H Ltd in their points of claim alleged, inter alia, that when C agreed on C Ltd's behalf to sell the indigo to H Ltd he intended to use the purchase money to pay J Ltd and knew that if the money was not used for production purposes and was paid instead to J Ltd, C Ltd could neither deliver the indigo to H Ltd nor repay the purchase money, that C Ltd defrauded H Ltd by paying the £110,000 to J Ltd and that the respondents, knowing of the circumstances, were parties to the fraud by accepting the £110,000. The respondents applied, by summons, to have the points of claim struck out as disclosing no cause of action. They contended (i) that a single transaction could not amount to 'carrying on a business with intent to defraud creditors' within the meaning of s 332(1), and alternatively (ii) that they could not knowingly be parties to the carrying on of C Ltd's business with intent to defraud C Ltd's creditors because they had no powers of management or control over the carrying on of the business and did not assist in it.

Held – (i) For the purposes of s 332(1) it did not matter that only one creditor was defrauded and that he was defrauded by one transaction, provided that the transaction could properly be described as a fraud on a creditor perpetuated in the course of carrying on business. C Ltd carried on its business with intent to defraud H Ltd if it accepted the purchase price in advance knowing that it could not supply the indigo and would not repay the £125,698·32 (see p 53 c to j and p 54 a, post).

(ii) A creditor was a party to the carrying on of a business with intent to defraud creditors if he accepted money which he knew had been procured by carrying on business in that way for the purpose of making the payment. It followed that the points of claim established a case for investigation. Accordingly the summons would be dismissed (see p 54 c, post).

Notes
For personal responsibility for fraudulent trading on the winding-up of a company, see 7 Halsbury's Laws (4th Edn) paras 1384-1386, 1410, and for cases on the subject, see 10 Digest (Reissue) 1031-1033, 6320-6328.
For the Companies Act 1948, s 332, see 5 Halsbury's Statutes (3rd Edn) 361.

Case referred to in judgment
Murray-Watson Ltd, Re (6th April 1977) unreported.

Cases also cited
Cyona Distributors Ltd, Re [1967] 1 All ER 281, [1967] Ch 889, CA.
Maidstone Buildings Provisions Ltd, Re [1971] 3 All ER 363, [1971] 1 WLR 1085.
R v Allsop (1977) 64 Cr App Rep 29, CA.

Adjourned summons
By an originating summons dated 24th March 1977, the applicants, Harrisons (London) Ltd ('Harrisons'), applied to the court for a declaration, under s 332 of the Companies Act 1948, that the respondents, Jimlou Ltd and William Jerome Gredley and Anthony James Alexander Helme, directors of Jimlou Ltd, and each of them, were knowingly parties to the carrying on of the business of Gerald Cooper Chemicals Ltd ('the company'), a company in creditors' voluntary liquidation, with intent to defraud creditors and for other fraudulent purposes and that each of them were responsible without any limitation of liability for the sum of £125,698.32 being money due and owing from the company to Harrisons, and payment by the respondents, and each of them, of the sum of £125,698·32. By a summons dated 4th May 1977, the respondents sought an order that the points of claim dated 20th April 1977 delivered by Harrisons pursuant to their summons be struck out as disclosing no cause of action or as being

frivolous and vexatious and an abuse of the process of the court. The facts are set
out in the judgment.

P J Crawford QC and *D J Richardson* for Harrisons.
E C Evans Lombe for the respondents.

Cur adv vult

22nd November.   **TEMPLEMAN J** read the following judgment: The applicants,
Harrisons (London) Ltd, claim a declaration under s 332 of the Companies Act 1948
against the respondents, Mr Gredley and Mr Helme and Jimlou Ltd. By this summons, the respondents seek to strike out points of claim delivered by Harrisons on
the grounds that the points of claim disclose no cause of action or no plausible hope
of success. Section 332(1) provides, inter alia:

> 'If in the course of the winding up of a company it appears that any business of
> the company has been carried on with intent to defraud creditors of the company
> ... or for any fraudulent purpose, the court, on the application of the official
> receiver, or the liquidator or any creditor or contributory of the company, may,
> if it thinks proper so to do, declare that any persons who were knowingly parties
> to the carrying on of the business in manner aforesaid shall be personally re-
> sponsible, without any limitation of liability, for all or any of the debts or other
> liabilities of the company as the court may direct.'

Harrisons are creditors of Gerald Cooper Chemicals Ltd, now in liquidation.
Harrisons claim that the business of the Cooper company was carried on with intent
to defraud creditors and that the respondents were knowingly parties to the carrying
on of the business of the Cooper company in this fraudulent manner. Harrisons seek
a declaration accordingly, and payment by the respondents of the debts and liabilities
of the Cooper company, or, at the least, payment of the sum of £125,698·32 to
Harrisons.

The points of claim contain 26 paragraphs and make a number of serious allegations
which are strenuously denied by the respondents. For the purpose of deciding
whether the points of claim ought to be struck out, it must be assumed that the
allegations can be proved. The tale which I now unfold is, however, only the tale as
told by Harrisons and may bear no resemblance to the true history of the Cooper
company.

The Cooper company was the brain-child of Mr Cooper, who was a director and
owned all the shares. In March 1976 the respondents agreed with Mr Cooper to
provide the capital sum of £150,000 to enable the Cooper company, through its
subsidiary Cooper Medical Products (UK) Ltd, to purchase and install plant for the
production of indigo at a factory in Poplar. In return for this initial capital, the
Cooper company agreed to pay £150,000 by 30th June 1976 to the respondents,
Jimlou, a company owned by Mr Gredley, and to pay a further £1·35 million to
Jimlou by 26th March 1977. These sums were expected to be available to the Cooper
company out of profits from the sale of indigo, a commodity then much sought
after by the makers of blue jeans.

The capital sum of £150,000 was duly provided by the respondents but proved
insufficient to finance the production of indigo. Mr Cooper raised money to finance
production by forward sales of indigo, accepting advance payments by customers
against promises of future deliveries of indigo. By the end of July 1976 production of
indigo had not started and the Cooper company was insolvent, and would remain
so unless further substantial sums became available by way of capital. The respondents, it is said, knew all this. On 4th August 1976 the respondents agreed to the
further deferment of the overdue payment of £150,000 which should have been
paid on 30th June 1976 to Jimlou. The deferment agreed was until 10th August 1976.

The respondents, according to the points of claim, well knew that there was no
prospect of Mr Cooper raising the moneys other than by purported forward sales of *a*
indigo by proforma invoices, but that, if money so paid in advance were applied to
the payment of Jimlou's debt rather than for production purposes, no indigo would
be available to satisfy the customer's order. Accordingly, if they pressed for payment
of the sum then owing to Jimlou, a fraud would be perpetrated on the customer,
or would-be customers, of the Cooper company.

On 19th August 1976, Mr Cooper, on behalf of the Cooper company, agreed to *b*
deliver 5,000 kilos of indigo to Harrisons during September 1976, and on 20th August
1976 Harrisons paid in advance the purchase price amounting to £125,698·32. The
points of claim do not allege that the business of the Cooper company was carried on
before 19th August 1976 with intent to defraud creditors. The points of claim do not
allege that the respondents knew about the agreement made between the Cooper
company and Harrisons on 19th and 20th August. The points of claim gloss over the *c*
conduct of Mr Cooper, but an essential part of Harrisons' case, which will be made
clear by amendment, is that when Mr Cooper agreed with Harrisons, he intended to
use their money to pay Jimlou, and knew that if he paid Jimlou he could neither
deliver indigo to Harrisons nor repay Harrisons their purchase price.

On the very day when Harrisons made the advance payment to the Cooper company, namely 20th August 1976, of a sum in excess of £125,000, the Cooper company *d*
paid £110,000 to Jimlou in part discharge of the sum of £150,000 which should have
been paid on 30th June 1976. Harrisons allege that the respondents knew that the
sum of £110,000 could only be, and was, part of an advance payment by a customer
of the Cooper company, and that the respondents knew that the payment to Jimlou
effectively and irrevocably rendered the Cooper company powerless either to
deliver the indigo for which the advance had been made, or to return to the customer *e*
the cash which the customer had innocently paid for indigo which he was not going
to get. Thus, by making payment to Jimlou, the Cooper company defrauded
Harrisons, and by accepting payment with knowledge of all the circumstances,
except the name of the defrauded customer, the respondents became parties to the
fraud on Harrisons.

Counsel for Harrisons and counsel for the respondents agree that if these allegations *f*
are substantiated, Jimlou became a constructive trustee of £110,000 for Harrisons.
Alternatively or additionally, though counsel for the respondents was not disposed
to agree, the respondents may be liable in damages to Harrisons for fraud. Counsel
for Harrisons submitted that if the respondents are liable in equity or common law
for money which the respondents knew to have been obtained by a fraud perpetrated
on a creditor by the Cooper company in carrying on their business, then Harrisons *g*
are entitled to use the machinery of s 332 instead of issuing more conventional
proceedings against the respondents as trustees or tortfeasors.

Counsel for the respondents submitted in the first place that the points of claim do
not establish that the business of the Cooper company was 'carried on with intent
to defraud creditors'. Counsel for the respondents submitted in the alternative
that the points of claim do not establish that the respondents were 'knowingly *h*
parties to the carrying on of the business' of the Cooper company. The requirements
of s 332 are not, therefore, capable of fulfilment, the points of claim must be struck
out, and Harrisons may, if they please, seek by the normal procedure of a writ and
statement of claim in the Chancery Division or the Queen's Bench Division any
more appropriate remedy which may be available, if they proceed with regularity
and manage to prove their allegations.   *j*

Counsel for the respondents submitted that one transaction cannot amount to the
carrying on of a business with intent to defraud creditors. For this submission he
relied on certain observations of Oliver J in *Re Murray-Watson Ltd*[1]. The learned judge
said:

1 (6th April 1977) unreported

'[Section 332] is aimed at the carrying on of a business . . . and not at the execution of individual transactions in the course of carrying on that business. I do not think that the words "carried on" can be treated as synonymous with "carried out", nor can I read the words "any business" as synonymous with "any transaction or dealing". The director of a company dealing in second-hand motor cars who wilfully misrepresents the age and capabilities of a vehicle is, no doubt, a fraudulent rascal, but I do not think that he can be said to be carrying on the company's business for a fraudulent purpose, although no doubt he carries out a particular business transaction in a fraudulent manner.'

In my judgment, when Mr Cooper on behalf of the Cooper company sought from Harrisons an order for indigo on advance payment terms, Mr Cooper was carrying on the business of the Cooper company. When the Cooper company accepted the advance payment of £125,698 odd, Mr Cooper knowing that there was no prospect, or no reasonable prospect or intention of supplying indigo, and no intention of returning the money to Harrisons, the business of the Cooper company was carried on fraudulently. The subsequent payment to Jimlou of £110,000 made the fraudulent carrying on of the business irremediable and constituted a fraud on the then creditor, Harrisons. The whole transaction between the Cooper company and Harrisons constituted the carrying on of the business of the Cooper company with intent to defraud a creditor of the company. Save that only one creditor was involved, the situation appears to meet the requirements of s 332 set forth by Oliver J in *Re Murray-Watson Ltd*[1] to which I have already referred, namely that the section is contemplating a state of facts in which the intent of the person carrying on the business is that the consequence of carrying it on (whether because of the way it is carried on or for any other reason) will be that creditors will be defrauded; 'intent', of course, being used in the sense that a man must be taken to intend the natural or foreseen consequences of his act.

In the example given by Oliver J the dealer was carrying on the business of selling motor cars. He did not carry on that business with intent to defraud creditors if he told lies every time he sold a motor car to a customer or only told one lie when he sold one motor car to one single customer. When the dealer told a lie, he perpetrated a fraud on a customer, but he did not intend to defraud a creditor. It is true that the defrauded customer had a right to sue the dealer for damages, and to the extent of the damages was a contingent creditor, but the dealer did nothing to make it impossible for the customer, once he had become a creditor, to recover the sum due to him as a creditor.

In the present case, the Cooper company was carrying on the business of selling indigo. In my judgment, they carried on that business with intent to defraud creditors if they accepted deposits knowing that they could not supply the indigo and were insolvent. They were carrying on business with intent to defraud creditors as soon as they accepted one deposit knowing that they could not supply the indigo and would not repay the deposit. It does not matter for the purposes of s 332 that only one creditor was defrauded, and by one transaction, provided that the transaction can properly be described as a fraud on a creditor perpetrated in the course of carrying on business. If the Cooper company had fraudulently supplied sub-standard indigo to Harrisons, the Cooper company would have committed a fraud on a customer, but by accepting a deposit knowing that they could not or would not supply indigo, and by using the deposit in a way which made it impossible for them to repay Harrisons, the Cooper company, in my judgment, committed a fraud on a creditor. If a mail order company advertises goods and solicits deposits with no intention of supplying the goods or of returning the money, and if one hundred customers in response to the advertisement pay over £100,000, the business of the company is plainly being carried

1   (6th April 1977) unreported

on with intent to defraud creditors of the company. If the company, as in the present case, solicits and obtains an advance of £100,000 from one customer, the situation is no different. It follows that if the points of claim are substantiated, the Cooper company was being carried on with intent to defraud creditors within the meaning of s 332.

Counsel for the respondents submitted in the alternative that the respondents could not be knowingly parties to the carrying on of the business of the Cooper company with intent to defraud creditors of the Cooper company because they had no powers of management or control over the carrying on of the business, and did not themselves assist in the carrying on of the business. I agree that a lender who presses for payment is not party to a fraud merely because he knows that no money will be available to pay him if the debtor remains honest. The honest debtor is free to be made bankrupt. But in my judgment a creditor is party to the carrying on of a business with intent to defraud creditors if he accepts money which he knows full well has in fact been procured by carrying on the business with intent to defraud creditors for the very purpose of making the payment. Counsel for the respondents said truly that s 332 creates a criminal offence and should be strictly construed. But a man who warms himself with the fire of fraud cannot complain if he is singed.

An application by a creditor under s 332 must be carefully regulated if injustice is not to result. The respondents to this summons under s 332 must not be placed in double jeopardy by the possibility of further proceedings under s 332 by the liquidator. Moreover, if an order is to be made under s 332, the court must know whether to order payment to the creditor applicant or to the liquidator. Harrisons should, therefore, ask the liquidator to elect whether to intervene to claim relief under s 332, either based on the transaction with Harrisons or based on any other transactions of the Cooper company which implicate the respondents. The liquidator should also be asked whether he wishes to contend that the whole or any part of any money for which the respondents may prove to be liable under s 332 should be paid to him and not to Harrisons. He should be informed that if he does not choose to intervene now he will not be able successfully to institute s 332 proceedings against the respondents in the future. But it is essential that the liquidator should be advised of the present proceedings. For all I know, the sum of £110,000 paid to Jimlou may have been directly or indirectly derived not simply and solely from Harrisons' money but from advance payment or other sums paid by other creditors in the like position. Of course, if the respondents know nothing of the operations of the Cooper company they will be safe both against Harrisons and against the liquidator.

All I decide now is that the points of claim appear to establish a case which invites investigation under s 332 and at Harrison's risk as to costs if they fail to establish the liability of one or more of the respondents under that section.

By a separate summons, Harrisons seek the appointment of a receiver of the assets and manager of the business of Jimlou. The grounds of this application are that Jimlou received the £110,000 as constructive trustees for Harrisons, and may part with that sum and dissipate their assets. I do not see how this wide relief could be appropriate when the liability of Jimlou remains at issue, and in any event it appears that Jimlou have already parted with the sum of £110,000. I make no order on this summons.

Order accordingly.

Solicitors: *Gumbiner & Co* (for the applicants); *Ashurst, Morris Crisp & Co* (for the respondents).

Jacqueline Metcalfe Barrister.

a

Maxim's Ltd and another v Dye

CHANCERY DIVISION
GRAHAM J
16th·MAY, 1st JUNE 1977

b   *Passing off – Trade name – Business carried on abroad but not in England – Business enjoying reputation and goodwill in England – Restaurant in Paris – Defendant opening
restaurant in England under name of plaintiff's restaurant and furnishing it in same style –
Whether plaintiff entitled to injunctions restraining defendant from using plaintiff's name
and passing off her business as that of plaintiff – Whether existence of goodwill and reputation
in England without carrying on business there sufficient to entitle plaintiff to relief.*

c
*European Economic Community – Restriction on freedom to provide services – Injury to
reputation and goodwill in England – Reputation of business carried on in another member
state – Prospective goodwill in relation to future business which might be set up in England –
Injunction having effect of protecting plaintiff's freedom to provide services in England –
EEC Treaty, art 59.*

d
The plaintiff, an English company, brought an action against the defendant alleging
in its statement of claim that since 1907 it had owned a famous restaurant in Paris
known as Maxim's which enjoyed fame and goodwill in England and was extensively
patronised by persons resident in England, that the English public understood
the name Maxim's to refer to the plaintiff's restaurant in Paris, that in December
e   1975 the defendant had opened a restaurant in Norwich under the name Maxim's
and furnished it in such a style, with cartoons and paintings by French artists, to
give it a period French atmosphere, that the defendant's restaurant was run to a much
lower standard than the plaintiff's restaurant and that the defendant's conduct in
operating her restaurant was calculated to injure the plaintiff's goodwill and reputation. The plaintiff had never had any business in England. The plaintiff claimed
f   injunctions to restrain the defendant from operating a restaurant under the name
Maxim's and from passing off or attempting to pass off in any other manner her
business as the plaintiff's business. The defendant failed to deliver a defence to the
claim and in default of a defence the plaintiff moved for judgment against her in the
terms of the relief claimed in the statement of claim.

g   **Held** – (i) The existence and extent of a plaintiff's reputation and goodwill in his
business was in every case a question of fact. A plaintiff could, therefore, establish that
he had goodwill in England in respect of a foreign business which the courts would
protect without it having to be shown that he carried on business in England (see
p 59 *a b*, post).
    (ii) Furthermore, a restaurant business was an 'activity of a commercial character'
h   within art 60[a] of the EEC Treaty, and therefore a 'service' to which art 59[b] applied.
To deny, solely on the ground that the plaintiff did not carry on a restaurant business
in England, legal protection against damage to the reputation in England of the
plaintiff's restaurant business in another member state of the community was a
restriction on 'freedom to provide services' within the community and as such prohibited by art 59. Accordingly, it would be contrary to art 59 to permit damage to the
j   plaintiff's existing reputation and goodwill in England which would damage his
prospective goodwill in relation to any future restaurant business he might set up in

---

a   Article 60, so far as material, provides: ' "Services" shall in particular include . . . (b)
    activities of a commercial character . . .'
b   Article 59 is set out at p 60 d, post

England, so making it more difficult for him to set up such a business in England (see p 60 e and j to p 61 b, post).

(iii) Since it had to be assumed that the plaintiff had proved that it had a reputation and goodwill in England derived from its restaurant business in Paris, the plaintiff was entitled to the relief claimed by reason of English law both before and after accession to the EEC Treaty (see p 61 c d, post).

Baskin-Robbins Ice Cream Co v Gutman [1976] FSR 545 followed.

Alain Bernadin et Cie v Pavilion Properties Ltd [1967] RPC 581 not followed.

Notes

For passing off a business, see 38 Halsbury's Laws (3rd Edn) 595-598, paras 996, 998, and for cases on the subject, see 46 Digest (Repl) 227-251, 1481-1626.

For the EEC Treaty, arts 59, 60, see 42A Halsbury's Statutes (3rd Edn) 1118.

Cases referred to in judgment

Alain Bernadin et Cie v Pavilion Properties Ltd [1967] RPC 581.
Baskin-Robbins Ice Cream Co v Gutman [1976] FSR 545.
Brestian v Try [1958] RPC 161, CA, 46 Digest (Repl) 232, 1516.
Coenen v Sociaal-Economische Raad [1976] 1 CMLR 30.
Globelegance BV v Sarkissian [1974] RPC 603.
Inland Revenue Comrs v Muller & Co's Margarine Ltd [1901] AC 217, [1900-3] All ER Rep 413, 70 LJKB 677, 84 LT 729, 45 Digest (Repl) 515, 1002.
Poiret v Jules Poiret Ltd (1920) 37 RPC 177.
R v Marlborough Street Stipendiary Magistrate, ex parte Bouchereau [1977] 3 All ER 365, [1977] 1 WLR 414, DC.
Sheraton Corpn of America v Sheraton Motels Ltd [1964] RPC 202.
Société Anonyme des Anciens Etablissements Panhard et Levassor v Panhard Levassor Motor Co Ltd [1901] 2 Ch 513, [1900-3] All ER Rep 477, 70 LJCh 738, 85 LT 20, 18 RPC 405, 46 Digest (Repl) 282, 1848.
Thieffry v Conseil de l'Ordre des Avocats à la Cour de Paris [1977] 3 WLR 453, ECJ.
Van Binsbergen (JHM) v Bestuur van de Berdrijfsvereniging Voor de Metaalnijverheid [1975] 1 CMLR 298.

Cases also cited

Collins Co v Brown (1857) 3 K & J 423.
Marengo v Daily Sketch [1948] 1 All ER 406, HL.
Oertli (T) AG v Bowman (London) Ltd [1959] RPC 1, HL.
Trego v Hunt [1896] AC 7, [1895-9] All ER Rep 804, HL.

Motion

By a writ dated 20th December 1976, the plaintiffs, Maxim's Ltd and Louis Vaudable, claimed against the defendant, Joan Grace Dye' trading as 'Maxim's', 'the New Maxim's' and 'the New Maxim's Late Night Restaurant', (1) an injunction to restrain the defendant by herself, her servants or agents from (i) operating any restaurant, not being the plaintiffs' restaurant or one connected therewith, under any name or style consisting of or including the word 'Maxim's' or any colourable imitation thereof; (ii) in any other manner passing off or attempting to pass off the defendant's business as and for the plaintiffs' business or a business connected therewith; (2) obliteration on oath of the name Maxim's on the defendant's premises at 13/14 The Walk, Norwich and any material the use of which would be in breach of the injunctions claimed; (3) an enquiry as to damages, alternately an account of profits and (4) any other relief. The first plaintiff served a statement of claim on 10th February 1977. The defendant having failed to serve a defence the plaintiffs by notice of motion dated 4th March 1977 sought judgment against her in the terms of minutes of order appended to the notice, namely an injunction in the terms set out in the writ, and obliteration within 14 days of service of the order on the defendant of the name Maxim's from her premises. The facts alleged in the statement of claim are set out in the judgment.

Peter Prescott for the plaintiffs.
The defendant did not appear.

Cur adv vult

1st June. **GRAHAM J** read the following judgment: These proceedings arise out of an action by the plaintiff to restrain the defendant from, inter alia, operating at 13/14 The Walk, Norwich, a restaurant under the name 'Maxim's' and from passing off the defendant's said restaurant business in that city as that of the plaintiff's well-known restaurant business of the same name in Paris or as a business connected therewith. The plaintiff, Maxim's Ltd, moves for judgment in default of defence and ask for an order as scheduled in the minutes of order appended to the notice of motion. In default of defence, the court will, in its discretion, give such judgment as the plaintiff appears entitled to on its statement of claim. The court cannot receive any evidence in such cases but will proceed on the statement of claim which must, of course, show a case for the order which the plaintiff seeks.

Before me service of the statement of claim and the notice of motion and minutes of order were duly proved and the material allegations in the statement of claim, which must be accepted as proved for present purposes, are as follows. (1) The plaintiff is an English company first registered in 1907 and has since that date owned the world famous Parisian restaurant known as 'Maxim's'. (2) The plaintiff's business enjoys an extensive fame and goodwill and the name Maxim's is taken by the public in this country as referring to the said business. (3) The plaintiff has its registered office in this country. Its restaurant in Paris is extensively patronised by persons resident in England and on past occasions some of such persons have written direct from England to the restaurant to book a table. (4) The goodwill is not confined to the city of Paris but extends to many countries of the world including this country. (5) In the past the plaintiff has obtained decisions in many countries and in particular in the United States of America and Switzerland against persons trying to set up restaurants under the name Maxim's in such countries. Furthermore, in or about June 1970 a restaurant named Maxim's was opened at 13/14 The Walk, Norwich, that is the same address at which the defendant now trades, by a company named Norwich (Maxim's) Ltd. In an action in the High Court of Justice, Chancery Division, between the present plaintiff and that company, the latter undertook, inter alia, not to operate any restaurant under the name Maxim's after 30th December 1973 and that they would obliterate permanently the name Maxim's on the premises. On such and other undertakings the action was stayed. (6) In or about December 1975 the defendant opened a restaurant at 13/14 The Walk, Norwich, under the name Maxim's as to which the following facts must be taken to be proved. There was a sign over the entrance bearing the word 'Maxim's' and one at the entrance bearing the words 'The New Maxim's'. The menu cards were headed 'The New Maxim's Late Night Restaurant', the premises are furnished in an Edwardian style red plush and brass rail decor with framed French cartoons by Toulouse Lautrec and like well-known left-bank artists so as to give a period French atmosphere to the establishment. (7) As a result of the foregoing, the defendant's business is calculated to cause loss and damage to the plaintiff and the defendant threatens and intends to persist in the conduct complained of unless restrained. (8) The defendant has refused to desist in spite of being asked in writing to do so and on or about 4th January 1977 by telephone she claimed she was entitled to call her restaurant Maxim's because she had registered the name at the registry of business names. Notwithstanding that it was explained to her that such registration did not confer any right to use the name, the defendant had not at the date of the statement of claim changed such name. (9) The defendant's restaurant is run to a much lower standard than the plaintiff's genuine restaurant

Maxim's and the conduct of the defendant is calculated to injure the goodwill and reputation of the plaintiff.

On these allegations, the truth of which for present purposes must be accepted, the plaintiff claims the injunctions asked for. Counsel for the plaintiff, whilst submitting that his client was entitled to the relief claimed, very properly pointed out that it might be argued by the defendant, if she had put in a defence and been represented before the court, that if the court followed the recent authority of *Alain Bernadin et Cie v Pavilion Properties Ltd*[1], often called the 'Crazy Horse' case, a decision of Pennycuick J on an application for an interlocutory injunction, then the injunctions asked for ought not be granted. This, of course, raised the question whether, even if all the matters alleged in the statement of claim are, as they must be, deemed to be proved, the court as a matter of law is entitled to make such a grant.

The judgment in the 'Crazy Horse' case[1], being an interlocutory proceeding, does not bind me in the present proceedings and in *Baskin-Robbins Ice Cream Co v Gutman*[2] I felt I was unable to adopt its reasoning and follow it as an authority. Before me the 'Crazy Horse' case[1] was carefully analysed by counsel for the plaintiff and he pointed out that it appeared possible from the report that the only cases cited to Pennycuick J were *Poiret v Jules Poiret Ltd & A F Nash*[3] and *Sheraton Corpn of America v Sheraton Motels Ltd*[4], and that the reference in the judgment[5] to *Inland Revenue Comrs v Muller & Co's Margarine Ltd*[6] might well have been quoted from the then current edition of Kerly on Trade Marks[7] where exactly the same passages are set out. He contended that if these passages in *Muller's* case[6] are given too narrow a meaning in defining the 'local' nature of goodwill then they give a wrong impression as to the ratio decidendi of the decision in that case. A study of the full speeches in that case makes it clear, he contended, that the House of Lords considered that, though of course, goodwill cannot exist in vacuo without an associated business, nevertheless its extent in any given case must be a question of fact. This is the view I myself had also expressed in the *Baskin-Robbins* case[2]. *Société Anonyme des Anciens Etablissements Panhard et Levassor v Panhard-Levassor Motor Co Ltd*[8], *Sheraton Corpn of America v Sheraton Motels Ltd*[4] and *Globelegance BV v Sarkissian*[9] were also cited to me, the first being, as I think, important as establishing that a foreign company with no place of business in England may nevertheless as a matter of fact have such a reputation in its name in England as to justify the grant of relief for passing off against a defendant setting up in this country under a similar name. The *Panhard* case[8] does not appear to have been cited to Pennycuick J. *Globelegance BV v Sarkissian*[9], a recent interlocutory decision of Templeman J, is also interesting. In that case there was sufficient user in this country for Templeman J to be able to distinguish it from the 'Crazy Horse' case[1] but it is, I think, clear from analysis of that case and his reference[10] to it being a strait-jacket which might have prevented him from giving relief to Mr Valentino in *Globelegance BV v Sarkissian*[9] that he considered the conclusions as to goodwill in the 'Crazy Horse' case[1] as unduly narrowing in their effect.

For my part, I feel unable legitimately to distinguish the case before me on the facts from those in the 'Crazy Horse' case[1]. True, the plaintiff is an English company

---

1   [1967] RPC 581
2   [1976] FSR 545
3   (1920) 37 RPC 177
4   [1964] RPC 202
5   [1967] RPC 581 at 583
6   [1901] AC 217 at 223, 224, 235, [1900-3] All ER Rep 413 at 415, 416, 423
7   9th Edn (1966), para 488
8   [1901] 2 Ch 513, [1900-3] All ER Rep 477
9   [1974] RPC 603
10 [1974] RPC 603 at 615

but it is clear it has not and never has had any business in this country. Nevertheless
a I am bound on the statement of claim to hold that as a fact the plaintiff has a reputation in this country by virtue of its restaurant in Paris. If it is in law correct to say
that a plaintiff cannot establish that he has goodwill in England which will be protected by our courts without actually showing that he has a business in England, then
of course that is the end of the matter and the plaintiff cannot recover here, but in
my judgment that is not the law. The true position is, I think, as I stated in *Baskin-*
b *Robbins Ice Cream Co v Gutman*[1] and I would like to quote my conclusion in that case
on the point:

> 'Some businesses are, however, to a greater or lesser extent truly international
> in character and the reputation and goodwill attaching to them cannot in fact
> help being international also. Some national boundaries such as, for example,
c > those between members of the EEC are in this respect becoming ill-defined and
> uncertain as modern travel, and Community rules make the world grow smaller.
> Whilst therefore not wishing to quarrel with the decisions in question, if they are
> read as I have suggested, I believe myself that the true legal position is best
> expressed by the general proposition, which seems to me to be derived from
> the general line of past authority, that that existence and extent of the plaintiffs'
d > reputation and goodwill in every case is one of fact however it may be proved and
> whatever it is based on.'

If writing the passage again I would, for purposes of clarity, add the words 'in his
business' after the words 'reputation and goodwill' towards the end of the quotation.
In circumstances such as the present it also seems to me that a plaintiff's existing good-
e will in this country which derives from and is based on a foreign business, such as one
in Paris or elsewhere in the European Community, may be regarded as prospective
but nonetheless real in relation to any future business which may later be set up by
the plaintiff in this country.

With considerations such as these in mind I therefore suggested at the end of the
hearing that counsel for the plaintiff might like to consider whether our accession to
f the EEC Treaty and the provisions of community law had, as it appeared to me they
might have, any and if so what application to his argument in this case. I ,therefore
adjourned the matter to enable it to be looked into and I should say that I am grateful for the clear argument which resulted since it does to my mind confirm the view
to which I had previously come, that I ought not to follow the reasoning in the 'Crazy
Horse' case[2] but should grant an injunction here. The views on community law
g expressed hereafter are of course my views, based on the argument addressed to me,
of what I think such law is.

The argument based on community law may be stated in the following propositions on the assumption that confusing similarity between the names of the plaintiff
and defendant is proved. (1) The proprietor of a business carried on in a limited part
of England, e g the London area, is entitled to bring a passing-off action against a
h person carrying on a business outside the London area provided the former's reputation extends to the area of the latter. This is an accepted principle of English law: see
e g *Brestian v Try*[3] and the other cases there quoted. (2) It follows from the 'Crazy
Horse' case[2] that the proprietor of a business carried on in France (but not in England
even though its reputation extends to England) is not entitled to bring a passing-off
action against a business carried on in England. (3) If proposition (2) is correct it
follows that English law discriminates between businesses in different member states
j of the community on the basis of their location, e g if reputation in England is proved

---

1   [1976] FSR 545 at 548
2   [1967] RPC 581
3   [1958] RPC 161

and the business from which it is derived is situated in England then passing-off relief will be given but if the business from which it is derived is situated in France it will not be given. Thus English law will permit damage to be done to the reputation of a business situated in France which it will forbid if the business is situated in England. If such is the effect of English law it will obstruct or make more difficult the provision in England by an existing French company or business of services similar to those it is providing in France. (4) If the above were correct, it would follow that the prohibitions of English law which make it so (a) though they may be prohibitions or restrictions relating to industrial property also 'constitute a means of arbitrary discrimination or disguised restriction on trade between Member States' contrary to art 36 of the EEC Treaty, (b) tend to distort competition contrary to art 3(f) of the treaty and are incompatible with the spirit of the treaty as set forth in the preamble since they are an obstacle to ensuring fair competition, (c) constitute a restriction on the free supply of services within the community contrary to art 59 of the treaty, which reads as follows:

'Within the framework of the provisions set out below, restrictions on freedom to provide services within the Community shall be progressively abolished during the transitional period in respect of nationals of Member States who are established in a State of the Community other than that of the person for whom the services are intended.

'The Council may, acting unanimously on a proposal from the Commission, extend the provisions of this Chapter to nationals of a third country who provide services and who are established within the Community.'

By art 60 of the treaty 'services' shall be considered to include 'activities of a commercial character'. It seems to me that essentially a restaurant business provides 'services' and carries on 'activities of a commercial character'. Reference is then made to *J H M van Binsbergen v Bestuur van de Berdrijfsvereniging Voor de Metaalnijverheid*[1]. This establishes that the transitional period during which directives under art 63 to implement art 59 were to be implemented has ended, and whether or not so implemented the provisions of art 59 became unconditional on the expiry of that period and are in force. Furthermore, they create rights in the individual which the national courts must enforce, as is also established in *Thieffry v Conseil de l'Ordre des Avocats à la Cour de Paris*[2], in respect of the analogous provisions of arts 52 et seq which deal with the right of establishment. In *Coenen v Sociaal-Economische Raad*[3] it is stated that art 59 describes the restrictions whose abolition is imposed as including those of nationality and residence. The same thing is said in the *Van Binsbergen* case[4].

It is to be noted that the cases above mentioned both relate to individuals or natural persons and it might, on its wording, be argued that art 59 is limited to natural persons and does not apply to companies. I do not think this is a correct argument for the following reasons. Articles 52 to 58 dealing with the right of establishment, by definition in art 58 (probably because the expression 'nationals' is used in art 52), place 'companies or firms' in the same position as 'natural persons' who are 'nationals' of member states. Article 59 also speaks of 'nationals' and by art 66 it is provided that the provisions of art 58 shall apply to the matters covered by Chapter 3, i e arts 59 to 66. It follows therefore that companies and firms are to be treated in the same way as individuals in art 59.

The denial of legal protection against damage to reputation and trade connection to a person purely on the ground that his business is established exclusively, for

---

1   [1975] 1 CMLR 298 at 313, 314, paras 18-27
2   [1977] 3 WLR 453
3   [1976] 1 CMLR 30 at 38, 39, paras 5-9
4   [1975] 1 CMLR 298 at 312, 314, paras 10, 25, 27

example, in France although he has a famous reputation in England is an instance of a requirement imposed on him which, making it as it does more difficult for him to conduct his business, is prohibited by art 59. There ought to be no requirement that he must trade in England in order to prevent his reputation there being tarnished or stolen. If, in fact, it is permissible for a third party to steal his reputation and start a business ahead of him under the same name in England, it may be very difficult, if not impossible, for him to start trading in England when, as he may, he later decides to do so.

It is in this sense and for the above reasons that earlier in this judgment I used the adjective 'prospective' as applied to his English goodwill in such circumstances. I should only add that in this case the plaintiffs are not only the company, Maxim's Ltd, but also Louis Vaudable, a natural person, so that even if the former is not entitled to rely on art 59, the latter clearly would be, though on the statement of claim his position is not clear and he is not, in fact, included in the claim for relief. On the fact, therefore, which must be presumed, that the plaintiff company has a reputation and goodwill in respect of the name Maxim's which derives from the restaurant business in Paris with that name they are, in my judgment, for reasons of English law, both before and after accession to the EEC Treaty, entitled to the relief for which they ask against the defendant.

I see no reason why the reality of the reputation in the United Kingdom should not be protected and I believe that our courts could properly be regarded as being out of touch with reality if they have not the power to protect such goodwill. I think that they always have had such power and, even if they did not, have it in the past they have it now by reason of community law, which since accession is part of our law.

In view of the fact that I consider the conclusion in this case should be the same whether based on our law before or after accession, it is not necessary for me to refer the matter to the European Court of Justice under art 177 to enable me to give a decision. I was asked not to do so in any event in view of the fear of the expense involved which was expressed to me in argument. Such fear does however prompt me to point out that the trial judge may be put into a very difficult position in a case where his view is that English law before accession conflicts with community law, which after accession will override English law. If the parties agree he can, of course, refer to the European Court the question whether his view of community law is correct and obtain a decision which will enable him to decide the case before him in England. If, however, the party or parties (and here there is only one which is a company and not an individual) do not feel able, by reason of expense, to agree to a reference, what is the judge to do? It might be argued that there is a question of jurisdiction involved if the judge is an inferior tribunal and if he acts without finding out what the community law is. Whether, however, he has jurisdiction or not he may well find it difficult to reconcile with his judicial oath a decision deliberately given in ignorance of the correct view of community law. In the case of an individual party the position is relatively simple because in *R v Marlborough Street Stipendiary Magistrate, ex parte Bouchereau*[1] it has been held that a reference to the European Court is a step in the proceedings before the magistrates' court and a legal aid order, under s 28(2) of the Legal Aid Act 1974, covers both proceedings here and before the European Court. No such provision for legal aid however is available when the party in question is a company. It is understood that the European Court itself has power to grant legal aid but it is not clear on what principles such aid will be granted nor to whom and in particular whether it will be granted to a small company which cannot itself justifiably be asked to bear the cost of finding out what the relevant community law is. The problem is likely to arise in the future in cases, certainly not infrequent, involving industrial property rights of all kinds where one or more of the parties are companies without adequate resources to meet the cost of reference. It is suggested

---

1   [1977] 3 All ER 365, [1977] 1 WLR 414

that a procedure should be worked out as soon as possible whereby legal aid can be obtained in a proper case and the reference made effectively without delay to enable the judge to receive the help he needs from the European Court.

Order accordingly.

Solicitors: *Linklaters & Paines* (for the plaintiffs).

Evelyn M C Budd Barrister.

R v Manchester City Stipendiary Magistrate, ex parte Snelson

QUEEN'S BENCH DIVISION

LORD WIDGERY CJ, PARK AND WATKINS JJ

9th MAY 1977

Criminal law – Committal – Preliminary hearing before justices – Discharge of defendant on committal proceedings – Commencement of fresh proceedings in respect of same offence – Procedure – Defendant discharged on committal proceedings because adjournment of proceedings to enable prosecution to complete their case refused and no evidence offered by prosecution – Prosecution commencing fresh committal proceedings in respect of same offence – Whether examining justices having jurisdiction to hear fresh committal proceedings – Whether prosecution obliged to proceed by preferring voluntary bill of indictment.

The applicant was charged with indictable offences under the Theft Act 1968 which were triable summarily and elected to be tried by a jury. When the committal proceedings came on for hearing, on 8th December 1976, the prosecution had not completed their case and the examining magistrate adjourned the proceedings until 13th January 1977. On 13th January the prosecution still had not completed their case and applied for a further adjournment. The magistrate refused to grant any further adjournment of the proceedings and, when the prosecution did not offer any evidence, he discharged the applicant under s 7(1)[a] of the Magistrates' Courts Act 1952. A short time afterwards when they had completed their case, the prosecution commenced fresh committal proceedings against the applicant in respect of the same offences. The applicant applied for an order prohibiting the magistrate from hearing the fresh proceedings on the ground that where committal proceedings had resulted in the discharge of the defendant further proceedings in respect of the same offence could be commenced only by preferring a voluntary bill of indictment.

Held – Although it was the general practice, where the defendant had been discharged on committal proceedings, for the prosecution to prefer a voluntary bill of indictment if they wished to proceed against him for the same offence, the examining magistrate had jurisdiction to hear fresh committal proceedings in respect of the same offence. The risk that there might be repeated committal proceedings in

---

a Section 7(1), so far as material, provides: '. . . if a magistrates' court inquiring into an offence as examining justices is of opinion, on consideration of the evidence and of any statement of the accused, that there is sufficient evidence to put the accused upon trial by jury for any indictable offence, the court shall commit him for trial; and, if it is not of that opinion, it shall, if he is in custody for no other cause than the offence under inquiry, discharge him.'

respect of the same offence was overcome by the discretion of the court to ensure
a that repeated committal proceedings were not vexatious or an abuse of the process
of the court. In the circumstances the commencement of fresh committal proceedings
against the applicant had not been vexatious or an abuse of the court's process and the
application would therefore be refused (see p 64 d to j, post).

Notes
b For discharge of the defendant by the examining justices, see 11 Halsbury's Laws
(4th Edn) para 156.
   For voluntary bills of indictment, see ibid paras 197, 198.
   For the Magistrates' Courts Act 1952, s 7, see 21 Halsbury's Statutes (3rd Edn) 192.

Cases cited
c *Atkinson v United States Government* [1969] 3 All ER 1317, [1971] AC 197, HL.
   R v Humphreys [1975] 2 All ER 1023, [1976] QB 191, CA.
   R v South Greenhoe Justices, ex parte Director of Public Prosecutions [1950] 2 All ER 42,
   [1950] 2 KB 558, DC.

Motion for prohibition
d This was an application by Allan Snelson for an order of prohibition to prohibit
John Coffey Esq, the stipendiary magistrate for the City of Manchester sitting as a
magistrates' court at Crown Square, Manchester, or any of the justices of the city,
from enquiring further as examining justices into offences under ss 9 and 25 of the
Theft Act 1968 alleged to have been committed on 28th October 1976 by the applicant,
and an order to stay all proceedings relating to the enquiry until after the hearing of the
e motion or further order. The ground on which relief was sought was, inter alia, that
the stipendiary magistrate had been wrong in law in holding that he could conduct
another enquiry as examining justice when the applicant had already been discharged
after previous enquiry into the same offences alleged against him. The facts are set
out in the judgment of Lord Widgery CJ.

f *David Brennan* for the applicant.
   Joyanne Bracewell for the prosecution.

LORD WIDGERY CJ. In these proceedings counsel moves on behalf of the
applicant for an order of prohibition to prohibit the stipendiary magistrate for the City
g of Manchester from enquiring further as an examining justice into offences alleged
to have been committed by the applicant under ss 9 and 25 of the Theft Act 1968 on
28th October 1976.
   The circumstances of the matter were that the applicant, with a co-defendant,
one Bhardwaj, appeared before the City Magistrates' Court on 24th November
1976. Neither defendant had appeared in the court in which committals were heard
h and, as deposed to in an affidavit before the court, committal proceedings could
not have been commenced on the first appearance of these men before the court.
They were in fact put to their election, and they were remanded on bail to 8th December when it was intended that committal proceedings should start.
   The prosecution were not ready by 8th December because the witness statements
were not complete. They had a total of seven witnesses from whom statements
j were required, and there were other difficulties. Accordingly both defendants were
remanded on bail again until 13th January 1977 for committal proceedings to take
place on that date, and the remand was at the request of the prosecution.
   Then, before 13th January 1977, the prosecution file was completed by the police and
submitted to the chief prosecuting solicitor. Again it was found by him not to be
wholly satisfactory and the prosecution decided to apply for an adjournment on

13th January. This in due course took place. On arrival on 13th January the prosecution were still not in a position to go ahead. The magistrate, perhaps not surprisingly getting a little tired of this procedure, concluded that he would not give an adjournment and accordingly when the parties were before the court on 13th January there was nothing which the prosecution could do except to offer no evidence, and under s 7 of the Magistrates' Courts Act 1952 the applicant and his co-defendant were discharged.

This liberty did not last long of course, because in quite a short time the prosecution were ready, and since their proceedings had been discharged they had to start again. They could no doubt have applied to a High Court judge for a voluntary bill but, for reasons which seemed good to them, they decided not to do that but to start committal proceedings afresh. Fresh committal proceedings were instituted. It is in relation to those fresh committal proceedings that the present application for prohibition arises because the applicant says that the prosecution have no power to bring forward again a summons involving committal proceedings in respect of these same charges against the history of the matter to which I have referred.

Counsel for the applicant bases his arguments in the main, I think, on the fact that an application for a voluntary bill would have been appropriate in this case had the prosecution sought to take advantage of it. He submits the practice now has become so settled to use a voluntary bill in this situation that it is wrong to go by any other procedure. He has to put his argument in that way because all the authorities show that no question of autrefois acquit arises by reason of the earlier discharge of this applicant. One need not go into the details or look at the books for that proposition because everybody accepts that it is so. Counsel for the applicant, as I say, seeks to avoid the apparent difficulty that autrefois acquit is not an argument available to him by saying that the practice has crystallised and in effect requires in these circumstances that a voluntary bill should be used.

As far as I am concerned, I have no doubt that counsel's argument is without substance. It may be true that in nine cases out of ten when this situation arises a voluntary bill is the convenient course and is taken. But in order to succeed before us counsel for the applicant has to show that the justices have no power to hear the second committal proceedings, and consequently that the prosecution are inviting the justices to go beyond their jurisdiction.

This seems to me to be quite wrong, and the only aspect of the whole case which has troubled me is the feeling that if the prosecution are right in their argument there seems to be a risk that a defendant might be prejudiced by repeated committal proceedings all failing, resulting in a committal being repeated time after time by further similar attempts.

I am satisfied that that particular difficulty is overcome, as counsel for the prosecution suggested, by saying that this court has a discretionary power to see that the use of repeated committal proceedings is not allowed to become vexatious or an abuse of the process of the court. If that point is reached (and whether or not it is reached is a matter of degree), then I have no doubt that it would be right for us to stop in by prohibition to prevent the repeated use of this procedure. We have not come to that point by a very long way, and I do not think counsel for the applicant has made out his case. I would refuse his application.

PARK J. I agree.

WATKINS J. I agree.

Application refused.

Solicitors: *Temperley, Taylor & Wilkinson*, Middleton (for the applicant); *D S Gandy*, Manchester (for the prosecution).

Lea Josse   Barrister.

Johnson v Inland Revenue Commissioners

COURT OF APPEAL, CIVIL DIVISION
STAMP, ORR AND SHAW LJJ
22nd, 23rd NOVEMBER 1977

Income tax – Husband and wife – Collection from wife of tax assessed on husband and attributable to wife's income – Notice requiring wife to pay the tax she would have had to pay if separately assessed – Time limit – Assessment on husband in time – Non-payment by husband of surtax – Assessments to surtax for years 1961-62 and 1965-66 – Notice served on wife in 1974 requiring her to pay that part of unpaid tax which would have been payable by her if she had been separately assessed – Whether time limit for making assessments applicable to notice – Whether notice effective – Taxes Management Act 1970, s 34 – Income and Corporation Taxes Act 1970, s 40(2).

The husband and wife were not separately assessed to tax. Within the time allowed assessments for surtax were made on the husband for the years 1961-62 and 1965-66. The assessments included surtax in respect of the wife's income. The husband failed to discharge those assessments and on 13th December 1974 a notice was served on the wife under the predecessor of s 40ᵃ of the Income and Corporation Taxes Act 1970 demanding payment from her of the sum of £4,235 as the amount of the surtax unpaid by the husband which would have been payable by the wife if in respect of the years 1961-62 and 1965-66 she had been separately assessed. It was common ground that if the wife had been separately assessed in those years an assessment made on her on 13th December 1974 for the tax demanded by the notice would have been out of time, and that, on appeal against the assessment under s 34 of the Taxes Management Act 1970, the assessment would have been discharged. The wife appealed against the demand to pay under the notice.

Held – Under the terms of s 40(2) of the 1970 Act the same consequences were to follow the service of a notice under s 40(1) as would have followed the making on the day of the service of the notice a separate assessment on the wife for the tax demanded by the notice. Since, if the wife had been separately assessed on 13th December 1974 to the tax demanded, the consequence would have been that, on appeal, the assessment would have been discharged as being out of time, it followed that, as the wife had appealed against the notice, it would be discharged and that she was not liable to pay the sum demanded. The appeal would therefore be allowed (see p 68 g to j and p 69 e f, post).

Decision of Foster J [1977] 1 All ER 390 reversed.

Notes
For the recovery from the wife of tax assessed on the husband, see 20 Halsbury's Laws (3rd Edn) 382, 383, para 695.

For the Income and Corporation Taxes Act 1970, s 40, see 33 Halsbury's Statutes (3rd Edn) 75.

Appeal
The taxpayer, Winifred Maud Elaine Johnson, appealed against the judgment of Foster J[1] given on 12th November 1976 whereby he upheld a determination made by the Commissioners for the Special Purposes of the Income Tax Acts that a notice served on the taxpayer under s 359 of the Income Tax Act 1952, the predecessor of s 40 of the Income and Corporation Taxes Act 1970, was effective to render the taxpayer liable to pay an amount of surtax attributable to her income which remained

---

a   Section 40, so far as material, is set out at p 67 a to j, post
1   [1977] 1 All ER 390, [1977] STC 18

unpaid under assessments in respect of the years 1961-62 and 1965-66 made on her husband who was now deceased. The facts are set out in the judgment of Stamp LJ. *a*

Harvey McGregor for the taxpayer.
Stewart Bates QC for the Crown.

STAMP LJ. This is an appeal from an order of Foster J[1] made on 12th November 1976. The order was made on appeal by the taxpayer by way of case stated from a *b* determination of the Commissioners for the Special Purposes of the Income Tax Acts and by the order of the learned judge that determination was affirmed. The question which arises and comes for determination can be shortly stated thus: whether a notice requiring the taxpayer to pay a sum which the Commissioners of Inland Revenue assert would have been payable by her if she had applied to be assessed for income tax separately from her husband was effective for the purpose *c* of making her liable to pay that sum.

The notice was given on 13th December 1974 and it is common ground that if the taxpayer had applied to be assessed separately from her husband an assessment made on 13th December 1974 would have been out of time.

Where a husband and wife each has income their incomes are put together for the purpose of computing the total liability to income tax. Unless they have applied *d* to be separately assessed, the assessment of tax is made on the husband. Section 37(1) of the Income and Corporation Taxes Act 1970 provides as follows:

'Subject to the provisions of this Chapter, a woman's income chargeable to income tax shall, so far as it is income for—(*a*) a year of assessment; or any part of a year of assessment . . . during which she is a married woman living with *e* her husband, be deemed for income tax purposes to be his income and not to be her income. . .'

It must, I think, follow that subject to the provisions of that chapter, a married woman living with her husband is under no liability to pay income tax in respect of her income. *f*

Section 38 of the 1970 Act provides:

'(1) If, within six months before the 6th July in any year of assessment, a husband or a wife makes an application for the purpose in such manner and form as the Board may prescribe, income tax other than surtax for that year shall be assessed, charged and recovered on the income of the husband and on the income of the wife as if they were not married, and all the provisions of the Income Tax *g* Acts with respect to the assessment, charge and recovery of income tax other than surtax shall, save as otherwise provided by those Acts, apply as if they were not married . . .
'(2) If, before the 6th July in the year next following the year of assessment, a husband or a wife makes an application for the purpose in such manner and form as the Board may prescribe—(*a*) surtax for that year shall be assessed, *h* charged and recovered on the income of the husband and on the income of the wife as if they were not married, and all the provisions of the Income Tax Acts with respect to the assessment, charge and recovery of surtax shall apply as if they were not married, and (*b*) the income of the husband and wife shall be treated as one in estimating total income for the purposes of surtax . . .'

j
Then there are provisions in that section to which I need not refer.

Among the provisions to which s 37 is subject are the provisions of s 40 of the 1970 Act which replaces s 359 of the Income Tax Act 1952. Section 40 is the section with

---

1 [1977] 1 All ER 390, [1977] STC 18

which the court is primarily concerned in this case, and I will have to read the greater part of it. It provides as follows:

'(1) Where—(a) an assessment to income tax (hereafter in this section referred to as "the original assessment") is made on a man, or a man's trustee, guardian, curator, receiver or committee, or on a man's executors or administrators, and (b) the Board are of opinion that, if an application for separate assessment under section 38(1) or 38(2) of this Act had been in force with respect to the year for which the assessment is made, an assessment in respect of, or of part of, the same income would have fallen to be made on, or on the trustee, guardian, curator, receiver or committee of, or on the executors or administrators of, a woman who is the said man's wife, or was his wife in that year of assessment, and (c) the whole or part of the amount payable under the original assessment has remained unpaid at the expiration of twenty-eight days from the time when it became due, the Board may serve on her, or, if she is dead, on her executors or administrators, or, if such an assessment as is referred to in paragraph (b) above could in the event therein referred to have been made on her trustee, guardian, curator, receiver or committee, on her or on her trustee, guardian, curator, receiver or committee, a notice—(i) giving particulars of the original assessment and of the amount remaining unpaid thereunder, and (ii) giving particulars, to the best of their judgment, of the assessment which would have fallen to be made as aforesaid, and requiring the person on whom the notice is served to pay the amount which would have been payable under the last-mentioned assessment if it conformed with those particulars, or the amount remaining unpaid under the original assessment, whichever is the less.

'(2) The same consequences as respects—(a) the imposition of a liability to pay, and the recovery of, the tax, with or without interest, and (b) priority for the tax in bankruptcy, or in the administration of the estate of a deceased person, and (c) appeals to the General or Special Commissioners, and the stating of cases for the opinion of the High Court, and (d) the ultimate incidence of the liability imposed, shall follow on the service of a notice under subsection (1) above on a woman, or on her trustee, guardian, curator, receiver or committee, or on her executors or administrators, as would have followed on the making on her, or on her trustee, guardian, curator, receiver or committee, or on her executors or administrators, as the case may be, of such an assessment as is referred to in paragraph (b) of that subsection, being an assessment which—(i) was made on the day of the service of the notice, and (ii) charged the same amount of income tax as is required to be paid by the notice, and (iii) fell to be made, and was made, by the authority who made the original assessment, and (iv) was made by that authority to the best of their judgment, and the provisions of the Income Tax Acts relating to the matters specified in paragraphs (a) to (d) of this subsection shall, with the necessary adaptations, have effect accordingly.'

Then there is a proviso to sub-s (2) which I need not set out. Subsection (3) I need not, I think, set out. Subsection (4) is perhaps not wholly irrelevant and I will read it:

'Where the amount payable under a notice given under subsection (1) above is reduced as the result of an appeal, or of the stating of a case for the opinion of the High Court—(a) the Board shall, if in the light of that result they are satisfied that the original assessment was excessive, cause such relief to be given by way of repayment or otherwise as appears to them to be just, but (b) subject to any relief so given, a sum equal to the reduction in the amount payable under the notice shall again become recoverable under the original assessment.'

Subsection (5) gives the Board and the inspector like powers of obtaining information and so on in connection with the notice as they have in relation to an original assessment.

It is common ground that, subject to the exceptions which are not relevant in the instant case, an assessment on a wife who is separately assessed, like an assessment *a* on a man, whether separately assessed or not, must be made within the time limited by the Taxes Acts. If not so made, objection may be taken to it on appeal against it on the ground that the time limited for making it has expired (see s 34 of the Taxes Management Act 1970). In the instant case the husband and wife were not separately assessed.

Within the time allowed assessments for surtax were made on the husband as *b* follows: 1961-62, date 20th November 1962, a main assessment of £8,551; 1961-62, date 17th February 1970, an additional assessment of £3,000; 1965-66, date 15th December 1966, a main assessment of £11,800. There have been some subsequent adjustments but nothing turns on the figures in this case and I do not think it is necessary to refer to them further.

The husband had not by 13th December 1974, so it appears from the stated case, *c* discharged any of the tax payable pursuant to the second and third assessments. It is common ground that had the wife been the subject of a separate assessment in respect of the years to which I have referred and an assessment had been made on her on 13th December 1974 that assessment would have been out of time and would have had to be discharged on appeal on the ground that the time limited for making it had expired. One of the 'consequences' (I take the word 'consequences' from sub-s *d* (2) of s 40) of that would have been that the taxpayer, who had then become a widow, would never have come under any liability to pay the tax which is now demanded. Nevertheless, on that day, which was many years after the wife had received the income in respect of which tax is sought to be recovered, notice was served on her under s 40 to pay forthwith the sum of £4,235, being the amount of the surtax which it was said would have been payable by her for the years 1961-62 and 1965-66 if she *e* had been assessed separately. That notice to pay was given pursuant to what was then s 359 of the Income Tax Act 1952, which is now s 40 of the 1970 Act, to which I have referred.

It is to be emphasised that prior to the service of the notice the taxpayer was under no liability to pay any part of the unpaid tax. Nor do the terms of sub-s (1) of s 40 impose any liability on the taxpayer to pay the unpaid tax. Subsection (1) only *f* authorises the giving of a notice calling on the wife to pay. It is only when one comes to sub-s (2) of s 40 that one finds the 'consequences' of the giving of the notice. That subsection provides that 'the same consequences' as respects the matters there speci- fied 'shall follow on the service of a notice under subsection (1) ... as would have followed on the making on [the woman of a separate assessment] ... being an assess- ment ... which ... was made *on the day of the service of the notice'*. So one must, in my *g* view, ask the question what consequences of such an assessment as is specified in s 40(1)(*b*), that is to say a separate assessment on the wife, would have followed had such an assessment been made on the day of the service of the notice.

As I have already indicated, had the parties been separately assessed and had the commissioners had the temerity to make an assessment on the taxpayer, and I quote sub-s (2), *'on the day of the service of the notice'*, i e on 13th December 1974, the *h* consequences which would have followed would have been the discharge of the assessment on appeal and an absence of any imposition of a liability on the taxpayer to pay any tax at all. Since under the very terms of sub-s (2) the same consequences as respects the imposition of a liability to pay and the recovery of the tax as to appeals are to follow the service of notices as would have followed the making of a separate assessment on the day of the service of the notice it must, in my judgment, follow *j* that the taxpayer, having duly appealed, never came under any liability to pay the sum demanded by the notice or any part thereof. On those short grounds this appeal must, in my judgment, succeed.

With all respect to the Special Commissioners and to the learned judge in the court below I venture to think that too much emphasis was placed on the terms of

sub-s (1) of s 40 and too little on the terms of sub-s (2) and that some confusion was
a introduced, as it was at one stage in this court, by discussion whether the notice itself
was out of time. There is a complete absence in the finding of the commissioners
and the judgment of the learned judge of any emphasis on the fact that the consequences which would ensue from the service of the notice are to be governed by
reference to a notional assessment made on the very day of the service of the notice.
The reference in sub-s (2) to the day of the service of the notice appears to me to be
b quite vital to this case. The learned judge in the court below paid particular attention
to the words 'original assessment' which, he remarked[1], '. . . you will find occurring
in almost every line of that section'. He thought that all s 40(2) was saying was that
the effect of the notice was not to raise any new assessment on the wife at all, but
to assume that the original assessment was not one assessment on the husband and
wife but two separate assessments, one on the husband and one on the wife, and then
c it imposed on the wife a liability to pay tax which she would have had to pay if there
had been a separate assessment on her. The learned judge went on to say[1]:

> 'One must look at sub-s (2), because the words "as would have followed on
> the making on her . . . being an assessment which" clearly show that what it is
> doing is not to say that there is to be any new assessment, but is simply passing
d > the liability to pay from the husband who has failed to pay to the wife who now
> is required to pay it under the notice. The amount which she has to pay is, of
> course, limited to that part which is attributable to her income which was
> originally included in the assessment which was made on the husband.'

That was really all the learned judge said in support of these findings.
As I have already indicated, I think that he failed to pay correct attention to the
e terms of sub-s (2) and I would allow the appeal.

ORR LJ. I agree.

SHAW LJ. I agree.
f

Appeal allowed. Leave to appeal to the House of Lords refused.

Solicitors: *J Memery & Co* (for the taxpayer); *Solicitor of Inland Revenue*

A S Virdi Esq Barrister.
g
───
1 [1977] 1 All ER 390 at 397, [1977] STC 18 at 25

Sheffield City Council v Graingers Wines Ltd   *a*

COURT OF APPEAL, CIVIL DIVISION
LORD DENNING MR, ORR AND SCARMAN LJJ
22nd, 23rd, 24th FEBRUARY 1977

Rates – Unoccupied property – Resolution for rating of unoccupied property – Rating **b**
provisions to come into operation on day specified in the resolution – Specified in the resolution –
Date not expressly stated in resolution – Rating authority's intention that rating should
start on 1st April 1974 – All public announcements stating that rating to start on that date –
Whether requirement that date should 'be specified in the resolution' complied with – General
Rate Act 1967, s 17, Sch 1.

                                                                          c

On 6th March 1974, at a meeting of the policy committee of the council, the city
treasurer recommended that a resolution should be passed under s 17(1)*ª* of the
General Rate Act 1967 that unoccupied properties in the council's area were to be
rated. A resolution was proposed that those properties should 'be rated in accordance with Section 17, as amended, and the 1st Schedule of' the 1967 Act. The discussion
at the meeting centred on whether the rating should start from 1st April, i e the com-   *d*
mencement of the next rating period. A few councillors who wished to defer a
decision on the matter put forward an amendment to the resolution. The amendment was defeated and the resolution passed. It did not however specify the date on
which the provisions of Sch 1 were to become operative. Later that day the minutes of
the meeting were forwarded to the council which, in the presence of the press,
approved the resolution. On 7th March the local newspapers announced that the   *e*
rating of unoccupied properties in the area was to take place straight away. Thereafter
the council, in accordance with their statutory obligation under s 17(3)*ᵇ* of the 1967
Act, caused a copy of the resolution to be inserted in a local newspaper and in the
London Gazette, and prefaced it with a statement that it was to take effect as from 1st
April. They also distributed a notice to the owners of unoccupied properties in the area
announcing that it had been resolved to rate those properties as from 1st April. They   *f*
then issued the rate demands. The defendants, who were the owners of one of the
unoccupied properties, refused to pay the rates in respect of it, contending that the
resolution of 6th March was invalid since it failed to comply with the mandatory
requirement in s 17(1) that the day on which the provisions of Sch 1 were to come into
operation should 'be specified in the resolution'.

                                                                          g

Held – On the true construction of s 17(1), the word 'specified' meant 'made clear', and
the resolution had, in the circumstances in which it had been passed, approved and
communicated to the general public, made it clear that the provisions of Sch 1 were
to come into operation on 1st April. It followed that the council had complied with the mandatory requirements of s 17(1) and that the defendants were   *h*
liable to pay the rates demanded in respect of their property (see p 72 *h*, p 73 *a* to *c*
and *g* to p 74 *f*, p 75 *h j*, p 76 *c d h j*, p 77 *d j* and p 78 *b*, post).

Notes
For the rating of unoccupied property, see Supplement to 32 Halsbury's Laws (3rd
Edn) para 51A.   *j*
    For the General Rate Act 1967, s 17, Sch 1, see 27 Halsbury's Statutes (3rd Edn) 93,
210.

---

a   Section 17(1), so far as material, is set out at p 75 *f*, post
b   Section 17(3) is set out at p 72 *h*, post

Section 17 and Sch 1 were amended, with effect from 4th March 1974, by s 15 of the
a Local Government Act 1974.

Case referred to in judgments
Reid v Dawson [1954] 3 All ER 498, [1955] 1 QB 214, [1954] 3 WLR 810, 53 LGR 24, CA,
2 Digest (Repl) 7, 14.

b **Appeal**
This was an appeal by the plaintiffs, the Sheffield City Council ('the council'),
against the judgment of Melford Stevenson J, dated 10th May 1976, dismissing their
claim against the defendants, Graingers Wines Ltd, for rates amounting to £1,188·29
due in respect of the defendants' factory and premises situated at Shepherd Street,
Sheffield, which were unoccupied for the purposes of s 17 of, and Sch 1, to the General
c Rate Act 1967, as amended, from 1st July 1974 to 15th October 1974. The facts are
set out in the judgment of Lord Denning MR.

Francis Radcliffe for the council.
Brian McCarthy for the defendants.

d **LORD DENNING MR.**   The councillors of the city of Sheffield have got into
trouble. Three years ago they determined to rate commercial properties which were
standing empty. In the old days they did not rate empty properties, but they determined to do so from 1st April 1974. There were 1,108 unoccupied commercial properties in the Sheffield area. They charged rates on them. The total amount due
for the year beginning 1st April 1974 was £373,289. Of that sum they collected
e £269,997. A balance remained yet to be paid of £103,292. Then someone concerned
with the Sheffield Chamber of Commerce said that the demand was unlawful; that
the officers of the city council had not got the procedure right. So they could not go
on to collect the outstanding £103,292; and it might be that the council would have
to pay back the sum of £269,997 which they had already collected. The point came
before Melford Stevenson J. He held that the city council had not complied with the
f legal requirements when they set out to rate unoccupied property. The council
appeal to this court.

Ever since the statute of Elizabeth I[1] empty properties were not liable to rates. But
in 1967, under the General Rate Act 1967, Parliament said that a rating authority
could resolve to rate unoccupied properties; and if they decided to do so, the provisions should come into operation on such day as may be specified in the resolution.
Note those words 'on such day as may be specified in the resolution'. They are in s 17
g of the General Rate Act 1967.

For six or seven years after that Act many local authorities did not take advantage
of that power. The reason was that at that time, if they did not rate unoccupied
properties, they would automatically get the money out of a government grant. So
there was no advantage to them in rating unoccupied properties. But then in 1974
the situation altered. It was generally realised that it was unfair to others that the
h owners of unoccupied properties should be free of rates. After all, the owners get
the advantage of many of the local services, such as the fire services and the police.
So they ought to pay their share of the rates. In consequence the local authorities
were deprived of the government grant which they had previously received. Thenceforward it was advantageous for the local authorities to rate unoccupied properties.
But they had to do it by a resolution; and they had to do it 'on such day as may be
j specified in the resolution'.

The point in this case is this. The Sheffield Chamber of Commerce say that the
Sheffield City Council did not specify the day in the resolution. They did not specify
1st April 1974. If their resolution is to be construed very formally, that may be right.

1   Poor Relief Act 1601 (43 Eliz I c 2)

The judge so held. But is that the right approach? Ought the resolution to be construed so formally?

Much of the discussion before the judge, and before us, was whether or not the provision in s 17 'on such day as may be specified in the resolution' was mandatory or directory. That is always a matter of impression. I do not think that approach is at all helpful here. I would simply ask whether or not the resolution did make sufficiently clear the day from which it was to operate.

I will now state the facts. Everything happened quite quickly because time was important. The relevant amending statute only came into force on 4th March 1974 under the Local Government Act 1974. In anticipation of it, I expect that the government department sent out a circular to local authorities. At any rate, on 6th March 1974 the policy committee of the Sheffield City Council had a special meeting. The city treasurer made a report on the new situation. He said that the council must come to its decision quickly so as to apply it from 1st April 1974; and that it had to pass a resolution before 31st March. He recommended that there should be the rating of the unoccupied properties. A resolution was put forward. An amendment was proposed. A vote was taken. The members were divided according to their political parties. The Labour members wanted to rate the unoccupied commercial premises (omitting ordinary domestic houses, shops with rooms above, lock-up garages and museums) as from 1st April. Four Conservative members proposed an amendment to try and get the plan deferred. It went to a vote. A dozen Labour members voted for it. Four Conservatives voted against it. The Labour councillors succeeded. The resolution was then put to the meeting and it was carried. This was the resolution:

> 'Resolved: (1) That every relevant hereditament, as defined in Paragraph 15 of the 1st Schedule of the General Rate Act 1967, excluding the following classes of property [that is all the private houses, and so forth] be rated in accordance with Section 17, as amended, and the 1st Schedule of the General Rate Act 1967 at a rate of 100% of the charge applying to occupied properties within the area.'

That is all I now read. It will be seen that it does not include the words 'as from 1st April 1974'. That was an error of the draftsman. He ought to have put in those words. The discussion had been on the one point, should the rating start from the 1st April 1974 or should it be deferred? It is clear that the resolution was intended to operate as from 1st April 1974. That was what was resolved. But the draftsman unfortunately missed out the words 'as from 1st April 1974'.

The minute was drawn up. The policy committee sent it forward on the same day to the city council; and they approved it. The press were there. They were under no misapprehension. They knew that the rating of unoccupied property was going to take place from 1st April 1974. On the next day, 7th March, the local papers all came out with the announcement that the rating of unoccupied properties was to take place straight away. The comment was: 'Won't this turn people away from coming to Sheffield?' So the newspapers made it known to the public at large that the charge was to operate from 1st April 1974.

There was more to be done. Section 17(3) said:

> 'As soon as may be after a resolution is passed by a rating authority under this section, the authority shall cause a copy of the resolution to be published in the London Gazette and in one or more newspapers circulated in the area of the authority.'

The Sheffield City Council did so; and in those publications, the omission was remedied. In the local newspaper The Morning Telegraph for Friday, 29th March 1974, the notice ran:

> 'Notice is hereby given that the Sheffield District Council at its meeting on the

6th day of March, 1974 made a Resolution in the following terms to take effect
a   *as from the 1st day of April, 1974* [and then it set out the resolution].'

It was signed 'S. Jones, Head of Administration and Legal Department'. There was a
notice in exactly the same terms in the London Gazette. So when it came to those
formal notifications to the public, words were inserted which made it clear that it was
intended to take effect from 1st April 1974.
b   In addition the Sheffield City Council issued a notice telling everybody what they
were doing in respect of the rating of unoccupied properties. They sent it round to all
the unoccupied and unused properties. The first sentence said:

> 'The Rating Authority has resolved that the provisions of schedule 1 of the
> General Rate Act 1967, as amended, with respect to the rating of unoccupied or
> unused buildings shall apply in the area of the City of Sheffield Metropolitan
c   > District from the 1st April 1974.'

So they told everyone concerned the correct date.
Then they issued all their rate demands. Most of the demands were met. Over a
quarter of a million pounds was paid in respect of them. Everything seemed to be in
order until 11 months later. Then someone, who was buying property, made an
d   enquiry at the council officers about the rates. He looked through the formal documents. He checked them and said: 'They have not fulfilled the statute. In their
formal resolution they have missed out the requirement "such day as may be specified
in the resolution". They have missed out the words "1st April 1974".' Maybe it was a
drafting mistake, but that does not matter. They have missed it out. They have got
it all wrong, so they cannot collect the extra £100,000-odd that is due and they will
e   have to pay back all they have collected.' The judge held that that objection was
correct. I think that is far too technical a way in which to construe the resolution. It is
a well known maxim of the law that documents and transactions are to be construed
so as to give them validity; and not perish or fall.
Let us see what would happen if the judge is right, if all this is held to fall to the
ground by reason of the drafting error. It means that all the people who have not
f   paid yet, the bad payers or the late payers, get off and do not have to pay that £100,000.
All those who have already paid may or may not get their money back. The burden
will have to be put back on to all the ordinary ratepayers of occupied properties. We
were told it might come to 60p in the pound. Some occupiers might have to pay a
very large additional sum in rates.
It is quite clear that the correct resolution was made by the members of the com-
g   mittee. It was intended by them to operate as from 1st April 1974. Apart from the
formal record, that was undoubtedly what they intended and what they resolved.
It seems to me that the formal record should be read in the context of the whole of
the minute including the discussion of the proposed amendment, and so forth.
When it is read as a whole the implication is clear, that it is to operate as from 1st
April 1974.
h   The matter does not stop there. The drafting error would not be known to the
general public. Whenever any communication was made to the general public of
the resolution, the position was made plain beyond doubt. The position was made
plain both to the press and the newspapers, who published it on 7th March, and then
to anyone who read the Morning Telegraph or the London Gazette. It was as plain
as can be there. It was plain to the owners of unused property who received the
j   circular which was sent round that the resolution was intended to operate as from
1st April 1974.
In those circumstances, it seems to me that there is only one reasonable interpretation to be put on this resolution, that it was to operate as from 1st April 1974,
and it was plain to anyone who had read anything about this resolution that it was
to be implemented from 1st April 1974. Also it was made as clear as was reasonably

necessary in the resolution itself. That was a sufficient compliance with the provisions
of the statute, even though they be construed as mandatory.   *a*

So on this ground (which was not discussed before the judge) we should hold that
this rating charge is good and operates from 1st April 1974. I would allow the appeal
accordingly. The rates have to be paid by this company, Graingers Wines Ltd.

ORR LJ.   I agree. In my judgment, it clearly was the intention of the council   *b*
policy committee at its meeting on 6th March 1974 that the rating of unoccupied
premises should begin on 1st April of that year. The committee had before them a
report by the city treasurer pointing out that, to take advantage of s 17 of the General
Rate Act 1967 from 1st April 1974 a resolution would have to be approved by the
district council by 31st March. At that same meeting of the policy committee an
amendment was proposed by a member of the minority group in the council, con-   *c*
sisting of four members in number, whereby a decision on this matter would have
been postponed, and that amendment was heavily defeated.

It is, in my judgment, equally clear that the intention of the council itself at its
meeting on the same evening was the same. The subsequent advertisements in the
two newspapers correctly expressed the intention that the rating should commence
on 1st April, and the only error made was that it did not include the fact that rating   *d*
was to commence from that date in the terms of the resolution itself as set out below
on the same advertisement.

For the reasons given by Lord Denning MR, I too have been satisfied that in all the
circumstances of this case there was a compliance with the requirement that the day
when the rating was to begin should be specified in the resolution. I think it would be
taking far too narrow a view in all the circumstances to hold that that requirement   *e*
had not been complied with.

I would only add that the argument advanced before Melford Stevenson J appears
to me to have been materially different, at least in its emphasis, from that which
has been advanced in this court. I too would allow this appeal.

SCARMAN LJ.   I agree.   The issue between the parties emerges clearly from the   *f*
pleadings. The Sheffield City Council claim in this action rates which they say are
due in respect of unoccupied factory premises, and they put their claim under s 17
of, and Sch 1 to, the General Rate Act 1967. The defendants, respondents in this
court, Graingers Wines Ltd, by their defence admit that there was a resolution of
6th March (made by the district council, the plaintiffs' predecessors) pursuant to
which they purported to resolve that the provisions of Sch 1 to the General Rate Act   *g*
1967 should apply to the Sheffield area, but contend that the resolution failed to
specify, as required by the section, any day on which the provisions of Sch 1 should
come into operation. In the premises, the defendants submit that the provisions
of Sch 1 were not in operation in Sheffield at the material time and that they are not
liable for the rates claimed.

The issue between the parties depends on a consideration of the statute and the   *h*
resolution. It was contended on behalf of the council before the trial judge, Melford
Stevenson J, that the true effect of s 17 was directory only, by which was meant that
so long as there was a substantial compliance with the requirements of the section it
would not matter if it were not strictly complied with. The defendants contended
that on a proper construction of the section it was mandatory in effect, i e that it had
to be strictly complied with by the council as rating authority.   *j*

We have had copious citation of authority on the problem of whether statutory
provisions are to be considered mandatory or directory and, indeed, the judge was
also provided with a copious citation of authority. The judge came to the conclusion
that s 17 of the General Rate Act 1967 was mandatory in character. I wholly agree
with him. It was a statute which conferred on the council a power by taking

certain action to impose a money burden, i e liability to a rate, on owners of certain
a property in their area. Without resort to the many cases to which our attention has
been drawn, it emerges as perfectly clear on authority that, if a power is given to
impose a financial burden on a member of the public, then the donee of that power,
in this case the council, must act strictly in accordance with the requirements
or conditions laid down by Parliament so that it may have the benefit of the exercise
of that power. Although, of course, it is not directly in line with this case, nevertheless
b that approach to a section such as s 17 is amply justified by the principle that lies
behind the Bill of Rights of 1688. It was referred to us in the course of argument,
and it does show the sort of approach that the courts should make to any statutory
provision which entitles a levy of money to be laid on the citizen. In the recital to the
Bill of Rights one finds that one of the grievances which was there to be redressed was
levying money for and to the use of the Crown by pretence of prerogative for other
c time and in other manner than the same was granted by Parliament. And in the
enacting part of the Bill of Rights one finds that levying money for or to the use of the
Crown by pretence of prerogative without grant of Parliament for longer time or in
other manner than the same is or shall be granted is illegal. It is quite clear that when
Parliament indicates a manner and the time in which a subordinate authority may
exercise a power of imposing a monetary burden on the citizen, Parliament will expect
d and intend that the conditions for the exercise of that power be strictly complied
with.

I therefore think that the judge was absolutely right to answer the question which
was argued before him in the way that he did and to hold that this section was mandatory in its effect.

The next question that arises, is, what is the true construction of this mandatory
e section? Section 17(1) was a re-enactment of s 20 of the Local Government Act 1966
when it entered the law for the first time, and so far as material provides:

'A rating authority may resolve that the provisions of Schedule 1 to this Act
with respect to the rating of unoccupied property—(a) shall apply . . . to their
area, and in that case those provisions shall come into operation, or, as the case
may be, cease to be in operation, in that area on such day as may be specified in
f the resolution.'

In other words, the subsection confers on the rating authority a power to apply in its
area the provisions of Sch 1 by resolution and the provisions of that schedule will
come into operation on the date to be specified in the resolution. Subsection (2)
provides:

g 'The day to be specified in a resolution under subsection (1) of this section shall
be . . . the first day of a rate period for that area beginning after the day on which
the resolution is passed.'

It was argued on behalf of the defendants in this court that because the resolution,
the terms of which I shall turn to later, did not expressly mention 1st April 1974 or,
h indeed, any other day, it was impossible to say that the resolution could comply with
the section since the section does require, and I agree that it does require, that the date
on which the schedule is to come into operation is to be specified in the resolution.
Counsel for the defendants submitted that it would not be good enough if the best
that could be said would be that the date was necessarily implied on the true construction of the resolution. I reject that argument. The word "specified" in my judg-
j ment means no more than "made clear", and there is Court of Appeal authority
for that view of the word. I refer to *Reid v Dawson*[1]. In that case the Court of Appeal
had under consideration the phrase 'during some specified period of the year' as it

1   [1954] 3 All ER 498, [1955] 1 QB 214

was used in the Agricultural Holdings Act 1948. An argument was addressed to the court on the basis that implication would not do since the Act required that the *a* period of the year be specified. That argument was rejected in terms by Morris LJ, and I quote one passage from his judgment. He said[1]:

> 'In regard to that part of the case, however, an additional argument has been addressed to us, that inasmuch as this further period was a period that arose by implication, then it was not for some specified period of the year; for it is said that if the period arises by implication it cannot be "specified". In my judgment, *b* that reasoning is not sound'

In my respectful opinion, that dictum of Morris LJ is extremely helpful in guiding one to a proper understanding of this section and, for myself, I construe the word 'specified' where it appears in s 17(1) and (2) as meaning no more than 'made clear'. Therefore the obligation imposed on the council which seeks to exercise the *c* power conferred by this section is to do so by a resolution which makes clear the date on which the provisions of Sch 1 to the Act are to come into operation.

I have already said that in my judgment the section has to be strictly complied with by the council if it seeks to impose the rate. The question therefore becomes: did the Sheffield District Council in its resolution of 6th March 1974 make clear, and by that it must mean, I think, make clear to the members of the public concerned, *d* that the effective date for the application of Sch 1 to the Act was 1st April 1974?

The section does provide that certain actions shall be taken by the council to give notice, i e to make clear the existence and terms of the resolution. The section also provides the enquiring citizen with an opportunity of discovering what the resolution was. The duty on the council is imposed by s 17(3), which provides:

> 'As soon as may be after a resolution is passed by a rating authority under this *e* section, the authority shall cause a copy of the resolution to be published in the London Gazette and in one or more newspapers circulating in the area of the authority.'

That obligation was carried out by the district council (or their successors the city council, because there was a changeover of authority about this time) by insertion *f* of advertisements in the Sheffield Morning Telegraph and the London Gazette. The terms of the advertisement are, in my judgment, extremely important since they do reveal perfectly plainly how the council was interpreting the resolution that was passed in March. The advertisement, which was in precisely the same terms in both the Morning Telegraph and the London Gazette, began with the words:

> 'Notice is hereby given that the Sheffield District Council at its meeting on the *g* 6th day of March, 1974, made a Resolution in the following terms to take effect as from the 1st day of April, 1974 [and then the terms of the resolution are set out].'

Of course the 'following terms' do not include any express reference to date. That *h* advertisement appeared over the signature of the head of the administration and legal department of the Sheffield District Council. It was the clearest possible intimation to anyone who should read it that a resolution had been passed to take effect from 1st April 1974, and that it was a resolution applying the provisions of Sch 1 to the area of the council. It is, in my judgment, some evidence, it may not be conclusive, but it is some evidence, of the nature of the resolution passed that it is described in the statutory advertisement as a resolution to take effect from 1st April *j* 1974.

The citizen who does not see the advertisement can, as I have already mentioned,

---

1   [1954] 3 All ER 498 at 501, [1955] 1 QB 214 at 220

apply to the local authority for a copy of the minutes of the resolution. This facility
a is made available by s 17(4), which provides:

> 'A document purporting to be a copy of the minutes of a resolution...and to be
> certified under the hand of the clerk of the authority as a true copy of the minutes
> of the resolution shall be evidence that the resolution was passed by the
> authority.'

b   The defendants in this case, Graingers Wines Ltd, did ask for a certified copy of the
resolution, and received a document which has been very much at the heart of the
case. That document is certified as a true copy of a resolution passed by the district
council at their meeting held on 6th March 1974. It contains a preamble to this
effect:

> 'The City Treasurer submitted a report on the mandatory and discretionary
c > provisions of the Local Government Act 1974, in relation to the rating of unoccu-
> pied or unused buildings [and then it records]: Resolved [and I leave out the
> immaterial words] That every relevant hereditament . . . be rated in accordance
> with Section 17, as amended, and the 1st Schedule of the General Rate Act 1967
> at a rate of [etc].'

d Pausing there, notice the present tense. That resolution is much more consistent
with an immediate imposition of a rate than a future one. It certainly does not
contemplate a definite or agreed period which will have to elapse before it comes
into force. When one bears in mind the terms of sub-s (2) that the first legal opportunity for this resolution to have effect would be 1st April 1974, then one can say that,
so far, the words of the resolution are completely consistent, its intention being to
e make these relevant hereditaments liable to rates as from the first possible opportunity, i e in law, as we know, 1st April 1974 (subject only to the moratorium of three
months granted by Sch 1 itself). But the certificate of the resolution produced by the
clerk contains more than the mere operative part of the resolution. I have already
referred to the preamble, but it also contained a recital of an attempt by a number of
councillors to get the matter deferred and, indeed, an amendment was proposed to
f defer the resolution, and this amendment as is set out in the certified copy of the
minutes of the resolution was rejected. For what it is worth, that piece of information,
made public in the way that I have indicated as part and parcel of the minutes containing the resolution is another indication that the resolution was intended to have the
most immediate effect that it could have in law.
        It is important to look at the surrounding circumstances of the resolution insofar as
g one may use them to interpret the resolution as they would be known not to the few
in the confidence of the council but to the general public, and we now see what the
general public did have. They had the two advertisements stating firmly and clearly
that the effective date of the resolution was 1st April 1974. They had on call the
minute of the resolution, a resolution which by an error in draftsmanship did not
mention expressly the date but the terms of which indicated that it was intended to
h impose the rate as soon as was lawfully possible. In my judgment, one has to ask
oneself, therefore, whether the resolution, interpreted in the factual matrix known
to the public, was such that it specified or made clear the date on which the provisions
of Sch 1 to the Act of 1967 was to be brought into operation. This point was not, I
think, really argued, at any rate, it certainly was not exposed clearly, to the trial
judge, but it has been fully argued in this court. Like Lord Denning MR and Orr LJ, I
j have come to the clear conclusion that the resolution properly construed in those
surrounding circumstances which it is legitimate to consider did specify the date on
which the schedule was to come into operation and the rate was to be imposed.
        Counsel, who has argued the case with very great skill on behalf of the respondent
citizen, has sought to counter that argument by saying that, if you look at the section
it is laying emphasis exclusively on the resolution, and if you look at all that material,

to which Lord Denning MR and I have referred, as to the publication of the resolution, you must isolate the resolution from its context and must focus on the purely formal *a* language of the resolution. Neither justice nor commonsense seems to me to require that we should make that violent and artificial extraction of the kernel from the nut in which it shelters.

In my judgment this resolution, notwithstanding its technical defect as a piece of draftsmanship, did in circumstances known to all concerned, or available to be known to all concerned, make clear the effective date on which the rate was to be *b* imposed by the council when it decided to exercise the power given to it by the section. For those reasons I also would allow the appeal.

Appeal allowed. Judgment for amount claimed. Leave to appeal to the House of Lords refused.

Solicitors: *Sharpe, Pritchard & Co*, agents for *Samuel Jones*, Sheffield (for the council); *c* *Lucas, Styring & Appleby*, Sheffield (for the defendants).

Christine Ivamy Barrister.

d

Wilson v Maynard Shipbuilding Consultants AB

COURT OF APPEAL, CIVIL DIVISION
MEGAW, BRIDGE AND WALLER LJJ
e
17th, 18th OCTOBER, 11th NOVEMBER 1977

Unfair dismissal – Excluded classes of employment – Employee who ordinarily works outside Great Britain – Work partly inside and partly outside Great Britain – Method to be applied in determining whether employee ordinarily works outside Great Britain – Whether employee who ordinarily works in Great Britain can also ordinarily work outside Great Britain during *f* *same period of employment – Whether proper to look at terms of contract or at what had happened during period of employment to determine whether employee 'ordinarily works outside Great Britain' –Trade Union and Labour Relations Act 1974, Sch 1, para 9(2).*

In July 1973 W was engaged by a shipbuilding company as a staff consultant on engineering matters. His contract of employment did not expressly state where he *g* would work but it was an implied term that he would work as required by the company in any country in which it had contracts. Between July 1973 and September 1975 he worked in Italy for 50 weeks and in the United Kingdom for 40 weeks. On 15th September 1975 he was dismissed. He made a complaint to an industrial tribunal, pursuant to Sch 1, para 4[a], to the Trade Union and Labour Relations Act 1974, claiming that his dismissal was unfair. The tribunal held that, since para 9(2)[b] of Sch 1 to *h* the 1974 Act excluded from the ambit of para 4 an employee who 'under his contract of employment . . . ordinarily works outside Great Britain', it had, by virtue of para 9(2), no jurisdiction to hear the complaint as he had worked more outside Great Britain than inside it during the period up to his dismissal. W appealed to the Employment Appeal Tribunal which affirmed the industrial tribunal's decision on the ground that para 9(2) applied to any employee who ordinarily worked outside Great Britain, *j* irrespective of whether he also ordinarily worked inside Great Britain. On appeal,

---

a Paragraph 4, is set out at p 80 *a b*, post
b Paragraph 9, so far as material, is set out at p 80 *c d*, post

Held – On the true construction of Sch 1, para 9, an employee could not, within the
a meaning of para 9(2), 'ordinarily work' under his contract of employment both inside
Great Britain and outside it during the same period of employment. Furthermore, in
deciding whether, for the purposes of para 9(2), an employee ordinarily worked
under his contract outside Great Britain, the tribunal had to look not at what had
actually happened during the period of employment up to his dismissal, but at the
express and implied terms of the contract to see where, having regard to the whole
b period contemplated by the contract, his base was to be, for, in the absence of special
factors leading to a contrary conclusion, it was the country where his base was to be
that would be treated as the place where he ordinarily worked under his contract of
employment. It followed that the industrial tribunal and the Employment Appeal
Tribunal had adopted the wrong approach to the determination of the question
where W ordinarily worked under his contract of employment. The appeal would
c therefore be allowed and the complaint remitted to the industrial tribunal for
reconsideration (see p 81 g, p 82 a and j to p 83 a and p 84 e to h, post).
Portec (UK) Ltd v Mogensen [1976] 3 All ER 565 overruled.

Notes
For the classes of employment excluded from the provisions relating to unfair dis-
d missal, see 16 Halsbury's Laws (4th Edn) para 618.
    For the Trade Union and Labour Relations Act 1974, Sch 1, paras 4, 9, see 44
Halsbury's Statutes (3rd Edn) 1787, 1793.

Cases referred to in judgment
Liverpool City Council v Irwin [1976] 2 All ER 39, [1977] AC 239, [1976] 2 WLR 562, 74
e   LGR 392, HL.
Maulik v Air India [1974] ICR 528, 9 ITR 348, NIRC; *affg* 9 ITR 257.
Portec (UK) Ltd v Mogensen [1976] 3 All ER 565, [1976] ICR 396, EAT.
Schuler (L) AG v Wickman Machine Tool Sales Ltd [1973] 2 All ER 39, [1974] AC 235,
    [1973] 2 WLR 683, [1973] 2 Lloyd's Rep 53, HL; *affg* [1972] 2 All ER 1173, [1972] 1
    WLR 840, CA, Digest (Cont Vol D) 123, *3613a*.
f
Case also cited
Roux International Ltd v Licudi [1975] ICR 424, 10 ITR 162.

Appeal
This was an appeal by Alan Wilson ('the employee') against the judgment of the
g Employment Appeal Tribunal given by Phillips J on 7th October 1976, dismissing
his appeal against a decision of an industrial tribunal (chairman Martin Jukes QC)
sitting in London on 29th January 1976, whereby the tribunal decided that it had no
jurisdiction to hear his complaint, made pursuant to Sch 1, para 4, to the Trade Union
and Labour Relations Act 1974, against the respondents, Maynard Shipbuilding
Consultants AB ('the employer'), alleging that he had been unfairly dismissed. The
h facts are set out in the judgment of the court.

Denis Orde for the employee.
Alexander Irvine for the employer.

                                                              Cur adv vult

j 11th November. **MEGAW LJ** read the following judgment of the court: This
appeal raises questions as to the construction of para 9(2) of Sch 1 to the Trade Union
and Labour Relations Act 1974. That schedule contains statutory provisions relating
to unfair dismissal. The concept of unfair dismissal, which is wider than, and in many
respects different from, the common law concept of wrongful dismissal, was originally enacted in the Industrial Relations Act 1971. Part II of Sch 1 to the 1974 Act

re-enacts the statutory provisions as to unfair dismissal which were contained in various sections of the repealed 1971 Act. Paragraph 4 of Sch 1 reads:

'(1) In every employment to which this paragraph applies every employee shall have the right not to be unfairly dismissed by his employer, and the remedy of an employee so dismissed for breach of that right shall be by way of complaint to an industrial tribunal under Part III of this Schedule, and not otherwise.

'(2) This paragraph applies to every employment except in so far as its application is excluded by or under any provision of this Schedule.'

The 'exclusions' foreshadowed by para 4(2) are enacted in para 9. We are not concerned with the exclusions set out in para 9(1). Paragraph 9(2) reads:

'Paragraph 4 above does not apply to any employment where under his contract of employment the employee ordinarily works outside Great Britain.'

Paragraph 9(3), which is relevant for the construction of para 9(2), provides:

'For the purposes of sub-paragraph (2) above a person employed to work on board a ship registered in the United Kingdom (not being a ship registered at a port outside Great Britain) shall, unless (a) the employment is wholly outside Great Britain, or (b) he is not ordinarily resident in Great Britain, be regarded as a person who under his contract ordinarily works in Great Britain.'

The importance of the decision we have to make as to the meaning and effect of these two sub-paragraphs is enhanced by the fact that language which in material respects is indistinguishable is used in the Employment Protection Act 1975, s 119(5) and (6). Section 119(5) provides:

'The following provisions of this Act do not apply to employment where under his contract of employment the employee ordinarily works outside Great Britain, that is to say, sections 22, 29, 35, 53, 57, 58, 59, 61, 64, 65, 70, 81, 99 and 100.'

The range of employees' rights and privileges thus excluded is extremely wide, as reference to the sidenotes of the sections enumerated suffices to show.

Following the language of the Act, we shall refer to the appellant as 'the employee'. We shall refer to the respondents, Maynard Shipbuilding Consultants AB, as 'the employer'.

The employee submitted to the industrial tribunal a claim against the employer for unfair dismissal. The employer contended that the industrial tribunal had no jurisdiction because of para 9(2) of Sch 1. The industrial tribunal, by its decision of 28th November 1975, upheld that submission. They held that the employee, under his contract of employment, ordinarily worked outside Great Britain. The employee appealed to the Employment Appeal Tribunal, which, in a judgment delivered by Phillips J on 7th October 1976, affirmed the decision of the industrial tribunal. The employee appeals to this court.

The employee had been employed since 1970 as a staff consultant on engineering matters, by an English company, H B Maynard & Co Ltd, the subsidiary of a United States corporation. In 1973 that contract was terminated as the result of the substitution of a new contract with a different employer, a Swedish company which is itself also a subsidiary of the American corporation. That company is 'the employer' for the purpose of this appeal. The contract was made by the acceptance by the employee on 27th November 1973 of the terms offered by the employer in a letter dated 2nd October 1973. The date of employment was expressed to be from 2nd July 1973. The contract contained no express term as to the place where the employee was to work. There were express terms which may be relevant. The employee was discharged by the employer with effect from 15th September 1975. This is the alleged unfair dismissal which the employee seeks to establish.

The industrial tribunal rejected an argument for the employee that the 1970
a contract, and what had happened thereunder as to place of work, were relevant
matters. They held that it was the 1973 contract which was relevant. That was a
conclusion of law. It is not now challenged. Another conclusion of law by the tribunal
which also is accepted by the employee, is that it was an implied term of the 1973
contract that the employee 'was to work as required in any country in which his
employers . . . had contracts'. The tribunal decided that 'the material time to look
b at [was] from July 1973, until he was discharged in September 1975'. Having already
found as a fact that during that period the employee had worked in Italy for 50 weeks
and in the United Kingdom (sic) for 40 weeks ('. . . and there was a period of holiday'),
the tribunal said:

c
> '. . . the applicant was working far more often outside the country than he was
> in England and . . . his work spanned more than one country. Accordingly we
> conclude that under this contract of employment the applicant ordinarily
> worked outside Great Britain.'

The tribunal's decision that the exclusion contained in para 9(2) barred the employee's right to assert unfair dismissal thus was based, and based solely, on the fact
that the employee had, during the period between the start of the employment and
d the dismissal, worked more weeks in Italy than in Great Britain.

Before the employee's appeal came on for hearing by the Employment Appeal
Tribunal, a judgment dealing with the construction of para 9(2) had been delivered
in another case before the appeal tribunal, *Portec (UK) Ltd v Mogensen*[1]. In that case
it had been held, in a judgment delivered by Bristow J[2], that—

e
> 'on the plain and ordinary meaning of its words, para 9(2) applies to anyone
> who, whether or not he ordinarily works inside Great Britain, ordinarily works
> outside.'

In other words, under para 9(2), an employee can 'ordinarily work', in respect of
the selfsame period of time, in two different countries; he can be ordinarily working
both in Great Britain and outside Great Britain. Even though he is ordinarily working
f in Great Britain, he may not have the statutory right as regards unfair dismissal,
because he may simultaneously be ordinarily working outside Great Britain. In his
judgment in the present case, Phillips J made it clear that the appeal tribunal regarded
itself as bound to follow that earlier decision. It was, it would seem, on the basis of the
correctness of the *Portec*[1] construction of para 9(2) that the decision of the industrial
tribunal in the present case was upheld.

g With all respect, we regard para 9(3) as showing that, in respect of the whole period
of employment contemplated by the contract or any given period within it, a person
cannot, during the selfsame period, be ordinarily working under his contract of employment both in Great Britain and outside Great Britain. 'Ordinarily works' cannot
have a different meaning in the two sub-paragraphs, (2) and (3), of para 9. In sub-para
(3) it must have the effect that an employee cannot ordinarily work both in and
h outside Great Britain in the same relevant period. Were it otherwise, sub-para (3)
would wholly fail in its intended purpose. It is intended to prevent British seamen
from being excluded from the right not to be unfairly dismissed, merely because they
may spend the greater part of their working time on board ship outside Great Britain.
This latter factor is intended to be rendered irrelevant by the provision of sub-para
(3) that seaman shall be 'regarded as a person who under his contract ordinarily
j works in Great Britain'. It must connote: 'and therefore does not ordinarily work
outside Great Britain'. Otherwise it would achieve nothing. For the obvious answer
would be: 'Never mind whether he is deemed ordinarily to work in Great Britain.

---

1   [1976] 3 All ER 565
2   [1976] 3 All ER 565 at 569

On the facts he ordinarily works outside Great Britain. Therefore para 9(2) does not operate to protect him'. He is excluded from the statutory right not to be unfairly *a* dismissed. Therefore we take the view that the judgment appealed from, following the earlier decision in *Portec (UK) Ltd v Mogensen*[1], is wrong. Unfortunately this is not the end of the difficulties thrown up by this case in relation to the deceptively simple-looking words of para 9(2). In deciding whether or not under his contract of employment the employee ordinarily works outside Great Britain, does one look to the terms of the contract or to what has actually happened during the employment? *b* What are the criteria by which the tribunal is to decide a disputed question as to where the employee 'ordinarily works under his contract of employment'?

As to the first of those questions, it is essential to bear in mind that para 9(2) is concerned, and concerned only, with cases in which the employment had not run its normal course to the end of the period, whatever it may have been, contemplated by the contract. The employee is claiming that the employment has been prematurely *c* terminated, unlawfully. It must be assumed, for the purposes of any question of construction of para 9(2), that the employee may be right in that claim. So if it were requisite or proper to look at what had actually happened, that investigation would be limited to looking at what had happened under a part only of the contemplated contractual period of employment; and the extent of that truncated period would have been defined by the unilateral, and possibly unlawful, act of the employer in *d* giving the dismissal notice. Thus, it could not be right, nor could it be the intended meaning of the words used in para 9(2), that one should decide the 'ordinarily works' ssue simply by reference to what had actually happened. Take an example. The contract by its express or implied terms provides that the employment should be for three years, of which the first year would be served abroad and the remaining two years in Great Britain. The employer gives notice, which the employee wishes to *e* claim was unfair dismissal, towards the end of the first year. It could not be said that the para 9(2) exclusion applies because of the fact that the employee had worked wholly abroad during the whole period that the employment had actually lasted. The answer is that one must look at the terms of the contract, express or implied. This was the view taken by Sir John Donaldson P in *Maulik v Air India*[2]. We think it must be right. *f*

This meaning conforms with the grammatical structure of para 9(2). The present tense is used: 'ordinarily works'. If it had been intended to relate the decision to what had happened up to the time of the dismissal, the present tense would be inappropriate. This construction also conforms, we believe, with good sense. It means that the question whether or not this important statutory right exists is settled at, and can be ascertained by reference to, the time of the making of the contract. *g* It is not liable to be varied by the unilateral act of the employer, the decision of the employer to give a dismissal notice at a time chosen by him, in the course of the performance of the contract. Of course, the terms of the contract may be varied, and, if they are varied in some relevant respect, it is the varied terms which have to be considered. But the question of variation, if it is raised in a case under para 9(2), has to be decided by the ordinary principles of the law of contract. A variation, *h* for example, cannot be unilateral, and it must be intended to affect the legal relations between the parties.

So the issue under para 9(2) must be answered by reference to the relevant terms of the contract of employment, express or implied. In the ordinary way, as the House of Lords has recently held (see, for example, *L Schuler AG v Wickman Machine Tool Sales Ltd*[3]) one may not look at what the parties did under the contract for the *j* purpose of construing its terms. There would seem, however, to be an exception to

---

1   [1976] 3 All ER 565
2   [1974] ICR 528
3   [1973] 2 All ER 39, [1974] AC 235

the strictness of that doctrine where there must be a relevant term, but what that
a term is cannot be ascertained otherwise than by looking at what the parties did.
See, for example, per Lord Kilbrandon in *L Schuler AG v Wickman Machine Tool Sales
Ltd*[1] and per Lord Wilberforce in *Liverpool City Council v Irwin*[2]. But such evidence,
if admissible in a particular case, must be treated with special care. For example, in
the present case the evidence that during the period of the contract which had elapsed
before the allegedly unfair dismissal the employee had been required to spend such
b and such time outside Great Britain and such and such time in Great Britain could
not be conclusive, and might have very small weight in the consideration of the
question where he would have been required to work if the contract had not been,
as the employee contends, wrongfully terminated at that point; or in the consideration of the question where, looking at the contract as a whole, the employee's base of
work was to be.
c   If the contract by its express or implied terms requires that the employee should do
his contractual work wholly, or substantially wholly, in Great Britain, the answer will
normally be simple. So, conversely, if under the contract the contractual work has to
be carried out wholly or substantially wholly outside Great Britain. This will dispose,
quite simply, of many cases. But what is to happen if, as in the present case, an
implied term of the contract leaves it to the employer's discretion as to whether the
d work shall be carried out wholly in Great Britain or wholly outside Great Britain or
for some period or periods in one place and for another period or other periods in
other places? Frankly, we do not think that those who were responsible for this
legislation realised the existence of this problem. But we have to try to give guidance
how such cases, of which the present case is one, ought to be approached so as to give
effect, as sensibly as is possible, to the words of para 9(2). If the guidance which we
e give is not in accordance with the intention of the legislation, or if it should involve
consequences which are regarded by the policy-makers as undesirable, or if it should
involve insoluble problems for the industrial tribunals who will have to consider such
questions, we express our urgent support for the plea which has already been made,
by Phillips J, in his judgment under appeal in this very case, that those who have the
responsibility for so doing should, as a matter of urgency, reconsider para 9(2). If
f amendment or clarification is required, para 11(2) and (3) of Sch 1 to the 1974 Act
provides a relatively simple procedure. Let it not be said that the Employment
Appeal Tribunal or this court is frustrating the intention of the legislature when both
those courts are urging that, if their interpretation of the words used should not
give effect to the intention of the legislature, the legislature should be invited urgently,
by a simple procedure, to clarify its intention.
g   In trying to ascertain the intention of the legislature, the court is entitled, and we
think bound, to have regard to the use of the phrase 'ordinarily works', as used by
the legislature in s 12 of the Contracts of Employment Act 1972. It cannot have been
intended to have a different meaning in para 9(2) of the 1974 Act from the meaning
which it plainly has in that section of the 1972 Act. In s 12 of the 1972 Act it plainly
contemplates that the employee may 'ordinarily work in Great Britain' even though
h for a period of his employment he is engaged in work wholly or mainly outside
Great Britain. It necessarily follows that, to decide where an employee 'ordinarily
works', one must look to the contract and to the whole contemplated period of the
contract, and not simply to some lesser period within that whole period. The decision
of the industrial tribunal in this case, based on the relative length of the periods
spent in work in Italy and Great Britain respectively up to the date of the dismissal,
j therefore cannot stand. From what we have said, however, it will be clear that we
have great sympathy with the industrial tribunal in the task with which it was faced
in this case.

---

1   [1973] 2 All ER 39 at 63, [1974] AC 235 at 272
2   [1976] 2 All ER 39 at 43, [1977] AC 239 at 253

By what criteria, then, is one to decide, looking at the contractual terms express or implied, where the employee 'ordinarily works' under that contract, where those *a* terms do not themselves provide and require that the place of work is to be, wholly or substantially wholly, in Great Britain, or wholly or substantially wholly, outside Great Britain? An employee may properly be regarded as 'ordinarily working' at a particular place under his contract of employment even though in the event, at the end of the employment, it should turn out that he had actually spent more of his working hours or days or weeks or months away from that place than in that place; *b* and even though the forecast (for what it might be worth) made at the time when the contract of employment was made would be that he would so spend his time. Thus, to take domestic examples, a meter-reader employed by a gas or electricity authority may spend much more of his time away from his base than in his base. But if the question were to arise where he 'ordinarily works', the answer, subject to consideration of any relevant contractual terms, might, at least, well be 'he ordinarily *c* works at the office which is his base'. So with a barrister who, if a time record were made, may be found to spend much more of his working life in courts and travelling to and from courts than in his chambers. Yet it might very well sensibly be said, if the question arose as to where he 'ordinarily works', that he 'ordinarily works' in his chambers. The same applies where an employee may under the terms of his contract be required to go out of Great Britain, either on journeys in discharge of his contractual *d* duties, like an air-pilot or a long-distance lorry driver, or to spend periods of time, longer or shorter in the discretion of his employer, working at some place or a number of different places outside Great Britain.

In such a case as the present it appears to us that the correct approach is to look at the terms of the contract, express and implied (with reference, it may be, to what has happened under the contract, for the limited purpose which we have expressed *e* above) in order to ascertain where, looking at the whole period contemplated by the contract, the employee's base is to be. It is, in the absence of special factors leading to a contrary conclusion, the country where his base is to be which is likely to be the place where he is to be treated as ordinarily working under his contract of employment. Where his base, under the contract, is to be will depend on the examination of all relevant contractual terms. These will be likely to include any such *f* terms as expressly define his headquarters, or which indicate where the travels involved in his employment begin and end; where his private residence, his home, is, or is expected to be; where, and perhaps in what currency, he is to be paid; whether he is to be required to pay national insurance contributions in Great Britain. These are merely examples of factors which, among many others that may be found to exist in individual cases, may be relevant in deciding where the employee's base is for the *g* purpose of his work, looking to the whole normal, anticipated, duration of the employment.

We allow the appeal and remit the application for reconsideration by the industrial tribunal.

Appeal allowed. Application remitted to industrial tribunal for reconsideration. Leave to *h* *appeal to the House of Lords refused.*

Solicitors: *Mincoff, Science & Gold*, Newcastle-upon-Tyne (for the employee); *Baker & Mackenzie* (for the employer).

                                         Christine Ivamy   Barrister.

a # Dunmore v McGowan (Inspector of Taxes)

COURT OF APPEAL, CIVIL DIVISION
STAMP, ORR AND EVELEIGH LJJ
8th FEBRUARY 1978

b *Income tax – Persons chargeable – Receipt of income – Person receiving income chargeable –
Interest on money – Deposit account in bank's name retained to satisfy taxpayer's liability to
bank under guarantee – Interest paid into account – Guarantee discharged – Deposit and
interest transferred to taxpayer – Whether taxpayer received interest on deposit when
credited – Income Tax Act 1952, s 148.*

c In 1965 the taxpayer entered into a written guarantee in favour of a bank guaranteeing
to pay all moneys owed to the bank by a company. In April 1967 the taxpayer opened
a deposit account in the name of the bank on his behalf ('the first deposit account'),
which was credited with various sums. On 5th June the taxpayer wrote to the bank
authorising them to transfer to a new deposit account ('the second deposit account')
in the bank's name a certain sum to be retained by them while he remained under
d any liability in respect of the guarantee. On 20th June interest was credited to the
first deposit account and in July the balance of the account including interest was
transferred to the new deposit account. Until July 1969 interest was periodically
credited to the second deposit account. That account was then closed, the loan to
the company having been paid off, and the taxpayer withdrew the balance. He was
assessed to income tax under Sch D, Case III, for the years 1967 to 1970 on the total
e interest on the ground that he had received or been entitled to the income on the first
and second deposit accounts, within s 148[a] of the Income Tax Act 1952. The taxpayer
appealed, contending that the money in the second deposit account was held by the
bank as trustee during the existence of the guarantee and that in any event, under the
terms of the June 1967 letter, he did not receive and was not entitled to any interest,
since he could not at any time claim it.

f **Held** – The whole of the interest paid enured immediately to the taxpayer's
benefit, regardless of the guarantee. If the interest had been resorted to under the
terms of the June letter, it would have reduced the personal liability of the taxpayer
pro tanto; since the interest was not called on, the taxpayer had been entitled to
withdraw it in full on the ending of the guarantee. There was no express arrangement
g between the bank and the taxpayer creating a trust of the money and no such relationship could be implied. It followed that the taxpayer was liable to tax on the interest.
Accordingly the appeal would be dismissed (see p 87 d and h to p 88 c and f g, post).

Whitworth Park Coal Co Ltd v Inland Revenue Comrs [1959] 3 All ER 703 considered.
· Per Curiam. The doctrine that 'receivability without receipt is nothing' is a doctrine
which can be pressed too far (see p 87 e, post).
h Decision of Brightman J [1976] 3 All ER 307 affirmed.

Notes
For interest of money on bank accounts within Sch D, Case III, see 20 Halsbury's Laws
(3rd Edn) 246-248, 257, 258, paras 450-453, 471.
For the Income Tax Act 1952, s 148, see 31 Halsbury's Statutes (2nd Edn) 145.
j For 1970-71 and subsequent years of assessment, s 148 of the 1952 Act has been
replaced by s 114(1) of the Income and Corporation Taxes Act 1970.

---

a Section 148 provides: 'Tax under Schedule D shall be charged on and paid by the persons
receiving or entitled to the income in respect of which tax under that Schedule is in this
Act directed to be charged.'

Case referred to in judgments

Whitworth Park Coal Co Ltd v Inland Revenue Comrs [1959] 3 All ER 703, [1961] AC 31, [1959] 3 WLR 842, 38 Tax Cas 531, HL, 28(1) Digest (Reissue) 265, 864.

Appeal

On 30th September 1965 the taxpayer, William Sydney Dunmore, entered into a written guarantee in favour of Lloyds Bank Europe Ltd. He guaranteed to pay on demand all moneys then or thereafter owing to the bank by Belmound Investments Ltd, a property company with which he was concerned, on any current or other account. The amount recoverable under the guarantee was limited to £50,000 with interest. On 1st April 1967 the taxpayer opened a deposit account with Lloyds Bank Europe Ltd with a credit of £2,000 ('the first deposit account'). The first deposit account was headed 'Lloyds Bank Europe Limited. Re W. S. Dunmore, Deposit Account at 7 days' notice—Interest allowed at half per cent over bank rate'. On 10th April 1967 a further £4,000 was credited to the first deposit account. On 24th May £2,000 was debited to the account. On 26th May £24,000 was paid into the first deposit account, thus producing a credit balance of £28,000. On 5th June the taxpayer addressed a letter ('the June letter') in the following terms to the bank:

> 'With reference to my guarantee in favour of the Bank on behalf of the above-mentioned Company dated the 30th September 1965, for the sum of £50,000, I authorise you to transfer to a Deposit Account in your name the sum of £4,000 plus £25,000 which you will be receiving from the Liquidator of Bardimore Investments Limited, representing my share of the proceeds of sale of Bardimore Investments Plot 4 of the Golden Valley Estate. These sums are to be retained by you whilst I remain under any liability under the aforementioned guarantee. You may at any time apply the amount for the time being standing to the credit of the said Deposit Account in or towards payment of any monies payable by me to you under the aforementioned guarantee.'

The taxpayer was unaware, when he signed the June letter, of the credits already made to the first deposit account. The credits of £4,000 and £24,000 which had already been made to the first deposit account represented the credits of £4,000 and £25,000 described in the June letter as anticipated future receipts. The first deposit account was in the name of and operable by the taxpayer. It was common ground between the parties that the interest to accrue on the moneys to be transferred to the new account mentioned in the June letter would be caught by the terms of the June letter, and that it would not be open to the taxpayer to require interest which might be credited on the moneys in the new deposit account to be paid to him. On 20th June 1967 interest amounting to £190 18s 6d was credited to the first deposit account. On 4th July 1967 the sum of £28,190 18s 6d, being the sum to the credit of the first deposit account, was transferred to the credit of a new deposit account headed 'Lloyds Bank Europe Limited. Re liability of W. S. Dunmore on behalf of Belmound Investments' ('the second deposit account'). Interest was thereafter periodically credited to this account, the last credit of interest being made on 31st July 1969. On that day, the loan to Belmound Investments Ltd having then or previously been paid off, the second deposit account was closed. A sum of £31,000 was withdrawn by the taxpayer, and the balance of £1,510 was placed to the credit of a third deposit account with Lloyds Bank Europe Ltd in the sole name of the taxpayer. The total interest accumulated in the second deposit account plus the £190 18s 6d credited to the first deposit account amounted to just over £5,000. Further assessments to income tax were made against the taxpayer under Sch D, Case III, for the years 1967-68, 1968-69 and 1969-70 in the sums of £200, each in respect of bank interest. The taxpayer appealed to the Commissioners for the General Purposes of the Income Tax for the Division of Croydon who, on 10th January 1975, determined the further assessments on the taxpayer in the sum of £1,109 for 1967-68, £2,431 for 1968-69 and

£1,540 for 1969-70. The taxpayer required the commissioners to state a case for the
a opinion of the High Court pursuant to s 56 of the Taxes Management Act 1970, the
question for the opinion of the court being whether on the facts found the sums of
interest credited to the deposit accounts were income in respect of which the taxpayer
was properly assessable to income tax. On 25th June 1976 Brightman J[1] dismissed
the taxpayer's appeal.

b *Marcus Jones* for the taxpayer.
C H McCall for the Crown.

STAMP LJ. This is an appeal by the taxpayer against an order of Brightman J[1] made
on 25th June 1976 when an appeal by the taxpayer by way of case stated from the
c General Commissioners for the Croydon District was dismissed, the learned judge
upholding the decision of the General Commissioners that tax was payable on some
interest payments referred to in the case stated.

The facts of the case and the judgment of the learned judge are fully stated in the
report of the case in the court below and it is unnecessary for me to set out the facts
or refer at length to the judgment; it is there for all to read.

d The point at issue clearly appears from Brightman J's judgment. It is a judgment
with which I fully agree and I would be content to accept it as my own. I will, however,
add a few remarks in deference to the submissions made by counsel for the taxpayer
in this court.

First of all, may I say this, that it appears to me that the doctrine that 'receivability
without receipt is nothing' is a doctrine which can be pressed too far. Much play was
e made in this court, as in the court below, of *Whitworth Park Coal Co Ltd v Inland
Revenue Comrs*[2] where the facts were wholly different. However, there is a passage on
which particular reliance was placed in which Viscount Simonds said[3]:

'Traders pay tax on the balance of profits and gains and bring money owed to
them into account in striking that balance, but ordinary individuals are not
f assessable and do not pay tax until they *get* the money, because until then it is not
part of their income. There may well be difficult border-line cases which do not
clearly fall into either or these classes . . .' [My emphasis.]

Of course, to some extent that remark, 'individuals . . . do not pay tax until they *get* the
money', begs the question: for what is meant by the word 'get'? Read in isolation it
does not take one very much further because one does not know without reading the
g whole of the *Whitworth* case[2] what precisely is meant by 'get', and when one finds the
facts of that case are wholly different from the facts of this case one does not obtain very
much assistance in solving the problem whether in the instant case the interest here
in question was in truth received.

However, as the judge pointed out in the instant case every penny of the interest in
question enured immediately to the benefit of the taxpayer and to the full extent of
h the interest. The judge went on to say[4]:

'Admittedly the money was locked up in the deposit account while the guarantee subsisted, but it was locked up in such a way that it enured to the taxpayer's
benefit at once, either as money coming to his hands or as reducing his liabilities.
Whatever might be the ultimate destination of the £347, it was in my judgment

j

1 [1976] 3 All ER 307, [1976] 1 WLR 1086, [1976] STC 433
2 [1959] 3 All ER 703, [1961] AC 31, 38 Tax Cas 531
3 [1959] 3 All ER 703 at 713, 714, [1961] AC 31 at 63, 38 Tax Cas 531 at 573
4 [1976] 3 All ER 307 at 313, [1976] 1 WLR 1086 at 1090, [1976] STC 433 at 439

received by the taxpayer on the day when it was credited to the second deposit account. On that day it swelled his estate to the extent of £347. I do not think that there is anything in this reasoning which is contrary to the logic of *Whitworth Park Coal Co Ltd v Inland Revenue Comrs*[1].'

I agree entirely. Just as the £28,000 deposited with the bank was a debt due by the bank to the taxpayer subject to any claims that might arise under the guarantee, so on the interest being credited to the deposit account did the interest acquire the same characteristics. The interest was received or 'got' when it was credited to the deposit account, an account of money which was at all times owed by the bank to the taxpayer, albeit charged in support of the guarantee.

Counsel for the taxpayer submitted that the taxpayer would only receive the interest credited to the account if the bank turned out to be solvent. In my view this confuses payment with receipt in the sense in which that word is used in the relevant parts of the Income Tax Acts. The interest which is credited to my deposit account is received by me at the date when it is so credited, notwithstanding that it may not be paid to me until a future date, and it is just as much mine whether it is or is not paid to me.

Counsel for the taxpayer also repeated the submissions made in the court below, that the bank became a trustee of the 'funds' (I put the word in inverted commas, it was the word used by counsel for the taxpayer) in which the taxpayer had only a contingent interest. Counsel for the taxpayer when asked what was the property of which the bank was a trustee submitted that the property consisted of what he called the totality of the accounts. I confess I found difficulty in appreciating the meaning of that expression but, however that may be, I am satisfied that the relationship between the bank and the taxpayer never became anything but the relationship of banker and customer.

Alternatively, it is said that the bank exercised control over what counsel for the taxpayer called the 'fund'. Again I confess I do not understand or appreciate that conception. There was no fund except a sum of money which historically had been deposited with the bank and for which the bank became liable (in one way or another either by discharging the amount due on the guarantee or by repayment to the taxpayer) to repay. I can see no fiduciary element in the transaction at all.

For the reasons given by Brightman J, and those short reasons, I would dismiss this appeal.

ORR LJ. I agree.

EVELEIGH LJ. I agree.

Appeal dismissed. Leave to appeal to the House of Lords refused.

Solicitors: *W S Dunmore* (for the taxpayer); *Solicitor of Inland Revenue.*

A S Virdi Esq Barrister.

---

1 [1959] 3 All ER 703, [1961] AC 31, 38 Tax Cas 531

Daniels and others v Daniels and others

CHANCERY DIVISION
TEMPLEMAN J
20th, 21st JULY 1977

b   *Company – Minority shareholder – Representative action – Negligence alleged against majority shareholders – Negligence resulting in profit to majority shareholders at expense of company – No fraud alleged – Majority shareholders directors of company – Directors alleged to have procured company to sell land to one of themselves – Action by minority shareholders alleging that sale at an undervalue – Statement of claim alleging that sale made in breach of duty and that directors had benefited from breach but not alleging fraud – Whether action maintainable by minority shareholders – Whether statement of claim should be struck out.*

The plaintiffs were minority shareholders in the third defendant ('the company'). The first and second defendants were majority shareholders and directors of the company. In October 1970 the company sold certain land to the second defendant *d*   for £4,250 on the instructions of the first and second defendants as directors. In 1974 the land was sold by the second defendant for £120,000. The plaintiffs brought an action against the defendants alleging that the price at which the land had been sold to the second defendant was well below its market value and that the first and second defendants knew that that was so, but had purported to adopt the probate value of the land although a probate value was usually much less than the open *e*   market value. The defendants applied to strike out the statement of claim as disclosing no reasonable cause of action since it did not allege fraud or any other ground that would justify an action by minority shareholders against the majority for damage caused to the company.

Held – The application would be dismissed. The confines of the rule that minority *f*   shareholders could not maintain an action on behalf of the company should not be drawn so narrowly that directors were able to make a profit out of their own negligence. Accordingly, minority shareholders were entitled to bring an action where the majority of the directors negligently, though without fraud, had benefited themselves at the expense of the company (see p 96 *b* to *f* and p 97 *b*, opst).

Alexander v Automatic Telephone Co [1900] 2 Ch 56 and *Cook v Deeks* [1916-17] All ER *g*   Rep 285 applied.

Foss v Harbottle (1843) 2 Hare 461 explained.

Atwool v Merryweather (1867) LR 5 Eq 464, *Turquand v Marshall* (1869) LR 4 Ch App 376 and *Pavlides v Jensen* [1956] 2 All ER 518 distinguished.

Notes

h   For the rule in *Foss v Harbottle*, see 7 Halsbury's Laws (4th Edn) para 713, and for when the court will interfere with the exercise of a company's powers, see ibid para 714, and for cases on the subject, see 9 Digest (Reissue) 643, 689-691, 3860-3867, 4094-4106.

Cases referred to in judgment

Alexander v Automatic Telephone Co [1900] 2 Ch 56, 69 LJCh 428, 82 LT 400, CA, 9 Digest *j*   (Reissue) 748, 4446.

Atwool v Merryweather (1867) LR 5 Eq 464n, 37 LJCh 35, 9 Digest (Reissue) 686, 4079.

Birch v Sullivan [1958] 1 All ER 56, [1957] 1 WLR 1247, 9 Digest (Reissue) 755, 4486.

Burland v Earle [1902] AC 83, 71 LJPC 1, 85 LT 553, 9 Digest (Reissue) 670, 4001.

Clinch v Financial Corpn (1868) LR 5 Eq 450; *affd and varied* LR 4 Ch App 117, 38 LJCh 1, 19 LT 334, 9 Digest (Reissue) 748, 4449.

Cook v Deeks [1916] 1 AC 554, [1916-17] All ER Rep 285, 85 LJPC 161, 114 LT 636, PC, 9 Digest (Reissue) 629, *3754.*

Foss v Harbottle (1843) 2 Hare 461, 67 ER 189, 9 Digest (Reissue) 689, *4094.*

Gray v Lewis, Parker v Lewis (1873) LR 8 Ch App 1035, 43 LJCh 281, 29 LT 12, 9 Digest (Reissue) 678, *4046.*

Heyting v Dupont [1963] 3 All ER 97, [1963] 1 WLR 1192, *affd* [1964] 2 All ER 273, [1964] 1 WLR 843, CA, 9 Digest (Reissue) 752, *4481.*

MacDougal v Gardiner (1875) LR 20 Eq 383; *rvsd* LR 10 Ch App 606, 32 LT 653, LJJ, subsequent proceedings 1 Ch D 13, 45 LJCh 27, 33 LT 521, CA, 9 Digest (Reissue) 643, *3860.*

Mason v Harris (1879) 11 Ch D 97, 48 LJCh 589, 40 LT 644, CA, 9 Digest (Reissue) 748, *4445.*

Menier v Hooper's Telegraph Works (1874) LR 9 Ch App 350, 43 LJCh 330, 30 LT 209, LJJ, 9 Digest (Reissue) 686, *4085.*

Mozley v Alston (1847) 1 Ph 790, 16 LJCh 217, 9 LTOS 97, 41 ER 833, LCC, 9 Digest (Reissue) 747, *4440.*

Pavlides v Jensen [1956] 2 All ER 518, [1956] Ch 565, [1956] 3 WLR 224, 9 Digest (Reissue) 755, *4485.*

Turquand v Marshall (1869) LR 4 Ch App 376, 38 LJCh 639, 20 LT 766, 33 JP 708, LC, 9 Digest (Reissue) 534, *3193.*

Cases also cited

Campbell v The Australian Mutual Provident Society (1908) 77 LJPC 117, PC.

Dominion Cotton Mills Co Ltd v Amyot [1912] AC 546, PC.

Harris v A Harris Ltd 1936 SC 183.

North-West Transportation Co Ltd v Beatty (1887) 12 App Cas 589.

Russell v Wakefield Waterworks Co (1875) LR 20 Eq 474.

Procedure summons

The plaintiffs, (1) Douglas Percy Daniels, (2) Gordon Eric Daniels and (3) Caroline Emma Soule, brought an action against the defendants, (1) Bernard Edwyn Daniels, (2) Beryl G Daniels and (3) Ideal Homes (Coventry) Ltd ('the company'), claiming, inter alia, (1) a declaration that the first and second defendants and each of them as directors of the company had been guilty of misfeasance and breach of trust in relation to the company by causing the company to sell certain freehold land to the second defendant, (ii) an order that the first and second defendants should pay damages to the company for the misfeasance, and (iii) an account of all profits made by the first and/or second defendant by reason of the sale and/or misfeasance and breach of trust and payment to the company of whatever should be found due on taking the account. By a summons dated 24th November 1976 the first and second defendants applied for an order that the statement of claim in the action be struck out as disclosing no reasonable cause of action or otherwise as an abuse of the process of the court. The facts are set out in the judgment.

David Richards for the first and second defendants.
W A Blackburne for the plaintiffs.

TEMPLEMAN J. This is an application to strike out a statement of claim as disclosing no reasonable cause of action. The authorised share capital of the third defendant company consists of 3,000 £1 ordinary shares and the three plaintiffs between them hold 1,348. They are, therefore, in a minority. The first two defendants, who are husband and wife, hold 1,651 shares and they are, therefore, in a majority. The first two defendants, according to the statement of claim, were in October 1970 the only directors of the company.

The plaintiffs' complaint appears from paras 3 and 4 of the statement of claim. Paragraph 3 alleges that in October 1970 the company sold certain land in Warwickshire to the second defendant for £4,250 on the instructions and by the direction of the directors, who were the first and second defendants. Paragraph 4 alleges that the price of £4,250 paid to the company by the second defendant was less than the current value of the land at the time of the sale, as the first and second defendants well knew or ought to have known. The particulars of that allegation are first that the first and second defendants purported to adopt a probate value made on the death, which took place on 8th June 1969, of the father of the plaintiffs and the first defendant; secondly, that 'probate values, being conservative in amount, are customarily less than the open market value obtainable as between a willing vendor and a willing purchaser'; thirdly, that in 1974 the land was sold by the second defendant for the sum of £120,000.

Putting it broadly, all the allegations will be denied by the defendants, if the action proceeds. But it is common ground that for the purpose of this application I must proceed on the basis that all the allegations in the statement of claim can be sustained.

Counsel for the first two defendants, who bring this application to strike out, says there is no cause of action shown because the statement of claim does not allege fraud and, in the absence of fraud, minority shareholders are unable to maintain a claim, on behalf of the company against a majority. For that proposition he referred first of all to the principles set out in *Foss v Harbottle*[1]. That case established the general proposition that minority shareholders cannot maintain an action on behalf of the company, subject to certain exceptions. The exceptions are four in number, only one of which is of possible application in the present case. The first exception is that a shareholder can sue in respect of some attack on his individual rights as a shareholder; secondly, he can sue if the company, for example, is purporting to do by ordinary resolution that which its own constitution requires to be done by special resolution; thirdly, if the company has done or proposes to do something which is ultra vires; and, fourthly, if there is fraud and there is no other remedy. There must be a minority who are prevented from remedying the fraud or taking any proceedings because of the protection given to the fraudulent shareholders or directors by virtue of their majority.

Counsel for the defendants says, and it is conceded, that the statement of claim in its present form does not allege fraud. Counsel for the plaintiffs says of course he is not alleging fraud because the plaintiffs do not really know what happened: all they know is what is set out in the statement of claim. There has been a sale at an undervalue and the second defendant has made a substantial profit; therefore, fraud is not pleaded. But, says counsel, when the authorities are considered, the rights of a minority are not limited to cases of fraud; they extend to any breach of duty. In the present case if the defendants sold at an undervalue then that was a breach of duty. As the plaintiffs cannot remedy the breach, save by a minority shareholders' action, they should be entitled to bring the action.

Foss v Harbottle[1] was a case in which there was no oppression by a majority. The next case in point of time to which I was referred was *Atwool v Merryweather*[2]. The exception of fraud in *Foss v Harbottle*[1] was emphasised, the reason being, according to Page Wood V-C[3]:

'If I were to hold that no bill could be filed by shareholders to get rid of the transaction on the ground of the doctrine of *Foss* v. *Harbottle*[1], it would be simply impossible to set aside a fraud committed by a director under such circumstances, as the director obtaining so many shares by fraud would always be able to outvote everybody else.'

1 (1843) 2 Hare 461
2 (1867) LR 5 Eq 464
3 LR 5 Eq 464 at 468

That was a case described as 'simple fraud'[1]. In the next case, *Clinch v Financial Corpn*[2], allegations were made of fraud and of acts which were said to be ultra vires. The charges of fraud were not sustained, but the minority shareholder was allowed to bring an action to restrain or correct an act which was ultra vires the company.

Then in *Turquand v Marshall*[3] Lord Hatherley LC in dealing with a loan to one of the directors said:

> 'There was no specific allegation of any impropriety in lending the money to him, nor was any specific relief prayed in this respect. It was within the powers of the deed to lend to a brother director, and however foolish the loan might have been, so long as it was within the powers of the directors, the Court could not interfere and make them liable. They were intrusted with full powers of lending the money, and it was part of the business of the concern to trust people with money, and their trusting to an undue extent was not a matter with which they could be fixed, unless there was something more alleged, as, for instance, that it was done fraudulently and improperly and not merely by a default of judgment. Whatever may have been the amount lent to anybody, however ridiculous and absurd their conduct might seem, it was the misfortune of the company that they chose such unwise directors . . .'

So that even a foolish and negligent loan to a director, if made in good faith and within the powers of the directors, does not enable a minority shareholder to recover in an action.

The next case, *Gray v Lewis*[4], is an instance of fraud creating an exception to the rule in *Foss v Harbottle*[5]. For example, James LJ said[6]:

> 'I think it is of the utmost importance to maintain the rule laid down in *Mozley* v. *Alston*[7] and *Foss* v. *Harbottle*[5], to which, as I understand, the only exception is where the corporate body has got into the hands of directors and of the majority, which directors and majority are using their power for the purpose of doing something fraudulent against the minority, who are overwhelmed by them . . .'

In *Menier v Hooper's Telegraph Works*[8] a minority shareholders' action was allowed where the majority intended to divide the assets of the company more or less between themselves to the exclusion of the minority. Mellish LJ said[9]:

> 'I am of the opinion that although it may be quite true that the shareholders of a company may vote as they please, and for the purpose of their own interests, yet that the majority of shareholders cannot sell the assets of the company and keep the consideration, but must allow the minority to have their share of any consideration which may come to them.'

In *MacDougall v Gardiner*[10], although the actual decision was reversed, Malins V-C said that there had to be something at least bordering on fraud to found a minority shareholders' action.

---

1   (1867) LR 5 Eq 464 at 467
2   (1868) LR 5 Eq 450
3   (1869) LR 4 Ch App 376 at 386
4   (1873) LR 8 Ch App 1035
5   (1843) 2 Hare 461
6   LR 8 Ch App 1035 at 1051
7   (1847) 1 Ph 790
8   (1874) LR 9 Ch App 350
9   LR 9 Ch App 350 at 354
10 (1875) LR 20 Eq 383

In *Mason v Harris*[1] Jessel MR, in an action to set aside a sale by a managing director to the company on the grounds of fraud, said:

'As a general rule the company must sue in respect of a claim of this nature, but general rules have their exceptions, and one exception to the rule requiring the company to be plaintiff is, that where a fraud is committed by persons who can command a majority of votes, the minority can sue. The reason is plain, as unless such an exception were allowed it would be in the power of a majority to defraud the minority with impunity. If the majority were to make a fraudulent sale and put the money into their own pockets, would it be reasonable to say that the majority could confirm the sale.'

In 1900 there was a case of rather wider import on which counsel for the plaintiffs relies, *Alexander v Automatic Telephone Co*[2]. In that case directors issued shares, and required some people who took up the shares to make payments in respect of those shares, but the directors did not themselves make payments on the shares which they had taken up. The headnote reads, in part[2]:

'if directors require other applicants for shares to make payments on application and allotment, and issue their own shares for which they have subscribed the memorandum without requiring any such payments to be made, and without disclosing to the other shareholders this difference between their position and that of the directors, they commit a breach of duty, even though in so doing they act without fraud, and in the belief that they are doing nothing wrong.'

A minority shareholders' action was allowed. Fraud was negatived and the basis for the action was given as 'breach of duty'. Lindley MR said[3]:

'The directors, in fact, so managed matters as to place themselves in a better position as regards payment than the other shareholders, and they did so without informing the other shareholders of the fact. This, the plaintiffs contend, was a breach of duty on the part of the directors to those who applied for and took shares upon the faith that the directors were not obtaining advantages at their expense. It is no answer to the plaintiffs' case so put to appeal to the contracts alone, for the charge is that the directors were guilty of a breach of duty in procuring those contracts and in taking advantage of them so as to benefit themselves at the expense of the other shareholders.'

Lindley MR further said[4]:

'The Court of Chancery has always exacted from directors the observance of good faith towards their shareholders and towards those who take shares from the company and become co-adventurers with themselves and others who may join them. The maxim "Caveat emptor" has no application to such cases, and directors who so use their powers as to obtain benefits for themselves at the expense of the shareholders, without informing them of the fact, cannot retain those benefits and must account for them to the company, so that all the shareholders may participate in them.'

That was a case which falls within the first exception to *Foss v Harbottle*[5], in that the

1   (1879) 11 Ch D 97 at 107
2   [1900] 2 Ch 56
3   [1900] 2 Ch 56 at 64, 65
4   [1900] 2 Ch 56 at 66, 67
5   (1843) 2 Hare 461

plaintiff shareholder could be said to be suing in respect of his individual rights as a shareholder to receive the same treatment as any other shareholder. But Lindley MR also considered the directors to be in breach of duty to the company[1]:

'The breach of duty to the company consists in depriving it of the use of the money which the directors ought to have paid up sooner than they did. I cannot regard the case as one of mere internal management which, according to *Foss* v. *Harbottle*[2] and numerous other cases, the Court leaves the shareholders to settle amongst themselves. It was ascertained and admitted at the trial that, when this action was commenced, the defendants held such a preponderance of shares that they could not be controlled by the other shareholders. Under these circumstances an action by some shareholders on behalf of themselves and the others against the defendants is in accordance with the authorities, and is unobjectionable in form.'

That was a case intermingled with the individual grievances of the shareholders in respect of their own rights, but contemplated an exception to *Foss* v *Harbottle*[2] going wider than fraud.

Shortly thereafter, in *Burland v Earle*[3], it was said that minority shareholders can sue in their own names, but must show that the acts complained of are either fraudulent or ultra vires. In particular, Lord Davey, who delivered the advice of the Judicial Committee, said[4]:

'It is an elementary principle of the law relating to joint stock companies that the Court will not interfere with the internal management of companies acting within their powers and in fact has no jurisdiction to do so. Again, it is clear law that in order to redress a wrong done to the company or to recover moneys or damages alleged to be due to the company, the action should primâ facie be brought by the company itself. These cardinal principles are laid down in the well-known cases of *Foss* v. *Harbottle*[2] and *Mozley* v. *Alston*[5] and in numerous later cases which it is unnecessary to cite. But an exception is made to the second rule, where the persons against whom the relief is sought themselves hold and control the majority of the shares in the company, and will not permit an action to be brought in the name of the company. In that case the Courts allow the shareholders complaining to bring an action in their own names. This, however, is mere matter of procedure in order to give a remedy for a wrong which would otherwise escape redress, and it is obvious that in such an action the plaintiffs cannot have a larger right to relief than the company itself would have if it were plaintiff, and cannot complain of acts which are valid if done with the approval of the majority of the shareholders, or are capable of being confirmed by the majority. The cases in which the minority can maintain such an action are, therefore, confined to those in which the acts complained of are of a fraudulent character or beyond the powers of the company. A familiar example is where the majority are endeavouring directly or indirectly to appropriate to themselves money, property, or advantages which belong to the company, or in which the other shareholders are entitled to participate ...'

The decision in this case turned on the fact that those against whom allegations were made were not, in fact, in control of the company.

---

1   [1900] 2 Ch 56 at 69
2   (1843) 2 Hare 461
3   [1902] AC 83
4   [1902] AC 83 at 93
5   (1847) 1 Ph 790

Then in 1916 minority shareholders were allowed to sue, although fraud in the true
a sense of the word was not sustained; fraud was pleaded but rejected. In *Cook v Deeks*[1]
directors obtained for themselves the benefit of a contract which might otherwise
have gone to the company. Fraud was expressly negatived. Lord Buckmaster LC
said[2]:

b
'It is quite right to point out the importance of avoiding the establishment of
rules as to directors' duties which would impose upon them burdens so heavy
and responsibilities so great that men of good position would hesitate to accept
the office. But, on the other hand, men who assume the complete control of a
company's business must remember that they are not at liberty to sacrifice the
interests which they are bound to protect, and, while ostensibly acting for the
company, divert in their own favour business which should properly belong to the
c   company they represent.'

Counsel for the defendants said that was really a case of constructive fraud, but express
fraud having been negatived, it seems to me that it established that an action will lie
where, without fraud, directors in a majority, 'divert in their own favour business
which should properly belong to the company they represent'[2].
d   Then in 1956 there was a case on which counsel for the defendants very strongly
relies and from which counsel for the plaintiffs asked me to differ. In *Pavlides v
Jensen*[3] it was alleged that directors had been guilty of gross negligence in selling a
valuable asset of the company at a price greatly below its true market value, and it was
alleged that the directors knew or well ought to have known that it was below market
value. Danckwerts J struck out the statement of claim as disclosing no cause of action
because no fraud was pleaded. The headnote says[4]:
e
'. . . since the sale of the asset in question was not beyond the powers of the
company, and since there was no allegation of fraud on the part of the directors
or appropriation of the assets of the company by the majority shareholders in
fraud of the minority, the action did not fall within the admitted exceptions to
the rule in *Foss* v. *Harbottle*[5] . . .'
f
Danckwerts J said[6]:

'On the facts of the present case, the sale of the company's mine was not beyond
the powers of the company, and it is not alleged to be ultra vires. There is no
allegation of fraud on the part of the directors or appropriation of assets of the
g   company by the majority shareholders in fraud of the minority. It was open to
the company, on the resolution of a majority of the shareholders, to sell the mine
at a price decided by the company in that manner, and it was open to the company
by a vote of the majority to decide that, if the directors by their negligence or
error of judgment had sold the company's mine at an undervalue, proceedings
should not be taken by the company against the directors.'
h
Counsel for the defendants relies very strongly on this decision as showing that,
whatever the exceptions to *Foss v Harbottle*[5] may be, mere gross negligence is not
actionable, and he says all that is pleaded in the present case is gross negligence at the
most. But in *Pavlides v Jensen*[3] no benefits accrued to the directors. Counsel for the

j 1 [1916] 1 AC 554, [1916-17] All ER Rep 285
     2 [1916] 1 AC 554 at 563, [1916-17] All ER Rep 285 at 290
     3 [1956] 2 All ER 518, [1956] Ch 565
     4 [1956] Ch 565 at 566
     5 (1843) 2 Hare 461
     6 [1956] 2 All ER 518 at 523, [1956] Ch 565 at 576

plaintiffs asks me to dissent from *Pavlides v Jensen*[1] but the decision seems to me at
the moment to be in line with the authorities, in what is a restricted exception to the
rule in *Foss v Harbottle*[2].

In *Birch v Sullivan*[3] the decision really went off on a point of pleading; moreover
the learned judge was not satisfied that the dissenting shareholders could not put
matters right by a meeting of the company. Finally I was referred to *Heyting v Dupont*[4].
But that was only an instance of the court refusing on its own initiative to hear an
action begun by minority shareholders where the *Foss v Harbottle*[2] exceptions did
not come into play.

The authorities which deal with simple fraud on the one hand and gross negligence
on the other do not cover the situation which arises where, without fraud, the directors and majority shareholders are guilty of a breach of duty which they owe to the
company, and that breach of duty not only harms the company but benefits the
directors. In that case it seems to me that different considerations apply. If minority
shareholders can sue if there is fraud, I see no reason why they cannot sue where the
action of the majority and the directors, though without fraud, confers some benefit
on those directors and majority shareholders themselves. It would seem to me quite
monstrous particularly as fraud is so hard to plead and difficult to prove, if the confines
of the exception to *Foss v Harbottle*[2] were drawn so narrowly that directors could
make a profit out of their negligence. Lord Hatherley LC in *Turquand v Marshall*[5]
opined that shareholders must put up with foolish or unwise directors. Danckwerts J
in *Pavlides v Jensen*[1] accepted that the forebearance of shareholders extends to directors who are 'an amiable set of lunatics'. Examples, ancient and modern, abound.
But to put up with foolish directors is one thing; to put up with directors who are so
foolish that they make a profit of £115,000 odd at the expense of the company is
something entirely different. The principle which may be gleaned from *Alexander v
Automatic Telephone Co*[6] (directors benefiting themselves) from *Cook v Deeks*[7] (directors diverting business in their own favour) and from dicta in *Pavlides v Jensen*[1]
(directors appropriating assets of the company) is that a minority shareholder who
has no other remedy may sue where directors use their powers intentionally or
unintentionally, fraudulently or negligently in a manner which benefits themselves
at the expense of the company. This principle is not contrary to *Turquand v Marshall*[5]
because in that case the powers of the directors were effectively wielded not by the
director who benefited but by the majority of independent directors who were acting
bona fide and did not benefit. I need not consider the wider proposition for which
counsel for the plaintiffs against some formidable opposition from the authorities
contends that any breach of duty may be made the subject of a minority shareholder's
action.

I am certainly not prepared to say at this stage of the game that the action brought
by the plaintiffs in the present instance is bound to fail. What the result of the action
will be I know not, but if the statement of claim is right, and the husband and wife
who control 60 per cent of the shares were responsible for a sale by the company to
the wife at an undervalue, which they knew or ought to have known, then a remedy
for the minority shareholders ought to lie.

Counsel for the defendants said that in any event the action does not lie against the
husband but only against the wife who took the property, but at the present moment
I do not know what the facts are, and the law on the consequences of the facts has not

---

1 [1956] 2 All ER 518, [1956] Ch 565
2 (1843) 2 Hare 461
3 [1958] 1 All ER 56, [1957] 1 WLR 1247
4 [1963] 3 All ER 97, [1963] 1 WLR 1192
5 (1869) LR 4 Ch App 376
6 [1900] 2 Ch 56
7 [1916] 1 AC 554, [1916-17] All ER Rep 285

been expounded. It seems to me to be more convenient to allow the action to continue
against both husband and wife. Counsel for the plaintiffs has had a warning shot
fired across his bows and he might succeed against one defendant and not against the
other and would then have to consider the question of costs. But in the present state
of affairs before discovery and further consideration I think the best thing to do is to
allow the action to take its normal course. The result is that I dismiss the present
application.

Application dismissed.

Solicitors: *J E Baring & Co* agents for *Brindley, Twist, Tafft & James*, Coventry (for the
defendants); *Rotherhams*, Coventry (for the plaintiffs).

Jacqueline Metcalfe Barrister.

Haydon v Kent County Council

COURT OF APPEAL, CIVIL DIVISION
LORD DENNING MR, GOFF AND SHAW LJJ
5th, 6th, 7th JULY, 18th NOVEMBER 1977

*Highway – Maintenance – Scope of duty to maintain – Duty to repair and keep in repair –
Removal of obstructions – Highway rendered dangerous by snow and ice – Footpath much
used by pedestrians – Highway authority informed of dangerous condition within four days of
onset of icy conditions – Authority acting promptly by gritting path – Plaintiff injured by
slipping on ice before gritting carried out – Whether duty to maintain wider than duty to
repair and keep in repair – Whether duty to maintain including duty to remove ice – Whether
highway authority in breach of duty to maintain – Highways Act 1959, s 44(1).*

*Highway – Obstruction – Removal – Civil liability for failure to remove obstruction – Snow
and ice on highway – Injury caused by failure to remove snow and ice – Whether highway
authority liable.*

A steep, narrow footpath, surfaced with tarmac, which was 400 feet above sea level,
led down to a village in the valley and was much used by pedestrians. It was a public
highway. It was known to become hazardous in icy conditions. On Sunday or Monday, 11th or 12th February 1973, wintry conditions set in and by Tuesday, 13th
February, the surface of the footpath was icy and dangerous. A local authority
workman who used the footpath on Wednesday evening, 14th February, reported its
slippery and dangerous condition to the local authority the following morning,
Thursday, 15th February. The authority immediately sent workmen to lay grit on the
footpath but before the grit had been laid the plaintiff, who lived in a cottage adjoining
the footpath, whilst walking down the path on the Thursday morning on her way
to work in the village, slipped on the ice and was injured. She brought an action
against the local authority as the highway authority for breach of duty to maintain the footpath under s 44(1)*ᵃ* of the Highways Act 1959, and claimed damages.

---

a Section 44(1), so far as material, provides: 'The authority who are for the time being the
highway authority for a highway maintainable at the public expense shall . . . be under a
duty to maintain the highway.'

The authority did not plead the statutory defence under s 1(2)[b] of the Highways
(Miscellaneous Provisions) Act 1961. The judge held that the failure of the authority *a*
to remove the ice or to grit the path before the accident occurred constituted a
breach of the duty to maintain the footpath and awarded the plaintiff damages.
The local authority appealed. The plaintiff contended that if she was not entitled
to recover damages for breach of duty under s 44(1), she was entitled to recover them
for breach of duty under s 129(1)[c] of the 1959 Act.

    b

Held – The appeal would be allowed for the following reasons—
    (i) (per Lord Denning MR) The duty to 'maintain' the highway under s 44(1) of the
1959 Act embraced only the duty to repair and keep in repair, even though the word
'maintain' was defined in s 295 of the 1959 Act as 'including' repair, and did not
include a duty to remove obstructions except when the obstruction had damaged the
surface of the highway, thereby rendering it out of repair and making it necessary to *c*
remove the obstruction to execute repairs. A transient obstruction caused, e g, by
snow and ice, which had not damaged the surface of the highway, could not give rise
to an action for breach of the duty to maintain the highway. The obligation to
remove such an obstruction arose under s 129(1) of the 1959 Act and, by virtue of
s 1(1)[d] of the 1961 Act, an action for damages for breach of the duty under s 129(1) did
not lie. It followed that, since the icy condition of the footpath did not constitute a *d*
breach of the duty to maintain, the plaintiff had no cause of action against the highway
authority (see p 103 *f*, p 104 *b*, p 105 *b* to *e* and p 106 *d*, post); *R v Heath* (1865) 6 B & S
578, *R v Greenhow (Inhabitants)* (1876) 1 QBD 703 and dicta of Lord Denning MR and
Diplock LJ in *Burnside v Emerson* [1968] 3 All ER at 743, 744 and of Cairns LJ in
Hereford and Worcester County Council v Newman [1975] 2 All ER at 681 applied.
    (ii) (per Goff and Shaw LJJ) The duty to maintain under s 44(1) of the 1959 Act was *e*
wider in scope than a duty to repair or keep in repair, and could include a duty to
clear obstructions such as snow and ice. However, the plaintiff had not established
breach of the duty to maintain the footpath having regard to the short interval of
time between the onset of the icy conditions and the accident, the fact that the highway authority when informed of the icy conditions had acted promptly to remedy
the conditions and the authority's heavy commitments to keep major highways and *f*
other important roads safe (see p 106 *f* to *h*, p 107 *f*, p 108 *a* to *d f h* and p 109 *b* to *g*,
post).

Notes
For the extent of the duty to maintain a highway, see Supplement to 19 Halsbury's *g*
Laws (3rd Edn) para 173, and for liability for non-feasance, see ibid, paras 227, 228;
for cases on the subject, see 26 Digest (Repl) 418-422, 1278-1309.
    For the Highways Act 1959, ss 44, 129, see 15 Halsbury's Statutes (3rd Edn) 195, 272.
    For the Highways (Miscellaneous Provisions) Act 1961, s 1, see ibid 485.

    h

Cases referred to in judgments
Acton District Council v London United Tramways [1909] 1 KB 68, 78 LJKB 78, 100 LT
    80, 70 JP 6, 7 LGR 20, DC, 26 Digest (Repl) 503, 1849.

---

b Section 1(2), so far as material, provides: 'In an action against a highway authority in respect
    of damage resulting from their failure to maintain a highway maintainable at the public *j*
    expense, it shall be a defence . . . to prove that the authority had taken such care as in all
    the circumstances are reasonably required to secure that the part of the highway to which
    the action relates was not dangerous for traffic.'
c Section 129(1) is set out at p 104 *b*, post
d Section 1(1) is set out at p 104 *f*, post

Anns v London Borough of Merton [1977] 2 All ER 492, [1977] 2 WLR 1024, 75 LGR 555, HL.

Burnside v Emerson [1968] 3 All ER 741, [1968] 1 WLR 1490, 133 JP 66, 67 LGR 46, CA, Digest (Cont Vol C) 410, *1309c.*

Cowley v Newmarket Local Board [1892] AC 345, 62 LJQB 65, 67 LT 486, 56 JP 805, 1 R 45, HL, 26 Digest (Repl) 419, *1290.*

Farrell v Alexander [1976] 2 All ER 721, [1977] AC 59, [1976] 3 WLR 145, HL.

Griffiths v Liverpool Corpn [1966] 2 All ER 1015, [1967] 1 QB 374, [1966] 3 WLR 467, 130 JP 376, CA, Digest (Cont Vol B) 329, *1278a.*

Hereford and Worcester County Council v Newman [1975] 2 All ER 673, [1975] 1 WLR 901, 73 LGR 461, 30 P & CR 381, CA, Digest (Cont Vol D) 375, *1166a.*

Inland Revenue Comrs v Hinchy [1960] 1 All ER 505, [1960] AC 748, [1960] 2 WLR 448, 38 Tax Cas 625, 39 ATC 13, [1960] TR 33, 53 R & IT 188, HL, 28(1) Digest (Reissue) 579, *2159.*

Latimer v AEC Ltd [1953] 2 All ER 449, [1953] AC 643, 117 JP 387, 51 LGR 457, HL, 24 Digest (Repl) 1065, *267.*

Maunsell v Olins [1975] 1 All ER 16, [1975] AC 373, [1974] 3 WLR 835, 30 P & CR 1, HL, Digest (Cont Vol D) 596, *8565a.*

R v Greenhow (Inhabitants) (1876) 1 QBD 703, 45 LJMC 141, 35 LT 363, 41 JP 7, DC, 26 Digest (Repl) 405, *1114.*

R v Heath (1865) 6 B & S 578, 12 LT 492, 122 ER 1309, DC.

R v High Halden (Inhabitants) (1859) 1 F & F 678, 175 ER 903, 26 Digest (Repl) 383, *918.*

Russel v Men of Devon (1788) 2 Term Rep 667, 100 ER 359, 26 Digest (Repl) 654, *2993.*

Thomas v Bristol Aeroplane Co Ltd [1954] 2 All ER 1, [1954] 1 WLR 694, 52 LGR 292, CA, 24 Digest (Repl) 1065, *269.*

Young v Davis (1862) 7 H & N 760, 31 LJ Ex 250, 6 LT 363, 158 ER 675; *affd* (1863) 2 H & C 197, 2 New Rep 205, 9 LT 145, 10 Jur NS 79, 159 ER 82, Ex Ch, 26 Digest (Repl) 418, *1280.*

Appeal

This was an appeal by the defendants, Kent County Council ('the highway authority') against the judgment of O'Connor J given on 2nd April 1976 whereby he held that the highway authority were liable to pay the plaintiff, Annie Edith Matilda Haydon, damages of £4,250 with interest in respect of injuries she sustained when she slipped and fell on the icy surface of a footpath on the ground that the authority were in breach of the duty to maintain the footpath imposed on them by s 44(1) of the Highways Act 1959. The ground of the appeal was that the mere presence of snow or ice on the footpath did not constitute failure to maintain the footpath within s 44(1) of the 1959 Act. By a respondent's notice the plaintiff gave notice that on the hearing of the appeal she would seek to affirm the judgment on the grounds (1) that if she were not entitled to recover damages for breach of s 44(1) of the 1959 Act, she was entitled to recover damages for breach of s 129(1) of the 1959 Act; (2) further or in the alternative, on the facts found by the judge she was entitled to recover damages for negligence against the highway authority in the sum assessed at the trial. The facts are set out in the judgment of Lord Denning MR.

Michael Turner QC and *Raymond Croxon* for the highway authority.
Michael Wright QC and *John Crowley* for the plaintiff.

Cur adv vult

18th November. The following judgments were read.

LORD DENNING MR. Mrs Haydon lives next to the Pilgrim's Way. That is by tradition the way taken by the pilgrims to visit the shrine of Thomas à Becket at Canterbury. It was in those days a grassy track running along the ridge of the North

Downs. From it paths ran down to the villages in the valleys below. All were at that time highways along which everyone was entitled to go. They have remained *a* highways ever since. But of very different kinds. At places the Pilgrim's Way is still only a grassy track. At others it has become metalled with stone. At yet others it is a motor road. Likewise with the ways down to the villages. Some are still only grass paths. They are trodden by ramblers for pleasure. Others have been surfaced with tarmac. They are used by the local folk for access to their houses and shops and by the children to go to school. Yet others have become metalled roads for transport of *b* all kinds.

All these developments come under our scrutiny in this case. It is at Kemsing near Sevenoaks. The Pilgrim's Way at this point is now a metalled road going along the high ground at a height of 400 feet above sea level. The village of Kemsing is in the valley 74 feet lower. It used to be a village, but it is now a town. There are several houses bordering the road along the Pilgrims' Way. They are called Pilgrim's Way Cottages. *c* Mrs Haydon lives in one of them.

The path needs close description. It is steep with a gradient of one in six. It is narrow with a width of about six or seven feet. It is bounded by garden fences and hedges. It is surfaced with tarmacadam. There are drains laid underneath. There are two or three houses beside it with access to it on foot. At the lower end is the Kemsing County Primary School. 400 or 500 children use it every day. So do many *d* residents and tradesmen. The path is only for people on foot. It is too narrow and too steep for vehicles. But it is much used because it is the one short way from the top to the bottom. It saves going a long way round by the roads.

In February 1973 there were wintry conditions. Snow fell and there was a hard frost. After two days this steep path had become very slippery and dangerous. On the Wednesday evening when people walked up it, they had to hold on to the *e* bushes and fence to save themselves from slipping over. On the Thursday morning Mrs Haydon set out from her home to go to work. She is a lady of 61 years of age. She lives at 7 Pilgrim's Way and worked in the village. She went down the footpath very carefully because it was so slippery. But, despite all her care, she slipped and broke her ankle. It was a bad break. It has mended, but there is a risk of ill effects.

She now claims damages from the Kent County Council. She says that they were *f* the highway authority and were liable by statute to maintain this footpath. She says that they ought to have made it safe by putting salt and grit down, just as they do with main roads and secondary roads. And as they did not do so, they are liable to her. She was supported by the headmaster of the primary school. He said that in winter when there is ice and snow about, the footpath becomes dangerous. When any frost comes on top of it, the children make slides down it. On numerous occasions children *g* had fallen and hurt themselves. So much so that he had asked the county ground staff for salt and they have provided it. Mrs Haydon was also supported by a council roadman who lives in Kemsing. He saw the place on the Wednesday evening, before Mrs Haydon's accident. He had gone up the path and found it so slippery and dangerous that he reported it to his superiors. On the next morning he put grit and salt on it but not in time to save Mrs Haydon. She fell down shortly before the roadmen *h* started work.

On the other hand, the highway authority say that they do everything possible to keep open all the main traffic routes. They have a warning system by which they get weather reports when snow or frost is expected. They send out lorries with salt and grit to keep clear the main traffic routes. But they simply have not the men or the lorries to go through all the footpaths. There are 4,000 miles of footpaths in *j* Kent. If they have a report about a particular footpath, they will clear it if they can spare the men for it. But they had no complaints about this footpath at Kemsing. So they had not done anything about it before their roadman reported it on the Thursday morning. And then it was cleared at once. But not in time to save Mrs Haydon from falling. Such are the facts. Now for the law.

Mrs Haydon relies on the duty imposed by ss 44 of the Highways Act 1959 which
a says that the highway authority shall be 'under a duty to maintain the highway'.
The word 'maintain' is defined in s 295, which says that 'maintenance' includes repair.
The judge said that this showed that 'maintain' meant more than physically repairing
the surface of the highway. It included 'the practice which local authorities adopt of
putting down salt and grit on the highway where there has been a fall of snow or icy
conditions'. He went on to enunciate this general proposition:

b
'Where there are pieces of highway, such as this, which have their own special
dangers in times of snow and frost, then in my judgment there is a duty on the
local authority to take reasonable steps to mitigate the danger of people falling
over and hurting themselves. That they failed to do in the present case, and the
plaintiff is entitled to succeed on liability.'

c   He awarded her £4,250 and interest.
The judgment has caused the highway authority some anxiety, for, if they have to
put down sand and grit on the many footpaths which become slippery in winter, it
would be a task beyond anything they have hitherto supposed to be their duty.
So they appeal to this court.
It is necessary to consider two statutes. The first is the Highways Act 1959 which
d imposes a duty on the highway authority to maintain at the public expense every
highway within its district. That is a duty owed to the public at large, but it gives no
cause of action to any individual who is injured by neglect to perform it. The second
is the Highways (Miscellaneous Provisions) Act 1961 which gives a cause of action to a
person who is injured. The two Acts must be considered quite separately. The
extent of the duty under the 1959 Act cannot be affected by the provisions of the 1961
e Act.

The construction of the Highways Act 1959
In construing the Highways Act 1959 it is important to observe that in its long
title it is described as an 'Act to consolidate with amendments certain enactments
relating to highways...'. Such an Act is to be construed very differently from an
f ordinary Act of Parliament and for a very good reason. The procedure in both
Houses is very different. What happened can be seen in Hansard. The discussion is
much shorter. The Bill is accepted in both Houses as being simply a re-statement of
the existing law, effecting no alteration therein, except insofar as those amendments
are drawn specifically to the attention of each House. So there is no debate except
on specific amendments. When this is appreciated, it is obvious that the courts must
g construe the Act on the principle stated by Lord Reid in *Inland Revenue Comrs v
Hinchy*[1]:

'... one must presume that such an Act makes no substantial change in the
previous law unless forced by the words of the Act to a contrary conclusion.
Therefore, in interpreting a consolidation Act it is proper to look at the earlier
h   provisions which it consolidated.'

That he proceeded to do. The same principle was applied by the majority of the
House in *Maunsell v Olins*[2] and commented on by Lord Wilberforce in *Farrell v
Alexander*[3]. So here we must look at the common law and at the previous Highways
Acts. I have done this. At common law the only obligation on the inhabitants at
j large was to repair and keep in repair. The indictment lay only for non-repair.
The various Highways Acts set up new highway authorities, but retained unaltered

---

1 [1960] 1 All ER 505 at 512, [1960] AC 748 at 768
2 [1975] 1 All ER 16, [1975] AC 373
3 [1976] 2 All ER 721, [1977] AC 59

all the substantive law as to their powers and duties and exemptions. A good instance
is to be found in s 298 of the 1959 Act. That makes it clear that the new highway   *a*
authorities were to be exempt from liability for non-repair just as the inhabitants at
large were exempt by common law. Another instance is s 129 of the 1959 Act which
imposes a duty to remove snow from the highway. It repeats word for word s 26
of the Highway Act 1835.

Coming now to s 44 of the 1959 Act, it seems to me that it puts in modern form the
duty at common law of the inhabitants of a parish to repair and keep in repair the   *b*
highways. It is described in the previous statutes as a duty to 'maintain' the highways
and is used as synonymous with 'repair and keep in repair'. Thus s 6 of the 1835 Act
said: 'That the Inhabitants of every Parish *maintaining* its own Highways . . .' shall
appoint a surveyor 'which Surveyor *shall repair and keep in repair* the several Highways
. . . which are now or hereafter may become liable to be repaired by the said Parish'.
And s 23 said that new highways like old ones 'for ever thereafter shall be *kept in*   *c*
repair by the parish'. In the Highway Act 1862, s 17 said that: '. . . The Highways
Board shall *maintain in good Repair* the Highways within their District' (emphasis
mine).

Every one of those previous sections treats 'maintain' as meaning 'repair and keep
in repair'. It follows that in the consolidation Act of 1959 it should be given that same
meaning.   *d*

Apart from the previous law

The judge did not have those statutes before him. He simply took the definition
in s 295 of the 1959 Act which says: 'maintenance' includes repair. He inferred that it
meant something else besides repair and thus came to include a duty to remove snow
and ice.   *e*

This seems to me to give too literal a meaning to the word 'includes'. That word is
itself ambiguous. According to the Shorter Oxford English Dictionary it may well
mean 'comprise' or 'embrace'. If one says that 'maintain' comprises or embraces repair, that only means that it embraces repair without necessarily embracing anything
else. In other words, Parliament only wanted to make clear that 'repair' was at any
rate to be covered by the word 'maintain' without committing itself to any additional   *f*
meaning. If the legislature had intended it to include also the removal of snow and
ice, they should have said so and not left us all to dispute about it. Especially when
it is remembered that previously, both under common law and the statutes, the
only obligation of a highway authority was to repair and keep in repair.

So I proceed on that basis. I think the most helpful approach is to take the key
words and state their meaning.   *g*

The word 'repair'

'Repair' means making good defects in the surface of the highway itself so as to
make it reasonably passable for the ordinary traffic of the neighbourhood at all
seasons of the year without danger caused by its physical condition. That is the combined effect of the statements of Blackburn J in *R v High Halden (Inhabitants)*[1], of   *h*
Diplock LJ in *Burnside v Emerson*[2] and Cairns LJ in *Hereford and Worcester County*
Council v Newman[3]. Thus deep ruts in cart roads, pot-holes in carriage roads, broken
bridges on footpaths or bushes rooted in the surface, make all these highways 'out of
repair'.

The word 'obstruction'   *j*

An 'obstruction' to a highway occurs when it is rendered impassable, or more

---

1   (1855) 1 F & F 678
2   [1968] 3 All ER 741 at 744, [1968] 1 WLR 1490 at 1497
3   [1975] 2 All ER 673 at 681, [1975] 1 WLR 901 at 911

difficult to pass along it by reason of some physical obstacle. It may be obstructed
a without it being out of repair at all. If a tree falls across a road, it may not injure the
surface at all, it may even straddle it without touching the surface, the road is then
'obstructed', but it is not out of repair. If a barbed-wire fence is across a footpath or
if bushes and branches overhang it the footpath is 'obstructed' but it is not out of
repair; see *Hereford and Worcester County Council v Newman*[1] by Cairns LJ. So also if a
highway is blocked by a fall of snow, or by a landslide without injuring the surface of
b the road the highway is 'obstructed' (as s 26 of the 1835 Act: s 129 of the 1959 Act says
so) but it is not out of repair.

The word 'maintain'
   The duty to 'maintain' (in the sense of repair and keep in repair) is an absolute duty.
This was emphasised by Diplock LJ in *Griffiths v Liverpool Corpn*[2], where he said:
c 'It was an absolute duty to maintain, not merely a duty to take reasonable care to
maintain . . .' In this respect it is like the duty to fence used by Factory Acts. If a
machine is not securely fenced, the occupier of the factory is liable, even though he
has not been negligent at all. So also if a highway is out of repair, there is a failure to
maintain, even though the highway authority has not been negligent at all.
   But this absolute duty is confined to a duty to repair and keep in repair. It was so
d stated by Diplock LJ himself a little later in *Burnside v Emerson*[3], when he said:

   'The duty of maintenance which was, by s 38(1) of the Highways Act 1959
   removed from the inhabitants at large of any area, and by s 44(1) of the same Act
   was placed on the highway authority, is a duty not merely to keep the highway
   in such a state of repair as it is at any particular time, but to put it in such good
   repair as renders it reasonably passable for the ordinary traffic of the neighbour-
e   hood at all seasons of the year without danger caused by the physical condition.'

Removal of obstructions
   'Maintain' does not, however, include the removal of obstructions, except when
the obstruction damages the surface of the highway and makes it necessary to remove
f the obstruction so as to execute the repairs. Obstructions which do *not* damage the
surface come under s 26 of the 1835 Act, now repeated in s 129 of the 1959 Act. But
obstructions which *do* damage the surface come under the duty to 'repair and keep
in repair'. That is shown by *R v Heath*[4] when properly understood. Mr Heath built
a cottage which obstructed a public footpath and damaged it. The highway authority
prosecuted him on indictment and he removed the obstruction. They then sought to
recover from him the costs of the prosecution and succeeded. This was not on the
g ground that removal of the obstruction was 'maintenance', but on the ground that the
duty of repair (i e of repairing the surface) could not be carried out unless the obstruction were removed and, therefore, the cost of getting the obstruction removed
was part of the cost of repair. That is how the case was explained by Cairns LJ in
Hereford and Worcester County Council v Newman[1], and I agree with him. It corresponds
h exactly with the ground on which Blackburn J[5] rests his decision. He said:

   '[Section 6 of the Highway Act 1835] imposed on the parish surveyor the duty to
   repair and keep in repair the highways within it, and for that purpose it may be
   necessary to institute a prosecution against some person who, by erecting an
   obstruction on a highway, prevents it from being kept in repair.'

j
1 [1975] 2 All ER 673 at 682, [1975] 1 WLR 901 at 911
2 [1966] 2 All ER 1015 at 1021, [1967] 1 QB 374 at 389
3 [1968] 3 All ER 741 at 744, [1968] 1 WLR 1490 at 1496, 1497
4 (1865) 6 B & S 578
5 *R v Heath* (1865) 6 B & S 578 at 589, 590

Likewise in *R v Greenhow (Inhabitants)*[1], there was a landslide which engulfed a road and partly destroyed the surface. It was held that the highway authority had to make *a* the road good as part of their duty to 'repair' the highway.

Section 129 of the 1959 Act

If the obstruction is, however, of a transient nature like snow or ice, or water, or something which does not damage the surface of the highway, then the duty of the highway authority is prescribed by s 129 (as amended) of the 1959 Act. It says: *b*

'(1) If an obstruction arises in a highway from accumulation of snow or from the falling down of banks on the side of the highway, or from any other cause, the highway authority for the highway shall remove the obstruction.

'(2) If a highway authority fail to remove an obstruction which it is their duty under this section to remove, a magistrates' court may, on a complaint made by any person, by order require the authority to remove the obstruction within such *c* period (not being less than twenty-four hours) from the making of the order as the court thinks reasonable, having regard to all the circumstances of the case . . .'

That section is very appropriate to deal with highways which get blocked or impeded by snow or ice, or by earth falling down from a bank, or by a tree falling down *d* and straddling the highway. It puts on the highway authority a duty to remove the obstruction; but it leaves it to the highway authority to carry out that duty at such time as it thinks best. To do it 'from time to time'. They have, therefore, a discretion save that, if they delay too long, they can be brought to book by a magistrate's order. By no shadow of argument can it be called an absolute duty. Nor does it give rise to a civil action for damages if it is not performed. *e*

The 1961 Act

Now I turn to the 1961 Act. It gave for the first time a cause of action to a person who was injured by a failure of a highway authority to maintain a highway. It gave it to him in case of 'non-repair' of a highway, but not in other cases. That is plain to my mind from the very wording of s 1(1) which says: *f*

'The rule of law exempting the inhabitants at large and any other person as their successor from liability for non-repair of highways is hereby abrogated.'

The purpose of that enactment is clear. Parliament were advised that under the existing law a highway authority was exempt from liability for non-repair of the highway. So it determined to remedy it by enacting that it should be liable for non- *g* repair. In every case from *Russel v Men of Devon*[2] onwards the law had been stated to be that no action will be against a highway authority by a person injured by its 'being out of repair'. In *Young v Davis*[3] Martin B said:

'There is no single instance of such an action against a surveyor of highways, although there must have been thousands of cases in which carts have been broken, houses have fallen down, and persons have been injured in consequence *h* of non-repair of highways.'

Likewise in *Cowley v Newmarket Local Board*[4]. In all cases the exemption under the existing law was from liability 'for non-repair' or 'for the way being out of repair'. Thus making the exemption for 'non-repair' co-extensive with the duty to 'repair and keep in repair'. *j*

---

1 (1876) 1 QBD 703
2 (1788) 2 Term Rep 667
3 (1862) 7 H & N 760 at 773
4 [1892] AC 345

The exemption being taken away, it follows that a highway authority is now
a liable to an action for non-repair of highways whereas previously it was exempt.
But there is nothing in s 1(1) of the 1961 Act to make a highway authority liable for
things which are not 'non-repair'. Thus, when there was snow or ice on the road,
it was not out of repair. As Cairns LJ said in *Hereford and Worcester County Council v
Newman*[1]: '. . . an icy road would not in my view be out of repair.' So the highway
authority are not liable for it.

b   In short, it is only for non-repair (in breach of their duty to maintain, i e to repair
and keep in repair) that a highway authority is liable. For any other cases of non-
feasance, the highway authority remains, as before, not liable to a civil action.

Extent of duty to maintain

In my opinion, therefore, the duty under s 44 of the 1959 Act 'to maintain the
c highway' is the equivalent of the duty at common law and in the 1835 Act 'to repair
and keep in repair'. It means that whenever there is a defect in the surface of the
highway, the highway authority is under a duty to repair it. But it does not mean
that the highway authority is under a duty to remove snow or ice whenever it makes
the highway slippery or dangerous. I adhere, therefore, to the view I expressed in
Burnside v Emerson[2]: '. . . an icy patch in winter, or an occasional flooding at any time
d is not in itself evidence of a failure to maintain.'

This is not to say that the highway authority have no duty to clear roads that are
snowed up or ice-bound. Of course they have a duty and they fulfil it as we all know
by their modern vehicles which spray salt and grit. But this duty does not arise out
of their duty to maintain under s 44. It arises out of their duty to remove obstructions
under s 129 and a breach of that duty does not give rise to a civil action for damages.

e   Any other view could lead to the most extraordinary consequences. If s 44 meant
that the highway authority were under a duty, an absolute duty, to remove snow and
ice, they would be given an impossible task. Section 44 applies to all highways without exception. It applies not only to major roads, but also to minor roads. It applies
to main roads and country lanes. It applies to by-ways, bridle paths and footpaths.
It applies to all such ways, no matter whether they are little used or much used.
f Every single one of them is likely to become slippery and dangerous when there is
snow and frost. Every one of them may have 'its own special dangers in times of
snow and frost', to use the judge's words. Every one of them must be made safe
without any exception if s 44 is given the wide meaning contended for. The section
gives no priority to main roads over country lanes; or to much-used footpaths over
little-used footpaths. If the highway authority were bound to clear all those of snow
g and ice whenever they become slippery or dangerous, they would require an army
of men with modern machines and tools stationed at innumerable posts and moving
forward in formation whenever there was a severe frost.

Section 1(2)(3) of the 1961 Act

Even in cases where the highway is out of repair (and thus not maintained in
h accordance with the absolute duty) the 1961 Act does not give an unqualified right
to damages to a person injured by the non-repair. The highway authority can escape
liability by proving that they took such care as was in all the circumstances reasonable
to secure that the highway was not dangerous. In the present case the highway authority did not plead that defence because they wanted, no doubt, a decision on the ambit
of their duty to 'maintain'. And the burden, once placed on them, may be difficult
j to displace. In this very case, the judge said that if they had, he would have held that
it was not made out. So it does not arise for our consideration.

---

1   [1975] 2 All ER 673 at 681, [1975] 1 WLR 901 at 917
2   [1968] 3 All ER 741 at 743, [1968] 1 WLR 1490 at 1494

Anns v London Borough of Merton[1]

A further point was mentioned. It was suggested that the highway authority had a general power to make highways safe by putting sand and grit on them and that they were under a duty to use reasonable care in the exercise of that power. Reliance was placed on *Anns v London Borough of Merton*[1]. But that is miles away. That case was concerned with powers, not duties. Here the statute prescribes the duty and the only task of the courts is to define the scope of the statutory duty. In any event, if there was any error in the highway authority, it was an error which lay within the policy area and not the operational level.

Conclusion

Until this case, I should have thought everyone knew that if he walked out on a road or footpath made slippery or dangerous with ice or snow, he did so at his own risk. If he fell down and broke his ankle or hurt himself, that was just 'one of those things' which happen just as if he slips on the path to his own front gate or on a private road. His broken ankle will, no doubt, be mended at the expense of the state under the National Health Service, and he will get compensation under the National Insurance Acts whilst he is out of work. But I see no possible justification for his claiming big damages from the highway authority on the footing that it was their fault. To my mind, they were under no such duty as the judge suggests. I would, therefore, allow the appeal and enter judgment for the council as highway authority.

GOFF LJ. I confess that I have not found it easy to arrive at a conclusion in this case, but in the end I have reached the same answer as Lord Denning MR, but not I regret to say for the same reasons.

It is clear that clearing ice off the highway or taking precautions to avoid accidents by gritting is not repair: see *Hereford and Worcester County Council v Newman*[2]. The statutory duty under s 44 of the Highways Act 1959 is, however, to repair and maintain, not repair only, and the question is, therefore, in my view whether although the footpath was not out of repair the defendants had failed to maintain it.

Now, the 1959 Act contains no definition of 'maintain'. All it says is that maintain includes repair: see s 295(1). So as Lawton LJ said in the *Worcester* case[3] repair and maintenance are not synonymous, and in my judgment maintenance must be in some respect wider than repair, which it includes. It is here that I find difficulty in seeing exactly what maintenance adds to repair, particularly in view of the cases which are not entirely easy to reconcile.

Lord Denning MR construes the word as meaning no more than 'keep in repair' but with respect, and having regard to his vast experience I must say with some trepidation, I cannot accept that. In my humble judgment an obligation is all one whether it is expressed to be 'to repair', or 'to keep in repair' or 'to repair and keep in repair'; see Foa, Landlord and Tenant[4]. Moreover, as a matter of the ordinary meaning of words there are, I think, many instances of preservation of a physical thing or of its functions which must be considered maintenance and not repair. Thus to strip down an engine, clean and oil it, is maintennace but not repair unless, and if and so far as, worn parts have to be amended or replaced.

What then I ask myself is comprehended by the word 'maintain' in relation to a highway which has become icy? None of the cases is precisely in point but there are a number of indications.

1 [1977] 2 All ER 492, [1977] 2 WLR 1024
2 [1975] 2 All ER 673, [1975] 1 WLR 901
3 [1975] 2 All ER 673 at 682, [1975] 1 WLR 901 at 911
4 8th Edn (1957), p 213

In *Acton District Council v London United Tramways*[1] Walton J said that the contention
a   that the removal of the snow was part of the duty of maintaining the tramway track
and keeping it in good condition could not be supported. In that case, however
the proviso to the relevant section, which referred to breaking up the road, pointed to
'maintain' being limited to want of repair of the road itself.
   In *Thomas v Bristol Aeroplane Co*[2] Somervell LJ said:

b   'My approach to this case, which is the same as that of the judge, is that this
        danger of finding surfaces icy is one of the incidents of winter in our country
        which everyone encounters, and it is one of those things which one has got to
        anticipate and take care of.'

He went on to say, however, that it would be very right and proper that if the icy
condition persists there should be a system in the works for gravelling or sanding the
c   surface, and he referred to the system which highway authorities have, but (1) in the
case before him the statutory obligation was to keep the way safe and (2) he did not
say that the highway authority would be liable if it did not have such a system. In
the same case Morris LJ said[3]:

d   'It seems to me, therefore, that the risks which resulted that morning at that
        time from the vagaries of the weather were no more than the risks which form
        a part of the ordinary incidents of daily life to which all are subject.'

Lord Porter in *Latimer v AEC Ltd*[4] said:

e   '... it becomes a question of the degree of temporary inefficiency which
        constitutes a breach of the employers' obligation, [but there he was dealing with
        a duty to keep the floor efficient and he went on to say:] ... But I cannot think
        the provision was meant to, or does, apply to a transient and exceptional con-
        dition.'

Finally, in *Burnside v Emerson*[5] a case dealing with flood water, which must be
f   comparable, Lord Denning MR said: '... an icy patch in winter or an occasional
flooding at any time is not in itself evidence of a failure to maintain.'
   The conclusion I reach is, therefore, that the statutory obligation to maintain does
include clearing snow and ice or providing temporary protection by gritting, but
whether there has been a breach of this duty is a question of fact and degree on the
facts of each particular case.
   If this be right then the question is what must be proved by a person who has
g   suffered injury in the way the plaintiff did to establish a breach of the statutory duty?
It cannot be that the plaintiff must negate the statutory defence under s 1(2) of the
1961 Act, since that would simply invert the statutory onus of proof, and in any
case the plaintiff would not know all the material facts.
   In my judgment the plaintiff must prove either as in *Burnside v Emerson*[6] that the
h   highway authority is at fault apart from merely failing to take steps to deal with
the ice, or, which is the point in this case, that having regard to the nature and importance of the works, sufficient time had elapsed to make it prima facie unreasonable
for the highway authority to have failed to take remedial measures. Then the highway
authority is liable unless it is able to make out the statutory defence.

j   1 [1969] 1 KB 68 at 72
    2 [1954] 1 WLR 694 at 696, cf [1954] 2 All ER 1 at 2
    3 [1954] 2 All ER 1 at 4, [1954] 1 WLR 694 at 698
    4 [1953] 2 All ER 449 at 452, [1953] AC 643 at 654
    5 [1968] 3 All ER 741 at 743, [1968] 1 WLR 1490 at 1494
    6 [1968] 3 All ER 741, [1968] 1 WLR 1490

The learned judge treated the statutory defence and the necessity for the plaintiff to make out a case beyond merely proving the dangerous condition due to the ice *a* as very much one composite thing, but in my view they are separate.

Accordingly in my judgment we ought to review the question whether as a matter of fact and degree sufficient was shown in this case to render the highway authority liable, apart from the statutory defence which was not pleaded and, therefore is out of the way. The interval of time between the onset of the icy conditions and the accident was really very short. It occurred on Thursday, 15th February, and the *b* meterological report shows that the bad conditions began on Monday or possibly Sunday and the surface had become frozen by the Tuesday. Moreover, although this was a much used path, and one which was known to become somewhat hazardous, one must not lose sight of the heavy commitments that the highway authority had to keep major highways and other important roads safe and clear, and Mr Robson's evidence was 'Normally when it snows it takes us approximately two to three days *c* to cover all the highways'. Further, the highways authority's attention had not on this particular occasion been drawn to the dangerous conditions existing on this path until the morning on which the accident occurred, and when it was they took prompt action and the roadman who reported it was sent at once to put down grit and salt.

In the end in my judgment the plaintiff did not discharge the onus on her.

I have also considered the alternative case of negligence at common law based on *d* *Anns v London Borough of Merton*[1] but I do not think that helps the plaintiff. If I am right in thinking that removing the ice or taking other protective steps was within the statutory duty to maintain, then I do not think the duty at common law can be any higher than the statutory one.

If, however, I am wrong on that then it seems to me the plaintiff cannot succeed because this lies within the discretionary field. It would have had to be shown that in *e* deciding to leave the footpaths and concentrate on the roads, the defendants had not properly exercised their discretion: see per Lord Wilberforce[2] and per Lord Salmon[3]. The learned judge found (a) a breach of duty under s 44 and (b) a failure to make out a defence under the 1961 Act because the highway authority should have had a place in its programme for this particular path. This however is not the same thing as saying that it had not exercised a bona fide discretion. The plaintiff did not in my *f* judgment begin to make that out.

For these reasons I agree that this appeal should be allowed.

SHAW LJ. The issue raised by this action is whether the accident which befell the plaintiff can be said to be attributable to a culpable failure on the part of the highway authority to maintain the footpath on which the plaintiff slipped when she encoun- *g* tered an icy patch in prevailing wintry conditions.

Section 44(1) of the Highways Act 1959 assigns to the appropriate highway authority the duty to 'maintain' a highway. The effect of this provision is to define the focus of responsibility and to fix the incidence of the cost and public expense of the general maintenance of a highway. What is the scope of maintenance is nowhere defined save insofar as s 295 of the 1959 Act says that it 'includes repair'. This is probably intended *h* to preclude disputation as to where the cost of repair is to fall and whence the means are to be provided. What seems to me clear is that 'maintenance' is wider in its scope than repair. In my view it must mean also more than 'keeping in repair' which is really an extension of the concept of repair.

Applying the primary canons of construction to what is an ordinary phrase, the ordinary meaning of 'to maintain' is to keep something in existence in a state which *j*

---

1 [1977] 2 All ER 492, [1977] 2 WLR 1024
2 [1977] 2 All ER 492 at 501, 505, [1977] 2 WLR 1024 at 1035, 1040
3 [1977] 2 All ER 492 at 506, 507, [1977] 2 WLR 1024 at 1041, 1042

enables it to serve the purpose for which it exists. In the case of a highway that
a purpose is to provide a means of passage for pedestrians or vehicles or both (according
to the character of the highway). To keep that purpose intact involves more than
repairing or keeping in repair. Thus permitting the use of a highway for activities
which would prevent or substantially impede movement to and fro, such as the
setting up of a market, or the erection of barriers might be regarded as failures to
maintain the highway in its function as a highway. It is true that s 129 of the 1959
b Act deals specifically with the removal of obstructions of a kind which may be said
to have arisen spontaneously but it seems to me that it is nonetheless an aspect of
maintenance. Section 129 is largely concerned with the mode of enforcement of the
duty to remove an obstruction. It is not without interest to compare the prodecure
prescribed under s 129 with that set out in s 59 in relation to what is described in
general terms as 'Enforcement of liability to maintain a highway' but which is mainly
c directed to cases of want of repair. Although the procedure prescribed in s 129
exhibits a greater sense of the need for promptness it does not insist on an arbitrary
or inflexible immediacy of action on the part of a highway authority. On the contrary
it takes account of relevant considerations of practicability.

I agree with what has been said as to the presence of an icy patch on a footpath not
constituting a want of repair. The plaintiff could not succeed on such a ground. In
d what other sense can it be asserted that the highway authority were guilty of a culpable breach of their duty to maintain the footpath? The icy patch cannot sensibly
be regarded as an obstruction for it did not render the path impassable though it may
have called for particular care in negotiating it. Even if it be regarded as having made
passing along the footpath hazardous in some degree, I cannot see how the failure to
deal immediately or promptly by some counter measure with the outcome of
e weather conditions on the footpath in question could be said to be culpable so as to
give rise to a liability on the part of the highway authority. I feel, as does Goff LJ,
that there may be extreme cases in special circumstances where a liability for failure
to maintain not related to want of repair may arise. Such cases are not readily brought
to mind although I would not wish to exclude them by confining the scope of maintenance to matters of repair and keeping in repair. What is clear is that the present
f case exhibits no such special or extreme features.

In arriving at his conclusion it seems to me that the learned judge imposed on
highway authorities in regard to their duty to maintain a highway a standard which
was more stringent and perhaps more extensive than the provisions of the Highways
Act 1959 require. I too would allow the appeal.

g *Appeal allowed. Leave to appeal to the House of Lords refused.*

Solicitors: *Hair & Co* (for the highway authority); *Argles & Court*, Maidstone (for the
plaintiff).

Gavin Gore-Andrews Esq Barrister.

Lord Glendyne v Rapley   *a*

COURT OF APPEAL, CIVIL DIVISION
LORD SCARMAN, MEGAW AND ROSKILL LJJ
9th, 23rd FEBRUARY 1978

b

Rent restriction – Agricultural worker – Agriculture – Livestock keeping – Animals kept for production of food – Keeping and rearing of pheasants for sport – Gamekeeper occupying cottage on agricultural holding – Gamekeeper employed to keep and rear pheasants for sport – Eighty per cent of birds killed sold – Whether gamekeeper employed to keep and rear livestock 'for the production of food' – Whether gamekeeper employed in 'agriculture' – Rent (Agriculture) Act 1976, s 1.   *c*

The defendant was employed by the plaintiff as a gamekeeper. His job was to keep and rear pheasants for sport. A term of his employment was that he should be entitled to occupy a cottage on the plaintiff's estate rent and rates free. He was paid and received holiday entitlement according to the agricultural wages legislation. *d* Although for convenience he was paid by the plaintiff's farm manager, he was not employed on the farm and his wages did not go through the farm books. The plaintiff sold 80 per cent of the birds killed and retrieved but he would not have kept pheasants at all if it had not been for the sport they provided. The defendant continued to occupy the cottage after he had ceased to be employed as gamekeeper and the plaintiff brought proceedings against him to recover possession. The defendant claimed that *e* he was an agricultural worker and therefore entitled to the protection of the Rent (Agriculture) Act 1976. The county court judge held that the defendant's job was to rear pheasants for sport not food, that his employment did not fall within the definition of 'agriculture' in s 1(1)[a] of the 1976 Act and that accordingly he was not entitled to security of tenure under the Act. The judge therefore granted the plaintiff an order for possession. The defendant appealed.

f

Held – The definition of 'agriculture' in s 1 of the 1976 Act did not include every rural or country activity but was intended to include all operations involved in farming land for commercial purposes of which one was the keeping and breeding of livestock for the production of food. Since the pheasants were kept for sport and not for the production of food, the defendant's employment was to promote a field sport *g* and not 'agriculture', as defined in s 1(1). Accordingly he was not entitled to security of tenure under the 1976 Act and the appeal would be dismissed (see p 111 *j* and p 112 *b* and *d* to *f*, post).

Notes
For the meaning of agriculture, see 1 Halsbury's Laws (4th Edn) para 1002, and for the *h* protection of agricultural workers from eviction, see ibid para 1624.
For the Rent (Agriculture) Act 1976, s 1, see 46 Halsbury's Statutes (3rd Edn) 53.

Cases cited
Kendall (Henry) & Sons (a firm) v William Lillico & Sons Ltd [1968] 2 All ER 444, [1969] 2 AC 31, HL.   *j*
Minister of Agriculture, Fisheries and Food v Appleton [1969] 3 All ER 1051, [1970] 1 QB 221, DC.

---

a   Section 1, so far as material, is set out at p 111 *j* to p 112 *a*, post

Peterborough Royal Foxhound Show Society v Inland Revenue Comrs [1936] 1 All ER 813,
   [1936] 2 KB 497.
R v Garnham (1861) 2 F & F 347, 175 ER 1090.
Smith v Coles [1905] 2 KB 827, CA.
Stephens, Re [1938] 2 KB 675.
Walters v Wright [1938] 4 All ER 116, DC.
Vellacott, Re [1922] 1 KB 466.

Appeal

The defendant, John Rapley, appealed against the order made by Mr F R N H Massey,
sitting as a deputy circuit judge, on 18th November 1977 in the Salisbury County
Court whereby he granted the plaintiff, the Right Honourable Robert Baron Glen-
dyne, possession against the defendant of Keeper's Cottage, Hurdcott, Barford St
Martin, nr Salisbury, Wiltshire. The facts are set out in the judgment of Lord
Scarman.

Michael Kolanko for the defendant.
Robert Pryor for the plaintiff.

LORD SCARMAN delivered the following judgment of the court: On 18th November 1977 Deputy Judge Massey, sitting in the Salisbury County Court, gave the plaintiff judgment against the defendant for possession of Keeper's Cottage, Hurdcott,
Barford St Martin. The defendant, who now appeals against the judgment, contends
that he is entitled, as an agricultural worker, to the protection of the Rent (Agriculture) Act 1976. The judge held that he was not employed in agriculture and, therefore,
not entitled to the protection of the Act. The only point raised in this appeal is
whether the defendant was employed in agriculture. If he was, his appeal succeeds.

    The defendant was employed by the plaintiff from 2nd June 1972 until 19th Sept-
ember 1977 as a gamekeeper. A term of his employment was that he should have a
house, i e Keeper's Cottage at Barford St Martin, rent and rates free. His rate of pay
was to be under the terms of the agricultural wages structure which is itself derived
from the Agricutural Wages Act 1948. The judge found that his job was to keep
and rear pheasants for sport, that, although paid for convenience by the plaintiff's
farm manager, he was not employed on the farm and that his wages did not go
through the farm books. The defendant himself told the judge that his job was
'to put birds in the air as targets for sportsmen'. On this evidence the judge concluded that the defendant's job was to rear pheasants not for food but for sport.
Though the plaintiff sold 80 per cent of the birds he and his guests shot, he would
not have kept pheasants at all had it not been for the sport they provided. Accordingly, the judge held that the defendant was not employed in agricultural and that
he was not entitled to the protection of the Act.

    The appeal turns on whether keeping and breeding pheasants for sport is within
the definition of agriculture to be found in s 1 of the Act. A number of cases in which
similar definitions in other Acts have been considered by the courts were cited to us.
They do not help, save to emphasise what might seem to be obvious, that not every
rural pursuit is an agricultural activity. The point turns on the definition itself.
Section 1, so far as relevant, is in these terms:

    '(1) In this Act—(*a*) "agriculture" includes—(i) ... livestock keeping and
    breeding ...
    '(2) For the purposes of the definitio.1 in subsection (1)(*a*) above ... "livestock"
includes any animal which is kept for the production of food, wool, skins or fur,

or for the purpose of its use in the carrying on of any agricultural activity, and for
the purposes of this definition "animal" includes bird but does not include fish.' *a*

'Agriculture', therefore, includes 'livestock keeping and breeding'; 'livestock' includes
'any animal which is kept for the production of food'; and 'animal' includes birds
but not fish.

The judge's finding that the plaintiff kept pheasants for sport, not food, clearly
puts the defendant's employment outside the express terms of the definition. But it
was urged before us that the definition was not intended to be exhaustive and that *b*
the Act should not be given a narrow meaning. Counsel for the defendant, developing
this submission, made the following points: (1) the definition is introduced by the
word 'includes'; (2) this 'inclusive' type of definition is used to enable the court to
construe in a broad and flexible way the term 'agriculture', so as to retain its essentially fluctuating nature; (3) keeping pheasants is part of the rural scene which includes
agriculture; it is truly an agricultural activity; (4) the word 'livestock' is similarly *c*
to be given a broad and flexible meaning; (5) the defendant's contract was drafted so
as to incorporate into it the rates of pay and holiday entitlement established under the
agricultural wages legislation. Finally, counsel for the defendant reminded us that
the Act has an important social purpose and should not be construed so as to introduce
refined and difficult distinctions into rural and farming operations and country life. *d*

These arguments are entitled to respect. They fail because plainly not every rural
or country activity is intended to be included in the definition of agriculture. Fishing,
for example, is clearly excluded. The definition is really directed towards including
all operations involved in farming land for commercial purposes of which the one
relevant to this appeal is the production of food. The finding that these pheasants
were kept for sport, although 80 per cent of those killed and retrieved were in fact
sold, is, in our judgment, conclusive. The defendant's employment was to promote *e*
not agriculture but a field sport. This is a country activity but not an agricultural
one. The appeal is, therefore, dismissed.

Appeal dismissed.

Solicitors: *Theodore Goddard & Co*, agents for *Batt, Broadbent & Beecroft*, Salisbury (for *f*
the defendant); *Young, Jones, Golding, Patterson* (for the plaintiff).

Mary Rose Plummer   Barrister.

Chelsea Land & Investment Co Ltd v Inland Revenue Commissioners

COURT OF APPEAL, CIVIL DIVISION
BUCKLEY, GOFF LJJ AND SIR DAVID CAIRNS
13th, 16th, 17th JANUARY 1978

Stamp duty – Relief – Reconstruction or amalgamation of companies – Acquisition of shares in existing company – Particular existing company – Existing company an unlimited company – Relief from capital duty and from transfer stamp duty sought – Whether necessary that particular existing company should be a limited liability company to obtain relief claimed – Whether transferee company entitled to relief claimed – Finance Act 1927, s 55(1)(b) – Finance Act 1930, s 41.

In June 1973 the taxpayer, a limited liability company incorporated in England, increased its capital for the express purpose of acquiring the whole of the issued share capital of Cadogan, another company incorporated in England, which was an unlimited company. The taxpayer accordingly acquired Cadogan's issued share capital, which consisted of 500,000 shares of £1 each, at the price of £5,344,000 and satisfied the price by issuing to shareholders in Cadogan 1,409,000 ordinary shares of £1 each in the taxpayer. The shares in Cadogan were transferred to the taxpayer and to its wholly-owned subsidiary by three instruments of transfer. The taxpayer claimed exemption (i) from capital duty in respect of the increase of capital, under s 55(1)(A)[a] of the Finance Act 1927, as amended by s 41[b] of the Finance Act 1930, and

---

a   Section 55(1), so far as material, provides: 'If in connection with a scheme for the reconstruction of any company or companies or the amalgamation of any companies it is shown to the satisfaction of the Commissioners of Inland Revenue that there exist the following conditions, that is to say—(a) that a company with limited liability is to be registered, or that since the commencement of this Act a company has been incorporated by letters patent or Act of Parliament, or the nominal share capital of a company has been increased; (b) that the company (in this section referred to as "the transferee company") is to be registered or has been incorporated or has increased its capital with a view to the acquisition either of the undertaking of, or of not less than ninety per cent. of the issued share capital of, any particular existing company; (c) that the consideration for the acquisition (except such part thereof as consists in the transfer to or discharge by the transferee company of liabilities of the existing company) consists as to not less than ninety per cent. thereof—(i) where an undertaking is to be acquired, in the issue of shares in the transferee company to the existing company or to holders of shares in the existing company; or (ii) where shares are to be acquired, in the issue of shares in the transferee company to the holders of shares in the existing company in exchange for the shares held by them in the existing company; then, subject to the provisions of this section,—(A) The nominal share capital of the transferee company, or the amount by which the capital of the transferee company has been increased, as the case may be, shall, for the purpose of computing the stamp duty chargeable in respect of that capital, be treated as being reduced by either—(i) an amount equal to the amount of the share capital of the existing company in respect of which stamp duty has been paid, or, in the case of the acquisition of a part of an undertaking, equal to such proportion of the said share capital as the value of that part of the undertaking bears to the whole value of the undertaking; or (ii) the amount to be credited as paid up on the shares to be issued as such consideration as aforesaid, whichever amount is the less; and (B) Stamp duty under the heading "Conveyance or Transfer on Sale" in the First Schedule to the Stamp Act, 1891, shall not be chargeable on any instrument made for the purposes of or in connection with the transfer of the undertaking or shares, nor shall any such duty be chargeable under section twelve of the Finance Act, 1895, on a copy of any Act of Parliament, or on any instrument vesting, or relating to the vesting of, the undertaking or shares in the transferee company . . .'

b   Section 41, so far as material, provides: 'Section fifty-five of the Finance Act, 1927 . . . shall—
(1) as from the commencement of this Act have effect as if the words "in respect of which

(*Continued on p 114*)

(ii) from conveyance or transfer duty in respect of the three instruments of transfer, under s 55(1)(B) of the 1927 Act. The Inland Revenue Commissioners decided that the taxpayer did not qualify under s 55(1) for the exemptions claimed because Cadogan was an unlimited company and therefore was not a 'particular existing company', within s 55(1)(b) of the 1927 Act. On appeal the judge[c] upheld the commissioners' decision on the grounds that a particular existing company, within s 55(1)(b), meant a company in respect of the capital of which capital duty, under ss 112 and 113 of the Stamp Act 1891, would have been payable and did not therefore include an unlimited company since capital duty was not exigible in respect of an unlimited company, and that s 41 of the 1930 Act had not altered the scope of the expression 'particular existing company' but merely provided that, in respect of capital duty, relief could be granted where the particular existing company though a limited company had not paid capital duty. The taxpayer appealed to the Court of Appeal.

Held (Sir David Cairns dissenting) – On the true construction of s 55(1) of the 1927 Act the expression 'any particular existing company' in s 55(1)(b) was to be construed, both before and after the date of the amendment to s 55(1)(A) introduced by s 41 of the 1930 Act, according to its natural meaning, as referring to an existing company of any kind which was incorporated in England, and the expression therefore included an unlimited company. In construing the expression it was necessary to consider the relief afforded by para (B) of s 55(1) as well as that afforded by para (A), and accordingly the fact that under para (A) as originally enacted exemption from capital duty could not have been obtained unless capital duty had been paid by the former or transferor company on its capital did not afford a logical reason for construing the expression 'particular existing company' as meaning a limited company only, for that requirement was irrelevant to the relief afforded by para (B). Furthermore the fact that in all the other references to 'company' in s 55(1)(a) and (b) that word meant a limited company did not render it inconsistent to construe the word 'company' in the expression 'particular existing company' as extending to an unlimited company since the other references were to the transferee or taxpayer company whereas the expression 'particular existing company' referred to the transferor or former company. The effect of the amendment introduced by s 41 of the 1930 Act was not to alter the character of a 'particular company' but merely to alter the extent to which exemption from capital duty was available under para (A) of s 55(1). It followed that Cadogan though an unlimited company was a particular existing company. Accordingly the appeal would be allowed (see p 121 g to j, p 122 a to e and p 124 c to h, post).

Nestlé Co Ltd v Inland Revenue Comrs [1953] 1 All ER 877 distinguished.

Decision of Fox J [1977] 3 All ER 23 reversed.

Notes

For relief from capital and transfer stamp duty on reconstruction or amalgamation of companies, see 7 Halsbury's Laws (4th Edn) paras 1556-1559, and for cases on the subject, see 10 Digest (Reissue) 1193-1195, 7424-7430.

For the Finance Act 1927, s 55, see 32 Halsbury's Statutes (3rd Edn) 229.

For the Finance Act 1930, s 41, see ibid 237.

For the Stamp Act 1891, ss 112, 113, see ibid 164, 165.

With effect from 1st August 1973, ss 112 and 113 of the 1891 Act and s 55(1)(A) of the 1927 Act have been repealed by s 59 of and Sch 22, Part V, to the Finance Act 1973.

(Continued from p 113)

stamp duty has been paid" in subsection (1) A (i) of the said section were not contained therein; and (2) be deemed to have effect up to the commencement of this Act as if after the said words there had been inserted the words "or relief has been allowed under the provisions of this section".'

c	[1977] 3 All ER 23

Case referred to in judgments

Nestlé Co Ltd v Inland Revenue Comrs [1953] 1 All ER 877, [1953] Ch 395, [1953] 2 WLR 786, 32 ATC 53, [1953] TR 79, 46 R & IT 232, CA; *affg* [1952] 1 All ER 1388, 9 Digest (Reissue) 181, 1107.

Cases also cited

Attorney-General v London Stadiums, Ltd [1949] 2 All ER 1007, [1950] 1 KB 387, CA.
Tillotson (Oswald) Ltd v Inland Revenue Comrs [1933] 1 KB 134, [1932] All ER Rep 965, CA.

Appeal

This was an appeal by the taxpayer, Chelsea Land and Investment Company Ltd, against the judgment of Fox J[1] given on 1st March 1977 whereby, on a case stated, he dismissed their appeal against the decision of the Inland Revenue Commissioners refusing to grant them relief from stamp duty in respect of an increase in capital and three instruments of transfer of shares executed pursuant to an agreement dated 25th June 1973 made between the taxpayer and Cadogan Holdings Co. The facts are set out in the judgment of Buckley LJ.

C N Beattie QC and *Gregory Hill* for the taxpayer.
Peter Gibson for the Crown.

BUCKLEY LJ. The facts of this case are set out in the case stated by the Commissioners of Inland Revenue under the Stamp Act 1891, s 13. It is unnecessary for me to recapitulate them beyond saying that the taxpayer, a limited company incorporated under the Companies Act 1948, in June 1973 increased its capital expressly with a view to the acquisition of the whole of the issued share capital of another company, to whom I shall refer as 'Cadogan', which was an unlimited company incorporated under the same Act in 1961. Cadogan had an authorised share capital of £500,000 divided into 500,000 shares of £1 each. The taxpayer acquired the issued share capital of Cadogan at the price of £5,344,000, which was satisfied by the issue to the shareholders in Cadogan of 1,409,000 ordinary shares of the taxpayer of £1 each, credited as fully paid up. The shares in Cadogan were transferred partly to the taxpayer and partly to a wholly-owned subsidiary company of the taxpayer by three instruments of transfer. The taxpayer claimed exemption under the Finance Act 1927, s 55(1)(A) from capital stamp duty under s 112 of the 1891 Act, in respect of the increase of capital, and under s 55(1)(B) of the same Act from ad valorem duty under the heading 'Conveyance or Transfer on Sale' in Sch 1 to the 1891 Act in respect of the three instruments of transfer.

The Inland Revenue Commissioners rejected both these claims to exemption on the ground that Cadogan, being an unlimited company, is not a 'particular existing company' for the purposes of s 55(1). The taxpayer appealed and Fox J[1], before whom the appeal came, dismissed it on 1st March 1977, upholding the commissioners' decision. The taxpayer now appeals to this court from the decision of Fox J.

The case turns entirely on the construction of s 55 of the 1927 Act. What does the word 'company' mean in the expression 'any particular existing company' used in s 55(1)(b)?

The learned judge, who was much influenced in this respect by the decision of this court in *Nestlé Co Ltd v Inland Revenue Comrs*[2], held that it means a company in respect

---

1 [1977] 3 All ER 23, [1977] STC 245
2 [1953] 1 All ER 877, [1953] Ch 395

of whose capital capital duty would be payable under ss 112 and 113 of the 1891 Act, and consequently does not extend to an unlimited company because no capital duty *a* is payable in respect of such a company.

In the Nestlé case[1] this court held that foreign companies (they were in fact companies incorporated in Northern Ireland) were not 'existing companies' for the purposes of s 55. I must consider that decision later, but first let me look at the frame and language of the section. In paras (*a*), (*b*) and (*c*) of sub-s (1) of s 55 there are set out the conditions which must be satisfied to bring the section into operation. From these *b* it is clear that the transferee company must be a company with limited liability and must have a share capital. All that is expressly stipulated in respect of the other company concerned (to which it will be convenient although somewhat inaccurate sometimes to refer as 'the transferor company') is that it must be a 'particular existing company'. Following the semicolon at the end of para (*c*) is the operative part of the subsection, divided into two paragraphs, paras (A) and (B). These contain two separate *c* exemptions from two different forms of tax. Paragraph (A) creates an exemption from capital duty and defines the extent of such exemption; para (B) wholly exempts from conveyance or transfer duty any conveyance or instrument of transfer involved in the transfer to the transferee company of the shares or undertaking transferred. In the form in which the section was originally enacted the extent of the exemption was restricted to the amount of the capital of the transferor com- *d* pany 'in respect of which stamp duty has been paid'. The effect of these words was that although the conditions stipulated in paras (*a*), (*b*) and (*c*) might have been satisfied in a particular case, no exemption would be available under para (A) unless the transferor company was one of a kind in respect of whose capital capital duty was exigible and had been paid. No exemption could be available where the transferor company was an unlimited company because capital duty is not exigible in respect of *e* such a company.

Paragraph (B) on the other hand contains no such limiting provision. The exemption under that paragraph is available whenever the conditions specified in paras (*a*), (*b*) and (*c*) have been satisfied.

The policy underlying these exemptions in the form in which they were originally enacted seems to have been, as regards capital duty, that the new share capital *f* brought into existence by the transferee company should in substance be regarded as substituted for, or a replacement of, the share capital of the transferor company acquired by the transferee company, or for the share capital of the transferor company the value of which immediately before the acquisition by the transferee company of the undertaking of the transferor company reflected the value of the undertaking acquired by the transferee company, and that the new share capital, regarded as such *g* a substitute or replacement, should not attract capital duty if such duty had already been paid on the capital of the transferor company. As regards conveyance or transfer duty, the policy seems to have been that the value of the shares issued by the transferee company (i e the value of the stake of the allottees of those shares in the transferee company after its acquisition of the shares or undertaking transferred to it) should be regarded as in substance equivalent to the value of those allottees' shares in the trans- *h* feror company immediately before the transaction; so that, regarding the transaction in a broad way, it seems to have been thought fair to treat it for tax purposes as one under which no beneficial interest passed.

In 1930 s 55 was amended by s 41 of the Finance Act 1930, which provides that s 55 of the 1927 Act should (1) as from the commencement of the 1930 Act have effect as if the words 'in respect of which stamp duty has been paid' in s 55(1)(A)(i) were *j* not contained therein; and (2) be deemed to have effect up to the commencement of the 1930 Act as if after those words there had been inserted the words 'or relief has been allowed under the provisions of this section'.

---

1 [1953] 1 All ER 877, [1953] Ch 395

The effect of the amendment was discussed in the *Nestlé* case[1], to which I shall come. Its effect was that it was no longer an express requirement of s 55 that to qualify for exemption from capital duty the transaction must be one in which the transferor company was of a kind in respect of whose capital capital duty was exigible. Capital duty was first imposed by the Customs and Inland Revenue Act 1888, so that companies incorporated before that year, or before the commencement of that Act, were not and have never been liable to capital duty on share capital created before then. Capital duty is not payable in respect of the capital of any unlimited company; nor is it payable by any company incorporated outside the United Kingdom. The duty is payable by companies incorporated in Northern Ireland because the 1891 Act forms part of the law of Northern Ireland, but in the case of companies incorporated in Northern Ireland after the establishment of the Northern Ireland Parliament it did so by virtue of Northern Ireland legislation, not directly by virtue of legislation at Westminster.

Yet another form of capital in respect of which capital duty is not exigible is capital exempted by s 55 of the 1927 Act. So before the 1930 amendment no exemption from capital duty could be obtained when the relevant capital of the transferor company was of any of these four kinds, viz capital existing before 1888, capital of an unlimited company, capital of a foreign company and capital which had been exempted from duty under s 55 of the 1927 Act. When Parliament amended s 55 in 1930, which of these kinds of capital did it intend to permit to be taken into account for the purposes of exemption under s 55(1)(A)?

Counsel for the taxpayer has contended that even before 1930 any company incorporated under English law could have come within the term 'any particular existing company' for the purposes of a claim to exemption from transfer duty under s 55(1)(B). He says that for the purposes of exemption under that paragraph there is no context justifying restriction of the word 'company' in the expression 'particular existing company' to a company incorporated with limited liability. The only limitation of its meaning is, he says, that it means a company incorporated under the law of this country.

In the *Nestlé* case[1] the taxpayer increased its capital for the purpose of acquiring the whole capital of four existing limited companies, of which two had been incorporated and registered in England and two had been incorporated and registered in Northern Ireland in 1946 and 1947 under the Companies Act (Northern Ireland) 1932. Exemption from capital duty under s 55 of the 1927 Act was claimed in respect of the whole increase of capital including that part which was issued in consideration of the transfer of shares of the Northern Ireland companies. The question for decision in this court was whether that part of the increase of capital qualified for exemption. No question arose in that case about exemption from transfer duty, although some reference was made to para (B) as part of the context in relation to which s 55(1) as a whole fell to be construed.

It was contended by the taxpayer in the *Nestlé* case[1] that 'company' in the expression 'particular existing company' in s 55(1)(b) should be construed as extending to any incorporate body or persona ficta which by analogy to an English joint stock company or otherwise might fairly be described as a company. This argument was similar to that propounded by counsel for the taxpayer in the present case, except that counsel necessarily concedes that the meaning of the word must be restricted to companies incorporated under the law of this country.

It should be noted that in the *Nestlé* case[1] the court was not concerned with any question other than whether on the true construction of s 55 a foreign company could be a transferor company for the purposes of the section, and that no reference was made throughout the case to unlimited companies. Indeed, for what it is worth, counsel for the Crown are reported as having submitted that under the 1891 Act,

ss 112 and 113, every company is chargeable with capital duty but that s 55 only
applied to companies incorporated in Great Britain. If this was indeed their sub-   a
mission it was mistaken, for ss 112 and 113 do not apply to unlimited companies, at
any rate unless and until such a company applies to be registered with limited
liability.

After stating the appellants' argument for a broad construction of the word 'company' and indicating that in the English language 'company' is a word capable of a
wide range of meaning, Evershed MR said[1]:   b

> 'I think that, when the general purpose of this section is borne in mind, one is
> inevitably carried back to s. 112 and s. 113 of the Stamp Act, 1891, to see what
> sort of creature Parliament is referring to as a company in s. 55(1) of the Finance
> Act, 1927. In other words, one must give a restricted and technical meaning to
> this word "company", and I think that its inevitable meaning, in this context, is a   c
> body corporate of the kind indicated in s. 112 and s. 113 of the Act of 1891, i.e., a
> body corporate incorporated under letters patent of Her Majesty or according to
> the laws general or special of Great Britain. By Great Britain I mean England,
> Wales and Scotland.'

Those last words, of course, refer to the fact that they were there concerned with
Northern Ireland companies.   d

At the end of that citation I think that Evershed MR made plain what he meant
by 'a body corporate of the kind indicated in s. 112 and s. 113'; that is to say, he considered that reference to those sections showed that the company concerned must be
a body corporate incorporated under English law, and no more than that.

On two subsequent occasions in his judgment Evershed MR emphasises that in his
view 'company' should be construed in s 55 as a company registered in accordance   e
with the laws of Great Britain[2]. There is nothing in his judgment to indicate that he
thought that reference to ss 112 and 113 of the 1891 Act imported or required any
further restriction on the meaning of the word.

In dealing with the 1930 amendment, Evershed MR said[2]:

> 'Three years later, in the Finance Act, 1930, s. 41, there was an amendment   f
> of that paragraph of a rather unusual nature. The difficulty to which the clause
> gave rise was twofold. Stamp duty was first imposed in 1888, and the whole of
> the share capital of an existing company might have been issued before 1888 and
> no duty ever have been paid in respect of it. The original form of words would
> exclude from benefit the acquisition of the shares of such a company. Further-
> more, it was quite likely that one amalgamation or reconstruction would follow   g
> another, and, if a company had once issued capital and had been granted relief in
> respect of that issue under this section and was afterwards itself acquired, this
> form of words would again quoad that share capital deprive the transferee company
> of the benefit. This is because, ex concessis, no stamp duty would have been
> paid in respect of that capital, since it would have been remitted under this sec-
> tion. Parliament, therefore, provided in the first place that, to the words "in re-   h
> spect of which stamp duty has been paid", there should be deemed to have been
> added "or relief has been allowed under the provisions of this section", and,
> secondly, that from the date of the passing of the Finance Act, 1930, neither
> the original qualification nor the one deemed to have been added should per-
> sist—in other words, from 1930, that the paragraph should read simpliciter,
> "an amount equal to the share capital of the existing company", without any   j
> qualification whatever (s. 41 of the Act of 1930). I have explained, at a little length,
> the nature of that amendment in order to make clear the extent to which use

---

1   [1953] 1 All ER 877 at 879, [1953] Ch 395 at 401
2   [1953] 1 All ER 877 at 880, [1953] Ch 395 at 403, 404

a
can legitimately be made of the words which were originally in the paragraph. I think it is legitimate to have regard to the form the paragraph originally took, as showing that, not only the transferee company, but also the existing company, was thought of as a company in respect of which this capital duty might have been leviable, a circumstance which would only come about in the case of a company incorporated under the local law of this country.'

b
Jenkins LJ said[1]:

'Section 55(1) of the Finance Act, 1927, is an enactment passed by the Parliament of the United Kingdom for the purpose of giving relief to certain companies fulfilling the conditions stated from the duty on the capital of companies imposed by an enactment of a similar character, that is to say, the Stamp Act, 1891. One would expect, therefore, that s 55(1), addressed as it is to that subject-matter,
c
would be concerned, and concerned only, with companies of the same kind, that is to say, companies incorporated under the general law of the United Kingdom. One must rightly, I think, in those circumstances, approach s. 55(1) with a strong bias towards the view that the companies referred to, whether they be transferee companies or particular existing companies, are companies within the meaning of the law of this country, and as such are companies which,
d
save in so far as they may have been exempted from it by the date of their incorporation, or relieved from it by some previous application of the provisions of s. 55(1), are amenable to the provisions of s. 112 and s. 113 of the Stamp Act, 1891, as regards stamp duty on their capital.'

e
As I read that last sentence, Jenkins LJ is saying that the companies to which s 55 applies are companies formed under English law and that that class of company comprises two sub-classes, those which are 'amenable' to ss 112 and 113 of the 1891 Act as regards capital duty, and those which are exempt from that duty by reason of their date of incorporation or an earlier exemption from capital duty under s 55. If it be accepted that by 'amenable' he meant liable to duty under ss 112 and 113, I think he is nevertheless saying that the word 'company' in s 55 is not restricted to
f
companies which are so liable, but extends for instance to companies incorporated before 1888 in respect of whose capital no liability to capital duty had arisen.

Jenkins LJ went on, in the next two paragraphs, to give reasons for thinking that foreign companies were not intended to be included in the meaning of the word 'company' in s 55 and says that they afford strong reasons for limiting the meaning of the words 'particular existing companies' in the way contended for by the Crown;
g
that is to say, to companies incorporated in Great Britain. He then said[2]:

'But the matter does not rest there, for, under s. 55(1) as originally framed, para. (A)(i) went on from the point down to which I have already read it with the words, "in respect of which stamp duty has been paid". Now that language, to my mind, said in so many words that the section was only concerned with cases in which the particular existing company was a company amenable to the pro-
h
visions of s. 112 or s. 113 of the Stamp Act, 1891. Those words were repealed by the Finance Act, 1930, s. 41 of which, as from the commencement of that Act, caused the provision in question to have effect as if the words "in respect of which stamp duty has been paid" were not contained therein, and provided further that the provision should be deemed to have effect up to the commencement of the Act of 1930 as if, after the said words, there had been inserted the words "or
j
relief has been allowed under the provisions of this section". Legitimate use has been made of that amendment in support of the appellant company's argument to suggest that, as from the date when the amendment took effect, s. 55, whatever

1   [1953] 1 All ER 877 at 882, [1953] Ch 395 at 407
2   [1953] 1 All ER 877 at 883, [1953] Ch 395 at 408, 409

its previous scope may have been, was enlarged in its application so as to include all the heterogeneous tribe of foreign corporations. I cannot, for my part, accept the view that this amendment caused, as it were by a side wind, so fundamental an alteration in the scope of s. 55(1). To my mind, it is amply satisfied by the consideration that companies incorporated before the date when the Customs and Inland Revenue Act, 1888 introduced duty on the capital of companies were not liable for that duty on their share capital created prior to that date, and that it may have been thought unfair that those companies should not participate in the benefit of the exemption for which they would otherwise have qualified. It is satisfied also by the further consideration that it was obviously unreasonable that a company should not be entitled to the benefit of the exemption with respect to the capital of a particular existing company which had secured relief from capital duty by some previous application of the benefits of s. 55(1).'

If, in the first passage I have cited from his judgment Jenkins LJ[1] had meant to say that only companies liable to capital duty were within s 55 as originally enacted, the amendment could not have enlarged that meaning of 'company' in sub-s (1)(b) and would not have had the effect of making exemption available when the transferor company was a pre-1888 company which had not increased its capital after 1888; for the section can only operate if the conditions in paras (a), (b) and (c) are satisfied, so that if a particular existing company must be one liable to capital duty, a pre-1888 company which had never increased its capital would not qualify as such. If it be suggested that a pre-1888 company would be 'amenable' to s 112 of the 1891 Act in the sense in which Jenkins LJ used that word because, if it were at any time after 1888 to increase its capital although it had not done so, it would be liable to capital duty, it seems to me that in a precisely similar sense an unlimited company is 'amenable' to the section, because it would be liable to capital duty if it were at any time to seek to register itself, as it could, with limited liability.

Jenkins LJ said that a consideration of the position relating to transfer duty carried the case no further. He said[2]:

'The problem is to discover, on a true construction of the section, what is meant by the phrase "particular existing company" and to follow that construction wherever it leads. It is nihil ad rem to say that "particular existing company" ought to be given some other meaning, because, if given that meaning, it will cause no difficulty in the application of one particular provision of the section.'

I could follow and agree with that reasoning if the provision relating to capital duty were only capable of a reasonable construction by concluding that a transferor company must be what Jenkins LJ called 'amenable' to ss 112 and 113 of the 1891 Act. There were strong reasons for holding that such a company must in respect of exemption from capital duty be a company incorporated under the laws of this country, and I accept that once that conclusion is reached it must follow that exemption from transfer duty can only be available where the transferor company is so incorporated; but this reasoning does not help me to solve the problem whether the transferor company must be registered with limited liability.

The ratio decidendi of the judgment of Hodson LJ in the Nestlé case[3] seems to me to lie in the second and third paragraphs of his judgment. He goes on to reinforce this view by referring to the words 'in respect of which stamp duty has been paid', and says[4]:

---

1 [1953] 1 All ER 877 at 882, [1953] Ch 395 at 407
2 [1953] 1 All ER 877 at 884, 885, [1953] Ch 395 at 410, 411
3 [1953] 1 All ER 877, [1953] Ch 395
4 [1953] 1 All ER 877 at 886, [1953] Ch 395 at 413

'I agree with the learned judge that the language supports a limited construction of the words "particular existing companies"; it shows that what is contemplated is an existing company which has paid stamp duty, and is, accordingly, a United Kingdom company. The section as a whole is not, I think, naturally to be read as, in the first place, including all companies by the words "particular existing companies" [I think he must have meant "particular existing company"] and, in the second place, providing a scheme for, so to speak, analysing the position to see whether or not a particular company is inside or outside.'

I do not think Hodson LJ can have meant to say that in paragraph (b) 'particular existing company' can only mean a company which has paid capital duty, for the effect of this would be that the 1930 amendment would not let in cases where the transferor company was a pre-1888 company which had not increased its capital after 1888. He was, I think, merely indicating that the measure of exemption under s 55 in its original form reinforced the other considerations which indicated that the transferor company could not be a foreign company.

Having regard to the particular facts of the Nestlé case[1], where all the companies were limited companies, and the particular nature of the question raised in that case, I do not consider that it in any way binds us in the present case. It seems to me to be right that the court there reached its conclusion on the basis that in the case of a statute creating fiscal exemptions the primary inference must be that the legislature meant the provisions to apply only to English companies, a view which was reinforced by consideration of the practical difficulties which would arise, at any rate in respect of capital duty, from a contrary view; secondly, that the 1930 amendment would only displace that primary inference if it could only be shown to have operative effect by treating s 55 in its original form as extending to cases in which the transferor company was a foreign company; thirdly, that this was not the case because para (2) of the amending section (s 41 of the 1930 Act) shows that one object of the amendment was to deal with transferor companies which had obtained exemption under s 55 at an earlier stage; and fourthly, that para (1) of s 41 of the 1930 Act was intended to achieve a wider relaxation of the terms of s 55 than was achieved by para (2), but that this was in fact achieved in relation to pre-1888 companies which had never paid capital duty. Therefore the 1930 amendment was not such as to displace the primary interpretation of s 55 as one restricted to companies incorporated under the law of this country. It was unnecessary for the court to probe any further into the possible operation of s 55. The reference made by the members of the court in the Nestlé case[1] to the sections of the 1891 Act seems to me to be directed solely to the question of whether it was possible to interpret s 55 as extending to transactions in which the transferor company was other than a company incorporated under the law of this country.

None of this seems to me to touch the question of whether a particular existing company within s 55(1)(b) can be an unlimited company. It is accepted that the transferee company must be a company with limited liability (see s 55(1)(a)) but I can see no compelling reason for holding that a 'particular existing company' mentioned in s 55(1)(b) need be a company with limited liability. Indeed, the circumstance that this paragraph does not say so points, as I think, the other way. The words 'any particular existing company' are wide words. Accepting that they must be read as referring to companies incorporated under the law of this country, why should they not bear their natural meaning of an existing company of any kind incorporated under the law of this country? True, if the company has no share capital, no exemption from capital duty will be available, but this will not result from placing a restricted meaning on 'particular existing company'; it will result from the measure of exemption imposed by para (A).

1   [1953] 1 All ER 877, [1953] Ch 395

Why, one may ask, if the 1930 amendment let in cases in which the transferor company was a pre-1888 company which had never paid capital duty, should it not *a* also let in cases in which the transferor company has never paid capital duty because it is an unlimited company having a share capital? Why should the provisions which are concerned with limiting the amount of exemption available in relation to capital duty restrict in any way the availability of exemption from transfer duty? I see no good reason for holding that 'any particular existing company' means anything other than any company incorporated under English law.   *b*

In the course of his judgment, Fox J said[1]: 'Further, it seems to me unlikely that Parliament would, by an amendment in this form, have intended to alter a fundamental basis as to the nature of the companies to which relief would be granted.' In this court certainly, and I believe in the court below, the argument presented by counsel for the taxpayer was not that the 1930 amendment had made an alteration in the fundamental basis of the nature of the companies to which relief would be *c* granted, for his contention is that in s 55(1)(*b*) the expression 'particular existing company' has always been an expression extending to a company of any kind incorporated under the law of this country. His argument has been that the effect of the amendment was not to alter the character of the companies to which the conditions of the operation of s 55 apply, but to alter the extent to which exemption was available under para (A). In my judgment, according to the true construction of s 55 that *d* argument of counsel for the taxpayer is correct and, as I have said, I think that on the true construction of the section 'any particular existing company' should be read and construed both before and after the date of the amendment as meaning 'any company incorporated under the law of this country'.

Accordingly, for these reasons I would allow this appeal.

e

GOFF LJ. As Buckley LJ has said, the facts of this case are very fully set out in the case stated, and moreover Buckley LJ has included in his judgment a brief résumé of them. It is therefore unnecessary for me to deal with the facts.

The question of law at issue in the case is the meaning of the word 'company' in the expression 'any particular existing company' in s 55(1)(*b*) of the Finance Act 1927. Counsel's argument for the taxpayer is simple and direct. He says, first, that there is *f* nothing ambiguous about that expression and, using the words in their natural and ordinary meaning, they exactly describe Cadogan which at the relevant time was existing, a company and a particular one.

Secondly, there is no reason why the words should be given any secondary, or different, meaning and no reason why 'company' should in that expression be confined to companies with limited liability.   *g*

It is true that in s 55(1)(*a*) there are three references to a company, all meaning a limited company, though only once so described, and it is also true that in s 55(1)(*b*) the expression 'the company' also means a limited liability company. But that, he submits, is no reason for applying the same restriction in construing the expression 'any particular existing company', for the subject-matter is different. In all the earlier instances s 55 is referring to a taxpayer company which at least, so far as para (A) is *h* concerned, must be a limited liability company, for the capital tax with which the section is dealing is, by ss 112 and 113 of the Stamp Act 1891, replacing the Customs and Inland Revenue Act 1888, imposed only on such companies; whereas the 'particular existing company' is relevant only for the purpose of determining whether the taxpayer company is eligible for, and qualifies for, relief; and there is no reason, in principle or logic, why for that purpose there should be any difference between *j* limited and unlimited companies.

Thirdly, although it is relevant to refer to ss 112 and 113 of the 1891 Act, yet that only shows that the subject-matter of s 55 as a whole is confined to companies subject

1 [1977] 3 All ER 23 at 31, [1977] STC 245 at 253

to the law of Great Britain and formed under that law, to which I shall refer as
a 'English companies'. It does not mean that one has to limit the word 'company'
in the expression in question to those which have limited liability, although that is an
essential condition of liability to the capital duty under those sections.

The Crown, on the other hand, say that 'company' in the expression in question
must mean a limited company, for the following reasons: (i) they rely upon the fact
that I have already mentioned, that in all other instances in s 55(1)(a) and (b) 'company'
b does mean a limited company only; (ii) s 55(1)(A) shows that the thinking behind
the exemption in the section as originally worded before the 1930 amendment was
that the transferee company would, either totally or to the proportionate extent of
the assets purchased with its increased capital, be in substance the same as the 'particular existing company', and it would be unfair that capital duty should be paid twice.
True, the particular existing company, even if limited, might not have paid capital
c duty, but that was covered by the formula prescribed by para (A), which would
preclude the transferee company from obtaining exemption in such a case; (iii) that
in any event this court is bound by the *Nestlé* case[1] to construe 'company' in that
expression as meaning a limited company only, since, although the actual decision
went no further than that 'company' in that expression means English companies
only, yet the ratio decidendi laid down a general principle that the word 'company' in
d that expression means a body corporate of the kind indicated in ss 112 and 113 of the
1891 Act: see, for example, per Evershed MR[2]. This must, so the argument runs,
confine it not only to English companies but also to those with limited liability
because it is only such companies with which ss 112 and 113 are dealing.

It is to be observed, however, as Buckley LJ has pointed out in his judgment, that
Evershed MR went on to say, after his reference to a body corporate of the kind
e indicated in ss 112 and 113 of the 1891 Act[2]:

'... i.e., a body corporate incorporated under letters patent of Her Majesty or
according to the laws general or special of Great Britain. By Great Britain,
I mean England, Wales and Scotland.'

f (iv) Even if that case does not actually bind us so to hold, still the Crown's construction
is consistent with the reasoning in that case, and that for the taxpayer company is not.

For myself, I do not think that there is anything in the *Nestlé* case[1] which does bind
us one way or the other on the question of construction whether the expression 'any
particular existing company' includes unlimited companies. Nor do I think the
reasoning leads to that conclusion, and care must, I think, be taken in considering the
judgments in that case not to give to any particular words or passages taken out of
g their context a meaning which I think they were not intended to have. In analysing
that case one must keep carefully in mind that the question whether unlimited
companies were included was neither relevant nor, I think, present to anyone's mind.

For my part, I accept counsel for the taxpayer's analysis of the reasoning in that case,
which was as follows: the court was concerned to decide whether the word 'company'
in the expression in question was confined to English companies or included foreign
h companies, in that case Northern Ireland companies, and they said in general in
United Kingdom legislation, particularly fiscal legislation, Parliament is prima facie
to be taken as dealing only with English companies, but one must look at the whole of
the relevant statutes. So the learned judges who constituted the court in that case
started with the sections imposing capital duty, ss 112 and 113, and found there indications that the word was indeed related only to English companies. Then they looked
j to the relieving Act itself, s 55 of the Finance Act 1927, to see whether it confirmed or

---

1   [1953] 1 All ER 877, [1953] Ch 395
2   [1953] 1 All ER 877 at 879, [1953] Ch 395 at 401

displaced that view, and found confirmation in para (A), because if that be extended to foreign companies all kinds of difficulties would present themselves. Finally, they *a* said, one must look at the amending Act, and if the only kind of company which could fall within the provisions of that Act must be a foreign company, that would displace the view so far reached, but they found it not so. An English company which had already obtained relief under s 55 would get the benefit of the amendment, but that would not go far enough, since s 55(2) deals expressly with that situation, whilst s 55(1) gives wider and general relief. However, a pre-1888 English company *b* could get relief under that section, and so the amending Act makes sense without including foreign companies. On that analysis the case imports no more than it actually decided.

Nor, in my judgment, does it mean that those two examples, pre-1888 companies and companies having had previous exemption, are the only possible cases outside limited liability companies which had paid duty of 'particular existing companies'.   *c*

In my view, in solving the problem presented in this case, we have to decide the question of construction involved for ourselves. In doing that, it seems to me that one must consider the impact of para (B) as well as para (A). Whilst the thinking behind para (A) must have been as stated in the reasons that I have recited under head (ii) of the Crown's argument, the thought behind para (B) cannot have been the same. It must have been that on an amalgamation or reconstruction, the shareholders in the *d* particular existing company are wholly, or pro tanto substantially and in effect, the owners of the transferee company, and therefore there is no real change of beneficial ownership; but that has nothing to do with whether the pre-existing company is limited or unlimited. The conditions which a company has to satisfy under paras (A) and (B) of s 55(1) govern relief both under paras (A) and (B) and the fact that under para (A) relief was not allowed unless capital duty had actually been paid does not *e* seem to me to afford any logical reason for construing those conditions so as for both purposes to require the particular existing company to be limited, which is wholly irrelevant to para (B).

Further, it does not seem to me inconsistent or a forced construction to give a different meaning to 'company', in the expression 'any particular existing company', from what it bears in the rest of paras (a) and (b) of s 55(1), since as I have observed *f* the subject-matter is different. Until one comes to that expression one is dealing with the taxpayer company, which must be limited, since otherwise para (A) cannot apply at all; but in the expression in question one is considering the former company, which is relevant only for the purpose of seeing what is involved in the concept of reconstruction or amalgamation.

In the result, therefore, in my judgment counsel for the taxpayer's short opening *g* premise is correct. Cadogan was, within the ordinary meaning of the words used, a particular existing company, and I see nothing in the terms of s 55, or the *Nestlé* case[1], or otherwise, to require us to depart from that ordinary meaning.

I agree entirely with Buckley LJ's judgment and with his careful, and very full, review of the judgments in the *Nestlé* case[1] and, for the reasons he has given and for those which I have endeavoured shortly to state in my own words, I too would allow *h* this appeal.

SIR DAVID CAIRNS. I regret that I cannot agree with Buckley and Goff LJJ that the appeal should be allowed. I can give my reasons very briefly.

It appears to me that the ratio decidendi of this court in *Nestlé v Inland Revenue* *j* *Comrs*[1] was that a foreign company was not a 'particular existing company' within s 55 of the Finance Act 1927, because s 55(1)(A) compelled the view that the particular

---

1   [1953] 1 All ER 877, [1953] Ch 395

a existing company must be a company liable to capital duty under s 112 or s 113 of the Stamp Act 1891.

Now only a limited company is liable to such duty. I find it impossible to read the language of the judgments taken as a whole as meaning that a company which, by some change in the law or by reason of its ability to change its character from that of an unlimited company to that of a limited company, could become amenable to capital duty could be such a 'particular existing company'.

b In those circumstances I am of the opinion that the decision of Fox J should be upheld.

Appeal allowed with costs in the Court of Appeal and below. Leave to appeal to the House of Lords conditional on the Crown not seeking to disturb the order as to costs in the Court of Appeal.

c
Solicitors: *May, May & Merrimans* (for the taxpayer); *Solicitor of Inland Revenue.*

J H Fazan Esq Barrister.

d

Biss v Lambeth, Southwark and Lewisham Health Authority

e COURT OF APPEAL, CIVIL DIVISION
LORD DENNING MR, GEOFFREY LANE AND EVELEIGH LJJ
21st OCTOBER, 15th NOVEMBER 1977

Practice – Dismissal of action for want of prosecution – Delay – Prejudice to defendant – Delay before issue of writ – Delay causing prejudice to defendant – Significant increase in f prejudice in consequence of delay after issue of writ – Threat of action hanging over defendant prejudicing conduct of his affairs – Action brought outside limitation period pursuant to leave of court – Delay in bringing action causing prejudice to defendant – Delay after issue of writ inordinate and inexcusable – Whether prejudice to defendant significantly increased by delay after issue of writ.

g Practice – Dismissal of action for want of prosecution – Inordinate delay without excuse – Delay before issue of writ – Writ claiming damages for personal injuries issued outside three year limitation period persuant to leave of court – Whether inordinate and inexcusable delay before issue of writ sufficiently prejudicial to defendants to justify dismissal of action for want of prosecution.

h The plaintiff was admitted to hospital in March 1965 suffering from multiple sclerosis. While in hospital the plaintiff contracted severe bed sores which she alleged were the result of negligent treatment by the nursing staff. In March 1966 her solicitors wrote to the defendants, the hospital authority, stating that a claim would be made against them by the plaintiff. Later in 1966 the plaintiff's legal aid certificate was discharged and the defendants heard nothing further about the plaintiff's proposed claim until j December 1974 when the plaintiff applied for leave under the Limitation Act 1963 to bring an action against the defendants out of time. Leave was granted and a writ was issued in February 1975 alleging negligence on the part of the defendants and claiming damages for personal injuries. The defendants denied liability but by that time they had already suffered prejudice in consequence of the ten years' delay, in that nurses had left the hospital, their notes had been destroyed and their memories had faded.

Pleadings closed on 23rd July and on 2nd December the defendants served on the
plaintiff a request for further and better particulars. That request was not complied   *a*
with. The plaintiff then instructed new solicitors who gave notice of change on 13th
September 1976. The solicitors were required by the plaintiff's legal aid certificate to
obtain counsel's opinion before setting the action down for trial. That necessitated a
further medical report but it could not be obtained because the plaintiff failed to
attend for an examination. No further steps were taken by the plaintiff and on 22nd
March 1976 the defendants issued a summons for an order that the action be dis-   *b*
missed for want of prosecution. The master granted the order but on appeal the
order was rescinded and the action ordered to proceed on the ground that, although
the plaintiff's delay since the issue of the writ had been inordinate and inexcusable,
the prejudice which the defendants had suffered had not been a result of that delay
but a result of the long delay before the issue of the writ. The defendants appealed.

c

Held – The appeal would be allowed for the following reasons—
(i) The prejudice that might be suffered by a defendant as a result of the plaintiff's
delay was not to be found solely in the death or disappearance of witnesses, or their
fading memories, or in the destruction of records, but might also be found in the
difficulty experienced in conducting his affairs with the propects of an action hanging
indefinitely over his head. In the circumstances, by having the action suspended   *d*
indefinitely over their heads, the defendants had been more than minimally prejudiced by the plaintiff's inordinate and inexcusable delay and contravention of rules
of court as to time since the issue of the writ, and that, added to the plaintiff's great
and prejudicial delay before the issue of the writ, justified the court in dismissing the
action for want of prosecution (see p 131 *d* to *h*, p 132 *e* to *g*, p 134 *d e* and p 135 *e*, post.)
(ii) In an action commenced after the expiry of the relevant limitation period, the   *e*
court had a discretion to dismiss the action for want of prosecution if the total delay
on the part of the plaintiff, including delay before the issue of the writ, had seriously
prejudiced the defendant, regardless of the fact that any delay since the issue of the
writ might have caused no, or no more than minimal, prejudice to him. In view
of the plaintiff's delay of almost ten years before issuing her writ and the serious
prejudice that had caused the defendants, the discretion should be exercised by   *f*
dismissing the action (see p 132 *d e*, p 134 *g h* and p 135 *e*, post).
Birkett v James [1977] 2 All ER 801 distinguished.

Notes
For the dismissal of actions for want of prosecution, see 30 Halsbury's Laws (3rd Edn)
410, para 771.   *g*
For the Limitation Act 1963, ss 1, 2, see 19 Halsbury's Statutes (3rd Edn) 103, 104.
For the Limitation Act 1975, s 1, see 45 ibid 848.

Cases referred to in judgments
Allen v Sir Alfred McAlpine & Sons Ltd, Bostic v Bermondsey and Southwark Group Hospital   *h*
Management Committee, Sternberg v Hammond [1968] 1 All ER 543, [1968] 2 QB 229,
[1968] 2 WLR 366, CA, Digest (Cont Vol C) 1091, 2262b.
Birkett v James [1977] 2 All ER 801, [1977] 3 WLR 38, HL.
India (President of) v John Shaw & Sons (Salford) Ltd [1977] Court of Appeal Transcript
383, [1977] The Times, 28th October.
Intended Action, Re an, Biss v Lewisham Group Hospital Management Committee [1975]   *j*
The Times, 13th February, 119 Sol Jo 204, CA.
Parker (William C) Ltd v F J Ham & Son Ltd [1972] 3 All ER 1051, [1972] 1 WLR 1583, CA,
Digest (Cont Vol D) 1057, 2262s.
Sweeney v Sir Robert McAlpine & Sons Ltd [1974] 1 All ER 474, [1974] 1 WLR 200, [1974]
1 Lloyd's Rep 128, CA, Digest (Cont Vol D) 1041, 1238e.

Thorpe v Alexander Fork Lift Trucks Ltd [1975] 3 All ER 579, [1975] 1 WLR 1459, CA,
a   Digest (Cont Vol D) 1042, *1238f.*
Tolson v Kaye (1822) 3 Brod & Bing 217, 6 Moore CP 542, 129 ER 1267, 32 Digest (Repl)
    368, 8.
Wallersteiner v Moir, Moir v Wallersteiner [1974] 3 All ER 217, [1974] 1 WLR 991, CA,
    Digest (Cont Vol D) 254, *204e.*

b **Cases also cited**
McCafferty v Metropiltan Police District Receiver [1977] 2 All ER 756, [1977] 1 WLR 1073,
    CA.
*Paxton (late an infant but now of full age) v Allsopp (administrator of the estate of Robert
    Graham Allsopp (deceased))* [1971] 3 All ER 370, [1971] 1 WLR 1310, CA.

c **Interlocutory appeal**
This was an appeal by the defendants, the Lambeth, Southwark and Lewisham Area
Health Authority (Teaching) (formerly the Lewisham Group Hospital Management
Committee), against the order of his Honour Judge Norman Richards QC, sitting as a
deputy High Court judge, made on 8th July 1977, allowing an appeal by the plaintiff,
Elizabeth Grace Biss, against the order of Master Waldman dated 3rd June 1977
d whereby he dismissed the action brought by the plaintiff against the defendants for
want of prosecution. The facts are set out in the judgment of Lord Denning MR.

Nicholas Merriman for the defendants.
Jeremy Roberts for the plaintiff.

e   *Cur adv vult*

15th November. The following judgments were read.

LORD DENNING MR. The plaintiff, Mrs Biss, suffers from multiple sclerosis.
f It struck her suddenly 12½ years ago. It was on Tuesday, 30th March 1965. She awoke
at home in the morning to find that she could not move her legs. She was taken to
Lewisham Hospital. She lay paralysed and helpless on her back. She wetted the bed.
Bed sores developed and were very painful. She was there for some months, then
home for a while, and then back again. But on 17th January 1966 she was transferred
to a special care centre at Stoke Mandeville in Buckinghamshire. She was there for a
year. They treated her so skilfully that the sores were healed, and she was able to
g walk again with the aid of sticks. But while at Stoke Mandeville she began to make all
sorts of accusations against the nursing staff at the Lewisham Hospital. She said they
had not looked after her properly; that the bed sores were due to negligent treatment;
that the nurses had never turned her in bed; that they had never given her a catheter
to help her not to wet the bed; and so forth. She went to solicitors. On 17th March
1966 they wrote to the defendants, the hospital board. On 1st July 1966 the solicitors
h for the board, having investigated her complaints, made a reply denying her charges.
I will read it, for it shows the case for the nurses:

'Every possible care was taken to prevent the development of blisters, and
later to cure them when they developed. Your Client was placed on a ripple
mattress to help relieve pressure areas, frequent attention to pressure areas was
j   given, and she was advised how to lie so as to remove pressure on the blisters.
However, we are instructed, and the records made at the time shew, that she
was very unco-operative and would not lie in the positions in which the nursing
staff put her. She received occupational therapy and was provided with a wheel
chair. Splints were provided to help to support her legs, and she received daily
physiotherapy. She was encouraged to walk again. She was advised against

returning home—which advice she ignored. She was advised not to return home, but she went against such advice and our Client allowed her to take the wheel chair home. She was advised [to] transfer to Stoke Mandeville, which she initially refused but later she went there.'

Despite that detailed reply, Mrs Biss still insisted that the nurses at Lewisham had been negligent. She got legal aid, with which a medical report was obtained and two opinions of counsel. These were to the effect that Lewisham Hospital were not guilty of negligence. So her legal aid certificate was discharged. That was in 1966.

In January 1967 she left Stoke Mandeville and went home. She walked about with sticks. Despite the advice which she had received, she still persisted in her complaints about the Lewisham Hospital. She approached her Member of Parliament and the newspapers and her local councillor. None of them took up her case. So the Lewisham Hospital quite understandably thought that the case was closed. There was no need to worry about it any more. But then about 1970 she joined the Multiple Sclerosis Society. They took up her case. Eventually a medical report was obtained from Dr Walsh, the director of the Stoke Mandeville Hospital. In a report of 30th July 1973 he said:

'Pressure sores commonly occur even in this country in patients suffering from multiple sclerosis and other spinal cord lesions and injuries. These pressure sores are usually due to inadequate nursing. There is a grave nursing shortage and particularly a shortage of highly skilled adequately trained nursing staff in the field ...'

Armed with that report, Mrs Biss once again applied for legal aid and got it. In due course in February 1975 she applied for leave under the Limitation Act 1963 to bring an action against the Lewisham Hospital. It was ten years since she left the hospital but still she applied for leave to sue them. The application was made ex parte, without the Lewisham Hospital being heard in their defence. Boreham J refused leave. But this court on 12th February 1975 (basing itself on the then current inter-pretation of the 1963 Act) gave leave[1]. That was, I now think, a mistake. At any rate, in pursuance of that leave, Mrs Biss's advisers issued a writ on 18th February 1975 against the Lewisham Hospital for damages for negligence 'between about April 1965 and January 1966'. So there it was. A writ issued ten years after the alleged negligence. The hospital denied negligence and relied on the Limitation Act 1939. On 9th July 1975 the plaintiff delivered a reply saying that the material facts were outside her knowledge until a year earlier than the writ and so she was not barred by the Statute of Limitations.

Pleadings were closed on 23rd July 1975. A summons for directions was issued and directions given on 11th November 1975. On 2nd December 1975 the hospital gave particulars of their defence and served on the plaintiff a request for further and better particulars. But Mrs Biss did not comply with it. Her then solicitor did nothing. Nine months passed. New solicitors were engaged. They gave notice of change on 13th September 1976. The legal aid certificate required them to get a further opinion of counsel before setting down the case for trial. For this purpose the solicitors wished to get a further opinion from Dr Walsh at Stoke Mandeville. Seeing that three years had passed since his previous opinion, Dr Walsh wanted to see Mrs Biss again at Stoke Mandeville, but she said she could not undertake the journey to Stoke Mandeville. Two or three times she said so. Eventually, on 28th January 1977, the solicitor to the hospital warned Mrs Biss's solicitors that, if some progress was not made fairly soon, they would apply to dismiss the case for want of prosecution. On 28th February 1977 they wrote saying:

---

1 *Re an Intended Action, Biss v Lewisham Group Hospital Management Committee* [1975] The Times, 13th February

'We are sure that our client would not wish to take unfair advantage of a
disabled opponent, but we are thinking in terms of taking instructions on whether
to apply for the action to be dismissed if you do not proceed with it in the near
future.'

Still Mrs Biss had not gone to Stoke Mandeville; and Dr Walsh had not given his
further medical report. So on 22nd March 1977 the hospital issued a summons to
dismiss for want of prosecution. On 3rd June Master Waldman acceded to the
hospital's request. He dismissed the action. But on 8th July 1977 Judge Norman
Richards QC held that the action was to proceed. The hospital now appeals to this
court.

The argument before us turned much on the recent decision of the House of Lords
in *Birkett v James*[1]. Counsel for Mrs Biss submitted that, as a result of that decision,
the crucial date was the date of the issue of the writ; and the crucial delay was the
delay since the issue of the writ. He said that, in order that a case should be dismissed
for want of prosecution, the delay since the writ must have been inordinate and
inexcusable, and that delay must have caused serious prejudice to the defendant,
or at any rate, prejudice which was 'more than minimal', in addition to any prejudice
that had been caused to the defendant before the issue of the writ.

Applying that proposition here, counsel for Mrs Biss relied on the plain fact that
the writ was issued, and lawfully issued, on 18th February 1975. He submitted that the
relevant delay since that date was the nine months from December 1975 to September
1976. He admitted that that delay was inordinate and inexcusable, but he submitted
that that delay did not add any extra prejudice, or, at any rate, no more than minimal.
So the action could not be dismissed.

The argument is formidable. It makes it necessary to consider the principles on
which the court should act. Before *Birkett v James*[1] there were two rival approaches
to these cases about dismissal for want of prosecution. One approach was on the
basis of public policy. It was in the public interest that, once a writ was issued, the
action should be brought to trial as quickly as possible and that long delay thereafter
might lead to the action being dismissed. On the simple principle interest reipublicae
ut sit finis litium I venture to quote what I said in *Allen v Sir Alfred McAlpine & Son
Ltd*[2]:

'... when the delay is prolonged and inexcusable, and is such as to do grave
injustice to one side or the other, or to both, the court may in its discretion
dismiss the action straight away ...'

I followed this up in *Sweeney v Sir Robert McAlpine & Sons Ltd*[3] by saying:

'... the court does not look merely at the delay since the writ ... The court
enquires whether the total delay has been such that a fair trial between these
parties cannot now be had.'

To which I added this proposition in *Thorpe v Alexander Fork Lift Trucks Ltd*[4]:

'... the plaintiff is not entitled to delay as of right for four years from the
accident, three years before issuing the writ and another year for service. He has
no such right. He is not entitled to delay at all. It is his duty, once the writ is
issued to serve it promptly and get on with it promptly.'

The rival approach was to concentrate on the delay since the issue of the writ.
A plaintiff, it was said, has a legal right to delay to the full period permitted by the

1   [1977] 2 All ER 801, [1977] 3 WLR 38
2   [1968] 1 All ER 543 at 547, [1968] 2 QB 229 at 245, 246
3   [1974] 1 All ER 474 at 476, [1974] 1 WLR 200 at 204
4   [1975] 3 All ER 579 at 581, [1975] 1 WLR 1459 at 1464

Statute of Limitations. So he can, as of right, delay issuing his writ for six years in the case of breach of contract and for three years in the case of personal injuries; and, *a* after issuing it, he has a further year allowed to him by the rules of court, for the service of it: see RSC Ord 6, r 8(2). Seeing that he has this legal right, so the reasoning goes, he is entitled to take advantage of it to the very last minute. No delay in issuing his writ during that period or serving it, no matter how inordinate and inexcusable it may be, and no matter how prejudicial it may have been, can of itself be a ground for dismissing his action for want of prosecution. No person should be penalised for doing *b* that which he has a legal right to do. His action cannot be dismissed for want of prosecution unless he has, since the issue and service of the writ, been guilty of inordinate and inexcusable delay; and that delay, the delay since the writ, has seriously prejudiced the defendant. If the defendant has not been prejudiced by the delay since the writ, the action cannot be struck out, no matter how much the defendant may have been prejudiced beforehand. That approach was adopted in *William C* *c* *Parker Ltd v F J Ham & Son Ltd*[1], and it has since been established to be the right approach. In *Birkett v James*[2] the House of Lords so declared. Their reasoning was based on the assertion that the plaintiff had a legal right to delay until the last moment of the permitted period[3]; whereas, I had taken the view that he had no legal right to delay even for that period. The only effect of the Statute of Limitations was to bar him completely. If he was foolish and indolent enough to delay unduly and unjustifi- *d* ably during the permitted period he ran a risk; for it could be taken into account later. Like a man with a seat belt; he is at liberty not to wear it; but, if he is foolish enough not to wear it, it can be taken into account later.

Coming back to the reasoning in *Birkett v James*[2] it leads to a difficulty which is exemplified by the present case. In most cases where the plaintiff takes advantage of the full period permitted by the Statute of Limitations, the prejudice to the defendant *e* has been done already before the issue of the writ. It is very rare that there is any additional prejudice since the issue of the writ, or, at any rate, the additional prejudice is no more than minimal. It is often during the first three or four years that witnesses die or disappear or forget what happened and that records and notes are lost or destroyed, especially when there is no letter before action. Take the case we had a few days ago brought by the Government of India[4]. The plaintiffs issued their writ *f* for breach of contract six years after the cause of action occurred. During that time one of the most important witnesses had died. The other had forgotten all about it. After the writ was issued, the plaintiffs took two years on pleadings and then inexcusably delayed for two more years. It was forcibly argued for the plaintiffs that this last delay caused no additional prejudice over and above that which occurred before the writ was issued. Everything would depend on the documents which had *g* come into existence ten years before. Yet we dismissed the action and the House of Lords refused leave to appeal. Then we had another case where a lay client sued a firm of solicitors for negligence in 1967. He did not issue the writ until six years later in 1973. The pleadings were closed in 1974, during which time the managing clerk of the solicitors had been drowned in an accident. Then the plaintiff delayed for a whole 13 months. It was forcibly argued that this last 13 months had caused no addi- *h* tional prejudice over and above that which had been caused before the pleading closed. Yet we dismissed the action. Take the present case. It is said with force that all the prejudice to the defendants occurred during the first three years. During that time Mrs Biss's solicitor had written a letter before action, but after receiving the detailed reply, had taken advice and dropped the claim; so the hospital thought no more about it. But then, after ten years, Mrs Biss issued a writ with the leave of the court. By that time *j*

---

1   [1972] 3 All ER 1051, [1972] 1 WLR 1583
2   [1977] 2 All ER 801, [1977] 3 WLR 38
3   See [1977] 2 All ER 801 at 806, 809, 818, [1977] 3 WLR 38 at 48, 51, 62
4   *President of India v John Shaw & Sons (Salford) Ltd* [1977] Court of Appeal Transcript 383

great prejudice had taken place. Nurses had left the hospital. One had gone to South
a Africa. Their nursing notes had been destroyed. Their memories must have failed
them, or at any rate an extra nine months would make their memories no worse.
So there was no additional prejudice since the issue of the writ or, at any rate, no
more than marginal. These arguments are so formidable that I am sure that the
House of Lords can never have envisaged such cases as these. If the approach established in *Birkett v James*[1] is carried to its logical conclusion, it would mean that in the
b many cases where the plaintiff takes advantage of the full period of limitation, so
that the defendant is hopelessly prejudiced before the writ is issued, then the plaintiff
can delay afterwards to an inordinate and inexcusable extent, with impunity. If the
defendant should take out a summons to dismiss for want of prosecution, the plaintiff
can say: 'My delay since writ has caused no additional prejudice, or at any rate no
more than minimal', so the court cannot dismiss the action. At most it can make a
c peremptory order, an 'unless' order, requiring the plaintiff to take the next step, as for
instance, to deliver a statement of claim in a specified time. The plaintiff can then
take that one step, and then start delaying all over again, just as he used to do in the
days before *Allen v McAlpine*[2].

Seeing that the House of Lords cannot have envisaged such cases as these, I feel we
must seek for some solution ourselves, so far as we can do so, consistently with what
d the House of Lords have said. The one solution that I see is that the prejudice to a
defendant by delay is not to be found solely in the death or disappearance of witnesses
or their fading memories or in the loss or destruction of records. There is much
prejudice to a defendant in having an action hanging over his head indefinitely, not
knowing when it is going to be brought to trial; like the prejudice to Damocles when
the sword was suspended over his head at the banquet. It was suspended by a single
e hair and the banquet was a tantalising torment to him. So in the *President of India* case[3],
which we heard the other day. The business house was prejudiced because it could not
carry on its business affairs with any confidence, or enter into forward commitments,
whilst the action for damages was still in being against it. Likewise the hospital here.
There comes a time when it is entitled to have some peace of mind and to regard the
incident as closed. It should not have to keep in touch with the nurses saying: 'We may
f need you to give evidence'; or to say to the finance department: 'We ought to keep
some funds in reserve in case this claim is persisted in'; or to say to the keepers of records: 'Keep these files in a safe place and don't destroy them as we may need them.'
It seems to me that in these cases this kind of prejudice is a very real prejudice to a
defendant when the plaintiff is guilty of inordinate and inexcusable delay since the
issue of the writ, and that it can properly be regarded as more than minimal. And
g when this prejudice is added to the great and prejudicial delay before writ (as the
House of Lords says it may be: see *Birkett v James*[4]) then there is sufficient ground
on which to dismiss the action for want of prosecution.

Applying this principle, I am clearly of opinion that this action should be dismissed
for want of prosecution. It would be an intolerable injustice to the hospital, and to
the nurses and staff, to have to fight it out 12 years after the incident, when they
h quite reasonably regarded it as closed 11 years ago.

In addition, it seems to me that in *Birkett v James*[1] the House of Lords only had in
mind actions that were commenced within the old periods of limitation, that is, six
years for breach of contract, and three years for personal injuries. They had not in
mind actions like the present for personal injuries which under the recent legislation
can be started more than three years after the accrual of the cause of action. It was
j the Limitation Act 1963 which first enabled some actions for personal injuries to be

---

1   [1977] 2 All ER 801, [1977] 3 WLR 38
2   [1968] 1 All ER 543, [1968] 2 QB 229
3   [1977] Court of Appeal Transcript 383
4   [1977] 2 All ER 801 at 809, 815, [1977] 3 WLR 38 at 51, 58

started after three years, but that did not give the plaintiff a legal right to do so. He could only start an action after the three years if the court gave him leave to do so: see s 1(1)(a). I know that in practice the court nearly always did give him leave, but still he had to get it. That Act is now replaced by the Limitation Act 1975, under which leave is no longer required. That Act now applies to this action here, because it is retrospective: see s 3(1). But even this 1975 Act does not give the plaintiff an unqualified legal right to start an action after three years. It depends on his state of knowledge: see s 2A(4)(b); or on whether it is equitable: see s 2D(1); and those are matters to be thrashed out later. He can issue his writ after three years, and then apply to the court to allow the action to proceed, notwithstanding that more than three years have elapsed. Counsel for Mrs Biss suggested that that is the way to deal with delay nowadays, to let it be considered later, applying all the considerations set out in s 2D(3). There is no room now, he said, for this court, on an application to dismiss, to take into account delay before writ. That must be dealt with later on the hearing of an application under s 2D. All that should be considered on the application to dismiss was, he submitted, the delay since the writ and the prejudice since the writ. Applied to this case the delay of nine months since the writ caused so little prejudice that the action should not be dismissed on that account.

I cannot accept that submission. It would submit the hospital to even greater injustice. They would have to go to trial, not only on the issue of negligence 12 years ago and the damage from it, but also on the issue of knowledge of the plaintiff and on whether it was equitable to allow the action to proceed having regard to all that had happened. If the House of Lords in *Birkett v James*[1] had had the 1975 Act in mind (which applies to all actions now pending for personal injuries), I cannot help feeling that they would have said that in all cases when the plaintiff seeks to take advantage of the 1975 Act the court can look at the totality of the delay and see whether the defendant was seriously prejudiced by it.

One word more. It is, I believe, accepted on all hands that if the plaintiff is guilty of inordinate and inexcusable delay before issuing the writ, then it is his duty to proceed with it with expedition after the issue of the writ. He must comply with all the rules of court and do everything that is reasonable to bring the case quickly for trial. Even a short delay after the writ may in many circumstances be regarded as inordinate and inexcusable, and give a basis for an application to dismiss for want of prosecution. So in the present case the delay of nine months was properly admitted to be inordinate and inexcusable. It is a serious prejudice to the hospital to have the action hanging over its head even for that time. On this simple ground I think this action should be dismissed for want of prosecution.

I would allow the appeal, accordingly.

GEOFFREY LANE LJ. From April 1965 until January 1966 the plaintiff was a patient in a hospital run by the defendants' predecessors. She had multiple sclerosis. During her stay there she contracted severe bed sores. During 1966 she consulted solicitors with a view to claiming damages in negligence against the hospital. Letters were written. Liability was denied. After counsel had advised her that she was unlikely to succeed, no further steps were taken until 1973. By then the plaintiff had joined the Multiple Sclerosis Society and they encouraged her to renew her claim. An opinion was obtained from Dr Walsh, the director of Stoke Mandeville Hospital, where she had been a patient in 1966. Thus, almost nine years after she had entered the defendants' hospital, she sought to issue a writ under the provisions of s 1 of the Limitation Act 1963. The judge refused leave, but her appeal to a division of this court was in February 1973 allowed. On 18th February 1975 the writ was issued and matters for a time proceeded expeditiously. In November came a summons for

---

1   [1977] 2 All ER 801, [1977] 3 WLR 38

directions. The master ordered the defendants to serve further and better particulars
a of their defence, and these were delivered on 2nd December 1975.
  Thereafter activity ceased. The plaintiff should have taken out a further summons
for directions. In August 1976 she changed her solicitors. There was a suggestion in
September 1976 from the new solicitors that the time had come for documents to be
inspected. They wished her to be seen again by Dr Walsh, but failed despite many
letters to gain her co-operation to this end. In January 1977 the defendants warned
b the plaintiff's solicitors that they might apply to dismiss the action. The warning was
repeated by letter dated 28th February 1977. It had no effect. Due entirely to the
plaintiff's own fault nothing happened. There was inordinate and inexcusable delay
and contravention of the rules as to time, but this post-writ delay added little or
nothing to the difficulties of the defendants in meeting the claim, which difficulties
had been caused by the original lapse of nine years.
c   On 22nd March 1977 the defendants' solicitors issued a summons for an order that
the action be dismissed for want of prosecution. The master made the order, but the
judge allowed the plaintiff's appeal, feeling that he was bound by the decision of the
House of Lords in *Birkett v James*[1] so to do.
  The effect of the Limitation Act 1975 has been to abolish the necessity of
obtaining leave ex parte to issue a writ after the expiry of the ordinary limitation
d period. The task of deciding whether it is a proper case under the provisions of that
Act in which to allow the action to continue is left to the trial judge, unless it is
ordered to be tried as a preliminary issue under RSC Ord 18.
  Where the writ has been issued within the normal period of three years applicable
to actions in tort then no difficulty arises in applying the principles set out in *Birkett v
James*[1]. It is in the case of actions such as the present, whether brought under the
e provisions of the 1963 Act or the 1975 Act, that difficulties arise. If *Birkett v James*[1] is
applied to such situations it seems prima facie that the longer the pre-writ delay, the
more unlikely it is that the action will be dismissed for want of prosecution. The
reason for this is that, in the nature of things, all or nearly all the prejudice to the
defendant in the shape of fading memories and lost documents will usually have taken
place before the writ was issued. The post-writ delay will only have increased those
f difficulties to a minimal extent. Lord Diplock in *Birkett v James*[2] said:

  'To justify dismissal of an action for want of prosecution some prejudice to the
  defendant additional to that inevitably flowing from the plaintiff's tardiness in
  issuing his writ must be shown to have resulted from his subsequent delay (beyond
  the period allowed by rules of court) in proceeding promptly with the successive
  steps in the action. The additional prejudice need not be great compared with
g that which may have been already caused by the time elapsed before the writ
  was issued; but it must be more than minimal . . .'

If one applies those words strictly to the present case it might seem that the action
should not be dismissed. If that is so it follows that the defendants may have to wait
until the trial of the action before they can obtain a ruling that the plaintiff's delay is
h such that the action should not continue. By that time they will no doubt have incurred
substantial costs which they may be unable to recover. I find it hard to believe that
the court should be powerless to intervene to prevent such a manifest injustice.
  The House of Lords in that case was not considering, and had no need to consider,
the situation which may arise under the later Limitation Acts and has arisen here.
j Secondly it is apt to be thought that the only way in which prejudice can be caused
to the defendants through delay is in relation to the non-availability of witnesses and
documents and the failing of memory. That is not so.

---

1 [1977] 2 All ER 801, [1977] 3 WLR 38
2 [1977] 2 All ER 801 at 809, [1977] 3 WLR 38 at 51

The principles are set out in the Supreme Court Practice[1] in a passage approved by Russell LJ in *William C Parker Ltd v F J Ham & Son Ltd*[2] as follows:

'. . . this power should not be exercised unless the Court is satisfied (1) that the default has been intentional and contumelious, e.g., disobedience to a peremptory order of the Court or conduct amounting to an abuse of the process of the Court (see *Wallersteiner* v. *Moir*[3]); or 2(a) that there has been inordinate and inexcusable delay on the part of the plaintiff or his lawyers, and (b) that such delay will give rise to a substantial risk that it is not possible to have a fair trial of the issues in the action or is such as is likely to cause or to have caused serious prejudice to the defendants either as between themselves and the plaintiff or between each other or between them and a third party.'

It is clear from this passage that the risk that a fair trial is not possible is only one aspect. Prejudice to the defendant is equally a ground on which the court can exercise its power.

As Lord Denning MR has already indicated, there are many ways in which defendants may be prejudiced by continued delay. A small business concern faced with a huge claim in damages may well suffer continuing financial stringency and loss each week that goes by through having to set aside funds against their contingent liabilities. In the present case the nurses whose competence and standards of care are in question are no doubt suffering at least some apprehension as to what may happen or be said at the trial. Why, one may ask, should they continue to have to suffer? That to my mind provides enough by way of prejudice to entitle one to say in accordance with *Birkett v James*[4] that extra prejudice beyond that caused by the pre-writ delay has occurred to the defendants here, justifying us in dismissing the action.

There are, however, other considerations. It is the duty of the court to prevent its procedures being used to create injustice. A plaintiff who issues a writ outside the normal limitation period under the terms of either the 1963 Act or the 1975 Act has only a defeasible right to continue the action. That right will ultimately depend on the decision of the judge at the trial. Whatever the merits of his claim he may find himself defeated because he cannot bring himself within the terms of the particular Act. The defendant meanwhile must expend time and money on preparing for trial. In these circumstances it is incumbent on the plaintiff to prosecute the action with diligence. If he fails to conform with the rules of court as to the various steps in the action and is guilty of serious and inexcusable delay, the court should have, and I believe has, the power in its discretion to dismiss the action for want of prosecution. It should not be necessary for the defendant to prove any additional post-writ prejudice. Such prejudice should in these circumstances be presumed.

Thus in cases where (1) the writ was issued after the normal period of limitation had expired, (2) the plaintiff has failed to comply with all the rules of court as to time, (3) the plaintiff has been guilty since the issue of the writ of serious and inexcusable delay, (4) the totality of the plaintiff's delay either made it substantially impossible for there to be a fair trial of the issues or alternatively has prejudiced the defendant, the court should be entitled in its discretion to dismiss the action.

I would accordingly allow the appeal and dismiss the action.

EVELEIGH LJ. The facts of this case are quite different from those in *Birkett v James*[4]. The limitation period had long expired at the date of the writ. The plaintiff may be able to issue another writ if this action is dismissed but she has no right to insist that the action should proceed, because she is outside the time limit imposed by

1 (1976) vol 1, p 425, para 25/1/3B
2 [1972] 3 All ER 1051 at 1052, [1972] 1 WLR 1583 at 1585 (approving the equivalent passage in the Supreme Court Practice 1973)
3 [1974] 3 All ER 217, [1974] 1 WLR 991
4 [1977] 2 All ER 801, [1977] 3 WLR 38

the Limitation Act 1975. The fact that she has been granted leave does not alter the
a position, for s 3(3) of the 1975 Act provides:

'It is hereby declared that a decision taken at any time by a court to grant, or
not to grant, leave under Part 1 of the Limitation Act 1963 (which, so far as it
relates to leave, is repealed by this Act) does not affect the determination of any
question in proceedings under this Act, but in such proceedings account may be
b taken of evidence admitted in proceedings under the said provisions repealed by
this Act.'

Therefore the plaintiff, although she was given leave, is in the position of having to
ask the court's discretion for her action to proceed by virtue of s 2D of the Limitation
Act 1939. Furthermore she was in such a position as from September 1975. One of
the factors which the court is directed to take into account in deciding whether or not
c it would be equitable to allow an action to proceed is, as stated in s 2D(3)(c)—

'the conduct of the defendant after the cause of action arose, including the
extent if any to which he responded to requests reasonably made by the plaintiff
for information or inspection for the purpose of ascertaining facts which were or
might be relevant to the plaintiff's cause of action against the defendant.'

d On 2nd December 1975 a request for further and better particulars of the statement
of claim was served on the plaintiff's solicitors. By the date of the summons to
dismiss the action, namely 22nd March 1977, no step whatsoever was taken by the
plaintiff to prosecute the action. In view of the above provision introduced by the
Limitation Act 1975 in my opinion the plaintiff's delay has been all the more inexcusable. I see nothing in the circumstances of this case which allows the plaintiff
e to contend that this court is precluded from dismissing the action because of the
decision in Birkett v James[1]. I agree for the reasons stated in the judgments of Lord
Denning MR and Geoffrey Lane LJ that this is a proper case for the court to exercise its
power to dismiss the action. In Birkett v James[2] Lord Edmund-Davies said:

'Thirdly, the law is intended to ensure that a person may with confidence feel
f that after a given time he may regard as finally closed an incident which might
have led to a claim against him, and it was for this reason that Lord Kenyon
described statutes of limitation as "statutes of repose"[3].'

In my view certainly by the beginning of 1977 the defendants and their colleagues
should be entitled to be free from the worry of this action.

g *Appeal allowed.*

Solicitors: *Levett, Son & Baldwin*, Bromley (for the defendants); *Lewis Silkin & Partners*
(for the plaintiff).

Gavin Gore-Andrews Esq   Barrister.

h

1 [1977] 2 All ER 801, [1977] 3 WLR 38
2 [1977] 2 All ER 801 at 816, [1977] 3 WLR 38 at 59
3 *Tolson v Kaye* (1822) 3 Brod & Bing 217 at 222, 223, per Dallas CJ

Hoskyn v Commissioner of Police for the Metropolis

HOUSE OF LORDS

LORD WILBERFORCE, VISCOUNT DILHORNE, LORD SALMON, LORD EDMUND-DAVIES AND LORD KEITH OF KINKEL

23rd, 24th JANUARY, 6th APRIL 1978

Criminal evidence – Compellability as witness – Spouse as witness for prosecution – Husband charged with crime of personal violence against wife – Wife called as witness for prosecution – Whether wife compellable witness against husband charged with a crime of violence against her.

The appellant was charged with wounding a woman with intent to do her grievous bodily harm, contrary to s 18 of the Offences against the Person Act 1861. Two days before the trial the appellant and the woman were married. At the trial the woman was called by the prosecution as a witness but was reluctant to give evidence against her husband. The trial judge ruled that she was not only a competent witness but also a compellable witness and he ordered her to give evidence. Part of her evidence, if believed, was highly damaging to the appellant. The appellant was convicted of the offence charged and appealed.

Held (Lord Edmund-Davies dissenting) – The wife of a defendant charged with a crime of violence against her was not a compellable witness against him. The appeal would therefore be allowed and the conviction quashed (see p 143 *a c*, p 147 *g*, p 148 *b* to *d*, p 152 *c d* and p 160 *c*, post).

Leach v R [1912] AC 305 applied.

R v Lapworth [1930] All ER Rep 340 overruled.

Notes

For evidence by a defendant's spouse, see 11 Halsbury's Laws (4th Edn) paras 470, 471, and for cases on the subject, see 14(2) Digest (Reissue) 646-648, 650, 651, 5216-5251, 5267-5277.

Cases referred to in opinions

Advocate (HM) v William Commelin or Comeling (1836) 1 Swin 291.

Bentley v Cooke (1784) 3 Doug KB 422, 99 ER 729.

Cartwright v Green (1803) 8 Ves 405, 2 Leach 952, 32 ER 412, LC, 15 Digest (Reissue) 1276, 10,975.

Director of Public Prosecutions v Morgan [1975] 2 All ER 347, [1976] AC 182, [1975] 2 WLR 913, 139 JP 476, 61 Cr App Rep 136, HL, 15 Digest (Reissue) 1212, 10,398.

Fernandez, Ex parte (1861) 10 CBNS 3, 30 LJCP 321, 4 LT 324, 7 Jur NS 571, 142 ER 349, 16 Digest (Repl) 87, 956.

Griggs's Case (1661) T Raym 1, 83 ER 1.

Leach v R [1912] AC 305, sub nom *Leach v Director of Public Prosecutions* 81 LJKB 616, 106 LT 281, 76 JP 203, 22 Cox CC 721, 7 Cr App Rep 157, HL; *rvsg* sub nom *R v Acaster and Leach* 7 Cr App Rep 84, CCA, 14(2) Digest (Reissue) 650, 5267.

R v Algar [1953] 2 All ER 1381, [1954] 1 QB 279, [1953] 3 WLR 1007, 118 JP 56, 37 Cr App Rep 200, CCA, 14(2) Digest (Reissue) 650, 5275.

R v All Saints, Worcester (Inhabitants) (1817) 6 M & S 194, 105 ER 1215, 22 Digest (Reissue) 435, 4323.

R v Azire (1725) 1 Stra 633, 93 ER 746, 14(2) Digest (Reissue) 646, 5229.

R v Carter (1976) 28 CCC (2d) 219.

R v Lapworth [1931] 1 KB 117, [1930] All ER Rep 340, 100 LJKB 52, 144 LT 126, 95 JP 2, 29 LGR 61, 29 Cox CC 183, 22 Cr App Rep 87, CCA, 14(2) Digest (Reissue) 647, 5234.

R v Lonsdale (1973) 15 CCC (2d) 201.

R v Lord Audley, Earl Castlehaven's Case (1631) 3 State Tr 401, Hut 115, 1 Hale PC 629,
a   123 ER 1140, HL, 15 Digest (Reissue) 1211, *10,383*.
R v Phillips [1922] SASR 276, 14(2) Digest (Reissue) 648, *4184*.
Reeve v Wood (1864) 5 B & S 364, 5 New Rep 173, 34 LJMC 15, 34 LJQB 24, 11 LT 449,
     29 JP 214, 11 Jur MS 201, 10 Cox CC 58, 122 ER 867, 14(2) Digest (Reissue) 646, *5220*.
Riddle v R (1911) 12 CLR 622, 14(2) Digest (Reissue) 651, *4203*.
Sharp v Rodwell [1947] VLR 82.
b   *Wakefield's Case* (1827) 2 Lew CC 1, 279, 2 Town St Tr 112, Mood & M 197, 168 ER 1154,
     14(2) Digest (Reissue) 647, *5237*.

Appeal

This was an appeal by Edward William Hoskyn against the decision of the Court of
Appeal, Criminal Division (Geoffrey Lane LJ, Cusack and Croom Johnson JJ) given
c   on 8th July 1977 dismissing the appellant's appeal against his conviction and sentence
on 8th October 1976 at the Central Criminal Court for the offence of wounding
Janis Ann Scrimshaw with intent to do her grievous bodily harm (count 4 of the
indictment), contrary to s 18 of the Offences against the Person Act 1861. The facts
are set out in the opinion of Lord Wilberforce.

d   *C F Ascher* for the appellant.
Richard Du Cann QC and *David Miller* for the Crown.

Their Lordships took time for consideration.

6th April. The following opinions were delivered.
e

LORD WILBERFORCE.   My Lords, the following point of law has been cetifiedt
as of general public importance: whether a wife is a compellable witness against
her husband in a case of violence on her by him. It arises on the appellant's appeal,
by leave of this House, against his conviction for wounding with intent to do grievous
f   bodily harm.
The appellant was charged at the Central Criminal Court inter alia (i) with assaulting one Bailey thereby occasioning him actual bodily harm, and (ii) with wounding
Janis Ann Scrimshaw (sic) with intent to do grievous bodily harm. The woman
concerned was so described because at the date of the alleged wounding and at the
date of the committal proceedings she was not married to the appellant and that was
g   her maiden name. The marriage only took place on 2nd October 1977, two days
before the trial was due to begin. However, at the trial, the appellant's wife she was
and so the point of law, which is of greater general importance than the particular
circumstances would suggest, arose and must now be decided.
At the trial, when Janis Hoskyn (as she had then become) was called by the Crown,
she showed herself unwilling to give evidence. There took place exchanges with
h   the learned judge, which, the Crown does not dispute, amounted in law to her
being treated as a compellable witness, and she gave evidence accordingly. It is
not necessary to go into the details of the evidence she gave: she did not give the
evidence expected of her by the Crown, was treated as a hostile witness and committed herself to a number of inconsistencies. In his summing-up, the learned
judge in effect advised the jury to disregard her evidence unless corroborated, but it
j   was given and was heard by the jury, and part of it, if believed, was highly damaging
to the appellant. The whole process, illustrative of what may be expected if one
spouse is to be treated as compellable to give evidence against the other, was in fact
unsatisfactory, so that one must doubt the expediency of the rule which gave rise to it.
The Crown accepts that, since the jury may well have taken it into account, it must
follow that if in law the spouse ought not to have been compelled to testify, the

conviction cannot stand. So, in relation to this charge of violence on her by her husband, ought she to have been treated as compellable?

My Lords, since most prosecutions for violence by a husband are initiated by the wife herself, the wife would normally be willing to give evidence against him (see for example *Director of Public Prosecutions v Morgan*[1]). On the other hand, cases must have occurred where, after a charge has been made and during the period before trial, a wife, in the interests of her marriage, has second thoughts and when it comes to the point does not wish to give evidence against her husband and will only do so under compulsion. So it is surprising that there is so little authority on the point which now concerns us. In English law there is only one direct authority, *R v Lapworth*[2], in which the Court of Criminal Appeal (Avory, Swift and Acton JJ) held that the wife was compellable. This case has held the field since 1931, and no doubt practice has followed it. The law which it stated was repeated in 1954 in a dictum by so great an authority as Lord Goddard CJ in *R v Algar*[3]. It was also accepted by the Criminal Law Revision Committee in its 11th report in 1972[4]. Your Lordships were naturally urged, therefore, not to bring about a change in the law but to leave any necessary reform to Parliament. As to this I would say two things. First, there are arguments, essentially of policy, either way. The argument for compellability has often been stated in the past, but in parallel with the recognition that the existing law is against compellability. Thus Wigmore[5]:

'In an age which has so far rationalized, depolarized, and de-chivalrized the marital relation and the spirit of Femininity as to be willing to enact complete legal and political equality and independence of man and woman, this marital privilege is the merest anachronism, in legal theory, and an indefensible obstruction to truth, in practice.'

And the Commissioners of Common Law Procedure[6] recommended that husband and wife should be competent and compellable to give evidence for and against another, inferentially accepting that the law was otherwise.

Secondly, our task is to ascertain and state the law as it is. We may and must both respect any decision and course of practice as evidence of what the law is, and we must try to understand the policy, which may by an evolving policy, behind the common law, but if a decision or course of practice is contrary to the common law, as, in relation to *R v Lapworth*[2] the appellant argues that it is, we must so declare.

My Lords, we start from two certain points. First, in principle, anyone who is a competent witness is a compellable witness (*Ex parte Fernandez*[7]). This general rule is a constitutional principle underlying our whole system of justice, but, as Willes J[8] in his judgment adds, it applies 'unless he can shew some exception in his favour . . .' The only certain exceptions seem to be the Sovereign and persons protected by diplomatic immunity, but, except that they show that the law recognises that certain persons, undoubtedly competent, may by virtue of their status not be compellable, these cases provide no analogy for the treatment of a wife. The case of a spouse is, however, capable of inclusion under the words 'some exception'; the question is whether it is so included. Secondly, a wife, at common law, was incompetent to give evidence against her husband. Broadly the incompetence according to the authorities can be said to rest on the doctrine of the unity of husband and wife, coupled with the

---

1   [1975] 2 All ER 347, [1976] AC 182
2   [1931] 1 KB 117, [1930] All ER Rep 340
3   [1953] 2 All ER 1381 at 1382, [1954] 1 QB 279 at 285
4   (1972) Cmnd 4991, para 144
5   A Treatise on the System of Evidence in Trials at Common Law (3rd Edn, 1940), para 2228 at p 232
6   (1853) 2nd Report, 13
7   (1861) 10 CBNS 3
8   10 CBNS 3 at 39

privilege against self-incrimination. The danger of perjury is also invoked[1], and the repugnance likely to be felt by the public seeing one spouse testifying against the other.

To this second rule as to competence limited exceptions have been recognised to exist. The clearest, and that relevant here, related to cases of rape or personal violence. This rests on the opinion of the judges given in *R v Lord Audley*[2], accepted by the House of Lords (followed by *R v Azire*[3] and *Bentley v Cooke*[4], per Lord Mansfield). The reason for it, quite evidently, and indeed as so stated, is that unless this were so the wife would have no protection except in the unlikely event of a third person being present.

Other possible exceptions, and these were the only exceptions, were cases of treason and cases of abduction. But the law on treason appears to be in some doubt[5] and the case of abduction, which must mean abduction of an unmarried girl whom the abductor afterwards marries, is not of frequent occurrence.

I need not cite authority at length to support the above. Dean Wigmore[6] declares that the history of the privilege not to testify against a spouse is involved 'in a tantalising obscurity'. But it was established by the time of Coke. In a passage disparaged by Wigmore[7] as mouthing 'a few Latin words of mediaeval scholasticism' and described by Bentham[8] as 'the grimgribber nonsensical reason', Coke[9] said in a passage written before *R v Lord Audley*[2]:

> 'Note, it hath been resolved, that a wife cannot be produced either for or against her husband, *quia sunt duæ animæ in carne una*, and it might be a cause of implacable discord and dissention between them, and a means of great inconvenience.'

The law similarly stated in Hale[10], Hawkins[11] and Blackstone[12]. I make only one further citation, from Gilbert on the Law of Evidence[13]:

> 'And it would be very hard that a Wife should be allowed as Evidence against her own Husband when she cannot attest for him; such a Law would occasion implacable Divisions and Quarrels, and destroy the very legal Policy of marriage that has so contrived it, that their interest should be but one; which it could never be if Wives were admitted to destroy the Interest of their Husbands, and the Peace of Families could not easily be maintained if the Law admitted any Attestation against the Husband.'

This passage it will be seen has moved from Coke's mediaeval doctrine of 'one flesh' to a more modern rationale derived from the unity of interest.

None of these authorities, or any authority until the 19th century, deals with the question of compellability in cases where the wife is competent. Indeed Gilbert[14], with reference to the case of high treason, says only that the wife is *admitted* as evidence

---

1 Hawkins, Pleas of the Crown (1824), p 600
2 (1631) 3 State Tr 401
3 (1725) 1 Stra 633
4 (1784) 3 Doug KB 422 at 423, 424
5 See 11 Halsbury's Laws (4th Edn) para 470, n 2
6 Evidence (3rd Edn, 1940), vol 8, para 2227
7 Ibid, para 2228
8 Ration Judic Evid (1827), vol 5, p 344
9 Co Litt 6b
10 Pleas of the Crown (1836) 1.301
11 Pleas of the Crown (1824), p 601
12 Commentaries, p 556
13 3rd Edn (1769), p 136
14 Law of Evidence (3rd Edn, 1769), p 136

against the husband. One would think that if she was compellable at all, under some notion of the public good, she would be so in this case, yet that she is is not suggested. The references in decided cases are sparse. In *Cartwright v Green*[1], a case in Chancery, Lord Eldon LC held that a wife, who was defendant to a bill in Chancery, was not compellable to answer on oath so as to show that her husband had been guilty of a criminal offence. '. . . the wife, if the act was a felony in the husband, would be protected: at all events she could not be called upon to make a discovery against her husband . . .' In *R v Inhabitants of All Saints, Worcester*[2] the issue was whether the wife was a competent witness on a proceeding under the Poor Laws as to the settlement of a pauper. It was decided that she was, on the ground that her evidence could not criminate her husband. But Bayley J[3] in his judgment added these words:

> 'It does not appear that she objected to be examined, or demurred to any question. If she had thrown herself on the protection of the Court on the ground that her answer to the question put to her might criminate her husband, in that case I am not prepared to say that the Court would have compelled her to answer; on the contrary, I think she would have been entitled to the protection of the Court.'

As to this passage the authoritative textbook Taylor on Evidence[4] says:

> 'But although by the common law rule of incompetency, the wife may be *permitted* to give evidence which may indirectly criminate her husband, it by no means follows that she can be *compelled* to do so; and the better opinion is that under it she may throw herself on the protection of the Court, and decline to answer any question which would tend to expose her husband to a criminal charge.'

Similarly Phillips and Anderson on Evidence[5] and Roscoe's Digest[6]. Other views are expressed in other textbooks.

The word 'compellability' itself seems to be of comparatively recent origin. It appears first in Lord Brougham's Evidence Act 1851. Section 2 of this Act made parties to proceedings 'competent and compellable' to give evidence. Section 3, dealing with criminal proceedings, maintained the protection of persons charged, and the husband or wife of such persons; none of these persons was to be competent or compellable to give evidence. It was said that the words 'competent and compellable' in s 2 should be read as 'competent *and therefore* compellable', so as to support the proposition that competency automatically involves compellability. I do not agree: on the contrary the formulation suggests that competency and compellability are two different things and s 3 suggests, or at least recognises, that a spouse can be competent without being compellable.

A great number of statutes (some 27) were passed between 1853, the date of Lord Brougham's second Law of Evidence Act[7], and the Criminal Evidence Act 1898, dealing with competency and compellability in a number of contexts. The Married Women's Property Act 1884, s 1, amending the Married Women's Property Act 1882, s 16, made both husband and wife, in criminal proceedings under that Act, competent and admissable witnesses and, except when defendant, compellable to give evidence' but neither this nor any other statute establishes a general rule. I think that the most that can be drawn from these statutes is that, as a matter of Parliamentary language, it was recognised that competency or compellability are distinct one from the other,

---

1   (1803) 8 Ves 405 at 410
2   (1817) 6 M & S 194
3   6 M & S 194 at 200
4   10th Edn (1906), para 1368
5   10th Edn (1852), p 73
6   11th Edn (1890), p 143
7   Evidence Amendment Act 1853

and that none of them affected, or threw any light on, what the common law was as to criminal proceedings by one spouse against the other either generally or in cases of violence.

The Criminal Evidence Act 1898 at last made persons charged with criminal offences and their wife or husband competent to give evidence. Section 4(1) provided:

> 'The wife or husband of a person charged with an offence under any enactment mentioned in the schedule to this Act may be called as a witness either for the prosecution or defence and without the consent of the person charged.'

The schedule listed five Acts to which the Punishment of Incest Act 1908 added a sixth. This section gave rise to the important case of *Leach v R*[1] which reached this House. The question was there directly raised whether the wife of a person charged under a scheduled Act (in that case the Punishment of Incest Act 1908) was a compellable witness. The Court of Criminal Appeal[2] (Lord Alverstone CJ, Hamilton and Bankes JJ) following various decisions in 1899 held that she was: 'S. 4 [of the 1898 Act] is sufficient to make a wife called for the prosecution an ordinary witness, and therefore compellable.'[3] On appeal this House took a different view. Their Lordships had the benefit of a full argument, which is reported, with some differences, both in the Criminal Appeal Reports[4] and in the Law Reports[1]. Their attention was drawn to the three common law exceptions to the rule of non-competence (violence, abduction, treason) and, according to one report[5], an analogy was sought to be drawn from what was said to be the common law:

> '. . . at common law the wife was a competent witness where personal injuries to herself were involved, but in such cases she was also at common law a compellable witness; the effect of making her a competent witness by statute must be the same',

an argument the House rejected. The opinion of the House was expressed in three speeches, delivered, it appears, without an interval for consideration. Earl Loreburn LC[6] referred to 'a fundamental and old principle . . . that you ought not to compel a wife to give evidence against her husband in matters of a criminal kind'. Lord Halsbury said[7]:

> ' . . since the foundations of the common law it has been recognized that [i e to compel a wife to give evidence against her husband] is contrary to the course of the law. . . If you want to alter the law which has lasted for centuries and which is almost ingrained in the English Constitution, in the sense that everybody would say, "To call a wife against her husband is a thing that cannot be heard of" . . .'

Lord Atkinson said[7]: 'The principle that a wife is not to be compelled to give evidence against her husband is deep seated in the common law of this country . . .' Lord Macnaghten, Lord Shaw of Dunfermline and Lord Robson agreed.

My Lords, it is certain that their Lordships were dealing with a point of statutory construction (of s 4 of the 1898 Act), that they were not called on to pronounce on the position at common law, and that anything they said, expressly or by implication, as to the latter would be outside what they were called on to decide. Nevertheless, I

---

1   [1912] AC 305
2   (1911) 7 Cr App Rep 84
3   7 Cr App Rep 84 at 89
4   (1912) 7 Cr App Rep 157
5   7 Cr App Rep 157 at 166, per Sir John Simon (Solicitor-General) arguendo
6   [1912] AC 305 at 309
7   [1912] AC 305 at 311

cannot believe that they would have used the strong and unqualified expressions which they did, if they had thought that there were special cases, outside the ambit of the statute, in which a wife was compellable. If they had so thought they would surely have thought it necessary to deal with the argument by analogy: '... it is true that the principle we are stating is not absolute: there are exceptions at common law, when the wife is competent and compellable, but that does not affect the position under statute', or at least to qualify in some way their general statements. And if they had been asked: 'What about the case where a wife was competent at common law? Does not the ordinary rule make her compellable?' they would surely have answered: 'No, because the considerations which led the law to treat her as competent do not in any way weaken the force of the principle we have stated that a wife ought not to be forced into the witness box, a principle of general application and fundamental importance.'

My Lords, when *R v Lapworth*[1] came to be decided in 1931, the Court of Criminal Appeal was content to distinguish *Leach v R*[2] as a case on a point of statutory construction. This they were formally entitled to do. Their own judgment as to the common law rests on two arguments, first the general argument that, in English law, all competent witnesses are compellable. This of course is true, but it does not resolve the particular question whether the wife of an accused person, who clearly enjoys a special status, is within or without this rule.

Secondly, they found on an observation during argument attributed by the Criminal Appeal Reports[3] to Lord Halsbury:

> 'I should have thought that if the known state of the law was that in order to confer competency you had to enact it, the fact that you simply used the word "competent" did not necessarily mean "against his or her will"',

and they argued[4]:

> 'I read that as meaning: if the known state of the law is such as to confer competency without a statute, then compellability follows as a matter of course from that fact.'

With all respect a complete non sequitur.

I respect the view of these experienced judges as to the practice, but against this they give no weight to such authority as can be found which I have cited, which, in the view of one respected author, led him to think that the 'better opinion' is against compellability. Nor do they examine in any depth, or indeed at all, the fundamental question which I think to be this: a wife is in principle not a competent witness on a criminal charge against her husband. This is because of the identity of interest between husband and wife and because to allow her to give evidence would give rise to discord and to perjury and would be, to ordinary people, repugnant. Limited exceptions have been engrafted on this rule, of which the most important, and that now relevant, relates to cases of personal violence by the husband against her. This requires that, as she is normally the only witness and because otherwise a crime would go without sanction, she be permitted to give evidence against him. But does this permission, in the interest of the wife, carry the matter any further, or do the general considerations, arising from the fact of marriage and her status as a wife, continue to apply so as to negative compulsion? That argument was in just this form put to the House of Lords and in a general form answered in the affirmative. It was not faced in *R v Lapworth*[1] at all.

---

1   [1931] 1 KB 117, [1930] All ER Rep 340
2   [1912] AC 305
3   *Leach v Director of Public Prosecutions* (1912) 7 Cr App Rep 157 at 166
4   [1931] 1 KB 117 at 122, [1930] All ER Rep 340 at 341

My Lords, after careful consideration I have reached the conclusion that *R v Lapworth*[1] was wrongly decided and must be overruled, that the general principles stated in *Leach v R*[2] apply and that the wife should be held non-compellable.

I will add that I have taken into account the position, so far as it has been made clear, in other jurisdictions. In Scotland the law has been clear since 1836 in favour of compellability: *H M Advocate v Commelin*[3]. In Australia, the High Court, on a New South Wales appeal, obiter it is true, but after a careful analysis of the authorities by Griffith CJ, expressed a view, before the English case of *Leach v R*[2], against compellability (*Riddle v R*[4]). The same view has been taken in South Australia (*R v Phillips*[5]). In Victoria, Gavan Duffy J following *Lapworth*[1] and not *Riddle*[4] expressed the opposite opinion[6].

In Canada a learned article by Dean Weir[7] suggested that *R v Lapworth*[1] should be followed, but since then judicial opinions have been expressed either way: *R v Lonsdale*[8] (compellable), *R v Carter*[9] (not compellable). In this state of authority it would be invidious to assert where the 'better opinion' is to be found.

I would allow the appeal and quash the conviction.

VISCOUNT DILHORNE. My Lords, can a wife be compelled to give evidence against her husband if he is charged with subjecting her to violence? That is the question to be decided in this appeal and it is surprising that at this time it should admit of argument.

The appellant was charged with wounding Janis Scrimshaw on 15th September 1975 contrary to s 18 of the Offences against the Person Act 1861. His trial started at the Central Criminal Court on Monday, 4th October 1976. It was announced that it would do so on Friday, 1st October and the appellant married her on 2nd October. It would make no difference to the answer to the question to be resolved if the violence had been alleged to have taken place after and not before the marriage. Mrs Hoskyn, as she had become, was reluctant to give evidence against her husband but, it is common ground, was compelled to do so, the learned judge feeling obliged to follow the decision in *R v Lapworth*[1] of the Court of Criminal Appeal.

It is now contended that that case was wrongly decided and that that court wrongly interpreted and failed to apply the decision of this House in *Leach v R*[2]. That court, it is said, should have held that the wife was a competent but not a compellable witness.

It is well established that ordinarily a person who is competent to give evidence is also compellable. He or she may of course be entitled to refuse to answer on the grounds that to do so might incriminate or for some other valid reason, but as a general rule under the common law, if one is competent, it follows that one is a compellable witness. Also the rule is well established that, subject to certain exceptions under the common law and made by statute, a wife cannot give evidence against her husband or a husband against his wife. Coke states[10]:

'. . . it hath been resolved that a wife cannot be produced either for or against her husband, *quia sunt duæ animæ in carne una*, and it might be a cause of implacable discord and dissention between them, and a means of great inconvenience.'

---

1   [1931] 1 KB 117, [1930] All ER Rep 340
2   [1912] AC 305
3   (1836) 1 Swin 291
4   (1911) 12 CLR 622
5   [1922] SASR 276
6   *Sharp v Rodwell* [1947] VLR 82 at 85
7   [1931] Can BR 216
8   (1973) 15 CCC (2d) 201
9   (1976) 28 CCC (2d) 219
10 Co Litt 6b

He did not say there were any exceptions to the rule, but three years later in 1631, when Lord Audley was tried by his peers for the rape of his wife, his wife was allowed *a* to give evidence against him, the judges resolving[1]—

'that in civil cases the Wife may not; but in a criminal cause of this nature, where the Wife is the party grieved and on whom the crime is committed, she is to be admitted a witness against her Husband.'

No question arose in that case as to whether an unwilling wife could be compelled *b* to do so; she was just admitted to give evidence.

In 1661 that decision was not followed, it being held that a wife could not be admitted to give evidence against her husband in any case excepting treason and Coke[2] was cited: *Mary Griggs's Case*[3]. But in *R v Azire*[4] a wife was 'allowed . . . to be a good witness for the King' against her husband, and in *Bentley v Cooke*[5] Lord Mansfield said: *c*

'There never has been an instance either in a civil or criminal case where the husband or wife has been permitted to be a witness for or against the other, except in case of necessity, and that necessity is not a general necessity, as where no other witness can be had, but a particular necessity, as where, for instance, the wife would otherwise be exposed without remedy to personal injury.' *d*

In *Wakefield's Case*[6] Hullock B in the course of his judgment said:

'A wife is competent against her husband in all cases affecting her liberty and person. This was decided in *Lord Audley's* case[1], having been, before that, for a long while doubted . . .'

e

See also *Reeve v Wood*[7].

In none of the cases to which I have referred, in which a wife was admitted to give evidence against her husband, is any suggestion to be found that the consequence of recognition of a wife as a competent witness was that she was also compellable.

Once competent it is argued that under the common law compellability follows. But I see no grounds for assuming that when this exception was made to the general *f* rule as enunciated by Coke, it had that consequence. A number of reasons have been put forward for the general rule. There were the two grounds stated by Coke[2]. Blackstone[9] in his Commentaries says:

'Upon this principle, of an union of person in husband and wife, depend almost all the legal rights, duties and disabilities that either of them acquire by the *g* marriage',

and he, while advancing other reasons for it, appears to base it primarily on this ground. Another reason put forward was that there is a natural repugnance to allowing a husband or wife to give evidence against the other. If there is force in this, there surely must be greater repugnance to compelling an unwilling wife to give *h* evidence against her husband.

The first case in which the compellability of a wife came under consideration

---

1   *R v Lord Audley* (1631) 3 State Tr 401 at 414
2   Co Litt 6b
3   (1661) T Raym 1
4   (1725) 1 Stra 633
5   (1784) 3 Doug KB 422 at 423, 424
6   (1827) 2 Lew CC 279 at 287
7   (1864) 5 B & S 364
8   Bk 1, p 442

j

appears to have been *R v Inhabitants of All Saints Worcester*[1]. There a wife was
admitted to give evidence. Objection was taken as to her competency. Lord Ellenborough CJ said[2]: 'I cannot discover any incompetence . . . She did not refuse to be
examined', and Bayley J said[3]:

> '. . . it appears to me that Ann Willis was a competent witness . . . It does
> not appear that she objected to be examined or demurred to any question. If
> she had thrown herself on the protection of the Court on the ground that her
> answer to the question put to her might criminate her husband, in that case I
> am not prepared to say that the Court would have compelled her to answer; on
> the contrary, I think she would have been entitled to the protection of the Court.'

If in 1817 it was held in some quarters that a wife who was competent was ipso facto
compellable, I cannot but think that Lord Ellenborough CJ and Bayley J would
have referred to it. What was said in that case certainly lends no support to the view
that competence on the part of a wife involves compellability; and no support for that
is to be found in Hale's Pleas of the Crown or in Hawkins's Pleas of the Crown or in
Blackstone.

In Taylor on Evidence[4] it is stated that although a wife may be permitted to give
evidence—

> 'it by no means follows that she can be *compelled* to do so; and the better
> opinion is that under it she may throw herself on the protection of the Court and
> decline to answer any question which would tend to expose her husband to a
> criminal charge.'

In the 19th century a large number of statutes were passed making in some cases a
married person competent and in others competent and compellable as a witness in
support of certain indictments. These statutes do not bear directly on the question
whether a married person competent to give evidence under the common law against
her husband in support of a criminal charge can be compelled to do so. But it is
perhaps surprising that this distinction between competence and compellability
should have been drawn by Parliament if it was thought that in every case, unless the
contrary were stated, competence at common law involved compellability. The
exhaustive researches made by counsel in this case have provided little, if any, material
to support that conclusion.

The Criminal Evidence Act 1898, by s 1, made the wife or husband of the person
charged a competent witness for the defence subject to the proviso that he or she
should not be called as a witness except on the application of the person charged.
Even if called, a married person was not compellable to disclose any communication
made by his or her spouse during the marriage. Section 4(1) provided that the husband or wife of the person charged could be called as a witness for the prosecution
or defence and without the consent of the accused if the charge was for one of the
offences specified in the schedule. Section 4(2) provided that nothing in the Act should
affect the case where the wife or husband of a person charged with an offence may at
common law be called as a witness without the consent of that person.

In *R v Acaster and Leach*[5] the Court of Criminal Appeal held that a person who
could be called by virtue of s 4(1) was compellable. On appeal to this House this
decision was reversed (*Leach v R*[6]). Although this decision was as to the construction of

1 (1817) 6 M & S 194
2 6 M & S 194 at 198
3 6 M & S 194 at 200
4 9th Edn (1895), p 892
5 (1911) 7 Cr App Rep 84
6 [1912] AC 305

s 4(1) of the Act, the report of the argument in this House in the Criminal Appeal
Reports[1] shows that the question was gone into very thoroughly and it is to my mind   a
inconceivable that the six members of this House who sat ignored the position at
common law. Lord Loreburn LC said[2] that it was—

> 'a fundamental and old principle to which the law has looked, that you ought
> not to compel a wife to give evidence against her husband in matters of a criminal
> kind.'
>   b

Lord Halsbury[3] said that he thought—

> 'that almost everybody in English life would recognise the fact that a wife
> ought not to be allowed to be called against her husband. It is not necessary to
> enter into that question; but what I mean is that those who are under the respon-
> sibility of passing Acts of Parliament would recognise a matter of that supreme   c
> importance as one to be dealt with specifically and definitely, and not to be left
> to an inference.'

In the Law Reports[4] this passage is reported in the same words. The next paragraph
of his speech, as reported in the Criminal Appeal Reports, includes the following
passage[3]—   d

> '. . . and I must say for myself, speaking as an ordinary person, I should have
> asked, when it was proposed to call the wife against the husband: 'Will you shew
> me an Act of Parliament that definitely says you may do so? because since the
> foundation of the common law it has been recognised that this is contrary to the
> course of the law'".'
>   e

In the report in the Law Reports, however, Lord Halsbury[5] is reported as having
said not ' Will you shew me an Act of Parliament that definitely says you may do so',
but 'Will you shew me an Act of Parliament that definitely says you may compel
her to give evidence?'
    Where there are differences between reports of judgments, it is the recognised   f
practice to prefer that in the Law Reports, as the report there published is likely to
have been revised by the judge. In this case there was no issue as to the wife being
allowed to be called, for the 1898 Act provided for that. The issue was, could she be
compelled to give evidence? and it is most improbable that Lord Halsbury was not
directing his observations to that question. Indeed it may be that the reference in the
preceding paragraph to her being 'allowed to be called' was an uncorrected error and   g
it may be that instead of those words there should have read 'compelled to give
evidence'.
    Lord Halsbury's question as stated in the Law Reports in relation to the position
when competence has been conferred by statute is, in my opinion, equally pertinent
in relation to competence arising under the common law in consequence of judicial
recognition of an exception to the general rule.   h
    In the same case Lord Atkinson said[5]:

> 'The principle that a wife is not to be compelled to give evidence against her
> husband is deep seated in the common law of this country, and I think if it is to be
> overturned it must be overturned by a clear, definite and positive enactment . . .'

                                                                                          j

1 (1912) 7 Cr App Rep 157
2 [1912] AC 305 at 308
3 7 Cr App Rep 157 at 170
4 [1912] AC 305 at 310, 311
5 [1912] AC 305 at 311

Up to this time there is an absence of any clear authority for the proposition that a wife can, in the circumstances in question, be compelled to give evidence and I see no justification in the light of the cases to which I have referred for drawing any such inference.

In 1931, however, in *R v Lapworth*[1] the question whether a wife could be compelled to give evidence against her husband on a charge of causing her grievous bodily harm arose for decision. She was reluctant to give evidence but was ordered to do so. He was convicted and appealed on the ground that she should not have been so directed. In the course of the argument the only cases referred to were *Leach v R*[2], the *Lord Audley* case[3] and *R v Phillips*[4], decided in South Australia, where Angus Parsons J held that a husband was not a compellable witness against his wife on a charge of wounding. This case followed the decision of the High Court of Australia in *Riddle v R*[5] where Griffith CJ[6] posed the question: 'Was a wife compellable at common law to give evidence against her husband?' and, after referring to *R v Inhabitants of All Saints, Worcester*[7] and Taylor on Evidence[8], he appears to have agreed with a view expressed in Taylor that the better opinion was that she was not.

In *R v Lapworth*[1] Avory J delivered the judgment of the court. He accepted that there was no direct authority on the point and said that that sometimes happened where it was recognised that a certain state of the law existed when it had never been called in question. It is perhaps unfortunate that *Riddle v R*[5] was not drawn to the court's attention. That court held that in *Leach*[2] the members of the House had not had present in their minds cases of violence by one spouse to another and that this House had no intention of including such cases in their observations.

I must say that it appears to me improbable that this House in *Leach*[2] did not have regard to cases of violence between spouses. I see no reason for the conclusion that their observations as to the non-compellability of wives as witnesses were not intended to apply to wives asked to testify against their husbands on charges of violence.

I do not regard this decision as satisfactory. It is perhaps particularly unfortunate that the observations of Bayley J in *R v Inhabitants of All Saints, Worcester*[9] and the passage from Taylor on Evidence[10] were not brought to the court's attention. That decison has, however, now stood for 46 years, though it may be that in the course of those years only a few occasions has a wife or husband been compelled against his or her will to give evidence. In the present case the learned judge allowed Mrs Hoskyn to be treated as a hostile witness and in his summing-up told the jury not to consider her a reliable witness. It may be that in a number of cases it has not been thought worthwhile by the prosecution to seek to secure that a wife or husband reluctant to give evidence is compelled to do so.

The conclusion to which I have come in the light of the authorities to which I have referred and to which the court in *R v Lapworth*[1] was not referred is that the decision in that case was wrong. In my view the fundamental principle was correctly stated by Lord Loreburn LC and Lord Atkinson in *Leach*[2] and I would conclude this speech with two citations and one observation. The first citation is from the reply by counsel in *Leach v R*[11]:

---

1   [1931] 1 KB 117, [1930] All ER Rep 340
2   [1912] AC 305
3   (1631) 3 State Tr 401
4   [1922] SASR 276
5   (1911) 12 CLR 622
6   12 CLR 622 at 627
7   (1817) 6 M & S 194
8   10th Edn (1906)
9   6 M & S 194 at 200
10 9th Edn (1895), p 892
11 (1912) 7 Cr App Rep 157 at 168, arguendo

'In the case of an ordinary person if he may be called as a witness, the usual consequences follow, i.e., he must give evidence, but the wife has never, as regards her husband, been in the position of an ordinary witness by reason of the common law, and she can no more be compelled than the prisoner himself can be compelled.'

The other citation is from the judgment of Griffith CJ in *Riddle v R*[1]:

'The old doctrine of the unity of husband and wife and the importance of preserving confidence between them, and the other reasons which have been variously given, have still a great deal of weight.'

If *R v Lapworth*[2] was rightly decided, a wife could be compelled at the instance of any prosecutor to testify against her husband on a charge involving violence, no matter how trivial and no matter the consequences to her and to her family. I find that very repugnant.

My conclusion therefore is that Mrs Hoskyn should not have been compelled to give evidence and as, though the judge said she was not a reliable witness, it is not possible to determine to what extent, if any, the jury had regard to what she said, in my opinion this appeal should be allowed and the conviction appealed from quashed.

LORD SALMON. My Lords, this appeal raises an important question of law: when a man is charged with committing a crime of violence against his wife, can she be compelled to give evidence for the Crown against her husband?

In the present case the appellant was convicted of wounding Janis Scrimshaw with intent to do her grievous bodily harm. At the time of the alleged offence the appellant and Janis Scrimshaw were not married. They were however lawfully married to each other before the trial. When she was called by the Crown to give evidence against her husband she made it plain that she did not wish to do so. The learned trial judge who considered, rightly, that he was bound by the Court of Criminal Appeal's decision in *R v Lapworth*[2] ruled that she was not only a competent but also a compellable witness. He told her that she must give evidence. She went into the witness box but apparently did not give the evidence which the Crown was expecting and leave was obtained to treat her as a hostile witness. On the appellant's appeal to the Court of Appeal that court considered itself, I think rightly, to be bound by *Lapworth*[2] and dismissed the appeal. It has been conceded by the Crown that, if *Lapworth*[2] was wrongly decided and the appellant's wife was accordingly wrongly compelled to give evidence, this appeal should be allowed and the appellant's conviction quashed.

At common law, the wife of a defendant charged with a crime, however serious, was not, as a general rule, a competent witness for the Crown. If a man were charged with murder, for example, much as it would be in the public interest that justice should be done, his wife, whatever vital evidence she might have been able to give, was not at common law a competent, let alone a compellable, witness at his trial.

This rule seems to me to underline the supreme importance attached by the common law to the special status of marriage and to the unity supposed to exist between husband and wife. It also no doubt recognised the natural repugnance of the public at the prospect of a wife giving evidence against her husband in such circumstances.

The only relevant exception to the common law rule that a wife was not a competent witness at her husband's trial was when he was charged with a crime of violence against her. There is some doubt whether this exception also applies when a husband is charged with treason, but this is not a matter relevant to this appeal.

---

1 (1911) 12 CLR 622 at 630
2 [1931] 1 KB 117, [1930] All ER Rep 340

The instant case turns solely on whether, at common law, the wife of a defendant charged with having committed a crime of violence against her is not only a competent but also a compellable witness against her husband.

The main argument on behalf of the Crown is that all persons who are competent witnesses normally are also compellable witnesses. And therefore, so the argument runs, in cases in which wives are competent witnesses it follows that they also must be compellable witnesses. This seems to me to be a complete non sequitur for it takes no account of the special importance which the common law attaches to the status of marriage. Clearly, it was for the wife's own protection that the common law made an exception to its general rule by making the wife a competent witness in respect of any charge against her husband for a crime of violence against her. But if she does not want to avail herself of this protection, there is, in my view, no ground for holding that the common law forces it on her.

In many such cases, the wife is not a reluctant or unwilling witness; she may indeed sometimes be an enthusiastic witness against her husband. On the other hand, there must also be many cases when a wife who loved her husband completely forgave him, had no fear of further violence, and wished the marriage to continue and the pending prosecution to fail. It seems to me altogether inconsistent with the common law's attitude towards marriage that it should compel such a wife to give evidence against her husband and thereby probably destroy the marriage. It is indeed remarkable that if a wife were a compellable witness, no single authority to that effect (prior to R v Lapworth[1]) has been drawn to the attention of this House. Counsel for the appellant and for the Crown, to whom this House is most indebted, have clearly made the most careful researches but have found no such authority. Nor have I. It is perhaps worth pointing out that at common law spouses are not the only persons who are competent but not compellable witnesses. Foreign ambassadors and the members of their suites also are competent but not compellable witnesses. This, of course, is because of the common law's regard for the comity of nations. There is, however, no reason to believe that it has any less regard for the institution of marriage and the special relationship between husband and wife.

None of the common law treatises support the view that a wife is a compellable witness in a case of violence by her husband against her; see Coke's Commentaries on Littleton[2], Hale's History of Pleas of the Crown[3] and Hawkin's Pleas of the Crown[4]. Gilbert on Evidence[5] and Taylor on Evidence[6] lend support to the view that at common law a wife may be a competent but never a compellable witness against her husband.

In R v Inhabitants of All Saints, Worcester[7] Bayley J said of a wife whom the court had decided was a competent witness:

'It does not appear that she objected to be examined, or demurred to any question. If she had thrown herself on the protection of the Court on the ground that her answer to the question put to her might criminate her husband, in that case I am not prepared to say that the Court would have compelled her to answer; on the contrary, I think she would have been entitled to the protection of the Court.'

That pronouncement was, no doubt, obiter, but coming from such a master of the

---

1   [1931] 1 KB 117, [1930] All ER Rep 340
2   Co Litt 6b
3   (1800) vol 1, p 301, vol 2, p 279
4   (1824) 2, c 46, ss 77, 80, 81
5   (1763), p 137
6   9th Edn (1895), paras 1363, 1369, 1370, 1453
7   (1817) 6 M & S 194 at 200

common law it deserves to be treated with the greatest respect: I regard it as being of the highest persuasive authority.

I now come to *Leach v R*[1] in the light of which I consider it impossible for the decision in *Lapworth*[2] to survive. In *Leach's* case[1] the appellant was tried for the crime of incest under the Punishment of Incest Act 1908. At the trial[3] the appellant's wife was called by the Crown. She objected to give evidence. The point was taken on her behalf that under s 4 of the Criminal Evidence Act 1898 she could not be compelled to give evidence against her husband. The learned trial judge ruled that she was a compellable witness and directed her to give evidence, which she did. The appellant was duly convicted. He appealed to the Court of Criminal Appeal which affirmed the learned trial judge's ruling and upheld the conviction. That decision was reversed in your Lordships' House.

The Criminal Evidence Act 1898, s 4, reads as follows:

'(1) The wife or husband of a person charged with an offence under any enactment mentioned in the schedule to this Act may be called as a witness either for the prosecution or defence . . .'

The Punishment of Incest Act 1908, s 4(4), reads: 'Section 4 of the Criminal Evidence Act, 1898, shall have effect as if this Act were included in the schedule to that Act.'

In my view, the whole argument on behalf of the appellant was based on the common law rule that a wife was not competent to testify against her husband except in a case in which he was charged with an act of criminal violence against her, and even then she could never be compelled to give evidence against him. Accordingly, so the argument ran, if a statute was introduced (and many had been in the 19th century) making the wife a competent witness against her husband, she could never be held to be a compellable witness unless the statute said so expressly. It was admitted on behalf of the appellant that the statute to which I have referred expressly made her a competent witness against him, but it was argued that it was impossible to construe the statute as making her a compellable witness by inference.

Lord Loreburn LC said[4]:

'. . . it is a fundamental and old principle to which the law has looked, that you ought not to compel a wife to give evidence against her husband in matters of a criminal kind.'

Lord Halsbury said[5]:

'. . . I should have asked, when it was proposed to call the wife against the husband, "Will you shew me an Act of Parliament that definitely says you may compel her to give evidence? because since the foundations of the common law it has been recognized that that is contrary to the course of the law." If you want to alter the law which has lasted for centuries and which is almost ingrained in the English Constitution, in the sense that everybody would say, "To call a wife against her husband is a thing that cannot be heard of," to suggest that that is to be dealt with by inference . . . seems to me to be perfectly monstrous.'

This apparently was an extempore speech since it seems to have been delivered on the same day as that on which the appeal was heard. I think it is implicit that Lord Halsbury must have been referring to calling a wife against her husband contrary to her will. Section 4 of the 1898 Act expressly made a wife competent to give evidence

---

1　[1912] AC 305
2　[1931] 1 KB 117, [1930] All ER Rep 340
3　(1911) 7 Cr App Rep 84
4　[1912] AC 305 at 309
5　[1912] AC 305 at 311

against her husband. This was never disputed. The whole point of the case was whether the Act compelled her to give evidence against him.

Lord Atkinson said[1]: 'The principle that a wife is not to be compelled to give evidence against her husband is deep seated in the common law of this country . . .' Lord Macnaghten, Lord Shaw of Dunfermline and Lord Robson all agreed. It seems to me that the finding that you could not infer into a statute a power to compel a wife to give evidence against her husband in a criminal matter was based on their Lordships' opinion that it was contrary to the common law to compel a wife to give such evidence and that such compulsion could be introduced into a statute only by plain and express words. Although their Lordships were only construing a statute, their ratio decidendi was based largely on their opinion as to the effect of the common law and therefore cannot in my view be regarded as merely obiter dicta. I regard *Leach's* case[2] as a binding authority for the proposition that a wife can never be a compellable witness against her husband unless expressly made so by statute. To suppose, as Avory J did in *Lapworth's* case[3], that this House cannot have had in mind the common law principle which permitted a wife to give evidence against her husband charged with inflicting injuries on her seems strange, particularly as that principle was clearly spelt out to their Lordships by counsel in opening the appeal[4].

My Lords, for the reasons I have explained, I respectfully disagree with Avory J when, in delivering the judgment of the court, he said[5]: 'Once it is established that she [the wife] is a competent witness, it follows that she is a compellable witness.' I also disagree with him when he says[5]:

> 'An observation made by Lord Halsbury in that case confirms me in the view of the law that I have expressed when he said[6]: "I should have thought that if the known state of the law was that in order to confer competency you had to enact it, the fact that you simply used the word 'competent' did not necessarily mean 'against his or her will.' "'

I should have thought that that observation of Lord Halsbury to which Avory J alluded, far from confirming the view he stated in *Lapworth's* case[3] completely destroys it.

I have no doubt that the decision in *Lapworth's* case[3] has been followed by trial judges, the Court of Criminal Appeal and the Court of Appeal (Criminal Division) in such cases as may have come before them since 1931 and were covered by *Lapworth*[3]. *R v Algar*[7], in which that great judge, Lord Goddard CJ, presided, is an example of such a case. But it must be remembered that the courts which decided those cases were bound by the decision in *Lapworth*[3]. This however is the first time that your Lordships' House has had an opportunity of considering *Lapworth's* case[3]. For my part I strongly disapprove of it for the reasons I have attempted to explain.

I have already said that in the instant case the Court of Appeal was bound by *Lapworth's* case[3] and was therefore compelled to follow it. I cannot however agree with the Court of Appeal when it sought to justify the decision in *Lapworth's* case[3] by saying:

> 'It must be borne in mind that the court of trial in circumstances such as this where personal violence is concerned . . . is not dealing merely with a domestic dispute between husband and wife, but it is investigating a crime. It is in the

---

1 [1912] AC 305 at 311
2 [1912] AC 305
3 [1931] 1 KB 117, [1930] All ER Rep 340
4 [1912] AC 305 at 306, arguendo
5 [1931] 1 KB 117 at 122, cf [1930] All ER Rep 340 at 341
6 *Leach v R* (1912) 7 Cr App Rep 157 at 166, arguendo
7 [1953] 2 All ER 1381, [1954] 1 QB 279

interests of the state and members of the public that where that is the case evidence of that crime should be freely available to the court which is trying the crime.'

If such a consideration could have been a justification for the decision in *Lapworth's* case[1] still more would it be a justification for making the wife a competent and compellable witness against her husband were he to be charged with murder, which clearly she is not.

Imagine also a case of incest in which a father has compelled his two daughters aged ten and 12 to have sexual intercourse with him. Surely that is a case far more serious than a husband's physical violence against his wife, and one in which the public weal, to say nothing of the weal of those young children, might reasonably be considered to require any competent witness to such a crime to be a compellable witness. Nevertheless when Parliament made a wife competent to give evidence against her husband charged with incest, it did not make her a compellable witness. This, in my view, was because Parliament did not see fit, even in such a case, to depart from the common law rule that a wife should not, in any circumstances, be compelled to give evidence against her husband: see *Leach's* case[2].

My Lords, for the reasons I have stated, I would overrule *Lapworth's* case[1], allow this appeal and quash the conviction.

LORD EDMUND-DAVIES. My Lords, when your Lordships' House is called on to determine a question of law regarding which there are no binding precedents and no authorities directly in point, and where it has accordingly to perform an act of law-making, I apprehend that the decision will largely turn on what is thought most likely to advance the public weal. That consideration is particularly important when questions arise regarding the administration of the criminal law. And while the particular facts of a case may not be decisive of the proper answer, they may be far from irrelevant to the purpose in hand. In other words, however elaborate the language employed in rationalising the conclusion arrived at in such hitherto uncharted circumstances, a declaration of what, in the opinion of this House, the law is will be largely influenced by the individual views of your Lordships recording what *should* be the law. And the facts of the particular case may have a potent influence in shaping one's notions of a commendable public policy. It is for that reason that I begin by adverting briefly to the facts which give rise to this appeal, as they appear from the depositions.

One evening in September 1975 a young woman, Janis Scrimshaw, was in a public house with her mother when she was called outside by the appellant, Edward William Hoskyn, with whom she had earlier in the year been on terms of friendship, but which she had later discontinued. Her mother remained inside, and shortly thereafter Janis suddenly fell through the door and into the bar, 'screaming and covered with blood'. When examined in a hospital casualty department, she was found to have sustained the following injuries inflicted by 'a sharp instrument': two stab wounds in the chest, penetrating the outer lining of the lung on each side; a 9 centimetre cut extending from the temple to her right ear; smaller cuts to her right lip and chin; and a 4½ centimetre cut to the left forearm.

She testified against the appellant before the examining justices and she named him as her assailant when submitting a claim to the Criminal Injuries Compensation Board. In February 1976 the appellant was committed for trial on a charge under s 18 of the Offences against the Person Act 1861 of wounding Janis Scrimshaw with intent to cause her grievous bodily harm. On Friday, 1st October he was warned to attend for

---

1   [1931] 1 KB 117, [1930] All ER Rep 340
2   [1912] AC 305

trial at the Central Criminal Court on the following Monday. On Saturday 2nd
October he married Janis Scrimshaw, and what happened when on Tuesday 5th
October his new bride was called for the prosecution and compelled to testify has
already been related in the speech by my noble and learned friend, Lord Wilberforce.
Following on his conviction and sentence to two years' imprisonment, Hoskyn unsuccessfully appealed to the Court of Appeal (Criminal Division) who, while refusing
leave to appeal to this House, certified the following point of law involved as one of
general public importance: 'Whether a wife is a compellable witness against her
husband in a case of violence on her by him'.

As appears from the speeches I have had the advantage of reading, your Lordships
are all of the opinion that the question demands a negative answer, and some of
your Lordships have described the idea that an affirmative answer is called for as
'repugnant' to the married state and, as such, entirely unacceptable. This attitude
may be contrasted with that adopted in the instant case by Geoffrey Lane LJ who,
after reviewing most of the legal authorities brought to light by the admirable
researches of the appellant's counsel, said:

> 'It must be borne in mind that the court of trial in circumstances such as this,
> where personal violence is concerned (and this case is a good example where
> wounding with a knife is concerned) is not dealing merely with a domestic dis-
> pute between husband and wife, but it is investigating a crime. It is in the interests
> of the state and members of the public that, where that is the case, evidence of
> that crime should be freely available to the court which is trying the crime. It
> may very well be that the wife or the husband, as the case may be, is the only
> person who can give evidence of that offence. In those circumstances, it seems
> to us that there is no reason in this case for saying that we should in any way
> depart from the ruling . . . in Lapworth[1] . . .'

What is the proper attitude and what, accordingly, the proper answer to the
certified question? Such legal learning as has a bearing, however remote, on the
matter has been extensively reviewed by your Lordships, and no purpose would be
served by my attempting it all over again, though I naturally propose to comment
on the views expressed by your Lordships in the light of the available material. There
is common agreement that there exists only one authority directly in point (R v
Lapworth[1]), and it follows that, as far as this House is concerned, we are engaged in
an act of law-making. I have the misfortune to think that the law as your Lordships
conceive it to be is inimical to the public weal, and particularly so at a time when
disturbing disclosures of great violence between spouses are rife. Nor am I able to
accept, as your Lordships have in fact said, that if spouses subjected to violence are to
become compellable witnesses against their attackers it must be left to Parliament
to say so. On the contrary, it is open to your Lordships to declare here and now that
such is already the law, were you minded to do so.

In a scene of great confusion, what stand rock-like are two unchallengeable propositions about the common law. They are:

1. That all competent witnesses are, virtually without exception, also compellable
witnesses. As Willes J said in Ex parte Fernandez[2]:

> 'Every person in the kingdom except the Sovereign may be called upon and is
> bound to give evidence to the best of his knowledge upon any question of fact
> material and relevant to an issue tried in any of the Queen's courts, unless he can
> shew some exception in his favour, such, for instance, as that suggested to

---

1   [1931] 1 KB 117, [1930] All ER Rep 340
2   (1861) 10 CBNS 3 at 39

exist in this case, namely, that to answer might put him in peril of criminal proceedings.'

As my noble and learned friend, Lord Wilberforce, has said, the only recognised exceptions to that proposition 'provide no analogy for the treatment of a wife'.
2. That although in earliest times spouses were wholly incompetent to give evidence against each other in any case, ever since Lord Audley's case[1] in 1631, where a wife was raped by a footman at her husband's instigation and in his presence, the common law has unquestionably been that a spouse is a competent prosecution witness in cases of assault or infringement of liberty perpetrated by the other party to the marriage. That this was a momentous development which was felt to undermine one of the most basic legal concepts is deducible from such writers as Gilbert CJ[2] who claimed with manifest (but, as it turned out, misplaced) relief that the decision:

'... hath since been exploded ... because it may be improved to dreadful purposes, to get rid of husbands that prove uneasy, and must be a cause of implacable quarrels if the husband chance to be acquitted.'

My Lords, the fundamental question is whether, as the appellant contends, one spouse who, though physically attacked by the other, is unwilling to testify for the prosecution can lawfully claim to be within any exception to the general rule that, being competent, he or she is therefore compellable. In my judgment the case law, the statutory history and the textbooks do not establish that the question must receive an affirmative answer. The epoch-making decision in Lord Audley's case[1] is sought to be explained away as arising simply ex necessitate, a spouse assaulted in secret having no redress were she denied a hearing in the courts. But the criminal law serves a dual purpose: to render aid to citizens who themselves seek its protection, and itself to take active steps to protect those other citizens who, though grievously in need of protection, for one reason or another do not themselves set the law in motion. And it does not follow that their failure should mean that, proceedings having nevertheless been instituted, the injured spouse should be less compellable as a Crown witness than one unrelated by marriage to the alleged assailant. I readily confess to a complete absence of any feeling of 'repugnance' that, in the circumstances of the instant case, Mrs Hoskyn was compelled to testify against the man who had three days earlier become her husband. And, agreeing as I do with the attitude of Geoffrey Lane LJ, I am regretfully unable to accept the view expressed by my noble and learned friend, Lord Salmon, that, '... if she does not want to avail herself of [the law's] protection, there is, in my view, no ground for holding that the common law forces it on her'.

Nor do I regard the obiter dicta of Bayley J in R v Inhabitants of All Saints, Worcester[3] as a clear pointer in the opposite direction, and I fear I must expatiate at some length in explaining why. The facts were widely different from those of the present case; it had nothing to do with physical violence, and no spouse was accused. But the differences by no means stop there. In proceedings of a quasi-criminal character for the removal of a female pauper, it was material to ascertain whether C had gone through a ceremony of marriage with her. As it was in the interests of one of the parties to establish that he had not, they called A to prove that she had some years earlier married C and that the marriage was still subsisting. It was beyond doubt that A was a competent witness in the removal proceedings, and in the course of his judgment Bayley J said[4]:

1　(1631) 3 State Tr 401
2　Evidence (6th Edn, 1801), p 120
3　(1817) 6 M & S 194
4　6 M & S 194 at 200, 201

'It does not appear that she objected to be examined, or demurred to any question. If she had thrown herself on the protection of the Court on the ground that her answer to the question put to her might criminate her husband, in that case I am not prepared to say that the Court would have compelled her to answer; on the contrary, I think she would have been entitled to the protection of the Court. But as she did not object, I think there was no objection arising out of the policy of the law, because by possibility her evidence might be the means of furnishing information, and might lead to enquiry, and perhaps to the obtaining of evidence against her husband. It is no objection to the information that it has been furnished by the wife.'

These words of a judge of outstanding quality are heavily relied on by your Lordships as a powerful indication that it is a mistake to equate competence at common law with compellability, as they have been by Taylor[1] and by some other (but by no means all) textbook writers who rely on them as their sole authority for that proposition. But in fact the case had nothing to do with competence or compellability to testify, but solely with privilege, and confusion between the three concepts is commonplace[2]:

'There are certain questions which a witness may refuse to answer if he so wishes. He is said to be privilged in respect of those questions. It should be clear, therefore, that competence without compellability (or bare competence) is not the same as privilege. Compellability is concerned with whether a witness can be forced by a party to give evidence at all. Privilege is concerned with whether a witness who is already in the box is obliged to answer a particular question. The protection of privilege is exactly the same whether the witness is barely competent and of his own free will elected to give evidence or the witness is compellable and was forced to give evidence. These distinctions are restated here as they have sometimes been lost sight of and the terms "not compellable" and "privileged" have been used interchangeably. An example of this is to be found in the Matrimonial Causes Act [1950], section 32(2). That subsection in fact creates a privilege, but the phrase used is "shall not be compellable".'

I have to say, with respect, that a similar confusion has arisen in relation to R v Inhabitants of All Saints, Worcester[3], for nowhere did Bayley J lend support to the proposition contended for by the present appellant. Bayley J said in terms that A had not incriminated C and that she was not competent to incriminate him. The case was therefore basically different from the instant appeal, for here there is no doubt as to the victim's competency to testify against her husband. Bayley J was following on the judgment of Lord Ellenborough CJ, who said[4]:

'I would observe that by the present decision the Court does not mean to break in on the rule, founded in the policy of the law, that husband and wife shall not be permitted to be witnesses for or against . . . each other.'

The charge which might conceivably be laid against C was obviously one of bigamy, and as to that A would not then have been a competent prosecution witness. Thus it is that Bayley J added[5]:

---

1   Evidence (1906, 10th Edn)
2   Cowen and Carter, Essays on the Law of Evidence (1956), p 220
3   (1817) 6 M & S 194
4   6 M & S 194 at 199
5   6 M & S 194 at 201, 202

'It has . . . been argued that the wife's evidence in this case might operate as a direct charge against her husband . . . but . . . nothing which the wife proved on this occasion could be the direct means of founding a prosecution against her husband, although it might afford the means of procuring evidence against him. But such a collateral consequence is not a sufficient objection . . . Therefore on the ground that the admission of this witness does not interfere with the policy of the law as it concerns marriage, I think she was competent.'

Abbott J, in his turn, said[1]:

'Her evidence upon this occasion can never be received against her husband, nor can the decision of the sessions be used against him. They can found neither a charge nor the evidence of any charge against him.'

The *All Saints, Worcester* case[2], in my judgment, has accordingly nothing to do with the compellability of a witness competent at common law: it deals merely with the entitlement of a witness, competent for some purposes but not for others, to be privileged not to answer certain questions put to her. A, being incompetent to testify against C if bigamy proceedings ensued, many judges would share the view of Bayley J (expressed in notably tentative language) that it would not be right to compel her to furnish material which might later form (however indirectly) the basis for such a criminal charge against her husband. But that has nothing to do with the certified question in this case. And no competent witness can refuse to go into the witness box simply on the ground that he might incriminate himself or another; he can only claim privilege after he has been sworn and specific questions put to him, so that the court may rule whether the claim is a tenable one.

My Lords, I propose to say but little about the argument that the wording of certain 19th century statutes lends support to the proposition that common law competence and compellability do not go hand in hand. They are wholly inconclusive, and I respectfully adopt the view expressed in the speech of my noble and learned friend, Lord Wilberforce, that none of them illuminates what was and is the position at common law in criminal proceedings where one spouse who has been the victim of the other's violence is sought to be called by the prosecution. It would be as unreliable to conclude from any of those statutes that competence at common law does not generally carry with it compellability as it would be to infer the converse from the fact, for example, that s 12 of the Prevention of Cruelty to Children Act 1904 provides that—

'In any proceeding against any person for an offence under this Act, . . . such person shall be competent but not compellable to give evidence, and the wife or husband of such person may be required to attend to give evidence as an ordinary witness in the case and shall be competent but not compellable to give evidence.'

And so, my Lords, we come at last to the decisions in *Leach v R*[3] and *R v Lapworth*[4]. Strong reliance is placed on obiter dicta in the former, and the latter is said to be wholly irreconcilable with them and therefore to be wrong. My Lords, my submission is that, dealing as they are with entirely different questions of law, they are not irreconcilable. I need not again relate the relevant facts, but there are features of the undoubtedly extempore views[5] expressed in the earlier case which require the

1 (1817) 6 M & S 194 at 203
2 6 M & S 194
3 [1912] AC 305
4 [1931] 1 KB 117, [1930] All ER Rep 340
5 See (1912) 22 Cox CC 721 at 723

closest scrutiny. In Leach[1] Lord Loreburn LC stressed at the outset that the only
question for determination was as to the meaning of the Criminal Evidence Act
1898 which, it is important to observe, provided by s 4(2) that:

'Nothing in this Act shall affect a case where the wife or husband of a person
charged with an offence may at common law be called as a witness without the
consent of that person.'

This followed directly on the provision in s 4(1), which, for the first time enabled the
spouse of a person charged with an offence under one of the enactments scheduled in
the Act to be called 'as a witness either for the prosecution or defence and without the
consent of the person charged'. The reference of Lord Loreburn LC[2] to 'a fundamental
and old principle to which the law has looked, that you ought not to compel a wife
to give evidence against her husband in matters of a criminal kind' is, I suggest, one
relating to the general *incompetence* of spouses as witnesses for the prosecution, for a
little later[3] the point is made that, but for s 4(1)—

'the wife could not have been *allowed* to give evidence, and the result of what
was that the wife could not have been compelled to do so, and was protected
against compulsion.'

My Lords, the speech of Lord Halsbury clearly proceeds on the basis (which I
have respectfully to submit was manifestly wrong) that a wife can never give evidence
in criminal proceedings unless an Act of Parliament expressly makes her competent
to do so. He said[4]:

'If you want to alter the law which has lasted for centuries and which is almost
ingrained in the English Constitution, in the sense that everybody would say,
"To call a wife against her husband is a thing that cannot be heard of," to suggest
that that is to be dealt with by inference and that you should introduce a new
system of law without any specific enactment of it, seems to me to be perfectly
monstrous.'

But, my Lords, 'monstrous' or not, we know that certainly from 1631 such had been
and remained the law of England in cases of personal violence by one spouse on
another. There remains the opinion expressed by Lord Atkinson[4]: 'The principle
that a wife is not to be compelled to give evidence against her husband is deep seated
in the common law of this country . . .' All that can be said about that pronouncement
is that it is based on no cited authority and that it was unnecessary for the determination of the only issue in that case, which was whether the husband or wife of the defendant can, in cases governed by s 4(1) of the 1898 Act, be compelled to give evidence
against his or her will.
   My Lords, it is not, I submit, right to regard these obiter dicta in Leach[1] as decisive
of the point in issue in the present case. For what it is worth, they were certainly not so
regarded by Mr Herman Cohen, a criminal lawyer who, within a few months of the
delivery of those speeches, thanking his 'learned friends, Dr. Kenny, Downing
Professor in the University of Cambridge, and Mr. S. Phipson, author of a well-known
work on Evidence, for suggestions', published a pamphlet entitled 'Spouse-Witnesses
in Criminal Cases'. After considering the speeches in Leach[1], the author wrote[5]:

---

1 [1912] AC 305
2 [1912] AC 305 at 309
3 [1912] AC 305 at 310
4 [1912] AC 305 at 311
5 Page 26

'The question, then, is, when by the common law a spouse-witness is admissible
for the Crown, is he or she compellable? There seems to be no binding authority
at all upon the point . . . The complete silence of the great common law writers
on the point seems to show that they took it for granted that a competent witness
for the Crown was compellable . . . "At common law," said Mr. (now Mr.
Justice) Rowlatt[1], "the wife was merely incompetent, the question of compellability could not arise; but once you get rid of incompetence, compellability
follows. If a man attempts to murder his wife, she would be compelled to go
into the box for the Crown. There is no substantive rule of common law that a
wife is not compellable to give evidence against her husband."
    'It is submitted that this reasoning, in the absence of other authorities, is
correct and that, in the case of the common law exception, when a spouse-
witness may be called, he or she is a compellable witness for the Crown.
    'The language of Lord Atkinson in giving judgment in Leach's case[2] seems,
at first sight, opposed to this view . . . But, it is submitted, the noble and learned
Lord is referring solely to the general rule applicable to the case under decision—a
point in relation to a statutory offence on which statute law is silent and the
common law must be invoked, not to the recognised common law exceptions, as
to which the argument for the Crown was: Once you go back to the general
common law and make the wife competent like anyone else, you make her an
ordinary witness liable to a subpoena.'

The general conclusion of the author in this short work is thus stated[3]:

    'A spouse-witness is only competent for the prosecution when the offence
    charged is within the schedule, as amended, of the Criminal Evidence Act; and
    in those cases which he or she is compellable. A spouse-witness is competent in
    the defence of the spouse in all criminal trials without exception. A spouse-witness
    is compellable for the prosecution or for the defence of the spouse, when the
    offence charged is personal injury (including threats and attempts) or forcible
    abduction and marriage, and only in those cases.'

My Lords, the last proposition preceded by nearly 30 years the decision of the
Court of Criminal Appeal in Lapworth[4], the only decision directly bearing on the
certified question in this appeal. The reputation of few criminal judges of this century
stands as high as Avory J[5] who gave the judgment of the court, and he expressed
himself as being—

    '. . . satisfied that in the case of LEACH[2] the learned Lords had not present to their
    mind the case which is now before this Court, where personal violence has been
    done by a husband to a wife. I am satisfied that in the general observations which
    they there made . . . they had no intention of including cases such as the one with
    which we have to deal today.'

Regarding the question there in issue, Avory J said[6]:

    '. . . I am satisfied that at common law . . . a wife was always a competent
    witness on a charge against her husband of having assaulted her. If it is once

1 (1912) 7 Cr App Rep 157 at 168
2 [1912] AC 305
3 Page 32
4 (1931) 22 Cr App Rep 87
5 22 Cr App Rep 87 at 90
6 22 Cr App Rep 87 at 89

established that she was competent, I think it follows that she was compellable
a at common law, and remains so under section 4, sub-section 2 of the Criminal
Evidence Act, 1898 . . . It has always been assumed in practice that in such cases
. . . it is the duty of the tribunal to ascertain the facts and, if necessary, to compel
her to give that evidence.'

Your Lordships, in effect, challenge that sequence of propositions which Avory J
b regarded as both self-evident and well-established. I must be allowed to say that your
reluctance to accept his view derives seemingly from a harking-back to the strong
opposition at common law to one spouse ever testifying against the other, an opposition
based on a variety of reasons, such as the unity of person, the fear of consequent discord
and dissension, and the natural repugnance created by such a prospect. But what, with
respect, appears to me to be inadequately recognised is the magnitude of the decision
c in 1631[1] that in cases turning on violence by one spouse to the other none of the
established arguments against testifying must be allowed to prevail. Once that
conclusion was arrived at, I see no objection or difficulty in holding that in such cases
as the present a spouse, being competent to testify, was also a compellable witness.

My Lords, if the proper conclusion is that the law on the certified question has
hitherto been uncertain, this House has now an opportunity to declare what that
d law is. In that event, I end as I began by inviting your Lordships to consider what
decision is likely to advance the public good. This House had only a few years ago to
deal with a case arising from events as horrible as those which led to Lord Audley's
conviction in 1631. Indeed, the facts in *Director of Public Prosecutions v Morgan*[2] were
startlingly similar, for there too a husband had procured other men to rape his wife.
It surely creates a revulsion going far beyond 'repugance' if the wronged wife at the
e last moment declined to testify against her husband and, in consequence, he and the
four other accused were acquitted, so inextricably did her evidence involve all five
accused. The noble and learned Lord, Viscount Dilhorne, has spoken of the repugnance created by a wife being compelled '. . . to testify against her husband on a charge
involving violence, no matter how trivial and no matter the consequences to her and
to her family'. For my part I regard as extremely unlikely any prosecution based on
f trivial violence being persisted in where the injured spouse was known to be a reluctant witness. Much more to the point, as I think, are cases such as the present, as
Morgan[2], and as others arising from serious physical maltreatment by one spouse
of the other.

Such cases are too grave to depend simply on whether the injured spouse is, or is
not, willing to testify against the attacker. Reluctance may spring from a variety of
g reasons and does not by any means necessarily denote that domestic harmony has
been restored. A wife who has once been subjected to a 'carve up' may well have
more reasons than one for being an unwilling witness against her husband. In such
circumstances, it may well prove a positive boon her to be directed by the court
that she has no alternative but to testify. But, be that as it may, such incidents ought
not to be regarded as having no importance extending beyond the domestic hearth.
h Their investigation and, where sufficiently weighty, their prosecution is a duty which
the agencies of law enforcement cannot dutifully neglect. In *R v Algar*[3] Lord
Goddard CJ said:

'At common law one spouse could not give evidence against the other except
in the case of offences against the person or liberty of the other party to the
j marriage. In such cases a spouse is both competent and compellable.'

---

1   *R v Lord Audley* (1631) 3 State Tr 401
2   [1975] 2 All ER 347, [1976] AC 182
3   [1953] 2 All ER 1381 at 1382, [1954] 1 QB 279 at 285

These words should not be regarded as being merely conforming to *Lapworth*[1], which was never cited in the case. And even if it had been, Lord Goddard CJ was never content to apply without explicit remonstrance decisions with which he disagreed. In expressing himself as he did, he was, I believe, drawing on his immense reservoirs of knowledge of the common law and of the long-standing practice of the courts. *Lapworth*[1] is the only authority cited to your Lordships which bears directly on the facts of this case, and Avory J claimed to be doing no more than asserting what had long been the law. The decision itself must surely have since been applied in countless cases without any known expressions of outrage or resentment. It is, with respect, a decision which should find favour with this House today.

My Lords, for these reasons I would dismiss this appeal.

LORD KEITH. My Lords, I have had the advantage of reading in draft the speech of my noble and learned friend, Lord Wilberforce. I agree with it, and for the reasons which he has stated I too would allow the appeal.

Appeal allowed.

Solicitors: *Voss & Son* (for the appellant); *Solicitor, Metropolitan Police.*

Mary Rose Plummer Barrister.

---

1   [1931] 1 KB 117, [1930] All ER Rep 340

Director of Public Prosecutions v Goodchild

HOUSE OF LORDS
LORD DIPLOCK, VISCOUNT DILHORNE, LORD SALMON, LORD FRASER OF TULLYBELTON AND
LORD SCARMAN
7th MARCH, 6th APRIL 1978

Drugs – Dangerous drugs – Cannabinol derivative – Unlawful possession – Possession of leaves and stalk separated from plant – Cannabinol derivative naturally present in the leaves and stalks – Whether possession of naturally occurring material containing cannabinol derivative as an unseparated constituent amounts to possession of a 'cannabinol derivative' – Misuse of Drugs Act 1971, s 5(2), Sch 2, Part IV.

The offence of unlawful possession of any controlled drug described in Sch 2 to the Misuse of Drugs Act 1971 by its scientific name is not established by proof of possession of naturally occurring material of which the described drug is one of the unseparated constituents. This is so whether or not the naturally occurring material is also included as another item in the list of controlled drugs. Accordingly possession of naturally occurring leaf and stalk of the plant cannabis sativa of which a cannabinol derivative, THC, is an unseparated constituent does not amount to possession of a 'cannabinol derivative', as defined in Sch 2, Part IV[a], to the 1971 Act, contrary to s 5(2)[b] of the 1971 Act (see p 165 c to e and p 166 a b and e to h, post).

Decision of the Court of Appeal, Criminal Division sub nom *R v Goodchild (No 2)* [1978] 1 All ER 649 reversed.

Notes

For controlled drugs and unlawful possession of them, see Supplement to 26 Halsbury's Laws (3rd Edn) paras 491B, 491C.3.

For the Misuse of Drugs Act 1971, ss 5, 37 and Sch 2, Part IV, see 41 Halsbury's Statutes (3rd Edn) 884, 909, 915.

The definition of 'cannabis' in the Misuse of Drugs Act 1971, s 37(1), was amended by the Criminal Law Act 1977, s 52.

Appeal

The appellant, Kevin John Goodchild, was charged on indictment, inter alia, with unlawful possession of cannabis, contrary to s 5(2) of the Misuse of Drugs Act 1971 (count 1), with unlawful possession of cannabis resin, contrary to s 5(2) of the 1971 Act (count 3) and with unlawful possession of a cannabinol derivative, contrary to s 5(2) of the 1971 Act (count 5). Each of those counts related to the same vegetable growth, namely some leaves and stalk only from a plant of the genus cannabis. At the trial at the Crown Court at Portsmouth before his Honour Judge Broderick QC in June and July 1976, following a ruling by the judge on a question of law, the appellant pleaded guilty and was convicted on count 1. The judge directed the jury to acquit him on count 3, on the ground that the leaves and stalk did not come within the definition of cannabis resin in s 37(1) of the 1971 Act. The appellant appealed against his conviction on count 1 and the Attorney-General referred the acquittal on count 3 to the Court of Appeal, Criminal Division[1] (Lord Widgery CJ, Talbot and Slynn JJ) which on 13th January 1977 allowed the appellant's appeal, quashed his conviction on count 1 and confirmed that he had been rightly acquitted on count 3.

---

a Part IV, so far as is material, is set out at p 163 j, post
b Section 5, so far as material, provides:
    '(1) ... it shall not be lawful for a person to have a controlled drug in his possession.
    '(2) ... it is an offence for a person to have a controlled drug in his possession in contravention of subsection (1) above ...'
1 [1977] 2 All ER 163

Because the Crown had obtained a conviction on count 1 it did not proceed at the original trial with the charge on count 5 which was ordered to lie on the file and not to be proceeded with without the leave of the court. Subsequently the court gave the Crown leave to proceed with the trial of count 5. At that trial, at the Crown Court at Portsmouth before the judge his Honour Judge McLellan on 3rd March 1977, rejected the submission of counsel for the appellant that on the expert evidence tendered, and the true construction of the 1971 Act, there was no case to go to the jury. Following that ruling the appellant changed his plea on count 5 to guilty of unlawful possession of a cannabinol derivative and was convicted and fined in respect of that offence. He appealed to the Court of Appeal, Criminal Division[1] (Lord Widgery CJ, Melford Stevenson and Slynn JJ), which on 1st July 1977 upheld the judge's ruling and dismissed the appellant's appeal against conviction on count 5. The appellant appealed to the House of Lords. The facts are set out in the opinion of Diplock Lord.

Randolph Boxall and *Roderick Cordara* for the appellant.
Ian Kennedy QC and *Michael de Navarro* for the Crown.

Their Lordships took time for consideration.

6th April. The following opinions were delivered.

LORD DIPLOCK. My Lords, as long ago as September 1975 the appellant was found to be in possession of about ¼lb of leaf and stalk of the cannabis plant. He was in due course charged on indictment with unlawful possession of controlled drugs contrary to s 5(2) of the Misuse of Drugs Act 1971. In three counts, which were laid in the alternative, the drugs were described as: (1) a Class B controlled drug, namely, cannabis, (2) a Class B controlled drug, namely cannabis resin, and (3) a Class A controlled drug, namely, a cannabinol derivative.

To understand what lies behind the application of these three different descriptions to the leaves and stalk of cannabis plant it is necessary to understand a little of the botany and pharmacognosy of the plant cannabis sativa, the botanical name for Indian hemp. It can be grown in a wide range of climates from tropical to temperate, including the United Kingdom, although its cultivation here is now prohibited by s 6 of the Misuse of Drugs Act 1971. It is one of the oldest of cultivated plants in Asia where its fibrous stalk is used for making rope and cloth and its seed for birdseed, fishbait and cattle food, and oil from the seed is used for soap and paint making. The plant contains hallucinogenic ingredients, of which the chemical names are cannabinol and other substances of closely related molecular structure known to chemists as cannabinol derivatives. Of these one of the most potent and important is the tetrahydro derivative of cannabinol known familiarly as THC.

Cannabis sativa is an annual. It grows to a height of 4 feet to 16 feet and flowers and fruits in October to November. The floral structure is formed at the top of the stems and is associated with a mass of small leaves known as vegetative tops. The lower parts of the plant also have a luxuriant growth of leaves which differ, and are to be distinguished, from the vegetative tops. The hallucinogenic ingredients are found in the resin of the plant. These are secreted in the hairs of trichomes on the leaves and on the flowering and fruiting tops. They are present in increasingly greater concentration as one moves from bottom to top of the plant. There is very little in the stem itself or in the ripe seeds. The concentration in the flowers is about two-and-a-half times, and in the vegetative tops is about twice, the concentration in the lower leaves. The resin can be extracted from the plant by brushing it off the leaves and flowers. The hallucinogenic ingredients, cannabinol and THC can then be extracted from the resin. The narcotic effect of the cannabis plant when subjected to no other treatment except drying thus varies with the portion of the plant that is used. The resin when separated from the plant contains a higher concentration of narcotic than the plant itself; while the highest narcotic content is to be found in cannabinol and cannabinol derivatives after they have been extracted from the resin.

The Misuse of Drugs Act 1971 specifies in Sch 2 what are the controlled drugs dealt with by the Act and allots them to three classes, A, B, and C. By s 5 it is an offence for a person to have a controlled drug in his possession. (This is subject to some exceptions that do not affect the instant case.) By s 25 and Sch 4 the maximum penalty on prosecution on indictment for having possession of a controlled drug is progressive according to the class of drug involved. It is a maximum of seven years imprisonment for a Class A drug, five years for a Class B drug and two years for a Class C drug.

Schedule 2 contains a list of more than a 120 different drugs. Most of these are in Class A, but cannabis and cannabis resin are listed in Class B. The majority of drugs in all three classes are synthetic substances only, that is to say they are man-made. All these are described in Sch 2 by their scientific name which, to a skilled chemist, would indicate their molecular composition. There are, however, a few drugs which also occur naturally in plants, in fungi or in toads. Apart from cannabis the most important of these are opium and its narcotic constituents, which include such well-known alkaloids as morphine, thebaine and codeine. 'Opium' is specified as a Class A drug under that name (which is not a scientific one). It consists of the coagulated juice of the opium poppy. All parts, except the seeds, of the opium poppy, are also included separately in the list of Class A drugs under the description 'Poppy-straw'; while morphine, thebaine and other alkaloids contained in opium appear as separate items in Class A, and codeine as an item in Class B. Cocaine occurs natually in coca leaf which is the leaf of a plant of the genus erythroxylon: 'Coca leaf' and 'Cocaine' appear as separate items in Class A.

These, together with cannabis are instances where a naturally occurring substance which contains drugs specified by their scientific names in Sch 2, is itself included as a separate item in the schedule. There are other drugs listed under their scientific names which also occur in nature, but the natural source from which they can be obtained is not itself specified as a controlled drug in the schedule. The following are examples.

Lysergamide and lysergide occur in nature in the stalks, leaves and stem of the flowering plant known as morning glory; mescaline is found in the flowering heads of the peyote cactus; psilocin and psilocybin are to be found in a toadstool sometimes called the Mexican magic mushroom; and bufotenine occurs in the common toadstool and in three other varieties of toadstool, in the stalks and leaves of a semi-tropical plant, and even as a secretion of the common toad and natterjack toad.

Cannabis and cannabis resin are defined respectively in s 37(1) as follows:

' "cannabis" (except in the expression "cannabis resin") means the flowering or fruiting tops of any plant of the genus *Cannabis* from which the resin has not been extracted, by whatever name they may be designated; "cannabis resin" means the separated resin, whether crude or purified, obtained from any plant of the genus *Cannabis*.'

They are included as items in the list of Class B drugs, but 'Cannabinol, *except where contained in cannabis or cannabis resin*' is an item in Class A; so is 'Cannabinol derivatives', an expression which is defined in Part IV of Sch 2 as meaning—

'the following substances, *except where contained in cannabis or cannabis resin*, namely tetrahydro derivatives of cannabinol and 3-alkyl homologues of cannabinol or of its tetrahydro derivatives.'

The italics here are my own.

Following on the lists of controlled drugs specified by name in each of the three classes are additional paragraphs designed to incorporate in the class closely related chemical analogues of the listed drugs, such as stereoisomers, esters, ethers and salts. In addition there is a paragraph which incorporates within the relevant class 'Any preparation or other product containing a substance or product for the time being specified in [the list of drugs] above.'

At the first trial of the appellant in the Crown Court in June 1976, the expert scientific evidence was given in the form of written statements. It was common ground that it was not proved that any part of the leaf and stalk of the cannabis plant that had been found in his possession consisted of flowering or fruiting tops, but that it was proved, though by qualitative analysis only, that some THC was present in the specimen that had been subjected to analysis. On this evidence the judge ruled that the material found in the appellant's possession was cannabis. The judge also ruled that the appellant had in his possession a cannabinol derivative, THC, since this had been identified as a constituent of that material, but that the appellant was not in possession of any cannabis resin.

In consequence of those rulings, the appellant pleaded guilty to the count of unlawful possession of the controlled Class B drug, cannabis. He pleaded not guilty to the count of being in unlawful possession of the Class A drug, 'a cannabinol derivative'. This count was left on the file; and the appellant was sentenced to a fine of £100 or six months' imprisonment in default of payment on the count of unlawful possession of cannabis.

His appeal to the Court of Appeal[1] against his conviction on this count was allowed on 13th January 1977, on the ground that the statutory definition of cannabis is restricted to the flowering or fruiting tops of the plant, and that leaf and stalk alone, in the absence of any such flowering or fruiting tops, does not fall within the definition. This was, in my view, obviously right. No argument to the contrary has been advanced before your Lordships' House.

The appellant underwent a second trial on the count remaining on the file which charged him with unlawful possession of 'a cannabinol derivative'. This was held in the Crown Court on 3rd March 1977 and was presided over by a different judge. He too ruled that possession of leaf and stalk of the cannabis plant which proved on analysis to contain traces of THC amounted to possession of 'a cannabinol derivative', within the meaning of s 5 of and Sch 2 to the 1971 Act. Faced by this ruling the appellant once more changed his plea to guilty and was sentenced to a fine of £25. Once more too he appealed to the Court of Appeal[2] which upheld the judge's ruling and certified that a point of law of general public importance was involved in the decision, namely:

'Whether on the true construction of the Misuse of Drugs Act 1971 a person in possession of some leaves and stalk only from a plant or plants of the genus cannabis may thereby be in possession of a cannabinol derivative naturally contained in those leaves, in contravention of s 5(1) of that Act.'

My Lords, the 1971 Act is a criminal statute. It makes it an offence to be in possession of any of a long list of drugs and makes the gravity of the offence depend on the class of listed drug into which the particular substance in his possession falls. Most, though not all, of the listed drugs in the three classes, A, B and C, are described by their precise chemical name and are synthetic substances which do not occur in the natural state. In the case of these drugs there is no room for doubt or ambiguity. Either a substance is the described synthetic drug (or a preparation or other product containing the described synthetic drug) or it is not. But there are some listed drugs

1 [1977] 2 All ER 163, [1977] 1 WLR 473
2 [1978] 1 All ER 649, [1977] 1 WLR 1213

which, although they can be synthesised, also occur in the natural state in plants,
a fungi or animals, and these include some of the most used narcotic drugs. It would
not in my view be a natural use of language to say, for instance, that a person was in
possession of morphine when what he really had was opium poppy-straw from which
whatever morphine content there might be in it had not yet been separated; nor
do I think it would be an apt use of language to describe poppy-straw as a 'preparation
or other product' containing morphine, since this expression is inappropriate to
b something that is found in nature as distinct from something that is man-made.
Regarded simply from the point of view of language the matter is in my view put
beyond doubt as respects the specific narcotic ingredients found in opium poppies
by the inclusion in the list, as separate items, of 'Opium' and 'poppy-straw', as well
as morphine, thebaine, codeine and several other specified alkaloids which are or
may be constituents of opium and of poppy-straw. A similar indication of the
c meaning of references in the schedule to specific drugs by their scientific names
is to be found in the inclusion as separate items of 'Cocaine' itself and 'Coca leaf'
which contains cocaine and from which cocaine can be extracted. I should conclude,
therefore, that prima facie a reference in Sch 2 to a specific drug by its scientific
name does not include a reference to any naturally occurring substance of which the
specific drug is a constituent but from which it has not yet been separated.
d   So prima facia one would not suppose that possession of naturally occurring leaf
and stalk of the plant cannabis sativa of which a cannabinol derivative, THC, was an
unseparated constituent could be charged under the 1971 Act as possession of a
'cannabinol derivative'.
      The argument to the contrary depends on the presence of the words of exception
which I have italicised in the description of cannabinol in the list of Class A drugs
e and in the definition of cannabinol derivatives in Part IV of Sch 2. These, it is suggested,
give rise to an inference that, but for the exception, cannabinol and cannabinol derivatives, notwithstanding that they were contained in the natural substances cannabis
or cannabis resin, would have fallen within the definition and that, accordingly
possession of cannabinol and cannabinol derivatives in however small a quantity
if contained in any naturally occurring material other than one falling within the
f statutory definition of cannabis or cannabis resin would constitute the offence of
possession of a Class A drug under the 1971 Act.
      My Lords, such inference as to the ambit of enacting words that can be derived
from the presence of a proviso or the exception is notoriously a weak one, since the
proviso or exception may have been inserted per majorem cautelam. In any event
it must give way whenever the consequences of applying it would be irrational or
g unjust. In the instant case the consequence, at the time when the appellant was
prosecuted, would have been that he would be liable to be convicted of the more
serious offence of unlawful possession of a Class A drug, whereas if what he had had
in his possession had included part of the flowering or fruiting tops of the cannabis
plant, and so contained a greater concentration of cannabinol derivatives, he could
only have been convicted of the lesser offence of possession of a Class B drug, to wit
h cannabis itself.
      I would construe the 1971 Act in such a way as to avoid this irrational and unjust
result. A man should not be gaoled on an ambiguity. I would allow the appeal and
quash the conviction of the appellant for the offence of unlawful possession of a
cannabinol derivative.
      The question directly involved in this appeal will not arise again in the future,
j as the definition of 'cannabis' has now been amended by s 52 of the Criminal Justice
Act 1977, so as to include the whole of the plant except the mature stalk and fibre
produced from it and the seeds. However, similar questions may arise in relation
to those other listed drugs described by their scientific names, but which also occur
naturally in plants or fungi or animals. As I have already indicated as a necessary
step in the reasoning which has led me to the conclusion in the instant appeal that

no offence was committed by the appellant, the offence of unlawful possession of
any controlled drug described in Sch 2 by its scientific name is not established by proof   *a*
of possession of naturally occuring material of which the described drug is one of the
constituents unseparated from the others. This is so whether or not the naturally
occurring material is also included as another item in the list of controlled drugs.

VISCOUNT DILHORNE. My Lords, I have had the advantage of reading the   *b*
speech of my noble and learned friend, Lord Diplock. I agree with it and only desire
to add a few observations.

When Parliament intended that plants and parts of plants should come within
the scope of the Misuse of Drugs Act 1971, it made its intention manifest, e g by the
definition of cannabis in s 37(1) as meaning the flowering or fruiting tops of any plant
of the genus cannabis from which the resin had not been extracted, and in Sch 2,   *c*
Part I, by the inclusion in Class A drugs of coca leaf and of poppy-straw, defined as
meaning all parts, except the seeds, of the opium poppy, after mowing.

No parts of any plants of the genus cannabis other than its flowering or fruiting
tops are mentioned in the 1971 Act, and in my view no parts other than flowering
or fruiting tops whether or not in their natural state they contain cannabinol derivatives, as defined in Part IV of Sch 2, come within the scope of the Act.   *d*

The definition of 'cannabinol derivatives' defines those words as meaning a number
of substances 'except where contained in cannabis or cannabis resin'. This definition
may suggest that it should be inferred that a cannabinol derivative contained in parts
of a plant other than the flowering or fruiting tops of the genus cannabis is covered
by the definition, but I do not think that any such conclusion can properly be drawn.
The draftsman, having defined cannabis and cannabis resin in s 37, no doubt felt   *e*
compelled to exclude the substances so defined from the definition of cannabinol
derivatives.

In my opinion this appeal should be allowed.

LORD SALMON. My Lords, I have had the advantage of reading in draft the speech   *f*
prepared by my noble and learned friend, Lord Diplock. I agree with it and would
also allow this appeal.

LORD FRASER OF TULLYBELTON. My Lords, I have had the advantage of
reading in draft the speech prepared by my noble and learned friend, Lord Diplock.   *g*
I agree with his conclusion and with the whole of the reasoning on which it is based.
I also would allow this appeal.

LORD SCARMAN. My Lords, I have had the advantage of reading in draft the
speech delivered by my noble and learned friend, Lord Diplock. I agree with it,   *h*
and for the reasons he gives would allow this appeal.

Appeal allowed. Conviction on count 5 quashed.

Solicitors: *Amphlett & Co*, agents for *Donnelly & Elliot*, Gosport (for the appellant);
Director of Public Prosecutions.   *j*

Mary Rose Plummer   Barrister.

a
Practice Direction

CHANCERY DIVISION

Family provision – Appeal – Appeal from master's decision – Application heard by master in chambers – Appeal by way of rehearing – Master to ensure record of proceedings taken –
b *Witnesses not to attend rehearing unless directed by judge.*

1. Applications under the Inheritance (Provision for Family and Dependants) Act 1975 are now frequently heard and disposed of by masters. The question arises how the case is to proceed if a party is dissatisfied with the master's decision.

2. It is open to the master, with the consent of the parties, to try the case in court
c under RSC Ord 36, r 9, and if he does so an appeal lies to the Court of Appeal under RSC Ord 58, r 3.

3. If, however, the case is heard in chambers a dissatisfied party must apply for an adjournment to the judge, in which case there must be a rehearing, normally in court.

4. Though the judge or the parties may require any cross-examination on affidavits
d or other oral evidence to be heard again in full, in most cases this should not be necessary if a full note or a transcript of the evidence before the master has been made.

5. A master hearing a case in chambers should therefore ensure, if possible, that the proceedings before him are recorded by a shorthand writer or a recording instrument. If he is unable to arrange this he should take as full a note as practicable of
e the oral evidence given before him. On the adjournment to the judge there should be sent to the judge, with the affidavits, a transcript or copy of the master's note of the oral evidence and a transcript or copy of the master's judgment.

6. No provision should be made for the attendance of witnesses at the rehearing before the judge unless a judge so directs. A party requiring such a direction should apply to the master to adjourn that question to a judge in chambers as a preliminary
f point.

By the direction of the Vice-Chancellor.

R E BALL
5th April 1978   Chief Master.

Director of Public Prosecutions v Camplin

a

HOUSE OF LORDS

LORD DIPLOCK, LORD MORRIS OF BORTH-Y-GEST, LORD SIMON OF GLAISDALE, LORD FRASER OF
TULLYBELTON AND LORD SCARMAN

20th, 21st FEBRUARY, 6th APRIL 1978

b

*Criminal law – Murder – Provocation – Self-control of reasonable man – Reasonable man –
Ordinary person of same sex and age as accused and sharing such of accused's characteristics
as would affect gravity of provocation to him – Unusual characteristics of accused – Age –
Young person – Whether proper to direct jury to ignore accused's age for purpose of determining whether reasonable man would have acted as accused had done – Homicide Act 1957,
s 3.*

c

The respondent, who was aged 15, went to the house of one K, a man in his fifties.
Whilst the respondent was there K buggered him. The respondent hit K over his
head with a pan and killed him. He was charged with murder. At his trial he put
forward the defence of provocation, pursuant to s 3[a] of the Homicide Act 1957, and
gave evidence (i) that the act of buggery had been forcibly committed on him by K   *d*
against his will, (ii) that afterwards he had become overwhelmed by shame and
(iii) that when he had heard K laughing at his sexual triumph, he had lost his self-
control and hit K with the pan. The jury were directed that the criterion to apply
where the defence of provocation was put forward was whether a reasonable man of
full age would in like circumstances have acted as the respondent had done. The respondent was convicted of murder, but the Court of Appeal[b] substituted a verdict of   *e*
manslaughter, holding that, where a person accused of murder raised the defence of
provocation, the 'reasonable man' test was designed to exclude from consideration
to the accused's advantage mental or physical abnormalities which might make him
exceptionally deficient in self-control, but youth, and the immaturity which accompanied youth, were not abnormalities; accordingly where the accused was of tender
years, the proper direction to the jury was to invite them to consider whether the   *f*
provocation was enough to have made a reasonable man of the same age as the
appellant act, in the same circumstances, as he had done. The Crown appealed to
the House of Lords.

Held – For the purposes of the law of provocation the 'reasonable man' was not
confined to the adult male; the expression meant an ordinary person of either sex,   *g*
not exceptionally excitable or pugnacious, but possessed of such powers of self-control
as everyone was entitled to expect that his fellow citizens would exercise in society
as it was today. Since the passing of the 1957 Act, the unqualified proposition that for
the purposes of the 'reasonable man' test any unusual characteristics of the accused
must be ignored no longer applied. Because the relevant characteristic of the respondent was that he was only 15 at the time of the killing, the judge ought not to   *h*
have instructed the jury to pay no account to his age, since they might have been of
the opinion that the degree of self-control to be expected of a boy of that age was less
than in an adult. In instructing the jury as he had done the judge had imposed a
fetter on the right and duty which s 3 of the 1957 Act accorded to them to act on their
own opinion on the matter. It followed that the appeal would be dismissed (see   *j*
p 173 j to p 174 a and e, p 175 b d and e, p 178 d and p 183 e and d, post).

Mancini v Director of Public Prosecutions [1941] 3 All ER 272, *Holmes v Director of Public*

---

a Section 3 is set out at p 173 *c* and *d*, post
b [1978] 1 All ER 1236

Prosecutions [1946] 2 All ER 124 and *Bedder v Director of Public Prosecutions* [1954]
a 2 All ER 801 explained.

Per Curiam. The proper direction for the jury on a charge of murder where the defence of provocation is raised is for the judge to state what the question is, using the very terms of s 3 of the 1957 Act; then to explain that the 'reasonable man' is a person having the power of self-control to be expected of an ordinary person of the sex and age of the accused but in other respects sharing such of the accused's characteristics
b as they think would affect the gravity of the provocation to him, and to explain that the question is not merely whether such a person would in like circumstances be provoked to lose his self-control but would also react to the provocation as the accused did (see p 175 *b* to *d*, p 177 *g* and *h*, p 178 *a* to *c*, p 182 *a* and *b* and p 183 *c* and *d*, post).

Per Lord Morris of Borth-y-Gest. It is for the court to decide whether, on a charge
c of murder, there is evidence on which a jury can find that the accused was provoked to lose his self-control; thereafter all questions are for the jury (see p 176 *j* to p 177 *a*, post).

Decision of the Court of Appeal, Criminal Division sub nom *R v Camplin* [1978] 1 All ER 1236 affirmed.

d **Notes**
For the defence of provocation on a charge of murder, see 11 Halsbury's Laws (4th Edn) paras 1163, 1164, and for cases on the subject, see 15 Digest (Reissue) 1118-1128, *9394-9489.*

For the Homicide Act 1957, s 3, see 8 Halsbury's Statutes (3rd Edn) 461.

Cases referred to in opinions
e *Bedder v Director of Public Prosecutions* [1954] 2 All ER 801, [1954] 1 WLR 1119, 38 Cr App Rep 133, HL, 15 Digest (Reissue) 1123, *9431.*

Holmes v Director of Public Prosecutions [1946] 2 All ER 124, [1946] AC 588, 115 LJKB 417, 175 LT 327, HL, 15 Digest (Reissue) 1124, *9441.*

Jones v Secretary of State for Social Services, Hudson v Secretary of State for Social Services [1972] 1 All ER 145, [1972] AC 944, [1972] 2 WLR 210, HL, Digest (Cont Vol D)
f *683, 4585b.*

Knuller (Publishing, Printing and Promotions) Ltd v Director of Public Prosecutions [1972] 2 All ER 898, [1973] AC 435, [1972] 3 WLR 143, 136 JP 728, 56 Cr App Rep 633, HL, 14(1) Digest (Reissue) 140, *966.*

Mancini v Director of Public Prosecutions [1941] 3 All ER 272, [1942] AC 1, 111 LJKB 84, 165 LT 353, 28 Cr App Rep 65, HL, 14(1) Digest (Reissue) 391, *3324.*

g *R v Broadfoot* (1743) 18 State Tr 1323, sub nom *Broadfoot's Case* Fost 154.

R v Hayward (1833) 6 C & P 157, 172 ER 1188, 15 Digest (Reissue) 1121, *9413.*

R v Lesbini [1914] 3 KB 1116, 84 LJKB 1102, 112 LT 175, 24 Cox CC 516, 11 Cr App Rep 7, CCA, 14(1) Digest (Reissue) 46, *211.*

R v McCarthy [1954] 2 All ER 262, [1954] 2 QB 105, [1954] 2 WLR 1044, 38 Cr App Rep 74, CCA, 14(1) Digest (Reissue) 52, *248.*

h *R v McGregor* [1962] NZLR 1096, 15 Digest (Reissue) 1122, *7191.*

R v Smith (Annie) (1914) 11 Cr App Rep 36, CCA, 15 Digest (Reissue) 1123, *9435.*

R v Welsh (1869) 11 Cox CC 336, 15 Digest (Reissue) 1119, *9407.*

Appeal
On 14th January 1977 in the Crown Court at Leeds before Boreham J the respondent, Paul Camplin, was convicted of murder and, being at the date of his conviction aged 16
j was, pursuant to s 53(1) of the Children and Young Persons Act 1933, as substituted by the Murder (Abolition of Death Penalty) Act 1965, s 1(5), sentenced to be detained during Her Majesty's pleasure. On 25th July 1977 the Court of Appeal, Criminal Division[1] (Bridge LJ, Willis and Crichton JJ) allowed the respondent's appeal against

1 [1978] 1 All ER 1236, [1977] 3 WLR 929

conviction. The Crown appealed to the House of Lords. The facts are set out in the opinion of Lord Diplock.

J Barry Mortimer QC and *Peter Charlesworth* for the Crown.
Geoffrey Baker QC and *James Stewart* for the respondent.

Their Lordships took time for consideration.

6th April. The following opinions were delivered.

LORD DIPLOCK. My Lords, for the purpose of answering the question of law on which this appeal will turn only a brief account is needed of the facts that have given rise to it. The respondent, Camplin, who was 15 years of age, killed a middle-aged Pakistani, Mohammed Lal Khan, by splitting his skull with a chapati pan, a heavy kitchen utensil like a rimless frying pan. At the time the two of them were alone together in Khan's flat. At Camplin's trial for murder before Boreham J his only defence was that of provocation so as to reduce the offence to manslaughter. According to the story that he told in the witness box but which differed materially from that which he had told to the police, Khan had buggered him in spite of his resistance and had then laughed at him, whereupon Camplin had lost his self-control and attacked Khan fatally with the chapati pan.

In his address to the jury on the defence of provocation, counsel for Camplin had suggested to them that when they addressed their minds to the question whether the provocation relied on was enough to make a reasonable man do as Camplin had done, what they ought to consider was not the reaction of a reasonable adult but the reaction of a reasonable boy of Camplin's age. The judge thought that this was wrong in law. So in this summing-up he took pains to instruct the jury that they must consider whether—

'the provocation was sufficient to make a reasonable man in like circumstances act as the defendant did. Not a reasonable boy, as [counsel for Camplin] would have it, or a reasonable lad; it is an objective test—a reasonable man.'

The jury found Camplin guilty of murder. On appeal the Court of Appeal, Criminal Division[1], allowed the appeal and substituted a conviction for manslaughter on the ground that the passage I have cited from the summing-up was a misdirection. The court held that[2]—

'the proper direction to the jury is to invite the jury to consider whether the provocation was enough to have made a reasonable person of the same age as the appellant in the same circumstances do as he did.'

The point of law of general public importance involved in the case has been certified as being:

'Whether, on the prosecution for murder of a boy of 15, where the issue of provocation arises, the jury should be directed to consider the question, under s 3 of the Homicide Act 1957, whether the provocation was enough to make a reasonable man do as he did by reference to a "reasonable adult" or by reference to a "reasonable boy of 15".'

My Lords, the doctrine of provocation in crimes of homicide has always represented an anomaly in English law. In crimes of violence which result in injury short of death, the fact that the act of violence was committed under provocation, which

---

1 [1978] 1 All ER 1236, [1977] 3 WLR 929
2 [1978] 1 All ER 1236 at 1242, [1977] 3 WLR 929 at 935

has caused the accused to lose his self-control, does not affect the nature of the offence
a of which he is guilty: it is merely a matter to be taken into consideration in determining the penalty which it is appropriate to impose: whereas in homicide provocation
effects a change in the offence itself from murder, for which the penalty is fixed by
law (formerly death and now imprisonment for life), to the lessor offence of mans-
slaughter, for which the penalty is in the discretion of the judge.

The doctrine of provocation has a long history of evolution at common law. Such
b changes as there had been were entirely the consequence of judicial decision until
Parliament first intervened by passing the Homicide Act 1957. Section 3 deals specifically with provocation and alters the law as it had been expounded in the cases,
including three that had been decided comparatively recently in this House, namely
Mancini v Director of Public Prosecutions[1], *Holmes v Director of Public Prosecutions*[2]
and *Bedder v Director of Public Prosecutions*[3]. One of the questions in this appeal is
c to what extent propositions as to the law of provocation that are laid down in those
cases, and in particular in *Bedder*[3], ought to be treated as being of undiminished
authority despite the passing of the Homicide Act 1957.

For my part I find it instructive to approach this question by a brief survey of the
historical development of the doctrine of provocation at common law. Its origin
at a period when the penalty for murder was death is to be found, as Tindal CJ,
d echoing Sir Michael Foster[4], put it in *R v Hayward*[5], in 'the law's compassion to human
infirmity'. The human infirmity on which the law first took compassion in a violent
age when men bore weapons for their own protection when going about their
business appears to have been chance medley or a sudden falling out at which both
parties had recourse to their weapons and fought on equal terms. Chance medley
as a ground of provocation was extended to assault and battery committed by the
e deceased on the accused in circumstances other than a sudden falling out. But with
two exceptions actual violence offered by the deceased to the accused remained the
badge of provocation right up to the passing of the 1957 Act. The two exceptions were
the discovery by a husband of his wife in the act of committing adultery and the discovery by a father of someone committing sodomy on his son; but these apart,
insulting words or gestures unaccompanied by physical attack did not in law amount
f to provocation.

The 'reasonable man' was a comparatively late arrival in the law of provocation.
As the law of negligence emerged in the first half of the 19th century he became the
anthropomorphic embodiment of the standard of care required by the law. It would
appear that Keating J in *R v Welsh*[6] was the first to make use of the reasonable man as
the embodiment of the standard of self-control required by the criminal law of per-
g sons exposed to provocation, and not merely as a criterion by which to check the
credibility of a claim to have been provoked to lose his self-control made by an accused
who at that time was not permitted to give evidence himself. This had not been
so previously and did not at once become the orthodox view. In his Digest of the
Criminal Law[7] and his History of the Criminal Law[8] Sir James Fitzjames Stephen
makes no reference to the reasonable man as providing a standard of self-control by
h which the question whether the facts relied on as provocation are sufficient to reduce
the subsequent killing to manslaughter is to be decided. He classifies and defines
the kinds of conduct of the deceased that alone are capable in law of amounting
to provocation and appears to treat the questions for the jury as being limited to (1)

j
1   [1941] 3 All ER 272, [1942] AC 1
2   [1946] 2 All ER 124, [1946] AC 588
3   [1954] 2 All ER 801, [1954] 1 WLR 1119
4   See *Broadfoot's Case* (1743) Fost 154
5   (1833) 6 C & P 157 at 159
6   (1869) 11 Co CC 336
7   (1877)
8   (1883)

whether the evidence establishes conduct by the deceased that falls within one of
the defined classes and, if so, (2) whether the accused was thereby actually deprived *a*
of his self-control.

The reasonable man referred to by Keating J[1] was not then a term of legal art nor
has it since become one in criminal law. He (or she) has established his (or her)
role in the law of provocation under a variety of different sobriquets in which the
noun 'man' is frequently replaced by 'person' and the adjective 'reasonable' by
'ordinary', 'average' or 'normal'. At least from as early as 1914 (see R v Lesbini[2]), *b*
the test of whether the defence of provocation is entitled to succeed has been a dual
one: the conduct of the deceased to the accused must be such as (1) might cause in any
reasonable or ordinary person and (2) actually causes in the accused a sudden and
temporary loss of self-control as the result of which he commits the unlawful act
that kills the deceased. But until the 1957 Act was passed there was a condition
precedent which had to be satisfied before any question of applying this dual test *c*
could arise. The conduct of the deceased had to be of such a kind as was capable
in law of constituting provocation; and whether it was or was not a question for the
judge, not for the jury. This House so held in Mancini[3] where it also laid down
a rule of law that the mode of resentment, as for instance the weapon used in the act
that caused the death, must bear a reasonable relation to the kind of violence that
constituted the provocation. *d*

It is necessary for the purposes of the present appeal to spend time on a detailed
account of what conduct was or was not capable in law of giving rise to a defence of
provocation immediately before the passing of the 1957 Act. It had remained much
the same as when Stephen was writing in the last quarter of the 19th century. What,
however, is important to note is that this House in Holmes[4] had recently confirmed
that words alone, save perhaps in circumstances of a most extreme and exceptional *e*
nature, were incapable in law of constituting provocation.

My Lords, this was the state of law when Bedder[5] fell to be considered by this House.
The accused had killed a prostitute. He was sexually impotent. According to his
evidence he had tried to have sexual intercourse with her and failed. She taunted him
with his failure and tried to get away from his grasp. In the course of her attempts to
do so she slapped him in the face, punched him in the stomach and kicked him in *f*
the groin, whereupon he took a knife out of his pocket and stabbed her twice and
caused her death. The struggle that led to her death thus started because the deceased taunted the accused with his physical infirmity; but in the state of the law
as it then was, taunts unaccompanied by any physical violence did not constitute
provocation. The taunts were followed by violence on the part of the deceased in
the course of her attempt to get away from the accused, and it may be that this *g*
subsequent violence would have a greater effect on the self-control of an impotent
man already enraged by the taunts than it would have had on a person conscious of
possessing normal physical attributes. So there might be some justification for the
judge to instruct the jury to ignore the fact that the accused was impotent when they
were considering whether the deceased's conduct amounted to such provocation as
would cause a reasonable or ordinary person to lose his self-control. This indeed *h*
appears to have been the ground on which the Court of Criminal Appeal[6] had
approved the summing-up when they said:

'... no distinction is to be made in the case of a person who, though it may
not be a matter of temperament is physically impotent, is conscious of that

j

1   (1869) 11 Cox CC 336 at 338
2   [1914] 3 KB 1116
3   [1941] 3 All ER 272, [1942] AC 1
4   [1946] 2 All ER 124, [1946] AC 588
5   [1954] 2 All ER 801, [1954] 1 WLR 1119
6   [1954] 2 All ER 801 at 803, [1954] 1 WLR 1119 at 1121

a impotence, *and therefore mentally liable to be more excited unduly* if he is "twitted" or attacked on the subject of that particular infirmity.'

This statement, for which I have myself supplied the emphasis, was approved by Lord Simonds LC speaking on behalf of all the members of this House who sat on the appeal; but he also went on to lay down the broader proposition that[1]:

b 'It would be plainly illogical not to recognise an unusually excitable or pugnacious temperament in the accused as a matter to be taken into account but yet to recognise for that purpose some unusual physical characteristic, be it impotence or another.'

Section 3 of the 1957 Act is in the following terms:

c 'Where on a charge of murder there is evidence on which the jury can find that the person charged was provoked (whether by things done or by things said or by both together) to lose his self-control, the question whether the provocation was enough to make a reasonable man do as he did shall be left to be determined by the jury; and in determining that question the jury shall take into account everything both done and said according to the effect which, in their opinion, it would have on a reasonable man.'

d My Lords, this section was intended to mitigate in some degree the harshness of the common law of provocation as it had been developed by recent decisions in this House. It recognises and retains the dual test: the provocation must not only have caused the accused to lose his self-control but also be such as might cause a reasonable man to react to it as the accused did. Nevertheless it brings about two important changes in the law. The first is it abolishes all previous rules of law as to what can or

e cannot amount to provocation and in particular the rule of law that, save in the two exceptional cases I have mentioned, words unaccompanied by violence could not do so. Secondly it makes it clear that if there was any evidence that the accused himself at the time of the act which caused the death in fact lost his self-control in consequence of some provocation however slight it might appear to the judge, he was bound to leave to the jury the question, which is one of opinion not of law, whether

f a reasonable man might have reacted to that provocation as the accused did.

I agree with my noble and learned friend, Lord Simon of Glaisdale, that since this question is one for the opinion of the jury the evidence of witnesses as to how they think a reasonable man would react to the provocation is not admissible.

The public policy that underlay the adoption of the 'reasonable man' test in the common law doctrine of provocation was to reduce the incidence of fatal violence

g by preventing a person relying on his own exceptional pugnacity or excitability as an excuse for loss of self-control. The rationale of the test may not be easy to reconcile in logic with more universal propositions as to the mental element in crime. Nevertheless it has been preserved by the 1957 Act but falls to be applied now in the context of a law of provocation that is significantly different from what it was before the Act

h was passed.

Although it is now for the jury to apply the 'reasonable man' test, it still remains for the judge to direct them what, in the new context of the section, is the meaning of this apparently inapt expression, since powers of ratiocination bear no obvious relationships to powers of self-control. Apart from this the judge is entitled, if he thinks it helpful, to suggest considerations which may influence the jury in forming their own opinions as to whether the test is satisfied; but he should make it clear

j that these are not instructions which they are required to follow: it is for them and no one else to decide what weight, if any, ought to be given to them.

As I have already pointed out, for the purposes of the law of provocation the 'reasonable man' has never been confined to the adult male. It means an ordinary person

1 [1954] 2 All ER 801 at 803, 804, [1954] 1 WLR 1119 at 1123

of either sex, not exceptionally excitable or pugnacious, but possessed of such powers
of self-control as everyone is entitled to expect that his fellow citizens will exercise *a*
in society as it is today. A crucial factor in the defence of provocation from earliest
times has been the relationship between the gravity of provocation and the way in
which the accused retaliated, both being judged by the social standards of the day.
When Hale was writing in the 17th century pulling a man's nose was thought to
justify retaliation with a sword; when *Mancini*[1] was decided by this House, a blow
with a fist would not justify retaliation with a deadly weapon. But so long as words *b*
unaccompanied by violence could not in common law amount to provocation the relevant proportionality between provocation and retaliation was primarily one of degrees
of violence. Words spoken to the accused before the violence started were not normally to be included in the proportion sum. But now that the law has been changed so
as to permit of words being treated as provocation, even though unaccompanied by
any other acts, the gravity of verbal provocation may well depend on the particular *c*
characteristics or circumstances of the person to whom a taunt or insult is addressed.
To taunt a person because of his race, his physical infirmities or some shameful
incident in his past may well be considered by the jury to be more offensive to the
person addressed, however equable his temperament, if the facts on which the taunt
is founded are true than it would be if they were not. It would stultify much of
the mitigation of the previous harshness of the common law in ruling out verbal *d*
provocation as capable of reducing murder to manslaughter if the jury could not take
into consideration all those factors which in their opinion would affect the gravity
of taunts and insults when applied to the person to whom they are addressed. So to
this extent at any rate the unqualified proposition accepted by this House in *Bedder*[2]
that for the purposes of the 'reasonable man' test any unusual physical characteristics
of the accused must be ignored requires revision as a result of the passing of the *e*
1957 Act.
    That he was only 15 years of age at the time of the killing is the relevant charac-
teristic of the accused in the instant case. It is a characteristic which may have its
effects on temperament as well as physique. If the jury think that the same power
of self-control is not to be expected in an ordinary, average or normal boy of 15 as in
an older person, are they to treat the lesser powers of self-control possessed by an *f*
ordinary, average or normal boy of 15 as the standard of self-control with which the
conduct of the accused is to be compared?
    It may be conceded that in strict logic there is a transition between treating age
as a characteristic that may be taken into account in assessing the gravity of the
provocation addressed to the accused and treating it as a characteristic to be taken
into account in determining what is the degree of self-control to be expected of the *g*
ordinary person with whom the accused's conduct is to be compared. But to require
old heads on young shoulders is inconsistent with the law's compassion of human
infirmity to which Sir Michael Foster ascribed the doctrine of provocation more than
two centuries ago. The distinction as to the purpose for which it is legitimate to take
the age of the accused into account involves considerations of too great nicety to
warrant a place in deciding a matter of opinion, which is no longer one to be decided *h*
by a judge trained in logical reasoning but by a jury drawing on their experience of
how ordinary human beings behave in real life.
    There is no direct authority prior to the Act that states expressly that the age of
the accused could not be taken into account in determining the standard of self-
control for the purposes of the reasonable man test, unless this is implicit in the
reasoning of Lord Simonds LC in *Bedder*[2]. The Court of Appeal distinguished the *j*
instant case from that of *Bedder*[2] on the ground that what it was there said must be
ignored was an unusual characteristic that distinguished the accused from ordinary

1 [1941] 3 All ER 272, [1942] AC 1
2 [1954] 2 All ER 801, [1954] 1 WLR 1119

normal persons, whereas nothing could be more ordinary or normal than to be aged

a 15. The reasoning in *Bedder*[1] would, I think, permit of this distinction between normal and abnormal characteristics, which may affect the powers of self-control of the accused; but for reasons that I have already mentioned the proposition stated in *Bedder*[1] requires qualification as a consequence of changes in the law affected by the 1957 Act. To try to salve what can remain of it without conflict with the Act could in my view only lead to unnecessary and unsatisfactory complexity in a question

b which has now become a question for the jury alone. In my view *Bedder*[1], like *Mancini*[2] and *Holmes*[3], ought no longer to be treated as an authority on the law of provocation.

In my opinion a proper direction to a jury on the question left to their exclusive determination by s 3 of the 1957 Act would be on the following lines. The judge should state what the question is, using the very terms of the section. He should then

c explain to them that the reasonable man referred to in the question is a person having the power of self-control to be expected of an ordinary person of the sex and age of the accused, but in other respects sharing such of the accused's characteristics as they think would affect the gravity of the provocation to him, and that the question is not merely whether such a person would in like circumstances be provoked to lose his self-control but also would react to the provocation as the accused did.

d I accordingly agree with the Court of Appeal that the judge ought not to have instructed the jury to pay no account to the age of the accused even though they themselves might be of opinion that the degree of self-control to be expected in a boy of that age was less than in an adult. So to direct them was to impose a fetter on the right and duty of the jury which the 1957 Act accords to them to act on their own opinion on the matter.

e I would dismiss this appeal.

LORD MORRIS OF BORTH-Y-GEST. My Lords, for many years past in cases where murder has been charged, it has been recognised by courts that there can be circumstances in which the accused person was so provoked that this unlawful act was held to amount to manslaughter rather than to murder. Due and sensibly

f regard to human nature and to human frailty and infirmity was being paid. In *R v Hayward*[4] this result was said to be 'in compassion to human infirmity'. But courts were careful to ensure that a plea of provocation should involve more than some easy explanation as to how a death had been caused. What was involved was that the accused had acted in 'heat of blood' or in a 'transport of passion' or in other words had lost his self-control and that this was the result of the provocation. But

g in addition to this and by way of limitation, courts introduced certain tests of reasonableness. Was it but natural for even a reasonable man to have been as much aroused as was the accused? Furthermore, might even a reasonable man have been induced in the violence of passion to do what the accused did?

These lines of approach were at different times expressed in different ways. In

h *R v Welsh*[5] Keating J, in his summing-up, used the following words:

'The question, therefore, is—first, whether there is evidence of any such provocation as could reduce the crime from murder to manslaughter; and, if there be any such evidence, then it is for the jury whether it was such that they can attribute the act to the violence of passion naturally arising therefrom, and likely to be aroused thereby in the breast of a reasonable man ... The law is,

j

1   [1954] 2 All ER 801, [1954] 1 WLR 1119
2   [1941] 3 All ER 272, [1942] AC 1
3   [1946] 2 All ER 124, [1946] AC 588
4   (1833) 6 C & P 159 at 159
5   (1869) 11 Cox CC 336 at 338

that there must exist such an amount of provocation as would be excited by the circumstances in the mind of a reasonable man, and so as to lead the jury to *a* ascribe the act to the influence of that passion . . . The law contemplates the case of a reasonable man, and requires that the provocation shall be such as that such man might naturally be induced, in the anger of the moment, to commit the act.'

When Keating J said that 'The law contemplates the case of a reasonable man' was he doing more than saying that the jury had to consider whether the accused had *b* reasonably been aroused and had reasonably been subject to a violence of passion? Could a reasonable man in the position of the accused have been 'excited by the circumstances'? Could such a person have done what the accused did? Those were all questions for the jury.

At a much later date, in *Holmes v Director of Public Prosecutions*[1], Viscount Simon said:
                                                                                        c
  'If, on the other hand, the case is one in which the view might fairly be taken (*a*) that a reasonable person, in consequence of the provocation received, might be so rendered subject to passion or loss of control as to be led to use the violence with fatal results, and (*b*) that the accused was in fact acting under the stress of such provocation, then it is for the jury to determine whether on its view of the facts manslaughter or murder is the appropriate verdict.'   *d*

Before the time when *Bedder v Director of Public Prosecutions*[2] came under consideration, the courts seemed to have created the conception of 'the reasonable man' as a mythical person seemingly not only detached from but also rather remote from the accused person and having certain attributes as laid down by the court as the courts directed juries to accept.
                                                                                        e
Who then or what then was the 'reasonable man'? If a reasonable man is a man who normally acts reasonably, it becomes important to consider the mind of the accused person when considering his reactions to some provocation. To consider the mind of some different person, and to consider what his reactions would have been if comparably provoked, could involve an unreal test. In the argument in *Bedder's* case[2] the question was raised as to the position of a dwarf. If at the date of *f* that case things said could have amounted to provocation and if grossly offensive things in relation to his stature had been said to a dwarf, had the jury to consider not whether the dwarf only acted as a reasonable dwarf might have acted in being subject to passion and in doing what he did, or must the jury consider what would have been the reactions of a man of normal physique if the things said had been said to him?

These questions in regard to the reasonable man must now be reviewed in the light *g* of the provisions of the 1957 Act. Those contained in s 2 in reference to persons suffering from diminished responsibility may merely be noted in passing. Those contained in s 3 are of supreme importance. That section provides as follows:

  'Where on a charge of murder there is evidence on which the jury can find that the person charged was provoked (whether by things done or by things *h* said or by both together) to lose his self-control, the question whether the provocation was enough to make a reasonable man do as he did shall be left to be determined by the jury; and in determining that question the jury shall take into account everything both done and said according to the effect which, in their opinion, it would have on a reasonable man.'
                                                                                        j
One big change enacted was that things said could, either alone or in conjunction with things done, constitute provocation. It will first be for the court to decide

---

1   [1946] 2 All ER 124 at 126, [1946] AC 588 at 597
2   [1954] 2 All ER 801, [1954] 1 WLR 1119

whether, on a charge of murder, there is evidence on which a jury can find that the
a person charged was provoked to lose his self-control; thereafter, as it seems to me,
all questions are for the jury. It will be for the jury to say whether they think that
whatever was or may have been the provocation, such provocation was in their view
enough to make a reasonable man do as the accused did. The jury must take into
account everything both done and said according to the effect which they think there
would have been on a reasonable man. Who then or what then is the 'reasonable man'
b who is referred to in the section? It seems to me that the courts are no longer entitled
to tell juries that a reasonable man has certain stated and defined features. It is for
the jury to consider all that the accused did; it is for them to say whether the provocation was enough to make 'a reasonable man' do as the accused did. The jury must
take into account 'everything both done and said'. What do they think would have
been the effect on a reasonable man? They must bring their 'collective good sense'
c to bear. As Lord Goddard CJ said in *R v McCarthy*[1]:

> 'No court has ever given, nor do we think ever can give, a definition of what
> constitutes a reasonable or average man. That must be left to the collective good
> sense of the jury, and what, no doubt, would govern their opinion would be the
> nature of the retaliation used by the provoked person.'

d So in relation to the facts in *Bedder's* case[2] apart from the painful physical kick, a jury
would now have to consider the effect of the things said on a reasonable man. If an impotent man was taunted about his impotence the jury would not today be told that an
impotent man could not be a reasonable man as contemplated by the law. The jury
would be entitled to decide that the accused man acted as 'a reasonable man' in being
provoked as he was and in doing 'as he did'.
e   It seems to me that as a result of the changes effected by s 3 of the 1957 Act a jury
is fully entitled to consider whether an accused person, placed as he was, only acted as
even a reasonable man might have acted if he had been in the accused's situation.
There may be no practical difference between, on the one hand, taking a notional independent reasonable man, but a man having the attributes of the accused and subject
to all the events which surrounded the accused, and then considering whether what
f the accused did was only what such a person would or might have done, and, on the
other hand, taking the accused himself with all his attributes and subject to all the
events and then asking whether there was provocation to such a degree as would or
might make a reasonable man do what he (the accused) in fact did.
   In my view it would now be unreal to tell the jury that the notional 'reasonable man'
is someone without the characteristics of the accused: it would be to intrude into
g their province. A few examples may be given. If the accused is of particular colour
or particular ethnic origin and things are said which to him are grossly insulting
it would be utterly unreal if the jury had to consider whether the words would have
provoked a man of different colour or ethnic origin, or to consider how such a man
would have acted or reacted. The question would be whether the accused if he was
provoked only reacted as even any reasonable man in his situation would or might
h have reacted. If the accused was ordinarily and usually a very unreasonable person,
the view that on a particular occasion he acted just as a reasonable person would or
might have acted would not be impossible of acceptance.
   It is not disputed that the 'reasonable man' in s 3 of the 1957 Act could denote
a reasonable person and so a reasonable woman. If words of grievous insult were
addressed to a woman, words perhaps reflecting on her chastity or way of life, a
j consideration of the way in which she reacted would have to take account of how
other woman being reasonable women would or might in like circumstances have
reacted. Would or might she, if she had been a reasonable woman, have done what
she did?

---

1 [1954] 2 All ER 262 at 265, [1954] 2 QB 105 at 112
2 [1954] 2 All ER 801, [1954] 1 WLR 1119

In the instant case the considerations to which I have been referring have application to a question of age. The accused was a young man. Sometimes in the summing- *a* up he was called a boy or a lad. He was at the time of the events described at the trial under 16 years of age: he was accountable in law for the charge preferred against him. More generally in the summing-up he was referred to as a young man; that would appear to me to have been appropriate. In his summing-up, however, the learned judge in referring to a reasonable man seemed to emphasise to the jury that the reasonable man with whom they must compare the accused could not be a *b* young man of the age of the accused but had to be someone older and indeed had to be someone of full age and maturity. In my view that was not correct. The jury had to consider whether a young man of about the same age as the accused but placed in the same situation as that which befell the accused could, had he been a reasonable young man, have reacted as did the accused and could have done what the accused did. For the reasons which I have outlined the question so to be considered *c* by the jury would be whether they considered that the accused, placed as he was, and having regard to all the things that they find were said, and all the things that they find were done, only acted as a reasonable young man might have acted, so that, in compassion, and having regard to human frailty, he could to some extent be excused even though he had caused death.

I consider that the Court of Appeal came to the correct conclusion and agreeing *d* with what my noble and learned friend, Lord Diplock, has said as to the direction to a jury, I would dismiss the appeal.

LORD SIMON OF GLAISDALE. My Lords, the accused, the respondent to this appeal, was indicted for murder. He pleaded guilty of manslaughter but not guilty of murder. His defence was provocation. He was found guilty of murder but *e* the verdict was quashed on appeal and a verdict of manslaughter was substituted. The Crown now appeals to your Lordships' House.

At the time of the offence the accused was 15 years of age. It was the common assumption of his counsel, of the trial judge, Boreham J, and of the Court of Appeal that the jury might have thought that the age of the accused could have been a factor affecting his self-control, in other words, that the jury might have held that a boy *f* of 15 was more liable to lose his self-control than a man of full age. It was for this reason that Boreham J, no doubt feeling constrained to do so by *Bedder v Director of Public Prosecutions*[1], directed the jury that, to justify a verdict of manslaughter, the provocation must be sufficient to make a reasonable *man* (expressly, not a reasonable boy or lad), in like circumstances to those of the accused at the time of the homicide, act as the accused did. And it was for this reason that the Court of *g* Appeal, distinguishing *Bedder*[1], allowed the appeal and submitted a verdict of manslaughter. Your Lordships must, I think, proceed on the same assumption for the purposes of this appeal.

In *Bedder*[1], the defendant, who was sexually impotent, had in vain attempted to have intercourse with a prostitute. The woman jeered at him for his impotence; *h* when he tried to hold her she slapped his face and punched him in the stomach, and as he pushed her back she kicked him in the private parts. He took a knife from his pocket and struck her two blows with it, which killed her. It was argued on his behalf that the 'reasonable man' (whom a long line of previous authorities since 1859 had established as the standard for measuring the self-control required where a defence of provocation was in question) should be invested with the physical qualities of the defendant (in that case, impotence), and that the question should be asked, *j* what would be the reaction of an impotent reasonable man in the circumstances? But the judge directed the jury in these terms[2]:

---

1   [1954] 2 All ER 801, [1954] 1 WLR 1119
2   [1954] 2 All ER 801 at 802, [1954] 1 WLR 1119 at 1121

a 'The reasonable person, the ordinary person, is the person you must consider when you are considering the effect which any acts, any conduct, any words, might have to justify the steps which are taken in response thereto, so that an unusually excitable or pugnacious individual, or a drunken one or a man who is sexually impotent is not entitled to rely on provocation which would not have led an ordinary person to have acted in the way which was in fact carried out.'

b This direction was upheld both in the Court of Criminal Appeal and in your Lordships House.

It is, I think, important to note what was the point of law certified by the Attorney-General for the consideration of this House, because it defines the scope of the decision. The crucial passage is as follows[1]:

c 'Where provocation is set up as the defence to a charge of murder, to what extent (if at all) it is relevant, in considering the effect on a reasonable man of the alleged provocation, that the accused suffers from a physical infirmity or disability likely to render a person similarly affected more susceptible to the provocation alleged than a person not so affected ...'

d Lord Simonds LC[2], with whose speeech the other members of the House agreed, gave three main reasons for dismissing the appeal. (1):

'It would be plainly illogical not to recognise an unusually excitable or pugnacious temperament in the accused as a matter to be taken into account but yet to recognise for that purpose some unusual physical characteristics, be it impotence or another.'

e (Lord Simonds LC's reference to 'unusually excitable or pugnacious' was a direct citation from the speech of Viscount Simon LC, with whom the rest of the House concurred, in *Mancini v Director of Public Prosecutions*[3], where, approving *R v Lesbini*[4], he said: ' ... an unusally excitable or pugnacious individual is not entitled to rely on provocation which would not have led an ordinary person to act as he did.') (2):

f 'Moreover, the proposed distinction appears to me to ignore the fundamental fact that the temper of a man which leads him to react in such and such a way to provocation, is, or may be, itself conditioned by some physical defect. It is too subtle a refinement for my mind, or I think, for that of a jury to grasp that the temper may be ignored but the physical defect taken into account.'

(3) To invest the hypothetical reasonable man with the peculiar characteristics of the accused would make nonsense of the test established by authority.

g 'If the reasonable man is then deprived in whole or in part of his reason, or the normal man endowed with abnormal characteristics, the test ceases to have any value.'[5]

When *Bedder*[6] was decided your Lordships' House was bound by the rule of precedent. *Bedder*[6] followed preceding authorities in your Lordships' House and the
h speech of Lord Simonds LC is closely reasoned in the light of those authorities. (It is presumably in consequence of this that some critics of the decision would wish to go back beyond 1859 and dispense with the 'reasonable man' test altogether.) Subsequent discussion of *Bedder*[6] has, however, shown that some of its implications constitute affronts to common sense and any sense of justice. By way of example only, a blow on the face might be quite insufficient to make an ordinary reasonable

j 1 (1954) 38 Cr App Rep 133 at 134
   2 [1954] 2 All ER 801 at 803, 804, [1954] 1 WLR 1119 at 1123
   3 [1941] 3 All ER 272 at 277, [1942] AC 1 at 9
   4 [1914] 3 KB 1116
   5 [1954] 2 All ER 801 at 804, [1954] 1 WLR 1119 at 1123
   6 [1954] 2 All ER 801, [1954] 1 WLR 1119

man lose his self-control, whereas if he has a severe abscess in his cheek the situation might be very different, but, according to Bedder¹, the abscess would have to be **a** disregarded. And it is accepted that the phrase 'reasonable man' really means 'reasonable person', so as to extend to 'reasonable woman' (see, specifically, Holmes v Director of Public Prosecutions²). So, although this has never yet been a subject of decision, a jury could arguably, consistent with Bedder¹ and its precedent authorities, take the sex of the accused into account in assessing what might reasonably cause her to lose her self-control. (A 'reasonable woman' with her sex eliminated is alto- **b** gether too abstract a notion for my comprehension or, I am confident, for that of any jury. In any case, it hardly makes sense to say that an impotent man must be notionally endowed with virility before he ranks within the law of provocation as a reasonable man, yet that a normal woman must be notionally stripped of her femi- ninity before she qualifies as a reasonable woman.) If so, this is already some quali- fication on the 'reasonable person' as a pure abstraction devoid of any personal **c** characteristics, even if such a concept were of any value to the law. This qualification might be crucial: take the insult 'whore' addressed respectively to a reasonable man and a reasonable woman. Nevertheless, as counsel for the appellant sternly and co- gently maintained, Bedder¹ would preclude the jury from considering that the accused was, say, pregnant (R v Annie Smith)³, or presumably undergoing menstruation or menopause.   **d**

Such refinements, anomalies and affronts to common sense invite courts to dis- tinguish an authority. In the instant case the Court of Appeal distinguished Bedder¹ on the ground that age is a universal quality not a personal idiosyncrasy. It is certainly not a 'physical infirmity or disability'. This distinction is, further, arguably justified by the implications of the 'reasonable woman' as a standard. It could be said that the law, in distinguishing from personal idiosyncrasy something universal like age, **e** was doing no more than it had already done in distinguishing implicitly something universal like sex.

Nevertheless, the distinction drawn by the Court of Appeal leads to great diffi- culties. If youth is to be considered (and, presumably, advanced years too), what about immaturity in a person of full years or premature senility? These would seem to fall on the other, on the Bedder¹ side, of the line. One calls to mind what Lord Reid **f** said in Jones v Secretary of State for Social Services, Hudson v Secretary of State for Social Services⁴: 'It is notorious that where an existing decision is disapproved but cannot be overruled courts tend to distinguished it on inadequate grounds.' The fine distinctions and the anomalies inherent in distinguishing Bedder¹ are such as, in judgment, to make it incumbent to face the issue whether Bedder¹ should be followed or is so inconvenient an authority that it should be regarded as no longer repre- **g** presenting the law. The latter course involves considerable retracing of judicial steps. In order to see where it would be necessary to go, it is undesirable to investigate the reasons for the various rules which have been evolved in the law of provocation.

The original reasons in this branch of the law were largely reasons of the heart and of common sense, not the reasons of pure juristic logic. The potentiality of provo- cation to reduce murder to manslaughter was, as Tindal CJ said in R v Hayward⁵, **h** 'in compassion to human infirmity'. But justice and common sense then demanded some limitation: it would be unjust that the drunk man or one exceptionally pug- nacious or bad-tempered or over-sensitive should be able to claim that these matters rendered him peculiarly susceptible to the provocation offered, where the sober and even-tempered man would hang for his homicide. Hence, I think, the development of the concept of the reaction of a reasonable man to the provocation offered, even **j**

1   [1954] 2 All ER 801, [1954] 1 WLR 1119
2   [1946] 2 All ER 124, [1946] AC 588
3   (1914) 11 Cr App Rep 36
4   [1972] 1 All ER 145 at 149, [1972] AC 944 at 966
5   (1833) 6 C & P 157 at 159

though it may have originally come into this branch of the law by way of testing the credibility of the claim of the accused (who could not at that time himself give evidence) that he had been so deprived of his self-control as to be incapable of forming the relevant intent. But it is one thing to invoke the reasonable man for the standard of self-control which the law requires; it is quite another to substitute some hypothetical being from whom all mental and physical attributes (except perhaps sex) have been abstracted.

Nevertheless, although your Lordships are no longer bound to follow a previous decision of your Lordships' House, and are free to retrace steps if it appears that the following of authority has led into a false position, and although the inconveniences, anomalies and injustices implicit in the *Bedder*[1] decision are now apparent after the lapse of a quarter of a century, I am most reluctant to urge your Lordships to overrule *Bedder*[1]. This partly for the reasons given by Lord Reid in *Knuller (Publishing, Printers and Promotions) Ltd v Director of Public Prosecutions*[2]. But these are reinforced in the instant case. The issue here involves important questions of public safety; and Parliament as a whole constitutes a more suitable matrix for the framing of legal rules which concern such issues. Moreover, the Criminal Law Revision Committee put out a working paper[3] which covers the issue involved in this appeal. The paper invited comments on provisional proposals for amendment of the law, and no doubt the committee will shortly be producing its final report. I feel great reluctance in taking any step which might pre-empt the consequent decision.

But there is one factor here which makes the instant situation a peculiar one. Section 3 of the Homicide Act 1957 has supervened on *Bedder*[1] and makes it incumbent to determine whether *Bedder*[1] has thereby been weakened as an authority, particularly in view of the unsatisfactory consequences of merely distinguishing *Bedder*[1]. Section 3 reads as follows:

'Where on a charge of murder there is evidence on which the jury can find that the person charged was provoked (whether by things done or by things said or by both together) to lose his self-control, the question whether the provocation was enough to make a reasonable man do as he did shall be left to be determined by the jury; and in determining that question the jury shall take into account everything both done and said according to the effect which, in their opinion, it would have on a reasonable man.'

The main changes effected by this section were first, to provide that words alone could constitute provocation in law and secondly, to make the issue one for the jury alone. I would also draw particular attention to the words, 'the jury shall take into account *everything* . . . according to the effect which, in their opinion, it would have on a reasonable man'.

The provision that words alone can constitute provocation accentuates the anomalies, inconveniences and injustices liable to follow from the *Bedder*[1] decision. The effect of an insult will often depend entirely on a characteristic of a person to whom the insult is directed. 'Dirty nigger' would probably mean little if said to a white man or even if said by one coloured man to another, but is obviously more insulting when said by a white man to a coloured man. Similarly, such an expression as 'Your character is as crooked as your back' would have a different connotation to a hunchback on the one hand and to a man with a back like a ramrod on the other. (I would, however, wish to emphasise that I do not suggest that a jury would necessarily, or even probably, consider such insults as I have cited in this speech as in themselves excusing homicidal violence, any more than it must be assumed that I think it likely that a jury would hold that a mid or late teenager was to be credited with any exceptional incapacity for

---

1   [1954] 2 All ER 801, [1954] 1 WLR 1119
2   [1972] 2 All ER 898 at 903, [1973] AC 435 at 455
3   Offences against the Person (August 1976, HMSO)

self-control as to excuse homicidal violence.) But if the jury cannot take into account the characteristic which particularly points the insult, I cannot see that they are taking 'into account everything . . . according to the effect . . . it would have on a reasonable man'. In my judgment the reference to 'a reasonable man' at the end of the section means 'a man of ordinary self-control'. If this is so the meaning satisfies what I have ventured to suggest as the reasons for importing into this branch of the law the concept of the reasonable man, namely to avoid the injustice of a man being entitled to rely on his exceptional excitability (whether idiosyncratic or by cultural environment or ethnic origin) or pugnacity or ill-temper or on his drunkenness (I do not purport to be exhaustive in this enumeration).

There is another respect in which the 1957 Act may have affected the rigour of the *Bedder*[1] doctrine and thus undermined its authority. There have been differences of opinion lately in your Lordship's House on how far one may have forensic recourse to a public or parliamentary report. I cite the working paper[2] to which I have referred of the Criminal Law Revision Committee (as I would an authoritative textbook) as an expression of view of the law, formed by a body of criminal lawyers of outstanding eminence and wide-ranging experience:

> 'In this country the law on this matter [provocation] has been indirectly affected by the introduction of the defence of diminished responsibility. It is now possible for a defendant to set up a combined defence of provocation and diminished responsibility, the practical effect being that the jury may return a verdict of manslaughter if they take the view that the defendant suffered from an abnormality of mind *and* was provoked. In practice this may mean that a conviction of murder will be ruled out although the provocation was not such as would have moved a person of normal mentality to kill.'

In the exceptional circumstances whereby the reasoning of a decision of your Lordships' House, and that of the authorities on which it was founded, has been undermined by a subsequent Act of Parliament (even though the decision has not been clearly and expressly abrogated), I think that your Lordships are justified in saying that *Bedder*[1] should no longer be followed. I think that the law as it now stands in this country is substantially the same as that enacted in the New Zealand Crimes Act 1961, s 169(2), as explained by the Court of Appeal of New Zealand in *R v McGregor*[3].

I think that the standard of self-control which the law requires before provocation is held to reduce murder to manslaughter is still that of the reasonable person (hence his invocation in s 3 of the 1957 Act), but that, in determining whether a person of reasonable self-control would lose it in the circumstances, the entire factual situation, which includes the characteristics of the accused, must be considered.

There is only one other matter which I would desire to add. It was suggested on behalf of the Director of Public Prosecutions that if what his counsel called the 'completely objective test' as established by *Bedder*[1] were modified, so that it was open to the jury to consider such mental or physical characteristics of the defendant as might affect his self-control in the relevant situation, the jury might require evidence as to how a person of reasonable self-control would be likely to react in such circumstances, or at least that it would be open to either side to call such evidence. In other words, evidence would be required, or alternatively be admissible, to show, for example, how a pregnant woman or a 15-year-old boy or a hunchback would, exercising reasonable self-control, react in the circumstances. I cannot agree. Evidence of the pregnancy or the age or the malformation would be admissible. But whether the defendant exercised reasonable self-control in the totality of the circumstances (which would include the pregnancy or the immaturity or the malformation) would

---

1 [1954] 2 All ER 801, [1954] 1 WLR 1119
2 Offences against the Person (August 1976, HMSO), para 53
3 [1962] NZLR 1096

be entirely a matter for consideration by the jury without further evidence. The
a jury would, as ever, use their collective common sense to determine whether the
provocation was sufficient to make a person of reasonable self-control in the totality
of the circumstances (including personal characteristics) act as the defendant did.
I certainly do not think this is beyond the capacity of a jury. I have heard nothing to
suggest that juries in New Zealand find the task beyond them.

My Lords, for the foregoing reasons I would dismiss the appeal.

b   I have had the privilege of reading in draft the speech prepared by my noble and
learned friend, Lord Diplock; and I agree with what he proposes as the appropriate
direction to the jury.

LORD FRASER OF TULLYBELTON. My Lords, I have had the advantage
of reading in draft the speech prepared by my noble and learned friend, Lord Diplock.
c I entirely agree with it, and for the reasons given by him I would dismiss the appeal.

LORD SCARMAN. My Lords, I have had the advantage of reading in draft the
speech delivered by my noble and learned friend, Lord Diplock. I agree with it,
and would dismiss the appeal.

d *Appeal dismissed.*

Solicitors: *Director of Public Prosecutions*; *Robbins, Olivey & Lake*, agents for *Rice-Jones
& Smiths*, Halifax (for the respondent).

Mary Rose Plummer Barrister.

e

Re D H Curtis (Builders) Ltd

CHANCERY DIVISION
f BRIGHTMAN J
29th, 30th JUNE, 1st, 28th JULY 1977

*Bankruptcy – Proof – Set-off – Mutual credits, mutual debts or other mutual dealings –
Claims arising otherwise than out of contract – Statutory debts due to Crown – Company in
voluntary liquidation – Crown owing excess input tax to company – Unpaid taxes in greater
sum owed to Crown – Whether right of set-off restricted to claims arising out of contract –*
g *Whether Crown entitled to set off statutory debts owed to it against excess input tax – Bankruptcy Act 1914, s 31.*

A limited company went into voluntary liquidation. The company was indebted to
the Crown for unpaid taxes. However, at the same time, the Crown owed the company a balance of excess input tax paid under s 3(2) of the Finance Act 1972. The
h liquidator applied by summons for a declaration that the Crown was not entitled
to set off the claim to unpaid taxes against its obligation to repay the excess input
tax, contending that, under s 31[a] of the Bankruptcy Act 1914, claims sought to be
set off had to be such as arose either directly or indirectly out of contract.

Held – On its true construction, s 31 of the 1914 Act was not restricted to mutual

j ────────────────────────────────
   a   Section 31, so far as material, provides: 'Where there have been mutual credits, mutual
       debts or other mutual dealings, between a debtor against whom a receiving order shall be
       made . . . and any other person proving or claiming to prove a debt under the receiving
       order, an account shall be taken of what is due from the one party to the other in respect
       of such mutual dealings, and the sum due from the one party shall be set off against any
       sum due from the other party . . .'

debts, mutual credits and mutual dealings which arose out of contract but extended to any mutual demands capable of being proved in bankruptcy. Accordingly the Crown was entitled to set off the statutory debts owed to it against its own obligation to repay the excess input tax and the liquidator's claim therefore failed (see p 190 c to g, p 191 e and p 192 e to g, post).

Dicta of Brett MR and Cotton LJ in *Re Asphaltic Wood Pavement Co* (1885) 30 Ch D at 222, 224 and *Mathieson's Trustee v Burrup, Mathieson & Co* [1927] All ER Rep 172 applied.

Jack v Kipping (1882) 9 QBD 113, dictum of Lord Russell of Killowen CJ in *Palmer v Day & Sons* [1895] 2 QB at 621 and *Tilley v Bowman Ltd* [1908-10] All ER Rep 952 explained.

Dictum of Vaughan Williams J in *Re Mid-Kent Fruit Factory* [1896] 1 Ch at 570, 571 disapproved.

Notes

For the circumstances in which a right of set-off is available to a creditor, see 3 Halsbury's Laws (4th Edn) para 753, and for cases on mutual credit and set-off in bankruptcy, see 4 Digest (Reissue) 428-462, 3736-3974.

For the Bankruptcy Act 1914, s 31, see 3 Halsbury's Statutes (3rd Edn) 80.

Cases referred to in judgment

Asphaltic Wood Pavement Co, Re, Lee & Chapman's Case (1885) 30 Ch D 216, 54 LJ Ch 460, 53 LT 65, CA, 10 Digest (Reissue) 1071, 6579.
Bailey v Finch (1871) LR 7 QB 34, 41 LJQB 83, 25 LT 871, 4 Digest (Reissue) 437, 3809.
Canada Cycle & Motor Agency (Queensland) Ltd, Re (1931) 4 ABC 27.
City Life Assurance Co Ltd, Re [1926] Ch 191, [1925] All ER Rep 453, 95 LJ Ch 65, 134 LT 207, 1925 B & CR 233, CA, 10 Digest (Reissue), 1267, 7986.
Davies, Re, ex parte Cleland (1867) LR 2 Ch App 808, 36 LJ Bcy 45, 17 LT 187, LJ, 5 Digest (Reissue) 1244, 9912.
Forster v Wilson (1843) 12 M & W 191, 13 LJ Ex 209, 152 ER 1165, 4 Digest (Reissue) 435, 3802.
Jack v Kipping (1882) 9 QBD 113, 51 LJQB 463, 46 LT 169, DC, 4 Digest (Reissue) 441, 3842.
Mathieson's Trustee v Burrup, Mathieson & Co [1927] 1 Ch 562, [1927] All ER Rep 172, 96 LJ Ch 148, 136 LT 796, [1927] B & CR 47, 4 Digest (Reissue) 438, 3815.
Mid-Kent Fruit Factory Ltd, Re [1896] 1 Ch 567, 65 LJ Ch 250, 74 LT 22, 3 Mans 59, 4 Digest (Reissue) 432, 3775.
Naoroji v Chartered Bank of India (1868) LR 3 CP 444, 37 LJCP 221, 18 LT 358, 4 Digest (Reissue) 447, 3877.
Palmer v Day & Sons [1895] 2 QB 618, 64 LJQB 807, 2 Mans 386, 15 R 523, 4 Digest (Reissue) 449, 3896.
Pollitt, Re, ex parte Minor [1893] 1 QB 455, 62 LJQB 236, 68 LT 366, 10 Morr 35, 4 R 253, CA, 4 Digest (Reissue) 434, 3789.
Tilley v Bowman Ltd [1910] 1 KB 745, [1908-10] All ER Rep 952, 79 LJKB 547, 102 LT 318, 17 Mans 97, 4 Digest (Reissue) 441, 3843.

Cases also cited

Atlantic Engine Co (1920) *Ltd (in liquidation) v Lord Advocate* 1955 SLT 17.
City Equitable Fire Insurance Co Ltd, Re (No 2) [1930] 2 Ch 293, [1930] All ER Rep 315, CA.
Daintrey, Re, ex parte Mant [1900] 1 QB 546, [1895-9] All ER Rep 657, CA.
Duncan & Wakefield's Assignment, Re (1932) 5 ABC 96.
Eberle's Hotels & Restaurant Co Ltd v Jonas & Brothers (1887) 18 QBD 459, CA.
Government of India v Taylor [1955] AC 491, HL.
Hiram Maxim Lamp Co, Re [1903] 1 Ch 70.
Laing (Liquidator of Inverdale Construction Co) v Lord Advocate 1973 SLT (Notes) 81.
Mathrick, Re (1941) 12 ABC 212.

McCann & Edwards' Deed of Arrangement, Re (1932) 4 ABC 105.
Metal Industries (Salvage) Ltd v Owners of the ST Harle 1962 SLT 114.
National Westminster Bank Ltd v Halesowen Presswork & Assemblies Ltd [1972] 1 All ER
    641, HL, *rvsg* [1970] 2 All ER 473, CA.
Peat v Jones & Co (1881) 8 QBD 147, CA.
Prescot, Re, ex parte Prescot (1753) 1 Atk 230, LC.
Rolls Razor Ltd v Cox [1967] 1 All ER 397, [1967] 1 QB 552, CA.
Thorne (HE) & Son Ltd, Re [1914] 2 Ch 438.
United States of America v Harden (1963) 41 DLR (2d) 721.

Adjourned summons
By an originating summons dated 26th November 1976, Gordon Alan Coombs, the
liquidator of D H Curtis (Builders) Ltd ('the company'), sought as against Her Majesty's
Commissioners of Customs and Excise (i) a declaration that the commissioners were
not entitled to set off against their obligation to repay the company a balance of excess
input tax under s 3(2) of the Finance Act 1972 amounting to £219·45 a claim by the
Inland Revenue Commissioners amounting to £106·65 and a claim by the Department
of Health and Social Security amounting to £112·80, and (ii) an order that the Customs
and Excise Commissioners repay to the company a sum of £219·45. The facts are
set out in the judgment.

Michael Crystal for the liquidator.
Peter Gibson for the commissioners.

Cur adv vult

28th July. **BRIGHTMAN J** read the following judgment: This company was
formed in 1971 to carry on the business of building contractors. Its registered office
is in England. It went into voluntary liquidation in October 1974. Among the creditors
of the company are the Commissioners of Inland Revenue and the Department of
Health and Social Security to whom taxes are owed. At the same time the Commissioners of Customs and Excise owe to the company a balance of £219 in respect of
input tax under s 3(2) of the Finance Act 1972. The position therefore is that the
company is indebted to the Crown through two departments for certain taxes and
the Crown through another department is indebted to the company for the repayment of another tax. The three debts all arise by statute and it is conceded that it
is irrelevant that three separate government departments are involved. Two statutory
debts are due from the company to the Crown and one statutory debt is due from the
Crown to the company. The question that arises is whether the Crown is entitled
to set off the statutory debts owed to it against its own obligation to repay £219 input
tax or whether the Crown is bound to pay the input tax to the company and is left
to prove in the liquidation for the statutory debts due to it. The case is in the nature
of a test case because the financial implications are small so far as this particular
liquidation is concerned. There are however other pending liquidations which may
be affected by the result of this case and matters have been so arranged as to ensure
that the creditors of the company with which I am concerned will not be prejudiced
by the cost of this litigation.
    There is one other preliminary matter which I should explain in order to avoid
misunderstandings. Section 35 of the Crown Proceedings Act 1947 enacted that rules
should be made for providing among other things that the Crown when sued in
the name of a government department should not, without leave of the court, be
entitled to avail itself of any set-off if the subject-matter thereof does not relate to
that department. This is regulated by RSC Ord 77, r 6. No such leave is sought by
the Crown in the case before me because, for reasons which it is unnecessary to develop,
the liquidator does not rely on the prohibition contained in the 1947 Act.
    I am left with the short question whether the Crown is or is not entitled to set off its

own claims against the liquidator's claim. The Crown's answer is that it is plainly so entitled by virtue of the clear wording of s 31 of the Bankruptcy Act 1914. Section 317 of the Companies Act 1948 applies this section to the winding-up of insolvent companies registered in England. The answer of the liquidator is that for over 80 years the law has been interpreted as confining the statutory right of set-off in insolvency to demands which arise out of contract. The Crown submits that the law has been wrongly interpreted, in a manner which is not binding on this court.

The debts provable in bankruptcy are described in s 30 of the Bankruptcy Act 1914. The debts due to the Crown[2] in the present case are so provable. It will be sufficient to read the first three subsections:

'(1) Demands in the nature of unliquidated damages arising otherwise than by reason of a contract, promise, or breach of trust shall not be provable in bankruptcy.

'(2) A person having notice of any act of bankruptcy available against the debtor shall not prove under the order for any debt or liability contracted by the debtor subsequently to the date of his so having notice.

'(3) Save as aforesaid, all debts and liabilities, present or future, certain or contingent, to which the debtor is subject at the date of the receiving order, or to which he may become subject before his discharge by reason of any obligation incurred before the date of the receiving order, shall be deemed to be debts provable in bankruptcy.'

The effect is that, subject to certain exceptions, all claims arising before the bankruptcy are provable except a claim in the nature of unliquidated damages arising out of a tort.

So far as set-off is concerned the law has for many years recognised the general principle that where there are mutual debts existing between a creditor and a bankrupt, the smaller debt is to be set against the larger debt and only the balance is to be accounted for by the creditor or relegated to proof in the bankruptcy. This principle can be traced back for at least 300 years: see Bailey v Finch[1]. It received statutory recognition in s 28 of the Bankruptcy Act 1731 which dealt with mutual credits and debts, and required the commissioners to state the balance of the account between the bankrupt and the other person. That section was replaced by s 3 of the Bankruptcy Act 1806, followed successively by s 50 of the Bankruptcy Act 1825, s 171 of the Bankruptcy Act 1849, s 39 of the Bankruptcy Act 1869, s 38 of the Bankruptcy Act 1883, and finally s 31 of the Bankruptcy Act 1914, all in much the same terms.

The starting point of the problem before me is Palmer v Day & Sons[2], decided under the 1883 Act. Section 38 of that Act read as follows:

'Where there have been mutual credits, mutual debts or other mutual dealings between a debtor against whom a receiving order shall be made under this Act, and any other person proving or claiming to prove a debt under such receiving order, an account shall be taken of what is due from the one party to the other in respect of such mutual dealings, and the sum due from the one party shall be set off against any sum due from the other party, and the balance of the account, and no more, shall be claimed or paid on either side respectively; but a person shall not be entitled under this section to claim the benefit of any set-off against the property of a debtor in any case where he had at the time of giving credit to the debtor, notice of an act of bankruptcy committed by the debtor, and available against him.'

Section 31 of the 1914 Act is in almost identical terms.

In Palmer v Day & Sons[2] the plaintiff was the trustee in bankruptcy of a householder. He sought to recover £31 from the defendants, a firm of auctioneers. The

---

1   (1871) LR 7 QB 34
2   [1895] 2 QB 618

bankrupt had instructed the auctioneers to sell his house and furniture. A sum of £24 was due to them in respect of their fees on the sale of the house, which in fact proved abortive, and £7 was due in connection with the sale of furniture. Certain pictures were bought in at the furniture sale and were consigned by the bankrupt to the auctioneers for sale on their own premises. Subsequently the householder went bankrupt. The auctioneers claimed to deduct the £31, due to them for fees, from the proceeds which they held from the sale of the pictures. The county court judge decided in favour of the auctioneers on the ground that there was a single contract, thereby enabling the auctioneers to exercise a lien over the proceeds of sale in respect of all their fees. There was an appeal to a divisional court of the Queen's Bench Division. Lord Russell of Killowen CJ delivered the reserved judgment of the court. The court decided first that there were two contracts, so that the auctioneers could not rely on a lien. The court then decided that there were mutual credits or mutual dealings between the bankrupt and the auctioneers, that is to say, a credit in their favour in respect of their fees and a credit in his favour in respect of the proceeds of sale. In the course of their judgment the court said in relation to s 38 of the Bankruptcy Act 1883[1]:

> 'The section in its present shape, however, has been held applicable to all demands provable in bankruptcy, and so to include claims as well in respect of debts as of damages liquidated or unliquidated provided they arise out of contract.'

Six months later *Re Mid-Kent Fruit Factory*[2] was argued in the Chancery Division. At the commencement of the liquidation of a bankrupt company, the company's solicitors owed £325 for services rendered. The solicitors had in their hands £93 being the balance remaining out of a sum of £289 handed to them by the company prior to the liquidation for the purpose of negotiating settlements with the company's creditors. The judge rejected a claim by the solicitors to use the £325 as a set-off expunging the liquidator's claim for £93, on the well-established principle that if money has been paid by the insolvent to a creditor in order that it be applied for a special purpose, the creditor is under an obligation to return the whole of any unused balance to the insolvent and is not entitled to use it to pay his own debt. Having disposed of the case on that ground, Vaughan Williams J said[3]:

> 'I propose to say a few words as to the law as it now stands, as that may be useful in future cases. The law as to mutual credits has been modified in the Bankruptcy Act, 1883, by the introduction of the words as to mutual dealings, and now many matters come within the section referring to mutual credits which would not have fallen within the corresponding section in the prior Acts. The necessity for mutuality, however, has not ceased to exist. At one time it was supposed that there must be mutual debts; then that there must be mutual transactions which must result in a debt; and then the proposition was widened, and it was said that it would be sufficient if the transactions were such as would probably result in a debt. Then came the Bankruptcy Act, 1883, the result of the provision in which is to include all mutual dealings between two parties. Still the characteristic of mutuality must always be present. The judgment of Lord Russell C.J. in *Palmer* v. *Day & Sons*[4] was cited to me, and, as I understand, for the purpose of shewing that in the present state of the law no such mutuality is necessary, and that every claim provable in bankruptcy necessarily falls within the mutual credit section. He did not, in my opinion, decide anything of the sort. When one looks at his words, it seems plain that he did not intend that. He says[1]: "The section in its present shape, however, has been held applicable to all

---

1 [1895] 2 QB 618 at 621
2 [1896] 1 Ch 567
3 [1896] 1 Ch 567 at 570, 571
4 [1895] 2 QB 618

demands provable in bankruptcy, and so to include claims as well in respect of debts as of damages liquidated or unliquidated *provided they arise out of contract.''* He there clearly limits the operation of the section by these few words.'

The learned judge was in fact mistaken in referring to the Bankruptcy Act 1883; it should have been the Bankruptcy Act 1869.

That statement of the law, though not essential to the case, not unnaturally led to the belief that under the English law of bankruptcy there can be no set-off of mutual credits, debts or dealings unless the claims on each side arise out of contract either directly or, as in *Jack v Kipping*[1], indirectly. The latter was a case where the purchaser of shares from a vendor, who became bankrupt, was held entitled to set off, against a claim for the unpaid price, his own claim in damages for the fraudulent misrepresentation which had induced him to buy the shares. The ratio was expressed as follows[2]:

'It seems to us that it would be inequitable to hold that, where a purchaser has had an article which turns out to be worthless palmed off on him by fraudulent misrepresentations, and the vendor has become bankrupt, he should be compelled to pay the agreed price to the trustee, and be left to recover back as much as he can in the shape of a dividend. It is said that such a fraudulent misrepresentation is a tort; but we think that it is not a personal tort, but a breach of the obligation arising out of the contract of sale.'

That seems to be the origin of the formula 'provided they arise out of contract', which formula is absent from the statute.

In *Tilley v Bowman Ltd*[3] a retail jeweller by a fraudulent misrepresentation induced a wholesale jeweller to sell him jewellery for £569 on credit. The retailer pawned the jewellery for £300, paid £182 off the purchase price and later went bankrupt. The wholesaler rescinded the contract, paid off the pawnbroker and recovered the jewellery. The trustee in bankruptcy of the retailer sued the wholesaler for the return of the £182 as money paid for a consideration which had failed. The wholesaler claimed to set off, as damages, the £300 paid to the pawnbroker. Following the decision in *Jack v Kipping*[1] Hamilton J upheld the set-off. In the course of his judgment he appears to have adopted the view of the law expressed by Vaughan Williams J[4] that s 38 had no application at all unless the cross-demands arose out of contract. This was not necessary to his decision.

The same principle was adopted and applied in the Australian case, *Re Canada Cycle and Motor Agency (Queensland) Ltd*[5]. The liquidator of a company claimed against a director certain sums which were alleged to have been wrongly paid out of the company's money in breach of duty. It was held that as the director's liability for misapplied money did not arise out of contract, the liquidator could not make use of his claim against the director for the purpose of reducing or expunging the director's own proof in the liquidation. This case was decided under s 82 of the then Australian Bankruptcy Act which is similar to the corresponding English enactment.

So far as the textbooks are concerned, the requirement that nothing can be set off unless it is a claim arising out of contract was stated in the first edition of Halsbury's Laws of England[6], and has been repeated in all subsequent editions[7].

Counsel for the liquidator in the course of a careful and well researched argument supported the proposition by submitting that it is a characteristic of the mutuality

1   (1882) 9 QBD 113
2   9 QBD 113 at 116, 117
3   [1910] 1 KB 745
4   [1896] 1 Ch 567
5   (1931) 4 ABC 27
6   2 Halsbury's Laws 211, 212, para 347
7   See now 3 Halsbury's Laws (4th Edn) para 751

required by s 31 of the 1914 Act and its predecessors that the claims on each side
sought to be set off must be such as result in pecuniary liabilities arising out of contract.
I am not clear as to the logical basis of that submission. In my view the word mutual
in this context connotes that comparable acts or events are to be found on both sides.
The type of acts or events seem to me to be immaterial provided that they are comparable, i e commensurable. If the liquidator's proposition is correct, it could lead to
some startling results. To take an example not far removed from the present case.
Suppose that a trader owed to the Commissioners of Customs and Excise at the end
of one quarter the sum of £1,000 in respect of value added tax on his outputs. Suppose
at the end of the next quarter there was a balance in the trader's favour of £1,000
in respect of value added tax paid on inputs. Suppose that the trader then went
bankrupt. Common sense would seem to suggest that the £1,000 owed *by* the
commissioners should be set off against the £1,000 owed *to* the commissioners.
Neither debt arises out of contract. According to the submission made to me, the
Crown would be compelled to pay the £1,000 to the trustee in bankrupty of the
trader and would be left to prove for the £1,000 due to it. Examples of that sort
can be multiplied. A has a judgment debt against B in tort for £1,000. Being a judgment debt, it is provable in bankruptcy. B obtains judgment against A in respect of
some other tort for £1,000. Neither sum has been satisfied when B goes bankrupt.
One would think that the one judgment debt should be set off against the other
judgment debt. In each of the examples I have given there are two debts which seem
to answer any ordinary test of mutuality. It would be surprising if s 31 of the 1914 Act
had to be construed in such a way as to exclude set-off.

The first question which I have to decide is whether I am bound by authority to
decide this case in favour of the liquidator. If not, I must then consider whether the
proposition advanced by the liquidator is supported by dicta which I cannot properly
disregard.

I do not think that the judgment read by Lord Russell of Killowen CJ in *Palmer v Day
& Sons*[1] contains much that assists the liquidator's case. The sentence on which the
liquidator relies is in two parts[2]. The first part is in favour of the Crown and against
the liquidator: 'The section in its present shape . . . has been held applicable to all
demands provable in bankruptcy . . .', ie generally speaking all debts and liabilities
except unascertained damages in tort. The second part of the sentence is framed as
consequential thereon· '. . . and so to include claims as well in respect of debts as of
damages liquidated or unliquidated provided they arise out of contract.' I am
inclined to think that this was not intended to be a precise and exhaustive analysis
of s 38, but rather a convenient verbal shorthand. As the court went on to consider
Jack v Kipping[3] it seems to me possible that what they meant was 'and so to include
claims as well in respect of debts as of damages liquidated or unliquidated provided,
in the latter case, that they arise out of contract'. It was unnecessary to the decision in
Palmer v Day & Sons[1] to interpret s 38 as excluding therefrom all claims not arising
out of contract since the cross-claims in that case did arise out of contract. Therefore
if, contrary to my view, the court was stating that s 38 should be construed as excluding all non-contractual cross-claims, that pronouncement would have been obiter.
The observations made by Vaughan Williams J in *Re Mid-Kent Fruit Factory*[4] are far
more specific and quite clearly support the liquidator's proposition. Vaughan
Williams J interprets the judgment of the divisional court as limiting the operation of
s 38 to claims which arise out of contract. But again this expression of view was
clearly obiter. Vaughan Williams J had already decided against set-off on the ground
that the solicitors had been handed the money for certain specific purposes only. In

---

1   [1895] 2 QB 618
2   [1895] 2 QB 618 at 621
3   (1882) 9 QBD 113
4   [1896] 1 Ch 567 at 570, 571

this respect the judge followed (without however mentioning it) the decision of the Court of Appeal in *Re Pollitt*[1], which had been relied on in argument, as indeed he was bound to do as the case was on all fours. There are many other cases decided on the same principle.

Tilley v Bowman Ltd[2] carries the matter no further. It was a decision which follows and was expressed to follow *Jack v Kipping*[3]:

'*Jack* v. *Kipping*[3] . . . is an authority which binds me, and accordingly seems to me to conclude the present case. The defendants' claim for damages for the fraudulent misrepresentation, which is in one sense a claim in respect of a tort, may be allowed to come within the mutual dealings clause upon the ground that, the claim of the trustee being in the nature of a claim under the contract, the misrepresentation which led to the contract was a mutual dealing as between the vendors and the bankrupt purchasers.'

I accordingly take the view that I am not compelled by authority to apply s 31 of the 1914 Act as permitting set-off only where mutual debts, mutual credits or mutual dealings arise out of contract.

I turn to the question whether I ought to follow the dictum of Vaughan Williams J although it is not binding on me. The view so expressed emanates from a judge of the highest authority and was intended by him to lay down the law. I believe I ought to follow what he has said and has apparently stood unchallenged for 80 years, unless I have an overwhelming conviction that it was not correct. In that event I am sure that my proper course is to decide this case according to my own conviction.

The purpose of set-off in insolvency is to do substantial justice between the bankrupt and his creditors. This has frequently been recognised. See *Forster v Wilson*[4]: 'The object of this clause [he meant s 50 of the Bankruptcy Act 1825] is not to avoid cross actions . . . but to do substantial justice between the parties . . .', a passage which was read with approval by Lord Cairns LJ in *Re Davies, ex parte Cleland*[5] and by Pollock MR in *Re City Life Assurance Co*[6]. If that is the purpose of set-off in bankruptcy, one would expect to find that any mutual demands capable of being proved in bankruptcy can be the subject-matter of set-off whether or not arising out of contract. Part II of the Bankruptcy Act 1914 has the cross heading 'Administration of Property' followed by the sub-heading 'Proof of Debts'. The first section in Part II is s 30 which describes those debts which can be proved in bankruptcy. Section 31 provides for the taking of an account where there have been mutual credits, mutual debts or other mutual dealings. A natural assumption would be that s 31 is intended to cover the same subject-matter as s 30. This was indeed so expressed in s 50 of the Bankruptcy Act 1825 and in s 171 of the Bankruptcy Act 1849; both sections ended with the words:

'. . . and what shall appear due on either Side on the Balance of such Account, and no more, shall be claimed or paid on either Side respectively; *and every Debt or Demand hereby made provable against the Estate of the Bankrupt may also be set off in manner aforesaid against such Estate*, provided that the Person claiming the Benefit of such Set-off had not, when such Credit was given, Notice of an Act of Bankruptcy by such Bankrupt committed.'

The intermediate words were not included in s 39 of the Bankruptcy Act 1869 which simply read:

1　[1893] 1 QB 455
2　[1910] 1 KB 745 at 752, 753, cf [1908-10] All ER Rep 952 at 954
3　(1882) 9 QBD 113
4　(1843) 12 M & W 191 at 203, 204
5　(1867) LR 2 Ch App 808 at 812, 813
6　[1926] Ch 191 at 216, [1925] All ER Rep 453 at 464

'. . . and the balance of such account , and no more, shall be claimed or paid on either side respectively; but a person shall not be entitled under this section to claim the benefit of any set-off against the property of a bankrupt in any case where he had at the time of giving credit to the bankrupt notice of an act of bankruptcy committed by such bankrupt and available against him for adjudication.'

Nevertheless, the Court of Appeal in Re Asphaltic Wood Pavement Co, Lee & Chapman's Case[1], does not seem to have considered that the omission of those words broke the link between the two sections. Brett MR said[2]:

'As between them this claim to damages can be proved in the winding-up. The moment I come to that conclusion, I must hold that the Bankruptcy Act, 1869, s. 39, applies, and that the claim of the Commissioners is to be treated by way of set-off, and they are entitled to say that they cannot be called upon to pay more than the amount which they owed the company diminished by that which the liquidator owed them for these damages.'

Cotton LJ said[3]:

'At the time when the company commenced its liquidation, it was under a contract which implied a liability to maintain these streets if it were required. It is now rendered impossible by the winding-up for the company to do that, and in my opinion, though no notice had been given before the commencement of the winding-up, that is properly a liability the damages for which are capable of being proved, and, if capable of being proved, are capable under the mutual credit clause of being set off against any claim by the liquidator as against the Commissioners.'

As a matter of construction of s 31 I cannot myself see any justification whatever for limiting its operation to mutual claims which arise out of contract. Counsel for the liquidator suggested that the section was inserted for the benefit of traders and for that reason was intended only to embrace cross-claims arising out of commercial transactions. He referred me to passages in a number of cases which he said linked s 31 with dealings between merchants. For example Naoroji v Chartered Bank of India[4], per Montague Smith J:

'The object of the enactment seems to me to have been, that, where merchants have had mutual dealings, each giving credit to the other, relying upon each other's solvency, in the event of the bankruptcy of one of them, the account shall be taken between them of all such credits and dealings as in the natural course of business would end in debts, and the balance shall be the debt due from the one to the other.'

I do not think that any of the cases mentioned to me afford sufficient support for the liquidator's proposition.

In Mathieson's Trustee v Burrup, Mathieson & Co[5] Clauson J applied s 31 to cross-claims which did not arise out of contract. A company called Burrup, Mathieson & Sprague Ltd, which I will call the old company, in June 1923 had assigned to the defendant company, which I will call the new company, the whole of its undertaking including book debts. The assignment also provided that the new company should discharge all the debts of the old company. Gerard Mathieson, who had been a director of the old company, entered into a service agreement with the new company. In

1   (1885) 30 Ch D 216
2   30 Ch D 216 at 222
3   30 Ch D 216 at 224
4   (1868) LR 3 CP 444 at 452
5   [1927] 1 Ch 562, [1927] All ER Rep 172

August 1925 Mathieson became bankrupt. In 1922 the Inland Revenue had assessed the old company in the sum of £3,000 excess profits duty. This liability arose as a result of the disallowance of the deduction for tax purposes of part of the remuneration paid by the old company to Mathieson for a period ending in 1920. Part of the £3,000, namely £2,150, had been paid by the old company to the Revenue after the date of the assignment but prior to the date of the receiving order. It was therefore a liability which the new company was bound to discharge under the terms of the assignment. The old company had a right under s 49(2) of the Finance Act 1916 to recover from Mathieson an amount equal to the excess profits duty so paid. That right was a book debt which passed to the new company under the terms of the assignment. In January 1926 Mathieson's trustee in bankruptcy sued the new company for £1,250 arrears of salary. The new company pleaded a right to set off against the £1,250 so claimed the sum of £2,150 which the new company was entitled to recover from Mathieson. The debt of £2,150 did not arise out of contract, but by statute. The only point of substance raised by the trustee in bankruptcy was that the cross-claim against the bankrupt was an equitable claim since the assignment by the old company had not been perfected at law. It was held that the bankruptcy jurisdiction depended on equitable principles and drew no distinction between an equitable and a legal right for the purposes of administration. In the course of his judgment Clauson J said this[1]:

> '. . . assuming there had been an assignment of this liability perfected at law from the old company to the new company, the position at the moment the bankruptcy commenced would be this: a legal claim by the director against the new company for salary; and on the other hand a legal claim by the new company against the director to be recouped the sum in question. If that had been the state of the facts, it would have been impossible to contend that s. 31 would not apply, and there would have been a set-off . . .'

It is right to say that counsel for the trustee in bankruptcy did not put the argument that there was no right of set-off because the old company's right did not arise out of contract. But if the liquidator's proposition in the case before me is correct Clauson J's decision in the Mathieson case[2] must have been wrong.

In my judgment s 31 of the 1914 Act does not apply only to mutual debts, mutual credits and mutual dealings which arise out of contract. Which the utmost respect to Vaughan Williams J, I prefer not to follow his dictum[3] which I am convinced was wrong. In my view it is impossible to reconcile it with the wording of s 31 or with the purpose of the bankruptcy jurisdiction. In disregarding the dictum of so eminent a judge I comfort myself with the thought that I am following in the footsteps of Clauson J, even if he did not realise that they diverged from those of his predecessor. Accordingly I decide this case against the claim of the liquidator.

Order accordingly.

Solicitors: *Gouldens*, agents for *Sargent & Probert* Exeter (for the liquidator); *Solicitor, Customs and Excise.*

Evelyn M C Budd   Barrister.

---

1 [1927] 1 Ch 562 at 568, [1927] All ER Rep 172 at 173
2 [1927] 1 Ch 562, [1927] All ER Rep 172
3 [1896] 1 Ch 567 at 570, 571

Delbourgo v Field (Inspector of Taxes)

COURT OF APPEAL, CIVIL DIVISION
STAMP, ORR AND EVELEIGH LJJ
19th, 20th JANUARY 1978

Income tax – Appeal – Settlement by agreement – Agreement – Inspector agreeing settlement in principle – Apportionment of sum between capital gains tax and income tax – Taxpayer bringing actions for damages for breach of agreement to purchase shareholding and for compensation for loss of office – Actions settled by payment to taxpayer of single sum – Taxpayer proposing apportionment of sum between claims – Inspector of taxes agreeing apportionment – No figures agreed – Inspector subsequently assessing entire sum to capital gains tax as award in respect of shares – Taxpayer claiming inspector bound by agreement in principle – Whether inspector and taxpayer having 'come to an agreement' – Taxes Management Act 1970, s 54(1).

In 1968 the taxpayer entered into two agreements with an investment trust ('Triumph'). By the first ('the vending agreement') he agreed to sell his shareholding in D Ltd on certain terms to Triumph, and by the second ('the service agreement') he agreed to serve for ten years as managing director of two of Triumph's subsidiary companies. Disputes arose between the taxpayer and Triumph and its two subsidiary companies. The taxpayer brought an action against them claiming damages for breach of both agreements. The two subsidiary companies counterclaimed for damages for breaches of the service agreement and brought an action against him claiming other relief. Both actions were settled on payment by Triumph of £399,357 to the taxpayer. No specific amount was allocated to either the taxpayer's claim in respect of the service agreement or the vending agreement. The taxpayer wrote to the inspector of taxes informing him of what had happened and suggesting that £70,000 of the payment should be attributed to loss of prospective earnings in relation to his managing directorships, but should be treated as a sum of £42,875 after deduction of tax, leaving as a gain for capital gains tax purposes a sum of £151,262. After further correspondence, the inspector wrote to the taxpayer saying: 'I am now prepared to accept your apportionment of this payment and propose assessing the £70,000 compensation payment under Schedule E ...' The taxpayer replied that he could not accept the inspector's proposed assessment under Sch E because on the taxpayer's reckoning the figure was £42,857. The inspector, after a further consideration of the documents, decided that the £399,357 was paid solely in settlement of the taxpayer's claim in respect of the vending agreement and therefore the whole of that sum was chargeable to capital gains tax. The taxpayer was accordingly assessed to capital gains tax on £399,357. He appealed contending that the correspondence between him and the inspector constituted an agreement that the capital gains computation would be made on the basis of the apportionment which he had suggested and that, by virtue of s 54(1)[a] of the Taxes Management Act 1970, the agreement had the same effect as if it were a determination of the commissioners. The Special Commissioners found that the parties had agreed that the £399,357 should be apportioned, but they dismissed the appeal on the ground that the parties had not, within the meaning of s 54(1), 'come to an agreement that the assessment under appeal should be treated as varied in a particular manner' because they had not agreed on the amount to be apportioned. On appeal,

Held – To come within s 54(1) as an agreement to vary, the agreement had to specify

---

a   Section 54(1) is set out at p 194 *j* to p 195 *b*, post the varied amount of the assessment or, at the very least, had to provide the commissioners with a basis from which the varied figure could be readily calculated. On *a* the evidence it provided neither a figure nor any basis from which one could be calculated. It followed that s 54(1) did not apply and the appeal would be dismissed (see p 196 *j* to p 197 *d* and *g*, post).

Decision of Foster J [1977] 1 All ER 323 affirmed.

Notes

For settlement of appeals by agreement, see 20 Halsbury's Laws (3rd Edn) 45, 680, 681, paras 64, 1342.

For the Taxes Management Act 1970, s 54, see 34 Halsbury's Statutes (3rd Edn) 1299.

Cases referred to in judgments

British Transport Commission v Gourley [1955] 3 All ER 796, [1956] AC 185, [1956] 2 WLR *c* 41, 220 LT 354, [1955] 2 Lloyd's Rep 475, 34 ATC 305, [1955] TR 303, 49 R & IT 11, HL, 17 Digest (Reissue) 88, 35.

Chambers v Hibbert (6th March 1970) unreported.

Appeal

The taxpayer, Raphael Jack Delbourgo, was assessed to capital gains tax for the years *d* 1968-69, 1969-70 and 1971-72 in respect of, inter alia, the disposal by him of shares in Delbourgo Ltd to Triumph Investment Trust Ltd. He appealed against the assessments. The Commissioners for the Special Purposes of the Income Tax Acts reduced the assessment for 1968-69 and discharged the assessments for 1969-70 and 1971-72. The Crown and the taxpayer both declared their dissatisfaction with the commissioners' decision and required them to state a case for the opinion of the High *e* Court pursuant to s 56 of the Taxes Management Act 1970. The questions of law for the opinion of the court were (i) as regards the taxpayer's appeal, whether the commissioners had erred in law in deciding that the appeal was not settled by agreement under s 54 of the 1970 Act, and (ii) as regards the Crown's cross-appeal, whether the commissioners had erred in law in discharging the assessments for 1969-70 and 1971-72. On 8th November 1976 Foster J[1] dismissed the appeal and the cross-appeal. The *f* taxpayer appealed against the dismissal of his appeal. The facts are set out in the judgment of Orr LJ.

The taxpayer appeared in person.
C H McCall for the Crown.

g

ORR LJ delivered the first judgment at the invitation of Stamp LJ. This is an appeal by a taxpayer, Mr Delbourgo, who has conducted his case in person, as he did before the learned judge, against an order made by Foster J[1] on 8th November 1976 affirming, on a case stated, a determination of the Special Commissioners whereby they rejected an argument by the taxpayer that assessments to capital gains tax made on him for the years 1968-69, 1969-70 and 1971-72 had been settled by agreement *h* under s 54 of the Taxes Management Act 1970 and, having invited the parties to agree figures on that basis, determined the assessment for the first of those years in the sum of £120,807 and discharged the assessment for the two later years.

Section 54(1) of the Act provides as follows:

'Subject to the provisions of this section, where a person gives notice of appeal *i* and, before the appeal is determined by the Commissioners, the inspector or *j* other proper officer of the Crown and the appellant come to an agreement, whether in writing or otherwise, that the assessment or decision under appeal

---

1 [1977] 1 All ER 323

should be treated as upheld without variation, or as varied in a particular manner or as discharged or cancelled, the like consequences shall ensue for all purposes as would have ensued if, at the time when the agreement was come to, the Commissioners had determined the appeal and had upheld the assessment or decision without variation, had varied it in that manner or had discharged or cancelled it, as the case may be.'

The facts of the case were briefly these. By the first (which I shall refer to as 'the vending agreement') of two agreements made in 1969 the taxpayer agreed to sell his shareholding in a company Delbourgo Ltd on certain terms to Triumph Investment Trust Ltd; and by the second agreement (which I shall call 'the service agreement') he agreed to serve two subsidiary companies of Triumph as managing director for ten years. Disputes later arose between the taxpayer and Triumph and two of its subsidiaries, as a result of which the taxpayer claimed damages for breach of both agreements and Triumph's subsidiaries counterclaimed for alleged breaches of the service agreement and also brought an action for other relief, but eventually both actions and the counterclaim were settled on payment by Triumph to the taxpayer of £399,357. Thereafter on 22nd April 1974 the taxpayer wrote to the inspector of taxes referring to the two agreements, the litigation and the compromise and to the problem of apportioning the sum received by him as between the two agreements and suggesting that £70,000 should be attributed to loss of prospective earnings but should be treated, on the authority of *British Transport Commission v Gourley*[1], as a sum of £42,875 paid after deduction of tax, leaving as a gain for the purpose of capital gains tax a sum of £151,262.

To that the inspector replied querying (and in my judgment rightly querying) the application of the *Gourley* principle[1] since tax would be payable on the sum received for loss of earnings and stating that on the taxpayer's apportionment of the total payment £329,357 would fall to be included in the capital gains computation and £70,000 would be assessable to income tax with an exemption for £5,000 of that sum.

On 2nd September 1974 the inspector wrote as follows:

'I am now prepared to accept your apportionment of this payment and propose assessing the £70,000 compensation payment under Schedule E for 1971-72 less £5,000 exempt under Section 187 [of the Income and Corporation Taxes Act 1970]. Please let me know . . .'

and then he made an inquiry, which I need not refer to in detail, about top slicing relief.

On 10th September the taxpayer wrote to the inspector:

'I note that you accept my apportionment of this payment, but I cannot accept your proposed assessment under Schedule E. My computation is in fact for £42,000 less £5,000.'

On 26th November the taxpayer's solicitors explained to the inspector that the amount of £42,000 was arrived at after calculating the total salary for the unexpired part of the service agreement but discounting it for accelerated payment and then deducting income tax.

On 2nd January 1975 the inspector wrote:

'I should make one point immediately. It has been accepted up to now that £70,000 represented compensation for loss of office. In this event the amount assessable both to Income Tax and Surtax will be £70,000 less £5,000 exempt',

that is, £65,000. I need not, I think, refer to the remainder of that letter.

On 23rd April the inspector wrote to the taxpayer's solicitors as follows:

---

1   [1955] 3 All ER 796, [1956] AC 185

'I have sought the opinion of my Head Office and they consider that the agreement of the 29 June 1971 must be taken at its face value, i e that the total payment of £399,357 was in full and final settlement of your client's entitlement in respect of the shares (the penultimate paragraph of my letter of the 2 January refers). No evidence has been produced to show that any part of the sum received was in respect of the service contract. Should such evidence be forthcoming I will of course consider the matter further. Summing up the view is now taken that [the taxpayer] dropped any claim for damages in respect of his service agreement and obtained £399,357 in respect of the shares. The whole of this amount is chargeable to capital gains tax. I trust that upon reconsideration you can agree.'

Before the Special Commissioners it was argued for the taxpayer that his letter of 22nd April 1974 contained a clear proposal that the total payment should be apportioned as to £42,875 to the service agreement and as to the balance to the sale of shares; that the inspector so agreed on 2nd September; and that accordingly there was an agreement that the capital gains computation would be made on the basis of that apportionment and that by virtue of s 54 of the Taxes Management Act 1970 such agreement had the same effect as if it were a determination of the commissioners.

For the inspector of taxes it was conceded that the inspector had agreed that the total payment made to the taxpayer should be apportioned but it was denied that there was any agreement that the amount apportioned to the service agreement was £42,875 and it was submitted that in any event s 54 did not apply.

The Special Commissioners found on the correspondence that by 2nd September 1974 the parties were agreed that the total sum should be apportioned but that all that was agreed was that there should be an apportionment, there being no agreement as to the amount to be apportioned and there being other matters outstanding which bore on the final computation, and they held that the parties had not in the relevant words of s 54 'come to an agreement that the assessment under appeal should be treated as varied in a particular manner' since in their view 'varied in a particular manner' must, as applied to an appeal against an assessment, mean a variation of the amount of the assessment and must be such as to produce an ascertained or immediately ascertainable figure.

On appeal Foster J upheld the Special Commissioners' decision, holding that there must be, as a result of an agreement under s 54, a figure arrived at which can be included in an assessment.

Against that decision the taxpayer now appeals to this court and he has put his arguments very clearly. One of them, which is referred to in the judgment of Foster J[1], was that the Taxing Acts are to be construed strictly against the Crown. But while I agree that Taxing Acts are to be construed strictly, I do not agree with the addition of the words 'against the Crown', which suggest that words are to be unduly restricted against the Crown, and I do not think that this argument can help the taxpayer in the present case. I would only add that any such statement of principle as I have quoted in this matter must be considered in the context of a tax system under which very often it is not the Crown that is claiming tax but the taxpayer who is seeking relief.

A further argument was that the word 'agreement' in s 54 should not be given a narrow legal meaning, but I do not think that anything turns on that word for the purposes of this appeal, in which it is common ground, on the finding of the commissioners, that the parties did in fact agree that the total payment should be apportioned between the sale and the service agreements and the question at issue is whether it was agreed that the assessment 'should be treated as varied in a particular manner' in which event the section says that the like consequences are to ensue as would have ensued if the commissioners had varied the assessment in that manner. These words, in my judgment, clearly involve that the agreement, if it is to fall within s 54, must be such that the commissioners, on the basis of the agreement reached,

_____
1   [1977] 1 All ER 323 at 332, [1977] STC 1 at 10

can, instead of determining the appeal, which they are relieved from doing if the agreement falls within s 54, substitute a different figure in place of the amount of the assessment. In the result, in my judgment, the agreement, to fall within the section, must be an agreement that the assessment is to be upheld or an agreement that it be discharged or an agreement that it is to be varied and, if it is an agreement to vary, it must specify what the varied amount of the assessment is to be or, at the very least, must provide the commissioners with a basis from which the varied figure can be readily calculated. In the present case the agreement provided neither a figure nor any basis on which a figure could be calculated and in my judgment it was not an agreement falling within the section.

In coming to this conclusion I derive some support from the unreported judgment (of which we have been provided with a transcript) of Buckley J in *Chambers v Hibbert*[1] in which he held that an agreement as to the basis on which an appeal should be allowed to proceed was not within the ambit of s 510(1) of the Income Tax Act 1952, which was the predecessor of the present s 54(1) of the 1970 Act.

For these reasons I am in complete agreement with the conclusion reached by the Special Commissioners and upheld by the judge and I would dismiss this appeal.

EVELEIGH LJ. I agree.

STAMP LJ. I agree that this appeal must be dismissed. As I read s 54, it contemplates a situation in which an appeal from an assessment is pending for determination by the appropriate commissioners and it contemplates an agreement which is intended to deal with the appeal and take the place of a decision of the commissioners. What is contemplated is that the assessment should be treated as upheld without variation or as varied in a particular manner or as discharged or cancelled and what is contemplated is that—

> 'the like consequences shall ensue for all purposes as would have ensued if, at the time when the agreement was come to, the Commissioners [and I emphasise these words] *had determined the appeal and had upheld the assessment or decision without variation, had varied it in that manner or had discharged or cancelled it*, as the case may be.'

That appears to me to contemplate a situation in which it is unnecessary to pursue the appeal, the agreement having got rid of that necessity. This can only be if the agreement is one which either is an agreement fixing the figure to be assessed or stating a mathematical formula for ascertaining that amount which will leave no room for any further argument as to the amount which falls to be substituted for the amount which has been assessed.

On those short grounds I too would dismiss the appeal.

Appeal dismissed. Leave to appeal to the House of Lords refused.

Solicitors: *Solicitor of Inland Revenue.*

A S Virdi Esq   Barrister.

---

1   (6th March 1970) unreported

R v Hull Prison Board of Visitors, ex parte St Germain and others

QUEEN'S BENCH DIVISION

LORD WIDGERY CJ, CUMMING-BRUCE LJ AND PARK J

5th, 6th DECEMBER 1977

Certiorari – Jurisdiction – Prison board of visitors – Exercise of disciplinary powers – Prisoners charged with breach of prison discipline – Adjudication by board of visitors – Allegation that board had acted contrary to natural justice in their adjudication – Whether certiorari would lie against board's decisions.

A disturbance occurred in a prison where the seven applicants were incarcerated. As a result the board of prison visitors, pursuant to their powers under the Prison Act 1952 and the rules made thereunder, heard charges against the applicants who had been involved in the acts of indiscipline. The board made various disciplinary awards against the applicants, including loss of remission. The applicants applied to the Divisional Court for orders of certiorari to quash the board's decisions on the ground that the board had failed to observe the rules of natural justice.

Held – Although the board of visitors was in the nature of a judicial body under a duty to act judicially and one which therefore, on the face of it, would be subject to the jurisdiction of the High Court by way of certiorari, that jurisdiction did not extend to disciplinary proceedings in a closed body which enjoyed its own form of discipline and rules and where there was power to impose sanctions within the scope of those rules given as part of the formation of the body itself. Accordingly, since the board of visitors sitting as a disciplinary body was part of the disciplinary machinery of the prison, they were not subject to the control of the High Court by way of certiorari. The applications would therefore be refused (see p 204 *a b* and *f* to p 205 *a c* and p 206 *a* to *c*, post).

Ex parte Fry [1954] 2 All ER 118 and dictum of Lord Denning MR in *Becker v Home Office* [1972] 2 All ER at 682 applied.

Ridge v Baldwin [1963] 2 All ER 66 and dictum of Lord Parker CJ in *R v Criminal Injuries Compensation Board, ex parte Lain* [1967] 2 All ER at 778 considered.

Notes

For bodies amenable to orders of certiorari, see 1 Halsbury's Laws (4th Edn) paras 148-152, and for cases on the jurisdiction to grant certiorari, see 16 Digest (Repl) 471-485, *2905-3038*.

Cases referred to in judgments

Becker v Home Office [1972] 2 All ER 676, [1972] 2 QB 407, [1972] 2 WLR 1193, CA, Digest (Cont Vol D) 729, *33b*.

Booth v Dillon (No 3) [1977] VR 143.

Fry, Ex parte [1954] 2 All ER 118, [1954] 1 WLR 730, 118 JP 313, 52 LGR 320, CA, 38 Digest (Repl) 258, *666*.

R v Church Assembly Legislative Committee, ex parte Haynes Smith [1928] 1 KB 411, [1927] All ER Rep 696, 97 LJKB 222, 138 LT 399, DC, 19 Digest (Repl) 240, *2*.

R v Criminal Injuries Compensation Board, ex parte Lain [1967] 2 All ER 770, [1967] 2 QB 864, [1967] 3 WLR 348, DC, 14(2) Digest (Reissue) 866, *7499*.

R v Electricity Comrs, ex parte London Electricity Joint Committee Co [1924] 1 KB 171, [1923] All ER Rep 150, 93 LJKB 390, 130 LT 164, 88 JP 13, 21 LGR 719, CA, 16 Digest (Repl) 433, *2381*.

Ridge v Baldwin [1963] 2 All ER 66, [1964] AC 40, [1962] 2 WLR 935, 127 JP 295, 61 LGR 369, HL, 37 Digest (Repl) 195, *32*.

Cases also cited

a Arbon v Anderson, De Laessoe v Anderson [1943] 1 All ER 154, [1943] KB 252.
Baldwin and Francis Ltd v Patents Appeal Tribunal [1959] 2 All ER 433, [1959] AC 663, HL.
Buckoke v Greater London Council [1971] 2 All ER 254, [1971] Ch 655, CA
Durayappah v Fernando [1967] 2 All ER 152, [1967] AC 337, PC.
Fraser v Mudge [1975] 3 All ER 78, [1975] 1 WLR 1132, CA.
b Gaiman v National Association for Mental Health [1970] 2 All ER 362, [1971] Ch 317.
Glynn v Keele University [1971] 2 All ER 89, [1971] 1 WLR 487.
Maynard v Osmond [1977] 1 All ER 64, [1977] QB 240, CA.
Morriss v Winter [1930] 1 KB 243.
Parke, Davis & Co v Comptroller-General of Patents, Designs and Trade Marks [1954] 1 All ER 671, [1954] AC 321, HL.
c R v Gaming Board for Great Britain, ex parte Benaim [1970] 2 All ER 528, [1970] 2 QB 417, CA.
R v Leeds Prison Governor, ex parte Stafford [1964] 1 All ER 610, [1964] 2 QB 625, DC.
R v Maguire (1956) 50 Cr App Rep 92, CCA.
R v Manchester Legal Aid Committee, ex parte R A Brand & Co [1952] 1 All ER 480, [1952] 2 QB 413, DC.
d R v Metropolitan Police Comr, ex parte Parker [1953] 2 All ER 717, [1953] 1 WLR 1150, DC.
R v Paddington Valuation Officer, ex parte Peachey Property Corpn [1965] 2 All ER 836, [1966] 1 QB 380, CA.
R v Secretary of State for the Home Department, ex parte Hosenball [1977] 3 All ER 452, [1977] 1 WLR 766, CA.
R v Secretary of State for War, ex parte Martyn [1949] 1 All ER 242, DC.
e Savundra, Re [1973] 3 All ER 406, [1973] 1 WLR 1147.
Selvarajan v Race Relations Board [1976] 1 All ER 12, [1975] 1 WLR 1686, CA.
Stevenson v United Road Transport Union [1977] 2 All ER 941, CA.

Motions for certiorari

f The applicants, Ronald St Germain, Michael Reed, Keith Saxton, Kenneth Anderson, James Joseph Pike, Peter Rajah and James Loff Lennon, each applied by way of motion for an order of certiorari to bring up and quash decisions of the Board of Visitors of Hull Prison in respect of each applicant in respect of charges framed against them arising out of a disturbance at Her Majesty's Prison Hull which took place between 8 p m on 31st August and 12 noon on 2nd September 1976, and in respect of which the prison visitors imposed punishments involving loss of privileges of various kinds. All the applicants complained, inter alia, that the prison visitors had failed *g* to comply with the rules of natural justice. The full nature of the charges considered by the prison visitors and the full grounds of the individual applications are not set out because at the beginning of the hearing of the applications counsel for the board raised the preliminary point of law that the remedy of certiorari would not go to a prison board of visitors in respect of their alleged failure to comply with the rules of natural justice in making their adjudications, and it is on that point that the case is *h* reported.

Andrew Collins for the applicant St Germain.
Ashraf Khan for the applicant Reed.
Michael Beloff for the applicants Saxton, Anderson, Pike and Lennon.
Peter Thornton for the applicant Rajah.
j Harry Woolf and Robert Owen for the board of visitors.

LORD WIDGERY CJ. Each of the matters before the court today arises out of a disturbance at Her Majesty's Prison Hull which took place between 20.00 hours on 31st August 1976 and 12.00 hours on 2nd September 1976. During that time a large number of prisoners were out of their cells; a substantial number were on the

roof throwing slates and the like down to ground level. This went on, as I have
already indicated, for some considerable time. Eventually peace was restored. Those   *a*
thought by the authorities to be the ringleaders were taken to other prisons, and
consideration was then no doubt given to what charges might be brought against the
rioters consequent on their conduct.

It suffices for present purposes to say that, in general, the nature of the charges was
not that of the normal criminal law but special language coming from the Prison Act
1952 and Prison Rules 1964[1]. The precise charges laid against St Germain (who is the   *b*
first applicant and is a good example of what happened) were, firstly, that he absented
himself without permission from 'A' Wing and, secondly, that during the course of
the disturbance he was concerned in a concerted act of indiscipline by being on
the segregation unit and 'A' Wing roofs with others. Those charges were heard before
the board of visitors, and they imposed punishments involving loss of privileges of
various kinds. That case is typical of all seven before us for present enquiry.   *c*

The charges having been framed, the various prisoners were confronted in various
prisons all over the country by the board of visitors from Hull. By that means the
same tribunal dealt with the whole, although they were dealt with in several different
places. The universal complaint of those before us today is that in the course of dealing
with them the visitors from Hull Prison failed to comply with the rules of natural
justice.   *d*

In the ordinary way that would immediately involve a consideration of the details
of the hearing before the board of visitors, but that is not appropriate in fact because
counsel for the board of visitors took an intial point to the effect that certiorari, which
is the remedy principally sought by the applicants, would not go to a prison board of
visitors in respect of their failure to comply with the rules of natural justice in making
an adjudication; and that is the issue, and the only issue, we are concerned to deal   *e*
with at the present stage.

The board of visitors is the creature of the Prison Act 1952. Section 6 provides:

> '(1) Rules made under section forty-seven of this Act shall provide for the
> constitution, for prisons to which persons may be committed directly by a court,
> of visiting committees consisting of justices of the peace appointed at such times,   *f*
> in such manner and for such periods as may be prescribed by the rules, by such
> courts of quarter sessions for counties or benches of magistrates for boroughs as
> the Secretary of State may by order direct.
>
> '(2) The Secretary of State shall appoint for every prison other than a prison
> mentioned in subsection (1) of this section a board of visitors of whom not less
> than two shall be justices of the peace.'
>   *g*

As we shall see in a moment, the powers of the board of visitors are diverse, but
they include disciplinary powers, and if we turn to the only other section of the Act
to which one needs to refer, s 47, provision is made for the Secretary of State to make
rules for the regulation and management of prisons, remand centres, detention
centres etc. By s 47(2) it is provided: *h*

> 'Rules made under this section shall make provision for ensuring that a person
> who is charged with any offence under the rules shall be given a proper oppor-
> tunity of presenting his case.'

Thus at an early stage in the language of the statute appears an oblique reference to
what we have collectively called the rules of natural justice.

That is the Act, and it is backed up by comprehensive rules, those appropriate to the   *j*
present time being the 1964 rules. The statutory instrument contains a section headed
'Offences against discipline'. Rule 47 details these special prison offences and it sets out

---

1   SI 1964 No 388

in 21 numbered paragraphs what one might call the prison disciplinary offences. Then
a rr 48, 49, 50, 51 and 52 all deal with the manner in which a disposal under these rules
is to take place. One finds, first of all, that there is power for the governor, within
certain limits, to impose his own penalties out of the range to which I have referred.
Then further provision is made in r 51 for more serious offences where the governor
cannot or will not deal with them alone, whereby, when a prisoner is charged with
such offences as escaping or attempting to escape, the governor informs the Secretary
of State and, unless otherwise directed, refers the charge to the board of visitors.
b It is at this point that the board of visitors come in in regard to disciplinary matters.
If the case is too serious for the governor, he refers it to the board of visitors, and they
take over the disciplinary charge themselves. There is a further provision for especially grave offences. There is a now obsolete rule about corporal punishment.
Rule 56 has been the subject of a good deal of debate in the course of the hearing,
c and I must mention it. Rule 56(1) provides:

'The Secretary of State may remit a disciplinary award or may mitigate it
either by reducing it or by substituting another award which is, in his opinion,
less severe.'

Rule 56(2), in its original form, provides:

d 'A disciplinary award, other than forfeiture of remission or postponement of
eligibility for release, may be remitted or mitigated by the person, committee or
board by whom the award was made.'

Importance was attached in the course of argument to that rule because it shows
there is further authority beyond the board of visitors, and it has been argued that
e that is precisely how it should be construed. I choose to regard it as a further right
of appeal, as it were, to the Secretary of State who can act on the appeal within the
limits that I have already mentioned.
Those are the visitors wearing their disciplinary hats, if one may use that phrase.
They come in again for a variety of other purposes in a number of other rules, beginning with r 88. I need not read r 88, but r 89 deals with visiting committees, and r 90
f deals with the appointment of members of visiting committees. When we get down
to r 92 we come across the board of visitors, which was the appropriate body at Hull
at the time in question. Rule 92(1) provides:

'A member of the board of visitors for a prison appointed by the Secretary of
State under section 6(2) of the Prison Act 1952 shall hold office for three years, or
such less period as the Secretary of State may appoint.'
g
We were told by counsel for the board of visitors (this is the only piece of information I am conscious of using which did not come from the papers in this case) that
in Hull at the relevant time there were 12 prison visitors, and so one immediately
realises that they must have become fairly familiar with the prison and its characters
over a period of time. The frequency of their attendances is dealt with in the
h 1964 rules and it is by no means a sinecure to be a member of the board of visitors.
For example, r 93(1) provides:

'The board of visitors for a prison shall meet at the prison once a month or, if
they resolve for reasons specified in the resolution that less frequent meetings
are sufficient, not fewer than eight times in twelve months.'

j Then provision is made for minutes and other matters of business like that. Under
r 94 we find the general duties of committees and boards:

'(1) The board of visitors for a prison shall satisfy themselves as to the state
of the prison premises, the administration of the prison and the treatment of the
prisoners.

'(2) The board shall inquire into and report upon any matter into which the Secretary of State asks them to inquire.

'(3) The board shall direct the attention of the governor to any matter which calls for his attention, and shall report to the Secretary of State any matter which they consider it expedient to report.'

So the matter goes on, and one visualises, as I say, constant visiting of the prison by these ladies and gentlemen, two of whom are justices of the peace and others who may or may not be similarly qualified.

So much for the board of visitors. They duly met, as I have already said, in a number of prisons about the country, and eventually dealt with some 180 complaints arising out of the riot. We must focus our attention from now onwards in the judgment entirely on counsel for the board of visitors' preliminary point. He says in the plainest terms that certiorari will not go to a board of visitors to quash a decision of the kind with which we are concerned here.

For quite a long time it seemed to me that the argument was going to turn on the fact that remission for a prisoner is a matter of grace and not a matter of right, and that we were going to be concerned with distinctions of that sort arising out of the precise form of order made. But at the end of the day I do not think that the argument put forward on behalf of the Crown by counsel for the board of visitors turns on whether we are dealing with rights or privileges because it seems to me that the argument would be equally effective in regard to either.

One must start this question of whether certiorari will or will not go with a recognition of the fact that there is not, and one may hope never will be, a precise and detailed definition of the exact sort of order which can be subject to certiorari. If we ever get to the day when one turns up a book to see what the limit of the rights of certiorari is it will mean that the right has become rigid, and that would be a great pity. Therefore, we approach it today, in my judgment, on the basis that there are no firm boundaries, and one has to look to such clear, useful and helpful pointers as, with the assistance of counsel, we have been able to derive from the authorities.

Let us look, first of all, at the arguments for certiorari going on the facts of this case. One looks at the circumstances and one visualises the board of visitors sitting very much like a bench of magistrates, one would think, and the applicant prisoner standing before them. With that mental picture, one can say it looks as though this is a case for certiorari. Instinctively one would think that this would be within the category to which the order applies.

That is reinforced by the view, which I hold at any rate, that the act which the board of visitors perform under this jurisdiction is a judicial act. One knows nowadays that it is not necessary to show a judicial act in order to get certiorari, but if the order is a judicial act it makes it that much easier to justify the making of the order. I should have thought that there was no question but that this was a judicial act for present purposes.

Thus fortified, I would go next to the House of Lords decision in *Ridge v Baldwin*[1] because this is in a sense where the modern approach to certiorari is to be found. There is one passage in Lord Reid's speech to which I would like to refer. He is dealing with the well known passage of Atkin LJ in *R v Electricity Comrs, ex parte London Electricity Joint Committee Co*[2] in 1924. Lord Reid said[3]:

'The matter has been further complicated by what I believe to be a misunderstanding of a much quoted passage in the judgment of ATKIN, L.J., in *R. v. Electricity Comrs.*[4]. He said: "The operation of the writs [of prohibition and certiorari] has

---

1   [1963] 2 All ER 66, [1964] AC 40
2   [1924] 1 KB 171, [1923] All ER Rep 150
3   [1963] 2 All ER 66 at 77, [1964] AC 40 at 74
4   [1924] 1 KB 171 at 205, [1923] All ER Rep 150 at 161

a
extended to control the proceedings of bodies which do not claim to be and
would not be recognised as, courts of justice. Whenever any body of persons
having legal authority to determine questions affecting the rights of subjects, and
having the duty to act judicially, act in excess of their legal authority, they are
subject to the controlling jurisdiction of the King's Bench Division exercised in
these writs." A gloss was put on this by LORD HEWART, C.J., in *R. v. Legislative
Committee of the Church Assembly*[1].'

b
Then he went on to deal with the facts of that case which are of no interest to us here,
and came to a few words of Salter J. Lord Reid said[2]:

'SALTER, J., put it in a few lines[3]: "The person or body to whom these writs are
to go must be a judicial body in this sense, that it has power to determine and
decide, and the power carries with it, of necessity, the duty to act judicially. I
c
think that the Church Assembly has no such power and, therefore, no such duty.'

Then he went on to deal with Lord Hewart CJ's gloss again, and I leave that passage
unread, and go on to the passage where he said[4]:

'I have quoted the whole of this passage because it is typical of what has been
said in several subsequent cases. If LORD HEWART, C.J., meant that it is never
d
enough that a body simply has a duty to determine what the rights of an individual should be, but that there must always be something more to impose on it
a duty to act judicially before it can be found to observe the principles of natural
justice, then that appears to me impossible to reconcile with the earlier authorities.'

Hence, as I say, I approach this on the footing that the board of visitors have a judicial
e
task to perform and proceeded to perform it.
I also proceed to a conclusion on this question keeping very much in mind what was
said in one of the more recent cases in this court concerned with the availability of
certiorari, and that is the case which first recognised that the Criminal Injuries Compensation Board was subject to control in this court by the prerogative orders. The
case is *R v Criminal Injuries Compensation Board, ex parte Lain*[5], and the passage I want
f
to refer to comes in the judgment of Lord Parker CJ where he said[6]:

'The position as I see it is that the exact limits of the ancient remedy by way of
certiorari have never been and ought not to be specifically defined. They have
varied from time to time, being extended to meet changing conditions. At one
time the writ only went to an inferior court. Later its ambit was extended to
statutory tribunals determining a lis inter partes. Later again it extended to cases
g
where there was no lis in the strict sense of the word, but where immediate or
subsequent rights of a citizen were affected. The only constant limits throughout
were that the body concerned was under a duty to act judicially and that it was
performing a public duty. Private or domestic tribunals have always been outside
the scope of certiorari . . .'

h
I mention that particularly because, if one wanted encouragement to extend the
scope of certiorari, one could hardly find a more powerful phrase to constitute that
encouragement than the one which I have just read.
What is to be said on the other side? In this case there seems to me to be one thing,
and one thing only, which is said on the other side, and that is that despite the prima

j
1   [1928] 1 KB 411 at 415, 416, [1927] All ER Rep 696 at 699
2   [1963] 2 All ER 66 at 77, [1964] AC 40 at 74
3   [1928] 1 KB 411 at 419, [1927] All ER Rep 696 at 701
4   [1963] 2 All ER 66 at 77, [1964] AC 40 at 75
5   [1967] 2 All ER 770, [1967] 2 QB 864
6   [1967] 2 All ER 770 at 778, cf [1967] 2 QB 864 at 882

facie case, as it were, already made out for saying that certiorari will go, yet there is an
exception, so the board of visitors would have us say, which prevents certiorari from *a*
going even though the circumstances otherwise appear entirely suitable and appropriate for it. That exception is where the order under challenge is an order made in
private, disciplinary proceedings where there is some closed body, and a body which
enjoys its own form of discipline and its own rules, and where there is a power to
impose sanctions within the scope of those rules donated as part of the formation of
the body itself. If one gets that situation, it is possible, in my judgment, on the *b*
authorities to say that certiorari will not go even though in other respects the case is
suitable for it.

The principal authority which moves me here is *Ex parte Fry*[1] which is a decision
of this court presided over by Lord Goddard CJ. The applicant applying for certiorari
was a fireman who had refused to clean the jacket of his superior officer, and that
gave rise to a certain amount of trouble, a disciplinary order, and an attempt to *c*
quash the order by certiorari. The passage which is of general concern and interest,
and to which therefore I want to refer, is in the judgment of Lord Goddard CJ where
he said[2]:

'It seems to me impossible to say that a chief officer of a force which is governed
by discipline, such as a fire brigade is, in exercising disciplinary authority over a *d*
member of the force, acting either judicially or quasi-judicially, any more than a
schoolmaster is when he is exercising disciplinary powers over his pupils. It is
true that there is an Act of Parliament, the Fire Services Act, 1947, but so there
is an Army Act, and there are the Queen's Regulations under the Army Act.
Under the Army Act a court-martial can be set up to deal with certain offences,
and a commanding officer has power to deal with certain disciplinary offences in *e*
the orderly room; there he is not sitting as a court but as an officer administering
discipline. I have never heard it suggested that this court can issue certiorari to
bring up his order, nor do I know of any case with regard to police officers, who
are also dealt with under regulations in matters of discipline, in which this court
has ever yet purported to exercise control over those bodies by the issue of the
writ of certiorari. Certiorari goes to courts, or to something which can fairly be *f*
said to be a court.'

The principle there that domestic discipline in the form of a disciplinary body is
something for the officer charged with the duty of maintaining discipline and not
something for the courts is a principle which, in my judgment, we should adhere to
and not allow to be wasted away. It is in no way inconsistent with the general
approach to certiorari. It sets aside those particular situations of disciplinary bodies *g*
and would, and does, in my judgment, open the way to refusing certiorari when an
order of such a disciplinary body is under review.

At first I thought this was a principle which would apply only to the governor. I
saw the governor equated with the commanding officer of the regiment in Lord
Goddard CJ's judgment, and it was not until the argument had progressed some
way that it seemed to me right that we should include in this principle the board of *h*
visitors. The reason why I think it is right to include them is because I think that
when they are sitting as a disciplinary body they are part of the disciplinary machinery
of the prison. I reject entirely any suggestion that the governor's decision should be
the subject of certiorari, and I cannot see myself how, if the governor is left out, the
board of visitors can be put in. I base that conclusion on the intimate character of the
relationship between the board of visitors and the prison, and on my understanding *j*
of the situation as showing that the visitors are an active part of the disciplinary
machine and not merely strangers brought in from outside to deal with a particular

1   [1954] 2 All ER 118, [1954] 1 WLR 730
2   [1954] 1 WLR 730 at 733, cf [1954] 2 All ER 118 at 119

charge or breach of discipline when it occurs. I am reinforced by the fact that there are traces in the European Commission on Human Rights of a similar approach to the existence of disciplinary remedies which are outside the normal remedies such as certiorari. Furthermore, we have been shown an authority[1] in Australia which also seems to me to recognise that there is a difference between the discipline of the unit, as it were, and other matters which may arise under certiorari.

I am conscious of the fact that Lord Denning MR is so right, if I may say so, in his judgment and the observation he made about this problem in *Becker v Home Office*[2] where he said:

'If the courts were to entertain actions by disgruntled prisoners, the governor's life would be made intolerable. The discipline of the prison would be undermined. The Prison Rules are regulatory directions only. Even if they are not observed, they do not give rise to a cause of action.'

I respectfully agree with that, and I think that is the last and final consideration which I would put forward as justifying the conclusion that certiorari in the present instance should not go.

CUMMING-BRUCE LJ. I agree and for the reasons stated by Lord Widgery CJ. I am moved by the consideration that by s 1 of the Prison Act 1952 all powers and jurisdiction in relation to prison and prisoners before the commencement of the Prison Act 1877 which were exercisable by any other authority shall be exercised by the Secretary of State. By s 47 the Secretary of State shall make rules for the regulation and management of prison and other penal establishments, and for the classification, treatment, employment, discipline and control of persons required to be detained therein. By s 6 boards of visitors are to be appointed with functions therein set out, functions that bring them close to the life of the prison.

Throughout my lifetime I have derived a growing delight as I have observed the rule of law extended to control institutions and individuals exercising public powers by the great writ of certiorari, the use of which has been steadily extending as is pointed out in the authorities cited by Lord Widgery CJ. I have no hesitation in recognising the activities of a board of visitors such as is disclosed in these papers as being activities of a judicial character leading, as they do, to an adjudication, a word used in the Prison Rules 1964 themselves. So I started certainly from the position that this was the sort of activity to which the rule of law from this court would extend by the writ of certiorari

But as the authorities were cited to us (and we have been taken extensively and rightly through the authorities, and referred to the textbooks that try to summarise their effect), it gradually became clearer and clearer to me that as a matter of common sense there would be very grave public disadvantages in allowing the writ to go either to a prison governor or to a board of visitors when exercising disciplinary functions.

A prison is an organisation wherein the officers under the governor's command seek to control the inmates, a body of men who are not there voluntarily and who, thanks to defects of character or the frustrations of life in confinement, are liable to acts of indiscipline and resentment of authority. Those responsible for controlling penal institutions have a task that no one readily envies.

Where breaches of discipline take place, as in a regiment in the army or in a ship in the Royal Navy, it is necessary that the commanding officer take disciplinary action quickly, firmly and justly, and that the disciplinary sanction that he determines, if any, shall be put into effect at once. Nothing is worse in an institution subject to discipline than that after a disciplinary sanction has been imposed it should be left

---

1 *Booth v Dillon (No 3)* [1977] VR 143
2 [1972] 2 All ER 676 at 682, [1972] 2 QB 407 at 418

action taken by the board of visitors. The 1964 rules themselves provide that discipinary measures shall be instituted as quickly as possible. In the case of the governor they have to be taken the very next day.

Against that background, I am satisfied that I recognise in the institution called a prison, being an institution operating pursuant to the 1952 Act and under the 1964 rules, the kind of institution in respect of which judicial control pursuant to a writ of certiorari would be inconsistent with the kind of disciplinary control that I find in the Act and the rules. It appears to me, after trying to discipline my own thought by looking at the great variety of different kinds of institution to which certiorari has or has not been applied, that the activities of a board of visitors and a prison governor in relation to the discipline of a prison are matters that Parliament sufficiently clearly did not intend to be subject to the control of this court as well as the Secretary of State.

There were many other arguments canvassed, but I hope it will not be thought disrespectful to the interesting submissions of all counsel on both sides if I say no more than give the reason that at the end of the day has brought me to my decision.

PARK J: I agree for the reasons given in both judgments.

Applications dismissed.

Solicitors: *George E Baker & Co*, Guildford (for the applicant St Germain); *Philip Hamer & Co*, Hull (for the applicant Reed); *Bindman & Partners* (for the applicant Saxton); *Douglas-Mann & Co*, agents for *Patterson, Glenton & Stracey-Donald Harvey & Co*, South Shields (for the applicants Anderson and Pike); *Hilary Kitchin* (for the applicant Rajah); *Bindman & Partners*, agents for *T I Clough*, Bradford (for the applicant Lennon); *Treasury Solicitor*.

N P Metcalfe Esq　Barrister.

P B Frost Ltd v Green

CHANCERY DIVISION
SLADE J
24th NOVEMBER 1977

Mortgage – Action by mortgagee for possession – Jurisdiction of High Court – Net annual value of property for rating – Property not liable to be rated – County court having exclusive jurisdiction if net annual value for rating less than county court limit – Mortgaged property comprising two hereditaments one of which not liable to be rated and the other having net annual value for rating below county court limit – Net annual value for rating of property not consisting of one or more hereditaments having separate net annual value – Property to be taken to have net annual value for rating equal to its value by the year – Whether annual value by the year of hereditament not liable to be rated to be taken as its net annual value for rating – Whether combined net annual value for rating of both hereditaments exceeding county court limit – Administration of Justice Act 1970, s 37(1) – County Courts Act 1959, ss 48, 200(2)(b).

By a legal charge dated 19th January 1977 the defendant, in consideration of a loan to him of £40,000 from the plaintiffs, charged by way of legal mortgage two separate parcels of land, one containing a freehold dwelling-house which he occupied and 12 acres or so of adjoining land, and the other some 218 acres of freehold agricultural land. He covenanted to repay the principal money lent on 19th April 1977 and to pay interest in equal half-yearly payments in January and July each year. The defendant failed to comply with a notice to repay the principal sum or to repay the first instalment of interest when it fell due. The plaintiffs took out a summons in the High Court claiming, inter alia, payment of all money due to them, and possession of the two parcels. The net annual value for rating of the parcel containing the dwelling-house was £742. The parcel containing the agricultural land however was not liable to be rated or included in any valuation list for rating purposes, although its value by the year was in excess of £258. It was contended on behalf of the defendant that the net annual value for rating of both parcels was £742 and therefore, under s 37(1)^a of the Administration of Justice Act 1970 and s 48(1)^b of the County Courts Act 1959, the High Court had no jurisdiction to hear the summons since the net annual value for rating of the mortgaged property was below the county court limit of £1,000.

Held – For the purposes of determining the county court's jurisdiction where a property comprised two hereditaments, one of which was not liable to be rated and therefore had no net annual value for rating, the net annual value for rating of the hereditament not liable to be rated was to be assessed by reference to s 200(2)(b)^c of the 1959 Act since the property was one which did 'not consist of one or more hereditaments having . . . a separate net annual value for rating'. Accordingly that part of the property which did not consist of a hereditament having a separate net annual value for rating was to be taken to have a net annual value for rating equal to its value by the year. Since the annual value by the year of the 218 acres was in excess of £258 it followed that, for the purpose of s 37(1) of the 1970 Act and s 48(1) of the 1959 Act, the mortgaged property had a net annual value for rating greater than £1,000 and therefore the High Court had jurisdiction to hear the summons (see p 211 e to h and p 212 b to d and g to j, post).

Notes

For jurisdiction of the courts in actions for the recovery of land, see 10 Halsbury's Laws (4th Edn) para 81, and for cases on the subject, see 13 Digest (Reissue) 425, 3536-3540.

For the Administration of Justice Act 1970, s 37(1), see 40 Halsbury's Statutes (3rd Edn) 1061.

For the County Courts Act 1959, s 200(2), see 7 ibid 423.

Case referred to in judgment

Trustees of Manchester Unity Life Insurance Collecting Society v Sadler [1974] 2 All ER 410, [1974] 1 WLR 770, 28 P & CR 10, 13 Digest (Reissue) 425, 3539.

Procedure summons

The plaintiffs, P B Frost Ltd, were mortgagees under a legal charge dated 19th January 1977 made between the defendant, William James Green, and the plaintiffs whereby the defendant had charged to the plaintiffs by way of legal mortgage two hereditaments, (1) the freehold dwelling-house occupied by the defendant known as Pickwell Manor, Melton Mowbray, Leicestershire, together with 12 acres or thereabouts of adjoining land other than a cottage known as Butler's Cottage, and (2) 218 acres or thereabouts of freehold agricultural land at Pickwell in Leicestershire, to secure the sum of £40,000 lent by the plaintiffs to the defendant. By an originating summons dated 29th July 1977, the plaintiffs sought, inter alia, payment of all money due, foreclosure or sale, and delivery up to them of vacant possession. At the hearing before the master, it was submitted on behalf of the defendant that, having regard to s 37 of the Administration of Justice Act 1970, the High Court had no jurisdiction to deal with the case, and the master accordingly adjourned it into court as a procedure summons. The facts are set out in the judgment.

C P F Rimer for the plaintiffs.
Stephen Hunt for the defendant.

---

a Section 37(1) is set out at p 209 *h*, post
b Section 48(1) is set out at p 210 *d*, post
c Section 200 is set out at p 211 *b* to *d*, post

SLADE J. This is an originating summons under which the plaintiffs claim possession as mortgagees of certain land against the defendant. Two questions are raised for my decision today. The first is: has this court jurisdiction to hear the case at all? It is the defendant's contention that only the county court has jursidiction to hear it. Secondly, if this court has jurisdiction to hear it, should the defendant be granted a stay of the order for possession to which, I think, it is common ground that the plaintiffs would otherwise be entitled? This judgment is directed solely to the first point, though the narrative will touch on some matters which are relevant only to the second.

The plaintiffs' title arises under a legal charge dated 19th January 1977 which was granted in their favour by the defendant. By this charge, in consideration of a loan of £40,000, the defendant charged by way of legal mortgage two separate hereditaments, namely a dwelling-house occupied by the defendant and known as Pickwell Manor, near Melton Mowbray, Leicestershire together with 12 acres or so of adjoining land and also a small cottage known as Butler's Cottage, of which possession is not now sought, and secondly, 218 acres or thereabouts of freehold agricultural land at Pickwell in Leicestershire, which comprises no dwelling-house. The first mentioned hereditaments, with the exception of the cottage, are shown coloured red on a plan annexed to the originating summons and I shall refer to them as 'the red land'.

By the legal charge, the defendant covenanted with the plaintiff that he would repay the principal money lent on 19th April 1977 and would pay interest at the rate of 17 per cent on the loan by equal half-yearly payments on 19th January and July in each year.

On 24th May 1977 the plaintiffs, acting by their former solicitors, gave written notice to the defendant requiring him to repay the principal sum and interest owing in respect of it, but this notice has not been complied with. On 19th July a first instalment of interest was due but this was not paid. On 29th July the plaintiffs issued the present originating summons, claiming first payment and also claiming, among other things, foreclosure or sale and also delivery up to them of vacant possession of the red land and of the 218 acres. Butler's Cottage, to which I have referred, although comprised in the mortgage, is subject to a tenancy and the plaintiffs do not seek to disturb that tenancy.

The application for possession was in due course supported by an affidavit sworn by Mr P B Frost, a director of the plaintiffs, in which he stated among other things that the amount due in respect of principal and interest was in the aggregate £43,000. It is now common ground, I think, that the amount due today is £45,793·96. Mr Frost also stated in this affidavit that the net annual value for rating of the manor house is £742. He continued:

'The mortgaged property also comprises some 218 acres of agricultural land, and although that land as such is not rated, its value of [sic] by the year for the purposes of Section 200(2) of the County Courts Act 1959 must on any footing be well in excess of £258·00. and accordingly I respectfully submit that this is a case where the County Court has no jurisdiction to deal with this application.'

The relevance of the figure of £258, as will appear, is that £258 when added to £742, makes £1,000.

The originating summons was served on the defendant in early August and a first hearing took place before Master Heward on 19th September, when counsel appeared for both parties. On that occasion, I understand, counsel who appeared for the defendant but had only been very recently instructed, took no point in relation to jurisdiction, but sought an adjournment on the ground that his client hoped to be able to redeem the mortgage within three weeks or so. Master Heward adjourned the matter to 14th October, with a view to giving the defendant time to redeem, and gave certain directions with regard to the filing of evidence. On 29th September a Mr Brian John Frost, a solicitor, swore an affidavit on behalf of the defendant, deposing to the fact that the defendant received in August 1977 an offer of approximately £700 per acre for the 218 acres, but was reluctant to accept it, since it would have meant the loss of his livelihood. He confirmed that the offer still remained open to him but that the defendant was determined, if possible, to enter into an agreement for the sale and lease back of the farm, which would enable him to continue farming. Then on 13th October an articled clerk in the firm of the defendant's solicitors swore an affidavit, to which he exhibited copies of the annual entries in the valuation list of the rating district comprising the land which is the subject of this present application. These entries show Pickwell Manor as including a house and two garages and as having a net annual value for rating of £742, but they contain no reference to the 218 acres. The deponent to this affidavit said: 'I can confirm that the farm land and buildings of approximately 218 acres, which the plaintiffs have requested possession, has a rateable value of nil.' In fact, I do not think this statement was strictly correct. The legal position, as I understand it, is that the 218 acres are not liable to be rated or to be included in any valuation list for rating purposes, because they comprise solely agricultural land (see s 26(1) of the General Rate Act 1967). It is not, I think, strictly accurate to say that land which is not liable to be rated at all has a 'rateable value of nil'.

On 14th October the restored originating summons came before Master Chamberlain. By that time no evidence had been filed showing that completion of any sale or sale and lease back of the 218 acres, as previously contemplated by the defendant, had taken place. The point taken by the defendant's counsel at that hearing was a quite different one. He submitted that, having regard to s 37 of the Administration of Justice Act 1970, the High Court had no jurisdiction to deal with the case at all. At the end of that hearing the master adjourned the matter into court as a procedure summons and that is how it comes before me today. He was, however, informed of certain further negotiations for sale and lease back and, in the light of that, he directed that the case should not be listed for 21 days and adjourned the whole of it so that, if the High Court had jurisdiction, any decision on suspension would be before the court.

To complete the references to the evidence, a further affidavit has been sworn by the defendant, on 17th November, in which he refers among other things to certain further offers which he has had for the purchase of the 218 acres, including one offer to purchase them at a price of £800 per acre on condition that the land is sold with vacant possession. No such offer, however, has yet been accepted by him.

It is, I think, common ground that the plaintiffs' title to possession has been made out in all the circumstances, subject only to the question of jurisdiction and to any question of suspending the operation of any order which it may see fit to make or postponing the date for delivery of possession. Section 37(1) of the Administration of Justice Act 1970 provides:

'Where a mortgage of land consists of or includes a dwelling-house and no part of the land is situated in Greater London, then, subject to subsection (2) below, if a county court has jurisdiction by virtue of section 48 of the County Courts Act 1959 or section 38 of this Act to hear and determine an action in which the mortgagee under that mortgage claims possession of the mortgaged property, no court other than a county court shall have jurisdiction to hear and determine that action.'

On the face of things, s 37(2) might appear to offer some assistance to the plaintiffs, since it provides that the section shall not apply to 'an action for foreclosure or sale in which a claim for possession of the mortgaged property is also made'. The claim for relief in the originating summons, as drafted, does include, inter alia, a claim for 'foreclosure or sale'. Walton J, however, in *Trustees of Manchester Unity Life Insurance Collecting Society v Sadler*[1] decided that the phrase 'an action for foreclosure'

1   [1974] 2 All ER 410, [1974] 1 WLR 770

within the meaning of s 37(2) meant an action in which the plaintiff was genuinely seeking the remedy of foreclosure. In the face of that decision, counsel for the plaintiffs accepted that the subsection would not avail him or his client, bearing in mind that foreclosure or sale was not the primary relief sought. Accordingly, attention falls to be focussed on s 37(1) of the 1970 Act.

The scheme of s 37(1), subject only to sub-s (2), is that the High Court has no jurisdiction to hear and determine any action in which a mortgagee of land claims possession of the mortgaged property in any case where three conditions are fulfilled, namely (i) the mortgage consists of or includes a dwelling-house; (ii) no part of the land is situate in Greater London; (iii) a county court has jurisdiction by virtue of s 48 of the County Courts Act 1959 or s 38 of the Administration of Justice Act 1970 to hear and determine the case. As counsel for the defendant pointed out, s 37(1) is mandatory in its terms. There is no dispute on the facts that the first two of the three conditions which I have mentioned are fulfilled here. The question arises in relation to the third. Counsel for the defendant places no reliance on s 38 of the 1970 Act. He claims, however, that the county court has jurisdiction to hear and determine the present proceedings by virtue of s 48 of the 1959 Act and accordingly that the third of the three conditions is fulfilled, just as much as the first and second, so as to deprive the High Court of jurisdiction.

I turn to s 48(1) of the 1959 Act which as amended by the Administration of Justice Act 1973, s 6 and Sch 2 reads:

'A county court shall have jurisdiction to hear and determine any action for the recovery of land where the net annual value for rating of the land in question is not above the county court limit.'

The county court limit referred to was fixed at £1,000 by the Administration of Justice Act 1973, s 6 and Sch 2, and remains, I understand, at that figure.

As will have appeared, the subject-matter of the present proceedings comprises first the red land, which has a 'net annual value for rating' of £742, and secondly the 218 acres, which strictly cannot be said to have any 'net annual value for rating', because they are not liable to be rated. This illustrates a problem which s 48(1) on the face of it raises because, according to its terms, it appears to be contemplating only land which has a 'net annual value for rating'. On its face and if read in isolation the section raises two obvious questions. First, how is it to be applied if the property which is the subject-matter of the action is not separately rated, but forms part of a larger piece of land, which *is* separately rated and thus does have a 'net annual value for rating'? Secondly, and even more significantly, how is the section to be applied, if the relevant property is not liable to be rated at all?

Touching on the second question, s 48(1) appears on its face to be fraught with potential anomalies. Let me take the case of an action relating solely to agricultural land, which as such is not liable to be rated. If one were to read the section in isolation, there would, I think, be two possible ways of applying it.

First, one could say that if the property was not liable to be rated at all, then its 'net annual value for rating' was nil. As I have indicated, however, such a construction would in my judgment involve attributing to the legislature an inaccurate use of terminology, in that there is a difference between a property not being liable to be rated at all and having a nil net annual value for rating. Furthermore, and perhaps more remarkably, this construction would mean that the county court would have absolutely limitless jurisdiction where the subject-matter of an action for the recovery of land comprised exclusively property not liable to be rated. Simply for example, if the mortgaged property solely comprised agricultural land worth £5 million, it would fall within the county court's jurisdiction.

The other possible way of construing s 48(1), if read in isolation, would be to say that, where the land in question is not liable to be rated, it necessarily has *no* 'net annual value for rating' within the meaning of the subsection; that therefore the

section is incapable of application to such land; and that therefore an action solely
for recovery of land which is not liable to be rated can never fall within the jurisdiction
conferred by s 48 of the 1959 Act.

Both these conclusions would seem so extraordinary and anomalous that common
sense would suggest that they could not be right. One therefore seeks to find elsewhere in the 1959 Act itself the answer to the problems raised. The answer in my
judgment, as counsel for the plaintiffs has submitted, is to be found in s 200, as amended by the Administration of Justice Act 1973, s 6 and Sch 2, which I should read in
full:

'(1) For the purposes of this Act, the net annual value for rating of any property
shall be determined as at the time when the relevant proceedings are commenced,
except in a case where it is otherwise expressly provided, and, subject to the
following subsection, by reference to the valuation list in force at the time in
question.

'(2) Where the property of which the value is in question does not consist of one
or more hereditaments having at the time in question a separate net annual
value for rating, the property or such part of it as does not so consist (a) shall
for the purpose of entitling a county court to exercise jurisdiction (but not for
any other purpose), be taken to have a net annual value for rating not exceeding
that of any such hereditament of which at the time in question it forms part; and
(b) subject to paragraph (a) above, shall be taken to have a net annual value for
rating equal to its value by the year.'

Section 200(1) is of no assistance or relevance in considering a case where all or part of
the land in question, such as the 218 acres in the present case, is not liable to be rated
at all, because the machinery for which it provides contemplates reference to a
'valuation list'. Section 200(2), however, in my judgment, does provide the answer
to the problems that would otherwise arise in attempting to apply s 48 in the untidy
case where the property sought to be recovered does not consist of one or more
separate hereditaments each having a separate 'net annual value for rating'. Paragraph (a) of s 200(2) covers the case where the relevant property or part of it does
not have a separate 'net annual value for rating', but forms part of a larger hereditament which does have such a value. It provides that in such a case, solely for purposes
of entitling a county court to exercise jurisdiction, the relevant property or part of it
shall be deemed to have a 'net annual value for rating' not exceeding that of the larger
hereditament of which it forms part. Paragraph (b) then goes on to cover any other
case where the property sought to be recovered does not consist of one or more
separate hereditaments each having a separate 'net annual value for rating'. In
particular, in my judgment, it covers the case where the property sought to be
recovered is or includes property which does not have a net annual value for rating
at all, because it is not liable to be rated.

Counsel for the defendant, in his ingenious argument, submitted that the legislature
in referring in s 200(2) to 'hereditaments' was referring solely to hereditaments liable
to be rated and that there was nothing in the subsection which indicated that any part
of s 200 is capable of applying to property which can have no 'net annual value for
rating'. He thus submitted that the present application concerns only one 'hereditament', within the meaning of s 200(2), namely the manor and its appurtenances, and
since they have a 'net annual value for rating' of only £742, the county court has
jurisdiction to deal with this action, under s 48(1) of the 1959 Act, which thus excludes
jurisdiction in the High Court in view of s 37(1) of the 1970 Act. I do not feel able to
accept this argument. It involves attributing a meaning to the word 'hereditaments'
in the context of s 200(2) far narrower than its natural meaning. Furthermore,
the word hereditament is defined in s 201 as including 'both a corporeal and an
incorporeal hereditament'; this definition contains no reference to rating purposes at
all. It is expressed to apply 'unless the context otherwise requires'. In my judgment,

however, the context does not otherwise require in s 200(2) of the 1959 Act. Indeed, in my judgment, the context positively requires that 'hereditaments' in s 200(2) should bear this ordinary meaning. For, by attributing to the word its ordinary meaning, it is possible to produce a consistent and coherent pattern, in interpreting ss 48 and 200 in conjunction with one another, and thereby avoid the two alternative anomalous results that would have otherwise ensued in the application of s 48, namely that, in the case of actions to recover land which was not liable to be rated, the county court's jurisdiction would be either unlimited in amount or would not exist at all.

I therefore conclude that s 200(2)(*b*) is apt to cover a case, such as the present, where the property in question comprises two hereditaments, one which is liable to be rated and the other which is not so liable and therefore, apart from s 200(2)(*b*), has no net annual value for rating.

Applying this interpretation to the facts of the case, what is the position? The application relates to two hereditaments, one being the red land and the other the 218 acres, which apart from s 200 have no net annual value for rating. The red land has a net annual value for rating of £742. The net annual value for rating of the 218 acres in accordance with s 200(2)(*b*) falls to be treated as being 'equal to its value by the year'. The phrase 'its value by the year' is not defined in the 1959 Act, but I would think that, in general terms, the meaning that should be attributed to the phrase would be one at least very similar to the formula provided by s 19(3) of the General Rate Act 1967 in relation to hereditaments other than houses or other non-industrial buildings. This reads:

'The net annual value of any other hereditament shall be an amount equal to the rent at which it is estimated the hereditament might reasonably be expected to let from year to year if the tenant undertook to pay all usual tenant's rates and taxes and to bear the cost of the repairs and insurance and the other expenses, if any, necessary to maintain the hereditament in a state to command that rent.'

There has, however, been no full argument before me as to the meaning of this phrase and I do not think it is necessary to pursue the point, for this short reason.

Mr P B Frost, in a passage from his affidavit which I have already quoted, has already deposed to the fact that the value of the 218 acres 'by the year' (by which he must have meant for the purposes of s 200(2)(*b*) of the 1959 Act) must be well in 'excess of £258'. This allegation has not been denied in any evidence sworn on behalf of the defendant. Furthermore, as I think counsel for the defendant sensibly accepts, for practical purposes it would probably be idle to deny it, bearing in mind that the court is here dealing with 218 acres of agricultural land, as to which the defendant has received according to his own evidence an offer to purchase at a price of £800 per acre.

In all the circumstances, I am satisfied that the 'net annual value for rating' of the 218 acres for the purposes of defining the county court's jurisdiction under ss 200(2)(*b*) and 48 of the County Courts Act 1959 must be and is substantially more than £258. Accordingly, I find that the 'net annual value for rating', for the purpose of those two sections, of the lands which are the subject of this application totals in the aggregate more than £1,000. I therefore conclude that the county court does not have jurisdiction to hear this application under s 48 of the 1959 Act. Accordingly, I must reject the defendant's submission that the jurisdiction of the High Court is excluded by s 37 of the Administration of Justice Act 1970. In my judgment, this court has jurisdiction to hear this case.

Order accordingly.

Solicitors: *Burchell & Ruston*, agents for *Gepp & Sons*, Chelmsford (for the plaintiffs), *Blacket, Gill & Langhams*, agents for *Peter M Cox & Co*, Melton Mowbray (for the defendant).

Jacqueline Metcalfe   Barrister.

Moriarty v McCarthy

QUEEN'S BENCH DIVISION
O'CONNOR J
9th, 10th OCTOBER 1977

Damages – Personal injury – Loss of future earnings – Marriage prospects – Young unmarried woman – Likelihood of marriage and consequent cessation of employment to care for family to be taken into account – Plaintiff aged 24 and working at date of accident – Injuries resulting in paraplegia – Appropriate multiplier in assessing damages for loss of earnings – Whether multiplier should be less than in case of man of same age.

Damages – Personal injury – Loss of amenities of life – Marriage prospects – Young unmarried woman – Loss of financial support of a husband – Loss of financial support during period when plaintiff unable to work because of family duties – Plaintiff unmarried woman aged 24 suffering paraplegia – Accident destroying prospect of marriage – Damages for loss of earnings reduced by four years' purchase to take account of probability that plaintiff would have married and been unable to work for a period because of family duties – Whether sum for loss of financial support of a husband during that period to be taken into account in assessing general damages.

The plaintiff, an attractive unmarried woman of 24, was involved in an accident which was caused by the defendant's negligence. She sustained severe injuries which resulted in paraplegia from the waist down. The prognosis was that for the rest of her life she would be confined to a wheelchair, and it was improbable that she would be able to get gainful employment. Before the accident the plaintiff was working as a machinist and it was agreed that her net loss of earnings was at the rate of £1,820 per annum. At the trial the only matter in issue was the assessment of the damages, in particular the effect of the loss of the plaintiff's prospects of marriage on the amount of damages to be awarded for loss of future earnings and on the amount of general damages to which she was entitled.

Held – (i) In assessing loss of future earnings in the case of a young woman, account had to be taken of the probability that she would have married and for a number of years would have had to give up gainful employment to bear and rear her children. Accordingly, although in the case of a young man aged 24 a multiplier of 15 would have been appropriate in calculating the damages for loss of earnings, in the plaintiff's case a multiplier of 11 would be applied to take account of the probability that she would have married and had children. It followed that the plaintiff should be awarded damages for loss of earnings of £20,000, i e £1,820 to which has been applied a multiplier of 11 (see p 217 c to e and p 218 a b, post); *Harris v Harris* [1973] 1 Lloyd's Rep 445 applied.

(ii) However, since for practical purposes the accident had destroyed the plaintiff's chance of marriage, there should be included as an element in her general damages a sum for loss of the amenity of financial support from a husband during the period that she would have been unable to work because of family duties. That loss should be valued in the same way as the four years' purchase lost, in comparison with a man of similar age, in calculating her damages for loss of earnings, i e at approximately £7,500. It followed that as £27,500 would be the right sum to award as general damages to a man aged 24 with injuries similar to the plaintiff's, she would be awarded general damages of £35,000, (see p 218 b to j, post).

Notes

For the measure of damages for personal injury, see 12 Halsbury's Laws (4th Edn) paras 1145-1158, and for cases on the subject, see 17 Digest (Reissue) 113-118, *168-199*.

Cases referred to in judgment

Cookson v Knowles [1977] 2 All ER 820, [1977] QB 913, [1977] 3 WLR 279, CA.
Grace v Lamoureaux (9th May 1977) unreported.
Harris v Harris [1973] 1 Lloyd's Rep 445, CA.
Jefford v Gee [1970] 1 All ER 1202, [1970] 2 QB 130, [1970] 2 WLR 702, [1970] 1 Lloyd's Rep 107, CA, Digest (Cont Vol C) 709, *182a*.
Parry v Cleaver [1969] 1 All ER 555, [1970] AC 1 [1969] 2 WLR 821, [1969] 1 Lloyd's Rep 183 HL, 36(1) Digest Reissue 320.

Action

By a writ issued on 28th February 1975, the plaintiff, Ann Moriarty brought an action against the defendant, John McCarthy, claiming damages for personal injury and consequential loss arising out of an accident on or about 28th November 1973 caused by the defendant's negligence in driving his car. The defendant admitted liability and the issue was as to the assessment of the damages. The facts are set out in the judgment.

John Wilmers QC for the plaintiff.
Graeme Hamilton for the defendant.

O'CONNOR J. In this action the plaintiff seeks to recover damages for personal injuries sustained by her in an accident which occurred on 27th October 1973. At that time she had been in England for a few months and was working as a machinist. The family came from Kerry but a few years ago had moved to Dublin, and she had come over to England to stay with a member of the family who was already over here, and to get work here.

In the accident she sustained exceedingly serious injuries. She had a broken back which has resulted in paraplegia, that is complete loss of the power to move or feel from the waist down, with no control of bladder and bowel, no sexual sensation, and she is a wheelchair case for the rest of her life. She is now 24 years of age. In addition, she had a severe injury to the head from which she has made a complete recovery, as I understand it. She also had a fractured pelvis which has aligned in reasonably good repair, but she is left, and I accept her evidence about this, with a painful back above the level controlled by the fractured vertebra, that is D 11. She gets pain in her back when she is sitting in her wheelchair and as far as I can see, there is no reason to suppose that it is going to get any better. She says she has learned to live with it; brave girl.

As far as the future is concerned, the condition is permanent. Unfortunately, the plaintiff simply cannot accept that. She spends hours a day exercising, or attempting to exercise, with the help of putting on calipers and seeking to exercise herself and use her legs, in the mistaken belief that some power may return to her and that she will be able to walk. Equally unfortunately, although I have not seen her, she seems to be encouraged in this belief by her mother with whom she is living. In time, it is to be hoped that she will come to accept the fact that she is not going to walk again.

She spent seven or eight months in Stoke Mandeville Hospital where she was trained, with the great expertise which that hospital is famous for, to learn the various techniques for trying to be able to evacuate her bowel and bladder at the right time. She learned the techniques of getting in and out of a wheelchair, of getting in and out of a motor car from the wheelchair; when a suitable bed is to be found, of moving from wheelchair to bed, and from wheelchair to lavatory pan.

Having left Stoke Mandeville in the summer of 1974, she spent some months somewhere in England, I have not been told where, and returned to her family in Dublin just before Christmas 1974. The set-up in Dublin was that at that time the family had a ground floor flat, and in it were mother and father (the mother is now aged 53), an elder brother who was at work, an elder sister who was at work, whom I have seen, and a younger sister who was still at school. At some stage, and it does not matter precisely when, about late 1975 or 1976, the family had to move from that flat and moved into a house. That is wholly inconvenient and inappropriate for looking after the plaintiff. It has only got one bathroom and lavatory in the house which is upstairs, and she has to be helped or carried and taken up the stairs by whichever member of the family is on hand if she is to make use of its facilities. Secondly, there are steps up to the house and you cannot get a wheelchair in and out of it without having somebody carry it down for you. At or about this time, the father who is an alcoholic asthmatic, retired to the family smallholding in Kerry where he has been living for the last year or more. That left in Dublin the other members of the family to whom I have referred.

The mother had never done any gainful work outside the home until she took a job as a waitress in June 1974. This was at the very moment when her daughter, Anne, was being discharged from Stoke Mandeville Hospital, and she worked for a few weeks, from the third week in June until early in August of 1974 when she stopped. Why she stopped, I do not know. At one stage it was suggested that she had given up the work in order to be available to receive and look after the plaintiff. That will not do, and it is quite obvious that no useful information is to be gleaned as to her motivation for taking work at that particular moment and, secondly, for stopping it within a few weeks. If it was intended to found a basis for a claim as to what her worth in looking after her daughter was, in my judgment it is a hopeless failure. All that can be said about it is that the mother apparently, if she wanted to, is capable of doing a job as a waitress and being paid for it, or if you prefer, a canteen assistant.

Since the plaintiff returned home she has effectively, of course, been looked after by her mother. Her mother is at home in any event because she has got to look after the other members of the family, but that will not be for ever. The boy is leaving her; he is about to get married. The elder of the two remaining daughters, whom I have seen, is 19; she is working in Dublin as an accountant's clerk, and it is reasonable to suppose that in due course she will leave home too, probably to get married. There is a younger daughter who is still at school, now aged 17, Patricia. I have not seen her, but the fact that she has remained at school shows that she has the educational ability to benefit from it. The sister whom I have seen left school at 14, that is Margaret Moriarty.

So there it is, that is the family set-up. Now, what is likely to happen in the future? Everybody appreciates that this plaintiff in a few minutes' time is going to be awarded a very large sum of money, and it may be that provision will be made for the family to remain in Dublin. It may be that they will decide that life in Kerry is better for everyone. I do not know. What is the Dublin situation? When the plaintiff went back to Dublin, she went into the care of the National Medical Rehabilitation Centre, Dun Laoghaire, under the care of Dr Gregg. She attended there daily; she was taken there by taxi at government expense, and taken home again. While she was there, they applied their minds to attempting to train her for some form of sedentary work. The agreed medical reports contain a long assessment of her abilities, but she is at the lower end of normal intellectual capacity. She is a nice looking girl, and she tried to learn typewriting and secretarial work but she did not seem to be very good at it. She could do some light assembly work if such work could be found for her and if she could get to it. She did indeed have a job which was made for her through the good offices of Dr Gregg, either in or very close to the rehabilitation centre, where she worked as a switchboard operator, I do not see in my mind a large office switchboard, but effectively answering the telephone in comparatively humble surroundings, and she tried to increase her abliity to use a typewriter. She only held that work for a few months in the latter part of 1975, and for a variety of reasons it came to an end.

While she was at Dun Laoghaire she also had driving lessons, because one of the developments for the treatment and mobilisation of paraplegics in the last 25 years has been that motor cars can be adapted for their use, providing hand controls, and certainly an invalid carriage can be driven by a paraplegic, and in Britain these are very often provided by the local authority or the national health service, or from public funds. Not so in the Republic of Ireland; if you want one, you have to buy it. She was given driving lessons at Dun Laoghaire. There is no precise record of how often, or when. The evidence is that she had something like a dozen, but she never got to the stage of passing a test. In 1976, in the Republic as elsewhere, money went short and there was no longer the provision of being able to bring the plaintiff from her home to the centre by taxi, and her treatment and rehabilitation at the centre came to an end. She had not got the money to go there under her own steam, and since the summer of 1976, that is for nearly 18 months, she has just been living at home.

That is the present set-up, and there is no doubt that her future is a difficult one to assess. On the one hand, it is said that when the damages which are to be awarded are available she will be able if she so wishes to go back to the rehabilitation centre and take advantage of its facilities. Note that its facilities are never going to restore the use of her legs, although she firmly believes that that is possible. Will they succeed in teaching her to drive a car? It may be a question mark hangs over that. She does not at the moment seem to me to be a person who wants to drive a car. She commented with some feeling that she did not want to drive a car and possibly do to another what had been done to her. She may, of course, change her mind in due course, because unless she mobilises herself the question of employment is simply non-existent.

Now, in Dublin (the evidence comes from Dr Gregg primarily) there is opportunity for paraplegics of this sort of age to get gainful employment which is within their capacity, namely of a secretarial or sedentary kind; light assembly work could be managed and certain secretarial work of various kinds. The evidence from Dr Gregg about it is that of the young paraplegics approximately 50 per cent have some kind of work. Well, having seen and heard the plaintiff, in my judgment the probability is that she is in the 50 per cent who do not get any gainful employment. I may be wrong about it, I hope that I am, but in compensating her I do not really regard it as on that she is ever going to make any worthwhile stab at earning money in outside employment. I do not think that that is in any way her fault; it is the way she is built. As I say, she may in due course get over her fears of mobilising herself with a motor car; she will certainly have the money to equip herself with one if she so wants, and it may be that in her own interests she will try and get work outside. But as I say, I do not think that that chance is sufficiently assessable to treat her as other than a person who has simply had her earning capacity destroyed.

The only other medical matter is that she has a normal expectation of life in all probability, but because of the very nature of paraplegia and the possibility that if one does not look after oneself one is more liable to contract infections, particularly of the bladder, with more serious consequences than to the ordinary citizen. The doctors are agreed that an allowance should be made of a ten per cent chance that her life expectancy has been shortened. For a girl of this age, in carrying out the necessary assessments of damages, that makes no difference.

I now turn to consider the various heads of damages. I do that because liability is admitted in the case, save that there is an agreement between the parties that the total award of damages should be reduced by 12½ per cent to allow for the possibility that had the issue been contested she might have been found partly to blame for travelling with a drunken driver.

Let me say at the outset, as I said in May 1977 in *Grace v Lamoureaux*[1], that in considering general damages in an inflationary period plaintiffs cannot expect to find themselves in a class which is shielded from the effects of inflation which the rest of their

1 (9th May 1977) unreported

fellow citizens battle with. When that is said and done, one must face the reality of the present day.

The difficulty in dealing with the main heads of damages really occurs because the law needs to be looked at with a little care in the case of a young woman. It is agreed that this plaintiff at the moment is suffering a net loss of earnings of £35 a week, that is £1,820 per annum. It has become conventional to assess the loss of earnings, or the damage to earning capacity, whichever way one likes to put it, as a separate head of damage and to quantify it. The reason for that is well-known because of the incidence of interest as propounded by the Court of Appeal in *Jefford v Gee*[1]. Since *Cookson v Knowles*[2], that is no longer the position. On the other hand, *Cookson v Knowles*[2], in the shape of a subsequent case, is on its way to the House of Lords, and I take the view that a trial judge today still ought to quantify the loss of earnings head separately.

If the plaintiff had been a man of 24 with an agreed net loss of earnings of £1,820 a year, nobody would quarrel with applying to it a multiplier of 15 and arriving at £27,500. When one is dealing with a young woman, it is said that a multiplier of 15 is too great, and the reason that that is said is this: if you look at the reality of the immediate pre-accident position, there was a girl who was working and earning money, but the probability was that in a given number of years, nobody can say how many, she would probably have got married, and not necessarily stopped working at once, but probably within a reasonable time have participated in the bearing and rearing of a family, and that at that time it is reasonably certain that she would have had to give up gainful employment outside the home, at least for a number of years. It is those considerations which led the court to say that for a young woman it is wrong to apply the same multiplier to this head of damage as for a man. The authority for that is most clearly stated in *Harris v Harris*[3] in the Court of Appeal. It is noticeable that in that case the plaintiff was not a paraplegic, but had a brain injury and a brain injury, I may say, which left her with sufficient capacity to have a number of 'O' levels, to be at a girls' public school and to be studying for 'A' levels. She had been aged only 12½ when the accident occurred, and was 17½ or 18, when judgment was given in her favour. In that case, the learned judge used a multiplier of 15 for the loss of earnings head. Now what is noticeable about that are two things. (1) she was only 18 and she had not yet taken her 'A' levels; she was a person who was likely to go, but for the accident, to university; and (2) she would not have been in gainful employment earning money for a period of something like five years after the date of the award, and the Court of Appeal rightly said that it appeared that the learned trial judge had not sufficiently taken into account the factor of acceleration in making the award a long time ahead. They also said that the multiplier of 15 was too high because of the factors to which I have already referred, of the lost opportunity of marriage, and asserted that the trial judge had already included that in the £20,000 which he had awarded by way of general damages for pain and suffering and loss of amenity. I may say that the loss of earnings in that case when multiplied out came to £22,500. In those circumstances, the defendants having appealed, the Court of Appeal said that the multiplier was too great and substituted for 15 a multiplier of ten. They had, therefore, done two things: (1) they had allowed for the acceleration and (2), having asserted that the lost opportunity of marriage had been fully compensated in the £20,000, made a further reduction in the loss of earnings head and cut it to ten years. There was no cross-appeal by the plaintiff in that case. I have not seen or read the judgment of the learned trial judge, but it is undoubted that the Court of Appeal assumed that the £20,000 head included full compensation for the loss flowing from the diminution of that plaintiff's chances of marriage.

1   [1970] 1 All ER 1202, [1970] 2 QB 130
2   [1977] 2 All ER 820, [1977] QB 913
3   [1973] 1 Lloyd's Rep 445

I now turn to apply these principles to the present case to see how they can be made to fit. As I have said, a man in this situation would unquestionably have a multiplier of 15 applied to it. What, then, for this plaintiff? In my judgment, if ten years' purchase or a multiplier of ten was right in *Harris v Harris*[1], then at least it ought to be a little bit more in the present case, because in the present case nothing is to be taken off for acceleration, for this girl was already at work and earning money, and had been, certainly in this country for a few months, and for all I know for some time in Ireland before that. So that matter does not apply, but the marriage one does, and I propose effectively to apply a multiplier of 11 to that head. There is an agreed net loss of earnings of £1,820, and, if my arithmetic is right, that comes to £20,000.

I then turn to consider the general damages. There are a number of conventional figures for this kind of injury, and most of the reported cases are for men. Now, let me suppose for a moment that for a man of this age by way of general damages, having had his full 15 years' purchase for loss of earnings, a fair figure to award would be £27,500. What then of the girl? Let us take the same rate of wages. He would get £27,500 and he would already have had £27,500 for his loss of earnings, making a total of £55,000. Is it then to be said that the girl is to end up with £27,500 plus only £20,000; £47,500. To my mind, the answer comes back No. What is wrong with this is that there is not a sufficient valuation for the head of her lost opportunity of marriage. The fact is that the accident which has destroyed her earning capacity has also for effective purposes destroyed her chances of marriage. On that head, as I have said, she is an attractive girl. I put entirely from this equation the possibility that she may be a target for fortune hunters. But that is not the point. She can conceive and, in due course deliver, I take it by Caesarean section, a child, but for practical purposes she has had her chances of marriage, perhaps it is wrong to say destroyed, but certainly grossly reduced, and on the economic head, one must face reality, the chances of finding a man who is prepared to take her on and support her, which is what this head is about, during the time that she cannot work because of her family duties, to my mind have gone. Why, then, should the defendant be relieved by some sleight of hand of compensating her for what her real loss is? If one had been able to say before the accident occurred, and suppose, for example, that she was a woman of fifty who had never married and who had said, 'Well, I have no intention of marrying or of ever getting married; I was happy in my work and I was going to go on doing it', the court would apply the same multiplier for her as they would for a man of equivalent age. It is only when one is dealing with young women that this problem arises; and that is in a society where most young women are working, and will work, and, as I have said, they may or may not return to work after family bearing and rearing, depending on the financial circumstances of the husband.

The support is gone. How is it to be valued? Well, why should it not be valued in the same way as the lost years' purchase? And I propose to put back the £7,500 into the award of general damages as an element in it, and I name it in case the case is looked at by the Court of Appeal so that they shall know what I have done; I put that back into the general damages, and it seems to me the answer to that is that, for a man at the present time, £27,500 in this case would have been about right, and I do not see why it should not be so for the girl. But her loss of amenity insofar as it is her loss of financial support from a possible husband is wholly different to that of a man, and I propose to put that money right back into the general damages and award her £35,000 by way of general damages.

That deals with the two major heads of damage. There now come a whole series of matters about which there has been some dispute and some agreement. Let me deal with the matters which are in dispute.

---

1   [1973] 1 Lloyd's Rep 445

One is the head of damage which is frequently called 'nursing care and attention' or, alternatively, 'a companion, a helper, in the home'. It is common ground that this young woman needs some help at home. It is being provided by her mother at the moment, and to some extent by the other members of the family. When she has been rehoused, as she will be (but that is a separate head which I will deal with in a moment) the living conditions will be such that there will be no reason why she cannot reasonably look after herself; namely she cannot do a great deal of heavy cleaning or a certain amount of cooking and so forth, but she will be able to move about in the house in her wheelchair, and she will be able to make use of the lavatory unaided; she will be able to have a bath if need be; she will be able to wheel herself out into the road and, if she is minded to learn how to drive a motor car, make herself reasonably independent. But she will need somebody to help, and she is entitled to a fair sum for the cost of such a person. There is no reason why she should not be left alone in the house from time to time, but it is common ground that she should have somebody sleeping there at night.

How is that to be evaluated? When one looks at the cases, one finds a whole band of different situations. Sometimes the patient requires actual nursing attendance, and evidence is led of the cost of providing that and, according to the age of the plaintiff, a multiplier is applied to the going rate of today. Sometimes the assistance is provided by a member of the family, usually a parent or sometimes a spouse, who gives up gainful employment in order to look after the injured plaintiff. If the value of the gainful employment surrendered is less than the cost of importing an outsider to provide the same services, it seems that the courts normally accept that that is a fair measure of the amount of money needed for this purpose. The cases show, and the law has been properly developed on this, that that is a fair way of doing it. The old idea that a parent or spouse was in duty bound to look after an injured spouse or child and get nothing for it has gone. Of course, family affection must count in this matter, and thus we find sometimes the head being valued at tiny sums of money where a parent has given up a job of £5 a week; sometimes we find the head being valued in large sums of money where either there is no parent or a greater job has been given up, and very little help is to be gained from examining the actual awards under this head of damage.

What is the reality of this case? The plaintiff's version of it is that I should say to myself that she needs resident domestic help for the rest of her life; that the present cost of getting unskilled resident help, for example, an unmarried mother and her child who have got to be housed and fed, the evidence from the witnesses was that in Dublin one would expect to pay a wage on top of £40 a week and, say the plaintiff's advisers, I should apply a multiplier of 15 at £2,000 per annum and arrive at another £30,000. Well, when I look at that, I am satisfied that that is quite unreal and I do not accept the evidence that nobody can be found in Dublin to come and live in, all found, and give a bit of help for less than £40 a week. The reality of it is that for many years the mother is in fact going to provide this service. The plaintiff is entitled, nevertheless, to be compensated for the true value of the services which she really needs. Doing the best I can under that head, it seems to me that for the present and for the future, that if I take a multiplicand of £1,000 I will be doing her no injustice, and I shall put the multiplier of 15 and award £15,000 under that head.

The next matter which has to be dealt with is the alteration and provision of a bungalow. As I have said, the accommodation in which the plaintiff is living at the moment is wholly unsuitable. The cases show that the capital cost of a new house cannot be awarded by way of damages. There have been various methods of trying to calculate the diminution in income if part of the award of general damages is in fact put into a house, and the various calculations have been done in the cases. I do not propose to do them here. I prefer to deal with the matter in the way in which it is regularly dealt with, namely to consider the additional cost of providing a suitable bungalow, either to convert an existing one or the extra cost if one builds a new one.

Again, a cursory glance through the relevant pages in Kemp and Kemp[1] will show that this is regularly done, and you will find if you look in that book that sometimes there has been an agreed figure of £8,000, sometimes there has been a figure of £7,000, sometimes it is very much less; it all depends where you start from. In the present case the evidence is all one way. This plaintiff starts from scratch. She is not going to get a ready-made council house provided for her because her financial position after the award which I am making puts her outside the category of persons who are so assisted in Ireland. She will, however, have ample money to equip herself with either a new or an existing bungalow, but she is entitled, in my judgment, to the cost of altering it in order to make it fit for her purposes. I have already stated what that is. The evidence is all one way that the cost in Ireland of doing that is of the order of £8,000, and I see no reason to suppose, particularly as I find that that is a figure which has been used in more than one case in this country, to consider that that is too high, and I propose to award her £8,000 under that head.

Now there are some small matters. Let me dispose at once of the claim that she should be provided for life with a motor car and have it running free of cost. It is suggested that I should provide her with enough money to have three motor cars over the next 15 or 20 years and to provide her with enough money to run all these cars, one at a time of course, for the rest of her life, making a deduction for the possibility that she may never buy a motor car and never drive a mile. It is said that her position is different from that of many plaintiffs in that she came from a walk of life where it was unlikely that she would ever be a car owner, either directly or as the wife of a car owner. I cannot accept that. It seems to me that the probability is if she had gone on working and got married that there would have been a family car around, and I do not see any reason to draw a distinction under that head. Just as the capital value of a house is not awarded as a separate item, so the capital value of a car is not to be awarded. What is to be awarded is the cost of adapting the car to fit it for use, and the agreed figure for that is £70. She is entitled to it, and in my judgment she is not entitled to anything by way of capital value of a car or anything towards the running of it, even if there had been any certainty that she was going to do so, and I will make no award under that head.

Another matter is future medical expenses in Ireland. Effectively, there are agreed figures. The evidence is that for hospital and specialist treatment there should be a provision of £180 per annum. The fact is that Dr Gregg expected her probably to require, for one reason or another, in-patient treatment for a short period in any year, but the fact is that she has never had a week of in-patient treatment since she returned to Ireland at Christmas 1974, and I do not think it is right, therefore, to apply a strict multiplier of 15 to £180. There is also an agreed figure of £36 per annum as the cost of a general practitioner to keep an eye on her. The defendant accepts that that is a fair figure, but when I lump those two heads together, as I think I should, I think that justice is done by awarding a total of £2,500 under those heads.

There is a very small item of a telephone. It is agreed that the defendant should pay for the cost of the rental of the telephone because she needs a phone in her house in case of emergency. Rental at £48 per annum and £100 for installation comes to £820, that is applying a 15 year multiplier, and I see no reason why she should not have that, and I assess that at £820.

There remains an agreed sum of special damage, which I do not propose to go into in any detail, of £9,896. She is entitled to a wheelchair; provision for a new wheelchair and something for running it, and I think if she has £600 under that head she is well compensated. When all those sums are added up, unless I have overlooked some particular head, and when somebody has worked out what 12½ per cent is to be deducted, I will enter judgment accordingly.

Counsel for the defendant submitted that the sum of £511 per annum which this

---

1   The Quantum of Damages (4th Edn, 1975), vol 1, pp 112-114

girl is receiving from the Irish State should be deducted from the loss of earnings calculation. Very properly, he drew my attention to the dictum of Lord Reid in *Parry v Cleaver*[1] (which is conveniently set out in Kemp and Kemp[2]) where Lord Reid, obiter, said:

> 'We do not have to decide in this case whether these considerations also apply to public benevolence in the shape of various uncovenanted benefits from the welfare state, but it may be thought that Parliament did not intend them to be for the benefit of the wrong-doer.'

The payment in Ireland is completely non-contributory, she has never contributed anything towards it. I do not know what its statutory provenance is, but it is a welfare payment which she is entitled to as a citizen of her country to which she has made no contribution. I apply Lord Reid's dictum to it, and it seems to me that it is not to be deducted.

Judgment for the plaintiff for £91,886, reduced by agreement, by 12½ per cent, to £81,400 including interest.

Solicitors: *Vizards* (for the plaintiff); *Stevensons* (for the defendant).

K Mydeen Esq Barrister.

First National Securities Ltd v Jones
and another

COURT OF APPEAL, CIVIL DIVISION
BUCKLEY, GOFF LJJ AND SIR DAVID CAIRNS
4th NOVEMBER 1977

Deed – Execution – Sealing – Need for physical seal or impression on paper – Document containing nothing more than indication of place were seal should be – Document in printed form purporting to be legal charge – Document merely containing printed circle enclosing letters 'L.S.' – Signature of mortgagor placed across circle – Attestation clause signed by witness stating that document 'signed sealed and delivered' by mortgagor in presence of witness – Whether document properly sealed and executed by mortgagor as his deed.

The plaintiffs, a bank, brought an action against the defendant relating to a loan alleged to have been made by the plaintiffs to the defendant and secured by a mortgage by the defendant of certain land. The plaintiffs claimed that under the mortgage a sum of upwards of £5,000 was owing. The legal charge which was alleged to constitute the mortgage was on a standard printed form of mortgage used by the plaintiffs for transactions of that kind. It was described as a 'Legal charge'; the names of the parties were given, the defendant being named as mortgagor, and the property to be charged was identified. The operative part of the document began with the words 'NOW THIS DEED WITNESSETH'. At the end were the words 'IN WITNESS whereof the Mortgagor has hereunto set his hand and seal the day and year first before written'. Beneath that was a circle printed on the document containing the letters 'L.S.', signifying locus sigilli, and against that was the ordinary place for the attesting witness to sign which had the legend 'SIGNED SEALED AND DELIVERED by the above-named Mortgagor in the presence of', followed by a space for the signature and

---

1 [1969] 1 All ER 555 at 558, [1970] AC 1 at 14
2 The Quantum of Damages (4th Edn, 1975), vol 1, p 161

address of the witness. The defendant's signature had been written across the circle containing the letters 'L.S.' and the attestation clause was signed by a witness. The plaintiffs' action was dismissed on the ground that the legal charge was not under seal and had not therefore been properly executed by the defendant as his deed. The plaintiffs appealed.

Held – It was not, as a matter of law, necessary for the due execution of a deed that there should be any physical seal attached to, or impression on, the paper. A document purporting to be a deed was capable in law of being such, even though it bore nothing more than an indication of where the seal should be. Since the mortgage document bore the printed letters 'L.S.' in a circle across which the defendant had placed his signature and an attestation clause signed by a witness to the effect that the document had been signed, sealed and delivered by the defendant in the witness's presence, that was sufficient evidence that the document had been executed by the defendant as his deed. The appeal would therefore be allowed (see p 225 *a b*, p 227 *e* to *h*, p 228 *b* to *g* and p 229 *b* and *f* to *j*, post).

Re Sandilands (1871) LR 6 CP 411 and dictum of Danckwerts J in *Stromdale and Ball Ltd v Burden* [1952] 1 All ER at 62 applied.

Re Balkis Consolidated Co Ltd (1888) 58 LT 300 explained.

National Provincial Bank of England v Jackson (1886) 33 Ch D 1 distinguished.

Notes

For validity of deeds where no seal is affixed, see 12 Halsbury's Laws (4th Edn) para 1325, and for cases on the subject, see 17 Digest (Reissue) 249, 250, *135-139*.

Cases referred to in judgments

Balkis Consolidated Co Ltd, Re (1888) 58 LT 300, 17 Digest (Reissue) 249, *137*.

National Provincial Bank of England v Jackson (1886) 33 Ch D 1, 55 LT 458, CA, 17 Digest (Reissue) 249, *136*.

Sandilands, Re (1871) LR 6 CP 411, sub nom *Re Mayer* 40 LJCP 201, 24 LT 273, 17 Digest (Reissue) 249, *135*.

Smith, Re, Oswell v Shepherd (1892) 67 LT 64, CA, 17 Digest (Reissue) 249, *138*.

Stromdale and Ball Ltd v Burden [1952] 1 All ER 59, [1952] Ch 223, 17 Digest (Reissue) 250, *139*.

Appeal

This was an appeal by the plaintiffs, First National Securities Ltd, of Harrow, Middlesex, against the judgment of Mr I B McLennon sitting as a deputy circuit judge at the Stourbridge County Court on 5th January 1977 affirming the decision of Mr Registrar J N Taylor and ordering that the plaintiffs' claim for possession of the defendants' property and payment of arrears of mortgage instalments be dismissed. The claim related to an agreement of 19th August 1974 between the plaintiffs and the defendants, Christopher Timothy Jones and his wife Shirley Jones, whereby, as security for a loan of £4,000 repayable by monthly instalments of £80·65 with interest at the rate of 20½ per cent per annum, the first defendant executed a legal charge on property situated at Chawnhill Close, Old Winford, Stourbridge, West Midlands, in favour of the plaintiffs. The facts are set out in the judgment of Buckley LJ.

Hedley Marten for the plaintiffs.
Joseph Ricardo for the defendants.

BUCKLEY LJ. This is an appeal from a decision of his Honour Deputy Judge McLennon, sitting at the Stourbridge County Court on 5th January 1977. The action relates to a loan alleged to have been made by the plaintiff company to the defendants and secured by a mortgage by the first defendant, who is the husband of the second defendant, of some land at Stourbridge, under which the plaintiffs claim that the sum of upwards of £5,000 is now owing. The action came before the registrar of the court, and was apparently dismissed on the ground that the legal charge constituting the mortgage was not under seal. The plaintiffs appealed from that decision to the judge. The matter came before Deputy Judge McLennon, and we have only an extremely exiguous note of the proceedings before him, which does not include any note of the reasons he gave for his decision, although it would seem from what we have been told by counsel that the learned judge did deliver a judgment. This is very unsatisfactory and is not a proper compliance with the practice, which requires that an appellant shall obtain either a copy of the learned judge's own note of the judgment or at any rate a copy of counsel's note of the judge's judgment, or a solicitor's note of the judge's judgment, agreed between the parties and submitted to the judge for his approval and included in the papers submitted to this court. That course unfortunately has not been adopted in the present case, as it should have been, and we have only had the advantage of having had read to us such notes as were taken by the solicitors who appeared in the county court, and it seems that the learned deputy county court judge dismissed the action on the same ground as that on which the registrar dismissed it, namely that the legal charge was not under seal, from which he concluded that the plaintiffs were unable to make out any right to relief.

The relief which was sought on the particulars of claim was, first, possession of the mortgaged property and, secondly, payment of all moneys due under the mortgage. Even if the mortgage was not duly executed as a deed, further questions would arise whether it could operate as an equitable mortgage, and in any event, even if the mortgage were wholly ineffective as a security, there would still be a right to the repayment of the loan, if indeed the loan was one which the plaintiffs had made to the defendants.

But the defendants put in defences. The defence of the first defendant was that the loan was never received by him: that it was sent in a way which he described as 'quite unethically' by the plaintiffs to a solicitor not known to the first defendant and without his authority or approval; and he asserts in his defence that the money was misappropriated by the plaintiffs and the solicitor to whom it is said to have been paid, and there is an allegation in the defence that the second defendant's signature on the document was forged.

The second defendant put in a defence saying that she had never received the moneys alleged to have been advanced and that the forms were not explained to her; that she was not in a position to repay anything because she was not in employment and that the forms were incomplete when she put her signature to them. The 'forms' there referred to may include perhaps the proposal form for the loan; one does not quite know what the documents are to which the lady is referring. But it would seem that apart from the formal affidavit evidence which has been put in by the plaintiffs, giving particulars of the state of the account, of the parties involved and so on, and exhibiting a copy of the legal charge, no evidence at all was adduced before the learned judge, for his note makes no reference to any oral evidence, and there was no other affidavit evidence as far as counsel has been able to inform us, apart from the plaintiffs' formal evidence that I have mentioned, which consists of one affidavit and two supplementary affidavits, the supplementary affidavits being concerned merely with bringing up to date the particulars of the state of the account. So apart from the question of whether the legal charge was ever duly executed by the mortgagor, that is the first defendant, no issue in the action seems to have been adjudicated on at all.

We heard argument about whether or not the legal charge can be said to have been duly executed. The position with regard to that is that the mortgage is a printed form of mortgage, the plaintiffs being a bank which carries on the business of making advances to borrowers and this is the standard form which they employ in connection with transactions of that kind. It is described as a 'legal charge' in heavy gothic type at the beginning of the document; the names of the parties are given, the mortgagor being the first defendant, and the customers, that is to say the persons to whom the advance was to be made, being the first defendant and the second defendant. It identifies the property to be charged and it refers to a pre-existing first mortgage. The operative part of the document starts with the accustomed words 'NOW THIS DEED WITNESSETH'. At the end of the document there are the words 'IN WITNESS whereof the Mortgagor has hereunto set his hand and seal the day and year first before written', and then beneath that there is a circle printed on the document containing the letters 'L.S.', signifying locus sigilli, and against that there is the ordinary place for the attesting witness to sign, which has the legend 'SIGNED SEALED AND DELIVERED by the above-named Mortgagor in the presence of', and then there is a space for the signature and address of the witness. Across the circle containing the letters 'L.S.' there is the signature of the first defendant; beneath that signature, partially over the circle, there is a signature which at any rate purports to be the signature of the second defendant, but it seems to me that she was not a necessary party to the document at all, because although the advance was being made to her and her husband, the mortgage was a mortgage created by the husband alone.

We have been referred to certain authorities on the subject of what constitutes good execution of a deed, the earliest of which is Re Sandilands[1]. This case related to the acknowledgment by certain married ladies in Australia of a deed as their act and deed. A special commission had been issued for taking acknowledgment of the deed at Melbourne by the ladies in question; the deed was sent out to them; it had no physical seal on it, but there were pieces of green ribbon attached to the places where the seals should have been. The attestation was in the usual form, 'Signed, sealed and delivered by', and the signatures were duly attested. There was a certificate of two commissioners, stating that the ladies in question appeared personally before them and produced the deed before them, acknowledging the same to be their respective acts and deeds. No physical seal was ever put on the documents; there were merely these pieces of green ribbon or tape. In those circumstances the Court of Common Pleas held that the deed had been sufficiently executed. Bovill CJ said that he thought there was prima facie evidence that the deed was sealed at the time of its execution and acknowledgment by the parties. I quote now from his judgment[2]:

'To constitute a sealing, neither wax, nor wafer, nor a piece of paper, nor even an impression, is necessary. Here is something attached to this deed which may have been intended for a seal, but which from its nature is incapable of retaining an impression. Coupled with the attestation and the certificate, I think we are justified in granting the application that the deed and other documents may be received and filed by the proper officer, pursuant to the statute.'

Byles J said that the sealing of a deed need not be by means of a seal; it may be done with the end of a ruler or anything else. Nor is it necessary that wax should be used. He went on to say[2]:

'The attestation clause says that the deed was signed, sealed, and delivered by the several parties; and the certificate of the two special commissioners says that the deed was produced before them, and that the married women "acknowledged the same to be their respective acts and deeds".'

He thought that there was prima facie evidence that the deed was sealed. Montague Smith J[2] concurred on the ground that the attestation was prima facie evidence

1   (1871) LR 6 CP 411
2   LR 6 CP 411 at 413

that the deed was sealed, and that there was no evidence to the contrary. So that authority appears to establish that for due execution of a deed it is not necessary to have any physical seal, or even any impression on the paper, as long as the evidence establishes that the document has been delivered by the relevant party as his act and deed; and, in the view of Montague Smith J at any rate, the attestation of the execution of the deed as being signed, sealed and delivered as the party's act and deed is prima facie evidence that the deed was sealed.

Next we were referred to a decision of North J in *Re Balkis Consolidated Co Ltd*[1]. This case related to a transfer of shares in a company, the regulations of which required that transfers should be made by deed. The question was whether a particular document of transfer which had been signed by a shareholder named Arnott was a transfer by deed. The document had been signed by Arnott at the offices of his stockbroker and was witnessed by a clerk of the stockbroker as having been signed, sealed and delivered by him. There was no seal on it, and no wafer or anything of that nature, but only a circular mark on the paper with the words 'Place for seal' printed within it. The evidence as to the execution of the document was conflicting, for Arnott himself swore on affidavit that he never had sealed or delivered the transfer, but the stockbroker gave evidence to the effect that Arnott did seal and deliver the transfer, or transfers, in the presence of his, the stockbroker's, clerk, and that whenever Arnott signed a blank transfer, as this was, he invariably put his finger on the printed seal. But that was denied by Arnott. This point emerged in the course of the hearing before North J when counsel for Arnott took the objection that the transfer had no seal on it and did not even appear to be a valid document. The application before the learned judge was an application for rectification of the register, to remove a registration of the name of the person into whose name the shares had been transferred by use of the blank transfer. The learned judge refused to make an order rectifying the register, saying that he was not satisfied that he had sufficient materials before him to enable him to decide the question, that is to decide whose name ought to be on the register, I take it. He said that the evidence whether any form of sealing was gone through was conflicting and that he was not satisfied that any document which was complete on the face of it was delivered to the applicant. He referred to *Re Sandilands*[2], which I have already mentioned, but he thought that that case did not assist him. He refused the motion to rectify the register, but he said[3]:

> '. . . if the applicants are advised to bring an action to have the question determined on fuller evidence, I will reserve the question of costs till that action is decided.'

So I think it is clear from the judgment of the learned judge that he was not then reaching a final conclusion that the document in the form in which it was could not be found to have been duly executed by Arnott and that, it will be remembered, was a situation in which there was merely a circular mark on the paper with the words 'Place for seal' printed within it.

Re Sandilands[2] has been further considered in a decision of this court, *National Provincial Bank of England v Jackson*[4]. There it was described by Lindley LJ[5] as being a 'good-natured decision', by which I imagine that he indicated that he thought the court had gone as far as it possibly could in *Re Sandilands*[2] in favour of holding that the document had been properly executed. Cotton LJ, in the first judgment delivered in *National Provincial Bank of England v Jackson*[6], said:

---

1   (1888) 58 LT 300
2   (1871) LR 6 CP 411
3   58 LT 300 at 301
4   (1886) 33 Ch D 1
5   33 Ch D 1 at 14
6   33 Ch D 1 at 10, 11

'This further is remarkable, that although these instruments are expressed to be signed, sealed, and delivered in the presence of the attesting witness, who was *a* one of R. *Jackson's* clerks, there is no trace of any seal, but merely the piece of ribbon for the usual purpose of keeping the wax on the parchment. In my opinion the only conclusion we can come to is that these instruments were never in fact sealed at all. They were somehow or other prepared by R. *Jackson*, but never in fact executed by him in such a way as to reconvey the legal estate. It is said, and said truly, that neither wax nor wafer is necessary in order to con- *b* stitute a seal to a deed, and that frequently, as in the case of a corporation party to a deed, there is only an impression on the paper; and *In re Sandilands*[1] was referred to, where an instrument had been forwarded from the colonies together with an official certificate of its having been duly acknowledged, and this was recognised by the Court as a deed although there was no seal but only the ribbon on it. That case is not now under appeal, but it is evident that the question was *c* merely as to what was the true inference of fact, and although perhaps, having regard to the certificate, it was right there to hold that the deed had been sealed, here in my opinion it would be wrong to do so. It is true that if the finger be pressed upon the ribbon that may amount to sealing, but no such inference can be drawn here [and these I think are important words] where the attesting witness who has given evidence recollects nothing of the sort, and when *Jackson* *d* had already committed one fraud in the matter and perhaps then intended another.'

As I have said, Lindley LJ[2] described the decision in *Re Sandilands*[1] as being a good-natured decision and thought that he would not have come to the same conclusion. I do not think Lopes LJ added anything. He said[3]:

e

'On the question as to the reconveyances I will add nothing, except to say that in my opinion they were inoperative for the reasons given by the Lords Justices.'

The most recent decision to which we have been referred is a decision of Danckwerts J in *Stromdale and Ball Ltd v Burden*[4], in which the learned judge said:

f

'Another point is taken which also depends on the defendant's evidence. It is said that, as she merely signed the document called "deed of licence" and never did any act amounting to sealing, it was not effectively executed as a deed. I was referred by counsel for the defendant to NORTON ON DEEDS[5] where the formalities required for the execution of deeds are discussed, and it is said there, quoting MONTAGUE SMITH, J. in *Re Sandilands*[6], that ". . . some act must be done 'with the *g* intention of sealing'." Reliance was also placed on *Re Smith*[7], in which the document intended to be a bond bore the words "sealed with my seal" and was stated in the attestation clause to have been "signed, sealed, and delivered," but there was no mark, wafer, or seal visible on the face of the document. It was held in that case that the document could not be treated as having been sealed. In the present case the defendant's evidence is very vague as to whether the wafer *h* seal was on the document when she signed it, and I think it is unlikely that the wafer seal had not been placed on it before she was asked by the solicitors' clerk to sign. If it was there when she signed, it seems to me that the document was

---

1 (1871) LR 6 CP 411
2 (1886) 33 Ch D 1 at 14
3 33 Ch D 1 at 15
4 [1952] 1 All ER 59 at 62, [1952] Ch 223 at 229, 230
5 2nd Edn (1928), pp 7, 8
6 LR 6 CP 411 at 413
7 (1892) 67 LT 64

j

effectively executed as a deed. Time was when the placing of the party's seal was the essence of due execution. Signature was not, indeed, necessary to make a deed valid: see Norton on Deeds[1]. But with the spread of education the signature became of importance for the authentification of documents and since 1925 it has become essential by reason of the provisions of the Law of Property Act, 1925, s. 73(1). Meticulous persons executing a deed may still place their finger on the wax seal or wafer on the document, but it appears to me that at the present day if a party signs a document bearing wax or wafer or other indication of a seal with the intention of executing the document as a deed, that is sufficient adoption or recognition of the seal to amount to due execution as a deed.'

In the present case we really have no evidence at all beyond the fact that in the first of the plaintiffs' affidavits, which the learned deputy judge may or may not have looked at (we cannot tell), there appears this statement: 'On the 20th day of September 1974 the Defendant executed a Legal Charge of the whole of the interest in the property in favour of the Plaintiffs', and then a true copy of the charge is exhibited. We have that exhibit, the features of which I have described, and we have no evidence to indicate in any other way whether the first defendant did or did not intend to deliver this document as his act and deed. But it is a very familiar feature nowadays of documents which are intended to be executed as deeds that they do not have any wax, or even wafer, seal attached to them, but have printed at the spot where formerly the seal would probably have been placed, a printed circle, which is sometimes hatched and sometimes has the letters 'L.S.' within it, which is intended to serve the purpose of a seal if the document is delivered as the deed of the party executing it.

In the present case there is not only the circle with the letters 'L.S.' within it on the document, printed as part of the printed version of the document, but also there is the feature that the mortgagor has placed his signature across that circle. In my judgment those features, and the attestation in the absence of any contrary evidence, are sufficient evidence to establish that the document was executed by the first defendant as his deed. On the material before us it seems to me that there was certainly no evidence before the learned judge on which he could have held that the document had not been so executed by the first defendant; and in the light of the authorities to which I have referred, I am of the opinion that the evidence sufficiently establishes that this legal charge was executed by the first defendant as a deed, and that the learned judge was mistaken in law in thinking that what was done did not amount to sufficient execution and delivery of the document as the mortgagor's deed. For these reasons it seems to me that the learned deputy county court judge reached a wrong conclusion in law, and that this appeal should be allowed.

There will remain the issues in the action appearing on the pleadings, which have never yet been investigated. I would allow this appeal and remit the action to the county court for retrial.

GOFF LJ. I agree. There are two questions of law which arise in determining whether the alleged legal charge of 20th September 1974 was duly executed as a deed. The first is whether, whatever the facts, there can be a deed when nothing is attached to the paper, but it has merely, as in the present case, a printed or written indication of the place where a seal should be affixed. The second is whether, if the document was in law capable of being a deed though it had no more than an indication of where the seal should be placed, there was any evidence on which the learned deputy county court judge could hold that it was not duly executed.

---

1   2nd Edn (1928), p 7

Re Balkis Consolidated Co Ltd[1], to which Buckley LJ has referred, was a case in which, when the document was produced in court, it was found that there was no seal on it and no wafer in the place of a seal, but only a circular mark on the paper with the words 'Place for seal' printed within it. But I do not read that case as a decision that therefore the document could not be a deed. Rather, I think, the reverse, because the learned judge reserved the question of whether it was a deed until the conflict of evidence which had manifested itself as to what in fact occurred had been resolved.

The dictum of Danckwerts J in *Stromdale and Ball Ltd v Burden*[2] strongly supports the view that an instrument having nothing physically affixed to it, but merely indicating where the seal should be, is capable of being executed as a deed, for the learned judge said:

'Meticulous persons executing a deed may still place their finger on the wax seal or wafer on the document, but it appears to me that at the present day if a party signed a document bearing wax or wafer [and then follow the important words] or other indication of a seal with the intention of executing the document as a deed, that is sufficient adoption or recognition of the seal to amount to due execution as a deed.'

In my judgment, in this day and age, we can, and we ought to, hold that a document purporting to be a deed is capable in law of being such although it has no more than an indication where the seal should be. *National Provincial Bank of England v Jackson*[3], which was a decison of this court, does not in any way preclude us from arriving at that conclusion, because it was a decision on the facts. In that case the attesting witness gave evidence and was unable to recollect any execution of the document by the parties concerned. Moreover, there were grounds for supecting fraud. Cotton LJ said[4]: 'In my opinion the only conclusion we can come to is that these instruments were never in fact sealed at all.' Lindley LJ, in the passage to which Buckley LJ has referred where he said that *Re Sandilands*[5] was a good-natured decision, went on to say[6]: '. . . but on the evidence in this case I certainly cannot come to that conclusion.' I think I need make only one further reference to authority, that is to refer to the judgment of Montague Smith J in the early case of *Re Sandilands*[7] itself, in which he relied on the apparent regularity of the attestation as being sufficient. In my judgment, therefore, the alleged legal charge was capable of being a deed, although it bore no seal and nothing was physically annexed to it.

Then it becomes a question of fact, and I turn to the second question, whether there was any evidence on which the learned deputy county court judge could reach the conclusion he did reach, that it was not duly executed as a deed. The papers contain the affidavit, to which Buckley LJ has referred, in which a witness on behalf of the plaintiffs swore that on 20th September 1974 the defendant executed a legal charge on the property in favour of the plaintiffs. We do not know whether that affidavit was laid before the learned deputy judge. If it were, of course, it contained positive evidence of the due execution of the deed. But, apart from that, the document itself was produced to the court. It describes itself as a deed, as Buckley LJ has observed, because the operative part is introduced with the common form words 'Now THIS DEED WITNESSETH AS FOLLOWS'. It contains an attestation clause in due form, 'SIGNED

---

1   (1888) 58 LT 300
2   [1952] 1 All ER 59 at 62, [1952] Ch 223 at 230
3   (1886) 33 Ch D 1
4   33 Ch D 1 at 11
5   (1871) LR 6 CP 411
6   33 Ch D 1 at 14
7   LR 6 CP 411 at 413

SEALED AND DELIVERED by the above-named Mortgagor in the presence of', and then it is signed by a witness, and it is signed by the first defendant and, as Buckley LJ has pointed out, signed over the very place where there appears the indication that there should be a seal, thus recognising the significance of that part of the instrument.

It seems to me that on the evidence before the learned judge it is clear that the first defendant recognised and accepted the document as his deed. Certainly I can see no evidence whatever on which to base a finding that he did not, and in my judgment, with all respect to the learned deputy judge, the conclusion which he reached is one which cannot be supported.

That, of course, is not the end of the dispute between the parties, because there appear to be issues as to what money, if any, was in fact advanced and as to the state of account between the parties. The origin of the relationship appears to be an agreement by the plaintiffs to lend a specific sum of money, namely £4,100, on certain terms providing for repayment by instalments, and the first defendant said in his pleading that the money was not paid to him, or for that matter to his wife, but was paid to a solicitor without the first defendant's knowledge or authority. There is a provision in the agreement that the moneys were to be paid to a solicitor against an undertaking to utilise moneys for the purchase of a share in Macs Motors, but the pleading says that the money was misappropriated, either by the plaintiffs or by the solicitor to whom it was paid, or both, and there may be questions between the parties whether the money was advanced, if so to whom it was advanced and if to a solicitor whether he was the agent of the plaintiffs or of the first defendant and what he did with the moneys he received. In any event the legal charge is not a charge covering that proposed advance only, but is an all-moneys charge in the usual form employed by banks, and therefore there will be a question whether there were any moneys secured by the legal charge by reason of the account between the bank and its customers, the first defendant and his wife. Those are all matters which remain to be investigated on a proper trial of the issues between the parties, and I agree with Buckley LJ that this action should be remitted to the county court for trial of those issues, but of course on the basis of our decision that the document was duly executed as a deed.

SIR DAVID CAIRNS. I agree that this appeal should be allowed and that the matter should be remitted to the county court for further hearing. I agree with the reasons that have already been given by Buckley and Goff LJJ for that conclusion.

For my part, I would say that even if the first defendant's signature had not been written over the circle containing the letters 'L.S.' I should have been prepared to hold that the document was a valid deed. In my judgment the present state of the law is accurately stated by Danckwerts J in the passage in *Stromdale and Ball Ltd v Burden*[1] which has already been referred to.

Moreover, while in 1888 the printed indication of a locus sigilli was regarded as being merely the place where a seal was to be affixed, I have no doubt that it is now regarded by most business people and ordinary members of the public as constituting the seal itself. I am sure that many documents intended by all parties to be deeds are now executed without any further formality than the signature opposite the words 'Signed, sealed and delivered', usually in the presence of a witness, and I think it would be lamentable if the validity of documents so executed could be successfuly challenged.

One further matter that I would mention is that when further consideration is given to the action in the county court, it will be necessary for the learned judge to consider whether any money judgment can be given, having regard to the limitation

---

1   [1952] 1 All ER 59 at 62, [1952] Ch 223 at 230

of the jurisdiction of the court as to amount in actions for money claimed under a contract, contained in s 39(2) of the County Courts Act 1959, unless indeed an agreement in writing has been made under s 42 of that Act.

Appeal allowed. Action remitted to the county court.

Solicitors: *Davis & Co*, Harrow (for the plaintiffs); *E H Grove & Co*, Halesowen (for the defendants).

J H Fazan Esq   Barrister.

Re C (minors) (wardship: jurisdiction)

COURT OF APPEAL, CIVIL DIVISION
STAMP, ORMROD LJJ AND SIR DAVID CAIRNS
28th, 29th APRIL, 3rd MAY 1977

Ward of court – Jurisdiction – Kidnapping – Peremptory order for return of wards to foreign jurisdiction – Refusal to make order – Welfare of children first and paramount consideration – Circumstances rendering it proper for English court to assume jurisdiction – Likelihood of foreign court ordering return of children to custody of natural parent in England – Children living with mother and stepfather in California – Death of mother – Natural father having remarried and living in England – Application by stepfather to Californian court for custody – Father removing children to England and making them wards of court – Application by stepfather for peremptory order for return of children to California – Whether court should make order.

In 1966 the father went to the United States on an immigrant's visa and, while there, met the mother; they were then both 19 years old. The mother became pregnant by him and in 1967 they married. Soon afterwards they set up home in England. They had three children, a girl, N, and two boys, J and A, who were born between 1967 and 1971. In August 1973 the mother left the father and, with his consent, returned with the children to her family in California. In 1974 the father visited them. In the same year the mother, with the children, went to live with another man ('the stepfather'). In 1975 the parents' marriage was dissolved. Custody of the children was given to the mother by consent. Shortly afterwards the mother married the stepfather and the father also remarried. During 1976 the father and his new wife visited the children. On 8th February 1977 the mother died suddenly. On 13th February the father heard the news of her death and, two days later, went to California with his own mother. On his arrival, the stepfather, the maternal grandmother and an aunt applied to the Superior Court of California for custody of the children and an interim order was made. On 21st March the court made an order for access in the father's favour which included staying access on the weekend of 26th and 27th March. During that weekend the father 'kidnapped' the children and brought them back to England to live with him and his wife. On 5th April the stepfather started proceedings in the High Court making the children wards of court and asked for a peremptory order that they be returned forthwith to California where proceedings were pending. At the hearing before the judge the father gave evidence that, from time to time, the stepfather smoked cannabis; that evidence was not disputed. The judge held that he was required to make a peremptory order for the return of the children to California unless he was satisfied that there was 'some obvious moral or physical danger involved in making such an order'. He concluded, however, that the facts of the case constituted 'such a serious moral danger to these children that their future ought to be considered by the English courts' for, as the children got older, 'they may acquire a habituation to the use of drugs'. Accordingly he refused to make a peremptory order for their return. The stepfather appealed. At the hearing of the appeal, the Court of Appeal had before it a report of the welfare officer of the Californian court which recommended that the petition of the stepfather, the maternal grandmother and the aunt be denied because it would not be 'detrimental for the children to live and be with their natural father . . .' The report continued: 'The laws of California give preference to a natural parent and we find [the father] able to function as parent to his children.'

Held – (i) The principles to be applied in kidnapping cases where the court was called on to make a peremptory order for the return of a child were exactly the same as in all other decisions relating to the welfare of children, i e the child's welfare was the first and the paramount consideration because it was of first importance and because it was the consideration which determined the course that was to be followed. Accordingly, the judge was wrong in holding that he was required to find some obvious moral or physical danger to the child before he would be justified in refusing to make a peremptory order (see p 234 *f g*, p 235 *c* to *g* and p 239 *j* to p 240 *a* and *g h*, post); dicta of Lord MacDermott in *J v C* [1969] 1 All ER at 820, 821 and of Buckley LJ in *Re L (minors) (wardship: jurisdiction)* [1974] 1 All ER at 924, 925 applied.

(ii) It appeared from the Californian welfare officer's report that there was a real risk of the children being taken back to California only to be sent back again to be placed in the care of their natural father. For that reason the proper course was for the English court to assume jurisdiction, the only justification for that being the likelihood that the Californian court would come to the same conclusion. In the circumstances it was clearly in the interests of the children that they should stay with their father not simply because he was their natural father, but more importantly because, unlike the stepfather, he was able to offer them a mother-substitute in his new wife and a stable home. The appeal would therefore be dismissed (see p 238 *d*, to p 239 *f* and p 240 *f* to *h*, post).

Notes
For the rights of the father and mother to custody, see 21 Halsbury's Laws (3rd Edn) 191-197, paras 425-432, and for cases on the subject, see 28(2) Digest (Reissue) 793-813, 1183-1290.

Cases referred to in judgments
B G, Re (1974) 11 Cal 3d 679, 114 Cal Rptr 444.
E (an infant), Re [1967] 1 All ER 329, [1967] Ch 287, [1967] 2 WLR 445; *affd* [1967] 2 All ER 881, [1967] Ch 761, [1967] 2 WLR 1370, CA, 28(2) Digest (Reissue) 801, 1236.
J v C [1969] 1 All ER 788, [1970] AC 668, [1969] 2 WLR 540, HL, 28(2) Digest (Reissue) 800, 1230.
L (minors) (wardship: jurisdiction), Re [1974] 1 All ER 913, [1974] 1 WLR 250, CA, Digest (Cont Vol D) 520, 1237a.
McKee v McKee [1951] 1 All ER 942, [1951] AC 352, PC, 28(2) Digest (Reissue) 801, 1235.
T (infants), Re [1968] 3 All ER 411, [1968] Ch 704, [1968] 3 WLR 430, CA, Digest (Cont Vol C) 152, 1185c.
T A (infants), Re (1972) 116 Sol Jo 78.

Appeal
The plaintiff, who was the stepfather of three children who had been made wards of court in proceedings commenced by the defendant, their natural father ('the father'), appealed against an order of his Honour Judge McLellan, sitting at Winchester as a deputy judge of the High Court, on 20th April 1977 dismissing an application by the

plaintiff for an order that the children be returned forthwith to the care and control
of the plaintiff, that the plaintiff be at liberty to remove the children from the juris- *a*
diction and that the children be dewarded. The facts are set out in the judgment of
Ormrod LJ.

John K Wood QC and *Anthony Coleman* for the plaintiff.
Barbara Calvert QC and *Andrew Massey* for the father.

b

ORMROD LJ delivered the first judgment at the invitation of Stamp LJ. This is a
case which can properly be called an extremely tragic one for everybody concerned.
It has caused the court a great deal of anxiety and worry; but I think it is right to say,
on the part of myself at any rate, that we are extremely grateful first to counsel,
who have helped us immensely on both sides, and also to Mr Chapman, the welfare *c*
officer, who made a most helpful report on this case in a very short period of time,
which has been of immense assistance to us.

The short facts are these. In 1966 the father of these three children emigrated to the
United States on an immigrant's visa and, while there, he met their mother. She
became pregnant by him; they were both very young, each of them only about 19,
and they got married on 26th March 1967. They both came back to England fairly *d*
soon afterwards, and in 1971 set up house together at Midanbury, Southampton.
They had three children who are the subject-matter of these proceedings: N, who was
born in 1967 and is nine; J, who was born in 1969 and is eight; and A, who was born in
1971 and is six. The marriage did not survive very long and in August 1973 they
parted. It seems to have been an unhappy marriage. We had some evidence to that
effect in the form of an affidavit from a friend of the mother's, which indicated that *e*
the marriage was an unsatisfactory one from the mother's point of view.

In 1973 the mother returned with the children, with the consent of the father, to
California, having transferred her interest in the matrimonial home to him. She
went back to her mother and her family, who were living in California. In 1974
the father paid a visit to California and saw the mother and the children. Also in
that year the mother began to live with Mr O'B, who is the plaintiff in these present *f*
proceedings, who became the stepfather of the children. They lived together in
San Francisco.

Eventually, on 10th March 1975, the marriage of the father and mother was dissolved by decree nisi, and custody was given to the mother by consent. There was
no formal order giving her leave to keep the children out of the jurisdiction, but
that was obviously part of the consent order. The decree was made absolute on 22nd *g*
April 1975. Very shortly after that the mother remarried the plaintiff and they
moved together to an address at Novato, California. Again about the same time, the
father remarried a young woman who is now herself about 19 years of age. She was
by upbringing a member of the Jehovah's Witness persuasion, and the father, either
immediately before or after the marriage, became converted to that persuasion also,
and they now are both practising Jehovah's Witnesses. *h*

In August 1976 the father and his new wife visited California for a few weeks and
saw the children from time to time. Then, on 8th February 1977, the great tragedy
occurred in these children's lives, because their mother suddenly died of a heart attack,
consequent on some existing heart disorder that she had. That left these children
in the care of the plaintiff, who is obviously extremely fond of them and they of him.
On 13th February the father was told of the mother's death and a couple of days later *j*
he arrived with his own mother in California. Almost immediately after his arriving
in California, the plaintiff and the maternal grandmother and the mother's sister,
all three, applied to the Superior Court of California in Marin County for an order for
custody of the children, no doubt stimulated by the arrival of the father. An interim
order for custody in favour of the plaintiff and the grandmother and aunt was made;

and on 12th March the procedure which is followed in the United States of taking
depositions of the witnesses on the opposing side by the advocate for the other party
took place. We have been supplied with copies of those depositions.

On 14th March the first hearing took place, which was largely a formality, because
the matter was assigned, according to the procedure in California, to the Department
of Social Services to investigate and report. Meanwhile, the interim order continued.
A week later, on 21st March, an order for access was made in favour of the father,
and that order for access included staying access on the weekend of 26th and 27th
March. During that weekend the father, in deliberate breach of the order of the
court in California, kidnapped the children; that is to say, he put them on a plane
and brought them back to England.

On 5th April the plaintiff caused an originating summons to be issued in the High
Court in England, making the children thereby wards of court. He also issued a
summons for leave to remove the children back to the United States forthwith;
in other words, he was then asking for a peremptory order that the children return
to California, where the proceedings were of course still pending. On that same day a
warrant of arrest was issued in the Californian court for the arrest of the father;
and we were told that extradition proceedings were started, I am not sure by whom.

On 6th April the matter came before his Honour Judge Stock QC, who adjourned
the summons but made an order for access by the plaintiff to the children, he being
now in England, and an order was made requiring the father to give particulars of any
criticism that he relied on of the plaintiff's character.

On 14th April the hearing began before his Honour Judge McLellan, that hearing
being a hearing of the plaintiff's summons for an order that the children be forthwith
returned to California. That summons was adjourned in the hope that the welfare
officer's report which had been ordered by the Californian court would be available
very shortly, but unfortunately it did not arrive in time for the adjourned hearing,
and the learned judge, reasonably in the circumstances, felt that he could wait no
longer than 20th April before embarking on a full hearing of the matter of the
plaintiff's summons for the children to be returned to California. At the conclusion
of the hearing, at which he heard a considerable body of evidence from both the
father and the plaintiff and others, the learned judge decided (I think reluctantly,
from reading his judgment) that he could not, in all the circumstances of the case,
make a peremptory order directing the return forthwith of these children to California
with the plaintiff, for reasons which I will come to in a moment. The appeal which is
now before this court is an appeal from that order made by his Honour Judge McLellan
on 20th April.

The case is one which is clearly a very difficult one from every point of view, not
least that of the potential conflict of jurisdiction between this court and the Californian
court, but it is perhaps right to say at this stage that the view of this court is that the
learned judge arrived at the right conclusion. It is also right to say that this court has
reached that conclusion on very different grounds from those which the learned
judge relied on and on much fuller information than he had, because we have had
the advantage of seeing now the welfare officer's report, prepared in California,
although it is quite correct to say that it was not complete because the children were
removed before the enquiries of the welfare officers in California were completed.
We also have before us, as I have said already, Mr Chapman's report on the condition
of the children here in England. The children have been, since their arrival in
England on 27th March, living at Southampton in their father's house with the father
and their stepmother and have just started school in England.

There are one or two matters in the judge's judgment on which I feel it is necessary
to say something, particularly in view of the fact that this judgment may find its
way in due course back to the court of California, and it is of paramount importance
that the two courts concerned in this matter do not misunderstand one another.
The learned judge in his judgment formed a very unfavourable view, it is right to

say, of the father and a favourable view of the plaintiff, generally speaking, although he made certain criticisms about him. He observed that he was 'a man materialistic and philistine to a marked degree, but with the material and emotional generosity that sometimes accompanies such a temperament and outlook', but he accepted his evidence wherever it conflicted with that of the father as being evidence of truth, and he made some very serious criticisms of the father himself. The father, of course, was highly vulnerable to criticism, because he had acted in a grossly improper way, in circumstances which I will refer to in a little more detail in a moment, in kidnapping these children unilaterally from the control of the Californian court. It is only natural that this court should be most reluctant to take over a case of this kind in the middle, when proceedings are pending in another jurisdiction.

In my judgment, the judge, although he referred to the leading authority in this court on this type of problem, that is Re L[1], did not in fact apply the principles therein set out. Re L[1] is now the locus classicus, as I think, for all problems relating to how the courts in England should deal with situations where children have been unilaterally taken from one jurisdiction to another and proceedings have been started in England in consequence. The judge eventually directed himself so far as the law is concerned in this way. Having referred to Re L[1], he said:

> 'First, as to kidnapping. The kidnapping of children is unfortunately easy and once it has been affected the children are effectively removed irrevocably to another country and jurisdiction. I am not all at sure that the superior courts have spoken the last word on the matter and where, as in this case, a child the subject of pending proceedings has been kidnapped from the jurisdiction of another civilised and orderly state I should have thought that there is a good deal to be said for ordering its immediate return, leaving it to the courts of that state to arrive at a just conclusion. However, that is not the law as I find it laid down for my guidance. A kidnapping is one, but only one, of the factors involved, and I must consider all the facts and matters in the case.'

So far, if I may say so with respect to the learned judge, he correctly follows Re L[1]. Then he goes on:

> 'I must, as I understand the matter, make a peremptory order for the return of these children unless I am satisfied that there is some obvious moral or physical danger involved in making such an order.'

That, in my respectful judgment, is a misdirection, and a serious one. The proposition established by Buckley LJ's long and most careful review of all the cases on this subject and his conclusion about them, particularly in the light of the House of Lords' decision in J v C[2], is set out quite clearly where he said this[3]:

> 'How, then, do the kidnapping cases fit these principles? Where the court has embarked upon a full-scale investigation of the facts, the applicable principles, in my view, do not differ from those which apply to any other wardship case. The action of one party in kidnapping the child is doubtless one of the circumstances to be taken into account, and may be a circumstance of great weight; the weight to be attributed to it must depend on the circumstances of the particular case. The court may conclude that notwithstanding the conduct of the "kidnapper" the child should remain in his or her care (McKee v McKee[4], Re E (an infant)[5] and Re T A (infants)[6], where the order was merely interim);

---

1 [1974] 1 All ER 913, [1974] 1 WLR 250
2 [1969] 1 All ER 788, [1970] AC 668
3 [1974] 1 All ER 913 at 925, [1974] 1 WLR 250 at 264
4 [1951] 1 All ER 942, [1951] AC 352
5 [1967] 2 All ER 881, [1967] Ch 761
6 (1972) 116 Sol Jo 78

a or it may conclude that the child should be returned to his or her native country
or the jurisdiction from which he or she has been removed (*Re T (infants)*[1]).
Where a court makes a summary order for the return of a child to a foreign
country without investigating the merits, the same principles, in my judgment,
apply, but the decision must be justified on somewhat different grounds. To
take a child from his native land, to remove him to another country where,
maybe, his native tongue is not spoken, to divorce him from the social customs
b and contacts to which he has been accustomed, to interrupt his education in his
native land and subject him to a foreign system of education, are all acts (offered
here as examples and of course not as a complete catalogue of possible relevant
factors) which are likely to be psychologically disturbing to the child, particularly
at a time when his family life is also disrupted.'

c The passage continues. I do not think I need read more.
The principles to be applied, therefore, in cases of this kind, where the court is
called on to consider whether or not to make an order for the peremptory return
of the child, are exactly the same as in all other decisions relating to the welfare of
children. Those principles were set out by Lord MacDermott in the very well-
known passage in *J v C*[2] which is quoted by Buckley LJ[3]. I will read it, in case this
d judgment finds its way to America:

'Reading these words[4] in their ordinary significance, and relating them to the
various classes of proceedings which the section has already mentioned, it seems
to me that they must mean more than that the child's welfare is to be treated as
the top item in a list of items relevant to the matter in question. I think they
connote a process whereby, when all the relevant facts, relationships, claims and
e wishes of parents, risks, choices and other circumstances are taken into account
and weighed, the course to be followed will be that which is most in the interests
of the child's welfare as that term has now to be understood. That is the first
consideration because it is of first importance and the paramount consideration
because it rules on or determines the course to be followed.'

f In other words, using for a moment the American terminology, all decisions relating
to the welfare and future of children have to be decided on the 'best interests' of
the children principle and no other glosses are to be put on that test. The learned
judge, in thinking that he had to find some obvious moral or physical danger was
clearly, in my judgment, putting on Buckley LJ's judgment a gloss which was
unwarranted.

g However, notwithstanding that gloss, he arrived at the conclusion to which he did;
and I must now say why. There had been evidence from the father, which had not
been disputed by the plaintiff, that from time to time the plaintiff (and I suppose his
friends) smoked what we call 'cannabis' and the Americans in the United States refer
to as 'marijuana'. The judge's conclusion on the evidence was that the plaintiff
was in no sense an addict, but smoked marijuana 'socially' (as one might describe it)
h from time to time. However, the judge took a very legalistic view of this, and at the
conclusion of his judgment said this:

'In the course of the arguments I put to counsel for the father the proposition
that there is known to be a sufficient disagreement in informed opinion in this
and other countries that however much the law of England disapproves of the

j 1 [1968] 3 All ER 441, [1968] Ch 704
2 [1969] 1 All ER 788 at 820, 821, [1970] AC 668 at 710, 711
3 [1974] 1 All ER 913 at 924, 925, [1974] 1 WLR 250 at 263
4 'Where in any proceeding . . . the custody or upbringing of an infant . . . is in question,
the court . . . shall regard the welfare of the infant as the first and paramount consideration
. . .': Guardianship of Infant Act 1925, s 1

consumption of cannabis other civilised states are entitled to make their own
domestic laws on this point and that if they are less stringent than those of
England it was a matter for their own domestic tribunals to give the appropriate
weight to facts which are not in dispute. I have said before, and I repeat, that I
do not disagree with the law of England. I did express a doubt as to whether the
law preventing the consumption of cannabis presented such a universal moral
imperative as to justify the English courts assuming final jurisdiction in a case
arriving before it in this way. Whatever may be the answer to this not unimportant and interesting question, after careful consideration and some hesitation I
have come to the conclusion that the facts of this case, which are not open to
serious dispute on this issue, are such that I am compelled to and do regard them
as constituting such a serious moral danger to these children that their future
ought to be considered by the English courts and that I ought not, as counsel for
the plaintiff has asked me to, make a peremptory order for the children's return.
As the children get older they may acquire a habituation to the use of drugs.'

That was the ratio decidendi, quite plainly, of the learned judge's decision. Speaking
entirely for myself, it is not a ratio decidendi which I myself would have adopted.
On the evidence as the learned judge accepted it, I would have formed the view that
the smoking of cannabis by the plaintiff, assuming that his version of it was correct,
was a matter to be taken into account in considering the future of these children,
but by no means a conclusive one. It would, of course, be otherwise if the judge had
found that his use of marijuana or cannabis had gone much further than the learned
judge thought it had. The judge went on to say:

'I have earlier mentioned the welfare report in the California court. No copy
of that report has yet come to hand but this morning a letter was handed to me
emanating from the Department of Health and Human Services of the county
of Marin in the State of California. This seems to indicate that provisionally at
any rate it would be reasonable to expect [the father] to succeed in his application
for custody in California. I am bound to say that this impression—and it is only
an impression—confirms my own impression—which again is only an impression,
that wherever the question of custody is litigated it is highly probable that
custody will be given to the natural father who is in a position to offer the children
a stable home and the assistance of a stepmother. However, I should make it
clear that this tentative view is not the basis on which I arrived at my decision.'

Having seen now the full welfare officer's report from California and our own welfare
officer's report, I have no hesitation in saying that that is the basis of my conclusion
in this case.

Before I leave the judge's judgment, there is one other matter which I think it is
right to mention; that is, that in dealing with the father, the judge, I think, took the
view that he had planned to kidnap these children from the outset. Certainly he
said:

'When he took advantage of the permission of the California court to put the
children on an aircraft and bring them to England, contrary to the order of that
court, I have no doubt that he knew full well what he was doing. I regarded his
attempts to explain his actions away in his evidence before me as blatant lies.
He went to America with a ticket. I have no doubt he intended to use it in this
way if he could not attain his ends legally. In general I did not regard his evidence
as candid. I have no doubt that he has abused his position whilst the children
have been in his care in England to influence their minds in favour of the tenets
of the Jehovah's Witnesses and against [the plaintiff] as an "evil" person, which
I do not think he is, much as I dislike some of his views and practices.'

In fairness to the father, two things should be said. The first is that he left England

with tickets to bring the children back to England at a time when there was no order
a of any court in existence which prevented him as their father from doing exactly
that. Secondly, it seems to me clear on the evidence that he and his mother set off
from England to do what, I would imagine, they would themselves have called
'bringing the children home', in view of the tragedy that had happened with the death
of their mother. It is perhaps an unfair stricture on the father to treat him as a person
who had planned to flout an order of the court from the outset. It is clear from his
b own evidence, and it would be difficult, I venture to think, not to accept his evidence
on this, having regard to his economic position, that the prolongation of proceedings
in California (and by that I do not mean to suggest for a moment that they were
unduly prolonged) put him and his mother into a financial difficulty of the gravest
possible kind, so that it was more and more unlikely that he would be able to stay
in California, or could afford to stay in California, any longer. No doubt he incurred
c enormous expense in obtaining legal representation in the proceedings and so on,
and it is very easy to see that by the end of March this year he must have been under
the greatest possible financial pressure to get back from California as quickly as
possible. I make those observations in fairness to him, because it would be wrong I
think, certainly unfair, if those points were not borne in mind.

I turn now to the first letter from the Californian welfare officer which is in our
d bundle. It is a letter from Mrs Marjorie Buckley, a social worker, dated 14th April
1977, addressed to the solicitors acting for the stepfather. The relevant paragraph
in the letter is this: having said that it was impossible to complete the report in time
to get it to England by the date of the hearing, 19th or 20th April, she says:

e
> 'It is my recommendation to the Marin County Superior Court that the petition
> of [the plaintiff, the maternal grandmother and the aunt] for guardianship of [the
> children] be denied on the basis that, in evaluating the information gathered
> concerning this matter, I did not find it would be detrimental for the children to
> live and be with their father . . .'

Now that we have the full report, that is the conclusion that is reached in the full
report itself, after a long account of what was said by various people to the welfare
f officer and all sorts of enquiries which she had made. The report in its final form,
final that is to say so far as this court is concerned, is this:

> 'Losing either their father or stepfather would be painful to the children. It
> would be hoped that [the plaintiff] and [the father] would be able to put aside
> the past so the children would be relieved of the conflicts which have surrounded
> them.'

g
Then this is the important part:

> 'We have not found it would be detrimental for the children to live and be with
> their natural father . . . The laws of California give preference to a natural
> parent and we find [the father] able to function as parent to his children. Recom-
> mendation: The Marin County Division of Public Social Services recommend]
h > that the petition of [the stepfather, the maternal grandmother and the aunts
> for the guardianship of [the children] be denied.'

The reason no doubt for that recommendation is to be found in the fact that the
welfare authorities could not find anything 'detrimental' in the children being
returned to their father.
j We were referred very helpfully to a report of a case called *Re B G*[1] in the Supreme
Court of California in June 1974. It is a judgment of the full court, in which there are
certain dissenting judgments. All I think I need for present purposes say about it is
this. The judgment traces the development of the law on the question of the standing

---

1   (1974) 11 Cal 3d 679

of a natural parent vis-à-vis a non-parent in claims for custody of children. The judgment demonstrates that the former law in California was that in order to give *a* the custody of a child to a non-parent it was necessary for the court to find as a fact that the parent was 'unfit' to exercise custody. Then apparently in 1969 the Family Law Act amended the existing law in California by deleting the requirement that it was necessary to prove unfitness to exercise custody and substituting for it a provision that the court must find that the award of custody to the parent would be 'detrimental' to the child, and that such an award to a non-parent was required to serve *b* the best interests of the child.

That is the present state of the law in California. Perhaps one might properly comment that the evolution of the law in California seems to be following very much the same lines as the law in England has already followed from the time before the first of the Guardianship of Infants Acts in 1886, when a claim by a father was almost irresistible by the mother or anybody else unless he was shown to be a person who *c* had totally unfitted himself to act as a parent, through a period after the Guardianship of Infants Acts 1886 and 1925 were passed, when the claim of a natural parent, particularly an unimpeachable natural parent, took precedence over the claims of any non-parent, to the present state of the law set out in *J v C*[1] by the House of Lords, which makes it clear that in England now the law requires the court, as I have already said, to make its decision based on the best interests of the children without gloss or *d* qualification. The Californian court seems to be very much in the state that this court was in before *J v C*[1] was finally decided by the House of Lords.

The importance of this consideration is this, that if this court decides that the proper order is to send these children back to California for their future to be decided by the Californian court, judging by the welfare officer's report and doing the best we can in a necessarily amateur way, it seems highly likely that the American court *e* will conclude that the plaintiff is unable to demonstrate that it would be 'detrimental' to the interests of these children to be placed in the custody of their father, in which case the Californian court would have to make an order for custody in the father's favour, which would mean that the children would be returned, or have to be returned, to this country once more. It cannot possibly be in the best interests of children to expose them to a real risk, call it balance of probabilities or whatever, *f* but I would prefer to speak of it as a real risk, of being taken back to California by the plaintiff, only to be sent back again here to be placed in the care of their natural father. It is only for that reason that, in my judgment, this court should assume jurisdiction, and it is for that reason that I agree that the order which the learned judge made was a right order, although I cannot agree with the grounds on which he made it. It is only in such a way that this court could justify this interference (as it were) *g* with the court in California, and the justification for it is that this court is coming to a decision which, so far as it can judge, the Californian court would be likely to reach itself.

Counsel for the plaintiff has tried to argue the case on the footing that he was appearing in the Californian court, trying to show that there was sufficient evidence here to establish 'detriment'. This is, of course, a difficult theoretical exercise, par- *h* ticularly before a court which does not know at all clearly how the word 'detriment' is interpreted in California. It has clearly got to be something more than 'not in the best interests of the children'.

The position as we find it in fact now is this, as I see it. The children had become and got completely used to their life in California, their friends and their relatives were there, and counsel for the plaintiff is perfectly justified in saying that they had *j* put down their roots in California. They clearly had. They were, all the evidence shows, happy there, and their memories of England must have been comparatively faint. It is also right to say that the death of their mother has been the most terrible

---

blow to each of them, and each of them no doubt is trying to deal with that blow in
the child's own particular way. Counsel for the plaintiff argues that what they need
above all things is continuity. Certainly one can understand that. However, the
great difficulty in the continuity argument is that they have been deprived by death
of the one element in their particular environment the continuity of which is essential
to them; and, without their mother, continuity (except in the most general sense)
is very difficult to maintain, particularly for the plaintiff who has not at the present
moment any female assistance in bringing them up with him, although he hopes to
get such assistance. The thing that stands out a mile to my mind is that, so far as
California is concerned, there is no visible mother-substitute for these children at the
time when they very badly need one. The aunt and the grandmother have made it
clear that they cannot, for various reasons, take on any close day-to-day role in
looking after these children, and so some woman would have to be found. On the
other hand, the father has a wife, a new wife, though, it is true, a very young woman
to take on so great a responsibility, but he has got a wife and a home which is a two-
parent home of an established kind. So he has a very powerful attraction in that
respect. I think it is also wrong of us wholly to overlook the fact that he is the children's
natural father. I do not mean to say that the scales should be weighted particularly
heavily. If other indications pointed to the plaintiff, I would not hesitate for my part
to make an order in favour of him; but the fact is that the father's reaction over these
children is a perfectly normal and natural reaction for a father whose children have
suddenly been partially orphaned by the death of their mother. From Mr Chapman's
report it is striking how N has taken to her stepmother. His impression (it is true, of a
fleeting visit) is that N is really quite content. She appears to be quite pleased with her
English school, and she actually expressed the view, in contrast to what she had said
before, that she did not want to go back to California. She referred to the whole
thing as a 'bore' and no doubt, poor child, she must feel at sea because she has lived
since her mother died in an atmosphere of almost constant conflict. J is clearly very
much disturbed and is adjusting with much greater difficulty; but A seems happy
enough, so far as anyone can tell.

On that state of the evidence, it seems to me, with respect to counsel for the plaintiff's
argument, very difficult to imagine how the court in California could find that it
would be 'detrimental' to these children to be entrusted to the care and custody of
their father.

The case is complicated by one matter which is always a difficulty, and that is, as I
have mentioned earlier, that the father and stepmother are Jehovah's Witnesses.
Counsel for the plaintiff is quite right in saying that if the children remain with the
father, they will be brought up as Jehovah's Witnesses. They are not by any means
alone in this world as children being brought up as Jehovah's Witnesses. It is unfortunate that this particular persuasion does seem prone to lead to controversies in
the courts from time to time, so that we are all very familiar with cases involving
this particular persuasion. But the court must approach it as it approaches any other
religious persuasion and do the best it can. There are certain aspects of the way of life
of Jehovah's Witnesses which do seem to people who are not members of the persuasion somewhat awkward, difficult and not very good for children. There is a
tendency to isolate them from other people at school to some extent. There is the
unfortunate feature that Christmas and birthdays are not celebrated in the way that
most people do, and a number of other matters. But these are all matters of relatively
light weight when the court is considering the welfare of the children in the sort of
circumstances in which we are in this court today. My conclusion would be that it
would be quite wrong to say, or for any court to say, that because the parents were
Jehovah's Witnesses, this represented a 'detriment', however that word is construed
in the American court.

The evidence, therefore, as it is before us, and I stress 'as it is before us' because we
are relying on the welfare officer's report, is heavily in favour of leaving the children

where they are, with their father. It is perfectly true that of course the fact that he took them unilaterally from California has produced a situation in which the children *a* have actually been living with him for a short period which they would not otherwise have done. This, of course, is unfortunate from the point of view of the plaintiff. I mean forensically unfortunate, because it enables the court and the children to look at two situations in terms of reality, as opposed to looking at one situation in terms of reality and the other in terms of hypothesis. Children are often able, I think, to judge between two real situations of which they have experience very much *b* better than they can judge between one which they have experienced and one which is put to them in the form of hypothesis. Mr Chapman's report indicates to me that the children, having regard to the appalling difficulties that they have had in the last couple of months, have really settled down remarkably well. I would regard it as plain that the best interests of the children are now that they remain where they are. I can well understand the attraction of the plaintiff, who might be able to give *c* them a much freer, easier, outgoing sort of life; but he has, as I think, immense problems to tackle himself. I would hesitate for a long time to put on him the burden of taking care of these three children, none of whom is related to him at all.

So, for all those reasons, I would dismiss the appeal from the learned judge's judgment. I would go further and say, having regard to the fact that we have now investigated the case as fully as one reasonably can, that we should now make an order *d* for care and control of these children in favour of their father. That they should remain wards, I have no doubt whatever; and, having regard to the difficulties that he and his present wife are likely to experience with the children, it seems to me to be a case for making a supervision order, possibly for a limited time, perhaps two years, not because the court has any desire (as it were) to look over the shoulders of the father and stepmother, but rather that there should be some experienced person *e* readily available to whom they can turn for advice if and when they need it. It is against that background that I would be in favour of making a supervision order.

As to questions of undertakings, it is perhaps convenient to leave those over for the time being; and access, too, though so far as access in California is concerned, my own feeling is that it might be more natural and less stressing for all concerned if access was approached on the footing primarily of access to their grandmother and aunt *f* in California, with the plaintiff as an incident to that, rather than (as it were) promoting the plaintiff to the centre of the stage, which might lead to further friction between him and the father.

For those reasons, I would dismiss the appeal and make the order I have indicated.

SIR DAVID CAIRNS. I agree that his appeal should be dismissed and that *g* an order should be made in the form indicated by Ormrod LJ. I find myself in complete agreement with everything that he has said in the course of his judgment. I have nothing to add.

STAMP LJ. I too find myself in complete agreement with everything that has been *h* said by Ormrod LJ and with the order which he suggests.

Appeal dismissed.

Solicitors: *Turner Peacock*, agents for *Moore & Blatch*, Southampton (for the plaintiff); *Ewing Hickman & Clark*, Southampton (for the father). *j*

A S Virdi Esq Barrister.

Newstead (Inspector of Taxes) v Frost

CHANCERY DIVISION
BROWNE-WILKINSON J
21st, 22nd, 23rd, 28th NOVEMBER 1977

Income tax – Foreign possessions – Income arising from possessions out of the United Kingdom – Partnership between taxpayer and Bahamian company – Partnership activities carried on outside United Kingdom – Taxpayer's motive for entering into partnership to avoid tax on overseas earnings – Object of partnership to exploit taxpayer's talents as television personality – Objects of company including 'all kinds of financial commercial trading or other operations' – Partnership genuine and carrying on genuine commercial trade of exploiting taxpayer's talents – Taxpayer entitled to 95 per cent of partnership profits – No part of profits remitted to United Kingdom – Whether income arising from partnership assessable to tax – Whether income arising from foreign possessions – Whether motive for entering into partnership overrode genuine commercial nature of partnership – Income and Corporation Taxes Act 1970, ss 109(2), 122(2)(b).

The taxpayer who had established himself in the United Kingdom as a television entertainer and author wished to exploit his talents abroad, particularly in the United States, but wished to remain resident in the United Kingdom. He sought advice on legitimate ways of reducing his United Kingdom tax liability on his prospective overseas earnings. A scheme was devised to achieve a tax saving whereby, in February 1967, the taxpayer entered into a 'partnership' agreement ('the agreement') with a Bahamian company. The company was an 'off-the-peg' company activated solely for the purpose of the agreement. The objects of the company authorised it, inter alia, to carry on and execute 'all kinds of financial commercial trading or other operations', and to enter into partnership with any person carrying on any business which the company was authorised to carry on. The objects of the agreement were to enter into the business of 'exploiting copyrights ... [and of] television and film consultants and advisers publicity agents and providers of publicity services ... throughout the world outside the United Kingdom', and also to enter into the 'business of producing television programmes, films ... and other entertainments'. The agreement provided that the 'partnership' business was to be carried on outside the United Kingdom and that the profits were to be divided as to 95 per cent to the taxpayer and as to five per cent to the company. During the relevant period all the 'partnership' activities, including the control and management of the 'partnership', took place outside the United Kingdom. The exploitation of the taxpayer's talents in the United States proved to be very successful. The profits of the 'partnership', which arose mainly from the taxpayer's United States activities, were divided in accordance with the agreement but no part of the taxpayer's share of them was remitted to the United Kingdom. In assessing the taxpayer to income tax for the years 1969-70 to 1971-72 the Crown proceeded on the footing that the taxpayer's share of the 'partnership' profits was in reality the profits of his trade, business or vocation. The General Commissioners held that the income received by him from the partnership was not assessable to United Kingdom tax on the grounds that it was possible for a partnership to exist between the taxpayer and the company, that during the relevant periods a genuine partnership between them had existed with the taxpayer providing the profit-earning contribution and the company providing administrative and secretarial services and financial and fiscal advice, that the taxpayer's activities outside the United Kingdom had been performed under the partnership and all of its activities had taken place outside the United Kingdom, that therefore the income in question had arisen from 'possessions out of the United Kingdom', within s 109(2)[a] of the Income and Corporation Taxes Act 1970, and was chargeable under

---

a   Section 109, so far as material, provides:
    '(1) Tax under Schedule D shall be charged under the Cases set out in subsection (2) below ...
    '(2) The Cases are— ... Case V—tax in respect of income arising from possessions out of the United Kingdom ...'

Case V of Sch D, but that as the income had been derived from the carrying on by the
taxpayer of his profession in partnership, within s 122(2)^b of the 1970 Act, he was
chargeable to tax in respect of the income under s 122(3)(b) of that Act, i e only
in respect of actual sums received by him in the United Kingdom. The Crown
appealed contending (a) that the taxpayer and the company were not in partnership
because it was ultra vires the company's objects to enter into the partnership; (b)
that even if there was a partnership the income in question was not income of that
partnership and therefore not income arising from 'possessions out of the United
Kingdom', within s 109(2) of the 1970 Act, because (i) a number of the partnership
activities were ultra vires the company, (ii) on its true construction the agreement
embraced only exploiting the copyrights and services of persons other than partners
and (iii) the object of the partnership was not to carry on a trade or business, but
to carry on a profession, i e the taxpayer's profession of television entertainer and
author, which the company, being an artificial person, could not carry on; and (c)
that, since the creation and operation of the partnership was a device designed solely
to avoid liability to United Kingdom tax which, if the taxpayer had conducted his
profession on his own account, he would have had to bear, the court ought to ignore
the existence of the partnership.

Held – The appeal would be dismissed for the following reasons—
  (i) The words describing the objects of the company, namely 'all kinds of financial
commercial trading or other operations', should be construed as authorising all
kinds of (a) financial operations, (b) commercial operations, (c) trading operations
and (d) other operations, and not authorising one activity answering the description
'financial commercial trading'. Accordingly the company had the power to carry
on the partnership business on its own account and was therefore authorised to enter
into the partnership agreement (see p 250 j to p 251 b, post).
  (ii) Since the objects of the partnership were to use and exploit the services of
producers, actors and directors, and not to carry on business as a producer, actor or
director, the company was entitled to be a partner in the partnership's business of
exploiting the taxpayer's talents, by providing administrative and secretarial experience and financial and fiscal advice. It followed that the income in question arose from
the partnership activities and therefore from possessions out of the United Kingdom
within s 109(2) of the 1970 Act (see p 251 j to p 252 a, post).
  (iii) A transaction which had been genuinely entered into and was a real as opposed
to a sham transaction had to be taken into account in determining tax liability even
if it had been entered into solely for tax purposes and was of an entirely artificial
nature. Where therefore a taxpayer had entered into a genuine partnership which
was carrying on a genuine commercial trade, the fact that the motive for entering into
the partnership was solely to avoid liability to United Kingdom tax did not preclude
his income from the partnership from being treated as falling within s 122(2)(b) of the
1970 Act, for tax liability was linked to the objective nature of a taxpayer's acts and
not to the subjective motive for doing the acts. It followed that as the partnership

---

b   Section 122, so far as material, provides:
      '(1) Subject to the provisions of this section and sections 123 and 124 below, income tax
    chargeable under . . . Case V of Schedule D shall be computed on the full amount of the
    income arising in the year preceding the year of assessment, whether the income has been
    or will be received in the United Kingdom or not . . .
      '(2) Subsection (1) above shall not apply— . . . (b) to any income which is immediately
    derived by a person from the carrying on by him of any trade, profession or vocation,
    either solely or in partnership . . .
      '(3) In the cases mentioned in subsection (2) above, the tax shall, subject to sections 123
    and 124 below, be computed— . . . (b) in the case of tax chargeable under Case V, on the
    full amount of the actual sums received in the United Kingdom in the year preceding the
    year of assessment from remittances payable in the United Kingdom . . .'

between the taxpayer and the company was genuine and the partnership was carrying on a genuine commercial trade, i e exploiting the taxpayer's talents, it could not be said, even though the taxpayer had entered into the partnership solely to avoid liability to United Kingdom tax, that it was a wholly non-commercial undertaking. Accordingly the taxpayer's income from the partnership fell to be treated as income to which s 122(2)(b) of the 1970 Act applied (see p 252 b to f and p 253 d to f, post); *Bishop (Inspector of Taxes) v Finsbury Securities Ltd* [1966] 3 All ER 105 and *FA & AB Ltd v Lupton (Inspector of Taxes)* [1971] 3 All ER 948 distinguished.

(iv) It followed that, although the taxpayer's income arose from possessions out of the United Kingdom, within s 109(2) of the 1970 Act, since it was derived by him from the carrying on of his profession in partnership, it was within s 122(2)(b) of the 1970 Act and was taxable, by virtue of s 122(3)(b), only to the extent to which it had been remitted to the United Kingdom (see p 254 c, post).

Per Curiam. It is not the law that each partner must, by himself, be physically capable of doing all the acts done by the partnership for it to be an effective partnership (see p 251 g h, post).

Notes

For tax in respect of income arising from possessions out of the United Kingdom, see 20 Halsbury's Laws (3rd Edn) 276-280, paras 500-506, and for cases in the subject, see 28(1) Digest (Reissue) 301-311, *1031-1082*.

For the existence of a partnership, see 20 Halsbury's Laws (3rd Edn) 237, para 431, and for cases on the subject, see 28(1) Digest (Reissue) 232, 234, 566, *710, 712, 723, 2084*.

For the tax liability of a partner, resident in the United Kingdom, of a partnership controlled abroad, see 20 Halsbury's Laws (3rd Edn) 299, 300, para 547, and for a case on the subject, see 28(1) Digest (Reissue) 301, *1031*.

For the Income and Corporation Taxes Act 1970, ss 109, 122, see 33 Halsbury's Statutes (3rd Edn) 154, 173.

Cases referred to in judgment

Bishop (Inspector of Taxes) v Finsbury Securities Ltd [1966] 3 All ER 105, [1966] 1 WLR 1402, 43 Tax Cas 591, 45 ATC 333, [1966] TR 275, HL, 28(1) Digest (Reissue) 461, *1661*.

Colquhoun v Brooks (1889) 14 App Cas 493, [1886-90] All ER Rep 1063, 2 Tax Cas 490, 59 LJQB 53, 61 LT 518, HL, 28(1) Digest (Reissue) 301, *1031*.

FA & AB Ltd v Lupton (Inspector of Taxes) [1971] 3 All ER 948, [1972] AC 634, [1971] 3 WLR 670, 47 Tax Cas 580, 50 ATC 326, [1971] TR 284, HL, Digest (Cont Vol D) 441, *207*.

Glasson (Inspector of Taxes) v Rougier [1944] 1 All ER 535, 26 Tax Cas 86, 28(1) Digest (Reissue) 239, *735*.

Cases also cited

Brighton College v Marriott [1926] AC 192, [1925] All ER Rep 6n, 10 Tax Cas 213, HL.

Carson (Inspector of Taxes) v Cheyney's Executor [1958] 3 All ER 573, [1959] AC 412, 38 Tax Cas 240, HL.

Cox v Hickman (1860) 8 HL Cas 268, 11 ER 431, HL.

Dickenson v Gross (Inspector of Taxes) (1927) 11 Tax Cas 614.

Edwards (Inspector of Taxes) v Bairstow [1955] 3 All ER 48, [1956] AC 14, 36 Tax Cas 207.

Esplen (William), Son and Swainston Ltd v Inland Revenue Comrs [1919] 2 KB 731.

Farrell (Surveyor of Taxes) v Sunderland Steamship Co Ltd (1903) 4 Tax Cas 605.

Fenston v Johnstone (1940) 23 Tax Cas 29.

Gardiner v Childs (1837) 8 C & P 345.

Gardner and Bowring, Hardy & Co Ltd v Inland Revenue Comrs (1930) 15 Tax Cas 602.

Griffith (Inspector of Taxes) v Harrison (J P) (Watford) Ltd [1962] 1 All ER 909, [1961] AC 1, 40 Tax Cas 281, HL.

Inland Revenue Comrs v Maxse [1919] 1 KB 647, 12 Tax Cas 41, CA.

Inland Revenue Comrs v McIntyre (Peter) Ltd 1927 SC 166, 12 Tax Cas 1006.

Inland Revenue Comrs v Mills [1974] 1 All ER 722, [1975] AC 38, 49 Tax Cas 367, HL.
Inland Revenue Comrs v Williamson (1928) 14 Tax Cas 335.
Loss v Inland Revenue Comrs [1945] 2 All ER 683.
Mason (Inspector of Taxes) v Innes [1967] 2 All ER 926, [1967] Ch 1079, 44 Tax Cas 326, CA.
Oglivie v Kitton (Surveyor of Taxes) 1908 SC 1003, 5 Tax Cas 338.
Ridge Securities Ltd v Inland Revenue Comrs [1964] 1 All ER 275, [1964] 1 WLR 479, 44 Tax Cas 373.
Rowley Holmes & Co v Barber [1977] 1 All ER 801, [1977] 1 WLR 371, EAT.

Case stated

1. At a meeting of the Commissioners for the General Purposes of the Income Tax for the Division of Kensington held on 18th, 19th, 20th and 21st February 1975, David Paradine Frost ('the taxpayer') appealed against the following assessments to income tax under Case II of Sch D in respect of profits of the trade, business or profession of entertainer: 1969-70, £30,000; 1970-71, £29,256 (additional); 1971-72, £115,398.

2. Evidence was given by the taxpayer and by Mr John Henry Gaffney who was, at the material time, vice-chairman of the Trust Corporation of Bahamas Ltd.

[Paragraph 3 listed the documents admitted or proved before the commissioners.]

4. Counsel on behalf of the Revenue agreed that for convenience the words 'partnership' and 'partner' could be used throughout the proceedings provided that was not taken as an admission of the existence of a partnership in fact or in law. The commissioners used the words in the case stated (but not in their conclusions in cl 10) similarly as a matter of convenience. Similarly for convenience the commissioners referred throughout to the provisions of the Income and Corporation Taxes Act 1970 ('the Taxes Act') as if they were in force at all material times.

5. The following facts were proved or admitted: (1) By 1966 the taxpayer had established himself as a very successful television personality in the United Kingdom, responsible among other matters for two very successful programmes, The Frost Report and The Frost Programmes. He held the controlling interest in a number of United Kingdom companies connected with television, films and the theatre and was also a successful author. (2) Before, during and after the years under appeal the taxpayer had been assessed under Sch D, Case II as a writer and entertainer in the United Kingdom and figures (apart from those which are in issue in these appeals) had been agreed on his behalf with the Revenue. (3) In 1966 the taxpayer was considering the exploitation of his talents outside the United Kingdom and particularly the possibility of substantial earnings in the United States. He accordingly sought advice as to the legitimate ways of reducing the tax liabilities which would ensue, indicating that he wished to remain resident in the United Kingdom and to be able to remit his earnings to the sterling area, if possible, while minimising tax liabilities. (4) As a result he instructed London solicitors, Messrs Harbottle and Lewis, to investigate the possibility of arrangements for partnership with a company in the Bahamas and the following events took place. (a) 4th January 1967: Messrs Harbottle & Lewis informed the trust corporation of Bahamas Ltd ('the trust corporation') that the taxpayers wished to proceed with a partnership agreement with a Bahamian company, and would like the name of the company to be Lysander. (b) Messrs Harbottle & Lewis forwarded to the trust corporation a letter, dated 17th January 1967, addressed to it by a Mr George Brightwell (a friend and colleague of the taxpayer) enclosing a cheque for £350 'as an outright and unconditional gift to be used by you and your colleagues in any manner you may wish'. The letter was marked 're David Frost-Lysander Enterprises'. The witness John Henry Gaffney had expected such a contribution. (c) 7th February 1967: Messrs Harbottle & Lewis sent to the trust corporation a draft of partnership agreement for the proposed partnership. (d) 8th February 1967: Pembina Investment Co Ltd a 'shell' company held by the trust corporation, changed its name to Leander Productions Ltd ('the company') (e) 17th February 1967: The document (referred to as an indenture of partnership between the taxpayer and the

company) was completed. (5) According to the partnership deed dated 17th February 1967 the business of the partnership was 'exploiting copyrights and interests in copyrights and in the business of television and film consultants and advisers, publicity agents and providers of publicity services and facilities throughout the world outside the United Kingdom'. Those objects were extended by agreement at a partnership meeting on 12th February 1969 to include 'the business of producing television programmes, films, stageplays and other entertainment and using and exploiting the services of producers, actors, directors, writers and artistes, and material and facilities which may be used for the production of television programmes, films, stageplays and other entertainments, and in the business of television films and stage advisers and agents.' (6) The indenture of partnership also provided that: (a) the business was to be known as Leander Enterprises and was to be carried on outside the United Kingdom; (b) both partners were to take an active part in the partnership business, but the company was to manage the day to day operation of the partnership business; (c) profits were to be divided 95 per cent to the taxpayer and five per cent to the company but the capital assets were to belong 99 per cent to the taxpayer and one per cent to the company; (d) subject to certain reserved matters, partnership decisions should be effective and binding if made by a simple majority of the votes of the partners; (e) the company should have two votes and the taxpayer one vote and that any one director of the company might represent the company in partnership matters. (7) The company was incorporated in Nassau pursuant to a request made by the trust corporation on 31st August 1966. The payment of £350 made by Mr Brightwell to the trust corporation had been accepted as a contribution to the J H Gaffney trust for charity (of which the witness Mr John Henry Gaffney was the settlor) out of which that trust had acquired from the trust corporation beneficial ownership of the company. (8) During the relevant period there were repeated changes in the constitution of the board of the company, the directors from time to time being officers of the trust corporation nominated to serve in that capacity as part of their duties and to give them training and experience. (9) In 1968 when it became apparent that Leander Enterprises would earn substantial sums from the United States, consideration was given to the incidence of United States tax. On the advice of the trust corporation two further companies were formed. Hellespont NV ('Hellespont') a company situate in Curacao in the Netherlands Antilles and, Tamarisk Investments Ltd ('Tamarisk') in the Bahamas. With effect from 1st January 1969 Leander Enterprises gave Tamarisk the benefit of the services and facilities of the partners on a non-exclusive basis in return for a variable fee, and on 15th March 1969 the company on behalf of Leander Enterprises entered into a contract with Hellespont under which Hellespont had the sole and exclusive benefit, as provided for in the agreement, of the exploitation in the United States of the assets of Leander Enterprises. The reason for those arrangements was that there was no double taxation convention applicable between the United States and the Bahamas, so that payments from the United States to the Bahamas of income receipts would have attracted withholding tax. Under a double taxation convention with the Netherlands, payments from the United States to Curacao avoided withholding tax. Tamarisk was owned by the J H Gaffney Trust for charity and in turn Hellespont was owned by Tamarisk. (10) By far the most important source of income for Leander Enterprises was a programme known as the David Frost Show, produced in the United States and broadcast five days a week from July 1969 until June 1972, each programme having a duration of 90 minutes. That programme was the subject of an agreement dated 15th March 1969 between Group W Productions Inc and Hellespont under which certain moneys were paid direct to the taxpayer in the United States, out of which he met expenses in that country, accounting to Leander Enterprises for any balance. The balance of moneys payable was paid to Hellespont in Curacao. Hellespont would then make payments to Tamarisk and to Leander Enterprises in the Bahamas, Tamarisk out of its receipts would pay a fee to Leander Enterprises, who thus received substantially the whole benefit of the money paid for the David Frost Show. (11) Although the David Frost Show provided the greater part of the income of Leander Enterprises there were also receipts derived from the taxpayer's appearances on other television shows, lectures and speeches, consultation fees, book royalties, personal appearances and similar activities. (12) The profits of Leander Enterprises after deducting all proper expenses were divided in accordance with the indenture of partnership, five per cent to the company and 95 per cent to the taxpayer. (13) No remittances to the United Kingdom were made by the taxpayer out of his 95 per cent share of the partnership profits. (14) All the income of the partnership originated in the activities of the taxpayer. The company contributed administrative and secretarial experience and financial and fiscal advice. (15) Leander Enterprises did not have premises of its own or the exclusive services of any office or administrative staff, but was entitled to an address and office facilities through the company who in turn without any exclusive office or staff, was provided with an address and office facilities by the trust corporation who dealt similarly with some 800 other companies. (16) The taxpayer at all times observed very carefully the distinction between his United Kingdom activities and his activities on behalf of Leander Enterprises outside the United Kingdom. As appears from his travel itinerary during the relevant financial years the taxpayer was completely out of the United Kingdom for an average of 247 days each year, and partially out of the United Kingdom for the average of a further 52 days each year.

    6. It was contended on behalf of the taxpayer: (1) that the partnership agreement of 17th February 1967 was made abroad; (2) that all partners meetings took place abroad and all decisions controlling or managing or relating to the partnership business were made abroad; (3) that all contracts made by the partnership or relating to the partnership business were made abroad; (4) that all activities that produced the partnership income took place abroad; (5) that using Hellespont and Tamarisk as go-between the partnership exploited its assets (in particular the services of the taxpayer) abroad (particularly in the United States); (6) that the taxpayer was always aware that his work abroad (particularly in the United States) was performed on behalf of the partnership and was distinct from the self-employed work that he carried on in the United Kingdom; (7) that there was in revenue law no antithesis between 'form' and 'substance'; it was necessary to look at the substance, i e at the legal reality of what the parties transacted; neither the Crown nor the taxpayer was entitled to say 'but if the parties had chosen some different transaction to reach substantially the same result, more tax, or less tax, would have been payable, therefore treat them as if they had chosen that different transaction'; (8) that in this case the legal reality and thus the substance was that; (a) a partnership existed; (b) all the taxpayer's activities outside the United Kingdom were performed under that partnership, and; (c) the income which is the subject of the assessments under appeal arose from 'possessions out of the United Kingdom within s 109(2) of the Taxes Act and so could only be charged under Case V of Sch D; (d) but as it was immediately derived from the carrying on by the taxpayer of his trade profession or vocation in partnership, within s 122(2)(b), he could only be assessed, under s 122(3)(b) of the Act, on actual sums received in the United Kingdom which were nil.

    7. It was contended on behalf of the Crown: (1) that there was a clear distinction for tax purposes between trade on the one hand and profession or vocation on the other hand and the activities of the taxpayer (a) as an author, or (b) as a television star, or (c) as a television and film consultant and adviser fell within the latter, the profits thereof depending wholly or mainly on the personal qualities of the author or consultant in question; (2) that as to the profession or vocation of authorship: (a) the taxpayer, pursuing that profession or vocation and assessed in years prior to those under appeal, under Sch D Case II in respect of the profits thereof, could not by unilateral decision alter that basis of assessment to some other basis, and in particular not to Case I of Sch D by claiming to have become either a trader in, or a part-

ner in the trade or exploiting, his own manuscripts; (b) it was as a matter of law impossible for a Bahamian 'shell' limited company such as the company to pursue the profession of authorship; (c) a purported partnership between such a company and an author, either 'to write books' or 'to exploit that author's MSS', could not be a genuine partnership because the purported partners could not be carrying on 'a profession or vocation in common'; and (d) hence the taxpayer's share of the profits of Leander Enterprises derived either (i) from the taxpayer's authorship or (ii) from his or the company's exploitation of such authorship, remained assessable on him under Case II of Sch D; (3) that as to the profession or vocation of a television star: The like contentions, mutatis mutandis, applied as in sub-cl (2) above: the essence of such profession or vocation was 'exploitation of personal appearances for reward' and it was impossible, as a matter of law, for a television star to sever his profits as such into (a) those derived from 'personal appearances on his own' incapable of being made or carried on in common with an inanimate shell such as the company, and (b) those derived from 'exploitation of such personal appearances'. In any case such exploitation was also incapable of being made or carried on in common with an inanimate shell such as the company; (4) that as to the profession or vocation of 'a television and film consultant and adviser': the like contentions, mutatis mutandis, applied as in sub-cl (2) above; (5) that as to the taxpayer's share of the profits earned ostensibly by Leander Enterprises and deriving from the taxpayer's activities 'as publicity agent(s) and provider(s) of publicity services and facilities': (a) insofar as what was actually done was the publicising of the taxpayer himself as 'author' or 'television star' or 'television and film consultant and adviser', these still fell to be assessed on him under Case II of Sch D. (b) insofar as what was done fell outside the exploitation of the taxpayer himself as 'author', 'television star', or 'television and film consultant and adviser', these might constitute profits of 'a trade or business' as distinct from 'a profession or vocation' but there was no evidence that anyone apart from the taxpayer had been so publicised etc; (6) that as to the taxpayer's share of the profits ostensibly earned by Leander Enterprises and deriving from other activities of the taxpayer, the like comments, mutatis mutandis, applied as under sub-cl (5) above; (7) that the commissioners were not bound by the name given by the parties to the arrangement and were fully entitled to hold that no partnership existed; (8) that even if that were not correct the income which was the subject of the assessments under appeal did not in any event arise from 'possessions out of the United Kingdom', within s 109(2) of the Taxes Act, so that Case V of Sch D was not in point and s 122(2)(b) and (3)(b) were both irrelevant; (9) that alternatively, if Case V of Sch D were capable of applying, only the residual profits of Leander Enterprises, after deducting all the profits derived from professional activities similar to those carried on by the taxpayer before and after the partnership existed could qualify as 'income arising from possessions out of the United Kingdom and those residual profits would derive from 'an artificial fiscal operation remote from trade' as distinct from 'a joint venture in the nature of trade'; alternatively, only such residual profits could be regarded as exempt from United Kingdom tax under s 122(2)(b) and (3)(b) aforesaid; and (10) that further and alternatively, s 153 of the Taxes Act did not apply to any of the profits of Leander Enterprises deriving from the professional activities of the taxpayer (a) because it applied only to a trade or business and not to a profession or vocation; (b) because 'control and management of the (partnership) business was (not) situated abroad' as the taxpayer at all material times retained real control of his relevant professional activities; and that such control followed the taxpayer's admitted residence in the United Kingdom the partnership was therefore controlled from the United Kingdom.

[Paragraph 8 listed the cases[1] cited to the commissioners.]

---

1   *Bishop (Inspector of Taxes) v Finsbury Securities Ltd* [1966] 3 All ER 105, [1966] 1 WLR 1402, 43 Tax Cas 591; *Carson (Inspector of Taxes) v Cheyney's Executor* [1958] 3 All ER 573, [1959] AC

(*Continued on p 248*)

9. The commissioners were also referred to the Partnership Act 1890 for the definition of a partnership ('the relationship which subsists between persons carrying on a business in common with a view to profit') and to the Income and Corporation Taxes Act 1970, ss 108, 109, 122, 152 and 153.

10. The commissioners, who heard the appeal came to the following conclusions:

'(1) We did not accept that the basis of assessment of the [taxpayer] was incapable of being changed from Case II of Schedule D.

'(2) We were not bound by the fact that the [taxpayer] and the company chose to call their arrangement a partnership but that on the authority inter alia of *Fenston v Johnstone*[1] we were entitled to consider whether or not a partnership had existed and functioned during the relevant years.

'(3) We found that it was possible for a partnership to exist between a television personality and a Bahamnian company. The case of *John Gardner and Bowring, Hardy & Co Ltd v Inland Revenue Comrs*[2] showed that there could be a partnership where each partner was undertaking a different function.

'(4) In the present case the [taxpayer] was providing that profit earning contribution to the partnership and the company through trust corporation the financial, administrative, secretarial and fiscal services and advisory contribution.

'(5) We found as a fact that during the relevant years there was a partnership between the [taxpayer] and the company.

'(6) We found as a fact that the partnership meetings took place as stated . . . and that all the activities of the partnership took place outside the United Kingdom.

'(7) We further found as a fact that control and management of the partnership business was situated abroad and therefore we decided that in the absence of any remittances to the U.K. sections 122(2)(b) and (3)(b) and sections 153(1) of the Income and Corporation Taxes Act 1970 applied.

'(8) We accordingly issued our notice of decision on 19th March 1975 in the following terms:

'1969-70 Schedule D assessment as entertainer in the sum of £30,000. This assessment is reduced to £11,189 less capital allowances £23 and so determined. 1970-71 Schedule D Assessment as Entertainer in the sum of £29,256. This assessment is discharged. 1971-72 Schedule D Assessment as Entertainer in the sum of £115,398. This assessment is reduced to £16,616 less capital allowances £17 and so determined.'

11. Immediately after the determination of the appeal dissatisfaction therewith was declared to the commissioners on behalf of the Crown as being erroneous in point of law, and in due course the commissioners were required to state a case for the opinion of the High Court pursuant to the Taxes Management Act 1970, s 56.

12. The question of law for the opinion of the court was whether there was evidence on which the commissioners could properly come to their decision and whether the decision was correct in law.

(Continued from p 247)

412, 38 Tax Cas 240, HL; *Colquhoun v Brooks* (1889) 14 App Cas 493, [1886-90] All ER Rep 1063, 2 Tax Cas 490, HL; *FA & AB Ltd v Lupton (Inspector of Taxes)* [1971] 3 All ER 948, [1972] AC 634, 47 Tax Cas 580, HL; *Farrell (Surveyor of Taxes) v Sunderland Steamship Co Ltd* (1903) 4 Tax Cas 605; *Fenston v Johnstone* (1940) 23 Tax Cas 29; *Gardner and Bowring, Hardy & Co Ltd v Inland Revenue Comrs* (1930) 15 Tax Cas 602; *Hall (George) & Son v Platt* (1954) 35 Tax Cas 440; *Inland Revenue Comrs v Maxse* [1919] 1 KB 647, 12 Tax Cas 41, CA; *Inland Revenue Comrs v McIntyre (Peter) Ltd* 1927 SC 166, 12 Tax Cas 1006; *Ogilvie v Kitton (Surveyor of Taxes)* 1908 SC 1003, 5 Tax Cas 338; *Ransom (Inspector of Taxes) v Higgs* [1974] 3 All ER 949, [1974] 1 WLR 1594, [1974] STC 539, HL; *Salomon v Salomon & Co Ltd* [1897] AC 22, [1895-9] All ER Rep 33, HL.

1 (1940) 23 Tax Cas 29
2 (1930) 15 Tax Cas 602

Conrad Dehn QC and *Brian Davenport* for the Crown.
D C Potter QC and *Andrew Park* for the taxpayer.

Cur adv vult

29th November.   **BROWNE-WILKINSON J** read the following judgment:
This case concerns assessments to income tax for the years 1969-70, 1970-71 and 1971-72, totalling rather over £174,000, made on Mr David Frost ('the taxpayer'), the well-known television entertainer. The taxpayer appealed against those assessments and the General Commissioners allowed his appeals, reducing the assessments to a total for the three years of just over £27,000. The question for me to decide is whether the General Commissioners' decision is right in law.

The facts are fully set out in the case stated and it is only necessary for me to set out the salient parts of the history. The taxpayer having established himself as a very successful television personality in this country, in 1966 was considering the possibility of extending his activities outside this country and particularly in the United States of America. He wished to remain resident in the United Kingdom, but was anxious to reduce the impact of United Kingdom income tax and surtax on his prospective overseas earnings. He accordingly instructed solicitors to advise: a scheme designed to achieve such tax saving was evolved and put into operation. The scheme was carried through by the taxpayer entering into a partnership agreement ('the agreement') dated 17th February 1967, in the Bahamas, which agreement purported to create a partnership between the taxpayer and a Bahamian company, Leander Productions Ltd ('the company').

Clause 1 of the agreement provided as follows:

'[The taxpayer] and the company (hereinafter severally called "a partner" and together called "the partners") will on and after the Seventeenth day of February 1967 (hereinafter called "the date") become and remain partners in the business of exploiting copyrights and interests in copyrights and in the businesses of television and film consultants and advisers publicity agents and providers of publicity services and facilities throughout the world outside the United Kingdom and such businesses shall be carried on under the name of Leander Enterprises.'

The objects for which the partnership was formed were subsequently extended to include—

'the business of producing television programmes, films, stage plays and other entertainment and using and exploiting the services of producers, actors, directors, writers and artistes, and material and facilities which may be used for the production of television programmes, films, stageplays and other entertainments, and in the business of television, films and stage advisers and agents.'

The agreement also provided, inter alia: (1) that the business was to be carried on outside the United Kingdom; (2) that the company was to manage the day-to-day operation of the partnership business; (3) that the profits of the partnership business were to be divided 95 per cent to the taxpayer and five per cent to the company; (4) that the capital assets of the partnership were to be divided 99 per cent to the taxpayer and one per cent to the company; and (5) that partnership decisions were to be decided by a majority, the company having two votes and the taxpayer one vote.

The company was an 'off-the-peg' company, previously incorporated by the Trust Corporation of Bahamas Ltd. A friend and colleague of the taxpayer made a donation of £350 to that trust corporation, which accepted it as a donation to the J H Gaffney Trust for Charity, and that charity in turn, used the £350 to acquire shares in the company. Having established this machinery, the taxpayer, purportedly on behalf of the partnership, made his services available for programmes in the United States. For purposes of United States tax, various intermediary companies were established between the partnership and those using the taxpayers services in the United States, but effectively the whole of the taxpayer's earnings in the United States were received by the partnership.

As is well known, the taxpayer's activities in the United States were outstandingly successful, particularly his programme 'The David Frost Show' which was broadcast on television in the United States five nights a week from July 1969 to June 1972, but he also operated in other spheres in the United States. The profits of the partnership were divided as agreed, but no part of the taxpayer's share of those profits was remitted to the United Kingdom.

The General Commissioners found as facts (and in these cases there is no right of appeal against their findings of fact): first, that during the relevant time there was a partnership between the taxpayer and the company; secondly, that the partnership meetings took place as stated in the minutes of the partnership (which were in evidence) and that all the activities in question took place out of the United Kingdom; and thirdly, that the control and management of the partnership business was situated abroad. On those findings the General Commissioners held that the income received by the taxpayer from the partnership (but not remitted to this country) was not assessable to United Kingdom tax.

The legal steps in reaching this conclusion are: (1) as was decided by the House of Lords in *Colquhoun v Brooks*[1], receipts representing a share of profits made by a partnership conducted wholly overseas fall to be treated as 'income arising from possessions out of the United Kingdom', and accordingly fall to be taxed (if at all) under Case V of Sch D; (2) by virtue of the Income and Corporation Taxes Act 1970, s 122(2)(b), tax is not chargeable under Case V of Sch D on income 'which is immediately derived by a person from the carrying on by him of any trade, profession or vocation, either solely or in partnership' unless such income is remitted to this country; therefore, (3) since the immediate source of the taxpayer's overseas income was his share of the partnership profits and the partnership was wholly controlled and conducted outside the United Kingdom, no tax is chargeable on those profits unless remitted to this country.

Before me, the Crown have sought to attack this result on a number of different grounds. First, they argue that although the parties may have thought they were in partnership, in law they could not have been since it was ultra vires the powers of the company to enter into this partnership. It is said that if the company could not conduct on its own account a business having the same objects as the partnership, it could not have power to enter into a partnership to achieve those objects. This argument (which was not advanced before the General Commissioners) requires me to construe the memorandum and articles of the company. The company's original name was 'Pembina Investment Co Ltd', and the first objects stated in its memorandum are of the kind one would expect from its name, namely to buy real and personal property. But object (6) is in these terms: 'To carry on business as bankers, capitalists, financiers, concessionaires and merchants and to undertake and carry on and execute all kinds of financial commercial trading or other operations and generally to undertake and carry out all such obligations and transactions as an individual capitalist may lawfully undertake and carry out.' The words 'to undertake and carry on and execute all kinds of financial commercial trading or other operations' would, on their face, authorise the company to carry on a business of the same kind as the partnership business. But counsel for the Crown submits that read in their context, as they must be, the words do not have that effect. He says that the earlier express reference to bankers, capitalists, financiers, concessionaires and merchants limits the ambit of authorised activities to those of the same genus.

I cannot accept this argument. I find it difficult to define what such genus could be. Moreover, I construe the words 'all kinds of financial commercial trading or other

---

1 (1889) 14 App Cas 493, [1886-90] All ER Rep 1063, 2 Tax Cas 490

operations' not as authorising one activity answering the description 'financial commercial trading' (whatever that may be), but as authorising all kinds of (a) financial operations (b) commercial operations (c) trading operations and (d) other operations. In my judgment, therefore, the company would have had power to carry on the partnership business on its own account and, since object (15) stated in its memorandum authorises it to 'enter into partnership . . . with . . . any company, firm or person . . . carrying on any business which this Company is authorised to carry on', the entry into the agreement was not, in my judgment, ultra vires the company.

The Crown's next main contention was that even if there was a partnership, the income in question was not the income of that partnership, and accordingly was not 'income arising from possessions out of the United Kingdom' within Case V. This main argument was itself put in a number of different ways which I will deal with under headings (a) to (c). (a) It was said that a number of the activities carried on by the partnership were ultra vires the powers of the company and that the company could not, as a partner, have done what it could not do on its own account, even if initially it had power to enter into the partnership. For the reasons I have already given, I do not think any of the partnership activities were ultra vires the company.

(b) It was next said that on its true construction the agreement did not embrace exploiting the taxpayer's copyrights or services but extended only to exploiting the copyrights and services of persons other than the partners. I am unable to see how this can be the right construction of the agreement. The words, on their face, are completely general and if they are to be limited in some way it can only be by an irresistible implication from the surrounding circumstances. But when one looks at the surrounding circumstances they lead in the opposite direction. This was agreement between a well-known television personality and a company which, although not owned or incorporated by the taxpayer, had been brought to life only by his intervention. Why, in these circumstances, should the taxpayer and the company have intended to exclude the taxpayer's copyrights or services from the ambit of the partnership activities? Moreover, even if I am wrong in my view of the true construction of the agreement, the parties did in fact exploit the taxpayer's copyrights and services. In the absence of any evidence to the contrary, it would be necessary to infer from the course of dealing an agreement that these were to be partnership activities.

(c) Finally on their second main contention, the Crown argue that the objects and activities of the partnership were to carry on not a trade or business, but a profession, namely the taxpayer's profession as a television entertainer and author, and that since the company, as an artificial person, cannot carry on such a profession, the income generated by the taxpayer's activities cannot have flowed from partnership activities. A number of cases were cited in support of the proposition that a limited company cannot carry on a profession. On the view I take of the matter, it is not necessary to express any view on this point. The submission appears to be based on an assumption that each partner must, by himself be physically capable of doing all acts done by the partnership. In my judgment, that is not the law. I could understand the proposition that a partnership between, say, a professional footballer and a limited company to play football for profit might be ineffective, since by physical incapacity one of the partners (the company) could not perform the sole partnership activity, that is to say playing football. But I can see no reason why in law there should not be a partnership between a limited company and a professional footballer to exploit the footballer's talents for the benefit of both. In the latter case, the object of the partnership is not to play football but to exploit the talent. One of the commonest types of partnership is one in which people of various skills join together in partnership with a view to each of them exercising their individual skills for the benefit of all the partners.

So here, in my judgment, the Crown cannot say, 'The object of the partnership is to carry on the taxpayer's profession'. The objects, which I have already read, show that the objects were not to carry on business as, for example, a producer, actor or director, but to use and exploit the services of producers, actors and directors. Therefore, I can see no legal reason why the company could not be a partner in the business of exploiting the taxpayer's talents providing, as the commissioners found that it did, administrative and secretarial experience and financial and fiscal advice. I therefore hold that this submission also fails.

The Crown's third main contention is that the creation and operation of the partnership was a device designed solely to avoid liability for United Kingdom tax which the taxpayer would have had to bear if he, as a United Kingdom resident, had conducted his chosen calling on his own account, and that accordingly the court should ignore the existence of the partnership. This contention has caused me the most difficulty. In general, I understand the law to be that tax is payable according to the true nature of the transactions which the taxpayer has entered into. If there are purported transactions by a taxpayer which are found, as a matter of fact, to be a mere sham, such transactions are ignored for tax purposes: they have no real existence, and tax is exigible on the basis of the true, not the dissembled, facts. But if transactions have been genuinely entered into and have a real existence, then the tax liability has to be determined taking account of those transactions, even if they were entered into solely for tax purposes and are of an entirely artificial nature. In the present case, the General Commissioners have found that the Bahamian partnership was a genuine partnership; and although there is no express finding to this effect, the only possible inference from the facts found is that the partnership was carrying on a genuine commercial trade, namely exploiting the talents of the taxpayer. Therefore, this is not a case where the court can ignore the partnership or its business as being a mere sham; nor, indeed, have the Crown so contended.

The Crown's contention is a narrower one. They say that, as there was no commercial reason for the Bahamian partnership, which was introduced solely to avoid United Kingdom tax, the taxpayer could not show that he brought himself within s 122(2)(b) of the Income and Corporation Taxes Act 1970 since on its true construction that section does not extend to income derived from the carrying on of a trade, profession or vocation in partnership where the only reason for the partnership is to secure a tax advantage. This contention is founded on two decisions of the House of Lords in 'dividend-stripping' cases; namely *Bishop (Inspector of Taxes) v Finsbury Securities Ltd*[1] and *FA & AB Ltd v Lupton (Inspector of Taxes)*[2]. In each of those cases the taxpayer was a dealer in shares but entered into certain extraordinary share transactions as a result of which it claimed to have incurred an allowable loss for tax purposes. There was no question of the transactions being shams, but in order to be allowed the losses the taxpayer had to show that the case fell within the words of s 341 of the Income Tax Act 1952, which allows losses 'Where any person sustains a loss in any trade'. The House of Lords in both cases held that the losses were not sustained in any trade, since the whole purpose of the share transactions was not to deal in shares but to obtain the fiscal advantage, and that did not constitute trading. As the headnote to the *Lupton* case[3] states: '*Held*, that all the transactions were tax devices and not trading transactions.'

The Crown contend by analogy in the present case that, although the income arose from the taxpayer carrying on a trade, profession or vocation, and although he was so carrying on his trade in partnership, since (as was conceded) the sole purpose of that trade being carried on in partnership rather than his sole name was to obtain the tax advantage, the income was not to be treated as falling within the true meaning of s 122(2)(b) of the 1970 Act. In my judgment, I must reject this third contention also. It is to be noted that in both the *Finsbury* case[1] and the *Lupton* case[2] their Lordships

---

1 [1966] 3 All ER 105, [1966] 1 WLR 1402, 43 Tax Cas 591
2 [1971] 3 All ER 948, [1972] AC 634, 47 Tax Cas 580
3 47 Tax Cas 580 at 581

stressed that if, looked at as a whole, the transaction was properly to be regarded as commercial, the fact that it contained elements directed to obtaining fiscal advantages would not deprive the transaction of being in the nature of trade: see, for example, per Lord Morris in the *Finsbury* case[1], and in the *Lupton* case[2], per Lord Morris, Lord Guest and Lord Dilhorne. The decision in both cases was that the transactions were wholly directed to obtaining the tax advantage and were in no way commercial, and therefore were not entered into in the course of trade. The decisions did not require the court to ignore any genuine trading: there was none. Moreover, Lord Donovan in the *Lupton* case[3] usefully points out that in deciding whether or not the transaction was properly described as trading, the court must look at the transaction as a whole, and not merely at isolated parts of the whole.

Accordingly, the decisions of the House of Lords were that in those cases the transactions were wholly non-trading transactions. The decisions did not involve saying that, despite the transactions having certain features of trading, those features were to be ignored because of a predominantly fiscal motive. If that be the right analysis of those decisions, in my judgment they do not cover the present case. The relevant question in this case is: was the income derived by the taxpayer from the carrying on by him of any trade, profession or vocation in partnership? The unchallengeable facts are that he was carrying on a trade for commercial reasons, and that he was doing so in partnership. It is impossible to say that the transaction as a whole, that is to say carrying on trade in the United States through the partnership, was a wholly non-commercial undertaking, and was undertaken solely to obtain a tax advantage.

If I were to accede to the Crown's argument, I would have to reject or ignore this genuine commercial objective simply because the machinery used to achieve it was adopted solely for fiscal purposes. That would be to go far beyond anything decided in the House of Lords decisions I have referred to, and in my judgment would be an undesirable and unwarrantable extension of the law. This was undoubtedly a tax avoidance scheme by the taxpayer and his advisers, but so long as Parliament continues to seek to deal with tax avoidance schemes by linking tax liability to the objective nature of the acts done as opposed to the subjective motive with which they are done, in my judgment it is not open to the court to make liability to tax depend on the motive leading a taxpayer to adopt one type of machinery for carrying on his lawful business rather than another.

The Crown advanced a further argument in opening the appeal which was not referred to in the closing speech, but which I should deal with. It was said that someone like the taxpayer carrying on a profession cannot alter the nature of his earnings so as to make them taxable otherwise than under Case II. I was referred to certain decisions on the taxable nature of receipts by an author, certain dicta in which, read out of context, lent some support to the contention. I accept that, for example, an author cannot escape liability to tax under Case II by selling the copyright of a book he has written and then claiming that the price paid is a capital sum and not Case II income: see *Glasson (Inspector of Taxes) v Rougier*[4]. It may be (but I express no view on the point) that, on that principle, when the taxpayer disposed of his future earnings outside the United Kingdom to the partnership he might have been assessed to tax on the value of the rights that he acquired under the agreement. But I do not accept that the taxpayer's income from the partnership forever thereafter has to be taxed under Case II, any more than if an author were to sell his copyright to a company in return for shares, the dividends payable in the future on those shares, as opposed to their immediate capital value, would fall to be taxed under Case II.

---

1   [1966] 3 All ER 105 at 111, [1966] 1 WLR 1402 at 1417, 43 Tax Cas 591 at 627
2   [1971] 3 All ER 948 at 955, 957, 962, [1972] AC 634 at 647, 650, 655, 47 Tax Cas 580 at 620, 623, 627
3   [1971] 3 All ER 948 at 964, [1972] AC 634 at 658, 47 Tax Cas 580 at 629
4   [1944] 1 All ER 353, 26 Tax Cas 86

I must also note an alternative formulation of the taxpayer's case put forward by counsel who appeared for him. He argued that since there was a partnership, s 152 of the Income and Corporation Taxes Act 1970 requires a partnership assessment to be made on the partners jointly; that this had not been done and that the assessments under appeal, being made on the taxpayer alone, were bad assessments. However, counsel for both parties were agreed that there was some doubt how far s 152 applies to overseas partnerships and, as it is not necessary for the decision of this case, I express no view on the alternative argument.

Finally, before me the Crown effectively conceded that if the income in question did arise from a valid Bahamian partnership, the decision of the House of Lords in *Colquhoun v Brooks*[1] established that such income arose from 'possessions out of the United Kingdom' for the purposes of Case V of Sch D. However, the Crown reserved the right to challenge that decision if this case proceeds to the House of Lords. I accordingly dismiss the appeal.

Appeal dismissed.

Solicitors: *Solicitor of Inland Revenue; Harbottle & Lewis* (for the taxpayer).

Rengan Krishnan Esq   Barrister.

Associated Bulk Carriers Ltd v Koch Shipping Inc
The Fuohsan Maru

COURT OF APPEAL, CIVIL DIVISION
LORD DENNING MR, BROWNE AND GEOFFREY LANE LJJ
20th, 21st JULY, 1st AUGUST 1977

Arbitration – Stay of court proceedings – Refusal of stay – No dispute between parties with regard to matter agreed to be referred – Claim for damages for breach of contract – Admission of liability but dispute as to quantum of damages – Substantial sum indisputably due to plaintiff – Amount unquantified – International arbitration agreement – Whether court entitled to refuse to stay proceedings so far as they related to sum indisputably due to plaintiffs – Arbitration Act 1975, s 1(1).

Practice – Summary judgment – No defence to part of claim – Damages for breach of contract – Admission of liability but dispute as to quantum of damages – Substantial sum indisputably due to plaintiff – Amount unquantified – Whether court having power to give summary judgment for sum indisputably due to plaintiffs – RSC Ord 14, rr 1(1), 3(1).

In August 1974 the plaintiffs let a motor vessel to the defendants on a time charter for five years, redelivery to take place on or after 29th July 1979. It was a term of the charterparty that any disputes arising out of the charter were to be put to arbitration in London. During the period of the charter the market rate for the vessel fell and the defendants used various devices to get out of the charter. On 11th April 1977 they purported to terminate the charterparty and to redeliver the vessel. The plaintiffs treated the defendants' conduct as a repudiation of the charterparty. On 11th

---

1   (1889) 14 App Cas 493, [1886-90] All ER Rep 1063, 2 Tax Cas 490

May they brought an action against the defendants claiming damages for wrongful repudiation amounting to some $4,000,000 representing 27 months' hire less the hire obtainable under a time charter for that period as at the date of repudiation, and applied for summary judgment under RSC Ord 14. The defendants admitted liability for wrongful repudiation but denied that the plaintiffs were entitled to the amount of damages claimed. They applied for an order under s 1(1)^a of the Arbitration Act 1975 that the proceedings should be stayed and the dispute referred to arbitration in accordance with the charterparty. The judge granted the defendants' application and dismissed the plaintiffs' application for summary judgment. The plaintiffs appealed, contending that, since they were entitled to a substantial sum of damages, the court had jurisdiction to give summary judgment for the sum that was indisputably due to them, the defendants having no defence to that part of the claim, within RSC Ord 14, rr 1(1)^b, and 3(1)^c, and, further, that since there was no dispute as to the defendant's liability, the court was not required by s 1(1) of the 1975 Act to refer their claim to that sum to arbitration.

Held (Lord Denning MR dissenting) – The appeal would be dismissed for the following reasons—

(i) Although it was plain that the plaintiffs were entitled to heavy damages for breach of contract, the amount of damages, i e the whole claim for damages, was in issue and therefore it could not be said that any definable or quantified part of the claim was not in fact in dispute. It followed therefore that it would not be true to say that 'there is not in fact any dispute between the parties with regard to the matter agreed to be referred', within s 1(1) of the 1975 Act, since the matter agreed to be referred was any dispute under the charterparty and there was a dispute as to the quantum of damages. Accordingly the court was bound to stay the proceedings under s 1(1) (see p 263 g to p 264 a and p 266 h j, post).

(ii) Even if the court had jurisdiction to refuse a stay, the plaintiffs were not entitled to summary judgment under RSC Ord 14 for it was impossible to identify or quantify any particular part of their claim which was indisputably due or in respect of which there was no defence. In effect the plaintiffs were asking the court to order an interim payment on account of the damages which they expected to obtain and the court had no power, either statutory or under its inherent jurisdiction, to make such an order (see p 264 d to g and p 266 a to g, post); *Moore v Assignment Courier Ltd* [1977] 2 All ER 842 applied; *Lazarus v Smith* [1908] 2 KB 266 distinguished.

Notes

For stay of court proceedings by a party to an arbitration agreement, see 2 Halsbury's Laws (4th Edn) paras 555, 556, and for cases on the subject, see 2 Digest (Repl) 477-498, 346-464.

---

a Section 1(1) is set out at p 259 b c, post
b Rule 1(1) provides: 'Where in an action to which this rule applies a statement of claim has been served on a defendant and that defendant has entered an appearance in the action, the plaintiff may, on the ground that that defendant has no defence to a claim included in the writ, or to a particular part of such a claim, or has no defence to such a claim or part except as to the amount of any damages claimed, apply to the Court for judgment against that defendant.'
c Rule 3(1) provides: 'Unless on the hearing of an application under Rule 1 either the Court dismisses the application or the defendant satisfies the Court with respect to the claim, or the part of a claim, to which the application relates that there is an issue or question in dispute which ought to be tried or that there ought for some other reason to be a trial of that claim or part, the Court may give such judgment for the plaintiff against that defendant on that claim or part as may be just having regard to the nature of the remedy or relief claimed.'

For summary judgment after appearance, see 22 Halsbury's Laws (3rd Edn) 759-765, paras 1621-1630.
For the Arbitration Act 1975, s 1, see 45 Halsbury's Statutes (3rd Edn) 33.

Cases referred to in judgments
Aries Tanker Corpn v Total Transport Ltd [1977] 1 All ER 398, [1977] 1 WLR 185, [1977] 1 Lloyd's Rep 334, HL.
Contract Discount Corpn Ltd v Furlong [1948] 1 All ER 274, CA, 50 Digest (Repl) 416, 1240.
Dawnays Ltd v F G Minter Ltd [1971] 2 All ER 1389, [1971] 1 WLR 1205, [1971] 2 Lloyd's Rep 192, CA, Digest (Cont Vol D) 85, 418b.
Ellis Mechanical Services Ltd v Wates Construction Ltd (1976) 2 Building Law Reports 57, CA.
Gilbert-Ash (Northern) Ltd v Modern Engineering (Bristol) Ltd [1973] 3 All ER 195, [1974] AC 689, [1973] 3 WLR 421, 72 LGR 1, HL, Digest (Cont Vol D) 86, 419d.
Henriksens Rederi A/S v T H Z Rolimpex, The Brede [1972] 2 Lloyd's Rep 511, affd [1973] 3 All ER 589, [1974] QB 233, [1973] 3 WLR 556, [1973] 2 Lloyd's Rep 333, CA, Digest (Cont Vol D) 829, 3514a.
Lagos v Grunwaldt [1910] 1 KB 41, [1908-10] All ER Rep 939, 79 LJKB 85, 101 LT 620, CA, 50 Digest (Repl) 279, 240.
Lazarus v Smith [1908] 2 KB 266, 77 LJKB 791, 99 LT 77, CA, 35 Digest (Repl) 258, 560.
Mareva Compania Naviera SA v International Bulkcarriers Ltd [1975] 2 Lloyd's Rep 509, CA.
Moore v Assignment Courier Ltd [1977] 2 All ER 842, [1977] 1 WLR 638, CA.
Nova (Jersey) Knit Ltd v Kammgarn Spinnerei GmbH [1977] 2 All ER 463, [1977] 1 WLR 713, [1977] 1 Lloyd's Rep 463, HL.

Interlocutory appeal
The plaintiffs, Associated Bulk Carriers Ltd ('the shipowners'), appealed against the order of Kerr J dated 23rd June 1977 in the Commercial Court, whereby (i) on an application by the defendants, Koch Shipping Inc ('the charterers'), he ordered that the action brought by the shipowners against the charterers be stayed under s 1 of the Arbitration Act 1975, and (ii) he dismissed an application by the shipowners for summary judgment under RSC Ord 14. The facts are set out in the judgment of Lord Denning MR.

Andrew Leggatt QC and *Roger Buckley* for the shipowners.
Richard Southwell QC and *Brian Davenport* for the charterers.

Cur adv vult

1st August. The following judgments were read.

LORD DENNING MR. The Fuohsan Maru is a Japanese motor vessel. She is a big bulk carrier and can carry 105,000 long tons of oil or of ore. She is owned by a Japanese company and time-chartered for a long period to Associated Bulk Carriers Ltd whom I will call 'the shipowners'.

In 1972 the shipowners let her on a time charter on the BP time form to the charterers for five years (one month more or less) from delivery. The charter hire was $2·59 cents per ton dead weight per month. She was delivered to the charterers on 29th August 1974. So under the time charter she could be redelivered at the earliest on 29th July 1979. There was a printed clause which said:

'This Charter shall be construed and the relations between the parties determined in accordance with the law of England. The High Court in London shall have exclusive jurisdiction over any dispute which may arise out of this Charter.'

But there was a typewritten clause which said:

'Any and all differences and disputes of whatsoever nature arising out of this Charter shall be put to arbitration in the City of London pursuant to the laws relating to arbitration there in force . . .'

Presumably the typewritten clause takes precedence over the printed clause.

From August 1974 the charterers duly operated the vessel and paid the charter hire regularly every month for nearly 2½ years. But by that time the tanker market had slumped to the bottom. By December 1976 the rate for this vessel had fallen from $2·59 to a little more than $1. So the charterers sought by every possible device to get out of the charter. They did it by making claims which the judge described as 'manufactured' for the purpose of avoiding payment of the hire. In December 1976 and January 1977 they made deductions from the monthly hire, alleging that the master had neglected to clean the holds. Then on 3rd March 1977, when she was in the US Gulf, they said that they intended to send her in ballast through the Suez Canal to the Persian Gulf and there load a full cargo of 105,000 tons of crude oil and to carry it back through the Suez Canal and deliver it in the Mediterranean. This was a spurious suggestion. She could not conceivably carry that cargo through the Suez Canal. The maximum draft through the Suez was 37 feet; and this 105,000 tons of cargo would require a draft of 51 feet. The vessel would, as the judge suggested, need 'wings' to carry her through the canal. When the shipowners pointed this out, the charterers changed the orders and said that they intended to send her to Port Walcott in Australia to load a cargo of ore and carry it via the Cape of Good Hope to Eleusis in Greece and there unload. But that too was a spurious suggestion manufactured by the charterers and formed another pretext for not paying. The shipowners found out that no one at Port Walcott had heard of any such shipment; and that there were no facilities for discharging ore at Eleusis. The charterers followed it up with an impudent claim; they said the shipowners were at fault. On 11th April 1977 they sent this telex to the shipowners:

'Charterers find themselves prevented by owners from employing vessel as intended. There being little prospect of economic alternative employment for the vessel, charterers regret they must treat owners inability to honour their charter obligations as bringing this charterparty to an end. The vessel is re-delivered to owners as of the time and date hereof.'

By that telex the real object of the charterers became plain. They were not going to pay any more of the hire and were making what seems to be the outrageous suggestion that the shipowners were at fault. The shipowners, on 22nd April, made this dignified reply:

'. . . we much regret you appear intent on forcing yet another repudiation situation—presumably in order to obtain some temporary relief from monthly financial commitments during the delay which will occur before litigation can be completed. We do not believe that your legal advisers can be supporting your present stance and thus you are acting in complete disregard of your legal obligations. We call upon you as charterers with a reputation to maintain to earnestly reconsider your attitude . . .'

The charterers replied that there was no question of their giving any further orders. So on 25th April the shipowners treated the charterers' conduct as a repudiation. They accepted it as of 25th April and held the charterers liable for all loss or damage arising therefrom.

The shipowners sought redress in the courts. They had already, on 14th March 1977, issued a writ claiming the hire due on 28th February 1977 amounting to

$290,182·61. On 15th March they got a Mareva¹ injunction. On 12th May 1977 they applied for summary judgment. The charterers then said they had a counterclaim for wrongful repudiation by the shipowners which exceeded the 28th February hire and they asked for the action to be stayed and for the whole claim and counterclaim to be sent to arbitration. Kerr J rejected the charterers' suggestion. He said that the counterclaim was 'not bona fide, but merely manufactured as a pretext for getting out of the Charterparty'. So he refused a stay and gave judgment for the February hire. The charterers did not appeal from that judgment. They paid the February hire.

On 11th May 1977 the shipowners issued a writ against the charterers claiming damages for wrongful repudiation of the charterparty. They based it on the hire payable under the charterparty for the remaining 27 months, less the hire obtainable under a time charter for that period as at the date of repudiation. Their claim would come to something approaching, if not exceeding, $4,000,000. The shipowners applied ex parte for a Mareva injunction and got it. They applied again for summary judgment under RSC Ord 14. The charterers retorted with a summons to stay under the Arbitration Act 1975.

The summonses were heard by Kerr J on 23rd June 1977. At this stage the charterers admitted that the shipowners were entitled to damages for repudiation. They no longer put forward their manufactured cross-claim for repudiation. So the only issue was what was the proper sum of damages to be awarded to the shipowners? The judge made this important finding:

'On the evidence before me it is overwhelmingly probable that the [ship-owners] are entitled to recover a very substantial sum . . . [Counsel for the charterers] has rightly accepted that it is in the highest degree probable that the [shipowners] will recover a substantial amount. To the extent that the [charterers] have sought to controvert the [shipowners'] evidence as to approximate or minimum amounts to which the [shipowners] are entitled, I find the [charterers'] evidence unimpressive—no more impressive than their conduct during the last few months of the charterparty . . . the [shipowners] have all the merits, and I suspect that the [charterers] have no merits whatsoever and are still trying to stave off the day of reckoning. I have to decide whether they have the law on their side. With reluctance I have come to the conclusion that they have . . . I must therefore grant the [charterers] the stay for which they ask.'

So there is the point. There is beyond doubt a big sum payable as damages by the charterers to the shipowners; but because it cannot be ascertained and put down as a definite figure, the shipowners are to get no judgment for any sum at all. The whole matter must be sent to arbitration which, as we all know, would mean a long delay. Arbitrators have little control over the speed of the arbitration. It takes a long time to get an appointment; and when that is done, if the debtor wants to avoid payment, he can put off the day of judgment indefinitely: by asking for more time for one thing or another, by saying he is not ready yet; and, even after an award, by asking for a case to be stated; and so forth. It is most regrettable. It means that defaulting parties can get time indefinitely. The solicitors for the shipowners, with all the responsibility which attaches to them as solicitors in the City of London, have put this on affidavit:

'This is not the first case in which the [charterers] have adopted unusual tactics in order to rid themselves of financially unfavourable charter commitments. In a number of cases . . . the [charterers] have terminated the Charter and have then used the delay regrettably inherent in arbitration proceedings to negotiate a discounted settlement.'

---

1   *Mareva Compania Naviera SA v International Bulkcarriers Ltd* [1975] 2 Lloyd's Rep 509

Arbitration Act 1975

It is against this background that I consider the effect of the Arbitration Act 1975. It does not apply to domestic arbitration agreements, but only to international arbitration agreements like this one. Under the Arbitration Act 1950 the courts have a discretion whether to stay the action or not. The 1975 Act takes away any discretion in the court. It makes it compulsory to grant a stay when the matter in dispute comes within the Act. The word 'shall' is used imperatively. I will read s 1(1) in full:

> 'If any party to an arbitration agreement to which this section applies, or any person claiming through or under him, commences any legal proceedings in any court against any other party to the agreement, or any person claiming through or under him, in respect of any matter agreed to be referred, any party to the proceedings may at any time after appearance, and before delivering any pleadings or taking any other steps in the proceedings, apply to the court to stay the proceedings; and the court, unless satisfied that the arbitration agreement is null and void, inoperative or incapable of being performed, or that there is not in fact any dispute between the parties with regard to the matter agreed to be referred, shall make an order staying the proceedings.'

The important words for the present purpose are 'any matter agreed to be referred', and 'there is not in fact any dispute between the parties in regard to the matter agreed to be referred'.

Seeing that this is a new Act on which questions will often arise, I venture to make these suggestions. (i) The first proposition is illustrated by the first action which I have described in respect of the February 1976 hire. It is this. When a creditor has a sum certain due to him, as to which there is no dispute, but the debtor seeks to avoid payment by making a set-off or counterclaim as to which there is a dispute, then the court can give summary judgment under RSC Order 14 for the sum due to the creditor, but it must send the set-off or counterclaim off to arbitration. If the set-off or counterclaim is bona fide and arguable up to or for a certain amount, the court may stay execution on the judgment for that amount. But in some cases it will not even grant a stay, even when there is an arguable set-off or counterclaim, such as when the claim is on a bill of exchange (see *Nova (Jersey) Knit Ltd v Kammgarn Spinnerei GmbH*[1] per Viscount Dilhorne) or for freight (see *Henriksens Rederei A/S v THZ Rolimpex, The Brede*[2] and the recent case of *Aries Tanker Corpn v Total Transport Ltd*[3]) Or, I would add, for sums due on architects' certificates when they are, by the terms of the contract, expressly or impliedly payable without deduction or further deduction (see *Dawnays Ltd v FG Minter Ltd*[4], a case in which that construction which this court put on it met with the approval of Lord Reid and Lord Morris of Borth-y-Gest in the House of Lords in *Gilbert-Ash (Northern) Ltd v Modern Engineering (Bristol) Ltd*[5]. The other Law Lords only differed on the construction of the agreement). (ii) Take a case where a creditor has an ascertainable sum due to him, such as for work done and materials supplied, but the sum is not exactly quantified. The creditor says that it comes to, say, £1,000. The debtor admits that a considerable sum is due, but says that it is no more than £800. Then the court can give judgment for the £800 and send the balance of £200 to arbitration: because the only matter in dispute then is £200 (see *Lazarus v Smith*[6] and *Contract Discount Corpn Ltd v Furlong*[7]). (iii) Take the same case of work done and material supplied, and suppose that the debtor admits that a

---

1 [1977] 2 All ER 463 at 470, [1977] 1 WLR 713 at 722
2 [1973] 3 All ER 589, [1974] QB 233
3 [1977] 1 All ER 398, [1977] 1 WLR 185
4 [1971] 2 All ER 1389, [1971] 1 WLR 1205
5 [1973] 3 All ER 195, [1974] AC 689
6 [1908] 2 KB 266
7 [1948] 1 All ER 274

considerable sum is due, but he declines to put a figure on it. The court should not allow him to obtain any advantage on that account. He should not be allowed to pay nothing. The court ought to give judgment for such sum as appears to the court to be indisputably due and to refer the balance to arbitration. This is established by the decision of this court in *Ellis Mechanical Services Ltd v Wates Construction Ltd*[1]. As it is not reported generally, I would like to refer to two or three extracts from the judgment in this case because they are particularly apposite here. In my own judgment I said[2]:

'There is a general arbitration clause. Any dispute or difference arising on the matter is to go to arbitration. It seems to me that if a case comes before the court in which, although a sum is not exactly quantified and although it is not admitted, nevertheless the court is able, on an application of this kind, to give summary judgment for such sum as appears to be indisputably due, and to refer the balance to arbitration, the defendants cannot insist on the whole going to arbitration by simply saying that there is a difference or a dispute about it.'

Lawton LJ put it with his usual common sense[3]. He said:

'If the main contractor can turn round, as the main contractor has done in this case and say "Well, I don't accept your account; therefore there is a dispute", that dispute must be referred to arbitration and the arbitration must take its ordinary long and tedious course. Then the sub-contractor is put into considerable difficulties. He is deprived of his commercial life blood. It seems to me that the administration of justice in our courts should do all it can to restore that life blood as quickly as possible ... In my judgment it can be avoided if the courts make a robust approach, as the master did in this case, to the jurisdiction under Order 14.'

Bridge LJ said[4]:

'To my mind the test to be applied in such a case is perfectly clear. The question to be asked is: is it established beyond reasonable doubt by the evidence before the court that at least £X is presently due from the defendant to the plaintiff? If it is, then judgment should be given for the plaintiff for that sum, whatever X may be; and in a case where, as here, there is an arbitration clause, the remainder in dispute should go to arbitration. The reason why arbitration should not be extended to cover the area of the £X is indeed because there is no issue, or difference, referable to arbitration in respect of that amount.'

(iv) Take a like case where the creditor is entitled to an ascertainable sum due to him, not for work done and materials supplied but for damages (such as, on a sale of goods when the buyer refuses to accept the goods, the difference between contract price and market price under s 50(2) of the Sale of Goods Act 1893). The buyer is clearly liable, but he says that the seller's calculation is wrong because the market price was different from what the seller alleges. In such a case if the buyer puts forward his own figure of the market price, the seller gets judgment for the admitted damages, and the balance goes to arbitration; because that is the only matter in dispute. If the buyer does not put forward his own figure of the market price, he should not get an advantage on that account. The court should give judgment for the amount which is indisputably due and send the balance to arbitration. The case is indistinguishable in principle from *Ellis Mechanical Services Ltd v Wates Construction Ltd*[1].

---

1   (1976) 2 Building Law Reports 57
2   2 Building Law Reports 57 at 61
3   2 Building Law Reports 57 at 63, 64
4   2 Building Law Reports 57 at 65

On principle therefore, it is my opinion that when the creditor is clearly entitled
a to substantial damages for breach of contract, and the only question outstanding
is how much those damages should be, then if the creditor quantifies them at £1,000
and the debtor quantifies them at £800, there is not in fact any dispute between the
parties as to the £800, but only as to the £200; so only the £200 need be referred to
arbitration. Now suppose that the debtor does not condescend to quantify the
damages, but stalls and says he will not, or cannot, calculate the damages. He
b should not be better off by his evasive action. If he will not give any figure at all
or gives a figure which is patently too low, then he cannot complain if the court
itself assesses the figure. In such a situation the court can and should assess the
figure of damages which it considers to be indisputable, and leave the balance as the
matter in dispute 'which is agreed to be referred'. That I think is the consequence of
Ellis Mechanical Services Ltd v Wates Construction Ltd[1] properly understood.
c   Returning to the facts in this case the shipowners are undoubtedly entitled to
damages from the charterer for wrongful repudiation of the charter. The charterer
admits it. The only question is the amount. I will not go into all the figures. The
shipowners calculate their damages by taking the charter hire at $2·59, and deducting
from it the hire obtainable on a time charter for the outstanding time as given by
the London Tanker Brokers Pound, that is, $1·01. That gives the damages as over
d $4,000,000. The charterers give their own calculation. On the basis of a consent
voyage rate they put the rate obtainable at $2·26; on a pure time charter they put it
at $1·88. The resulting figure of damages is: in the one calculation $833,564; in the
other calculation $1,786,995·57. There are some adjustments to be made for minor
claims by the charterers. In addition the charterers put forward all sorts of arguments
to reduce the figure—making bricks without straw just as the defendants sought to in
e *Ellis Mechanical Services Ltd v Wates Construction Ltd*[1]. I am quite clear that the
charterers' lowest figure of damage, $833,564, is patently too low, especially when it is
remembered that in December 1976 the charterers offered that the charter should be
cancelled on them paying $1,500,000; and in February 1977 $2,000,000.
   In all the circumstances it seems to me that $1 million is indisputably payable by
way of damages; and it is only the excess of $3,675,000 which is in dispute. So far as
f the Arbitration Act 1975 is concerned, then I would only stay the action in respect of
that balance.

RSC Order 14.
   Alongside the 1975 Act, there is a parallel problem under RSC Ord 14. It is said
that judgment can only be given for the whole or part of a claim if it is a 'liquidated
g demand'. I agree that that is the case in respect of judgment in default of appearance:
see RSC Ord 13, r 1; and in default of pleading: see RSC Ord 19, r 2. But those two
rules have a historical origin. They are a survival from the old counts in indebitatus
assumpsit. Anything that could be sued for under those counts comes within the
description of a 'debt or liquidated demand': see *Lagos v Grunwaldt*[2], per Farwell LJ.
Hence it has invariably been held that a demand on a quantum meruit for money
h due for work done and material supplied, even though strictly speaking it is unliquidated, is always recoverable as a 'debt or liquidated demand'. Those words
are not, however, to be found in RSC Ord 14, r 1. I see no reason why Ord 14 should
be confined to cases where the writ is indorsed for a claim for a debt or liquidated
demand. It is daily practice to apply Ord 14 to claims for a sum for work done and
material supplied, and then for judgment to be given for such part of it as is admitted
j to be payable: or for such part of it as on the evidence can be said to be indisputably
due. Such is simple justice to the builder who has done the work and ought to be
paid. It would be a disgrace to the law if the customer could resist paying anything

---

1   (1976) 2 Building Law Reports 57
2   [1910] 1 KB 41 at 48, [1908-10] All ER Rep 939 at 942

by simply saying, 'There is no certainty that that is the correct figure'. Similarly, when there is a sum which can only be ascertained on the taking of an account. If *a* the debtor, who is himself in a position to calculate the amount, admits that something is owing, but he is not sure what it is, the court can give judgment for such sum as it can say is indisputably due: see *Contract Discount Corpn Ltd v Furlong*[1]. I see no distinction in principle between those cases and the present case. The case of *Moore v Assignment Courier Ltd*[2] is quite distinguishable because the defendants had put in a defence that went to the whole of the claim. So it did not fall within RSC Ord 14. *b* That was the ground of the decision.

I come back to the words of RSC Ord 14, rr 1 and 3. These make it clear that when the defendant has no defence to a claim or 'a particular part' of such a claim, the court can give such judgment 'on that claim or part as may be just'. I see no reason why this should not apply to a claim for unliquidated damages, just as it does to a claim on a quantum meruit, or a sum due on account. Take again a contract for the sale of *c* goods when the damages depend on a calculation of the difference between contract price and market price, or a claim under a charterparty for damages for repudiation when the damages depend on a calculation of the difference between the contract rate of hire and the market rate. In such a case the market rate may be a matter of dispute or difference, but usually between defined limits. The court can readily ascertain the minimum figure for which the defendant is liable. It should be able to *d* give judgment accordingly.

Counsel for the charterers stressed the words in RSC Ord 14, r 1, 'except as to the amount of damages claimed', and argued that when there was an interlocutory judgment for damages to be assessed, there was never any power to give judgment for part. But I read those words as applying to such part of the damages as to which there is a dispute. It does not apply to that part of the damages which is indisputably *e* due.

Counsel for the charterers also argued that a judgment for part of the damages (even the indisputable part) would be in effect a judgment for an interim payment; and the court would not have power to give such a judgment. It was first introduced, he said, by the Administration of Justice Act 1969, and it had only been applied to personal injury cases. I cannot accept this argument either. When the court gives *f* judgment for a sum which is indisputably due, it is not ordering an interim payment properly so called. It is a judgment for a sum which is indisputably due.

Conclusion

Every judge concerned in this case has felt that there ought to be power to give judgment for the shipowners for a substantial sum, but has felt that under the rules *g* there is no power to do it, and that we must await an amendment of the rules. This treats the powers of the courts, in matters of practice and procedure, to be limited by the rules. It is said, 'Unless it is found in the rules, there is no power'. I do not agree. Long before the Rule Committee was established the judges had inherent power over all matters of practice and procedure. All the rules were made by them. They retain this power still. As I have often said, the courts are masters of their own *h* procedure and can do what is right even though it is not contained in the rules. Rather than wait for the Rule Committee to act, it seems to be much better for the courts to do what is necessary as and when the occasion arises. Take this very case. If the shipowners fail to get anything in this case the charterers will once more have succeeded by this latest manoeuvre, by not admitting any figure, in depriving the shipowners of their just claim for years to come. The charterers will be rubbing their *j* hands with joy. At last they have found a good way out of payment. For myself I

---

1 [1948] 1 All ER 274
2 [1977] 2 All ER 842 at 845, [1977] 1 WLR 638 at 641

would not allow this. I would allow the appeal and enter judgment for the sum
a which on the evidence appears to me to be indisputably due. I would assess it at
$1,000,000.

I would allow the appeal accordingly.

BROWNE LJ. I wish I could agree with Lord Denning MR, but I am afraid I
cannot. In my judgment this appeal must be dismissed. Kerr J thought that the
b shipowners had all the merits and I have heard nothing which gives me the slightest
reason to doubt that he was right. But I am driven to the conclusion that he was also
right in holding that the charterers have the law on their side.

The arbitration clause in the charterparty (cl 53) provides:

'Any and all differences and disputes of whatsoever nature arising out of this
Charter shall be put to arbitration in the City of London pursuant to the laws
c relating to arbitration there in force . . .'

By s 1(1) of the Arbitration Act 1975:

'If any party to an arbitration agreement to which this section applies . . .
commences any legal proceedings in any court against any other party to the
agreement . . . in respect of any matter agreed to be referred, any party to the
d proceedings may . . . apply to the court to stay the proceedings; and the court,
unless satisfied that . . . there is not in fact any dispute between the parties with
regard to the matter agreed to be referred, shall make an order staying the
proceedings.'

It is not in dispute that by virtue of s 1(2) and (4) this arbitration agreement is one
e to which the section applies. The section is mandatory, and the court must stay
unless the case falls within one of the exceptions in the section; the court has no
discretion to refuse a stay, nor can it impose conditions (e g as to payment to the
other party or into court), as counsel for the shipowners concedes.

Where a claim (admittedly within the arbitration agreement) consists of separate
identifiable and quantified items, for example the case put by Kerr J of an admitted
f claim for freight and a disputed claim for demurrage, the court would in my view
be entitled to hold that there was 'not in fact any dispute' as to the admitted item and
to refuse a stay in respect of that part of the claim. In *Ellis Mechanical Services Ltd v
Wates Construction Ltd*[1], the claim was for a specified sum, and this court took the
view that £X, part of that sum, was 'indisputably due'. I think that in such a case
also the court would be entitled to refuse a stay in respect of £X and let the rest go
g to arbitration. But in such cases there is by admission, or can be by a decision of the
court, a quantified sum as to which 'there is not in fact any dispute'.

In the present case it is plain that the shipowners are entitled to heavy damages
for breach of contract, but there is no such quantified sum. Counsel for the shipowners at various stages in his argument put forward various differing figures as the
minimum amount 'indisputably due', but in my view it is impossible to say that any
definable and quantified part of the shipowners' claim is 'indisputably due'. As Kerr J
h said, 'the difficulty of doing it [i e putting forward such a minimum figure] in itself
demonstrates the difficulty in which the court is placed'. In fact during his final speech
counsel for the shipowners put forward a figure lower than the $1,000,000 to which
Lord Denning MR has referred; he put forward a figure of $833,564. Kerr J held that
the issue of liability was res judicata and that there was no issue as to liability in this
j action. The charterers have now admitted liability, but by virtue of RSC Ord 18,
r 13(4), the amount of damages, that is the whole claim for damages, is in issue.
On the facts of this case, I cannot say that any definable or quantified part of the claim
is not in fact in dispute. I agree with what Kerr J said:

---

1   (1976) 2 Building Law Reports 57

'I cannot possibly conclude that there is no dispute in respect of the matter agreed to be referred. The matter agreed to be referred is any dispute under the *a* charterparty, and there is a dispute as to the [shipowners'] quantum of damages.'

Like Kerr J, I reach this conclusion with reluctance, but in my judgment the court has in this case no choice under s 1(1) of the 1975 Act but to grant the stay, and I would dismiss the appeal.

The question what would have been the position if the 1975 Act did not apply *b* therefore does not arise, but it was fully argued and I think I should deal with it. RSC Ord 14, r 1, deals with two situations: (a) where a defendant has no defence to a claim included in the writ or to a particular part of such a claim; (b) where a defendant has no defence to such a claim or part except as to the amount of any damages claimed. Corresponding references to the claim or the part of a claim appear in RSC Ord 14, rr 3(1) and 4(3).

In *Lazarus v Smith*[1] this court (presumably applying (a)) held that it was right to *c* give judgment under RSC Ord 14 for the admitted part of a larger (quantified) debt. In *Ellis Mechanical Services Ltd v Wates Construction Ltd*[2] both the total amount claimed and the part of it which this court held to be 'indisputably due' were quantified; the sum for which judgment was given under RSC Ord 14 (presumably again under (a)) was retention money forming part of sums certified by the engineers. *d*

But in the present case I think the shipowners are in the same difficulty under RSC Ord 14 as under s 1 of the 1975 Act. It is impossible to identify or quantify any particular part of their claim in respect of which there is no defence or which is 'indisputably due'. It seems to me that what the shipowners are really doing is to ask the court to order an interim payment on account of the damages which they expect to recover. In *Moore v Assignment Courier Ltd*[3] this court held that there is no inherent *e* power to make such an order. The court referred to s 20 of the Administration of Justice Act 1969 which gave power to the Rule Committee to make rules enabling the court to make orders requiring interim payments. That power is quite general, but the only rules so far made under it are RSC Ord 29, rr 9 to 17, which apply only to claims for damages in respect of death or personal injuries. Although it was held in *Moore's* case[3] that RSC Ord 14 did not there apply, I think we are bound *f* by that decision (with which I entirely agree) to hold that we have no power to order an interim payment in the present case.

Even if the 1975 Act did not apply in this case, I should feel bound to hold that the court has no power to give any judgment or make any order for payment to the shipowners of any part of the damages to which they will no doubt ultimately be held to be entitled. *g*

It may be that the Rule Committee will think it right to consider whether there should be any extension of the power to order interim payments on account of damages.

GEOFFREY LANE LJ (read by Browne LJ). The shipowners claimed before Kerr J to be entitled to summary judgment under RSC Ord 14 against the charterers *h* for damages for breach of a long-term charterparty. The charterers claimed that there was a dispute as to liability and quantum and that under the terms of the charterparty the dispute had to be referred to arbitration by virtue of s 1(1) of the Arbitration Act 1975. The learned judge had no difficulty in deciding that the charterers had no defence to the claim so far as liability was concerned, and indeed they have since the hearing formally admitted it. It is clear that the charterers, ever since *j*

---

1   [1908] 2 KB 266
2   (1976) 2 Building Law Reports 57
3   [1977] 2 All ER 842, [1977] 1 WLR 638

the terms of the charterparty became burdensome to them, have used every subter-
a fuge and device available to them in an attempt to avoid or delay the necessity of
paying to the shipowners the very large sum by way of damages to which the shipowners are undoubtedly entitled. The charterers are devoid of merit and deserve
no sympathy. The shipowners submit that in these circumstances the charterers
should be ordered at once to pay such portion of the as yet unascertained amount of
damages as can properly be described as 'indisputably due' and that the proceedings
b should then be stayed and the remaining question (namely to how much more the
shipowners are entitled by way of damages) referred to arbitration.

   Although the question under RSC Ord 14 and that under the 1975 Act are technically separate and distinct, they seem to me to depend in each case on the same
consideration. Can it be said that this is a proper case under RSC Ord 14 for the
charterers to be ordered to pay a portion of the claim to the shipowners, leaving the
c balance to be assessed? Such orders are of course made every day in appropriate
circumstances: see for example *Lazarus v Smith*[1]. It has however been the practice
to confine such an order to cases where the amount ordered to be paid has already
been ascertained or is capable of being ascertained by mere calculation without
further investigation, or is admittedly due. So far as we have been told the only
possible exception has been in the case of claims on a quantum meruit which under
d Ord 14 are treated prima facie as a liquidated demand.

   We were referred to *Ellis Mechanical Services Ltd v Wates Construction Ltd*[2], a decision
of this court. Lord Denning MR is reported as follows:

   'It seems to me that if a case comes before the court in which, although a sum
   is not exactly quantified and although it is not admitted, nevertheless the court
   is able, on application of this kind, to give summary judgment for such sum as
e appears to be indisputably due, and to refer the balance to arbitration, the
   defendants cannot insist on the whole going to arbitration by simply saying that
   there is a difference or a dispute about it. If the court sees that there is a sum
   which is indisputably due, then the court can give judgment for that sum and
   let the rest go to arbitration, as indeed the master did here.'

f Taken at its face value that statement, part of a judgment with which Lawton LJ
agreed, would cover the circumstances of the present case. But an examination of the
facts in that case shows that the sum claimed by the plaintiffs as being immediately
payable to them (£52,437) was retention money retained against them according to
the terms of the contract and was payable for work that had already been done.
It therefore fulfilled all the necessary conditions for a typical Ord 14 payment.

g How different the present case is can be judged from the way in which matters have
been pleaded and argued. There is in the writ as amended no mention of any sum
other than the total amount claimed, namely some $4,000,000, and no mention of any
sum which is 'indisputably due'. Apparently no such sum was put before the judge
who was left to make his own calculations to that end if he wished.

   Before us, after much prompting from the court, various figures between about
h $850,000 and $2,000,000 were suggested, but that is as near as one was taken to the
'indisputably due' amount until counsel for the shipowners came to his reply, when
the following possibilities were put forward, namely $833,564 or $1,786,995[3]. That
was the first mention which had been made of those particular figures. The charterers
had had no opportunity of considering them or of addressing the court on them, and,
as I understand it, the court was being asked somehow to select, on the basis of the
j two figures, the sum for which it should give judgment under RSC Ord 14, staying

1   [1908] 2 KB 266
2   (1976) 2 Building Law Reports 57 at 61
3   The figures are based on the charterers' suggested rates of hire for a consent voyage and
     for a pure time charter.

the action as to the balance and allowing that dispute to go to arbitration. Despite the obvious temptation to decide this question in favour of the wholly meritorious *a* plaintiffs against defendants who have less than no merits, it seems to me quite impossible to do so for two principal reasons. First, even in circumstances where such an order can properly be made the plaintiff must assert and prove what he alleges to be the figure 'indisputably due'. However unmeritorious the defendants may be, they are entitled to know the allegation they have to meet at a stage in the proceedings when they are in a position to meet it. Secondly, quite apart from that *b* narrow ground, the shipowners are in truth asking the court not to give judgment under RSC Ord 14 for a specified ascertained sum as to which there can be no legitimate dispute, but to make an interim award on account of future damages so that the shipowners shall not be kept out of their money by the procrastination of the charterers. The difficulties which the shipowners experienced in trying to particularise the sum claimed were largely due to this.   *c*

However desirable it may be that such a power should exist in the hands of the court, it is not legitimate for the court to confer the power on itself in purported exercise of its inherent jurisdiction to control its own procedure. So much is clear from s 20(1) of the Administration of Justice Act 1969 which reads as follows:

> 'The power to make rules of court under section 99 of the Judicature Act 1925, *d*
> and the power to make county court rules under section 102 of the County Courts
> Act 1959, shall each include power by any such rules to make provision for enabl-
> ing the court in which any proceedings are pending, in such circumstances as may
> be specified in the rules, to make an order requiring a party to the proceedings to
> make an interim payment of such amount as may be specified in the order,
> either by payment into court or (if the rule so provides) by paying it to another
> party to the proceedings.'   *e*

In exercise of that power the Rule Committee provided by RSC Ord 29 that interim payments may be made in cases involving claims in respect of personal injuries or death.   As Megaw LJ, pointed out in *Moore v Assignment Courier Ltd*[1] Parliament by enacting s 20 of the 1969 Act made it clear that the existing powers of the rule *f* committee were not wide enough to enable the committee to authorise interim payments. The relevant existing powers were contained in s 99 of the Supreme Court of Judicature (Consolidation) Act 1925:

> 'Rules of court may be made under this Act for the following purposes:—(a) For
> regulating and prescribing the procedure . . . and the practice to be followed in
> the Court of Appeal and the High Court respectively in all causes and matters
> whatsoever . . .'   *g*

Thus Parliament in enacting s 20(1) of the 1969 Act made it clear that the ordering of interim payments is not a matter of mere procedure in which the court is entitled to do as it thinks fit. The judge was right in his conclusion.

By the same token the charterers' claim under s 1 of the Arbitration Act 1975 succeeds. Damages are in issue by virtue of RSC Ord 18, r 13. The shipowners as *h* already described have failed to show that any identifiable or specific part of those damages is not in dispute. That being so the court has no option but to make an order staying proceedings and allowing the dispute to be put to arbitration in accordance with the relevant clause in the charterparty.

I agree with Browne LJ that the appeal should be dismissed.

Appeal dismissed.   *j*

Solicitors: *Ince & Co* (for the shipowners); *Coward Chance* (for the charterers).

Gavin Gore-Andrews   Barrister.

---

1   [1977] 2 All ER 842 at 848, [1977] 1 WLR 638 at 645

a # Brotherton v Inland Revenue Commissioners
Mears v Inland Revenue Commissioners

COURT OF APPEAL CIVIL DIVISION
STAMP, ORR AND SHAW LJJ
b 30th NOVEMBER, 1st DECEMBER 1977

*Settlement – Contingent interest – Contingent interest distinguished from vested interest liable
to be divested – Ownership of income from trust fund – Trustees to hold trust fund until
beneficiary attained age of 30 – Direction to accumulate up to age of 22 – Beneficiary between
age of 22 and 25 not entitled to direct trustees to pay income – Gift over on failure or deter-*
c *mination of the trust – Contrary intention – Whether beneficiary's interest vested or contingent.*

By a settlement made in 1942, the settlor set up a trust fund for the benefit of his son
and daughter who were then both minors. Clause 3 of the settlement directed the
trustees to hold 'one moiety of the Trust Fund in trust for the Son if and when he shall
attain the age of Thirty years but if he shall die under that age then upon the trusts and
d subject to the powers and provisions hereinafter declared and contained concerning
the other moiety of the Trust Fund and so as to form therewith a single fund for all
purposes'. Clause 4 directed the trustees to hold the other moiety of the trust fund in
trust for the daughter on terms corresponding to those relating to the son's moiety.
Clause 5 provided: 'So long as the Son or the Daughter shall be under the age of
Twenty two years the whole of the income of his or her moiety of the Trust Fund shall
e be accumulated by way of compound interest by investing the same and the resulting
income thereof as aforesaid and so long as he or she shall be over the age of Twenty
two years but under the age of Twenty five years the provisions of Section 31 of the
Trustee Act 1925 shall have effect as if he or she were under the age of Twenty one
years to the intent that he or she shall not be entitled to direct the Trustees to pay the
income of his or her moiety aforesaid to him or her.' In the event of failure or deter-
f mination of the trusts there was an ultimate gift over to charity. The settlor died in
1949 when the son and daughter were still both minors. The daughter attained the
age of 21 in 1960 and the son attained that age in 1962. By virtue of s 164 of the Law of
Property Act 1925, the direction in cl 5 of the settlement to accumulate the income
of the son's and the daughter's respective moieties of the trust fund up to the age of 22
was void in that it extended the permissible period of accumulation beyond the age of
g 21. Assessments to surtax were made on the son and the daughter in respect of the income
which had accrued during the 12 months between their respective 21st and 22nd
birthdays, on the basis that, in view of the gift over in the event of their dying under the
age of 30, the settlement had to be construed, in the absence of a contrary intention, as
giving each of them a vested interest liable to be divested on failing to attain that age,
with the result that they were the persons to whom, by virtue of s 164, the income
h accruing in their respective 22nd years was to go and by whom it was to be received.
The son and daughter appealed, contending that their interests were contingent, since
the express direction to accumulate, although invalid, constituted a contrary intention
on the settlor's part to earlier vesting, and that consequently the income of the trust
fund during their respective 22nd years did not belong to them but was undisposed
of by the settlement and resulted to the settlor's estate. Foster J[a] allowed the appeal.
j The Crown appealed against his decision.

Held – On the true construction of the settlement the son and daughter each took a

a [1977] STC 73

vested interest liable to be divested in the event of death under the age of 30. It
followed that the income belonged to them in the 12 months between their respective   *a*
21st and 22nd birthdays and that the assessments had been properly made. Accordingly the appeal would be allowed (see p 272 *d e* and *g*, post).
   Phipps v Ackers (1842) 9 Cl & Fin 583 applied.

Notes

For the rule in *Phipps v Ackers*, see 39 Halsbury's Laws (3rd Edn) 1124, 1125, para 1660,   *b*
for contingent gifts over, see ibid 1127, 1128, para 1664, and for cases on the subject,
see 49 Digest (Repl) 974-979, 9154-9178.
   For the Law of Property Act 1925, s 164, see 27 Halsbury's Statutes (3rd Edn) 587.
   For the Trustee Act 1925, s 31, see 38 ibid 137.

Cases referred to in judgments   *c*

Edwards v Hammond (1684) 3 Lev 132, 1 Bos & P (NR) 324n, 83 ER 614, 49 Digest (Repl)
   968, 9120.
Heath, Re, Public Trustee v Heath [1936] Ch 259, [1935] All ER Rep 677, 105 LJCh 29, 154
   LT 536, 49 Digest (Repl) 1037, 9711.
Kilpatrick's Policies Trusts, Re, Kilpatrick v Inland Revenue Comrs [1966] 2 All ER 149,
   [1966] Ch 730, [1966] 2 WLR 1346, CA, Digest (Cont Vol B) 245, 137*a*.   *d*
Mallinson Consolidated Trusts, Re, Mallinson v Gooley [1974] 2 All ER 530, [1974] 1 WLR
   1120, Digest (Cont Vol D) 813, 2715*b*.
Phipps v Ackers (1842) 9 Cl & F 583, [1558-1774] All ER Rep 381n, 4 Man & G 1107, 8
   ER 539, HL, 49 Digest (Repl) 975, 9163.
Ransome's Will Trusts, Re, Moberley v Ransome [1957] 1 All ER 690, [1957] Ch 348, [1957]
   2 WLR 556, 49 Digest (Repl) 1044, 9768.   *e*

Appeal

The Crown appealed against an order of Foster J[1] made on 19th November 1976
whereby he allowed appeals by the taxpayers, David Ratcliffe Brotherton and Anne
Ratcliffe Mears, by way of cases stated from the determination of the Commissioners
for the Special Purposes of the Income Tax Acts and ordered that the cases be remitted   *f*
to the commissioners for them to adjust, in accordance with his judgment, the
assessments to surtax made on the taxpayers. The facts are set out in the judgment of
Stamp LJ.

Jonathan Parker for the taxpayers.
Peter Gibson for the Crown.   *g*

STAMP LJ.   The question which arises in these appeals, which are appeals by the
Crown, is whether some considerable sums of income which accrued under a settlement between the respective 21st and 22nd birthdays of the primary beneficiaries
under the settlement belonged to them or were undisposed of by the settlement and   *h*
resulted to the settlor's estate. Only if the income belonged to the taxpayers is the
claim of the Crown for surtax thereon well founded. If the income did not belong
to the two primary beneficiaries it is common ground that it goes back, or went back,
to the settlor's estate, the settlor's having died between the date of the settlement
and the date when the elder of the two beneficiaries attained the age of 21.
   The facts were shortly stated by the learned judge in the court below[1], and I take my   *i*
recital of them from his judgment with one or two slight modifications. On 12th
February 1942 Mr C F R Brotherton ('the settlor') made a settlement of £5,000, later
increased very, very considerably, for the benefit of the two principal beneficiaries,

---

1   [1977] STC 73

David and Anne Brotherton (as they then were; Anne is now a married lady). They
a were the settlor's children. Anne was born on 2nd October 1939 and attained the age
of 21 on 2nd October 1960. David was born on 20th April 1941 and attained the age of
21 on 20th April 1962. The settlor died in 1949. Both David and Anne have attained
the age of 30 and have vested interests in the capital of their shares. For the tax year
1962-63 David was assessed for surtax on a sum of £46,692 and for the year 1963-64
on a sum of £49,916. For the year 1960-61 Anne was assessed for surtax on a sum of
b £19,969 and for the year 1961-62 on a sum of £46,948. These figures were subject to
some adjustment when the matter came before the Special Commissioners, but
nothing turns on the figures, which in any event may not have been stated quite
correctly by the learned judge. Nothing turns on that.

The taxpayers, David and Anne, appealed against the assessments to the Commissioners for the Special Purposes of Income Tax Acts who, subject to adjustments,
c confirmed the assessments. The taxpayers each appealed by way of case stated from
that decision. The appeal came before Foster J on 19th November 1976, when he
allowed the appeal, holding that the sums in question were undisposed of by the
settlement and did not form part of the respective taxpayers' income. From that
decision the Crown now appeals.

It is common ground that the question turns entirely on the construction of the
d settlement, the relevant terms of which I shall now read. As I have said, it was made
on 12th February 1942. It recites that the settlor—

'. . . is desirous of making such settlement as hereinafter appearing for the
benefit of his infant children David Ratcliffe Brotherton (hereinafter called "the
Son") and Anne Ratcliffe Brotherton (hereinafter called "the Daughter").'

e It recites the setting up of the trust fund and then provides that the trustees shall
hold one moiety of the trust fund which has been thereby directed to be set up from
the sum of £5,000 and any further investments for the time being representing the
same and all other property (if any) from time to time given to or acquired by the
trustees—

f '. . . In trust for the Son if and when he shall attain the age of Thirty years but
if he shall die under that age then upon the trusts and subject to the powers and
provisions hereinafter declared and contained concerning the other moiety of
the Trust Fund and so as to form therewith a single fund for all purposes.'

Then by cl 4 it is provided that:

g 'THE TRUSTEES shall hold the other moiety of the Trust Fund in trust for the
Daughter if and when she shall attain the age of Thirty years but if she shall die
under that age then Upon the trusts and subject to the powers and provisions
hereinbefore and hereinafter declared and contained concerning the other
moiety of the Trust Fund and so as to form therewith a single fund for all
purposes.'

h Clause 5 provides:

'So long as the Son or the Daughter shall be under the age of Twenty two years
the whole of the income of his or her moiety of the Trust Fund shall be accumulated by way of compound interest by investing the same and the resulting income thereof as aforesaid and so long as he or she shall be over the age of Twenty
j two years but under the age of Twenty five years the provisions of Section 31 of
the Trustee Act 1925 shall have effect as if he or she were under the age of Twenty
one years to the intent that he or she shall not be entitled to direct the Trustees to
pay the income of his or her moiety aforesaid to him or her.'

Then there is an ultimate trust for a charity, I think (it does not matter which it is for), 'IF all the trusts hereinbefore declared concerning the Trust Fund shall fall or determine'.

It is common ground that the direction to accumulate the income of his or her moiety of the trust fund so long as the son or the daughter shall be under the age of 22 years offended s 164 of the Law of Property Act 1925 in that it extended the admissible period of accumulation from a period down to the date when the child attained the age of 21 to the date when the child attained the age of 22. So the question is to whom did the income belong in his or her 22nd year.

It is common ground that under s 164 of the Law of Property Act 1925 that income is to go to and be received by the person or persons who would have been entitled thereto if the accumulation had not been directed. It is common ground that if the trust in favour of each of the taxpayers contained in cll 3 and 4 of the settlement conferred a vested interest on the son and daughter respectively, he or she would have been the person designated by s 164 as the person to whom the income accruing in his or her 22nd year was to go and be received by. So the great question is whether each of the taxpayers took a vested interest liable to be divested or a contingent interest.

It is clear that but for the provisions contained in cl 5 of the settlement each taxpayer would have taken a vested interest liable to be divested in the event of death under the age of 30. It was a rule of construction that—

'If real estate be devised to A. "if," or "when," he shall attain a given age, with a limitation over in the event of his dying under that age, the attainment of the given age is held to be a condition subsequent and not precedent, and A. takes an immediate vested estate, subject to be divested upon his death under the specified age.'

The rule is so stated in Hawkins on Wills[1], citing, inter alia, *Edwards v Hammond*[2] and *Phipps v Ackers*[3] for that proposition. I say it *was* the rule because since the third edition of Hawkins it has been held that the rule applies not only to a devise of real estate but to a bequest of personalty and also to a trust under an inter vivos instrument. The rule was stated in the House of Lords by Tindal CJ in *Phipps v Ackers*[4] in these terms:

'The second class of cases [and this is admitted to be among that class of case] goes on the principle that the subsequent gift over in the event of the devisee dying under 21, sufficiently shows the meaning of the testator to have been that the first devisee should take whatever interest the party claiming under the devise over is not entitled to, which of course gives him the immediate interest, subject only to the chance of its being devested on a future contingency.'

As I have said, the rule has been applied to gifts of personalty (see the decision of Farwell J in *Re Heath*[5] and of this court in *Re Kilpatrick's Policies Trusts*[6]) and to trusts contained in an inter vivos instrument (see *Re Kilpatrick's Policies Trusts*[6]). The rule was criticised in *Re Mallinson Consolidated Trusts*[7] and by Foster J[8] in the instant case, who described it as one which is out of date, makes no sense now and should have been abolished long ago. If however, as has been assumed in this case, the application of the rule would operate to frustrate a resulting trust of income and to pass the income to the persons for the benefit of whom the settlement was made, the rule will perhaps not have lived in vain.

---

1   3rd Edn (1925), p 286
2   (1684) 3 Lev 132
3   (1842) 9 Cl & F 583, [1558-1774] All ER Rep 381
4   9 Cl & F 583 at 591, 592, [1558-1774] All ER Rep 381 at 384
5   [1936] Ch 259 [1935] All ER Rep 677
6   [1966] 2 All ER 149, [1966] Ch 730
7   [1974] 2 All ER 530, [1974] 1 WLR 1120
8   [1977] STC 73 at 80

It is conceded on behalf of the Crown that, like all rules of construction, the rule in
a *Phipps v Ackers*[1] will yield to an indication of an intention that it shall not apply. The
learned judge in the court below summarised[2] the submissions on behalf of the
taxpayers in this regard as follows:

> 'For the [taxpayers], it was submitted: (1) that if the court approaches the
> settlement without the rule in mind, the words "if and when" clearly show that
> *b* the interest is a contingent interest; (2) that the court, bearing in mind the rule,
> should not look at paras 3 and 4 of the settlement in isolation and say the rule
> applies, and then pose the question whether para 5 shows a contrary intention; (3)
> that para 5 contains three signposts leading to the conclusion that the interest
> given was contingent: first, the [taxpayers] were not entitled to any income until
> they reached, respectively, the age of 22 years; secondly, that thereafter, until they
> *c* reached the age of 25 years, they were only entitled to be maintained under s 31 of
> the Trustee Act 1925, and the remainder of the income had to be accumulated;
> and, thirdly, the last two lines of para 5, "to the intent that he or she shall not be
> entitled to direct the Trustees to pay the income of his or her moiety aforesaid
> to him or her", inevitably point to the conclusion that the intention of the settlor
> was to give a contingent interest.'

d   The learned judge accepted one or more of these submissions, and I venture to
think that in so doing he failed to distinguish between the gift of capital and the
provisions regarding the intermediate income. The rule in *Phipps v Ackers*[1] of course
applies to the gift of capital. The first question is whether each of the beneficiaries was
entitled to a vested or contingent interest, and for my part I find great difficulty in
seeing how the construction of the clauses by which the capital is given can be affected
e by the directions which the settlor gave as to the destination of the intermediate
income.
In this court counsel for the taxpayers, in a persuasive argument, very properly
emphasised (and this again is, I think, common ground) that it is crucial to the application of the rule in *Phipps v Ackers*[1] that the gift over in the event of the primary
beneficiary's dying under the specified age should be capable of being construed as
f indicating that the primary beneficiary should take whatever interest the person
claiming under the gift over is not entitled to, that is to say the immediate interest
subject only to the chance of divesting on a future contingency. It is counsel for the
taxpayers' submission that the directions in cl 5, and more particulary the direction to
accumulate, were more consistent with an intention to create contingent interests than
with an intention to create vested interests and that on reading the settlement as a
g whole the settlor is shown to have intended a contingent interest only. Again I venture to think that this submission fails to distinguish between the gift of the fund itself
and the provisions regarding the destination of the income pending the fund's becoming absolutely vested in a beneficiary. Counsel for the taxpayers was bound to concede
that a direction to accumulate is, if for no other reason than because s 31 contemplates
just such a situation, not inconsistent with the existence of a vested interest in the fund,
h and once that concession is made it seems to me to follow that the disposition of
income cannot really affect the question whether the gift of a fund itself is or is not
vested and liable to be divested. Counsel for the taxpayers however, pursuing his
submissions, submitted that the provisions of cl 5 were at least more consistent with a
contingent gift of capital than with a vested interest liable to be divested. For my
part I cannot accept that view of the words used in cl 5 of the settlement.
j   Let me turn back for a moment to indicate my views on it. It starts by directing
that—

---

1   (1842) 9 Cl & F 583, [1558-1774] All ER Rep 381
2   [1977] STC 73 at 80

'So long as the Son or the Daughter shall be under the age of Twenty two years the whole of the income of his or her moiety of the Trust Fund shall be accumulated . . .'

The reference to 'the whole of the income of his or her moiety' is in my view just as consistent with the existence of a vested interest in capital as with the existence of a contingent interest, and the reference to 'his or her moiety' certainly suggests that the settlor regards himself as having given the income as well as the capital of the moiety for the benefit of the son or the daughter as the case may be. The words 'of his or her moiety' are repeated at the end of the clause and, I think, have to be introduced into the second limb of cl 5, which provides that—

'so long as he or she shall be over the age of Twenty two years but under the age of Twenty five years the provisions of Section 31 of the Trustee Act 1925 shall have effect [I think one must introduce the words "in relation to his or her moiety" at that point to make sense of the provision] as if he or she were under the age of Twenty one years to the intent that he or she shall not be entitled to direct the Trustees to pay the income of his or her moiety aforesaid to him or her.'

That looks to me very much like a direction taking away the income to which the settlor thought the son or daughter would be entitled but for the direction he has made, and is at least as consistent with the son's and daughter's having been given vested interests as with their having been given contingent interests. I find nothing in cl 5 which leads me to the conclusion that the wording of cll 3 and 4 should be construed otherwise than in the sense required by the rule in *Phipps v Ackers*[1]. I can find nothing in cl 5 which suggests to me that the settlor intended either of the taxpayers to have an interest which was otherwise than vested but liable to be divested. For those reasons I would allow the appeal.

I must however add one thing. Nothing in this judgment is to be taken as an expression of approval of the view that if on the true construction of the settlement the interests of the primary beneficiaries be contingent only he or she would not have been entitled to the income here in question. The question would be whether s 31 would have applied to so much of the income as was not subject to a valid direction to accumulate. That question has not been explored, the Crown accepting that the decision in *Re Ransome*[2] was correct and binding. I would not wish to throw any doubt on that decision, but it is right to say it has not been considered.

ORR LJ. I entirely agree and would allow this appeal for the reasons given by Stamp LJ. I would add only my tribute for the very able arguments we have heard on both sides.

SHAW LJ. I agree.

Appeal allowed; case remitted to Special Commissioners. Leave to appeal to the House of Lords refused.

Solicitors: *Simpson, Curtis & Co*, Leeds (for the taxpayers); *Solicitor of Inland Revenue*.

A S Virdi Esq Barrister.

---

1   (1842) 9 Cl & F 583, [1558-1774] All ER Rep 381
2   [1957] 1 All ER 690, [1957] Ch 348

Re Associated Travel Leisure and Services Ltd (in liquidation)

CHANCERY DIVISION
TEMPLEMAN J
12th, 21st OCTOBER 1977

Company – Compulsory winding-up – Liquidator – Appointment of solicitor – Sanction of court or of committee of inspection – Retrospective sanction – Validity – Liquidator appointing solicitors to recover substantial debt due to company – Sanction of court or committee not obtained beforehand – Liability of liquidator for solicitor's costs – Whether court or committee having power to sanction appointment retrospectively – Whether court having power to relieve liquidator of consequences of unauthorised appointment in proper case – Companies Act 1948, ss 245(1), 246(3).

On 16th January 1975 the liquidator of a company, without the prior sanction of the court or the committee of inspection required under s 245(1)[a] of the Companies Act 1948, instructed solicitors to issue proceedings and to proceed to collect a debt due to the company, requesting them to treat the matter as urgent because there was a danger that the debtor might become insolvent. The solicitors speedily recovered £15,800 for the company, and submitted a bill of £124·60. On 18th June 1976 the committee of inspection purported to sanction the appointment. The taxing master, whilst considering the solicitors' bill of costs to be clearly modest and reasonable, disallowed the whole of the bill because he was not satisfied that s 245(1) had been complied with. On a review of the taxation, the question arose whether, under s 245(1), the sanction could be given retrospectively and, if not, whether the court had power to relieve the liquidator of the consequences.

Held – (i) Section 245(1)(c) did not authorise a liquidator to appoint a solicitor without first obtaining the sanction of the court or the committee of inspection; the sanction could not be obtained retrospectively so as to authorise the prior appointment of a solicitor. Accordingly the liquidator was liable to meet the solicitor's bill (see p 275 b to e, post).

(ii) However, the court had power, either under s 246(3) or under its inherent jurisdiction, to give retrospective sanction in a proper case to action taken under s 245(1) without the proper sanction. Since the liquidator had incurred a liability to the solicitors for £124·60 and the benefit of that expenditure, admittedly necessary and reasonable, had accrued to the company, the case was a proper one in which to authorise the liquidator to retain out of the assets of the company as part of the expenses of the winding-up sum of £124·60 as indemnity against the claim of the solicitors against the liquidator for the services rendered (see p 275 e to h, post).

Notes

For liquidator's powers, see 7 Halsbury's Laws (4th Edn) para 1122.

For employment of a solicitor by liquidator, see ibid para 1125, and for cases on the subject, see 10 Digest (Reissue) 998, 999, 6055-6066.

For the Companies Act 1948, s 245(1), see 5 Halsbury's Statutes (3rd Edn) 305.

---

a   Section 245(1), so far as material, provides: 'The liquidator in a winding up by the court shall have power, with the sanction either of the court or of the committee of inspection . . . (c) to appoint a solicitor to assist him in the performance of his duties . . .'

Case referred to in judgment

Banque des Marchands de Moscou (Koupetschesky), Re [1953] 1 All ER 278, [1953] 1 WLR   a
172, 10 Digest (Reissue) 1397, 8960.

Review of taxation

On 16th January 1975 the liquidator of Associated Travel Leisure and Services Ltd, a
company being compulsorily wound up by the court, instructed solicitors to collect a
debt due to the company. The solicitors carried out their instructions and duly   b
received £15,800 for the benefit of the liquidation estate and rendered a bill of costs
amounting to £124·60 to the liquidator. On 18th June 1976 the committee of inspection purported to sanction retrospectively the liquidator's employment of the
solicitors. In September 1976 the liquidator referred the solicitors' bill of costs for
taxation pursuant to the Companies (Winding-up) Rules 1949. The taxing master,
after hearing representations from the solicitors and the Official Receiver, disallowed   c
the bill of costs and on a review confirmed his decision. The liquidator applied for a
review of the master's taxation by a judge pursuant to RSC Ord 62, r 35(1). The
review was heard in chambers but judgment was delivered in open court. The facts
are set out in the judgment.

Robert Francis for the liquidator.   d
The Official Receiver as amicus curiae.

Cur adv vult

21st October. **TEMPLEMAN J** read the following judgment: Section 245 (1) of   e
the Companies Act 1948 authorises the liquidator in a winding-up by the court to
exercise certain defined powers 'with the sanction either of the court or of the committee of inspection'. The question is whether that sanction may be given retrospectively and if not whether a liquidator may, in a proper case, be relieved of the
consequences.

The powers conferred by s 245(1) include power '(c) to appoint a solicitor to assist him   f
in the performance of his duties'. In the present case the liquidator instructed a firm
of solicitors on 16th January 1975 to issue proceedings and to proceed to collect a debt
due to the company. The liquidator requested the solicitors to treat the matter as
urgent because there was a danger that the debtor might become insolvent. The
solicitors, acting speedily and efficiently, recovered for the company the sum of
£15,800 and submitted a bill of £124·60, described by the taxing master and acknow-   g
ledged to be modest and reasonable. On 18th June 1976 the committee of inspection
purported to sanction the appointment of the solicitors on 16th January 1975.

Counsel for the liquidator argued that 'sanction' means not only approval in advance
but also recognition, confirmation or ratification in arrears. He relied in the first
instance on dictionary definitions of the word 'sanction', which show that sanction
can mean prior approval, but can also mean ratification. Counsel for the liquidator   h
also relied on the legislative history which preceded the enactment of s 245(1). By
s 12(4) of the Companies (Winding up) Act 1890 the liquidator of a company being
wound up by order of the court was authorised with the sanction either of the court
or of the committee of inspection to—

'employ a Solicitor or other agent to take any proceedings or do any business
which the liquidator is unable to take or do himself. The sanction aforesaid must   i
be a sanction obtained before the employment, except in cases of urgency, and in
such cases it must be shown that no undue delay took place in obtaining the
sanction.'

Section 245(1) of the 1948 Act refers to the appointment and not the employment

of a solicitor and omits the express direction that, subject to certain specified excep-
a tions, the sanction must be obtained before the event. Counsel for the liquidator
argued that the failure in the 1948 Act to make any positive direction with regard to
the timing of the sanction indicates that the legislature were by 1948 content to
allow the liquidator to obtain the necessary sanction before or after the appointment
of a solicitor. In my judgment however the 1948 Act cannot safely be construed by
implication from the different provisions of the 1890 Act.

b   The representative of the Official Receiver appeared to argue for the assistance
of the court against the contentions put forward on behalf of the liquidator. He
argued that the liquidator is limited to the express powers conferred on him by
statute. By s 245(1) the liquidator cannot 'appoint' a solicitor without the sanction of
the court or the committee of inspection. The solicitors in the present case were not
validly 'appointed' until 18th June 1976. Nothing which the solicitors did before
c 18th June 1976 was authorised under s 245(1). I agree with the Official Receiver's
analysis. Moreover, s 245(1) contains a series of powers of considerable importance
which merit the approval of the committee of inspection or of the court being first
obtained. If a liquidator could exercise the powers conferred by s 245(1), and subsequently obtain the sanction of the committee of inspection, the creditors would lose
the benefit of the independent advice of the liquidator who would be personally con-
d cerned to defend the action which he had already taken. It is particularly important
that the committee of inspection should receive the unbiased advice of the liquidator
before sanctioning the exercise of any power conferred by s 245(1). If a liquidator appoints a solicitor without first obtaining the sanction of the court or the committee of
inspection, pursuant to s 245(1), the liquidator will be personally liable to the solicitor
for breach of an implied warranty of authority that the necessary sanction had been
e obtained. Thus in the present case the liquidator would have to meet the solicitors'
bill.

        By s 242(2) of the 1948 Act and r 159 of the Companies (Winding-up) Rules 1949[1]
the court has power to direct remuneration to be paid to a liquidator other than the
official receiver. By s 246(3) of the 1948 Act, the liquidator may apply to the court
for directions in relation to any particular matter arising under the winding-up.
f Either under s 246(3) or under its inherent powers, the court may authorise the
liquidator to make a variety of payments, including even an ex gratia payment:
see *Re Banque des Marchands de Moscou (Koupetschesky)*[2].

        In the present case the liquidator has incurred a liability of £124·60 to the solicitors
and the benefit of that expenditure, admittedly necessary and reasonable, has accrued
to the creditors. In these circumstances I authorise and direct the liquidator to retain
g out of the assets of the company as part of the expenses of the winding-up the sum of
£124·60 as an indemnity against the claim of the solicitors against the liquidator for
the services rendered by the solicitors. In the result, the court has power to give a
retrospective sanction in a proper case to action taken under s 245(1) without the
prior sanction of the committee of inspection or of the court. I do not think the result
will be either inconvenient or expensive. A liquidator should obtain prior sanction
h and if he does not do so he will have to satisfy the court that his expenditure should
be allowed.

Order accordingly.

Solicitors: *Stephenson Harwood & Tatham.*

j

                                        Jacqueline Metcalfe   Barrister.

---

1   SI 1949 No 330
2   [1953] 1 All ER 278, [1953] 1 WLR 172

Holt Southey Ltd v Catnic Components Ltd

CHANCERY DIVISION

GOULDING J

8th, 10th NOVEMBER 1977

Company – Compulsory winding-up – Petition by creditors – Disputed debt – Admission that part of sum prospective debt – Demand for payment of £39,068 served on company – Company denying any part of that sum due–Company admitting that £20,000 of that sum was prospective debt – Whether company entitled to injunction restraining presentation of petition – Companies Act 1948, s 224(1).

The defendants served on the plaintiff company a demand, under s 223 of the Companies Act 1948, requiring it to pay the sum of £39,068·15 which they said was due to them. The company alleged, inter alia, that the defendants had arranged to allow it credit of £20,000 in respect of goods sold and delivered to it and that by virtue of the arrangement the defendants were precluded from claiming payment in respect of that amount at present. The company issued a writ claiming an injunction restraining the defendants from presenting a petition to wind up the company based on the debt of £39,068·15, and, by notice of motion, sought an injunction restraining them from doing so until the trial of the action or further order. On the hearing of the motion.

Held – The defendants, as prospective creditors in respect of the £20,000, would be entitled to present a petition under s 224(1)ᵃ of the 1948 Act and they ought not to be deprived of their right to do so by virtue of the fact that on the evidence there was a substantial dispute as to the sum demanded. They did not have to establish for the purposes of the motion, that they could satisfy proviso (c) to s 224(1) and make a prima facie case that the company was unable to pay its debts. Furthermore, they should not be restrained from presenting a petition otherwise than as prospective creditors. Once it was shown that a person had locus standi to present a petition, it was for the Companies Court to determine the validity of any allegations that might be made in the petition. It followed that the motion would be dismissed (see p 278 h j, p 279 g h to p 280 a and d to p 281 a, post).

Mann v Goldstein [1968] 2 All ER 769 and *Bryanston Finance Ltd v de Vries (No 2)* [1976] 1 All ER 25 considered.

Notes

For injunctions to restrain a winding-up petition generally, see 7 Halsbury's Laws (4th Edn) para 1004, and for cases on the subject, see 10 Digest (Reissue) 934, 935, 5457–5463.

For the Companies Act 1948, ss 223(1), 224, see 5 Halsbury's Statutes (3rd Edn) 292, 293.

Cases referred to in judgment

Bryanston Finance Ltd v de Vries (No 2) [1976] 1 All ER 25, [1976] Ch 63, [1976] 2 WLR 41, CA.

Cadiz Waterworks Co v Barnett (1874) LR 19 Eq 182, 44 LJCh 529, 31 LT 640, 10 Digest (Reissue) 934, 5457.

Imperial Guardian Life Assurance Society, Re (1869) LR 9 Eq 447, 39 LJCh 147, 10 Digest (Reissue) 934, 5455.

Mann v Goldstein [1968] 2 All ER 769, [1968] 1 WLR 1091, 10 Digest (Reissue) 935, 5463.

Niger Merchants Co v Capper (1877) 18 Ch D 557n, 10 Digest (Reissue) 934, 5459.

---

a   Section 224(1), so far as material, is set out at p 279 e and f, post

Motion

By a writ issued on 25th October 1977, the plaintiffs, Holt Southey Ltd, brought an action against the defendants, Catnic Components Ltd, claiming an injunction restraining the defendants, whether by their officers, servants, agents or otherwise howsoever, from presenting a petition to wind up the plaintiffs based on a debt of £39,068·15 alleged by the defendants to be due from the plaintiffs to the defendants in a demand dated 16th September 1977. By notice of motion, dated 25th October 1977, the plaintiffs sought an injunction restraining the defendants from presenting such a petition until the trial of the action or further order. The facts are set out in the judgment.

L F R Cohen for the plaintiffs.
Robin Potts for the defendants.

GOULDING J. I now have to give judgment on a motion in an action between two companies. The plaintiff seeks by the motion to restrain the defendants until trial or further order, from presenting a petition in the Companies Court to wind up the plaintiff, based on a debt of £39,068·15 alleged by the defendant to be due from the plaintiff to the defendant in a demand dated 16th September 1977. That was a demand served in pursuance of s 223 of the Companies Act 1948 for the evident purpose of founding a winding-up petition.

The circumstances in which this court will restrain the presentation of a winding-up petition in the Companies Court, or possibly the taking of some step in prosecuting the petition if already presented, are to be found in a case decided by Ungoed-Thomas J, *Mann v Goldstein*[1]. Ungoed-Thomas J said[2]:

> 'When the debt is disputed by the company on some substantial ground (and not just on some ground which is frivolous or without substance and which the court should, therefore, ignore) and the company is solvent, the court will restrain the prosecution of a petition to wind up the company. As Sir Richard Malins, V.-C., said in *Cadiz Waterworks Co. v. Barnett*[3], of a winding-up application, "... it is not a remedy intended by the legislature, or that ought ever to be applied, to enforce payment of a debt where these circumstances exist—solvency and a disputed debt." As Sir George Jessel, M.R., said in the judgment from which I have already quoted [a judgment in *Niger Merchants Co v Capper*[4]] "When a company is solvent, the right course is to bring an action for the debt: ..." So, to pursue a winding-up petition in such circumstances is an abuse of the process of the court.'

I may interject at that point that it appears, from the judgment in *Mann v Goldstein*[1] itself, that in such an application as the present the solvency of the company is not something that has to be proved in order to restrain the prosecution of a petition based on a substantially disputed debt.

The other passage I want to read from Ungoed-Thomas J's judgment is the following[5]:

> 'For my part, I would prefer to rest the jurisdiction directly on the compara-tively simple propositions that a creditor's petition can only be presented by a creditor, that the winding-up jurisdiction is not for the purpose of deciding a

---

1   [1968] 2 All ER 769, [1968] 1 WLR 1091
2   [1968] 2 All ER 769 at 773, [1968] 1 WLR 1091 at 1096
3   (1874) LR 19 Eq 182 at 194
4   (1877) 18 Ch D 557n at 559
5   [1968] 2 All ER 769 at 775, [1968] 1 WLR 1091 at 1098, 1099

disputed debt (that is, disputed on substantial and not insubstantial grounds) since, until a creditor is established as a creditor he is not entitled to present the petition and has no locus standi in the Companies Court; and that, therefore, to invoke the winding-up jurisdiction when the debt is disputed (that is, on substantial grounds) or after it has become clear that it is so disputed is an abuse of the process of the court.'

It has been suggested by counsel for the defendant in the present case that those observations in *Mann v Goldstein*[1] have to be read with some modification or, at any rate, in a different light because of the observations of the Court of Appeal in *Bryanston Finance Ltd v de Vries (No 2)*[2]. I do not think that that is so. The two cases seem to me entirely consistent. *Bryanston Finance Ltd v de Vries (No 2)*[2] emphasised that the High Court is not to interfere with the subject's right to present a petition to the Companies Court, unless it is clear that such a petition, if presented, would be an abuse of that court's process. The hardship to the would-be petitioner in being denied his prima facie right of petitioning and in perhaps being forced into a multiplicity of proceedings has to be remembered just as much as the hardship to the company if an illfounded and unjustified petition is presented against it and advertised. But there is nothing in that emphasis that is in the least inconsistent to my mind with what Ungoed-Thomas J said.

The basis of *Mann v Goldstein*[1], as I understand it, is that it is plainly an abuse of the process of the Companies Court for someone to petition in the capacity of a creditor who is not a creditor. Once that is seen, there is no possible conflict between *Bryanston Finance Ltd v de Vries (No 2)*[2] and *Mann v Goldstein*[1]. That is why, where the would-be petitioner cannot show his qualification as a creditor without a preliminary action to get judgment on a truly disputed debt, this court will restrain him from using the machinery of the Companies Court.

It was also suggested by counsel for the defendant that possibly one had to approach the matter in a rather different manner in a case such as the present, where no petition has yet been presented, to a case such as *Mann v Goldstein*[1], where the petition had been presented and the respondent company was seeking to restrain advertisement or other steps in prosecuting the petition. I do not think it right or necessary to draw any such distinction. In that connection I remember what Buckley LJ said in *Bryanston Finance Ltd v de Vries (No 2)*[3]:

'It has long been recognised that the jurisdiction of the court to stay an action in limine as an abuse of process is a jurisdiction to be exercised with great circumspection and exactly the same considerations must apply to a quia timet injunction to restrain commencement of proceedings. These principles are, in my opinion, just as applicable to a winding-up petition as to an action.'

My brief survey of the authorities cited therefore leaves me persuaded that I ought to take the judgment in *Mann v Goldstein*[1] as the criterion for deciding the present application. So I have to ask myself, is the debt relied on by the defendant disputed by the plaintiff on some ground which is substantial as opposed to a ground which is frivolous or insubstantial.

I shall not take time to read through the affidavits on either side. It is in my judgment impossible to say that the dispute raised by the plaintiff is either frivolous or insubstantial, if one assumes the sincerity of the evidence filed on the plaintiff's behalf. Although circumstances have been pointed out which raise a need for caution and possible suspicion on some details of the evidence, it is quite impossible for me to say it is not honest on mere suspicions from an examination of allegations on paper.

1   [1968] 2 All ER 769, [1968] 1 WLR 1091
2   [1976] 1 All ER 25, [1976] Ch 63
3   [1976] 1 All ER 25 at 36, [1976] Ch 63 at 78

It would follow so far, I think, that in accordance with the principles stated by Ungoed-Thomas J I ought to restrain the presentation of a petition pending the trial of this action. The result would presumably be that the defendant would have to seek a judgment in some other action before proceeding further.

However, a further and different point has been raised by counsel for the defendant which I shall have to consider. Part of the dispute between the parties is that the plaintiff alleges an arrangement, apparently of a somewhat complicated character (and it may involve other parties) by which the defendant allowed a credit of £20,000 in respect of goods sold and delivered to the plaintiff. That is why the plaintiff contends that as to that amount at any rate, and there are other answers as to the balance, the sum of £39,000 odd specified in the statutory demand was not and is not due. The terms of the arrangement are not precisely formulated, but are alleged, as I have said, to preclude the defendant from claiming payment of £20,000 in respect of goods sold and delivered at present.

Counsel for the defendant points to the rights given to a contingent or prospective creditor under the 1948 Act. It will be remembered that one, and the most usual, ground for the winding-up of a company by the court is that the company is unable to pay its debts. It will also be remembered that, by s 223(d) of the 1948 Act—

'... in determining whether a company is unable to pay its debts, the court shall take into account the contingent and prospective liabilities of the company.'

In the next section, s 224(1), the Act provides that—

'An application to the court for the winding up of a company shall be by petition [and that the petition may be presented by, among others,] any creditor or creditors (including any contingent or prospective creditor or creditors) ...'

Then there is a proviso, proviso (c) of s 224(1), that—

'... the court shall not give a hearing to a winding-up petition presented by a contingent or prospective creditor until such security for costs has been given as the court thinks reasonable and until a prima facie case for winding up has been established to the satisfaction of the court ...'

Counsel for the defendant says that even if the plaintiff is wholly right in its assertions, yet the defendant is at liberty to petition with regard to the prospective debt of £20,000, subject of course, if that is the only good ground for a petition, to satisfying the Companies Court by some evidence other than the demand already served that there is a prima facie case for winding-up. Only after that preliminary matter has been pursued before the registrar of the Companies Court can the petition be heard. Counsel for the defendant says that it is wrong for this court to curtail the defendant's statutory right to petition when, even on the plaintiff's showing, the defendant is a qualified creditor for that purpose.

Counsel for the plaintiff suggests that I ought not to listen to such a contention, at any rate until there is some evidence before me that the defendant as a prospective creditor could satisfy the proviso in s 224 of the 1948 Act and make a prima facie case that the plaintiff is unable to pay its debts. I do not think, consistently with *Mann v Goldstein*[1], that it would be right for me to go into the question whether the defendant, as a prospective creditor, could satisfy the proviso. The basis of *Mann v Goldstein*[1] was that the would-be petitioner was not shown to be a creditor at all, and therefore it would be an abuse for him to present a petition. It is a step further in the interference by this court with the proceedings of the Companies Court if it is to be said that,

---

1   [1968] 2 All ER 769, [1968] 1 WLR 1091

although qualified to present a petition, the would-be petitioner could not get it on for hearing because he could not satisfy some requirement of the Companies Court, and therefore he ought not to be allowed to present it.

I am very loath to extend the scope of proceedings of this kind, where the High Court seeks to control proceedings in the Companies Court, and I am particularly influenced in this respect by a passage in *Mann v Goldstein*[1]:

'So if a person is entitled to present a petition, then the company's inability to pay its debts is the very matter which it is appropriate for the Companies Court to enquire into and decide in the exercise of its jurisdiction to make a winding-up order.'

I also remember what Buckley LJ said in *Bryanston Finance Ltd v de Vries (No 2)*[2]. He said:

'In my judgment, the fact that the second action is an action designed to prevent the commencement of proceedings in limine is such a special factor. In such a case the court should not, in my judgment, interfere with what would otherwise be a legitimate approach to the seat of justice unless the evidence is sufficient to establish prima facie that the plaintiff will succeed in establishing that the proceedings sought to be restrained will constitute an abuse of process.'

Thus it seems to me that the point taken by counsel for the defendant is a good one and that at least I ought not to prevent the presentation of a petition based on a prospective debt.

Then counsel for the plaintiff makes an alternative submission, assuming I get to the point (at which I have in fact arrived) of holding that there is a substantial dispute regarding the debt alleged in the statutory demand, but at the same time thinking that I ought not to ignore the defendant's locus standi as a prospective creditor for a sum admitted in that respect. Counsel for the plaintiff suggests that I ought, nonetheless, to restrain the defendant until further order from presenting a winding-up petition otherwise than as a prospective creditor. He asks me also to restrain the advertisement of a petition presented on that footing until prior notice has been given to the plaintiff.

I have hesitated over that application, but it seems to me that I ought not to accede to it. As I have said, I am very loath to extend this type of proceeding. As I have also said more than once, I think the basis of *Mann v Goldstein*[3] is that it is an abuse for a person who is not qualified as a petitioner under the terms of the 1948 Act to present a petition. If he is qualified, it seems to me that the only satisfactory course is to leave the Companies Court itself to weigh up and decide by its own process all the allegations that may be made in the petition. It was said by James V-C in *Re Imperial Guardian Life Assurance Society*[4] quoted in *Mann v Goldstein*[5] that 'A winding-up petition is not to be used as machinery for trying a common law action', and that of course is the whole basis of the application before me. But that does not mean that the Companies Court may not have to decide on the validity or terms of an alleged liability once the petitioner has established his locus standi to petition before that court.

As I say, after some hesitation I conclude that, once I am satisfied that I should not restrain a petition altogether, I ought not to attempt to dictate the allegations that

---

1 [1968] 2 All ER 769 at 772, [1968] 1 WLR 1091 at 1095
2 [1976] 1 All ER 25 at 36, [1976] Ch 63 at 78
3 [1968] 2 All ER 769, [1968] 1 WLR 1091
4 (1869) LR 9 Eq 447 at 450
5 [1968] 2 All ER 769 at 773, [1968] 1 WLR 1091 at 1097

may or may not be put in. It must be left to the Companies Court to do its own work in that respect. Accordingly, the motion fails.

Order accordingly.

Solicitors: *Fulwell & Partners*, Bristol (for the plaintiff); *Clifford-Turner* (for the defendant).

Evelyn M C Budd Barrister.

Victoria Square Property Co Ltd v London Borough of Southwark

COURT OF APPEAL, CIVIL DIVISION
MEGAW, BRIDGE AND WALLER LJJ
27th, 28th OCTOBER, 11th NOVEMBER 1977

Housing – House unfit for human habitation – Premises beyond repair at reasonable cost – Purchase in lieu of demolition – Power of local authority to purchase house which is or can be rendered capable of providing accommodation which is adequate for the time being – Extent of power – Whether limited to power to acquire house for purpose of providing temporary accommodation pending demolition – Whether including power to purchase house with a view to restoring it for purpose of long-term occupation – Housing Act 1957, s 17(2).

The owners of a small house in the local authority's area let it to a tenant under an agreement to which s 6^a of the Housing Act 1957 applied. The local authority were not satisfied that the house was fit for human habitation and they served on the owners a notice under s 9 requiring them to execute an extensive schedule of works in order to restore it to the standard of fitness prescribed by s 4. The owners appealed, under s 11, against the notice, contending, inter alia, that the house was not capable of being rendered fit for human habitation at reasonable expense. The county court judge allowed the appeal and quashed the notice. The local authority thereupon decided to purchase the house compulsorily under s 12(1)^b and to execute the works themselves. They made a compulsory purchase order and then realised that they had not obtained from the county court judge at the hearing an express finding under s 11(3) that the house was not capable of being rendered fit for human habitation at reasonable expense. Since such a finding was an essential precondition to a compulsory purchase order under s 12, they requested the county court judge to make the necessary finding. The judge refused to do so and the local authority, recognising that the compulsory purchase order could not be confirmed by the Minister without it, withdrew the order. The local authority then adopted the procedure provided by the Act for use where a housing authority were satisfied that a house was unfit for human habitation and incapable of being rendered fit at reasonable expense. They

---

a Section 6, so far as material, provides: '. . . (2) . . . in any contract to which this section applies there shall, notwithstanding any stipulation to the contrary, be implied a condition that the house is at the commencement of the tenancy, and an undertaking that the house will be kept by the landlord during the tenancy, fit for human habitation . . .'
b Section 12(1) provides: 'Where a person has appealed against a notice under this Part of this Act requiring the execution of works to a house, and the judge or court in allowing the appeal has found that the house cannot be rendered fit for human habitation at a reasonable expense, the local authority may purchase that house by agreement or may be authorised by the Minister to purchase it compulsorily; and the First Schedule to this Act shall apply in relation to a compulsory purchase under this section.'

served on the owners a notice under s 16^c specifying a time and place at which they would consider the condition of the house and any offer which the owners might wish to submit with respect to the carrying out of works. The owners did not serve, under s 16(3), a notice of intention to execute works, but they offered a formal undertaking, pursuant to s 16(4), that the house would not be used for human habitation until the local authority were satisfied that it had been rendered fit for that purpose and cancelled the undertaking. The local authority refused to accept the undertaking and served on the owners, pursuant to s 19, a notice of their determination to purchase the house under s 17(2)^d. The owners appealed, under s 20, against the notice. The judge found (1) that the local authority's intention on acquiring the house was to rehouse the sitting tenant and to render the house fit for occupation for more than 30 years by carrying out not only the works specified in the s 9 notice but also additional work to bring it up to an even higher standard of fitness; (2) that their reasons for wanting to acquire the house were (a) to avoid the loss of residential accommodation which would result if it was not rehabilitated and occupied, and (b) to ensure that it was occupied by a person on their waiting list; (3) that the owners would suffer a financial loss if the local authority compulsorily acquired the house under s 17(2). He held (i) that the local authority had no power under s 17(2) to acquire it for the purpose of obtaining a permanent addition to their housing stock; and (ii) that, in any event, even if they had power to do so under s 17(2), he would, having weighed the local authority's reasons against, inter alia, the financial implications for the owners, have exercised his discretion under s 20(3)^e to set aside the s 19 notice and required the local authority to accept the undertaking offered by the owners under s 16(4). The local authority appealed.

Held – The appeal would be dismissed for the following reasons—

(i) Section 17(2) merely conferred on a local authority power to acquire a property so that they could use it to provide temporary housing accommodation pending its demolition, notwithstanding that its condition fell short of the standard of fitness for human habitation prescribed by the Act. The subsection could not be stretched to cover an acquisition made with the intention of restoring a property for the purpose of long-term occupation. It followed that the local authority were not entitled under s 17(2) to purchase the house for the purpose of obtaining a permanent addition to this housing stock (see p 286 e to g, p 287 g to p 288 a, p 289 c, p 291 c d and p 292 c d, post).

(ii) In any event the judge's exercise of his discretion under s 20(3) could not be impugned for he had not acted on any wrong principle; he had taken into account the relevant matters, he had not had regard to irrelevant matters and he had not acted unreasonably (see p 289 j, p 291 b to d and p 292 a to c and j to p 293 d, post).

Notes

For the purchase of unfit houses in lieu of demolition, see 19 Halsbury's Laws (3rd Edn) 620, 621, para 1000.

For the Housing Act 1957, ss 4, 6, 9, 11, 12, 16, 17, 19, 20, see 16 Halsbury's Statutes (3rd Edn) 117, 118, 121, 125, 126, 130, 132, 135.

Cases cited

Croydon Corpn v Thomas [1947] 1 All ER 239, [1947] KB 386, DC.
Fletcher v Ilkeston Corpn (1931) 96 JP 7, CA.
Pocklington v Melksham Urban District Council [1964] 2 All ER 862, [1964] 2 QB 673, CA.
R v Kerrier District Council, ex parte Guppys (Bridport) Ltd (1976) 75 LGR 129, CA.
Salford City Council v McNally [1975] 2 All ER 860, [1976] AC 319, HL.
Stepney Borough Council v Joffe [1949] 1 All ER 256, [1949] 1 KB 599, DC.

c   Section 16, so far as material, is set out at p 284 b to f, post
d   Section 17(2) is set out at p 284 h, post
e   Section 20(3) is set out at p 284 j to p 285 a, post

Appeal

This was an appeal by the Southwark London Borough Council ('the local authority') against an order of his Honour Judge McDonnell, dated 20th May 1977, (i) allowing an appeal by the respondents, Victoria Square Property Co Ltd, the owners of a house at 37 Landells Road, London SE22, against a notice of determination to purchase, dated 28th September 1976, served on them by the local authority, and (ii) ordering the local authority to accept an undertaking by the owners not to use the house for human habitation until the local authority, on being satisfied that it had been rendered fit for that purpose, cancelled the undertaking. The facts are set out in the judgment of Bridge LJ.

Anthony Scrivener QC and *William Birtles* for the local authority.
Richard Fawls for the owners.

Cur adv vult

11th November. The following judgments were read.

BRIDGE LJ read the first judgment at the invitation of Megaw LJ. This is an appeal by the local authority from an order of his Honour Judge McDonnell made in the Lambeth County Court on 20th May 1977, the effect of which was to quash a notice of determination to purchase from the owners a three-bedroomed terrace house. The purchase notice had been served by the local authority pursuant to ss 17(2) and 19 of the Housing Act 1957. The owners appealed to the county court under s 20. On the hearing of that appeal the county court judge made the order against which appeal is now brought to this court.

To understand the history of the litigation between the parties it is necessary first to consider the general scheme of Part II of the 1957 Act and to set out the particular provisions on which the decision of this appeal turns. The heading of Part II is 'Provisions for Securing the Repair, Maintenance and Sanitary Condition of Houses'. Section 4 prescribes a statutory standard of fitness for human habitation of dwelling-houses. Section 6 provides that on the letting of certain classes of house, within which the house in question in this case falls, there shall be implied a statutory condition that the house is at the commencement of the tenancy, and an undertaking that the house will be kept by the landlord during the tenancy, fit for human habitation. The main provisions of Part II impose on a local authority a statutory obligation to deal with houses in their area found to be unfit for human habitation in one or other of two ways. The first procedure is that contained in the fasciculus of sections, ss 9 to 15. These sections are headed 'Unfit premises capable of repair at reasonable cost'. The procedure which they embody may conveniently be called the rehabilitation procedure, since the object is that houses to which the procedure is applied shall be repaired to the appropriate standard of fitness for human habitation. The alternative procedure is that contained in the fasciculus of ss 16-32 which are headed 'Unfit premises beyond repair at reasonable cost'. This procedure may appropriately be called the demolition procedure, since demolition of the unfit houses to which the procedure is applied will be the normal end result.

The rehabilitation procedure begins with the service of a notice on the owner of the house in question requiring him to carry out such works of repair as the notice specifies in order to restore the premises to a condition of fitness. The recipient of the notice can appeal to the county court against it under s 11 on the ground, inter alia, that the house is not capable of being rendered fit for human habitation at a reasonable expense. If the judge allows an appeal against a s 9 notice, he is required, if requested by the local authority so to do, to make a finding whether the house can or cannot be rendered fit for human habitation at a reasonable expense (s 11(3)).

If the judge has made a finding that the house cannot be rendered fit for human habitation at reasonable expense, but the local authority are still of the opinion that repair of the house to restore it to a state of fitness is an appropriate course, they are empowered under s 12 to purchase the house either by agreement or compulsorily. The compensation to the owner on such an acquisition is the site value of the property. Having effected such an acquisition the local authority are obliged by s 12(3) themselves to carry out the works specified in their notice under s 9 as necessary to restore the house to a condition of fitness for human habitation.

The alternative demolition procedure begins under s 16. The important provisions are the following. Section 16(1) provides:

'Where a local authority, on consideration of an official representation, or a report from any of their officers, or other information in their possession, are satisfied that any house—(a) is unfit for human habitation, and (b) is not capable at a reasonable expense of being rendered so fit, they shall serve upon [any person interested in the house] notice of the time . . . and place at which the condition of the house and any offer with respect to the carrying out of works, or the future user of the house, which he may wish to submit will be considered by them.'

Section 16(3) enacts formal requirements with respect to any offer to carry out works to the house. Section 16 continues:

'(4) The local authority may if, after consultation with any owner or mortgagee, they think fit so to do, accept an undertaking from him, either that he will within a specified period carry out such works as will in the opinion of the authority render the house fit for human habitation, or that it shall not be used for human habitation until the authority, on being satisfied that it has been rendered fit for that purpose, cancel the undertaking.

'(5) Nothing in [the Rent Act 1968] shall prevent possession being obtained of any premises by any owner thereof in a case where an undertaking had been given under this section that those premises shall not be used for human habitation.'

Section 17(1) provides:

'If no such undertaking as is mentioned in the last foregoing section is accepted by the local authority, or if, in a case where they have accepted such an undertaking—(a) any work to which the undertaking relates is not carried out within the specified period, or (b) the premises are at any time used in contravention of the terms of undertaking, then subject to the provisions of this section, the local authority shall forthwith make a demolition order for the demolition of the premises to which the notice given under the last foregoing section relates . . .'

The proviso authorises the making of a closing order instead of a demolition order in certain cases. Section 17(2) provides:

'Where a local authority would under the foregoing subsection be required to make a demolition or closing order in respect of a house they may, if it appears to them that the house is or can be rendered capable of providing accommodation which is adequate for the time being, purchase the house instead of making a demolition or closing order.'

Section 19 provides for service of notice of a determination to purchase. Section 20 gives a right of appeal to the county court against such a notice. Section 20(3) provides:

'On an appeal to the county court under this section the judge may make such order either confirming or quashing or varying the order or notice as he thinks fit and may, if he thinks fit, accept from an appellant any such undertaking as

a
might have been accepted by the local authority, and any undertaking so accepted by the judge shall have the like effect as if it had been given to and accepted by the local authority under this Part of this Act.'

Section 29(1) and (2) authorise acquisition of a house pursuant to a purchase notice, by agreement or compulsorily at site value. Section 29 continues:

b
'(3) A local authority by whom a house is purchased under this section may carry out such works as may from time to time be required for rendering and keeping it capable of providing accommodation of a standard which is adequate for the time being pending its demolition by the authority.

'(4) In respect of any house purchased under this section the local authority shall have the like powers as they have in respect of houses provided under Part V of this Act, and section six of this Act shall not apply to a contract for the letting by

c
a local authority of any such house.'

The history of the dispute between the local authority and the owners in this case begins with the service of a notice under s 9 of the 1957 Act dated 26th June 1975, requiring them to carry out an extensive schedule of works on the house. The owners appealed to the county court against this notice on the ground, inter alia, that the

d
premises were not capable of being rendered fit for human habitation at a reasonable expense. On 17th October, 1975, in the Lambeth County Court, her Honour Judge Cooper allowed that appeal and quashed the s 9 notice. It is not wholly clear, but it would seem a probable inference that her ground for so doing was that the owners has succeeded in establishing the ground referred to. The local authority decided to proceed by way of acquisition under s 12 of the 1957 Act and themselves carry

e
out the scheduled works. There being no purchase by agreement, on 24th February 1976 the local authority made a compulsory purchase order. They then appreciated that they had not obtained from Judge Cooper at the hearing of the appeal an express finding under s 11(3) that the premises were not capable of being rendered fit for human habitation at a reasonable expense. Such a finding was a necessary foundation to support the compulsory purchase order they had made. Accordingly the local

f
authority applied to the county court with a request for an express finding under s 11(3). For some reason which it is not easy to understand, this application was, on 30th April 1976, dismissed by her Honour Judge Cooper. It would be quite wrong to criticise the learned judge in any way, since we do not know what were the reasons which prompted her to dismiss the application. But I feel bound to say that I feel much sympathy with the local authority in the difficulties in which this decision of

g
the county court judge placed them. They were proceeding perfectly properly in seeking to acquire the property in order to carry out the works themselves pursuant to s 12. But when they were thwarted in this proceeding by their inability to obtain the necessary finding of fact to validate the s 12 compulsory purchase, they understandably felt obliged to resort to a different procedure. It is from this frustration of the proposed compulsory purchase under s 12 that all the local authority's later

h
problems stem. Recognising in fact that the compulsory purchase order could not now be confirmed, the local authority naturally withdrew it.

The second stage of the history begins with the service on 29th June 1976 of a notice specifying a time and place pursuant to s 16 at which the local authority would consider the condition of, and any offers with respect to, the house. The premise on which this notice was served was necessarily that the local authority were now satis-

j
fied, contrary to the view on which they had previously proceeded, that the house was not capable of being rendered fit for human habitation at a reasonable expense. No notice of an intention to carry out works was served by the owners pursuant to s 16(3). However, at the time and place specified in the s 16 notice the owners did offer a formal undertaking pursuant to s 16(4) that the house would not be used for human habitation until the local authority, being satisfied that it had been rendered fit for that

purpose, cancelled the undertaking. This undertaking was not accepted by the local authority. On 28th September 1976 the local authority served on the owners pursuant to s 19 a notice of their determination to purchase the house under s 17(2). The owners appealed against this notice under s 20.

The hearing of the appeal before Judge McDonnell was on 21st April 1977. He delivered his reserved judgment in writing on 20th May. The essential facts were not in dispute. The local authority's intention was, as it has always been, that works to the house should be carried out to restore it to a state of fitness for human habitation. They were proposing on acquisition to rehouse the sitting tenant, who would require only single bedroom accommodation, and then to carry out at the house not only the works which had been specified in their original notice under s 9 but other works to bring the house to a still higher standard. After the works were carried out, the house, it was estimated, would have a useful life of not less than 30 years. The judge concluded, first, that the acquisition was not within the powers conferred on the local authority by s 17(2), but that, secondly, if, contrary to his conclusion on the first point, the purchase was within the powers of the local authority, he would in the exercise of his discretion set the notice aside and accept the undertaking offered by the owners pursuant to s 16(4).

The learned judge expressed his conclusion on the question of vires in these terms:

'I hold that a local authority are only entitled to purchase property under s 17(2) for the purpose of using it temporarily pending demolition ... In my judgment the local authority were not entitled to use their powers under the subsection for the purpose of obtaining a permanent addition to their housing stock.'

The first question we have to decide on this appeal is whether this was a correct conclusion on the true construction of the relevant provisions of the 1957 Act. It is quite clear that the primary purpose of an acquisition under s 17(2) is to enable the local authority to use a house to provide temporary housing accommodation not-withstanding that its condition falls short of the standard of fitness for human habi-tation prescribed by the Act. This emerges from consideration of the phrases in s 17(2) 'is or can be rendered capable' and 'adequate for the time being', from the words in s 29(3) 'pending its demolition by the authority', and from the provision in s 29(4) excluding the statutory implied condition of fitness for human habitation from any letting of the house. But is the power conferred by s 17(2) limited to cases where the purpose of the local authority is to use the house only for a limited period and in a condition affording such a limited standard of accommodation? Counsel's argument in support of the appeal for the local authority is essentially a simple one. He submits that, once the authority have acquired the house under s 17(2), there is nothing in the statutory provisions to limit the scale of the works which the authority may carry out by way of repair or improvement of the house, the standard of accommodation which they may use it to provide, or the period of time for which it may be retained for use as housing accommodation 'pending demolition'. He relies in particular on the applica-tion by s 29(4) to houses acquired in this way of the powers of Part V of the 1957 Act. These include power under s 92(1)(d) to alter, enlarge, repair or improve any house which has been acquired by the local authority. It is said that the standard to which a house acquired under s 17(2) is to be repaired or improved and the length of time which it is to be retained are both matters of degree and that accordingly it would be impossible to draw a line at any point on the scale and to say that by proceeding beyond that point the local authority would be acting ultra vires. Thus it follows, so runs the argument, that even in a case where, as here, the declared purpose of the local authority which underlies the proposed acquisition is not to use the house to pro-vide temporary accommodation of a standard falling short of fitness for human habitation but to bring it up to the full statutory standard of fitness and retain it as part of the local authority's permanent housing stock, it cannot be said that the purchase is beyond the power of the section.

To my mind the most helpful approach to the problem of construction involved
a is to compare the provisions in ss 17 and 29, with which we are directly concerned,
with the comparable provisions found in Part III of the Act, dealing with clearance
areas, which also provide for postponement of clearance and the use of unfit houses
during a period of postponement to provide housing accommodation. Whereas
Part II of the Act provides quite different procedures for dealing with individual
unfit houses according to whether they can or cannot be rendered fit for human
b habitation at a reasonable expense, the clearance area procedure under Part III
ignores this distinction. If included in a clearance area, unfit houses are liable to be
demolished or acquired at site value even though they could be rendered fit for human
habitation at a quite modest expense. The starting point of the procedure is a decision
by the local authority under s 42 that all the houses in the area are unfit for human
habitation and that the most satisfactory method of dealing with the conditions in
c the area is the demolition of all the buildings in it. The local authority may then
proceed either by making clearance orders, requiring the owners to demolish their
properties, or by acquiring them for demolition by the local authority. In both
these procedures the Act makes provision for postponement of demolition and for
the use of the unfit properties to provide housing accommodation pending demolition.
In the course of the argument our attention was invited in detail to the provisions
d of s 46, under which houses subject to clearance orders may be given temporary
reprieve. I find, however, that the more illuminating section for present purposes
is s 48, which contains the relevant provisions relating to houses in a clearance area
which have been acquired by the local authority. It provides:

'(1) Notwithstanding anything in the foregoing provisions of this Part of this
Act a local authority by whom an area has been decided to be a clearance area
e may postpone, for such period as may be determined by the authority, the demolition of any houses on land purchased by or belonging to the authority within that
area, being houses which in the opinion of the authority are or can be rendered
capable of providing accommodation of a standard which is adequate for the time
being, and may carry out such works as may from time to time be required for
rendering or keeping such houses capable of providing such accommodation
f as aforesaid pending their demolition . . .
'(4) In respect of any houses retained by a local authority under this section
for temporary use for housing purposes the local authority shall have the like
powers as they have in respect of houses provided under Part V of this Act and
section six of this Act shall not apply to a contract for the letting by a local
authority of any such houses.'

g Looking at these provisions in the context of the clearance area procedure and bearing
in mind that the houses in question have been acquired at site value and subject to an
express obligation on the local authority under s 47 either to demolish them or to
secure their demolition, it is clear to my mind beyond all argument that Parliament
cannot possibly have intended by the language used in s 48 to frustrate the whole
h procedure and enable the local authority to go back on their own declared belief,
which was its starting point, that the most satisfactory method of dealing with the
conditions in the area was to demolish all the buildings, by empowering the authority,
after acquisition, to carry out works to restore the houses to a state of fitness for
human habitation, to add them to their permanent housing stock, and thus to obviate
the necessity for demolition. I would therefore give a strictly limited construction
j to these provisions defining the power of a local authority to postpone demolition
of houses in a clearance area after acquisition. Having reached this conclusion, I ask
myself whether there can be any justification for giving a different and wider construction to the corresponding provisions in Part II of ss 17(2) and 29, which define the
power of a local authority to purchase a condemned house for the purpose of its use
as housing accommodation pending demolition. The correspondences of language

between the two sets of provisions are, in my judgment, too numerous and too striking to admit of different interpretations being applied to them. In both cases the power is dependent on the opinion of the authority that the houses 'are or can be rendered capable of providing accommodation of a standard which is adequate for the time being'. In both cases the local authority is empowered to 'carry out such works as may from time to time be required for rendering or keeping such houses capable of providing such accommodation'. In both cases the powers are exercisable 'pending' the demolition of the houses. In both cases the powers of a housing authority under Part V of the Act, which include of course the important and necessary powers of housing management, are made applicable. In both cases the statutory implied condition of fitness for human habitation is excluded from any letting of the houses. The only difference in the language in which the two sets of provisions are expressed which could be of any possible significance is the reference in s 48(4) to 'houses retained by a local authority under this section for temporary use for housing purposes'. But this does no more than make explicit what is already clearly implicit in the language of s 48(1). I cannot believe that this express reference to temporary use was intended to introduce into s 48 a limitation on the local authority's powers to which they would not otherwise be subject.

I find other indications to support the view that s 17(2) should be given a limited construction. One is in the anomaly which would otherwise arise from the continued exclusion of the statutory implied condition of fitness for human habitation from lettings of houses after they had been restored to a condition of fitness. If Parliament had ever contemplated that houses acquired under s 17(2) might be so restored, I would expect to find a provision in s 29 that the exclusion of s 6 should cease to operate after such a restoration.

A more important consideration is, I think, that, if given this limited construction, s 17(2) can still fit aptly into the general scheme of Part II of the Act and will in no way inhibit a local authority from achieving their proper purposes if they operate the statutory machinery sensibly and correctly. In deciding in relation to a particular house falling to be dealt with under Part II whether to proceed under s 9 or s 16 the local authority are not, in my judgment, under any obligation to undertake a precise and detailed examination of the economic factors to which s 39 directs attention in order to reach a positive conclusion one way or the other as to whether, objectively considered, the house can be rendered fit for human habitation at a reasonable expense. This is because an affirmative decision to that effect on the part of the local authority is not required as a condition for operating the procedure under s 9. A local authority may serve a notice under that section 'unless they are satisfied that it is not capable at a reasonable expense of being rendered so fit'. In practice I apprehend that all a local authority need decide at this stage is whether, if they acquired the house at site value, it would be economically viable from their point of view to carry out the works necessary to make it fit for human habitation. If they decide that it would not, that will inevitably lead to the conclusion that the house cannot be rendered fit for human habitation at a reasonable expense and indicate that the procedure under s 16 will be appropriate. But if the local authority wish to see the house made fit and are prepared to acquire it and make it fit themselves if necessary, I can see no reason why they should not proceed under s 9 without examining the economic question further, leaving it to the owner to exercise his right of appeal if he contends that the house cannot be made fit at a reasonable expense. If an appeal succeeds on that ground, the local authority will then be in a position to implement their own intention to acquire and carry out the necessary works in excercise of the powers conferred on them by s 12. If this is the correct view of how, in practice, Parliament contemplated that the machinery under Part II should be operated, it accounts for the striking similarities between the provisions of s 17(2) and s 29 in Part II and the provisions of ss 46 and 48 in Part III. Just as Parliament never contemplated under Part III that a temporary postponement of demolition could lead to a reversal of the

original decision to demolish, so too, in the procedure under Part II beginning under
s 16, it is, I think, implicit that Parliament regarded the initial decision that a house
could not be rendered fit for human habitation at a reasonable expense as a decision
necessarily leading to demolition or closure and a decision in that respect which
would not be liable to be reversed, even though, as under Part III, the demolition or
closure might properly be postponed for a limited period. This view of the practical
working of Part II is really borne out by what happened in the instant case. The local
authority always intended that either the owners or they themselves should carry
out the works necessary to render this house fit for human habitation. But for the
procedural mishap which unfortunately befell them in the first county court proceedings, they would, subject to obtaining confirmation of their compulsory purchase
order, have achieved their objective perfectly normally under s 12. Finding that
s 12 is tailor-made to empower an acquisition for the very purpose which the local
authority are here seeking to achieve, I feel neither surprise nor regret to discover,
as I hold, that the language of s 17(2), which comtemplates quite a different purpose,
cannot properly be stretched to cover the same ground as s 12.

For these reasons I think the learned county court judge reached a correct conclusion on the construction of the statute and that the proposed acquisition was
ultra vires. I would dismiss the appeal on this ground.

I turn to consider the alternative basis of the judge's decision, i e that, if the determination to purchase was within the powers of the local authority, he would
nevertheless, in the exercise of his discretion, accept the owner's proffered undertaking under s 16(4) and allow their appeal against the purchase notice on that ground.
Various limitations have been suggested in argument on the judge's powers under
s 20(3). I hope I will not be thought discourteous if I do not examine these in detail.
It is difficult to imagine what language the legislature could have used to confer on
the judge any wider power to review the decision taken by the local authority than by
providing that he 'may make such order either confirming or quashing or varying
the order or notice as he thinks fit and may, if he thinks fit, accept from any appellant
any such undertaking as might have been accepted by the local authority'. In my
judgment those words clearly empower the judge to decide for himself, first,
whether in all the circumstances it is appropriate to accept an owner's undertaking
under s 16(4), in which case no further question will fall for decision under s 17, and
secondly, if no such undertaking is accepted, whether the local authority's decision
under s 17 to make a demolition or closing order or to purchase, as the case may be,
should on its merits be supported or reversed. In making these decisions the judge is
to exercise his own discretion, giving such weight to the reasons which have prompted
the local authority's decision as he thinks to be warranted by their intrinsic validity
and force when balanced in the scales against all relevant objections advanced on
behalf of the appellant. This was precisely the approach of the learned judge. He said:

'I hold that the court should approach the matter completely afresh and use
its own judgment as to which result would be best in all the circumstances and I
hold that I should give no weight to the fact that the [local authority] have decided upon a particular course of action but should consider their reasons for
doing so on their merits and weigh them against the arguments of the property
owners.'

This approach cannot be faulted. In this court the judge's discretionary decision
can only be attacked if it is shown to be erroneous in point of law. Having regard to
the nature of the discretion exercised, this burden could only be discharged by showing
that the judge acted on some wrong principle, failed to take account of relevant
matters, took account of irrelevant matters, or reached a conclusion so manifestly
unreasonable that it could not properly have been reached by a reasonable judge
correctly directing himself in law.

The two main passages in the judgment where the judge considers the merits are the following. The first is where the judge said:

'The [local authority's] reasons for wanting to acquire the property compulsorily are (a) to avoid a loss of residential accommodation, which will result if and in so far as the house is not rehabilitated and occupied, and (b) to exercise control over who occupies the house, in other words to ensure that it should be occupied by persons on their own housing waiting list.
'The following figures were agreed:

Present value with a sitting tenant	£1,000-£1,500
Site value	£700 -£1,000
Value with vacant possession but subject to a closing order	£5,500-£6,000
Cost of works to bring up to full standard	£4,000
Value with vacant possession and brought up to full standard	£10,500-£11,000

'If the property is acquired under section 17(2) the compensation to be paid under section 29(2) is the site value. It therefore follows that if the appeal is dismissed the [owners] will suffer an immediate loss of £300-£500 and will be deprived of the opportunity of making a further gain of £4,500 by sale in the market after the tenant has left. If the appeal is allowed and a closing order made then the [owners] will have the opportunity of making a profit of £4,500 by selling the property and their purchasers will have the opportunity of making a profit of a further £1,000 if they do the works necessary to bring the property up to full standard.'

The other passage is where the judge said:

'I fully appreciate [the local authority's] desire to ensure that as many people as possible are housed. I also fully accept the desirability of ensuring that as many houses as possible are rehabilitated rather than demolished. I accept [the local authority's] view that it would not be economically sensible to do the work required to make the house suitable for occupation for a period of no more than 5 or 7 years. I do not attach any weight to the [owners'] offer to procure that any person to whom they sell the property should covenant to do work necessary to bring it up to full standard. If an undertaking that the house will not be used for human habitation until the local authority are satisfied that it has been rendered fit for that purpose is given there is a very strong probability that the house will be rehabilitated and occupied either by a tenant or owner-occupier. Balancing the financial detriment to the [owners] against the [local authority's] desire that the house should be made available not merely for occupation but for occupation by its own tenant I am of opinion that in all the circumstances the owners' interest should prevail and that an undertaking not to use the house for human habitation until the [local authority] cancel the undertaking should be accepted.'

Counsel for the local authority has submitted both that, in reaching this decision' the judge failed to take account of relevant matters and that the decision was so unreasonable that this court should reverse it. I do not examine the arguments in support of these submissions in detail, because they are, in my judgment, without foundation.

The main argument advanced by counsel for the local authority on this part of the case was that, in regarding the financial detriment to the owners, the judge was taking account of an irrelevant matter. The acceptance of the owner's undertaking under s 16(4) enables them to evict their sitting tenant, whom the local authority are then obliged to rehouse. The large financial gain which this brings to the owners is an

adventitious consequence of the fact that the house had been allowed to fall into
disrepair. The fact that confirmation of the local authority's decision to purchase
would deny this windfall to the owners cannot, so runs the argument, be a proper
matter to influence a decision in favour of the owners and against the local authority.
As an argument on the merits this has much force. But as an argument to impugn
the judge's decision as erroneous in law it is fallacious, because it confuses relevance
with weight. In deciding on the merits whether or not it is just to exercise a compulsory power of expropriation, the financial implications of the decision for the property
owner must always be relevant. What weight should be given to the financial
implications of the decision in any particular case is quite another matter. In some
cases they may be decisive, in others their weight in the scale may be negligible.

For these reasons I am of the opinion that even if the judge was wrong in his decision
on the question of vires, his decision on the merits to allow the owner's appeal and
accept their undertaking under s 16(4) can in no way be impugned. I would dismiss
the appeal on this ground also.

WALLER LJ. I agree. I would only add a word about the exercise of the discretion.
The judge, in the course of his judgment and in considering how the discretion
should be exercised, said:

> 'In the present case the [local authority] have a very considerable direct in-
> terest and have avowedly exercised their power in order to acquire an addition
> to their housing stock. In these circumstances I hold that the court should
> approach the matter completely afresh and use its own judgment as to which
> result would be best in all the circumstances and I hold that I should give no
> weight to the fact that the [local authority] have decided on a particular course
> of action but should consider their reasons for doing so on their merits and
> weigh them against the arguments of the property owners.'

Whether it is right to express, as the judge did, that the local authority have a 'very
considerable direct interest', the local authority certainly have a duty to consider the
housing requirements in their borough. To that extent they have, on behalf of the inhabitants of the borough, an interest to see that the housing needs of those inhabitants
are looked after both in quality and, so far as they can be in quantity. The interest
is a public one and it is clear that the judge had a complete discretion to balance the
needs of the inhabitants on the one hand with justice to the person having control of
the house on the other.

How is the balance to be judged? The judge is exercising a discretion under the
Housing Act 1957. If the local authority makes a demolition or closing order, then
under s 30—

> 'Any person may represent to [the local authority] that the house has been
> well maintained and that the good maintenance of the house is attributable
> wholly or partly to work carried out by him or at his expense.'

There is then a power in the local authority to make such payment as is authorised
by Sch 2, Part I. Thus, if the owner has maintained his property well he will get, in
addition to the site value, a well maintained grant which will increase to some extent
the amount of his compensation. The local authority no doubt would have to consider whether it is just that another house owner whose house was in bad repair
and not fit for human habitation and who would not qualify for a well maintained
grant, should nevertheless, because of the action of the local authority itself, be able
to get vacant possession of his house and by that action and because of the very poor
condition of the house possibly obtain (as in this case) five times the site value by
selling the house. On the other hand there may be counterbalancing advantages
which should be taken into account, for example the probable condition of the house

if it is improved by a private developer or the possibility that private funds will
complete the improvements and therefore the cost will not be a burden on the rate- *a*
payers. No doubt the county court judge on appeal would have similar considerations in mind when exercising his discretion.

Whether the grounds on which he said he would have exercised the discretion in the
way he did are clear or not, this is a matter on which the judge has a wide discretion,
and provided that he has not misdirected himself, or taken into account considerations
which he ought not to have done, this court cannot interfere. Accordingly, even if the *b*
local authority had succeeded on the main question of whether they had the power
to purchase the house, I would have been in favour of dismissing the appeal because
the arguments for the local authority have not persuaded me that the judge exercised
his discretion on wrong principles or had taken matters into account which he ought
not to have done.

c

MEGAW LJ. On the first issue, as to the extent of the power conferred on the local
authority by s 17(2) of the Housing Act 1957, I agree with the reasons and the conclusion expressed in the judgment of Bridge LJ.

I should have felt concern at the consequences of that conclusion in limiting the
scope of the local authority's powers in carrying out their difficult and important *d*
duties as a housing authority, if I had thought that s 12 had not, as a matter of law, been
available to the local authority in this and similar cases, enabling them to purchase
the property compulsorily, subject to the authorisation of the Minister as provided
in the section. However, even if I were wrong as to the availability of s 12, I should
have thought that it would be a matter for the legislature to consider, and, if as a
matter of policy it was thought right, to amend the Act, rather than for the court to *e*
put on it an interpretation which I do not think is justified by the legislation in its
present form.

It is most unfortunate that at an earlier stage in the present case something appears
to have gone wrong; so that the judge who was then dealing with the matter apparently declined to include a finding, whether affirmative or negative, which s 11(3)
provides shall be included on the request of the local authority. But, as Bridge LJ *f*
has said, it would not be right or possible for us to investigate why that happened;
and therefore nothing that I say is to be taken as attributing blame to anyone. If,
perchance, it arose out of some question as to the time when the application should
be made, and I do not know whether or not any such question arose, it would be desirable that those who are responsible for the County Court Rules should urgently consider whether the rules should provide for this matter. However that may be, if it had *g*
not been for some error or misunderstanding on someone's part, and if the judge on a
request made under s 11(3) had made an affirmative finding, I see no good reason why
the s 12 procedure should not have been appropriate. The section expressly contemplates that the procedure may be used by the local authority when the court
has found that the house cannot be rendered fit for human habitation at a reasonable
expense. The local authority cannot be debarred legally, nor, I should have thought, *h*
morally, from using the procedure, whether it itself agrees or disagrees with the
court's finding in that respect, if the local authority takes the view that its duties as
housing authority make it desirable that the result should be achieved which s 12 is
intended to make possible.

The second issue, then, does not require decision. If it had arisen, I should have
felt bound to hold that no issue of law is shown to exist and that therefore this court *j*
would have no jurisdiction to interfere.

The jurisdiction of this court on appeal from the county court is statutory. The only
statutory provision conferring jurisdiction which could be relevant in this case is s 108
of the County Courts Act 1959. It provides for an appeal on a point of law. An exercise of a discretion by the judge of a county court may, it has long since been held,

involve a question of law. It will do so if the discretion has been exercised on a wrong principle. It will have been exercised on a wrong principle if it appears that the judge in exercising his discretion has taken into account some matter as being material which he ought not to have taken into account; or has failed to take into account some matter which would have been material and which he ought to have taken into account; or that, although no such error can be specifically identified, the exercise of the discretion is so unreasonable that it can be explained only on the basis that the judge must have erred in principle. This court's jurisdiction, as given by Parliament, in a case such as this is thus much less extensive than the jurisdiction given by Parliament to the county court, when it is dealing with the first appeal to the courts, by the very wide words of s 20(3) of the Housing Act 1957.

While I doubt whether, on the hypothesis that my view on the first issue were wrong, I should myself have thought it right, on the material before the learned judge, to have exercised the discretion given to him in the same way as he exercised it, I am unable to hold, following the criteria which I have stated, that there has been shown to be an error in point of law.

I would dismiss the appeal.

Appeal dismissed. Leave to appeal to the House of Lords refused.

Solicitor: *J B Parker* (for the local authority); *Stafford Clark & Co* (for the owners).

Christine Ivamy   Barrister.

Practice Direction

EMPLOYMENT APPEAL TRIBUNAL

Employment Appeal Tribunal – Practice – Appeals – Appeals out of time – Institution of appeals – Appeals not appearing to disclose arguable points of law – Interlocutory applications – Meetings for directions   Right to inspect and copy certain documents – Listing of appeals – Admissibility of documents – Complaints of bias – Exhibits and documents for use at hearing.

The practice direction[1] dated 7th January 1977, as amended on 9th March 1977[2], is hereby revoked and replaced by the following.

1. The Employment Appeal Tribunal Rules 1976[3] came into operation on 30th March 1976.

2. By virtue of para 15(2) of Sch 6 to the Employment Protection Act 1975, the Employment Appeal Tribunal has power, subject to the 1976 rules, to regulate its own procedure.

3. Where the 1976 rules do not otherwise provide the following procedure will be followed in all appeals to the appeal tribunal.

4. *Appeals out of time*—(a) By virtue of r 3(1) of the 1976 rules every appeal under s 88 of the 1975 Act to the appeal tribunal shall be instituted by serving on the tribunal, within 42 days of the date on which the document recording the decision or order appealed from was sent to the appellant, a notice of appeal as prescribed in the 1976 rules. (b) Every notice of appeal not delivered within 42 days of the date on which the document recording the decision or order appealed from was

---

1   [1977] 1 All ER 478, [1977] 1 WLR 145
2   [1977] 1 All ER 880, [1977] 1 WLR 317
3   SI 1976 No 322

sent to the appellant must be accompanied by an application for an extension of time,
setting out the reasons for the delay. (c) Applications for an extension of time for
appealing cannot be considered until a notice of appeal has been presented. (d) Unless
otherwise ordered, the application for extension of time will be heard and determined
by the registrar on a date appointed by him pursuant to r 9 of the 1976 rules. (e) In
determining whether to extend the time for appealing, particular attention will be
paid to the guidance contained in *Practice Note (Marshall v Harland & Wolff Ltd)*[1] and
to whether any excuse for the delay has been shown. (f) It is not necessarily a good
excuse for delay in appealing that legal aid has been applied for, or that support is
being sought e g from the Equal Opportunities Commission or from a trade union.
In such cases the intending appellant should at the earliest possible moment, and at the
latest within the time limited for appealing, inform the registrar, and the other party,
of his intentions, and seek the latter's agreement to an extension of time for appealing.
(g) Time for appealing runs from the date on which the document recording the
decision or order of the industrial tribunal was sent to the appellant, notwithstanding
that the assessment of compensation has been adjourned, or an application has been
made for a review. (h) In any case of doubt or difficulty, notice of appeal should be
presented in time, and an application made to the registrar for directions.

  5. *Institution of appeal*—(a) Subject to r 3(2) of the 1976 rules, if it appears to the
registrar that a notice of appeal gives insufficient particulars or lacks clarity either as
to the question of law or the grounds of an appeal, the registrar may postpone his
decision under that rule pending amplification or clarification of the notice of appeal,
as regards the question of law or grounds of appeal, by the intended appellant. (b)
Upon the hearing of an appeal an appellant will not ordinarily be allowed to contend
that 'the decision was contrary to the evidence' or 'there was no evidence to support
the decision', or to advance similar contentions, unless full and sufficient particulars
identifying the particular matters relied on have been supplied to the appeal tribunal.
(c) In any case where it appears to the registrar that the question raised by a notice
of appeal, or the grounds of appeal stated therein and any further particulars given
under (a) above, do not give the appeal tribunal jurisdiction to entertain the appeal,
he will notify the appellant accordingly, informing him of the reasons for his decision.
(d) Where the appellant, having been notified of the registrar's decision under r 3(2),
serves a fresh notice of appeal under r 3(3) within the time limited by that rule, the
registrar may consider such fresh notice of appeal with regard to jurisdiction as though
it were an original notice of appeal lodged pursuant to r 3(1). (e) Where an appellant
is dissatisfied with the reasons given by the registrar for his opinion that the grounds of
appeal stated in the notice of appeal do not give the appeal tribunal jurisdiction to
entertain the appeal, the registrar will place the papers before the president or a judge
for his direction. (f) It will not be open to the parties to reserve a right to amend,
alter or add to any pleading. Any such right is not inherent and may only be exercised
if permitted by order for which an interlocutory application should be made as soon
as the need for alteration is known.

  6. *New procedure*—(a) Where an appeal has not been rejected pursuant to r 3(2)
but nevertheless the appeal tribunal considers that it is doubtful whether the grounds
of appeal disclose an arguable point of law, the president or a judge may direct that
the matter be set down before a division of the appeal tribunal for hearing of a preliminary point to enable the appellant to show cause why the appeal should not be
dismissed on the ground that it does not disclose an arguable point of law. (b) The
respondent will be given notice of the hearing but since it will be limited to the
preliminary point he will not be required to attend the hearing or permitted to take
part in it. (c) If the appellant succeeds in showing cause, the hearing will be adjourned
and the appeal will be set down for hearing before a different division of the appeal
tribunal in the usual way. (d) If the appellant does not show cause, the appeal will be

---

1   [1972] ICR 97

dismissed. (e) The decision as to whether this procedure will be adopted in any particular case will be in the discretion of the president or a judge.

7. *Interlocutory applications*—(a) Every interlocutory application made to the appeal tribunal will be considered in the first place by the registrar who will have regard to the just and economical disposal of the application, and to the expense which may be incurred by the parties in attending an oral hearing. (b) The registrar will submit a copy of the application to the other side together with notice of the time appointed for the hearing, and will indicate in the notice of appointment that if it is not intended to oppose the application it may be unnecessary for the parties to be heard and that the appropriate order may be made in their absence. Where the application is opposed the registrar will also in appropriate cases give the parties an opportunity of agreeing to the application being decided on the basis of written submissions. (c) Save where the president or a judge directs otherwise, every interlocutory application to strike out pleadings or to debar a party from taking any further part in the proceedings pursuant to r 9 or r 15 will be heard on the day appointed for the hearing of the appeal, but immediately preceding the hearing thereof.

8. *Meeting for directions*—On every appeal from the decision of the certification officer, and, if necessary, on any other appeal, so soon as the answer is delivered, or if a cross-appeal, the reply, the registrar will appoint a day when the parties shall meet on an appointment for directions and the appeal tribunal will give such directions, including a date for hearing, as it deems necessary.

9. *Right to inspect the register and certain documents and to take copies*—Where, pursuant to the direction dated 31st March 1976, a document filed at the appeal tribunal has been inspected and a photographic copy of the document is bespoken, a copying fee of 25p for each page will be charged.

10. *Listing of appeals*

A. *England and Wales*—When the respondent's answer has been received and a copy served on the appellant both parties will be notified in writing of a date, between four and six weeks ahead, after which the hearing will take place. In the same letter the parties will be invited to apply for a date to be fixed for the hearing. For that purpose an application form will be enclosed, to be returned to the listing officer within 14 days on which solicitors (or if appropriate litigants in person) will be able to specify any dates they wish to be avoided. The date that has been fixed will then be notified to the parties with as much notice as possible. If the application form is not returned to the appeal tribunal within 14 days a party will have no right to ask for a fixed date. The case will in due course be listed for hearing (i e in the warned list) and once this has been done it will be liable to be listed at a day's notice, though in practice it is hoped to be able to give much longer notice than that in the majority of cases. (Where either of the parties is appearing in person at least a week's notice will be given.) The warned list will appear weekly in the daily cause list and it will also be displayed in room 6 at the Royal Courts of Justice. The onus will be on solicitors' or counsels' clerks to watch the warned list; no date will be able to be vacated except by formal application to the tribunal. The warned list will accordingly contain (a) cases fixed for hearing during the coming week, with the date on which they are to be heard; (b) cases where the 'not before date' has passed, no application has been made for a fixed date, and the date of hearing has not yet been fixed. Cases where the 'not before date' has not yet been reached, or cases in which an application has been made for a fixed date but the date has not yet been fixed, and cases that have been fixed for hearing beyond the following week will not be included in the warned list. Normally a case estimated to take half a day or less will be listed together with another of the same duration for one court in one day, and when two or more courts are sitting 'floaters' will also be listed as appropriate.

B. *Scotland*—When the respondent's answer has been received and a copy served on the appellant both parties will be notified in writing that the appeal will be ready for hearing in approximately six weeks. The proposed date of hearing will be notified to the parties three or four weeks ahead. Any party who wishes to apply for a different date must do so within seven days of receipt of such notification. Thereafter a formal notice of the date fixed for the hearing will be issued not less than 14 days in advance. This will be a peremptory diet. It will not be discharged except by the judge on cause shown.

11. *Admissibility of documents*—(a) Where, pursuant to r 9 or r 13, an application is made by a party to an appeal to put in at the hearing of the appeal any document which was not before the industrial tribunal, including a note of evidence given before the industrial tribunal (other than the chairman's note), the application shall be submitted in writing with copies of the document(s) sought to be made admissible at the hearing. (b) The registrar will forthwith communicate the nature of the application and of the document(s) sought to be made admissible to the other party and, where appropriate, to the chairman of the industrial tribunal, for comment. (c) A copy of the comment will be forwarded to the party making the application by the registrar who will either dispose of it in accordance with the 1976 rules or refer it to the appeal tribunal for a ruling at the hearing. In the case of comments received from the chairman of the industrial tribunal a copy will be sent to both parties.

12. *Complaints of bias etc*—(a) The appeal tribunal will not normally consider complaints of bias or of the conduct of an industrial tribunal unless full and sufficient particulars are set out in the grounds of appeal. (b) In any such case the registrar may enquire of the party making the complaint whether it is the intention to proceed with the complaint in which case the registrar will give appropriate directions for the hearing. (c) Such directions may include the filing of affidavits dealing with the matters on the basis of which the complaint is made or for the giving of further particulars of the complaint on which the party will seek to rely. .(d) On compliance with any such direction the registrar will communicate the complaint together with the matters relied on in support of the complaint to the chairman of the industrial tribunal so that he may have an opportunity of commenting on it. (e) No such complaint will be permitted to be developed on the hearing of the appeal, unless the appropriate procedure has been followed. (f) A copy of any affidavit or direction for particulars to be delivered thereunder will be communicated to the other side.

13. *Exhibits and documents for use at the hearing*—(a) The appeal tribunal will prepare copies of all documents for use of the judges and members at the hearing in addition to those which the registrar is required to serve on the parties under the 1976 rules. In Scotland a copy of the chairman's notes will not be supplied to the parties except on application to the appeal tribunal on cause shown. (b) There is no inherent right to a copy of the chairman's notes but in England and Wales copies will be sent to the parties as soon as they are available, unless in the discretion of the appeal tribunal all or part of such notes is considered to be unnecessary for the purposes of the appeal. A chairman's notes are supplied for the use of the appeal tribunal and not for the parties to embark on a 'fishing' expedition to establish further grounds of appeal. (c) It will be the responsibility of the parties or their advisers to ensure that all exhibits and documents used before the industrial tribunal, and which are considered to be relevant to the appeal, are sent to the appeal tribunal immediately on request. This will enable the appeal tribunal to number and prepare sufficient copies, together with an index, for the judges and members at least a week before the day appointed for the hearing. (d) A copy of the index will be sent to the parties or their representatives prior to the hearing so that they may prepare their bundles in the same order.

PHILLIPS J
President.

3rd March 1978

The Nowy Sacz
Owners of the ship Olympian v Owners of the ship Nowy Sacz

COURT OF APPEAL, CIVIL DIVISION

STEPHENSON, SHAW LJJ AND SIR DAVID CAIRNS, ASSISTED BY NAUTICAL ASSESSORS

14th, 15th, 16th MARCH, 1st APRIL 1977

Shipping – Collision regulations – Overtaking vessel – Vessel coming up with another vessel more than two points abaft her beam – Coming up with – Risk of collision – Degree of proximity required – Need to establish risk of collision exists before overtaking rule applies – Overtaking vessel ceasing to be more than two points abaft overtaken vessel's beam before risk of collision arising – Vessels on converging courses – Whether overtaking vessel to be regarded as 'coming up with' other vessel before risk of collision had arisen – Whether overtaking rule or crossing rule applicable – Whether overtaking or overtaken vessel under duty to give way – Collision Regulations (Ships and Seaplanes on the Water) and Signals of Distress (Ships) Order 1965 (SI 1965 No 1525), rr 19, 24.

On a fine night in open sea the plaintiffs' ship, the Olympian, was proceeding at 14½ knots on a course 331 degrees (true) and the defendants' ship, the Nowy Sacz, was proceeding at 12½ knots on a course 341 degrees (true). At 02.45 the ships were about three miles apart and the masthead lights of the Olympian, bearing 25 degrees to 30 degrees abaft the starboard beam of the Nowy Sacz, were seen by the latter's officer of the watch. At that time the officer of the watch of the Olympian had not yet seen any lights of the Nowy Sacz. At 03.00 the officer of the Nowy Sacz was able to see the red light of the Olympian as she passed two points abaft the beam. At the same time the officer of the Olympian could see both the masthead and green lights of the Nowy Sacz. At 03.30 the ships were about a mile apart and the Olympian was approximately abaft the beam of the Nowy Sacz. From that moment onwards there was a risk of collision. At 03.45 the Olympian was about 30 degrees forward of the Nowy Sacz's beam. At 03.56½, when the ships were one to two cables apart, the engines of the Nowy Sacz were put half astern and then full astern, and that or interaction caused her to turn to starboard. At about the same time the wheel of the Olympian was put hard to starboard and at 03.58 the two ships collided. In an action by the plaintiffs for damages the defendants contended that since prior to the collision the Olympian had been 'coming up with' the Nowy Sacz from more than two points abaft the beam, r 24[a] (the overtaking rule) of the Collision Regulations applied, and not r 19[b] (the crossing rule) and that in consequence the Olympian, as the overtaking ship, should have kept out of the way of the Nowy Sacz. The judge held that r 24 only applied if a risk of collision existed before the overtaking ship ceased to be more than two points (22½ degrees) abaft the beam of the overtaken ship, and that, since prior to 03.00 there had been no such risk, r 19 applied. He concluded therefore that, in accordance with r 19, the Nowy Sacz should have kept out of the way of the Olympian and had been mainly to blame for the collision but that the Olympian had been guilty of contributory negligence in failing to take avoiding action in time. He assessed responsibility for the collision at 75 per cent against the Nowy Sacz and 25 per cent against the Olympian. The defendants appealed.

Held – (i) Rule 24 applied whenever one vessel was 'coming up with' another vessel from more than two points abaft the beam even though at that time no risk of

---

a   Rule 24, so far as material, is set out at p 300 *j* to p 301 *a*, post
b   Rule 19 is set out at p 300 *h*, post

collision had arisen. A vessel was to be regarded as 'coming up with another vessel', within r 24, when the two vessels were in sight of each other and there was some degree of proximity between them (see p 303 *b c* and *g h*, p 305 *b c* and *f* and p 306 *d e*, post).

(ii) Since by 03.00 the two vessels had been in sight of each other and less than three miles apart, the Olympian was at that time 'coming up with' the Nowy Sacz, and as she was doing so from more than two points abaft the Nowy Sacz's beam, she was an overtaking ship within r 24. It followed that r 24 applied and the Olympian should have kept out of the way of the Nowy Sacz. The appeal would therefore be allowed and the responsibility for the collision apportioned 75 per cent against the Olympian and 25 per cent against the Nowy Sacz (see p 306 *g* to *j*, post).

The Franconia (1876) 2 PD 8, *The Seaton* (1883) 9 PD 1, *The Beryl* (1884) 9 PD 137 and *The Main* (1886) 11 PD 132 applied.

The Banshee (1887) 57 LT 841 and *The Manchester Regiment* [1938] P 117 not followed.

Notes

For crossing and overtaking vessels, see 35 Halsbury's Laws (3rd Edn) 653-661, paras 978-989, and for cases on crossing vessels and overtaking vessels, see 42 Digest (Repl) 854-858, 879-881, 6408-6450, 6659-6680.

For the Collision Regulations (Ships and Seaplanes on the Water) and Signals of Distress (Ships) Order 1965, rr 19, 24, see 20 Halsbury's Statutory Instruments (3rd Reissue) 128.

Cases referred to in judgments

Auriga, The [1977] 1 Lloyd's Rep 384.

Banshee, The (1887) 57 LT 841, 6 Asp MLC 221, CA, 42 Digest (Repl) 880, 6675.

Beryl, The (1884) 9 PD 137, 53 LJP 75, 51 LT 554, 5 Asp MLC 321, CA, 42 Digest (Repl) 857, 6440.

Franconia, The (1876) 2 PD 8, 35 LT 721, 3 Asp MLC 295, CA, 42 Digest (Repl) 879, 6659.

Main, The (1886) 11 PD 132, 55 LJP 70, 55 LT 15, 6 Asp MLC 37, CA, 42 Digest (Repl) 828, 6042.

Manchester Regiment, The [1938] P 117, 107 LJP 63, 159 LT 227, 19 Asp MLC 189, 60 Ll L Rep 279, 42 Digest (Repl) 869, 6553.

Roanoke, The [1908] P 231, 77 LJP 115, 99 LT 78, 11 Asp MLC 253, CA, 42 Digest (Repl) 856, 6433.

Seaton, The (1883) 9 PD 1, 53 LJP 15, 49 LT 747, 5 Asp MLC 191, 42 Digest (Repl) 879, 6662.

Young v Bristol Aeroplane Co Ltd [1944] 2 All ER 293, [1944] KB 718, 113 LJKB 513, 171 LT 113, 37 BWCC 51, CA; *affd* [1946] 1 All ER 98, [1946] AC 163, 115 LJKB 63, 174 LT 39, 79 Ll L Rep 35, 38 BWCC 50, HL, 30 Digest (Reissue) 269, 765.

Cases also cited

Australia (Steamship) (Owners) v Owners of Steamship Nautilus, The Australia [1927] AC 145, [1926] All ER Rep 461, HL.

British Fame (Steamship) (Owners) v Owners of Steamship Macgregor [1943] 1 All ER 33, [1943] AC 197, HL.

Canning (Steamship) (Owners) v Owners of Steamship The Bellanoch [1907] AC 269, HL.

Thuroklint (Owners) v Koningin Juliana (Owners), The Koningin Juliana [1975] 2 Lloyd's Rep 111, HL.

Orduna (Steamship) (Owners) v Shipping Controller [1921] 1 AC 250, HL.

Peckforton Castle, The (1877) 3 PD 11, CA.

Savina, The [1976] 2 Lloyd's Rep 123, HL.

Toni, The [1974] 1 Lloyd's Rep 489, CA.

Appeal

a This was an appeal by the defendants, the owners of the ship Nowy Sacz, against a decision of Brandon J[1] on 28th May 1976 whereby he found that the collision between the Nowy Sacz and the ship Olympian, owned by the plaintiffs, which had occurred on 14th February 1972, had been caused by the fault of both ships, and ordered, inter alia, that the damages arising from the collision should be borne as to one-quarter by the plaintiffs and as to three-quarters by the defendants. The facts are set out in **b** the judgment.

Barry Sheen QC and *David Steel* for the defendants.
Gerald Darling QC and *R J Kay* for the plaintiffs.

Cur adv vult

c 1st April. **SIR DAVID CAIRNS** read the following judgment of the court: This is an appeal from the judgment of Brandon J[1] in an action arising from a collision between the plaintiffs' ship Olympian and the defendants' ship Nowy Sacz. The collision occurred shortly before 04.00 on 14th February 1972 in the Atlantic Ocean some miles south of Cape St Vincent. The night was fine and the ships had been in **d** sight of each other for about an hour. The stem and starboard bow of the Nowy Sacz struck the port quarter of the Olympian. Both ships were damaged, but not sufficiently to prevent them from continuing their voyages.

The Olympian is a Cypriot ship, a single screw motor ship 520 feet in length. The Nowy Sacz is a Polish ship, a single screw motor ship 357 feet in length. The Olympian was on a voyage from Malta to West Germany and the Nowy Sacz on a voyage from Casablanca to Gdynia. The courses of both ships were roughly in a north-westerly **e** direction. The Olympian was at one stage well aft of the Nowy Sacz but was making a faster speed and at the time of the collision had overtaken her on her starboard side. The main issue was whether the situation was such as to bring into play the crossing rules, as the plaintiffs contended, or the overtaking rules, as the defendants contended.

f The judge held that the crossing rules applied and that the main blame for the collision lay on the Nowy Sacz for failing to keep out of the way of the Olympian. However, he found that a situation arose when the Olympian should have gradually altered course to starboard away from the Nowy Sacz and that by failing to take such action at an early stage, and so becoming obliged to go hard to starboard very shortly before the collision the Olympian was guilty of a fault which contributed to the casualty.

g The learned judge assessed the degrees of responsibility as three-quarters against the Nowy Sacz and one-quarter against the Olympian. The defendants appeal, contending by their notice of appeal that the Olympian was solely to blame or alternatively that her degree of fault was more than a quarter. In argument, however, counsel for the defendants limited himself to the contention that the proportions assessed by the judge should be reversed. The plaintiffs by a respondents' notice **h** supported the judge's assessment of proportions of fault either on the facts as found by him or alternatively on the basis that he should have made a different finding as to the course of the Olympian. This latter contention was, however, only faintly relied on at the hearing.

No witnesses from the Olympian were available at the trial but signed statements **j** from her master, chief officer, second officer, third engineer and two quartermasters were put in evidence. From the Nowy Sacz the second officer and a seaman were called and statements from the master and chief officer were put in. On each ship the second officer was at the material time the officer of the watch. The judge found

---

1 [1976] 2 Lloyd's Rep 682

the evidence of the second officer of the Nowy Sacz to be substantially true and reliable.

The course of the Nowy Sacz at all material times was said to be 341 degrees (true). This was not challenged and was found by the judge to be so. The evidence from the Olympian was that her course was 290 degrees (true). If that had been right the situation would clearly have been one to which the crossing rules applied. But the judge found that the angle between the courses was only about 10 degrees, i e that the Olympian's course was about 331 degrees (true). He set out fully his reasons for reaching that conclusion and we can see no ground for differing from him on it. He also found that the respective speeds until very shortly before the collision were about 14½ knots for the Olympian and about 12½ knots for the Nowy Sacz. While it is difficult to reconcile findings which he made about the bearings at different times with these speeds having been maintained without any variation, there is no doubt that the Olympian's general speed was something like two to 2½ knots faster than that of the Nowy Sacz. So, with the two courses converging at a narrow angle and the Olympian proceeding faster than the Nowy Sacz it looks on the face of it like an over-taking situation. The judge, however, held that on the correct interpretation of the Collision Regulations, in accordance with judicial authorities, it was the crossing rules and not the overtaking rules that applied.

We can summarise quite briefly the further essential findings of fact made by the learned judge, all of which we accept. At about 02.45 the second officer of the Nowy Sacz saw the masthead lights of the Olympian bearing about 25 degrees to 30 degrees abaft the starboard beam and distant about three miles. At that time the second officer of the Olympian had not yet seen any lights of the Nowy Sacz. At about 03.00 the red light of the Olympian became visible to the second officer of the Nowy Sacz as she passed into the green sector of the Nowy Sacz (i e passed the bearing of two points abaft the beam). The second officer of the Olympian was then seeing the masthead and green lights of the Nowy Sacz. At about 03.30 the Olympian was about abeam of the Nowy Sacz and about a mile away. At about 03.45 she was bearing about 30 degrees forward of the Nowy Sacz's beam. When the Olympian was one to two cables away the engines of the Nowy Sacz were put half astern and then full astern. At about the same time the wheel of the Olympian was put hard to starboard. This was only about 1½ minutes before the collision. Both ships went to starboard to about the same extent, the Olympian because of her wheel action and the Nowy Sacz because of interaction or the effect of her engines having been put astern. The ships collided at about 03.58.

Now, the revelant rules are in Part D of the Collision Regulations. That part is prefaced by four preliminary paragraphs, of which the first and fourth read as follows:

'1. In obeying and construing these Rules, any action taken should be positive, in ample time, and with due regard to the observance of good seamanship . . .
'4. Rules 17 to 24 apply only to vessels in sight of one another.'

The rule which specifically deals with ships on crossing courses is r 19, which provides:

'When two power-driven vessels are crossing, so as to involve risk of collision, the vessel which has the other on her own starboard side shall keep out of the way of the other.'

The rule which specifically deals with the situation when one ship is overtaking another is r 24, which provides:

'(a) Notwithstanding anything contained in these Rules, every vessel over-taking any other shall keep out of the way of the overtaken vessel.
'(b) Every vessel coming up with another vessel from any direction more than 22½ degrees (2 points) abaft her beam, i.e., in such a position, with reference to the vessel which she is overtaking, that at night she would be unable to see

either of that vessel's sidelights, shall be deemed to be an overtaking vessel; and no subsequent alteration of the bearing between the two vessels shall make the overtaking vessel a crossing vessel within the meaning of these Rules, or relieve her of the duty of keeping clear of the overtaken vessel until she is finally past and clear . . .'

Paragraph (c) is not relevant.

Whether the situation is one of crossing or of overtaking, rr 21 to 23 specify the duties of the respective ships:

'Rule 21 Where by any of these Rules one of two vessels is to keep out of the way, the other shall keep her course and speed. When, from any cause, the latter vessel finds herself so close that collision cannot be avoided by the action of the giving-way vessel alone, she also shall take such action as will best aid to avert collision (see Rules 27 and 29).

'Rule 22 Every vessel which is directed by these Rules to keep out of the way of another vessel shall, so far as possible, take positive early action to comply with this obligation, and shall, if the circumstances of the case admit, avoid crossing ahead of the other.

'Rule 23 Every power-driven vessel which is directed by these Rules to keep out of the way of another vessel shall, on approaching her, if necessary, slacken her speed or stop or reverse.'

All the above rules are subject to the provisions of r 27 which provides:

'In obeying and construing these Rules due regard shall be had to all dangers of navigation and collision, and to any special circumstances, including the limitations of the craft involved, which may render a departure from the above Rules necessary in order to avoid immediate danger.'

The contest in this case has resolved around one question of law and one question of fact. The question of law is: does r 24 operate only when the positions, courses and speeds of the ships are such as to involve a risk of collision? If that question is to be answered in the affirmative then the question of fact is: was a risk of collision involved in this case before the Olympian had ceased to be more than two points abaft the beam of the Nowy Sacz? The judge held that the answer to the question of law was Yes and the answer to the question of fact was No. There is no doubt, because of the terms of the latter part of r 24(b), that if once that rule applied the Olympian was the give-way ship from then onwards, whereas if r 24 did not apply the Nowy Sacz was the give-way ship. On this appeal the defendants say that the judge was wrong on the law and, if he was right on the law, he was wrong on the facts.

In considering the question of law the first point that strikes one is that whereas eight of the Steering and Sailing Rules, including r 24, are by reason of preliminary para 4 to apply only to vessels in sight of one another and four of them, including r 19, are by their express provisions applicable only when vessels are proceeding so as to involve risk of collision; this second condition is not contained in r 24. There is, however, impressive judicial authority for implying that condition in r 24.

In The Banshee[1] (Lord Esher MR, Lindley and Lopes LJJ) it was held, reversing Butt J, that the rule did not apply when one ship, gaining on another, was 800 yards away from it. Lord Esher MR said[2]:

'Now at what period of time is it that the Regulations begin to apply to two ships? It cannot be said that they are applicable however far off the ships may be. Nobody could seriously contend that, if two ships are six miles apart, the Regulations for Preventing Collisions are applicable to them. They only apply at a

---

1   (1887) 57 LT 841
2   57 LT 841 at 842

time when, if either of them does anything contrary to the Regulations, it will
cause danger of collision. None of the Regulations apply unless that period of
time has arrived. It follows that anything done before the time arrives at which
the Regulations apply is immaterial, because anything done before that time
cannot produce risk of collision within the meaning of the Regulations.'

The Banshee[1] was followed by Merriman P in The Manchester Regiment[2]. The circumstances were rather odd. The Manchester Regiment was performing the operation of adjusting compasses, which involved making a series of right-angled turns.
The Clan MacKenzie was approaching and when two or three miles distant was two
points abaft the beam of the Manchester Regiment. Later, the Manchester Regiment,
having executed a turn to starboard, the ships' courses were at right angles and then
they collided. Merriman P held that the crossing rules applied and not the overtaking
rules. He quoted the passage from Lord Esher MR's judgment which I have read
and went on[3]:

'There is nothing in any of these observations, by which I am bound, which
hints at any difference between the overtaking rule and the other rules as to
the moment at which they apply. The test is stated in different forms, but with
no difference in substance, and it is applied universally; nor is there anything
in the case of The Banshee[1] itself to give the slightest warrant for Mr Carpmael's
contention that mere visibility is the test for the applicability of rule 24. Indeed
in the circumstances of that case the Court of Appeal held that, though the
vessels had been in sight of each other for some time, the Regulations had not
begun to apply when the overtaking was within 800 yards of the overtaken
vessel. But although 800 yards was taken in that case as being a distance at which
the rules had not begun to apply, I appreciate that that finding is not to be
applied arbitrarily; for example, nothing is said in the report about the relative
speeds of the vessels, though it appears that both were small ships. It is obvious
that the distance astern at which the overtaking rule becomes applicable must
vary according to circumstances. Eight hundred yards astern may be a long
distance between two tramps steaming respectively at six and seven knots,
but it would be a very short distance if the Queen Mary, at speed, was overhauling
one of them. Likewise the lateral interval between the courses would be a
factor of importance. It is the principle laid down in The Banshee[1] and the other
cases which matters.'

The plaintiffs' case is that this court is bound by The Banshee[1] and if, for any
reason, it can be distinguished, the court should follow the decision in The Manchester
Regiment[2] because it has stood unquestioned for nearly 40 years. Counsel for the
plaintiffs conceded that if the matter were free from authority a different view might
well be taken. Counsel for the defendants contended that the a priori reasons for not
implying into r 24 the condition of a risk of collision being involved are so strong
that the court should not make any such implication unless absolutely bound to do so,
that The Banshee[1] is distinguishable, or if not, is in conflict with other authorities
which are to be preferred, and that The Manchester Regiment[2] was either wrongly
decided or is to be limited to its very exceptional facts.

Considering the matter apart from authority, it is indeed a striking feature of the
rules that in every other rule which prescribes which vessel is to keep out of the way
of another the qualification 'so as to involve risk of collision' is expressed (see r 17,
sailing vessels; r 19, power-driven vessels crossing; r 20, power-driven and sailing
vessels). A similar qualification occurs in a rule requiring both vessels to alter course
(r 18, vessels meeting end-on).

1　(1887) 57 LT 841
2　[1938] P 117
3　[1938] P 117 at 129, 130

The latter part of r 24(b) contemplates that there may be alterations of bearing after the rule has begun to apply. Since a constant bearing between two ships points to a risk of collision and an alteration of bearing points against such a risk, this part of the rule suggests that the rule applies before there is a risk of collision.

The only indication in the rule itself that it does not begin to apply as soon as the vessels are in sight of one another is in the words 'coming up with'. In The Auriga[1] Brandon J took the view that these words involved a certain degree of proximity in space or time between the ships. He was supported in that opinion, insofar as it was a question of construction which would be put on the words by seamen, by the Elder Brethren who advised him. We put to our assessors the question: do you consider that the words 'coming up with another vessel' import the concept of proximity in space or time? They answered: 'In space'. We would give the same answer as a matter of ordinary English. If, therefore, ships came in sight of each other when many miles apart, we think it would be wrong, whatever their relative positions and courses may have been, to say that one was 'coming up with' the other. It does not, however, follow that for one to be coming up with the other there must be a risk of collision between them. For instance, if two ships are on parallel courses and one is abaft the other and travelling faster, we think a time would come when the faster ship should be considered to be coming up with the other, provided that the courses were not more than a few cables apart, even though if each ship maintained its course there would be no risk of collision. Butt J held in The Seaton[2] that the overtaking rules applied when two ships were on courses so nearly parallel as to involve no risk of collision, and applied at a time when the ships were three or four miles distant from each other.

To obtain help as to the stage at which, on the facts of the present case, a seaman would consider that the Olympian was coming up with the Nowy Sacz we put to our assessors, in accordance with the request of counsel for the defendants, this question:

> 'Assume the following facts: 1. Nowy Sacz on course 341° at speed 12½ knots. 2. Olympian on course converging with that of Nowey Sacz at speed of 14½ knots. 3. When Nowy Sacz came into sight her stern light was visible to Olympian and red light of Olympian to Nowy Sacz. Would a competent mariner consider that Olympian was coming up with Nowy Sacz? Answer: Yes.'

Again, we should take the same view, as a matter of ordinary English. As will appear hereafter we are of opinion (as was Brandon J and as were the assessors advising us) that the risk of collision arose at a later stage than this. It follows that in our opinion the time when one vessel can be said to be 'coming up with' another, while it does involve an element of proximity, may be before the time when there is a risk of collision.

A good reason for holding that r 24 applies before there is a risk of collision is that it is the object of the regulations not only to avoid collisions but to avoid the risk of collisions. Indeed, in The Beryl[3] this court interpreted the words 'so as to involve risk of collision' in the crossing rule as bringing the rule into play before there was a risk of collision (see per Brett MR[4] and per Bowen LJ[5]).

In The Franconia[6] Brett JA gave this definition:

> 'Can we, then, form a definition of the difference between crossing ships and overtaking ships? It seems to me that this may be a very good definition—I will

1   [1977] 1 Lloyd's Rep 384
2   (1883) 9 PD 1
3   (1884) 9 PD 137
4   9 PD 137 at 140
5   9 PD 137 at 144
6   (1876) 2 PD 8 at 12

not say that it is exhaustive, or that it may not on some occasion be found to be short of comprising every case, but I think it is a very good rule—that if the ships are in such a position, and are on such courses and at such distances, that if it were night the hinder ship could not see any part of the side lights of the forward ship, then they cannot be said to be crossing ships, although their courses may not be exactly parallel. It would not do, I think, to limit the angle of the crossing too much, but a limit to that extent it seems to me is a very useful and practical rule. And then if the hinder of two such ships is going faster than the other she is an overtaking ship.'

The Main[1] was decided at a time when the regulations, by art 11, required a stern light to be displayed only when a ship was being overtaken. The headnote reads as follows:

'A ship is "being overtaken" within the meaning of art. 11 when another is going faster than, and is coming nearer to her, on a course which may ultimately lead to a position of danger, and when the following ship is within the space not covered by the lights of the first ship, and is thus in a position in which these lights cannot be seen by those on board the following ship. The light prescribed in art. 11 must be shewn within a reasonable time before the overtaking ship gets into a position of danger, and after the overtaken ship has become aware that the overtaking ship is approaching in a manner before stated. *The Franconia*[2] approved.'

Lord Herschell LC, presiding in the Court of Appeal, said[3]:

'It has been contended on behalf of the defendants that a ship is being overtaken by another, within the meaning of this article, when a ship is approaching another in a position in which she is unable to see the lights of the vessel which is ahead of her, and which she is approaching. On the other hand, it has been contended for the plaintiffs that a vessel is only being overtaken when the course of the overtaking ship is such that if it be left unchanged a collision will ensue. The latter is, I think, certainly too narrow a construction; it would be a dangerous construction to put not only on this article, but also on art. 20.'

Corresponding with present r 24(*a*), Lord Esher MR said[4]:

'The rule therefore laid down in *The Franconia*[2] is a sound working one, and I agree with it as a definition, though not an exhaustive one, of what constitutes an overtaking or an overtaken vessel within the meaning of art. 11. Then it also follows that the light must be exhibited within a reasonable time.'

Fry LJ said[5]:

'A ship, it appears to me, is being overtaken when she is a ship towards which there is another ship going at a greater speed than the first, in such a direction as to approach the first ship. But that definition is not enough in order to enable us to determine whether the second is an overtaking ship or not. We must therefore inquire what must be the position of one ship to the other in order to bring her into the position of an overtaking ship, and the other into that of a ship being overtaken. The answer to that inquiry is to be found in the Regulations themselves. The Regulations before art. 11, provide that every sea-going ship shall carry lights which cover twenty points of the whole area, thus leaving a space in which the lights exhibited do not shew. Now art. 11 introduces an additional light, and it seems most reasonable that that light should be used

1 (1886) 11 PD 132
2 (1876) 2 PD 8
3 11 PD 132 at 135
4 11 PD 132 at 139
5 11 PD 132 at 140

a for the purpose of giving notice to a vessel within the area not covered by the other lights. Taking that view, it appears to me that one vessel may be said to be overtaking the other when she is within the space not covered by the green or red light, and is approaching the other ship. Equally, the other vessel is being overtaken when there is within that space another ship drawing nearer to her.'

b These passages were part of the ratio decidendi. A ship which is an overtaking ship for the purpose of one rule must also be an overtaking ship for the purpose of another rule in the same part of the same regulations. Indeed Lord Herschell made it clear that the same construction should be applied to both rules. I regard The Main[1] as authority for the proposition that art 20 (now r 24) comes into effect before a risk of collision is involved.

This does not mean that it necessarily comes into effect as soon as the vessels are in sight of one another. As Brandon J pointed out in The Auriga[2], as soon as r 24 applies *c* to one ship, r 21 applies to the other and inhibits her from altering course or speed. It was contended by counsel for the defendants that this would cause no real difficulty to the overtaken ship because, as was held in The Roanoke[3], a ship carrying out a proper manoeuvre, the nature of which was known to the other ship, could continue the manoeuvre notwithstanding that she was the stand-on ship and that the man- oeuvre involved a reduction in speed. That was a case on special facts because the *d* manoeuvre involved was slowing down to pick up a pilot, which would be well- known to the other ship because the appropriate flag signal was being shown. We put to our assessors this question:

> 'Do you consider that if r 24 were to apply whenever ship A has ship B bearing more than two points abaft her beam and proceeding at a higher speed
> *e* and in something like the same direction, this would give rise to substantial difficulties for those navigating ship A?'

and received the answer No. The question was perhaps too general in its terms and we should not be willing to accept that the early application of the rule would never cause substantial difficulties for those navigating the overtaking ship but we would accept that it is not necessary, in order to avoid such difficulties, to confine the rule *f* to a time after the risk of collision has arisen.

Our conclusion at this stage is that on the construction of the regulations, and giving to r 24 the meaning most consonant with the general purposes of the regula- tions, it should be held to apply before a risk of collision has developed.

What, then, is the effect of the authorities? It appears to us that The Banshee[4] is in conflict with The Main[1] and that it is open to this court, on the principle of *g* Young v Bristol Aeroplane Co[5], to decide which it should follow. We consider that we should follow The Main[1] because, in addition to the reasons we have already given for preferring a construction which would make the rule effective before there is a risk of collision, we are of opinion that that is more in keeping with The Franconia[6], The Beryl[7] and The Seaton[8] than the other construction. If, contrary to our view, The Main[1] is to be regarded as an authority only on the interpretation of the old art 11, *h* then the question arises whether The Banshee[4] is conclusive of the question of law in this case.

A ground on which it seems to us that it is possible to distinguish The Banshee[4] from the present case is that at the time when it was decided the predecessor of r 24 did not contain para (b) or any other definition of overtaking. It was no doubt open to this court in The Banshee[4] to qualify the Franconia[6] definition by adding a modifi-

j
1 (1886) 11 PD 132
2 [1977] 1 Lloyd's Rep 384 at 394
3 [1908] P 231
4 (1887) 57 LT 841
5 [1944] 2 All ER 293, [1944] KB 718
6 (1876) 2 PD 8
7 (1884) 9 PD 137
8 (1883) 9 PD 1

cation which would not have been relevant in the circumstances considered in *The Franconia*[1]. What is significant, however, is that when the regulations were amended and a definition of what is meant by an overtaking vessel was introduced no reference was made to risk of collision. Seeing that r 24(b) is clearly based on judicial decision it seems to us highly probable that the definition is intended to be a complete one rather than that resort should have to be had to other cases to put a gloss on it. For this reason, we are of opinion that the court is not bound by *The Banshee*[2].

The Manchester Regiment[3] was decided after r 24 had been put into its present form. *The Banshee*[2] was followed without its being suggested that it was not applicable under the amended rule. But the case was a very unusual one on its facts; to have held the Clan MacKenzie to have been an overtaking ship would have been something of an absurdity. One reason given[4] by Merriman P for his decision, namely that the words 'notwithstanding anything contained in these Rules' lent support to his decision is admittedly difficult to follow. It is obvious that both Merriman P and Brandon J regarded that the condition introduced by *The Banshee*[2] as being based on an implication which is necessary in order to give a sensible effect to r 24. We recognise that great weight is to be given to the specialised knowledge and understanding of those learned judges in relation to navigation. We have hesitated long as to whether it is open to this court, and right for this court, to differ from them. But having formed a clear view we have decided that it is our duty to express it and to give effect to it.

We would hold accordingly that r 24 begins to operate before there is a risk of collision and as soon as it can properly be said that the overtaking ship is coming up with the overtaken ship. When exactly that will be may not always be easy to determine but we see no reason to suppose that it will be any more difficult than the decision as to when the situation involves a risk of collision.

It is not strictly necessary for us to reach a conclusion as to when the risk of collision arose but in case that question should be material we put to our assessors this question:

'Assume the following facts: at 03.00 the Olympian about two points abaft the beam of the Nowy Sacz, the distance between the ships a little over two miles, with closing speed about 2 to 2½ knots; at 03.30 the Olympian about a beam of Nowy Sacz and the distance reduced to about a mile. At what stage could it fairly be said that a risk of collision arose?'

Their answer was: 'About 03.30 when Olympian was about abeam of Nowy Sacz and continuing to close.' This is the same advice what was given by the Elder Brethren in the court below and is in accordance with Brandon J's own view. We would accept it as correct.

Brandon J found that the Olympian was in sight of the Nowy Sacz by about 02.45 and, on a balance of probabilities, that the Nowy Sacz was in sight of the Olympian at some time between 02.45 and 03.00. These findings were in accordance with the evidence and we accept them. By the time the vessels were in sight of each other and less than three miles apart we are of opinion that the Olympian was coming up with the Nowy Sacz. If follows that from that time the Nowy Sacz was, in our judgment, the stand-on ship and the Olympian was the give-way ship.

Counsel for the defendants contended that in those circumstances the Olympian should be held three-quarters to blame and the Nowy Sacz one-quarter. Counsel for the plaintiffs advanced no argument to the contrary and in our judgment that would be the right proportion.

We allow the appeal accordingly.

Appeal allowed. Leave to appeal and cross-appeal to the House of Lords granted.

Solicitors: *Elborne Mitchell & Co* (for the defendants); *Holman, Fenwick & Willan* (for the plaintiffs).   L I Zysman Esq Barrister.

1   (1876) 2 PD 8
2   (1887) 57 LT 841
3   [1938] P 117
4   [1938] P 117 at 128

Laundon v Hartlepool Borough Council

COURT OF APPEAL, CIVIL DIVISION
STEPHENSON, ORR AND CUMMING-BRUCE LJJ
29th APRIL, 13th MAY 1977

Housing – Compulsory purchase – Compensation – House wholly or partly occupied as private dwelling – Occupied as private dwelling – Occupied as private dwelling throughout qualifying period – House purchased during qualifying period – Purchaser not taking up residence in house until one month after vendor ceased to reside in house – Furniture bought by purchaser from vendor in house from date vendor ceased to reside – Purchaser decorating house in month before he took up residence – Whether during month house occupied 'as a private dwelling' – Whether presence of furniture in house imparting quality of occupation as a dwelling house – Housing Act 1969, Sch 5, para 1(1)(b).

From a date before 6th April 1971 until 27th October 1972, G was the owner and occupier of a house. He sold the house to the claimant and on 27th October ceased to live in it. When he departed on 27th October G left in the house certain items of furniture which he had sold with the house to the claimant. On 6th November the keys of the house were handed to the claimant and on 15th November the claimant paid the purchase price. Between 6th November and 25th November the claimant did not reside at the house but visited it to carry out decorations to prepare it for use as his residence. On 25th November he and his wife began to reside in the house. The furniture left by G remained in the house throughout the period 27th October to 25th November. On 5th April 1973 the acquiring authority made a clearance order, under the Housing Act 1957, in respect of the area in which the house was situated, and on 6th April a compulsory purchase order was made in respect of the house. The claimant claimed that the compensation payable to him for the compulsory purchase included an owner-occupier's payment under Sch 5, para 1(1)[a], to the Housing Act 1969, since 'throughout the qualifying period' the house had been wholly or partly 'occupied as a private dwelling', within para 1(1)(b) of Sch 5. The qualifying period for the purpose of para 1(1)(b) was, by virtue of Sch 5, para 5[b], the period of two years prior to the date of the clearance order, i e from 6th April 1971 to 5th April 1973. The acquiring authority referred the claim to the Lands Tribunal. The authority conceded that from 27th October to 25th November the house had been 'occupied', by virtue of the presence of the furniture, but contended that it had not been 'occupied as a private dwelling'. The tribunal upheld that view and decided that the claimant was not entitled to an owner-occupier's payment. The claimant appealed, contending that the court was required to look at the character of the occupation of the house throughout the qualifying period, which was as a private dwelling, and since it had been conceded that he was in occupation between 27th October and 25th November, by virtue of the presence of the furniture, the character of that occupation was as a private dwelling, and the fact that during that period he had not been in residence because he was decorating the house did not destroy the character of his occupation of it as a private dwelling.

Held – (i) Where there had been a sale of a house during the qualifying period the purchaser did not become the occupier of the house 'as a private dwelling', within para 1(1)(b) of Sch 5, until he had taken up personal residence in the house, and during the period when the house was empty except for furniture which the purchaser had bought from the vendor the house was not occupied as a private dwelling, for the

---

a Paragraph 1 is set out at p 309 *d* to p 310 *a*, post
b Paragraph 5, so far as material, is set out at p 310 *a*, post

mere presence of the furniture in the house did not, even though it constituted 'occupation', impart to that occupation the quality of occupation as a private dwelling *a* (see p 312 *b* to *e* and *g*, p 313 *h* and p 314 *a b* and *f*, post).

(ii) Where, however, the gap between the successive residential occupations of the vendor and purchaser was not more than one week or 10 days the de minimis rule would apply and such a gap would be too insignificant to destroy the quality of occupation as a private dwelling; but a period of a month or just under would be too long a period to be disregarded under that rule. Consequently the period 27th October *b* to 25th November was too long to be disregarded, and it followed that, as the claimant had not been personally resident in the house during that period, it had not been 'occupied as a private dwelling' throughout the qualifying period and the claimant was not therefore entitled to an owner-occupier payment. Accordingly the appeal would be dismissed (see p 312 *f* and p 314 *d* to *f*, post).

c

Notes

For payment to the owner-occupier of a house on compulsory purchase, see 8 Halsbury's Laws (4th Edn) para 314.

For the Housing Act 1969, s 68 and Sch 5, see 16 Halsbury's Statutes (3rd Edn) 530, 541.

Case referred to in judgments

d

Arbuckle Smith & Co Ltd v Greenock Corporation [1960] 1 All ER 568, [1960] AC 813, [1960] 2 WLR 435, 124 JP 251, 58 LGR 155, HL, Digest (Cont Vol A) 1278, *13a*.

Appeal

On the compulsory acquisition of his house, 21 Talbot Street, Hartlepool, under the Housing Act 1957 the claimant, David Laundon, claimed that he was entitled, under *e* s 68 of and Sch 5 to the Housing Act 1969, to an owner-occupier's payment of £1,226. The acquiring authority, Hartlepool Borough Council, referred to the Lands Tribunal the amount of the compensation which was payable to the claimant. The claimant had purchased the house during the 'qualifying period' as defined by Sch 5, para 5, to the 1969 Act. On 2nd July 1975 the tribunal (V G Wellings Esq QC) found as a fact that for a period of ten days during the qualifying period the house was unoccupied although used for the storage of furniture which had been included in the sale of the house to the claimant, and on that finding determined that the house had not been wholly or partly occupied as a private dwelling throughout the qualifying period, within para 1(1) of Sch 5, and consequently the claimant was not entitled to an owner-occupier's payment. The claimant appealed on the ground that the tribunal's determination had been erroneous in law in that the finding that the house was *g* unoccupied for ten days, though used throughout that period for the storage of furniture, did not constitute an interruption in the qualifying period for the purpose of entitlement to an owner-occupier's payment. The facts are set out in the judgment of Orr LJ.

William Glover QC and *John Grove* for the claimant.   *h*
John Newey QC and *Jim Williams* for the acquiring authority.

Cur adv vult

13th May. **ORR LJ** read the first judgment at the invitation of Stephenson LJ. This is an appeal by the claimant, the owner of a house at 21 Talbot Street, West Hartlepool, against a decision of the Lands Tribunal (Mr V G Wellings QC) dated 2nd July 1975, whereby it was held that the claimant, while admittedly entitled to receive as compensation for the compulsory purchase of that house pursuant to a closure order the sum of £24 assessed (and as a figure not in dispute) by the district valuer as the site value of the house, was not entitled to receive by way of further compensation as an owner-occupier's supplement under the provisions of s 68 of and Sch 5 to the Housing Act 1969 a further sum of £1,226 assessed (and also as a figure not in dispute) by the district valuer as the difference between the site value of the house and its full compulsory purchase value (or market value).

The events relevant to the compulsory acquisition of the house are that on 5th April 1973 the area in which it is situated was declared by the acquiring authority to be a clearance area under the provisions of the Housing Act 1957; on 6th April 1973 a compulsory purchase order was made under the 1957 Act in respect of this and other houses within the area; that order was on 18th December 1973 confirmed by the Secretary of State; and on 12th December 1973 notification of the order was sent to the claimant together with a notice to treat, following which compensation claim forms were submitted by the claimant's solicitors to the local authority and enquiries were made on the acquiring authority's behalf with a view to determining the claimant's entitlement to the supplement.

The relevant statutory provisions with reference to the supplement may be summarised as follows. Section 68 of the Housing Act 1969, enlarging provisions contained in the 1957 Act as to payment of compensation in respect of unfit houses purchased or demolished, enacts that the provisions of Sch 5 to the 1969 Act shall have effect with respect to certain payments to be made in certain circumstances in respect of owner-occupied houses. Schedule 5, para 1, provides as follows:

'(1) Where a house has been purchased at site value in pursuance of a compulsory purchase order made by virtue of Part II or Part III of the Act of 1957 or in pursuance of an order under paragraph 2 of Schedule 2 to the Land Compensation Act 1961, or has been vacated in pursuance of a demolition order under Part II of the Act of 1957, a closing order under section 17 of that Act or a clearance order, then, if—(a) the relevant date is later than 23rd April 1968; and (b) on the relevant date and throughout the qualifying period the house was wholly or partly occupied as a private dwelling and the person so occupying it (or, if during that period it was so occupied by two or more persons in succession, each of those persons) was a person entitled to an interest in that house or a member of the family of a person so entitled; the authority concerned shall make in respect of that interest a payment of an amount determined in accordance with paragraphs 2 and 3 of this Schedule.

'(2) Where an interest in a house purchased or vacated as mentioned in sub-paragraph (1) of this paragraph was acquired by any person (in this sub-paragraph referred to as the first owner) after 23rd April 1968 and less than two years before the relevant date, and a payment under sub-paragraph (1) of this paragraph in respect of that interest would have fallen to be made by the authority concerned had the qualifying period been a period beginning with the acquisition and ending with the relevant date, the authority concerned shall make to the person who was entitled to the interest at the date the house was purchased or vacated a payment of the like amount, if—(a) the authority are satisfied that before acquiring the interest the first owner had made all reasonable enquiries to ascertain whether it was likely that the order, notice or declaration by reference to which the relevant date is defined in paragraph 5(1) of this Schedule would be made or served within two years of the acquisition and that he had no reason to believe that it was likely; and (b) the person entitled to the interest at the date when the house was purchased or vacated was the first owner or a member of his family.

'(3) Where during a part of the qualifying period amounting, or during parts thereof together amounting, to not more than one year a person previously in occupation of the whole or part of the house was not in occupation thereof by reason only of a posting in the course of his duties as a member of the armed forces of the Crown or of a change in the place of his employment or occupation he shall be deemed for the purposes of this paragraph to have continued in occupation during that part or those parts.'

Schedule 5, para 5, defines the 'qualifying period' for the purposes of para 1 as 'the period of two years ending with the relevant date' which in this case was 5th April 1973, being the date of the clearance order. Accordingly the issue in the case has been whether 'throughout' the period from 6th April 1971 to 5th April 1973, the house in question was wholly or partly occupied as a private dwelling.

The relevant facts found by the Lands Tribunal as to the house, 21 Talbot Street, were as follows. It was owned and occupied by a Mr Galloway, who sold it to the claimant, from before 6th April 1971 (the commencement of the qualifying period) until 27th October 1972 when Mr Galloway ceased to live in the house but left in it certain items of furniture which were sold along with the house to the claimant, but the tribunal made no finding as to the date of the contract of sale. On 6th November 1972, the keys of the house were handed to the claimant who thereafter visited the house for the purpose of redecorating it for residential occupation. The purchase price was paid on 15th November. On 25th November, the claimant and his wife began to live in the house and from that date there is no doubt that it was wholly occupied by them as a private dwelling, but the question at issue in the case is whether this requirement was satisfied during the two short periods to which I have already referred, the first from 27th October to 6th November 1972, when the vendor had ceased to live in the house and it was occupied only by the items of furniture, and the second from 6th to 25th November when the claimant did the decorative work and the furniture left by the vendor remained in the house.

On this material the tribunal held that the claimant was not entitled to the owner-occupier supplement and came to a similar conclusion as respects five other references all involving sales of houses and gaps of varying length, the longest over a year, between the vendor ceasing and the purchaser beginning to reside at the house in question, and some of them also involving the factors of furniture left by the vendor and/or decorative or other work done by the purchaser in the house before he began to reside in it.

At the conclusion of the hearing, in response to a request made by the solicitor for the acquiring authority that guidance should be given as to the approach to be made to para 1(2) of Sch 5 in case any of the claimants should wish to make a claim for compensation under that provision, the tribunal observed that the several claimants appeared to fulfil all the conditions of that provision save that each of them would have to show that before acquiring his interest he had made all reasonable enquiries and had no reason to believe that it was likely that the order, notice or declaration in question would be made or served within two years of his acquisition, but that the acquiring authority had not so far been asked to say that it was satisfied as to these matters which were for the acquiring authority to determine, there being, as the tribunal understood the law, no provision for review of the decision either by the tribunal or by the courts.

In rejecting the various applications the tribunal said that in its view the word 'occupied' in Sch 5 bore its ordinary meaning which was not limited to personal occupation but included occupation enjoyed vicariously through, inter alia, furniture by the exercise of control over the subject-matter, but the question at issue was not confined to occupation. It was whether the house 'throughout' the qualifying period was wholly or partly occupied 'as a private dwelling'. In the tribunal's view the word 'throughout' meant that there must be no break in residential occupation, any injustice to which this requirement might give rise being alleviated in a proper case by para 1(2).

As respects the claimant's case the tribunal concluded that the gap of ten days between 27th October and 6th November 1972 during which the house was 'completely unoccupied' was in itself sufficient to destroy the claimant's claim, but added

that there was also the further period from 6th to 25th November before the
a claimant's occupation became residential in quality.

Against this decision the claimant now appeals and it has not been in dispute in the
appeal that the tribunal was right in holding as it had clearly done that the house
was during the two periods in question 'occupied' by virtue of the presence of the
furniture and that in later referring to the house as being 'completely unoccupied'
during the first period the tribunal must have meant that it was unoccupied apart
b from the furniture.

The sole issue in the appeal has therefore been whether the tribunal was right in
holding that during the two periods in question the house, although occupied, was not
occupied as a private dwelling, and on this issue counsel for the claimant conceded
that the fact that the claimant during the second period did the decorative work
could add nothing to his case. In my judgment this concession was plainly right on the
c authority of *Arbuckle Smith & Co Ltd v Greenock Corpn*[1] where the House of Lords drew
a clear distinction between user of premises for the purpose for which they are
occupied and work done in preparation for such user.

Having made this concession counsel for the claimant's argument was that the words
'throughout the qualifying period' in para 1(1) of Sch 5 involve the court in looking
at the user made of the house by occupiers throughout the period; that the house
d never had been occupied other than as a private dwelling; that the claimant having
been found to be in occupation by virtue of the furniture, the only possible character
of the occupation must have been as a private dwelling; and that if, as counsel for the
acquiring authority accepted, the character of the occupation as a private dwelling,
once established, is not destroyed by temporary absence of the occupier on holiday
or for other reasons, the word 'throughout' cannot mean at every instant during the
e qualifying period.

Counsel for the acquiring authority relied on a number of dictionary meanings of
the word 'throughout'. He accepted that once an occupant has begun to reside in
premises he can temporarily absent himself on holiday or for other reasons without
ceasing to occupy the premises as a private dwelling, but contended that before
residence begins it cannot be said that the premises are occupied as a private dwelling.
f He accepted that a short gap between residential occupations could be treated as de
minimis but claimed that de minimis in the present context would be no more than
one day, and that any hardship arising where there has been, as here, a longer gap is
alleviated by para 1(2) of Sch 5, which would apply in the present case provided
the claimant can satisfy the requirements already mentioned.

I have not found the case an easy one to determine. It is clear from the terms of
g para 1(1)(a) of Sch 5, which refers to occupation by two or more persons in succession,
that Parliament must have contemplated that there could be sales of the property
in question and it seems unrealistic to suppose that the purchaser would always, or
even in most cases, take up residence on the very day the vendor leaves, but the effect
of counsel for the acquiring authority's argument is that if the purchaser does not do
so the right conferred by para 1(1) of Sch 5 is not acquired and the purchaser can only
h rely on the more restricted rights under para 1(2) and with no right of appeal against
the decision. On the other hand I can well understand that if the entry of the purchaser can be delayed indefinitely, or for a substantial period, the evil which the
legislature wished to prevent might well arise in that a purchaser who never intended
to occupy the house but only to make a profit by resale in what he believed, on the
supposition that a clearance order was going to be made, to be a rising market, would
j be given time to negotiate a resale. It is true that he would probably have to pay
his vendor, but he might be prepared to do so, or the vendor might be prepared to
wait for his money, it may be on terms that he should have some share in the resale
profit. I do not suggest for a moment that anything of this kind underlay the present

---

1 [1960] 1 All ER 568, [1960] AC 813

case but only that evils of this kind could arise and that for this reason Parliament may well have taken the view that such cases should be dealt with under para 1(2).

For these reasons the construction of para 1(1) of Sch 5 which I should wish to adopt is that which will provide a reasonable protection against the abuses which Parliament clearly had in mind but which will not impose on a purchaser such a time limit for the taking up of residential occupation as may in practice be impossible for bona fide purchasers to comply with. I would also, so far as possible, wish to adopt a construction which will not involve artificialities or the attribution of decisive importance to chance factors. As to this last matter it seems to me surprising that a purchaser's ability to become an occupier of a house as a private dwelling without going to live in it should depend on the chance factor of the vendor having items of furniture which the purchaser wishes to buy, but it is in my judgment an even stronger objection to counsel for the claimant's argument that if the purchaser can obtain residential status by virtue of the items of furniture involved in this case there appears to be no reason why this situation should not continue indefinitely and so give rise to the evils which the legislature was clearly concerned to prevent.

Apart, however, from these considerations I am unable, with great respect to the contrary view, to accept that because the presence of furniture involves, as in law it undoubtedly does, that the house is occupied, it also follows in this case that the house was occupied as a private dwelling. This question is not answered in my judgment by reference to the past history of the house or on the basis of a presumption of continuance. The question is whether over the two periods in question it was being occupied as a private dwelling and in my judgment the answer is that it was not, but was being occupied as a temporary repository for the items of furniture, and factors such as temporary absence on holiday or otherwise, which would be relevant on the question whether an established residential occupation has continued through a period of physical absence, are not in my judgment material when the question is whether a new residential occupation has commenced.

On this critical issue in the appeal I therefore accept counsel for the acquiring authority's argument but I part company from him on the issue of what, in the present context, would be de minimis. In my judgment de minimis would apply, in this and at least most other cases of this kind, to a gap of up to a week between residential occupations and might apply to a ten day gap, but in my judgment it could not cover the gap of just under a month between 27th October and 25th November.

For these reasons I would dismiss this appeal.

CUMMING-BRUCE LJ. I agree with the reasoning and conclusion of Orr LJ. I accept without qualification his approach to the construction of the Sch 5 to the Housing Act 1969 and his decision that the claimant could add nothing to his case by reliance on the period from 6th to 25th November when he was doing decorative work in preparation for his residence in the house.

As a consequence of the ground relied on in the notice of appeal, and the ensuing question on which the decision of this court is desired, the argument in this court focussed on the narrow and somewhat abstract issue whether a house empty save for some items of furniture was occupied as a private dwelling house within the meaning of Sch 5. The claimant's advisers fastened on the contradiction between the decision that 'occupied' in para 1(1)(b) of Sch 5 could be constructive occupation by furniture and the determination in the case that there was a gap for ten days in which the house was completely unoccupied. Having established that the Lands Tribunal has decided as a matter of construction that 'occupied' in the paragraph has a broad meaning which includes occupation enjoyed vicariously through furniture (against which there is no cross-appeal), counsel for the claimant posed the problem: what was the house occupied as? Which leads to the reasoning: it was occupied by the vendor as a private dwelling, and after sale by the purchaser (the claimant) as a private dwelling.

The furniture was there to facilitate use of the house as a private dwelling. It is absurdly artificial to hold that for ten days the occupation of the house had changed its character, if only because no one suggests that the house was ever contemplated by anyone as being occupied save as a private dwelling.

This leads remorselessly to the conclusion that the vendor's vicarious occupation of the house by furniture was an occupation as a private dwelling. In my view there is a fallacy in the reasoning which can be traced to the way in which the question for decision has been put. The presence of the furniture in the otherwise empty house has been isolated from the rest of the facts, and a pyramid of legal abstraction has been constructed on this narrow foundation.

I prefer to recite the facts as far as known (which is not very far) and to examine at each stage whether it is common sense to regard the house as occupied as a private dwelling. But first I try to picture what usually may happen when there is a transfer of ownership of a privately occupied dwelling-house, for the draftsman must have intended the words he selected to be apt for what happens in most ordinary situations of change in occupation.

First the vendor has to move out in order to give vacant possession. (i) He may personally depart taking his furniture with him on the same day so that the house is empty. (ii) He may depart himself, but arrange for his furniture to follow him a short time later. (iii) Or he may personally depart, but leave all or some of his furniture behind for acquisition by a purchaser or disposal on the market. In (i) the vendor's residence (occupation as a private dwelling) clearly ends when he goes with his furniture. In (ii) it can fairly be said that he is winding up his residence in the house over a short period of time, and that his occupation of the house as a private dwelling does not end until he has finished removing his furniture. In (iii), however, his use of the house as a private residence ends when he personally departs. The house is thereafter being used as a means towards disposal of the furniture. Whatever it is being used for, it is not as the vendor's private dwelling. The vendor may alternatively move out personally with his furniture and put in decorators or builders to improve the house before he puts it on the market or while it is on the market. This is vicarious occupation of the house by the vendor, for the purpose of preparing it for use as a dwelling house again after the decorators or builders have done their work.

Secondly the purchaser has to move in. He may set about it in much the same way as the vendor, mutatis mutandis. (i) He may arrive with his furniture and para- phernalia. (ii) He may camp in the house and wait for the arrival of his furniture in a few days' time. (iii) He may install his furniture over a period of days and take up residence when the house is ready for him. In cases (i) and (ii) his occupation as a private dwelling is complete on the first day. In case (iii) the process of occupation as a private dwelling begins with the arrival of the first instalment of furniture, and is completed when he takes up his residence personally in the house. Or he may deco- rate or repair in order to prepare the empty or nearly empty house for use as a private dwelling, and move in when the work is done. On the ordinary use of language he does not make the house his home, his dwelling, until he moves in himself or, at least, having begun the process of moving in by installing his furniture, continues the process without undue break in time until he personally takes up residence.

So to the facts of the instant case to see what happened. The vendor personally moved out, apparently taking some of his furniture but leaving behind what he did not want, intending to dispose of it by sale to the claimant or otherwise. When the vendor thus moved out with the furniture he wanted, he ceased to occupy the house as his private dwelling. The claimant at an uncertain date agreed to buy the furniture as part of the bargain for purchase of the house. He obtained possession of the house and furniture on 6th November, and paid for it on 15th November. If on 6th Novem- ber he had personally taken up residence in the house, or had begun the process of moving the rest of his belongings into the house, it might be fairly said that the pro- cess of his occupation of the house as his dwelling began on 6th November. But on the facts that did not happen. On 6th November he began decoration of the house to prepare it for his use as his residence, and did not move in until 25th November. *a* So looking backwards in time from 25th November, it is quite unreal to hold that the presence of the furniture in the house with effect from 27th October had any causative effect on his occupation of the house as his residence until 25th November. It must be the purchaser's installation or use of the furniture in the house which imparted to the occupation of the house a quality of occupation as a private dwelling. On the facts that did not begin to happen until 25th November. Between 25th October and 6th *b* November the existence in the house of the furniture which the vendor was selling to the claimant did not begin the process by which the claimant imparted to the house the quality of occupation as his private dwelling.

Counsel for the acquiring authority has conceded that where a house is occupied as a private dwelling, the continuity of such occupation is not broken if the householder goes away on a short holiday or is absent for brief intervals such as usually occur to *c* many people living at home. But he submits that the essential feature of such situations is that the house has already been occupied by the owner-occupier as his dwelling-house, and does not assist a purchaser to claim that a house is his dwelling for a similar period of time before he has established himself in it as his home. I accept this distinction.

That is sufficient to dispose of this appeal. But I would add a reference to the room *d* for the de minimis rule. It may frequently happen that the vendor vacates the house a few days before the date for vacant possession, or that the purchaser does not begin to establish his residence in the house until a few days after that date. The acquiring authority has regarded what it describes as such short gaps in residential user as too insignificant to destroy occupation throughout the qualifying period. I agree with this approach. If the effect of the practical arrangements made by vendor or pur- *e* chaser, or both of them, is to leave the house vacant for a week, I would not regard the continuity of occupation as a private dwelling throughout the period as thereby broken. And if there is an unforeseen accident which adds a day or two to that week that might reasonably be disregarded too. But 28 days is too long to be disregarded by resort to the de minimis rule.

f

STEPHENSON LJ. I had prepared a judgment of my own, but I agree so fully with both judgments delivered by Orr and Cumming-Bruce LJJ that I propose to add only this: I find some support for the decision of the Lands Tribunal in Sch 5, para 1(3) to the Housing Act 1969. That sub-paragraph refers to 'a person previously in occupation' of the house, who during a part or parts of the qualifying period is not *g* in occupation himself by reason of a posting in the armed forces or a change in the place of his employment or (in another sense) occupation. Such a person would not necessarily, or perhaps usually, move his furniture out of the house, yet the sub-paragraph regards him as not in occupation during the part or parts of the qualifying period when he is away on army duty or in his new place of work.

I concur in dismissing the appeal, and the question stated by the member of the *h* tribunal will be answered in the affirmative, namely that the tribunal was correct in law in holding that the house had not been wholly or partly occupied as a private the claimant to the owner-occupier's payment in accordance with s 68 of and Sch 5 to the 1969 Act.

Appeal dismissed. Leave to appeal to House of Lords refused. *i*

Solicitors: *Sinclair Roche & Temperley*, agents for *Tilly Bailey & Irvine*, Hartlepool (for the claimant); *Borough Solicitor*, Hartlepool Borough Council (for the acquiring authority).

L I Zysman Esq Barrister.

R v West London Supplementary Benefits Appeal Tribunal, ex parte Wyatt

QUEEN'S BENCH DIVISION
LORD WIDGERY CJ, PARK AND MAY JJ
28th NOVEMBER 1977

Supplementary benefit – Entitlement – Requirements – Requirements excluding medical, surgical, optical, aural or dental requirements – Medical requirements – Electrically operated special aids – Whether cost of electricity to operate special aids a 'medical . . . requirement' – Whether cost an 'exceptional circumstance' for which benefit may be awarded – Supplementary Benefits Act 1976, ss 1(3), 3(1), Sch 1, para 4(1).

The applicant and his wife, who were in ill health, had been provided with various items of electrical equipment, which included electric hoists, an electric wheelchair and an electrically operated remote control system, to alleviate their situation. These had been provided in part by the local authority, in part by the area health authority and in part by the Department of Health and Social Security. An application for supplementary benefit to cover the cost of running the special aids was rejected by the Supplementary Benefits Commission whose decision was upheld by a supplementary benefits appeal tribunal on the ground that the provision of electricity for the operation of the special aids was a 'medical . . . requirement', within s 1(3)[a] of the Supplementary Benefits Act 1976, and hence excluded from the applicant's requirements to be taken into account for the purpose of calculating the amount of benefit to which he was entitled under the 1976 Act. The applicant sought an order of certiorari to quash the commission's decision.

Held – The application would be granted for the following reasons—
(i) It could not be said that the running costs of the special aids necessarily all came within the expression 'medical . . . requirements' in s 1(3) of the 1976 Act without considering each particular piece of equipment separately, the purpose for which it was used and, perhaps, by whom it had been originally provided, and the tribunal were wrong to say that the running costs all came within that expression (see p 316 *j* to p 317 *h* and *h*, post).
(ii) Alternatively, the commission had a discretion under s 3(1)[b] of or para 4(1)[c] of Sch 1 to the 1976 Act to make exceptional payments in exceptional circumstances if it considered it appropriate and in so doing it was not restricted by the provisions of s 1(3) (see p 317 *e* to *h*, post).

Per Curiam. Supplementary benefit is the ultimate source of financial assistance which, subject to the provisions of the 1976 Act, is available to the ordinary citizen who may need it, and where assistance is available from no other source the 1976 Act should where possible be construed so as to bring the citizen's needs within its scope (see p 317 *b c*, post).

Notes
For right to supplementary benefit, see Supplement to 27 Halsbury's Laws (3rd Edn) para 930A.

---

a Section 1(3) is set out at p 316 *h*, post
b Section 3(1) provides: 'Where it appears to the Commission reasonable in all the circumstances they may determine that supplementary benefit shall be paid to a person by way of a single payment to meet an exceptional need.'
c Paragraph 4(1), so far as material, provides: 'Where there are exceptional circumstances—
(a) supplementary benefit may be awarded at an amount exceeding that, if any, calculated in accordance with . . . this Schedule . . . as may be appropriate to take account of those circumstances.'

For the Supplementary Benefits Act 1976, ss 1, 3, Sch 1, para 4, see 46 Halsbury's
Statutes (3rd Edn) 1048, 1049, 1077.

Case referred to in judgment
R v Peterborough Supplementary Benefits Appeal Tribunal, ex parte Department of Health
and Social Security (11th February 1977) unreported.

Motion for certiorari
This was an application by way of motion by Robert Ernest Wyatt for an order of
certiorari to bring up and quash a decision of the West London Supplementary
Benefits Appeal Tribunal dated 24th May 1977 confirming a decision of the Supplementary Benefits Commission that no grant could be made to the applicant for the
running costs of special aids provided for the applicant's wife. The London Borough
of Hillingdon was joined as being interested in the proceedings as the social services
authority for the area. The facts are set out in the judgment of May J.

Julian Gibson-Watt for the applicant.
Harry Woolf for the Supplementary Benefits Commission.
Richard Walker for the London Borough of Hillingdon.

MAY J delivered the first judgment at the invitation of Lord Widgery CJ. In this
matter counsel moves on behalf of the applicant for an order of certiorari to remove
to this court for the purpose of its being quashed a decision of the West London
Supplementary Benefits Appeal Tribunal of 24th May 1977 that no grant could be
made to him in respect of certain running costs to which I shall refer in a moment.
      The facts of this case can be very shortly stated. Unfortunately, both the applicant
and his wife are in ill health, the wife especially. In order to alleviate her situation, the
household, and she in particular, have been provided with various items of electrical
equipment, for instance electric hoists, an electric wheelchair, a ripple mattress and
cushion and an electrically operated remote control system. These have been provided in part by the local authority, in part by the area health authority, and in part
by the Department of Health and Social Security. Being electrical equipment, they
require a supply of electricity to operate them. Effectively, the issue in this case as the
court sees it, is who is ultimately to pay for the electricity used to operate these
various pieces of equipment.
      The decision of the tribunal was given on an application by Mr Wyatt for supple-
mentary benefit under the Supplementary Benefits Act 1976, on appeal from an
original decision of the Supplementary Benefits Commission of 7th March 1977. The
tribunal decided that the running costs of the special equipment were excluded,
that is to say that they could not be taken into account in assessing any supplementary
benefit payable to Mr Wyatt, in these terms: 'The tribunal were satisfied that the
running costs of the special aids under appeal were excluded under s 1(3) of the
Supplementary Benefits Act 1976 and that no grant could be made.'
      I turn immediately therefore to that statutory provision. Section 1(3) of the 1976
Act provides: 'The requirements of any person to be taken into account for the
purposes of this Act do not include any medical, surgical, optical, aural or dental
requirements.'
      If one combines the reason for the tribunal's decision which I have just quoted with
that statutory provision, it is at once apparent that the tribunal were taking and
expressing the view that the provision of electricity for the operation of all the various
appliances was a 'medical requirement', and thus could not be included in Mr Wyatt's
'requirements' for the purpose of performing the arithmetical calculation which
underlies the whole scheme set up by the 1976 Act.
      In my view, without considering each particular piece of equipment separately,

the purposes for which it is used and, it may well be, by whom it was originally
a supplied, it cannot be said that the running costs of these special aids must all come
within the phrase 'medical requirements' in s 1(3) of the 1976 Act. Some may; some
may not. But I think that it was wrong for the tribunal to refuse to take into account
the running costs of these special aids on the basis that in any event and on any view
these must fall within the provisions of s 1(3). Thus, in my judgment, on the face of
the tribunal's decision alone this application must succeed.

b   I would add this. As has been said in argument, supplementary benefit is the
ultimate source of financial assistance which, subject to the provisions of the 1976
Act, is available to the ordinary citizen who may need it. For instance, for medical
purposes it is available, if at all, only after recourse has been had to the national
health service, to which reference has been made in the course of the argument. It is
available, if at all, only after the provision of the relevant equipment itself under other
c legislation which applies to the local authorities. But if and to the extent that in
circumstances such as the present these electrical running costs cannot be obtained
from any other authority, I think it only right that one should seek to construe the
1976 Act if one can in such a way that these costs are within its scope either as a 'requirement' not excluded under s 1(3), or, alternatively, under para 4 of Sch 1 to the 1976
Act.

d   Insofar as this last statutory provision is concerned, our attention was drawn to
*R v Peterborough Supplementary Benefits Appeal Tribunal, ex parte Department of Health
and Social Security*[1], a decision of this court of 11th February 1977. It was a decision on
the Supplementary Benefit Act 1966 but counsel for the Supplementary Benefits
Commission submitted that, having regard to the judgment of Michael Davies J in
that case, the limitations in s 1(3) of the 1976 Act should apply not only to paras 1 to 3
e but also to para 4 of Sch 1 to the Act. In the *Peterborough* case[1] in fact the court had to
consider ss 6 and 7 of the 1966 Act, which have now effectively become ss 1(3) and 3 of
the 1976 Act. Section 3 permits the Supplementary Benefits Commission to make a
lump sum payment rather than weekly payments in exceptional circumstances,
and, as Michael Davies J held on s 7 of the 1966 Act in the *Peterborough* case[1], in considering whether or not to make such a lump sum payment rather than a weekly
f one, which is the normal basis of operating the supplementary benefits scheme, I
think that the 'requirements' referred to in s 1(3) are to be disregarded.

But the *Peterborough* decision[1] did not deal with, and in my judgment ought not to
be treated as applying to, para 4 of Sch 1 to the 1976 Act. I think that that provides the
Supplementary Benefits Commission with the ultimate discretion to make exceptional payments if it considers it appropriate, and that when it is considering whether
g or not to do so it is not restricted by the provisions of s 1(3) of the 1976 Act.

On either approach, therefore, in my judgment, the decision of the tribunal as it
appears on its face was wrong, and I would allow this application.

PARK J. I agree.

h **LORD WIDGERY CJ.** I agree also.

Application allowed; order of certiorari granted.

Solicitors: *Nicholas Warren* (for the applicant); *Solicitor, Department of Health and Social
Security; Solicitor, London Borough of Hillingdon.*

j
                                                        Lea Josse Barrister.

---

1   (11th February 1977) unreported

Re L (a minor) (wardship proceedings)

COURT OF APPEAL, CIVIL DIVISION
ROSKILL AND ORMROD LJJ
9th NOVEMBER 1977

Ward of court – Jurisdiction – Registrar – Application for care and control of minor – Order ***b***
made by district registrar without referring matter to appropriate county court judge –
Proper practice to refer matter to appropriate judge.

Ward of court – Practice – Hearing – Notice of hearing – Notice sent to mother of minor
and not to solicitors on record – Whether desirable.

A grandmother commenced wardship proceedings in a district registry. The mother,
who had been divorced from the father and who was interested in the proceedings,
had instructed solicitors who were the solicitors on the record. Notice of the proposed
hearing was given directly to the mother instead of her solicitors who were only
told of the hearing by the mother 75 minutes before it was due to begin. An articled
clerk, the only person the mother could find at the time in the solicitor's office, ***d***
appeared before the deputy registrar who indicated that he was minded to grant
an order to the grandmother in the terms of the originating application solely on the
basis of the affidavit evidence before him and on the report of the court welfare
office. He ordered that the child remain a ward of court during his minority and that
he remain in the care and control of the grandmother until further order. The
mother appealed. ***e***

Held – Even though the deputy registrar had jurisdiction under RSC Ord 90, r 12*[a]*,
to make such an order, the way in which he had exercised it was contrary to practice:
he should have first have given directions for the hearing to proceed before the
appropriate judge dealing with such business in the district registry. Furthermore,
it was quite wrong to have given notice of the proposed hearing directly to the mother ***f***
instead of to the solicitors on the record. Accordingly, the appeal would be allowed
and the matter would be remitted to the registry to be dealt with by the appropriate
county court judge (see p 319 *d* to *f* and p 320 *b* to *d* and *h*, post).
Per Ormrod LJ. RSC Ord 90, r 12, which gives a registrar the same jurisdiction
to make an order, inter alia, for care and control in wardship proceedings as that
of a judge in chambers, is totally inconsistent with r 92*[b]* of the Matrimonial Causes ***g***
Rules 1977, which limits the jurisdiction, except by consent, of a registrar in custody
cases arising after a divorce to making orders relating to the quantum of access
(see p 320 *e* to *g*, post).

---

a Rule 12, so far as material, provides: '(1) In proceedings to which this Part of this Order
applies a registrar may transact all such business and exercise all such authority and ***h***
jurisdiction as may be transacted and exercised by a judge in chambers . . .'
b Rule 92, so far as material, provides:
'(1) Subject to paragraph (2), an application for an order relating to the custody or
education of a child, or for an order committing him to the care of a local authority under
section 43 of the [Matrimonial Causes Act 1973] or providing for his supervision under
section 44 of that Act, shall be made to a judge.
'(2) An application by the petitioner or the respondent for—(a) an order in terms agreed ***j***
between the parties relating to the custody or education of a child, or (b) access to a child
where the other party consents to give access and the only question for determination is the
extent to which access is to be given, may be made to the registrar who may make such
order on the application as he thinks fit or may refer the application or any question arising
thereon to a judge for his decision . . .'

Notes

a For the duties and powers of registrars, see 13 Halsbury's Laws (4th Edn) paras 515, 933.

Appeal

The minor's mother appealed against an order made by Mr Deputy District Registrar Dobbie at Newcastle-upon-Tyne on 22nd September 1977 that the minor remain a ward of court during his minority and that care and control of the minor remain *b* with his paternal grandmother, who had commenced the wardship proceedings in relation to the minor. The facts are set out in the judgment of Roskill LJ.

R A Percy for the mother.
Isobel Plumstead for the grandmother.

c

ROSKILL LJ. This is an appeal by a mother from an order made by the deputy district registrar at Newcastle-upon-Tyne on 22nd September 1977 in wardship proceedings which the minor's grandmother had started in the Newcastle district registry a short while before. The learned deputy district registrar ordered that the *d* child remain a ward of court during his minority, and further that he remain in the care and control of the grandmother until further order. When Ormrod LJ and I first read these papers we wondered whether the deputy district registrar had any jurisdiction to make such an order. We are indebted to counsel for the grandmother for having drawn our attention to the relevant provisions of RSC Ord 90 r 12 which suggests that technically such an order may be within the jurisdiction of the deputy district registrar.

e However, even assuming that there was jurisdiction, it seems to us that it is contrary to practice that the jurisdiction of the court should have been exercised in the way it was. This is plainly a matter in which, in accordance with the usual practice, the registrar should first have given directions for the hearing to proceed before the appropriate judge dealing with such business in that district registry. That omission *f* seems to us a regrettable failure in the administration of justice.

Unfortunately, the matter does not stop there. The baby's mother, who, of course, was very interested in the proceedings, as was the baby's father from whom the mother was divorced (those two persons had apparently married when they were sixteen) had instructed solicitors in Newcastle, and those solicitors were the solicitors on the record. For some extraordinary reason which, for myself, I find almost impossible to understand, the court at which this order was made by the deputy district *g* registrar gave notice of the proposed hearing directly to the mother instead of to the solicitors on the record. Those solicitors were only told of the hearing by the mother at 10 o'clock in the morning of 22nd September. At that time the only person the mother could find in the solicitors' office was an articled clerk, who seems to me to have dealt with the matter very promptly and admirably. The mother *h* told the articled clerk that she had received a notification directly from the court to say that the proceedings were to be heard on 22nd September, that self-same day, at 11.15 am, that is to say 75 minutes after the mother had arrived in the solicitors' office. Mr Lamb, the articled clerk, stated in his affidavit:

> 'It was most embarrassing that the court should give notice in this manner to the
> *j* [mother] even although my principals were on the record and certainly up until
> that time no notification of any adjourned hearing date had been given to them
> either by the Court or by the [grandmother's] solicitors.'

Mr Lamb went round and appeared before the deputy district registrar. In his affidavit he gives an account of what happened. He was obviously in a most difficult position. It seems that the deputy district registrar at once indicated that he, Mr

Lamb, had a difficult task in front of him. To quote from para 16 of Mr Lamb's affidavit, the deputy district registrar—

'. . . indicated in clear terms to me that he was minded to grant an Order to the [grandmother] in terms of the Originating Application on the basis alone of the affidavit evidence before him and the Court Welfare Officer's report.'

Without wishing to criticise, this really was a most extraordinary way of exercising one of the most sensitive jurisdictions which a court has, namely applications concerning the custody, care and control of a very young infant following a divorce. This court must express its strong disapproval of the way this matter was dealt with.

The only thing that we can do in these circumstances is to set aside the deputy district registrar's order, and order that this matter be remitted forthwith to the Newcastle District Registry there to be dealt with by the appropriate county court judge. Counsel for the mother has told us that both his Honour Judge Smith QC and his Honour Judge Lyall Wilkes regularly deal with matters such as this in that registry, there doing the work of Family Division judges. In those circumstances we think they should be approached instantly, and when I say 'instantly' I mean instantly, with a view to asking one or other of them if he would be good enough to give the earliest possible date for the hearing of this application, so that this matter may then be dealt with properly. It is regrettable that what has happened should have happened because the extra expenditure of public money must be not inconsiderable. The appeal will be allowed and the matter remitted accordingly.

ORMROD LJ. I just want to add one thing. This is to draw the attention of the rules committee to the wording of RSC Ord 90, r 12. This, as it is drafted at present, is totally inconsistent with the Matrimonial Causes Rules 1977[1], r 92. We have this apparently absurd anomaly that in custody cases arising after a divorce, registrars have no jurisdiction to make orders relating to custody or education. Indeed, they have only a jurisdiction, except by consent, to make orders relating to the quantum of access. They have no jurisdiction to make an order as to access where one party is maintaining that there should be no access at all. So that under the Matrimonial Causes Rules 1977 in, I suppose 95 per cent of cases involving children the registrar's jurisdiction has been expressly limited. Then by some extraordinary oversight RSC Ord 90, r 12 purports to give a registrar jurisdiction to make an order for care and control in wardship proceedings. That is something of which I have never heard in the whole of my experience. I can understand the learned deputy district registrar in this case being misled by the rule, if he was aware of it. There is a footnote in The Supreme Court Practice[2] which says that this generally will be a matter for a judge save where the parties consent to the order. This ambiguity ought to be cleared up as soon as convenient by the rules committee. Otherwise I agree with what Roskill LJ has said.

Appeal allowed.

Solicitors: *Bindman & Partners*, agents for *Allan Henderson, Beecham & Lee*, Newcastle-upon-Tyne (for the mother); *Stanford & Lambert*, Newcastle-upon-Tyne (for the grandmother).

A S Virdi Esq   Barrister.

---

1   SI 1977 No 344
2   1976, vol 1, para 90/12/1, p 1312

a

W T Ramsay Ltd v Inland Revenue Commissioners

CHANCERY DIVISION

GOULDING J

b 22nd, 23rd FEBRUARY, 2nd MARCH 1978

*Capital gains tax – Disposal of assets – Debt – Debt on a security – Security – Need for docu-
ment or certificate issued by debtor – Loan by taxpayer company to subsidiary – Loan not
secured on assets of subsidiary – Subsidiary not issuing document or certificate constituting
marketable security – Whether loan a 'debt on a security' – Finance Act 1965, Sch 7, paras*

c *5(3)(b), 11(1).*

The taxpayer company, having made a large capital gain from the sale of a farm,
entered into a tax avoidance scheme to create an allowable loss to offset that gain. In
pursuance of the scheme, on 23rd February 1973, the taxpayer company acquired the
whole of the issued shares of C Ltd, a specially incorporated investment company, for
about £185,000. By a letter of the same date the taxpayer company offered to make two
d loans('loan L1' and 'loan L2') to C Ltd, each of £218,750, repayable at par after 30 and
31 years respectively. C Ltd was entitled to repay the loans earlier at par or marketable
value, whichever was the higher, and was obliged to do so if it went into liquidation.
Both loans carried interest at 11 per cent, but the taxpayer company had the right,
exercisable on one occasion only, to decrease the interest rate on one of the loans and
to increase correspondingly the interest rate on the other. The offer was accepted
e orally by C Ltd and later the oral acceptance was evidenced by a statutory declaration made by a director of C Ltd. The taxpayer company then paid a total of £437,500
to C Ltd. On 2nd March 1973 the taxpayer company reduced the interest rate on
loan L1 to zero and increased the rate on loan L2 to 22 per cent, and sold loan L2 to a
finance company at its approximate market value of £391,481. In due course, after
further loan and share transactions, loan L1 was repaid at par, and the taxpayer
f company incurred a capital loss of about £175,000 in respect of the shares. Loan L2
was repaid at a premium. In computing its corporation tax for the accounting period
ended 31st May 1973, the taxpayer company claimed that loan L2, not being a debt
evidenced in a document as a security, was not a 'debt on a security' within paras
11(1)[a] and 5(3)(b)[b] of Sch 7 to the Finance Act 1965, and accordingly the capital profit
of £172,731 arising on the sale thereof was not a chargeable gain. The Special Com-
g missioners rejected the taxpayer company's claim, holding that the words 'on a
security' referred to the quality of the debt; that if the debt was of a quality with
which a document or written evidence of title was normally associated, the absence
of such a document or evidence did not render the debt any the less a debt on a
security; and that loan L2 being such a debt, the gain arising on the sale thereof was
h not exempt from liability to corporation tax. The taxpayer company appealed.

Held – There could be no 'debt on a security' within para 11 of Sch 7 to the 1965 Act
unless there was a 'security' within the meaning and for the purposes of para 5 of that
schedule. The essential feature of a security, in the context of para 5, was a document or a certificate issued by the debtor which would represent a marketable
security or which would enable it to be dealt in and, if necessary, converted into
j shares or other securities. No such document had been issued by C Ltd to the taxpayer
company as security for the loans. Accordingly loan L2 was not a 'debt on a security',
within para 11(1) of Sch 7 to the 1965 Act, and the gain accruing to the taxpayer com-

---

a Paragraph 11(1) is set out at p 330 *a* and *b*, post
b Paragraph 5(3) is set out at p 330 *c* and *d*, post

pany on the sale thereof was not within the charge to tax by virtue of that paragraph. The appeal would therefore be allowed (see p 338 e to h and p 339 a and b, post).   a

Dicta of the Lord President (Lord Emslie) and of Lord Wilberforce in *Aberdeen Construction Group Ltd v Inland Revenue Comrs* [1977] STC at 309 and [1978] 1 All ER at 968 applied.

Notes
For the treatment of a debt on a security for the purposes of capital gains tax, see   b
5 Halsbury's Laws (4th Edn) para 104.

For the Finance Act 1965, Sch 7, paras 5 and 11, see 34 Halsbury's Statutes (3rd Edn) 953, 956.

Cases referred to in judgment
Aberdeen Construction Group Ltd v Inland Revenue Comrs [1978] 1 All ER 962, [1978] 2   c
WLR 648, [1978] STC 127, HL; varying [1977] STC 302, CS.
Agricultural Mortgage Corpn Ltd v Inland Revenue Comrs [1978] 1 All ER 248, [1978]
2 WLR 230, [1978] STC 11, CA.
Cleveleys Investment Trust Co v Inland Revenue Comrs 1971 SC 233, 47 Tax Cas 300,
50 ATC 230, [1971] TR 205, CS, Digest (Cont Vol D) 482, 1453b.
Reed International Ltd v Inland Revenue Comrs [1975] 3 All ER 218, [1976] AC 336, [1975] 3   d
WLR 413, [1975] STC 427, 54 ATC 238, [1975] TR 197, HL, Digest (Cont Vol D) 100,
8871b.

Case stated
1. At a meeting of the Commissioners for the Special Purposes of the Income Tax Acts held on the 19th, 20th and 21st January 1976 W T Ramsay Ltd ('the taxpayer   e
company') appealed against an assessment to corporation tax in the sum of £176,552
for the period ended 31st May 1973.

2. Shortly stated the question for decision was whether by means of a scheme known as 'the capital loss scheme' the taxpayer company had created a capital loss in respect of a transaction in shares in Caithmead Ltd.

3. Mr N D Pilbrow, a chartered accountant and managing director of Dovercliff   f
Consultants Ltd, gave evidence before the commissioners.

[Paragraph 4 listed the documents proved or admitted before the commissioners.]

5. As a result of the evidence both oral and documentary adduced before the commissioners they found the following facts proved or admitted: (1) The taxpayer company was incorporated in the United Kingdom on 7th July 1961 and was at all material times resident in the United Kingdom and farming at Scotton, Lincolnshire,   g
on property of which (until 6th November 1972) it owned the freehold. In the 12 month accounting period ended 31st May 1973 the taxpayer company sold the freehold and took a lease of the farm from the purchaser, making a capital profit of £192,710. That resulted in chargeable gains of £187,977 (before deducting any allowable losses). (2) In order to create a capital loss to set off against this capital gain the taxpayer company embarked on a scheme to create two new assets one of which,   h
being exempt from capital gains tax, would be contrived to increase at the expense of the other which was not so exempt. The latter would then be extinguished with the intention of creating a loss. All the following steps were taken in pursuance of a scheme summarised in a letter to the taxpayer company from Dovercliff Consultants Ltd ('Dovercliff') dated 23rd February 1973 as follows:

'Dear Sirs   i

'Exempt Debt/Capital Loss Scheme ("the Scheme")
'We now enclose the joint Written Opinion of Tax Counsel Mr George Graham QC and Mr Andrew Park together with Company Counsel, Mr Michael Wheeler QC's opinion.

'This document is sent and the information set out hereunder is furnished to you subject to and in accordance in all respects with the terms of your written undertaking to us dated the 23rd day of February 1973. It is essential both from our point of view in order to protect the Scheme and from your point of view to maximize the chances of success of the Scheme, that it suffers the minimum of exposure and that the implementation of the Scheme is carried out through our offices or those of our duly authorised representatives.

'The enclosure to this letter sets out the detailed steps to be taken to implement the Scheme. These however can be briefly summarised as under (which will be subject to minor variations in the case of a corporate taxpayer):—(a) The taxpayer ("T") acquires a company ("X Limited") and appoints himself and two nominees as directors. For the convenience of the Scheme and in certain circumstances to comply with the financing requirements of the Scheme, a representative of this company will be one of the nominated directors. (b) The subscriber shares are allotted to T and his nominees. (c) X Limited makes a rights issue, the rights shares being payable as to £5 upon application and the balance of the subscription price being payable on call. (d) T then offers to make two loans to X Limited ("L1 and L2") L1 being repayable on demand at the expiration of 30 years and L2 being repayable on demand at the expiration of 31 years, in each case at par. X Limited will be at liberty to repay either of the loans at any time and is obliged to do so if it goes into liquidation and the terms of the loans are that if either of them is repaid prematurely by X Limited; the amounts to be repaid will be whichever is the higher of the face value of the loan or the market value of the loan on the assumption that it would remain outstanding for the full period. (e) Each loan will carry interest at the rate of 11% per annum payable quarterly and T reserves the right, exercisable on one occasion only and only while both L1 and L2 remain in his beneficial ownership, to decrease the interest rate on one of the loans and to increase correspondingly the interest rate on the other loan. (f) T will after receiving one payment of interest on both the loans exercise the right reserved to him and will direct that the rate of interest on L1 should be reduced to nil and that the rate of interest on L2 should be correspondingly increased to 22% per annum. (g) Following this, X Limited will call up the amount of capital outstanding on the 98 shares issued to T by way of rights. (h) T will then sell L2 to a finance company ("F") for its market value, less a discount equal to 0.5% thereof, and contemporaneously therewith and conditional thereon will grant an option to F to purchase at market value either or both of L1 and the shares in X Limited, such option to be exercisable at any time while L2 remains outstanding in F's beneficial ownership and then only if X Limited is asked by F to redeem L2 and declines to do so within 14 days of such request. The option will contain undertakings by T that the assets of X Limited will not be depleted, to secure the appointment to the Board of X Limited of a director nominated by F and to alter the bank mandate of X Limited so that X Limited's bank account cannot be operated without the signature of the director nominated by F. (j) U Limited (a wholly-owned subsidiary of X Limited) will then purchase L2 from F and the option granted by T to F will lapse. (k) U Limited will then go into a members' voluntary liquidation and the liquidator will distribute its sole asset (L2) to X Limited. (l) X Limited will then go into a members' voluntary liquidation and L1 will be repaid to T at par. (m) The value of T's shareholding in X Limited will as a result of the repayment of L2 at a premium and the repayment of L1 at par be reduced, thereby giving rise to a capital loss. (n) T will then exchange the shares of X Limited with Z Limited for the allotment and issue by Z Limited of its loan stock of nominal value equal to the market value of the shares in X Limited. (o) T will then sell for cash Z Limited's loan stock to H Limited for its nominal value and the Scheme so far as T is concerned will have been completed.

'We should point out the following: (i) The Scheme is a pure tax avoidance scheme and has no commercial justification insofar as there is no prospect of T making a profit; indeed he is certain to make a loss representing the cost *a* of undertaking the Scheme. (ii) Nevertheless, every transaction in the Scheme will be genuinely carried through, and will in fact be exactly what it purports to be. (iii) Although the Scheme is a scheme in the sense of a preconceived series of steps, T should understand before deciding to embark upon the Scheme, that there is no binding arrangement or undertaking to the effect that once the first step has been taken, then every other step must be taken in its appointed order. *b* It is reasonable for T to assume that all steps will in practice be carried out, but as a matter of law, T is free to withdraw at any time, and so are all the other contemplated parties to the Scheme. If any party does withdraw, T will have no redress. (iv) It will be essential for T to provide the necessary finances for the share subscriptions and the loans, either out of his own resources or by entering into suitable borrowing arrangements. *c*

'Our fee is 8% of the required capital loss; of this 6⅞% is payable as soon as T embarks on the scheme, the balance being incorporated in the profit realised by the purchaser of L2; if T decides voluntarily not to carry through the entire scheme, then no refund will be made. However if any party over whom T has no control decides that it does not wish to embark upon the scheme or having so embarked, withdraws voluntarily, then a refund of the fee will be made, less a *d* deduction in respect of the costs incurred.

'Finally, we would point out that we do not undertake any enforceable obligation to procure the implementation of the entire scheme.

'There is no guarantee that the anticipated tax relief will result from the implementation of the scheme and we can accept no responsibility or liability whatsoever for any expense or loss incurred as a result of the scheme being embarked *e* upon. The decision to enter the scheme should be taken on the advice of T's accountant, solicitor or other professional adviser.

'Please sign and return the enclosed copy of the letter by way of acknowledgement that you accept fully the points raised therein.

'Yours faithfully . . .'

f

(3) On 23rd February 1973 the taxpayer company applied for and was allotted two preferred ordinary shares in a newly formed investment company named Caithmead Ltd ('Caithmead') at a cost of £40. Caithmead had been incorporated on 16th October 1972. On the same day, Caithmead made a rights issue of 34 preferred ordinary shares for each of the two shares already issued; the terms were a premium of £2,719·50 per share, £5 payable on application, the balance on call. On the same *g* day, the taxpayer company resolved to take up its rights and make the required payment of £340 in respect of the 68 shares in question, and the said shares were duly issued and allotted. Consequently the taxpayer company was the beneficial owner of all the preferred ordinary shares of Caithmead. (4) On the same day (23rd February 1973), the taxpayer company offered to make two loans ('L1' and 'L2') to Caithmead, each of £218,750. In preparation for this, and also for the call on its shares, the tax- *h* payer company had earlier negotiated for itself a loan facility with a bank, Slater Walker Ltd. The security provisions for this facility included assignments of the right to repayment of L1 and L2. The terms of L1 and L2 were as follows: (a) L1 repayment after 30 years at par: L2 repayment after 31 years at par: except that Caithmead would be entitled to make earlier repayment if desired and would be obliged to do so if it went into liquidation; (b) if either loan were repaid before its maturity *j* date, then it had to be repaid at par or at its market value on the assumption that it was to be repaid only upon its maturity date—whichever was the higher; (c) both loans to carry interest at 11 per cent per annum payable quarterly on 1st March, 1st June, 1st September, 1st December each year, the first such payment on 1st March 1973; (d) the taxpayer company was to have the right, exercisable on one occasion

only, and then only if it was still the beneficial owner of both L1 and L2, to decrease
the interest rate on one of the loans and to increase correspondingly the interest
rate on the other. The offer having been made, by letter, was accepted orally by
Caithmead on the same day. The oral acceptance was evidenced by a statutory declaration made on 23rd February 1973 by George William Livingstone, a director
of Caithmead. On the same day, the taxpayer company paid £437,500 to Caithmead
out of a loan facility provided by Slater Walker Ltd. (5) On 2nd March 1973, the taxpayer company, having received from Caithmead an interest payment of £452·22 in
respect of L1 and L2, exercised its right to reduce the interest rate on L1 to zero and to
increase the interest rate on L2 to 22 per cent and it so notified Caithmead, by letter.
Later on the same day, Caithmead called on the taxpayer company to pay the balance
of £184,654 due in respect of the 68 preferred ordinary shares. The taxpayer company
paid the said balance. (6) Following the above, and on the same day, the taxpayer company made a written offer to Masterdene Finance Ltd ('Masterdene'), a finance company resident in the United Kingdom, being a wholly-owned subsidiary of Dovercliff,
to sell L2 to it at a discount of five per cent plus £300 from a previously ascertained
market value of £393,750. By a separate letter the taxpayer company made a second
offer which was conditional on acceptance of the first offer; that was to grant to Masterdene an option to purchase from the taxpayer company at specified prices based on
market values, L1 and the taxpayer company's holding in Caithmead. Such option
would only be exercisable in the event that Caithmead declined to redeem L2 when so
requested by Masterdene, at a time when Masterdene was still the beneficial owner
of L2. (This option was never exercised.) Masterdene accepted both offers orally
on the same day, and paid the sum of £391,481 to the taxpayer company. It also gave
notice to Caithmead of this assignment of L2 and of the grant of the option. (7)
Meanwhile, on 23rd February 1973, Caithmead had made an application to Caithrole
Ltd ('Caithrole'), an investment company incorporated on 17th October 1972, to
acquire its entire authorised share capital of 100 ordinary shares at a premium of
£3,946·13 each, the price being payable as to 50p per share on application and the
balance on 9th March. That application had been accepted on that same day and the
sum of £50 duly paid. Now, on 2nd March, the directors of Caithmead having considered that a resolution to wind up Caithmead would be passed if the remaining
steps were taken in implementation of the proposed scheme, deposed to a declaration
of solvency in respect of Caithmead; the directors of Caithrole, after similar consideration regarding a future winding up resolution in respect of Caithrole, deposed
to a declaration of solvency in respect of Caithrole. (8) On 9th March payment
was made by Caithmead to Caithrole of the balance of £394,663 owing on the Caithrole shares, and Masterdene made a written offer to Caithrole to sell L2 at a price of
£394,673. On the same day, this offer was orally accepted, payment was made by
Caithrole to Masterdene and Caithrole notified Caithmead of this assignment of L2.
This assignment caused the former option (referred to in (6) above) to lapse. (9)
On the same day (9th March): (a) an extraordinary general meeting of Caithrole
was held and a winding up resolution was passed by Caithrole. (b) Mr N P Pilbrow
was appointed liquidator of Caithrole and as such liquidator he at once wrote to the
directors of Caithmead pointing out that Caithmead was indebted to Caithrole,
(i e L2) but suggesting that since Caithmead was entitled to all the assets of Caithrole
(there being no creditors), the liquidation distribution might be effected by simply
extinguishing the indebtedness both as to capital and interest. The directors of
Caithmead gave their written agreement to this forthwith. (c) Immediately following
steps (a) and (b) above, an extraordinary general meeting of Caithmead was held
and a winding up resolution was passed by Caithmead. (d) Mr N D Pilbrow was appointed liquidator of Caithmead and as such liquidator Mr Pilbrow notified the taxpayer company that L1 had become repayable at par and instructions were given to
Caithmead's bankers to pay the sum of £218,750 to the taxpayer company. (10)
Following the above, the taxpayer company approached T J Nicholas Holdings Ltd,

which had a small holding of deferred shares in Caithmead, and offered to sell its 70 preferred ordinary shares. By a written reply, T J Nicholas Holdings Ltd offered to take the said shares in exchange for its own eight per cent unsecured loan stock 2027, the terms being £134·10 of such stock for each Caithmead share, making a total of £9,387. The taxpayer company accepted this offer on the same day and at once executed a transfer of its Caithmead shares in favour of T J Nicholas Holdings Ltd, which company thereupon notified the liquidator of Caithmead accordingly. T J Nicholas Holdings Ltd issued the said loan stock to the taxpayer company. It was common ground that the 'roll-over' provisions applied to the last mentioned transaction: Sch 7, para 4, to the Finance Act 1965. (11) On the same day (9th March), the taxpayer company disposed of its T J Nicholas Holdings Ltd issue of loan stock by selling the same to Guardclose Ltd in consideration of a cash sum of £9,387, which payment was made to the credit of the taxpayer company's banking account. (12) T J Nicholas Holdings Ltd was the wholly-owned subsidiary of Guardclose Ltd which was not connected with other companies herein mentioned, its shares being in the beneficial ownership of a Mr T J Nicholas. (13) Mr Pilbrow gave evidence before us from which we find the following facts. He was managing director of Dovercliff and conducted their business at the material times. The principal activity of Dovercliff was the operation of the capital loss scheme. The taxpayer company had been introduced to Dovercliff by an estate agent. Masterdene was a wholly-owned subsidiary of Dovercliff and he was a director thereof. He became liquidator of Caithmead and Caithrole when they went into liquidation. Apart from the transaction referred to above and in the documents listed in para 4 of this case there were no other transactions entered into in connection with the capital loss scheme. The financial benefits to Dovercliff consisted of the sums mentioned in the letter from Dovercliff set out in para 5 above. Masterdene made a profit of 1⅛ per cent of the capital loss to be manufactured by the scheme less some small expenses. He agreed that a purchaser such as the taxpayer company bought the capital loss scheme as a whole and entered it in anticipation that all transactions would be completely envisaged by the letter from Dovercliff to the taxpayer company setting out the scheme but so far as it was possible to do so each step in the scheme was made independent as envisaged by that letter. The accounts of Caithmead had been prepared on the wrong basis initially for the year 1973. The share premium account was not correct. Instead of the figure of £9,041, the current figure to be included in the share premium account was £184,964 and he produced amended accounts on this basis.

6. It was contended on behalf of the taxpayer company: (a) that by the letter from Dovercliff to the taxpayer company it was made an express condition of the scheme that each step would be independent of other steps; and that once the first step had been taken the taxpayer company was free to withdraw at any time and so were all the other contemplated parties to the scheme. Every transaction in the scheme was a genuine transaction and took effect in law accordingly; (b) that the consideration of £184,654 paid for the calls on the 68 Caithmead shares was a proper commercial consideration; (c) that the loans L1 and L2 were not 'debts on a security' and accordingly when they were disposed of no chargeable gain accrued: Sch 7, para 11, to the 1965 Act; and (d) that the taxpayer company had incurred a loss in respect of the transaction in the Caithmead shares being the difference between the cost (which was wholly and exclusively incurred for the acquisition) and the disposal of the T J Nicholas Holdings Ltd loan stock.

7. It was contended on behalf of the Crown: (a) that, having regard to the admitted artificial nature of the scheme and the circular movement of the moneys provided by Slater Walker Ltd, the consideration paid for the Caithmead shares was not 'consideration in money's worth given . . . wholly and exclusively for the acquisition of the [shares]', but was given wholly or in substantial part for the implementation of the tax avoidance scheme; (b) that alternatively the loans L1 and L2 were 'debts on a security' within Sch 7, para 5, to the 1965 Act. They were accordingly not exempted by Sch 7, para 11; alternatively (c) that the scheme necessarily involved

such abuses of the Companies Act as to be ineffective: for example it was inevitable and intended from its formation that Caithmead's capital would be returned to the members in an unauthorised form; alternatively (d) that the entire scheme was artificially created to manufacture a 'loss' for capital gains tax purposes and was ineffective for tax purposes.

[Paragraph 8 listed the cases[1] cited to the commissioners.]

9. The commissioners who heard the appeal took time to consider their decision and gave it in writing on 30th January 1976 as follows:

'1. The object of the tax avoidance scheme ... was, as the [taxpayer company] admitted, to manufacture a loss which would reduce a chargeable gain of £187,977 which had accrued to the [taxpayer company] on the sale of a freehold farm.

'2. (a) We deal first with the Crown's contention that the scheme should be looked at as a whole; that (ignoring the profit taken by Masterdene Finance Limited on the sale of L2 and small sums of tax and interest paid) moneys provided by Slater Walker Limited on the terms of the Facility Letter went round in a circle; that when the scheme had been implemented the [taxpayer company] owned nothing that it did not own before, and so far as that company was concerned the scheme achieved nothing inasmuch as it produced nothing. Moneys paid out by the [taxpayer company] were not therefore paid wholly and exclusively for the acquisition of any asset and were therefore not allowable deductions within paragraph 4(1) Schedule 6 Finance Act 1965. All that the [taxpayer company] acquired was what was to be found in A2 of the agreed bundle. (b) We take the view that it is not open to us to ignore the several steps in the scheme and so treat it as ineffective. The requisite payments were duly made; the companies, Caithmead Limited and Caithrole Limited, were properly incorporated and duly issued their shares; the two loans L1 and L2 were actually paid and the money banked. Each step in the scheme was fully documented and, although the scheme was such that the party interested in the next step was in a position to secure that that step would in fact follow, there was no binding arrangement between the parties that once the first step had been taken all the other steps would necessarily follow. Capital gains tax is concerned with assets, their acquisition and disposal. In our view the shares in Caithmead and Caithrole, and the two loans, were all assets for the purposes of the tax and moneys paid under the scheme for their acquisition were wholly and exclusively so paid. The relevant statutory provisions must accordingly be applied to the several dealings with those assets as though those dealing were independent of one another. We reject the Crown's first contention.

'3. We proceed to consider the matter on the basis that each step must be taken at its face value and to have taken effect as it purported to take effect. (a) In view of the decision in *Commissioners of Inland Revenue v Montgomery*[2] it was

---

1   *Bentleys, Stokes & Lowless v Beeson* [1952] 2 All ER 82, CA; *Black Nominees Ltd v Nicol (Inspector of Taxes)* [1975] STC 372; *British India Steam Navigation Co Ltd v Leslie* (1881) 7 QBD 165; *Broderip v Salomon* [1895] 2 Ch 323, rvsd sub nom *Salomon v Salomon & Co Ltd* [1897] AC 22, [1895-9] All ER Rep 33; *Cleveleys Investment Trust Co v Inland Revenue Comrs* 1971 SC 233, 47 Tax Cas 300, CS; *Cleveleys Investment Trust Co v Inland Revenue Comrs (No 2)* [1975] STC 457; *Inland Revenue Comrs v Europa Oil (NZ) Ltd* [1971] AC 760, PC; *Inland Revenue Comrs v Montgomery* [1975] 1 All ER 664, [1975] Ch 266, [1975] STC 182; *Johnson v Jewitt (Inspector of Taxes)* (1961) 40 Tax Cas 231, CA; *Lemon v Austin Friars Investment Trust Ltd* [1926] Ch 1, [1925] All ER Rep 255, CA; *Littlewoods Mail Order Stores Ltd v McGregor (Inspector of Taxes)* [1969] 3 All ER 855, [1969] 1 WLR 1241, 45 Tax Cas 519, CA; *Ransom (Inspector of Taxes) v Higgs* [1974] 3 All ER 949, [1974] 1 WLR 1594, [1974] STC 539, HL; *Westminster (Duke) v Inland Revenue Comrs* [1936] AC 1, [1935] All ER Rep 259, 19 Tax Cas 490, HL.

2   [1975] 1 All ER 664, [1975] Ch 266, [1975] STC 182

not open to the Crown to contend that the moneys paid to the [taxpayer company]
by Masterdene for L2 were, having regard to the scheme as a whole, derived *a*
from the shares in Caithmead and that there was therefore a deemed disposal
of assets within section 22(3) Finance Act 1965. (b) It was agreed between the
parties that the price paid by Masterdene for L2 was equal to the market value
of L2 and that no question regarding the value of L2 was therefore in issue under
Section 22(4) Finance Act 1965. (c) The question which we therefore have to
decide is whether L1 and L2, and in particular L2, are "debts on a security" *b*
within paragraphs 11(1) and 5(3)(b) Schedule 7 Finance Act 1965.
     '4. (a) L1 and L2 came into existence as a result of a written offer made by the
[taxpayer company] to Caithmead on 23 February 1973 and orally accepted by
Caithmead on the same day. The oral acceptance was recorded in a statutory
declaration made by George William Livingstone, a director of Caithmead, also
on the same day. (b) The Crown contended that L2 was "stock or similar *c*
security" within paragraph 5(3)(b) Schedule 7 Finance Act 1965 and in particular
that, as it was evidenced by the above mentioned statutory declaration of
Mr Livingstone, there was a sufficient instrument to constitute a "debenture"
within the meaning attributed to that word by Lindley J in *British India Steam
Navigation Company v Commissioners of Inland Revenue*[1]. The statutory declaration
was not however expressed to be made on behalf of Caithmead and we doubt *d*
whether it can be construed as an acknowledgment of indebtedness by that
company. Nor could we treat the written acknowledgment by Caithmead of
the alteration of the interest rates on L1 and L2 as written acknowledgments of
those debts. (c) For the [taxpayer company] reliance was placed in particular
on the observation of Lord Migdale in his dissenting judgment in *Cleveleys
Investment Trust Co v Commissioners of Inland Revenue*[2] that "debt on a security" *e*
means debt evidenced in a document as a security and it was contended that there
was no such document in the present case. However, no views were expressed on
the question by The Lord President (Clyde) or by Lord Johnston. Lord Cameron
observed that once the terms of paragraph 5 were examined it became abundantly plain that the word "security" in paragraph 11(1) is a substantive and
refers to those securities which are or can be subject to a conversion. Lord *f*
Cameron did not say whether a document was essential to the creation of a
security. In *Cleveleys's* case[2] the loan in question was of a temporary character
only and was held to be an integral part of a transaction whereunder (inter alia)
the amount advanced was to be used to acquire shares in the borrowing company.
In the present case, the arrangement is very different. L1 and L2 were not loans,
pure and simple. They were expressed to be repayable at par after 30 years and *g*
31 years respectively and meanwhile were to carry interest at 11%. The borrowing company, Caithmead, was to be entitled to make earlier repayment, if
desired, at par or market value whichever should be the higher and would be
obliged so to repay if it went into liquidation. Caithmead was an investment company and the [taxpayer company] gave a warranty to Masterdene that it had not
traded. In our view the loans were intended to and did form part of the perma- *h*
nent loan and capital structure of Caithmead. They were so treated in the Report
and Accounts 1973 presented to the company on 8 February 1974 after it had gone
into liquidation, L2 being referred to in the Balance Sheet as at 9 March 1973 as
"Unsecured Loan 2004." Applying the test favoured by Lord Cameron in *Cleveleys's*
case[2], and having regard to the context in which the word "security" appears, we
are of the opinion that the unsecured loans, L1 and L2, being part of Caithmead's *j*
loan capital structure, were of a type which, unlike short term or trading debts,
are investments and could be the subject of a conversion such as is contemplated

---

1   (1881) 7 QBD 165
2   1971 SC 233, 47 Tax Cas 300

by paragraph 5(1) of Schedule 7 and in respect of which it would have been appropriate to issue a document evidencing title to the loan. It does not seem to us that Parliament could have intended that the question should be dependent upon the formality of the issue of a certificate or other evidence of title. Issue of such evidence could readily be dispensed within many cases without prejudicing the rights of the parties or altering the quality of the loan. In our opinion the words "on a security" refer to the quality of the debt and if that debt is of a quality with which a document or written evidence of title is normally associated the absence of such document or evidence does not render the debt any the less a debt on a security. We therefore conclude that the loans were "loan stock or similar security" of Caithmead within paragraph 5(3)(b) and that L2 was a "debt on a security". In our opinion therefore a chargeable gain accrued on the disposal on 2 March 1973 of L2 by the [taxpayer company] to Masterdene Finance Limited.

'5. We are unable to accept the Crown's contention that the scheme was in law an abuse of the Companies Acts and that the several steps comprised therein were of no effect.

'6. We therefore dismiss the appeal in principle and adjourn it for the figures to be agreed.'

10. Figures were agreed between the parties and on 12th October 1976 the commissioners adjusted the assessment accordingly.

11. The taxpayer company immediately after the determination of the appeal declared its dissatisfaction therewith as being erroneous in point of law and on 14th October 1976 required the commissioners to state a case for the opinion of the High Court pursuant to the Taxes Management Act 1970, s 56.

12. The questions of law for the opinion of the court were: (a) whether on the true construction of the expressions 'security' and 'the debt on a security' in the Finance Act 1965, Sch 7, paras 5(3)(b) and 11(1) and in the events that happened, the loan L2 was 'the debt on a security'; (b) whether a chargeable gain accrued to the taxpayer company on its disposing of L2 to Masterdene (para 5(6) above).

D C Potter QC and *David C Milne* for the taxpayer company.
Peter Millett QC and *Brian Davenport* for the Crown.

Cur adv vult

2nd March.   **GOULDING J** read the following judgment: This is an appeal from a decision of the Special Commissioners whereby they dismissed an appeal by a company called W T Ramsay Ltd ('the taxpayer company') against an assessment to corporation tax for an accounting period ending on 31st May 1973 in the sum of £176,522.

In circumstances which I need not describe, the taxpayer company took part in an elaborate series of transactions, a great part of which I need not recount, with the sole object of reducing its liability to corporation tax in respect of chargeable gains. The Special Commissioners accepted the successive operations as real and effective transactions. It has not been argued before me that in so doing they committed any error of law. In the course of carrying out its plan to escape tax, the taxpayer company lent a sum of £218,750 to a company named Caithmead Ltd, in which the taxpayer company also became interested as a shareholder. At a later date, and after some intermediate transactions, the taxpayer company sold the debt of Caithmead Ltd to a third party, receiving £391,481 as its price. The taxpayer company thus made a gross capital profit of £172,731. The only question before me is whether the Special Commissioners were right in law in holding that such profit, subject to any allowable deductions, was a chargeable gain. Corporation tax for this purpose follows the principles applying for capital gains tax, and it is common ground that the question depends on the interpretation of two paragraphs in Sch 7 to the Finance Act 1965 and on their proper application to the facts of this case.

I will read the paragraphs at once, but I shall defer an examination of their meaning until I have stated the facts in more detail. The first is paragraph 11(1):

'Where a person incurs a debt to another, whether in sterling or in some other currency, no chargeable gain shall accrue to that (that is the original) creditor or his personal representative or legatee on the disposal of the debt, except in the case of the debt on a security (as defined in paragraph 5 of this Schedule).'

Paragraph 5 of Sch 7 deals with the conversion of securities. Sub-paragraph (3) thereof contains the relevant provisions as to interpretation, and I had better read the whole of it:

'For the purposes of this paragraph—(a) "conversion of securities" includes—(i) a conversion of securities of a company into shares in the company, and (ii) a conversion at the option of the holder of the securities converted as an alternative to the redemption of those securities for cash, and (iii) any exchange of securities effected in pursuance of any enactment (including an enactment passed after this Act) which provides for the compulsory acquisition of any shares or securities and the issue of securities or other securities instead, and (b) "security" includes any loan stock or similar security whether of the Government of the United Kingdom or of any other government, or of any public or local authority in the United Kingdom or elsewhere, or of any company, and whether secured or unsecured.'

It should be remembered in construing the 1965 Act that the same tests which distinguish a gain as a chargeable gain are used to distinguish a loss as an allowable loss.

Next I must recite the documentary evidence regarding the origin of the debt in question and its subsequent history. The first document is a letter from the taxpayer company to Caithmead Ltd dated 23rd February 1973. I need not read it, for its terms are repeated in the next document, being minutes of a directors' meeting of Caithmead Ltd held on the same day. The loan by the taxpayer company with which this case is concerned is referred to in the letter and the minutes as 'L2'. I shall read the minutes:

'1. The Minutes of the last Meeting of the Board of Directors were read and IT WAS RESOLVED that the same be confirmed.

'2. The Board considered a letter of offer of two loans made to the Company by [the taxpayer company] upon the terms and conditions set out in the aforesaid letter which terms and conditions are summarised hereunder: (a) Each loan (hereinafter referred to as 'L1' and 'L2' respectively) is to be for the sum of £218,750. (b) The lender is to be entitled to demand repayment of L1 at par 30 years from the date of the letter of offer and of L2, also at par, 31 years from the date of the letter of offer. (c) The Company is to be at liberty to repay either loan at any earlier time, and is obliged to do so if it goes into liquidation before the right to demand repayment of either of the loans accrues to the lender. (d) If either L1 or L2 is repaid prematurely (i e before 30 years in the case of L1 and before 31 years in the case of L2 computed in each case from the date of the letter of offer) the amount to be repaid will be whichever is the higher of: (i) the face value of the loan (£218,750) or (ii) the market value of the loan on the assumption that it would remain outstanding for the full period of 30 or 31 years. Each of L1 and L2 is to carry interest at the rate of 11% per annum payable quarterly on March 1, June 1, September 1, and December 1, the first of such payments to be made on March 1, 1973. (e) The lender reserves the right to itself, exercisable on one occasion only and only while both L1 and L2 remain in its beneficial ownership, to decrease the interest rate on one of the loans and to increase correspondingly the interest rate on the other loan. Due consideration having been given to the terms upon which L1 and L2 were to be made available to the Company IT WAS RESOLVED that [the taxpayer company] be notified orally by Mr G. W. Livingstone that its offer is accepted.

[I interrupt my reading to mention that Mr Livingstone was a director of Caithmead Ltd present at the meeting. The minutes continue:] The meeting was then adjourned so that Mr G. W. Livingstone could notify [the taxpayer company] orally of the Company's acceptance. After the adjournment:

'3. The meeting was then joined by Mr Robert Bicket Ramsay and Mr G. Livingstone informed the Meeting that he had communicated orally to Mr R. B. Ramsay of [the taxpayer company] the Company's acceptance of L1 and L2 upon the terms set forth in [the taxpayer company's] letter to the Company. Mr R. B. Ramsay confirmed that he had received such oral acceptance on behalf of [the taxpayer company] and produced a letter to Slater Walker Limited who had agreed to make the necessary finance available to [the taxpayer company] to pay to the Company's bank account an amount of £437,500 representing L1 and L2.

'4. Consideration was then given as to how best to invest the funds now available to the Company. The Company considered investing part of the aggregate total of L1 and L2 amounting to £394,713 in acquiring the entire authorised share capital of Caithrole Limited by subscribing for the 100 shares of £1 each at a premium of £3946·13, the price being payable as to £0·50 per share on application and the balance on the 9th day of March 1973. It was resolved that an application be made for such shares and that the Secretary despatch a written application therefor and to instruct the Company's bankers to remit the sum of £50 immediately to Caithrole Limited's bankers.

'5. The Board was undecided as to how to invest the balance of the monies available to it and accordingly it was resolved that the sum of £437,400 be placed on temporary deposit with the Company's bankers pending a decision as to a more permanent form of investment.

'6. There being no other business to be transacted, the Meeting closed.'

On the same day, as appears from other minutes, the directors of the taxpayer company instructed the taxpayer company's banker, Slater Walker Ltd, to transfer £437,500 to the credit of Caithmead Ltd. On the same day also Mr Livingstone made a statutory declaration recording what had taken place.

Some days later, on 2nd March 1973, a letter was addressed by the taxpayer company to Caithmead Ltd in the following terms:

'Loans L1 and L2. Reference is made to our letter of offer relating to L1 and L2 which was orally accepted by you on the 23rd day of February 1973. In exercise of the right which we reserved unto ourselves under paragraph number 6 of our letter we here by direct that the rate of interest on L1 shall be reduced to nil and that the rate of interest on L2 shall be correspondingly increased to 22%. Kindly acknowledge receipt of this letter and at the same time confirm to us that you will act in accordance with the direction herein contained.'

The desired acknowledgment and confirmation were given by Caithmead Ltd in writing and bear the same date, 2nd March. On that day also Mr R B Ramsay, a director of the taxpayer company, made a statutory declaration on behalf of the taxpayer company exhibiting and identifying copies of the taxpayer company's original letter of 23rd February, Mr Livingstone's statutory declaration and the two letters of 2nd March.

A third letter of the same date was written by the taxpayer company to a company named Masterdene Finance Ltd, which was a subsidiary of Dovercliff Consultants Ltd, the adviser under whose guidance the taxpayer company was acting throughout this history. It said this:

'We enclose herewith a copy of Mr Robert Bicket Ramsay's Statutory Declaration dated the 2nd day of March, 1973 . . . and your attention is drawn to [the letter of 23rd February from the taxpayer company to Caithmead] and to the loans therein offered to be made which are therein and are hereinafter save where the context otherwise requires referred to as L1 and L2. We are informed that the market value of L2 is £393,750 and we hereby offer to sell to you the benefit of the right to repayment of L2 at that price less a discount of the aggregate of .5% thereof and £300. This offer remains open for acceptance for a period of seven days and thereafter will lapse. L2 is subject to a charge in favour of Slater Walker Limited and we enclose a copy of a letter from the bank undertaking to release its charge upon payment of the amount therein specified. We undertake to use so much of the purchase consideration as the mortgagee requires to release L2 from such charge. We declare that nothing herein contained imposes upon us any obligation to procure the debtor company to repay L2 to you. If you wish to accept this offer on the term set out in this letter please signify your acceptance orally to us and transfer the sum of £391,481 to Slater Walker Limited for the credit of our account with them.'

It appears from subsequent minutes and correspondence that Masterdene Finance Ltd accepted the offer and authorised payment of the purchase money on that same busy Friday, 2nd March 1973.

The sale of L2 by the taxpayer company was a disposal of a debt by the original creditor. Reference to the provisions I have already read from the Finance Act 1965 shows that the profit accruing to the taxpayer company from the sale is not a chargeable gain for tax purposes unless the debt was a 'debt on a security' within the meaning of those provisions. The Special Commissioners upheld the Crown's contention that it was. They expressed themselves as follows:

'For the [taxpayer company] reliance was placed in particular on the observation of Lord Migdale in his dissenting judgment in *Cleveleys Investment Trust Co v Commissioners of Inland Revenue*[1] that "debt on a security" means debt evidenced in a document as a security and it was contended that there was no such document in the present case. However, no views were expressed on the question by The Lord President (Clyde) or by Lord Johnston. Lord Cameron observed that once the terms of paragraph 5 were examined it became abundantly plain that the word "security" in paragraph 11(1) is a substantive and refers to those securities which are or can be subject to a conversion. Lord Cameron did not say whether a document was essential to the creation of a security. In *Cleveleys's* case[1] the loan in question was of a temporary character only and was held to be an integral part of a transaction whereunder (inter alia) the amount advanced was to be used to acquire shares in the borrowing company.

'In the present case, the arrangement is very different. L1 and L2 were not loans, pure and simple. They were expressed to be repayable at par after 30 years and 31 years respectively and meanwhile were to carry interest at 11%. The borrowing company, Caithmead, was to be entitled to make earlier repayment, if desired, at par or market value whichever should be the higher and would be obliged so to repay if it went into liquidation. Caithmead was an investment company and the [taxpayer company] gave a warranty to Masterdene that it had not traded. In our view the loans were intended to and did form part of the permanent loan and capital structure of Caithmead. They were so treated in the Report and Accounts 1973 presented to the Company on 8 February 1974 after it had gone into liquidation, L2 being referred to in the Balance Sheet as at 9 March 1973 as "Unsecured Loan 2004". Applying the test favoured by Lord Cameron in *Cleveleys's* case[1], and having regard to the context in which the word "security" appears, we are of the opinion that the unsecured loans, L1 and L2, being part of Caithmead's loan capital structure, were of a type which, unlike short term or trading debts, are investments and could be the subject of a conversion such as is contemplated by paragraph 5(1) of Schedule 7 and in respect of which it would have been appropriate to issue a document evidencing title to the loan. It does not seem to us that Parliament could have intended that the question should be dependent upon the formality of the issue of a certificate or other evidence of title. Issue of such evidence could readily be dispensed with in many cases without prejudicing the rights of the parties or altering the quality of the loan. In our opinion the words "on a security" refer to the quality of the debt and if that debt is of a quality with which a document or written evidence of title is normally associated the absence of such document or evidence does not render the debt any the less a debt on a security. We therefore conclude that the loans were "loan stock or similar security" of Caithmead within paragraph 5(3)(b) and that L2 was a "debt on a security". In our opinion therefore a chargeable gain accrued on the disposal on 2 March 1973 of L2 by the [taxpayer company] to Masterdene Finance Limited.'

The only authority which has been cited to me on the interpretation of the statutory provisions consists of two Scottish cases. In the first of them, *Cleveleys Investment Trust Co v Inland Revenue Comrs*[1], referred to in the Special Commissioners' decision, the taxpayer was an unlimited company carrying on the business of investing its money in stocks and shares. It contemplated investing in a limited company engaged in manufacturing industry and referred to shortly as 'Falkirk'. To help Falkirk, the taxpayer lent it £25,000 against a bill of exchange payable in a few months' time, a promise to pay interest and an undertaking by Falkirk and its directors to allot 51 per cent of Falkirk's ordinary share capital to the taxpayer on completion of a scheme of capital reconstruction. Those obligations were put into writing and signed by the directors of Falkirk. Falkirk failed, the money was wholly lost and the taxpayer claimed an allowable loss for the purpose of corporation tax.

Before the First Division of the Court of Session the taxpayer succeeded on the ground that the whole arrangement conferred on it an asset (subsequently lost) which was not a mere debt. It had argued in the alternative that the asset was a debt on a security, and two of the learned judges made observations on the meaning of that expression. Lord Migdale, who differed from his fellow judges on the main question, said[2]:

'The word "security" has two meanings. It may refer to some property deposited or made over or some obligation entered into by or on behalf of a person in order to secure his fulfilment of an obligation he has undertaken. Or it may refer to a document held by a creditor as evidence or a guarantee of his right to repayment. (See Shorter Oxford English Dictionary, vol. 2.) I think that the words "the debt on a security" refer to an obligation to pay or repay embodied in a share or stock certificate issued by a government, local authority or company which is evidence of the ownership of the share or stock and so of the right to receive payment. This reading of this section enables me to give some effect to the words "whether secured or unsecured". If I take the words "security" and "secured" as meaning the same thing, these last words, "whether secured or unsecured", have no meaning at all. "The debt on a security" means debt evidenced in a document as a security. I cannot see any similarity between the letter of acceptance or the bill of exchange in this case and loan stock or, for that matter, an unsecured debenture. On any view I cannot see how it can be said that repayment of the debt of £25,000 was secured in any sense. The written acknowledgement of the loan and the bill of exchange may make it quicker for the Appellants to get repayment of their advance, but neither document helps

---

1   1971 SC 233, 47 Tax Cas 300
2   1971 SC 233 at 243, 244, 47 Tax Cas 300 at 315

them to get it or affords them any right against Falkirk over and above its obligation to repay, and neither document would enable Falkirk to go against any third party for payment.'

Lord Cameron said[1]:

'In my opinion there can be no doubt that, if this loss of the money advanced by the Appellant to Falkirk under the arrangement can be treated in isolation as disposal of a debt, and thus as disposal of an asset, part of the Appellant's property, then the Crown must succeed and the decision of the Special Commissioners stand. The argument to the effect that by virtue of the bill of exchange this was a secured debt seems to me irrelevant and without support in the Statute and the passage on which the Appellant relied in Sch. 7, para. 11. If Parliament had meant to designate or distinguish a secured debt in the final phrase of para. 11(1) I find it difficult to see, in the first place, why such a phrase as "the debt on a security" should be used; second, why it should be necessary to give a special and limited meaning to the substantive "security"; and, further, what distinction in substance could be drawn between a debt secured and a debt unsecured to justify exemption from liability in the one case and not in the other on disposal by an original creditor. This difficulty becomes all the more pressing when the definition of the word "security" in para. 5(3) is examined. The use of the words "secured or unsecured" in that sub-paragraph seem to me to demonstrate that, whatever else it may mean, the phrase "the debt on a security" is not a synonym for a secured debt. Once the terms of para. 5 are examined it becomes abundantly plain that the word "security" in para. 11(1) is a substantive and refers to those securities which are or can be subject to a conversion. I would also draw attention to the fact that the word "security" is also defined in para. 6 of Part I of Sch. 11 and in para. 7(1) of that Schedule, and this seems to me to make it very clear that the word "security" as used in para. 11 of Sch. 7 is given precisely that limited and specialised meaning which is stamped upon it by para. 5(3), to which I have already referred.'

That decision was pronounced in 1971. Nearly six years later the Court of Session had to consider the second case, *Aberdeen Construction Group Ltd v Inland Revenue Comrs*[2]. There, the taxpayer, a holding company, had lent large sums of money to a trading subsidiary, referred to shortly as 'Rock Fall'. The loan was unsecured. The taxpayer released it outright as one of the terms of a sale of the entire issued share capital of Rock Fall. A profit accrued to the taxpayer on the sale of the shares, considered in isolation, and it sought (among other arguments) to set off an allowable loss on the loan against the chargeable gain on the shares. The court unanimously rejected that contention, holding that the loan was not a debt on a security, and therefore its disposal could not produce an allowable loss or a chargeable gain.

Lord Emslie, the Lord President, said[3]:

'To be a debt on a security one must have "a security" on which there is a debt. What then is "a security" within the meaning of para 11(1)? Reference to para 5(3) of Sch 7 shows that it is concerned with "conversion of securities" and with the word "security" itself and the subsection provides in particular as follows. [The learned Lord President then read the definition of 'security' from para 5(3). He continued:] On a proper construction of that subsection I am persuaded that what is in contemplation is the issue of a document or certificate by the debtor institution which would represent a marketable security, as that expression is commonly understood, the nature and character of which would remain

---

1   1971 SC 233 at 244, 47 Tax Cas 300 at 318
2   [1977] STC 302
3   [1977] STC 302 at 309

constant in all transmissions. Support for this view is to be found in the opinions of Lords Migdale and Cameron in *Cleveleys Investment Trust Co v Inland Revenue Comrs*[1], in which they offer their interpretation, obiter, on the meaning of "security" for the purposes of para 11(1).'

Lord Emslie then read part of what I have read from the judgments of Lord Migdale[2] and Lord Cameron[3] in the earlier case. He concluded on this point by saying:

'In the present case, accordingly, I am quite unable to regard the loans of £500,000 to Rock Fall as "a debt on a security" within the meaning of para 11(1). They were, in my opinion, no more than simple unsecured debts and a loss on their disposal does not qualify as an allowable loss.'

To similar effect is the judgment of Lord Johnston[4]. He said:

'It was then contended, first, that the loan of £500,000 was a "debt on a security" in terms of para 11(1) of Sch 7 to the 1965 Act and was an allowable loss. Despite the promise of a definition of the phrase in para 5 of Sch 7, there is no such definition. But, as Lord Cameron said in *Cleveleys Investment Trust Co v Inland Revenue Comrs*[3]: "... whatever else it may mean the phrase 'the debt on a security' is not a synonym for a secured debt". But while it may not be necessary that the debt be secured it is clear that the debt by itself will not suffice. I agree with the Lord President that what appears to be in contemplation is the issue of a document by the debtor which would represent a marketable security. No such document was issued to the taxpayer company by Rock Fall so far as the case shows and accordingly I reject this contention."'

So, too, said Lord Avonside[5]:

'When one looks at the definition of "security" contained in para 5(3)(*b*) it is to my mind plain that the creditor in such a debt must be issued some kind of "voucher". I use the word neutrally, which acknowledges the debt on which it is charged. In this case it is perfectly true to say that at any time they wished the taxpayer company could have made their loan of £500,000 a debt on a security. They wholly owned Rock Fall; they could have, for example, issued debentures against the £500,000 or adopted various different means of creating a debt on a security. But the simple fact is that they did not do so. The loan throughout its existence was a simple loan and the question of charge does not arise.'

The *Aberdeen Construction* case[6] was carried to the House of Lords. Before I turn to the speeches there, it is worth summarising what can be drawn from the two decisions in Scotland. First of all, all three learned judges held in the *Aberdeen Construction* case[7], and Lord Migdale was of opinion in the earlier case, that the idea of a debt on a security requires the issue by the debtor of some kind of document of title or certificate of the debt which would (in the phrase of the Lord President (Lord Emslie) and Lord Johnston) represent a marketable security. Secondly, Lord Cameron in the *Cleveleys Investment* case[1] took the view that the debts in question are debts on securities which are or can be subject to a conversion.

The taxpayer's appeal to the House of Lords in the *Aberdeen Construction* case[6] was in part successful, but not on the point with which I am concerned. On that

1   1971 SC 233, 47 Tax Cas 300
2   1971 SC 233 at 243, 244, 47 Tax Cas 300 at 315
3   1971 SC 233 at 244, 47 Tax Cas 300 at 318
4   [1977] STC 302 at 313
5   [1977] STC 302 at 314, 315
6   [1978] 1 All ER 962, [1978] 2 WLR 648, [1978] STC 127
7   [1977] STC 302

point, Lord Wilberforce made the most extensive of their Lordships' observations. He said[1]: .

'The Crown claims that the disposal of this debt is prevented from giving rise to a gain (or a loss) by Sch 7, para 11(1), which, as between the original debtor and creditor, does so prevent "except in the case of the [sic] debt on a security (as defined in paragraph 5 of this Schedule)". Reference to para 5 plunges us at once into a thicket. [Lord Wilberforce read paragraph 5(3)(b), and continued:] This raises several difficulties. First, the sub-paragraph does not provide a definition except by inclusion, so the question must arise whether the reference in para 11 is limited to what is specifically mentioned as included, or to some wider class. Second, if it defines anything, it defines "security" not "debt on a security", and in view of the words "whether secured or unsecured" the latter must include some unsecured debts. As Lord Cameron said in Cleveleys Investment Co v Inland Revenue Comrs[2] "whatever else it may mean, the phrase 'the debt on a security' is not a synonym for a secured debt". But which unsecured debts come within the exclusion in para 11 and which do not is not stated and I find it impossible to discover any principle on which to state a discrimen. The general subject of company indebtedness, or of loans to companies seems to be one as to which the legislative mind is clouded. The courts have had difficulties over the subject of "funded debt" as to which this House felt obliged to differ from the Court of Appeal (Reed International Ltd v Inland Revenue Comrs[3]). They have had difficulties over "loan capital" and "issue of loan capital" (Agricultural Mortgage Corpn v Inland Revenue Comrs[4]). In that case money was borrowed by the company for capital purposes, the purpose being to enable it to make loans to other persons. The members of the court thought that the money borrowed had the character of loan capital. "The money was required for capital purposes; and it was borrowed money" (per Scarman LJ[5]). But they did not consider that there had been an "issue". The decisions were on different statutes inter se and from the Finance Act 1965 and it is difficult to find any clear common principle underlying them, but taking such guidance as they do provide leads me to think that the only basis on which a distinction can be drawn is between a pure unsecured debt as between the original borrower and lender on the one hand and a debt (which may be unsecured) which has, if not a marketable character, at least such characteristics as enable it to be dealt in and if necessary converted into shares or other securities. This is indeed lacking in precision but no more can be drawn from the statutory provisions than the draftsmen have put in, and that is both meagre and confusing. In agreement with the Court of Session I can find nothing here except an unsecured loan subsisting as between the original debtor and creditor given the description of loan capital, whether correctly or not but with no quality or characteristic which brings it within whatever special category is meant by debt on a security. I cannot therefore accept this argument.'

Before leaving Lord Wilberforce's speech, I should mention that neither party has relied before me on either of the two decisions on different statutes from which he indicated that he had drawn some slight, and perhaps obscure, guidance. Lord Dilhorne[6], except on another point, said that he agreed with, and had nothing to

---

1 [1978] 1 All ER 962 at 967, 968, [1978] 2 WLR 648 at 653, 654, [1978] STC 127 at 132, 133
2 1971 SC 233 at 244, 47 Tax Cas 300 at 318
3 [1975] 3 All ER 218, [1975] 3 WLR 413, [1975] STC 427
4 [1978] 1 All ER 248, [1978] 2 WLR 230, [1978] STC 11
5 [1978] 1 All ER 248 at 264, [1978] 2 WLR 230 at 247, [1978] STC 11 at 27
6 [1978] 1 All ER 962 at 969, [1978] 2 WLR 648 at 654, [1978] STC 127 at 134

add to, the speeches of Lord Wilberforce and Lord Russell. Lord Fraser had this
to say[1]:

'Schedule 7, paras 5 and 11 provide in effect that no chargeable gain or allowable
loss shall accrue to the original creditor in a debt except in the case of a "debt on a
security". For the reasons given by the learned judges of the First Division and
by my noble and learned friends, Lord Wilberforce and Lord Russell of Killowen,
I find it impossible to say that Aberdeen's loan to Rock Fall was a debt "on a
security", whatever the exact meaning of the expression may be.'

Lord Russell read paras 11(1) and 5(3)(b), and continued[2]:

'I find these provisions particularly obscure and on any construction cannot find
a rational explanation. There may be a temptation to take advantage of that
very obscurity so as to reach a construction favourable to the stricken taxpayer
company; but it must be borne in mind that the provision works both ways,
and to find in this case an allowable loss is to find in another case a chargeable
gain, though not perhaps of such hardship. Paragraph 11(1) deals with the disposal of a debt asset, but only where such disposal is made by the original creditor
(or his legatee): such disposal might, for example in the case of a debt expressed
in a foreign currency, result, on disposal by the original creditor (or his legatee),
in a capital gain, but that gain is not to be a chargeable gain; and a parallel
loss is not an allowable loss. But those provisions do not cover all debts, for there
is excepted "the case of the debt on a security (as defined in paragraph 5 of this
Schedule)". (I do not know why "the debt"; I take the phrase simply to mean
"a debt", the language used in sub-para (2).) If the taxpayer company are to
succeed on the third contention they must bring the £500,000 debt into the
exception, the taxpayer company being the original creditor. In the ordinary
sense of the phrase this cannot be said to be a debt on a security; it was not
secured on any property or in any way. Can it be said to be a debt "on a security"
in the extended meaning given to the word "security" by para 5(3)(b)? That
word embraces "any loan stock or similar security . . . of any company . . .
whether secured or unsecured". Can it fairly be said that we have a case of
"loan stock" or of a security "similar to loan stock"? The debt was of course a
loan, or series of loans, to Rock Fall, and figured in Rock Fall's balance sheet
as such as one item under the head of "Capital Employed"; this was a suitable
accountancy niche having regard to the purposes for which the loans were made
and to which they were put. But in my opinion this was not a case of loan stock,
which suggests to my mind an obligation created by a company of an amount
for issue to subscribers for the stock, having ordinary terms for repayment with
or without premium and for interest. The series of loans by the taxpayer company to Rock Fall ultimately in total outstanding amounting to £500,000 are
not within that concept; nor can they fairly be described as "similar security".
They were simply loans by Aberdeen, initially when Rock Fall was not a
subsidiary and for the greater part when it was.'

Finally, Lord Keith[3] simply agreed with the speech of Lord Wilberforce.
    Those speeches in the House of Lords, other than that of Lord Fraser, neither
expressly affirm nor expressly disapprove the Court of Session's view that there is
no debt on a security without the issue of a document by the debtor. Do they overrule it by implication? The following points seem to me to indicate an answer to
that question. First, Lord Wilberforce (with the general concurrence of Lord Dilhorne

1   [1978] 1 All ER 962 at 972, 973, [1978] 2 WLR 648 at 658, [1978] STC 127 at 137, 138
2   [1978] 1 All ER 962 at 974, 975, [1978] 2 WLR 648 at 660, 661, [1978] STC 127 at 139, 140
3   [1978] 1 All ER 962 at 975, [1978] 2 WLR 648 at 661, [1978] STC 127 at 140

and Lord Keith) distinguished a debt on a security from a pure unsecured debt as having if not a marketable character, at least such characteristics as enable it to be dealt in, and if necessary converted into shares or other securities. He must, I think, have contemplated conversion in the context of securities that can be dealt in, for any debt of a company is in one sense capable of conversion into shares, namely if the creditor applies it in payment for an allotment. In all ordinary experience, one of the universal characteristics of securities that are dealt in the sense that I think Lord Wilberforce intended, 'marketable or quasi-marketable securities', as I would call them, is the existence of a certificate or bond or other written evidence of the creditor's rights, executed by or on behalf of the debtor. It is therefore, in my judgment, at least an over-bold or unsafe inference to suppose that Lord Wilberforce meant implicitly to over-rule the unanimous opinion of the court below.

Secondly, Lord Fraser expressly approved the reasons given by the judges of the First Division. He found nothing inconsistent in adopting, in the same breath, those of Lord Wilberforce and Lord Russell, and they for their part did not think it necessary to express any disagreement with Lord Fraser.

Thirdly, Lord Russell described loan stock as an obligation created by a company of an amount for issue to subscribers for the stock. Issue here, in my opinion, contemplates the provision of a document of title, and there is nothing to suggest that Lord Russell would give any very liberal construction to the words 'or similar security'.

Thus I have before me a plain judgment of the appellate revenue court of Scotland which, on a question of this sort, I must regard as practically binding on me unless it has been overruled. I have one speech in the House of Lords approving that judgment and four which neither affirm nor deny it expressly, and whose implications in my opinion incline rather to accept than to reject it. It is therefore my duty to follow the decision of the *Aberdeen Construction* case[1] in the First Division, and I do so without reluctance, for I find the Lord President's reasoning compelling. The language of the 1965 Act shows beyond doubt, to my mind, that there can be no debt on a security within para 11 of Sch 7 unless it is on (which may be paraphrased as 'supported by') something that is a security within the meaning, and (should they arise) for the purposes of para 5. The imperative requirement of an underlying security may just possibly explain the use in para 11(1) of the definite article that Lord Russell found puzzling.

To see what is meant by such a security, look at the whole of para 5 in its context as a sequel to para 4. In my view it then becomes tolerably clear that such a loan as L2 was not intended to be within the term 'security'. It has certain marks that may also be found in a company's loan stock, notably detailed terms as to the time and conditions of repayment and as to interest in the meantime, and the possibility (like any long-term debt at a fixed rate of interest) of appreciating in value to the creditor, but it lacks the essential feature described by the Lord President[2] as 'the issue of a document or certificate by the debtor institution which would represent a marketable security, as that expression is commonly understood', or, in Lord Wilberforce's wider phrase[3], 'such characteristics as enable it to be dealt in and if necessary converted into shares or other securities'.

The Special Commissioners were not willing to construe Mr Livingstone's statutory declaration as the equivalent of a debenture issued by Caithmead Ltd. I agree with them in that, and indeed I have not been pressed to say they were wrong in that respect. Their dismissal of the taxpayer company's appeal cannot however stand. In my judgment, they erred in law in holding L2 to be a debt on a security within the

1 [1977] STC 302
2 [1977] STC 302 at 309
3 [1978] 1 All ER 962 at 968, [1978] 2 WLR 648 at 653, [1978] STC 127 at 133

1965 Act. That conclusion is no criticism of them, for they sat before the *Aberdeen Construction* case[1] was heard by the Court of Session.

I turn to the questions of law propounded at the end of the case stated. The first is whether on the true construction of the expressions 'security' and 'the debt on a security' in the Finance Act 1965, Sch 7, paras 5(3)(*b*) and 11(1) and in the events that happened, the loan L2 is 'the debt on a security'. I answer that No. The second question is whether a chargeable gain accrued to the taxpayer company on its disposing of L2 to Masterdene. That also I must, in consequence, anwer No. I accordingly allow the appeal and remit the matter to the Special Commissioners to adjust the assessment in accordance with my opinion.

Appeal allowed.

Solicitors: *Slowes* (for the taxpayer company); *Solicitor of Inland Revenue.*

Rengan Krishnan Esq Barrister.

SA Consortium General Textiles v Sun & Sand Agencies Ltd

QUEEN'S BENCH DIVISION

PARKER J

31st JANUARY, 14th FEBRUARY 1977

COURT OF APPEAL, CIVIL DIVISION

LORD DENNING MR, GOFF AND SHAW LJJ

29th, 30th JUNE, 1st, 4th JULY 1977

Conflict of laws – Foreign judgment – Registration in England – Judgment unenforceable in country of original court – Formal defect in judgment – Judgment liable to be set aside on appeal – Judgment in default obtained against English company in French court – French judgment failing to comply with formal requirements of French Code of Civil Procedure – Whether judgment could 'be enforced by execution' in France – Whether judgment registrable in England – Foreign Judgments (Reciprocal Enforcement) Act 1933, s 2(1)(b).

Conflict of laws – Foreign judgment – Registration in England – Jurisdiction of foreign court – Agreement by defendant to submit to jurisdiction – English defendant – French company threatening to bring claim against English company in England for contract debt – English company's solicitor suggesting that under terms of contract French court had jurisdiction – French company bringing claim in French court and obtaining judgment by default – Whether English company had 'agreed . . . to submit to the jurisdiction of' the French court – Foreign Judgments (Reciprocal Enforcement) Act 1933, s 4(2)(a)(iii).

Conflict of laws – Foreign judgment – Registration in England – Jurisdiction of foreign court – Submission by defendant to jurisdiction by voluntarily appearing in proceedings otherwise than for purpose of protecting property or contesting jurisdiction – Appeal by defendant – Judgment obtained against defendant by default – Defendant giving notice of appeal against judgment – Notice of appeal not denying jurisdiction of court – Whether defendant had 'submitted to the jurisdiction of [the foreign] court by voluntarily appearing in the proceedings otherwise than for the purpose of . . . contesting the jurisdiction of that court' – Foreign Judgments (Reciprocal Enforcement) Act 1933, s 4(2)(a)(i).

1 [1977] STC 302

Conflict of laws – Foreign judgment – Registration in England – Sum of money payable thereunder not being a sum payable in respect of taxes or of a fine or other penalty – Fine or other penalty – Damages for unreasonable resistance to claim – French proceedings – Résistance abusive – Head of damage intended to compensate plaintiff for such matters as loss of use of capital – Judgment obtained against English company in France for damages for résistance abusive in resisting a plain claim – Whether damages for résistance abusive constituting a 'fine or other penalty' – Whether enforcement contrary to public policy – Whether judgment registrable in England – Foreign Judgments (Reciprocal Enforcement) Act 1933, ss 1(2)(b), 4(1)(a)(v).

The plaintiffs were a French textile company with a head office in Lille and branches at Lille, Paris and elsewhere. In 1974 the Lille and Paris branches both sold clothing under separate contracts to the defendants, who were clothing wholesalers in England. The Lille contract was worth Fr 448,955 and the invoice from that branch stated that all disputes were to be referred to the Commercial Court at Lille. The Paris contract was worth Fr 280,489 and £6,989 and the invoice in respect of it stated that all disputes were to be referred to the Commercial Court at Paris. The goods were delivered but the defendants failed to pay the amounts invoiced, and the plaintiffs instructed London solicitors to collect the amounts due. The solicitors wrote to the defendants threatening to issue proceedings in England unless the debt was paid within seven days. The defendants passed the letter over to their own solicitor in London who telephoned the plaintiffs' solicitors on 15th July 1975 pointing out that the plaintiffs' notepaper stated that all disputes were to be brought before the Commercial Court at Lille. The following day the defendants' solicitor wrote to the plaintiffs' solicitors again suggesting that the matter came within the jurisdiction of the Lille court and that the jurisdiction of the English courts had been ousted. On the same day the plaintiffs instituted proceedings in the Lille court to recover the whole amount owing under the Lille and Paris contracts together with interest and Fr 10,000 for 'résistance abusive', a head of damage which could be awarded under French law against a defendant who had unreasonably refused to pay a plain claim. The French writ was duly served on the defendants who ignored it. On 14th October the plaintiffs obtained judgment in the Lille court for the whole amount claimed and costs. Article 479 of the French Code of Civil Procedure provided that a judgment obtained in default of appearance against a party residing abroad was to state expressly the steps taken to bring the original summons to the defendant's knowledge. The judgment of the Lille court, however, simply recited that the defendants had been regularly summoned to appear at the hearing. On 29th January 1976 the defendants were given notice of the judgment and of their right to appeal to the appeal court at Douai within three weeks, but chose to ignore the notice and a reminder sent on 2nd March. On 5th August the plaintiffs issued a summons in the High Court to register the judgment of the Lille court under s 2(1)ᵃ of the Foreign Judgments (Reciprocal Enforcement) Act 1933. The summons was heard on 14th October by a master who ordered registration of that part of the judgment relating to the Lille contract but not that relating to the Paris contract or the Fr 10,000 for 'résistance abusive'. In December 1976 the defendants applied to the President of the Court of Appeal at Douai for leave to appeal out of time against the Lille judgment. The application was dismissed and they filed a notice of appeal to the appeal court

---

a　Section 2(1), so far as material, provides: 'A person, being a judgment creditor under a judgment to which this Part of this Act applies, may apply to the High Court at any time within six years after the date of the judgment, or, where there have been proceedings by way of appeal against the judgment, after the date of the last judgment given in those proceedings, to have the judgment registered in the High Court, and on any such application the court shall . . . order the judgment to be registered: Provided that a judgment shall not be registered if at the date of the application . . . (*b*) it could not be enforced by execution in the country of the original court.'

at Douai. On 14th February 1977 the judge allowed an appeal by the plaintiffs against
a the master's order and ordered the whole of the judgment of the Lille court to be
registered as a foreign judgment. The defendants appealed, contending (i) that under
s 2(1)(*b*) of the 1933 Act the judgment of the Lille court was not registrable in England
because it could not be enforced by execution in the country of the original court
by reason of the failure to comply with art 479 of the French Code of Civil Procedure;
(ii) that under s 4(1)(*a*)(ii)^*b* the registration of that part of the judgment relating to
b the Paris contract should be set aside because the Lille court had no jurisdiction in
respect of the Paris contract; (iii) that under ss 1(2)(*b*)^*c* and 4(1)(*a*)(v)^*d* the sum awarded
for 'résistance abusive' was not registrable because it was in the nature of a fine or
other penalty, or alternatively its enforcement would be contrary to public policy
in England; and (iv) that under s 5(1)^*e* the judge should have exercised his discretion
to set aside the registration or adjourn the application pending the outcome of the
c defendants' appeal to the appeal court at Douai.

Held (Goff LJ dissenting in part) – The appeal would be dismissed for the following
reasons—
(i) There was no reason to interfere with the trial judge's decision not to exercise his discretion under s 5(1) to set aside the registration of the Lille judgment or
d adjourn the application pending the outcome of the appeal to the Douai court because
(per Lord Denning MR) full faith and credit ought to be given to the French judgment;
(per Goff and Shaw LJJ) the judge had not been shown to have acted on a wrong
principle; and (per Goff LJ) the defendants had been guilty of long delays, they had
chosen to take no part in the Lille proceedings even though the Lille court had
undoubted jurisdiction over at least part of the claim, and registration would not
prevent them from having the Lille judgment reversed or counterclaiming in France
e which in any event was likely to be difficult and was certainly not imminent (see p 353
d to *f*, p 359 *h* to p 360 *h* and p 362 *d*, post); *Ferdinand Wagner (a firm) v Laubscher
Brothers & Co (a firm)* [1970] 2 All ER 174 applied.
(ii) The judgment of the Lille court was good until set aside on appeal and the fact
that it might be voidable for failure to comply with the formal requirements of art
f 479 of the French Code of Civil Procedure did not make it a nullity so that it was not
therefore barred from registration as a judgment which 'could not be enforced by
execution in' France, within proviso (*b*) to s 2(1) of the 1933 Act (see p 353 *b c*, p 356
h j and p 360 *j* to p 361 *b*, post).
(iii) The judgment of the Lille court for Fr 10,000 in respect of 'résistance abusive'
was correctly registered because it was in the nature of compensatory damages for
g such matters as loss of use of capital and was therefore not a 'fine or other penalty',
within s 1(2)(*b*), nor was it 'contrary to public policy' under s 4(1)(*a*)(v) to enforce it
(see p 354 *j* to p 355 *b*, p 359 *h* and p 362 *d* to *f*, post).
(iv) (Goff LJ dissenting) The judge was right to register the whole judgment of
the Lille court including that part relating to the Paris contract because—

---

b Section 4(1)(*a*)(ii) is set out at p 348 *a* and *b*, post
c Section 1(2), so far as material, provides: 'Any judgment of a superior court of a foreign
country to which this Part of this Act extends, other than a judgment of such a court given
on appeal from a court which is not a superior court, shall be a judgment to which this
Part of this Act applies, if . . . (*b*) there is payable thereunder a sum of money, not being a
sum payable in respect of taxes or other charges of a like nature or in respect of a fine or
other penalty.'
d Section 4(1)(*a*)(v), so far as material, provides: '(1) On an application in that behalf duly made
by any party against whom a registered judgment may be enforced, the registration of the
judgment—(*a*) shall be set aside if the registering court is satisfied . . . (v) that the enforcement of the judgment would be contrary to public policy in the country of the registering
court.'
e Section 5(1) is set out at p 345, post

(a) It was to be inferred from the statements by the defendants' solicitor in the telephone conversation of 15th July and his letter of 16th July to the effect that the dispute came within the jurisdiction of the Lille court, that the defendants 'had agreed . . . to submit [the whole claim] to the jurisdiction of that court', within s 4(2) (a)(iii)*f* (see p 354 *c* and p 361 *d* to *g*, post).

(b) Furthermore the defendants' notice of appeal to the appeal court at Douai by not denying the Lille court's jurisdiction over the Paris contract was for the purposes of s 4(2)(a)(i), a submission 'to the jurisdiction of the [Lille] court by voluntarily appearing in the proceedings otherwise than for the purpose . . . of contesting the jurisdiction of that court', and therefore the Lille court was deemed to have had jurisdiction over the whole claim for the purposes of s 4(1)(a)(ii) of the 1933 Act (see p 354 *e* to *g* and p 361 *g h*, post); dictum of Denning LJ in *Re Dulles' Settlement Trusts, Dulles v Vidler* [1951] 2 All ER at 72 applied; *Henry v Geopresco International Ltd* [1975] 2 All ER 702 distinguished.

Per Goff and Shaw LJJ, Lord Denning MR dissenting. Submission to the 'jurisdiction of . . . the courts of the country of that court', within s 4(2)(a)(iii), can arise only where there is an express submission in general terms to the courts of a country rather than to an individual court (see p 357 *f h* and p 362 *c d*, post).

Notes

For submission, and agreement to submit, to the jurisdiction of a foreign court, see 8 Halsbury's Laws (4th Edn) paras 720, 721, and for cases on the subject, see 11 Digest (Reissue) 592-595, 1407-1422.

For the Foreign Judgments (Reciprocal Enforcement) Act 1933, ss 1, 2, 4, 5, see 6 Halsbury's Statutes (3rd Edn) 365, 336, 368, 370.

Cases referred to in judgments

Cassell & Co Ltd v Broome [1972] 1 All ER 801, [1972] AC 1027, [1972] 2 WLR 645, HL, 17 Digest (Reissue) 82, 17.

Dulles' Settlement Trusts, Re, Dulles v Vidler [1951] 2 All ER 69, [1951] Ch 842, CA, 28 (2) Digest (Reissue) 789, 1172.

Guiard v De Clermont & Donner [1914] 3 KB 145, 83 LJKB 1407, 111 LT 293, 11 Digest (Reissue) 593, 1411.

Henry v Geopresco International Ltd [1975] 2 All ER 702, [1975] 2 Lloyd's Rep 148; sub nom *Henry v Geopresco International Ltd* [1976] 1 QB 726, [1975] 3 WLR 620, CA, Digest (Cont Vol D) 108, 1413a.

Huntington v Attrill [1893] AC 150, 62 LJPC 44, 68 LT 326, 57 JP 404, PC, 11 Digest (Reissue) 600, 1466.

Macartney, Re, Macfarlane v Macartney [1921] 1 Ch 522, 90 LTCh 314, 124 LT 658, 11 Digest (Reissue) 581, 1356.

Rookes v Barnard [1964] 1 All ER 367, [1964] AC 1129, [1964] 2 WLR 269, [1964] 1 Lloyd's Rep 28, HL, 17 Digest (Reissue) 81, 14.

Wagner (Ferdinand) (a firm) v Laubscher Brothers & Co (a firm) [1970] 2 All ER 174, [1970] 2 QB 313, [1970] 2 WLR 1019, CA, 11 Digest (Reissue) 623, 1620.

Cases also cited

Esdale v Bank of Ottawa (1920) 51 DLR 485 (Alta CA).

Nouvion v Freeman (1889) 15 App Cas 1, 59 LJCh 337, HL.

Raulin v Fischer [1911] 2 KB 93, 80 LJKB 811.

Scott v Pilkington (1862) 2 B & S 11, 6 LT 21.

Westinghouse Electric Corpn Uranium Contract Litigation MDL Docket No 235, Re [1977] 3 All ER 703, [1977] 3 WLR 430, CA.

---

f Section 4(2), so far as material, is set out at p 348 *d* and *e*, post

Westinghouse Electric Corpn Uranium Contract Litigation MDL Docket No 235 (No 2), Re
[1977] 3 All ER 717, [1977] 3 WLR 492, CA.

Appeal and cross-appeal
The defendants, Sun & Sand Agencies Ltd ('the English company'), appealed against
so much of the order of Master Warren given in chambers on 14th October 1977 as
ordered that part of a judgment of the Tribunal de Commerce de Lille, France,
in favour of the plaintiffs, SA Consortium General Textiles ('the French company'),
against the defendants and dated 14th October 1975 be registered in the High Court.
The plaintiffs cross-appealed against so much of the master's order as ordered that
the remaining part of the judgment of the Tribunal de Commerce should not be so
registered. The hearing of the appeal and cross-appeal took place in chambers but
the judgment was delivered in open court. The facts are set out in the judgment of
Parker J.

Mr Antony St John Davies, solicitor, for the French company on the hearing of the
     summons.
Robin Widdison for the plaintiffs on the delivery of judgment in open court.
Colin Ross-Munro QC and *Aron Owen* for the English company.

Cur adv vult

14th February. **PARKER J** read the following judgment: This is an appeal and
cross-appeal from an order of Master Warren made on 14th October 1976 by which it
was ordered, first, that a certain judgment of the Tribunal de Commerce de Lille
('the Lille court') in favour of a French company, SA Consortium General Textiles,
against an English company, Sun & Sand Agencies Ltd, and dated 14th October
1975 be registered as to part under Part I of the Foreign Judgments (Reciprocal
Enforcement) Act 1933; secondly, that an issue as to interest be stated and tried;
thirdly, that there be a stay of execution for 14 days, to be continued until determination of any appeal or further order should notice of appeal be given within
that time; and fourthly, that both parties should bear their own costs.
     The appeal raises a number of points under the above-mentioned Act to which I
will refer as 'the 1933 Act' and both parties agreed that it was desirable that I should
deliver judgment in open court. The facts are a little complex and the arguments
advanced make it necessary that I should set them out in some detail. The story
begins in 1974, when the French company sold a number of parcels of clothing to
the English company.
     One group of these parcels was to be delivered by a department of the French
company called the Coframaille department; the other group of these parcels was
to be delivered by another department of the French company called the Pigeon
Voyageur department. The invoices in respect of the goods to be delivered by the
Coframaille department contained a provision that the Tribunal de Commerce de la
Seine ('the Paris court') should have exclusive jurisdiction in the event of disputes.
The invoices in respect of the goods to be delivered by the Pigeon Voyageur department
also contained an exclusive jurisdiction clause but in those invoices the selected court
was the Lille court. It is accepted by both parties that these clauses were valid and
binding provisions.
     On 16th July 1975 the French company issued proceedings in the Lille court claiming
Fr 729,444·13 and £6,989 in respect of the price of goods sold and delivered. This
claim related, as to Fr 280,489·13, to goods delivered by the Coframaille department
and, as to the balance of Fr 448,955 and £6,989, to goods delivered by the Pigeon
Voyageur department. Additionally the French company claimed Fr 10,000 in respect
of something called 'abusive opposition' and expenses. 'Abusive opposition', in
French, 'résistance abusive', is a head of damage which, in France, may be awarded

where a defendant has unreasonably refused to pay a plain claim. A translation of the document by which these proceedings were initiated and which for convenience I shall call 'the French writ' is an exhibit to the affidavit of a Mr Muller sworn on behalf of the English company on 7th October 1976.

The French writ was duly served on the English company but for reasons which no doubt seemed good to them they chose not to appear on the hearing and the result was that on 14th October 1975 the Lille court gave judgment against them for the full amount claimed together with interest and costs. The appropriate amount of interest was, at the time when the matter came before Master Warren, in dispute. I shall deal with it when I have disposed of all other matters arising on the appeals, but interest I am told is now agreed.

Before relating events which occurred subsequently to the judgment of the Lille court it is necessary that I should mention briefly two matters. Firstly, the English company's address is 12 Dryden Chambers, 119 Oxford Street and letters addressed simply to them at Dryden Chambers do not, or perhaps more strictly, may not, get delivered. Secondly, French law provides two methods by which a party outside the jurisdiction may be served with or notified of a judgment, both of which methods appear to operate concurrently. One method is for the judgment or notification thereof to be posted directly to the defendant by an official process server called a 'huissier' The other is for the judgment to be filed with an institution called the Parquet which then despatches it to the French Consulate General in the country in which the defendant is resident, which, on receiving it, notifies the defendant by letter that it is available for collection. Both these methods apply also in the case of service of the 'writ'.

What happened in the case of the Lille judgment was that the 'huissier' omitted the number when sending the judgment or notification thereof to the English company with the result that it never reached them. It was eventually returned to the 'huissier' and the returned envelope was produced in evidence as an exhibit to an affidavit of Mr Anthony St John Davies sworn on 12th October 1976. The first of the two methods therefore failed to bring the judgment to the notice of the English company. The second method was also put into operation. The judgment was filed on 10th December 1975. The Consulate General received the judgment and, on 29th January 1976, wrote to inform the English company that it was available for collection. A reminder was sent on 2nd March 1976. Both the letter and reminder remained unanswered but were apparently not returned. It appears probable from the heading of a letter from the Consulate General to the French company's solicitors dated 12th May 1976 that both were addressed like the huissier's letter, simply to Dryden Chambers, the number being omitted, and I was originally informed that the first that the English company knew of the judgment was when the French company's solicitors sent them a copy under cover of a letter dated 26th April 1976. Later in the hearing however the English company produced a copy of a letter from their solicitors to the French company's solicitors dated 7th June 1976 which makes it appear that the letter of notification and reminder from the consulate were in fact received. The material passage in the letter reads:

> 'I have already indicated that my clients have never been served with a copy of the Judgment, giving them a right of appeal and that assertion is clearly supported by your own documents. These indicate that whereas the Assignation [i e the French writ] was sent by post to my clients' registered office and a copy sent to the French Consulate for onward transmission, this procedure was not followed in the case of the Judgment. All that happened was that a copy was sent to the Consulate whose letters were ignored. With the greatest possible respect that cannot be said to constitute good service.'

Having regard to the terms of that letter and the fact that the letter and reminder from the consulate were not returned I find that both letter and reminder were

received and accordingly that the English company were aware of the judgment
a shortly after 29th January 1976. One cannot ignore letters which one has not received.
According to the formal notification of judgment, the English company had three
months from its heading date, which was 10th December 1975, in which to appeal
to the Court of Appeal at Douai. Time for appeal thus expired on 10th March 1976,
that is to say prior to the date on which the English company received notice of
the judgment from the French company's solicitors but after the date on which I
b find they had received notice from the Consulate General.

The next material event is that the French company applied to register the Lille
judgment under the 1933 Act. The application was originally made ex parte but a
summons was as I understand it directed under RSC Ord 71, r 2(1). This was issued on
5th August and service was accepted by the English company's solicitors on 12th
August 1976. Before that summons could be heard the English company instituted
c proceedings against the French company in the Paris court claiming, in respect of
the same Coframaille goods which had been included in the claim in the Lille court,
sums which totalled the equivalent of some £83,000.

It was in this state of affairs that the French company's summons came before
Master Warren on 14th October 1976 and that the order which I have mentioned was
made. The part of the judgment then ordered to be registered was that relating to
d the Pigeon Voyageur goods. The parts relating to the Coframaille goods and the
'résistance abusive' were not ordered to be registered. From Master Warren's order
the English company gave notice of appeal dated 20th October and the French
company gave notice of appeal dated 27th October. By their notices the English
company and French company respectively seek orders, in effect, rejecting the
application to register in its entirety and registering it in whole instead of in part.

e Since then further events have occurred and further affidavits have been filed.
The further events are as follows. (1) In November the French company filed a
defence in the proceedings which had been instituted by the defendants in the Paris
court. This was not put in evidence. (2) On 9th December the English company,
as a result of advice from their lawyers in Lille, applied to the President of the Court
of Appeal at Douai for leave to appeal out of time from the Lille judgment. (3) On
f 23rd December the President dismissed the application with costs on the ground
that as the English company had had knowledge of the Lille judgment since 26th
April 1976 and had made no application for seven months thereafter but had instead
commenced parallel proceedings in the Paris court they were not entitled to relief
under the terms of the relevant provisions of French law. (4) On 25th January 1977
the English company filed notice of appeal to the full court at Douai against the Lille
g judgment, having been advised that that judgment was either a nullity or suffered
from a material defect which would prevent time for appeal from running. The
basis of this advice is set out in an affidavit of Guy Reginald Pierre Picarda, a member
of the English Bar and a practising advocate of the Court of Appeal in Paris, which was
sworn on 27th January 1977.

Having set out the facts I now turn to consider the two appeals. I shall deal first with
h the appeal by the English company. That appeal is founded simply on the provisions
of s 5(1) and (2) of the 1933 Act. Those subsections provide as follows:

'(1) If, on an application to set aside the registration of a judgment, the applicant
satisfies the registering court either that an appeal is pending, or that he is entitled
and intends to appeal, against the judgment, the court, if it thinks fit, may, on
j such terms as it may think just, either set aside the registration or adjourn the
application to set aside the registration until after the expiration of such period as
appears to the court to be reasonably sufficient to enable the applicant to take
the necessary steps to have the appeal disposed of by the competent tribunal.
'(2) Where the registration of a judgment is set aside under the last foregoing
subsection, or solely for the reason that the judgment was not at the date of the

application for registration enforceable by execution in the country of the original court, the setting aside of the registration shall not prejudice a further application to register the judgment when the appeal has been disposed of or if and when the judgment becomes enforceable by execution in that country, as the case may be.'

It will be seen that those subsections in terms deal with an application to set aside a registration but it was accepted by Mr Davies for the French company that the appeal should be treated as an application to set aside the registration of that part of the judgment ordered to be registered. Counsel for the English company contended that an appeal from the judgment having been filed I have a discretionary power either to allow the appeal and thus in effect set aside the registration or to adjourn the appeal for such period as will allow their appeal to be disposed of by the appeal court at Douai and that I may do so on such terms as I think just. This proposition was accepted by Mr Davies, the contest so far as the English company appeal is concerned, is therefore limited to the question whether I should or should not exercise the discretion which admittedly exists.

It is submitted on behalf of the English company that I should do so because the Lille judgment may be either defective or a nullity, because with respect to the Pigeon Voyageur part of the claim in the Lille court, which alone the master ordered to be registered, the defendants have a counterclaim for defective goods, and because, in addition, the English company claim in respect of the Coframaille goods may result in a set-off against the Pigeon Voyageur claim. To exercise the discretion will, it is contended, do no harm to the French company because they can always re-register as a result of s 5(2) of the 1933 Act. The most that will happen is that there will be some delay.

Mr Davies on the other hand submits that this is a case in which the French company have already been kept out of their money for a long time, that the English company are merely seeking to gain yet further time, that they have known of the judgment since at least 26th April 1976 and that as to the part of the judgment ordered to be registered the Lille court had undoubted jurisdiction.

I am satisfied that this is not a case in which I should exercise my discretion. The English company admittedly received the French writ and were thus aware that the claim included both Pigeon Voyageur and Coframaille goods. There was no question but that the Lille court had jurisdiction to entertain the part of the claim which has been ordered to be registered and which related to the Pigeon Voyageur goods. In the light of this knowledge the English company chose not to contest the action and thereafter ignored letters notifying them of the judgment. Additionally it is to be noted that when applying to the President of the Court of Appeal in Douai for leave to appeal they stated incorrectly that they had had no knowledge of the judgment until the issue of the summons for leave to register on 5th August 1976. This was untrue for, quite apart from the letters of the Consulate General, they had actually had a copy of the judgment since 26th April 1976, and their solicitors had been in correspondence about the matter thereafter. The letter of 7th June 1976, indeed, specifically refers to s 1(3) of the 1933 Act thus making it plain that the possibility that the Lille judgment might be registered was present to their solicitors' minds long before the summons for leave to register was issued. That same letter is also of relevance in relation to the suggested counterclaim in respect of the Pigeon Voyageur part of the claim. The letter is dealing with the whole position. It specifically mentions a counterclaim in respect of Coframaille but makes no mention of any such claim in respect of Pigeon Voyageur. The English company have produced no evidence of the existence of any such counterclaim save para 8 of Mr Muller's affidavit of 26th January 1977 in which he says no more than 'the [English company] have a counterclaim based on deliveries of defective merchandise'. No details whatsoever are given.

In the light of the foregoing I am not prepared to exercise my discretion in favour
of the English company. Matters must in my judgment be allowed to take their
course in respect of the Pigeon Voyageur part of the claim and accordingly the
English company's appeal is dismissed. This will not of course prevent them from
asserting any counterclaim which the Lille court sees fit to entertain.

Turning to the French company's appeal there are two matters which arise for
consideration namely: (1) should the Coframaille part of the judgment be registered?
(2) should the Fr 10,000 for 'abusive resistance' be registered?

I take the second point first. It arises out of s 1(2)(b) of the 1933 Act which in effect
prevents registration of any sum which is 'in respect of a fine or penalty'. Put in
their shortest forms the rival arguments are these: on the part of the French company that the words 'fine or penalty' refer only to fines or penalties of a public nature
and do not cover such private rights; on the part of the English company that the words
cover such matters as contractual penalties and exemplary damages, to which damages for 'résistance abusive' may be likened. In support of the former contention I was
referred to *Huntington v Attrill*[1]. That was a case in the Privy Council on appeal from
Canada in which, in an action to enforce a foreign judgment, the defence was that the
original action was for a penalty and therefore the judgment ought not to be enforced
by reason of the rule of international law which prohibits the courts of one country
from enforcing the penal laws of another. The passage[2] relied on appears in the advice
of the Judicial Committee. In my judgment that case is of some but only limited
assistance when the problem is the construction of s 1(2)(b). That provision is covering
at least in part matters which are the subject of the international rule and the case
cited may therefore throw some light on the reason for the presence of the provision.
In the end however it is the words in their context which have to be considered.
In support of the English company's contention certain passages in *Cassel & Co Ltd v
Broome*[3] were referred to in which exemplary damages were referred to as a penalty.
In my judgment such passages are of no assistance in the construction of this particular
provision.

The nature of that which is recoverable under the heading 'résistance abusive' is
in my judgment damages. It bears some similarity to exemplary damages and some
to the interest which may be awarded on debts or damages in civil actions in this
country. Both are in some sense penalties, the one for conduct generally the other
for delay in paying just dues. Both are heads of damage recoverable by a private
individual against another in respect of a civil wrong. Neither bears the least similarity
to taxes or other charges of a like nature or to a fine which are other matters mentioned in s 1(2)(b). It is moreover significant that the phrase used is 'fine or other
penalty'. Damages for 'résistance abusive' does not in my mind come anywhere near
'fine' as used in the subsection. Can they then be described as an 'other penalty'.
In my judgment they cannot. They are no more a penalty of the type contemplated
than is interest on damages or indeed exemplary damages. In my judgment the
penalties referred to are those recoverable for some public wrong and not by an
individual in a civil action for breach of a private right. It follows therefore that I
would allow the French company's appeal as to the Fr 10,000 unless to do so would
involve, as to part, registering something properly attributable to a claim itself un-
registerable by reason of lack of jurisdiction in the foreign court. To this matter I
will return later.

I turn now to consider whether the French company's appeal, insofar as it relates
to the Coframaille part of the judgment of the Lille court, should be allowed and
that part of the judgment also registered. For the consideration of this part of the

1   [1893] AC 150
2   [1893] AC 150 at 156
3   [1972] 1 All ER 801, [1972] AC 1027

French company's appeal it is necessary to refer to certain of the provisions of s 4 of the 1933 Act. I will refer first to section 4(1). That reads as follows:

'On an application in that behalf duly made by any party against whom a registered judgment may be enforced, the registration of the judgment—(a) shall be set aside if the registering court is satisfied . . . (ii) that the courts of the country of the original court had no jurisdiction in the circumstances of the case . . .'

On behalf of the English company it is contended that the Lille court had no jurisdiction in respect of the claim relating to the Coframaille goods by reason of the clause in the Coframaille invoices giving exclusive jurisdiction to the Tribunal de la Seine and that this satisfies s 4(1)(a)(ii) and would therefore result in them being entitled to have the judgment set aside if already registered and thus in the circumstances to bar registration.

The French company's counter to this is based on s 4(2) which, so far as material, provides:

'For the purposes of this section the courts of the country of the original court shall, subject to the provisions of subsection (3) of this section, be deemed to have had jurisdiction—(a) in the case of a judgment given in an action in personam— (i) if the judgment debtor, being a defendant in the original court, submitted to the jurisdiction of that court by voluntarily appearing in the proceedings other- wise than for the purpose of protecting, or obtaining the release of, property seized, or threatened with seizure, in the proceedings or of contesting the juris- diction of that court; or . . . (iii) if the judgment debtor, being a defendant in the original court, had before the commencement of the proceedings agreed, in respect of the subject matter of the proceedings, to submit to the jurisdiction of that court or of the courts of the country of that court . . .'

The French company submits that when the English company applied to the President for leave to appeal against the Lille judgment they voluntarily submitted to the jurisdiction of the Lille court by voluntarily appearing in the proceedings other- wise than for the purpose of contesting the jurisdiction of that court and accordingly that it must under s 4(2)(a)(i) be deemed to have had jurisdiction.

They further submit that the English company had, before the commence- ment of the proceedings, agreed in respect of the subject-matter of the proceedings to submit to the jurisdiction of a French court, namely the Paris court, and that, this being so, if the Lille court exceeded its jurisdiction that is a matter for the French courts and not for the courts of this country.

In support of the first submission the plaintiffs relied on *Henry v Geopresco Inter- national Ltd*[1]. In that case the judgment of the Court of Appeal was delivered by Roskill LJ and the passage on which the French company principally relied reads[2]:

'For our part we think that where any issues arise for decision at any stage of the proceedings in the foreign court and that court is invited by the defendant as well as by the plaintiff to decide those issues, "the merits" are voluntarily submitted to that court for decision so that that submission subsequently binds both parties in respect of the dispute as a whole, even if both would not have been so bound in the absence of that voluntary submission. Were that not so, the submission of a preliminary issue (whether of fact or of law) to a foreign court for decision would not be a voluntary submission to the jurisdiction of that court, and if a defendant lost on that issue he could nonetheless thereafter chal-

---

1   [1975] 2 All ER 702, [1976] 1 QB 726
2   [1975] 2 All ER 702 at 720, 721, [1976] 1 QB 726 at 749

a   lenge the jurisdiction of that court to try the remaining issues—a proposition which we venture to think cannot be sustained.'

For the English company it was pointed out that this was a case which did not concern the 1933 Act but related to the common law position.

The French company's contention is founded on the fact that the application for leave to appeal was not limited to a challenge of the Lille court's jurisdiction to deal
b   with the Coframaille claim but was completely general. This is, as a fact, plainly correct. The application recites the overall judgment without drawing any distinction between the Coframaille and Pigeon Voyageur parts thereof. It states that the English company, considering the claim ill-founded, wish to exercise their rights under French jurisdiction and request that they be authorised to appeal against the judgment.

On any such appeal the defendants would be able to contend, and counsel for the
c   English company stated that they would in fact contend, inter alia, both that the Lille court had no jurisdiction in respect of the Coframaille part of the claim and that in any event it should be reduced or extinguished or even over-topped by the suggested counterclaim. Had the English company raised both these matters originally there could, in my judgment, have been no doubt that there was a voluntary submission otherwise than for the purpose of contesting the Lille court's jurisdiction
d   within the plain meaning of those words in s 4(2)(*a*)(i) but if there were any doubt about the meaning I would adopt the reasoning in the *Geopresco* case[1] to resolve that doubt. It would be an absurdity if the English company could be permitted to say: 'our counterclaim if we establish it will over-top the claim. We will therefore have it tried but if we do not like the answer we will say there was no jurisdiction and the judgment cannot be registered.' Does it make any difference that the voluntary
e   submission followed instead of preceding the judgment? In my judgment it does not and accordingly I hold that the Coframaille part of the judgment is registrable.

Should it then be registered or should I in this case exercise the discretion to refuse or adjourn in the light of the pending appeal? For the like reasons as I have given for declining to exercise that discretion in the case of the Pigeon Voyageur part of the claim and for one additional reason I decline to do so. The additional reason is this.
f   On 9th July 1975, some seven days before issue of the French writ, the French company's solicitors wrote to the English company presenting claims in respect of both the Coframaille and the Pigeon Voyageur goods and stating that if the claims were not paid within seven days they had instructions to issue proceedings. This letter was passed by the English company to their solicitors who on 16th July, on which day the French writ was in fact issued, wrote as follows: '. . . it would seem that your clients have omitted to inform you that their dispute with my clients comes within
g   the jurisdiction of the Lille court.' The French writ was of course not issued in reliance on this letter but when one finds a party complaining of absence of jurisdiction when its initial stand was that the court had jurisdiction, when it had knowledge of the original proceedings, when, although these proceedings were, admittedly, within jurisdiction as to part, it chose neither to defend that part nor to challenge jurisdiction on the remainder, when it had knowledge of the judgment long before the time when
h   it asserted in writing to the French Court of Appeal that it had such knowledge, it is not in my judgment entitled to the benefit of discretionary relief.

My conclusion on this point results in there being no problem with regard to apportionment of the Fr 10,000 in respect of 'résistance abusive' and in it being unnecessary for me to deal with the French company's alternative point under s 4(2)(*a*)
j   (iii). I therefore express no concluded view on that point. It appears to me however that the subsection requires an agreement to submit to the jurisdiction either to a particular court or generally to the courts of the country in question. In the present case there was an agreement to submit to the jurisdiction of a particular court,

1   [1975] 2 All ER 702, [1976] 1 QB 726

the Paris court not the Lille court, and there was no agreement to submit generally
to the courts of France. Despite Mr Davies's forceful argument that an agreement a
to submit to the jurisdiction of the Paris court grounds jurisdiction in *any* French
court for the purposes of the 1933 Act I would have held against the French company
on this point had it been necessary to do so.

I should refer briefly to Mr Picarda's affidavit with regard to French law. I have
not found it necessary to deal with it in any detail for it does no more than establish
either (a) that the Lille judgment is possibly a nullity, in which case the French b
company would have to begin all over again, or (b) that it is defective in a manner
which has the effect of preventing time for appeal from running until the defect
is cured. These matters will no doubt be ventilated in the appeal which has been
entered in the Court of Appeal at Douai. In the event of either suggestion being
upheld the effect will delay very considerably the French company's right of recovery
on the Pigeon Voyageur part of the claim to which no defence and no counterclaim c
of substance has been shown to exist.

In the end I have no hesitation in reaching the conclusion that the English company
are by their manoeuvrings doing no more than seeking to put off the evil hour and
that justice will be served by letting the full judgment be registered and leaving the
English company to establish any counterclaims or claims which they may have in
the appropriate French courts. In the result the English company's appeal will be d
dismissed, the cross-appeal will be allowed and the order of Master Warren varied
so as to order registration of the whole judgment. There remains only the question
of interest. The parties have now agreed as to the proper sum to be included in the
registration in respect of interest and therefore that sum, when it has been notified to
the court, will also be ordered to be registered. The English company's appeal will
therefore be dismissed and the French company's appeal will be allowed in the e
manner I have stated.

English company's appeal dismissed; French company's cross-appeal allowed.

Solicitors: *O H Parsons* (for the English company); *Lee, Bolton & Lee* (for the French
company). f

K Mydeen Esq Barrister.

Appeal

The English company appealed against the order of Parker J.

g

Kenneth Rokison QC and *Aron Owen* for the English company.
Brian Neill QC and *Thomas Shields* for the French company.

Cur adv vult

4th July. The following judgments were read.

LORD DENNING MR. In this case a French company have obtained judgment h
in France against an English company, and seek to register the judgment here in
England so that it can be enforced here. It involves several technical points.

The facts are these. There is a large textile firm in France called the SA Consortium
General Textiles. I will call it 'the French company'. Its head office is at Lille, but it
has several branches. One of them is called Pigeon Voyageur which carries on at
Lille. The other is called Coframaille which carries on at Paris. In 1974 the Lille j
branch (Pigeon Voyageur) of the French company supplied thousands of trousers to
English merchants called Sun & Sand Agencies Ltd. I will call them 'the English
company'. They resold them to big retailers in London. The Paris branch (Coframaille) of the French company supplied thousands of T-shirts to the same English
company, likewise for resale. The invoices contained printed conditions. The Lille

branch had a condition saying that all disputes were to be referred to the Commercial
a   Court at Lille ('the Lille court'): 'Toute contestation sera du ressort du Tribunal de
Commerce de LILLE même en cas d'appel en garantie ou de pluralité de défendeurs.'
The Paris branch had a condition saying that all disputes were to be referred to the
Commercial Court at Paris ('the Paris court'): 'Le Tribunal de Commerce de la
Seine est seul compétent pour toutes contestations.'
    The goods were delivered. The sum payable by the English company amounted to
b   Fr 448,955 to the Lille branch and Fr 280,489 to the Paris branch. That came to about
£50,000 or £60,000 in sterling. The debt was guaranteed by Mr Muller, a director of
the English company, up to a total of £100,000. The sums not having been paid, the
French company instructed London solicitors to collect it. On 9th July 1975 the
solicitors wrote to the English company at their business address 12 Maddox Street,
London W1.   They specified the sums payable to the two branches, and said that
c   unless the money was paid within seven days they would issue proceedings against
the English company in the High Court here in England.
    I pause here to say that (if we were to forget for the moment the jurisdiction
clauses) it was entirely proper for the French company to bring proceedings in
England. Under the Brussels Convention relating to the enforcement of judgments[1],
which is to come into effect before long, the general principle in Europe is that a
d   creditor must seek out the debtor and sue him in the debtor's country.
    The English company passed this letter to their London solicitor. On 15th July 1975
he telephoned to the London solicitors for the French company who made a note of
the conversation. The English company's solicitor pointed out that on the notepaper
of CGT Lille (the French company) 'it was clearly stated that all disputes must be
brought before the [Lille court], and that therefore any action brought in England
e   could be stayed'. On the next day, 16th July, the solicitor for the English company
wrote to the solicitors for the French company:

    '[The English company] and their Managing Director, Mr. Muller, have asked
    me to deal with your letter of 9th July and, as mentioned over the telephone
    yesterday, it would seem that your clients have omitted to inform you that
    their dispute with my clients comes within the jurisdiction of the Lille Court:
f   see, for example, the copy letter herewith from Pigeon Voyageur dated 27th
    March 1975. In these circumstances, it seems to me that the jurisdiction of the
    High Court here in England has been ousted and perhaps you will be good enough
    to consider the matter further with your clients.'

    It is clear from that telephone communication and letter that the English company
g   objected to proceedings being brought in England. It said that the High Court in
England had no jurisdiction. The French company accepted that point of view.
Instead of taking proceedings in England, it took proceedings in France. On 16th
July 1975 the French company issued a writ against the English company in the Lille
court claiming the two sums due respectively, Fr 280,489 due to the Paris branch and
Fr 448,955 due to the Lille branch together with interest; and in addition Fr 10,000
h   on the ground that the English company were wrongly resisting payment. This claim
for Fr 10,000 was formulated in French in these words: 'La résistance abusive de la
Société débitrice cause a ma requérante un préjudice qui ne saurait être fixé à moins de
10,000·00 F.F.'
    By that French writ the English company was summoned to appear before the
Lille court on 30th September 1975. Notice of the writ was served out of the juris-
j   diction by the method prescribed by French law, namely by being sent by registered

---

1   Brussels Convention on Jurisdiction and the Enforcement of Civil and Commercial Judg-
    ments, art 2. Council of Europe, The practical guide to the recognition and enforcement
    of foreign judicial decisions in civil and commercial law (Strasbourg, 1975), p 105. The
    convention is dated 27th September 1968

letter to the English company at their registered office, 12 Dryden Chambers, 119 Oxford Street, London, on 12th August 1975 and a reminder on 12th September *a* 1975. The English company received the copy writ but, on the advice of their lawyers, ignored it. The English company did not appear on 30th September 1975 before the French court. They let the proceedings in France go by default.

So, there being no appearance, the Lille court, on 14th October 1975, entered judgment in default of appearance against the English company for the total sum of Fr 729,444·13 and interest and the sum of Fr 10,000 for damages. It added: 'Since the *b* case is pressing, [the court] ordains the provisional enforcement of this judgment, notwithstanding appeal, and without security.' In other words, it ordered the judgment to be enforced and there was to be no stay of execution.

On 10th December 1975 the Lille court sent a copy of that judgment by registered post to the English company, adding: 'You may appeal against this judgment before the Appeal Court of DOUAI within THREE MONTHS reckoning from the date [of service]'; *c* and a copy was sent to the French consulate in London for them to notify the English company. The letter sent direct to the English company was not delivered because the address was given as 'Dryden Chambers' whereas it should have been '12 Dryden Chambers'. But that omission was made good because a like notice was sent by the French Consul-General in London; and he notified the English company of it. He gave the English company written notice of it on 29th January 1976 and a reminder *d* on 2nd March. The English company certainly got it. But they ignored that judgment also. They did not appeal within the three months that were allowed.

On those facts it is apparent that the English company ignored the French proceedings. They did not appear or appeal. So on the face of it, the French judgment was a good judgment. Accordingly, on 5th August 1976 the French company applied to the High Court of England to have the judgment of 14th October 1975 registered *e* in the High Court here under s 2(1) of the Foreign Judgments (Reciprocal Enforcement) Act 1933.

The English company then for the first time did something. They opposed the registration in England. They also instructed lawyers in Lille to apply to the Lille court for leave to appeal out of time from the judgment of 14th October 1975. On 23rd December 1976 the President of the court of Douai, sitting in chambers, dis- *f* missed the application. On 25th January 1977 the English company asserted that it could appeal without leave and entered an appeal to the full court at Douai.

Another step was taken by the English company. On 27th October 1976 they issued a writ against the French company in the Paris court in which they claimed damages in respect of the T-shirts supplied by the Paris branch. They claimed a sum of some £80,000 sterling which would overtop the purchase price of the T-shirts. Such are *g* the facts.

Section 2(1)(b) of the Foreign Judgments (Reciprocal Enforcement) Act 1933

Seeing that the judgment of the Lille court was apparently in good order, it would seem a plain case for registration under s 2(1) of the 1933 Act but the English company rely on the provisions contained in s 2(1)(b). They say that the judgment of the *h* Lille court should not be registered in the High Court here because 'it could not be enforced by execution in the country of the original court', that is in France.

This contention is based on the form of the judgment of 14th October 1975. It was a judgment by default; and under the French Code of Civil Procedure—

> 'When a judgment by default is given against a party residing abroad it should state expressly the steps taken with a view to bringing the original summons to *j* the knowledge of the defendant.'

(That is art 49 of the 1972 Code now replaced by art 479 of the 1976 Code.) In this case the judgment of 14th October 1975 simply recited: 'Whereas the above mentioned company was regularly summoned to appear at the hearing on 30th September';

but it was said that, in order to comply with art 49, it should have stated that the
a summons 'was sent by registered letter' etc, setting out each of the steps which had
been taken to bring the original summons to the knowledge of the defendants.
It was suggested that this failure to state expressly the steps made the judgment a
nullity.

This contention was not, in my judgment, substantiated. Reading the evidence
of the French lawyers, it is plain that a failure to mention those steps in the recital
b did not make the judgment a nullity. It only made it voidable. It would not render
it a nullity unless on appeal a competent court declared it to be so. Furthermore,
it seems to me on the evidence that the required steps had in fact been taken and the
omission to mention them in the recital did not prejudice the defendants in any way.
The French courts would not declare it a nullity.

In these circumstances, it seems to me that the Lille judgment could be enforced
c by execution in the French courts. So s 2(1)(b) is no bar.

Section 5(1) of the 1933 Act

The English company also relied on s 5(1) which says that if an appeal is pending
against the Lille judgment 'the court, if it thinks fit, may, on such terms as it thinks
ust, either set aside the registration or adjourn the application'.
d   The English company did on 25th January 1977 lodge an appeal to the Full Court
at Douai on the same grounds as I have mentioned, namely the failure to comply
with art 49. They also say that they have a cross-claim on the ground that the goods
were defective. Counsel for the English company urged us to say that the grounds
were arguable and that on this account the court should exercise its discretion in
favour of the English company. I cannot accept this argument. We considered a
e similar argument in *Ferdinand Wagner (a firm) v Laubscher Brothers & Co (a firm)*[1] and
rejected it. It seems to me that we ought to give full faith and credit to the French
judgment, even though there may be arguable grounds for disputing it or raising a
counterclaim against it. This is reinforced by the European Convention which requires
each of the member states to take proper steps to enforce the judgments of other
member states. I agree with Parker J on this point. I do not think there is any reason
f why the discretion in this case should be exercised in favour of the English company.

Section 4(2)(a)(i) and (iii) of the 1933 Act

Section 4(1)(a)(ii) says that a registration may be set aside if 'the courts of the country
of the original court had no jurisdiction in the circumstances of the case'. The English
company admitted that the Lille court had jurisdiction in respect of the part of the
g judgment in respect of the Lille branch (the Pigeon Voyageur and CGT). This was
because the condition on the printed invoice of the Lille branch was a voluntary
submission to the jurisdiction of the Lille court in respect of the Fr 448,995 due to the
Lille branch. But the English company said that the Lille court had no jurisdiction
in respect of the Fr 280,489 due to the Paris branch (Coframaille), because the
English company had never submitted to the jurisdiction of the Lille court in that
h regard, but only to the Paris court. The master accepted that contention, and only
registered the part in respect of the Lille branch and not in respect of the Paris branch,
but Parker J rejected the contention. He registered the whole judgment.

So the question is whether the French courts had jurisdiction in respect of the
Paris debt. I will deal with this in two parts. First, s 4(2)(a)(iii) says that a defendant
j is deemed to have submitted to the jurisdiction of the original court—

'if the judgment debtor, being a defendant in the original court, had before
the commencement of the proceedings agreed, in respect of the subject matter

---

1 [1970] 2 All ER 174, [1970] 2 QB 313

of the proceedings, to submit to the jurisdiction of that court or of the courts of
the country of that court.'

I would construe those last nine words widely so as to read them: 'of *any* of the
courts of the country of that court.' That meets the intendment of the 1933 Act. It
may fairly be assumed that each of the courts of a country applies the same law, that is,
the law of the country itself. So a submission to the jurisdiction of any one of the
courts of that country should be treated as equivalent to a submission to the jurisdiction of any of the other courts of the country. In this case, therefore, when the
English company agreed to submit the dispute with the Paris branch to the Paris
court, it must be taken to be equivalent to a submission to any of the courts of France,
including the Lille court.

Alternatively I would read the telephone conversation of 15th July 1975 as an
agreement to submit to the jurisdiction of the Lille court. The English solicitors, by
asserting that '*all* disputes must be brought before the Tribunal de Commerce de
Lille' must be understood as implying that the English company would submit to
the tribunal in respect of all disputes between them.

Take next s 4(2)(*a*)(i). It says that a defendant is deemed to have submitted to the
jurisdiction—

'if the judgment debtor, being a defendant in the original court, submitted to
the jurisdiction of that court by voluntarily appearing in the proceedings otherwise than for the purpose . . . of contesting the jurisdiction of that court.'

The English company did not appear in the original court at Lille but it did appear
in the appeal court at Douai. It made an application to the appeal court and lodged
an appeal against the judgment of the original court. That application to the appeal
court was in my view a submission to the jurisdiction of the original court, because it
sought to upset it. By inviting the appeal court to decide in its favour on the merits,
it must be taken to have submitted to the jurisdiction of the original court. If the
appeal court decided in its favour, it would have accepted the decision. So also if it
decided against it, thus upholding the original court, it must accept the decision. It
cannot be allowed to say that it would accept the decision of the appeal court if it was
in its favour, and reject it if it was against it. In my opinion, therefore, by appealing to
the appeal court, the English company was submitting to the jurisdiction of the
original court. This is in accord with what I said in *Re Dulles' Settlement Trusts, Dulles v
Vidler*[1]. It is unaffected by *Henry v Geopresco International Ltd*[2]. I would hold that there
is jurisdiction in respect of the whole of the amount due to both branches.

The Fr 10,000

The English company urged that the judgment for Fr 10,000 should be excluded
because it was a sum payable 'in respect of a fine or other penalty' within s 1(2)(*b*);
or that the enforcement of it 'would be contrary to public policy' in England under
s 4(1)(*a*)(v).

This objection was based on the description given to the claim as being made on
account of 'résistance abusive', which may be translated as damages for unjustifiable
opposition to the plaintiffs' claim. It was said that the Fr 10,000 were claimed as
punitive or exemplary damages which amounted to a penalty and would have been
outlawed in England by *Rookes v Barnard*[3] and *Cassell & Co Ltd v Broome*[4], and therefor it should not be enforced as part of a foreign judgment.

I cannot accept this view. The word 'penalty' in the 1933 Act means, I think, a sum
payable to the state by way of punishment and not a sum payable to a private indivi-

---

1   [1951] 2 All ER 69 at 72, [1951] Ch 842 at 850
2   [1975] 2 All ER 702, [1976] 1 QB 726
3   [1964] 1 All ER 367, [1964] AC 1129
4   [1972] 1 All ER 801, [1975] AC 1027

dual, even though it is payable by way of exemplary damages. Likewise I see nothing
a contrary to English public policy in enforcing a claim for exemplary damages, which
is still considered to be in accord with public policy in the United States and many of
the great countries of the Commonwealth.

In any case, as I read the claim for Fr 10,000, it is not a claim for exemplary damages,
but it is a claim for compensatory damages, so as to compensate the plaintiff for
losses not covered by an award of interest, such as loss of business caused by want of
b 'cash flow', or for costs of the proceedings not covered by the court's order for costs.
So it seems to me that the Fr 10,000 item formed part of a perfectly proper judgment.

Conclusion

The long and the short of the case is that in July 1975 the French company proposed
to issue proceedings against the English company in the High Court in England;
c but the English company objected to that course, saying in effect that they should be
brought in the Lille court. Then, when the French company did issue proceedings
against the English company in that court, the English company simply ignored
them. As a consequence, judgment was entered by default against the English company in the Lille court. Then, when the French company quite properly sought to
register that judgment in England, the English company took all sorts of objections,
d technical objections as I see them, against the enforcement of it. I do not think we
should uphold these technical objections. We should give full faith and credit to
the judgment of the French court, just as we would expect them to give full faith
and credit to a judgment of an English court. I agree with the decision of the judge.
I think the whole of his judgment should be registered in England and enforced in
England. I would dismiss the appeal accordingly.

e

GOFF LJ. In this case I regret to find myself in disagreement with Lord Denning MR
as to part of this case, and I fear that I shall be found equally in disagreement with
Shaw LJ.

The first question which arises is as follows. It is said that the judgment is not
f registrable at all, having regard to proviso (b) to s 2(1) of the Foreign Judgments
(Reciprocal Enforcement) Act 1933. That proviso reads:

'. . . that a judgment shall not be registered if at the date of the application
. . . (b) it could not be enforced by execution in the country of the original court.'

g It is not suggested that, if the judgment be valid, it is of a kind in respect of which
execution is not possible or permissible. What is said is that the judgment is defective.
That is a purely technical objection. French law prescribes specifically how notice of
the commencement of proceedings is to be served where the defendant is resident out
of their jurisdiction. Those steps were complied with properly and the service was as
a matter of fact effective. The judgment, given in default because the English company
h refused to have anything to do with the proceedings, opened with a recital that the
company was regularly summoned to appear at the hearing. Mr Picarda, an expert
witness on French law, has made an affidavit in which he says in para 3:

'I am of the opinion that the Judgment of the Commercial Court of Lille,
France, dated the 14th October 1975 . . . is materially defective and possibly a
j nullity insofar as the Court failed to observe one of the express legal requirements
of the French Code of Civil Procedure (CPCN) relating to Judgments "réputés
contradictoires", namely that where such Judgment is given against a party
resident abroad, the Court by Article 479 of the CPCN must state expressly what
steps have been taken with a view to giving "knowledge" (connaissance) of the
Originating Summons to the defendant.'

Later in para 4 of the same affidavit he says:

'All the Court did was to repeat the standard formulae used in judgments in   **a**
France when both parties reside there and service is effected in France, namely:
"Whereas the above named defendant was duly served with notice to appear at
the hearing of the 30th September, extended to the date hereof".'

So what he is saying is that not only must the proper steps be taken, as they were,
but the judgment must recite that they were taken.   **b**
The affidavit is somewhat ambiguous because it uses the expression 'is materially
defective and possibly a nullity', but para 9 of the same affidavit appears to me to
show what Mr Picarda really meant, because he refers there to the judgment being
'voidable for a material omission of the statement required to be made under Art
479 CPCN . . . '

The French company's English solicitor, Mr Davies, stating the result of enquiries   **c**
which he made of another French advocate, Maître Racca, swore an affidavit to the
following effect, and I commence reading at para (5)(b):

'Failure to comply with technical formalities will only result in proceedings
being treated as a nullity if it is so declared by a competent Court to whom an
Appeal is made. (c) Special considerations affect any proceedings sought to annul   **d**
an actual Judgment on the grounds of procedural irregularity. Nullity will not
be declared where the procedural irregularity is a failure to mention the carrying
out of some procedural step if in practice that procedural step was duly carried
out. (d) In any event there is a general principle of French Law "Pas de Nullité
sans griefs" eg. if it is sought to nullify a Judgment for procedural irregularity
the Applicant must prove that he has suffered damage or his case has in some way   **e**
been prejudiced by reason of such irregularity. (6) It follows therefore that in
the view of Maître Racca the appeal to the Court of Douai has no chance of
success because, (a) The only defect alleged is the failure to set out the method
by which the service of the Writ was effected. (b) It is quite clear that the Writ
was properly served as is conceded. (c) That the Defendants have in no way been
prejudiced by this procedural irregularity as has been conceded by Counsel on   **f**
their behalf. (7) Maitre Racca therefore advises that in this Case notwithstanding
failure to comply with Article 49 of the 1972 Code or Article 479 of the new Code
the Lille Judgment is valid unless and until set aside by a competent Court of
Appeal.'

Paragraph (7) does not appear to be wholly consistent with para (6), but I think it is   **g**
clear that Mr Davies interpreted the maître's advice as meaning that on the facts of
this case it was impossible to have the judgment set aside. But Maitre Picarda was
in court, and we were informed that he said he did not agree that the judgment could
not be set aside on the grounds postulated by him even though the failure to recite the
steps taken had not resulted in prejudice. So the evidence that it is unassailable is
perhaps open to question, as there is a conflict about that between the French legal   **h**
advisers, but it is clearly common ground that the judgment can only be attacked,
if at all, on appeal. It is, therefore, good until set aside. Accordingly, in my view, the
judgment does not come within the proviso, but the matter will fall to be further
considered in respect of the exercise of discretion when I turn to s 5.

Before I come to that section, however, there are two other questions with which I
must deal, and the first is the aspect of this case on which unhappily I am unable to   **j**
agree with Lord Denning MR. The English master divided the judgment into two
parts, and he registered it so far as it concerned the Pigeon Voyageur part of the claim,
which by the original agreement between the parties had been consigned to the
Lille court, but refused to register the Coframaille claim, which had been consigned
to the Paris court. The question is: was that right?, and it turns on sub-ss (1)(a)(ii) and

(2)(*a*)(i) and (iii) of s 4 taken in conjunction with s 2(5). Section 4(1)(*a*)(ii), so far as material, says:

'. . . the registration of the judgment—(*a*) shall be set aside if the registering court is satisfied . . . (ii) that the courts of the country of the original court had no jurisdiction in the circumstances of the case.'

Section 2(5) is in these terms:

'If, on an application for the registration of a judgment, it appears to the registering court that the judgment is in respect of different matters and that some, but not all, of the provisions of the judgment are such that if those provisions had been contained in separate judgments those judgments could properly have been registered, the judgment may be registered in respect of the provisions aforesaid but not in respect of any other provisions contained therein.'

The jurisdiction originally agreed between the parties was in a particular French court: the Lille court so far as it concerned the Pigeon Voyageur part of the case, and the Paris court so far as it concerned the Coframaille part of the case. It is said that that was a submission to a particular court and not generally and, therefore, the Coframaille part is bad because s 4(1)(*a*)(ii) requires that the submission should have been to the courts of the country of the original court, although, of course, the Pigeon Voyageur part will stand under ss 4(2)(*a*)(iii) and 2(5). That, in my view, is correct, unless any of the provisions of s 4(2) apply to the Coframaille claim, for if they do, then it is provided that for the purposes of this section the courts of the country of the original court shall, subject to the provisions of s 4(3), which are not material, be deemed to have had jurisdiction.

On the other hand, it was argued, so long as by the agreement between the parties any French court had jurisdiction, they all had, so that the agreement that the Coframaille part should be cognisable by the Paris court gave jurisdiction to the Lille court. I cannot accept that. It appears to me to be quite inconsistent with the distinction drawn in s 4(1) and (2) between the original court and the courts of the country. In my view, therefore, unless there be something within s 4(2) to bring the Coframaille part of the case within the section and make it registrable, the master was right not to register that part of the judgment.

It was submitted, however, that there was some such thing, namely that the case fell within paras (i) and (iii) of s 4(2)(*a*). Paragraph (iii) says:

'if the judgment debtor, being a defendant in the original court, had before the commencement of the proceedings agreed, in respect of the subject matter of the proceedings, to submit to the jurisdiction of that court or of the courts of the country of that court.'

It is clear, in my view, that there was never any agreement to submit to the courts of the country. The question is, was there an agreement to submit the Coframaille part of the case to the Lille court? The case was based on a telephone conversation between the solicitors for the parties on 15th July 1975, the day before the French summons was issued, which conversation is referred to in the letter of 16th July 1975, which Lord Denning MR has mentioned. We have had the advantage of seeing Mr Davies's attendance note of that telephone conversation, which reads as follows:

'Mr. Berger on his telephoning to point out that on the writing paper of C.G.T. Lille it was clearly stated that all disputes must be brought before the Tribunal de Commerce de Lille and that therefore any action brought in England could be stayed. We promised therefore to do nothing further until we heard from him.'

It was argued that 'agreed' in s 4(2)(*a*)(iii) means no more than consented. That is probably right, but in my view it is unnecessary to decide that question because, in my judgment, this conversation could not be an agreement within the paragraph on any construction. All it did was to record that there had been an agreement that all disputes must be brought before the Lille court, but that was an error. There was no such agreement, and this conversation did not purport to make one. Even if it were proved, which it was not, that the letter of 16th July was received before the commencement of the proceedings, which it could not have been unless delivered by *hand*, still the letter carries the matter no further.

It was then suggested that there might be an estoppel. There clearly could be none arising out of the telephone conversation or the letter, because it is clear that, in commencing the proceedings in Lille, the French company were not relying on either. This must be so both from the dates and from the fact, as evidenced from the attendance note, that Mr Davies was awaiting hearing further from the English company's solicitors.

It did cross my mind that there might be an estoppel arising subsequently from the failure of the English company to indicate in any way that what was said on the telephone and in the letter was wrong. But apart from any question whether that would estop the English company from denying that there was an agreement prior to the commencement of the proceedings, there is absolutely no evidence that the French company continued the proceedings in Lille in reliance in any way on such non-correction. In my judgment, therefore, the case does not fall within s 4(2)(*a*)(iii).

I turn then to consider s 4(2)(*a*)(i), and here there are two relevant matters. First, the application to the President of the Court at Douai for leave to appeal out of time; and, secondly, the actual appeal which has now been made to that court. · It was argued for the English company that an appeal, even on the merits, can never be a submission to the judgment of the inferior court though it may of couse be a submission to the judgment of the foreign court of appeal, and reliance was placed on *Guiard v de Clermont & Donner*[1]. That case is distinguishable because there the judgment of the court below had been set aside; and, as Lawrence J said[2], it was dead. It seems that what is registered is the original judgment and not that of the court of appeal: see the language of s 2(1), which is in these terms:

'A person, being a judgment creditor under a judgment to which this Part of this Act applies, may apply to the High Court at any time within six years after the date of the judgment, or, where there have been proceedings by way of appeal against the judgment, after the date of the last judgment given in those proceedings, to have the judgment registered in the High Court.'

In *Ferdinand Wagner (a firm) v Laubscher Brothers & Co (a firm)*[3] it was the original judgment affirmed by the foreign court of appeal which was ultimately registered. Therefore, it would seem that an appeal on the merits would be sufficient, but in my judgment, it is unnecessary to decide that point.

So far as the actual appeal now pending is concerned, the grounds have not yet been stated, and Mr Picarda says in para 2 of his second affidavit:

'Although I am instructed that the grounds of Appeal have not yet been lodged the fact of the Appeal itself does not mean that the [English company] have thereby retrospectively submitted the merits of the Coframaille claim to the Lille Court or that the Appeal relates to the said merits. It is open to the [English company] in the event to challenge the jurisdiction of the Lille Court in respect of the Coframaille Claim.'

On the evidence before us that is not challenged, and it is, therefore, impossible to

1 [1914] 3 KB 145
2 [1914] 3 KB 145 at 155
3 [1970] 2 All ER 174, [1970] 2 QB 313

say so far as the Coframaille part of the case is concerned that the English company has by appealing taken part in the proceedings for a purpose other than that of disputing the jurisdiction, and that is what has to be shown.

.I have been more concerned about the application for leave to appeal since it might be said that that did recognise the validity of the judgment because it presupposed the time for appeal had run, but I think that is too narrow a view. Here again in my view, the English company did not commit themselves. They failed to get leave, and that was that. But, had they got it, they might have appealed against the Coframaille part of the judgment on the question of jurisdiction only. It was pointed out that the application draws no distinction between the two parts of the claim, and it was based simply on the untruthful statement that they had not had notice of the judgment, and, it was urged, that if they had intended, if allowed to appeal, to limit it so far as Coframaille is concerned to the question of jurisdiction they should have made some reservation to that effect. I do not think that was necessary at that stage. Accordingly, in my judgment, the master was right to divide the claim into two parts and to refuse registration of the Coframaille part, and I would allow the appeal to that extent.

The other question is whether registration should be refused of the whole or part of the judgment, as the case may be, so far as concerns the damages or award of compensation for 'résistance abusive' as being a tax or other charge of a like nature or a fine or penalty within s 1(2)(b) or contrary to public policy within s 4(1)(a)(v). Counsel for the English company argued that the words have a wide meaning and, therefore, embrace such an award because, so the argument ran, it is not compensation or an estimate of damages, and he stresses that it was given in addition to interest. Alternatively, he says it is akin to exemplary damages and not within any of the categories laid down in *Rookes v Barnard*[1], and, therefore, it is contrary to public policy, because in *Re Macartney, Macfarlane v Macartney*[2] it was established that it is the policy of the law not to extend these categories.

Counsel for the French company argued, per contra, that the words have a narrow meaning, and are merely declaratory of the common law[3]:

'The court has no jurisdiction to entertain an action—(1) for the enforcement, either directly or indirectly, of a penal, revenue, or other public law of a foreign State; or (2) founded upon an act of State.'

In any event, he says they are aggravated damages, not exemplary damages, and, even if they are the latter, still no question of public policy is involved: it is merely a question of the circumstances in which an English court today in an English case will award exemplary damages; that is not a question of public policy.

The judgment describes this award as damages, and the French summons specifies the nature of the claim. It is translated as a tort, but the original which we have seen shows that to be a bad translation. The French word is 'préjudice'. In my judgment, therefore, this was a further award of damages or compensation. It is not a fine or other penalty within the section and no question of public policy arises.

I come then to the last matter, the exercise of discretion under s 5, and I agree with Lord Denning MR and the judge below that the discretion should not be exercised in the English company's favour. I would not in any case refuse registration under this section. The question I have considered is: should we adjourn pending the appeal which has now in fact been started, and I have no hesitation in reaching the conclusion that we should not, for which there appear to me to be a number of unassailable reasons. The first is that the trial judge exercised his discretion that

1 [1964] 1 All ER 367, [1964] AC 1129
2 [1921] 1 Ch 522 at 527, 528
3 Dicey and Morris, The Conflict of Laws (9th Edn, 1973), p 75, r 3

way, and he has not been shown to have acted on a wrong principle. Secondly, the Lille court had undoubted jurisdiction as to the Pigeon Voyageur claim, and the English company chose to take no part in the proceedings at all and did not set up any defence or counterclaim if it had one. The whole proceeding was ignored. That was done on advice, and it may be unfortunate advice, but the English company cannot shelter behind that. Their conduct in that regard has simply caused the French company long delay and added expense. Thirdly, the judgment was given on 14th October 1975, but it was not until the case was before us that anything like a detailed statement of defence or counterclaim was produced, so there was more delay.

It is suggested that as the claim which the English company now desire to set up could have been brought before the court in the Lille action, they are now barred unless the judgment can be and is set aside. That may be so under French law or it may not, but in my judgment for present purposes that is an irrelevant consideration, since registration will not make the judgment less vulnerable nor will adjournment protect it. If they have lost their rights, they have, but apart from that, the registration of the judgment will not prevent them enforcing their claims by separate proceedings, and that is the fourth reason for refusing an adjournment.

The fifth is that before they can get an appeal on the merits on its feet at all they have to succeed in France on two purely technical points. The first, as Lord Denning MR has already stated and I have referred to it further in my judgment, is the non-statement of the mode of service of the summons, and the second is very similar. By French law the huissier or process server had to serve notice of the judgment by registered post. It is said that he did not do so effectively, although he addressed the letter as was proper to the registered office of the English company, because although he had the address correct in every other particular he omitted the street number, although he knew it. The evidence at present seems to show the result of that small omission was that it proved impossible to deliver the notice at all despite two separate attempts. I find that difficult to understand, and I am tempted to think that the letter found its way to the proper place and that somebody there refused to accept it. I cannot, however, draw that inference on the evidence as it stands, having regard to the affidavit which has been sworn by the company's accountant, a Mr Winter, whose office is the registered office of the company. That may have to be explored in the Douai proceedings, but the fact remains that both these points are purely technical and the appeal has to succeed on those preliminary technical points before, if I may use the expression, it can get off the ground.

The sixth reason I would advance is that the hearing is not even imminent. There is an appointment for September, no earlier, and that is merely a preliminary one to fix the date for the actual hearing of the appeal. I realise the force of the objection which has been urged on us that, if we allow registration, the French company can then levy execution here and the English company can only pursue such remedies as are open to them and seek repayment in France. In many cases that would have great weight, but not in my judgment on the facts of the present case where, as I see it, the English company and their advisers have brought the troubles on themselves.

I would therefore allow the appeal to the extent I have mentioned by dividing the judgment into two parts and rescinding the registration of the Coframaille part, but I would refuse the appeal as to the residue of the judgment.

SHAW LJ. Subject to what is in this case an immaterial qualification I agree with the conclusions and the reasons stated in the judgment of Lord Denning MR. I need only therefore consider in any detail those aspects of this appeal in regard to which Goff LJ differs from those conclusions.

It seems clear enough that the judgment it is sought to register is under French law voidable and not void; accordingly it cannot be disregarded unless and until it is declared a nullity by the appellate court at Douai. Although the evidence before this court does not enable a definite concluded view to be reached, it seems to me at least very unlikely that the failure to comply with the formal requirements of art 479 of the 1976 Code could, in the circumstances of this case, have the ultimate consequence of causing the judgment to be vitiated and declared a nullity. The English company cannot point to any detriment to them of a material kind which has resulted from the omission from the judgment of the requisite statement as to the mode of service pursued. This is the more so having regard to the fact that they had made, on legal advice, a deliberate decision to ignore any proceedings in the French courts. It is sufficient to say that the judgment stands for the time being.

Irrespective of this view as to the status of the judgment, there is the crucial question of whether or not there was on the part of the English company a submission to the jurisdiction of the Lille court in regard to the Coframaille transaction. Section 4(2)(a)(iii) speaks of the judgment debtor having 'agreed in respect of the subject matter of the proceedings' that the particular court should have jurisdiction. In this context it seems to me that 'agreed' must mean expressed willingness or consented to or acknowledged that he would accept the jurisdiction of the foreign court. It does not require that the judgment debtor must have bound himself contractually or in formal terms so to do.

In their letter of 16th July 1975 the English company's then solicitor referred to a telephone conversation in which he had told the French company's solicitors 'that their dispute with my clients comes within the jurisdiction of the Lille Court'. That dispute comprehended at that date the Coframaille contract as well as the Pigeon Voyageur one. The terms of that letter amount, in my judgment, reiterating as they do a conversation the day before, to an invitation to the French company to institute proceedings at Lille in respect of the Pigeon Voyageur and the Coframaille business. Semantic analysis is an incongruous exercise when dealing with commercial disputes and it seems to me that the practical requirements of commerce are more significant in such a situation than canons of construction. It is true that it was not this invitation which encouraged the French company to start a comprehensive action in Lille, but at least it disarmed further consideration as to whether that was the proper venue for the overall dispute. The inference that the prospective defendants were ready to submit to the jurisdiction of the Lille court in regard to all matters in dispute between them and the French company, and that their solicitor meant to convey this, is rendered easily acceptable by the consideration that if the English company were to be sued at all, it would be advantageous and not disadvantageous to them to have to face proceedings in one court at one and the same time rather than in two different courts.

Even if this is wrong, there is the further demonstration of unqualified submission to the jurisdiction of the Lille court, in the English company's application to the appeal court at Douai for leave to appeal against the judgment of the Lille court, which judgment of course dealt with both transactions. The recitals in the notice of appeal make it abundantly clear that both constituents of that judgment are to be called in question. There is not the least hint that the Coframaille judgment is to be impugned on any ground different from that relating to Pigeon Voyageur. An unqualified notice of appeal which does not differentiate between one part of the judgment and another should be taken as asking the appellate court to regard itself as seised of all aspects of the prospective appeal including the merits.

There are no fewer than nine separate recitals in the notice of appeal. It would have been elementary and proper if jurisdiction was to be called in issue to have added a tenth recital, namely 'whereas the parties had agreed in relation to the Coframaille transaction that the Tribunal de la Seine should have exclusive jurisdiction to try any dispute arising therefrom'. No such indication is given anywhere in the notice of appeal which is at large and must be regarded as going to all the merits even if jurisdiction is to be called into question as well. Thus the eighth recital avers that the applicant wishes to exercise his rights before the French jurisdiction, holding the view that the claim of CGT is ill-founded. That, as it seems to me, is indicating in plain terms that what is going to be sought on appeal is leave to attack the judgment on the whole of the merits arising out of both transactions to which that judgment related.

Counsel for the English company has yet another string to his bow. He contended that the phrase 'in the proceedings' where it appears in s 4(2)(*a*)(i) must be read as meaning 'in the proceedings in the original court'. For myself I see no warrant for this proposition. The expression 'proceedings' comprehends the whole course of litigation relating to a particular subject-matter whether in the court of first instance or appeal to a superior tribunal. If this simple proposition is not in itself sufficiently convincing, it is reinforced by the use in s 4 of the phrase 'proceedings in the original court', which appears in sub-s (2)(*a*)(ii), and the phrase 'the proceedings in that court', which appears in sub-s (2)(*a*)(v). This is a clear demonstration, so it seems to me, that the phrase 'the proceedings' where it appears without qualification in sub-s (2)(*a*)(i) is not to be understood in any restricted sense but refers to the whole course of the proceedings in a given litigious process.

I am in agreement with Goff LJ as to the proper construction of s 4(2)(*a*)(iii), namely that 'submission to the courts of that country' can arise only where there is an express submission in general terms to the courts of a country rather than to individual courts.

As to the question of discretion, so far as it arises on this application, if one regards it as an application to set aside a registration, I see no reason to depart from the view expressed in that regard by Parker J. I am also of the view, in relation to the Fr 10,000 award in respect of résistance abusive' that this is purely compensatory. It represents damage other than loss of interest which flows from a failure of a party to a mercantile transaction to pay in accordance with his obligations. Deprivation of the use of capital may be disruptive of a business and may involve loss beyond mere interest on capital.

I would accordingly dismiss the appeal in its entirety.

Appeal dismissed. Leave to appeal to the House of Lords refused.

Solicitors: *Linklaters & Paines* (for the English company in the Court of Appeal); *Lee, Bolton & Lee* (for the French company).

Sumra Green   Barrister.

Hudgell Yeates & Co v Watson

COURT OF APPEAL, CIVIL DIVISION
MEGAW, BRIDGE AND WALLER LJJ
20th, 21st, 24th OCTOBER, 3rd, 30th NOVEMBER 1977

Solicitor – Partnership – Dissolution – Lapse of practising certificate – Unlawful for person to act as a solicitor without a practising certificate – Partner inadvertently allowing practising certificate to lapse – Whether partnership dissolved by operation of law – Whether partnership reconstituted between remaining partners – Partnership Act 1890, s 34.

Solicitor – Costs – Recovery – Unqualified person – Partnership – Partner allowing practising certificate to lapse – Costs incurred in respect of work done by another partner during period of disqualification – Action to recover costs – Whether by virtue of partnership work to be treated as work done by disqualified partner – Whether other partner precluded from recovering costs in respect of work done – Solicitors Act 1957, s 18(2)(b).

In January 1973 the defendant instructed J, a partner in the plaintiffs, a firm of solicitors, to act for him in the conduct of certain litigation. J passed the defendant to another partner, G, who, together with a managing clerk who was supervised by and responsible to G, conducted the defendant's litigation between January and December 1973. There was a third partner in the firm, S, who worked at a different office of the firm's from that in which G and J both worked. S took no part in the defendant's affairs. S inadvertently failed to renew his practising certificate for 1973 until 2nd May 1973 and for the period 1st January to 1st May 1973 ('the relevant period') did not hold a current practising certificate. He was therefore, by virtue of s 1 of the Solicitors Act 1957, during that period disqualified from acting as a solicitor. The defendant failed to pay the plaintiff's bill of costs which covered the period 2nd January to December 1973. In May 1974 the plaintiffs, suing in the names of S and the other two partners, brought an action against the defendant to recover the costs under the bill and obtained judgment against him. On appeal, the defendant contended, inter alia, that, because S had been disqualified from practising as a solicitor during the relevant period, the plaintiffs were precluded by s 18(2)(b)[a] of the 1957 Act from recovering costs in respect of work done for the defendant during that period, since work done by one of the partners, or by an employee under his supervision, was work done by him as agent for all the partners.

Held (Bridge LJ dissenting) – The defendant's contention failed for the following reasons—

(i) When S's practising certificate lapsed the existing partnership between himself and the remaining partners was automatically dissolved under s 34[b] of the Partnership Act 1890, since it was illegal for an unqualified person to be a member of a solicitors' partnership. Accordingly the partnership had been reconstituted during the relevant period as a partnership between the remaining partners. Furthermore J and G were not estopped from denying that S had been a partner during the relevant period for, although they had held S out as being a partner, the defendant had not instructed the firm in reliance on the representation that S was a partner. Accordingly, since no work had been done for the defendant by, or under the supervision of, S during the relevant period, J and G as the remaining partners were entitled to recover their costs for the work done for him during that period (see p 372 f to p 373 a, p 374 a and e to g and p 375 b and e to h, post); dicta of Lord Ashbourne LC in *Martin v Sherry* [1905] 2 IR at 65, 67 applied.

---

a Section 18(2), so far as material, is set out at p 366 j, post
b Section 34 is set out at p 368 f, post

(ii) In any event (per Waller J) the references in s 18(2)(*b*) of the 1957 Act to an 'unqualified person' were references to an individual; it was only the individual who was made incapable of maintaining the action. Since the plaintiffs' claim included nothing for work done by S acting as a solicitor, or by an employee of the firm acting under his supervision, they were entitled to recover costs for work done during the relevant period (see p 370 *f g* and *j*, p 371 *a* and p 373 *b c* and *e*, post).

Notes

For the effect of practising without a certificate, see 36 Halsbury's Laws (3rd Edn) 37, 38, para 55, and for cases on the subject, see 43 Digest (Repl) 40-44, *201-321*.

For the Solicitors Act 1957, s 18, see 32 Halsbury's Statutes (3rd Edn) 31.

For the Partnership Act 1890, s 34, see 24 Halsbury's Statutes (3rd Edn) 518.

Section 18 of the 1957 Act was replaced by the Solicitors Act 1974, s 25, on 1st May 1975.

Cases referred to in judgments

Fowler v Monmouthshire Railway and Canal Co (1879) 4 QBD 334, 48 LJQB 457, 41 LT 159, DC, 43 Digest (Repl) 41, *222*.

Freeman v Cooke (1848) 2 Exch 654, [1843-60] All ER Rep 185, 6 Dow & L 187, 18 LJEx 114, 12 LTOS 66, 12 Jur 777, 154 ER 652, 21 Digest (Repl) 366, *1090*.

Hill v Clifford, Clifford v Timms, Clifford v Phillips [1907] 2 Ch 236, 76 LJCh 627, 97 LT 266, CA; *on appeal* [1908] AC 12, 15, HL, 21 Digest (Repl) 232, *257*.

Martin v Sherry [1905] 2 IR 62, CA, 43 Digest (Repl) 407, **1384*.

R v Kupfer [1915] 2 KB 321, 84 LJKB 1021, 112 LT 1138, 79 JP 270, 24 Cox, CC 705, 11 Cr App Rep 91, CCA, 2 Digest (Repl) 274, *636*.

Scarf v Jardine (1882) 7 App Cas 345, [1881-5] All ER Rep 651, 51 LJQB 612, 47 LT 258, HL, 36(2) Digest (Reissue) 658, *555*.

Stevenson (Hugh) & Sons Ltd v Aktiengesellschaft für Cartonnagen-Industrie [1918] AC 239, [1918-19] All ER Rep 600, 87 LJKB 416, 118 LT 126, HL, 2 Digest (Repl) 274, *637*.

Cases also cited

Green v Hoyle, Ashford v Hoyle [1976] 2 All ER 633, [1976] 1 WLR 575, DC.

Heywood v Wellers (a firm) [1976] 1 All ER 300, [1976] QB 446, CA.

Rawlinson v Moss (1861) 30 LJCh 797, 4 LT 619.

Sweeting, Re [1898] 1 Ch 268.

Appeal

In May 1974 the plaintiffs, Hudgell Yeates & Co (a firm), brought an action in Woolwich County Court against the defendant, John James Watson, claiming the sum of £575·10 as costs incurred by them in conducting litigation on behalf of the defendant. The defendant served a defence and counterclaim alleging that the plaintiffs had been negligent in the conduct of the litigation and claimed damages for negligence in the sum of £750. On 16th July 1976 his Honour Judge White gave judgment in the action whereby he rejected in the main the defendant's allegation of negligence but found that in one respect the plaintiffs had been negligent in conducting the litigation and that the value of the work rendered useless by that negligence was £49·70. The judge held that that sum was to be deducted from the plaintiffs' claim, and entered judgment for the plaintiffs for £512·90 with interest on that sum at ten per cent. The defendant appealed on the following, among other, grounds: (ground 1) that the amount which the judge had deducted from the plaintiffs' claim in respect of their negligence was inadequate and (ground 6) that in the circumstances the plaintiffs were not entitled to recover their costs of conducting the litigation because of s 18 of the Solicitors Act 1957. The facts are set out in the judgment of Bridge LJ.

The defendant appeared in person.

Peter Irvin for the plaintiffs.

Alastair Hill for the Law Society.

Cur adv vult

30th November. The following judgments were read.

BRIDGE LJ delivered the first judgment at the invitation of Megaw LJ. This is the defendant's appeal from a judgment given against him in the Woolwich County Court by his Honour Judge White on 16th July 1976 for £659·40. The plaintiffs are a firm of solicitors. In the action they sued to recover their costs incurred in conducting litigation on behalf of the defendant. The defendant had at one time been employed by the plaintiffs as a managing clerk. He left them and went to work for a body called the National House Owners Society ('the society'), being an organisation which offered a cut-price conveyancing services to the public. At about the end of 1972 he fell out with the society and ceased to work for them. The ensuing dispute led to litigation in which the defendant instructed the plaintiffs to act for him. A High Court action was commenced against the defendant by a Mr Michael Hickmott (suing on behalf of himself and all other members of the society) by writ dated 5th January 1973. On 9th April 1973 the defendant served a defence and counterclaim, bringing in three additional parties as defendants to the counterclaim. These were Jacquie Hickmott and Basil Lambert Blower (sued as trustees of and representing the society) and Sydney George Carter (sued as president and representing the society alternatively as an individual person). The plaintiffs acted for the defendant in relation to these proceedings from their commencement until some time in December 1973. They were initially paid by the defendant £50 on account of costs. They eventually ceased to act for the defendant because of his failure to make any further payment. On 25th June 1973 the plaintiffs delivered a bill of costs in the sum of £447·60. On 23rd April 1974 they delivered a further bill in the sum of £165. On 29th May 1974 the plaintiffs commenced the present proceedings in the Woolwich County Court claiming £575·10, being the aggregate of the two bills less the £50 paid on account. The defendant served a defence and counterclaim alleging that the plaintiffs had been negligent in the work they did for him. By way of defence he contended that by reason of the plaintiffs' negligence the litigation in which he had engaged had been wholly fruitless. He further sought to recover on his counterclaim damages in the sum of £750, presumably on the footing that if the litigation had been properly conducted this was the sum which he would have recovered in the High Court action on his counterclaim.

The hearing in the Woolwich County Court began on 12th July 1976 and occupied four days. The defendant conducted his case in person. On 16th July Judge White gave a careful judgment in writing. In the main he rejected the case of negligence advanced by the defendant. He did, however, find that the plaintiffs had been negligent in one respect at a certain point in the proceedings. He held that the amount included in the plaintiffs' claim for costs referable to the steps rendered abortive by this negligence was £49·70. He deducted this amount from the total of the plaintiffs' claim and gave judgment for the balance of £512·90. He also awarded interest on this sum at ten per cent per annum calculated from the respective dates when the two bills of costs were delivered. This brought the total amount of the judgment up to the figure already mentioned of £659·40.

[His Lordship considered the issue raised by ground 1 of the defendant's notice of appeal, that the judge had underestimated the amount to be deducted from the plaintiffs' claim in respect of their negligence as found by the judge and said that he would allow the appeal in relation to that ground to the extent of ordering a retrial limited to the issue of the quantum of damage which had flowed from the plaintiffs' negligence as found by the judge, and the retrial would determine the proper amount which was to be deducted from the plaintiffs' claim. His Lordship continued:]

Finally, the defendant takes a further objection under s 18 of the Solicitors Act 1957. The point arose in this way at the trial. On the evening before the last day of the hearing, the defendant discovered that the name of one of the partners of the plaintiffs, Mr Laurence Arthur Smith, did not appear in the Law List for 1973. Although the point was not covered by his pleaded defence, he was not prevented from taking it. He relied on s 17(2) of the 1957 Act, the effect of which is that the absence from the Law List of the name of any person is to be prima facie evidence that that person is not qualified to practise as a solicitor under a practising certificate for the current year. The plaintiffs met the point by the production to the judge of Mr Smith's practising certificate for 1973. The judge held this to be a complete answer to the defendant's objection. It appears to have been overlooked by everyone that in fact Mr Smith's practising certificate for 1973 was not issued until 2nd May 1973. It is now common ground that that was the fact and that from the date when the plaintiffs were first instructed by the defendant until 2nd May 1973, Mr Smith held no practising certificate and was therefore not qualified pursuant to the provisions of s 1 of the 1957 Act.

When this matter was first raised in this court it was pointed out to the defendant by the court that the objection, even though taken at the trial, was still not covered by his pleading as it stood and therefore, on well-settled principles, could not be pursued without an amendment of the pleadings. The defendant in due course applied for and was granted leave to amend his defence by adding the following paragraphs:

'4. One of the plaintiffs, namely L.A. Smith, was not in the Law List 1973 and not qualified to act as a solicitor for the purposes of the Solicitors Act 1957.
'5. The said L.A. Smith not being a qualified person for the purposes of the Solicitors Act, 1957, the plaintiffs were not entitled to render me an account for work carried out by them as solicitors or to recover any costs'.

The defendant has argued that under s 17(2) of the 1957 Act the prima facie inference that a person is unqualified arising from the absence of his name from the Law List can only be rebutted by the production of a certified extract from the Law Society's roll. The argument is misconceived. The section provides that such a certified extract 'shall be evidence of the facts appearing in the extract'. This clearly does not exclude proof of those same facts by other means. In any event, however, the matter has now been set at rest by the production to this court of a certified extract from the roll which shows, as already stated, that Mr Smith held a practising certificate for 1973 but only from 2nd May onwards. Mr Smith did not, however, at any time play any personal part in the High Court litigation in which the plaintiffs were acting for the defendant or assume any personal responsibility in relation to it. Indeed he worked at a different office of the plaintiffs' from that from which all business relevant to the defendant's affairs was conducted. We have now to decide whether, in these circumstances, Mr Smith's lack of a practising certificate precludes the plaintiffs from recovering costs in respect of work done for the defendant before 2nd May 1973.

Section 18 of the Solicitors Act 1957 provides:

'(1) No unqualified person shall act as a solicitor, or as such sue out any writ or process, or commence, carry on or defend any action, suit or other proceeding, in the name of any other person or in his own name, in any court of civil or criminal jurisdiction . . .
'(2) If any person contravenes the provisions of this section, he shall— . . . (b) be incapable of maintaining any action for any costs in respect of anything done by him in the course of so acting . . .'

Section 23 of the 1957 Act provides: 'No costs in respect of anything done by any unqualified person acting as a solicitor shall be recoverable in any action, suit or matter by any person whomsoever.' It has been held[1] under this provision that a successful party to litigation cannot recover under an order for payment of his costs by the opposite party costs in respect of work done by his solicitor at a time when the solicitor was uncertificated, whether or not the litigant knew that his solicitor held no certificate. At first blush this seems harsh, but its rationale is no doubt to prevent a party litigant recovering from another party costs which he himself cannot be made liable to pay.

By definition in s 86(1) of the 1957 Act, 'costs' includes disbursements. But the rigour of s 18(2)(b) and s 23 as applicable to disbursements has been mitigated by s 23A of the 1957 Act, introduced by amendment by the Solicitors Act 1965, which enables an uncertificated solicitor to recover moneys properly 'paid or to be paid . . . on behalf of a client'.

It is surprising that there is no clear authority on the application of these provisions to a situation such as arises in the instant case, where one partner in a firm of solicitors, not personally concerned in the matter in which the disputed costs were earned, has inadvertently allowed his practising certificate to lapse.

Provisions to the like effect as those which we have to construe have been on the statute book for a very long time. But the only authority directly in point is a decision of the Irish Court of Appeal, *Martin v Sherry*[2]. A father and son, who were both solicitors, worked together. Inadvertently the son failed to renew his practising certificate in due time. While the son was unqualified, because he held no current certificate, the father acted in litigation for the successful plaintiff. The defendant sought to resist an order for costs against him under a provision corresponding to s 23 of the 1957 Act on the ground that the father and son were partners. The tenor of the judgments shows the court evincing understandable distaste for this defence. They held that it failed on the ground that there was in fact no partnership between the father and the son. Lord Ashbourne LC said[3]:

> 'Nothing was proved to establish a partnership between them: there was no deed of partnership, but his name was added to that of his father in the conduct of the business . . . What was the position of the son in this case?   There was no deed of partnership; there was no division of profits; there was nothing but the addition of the son's name to the father's in the business and in legal documents. I think the partnership was merely verbal or titular, and there was nothing to prove its existence except some payments made by the father to the son, to keep him going'.

Holmes LJ said[4]:

> 'The ground on which I am prepared to dismiss this appeal is the view I take of the position of Mr. John Peel in his father's office. I have carefully considered Mr. Joshua Peel's candid affidavit, and I have formed the opinion that his son is in no sense of the word a partner in the business.'

Although nothing was expressly indicated as to what the result would have been had there been a partnership between the father and the son, the implication from the judgments is that, at least in that situation, their Lordships would have found it difficult to uphold the judgment in favour of the plaintiff for the recovery of his costs. It is perhaps of particular significance to note the observations of Holmes LJ, where he said[5]:

1   *Fowler v Monmouthshire Railway and Canal Co* (1879) 4 QBD 334
2   [1905] 2 IR 62
3   [1905] 2 IR 62 at 66, 67
4   [1905] 2 IR 62 at 68
5   [1905] 2 IR 62 at 69

'Considerable difficulty was created in my mind by the first paragraph of Mr. Joshua Peel's affidavit, which states that the two gentlemen were the plaintiff's solicitors on the record; but on reflection I think that it would be unjust to fasten on these words a meaning which would be inconsistent with the true facts.'

We have had the benefit of a powerful submission by counsel, appearing in response to a request from the court that the Law Society should instruct counsel to assist us as amicus curiae, as well as the submissions of counsel for the plaintiffs.

The essence of the first submission they both make is that the two relevant phrases, in s 18(2)(b) of the 1957 Act, 'anything done by him in the course of so acting', and in s 23, 'anything done by any unqualified person acting as a solicitor', should be construed as applying only to personal acts of the uncertificated partner, or, insofar as the disputed costs are referable to the activities of managing clerks or other employees of the firm, to such activities as were carried on under the supervision of the uncertificated partner acting as the solicitor who assumed responsibility for the conduct of the business in question. The submission has the attraction of directness and simplicity, and no doubt there is much to be said for the view that the construction contended for allows sufficient scope to the operation of the provisions in question to cover the principal, if not the only, mischief at which they are aimed, viz the protection of the public against the conduct of legal proceedings otherwise than under the supervision of a properly qualified solicitor. But to construe the words in this way seems to me to fly in the face of the fundamental principle of agency applicable to partners, as expressed in s 5 of the Partnership Act 1890, that 'Every partner is an agent of the firm and his other partners for the purpose of the business of the partnership . . .' It must follow from the application of this principle that an act done by one partner in the conduct of the firm's business is an act done by all the others. Likewise the acts of the managing clerk or other employee of the firm are not done as agent only of the partner responsible for the supervision of the particular business in question but as agent for all the partners alike. I am driven by this consideration to reject the first submission advanced by both counsel.

The second submission we have to consider rests on the application of s 34 of the Partnership Act 1890, which provides:

'A partnership is in every case dissolved by the happening of any event which makes it unlawful for the business of the firm to be carried on or for the members of the firm to carry it on in partnership.'

The lapse of Mr Smith's certificate was an event, it is contended, which effected the automatic dissolution of the pre-existing partnership. So long as Mr Smith was uncertificated the other partners should be regarded as carrying on the business of a newly constituted firm of which he was not a member. When his new certificate was issued, the firm was once again reconstituted to include him and he should be regarded as a plaintiff in the present proceedings only in respect of the claim for costs relating to work done after 2nd May 1973. This is an ingenious and, at first blush, compelling way of avoiding the harsh consequences of penalising innocent partners for an oversight by one member of their firm. It has the particular merit, in the instant case, that on the facts it was clearly a matter of complete indifference to the defendant whether or not Mr Smith was at any time a member of the firm acting for him.

The operation of s 34 of the 1890 Act is easy enough to understand when the event which would make it unlawful for the members of a firm to continue their partnership is known to and recognised by them, as would occur for instance when one partner in a firm was struck off the roll of solicitors. But I find the concept of automatic dissolution and the relevant effects of s 34 much more difficult to understand when the event occasioning the statutory dissolution goes unnoticed by all the partners, being due to mere inadvertence by one of them, and consequently they all

continue to act in relation to the conduct of the partnership business as if the original
partnership continued in existence. It would be surprising if, in these circumstances,
when the unlawfulness of continuing to operate the partnership subsequently came
to light, the partners could rely on s 34 to relieve them of all the disabling consequences of having done so. However that may be, the critical question for present purposes
is whether, notwithstanding that throughout the period during which Mr Smith
was uncertificated the business of the firm was conducted on the footing that he was
still a member of it, the other partners can rely on s 34 as leading to the conclusion
that they were the sole principals for whom Miss Griffiths, as the supervising partner,
Mr Frost as managing clerk, and any other employee concerned, were acting as
agents in the conduct of the defendant's litigation and that consequently costs claimed
in respect of work done before 2nd May 1973 are not in respect of anything done by
Mr Smith.

Throughout the relevant period Mr Smith was held out as being a partner in the
firm. There can be no doubt, therefore, that he continued as a principal to be subject
to all liabilities incurred by the firm. But equally it must have been the intention of
all parties concerned that he should continue to enjoy the rights of a principal and to
participate in the fruits of the labours of all the partners in the firm as well as those of
its employees. This being the factual position it is not, in my judgment, possible to
rely on the operation of s 34 of the Partnership Act 1890, as having terminated the
vital relationship of principal and agent between Mr Smith and his partners the
existence of which is decisive in determining affirmatively that, for the purpose of ss
18(2)(b) and 23 of the Solicitors Act 1957, the conduct of the defendant's litigation
was 'done by him in the course of acting as a solicitor'.

If a solicitor, A, practised in his own name but employed B, another solicitor, as a
salaried assistant, it is clear that no costs could be recovered in respect of litigation
carried on at a time when A held no practising certificate, notwithstanding that B
had had the entire conduct of the litigation without supervision from A and that the
client had been aware of and content with this situation. A's name would be on the
record as the solicitor acting. It would be clear throughout that B was acting as agent
for A as principal. In these circumstances, whatever was done in the conduct of the
litigation would be done by A acting as a solicitor. I find it impossible to see any
valid distinction in principle between this situation and the situation where A and B
are not employer and employee but are partners. In this latter case the names of A
and B or the name of their firm would be on the record. Here again it would be clear
that B was acting not solely on his own behalf, but on behalf of himself and A as
joint principals. Here again what was done in the conduct of the litigation would
be done by both A and B and thus, A, being unqualified, would fall within the disabling provisions of s 18(2)(b) and s 23 of the 1957 Act. B could not circumvent this
by claiming, contrary to the fact, that he was acting on his own account and in his own
name alone.

I reach this conclusion with reluctance on the merits of the present case. But I
derive some consolation from the consideration that the construction I have put on
ss 18(2)(b) and 23 of the 1957 Act at least produces a clear-cut rule which it is perfectly simple to apply. On the contrary construction it might in many cases be
extremely difficult to decide how far an uncertificated solicitor had participated
personally in or assumed supervisory responsibility for some business conducted by
his firm on behalf of a client and, in a case of partial participation, to quantify the
extent to which the claim for costs ought to be abated. The rule resulting from the
construction which seems to me correct may be a harsh one in these days when
solicitors tend to practise in very large partnerships. But the essential harshness lies
in a statutory provision which, on any construction, may seriously penalise an individual solicitor for the venial fault of failing to renew his practising certificate
in due time. This harsh doctrine is accentuated in degree, but is no different in kind,
if, on the true construction of the statute, solicitors who practise in partnership are

put in a position where they have a similar responsibility to ensure due renewal of their partners' as of their own practising certificates.

For the reasons given I would allow the appeal on this further point and order a retrial of the issue of quantum on the footing that the plaintiffs are not entitled to any profit costs in respect of work done before 2nd May 1973.

WALLER LJ, having considered the issue raised by ground 1 of the notice of appeal as to the amount to be deducted from the plaintiffs' claim for their negligence, said that he would dismiss the appeal in relation to that ground since the figure of £49·70 deducted from the claim by the judge, as being the amount of the costs thrown away by the plaintiffs' negligence, was a proper deduction. His Lordship continued: I next consider the submission by the defendant that the plaintiffs are not entitled to sue for their fees because of the provisions of s 18(2) of the Solicitors Act 1957. Bridge LJ has stated the circumstances in which this defence arose. It is sufficient for me to state that the plaintiffs' bill covered the period 2nd January 1973 to a date in December 1973; that the defendant originally consulted Mr James, a partner at the Blackheath Village office, who later passed the defendant to Miss Griffiths, another partner at the Blackheath Village office, who dealt with litigation matters. There was another partner, Mr Smith, who worked at a different office and who did no work at the Blackheath Village office. Mr Smith did not have a practising certificate from 1st January 1973 to May 1973. Consequently by virtue of s 1 of the 1957 Act he was not qualified to act as a solicitor.

The question raised by the defendant was of such importance that the Law Society were invited to instruct counsel as amicus curiae. Mr Hill appeared as amicus, and the clear and balanced way in which he put his arguments was of great assistance. Section 18(1) provides:

> 'No unqualified person shall act as a solicitor, or as such sue out any writ or process, or commence, carry on or defend any action, suit or other proceeding, in the name of any other person or in his own name, in any court of civil or criminal jurisdiction, or act as a solicitor in any cause or matter, civil or criminal, to be heard or determined before any justice or justices . . .'

The words of the subsection are concerned with a person acting as a solicitor. Practising certificates are issued to individuals and are not issued to firms so, while 'person' may include the plural, the prima facie meaning in this subsection is singular and does not include the firm. The other partners of the plaintiff firm were all qualified. Then s 18(2) reads: 'If any person contravenes the provisions of this section, he shall—(a) be guilty of a misdemeanour and of contempt of the court in which the action . . . is brought or taken and may be punished accordingly . . .' Again, this would appear to refer only to the person who has not got a practising certificate. That the position of the innocent partner who has a practising certificate is unaffected is shown by s 34 of the 1957 Act which, in sub-s (1), reads:

> 'No solicitor shall wilfully and knowingly act as agent in any action or in any matter in bankruptcy for any unqualified person, or permit his name to be made use of in any such action or matter upon the account of or for the profit of any unqualified person, to send any process to any unqualified person, or do any other act enabling any unqualified person to appear, act or practise in any respect as a solicitor in any such action or matter.'

This section lends support to the view I have tentatively expressed, namely, that an innocent person is unaffected. Section 18(2)(b) reads:

> 'If any person contravenes the provisions of this section, he shall . . . (b) be incapable of maintaining any action for any costs in respect of anything done by him in the course of so acting.'

Again, the plain meaning of these words would appear to be that it is 'anything done by him' whilst as an unqualified person acting as a solicitor for which he cannot maintain an action.

Section 23 of the 1957 Act is also relevant, and reads: 'No costs in respect of anything done by any unqualified person acting as a solicitor shall be recoverable in any action, suit or matter by any person whomsoever.' Again, there is a phrase 'anything done by any unqualified person acting as a solicitor'.

Section 23A of the 1957 Act deals with a solicitor acting 'without holding a practising certificate in force'. In this section the phrase is, again, 'anything done by the solicitor while acting for the client'. So here also it is 'the solicitor', an individual, with whom the section is concerned.

The only decision of direct relevance to s 18 of the 1957 Act is *Martin v Sherry*[1], already referred to by Bridge LJ. Holmes LJ clearly based his decision on the absence of a partnership and, while remaining unconvinced by argument on the basis of an existing partnership, expressly left it open for consideration at some later date. As I read Lord Ashbourne LC's judgment, however, he did not take quite the same view. He said[2]:

> 'Now, there are many kinds of partnership, as everyone knows. There may be a partner only in name, or a partner without having his name in the firm; there may be a sleeping partner, or a partner who is only a clerk. What was the position of the son in this case? There was no deed of partnership; there was no division of profits; there was nothing but the addition of the son's name to the father's in the business and in legal documents. I think the partnership was merely verbal or titular, and there was nothing to prove its existence except some payments made by the father to the son, to keep him going. It is true that the son ceased to be a solicitor entitled to recover costs during the time that his license duty was not paid; but the son is not seeking to recover any part of the costs, and the argument put forward here was that while the son was not licensed till October, 1902, that would suspend a partnership, and that we should regard it as suspended.'

Counsel for the Law Society echoed those words when he submitted that there was a notional dissolution of the partnership when one partner failed to renew his certificate.

Section 34 of the Partnership Act 1890, to which counsel for the plaintiffs drew our attention, reads as follows:

> 'A partnership is in every case dissolved by the happening of any event which makes it unlawful for the business of the firm to be carried on or for the members of the firm to carry it on in partnership.'

When the words of the section say 'A partnership is . . . dissolved' by the happening of an event making it illegal, does the fact that the partners were unaware of the circumstances make any difference? There are three cases to which I would refer which give some assistance about this. In *Hill v Clifford*[3], which was an action for dissolution of a dentists' partnership when one of the partners had been struck off the register, Sir Gorell Barnes P said[4]:

> 'There is a further point in this and the other two cases which is worth referring to, though it is not necessary to give any positive opinion upon it. By s 34 of the Partnership Act, 1890, a partnership is in every case dissolved by the happening of any event which makes it unlawful for the business of the firm to be carried

---

1 [1905] 2 IR 62
2 [1905] 2 IR 62 at 66, 67
3 [1907] 2 Ch 236
4 [1907] 2 Ch 236 at 255

on or for the members of the firm to carry it on in partnership. As the Cliffords have ceased to be registered or entitled to be registered under the Act, and can no longer call themselves dentists and are liable to penalties if they do, it may perhaps be said that an event has happened which makes it unlawful for the business of the firm to be carried on by them, and that this may be so even though the defendants' names do not appear in the style of the firm . . . It is idle to say that the partners can still do work of the kind performed by dentists without calling themselves dentists. The deed is a deed for a partnership as dentists, which cannot really be carried on any longer.'

The case was decided on other grounds, but in this dictum Sir Gorell Barnes P was anticipating the argument put forward in this case.

In *R v Kupfer*[1], a case of a partnership dissolved by the outbreak of war, Lord Reading CJ said:

'We assume that the partnership came to an end by operation of law as soon as war was declared. There can be no partnership between enemies of this country and a subject of this country when war has once been declared. Commercial intercourse is prohibited, and immediately that prohibition comes into force it is impossible for the relationship of partners to subsist, at any rate during the war. The partnership was therefore at an end . . . But giving full effect to the law—and we assume not only that the partnership came to an end, but that the prisoner knew that it did so because he was presumed to know the law— what is the position?'

So that Lord Reading CJ clearly took the view that the moment the partnership became illegal it was dissolved. And, inferentially, dissolved whether the partners knew or not. It is true that in that case the facts were known and knowledge of the law was to be presumed, whereas in the present case there is no evidence as to whether the facts were known or not. Nevertheless in my opinion this does not affect the principle. See also *Hugh Stevenson & Sons Ltd v Aktiengesellschaft für Cartonnagen-Industrie*[2], another case of an enemy alien. Although these cases do not decide the question they do tend to show that the knowledge or otherwise of partners does not affect the dissolution. It takes place by force of law.

If the partnership was dissolved by force of law and since it is illegal for someone who is not qualified to be in partnership with a solicitor, it is inevitable in my view that if there is a partnership of solicitors it cannot include the unqualified man. I do not find the effect of s 5 of the Partnership Act 1890 to provide any obstacle to the view that I have expressed. Proceedings were started in the name of the plaintiff firm. If that was a partnership it could not contain an unqualified man. If it was not a partnership, then the only person acting as a solicitor would be the person in charge of the litigation, namely Miss Griffiths.

The 1957 Act is concerned with status. If solicitors enter into partnership they do so in order to share the profits and bear the financial adversities in common; also to share the abilities and expertise of the partners. But the partnership remains a group of individuals, each with a practising certificate, and it does not and cannot have a practising certificate for the partnership as a whole.

I do not find the doctrine of holding out to be inconsistent with this view. 'The doctrine of holding out only applies in favour of persons who have dealt with a firm on the faith that the person whom they seek to make liable is a member of it.'[3] The fact, if it be the fact, that Mr Smith was held out as being a partner might well make the other partners liable for his actions in contract because they were holding

---

1 [1915] 2 KB 321 at 338
2 [1918] AC 239, [1918-19] All ER Rep 600
3 Lindley on the Law of Partnership (13th Edn, 1971), p 108

him out as a partner. Similarly, insofar as he was holding himself out as a partner he would be making himself liable for the debts of the firm. But in each case this would not be because he was a partner but because on the facts he was being held out. When the different question is asked, was there a partnership so that the acts of the others must have been the acts of Mr Smith, my answer is No. There was no partnership. Accordingly s 5 of the Partnership Act 1890 has no application.

In my judgment references in s 18(1) and (2) of the 1957 Act are to an individual. In sub-s (1) 'No unqualified person' refers to an individual. In sub-s (2) 'any person' refers to an individual and is not to be interpreted as 'any person or persons'. It is only the individual who is made incapable of maintaining an action, and even then only for acts done in contravention of the section.

In this case the unqualified person was Mr Smith. There was nothing done by him acting as a solicitor and, subject to a possible argument based on the relationship of the managing clerk, this claim does not include any costs for anything done by him acting as a solicitor.

In some cases there may be difficult questions of fact to determine where much of the work is being done by a managing clerk. In this case much of the work was done by the managing clerk, Mr Frost, who was employed by the partnership. Counsel for the Law Society submitted that for every action as managing clerk there was a partner responsible. The work was always being done by an individual solicitor although it might be through a managing clerk working on his behalf. Although the partnership would employ the managing clerk, a partner would be responsible for his work in any particular case. It is the partner who is acting as a solicitor, not the partnership. In some circumstances, if the managing clerk were responsible to more than one partner difficult questions of fact might arise. In this case, however, the position is clear because at all times Mr Frost was being supervised by, and was responsible to, Miss Griffiths. Mr Smith was not acting through Mr Frost, nor was he doing any work acting as a solicitor for the defendant.

It was argued that the fact that the plaintiffs were suing in the name of the partnership indicated that the profit was being taken by all members of the partnership. There is no evidence to show what arrangements exist between the partners for sharing profit, and no inference can be drawn on this question. Mr Smith was undoubtedly qualified for part of the period covered by the claim, that is to say from 2nd May onwards, and he is properly a party thereafter. The fact that by s 34 of the Partnership Act 1890 he was probably not a partner during the earlier period when he was not a qualified person does not prevent him from being a partner and suing for the later period.

If the opinion which I have expressed above is correct it will avoid a situation which would be grossly unfair. Counsel for the Law Society has pointed out that there are some firms in the Law List with over a hundred partners. Lord Ashbourne LC, in *Martin v Sherry*[1], which I have already mentioned, dealing with the corresponding section to s 28 of the 1957 Act, said:

> 'That section is sought to be used in this case not only to prevent an unregistered solicitor from recovering costs, but to prevent a fully registered solicitor from recovering costs. It is noteworthy that the term "partner," or "partnership," is not to be found in the section; but I venture to think that the Legislature would be surprised if they heard this section used as the foundation of the argument addressed to us.'

That was a case where it was argued that one qualified man could not recover costs because another man was unqualified, that is to say had not got his practising certificate. How much more surprising it would be if 99 solicitors who are completely

---

1   [1905] 2 IR 62 at 65

innocent would be unable to recover costs because one partner was not qualified, even if it were no fault of his own.

On the facts of this case, since Mr Smith at no time took any part vis-à-vis the defendant in any matter covered by the plaintiffs' bill it follows that there are no costs claimed 'in respect of anything done by him in the course of' acting as a solicitor. Accordingly in my opinion the defendant's submission fails.

Apart from these two matters I agree with the judgment of Bridge LJ, which he has already delivered.

MEGAW LJ. I agree with the judgment of Bridge LJ on all the issues except the issue as to the effect on the plaintiffs' claim of the failure of Mr Smith to ensure that his practising certificate was renewed. [His Lordship first considered the issue raised by ground 1 of the notice of appeal and said that he agreed with Bridge LJ that the defendant was entitled to a new trial on the issue. His Lordship continued:] I now turn to the issue in respect of the practising certificate. On that issue I agree with the conclusion expressed by Waller LJ. But I think it right to express my reasons in my own words.

It would be extraordinary if, because of an accidental lapse by a partner in a firm of solicitors to ensure the renewal of his practising certificate over a period of a few months, the firm should as a matter of law necessarily and automatically be disentitled to recover any profit costs for any work done by any partner during that period. But that result, however fantastic, is not an argument against the defendant's submission if that submission is right in law.

The answer to the defendant's submission, on the facts of this case is, in my opinion, provided by reference, first, to the provisions of the Partnership Act 1890 to which counsel for the plaintiffs drew our attention. Section 34 of the 1890 Act, which Bridge and Waller LJJ have already read, produces the result, on the facts of this case, that the existing partnership was dissolved on 1st January 1973. Thereafter a solicitors' partnership including Mr Smith could not legally be created until he again became a qualified person by holding a current practising certificate. That does not mean that the remaining partners in the plaintiff firm could not be, or were not, thereafter partners lawfully carrying on the business of solicitors in partnership with one another. Though none of them realised it, by operation of law the old partnership was dissolved, and a new partnership came into being by conduct. Mr Smith was not a partner. By statute, the partnership, including him as a partner, was dissolved. What is dissolved by statute cannot be recreated by the courts. Though Mr Smith, no doubt unconscious of the problem, as were the remaining partners, continued to act as though he were a partner, he was not a partner, for statute precluded him; and no conduct of his could override the statute so as to bring him in again as a partner by conduct, so long as he was not a qualified person. For the strict purposes of the 1890 Act, he was not a partner.

But, of course, Mr Smith held himself out as being a partner; and the remaining partners in the new partnership, reconstituted by conduct, held Mr Smith out as being a partner. They did so in ignorance of the statutory bar on his being a partner. But that does not make it one whit the less a plain holding out.

But what is the effect of a holding out of someone as being a partner? A holding out is relevant, and relevant only, as an estoppel. As it is put in Lindley on the Law of Partnership[1]:

> 'The doctrine that a person holding himself out as a partner, and thereby inducing others to act on the faith of his representations, is liable to them as if

1   13th Edn (1971), p 100

he were in fact a partner is nothing more than an illustration of the general principle of estoppel by conduct.'

For an estoppel to exist it is necessary to show, not only that there has been an unequivocal representation (here the holding out), but also that the person seeking to assert an estoppel has acted on the faith of the representation: *Freeman v Cooke*[1] This requirement is stressed by Lord Blackburn in his speech in *Scarf v Jardine*[2] where he says: 'I put emphasis on those last words "against those who acted upon the faith that the authority continued".'

In the present case, the defendant cannot say that he, in January 1973, instructed the plaintiff firm on the faith of the representation, the holding out, that Mr Smith was a partner; nor that he suffered any detriment. His own case, as was pointed out to us by counsel for the plaintiffs, was that he instructed one particular partner, Mr James, who has since died. That is made clear from a passage in the judge's notes of the hearing. The defendant had been invited by the judge to outline his case to assist the court with the issues. The defendant said:

'2. *Retainer*. I contend that there was a personal retainer to Mr James. 3. *Breach of contract*. The contract with Mr James carried an implied term that he would conduct the action in my best interests . . .'

The defendant's case, then, was that he was in contract with Mr James, and Mr James alone, or at least that that was his intention and understanding, and that Mr James had broken that contract, personal to him, by handing over the conduct of the defendant's business to others in the firm. The defendant did not persuade the judge that his instructions were to be treated as having been instructions to Mr James alone. But for this purpose, that does not matter. The defendant, having asserted that that was his intention and understanding, cannot now turn round and say: 'But I acted on the holding out of Mr Smith as a partner in giving, and thereafter continuing, my instructions to the plaintiff firm.' His own case was to the contrary. There is no reason why he should be disbelieved, to his own advantage, as to his own instructions and understanding, even though it did not avail him for the purpose for which he put it forward.

So though there was a holding out, a continued holding out, of Mr Smith as being a partner when he was not, there is no estoppel in favour of the defendant on the facts of this case. It is not that the defendant is estopped from alleging the holding out. He is not. It is that the holding out was irrelevant because the defendant's own assertion as to his state of mind involves that he did not rely on it. We are not here concerned with any question as to the burden of proof, or as to presumptions, in relation to reliance on a holding out. As the defendant did not rely on the holding out and as, in law, Mr Smith was not a partner, the partners in the new partnership which had come into existence before the defendant gave his instructions, are not contaminated so as to lose their entitlement to profit costs for work done, not being work done by Mr Smith, by reason of any question of partnership between them and the temporarily unqualified Mr Smith.

We do not, therefore, have to consider what the position would have been if the defendant had, or was to be deemed to have, relied on the holding out of Mr Smith as a partner.

Of course, if Mr Smith himself had done any of the work for which it is sought to charge the defendant during the period of his disqualification, or if such work had been done by persons under his supervision, the plaintiffs would not have been entitled to recover profit costs in respect of such work. Whether it would have gone further and they would not have been entitled to recover any profit costs at all, I

---

1   (1848) 2 Exch 654
2   (1882) 7 App Cas 345 at 357

need not stay to consider. For on the facts of this case none of the work was done by Mr Smith or under his supervision. He worked in a different office and had nothing whatever to do with the defendant's affairs.

There remains the purely technical question whether the action is properly constituted. The plaintiffs include Mr Smith. I should have had no hesitation, if I had thought it necessary, in allowing an amendment to delete Mr Smith's name as a plaintiff and to make a corresponding amendment to the order of the court. How the remaining plaintiffs would have dealt with the sum recovered as between themselves, or as between themselves and Mr Smith, would have been a matter for them. But, again in the circumstances of this case, I do not think such an amendment is required. It would be purely technical. Mr Smith became a partner again, by the conduct of himself and the other plaintiffs, immediately on the issue, belatedly, of his practising certificate on 2nd May 1973. He could therefore properly have been joined by the defendant (as indeed he was, by the counterclaim) as a party in respect of any claim for negligent work. Being capable of being made a defendant by counterclaim, he is entitled to be plaintiff, in respect of work done after 2nd May 1973.

The result is that the appeal will be allowed on one issue only, and this court will, in accordance with its powers under RSC Ord 59, r 11(3), direct a new trial on that specific question, and on that question only, without interfering with the finding or decision on any other question.

Subject to the question of costs, on which we shall hear such submissions as the parties wish to make, the order of the court will be: (1) The appeal will be allowed to the extent hereinafter shown. (2) The findings and decisions in the judgment appealed from shall not be interfered with other than in respect of the question mentioned in para (3) hereunder and in respect of the amount of the judgment to be entered for the plaintiffs consequential on the findings and decisions of the said question. (3) There shall be a new trial on the question as to the sum to be deducted from the plaintiffs' claim by reason of the negligence of the plaintiffs as found by the learned judge in the judgment appealed from. (4) Subject as aforesaid, the judgment appealed from should be affirmed.

Appeal allowed in part. Order accordingly. Leave to appeal to the House of Lords refused.

9th March 1978. The Appeal Committee of the House of Lords refused leave to appeal.

Solicitors: *Hudgell Yeates & Co; The Law Society.*

Mary Rose Plummer Barrister.

R v Camberwell Green Justices, ex parte Christie

QUEEN'S BENCH DIVISION
LORD WIDGERY CJ, O'CONNOR AND LLOYD JJ
27th JANUARY 1978

Criminal law – Committal – Preliminary hearing before justices – Joinder of two or more accused – Separate defendants alleged to have committed separate offences – Offences ones which could properly be tried together on indictment – Magistrate proceeding with concurrent committal proceedings against defendants despite their wish to have separate committal proceedings – Whether permissible.

Where separate offences alleged to have been committed by separate defendants can properly be tried together on indictment, it is permissible as a matter of practice for a magistrates' court sitting as examining justices to insist that the committal proceedings against the defendants be heard and determined together as concurrent proceedings without obtaining the consent of the defendants (see p 380 *a b* and *d e*, post).

R v Assim [1966] 2 All ER 881 applied.

Aldus v Watson [1973] 2 All ER 1018 distinguished.

Notes

For committal for trial of defendant, see 11 Halsbury's Laws (4th Edn) para 156, for joinder of two or more defendants, see ibid, para 215; and for cases on the subject, see 14(1) Digest (Reissue) 290-293, *2199-2244*.

For the Magistrates' Courts Act 1952, s 7, see 21 Halsbury's Statutes (3rd Edn) 192.

Cases referred to in judgments

Aldus v Watson [1973] 2 All ER 1018, [1973] QB 902, [1973] 2 WLR 1007, 137 JP 684, [1973] RTR 466, DC, Digest (Cont Vol D) 634, *644a*.

R v Assim [1966] 2 All ER 881, [1966] 2 QB 249, [1966] 3 WLR 55, 130 JP 361, 50 Cr App Rep 224, CCA, 14(1) Digest (Reissue) 202, 2232.

Cases also cited

Atkinson v United States Government [1969] 3 All ER 1317, [1971] AC 197, HL.
Brangwynne v Evans [1962] 1 All ER 446, [1962] 1 WLR 267, DC.
R v Groom [1976] 2 All ER 321, [1976] 2 WLR 218, CA.
R v Lockett, Grizzard, Gutwirth and Silverman [1914] 2 KB 720, CCA.

Motions for prohibition, mandamus and certiorari

The applicant, Sylvia Christie, moved for (i) an order of prohibition prohibiting the metropolitan stipendiary magistrate sitting at Camberwell Green Magistrates' Court (Maurice Guymer Esq) from proceeding or further proceeding with the hearing and determination of committal proceedings under s 7 of the Magistrates' Courts Act 1952 in which the applicant was charged with an offence under s 1 of the Children and Young Persons Act 1933 together with Keith Fraser who was charged with murder; (ii) an order of mandamus directing the metropolitan stipendiary magistrate to hear and determine the committal proceedings of the applicant and Keith Fraser separately; (iii) an order of certiorari to remove into the High Court and quash a decision of the metropolitan stipendiary magistrate sitting on 5th December 1977 that the committal proceedings in relation to the applicant and Keith Fraser be heard concurrently. The facts are set out in the judgment of Lord Widgery CJ.

A Shaw for the applicant.
Michael Worsley and *Allan D Green* for the Crown.

LORD WIDGERY CJ. In these proceedings counsel moves on behalf of the applicant for an order of prohibition to prohibit Mr Guymer, the metropolitan stipendiary magistrate at Camberwell Green, from proceeding or further proceeding with the hearing and determination of committal proceedings under s 7 of the *a* Magistrates' Courts Act 1952 in which the applicant is charged with an offence under s 1 of the Children and Young Persons Act 1933 together with Keith Fraser who is charged with murder. That is the order of prohibition which is sought. Then the applicant seeks an order of mandamus directing the said metropolitan stipendiary magistrate sitting as aforesaid to hear and to determine the said committal proceedings of the applicant and the said Keith Fraser separately. Finally, there is sought an *b* order of certiorari to remove into this court with a view to its being quashed a decision made by the said metropolitan magistrate sitting as aforesaid on 5th December 1977 that the committal proceedings in relation to the application and the said Keith Fraser be heard concurrently.

The background to the case so far as is necessary to consider the point of law involved is quite simple. The applicant was living at the material time with Keith *c* Fraser. There was a child of that union also called Keith Fraser. There were other children born of a union between the applicant and her husband, but they are irrelevant for present purposes. Keith Fraser also had one child of a previous relationship.

The charges brought against the applicant and Keith Fraser relate to the prosecution allegation that, this child having died on 11th September 1977, Keith Fraser was guilty *d* of the murder of the child. Furthermore, there is an information laid against the applicant that under s 1 of the Children and Young Persons Act 1933 she was a party to wilful ill-treatment of the child.

The point at issue is quite a short one. The magistrate has made it clear that he intends to proceed with committal proceedings relative to both the applicant and Keith Fraser, notwithstanding the fact that they do not wish to be so joined in com- *e* mittal proceedings. This case raises in stark form the question whether the magistrate can insist on concurrent committal proceedings where there are two informations, and where the defences are separate and where the defendants in the proceedings are unwilling that those proceedings should be concurrent.

Counsel for the applicant has put his argument very compactly. He says, as is undoubtedly the case, that the Magistrates' Courts Act 1952 is a statute conferring *f* power on the magistrates' court, and that if one wants to see whether a magistrates' court has a power to do or not to do a certain thing then one should look at the Act and the rules to see whether the power is conferred. He submits that if the power is not conferred, then the court does not enjoy that power. He says, and there is no doubt about this, that there is nothing in the 1952 Act, or indeed in any other Act, to indicate that the magistrate has power to conduct concurrent committal pro- *g* ceedings. Indeed one may observe there is no such provision which says he has not either, but that is the state of the statutory provisions, and counsel for the applicant's argument that that means in the absence of express power his contention should succeed is clear enough to follow.

There is only one authority which is appropriately cited at this point, this being an area in which there is a considerable dearth of authority. That is *Aldus v Watson*[1]. *h* I do not find it necessary to go through the facts of that case in detail. There were a number of defendants who had been riding motor cycles in a fashion which would disturb and incommode other road users. In the end they were charged with an offence of using the road without due consideration for other road users. They were tried by the justices, and on conviction appealed to this court which allowed the appeal on the ground that the justices had no power to order a joint trial of defendants *j* who were charged on separate informations unless the defendants consented to be tried jointly. Accordingly, the justices were wrong in trying the informations together and the convictions should be quashed.

1 [1973] 2 All ER 1018, [1973] QB 902

Understandably, counsel for the applicant attaches importance to this case. He says that was a situation where justices were contemplating summary trial of two or more persons concurrently and the authorities say they cannot do it. It is a short step, he would say, from there to a situation like the present where someone wants the justices to conduct committal proceedings concurrently, and where on counsel for the applicant's argument they are unable to do it.

He also seeks to say that, unless his submission is acceded to here, there will be an incompatability between the 1952 Act and the usage of the magistrates. He chooses as his most vivid illustration of that s 18 of the 1952 Act, which provides that proceedings may begin before a magistrate as committal proceedings and subsequently become a summary trial. He said that if the two defendants can be combined in concurrent committal proceedings initially, it may not be long before an order is made whereby a summary trial is substituted, and then the difficulty presented by *Aldus v Watson*[1] will be immediately apparent, because under *Aldus v Watson*[1] a concurrent summary trial will be unlawful. Therefore, says counsel, one will get into a very distinct difficulty if his submission is not right.

Counsel for the Crown, on the other hand, recognising that there is very little authority here, makes, as I understand it, his main point that we are not dealing here with matters of substantive law. We are dealing here with matters of practice. He says that, if and insofar as we are dealing with matters of practice, then it is permissible for the courts to work out their own practice in their own way, and it is not necessary to find specific statutory authority for the doing of acts which are properly to be classified as part of the general practice. He cites as his principal authority in the case the decision in *R v Assim*[2]. *R v Assim*[2] dealt with the joinder of offences and offenders on indictment, and the principle for which it is constantly referred to is accurately expressed in the headnote, which is itself an exact copy of a passage in the judgment of the court. This is what it says[3]:

'Questions of joinder, whether of offences or of offenders, are matters of practice on which the Court has, unless restrained by statute, inherent power both to formulate its own rules and to vary them in the light of current experience and the needs of justice. There has never been a clear, settled and general practice based on principle with regard to the occasions when joinder of offenders is in practice correct. As a general rule it is no more proper to have tried by the same jury several offenders on charges of committing individual offences that have nothing to do with each other than it is to try together distinct offences committed by the same person. Where, however, the matters which constitute the individual offences of the several offenders are, on the evidence, so related, whether in time or by other factors, that the interests of justice are best served by their being tried together, then they can properly be the subject of counts in one indictment and can, subject always to the discretion of the Court, be tried together. Such a rule includes, but is not limited to, cases where there is evidence that the several offenders acted in concert. Joint trials are appropriate to incidents which, irrespective of there being a joint charge in the indictment, are contemporaneous (as in cases relating to affray), or successive (as in protection racket cases), or linked in a similar manner (as in the case of two individual defendants committing perjury in the same trial with regard to the same or a closely related fact) but the operation of the rule is not limited to such cases.'

That principle that joinder is a matter of practice, if established, goes a very long way to solving all the problems which have arisen in this case. I think that it is proper for us to accept the decision in *R v Assim*[2] as laying down a principle that these are matters of practice, and I think that from there we can enquire into whether there is an

---

1 [1973] 2 All ER 1018, [1973] QB 902
2 [1966] 2 All ER 881, [1966] 2 QB 149
3 50 Cr App Rep 224 at 224, 225

established practice of joinder in committal proceedings which will by virtue of the *Assim*[1] doctrine become authoritative properly to be followed by individual courts.   a
There seems to me to be no answer to the contention that the experience of practice is overwhelming that where two offences, which can properly be tried together on indictment, are the subject of committal proceedings, they can be the subject of concurrent committal proceedings without the necessity of obtaining the consent of the parties concerned. When one goes beyond that test of asking whether the two offences could appear together in the same indictment, it may be that other practical   b rules supersede, but that is the situation in the case before us. Since it cannot be challenged that both the defendants in these two informations could be tried together, it seems to me that we can properly adopt the principle that where the two offences could be tried together then they could be the subject of concurrent committal proceedings as well.

I would not think it necessary to go beyond that today, and indeed I think it is   c probably wise not to be too far reaching in dicta which are concerned with matters of practice. Practice should vary from time to time, and the variation and correction of practice should not be restricted by excessively wide judgments already appearing in the law reports.

I content myself, therefore, with a limited approach to this problem, finding what is sufficient to answer the question posed to us, that as a matter of practice it is per-   d missible to join in one committal proceeding two or more proceedings if those proceedings could be joined together in an indictment. Applying that principle to the present case, the magistrate was entitled to do as he did, and I would refuse the applications.

O'CONNOR J.   I agree.   e

LLOYD J.   I also agree.

Motions dismissed.

Solicitors: *Wilford McBain* (for the applicant); *Director of Public Prosecutions.*

N P Metcalfe Esq   Barrister.

Tan Keng Hong and another v New India Assurance Co Ltd

PRIVY COUNCIL
LORD SALMON, LORD EDMUND-DAVIES, LORD RUSSELL OF KILLOWEN, LORD SCARMAN AND   g
SIR HARRY GIBBS
17th, 18th OCTOBER, 19th DECEMBER 1977

Motor insurance – Exception – Passenger other than one carried by reason of or in pursuance of a contract of employment – By reason of contract of employment – Passenger's contract of employment containing no provision for him to obtain lift – Forester whose duty it was to   h *inspect lorry loads of logs requesting lift from driver of timber lorry for personal reasons – Forester's contract making no provision for him to obtain lifts on timber lorries – Driver giving lift to forester because he thought it might help his employer – Lorry overturning and killing forester – Driver and employer ordered to pay damages to forester's estate – Whether forester being carried 'by reason of . . . [his] contract of employment' – Whether insurer liable under policy to indemnify driver and employer.*

A company owned a timber concession and saw mill in Malaysia. The timber concession logging area was some 32 miles from the saw mill. A driver employed by the company took one of the company's lorries, loaded with logs, from the logging

1   [1966] 2 All ER 881, [1966] 2 QB 149

area on a journey to the saw mill. The use of the lorry was covered by an insurance
policy which provided, inter alia, that the insurer would indemnify the company
against sums payable in respect of death or bodily injury in the event of an accident
caused by or arising out of the use of the vehicle, subject however to certain exceptions
one of which provided that the insurer would not be liable in respect of death of or
injury to a passenger 'other than a passenger carried by reason of or in pursuance of a
contract of employment'. Before setting out for the saw mill, the driver proceeded to
a government checking station where the logs were checked by the Forestry Department to ascertain that royalties due in respect of them had been paid. Once that had
been done he set out for the saw mill. On the way he was stopped by a government
forester who asked him for a lift. The forester was one of the foresters employed by
the Forestry Department to inspect lorry loads of logs at checking stations or on their
way to saw mills but at the time he was not on duty and required the lift for personal
reasons. The forester's contract of employment contained no provision, express or
implied, for him to obtain lifts in timber lorries for his own convenience. The driver
agreed to give him a lift because he feared that if he refused the forester might be
displeased with him and the company and might in the future be ill-disposed towards
them when inspecting their logs. In the course of the journey the lorry overturned
and the forester was killed. The administrators of his estate brought an action against
the driver and the company claiming damages for negligence and obtained judgment
for $21,600 against them. The driver and the company in turn claimed an indemnity
against the insurers in respect of the damages so awarded under the motor insurance
policy, contending that the exception in the policy did not apply since the forester
had been carried 'by reason of' his contract of employment in that, but for that
contract, the driver would not have given him a lift.

Held – The words 'by reason of . . . a contract of employment' in the exception
had to be read in conjunction with the words 'in pursuance of' and so were to be construed as meaning that the passenger was being carried because his contract of employment expressly or impliedly required him, or gave him the right, to travel as a
passenger in the motor vehicle concerned. Whether a passenger was being carried by
reason or in pursuance of a contract of employment within the exception depended
solely on the terms of his employment. Since there was no term in the forester's
contract of employment, either express or implied, which required or entitled him to
travel in the company's lorry, he did not fall within the exception in the policy and
the insurers were therefore not liable to indemnify the driver or the company in
respect of the damages which had been awarded against them (see p 383 e f, and p 384
f to h, post).

Izzard v Universal Insurance Co [1937] 3 All ER 79 and *McSteen v McCarthy* [1952]
NI 33 applied.

Notes
For risks required to be insured in relation to motor vehicles, see 25 Halsbury's Laws
(4th Edn) paras 760-763, and for cases on the subject, see 29 Digest (Repl) 547, 548,
3725-3727.

Cases referred to in judgment
Izzard v Universal Insurance Co Ltd [1937] 3 All ER 79, [1937] AC 773, 106 LJKB 460,
    157 LT 335, 42 Com Cas 352, 58 Ll L Rep 121, HL, 29 Digest (Repl) 547, 3725.
McSteen v McCarthy [1952] NI 33, 29 Digest (Repl) 542, *2374.
St Helens Colliery Co Ltd v Hewitson [1924] AC 59, [1923] All ER Rep 249, 93 LJKB 177,
    130 LT 291, HL, 34 Digest (Repl) 385, 2874.

Appeal
This was an appeal by the defendants, Tan Keng Hong and Yoong Leok Kee Corpn
Ltd, against the judgment of the Federal Court of Malaysia (Suffian CJ, Gill and Ong
FJJ) dated 2nd March 1974, dismissing their appeal against the judgment of the High
Court of Malaya at Seremban (Wan Suleiman J) dated 23rd October 1973 whereby,

judgment having been entered for the plaintiffs, Fatimah binti Abdullah and Mohd Yusof bin Ibrahim, as administrators of the estate of Ibrahim bin Kimpal deceased, on the plaintiff's claim against the appellants for damages arising out of a fatal accident, the appellant's claim in third party proceedings against the respondent, New India Assurance Co Ltd, for an indemnity under a policy of insurance, in respect of the damages and costs awarded to the plaintiffs, was dismissed. The facts are set out in the judgment of the Board.

Nigel Murray for the appellants.
George Newman for the respondent.

LORD SALMON. On 1st June 1963 a forester in the employment of the Forestry Department was being given a lift in a lorry owned by the second appellant and driven by the first appellant when the lorry overturned and the forester was killed. The administrators of his estate sued both appellants against whom they obtained judgment for $21,600 damages and costs on the ground that the accident and death had been caused by their negligence. The appellant's appeal from the judgment both on liability and quantum was dismissed. The appellants however had brought in their insurers as third parties, claiming an indemnity from them in respect of the damages and costs awarded to the deceased's estate. This claim was dismissed by the trial judge and so was the appeal from his judgment. The appellants now appeal to this Board against the dismissal of their appeal by the Federal Court.

The facts lie within a short compass. The second appellant has a timber concession in the jungle at Bukit Tinggi and a saw mill about 32 miles away in Seremban. On the day of the accident, the second appellant's lorry had been fully loaded with logs at Bukit Tinggi and had been driven to the government forest checking station in Kuala Pilah about ten or 12 miles away. Here the logs were checked by the Forestry Department. This check satisfied the department that the royalties due in respect of the logs had been paid. After leaving Kuala Pilah the lorry was on the road to the second appellant's saw mill at Seremban when it was stopped by the deceased forester who asked for a lift into Seremban. The driver told him to get into the lorry and continued his journey towards Seremban. It was in the course of this journey that the fatal accident occurred.

Prior to the accident, it was not unusual for timber lorries to give lifts to foresters, both to the logging areas and to Seremban. The deceased was one of the foresters whose duty it was to inspect lorry loads of logs at checking stations or on their way to saw mills in order to ensure that the royalties due on the logs had been paid. It will be remembered that the second appellant's lorry load of logs had been duly examined and passed at a checking station shortly before the deceased forester was given a lift. There was no evidence that the deceased forester was on duty at the material time, nor that he was going to Seremban other than for private puposes. The learned trial judge's finding was that he was merely getting a free lift into town; and there was certainly no evidence to the contrary. The trial judge also accepted the driver's evidence to the effect that he agreed to give the forester a free lift because he feared that if he refused to do so it might annoy the forester and cause him to create difficulties for the second appellant in the future.

It is now necessary to consider the relevant provisions of the policy of insurance. Section II of that policy provides that:

'The Company [the insurer] will subject to the Limits of Liability indemnify the Insured [the second appellant and its servant the first appellant] in the event of accident caused by or arising out of the use of the Motor Vehicle . . . against all sums including claimant's costs and expenses which the Insured shall become legally liable to pay in respect of (a) death of or bodily injury to any person . . .'

The relevant 'Exceptions to Section II' read as follows:

'The Company shall not be liable in respect of . . . (ii) death of or bodily injury to any person in the employment of the Insured arising out of and in the course of such employment (iii) death of or bodily injury to any person (other than a passenger carried by reason of or in pursuance of a contract of employment) being carried in or upon . . . the Motor Vehicle at the time of the occurrence of the event out of which any claim arises.'

The result of this appeal must depend on whether the deceased forester, when he met his death, was 'a passenger carried by reason of or in pursuance of a contract of employment'. There is nothing to suggest, nor has it been argued, that the forester's contract of employment made any provision, express or implied, for him to obtain lifts in timber lorries for his own convenience. Counsel for the appellants conceded that at the material time he was not being carried '*in pursuance of* [his] *contract of employment*'. He contended, however, that the deceased was being carried '*by reason of* . . . [his] *contract of employment*' because, but for that contract, the first appellant would not have given him a lift. He did so only because he feared that, if he refused, the forester would be displeased with him and his employer and might in the future be ill-disposed towards them when inspecting their logs. If that ingenious and novel argument is sound, it would open up a very wide and hitherto unsuspected escape route from the clause in insurance policies designed to exclude from the risks insured the risk of the death of or injury to passengers in the insured's motor vehicle. Any insured would be able to say every time, e g when he gave a lift to the buyer or an executive of a customer with whom he did or hoped to do business, that his passenger was being carried 'by reason of . . . [his] contract of employment' within the meaning of those words as used in the policy of insurance.

Their Lordships are unable to accept a construction of the insurance policy which leads to such results and which, not only lacks any authority, but is as irreconcilable with existing authorities as it is with common sense. In their Lordships' view the words 'by reason of . . . a contract of employment' must be read in conjunction with the words 'in pursuance of', and, properly construed, mean because the contract of employment expressly or impliedly requires the employee or gives him the right to travel as a passenger in the motor vehicle concerned. It does not mean that the passenger was being carried because the driver of the vehicle thought that by reason of the passenger's employment he might gain some business advantage by doing the passenger the favour of giving him a lift.

The leading case on this subject is *Izzard v Universal Insurance Co Ltd*[1]. Lord Wright, with whose speech Lord Atkin, Lord Thankerton, Lord Russell of Killowen and Lord Roche concurred, said[2]:

'I think the Act [the language of which is the same as that of the policy] is dealing with persons who are on the insured vehicle for sufficient practical or business reasons, and has taken a contract of employment in pursuance of which they are on the vehicle as the adequate criterion of such reasons.'

Lord Wright was, in their Lordships' view, using the word 'practical' as being synonymous with 'business' reasons. In the present case, on the facts as found, the deceased forester was certainly not on the lorry for business reasons but for personal reasons, i e his own personal convenience. Nor, as already indicated, is there anything to suggest that his contract of employment, so far as he or his employers were concerned, could have any connection with his presence on the lorry.

Lord Wright went on to point out that the words 'contract of employment' could, perhaps in exceptional cases, apply to a contract of employment between the passenger and the insured owner of the vehicle but they would certainly apply to a contract of employment between the passenger and the person whose goods were being carried on an insured carrier's vehicle if, e g, the employer had ordered

---

1   [1937] 3 All ER 79, [1937] AC 773
2   [1937] 3 All ER 79 at 83, [1937] AC 773 at 782

his employee to accompany the goods in order to look after them in transit and see to their unloading on delivery. In such circumstances, the passenger would clearly be on the vehicle 'by reason of or in pursuance of his contract of employment.' In *Izzard's* case[1] the plaintiff was killed whilst being driven home from work in a lorry whose owner was not his master. The lorry owner was covered by a policy virtually identical with the policy in the present case. It was a term of Izzard's employment that the lorry in which he was killed should be at his disposal when returning from work at weekends. The House of Lords unanimously held that he was a passenger being carried by reason of or in pursuance of his contract of employment, and that the insured being bankrupt the insurers were liable to pay the deceased's widow £850 damages for which she had obtained judgment against the insured.

In *McSteen v McCarthy*[2] the plaintiff was injured whilst travelling in his employer's lorry on his way home after his work was done. The employer was insured under a policy which, as in *Izzard's* case[1], was identical with the one on the present case. The reason an employer is rarely able to claim under his policy of insurance in respect of injury sustained by anyone in his employ whilst being carried on one of his vehicles is that the accident causing such an injury would usually arise out of and in the course of the passenger's employment; and the insurers would accordingly be protected by exception (ii). In *McSteen's* case[2], however, the plaintiff employee was injured whilst being driven home; and accordingly could not have been held to have been injured in the course of his employment: see *St Helen's Colliery Co Ltd v Hewitson*[3]. In *McSteen's* case[4] Lord MacDermott CJ found that—

> 'though the plaintiff was not obliged to travel back on his employer's lorry he was entitled to do so if he wished. As one would expect there was no formal agreement entered into about this, but the plaintiff, as the defendant must have known, lived in Belfast and . . . it was understood between them when the plaintiff agreed to do this . . . work that he would be allowed to travel back in the defendant's lorry when the job was finished . . . I am . . . of opinion that the plaintiff's right to travel back on the lorry cannot be dissociated from his employment and that he was "a passenger carried by reason of or in pursuance of a contract of employment" within the meaning of exception [(iii)].'

These two authorities and all the others to which reference was made in argument make it plain that whether a passenger is carried by reason of or in pursuance of a contract of employment within the meaning of exception (iii), depends solely on the terms of the passenger's employment. In the present case, there is no term of the forester's contract of employment, express or implied, which required or entitled him to travel on the second appellant's lorry. It is true that there was no prohibition in his contract of employment against asking for and accepting a lift in a timber lorry or, for that matter, in any other vehicle. The absence of such a prohibition cannot be seriously regarded as any evidence that he was being carried in the lorry by reason of his contract of employment within the meaning of those words in exception (iii). Still less, in their Lordships' view, can the fact that the lorry driver gave him a lift because he thought that, by reason of the forester's employment, it might be good for business to do so.

Their Lordships will advise His Majesty the Yang di-Pertuan Agong that the appeal should be dismissed with costs.

Appeal dismissed.

Solicitors: *Philip Conway, Thomas & Co* (for the appellants); *Coward Chance* (for the respondent).

Mary Rose Plummer Barrister.

---

1 [1937] 3 All ER 79, [1937] AC 773
2 [1952] NI 33
3 [1924] AC 59, [1923] All ER Rep 249
4 [1952] NI 33 at 35, 36

Union Transport Finance Ltd v British Car Auctions Ltd

COURT OF APPEAL, CIVIL DIVISION
CAIRNS, ROSKILL AND BRIDGE LJJ
16th FEBRUARY 1977

Conversion – Possession – Right to immediate possession – Hire-purchase owner – Hire-purchase agreement giving owner right to terminate hiring by notice on hirer committing any breach of agreement – Hirer in breach of agreement by instructing auctioneers to sell car – Hirer not disclosing to auctioneers that car subject to hire-purchase agreement – Sale of car by auctioneers to innocent third party – Owner, knowing nothing of sale, subsequently serving notice of default on hirer for failure to pay instalment – Owner learning of disappearance of hirer and car – Owner suing auctioneers for conversion – Whether action maintainable – Whether owner having at time of sale by auctioneer right to immediate possession of car – Whether hire-purchase agreement terminable only by notice.

On 7th February 1973 the plaintiffs bought a motor car and let it on hire purchase to S, who paid a deposit for it. The hire-purchase agreement provided, inter alia, (i) that S would pay the balance of the hire in 36 monthly instalments starting on 7th March 1973; (ii) by cl 1(c), that he would not remove, or allow to be removed, the current identification marks on the car; (iii) by cl 1(f), that he would not, without the plaintiffs' prior consent, part with possession or control of the car or sell it or offer it for sale; (iv) by cl 3 (a), that unless and until the whole of the sums due under the agreement had been paid and purchase had been made the car would remain the absolute property of the plaintiffs and S would not have any right or interest in it other than that of hirer; and (v) by cl 3(b), that if S made any default in the monthly rentals or committed any other breach of the agreement the plaintiffs had 'the right at any time to declare the hiring to be terminated by forwarding a notice of default to [S's] last known address' and to take action to retain possession of the car and recover against S the amount then owing. S altered the car's registration number and on 19th February instructed the defendants, a firm of car auctioneers, to sell it, without disclosing to them that it was still the subject of a hire-purchase agreement. On 22nd February the defendants sold the car for £1,045 and on 28th February paid the proceeds, less their commission, to S. On 11th April the plaintiffs, knowing nothing of S's dishonest activities but only that he had not paid the monthly instalments due on 7th March and 7th April, served a notice of default at S's last known address stating that unless the outstanding instalments were paid within seven days the hiring of the car would be terminated forthwith and steps would be taken to recover it. By that time both the car and S had disappeared. Having learned what had happened the plaintiffs brought an action against the defendants claiming damages for the conversion of the car. The trial judge ordered judgment to be entered for the plaintiffs for £1,045. The defendants appealed, contending (i) that in the circumstances they could not be guilty of conversion; (ii) that, in any event, even if they could, the plaintiffs' action was not maintainable because the plaintiffs were not entitled at the time of the sale to immediate possession of the car, as their right to enter into possession was, by virtue of the terms of the hire-purchase agreement, exercisable only after notice had been given under cl 3(b) to terminate the agreement.

Held – The appeal would be dismissed for the following reasons—

(i) On the facts it was not open to the defendants to assert that they were incapable as a matter of law of being guilty of conversion (see p 387 *f*, p 391 *e* and p 392 *c*, post); *Hollins v Fowler* [1874-80] All ER Rep 118 applied.

(ii) On the true construction of the agreement, cl 3(b) merely gave the plaintiffs an additional right; it did not restrict their common law right to terminate the bailment without notice if S acted in a way which was repugnant to the terms of the agreement. On the evidence the agreement had been terminated and the plaintiffs had acquired the right to immediate possession as soon as S, in breach of cl 1(c) and (f), instructed the auctioneers to sell the car bearing a new registration number (see p 390 f to j, p 391 e to j and p 392 c, post); *North Central Wagon and Finance Co Ltd v Graham* [1950] 1 All ER 780 applied.

Notes
For an auctioneer's liability for conversion, see 2 Halsbury's Laws (4th Edn) para 727, and for cases on the subject, see 3 Digest (Repl) 49, 50, 342-358.

Cases referred to in judgments
Hollins v Fowler (1875) LR 7 HL 757, [1874-80] All ER Rep 118, 44 LJQB 169, 33 LT 73, 40 JP 53, 3 Digest (Repl) 354.
North Central Wagon and Finance Co Ltd v Graham [1950] 1 All ER 780, [1950] 2 KB 7, CA, 26 Digest (Repl) 670, 57.

Appeal
By a writ issued on 25th April 1974, the plaintiffs, Union Transport Finance Ltd, brought an action against the defendants, British Car Auctions Ltd, claiming damages for the conversion of an Audi 100 LS motor car, registration number CFH 138 J. At the trial of the action on 10th May 1976 Lawson J ordered that judgment be entered for the plaintiffs in the sum of £1,045. The defendants appealed against the order. The facts are set out in the judgment of Roskill LJ.

Gerald Owen QC and *Thayne Forbes* for the defendants.
R L Denyer for the plaintiffs.

ROSKILL LJ delivered the first judgment at the invitation of Cairns LJ. This is an appeal by the defendants from a judgment of Lawson J given by him at Bristol on 10th May 1976. The appeal has, if I may say so, been admirably argued by both counsel for the defendants, but, for my part, I have no doubt but that the learned judge's decision was right. The problem that we have to consider is the all too familiar one of which of two innocent parties has to suffer for the fraud of a third.

The plaintiffs in the action are Union Transport Finance Ltd, a well-known hire-purchase finance company, and, indeed, as their documents show, a subsidiary of the even better known Wagon Finance Corpn Ltd. The defendants are a well-known firm of car auctioneers, who we are told have passing through their hands throughout the length and breadth of this country many scores of thousands of cars every year. The trouble arose because on 7th February 1973 the plaintiffs, in accordance with what to them was no doubt a perfectly ordinary hire-purchase transaction, bought an Audi car, the number of which was CFH 138 J, from a firm of dealers for the purpose of letting it on hire-purchase to a gentleman who gave the not very unusual name of Harry Smith. Mr Smith told them that he was a surveyor, and a contract was entered into on that date in the usual hire purchase transaction form providing for a sum to be paid down and for some 36 monthly instalments to be paid, the first payment to be made later, namely on 7th March 1973. I need not take up time by reading the whole of the contract. The relevant contractual details regarding the car, the number of the car, the deposit, the cash price and the instalments are set out in the agreement.

The next day Mr Smith (as he was thought to be) taxed the vehicle. On 13th February the plaintiffs, in accordance with the usual practice, informed Hire Purchase Information Ltd. On 19th February 1973 Mr Smith, who by this time appears to have changed his name to Smithers, entered that car for auction with the defendants, not under its original number, but under number CFH 738 J, presumably having done the necessary physical alterations to the number plates. He did not reveal that there were any outstanding hire-purchase instalments. On 22nd February the defendants sold the car at an auction at Alexandra Palace for £1,045, from which they deducted their commission of just under £60. On 28th February 1973 they sent Mr Smithers, as by then he was, a cheque for the difference.

Down to that time, of course, the plaintiffs knew nothing about Mr Smithers's or Mr Smith's, dishonest activities. But come 7th March, which was the day for the payment of the first instalment, strangely enough none was forthcoming. Nor was any instalment forthcoming on the next monthly date, 7th April. The plaintiffs accordingly, as one would expect, on 11th April served a notice of default in respect of those two instalments. That letter reads thus:

'We cannot trace a reply to previous reminders and unless the above amount [which by this time was £90] is paid in full within seven days from the serving of this notice by normal postal delivery the hiring of the above goods will be terminated forthwith and steps taken to recover our property together with your full liability under the terms of the hire purchase agreement.'

We were told by counsel that the vehicle had been bought by someone called Yates. He plays no part in this story. Whatever his part was, he was a completely innocent purchaser. We are told that he subsequently resold it, and the vehicle has now irretrievably disappeared. The sins of Mr Smith, or Smithers, in due course were found out, and in yet another name, that of Day, in August 1973, he was sent to prison for obtaining this vehicle by dishonest representations. He might well, I should have thought, have been charged with the theft of the vehicle, although whether he was or not does not matter, nor is it clear from the papers.

That being the factual background of the matter, the action came before Lawson J at Bristol on agreed facts. There was no oral evidence adduced before the learned judge, and he was invited to decide on those facts whether or not the defendants were guilty of conversion.

The defendants took two points in reply to the plaintiffs' claim. First, and I can deal with this quite shortly, they said that auctioneers who act as they acted on this occasion are not in law guilty of conversion; and secondly, they said: 'Even if in law we as auctioneers can be guilty of conversion, you, the plaintiffs, on the date when we resold the car, 22nd February 1973, had no right to immediate possession, and, therefore, you cannot maintain this action for conversion against us.' Those were the issues which Lawson J had to try.

I can, I hope without any discourtesy to counsel for the defendants, dispose of the first point speedily. The learned judge had no doubt, and he, too, dealt with this point very shortly, that before him it was not open to the defendants to assert that they were incapable as a matter of law of being guilty of conversion. The same position, as I think, obtains in this court. Counsel for the defendants reserved his clients' right if this matter were to go to the House of Lords to re-open what has been long thought to be the law, ever since *Hollins v Fowler*[1] about 100 years ago, and to put the matter to the test in the highest tribunal. I mention for the sake of completeness that the point that an auctioneer cannot in such circumstances as these be guilty of conversion, might have been, but was not, taken in this court in a case to which I shall refer in more detail in a moment, *North Central Wagon and Finance Co Ltd v Graham*[2]. If one looks at the statement of facts[3] one sees that the defendant, Mr Graham, was an auctioneer against whom, as in the case of the present appellants, no allegation whatever of want of good faith was made. But counsel for Mr Graham did not take the point which it is sought to keep open in the present case.

I now turn to the second point that has been pressed on us in this court. It is, I apprehend, an elementary branch of the law of tort, first, that an action for conversion depends on injury to the right to possession; and secondly, as Asquith LJ put it in *North Central Wagon and Finance Co Ltd v Graham*[4]—

1   (1875) LR 7 HL 757, [1874-80] All ER Rep 118
2   [1950] 1 All ER 780, [1950] 2 KB 7
3   [1950] 1 All ER 780, [1950] 2 KB 7 at 7, 8
4   [1950] 1 All ER 780 at 781, 782, [1950] 2 KB 7 at 11

'When a bailor and lessor on hire purchase wants to sue in conversion by reason of the wrongful sale by the bailee, it is essential for him to show that he is *a* entitled at the time of the sale to immediate possession of the goods.'

The hire-purchase finance agreement between the plaintiffs and Mr Smith contained a large number of clauses. It is not necessary for me to read more than a few in order to make plain the point that was argued before Lawson J and has been argued again in this court. If one looks at cl 1 one finds a number of covenants under the letters (a), *b* (b) and (c) and through to (k) on the part of the hirer. Clause 1(c) provides:

'To keep the goods in good repair and working condition . . . and not to remove or allow to be removed their present identification marks.'

Clause 1(f) provides:

'Not without the previous consent of the owner to part with the possession or *c* control of the goods . . . and not to sell or offer for sale nor assign pledge mortgage underlet give away or otherwise in any way legally or equitably deal or attempt to deal with either the goods or option to purchase herein contained or other interest of the hirer hereunder.'

Pausing there, there can be no doubt that Mr Smith's actions, first in altering the *d* number plate by substituting the figure '7' for the figure '1', as I mentioned earlier, was a breach of cl 1(c), and then in handing over the car to the defendants as auctioneers for sale was a breach of cl 1(f).
Clause 3 provides:

'(a) Unless and until the whole of the sums due under this agreement shall have *e* been paid and purchase been made under clause 2(2) hereof the goods shall remain the absolute property of the owner and the hirer shall not have any right or interest in the same other than that of hirer under this agreement. (b) Should the hirer make default in any monthly rentals as agreed or commit any other breach of this agreement [or] be adjudicated bankrupt . . . the owner shall have the right at any time to declare the hiring to be terminated by forwarding a *f* notice of default to the hirer's last known address and take action to retake possession of the goods and to recover against the hirer or his estate the amount stated in clause 3(f) hereof . . . '

I need not read sub-cll (c), (d), (e) or (f), but I mention that sub-cl (f) deals with what is the liability of the hirer.
Stated in a sentence, the argument of the defendants is this. 'True, Mr Smith *g* acted dishonestly on 22nd February in handing this car over, but you, the plaintiffs, the legal owners, have no right to sue us, the defendants, in conversion, because as at the date when we sold this car and would be liable in conversion if an action for conversion lies against us at all, you had no right to immediate possession, and therefore your action is not maintainable against us.' I hope that I do counsel for the defendants' argument no injustice if I say that in the ultimate analysis, however he sought to *h* put it, in the end one comes back to the same point: on the true construction of the clauses to which I have referred in this agreement, is there anything to bar the plaintiffs from bringing this agreement to an end in any other way than as is there provided, and thus acquiring an immediate right to possession? That was the question before Lawson J, and it has been repeated in this court. The learned judge well summarised the point in his judgment when he said: *j*

'Counsel on behalf of the defendants submits this: that having regard to the terms of the hire purchase agreement and, specifically, the terms of cl 3(b) of the hire purchase agreement, unless and until the bailors, the plaintiffs in this action, have served a notice of termination, the right to immediate possession remains in the bailee, and that they, therefore, the bailors, the plaintiffs here, had no right to immediate possession because they had not in fact served a notice of termination under cl 3(b) as is the fact, of course; the position being that on 22nd February, as far as they, the owners of the car, were concerned [Mr Smith] was not in arrears of any instalment.'

There will have been observed as I read that passage from the learned judge's judgment the words 'the right to immediate possession remains in the bailee'. When counsel for the defendants read that passage all three members of this court intervened to ask whether that did represent his argument. He frankly said that it did, and that it was an essential part of his argument that at that point of time the bailee, Mr Smith, alone had the right to immediate possession. I will come back to that point later.

Reliance was placed on the decision in *North Central Wagon and Finance Co Ltd v Graham*[1], and counsel for the defendants laid much stress on the first of the judgments in that case delivered by Asquith LJ. The second judgment was given by Cohen LJ, and Singleton LJ merely said[2], 'I agree'. When one looks at Asquith LJ's judgment, it seems that he looked at the matter from the point of view of whether the particular hire-purchase agreement there before the court had the effect contended for by the defendants (a view which had been accepted by the trial judge, Lewis J) of preventing the plaintiff bailors from claiming to be entitled to sue for conversion as being the persons immediately entitled to possession. Asquith LJ[3] went through the agreement in some detail, and he reached the conclusion[4] that that agreement on its true construction did not operate to prevent the plaintiffs from immediately terminating the agreement apart from its express provisions and thus claiming to be the persons entitled to immediate possession and thus to sue for conversion.

Cohen LJ, who began his judgment by saying that he agreed with Asquith LJ, and for the same reasons, then approached the matter somewhat differently, and, as I venture to think, on a rather wider basis. Cohen LJ referred[5] to a passage in the then current edition of Halsbury's Laws of England which[6] reads thus:

' "The act of the bailee in doing something inconsistent with the terms of the contract terminates the bailment, causing the possessory title to revert to the bailor and entitling him to maintain an action of trover." That view is stated in somewhat similar language in the following passage in POLLOCK AND WRIGHT ON POSSESSION IN THE COMMON LAW[7]: "Any act or disposition which is wholly repugnant to or as it were an absolute disclaimer of the holding as bailee re-vests the bailor's right to possession, and therefore also his immediate right to maintain trover or detinue even where the bailment is for a term or is otherwise not revocable at will, and so *a fortiori* in a bailment determinable at will." '

Cohen LJ then went on to say[8]:

'Those passages, which seem to me, if I may respectfully say so, to be a correct statement of the law, definitely support the view which my brother has expressed, namely, that the plaintiffs are in a position to maintain an action in trover. Counsel for the defendant says that they only apply where the contract is silent on the subject, and that here the contract provides what is to happen in the event of a breach of any stipulation and merely gives the right to terminate the

1   [1950] 1 All ER 780, [1950] 2 KB 7
2   [1950] 1 All ER 780 at 784, [1950] 2 KB 7 at 16
3   [1950] 1 All ER 780 at 783, [1950] 2 KB 7 at 13
4   [1950] 1 All ER 780 at 783, [1950] 2 KB 7 at 14
5   [1950] 1 All ER 780 at 784, [1950] 2 KB 7 at 15
6   1 Halsbury's Laws (2nd Edn) 736, para 1211
7   Page 132
8   [1950] 1 All ER 780 at 784, [1950] 2 KB 7 at 15, 16

contract. That, he says, is something distinct from a right to enter into possession, and the latter right is only exercisable after notice has been given to terminate the contract. As I have said, I do not so construe the contract, and I am glad to find that the construction which I place on it accords with the view of what the law would be in the absence of express provision and, if I may say so respectfully, with what is a very reasonable position in the circumstances of the case.'

Cohen LJ was there presumably founding on what he thought was the position at common law. He then went on to say[1] that Mr Elwes, whose argument in that case must have resembled counsel for the defendants' argument in the present case, could not escape from the common law position by relying on the language of the contract there in question.

The learned judge in the present case drew attention to what counsel for the defendants had said, namely that the current edition of Halsbury's Laws of England[2] stated the law rather differently from the statement in the passage I have just read from the second edition[3]. However that may be, as my Lord pointed out during the argument, it seems plain that this court, in the persons of Cohen and Singleton LJJ, expressly approved that statement of the law in the second edition. We therefore should follow that statement whatever may be stated in the fourth edition, to which we have not been referred beyond the reference to that passage in Lawson J's judgment.

It seems to me that there is no room for doubt that the position at common law is this: if the bailee acts in a way which, to use the phrase used in argument, destroys the basis of the contract of bailment, the bailor becomes entitled at once to bring that contract to an end, and thus at once acquires the right to immediate possession of the article bailed. That is consistent with what is stated in the second edition of Halsbury[3] and in their classic work on Possession by Sir Frederick Pollock and the first Wright J.

In those circumstances, it seems to me that the only question that remains for consideration is whether the provisions of the present contract affect the basic common law position. Counsel for the defendants strenuously argued that they do. He contends that because there is this express contractual right to bring this contract to an end only after notice of termination, there is no room for the survival as between the plaintiffs and Mr Smith of the basic common law rule, and, indeed, the phrase he used in argument was that 'Clause 3 ousts the common law rule'. I think, with respect, that this argument is misconceived for a number of reasons. When one looks at these clauses one can see why they are there. They give a modicum of protection to the hirer but they also give certain specific contractual rights to the bailor in the happening of certain events. They give him the right to bring the contract to an end and to re-take possession in the event of certain things happening. But they do not expressly deprive the bailor of any other rights that he may have at common law; and still less, in my view, do these clauses, either expressly or impliedly, confer any right, possessory or otherwise, on the bailee which would lead to a conclusion different from that which would follow at common law if the bailee deliberately, as happened here, tears up the contract of bailment by fraudulently selling the car through an auctioneer, to an innocent third party. Therefore, it seems to me, following the reasoning in *North Central Wagon and Finance Co Ltd v Graham*[4], that even if there be room in principle for the existence of a contract which may contract out of the basic common law rule, it would require very clear language to deprive the bailor, of his common law rights in circumstances such as these. In the case of the present contract the language used is nothing like strong enough to achieve that result.

I mentioned a few moments ago a passage in the judgment of Lawson J in which,

---

1   [1950] 1 All ER 780 at 784, [1950] 2 KB 7 at 15
2   2 Halsbury's Laws (4th Edn) para 1585
3   1 Halsbury's Laws (2nd Edn) 736, para 1211
4   [1950] 1 All ER 780, [1950] 2 KB 7

in setting out counsel for the defendants' argument, he referred to the fact that it had
been contended that the right to immediate possession remained in the bailee, Mr
Smith. With respect to counsel for the defendants, that seems to me to be an impossible argument. I ventured to ask counsel for the defendants in whom he claimed the
possessory title lay at the moment when the hammer fell and this car purported to
be sold. As I understood him, he replied that it would then pass to the innocent
purchaser, and would remain his as a possessory title unless and until it came to an
end on the termination of the contract of hire-purchase by the giving of the appropriate notice. That argument involves that the innocent purchaser has a defeasible
possessory title; which, being defeasible, would suddenly come to an end on the true
owner, the person in whom the legal title was vested, giving notice to determine the
contract, to which the innocent purchaser would not be a party and of which he would
never have heard. I venture, with respect, to think that that cannot possibly be right
in principle.

During the argument Cairns LJ referred to the well-known Latin tag 'nemo dat
quod non habet' which may be translated into English as: 'You cannot give what you
have not got'. In the present case, it seems plain that Mr Smith had nothing beyond a
possessory title which he acquired when the agreement was entered into and he took
delivery of the car, but which he lost the moment he destroyed the agreement by
acting dishonestly, and that, therefore, he could not convey any title possessory or
otherwise, either to the auctioneer or to the innocent purchaser.

For those reasons, which I have given at some length in deference to the argument
for the defendants, it seems to me clear that Lawson J gave the right answer, and I
would dismiss the appeal.

BRIDGE LJ. I agree. I take as a safe starting point the classic statement of principle
from Pollock and Wright on Possession in the Common Law[1], cited with approval
by Cohen LJ in the passage which Roskill LJ has read from *North Central Wagon and
Finance Co Ltd v Graham*[2], and I make no apology for repeating it:

> 'Any act or disposition which is wholly repugnant to or as it were an absolute
> disclaimer of the holding as bailee revests the bailor's right to possession, and
> therefore also his immediate right to maintain trover or detinue [and I pause to
> emphasise the concluding words] even where the bailment is for a term or is
> otherwise not revocable at will . . .'

I emphasise those concluding words because it seems to me that it would make no
difference to this statement of principle if they were altered to read: 'even where the
bailment is otherwise only terminable by notice.' Of course I accept, as does Roskill
LJ, that in theory it would be perfectly possible to introduce into a contract of bailment a term expressly limiting the manner in which the bailee's right to possession
as against the bailor could be terminated; in other words, an express term excluding
the application of the principle of law cited. It seems to me that it would require the
clearest express terms to have that effect. A clause which merely gives a right to
terminate by notice for any breach of the contract of bailment could not possibly, in
my judgment, be construed as having that effect. Its purpose is to enhance the rights
of the bailor and not to curtail them. It gives him a right to terminate on any breach
by the bailee of the contract of bailment, whether the breach by the bailee is a
repudiation or not, for example, for a non-repudiatory breach by default in making
punctual payment of hire. But it cannot possibly be construed as restricting his
right to terminate the bailment without notice on the happening of a breach which is a
repudiation.

I would only add that we were referred in the course of the argument to a passage

---

1 Page 132
2 [1950] 1 All ER 780 at 784, [1950] 2 KB 7 at 15

from Mr Goode's textbook on Hire Purchase Law and Practice[1], where the following appears: *a*

'Where, however, the agreement contains express provisions as to the mode of termination by the owner *e.g.* by notice to the hirer—this excludes the common law rule, and the owner's repudiation will not be effective to terminate the agreement unless the method stipulated in the agreement is followed.'

The footnote cites as authority for that proposition *North Central Wagon and Finance Co*   *b*
Ltd v Graham[2]. With great respect, it seems to me that that case is no authority for that proposition, and that that proposition is not an accurate statement of the law. I agree that the appeal should be dismissed.

CAIRNS LJ. I am in complete agreement with the judgments which have been   *c*
delivered and with the reasons given by Roskill and Bridge LJJ, and I too would dismiss the appeal.

Appeal dismissed. Leave to appeal to House of Lords refused.

Solicitors: *Cripps, Harriers, Willis & Carter*, agents for *Clive Fisher & Co*, Addlestone   *d*
(for the defendants); *Meade-King & Co*, Bristol (for the plaintiffs).

Christine Ivamy Barrister.

e

R H Willis and Son (a firm) v British Car Auctions Ltd

COURT OF APPEAL, CIVIL DIVISION
LORD DENNING MR, ROSKILL AND BROWNE LJJ   *f*
13th, 14th, 15th DECEMBER 1977, 13th JANUARY 1978

Conversion – Auctioneer's liability – Provisional bid – Auctioneer effecting sale by private treaty – Car under hire-purchase entered for sale at auction – Seller having no title – Reserve price not reached – Auctioneers accepting provisional bid from highest bidder – Auctioneers arranging sale between highest bidder and seller – Sale completed by auctioneers under their conditions for sale under the hammer – Auctioneers using same documents as for sales under the hammer – Whether sale made by auctioneers or by private treaty between seller and highest bidder – Whether auctioneers liable in conversion to owners under hire-purchase agreement.   *g*

The plaintiffs, a firm of motor car dealers, sold a car on hire-purchase to C for a total hire-purchase price of £625. C paid an initial deposit of £350 leaving a balance of   *h*
£275 to be paid by instalments over a six month period. The hire-purchase agreement contained the usual warning that the goods would not become C's property until he had made all the payments. In breach of the agreement and while instalments amounting to £275 remained outstanding C entered the car in a car auction run by the defendant auctioneers. C falsely stated that the car was not the subject of any outstanding hire-purchase agreement and fixed a reserve price of £450 on the   *j*
car. The auctioneers put the car up for auction under their usual conditions of sale but it failed to reach the reserve price. The highest bid received was £410 from W

---

1 2nd Edn (1970), p 277
2 [1950] 1 All ER 780, [1950] 2 KB 7

whereupon the auctioneers followed their 'provisional bid' procedure. They obtained W's signature to a purchase slip acknowledging that he had 'purchased/provisionally purchased' the car 'at the price shown and in accordance with the Conditions of Sale as Exhibited'. The purchase slip was the same document that would have been used if the car had been sold under the hammer. It contained a space for the price '+£2 for Indemnity Policy'. Under the auctioneers' conditions of sale a purchaser was required to take out such a policy 'against any loss he may suffer . . . through any defect in title of the seller'. The auctioneers then called C, asked him if he would accept £410 for the car, and when he agreed the auctioneers followed the same procedure as if the car had been sold under the hammer. They made out an invoice to W for £410 plus the indemnity fee of £2 plus ten per cent value added tax, debited his account for that amount and gave him a purchase slip authorising him to take the car away. The next day after ascertaining that the car was not under hire-purchase from a finance company the auctioneer paid C the £410 less their commission and charges. A few days later C was adjudged bankrupt. The plaintiffs brought an action in the county court against the auctioneers alleging conversion and claiming £275 being the outstanding hire-purchase instalments on the car, contending that they had not themselves sold the car, either under the hammer or by private treaty, but had merely acted as a conduit pipe in bringing together buyer and seller.

Held – The provisional bid procedure adopted by the autioneers was indistinguishable in its essential nature and legal consequences from a sale under the hammer and therefore, applying the principles relating to sales under the hammer, the auctioneers in selling a chattel to which the purported seller had no title were liable in conversion to the plaintiffs as the true owners of the car. Accordingly the plaintiffs were entitled to judgment (see p 396 c to e, p 397 d to f, p 398 a h and p 399 a, post).

Hollins v Fowler [1874-80] All ER Rep 118, Cochrane v Rymill (1879) 40 LT 744, Barker v Furlong [1891] 2 Ch 172, Consolidated Co v Curtis & Son [1892] 1 QB 495, Union Transport Finance Ltd v British Car Auctions Ltd p 385, ante, applied.

National Mercantile Bank v Rymill (1881) 44 LT 767 distinguished.

Turner v Hockey (1887) 56 LJQB 301 disapproved.

Notes

For an auctioneer's liability for conversion, see 2 Halsbury's Laws (4th Edn) para 727, and for cases on the subject, see 3 Digest (Repl) 49, 50, 342-358.

Cases referred to in judgments

Barker v Furlong [1891] 2 Ch 172, 60 LJCh 368, 64 LT 411, 3 Digest (Repl) 49, 342.

Central Newbury Car Auctions Ltd v Unity Finance Ltd [1956] 3 All ER 905, [1957] 1 QB 371, [1956] 3 WLR 1068, CA, 21 Digest (Repl) 484, 1713.

Cochrane v Rymill (1879) 40 LT 744, 43 JP 572, 3 Digest (Repl) 49, 347.

Consolidated Co v Curtis & Son [1892] 1 QB 495, 61 LJQB 325, 56 JP 565, 3 Digest (Repl) 50, 353.

Hollins v Fowler (1875) LR 7 HL 757, [1874-80] All ER Rep 118, 44 LJQB 169, 33 LT 73, 40 JP 53, HL; affg (1872) LR 7 QB 616, Ex Ch, 46 Digest (Repl) 460, 102.

Morris v Ford Motor Co Ltd [1973] 2 All ER 1084, [1973] QB 792, [1973] 2 WLR 843, [1973] 2 Lloyd's Rep 27, CA, Digest (Cont Vol D) 370, 1949a.

Moorgate Mercantile Co Ltd v Twitchings [1976] 2 All ER 641, [1977] AC 890, [1976] 3 WLR 66, HL.

National Mercantile Bank v Rymill (1881) 44 LT 767, CA, 3 Digest (Repl) 50, 351.

Post Office v Norwich Union Fire Insurance Society Ltd [1967] 1 All ER 577, [1967] 2 QB 363, [1967] 2 WLR 709, [1967] 1 Lloyd's Rep 216, CA, Digest (Cont Vol C) 573, 3588a.

Turner v Hockey (1887) 56 LJQB 301, DC, 3 Digest (Repl) 50, 352.

Union Transport Finance Ltd v British Car Auctions Ltd p 385, ante, CA.

Cases also cited

Caxton Publishing Co Ltd v Sutherland Publishing Co [1938] 4 All ER 389, [1939] AC 178,   a
HL.
Douglas Valley Finance Co Ltd v S Hughes (Hirers) Ltd [1966] 3 All ER 214.
Henderson v Henry E Jenkins & Sons [1969] 3 All ER 756, [1970] AC 282, HL.
Hesperides Hotels Ltd v Aegean Turkish Holidays Ltd [1978] 1 All ER 277, [1977] 3 WLR
656, CA.
Oakley v Lyster [1931] 1 KB 148, [1930] All ER Rep 234, CA.   b
Stephens v Elwall (1815) 4 M & S 259.
Underwood (A L) Ltd v Bank of Liverpool [1924] 1 KB 775, 93 LJKB 690, CA.

Appeal

This was an appeal by the defendants, British Car Auctions Ltd ('the auctioneers'),
against the judgment of his Honour Judge Sheldon given at Aldershot and Farnham   c
County Court on 1st November 1976 in favour of the plaintiffs, R H Willis and Son (a
firm), awarding them £275 for conversion of a Ford motor car. The facts are set out
in the judgment of Lord Denning MR.

David Friedman for the auctioneers.
Jonathan Fulthorpe for the plaintiffs.   d

Cur adv vult

13th January. The following judgments were read.

LORD DENNING MR. There is a firm of motor car dealers in Southampton called
R H Willis and Son. They sell secondhand cars. In May 1973 Mr Croucher, the   e
licensee of a local public house, the City Arms at Nursling, wanted to buy one of
their cars. It was a Ford Mustang eight years old. The cash price was £600. But he
had not got that sum available. So the dealers allowed him to have it on hire-purchase
terms at the hire-purchase price of £625. He paid £350 in cash or in part exchange,
and agreed to pay the balance of £275 by monthly instalments over the next six
months. He signed the hire-purchase agreement in a familiar form. It contained
this warning to Mr Croucher: 'The goods will not become your property until you
have made all the payments. You must not sell them before then.'
    Mr Croucher did not heed this warning. He was in financial difficulties with
bankruptcy staring him in the face. He decided to raise some money by selling the
car. He took it 50 miles away to Farnham in Surrey and put it into the car auction
there. It was run by British Car Auctions Ltd. He put on it the reserve price of £450   g
net. He told the auctioneers that it was his own car and that it was not subject to any
outstanding hire-purchase. He signed the entry form to that effect.
    The auction was held subject to the auctioneers' usual 'Conditions of Sale' which
were plainly exhibited and also announced by the auctioneer. The car was entered as
lot 67 and put up for sale. It did not reach the reserve price of £450. The highest
bid was £410. This was, however, not so very far short of the £450. So the auctioneers   h
treated it as a 'provisional bid'; and followed their usual practice in regard to provisional bids. A clerk went down amongst the people and spoke to the man who had
made the bid of £410. The clerk said to him: 'Will you stand on your bid?' He said
'Yes'. He was a Mr Worth of Hillingdon near London. The auctioneers knew him
because he had an account with them. The clerk then called over the loudspeaker
system saying: 'Will the vendor and highest bidder of lot 67 please come to the   j
provisional bid office.' That was an office specially set up to deal with such provisional bids. Mr Worth went to the office. So did Mr Croucher; or if not, the auctioneers spoke to him on the telephone. The auctioneers told Mr Croucher that Mr
Worth had bid at £410: 'Will you accept it?' Mr Croucher said: 'Yes, but only if you
will reduce your commission.' The auctioneers said: 'Our usual commission is five per

cent. That is £20·50 on £410. But we will reduce it to £15 if you will accept the £410.'
Mr Croucher said: 'I am agreeable to sell the car on those terms.'

The auctioneers then treated the sale as concluded subject to the conditions of sale
exhibited in the sale room. They filled in the entry form describing the car as sold for
£410 and their commission as £15. They made out an invoice for the car to Mr
Worth for £410 and in accordance with their conditions of sale added an indemnity
fee of £2 plus 'V.A.T. @ 10%', making a sum of £412·20. They debited Mr Worth's
account with that sum and gave him a purchase slip authorising him to take the car
away. He did so.

Next day the auctioneers checked with Hire Purchase Information Ltd ('HPI
Ltd') so as to see if any of the finance companies had advanced any money on the car.
HPI Ltd said they had no entry against it. So the auctioneers regarded Mr Croucher
as having a good title to the car. They paid him the £410, less £15 commission, 50p
service charge, and £1·55 to check HPI Ltd, making £392·95.

A few days later Mr Croucher was made bankrupt. He had not paid the instalments due on the car. So R H Willis and Sons, the car dealers, sought to have recourse
against someone or other. The purchaser had disappeared, so we are told: and so had
the car. So they came down on the auctioneers. They said that the auctioneers were
liable in conversion and they claimed from the auctioneers the £275 outstanding
instalments on the car. R H Willis and Sons issued their plaint in the county court
on 5th November 1973. The case was adjourned for a long time awaiting the decision
of the House of Lords in *Moorgate Mercantile Co Ltd v Twitchings*[1]. It was then restored
for hearing on this one point: were the auctioneers liable in conversion? The county
court judge held that they were. The auctioneers appeal to this court. They want
to know how they stand in regard to 'provisional bids' which are now an established
feature of their trade.

The question that arises is the usual one: which of the two innocent persons is to
suffer? Is the loss to fall on the motor car dealers? They have been deprived of the
£275 due to them on the car. Or on the auctioneers? They sold it believing that Mr
Croucher was the true owner. In answering that question in cases such as this, the
common law has always acted on the maxim: nemo dat quod non habet. It has
protected the property rights of the true owner. It has enforced them strictly as
against anyone who deals with the goods inconsistently with the dominion of the
true owner. Even though the true owner may have been very negligent and the
defendant may have acted in complete innocence, nevertheless the common law held
him liable in conversion. Both the 'innocent acquirer' and the 'innocent handler'
have been hit hard. That state of the law has often been criticised. It has been proposed that the law should protect a person who buys goods or handles them in good
faith without notice of any adverse title, at any rate where the claimant by his own
negligence or otherwise has largely contributed to the outcome. Such proposals have
however been effectively blocked by the decisions of the House of Lords in the last
century of *Hollins v Fowler*[2], and in this century of *Moorgate Mercantile Co Ltd v Twitchings*[1], to which I may add the decision of this court in *Central Newbury Car Auctions Ltd v
Unity Finance Ltd*[3].

In some instances the strictness of the law has been mitigated by statute, as for
instance, by the protection given to private purchasers by the Hire Purchase Acts.
But in other cases the only way in which the innocent acquirers or handlers have been
able to protect themselves is by insurance. They insure themselves against their
potential liability. This is the usual method nowadays. When men of business or
professional men find themselves hit by the law with new and increasing liabilities,
they take steps to insure themselves, so that the loss may not fall on one alone, but

---

1   [1976] 2 All ER 641, [1977] AC 890
2   (1875) LR 7 HL 757, [1874–80] All ER Rep 118
3   [1956] 3 All ER 905, [1957] 1 QB 371

be spread among many. It is a factor of which we must take account: see *Post Office v Norwich Union Fire Insurance Society Ltd*[1] and *Morris v Ford Motor Co Ltd*[2].

Sales under the hammer

The position of auctioneers is typical. It is now, I think, well established that if an auctioneer sells goods by knocking down his hammer at an auction and thereafter delivers them to the purchaser—then although he is only an agent—then if the vendor has no title to the goods, both the auctioneer and the purchaser are liable in conversion to the true owner, no matter how innocent the auctioneer may have been in handling the goods or the purchaser in acquiring them: see *Barker v Furlong*[3] per Romer J and *Consolidated Co v Curtis & Son*[4]. This state of the law has been considered by the Law Reform Committee in 1966[5] as to innocent acquirers; and in 1971[6] as to innocent handlers. But Parliament has made no change in it; no doubt it would have done so in the Torts (Interference with Goods) Act 1977 if it had thought fit to do so.

Provisional bids

Such is the position with sales 'under the hammer'. What about sales which follow a 'provisional bid'? I see no difference in principle. In each case the auctioneer is an intermediary who brings the two parties together and gets them to agree on the price. They are bound by the conditions of sale which he has prepared. He retains the goods in his custody. He delivers them to the purchaser on being paid the price. He pays it over to the vendor and deducts his commission. So in principle, I think that on a 'provisional bid' an auctioneer is liable in conversion, just as when he sells under the hammer. There are two decisions, however, which suggest a difference. Each followed a dictum of Bramwell LJ in *Cochrane v Rymill*[7]. One is the decision of the Court of Appeal in *National Mercantile Bank Ltd v Rymill*[8]. The other is the decision of the Divisional Court in *Turner v Hockey*[9]. In those two cases it was held that the auctioneer was not liable in conversion, because he had not actually effected the sale. It had been made by the parties themselves. I doubt whether those decisions are correct. Although the auctioneer had not actually effected the sale, his intervention in each case was an efficient cause of the sale and he got his commission for what he did. To my mind those two decisions are a departure from the principles stated by Blackburn J in *Hollins v Fowler*[10]. That is the principle which should guide us, especially as it was inferentially accepted by the House of Lords. I cannot help thinking that in those two cases the courts were anxious to protect the auctioneer, as an innocent handler, from the strictness of the law. In doing so they introduced fine distinctions which are difficult to apply. I do not think we should follow those two cases today, especially when regard is had to the insurance aspect to which I now turn. It is clear that the auctioneers insure against both kinds of sale equally. On every one of the sales, under the hammer or on provisional bids, the auctioneers charge an 'indemnity fee' to the purchaser. He has to pay a premium of £2 on each vehicle purchased. In return for it the auctioneers, British Car Auctions Ltd, through an associate company, the Omega Insurance Co Ltd, insure the purchaser against any loss he may

---

1 [1967] 1 All ER 577 at 580, [1967] 2 QB 363 at 375
2 [1973] 2 All ER 1084 at 1090, 1091, [1973] QB 792 at 801
3 [1891] 2 Ch 172 at 181
4 [1892] 1 QB 495
5 Law Reform Committee Twelfth Report (Transfer of Title to Matters), April 1966 (Cmnd 2958)
6 Law Reform Committee Eighteenth Report (Conversion and Detinue), September 1971 (Cmnd 4774)
7 (1879) 40 LT 744 at 746
8 (1881) 44 LT 767
9 (1887) 56 LJQB 301
10 (1875) LR 7 HL 757 at 766, 767

suffer through any defect in title of the seller. So if the true owner comes along
and retakes the goods from the purchaser or makes him pay damages for conversion,
the auctioneers (through their associate company) indemnify the purchaser against
the loss. The premium thus charged by the auctioneers (through their associate
company) is calculated to cover the risk of the seller having no title or a defective
title. That risk is the same no matter whether the true owner sues the auctioneer
or the purchaser. The auctioneer collects £2 from every purchaser to cover that risk.
We are told it comes to £200,000 a year. Seeing that they receive these sums, they
ought to meet the claims of the true owners out of it. This system is the commercial
way of doing justice between the parties. It means that all concerned are protected.
The true owner is protected by the strict law of conversion. He can recover against
the innocent acquirer and the innocent handler. But those innocents are covered by
insurance so that the loss is not borne by any single individual but is spread through
the community at large. The insurance factor had a considerable influence on the
Law Reform Committee. In view of it they did not recommend any change in the
law[1]. So also it may properly have an influence on the courts in deciding issues
which come before them.

Conclusion

My conclusion is that, where goods are sold by the intervention of an auctioneer,
under the hammer or as a result of a provisional bid, then if the seller has no title,
the auctioneer is liable in conversion to the true owner. I would dismiss the appeal
accordingly.

ROSKILL LJ. I have had the opportunity of reading in draft the judgments of
Lord Denning MR and of Browne LJ. Like them and like his Honour Judge Sheldon, I
am clearly of the view that a sale pursuant to the auctioneers' provisional bid procedure is indistinguishable in its essential nature and legal consequences from a sale by
them under the hammer. That being so, none of the interesting questions of law
which were argued before us with conspicuous ability by both counsel arises for
decision and I do not find it necessary to consider those arguments in detail. If *National
Mercantile Bank Ltd v Rymill*[2] be correctly reported, I find the decision difficult to
reconcile with the decision of the House of Lords in *Hollins v Fowler*[3], and in particular
with the opinion of Blackburn J[4] advising the House in that case. But on any view I
think that the former case is clearly distinguishable from the present, as Browne LJ
says. I also entirely agree with the criticism made of *Turner v Hockey*[5] to which he
refers. It seems to me that that case, if correctly reported, was wrongly decided. For
the reasons Browne LJ gives, which I think are substantially the same as those given by
the county court judge in his most careful and clear judgment, I would dismiss this
appeal.

BROWNE LJ. Counsel for the auctioneers rightly accepted on behalf of British
Car Auctions Ltd (at any rate as far as this court is concerned): (a) that at the relevant
time the plaintiffs were entitled to immediate possession of this car and were therefore entitled to sue in conversion (see the decision of this court in *Union Transport
Finance Ltd v British Car Auctions Ltd*[6]); (b) that when an auctioneer sells under the
hammer a chattel to which the purported seller has no title he is guilty of conversion

1   See Cmnd 4774, para 48, note 2
2   (1881) 44 LT 767
3   (1875) LR 7 HL 757, [1874-80] All ER Rep 118
4   LR 7 HL 757 at 766, 767
5   (1887) 56 LJQB 301
6   Page 385, ante

see *Cochrane v Rymill*[1], *Barker v Furlong*[2], *Consolidated Co v Curtis & Son*[3], *Union Transport Finance Ltd v British Car Auctions Ltd*[4]); (c) that for this purpose there is no distinction between a sale by an auctioneer under the hammer and a sale by an auctioneer by private treaty.

In this case, there was no sale under the hammer. Counsel for the auctioneers submits that there was no sale by the auctioneers by private treaty, and that what the auctioneers did, something less than a sale by them, did not amount to conversion of the car by them. We had a long, able and interesting argument about the nature of the action of conversion, about the meaning and scope of such metaphorical (and I think unhelpful) phrases as 'conduit pipe' (or 'mere conduit pipe') and 'ministerial acts', about the meaning of 'mere asportation' and about the authorities on these problems.

But if on the facts of this case there was a sale of the car by the auctioneers none of these interesting problems arise.

Very naturally, by the time of the hearing no one from the auctioneers could remember anything about this particular transaction, and it can only be assumed that it was carried out in accordance with the auctioneers' usual practice as described by Mr Plumridge in his evidence. Mr Plumridge agreed that the intention of the auctioneers' fairly elaborate 'provisional bid' system was for a sale to take place 'because we are in commerce to make money and we are delighted if a sale can be agreed so that we can earn the negotiating fee'. He was asked: 'So would you accept my proposition that this provisional sale system could be, as it maybe is, designed to help you sell cars and make money?' and answered: 'Yes, I do'. When a car is put up for auction and fails to reach the reserve, Mr Plumridge said (rightly I think) that the auctioneers were then without instructions as auctioneers. As he said, '[It] brings it into the realm of private treaty sale'. But even before they get further instructions, the rostrum clerk goes to the highest bidder, taking with him the purchase slip. This is the same document as that which would be used if the car had been sold under the hammer, and contains the following, to be signed by the purchaser: 'I acknowledge having purchased/provisionally purchased this Lot at the price shown and in accordance with the Conditions of Sale as Exhibited'; these are of course the conditions of sale to be incorporated in a contract between the auctioneers and the purchaser. It also contains a space for the price, and '+£2 for Indemnity Policy with the Omega Insurance Company Ltd.'; this refers to cl 20 of the conditions of sale, which requires the purchaser to take out a policy with Omega (a company associated with the auctioneers) 'AGAINST ANY LOSS HE MAY SUFFER . . . THROUGH ANY DEFECT IN TITLE OF THE SELLER . . .' When this 'provisional sale' was completed, the same entry form was used as if it had been sold under the hammer. The seller gets the same 'guarantee' of his money from the auctioneer. The same insurance is effected. If the sale takes place on the same day, the auctioneers are entitled to the same commission from the seller (cl 9 of the conditions of entry), though in practice they are prepared to negotiate a reduction of their commission or 'negotiating fee' as they did in this case. The invoice really seems to me conclusive in itself. It is headed 'British Car Auctions Limited'; it bears their value added tax registration number and charges value added tax; and it includes £2 for the insurance premium.

I am clearly of opinion that this car was sold by the auctioneers to Mr Worth. Accordingly, they are in my judgment liable to the plaintiffs in conversion.

On my view of the facts, the difficult questions raised in argument do not arise, and I think it would be wrong to express any detailed conclusions about them which

---

1　(1879) 40 LT 744
2　[1891] 2 Ch 172
3　[1892] 1 QB 495
4　Page 385, ante

would be obiter. I will only say: (a) whether or not *National Mercantile Bank Ltd v Rymill*[1] was rightly decided, it is in my view clearly distinguishable from the present case on the facts; (b) I entirely agree with the criticisms of *Turner v Hockey*[2] made by Collins J in *Consolidated Co v Curtis & Son*[3].

The auctioneers have entirely failed to satisfy me that the judge's finding that they sold the car was wrong. I think it was right. I would therefore dismiss this appeal.

Appeal dismissed. Leave to appeal to the House of Lords refused.

Solicitors: *Cripps, Harries, Willis & Carter*, agents for *Clive Fisher & Co*, Addlestone (for the auctioneers); *Hepherd, Winstanley & Pugh*, Southampton (for the plaintiffs).

Sumra Green　Barrister.

Stubbs v Assopardi and another

COURT OF APPEAL, CIVIL DIVISION
MEGAW, LAWTON AND SHAW LJJ
8th, 20th DECEMBER 1977

Rent restriction – Furnished letting – Extension of protection to furnished tenancies – Statutory exception – Furnished tenancies granted on or after commencement date protected except where resident landlord – Exception excluded where fixed term tenancy granted to person who immediately before it was granted was tenant under earlier tenancy which 'by virtue of this section' was not a protected tenancy – Transitional provision – Earlier tenancy granted before commencement date deemed to be granted on that date – Resident landlord granting tenant two successive fixed term tenancies of furnished premises – First tenancy unprotected when granted – Statute extending protection to furnished premises before termination of first tenancy and commencement of second – Whether second tenancy protected – Whether first tenancy not a protected tenancy 'by virtue of this section' – Rent Act 1968, s 5A(1)(5) – Rent Act 1974, Sch 3, para 1.

On 1st July 1973 the plaintiff, by a written agreement, let a furnished flat in the house in which she resided to the defendant for a period of two years expiring on 30th June 1975 ('the first tenancy'). When the first tenancy was granted the defendant was not a protected tenant as s 2(1)(b) of the Rent Act 1968 excepted furnished tenancies from the protection of the Act. On 1st July 1975, on the expiry of the first tenancy, the plaintiff let the flat to the defendant for a further period of 11 months expiring on 30th May 1976 ('the second tenancy'). After the second tenancy expired, the plaintiff brought proceedings in the county court to recover possession of the flat. The county court judge made an order for possession to be given up within six weeks. The defendant appealed to the Court of Appeal. The question arose whether the defendant was entitled to claim the protection of the Rent Acts 1968 and 1974 by virtue of s 1(1)(a)[a] of the 1974 Act, which had come into force on 14th

---

1　(1881) 44 LT 767
2　(1887) 56 LJQB 301
3　[1892] 1 QB 495 at 502, 503
a　Section 1(1), so far as material, provides: 'On and after the commencement date,—(a) a tenancy of a dwelling-house shall no longer be prevented from being a protected tenancy for the purposes of the Rent Act by reason only that, under the tenancy, the dwelling-house is bona fide let at a rent which includes payments in respect of the use of furniture . . .'

August 1974 (i e in the course of the first tenancy) and which retrospectively extended the protection of the Rent Acts to furnished tenancies. A new section, s 5A, was added to the 1968 Act by s 2(3) of, and Sch 2, Part 1, para 1 to, the 1974 Act. Section 5A(1)[b] excluded furnished tenancies from the protection of the Rent Acts if there was a resident landlord. The defendant contended that the plaintiff was unable to rely on s 5A(1) because s 5A(5)(b)[c] provided that the exclusion in s 5A(1) was not to apply where the tenancy (i e the second tenancy) was for a term of years certain and was granted to a person who, immediately before it was granted, was the tenant under an earlier tenancy (i e the first tenancy) of the dwelling and 'by virtue of this section that earlier tenancy was not a protected tenancy'. The plaintiff contended that it was not 'by virtue of' s 5A that it was not protected but by virtue of Sch 3, para 1(1)[d], to the 1974 Act, and therefore the exclusion from protection contained in s 5A(1) applied nevertheless. Schedule 3, para 1(1), provided that in any case where before the commencement date of the 1974 Act a dwelling was subject to a tenancy which was a furnished letting and the dwelling formed part only of a building and on that date the interest of the lessor under the furnished letting belonged to a resident landlord, and, apart from that paragraph, the furnished letting would, on the commencement date, become a protected tenancy, the Act should apply, subject to Sch 3, para 1(2), as if the tenancy had been granted on the commencement date and as if the condition in s 5A(1)(b) of the 1968 Act were fulfilled in relation to the grant of the tenancy. Schedule 3, para 1(2), provided, inter alia, that in the application of the 1968 Act to a tenancy by virtue of that paragraph, s 5A(5) should be omitted.

Held – On the true construction of the 1974 Act, it was not 'by virtue of s 5A' that the first tenancy was 'not a protected tenancy', but by virtue of the statutory fiction created by Sch 3, para 1, to the 1974 Act (whereby a furnished tenancy granted before the commencement date of the 1974 Act was to be treated as granted on that date) that the first tenancy was deprived of the protection which it would otherwise have had under s 1(1)(a) of that Act and was brought within s 5A(1) of the 1968 Act. It followed that, since the second requirement in s 5A(5) had not been fulfilled, the defendant was not a protected tenant and the plaintiff was entitled to an order for possession (see p 403 c to j and p 404 b to e, post).

Notes

For exclusion of protected status where landlord's interest belongs to resident landlord, see Supplement to 23 Halsbury's Laws (3rd Edn) para 1523A.

For the Rent Act 1968, s 5A, see 44 Halsbury's Statutes (3rd Edn) 628, 629.

For the Rent Act 1974, Sch 3, para 1, see ibid 631.

As from 29th August 1977, s 5A of the 1968 Act has been replaced by s 12 of, and Sch 2, Part I, to the Rent Act 1977, and Sch 3, para 1, to the 1974 Act has been replaced by Sch 24, para 6, to the 1977 Act.

Appeal

This was an appeal by the second defendant, Jeffrey Adams, against an order of his Honour Judge Curtis-Raleigh made in the Bloomsbury and Marylebone County Court on 18th March 1977 whereby he ordered that the plaintiff, Anna Maria Josepha Stubbs, should recover possession against the defendants, Lydia Assopardi and Jeffrey Adams, of the ground floor flat at 13 Norland Square, London W11, of which the plaintiff was the landlord. The facts are set out in the judgment of the court.

Derek Wood for Mr Adams.
The plaintiff appeared in person.

---

b Subsection (1), so far as material, is set out at p 402 b, post
c Subsection (5), so far as material, is set out at p 402 d, post
d Paragraph 1, so far as material, is set out at p 402 j to p 403 b, post

Cur adv vult

20th December. **MEGAW LJ** read the following judgment of the court: The plaintiff claimed against the defendants, Miss Assopardi and Mr Adams, possession of the ground floor flat at 13 Norland Square, London W11. The particulars of claim as formulated by the plaintiff in the Bloomsbury and Marylebone County Court averred that by an agreement in writing dated 1st July 1975 the flat had been let to the defendants, furnished, at a rent of £60·68 per month, for 11 months, which fixed-term tenancy had expired on 1st June 1976.

In this court some point was sought to be made on behalf of the plaintiff to the effect that Mr Adams was not a party to the agreement because, though he had signed it as a party, the agreement on its first page recorded Miss Assopardi alone as 'the tenant'. We did not allow any such issue to be raised. It would have been inconsistent with the plaintiff's own pleading, and it had not been taken in the county court, where it had been accepted or assumed that Mr Adams was a party and no question had been raised below as to any special considerations which might arise with regard to a joint tenancy, and no facts were put in evidence which would give rise to any question with regard thereto. We say no more on that point.

At the hearing in the county court before Judge Curtis-Raleigh the relevant facts were not in dispute. They are clearly and succinctly set out by the learned judge in the first paragraph of his judgment as follows:

> 'In this case the landlord plaintiff claims possession of ground floor flat, 13 Norland Square W11, which was let to the defendants under two successive agreements in writing, the first from 1st July 1973, for a term of two years expiring on 30th June 1975, followed immediately by a tenancy for a fixed term of 11 months from 1st July 1975. Both the lettings were lettings of premises which were fully furnished. The landlord was a resident landlord.'

When the agreement of 1st July 1973 (which we shall call 'the first tenancy') was made, the defendants were not protected tenants, because the tenancy was of furnished premises and s 2(1)(b) of the Rent Act 1968, as it then stood, excepted such a tenancy, so that it was not a protected tenancy. This was so, irrespective of the fact that the plaintiff was what the judge described as 'a resident landlord'. The Rent Act 1974 came into force on 14th August 1974, and was thus in force when the first tenancy ended and when, immediately thereafter, the tenancy brought into being by the agreement of 1st July 1975 (which we shall call 'the second tenancy') commenced.

The issue, and the only issue, which arises on this appeal is whether, on the facts stated above and on the true construction of certain provisions of the 1974 Act, the defendants were, when the proceedings were brought and at the time of the hearing, protected tenants. Their defence to the claim for possession was expressed thus in para 8 of their defence:

> 'The defendants aver that the said agreement of 1st July 1975 was a second and immediately successive fixed-term agreement subsequent to the agreement of 1st July 1973 and claim the protection of s 5A(5)(b) of the Rent Act 1968, as inserted by Sch 2, Part I, para 1 of the Rent Act 1974.'

In the county court the judge allowed the plaintiff's husband to make submissions on her behalf, since it was said that the plaintiff herself had not a sufficient command of the English language. We allowed the same course to be followed on the hearing of the appeal.

The judge held in favour of the plaintiff and granted an order for possession. Mr Adams appealed to this court. He was represented in this court by Mr Wood, who did not appear in the county court. We would pay tribute to the admirable clarity and fairness of Mr Wood's exposition of extremely complex and highly technical statutory provisions.

Section 1(1)(*a*) of the 1974 Act extends Rent Act protection to furnished tenancies. That extension applied not only to tenancies created after the coming into force of the Act but also to already existing tenancies. However, s 2(3) provides for the insertion in the 1968 Rent of a new s 5A, which introduces the concept of a 'resident landlord' as a relevant factor in excluding the protected status of furnished tenancies. Its terms are set out in para 1 of Sch 2 to the 1974 Act. Subsection (1) of that new section of the 1968 Act, so far as it is relevant in the present appeal, reads:

'Subject to subsection (5) below, a tenancy of a dwelling-house which is granted on or after the commencement date [i e 14th August 1974] . . . shall not be a protected tenancy at any time if— . . . (*b*) the tenancy was granted by a person who, at the time that he granted it, occupied as his residence another dwelling-house which also forms part of that building . . .'

If it rested there, the defendants in this case would not be protected tenants. The second tenancy, of 1st July 1975, was granted after the commencement date of the 1974 Act; and, as appears from the undisputed facts set out above, the landlord was a 'resident landlord', that is, he fulfilled the requirements of para (*b*) above. But the provisions of sub-s (1) of s 5A are expressly made subject to sub-s (5), which, so far as relevant, reads as follows:

'This section does not apply to a tenancy of a dwelling-house which forms part of a building if— . . . (*b*) the tenancy is a tenancy for a term of years certain and is granted to a person who, immediately before it was granted, was the tenant under an earlier tenancy of that dwelling-house . . . and, by virtue of this section, that earlier tenancy was not a protected tenancy . . .'

So the exclusion of the tenancy from being a protected tenancy, which s 5A(1) would otherwise achieve in respect of a post-14th August 1974 tenancy, is itself excluded if the requirements of s 5A(5) are fulfilled. There is no doubt but that in the present case all the requirements contained in sub-s (5)(*b*) are met, save only for one possible exception. The second tenancy is a tenancy for a term of years certain. The provision for 11 months duration, it is not disputed, satisfies that requirement. That second tenancy was granted to a person who, immediately before it was granted, was the tenant under an earlier tenancy (the first tenancy) of that dwelling-house (the ground floor flat). There is no doubt that that first tenancy was not a protected tenancy. The one and only ground on which it could be suggested, and the ground on which the judge held, that the requirements of sub-s (5)(*b*) were not fulfilled is that it was not 'by virtue of this section' (i e s 5A) that the first tenancy was not a protected tenancy but that, instead, it was 'by virtue of' something else. The 'something else' which the judge held to be relevant and effective was the transitional provisions of the 1974 Act as set out in para 1 of Sch 3.

The purpose of the transitional provisions was to ensure that a resident landlord who before the commencement of the 1974 Act had granted a furnished tenancy, which was still in effect at the commencement of the Act, should be in no worse position than a resident landlord who granted such a tenancy on or after the date of the commencement of the Act. The tenancy granted on or after the commencement of the Act would not be protected because of the new s 5A inserted in the 1968 Act. But in the absence of transitional provisions a pre-commencement date tenancy would be protected because of s 1(1) of the 1974 Act, coupled with the fact that the new s 5A(1) would not provide an exemption since it was expressed to be applicable to a tenancy granted on or after the commencement date.

The relevant transitional provisions, in Sch 3, para 1(1) and (2), so far as they are material, were as follows:

'(1) In any case where—(*a*) before the commencement date a dwelling was subject to a tenancy which is a furnished letting, and (*b*) the dwelling forms part only of a building . . . and (c) on that date the interest of the lessor . . . under the furnished letting—(i) belongs to a person who occupies as his residence another dwelling which also forms part of that building . . . and (d) apart from this paragraph the furnished letting would, on the commencement date, become a protected furnished tenancy, the Rent Act shall apply, subject to sub-paragraph (2) below, as if the tenancy had been granted on the commencement date and as if the condition in paragraph (b) of section 5A(1) of the Rent Act 1968 were fulfilled in relation to the grant of the tenancy.'

(Paragraph (b) of s 5A(1) has been set out earlier. It defines what we have called 'the resident landlord').

'(2) In the application of the Rent Act 1968 to a tenancy by virtue of this paragraph—(a) subsection (5) of section 5A shall be omitted; and (b) in section 102A any reference to section 5A of that Act shall be construed as including a reference to this paragraph.'

The transitional provisions are plainly relevant and material. If it were not for them, the first tenancy would have had the status of a protected tenancy. It would have been made such by s 1(1) of the 1974 Act. It would not have been deprived of that status by s 5A, because s 5A is concerned with tenancies granted on or after the commencement date. The first tenancy was granted before that date. The way in which the relevant transitional provisions (Sch 3, para 1(1) and (2)) achieve their object is by introducing a statutory fiction. The fiction is that the relevant tenancy was granted on the commencement date, although in fact it was granted earlier. It is thus brought within s 5A, and it thus loses its protected status. Schedule 3, para 1(1), expressly provides that s 5A shall apply. We say 'expressly', because there can be no doubt but that the words used, 'the Rent Act shall apply', in the context, mean the Rent Act including the new s 5A. Not only s 15(3) of the 1974 Act, but also the references, in the immediately following provisions of para 1(1) and (2) of Sch 3, to s 5A put it beyond doubt that that is so.

But that does not solve the essential question, which is: is the absence of protected status of the first tenancy 'by virtue of this section' within the meaning of that phrase in s 5A(5)(b), or is it 'by virtue of' the transitional provisions?

If it were not for the statutory fiction created by para 1(1) of Sch 3, s 5A would not apply and the first tenancy would thus be protected. Hence it can be said that it is 'by virtue of' those transitional provisions that the first tenancy does not have a protected status. But the machinery by which the transitional provisions operate to deprive the first tenancy of its protected status is by applying s 5A (less sub-s (5) thereof). Hence it could also be said that it is 'by virtue of section 5A' that the first tenancy does not have a protected status. Which of the two is the one to choose, for choose one must?

In the absence of any further guidance from the context, we should have inclined to the view that the choice should be the transitional provisions. In some respects it is like a choice of the real or effective cause where there are competing causes. To our mind, it is the statutory fiction, created by the transitional provisions, which would be the real or predominant cause of the first tenancy not being protected. If one has to choose between them, as one must, it is by virtue of that statutory fiction, rather than by virtue of the resulting application of s 5A, that the first tenancy does not have protected status.

We are confirmed in this view by two elements in the wording of the relevant transitional provisions. First, the opening words of para 1(2) of Sch 3 are: 'In the application of the Rent Act 1968 to a tenancy *by virtue of this paragraph* . . .' The Act thus stresses that the application of s 5A is 'by virtue of' these transitional provisions. To our mind, that tends to show that the legislature, in using the phrase 'by virtue of this section' in s 5A(5)(b), did not contemplate or intend that it should apply to a case where 'this section' itself had been made applicable, as the legislature itself has expressly said, 'by virtue of' the transitional provisions.

The second element is one which is stressed by the judge in his judgment as being, we believe, the main reason for his conclusion as to the construction of the Act: that is, the wording of para 1(2)(b) of Sch 3. It reads: '. . . in section 102A any reference to section 5A of that Act shall be construed as including a reference to this paragraph'. The judge says: 'Section 5A should not be read in conjunction with Sch 3, because when it has to be read in conjunction with the schedule the Act says so: see para 1(2)(b) of Sch 3.'

In one sense, of course, s 5A has to be read 'in conjunction with' Sch 3, because para 1(1) of Sch 3 provides that that section shall apply. But we agree with what we understand to be the reasoning of the judge. The new s 102A(1), introduced by para 4 of Sch 2 to the 1974 Act, contains the words 'If and so long as a tenancy is, by virtue only of section 5A of this Act, precluded from being a protected tenancy . . .' The legislature in enacting the transitional provisions, which make s 5A applicable in certain cases where it would not otherwise apply, has thought it right, in relation to those words used in s 102A 'by virtue only of section 5A of this Act', expressly to provide that those words are to be construed as containing a reference to the transitional provisions in Sch 3, para 1. There is no such provision, no corresponding words or formula, in relation to the corresponding words 'by virtue of this section' where those words occur in s 5A(5)(b). Therefore the legislature did not intend those words in s 5A(5)(b) to be read as 'including a reference to' the transitional provisions. Counsel for Mr Adams submits that this argument, which appealed to the judge, involves placing undue weight on the doctrine 'expressio unius, exclusio alterius'. We do not think so. Like the judge, we regard it as a powerful indication of the intention of the legislature, which, as is normally the principle of our law, has to be derived from the words used.

Counsel for Mr Adams criticised the judge's careful judgment in two other respects. The first was the passage in which the judge said:

'This tenant was the tenant under an earlier tenancy and the only question is whether it became unprotected by virtue of s 5A. The answer is No, because it was granted before s 5A came into force.'

We do not think that this was an error. At that point the judge was looking at the question without reference to the transitional provisions.

The other respect in which he criticised the judgment was the judge's 'cross-check' of his conclusion with his view of 'what the legislature might reasonably be expected to want to achieve'. We feel quite unable to express any confident view, one way or the other, as to the construction which would be more likely to fit in with the actual intention of the legislature. In any event, however, it is clear that the judge's 'cross-check' was not in any way the basis of his judgment. But in our opinion his decision on the question of construction was right.

We therefore dismiss the appeal.

Appeal dismissed. Stay of execution of order for possession for 28 days from 20th December 1977.

Solicitors: *Douglas-Mann & Co* (for Mr Adams).

Mary Rose Plummer   Barrister.

Mahesan v Malaysia Government Officers' Co-operative Housing Society Ltd

PRIVY COUNCIL

LORD DIPLOCK, LORD EDMUND-DAVIES AND LORD SCARMAN

4th, 5th OCTOBER, 28th NOVEMBER 1977

Agent – Secret commission – Bribe – Remedies of principal against bribed agent – Recovery of amount of bribe as money had and received or claim for damages for fraud in respect of loss sustained – Whether principal required to elect between remedies – Whether principal entitled to recover both bribe and damages.

The appellant was a director and employee of a housing society ('the society') in Malaysia whose object was to provide housing for government employees. He connived with one M in the purchase by M of certain land in Penang and its resale to the society in that shortly before M purchased the land the appellant inspected it, found that it was suitable for the society's purposes and knew that it was available for purchase at the price of $456,000, but nevertheless arranged with M that M should purchase the land at that price and resell it to the society for the price of $944,000. Between the purchase by M and the resale to the society, M incurred expenses amounting to $45,000 in evicting squatters from the land. He therefore made out of the sale to the society a gross profit of $488,000 and a net profit of $443,000. M passed to the appellant as a bribe for his connivance in the transaction one-quarter of the gross profit on the sale to the society, namely the sum of $122,000. M escaped to India before the society discovered the facts relating to the transaction. The appellant was convicted under the Prevention of Corruption Act 1961. The society also brought civil proceedings against him in which it claimed relief under two separate heads, (i) recovery of the amount of the bribe, i e $122,000, and (ii) damages quantified at $488,000, being the difference between the price it had paid for the land and the price M had paid for it, in respect of the loss it had sustained in consequence of the appellant's fraudulent breach of duty. The trial judge granted the relief claimed under head (i) and gave judgment for the society for $122,000, but refused to grant any relief under head (ii) on the ground that land prices were rising in Malaysia and the society had failed to prove that it had paid more than a fair market price for the land. The appellant appealed to the Federal Court of Malaysia against the judgment for $122,000. The society cross-appealed against the refusal to grant damages under head (ii) of its claim. The Federal Court dismissed the appellant's appeal and allowed the society's cross-appeal holding that the appellant was in breach of his duty as the society's director and employee in regard to the transaction, that prima facie the measure of the damages was $488,000, but that the sum of $45,000 incurred in evicting the squatters was to be deducted therefrom. Accordingly the court gave judgment for the society under head (ii) for $443,000, in addition to giving judgment under head (i) for $122,000. The appellant appealed to the Privy Council.

Held – At common law the principal of a bribed agent had, as against both the bribed agent and the briber, the alternative remedies of (a) claiming the amount of the bribe as money had and received or (b) claiming damages for fraud in the amount of the actual loss sustained in consequence of entering into the transaction in respect of which the bribe had been given; but he could not recover both and had to elect between the alternative remedies although he was not required to make the election until the time for entry of judgment in his favour on one or other of the alternative causes of action. It followed that the society was bound to elect between the claim to recover the bribe and the claim for damages for fraud. Since it would clearly have elected in favour of the latter, the judgment of the Federal Court would be varied by entering judgment for the society for $443,000 only, with interest, and to that extent the appeal would be allowed (see p 408 f, p 410 d to g, p 411 f to j and p 412 d e, post).

United Australia Ltd v Barclays Bank Ltd [1940] 4 All ER 20 applied.

Dicta of Lord Esher MR, Lindley and Lopes LJJ in Salford Corpn v Lever [1891] 1 QB at 177, 180, 181 disapproved.

Notes

For secret profits and bribes, see 1 Halsbury's Laws (4th Edn) paras 789-792, and for cases on the subject, see 1 Digest (Repl) 545-547, 548-551, 1691-1707, 1712-1727.

Cases referred to in judgment

Bagnall v Carlton (1877) 6 Ch D 371, 47 LJCh 30, 37 LT 481, CA, 43 Digest (Repl) 399, 4274.

Boston Deep Sea Fishing and Ice Co v Ansell (1889) 39 Ch D 339, [1886-90] All ER Rep 65, 59 LT 345, CA, 1 Digest (Repl) 551, 1726.

Fawcett v Whitehouse (1829) 1 Russ & M 132, 8 LJOSCh 50, 39 ER 51, 1 Digest (Repl) 545, 1691.

Grant v Gold Exploration and Development Syndicate Ltd [1900] 1 QB 233, 69 LJQB 150, 82 LT 5, CA, 1 Digest (Repl) 553, 1740.

Hovendon & Sons v Millhoff (1900) 83 LT 41, [1900-3] All ER Rep 848, 16 TLR 506, CA, 1 Digest (Repl) 553, 1738.

Reading v Attorney-General [1951] 1 All ER 617, [1951] AC 507, HL; affg sub nom Re Reading's Petition of Right [1949] 2 All ER 68, sub nom Reading v R [1949] 2 KB 232, CA, 1 Digest (Repl) 549, 1720.

Salford Corpn v Lever [1891] 1 QB 168, 60 LJQB 39, 63 LT 658, 55 JP 244, CA, 1 Digest (Repl) 549, 1718.

United Australia Ltd v Barclays Bank Ltd [1940] 4 All ER 20, [1941] AC 1, 109 LJKB 919, 164 LT 139, 46 Com Cas 1, HL, 45 Digest (Repl) 317, 275.

Appeal

This was an appeal by the defendant, T Mahesan, son of Thambiah, against the judgment of the Federal Court of Malaysia (Azmi LP, Suffian FJ and Syed Othman J) dated 28th February 1974, whereby the court (i) dismissed the appellant's appeal against the judgment of the High Court of Malaysia at Kuala Lumpur (Abdul Hamid J) dated 5th June 1972 awarding the Malaysia Government Officers' Co-operative Housing Society Ltd ('the housing society') $122,000 with interest, being the amount of a secret commission received by the appellant whilst a director and employee of the housing society in respect of a transaction relating to the purchase of land by the society, and (ii) allowed the housing society's cross-appeal against the dismissal by Abdul Hamid J of its claim for damages of $488,000 in respect of the excess payment it had made in purchasing the land. The facts are set out in the judgment of the Board.

Charles Fletcher Cooke QC and Nigel Murray for the appellant.
Robert Gatehouse QC and Raja Aziz Addruse (of the Malaysian Bar) for the housing society.

LORD DIPLOCK.   The facts of this case found by the trial judge are recounted in his judgment. His findings were accepted by the Federal Court. These are thus concurrent findings of fact, with which their Lordships, in accordance with their well-established practice, do not interfere. For the purpose of the questions of law which arise the relevant facts may be stated very shortly.

The appellant was a director and employee of the respondent ('the housing society'). Its object was to provide housing for government employees. In connection with a transaction involving the purchase of land in Penang from one Manickam, the appellant received from him a bribe amounting to $122,000. Shortly before this sale the appellant and Manickam had inspected the land together. The appellant had found it to be suitable for the housing society's purposes and Manickam had purchased it from its former owners at a price of $456,000. He resold it to the housing society for $944,000, thus realising a gross profit of $488,000, one quarter of which he passed on to the appellant. Between the purchase and the resale expenses amounting to $45,000 had been incurred by Manickam in removing squatters from the land; so the net profit that was made out of the housing society was $443,000. This represents the loss sustained by the housing society as a consequence of the appellant's fraudulent breach of duty in failing to inform his employers when he inspected it that the land was available at the price of $456,000, and in conniving with Manickam in the purchase of it by the latter and his resale of it to the housing society at more than double what he had paid for it.

The facts relating to the transaction were eventually discovered. Manickam escaped to India but the appellant was apprehended and brought to trial in the High Court, Kuala Lumpur. He was convicted of two offences of corruption under s 4(a) of the Prevention of Corruption Act 1961. He was sentenced to seven years' imprisonment and ordered under s 13 of that Act to pay to the housing society a penalty of $122,000, being the amount of the bribe.

Within a few days of the appellant's conviction the housing society brought the present action against him in the High Court of Kuala Lumpur. Relief was claimed under two separate heads: (1) recovery of the amount of the bribe the appellant had received, i e $122,000, and (2) damages for the loss sustained by the housing society in connection with the purchase of the land, which it quantified at $488,000.

The trial judge, Abdul Hamid J, granted the relief claimed under head (1); he gave judgment in favour of the housing society for $122,000 together with interest. He refused any relief under head (2) on the ground that the housing society had failed to prove that it had sustained any loss on the transaction. He apparently took the view that prices of land in Malaysia were rising and that the housing society had failed to adduce satisfactory evidence that it had paid for the land more than its fair price in the open market at the time of the purchase.

Both parties appealed to the Federal Court; the appellant appealed against so much of the judgment as was awarded $122,000 and interest against him under head (1); the housing society cross-appealed against the rejection of its claim under head (2). That court dismissed the appellant's appeal. It was an appeal on fact alone. The Federal Court examined the transcript of the evidence in detail. It upheld the learned judge's findings. So the judgment under head (1) for the recovery of the amount of the bribe received by the appellant stands and as already indicated is one which their Lordships will not permit to be re-opened.

The court allowed the cross-appeal of the housing society. It held that, on the evidence, if the appellant had been mindful of his duty as director and employee of the housing society, the society could have purchased the land itself at the time when the appellant inspected it and at the price of $456,000 which Manickam had given for it, instead of $944,000 at which he sold it to the society. In their Lordships' view this finding which is one of fact was fully justified. The Federal Court held that the difference between these two prices, i e $488,000, was prima facie the measure of the damages to which the housing society was entitled under head (2), but that there ought to be deducted from that amount a sum of $45,000 which, as the evidence disclosed, had been expended on evicting squatters from the land. Accordingly the court gave judgment for the housing society on the cross-appeal for $443,000. This is in addition to $122,000, the amount of the bribe, ordered to be paid under the judgment of Abdul Hamid J in consequence of the dismissal of the appellant's appeal under head (1). It is also in addition to the penalty in the like amount already ordered to be paid by the appellant to the housing society in the criminal proceedings, of which it had actually received $13,000 as proceeds of execution.

In assessing the damages under head (2) at $443,000 the Federal Court made no allowance for the fact that the housing society had already been adjudged entitled to recover the amount of the bribe from the appellant under head (1), thus reducing its actual loss as a result of his dishonest breach of duty by $122,000 to $321,000. The judgment of the Federal Court thus gave to the housing society in the civil action *double* recovery of the amount of the bribe that he had received; or, if account is also taken of the statutory penalty ordered to be paid to it in the criminal proceedings, *treble* recovery of that sum.

The order made in the criminal proceedings does not affect the rights of the principal against the agent in the civil proceedings. Section 30 of the Prevention of Corruption Act 1961 so provides. The question of law which has caused their Lordships difficulty in this appeal is whether or not in civil proceedings the amount of the bribe can be recovered from the dishonest agent twice over. In allowing double recovery the Federal Court treated the question as governed in Malaysia by the common law and principles of equity in force in England in 1956, the relevant date for the purpose of their acceptance as basic law in Malaysia. They did not consider that s 30 of the Prevention of Corruption Act 1961 made any relevant alteration to the civil liability of a bribed agent to his principal as it had been prior to the Act. They accordingly applied the principles stated in two judgments of the English Court of Appeal at the turn of the century: *Salford Corpn v Lever*[1] and *Hovenden & Sons v Millhoff*[2]. On the face of them the statements relied on by the Federal Court justify double recovery of the bribe from the agent who received it. They were, however, obiter. The actions in which they were made were actions by the principal against the giver of the bribe against whom there was no question of double recovery. They were not actions against the agent; and there does not appear to be any reported case of an action by a principal against his bribed agent in which double recovery of the amount of the bribe was obtained.

In their Lordships' view, these dicta, notwithstanding the eminence of the judges by whom they were made, are in conflict with basic principles of English law as they have been developed in the course of the present century. They call for re-examination in their historical setting.

By the early years of the 19th century it had become an established principle of equity that an agent who received any secret advantage for himself from the other party to a transaction in which the agent was acting for his principal was bound to account for it to his principal: *Fawcett v Whitehouse*[3]. The remedy was equitable, obtainable in the Court of Chancery, and there appears to be no reported case at common law for the recovery of a bribe by a principal from his agent before the Judicature Act 1875. No precedent for such a count is to be found in the third edition of Bullen and Leake's Precedents of Pleadings, published in 1868. Nevertheless by 1888, Bowen LJ[4] felt able to say that the bribe was recoverable at common law as money had and received by the agent to the use of the principal had:

'... the law implies a use, that is to say, there is an implied contract, if you put it as a legal proposition—there is an equitable right, if you treat it as a matter of equity—as between the principal and agent that the agent should pay it over,

---

1 [1891] 1 QB 168
2 [1900-3] All ER Rep 848
3 (1829) 1 Russ & M 132
4 *Boston Deep Sea Fishing and Ice Co v Ansell* (1889) 39 Ch D 339 at 367, 368, [1886-90] All ER Rep 65 at 75

a which renders the agent liable to be sued for money had and received, and there is an equitable right in the master to receive it, and to take it out of the hands of the agent, which gives the principal a right to relief in equity.'

This right of the principal to recover the amount of the bribe from the agent does not depend on his having incurred any loss as a result of his agent's conduct: *Reading v Attorney-General*[1]. But the giving of the bribe was treated in equity as constructive
b fraud on the part of the giver and where it was given in connection with a contract between the principal and the briber the principal was entitled to rescission of the contract. This equitable right was additional to his right to recover the bribe from the agent.

In *Bagnall v Carlton*[2] the principal brought an action against the briber for rescission of the contract in respect of which the bribe had been given and against the agent for
c recovery of the bribe. He compromised the action against the briber on terms that he was paid a sum of money by the briber and the contract remained afoot. It was held that this did not affect the principal's right to recover the bribe from the agent. There is nothing in the report to indicate how the amount paid under the compromise was arrived at. So far as the agent was concerned it was res inter alios acta. No question of double recovery against him was involved.

d *Bagnall v Carlton*[2] was, however, followed by *Salford Corpn v Lever*[3]. Again it was an action brought by the principal against the briber, but not in this case for rescission of the contracts for sale in respect of which the bribes were given but for damages for fraud. Rescission was not available as the goods which were the subject of the sales had been consumed. It was established by the evidence that the briber had sold the goods at prices which exceeded the market prices by the amount of the bribes; so
e the amount of the bribes was also the measure of the damage caused to the principal by the briber's fraud. The principal had previously brought an action in the Chancery Division against the agent for recovery of the bribe and had compromised this on terms that the agent should co-operate with him for the purpose of his suing the bribers and would put up security in the sum of £10,000 which would be released progressively by the amounts recovered by the principal by way of damages from
f the bribers.

In the action against the briber the latter relied on the compromise with the agent as amounting to the release of a joint tortfeasor. The Court of Appeal (Lord Esher MR, Lindley and Lopes LJJ) held that it was not, on the ground, among others, that the principal's cause of action for recovery of the bribe from the agent was a separate and different cause of action from his cause of action against the briber for damages
g for fraud. *Bagnall v Carlton*[2] was cited as authority for this proposition. The terms of the compromise of the action against the agent were such that no question of double recovery of any of the bribes could arise, nor was the agent a party to the action against the briber. Nevertheless all three members of the court expressed the opinion accurately summarised in the headnote as follows[3]:

h 'Where an agent, who has been bribed so to do, induces his principal to enter into a contract with the person who has paid the bribe, and the contract is disadvantageous to the principal, the principal has two distinct and cumulative remedies: he may recover from the agent the amount of the bribe which he has received, and he may also recover from the agent and the person who has paid the bribe, jointly or severally, damages for any loss which he has sustained by
j reason of his having entered into the contract, *without allowing any deduction in*

1 [1951] 1 All ER 617, [1951] AC 507
2 (1877) 6 Ch D 371
3 [1891] 1 QB 168

respect of what he has recovered from the agent under the former head, and it is immaterial whether the principal sues the agent or the third person first.'   a

The liability of the briber to the principal for damages for the loss sustained by him in consequence of entering into the contract in respect of which the bribe was given is a rational development from his former right in equity to rescission of the contract. The cause of action against the briber was stated by Lord Esher MR and Lopes LJ to be fraud, and, since the agent was necessarily party to the bribery, it follows that the   b
tort was a joint tort of briber and agent for which either or both could be sued. But fraud is a tort for which the damages are limited to the actual loss sustained; and if the principal has recovered the bribe from the bribed agent the actual loss he has sustained in consequence of entering into the contract is reduced by that amount. The words that their Lordships have caused to be italicised in the citation from the headnote were unnecessary to the actual decision of the case and appear to be in   c
conflict with established principles of the law of tort.

Although as a matter of decision the *Salford* case[1] was concerned only with the liability of the briber, the dicta summarised in the headnote deal also with the liability of the agent. It was accurate to say that the principal had two distinct remedies against the agent, one for money had and received and the other for the tort of fraud; but it was flying in the face of a long line of authority to say that these two remedies were   d
not alternative but cumulative. The authorities to this effect are discussed at length in the speeches in *United Australia Ltd v Barclays Bank Ltd*[2], a case in which the House of Lords confirmed the principle that where the same facts gave rise in law to two causes of action against a single defendant, one (formerly lying in assumpsit) for money had and received and the other for damages for tort, the plaintiff must elect between the remedies. It held, however, that such election was not irrevocable until   e
judgment was recovered on one cause of action or the other. The House of Lords also held that where the same facts gave rise in law to a cause of action against one defendant for money had and received and to a separate cause of action for damages in tort against another defendant, judgment recovered against the first defendant did not prevent the plaintiff from suing the other defendant in a separate action: but that to the extent that the judgment was actually satisfied this constituted satisfaction   f
pro tanto of the claim for damages in the cause of action against the second defendant.

Insofar as what was said in the *Salford* case[1] conflicts with this, in their Lordships' opinion it can no longer be regarded as good law and the words that are italicised in the citation of the headnote are wrong.

In the *Salford* case[1] the principal's cause of action against the briber was described by the majority of the court as being fraud, as was his second cause of action against   g
the agent. Damage is the gist of an action in fraud and any loss proved to have been sustained by the principal in consequence of entering into the contract in respect of which the bribe was given might be less or greater than the amount of the bribe. This would no doubt affect the principal's choice of whether to seek judgment against the agent for the amount of the bribe as money had and received or to seek damages for fraud against him, but by the law laid down in the *Salford* case[1] there would be   h
no such right of election against the briber. The principal's only cause of action against him was for damages for fraud.

In subsequent cases, however, there developed differences of opinion between members of the Court of Appeal as to whether or not the principal had an alternative cause of action for money had and received against the briber too, as well as against the bribed agent. In *Grant v Gold Exploration and Development Syndicate Ltd*[3] Collins   j
LJ was of opinion that there was such a cause of action against the briber. A L Smith

1 [1891] 1 QB 168
2 [1940] 4 All ER 20, [1941] AC 1
3 [1900] 1 QB 233

and Vaughan Williams LJJ doubted this, and preferred to express their judgments as damages for fraud, holding that the principal had proved a loss up to the amount of the bribes. However, in *Hovenden & Sons v Millhoff*[1] A L Smith and Vaughan Williams LJJ recanted and a new chapter was opened in the law of civil remedies for bribery. The Court of Appeal (A L Smith, Vaughan Williams and Romer LJJ) allowed the appeal and entered judgment for the principal against the briber for the amount of the bribe. Romer LJ[2], whose judgment was cited by the Federal Court in the instant case, laid down three rules which, if correct, would have the effect of making bribery a wrong committed by the principal which is sui generis and defies classification. The rules were: firstly, that the motive of the briber in giving the bribe is not relevant; secondly that, there is an irrebuttable presumption that the agent was influenced by the bribe, and thirdly—

'if the agent be a confidential buyer of goods for his principal from the briber, the court will assume as against the briber that the true price of the goods as between him and the purchaser must be taken to be less than the price paid to, or charged by, the vendor by, at any rate, the amount or value of the bribe. If the purchaser alleges loss or damage beyond this, he must prove it.'

These rules refer to three of the elements in the tort of fraud, the motive, the inducement, and the loss occasioned to the plaintiff, but go on to say that the existence of the first two elements and of the third up to the amount of the bribe are to be irrebuttably presumed. This is merely another way of saying that they form no part of the definition of bribery as a legal wrong. To the extent that it is said that there is an irrebuttable presumption of loss or damage to the amount of the value of the bribe this is another way of saying that, unlike in the tort of fraud, actual loss or damage is *not* the gist of the action. But then to go on to say that actual loss in excess of the amount of the bribe can be recovered only if it is proved, is to produce a hybrid form of legal wrong of which actual damage *is* the gist of part only of a single cause of action.

On analysis, what these rules really describe is the right of a plaintiff who has alternative remedies against the briber (1) to recover from him the amount of the bribe as money had and received, or (2) to recover, as damages for tort, the actual loss which he has sustained as a result of entering into the transaction in respect of which the bribe was given; but in accordance with the decision of the House of Lords in *United Australia Ltd v Barclays Bank Ltd*[3] he need not elect between these alternatives before the time has come for judgment to be entered in his favour in one or other of them.

This extension to the briber of liability to account to the principal for the amount of the bribe as money had and received, whatever conceptual difficulties it may raise, is now and was by 1956 too well established in English law to be questioned. So both as against the briber and the agent bribed the principal has these alternative remedies: (1) for money had and received, under which he can recover the amount of the bribe as money had and received, or (2) for damages for fraud, under which he can recover the amount of the actual loss sustained in consequence of his entering into the transaction in respect of which the bribe was given, but he cannot recover both.

As stated earlier, in Malaysia s 30 of the Prevention of Corruption Act 1961 deals with civil remedies for bribery. It is as follows:

'(1) Where any gratification has in contravention of this Act been given by

---

1   (1900) 83 LT 41, [1900-3] All ER Rep 848
2   83 LT 41 at 48, [1900-3] All ER Rep 848 at 851
3   [1940] 4 All ER 20, [1941] AC 1

any person to an agent, the principal may recover as a civil debt the amount or the money value thereof either from the agent or from the person who gave the gratification to the agent, and no conviction or acquittal of the defendant in respect of an offence under this Act shall operate as a bar to proceedings for the recovery of such amount or money value.

'(2) Nothing in this section shall be deemed to prejudice or affect any right which any principal may have under any written law or rule of law to recover from his agent any money or property.'

Subsection (1) which refers to the principal's right to recover the amount of the gratification as a civil debt either 'from the agent or from the person who gave the gratification to the agent' gives statutory recognition to the right of the principal at common law to recover the amount of the bribe from either the briber or the agent, as money had and received. Subsection (2) in their Lordships' view does no more than preserve the right of the principal to recover from the bribed agent as damages for fraud and loss in excess of the amount of the bribe, he has actually sustained in consequence of entering into the transaction. In their Lordships' view, the Federal Court was right in its assumption that these statutory provisions do not affect what had previously been the rights of the principal at common law.

It follows that in the instant case the housing society was bound to elect between its claim for $122,000 under s 30(1) of the Prevention of Corruption Act 1961 and its claim for $433,000 damages for fraud. Since it would clearly have elected the latter, judgment should be entered for that sum with interest thereon at 5½ per cent from 22nd February 1965. The appeal should be allowed to that extent. There should be no order as to costs of this appeal and the orders for costs made below should remain undisturbed. Their Lordships will report their opinion to His Majesty the Yang Di-Pertuan Agong accordingly.

Appeal allowed in part.

Solicitors: *Graham Page & Co* (for the appellant); *Coward Chance* (for the housing society).

Mary Rose Plummer   Barrister.

Hart v A R Marshall & Sons (Bulwell) Ltd

EMPLOYMENT APPEAL TRIBUNAL

PHILLIPS J, MR M L CLEMENT-JONES AND MR S C MARLEY

7th DECEMBER 1976, 26th JANUARY 1977

Master and servant – Contract of service – Frustration – Short-term periodic contract – Absence from work because of illness – Employer taking no steps to dismiss employee – Employee key worker – Employer waiting four months and then engaging new permanent member of staff to undertake employee's duties – Employer continuing to receive medical certificates from employee without comment – Employee declared fit after 21 months and returning to work – Employee told no work available – Whether employee having been dismissed – Whether contract having previously come to an end by frustration.

In 1968 the appellant entered into permanent employment with the respondents as a night service fitter. He was one of two such fitters, who, together with two other fitters, were key workers without whom the respondents could not carry on their business for any lengthy period. In April 1974 the appellant contracted industrial dermatitis and as a result was off work. From April until August the employers managed to keep the night service going but found that they could continue no longer than that with the temporary arrangement and so they took T into their employment on a permanent basis to perform the work previously done by the appellant. However, nothing was said to the appellant about his future employment with the respondents and he regularly took medical certificates which were received by the respondents without comment. In January 1976 the appellant was declared fit by his doctor. He took his final certificate to the respondents and was told by the manager to wait. After some delay, the manager told him that there was no work for him. He was given his P45 certificate and some holiday pay due to him. The appellant complained to an industrial tribunal that he had been unfairly dismissed. The complaint was dismissed on the ground that his contract of employment had come to an end by frustration. On appeal, the appellant contended that a contract which could be terminated at short notice could not be treated as having come to an end by operation of law in a case when the employer had not dismissed the employee.

Held – An employer's failure to dismiss an absent employee was an important factor to be taken into account in determining whether a short-term periodic contract of employment had been frustrated, for the court would be reluctant to declare that such a contract had come to an end by operation of law when the employer himself had taken no steps to dismiss him. However, it was not conclusive. The proper test in such cases was to determine whether the period of absence was such that the employer could not reasonably be expected to wait for the employee's return any longer. At the date when the respondents engaged T to do the key work formerly done by the appellant they could not reasonably have been expected to wait for the appellant's return. Accordingly his contract of employment had come to an end by operation of law and the appeal would be dismissed (see p 415 *e f* and p 416 *b* and *e* to p 417 *a*, post).

Notes

For the dismissal of an employee on the ground of his illness, see 16 Halsbury's Laws (4th Edn) para 645, and for cases on the subject, see 34 Digest (Repl) 81, 82, 530-533.

For the doctrine of frustration generally, see 9 Halsbury's Laws (4th Edn) paras 450-459.

Cases referred to in judgment

Egg Stores (Stamford Hill) Ltd v Leibovici [1977] ICR 260, EAT.

Evenden v Guildford City Association Football Club Ltd [1975] 3 All ER 269, [1975] QB 917, [1975] 3 WLR 251, [1975] ICR 367, CA, Digest (Cont Vol D) 677, 816Add(i).

Hebden v Forsey & Son [1973] ICR 607, NIRC, Digest (Cont Vol D) 675, 816Ay.
Marshall v Harland & Wolff Ltd [1972] 2 All ER 715, [1972] 1 WLR 899, [1972] ICR 101, **a**
NIRC, Digest (Cont Col D) 662, 816Adk.
Spencer v Paragon Wallpaper Ltd [1977] ICR 301, EAT.
Terry v East Sussex County Council [1977] 1 All ER 567, 75 LGR 111, [1976] ICR 536,
EAT.

Appeal   **b**
This was an appeal by Mr R N Hart against the decision of an industrial tribunal
(chairman Miss N Healey) sitting at Nottingham on 2nd April 1976 which dismissed
his application for compensation for unfair dismissal against A R Marshall & Sons
(Bulwell) Ltd ('the employers'). The facts are set out in the judgment of the appeal
tribunal.

                                                                                             c
Eldred Tabachnik for Mr Hart.
F B Smedley for the employers.

                                                                       Cur adv vult

26th January. **PHILLIPS J** delivered the following judgment of the appeal tribunal:
We are concerned in this appeal with the troublesome question of the circumstances **d**
in which it can be said that a short-term periodic contract of employment has come
to an end by operation of law on the ground of frustration. Mr Hart complained to
an industrial tribunal that he had been unfairly dismissed on 27th January 1976.
On 2nd April 1976 an industrial tribunal sitting at Nottingham rejected this complaint
on the ground that he had not been dismised since his contract of employment had
come to an end by operation of law, i e it had been frustrated. From that decision **e**
he now appeals. We are not agreed on the answer, and this judgment, except where
otherwise stated, is the judgment of the majority.

The facts found by the tribunal are simple. After various periods of service between
1948 and 1968 with his employers (the respondents), Mr Hart entered their permanent
employment as a night service fitter in October 1968. He was one of two night fitters
working five nights a week on shifts which varied in alternate weeks. The tribunal **f**
expressly found that these two, together with two other fitters who were employed,
were 'undoubtedly key workers without whom the company could not carry on its
business for any lengthy period'. The decision gives no details of the size of the employers' business, but we were told in answer to our enquiries that the business was
carried on in a substantial way, employing a large number of men, with several
premises and owning a substantial number of vehicles.

In April 1974 Mr Hart contracted industrial dermatitis. In January 1976 he had **g**
recovered, and his doctor signed him off. He took his final certificate to the employers
and was told by them, after some delay, that there was no work for him. He was
given his P45 and six days' holiday pay. In the period between the time when he fell
ill and January 1976 Mr Hart had regularly taken to his employers medical certificates
of his unfitness to work and those certificates had been received without comment. **h**

In their reasons the tribunal point out that much of the trouble in this case arose
from the inefficiency of the employers. For example, the contract of employment
of Mr Hart had disappeared, and no copy of it or evidence of its terms was put before
the tribunal. (The case proceeded on the footing that the contract contained no
terms regulating the position when an employee was sick, that an absent employee
was not entitled to be paid, and that Mr Hart was not entitled to any longer notice **j**
than that prescribed by the Contracts of Employment Act 1972.) Medical certificates
were received by some member of the staff and apparently filed, and 'there was no
liason of any sort. If this company had conducted its business properly this position
would not have arisen'. The tribunal found in the same paragraph that Mr Hart was a
key worker, and that from the commencement of his absence in April 1974 until

August 1974 the employers managed to keep the night service going. They further
a found that it would not have been reasonable in the circumstances to expect the
employers to continue longer than that with temporary arrangements and that in
August 1974 the employers took on a Mr Twells in that capacity, who was still in
their employment.

The decision of the National Industrial Relations Court in *Marshall v Harland &*
Wolff Ltd[1] is the most authorative recent statement of the law relating to frustration
b in the case of a short-term periodic contract of employment. In *Egg Stores (Stam-*
ford Hill) Ltd v Leibovici[2] the Employment Appeal Tribunal followed *Marshall v*
Harland & Wolff Ltd[1]. However, in that case[3], we drew attention to some of the
difficulties which arise in applying the doctrine to the case of contracts of employment
which can be determined at short notice, and suggested that in such cases the test or
question posed by Sir John Donaldson P in *Marshall v Harland & Wolff Ltd*[4] is more
c easily asked than answered. We pointed out[5] that in such cases—

> 'Often it will be extremely relevant to note that the employer has not thought
> it right to dismiss the absent employee. The reason may be that he does not think
> that a sufficient length of time has elapsed to make it a proper course to take.
> If so, that view, represented by his failure to take action, will be one (but not the
> only) fact to be taken into consideration in deciding whether the contract has been
d frustrated.'

Accordingly, in summarising the factors that we thought ought to be taken into
account in such cases we added, 'the acts and the statements of the employer in
relation to the employment, including the dismissal of, or failure to dismiss, the
employee'[6]. After all, if the employer has not dismissed the employee on the ground
e that he cannot reasonably be expected to wait any longer for his return, why should
the court declare that the contract of employment has terminated by operation of
law?

It seems to us that considerable importance attaches to the failure of an employer
in such circumstances to dismiss the employee. We have wondered whether in truth
the doctrine of frustration has anything much to do with short-term periodic con-
f tracts of employment, for there is no doubt that the concept is alien to both employers
and employees, and is often not matched by the reality of the situation as they see it.
The automatic ending of a contract by operation of law in a case where the subject-
matter is destroyed is easily understood and matches experience. So is the case where
a sudden calamity overtakes an employee which there and then renders any future
service by him impossible. But in the case of an illness of uncertain duration the situa-
g tion is quite different and neither employer nor employee thinks in terms approaching
those underlying the concept of frustration.

However, experience shows that in a surprisingly large area of industry formal contracts of employment, and standard terms and conditions, still do not exist or if they
do, make no provision for the rights of the parties during a prolonged period of illness
of an employee. Very often, as in the present case, no wages are paid during sickness
h nor are any other formal arrangements made. In such cases the employee is in a sort of
limbo. It seems that from the employer's point of view there is a reluctance to dismiss
an employee when he is away sick because to do so may seem harsh. From the employee's point of view it may seem preferable not to be dismissed, albeit that no wages
are being paid, because there is a hope that one day he will be able to return to work,

j 1 [1972] 2 All ER 715, [1972] 1 WLR 899
2 [1977] ICR 260
3 [1977] ICR 260 at 264
4 [1972] 2 All ER 715 at 719, [1972] 1 WLR 899 at 904
5 [1977] ICR 260 at 264, 265
6 [1977] ICR 260 at 265

though not necessarily to the same job. Experience in such cases shows that the parties very often drift along in this situation for long periods of time during which *a* the employee has ceased to do any work, or to be able to do any work, but has not been formally dismissed. The legal position seems to be that the employee is still employed although he is not in receipt of wages, and that his employment continues until he is dismissed or the contract is frustrated and comes to an end by operation of law. In these circumstances, while we think it right to attach considerable importance in a case of this kind to the failure by the employer to dismiss the employee, it is, *b* we think, impossible to say that unless the employee is dismissed the contract must always be taken to continue. To do so would be tantamount to saying that frustration cannot occur in the case of short-term periodic contracts of employment. We do not read the judgment of Sir Hugh Griffiths in *Hebden v Forsey & Son*[1] as going as far as that. In truth the employers are in a difficulty in this connection. First of all, if they dismiss the employee prematurely they may be said to have dismissed him unfairly; *c* here we have suggested that the test is whether the employer can reasonably be expected to wait any longer (*Spencer v Paragon Wallpapers Ltd*[2]). Secondly, if the employer takes on a temporary replacement pending the recovery of the sick employee, there is a risk that he will be obliged to pay him compensation if he dismisses him when the sick employee has recovered; and even if he guides himself by our decision in *Terry v East Sussex County Council*[3] he is probably buying litigation. *d*

Furthermore, we are very conscious of the fact, and attach much importance to it, that if frustration can never occur in such cases employers will feel obliged to dismiss employees in cases where they at present do not do so. In the long run, it is the employees who would be the losers.

In our judgment it comes to this. The failure of the employer to dismiss the employee is a factor, and an important factor, to take into account when considering *e* whether the contract of employment has been frustrated. But it is not conclusive. The important question, perhaps, is to look to see what was the reason for the failure. It may be due to the fact that the employer did not think that the time had arrived when he could not reasonably wait any longer, in which case it is a piece of evidence of the greatest value. Or it may be a case where the failure to dismiss is attributable to the simple fact that the employer never applied his mind to the question at all. *f* It is quite obvious that in the present case the employers felt, and the tribunal found correctly, that they could not wait any longer, for they engaged Mr Twells to do the work previously done by Mr Hart, and the tribunal have found that this was key work. It seems to us that the reason why the employers never dismissed Mr Hart was that the relationship after he fell sick was being conducted in the casual manner which, as we have indicated earlier in this judgment, is not uncommon in such cases. *g*

In *Hebden v Forsey & Son*[4] Sir Hugh Griffiths said:

'Another matter which weighed with the tribunal was that they regarded the employee as a "key man" in that he was one of only two sawyers. If it had been essential to replace the employee this would of course have been a factor to take into consideration in considering whether the period due to incapacity frustrated *h* the contract. But the short answer is that the employers never did replace him and that being so it is not a consideration that assists in determining the question of frustration.'

In the present case there is an express finding that Mr Hart occupied a key position, that he was a key worker, that it would not have been reasonable in the circumstances to expect the employers to continue longer with temporary arrangements, and that *j*

---

1   [1973] ICR 607 at 609, 610
2   [1977] ICR 301
3   [1977] 1 All ER 567
4   [1973] ICR 607 at 610

it was in those circumstances that they took on a replacement in the person of Mr
a Twells. Thus the employers could at that stage have dismissed Mr Hart without
acting unfairly.

Counsel for Mr Hart complains that there is no evidence that Mr Twells would only
come on a permanent basis and there was no reason why he should not have been employed on a temporary basis. But there is no evidence as to whether this question was
gone into, and we have already pointed out the difficulties in cases of this kind of em-
b ploying temporary replacements. Furthermore, although we do not know what an
enquiry as to the prognosis of Mr Hart's condition in August 1974 would have shown,
we do now know that in fact he was not able to return until January 1976, so that in
practice it is clear that it would have been difficult if not impossible to provide a temporary substitute. Counsel for Mr Hart further complains that the tribunal elevated
the factor concerning the key nature of Mr Hart's employment to an importance
c greater than that which it deserved, and ignored other factors. In particular, he says
that the decision, read correctly, shows that the tribunal ignored the continued receipt
of medical certificates, the delivery of the P45 and the payment of holiday pay as factors bearing on the question of frustration, and took these matters into account only in
connection with the question whether there might be inferred the creation of a new
contract. If the tribunal did ignore these matters in relation to the question of frus-
d tration, we think that they were wrong to do so, but it does not seem to us that this
led them into error. The P45 was a document which had to be rendered in any
event when Mr Hart recovered, for he would require it when seeking other employment. The notes of evidence do not properly explain the holiday pay, but we have
been into it and we do not think that it is possible to deduce from the fact of the
payment any recognition by the employers of the continued existence of the contract
e of employment after its supposed frustration. More important is the continued
receipt of medical certificates. It seems to us quite clear that this occurerd on a casual
basis, that they were received as part of the routine of the employers' office, and that
this is no more than a manifestation of the not uncommon relationship which continues when a man falls sick and remains absent from work for a very long period
which we have noticed earlier in this judgment. We do not think that these acts are
f inconsistent with the contract having come to an end. Employees like to keep in
touch, and employers are content that they should, in case in the future there may
be some opportunity or re-employment. Mr Hart's particular job as a night service
fitter had been filled. He could not be required to do a different job without his
consent; accordingly the continued receipt of the medical certificates could not have
indicated an intention to keep him on in his old job, even if the management had been
g aware of what was happening, as to which there was no evidence. Furthermore, Mr
Hart knew that his job had been filled. It seems clearly to be a case of 'keeping in
touch' in case, when he was recovered, there was work for him to do.

It seems to us that this is one of the comparatively rare cases where it can be said
that a short-term periodic contract of employment has been frustrated. Mr Hart was
away from work from April 1974 until January 1976. He occupied a key position.
h The employers required a replacement, and that replacement was engaged in August
1974. Those are findings of fact which are binding on us, and it seems to us that the
industrial tribunal were amply justified on that material in reaching the decision
which they did.

Counsel for Mr Hart's alternative contention was that the employers were precluded
by their conduct from alleging that the contract of employment had been frustrated.
j He relied on a case of waiver or estoppel, citing the decision of the Court of Appeal
in *Evenden v Guildford City Association Football Club Ltd*[1]. He contended that there was
here a representation by conduct, the acceptance of the medical certificates indicating
the continuing relationship of employer and employee, the former being interested in

---

1 [1975] 3 All ER 269, [1975] QB 917

monitoring Mr Hart's progress, that the representation was intended to be acted on
and that it was acted on by Mr Hart. He submitted that it was no longer necessary *a*
in such a case for there to be a pre-existing contractual relationship between the
parties, nor for the representee to have acted to his detriment. There are a number of
difficulties here, but it is sufficient, we think, to dispose of the contention, to say that
there is no evidence whatever that Mr Hart acted on any such representation (if there
was one), whether to his detriment or otherwise.

Mr Marley takes a different view. While accepting that the employers could have *b*
dismissed Mr Hart when they engaged Mr Twells, Mr Marley felt that the vital facts
were that the employers did not do so, and retained him on their books by accepting
medical certificates and holding moneys due to him. Thus they lost the opportunity to
dismiss him. On being declared fit for work Mr Hart took his final certificate to the
employers and saw the manager, who requested him to wait. After a while the
manager came out and told Mr Hart there was no work for him and they would for- *c*
ward the P45 and any money due to him. Mr Hart visited the employers on two
further Thursdays over a period of three weeks before being handed his P45 and
holiday money due to him. In none of this was Mr Hart at fault. Support for this view
could be found in the words of Sir Hugh Griffiths in *Hebden v Forsey & Son*[1]: 'But the
absence of any move by the employer to terminate the contract during a period of
incapacity is a powerful indication that the contractual relationship survives.' *d*

Appeal dismissed. Leave to appeal to the Court of Appeal granted.

Solicitors: *Pattinson & Brewer* (for Mr Hart); *Rotheras*, Nottingham (for the employers).

Salim H J Merali Esq Barrister. *e*

Re Ashbourne Investments Ltd *f*

CHANCERY DIVISION
TEMPLEMAN J
14th, 15th DECEMBER 1977

Company – Investigation by Board of Trade – Restrictions on transfer etc of shares – Order *g*
directing that restrictions should cease – Order for purpose of permitting transfer continuing
restriction on payment of any sum due on those shares – Takeover of company during in-
vestigation – Restriction on transfer of shares preventing acquiring company complying with
statutory directions to effect transfer of shares to itself – Acquiring company applying to
court for release of shares from restriction on transfer and for an order restricting payment
of the purchase price to former owners of shares without sanction of court – Whether price of *h*
shares a sum 'due from the company on those shares' – Whether court having power to impose
restriction on purchase price – Companies Act 1948, s 174(2)(a)(d)(4).

In July 1975 the Secretary of State appointed inspectors, pursuant to the Companies
Act 1948, to investigate the affairs and ownership of a company ('Ashbourne').
The investigation disclosed that 465,500 shares in Ashbourne ('the restricted shares')
were registered in the name of agents ('Montagu') who were acting for a Swiss bank *j*
which had purchased the shares on behalf of a customer. The Swiss bank, acting under
Swiss law, declined to disclose the customer's name without his consent which he

1 [1973] ICR 607

refused to give. In consequence, in December 1975 the Secretary of State ordered
a that the restricted shares were to be subject until further order to the restrictions
imposed by s 174(2)^a of the 1948 Act. Those restrictions included, by s 174(2)(*a*),
that any transfer of the restricted shares was to be rendered void. Meanwhile another
company ('Incentive') made a successful takeover bid for all the shares in Ashbourne
and acquired all of Ashbourne's shares except the restricted shares which amounted
to just over five per cent of Ashbourne's share capital. On the takeover, Incentive
b became bound, by virtue of s 209^b of the 1948 Act, to acquire the restricted shares at
their takeover price of £97,755, and to present to Ashbourne a transfer of the shares
executed on behalf of Montagu and to pay Ashbourne the consideration of £97,755 for
the shares. Section 209 also required Ashbourne to register Incentive as the holder of
the shares and to pay the consideration into a separate account to be held for the
benefit of the former owners of the shares. So long as the restrictions imposed by
c s 174(2) were in force the directions under s 209 to transfer the shares to Incentive
could not be complied with and so the object of the takeover, i e the acquisition of all
of Ashbourne's shares, was frustrated with the consequence that Incentive and its
shareholders were liable to suffer serious financial loss. If, however, the restrictions
imposed by s 174(2) were to be wholly released the investigation of Ashbourne's affairs
so far as it related to the ownership of the restricted shares would be abortive.

d _____

a Section 174, so far as material, provides:

'(2) So long as any shares are directed to be subject to the restrictions imposed by this
section—(*a*) any transfer of those shares, or in the case of unissued shares any transfer of the
right to be issued therewith and any issue thereof, shall be void . . . (*c*) no further shares
e shall be issued in right of those shares or in pursuance of any offer made to the holder
thereof; (*d*) except in a liquidation, no payment shall be made of any sums due from the
company on those shares, whether in respect of capital or otherwise.

'(3)Where the Board of Trade make an order directing that shares shall be subject to the
said restrictions . . . any person aggrieved thereby may apply to the court and the court
may, if it sees fit, direct that the shares shall cease to be subject to the said restrictions.

'(4) Any order (whether of the Board of Trade or of the court) directing that shares shall
f cease to be subject to the said restrictions which is expressed to be made with a view to
permitting a transfer of those shares may continue the restrictions mentioned in paragraphs
(*c*) and (*d*) of subsection (2) of this section, either in whole or in part, so far as they relate to
any right acquired or offer made before the transfer . . .'

b Section 209, so far as material, provides:

'(1) Where a scheme or contract involving the transfer of shares . . . in a company (in
this section referred to as "the transferor company") to another company . . . (in this
g section referred to as "the transferee company"), has, within four months after the making
of the offer in that behalf by the transferee company been approved by the holders of not
less than nine tenths in value of the shares whose transfer is involved . . . the transferee
company . . . shall . . . be entitled and bound to acquire those shares on the terms on which,
under the scheme or contract, the shares . . . are to be transferred to the transferee
company . . . .

h   '(3)Where a notice has been given by the transferee company under subsection (1) of this
section . . . the transferee company shall, on the expiration of one month from the date on
which the notice has been given . . . transmit a copy of the notice to the transferor company
together with an instrument of transfer executed on behalf of the shareholder by any person
appointed by the transferee company and on its own behalf by the transferee company,
and pay or transfer to the transferor company the amount or other consideration representing the price payable by the transferee company for the shares which by virtue of this
j section that company is entitled to acquire, and the transferor company shall thereupon
register the transferee company as the holder of those shares . . .

'(4) Any sums received by the transferor company under this section shall be paid into a
separate bank account, and any such sums and any other consideration so received shall be
held by that company on trust for the several persons entitled to the shares in respect of
which the said sums or other consideration were respectively received . . .'

Incentive and Ashbourne applied to the court, under s 174(3) and (4), for release of   *a*
the restricted shares from the restriction on transfer imposed by s 174(2)(*a*) in order
to permit transfer of the shares to Incentive, and for an order that the £97,755 payable
by Incentive to Ashbourne for the shares should be paid into a separate account and
that no part of the money should be paid out by Ashbourne without the sanction
of the court. Montagu, who were respondents to the application, contended that
the £97,755 was not a sum due from Ashbourne on the restricted shares, within
s 174(2)(*d*), since it was not a dividend or a payment of capital made on a reduction of   *b*
capital or on the redemption of shares and that accordingly, if the court were to release
the restriction on transfer of the shares, it could not, by virtue of s 174(4), retain the
other restrictions imposed by s 174(2), in particular the restriction imposed by
s 174(2)(*d*) on payment of the sums due from Ashbourne to the former owners of the
shares.

                                                                                          c

Held – The words 'payment . . . of any sums due from the company' in s 174(2)(*d*) were
not limited to payment of dividends or of capital on a reduction of capital or on
redemption of shares, for s 174(4) was clearly designed to enable the transfer of shares
by release of the restriction on transfer imposed by s 174(2)(*a*) while still enabling
payment of the price for the shares to the former owners to remain frozen. It followed   *d*
that the sum of £97,755, when received by Ashbourne, would constitute a sum due
from Ashbourne on the restricted shares, within s 174(2)(*d*), and that the court was
entitled to make an order under s 174(4) directing a partial release of the shares from
the restrictions imposed by s 174(2), so as to permit their transfer to Incentive, while
retaining the restriction on payment of sums due from Ashbourne under s 174(2)(*d*)   *e*
thus restricting payment of the £97,755 to Montague during the investigation into
Ashbourne's affairs (see p 422 *h* to p 423 *b*, post).

Notes
For imposition of restrictions on shares in connection with an investigation of the
ownership of a company, see 7 Halsbury's Laws (4th Edn) para 979.   *f*
    For the Companies Act 1948, s 174, see 5 Halsbury's Statutes (3rd Edn) 250.

Cases cited
Blue Metal Industries Ltd v Dilley [1969] 3 All ER 437, [1970] AC 827, PC.
Serrao v Noel (1885) 15 QBD 549, CA.
                                                                                          g

Motion
This was an originating motion by Incentive Investments Ltd ('Incentive') and Ashbourne Investments Ltd ('Ashbourne') claiming the following relief under s 174(3)
and (4) of the Companies Act 1948: that with effect from the payment by Ashbourne
of the sum of £97,755 into a separate bank account to be opened and maintained by   *h*
them for the purpose, (i) no payment of any kind whatsoever to or in favour of any
person whatsoever should be made out of the bank account, whether from the cash
sum of £97,755 or from any interest which might accrue thereon without the prior
sanction in that behalf of a further order of the court, and (ii) that save only as otherwise provided by para (i), and with a view to permitting the transfer of 465,500
shares to Incentive pursuant to s 209(3) of the 1948 Act, the 465,500 shares should   *j*
cease to be subject to the restrictions to which they were made subject by an order
dated 22nd December 1975 made by the Secretary of State pursuant to s 174(1) and
(2) of the 1948 Act. The 465,500 shares were registered in the name of the first respondent, Samuel Montagu & Co (Nominees) Ltd ('Montagu'). Montagu were agents
acting for Julius Bär & Co, Zurich, a Swiss Bank, who had purchased the shares on

behalf of a customer or customers. The second respondent was the Secretary of State
for Trade. The facts are set out in the judgment.

William Stubbs for Incentive and Ashbourne
Oliver Weaver for Montagu.
Peter Gibson for the Secretary of State.

TEMPLEMAN J. The question which arises on this application is whether moneys
payable pursuant to s 209(3) of the Companies Act 1948 in respect of shares acquired
under that section are, or can be made, the subject of a restraining order under s 174
until the beneficial owners of the shares identify themselves.

On 10th July 1975 the Secretary of State in pursuance of powers conferred on him
by ss 164 and 172 of the Companies Act 1948 appointed inspectors to investigate the
affairs of Ashbourne Investments Ltd ('Ashbourne') and to investigate the ownership
of the company, and to report. By ss 167(1) and 172(1) it is the duty of any persons
financially interested in the success of Ashbourne to give to the inspectors all assistance in connection with the investigations which they are reasonably able to give.
The inspectors' investigations, and the evidence on this application, disclose that
465,500 shares in Ashbourne (which I shall refer to as 'the restricted shares') were and
are registered in the name of Samuel Montagu & Co (Nominees) Ltd. Samuel
Montagu are agents acting for Julius Bär & Co Ltd, a Swiss bank. That Swiss bank
purchased the shares on behalf of a customer, or customers; the Swiss bank, relying
on Swiss law, declined to disclose the name of the customer without the consent of the
customer, and the customer has refused to give his consent.

By s 174(1) of the 1948 Act where, in connection with an investigation, it appears
to the Secretary of State that there is difficulty in finding out the relevant facts about
any shares, and that the difficulty is due wholly or mainly to the unwillingness of
the persons concerned, or any of them, to assist the investigation as required by the
1948 Act, the Secretary of State may by order direct that the shares shall until further
order be subject to the restrictions imposed by the section. On 22nd December 1975
the Secretary of State, in pursuance of the powers conferred on him by s 174, directed
that the restricted shares which he identified as being registered in the name of
Samuel Montagu and held for the account of the Swiss bank should be subject to all
the restrictions which are authorised by s 174. The first of those restrictions is that
any transfer of the shares is rendered void.

In the meantime the applicant, Incentive Investments Ltd ('Incentive'), made a
successful takeover bid for all the shares in Ashbourne, and they have now acquired
all the shares except the restricted shares which amount to just over five per cent of
the issued ordinary share capital of Ashbourne. The object of the takeover by Incentive is frustrated, and serious financial loss and damage, not to mention inconvenience,
are being caused and will continue to be caused to Incentive and its shareholders
unless the restricted shares can be acquired, whereupon Ashbourne will become a
wholly owned subsidiary of Incentive. So s 174, which was intended to procure
compliance with the investigatory needs of the Secretary of State and his inspectors,
is at the moment having an adverse effect on Incentive who, of course, know nothing
about the ownership of the shares.

By s 209(1) of the 1948 Act, Incentive, on making the takeover bid, became entitled
and bound to acquire, inter alia, the restricted shares at the takeover price which in
the case of the restricted shares amounts in aggregate to £97,755. Section 209(3) in
these circumstances directs Incentive to present to Ashbourne a transfer of the
restricted shares executed on behalf of Samuel Montagu by a person appointed by
Incentive, and also directs Incentive to pay to Ashbourne the sum of £97,755, and
thereupon the section requires Ashbourne to register Incentive as the holder of the
restricted shares. Those directions cannot be carried out for the moment because of

the bar imposed by s 174 and the order made thereunder. If the directions could be complied with, then by s 209(4) the sum of £97,755 which would be received by Ashbourne is directed to be paid by Ashbourne into a separate bank account and held by Ashbourne for the several persons entitled to the shares in respect of which the £97,755 is received. The machinery of s 209 and the completion of the takeover are held up so long as s 174 makes void any transfer of the restricted shares.

Section 174 itself includes provision for a release of the restrictions, either by the Secretary of State or by the court, and on this application Incentive and Ashbourne are the applicants asking for a release of the restrictions, and the Secretary of State and Montagu are the respondents. There is this dilemma that if the restrictions are not released, Incentive will continue to suffer loss and the object of the takeover bid will continue to be frustrated, but if the restrictions are wholly released than the statutory investigation so far as it relates to the restricted shares will be abortive.

Section 174, in addition to rendering a transfer void (a provision to be found in s 174(2)(a)), contains other restrictions which are material. Section 174(2)(c) says that no further shares shall be issued in right of the restricted shares or in pursuance of any offer made by the holder thereof, and sub-s (2)(d) directs that no payment shall be made of any sums due from the company, that is Ashbourne, on the restricted shares, whether in respect of capital or otherwise. Section 174(4) enables the Secretary of State or the court to lift some restrictions while maintaining others. Subsection (4) says that any order directing that shares shall cease to be subject to the restrictions which is expressed to be made with a view to permitting a transfer of those shares may continue the restrictions mentioned in paras (c) and (d) of sub-s (2) either in whole or in part, so far as they relate to any right acquired or offer made before the transfer. I am now asked to release the restrictions imposed by s 174, in the words of sub-s (4) 'with a view to permitting a transfer' of the restricted shares so that they can be transferred to Incentive, but to continue in relation to the sum of £97,755 the restrictions specified in s 174(2)(d), which forbids any payment being made of sums due from the company, that is Ashbourne, on the restricted shares. If that can be done, Ashbourne will retain the sum of £97,755 until the customer identifies himself and asks for the remaining restrictions to be lifted. All he has to do is to come along and ask for the money.

Montagu, for reasons which I am bound to say are not clear to me, chose to appear by counsel to argue that I have no power to do what I am asked to do. What is said is that the sum of £97,755 is not a sum due from Ashbourne on the restricted shares, and I must in this dilemma either release all the restrictions imposed by s 174, thus allowing the Swiss bank and the customer to continue to frustrate the investigations and flout our law, or else I must retain all the restrictions and, with the laudable object of enforcing our law, inflict and continue to inflict quite unjustified harm and loss on Incentive.

Counsel for Montagu argued that the further shares mentioned in para (c) are limited to bonus shares and rights issues, and he said the payments in para (d) are limited to dividends and payments made on a reduction authorised by the court of share capital, so that some capital goes back to the shareholders, and to payments of capital made in respect of redeemable shares when they are redeemed. No doubt s 174(2)(d) does encompass the kind of payments which counsel indicated. But in my judgment that does not show that it is limited to those payments, and that is the only effect of the operation of the section.

Section 174(4) is clearly designed to enable shares to be transfered while also enabling payment of sums due from Ashbourne to be frozen. Section 209 provides that on a transfer of the restricted shares to Incentive a payment shall be made by Incentive to Ashbourne in respect of the restricted shares, and Ashbourne are under a duty imposed by the section to pay that sum to the former owners of the shares. It seems to me that the sum of £97,755 is indeed a sum which, when it is received, will be due from Ashbourne on or in respect of the restricted shares. If this is not the case, it is difficult to see how s 174(4) can have any wide useful purpose and it is impossible to reconcile the requirements of s 209, which are designed to enable company amalgamations to take place, on the one hand, with the requirements of s 174 on the other. I do not find the Act to be so frustrating.

Accordingly I intend to make an order under s 174(4) directing a partial release with a view to permitting a transfer of the shares. I continue the restriction mentioned in sub-s (2)(d) and I declare that the payment of a sum of £97,755 is a payment within the meaning of sub-s (2)(d) and that no payment is to be made. If necessary I will impose an injunction on Ashbourne not to pay any of that money out to anybody until the restriction is lifted either by the Secretary of State or by the court.

Order accordingly.

Solicitors: *Halliwell, Landau & Co*, Manchester (for Incentive and Ashbourne); *Travers Smith, Braithwaite & Co* (for Montagu); *Treasury Solicitor.*

Jacqueline Metcalfe Barrister.

R v Secretary of State for the Home Department, ex parte Hussain

QUEEN'S BENCH DIVISION
LORD WIDGERY CJ, PARK AND PETER PAIN JJ
4th MAY 1977

COURT OF APPEAL, CIVIL DIVISION
MEGAW, ORR AND GEOFFREY LANE LJJ
25th, 26th MAY 1977

Immigration – Detention – Illegal entrant – Burden of proof that entry illegal – Entrant obtaining indefinite leave to enter and remain in United Kingdom – Leave obtained in consequence of fraud – Illegal entrant returning to United Kingdom with new passport after short visit abroad – Immigration officer accepting false explanation for passport – Officer granting indefinite leave to stay and stamping passport accordingly – Entrant subsequently detained as illegal entrant – Whether grant of indefinite leave on face of passport proof that entrant in United Kingdom legally – Whether sufficient for Secretary of State to show that on evidence as a whole he had reasonable grounds for concluding entry illegal – Immigration Act 1971, Sch 2, para 16(2).

Until 1970 the applicant lived in Lahore. In November 1970 he came to the United Kingdom and obtained leave to enter for the limited period of two months under the name of Ijaz Ahmed Lodhi on a passport which had been issued in that name in Lahore. The photograph on the application form for the passport was that of the applicant. The applicant remained in the United Kingdom illegally after the expiration of the two months and set up in business in Leeds. In 1972 he applied to the Pakistani consulate in Bradford for a new passport in the name of Safder Hussain and a passport in that name was issued to him. The Pakistan authorities certified that the passport was genuine. The passport did not refer to any previous passport. On 26th May 1974 the applicant went to Germany for a short visit. When he returned to the United Kingdom on 29th May he was interviewed by an immigration officer who enquired why his passport did not contain any entry or endorsement explaining his previous residence in the United Kingdom. The applicant told the immigration officer that initially he had entered the United Kingdom as an adopted child and, being a child, had not required a passport and had entered, legally, without one. The officer accepted that statement, which was consistent with the passport being the first passport of a person who had come to the United Kingdom as a child, and gave the applicant indefinite leave to enter and endorsed the passport accordingly. In November 1976 the applicant was detained in prison as an illegal entrant, pursuant to para 16(2)[a] of Sch 2 to the Immigration Act 1971, prior to being returned to Pakistan. He applied to the Divisional Court for a writ of habeas corpus contending that he had established a prima facie case that his detention was illegal because he had shown that his passport had been stamped with indefinite leave to enter on his return from Germany. The Secretary of State asserted that the applicant's true name was Lodhi and that he had falsely assumed the identity of another person, i e Safder Hussain, in order to obtain indefinite leave to enter. The Divisional Court refused the application on the ground that there was evidence on which the Secretary of State could properly conclude that there had been fraudulent use of the passport by the applicant to gain indefinite leave to enter and that once that had been shown it followed that his detention was valid. The applicant appealed. At the hearing of the appeal further evidence came to light which indicated that there was a possibility that the applicant really was Sadfer Hussain. In those circumstances the applicant contended that he had discharged such burden of proof as rested on him and that the Secretary of State had failed to show that the grant of indefinite leave was other than a proper exercise of the immigration officer's discretion and binding on the Secretary of State.

Held – Where on the evidence taken as a whole the Secretary of State had reasonable grounds for concluding that an entrant to the United Kingdom was there illegally in contravention of the 1971 Act, the court would not interfere with his detention as an illegal entrant. In the instant case, if the applicant's name was Lohdi, the passport he presented to the immigration officer in 1974 was not a valid passport in relation to him since it was in another name. If on the other hand the applicant's name was Hussain, then, although on the face of the passport he had obtained permission to stay indefinitely in the United Kingdom, the evidence as to what he had told the immigration officer regarding his initial entry to the United Kingdom indicated that the permission to stay indefinitely had been obtained by fraud or misrepresentation and was therefore of no effect. Accordingly, the Secretary of State was entitled to conclude that the applicant was an illegal entrant. The appeal would therefore be dismissed (see p 429 e f, p 430 a to d, p 431 b c and f to h and p 432 a, post).

Per Orr and Geoffrey Lane LJJ. Where a person is being detained under para 16 of Sch 2 to the 1971 Act it is for him to set up a prima facie case that his detention is illegal. The obligation of the court is to be satisfied that the Secretary of State has approached the case in good faith and that there is adequate evidence to justify the conclusion which the Secretary of State has reached (see p 429 b to e and p 430 d, post).

Notes

For illegal entry, see 4 Halsbury's Laws (4th Edn) para 1027, and for detention of persons liable to removal from the United Kingdom, see ibid, para 1009.

For the Immigration Act 1971, Sch 2, para 16, see 41 Halsbury's Statutes (3rd Edn) 67.

Case referred to in judgments

R v Secretary of State for Home Affairs, ex parte Badaiki [1977] The Times, 4th May, DC.

---

a   Paragraph 16(2) provides: 'A person in respect of whom directions may be given under any of paragraphs 8 to 14 [of Sch 2] may be detained under the authority of an immigration officer pending the giving of directions and pending his removal in pursuance of any directions given.'

Cases also cited
Hassen (Wajid), Re [1976] 2 All ER 123, [1976] 1 WLR 971, DC.
Joyce v Director of Public Prosecutions [1946] AC 347, [1946] 1 All ER 186, HL.
Khan v Secretary of State for the Home Department [1977] 3 All ER 538, [1977] 1 WLR 1466, CA.
R v Brailsford [1905] 2 KB 730, DC.
R v Secretary of State for the Home Department, ex parte Mughal [1973] 3 All ER 796, [1974] QB 313, CA.

Motion
This was an application by Sadfer Hussain for a writ of habeas corpus directed to the Secretary of State for the Home Department to procure the applicant's release from Armley Prison where he was detained pursuant to an order of an immigration officer made under para 16(2) of Sch 2 to the Immigration Act 1971. The facts are set out in the judgment of Lord Widgery CJ.

Mukhtar Hussain for the applicant.
Harry Woolf for the Secretary of State.

LORD WIDGERY CJ. In these proceedings counsel moves on behalf of an applicant now known as Safder Hussain for a writ of habeas corpus. The applicant is at present detained in Armley Prison under the order of an immigration officer acting under the Immigration Act 1971, whereby under para 16 of Sch 2 to that Act the immigration officer has ordered the detention of the applicant as a preliminary to his being returned to his native country.

There is a very sharp conflict between the parties here as to what the past history of this man is, and the most convenient way of expressing the problem is to take the two stories, the one relied on by the Home Office and the one relied on by the applicant, to see how they compare and to see how far they are supported by external documents.

The Home Office case is that in about 1970 there came to this country a Commonwealth citizen who was armed with a passport issued in Lahore, and which named him as Ijaz Ahmed Lodhi. The passport application, which is of course retained in the file at Lahore and which is available for inspection by representatives of the Home Office, has attached to it a photograph and the photograph is unquestionably a photograph of the present applicant who, as I have already said, passes under the name of Safder Hussain.

The Home Office case is that, having acquired himself a passport in the name of Lodhi, the applicant came to this country and was permitted to stay for a limited period of two months. Enquiries have shown that there was no record of Lodhi ever having left this country, either within the two months or at all. But, according to the Home Office case, the reason why we hear no more of Lodhi is because the applicant has abandoned that name and that personality, and has taken over a new one. Indeed it is quite clear that a new passport has been issued by the Pakistani authorities in Bradford to the applicant and that that passport was issued in 1972.

The Home Office say that this is all part of the same plan. Having arrived here under the Lodhi passport, and having found that his period for remaining in the country was limited, he now seeks to set up the alternative identity and procures for himself in Bradford that Pakistani passport in the name of Safder Hussain.

Of course nothing immediately followed the issue of that passport until the time came for the applicant to want to use it. The Home Office account of the matter, which counsel for the Secretary of State invites us to accept, is that this passport was used once and briefly only by the present applicant who went to Germany for three days in 1974. He undoubtedly did go to Germany for three days in 1974, and it is quite evident that he used the passport to which I have referred because the appropriate immigration stamps are on it. Also on the new passport are words of great significance, because immediately under the stamp which records the applicant's return through Dover from his visit to Germany are these words: 'Given leave to enter the United Kingdom for an indefinite period.

To those who seek to enter this country and make new lives here those words on the passport are gold-dust, and the contention of the Home Office is that this is again all part and parcel of a clever fraud and this was a way of getting the applicant's passport which would contain the endorsements necessary to set his mind at rest for ever on any question whether he could remain in this country or not. The account which we are invited to accept by the Home Office is that this visit to Germany may have been deliberately for this purpose only, it matters not, but that coming back the applicant must have been recognised in the Home Office files under the name of Safder Hussain as a person who was entitled to reside here, and it is on that account that the magic words have been added to the stamp as I have described.

If that story is correct, if that is a proper way of looking at it, then the applicant used a false passport fraudulently in order to obtain a right to remain in this country indefinitely. If that is the right interpretation, then I personally have no doubt that the immigration officer was entitled to make an order under para 16 of Sch 2 to the 1971 Act justifying the present detention and thus resulting in a repudiation of the application for habeas corpus. That is one side of the story.

The other side of the story as told by the applicant is this. He says that he was brought to this country and came in about 1970 (the date is not very important) by an Uncle Shafi. He says that Uncle Shafi made all the arrangements and that he, the applicant, had nothing to do with them at all. He was brought over by Uncle Shafi without a passport. This is a strange story because of course mistakes do happen, and we see a great many of them in this court. Even so, it would have been very unusual for this young man, then about 20, to come in with Uncle Shafi and to have been permitted to enter if he had not come armed with a passport. However, that is what he says.

Having arrived here without a passport, feeling embarrassed by not having one he says he applied for one, as we have seen, in Bradford in 1972, and he says that the passport which was then issued to him is a perfectly genuine passport. When he came back from Germany he presented it to the immigration officer and the immigration officer stamped it with the words which I have indicated, thus giving him the right to remain in this country indefinitely and completely nullifying any power which the Secretary of State might have to detain him under para 16 of Sch 2.

Where do we stand in regard to those matters? First of all, it must be borne in mind that the governor having returned that he was holding this person under para 16, it is for the applicant to set up a prima facie case to discharge that burden. Counsel on his behalf says that the prima facie case is set up when it is shown that the applicant came back through Dover, presented his passport and had it stamped with the words, as I have referred to them, sanctioning his continued living in this country.

In my judgment all that goes to nought if it can be shown that there is evidence on which the Secretary of State could properly conclude that there was here a fraud on the lines which I have indicated. Questions of fact in these matters are ultimately questions of fact for the Secretary of State. There are limits to the extent to which this court can go and, as I see it, our obligation at the moment is to be satisfied that the Home Office approach to the problem is one taken in good faith. Further, we have to decide whether there is or is not adequate evidence here to justify the sort of conclusion which the Secretary of State has reached.

In my judgment there is such evidence. I take no time to consider whether the approach is in good faith because there is no suggestion that it was not. I look at the second question and ask myself whether the Secretary of State had before him the sort of material on which a conclusion of fraud could be justified. I am satisfied that there was such material.

One begins in the first place with the very odd situation that the applicant undoubtedly came over to this country initially in the name of Lodhi. I do not see how one can doubt that now in view of the fact his photograph appears on the passport application in the name of Lodhi. One asks why indeed should he have done that unless Lodhi was his proper name. Everything points to the fact that Lodhi was his proper name, and he wished to get rid of it because it had become an encumbrance as soon as he realised that in the name of Lodhi he could only get permission to stay in this country for such a short term as about two months.

Then there is the strange situation that the passport should contain an endorsement authorising a stay for an indefinite time. Those of us sitting in this court must not make the mistake of becoming experts in immigration law, but we cannot fail to realise that the immigration authorities do not stamp a Commonwealth citizen's passport with permission for him to stay in this country for the rest of his life unless there is some reason for it, and it is quite beyond belief that he should have appeared in Dover in the ordinary way, and, instead of just being allowed to come back into this country for a limited period, should have been given the right to remain here for ever. It does not make sense, if one may use the vernacular in that way.

When one looks at those matters against the general background of this case and the strange pointers which have been unearthed in the enquiries which have been made, I am satisfied that the Secretary of State had before him material on which, if he thought right, he could form the view which he did that this was a fraudulent use of the passport. Once one gets to that stage, it follows that the Secretary of State's power is valid, the detention is valid, and the application is unfounded and must in my judgment be refused.

PARK J. I agree.

PETER PAIN J. I agree.

f   Application refused.

Solicitors: *Clintons*, agents for *Kuit Steinart Levy & Co*, Manchester (for the applicant); *Treasury Solicitor*.

N P Metcalfe Esq   Barrister.

Appeal
The applicant appealed.

Benet Hytner QC and *Mukhtar Hussain* for the applicant.
T Scott Baker for the Secretary of State.

GEOFFREY LANE LJ delivered the first judgment at the invitation of Megaw LJ. This is an appeal from an order of the Divisional Court of 4th May 1977 whereby they refused a motion by the applicant for a writ of habeas corpus. The facts are somewhat unusual, even in this context. The applicant, in an affidavit sworn on 17th December 1976, deposes that he was born on 8th December 1953; that he lived in Lahore until about Autumn 1971, and has always been known as Safder Hussain. It is, however, not disputed that on 14th November 1970 (that is, a year earlier than his sworn statement suggests) he came to this country from Pakistan under the name of Ijaz Ahmed Lodhi. It is likewise not disputed that there was produced to the immigration officer on that occasion a passport in that name of Lodhi and that under that name the applicant was given leave to enter the United Kingdom and to stay for two months. There is before us the application form in respect of the Lodhi passport. Suffice it to

say that the age, address and other particulars of Lodhi do not tally with the information about himself appearing in the applicant's affidavit. There is no doubt that
Lodhi and the applicant are one and the same person. This is established by the
photograph on the application form for the passport and also by admissions made to
this court. The applicant seeks in his affidavit to explain these matters by saying that
he was only 18 when he first came to England in 1970 and that he was brought here
by a friend of the family called Uncle Shafi; that Uncle Shafi made all the arrangements
about the visit to this country; that he, the applicant, knew nothing of any application
for a passport, indeed he went so far as to swear that he was not the holder of a
passport at all at that time; that he was not interviewed when he arrived at Heathrow;
and that as far as he knew no conditions were imposed on his entry. In a later affidavit
he seeks to qualify those statements by saying that he did not physically have a
passport in his possession, although a passport had been issued to him: it was in
Uncle Shafi's physical possession.

Despite the limit on his stay, he remained here, and did so, therefore, illegally. We
are dependent on his own account of events for what happened thereafter. According
to that account he moved to Leeds in 1972 and has remained there, at various addresses,
ever since, and has set himself up in business there and is in the process of buying a
house.

In 1972 he applied to the Pakistani consulate in Bradford for a fresh passport. This
was issued to him on 3rd February 1972. It is certified by the Pakistan authorities to
be a genuine passport. There is no mention on that document of any earlier passport.
It is issued in the name of Safder Hussain. On 26th May 1974 he went on a short visit
to Germany. He returned on 29th May, three days later, and his passport was then
stamped by the immigration officer 'Given leave to enter the United Kingdom for an
indefinite period'. Nothing else happened until November 1976, when the applicant
was arrested and detained in Armley Prison under the order of an immigration
officer acting under the Immigration Act 1971, Sch 2, para 16, as a preliminary step to
returning the applicant to Pakistan.

The contentions put forward on behalf of the Secretary of State before the Divisional
Court were (briefly) that the applicant assumed the identity of Safder Hussain and
assumed it falsely in order to obtain the indefinite leave to stay on the strength of the
new name which was not his but was that of another real person. Some support to
the idea that Lodhi was the true name, and Hussain the false, was lent by the discovery amongst the possessions of the applicant of a woman's passport in the name of
Lodhi. However, since the hearing before the Divisional Court two new pieces of
evidence have emerged. The first is what purports to be a birth certificate of Safder
Hussain, emanating from the municipal corporation of Multan, Pakistan, with a duly
attested translation. This contains particulars which coincide with the particulars
on the new passport. The applicant swears that that is his birth certificate.

The second piece of evidence is an affidavit from a gentleman called Safder Hussain
Malik, who was named Safder Hussain at birth. This man, it had been suggested by
the immigration officer in his affidavit originally, was the person whom the applicant
was seeking (so to speak) to impersonate. It is clear from Malik's affidavit that he did
not hold a passport in 1974, having returned his to the Home Office in 1973 on his
application for British citizenship. Thus there is doubt at this stage whether the
earlier theory propounded by the Home Office now holds good. In other words
there is a possibility that the applicant is in reality Safder Hussain.

Counsel for the applicant, who has presented the arguments on his behalf with
commendable clarity and force, submits that in these circumstances his client has
discharged such burden of proof as rests on him and that the Secretary of State has
failed to show that the permission to stay in the United Kingdom indefinitely, which
appears on the passport, was other than a proper exercise of the immigration officer's
discretion, uninfluenced by any misrepresentation on the part of the applicant. He
relies to some extent on the judgment of Peter Pain J on 3rd May 1977 in *R v Secretary*

of State for Home Affairs, ex parte Badaiki[1], the material part of which reads as follows:

'If the Secretary of State wishes to show that in fact he [that was the applicant in that case] was not given leave to enter within the meaning of the Immigration Act 1971 but was let in by virtue of some mistake, then I feel that the burden lies on the Secretary of State to establish that.'

Counsel for the applicant submits that the judgment of Lord Widgery CJ in the instant case is inconsistent with that passage and was wrong. What Lord Widgery CJ said in the Divisional Court in this case was as follows:

'Where do we stand in regard to those matters? First of all, it must be borne in mind that the governor having returned that he was holding this person under para 16, it is for the applicant to set up a prima facie case to discharge that burden. Counsel on his behalf says that the prima facie case is set up when it is shown that the applicant came back through Dover, presented his passport and had it stamped with the words, as I have referred to them, sanctioning his continued living in this country. In my judgment all that goes to nought if it can be shown that there is evidence on which the Secretary of State could properly conclude that there was here a fraud on the lines which I have indicated. Questions of fact in these matters are ultimately questions of fact for the Secretary of State. There are limits to the extent to which this court can go, and, as I see it, our obligation at the moment is to be satisfied that the Home Office approach to the problem is one taken in good faith. Further, we have to decide whether there is or is not adequate evidence here to justify the sort of conclusion which the Secretary of State has reached.'

That passage in my view represents the correct approach to this problem. If what Peter Pain J said in the earlier case is inconsistent with those views of Lord Widgery CJ then the judgment of Peter Pain J is to that extent in error.

The true view, as I see it, is this. If, on the evidence taken as a whole, the Secretary of State has grounds, and reasonable grounds, for coming to the conclusion that the applicant is here illegally, in contravention of the terms of the 1971 Act, this court will not interfere. Put into the terms of the present case, was the indefinite permission given by the immigration officer at Dover in May 1974 a proper exercise of discretion by which the Secretary of State is bound, or was it a decision brought about by deception, misrepresentation or fraud of the applicant? If it was, then the applicant cannot rely on it and the Secretary of State was entitled to act as he did and this appeal would fail.

To find the answer to this question one must turn to the affidavit of Mr Hatch, the immigration officer who dealt with the re-entry of the applicant into this country on 29th May 1974 after the short visit to Germany. He cannot, of course, remember interviewing the applicant, but he is able to say what his practice would have been in the particular circumstances of this case. What he says in his affidavit is as follows:

'I cannot remember the interview or the applicant but the description of the steps which I took contained in para 6 of the applicant's affidavit are typical of the steps which I would have taken when interviewing a returning Pakistani national. I would have asked the applicant several questions about his background and would have noticed that the passport was issued in Bradford and did not bear an endorsement that it succeeded a previous passport which had been lost. The applicant's statement that he had been adopted and brought to England would be consistent with the passport being the first passport of a child who had come to the United Kingdom as a child who did not need a passport because of his age. This was quite a common occurrence, particularly when the family had come to the United Kingdom in the 1960's.'

1 [1977] The Times, 4th May

Taking that affidavit with that of the applicant to which I have already made reference, it is plain beyond doubt, to my mind, that Mr Hatch *must* have asked the applicant about his original entry into this country and that the applicant *must* have told him that he had come in without a passport because he was too young to require one: that is, that he was here legally. The truth, as the applicant knew, was the opposite. In those circumstances, what appears to have been on the face of it a permission to stay here indefinitely was a permission obtained by fraud or misrepresentation and was therefore of no effect. The decision of the Divisional Court, although based on different grounds, was correct; and this appeal accordingly, to my mind, fails.

I should perhaps add this. If the applicant really is Ijaz Ahmed Lodhi, if his original entry into the United Kingdom was a genuine one, as may be the case, then the whole of his subsequent behaviour, the application for a passport in the name of Safder Hussain of Bradford and so on, is a fraud. On that basis, there is no doubt at all that the Secretary of State was entitled to take the steps he did; indeed the contrary is not argued by counsel for the applicant. Accordingly, I would dismiss this appeal.

ORR LJ. I agree that this appeal should be dismissed for the reasons given by Geoffrey Lane LJ, and would only add that if there be an inconsistency between the statements of the law made by Peter Pain J in the *Badaiki* case[1] and by Lord Widgery CJ in the present case, I too would accept the statement of Lord Widgery CJ as correct.

MEGAW LJ. Counsel for the applicant's main submission is that an important question of principle is involved in this appeal. With all respect to his clear and careful argument, I do not think that any doubtful question of principle arose in the decision of the Divisional Court on the material which was before it, or now arises on the material before us, including the further affidavits which we gave leave to be adduced in this appeal.

In his judgment Lord Widgery CJ expressed his own conclusions of fact, with which the other members of the court agreed, on the evidence which the Divisional Court had before it. Those conclusions included the conclusion that the applicant was Ijaz Ahmed Lodhi. If that were right, it would be the end of the matter. For it would inevitably follow that the passport which the applicant produced, in the name of Safder Hussain, when he presented himself at Dover on 29th May 1974, after his three day visit to Germany, was not a valid passport in relation to the applicant. It was in a name which was not, on that hypothesis, the applicant's name. The applicant, of course, would have known his own name and the falsity of the passport. The leave to enter given by the immigration officer would unquestionably have been obtained by the applicant's fraud; and that, as I say, would be the end of the matter. On that premise, as I understand it, counsel for the applicant would not dispute that conclusion.

In this court, the fresh evidence adduced on behalf of the applicant included an affidavit exhibiting what is said to be a certified copy of the applicant's birth certificate and which, it is said, shows that the applicant is Safder Hussain and is, and at all times was, properly so called. At any rate, it is said, the new evidence makes it probable that that is so. Let it be assumed that it is so. On that assumption, we have different evidence before us from the evidence on which the Divisional Court reached its conclusions of fact: materially different, I am prepared to assume, in respect of the true identity of the applicant.

An inevitable consequence of the making of that assumption is that the applicant's

---

1 [1977] The Times, 4th May

original entry into this country on 14th November 1970 was obtained by the production of a passport which gave a name which was not the applicant's true name. He, Safder Hussain, entered the United Kingdom as the result of the production of a passport describing him as Ijaz Ahmed Lodhi. I am afraid that the applicant's original assertion in his first affidavit in these proceedings, stating that he entered on that occasion without having a passport at all, is a falsehood, and that his subsequent assertion that, although there was a passport, he did not himself have it or know of its falsity in relation to his true identity, is simply not acceptable.

If the true conclusion were that the whole sequence of events, the original entry under the false name of Lodhi, the obtaining thereafter, with the assistance of 'Uncle Shafi', of a passport in the name of Safder Hussain, and the journey to Germany and the return to England on the new passport, was a connected plan, then so far as the May 1974 leave to enter and remain is concerned, it would, in my judgment, plainly be vitiated as a result of its being the intended end-product of a fraudulent scheme. The initial entry on the false passport could not be divorced from, or treated as irrelevant to, the subsequent obtaining of the leave on a different passport in May 1974. But I am prepared to assume, for the purposes of this appeal, that it would not, on the evidence, be right to conclude that there was, from the outset, this fraudulent scheme.

However, what the evidence, including the fresh evidence now before the court, shows beyond any real doubt is that when the applicant was seeking entry at Dover in May 1974 he made a materially false statement; he gave some false explanation, which (so far as that is relevant) he must have known to be false, as to how it came about that his Pakistani passport did not contain any entry or endorsement explaining his previous residence in the United Kingdom. He knew that he had entered the United Kingdom some three and a half years earlier on a false passport. It is plain on the applicant's own evidence (para 6 of his first affidavit) that the immigration officer did in fact question him about the present passport. I read from para 6 of the original affidavit, where the applicant deposes: 'I was asked when I had originally come to England and I told him and I described to the officer how I had been "adopted" by Mohammed Shafi and brought to England by him.' It is plain from the immigration officer's affidavit that there was such a questioning of the applicant. It would seem most probable that the applicant's answer was to say, or to use words intended to convey the impression that, he had originally entered the United Kingdom without a passport, as an adopted child. It is plain that the applicant's answer, whatever its precise terms, to the question which he was undoubtedly asked, was a statement which was deliberately, and knowingly, intended to make the immigration officer believe that something was true which was in fact false and, to the knowledge of the applicant, materially false.

This is not a case of a mere negative failure to tell the truth. There was a positive untruth, and a material one, in the sense that it was because the immigration officer believed that untrue statement that he gave the leave which he did give. That being so, making the assumption as to the applicant's identity which we are asked to make on the fresh evidence, the applicant's leave to enter in May 1974 was obtained by fraud, and the leave then given and stamped on his passport cannot avail him. Whether or not the result would have been the same on different facts, we do not have to consider.

In these circumstances, I do not find it necessary to discuss the suggested question of principle as to burden of proof, which was so ably and strenuously argued by counsel for the applicant. If indeed (as I very much doubt) there is a difference of principle in the decision of the Divisional Court in the present case, decided on 4th May 1977, as contrasted with the decision of the same court given on the previous day in *R v Secretary of State for Home Affairs, ex parte Badaiki*[1], that may have to be considered

---

1   [1977] The Times, 4th May

hereafter. But it does not fall to be decided for the purposes of the decision of the present appeal. I have been prepared to consider this appeal on the basis which *a* counsel for the applicant submits should have been, but as he says was not, followed by the Divisional Court: that is, on the basis of the court itself assessing the evidence. I agree that the appeal should be dismissed.

Appeal dismissed.

Solicitors: *Clintons*, agents for *Kuit Steinart Levy & Co*, Manchester (for the applicant); *b* *Treasury Solicitor*.

Mary Rose Plummer Barrister.

Practice Direction

FAMILY DIVISION

Husband and wife – Matrimonial order – Appeal to High Court against order of magistrates – Appeal against amount of weekly payments – Determination of appeal by single judge instead of Divisional Court – Hearing of appeal at a divorce town – Procedure – RSC Ord 90, r 16 (as amended by RSC (No 3) 1978, r 14).

With effect from 1st June 1978 RSC Ord 90, r 16, is amended[1]. Unless the President otherwise directs, an appeal under the Matrimonial Proceedings (Magistrates' Courts) Act 1960 to the Family Division of the High Court may be determined by a single judge, instead of by a Divisional Court, in cases where the appeal relates only to the amount of any weekly payment ordered to be made. The President may also direct that such an appeal be heard and determined by a single judge at 'a divorce town' *e* within the meaning of the Matrimonial Causes Rules 1977[2]. Consequential amendments are made to RSC Ord 90, r 16, concerning the number of copy documents required to be lodged where the appeal is to quantum only.

The practice to be followed in respect of any such appeal to a single judge of the Family Division will be that contained in the Practice Direction dated 11th May 1977[3] subject to the following modifications: (i) one copy only of the various documents *f* in support of the appeal need be lodged, unless the President directs that an appeal which has been listed before a single judge shall instead be heard by a Divisional Court when the Clerk of the Rules will notify the appellant's solicitor (or the appellant if acting in person) and request that he do lodge the additional copies required by RSC Ord 90, r 16, and the Practice Direction dated 11th May 1977[3] prior to the date fixed for the hearing; (ii) any request to fix an appeal for hearing by a single judge at a *g* place other than at the Royal Courts of Justice should be made in writing to the Clerk of the Rules; (iii) where the President directs that the appeal be heard at a divorce town as defined by the Matrimonial Causes Rules 1977, the Clerk of the Rules will inform the appellant of the relevant town and will refer the papers to the listing officer of the appropriate Circuit Office for a date of hearing to be fixed and notified to the appellant.

It should be noted that every appeal under the Matrimonial Proceedings (Magistrates' Courts) Act 1960 must continue to be entered in the Principal Registry.

The Registrar's Direction dated 16th December 1971 (Divisional Court appeal: date of hearing) is hereby cancelled.

R L BAYNE-POWELL *h*
22nd May 1978   Senior Registrar.

1   Rules of the Supreme Court (Amendment No 3) 1978, SI 1978 No 579, r 14
2   SI No 344, r 2(2)
3   [1977] 2 All ER 543, [1977] 1 WLR 609

Property and Reversionary Investment Corporation Ltd v Templar and another

COURT OF APPEAL, CIVIL DIVISION
ROSKILL AND CUMMING-BRUCE LJJ
20th JUNE 1977

Court of Appeal – Time for appeal – Extension of time for appeal – Discretion – Factors to be considered – Special circumstances – Overruling decision by superior court in an analogous case – Rent review clause in lease – Clause construed by judge – Subsequent decision by superior court showing construction of clause to be wrong – Whether decision by superior court constituting special circumstances for extending time for appeal – Whether unjust that parties' obligations under lease should be governed by erroneous decision of judge.

The landlords granted the tenants a lease of property for 21 years from 25th March 1965 at an initial yearly rent of £1,656. The lease entitled the landlords periodically to seek a rent review and laid down the procedure to be taken to entitle them to such a review. In 1972 the landlords brought an action against the tenants claiming a rent increase in accordance with the review provisions of the lease. On 1st November 1974 the judge dismissed the action on the ground that on the true construction of the lease time was of the essence of the rent review clauses and as the landlords had failed to comply with certain procedural steps within the time prescribed by those clauses they had lost their entitlement to a rent review. That decision was in accordance with decisions in the Court of Appeal. However on 23rd March 1977 the House of Lords[a] decided that those decisions were erroneous and that the presumption was that time was not of the essence in a rent review clause. The parties were agreed that if the landlords were allowed to appeal to the Court of Appeal against the judge's decision it would, in the light of the decision in the House of Lords, be held to be wrong. In June 1977 the landlords applied to the Court of Appeal for leave to appeal against the judge's decision out of time contending that the contractual relationship of the parties under the lease ought not to be governed by a decision which the parties were agreed was erroneous. The tenants opposed the application and contended that the landlords should receive only the initial yearly rent until the next rent review could be invoked in 1979, but undertook that when the next rent review was invoked they would not plead issue estoppel and would accept that the landlords would then be entitled to claim a rent review in accordance with the House of Lords' decision.

Held – For a party to obtain leave to appeal out of time it was not sufficient for him to state that there had been a subsequent decision of a superior court which showed that the decision against which he sought to appeal was wrong: he had to show that there were special reasons why he should be allowed to argue that the decision should not stand. In all the circumstances it would not be just that the parties should have their future contractual obligations governed by a construction of the lease which the decision of the House of Lords had shown to be erroneous. These were, therefore, special circumstances which justified an appeal out of time and, on the landlords' undertaking that if the appeal succeeded they would not claim any

---

a   *United Scientific Holdings Ltd v Burnley Borough Council* [1977] 2 All ER 62

increased rent in respect of any date before Midsummer Day 1978, leave to appeal out of time would be granted (see p 435 *f h j* and p 436 *a b d* and *e*, post).

Dictum of Lord Greene MR in *Re Berkeley, Borrer v Berkeley* [1944] 2 All ER at 397 applied.

Notes

For extension of time for appeal, see 30 Halsbury's Laws (3rd Edn) 463, para 877, and for cases on the subject, see 51 Digest (Reissue) 805-808, 3620-3643.

Cases referred to in judgments

Berkeley, Re, Borrer v Berkeley [1944] 2 All ER 395, [1945] Ch 1, 171 LT 303, CA, 51 Digest (Repl) 807, 3635.

Cheapside Land Development Co Ltd v Messels Service Co [1977] 2 All ER 62, [1977] 2 WLR 806, 75 LGR 407, HL; *rvsg* [1976] Court of Appeal Transcript 225.

Gatti v Shoosmith [1939] 3 All ER 916, [1939] Ch 841, 108 LJCh 380, 161 LT 208, CA, 51 Digest (Repl) 806, 3631.

United Scientific Holdings Ltd v Burnley Borough Council [1977] 2 All ER 62, [1977] 2 WLR 806, 75 LGR 407, HL; *rvsg* sub nom *United Scientific Holdings Ltd v Burnley Corpn* [1976] 2 All ER 220, [1976] Ch 128, [1976] 2 WLR 686, 74 LGR 316, CA.

Application

The plaintiffs, Property and Reversionary Investment Corpn Ltd ('the landlords'), applied for leave to appeal out of time against a judgment of his Honour Judge Fay QC given on 1st November 1974 dismissing their action claiming an increased rent under a rent review clause contained in a 21 year lease from 25th March 1965 granted to the defendants, Mr and Mrs Templar ('the tenants'). The facts are set out in the judgment of Roskill LJ.

William Goodhart for the landlords.
David Hunt for the tenants.

ROSKILL LJ. In 1972 the landlords issued proceedings against their lessees ('the tenants') in connection with a rent review clause in a lease entered into for 21 years from 25th March 1965 at an initial yearly rental of £1,656.

These proceedings came before his Honour Judge Fay QC sitting as a deputy judge of the Queen's Bench Division, and Judge Fay determined these proceedings in favour of the tenants. That decision was given on 1st November 1974 when the learned judge dismissed the landlords' action on the ground that the steps to obtain the rent increase had not been timeously initiated before 25th March 1972. We have not seen a transcript of his judgment, but it would seem that he followed the line of cases then prevailing and took the view that time was of the essence, and as the landlords had failed to comply with their obligations under the lease, properly construed, they had lost their entitlement under the rent review clause.

That, broadly speaking, was in line with the view taken in two decisions of this court, first in *United Scientific Holdings Ltd v Burnley Borough Council*[1] and secondly in *Cheapside Land Development Co Ltd v Messels Service Co*[2]. But on 23rd March 1977 the House of Lords[3] declared those two decisions to have been erroneous.

Counsel for the landlords has therefore claimed, and counsel for the tenants has agreed that we may assume (though he has made no admission) that, in the light of

1 [1976] 2 All ER 220, [1976] Ch 128
2 [1976] Court of Appeal Transcript 225
3 [1977] 2 All ER 62, [1977] 2 WLR 806

the decision of the House of Lords, Judge Fay's judgment if appealed to this court would be held to be wrong. We express no view whether that is right.

It is in the light of that present position that the landlords have now applied to this court for leave to appeal out of time. They are, of course, a long way out of time for it is now some two and a half years since Judge Fay gave this decision. But it is said by counsel for the landlords that the reason why this court should now give leave to appeal out of time is because this is a case where the parties are in a continuing contractual relationship and that it is wrong that that relationship should still continue and will continue, under the 21 years' lease until 1986, to be governed by a decision of Judge Fay which, on the assumption I have already mentioned, is to be treated as erroneous.

Counsel for the landlords relied on a decision of this court Re Berkeley, Borrer v Berkeley[1]. In that case there had been earlier decisions at first instance. Then there was a subsequent decision of this court which showed that the earlier decisions were wrong, and it was sought to appeal out of time against the second of those decisions. Lord Greene MR said[2]:

'It seems to me that the principle to be extracted is this. It is not sufficient for a party to come to the court and say: "A subsequent decision of a superior court has said that the principle of law on which my case was decided was wrong." The court will immediately say to him: "That bald statement is not enough for you. What are the circumstances? What are the facts? What is the nature of the judgment? Who are the parties affected? What, if anything, has been done under it?" In other words, the whole of the circumstances must be looked at. If the court, in the light of those circumstances, considers it just to extend the time, then it will do so. That seems to me to be the proper principle, and it is entirely in accordance with the view taken by this court in Gatti v. Shoosmith[3], the most recent case under this rule.'

It is therefore plain that it is not enough for counsel for the landlords to say that the recent decision of the House of Lords clearly shows that Judge Fay's decision was wrong. He must show there are special reasons why he should be allowed to argue that the judgment should not stand.

At one point he sought to contend that the landlords might be in a difficult position when next the rent review clause could be invoked in 1979 and said that notwithstanding the decision of the House of Lords, they would be bound to comply with Judge Fay's judgment, there being, as he contended, issue estoppel between the parties. Counsel for the tenants did not accept that, and indeed offered an undertaking that no question of issue estoppel would be raised in 1979 and that the tenants would accept that the landlords would be then entitled to base their claim for rent review in accordance with the decisions of the House of Lords.

We cannot speculate as to the future. The real point here, as counsel for the landlords ultimately accepted, is whether it is right that these parties should have this continuing contractual relationship governed by a lease the terms of which have assumedly been erroneously construed in the court below.

I think that notwithstanding counsel for the tenants' submissions that the landlords should be left to receive the lower rent for the next 18 months or so and thereafter become entitled to claim the higher rent in accordance with the House of Lords decision, there are special circumstances which justify leave to appeal out of time.

Counsel for the landlords, very properly in the light of Re Berkeley[1], accepted that

---

1   [1944] 2 All ER 395, [1945] Ch 1
2   [1944] 2 All ER 395 at 397, [1945] Ch 1 at 4
3   [1939] 3 All ER 916, [1939] Ch 841

he could not claim any new rent retrospectively, even if the appeal out of time ultimately succeeded. That is clearly right, and on his undertaking not to claim any increased rent if the appeal succeeds before any date before Midsummer Day next, I take the view that leave to appeal out of time should be given, and accordingly I would allow the motion.

CUMMING-BRUCE LJ. I agree and would only add this. The court has considered whether there are special circumstances which bring into play the principles described by Lord Greene MR in *Re Berkeley*[1], where he stated that the court has to look at all the circumstances, and here the context of this application is that there is a lease whereby the landlords have a right to seek a rent review periodically to keep in step with the market movements of such a lease, which included clauses defining the substantive obligations of the parties and a clause, or clauses, laying down the procedural steps required to enable the landlords to avail themselves of their rights for rent review.

What was decided in this case by the learned judge was that there had been a procedural default by the landlords in relation to certification in the time limited by the lease for a review of rent, and as a result of that decision, the landlords lost their right to the rent review that they would otherwise have had under the lease.

Now that the House of Lords has decided that the proper construction of the contract is other than that decided by the learned judge, I agree that there are special circumstances here because it does not seem just that future obligations between the parties to the lease should depend on the construction now shown to be wrong.

Leave to appeal out of time.

Solicitors: *Hicks, Arnold, Rose, Johnson* (for the landlords); *Barry Lewis* (for the tenants).

N Hoon Esq   Barrister.

---

1   [1944] 2 All ER 395 at 397, [1945] Ch 1 at 4

Drane v Evangelou and others

COURT OF APPEAL, CIVIL DIVISION
LORD DENNING MR, LAWTON AND GOFF LJJ
10th, 11th NOVEMBER 1977

Damages – Exemplary damages – Trespass to land – Landlord unlawfully evicting tenant from demised premises – Tenant suing for interference with right to quiet enjoyment – Facts pleaded sufficient to warrant claim for trespass – Landlord seeking to obtain premises from tenant unlawfully for own purposes – Whether circumstances justifying award of exemplary damages for trespass.

Pleading – Departure – Legal consequences of pleaded facts – Pleading setting out material facts and alleging interference with right to quiet enjoyment of premises – Facts pleaded sufficient to warrant claim for trespass – Judge in course of trial raising issue of trespass – Whether judge entitled of his own motion to raise issue – Whether defendant taken by surprise.

County court – Practice – Exemplary damages – Need to plead claim for exemplary damages – Claim for exemplary damages required to be pleaded in High Court – No equivalent rule applying to county court – Whether claim for exemplary damages in county court required to be pleaded.

The plaintiff was the tenant of a furnished flat owned by the defendant and let to the plaintiff at a rent of £25 per week. In July 1975 the plaintiff applied to a rent officer to fix the rent. Before the rent was fixed the defendant served a notice to quit on the plaintiff which was ineffective because of the statutory protection from eviction afforded to the plaintiff. On 8th October the rent officer fixed the rent of the flat at £16 per week. On 14th October, while the plaintiff was out, three associates of the defendant entered the premises, put the plaintiff's belongings outside in the back yard and prevented him from entering the flat. The defendant's parents-in-law moved into the flat while the plaintiff was forced to reside with friends and store his belongings in a garage. On 28th October the plaintiff issued a claim in the county court alleging that 'the defendant had interfered with the right of the plaintiff . . . to quiet enjoyment of the . . . premises by unlawfully evicting [him] from the . . . premises' and seeking (i) an order for delivery up of possession to the plaintiff, (ii) injunctions to restrain the defendant from preventing the plaintiff gaining re-admittance to the flat, from interfering with the plaintiff's right to quiet enjoyment of the premises, and from harassing the plaintiff, and ordering the defendant's parents-in-law to quit the flat, and (iii) damages limited to £1,000. On 31st October the plaintiff obtained an injunction compelling the defendant to restore him to the property. The defendant refused to comply with it or with a further injunction until the plaintiff instituted committal proceedings for breach of the injunction. On 1st January 1976 the plaintiff regained possession of the flat having been kept out of occupation for a period of ten weeks. On 14th September 1976 the plaintiff's action was heard in the county court. At the end of the evidence the defendant submitted that the claim was for breach of a covenant for quiet enjoyment and that exemplary damages could not be awarded. The judge stated that the facts were sufficient to found a claim in trespass and awarded damages of £1,000 to the plaintiff. The defendant appealed, contending, inter alia, that the plaintiff was not entitled to exemplary damages because the particulars of claim had not pleaded a claim in trespass and had not expressly claimed exemplary damages.

Held – The appeal would be dismissed for the following reasons—

(i) The judge was entitled of his own motion to raise the issue of trespass even though it had not been pleaded, because the facts were sufficient to warrant a claim for trespass and as they were set out in the particulars of claim the defendant could not claim that he had been taken by surprise when the judge raised the issue (see p 440 *d e*, p 441 *h*, p 442 *c g* and p 443 *e*, post); dictum of Lord Denning MR in *Re Vandervell's Trusts (No 2)* [1973] 3 All ER at 213 applied.

(ii) A claim for exemplary damages did not have to be specifically pleaded in the county court because there was no rule in the county court rules equivalent to RSC Ord 18, r 8(3), which required a claim in the High Court for exemplary damages to be specifically pleaded. Furthermore, in the county court the defendant had not raised the defence that exemplary damages should be specifically pleaded and therefore would not be permitted to raise it on appeal (see p 440 *g h*, p 441 *h* and p 443 *e*, post).

(iii) The defendant's conduct in unlawfully evicting the plaintiff in the manner in which he did was a grave wrong which justified an award of £1,000 damages either as exemplary damages because the defendant had acted with a cynical disregard of the plaintiff's rights in seeking to gain, at the expense of the plaintiff, property which he coveted and which he could not otherwise obtain and because it was a case in which it was necessary to teach the defendant that tort did not pay, or (per Lawton and Goff LJJ) as aggravated damages. Although the judge had not approached the award of exemplary damages in the same way as a jury should be directed to approach such an award, the award was not excessive in the circumstances (see p 441 *b* to *h*, p 442 *d e*, p 443 *a* to *e* and *j* and p 444 *f* to *h*, post); dictum of Lord Devlin in *Rookes v Barnard* [1964] 1 All ER at 411 applied.

Notes

For exemplary damages, see 12 Halsbury's Laws (4th Edn) para 1190, and for cases on the subject, see 17 Digest (Reissue) 80-83, 11-17.

Cases referred to in judgments

Cassell & Co Ltd v Broome [1972] 1 All ER 801, [1972] AC 1027, [1972] 2 WLR 645, HL; affg sub nom *Broome v Cassell & Co Ltd* [1971] 2 All ER 187, [1971] 2 QB 354, [1971] 2 WLR 853, CA, 17 Digest (Reissue) 83, 17.

McCall v Abelesz [1976] 1 All ER 727, [1976] QB 585, [1978] 2 WLR 151, 31 P & CR 256, CA.

Rookes v Barnard [1964] 1 All ER 367, [1964] AC 1129, [1964] 2 WLR 269, [1964] 1 Lloyd's Rep 28, HL, 17 Digest (Reissue) 81, 14.

Vandervell's Trusts (No 2), Re, White v Vandervell Trustees Ltd [1974] 3 All ER 205, [1974] Ch 269, [1974] 3 WLR 256, CA, Digest (Cont Vol D) 1008, 909a.

Cases also cited

Asinobi v Chake (9th December 1971) unreported, CA.
Mafo v Adams [1969] 3 All ER 1404, [1970] 1 QB 584, CA.
McCready v Rann [1970] The Times, 24th October.
Olidawura v Fulmyk (17th January 1975) unreported, Shoreditch County Court.
Perera v Vandiyar [1953] 1 All ER 1109, [1953] 1 WLR 672, CA.

Appeal

By amended particulars of claim dated 10th December 1975, Anthony Malcolm Drane ('the tenant') claimed, inter alia, (i) an order that George Evangelou ('the landlord') deliver up possession of premises at 172a Bowes Road, New Southgate, London N11, to the tenant and be restrained from preventing the tenant from gaining re-admittance to the premises, (ii) an injunction restraining the landlord, his servants or agents from interfering with the right of the tenant and his de facto wife, Ann Watts, to quiet enjoyment of the premises and from harassing the tenant and Ann Watts, (iii) an injunction ordering the second and third defendants, Panayiotou (male) and Panayiotou (married woman), to quit their unlawful occupation of the premises and not to re-enter into occupation, and (iv) damages limited to £1,000. On 14th September 1976 in the Barnet County Court his Honour Judge Lonsdale awarded the tenant £1,000 damages against the landlord and the second defendant and ordered that certain injunctions against the landlord and the second and third defendants made on 31st October and 19th December 1975 remain in force. The landlord appealed against the award of damages. The facts are set out in the judgment of Lord Denning MR.

Edward Cousins for the landlord.
S Anthony Eaton for the tenant.

LORD DENNING MR. 'Monstrous behaviour'—that is how the judge described it. He said that it called for exemplary damages. He awarded £1,000. The defendant appeals. These are the facts.

Mr George Evangelou is the owner of a leasehold house, 172a Bowes Road, New Southgate. He let a maisonette in it to a young man, Mr Anthony Malcolm Drane, who lived there with a woman, Ann Watts, not his wife, but who lived with him as if she was his wife. The maisonette was let to them furnished at a rent of £25 a week inclusive of rates from 31st August 1974.

On 11th July 1975 the tenant, Mr Drane, applied to the rent officer for a revision of the rent. This annoyed the landlord, Mr Evangelou, greatly. So on 21st August 1975 the landlord gave the tenant notice to quit. That was not effective because the tenant was protected by statute from eviction. On 8th October 1975 the rent officer fixed the rent and adjudged it be £16 a week exclusive. Note the date, 8th October 1975.

Six days later, on 14th October, the landlord behaved atrociously. He waited until the young couple were out, when the tenant had taken Ann Watts to college in the morning, and then got three men to invade the maisonette. The judge described what the tenant found on his return:

> 'When he came back a little later, I think at 9.30, there he found that a large Greek Cypriot was barring the entrance; all his belongings had been put outside in the backyard; the lock of the door had been hammered in; the door was bolted on the inside; about four to five people were inside his premises and two women among them ... some of their belongings were broken and books were damaged.'

The tenant called the police. They told Mrs Evangelou, the landlord's wife, that she was committing an offence and that it would be reported to the town hall. Nevertheless she did not let the tenants back into their maisonette. They had to go and stay with friends. They stored some of their belongings in their friends' garage, and slept on the living room floor of their friends' house.

The tenant went to the county court and asked for an injunction so that he and Ann Watts could be restored to their premises. The judge on 31st October 1975 granted an injunction against the landlord. But the landlord did not obey it. He had moved his wife's father and mother into the maisonette. The landlord or his in-laws appealed to this court. This court heard the appeal on 27th November 1975 and rejected it. Lawton LJ, giving the judgment of the court, said:

> 'I am surprised that this appeal has been made to this court. The defendant's behaviour was reprehensible ... it is right and just that the plaintiff should be put back where he is entitled to be ... this court should take every step it can to see that landlords who behave like the defendant in this case has behaved should get no benefit whatsoever from what they have done.'

So the appeal was dismissed on 27th November 1975. Still the landlord did not go out. The tenant had to apply again for an injunction to the county court on 19th December 1975. The landlord and his in-laws were ordered to leave by 6 p m on Saturday, 21st December. They gave the tenant a key, but it did not fit. So he could not get in. On 23rd December the tenant applied to commit them for contempt. That at least brought results. The in-laws left. It was only then, on 23rd December, that the in-laws and the landlord went out. The tenant had been kept out for ten weeks. The tenant eventually moved in on 1st January 1976. He found everything dirty and damaged and went on with his action for damages. He was awarded exemplary damages in the sum of £1,000.

Now there is an appeal to this court. The first point taken on behalf of the landlord was a pleading point. The particulars of claim alleged that the landlord 'had interfered with the right of the [tenant] and his de facto wife Ann Watts to quiet enjoyment of the said premises by unlawfully evicting them from the said premises on Tuesday 14th October 1975'. Counsel for the landlord submitted that that claim was for breach of a covenant for quiet enjoyment. He cited a passage from Woodfall[1]: 'Since the claim is in contract, punitive or exemplary damages cannot be awarded.' The judge at once said: 'What about trespass? Does the claim not lie in trespass?' Counsel for the landlord urged that trespass was not pleaded. The judge then said: 'The facts are alleged sufficiently so it does not matter what label you put on it.' The judge was right. The tenant in the particulars of claim gave details saying that three men broke the door, removed the tenant's belongings, bolted the door from the inside; and so forth. Those facts were clearly sufficient to warrant a claim for trespass. As we said in *Re Vandervells Trusts*[2]:

> 'It is sufficient for the pleader to state material facts. He need not state the legal result. If, for convenience, he does so, he is not bound by, or limited to, what he has stated. He can present, in argument, any legal consequence of which the facts permit.'

Another pleading point was not taken before the county court but was taken before us. It was said that the particulars of claim did not expressly claim exemplary damages and therefore they could not be awarded. In *Broome v Cassell & Co Ltd*[3] we said that exemplary damages need not be pleaded expressly. In the House of Lords Lord Hailsham LC said[4] he was content to accept the view of the Court of Appeal but he thought the practice should be altered. As a result of his words, the Rules of the Supreme Court have been amended. RSC Ord 18, r 8(3), says: 'A claim for exemplary damages must be specifically pleaded together with the facts on which the party pleading relies.'

Does that amendment apply to the county court? In my opinion it does not. The County Court Rules have not been amended. So it is not necessary in the county court to plead exemplary damages. The old practice still applies there, where exemplary damages can be awarded, even though not pleaded. In any case this point was not raised in the county court. So it cannot be raised here. If it had been raised in the county court, I am quite sure it would have been met immediately by an amendment to claim exemplary damages.

The next point was one of susbtance. Counsel for the landlord submitted that it was not open to the judge to award exemplary damages. He has taken us through Lord Devlin's judgment in *Rookes v Barnard*[5]. He said that the general principle nowadays is that in a civil action damages are awarded by way of compensation for damage actually done or for any aggravation by way of injured feelings of the

1 27th Edn (1968), para 1338
2 [1974] 3 All ER 205 at 213, [1974] Ch 269 at 321, 322
3 [1971] 2 All ER 187 at 197, [1977] 2 QB 354 at 378
4 [1972] 1 All ER 801 at 834, [1972] AC 1027 at 1083
5 [1964] 1 All ER 367 at 410-412, [1964] AC 1129 at 1226-1230

plaintiff; but the court cannot in the ordinary way award punitive damages over and above that which is compensation: because punishment is the prerogative of the criminal courts and should have no place in the civil courts.

That exclusion of exemplary damages has not found favour in the other common law countries, such as Canada, Australia, New Zealand and the United States of America. But since *Cassell & Co Ltd v Broome*[1] it must be accepted in England. Lord Devlin acknowledged that there are some categories of tort in which exemplary damages may still be awarded. This case seems to me to come within the second category. Lord Devlin said[2]:

> 'This category is not confined to moneymaking in the strict sense. It extends to cases in which the defendant is seeking to gain at the expense of the plaintiff some object,—perhaps some property which he covets,—which either he could not obtain at all or not obtain except at a price greater than he wants to put down. Exemplary damages can properly be awarded whenever it is necessary to teach a wrongdoer that tort does not pay.'

To my mind this category includes cases of unlawful eviction of a tenant. The landlord seeks to gain possession at the expense of the tenant, so as to keep or get a rent higher than that awarded by the rent tribunal, or to get possession from a tenant who is protected by the Rent Acts. So he resorts to harassing tactics. Such conduct can be punished now by the criminal law. But it can also be punished by the civil law by an award of exemplary damages. In the recent case of *McCall v Abelesz*[3] it was held that the provisions of the Rent Act 1965 against harassment only created a criminal offence; but I said[4]: '... I see no need to give any new civil remedy for harassment. As I understand it, the law already gives a perfectly good civil action for damges.' So in a case of this kind damages can be awarded not only by way of compensation but also by way of exemplary damages.

It was said that, in any event, the sum of £1,000 was far too high even as exemplary damages. It was suggested that this sum is out of scale altogether. In my opinion a sum awarded by the way of exemplary damages is not to be weighed in nice scales. It is a question for the judge, having heard all the evidence, to award such sum as he thinks proper. As this case unfolded before us, the circumstances in which this young couple were forced out of the house, the in-laws being pushed in, the landlord or the in-laws not complying with the injunction and not leaving until there was an application to commit, it did seem to me a case in which, in Lord Devlin's words, it was necessary 'to teach the landlord a lesson'. The judge thought £1,000 was appropriate. No doubt he felt strongly about it. So would any jury or any judge. I do not think we should interfere with the sum of £1,000.

There was a point about the costs. The judge said that it was not a case where he could bind the registrar to the higher scale, and he would give him a discretion to award a higher sum under CCR Ord 47, r 21(2). This is not a matter on which it would be right to alter the judgment of the county court judge.

This appeal should be dismissed.

LAWTON LJ. I agree with the judgment delivered by Lord Denning MR and have only two comments to make.

The first relates to what I understood counsel for the landlord to be complaining about, namely that in all the circumstances of the case the landlord was not fairly treated by the learned judge. Counsel for the landlord opened the matter before

1 [1972] 1 All ER 801, [1972] AC 1027
2 [1964] 1 All ER 367 at 411, [1964] AC 1129 at 1227
3 [1976] 1 All ER 727, [1976] QB 585
4 [1976] 1 All ER 727 at 730, [1976] QB 585 at 594

this court by telling us that the learned judge of his own motion had raised the question of trespass whereas the tenant was alleging breach of covenant for quiet enjoyment, and also of his own motion raised the question of exemplary damages. Had that been so, I would have felt some difficulty about this case but, on a close examination of the pleadings and of the judge's note, the course of events seems to have been this. The pleadings were drawn by a firm of solicitors, and they were none the worse for that. Paragraph 3 of the pleadings was in these terms:

'The [landlord] has interfered with the right of the [tenant] and his de facto wife Ann Watts to the quiet enjoyment of the said premises by unlawfully evicting them from the said premises on Tuesday 14th October 1975.'

There then followed detailed particulars of what had happened. I do not read that paragraph as a claim for breach of an implied covenant for quiet enjoyment. Anyway, if that is what it did amount to, which I do not think it did, what was done was to set out in para 3 of the particulars of claim the facts on which the court was asked to adjudge. The landlord was not in any way taken by surprise when the judge raised the question, in circumstances to which I shall refer later, of trespass. Facing the landlord on the pleadings was an allegation of trespass. What is more, if the landlord's advisers had had *Rookes v Barnard*[1] in mind, which counsel for the landlord said he did to some extent although he did not take the report of *Rookes v Barnard*[9] to the court, they should have appreciated, and probably did appreciate straight away, that the tenant was going to allege that this was a case for exemplary damages. I agree with what Lord Denning MR has said that on the facts this case comes fairly and squarely within the second category to which Lord Devlin referred in his speech in *Rookes v Barnard*[2].

It seems from the judge's note that at the end of the evidence counsel for the landlord raised with him the matter of exemplary or punitive damages. The judge has a note to that effect. Counsel had with him Woodfall on Landlord and Tenant[3] and invited the judge's attention to the fact that exemplary damages should not be given for breach of a covenant for quiet enjoyment. Then the learned judge said: 'What about trespass?' or words to that effect. So the landlord was not in any way taken by surprise. This was not a case, as I understood counsel for the landlord to be suggesting, in which the judge of his own motion raised in his judgment for the first time the question of trespass. The landlord, through counsel, did have an opportunity during the trial of inviting the judge's attention to any argument he might have been able to put forward on the basis of *Rookes v Barnard*[1]. He did not do so. In my judgment it is now too late for the landlord to submit that his counsel was taken by surprise and never had an opportunity at the trial of advancing the kind of argument which counsel for the landlord has put before this court. The judge did not treat the landlord unfairly.

The second ground of counsel for the landlord's complaint, as I understand it, is that the learned judge did not go through the mental processes which he should have gone through in strict compliance with *Rookes v Barnard*[1] before awarding exemplary damages. Counsel for the landlord pointed out that there is no indication in the notes taken by counsel of a short judgment that the judge made any attempt to assess the amount of the aggravated damages to which the tenant would have been entitled and then to ask himself the question: 'is the amount which I would award for aggravated damages sufficient to deal with the facts of this particular case?' I find it necessary to remind myself that this was a judgment delivered in the county court; it was not a judgment after a trial in the High Court. It was a judgment given by a judge who may or may not have had full library facilities available to him, and he certainly did not have *Rookes v Barnard*[1] brought to his

1 [1964] 1 All ER 367, [1964] AC 1129
2 [1964] 1 All ER 367 at 410, 411, [1964] AC 1129 at 1226, 1227
3 27th Edn (1968)

attention by counsel on either side. He was doing his best in all the circumstances. It seems to me that my task here is to look at the facts and to start by asking the question what sort of sum would it have been proper to award for aggravated damages in this case, which undoubtedly was one for aggravated damages. Counsel for the landlord at times seemed to be suggesting that this was a comparatively minor dispute between a landlord and a tenant. I emphatically disassociate myself from that. To deprive a man of a roof over his head is, in my judgment, one of the worst torts which can be committed. It causes stress, worry and anxiety. It brings the law into disrepute if people like the landlord can act with impunity in the way he did. Indeed I would add that when the police arrived they said that they were going to report the matter to the town hall. If they did, it is surprising that this landlord was not prosecuted for an offence under s 30 of the Rent Act 1965. Parliament has said that this kind of conduct is sufficiently serious to be made a criminal offence. It follows, in my view, that the court is entitled to approach cases of this kind on the basis that a very grave wrong indeed has been done to the tenant who is evicted in the sort of way that this tenant was evicted.

I myself would not have regarded the sum awarded, namely £1,000, as excessive for aggravated damages. But even assuming it was, I would ask myself the question whether the judge was entitled to add something for exemplary or punitive damages. If there ever was a case where a landlord like this landlord should be taught a lesson, it is this case. I cannot envisage any court saying that such sum as was added for exemplary damages making up a total of £1,000 was so excessive that this court ought to interfere. I would dismiss the appeal.

GOFF LJ. I entirely agree with both judgments which have been given, and it is not necessary for me to do more than add a few brief observations. First, on the question whether the case fell within the second category in *Rookes v Barnard*[1] Counsel for the landlord relied on the fact that Lord Devlin said[2]:

> 'Where a defendant with a cynical disregard for a plaintiff's rights has calculated that the money to be made out of his wrongdoing will probably exceed the damages at risk, it is necessary for the law to show that it cannot be broken with impunity.'

Counsel for the landlord had argued that this could not be a case for exemplary damages, because there was no calculation by the landlord of actual money which he hoped to make out of the conduct in which he was engaged. But Lord Devlin was very careful to see that his words should not be construed in that narrow sense because he went on at once to say in terms[3]:

> 'This category is not confined to moneymaking in the strict sense. It extends to cases in which the defendant is seeking to gain at the expense of the plaintiff some object,—perhaps some property which he covets,—which either he could not obtain at all or not obtain except at a price greater than he wants to put down.'

That is an exact description of what happened in this case. The landlord wanted the flat for his in-laws and he could not get it because he had a statutory tenant, so he took the law into his own hands and caused two or three men to break into the premises and remove the plaintiff's goods. I desire also to stress Lord Devlin's words at the end of that passage[3]: 'Exemplary damages can properly be awarded whenever it is necessary to teach a wrongdoer that tort does not pay', and I add as it is in this case.

---

1 [1964] 1 All ER 367 at 410, [1964] AC 1129 at 1226
2 [1964] 1 All ER 367 at 410, 411, [1964] AC 1129 at 1227
3 [1964] 1 All ER 367 at 411, [1964] AC 1129 at 1227

Clearly in any event it was a case in which the learned county court judge was entitled to award aggravated damages, and I would draw attention to a few words of Lord Devlin[1]:

'This conclusion will, I hope, remove from the law a source of confusion between aggravated and exemplary damages which has troubled the learned commentators on the subject. Otherwise, it will not, I think, make such difference to the substance of the law or rob the law of the strength which it ought to have. Aggravated damages in this type of case can do most, if not all, of the work that could be done by exemplary damages.'

The only other point on which I would like to make any observations is the question of quantum and how an appellate court should look at the matter. Both sides relied on a further passage[2] in Lord Devlin's speech, in which he said:

'Thus a case for exemplary damages must be presented quite differently from one for compensatory damages; and the judge should not allow it to be left to the jury unless he is satisfied that it can be brought within the categories which I have specified [as, of course, it was in this case]. But the fact that these two sorts of damage differ essentially does not necessarily mean that there should be two awards [those are important words]. In a case in which exemplary damages are appropriate, a jury should be directed that if, but only if, the sum which they have in mind to award as compensation (which may of course be a sum aggravated by the way in which the defendant has behaved to the plaintiff) is inadequate to punish him for his outrageous conduct, to mark their disapproval of such conduct and to deter him from repeating it, then it can award some larger sum. If a verdict given on such direction has to be reviewed on appeal, the appellate court will first consider whether the award can be justified as compensation, and, if it can, there is nothing further to be said. If it cannot, the court must consider whether or not the punishment is in all the circumstances, excessive.'

It is contended that the learned judge did not analyse the matter in the way in which it is there said a jury should be directed, but this is not a jury trial. It is a county court decision, and I think the crux of that passage for present purposes is where it is said[2]:

'. . . the appellate court will first consider whether the award can be justified as compensation, and, if it can, there is nothing further to be said. If it cannot, the court must consider whether or not the punishment is, in all the circumstances, excessive.'

For my part I would have thought that the award could be justified as compensation with the addition of aggravated damages; but, assuming in the landlord's favour that that is not so, I have not the slightest doubt that the aggregate included an element of punishment which was not in the circumstances excessive. The conduct of the landlord was completely outrageous and, in my judgment, the sum which the county court judge awarded was fully justified. I would dismiss the appeal.

Appeal dismissed.

Solicitors: *Griffinhoofe & Co* (for the landlord); *Pegden & Co* (for the tenant).

Gavin Gore-Andrews Esq   Barrister.

---

1   [1964] 1 All ER 367 at 412, [1964] AC 1129 at 1230
2   [1964] 1 All ER 367 at 411, [1964] AC 1129 at 1228

Batty and another v Metropolitan Property Realizations Ltd and others

COURT OF APPEAL, CIVIL DIVISION

MEGAW, BRIDGE AND WALLER LJJ

31st OCTOBER, 1st, 2nd, 7th, 8th NOVEMBER 1977

Contract – Construction – Warranty – Fitness of house for habitation – Warranty by property developers that house built in efficient and workmanlike manner and of proper materials and so as to be fit for habitation – Foundations of house and bricks and mortar properly constructed – House liable to collapse at any time owing to defective support from adjoining land – Defect discoverable before house built – Whether property developers liable for breach of warranty – Whether house built 'so as to be fit for habitation'.

Damages – Contract and tort – Power of court to enter judgment for damages for breach of contract and tort – Facts giving rise to breach of contract also constituting breach of common law duty of care – Sale of house by property developers – Warranty that house fit for habitation – House liable to collapse at any time due to defective support from adjoining land – Defect discovered after sale of house – Defect discoverable before house built – Purchasers suing property developers in contract and tort – Purchasers obtaining judgment in their favour for breach of contract – Whether court having power also to enter judgment for purchasers in tort.

Negligence – Duty to take care – Builder – Extent of duty – Duty to potential occupier of house which he builds – Defective support from adjoining land – Builder constructing house financed by development company on land owned by company – Builder and company inspecting site before decision to build taken – Foundations of house and bricks and mortar properly constructed – House sold by company to purchaser – House liable to collapse at any time owing to defective support from adjoining land – Defect discoverable before house built – Purchaser suing builder for negligence – Liability of builder.

Negligence – Damage – Nature of damage giving rise to cause of action – Negligence in construction of house – Present or imminent danger to health or safety of occupier – House built on top of hill – Garden on slope of hill – Foundations of house and bricks and mortar properly constructed by builder – House liable to collapse at any time owing to instability of hillside – Part of garden damaged in landslip – Danger to house having adverse mental and physical effect on occupier – Whether occupier having cause of action against builder for negligent construction of house.

In the late 1960s a local authority sold some land to a firm of builders who in turn sold it to a development company. The land consisted of a plateau and a steep slope which dropped down from it at a gradient of 1:3 to a stream. Representatives of the builders and the development company inspected it with a view to deciding, inter alia, whether it would be safe and suitable for housebuilding. Thereafter the development company and the builders agreed that the builders should construct a number of houses on the land and that the development company would finance the building of and find purchasers for them. In 1971, after the houses had been built, the development company granted to Mr and Mrs B a 999 year lease of one of the houses and the adjoining garden. The house and part of the garden were on the plateau. The rest of the garden was on the side of the steep slope. The contract between Mr and Mrs B and the development company contained a warranty by the development company that the house had been built 'in an efficient and workmanlike manner and of proper materials and so as to be fit for habitation'. After the lease had been granted the development company sold the reversion to the builders. In 1974 there was a severe slip of the natural strata of the hillside. It did not directly damage Mr and Mrs B's house or its foundations but it did cause direct damage to part of their garden. Mr and Mrs B brought an action against (1) the development company, (2) the builders, and (3) the local authority, claiming damages for actual and anticipated loss and damage to their house and garden and consequential loss and damage and personal injuries arising therefrom due to (i) the development company's negligence and breach of contract, (ii) the builders' negligence, and (iii) the local authority's negligence and/or breach of statutory duty in respect of its duties with regard to inspection of the foundations. The trial judge found that the foundations of the house and the bricks and mortar were properly constructed but that the house was doomed from the outset, and in consequence was unfit for habitation and unsaleable, because the land on which it relied for support was unstable due to the presence of a layer of varved clay in the boulder clay of the hillside; that the presence of the varved clay was the principal cause of the 1974 landslip; that at some time, not later than ten years from the date of the trial, and possibly much earlier, the movement on the hillside on the slope adjacent to the house would cause the house to collapse; and that the development company and the builders should have taken advice from surveyors or soil mechanics experts when they inspected the site and that if they had consulted such persons the instability of the hillside would have been detected then and the houses would almost certainly not have been built. Mr and Mrs B succeeded (1) against the development company on their claim in contract but not in tort, and (2) against the builders on their claim against them. They failed on their claim against the local authority. The judge awarded Mr and Mrs B jointly against both the development company and the builders £13,000 and he awarded Mrs B £250 damages for the effect of the foreseeable disaster on her health and peace of mind. He indicated that he would have entered judgment for Mr and Mrs B against the development company on their claim in negligence but that he was prevented from doing so because it was procedurally impossible for him to enter judgment in tort for a plaintiff who on the same facts had obtained judgment in contract. The development company and the builders appealed, and Mr and Mrs B cross-appealed asserting that, as against the development company, the judge ought to have entered judgment on their claim in tort as well as in contract. The development company contended (1) that the obligation imposed by the warranty 'and so as to be fit for habitation', although expressed as a separate warranty, was co-ordinate with the two warranties which preceded it in the clause and ought to be read as though it were expressed as 'and so as to be fit for habitation so far as compliance with the two preceding warranties can achieve that result', and (2) that the right of a plaintiff who sued in contract, where the facts giving rise to a breach of contract would also constitute a breach of common law duty apart from the contract, to have judgment entered under both heads was limited to cases where (i) the common law duty was owed by one who conducted a common calling and (ii) the duty was owed to a client by a professional man in respect of a professional skill. The builders contended, inter alia, (a) that a builder's duty of care to a potential occupier of a house which he built was limited, by reference to his statutory duty under the building regulations, to defects in, or observable on, the actual site on which the house was built, and he was not required to look for or to take any action in relation to any defects that might exist on neighbouring land which was not available to him in connection with his operations and was not otherwise owned by him or in his possession, (b) that if a builder's duty of care did extend to such land, it applied only to defects which were discoverable without subsoil investigation, (c) that their duty of care was no higher by reason of the particular relationship between them and the development company arising from their joint inspection of the land and the arrangements in regard to the building on it than that attaching to any other builder who built for a development company under a building contract, and (d) that no cause of action for breach of duty of care arose (i) in respect of damage to the house itself or, alternatively, (ii) until the house itself was damaged or was in such a state as to constitute a present or imminent danger to the health or safety of the occupier.

Held – (1) The development company's appeal would be dismissed because (i) on the true construction of the warranty it was broken if the house was unfit for habitation by reason of defective support from the adjoining land which a suitably qualified expert could have discovered before the building of the house was undertaken, and (ii) on the evidence the warranty had been broken in that way and its breach was the cause of the house becoming valueless and the cause of Mrs B's personal loss (see p 451 *d* to *g* and p 459 *e f*, post).

(2) Mr and Mrs B's cross-appeal would be allowed because the fact that they had obtained judgment against the development company for breach of contract did not preclude them from the entitlement which would have existed apart from contract to have judgment in tort entered in their favour; a plaintiff's right in such circumstances to have judgment entered on both heads was not limited to cases where a common law duty was owed by one who conducted a common calling or where the duty was owed to a client by a professional man in respect of his professional skill. It was the development company's common law duty to a prospective occupier to examine with reasonable care the site on which it was considering to build a house, and the land adjoining it, to see whether a house fit for habitation could safely be built there. The development company had been in breach of that duty. Accordingly judgment would be entered for Mr and Mrs B against the development company on their claim for damages for negligence as well as for breach of contract (see p 453 *b* to p 454 *a* and p 495 *e f*, post); *Esso Petroleum Co Ltd v Mardon* [1976] 2 All ER 5 applied; *Bagot v Stevens Scanlan & Co* [1964] 3 All ER 577 considered.

(3) The builders' appeal would be dismissed for the following reasons—

(i) They owed a duty to a potential occupier to act as a careful and competent builder would have acted in examining and investigating the land on which they proposed to build the house. The existence of the duty did not depend on whether defects affecting the land were on land which the builders owned or of which they had possession (see p 455 *d* to *f* and p 459 *e f*, post); *Donoghue v Stevenson* [1932] All ER Rep 1 applied; dictum of Lord Wilberforce in *Anns v London Borough of Merton* [1977] 2 All ER at 498, 499 considered.

(ii) In the circumstances the builders' duty extended to the land adjoining the house and included the duty of making a subsoil investigation (see p 455 *f* to *h* and p 459 *e f*, post).

(iii) The builders could not rely on the inspection of the land made by the development company's representative to absolve them from liability to Mr and Mrs B because the decision to build on the site had been a joint one, taken by both the development company and the builders (see p 456 *a* to *d* and p 459 *e f*, post).

(iv) On the facts Mr and Mrs B had a cause of action against the builders for breach of duty (a) because the landslip in 1974 had caused physical damage to part of Mr and Mrs B's property (ie the garden), and (b) in any event because the state of the house at the time the action was brought was such that it constituted an imminent danger to the health and safety of Mr and Mrs B (see p 457 *f* to p 458 *b* and p 459 *e f*, post); *Donoghue v Stevenson* [1932] All ER Rep 1 and dictum of Lord Wilberforce in *Anns v London Borough of Merton* [1977] 2 All ER at 504, 505 applied; dictum of Stamp LJ in *Dutton v Bognor Regis United Building Co Ltd* [1972] 1 All ER at 490 considered.

Notes

For the duty to take care and the standard of care, see 28 Halsbury's Laws (3rd Edn) 7-12, paras 4-9, and for cases on the subject, see 36(1) Digest (Reissue) 17-32, 39, 34-103, 115-123.

Cases referred to in judgments

Anns v London Borough of Merton [1977] 2 All ER 492, [1977] 2 WLR 1024, 75 LGR 555, HL.

Bagot v Stevens Scanlan & Co [1964] 3 All ER 577, [1966] 1 QB 197, [1964] 3 WLR 1162, [1964] 2 Lloyd's Rep 353, Digest (Cont Vol B) 68, 486Aa.

Donoghue v Stevenson [1932] AC 562, [1932] All ER Rep 1, 101 LJPC 119, 147 LT 281, 37 Com Cas 350, HL, 36(1) Digest (Reissue) 144, 562.

Dutton v Bognor Regis United Building Co Ltd [1972] 1 All ER 462, [1972] 1 QB 373, [1972] 2 WLR 299, 36 JP 201, [1972] 1 Lloyd's Rep 227, 70 LGR 57, CA, 36(1) Digest (Reissue) 30, 98.

Esso Petroleum Co Ltd v Mardon [1976] 2 All ER 5, [1976] QB 801, [1976] 2 WLR 583, [1976] 2 Lloyd's Rep 305, CA, 36(1) Digest (Reissue) 31, 99.

Hedley Byrne & Co Ltd v Heller & Partners Ltd [1963] 2 All ER 575, [1964] AC 465, [1963] 3 WLR 101, [1963] 1 Lloyd's Rep 485, HL, 36(1) Digest (Reissue) 24, 84.

Home Office v Dorset Yacht Co Ltd [1970] 2 All ER 294, [1970] AC 1004, [1970] 2 WLR 1140, [1970] 1 Lloyd's Rep 453, HL, 36(1) Digest (Reissue) 27, 93.

SCM (United Kingdom) Ltd v W J Whittall & Son Ltd [1970] 3 All ER 245, [1971] 1 QB 337, [1970] 3 WLR 694, CA, 36(1) Digest (Reissue) 28, 94.

Spartan Steel & Alloys Ltd v Martin & Co (Contractors) Ltd [1972] 3 All ER 557, [1973] QB 27, [1972] 3 WLR 502, CA, 17 Digest (Reissue) 149, 403.

Weller & Co v Foot and Mouth Disease Research Institute [1965] 3 All ER 560, [1966] 1 QB 569, [1965] 3 WLR 1082, [1965] 2 Lloyd's Rep 414, 36(1) Digest (Reissue) 45, 143.

Cases also cited

Gallagher v N McDowell Ltd [1961] NI 26.

Hancock v B W Brazier (Anerley) Ltd [1966] 2 All ER 901, [1966] 1 WLR 1317, CA.

Jackson v Mayfair Window Cleaning Co Ltd [1952] 1 All ER 215, CA.

Lister v Romford Ice & Cold Storage Co Ltd [1957] 1 All ER 125, [1957] AC 555, HL.

Rivtow Marine Ltd v Washington Iron Works [1973] 6 WWR 692, Can SC.

Sharpe v E T Sweeting & Son Ltd [1963] 2 All ER 455, [1963] 1 WLR 665.

Young and Marten Ltd v McManus Childs Ltd [1968] 2 All ER 1169, [1969] 1 AC 454, HL.

Appeal

By a writ issued on 18th July 1974 the plaintiffs, Raymond Batty and Helga Batty, brought an action against the first defendants, Metropolitan Property Realizations Ltd, the second defendants, Trippier Construction Ltd, and the third defendants, Rossendale District Council, claiming damages for the loss and damage actual and anticipated to the plaintiffs' dwelling-house, 33 Redwood Drive, Rawtenstall, Rossendale, Lancashire, and to the surrounding land, and consequential loss and damage and personal injuries arising therefrom due to (1) the first defendant' negligence, breach of contract, breach of statutory duty and /or breach of express and implied covenants contained in a lease dated 16th August 1971 and made between the plaintiffs and the first defendants, and/or (2) the second defendants' negligence and/or breach of statutory duty, and/or (3) the third defendants' negligence and/or breach of statutory duty. On 1st July 1976 Crichton J sitting at Manchester entered judgment for the plaintiffs (i) against the first defendants on their claim in contract, and (ii) against the second defendants on their claim against them. He awarded the plaintiffs jointly against both the first and the second defendants damages of £13,000 and he also awarded the second plaintiff, Mrs Batty, damages of £250. He dismissed the plaintiffs' claim against the third defendants. The first and second defendants appealed. The plaintiffs gave notice, under RSC Ord 59, r 6(2), that at the hearing of the appeal they would contend that the judge should have entered judgment for them against the first defendants on their claim in tort as well as in contract. The facts are set out in the judgment of Megaw LJ.

Douglas Brown QC and *Andrew Gilbart* for the first defendants.
J Martin Collins QC and *John Hoggett* for the second defendants.
B A Hytner QC and *Anthony Jolly* for the plaintiffs.

MEGAW LJ. In August 1971 the two plaintiffs, Mr Raymond Batty and his wife, Mrs Helga Batty, took from the first defendants, Metropolitan Property Realizations Ltd, on a 999 year lease, a house and garden. The house had just been built, being one of a number of houses on the same estate, at Rawtenstall, in the district of Rossendale, in North-East Lancashire. They paid £5,250 as consideration for what was in all respects other than a legal technicality a purchase by them of the house. The house became known as 33 Redwood Drive.

The house had been built by the second defendants, Trippier Construction Ltd, under arrangements made by them with the first defendants, who are a development company. The land on which the house was built, along with neighbouring land on which other houses were built at about the same time, was sold by the second defendants, who had earlier bought it from the local authority, the third defendants, the Rossendale District Council. It was sold by the second defendants to the first defendants. Under their contract with the first defendants, the second defendants proceeded to build this house and other houses. When this house had been completed and leased to the plaintiffs on a 999 year lease, the first defendants sold the reversion to the second defendants. Thus, in effect the building of the house and its disposition was a co-operative effort by the first defendants and the second defendants, the second defendants doing the building, the first defendants providing the finance and being the party with whom the purchasers of the house, the plaintiffs, entered into contractual relations. Both the first defendants and the second defendants, through their representatives, had inspected the site, and also had walked over the surrounding territory in 1969 and 1970, before the decision to build was taken and, therefore, before the building had started. The object of such inspection was to decide, by reference to various considerations, including the safety and suitability of the site for housebuilding, whether or not they or either of them would undertake, or become involved in, housebuilding in that area. They decided to build, on the basis, as between them, which I have just very summarily outlined.

The house was built on a sort of plateau, as it has been described, at the top of a steep slope which fell down at a gradient of about 1 : 3 to a stream, called the Balladen Brook, which ran in the bottom of the valley below the house. The front of 33 Redwood Drive faced on Redwood Drive, with a small front garden between the house and the road. At the back of 33 there was a piece of land, bought by the plaintiffs along with the house, which was intended to provide a garden at the back. It was somewhere down that garden that the relatively level area (it was only relatively level) which I have called 'the plateau' changed its inclination to the 1:3 slope which was the general inclination of the slope falling from there towards the stream. The total area covered by the house, 33 Redwood Drive, and the land sold with it was about 100 feet from front to back (from Redwood Drive to the bottom of the front garden) and about 40 feet from side to side in width.

Coloured photographs which we have seen give a reasonably clear impression of the general nature of the ground in and about the house and its neighbourhood. They show the steepness and roughness of the hillside on both sides of the valley. I shall not attempt to describe the topography further, as it is unnecessary to do so for the purposes of this appeal.

That was in 1971. The plaintiffs bought their house and moved into it and made it their home. In 1974 there was a severe slip of the natural strata of the hillside. It did not directly or immediately damage the plaintiffs' house or its foundations, although it did cause direct damage to a part of the back garden. As a result, urgent investigations were undertaken and legal proceedings were begun by the plaintiffs against three defendants, the two already mentioned and, as the third defendant, the Rossendale District Council, the local authority.

The gravity of that litigation, its seriousness for the parties, will become apparent when I recount that it was held by Crichton J, from whose judgment this appeal is brought, that the plaintiffs' house is doomed; and the finding on that issue, although it was the subject of much conflicting evidence at the trial, is not now disputed or challenged. At some time not later than ten years from the date of the trial, possibly much earlier, the movement of the strata on the hillside on the slopes adjacent to the plaintiffs' house will cause the foundations of that house to slide down the hill and the house will be in ruins. Already, of course, in those circumstances, the house is unsaleable.

The reason, or at least the principal reason, as found by the learned judge, for this very grave and disastrous prognosis is the presence in the boulder clay, which is the principal constituent of the hillside, of a layer of what is described technically as varved clay. I do not need to go into the technical or geological details. They are not relevant for the purposes of the decision of the appeal.

The plaintiffs' claim against the first defendants was in tort, for negligence, and for breach of contract. Against the second defendants the claim was in tort for negligence, on what I may call *Donoghue v Stevenson*[1] principles. Against the third defendants, the local authority, it was for negligence or breach of statutory duty, in respect of the local authority's duties with regard to inspection of the foundations. It was, however, held by the judge, and it does not appear to have been really in dispute, that the foundations as such were perfectly properly constructed, as were the bricks and mortar of the house itself. The only defect, but, in the circumstances, a very grave matter, was the nature of the land on which the house relied for its support. It was unstable, and by its instability the house was, from the outset, doomed. Thus, for that reason, and for that reason alone, the house was unfit for human habitation, because in a foreseeable, and short, time it would collapse, through the movement of the hillside.

The plaintiffs succeeded before the judge against the first defendants, although on their claim in contract only, and against the second defendants on the sole claim against them in tort. They failed against the third defendants. The judge awarded the plaintiffs, jointly against both the first and the second defendants, £13,000, and he also awarded Mrs Batty £250 for the consequences of her distress, the effect on her, physical and mental, of these events. Those sums were agreed by the parties as being the appropriate sums for damages, subject to liability.

The first and second defendants both appeal. There is a cross-notice on behalf of the plaintiffs, asserting that, as against the first defendants, the judge ought to have entered judgment on the claim in tort, as well as on the claim in contract. That would not have affected the amount to be awarded in the judgment, but it may be of practical importance to the plaintiffs nonetheless. There is no cross-appeal by the plaintiffs as regards the dismissal of their claim with costs against the third defendants.

Counsel for all the parties concerned have, if I may say so, presented their submissions in this court with admirable clarity and conciseness, both on the issues of fact and on the issues of law which they desire to raise. I shall seek to emulate their conciseness. In particular, I do not propose to set out or summarise in any detail the evidence on the various questions of fact which were in issue before us, for it appears to me that the conclusions of the learned judge on all those issues, as set out in his judgment, are not only supported by some evidence, but they are supported by evidence which fully justifies the judge's conclusions thereon. If anyone should wish to look in more detail at the evidence, they will find it summarised, with the judge's conclusions thereon, in his judgment.

The first ground of appeal argued by counsel for the first defendants is concerned with the terms of the contract of sale, or, rather, the contract relating to the 999 years' lease, between the first defendants and the plaintiffs. That contract was made in writing on 9th August 1971. It is contained in two related documents. The relevant term provides as follows, under the heading 'The Vendor's Obligations':

---

1   [1932] AC 562, [1932] All ER Rep 1

'3. The Vendor hereby warrants that the dwelling has been built or agrees that it will be built: (1) in an efficient and workmanlike manner and of proper materials and so as to be fit for habitation . . .'

That the house was not fit for habitation when the contract was made and when the plaintiffs took possession cannot, in my judgment, be disputed, on the, now unchallenged, facts which I have mentioned. How, then, do the first defendants seek to escape liability for breach of contract under this warranty? On behalf of the plaintiffs it was conceded that the warranty was not absolute; in this sense, that if there were, for example, some undetectable geological fault, at some distance away, which, after the house was built, caused an earth tremor, damaging or destroying the house, that would not be within the warranty. But if the instability of the hillside could have been detected by experts, but was not detected, and if as a result the house was, when handed over, unfit for habitation, that, say the plaintiffs, is a breach of warranty. For the first defendants it is said that the obligation imposed by the warranty 'and so as to be fit for habitation', although expressed as a separate warranty, co-ordinate with the two warranties which precede it in the clause, ought to be read as though it were expressed as 'and so as to be fit for habitation *so far as compliance with the two preceding warranties can achieve that result*'.

I am afraid that I cannot accept that construction. It is unnecessary, as I see it, in this appeal to seek to define whether, and, if so, to what extent, the warranty of fitness for habitation falls short of an absolute warranty. I am satisfied that on the facts of this case the warranty, on its true meaning, was broken. The warranty would be broken if the house is unfit for habitation, and is so unfit by reason of defective support from the adjoining land which a suitably qualified expert could have discovered before the building of the house was undertaken. The judge has found, and in my opinion unassailably found, that the lack of fitness for habitation, the instability of the hillside which spelled the not far distant doom of the house from the outset of its life, could have been discovered by expert examination.

I need do no more than refer to the evidence of Mr Townsend, the first defendants' development director, the only witness to be called on behalf of the first defendants. He, in cross-examination by counsel for the plaintiffs, very fairly and very frankly made admissions as to what he should have realised as a result of his visits to the site: the need for further investigation.

The judge was right to hold that the warranty was broken, and that the breach of the warranty was the cause of the house having become valueless, and the cause of Mrs Batty's personal loss.

For the first defendants it was further submitted, by reference to the evidence, that, while the judge held that on the facts known to them the first defendants should have conducted investigation into the stability of the hillside, the judge failed to give a clear answer to the question: what sort of investigation were the first defendants under a duty to carry out, having regard to whatever were the symptoms which they should have observed and which should have put them on warning? Counsel has, properly, taken us in particular to those passages in the evidence which deal with certain slips on the hillside which were regarded by some of the witnesses as being one of the factors which ought to have led to investigation. It was stressed by counsel for the first defendants that the judge ought, on the evidence, to have regarded these factually as having been at the relevant time what he called 'shallow slips', and that, being shallow slips, that meant that the investigation which ought to have been conducted, having regard to the symptoms, was not an investigation (to use the modern phrase, which may perhaps for once be appropriate here) in depth, in order to ascertain what the subsoil contained. In my judgment there is no fault that can properly be found in respect of the learned judge's conclusions on the evidence.

It was suggested that this court should look at the evidence and form its own conclusion. If this court were to agree with the judge on the evidence that some investigation was required, in accordance with the legal duty resting on the first defendants under their contract, then this court would have to go on to consider for itself what sort of investigation was required and what such investigation would have disclosed. The right conclusion, it was submitted, having regard to the evidence in relation to the possibly shallow slips and various other matters, would be that such investigation would not have disclosed anything relevant. To that argument there appears to me to be one simple answer, offered on behalf of the plaintiffs. That was that it was clear, on evidence accepted by the judge and which he was plainly entitled to accept, seeing and hearing the witnesses, that, if the defendants had through that investigation, any investigation, of the stability of the hillside failed to discover a cause of the symptoms which had led them to investigate they would not have allowed the building of the house to proceed. So any investigation, whatever it was and however short it properly went, would, on that basis, have resulted in the houses not being built. But no investigation was undertaken at all. I think that is right. But I am further satisfied, as was also submitted on behalf of the plaintiffs, that on the evidence the judge rightly held that the investigation which ought to have been undertaken would not, indeed, have produced merely a negative result of finding no cause for the symptoms, but would have shown, and shown clearly, that there was no safety margin from the point of view of the stability of the relevant ground; and, in the absence of a safety margin, no reasonable builder or developer would erect a building.

In this context I refer to two passages in the learned judge's judgment. The judge had already summarised the evidence as to what would have been seen on the ground by way of warning symptoms at the time when the building of the houses was being considered. His findings as to what those symptoms would be were, in my judgment, fully justified. The judge said:

'That is the state of the evidence. Where does it lead us to? I think it leads us in this direction, that these cracks [I pause there to say that the word 'cracks' there may not be entirely accurate, or comprehensive, because I have no doubt that the learned judge intended to include other symptoms which he had held to exist] on the other side of the valley and at the toe of the slope on "our" side should have put Mr Townsend and Mr Trippier on enquiry. If they had been put on enquiry—this is on the point of the cause of this situation—the probability would be that some instability would have been found whereby houses would not have been built. That I will deal with later. But at the moment I merely find that these cracks which existed, in my judgment, in 1970 and 1971 should have put the only people who investigated that valley on their enquiry.'

Then the learned judge said:

'The evidence—I will come to the question of duty—leads me to the belief that further steps should have been taken in the sense of consulting either surveyors or soil mechanics experts and also to the view that had those persons been consulted, having regard to the situation in that valley, it would be unlikely and improbable that houses would have been built in the position that the plaintiffs' house was built.'

Counsel for the first defendants in the course of his argument accepted that in order to succeed in his appeal, he had to upset that finding. I do not think that counsel's careful submissions on the evidence, with all respect to him, begin to show that that finding was wrong.

I turn to the plaintiffs' cross-notice affecting the first defendants. That is a cross-notice whereby it is asked that this court should include in the judgment against the first defendants judgment based on tort, the learned judge having refused to enter judgment for the plaintiffs other than on the basis of breach of contract.

Crichton J, as I understand his judgment, thought that he was bound so to hold on
a his reading of a passage in the judgment of Diplock LJ, sitting as a judge of first
instance, in *Bagot v Stevens Scanlan & Co Ltd*[1]. The learned judge, having cited that
case, went on to say: 'I have also had regard in that respect to the case of *Esso Petroleum Co Ltd v Mardon*[2]. But I do not find that this case detracts in any degree from
the finding of Diplock LJ, as he then was.'

I fear that I feel bound to disagree with the learned judge's view that *Esso Petroleum*
b *Co Ltd v Mardon*[4] does not affect the position. We in this court are bound by what
was said in *Esso Petroleum Co Ltd v Mardon*[2], insofar as what was said was ratio decidendi.
There can, I think, be no doubt, subject to one possible distinction which counsel
for the first defendants sought to persuade us in his reply to be a relevant distinction,
that the ratio decidendi of *Esso Petroleum Co Ltd v Mardon*[2] necessarily requires that
in a case such as the present we should hold that the mere fact that the plaintiffs have
c obtained judgment for breach of contract does not preclude them from the entitlement which would have existed, apart from contract, to have judgment entered in
their favour also in tort. I refer to the judgment of Lord Denning MR[3]. I do not
propose to read it. The sense of it appears to me to be entirely clear, and, incidentally,
to have included Lord Denning MR's view that *Bagot v Stevens Scanlan & Co*[1] had been
decided without Diplock LJ who decided it having had cited to him a number of
d relevant authorities.

The distinction to which I have referred which counsel for the first defendants
seeks to make is this: that the right of a plaintiff who sues in contract, where the
facts giving rise to the breach of contract would also constitute a breach of common
law duty apart from contract, to have the judgment entered on both heads, is limited
to cases where the common law duty is owed by one who conducts a common calling
e and thus is under a special type of legal liability, and to cases where the duty is
owed by a professional man in respect of his professional skill. Counsel for the first
defendants contends that, although there is no affirmative authority for limiting
the right in that way, it ought to be treated as being so limited because there is no
case in the English books, going back over many years, which shows that the right
has been allowed, or possibly even claimed, in cases other than the special types of
f cases to which he referred, and in particular the professional skill type of case. In
Esso Petroleum Co Ltd v Mardon[2] the right was held to arise in a case where the breach
of duty was a breach by an architect involving his professional skill. I see no reason,
in logic or on practical grounds, for putting any such limitation on the scope of the
right. It would, I think, be an undesirable development in the law if such an artificial distinction, for which no sound reason can be put forward, were to be held
g to exist. In my judgment the plaintiffs were entitled here to have judgment entered
in their favour on the basis of tortious liability as well as on the basis of breach of
contract, assuming that the plaintiffs had established a breach by the first defendants
of their common law duty of care owed to the plaintiffs. I have no doubt that it
was the duty of the first defendants, in the circumstances of this case, including the
fact of the joint responsibility which they undertook in arranging for the erection of
h this house on this site, apart altogether from the contractual warranty, to examine
with reasonable care the land, which in this case would include adjoining land, in
order to see whether the site was one on which a house fit for habitation could safely
be built. It was a duty owed to prospective buyers of the house. How wide or deep
the examination had to be, to comply with the duty, would depend on the facts of
the particular case, including the existence and nature of any symptoms which might
j give cause for suspecting the possibility of instability. It is clear from the facts found
by the judge that, if he had thought that a finding of tort was procedurally permissible,

---

1   [1964] 3 All ER 577, [1966] 1 QB 197
2   [1976] 2 All ER 5, [1976] QB 801
3   [1976] 2 All ER 5 at 14-16, [1976] QB 801 at 818-820

he would have held, on his assessment of the evidence, that the first defendants were in breach of that duty. Accordingly, I would accept the cross-notice and would *a* direct that judgment be entered for the plaintiffs against the first defendants for the tort of negligence as well as for the breach of contract.

I should add that counsel for the plaintiffs contended as an alternative ground, apart from what I may call the *Esso Petroleum Co Ltd v Mardon*[1] ground, that he should be entitled to such a judgment in this case because on the facts of this case it would be the proper view to treat the tort and the breach of contract as being truly independent *b* of one another. Counsel for the first defendants in his reply submitted that that would not be a proper basis. He suggested that if it were to be upheld it would startle bankers, and also that it would be a wrong concept of the time by reference to which the duty arises. In the circumstances, I do not propose to offer any view one way or the other on that dispute. It is unnecessary to do so, because of my view that apart from that alternative ground the plaintiffs are entitled to their judgment in *c* tort.

I now turn to the appeal by the second defendants, the builders. Counsel for the second defendants very helpfully and clearly put his argument in the form of six submissions. The first submission was this. A builder should not be taken to be under any duty of care in relation to defects in or observable only on land which is not available to him in connection with his operations and is neither owned by him *d* nor is in his possession.

Counsel for the second defendants, properly and as I think inevitably, conceded that, as he put it, 'in general terms a duty situation can arise between a builder and an occupier with whom the builder is not in privity of contract'. A duty of the *Donoghue v Stevenson*[2] type can arise, it is contended, in relation to realty. But counsel for the second defendants contends that the duty extends only to defects, to symptoms *e* of possible instability, for example, affecting properly built foundations, where those defects are in, or observable on, the actual site on which the house is to be built. If defects exist on neighbouring land which is not in his ownership or possession, or in respect of which he would require someone else's permission to go on it, there is no duty, it is said, to look for or to observe or to take any action in relation to such symptoms. *f*

For this submission, counsel for the second defendants relies on a passage in Lord Wilberforce's speech in *Anns v London Borough of Merton*[3]. The passage on which he relies in this context reads as follows[4]:

> 'Through the trilogy of cases in this House, *Donoghue v Stevenson*[2], *Hedley Byrne & Co Ltd v Heller & Partners Ltd*[5] and *Home Office v Dorset Yacht Co Ltd*[6], *g* the position has now been reached that in order to establish that a duty of care arises in a particular situation, it is not necessary to bring the facts of that situation within those of previous situations in which a duty of care has been held to exist. Rather the question has to be approached in two stages. First one has to ask whether, as between the alleged wrongdoer and the person who has suffered damage there is a sufficient relationship of proximity or neighbourhood such *h* that, in the reasonable contemplation of the former, carelessness on his part may be likely to cause damage to the latter, in which case a prima facie duty of care arises. Secondly, if the first question is answered affirmatively, it is necessary to consider whether there are any considerations which ought to negative, or to reduce or limit the scope of the duty or the class of person to whom it is

---

1 [1976] 2 All ER 5, [1976] QB 801
2 [1932] AC 562, [1932] All ER Rep 1
3 [1977] 2 All ER 492, [1977] 2 WLR 1024
4 [1977] 2 All ER 492 at 498, 499, [1977] 2 WLR 1024 at 1032
5 [1963] 2 All ER 575, [1964] AC 465
6 [1970] 2 All ER 294, [1970] AC 1004

owed or the damages to which a breach of it may give rise (see the *Dorset Yacht case*[1], per Lord Reid). Examples of this are *Hedley Byrne & Co Ltd v Heller & Partners Ltd*[2] where the class of potential plaintiffs was reduced to those shown to have relied on the correctness of statements made, and *Weller & Co v Foot and Mouth Disease Research Institute*[3] and (I cite these merely as illustrations, without discussion) cases about "economic loss" where, a duty having been held to exist, the nature of the recoverable damages was limited (see *SCM (United Kingdom) Ltd v W J Whittall & Son Ltd*[4], *Spartan Steel & Alloys Ltd v Martin & Co (Contractors) Ltd*[5]).'

Counsel for the second defendants contends that there is a consideration which ought to reduce the scope of the builder's *Donoghue v Stevenson*[6] duty to a potential occupier of the house which he builds. That is on the basis of Lord Wilberforce's 'Secondly': 'whether there are any considerations which ought to negative, or to reduce or limit the scope of the duty.' The scope, says counsel for the second defendants, ought to be limited by reference to the builder's statutory duty under the building regulations. If he builds foundations which comply in all respects with those regulations and any other statutory provisions, and the defects are outside the area of the foundations themselves, then the builder has no further duty.

With all respect to counsel for the second defendants' argument, I do not accept it. Of course, the question whether or not there has been a breach of the duty will depend on all relevant considerations going to the question: did the builder act as a competent and careful builder would have acted in what he did or did not do by way of examination and investigation? But I see no reason why, as a matter of law, or, by reference to any question of policy considerations, as a matter of the existence of the duty, it should depend on whether or not the symptoms, the observable defects, are on land of which the builder has ownership or in respect of which he has a legal right of entry without requiring some other person's permission. I would reject that first submission.

The second submission made by counsel for the second defendants was this. If a builder is under any such duty, it should be limited to defects which are discoverable without subsoil investigation. The way that he put his submission was: if there is a duty on the builder, it is not a very heavy one. It would not include subsoil investigation. If a builder knows that what he sees would endanger the stability of the house, it is difficult to say there is not a duty. Counsel for the second defendants, on being asked by a member of the court why should that not apply also if he ought to have known, submitted that that would put too high a burden on a builder, and that it is undesirable that the law should put such a duty on him. He accepted, as I understood it, that this submission of his must mean that he is submitting that a builder is under no duty to look at adjoining land; if, however, he does know, although he had no duty to look, of something on the adjoining land which indicates a danger without further investigation, he might be under a duty. I see no reason for limiting the duty as a matter of law in the manner in which it is suggested by that submission.

The third submission was that the second defendants were not under any higher duty than that attaching to any other builder who builds for a development company under a building contract. The argument as developed by counsel for the second defendants was that the second defendants here were under no higher obligation than if they had been retained as builders by contractors at arm's length. That is,

1   [1970] 2 All ER 294 at 297, 298, [1970] AC 1004 at 1027
2   [1963] 2 All ER 575, [1964] AC 465
3   [1965] 3 All ER 560, [1966] 1 QB 569
4   [1970] 3 All ER 245, [1971] 1 QB 337
5   [1972] 3 All ER 557, [1973] QB 27
6   [1932] AC 562, [1932] All ER Rep 1

their duty is no higher because of the particular circumstances here of the relationship between the developers and the builders and what happened between them in *a* relation to the inspection of the site before the building started and their arrangements in regard to the building and what was to happen in relation to it. It may well be that on certain facts a builder would be entitled to rely on an examination which he knew or reasonably supposed had been made by others on whose competence the builder could properly and reasonably rely. But in this case, on the evidence, the true view is that the decision to build on this site was a joint decision of the builders *b* and the developers, the second defendants and the first defendants. In my judgment, if one is a party to the decision to build on the particular site such as were shown in the evidence to exist in this case, the *Donoghue v Stevenson*[1] duty applies. Indeed, I have difficulty in seeing how, as was a part of counsel for the second defendants' argument at one stage, the fact that there was here an intervening contract, the contract for the 999 year lease between the first defendants and the *c* plaintiffs, can affect the question whether the second defendants are under a *Donoghue v Stevenson*[1] type of liability. For in *Donoghue v Stevenson*[1] itself the whole question of the manufacturer's liability was considered, and decided to exist, despite the existence of an intervening contract between the retailer and the purchaser of the goods.

I would reject the third submission, on the facts of this case. Again, in my view, *d* it is not a question of the existence of the duty. It is a question whether, in a particular case, on the facts of that case, it has been broken.

The fourth submission was this. If a builder is to be taken to be under any such duty, then no cause of action for breach of it arises (a) in respect of damage to the house itself or alternatively (b) until the house itself is damaged or is in such a state as to present present or imminent danger to the health or safety of the occupier. *e* This submission, essentially, as I see it, is founded on a question which was raised and the view which was expressed by Stamp LJ in *Dutton v Bognor Regis United Building Co Ltd*[2]:

'What causes the difficulty—and it is I think at this point that the court is asked to apply the law of negligence to a new situation—is that whereas the builder had, as I will assume, no duty to the plaintiff not carelessly to build a *f* house with a concealed defect, yet it is sought to impute a not dissimilar duty to the defendant council. At this point I repeat and emphasise the difference between the position of a local authority clothed with the authority of an Act of Parliament to perform the function of making sure that the foundations of a house are secure for the benefit of the subsequent owners of the house and a builder who is concerned to make a profit. So approaching the matter there is in *g* my judgment nothing illogical or anomalous in fixing the former with a duty to which the latter is not subject. The former by undertaking the task is in my judgment undertaking a responsibility at least as high as that which the defendant in the *Hedley Byrne* case[3] would in the opinion of the majority in the House of Lords have undertaken had he not excluded responsibility.'

h
I pause here to say that obviously this fourth proposition cannot be treated as entirely independent of the first of the propositions of counsel for the second defendant, with which I have already dealt.

The doubt which was raised by that passage in that judgment of Stamp LJ was, as I see it, put at rest by passages in the speech of Lord Wilberforce in *Anns v London Borough of Merton*[4]. Lord Wilberforce said[5]:

j

1   [1932] AC 562, [1932] All ER Rep 1
2   [1972] 1 All ER 462 at 490, [1972] 1 QB 373 at 415
3   [1963] 2 All ER 575, [1964] AC 465
4   [1977] 2 All ER 492, [1977] 2 WLR 1024
5   [1977] 2 All ER 492 at 504, [1977] 2 WLR 1024 at 1038

'*The position of the builder.* I agree with the majority in the Court of Appeal
in thinking that it would be unreasonable to impose liability in respect of defective foundations on the council, if the builder, whose primary fault it was, should
be immune from liability. So it is necessary to consider this point, although it
does not directly arise in the present appeal. If there was at one time a supposed
rule that the doctrine of *Donoghue v Stevenson*[1] did not apply to realty, there is no
doubt under modern authority that a builder of defective premises may be
liable in negligence to persons who thereby suffer injury . . .'

So far, Lord Wilberforce has agreed that it would be unreasonable to impose
liability for defective foundations on a council if the builder were immune. Then
Lord Wilberforce went on to say[2]:

'But leaving aside such cases as arise between contracting parties, when the
terms of the contract have to be considered . . . I am unable to understand why
this principle or proposition should prevent recovery in a suitable case by a
person, who has subsequently acquired the house, on the principle of *Donoghue
v Stevenson*[1]: the same rules should apply to all careless acts of a builder: whether
he happens also to own the land or not. I agree generally with the conclusions of
Lord Denning MR on this point (*Dutton's* case[3]). In the alternative, since it is
the duty of the builder (owner or not) to comply with the byelaws, I would be
of opinion that an action could be brought against him, in effect, for breach of
statutory duty by any person for whose benefit or protection the byelaw was
made. So I do not think that there is any basis here for arguing from a supposed
immunity of the builder to immunity of the council.'

The argument that the local authority should not be liable because it would be
unreasonable that it should be held liable when the builder was not held liable
was rejected, because Lord Wilberforce saw no reason why the builder should not
be held liable. True, he specifically referred to a case where there was a breach of
statutory duty, non-compliance with the building regulations, but that was the
particular question arising in that case. I see no logical or practical reason for so
confining it; nor, in my view, did Lord Wilberforce so intend.

As to the question of the nature of the damage which gives rise to the cause of
action, it seems to me that an answer given by counsel for the plaintiffs was a simple
and full answer. If it indeed is necessary that it should be shown that there has been
physical damage to the property before the action will lie against the builder, in the
present case there was physical damage to the property in the landslide, or landslip,
of 1974. True, the foundations of the house for the time being remained undisturbed.
True, the bricks and mortar of the house, as the judge has found, remained undamaged. But there was physical damage to the garden, a part of the property
conveyed. If physical damage be necessary in order to found the action, there was
physical damage. But, apart from what might be regarded as that possibly accidental
element here, there is, I think, a wider reason why the proposition of counsel for the
second defendants should not succeed on the facts of this case.

Again I refer to the speech of Lord Wilberforce in *Anns v London Borough of Merton*[4].
Lord Wilberforce was dealing with the question 'When does the cause of action arise?',
and he used this sentence: 'It can only arise when the state of the building is such that
there is present or imminent danger to the health or safety of persons occupying it.'
Was there not here imminent danger to the health or safety of persons occupying
this house at the time when the action was brought? Indeed, Mrs Batty, one of the

1 [1932] AC 562, [1932] All ER Rep 1
2 [1977] 2 All ER 492 at 504, 505, [1977] 2 WLR 1024 at 1038, 1039
3 [1972] 1 All ER 462 at 471, 472, [1972] 1 QB 373 at 392-394
4 [1977] 2 All ER 492 at 505, [1977] 2 WLR 1024 at 1039

plaintiffs, has been awarded damages for the consequences to her health and peace
of mind of the foreseen disaster. Why should this not be treated as being a case of
imminent danger to the safety and health of people occupying the house? No one
knows, or can say with certainty, not even the greatest expert, whether the foundations of the house will move and the house perhaps suddenly tumble tomorrow, or in
a year's time, or in three years' time, or in ten years' time. The law, in my judgment,
is not so foolish as to say that a cause of action against the builder does not arise in
those circumstances because there is no *imminent* danger. I would reject that
submission.

The fifth submission made by counsel for the second defendants is one that goes to
the facts. It is this: in any event the state of the terrain was not such as to render it
careless for the second defendants not to require further investigation prior to the
commencement of the building. Counsel for the second defendants has properly
taken us to passages in the evidence, in addition to the passages to which we had been
referred by counsel for the first defendants, going to the question of what would have
been seen on the site and the neighbourhood of the site at the relevant time before
building started, and of the evidence of what that ought to have conveyed to a reasonably careful builder observing those symptoms. Once again, I do not propose to go
into the evidence on those matters, helpful though counsel's references to it were.
I am quite satisfied that on the evidence the judge was right in his finding that the
symptoms were such that investigation was called for by a reasonably careful builder,
and that if the investigation which was called for by reason of those symptoms had
been made the house would not have been built.

The sixth and last of the submissions made by counsel for the second defendants is
this. The plaintiffs' house has not suffered damage and is not in such a state as to produce present or imminent danger to the plaintiffs' health or safety. Counsel made it
clear that he was not challenging the judge's finding that the house was likely to be
engulfed or the judge's finding that it is now valueless. This is really related to the
fourth submission, with which I have already dealt, and in that I have said all that I
think it is necessary to say and all that I am minded to say referring to this proposition.

I would therefore dismiss the appeals of the first and second defendants; and, by
reference to the plaintiffs' cross-notice, I would direct that judgment be entered for
the plaintiffs against the first defendants for liability in tort as well as for liability in
contract.

BRIDGE LJ. I fully agree; and I add only a very short postcript to the passage
in Megaw LJ's judgment dealing with the fourth submission of counsel for the second
defendants. Amongst the propositions enunciated by him in support of his argument
that the damage claimed by the plaintiffs in this case was of a nature irrecoverable
against the second defendants was the contention that a party liable for negligence
of the *Donoghue v Stevenson*[1] variety is liable only for damage consequential on having
put into circulation the dangerous article which foreseeably was likely to cause injury
and not for the loss of the value of that article itself. He relied in particular on a
passage from the judgment of Stamp LJ in *Dutton v Bognor Regis United Building Co
Ltd*[2], from which Megaw LJ has quoted, where the point was succintly put earlier in
the judgment[3]:

'It is pointed out that in the past a distinction has been drawn between constructing a dangerous article and constructing one which is defective or of inferior
quality. I may be liable to one who purchases in the market a bottle of ginger
beer which I have carelessly manufactured and which is dangerous and causes
injury to person or property; but it is not the law that I am liable to him for

1 [1932] AC 562, [1932] All ER Rep 1
2 [1972] 1 All ER 462 at 490, [1972] 1 QB 373 at 415
3 [1972] 1 All ER 462 at 489, [1972] 1 QB 373 at 414

a   the loss he suffers because what is found inside the bottle and for which he has paid money is not ginger beer but water.'

So it is argued here that whilst, if the defective house fell down and physically injured the plaintiffs, or indeed anyone else, that would impose a *Donoghue v Stevenson*[1] liability on the second defendants, the fact that the house itself has become valueless, and indeed incapable of repair at economic cost, is not a loss which the plaintiff can *b*   recover from the second defendants. This argument, to my mind, like the other arguments to which Megaw LJ has adverted, is really untenable, in the light of the speech of Lord Wilberforce in *Anns v London Borough of Merton*[2], with which, as I understand it, all the rest of their Lordships agreed. As Megaw LJ has pointed out, Lord Wilberforce[3] expressed his agreement with the view which had been indicated by the Court of Appeal that it would be unreasonable to impose liability on the local *c*   authority if the builder whose primary fault had caused the defect in the building was to be immune from liability. He was considering what damages were recoverable against the local authority. In the context of what he had said[3], in principle what he said must equally be applicable to the question of what damages are, in the *Donoghue v Stevenson*[1] situation, recoverable from the builder. Lord Wilberforce said[4] in terms:

d   'Subject always to adequate proof of causation, these damages may include damages for personal injury and damage to property. In my opinion they may also include damage to the dwelling-house itself . . .'

In my judgment that sets at rest the doubts raised by the judgment of Stamp LJ in *Dutton v Bognor Regis United Building Co Ltd*[5].

e   I agree, for all the reasons given by Megaw LJ, that the appeals should be dismissed, and the cross-notice allowed as he indicated.

WALLER LJ. I agree with both judgments which have been delivered, and do not desire to add anything to them.

f   *Appeals dismissed. Cross-notice allowed. Judgment to be entered for plaintiffs against first defendants for liability in tort as well as for liability in contract. First defendants awarded 50:50 contribution as against second defendants.*

Solicitors: *Tobin & Co* (for the first defendants); *Thicknesse & Hull*, agents for *Bannister, Preston & Ormerod*, Manchester (for the second defendants); *Gregory Rowcliffe & Co*, *g*   agents for *Whiteside & Lord*, Rawtenstall, Rossendale (for the plaintiffs).

Mary Rose Plummer   Barrister.

---

1   [1932] AC 562, [1932] All ER Rep 1
h   2   [1977] 2 All ER 492 at 498, 499, [1977] 2 WLR 1024 at 1032
3   [1977] 2 All ER 492 at 504, [1977] 2 WLR 1024 at 1038
4   [1977] 2 All ER 492 at 505, [1977] 2 WLR 1024 at 1039
5   [1972] 1 All ER 462 at 490, [1972] 1 QB 373 at 415

R v Atkinson (Leslie)

COURT OF APPEAL, CRIMINAL DIVISION
VISCOUNT DILHORNE, LORD SCARMAN AND CUSACK J
8th DECEMBER 1977

Criminal law – Trial – Plea – Plea-bargaining – Pre-trial review – Judge suggesting to counsel during pre-trial review that plea of guilty would result in non-custodial sentence – Judge emphasising that such plea to be made only if accused guilty – Accused pleading not guilty – Accused convicted and given custodial sentence – Whether judge's suggestion amounted to plea-bargaining – Whether sentence proper.

The appellant was charged with handling stolen goods. At a pre-trial review of the appellant's case in open court some two months before sentence was passed the trial judge suggested to counsel that a plea of guilty would result in a non-custodial sentence but that such a plea should be made only if the appellant was in fact guilty. Counsel conveyed the judge's views to the appellant. The appellant pleaded not guilty, the trial proceeded and he was convicted. The judge then sentenced him to an immediate term of imprisonment. On appeal against sentence,

Held – Although there was no general rule that there must never be any communication outside the trial, either openly or privately, between the judge and those representing the Crown and the defence, such a course was exceptional and should not be taken beyond the established limits. The appearance of justice was a part of the substance of justice and it was wrong if an accused person or the general public could derive the impression that it was possible to achieve a bargain with the court whereby the accused person would secure a more favourable sentence in return for a plea of guilty. Although the judge had no doubt had no intention of making a bargain with the appellant as to plea, it might well have appeared to the appellant that he was being offered relief from a sentence of immediate imprisonment if he should decide to plead guilty. Accordingly the appeal would be allowed and the sentence varied so as to enable the appellant to be released immediately (see p 462 *b c* and *g* and p 463 *b* to *d*, post).

Dictum of Lord Parker CJ in *R v Turner* [1970] 2 All ER at 285 applied.

Notes

For a defendant's free choice of plea, see 11 Halsbury's Laws (4th Edn) para 248.

Cases referred to in judgment

R v Cain [1976] Crim LR 464, CA.
R v Turner [1970] 2 All ER 281, [1970] 2 QB 321, [1970] 2 WLR 1093, 134 JP 529, 54 Cr App Rep 352, CA, 14(1) Digest (Reissue) 332, 2622.

Appeal

On 13th October 1977 in the Crown Court at Beverley before his Honour Judge Pickles, the appellant, Leslie Atkinson, was convicted of handling stolen goods, contrary to s 22(1) of the Theft Act 1968, and sentenced to six months' imprisonment. He appealed against sentence on the grounds, inter alia, that the trial judge had erred in imposing an immediate prison sentence after indicating in open court that he saw no reason for any sentence to involve immediate imprisonment and by considering the offence aggravated by the appellant's plea of not guilty so as to entitle him to pass an

immediate prison sentence when not otherwise appropriate. The facts are set out
a in the judgment of the court.

R A Stevenson for the appellant.

b **LORD SCARMAN** delivered the following judgment of the court: This appeal
against sentence reveals a disturbing situation which, it is the view of this court,
should be stopped from recurring.

The short facts are these. On 13th October 1977 at the Beverley Crown Court,
the appellant was convicted of an offence of handling stolen goods, namely a bicycle,
and was sentenced to six months' imprisonment. The facts of the offence do not
c matter for the purposes of the judgment of this court. Suffice it to say that it was
plainly an offence in respect of which there must always be room for doubt, before
one is acquainted with the full facts, whether the offender should be sent to prison.

On 22nd August 1977, some two months or less before sentence was passed, the
learned judged conducted what is called a pre-trial review. In the course of the
pre-trial review (we have been furnished with a transcript of what occurred) the
d learned judge asked counsel for the appellant whether the appellant was afraid that
he was going to be sent to prison. Counsel said that he had had no instructions on
that matter. The judge then said that he had seen his record and 'at the present time',
that is on 22nd August, he could see no reason why the appellant should have to go
to prison. He could see no reason why the offence should involve immediate
imprisonment. He then went on to say to counsel:
e

> 'Have a word with him. If he decides, on your advice—and on the strict under-
> standing that he only pleads guilty if he is guilty—if he decides to change his
> plea, for example, to the second count, we can dispose of it all today, and he
> would be out in the sunshine, but he must only plead guilty if he is guilty. Stand
> it down for the time being.'
f

That was a clear indication, which no doubt was faithfully conveyed to the appellant, that if he pleaded guilty there would be no question of his going to prison.
Although the learned judge no doubt had no intention of making a bargain with the
defence as to plea, it may well have appeared to the appellant that he was being
offered the relief from a sentence of immediate imprisonment if he should decide
g to plead guilty. He decided, however, to plead not guilty. There was a trial and he
was convicted.

When the trial judge came to pass sentence, he said to counsel for the appellant,
in the course of his mitigation:

> 'And I observe that I there indicated [the learned judge was referring to the
h > pre-trial review] that, on the basis of a plea of guilty, be it noted—which, of course,
> would have been the only possibility at that stage of dealing with it—that I
> hadn't in mind sending this man to prison. But he has not pleaded guilty, has
> he? And the position of a man who pleads guilty is one thing, because he can
> say, "Well, I am sorry. I am showing, by pleading guilty, I am not going to put
> the public to further expense." A man who is found guilty, having denied it,
j > is in a far different position, is he not?'

Then the trial judge proceeded to pass the sentence of six months and in his remarks
to the appellant, before passing sentence, he said:

> 'Well, now, if you had pleaded guilty, I would, of course, have borne that in

mind, because it would have shown to me that at least you regretted what you
had done, that you were sorry, that you were realising the error of what you had　*a*
done and promising to do better in future; but I am unable to reduce your sentence on that account, because you have not pleaded guilty. You have chosen,
which was your right, to contest the matter to the end.'

Of course the trial judge was not striking any bargain with the defence. He was
indicating the difference in sentence that a man can on occasions secure in his favour　*b*
by a plea of guilty. But in this sensitive area, the appearance of justice is part of the
substance of justice and it will not do if a prisoner or the general public derive the
impression that it is possible, either openly in a pre-trial review, as in this case, or
by private discussion between counsel and judge, to achieve a bargain with the
court.

Plea-bargaining has no place in the English criminal law. It is found in some　*c*
systems of law in which the prosecution are entitled to make submissions as to the
character or length of the sentence. In such systems of law it is possible for a bargain
to be driven between the defence and the prosecution, but never, so far as my researches have gone, with the court itself. In our law the prosecution is not heard on
sentence. This is a matter for the court, after considering whatever has to be said on
behalf of an accused man. Our law having no room for any bargain about sentence　*d*
between court and defendant, if events arise which give the appearance of such a
bargain, then one must be very careful to see that the appearance is corrected.

The appearance of plea-bargaining emerged in this case in the course of a pre-trial
review. It is a little surprising perhaps, if one does not know the full circumstances,
that a case as simple as this should require a pre-trial review which, one would expect,
would be directed towards identifying in a complex case the issues on which the　*e*
court would have to adjudge. Nevertheless it should not be thought that we are in
any way criticising the practice of pre-trial review in criminal cases. It is well known
that crown courts throughout the country have tremendous problems in the expedition of their cases and in organising their lists, and it may indeed be helpful, even in a
simple case such as this, for the court to know whether there is going to be a plea of　*f*
guilty or whether the matter will proceed to trial. But such useful devices as a pre-
trial review must not be used by the court to indicate to an accused man that he may
be treated one way if he pleads not guilty but in another way if he pleads guilty.

It is not possible to lay down, neither would we think is it desirable to lay down,
any general rule that there must never be any communication outside trial, either
openly or privately, between judge and those representing the Crown and the　*g*
accused. But we would emphasise that this exceptional course should never be taken
beyond the limits set in *R v Turner*[1]. Lord Parker CJ giving the judgment of the court
in that case set out a practice direction[2]. It is unnecessary to repeat its terms, since
they are well known.

There has been some doubt, we are aware, whether *R v Turner*[1] represents the
correct practice today. We say no more than that we have no doubt at all that it　*h*
does, and in particular we would draw attention to the very short practice direction[3]
which was issued after the publication of the decision in *R v Cain*[4]. The court in that
case might have appeared to have said some words in qualification of the practice
direction issued by Lord Parker CJ in *R v Turner*[2], but subsequent to the decision
a Practice Direction[3] was issued in these terms: 'The decision in *R v Cain*[4] has been

j

1　[1970] 2 All ER 281, [1970] 2 QB 321
2　[1970] 2 All ER 281 at 285, [1970] 2 QB 321 at 326, 327
3　[1976] 1 WLR 799
4　[1976] Crim LR 464

subject to further consideration by the Court of Appeal. In so far as it is inconsistent
a with *R v Turner*[1] the latter decision should prevail.'

The attention of this court has been drawn by the registrar to a case reported in
The Times newspaper of 7th December 1977, in which the Court of Appeal freed a
prisoner, in its own words, to 'save the good face of justice', there being a suggestion
in that case of plea-bargaining. One must get the problem into its correct perspective.
It is not for one moment suggested that a judge should not communicate with
b counsel. It is to be observed, greatly to his credit, that everything the judge did in
the present case he did in open court in full view of the public. But unfortunately
what he did could very well give the impression to this appellant, as well as to other
defendants, that there was a bargain: if you plead guilty, one result; if you plead not
guilty, another. Some, including the accused, might well think pressure was being
exerted on him to plead guilty. It is that which is so damaging to the face of justice; it
c is that which leads this court to reach the conclusion that this sentence of six months,
even if it be sustainable in other respects, must be quashed.

The question remains: what is the appropriate sentence? The appellant has been
in prison for a short time and, in the view of this court, justice will be served if there
be substituted for the sentence of six months such sentence as will enable him to be
released at once.

d

Appeal allowed. Sentence varied.

Solicitor: *Registrar of Criminal Appeals.*

e
                                         N P Metcalfe Esq Barrister.

---

1   [1970] 2 All ER 281, [1970] 2 QB 321

Practice Directions   a

PATENTS COURT

Patent – Patents Court – Appeal from Comptroller-General of Patents, Designs and Trade Marks – Constitution of court – Patents Act 1977, s 97(2).

                                                       b

Section 97(2) of the Patents Act 1977, which comes into operation on 1st June 1978, provides that for the hearing of appeals from the Comptroller-General of Patents, Designs and Trade Marks the Patents Court may consist of one or more judges in accordance with directions given by or on behalf of the Lord Chancellor.

For the hearing of such appeals the Patents Court will consist of a single judge unless, in any particular case, the senior judge of the court or, in his absence, another   c
nominated judge directs that it shall consist of two judges.

Given on behalf of the Lord Chancellor.

                                                      GRAHAM J
23rd May 1978   Senior Judge of the Patents Court.

                                                       d

PATENTS COURT

Patent – Patents Court – Appeal from Comptroller-General of Patents, Designs and Trade   e
Marks – Practice – Appeal to be brought by originating motion – Fees – Registrar of Patent Appeals – Proper officer – RSC Ord 104 (as inserted by RSC (No 3) 1978, r 12), r 14(1)(9)(17).

    1. Under RSC Ord 104[1], r 14(17), the Chief Master has nominated Mr D F James, at present the Registrar of the Patents Appeal Tribunal, to be the 'proper officer' of the Patents Court for the purposes of appeals from the Comptroller-General of   f
Patents, Designs and Trade Marks. He will be known as the Registrar of Patent Appeals. The registrars of the Chancery Division will continue to perform their present duties in infringement actions and other patent business.

    2. (a) Appeals from the comptroller must be brought by originating motion (RSC Ord 104, r 14(1)). The originating motion (in r 14 called 'notice of appeal') is issued by lodging copies with the Registrar of Patent Appeals (room 152). If the Registrar of   g
Patent Appeals and his deputy are not available, the copies may be lodged in the Chief Master's Secretariat (room 169). (b) Two copies of the originating motion (notice of appeal) will be required, one of which must be stamped with a £10 fee (fee 8) and the other of which will be sealed and returned to the appellant. (c) A respondent's notice under RSC Ord 104, r 14(9), asking that the decision of the comptroller be varied, must be stamped £5 (fee 36).   h

By the direction of the Vice-Chancellor and with the concurrence of the Senior Judge of the Patents Court.

                                                      R E BALL
18th May 1978   Chief Master.

                                                      j

  1 Inserted by the Rules of the Supreme Court (Amendment No 3) 1978, SI 1978 No 579, r 12

a
Dixon and another v British Broadcasting Corporation
Throsby v Imperial College of Science and Technology
b
Gwent County Council v Lane

EMPLOYMENT APPEAL TRIBUNAL
PHILLIPS J, MR J JACK AND MR J G C MILLIGAN
19th MAY, 7th, 8th, 26th JULY 1977

c

Unfair dismissal – Dismissal – Expiry of contract for fixed term without renewal of term – Contract for a fixed term – Contract liable to be determined by notice – Contract for a term which is to expire on a fixed date subject to earlier determination on either party giving notice – Whether a 'contract . . . for a fixed term' – Trade Union and Labour Relations Act 1974, Sch 1, para 5(2)(b).

d

A contract of employment for a period which is to expire at a date fixed by the contract is a 'contract . . . for a fixed term', within para 5(2)(b)ᵃ of Sch 1 to the Trade Union and Labour Relations Act 1974, even though the contract is one which makes provision for determination at an earlier date on either party giving notice. Accordingly, where a person is employed under such a contract and the term expires
e
without being renewed under the same contract, he is, by virtue of para 5(2)(b), to be treated, for the purposes of the 1974 Act, as having been dismissed by his employer (see p 470 e to j and p 471 b, post).

British Broadcasting Corpn v Ioannou [1975] 2 All ER 999 distinguished.

It is possible for a person to have two quite separate contracts of employment with the same employer and for one to be terminated and the other not (see p 471 h and j,
f
post).

Notes

For the circumstances in which a person employed under a fixed term contract is to be treated as having been dismissed, see 16 Halsbury's Laws (4th Edn) para 616.

For the Trade Union and Labour Relations Act 1974, Sch 1, para 5, see 44 Halsbury's
g
Statutes (3rd Edn) 1788.

Cases referred to in judgment

British Broadcasting Corpn v Ioannou [1975] 2 All ER 999, [1975] QB 781, [1975] 3 WLR 63, [1975] ICR 267, CA, Digest (Cont Vol D) 282a.

Goodrich v Paisner [1956] 2 All ER 176, [1957] AC 65, [1956] 2 WLR 1053, HL, 31(2)
h
Digest (Reissue) 1010, 8034.

London Transport Executive v Betts (Valuation Officer) [1958] 2 All ER 636, [1959] AC 213, [1958] 3 WLR 239, 122 JP 380, 56 LGR 371, 51 R & IT 49, HL.

Magor and St Mellon's Rural District Council v Newport Corpn [1951] 2 All ER 839, [1952] AC 189, 115 JP 613, 50 LGR 133, HL, 44 Digest (Repl) 267, 932.

Martin v Lowry [1926] 1 KB 550, CA; *affd* [1927] AC 312, 96 LJKB 379, 136 LT 580,
j
11 Tax Cas 297, HL, 28(1) Digest (Reissue) 26, 97.

102 Social Club and Institute Ltd v Bickerton [1977] ICR 911, EAT.

Terry v East Sussex County Council [1977] 1 All ER 567, [1976] ICR 536, 75 LGR 111, EAT.

Vokes Ltd v Bear [1974] ICR 1, NICR.

---

a   Paragraph 5, so far as material, is set out at p 467 c and d, post

Cases also cited
Inland Revenue Comrs v Hinchy [1960] 1 All ER 505, [1960] AC 748, HL.   *a*
Jones v Secretary of State for Social Services, Hudson v Secretary of State for Social Services
[1972] 1 All ER 145, [1972] AC 944, HL.
Taylor v Minister of Defence [1977] IRLR 214.
Winder v Cambridgeshire County Council [1977] The Times, 24th May.

Appeals   *b*
Leonard David Dixon and B Constanti appealed against the decision of an industrial
tribunal (chairman G H L Rhodes Esq) sitting at Manchester on 29th October 1976
rejecting their complaints of unfair dismissal against the British Broadcasting Corporation ('the BBC').

Peter W Throsby appealed against the decision of an industrial tribunal (chairman
Sir John Clayden) sitting in London on 21st January 1977 rejecting his complaints of   *c*
unfair dismissal against Imperial College of Science and Technology ('Imperial
College').

Gwent County Council appealed against the decision of an industrial tribunal
(chairman David Powell Esq) sitting at Cardiff on 9th December 1976 granting an
application by Lyndon Paul Lane for compensation for unfair dismissal.

The facts are set out in the judgment of the appeal tribunal which delivered a single   *d*
judgment in respect of all the appeals.

J Hand for Mr Dixon and Mr Constanti.
T R A Morrison for the BBC.
Mr L J Sapper for Mr Throsby.
Alexander Irvine for Imperial College.   *e*
Richard A Jones for Gwent County Council.
Mr Lane appeared in person.

Cur adv vult

26th July. **PHILLIPS J** read the following judgment of the appeal tribunal: In 1975   *f*
the Court of Appeal in *British Broadcasting Corpn v Ioannou*[1] decided that a 'fixed term'
in the expression 'contract for a fixed term of two years or more' in s 30 of the Industrial Relations Act 1971 and s 15 of the Redundancy Payments Act 1965—

'is one which cannot be unfixed by notice. To be a "fixed term", the parties
must be bound for the term stated in the agreement; and unable to determine   *g*
it by notice on either side. If it were only determinable for misconduct, it would,
I think, be a "fixed term"—because that is imported by the common law anyway.
But determination by notice is destructive of any "fixed term".'

The other judgments are to the same effect. There is no doubt that this statement
formed one of the grounds of the decision in the case and is binding on us.

Section 30 (which has been repealed and replaced by para 12 of Sch 1 to the Trade   *h*
Union and Labour Relations Act 1974) as re-enacted provides as follows:

'Paragraph 4 above does not apply—(*a*) to dismissal from employment under a
contract for a fixed term of two years or more, where the contract was made
before 28th February 1972 and is not a contract of apprenticeship, and the dismissal consists only of the expiry of that term without its being renewed, or (*b*)   *j*
to dismissal from employment under a contract for a fixed term of two years
or more, where the dismissal consists only of the expiry of that term without
its being renewed, if before the term so expires the employee has agreed in

---

1   [1975] 2 All ER 999 at 1005, [1975] QB 781 at 786, per Lord Denning MR

a   writing to exclude any claim in respect of rights under that paragraph in relation
     to that contract.'

     The decision in *British Broadcasting Corpn v Ioannou*[1] has been used as a means by
     which to circumvent the provisions relating to redundancy payments (Redundancy
     Payments Act 1965) and unfair dismissal (Trade Union and Labour Relations Act 1974,
     replacing the Industiral Relations Act 1971). These appeals concern claims by em-
b   ployees for compensation for unfair dismissal. Before such a claim can succeed an
     employee must establish that he has been dismissed. Since it is possible for employ-
     ment to come to an end without there being dismissal, it is necessary to define 'dis-
     missal' for the purpose of such claims, and the current definition is contained in
     para 5 of Sch 1 to the Trade Union and Labour Relations Act 1974. Paragraph 5
     provides in part as follows:

c   '(1) In this Schedule "dismissal" and "dismiss" shall be construed in accord-
         ance with the following provisions of this paragraph.
         '(2) Subject to sub-paragraph (3) below, an employee shall be treated for the
         purposes of this Act as dismissed by his employer, if, but only if,—(a) the contract
         under which he is employed by the employer is terminated by the employer,
         whether it is so terminated by notice or without notice, or (b) where under that
d   contract he is employed for a fixed term, that term expires without being re-
         newed under the same contract, or (c) the employee terminates that contract,
         with or without notice, in circumstances such that he is entitled to terminate it
         without notice by reason of the employer's conduct . . .'

     To all intents and purposes it may be said that the definition is the same as that
e   for the purposes of the Redundancy Payments Act 1965, s 3, and nothing in these
     appeals turns on its legislative history, which might be relevant for the construction
     of para 5(2)(c) of Sch 1. If 'fixed term' in para 5(2)(b) is given the same meaning
     as that given by the Court of Appeal in *British Broadcasting Corpn v Ioannou*[1] to the
     same expression in para 12, it is impossible for an employee employed under a
     contract of employment expiring at a fixed date, which was subject to prior
f   determination if notice had been given, to establish that he was dismissed.
     After the decision in that case it was quickly and widely seen that here was a way
     to avoid the provisions of the Act. Many employers have taken advantage of this.
     Some have drafted their contracts of employment specifically for that purpose;
     others have taken advantage of the fact that the contract of employment happened to
     be in that form. Most industrial tribunals have found in the employers' favour on
g   this point. Many further cases are pending before industrial tribunals, and there are
     many appeals pending to the appeal tribunal. Before the hearing of the first of these
     appeals it was decided that judgment would be postponed until the argument on
     the last of the three had been completed, and that then a single judgment would be
     given. Between them, these appeals seem to illustrate the problem in a representative
     way. There are certain specific additional points peculiar to one or more appeals,
h   and these we shall deal with separately, and later, in this judgment.
     Mr Dixon and Mr Constanti were employed as 'house services attendants' being
     principally engaged on duties of a portering nature. Mr Throsby was employed as a
     lecturer and was also the warden of a hall of residence. Mr Lane was a lecturer at a
     college of further education. What they all have in common is that, although they
     were all employed under contracts which expired on a particular day (and which
j   were therefore 'fixed' in that sense), in each case the contract provided that the con-
     tract of employment might be terminated before the date of expiry by an appro-
     priate notice. For present purposes it is not necessary to say more about the facts.
     There is no doubt that in each case the contract, following the decision of the Court of

---

1   [1975] 2 All ER 999, [1975] QB 781

Appeal, was not a contract for 'a fixed term' within para 12 of Sch 1. The question
which arises in those appeals is whether in those circumstances they were dismissed   *a*
within para 5(2)(*b*), when their contracts of employment were not renewed, no notice
having been given, and the date of expiry having been reached.

At the end of the argument on the hearing of these appeals we are satisfied that the
contention advanced on behalf of the employers, if sustained, would have disastrous
consequences. It would lead to the result that the provisions relating to unfair
dismissal could be evaded in any case where an employer could persuade an employee   *b*
to sign a contract of employment under a contract for an 'apparent fixed term',
the expression used during the argument to describe a contract for a term subject
to a provision permitting prior determination. Nor can we see that there is any need
for such an arrangement in any case. Even in the case of such employers as schools,
universities, and so on, who habitually employ teachers and lecturers on a temporary
basis there is no need for it, since the employer will in any event be protected if he   *c*
can show that there was a genuine need for a short-term contract of employment
and that it is reasonable not to re-employ the employee: see *Terry v East Sussex
County Council*[1]. The same principle applies to the employment by bodies such as
the BBC of lecturers, broadcasters and others on short-term engagements. Beyond
doubt there is no need for such an arrangement in the case of 'house services at-
tendants' such as Mr Dixon or Mr Constanti. Probably in such cases it is convenient   *d*
for the employers to be able to have an unfettered say whether they renew the
employment of temporary employees; but that is not the intention of the 1974
Act which is that in all cases except those where there is an express exclusion (as
there is in Sch 1, para 12) the matter, in case of dispute, should be left to the ruling
of the industrial tribunal. Equally, we reject the somewhat faint suggestion advanced on behalf of the BBC that because the contracts of employment of Mr Dixon   *e*
and Mr Constanti were for an apparent fixed term the matter was outside the control of the BBC, who were obliged to take the point that they had not been dismissed inasmuch as it went to jurisdiction. The answer is that there was nothing
in the world to prevent them, had they so wished, from giving the notice under
the contract instead of merely allowing it to expire without being renewed.   Not
only would the results be disastrous, but we are satisfied that they were not in-   *f*
tended. It is sometimes said that it is only possible to know what is intended by an
Act of Parliament by reading the words of the Act and that what is intended is what
the words say. In an ordinary case, no doubt this is true; but in the instant case it
can be asserted without any doubt whatever that this result is wholly unintended, and,
as will appear later, specifically inconsistent with other provisions of the Act. Finally,
we are satisfied that if it is permissible to construe para 5(2)(*b*) in a way which   *g*
will avoid these consequences there will be no corresponding disadvantage to the
obvious advantage to be obtained from so doing.

However, the contention of the employers' as advanced by their counsel is simple
and powerful. *British Broadcasting Corpn v Ioannou*[2], they say, is binding on us, and
is an authoritative ruling as to the meaning of the expression 'fixed term'.   In
accordance with ordinary principles of statutory construction that expression must   *h*
have the same meaning wherever used, particularly when used in the same Act and,
indeed, used in para 5(2)(*b*) which is specifically linked with para 12. If the results
of this are surprising (and they concede that they are) then the remedy lies with the
legislature and not with the courts; and we have been reminded with varying degrees
of delicacy of the dangers and impropriety of exceeding our powers. By way of
example we have been reminded of the words of Lord Denning in *London Transport*   *j*
Executive v Betts[3]:

---

1   [1977] 1 All ER 567
2   [1975] 2 All ER 999, [1975] QB 781
3   [1958] 2 All ER 636 at 655, [1959] AC 213 at 247

'But when it is pointed out that, if that meaning is adopted, it will lead to an absurdity in the statute—that it leaves a gap which Parliament cannot have intended—then it is said you must fill in the gap by writing into the statute words which are not there and by altering other words. At that point in the argument you come face to face, not with a particular precedent on this Act, but with a fundamental principle on all Acts, which is this—the judges have no right to fill in gaps which they suppose to exist in an Act of Parliament, but must leave it to Parliament itself to do so: see *Magor & St. Mellons Rural District Council v. Newport Corpn.*[1] No court is entitled to substitute its words for the words of the Act: see *Goodrich v. Paisner*[2].'

This is the difficulty at the heart of the matter, and we have given it serious and careful consideration.

It seems to us that it is an over-simple approach to say that 'fixed term' had been given a specific meaning by the Court of Appeal, that 'fixed term' is used in para 5(2)(b) and that if that paragraph is construed on that basis the result for which the employers contend must follow. The context and the purpose of the provisions are of vital importance in reaching a proper conclusion. The rule that particular words used in one enactment, or one part of one enactment, have the same meaning is not of universal application. In *Martin v Lowry*[3] Atkin LJ said:

'If one could adopt as a rigid canon of construction an assumption that in any statute the same word is always used with the same meaning, one's task would perhaps be easier: but it is plain that the assumption is ill-founded: and particularly so in regard to the Income Tax Acts. We must have regard to the context. When the history of the Income Tax Acts is looked at, the meaning of the words in question becomes plain.'

In this connection it is important to note that para 5(2)(b), unlike para 12, is concerned with the moment of cessation of employment and with the determination of the question whether that cessation has occurred as the result of dismissal. The enquiry therefore is necessarily directed to the last moment of the life of the contract of employment. Paragraph 12, on the other hand, although it excludes from para 4 certain acts of dismissal, is not specifically aimed at the moment of dismissal, but is concerned with the nature of the contract of employment in question. It seems to us that it is here that there is to be found the key to the solution of the problem.

Before saying more of this, it is necessary to notice one or two other factors which suggest that the result contended for by the employers is not one properly to be derived from the decision of the Court of Appeal in *British Broadcasting Corpn v Ioannou*[4]. At the end of the hearing in that case the matter was remitted to the industrial tribunal for the case to be determined on the merits. This could only be done on the basis that Mr Ioannou had been dismissed, for if he had not been he could not have claimed to have been unfairly dismissed. On the remission the industrial tribunal in its final decision on 11th August 1975 (para 10) specifically found: 'This was a non-renewal of a contract, which amounts to a dismissal under s 23(2)(b) of the Industrial Relations Act and s 3(1)(b) of the Redundancy Payments Act.' This was plainly the result contemplated and intended by the Court of Appeal, and, whatever may be said about whether the employers' contention in the present appeals is in accordance with the reasoning of the Court of Appeal, it is certainly contrary to the actual decision; furthermore, it is contrary to the underlying philosophy of the judgments of the Court of Appeal. Paragraph 12 is concerned with the exclusion of certain contracts for a fixed term from the provisions of para 4, which confer on employees the

1 [1951] 2 All ER 839, [1952] AC 189
2 [1956] 2 All ER 176, [1957] AC 65
3 [1926] 1 KB 550 at 561
4 [1975] 2 All ER 999, [1975] QB 781

right not to be unfairly dismissed. The Court of Appeal were concerned with the question whether the exclusion applied to an apparent fixed term or was limited to a true fixed term, the assumption being that if para 12 did not apply to an apparent fixed term the employee would enjoy under para 4 the right not to be unfairly dismissed. Yet the reasoning of the Court of Appeal leading to the conclusion that para 12 only applies to a true fixed term is being used in the present appeals by the employers to support the contention that an employee under a contract of employment for an apparent fixed term does not have the right not to be unfairly dismissed. Thus, if the contention of the employers is correct, the Court of Appeal will have been instrumental in producing a result inconsistent not only with the intended decision but also with the reasoning of the decision.

It was stated earlier that the results, if the contention of the employers were correct, would be to produce inconsistency between one part of the Act and another. Paragraph 4 confers in general terms the right of an employee in employment to which para 4 applies not to be unfairly dismissed. There follow various exclusions: excluded classes of employment (para 9); exclusion of certain contracts for a fixed term (para 12); exclusion in respect of dismissal procedures agreement (para 13). The contention of the employers would lead to the conclusion in practice that there would be a large additional class of exclusions, that is to say, the cases of the non-renewal of apparent fixed term contracts of employment. It seems very improbable that it could have been intended to bring this about by the way in which the definition of dismissal contained in para 5 operates in particular cases. It is true that there may be a cessation of employment without there being a dismissal, and that the definition of dismissal in para 5, as is stressed on behalf of the employers, is exhaustive and leaves no room for the application of general principles. But had it been intended to exclude from the Act the case of employees employed under apparent fixed term contracts, when the contracts were not renewed, no doubt it would have been expressly so provided by provisions similar to the later exclusion provisions, such as para 13, and not by the capricious operation of para 5(2)(*b*).

As indicated earlier in this judgment, it seems to us that the answer to the problem lies in realising that paras 12 and 5(2)(*b*) are dealing with different problems, and that in applying para 5(2)(*b*) it is essential to remember that one is considering the situation as it is at the moment the contract of employment comes to an end by non-renewal. For that moment to have arrived it must follow that the power to terminate the contract by notice has not been exercised. From the last moment when it ceased to be possible to exercise the power of termination it follows that the contract of employment must (subject to exceptional cases such as death or frustration etc, which are irrelevant for present purposes) continue until it expires by effluxion of time. If one enquires at that time why the contract of employment has ceased, the answer will be, and can only be, that it has ceased because the term was not determined earlier by notice and has come to an end. In these circumstances it seems right to say, in terms of para 5(2)(*b*), that what has expired without being renewed is a fixed term, considered, that is, at the moment of expiry, and bearing in mind the purpose of the provision. This is the reasoning adopted by the industrial tribunal in *Gwent County Council v Lane* and we are much indebted to Mr Powell, the chairman, for pointing the way to the solution of the problem. We think that that is the correct answer, which we prefer to those given by the other industrial tribunals which have upheld the contention of the employers.

We recognise that it cannot be said that all the language in the relevant provisions is entirely consistent. For example, counsel for Imperial College points out that the word 'that' in para 5(2)(*b*) refers back to para 5(2)(*a*) which requires one to look at the contract under which the employee is employed by the employer, and that it could be said that at an earlier point in time, in accordance with the decision of the Court of Appeal, the contract under which he is employed is for a fixed term as interpreted in that case. We see the force of this, but we do not regard it as conclusive against the view which we have preferred. That view, based as it is on assessing the situation at the moment of the cessation of the employment, makes it irrelevant to consider the earlier stages of the contract of employment, which cease to be important once the last moment for serving notice of prior determination has passed.

It follows that we are satisfied, and so hold, that where a contract of employment for an apparent fixed term is not renewed the employee is entitled to say that he has been dismissed, and so to put forward a claim (to be heard on the merits) for compensation for unfair dismissal. We turn now to the individual appeals.

Dixon v British Broadcasting Corpn, Constanti v British Broadcasting Corpn

There are no complications in these cases, and accordingly the order is that the appeals be allowed, and the cases be remitted to be heard by such industrial tribunal as the regional chairman may determine.

Throsby v Imperial College of Science and Technology

As already explained, Mr Throsby was a lecturer and also held the appointment as warden of a hall of residence. That appointment was not, and is not, due to expire until 30th September 1977. He has been informed by Imperial College that it is not intended to renew that appointment on its expiry. It is in respect of that prospective alleged termination of employment that he seeks compensation, but it seems to us that his application is premature. It is well settled that generally speaking an application cannot be made before the effective date of termination of the contract of employment, which cannot be before 30th September 1977. A recent amendment in the legislation (Employment Protection Act 1975, Sch 16, Part III, para 21) has gone some way to overcoming this difficulty. However, it does not seem to us to apply in the present case since the case must be one where the dismissal is with notice, para 21(4A) of Sch 1, as added by the amendment. Accordingly, if Mr Throsby is employed as warden under a separate contract of employment, and that contract is not renewed on its expiry on 30th September 1977, he will then be able to claim that he has been dismissed as a result of its non-renewal, within para 5(2)(*b*), and he will be able to commence proceedings. Although Mr Throsby has succeeded on the principal point in the appeal, inasmuch as these proceedings cannot continue for the reason stated above, it appears, subject to any further argument, that the proper order is that the appeal be dismissed. This, of course, is without prejudice to any later proceedings he may bring.

There is involved in Mr Throsby's appeal, and in the cross-appeal by Imperial College, a wholly separate point, which no doubt will be raised if and when further proceedings are commenced. Furthermore, Mr Sapper on behalf of Mr Throsby sought to raise on the appeal a new point, not taken before the industrial tribunal or in the notice of appeal, and in the event of further proceedings that too will be open. We do not propose to say much about these matters, but there is one topic on which we have heard argument and reached a view which it may be useful to express as it may be of some assistance in any further proceedings.

The industrial tribunal came to the conclusion that a person cannot be an employee of his employer in two ways simultaneously, so that if he were to be dismissed in one his relationship could continue in another. This was relevant because Mr Throsby was a lecturer, and also the warden of a hall of residence. It seems to us that this statement by the industrial tribunal is much too wide, and we see no reason in principle why a man should not have two quite separate contracts of employment with the same employer, or why it is not possible to terminate one only. However, counsel for Imperial College has put the matter somewhat more cautiously and submits that even if it is possible, as we have held, for a man to be employed by an employer under two contracts of employment, on all the facts of the present case there was here only one contract of employment, and that inasmuch as Mr Throsby's contract as a lecturer has not been terminated he cannot complain of unfair dismissal in respect of his contract as warden, because they are all part and parcel of the same contract. The position, says counsel, is similar to that where an employee is given additional duties to undertake. He relies in particular on the fact that it is a condition of being appointed warden that the appointee shall also be a lecturer. Mr Sapper replies that that does not necessarily make one contract, but that the existence of the contract as lecturer is merely a qualification for the separate appointment as a warden. We do not find that there is sufficient material before us on which we could answer this question, though there are some indications that the appointment as warden was in some senses separate. We do not mean, however, to express any view, as a great deal more evidence would be necessary before the question could be decided. All we are definitely deciding is that there is no reason in principle why there should not be in such cases two separate contracts of employment. It may be that in the event of further proceedings by Mr Throsby on this question, attention will have to be given to the question whether his service as warden, for which he received an honorarium, was as employee or office holder: see 102 Social Club v Bickerton[1].

Gwent County Council v Lane

Here we agree with the industrial tribunal that Mr Lane was dismissed within para 5(2)(b). The industrial tribunal found that the reason for the dismissal was redundancy. This was very faintly challenged on appeal, but there was evidence to support this finding, and it is not open to review on an appeal on a point of law only. The industrial tribunal went on to find that Mr Lane had been unfairly dismissed. As already explained, he had been employed as a lecturer at a college of further education. His appointment was for an academic year, and was not renewed at the end of the period of appointment. The appointment expressly described it as a 'temporary appointment'. There had always been some uncertainty whether it would be renewed, because it was dependent on the availability of public money required for the further support of the Training Services Agency, and it was always doubtful whether this would be forthcoming. The finding of unfair dismissal is based on the proposition, accepted by the industrial tribunal, that when a temporary contract of employment in the academic field ceases because it is not renewed it is the duty of the employing authority, just as it would be in the case of a redundancy in industry (*Vokes v Bear*[2]), to assist the employee by considering him for appointments which they may have available.

While accepting that some such duty exists, we think that the industrial tribunal stated it too highly. Furthermore, when drawing the analogy with the ordinary industrial case, they seem to overlook the fact that the ordinary industrial case is not that of the temporary employee, but usually that of the permanent employee, where somewhat different considerations apply. It seems to us that what is required in a particular case will depend entirely on the circumstances of that case, and that it is very important to see whether one is dealing with a case of a temporary employee whose employment has been known to be temporary and non-renewable from the outset (say, a teacher taken on specifically for a single term) or with an employee who, although employed as a temporary on (say) an annual basis, has had his contract of employment renewed year after year. While we accept that consideration for the needs of the employee should be given according to what is proper in the circumstances, it seems to us that there is a danger, if the duty is pitched too high, that the reasonable discretion of the appointing body or committee or sub-committee will be unduly hampered and that the recruitment of new blood will be unreasonably restricted. In particular, we feel that the industrial tribunal were not right when they said that before other posts were advertised the claims of the temporary employee, in this case Mr Lane, should be considered, and that if he were suitable he should

1 [1977] ICR 911
2 [1974] ICR 1

have been engaged in preference to advertising the post generally. This appears to amount to a rule that a comparatively short-term temporary employee whose contract has not been renewed has some kind of right to priority of appointment to an available suitable post over and above any other suitable candidate. We think that this is going too far. Certainly, we think that even if in a particular case the circumstances seem to justify such a conclusion it would require careful examination of the evidence to see what the practical consequences of such a rule would be.

However, there is little doubt that the employers in the present case, having decided, regretfully, that they could not renew Mr Lane's contract of employment, did not do very much to assist him in relation to other posts which they might have had available. Inasmuch as we have concluded that the industrial tribunal did not take a wholly correct approach to this question, and the evidence is not available which would make it possible for us to decide the question for ourselves, the technically correct course would be to remit the case for this matter to be further heard; but the amount of compensation awarded is small, the employers are more interested in the principle of this case than the detail, and they have not pressed us to remit it. Accordingly, in all the circumstances it seems to us that the justice of the matter is that the award should be allowed to stand. The order accordingly is that the appeal be dismissed.

Leave to appeal is granted in all cases.

For completeness, we should record that several submissions were made to the effect that where an apparent fixed term contract is not renewed on expiry the contract of employment is terminated by the employer, within para 5(2)(a), inasmuch as it was open to the employer to renew it and he has not done so and has thereby terminated it. This argument seems to us to be untenable.

Appeals of Mr Dixon and Mr Constanti allowed. Case remitted to the industrial tribunal for rehearing. Leave to appeal to the Court of Appeal granted.

Appeal of Mr Throsby dismissed. Leave to appeal to the Court of Appeal granted.

Appeal of Gwent County Council dismissed. Leave to appeal to the Court of Appeal granted.

Solicitors: *Casson & Co*, Salford (for Mr Dixon and Mr Constanti); *Solicitor, BBC; Trowers, Still & Keeling* (for Imperial College); *Solicitor, Gwent County Council.*

Salim H J Merali   Barrister.

Hatt & Co (Bath) Ltd v Pearce

COURT OF APPEAL, CIVIL DIVISION
MEGAW AND ROSKILL LJJ
3rd FEBRUARY 1978

County court – Jurisdiction – Injunction – Jurisdiction to grant injunction if claim for injunction ancillary to claim for specific relief – Plaintiffs alleging breach of restrictive covenant in contract and claiming £1 damages and injunction – Whether claim for injunction ancillary to claim for specific relief – Whether jurisdiction to grant injunction – County Courts Act 1959, s 74(1).

In 1974 the defendant entered into a contract of employment with the plaintiffs, a firm of hairdressers in the City of Bath, to be employed by them as an apprentice in the hairdressing business. The contract contained a restrictive covenant that the defendant would not work in any hairdressing establishment within one mile of the plaintiffs' establishment for a period of 12 months after completing her apprenticeship. The defendant's apprenticeship expired in August 1977. In October 1977 the defendant left the plaintiffs' employment on agreed notice and shortly after entered the employment of another firm of hairdressers in Bath at premises about half a mile distant from the plaintiffs' establishment. The plaintiffs commenced proceedings against the defendant in the county court alleging breach of contract and claiming damages of £1 for loss of goodwill and an injunction to restrain the defendant from continuing to work as a hairdresser with the other firm. The plaintiffs limited their claim for damages to £1 because they believed that the defendant would not be able to pay substantial damages if they were awarded against her. Pending the trial of the action the plaintiffs applied for an interlocutory injunction. The defendant contended that the county court judge had no jurisdiction under s 74(1)[a] of the County Courts Act 1959 to grant an interlocutory injunction because, having regard to the amount of damages claimed and the general nature of the action, the claim for the injunction was not ancillary to the claim for damages but was the essence of the relief claimed. The county court judge rejected that contention and granted an injunction. The defendant appealed.

Held – The duty of the county court judge when deciding whether he had jurisdiction to grant an injunction ancillary to some other claim for relief was to establish whether the other claim was for specific relief which was properly within the jurisdiction of the court. If the claim for specific relief was for a small amount of damages, the judge nevertheless had jurisdiction to grant an injunction if the claim for damages was genuine. The judge was not required to weigh or balance the importance of the claim for the injunction against the importance of the claim to specific relief in deciding whether the one was ancillary to the other. The plaintiffs' claim for £1 damages was a proper claim for specific relief within the jurisdiction of the county court and therefore the county court judge had jurisdiction to grant the injunction sought. Accordingly the appeal would be dismissed (see p 479 b to d and h, p 480 c and p 481 g to p 482 b and g, post).

Notes

For the ancillary and interlocutory jurisdiction of the county court, see 10 Halsbury's Laws (4th Edn) paras 58, 59, and for cases on the subject, see 13 Digest (Reissue) 407, 408, 3394-3403.

For the County Courts Act 1959, s 74, see 7 Halsbury's Statutes (3rd Edn) 349.

---

a Section 74(1), so far as material, is set out at p 476 *j*, post

Cases referred to in judgments

Arnbridge (Reading) Ltd trading as Manpower (Reading) v Hedges [1972] The Times, 17th March, [1972] Court of Appeal Transcript 74A.
Birkett v James [1977] 2 All ER 801, [1978] AC 297, [1977] 3 WLR 38, HL.
Burns v Rodgers [1977] Court of Appeal Transcript 342.
De Vries v Smallridge [1928] 1 KB 482, [1927] All ER Rep 613, 97 LJKB 244, 138 LT 497, CA, 13 Digest (Reissue) 407, *3394.*
Ipswich Group Hospital Management Committee v British Broadcasting Corpn [1972] The Times, 2nd March, [1972] Court of Appeal Transcript 52.
Kenny v Preen [1962] 3 All ER 814, [1963] 1 QB 499, [1962] 3 WLR 1233, CA, 31(1) Digest (Reissue) 363, *2892.*
R v Cheshire County Court Judge and United Society of Boilermakers, ex parte Malone [1921] 2 KB 694, [1921] All ER Rep 344, 90 LJKB 772, 125 LT 588, sub nom *R v Parsons, ex parte Malone* 37 TLR 546, CA, 13 Digest (Reissue) 408, *3401.*
Thompson v White [1970] 3 All ER 678, [1970] 1 WLR 1434, 13 Digest (Reissue) 407, *3396.*
Watts v Waller [1972] 3 All ER 257, [1973] QB 153, [1972] 3 WLR 365, 24 P & CR 39, CA, 13 Digest (Reissue) 424, *3524.*
Wong v Beaumont Property Trust Ltd [1964] 2 All ER 119, [1965] 1 QB 173, [1964] 2 WLR 1325, CA, 13 Digest (Reissue) 422, *3515.*

Cases also cited

F (infants) (adoption order: validity), Re [1977] 2 All ER 777, [1977] Fam 165, CA.
White (Marion) Ltd v Francis [1972] 3 All ER 857, [1972] 1 WLR 1423, CA.

Interlocutory appeal

This was an appeal by the defendant, Vivien Mary Pearce, against an interlocutory order made by his Honour Judge Russell in the Bath County Court on 30th November 1977 whereby the defendant was restrained until trial of the action or until further order from carrying on either as principal or as manager, agent or servant or in any other hairdressing capacity whatsoever or in being in any way engaged or concerned or interested in the business of ladies hairdresser within one mile of 8, 9 and 10 The Corridor, Bath, in breach of an agreement between the plaintiffs, Hatt & Co (Bath) Ltd, and the defendant. The facts are set out in the judgment of Megaw LJ.

James Wigmore for the defendant.
Harold Burnett for the plaintiffs.

MEGAW LJ. This is an appeal from an interlocutory order made by his Honour Judge Russell in the Bath County Court on 30th November 1977. The action out of which the appeal arises was between the plaintiffs, who, we are told, are an old-established firm of hairdressers carrying on that business in the City of Bath, and the defendant. The defendant is a young lady who, while she was still a minor, entered into a contract of employment with the plaintiffs to be employed by them as an apprentice in the hairdressing business. The actual date which appears on the relevant contract, I think I am right in saying, is 5th August 1974. It was, I believe, round about that date that the defendant began her work with the plaintiffs, but I think there is some reason to suppose that the agreement was actually made by oral discussion some time later, perhaps in November 1974, and was then ante-dated to 5th August 1974. Nothing turns on that ante-dating, at least for the purposes of this appeal. Let me also say at this stage, as covering everything that I am going to say hereafter, that, as this is an interlocutory appeal, in a matter which will or may have to be determined at a hearing hereafter, on evidence which may conceivably be different from the evidence, such as it is, that is before us on this interlocutory application, nothing that I say is to be taken as indicating any kind of final view on any issue of fact or law that may fall to be considered.

The defendant continued to work under that contract for some time; but on 17th October 1977 she left the plaintiffs' employment. I think by agreement between the parties, she was not required to give the full period of notice that would have been required under the contract. Nothing turns on that.

The contract of employment contained a term which provided restrictions on the defendant's future employment, for a period of one year after she should leave the service of the plaintiffs, in relation to work in a hairdressing establishment within a specified distance from the place where the plaintiffs carried on their business. We are not concerned, as I see it, in this appeal with any of the details or provisions of that contract. It is in issue between the plaintiffs, quite plainly, as to whether the provision as to limitation on the defendant's scope of employment after leaving the service of the plaintiffs is or is not valid in accordance with principles applied by the courts in relation to the doctrine of restraint of trade. The defendant then took, or was about to undertake, other employment which the plaintiffs allege involves a breach of that term of the contract.

The plaintiffs then issued a plaint, followed by particulars of claim, on 11th November 1977, in the Bath County Court; and they gave notice straight away that they would be seeking to obtain an interlocutory injunction, pending the hearing of the action in the county court, to restrain the defendant from undertaking the other employment. That application for an interlocutory injunction came before Judge Russell on 25th November. The defendant submitted that the county court judge had no jurisdiction to grant that interlocutory relief.

In the particulars of claim the plaintiffs claimed an injunction to restrain the defendant from carrying on her employment with another firm, and the sum of £1 for damages. The particulars of claim set out the alleged breach of contract and asserted that 'By reason of the premises the plaintiff has suffered damage. It has lost goodwill for which it demands the sum of £1 damages'. The pleading goes on to say: 'The defendant threatens and intends unless restrained from so doing to continue to commit the breach of the said agreement.' And so the prayer was as I have indicated.

There were affidavits before the learned judge on behalf of the parties. The only passage in any of the affidavits to which I need make reference is in para 12 of an affidavit put in on behalf of the plaintiffs sworn by Mr Eric Stanley Davis on 30th November 1977. That paragraph reads:

> 'Although an agreement for damages [there must be something wrong there: I think it means 'a claim for damages'] in this action has been limited to £1 this in no way represents the likely damage to the plaintiff company but only the realisation that if a substantial award of damages was allowed the defendant would not be able to pay them.'

The submission to the learned judge, which has been repeated in this court, on the question of jurisdiction was this. It is said that it is a principle of law, to be deduced from cases decided by this court, that the county court has no jurisdiction to entertain an application for an injunction unless the claim for the injunction is ancillary to some other claim which would properly be before the court within what I may call its specific jurisdiction. If one takes, for example, s 39 of the County Courts Act 1959, it provides that the county court shall have jurisdiction to hear and determine any action founded on contract or tort where the debt due or the damage claimed is not more than £1,000. Then, of course, there are various other sections giving county courts jurisdiction in other types of litigation. Then comes s 74(1) of the 1959 Act, which provides:

> 'Every county court, as regards any cause of action for the time being within its jurisdiction, shall—(a) grant such relief, redress or remedy or combination of remedies either absolute or conditional . . . as ought to be granted or given in the like case by the High Court and in as full and ample a manner . . .'

For what it may matter, the marginal note to that section is: 'General ancillary
a jurisdiction.'
The submission which was made to the county court judge and which was again
put forward very clearly and emphatically by counsel for the defendant in this court,
was that in the present case the claim for an injunction was the primary, or effective,
or main claim: it was the essence of the relief claimed; and although, indeed, there
was in the particulars of claim a claim for damages, limited to £1, both because of the
b smallness of the amount and because of the general nature of the action that claim
for damages was ancillary to the claim for the injunction and not vice versa. Therefore, it is said, the county court had no jurisdiction. If any such claim, framed in that
way, were to be heard by the courts, it would, it was submitted, have to be presented
and pursued in the High Court and not in the county court.
The foundation of counsel for the defendant's argument is a decision of this court, a
c court consisting of Lord Denning MR, myself and Stamp LJ, in *Arnbridge (Reading)*
Ltd trading as Manpower (Reading) v Hedges[1]. It has been reported, at any rate so far
as the researches of counsel go, only in The Times newspaper. We have had before us
the transcript of the judgments. The leading judgment, with which the other two
members of the court simply expressed their agreement, was given by Lord Denning
MR. It was a case in which the plaintiff company, Arnbridge (Reading) Ltd, had gone
d before the county court judge at Swindon to apply for an interlocutory injunction
to restrain the three defendants from conducting a business which they had recently
opened at Swindon. The defendants had attended by their solicitor and had asked for
an adjournment to answer the affidavit. That adjournment had been refused, and
the county court judge had granted an injunction restraining the defendants from
entering into any dealings with any person who at any time during the course of their
e employment by the plaintiff was a customer of the plaintiff in relation to the defendants' business as an employment bureau and a supplier of labour. Lord Denning MR
said:

> 'Reading through the particulars of claim, it seems plain to me that the essence
> of these proceedings before the county court judge was for an injunction. True
> it is that there is a sentence at the end of the particulars of claim claiming "that
f the plaintiffs have suffered and will suffer loss and damage". But that is not
> sufficient to give the county court judge jurisdiction to grant an injunction. It has
> been settled for years that in the county court a claim for an injunction is only
> permissible when it is ancillary to a claim for damages. This case seems to be the
> reverse: the substantial claim is for an injunction and the ancillary claim is only
> for damages. Only a week or two ago some plaintiffs did likewise. They went to
g the county court for an injunction, whereas they ought to have gone to the High
> Court. I deprecate this course. I hope we have seen the last of these excursions
> to the county court.'

The case of 'only a week or two ago' to which Lord Denning MR was referring was,
no doubt, *Ipswich Group Hospital Management Committee v British Broadcasting Corpn*[2],
h which is reported in The Times newspaper. In the following paragraph of Lord
Denning MR's judgment (which I need not read) he made it perfectly clear that,
apart from the question that he had dealt with in the preceding paragraph, the case
was one in which an injunction ought not to have been granted. Material information
had not been made available to the county court judge which ought to have been
made available to him by the plaintiffs; and when the matter came before this court
j it became apparent that the agreement which was relied on as founding the injunction had not been made with the particular plaintiff company at all but with a
different legal entity. So, Lord Denning MR said: 'This claim for an injunction is as

1 [1972] The Times, 17th March
2 [1972] The Times, 2nd March

full of holes as a colander. The injunction ought not to have been granted'; and he went on to say: 'If an application is to be renewed, it must not be done in the county *a* court. The case must be transferred to the High Court and dealt with by a judge here in London.'

I do not propose to go through the various other, earlier, authorities to which we were, properly, referred by counsel, starting with the decision of this court in *De Vries v Smallridge*[1], in which the relevant County Courts Act was the 1888 Act. There was no section in the 1888 Act corresponding to s 74 of the 1959 Act. But, as was *b* helpfully[2] pointed out to us by counsel, there was a section in a Judicature Act[2] which had application to the County Courts Act 1888, which was to substantially the same effect as s 74 of the 1959 Act.

We were referred also to *Kenny v Preen*[3], *Wong v Beaumont Property Trust Ltd*[4], *Watts v Waller*[5], *R v Cheshire County Court Judge and United Society of Boilermakers, ex parte Malone*[6] and to a relatively recent judgment of Brightman J, *Thompson v White*[7]. *c* I mention those cases to show that they were not overlooked by counsel in their careful submissions to us on this jurisdiction issue.

In *Kenny v Preen*[3] this court altered the judgment of the county court judge, who had awarded to the plaintiff damages of £100 and an injunction. This court held that the only legal wrong for which damages were recoverable was a breach of contract and that the only damages that could be recovered were nominal damages; accordingly, *d* they altered to 40s od the damages which the county court judge had held to be £100. Nevertheless in that case, as is clear from the judgment of Pearson LJ, the court saw no reason why that should be regarded as having deprived the county court judge of jurisdiction to grant the injunction: the mere fact that the only damages recoverable were nominal did not prevent the county court judge from having had jurisdiction to grant an injunction. *e*

To that, which at first sight would appear to be a complete answer to counsel for the defendant's proposition in the present case, counsel ingeniously makes the reply that what is relevant for present purposes is not what the court ultimately decides to be the amount of damages to which the plaintiff is entitled but is the amount which he has seen fit to claim in his proceedings. In many instances in the County Courts Acts and rules, it is the amount claimed which is determinant in reference to limita- *f* tion of amounts of money. Therefore, counsel for the defendant submits, in doing the task which he says is necessary in a case of this sort, namely weighing and balancing to see whether the claim for damages is ancillary to the claim for an injunction, or the claim for an injunction is ancillary to the claim for damages, one takes into account in the scale, in relation to damages, not the amount that is recoverable or recovered, but the amount that is claimed. To my mind that is a not very attractive doctrine *g* in relation to the issue in this appeal, for obvious reasons. But even if it were right it does not, I think, enable counsel for the defendant to succeed in his proposition.

In the other case to which I have referred, *Wong v Beaumont Property Trust Ltd*[4], the amount of damages which this court held the plaintiff entitled to recover was the sum of £10 and no more, the claim in that case having been framed as a claim for damages 'not exceeding £400'. The court saw no difficulty about the upholding of the *h* injunction which had been granted, even though the damages were only the sum of £10. But, says counsel for the defendant, one has got to take a true view in each case of what is the real relief which is being asked for: if one finds that in essence the

1 [1928] 1 KB 482, [1927] All ER Rep 613
2 Supreme Court of Judicature Act 1873, s 89
3 [1962] 3 All ER 814, [1963] 1 QB 499
4 [1964] 2 All ER 119, [1965] 1 QB 173
5 [1972] 3 All ER 257, [1973] QB 153
6 [1921] 2 KB 694, [1921] All ER Rep 344
7 [1970] 3 All ER 678, [1970] 1 WLR 1434

primary relief that the plaintiff is seeking to obtain is an injunction and that the damages are less essential, so that the injunction is the primary remedy, then the county
court, in a matter of this sort, has no jurisdiction. That, says counsel for the defendant,
is the only possible meaning to be given to the judgment of Lord Denning MR in the
Arnbridge case[1] by reference to the paragraph which I have read, beginning 'Reading
through the particulars of claim'. I do not accept that that is so. I do not think that
Lord Denning MR, or the other members of the court concurring with him in that
case, were expressing or intending to express the view that, if the claim for damages
in any particular case, though genuine, was small in amount, that necessarily or
inevitably, or even probably, produced the result that the county court would have
no jurisdiction to grant an injunction.

To my mind, counsel for the plaintiff is right. He is content, for the purposes of this
appeal, to make the assumption that the law is that the county court judge's jurisdiction to grant an injunction is properly regarded as applying where the grant of the
injunction is ancillary to some other relief that is claimed as being specific relief
within the ordinary jurisdiction of the county court. But, says counsel for the plaintiff,
that does not mean that one looks at the size of the claim for damages and determines
the matter in that way, or that one has to do any weighing and balancing such as
counsel for the defendant suggested in order to decide on this question of jurisdiction.
It would be most unsatisfactory, indeed it would be lamentable, if, in a matter of
this sort, that kind of exercise had to be performed for the purpose of arriving, not at
the question of the ultimate merits, but at the question, to be decided immediately,
as to whether the court had jurisdiction at all. It would further, to my mind, be a
lamentable consequence if the law were such that, in any action in respect of an
allegation by a plaintiff of a breach of covenant which the defendant says is a covenant
unenforceable as in restraint of trade, the county court did not have jurisdiction but
the parties had to come to London to the High Court merely because of some assessment of the relative weight to be attached to the claim by the plaintiff for damages
compared with that for the injunction. To my mind there is nothing in the *Arnbridge*[1],
case, properly considered, which leads to such a conclusion. No doubt it is very right
and proper that the jurisdiction of the county court in relation to the granting of injunctions should be treated by the county court judge before whom the application is
made with care; and in such cases as *Ipswich Group Hospital Management Committee v
British Broadcasting Corpn*[2] and *Arnbridge (Reading) Ltd trading as Manpower (Reading)
v Hedges*[1] appear to have been it would have been wholly inappropriate for the
county court judge to have accepted jurisdiction and granted an injunction. In such
cases, as the court indicated, the proper course for the county court judge would have
been to have said: 'I will not grant you an injunction. If you wish to obtain an injunction in circumstances such as these, you must start your proceedings in the High
Court or have them transferred there.' But that does not involve acceptance of the
principle which counsel for the defendant sought to assert.

For those reasons, I would reject the claim that the county court judge did not have
jurisdiction. I think he was right to accept jurisdiction, in the circumstances of this
case, on the basis of the relevant facts as he then saw them to be, particularly in
relation to the claim as asserted.

That is not, however, the end of the matter, because in this appeal counsel for the
defendant has further sought to submit that, even if he were wrong on the question
of jurisdiction, nevertheless the county court judge, having jurisdiction, had exercised
his discretion wrongly in granting the injunction to the plaintiffs. Counsel for the
defendant has taken us through his various points set out in the ground of appeal,
most of which are asserting that the learned judge failed to give sufficient weight
to this factor, that factor and the other factor. I would refer, without citing the passage,

---

1   [1972] The Times, 17th March
2   [1972] The Times, 2nd March

to what has recently been said by Lord Diplock in his speech in the House of Lords in
Birkett v James[1]. Though Lord Diplock there refers to the exercise of discretion by
judges of the High Court, I think that is useful also as providing at least some guidance
in relation to appeals to this court from the exercise of discretion by county court
judges in matters of the present nature.

In this case I am unable, despite counsel for the defendant's attractive argument, to
hold that the judge has erred in principle by giving weight to something which he
ought not to have taken into account or by failing to give weight to something which
he ought to have taken into account; nor that his decision in the exercise of his discretion could be regarded as unreasonable or plainly wrong. The fact, to which
counsel referred us, that a division of this court last term, in another interlocutory
appeal relating to an interlocutory injunction[2], in a case of an employee in a hairdressing business, arrived at the conclusion that in that case the learned judge had
erred in principle in granting an injunction is not of assistance in the present case.
I would, accordingly, dismiss the appeal.

ROSKILL LJ. I agree that this appeal should be dismissed. If ever there were a
case which ought to be tried in the local county court, in this case Bath, it is the
present. The plaintiffs are an old-established firm of hairdressers in that city. The
defendant is a hairdresser who was formerly employed by the plaintiffs in that city
and is now employed by another firm in that city. The contract between the plaintiffs
and the defendant which the defendant is alleged to have broken contained a restrictive covenant. The geographical limitation of that restrictive covenant is one mile
from the plaintiffs' office, which we are told is in the centre of Bath. Everything in
this case, therefore, concerns that city, and obviously that is by far the best place for
this case to be determined. But it has been strenuously argued by counsel for the
defendant that the learned county court judge had no jurisdiction to grant the
interlocutory injunction which the plaintiffs sought and obtained. With all respect, I
think that submission is untenable.

I quote, without disrespect to counsel's excellent argument, from the judgment of
Scrutton LJ in *R v Cheshire County Court Judge and United Society of Boilermakers, ex parte
Malone*[3], where he said:

> 'This is one of those cases which, though a lawyer may find it interesting, a
> layman like the plaintiff finds heart-breaking, because, wanting to find out
> whether he has been properly expelled from his society, he finds the case decided
> against him on a ground which he cannot understand. The reason of that is that
> to the lawyer the point which is being argued is whether a Court with limited
> jurisdiction, the county court, has or has not the powers which the plaintiff asks it to
> exercise; whereas it is quite clear that if the case had been brought before the
> High Court, the High Court could have given the relief for which the plaintiff
> asks, and we are going to hold that the county court could not give him that
> relief because of the limited terms of its jurisdiction created by statute.'

That is the result for which the defendant, through her counsel, contends. If, of
course, the argument is well-founded, it is our duty to give effect to it. But I am bound
to say that I find the argument basically unsound and I would only give effect to it if
the authorities compelled that result. To my mind, the more recent authorities
cannot and do not compel it. Of course, when county courts were established in the
middle of the last century they had limited jurisdiction. When they were first
established in the late 1840s they were courts designed for dealing with small claims.

1 [1977] 2 All ER 801 at 804, [1978] AC 297 at 317, 318
2 *Burns v Rodgers* [1977] Court of Appeal Transcript 342
3 [1921] 2 KB 694 at 704, 705

They then had very limited jurisdiction indeed. Gradually, over the last century and
a half, their jurisdiction has been immensely widened, the last widening, in terms of
money, having been very recent[1]. And, of course, as the years passed and as in the
High Court the fusion of law and equity came about, so the county courts acquired
jurisdiction to deal with matters of equity such as the grant of injunctions, just as they
could deal with common law claims for debt or damages. The present statutory
position, as Megaw LJ has pointed out, is regulated by ss 39 and 74 of the County Courts
Act 1959. Neither of those provisions was on the statute book at the time when two
of the most important cases in this field, *R v Cheshire County Court Judge and United
Society of Boilermakers, ex parte Malone*[2] and *De Vries v Smallridge*[3], were decided by
this court. Nonetheless, in those cases and in the subsequent cases, such as *Kenny v
Preen*[4], one can detect a consistent strain of judicial authority which has regarded the
grant of an injunction as something ancillary to the grant of relief in connection
with matters which are within the basic jurisdiction of the county court such as (and
this is by way of illustration and not limitation) a claim for damages or debt, and in
particular a claim for damages for breach of contract.

Accordingly, it seems clear on the authorities that, notwithstanding what is now
the apparently unrestricted language of s 74 of the 1959 Act, a plaintiff who went
to a county court and sought an injunction without more and without attaching
his claim for an injunction to any other form of relief within the jurisdiction of the
county court under s 39, might find himself met with a plea in bar, namely that that
court had no jurisdiction. But the question arises, and has had to be considered
in a number of cases of which one of the most recent is the decision of this court
on 14th March 1972 in *Arnbridge (Reading) Ltd trading as Manpower (Reading) v
Hedges*[5], how does one detect whether or not, where there purports to be a claim
for an injunction linked with a claim for damages, this principle has been complied
with or broken?

It is suggested, on the strength of a passage in the judgment of Lord Denning MR in
the *Arnbridge* case[5], that the court has almost to do a balancing operation and see
which part of the claim is the more important, the claim for an injunction or the claim
for damages, and, if it be that the claim for an injunction is more important than the
claim for damages, the court has no jurisdiction, whereas, if the claim for damages is
more important than the claim for an injunction, the court has got jurisdiction.
With respect to that argument, I do not think that the passage in the judgment of
Lord Denning MR bears that interpretation; and I cannot think that the other two
members of the court, Megaw and Stamp LJJ, could have thought that it was capable
of that interpretation since otherwise they would not have expressed almost mono-
syllabic agreement with the judgment of Lord Denning MR. The true principle
seems to me much plainer and much simpler. One has to look first of all to see
whether there is a claim within the jurisdiction of the county court. To my mind
there is here, when one looks at the particulars of claim, a perfectly good claim for
damages for breach of contract, which is within the jurisdiction of the county court.
It is alleged in para 2 of the particulars of claim that the defendant has become employed with another firm 'in breach of the said agreement'; and in para 3 it is alleged
that 'By reason of the premises [which means the plea in para 2] the plaintiff has
suffered damage. It has lost goodwill for which it demands the sum of £1 damages'.
Then in para 2 of the prayer in the particulars of claim there is a claim for damages
limited to £1.

It is said that because that claim for damages is very small it must mean that the

1 County Courts Jurisdiction Order 1974, SI 1974 No 1273, art 2
2 [1921] 2 KB 694, [1921] All ER Rep 344
3 [1928] 1 KB 482, [1927] All ER Rep 613
4 [1962] 3 All ER 814, [1963] 1 QB 499
5 [1972] The Times, 17th March

claim for an injunction outweighs the claim for damages and therefore cannot properly be called ancillary to that claim. I do not think that the court can properly at any   *a* stage, least of all in an interlocutory stage, do a balancing operation of the kind, to which Megaw LJ has referred, which was contended for by counsel for the defendant. The duty of the court is to see whether the requirements of the statute have been satisfied. Where, as in the present case, there is a perfectly good plea of a claim for damages, I cannot see that the jurisdiction of the court, which would, be concession, exist if the claim for damages were for, say, £100 or £200 or £500, suddenly ceases to   *b* exist because the plaintiffs, for reasons which they explain in their affidavit, have limited their claim to £1. The passage in the judgment of Lord Denning MR in the *Arnbridge* case[1] seems to me, when one reads it as a whole, and particularly reads the last paragraph with the second paragraph, to have been based fundamentally on the fact that in that case there was no bona fide claim for damages. It is clear that the plaintiffs there were not entitled to the injunction which the county court judge had   *c* granted. Accordingly, remembering that, as Megaw LJ has just said, that case followed shortly after the *Ipswich Hospital Group Management Committee* case[2], to which Lord Denning MR impliedly referred, it seems to me that that case does not support the principle for which counsel for the defendant contended in this court.

For those reasons, I think that the learned county court judge plainly had jurisdiction to grant this injunction. Was he wrong so to grant it? Megaw LJ has pointed out   *d* that the House of Lords recently, in *Birkett v James*[3], has emphasised that this court ought not to interfere with the exercise of discretion by a judge of first instance, whether in the county court or the High Court, unless it can be shown that the judge has in some way gone wrong in principle.

Counsel for the defendant took us through the grounds of appeal in this case. Those grounds of appeal, fully and clearly drawn as one would expect, simply indicate   *e* the various factors which a judge has to take into account in exercising his discretion. There is nothing whatever, save the bare fact that the judge did not refuse the injunction as the defendant would have had him do, to suggest that the learned judge did not have all those matters in mind. He weighed them in the balance, but found them wanting and thought that the scale tipped in favour of the plaintiffs so far as the granting of interlocutory relief was concerned. I can only say that so far as I can judge,   *f* on the matter as it was put before the judge I would have reached the same conclusion. But whether or not I would is irrelevant, for it was a matter for the learned county court judge. I think he had jurisdiction to do that which he did, and we cannot and should not interfere with his exercise of his discretion.

I too would dismiss this appeal.

   g

Solicitors: *Hextall Erskine & Co*, agents for *Cartwrights*, Bath (for the defendant); *Stone, King & Wardle*, Bath (for the plaintiffs).

Mary Rose Plummer   Barrister.

1   [1972] The Times, 17th March   *h*
2   [1972] The Times, 2nd March
3   [1977] 2 All ER 801 at 804, [1978] AC 297 at 317, 318

Shallow v Shallow

COURT OF APPEAL, CIVIL DIVISION

STAMP, ORR AND ORMROD LJJ

6th, 20th OCTOBER 1977

Divorce – Financial provision – Periodical payments – Calculation – Amount payable to wife and children – Amount left for husband to live on – Husband not to be reduced below subsistence level – Relevance of formula used by Supplementary Benefits Commission in assessing contribution required from husband for support of dependent relative – Amount husband permitted to retain under formula not to be equated with subsistence level – Whether permissible to have regard to formula – Whether calculation under formula an alternative to calculation under 'one-third' rule – Matrimonial Causes Act 1973, s 25(1).

The former husband had a net weekly income of £62·44. The registrar ordered him to pay to his former wife and the two children of the marriage periodical payments totalling £30·50 per week which left the husband, who was a single man, with £31·94 per week to live on. He appealed against the order to a judge who dismissed the appeal on the grounds that the wife needed the amount ordered and that, although the amount left for the husband to live on was less than the amount which the Supplementary Benefits Commission would have permitted him to retain in accordance with their formula for the purposes, if they had claimed contribution from him for the support of his family, that formula should be rejected since the husband was able to afford the amount of the order. The husband appealed contending that in fixing the amount of an order for maintenance or periodical payments in a low income case the courts should adopt as a guideline, as an alternative to the 'one-third' rule, the formula applied by the commission.

Held – The appeal would be dismissed for the following reasons—

(i) In fixing the amount of an order for periodical payments it was permissible, and might be useful in low income cases, to have regard to the formula applied by the commission to determine the amount a husband was required to contribute to a dependent relative, provided that the formula was properly applied. The amount a husband was permitted to retain under the formula was not to be equated with subsistence level for it was no more than a negotiating figure used by the commission in seeking contribution from a husband. Although in some circumstances the formula might be a useful alternative to the one-third rule, in either case, the resulting figure was to be regarded merely as a starting point which was to be adjusted according to the circumstances to give effect to the principles laid down in s 25 of the Matrimonial Causes Act 1973 (see p 486 *f g* and p 487 *c* to *e*, post).

(ii) Since the current subsistence level for a single man was £12·70 a week plus a rent allowance, to apply the commission's formula in the instant case in fixing the amount of the order would have resulted in leaving the husband with about £15 a week above his subsistence level to live on whereas the wife and children would have been left about £2 a week below their subsistence level. Since that could not be regarded as an equitable division of the available income, the judge had been right to reject the formula, and the registrar's order was both reasonable and proper (see p 486 *h* and p 488 *c* to *h*, post); *Ashley v Ashley* [1965] 3 All ER 554 applied; dictum of Sir George Baker P in *Smethurst v Smethurst* [1977] 3 All ER at 1114, 1115 explained.

Per Curiam. The practice of presenting the relevant figures in the form of schedules ought to be followed in all matrimonial cases even where the case is a simple one (see p 488 *h* and *j*, post).

Notes

For calculation of the amount to be awarded in making financial provision after a   *a*
decree of divorce and assessment of the parties' needs, see 13 Halsbury's Laws (4th Edn
paras 1066, 1087.

For the Matrimonial Causes Act 1973, s 25, see 43 Halsbury's Statutes (3rd Edn) 567.

Cases referred to in judgment

Ashley v Ashley [1965] 3 All ER 554, [1968] P 582, [1965] 3 WLR 1194, 130 JP 1, DC,   *b*
27(2) (Reissue) 975, 7840.

Barnes v Barnes [1972] 3 All ER 872, [1972] 1 WLR 1381, Digest (Cont Vol D) 418, 6603a.

Kershaw v Kershaw [1964] 3 All ER 635, [1966] P 13, [1964] 3 WLR 1143, 128 JP 589,
DC, 27(2) Digest (Reissue) 974, 7829.

Smethurst v Smethurst [1977] 3 All ER 1110, [1977] 3 WLR 472, DC.

Appeal   *c*

This was an appeal by Clayton Vanence Shallow ('the husband') against an order of
his Honour Judge Peck sitting at Reading County Court made on 9th May 1977
dismissing his appeal against an order of Mr Registrar Thorne made on 15th March
1976 whereby he was ordered to pay periodical payments to Gloria Shallow ('the
wife') during their joint lives until she remarried or further order at the rate of £12   *d*
per week and periodical payments for the two children of the marriage until they
respectively attained the age of 17 or further order at the rate of £5 per week for
each child, and to pay the mortgage instalments and rates on the former matrimonial
home. The grounds of the appeal were (i) that the judge had been wrong in law in
failing to have regard to the guidelines issued to officers of the Supplementary
Benefits Commission, (ii) that the judge had misdirected himself in failing to take   *e*
account of mortgage repayments and rates paid by the husband in respect of the
matrimonial home occupied by the wife and (iii) that the judge had been wrong in
law in making an order which would depress the husband below subsistence level.
The facts are set out in the judgment of the court.

J H Inskip QC and *Charles Pugh* for the husband.   *f*
Basil Hillman for the wife.
Harry Woolf as amicus curiae.

Cur adv vult

g

20th October.   **ORMROD LJ** delivered the following judgment of the court:
This is an appeal by a former husband against an order for periodical payments.
On 15th March 1976 Mr Registrar Thorne ordered him to pay £12 a week to his
former wife and £5 a week to each of two children, he continuing to pay the mortgage instalments and rates on the former matrimonial home which together came
to £8·50 per week. His total liability under that order therefore amounts to £30·50   *h*
per week. An appeal, well out of time, was dismissed by his Honour Judge Peck
at the Reading County Court on 9th May 1977, but he gave leave to appeal to this
court. Since the appeal appeared to turn on certain aspects of the administration
of supplementary benefits, the court asked the Attorney-General for his assistance
as amicus curiae; counsel has appeared on his behalf and has provided the court
with much useful information which has clarified the position and removed a number   *j*
of potential misunderstandings.

The grounds of appeal, as drafted, state: (1) the learned judge was wrong in law
in failing to have regard to the guidelines issued to the officers of the Supplementary
Benefits Commission; ground (2) does not matter; (3) the order was such as would
depress the husband below subsistence level.

In a written note of his reasons for dismissing the appeal the learned judge said that the wife clearly needed the amount ordered by the registrar and that although the husband was left with less than the 'supplementary benefit scale', he could afford the amount and that the order accordingly should stand. The first ground of appeal is therefore unsustainable because the judge did have 'regard to' the so-called supplementary benefit scale but decided not to adopt it in this particular case.

On the figures, which have been agreed by counsel in this court (they differ appreciably from those used by the judge), the position is that the husband has a gross annual income of £3,960 a year which, after tax and allowances, leaves him with a net weekly income of £62·44. The order in the aggregate amounts to £30·50, leaving the husband, who is a single man, with £31·94 to live on. Since this is rather more than the wife has on which to keep herself and the two children, it is absurd to suggest that the husband has been reduced below the subsistence level unless that phrase has acquired some purely technical meaning. The other ground of appeal therefore appears equally unsustainable. Counsel for the husband in this court was, as he recognised, in great difficulty, but he has developed his client's case as well as it could be put. His argument, for which the court is grateful, really amounts to saying that the court ought to adopt the practice which the Supplementary Benefits Commission use to determine the liability of the 'liable relative' to contribute to the support of his dependants, and he based his submission on a decision of the Divisional Court earlier this year in a case called *Smethurst v Smethurst*[1]. But for some observations of Sir George Baker P in that case, counsel for the husband conceded that the appeal would have been unarguable.

The matter arose originally from the Report of the Committee on One-Parent Families[2], which is conveniently referred to as the Finer Report. That report called attention to the differences between the practice of the courts and of the Supplementary Benefits Commission in assessing the liability of husbands and ex-husbands for the support of their families and suggested, expressly or by implication, that the courts might bring their practice more into line with that of the commission. The Finer Report[3] disclosed for the first time to the public the existence of a formula used by the Supplementary Benefits Commission for their own purposes in such cases. This formula contains three factors: (1) husband's rent; (2) amount which would be payable in supplementary benefits to him if he had no other resources for himself and dependants (if any); (3) one-quarter of his net income (i e gross income less tax and national insurance contributions).

For certain purposes only (which are referred to in more detail later) the Supplementary Benefits Commisssion consider that the husband should be permitted to retain an amount equal to the aggregate of those three sums for his own use and so limit their claim for contribution to the remainder of his income. This formula is called in the notice of appeal 'guidelines' and in the judge's reasons the 'supplementary benefit scale'.

Smethurst v Smethurst[1] is the first case in which reference had been made to it. In the course of giving judgment in that case (which raised a number of quite different issues) Sir George Baker P said this[4]:

> 'Another way of looking at this matter is to consider whether, and if so how far, the husband is on or above subsistence level. If the Supplementary Benefits Commission were seeking a contribution from this man, they would apply the formula, which is to be found in the Finer Report[5]. The report[6] stated: "Nothing could exceed the confusion created by three modes of assessment of a liability,

---

1   [1977] 3 All ER 1110, [1977] 3 WLR 472
2   (1974) Cmnd 5629
3   Ibid, vol 1, pp 136, 137, para 4.188
4   [1977] 3 All ER 1110 at 1114, 1115, [1977] 3 WLR 472 at 477
5   (1974) Cmnd 5629, vol 1, pp 136-138, paras 4.188-4.190.
6   Ibid, p 138, para 4.190

all different from each other, and two of them employed in courts of law acting in ignorance of the third mode which the Supplementary Benefits Commission use in making decisions which affect the very same group of people." I am not aware of this approach having been used before in the courts, but I see no reason why it should not be, and to my knowledge magistrates are considering it. The Supplementary Benefits Commission formula is as follows: the husband and his wife would have an allowance of £20·65 a week; the child would have the benefit of £4·35 and there would be a rent allowance of £8·64. In addition to that, the Supplementary Benefits Commission would allow the husband, as what I suppose might be called an "incentive allowance", one-quarter of his net income or £5 whichever be the greater. In the present case that would be £10 and the total of these four items is £43·64. So as the husband's net income is £40 a week, it would seem that the Supplementary Benefits Commission would not seek to recover anything from him in the present case, or at best a very small sum if, I do not know if this is right or not, they took his gross instead of his net income. I suspect they take his net, because they assess the quarter on his net earnings.'

The significant part of those observations is the first sentence, in which Sir George Baker P appears to be equating the figure which was produced by the formula with 'subsistence level', a phrase which at once calls to mind the line of authority, beginning with *Kershaw v Kershaw*[1] and *Ashley v Ashley*[2] in which it was said that, except in unusual circumstances, orders for maintenance or periodical payments should not reduce the husband below 'subsistence level'. Sir Jocelyn Simon P related 'subsistence level' closely to the amount which would be payable in supplementary benefits to the husband if he had no other resources for the support of himself and his dependants, if any[3]. Those cases were approved in principle in more general terms by this court in *Barnes v Barnes*[4]. If therefore, the product of the formula is now to be equated with 'subsistence level', and the principle in *Ashley v Ashley*[2] applied to it, something very like 'protected earnings' will be imported into the process of assessing liability for maintenance and periodical payments. This presumably was what was in the mind of counsel for the husband when he drafted the third ground of appeal in the present case. It is, however, unnecessary to pursue the point further because, as counsel for the Attorney-General has demonstrated very clearly, the formula has nothing to do with subsistence levels. It produces, in fact, nothing more than a negotiating figure for the use of the commission's officers when seeking contributions from 'liable relatives'. If a liable relative makes an offer which is more or less consistent with the product of the formula, the officers can accept it as reasonable and one which, experience shows, is more likely to be paid regularly than a higher sum imposed on the liable relative. If, on the other hand, the commission itself undertakes to enforce an order for periodical payments or maintenance made by a court, it seeks enforcement of the full amount of the order.

The subsistence level, in the language of *Ashley v Ashley*[2], therefore remains what it was, namely approximately the current amount of supplementary benefit appropriate to a single man or a man with dependants, as the case may be. These amounts are prescribed by the government from time to time and are available in the form of a statutory instrument. The current level for a single man is £12·70 plus a rent allowance. Counsel for the Attorney-General drew particular attention to a paragraph in the annual report of the commission which explains the basis of these amounts. The paragraph reads as follows:

---

1   [1964] 3 All ER 635, [1966] P 13
2   [1965] 3 All ER 554, [1968] P 582
3   [1965] 3 All ER 554 at 558, 559, [1968] P 582 at 590, 591
4   [1972] 3 All ER 872, [1972] 1 WLR 1381

a   'For better or worse, the supplementary benefit scale rates are the nearest thing Britain has to a definition of the minimum standard of living which this country is for the moment prepared to tolerate. If such a minimum standard is to be a defence against poverty, it must enable people to participate in the social system to which their fellow citizens belong. That means that the scale rates for a family of a given size should not fall too far below the incomes of similar families with a breadwinner in low paid work, and they should keep pace year by *b*   year with changes in the average worker's earnings and living standards.'

Faced with these difficulties, counsel for the husband limited his argument to the proposition that courts when fixing the amount of orders for periodical payments or maintenance should adopt the formula as a guideline as an alternative to the one-third rule in low income cases. Counsel for the Attorney-General suggested *c*   that it might be found useful in such cases, as indeed it may be. Like the one-third rule it is, in essence, a ranging shot which suggests a figure which can then be considered in detail in the light of all the circumstances of the particular case. But it must be properly applied if it is not to mislead.

The third term of the formula is one-quarter of net earnings after tax, not after deducting travelling and other expenses. In contrast, it is usual, in applying the one-*d*   third rule, to deduct from the respective incomes charges on income and expenses which can properly be treated as deductions, before aggregating the two incomes and calculating the sum required to bring the wife's income up to one-third of the joint income. In neither case should the resulting figure be regarded as anything more than a starting point, to be adjusted according to circumstances, to give effect in matrimonial causes to the principles laid down by Parliament in s 25 of the *e*   Matrimonial Causes Act 1973.

A comparison of the two methods, using the agreed figures in the instant case, is of some interest. On the one-third basis the husband's gross weekly income is approximately £75 per week, from which national insurance contribution is to be deducted (£228 per annum or £4·25 per week) together with something for travel-*f*   ling and other expenses of earning his income leaving, say, £68. The wife has no income except £3 per week child benefit. The aggregate is therefore £71, one-third of which is £24, from which £3 is to be deducted, leaving £21 as the starting point for the wife's own order. This is close to the registrar's figure of £20·50 (made up as to £12 plus £8·50 mortgage repayments and rates) for the wife herself.

On the Supplementary Benefits Commission formula the calculation is:

g

	£,	
Rent	9·50	
Supplementary		
benefit (rate for		
single man)	12·70	(total £22·20)
One-quarter of net		
income (¼ × £62)	15·50	
	———	
	37·70	
	════	

h

j

This leaves a balance of £24·30 (£62 minus £37·70) as the figure which the commission would be content to collect from a 'liable relative'.

The position looks rather different from the wife's point of view. On current scales her so-called 'subsistence level' is:

$£$

	$£$	
Rent	8·50	a
Supplementary benefit for herself	12·70	
Supplementary benefit for each child ($£4·35 × 2$)	8·70	

29·90 (of which $£3$ per week is
payable as child benefit)

On the one-third basis the husband has half his net income for himself while maintaining the wife and two children on the other half at a few pence above their so-
called subsistence level, while he himself is between $£9$ and $£10$ a week above his
'subsistence level'.

On the formula, the husband is about $£15$ a week above his 'subsistence level'
and the wife and children about $£2$ a week below theirs. This can scarcely be regarded
as an equitable or reasonable division of the available income.   Moreover, it would
have the effect of transferring part of his liability to the taxpayer since the wife would
be entitled to receive supplementary benefit at the rate of about $£2$ per week. (Her
total income, out of which she would have to pay mortgage instalments and rates,
would be $£24·30$ from the husband plus child benefit at $£3$ a week; that is, $£27·30$
as against a 'subsistence level' of $£29·90$.) It is, therefore, obviously impossible to
contend that in the instant case the formula produces a more equitable result than
the one-third approach.   On other sets of facts and figures the position may be reversed, particularly where the husband's income is lower or his liabilities higher
than in the present case, but this can only be determined by making both calculations and relating the results to the facts of the case. The learned judge was clearly
right in the present case to reject the result of the formula.

Counsel for the husband advanced three general arguments in support of the formula.
Echoing the Finer Report[1], he urged the advantages of uniformity of approach.
But this proves largely illusory because former husbands are not 'liable relatives',
so that the Supplementary Benefits Commission cannot recover contributions from
them and consequently do not have occasion to use the formula in cases where the
parties are divorced. Secondly, he urged that men are more likely to keep their
payments up to date if their orders are smaller. That may or may not be so as a
general proposition. Thirdly, he suggested that it is desirable to provide an incentive to
men to continue in work. In the present case the probability of the husband giving up
his job and a net income (after payment of the amount due under the order) of about
$£31$ per week for supplementary benefit at the rate of $£22$ per week seems remote.

In these circumstances this appeal must inevitably be dismissed on all grounds,
with the result that the registrar's order, which was plainly a reasonable and proper
one, stands.

In conclusion the court would like to express its thanks to the Attorney-General
and to counsel for him for their assistance in this case and to counsel for the parties
for taking the trouble to work out and agree the relevant figures and present them
in the form of schedules, which have been of great assistance. This is a practice which,
as this court has said before, ought to be followed in all cases of this kind, even comparatively simple ones. It shortens the proceedings and avoids the guesswork which
is otherwise unavoidable.

The appeal is therefore dismissed.

Appeal dismissed.

Solicitors: *Amery-Parkes & Co*, agents for *Rowberry Morris & Co*, Reading (for the
husband); *Hartley, Russell, Crowley & Co*, Reading (for the wife); *Treasury Solicitor.*

A S Virdi Esq Barrister.

1 (1974) Cmnd 5629

Multiservice Bookbinding Ltd and others v Marden

CHANCERY DIVISION
BROWNE-WILKINSON J
3rd, 4th, 5th, 6th, 9th, 11th MAY 1977

Money – Loan – Repayment of loan index-linked to foreign currency – Enforceability – Public policy – Mortgage – Parties within United Kingdom – Principal and interest due under mortgage to be repaid in sterling – Clause in mortgage index-linking sums concerned to Swiss franc – Whether index-linking of money obligation contrary to public policy – Whether clause void or unenforceable.

Mortgage – Redemption – Relief against contractual terms in mortgage transaction – Circumstances in which court will grant relief – Terms unfair and unconscionable – Mortgage to secure borrowed money – Mortgagor required to repay mortgagee principal and interest in sterling – Clause in mortgage index-linking to Swiss franc actual amount to be repaid – Depreciation of sterling against Swiss franc – Principal and interest to be repaid far exceeding in value nominal amount of sum lent – Whether clause unfair and unconscionable and therefore unenforceable.

In 1966 the plaintiffs, a small but prosperous company, needed cash to enable them to buy larger premises, costing £36,000, so that they could expand their business. They approached the defendant, who had £36,000 available, with a view to obtaining a loan. The defendant told them that he wanted to use the money in a way which would preserve its real purchasing power and would provide security for his retirement. He said that he would be willing to lend them the £36,000 provided that their liability to repay the capital and interest was linked to the value of the Swiss franc. Each side instructed separate solicitors who agreed a form of mortgage which was executed on 7th September 1966. The mortgage deed provided, inter alia, (i) that the plaintiffs would pay interest, at two per cent above bank rate, quarterly in advance on the whole of the £36,000 throughout the period of the loan notwithstanding the capital repayments; (ii) that arrears of interest would be capitalised after 21 days; (iii) that the loan could not be called in nor the mortgage redeemed during the first ten years of its life; and (iv) in cl 6 ('the Swiss franc uplift' provision) that any sum paid on account of interest or in repayment of the capital sum should be increased proportionately or decreased proportionately if at the close of business on the day preceding the day on which payment was to be made the rate of exchange between the Swiss franc and the pound sterling should vary by more than three per cent from the rate of 12·07⅝ francs to the pound sterling prevailing on 7th September 1966. In the decade which followed the pound greatly depreciated in value against the Swiss franc. In February 1976 the plaintiffs gave the defendant notice of their intention to redeem on 7th September 1976. They then brought a redemption action claiming the usual accounts which were duly ordered. When the redemption statement was prepared the rate of exchange was just over 4 Swiss francs to the pound. Although £24,355·57 had by then been repaid on capital account, the repayments had operated to reduce the nominal amount of the debt by only £15,000, leaving £21,000 nominal still to be discharged, which, after adding the Swiss franc uplift, meant that a further actual payment of £63,202·65 would be required, with the result that the defendant, who had advanced £36,000 in 1966, would receive £87,588·22 in repayment of capital. The combined effect of a high minimum lending rate and cl 6 of the mortgage deed had had a similar effect on the interest payable. The interest due totalled £45,380 (i e £31,051 basic interest + £14,329 Swiss franc uplift) which meant that the average rate of interest over the ten year period was 16·01 per cent. The plaintiffs applied to the court for the determination of the following questions which arose in taking the accounts: (i) whether cl 6 was void or unenforceable as being contrary to public policy; (ii) whether cl 6 or the terms of the mortgage, taken together, were unreasonable and as such unenforceable.

Held – (i) An index-linked money obligation in a contract made between two parties within the United Kingdom was not contrary to public policy; cl 6 was not therefore void or unenforceable as being contrary to public policy (see p 496 g, p 497 e and p 504 c, post); dictum of Denning LJ in *Treseder-Griffin v Co-operative Insurance Society Ltd* [1956] 2 All ER at 36 not followed.

(ii) The test of the enforceability of the terms of the mortgage was not whether they were reasonable but whether they were unfair and unconscionable. The court would hold that a bargain was unfair and unconscionable only where it was shown that one of the parties to it had imposed objectionable terms in a morally reprehensible manner. On the evidence there was nothing unfair, oppressive or morally reprehensible in the terms of the mortgage. The defendant had struck a hard bargain but had done nothing that he was not entitled to do by stipulating that he should be repaid the real value of the loan and had not been guilty of any sharp practice. The plaintiffs had entered into the bargain with their eyes open, with the benefit of independent advice and without any compelling necessity to accept the £36,000 on the terms offered. They were accordingly bound to comply with all the terms of the mortgage (see p 497 g, p 499 h j, p 502 a b and h j, p 503 e and p 504 c, post); *Kreglinger v New Patagonia Meat & Cold Storage Co Ltd* [1911-13] All ER Rep 970 and *Knightsbridge Estates Trust Ltd v Byrne* [1938] 3 All ER 618 applied; *Cityland & Property (Holdings) Ltd v Dabrah* [1967] 2 All ER 639 considered.

Notes

For the circumstances in which a bonus in addition to the sum advanced may be claimed by the mortgagee, see 27 Halsbury's Laws (3rd Edn) 238, para 428, and for cases on the subject, see 35 Digest (Repl) 407, 1022-1026.

Cases referred to in judgment

Biggs v Hoddinott [1898] 2 Ch 307, [1895-9] All ER Rep 625, 67 LJCh 540, 79 LT 201, CA, 35 Digest (Repl) 408, 1043.

Booth v Salvation Army Building Association Ltd (1897) 14 TLR 3, 35 Digest (Repl) 407, 1031.

Case of Mixed Money (1605) 2 State Tr 113, Davies's Rep 18, 80 ER 507, 11 Digest (Reissue) 751, 640.

Chambers v Goldwin (1804) 9 Ves 254, 1 Smith KB 252, 32 ER 600, 35 Digest (Repl) 420, 1127.

Cityland & Property (Holdings) Ltd v Dabrah [1967] 2 All ER 639, [1968] Ch 166, [1967] 3 WLR 605, Digest (Cont Vol C) 715, 625a.

Davis v Symons [1934] Ch 442, [1934] All ER Rep 136, 103 LJCh 311, 151 LT 96, 35 Digest (Repl) 408, 1046.

Knightsbridge Estates Trust Ltd v Byrne [1940] 2 All ER 401, [1940] AC 613, 109 LJCh 200, 162 LT 388, HL; affg [1938] 4 All ER 618, [1939] Ch 441, 108 LJCh 105, 160 LT 68, CA; rvsg [1938] 2 All ER 444, [1938] Ch 741, 35 Digest (Repl) 408, 1047.

Kreglinger v New Patagonia Meat & Cold Storage Co Ltd [1914] AC 25, [1911-13] All ER Rep 970, 83 LJCh 79, 109 LT 802, HL, 35 Digest (Repl) 280, 20.

New Brunswick Railway Co v British & French Trust Corpn Ltd [1938] 4 All ER 747, [1939] AC 1, 108 LJKB 115, 160 LT 137, 44 Com Cas 82, HL, 35 Digest (Repl) 186, 21.

R v International Trustee for the Protection of Bondholders Aktiengesellschaft [1937] 2 All ER 164, [1937] AC 500, 106 LJKB 236, 156 LT 352, 42 Com Cas 246, HL, 35 Digest (Repl) 186, 20.

Stanwell Park Hotel Co Ltd v Leslie (1952) 85 CLR 189, Aust HC.

Treseder-Griffin v Co-operative Insurance Society Ltd [1956] 2 All ER 33, [1956] 2 QB 127,
[1956] 2 WLR 866, [1956] 1 Lloyd's Rep 377, CA, 35 Digest (Repl) 190, 35.
White & Carter (Councils) Ltd v McGregor [1961] 3 All ER 1178, [1962] AC 413, [1962] 2
WLR 17, HL, 12 Digest (Reissue) 433, 3126.

Cases also cited

Ashworth v Lord (1887) 36 Ch D 545.
Bradley v Carritt [1903] AC 253, [1900-3] All ER Rep 633, HL.
Charles v Jones (1886) 33 Ch D 80, CA.
Commonwealth Savings Plan Ltd v Triangle C Cattle Co Ltd (1966) 55 WWR 52.
Cotterell v Stratton (1872) LR 8 Ch App 295.
Cottrell v Finney (1874) LR 9 Ch App 541.
Davis Contractors Ltd v Fareham Urban District Council [1956] 2 All ER 145, [1956] AC
696, HL.
Federal Commerce and Navigation Co Ltd v Tradax Export SA [1977] 1 All ER 79, [1977]
QB 937, CA.
Gledhow Autoparts Ltd v Delaney [1965] 3 All ER 288, [1965] 1 WLR 1366, CA.
Great Western Railway Co v Mostyn (Owners), The Mostyn [1928] AC 57, [1927] All ER
Rep 113, HL.
Harper v National Coal Board [1974] 2 All ER 441, [1974] QB 614, CA.
Lloyd's Bank Ltd v Bundy [1974] 3 All ER 757, [1975] QB 326, CA.
Lomax (Inspector of Taxes) v Peter Dixon & Son Ltd [1943] 2 All ER 255, [1943] 1 KB 671,
CA.
London Chartered Bank of Australia v White (1879) 4 App Cas 413, PC.
National Bank of Australasia v The United Hand-in-Hand and Band of Hope Co (1879) 4 App
Cas 391, PC.
Noakes & Co Ltd v Rice [1902] AC 24, [1900-3] All ER Rep 34, HL.
Salt v Marquess of Northampton [1892] AC 1, HL.
Samuel v Jarrah Timber & Wood Paving Corpn [1904] AC 323, HL.
Schroeder (A) Music Publishing Co Ltd v Macaulay [1974] 3 All ER 616, [1974] 1 WLR 1308,
HL.
Scruttons Ltd v Midland Silicones Ltd [1962] 1 All ER 1, [1962] AC 446, HL.
Teh Hu, The [1969] 3 All ER 1200, [1970] P 106, CA.

Adjourned summons

In March 1976 the plaintiffs, Multiservice Bookbinding Ltd, Eugene Louis Mara and
Margaret Lillian Marie-Therese Tatiana Mara, brought an action against the defendant,
Stephen Marden, claiming, under RSC Ord 88, r 1, (i) an account of what (if anything)
was due from the plaintiffs to the defendant under and by virtue of a legal charge
dated 7th September 1966 and made between the plaintiffs and the defendant whereby premises situated at Thornhill Road in the county of Greater London, N1, were
charged, and (ii) an order that on payment by the first plaintiff to the defendant of
any sum found due on the taking of the account the first plaintiff might be at liberty
to redeem the mortgaged property. On 11th May 1976 an order was made directing
an account to be made of what was due to the defendant under and by virtue of the
legal charge. By a summons dated 8th July 1976 and amended on 30th August 1976,
the plaintiffs applied to the court for the determination of the following question, pursuant to RSC Ord 44, r 20: whether on the true construction of cl 6 of the legal charge
any sum paid under it (being a sum the amount of which was increased or decreased
in accordance with the rate of exchange between the Swiss franc and the pound
sterling at the material time) in repayment of the capital sum or other moneys
thereby secured was to be credited as repaying the capital sum or moneys secured to
the extent of the amount of the payment before calculating such increase or decrease
and having regard to all the material facts whether (i) the provisions of cl 6 were (a)
void or (b) unenforceable, on the ground that they were contrary to public policy, and

(ii) if not so void or unenforceable, the provisions ought to be enforced by the court (a) in whole or (b) in part and if in part to what extent. The facts are set out in the judgment.

E G Nugee QC and *J Leigh Mellor* for the plaintiffs.
John Wilmers QC and *Gavin Lightman* for the defendant.

Cur adv vult

11th May. **BROWNE-WILKINSON J** read the following judgment: This case concerns a loan on mortgage by the defendant to the plaintiff company in September 1966, the most striking feature of which is that the sum repayable by way of principal and interest is variable, the amount payable being linked to an index. The amount payable is expressed in pounds sterling, but the amount varies proportionately to the variation in the rate of exchange as between the pound and the Swiss franc.

In 1966 the plaintiff company which carried on business as bookbinders and providers of after-print services, was in need of larger premises. Its directors and then sole shareholders, Mr and Mrs Mara, found a suitable property in Thornhill Road, north London, for sale for £36,000. The plaintiff company was unable to find this money itself or to borrow it from other sources. One of its employees, Mr Sebastian, introduced the plaintiffs to the defendant, who had money available. The defendant had recently sold his and his late wife's interest in his business for £100,000. He planned to invest this money in a way which would provide security for his retirement. Having used part in buying a house and stock exchange investments, he had some £40,000 remaining and was considering investing this remainder in buying real property. When approached for a loan by the plaintiffs he told them of his investment plans and stated the terms he would require clearly, including the provision whereby the liability of the plaintiffs would be linked to the value of the Swiss franc in order to safeguard him against a decline in the purchasing value of the pound sterling. Each side instructed separate solicitors who agreed a form of mortgage which was executed on 7th September 1966. This mortgage is made between the plaintiff company of the first part, Mr and Mrs Mara (as sureties) of the second part and the defendant of the third part. After reciting the agreement to lend £36,000, which was defined as the capital sum, the mortgage provided as follows:

'1. (a) In consideration of the capital sum now paid by the Lender to the Company at the request of the Sureties (the receipt whereof the Company hereby acknowledges) the Company and the Sureties hereby jointly and severally covenant with the Vendor (i) On the First day of December One thousand nine hundred and sixty six to repay the capital with interest thereon from the date hereof at the yearly rate equal to Bank Rate and further if the capital sum shall not be so paid to pay to the Lender during the first five years of the continuance of this security interest on the capital sum at the rate aforesaid and thereafter at the yearly rate of two per centum above Bank Rate or such lesser rate as may be agreed between the Lender and the Company Provided that for the purpose of calculating interest hereunder Bank Rate shall be taken as that prevailing at the date upon which each particular quarterly payment shall become due. (ii) If any interest due under the covenant hereinbefore contained shall at any time be in arrear for twenty one days after the quarterly day hereby appointed for payment thereof then and in every such case the interest so in arrear shall be converted into capital and be added to the capital sum (or such part thereof as shall be outstanding) as on the day the same became due as if the same had been money advanced by the Lender to the company on that day and every sum of money converted into capital as aforesaid shall be payable by the Company to the Lender

on demand and shall in the meantime bear interest at the rate and be payable on
the quarterly days aforesaid which interest shall if in arrear be converted into
capital under this Clause.

'(b) If and so long as—(i) The Company shall pay to the Lender by equal
quarterly instalments in advance on the First day of September, the First day of
March and the Fist day of June [sic] in each year interest on the capital sum hereby
secured (less tax) and the annual sum set out in the First Schedule hereto in
repayment of the capital sum the first payment of interest to be made on the
Seventh day of September One thousand nine hundred and sixty six in respect of
the period from the date hereof to the Thirtieth day of November One thousand
nine hundred and sixty six inclusive. (ii) The Company shall perform and observe
all its obligations hereunder. (iii) The Sureties (or other persons approved by
the Lender in writing) are the beneficial owners of the majority of the issued
ordinary share capital of the Company then the Lender will accept payment of
the quarterly instalments in repayment of the capital sum and in payment of the
interest thereon and will not enforce the security hereby constituted: Provided
always and it is hereby agreed and declared that the interest hereunder shall be
calculated on the whole of the capital sum secured hereby until repayment
thereof without reduction by reason of any repayment of part of the capital sum
Either the Lender or the Company may by giving at least six months' prior
written notice to the other expiring on the tenth anniversary hereof or upon any
subsequent date require the redemption of this Legal Charge by the Company
paying to the Lender the whole of the capital sum interest and other monies
hereby secured accrued up to and outstanding at the date of redemption and
upon the expiration of such notice the Company will so redeem this Legal Charge
and the Lender will accept such payment as aforesaid.'

It will be seen that in sub-cl (b) there is a reference to payment of the annual sum set
out in the first schedule thereto. Those sums together total £36,000 being the principal
and provide for repayments by instalments, no instalments being payable in the first
two years, thereafter annual sums at an increasing rate becoming payable until from
the ninth year onwards the annual rate of repayment is £3,000 per annum. By cl 2 of
the mortgage the company charged the premises mentioned in the schedule which
were the Thornhill Road properties—

'together with the fixtures and fittings now affixed to the premises and the
goodwill of the business of book-binders carried on by the company thereon . . .
with payment to the Company in accordance with the covenants herein contained
of all the capital sum interest and other monies hereby covenanted to be paid.'

Clause 4(a) of the mortgage contained a covenant to keep the buildings in repair.
Clause 4(c)(vii) was a covenant not to create any further charge on the mortgaged
property. Clause 4(d) provided that if the plaintiffs defaulted in performing the
covenants, the defendant could perform them and all expenses incurred by the
defendant were to be payable by the company on demand and in the meantime
charged on the property. Clause 5 varied the statutory powers of the mortgagee and
in particular provided that a receiver could manage the plaintiff company's business
and his expenses, together with interest, should be charged on the property. Then
cl 6 is in these terms:

'IT is a condition of the advance of the capital sum and is hereby agreed that any
sum to be paid hereunder on account of interest or in repayment of the capital
sum or other monies hereby secured shall be increased or decreased proportionately if at the close of business on the day preceding the day on which payment
is made the rate of exchange between the Swiss France and the Pound Sterling
shall vary by more than three per cent from the rate of 12·07 ⅝ francs to £1
prevailing at the date hereof. For this purpose (unless the parties agree to adopt a

different basis of calculation) the rate of exchange means the closing middle rate
on the London market as published in "The Times": Provided that if for a rele-   *a*
vant date closing rates are not so published or are published but in the opinion of
either party do not fairly represent the closing rates actually quoted or obtainable
in London or in the event of any disagreement between the parties as to the rate
of Exchange on any date the Certificate of the Westminster Bank Limited as to
the rate to be taken for the purpose of this clause . . . shall be final and binding on
the parties hereto for the purpose of this Legal Charge.'   *b*

Although, as I have read, the mortgage provided for interest at bank rate only and not
two per cent above for the first five years, it is common ground that I should treat the
interest payable as being two per cent above bank rate throughout, because Mr and
Mrs Mara agreed to increase Mr Sebastian's salary for five years by an amount approximately equal to the extra two per cent interest. The parties have treated references   *c*
to the bank rate as being references to the minimum lending rate.

It will be seen that the mortgage has the following features, not all of which are
common form: (1) the sum advanced was 100 per cent of the purchase price of the
property; (2) interest is payable quarterly in advance, on the whole sum of £36,000
throughout the period of the loan, notwithstanding the capital repayments which
were to be made from the third year onwards; (3) arrears of interest are capitalised   *d*
after 21 days, that is the mortgage provides for interest on interest; (4) the loan could
not be called in, nor was the mortgage redeemable during the first ten years; (5) The
provision of cl 6 for revalorising the loan (which is conveniently called the Swiss franc
uplift) applied not only to principal but also to interest and other monies secured by
the mortgage; (6) although six months notice of redemption had to be given, the
exact amount required to redeem could not be calculated until the day before actual   *e*
payment, since the calculation of the Swiss franc uplift depends on the rate of exchange
on that day.

Since 1966 the pound sterling has greatly depreciated as against the Swiss franc.
The September 1966 rate of exchange stated in the mortgage was just over 12 Swiss
francs to the pound. The rate at the beginning of October 1976 (when a redemption
statement was prepared) was just over 4 Swiss francs to the pound. Although by 15th   *f*
October 1976 some £24,355·57 had been repaid on capital account, these repayments
had operated to reduce the nominal amount of the debt by only £15,000. This left
£21,000 nominal to be discharged, which, after adding the Swiss franc uplift, would
require a further actual payment of £63,202·65. Accordingly, if redemption had
occurred on 15th October 1976, the defendant who had advanced £36,000 in 1966
would have received £87,588·22 in repayment of capital.   *g*

The combined effect of a high minimum lending rate and cl 6 has had a similar
effect on the interest payable. Down to 15th October 1976 interest due totalled
£45,380, made up as to £31,051 basic interest plus the Swiss Franc uplift of £14,329.
The average rate of interest over the whole ten years would have been 16·01 per cent.

As a final illustration, if one treats £36,000 as the principal and all other payments
(including the Swiss franc uplift element on capital repayments) as being charges on   *h*
the loan, the average annual rate of these charges (expressed as a percentage of the
capital outstanding) over the ten years would be 33·33 per cent. I emphasise that this
figure is only right if you artificially treat the Swiss franc uplift paid on the capital
repayments as a charge on the loan.

In these circumstances it is not surprising that the plaintiffs sought to redeem as
soon as they were able. By letter dated the 24th February 1976 they duly gave notice   *j*
to redeem on 7th September 1976. At the date of the notice it was impossible to
calculate the sum required for redemption, since the rate of exchange on 6th September 1976 was of course unknown. In fact between the date on which notice was
given and 15th October 1976 (the date down to which a redemption statement was
eventually made up) the amount required to pay off the outstanding capital (£21,000

nominal) increased by some £14,500, due to a further sharp depreciation of the

a pound against the Swiss franc.

However there is another side to the coin. Although the evidence is that in 1966 the plaintiff company was prosperous, its growth in the last ten years has been considerable. Comparing the years 1965-66 and 1975-76, turnover has risen from £39,323 to £184,879; profits (after charging directors emoluments and interest on the loan) from £674 to £14,759; directors remuneration from £5,000 to £21,898. It would be

b wrong to attribute these increases entirely to the new premises acquired in 1966; much must be due to the skill and hard work of Mr and Mrs Mara and the extra working capital introduced by them. But at least part of the increase must have been due to the availability of the larger premises, purchased with the loan made by the defendant. Perhaps most relevantly the property itself now stands in the books of the plaintiff company at a value of £93,075 (after deducting moneys expended since 1966).

c The last valuation was made in 1971-1972 before both the peak and the decline of the property market. It is therefore realistic to treat the property as being worth rather less than its book value. But at the very lowest, it has doubled in value and in my judgment there is not likely to be much difference between the capital growth, in terms of sterling, of the loan (from £36,000 to £87,588) and the capital growth of the property purchased by means of that loan. In making this assessment I have ignored

d the impact of tax on the parties (which is likely to bear more heavily on the plaintiffs) because in my judgment it is not relevant to any issue I have to consider.

On 15th March 1976, the plaintiffs started a redemption action claiming the usual accounts. These accounts were directed by an order dated 11th May 1976. On 16th June 1976 the plaintiffs took out a summons to determine two questions arising in taking the accounts, namely (a) whether the provision for the Swiss franc uplift in

e cl 6 is void or unenforceable as being against public policy; and (b) whether on some other ground the provisions of cl 6 should not be enforced. In fact the case as argued has been treated by both sides as embracing the wider question whether all the terms of the mortgage (taken together) are such as to be enforceable and if so to what extent.

I deal first with the question of public policy. The plaintiffs' case on this issue is

f based entirely on certain statements made by Denning LJ in *Treseder-Griffin v Co-operative Insurance Society Ltd*[1]. That case concerned the effect of a clause in a long lease which provided for the payment 'yearly during the said term either in gold sterling or Bank of England notes to the equivalent value in gold sterling the rent of £1,900 . . . by equal quarterly payments . . .' The main point at issue was one of construction, which does not touch the present case. But in the Court of Appeal

g Denning LJ said this[2]:

> 'This is the first case, so far as I know, to come before our courts where the parties have inserted a "gold clause" in a domestic contract where all the parties are within our own country. In external transactions it is, of course, quite common for parties to protect themselves against a depreciation in the rate of exchange by

h means of a gold clause. But in England we have always looked on a pound as a pound, whatever its international value. We have dealt in pounds for more than a thousand years—long before there were gold coins or paper notes—in all our dealings we have disregarded alike the debasement of the currency by kings and rulers or the depreciation of it by the march of time or events. This is well shown by the *Case of Mixed Money*[3]. Creditors and debtors have arranged for

j payment in our sterling currency in the sure knowledge that the sum they fix will be upheld by the law. A man who stipulates for a pound must take a pound

---

1   [1956] 2 All ER 33, [1956] 2 QB 127
2   [1956] 2 All ER 33 at 36, [1956] 2 QB 127 at 144
3   (1605) 2 State Tr 113

when payment is made, whatever the pound is worth at that time. Sterling is *a*
the constant unit of value by which in the eye of the law everything else is
measured. Prices of commodities may go up or down, other currencies may
go up and down, but sterling remains the same.'

Then, after referring to an example of that principle, he goes on[1]:

'The principle which I have stated is so well established that it is disturbing to
find a creditor inserting a gold clause in a domestic transaction. I am not al- *b*
together sure that it is lawful. In the United States gold clauses are declared by
the joint resolution of Congress to be contrary to public policy (see *R. v. International Trustee for Protection of Bondholders Aktiengesellschaft*[2]). In Canada they are
rendered inoperative by the Gold Clauses Act, 1937 (see *New Bruswick Ry. Co. v.
British & French Trust Corpn., Ltd.*[3]). Many other countries have like legislation.
In France, ever since the Franco-Prussian War, the Cour de Cassation has ruled *c*
that gold clauses are invalid in the case of internal contracts for payments in
France by the French people; but they are valid in the case of international
payments, i.e., those which involve a traffic across international frontiers. Those
countries do it, I suppose, to protect their own currencies. If we are now to hold
gold clauses valid in England for internal payments, we may be opening a door
through which lessors and mortgagees, debenture-holders and preference share- *d*
holders, and many others, may all pass. We might find every creditor stipulating
for payment according to the price of gold: and every debtor scanning the bullion
market to find out how much he has to pay. What then is to become of sterling? It
would become a discredited currency unable to look its enemy inflation in the
face. That should not be allowed to happen.'

Morris LJ (who with Denning LJ constituted the majority of the Court of Appeal *e*
on the construction point) expressed no view on the public policy point. Harman LJ
(who dissented on the construction point)[4] expressly said that such a clause was not
unlawful even in a domestic contract.

Counsel for the plaintiffs contended that the remarks of Denning LJ formed a
separate ground of decision which was binding on me. I cannot think this is right.
Denning LJ prefaces the material passage by the words, and I quote[5], 'I am not *f*
altogether sure that it is lawful'. These are not words of decision but of doubt.
Therefore in my opinion Denning LJ's dictum is not strictly binding on me. But of
course it carries great weight.

I have had the point elaborately argued before me by distinguished counsel, and
after considering the arguments I do not feel that in the year 1977 I can declare that
an index-linked money obligation is contrary to public policy. The reasons which *g*
lead me to this view are as follows: (1) If, as Denning LJ says, the evil to be guarded
against is that sterling will become discredited, this evil will flow not only from
indexing by reference to the price of gold or Swiss francs, but equally from any other
form of indexing, for example an obligation quantified by reference to the cost of
living index. The evil lies in the revalorisation of the pound sterling by reference to
any other yardstick, not in the nature of the yardstick itself. (2) Today a large number *h*
of obligations originally expressed in pounds sterling are varied by reference to an
external yardstick. Long-term commercial contracts frequently include index
linked obligations, as do many contracts of employment. The rent payable under
certain leases has for centuries been made variable dependent on the price of corn.
More important, Parliament itself has authorised the linking of public service pensions
to the cost of living and the issue of savings bonds similarly linked. It would be *j*

1   [1956] 2 All ER 33 at 36, 37, [1956] 2 QB 127 at 145
2   [1937] 2 All ER 164, [1937] AC 500
3   [1938] 4 All ER 747, [1939] AC 1
4   [1956] 2 All ER 33 at 48, [1956] 2 QB 127 at 163
5   [1956] 2 All ER 33 at 36, [1956] 2 QB 127 at 145

strange if Parliament had authorised transactions contrary to public policy. (3)
a Denning LJ treated the process of index-linking as being a cause, not a symptom, of
inflation. I know nothing of economics but it has been demonstrated to me that
economists are not agreed that indexing has a deleterious effect in promoting inflation. It would in my judgment be wrong for the courts to declare that a particular
class of transaction is against the public interest even though there is a body of better-
informed opinion that takes the view that no harm is caused. It is for Parliament,
b with all its facilities for weighing the complex issues involved, to make a policy
decision of this kind. (4) It seems to me that, even if there are good grounds for
saying that indexing causes inflation, there may well be counter-availing considerations which would have to be weighed. In any economy where there is inflation
there are few inducements to make long-term loans expressed in a currency the
value of which is being eroded. It is at least possible that, unless lenders can ensure
c that they are repaid the real value of the money they advanced (and not merely a
sum of the same nominal amount but in devalued currency) the availability of loan
capital will be much diminished. This would surely not be in the public interest. (5)
Shortly after 1956, the Cour de Cassation in France reversed its policy (referred to by
Denning LJ) and allowed index-linked obligations even in domestic contracts. Index-
linked obligations were held valid by the High Court of Australia in *Stanwell Park*
d *Hotel Co Ltd v Leslie*[1].

Therefore I feel unable to follow the obiter dictum of Denning LJ. I need hardly
say that I do so with considerable diffidence; but I receive some comfort from the
fact that since he expressed his views we have experienced 20 years of inflation and,
on the somewhat analogous question whether a judgment of an English court can be
expressed otherwise than in pounds sterling, he has departed from the nominalist
e principle which underlies his remarks in the *Treseder-Griffin* case[2]. In my judgment,
cl 6 of the mortgage is not contrary to public policy.

I turn then to the question whether the mortgage is unconscionable or unreasonable.
The plaintiffs' starting point on this aspect of the case is a submission that a lender on
mortgage is only entitled to repayment of principal, interest and costs. If the lender
additionally stipulates for a premium or other collateral advantage the court will not
f enforce such additional stipulation unless it is reasonable. Then it is submitted that
cl 6 (providing for the payment of the Swiss franc uplift in addition to the nominal
amount of capital and interest) is a premium which in all the circumstances is unreasonable. Alternatively it is said that the terms of the mortgage taken together
are unreasonable. In my judgment the argument so advanced is based on a false
premise. Since the repeal of the usury laws there has been no general principle that
g collateral advantages in mortgages have to be 'reasonable'. The law is fully explained
by the House of Lords in *Kreglinger v New Patagonia Meat and Cold Storage Co Ltd*[3] and
in particular in the speech of Lord Parker. In that case money had been advanced on
mortgage by woolbrokers to meat preservers, and in the same document the meat
preservers gave the woolbrokers a right of first refusal over any sheepskins to be sold
by the meat preservers, such right to last for five years. The mortgage having been
h redeemed within the five years, the meat preservers claimed that the right of first
refusal was unenforceable as being a collateral stipulation. It was common ground
that the arrangement was fair and reasonable.

In his speech Lord Parker reviews the whole of the law relating to clogs on the
equity of redemption and collateral advantages. He says this[4]:

j   'My Lords, there is another point which has some importance, namely, the
terms upon which equity allowed redemption after the estate had become

---

1   (1952) 85 CLR 189
2   [1956] 2 All ER 33, [1956] 2 QB 127
3   [1914] AC 25, [1911-13] All ER Rep 970
4   [1914] AC 25 at 49, 50, [1911-13] All ER Rep 970 at 980, 981

absolute at law. Except in the case of mortgages to secure moneys advanced by
way of loan, to which I shall presently refer, equity only allowed redemption on   *a*
the mortgagor giving effect so far as he could to the terms on which by the
bargain between the parties he had a contractual right to redeem the property.
Equity might, and most frequently did, impose further terms, e.g., payment of
interest up to the date of redemption and proper mortgagees' costs. But except
in the case of mortgages to secure moneys advanced by way of loan, I can find no
trace in the authorities of any equitable right to redeem without giving effect   *b*
as far as possible to the terms of the bargain. This is consistent with the principle
underlying the rule as to clogging the equity. In relieving from penalties or
forfeitures equity has always endeavoured to put the parties as far as possible
into the position in which they would have been if no penalty or forfeiture had
occurred. It is only in the case of mortgages to secure moneys advanced by way of
loan that there was ever any equity to redeem on terms not involving perfor-   *c*
mance of the bargain between the parties. The reason for this exception will
appear presently.'

He then further considers certain other points and turns to consider the case of
mortgages to secure borrowed money, and I quote[1]:

'My Lords, I now come to the particular class of mortgages to which I have   *d*
already referred, that is to say, mortgages to secure borrowed money. For the
whole period during which the Court of Chancery was formulating and laying
down its equitable doctrines in relation to mortgages there existed statutes
strictly limiting the rate of interest which could be legally charged for borrowed
money. If a mortgagee stipulated for some advantage beyond repayment of his
principal with interest, equity considered that he was acting contrary to the   *e*
spirit of these statutes, and held the stipulation bad on this ground. There thus
arose the rule so often referred to in the reported decisions, that in a mortgage
to secure borrowed money the mortgagee could not contract for any such
advantage. There was said to be an equity to redeem on payment of principal,
interest, and costs, whatever might have been the bargain between the parties,
and any stipulation by the mortgagee for a further or, as it was sometimes called,   *f*
a collateral advantage came to be spoken of as a clog or fetter on this equity. It
is of the greatest importance to observe that this equity is not the equity to redeem
with which I have hitherto been dealing. It is an equity which arises ab initio, and
not only on failure to exercise the contractual right to redeem. It can be asserted
before as well as after such failure. It has nothing to do with time not being of
the essence of a contract, or with relief from penalties or with repugnant con-   *g*
ditions. It is not a right to redeem on the contractual terms, but a right to redeem
notwithstanding the contractual terms, a right which depended on the existence
of the statutes against usury and the public policy thought to be involved in those
statutes. Unfortunately, in some of the authorities this right is spoken of as a
right incidental to mortgages generally, and not confined to mortgages to secure
borrowed money. This is quite explicable when it is remembered that a loan is   *h*
perhaps the most frequent occasion for a mortgage. But is, I think, none the less
erroneous. I can find no instance of the rule which precludes a mortgagee from
stipulating for a collateral advantage having been applied to a mortgage other
than a mortgage to secure borrowed money, and there is the authority of Lord
Eldon in *Chambers* v. *Goldwin*[2] for saying that this rule was based on the usury
laws. The right (notwithstanding the terms of the bargain) to redeem on pay-   *j*
ment of principal, interest, and costs is a mere corollary to this rule, and falls
with it. It is to be observed that stipulations for a collateral advantage may be

1   [1914] AC 25 at 54-56, [1911-13] All ER Rep 970 at 983, 984
2   (1804) 9 Ves 254

classified under two heads—first, those the performance of which is made a term of the contractual right to redeem, and, secondly, those the performance of which is not made a term of such contractual right. In the former case in settling the terms on which redemption was allowed the Court of Chancery entirely ignored such stipulations. In the latter case, so far as redemption was concerned, the stipulations were immaterial, but it is said that in both cases the Court of Chancery would have restrained an action at law for damages for their breach. This is possible, though I can find no instance of its having been done, but clearly on a bill for an injunction to restrain an action at law the plaintiff would have to show some equity entitling him to be relieved from his contract, and such equity could, I think, have been based only on the usury laws, or the public policy which gave rise to them. The last of the usury laws was repealed in 1854, and thenceforward there was, in my opinion, no intelligible reason why mortgages to secure loans should be on any different footing from other mortgages. In particular, there was no reason why the old rule against a mortgagee being able to stipulate for a collateral advantage should be maintained in any form or with any modification. Borrowers of money were fully protected from oppression by the pains always taken by the Court of Chancery to see that the bargain between borrower and lender was not unconscionable. Unfortunately, at the time when the last of the usury laws was repealed, the origin of the rule appears to have been more or less forgotten, and the cases decided since such repeal exhibit an extraordinary diversity of judicial opinion on the subject. It is little wonder that, with the existence in the authorities of so many contradictory theories, persons desiring to repudiate a fair and reasonable bargain have attempted to obtain the assistance of the Court in that behalf. My Lord, to one who, like myself, has always admired the way in which the Court of Chancery succeeded in supplementing our common law system in accordance with the exigencies of a growing civilization, it is satisfactory to find, as I have found on analysing the cases in question, that no such attempt has yet been successful. In every case in which a stipulation by a mortgagee for a collateral advantage has, since the repeal of the usury laws, been held invalid, the stipulation has been open to objection, either (1) because it was unconscionable, or (2) because it was in the nature of a penal clause clogging the equity arising on failure to exercise a contractual right to redeem, or (3) because it was in the nature of a condition repugnant as well to the contractual as to the equitable right.'

Then he says words much to the same effect[1]:

'My Lords, after the most careful consideration of the authorities I think it is open to this House to hold, and I invite your Lordships to hold, that there is now no rule in equity which precludes a mortgagee, whether the mortgage be made upon the occasion of a loan or otherwise, from stipulating for any collateral advantage, provided such collateral advantage is not either (1) unfair and unconscionable, or (2) in the nature of a penalty clogging the equity of redemption, or (3) inconsistent with or repugnant to the contractual and equitable right to redeem.'

It is not suggested in this case that any of the terms of the mortgage clog the equity of redemption or are inconsistent with the right to redeem. Therefore on Lord Parker's test, if the plaintiffs are to be excused from complying with any of the terms of the mortgage they must show that the term is, and I quote[2], 'unfair and unconscionable'; the test is not one of reasonableness.

Lord Parker's reasoning is entirely consistent with that of Lord Haldane LC, who

---

1   [1914] AC 25 at 60, 61, [1911-13] All ER Rep 970 at 986, 987
2   [1914] AC 25 at 61, [1911-13] All ER Rep 970 at 987

states[1] that since the repeal of the usury laws 'a collateral advantage may now be stipulated for by the mortgagee provided that he has not acted unfairly or **a** oppressively'.

In the *Kreglinger* case[2] the exact question whether the true test was 'unconscionableness' or 'unreasonableness' did not arise for decision because it was conceded that the bargain was a reasonable one in that case. But in my judgment the exact point was decided by the Court of Appeal in *Knightsbridge Estates Trust Ltd v Byrne*[3]. In that case the borrower and lender were both large companies. The terms of the **b** mortgage provided for repayment of principal by instalments over 40 years. The borrower wished to redeem by paying off the whole debt much sooner. At first instance, Luxmoore J[4] held that they were so entitled to redeem since the terms of the mortgage were such that they were, and I quote, 'onerous and unreasonable'. The Court of Appeal reversed his decision. Greene MR, having stated that a postponement of a right to redeem was not a clog on the equity of redemption (i e the **c** case did not fall within the second or third of Lord Parker's categories), says this[5]:

> 'Moreover, equity may give relief against contractual terms in a mortgage transaction if they are oppressive or unconscionable, and in deciding whether or not a particular transaction falls within this category the length of time for which the contractual right to redeem is postponed may well be an important considera- **d** tion. In the present case no question of this kind was or could have been raised. Equity, however, does not reform mortgage transactions because they are unreasonable. It is concerned to see two things, (i) that the essential requirements of a mortgage transaction are observed, and (ii) that oppressive or unconscionable terms are not enforced. Subject to this, it does not, in our opinion, interfere.'

In commenting on the use of the word 'reasonable' by Romer J in *Biggs v Hoddinott*[6], **e** Greene MR says this[7]:

> 'We do not think that the word "unreasonable" should be interpreted as meaning that the court is to disregard the bargain made by the parties merely because it comes to the conclusion that it is an unreasonable one. A postpone- ment of the right of redemption may be the badge of oppression, or it may be **f** unreasonable in the sense that it renders the right of redemption illusory. We doubt whether ROMER, J., meant more than this.'

Again in commenting on *Davis v Symons*[8] (in which Eve J referred to the stipulation as being 'extravagant and oppressive' but also used the word 'reasonable') Greene MR did not dissent from the former test but stated that if the word 'reasonable' meant something less than oppressive it was not a correct test. Finally, the Court of Appeal **g** overruled the decision of Luxmoore J on this point, and said[9]:

> 'In our opinion, if we are right in thinking that the postponement is by itself unobjectionable, it cannot be made objectionable by the presence in the mortgage deed of other provisions, unless the totality is sufficient to enable the court to say that the contract is so oppressive or unconscionable that it ought not to be **h** enforced in a court of equity. If such other provisions are collateral advantages

---

1 [1914] AC 25 at 37, [1911-13] All ER Rep 970 at 974
2 [1914] AC 25, [1911-13] All ER Rep 970
3 [1938] 4 All ER 618, [1939] Ch 441
4 [1938] 2 All ER 444 at 459, [1938] Ch 741 at 768
5 [1938] 4 All ER 618 at 626, [1939] Ch 441 at 457
6 [1898] 2 Ch 307, [1895-9] All ER Rep 625
7 [1938] 4 All ER 618 at 628, [1939] Ch 441 at 459
8 [1934] Ch 442, [1934] All ER Rep 136
9 [1938] 4 All ER 618 at 630, [1939] Ch 441 at 463

which are inadmissible upon the principles laid down by LORD PARKER in the passage cited above, they will, of course, fall to be dealt with as such.'

In my judgment the Court of Appeal in overruling the decision of Luxmoore J based on the unreasonableness of the term made a decision, first that if a postponement of the right to redeem is not objectionable on the grounds that it is a clog on the right to redeem, it is enforceable like any other stipulation unless it falls into Lord Parker's first category as being oppressive or unconscionable; and secondly that mere unreasonableness does not make a term oppressive or unconscionable. *Knightsbridge Estates Trust Ltd v Byrne*[1] went to the House of Lords where the decision of the Court of Appeal was upheld on other grounds, but so far as I can see no doubt was thrown on the reasoning of the Court of Appeal.

I have dealt with these authorities at some length because the sheet anchor of counsel for the plaintiffs' argument that mere unreasonableness is sufficient to invalidate a stipulation is the use of the word 'unreasonable' by Goff J in *Cityland & Property (Holdings) Ltd v Dabrah*[2]. In that case the plaintiff company was the freehold owner of a house of which the defendant had been the tenant for 11 years. His lease expired and the plaintiff company sold the freehold to him for £3,500, of which the defendant paid £600 in cash and the balance of £2,900 was left by the plaintiff company on mortgage. The mortgage was in unusual terms in that it contained simply a covenant to pay, by instalments, the sum of £4,553, that is to say, a premium of 57 per cent over the sum advanced. No explanation was given as to what this premium represented. The defendant defaulted in paying his instalments after only one year, and the plaintiff was seeking to enforce his security for the full sum of £4,553 less payments actually made. Not surprisingly Goff J refused to permit this on the grounds that the excess over £2,900 was an unlawful premium. Bearing in mind the relative strength of lender and borrower, the size of the premium and the lack of any explanation or justification for it, the premium in that case was unconscionable and oppressive. The difficulty arises from a passage in the judgment, where after reviewing the authorities, including citations at length from Lord Parker's speech in the *Kreglinger* case[3], the learned judge quoted this passage from Halsbury's Laws of England[4]:

'. . . but a contract for payment to the mortgagee of a bonus in addition to the sum advanced is valid if the bonus is reasonable and the contract was freely entered into by the mortgagor.'

Having quoted that passage Goff J went on[5]:

'It follows from those authorities that the defendant cannot succeed merely because this is a collateral advantage, but he can succeed if, and only if, on the evidence the bonus in this case was, to use the language of LORD PARKER[6], ". . . unfair and unconscionable", or, to use the language used in HALSBURY[4], "unreasonable", and I therefore have to determine whether it was or was not.'

There are other passages in the judgment where the learned judge seems to treat the words 'unreasonable' and 'unconscionable' as being interchangeable. But in that case it was unnecessary for Goff J to distinguish between the two concepts, since on either test the premium was unenforceable. I do not think that Goff J intended to cut down the obvious effect of the *Kreglinger* case[3] in any way. Moreover, the decision of the Court of Appeal in *Knightsbridge Estates Trust Ltd v Byrne*[7] was not cited to him.

---

1 [1940] 2 All ER 401, [1940] AC 613
2 [1967] 2 All ER 639, [1968] Ch 166
3 [1914] AC 25, [1911-13] All ER Rep 970
4 27 Halsbury's Laws (3rd Edn) 238, para 428
5 [1967] 2 All ER 639 at 647, [1968] Ch 166 at 180
6 [1914] AC 25 at 61, [1911-13] All ER Rep 970 at 987
7 [1938] 4 All ER 618, [1939] Ch 441

I therefore approach the second point on the basis that, in order to be freed from the necessity to comply with all the terms of the mortgage, the plaintiffs must show *a* that the bargain, or some of its terms, was unfair and unconscionable; it is not enough to show that, in the eyes of the court, it was unreasonable.

In my judgment a bargain cannot be unfair and unconscionable unless one of the parties to it has imposed the objectionable terms in a morally reprehensible manner, that is to say, in a way which affects his conscience.

The classic example of an unconscionable bargain is where advantage has been *b* taken of a young, inexperienced or ignorant person to introduce a term which no sensible well-advised person or party would have accepted. But I do not think the categories of unconscionable bargains are limited; the court can and should intervene where a bargain has been procured by unfair means.

Counsel for the plaintiffs submitted that a borrower was, in the normal case, in an unequal bargaining position vis-à-vis the lender, and that the care taken by the courts *c* of equity to protect borrowers (to which Lord Parker referred in the passage I have quoted) was reflected in a general rule that, except in the case of two large equally powerful institutions, any unreasonable term would be 'unconscionable' within Lord Parker's test. I cannot accept this. In my judgment there is no such special rule applicable to contracts of loan which requires one to treat a bargain as having been unfairly made even where it is demonstrated that no unfair advantage has *d* been taken of the borrower. No decision illustrating counsel for the plaintiffs' principle was cited. However, if, as in the *Cityland* case[1], there is an unusual or unreasonable stipulation the reason for which is not explained, it may well be that in the absence of any explanation, the court will assume that unfair advantage has been taken of the borrower. In considering all the facts, it will often be the case that the borrower's need for the money was far more pressing than the lender's need to lend; *e* if this proves to be the case, then circumstances exist in which an unfair advantage could have been taken. It does not necessarily follow that what could have been done has been done; whether or not an unfair advantage has in fact been taken depends on the facts of each case.

Applying those principles to this case, first I do not think it is right to treat the Swiss franc uplift element in the capital repayments as being in any sense a premium or collateral advantage. In my judgment a lender of money is entitled to ensure that he is repaid the real value of his loan and if he introduces a term which so provides, he is not stipulating for anything beyond the repayment of principal. I do not think equity would have struck down cl 6 as a collateral advantage even before the repeal of the usury laws. The decision in *Booth v Salvation Army Building Association*[2] turned on quite different considerations. It is in my opinion correctly explained by Professor *g* Waldock in his Law of Mortgages[3] as a decision that any additional sum expressed to be payable on redemption or default is not recoverable since it is a clog on the equity of redemption.

Secondly, considering the mortgage bargain as a whole, in my judgment there was no great inequality of bargaining power as between the plaintiffs and the defendant. The plaintiff company was a small but prosperous company in need of cash *h* to enable it to expand; if it did not like the terms offered it could have refused them without being made insolvent or (as in the *Cityland* case[1]) losing its home. The defendant had £40,000 to lend, but only, as he explained to the plaintiffs, if its real value was preserved. The defendant is not a professional moneylender and there is no evidence of any sharp practice of any kind by him. The plaintiffs were represented by independent solicitors of repute. Therefore the background does not give rise to any presupposition that the defendant took an unfair advantage of the plaintiffs.

1 [1967] 2 All ER 639, [1968] Ch 166
2 (1897) 14 TLR 3
3 2nd Edn (1950), pp 182, 183

Counsel for the plaintiffs' main case is based on the terms of the mortgage itself.
a He points to the facts that (1) the defendant's principal and interest is fully inflation
proofed; (2) that interest is payable at 2 per cent above minimum lending rate; and
(3) that interest is payable on the whole £36,000 throughout the term of the loan.
He says that although any one of these provisions by itself might not be objectionable,
when all these are joined in one mortgage they are together 'unfair and unconscionable'. He adds further subsidiary points, amongst them that it is impossible to
b know the sum required for redemption when notice to redeem has to be given;
that interest is payable in advance; that no days of grace were allowed for paying
the instalments of capital and any expenses incurred by the lender are charged on the
property and therefore under cl 6 are subject to the Swiss franc uplift even though
incurred long after 1966. He also contends that if there were capitalised arrears of
interest, the Swiss franc uplift would be applied twice, once when the arrears are
c capitalised and again when the capitalised sum is paid; but in my opinion this is not the
true construction of the mortgage.

However, counsel for the plaintiffs' other points amount to a formidable list and
if it were relevant I would be of the view that the terms were unreasonable judged
by the standards which the court would adopt if it had to settle the terms of a mortgage.
In particular I consider that it was unreasonable both for the debt to be inflation
d proofed by reference to the Swiss franc and at the same time to provide for a rate of
interest two per cent above bank rate (a rate which reflects at least in part the unstable
state of the pound sterling). On top of this interest on the whole sum advanced was
to be paid throughout the term. The defendant made a hard bargain. But the test is
not reasonableness. The parties made a bargain which the plaintiffs, who are businessmen, went into with their eyes open, with the benefit of independent advice, without
e any compelling necessity to accept a loan on these terms and without any sharp
practice by the defendant. I cannot see that there was anything unfair or oppressive
or morally reprehensible in such a bargain entered into in such circumstances. The
need for the defendant to invest his money in a way which preserved its real purchasing power provides an adequate explanation of all the terms of the mortgage,
except the provision which would apply the Swiss franc uplift to expenses defrayed in,
f say 1975, for which there can be no possible justification. It is common ground that
this was not an intended result (and therefore it cannot reflect on the morality of the
defendant's behaviour) and the defendant has stated that he would not apply the
Swiss franc uplift to money other than the principal and interest. It is not necessary
for me, therefore, to decide whether cl 6 would be permitted to apply to such
expenditure.

g In opening, counsel for the plaintiffs advanced the contention that even if at the date
the mortgage was entered into, it was unobjectionable the court would not now
enforce it in its full rigour because the dramatic fall in the value of the pound was not
foreseen in 1966 and hardship would be caused to the plaintiffs. I am not sure that
such contention was persisted in, but I know of no such dispensing power vested in the
court and I agree with counsel for the defendant that, if there was such a power, the
h doctrine of frustration of contracts and all the legal difficulty that it has caused would
have been unnecessary. A contract is not frustrated just because the parties had not
foreseen the event which occurred, but only if the provisions of the contract do not
cover that event.

If equity could, ever since 1875, have relieved a party from the harsh consequences
of unforeseen events, one would expect the point at least to have been argued in
j some case; but I have not been referred to any such case. On the contrary in *White
& Carter (Councils) Ltd v McGregor*[1] Lord Hodson said this:

'It is trite that equity will not rewrite an improvident contract where there is

---

1   [1961] 3 All ER 1178 at 1193, [1962] AC 413 at 445

no disability on either side. There is no duty laid on a party to a subsisting contract to vary it at the behest of the other party so as to deprive himself of the benefit given to him by the contract. To hold otherwise would be to introduce a novel equitable doctrine that a party was not to be held to his contract unless the court in a given instance thought it reasonable so to do. In this case it would make an action for debt a claim for a discretionary remedy. This would introduce an uncertainty into the field of contract which appears to be unsupported by authority either in English or Scottish law save for the one case on which the Court of Session founded its opinion and which must, in my judgment, be taken to have been wrongly decided.'

Therefore although I have considerable sympathy for Mr and Mrs Mara who will obviously suffer considerable hardship as a result of the unforeseen fall in the value of the pound sterling, I must declare that the whole of the provisions of cl 6 of the mortgage are valid and enforceable.

Declaration accordingly.

Solicitors: *S R Freed & Co* (for the plaintiffs); *Turner Peacock* (for the defendant).

Hazel Hartman Barrister.

Steel v Union of Post Office Workers and others

EMPLOYMENT APPEAL TRIBUNAL
PHILLIPS J, MRS D EWING AND MR T H GOFF
16th JUNE, 11th JULY 1977

Sex discrimination – Discrimination – Requirement or condition such that proportion of people of one sex who can comply with it considerably smaller than proportion of people of other sex – Justifiable requirement irrespective of sex – Employment – Onus on employer of showing that requirement justifiable – Need to show requirement necessary and not merely convenient – Need for requirement to be weighed against discriminatory effect – Sex Discrimination Act 1975, s 1(1)(b)(ii).

A basic distinction was made by the Post Office between 'temporary' and 'permanent' postmen. There was a seniority roll for permanent postmen and an individual was placed on it with seniority dating from the date of his appointment as a permanent postman. Before 1st September 1975 a postwoman could not attain permanent status. In preparation for the coming into force of the Sex Discrimination Act 1975, and as a result of an agreement between the Post Office and the postal workers' trade union, the restriction was abandoned. Accordingly, on 1st September the appellant, who had been employed as a 'temporary' postwoman by the Post Office since 1961, was raised to the status of a permanent postwoman, her seniority as such dating from that date. In March 1976 the Post Office invited applications from permanent postal employees to fill a situation that had become vacant. The normal practice of the Post Office in selecting a suitable candidate for the situation to be filled was based on seniority. Accordingly they selected a male postman who, although younger than the appellant, had attained the status of permanent postman on 9th July 1973. The appellant complained to an industrial tribunal, alleging that the Post Office had unlawfully discriminated against her under the 1975 Act. The tribunal dismissed her complaint and she appealed, contending that the rule as to seniority was a requirement or condition such that the proportion of woman who could comply with it was considerably smaller than the proportion of men who could do so, and was one which could not be justified and was to her detriment, within s $1(1)(b)(ii)^a$ of the 1975 Act.

Held – (i) In order to show that a requirement or condition which applied to a woman was one which was justifiable irrespective of the sex of the person to whom it applied, within s $1(1)(b)(ii)$ of the 1975 Act, a heavy onus rested on the employer to satisfy the tribunal that the case was a genuine one where it could be said that the requirement or condition was necessary. In deciding whether the employer had discharged that onus the tribunal had to take into account all the circumstances, including the discriminatory effect of the requirement or condition if it was permitted to continue, and was required to weigh the need for the requirement or condition against that effect. In distinguishing between a requirement or condition which was necessary and one which was merely convenient it was relevant to consider whether the employer could find some other and non-discriminatory method of achieving his object (see p 510 *a* to *c* and *g* and p 508 *g* to *j*, post); dictum of Phillips J in *Snoxell v Vauxhall Motors Ltd* [1977] 3 All ER at 778, 779 applied.

(ii) The appellant was entitled to succeed in her claim unless the Post Office could show that the seniority rule was justifiable irrespective of the sex of the person to whom it was applied. Accordingly the appeal would be allowed and the case remitted to an industrial tribunal (see p 509 *j* and p 511 *f*, post).

Notes

For discrimination against employees and applicants on the grounds of sex, see 16 Halsbury's Laws (4th Edn) para 771:5.

For the Sex Discrimination Act 1975, ss 1, 6, see 45 Halsbury's Statutes (3rd Edn) 227, 229.

Cases referred to in judgment

Corning Glassworks v Brennan (1974) 417 US 188, 41 L Ed 2d1, US SC.
Griggs v Duke Power Co (1971) 401 US 424, US SC.
Peake v Automotive Products Ltd [1977] QB 780, [1977] 2 WLR 751, [1977] ICR 480, EAT; rvsd [1978] 1 All ER 106, [1977] 3 WLR 853, [1977] ICR 968, CA.
Snoxell v Vauxhall Motors Ltd [1977] 3 All ER 770, [1978] QB 11, [1977] 3 WLR 189, [1977] ICR 700, EAT.

Appeal

This was an appeal by Mrs L B Steel against the decision of an industrial tribunal (chairman John Prosser Esq) sitting at Cardiff on 21st September 1976 dismissing her complaint against the Post Office and the Union of Post Office Workers ('the union'), whereby she alleged that the Post Office and the union had unlawfully discriminated against her. The facts are set out in the judgment of the appeal tribunal.

Michael Beloff for Mrs Steel.
James Goudie for the Post Office.
Mr J R Fraser for the union.

Cur adv vult

11th July.   **PHILLIPS J** read the following judgment of the appeal tribunal: Mrs Steel entered the employment of the Post Office on 6th November 1961, and has

---

a Section (1) is set out at p 508 *c* and *d*, post

remained so employed since that date. The Post Office has undergone various changes in status and organisation but nothing turns on that. On 30th April 1976 *a* she complained to an industrial tribunal that the Post Office and her trade union, the Union of Post Office Workers ('the union'), had unlawfully discriminated against her on the ground of her sex in the field of employment within Part II of the Sex Discrimination Act 1975. An industrial tribunal sitting at Cardiff on 21st September 1976, by a decision entered on 1st October 1976, dismissed her complaint. Mrs Steel was not represented on the hearing before the industrial tribunal, and in the course of *b* her remarks she explained that she had no complaint against the Post Office, but that her complaint was against her union which had made with the Post Office an agreement relating to the seniority of female postal workers which discriminated against her and other women. The industrial tribunal decided the case on the narrow ground that Mrs Steel was making no complaint against the Post Office and that her complaint aginst the union was misconceived. In the result the industrial tribunal *c* never considered the terms of the 1975 Act, or the possibility of its application to the facts of the case before it, and concluded the reasons for its decision in these words:

'We will only add that although she fails against both Respondents, we can understand Mrs Steel's feelings, with regard to the rules to seniority, particularly as she has been working as a post-woman since 6 November 1961. Having *d* said that however, we must say no more because such matters are entirely for the union, its members and the General Post Office.'

We are satisfied that this was the wrong approach, and that it is erroneous to say 'such matters are entirely for the union, its members and the General Post Office'. Such matters are for the industrial tribunal to decide in accordance with the terms of the 1975 Act.

There is no dispute on the facts, and where there is any deficiency in the decision *e* of the industrial tribunal it has been made good on the hearing of the appeal by admissions made by the parties. A basic distinction in the Post Office is between temporary and permanent postmen. Permanent postmen are sometimes described as 'long-term' postmen or as having long-term status. The meaning is the same, and 'permanent' or 'long-term' is used in the sense of 'established'. There are three kinds *f* of postmen: 'temporary part-time', 'temporary full-time' and 'permanent full-time'. There is a seniority roll for permanent full-time postmen, and an individual is placed on it with seniority dating from the date of his appointment as a permanent full-time postman. Prior to 1st September 1975 a postwoman could not attain permanent status. With effect from 1st September 1975, in preparation for the coming into operation of the 1975 Act on 29th December, and as a result of an agreement made *g* between the Post Office, the union and the Post Office Management Staffs Association this restriction was abandoned and it was agreed that thenceforth full-time postwomen would be employed on the same terms and conditions as full-time postmen. Consequent on the agreement postwomen with sufficient service as temporary full-time postwomen then became permanent full-time postwomen, their seniority dating from the day they attained that status. Mrs Steel had thus *h* been unable, before 1st September 1975, to become a permanent full-time post-woman although she had since November 1961 served continuously as a temporary full-time postwoman. As a result of the agreement referred to above, on 1st September 1975 she became a permanent full-time postwoman, her seniority as such dating from that date. Seniority is important for a number of purposes, including the allotting of 'walks'. A postal walk is the name given to the arrangement or round according to which a particular delivery is made in a particular district, and is the way in which duties are allotted to individual postmen. Though the enjoyment of a particular walk does not bring with it, directly at least, any financial advantage, some walks are preferable to others and it is an undoubted advantage to be able to obtain the walk of one's choice.

In March 1976, in accordance with normal practice, the Post Office advertised on
a the notice board in the office in Newport where Mrs Steel worked a vacant walk
and invited applications. Mrs Steel applied as did a number of others including a
Mr Moore. Mr Moore had become a permanent full-time postman on 9th July 1973
and was therefore senior to Mrs Steel. In accordance with normal practice to allot
walks by seniority the vacant walk was allotted to Mr Moore. Mrs Steel is a lady in
her fifties; Mr Moore is a much younger man. It was agreed that Mrs Steel in all
b probability would have become a permanent full-time postwoman in the mid-1960s
had that status been open to a woman, and that the only reason why the walk went
to a much younger man in the person of Mr Moore was that Mrs Steel was a woman,
in the sense that being a woman she had been prevented from becoming a permanent
full-time postwoman. In this situation Mrs Steel directed most of her complaints
against the union, rather than the Post Office, and, as we explained, it was for this
c reason that the industrial tribunal, concluding that no remedy was available against
the union, dismissed her claim against the Post Office. The substance of her complaint
against the union was that in negotiating the agreement referred to above they had
made no provision by which women who had at last become eligible to be permanent
full-time postwomen should receive some credit in terms in seniority for long previous service as temporary full-time postwomen.
d   Before turning to consider the terms of the 1975 Act, it is helpful to consider in
a general way the merits of Mrs Steel's complaint. It seems to us that she has indeed
something to complain of, as do other postwomen in a similar situation. Undoubtedly
prior to 1st September 1975 there was discrimination against postwomen on the
ground of their sex. Though the effect of the agreement has been to eliminate
it for the future, the form of the agreement is such that its effects will linger on for
e many years. Thus in any competition for a walk some years to come the most
mature postwomen will be at a disadvantage compared with comparatively youth-
ful postmen whose seniority will be greater albeit that their total years of service
are considerably less. The Post Office accept that this is the consequence of the
agreement made with the union, but excuse themselves by saying that the results
of which Mrs Steel, and other women, complain flow from past acts of discrimina-
f tion ante-dating the coming into effect of the 1975 Act, and point out correctly that
with the passage of years the effects will diminish and finally cease. In effect the
attitude of the Post Office is the not uncommon one of supporting sex equality,
but not yet. The attitude of the union is similar, and it is probably fair to suppose
that their reluctance to give postwomen added seniority in deference to their pre-
1st September 1975 service as temporary part-time postwomen is not unconnected
g with the fact that many of their members are men who would suffer a loss in seniority
if women were to gain. There is no doubt that the 1975 Act does not operate retrospectively, but some acts of discrimination may be of a continuing nature and it
would seem to us to be in accordance with the spirit of the Act if it applied as far as
possible to remove the continuing effects of past discrimination. Of course, we accept
that whether it has this effect or not must depend on the terms of the Act. We
h proceed to consider the case as put on behalf of Mrs Steel by counsel.
    The scheme of the 1975 Act is that Part I defines discrimination to which the Act
applies, and later Parts declared unalwful certain acts of discrimination so defined,
different Parts dealing with discrimination in different fields. Part II concerns discrimination in the employment field. We have no doubt that if there was discrimination by
the Post Office as defined in Part I it was rendered unlawful under s 6(2) which
j provides:

'It is unlawful for a person, in the case of a woman employed by him at an
establishment in Great Britain, to discriminate against her—(a) in the way he
affords her access to opportunities for promotion, transfer or training, or to any
other benefits, facilities or services, or by refusing or deliberately omitting to

afford her access to them, or (b) by dismissing her, or subjecting her to any other detriment.'

It seems clear to us that a successful application for a walk is a 'transfer' or 'other benefit' or a 'facility': see *Peake v Automotive Products Ltd*[1]. It may also be that s 6(1)(a) would apply, though this is perhaps more doubtful, for while it seems to us clear that the words 'offer' and 'employment' in that subsection should not be construed technically it may be objected that Mrs Steel was already in the employment of the Post Office so that the offer of a walk was not the offer of employment. The more difficult question is whether there was an act of discrimination to which the 1975 Act applies as defined in Part I.

Counsel for Mrs Steel relied on s 1(1)(b) and not s 1(1)(a). Section 1(1) provides:

'A person discriminates against a woman in any circumstances relevant for the purposes of any provision of this Act if—(a) on the ground of her sex he treats her less favourably than he treats or would treat a man, or (b) he applies to her a requirement or condition which he applies or would apply equally to a man but— (i) which is such that the proportion of women who can comply with it is considerably smaller than the proportion of men who can comply with it, and (ii) which he cannot show to be justifiable irrespective of the sex of the person to whom it is applied, and (iii) which is to her detriment because she cannot comply with it.'

It is said here that the Post Office applied the requirement or condition that the successful applicant for a walk must be the most senior in the roll of permanent full-time postmen, and that this requirement or condition was applied equally to men and women, but within s 1(1)(b)(i) was a requirement or condition such that the proportion of women who could comply with it was considerably smaller than the proportion of men who could comply with it. This was conceded by counsel for the Post Office. It was further contended for Mrs Steel that the requirement or condition was to her detriment because she could not comply with it within s 1(1)(b)(iii). Counsel for the Post Office did not formerly concede this, but in our judgment counsel for Mrs Steel's contention is correct. The time to consider the matter is that at which the requirement or condition has to be fulfilled, and it is nothing to the point that in the fullness of time Mrs Steel would or might be able to do so.

The difficult question is whether the Post Office can show the requirement or condition of seniority to be justifiable irrespective of the sex of the person to whom it is applied, within s 1(1)(b)(ii). The purpose of s 1(1)(b)(ii) is clear enough. There may be discrimination by indirect means by requiring a condition equally of men and women, but one which few women but most men can satisfy. A requirement that a candidate should be six foot high, or capable of lifting two hundred pounds, or have a degree in engineering in practice would rule out more female applicants than male. It is discriminatory unless the employer (in this case) can show it to be justifiable irrespective of sex. There is no doubt that the onus of proof here lies on the employer, and that it is a heavy onus in the sense that before it is discharged the industrial tribunal will need to be satisfied that the case is a genuine one, somewhat in the way that it must when a not dissimilar case is made by an employer under s 1(3) of the Equal Pay Act 1970 (as amended). The question is what considerations are relevant and proper to be taken into account when determining whether the requirement or condition was justifiable; in particular, is it sufficient merely to take into account the needs of the enterprise for the purpose of which the requirement or condition has been imposed, or is it necessary to look at all the circumstances including the discriminatory effect of the requirement or condition? We are satisfied that the latter is the case and that the industrial tribunal has to weigh up the needs of the enterprise against the discriminatory effect of the requirement or condition. Were it not so, many acts

1   [1977] QB 780

prima facie discriminatory would be allowed when there was no overriding need.
a   Furthermore, it is necessary as far as possible to construe the 1975 Act and the 1970 Act so as to form a harmonious code. Under Part II of the 1975 Act a case 'in the employment field' which could be brought under the 1970 Act must be brought under that Act and not the 1975 Act. Suppose the case of a woman employed on like work with a man in the same employment, the man being paid more than the woman, the difference being due to an increment payable in respect of such and such number
b   of years seniority. Prima facie the woman would be entitled under the 1970 Act to succeed in a claim to be paid the same as the man, and the only answer to such a claim by the employer could be under s 1(3); in other words he would claim that the variation between the woman's contract and the man's contract was genuinely due to a material difference (other than the difference of sex) between her case and his, namely that he had greater seniority than she. But suppose that her seniority was only less than his
c   because, as a result of a discriminatory rule in force up to 29th December 1975 women could not qualify for the same seniority as men. It is not at all clear in such a case that the employer's contention under s 1(3) would succeed. Dealing with a similar problem in *Snoxell v Vauxhall Motors Ltd*[1] we said:

d   'Putting these arguments side by side it can be seen that the solution depends on whether, in analysing the history of the difference in treatment of Miss Snoxell and Mrs Davies on the one hand and the 'red circle' male inspectors on the other, one stops at the moment of the formation of the 'red circle' or looks further back to see why Miss Snoxell and Mrs Davies were not within it. The arguments presented to us have, not surprisingly, considered questions of causation, and it has been said that the inability of Miss Snoxell and Mrs Davies
e   to join the 'red circle' was, or was not, the effective cause of the current variation in the terms of their contracts of employment. It seems to us that this earlier discrimination can be said to be an effective cause of the current variation. But we would put the matter more broadly. The onus of proof under s 1(3) is on the employer and it is a heavy one. Intention, and motive, are irrelevant; and we would say that an employer can never establish in the terms of s 1(3) that the
f   variation between the woman's contract and the man's contract is genuinely due to a material difference (other than the difference of sex) between her case and his when it can be seen that past sex discrimination has contributed to the variation. To allow such an answer would, we think, be contrary to the spirit and intent of the 1970 Act, construed and interpreted in the manner we have already explained. It is true that the original discrimination occurred before 29th December 1975, and accordingly was not then unlawful; nonetheless it
g   cannot have been the intention of the 1970 Act to permit the perpetuation of the effects of earlier discrimination.'

As we then went on to point out, this line of thought is in conformity with the approach of the Supreme Court of the United States to similar problems: see *Corning Glassworks v Brennan*[2].
h   Owing to the way in which the case went before the industrial tribunal, this is a matter on which they have made no finding, and on which the parties may wish to call further evidence. In these circumstances we have reluctantly come to the conclusion that it would be wrong for us to decide the question for ourselves; accordingly we shall remit the case for further hearing on this point. To summarise the position so as to avoid any doubt, we are satisfied that Mrs Steel is entitled to succeed
j   in her claim against the Post Office under ss 1(1)(*b*) and 6(2)(*a*) unless the Post Office can show that the seniority rule was justifiable irrespective of the sex of the person to whom it is applied.

1   [1977] 3 All ER 770 at 778, 779, [1978] QB 11 at 28
2   (1974) 417 US 188

It may be helpful if we add a word of detail about what we consider to be the right approach to this question. First, the onus of proof lies on the party asserting this *a* proposition, in this case the Post Office. Secondly, it is a heavy onus in the sense that at the end of the day the industrial tribunal must be satisfied that the case is a genuine one where it can be said that the requirement or condition is necessary. Thirdly, in deciding whether the employer had discharged the onus the industrial tribunal should take into account all the circumstances, including the discriminatory effect of the requirement or condition if it is permitted to continue. Fourthly, it is necessary *b* to weigh the need for the requirement or condition against that effect. Fifthly, it is right to distinguish between a requirement or condition which is necessary and one which is merely convenient, and for this purpose it is relevant to consider whether the employer can find some other and non-discriminatory method of achieving the object.

Turning to the facts of this case, it will be right to enquire whether it is necessary *c* to allot walks by seniority or whether some other method is feasible, to consider whether the seniority roll could not be revised so as to give the women some credit for their part-time service, and to consider the extent of the disadvantage which the women suffer under the present system in terms of numbers and likely duration. Assistance may be obtained from the judgments in the Supreme Court of the United States in *Griggs v Duke Power Co*[1]. Although the terms of the Act there in question *d* are different from those of the 1975, Act, it seems to us that the approach adopted by the court is relevant. In particular, the passage is helpful where it is said[2]:

'Congress has now provided that tests or criteria for employment or promotion may not provide equality of opportunity merely in the sense of the fabled offer of milk to the stork and the fox. On the contrary, Congress has now required *e* that the posture and condition of the job-seeker be taken into account. It has —to resort again to the fable—provided that the vessel in which the milk is proffered be one all seekers can use. The Act proscribes not only overt discrimination but also practises that are fair in form, but discriminatory in operation. The touchstone is business necessity. If an employment practice which operates to exclude Negroes cannot be shown to be related to job performance, the *f* practice is prohibited.'

A similar approach seems to us to be proper when applying s 1(*b*)(ii) of the 1975 Act. In other words a practice which would otherwise be discriminatory (which is the case here) is not to be licensed unless it can be shown to be justifiable, and it cannot be justifiable unless its discriminatory effect is justified by the need, not the convenience, of the business or enterprise. During the course of the argument on the hearing of the *g* appeal we suggested to counsel for Mrs Steel that it might be that his case could be brought under ss 1(1)(*a*) and 6(2), relying on the following analysis: the Post Office treated Mrs Steel less favourably on the ground of her sex than they treated Mr Moore (s 1(1)(*a*)) in the way in which they afforded her access to opportunities for transfer or other benefits (s 6(2)(*a*)) *in that* they afforded such access on the basis of a system which so operated that she and other women were at a disadvantage *h* compared to him and other men because she was a woman and he was a man.

Counsel for Mrs Steel was unwilling to embrace this way of putting his case, though he did not formally reject it, and counsel for the Post Office submitted that it was ill-founded. In these circumstances we say no more about it.

Turning to the position of the union, which was represented by one of its officials, Mr Fraser, it cannot be said as a matter of law that a claim such as that brought by *j* Mrs Steel cannot succeed, because s 42(1) provides a remedy against a person who

---

1   (1971) 401 US 424
2   401 US 424 at 431

knowingly aids another person to do an act made unlawful by the 1975 Act; and s 12
a makes it unlawful for a trade union to discriminate against one of its members.
On the other hand there was no evidence before the industrial tribunal on the basis
of which an order under either of those sections could be made against the union,
and it does not seem to us that any useful purpose would be served on the remission
by leaving the union as a party for the purpose at this stage of opening up a wider
enquiry. Mrs Steel's case against the union was based on the fact that they were parties
b to the agreement under which women for the first time were enabled to become
permanent full-time postwomen, and (as she believes) responsible for not including
or permitting to be included in that agreement a provision by which women so made
permanent for the first time might receive some added seniority. But at the end
of the day it was the Post Office who had to make the decisions and made the decisions.
They cannot and have not sought to shield behind the union. It seems to us that if
c the Post Office fail in their case under s 1(1)(b)(ii) an effective order may properly
be made against them, and that if they succeed the union could not be in any worse
position. Accordingly so far as the union is concerned the appeal will be dismissed.

   During the course of the hearing of the appeal we were informed that there are
many other cases pending before industrial tribunals, to which the Post Office are
party, raising matters similar to that in issue in the present appeal. Assuming that
d the issues in the various cases (or some of them) are the same, it seems desirable
that at least one of them, perhaps this one, should be decided on the basis of full
evidence and full legal argument. It may be, we cannot of course say for certain,
that the evidence will be voluminous as the Post Office may wish to explain the
extent of the problem, the workings of the seniority system and so on, and the
claimant may wish to explain the extent of the discrimination if the practice com-
e plained of is allowed to persist. In these circumstances it is desirable if possible that
the claimant should be legally represented as well as the Post Office. We do not
know what is the position of Mrs Steel in this respect. So, without making any formal
order, we would invite the parties to communicate with the Equal Opportunities
Commission and the President of the Industrial Tribunals as the most compendious
way of proceeding.
f   The order is: in *Steel v Union of Post Office Workers*, the appeal is dismissed; in
Steel v Post Office, the appeal is allowed. The case is remitted to such industrial tribunal
as the President of Industrial Tribunals may direct, to be determined in accordance
with this judgment and such further evidence as the parties may call.

   Order accordingly.

g
   Solicitors: *Bindman & Partners* (for Mrs Steel); *Solicitor, Post Office*.

                                        Salim H J Merali Esq Barrister.

Director of Public Prosecutions v Anderson

HOUSE OF LORDS

LORD WILBERFORCE, LORD DIPLOCK, LORD SALMON, LORD FRASER OF TULLYBELTON AND LORD KEITH OF KINKEL

25th APRIL, 24th MAY 1978

Criminal law – Trial – Other offences taken into consideration – Application – Admission of other offences – Procedure to be followed for obtaining accused's consent to other offences being taken into consideration – Accused himself must give express and unequivocal assent.

Criminal law – Bankruptcy order – Financial limit on jurisdiction to make order – Aggregate of loss or damage from offences of which accused convicted and other relevant offences – Offences which the court takes into consideration in determining sentence – Prosecution proceeding on sample counts – List of outstanding offences of similar nature submitted to defendant – Defendant convicted on sample counts – Outstanding offences taken into consideration in passing sentence – Whether offences taken into consideration 'other relevant offences' – Whether court entitled to take account of loss or damage from outstanding offences in determining aggregate of loss or damage without defendant's consent – Powers of Criminal Courts Act 1973, s 39(1)(2).

The appellant was charged and convicted on 13 counts on an indictment which involved offences of obtaining money by deception from his employers to the value of £7,112. The particular offences selected for inclusion in the indictment were sample counts. A schedule to the indictment set out 20 alleged similar offences involving some £19,600 which were not proceeded with by the Crown. Those offences were taken into consideration by the trial judge for the purpose of determining the appropriate sentence to pass. The appellant did not, however, give his consent to their being taken into consideration for that purpose. The judge sentenced the appellant to a term of imprisonment and also made a criminal bankruptcy order against him under s 39(1)[a] of the Powers of Criminal Courts Act 1973, stating that in doing so he was taking into consideration the amounts obtained by the appellant by the 20 alleged offences in the schedule to the indictment, which he regarded as having been proved. The appellant appealed against the making of the criminal bankruptcy order contending that the trial judge had no jurisdiction to make it since the offences charged on the indictment did not involve loss or damage exeeding £15,000 as required by s 39(1)(b) of the 1973 Act.

Held – The appeal would be allowed for the following reasons—

(i) Where a person had been convicted of an offence, the practice of taking into consideration outstanding offences which remained to be tried in determining sentence was not to be followed except with the express and unequivocal assent of the offender himself. He was to be informed explicity of each offence which the judge proposed to take into consideration and should explicitly admit that he had committed them and should state his desire that they should be taken into consideration in determining the sentence (see p 514 *e* and p 515 *j* to p 516 *a* and *g* to *j*, post); *R v Syres* (1908) 1 Cr App Rep 172 explained.

(ii) The same procedure should be followed where a person had been charged with sample counts. Only if the offender had been given an opportunity after the verdict to consider the schedule of other offences which he was alleged to have committed, had been explicitly asked by the judge which of them he admitted and whether he wished them to be taken into consideration, and agreed to that being done, might such offences be included in calculating the amount for which a criminal bankruptcy

---

a Section 39(1) is set out at p 515 *d* and *e*, post

order under s 31 or a compensation order under s 35 of the 1973 Act be made (see p 514 e and p 516 e to j, post).

(iii) Because the procedure for ascertaining the appellant's consent to the 20 alleged offences being taken into consideration had not at any stage been adhered to, the trial judge had no right to take them into consideration in determining sentence and they could not therefore be included in calculating the amount for which a criminal bankruptcy order might be made. Accordingly the appeal would be allowed and the criminal bankruptcy order set aside (see p 514 e g and p 516 a to c and g to j, post).

Per Lord Wilberforce. Because of the restrictive terms of the legislation dealing with the criminal bankruptcy jurisdiction, if the criminal bankruptcy procedure is to be workable without the necessity of multiplying charges, it would seem that either the sum of £15,000 should be changed or a wider discretion as to the existence or apparent existence of losses other than those involved in the offences of which the accused is convicted, must be given to the trial judge (see p 514 f and g, post).

Decision of the Court of Appeal, Criminal Division sub nom R v Anderson p 8 ante, reversed.

Notes
For criminal bankruptcy orders, see 11 Halsbury's Laws (4th Edn) para 803.

For the Powers of Criminal Courts Act 1973, s 39, see 43 Halsbury's Statutes (3rd Edn) 334.

Case referred to in opinions
R v Syres (1908) 1 Cr App Rep 172, 73 JP 13, CCA, 14(2) Digest (Reissue) 676, 5563.

Appeal
This was an appeal by Keith Anthony Anderson against the decision of the Court of Appeal, Criminal Division[1] (Ormrod LJ, Thompson and Jupp JJ) given on 15th November 1977 dismissing the appellant's appeal against the making by his Honour Judge McKinnon QC on 25th October 1976 at the Central Criminal Court of a criminal bankruptcy order against the appellant under s 39(1) of the Powers of Criminal Courts Act 1973 in the sum of £26,754·61 in respect of damage flowing from offences committed by the appellant. The facts are set out in the opinion of Lord Diplock.

Kenneth Bagnall QC and *John Foy* for the appellant.
P C Mott for the Director of Public Prosecutions.

Their Lordships took time for consideration.

24th May. The following opinions were delivered.

LORD WILBERFORCE. My Lords, this appeal concerns the right of the Crown Court to make a criminal bankruptcy order against a person who has been convicted of an offence before it. The jurisdiction, introduced by the Criminal Justice Act 1972, ss 9 and 10, and now contained in the Powers of Criminal Courts Act 1973 is an extremely useful one. It enables a speedy procedure, controlled by the Director of Public Prosecutions acting as Official Petitioner in Bankruptcy, to be put in motion through which steps can be taken to enable property, obtained by the convicted person by his criminal act, to be traced and recovered, without the necessity for the individuals who have suffered loss or damage to take slower and more expensive civil proceedings under the Bankruptcy Act 1914.

Unfortunately, this beneficial legislation has been conferred in restrictive terms:

1　Page 8 ante

in this it follows the pattern set by the Theft Act 1968, s 28, and in the sections dealing with compensation orders (ss 35 to 38 of the 1973 Act). In these respects English law has always lagged behind other systems in enabling persons suffering loss as the result of criminal conduct to recover their property, or compensation for the loss of it, in one set of proceedings rather than in two.

The criminal bankruptcy jurisdiction may, under s 39(1)(b), only be exercised where the amount or aggregate amount of the loss or damage caused by the offence and other relevant offences exceeds £15,000, other relevant offences being defined as offences of which the person in question is convicted in the same proceedings or which the court takes into consideration in determining his sentence.

Many cases of criminal dishonesty which come before the courts consist of numerous small crimes, either against one person, for example an employer, as in this case, or against numerous members of the public. It may take a large number of these individual offences to make up an aggregate loss of £15,000. So there is a dilemma: either the prosecution must bring in a large number of charges in similar form each of which must be proved or admitted, or specimen charges may be brought of sufficient number to indicate a system. The former alternative is obviously undesirable, in the interest of the administration of justice. The latter, which is the procedure commonly adopted, has the disadvantage that the amounts involved may not add up to £15,000 so that the persons suffering loss are prejudiced.

A third alternative was that adopted in this case: specimen charges were brought totalling some £7,000 but the judge said that he took into account amounts obtained by other invoices, though these were not charged, nor admitted, nor consented to be 'taken into consideration'.

The Court of Appeal endeavoured to uphold this procedure, and I sympathise with them. But there can be no doubt that it is invalid. My noble and learned friend, Lord Diplock, whose opinion I have had the benefit of reading in advance, and with which I wholly agree, demonstrates why this is so. I have ventured to add these observations because, as the judgment of the Court of Appeal, and the order made by the trial judge, make clear, an unsatisfactory situation is produced if, as is now seen to be inevitable, the expression 'taken into consideration' is given its correct meaning. Indeed it may be the case that the expression has been used in relation to s 28 of the Theft Act 1968, and in relation to compensation orders, and criminal bankruptcy orders, in the belief that a different and looser meaning could be attributed to it. If so, this case may show a need to reconsider the relevant provisions. If the criminal bankruptcy procedure is to be workable, without the necessity to multiply charges, it would seem that either the sum of £15,000 should be changed, or that a wider discretion as to the existence, or apparent existence, of other losses than those involved in the offences on which the person concerned was convicted, must be given to the trial judge.

The appeal must clearly be allowed and the order set aside.

LORD DIPLOCK. My Lords, the appellant was convicted at the Central Criminal Court on each count of an indictment which consisted of 13 counts. Eight of these charged him with obtaining money from his employers by deception, one charged him with an attempt to do so, and the other four with forging documents which he had used for the purposes of the deception. The total amount which he had obtained by the offences of which he was convicted was £7,112·01.

The nature of the swindle which he had carried out was simple. He was put in charge by his employers of a small department of their business known as the graphic department, and he had authority to sub-contract work which the department had not time to do itself. His contract required him to devote the whole of his time to the work of his employers and not to undertake work of any kind or accept any fee

or remuneration from any other source. What he did was to pretend to have sub-
a contracted work which he had done himself and to present and obtain payment of
invoices for it in the name of 'KBS Graphics', which he used as a pseudonym.
The particular offences selected for inclusion in the indictment were what have
become known as 'sample' counts. There were in fact another 20 similar instances
of the appellant's obtaining money by means of invoices in the name of 'KBS Graphics'.
These were introduced in evidence at the trial, presumably as evidence of system,
b for I know no other legal basis on which such evidence would be admissible. The
total amount involved in these additional invoices, which were not the subject of any
charge, was £22,878·20 and when added to the £7,112·01 lost by his employers as a
result of those offences of which he was convicted, made up a grand total of £29,990·21.
After the jury's verdict of guilty on all counts of the indictment, the judge expressed
his intention of making a criminal bankruptcy order against the appellant under s 39
c of the Powers of Criminal Courts Act 1973. That section, so far as is relevant to the
instant appeal is as follows:

> '(1) Where a person is convicted of an offence before the Crown Court and it
> appears to the court that—(a) as a result of the offence, or of that offence taken
> together with any other relevant offence or offences, loss or damage (not attribu-
> table to personal injury) has been suffered by one or more persons whose identity
d > is known to the court; and (b) the amount, or aggregate amount, of the loss or
> damage exceeds £15,000; the court may, in addition to dealing with the offender
> in any other way (but not if it makes a compensation order against him), make a
> criminal bankruptcy order against him in respect of the offence or, as the case
> may be, that offence and the other relevant offence or offences.
> '(2) In subsection (1) above "other relevant offence or offences" means an
e > offence or offences of which the person in question is convicted in the same
> proceedings or which the court takes into consideration in determining his
> sentence.'

The amount of the loss resulting from the only offences of which the appellant was
convicted was £7,112·01. This falls far short of the £15,000, which is the minimum
f amount required to justify a criminal bankruptcy order. The judge, however,
stated expressly that he took into consideration also the amount obtained by the
appellant by the other 20 invoices. These, he said, he regarded as having been proved,
notwithstanding that they had not been the subject of any charge against the appellant
who had never pleaded to them nor admitted them nor consented to their being
taken into consideration by the judge in determining the sentence he would pass.
g My Lords, in referring to cases taken into consideration in determining sentence,
which the draftsman of the Act did in s 39(2) and also in s 35(1) which relates to
compensation orders, he was using what has become a well-known term of legal art.
It refers to a practice, which apparently has existed since the turn of the century and
which received in 1908 the express approval of the newly created Court of Criminal
Appeal in *R v Syres*[1]. The laudable object of the practice is to give to a convicted
h offender the opportunity when he has served his sentence to start with a clean sheet
and not to be arrested at the prison gates for some other offence which he committed
before the particular offence which was the cause of his conviction. In effect, this
practice involves the convicted offender who has been convicted of one offence in
being punished for other offences for which he has never been formally arraigned,
tried or convicted and to which he has never formally pleaded guilty.
j If justice is to be done it is essential that the practice should not be followed except
with the express and unequivocal assent of the offender himself. Accordingly, he
should be informed explicitly of each offence which the judge proposes to take into

---

1 (1908) 1 Cr App Rep 172

consideration; and should explicitly admit that he committed them and should state his desire that they should be taken into consideration in determining the sentence *a* to be passed on him.

In the instant case, none of this was done. The appellant did not give evidence at his trial. He did not admit any offence in respect of the sums of money referred to in any of the 20 invoices which were not the subject of any count in the indictment. He was never asked whether he did so nor whether he wanted any of these alleged offences to be taken into consideration. In these circumstances, the judge, in my *b* view, clearly had no right to take them into consideration in determining the sentence. It follows that the amount of money involved in the 20 invoices cannot be added to the amounts involved in those offences of which he was convicted so as to reach the minimum limit of £15,000 required to justify the making of a criminal bankruptcy order. I would accordingly allow the appeal and set aside the criminal bankruptcy order. *c*

Nothing that I have said should be understood as discouraging the practice of limiting the charges in an indictment to a limited number of 'sample' counts in cases where, as in the instant case, the accused has adopted a systematic dishonest practice. Your Lordships were told that, where sample counts are used, it is customary to provide the defence with a list of all the similar offences of which it is alleged that those selected as the subject of the counts contained in the indictment are samples. *d* In appropriate cases it may be that evidence of all or some of these additional offences is led by the prosecution at the trial as evidence of 'system', as was apparently done in the instant case. In other cases, the additional offences in the schedule are not referred to until after a verdict of guilty has been returned. The judge is then told of the total amount involved in the systematic offences of which those charged in the indictment have been selected by the prosecution as samples. Where sample *e* counts are used it is, in my view essential that the ordinary procedure should be followed for taking other offences into consideration in determining sentence. The accused should be given an opportunity after the verdict to consider the schedule of other offences which he is alleged by the prosecution to have committed and should be explicitly asked by the judge which of them he admits and whether he wishes them to be taken into consideration. Only if he agrees to that course may such *f* offences be included in calculating the amount for which a criminal bankruptcy order may be made under s 39 of the Act or a compensation order under s 35.

LORD SALMON. My Lords, I am completely in agreement with my noble and learned friend, Lord Diplock, that this appeal should be allowed for the reasons which he states. I wish only to emphasise that, in cases such as the present, nothing in my *g* noble and learned friend's speech would justify the prosecution increasing the number of counts included in the indictment. In my opinion, far too many indictments contain far too many counts; and this leads to wholly unnecessary prolongation of trials, resulting in a shocking waste of public time and money.

LORD FRASER OF TULLYBELTON. My Lords, I have had the advantage of *h* reading the speech of my noble and learned friend, Lord Diplock, and I agree with it. For the reasons given by him I would allow this appeal.

LORD KEITH OF KINKEL. My Lords, I agree with the speech of my noble and learned friend, Lord Diplock, which I have had the opportunity of reading in draft, and for the reason which he gives I would allow the appeal.

Appeal allowed.

Solicitors: *Duke-Cohan & Co* (for the appellant); *Director of Public Prosecutions*.

Mary Rose Plummer Barrister.

Warnford Investments Ltd v Duckworth and others

CHANCERY DIVISION
MEGARRY V-C
16th, 17th NOVEMBER, 21st DECEMBER 1977

Company – Voluntary winding-up – Disclaimer of onerous property – Lease – Disclaimer of lease by liquidator – Company assignee from original lessee – Lessor claiming from original lessee rent falling due after disclaimer – Whether original lessee liable for rent notwithstanding disclaimer – Companies Act 1948, s 323(2)(7).

Bankruptcy – Disclaimer of onerous property – Lease – Disclaimer of lease by trustee in bankruptcy – Assignee from original lessee becoming bankrupt – Lessor claiming from original lessee rent falling due after disclaimer – Whether original lessee liable for rent notwithstanding disclaimer – Bankruptcy Act 1914, s 54.

Where a lease has been assigned to a company which afterwards goes into liquidation, and the liquidator, acting under s 323[a] of the Companies Act 1948, disclaims the lease, leaving the lease without an owner until a vesting order is made under s 323(6) of the 1948 Act, the disclaimer does not destroy the lease. Accordingly, the original lessee remains directly and primarily liable to the lessor for the rent throughout the remainder of the term of the lease and is not by virtue of the assignment reduced to being a mere surety for the discharge by the company of the obligations under the lease. The release of the original lessee from liability under the lease cannot be said to be 'necessary for the purpose of releasing' the company and its property from liability within s 323(2) of the 1948 Act, since under s 323(7) of the 1948 Act either the original lessee, if he remained liable for the rent, or the lessor, if the original lessee were released from liability, would be entitled to prove for the rent in the liquidation. The position is the same where the assignment is to an individual who becomes bankrupt and whose trustee in bankruptcy disclaims the lease under s 54[b] of the Bankruptcy Act 1914 (see p 525 d h, p 526 c to f and j to p 527 a and c to e and p 528 d e and h j, post).

Smyth v North (1872) LR 7 Exch 242, *Harding v Preece* (1882) 9 QBD 281 and *Hill v East and West India Dock Co* (1884) 9 App Cas 448 applied.

Stacey v Hill [1901] 1 KB 660 distinguished.

Notes
For the effect of disclaimer of a lease by a liquidator, see 7 Halsbury's Laws (4th Edn) para 1344.

For the Companies Act 1948, s 323, see 5 Halsbury's Statutes (3rd Edn) 352.

Cases referred to in judgment
Auriol v Mills (1790) 4 Term Rep 94, 100 ER 912, 31(2) Digest (Reissue) 715, 5867.

Cock, Re, ex parte Shilson (1887) 20 QBD 343, 57 LJQB 169, 58 LT 586, 5 Morr 14, DC, 5 Digest (Reissue) 1020, 8195.

Finley, Re, ex parte Clothworkers' Co (1888) 21 QBD 475, 57 LJQB 626, 60 LT 134, 5 Morr 248, CA, 5 Digest (Reissue) 1009, 8106.

Harding v Preece (1882) 9 QBD 281, 51 LJQB 515, 47 LT 100, 46 JP 646, 5 Digest (Reissue) 1013, 8145.

Hill v East and West India Dock Co (1884) 9 App Cas 448, 53 LJCh 842, 51 LT 163, 48

---

a Section 323, so far as material, is set out at p 519 *f* and *g*, post
b Section 54, so far as material, is set out at p 519 *h* to p 520 *a*, post

JP 788, HL; *affg* sub nom *East and West India Dock Co v Hill* (1882) 22 Ch D 111, 5 Digest (Reissue) 1014, *8146*.

Katherine et Cie Ltd, Re [1932] 1 Ch 70, [1931] All ER Rep 125, 101 LJCh 91, 146 LT 226, [1931] B & CR 121, 10 Digest (Reissue) 996, *6040*.

Levy, Re, ex parte Walton (1881) 17 Ch D 746, [1881-5] All ER Rep 548, 50 LJCh 657, 45 LT 1, CA, 5 Digest (Reissue) 1005, *8062*.

Morris (D) & Sons Ltd v Jeffreys (1932) 148 LT 56, [1932] All ER Rep 881, 5 Digest (Reissue) 1015, *8155*.

Moule v Garrett (1872) LR 7 Exch 101, [1861-73] All ER Rep 135, 41 LJEx 62, 26 LT 367, Ex Ch; *affg* LR 5 Exch 132, 31(2) Digest (Reissue) 730, *6018*.

Smyth v North (1872) LR 7 Exch 242, 41 LJ Ex 103, 5 Digest (Reissue) 1013, *8144*.

Stacy v Hill [1901] 1 KB 660, 70 LJKB 435, 84 LT 410, 8 Mans 169, CA; *affg* 69 LJQB 796, 5 Digest (Reissue) 1014, *8154*.

Thompson and Cottrell's Contract, Re [1943] 1 All ER 169, [1943] Ch 97, 112 LJCh 109, 168 LT 155, 5 Digest (Reissue) 1012, *8127*.

Wolveridge v Steward (1833) 1 Cr & M 644, 3 Moo & S 561, 3 Tyr 637, 3 LJEx 360, 149 ER 557, Ex Ch, 31(2) Digest (Reissue) 731, *6021*.

Cases also cited

Downer Enterprises Ltd, Re [1974] 2 All ER 1074, [1974] 1 WLR 1460.
Nottingham General Cemetery Co, Re [1955] 2 All ER 504, [1955] Ch 683.
Yeovil Glove Co, Re [1964] 2 All ER 849, [1965] Ch 148, CA.

Action

By a writ issued on 14th April 1977, the plaintiffs, Warnford Investments Ltd, brought an action against the defendants, Anthony John Stanhope Duckworth, Philip Charles Curtis, John Hanbury Pawle and James Dundas Hamilton. By their statement of claim the plaintiffs alleged that by a lease dated 8th October 1971 the plaintiffs had demised to the defendants premises forming part of the building known as Warnford Court, Throgmorton Street, London EC2 for the term of 20 years from 29th September 1971; that the lease contained a covenant whereby the defendants covenanted jointly and severally with the plaintiffs, inter alia, to pay to the plaintiffs rent for the premises during the term at the rate of £7,300 per annum by equal quarterly payments in advance on the usual quarter days, a service rent at the rate of £180 per annum by equal quarterly payments in advance on the usual quarter days, and certain further or additional rent; that by a deed of assignment dated 31st October 1974 the defendants had assigned the premises to LMB (Metals) Ltd (formerly known as London Metal Brokers Ltd) ('the company') for the unexpired residue of the term granted by the lease; that on 14th March 1976 the company had gone into creditor's voluntary liquidation; that the liquidator of the company by writing under his hand dated 1st March 1977 had disclaimed the lease and that rent, services rent and further or additional rent were in arrears and unpaid in the total sum of £4,161·92 and that sum was due and owing to the plaintiffs by the defendants. The plaintiffs therefore claimed that sum from the defendants. Part of the rent, services rent and further or additional rent claimed had become due after 1st March 1977, i e after the liquidator had disclaimed the lease. By their defence the defendants alleged that in law the effect of the disclaimer was to determine the lease, or, in the alternative, to determine the defendants' obligations thereunder.

Martin Buckley for the plaintiffs.
David Oliver for the defendants.

Cur adv vult

21st December. **MEGARRY V-C** read the following judgment: The facts in this case are simple and undisputed. I cannot say the same for the law; for I have to decide a point which has lain unresolved for over 75 years. The plaintiffs granted a lease of business premises to the defendants. With the plaintiffs' consent, the defendants later assigned the lease to a company. The company then went into a creditors' voluntary liquidation; and in due course the liquidator of the company disclaimed the lease. The plaintiffs then sued the defendants (who are, of course, the original lessees) for rent falling due after the date of the disclaimer. Originally there was also a claim for rent due prior to that date, but this rent has now been paid. The short point is thus whether the original lessees are liable for rent which falls due after they have assigned the lease to a company and the liquidator of the company has disclaimed the lease. Had the assignee been an individual who had then become bankrupt, the same point would have arisen in relation to a disclaimer of the lease by his trustee in bankruptcy.

The starting point is that at common law an original lessee remains liable on the covenants of the lease throughout the term despite any assignments of it. Any claim for immunity must therefore be based on statute; and today the relevant statutory provisions are, with the necessary modifications for the two systems of company liquidation and bankruptcy, virtually identical; see the Companies Act 1948, s 323, and the Bankruptcy Act 1914, s 54. The bankruptcy history is the longer. I begin with the Bankruptcy Act 1869, In this, s 23, a section which substantially repeated earlier legislation, contained provisions for disclaimer which were somewhat different in form. The Bankruptcy Act 1883 materially changed the wording (see s 55(2)), and that wording was carried into the present enactment, the Bankruptcy Act 1914, s 54. On the other hand, not until the Companies Act 1929, s 267, was there any corresponding provision for companies; and that section, with immaterial variations, was in the language of the Bankruptcy Act 1914, s 54. The Companies Act 1948, s 323, in substance repeated these provisions of the 1929 Act. There are thus only two forms of wording to consider, that of bankruptcy prior to the 1883 Act, and that of bankruptcy and liquidation since the 1883 and 1929 Acts respectively. I say this because of the need to consider certain authorities in bankruptcy prior to the 1883 Act.

I turn to the statutes. Section 323(2) of the Companies Act 1948 runs as follows:

'The disclaimer shall operate to determine, as from the date of disclaimer, the rights, interest and liabilities of the company, and the property of the company, in or in respect of the property disclaimed, but shall not, except so far as is necessary for the purpose of releasing the company and the property of the company from liability, affect the rights or liabilities of any other person.'

Then sub-s (7) provides as follows:

'Any person injured by the operation of a disclaimer under this section shall be deemed to be a creditor of the company to the amount of the injury, and may accordingly prove the amount as a debt in the winding up.'

As so many of the authorities are on bankruptcy, I think that I should read the corresponding provisions of the Bankruptcy Act 1914, s 54. Subsection (2) is as follows:

'The disclaimer shall operate to determine, as from the date of disclaimer, the rights, interests, and liabilities of the bankrupt and his property in or in respect of the property disclaimed, and shall also discharge the trustee from all personal liability in respect of property disclaimed as from the date when the property vested in him, but shall not, except so far as is necessary for the purpose of releasing the bankrupt and his property and the trustee from liability, affect the rights or liabilities of any other person.'

Then there is sub-s (8), which corresponds to sub-s (7) of the Companies Act 1948, s 323:

'Any person injured by the operation of a disclaimer under this section shall be deemed to be a creditor of the bankrupt to the extent of the injury, and may accordingly prove the same as a debt under the bankruptcy.'   **a**

I do not think that I need do more than merely mention sub-s (6) of each section, under which the court has wide powers of making a vesting order in respect of disclaimed leases and other property. I should add that there has been no suggestion that any difference in substance arises from the minor differences in wording which make the provisions appropriate to each system.   **b**

So far as is relevant to the case before me, these provisions have to be considered in two main categories, namely, in relation to the liability of the original lessee under a lease (which is what arises for decision in this case), and in relation to the liability of a surety who has guaranteed payment of the rent due under a lease. Within each category there are of course sub-categories. One of the difficulties is that the only decisions in the first category, that of the original lessee, were reached on the statutory   **c**   language that obtained before the Bankruptcy Act 1883. On the new language, there are decisions on suretyship, as well as on disclaimer and other matters, but none on the liability of the original lessee to the reversioner, which is the point before me. The broad effect of the submissions of counsel for the defendants, who are the original lessees, is that the decisions on suretyship on the new language should also apply to original lessees under a lease which has been assigned. If they do, the original lessee,   **d**   ceases to be liable for rent when the lease has been disclaimed by the assignee's trustee in bankruptcy. On the other hand, counsel for the plaintiffs, the lessors, contends that the old decisions that the original lessee remains liable to the lessor for rent despite the bankruptcy of the assignee and the disclaimer of the lease still apply, notwithstanding the change of statutory language; for the new language reinforces rather than destroys the effect of the old decisions. I propose first to consider the old decisions on the   **e**   position of an original lessee.

In *Smyth v North*[1] the assignee of a lease became bankrupt, and his trustee in bankruptcy disclaimed the lease. The lessor then sued the original lessee for rent. The claim was in fact for rent due prior to the disclaimer, but the case seems to have been considered on a basis which involved liability for future rent. The statute in force was the Bankruptcy Act 1869, s 23, which provided that a disclaimed lease was to be   **f**   'deemed to have been surrendered'. The Act contained nothing to correspond with the concluding 'but' clause of the present Bankruptcy Act 1914, s 54(2), and Companies Act 1948, s 323(2). Bramwell B dissented, but the majority of the court, consisting of Martin and Pigott BB, held that the section had to be construed so as to affect only the relations between the bankrupt and his trustee and the lessor, and not those concerning third parties, such as the original lessee. The word 'surrender' was thus   **g**   construed in a restricted sense. Pigott B said[2]:

> 'I think, therefore, that the Act only applies as between the bankrupt and his creditors; when he is the assignee of a lease, the relation of the lessor and the original lessee is not disturbed, and the lessee must seek his remedy in the clauses at the end of the section, which gives the Court power to make orders for the   **h**   delivery of possession of the disclaimed property to persons interested in it, and allow persons injured by the operation of the section to prove against the estate.'

In *Hill v East and West India Dock Co*[3] the basic facts were the same, save that the lessor's claim included rent which had accrued due since the disclaimer, and so the point necessarily arose for decision. The case was decided on the same statutory   **j**   provisions. With Lord Bramwell dissenting, the House of Lords affirmed the decision

---

1   (1872) LR 7 Exch 242
2   LR 7 Exch 242 at 246
3   (1884) 9 App Cas 448

of the Court of Appeal, which itself had affirmed the decision of Hall V-C. In effect,
a the view taken by the majority in *Smyth v North*[1] was approved. In the leading speech,
Earl Cairns[2] observed that of course Parliament could have enacted that the deemed
surrender of the lease should put an end to it for all purposes, but that it was difficult
to see on what principle Parliament could have enacted—

b
> 'that a solvent man who has entered, with his eyes open, into a covenant
> with the owners of property to pay rent to them and to be liable to them for that
> rent and for other covenants, and who upon an assignment has recognised that
> liability and has stipulated that it shall continue, shall nevertheless be delivered
> from that liability, not by reason of anything which has passed between him
> and the lessors, but from a misfortune which has happened to the lessors,
> namely that the person to whom the lease has been assigned has become a
> bankrupt.'

c
The purpose of the statute was to discharge the bankrupt, and not others, and so
the word 'surrender' should be construed in a restricted sense. As Lord Blackburn
said[3], the deemed surrender meant 'shall be surrendered so far as is necessary to
effectuate the purposes of the Act and no further'; to do otherwise would be 'to work
a cruel hardship' on the lessors. These words were spoken on 3rd April 1884, over
d seven months after the Bankruptcy Act 1883 had received the Royal Assent on 25th
August 1883, so that they were too late to have affected the drafting of the Act;
but the decisions of Hall V-C and of the Court of Appeal (consisting of Lord Selborne
LC, Jessel MR and Cotton LJ) had been given in 1882 (*East and West India Dock Co v
Hill*[4]), and so the draftsman of the 1883 Act would have had the assistance of those
authorities.
e   I should also mention *Harding v Preece*[5]. There, the trustee in bankruptcy of an
assignee of a lease disclaimed the lease. The original lessee then paid rent to the lessor,
and claimed reimbursement from a person who had covenanted with him to be
surety for the rent for the rest of the term. A Queen's Bench Divisional Court held
that the surety was liable to the original lessee, for despite the disclaimer the original
lessee remained liable to the lessor for t᷄ ᷄ rent. There were also other cases, not
f directly concerned with rent, which pointed in the same direction. In *Re Levy, ex
parte Walton*[6] the original lessees of property granted an underlease and later became
bankrupt. Their trustee in bankruptcy sought leave to disclaim the lease, and the
Court of Appeal upheld the decision of the registrar that unconditional leave to
disclaim should be given. The Court of Appeal made it pla᷄᷄ that the disclaimer
would not affect the right of the lessor to distrain for rent or re-enter for breach of
g covenant, and that the statutory provision for a deemed surrender must be restrictively construed so as to avoid that James LJ[7] trenchantly called 'the most grievous
injustice, and the most revolting absurdity'.
   It was in those circumstances that the 1883 Act was enacted. The new provision
about disclaimer, s 55, avoided any reference to the deemed surrender which had been
so much construed by the courts, and substituted the present formula about a dis-
h claimer determining the rights, interests and liabilities of the bankrupt. It also set
out explicitly something which had nowhere appeared in the former legislation but
had been in effect construed into it by the courts, namely, the provision that the disclaimer was not to affect the rights or liabilities of anybody save the bankrupt and his

j
1   (1872) LR 7 Exch 242
2   (1884) 9 App Cas 448 at 454
3   9 App Cas 448 at 458
4   (1882) 22 Ch D 14
5   (1882) 9 QBD 281
6   (1881) 17 Ch D 746
7   17 Ch D 746 at 757

trustee, except so far as this was necessary for the purpose of releasing the bankrupt, his property and his trustee from liability. In this way the legislature sought to make explicit what the courts had held to be implicit for the purposes of avoiding injustice and absurdity. If that had been all, I should have said that it was clear beyond a peradventure that the legislature had resoundingly approved of the law which was shortly to find its final expression by the House of Lords in *Hill v East and West India Dock Co*[1], and had succeeded in making that law explicit. But that was not to be all.

The subsequent cases that have been cited to me fall into two main categories, which for brevity I may call the leave to disclaim cases and the surety cases. The latter, with *Stacey v Hill*[2] in the forefront, are much the most important in the present case. Of the leave to disclaim cases, I shall mention only *Re Katherine et Cie Ltd*[3]. There, a company was the original lessee, and there were guarantors for the payment of rent to the lessors. When the company went into liquidation, the liquidator sought leave to disclaim the lease; but Maugham J refused to grant it. On the basis of *Stacey v Hill*[2], the disclaimer would injure the lessors by depriving them of the benefit of the guarantees. Furthermore, the disclaimer was not required to relieve the liquidator of any liability under the lease, for, unlike a trustee in bankruptcy, a liquidator does not have the lease vested in him, and so does not become liable on it. I do not think that the case provides any real assistance on the question that is before me, except, perhaps, on a point in *Stacey v Hill*[2] that I shall consider later.

I turn to the surety cases. As I have indicated, the leading authority is *Stacey v Hill*[2], a decision of the Court of Appeal; and this was counsel for the defendants' sheet anchor. The facts were simple. L had granted a lease to T, and G had entered into an agreement with L that he, G, would guarantee the payment of any rent that was 21 days in arrear, up to a stated limit. There had been no devolution of either the lease or the reversion, and T became bankrupt. His trustee in bankruptcy disclaimed the lease, and L sued G for a quarter's rent falling due after the disclaimer. The Court of Appeal unanimously affirmed the decision of Phillimore J in holding that G was not liable. While considering my judgment I found that although the Law Reports do not reveal it, the decision at first instance was in fact reported: *Stacey v Hill*[4]. Ever since this decision, questions have been raised whether it is the law that although on disclaimer of a lease a guarantor of the rent will be discharged if the lease was vested in the original lessee, the original lessee will nevertheless remain liable to the lessor if the lease was vested in an assignee. The decision was much discussed in argument before me, and as the point has now at last arisen for decision I must examine the judgments in the light of the arguments.

Counsel for the defendants contended that the basis for the decision was that the object of the statute was to release the bankrupt and his property as much as possible, and that the section should operate so as to effectuate this purpose. Accordingly, just as the guarantor was held in *Stacey v Hill*[2] to have been released by the disclaimer, so here the original lessees should be held to have been released. He accepted that if the defendants (the original lessees) were held liable, then under s 323(7) of the Companies Act 1948 they could prove the liquidation, whereas if they were held not liable it was the plaintiffs (the original lessors) who could prove in the liquidation. Thus in neither case would the company's property escape. But he said that as between the lessors and the lessees, the lessors were better able to mitigate their losses, for they were free from the lessees' covenants in the lease and so could relet the property free from any restrictions which would reduce the rent recoverable. On the other hand, if the lessees were to take a vesting order, they would take the lease with all its restrictions, and so would be likely to prove for a greater sum in the liquidation.

1 (1884) 9 App Cas 448
2 [1901] 1 KB 660
3 [1932] 1 Ch 70, [1931] All ER Rep 125
4 (1900) 69 LJKB 796

This last point was founded on the assumption that the lessors were freeholders, an assumption that proved to be false when the lease was examined; for the lease contains many references to the lessors' superior lessors, so that the lessors are evidently mere leaseholders and not freeholders. True, the head lease may in fact contain less burdensome restrictions than the lease; but I certainly will not assume this to be the case, and there is nothing in evidence before me to suggest that this is so. Even if it were the case, I would reject the contention; for I do not think that the statute is directed to fine distinctions of fact which depend on the relative amounts for which proof could be made. On behalf of the plaintiffs, the lessors, counsel disputed the reading of *Stacey v Hill*[1] that counsel for the dependants put forward, and contended that the case applied only where it was the original lessee who was bankrupt, and the lease was disclaimed while it was vested in him.

With that, I can turn to consider the case. The starting point, I think, is that it seems perfectly clear that when a lease is disclaimed there are very real distinctions between the case where it is vested in the original lessee and the case where it is vested in an assignee. A major distinction is that in the first case disclaimer terminates the lease, which ceases to exist, whereas in the second case the lease continues to exist despite the disclaimer, and it may be made the subject of a vesting order under the Bankruptcy Act 1914, s 54(6) or the Companies Act 1948, s 323(6). The position in the first case plainly appears in *Stacey v Hill*[2]. Sir Archibald Smith MR says that the effect of the disclaimer is that—

> 'the lease is put an end to altogether as between the lessor and the bankrupt lessee, the intention being that the bankrupt shall be altogether freed from any obligation arising under or in relation to it; and, consequently, no other person being interested in the lease, it ceases to exist. As the lease is determined, no rent can, subsequently to the disclaimer, become due under it: the reversion on the term is in effect accelerated; and the lessor gets back his property, and can let it to another tenant, for aught I know, at a higher rent.'

See also per Romer LJ[3]; *Re Finley, ex parte Clothworkers' Co*[4]; *Re Thompson and Cottrell's Contract*[5]. As Collins LJ pointed out in *Stacey v Hill*[6], this case stands entirely outside the cases 'in which the rights of the lessor against the original lessee survived'. In the second case, where the disclaimed lease was vested in an assignee, the lease was described by Uthwatt J in *Re Thompson and Cottrell's Contract*[7] as being 'something like a dormant volcano. It may break out into active operation at any time'. The activating event is the making of a vesting order. Such a lease continues in existence despite the disclaimer, which merely releases the bankrupt and his estate from liability under it. In considering the liability of the original lessee under a lease, there is clearly likely to be a real difference between the case where the lease is at an end, and the case where the lease, though cataleptic, still exists.

Where it is the original lessee who is bankrupt, so that the lease comes to an end on disclaimer, a basic reason for holding that a guarantor of the rent is discharged from liability on his guarantee is that such a liability ends with the termination of the obligation that is the subject of the guarantee. If there is no obligation to pay future rent, there can be no liability on a guarantee of the payment of that future rent. Collins LJ put it that way in *Stacey v Hill*[8]. He referred to the liability of the

1 [1901] 1 KB 660
2 [1901] 1 KB 660 at 664
3 [1901] 1 KB 660 at 667
4 (1888) 21 QBD 475 at 485
5 [1943] 1 All ER 169 at 171, [1943] Ch 97 at 99
6 [1901] 1 KB 660 at 665
7 [1943] Ch 97 at 100, cf [1943] 1 All ER 169 at 172
8 [1901] 1 KB 660 at 666

principal debtor, the lessee, as having been put an end to by statute, and then said:

'The liabilities of a surety are in law dependent upon those of the principal debtor, and I do not see how it can be said that in such a case as this the liabilities of the latter are determined without incidentally saying that those of the former are determined also. The lessor in this case is, upon the disclaimer, entitled to resume possession of the premises. That being so, how can he treat himself as a person to whom the lessee is still tenant; and, unless he can do so, how can the surety be liable? I do not see how the lessor can possibly be entitled to the premises, and have the right to relet them, and yet retain the liability of the defendant as surety for the bankrupt lessee. Under the earlier bankruptcy law, before the power of disclaimer was introduced, the bankrupt remained liable: *Auriol* v. *Mills*[1], and the surety, if compelled to pay the rent, could have obtained repayment from him; so that the bankrupt was not discharged. I think that what the Legislature intended in such a case as this was that the lease should be determined by the disclaimer as between the lessor and the lessee, and therefore incidentally as regards the surety, with the result that the bankrupt lessee is discharged and incidentally the surety also: and the lessor, getting back his land, can let it to some solvent tenant, and has a right to prove as against the bankrupt's estate for possible loss by reason of not being able to let the land on such favourable terms.'

Counsel for the defendants was driven to contending that this was wrong, and that it was not supported by the other judgments. I do not think that this is so. Romer LJ ended his very short judgment by saying[2]:

'The section does not operate so as to cast upon third persons liabilities different in kind from what they were under before the disclaimer. Here, if the appellant was right in his contention, the section would so operate. For the defendant has only agreed to be liable as surety for the payment of rent by a lessee under a lease: and yet the appellant seeks to make him liable to pay money, though there is no rent payable, no lease, and no person in the position of lessee.'

That passage seems to me to be a sufficient recognition of the fact that the liability of a surety for the rent comes to an end with the discharge of the principal liability for the rent. Sir Archibald Smith MR[3] also pointed out that 'the guarantee is on the face of it for payment of rent "in arrear". But, how can rent be "in arrear" after the date of the disclaimer, the lease being then at an end as against the lessee?' At first instance, I think that Phillimore J took the same view. Counsel had argued that by disclaimer the lease had come to an end, and in his judgment Phillimore J said this[4]:

'From the date of the disclaimer the rent was gone. This case is distinguishable from *Harding* v. *Preece*[5] and *Hill* v. *East and West India Dock Co.*[6] In those cases it was held that the disclaimer by the trustee in bankruptcy of the assignee of the lease did not destroy the original term. But in the present case the original lessee became bankrupt, and the effect of the disclaimer was to release the lessee, his property, and the trustee from liability to pay rent. As the defendant's guarantee only extended to the payment of rent in arrear, there is no liability under the guarantee for any rent after the date of the disclaimer.'

---

1 (1790) 4 Term Rep 94
2 [1901] 1 KB 660 at 667
3 [1901] 1 KB 660 at 664, 665
4 (1900) 69 LJQB 796 at 797
5 (1882) 9 QBD 281
6 (1884) 9 App Cas 448

The judgment of Phillimore J seems to me to be valuable in that in substance it distinguishes *Harding v Preece*[1] and *Hill v East and West India Dock Co*[2] not on the ground that they were decided on the old language of the previous statutes but on the ground of the difference between a disclaimer that destroys the term, and so the liability for the rent, and a disclaimer that leaves the term in being and, with it, the liability for the rent of all save the bankrupt, his estate and his trustee in bankruptcy. The judgments in the Court of Appeal do not mention the two cases distinguished by Phillimore J; but they cannot have been overlooked, since they were the only cases cited in the judgment appealed from, and they were also cited in argument in the Court of Appeal. I also observe that in *Re Katherine et Cie Ltd*[3], which I have already mentioned, Maugham J treated *Stacey v Hill*[4] as being a decision on the liability of guarantors falling with the termination of the principal obligation. I may add that in *D Morris & Sons Ltd v Jeffreys*[5], which follows *Stacey v Hill*[4], Swift J plainly put the decision in *Stacey v Hill*[4] on the point that if the principal is discharged, then the surety must also be discharged. The guarantee in that case was a simple guarantee of the rent, and not merely of rent in arrears; but it was held that this made no difference.

I do not think that I need examine any other cases at this point, though I shall have to refer to some other decisions. With the contentions and the authorities in mind, I propose to consider the position by stages, proceeding from the general to the particular. For brevity, I shall in general speak merely in terms of bankruptcy, since there is no material difference in company law.

(1) Generally speaking, an original lessee prima facie remains liable to the reversioner for payment of the rent throughout the term, even after it has been assigned. This is a direct and primary liability, though after an assignment it is normally accompanied by rights of indemnity against the first assignee, and also, where there have been further assignments, against the assignee in whom the lease is for the time being vested. I shall turn to these rights in due course.

(2) There are authorities, not explored in the argument before me, for describing the liability of an original lessee after the lease has been assigned as being that of a surety for the performance of the obligations of the lease by the assignee in whom the lease is vested: see, for example, *Wolveridge v Steward*[6]; *Moule v Garrett*[7]. At first blush, such language might be thought to give some encouragement to the defendants. If the lessee is a mere surety for the rent, would that not bring the defendants within the cover of *Stacey v Hill*[4]? However, I think it is important to consider such statements in their context, and not to read too much into them. As between the lessee and the assignee, such statements reflect the fact that the assignee takes the lease subject to its burdens, and he is under a duty to discharge them. His is the primary duty, and if he fails in his duty and the lessee has to pay, the lessee, like a surety, has the right to be reimbursed by the assignee. That is the position as between the lessee and the assignee which was being considered in the cases. But as between the lessee and the lessor, the position is quite different. The assignment of the lease does nothing to disturb the direct liability of the lessee to the lessor under the lease for the whole of the term. The assignment does not, in my judgment, prevent the lessee from remaining directly and primarily liable to the lessor, or reduce him to being a mere surety towards the lessor for the discharge of the obligations of the lease by the assignee.

---

1 (1882) 9 QBD 281
2 (1884) 9 App Cas 448
3 [1932] 1 Ch 70 at 73, [1931] All ER Rep 125 at 126
4 [1901] 1 KB 660
5 (1932) 148 LT 56, [1932] All ER Rep 881
6 (1833) 1 Cr & M 644 at 660
7 (1870) LR 5 Exch 132 at 138, *affd* LR 7 Exch 101, [1861-73] All ER Rep 135

(3) Generally speaking, the guarantor of rent due under a lease is in a very different position towards the lessor from that of an original lessee. Like any other guarantor, from the start the liability of a guarantor is merely collateral, or accessory, or secondary: the terms used in the authorities vary. There never is a period when the guarantor alone is liable to the lessor for the rent, in the way that initially the lessee alone is liable for it to the lessor. Instead, the guarantor is merely liable to pay if the principal debtor does not. It follows that once the liability of the principal debtor for future payments is at an end, so also is the liability of the surety.

(4) With these basic propositions in mind, I turn to disclaimer in bankruptcy. *Stacey v Hill*[1] seems to me to be a clear example of the liability of a surety perishing when there ceases to be any primary liability to make any further payments. Where there has been no assignment of a lease, and the lease is disclaimed on the bankruptcy of the original lessee, the lease is at an end, and so is any obligation of the lessee under it to pay any further rent. It follows that the liability of anyone who has guaranteed the payment of that rent is also at an end. With no lease in existence, and with the reversioner able to do as he wishes with the property, free from the lease, the surety cannot and ought not to be made liable for any more rent.

(5) On the other hand, where the lease has been assigned, and the bankruptcy is that of the assignee in whom the lease is vested, and not of the original lessee, the position of the original lessee is very different. The disclaimer does not destroy the lease, but leaves it in existence, though without an owner until a vesting order is made. The original lessee is a person who as principal, undertook towards the lessor, the obligations of the lease for the whole term; and there is nothing in the process of assignment which replaced this liability by the mere collateral liability of a surety who must pay the rent only if the assignee does not. The bankruptcy of the assignee has for the time being destroyed the original lessee's right against the assignee to require him to discharge the obligations of the lease, and it has impaired the lessee's right of indemnity against him when he has to discharge the obligations himself; but it has not affected his primary liability towards the lessor, which continues unaffected. At no time does an original lessee become a mere guarantor to the lessor of the liability of any assignee of the lease.

(6) *Hill v East and West India Dock Co*[2] firmly established that prior to the Bankruptcy Act 1883 the original lessee remained liable to the reversioner, notwithstanding an assignment and subsequent disclaimer. I think that it is clear that the new wording in the 1883 Act was not only intended to confirm the law laid down in *Hill v East and West India Dock Co*[2], but also actually did so. Lord Cairns[3] observed that the legislature had replaced the old enactment by an enactment 'of a very different and much more explicit kind', and that the question before him was one which 'cannot ... very well occur again'. In *Re Cock, ex parte Shilson*[4], Cave and A L Smith JJ made it clear that on the point that I am concerned with there was no doubt that the new provision was a re-enactment of the old provision as explained by the cases. In my judgment, the present wording is both more apt and more explicit for producing the result that in *Hill v East and West India Dock Co*[2] was achieved on the old wording. If the draftsman had intended to reverse or alter the law laid down in that case he could scarcely have chosen more inept language for his purpose; and counsel for the defendants was unable to advance any reasons why Parliament should have wished to reverse or alter the law which the courts had wrested out of the old statutory language in order to avoid hardship and injustice.

(7) Despite the doubts and uncertainties that have from time to time been expressed about the ambit of *Stacey v Hill*[1] and its effect, I do not think that, when properly

---

1   [1901] 1 KB 660
2   (1884) 9 App Cas 448
3   9 App Cas 448 at 453
4   (1887) 20 QBD 343 at 346

considered, it has affected the position of an original lessee who has assigned the lease, as in the case now before me. The two essential differences are that *Stacey v Hill*[1] concerned the disclaimer of a lease which had never been assigned, and the liability of a surety for the rent, whereas the case before me concerns the disclaimer of a lease after it had been assigned, and the liability of the original lessee for the rent. As I have indicated, these differences produce entirely different results. In particular, there is a marked difference between a lease which has been terminated by the disclaimer, and a lease which continues to exist despite the disclaimer, and also between the collateral liability of a surety and the principal liability of an original lessee.

(8) These differences are of importance in relation to the release of the bankrupt and his estate. Under s 54(2) of the Bankruptcy Act 1914 the disclaimer will not release anybody save the bankrupt except so far as it is necessary to do so 'for the purpose of releasing the bankrupt and his property and the trustee from liability'. For an original lessee to be released, he must show that his release is necessary for this purpose. I shall consider this first, before turning to the case of a surety.

(a) Where the lease has been assigned, I can see nothing which requires the original lessee to be released from liability in order to release the bankrupt, his property or his trustee. Whether he is released or not, the lease continues in existence, and rent under it continues to fall due. If it were to be held that the lessee remains liable for the rent, he could prove for it in the bankruptcy as an 'injury' under s 54(8) of the 1914 Act. If instead it were to be held that the lessee is released from liability for the rent, then it is the lessor who could prove for it in the bankruptcy, also as an 'injury' under s 54(8). The release of the lessee could thus in no way be said to be 'necessary for the purpose of releasing' the bankrupt, his property or his trustee from liability, for it would not achieve any release. I shall not complicate matters at this stage by examining the effect of the original lessee's rights of indemnity against assignees: I shall reserve this for a subsequent paragraph.

(b) Where the lease has not been assigned, the position is entirely different. On disclaimer, the lease is at an end, and the bankrupt lessee is, of course, released. If it were to be held that a surety for the rent remains liable for the rent, he could then prove in the bankruptcy under s 54(8). If instead it were to be held that the surety is released from liability for the rent, the lessor normally could not prove for it; for the lease is at an end, and he is free to let the land anew. If he promptly relets it for the same or a greater rent, he is not 'injured' within sub-s (8) of s 54, and so he will be unable to prove for anything. If he cannot relet it promptly and then only for a lower rent, he is 'injured' to the extent of the shortfall in rent, but no further: see, for example, *Stacey v Hill*[2]. In short, the release of the surety can properly be said to be 'necessary for the purpose' of releasing the bankrupt, his property and his trustee from liability, either wholly or in part.

(9)(a) I must now consider the effect of the original lessee's rights of indemnity against assignees that I mentioned in para (8)(a) above. Where the lease has been assigned and the original lessee has to pay the rent, he will usually have an alternative to proving for it in the bankruptcy. This will arise where (unlike the present case) the lease has been assigned more than once, and the bankrupt is not the first assignee but a subsequent assignee. In such a case the original lessee, on being held liable to the lessor, may well prefer to claim against the first assignee under a covenant for indemnity (either express, or implied by virtue of the Law of Property Act 1925, s 77(1)(c)) instead of proving in the bankruptcy of the subsequent assignee and merely receiving a dividend in it. The first assignee may then turn round in the same way against the second assignee, and so on down the line as far as the penultimate assignee, who will then merely have his right of proof in the bankruptcy.

(b) Thus far, with an unbroken chain of assignees who are liable, the final result is

---

1   [1901] 1 KB 660
2   [1901] 1 KB 660 at 666

not greatly different from the case where it is the original lessee who proves in the bankruptcy: in each case there will be someone who proves the bankruptcy. But let the chain of indemnities be broken, and at once a difference appears; for then there may be nobody who can, or is likely to, prove in the bankruptcy. The original lessee may receive his indemnity from the first assignee; and if he does he cannot, of course, prove in the bankruptcy. The burden of the indemnity may then be passed down the line as far as the break; but, subject to what I shall say in a moment, there it stops. The penultimate assignee, not having been made liable, cannot prove in the bankruptcy, and probably nobody else can, at any rate under the chain of indemnities. In such a case there is no ground for releasing the original lessee from liability: indeed, there is every reason for holding him liable, since to hold him liable will mean that there may be nobody who will prove in the bankruptcy, whereas to hold him not liable would mean that the lessor could prove in the bankruptcy.

(c) That, however, has to be qualified by the possibility that even in that case there might be some person with a right of proof in the bankruptcy. It may be that the last assignee in the chain of indemnities before it broke would be held to have a quasi-contractual right of indemnity against the assignee in whom the lease was vested when he became bankrupt, a right analogous to the original lessee's right to an indemnity against him which was recognised in *Moule v Garrett*[1]; and this would give him a right of proof in the bankruptcy. If this is so, once again the final result would not be greatly different from the case when it is the original lessee who proves in the bankruptcy: there would be somebody who could prove in it.

(d) From what I have said it will be seen that the rights of indemnity of the original lessee do not affect the basic position that the release of the original lessee is not necessary for the purpose of releasing the bankrupt, his property or his trustee. Such a release would either not improve the position of the bankrupt's estate or else, under sub-para (b) above, would worsen it. I should add that no points under the matters discussed in this paragraph arise directly for decision, and they were understandably not put forward in argument. I have, however, thought it right to consider them, since the result reached in a case in which there has been only one assignment ought at least to be compatible with the result that would be achieved in the case of multiple assignments; and if there were some inconsistency in principle, then that would be a ground for reconsidering any provisional conclusions reached in the case of a single assignment. The result of having considered multiple assignments is, however, one which does not suggest any incompatibility, and, indeed, so far as it goes, appears to me to reinforce the conclusion that I have reached in the case of a single assignment.

I do not think that I need consider any other matters. Indeed, I am very conscious that this is a long judgment for a case in which the point in issue is so short. Much of the length is due to complexities of law which I found difficult to discuss with brevity without becoming cryptic. I can, however, express my conclusion in a very few words. For the reasons that I have given, I hold that the original lessees under a lease remain liable to the lessors for the rent which falls due even after the term has been assigned to a company and the liquidator of the company has disclaimed the lease. Accordingly, I hold that in the case before me the plaintiffs are entitled to the sum claimed by the writ in respect of the rent that is still unpaid. I will only add that for the reasons that I have given the result would have been the same if the assignment had been to an individual and the lease had been disclaimed by his trustee in bankruptcy. I shall hear counsel on the question of interest and the details of the order.

Judgment for the plaintiffs.

Solicitors: *M L Spector* (for the plaintiffs); *Norton, Rose, Botterell & Roche* (for the defendants).

Hazel Hartman   Barrister.

---

1   (1872) LR 7 Exch 101, [1861-73] All ER Rep 135

Lloyd v Sadler and others

COURT OF APPEAL, CIVIL DIVISION

MEGAW, LAWTON AND SHAW LJJ

8th, 9th, 12th DECEMBER 1977, 19th JANUARY 1978

Rent restriction – Statutory tenancy – Protected tenant in occupation on termination of protected tenancy – Joint tenancy – One only of two joint tenants in occupation on termination of protected tenancy – Whether both joint tenants constituting 'the protected tenant' – Whether necessary that both joint tenants should be in occupation on termination of protected tenancy – Whether tenant remaining in occupation capable of becoming the statutory tenant – Rent Act 1968, s 3(1)(a).

On the true construction of s 3(1)(a)[a] of the Rent Act 1968, which provides that on the termination of the protected tenancy of a dwelling-house, the protected tenant, if still in occupation is to become the statutory tenant, the words 'the protected tenant' include one or some of a number of joint tenants. Accordingly, if two persons are joint tenants of a house or flat under a protected tenancy and one of them ceases to occupy the house or flat during the period of the tenancy, the other is to be regarded as 'the protected tenant' for the purpose of s 3(1)(a) and therefore, if still in occupation when the tenancy comes to an end, will thereupon become the statutory tenant (see p 532 *b* to *d*, p 535 *b* to *d*, p 537 *a* and *h*, and p 538 *a* to *c* and *g* to *j*, post).

Howson v Buxton [1928] All ER Rep 434 applied.

T M Fairclough & Sons Ltd v Berliner [1930] All ER Rep 170, *McIntyre v Hardcastle* [1948] 1 All ER 696, *Re Lower Onibury Farm, Lloyds Bank Ltd v Jones* [1955] 2 All ER 409 and *Jacobs v Chaudhuri* [1968] 2 All ER 124 distinguished.

Notes

For protected tenancies, see Supplement to 23 Halsbury's Laws (3rd Edn) para 1494A.

For the Rent Act 1968, s 3, see 18 Halsbury's Statutes (3rd Edn) 788.

As from 29th August 1977, s 3 of the 1968 Act has been replaced by the Rent Act 1977, s 2.

Cases referred to in judgments

Baker v Lewis [1946] 2 All ER 592, [1947] KB 186, [1947] LJR 468, 175 LT 490, CA, 31(2) Digest (Reissue) 1092, 8515.

Davis v Johnson [1978] 1 All ER 841, [1978] 2 WLR 182, CA.

Fairclough (TM) & Sons Ltd v Berliner [1931] 1 Ch 60, [1930] All ER Rep 170, 100 LJCh 29, 144 LT 175, 31(2) Digest (Reissue) 831, 6880.

Feyereisel v Parry [1952] 1 All ER 728, sub nom *Feyereisel v Turnidge* [1952] 2 QB 29, CA, 31(2) Digest (Reissue) 1007, 8018.

Howson v Buxton (1928) 97 LJKB 749, [1928] All ER Rep 434, 139 LT 504, CA, 2 Digest (Repl) 80, 452.

Jacobs v Chaudhuri [1968] 2 All ER 124, [1968] 2 QB 470, [1968] 2 WLR 1098, 19 P & CR 286, CA, 31(2) Digest (Reissue) 955, 7761.

Lower Onibury Farm, Re, Lloyds Bank Ltd v Jones [1955] 2 All ER 409, [1955] 2 QB 298, [1955] 3 WLR 5, 53 LGR 433, CA, 2 Digest (Repl) 46, 238.

McIntyre v Hardcastle [1948] 1 All ER 696, [1948] 2 KB 82, [1948] LJR 1249, CA, 31(2) Digest (Reissue) 1092, 8516.

Newman v Keedwell (1977) 244 Estates Gazette 469.

Powell v Cleland [1947] 2 All ER 672, [1948] 1 KB 262, [1948] LJR 250, CA, 31(2) Digest (Reissue) 1091, 8504.

---

a   Section 3(1), so far as material, is set out at p 530 *j*, post

Turley v Panton (1975) 29 P & CR 397, 236 Estates Gazette 197, DC, Digest (Cont Vol D) 596, 8737a.

Cases also cited
Dealex Properties Ltd v Brooks [1965] 1 All ER 1080, [1966] 1 QB 542, CA.
Farrell v Alexander [1976] 2 All ER 721, [1977] AC 59, HL.
Maunsell v Olins [1975] 1 All ER 16, [1975] AC 373, HL.

Appeal
This was an appeal by the plaintiff, John Michael Lloyd ('the landlord'), against the order made by his Honour Judge McIntyre QC in the West London County Court on 23rd March 1977 whereby he dismissed the landlord's claim against the defendants, Gloria Sadler ('the tenant') and her licensees, Joanna Tait, Clare Watson and Judith Lowe, for possession of premises known as the top floor flat, 22 Cottesmore Gardens, London, W8, of which the landlord was the leasehold owner. The facts are set out in the judgment of Megaw LJ.

David Neuberger for the landlord.
William Birtles for the tenant and her licensees.

Cur adv vult

19th January. The following judgments were read.

MEGAW LJ. The relevant facts are simple. The question of law which arises on them is of importance, with possibly wide-ranging effects.

By an agreement in writing a tenancy of the top floor flat, 22 Cottesmore Gardens, London W8, was granted by the landlord to Miss G Sadler and Miss M Lunt from 27th December 1975 to 25th December 1976. The tenancy was a protected tenancy under the Rent Act 1968. On about 28th October 1976 Miss Lunt left the flat in order to get married. She did not intend to resume, and she did not in fact resume, occupation of the flat. Miss Sadler remained in occupation of the flat during the remainder of the contractual tenancy, and she continued in occupation after 25th December 1976 when the contractual tenancy ended. In January 1977 the landlord started proceedings in the West London County Court, claiming possession of the flat. The defendants were Miss Sadler and three other ladies whom Miss Sadler had brought in to live in the flat as her licensees. No separate question arises as to them. Their right to stay in occupation stands or falls with that of Miss Sadler. So much for the relevant facts.

The question of law also can be simply stated. Was Miss Sadler a statutory tenant and thus entitled to the security of tenure given to statutory tenants by the Rent Acts, despite the fact that Miss Lunt, before the contractual tenancy had ended, had ceased, permanently, to occupy the flat?

The contractual tenancy was a joint tenancy of Miss Sadler and Miss Lunt. The contractual tenancy ended on 25th December 1976. The right of Miss Sadler to remain in possession thereafter, if it existed at all, could exist only because she had become the statutory tenant under s 3(1) of the Rent Act 1968. (That was the statute in force at the time. The corresponding provision of the new Act, s 2(1) of the Rent Act 1977, is identical.) Section 3(1)(a) of the 1968 Act provides:

'after the termination of a protected tenancy of a dwelling-house the person who, immediately before that termination, was the protected tenant of the dwelling-house shall, if and so long as he occupies the dwelling-house as his residence, be the statutory tenant of it . . .'

The landlord contended that the contractual, admittedly protected, tenancy was a joint tenancy; and that, as a result of the doctrine of joint tenancy in the law of property, anything that had to be done in connection with the joint tenancy, to have any legal effect, had to be done by the joint tenants; that is, by all the individuals acting collectively. One of the joint tenants, it was submitted (otherwise than when in law one joint tenant could be treated as acting as agent for them all), could not achieve any result recognised by law, he could not act validly, by anything which he himself did as an individual. Hence Miss Sadler's continuance in occupation of the flat after the end of the contractual tenancy did not, in law, produce the result that 'the protected tenant . . . occupies the dwelling-house as his residence'. Hence there was no statutory tenant. Miss Sadler did not achieve that status in law. That submission by the landlord was rejected by Judge McIntyre in his judgment delivered on 23rd March 1977. The landlord appeals to this court.

This case has brought to light two remarkable facts. First, the Rent Acts through all their long history have never made any relevant express provision relating to joint tenants or joint tenancies, whether protected or statutory. Secondly, and perhaps even more strangely, there seems to have been no previous case decided by any court, or at least no reported case, in which a question such as falls to be decided in the present case has been raised for consideration on s 3(1) of the 1968 Act or its predecessors. Yet there must have been, over the years, thousands of instances in which one of two joint tenants has ceased to occupy the dwelling-house before the end of the contractual tenancy, and the other original joint tenant has continued to live there, on the assumption that he has become the statutory tenant. If the landlord's submission is right, that assumption has been wrong. Similar instances must have arisen thousands of times where two or more persons have duly become 'the statutory tenant', and thereafter one or more of them has, or have, died or ceased to occupy the house as his, or their, residence. What is the effect on the legal status of the person, or persons, remaining in occupation? Does the statutory security of tenure cease?

I do not think that the absence of previous litigation helps one way or the other towards a decision of the issue. But the fact that there are likely to be very many cases with facts similar to those of the present case shows the practical importance of this issue. Whatever the answer be, it must affect many people, landlords and tenants, in a matter of great importance to them. If the landlord's submissions in the present case are wrong, the result may be a measure of prejudice to landlords. It would mean that a landlord who looked to two persons as both being liable to him for the rent might find that when the contractual tenancy ended there was only one person who was liable to him for the rent. On the other hand, if the landlord's submissions are right, the potential prejudice to joint tenants would be very much more serious; that is, the value of their legal rights as compared with what those legal rights would be if the landlord's submissions are wrong.

In view of the importance of the issue, it may be helpful to set out the landlord's submissions as they were conveniently summarised by his counsel in nine propositions, in the course of his very clear and careful argument: (1) The grant to Miss Sadler and Miss Lunt of a contractual tenancy resulted in Miss Sadler and Miss Lunt being joint tenants. (2) Therefore 'the tenant' under the contractual tenancy was Miss Sadler and Miss Lunt. (3) The contractual tenancy was a protected tenancy. (4) Therefore 'the protected tenant' was Miss Sadler and Miss Lunt. (5) On the determination of a protected tenancy a statutory tenancy can only arise 'if . . . he occupies the dwelling-house as his residence'. (6) The 'he' in the above quotation clearly refers to 'the person who . . . was the protected tenant'. (7) On the determination of the protected tenancy in this case it cannot be said that Miss Sadler and Miss Lunt were occupying the dwelling-house as their residence. (8) Therefore the protected tenant was not occupying the premises in question on the determination of the protected tenancy in this case. (9) Therefore no statutory tenancy can arise.

If the ordinary law as to joint tenancy, as it affects rights of property, is to be treated as applicable in all its strictness to s 3(1)(a) of the 1968 Act, the logic of counsel for the landlord's propositions appears to me to be unassailable. I agree with the view expressed by Judge McIntyre that s 1(1)(b) of the Interpretation Act 1889 is not of assistance one way or the other.

I have come to the conclusion that, on the true construction of s 3(1)(a) of the 1968 Act, the ordinary law as to joint tenancy does not have to be, and ought not to be, applied in all its strictness. I base that opinion, primarily at least, on the judgment of Scrutton LJ in *Howson v Buxton*[1]. It is not a direct authority. There is no direct authority. There are various decided cases to which we were properly referred as providing guidance by analogy, or as illustrating the general rule as to a joint tenancy. Some of them, or dicta in them, certainly lend support to the submissions on behalf of the landlord; but I find the most helpful guidance in *Howson v Buxton*[1]. It appears to me to decide that, where an Act of Parliament refers to 'the tenant', and the letting is to two or more persons jointly, it is permissible for the court to hold, if so to do makes better sense of the relevant statutory provision in its particular context, that one of those persons, by himself, may for certain purposes be treated as being 'the tenant'. So here Miss Sadler can be treated, and should on the facts be treated, as having been 'the protected tenant' immediately before the termination of the contractual tenancy, and as being 'the statutory tenant' thereafter. Hence she has security of tenure under the Act.

I do not propose to discuss at length the cases which I have mentioned. I shall refer to them briefly. In *T M Fairclough & Sons Ltd v Berliner*[2], Maugham J held that, where there are joint lessees, relief against forfeiture cannot be granted on the application of one person only. Otherwise, the joint tenant, who did not join in the application for relief, might find himself saddled with the continuance of obligations under an onerous lease, from which he would prefer to be free. In *Re Lower Onibury Farm, Lloyds Bank Ltd v Jones*[3], a covenant in a lease of a farmhouse and cottages provided that the tenant should 'at all times personally inhabit the farmhouse and cottages with his family and servants'. The tenant was defined to include the named tenant's executors and assigns. The lessee died. His trustees were his widow and another. The widow resided in the farmhouse until her death. The other trustee did not. It was held that this was a breach of covenant.

In *McIntyre v Hardcastle*[4], another decision of this court, it was not the tenant, but the landlord, who was a joint personage. The joint landlord consisted of two sisters. The case concerned what is now, in the 1968 Act, Case 8 in Part I of Sch 3: 'the dwelling-house is reasonably required by the landlord as a residence for (a) himself, or (b) any son or daughter of his, or (c) his father or mother . . .' It was held, following a dictum of Asquith LJ in *Baker v Lewis*[5], that, where there were joint landlords, 'himself' in para (a) should be read as 'themselves'; 'any son . . . of his' in para (b) should be read as 'any son . . . of theirs'; and so on. That was a strict construction of 'the landlord', adverse to the interest of landlords. Not unnaturally, counsel for the landlord in this case says in effect (though he did not put it so inelegantly), 'What is sauce for the landlord is sauce for the tenant'.

In *Turley v Panton*[6] a Divisional Court of the Queen's Bench Division held that a rent tribunal did not have jurisdiction to determine an application made by one person alone, he being one of a number of joint lessees under Part VI of the Rent Act 1968. The possibility of an unfair result to the others of the joint lessees, if such an

---

1 (1928) 97 LJKB 749, [1928] All ER Rep 434
2 [1931] 1 Ch 60, [1930] All ER Rep 170
3 [1955] 2 All ER 409, [1955] 2 QB 298
4 [1948] 1 All ER 696, [1948] 2 KB 82
5 [1946] 2 All ER 592 at 595, [1947] KB 186 at 193
6 (1975) 29 P & CR 397

application could validly be made without their concurrence, was stressed by the court. *Jacobs v Chaudhuri*[1] was a decision of this court. It was a decision, not in relation to security of tenure of living accommodation under the Rent Acts, but in relation to security of tenure of business premises under the Landlord and Tenant Act 1954. The letting of the business premises was to two persons who were in partnership. During the currency of the contractual lease the partnership was dissolved, and one of the two partners by agreement between them (the landlord not being a party to the agreement) took over the business as his own. He applied, in his own name alone, for a new tenancy under s 26 of the 1954 Act. It was held by a majority, Harman and Winn LJJ, Davies LJ dissenting, that the county court had no jurisdiction under the 1954 Act to entertain such an application, made by one individual, when the contractual tenancy had been granted as a joint tenancy to two persons. The majority distinguished *Howson v Buxton*[2]. Davies LJ thought that, though of course *Howson v Buxton*[2] was not direct binding authority in relation to this different statute and these different facts, the principle of Scrutton LJ's judgment was applicable by analogy.

The legislature promptly amended the 1954 Act. The Law of Property Act 1969 introduced two new sections into the Landlord and Tenant Act 1954. By s 13 it introduced a new section, s 43A, to overcome a technical defect in the county court's jurisdiction, using the draftsman's normal wording to achieve that purpose: the same form of wording (though I do not think this was called to the court's attention in a recent case[3]) as is used in s 1(1) of the Domestic Violence and Matrimonial Proceedings Act 1976.

The other new section introduced by the 1969 Act was s 41A, which showed that, to put it very broadly, Parliament preferred the view of Davies LJ to the view of the majority. But the fact that Parliament thought it right to include in the new s 41A a detailed code of provisions affecting joint tenants of business premises makes it probable, I think, that it was, indeed, an inadvertent gap which the legislature had left in the earlier legislation, rather than that the court had misinterpreted the meaning actually intended by Parliament to be expressed by the words used in the 1954 Act. If that assessment is right, it tends, in my opinion, strongly to support the view that the absence of express provisions in the Rent Acts as to the effect of joint tenancies is also, equally, an inadvertent gap. If so, and if this court's decision in this case accords with what Parliament would have enacted, had its intention been directed to the particular problem which has arisen in this case, it would, I firmly believe, be far better in the general interest that those parts of the gap which still remain, I suspect that those which remain are neither few nor unimportant, particularly as regards statutory joint tenancies, should be filled as the legislature would wish by an early and comprehensive Act of Parliament. They should not be left to be filled in, piecemeal, by the courts over the years, at random as cases happen to arise and happen to be taken to various stages of appeal. Such a code of judge-made law, however admirable it might prove to be in the end, would be built up slowly, probably erratically (because the various problems would not come up for decision in any logical order) and, most certainly, at no small cost in terms of human stress and anxiety and, in some cases, financial hardship to a large number of individual persons, who, to their misfortune, would happen to be the litigants on whose troubles the edifice of judge-made law would be built. In my opinion, there can be no doubt which would be the more efficient, sensible and humane way of filling any remaining gaps in the law as to the effect of joint tenancies in the Rent Acts.

The decision in *Jacobs v Chaudhuri*[1] is no longer law. But that does not necessarily

---

1 [1968] 2 All ER 124, [1968] 2 QB 470
2 (1928) 97 LJKB 749, [1928] All ER Rep 434
3 *Davis v Johnson* [1978] 1 All ER 841, [1978] 2 WLR 182

mean that the reasoning of the majority in that case is to be disregarded when the court has to interpret other statutory provisions in respect of which it is suggested that there is an analogy. However, in the present case I think it tends rather in the other direction. It is not, I believe, fanciful to suggest that the reaction of the legislature to the decision in *Jacobs v Chaudhuri*[1] tends to show that the legislature's approach to the problem of joint tenants in the 1954 Act, if it had specifically directed its mind to the problem at that time, would have been consonant with Scrutton LJ's approach in *Howson v Buxton*[2].

Before coming to *Howson v Buxton*[2], I should mention another case, very recently decided, to which we were referred: *Newman v Keedwell*[3]. It was a case arising under s 24(1) of the Agricultural Holdings Act 1948. Fox J delivered, if I may say so, a very clear and careful judgment, in the course of which he discussed *Jacobs v Chaudhuri*[1] and *Howson v Buxton*[2]. But, by reason of the nature of the issues in that case, I do not think that it assists on the issue which we have to decide.

Howson v Buxton[2] was a case which arose under s 12 of the Agricultural Holdings Act 1923 under which 'the tenant' of an agricultural holding was given certain rights of compensation in the event of a termination of the tenancy. In *Howson v Buxton*[2] there was a joint tenancy. It was held that, notwithstanding the doctrine of joint tenancy, a claim for compensation founded on a notice given by one only of two joint tenants was valid so as to give jurisdiction to the statutory arbitrator; and that one of the two joint tenants was entitled to recover compensation in respect of a loss which affected him alone, and did not effect also the other of the joint tenants. The relevant provisions of s 12 of the 1923 Act (the emphasis is mine) are:

'(1) Where *the tenancy* of a holding terminates by reason of a notice to quit given by the landlord, and in consequence of such notice *the tenant* quits the holding, then . . . compensation for the disturbance shall be payable by the landlord to *the tenant* . . .

'(6) The compensation payable under this section shall be a sum representing such loss or expense directly attributable to the quitting of the holding as *the tenant* may unavoidably incur upon or in connection with the sale or removal of *his* household goods, implements of husbandry . . .

'(7) Compensation shall not be payable under this section . . . (b) unless *the tenant* has . . . given notice in writing to the landlord of *his* intention to make a claim for compensation . . .'

The subject-matter obviously differs greatly from the subject-matter of s 3(1)(a) of the Rent Act 1968. But the relevance is the statutory reference to 'the tenant', 'his goods', 'his intention', coupled with the same absence of any specific provision for cases where the tenancy is joint. In *Howson v Buxton*[2] it was held by Scrutton LJ, with the concurrence of Sankey LJ, who expressly agreed 'for the reasons given by Scrutton, L.J.', that it was permissible for the court to hold that the statutory requirements which had to be fulfilled by 'the tenant' could validly and effectively be fulfilled by the individual act of one of the joint tenants. Thus, one of the two joint tenants could, acting by and for himself alone, give the requisite statutory notice. He could, without the concurrence or co-operation of the other participant in the joint tenancy, become entitled to the compensation which under the statute was payable to 'the tenant'. Even though it was a joint tenancy, 'his goods' could be construed to mean 'the goods which belong exclusively to one of the two joint tenants'. It did not have to be read as though, whether by the operation of the Interpretation Act 1889 or otherwise, it said 'their goods'. It will be remembered that in proposition 7 of counsel for the landlord's propositions, set out above, it was asserted as a

1 [1968] 2 All ER 124, [1968] 2 QB 470
2 (1928) 97 LJKB 749, [1928] All ER Rep 434
3 (1977) 244 Estates Gazette 469

step in his argument that the statutory tenancy could arise only if the dwelling-house could be said to be '*their* dwelling-house', that is, the dwelling-house occupied by Miss Sadler *and* Miss Lunt. Yet in *Howson v Buxton*[1] 'his goods' (the goods of 'the tenant') applied to goods in respect of which the other joint tenant had no right of ownership.

In my opinion, the judgment of Scrutton LJ in *Howson v Buxton*[1] shows that, where the strict application of the doctrine of joint tenancy would lead to unreasonable results, or results which the legislature is unlikely to have intended, it is permissible for the court to conclude that the legislature did not so intend; but that, instead, in such a case, the phrase 'the tenant', where there is a joint tenancy, is to be read as meaning 'the joint tenants or any one or more of them'. There is thus authority that the doctrine of joint participation by joint tenants is not a sacrosanct or immutable doctrine of statutory interpretation, where such phrases as 'the tenant' and 'the tenancy' are used. Where, then, is the line to be drawn? When does a suggested exception become a heresy? In the present case I believe that, for the purposes of s 3(1)(*a*) of the 1968 Act, the freedom from strict doctrinal restraint should, as in *Howson v Buxton*[1], be held to apply.

I would therefore hold that Miss Sadler became a statutory tenant on the expiration of the contractual tenancy on 25th December 1976, and that she so remains. I would dismiss the appeal.

LAWTON LJ. The issue which has to be decided in this appeal can be stated as follows: if a landlord lets a dwelling-house to two persons as joint tenants so as to create a protected tenancy and on the termination of that tenancy only one of the two joint tenants is in occupation, can that tenant be the statutory tenant for the purposes of the Rent Act 1968? The same question would arise under the Rent Act 1977, which repealed the 1968 Act, but re-enacted the relevant provisions of the 1968 Act. The answer to this question is likely to affect many tenants, particularly in areas where young people often join together to share accommodation. When they do, it may be prudent for landlords to grant them joint tenancies so as to have more than one tenant liable for the rent. Marriage, a change of job, graduation in the case of university students and diverse personal reasons may result in one tenant moving out. Surprisingly, there is no reported case bearing directly on the question which arises for consideration.

By an agreement in writing made on 21st November 1975 between the landlord and 'The Misses G. Sadler and M. Lunt', the landlord let to them the top flat at 22 Cottesmore Gardens for a period starting on 27th December 1975 and ending on 25th December 1976 at a rent of £34.32 per week. This agreement created a protected tenancy under the Rent Act 1968. The two ladies went into occupation. On 28th October 1976 Miss Lunt left to get married. She has never resumed occupation and at no material time has had any intention of doing so. Miss Sadler went on living in the flat and is still doing so. She claims that she was entitled to do this because on the termination of the contractual tenancy she became the statutory tenant pursuant to s 3(1)(*a*) of the 1968 Act, which is in these terms:

'Subject to sections 4 and 5 below—(*a*) after the termination of a protected tenancy of a dwelling-house the person who, immediately before that termination, was the protected tenant of the dwelling-house shall, if and so long as he occupies the dwelling-house as his residence, be the statutory tenant of it ...'

(Sections 4 and 5 have no relevance in this appeal.)

---

1   (1928) 97 LJKB 749, [1928] All ER Rep 434

The landlord submitted that this is not so because when s 1(1)(b) of the Interpretation Act 1889 is applied to the construction of s 3(1)(a), immediately before the termination of the tenancies, the two ladies, being, as they were, joint tenants, were 'the protected tenant' and after termination they, acting together, could claim to be 'the statutory tenant' if they both occupied the flat as their residence. Miss Sadler, by herself, could not claim to be the statutory tenant. Counsel for the landlord said that this was the plain meaning of the words used in s 3(1)(a). Moreover, this suggested construction, he said, falls in with the general principle of the law that when joint tenants are empowered or permitted by statute or agreement to acquire a benefit they must act together; one cannot act on his own. As a general principle this is so. Thus, one of two joint tenants cannot by himself claim relief from forfeiture: see *T M Fairclough & Sons Ltd v Berliner*[1]. In *Jacobs v Chaudhuri*[2] this court adjudged that on the true construction of s 24(1) of the Landlord and Tenant Act 1954, one of two or more joint tenants was not 'the tenant' that within the meaning of that section. In *Turley v Panton*[3] the Divisional Court held in the case of a joint tenancy an application to a rent tribunal had to be made by all the tenants acting together; one tenant could not apply on his own. Trustees of a deceased tenant must, acting together, do what he was required by covenant to do: see *Re Lower Onibury Farm, Lloyds Bank Ltd v Jones*[4]. Joint beneficial owners also must act together. Thus where there were joint beneficial owners of a dwelling-house to which the Rent and Mortgage Interest Restrictions (Amendment) Act 1933 applied both had to bring themselves within the provisions of that Act (now Case 9 in Sch 15 to the Rent Act 1977) which enabled a landlord to claim possession for himself or his son or daughter: see *McIntyre v Hardcastle*[5]. The only case which counsel for the plaintiff found which did not fit into this pattern was *Howson v Buxton*[6]. He submitted that it was not clear what its ratio decidendi was, as Greer LJ did not agree with Scrutton LJ's reasons for judgment and Sankey LJ seems to have qualified somewhat his assent to what Scrutton LJ had said. I shall return to this case later.

Counsel for the tenant submitted that s 3(1)(a) should be construed so as to follow what Denning LJ (as he then was) in 1952 called the guiding light through the darkness of the Rent Acts: see *Feyereisel v Parry*[7]. This lights up one of the main objects of these Acts, which always has been and still is to give tenants a personal right to security of tenure. Individuals are not to be turned out of their homes without an order of the court; and courts are not to make orders having this effect except on certain specified grounds. Further, the right to security of tenure which tenants enjoy after the termination of their contractual tenancies does not confer on them estates in land, as does a successful claim for relief against forfeiture or for the grant of a new business tenancy. The effect of the Law of Property Act 1925 has to be considered in such cases. A claim to be the statutory tenant is one for the enjoyment of a personal right. The Rent Acts are not in pari materia with the Law of Property Act 1925: see *Powell v Cleland*[8]. It follows, submitted counsel for the tenant, that s 3(1)(a) must be construed, as far as the words used will allow, in such a way as to safeguard the security of tenure of individuals. The only individual making the claim to enjoy the rights of the statutory tenant was Miss Sadler. Immediately before the termination of the protected tenancy she was one of the two joint tenants. Miss Lunt did not want the protection of the Rent Act 1968 but Miss Sadler did; and the fact that Miss Lunt had already moved out did not lessen her need for the security of

---

1　[1931] 1 Ch 60, [1930] All ER Rep 170
2　[1968] 2 All ER 124, [1968] 2 QB 470
3　(1975) 29 P & CR 397
4　[1955] 2 All ER 409, [1955] 2 QB 298
5　[1948] 1 All ER 696, [1948] 2 KB 82
6　(1928) 97 LJKB 74, [1928] All ER Rep 434
7　[1952] 1 All ER 728 at 773, [1952] 2 QB 29 at 37
8　[1947] 2 All ER 672 at 676, [1948] 1 KB 262 at 273

tenure which the Act gave 'the tenant'. As the Act gives protection to persons, not to legal concepts such as joint tenants, I am entitled, in my judgment, to construe s 3(1)(a) so as to allow one of two joint tenants to become 'the statutory tenant'.

I am fortified in this opinion by what Scrutton LJ decided in *Howson v Buxton*[1]. In that case this court was required to construe s 12 of the Agricultural Holdings Act 1923, and in particular sub-s (7)(b). That section gave 'the tenant' of an agricultural holding certain rights of compensation for disturbance, including a right to compensation arising in connection with the sale or removal of household goods, implements of husbandry, farm stock and the like. The subsection provided as follows:

> 'Compensation shall not be payable under this section . . . (b) unless the tenant has, not less than one month before the termination of the tenancy, given notice in writing to the landlord of his intention to make a claim for compensation under this section.'

There were two joint tenants but only one of them did the farming and owned that which is often called the dead and live stock. On the termination of the tenancy, only the farming tenant gave notice of an intention to claim compensation under sub-s (7)(b). The question for decision was whether his notice was effective. The same point was taken on behalf of the landlord as in this case, namely that when the Act used the words "the tenant" and said that the tenant must give notice, as the tenancy was a joint one, the notice had to be given by the whole, and that notice by one of two joint tenants would not do. Scrutton LJ[2] pointed out that the Act 'continually used the phrase "tenant" without any nice consideration of what would happen if there were more than one tenant'. The same can be said of the Rent Act 1968 and its predecessors. He then looked at what was the object of s 12 and the mischief which Parliament intended to deal with and to provide a remedy for. The object was to give compensation to persons who had suffered a specified kind of loss on the termination of their tenancy. Only one of two joint tenants might suffer loss. If, as the landlord contended, sub-s (7)(b) had to be construed as meaning the goods of both joint tenants, then loss of the goods of only one would not support the claim. 'That argument', said Scrutton LJ[3], 'seems to me so contrary to the mischief which the Act intends to remedy that I am justified in concluding, as I do, that the Act avoids it'. Greer LJ[4] agreed with Scrutton LJ that the appeal should be dismissed but he said that he did so on different grounds which made it unnecessary for him to consider whether he agreed or disagreed with the reasons the other had given. Sankey LJ had reasons of his own for dismissing the appeal, but at the end of his judgment he said[5]:

> 'I agree, for the reasons given by Scrutton, L.J., that the proper construction of the section as applicable to the facts in this case, is the one contended for by the respondent.'

The use of the words 'as applicable to the facts in this case' does not, in my judgment, qualify in any way his agreement on this point with Scrutton LJ. It follows that the agreed construction was the ratio decidendi. I approach the construction of s 3(1)(a) in the same way as the majority approached that of s 12(7)(b) of the Agricultural Holdings Act 1923.

The object of the Rent Act 1968 was to give security of tenure to persons; and one of two joint tenants might have wanted it and the other might not. The mischief for which Parliament provided a remedy was eviction for reasons other than those which the Act deemed good. If Miss Sadler has to leave the flat because Miss Lunt did not want to stay there any longer that it not a reason which was specified in the

1   (1928) 97 LJKB 749, [1928] All ER Rep 434
2   97 LJKB 749 at 753, [1928] All ER Rep 434 at 437
3   97 LJKB 749 at 754, [1928] All ER Rep 434 at 437
4   97 LJKB 749 at 754, [1928] All ER Rep 434 at 438
5   97 LJKB 749 at 757, [1928] All ER Rep 434 at 441

Act. I am satisfied that s 3(1)(a) can be construed so that one of two joint tenants can become 'the statutory tenant'. Any other construction would defeat one of the objects of the Act. In deciding as I do, I have not overlooked the fact that under the contractual tenancy the landlord could look to both Miss Sadler and Miss Lunt for payment of the rent. On my construction he can only look to Miss Sadler; but if she fails to pay she loses her personal right to security of tenure and the plaintiff will be able to get possession. The 1968 Act took away many of a landlord's rights at common law and was intended to do so for the benefit of tenants. The loss of a right to sue one of two joint tenants after the termination of a contractual tenancy is a minor matter compared to the restriction of the right to possession which the Act imposes on landlords.

I too would dismiss the appeal.

SHAW LJ. I agree. The answer to the question whether a joint tenant is entitled independently to assert or to pursue a right which is conferred by the joint tenancy or which develops from it must depend on the context in which the question arises. It is only on this basis that the numerous authorities cited in the course of the hearing of this appeal are to be reconciled.

Joint tenants do not constitute a collective entity in law; but since their respective interests in the subject-matter of their tenancy are identical and concurrent they must in general concur in the assertion and enforcement of rights which arise directly from that tenancy, for those rights must reside in each of the joint tenants. It does not, so it appears to me, necessarily follow that this principle must apply to the assertion of rights which are not founded on the grant itself but which are derived collaterally from the operation of some enactment. In such a case the purpose of the statutory provisions out of which the purported right emerges must be taken into account. The nature of the right which the statute creates may involve an individual or personal factor so that it would be apt to one joint tenant but not to others. The identity of interest which subsists during the term of the grant is not bound to persist in a statutory appendage to it. Whether it does or not must depend on the benefit or relief or protection which the statute confers or creates.

As has been emphasised in the preceding judgments, the primary object of s 3(1)(a) of the 1968 Act is to provide security of tenure after the term granted by a protected tenancy has expired. Such security is a matter of personal and individual interest. Even though that interest is not shared by or common to all the erstwhile joint tenants, one or some of them may be in need of the security which the statute affords.

For these reasons I would be disposed to regard 'the tenant' where the phrase appears in s 3(1)(a) as meaning any tenant and therefore as including one of a number of joint tenants unless the language of the subsection precludes such a construction and makes it wholly untenable. I see no insuperable semantic obstacle which stands in the way of such a construction. The only substantial objection is that it may impose some deprivation on the landlord; but s 3 is so designed as to bring that about in any case which falls within its scope. If a joint tenant dies during the term of a protected tenancy his survivors will unquestionably be entitled to qualify as statutory tenants although the potential sources for payment of rent will have been reduced in number. Moreover the ultimate recourse of the landlord where a statutory tenancy arises and there is default by the tenant or tenants is an action for possession. The prospect of some possible detriment to a landlord is not sufficiently formidable to deflect the interpretation of s 3(1)(a) from its plain objective.

I would dismiss the appeal.

Appeal dismissed. Leave to appeal to the House of Lords refused.

Solicitors: *Halsey, Lightly & Hemsley* (for the landlord); *Tyrer, Roxburgh & Dawson* (for the tenant and her licensees).

Mary Rose Plummer Barrister.

Dodds and another v Dodds

QUEEN'S BENCH DIVISION
BALCOMBE J
21st, 22nd JUNE, 28th JULY 1977

Fatal accident – Action – Right of action – Effect of negligence of one dependant on rights of other dependants – Claim on behalf of child in respect of father's death – Death caused by negligence of mother – Whether validity of child's claim affected by mother's negligence – Fatal Accidents Act 1846, s 2.

Fatal accident – Damages – Pecuniary loss – Calculation – Dependency of child – Death of father – Expenditure of family drawn from pool consisting of both parents' earnings – Dependency to be calculated by adding together expenditure exclusively on child and expenditure on family as a whole and calculating father's contribution to that total – Division of pecuniary loss between period before trial and period after trial – Interest.

Fatal accident – Damages – Benefits excluded in assessing damages – Dependency of child – Earnings of mother after father's death – Mother supporting child from earnings – Mother taking up full-time work after death of father – Prior to death mother working part-time and contributing her earnings to family pool – Whether mother's earnings after death to be taken into account in calculating dependency.

Fatal accident – Damages – Multiplier – Date at which multiplier to be determined – Determination at date of trial – Dependency of child – Child aged 12½ at date of trial – Appropriate multiplier five.

In May 1973 the deceased suffered fatal injuries in an accident which occurred when he was a passenger in a car driven by his wife. The wife admitted liability for the accident. At the date of death the deceased was aged 29 and in good health, and had one child, a son aged 8½. He was employed by a company and his take-home pay was £1,560 per annum. His wife was in part-time work as a school cook and earned £328 net per annum. She intended to take up full-time work when the son was aged 12. The wife put her earnings into the family pool and out of the joint family income of £1,888 per annum, £375 per annum was expended on the son, on his food, clothing, holidays etc, and £496 per annum on the family as a whole, on rent, mortgage instalments, rates, repairs to the home and like expenditure. After the deceased's death the wife trained to be a typist and at the date of trial in June 1977 was in full-time employment as a typist and earning £2,080 net per annum. She used her earnings to support the son and despite the deceased's death the son's standard of life had not materially changed. The deceased had had good prospects and at the date of the trial would have been earning £4,720 net per annum which if taken together with the wife's earning would have produced a family income of £6,800 per annum. Moreover on the deceased's promotion the family would have moved from the North of England to the South and lived in a better house. They would also have had the use of a company car. The administrators of the deceased's estate claimed damages under the Fatal Accidents Act 1846 to 1959 on behalf of the son as a dependant. On the claim the questions arose (i) whether the fact that the deceased's death was caused by the negligence of another dependant, the wife, affected the son's claim, (ii) whether the son had suffered any fininical loss as a result of the deceased's death, (iii) whether the benefit derived by him from the wife's current earnings was to be brought into account in assessing his dependency, (iv) what was the appropriate method of dividing the damages between the period before the trial and the period after the trial and (v) what multiplier was to be applied.

Held – (i) The negligence of one dependant could not affect the claim of another

dependant under the Fatal Accident Acts since, under s 2[a] of the Fatal Accidents Act
1846, the remedy in damages was given to individual dependants and not to the
dependants as a group, and each dependant was to be regarded as a separate plaintiff.
It followed that the validity of the son's claim was not affected by the wife's negligence
(see p 544 e and p 545 d h, post); *Mulholland v McCrea* [1961] NI 135 applied.

(ii) The son's dependency at the date of the deceased's death was to be assessed by
adding together the expenditure on him exclusively, which was £375, and the expenditure on the family as a whole, which was £496 i e a total of £871 which in view of
the incompleteness of the figures would be rounded up to £900, which amounted to
just under half of the joint family income of £1,888 per annum. The dependency was
therefore the amount of the deceased's contribution to the £900 per annum which
was £743 per annum, and whilst the wife was working part-time that sum was the
amount of the dependency (see p 546 c to f, post); *Hay v Hughes* [1975] 1 All ER 257 and
K v JMP Ltd [1975] 1 All ER 1030 applied.

(iii) Whether benefits were to be taken into account as gains in assessing a dependency under the Fatal Accident Acts, apart from the benefits required to be taken
into account by statute, was a question of fact to be decided in the light of what was
fair in all the circumstances. Where before a husband's death the wife had put her
earnings into the family pool, her earnings after his death were to be taken into
account in assessing the dependency. On that basis the combined family income
at the date of trial would have been £6,800 per annum but since it was likely that
more of that income would have been spent on luxuries, e g on entertainments and
travel, and less would have been spent on items directly benefiting the son, his
dependency from the date of the trial should be estimated at less than half of the
estimated joint family income of £6,800 and from the date would be estimated
at £2,750 per annum. The deceased's contribution to that sum would have been
£1,908 which was therefore the amount of the dependency from the date of the trial
(see p 546 g to j and p 547 c to e, post); *Cookson v Knowles* [1977] 2 All ER 820 applied.

(iv) The multiplier, which was intended to reflect that an award was a lump sum in
respect of future annual loss and the contingencies that might have occurred, was to
be determined at the date of trial since that was the point of time from which the
court looked forward in assessing the award. Since the son was aged 12½ at the date
of trial and would have been dependant on the deceased until he was 18, a period of
about six years, the multiplier would be fixed at the figure of five (see p 547 g to j, post);
Cookson v Knowles [1977] 2 All ER 820 considered.

(v) It followed that the award for the son's pecuniary loss up to the date of trial
would be £7,628·50, i e 47·5 per cent of the £16,060 which would have been the
deceased's total net remuneration from his death until the trial. That award would
bear interest at half the appropriate rate of interest, which was the rate payable on
money in court placed on short term investment account taken as an average over
the period from the date of death to the date of trial. The award for the pecuniary
loss from the date of trial would be £9,540, i e 5 × £1,908 (see p 548 a b, post).

Per Curiam. The courts can, and should, put a monetary value on the loss of opportunities resulting from death such as, in the instant case, loss of the opportunity to
move to the South of England and to have the use of a company car (see p 545 g, post).

Notes

For the measure of damages under the Fatal Accidents Acts, see 12 Halsbury's Laws
(4th Edn) para 1150, and for cases on the subject, see 36(1) Digest (Reissue) 360-365,
1456-1483.

For interest payable on damages, see 12 Halsbury's Laws (4th Edn) para 1204.

For the Fatal Accidents Act 1846, s 2, see 23 Halsbury's Statutes (3rd Edn) 781.

As from 1st September 1976, s 2 of the 1846 Act has been replaced by ss 1(2),(3)
and 2(1) of the Fatal Accidents Act 1976.

---

a Section 2, so far as material, is set out at p 544 *f*, post

Cases referred to in judgment

Benjamin v Currie [1958] VR 259.

Cookson v Knowles [1977] 2 All ER 820, [1977] QB 913 [1977] 3 WLR 279, CA.

Davies v Powell Duffryn Associated Collieries Ltd [1942] 1 All ER 657, [1942] AC 601, 111 LJKB 418, 167 LT 74, HL, 36(1) Digest (Reissue) 368, *1484*.

Hay v Hughes [1975] 1 All ER 257, [1975] QB 790, [1975] 2 WLR 34, [1975] 1 Lloyd's Rep 12, CA, 36(1) Digest (Reissue) 370, *1491*.

Howitt (Widow and administratrix of Richard Arthur Howitt) v Heads [1972] 1 All ER 491, [1973] 1 QB 64, [1972] 2 WLR 183, 36(1) Digest (Reissue) 364, *1480*.

Jefford v Gee [1970] 1 All ER 1202, [1970] 2 QB 130, [1970] 2 WLR 702, [1970] 1 Lloyd's Rep 107, CA, Digest (Cont Vol C) 709, *182a*.

Jenner v West (Allen) & Co Ltd [1959] 2 All ER 115, [1959] 1 WLR 554, CA, 36(1) Digest (Reissue) 372, *1498*.

K v JMP Co Ltd [1975] 1 All ER 1030, [1976] QB 85, [1975] 2 WLR 457, 36(1) Digest (Reissue) 361, *1463*.

Mulholland v McCrea [1961] NI 135, 36(1) Digest (Reissue) 387, **3134*.

Trueman v Hydro Electric Power Commission of Ontario (1923) 53 OLR 434, [1924] 1 DLR 406.

Action

By a writ dated 11th February 1976 the plaintiffs, James Foster Dodds and Lilian Dodds, the administrators of the estate of James Foster Dodds deceased, claimed against the defendant, Agnes Dodds ('Mrs Dodds'), the deceased's widow, damages under the Fatal Accidents Acts 1846-1959 on behalf of the deceased's son, Gary Dodds who was born on 31st October 1964, and damages under the Law Reform (Miscellaneous Provisions) Act 1934 for the benefit of the deceased's estate, in respect of fatal injuries sustained by the deceased on 4th May 1973 by reason of Mrs Dodd's admitted negligence in driving a motor car. The damages under the 1934 Act were agreed. The action was heard at Nottingham District Registry and judgment was given in London. The facts are set out in the judgment.

Iain McCullough QC, R Maxwell and *Nigel Baker* for the plaintiffs.
Donald Herrod QC, Calder Jose and *John Bassett* for Mrs Dodds.

Cur adv vult

28th July. **BALCOMBE J** read the following judgment: On 4th May 1973 James Foster Dodds was a passenger in a motor car driven by his wife, the defendant, Agnes Dodds. They were driving south along the M1 motorway when the car crossed the central reservation into the northbound carriageway and collided with a lorry. In the accident Mr Dodds suffered injuries from which he died on the same day. In this action the plaintiffs, as administrators of the estate of Mr Dodds, claim damages under the Fatal Accidents Acts 1846 to 1959 and under the Law Reform (Miscellaneous Provisions) Act 1934. Liability is admitted and the only issue which I have to decide is the quantum of damages. Further, the damages under the Law Reform (Miscellaneous Provisions) Act 1934 have been agreed at £163 for funeral expenses and £750 for loss of expectation of life.

Mr and Mrs Dodds had one son, Gary Dodds, who was born on 31st October 1964. Accordingly, he was 8½ at the time of the accident: he is now 12½. He is the dependant on whose behalf the claim under the Fatal Accidents Acts is made, it being conceded that as the widow was wholly to blame for the accident, she has no claim at all as a dependant. (I should say here that I was told that, as I would have expected, the defence has been conducted by Mrs Dodds' insurers. Mrs Dodds has, for the purposes of the action, been advised by separate solicitors and, by agreement between the parties, was in fact called as a witness for the plaintiffs.)

At the time of his death Mr Dodds was aged 29, in good health and with normal
expectation of life; his wife was aged 28 and they had been married for nine years. Mr
Dodds had been born and brought up in Sunderland, the only son of a man who is
now a skipper with the Sunderland Pilotage Authority. Mr Dodds left school at the
age of 15, but he was a very bright youngster who was keen to better himself and he
attended technical college, at first part-time on a day release scheme, and subsequently
full-time. He acquired various technical qualifications, principally the City and
Guilds' certificates for electrical fitters and electrical technicians. These would not be
regarded as senior qualifications such as Higher National Certificates or Ordinary
National Certificate. From time to time he changed his job so as to improve his
position until finally in September 1969 he entered employment as a service engineer
with Centri-Spray International, a company based in Croydon, and carrying on
business in the manufacture and installation of industrial washing and automatic
handling equipment for the automobile industry. In the course of this work Mr
Dodds travelled extensively, both in the United Kingdom and overseas and came
home to his wife and son in Sunderland only about one weekend in three. During
the boy's school holidays he and his mother would join Mr Dodds, sometimes in
London, sometimes abroad.

In February 1973 the assistant service manager of Centri-Spray International, Mr
Daley, was promoted to service manager, and Mr Dodds was chosen, out of the 15
service engineers employed by the company, to succeed Mr Daley as assistant service
manager. Mr and Mrs Dodds then decided to move from Sunderland and to buy a
house in or near Croydon. In Sunderland they lived in a rented council flat. In Croydon
they were looking for a three bedroom semi-detached house on a modern estate in
the £15,000 price bracket; as they had no savings they would have required a 95 per
cent mortgage. Before they found such a house Mr Dodds was killed and his widow
and son have remained in Sunderland.

On his appointment as assistant service manager Mr Dodds became entitled to a
salary of £3,000 per annum. He also received a mileage allowance for the use of his
own car on company business. In March 1973 he bought his wife an old car for some
£30 to £35, and he paid the tax and insurance on it for her. She paid for her own petrol
out of her earnings as a part-time school cook. For this she received a wage of £8
per week during school terms, and a retainer of £4 per week during school holidays,
giving her a take-home pay of £328 per annum.

Further, Mr Dodds had good prospects of promotion. Mr Daley, who also gave
evidence before me, left Centri-Spray International in the autumn of 1973 to start up,
with two other former employees of Centri-Spray, their own company in the same
field, namely Eurowide Engineering Ltd. Mr Daley was confident that Mr Dodds
would have succeeded him as service manager, although not necessarily at the same
salary (£5,500 per annum) as he (Mr Daley), an older and more experienced man,
was then earning. In 1975 Centri-Spray International ran into financial difficulties
and went into voluntary liquidation and a number of their employees were taken on
by Eurowide Engineering. Mr Daley, who had a very high opinion of Mr Dodds'
abilities, and who discounted his lack of higher paper qualifications, would have been
anxious to obtain his services as service manager, for which he would today be receiving a salary of £6,800 per annum together with the use of a comparatively expensive company car, a Ford Granada Ghia was mentioned, and expenses. Eurowide
Engineering Ltd has prospered, its turnover is now over £1m per annum with 62 per
cent of its trade overseas, and although its products are used exclusively by the motor
car industry, Mr Daley had no worries about its future.

I also heard evidence from Mr Robert Gouldrey, the managing director of Reward
Regional Surveys Ltd, whose business, as the name indicates, is the provision of
information to management of salary levels payable to employees. He was called by
Mrs Dodds. On the assumption that Mr Dodds would have been appointed service
manager of Centri-Spray International in November 1973 at an initial salary of

£5,000 per annum, Mr Couldrey was of the opinion that this would have been in-
a creased to £5,500 in May 1974 (six months after the appointment) and would have
stayed at this rate until May 1975. An increase of 20 per cent, to £6,600, would then
have been likely in view of the general escalation of earnings at that time. This
would have been increased to £6,912 in May 1976 (under phase 1 of the social contract)
and to £7,128 in May 1977 (under phase 2). Since these figures approximate closely
to what Mr Daley said that Mr Dodds would have earned had he been employed by
b Eurowide Engineering Ltd, I accept them. On the basis of these figures Mr Ball, a
chartered accountant called by Mrs Dodds, produced a statement showing that the
net remuneration that Mr Dodds could have expected to receive from the date of his
death to the date of the hearing, after deduction of income tax and other compulsory
outgoings, was £16,060. Counsel for the plaintiffs did not quarrel with these figures,
except to say that they took no account of the cash value to Mr Dodds, and hence to
c his dependants, of the use of an expensive company car.
      The evidence before me as to the way in which the family income was utilised is
incomplete. In the first place, since Mr Dodds' promotion to assistant service manager
had only occurred three months before his death, his increased salary had not affected
the family's pattern of spending. Further, Mrs Dodds was unable to recollect with
any degree of particularity how the money was spent. However, she was able to say
d that her husband used to give her housekeeping of £20 per week out of a take-home
pay which she put at £30 per week or £1,560 per annum. From this, together with
her own income of £328 per annum, she paid the following items per annum:
rent and rates £182; electricity £78; washing machine hire-purchase £48; life insurance £39; food £325; household items £52; petrol for her own car £50; travel and
Gary's swimming £100; clothes for herself £150; clothes for Gary £100; television
e £96; making a total of £1,220. In addition Mr Dodds paid, per annum: hire-purchase
on his car £288; tax and insurance on her car £62; telephone £40; weekend entertainments for himself and Mrs Dodds £100; tapes (for Mr Dodds) £24; making a
total of £514, which together with the £1,220 paid by Mrs Dodds gives a total of
£1,734 per annum. There were other items, e g Mr Dodds' own clothes, for which
Mrs Dodds was unable to give figures, and clearly the list of expenditure is incomplete.
f   Had the move to Croydon taken place the pattern of spending would have changed.
In particular, there would have been no rent payable, but instead there would have
been a liability to pay mortgage instalments (calculated on a 95 per cent mortgage
on a £15,000 house) of £1,189 per annum. This figure includes tax relief of approximately £50 per month: during later years, as the interest element of each instalment
became less, the relief would have progressively decreased.
g   Mrs Dodds, whose evidence I accept without hesitation, told me that she and her
husband were very concerned for Gary's education and had talked of the possibility
of sending him to a private, fee-paying school. This evidence was confirmed by Mr
Dodds senior, the deceased's father, who said that his son had discussed Gary's education with him (Gary's grandfather). Further, Mrs Dodds said that she and her husband
had decided to have no more children and that until Gary was aged 12 or thereabouts
h she expected to continue her part-time work, but would then have hoped to obtain
full-time employment. Mr Dodds was in good health and had few vices, he was a
light drinker and had given up smoking some eight months before his death. The
picture clearly emerges of a keen and industrious young man, a hard worker, anxious
to better himself, and to provide to the best of his ability for his wife and son. Both
his mother and grandfather say that Gary is a bright and observant boy, a fact con-
j firmed by his IQ scales when tested in 1974, and I find as a fact that his father would
have supported him to stay at school at least until the age of 18, and possibly further.
      In the event, Mrs Dodds and Gary have remained in Sunderland. Gary has stayed
within the state system of education and has just finished his first year at Monkwear-
mouth Comprehensive School. He felt his father's death greatly, and for a time this
caused him to have behavioural problems, but these have now been resolved. Mrs

Dodds after her husband's death went to college to learn typing; she now has a job as a typist at a gross wage of £53 per week with a take-home pay of £41 per week. She also has her state widow's pension and a pension from Centri-Spray International. She does her best to compensate Gary for the loss of his father and ensures that he is well clothed and well fed; if anyone goes short it is her rather than Gary. Compared with his position as at the date of his father's death she does not consider that Gary has suffered materially, except that holidays are no longer taken abroad but rather in holiday camps in England. She runs a car, although not a Granada Ghia, and sometimes takes Gary out in it at weekends.

On these facts the following questions have to be answered: (1) Does the fact that Mr Dodds' death was caused by the negligence of his widow, who would be a dependant with a claim under the Fatal Accidents Acts, affect the claim of the other dependant, his son? (2) What financial loss, if any, has Gary suffered as a result of his father's death? (3) Does Gary derive any benefit from his mother's present earning capacity which should be brought into account against any loss that he may have suffered? (4) How should any damages be divided as between the period from the date of death until trial, and any period thereafter? (5) What multiplier should be applied in calculating damages, and from what period should that multiplier be determined?

I consider the answers to these questions separately as follows:

(1) I was told by counsel, both of whom have considerable experience in this field of the law, that they know of no English decision on this point. However, the point has been considered by the learned editors of textbooks. Winfield and Jolowicz on Tort[1] Clerk and Lindsell on Torts[2], Glanville Williams on Joint Torts and Contributory Negligence[3] and McGregor on Damages[4] all take the view that the negligence of one dependant should not affect the rights of the other, non-negligent, dependants. This view is based on the reasoning that the remedy under the Fatal Accidents Acts is given to individuals, not to the dependants as a group, and each dependant can therefore be regarded, for this purpose, as if he were a separate plaintiff. This appears from s 2 of the Fatal Accidents Act 1846 which, so far as material, provides:

'Every such action [under s 1] shall be for the benefit of the wife, husband, parent, and child of the person whose death shall have been so caused . . . and in every such action the jury may give such damages as they may think proportioned to the injury resulting from such death to the parties respectively for whom and for whose benefit such action shall be brought . . .'

Although there is no English decision on the point, there are decisions of persuasive authority in other jurisdictions. Thus in *Trueman v Hydro Electric Power Commission of Ontario*[5], the appellate division of the Ontario Supreme Court held that the right of action given by the Fatal Accidents Act, RSO 1914, ch 151, which for all relevant purposes was the same as the English Fatal Accidents Act 1846, was a personal not a representative right in each beneficiary to sue, through the executor or administrator as nominal plaintiff if there were one, or otherwise if not. So a beneficiary whose negligence contributed to the accident in which the death occurred was precluded from recovering damages by contributory negligence (then, as in England at the time, an absolute bar). See in particular the judgments of Hodgins JA[6] and of Ferguson JA[7]. It is worthy of note that in that case at first instance the damages had

---

1 10th Edn (1975), pp 510, 511
2 14th Edn (1975), para 425
3 (1951), pp 443, 444
4 13th Edn (1972), pp 801, 841
5 [1924] 1 DLR 406
6 [1924] 1 DLR 406 at 420
7 [1924] 1 DLR 406 at 421

been assessed at $4,000, apportioned as to $2,000 to the one dependant who was found guilty of contributory negligence and as to $1,000 each to the other two dependants against whom there was no such finding. The judge at first instance had dismissed the action as to the claim of the first dependant because of his contributory negligence, and it was his appeal against this judgment that was before the appellate division; there was no cross-appeal by the defendant against the damages awarded to the non-negligent dependants. To the like effect is the Australian case of *Benjamin v Currie*[1] and in *Mulholland v McCrea*[2] before the Court of Appeal of Northern Ireland, the non-negligent dependants' claim was again allowed in full, and against this there was no cross-appeal, the appeal being by the plaintiff (widower) against the reduction of the amount of his damages on the ground of his contributory negligence. In the course of his majority judgment Lord MacDermott CJ said[3]:

> 'I respectfully agree with the conclusion reached by the majority in *Trueman's* case[4]. Once it is accepted, as in my opinion it now must be accepted, that the claim of a dependant to recover the loss caused by the death of a deceased person is a personal and individual claim, I can find no ground for ignoring the negligence of the claimant which has contributed to the cause of death . . .'

The converse of this argument is that the negligence of one dependant cannot affect the personal and individual claims of the other, non-negligent, dependants.

In my judgment, therefore, the validity of Gary's claim as a dependant under the Fatal Accidents Acts is not affected by the fact that it was his mother, another dependant, who was responsible for the death of the deceased. Indeed, I did not understand counsel for Mrs Dodds, i e in effect for the insurers standing behind her, to contend seriously to the contrary; his principal argument was a more subtle one, and that I consider later.

(2) Counsel for Mrs Dodds sought to argue that Gary has lost little in material terms. His standard of life is much the same as it was before the accident. Admittedly he still lives in Sunderland rather than in Croydon, and houses in Sunderland are cheaper than those in Croydon (on the evidence before me a house in Sunderland costs half the price of its equivalent in Croydon) but, submitted counsel for Mrs Dodds, how can that difference be evaluated in monetary terms? Similarly, how can one assess the loss to Gary of having to travel in a Ford Capri rather than in a Ford Granada Ghia? While I do not find this argument wholly unattractive, it is now far too late for it to stand any chance of success in a court of first instance. Many cases over the years have decided that the courts can, and should, put a monetary value on the loss of opportunities such as those mentioned above.

Counsel for Mrs Dodds further submitted that it is unfair and contrary to the principles of natural justice that the widow, who was wholly responsible for the accident and therefore has no claim in her own right, should benefit indirectly from the damages awarded to her son. In my judgment the answer to this plea is that it would be unfair and unjust to deprive the son of any part of the damages to which by law he is entitled merely because it is his mother who was the tortfeasor.

Counsel for the plaintiffs invited me to assess Gary's loss by adopting the method used by the Court of Appeal in *Hay v Hughes*[5] (see in particular the judgment of Buckley LJ[6]) and in *K v JMP Co Ltd*[7]. That is to divide the family expenditure into

1   [1958] VR 259
2   [1961] NI 135
3   [1961] NI 135 at 150
4   [1924] 1 DLR 406
5   [1975] 1 All ER 257, [1975] QB 790
6   [1975] 1 All ER 257 at 269, 270, [1975] QB 790 at 812
7   [1975] 1 All ER 1030, [1976] QB 85

four columns. The first column consists of those items which benefit the father
exclusively, the second column consists of those which benefit the mother exclusively,   *a*
the third column consists of those which benefit the child exclusively and the fourth
column consists of those which benefit the whole family. Under the third column
(the child's) are listed food, outings, holidays, pocket money, presents, sports, pets,
clothes and the child's use of the family car(s). Under the fourth column (the whole
family) are listed rent or mortgage instalments, rates, repairs, decoration to the
family house, heating and lighting, telephone, furniture, television, newspapers,   *b*
garden, window cleaning, and insurance of the house and contents. In my judgment
this approach has the approval of the Court of Appeal in the cases cited and I adopt
it in the present case. Counsel for the plaintiffs went on to submit that the adoption
of this method in practice leads to the result that half the father's net income is for the
benefit of the child or children of the family. Whether or not that was the fraction
derived from the evidence in other cases I know not, but it seems to me to be irrele-   *c*
vant. I have to decide Gary's dependancy in this case on the evidence before me.
On that evidence I attribute £375 of the expenditure to Gary and £496 to the whole
family, a total of £871. Because, as I have already said, the figures for the expenditure
were inevitably incomplete, I round this up to a dependancy of £900 per annum.
Expressed as a fraction of the joint take-home pay of husband and wife this is just
under half, and the father's contribution to it was $1,560/1,888 \times £900 = £743$. Or, put   *d*
another way, on these figures, Gary's dependency amounted to 47·5 per cent of his
father's take-home pay.

Of course, as the father's income increased, the mother's contribution to the joint
family income, so long as she only worked part-time, became proportionately less.
Further, if the move to Croydon had taken place, a greater proportion of the family
income would have been used, by way of mortgage instalments, to pay for the family   *e*
home. This would be a fourth column item, benefiting Gary. Gary would also have
derived some benefit from the father's ability to use a company car. On the other
hand, Gary would not have benefited from increased expenditure on such items as
weekend entertainments for his parents. Giving the matter the best consideration I
can, I find that Gary's dependancy would have continued to represent 47·5 per cent of
his father's income, so long as his mother continued to work only part-time.   *f*

(3) The rule that damages under the Fatal Accidents Acts are to be assessed by
ascertaining the balance of loss and gain to a dependant is well established; see e g
Davies v Powell Duffryn Associated Collieries Ltd[1]. Further, statute requires that certain
benefits are not to be taken into account on the 'gains side' of the equation; see e g
s 2 of the Fatal Accidents Act 1959. Thus the pensions which Mrs Dodds receives are
to be ignored.   *g*

Unfortunately, apart from these statutory exceptions, there is no test which enables
the court to decide what benefits should be taken into account as gains for this purpose;
the question is a jury question to be answered in the way which seems fair in the light
of all the circumstances of the case; see *Hay v Hughes*[2], per Buckley and Ormrod
LJJ. The particular benefit about which there has been much discussion in the
present case is the benefit which Gary derives from his mother's earnings as a whole-   *h*
time typist. In *Howitt v Heads*[3] Cumming-Bruce J, held that the court should make
no deduction in respect of the widow's capacity to earn. The validity of that decision
has been doubted by the Court of Appeal in *Cookson v Knowles*[4]. Certainly in a case
where, as here, the wife's earnings before her husband's death came into the family
pool, the judgment in *Cookson v Knowles*[4] makes it clear that the wife's earning
capacity after her husband's death must be taken into account.   *j*

---

1   [1942] 1 All ER 657, [1942] AC 601
2   [1975] 1 All ER 257 at 272, 275, [1975] QB 790 at 815, 818
3   [1972] 1 All ER 491, [1973] 1 QB 64
4   [1977] 2 All ER 820, [1977] QB 913

Counsel for Mrs Dodds sought to persuade me that the widow's earnings now used
a to support Gary should be taken into account as 'gains' resulting from Mr Dodd's
death on the basis that they are payments voluntarily made by a tortfeasor in an
attempt to mitigate the damage she has caused. This is the subtle argument to which
I referred earlier. Some support for this submission can be obtained from the decision
of the Court of Appeal in *Jenner v Allen West & Co Ltd*[1], where it was held that a
voluntary pension paid to a widow by employers who were in breach of their statutory
b and common law duties, which breaches resulted in their employee's death, was to be
taken into account in assessing the damages under the Fatal Accidents Acts. However,
I accept counsel for the plaintiffs' submission that there is no evidence before me to
suggest that Mrs Dodds works because she is conscious of being a tortfeasor who
wants to make up to her son the loss she has caused him; she works simply as a widow
who has a child to support. Accordingly, so far as I take into account the widow's
c earning capacity it is on the general basis indicated by *Cookson v Knowles*[2].
I have already said that Mrs Dodds expected to be able to work full-time when
Gary was 12 or a little over. Gary is now 12½, so it is convenient to take this as the date
when Mrs Dodds might have been expected to take up full-time work with a take-
home pay which I put at £40 per week or £2,080 per annum. From the evidence of
Mr Ball I find that the deceased's take-home pay would now be £4,720 per annum.
d Accordingly, the combined family income would be £6,800 per annum, plus whatever value should be attributed to the use of a company car. If Gary's dependancy
had remained at half, it would be in excess of £3,400 per annum. However, as the
family income increased to this extent it is probable that more would have been
spent on luxuries, such as entertainments and travel, and less on items from which
Gary would directly benefit, and I therefore estimate his dependency at £2,750 per
e annum. The deceased's contribution would have been 4,720/6,800 × £2,750 = £1,908
per annum.
(4) The Court of Appeal in *Cookson v Knowles*[2] has said that damages under the
Fatal Accidents Acts should now be divided into two parts. The first part is the
pecuniary loss up to the date of trial on which interest should run at half rate (like
damages in personal injury cases). The second part is the pecuniary loss from the
f date of trial onwards on which no interest is payable.
(5) The multiplier. In *Cookson v Knowles*[2] the multiplier (calculated as at the date of
death) had been fixed as 11 at the trial. Two and a half years had elapsed between
the date of death and the date of trial, and the Court of Appeal took a multiplier of
8½, being 11 less 2½. I do not understand the reason for doing this. Since the multiplier
is intended to reflect the fact that a lump sum award is being made in respect of
g future annual loss, and to reflect all contingencies, e g that either the deceased or the
dependant may not have survived the relevant period, it seems to me to follow that
the multiplier must necessarily be determined as at the point of time from which
one is looking forward, i e the date of trial according to the second part of the rule in
Cookson v Knowles[2]. It does not appear from the judgment in *Cookson v Knowles*[2]
that this question, the time at which the multiplier is to be fixed, was the subject of
h argument and I have not had the advantage of seeing a report of the case containing
the argument of counsel. I can only assume that this part of the judgment was given
per incuriam and I propose to fix the multiplier as at the date of the trial. At that
date Gary was 12½ and on the evidence I find that he would have been dependent on
his father at least until the end of the summer following his 18th birthday, a period
of six years. I fix the multiplier at five. In doing so, I have not acceded to counsel
j for the plaintiffs' formal request that I should take account of future inflation. In
this court I am bound to hold that future inflation must be disregarded; see *Cookson
v Knowles*[2].

1   [1959] 2 All ER 115, [1959] 1 WLR 554
2   [1977] 2 All ER 820, [1977] QB 913

The result of the foregoing is that I award damages under the Fatal Accidents Acts as follows: (1) For the pecuniary loss up to the date of trial the sum of £7,628·50 (being 47·5 per cent of £16,060) together with interest at half the appropriate rate. The appropriate rate of interest should be determined as that payable on money in court placed on short term investment account taken as an average over the period between 4th May 1973 and 21st June 1977; see *Jefford v Gee*[1]. (2) For the pecuniary loss from the date of trial I award the sum of £9,540 (being 5 × £1,908). (3) As already mentioned I award damages under the Law Reform (Miscellaneous Provisions) Act 1934 of £913. It is accepted on behalf of Mrs Dodds that these do not fall to be deducted from the damages under the Fatal Accidents Acts.

Judgment for the plaintiffs accordingly.

Solicitors: *Blyth, Dutton, Robins, Hay*, agents for *Hopkin, & Sons* Mansfield (for the plaintiffs); *Cecil Godfrey & Son*, Nottingham (for Mrs Dodds).

Janet Harding Barrister.

McKay (formerly Chapman) v Chapman

FAMILY DIVISION

LIONEL SWIFT QC SITTING AS A DEPUTY JUDGE OF THE HIGH COURT

10th, 21st NOVEMBER 1977

Divorce – Financial provision – Application – Application subsequent to petition or answer – Leave of court – Application by petitioner for lump sum for children – Court not having power at time of divorce to order lump sum for children – Petitioner applying under retrospective operation of statutory powers – Petitioner applying without leave as a person who has the custody of a child under an order of the court – Whether petitioner required to obtain leave – Whether petitioner 'any person who has the custody . . . of a child . . . under an order of the . . . court' – Matrimonial Causes Rules 1977 (SI 1977 No 344), r 69(b).

Divorce – Financial provision – Application – Nature of relief claimed – Duty of party to particularise relief – Application subsequent to petition for lump sum for children – Prayer in petition for 'child maintenance, a lump sum and/or a secured provision' – Whether court having power to award a lump sum for children – Matrimonial Causes Rules 1977 (SI 1977 No 344), r 68(1)(2)(a).

A wife presented a petition for divorce in March 1969 claiming, inter alia, custody of the three children and in the prayer 'such sums by way of alimony pending suit, maintenance, child maintenance, a lump sum and/or a secured provision as may be just'. Under the Matrimonial Causes Act 1965 which was then in force it was not open to the wife to apply for a lump sum for the children. The decree was made absolute in December 1970, the wife having obtained orders for periodical payments for herself and each of the children and, by agreement, custody of the children and a transfer of the matrimonial home. In September 1976 the wife issued a summons seeking an order against her husband for a lump sum for the children, pursuant to s 23 of the Matrimonial Causes Act 1973. The preliminary issue was raised whether the wife was entitled to make such an application without first obtaining the leave of the

1   [1970] 1 All ER 1202, [1970] 2 QB 130

a court and if not, whether it was appropriate that leave should be given. The husband contended that the application, being made by the petitioner in the original divorce proceedings, should, under r 68(1)^a of the Matrimonial Causes Rules 1977, have been made in the petition and, as it had not been, leave was required under r 68(2)(a). The wife contended that she was entitled to make the application without leave either because the terms of her petition were wide enough to include an application for a lump sum for the children or because she was to be regarded as included in the cate-
b gory of 'any person who has the custody or the care and control of a child of the family under an order of the . . . court', within the meaning of r 69(b)^b, and as such entitled to apply for the order sought as of right. Alternatively the wife contended that if leave was required it was a proper case for leave.

c **Held** – The application would be dismissed for the following reasons—
   (i) At the time of the filing of the petition in March 1969, the court's power, under s 34(3) of the 1965 Act, to order payment of a lump sum for the benefit of children was limited to ordering payment of a lump sum by way of security, and the prayer in the petition, read in the light of the contemporaneous legislation, could not be read to cover a prayer for payment of a lump sum to the children. In any event
d the terms of the prayer were inadequate to cover a lump sum for the children because neither 'child maintenance' nor 'lump sum and/or a secured provision' covered a prayer for a lump sum for the children (see p 553 f to h and p 554 a, post); *Wilson v Wilson* [1975] 3 All ER 464 applied.
   (ii) The wife could not avoid the mandatory requirements put on petitioners and respondents by r 68(1) by seeking to make an application under r 69(b) because, although she had custody of the children, she was a petitioner and not 'any person'
e who had custody, since the term 'any person' was to be interpreted as ejusdem generis with the other persons or parties specified in the rule, all of whom were distinguished by not being the petitioner or respondent and therefore not able to apply for ancillary relief in the petition or answer. Accordingly the wife was required to obtain the leave of the court under r 68(2)(a) before making the application (see p 555 f and j,
f post); *Chaterjee v Chaterjee* [1976] 1 All ER 701 applied.
   (iii) The wife's application for leave would be refused because it was to be inferred that at the time of the divorce the parties had arranged the disposition of capital on the basis that no further claims would be made on the husband, that there was no finan-cial need on the part of the children that could not adequately be met by a periodical payments order, and that there was no evidence that the father had failed to comply with the existing periodical payments or would fail to comply with an increased order
g in the future or that the husband was so unreliable that a lump sum was desirable to secure the children's future (see p 556 a to h, post); *Chaterjee v Chaterjee* [1976] 1 All ER 709 and *Chamberlain v Chamberlain* [1974] 1 All ER 33 applied.

Notes
h For the powers of the court to make financial provision for parties after divorce, and the kinds of orders which may be made, see 13 Halsbury's Laws (4th Edn) paras 1051 et seq, for the procedure on making an application for financial provision after divorce, see ibid para 1069, and for the persons who may apply for financial provision in respect of children, see ibid para 1162.

j ───────────────────────────────────

a   Rule 68, so far as material, is set out at p 554 b and c, post
b   Rule 69, so far as material, provides: 'Any of the following persons, namely . . . (b) any person who has the custody or the care and control of a child of the family under an order of the High Court or a divorce county court . . . may apply for an order for ancillary relief as respects that child by notice in Form 11.'

Cases referred to in judgment

Chamberlain v Chamberlain [1974] 1 All ER 33, [1973] 1 WLR 1557, CA, Digest (Cont Vol D) 426, 6962Abb.

Chaterjee v Chaterjee [1976] 1 All ER 719, [1976] Fam 199, [1976] 2 WLR 397, CA.

Doherty v Doherty [1975] 2 All ER 635, [1976] Fam 71, [1975] 3 WLR 1, CA, Digest (Cont Vol D) 423, 6843a.

H v H [1966] 3 All ER 560, 27(2) Digest (Reissue) 843, 6710.

Wilson v Wilson [1975] 3 All ER 464, [1976] Fam 124, [1975] 3 WLR 537, CA, Digest (Cont Vol D) 423, 6843b.

Cases also cited

Jones v Jones [1971] 3 All ER 1201, CA.

L v L [1961] 3 All ER 834, [1962] P 101, CA.

Marsden (J L) v Marsden (A M) [1973] 3 All ER 851, [1973] 1 WLR 641.

Powys v Powys [1971] 3 All ER 116, [1971] P 340.

Application

This was an application by a summons dated 6th September 1976 issued out of a district registry by Wendy Ann Chapman ('the wife') for an order for lump sum provision for the three children of her marriage to Rodney James Chapman ('the husband'). The wife had obtained a decree nisi from the husband on 21st December 1970 and now sought a variation of the orders made on the decree nisi. The wife sought to make the application without leave as a person who had custody of the children or with leave if leave was required. The summons was transferred to the Principal Registry. The hearing was in chambers with judgment in open court. The facts are set out in the judgment.

Barry Green for the wife.
Alan Ward for the husband.

Cur adv vult

21st November. **LIONEL SWIFT QC** read the following judgment: In this matter the petitioner, the former wife, seeks an order for payment by the respondent, the former husband, of a lump sum to or for the benefit of the three children of the family, pursuant to s 23 of the Matrimonial Causes Act 1973. I have been asked to decide as a preliminary matter whether the wife is entitled to make such an application as of right; and if she is not, whether this is an appropriate case in which to grant her leave to do so. For convenience, I shall refer to the parties as 'the husband' and 'the wife'.

The wife contends that she is entitled to make such an application without leave either because the terms of her petition filed in 1969 are sufficiently wide to bring the application within r 68(1) of the Matrimonial Causes Rules 1977[1], a contention counsel frankly said he could argue but faintly, or because, having custody of the children, she is 'a person' within r 69. Additionally and in the alternative, the wife contends it is a proper case in which to grant her leave pursuant to r 68(2). The husband contends that leave is necessary and that it ought not to be granted.

The facts

The parties were married on 12th November 1960 and there are three children of the family, two girls aged 15 and 12 and a boy of 14. The wife left the husband in December 1967 and the husband and wife have never since lived together. In March

---

1 SI 1977 No 344

1969 the wife presented a petition for divorce in the exercise of the court's discretion
a based on an allegation of adultery with a named woman. In her petition, the wife
claimed custody of the children, and in respect of ancillary relief the prayer in the
petition was: 'That the Respondent do pay to the Petitioner such sums by way of
alimony pending suit, maintenance, child maintenance, a lump sum and/or a secured
provision as may be just.' In September 1969 the husband filed an answer in which
he admitted adultery with the woman named and alleged adultery by the wife
b and cross-prayed for a divorce in the exercise of the court's discretion.

In an affidavit sworn in November 1970 the wife sought leave of the court to conclude and implement an agreement which had been reached between the parties.
The agreement provided that the suit would proceed on the prayer of the petition;
the wife would have custody of the children with provision to obtain leave to take them
out of the jurisdiction; the husband would pay alimony and thereafter maintenance for
c the wife and maintenance for the three children in sums which together amounted to
£25 odd a week; the wife should have all child relief for tax purposes so long as she
remained liable to United Kingdom income tax; the husband would transfer to
the wife the house in which she was then living with the children (and I quote) 'such
transfer to be in lieu of and in full and final settlement of the [wife's] claim for a lump
sum and in full and final settlement of any and all claims [the wife] might have against
d [the husband] under the Married Woman's Property Act 1882'. In her affidavit the
wife deposed: 'I am advised by my solicitors and verily believe that the course proposed meets the justice of the case and I am satisfied that the financial provision made
for me and children by [the husband] will enable me properly to provide a secure
home for them.' On 21st December 1970 the parties were given leave to implement
the agreement which they had reached; the wife obtained a decree nisi and custody
e of the children with leave to take them to Australia. She also obtained orders for
periodical payments for herself and each of the three children in a total sum which
amounted to a few pence below the sum in the agreement between the parties.
The orders were by consent and nothing turns on the differences of a few pence.
Pursuant to leave the decree was made absolute on 23rd December 1970. About six
weeks later the wife emigrated with the children to Australia. In October 1971 she
f married in Australia, Robin Daniel McKay from whom she separated more than
2½ years ago. By that marriage she has a daughter now aged five.

On 30th July 1976 the wife issued a summons for variation of the periodical payments in favour of the children. On 2nd May 1977 the registrar made an interim
order increasing periodical payments for the children to £10 a week each. There
is a dispute as to the date from which that order is to run, but that is not for my
g decision at this stage. On 6th September 1976 the wife issued a summons which
referred to the prayer in her petition and sought lump sum provision for the children.

From an affidavit sworn by the wife in February 1977 the following matters appear.
The wife lives with the three children of the family and her daughter by her second
marriage in a house which she owns in Labrador, Gold Coast, in Australia. She values
the house at $40,000 Australian, £25,000 sterling (I was asked to take £1 as equal to
h $1·6 Australian). She has a motor car on hire-purchase which is worth $5,000 Australian
and which she says is an absolute necessity bearing in mind the distances which she
inevitably has to cover for shopping and taking the children to and from school.
She anticipates that the motor car will shortly be repossessed as she is unable to
keep up the hire-purchase payments on it. She has debts totalling $1,500 Australian
and inclusive of the car her net capital worth is approximately £25,000 sterling.
j Immediately before emigrating to Australia the wife obtained three modest endow-
ment life assurance policies on her life for the benefit of each of the children, maturing
when each of them attains the age of 21. The premiums amount to £208·44 per
annum.

After her marriage to Mr McKay in October 1971 the husband reduced the maintenance he paid to £19 a week, ceasing to pay the periodical payments of £7·50 a

week for the wife but increasing the sum for the three children by £1 in all. Until the interim order to which I have referred, the wife was receiving in Australia the sum *a* of 763·56 (per annum), being £988 (the total payments made by the husband) less the insurance premiums and approximately £16 a year bank charges to remit the moneys. She receives from Mr McKay an allowance of $5,000 Australian per annum, i e approximately £60 per week. She says that her Australian lawyers have advised her that under Australian law, which governs her husband's liability towards her (he is a deep sea diver living in Trinidad), the allowance made by Mr *b* McKay is reasonable.

At the time of the affidavit the wife had negligible sums in English bank accounts which were the accumulation of the maintenance received from the husband held there for remission. She has received tax assessments from the United Kingdom Inland Revenue authorities for the years 1971-72 and 1973-74 totalling some £1,200. She has been informed by her solicitor that certain items in the assessments are *c* incorrect but that from the year 1972-73 onwards it is possible that she will be liable for United Kingdom income tax on the whole of the maintenance paid by the respondent. The wife says she has no assets whatsoever out of which to meet this liability. She says that she is unable to work in Australia because of her own medical condition and that of her youngest child. Exhibited to her affidavit is a medical report dated September 1976 to the effect that she is suffering from anxiety depression caused by a *d* number of factors including coping with family problems, including a severe behavioural problem with the daughter then aged 14, and a broken second marriage. Her daughter by Mr McKay is a hyper-active child. The wife is said to suffer from recurrent peptic ulceration of the stomach which is aggravated by her current family problems. The wife says that she had until the interim order a total income of £75 a week for the upkeep of her house and the maintenance of herself and the four children *e* but outgoings of about £140 a week. In consequence she has had to claim social security benefit which has been granted to her temporarily pending the outcome of her application at the rate of $54 Australian a week.

In her affidavit in support of her application the wife records that the husband has never made any capital settlement whatsoever on the children themselves. Rightly or wrongly, she regarded the total maintenance paid to her as available for the *f* children and considered the conveyance of the house as her own matrimonial settlement. She asserts that even on the most pessimistic view the husband is a man with very substantial capital assets and it is reasonable to expect a father wealthy in capital to make a capital settlement on his children. She says that in the situation in which the children presently find themselves their most desperate need is for a feeling of security which the existence of a capital fund would provide, and that the income of *g* such a capital fund could be applied towards their maintenance and education pending majority. They would then have the knowledge that their early adult years and their start on adult life were reasonably secured also. At some length, and not surprisingly, she challenges the accuracy of the husband's affidavit.

I now turn to the husband. Since the divorce he has remarried on a date I am not given and has had a child, Cara, aged eighteen months. He runs a farm. It is not *h* possible on his affidavit to reach any reliable conclusion as to his capital. He owns several properties. Allowing the farm at something under the asking price of £130,000 and in respect of which he says the highest offer he has received is £75,000, he has properties which at first sight appear to be worth approximately £175,000. In addition, as a result of a sale of shares in a transport company and a property company he says there is a sum of £220,000 due to him, of which £20,000 is now due but there *j* is a claim against him for £135,000. A further sum of £200,000 is payable to him if and when planning permission is obtained for the use of certain quarry lands previously owned by the company whose shares he has sold. The husband says that he has provided in a will dated May 1976 for gifts of £2,500 to each of the three children of the family. He says that he is prepared to increase the maintenance payable to

the children and had proposed an increase of £8 per week each, but that a lump sum
a is not appropriate. With regard to income, the husband asserts that his profits before
taxation is approximately £21,000 a year but his loss in the year ending November
1976 will be between £20,000 and £25,000.

If a full investigation of the husband's means were to be carried out, there is at
least a chance that the estimates in his affidavit would be proved to be on the low
side, and I am content for the purpose of this application to take him as a man who
b if ordered to do so would be able to find a substantial capital sum running into five
figures at least. He says that his capital and income position is not satisfactory due
to the current poor economic conditions and property market, and that his circumstances
will not improve until he can sell the farm, when he hopes in fact he can invest the
proceeds in a new business which would require the use of all available capital.
There is no suggestion on behalf of the wife that at the time when financial arrange-
c ments were made on the divorce she was in any way misled as to the husbands means,
or that the husband has not complied timeously and properly with the orders which
have been made for periodical payments.

The prayer in the petition

Counsel for the husband accepts, as he must, that s 23 of the Matrimonial Causes Act
d 1973 is retroactive in its effect so that in a proper case the court could order a lump sum
payment to be made to the children of the family, although ss 21, 23 and 24 of the
1973 Act and their predecessors, ss 2, 3 and 4 of the Matrimonial Proceedings and
Property Act 1970, came into operation after the petition was filed in this suit:
Chaterjee v Chaterjee[1].

It is common ground that if the terms of the prayer in the petition are wide enough
e to include the claim for a lump sum for the children no leave is necessary.

At the time when the wife's petition was filed there was no power in the court to
order the payment of a lump sum to or for the benefit of a child of the family. Power
to order a lump sum for a wife was contained in s 16 of the Matrimonial Causes Act
1965. But in the case of a lump sum for the benefit of children, the court's power was
limited to ordering such sum by way of security, under s 34(3) of the 1965 Act. The
f Law Commission referred to the cryptic nature of the court's powers at that time in
its report[2], and recommended that the position should be spelt out more clearly.
Subsequent to the report the wider powers enabling the court to order a lump sum
were contained in s 3 of the Matrimonial Proceedings and Property Act 1970. So at the
time when the petition was filed in March 1969 the terms of the prayer could not
properly have been meant or read to cover a prayer for the payment of a lump sum
g to the children of the family. Section 3 of the 1970 Act came into force on 1st January
1971 (see s 43(2)). At the time of the divorce, therefore, there was no power to order a
lump sum in favour of the children. For those reasons alone I would conclude that
the terms of the prayer of the petition were not intended to and did not include
payment of a lump sum to or for the benefit of the children of the family. It is therefore not necessary to consider the effect of the other words in the prayer of the petition.
h If it were necessary to do so, then with some hesitation I conclude that in any event
the terms of the prayer would be inadequate to cover a lump sum for the children.
In *Doherty v Doherty*[3] Ormrod LJ expressed the view that an application for maintenance would be adequate to include a lump sum, where to have construed the
notice otherwise would have allowed a genuine claim to be defeated by a technical
defect and there was no question of the husband being lulled into a false sense of
j security. But in the later case of *Wilson v Wilson*[4] a prayer for periodical payments

1 [1976] 1 All ER 709, [1976] Fam 199
2 Report on Financial Provision in Matrimonial Proceedings, Law Com No 25, 24th July 1969,
   para 33
3 [1975] 2 All ER 635 at 641, [1976] Fam 71 at 80
4 [1975] 3 All ER 464, [1976] Fam 124

only was held not wide enough to entitle the court to make a lump sum order without leave of the court. Since the prayer in the petition itemises maintenance, lump sum and secured provision, it would be wrong to interpret 'child maintenance' as including a lump sum sum for the children, or the lump sum in the prayer as including such a sum for the children.

Rules 68 and 69 of the Matrimonial Causes Rules 1977
Rule 68 provides:

'(1) Any application by a petitioner ... for ... (b) a financial provision order ... shall be made in the petition ...
'(2) Notwithstanding anything in paragraph (1), an application for ancillary relief which should have been made in the petition ... may be made subsequently —(a) by leave of the court ... or at the trial ...
'(3) An application by a petitioner ... for ancillary relief, not being an application which is required to be made in the petition ... shall be made by notice in Form 11.'

In these rules a financial provision order means any of the orders mentioned in s 21(1) of the 1973 Act except an order under s 27(6) of that Act (see r 2). An order for payment of a lump sum in favour of children of the family is an order mentioned in s 21(1).

I accept the argument of counsel for the husband that r 68(1) is mandatory. That seems to follow from the use of the word 'shall' in r 68(1) and the necessity for leave of the court pursuant to r 68(2) in the event that r 68(1) has not been complied with. Furthermore, although it is difficult to regard a claim for a lump sum for children as one which 'should have been made in the petition' inasmuch as such a claim could not have been made at the time of this petition, the correct view is that in applying this rule leave must be obtained by the wife in order to make a claim for a lump sum: *Chaterjee v Chaterjee*[1]. So if the wife is limited to an application pursuant to r 68 leave is necessary.

The wife asserts that she is entitled to claim a lump sum for the children, without leave pursuant to r 69, because she qualifies as a person who may apply for an order for ancillary relief as respects the children of the family, within r 69(b) as a person who has the custody of children of the family under an order of the High Court, and counsel for the wife contends that a petitioner or respondent who has custody of a child of the family can be within both rr 68 and 69.

The argument for the wife is that it cannot be right or reasonable that the power to claim a lump sum for a child, where there is no claim for it in the petition or answer, depends on the identity of the person who has his custody; that leave should be necessary if the petitioner or the respondent has custody, but unnecessary if the child is in the custody of, say, a grandparent. Furthermore, counsel for the wife refers to legislative provisions which he contends show that in matters of procedure, claims for ancillary relief for children are treated differently from and more generously than those of the adult parties, and accordingly r 69 is to be read as supplementing r 68 and not as exclusive of it. He thus refers to s 23(4) of the Matrimonial Causes Act 1973 which provides that:

'The power of the court under subsection (1) or (2)(a) above to make an order in favour of a child of the family shall be exercisable from time to time; and where the court makes an order in favour of a child under subsection (2)(b) above, it may from time to time, subject to the restrictions mentioned in subsection (1) above, make a further order in his favour of any of the kinds mentioned in subsection (1)(d), (e) or (f) above.'

---

1   [1976] 1 All ER 719 at 123, [1976] Fam 199 at 206

There is no similar provision relating to the adult parties. Similarly, counsel for the
wife refers to s 31(5) of the 1973 Act. The implication in the present s 31(5) is, as
the husband's counsel agrees, that on an application for the variation of a periodical
payments order in favour of a child, the court can make an order for payment
of a lump sum. In H v H[1] Sir Jocelyn Simon P held that s 31(1) of the 1965 Act enacted a new power to order a lump sum in variation proceedings. Section 9(5) of
the Matrimonial Proceedings and Property Act 1970 reversed that ruling as regards
orders in favour of spouses (see Chaterjee v Chaterjee[2], per Ormrod LJ), but neither s 9(5)
nor s 31(5) of the 1973 Act curtailed the power of the court to order a lump sum on an
application to vary a periodical payments order in favour of children. The omission
to curtail the court's powers in this regard was deliberate (see the Law Commission's
Report[3]).

It is agreed by the parties that s 31(5) of the 1973 Act does not apply to this application, since the order for periodical payments falls within para 17 of Part III of Sch 1
to the 1973 Act. But the wife's counsel refers to the present s 31(5) in his argument
that the wife qualifies under r 69. He says that as a lump sum can now be ordered
on an application for the variation of a periodical payments order in favour of a child
it is a strong indication that r 69 should be given its literal effect and, as I understand
his argument, that the provision as to leave in r 68(2) so far as it relates to a claim for
ancillary relief for a child, by a petitioner or respondent who has custody, is rendered
otiose. Furthermore, counsel for the wife says that there is nothing in s 26 of the
Matrimonial Causes Act 1973 or its predecessor, s 24 of the Matrimonial Proceedings
and Property Act 1970, both of which provide for the making of rules of court,
which prevents the interpretation of the rules for which he contends. Counsel says
that s 26(2) is discretionary (the words are 'Rules of court may provide . . .') and that
this legislation does not prevent r 69 from having effect according to its express terms.
None of this, says counsel for the wife, is surprising. It is to be expected that a person
having custody of a child, even though he or she has been petitioner or respondent,
should be able to seek a lump sum or other ancillary relief for the child without leave.

Attractive as these arguments are, I am unable to accept that a petitioner who has
custody does come within r 69, enabling her to make an application for a lump sum
for the children where no such application had been made in the petition. Rule 68(1)
is mandatory and the wife comes within that rule. There would be no purpose in
making it mandatory for such applications if r 69 covered the same applications.
In the great majority of cases, claims for ancillary relief for children are made by
the petitioner and the respondent, and there are many considerations for the rule
that notice should be given in the pleadings, when there are pleadings, that such
claims may be made. Rule 69 is aimed at an entirely different class, and 'any person'
in r 69(b) must, as I think, be interpreted as ejusdem generis with the other persons
or parties in the rule. Although the effect of s 31(5) of the 1973 Act enables a lump
sum to be ordered on an application for a variation of periodical payments for a child,
the section does not apply to this application, and it must, I think, be open to question
how far it is appropriate to refer to s 31(5) by way of analogy, when the court is
considering an application for leave to apply for a lump sum under s 23 of the 1973
Act.

In the result, I hold that the wife must obtain leave before she can apply for a lump
sum for the children.

Leave

The proper approach in determining whether or not to grant leave is that the court
ought not to refuse leave to apply in any case in which on the evidence the applicant
has or appears to have reasonable prospects of obtaining the relief claimed or a

1   [1966] 3 All ER 560
2   [1976] 1 All ER 719 at 724, [1976] Fam 199 at 207
3   Report on Financial Provision in Matrimonial Proceedings, Law Com No 25, 24th July 1969

seriously arguable case: *Chaterjee v Chaterjee*[1]. I accept that the court should be more
ready to grant leave where the proposed application is for the benefit of children. *a*
Bearing in mind, however, all the helpful dicta in *Chaterjee v Chaterjee*[1], I have come
to the conclusion that leave ought not to be granted. I take all the circumstances
into account in reaching that conclusion, and especially the following: (i) Although
no separate lump sum provision was made for the children at the time, the inference
is that the parties arranged their affairs so far as they related to the disposition of
capital at the time of the divorce. It is true that the wife could not then have claimed *b*
a lump sum for them. In making that disposition the parties contemplated that the
wife would have custody of the children, that she would go to Australia, and that the
children would live with her. Since then the husband has certainly rearranged his
finances to some degree at least and has, so far as I am aware, had neither knowledge
nor warning that any claim would be made on him for further capital. This is
very far from being a decisive or even a substantial consideration(*Chaterjee v Chaterjee*[2]) *c*
especially as in this case the children were not in any sense parties to the agreement
and the husband hopes to sell the farm and have available capital. But these matters
are relevant. (ii) As regards the criteria in s 25(2) of the Matrimonial Causes Act 1973,
I am not satisfied that there is any financial need on the part of these children which
cannot be adequately met and is properly to be dealt with by an order for periodical
payments which may be substantial. So far as the wife's need for social security *d*
benefits reflects a need on the part of the children, that can be remedied by a periodical
payments order. There is no suggestion that the disability of the youngest daughter
requires any capital payment for treatment or otherwise, nor any evidence that their
further education or training requires a capital payment. The wife's debt on the car
does not appear to be arrears. If the car is repossessed and additional moneys are
required for the children's travelling, they can be obtained by way of periodical *e*
payments. I do not think that the wife's debt of $1,500, or her potential liability
for United Kingdom income tax, give ground for holding she has a reasonable prospect of obtaining a lump sum for the children. (iii) The children are now living in
Australia with their mother who has the added responsibility of another child.
On the evidence, the mother has no financial resources beyond the value of her own
home and the mother does not enjoy good health. However, there is no evidence *f*
that the father has failed to comply with any order for periodical payments. There
is apparently no difficulty about the remission of money to Australia. (iv) The wife
contends that the children should have a nest egg and that the implication in the
husband's affidavit is that he is rich a man in whose capital the children would have
shared had the marriage continued. But having regard to his compliance with
previous orders, it appears to me that it would not be reasonable to require the father *g*
at this stage to make a capital payment for the children. In so holding I have in mind
the decision in *Chamberlain v Chamberlain*[3] and in particular the dicta of Scarman
LJ. (v) I am not satisfied that the husband's affidavit, although open in my view to
criticism and comment, shows the husband to be so lacking in assets or so unreliable
as an investor, as contended by the wife, to make it appropriate to consider that he
should pay a lump sum in order to secure the children's future position. *h*
    In the circumstances I do not grant leave and I dismiss the wife's application for leave.

Application dismissed.

Solicitors: *Brutton & Co*, Winchester (for the petitioner); *Buss*; *Stone & Co*, Tunbridge
Wells (for the respondent).

Georgina Chambers Barrister.

1   [1976] 1 All ER 719, [1976] Fam 199
2   [1976] 1 All ER 719 at 725, [1976] Fam 199 at 207
3   [1974] 1 All ER 33 at 38, [1973] 1 WLR 1557 at 1564, 1565

Daulia Ltd v Four Millbank Nominees Ltd

a

COURT OF APPEAL, CIVIL DIVISION
BUCKLEY, ORR AND GOFF LJJ
27th, 28th, 29th JULY, 4th OCTOBER, 24th NOVEMBER 1977

b *Sale of land – Contract – Memorandum – Contract for the disposition of an interest in land –
Oral contract to enter into formal written contract for sale of land – Vendor refusing to
complete – No note or memorandum evidencing oral contract – Whether purchaser able to sue
on oral contract – Whether oral contract a 'contract for the . . . disposition of . . . [an] interest
in land' – Law of Property Act 1925, s 40(1).*

c *Contract – Offer and acceptance – Acceptance – Unilateral contract – Offer by offeror to
enter into written contract if offeree performed stipulated conditions – Whether offeror
entitled to withdraw offer once offeree had embarked on performance of conditions.*

The defendants were mortgagees of a portfolio of properties which, the mortgagor
being in default, they were entitled to sell. The plaintiffs were anxious to purchase
d the properties and made several unsuccessful offers. However, on 21st December
1976, the parties agreed terms and further agreed to exchange contracts the next
day. When the plaintiffs attended the defendants' offices on 22nd December to
exchange contracts the defendants, who had in the meantime found another purchaser at a substantially increased price, refused to complete the sale. The plaintiffs
brought an action against the defendants claiming damages for breach of contract.
e The plaintiffs alleged that on 21st December an agent of the defendants' had promised
the plaintiffs that if the plaintiffs procured a banker's draft for the deposit, attended
at the defendants' offices at 10 o'clock the next morning and there tendered to the
defendants the plaintiffs' part of the contract engrossed and signed together with the
banker's draft, the defendants would enter into a contract ('the written contract')
with the plaintiffs for the sale of the properties. The plaintiffs further alleged that the
f agent's promise and the plaintiffs' performance of the conditions stipulated constituted a contract ('the oral contract') and that by refusing to accept the plaintiffs'
tender of the engrossed and signed contract and banker's draft the defendants were
in breach of the oral contract. On a motion by the defendants under RSC Ord 18,
r 19, have the action struck out, the plaintiffs contended that the oral contract was
not a 'contract for the . . . disposition of . . . [an] interest in land' and therefore did not
require to be evidenced by a 'note or memorandum' for the purposes of s 40(1)[a]
g of the Law of Property Act 1925. Nevertheless the action was struck out. The plaintiffs
appealed.

Held – (1) The oral contract pleaded by the plaintiffs was, if the facts were proved, a
valid unilateral contract by which the defendants had offered that they would enter
into the written contract if the plaintiffs fulfilled the conditions of presenting them-
h selves at the time and place appointed and being then and there ready and able to enter into the written contract, and the plaintiffs by fulfilling those conditions had
accepted the offer. Actual exchange of the written contracts was not part of the conditions which the defendants had stipulated in making their offer and was not therefore a necessary element in the formation of the oral contract (see p 560 *j* to p 561 *a*,
p 566 *c d* and p 570 *g h*, post).

j
_____

a Section 40(1), so far as material, provides: 'No action may be brought upon any contract
for the sale or other disposition of land or any interest in land, unless the agreement upon
which such action is brought, or some memorandum or note thereof, is in writing, and
signed by the party to be charged or by some other person thereunto by him lawfully
authorised.'

(2) The appeal would, however, be dismissed for the following reasons—
(i) The oral contract was a contract for the disposition of an interest in land, within *a*
the meaning of s 40(1), because it was either (a) a contract that, apart from the application of s 40, would itself be specifically enforceable as a contract relating to the sale of
land, or (b) a contract which, although not itself specifically enforceable, would
if performed create a proper written contract which would be specifically enforceable.
In both cases, the contract if so enforced would give the plaintiffs an equitable interest
in land and the oral contract was therefore a contract for the creation of, and con- *b*
sequently for the disposition of, an interest in land, and as such, was required by s 40
to be in writing before an action could be brought on it (see p 562 *f* to *h*, p 563 *a b*,
p 564 *e*, p 567 *b* to *e*, p 568 *c* and p 570 *g h*, post); *Union Car Advertising Co v Boston
Elevated Railway Co* (1928) 26 F 2d 755, *Sarkisian v Teale* (1909) 88 NE 333 and *McLachlan
v Village of Whitehall* (1906) 99 NYS 721 applied; *Warlow v Harrison* [1843-60] All ER
Rep 620, *Rainbow v Howkins* [1904] 2 KB 322 and *Wood v Midgley* (1854) 5 De GM & G *c*
41 distinguished; *Johnston v Boyes* [1899] 2 Ch 73 disapproved.
(ii) The oral contract was not saved from the effect of s 40 by the doctrine of part
performance because the alleged acts of part performance relied on by the plaintiffs
were those acts done by them to satisfy the conditions of the unilateral offer made by
the defendants and which led to the formation of the oral contract. These acts had
to be considered in isolation from the oral contract and, when so considered, the *d*
alleged acts suggested that the parties contemplated making a contract rather than
that there was a contract already in existence in pursuance of which the acts had
been performed (see p 564 *g h* and p 570 *f g* and *h*, post); dictum of Lord Reid in
Steadman v Steadman [1974] 2 All ER at 981, 982 applied.
Per Curiam. In a unilateral contract, although the offeror is entitled to require full
performance of the condition which he has imposed and although short of that he is *e*
not bound, once the offeree has embarked on performance of the condition there is an
implied obligation on the part of the offeror not to prevent performance and he cannot
revoke his offer (see p 561 *b c*, p 566 *a* to *c* and p 570 *g h*, post).
Per Buckley and Orr LJJ. *Law v Jones*[b] did not decide that a letter written 'subject to
contract' or forming part of a correspondence conducted subject to a 'subject to
contract' stipulation can constitute a note or memorandum of an oral agreement
to which it relates sufficient to satisfy the Statute of Frauds, at any rate so long as the
'subject to contract' stipulation remains operative. What it did decide was that, if
the parties subsequently enter into a new and distinct oral agreement, the facts may
be such that the earlier letter may form part of a sufficient note or memorandum of
the later oral agreement notwithstanding that it was 'subject to contract' in relation
to the earlier bargain (see p 570 *b* to *d* and *g* to *h*, post); *Law v Jones* [1973] 2 All ER 437 *g*
explained.

Notes

For the need for a note or memorandum in writing if action is to be brought on a
contract of sale of land, see 34 Halsbury's Laws (3rd Edn) 207-210, paras 346-348, and
for cases on the subject, see 40 Digest (Repl) 21-38, *82-205* and Digest (Cont Vol D) *h*
115-116, 602*a*-602*b*.
For acceptance of a unilateral offer, see 9 Halsbury's Laws (4th Edn) para 252.
For the Law of Property Act 1925, s 40, see 27 Halsbury's Statutes (3rd Edn) 399.

Cases referred to in judgments

Boyd v Greene (1895) 162 Mass 566, 39 NE 277.
Buxton v Rust (1872) LR 7 Exch 279, 41 LJEx 173, 27 LT 210, Ex Ch, 12 Digest (Reissue)
171, 1009.
Carlill v Carbolic Smoke Ball Co [1893] 1 QB 256, [1891-4] All ER Rep 127, 62 LJQB 257,
67 LT 837, 57 JP 325, 4 R 176, CA, 12 Digest (Reissue) 66, 342.

b [1973] 2 All ER 437

Hillas & Co Ltd v Arcos Ltd (1932) 147 LT 503, [1932] All ER Rep 494, 38 Com Cas 23, HL,
a 39 Digest (Repl) 448, *34.*
Johnston v Boyes [1899] 2 Ch 73, 68 LJCh 425, 80 LT 488, 12 Digest (Reissue) 579, *4051.*
Kingswood Estate Co Ltd v Anderson [1962] 3 All ER 593, [1963] 2 QB 169, [1962] 3 WLR
    1102, CA, 13 Digest (Reissue) 428, *3550.*
Law v Jones [1973] 2 All ER 437, [1974] Ch 112, [1973] 2 WLR 994, 26 P & CR 42, CA,
    Digest (Cont Vol D) 795, *120a.*
b *McLachlin v Village of Whitehall* (1906) 99 NYS 721.
Rainbow v Howkins [1904] 2 KB 322, 73 LJKB 641, 91 LT 149, DC, 3 Digest (Repl) 4, *17.*
Sarkisian v Teele (1909) 201 Mass 596, 88 NE 333.
Steadman v Steadman [1974] 2 All ER 977, [1976] AC 536, [1974] 3 WLR 56, 29 P & CR
    46, HL, Digest (Cont Vol D) 794, *81a.*
Thirkell v Cambi [1919] 2 KB 590, 89 LJKB 1, 121 LT 532, 24 Com Cas 285, CA, 12
c Digest (Reissue) 170, *1005.*
Tiverton Estates Ltd v Wearwell Ltd [1974] 1 All ER 209, [1975] Ch 146, [1974] 2 WLR
    176, 27 P & CR 24, CA, Digest (Cont Vol D) 116, *602b.*
Union Car Advertising Co Inc v Boston Elevated Railway Co (1928) 26 F 2d 755.
Warlow v Harrison (1859) 1 E & E 309, [1843-60] All ER Rep 620, 29 LJQB 14, 1 LT 211,
    6 Jur NS 66, 120 ER 925, Ex Ch; *rvsg* 1 E & E 295, 120 ER 920, 3 Digest (Repl) 47,
d *331.*
Wood v Midgley (1854) 5 De GM & G 41, 2 Eq Rep 729, 23 LJCh 553, 43 ER 784; *rvsg*
    2 Sm & G 115, 65 ER 327, 12 Digest (Reissue) 188, *1125.*

Appeal

The plaintiffs, Daulia Ltd, appealed against the judgment of Brightman J given on
31st March 1977 whereby he ordered that the plaintiffs' writ and statement of claim
e in their action for damages for breach of contract against Four Millbank Nominees
Ltd ('the defendants') and Slaughter & May, the defendant's solicitors, be struck out
pursuant to RSC Ord 18, r 19, as disclosing no reasonable cause of action or as being
scandalous, frivolous or vexatious or otherwise an abuse of the process of the court
and that the action be dismissed. The facts are set out in the judgment of Goff LJ.

f *Gerald Godfrey QC* and *Norman Primost* for the plaintiffs.
Leonard Hoffman QC and *Michael Driscoll* for the defendants.
Slaughter & May were not represented.

Cur adv vult

24th November. The following judgments were read.

g **GOFF LJ** (delivering the first judgment at the invitation of Buckley LJ). This is an
appeal from an order dated 31st March 1977 of Brightman J made on a motion under
RSC Ord 18, r 19, whereby he directed that as against Four Millbank Nominees Ltd
('the defendants') the statement of claim should be struck out and the action
dismissed with costs.

The plaintiffs were keen to buy certain commercial and residential properties from
h the defendants who were in a position to sell those properties as mortgagees. The
plaintiffs never in fact succeeded in obtaining an exchange of contracts or any other
written agreement for sale and purchase, but they claim they did obtain a unilateral
contract by the defendants that they would enter into a written contract of sale
on certain agreed terms and the plaintiffs claim damages for breach of that unilateral
contract.

j The facts on which they base that claim are extensively set forth in the re-amended
statement of claim but I need only refer to them quite briefly. I take them from the
following paragraphs of the re-amended statement of claim:

'7. On Tuesday, 21st December 1976 the terms of the proposed sale between
the Plaintiffs and the [defendants] were finally agreed between one Shebson
acting on behalf of the Plaintiffs and the said Langley [who was acting on behalf

of the defendants] whereby the Plaintiffs were to purchase the said properties from the [defendants] for a price of £825,000 payable by a deposit of £41,250 which *a* said deposit was to be payable by a Bankers Draft and the balance of £783,750 was to be payable on completion. The said terms were partly oral and partly in writing. Insofar as they were in writing they were contained in the draft Contracts which the Plaintiffs and the [defendants] already had. Insofar as they were oral, they had been agreed on the telephone between the said Shebson and the said Langley, and the said oral terms were evidenced by Riders to the *b* said Contract sent by the said Shebson to the said Langley on Tuesday, 21st December 1976.

'8. On the afternoon of Tuesday, 21st December 1976 one Osgoodby acting on behalf of the [defendants] promised the said Shebson acting on behalf of the Plaintiffs that the [defendants] would enter into a contract for the sale of the said properties with the Plaintiffs if the Plaintiffs procured a Bankers Draft *c* for the said deposit, attended at the [defendants'] offices before 10.00 a.m. on Wednesday, 22nd December 1976, at 4 Millbank and tendered to the [defendants] the Plaintiffs' part of the contract in the terms already agreed and the said Bankers Draft.

'9. In reliance on the said promise the Plaintiffs procured the Bankers Draft for the said deposit, executed and signed their part of the said contract for sale *d* in the terms already agreed.

'10. The Plaintiffs duly attended at the [defendants'] said offices before 10.00 a.m. on Wednesday, 22nd December 1976 with their said deposit and their said part of the contract for sale ready for tender to the [defendants] But the [defendants] refused to exchange their part of the said contract for sale with the Plaintiffs.'

e

Brightman J held that those facts disclosed no cause of action, and the plaintiffs now appeal to this court. Under this procedure the facts so pleaded must be taken as admitted, and they give rise to three questions of law: (a) Do they establish a valid unilateral contract? If they do, then there is no question but that they disclose a breach. (b) If the answer to (a) is 'Yes' then is that contract unenforceable for want of a written note or memorandum to satisfy s 40 of the Law of Property Act 1925, *f* unless there be sufficient acts of part performance to take the case out of the statute? (c) If s 40 applies are there such acts?

It is well settled that it is only in plain and obvious cases that the court should exercise its powers under the summary process provided by RSC Ord 18, r 19, and it was suggested that these questions should not be resolved by us but should in any event go to trial. I am satisfied, however, that so far as the facts are concerned the *g* plaintiffs' position cannot be improved by evidence beyond that in which they stand on the facts pleaded which for the purposes of this motion and appeal are taken to be admitted. Further the points of law have been very fully argued before us, and I have no doubt that we ought to determine them now.

I therefore turn to the first question. Was there a concluded unilateral contract by the defendants to enter into a contract for sale on the agreed terms?

h

The concept of a unilateral or 'if' contract is somewhat anomalous, because it is clear that, at all events until the offeree starts to perform the condition, there is no contract at all, but merely an offer which the offeror is free to revoke. Doubts have been expressed whether the offeror becomes bound so soon as the offeree starts to perform or satisfy the condition, or only when he has fully done so. In my judgment, however, we are not concerned in this case with any such problem, because in my *j* view the plaintiffs had fully performed or satisfied the condition when they presented themselves at the time and place appointed with a banker's draft for the deposit and their part of the written contract for sale duly engrossed and signed, and the retendered the same, which I understand to mean preferred it for exchange. Actual exchange, which never took place, would not in my view have been part of the

satisfaction of the condition but something additional which was inherently necessary
a to be done by the plaintiffs to enable, not to bind, the defendants to perform the
unilateral contract.

Accordingly in my judgment, the answer to the first question must be in the
affirmative.

Even if my reasoning so far be wrong the conclusion in my view is still the same for
the following reasons. Whilst I think the true view of a unilateral contract must
b in general be that the offeror is entitled to require full performance of the condition
which he has imposed and short of that he is not bound, that must be subject to one
important qualification, which stems from the fact that there must be an implied
obligation on the part of the offeror not to prevent the condition becoming satisfied,
which obligation it seems to me must arise as soon as the offeree starts to perform.
Until then the offeror can revoke the whole thing, but once the offeree has embarked
c on performance it is too late for the offeror to revoke his offer.

This brings me to the second question. There are certain English cases touching
this matter, but none precisely in point. The plaintiffs rely strongly on *Warlow v
Harrison*[1] and *Johnston v Boyes*[2]. In the former an auctioneer knocked down as sold
for 61 guineas, which was bid by the owner, a pony which according to the particulars
was to be sold without reserve, and the auctioneer, not the vendor, was sued for
d damages by the plaintiff who was the highest independent bidder at 60 guineas.
In the Court of Queen's Bench[3], Lord Campbell held that there was no contract
because the vendor had revoked the auctioneer's authority to accept the plaintiff's
bid, and therefore no question of the impact of s 17 of the Statute of Frauds arose.
The Exchequer Chamber agreed with this conclusion on the pleadings as they stood,
but allowed an amendment, and held the defendant liable; per Martin B[4] as on a
e contract that the sale should be without reserve, and per Willes and Bramwell JJ[5] on
a breach of warranty of authority to sell without reserve. Martin B said[6]:

> 'Upon the same principle, it seems to us that the highest bonâ fide bidder at an
> auction may sue the auctioneer as upon a contract that the sale shall be without
> reserve. We think the auctioneer who puts the property up for sale upon such a
f > condition pledges himself that the sale shall be without reserve; or, in other
> words, contracts that it shall be so; and that this contract is made with the
> highest bonâ fide bidder; and in case of breach of it, that he has a right of action
> against the auctioneer. The case is not at all affected by the 17th section of the
> Statute of Frauds, which relates only to direct sales, and not to contracts relating
> to or connected with them.'

g This case affords support for the plaintiffs' contention as far as it goes, but it is distinguishable, since there the action was against the auctioneer, not the vendor, and
it was not on a contract by the auctioneer that he himself would sell to the highest
bidder but that his principal would do so.

Warlow v Harrison[1] was approved by Cozens Hardy J in *Johnston v Boyes*[7], where he
h related it to the vendor himself, saying:

> 'A vendor who offers property for sale by auction on the terms of printed
> conditions can be made liable to a member of the public who accepts the offer
> if those conditions be violated: see *Warlow v. Harrison*[1], and the recent case of

j 1 (1859) 1 E & E 295, [1843-60] All ER Rep 620
    2 [1899] 2 Ch 73
    3 1 E & E 295
    4 1 E & E 301 at 316, [1843-60] All ER Rep 620 at 622
    5 1 E & E 301 at 318, [1843-60] All ER Rep 620 at 623
    6 1 E & E 301 at 316, 317, [1843-60] All ER Rep 620 at 622
    7 [1899] 2 Ch 73 at 77

Carlill v. Carbolic Smoke Ball Co.[1] Nor do I think that the Statute of Frauds would afford any defence to such an action. The plaintiff is not suing on a contract to purchase land: she is suing simply because her agent, in breach of the first and second conditions of sale, was not allowed to sign a contract which would have resulted in her becoming the purchaser of the land. I think this conclusion results from the decision of the Exchequer Chamber in *Warlow v. Harrison*[2].'

This, however, was merely obiter because not only was the action once again not against the vendor but against the auctioneer, but also the court held that there could be no liability anyway, quite apart from the effect of the statute, because the plaintiff's agent had not tendered cash, but only a cheque, which the auctioneer was not bound to accept. The case is in any event unsatisfactory because the complaint made was that the auctioneer had refused to allow the plaintiff's agent to sign a memorandum on her behalf, but that would not have been of any use to her. What was required was a note or memorandum signed by or on behalf of the vendor.

On the other hand *Rainbow v Howkins*[3], so far as it goes, tells against the plaintiffs but again it is distinguishable, because the action was brought on the ground that the auctioneer was personally liable as if he were vendor under a contract of sale not on a collateral contract, and alternatively for breach of warranty of authority, but it was held that he could not be sued on the first ground because of the statute, and could not be sued for breach of warranty of authority, because there was none since, apart from the statute, he had effectively bound the vendor. Counsel for the defendants also relied on *Wood v Midgley*[4]. That, however, was not a case of an agreement to enter into a written agreement but of a concluded oral agreement for sale with a concurrent or collateral agreement to reduce it to writing, so that again is distinguishable.

In these circumstances in my judgment it is necessary to consider how the matter stands in principle. As I see it the question is whether the unilateral contract is, and I quote these words from s 40 'a contract for the sale or other disposition of land or any interest in land'. It is clear to me that ex hypothesi it is not a contract for the sale of land or any interest in land because it is a separate and independent contract to enter into such a contract.

In my judgment, however, it is equally clearly a contract for some other disposition of an interest in land. It is not necessary in my view that the interest in land to be disposed of should actually exist at the time of the contract. I cannot doubt that a contract for valuable consideration to grant an easement over Blackacre would be a contract for the disposition of an interest in land within the meaning of the section.

Now, in the present case we have a contract to enter into a proper written contract for the sale of land. Such a contract if entered into would be specifically enforceable and would therefore give the plaintiffs a right to the land in equity and so would create and give them an equitable interest in the land. It follows in my judgment that the unilateral contract was a contract to dispose of an interest in land, because it was a contract to do something which would have that effect in law.

The plaintiffs say 'But we are not claiming specific performance; only damages'. That, however, in my view is an irrelevant consideration for two reasons. The first, which is I think conclusive, is that we are not concerned with whether the 'unilateral contract' could be specifically enforced so as actually to create an interest in land, but whether it is a contract to do that which, if done, would create such an interest. The words of the section look only to the contract. The second is that the plaintiffs cannot escape the impact of the section by limiting the nature of the relief they seek, and, moreover, the damages for breach of the unilateral contract must, as I see it,

1   [1893] 1 QB 256, [1891–4] All ER Rep 127
2   (1859) 1 E & E 301, [1843–60] All ER Rep 620
3   [1904] 2 KB 322
4   (1854) 2 Sm & G 115; *rvsd* 5 De GM & G 41

be exactly the same as damages for breach of the contract of sale would have been
a if contracts had been exchanged and then broken by the plaintiffs.

If, however, contrary to my view it be necessary that the unilateral contract should
be one capable of specific performance, in my judgment it is so, notwithstanding the
decision of Stirling J on motion in *Johnston v Boyes*[1], which with all respect to that
learned judge is in my view incorrect. For this purpose one must regard the matter
apart from s 40, for if one postulates that the section applies one begs the whole
b question. So regarded, I cannot see how a vendor can escape an order for specific
performance by agreeing (with sufficient particularity to be effective in law) to agree
to sell rather than by a direct agreement to sell.

The dictum of Lord Wright in *Hillas & Co Ltd v Arcos Ltd*[2] 'a contract *de præsenti* to
enter into what, in law, is an enforceable contract, is simply that enforceable contract,
and no more and no less', with which I respectfully agree, does not directly apply,
c because prior to exchange of contracts which never took place the plaintiffs were not
themselves bound to purchase or to enter into a contract to purchase. They could have
resiled at the very last moment, even after tender, so that this was not a contract
between A and B to make a contract between A and B, but a unilateral contract by
A to enter into a particular contract with B, but in my view the principle must be
the same.

d I am fortified in this conclusion by the American case of *Union Car Advertising Co v
Boston Elevated Railway Co*[3], a decision of the Circuit Court of Appeals, First Circuit.
Counsel for the plaintiffs pointed out that although the court said that[4]—

> 'it was virtually conceded by the plaintiff at the argument that under the law
> of Massachusetts an oral contract to execute a written contract for the sale or
e > transfer of an interest in land is within the statute of frauds and invalid'

the case before the court was not such a case but one of a contract not to be performed within the year. Therefore, he said, this American decision does not help
because the position with regard to a contract for the sale or other disposition of an
interest in land was not before the court, and anyway the court was dealing only
with the law of Massachusetts.

f So far as the second point is concerned the case is nonetheless persuasive authority,
and as to the first, the citations in the judgment from other cases show that the
concession was in truth in accordance with the law of that State, and show that law
to be founded on reasoning which commends itself to me and entirely accords with
my own.

Thus in *Sarkisian v Teele*[5] where the subject-matter was an oral contract to execute
g an unsigned written contract to sell stock in trade and to let the business premises,
the court said[6]:

> 'If the bill is considered as seeking to enforce an oral promise by the defendant
> to enter into the formal writing, as containing all the essential elements of the
> contract, it cannot be maintained . . . By the statute of frauds such an agreement
h > was required to be in writing, and an oral promise to execute a contract em-
> bodying these terms also comes within the statute.'

Further in *McLachlin v Village of Whitehall*[7]: '. . . the trustees of the defendant village
entered into an oral contract wherein it was agreed that if the plaintiff would in-

---

j 1   [1899] 2 Ch 73
2   (1932) 147 LT 503 at 515, [1932] All ER Rep 494 at 505
3   (1928) 26 F 2d 755
4   26 F 2d 755 at 759
5   (1909) 88 NE 333
6   88 NE 333 at 334
7   (1906) 99 NYS 721

crease his plant, so that he could furnish incandescent lights for private houses in the
village, the trustees would renew . . .' the written contract he then had for lighting   *a*
its street, which would otherwise expire in 1897. In that case the court said[1]:

> 'The question is therefore presented whether damages can be recovered
> for the breach of an oral agreement to enter into a contract which, under the
> statute of frauds, is required to be in writing. It is true that the oral agreement
> to enter into the written contract might be fully performed within a year or   *b*
> within a day. The action is not in form one to recover damages for a breach of
> contract for lighting the streets and public places for a term of five years, but for
> damages consequent upon a breach of the verbal agreement to award such a
> contract to the plaintiff. The damages, however, claimed as consequent upon
> such breach are none other than the same damages as would have been recover-
> able for a breach of the contract for lighting if it had been awarded to the plain-   *c*
> tiff . . . It is conceded that a contract for lighting for a term of five years would be
> void if not in writing, but if an oral agreement to enter into such a written con-
> tract is not also void, where the damages claimed for the breach of the oral
> agreement are not independent of it, but necessarily are the same as those which
> would arise from the breach of the written contract, the door would be open for
> the practical nullification of the statute of frauds in a large class of cases.'   *d*

The law is similarly stated in the American Jurist[2]:

> 'The general rule is that an oral agreement to reduce to writing a contract
> which is within the scope of the operation of the Statute of Frauds or to sign an
> agreement which the Statute of Frauds requires to be in writing is invalid and
> unenforceable.'
   e

In my judgment, therefore, the unilateral contract in this case is prima facie
unenforceable, and I turn to the third question.

The plaintiffs rely on all and every of the acts done by them to satisfy the conditions
of the 'unilateral contract', as being also sufficient acts of part performance. The
defendants say that cannot be so because nothing can be part performance if done   *f*
before there is any binding contract. Counsel for the defendants puts his case as
high as saying that by definition there can never be part performance of a unilateral
contract. I doubt whether that is right as a general principle, since in most cases the
performance of the condition by the offeree is also the discharge of all his obligations
and is certainly done pursuant to the inchoate contract. I think in many cases the
offeree's acts may amount to part performance, though I doubt whether in this case
they caused sufficient prejudice to the plaintiffs to raise an equity on which the   *g*
defendants could be charged.

In my view, however, it is unnecessary to decide these questions since in my judgment the case fails because none of the alleged acts of part performance of themselves
suggest that there was any contract between the parties. Indeed they point to the
exact opposite and suggest that the parties were about to make or contemplated
making a contract. It is only if one first looks to see what the oral contract is, and   *h*
finds that it is a unilateral contract, such as pleaded in this case, that the acts can
begin to be regarded as part performance, but that is an enquiry which one is not
permitted to make: see per Lord Reid in *Steadman v Steadman*[3], where he said:

> 'I think that there has been some confusion between this supposed rule and
> another perfectly good rule. You must not first look at the oral contract and   *i*
> then see whether the alleged acts of part performance are consistent with it.

---

1   (1906) 99 NYS 721 at 722, 723
2   2nd Edn (1974), vol 72, p 568
3   [1974] 2 All ER 977 at 981, 982, [1976] AC 536 at 541, 542

You must first look at the alleged acts of part performance to see whether they prove that there must have been a contract and it is only if they do so prove that you can bring in the oral contract . . . In my view, unless the law is to be divorced from reason and principle, the rule must be that you take the whole circumstances, leaving aside evidence about the oral contract, to see whether it is proved that the acts relied on were done in reliance on a contract: that will be proved if it is shown to be more probable than not.'

Lord Salmon appears to have taken a contrary view where he said[1]:

'In the present case the payment of £100 by the husband to his wife who had divorced him—looked at without regard to its surrounding circumstances— would not be any evidence of any contract, let alone of a contract concerning land.'

The other members of the court did not state the position so specifically one way or the other, but both Viscount Dilhorne and Lord Simon[2] accepted the statement in Fry on Specific Performance[3]:

'The true principle however of the operation of acts of part performance seems only to require that the acts in question be such as must be referred to some contract, and may be referred to the alleged one; that they prove the existence of some contract and are consistent with the contract alleged,'

approved by Upjohn LJ in *Kingswood Estate Co Ltd v Anderson*[4]. Here, of course, the acts do not prove any contract.

The plaintiffs argue that whilst one may not look to see what oral contract is alleged, one may look at the promise made as part of the surrounding circumstances and then the alleged acts of part performance are explained and shown to be referable to the existence of a contract; but that, with all respect, I reject as too subtle, and in reality looking to and examining the alleged acts of part performance in the light of the alleged contract.

For these reasons in my judgment the plaintiffs fail on the third question also, and I would dismiss this appeal, although I do so with considerable regret as the defendants' conduct appears to me to be unmeritorious.

BUCKLEY LJ. I agree. The plaintiffs and the defendants were in negotiation for the purchase by the former from the latter of a considerable number of properties in London described as the Gill Portfolio. It is common ground, however, that at no time was there a contract between them in this respect. It was the intention of the parties that the formation of a contract of sale should await the exchange of formal written agreements. The plaintiffs sue on an alleged contract, partly oral and partly by conduct, arising out of the promise alleged in para 8 of the re-amended statement of claim and the plaintiffs' conduct alleged in paras 9 and 10 thereof. It is claimed that the defendants thus became bound to enter into a formal written agreement of sale in terms which had already been agreed (though not contractually) between the parties when the contract sued on was made. The issues consequently are (1) whether the facts pleaded in paras 8, 9 and 10 of the re-amended statement of claim are such as would give rise to a contract; (2) whether a plea under the Law of Property Act 1925, s 40, could afford a good defence to an action on such contract; and (3) if so, whether in the present case there was any sufficient part performance to take the case out of s 40.

Brightman J seems to have accepted that the answer to the first question should

1 [1974] 2 All ER 977 at 1007, [1976] AC 536 at 571
2 [1974] 2 All ER 977 at 992, 999, [1976] AC 536 at 553, 561
3 6th Edn (1921), p 278
4 [1962] 3 All ER 593 at 604, [1963] 2 QB 169 at 189

be affirmative. In this court it has been suggested that the plaintiffs' conduct alleged in paras 9 and 10 did not fully satisfy the conditions on which the defendants' alleged promise was conditional, because it is not in terms alleged that the plaintiffs in fact tendered the plaintiffs' part of the written agreement. I would not regard this as an adequate ground for striking out the statement of claim; for if, as seems probable, the defendants' declaration on 22nd December 1976 of an intention not to exchange agreements stultified the plaintiffs' intention then to tender its part for exchange, the defendants could not, in my judgment, rely on any failure of the plaintiffs to make actual tender as a defence to a claim of breach of contract. The defendants' offer to exchange contracts must have been subject to an implied obligation that the defendants would not render the performance by the plaintiffs of the acts necessary for acceptance impossible, and I agree with Goff LJ that the defendants could not withdraw their offer once the plaintiffs had embarked on those acts.

In my opinion, the re-amended statement of claim is capable of supporting a conclusion that a contract was made on 22nd December 1976 under which the defendants became bound to enter into a written agreement of sale of the properties to the plaintiffs on the terms which, as alleged in para 7 of the re-amended statement of claim, had been finally agreed on the previous day.

The learned judge, in an interesting analysis of the position in the present case, reached the conclusion that, on the basis that a contract to exchange agreements existed, that contract was itself a contract for the sale of land, and that no distinction could be drawn between the contract to exchange agreements and the contract which would result from such exchange. If the judge was right, it must follow that he was also right in concluding that the contract to exchange agreements must fall within the operation of s 40 and be unenforceable for lack of writing unless there was sufficient part performance to take the case out of the section.

As I said, however, at the beginning of this judgment, it was, and I think still is, common ground between the parties that there never has been any contract of sale in the present case. If this is the case, any contract there may have been was merely a contract to do something, viz exchange of agreements, the doing of which would bring a contract of sale into existence. As I read the learned judge's judgment, he held that the contract to exchange agreements should be treated as, and indeed was in truth, a contract for the sale of land.

The plaintiffs contend that this is not good law and that the contract to exchange agreements is a contract to do a particular act which is distinct from the contract of sale which would result from the doing of that act.

If it be accepted that the intention of the parties was at all relevant times that there should be no contract of sale until formal agreements had been exchanged, there can have been no contract of sale on 22nd December 1976, for no agreements were then exchanged. In these circumstances, either no contract was made on that day or it was a contract which was not a contract of sale. If no contract was made, this can, I think, on the pleaded facts only have been because the promise alleged in para 8 of the re-amended statement of claim was not in truth a promise at all by reason of the 'subject to contract' character of the dealings between the parties in relation to the sale negotiations. The learned judge expressed the view that the exhibited correspondence showed clearly that the negotiations for the sale were intended to be subject to contract, and this has not been questioned in this court. The judge went on to say that it was theoretically possible that on 21st December 1976, that is on the occasion to which para 8 of the re-amended statement of claim refers, Mr Osgoodby on behalf of the defendants made an offer in the terms pleaded in para 8 which was not subject to contract. If the case were to turn on the question of fact whether the so-called promise was a part of 'subject to contract' negotiations or was an offer capable of acceptance having contractual effect, that question ought, I think, to go to trial. If the promise was subject to contract, no contract would have arisen from the plaintiffs' acts pleaded in paras 9 and 10 of the re-amended statement

of claim; if, on the other hand, it was not subject to contract, is any contract which
a may have arisen by reason of the plaintiffs' acceptance by conduct an enforceable
contract? In other words, would s 40 apply to it?

As I have already said, if the learned judge was right in his view of the effect of
the contract, s 40 must apply; but let me assume that, for whatever reason, that
view is incorrect and the contract was no more than a contract to exchange agreements. In my view such a contract would be one which the court could order to be
b specifically performed; for, although not a contract of sale of land, it would undoubtedly be a contract relating to a sale of land. At the risk of drawing too fine a distinction, one might say that, though not a contract of sale, it would be a contract for sale.
Such a contract, it seems to me, would be specifically enforceable, for the common
law remedy of damages would be inadequate. The injury suffered by the plaintiffs
in consequence of the failure to implement the contract to exchange agreements
c and the damages recoverable in respect of it would, I think, be precisely the same
as the injury resulting from, and the damages recoverable in consequence of, a
breach of the contract which would arise from the exchange of agreements. The
performance of the contract for an exchange of agreements would bring a contract
of sale into existence. The latter contract would confer an equitable interest in the
land on the purchaser. So I agree with Goff LJ that the contract to exchange agree-
d ments is a contract for the creation of, and consequently for the disposition of, an
interest in land within s 40 of the Law of Property Act 1925. Moreover, if specifically
enforceable, the contract to exchange agreements must have itself given rise to an
equitable interest in land.

We were referred to a number of American cases which will be found collected
and discussed in *Union Car Advertising Co Inc v Boston Elevated Railway Co*[1], a decision
e of the Circuit Court of Appeals, First Circuit. In one of these, *Boyd v Greene*[2], it was
said that an oral contract to execute a valid written agreement to convey land is as
much within the Statute of Frauds as an oral contract to execute and deliver a conveyance of land. In another, *Sarkisian v Teele*[3], it was held that an oral promise to
execute a contract to sell stock in trade and to lease a store to the plaintiff came
within the statute. Yet another, *McLachlin v Village of Whitehall*[4], was concerned
f with an oral promise made on behalf of the defendants to renew an expiring contract
for lighting the streets of the village for a further period of five years. The appellate
court decided in favour of the defendants saying[5]:

> 'It is conceded that a contract for lighting for a term of five years would be
> void if not in writing, but if an oral agreement to enter into such a written
> contract is not also void, where the damages claimed for the breach of the oral
g > agreement are not independent of it, but necessarily are the same as those which
> would arise from the breach of the written contract, the door would be open
> for the practical nullification of the statute of frauds in a large class of cases.'

The first and third of these three cases appear to have been cases relating to agreements to enter into a written contract where no contract already existed. *Sarkisian v
h Teele*[3], on the other hand, seems to have been a case of an agreement to render an
existing unenforceable agreement enforceable by reducing it to writing signed by
the parties. It seems to me, however, that there can be no valid distinction for the
relevant purpose between cases of these two classes. In each case the oral agreement,
if performed, will result in there being an enforceable contract where formerly
there was none. In the American Jurist[6] the matter is stated in these terms:

j 1 (1928) 26 F 2d 755
2 (1895) 162 Mass 566 at 569, 39 NE 277 at 278
3 (1909) 88 NE 333
4 (1906) 99 NYS 721
5 99 NYS 721 at 723
6 2nd Edn (1974), vol 72, p 568

'The general rule is that an oral agreement to reduce to writing a contract which is within the scope of the operation of the Statute of Frauds, or to sign an agreement which the Statute of Frauds requires to be in writing, is invalid and unenforceable. Neither promise is enforceable unless the statute is satisfied. In other words a parol agreement invalid under the statute is not aided by a further parol agreement to reduce the principal agreement to writing. To allow the enforcement of such an agreement would be tantamount to taking the main contract out of the statute, and as has been said, it is absurd to say that an oral promise in relation to certain subject matter is invalid, but that a promise that the party will thereafter bind himself with respect to the subject matter is valid. Such a construction would be a palpable evasion of the statute and let in all of the evils against which it is directed.'

This appears to deal with the matter on the basis of the general policy of the Statute of Frauds. I prefer, however, to base my decision in the present case on the view that the unwritten contract comes within the terms of s 40 of the Law of Property Act 1925 as a contract for a disposition of an interest in land.

We were referred, among other English authorities, to *Wood v Midgley*[1] where a purchaser, having promised to sign a written agreement on the following day, then refused to sign. A written receipt for a deposit paid by the purchaser was held to be an insufficient memorandum for the purposes of the Statute of Frauds. The plaintiff's bill contained no allegation to the effect that the purchaser's conduct was fraudulent. The defendants' demurrer to the plaintiff's bill was allowed. That case does not, in my judgment, assist us much in the present one. The plaintiff's action was for specific performance of the contract of sale, not for relief in respect of the oral promise to sign. In *Johnston v Boyes*[2], the defendants offered freehold land for sale under conditions providing that the highest bidder should be the purchaser. The plaintiff's husband, Johnston, bid on her behalf and the property was knocked down to him as the highest bidder. He thereupon tendered his own cheque in payment of the deposit. One of the defendants recognised him as a man who was impecunious and entirely dependent financially on his wife. On the vendor's instructions the auctioneer refused to accept the cheque or to permit Johnston to sign any agreement. The property was at once put up for resale and resold. The plaintiff sued for damages for breach of an alleged contract that the highest bidder at the auction should be the purchaser of the property. Cozens-Hardy J said[3]:

'A vendor who offers property for sale by auction on the terms of printed conditions can be made liable to a member of the public who accepts the offer if those conditions are violated: see *Warlow* v. *Harrison*[4] and the recent case of *Carlill* v. *Carbolic Smoke Ball Co.*[5] Nor do I think that the Statute of Frauds would afford any defence to such an action. The plaintiff is not suing on a contract to purchase: she is suing simply because her agent, in breach of the first and second conditions of sale, was not allowed to sign a contract which would have resulted in her becoming the purchaser of the land.'

The reference to Johnston not being allowed to sign a contract was, as Goff LJ has pointed out, inappropriate to anything which the learned judge had to decide. In my view his language must be read as referring elliptically to the refusal by the defendants through their agent, the auctioneer, to enter into a written contract of sale with Johnston as the agent of the plaintiff. It is true that the case was eventually

---

1   (1854) 5 De GM & G 41
2   [1899] 2 Ch 73
3   [1899] 2 Ch 73 at 77
4   (1859) 1 E & E 301, [1843-60] All ER Rep 620
5   [1893] 1 QB 256, [1891-4] All ER Rep 127

decided on the footing that the defendants could not be compelled to accept Johnston's cheque in payment of the deposit, but for my part I doubt whether it is correct
to say that the passage which I have cited from the learned judge's judgment was
obiter. Having decided in the passage which I have cited that there was an enforceable
contract, he went on to say[1]: 'It is, therefore, necessary to consider whether the
facts proved have established a breach of the contract alleged by the plaintiff.' He
went on to hold that the vendors were not bound to accept Johnston's cheque or to
wait for cash until the next day. They were accordingly under no obligation to sign
the contract and were not in breach of the contract sued on. Consequently I think
that the passage which I have cited is authority which tends to support the plaintiffs'
contention in the present case; but it does not appear to have been suggested to
Cozens-Hardy J in that case that the contract with which he was concerned might
have come within the Statute of Frauds as a contract for the transfer of an equitable
interest in land. He referred only to a contract to purchase land. Although he held
that the statute was not applicable to the contract there in question, he did not do so
on the ground on which I would hold that the contract sued on in the present case
does fall within s 40.
    In the course of the argument we were referred to a passage in the judgment of
Lord Denning MR, in *Tiverton Estates Ltd v Wearwell Ltd*[2], commenting on the earlier
decision of this court in *Law v Jones*[3]. Although this is not an occasion for an extended
discussion of the decisions in those two cases, *Law v Jones*[3] appears to have occasioned
so much misunderstanding that perhaps I may be permitted to make certain explanatory observations about it. I would emphasise, however, that these remarks
have no bearing on the decision of the present case. Contrary to what some statements about *Law v Jones*[3] appear to suggest, it was not a decision on the effect of the
words 'subject to contract'; nor, apart possibly from what I said in that case[4] which,
as I expressly stated, did not arise for decision, can I discover any statement in the
judgments in *Law v Jones*[3] on the topic of 'subject to contract' which was novel.
It is important to realise that there were two distinct sets of negotiations and two
bargains in that case. The first was for a sale at £6,500, which never came to anything
because the vendor resiled from it before it was put into writing. The second was for
a sale at £7,000 and was the subject of the letter of 17th March 1972, the bargain
having been made on 13th March 1972. The question for decision was whether that
letter, read in conjunction with documents linked to it by reference, afforded a
sufficient note or memorandum of the oral contract of 13th March to satisfy s 40
of the Law of Property Act 1925. It would be most presumptuous of me to suppose,
in the light of the judgments in *Tiverton Estates Ltd v Wearwell Ltd*[5], that I may not
have been mistaken in the view on this question which I expressed in *Law v Jones*[3], but
I have reread my judgment in that case most carefully in the light of those observations and I can find no reason for modifying my opinion in any respect. The
judgments in *Tiverton Estates Ltd v Wearwell Ltd*[5] rely strongly on *Buxton v Rust*[6] and
Thirkell v Cambi[7]. These were both cases in which a written document relied on to
satisfy s 17 of the Statute of Frauds denied liability but admitted the existence of a
contract. Documents of this character give rise, in my opinion, as I explained in
Law v Jones[3], to special considerations and do not establish that in every case a note
or memorandum to satisfy s 40 must acknowledge the existence of a contract. I
remain of the opinion that the 'offer cases' can only be fitted into the pattern of

---

1   [1899] 2 Ch 73 at 77
2   [1974] 1 All ER 209 at 216, [1975] Ch 146 at 159
3   [1973] 2 All ER 437, [1974] Ch 112
4   [1973] 2 All ER 437 at 446, [1974] Ch 112 at 126
5   [1974] 1 All ER 209, [1975] Ch 146
6   (1872) LR 7 Exch 279
7   [1919] 2 KB 590

authority if the section does not require the written note or memorandum to acknowledge expressly or by implication the existence of a contract. I am unable to understand how, outside the private world of the White Queen, a document written at a time when ex hypothesi no contract exists can acknowledge the existence of a contract made at a later date. With deference to the view expressed by Russell LJ in *Law v Jones*[1], the fact that a written offer is a continuing offer until withdrawn or accepted does not meet this point. I may perhaps add that I see no reason to dissent from what Lord Denning MR said in *Tiverton Estates Ltd v Wearwell Ltd*[2], but I do not regard that proposition as fitting the facts in *Law v Jones*[3].

Law v Jones[3] did not decide that a letter written 'subject to contract' or forming part of a correspondence conducted subject to a 'subject to contract' stipulation can constitute a note or memorandum of an oral agreement to which it relates sufficient to satisfy the Statute of Frauds, at any rate so long as the 'subject to contract' stipulation remains operative. What it did decide was that, if the parties subsequently enter into a new and distinct oral agreement, the facts may be such that the earlier letter may form part of a sufficient note or memorandum of the later oral agreement notwithstanding that it was 'subject to contract' in relation to the earlier bargain. It also, of course, decided the quite different point that a written note or memorandum to satisfy the statute need not acknowledge the existence of the contract, although it must record all its essential terms. In that respect *Law v Jones*[3] and *Tiverton Estates Ltd v Wearwell Ltd*[4] are undoubtedly in conflict.

To revert to the present case, for reasons which I have given, I am of the opinion that, whether the learned judge was right or mistaken in his view of the character and effect of the unwritten contract which is sued on, it falls within the operation of the Law of Property Act 1925, s 40. It is consequently necessary to consider the question of part performance.

The acts relied on as constituting part performance are those alleged in para 9 of the re-amended statement of claim. Having regard to the surrounding circumstances other than the unwritten contract, were these acts such as to suggest that it is more likely than not that they were done in pursuance of some contract? (*Steadman v Steadman*[5].) In my judgment they were not. I agree with Goff LJ in thinking that, if one ignores the unwritten contract, the natural conclusion to draw from the acts must be that they were done not in pursuance of a contract but in contemplation of making a contract.

For these reasons I agree that this appeal must fail. I do so with some regret, for it seems to me that this is another case of a kind which has become all too common recently, when property values have been very volatile, in which a vendor has taken advantage of s 40 in circumstances in which justice and probity should have induced the vendor to honour his bargain.

ORR LJ. I agree, also with some regrets, and for the reasons given by Goff and Buckley LJJ, that this appeal should be dismissed.

I would only add that I entirely agree with the observations made by Buckley LJ with reference to *Law v Jones*[3].

Hoffman QC for the defendants then addressed the court with leave of Buckley LJ: As your Lordships probably know, the defendants are the alter ego of the Crown Agents, and for reasons which your Lordships will appreciate, they may be somewhat sensitive about this sort of remark.

In the first place, my Lords, the defendants were selling as mortgagees and they

---

1   [1973] 2 All ER 437 at 440, [1974] Ch 112 at 119, 120
2   [1974] 1 All ER 209 at 218, [1975] Ch 146 at 160
3   [1973] 2 All ER 437, [1974] Ch 112
4   [1974] 1 All ER 209, [1975] Ch 146
5   [1974] 2 All ER 977, [1976] AC 536

have, as your Lordships will have seen, entered into contract negotiations to sell at
a the price in the draft contract. On the evening before exchange was due to take place,
the defendants were told by the mortgagors that the mortgagors had found a purchaser for a substantially increased price, and in fact had entered into a contract
themselves to sell to that purchaser at the increased price. The defendants were
told that if they proceeded with the sale to the plaintiffs at that price they would be
held liable for breach of their duty as mortgagees, in accordance with *Cuckmere Brick*
b *Co Ltd v Mutual Finance Co Ltd*[1], in failing to take proper care to secure the best price.
In those circumstances, my Lords, the defendants felt that they could not go ahead
with the transaction with the plaintiffs.

Of course, before your Lordships the allegations which were made in the statement
of claim as to the promises which were made etc have had to be accepted; that is
the hypothesis on which we have proceeded, and so we have taken the procedural
c step of seeking to strike out from the statement of claim that which may disclose a
cause of action, thereby short-circuiting the trial. Your Lordships have found that
step to be justified, but none of those allegations has been investigated.

Appeal dismissed.

Solicitors: *Kaufmann, Kramer & Shebson* (for the plaintiffs); *Clifford-Turner* (for the
d defendants).

J H Fazan Esq Barrister.

Re Bucks Constabulary Widows' and Orphans'
e # Fund Friendly Society
Thompson v Holdsworth and others

CHANCERY DIVISION
MEGARRY V-C
f 26th, 27th APRIL 1977

Friendly society – Dissolution – Division or appropriation of funds – Division or appro-
priation otherwise than to effect objects of society – Instrument of dissolution providing for
division or appropriation of funds among bodies having no claim by law on society's funds –
Adequate provision made for satisfying members' claims – Whether disposal of society's
funds to body or person having no claim by law on funds permitted – Friendly Societies Act
g *1896, s 79(4).*

The objects of a registered friendly society ('the society') were the relief of widows
and orphans of deceased members of the Bucks Constabulary, insurance of moneys
to be paid on the death of a member of that constabulary and the relief of members
of the constabulary during sickness and infirmity. In April 1968 the Bucks Constabu-
h lary was amalgamated with other constabularies to form the Thames Valley Constabulary. In October 1968 the society resolved that it should be wound up, that
annuities should be purchased for the beneficiaries of the society and that assets of the
society should be transferred to the benevolent fund of the Thames Valley Constabulary ('the Thames Valley fund') to purchase for beneficiaries of the society the right
of entry into the Thames Valley fund. Accordingly in December 1968 an instrument
i of dissolution was sent to members of the society which provided, by para 5, that after
j payment of debts and the expenses of dissolution, the funds and property of the
society were to be applied in the purchase of the annuities, the grant of £40,000 to the
Thames Valley fund (para 5(2)), and the donation of the balance of the society's
assets to the Bucks funds, a fund for the benefit of serving members of the former

_____

1 [1971] 2 All ER 633, [1971] Ch 949

Bucks Constabulary (para 5(3)). The instrument of dissolution was signed by a sufficient majority of the members of the society and the society was dissolved on 14th October 1969. The annuities were purchased and £40,000 was paid to the Thames Valley fund. The balance of the society's funds, amounting to some £30,000, remained in the hands of the sole trustee of the society. He took out a summons to determine whether by virtue of s 79(4)[a] of the Friendly Societies Act 1896 and para 5(2) and (3) of the instrument of dissolution he was authorised to dispose of the balance to the Thames Valley fund and the Bucks fund. The trustees of those funds contended that as adequate provision had been made for members of the society by the purchase of the annuities, s 79(4) allowed a disposition of the balance of the society's funds to be made to the Thames Valley fund and the Bucks fund even though they were bodies which were not entitled under the general law to benefit from the society's funds.

Held – Where on the dissolution of a registered friendly society the claims of those entitled to benefit from the funds of the society had been adequately satisfied, the 'division or appropriation' of the society's funds otherwise than for the purpose of effecting the objects of the society authorised by s 79(4) of the 1896 Act to be made by the instrument of dissolution was limited to provision for division or appropriation of the funds among those who were entitled by law to claim on the funds, and s 79(4) did not authorise a disposition of the funds to those who were not so entitled. Since, on the evidence, neither the Thames Valley fund nor the Bucks fund had any claim on the society's funds, the division or appropriation of the funds among them which the instruments of dissolution purported to authorise was not authorised by s 79(4), and the summons would be answered accordingly (see p 575 c and e and g to j, post).

Notes
For the dissolution of friendly societies, see 19 Halsbury's Laws (4th Edn) paras 303-313.
For the Friendly Societies Act 1896, s 79, see 14 Halsbury's Statutes (3rd Edn) 306.
The Friendly Societies Act 1896, except s 22, and ss 62 and 64 to 67 in certain respects, was repealed by the Friendly Societies Act 1974, a consolidating measure. Section 79 of the 1896 Act is replaced by s 94 of the 1974 Act.

Summons
The plaintiff, George William Thompson, the trustee of the Bucks Constabulary Widows' and Orphans' Fund Friendly Society ('the society') took out a summons dated 14th June 1973 for the court's determination of certain questions, question 1 of which was whether by virtue of the execution by members of the society of instruments of dissolution and by virtue of the Friendly Societies Act 1896 the plaintiff as trustee of the society was effectively authorised to dispose of the funds and property of the society in accordance with para 5 of the said instruments of dissolution. The defendants to the summons were (1) David Holdsworth, the trustee of the Thames Valley Constabulary Benevolent Fund, (2) George Hugh Whitton Wilkinson, a trustee of the Bucks Constabulary Benevolent Fund, (3) Hywel Wyn Edwards and (4) the Treasury Solicitor. The facts are set out in the judgment of Megarry V-C.

Robert Reid for the plaintiff.
Kenneth J Farrow for the first defendant.
Miss Elizabeth Appleby for the second defendant.
Richard McCombe for the third defendant.
John Knox for the fourth defendant.

MEGARRY V-C. The originating summons before me asks a number of questions. It is common ground, however, that at this stage it is desirable I that

___
a Section 79(4) is set out at p 514 e f, post

should answer only the first of these. The summons concerns the Bucks Constabulary Widows' and Orphans' Fund Friendly Society, a society registered under the Friendly Societies Act 1896. I shall call it 'the society'. The objects of the society are stated in r 3 of the society's rules. This reads as follows:

> 'Objects. 3. The object of the fund shall be to provide by the voluntary contributions of the members for the following purposes—(1) The relief of widows and orphans of deceased members. (2) Insuring money to be paid on the death of a member. (3) The relief of members during sickness or infirmity.'

On 1st April 1968 the Bucks Constabulary was amalgamated with a number of other constabularies to form the Thames Valley Constabulary; and on 31st October 1968 the final meeting of the society was held. It was resolved to wind up the society. Subscriptions were to cease to be payable after 31st December 1968, benefits were to continue to be paid until the dissolution of the society took effect, annuities were to be purchased for the present beneficiaries, and assets were to be transferred to the Thames Valley Constabulary Benevolent Fund which would purchase the right of entry for all present and future beneficiaries of the society. I shall call that fund 'the Thames Valley fund'.

In December 1968 a letter setting out the gist of these resolutions was sent to every member of the society. The letter stated that about £35,000 would be required for the purchase of annuities, and another £40,000 for the purchase of entry into the Thames Valley fund. That would leave some £12,000, and this, it was proposed, would be transferred to the Bucks Constabulary Benevolent Fund (which I shall call 'the Bucks fund') for the benefit of serving members of the former Bucks Constabulary. An 'Instrument of Dissolution' accompanied the letter. This provided for the dissolution of the society, and contained a paragraph, para 5, which is the subject of the dispute before me. This runs as follows:

> '5. The funds and property of the Society shall be appropriated and divided in the following manner after the payment of all debts and the expenses of dissolution:—1) Purchase of annuities of 16/-d per week for all widows and 2/-d per week for children below the age of 16 years. 2) Grant to the Thames Valley Constabulary Benevolent Fund of the sum of £40,000. 3) The balance remaining after paying all the expenses to be donated to the Bucks Constabulary Benevolent Fund.'

No question arises on sub-para (1) of this, but the efficacy of sub-paras (2) and (3) is in issue.

It was accepted that the instruments of dissolution were duly signed and returned by a sufficient majority of the members of the society to satisfy s 78(1)(c) of the Friendly Societies Act 1896: and the Registrar of Friendly Societies caused a notice of dissolution of the society to be advertised in the London Gazette on 14th October 1969. There was no challenge to this, and accordingly, by virtue of s 79(6) of the 1896 Act, the society was legally dissolved from that date. All the annuities have been purchased, the £40,000 has been paid to the Thames Valley fund, and the balance of the funds of the defunct society remain in the hands of the sole trustee of that society. They are worth some £30,000 at present. The summons was taken out by that trustee as plaintiff.

Put shortly, question 1 in the summons is whether by virtue of the 1896 Act and the execution of the instruments of dissolution the plaintiff was effectively authorised to dispose of the funds and property of the society in accordance with para 5 of the instruments of dissolution. Counsel who appeared on behalf of the first defendant, the trustee of the Thames Valley fund, and on behalf of the second defendant, a trustee of the Bucks fund, both said that the right answer to question 1 of the summons was 'Yes'. On the other hand, counsel who appeared on behalf of the third defendant, a person claiming to be beneficially interested in the funds and property

of the society, said that the answer was 'No, except as to para 5(1), relating to the
purchase of the annuities'. Counsel who appeared for the Treasury Solicitor and who
was interested in the cause of bona vacantia said that he was instructed not to oppose
the contention of counsel for the first and second defendants, and to leave this to
the court; but he helpfully made certain submissions designed to avert the right
decision being supported by wrong reasons. It was common ground that the point
was devoid of authority.

The arguments in the main centered on s 79(4) of the 1896 Act. Section 78(1) provides for the methods whereby a registered friendly society may be dissolved. One
method is in accordance with the rules, another is by instrument of dissolution,
and the third is by an award of the registrar. In the present case the only rule of
the society on the point, r 31, merely echoes the statutory provisions as to an instrument of dissolution. Section 79 of the 1896 Act then provides in detail for instruments of dissolution, and s 80 similarly provides in detail for dissolution by award.
I must read parts of s 79. This begins as follows:

> 'When a registered society or branch is terminated by an instrument of dis-
> solution:—(1) the instrument shall set forth—(a) the liabilities and assets of the
> society or branch in detail; and (b) the number of members and the nature of
> their interests in the society or branch; and (c) the claims of creditors (if any),
> and the provision to be made for their payment; and (d) the intended appro-
> priation or division of the funds and property of the society or branch, unless the
> appropriation or division is stated in the instrument of dissolution to be left to
> the award of the chief registrar.'

I can pass over sub-ss (2) and (3), and then there is sub-s (4) of s 79:

> 'The instrument shall not in the case of a registered friendly society or branch
> direct or contain any provision for a division or appropriation of the funds of
> the society or branch, or any part thereof, otherwise than for the purpose of
> carrying into effect the objects of the society or branch as declared in the rules
> thereof, unless the claim of every member or person claiming any relief, annuity,
> or other benefit from the funds thereof is first duly satisfied, or adequate
> provisions are made for satisfying those claims.'

I do not think I need read the remaining subsections.

The main thrust of the arguments has been on the meaning of the words 'division
or appropriation' in sub-s (4). Are they wide enough to allow a disposition of the funds
to be made to some extraneous body or person, or are they to be construed narrowly
so as merely to relate to the machinery which gives effect to existing rights in the
funds? In short, are the words dispositive, permitting the instrument to authorise a
disposition, or are they merely administrative? A subsidiary question is whether the
subsection is purely restrictive or negative in its effect, or whether it confers any
positive authority. I propose to consider the subsection by stages.

I shall take the latter point first. It seems to me that the subsection must be intended to have some positive operation. Section 79(1)(d) requires the instrument
of dissolution to 'set forth . . . the intended appropriation or division of the
funds', but it confers no positive authority to make any appropriation or division.
Subsection (4), it is true, is at the outset framed in the language of prohibition ('the
instrument shall not . . .'), but then it concludes with the 'unless' clause. To say
that a thing shall not be done unless a condition is satisfied seems to me to carry
with it the implication that if the condition is satisfied then there is authority to do
the thing. That, I think, is to some extent supported by the absence of any other
provision which could be treated as conferring authority to make the appropriation
or division which s 79(1)(d) requires to be stated as being the intention. In the present
case, the 'unless' clause in s 79(4) is admittedly satisfied by the provisions for annuities
and so on that have been made. On that footing, s 79(4) authorises a division or

appropriation for some purpose other than that of carrying into effect the objects of
a the society. As ex hypothesi the instrument of dissolution is bringing the society to
an end, it is natural enough for the statute to authorise it to provide for a division
or appropriation for some purpose other than carrying the objects of the society
into effect.

What, then, is the ambit of the phrase 'division or appropriation', construed in its
context? The word 'division' calls for an answer to the question 'among whom?',
b just as the word 'appropriation' invites the question 'to whom?' I appreciate that,
as counsel for the second defendant pointed out, dictionaries show that the verb
'to appropriate' has meanings such as 'to make over to any one as his own', and that
the noun 'appropriation' has as one of its meanings 'taking to one's own use'. Nevertheless, I have to construe the word in its context; and one feature of this is that
'appropriation' is linked to 'division'. As a phrase, 'division or appropriation' seems
c to me to be directed more to the parcelling out of the property in question among
those who have some claim to it than to laying down that persons who previously
had no claim to it shall be given a right to it.

That view is, I think, reinforced by s 80(3). That subsection is dealing (inter alia)
with the case where the funds of a society are insufficient to meet the existing claims
on them. In such a case, the registrar may award that the society be dissolved and its
d affairs wound up; and he is to direct in what manner the assets of the society 'shall be
divided or appropriated'. In such a case it is inconceivable that Parliament meant to
give the registrar a discretion to direct the assets to be distributed to anyone except
those who had a claim on them. In other words, as between those who have such a
claim the registrar is to direct what the division or appropriation is to be: it is not
that the division or appropriation is to determine who is to have a claim but that
e as between those who already have claims the division or appropriation is to decide
who will get what.

When one comes back to s 79(4), I think that the words 'division or appropriation'
are used in a similar sense. Counsel for the Treasury Solicitor helpfully pointed out
that a friendly society might have charitable objects; it might be analogous to a
members' club; or it might be in neither category. If when it was dissolved there
f were surplus funds, then in the first case questions of cy-près application would arise;
in the second, the members would have a claim to the surplus; and in the third,
subject to any resulting trust for identifiable donors, questions of bona vacantia
would arise. Furthermore, the rules might make provision for the destination of the
surplus funds. In short, the question of the persons entitled was one that fell to be
determined according to the general law. Once the claim of all those who were en-
g titled to any benefit had been satisfied, s 79(4) authorises making provision for a
division or appropriation among those entitled under the general law even though
this would not be carrying into effect the objects of the society: but it does not
authorise giving the property to those who are not entitled to it under the general law.

In their essentials I think that these submissions are right. As I have said, there
was no challenge to the validity of para 5(1) of the instrument of dissolution, relating
h to the purchase of annuities; but both sub-paras (2) and (3) were challenged. As
the evidence stands, I do not see how I can say that these sub-paragraphs operated
merely as a division or appropriation among those with rights under the general
law. Accordingly, subject to anything that may be said on the form of the order,
I propose to answer question 1 in the summons by saying 'No, apart from sub-
para (1) thereof.'

j *Answer accordingly.*

Solicitors: *Sharpe, Pritchard & Co*, agents for *Boyle & Ormerod*, Aylesbury (for the
plaintiff and the second and third defendants); *Russell, Jones & Walker* (for the first
defendant); *Treasury Solicitor.*

Hazel Hartman Barrister.

Massey v Crown Life Insurance Co

COURT OF APPEAL, CIVIL DIVISION

LORD DENNING MR, LAWTON AND EVELEIGH LJJ

2nd, 3rd, 4th NOVEMBER 1977

Unfair dismissal – Excluded classes of employment – Employment under contract for services – Employer and manager agreeing for tax purposes that manager to be self-employed in the future – Inland Revenue accepting arrangement – Manager operating under firm name rather than own name – Manager continuing to perform same duties as before – Manager dismissed and bringing claim for unfair dismissal – Whether manager an individual who has entered into or worked under a contract of employment – Whether manager an' employee' – Trade Union and Labour Relations Act 1974, s 30(1), Sch 1, para 4(1).

Master and servant – Contract of service – Distinction between contract of service and contract for services – Declaration of parties – Intention of employer and manager to change manager's status to self-employed for tax purposes – Genuine agreement with explicit terms – Whether parties' agreement conclusive in determining status of manager.

The appellant was employed as a branch manager by the respondents, an insurance company, from 1971 until 1973 under two contracts, under one of which he was treated as an employee and under the other as a general agent. Under his contract as an employee the appellant was paid wages by the respondents from which PAYE tax and contributions to the respondents' pension scheme were deducted, and he received a memorandum under the Contracts of Employment Act 1963. Under the general agency contract the appellant was a freelance agent paid on commission only and free to work for other insurance brokers. In 1973 the appellant, who wished to be taxed as a self-employed person, approached the respondents with a view to coming to a new arrangement with them. The respondents agreed and the parties entered into a new agreement whereby the appellant called himself 'John L Massey and Associates', a name which he registered under the Registration of Business Names Act 1916. Under the new agreement John L Massey and Associates were appointed manager of the appellant's branch, the appellant was repaid his contributions from the respondents' pension fund, and was thereafter paid by the respondents without tax or other deductions being made. The appellant arranged with the Inland Revenue to be treated as a self-employed person for tax purposes. Under the agreement John L Massey and Associates were allowed to employ other persons in the course of their work, but the appellant's duties vis-à-vis the respondents remained almost identical to his previous duties. In 1975 the appellant was dismissed by the respondents with one month's notice. The appellant made a complaint to an industrial tribunal of unfair dismissal. The tribunal considered, as a preliminary issue, whether the appellant was entitled to make a claim for unfair dismissal under the Trade Union and Labour Relations Act 1974, para 4 of Sch 1 to which extended the right not to be unfairly dismissed only to an 'employee', which by s 30(1)[a] was defined as 'an individual who has entered into or [has worked under] a contract of employment'. A contract of employment was further defined as a 'contract of service . . . whether it is express or implied and (if it is express) whether it is oral or in writing'. The tribunal held that the work which the appellant performed for the respondents was not performed under a contract of employment. The appellant appealed to the Employment Appeal Tribunal which dismissed his appeal. He appealed to the Court of Appeal contending that his relationship with the respondents had remained throughout that of employer and employee regardless of what he chose to call himself or the way in which he was assessed to tax.

---

a Section 30(1), so far as material, is set out at p 578 c, post

Held – The appellant could not say that for the purpose of claiming tax advantages he was not an employee and then say that for the purpose of claiming compensation for unfair dismissal he was an employee. The 1973 agreement was a genuine transaction which had been aimed to effect, and did in fact effect, a change in the appellant's status from that of an employee to that of a self-employed person, and he was not therefore an 'employee' within the meaning of s 30 of the 1974 Act and could not bring a claim for unfair dismissal under the Act. Accordingly the appeal would be dismissed (see p 580 *b c* and *g h*, p 581 *a* and *c* to *e*, p 582 *f* to *j* and p 583 *a*, post).

Ferguson v John Dawson & Partners (Contractors) Ltd [1976] 3 All ER 817 distinguished.

Notes

For the right of an employee not to be unfairly dismissed, see 16 Halsbury's Laws (4th Edn) para 615.

For the distinction between a contract of service and a contract for services, see ibid para 501.

For the Trade Union and Labour Relations Act 1974, s 30(1), Sch 1, para 4, see 44 Halsbury's Statutes (3rd Edn) 1781, 1787.

Cases referred to in judgments

Alexander v Rayson [1936] 1 KB 169, [1935] All ER Rep 185, 105 LJKB 148, 154 LT 205, CA.

Construction Industry Training Board v Labour Force Ltd [1970] 3 All ER 220, 5 ITR 290, DC, Digest (Cont Vol C) 685, 226a.

Davis v New England College of Arundel [1977] ICR 6, EAT.

Ferguson v John Dawson & Partners (Contractors) Ltd [1976] 3 All ER 817, [1976] 1 WLR 1213, [1976] 2 Lloyd's Rep 669, CA.

Global Plant Ltd v Secretary of State for Social Services [1971] 3 All ER 385, [1972] 1 QB 139, [1971] 3 WLR 269, Digest (Cont Vol D) 707, 6c.

Graham (Maurice) Ltd v Brunswick (1974) 16 KIR 158, DC.

Inland Revenue Comrs v Duke of Westminster [1936] AC 1, [1935] All ER Rep 259, 104 LJKB 383, 153 LT 223, sub nom *Westminster (Duke) v Inland Revenue Comrs* 19 Tax Cas 490, HL, 28(1) Digest (Reissue) 507, 1845.

Ready Mixed Concrete (South East) Ltd v Minister of Pensions and National Insurance [1968] 1 All ER 433, [1968] 2 QB 497, [1968] 2 WLR 775, Digest (Cont Vol C) 722, 6b.

Stevenson Jordon and Harrison Ltd v MacDonald and Evans [1952] 1 TLR 101, 69 RPC 10, CA, 28(2) Digest (Reissue) 1086, 906.

Cases also cited

Challinor v Taylor [1972] ICR 129, 116 Sol Jo 141.

Comrs of Customs and Excise v Pools Finance (1937) Ltd [1952] 1 All ER 775, CA.

Evenden v Guildford City Association Football Club Ltd [1975] 3 All ER 269, [1975] QB 917, CA.

Hammett v Livingstone Control Ltd (1970) 5 ITR 136.

Market Investigations Ltd v Minister of Social Security [1968] 3 All ER 732, [1969] 2 QB 173.

Morren v Swinton and Pendlebury Borough Council [1965] 2 All ER 349, [1965] 1 WLR 576, DC.

Napier v National Business Agency Ltd [1951] 2 All ER 264, 44 R & IT 413, CA.

Watling v William Bird & Son Contractors Ltd (1976) 11 ITR 70.

Appeal

This was an appeal by John Linnell Massey against a decision of the Employment Appeal Tribunal (Kilner Brown J, Mr A C Blyghton and Mr A J Nicol) dated 30th November 1976, dismissing his appeal against a decision of an industrial tribunal (chairman C H A Lewes) whereby the tribunal determined, on a preliminary issue, that the appellant could not pursue a claim for unfair dismissal against the respondents,

Crown Life Insurance Co, because he was not 'employed' by them at the date of his
dismissal. The facts are set out in the judgment of Lord Denning MR.   a

Alistair Sharp for the appellant.
Anthony Boswood for the respondents.

LORD DENNING MR. John Massey was the manager of the Ilford branch of the
Crown Life Insurance Co of Canada. He was employed there from 1971 until 1975.   b
On 17th November 1975 the company gave him one month's notice to terminate his
agreement. He claims that he was unfairly dismissed and is entitled to compensation
under the Trade Union and Labour Relations Act 1974.

A man can only claim compensation for unfair dismissal if he is an employee employed
under a contract of service. That appears from s 30(1) of the Act. It defines an 'employee' as
'an individual who has entered into or [has worked under] a contract of employment   c
. . .'; and it defines 'contract of employment' as 'a contract of service or of apprenticeship . . .' So it is essential that the person concerned should be an 'employee'
under 'a contract of service'.

For the last 100 years the law has drawn a distinction between a 'contract of service'
on the one hand and a 'contract for services' on the other; or, as it is sometimes put,   d
between a master and servant relationship on the one hand, and between an employer and an independent contractor on the other. The distinction is important in
the common law. A master is liable for all the wrongdoings of his servant in the
course of his employment; but an employer is not liable for all the wrongdoings of
an independent contractor. The distinction has also very important consequences
under the statute law. In many trades and occupations, the employer is liable to   e
pay taxes and insurance contributions and so forth in respect of servants who are
employed under contracts of service; but not for independent contractors who are
employed under contracts for services.

I will not today attempt to formulate the distinction except to repeat what I said in
Stevenson Jordan and Harrison Ltd v MacDonald and Evans[1]:

> 'It is often easy to recognize a contract of service when you see it, but difficult   f
> to say wherein the difference lies. A ship's master, a chauffeur, and a reporter
> on the staff of a newspaper are all employed under a contract of service; but a
> ship's pilot, a taxi-man, and a newspaper contributor are employed under a
> contract for services.'

In recent years the distinction has often come before the courts in one context or   g
another. Modern cases start with *Ready Mixed Concrete (South East) Ltd v Minister of
Pensions and National Insurance*[2] and go on to *Construction Industry Training Board v
Labour Force Ltd*[3]; then *Global Plant Ltd v Secretary of State for Social Services*[4] on to
Maurice Graham Ltd v Brunswick[5]; then *Ferguson v John Dawson & Partners (Contractors)
Ltd*[6], and finally *Davis v New England College of Arundel*[7]. So there is the distinction
running through the common law and running through the statute law, and here we   h
have it again. What was the position of Mr Massey? He was the manager of the
Ilford branch of the insurance company. For a couple of years, from 1971 to 1973,
the company treated him as though he were a servant. They gave him a memorandum under the Contracts of Employment Act 1963. They paid him wages; and,

1 (1952) 1 TLR 101 at 111, per Denning LJ
2 [1968] 1 All ER 433, [1968] 2 QB 497
3 [1970] 3 All ER 220
4 [1971] 3 All ER 385, [1972] 1 QB 139
5 (1974) 16 KIR 158
6 [1976] 3 All ER 817, [1976] 1 WLR 1213
7 [1977] ICR 6

before paying him, they deducted the tax, they deducted the stamp, and they deduc-
a ted graduated pension contributions from the amount they paid him. Further, they
had a pension scheme of their own and he had to make contributions towards his
pension. Being regarded as a servant, he was taxed for his income tax payments under
Sch E.

But then in 1973 Mr Massey went to his accountant who advised him to change his
relationship with his employers. The accountant said: 'I think you would be much
b better off if you so arranged your affairs as to be self-employed instead of being a
servant. Then you will come under Sch D instead of Sch E.' That is what was proposed. Instead of wages subject to deductions, the company would pay him the full
amount each week but they would not deduct tax or national insurance contributions
or anything like that. He would get the full amount. It would be for him to account
for tax to the Inland Revenue under Sch D.

c He went to his employers, the Crown Life Insurance Co, and told them: 'I have
been advised by my accountants to change over to Sch D. Will you agree?' They said:
'Oh, yes; we are agreeable.' So it was put through. They did it in this way. Instead
of calling him 'Mr John L Massey', he was called 'John L Massey and Associates'.
It was really just the same man under another name. He registered that new name
under the Registration of Business Names Act 1916. With that new name he entered
d into a new agreement with the Crown Life. So far as his duties were concerned, it
was in almost identical terms to the previous agreement. As a result of that new
agreement, he said he was no longer a servant, he was an independent contractor.
He was therefore liable to be taxed under Sch D. The position was placed before the
Inland Revenue, and the Inland Revenue seem to have thought it was all right.

In order to get it regularised, the company wrote a letter to the inspector of taxes.
e It said:

> 'Re: J. L. Massey ... I am enclosing a Form P.45 [that is the one you have for
> employees] in respect of the above named who is the Manager of our Ilford
> Division and who resigned from his Agreement on the 1st September 1973.
> I would advise you that Mr. Massey has now formed a Company called John L.
> Massey and Associates, and they have been appointed Manager of our Ilford
f > Division with effect from the 2nd September 1973. All future remuneration will
> be paid to John L. Massey and Associates, and in view of the fact that they are a
> Company no tax deductions will be made by us. If there is any further infor-
> mation you require, please do not hesitate to contact me.'

That letter was not accurate. Mr Massey had not formed a company. He was just
g himself calling himself by a new name. But at any rate the company let the tax
people see the two agreements. After seeing them, the tax people were quite content
that Mr Massey should change over to a Sch D basis. The insurance company paid
him the gross amount without any deductions thereafter. In consequence he himself
would be liable under Sch D for tax on the gross amount, and he would have to pay
tax under that schedule. So the accounts were conducted from 1973 to 1975.

h Then in November 1975 Mr Massey was dismissed. Thereafter he said: 'I want to
claim for unfair dismissal.'

A claim for unfair dismissal was quite admissible if he was employed by the company under a contract of service, but not if he was employed under a contract for
services. So here he was claiming as a servant whereas, for the last two years, he had
been paid on the basis that he was an independent contractor.

j The law, as I see it, is this: if the true relationship of the parties is that of master and
servant under a contract of service, the parties cannot alter the truth of that relationship by putting a different label on it. If they should put a different label on it,
and use it as a dishonest device to deceive the Inland Revenue, I should have thought
it was illegal and could not be enforced by either party and they could not get any
advantage out of it, at any rate not in any case where they had to rely on it as the

basis of a claim: see *Alexander v Rayson*[1]. An arrangement between two parties to put forward a dishonest description of their relationship so as to deceive the Inland Revenue would clearly be illegal and unenforceable. On the other hand, if their relationship is ambiguous and is capable of being one or the other, then the parties can remove that ambiguity, by the very agreement itself which they make with one another. The agreement itself then becomes the best material from which to gather the true legal relationship between them. This is clearly seen by referring back to the case of *Inland Revenue Comrs v Duke of Westminster*[2]. The Duke had a gardener and paid him for his work a weekly sum. But, in order to avoid tax, his solicitors drew up a deed in which it was said that his earnings were not really wages, but were an annual payment payable by weekly instalments. The House of Lords held that, to find out what the true relationship was and what the true nature of these payments were, you had to look at the deed. Lord Tomlin said[3]: 'Every man is entitled, if he can, to order his affairs so that the tax attaching under the appropriate Acts is less than it is otherwise would be.' The gardener did the same work as before but the legal relationship was changed by th_ _'ed drawn up by the solicitors.

Likewise in this present case Mr Massey, as the tribunal found, worked under the new agreement in 1973 exactly as he worked under the previous agreement. The practical difference, they said, was that Mr Massey ceased to be a member of the company's pension scheme, and the pension contributions he had made under the previous agreement were returned to him. But otherwise everything went on just the same as before.

It seems to me on the authorities that, when it is a situation which is in doubt or which is ambiguous, so that it can be brought under one relationship or the other, it is open to the parties by agreement to stipulate what the legal situation between them shall be. That was said in *Ready Mixed Concrete (South East) Ltd v Minister of Pensions and National Insurance*[4] in 1968 by MacKenna J. He said[5]:

'If it were doubtful what rights and duties the parties wished to provide for, a declaration of this kind might help in resolving the doubt and fixing them in the sense required to give effect to that intention.'

So the way in which they draw up their agreement and express it may be a very important factor in defining what the true relation was between them. If they declare that he is self-employed, that may be decisive.

Coming back to this case, for myself I have considerable doubt whether Mr Massey was really a servant from 1971 to 1973. It looks to me much more as if he was even in that time a commission agent. He could take on other work. He did in fact work for another insurance broker. He was paid on commission. He received a minimum sum but over and above that he was paid on commission as many commission agents are. So I think it is very doubtful whether he was under a contract of service from 1971 to 1973. But I am perfectly clear that afterwards in 1973, when this agreement was drawn up and recast, although the same work was done under it, the relation was no longer a master and servant relationship. It was an employer and independent contractor relationship. The change to 'John L Massey and Associates' was an unnecessary complication. It is significant that the tribunal found that both sides agreed that the agreement was, and was intended to be, a genuine transaction and not something which was done solely for the purposes of deceiving the inspector of taxes. They said: 'Had we thought otherwise, we would have held the agreement to be tainted with illegality with the consequence that it would have been void.'

---

1   [1936] 1 KB 169, [1935] All ER Rep 185
2   [1936] AC 1, [1935] All ER Rep 259
3   [1936] AC 1 at 19, [1935] All ER Rep 259 at 267
4   [1968] 1 All ER 433, [1968] 2 QB 497
5   [1968] 2 QB 497 at 513

It seems to me that those findings of the industrial tribunal were well-justified in
a the circumstances of this case. Mr Massey was not an employee. He was not employed under a contract of service so as to be able to avail himself of the unfair
dismissal provisions in the 1974 Act.

I would only say a word about the recent case of *Ferguson v John Dawson & Partners
(Contractors) Ltd*[1]. That case turned on its facts. Boreham J held that the real relationship of the parties was that of master and servant and that they had put the wrong
b label on it be regarding him as working on 'the lump'. The majority of this court
accepted that view. But Lawton LJ[2] thought that the partners had deliberately
put the right label on their relationship. The man was on 'the lump'. He had had all
the benefits of it by avoiding tax. It was contrary to public policy that, when he had
had an accident, he could throw over that relationship and claim that he was only
a servant.

c   In most of these cases, I expect that it will be found that the parties do deliberately
agree for the man to be 'self-employed' or 'on the lump'. It is done especially so as to
obtain the tax benefits. When such an agreement is made, it affords strong evidence
that that is the real relationship. If it is so found, the man must accept it. He cannot
afterwards assert that he was only a servant.

In the present case there is a perfectly genuine agreement entered into at the
d instance of Mr Massey on the footing that he is 'self-employed'. He gets the benefit of
it by avoiding tax deductions and getting his pension contributions returned. I do
not see that he can come along afterwards and say it is something else in order to
claim that he has been unfairly dismissed. Having made his bed as being 'self-employed', he must lie on it. He is not under a contract of service.

I agree entirely with the industrial tribunal and with the Employment Appeal
e Tribunal that he does not qualify to claim for unfair dismissal in this case, and I
would dismiss the appeal.

LAWTON LJ. In the administration of justice the union of fairness, common sense
and the law is a highly desirable objective. If the law allows a man to claim that he is
a self-employed person in order to obtain tax advantages for himself and then allows
f him to deny that he is a self-employed person so that he can claim compensation,
then in my judgment the union between fairness, common sense and the law is
strained almost to breaking point. The appellant in this case is asking this court to
adjudge that he is entitled to make claims with two different voices. The problem,
it seems to me, is this: what was the status of the appellant at the material time in
November 1975? At that time, for his own purposes, he had been claiming for over
g two years that he was a self-employed person and, if he was such, he could not claim
compensation for unfair dismissal. The problem turns in my judgment on the
surrounding facts and the terms of the contract.

I will start with the surrounding facts. In 1971 the appellant came into a business
relationship with the respondents, a large life insurance office. He entered into two
contracts in June 1971. The first appointed him to be manager. From then until the
h summer of 1973 the respondents treated him under that contract as an employee.
But on the same day as he entered into a contract to be manager, he entered into
another contract with the respondents to be a general agent. Clause 19 of that contract relating to general agency contains this provision: 'Nothing contained herein
shall be construed to create the relationship of employer and employee between the
Company and the General Agent.' Counsel for the respondents has told us, and it is
j almost certainly accurate and I would accept it as such, that in the world of insurance
it is very common indeed to have freelance agents. The contract relating to general
agency clearly made the appellant a freelance agent. The consequence of these two

---

1   [1976] 3 All ER 817, [1976] 1 WLR 1213
2   [1976] 3 All ER 817 at 828, [1976] 1 WLR 1213 at 1226

contracts running at the same time was that the appellant was wearing two hats, one as an employee and the other as a self-employed person. I can readily understand that by the summer of 1973 he felt that is was inconvenient for him to wear two hats, and somebody (maybe those with whom he worked or his accountant alerted) him to the advantages of wearing only one hat, namely that of being a self-employed person.

The fact that he had been wearing two hats for two years indicates to me that there was some ambiguity about his position with the respondents, and he was entitled, in my judgment, in the summer of 1973 to get that ambiguity cleared up. He did so, and the evidence shows that it was he who approached the respondents to be allowed to wear only one hat. They agreed that after the summer of 1973 he should only wear one hat. In order to ensure that he did wear only one hat, both he and the respondents entered into a new written agreement. It contains a large number of terms and, as counsel for the respondents pointed out to us, some of those terms (for example, the one which would have allowed his business of John L Massey and Associates to employ other persons in the course of his work as proprietor of the company) were fundamentally inconsistent with his being after the summer of 1973 merely an employee.

It is the existence of that written contract with its detailed terms which, in my judgment, distinguishes this case from *Ferguson v John Dawson & Partners (Contractors) Ltd*[1]. It is relevant perhaps to point out that in *Ferguson v John Dawson & Partners (Contractors) Ltd*[1] there was very little evidence indeed as to what the contract was. Such evidence as there was came from the defendants' foreman. According to the report of that case[2] all that happened was this. The foreman said: 'I did inform him that there were no cards, we were purely working as a lump labour force'; and, as Megaw LJ in his judgment pointed out, that being the situation, the court had to imply terms, and the terms which had to be implied were consistent solely with the relationship of master and servant. This case is entirely different. There are explicit terms; and it is interesting to note once again that, contemporaneously with the new agreement, there was executed an agreement which appointed the appellant to be general agent.

It clearly established that the parties cannot change a status merely by putting a new label on it. But if in all the circumstances of the case, including the terms of the agreement, it is manifest that there was an intention to change status, then in my judgment there is no reason why the parties should not be allowed to make the change. In this case, there seems to have been a genuine intention to change the status, and I find that the status was changed. It follows that there having been a change of status, the appellant cannot now say that there was not one.

In this connection it is relevant to see how the industrial tribunal approached the matter. They, like this court, were suspicious of the arrangement which was made in the summer of 1973. I must confess that, when I heard the facts of this case recounted by counsel on behalf of the appellant, I was equally suspicious. It seemed nothing more than a device to deceive the Inland Revenue in order to get a tax advantage. The industrial tribunal went into the facts and in the end came to the conclusion (and it is understandable once the full facts are discovered) that there had been a genuine attempt to make an agreement changing the appellant's status, and they excluded illegality. If there was no illegality, and it was a genuine arrangement, there could be only one consequence under the terms of the contract: the appellant changed his status. In those circumstances I can see nothing wrong with the approach which the appeal tribunal made. There was evidence to justify that approach and, in the circumstances, there can be no reason why this court should interfere with the findings of the industrial tribunal.

I too would dismiss the appeal.

1   [1976] 3 All ER 817, [1976] 1 WLR 1213
2   [1976] 3 All ER 817 at 822, [1976] 1 WLR 1213 at 1220

a **EVELEIGH LJ.** I agree with both judgments and have nothing to add.

Appeal dismissed. Leave to appeal to the House of Lords refused.

Solicitors: *Rosling, King, Aylett & Co* (for the appellant); *Coward Chance* (for the respondents).

Sumra Green   Barrister.

b

Gibson v Manchester City Council

COURT OF APPEAL, CIVIL DIVISION
c LORD DENNING MR, ORMROD AND GEOFFREY LANE LJJ
17th JANUARY 1978

Sale of land – Contract – Formation – Exchange of contracts – Necessity for exchange – Concluded contract before exchange – Intention of parties – Offer by council in printed form to sell council house to sitting tenant – Tenant completing and returning application to purchase but
d asking for reduction of purchase price on account of repairs required – Council advising that state of property taken into account in establishing purchase price – Tenant asking council to continue with sale in accordance with application – Council refusing to proceed with application following change in policy – Whether offer made by council and accepted by tenant – Whether conduct of parties and correspondence between them disclosed a contract for purchase by tenant – Whether parties ad idem – Whether contract binding on council although not
e reduced to formal written document.

In November 1970 the defendant city council adopted a policy of selling council houses to sitting tenants. The plaintiff who was renting a council house applied on a printed form supplied by the council for details of the price of the house and mortgage terms available from the council. The plaintiff paid a £3 administration fee and on *f* 10th February 1971 the city treasurer wrote to the plaintiff: 'I refer to your request for details of the cost of buying your Council house. The Corporation may be prepared to sell the house to you at the purchase price of £2,725 less 20% = £2,180 (freehold).' The letter then gave details of the mortgage likely to be made available to the plaintiff and went on: 'This letter should not be regarded as a firm offer of a mortgage. If you would like to make formal application to buy your Council house please *g* complete the enclosed application form and return it to me as soon as possible.' The application form was headed 'Application to buy a council house' and concluded with a statement: 'I . . . now wish to purchase my Council house. The above answers [i e the answers in the application form] are correct and I agree that they shall be the basis of the arrangements regarding the purchase . . .' The plaintiff completed the application form except for the purchase price and returned it to *h* the council under cover of a letter dated 5th March asking whether the council would repair a path 'or alternatively would you deduct an amount of money from the purchase price and I will undertake the repairs myself'. The council's housing manager replied on 12th March that the general condition of the property had been taken into account in fixing the purchase price. On 18th March the plaintiff wrote to the council: 'Ref your letter of 12th March . . . In view of your remarks I would *j* be obliged if you will carry on with the purchase as per my application already in your possession.' Thereafter the plaintiff's house was removed from the council's maintenance list and placed on their house purchase list. In May 1971 following the local government elections there was a change in control of the council and on 7th July the council resolved to discontinue the scheme for the sale of council houses forthwith and to proceed only with those sales where there had been an exchange of

of contracts. On 27th July the council wrote to the plaintiff to advise him that the
council was unable to proceed further with his application to purchase. The plaintiff **a**
brought an action alleging that there was a binding contract for the sale of the house
and asking for specific performance of the contract.

Held (Geoffrey Lane LJ dissenting) – Although the transaction had not been reduced
to a formal written document, it was clear from the correspondence as a whole and
the conduct of the parties that they were ad idem as to the essential terms of the **b**
contract, and (per Ormrod LJ) having regard to the fact that the court was dealing
with a policy decision by a local authority to sell council houses to tenants and not
an alleged contract of sale between two private individuals, and construing the
council's letter of 10th February 1971 in the light of the background to the transaction,
the circumstances, the relationship established between the parties, and the fact that
there was no outstanding contingency against which the council were refraining from **c**
committing themselves, the statement in the city treasurer's letter of 10th February
'The Corporation may be prepared to sell the house to you' meant 'The Corporation
are prepared to sell the house to you' and was a firm offer which the plaintiff by his
letter of 18th March requesting the council to carry on with the purchase had accepted.
Since there was a concluded contract for the sale of the property and it was sufficiently
evidenced in writing, the plaintiff was entitled to specific performance. The appeal **d**
would therefore be dismissed (see p 586 *h j*, p 587 *d* and *j*, p 588 *c d* and *f*, p 589 *c* and *e*
to *g* and *j* to p 590 *b* and *f*, post).

Brogden v Metropolitan Railway Co (1877) 2 App Cas 666 and *Storer v Manchester City
Council* [1974] 3 All ER 824 applied.

Notes
For the formation of a contract from the intention of the parties, see 9 Halsbury's **e**
Laws (4th Edn) para 263, and for cases on the subject, see 12 Digest (Reissue) 58-60,
300-313.

For the formation of contracts for the sale of land, see 34 Halsbury's Laws (3rd Edn)
205, para 342, and for cases on the subject, see 40 Digest (Repl) 11-14, *1-38*.

Cases referred to in judgments **f**
Brogden v Metropolitan Railway Co (1877) 2 App Cas 666, HL, 12 Digest (Reissue) 60, *313*.
Hyde v Wrench (1840) 3 Beav 334, 4 Jur 1106, 49 ER 132, 12 Digest (Reissue) 71, *360*.
Storer v Manchester City Council [1974] 3 All ER 824, [1974] 1 WLR 1403, 73 LGR 1,
   CA, Digest (Cont Vol D) 793, *26a*.

Appeal **g**
This was an appeal by the defendants, Manchester City Council, against the order of
his Honour Judge Bailey, sitting in the Manchester County Court, made on 15th
December 1976, whereby it was ordered that there should be specific performance of
an agreement for the sale of a council house to the plaintiff, Robert Gibson, provided a
good title were made to the property, and that all future hearing of the action be
adjourned generally. The grounds of the appeal were (1) that the judge was wrong in **h**
law in holding that a letter dated 10th February 1971 from the city treasurer which
was relied on by the plaintiff as constituting an offer by the defendants to the plaintiff
(a) constituted any such offer and (b) satisfied the requirements of the Law of Property
Act 1925, s 40; (2) that accordingly (a) the defendants never made any offer to the
plaintiff, (b) the plaintiff never accepted any such offer, (c) no contract came into
existence between the plaintiff and the defendants, and (d) the requirements of s 40 **j**
were not satisfied in relation to any such contract. The facts are set out in the judgment
of Lord Denning MR.

H E Francis QC and *A W Simpson* for the council.
George Carman QC and *Bruce Caulfield* for the plaintiff.

LORD DENNING MR. This is a test case affecting some 350 tenants of council
a houses in the City of Manchester. The council tenant is Mr Robert Gibson. He is a
senior clerk in the works department of the corporation. He has been with them for
many years.

In 1968 Manchester began to sell houses to council tenants. But at that time it was
very restricted. Only one-quarter of one per cent of their houses were allowed to
be sold to council tenants. Mr Gibson was one of the very first who applied to buy
b his house. But there was a long list of applicants, and his name did not come up at
that time. In June 1970 the restriction was lifted. Thenceforward the corporation was
enabled to sell its houses to council tenants without any restriction at all.

Mr Gibson himself followed all the prescribed procedures. He made his application
in good time and in good order. He was entitled to beneficial terms because of his
long tenure. He was able to buy his house at 20 per cent below the market price,
c and also to have a mortgage from the corporation on favourable terms.

All was going well with his application until May 1971. Then, to his dismay,
things went wrong for Mr Gibson. There was a change in the control of the Manchester Corporation. Previously the Conservatives had been in control. Afterwards
Labour gained control. Under the Conservatives the policy of the corporation had
been to sell council houses to tenants, but when the Labour administration took over
d in May 1971 that policy was reversed. The Labour controlled administration decided
not to sell council houses to tenants. They realised however they could not go back
on existing contracts. So they gave instructions to their officers that they were to
fulfil existing contracts but not to make any fresh contracts. The new Labour controlled administration said to the town clerk: 'You must fulfil those contracts by
which we are legally bound, but not those by which we are not legally bound.'

e We have had cases arising out of this new policy. In 1974 there was *Storer v Manchester City Council*[1]. There were about 120 tenants like Mr Storer. The corporation
argued: 'The contracts have not formally been exchanged. So we are not legally
bound to sell council houses to Mr Storer and the other tenants.' This court held that,
although there was not an actual exchange of contracts, nevertheless there was an
agreement with a sufficient note or memorandum to satisfy the Statute of Frauds.
f So the corporation were liable to sell the houses to those 120 tenants.

Now we have Mr Gibson and 350 tenants like him. The arrangements have not
gone nearly as far as in Mr Storer's case. The question is whether there was a concluded contract. The county court judge held that there was and he ordered it to be
specifically performed. The corporation appeal to this court.

So I must go through the material letters, to see whether there was a concluded
g contract between the parties. In November 1970 the corporation sent to the tenants a
brochure. It gave details of the scheme which they were inaugurating for the purchase by the tenants of those houses, giving favourable terms as to price and as to
mortgages. Mr Gibson immediately replied. He paid £3 as the administration fee.
He sent forward his application on the printed form:

h   'Please inform me of the price of buying my Council house. I am interested in
        obtaining a mortgage from the Corporation to buy the house. Please send me
        the details . . .'

He gave his name, and said that he had been a tenant of this house for 12 years or
more.

On 10th February 1971 the corporation sent to him the first of what I may call the
j contract documents. The city treasurer wrote saying:

        'I refer to your request for details of the cost of buying your Council house.
        The Corporation may be prepared to sell the house to you at the purchase price
        of £2,725 less 20%=£2,180 (freehold).'

---

1 [1974] 3 All ER 824, [1974] 1 WLR 1403

(That 20 per cent was a discount allowed to Mr Gibson because of his tenancy.)
The letter continued:

'The details which you requested about a Corporation mortgage are as follows:
'Maximum mortgage the Corporation may grant:
£2,177 repayable over 20 years.
'Annual fire insurance premium: £2·45
'Monthly repayment charge, calculated by:—
'(i) flat rate repayment method   £19·02

[After some further details, the letter said:] This letter should not be regarded
as a firm offer of a mortgage. If you would like to make a formal application to
buy your Council house, please complete the enclosed application form and
return it to me as soon as possible.'

That is just what Mr Gibson did. He filled in his application form and returned the
form. But he left the purchase price blank and wrote a covering letter of 5th March
1971. In it he said that there were various defects in the house, particularly in the
tarmac path. He said that there was a lot of work to be done and he wanted either
the price to be lowered or the corporation to repair the premises.

The corporation replied on 12th March 1971 in the following terms:

'Dear Sir, I refer to your letter concerning certain repairs to the path. Account
is taken of the general condition of the property at the time of the survey and
valuation and the price is fixed accordingly, allowing for such defects as there
may be. I regret I cannot authorise repairs of this nature at this stage.'

So there it was. Mr Gibson's suggestion was not accepted by the corporation. They
said, in effect, that they would stand by their offer in the letter of 10th February
1971 but would not modify it. In reply, on 18th March 1971 Mr Gibson wrote this
letter:

'Ref your letter of 12th March . . . In view of your remarks I would be obliged
if you will carry on with the purchase as per my application already in your
possession.'

It seems to me clear that, by writing that letter, Mr Gibson discarded the suggestion
which he had made in the covering letter. He returned to the simple application
which was already in their possession, of which they had intimated their acceptance.
As I view this letter of 12th March 1971, they had intimated that they would accept
his application if he did not press this point about repairs.

We have had much discussion as to whether Mr Gibson's letter of 18th March 1971
was a new offer or whether it was an acceptance of the previous offer which had been
made. I do not like detailed analysis on such a point. To my mind it is a mistake to
think that all contracts can be analysed into the form of offer and acceptance. I
know in some of the textbooks it has been the custom to do so; but, as I understand
the law, there is no need to look for a strict offer and acceptance. You should look
at the correspondence as a whole and at the conduct of the parties and see therefrom
whether the parties have come to an agreement on everything that was material.
If by their correspondence and their conduct you can see an agreement on all material
terms, which was intended thenceforward to be binding, then there is a binding
contract in law even though all the formalities have not been gone through. For that
proposition I would refer to *Brogden v Metropolitan Railway Co*[1].

It seems to me that on the correspondence I have read (and, I may add, on what
happened after) the parties had come to an agreement in the matter which they
intended to be binding. Let me say what happened afterwards. Mr Gibson telephoned to the department and was told that his case was being dealt with. He did

1   (1877) 2 App Cas 666

much work on the house in the belief that all was well. The corporation took the house off the list of maintenance to tenants and put it on the list of owner-owned houses where the owners had to do the maintenance themselves. Then on Wednesday, 26th May 1971 there was an announcement in the newspapers that all transactions might be stopped. He wrote on Friday 28th May, this letter to the corporation:

'...I have already put glass doors on internally at considerable expense and have made enquiries ref replacement of certain W [window] Frames. It seems rather a high handed decision to take at this stage of the proceedings, with little or no consideration for the feelings of the unfortunate tenant.'

The housing manager replied that all applications were being held in abeyance. Mr Gibson wrote on 25th June saying:

'...when the Tory Council took control, we were contacted by phone to let us know of the change in the situation and that it was in order for us to go ahead with alterations... I realise that it was done verbally but nevertheless the message was passed and I feel sure that your officers will not deny that it was so.'

The whole story shows to my mind quite clearly that the parties were agreed and intended the agreement to be binding; and, if there had been no change in the control of the local authority, there can be no doubt whatever that this sale would have gone through.

Mr Gibson followed the matter up. He went to two local councillors who took it up with the town clerk. In a letter of 2nd July the town clerk wrote to Councillor Goldstone, saying:

'In the course of time Mr. Gibson's application was dealt with by the City Estates and Valuation Officer, and also by the City Treasurer, who forwarded to him details of the purchase price, *the amount of mortgage which could be offered and the various methods for repayment. Mr. Gibson accepted this offer*, but before the papers could be passed to me for preparation of the formal Contract the local elections intervened.'

It is as plain as can be from that letter from the town clerk that he regarded everything as agreed.

On 4th August 1971 the town clerk wrote this to Councillor Silverman:

'Although Mr. Gibson's application had been processed by the Housing, City Estates and Valuation Officers and City Treasurer's Departments, formal contracts had not been prepared and exchanged prior to the suspension of the scheme for the sale of Council houses on the 14th May last. Accordingly, in view of the decision of the Council on the 7th July 1971, the sale of this property will not be proceeding. [Then there followed a note about repairs]: Following the Council decision of the 7th July referred to above, the Direct Works Department were instructed to deal with repairs to all Council houses, except those where they had been notified that sales were proceeding. This property, therefore, will now have been replaced on the maintenance list.'

That shows that the house had been taken off the maintenance list on the footing that the sale was proceeding; and it was put on it again after the Labour administration cancelled the sale.

It seems to me as plain as can be that there was a complete agreement of all the essential terms of this contract. As the county court judge said: 'What more was the plaintiff to do? What more were the defendants to do? In my view the contract was complete'; and so it was.

It has been argued before us: 'It was not complete in regard to the terms. If all the documents had been completed as expected, there would have been a simple

short agreement which included a clause[1] saying *"Deeds* of Conveyance or Transfer
and Mortgage to be in the Corporation's standard forms including conditions against
use except as a private dwelling-house and against advertising and a restriction not
to sell or lease the property for five years".'

It seems to me that such a clause is to be imported into the correspondence; or
alternatively, when granting specific performance, the court in its discretion should
include such a clause. The order should be for specific performance of an agreement
for the sale of a council house containing the clauses in the form in general use in
Manchester. It is a contract for sale on the terms of the usual agreement for selling
a council house. It seems to me, as it did to the judge, that Mr Gibson ought not to
have his expectations ruined by reason of the change of policy by the local government administration. To my mind there was a concluded contract, sufficiently
evidenced by writing, which he is entitled to have specifically performed.

I would agree with the county court judge and would dismiss the appeal.

ORMROD LJ. I agree with the judgment of Lord Denning MR and would only
add a little on my own behalf.

In my judgment there are two ways in which this case can be approached. The
first is to consider whether the parties to the alleged contract had reached a consensus
for the sale of 174 Charlestown Road by the council to the plaintiff. To answer that
question, it seems to me that one must look at the whole of the dealings between
these parties. The plaintiff had been anxious to buy his council house for a long time.
The council had been conducting a very limited sale of council houses for some years,
limited by the government restrictions. In June 1970 the restrictions were removed,
and the documents which are in the bundle before us show that the council reacted
rapidly to that change of policy which freed them not only to sell council houses
without restriction in number, but also enabled them to sell freeholds. They clearly
went ahead with the intention of selling council houses to council tenants, and they
published the brochure to which Lord Denning MR has referred already.

It is necessary in considering this case, in my judgment, to remember that this is
not a sale or an alleged contract of sale between two private individuals or between
an individual and some form of industrial or commercial concern. We are dealing
here with a policy decision by a council (a local authority) to sell council houses to
tenants.

The reason I say that is this: the council knew the tenant; they were proposing to
sell at an extremely attractive price; they were prepared to offer very reasonable
mortgage terms; and, of course, the reason for that was that the individual tenant
concerned, instead of continuing to pay his rent to the council, if he bought the house
and took on a mortgage, would continue to pay his mortgage instalments to the
council, so the two parties would continue in a fairly close relationship not so very
different in day to day practical terms from what it was before the sale except that the
responsibility for repairs and so on would be shifted to the tenant. It is against that
background that we have to consider this matter.

In November the brochure was published which was an open invitation to tenants
to offer to buy their houses. It gave full details as to how to set about it. The plaintiff
reacted immediately to that, filled in the form which was contained in the brochure,
and applied to the council, asking the price:

'Please inform me of the price of buying my Council house. I am interested in
obtaining a mortgage from the Corporation to buy the house. Please send me
details about the monthly repayments based on the following method,'

and he picked the flat rate repayment method and filled in a few more details which

---

1   Cf *Storer v Manchester City Council* [1974] 3 All ER 824 at 826, [1974] 1 WLR 1403 at 1406

the council wanted to make sure that he qualified as a purchaser. Then he was
asked to pay a £3 administration fee, which he paid, and he received in return the
letter of 10th February 1971, which informed him that—

> 'The Corporation may be prepared to sell the house to you at the purchase
> price of £2,725 less 20% = £2,180 (freehold).'

The letter then went on to say that the council might grant a mortgage of £2,177
repayable over 20 years. I will come back to that document later.

The plaintiff, after querying the price because of what he said about his drive or
pathway, sent the form in, giving his name, and applying for a loan on the terms which
had been indicated already, and the matter then proceeded through the normal
channels. The price was finally agreed in the letter of 18th March 1971 from the
plaintiff, who had by this time received a note from the council to say that the valuation they had put on the house took account of the fact that certain repairs were required. So, having been assured of that, he wrote the letter which, to my mind, is
the acceptance of the offer. He said:

> 'In view of your remarks I would be obliged if you will carry on with the
> purchase as per my application already in your possession.'

Thereafter the whole matter was placed in the council's pipeline, and it proceeded
slowly.

The only difference, as I see it, between this case and *Storer's* case[1] is that the plaintiff's file was a good way further back along the pipeline than Mr Storer's. There is
absolutely nothing to indicate that, if the plaintiff's file had reached the point in the
pipeline that Mr Storer's had on the date that Mr Storer's did, he would not have
received exactly the same documents as Mr Storer received and that the contract
would not have proceeded. It seems to me clear that the parties were ad idem on the
proposition that the council would sell and the plaintiff would buy this house at
the price of £2,180. It is equally clear in fact that both sides assumed that he would
raise this money by means of a mortgage supplied by the council on the terms of a
flat rate mortgage. There is nothing whatever to indicate that there was any doubt
in the minds of the council as to whether he was a suitable person to be given a
mortgage. In fact, quite obviously they knew perfectly well that he was a suitable
person because he was an employee of theirs, they knew all about him, and it was
inconceivable that they would have refrained from granting him a mortgage on the
terms they had indicated. For those reasons, I respectfully agree with Lord Denning
MR that the right conclusion to draw from those facts is that these parties were ad
idem on the question of sale.

The other way of looking at it is to analyse the documents more precisely. If
one does that, then one must look primarily at the document of 10th February 1971
that is the council's letter. That letter, looked at strictly, deals with two propositions,
connected but separate. The first is the question of the sale of the house and the
price. The second is the question of mortgage, the amount of the mortgage and the
amount of the monthly repayments. Those are dealt with in separate paragraphs.

Dealing with the question of sale, the first paragraph is the crucial one. That reads:

> 'I refer to your request for details of the cost of buying your Council house.
> The Corporation may be prepared to sell the house to you at the purchase price of
> £2,725 less 20%=£2,180 (freehold).'

Had that paragraph read: 'The Corporation *are* prepared to sell the house to you at
the purchase price . . .', it would be difficult, it seems to me, to contend that that was
not a firm offer which was capable of acceptance by the plaintiff; and, if accepted by

---

1   [1974] 3 All ER 824, [1974] 1 WLR 1403

the plaintiff, would constitute a contract. The question is: does the use of the phrase 'may be' instead of 'are' in that paragraph make all the difference between a contract and no contract? That depends, it seems to me, on whether or not there was any outstanding contingency against which the council were refraining from committing themselves. As far as I can see, there was, so far as the sale of the property was concerned, no outstanding contingency at that time at all. That being so, the use of the phrase 'may be' cannot make any difference, and I would be prepared to construe that paragraph as meaning: 'The Corporation *are* prepared to sell', construing it in the light of the background, the circumstances and the relationship which had been established between the parties.

That conclusion, I think, is supported by reference to the second part of the letter When one comes to look at that part of the letter dealing with mortgage arrangements, it reads: 'The details you requested about a Corporation mortgage are as follows:— Maximum mortgage the Corporation may grant: £2,177 repayable over 20 years.' There again that could be of course a statement that the council cannot advance more, that they are not allowed to advance more, than £2,177, or it may mean that the council may probably grant a mortgage in that sum; and, when one looks at the penultimate paragraph of the letter, one finds it ending in what seems to me to be a highly significant sentence: 'This letter should not be regarded as a firm offer of a mortgage.' There is an old Latin principle which covers that situation very clearly. In a letter like that it seems to me that a clear distinction must be drawn between the use of the word 'may' in relation to the sale and 'may' in relation to the granting of a mortgage, in the light of that later sentence. Of course, there was a reason for that because the corporation, although they must have known about the plaintiff's general situation, had not got all the details. If the plaintiff had been an ordinary council tenant and not an employee, they would have needed some information about his means before deciding to grant the mortgage. That further information they received in his form supplied by the council which he filled in and sent. So counsel for the defendants, I think, is right in arguing that there was no binding contract on the part of the council to grant a mortgage, but I think he is wrong in his submission that there was no binding contract of sale.

Whether the plaintiff will be in a position to proceed with the purchase if he does not get a council mortgage is another matter, but it is a matter for him to decide. What we have to decide is whether there was a contract to sell the prop rty; and, for the reasons which I have given, in my judgment there was, and I think   nty court judge was right, and I too would dismiss the appeal.

GEOFFREY LANE LJ. Lord Cairns LC in *Brogden v Metropolitan Railway Co*[1], to which reference has already been made, says this:

> 'My Lords, there are no cases upon which difference of opinion may more readily be entertained, or which are always more embarrassing to dispose of, than the cases where the Court has to decide whether or not, having regard to letters and documents which have not assumed the complete and formal shape of executed and solemn agreements, a contract has really been constituted between the parties.'

Unhappily I find myself in embarrassing disagreement with the judgments which have been delivered in this case by Lord Denning MR and Ormrod LJ.

Nobody has anything but sympathy for the plaintiff and the 349-odd other tenants who have found themselves caught in the cross-fire between the Tory Party faction and the Labour Party faction on the Manchester City Council. No doubt all those ladies and gentlemen have for many years been expecting, and expecting confidently,

---

1   (1877) 2 App Cas 666 at 672

that in due course they would be able to buy their council houses, of which they are tenants, at advantageous terms from the council. No doubt, on any view, the plaintiff at least got very close indeed to succeeding in that ambition. But what has to be decided as an unadorned question, not influenced by sympathy or politics, is whether it can truly be said that there was an offer by the council to sell and an unconditional acceptance by the plaintiff to buy, enabling a formal contract to be drawn without further reference to the parties and containing all the material terms which would eventually have to find their way into that contract.

Counsel for the plaintiff suggests that it is a mistake to think that all contracts have to be analysed into offer on the one hand and acceptance on the other. The true question, he suggests, is this: have the parties come to an agreement on everything which is material between them? In my judgment, on either of those two views, the council are entitled to succeed.

It is said by the plaintiff that agreement is to be found in the correspondence which passed between the parties over the months and, in particular, the letters and so on which went to and fro in February and March 1971. Indeed, there is no need to go back further in the history of these events than November 1970 when the housing manager sent a letter to the plaintiff, amongst others headed 'Sale of council houses' and containing this paragraph:

> 'You will note that under the new scheme you are required to forward an administration fee of £3 together with your request to purchase, but I must emphasise that this fee is treated as a payment towards the cost of the dwelling when the purchase is completed. The fee is not returnable if you decide not to proceed with the purchase. [Then the next paragraph but one:] I am, therefore, enclosing a copy of the brochure which has been prepared giving full details of the new scheme and I should be obliged if you would complete the form which comprises the last page and return it to me together with the £3 fee.'

We have been shown a copy of the brochure, and it is sufficient for the purpose of this case to say that in that brochure there is no mention of any special terms which might possibly find their way into the eventual contract between the parties.

The form was duly completed and sent back by the plaintiff, and received by the council on 2nd December 1970. The form, addressed to the housing manager, said:

> 'Dear Sir, Please inform me of the price of buying my Council house. I am interested in obtaining a mortgage from the Corporation to buy the house. Please send me details about the monthly repayments.'

and so on. Then there is the document already referred to by Lord Denning MR and Ormrod LJ which is said by the plaintiff to be the offer by the council, namely, the first of the potentially contractual documents in this case. It is dated 10th February 1971 and is written not by the town clerk, as one would expect had this truly been a formal offer by the council, but by the city treasurer, Mr Page; and again, not surprisingly because it comes from the city treasurer, it is aimed primarily, if not entirely, at the financial aspects of this transaction, and it reads as follows:

> 'Purchase of Council House [then it gives a reference number and reads on:] I refer to your request for details of the cost of buying your Council house. The Corporation may be prepared to sell the house to you at the purchase price of £2,725 less 20% = £2,180 (freehold). The details which you requested about a Corporation mortgage are as follows.'

then he sets out the amount that the corporation 'may' grant, the annual fire insurance premium, and the monthly repayment charge on the mortgage if the plaintiff should require it. As Ormrod LJ has pointed out, at the end of the penultimate paragraph it says: 'This letter should not be regarded as a firm offer of a mortgage.' Then it reads:

'If you would like to make formal application to buy your Council house, please complete the enclosed application form and return it to me as soon as possible.'

It is said that that letter constitutes a firm offer to sell.

It is largely a matter of impression, but, although to Lord Denning MR and Ormrod LJ it appears perfectly plain that that was a firm offer, to me it appears equally plain that it was not. First of all, the words used 'may be' in the first paragraph and 'may grant a mortgage' and finally the expression 'If you would like to make a formal application to buy your Council house' are strange words to use if this was indeed a formal offer on behalf of the council. It is, in my judgment, no more than one would expect of a letter coming from the city treasurer. It is a letter setting out the financial terms on which it may be the council will be prepared to consider a sale and purchase in due course.

Secondly, the letter makes no mention at all of the special conditions which were undoubtedly in due course going to be included in the formal contract and the conveyance. If one looks at the report by the town clerk dated 3rd August 1970, one sees that it sets out the terms which the council at that stage at any rate intended should be included in the contracts of sale to the tenants who were wishing to purchase their houses. Counsel for the plaintiff suggests that there were only matters of form or procedure outstanding and that all the material matters were agreed between the parties. I find myself unable to agree with that contention when I look at this report. It sets out in para 2 the fact that it intends to detail a summary of the conditions of sale, and then in para 3 it appears to set out the terms subject to which the tenancies have been created and indicates there, without going into it in unnecessary detail, which of those terms it is intended to include in the contract of sale. Just to take one or two examples, there is intended to be included a restrictive covenant that the house shall be used as a private dwelling-house only, that there shall be no advertising, that the purchaser shall not obstruct accesses, and so on. It seems to me that none of those matters could possibly be described as matters merely of procedure. They are matters closely affecting the rights which the proposed purchaser will eventually enjoy over his property. It was suggested by counsel for the plaintiff that it would be very unlikely that any purchaser applying for planning permission to use the premises other than as a private dwelling-house would receive such permission. That, it seems to me, is not a consideration which can possibly affect the decision in this case.

It seems to me for all those reasons that it is quite impossible to treat this letter of 10th February as being a firm offer made by the council, and it is interesting to observe the further words which Lord Cairns LC uses once again in the *Brogden* case[1] in the remainder of the paragraph, the beginning of which I have read:

'But, on the other hand, there is no principle of law better established than this, that even although parties may intend to have their agreement expressed in the most solemn and complete form that conveyancers and solicitors are able to prepare, still there may be a *consensus* between the parties far short of a complete mode of expressing it, and that *consensus* may be discovered from letters or from other documents of an imperfect and incomplete description.'

Up to that point the passage supports the plaintiff's contention, but note these final words: 'I mean imperfect and incomplete as regards form.'

If that view of the letter of 10th February is correct then that is an end of the matter, but it is worthwhile perhaps considering what happened thereafter. The response to the letter from the plaintiff was to send back the formal document, which again be it noted is headed not 'Acceptance' but 'APPLICATION TO BUY A COUNCIL HOUSE and APPLICATION FOR A MORTGAGE'. It is a document which was supplied of course by the

---

1   (1877) 2 App Cas 666 at 672

council for the plaintiff to fill in. 'Section A: Application to buy a council house':
there again, not an agreement to accept the council's offer. And therein various
particulars are set out, namely, the wife and her work and her income. Then:
'Section C: Certificates to be completed by all applicants. I have read the explanatory leaflet on how to buy my Council house', that is the brochure to which I have
referred—

'and your letter stating the costs involved, and now wish to purchase my
Council house. The above answers are correct and I agree that they shall be the
basis of the arrangements regarding the purchase and, if appropriate, the loan
between myself and the Manchester Corporation.'

But in the covering letter which accompanied that completed form the plaintiff is
making a counter-suggestion. He says this:

'I would therefore like your assurance that Direct works will not exclude these
premises when re-surfacing or re-laying starts, or alternatively would you
deduct an amount of money from the purchase price and I will undertake the
repairs myself. Whichever decision you arrive at I would like to make an initial
cash payment of £500—so I would be obliged if you will let me have the figures
to allow for the deposit mentioned. I have left the purchase price blank on the
application form until I hear from you.'

What he is suggesting there in short is that the price of these premises to him should
not be that which the council have put forward but that an allowance should be made
for his repairing the drive or alternatively there should be an obligation on the
council to make recompense in kind by repairing his drive themselves by direct
labour.

That seemed to me quite plainly to be a counter-offer. The reply which the council
sent is this:

'Dear Sir, I refer to your letter concerning certain repairs to the path. Account
is taken of the general condition of the property at the time of the survey and
valuation and the price is fixed accordingly, allowing for such defects as there
may be. I regret I cannot authorise repairs of this nature at this stage.'

Then on 18th March there was another letter back from the plaintiff in answer to
that:

'Ref your letter of the 12th March . . . In view of your remarks I would be
obliged if you will carry on with the purchase as per my application already in
your possession.'

It is suggested that that letter of 18th March from the plaintiff was appropriate to
revive, so to speak, the original offer, if there was one, by the council, and that one can
accordingly disregard the counter-offer and rejection which took place in the interim.
The matter is dealt with conveniently in Cheshire and Fifoot's Law of Contract[1] in
these terms, which I will read:

'Whatever the difficulties, and however elastic their rules, the judges must,
either upon oral evidence or by the construction of documents, find some act
from which they can infer the offeree's intention to accept, or they must refuse to
admit the existence of an agreement. This intention, moreover, must be conclusive. It must not treat the negotiations between the parties as still open to
the process of bargaining. The offeree must unreservedly assent to the exact
terms proposed by the offeror. If, while purporting to accept the offer as a

---

1   9th Edn (1976), p 33

whole, he introduces a new term which the offeror has not had the chance of examining, he is in fact merely making a counter-offer. The effect of this in the eyes of the law is to destroy the original offer. Thus in *Hyde* v. *Wrench*[1], "the defendant on June 6th offered to sell an estate to the plaintiff for £1,000. On June 8th, in reply, the plaintiff made an offer of £950, which was refused by the defendant on June 27th. Finally, on June 29th, the plaintiff wrote that he was now prepared to pay £1,000". It was held that no contract existed. By his letter of June 8th the plaintiff had rejected the original offer and he was no longer able to revive it by changing his mind and tendering a subsequent acceptance.'

It seems to me that that passage applies precisely to the circumstances in this case and, accordingly, even if the letter did amount to an offer, the plaintiff has failed to take advantage of it for the reasons which I have endeavoured to indicate.

The decision of this court in *Storer* v *Manchester City Council*[2], which was relied on by the judge seems to me to provide if anything good support for the council's case rather than the plaintiff's case. If I may just read a passage from Lord Denning MR's judgment[3], it reads as follows:

'On 11th February 1971 Mr Storer filled in an application form to buy a council house. He said: "I . . . now wish to purchase my Council house". In it he asked for a loan on mortgage. On 9th March 1971, the city treasurer wrote to him: "The Corporation will lend £2,279 repayable over 25 years with interest at 8½% . . . the total monthly instalment payable will be . . . £14·98." On the same day, 9th March 1971, the town clerk himself wrote a letter which is of crucial importance in the case.'

Note that superadded in that case to the treasurer's letter was this one from the town clerk, the counterpart of which does not exist in the case we are considering here today. That letter ran as follows[4]:

'Dear Sir, *Sale of Council Houses.* I understand you wish to purchase your Council house and enclose the Agreement for Sale. If you will sign the Agreement and return it to me I will send you the Agreement signed on behalf of the Corporation in exchange. From the enclosed list of Solicitors, who are prepared to act for you and advise you on the purchase, please let me know the name of the firm that you select, as soon as possible.'

Lord Denning MR continued:

'Enclosed with that letter there was a form headed: "City of Manchester. Agreement for sale of a Council House." The Corporation had filled in various details, such as the name of the purchaser, the address of the property, the price, the mortgage, amount, and the monthly repayments. There was this item left blank: "7. Date when your tenancy ceases and mortgage repayments will commence," followed by these clauses: "8. *Freehold* to be conveyed or transferred by the Corporation. 9. There will be no abstract or investigation of title . . . 10. *Deeds* of Conveyance or Transfer and Mortgage to be in the Corporation's standard forms including conditions against use except as a private dwelling-house and against advertising and a restriction not to sell or lease the property for five years. 11. *Warning.* As from the date mentioned in 7 above the property is at your risk. If you are taking a mortgage from the corporation it will be insured for you but the cost recharged to you. *If you are not taking a Mortgage insure it at once.* Your

---

1   (1840) 3 Beav 334
2   [1974] 3 All ER 824, [1974] 1 WLR 1403
3   [1974] 3 All ER 824 at 826, [1974] 1 WLR 1403 at 1406
4   [1974] 3 All ER 824 at 826, [1974] 1 WLR 1403 at 1406, 1407

responsibility for repairs and for payment of rates also start from that day. My solicitors are . . ." Mr Storer filled in that form. He filled in the name of solicitors, Messrs Hargreaves & Co. He signed the form himself and returned it on 20th March 1971. So he had done everything which he had to do to bind himself to the purchase of the property. The only thing left blank was the date when the tenancy was to cease.'

None of the documents which in that case were held to be the contractual documents even exist in the present case. It is of course bad luck that the 'Storer' line of cases should fall on one side of the line and the 'Gibson' type of case on the other, but bad luck is proverbially fertile ground for bad law.

It seems from what I have endeavoured to indicate that the plaintiff, however much sympathy one may feel for him, has totally failed to establish on any view the necessary ingredients of a contract, and for those reasons I respectfully differ from Lord Denning MR and Ormrod LJ and I would allow the appeal.

Appeal dismissed. Leave to appeal to the House of Lords granted on terms.

Solicitors: *Leslie Boardman*, Manchester (for the defendants); *Hargreaves & Co*, Manchester (for the plaintiff).

Sumra Green Barrister.

Re Beaney (deceased)

CHANCERY DIVISION
MARTIN NOURSE QC SITTING AS A DEPUTY JUDGE OF THE HIGH COURT
4th, 5th, 6th, 11th OCTOBER 1977

Gift – Inter vivos – Mental capacity to make gift – Degree of understanding required – Degree of understanding relative to importance of gift in relation to donor's other assets – Effect of gift to dispose of donor's only asset of real value and pre-empt devolution of estate under will or on intestacy – Donor understanding nature of transaction but not understanding effect on devolution of estate on her death – Validity of gift.

X, a widow, had three grown-up children, a son, P, and two daughters, V and G. She had her own house. In 1971 her mental condition deteriorated considerably and V, who was unmarried, went to live with her so that she could look after her. All three children were on good terms with X, and P and G, who were both married, visited her regularly. On 7th May 1973 she was admitted to hospital. She was then in an advanced state of senile dementia. V was anxious that the house should be transferred into V's name so that, if necessary, it could be sold, or otherwise dealt with, to make provision for X's maintenance. She raised the matter with X who, she said, assented to the suggestion. On 16th May V, X's solicitor and a family friend, took to the hospital, for X's signature, a deed transferring the house to V. The house was the only asset of any value which X possessed. The solicitor explained to X that if she executed the deed she would be giving the house to V absolutely, and asked her whether she understood what would happen and whether that was what she wanted. She answered in the affirmative and signed the deed. The solicitor however did not inform her that the effect of the deed would be to deprive P and G of any real interest in her estate. P and G knew nothing of the deed of transfer until X died intestate a year later. As the administrators of her estate, they brought an action against V, claiming, inter alia, a declaration that the deed was void and of no effect on the ground that X was of unsound mind when she signed it and accordingly incapable of understanding its effect. In her defence, V contended that the deed was valid in that it was sufficient if X understood that she was making a gift, that the subject-matter of the gift was the house and that the person to whom she was giving it was V.

Held – (i) The degree of understanding required for the making of a valid inter vivos gift was relative to the transaction to be effected. If the subject-matter and value of the gift were trivial in relation to the donor's other assets a low degree of understanding was sufficient, but, if the effect of the gift was to dispose of the donor's only asset of value and to pre-empt the devolution of his estate under his will or on his intestacy, the degree of understanding required was as high as that required for a will and the donor had to understand the claims of all potential donees and the extent of the property to be disposed of. It followed that, in the circumstances, X had not made a valid transfer of the house to V, and P and G were entitled to a declaration that the deed of transfer was void and of no effect (see p 600 *j* to p 601 *a* and *g* to *j*, post); dictum of Dixon CJ in *Gibbons v Wright* (1954) 91 CLR at 438 applied.

(ii) In any event, even if the degree of understanding required in respect of the deed of transfer had not been as high as that required for a will, P and G would have still been entitled to a declaration that the deed of transfer was void and of no effect because the evidence showed that at the time of making the transfer X was incapable of understanding that she was making an absolute gift of the house to V (see p 602 *g* and *j*, post).

Notes

For the capacity of mentally disordered persons to execute deeds, see 29 Halsbury's Laws (3rd Edn) 411, 412, para 802, and for cases on the subject, see 33 Digest (Repl) 591-592, 73-92.

Cases referred to in judgment

Ball v Mannin (1829) 3 Bli NS 1, 1 Dow & Cl 380, 4 ER 1241, HL, 33 Digest (Repl) 592, 83.
Birkin v Wing (1890) 63 LT 80, 33 Digest (Repl) 588, 46.
Gibbons v Wright (1954) 91 CLR 423, [1954] ALR 383, 33 Digest (Repl) 596, *31.
Manches v Trimborn (1946) 115 LJKB 305, 174 LT 344, 6 Digest (Repl) 89, 694.
Marshall, Re, Marshall v Whately [1920] 1 Ch 284, [1920] All ER Rep 190, 89 LJCh 204, 122 LT 673, 33 Digest (Repl) 601, 177.
Walker, Re [1905] 1 Ch 160, 74 LJCh 86, 91 LT 713, CA, 33 Digest (Repl) 601, 176.

Action

By a writ issued on 12th September 1975, the plaintiffs, Peter Frederick Beany ('Peter') and Gillian Rosemary Bannister ('Gillian'), as administrators of the estate of Maud Beaney deceased, brought an action against the defendant, Valerie Anne Beaney, ('Valerie') claiming, inter alia, a declaration that a deed of transfer, dated 16th May 1973, transferring the freehold property known as 74 Avenue Crescent, Cranford, Middlesex, from the deceased to the defendant, was void and of no effect. The facts are set out in the judgment.

T L G Cullen for Peter and Gillian.
P St J Langan for Valerie.

Cur adv vult

11th October. **MARTIN NOURSE QC** read the following judgment: This action, as it now stands, is one for a declaration that a voluntary transfer of a freehold house made in May 1973 was void and of no effect. There are also claims for consequential relief. The sole ground on which the action is based is that the transferor, the late Mrs Maud Beaney, was not of sound mind or understanding at the date the transfer was made and was incapable of understanding its effect. Like many disputes of its kind, it is one between two sides of the same family. I may lament that fact, but it does not discharge me from deciding it in favour of one side or the other. I say at once that, human nature being what it is and in the circumstances which I shall relate, I well understand how it is that both sides have taken up the entrenched positions in which they now find themselves.

Mrs Beaney was born on 7th May 1909. She was married to the late Mr Frederick Beany. He was employed by the Cement Marketing Co Ltd, which is the selling company in the Blue Circle Cement Group. In 1935 he purchased the property which is the subject-matter of the dispute in this action, 74 Avenue Crescent, Cranford, Middlesex. The house is semi-detached with three bedrooms. I was not told what Mr Beaney paid for it, but I was told that his parents helped him with the purchase. No doubt, in those days, the price was reckoned in hundreds, but its value today may well be £15,000 or thereabouts.

Mr and Mrs Beaney had three children and, as frequently happened with couples of their generation where the husband went off to serve in the Second World War, they had a pre-war family and a post-war family. Their eldest child is the defendant, Valerie Anne Beaney. She has not married and is now aged 38. She has had a number of different occupations, but told me that she would describe herself as a calligrapher. The second child is Gillian Rosemary. She is the second plaintiff. She is now aged 28 and is married to Mr James Bannister. The third child is Peter Frederick Beaney. He is the first plaintiff. He is now aged 27. He is also married, the name of his wife being Linda Ann Beaney. All three children, together with Mr Bannister and Mrs Peter Beancy, have given evidence in this case.

At the beginning of the 1960s Mr and Mrs Beaney and their three children were living at home. Between September 1963 and June 1966 Valerie lived mostly away from home, first at Cudham in Kent, then in Birmingham and finally in Ealing. She then spent about two years living at home, when she was working for the United Biscuit Co. She then again lived mostly away from home, doing a number of different jobs, until the beginning of 1971. Valerie did not get on well with her father during the 1960s. She told me that she felt he had been upset when she failed to obtain her National Diploma of Design in 1961. However, this had no effect on her relationship with her mother, which I shall describe in greater detail later.

Meanwhile, in 1967, the second daughter, Gillian, who was then about 18, had left home and she was married to Mr Bannister in 1968. Mr Beaney did not approve of the marriage, but again this does seem to have affected Gillian's relationship with her mother.

Mr Beaney died on 8th March 1971. Shortly before his death Valerie had come back to live at 74 Avenue Crescent. She has lived there ever since.

Mr Beaney died intestate. I was told that apart from the house he had perhaps £500 to £600 in savings. The house was at that time valued at £4,500 or somewhat less. Mrs Beaney took out letters of administration to his estate. She was the sole person entitled to his property on his intestacy. On 28th August 1971 she assented to the vesting of the house in herself absolutely.

In October 1971 the son, Peter, who was then about 21, was married and he and his wife set up home on their own. That left Mrs Beaney and Valerie as the sole occupants of 74 Avenue Cresent, but both Gillian and Peter continued to visit their mother regularly during the remainder of her lifetime. Both daughters said that Peter was their mother's favourite, but I am satisfied on the evidence that all three children were at all times on normal good terms of affection with their mother.

I will now deal with Mrs Beaney's physical and mental health up to the beginning of 1973, that being a period as to the events of which there is no serious dispute between the parties.

In 1949, shortly after the birth of Gillian, Mrs Beaney contracted diabetes, a condition from which she continued to suffer until her death. She was then aged about 40. In 1959 she had a stroke. She appears to have made good recovery from that. The evidence was that she was quite normal for most of the 1960s. At the end of the 1960s, or at the beginning of the 1970s, her mental condition began to deteriorate and it seems that the deterioration got progressively worse after the death of her husband in March 1971. Her mental condition was ultimately that known as gross cerebral atrophy or, in more common parlance, senile dementia. This condition was no doubt aggravated by her diabetes.

On 16th October 1972 Valerie signed a form of application to the Department of Health and Social Security for her to be appointed to act on behalf of Mrs Beaney for the purpose of receiving the latter's pension. The form was completed by somebody in the department from information provided by Valerie. The nature of Mrs Beaney's incapacity was stated on the form to be pre-senile dementia. The form contemplated that the investigating officer would have asked to see certificates or other adequate evidence of incapacity, and I have no doubt that a doctor's certificate was duly produced. Valerie thought that she had first gone to see the people in the department earlier in 1972, but I do not think it necessary to make a detailed consideration of Mrs Beaney's mental capacity before October 1972.

On the following day, 17th October, Mrs Beaney was admitted to the West Middlesex Hospital, where she stayed for three weeks. There was no medical evidence as to her condition during this period, but both Peter and his wife visited her there and gave evidence as to her state of mind. Peter said that her memory was virtually nil. She was in a very bad state, imagining things all the time. She used to think there were mice upstairs. She could not sleep very well. She was complaining about bombs being planted in the hospital by the IRA, that there was a hole in the floor outside the ward and so forth. Peter's wife said that she paid two visits. She said that Mrs Beaney moaned about cannons going off and said that they were fighting up in the television room.

It is clear that after Mrs Beaney came out of the West Middlesex Hospital her condition did not improve. Valerie said that she was definitely not capable of looking after herself at that time. She could not cook for herself. She could not really dress herself. Valerie added that at times it was possible to have a sensible discussion with her, but with the implication that this was unusual. Both Mrs Beaney and Valerie had 'flu over Christmas. Valerie said that Mrs Beaney got worse mentally during the early months of 1973. Valerie, not unnaturally, found that the strain of looking after her mother was getting worse.

I am satisfied by all this evidence that from October 1972 onwards Mrs Beaney was in an advanced state of senile dementia and that her condition was progressively deteriorating.

On 22nd March 1973 Mrs Beaney executed a general power of attorney in favour of Valerie. It appears that the suggestion that this be done had first been made about a year earlier by Mrs Beaney's bank manager. She was physically able to sign her cheques, but there must have been doubts about her mental capacity to do so. Later, it appears that the same suggestion was made by the Rev Howard Joad, an old family friend, and possibly also by Mr Robert Gellatly, an old friend of Mr Beaney's at work and with whom he had played cricket, football and table tennis. In due course they both attested Mrs Beaney's execution of the power. I was also told that on 19th March a consultant psychiatrist had seen Mrs Beaney at home and had told Valerie that her mother's senility was greatly advanced and rapidly increasing.

Accordingly, Valerie decided to go ahead with the power of attorney and she had it drawn up by the same solicitor as had acted for Mrs Beaney in the administration of Mr Beaney's estate in 1971. This was Miss Margaretta Bray, the sole principal of the firm of Worrell, Fordyce & Lys, then of London. She was to play an important part in the later history of this case.

The evidence surrounding the execution of the power of attorney further confirms
a the serious mental condition in which Mrs Beaney then was.
I now come to April 1973. Easter that year was on 22nd April. It was arranged that
Valerie should take Mrs Beaney to stay with Peter and his wife. The visit started
on Monday 16th April and the original intention was that it should last for a week,
that is to say until Easter Monday or thereabouts. However, the visit was not a success.
To begin with Mrs Beaney was in a very poor way, exhibiting many of the behavioural
b lapses characteristic of someone in her condition. I think it possible that Peter had
not realised until he had her in the house to what a bad stage she had got. I think
he was very upset by what he saw. Then there was a row, possibly more than one,
between Valerie and Peter's wife, that is Linda. The evidence of the latter on this
point, which I accept, was that there was a row about the third day of the visit. She
said that she and her husband had been out dancing and when they came back
c they found that Valerie had been cooking and ironing, that the place was in a mess
and that something had got burned by the iron. The immediate result was that
Linda walked out of the house and went off to her mother's. I think that this must
have happened on the Thursday night. In any event, Valerie took Mrs Beaney home
early on the Saturday morning and I infer that their departure was hastened, if not
actually caused, by the events which I have described.
d A more important matter was dealt with at some length in the evidence. Although
it does not have any direct relevance to the issues in this action, I think I ought to say
something about it. Valerie said that during this visit there was a discussion between
her and Peter and his wife about the future of the house and that Peter said that
she should have it for all she had done for their mother. She said that he was in a
very emotional state. She said that the conversation took place downstairs at about
e eight o' clock on the first evening of the visit after Mrs Beaney had gone up to bed.
Peter categorically denied that there was any discussion about the future of the
house. His wife, however, said that there was a discussion late one night up in their
bedroom, but that there were no mention of the house, only of money. She thought
that the discussion took place the night before the row.
The evidence was full of conflicts and very confusing. However, Peter's wife
f said that money was mentioned and I think it unlikely that money would have been
discussed in isolation from the house. After all, as I shall mention shortly, the house
was Mrs Beaney's only asset of any value and it is highly unlikely that it would have
been excluded from any discussion about her property. However, I am not persuaded
that there was anything in the nature of an agreement as to what should happen.
Peter's wife said that she was disgusted that this topic should be raised while Mrs
g Beaney was still alive and I think that that is probably how the matter was left. On
the other hand, I am prepared to accept that by the end of the visit Valerie, about
whose recollection I shall have more to say later, did think that Peter wanted her to
have the house, or at least the major share in it.
On Monday, 7th May, just over two weeks after she had returned home, Mrs
Beaney was admitted to the National Hospital for Nervous Diseases in Queen Square,
h London WC1. She stayed there for two weeks until Monday, 21st May. It was during
this period, on Wednesday, 16th May, that she executed the disputed transfer. I will
deal with the evidence relating to this very important period later.
On 29th May, eight days after her discharge from Queen Square, Mrs Beaney was
admitted to the Springfield Mental Hospital, a long-term mental hospital, where she
remained for most of the time until her death. In fact, she died in St George's Hospital,
j Tooting, having been removed there from Springfield for the second time on the
breaking of a leg. The date of her death was 19th June 1974.
Peter and Gillian both said that they first heard of the transfer of the house to
Valerie after Mrs Beaney's death through a telephone call from Valerie to Gillian.
For reasons which I will give later I accept their evidence on this point. In any event,
on 9th July there was a meeting of all three children at Miss Bray's office to discuss

the position. Shortly afterwards Peter and Gillian sought separate advice and there was correspondence between solicitors which culminated in the issue of the writ in this action on 12th September 1975. Meanwhile, Mrs Beaney having also died intestate, on 4th July 1975, Peter and Gillian had obtained a grant of letters of administration to her estate. If the transfer was ineffectual, the house will form part of Mrs Beaney's estate and, subject to administration, the three children will be beneficially entitled to it in equal shares. The estate was sworn at £15,151 gross, of which £14,000 presented the value of the house and the balance cash and personal effects. It is therefore clear that the house was Mrs Beany's only asset of value.

Before dealing with the events of May 1973 I will state my views as to the principles of law applicable to this case.

There appears to be no authority which deals clearly with the degree or extent of understanding required for the validity of a voluntary disposition made by deed. The reason for this, no doubt, is that it is unusual for a person who is, or may be, of unsound mind to make a gift of any substance without his affairs having first been subjected to the jurisdiction of the Court of Protection. It is established that a patient cannot, even during a lucid interval, make a valid disposition of his property inter vivos, since that would raise a conflict with the court's control of his affairs. The case of a will is different. A patient can make a valid will during a lucid interval. That is because a will does not take effect until death, at which time the Court of Protection has no further concern for his affairs. There is therefore no conflict of control. The distinction was discussed and affirmed by the Court of Appeal in Re Walker[1]; see also Re Marshall, Marshall v Whately[2]. Mrs Beaney was not a patient of the Court of Protection. I must therefore consider the position on general principles.

The test in regard to deeds was stated in general terms by the House of Lords in Ball v Mannin[3]. From that decision may be extracted the principle that the question in each case is whether the person concerned is capable of understanding what he does by executing the deed in question when its general purport has been fully explained to him. Both counsel for Peter and Gillian and counsel for Valerie accept that this is the correct test. They differ, and the difference could be important, over the degree or extent of understanding required before a voluntary disposition of the nature found in the present case is valid.

The rival contentions are these. Counsel for Valerie says that it was only necessary for Mrs Beaney to understand, first, that she was making a gift, secondly, that the subject-matter of the gift was the house, and, thirdly, that the person to whom she was giving it was her daughter Valerie. That is the narrow view. Counsel for Peter and Gillian, on the other hand, says that this is not enough. He says that it was also necessary for Mrs Beaney to understand that she was giving away her only asset of value, and was thus depriving her other two children of any real interest in her estate. In other words, counsel for Peter and Gillian says that the degree of understanding required in a case such as this is the same as that required for the making of a valid will, where it is established that a high degree is required, including an understanding of the claims of all potential beneficiaries and the extent of the property to be disposed of. That is the broad view. The reason why the distinction may be important is that, although it was explained to Mrs Beaney that she was making a gift of her house to Valerie, she was never told that its effect would be to deprive her other two children of any real interest in her estate. Accordingly, if counsel for Peter and Gillian is right, that is an end of the case and Peter and Gillian must succeed.

Authority apart, and with regard to the present case, I would be surprised to find that the law allowed a lower degree of understanding on the part of Mrs Beaney for the execution of the transfer dated 16th May 1973 than it would have required for her

---

1   [1905] 1 Ch 160
2   [1920] 1 Ch 284, [1920] All ER Rep 190
3   (1829) 3 Bli NS 1

to make a will on the same date. In either case she was in practice, or would have been
in fact, disposing of the whole of her estate. In either case I would have thought it
necessary for her to understand that that was what she was doing and to appreciate
the claims of the other potential beneficiaries, namely her two younger children.

Is there any authority which runs against this view? I think not. A case which has
been cited for the general proposition that the degree of understanding required for
testamentary capacity is somewhat different from that required for the execution of a
deed (see Halsbury's Laws of England[1]) is *Birkin v Wing*[2]. But that was a case of a
contract, which, although no doubt analogous to the case of a deed made for consideration, may be a long way from one of a gift. Further, Kekewich J, having said
that there was normally a great difference between contractual and testamentary
capacity, gave the example of an exceptional contract for which the mental capacity
required might be quite as large as for a will. He then considered other possible
cases and stated his conclusion to be that you must take all the circumstances into
consideration. In *Manches v Trimborn*[3], another contract case, Hallett J said that the
question of what mental capacity was necessary in any particular matter in order to
render the consent of the party concerned a real consent differed with the nature of
the transaction. He then contrasted capacity for the purposes of criminal liability at
one end of the scale with testamentary capacity at the other, but said that in between
those two extremes, there might be all sorts of different degrees of mental capacity
required in order to render a consent to a given transaction a real consent. Finally,
counsel for Valerie, for whose researches I am grateful, referred me to *Gibbons v
Wright*[4], a decision of the High Court of Australia presided over by Dixon CJ. That
was a case where the instruments in question were deeds made for consideration.
A large part of the judgment was concerned with the question whether such a
deed, if made by a person without sufficient mental capacity, is void or merely
voidable. The facts of the present case make it unnecessary for me to consider whether
that distinction could be material in the case of a voluntary disposition, and I express
no view on that point. However, the judgment is of value for its review of the cases
(including those to which I have referred) and its statement[5] that the principle is—

'that the mental capacity required by the law in respect of any instrument is
relative to the particular transaction which is being effected by means of the
instrument, and may be described as the capacity to understand the nature of
that transaction when it is explained.'

In the circumstances, it seems to me that the law is this. The degree or extent of
understanding required in respect of any instrument is relative to the particular
transaction which it is to effect. In the case of a will the degree required is always high.
In the case of a contract, a deed made for consideration or a gift inter vivos, whether
by deed or otherwise, the degree required varies with the circumstances of the transaction. Thus, at one extreme, if the subject-matter and value of a gift are trivial in
relation to the donor's other assets a low degree of understanding will suffice. But, at
the other, if its effect is to dispose of the donor's only asset of value and thus for
practical purposes to pre-empt the devolution of his estate under his will or on his
intestacy, then the degree of understanding required is as high as that required for a
will, and the donor must understand the claims of all potential donees and the extent
of the property to be disposed of.

On this view, and in the circumstances which I have mentioned, Peter and Gillian
must succeed. However, in case I am wrong, and the narrower view is correct, I must

---

1   29 Halsbury's Laws (3rd Edn) 412, 413, para 804
2   (1890) 63 LT 80
3   (1946) 115 LJKB 305
4   (1954) 91 CLR 423
5   91 CLR 423 at 438

now consider the events of May 1973 in detail, in order to see whether Valerie has established that Mrs Beaney did know that she was making a gift of the house to her. *a* [His Lordship then considered the evidence as to the conversation of 7th May and certain other matters and continued:] On 16th May there met at the hospital Valerie, Miss Bray and Mr Gellatly. Miss Bray did not think that she had ever met Mrs Beaney before. She certainly had not met Mr Gellatly. Miss Bray said that Mr Gellatly was there because she felt that, as she had not taken instructions directly from Mrs Beaney, it was desirable that there should be someone else there who could say from *b* his own knowledge that Mrs Beaney did wish to make the transfer. Her first suggestion had been that there should be a medical witness, but Valerie said that when she went to the ward sister they were not interested. Valerie then got Mr Gellatly to come.

The three of them went into the ward together. The first thing they had to do was to find Mrs Beaney, who was not anywhere near her bed. After preliminaries, *c* including the introduction of Miss Bray to Mrs Beaney, they all sat round Mrs Beaney's bed. Valerie told her mother that Miss Bray had come to see about the house. Miss Bray then produced the transfer and told Mrs Beaney that if she executed it it would have the effect of giving the house to Valerie absolutely. Miss Bray said that she asked Mrs Beaney certain questions, but that they were all susceptible of the answer 'Yes' or 'No'. She asked her whether she understood what would happen and *d* whether that was what she wanted. The questions were put to her twice and on both occasions she answered or nodded affirmatively. All three persons present said they thought Mrs Beaney understood what she was doing. Apparently she signed quite easily and, before she did so, she tried out her signature once or twice on the back of an envelope. Valerie said that her mother seemed more alert than usual; she had been apprehensive about it and was surprised that it went so easily. Mr Gellatly, *e* who knew Mrs Beaney well by this time, said that his general impression was that he had certainly known Mrs Beaney worse. He was quite sure that she understood what they were talking about. At one point, possibly more than once, Miss Bray asked Mr Gellatly whether Mrs Beaney wished to make the gift to Valerie and he said he thought she did. However, he had not seen Mrs Beaney for two weeks or so beforehand and I do not see how he could have been in a better position to know *f* what Mrs Beaney's intentions were than Miss Bray herself. It seems that Mrs Beaney did not in fact recognise Mr Gellatly on this occasion. So much for the evidence of the three persons who were present when Mrs Beaney executed the transfer. [His Lordship then considered the medical evidence, and the evidence of members of the family who had visited Mrs Beaney at the hospital, and continued:] In all the circumstances, I might be prepared to accept that Mrs Beaney knew that the transfer had something *g* to do with the house and that she knew that its effect was to do something which her daughter Valerie wanted. But I am quite satisfied on the evidence, and I find as a fact, that she was not capable of understanding, and did not understand, that she was making an absolute gift of the property to Valerie. I should add that the evidence of Valerie herself about the conversation with her mother on 7th May would make it very difficult, if not impossible, for me to find that Mrs Beaney had intended to *h* make an outright gift of the property to her. That conversation, which had been the only recent conversation on the subject, assuming Mrs Beaney had understood its import, would have led her to believe only that the property was to be put into Valerie's name in case it was necessary to sell it or deal with it for Mrs Beaney's maintenance. That is something entirely different from an outright gift.

In the circumstances, even if the narrow view of the law is correct, my findings of *j* fact entitle Peter and Gillian to succeed in the action.

I wish to make two further points. First, counsel for Peter and Gillian, as he was perfectly entitled to do, offered some criticisms of Miss Bray for the way in which she handled the transfer. However, a criticism by the court, particularly of a solicitor, is of a different order and I wish to make it clear that I have not considered whether any such criticism would be justified or not. Miss Bray did not come here to answer for her own conduct. She came here to give evidence in an action between other parties, and that she did fairly and with candour.

Secondly, I would like to say a little more about Valerie herself. During the course of her evidence she told me with great emotion that from 1949 she had been bound up with her mother's health. She described an incident soon after Mrs Beaney had contracted diabetes in that year. Her mother said she did not want her to go out and play with her friends, but that she wanted her to stay in and help her. Valerie was then aged about nine. Valerie said that from 1949 onwards she felt that a burden had been placed on her to look after her mother. I would like to say that so far as the evidence given in this court is concerned there has been nothing which could persuade me that Valerie did not fully and faithfully discharge that burden, particularly after her father's death. I believe that she was very close to her mother in her last years, so close in fact that she has not been able to distinguish between her own wishes and what she believes her mother would have wished. I am quite certain that Valerie genuinely thought that her mother wished her to have the house and I do not believe that she thought she was doing anything wrong in procuring the execution of the transfer. I observe that there was no alternative claim made in the action based on unconscionable dealing or anything like that. It is to the credit of Valerie that such a claim was not made, and, indeed, it was rightly not made, because I do not see that it could have succeeded. As to Valeries' recollection of events, I have had firmly to reject it on one point. She said in her evidence that on the morning of 16th May she made telephone calls to both Gillian and Peter, informing them that the transfer was going to be made that afternoon. However, both the other children denied this and, without going into detail, it is clear that I must accept their evidence on this point. Counsel for Peter and Gillian, quite rightly, did not accuse Valerie of deliberately trying to mislead me. My belief is that she may have intended to let them know what was happening, later that she realised that she ought to have done so and finally that she came to believe that she had. I think that counsel for Peter and Gillian was quite right in saying that there were certain parts of her evidence which showed that she was a witness whose recollection could genuinely be affected by later events and subsequent consideration of what would have been the right thing to do. At the same time, I do not think that just because Valerie did not let the others know she acted in an underhand manner. As I have already said, I think that after April 1973 she had got it into her head that Peter at least was quite content that she should have the house, or at least the major share in it. She may have been quite wrong about this, but that does not mean that she was deceitful.

Finally I should say that I have great sympathy for Valerie. It may very well be that if Mrs Beaney had been of sound mind and understanding she would indeed have wanted Valerie to have the house, so she could go on living there after her death. The two younger children are married with their own houses, their own families and their own lives. It would have been perfectly understandable if Mrs Beaney had wanted to do as much as she could to provide security for her eldest daughter. But that, unfortunately, is not the question in this action. I have to view the facts as they stand, and it is clear that the transfer cannot be maintained.

The claim for a declaration succeeds and I will now hear counsel on questions of consequential relief.

Declaration granted.

Solicitors: *Owen, White & Catlin* (for Peter and Gillian); *Bower, Cotton & Bower* (for Valerie).

Tokunbo Williams Barrister.

Cookson v Knowles

HOUSE OF LORDS

LORD DIPLOCK, VISCOUNT DILHORNE, LORD SALMON, LORD FRASER OF TULLYBELTON AND
LORD SCARMAN

13th, 14th, 15th MARCH, 24th MAY 1978

*Fatal accident – Damages – Pecuniary loss – Calculation – Division of award into two parts –
Pre-trial loss and post-trial loss – Pre-trial loss to be calculated arithmetically – Post-trial loss
based on deceased's estimated earnings at date of trial and appropriate multiplier.*

*Interest – Damages – Personal injury – Fatal accident – Pre-trial loss and post-trial loss –
Interest on award for pre-trial loss at half-rate – No interest for post-trial loss.*

In December 1973 the plaintiff's husband was killed in a motor accident for which the
defendant was responsible. At the date of his death the husband was aged 49 and was
in steady employment as a wood-work machinist. If he had lived, he would have
qualified for a retirement pension at the age of 65, at which age he might have been
expected to cease working. The plaintiff, who was aged 45 at the date of her husband's
death, brought an action against the defendant for damages under the Fatal Accidents
Acts 1846 to 1959. The trial of the action took place in May 1976. In calculating the
damages to be awarded the judge took the plaintiff's dependency at the date of trial
as being £2,250 per annum and applied a multiplier of 11, giving a capital sum of
£24,750. He then awarded interest at nine per cent (the short term investment rate)
on the whole of that amount from the date of death until the date of judgment
(£5,412). The defendant appealed to the Court of Appeal[a] which held (i) that, in
view of the increase in the annual rate of inflation in the 1970s, awards under the
Fatal Accidents Acts were to be divided into two parts, the first part being the actual
pecuniary loss of the dependant up to the date of the trial, calculated arithmetically
like special damages, and the second part being the future pecuniary loss to the
dependant from the date of the trial onwards, calculated by taking the earnings
which the deceased would have been receiving at the date of the trial and then
applying the appropriate multiplier; (ii) that in determining the multiplier no regard
was to be had to the possibility of future inflation; (iii) that interest was to be awarded
in respect of the first part of the award only and was to be calculated at half the short
term investment rate; and (iv) that no interest was to be awarded in respect of the
second part of the award. They calculated that the plaintiff's dependency at the
date of the husband's death was £1,614 and at the date of trial £1,980, owing to
increases in wages during the 2½ years that had elapsed since December 1973, and
awarded her (i) £4,492 (2½ × £1,797 average annual dependency) for the actual
pecuniary loss, which, with interest at 4½ per cent, came to a total of £4,997, and
(ii) £16,830 for the pecuniary loss from the date of trial onwards (8½ × £1,980 with no
interest), making a total award of £21,827. The plaintiff appealed contending (i)
that in the current financial climate the possibility of future inflation should no
longer be disregarded in assessing damages and that the award should be increased
to make an allowance for inflation after the date of the trial, and (ii) that interest
should be given on the post-trial as well as the pre-trial damages.

Held – (i) In the current financial climate a more reliable assessment of the loss
sustained by a dependant as a result of the deceased's death could be obtained in
normal fatal accident cases if the damages were split into two parts (a) the pecuniary
loss which it was estimated had been sustained by the dependant from the date of
death until the date of trial ('the pre-trial loss'), and (b) the pecuniary loss which it

was estimated the dependant would sustain from the trial onwards ('the future loss')
for which the proper multiplicand was the figure to which it was estimated the annual
dependency would have amounted by the date of the trial, and damages should
as a general rule be assessed in that way in such cases. No additional allowance
was to be made for future inflation after the date of the trial because inflation would
be counterbalanced by the higher rates of interest that would be given if the sum
awarded were invested in gilt-edged securities, where the rate of tax on the dependant's gross income was low. In normal cases interest on the pre-trial loss should
be awarded for the period between the date of death and the date of trial at half
the short term interest rates current during that period, but no interest should
be awarded on the future loss (see p 607 f to h, p 611 c to e and h to p 612 a and d to
g and j to p 613 b, p 614 b to f, p 615 c and f to p 616 b and g and p 617 c d, post); dictum
of Lord Diplock in *Mallett v McMonagle* [1969] 2 All ER at 190 and of Lord Pearson
in *Taylor v O'Connor* [1970] 1 All ER at 378 followed; *Jefford v Gee* [1970] 1 All ER 1202
considered.

(ii) On the evidence the plaintiff's case was a 'normal' one and the Court of Appeal
had applied the correct principles in assessing damages and awarding interest on the
first part of the award only; it followed that there were no grounds for interfering
with their decision and the appeal would be dismissed (see p 607 c, p 609 f, p 611 e
and h to p 612 a and g and j to p 613 b, p 615 f to p 616 b and g and p 617 c d, post).

Per Curiam. (i) The same principles regarding the effect of the prospect of continuing
inflation on the assessment of damages for future loss of dependency in fatal accident
cases apply pari passu to claims for loss of future earnings (or earning power) in
personal injury actions, and the same principles regarding the award of interest
on the two components of the total claim to damages in fatal accident cases also
apply to claims for loss of earnings in personal injury actions, where the corresponding
first component is the loss of earnings up to the date of the trial claimed under the
head of special damage (see p 612 h to p 613 b and p 617 d, post).

(ii) In exceptional cases, where the annuity is large enough to attract income tax at a
high rate, it might be appropriate to increase the multiplier or to allow for future
inflation in some other way (see p 612 j to p 613 b, p 616 b c and p 617 d, post).

Decision of the Court of Appeal [1977] 2 All ER 820 affirmed.

Notes

For interest payable on damages, see 12 Halsbury's Laws (4th Edn) para 1204.

For the measure of damages under the Fatal Accidents Acts, see 12 Halsbury's Laws
(4th Edn) para 1150, and for cases on the subject, see 36(1) Digest (Reissue) 360-365,
1456-1483.

For the Fatal Accidents Acts 1846 to 1959, see 23 Halsbury's Statutes (3rd Edn) 778,
780, 801.

As from 1st September 1976, the Fatal Accidents Acts 1846 to 1959 have been
replaced by the Fatal Accidents Act 1976.

Cases referred to in opinions

General Tire and Rubber Co v Firestone Tyre and Rubber Co Ltd [1975] 2 All ER 173,
[1975] 1 WLR 819, HL, 36(2) Digest (Reissue) 1299, 3874.

Jefford v Gee [1970] 1 All ER 1202, [1970] 2 QB 130, [1970] 2 WLR 702, [1970] 1 Lloyd's
Rep 107, CA, Digest (Cont Vol C) 709, 182a.

Macrae v Reed and Mallick Ltd 1961 SC 68.

Mallett v McMonagle [1969] 2 All ER 178, [1970] AC 166, [1969] 2 WLR 767, [1969] 1
Lloyd's Rep 127, HL, 17 Digest (Reissue) 219, 910.

Ruby v Marsh (1975) 132 CLR 642, 6 ALR 385.

Smith v Middleton 1972 SC 30.

Taylor v O'Connor [1970] 1 All ER 365, [1971] AC 115, [1970] 2 WLR 472, 49 ATC 37,
[1970] TR 37, HL, 36(1) Digest (Reissue) 362, 1472.

Young v Percival [1974] 3 All ER 677, [1975] 1 WLR 17, [1975] 1 Lloyd's Rep 130, CA, 36(1) Digest (Reissue) 363, *1473*.

Appeal and cross-appeal
Audrey Cookson, the widow of Frank Cookson deceased and the administratrix of his estate, appealed against an order of the Court of Appeal[1] (Lord Denning MR, Lawton and Bridge LJJ), dated 3rd June 1977 and corrected under RSC Ord 20, r 11, on 29th July 1977, allowing an appeal by the respondent, Edward John Knowles, against an order of Reeve J, dated 22nd June 1976, and ordering that damages of £24,750 and interest of £5,412, awarded in respect of the death of the deceased due to the negligent driving of the respondent, be reduced to damages of £21,322 and interest of £505. The respondent cross-appealed. The facts are set out in the opinion of Lord Diplock.

C D R Rose QC and *Anthony Jolly* for the appellant and cross-respondent.
Piers Ashworth QC and *Michael Kershaw* for the respondent and cross-appellant.

Their Lordships took time for consideration.

24th May. The following opinions were delivered.

LORD DIPLOCK. My Lords, in the instant case the Court of Appeal[1], speaking through Lord Denning MR, has laid down guidelines for the assistance of judges on whom there falls the task of assessing damages in cases brought under the Fatal Accidents Act 1976. These complement some earlier guidelines for the assessment of damages in personal injury cases which had been laid down by the Court of Appeal in *Jefford v Gee*[2]. The trial in *Jefford v Gee*[2] had taken place at a time when the relevant statutory provision empowering courts to award interest on damages was s 3 of the Law Reform (Miscellaneous Provisions) Act 1934. By the time the appeal was heard that section had been amended by s 22 of the Administration of Justice Act 1969.
    As was correctly stated by Lord Denning MR in *Jefford v Gee*[2], the effect of the amendment was not to alter the principles which the court should apply when awarding interest on damages in cases where it decided to do so. What the amendment did was to oblige the court to award interest in all actions for personal injuries or fatal accidents unless it was satisfied that there were special reasons why no interest should be given.
    The section as amended gives to the judge several options as to the way in which he may assess the interest element to be included in the sum awarded by the judgment. He may include interest on the whole of the damages or on a part of them only, as he thinks appropriate. He may award it for the whole or any part of the period between the date when the cause of action arose and the date of judgment and he may award it at different rates for different parts of the period chosen.
    The section gives no guidance as to the way in which the judge should exercise his choice between the various options open to him. This is all left to his discretion; but like all discretions vested in judges by statute or at common law, it must be exercised judicially or, in the Scots phrase used by Lord Emslie in *Smith v Middleton*[3], in a selective and discriminating manner, not arbitrarily or idiosyncratically, for otherwise the rights of parties to litigation would become dependent on judicial whim.
    It is therefore appropriate for an appellate court to lay down guidelines as to what matters it is proper for the judge to take into account in deciding how to exercise the discretion conferred on him by the statute. In exercising this appellate function,

---

1   [1977] 2 All ER 820, [1977] QB 913
2   [1970] 1 All ER 1202, [1970] 2 QB 130
3   1972 SC 30 at 37

the court is not expounding a rule of law from which a judge is precluded from depar-
a ting where special circumstances exist in a particular case; nor indeed, even in cases
where there are no special circumstances, is an appellate court justified in giving
effect to the preference of its members for exercising the discretion in a different
way from that adopted by the judge if the choice between the alternative ways of
exercising it is one on which judicial opinion might reasonably differ.

If a discretion to differentiate in an award of interest on damages between one
b component of the full amount of the award and another is to be exercised judicially,
this calls for an analysis of the nature and manner of assessment of the different kinds of
loss and injury sustained in personal injury and fatal accident cases. Such an analysis
was undertaken by the Court of Appeal in *Jefford v Gee*[1]. Although it was an action
for personal injuries by a living plaintiff, the judgment of the court dealt also with
fatal accident cases, although this could only be obiter.

c The instant case is a typical fatal accident case. There are no special features about
it that distinguish it from the general run of fatal accident cases so far as concerns
awarding interest on damages. The deceased, the husband of the plaintiff, was
killed in a motor accident in December 1973. He was then aged 49 and was in steady
work as a wood-work machinist. Had he lived it would have been 16 years before
he reached the age of 65 when he would have qualified for a retirement pension and,
d in the ordinary course, might have been expected to cease working. The plaintiff
was aged 45 and it was held by the Court of Appeal and is now common ground
that her dependency at the date of death can be taken as £1,614 a year and that by
the date of the trial in June 1976 the dependency as it would have been by then can
be taken as £1,980 a year, owing to increases in wages during the 2½ years that had
elapsed since December 1973.

e The judge assessed damages by applying to the dependency at the date of trial
which he had reckoned at £2,250 per annum a multiplier of 11 years purchase. This
comes to £24,750. He awarded interest on the whole of that amount from the date
of death until the date of judgment at nine per cent, the short term investment rate.
This came to an additional sum of £5,412. In so doing, he was following the guidelines
for fatal accident cases laid down obiter in *Jefford v Gee*[1].

f On appeal, the Court of Appeal varied those guidelines. They held that for the
purpose of awarding interest on damages the damages should be divided into two
parts, one assessed by reference to the assumed dependency during the period
between the date of death and the date of trial, and the other by reference to the
assumed future dependency from the date of trial onwards. On the former part,
interest should be awarded at half the short term investment rate, but on the latter
g part in respect of future dependency no interest should be allowed. The court also
took occasion, although this could only be obiter, to vary the guidelines for personal
injury cases laid down in *Jefford v Gee*[1] by holding that damages for non-economic
loss, ie pain and suffering and loss of amenities, should be assessed on the scale at
which such damages were currently being assessed at the date of trial, but that no
interest should be allowed on this part of the damages. Both these changes were
h said to be required by reason of the increase in the annual rate of inflation since the
decision in *Jefford v Gee*[1].

My Lords, in general I agree with the judgment of the Court of Appeal in the
instant case and, except in one respect, with the reasoning of that judgment and of
the earlier judgment in *Jefford v Gee*[1]. Two separate though related questions are
involved in the appeal to your Lordships' House. The first is whether and, if so, how
j should the prospect of continued inflation after the date of trial be dealt with in
assessing the capital sum to be awarded by way of damages in fatal accident and
personal injury cases. The second is whether in such actions, where there are no

---

1   [1970] 1 All ER 1202, [1970] 2 QB 130

unusual circumstances, interest should be awarded on the whole or part of that capital sum and, if the latter, on what part.

When the first Fatal Accidents Act was passed in 1846, its purpose was to put the dependants of the deceased, who had been the bread-winner of the family, in the same position financially as if he had lived his natural span of life. In times of steady money values, wage levels and interest rates this could be achieved in the case of the ordinary working man by awarding to his dependants the capital sum required to purchase an annuity of an amount equal to the annual value of the benefits with which he had provided them while he lived, and for such period as it could reasonably be estimated they would have continued to enjoy them but for his premature death. Although this does not represent the way in which it is calculated such a capital sum may be expressed as the product of multiplying an annual sum which represents the 'dependency' by a number of years' purchase. This latter figure is less than the number of years which represents the period for which it is estimated that the dependants would have continued to enjoy the benefit of the dependency, since the capital sum will not be exhausted until the end of that period and in the meantime so much of it as is not yet exhausted in each year will earn interest from which the dependency for that year could in part be met.

The number of years' purchase to be used in order to calculate the capital value of an annuity for a given period of years thus depends on the rate of interest which it is assumed that money would earn, during the period. The higher the rate of interest, the lower the number of years' purchase. Thus to give an illustration that is relevant to the instant case, the capital value of an annuity for the full 16 years which would have elapsed if the deceased had lived to work until he was 65 would require the 11 years' purchase adopted as multiplier by the judge at an assumed interest rate (whether he worked it out or not) of 4¾ per cent; whereas it would need only seven years as multiplier if the assumed interest rate were 12 per cent.

Today the assessment of damages in fatal accident cases has become an artificial and conjectural exercise. Its purpose is no longer to put dependants, particularly widows, into the same economic position as they would have been in had their late husband lived. Section 4 of the Fatal Accidents Act 1976[1] requires the court in assessing damages to leave out of account any insurance money or benefit under national insurance or social security legislation or other pension or gratuity which becomes payable to the widow on her husband's death, while s 3(2) forbids the court to take into account the remarriage of the widow or her prospects of remarriage. Nevertheless, the measure of the damages recoverable under the statute remains the same as if the widow were really worse off by an annual sum representing the money value of the benefits which she would have received each year of the period during which her husband would have provided her with them if he had not been killed. This kind of assessment, artificial though it may be, nevertheless calls for consideration of a number of highly speculative factors, since it requires the assessor to make assumptions not only as to the degree of likelihood that something may actually happen in the future, such as the widow's death, but also as to the hypothetical degree of likelihood that all sorts of things might happen in an imaginary future in which the deceased lived on and did not die when in actual fact he did. What in that event would have been the likelihood of his continuing in work until the usual retiring age? Would his earnings have been terminated by death or disability before the usual retiring age or interrupted by unemployment or ill-health? Would they have increased, and if so, when and by how much? To what extent if any would he have passed on the benefit of any increases to his wife and dependent children? Would she have gone out to work when the children had grown older and made her own contribution to the family expenses in relief of his?

Looked at from a juristic standpoint, it may be accurate to say, as did the majority

1 The Fatal Accidents Acts 1846 to 1959 are consolidated in the 1976 Act

of the High Court of Australia in *Ruby v Marsh*[1], that the entirety of the damage is
a sustained by the widow at the moment that her husband dies; but what she loses
then is only the expectancy of the benefits which he would have provided for her in
future years if he had lived. Looked at realistically her loss of the benefit for each
year is not suffered until the year in which it would have been received; and at
the date of death the present value of that future loss is such a sum as would grow
to the money value of the benefit if it were invested at compound interest at current
b rates until the year in which it would have been received.

So if it be assumed that apart from any other factors, owing to future rises in the
general level of wages consequent on monetary inflation, the value in inflated currency
of the benefits provided to his wife by the deceased would have progressively increased if he had lived, it would be possible by this means to calculate the total capital
value at the date of death of the deceased of yearly sums of amounts which did not
c remain constant but varied from time to time or increased progressively for each
successive year during the term of the annuity.

As regards any such assumption for the period after the trial, it can only be conjectural, since it involves in addition to the prospects of continuing monetary inflation,
the various speculative factors particular to the deceased which I have previously
mentioned. For the period between the death and trial, however, there will be some
d hard facts available which reduce, though they cannot eliminate, reliance on conjecture. Thus if it can be proved, as it was in the instant case, that if the deceased had
continued in good health in his existing employment for the 2½ years that had elapsed
between his death and the date of trial his wages would have risen by some 27 per cent
(which represents a rate of 10 per cent per annum compound over the 2½ years)
and the judge feels justified on the evidence in assuming a likelihood, which, however,
e necessarily falls short of certainty, that the dependency during that period would
have increased proportionately, there is a relatively firm foundation on which to
base an assessment of the value of the benefits lost by the widow up to the date
of trial.

I agree therefore with that part of the decision of the Court of Appeal that holds
that, as a general rule in fatal accident cases the damages should be assessed in two
f parts, the first and less speculative component being an estimate of the loss sustained
up to the date of trial, and the second component an estimate of the loss to be
sustained thereafter.

In so deciding the Court of Appeal assigned as the reason for assessing the damages
in two parts not the greater reliability of the assessment of the loss suffered by the
widow during the period up to the date of trial, but the fact that only by this method
g does one obtain as a starting point for estimating the loss to be suffered by the widow
in future years after the trial, a figure for 'the dependency' greater than that existing
at the date of death by an amount that reflects the influence of inflation on the general
level of wages since the deceased's death. It is at this point in the reasoning that, with
respect, I part company with them.

What they in fact did was to assess the annual dependency during the 2½ years
h up to the trial at the mean figure of £1,797 accepted by the court as applicable
during that period. For the remaining period of dependency after the date of trial
they applied a multiplier of 8½ years' purchase (viz the judge's 11 years minus 2½)
to the figure of £1,980 to which they accepted the dependency would have risen by
the date of the trial. By calculating the future dependency in this way and using a
j figure 27 per cent higher than the dependency at the date of death, they considered
that effect would be given to the increase in the general rate of wages owing to
inflation which had actually occurred between the date of death and the date of
trial; but apparently they did not think that their calculations made any allowance

---

1   (1975) 132 CLR 642

for the possibility of continuing inflation thereafter. In this, they were in my view
mistaken.   a

In *Mallet v McMonagle*[1], when the rate of inflation was running at an average rate
of three to 3½ per cent per annum, I suggested that its effects could be offset, to some
extent at any rate, by prudent investment in buying a home, in growth or in short
term high interest yielding securities; and I went on to give some examples of the
effects of interest rates on the capital value of annuities. High rates are obtainable in
times of inflation because the interest sought by a lender represents not only what he   b
would require in times of stable currency for foregoing the use of his money for a year,
but also an additional sum that is sufficient to restore to him in depreciated currency
the buying power which his money represented when he lent it.

I had supposed that what I myself had said in 1970[2] and Lord Pearson had repeated
in 1971 in *Taylor v O'Connor*[3], that the rate of inflation could be largely offset by
prudent investment policy, would no longer hold good once inflation was proceeding   c
at rates as high as those that have been current in the last three or four years. This
has proved to be the case with investment in equities and growth stocks; but, as has
been demonstrated by arithmetical tables produced by the respondent, it has not
been so in the case of investment in fixed interest bearing securities at any rate if the
rate of tax on the dependant's gross income is low. The rate of return on these
securities between the dates of death and trial has been of the order of 14 per cent   d
gross; thus giving to an investor in the tax bracket which would have been applicable
to the plaintiff in the instant case a net return of 12 per cent. This is the relevant type
of investment which is to be assumed for the purpose of calculating the present
value of an annuity. At this net rate of interest the multiplier of 11 years' purchase
adopted by the judge and split into 2½ and 8½ years by the Court of Appeal is sufficient
to provide an annuity for the whole period of 16 years of a constant amount between   e
55 per cent and 60 per cent greater than the annual sum found by the Court of Appeal
to be the dependency at the date of death and some 24 per cent greater than the
assumed dependency at the date of trial.

So far as inflation and increasing wages would affect dependency in future years,
however, the effects are progressive. If allowance is to be made for future inflation a
more relevant calculation would be of the capital cost of an annuity which increased   f
from one year to another throughout the period. In the instant case the product of
11 years' purchase of a sum of £1,614 which was found by the Court of Appeal to be
the dependency at the date of the deceased's death would produce at an assumed
net rate of interest of 12 per cent a capital sum sufficient to purchase an annuity
starting at £1,614 and increasing by £180 in each successive year throughout the
whole period of 16 years. For the first 2½ years between death and trial this gives   g
figures which are not very far off what the evidence showed to be the actual rate of
increase of wages during that period in the kind of work in which the deceased had
been employed. They take three years instead of 2½ to reach £1,980. For the remaining
13½ years which would have elapsed before the deceased would have reached normal
retiring age the capital sum would provide for continuing annual increases of the
same amount rising in the last year to a dependency of £4,314. Since the annual   h
rise is constant and inflation operates at a compound rate this calculation provides
for a diminishing rate of future inflation. On the other hand, it makes no allowance
for the various hazards of working life that may have ended, interrupted or reduced
the earning power of the deceased before he reached normal retiring age of 65.

My Lords, calculations such as these are artificial, but so is the measure of damages
called for by the Fatal Accidents Act 1976. The kinds of security with which the   j
calculations are concerned are not typical of the way in which a dependent widow

---

1 [1969] 2 All ER 178, [1970] AC 166
2 *Mallett v McMonagle* [1969] 2 All ER 178 at 190, [1970] AC 166 at 175
3 [1970] 1 All ER 365 at 378, 379, [1971] AC 115 at 142

(who will have other sources of income as well) is likely to invest the damages she
a receives; but they represent the kinds of security most appropriate for providing
the annuity on the capital cost of which the assessment of damages in fatal accident
cases has to be based. They demonstrate that even in periods of inflation much
higher than those contemplated at the time of *Mallett v McMonagle*[1] and *Taylor v
O'Connor*[2], the greater part of its effect on the real value of damages recovered in
respect of future annual loss would be counteracted by a compensating increase in
b interest rates.

Quite apart from the prospects of future inflation, the assessment of damages in
fatal accident cases can at best be only rough and ready because of the conjectural
nature of so many of the other assumptions on which it has to be based. The conventional method of calculating it has been to apply to what is found on the evidence to be
a sum representing 'the dependency', a multiplier representing what the judge con-
c siders in the circumstances particular to the deceased to be the appropriate number
of years' purchase. In times of stable currency the multipliers that were used by
judges were appropriate to interest rates of four per cent to five per cent whether the
judges using them were conscious of this or not. For the reasons I have given I adhere
to the opinion Lord Pearson[3] and I[4] had previously expressed, which was applied
by the Court of Appeal in *Young v Percival*[5], that the likelihood of continuing inflation
d after the date of trial should not affect either the figure for the dependency or the
multiplier used. Inflation is taken care of in a rough and ready way by the higher rates
of interest obtainable as one of the consequences of it and no other practical basis of
calculation has been suggested that is capable of dealing with so conjectural a factor
with greater precision.

I turn then to the question of interest on the two components in the award of
e damages; the loss of the dependency sustained by the widow up to the date of trial,
and the future loss of the dependency after that date. I can deal with the matter
shortly, for I agree with the result reached by the Court of Appeal. Once it has been
decided to split the damages into two components which are calculated separately,
the starting point for the second component, the future loss (which I will deal with
first), is the present value not as at the date of death but *at the date of the trial* of an
f annuity equal to the dependency starting then and continuing for the remainder of
the period for which it is assumed the dependency would have enured to the benefit
of the widow if the deceased had not been killed. To calculate what would have been
the present value of that annuity at the date of death, its value at the date of trial
would have to be discounted at current interest rates for the 2½ years which had
elapsed between the death and trial. From the juristic standpoint it is that discounted
g amount and no more to which the widow became entitled at the date of her husband's
death. Interest on that discounted figure to the date of trial would bring it back
up to the higher figure actually awarded. To give in addition interest on that higher
figure would be not only to give interst twice but also to give interest on interest.

On the other hand the first component of the total damages, the loss of dependency up to the date of trial, is in respect of losses that have already been sustained
h over a period of 2½ years before the award is made. Had her husband lived the
widow would have received the benefit of the dependency in successive instalments
throughout that period. A rough and ready method of compensating her for the
additional loss she has sustained by the delay in payment of each instalment (which
ranges from 2½ years to none) is that adopted by the Court of Appeal, viz to give
interest for the whole of the period but at half the short term investment rate on
j the mean annual amount which represents the assumed dependency during that

---

1 [1969] 2 All ER 178, [1970] AC 166
2 [1970] 1 All ER 365, [1971] AC 115
3 [1970] 1 All ER 365 at 379, [1971] AC 115 at 143
4 [1969] 2 All ER 178 at 190, [1970] AC 166 at 175
5 [1974] 3 All ER 677 at 686-688, [1975] 1 WLR 17 at 27-29

period. Looked at from the juristic standpoint the justification for giving interest at only half the current rate is that the amount that the widow became entitled to at the date of her husband's death in respect of the instalments of the dependency which would have enured to her benefit up to the date of trial, would be the present value of each successive instalment as *at the date of death*. To calculate that value the nominal amount of the first instalment after the death would not need to be discounted at all, that of the median instalment would need to be discounted at current rates, but for half the period only between date of death and trial while that of the last instalment would need to be discounted at current rates for the whole of the period. The discounted figure for the sum of the instalments which represents their present value as at the date of death would thus be less than the sum actually awarded by an amount which represents the discount at current rates of interest on the nominal amount of each instalment for a period which over all the instalments averages approximately half the period between the date of death and trial. So, in effect, interest for half the period has already been included in an award of the sum of the nominal amounts of the instalments due up to the date of trial. To give interest on the sum of the instalments for the whole of that period instead of only half would be to give interest twice. This may be avoided either by halving the period for which interest is given at current rates or by giving interest for the whole period at half the current rates, as suggested by the Court of Appeal.

To summarise: for the reasons I have given, which follow largely on the arithmetical basis for the assessment of damages which is called for by the provisions of the Fatal Accidents Act 1976 I consider that—

1. In the normal fatal accident case, the damages ought, as a general rule, to be split into two parts:

(a) the pecuniary loss which it is estimated the dependants have already sustained from the date of death up to the date of trial ('the pre-trial loss'), and

(b) the pecuniary loss which it is estimated they will sustain from the trial onwards ('the future loss').

2. Interest on the pre-trial loss should be awarded for a period between the date of death and the date of trial at half the short term interest rates current during that period.

3. For the purpose of calculating the future loss, the 'dependency' used as the multiplicand should be the figure to which it is estimated the annual dependency would have amounted by the date of trial.

4. No interest should be awarded on the future loss.

5. No other allowance should be made for the prospective continuing inflation after the date of trial.

I would dismiss this appeal and the respondent's cross-appeal.

The instant case is concerned with damages in fatal accident cases only but the Court of Appeal took occasion to deal also, though obiter, with damages in personal injury cases and your Lordships have been invited to follow suit. It is evident that what I have earlier said about the effect of the prospect of continuing inflation on the assessment of damages for future loss of the dependency in fatal accident cases would apply pari passu to claims for loss of future earnings (or earning power) in personal injury actions; what I have said about awarding interest on the two components of the total claim to damages in fatal accident cases, would also apply to claims for loss of earnings in personal injury actions, where the corresponding first component is the loss of earnings up to the date of trial claimed under the head of special damage. The question of damages for non-economic loss which bulks large in personal injury actions, however, does not arise in the instant case. It has not been argued before your Lordships and I refrain from expressing any view about it.

VISCOUNT DILHORNE. My Lords, I have had the advantage of reading in

draft the speeches of my noble and learned friends, Lord Diplock and Lord Fraser of
Tullybelton. I agree with them and would dismiss this appeal, and the cross-appeal.

LORD SALMON. My Lords, I agree that this appeal and cross-appeal should both
be dismissed broadly on the grounds stated by my noble and learned friend, Lord
Fraser of Tullybelton, with which I completely concur.

There is one matter that I should like to emphasise, namely that in my view it is
impossible to lay down any principles of law which will govern the assessment of
damages for all time. We can only lay down broad guidelines for assessing damages
in cases where the facts are similar to those of the instant case and where economic
factors remain similar to those now prevailing. For example, it was at one time
regarded as axiomatic that, in assessing damages in cases of death, for loss of earnings,
or maintenance, it could safely be assumed that if a substantial part of the sum
awarded was invested in equities, the plaintiff would be amply protected against
inflation because this would be balanced by the rise in equities which would automatically follow inflation. This theory which was regarded by most financial experts as being
beyond doubt is now exploded. But it has not made much difference because sums
awarded as damages, if invested in gilts, now produce interest up to the rate of 14
per cent a year. And so, although in assessing damages the courts still use about the
same multiplicand and multiplier as formerly, the result, by chance, is much the
same. Just as the price of equities ceased to keep pace with inflation so, one day,
may the interest rates of gilts. I entirely agree with Lord Reid when he said in
Taylor v O'Connor[1] that in assessing damages it would 'be quite unrealistic to refuse
to take it [inflation] into account at all'. Inflation, however, is only relevant insofar
as it increases wages. Wages may keep pace with inflation or they may lag behind or
overtake it. If inflation ceases, as it might, to increase interest rates just as it has
failed to increase the capital value of equities, yet it increases the rate of wages, the
whole basis of assessing damages for loss of wages or maintenance will have to be
reconsidered; and the instant case will become as outdated as *Jefford v Gee*[2].

LORD FRASER OF TULLYBELTON. My Lords, three questions are raised in
this appeal. The first relates to the basis on which damages under the Fatal Accidents
Acts 1846 to 1959, and now under the Fatal Accidents Act 1976, ought to be assessed,
and in particular whether it should be similar to the basis used for assessing damages
for personal injuries. The second is whether the prospect of future inflation should be
taken into account in assessing damages under the Acts and, if so, how that should be
done. The third question relates to the principles on which the discretionary power of
the court to award interest on the principal sum of damages under the Acts ought to be
exercised. The questions are separate but to some extent are related to one another.

On the first question the most important point is whether the damages ought to be
assessed as at the date of death or as at the date of trial. In strict theory I think there is
no doubt that they should be assessed as at the date of death, just as in theory they are
assessed at the date of injury in a personal injury case. But the damages awarded to
dependants under the Fatal Accidents Acts for loss of support during what would (but
for the fatal accident) have been the remainder of the deceased person's working
life have to be based on estimates of many uncertain factors, including the length of
time during which the deceased would probably have continued to work and the
amount that he would probably have earned during that time. The court has to make
the best estimates that it can having regard to the deceased's age and state of health
and to his actual earnings immediately before his death, as well as to the prospects of
any increases in his earnings due to promotion or other reasons. But it has always

---

been recognised, and is clearly sensible, that when events have occurred, between the
date of death and the date of trial, which enable the court to rely on ascertained   *a*
facts rather than on mere estimates, they should be taken into account in assessing
damages. Thus if a dependant widow has died between the date of the injured man's
death and the date of the trial or if (before the Fatal Accidents Act 1976, s 3(2) became
law) she had remarried, the fact would be taken into account, just as medical evidence
of facts relating to the injuries of an injured person up to the date of trial is taken into
account in preference to prognosis made immediately after the accident. Similarly   *b*
if the rate of wages paid to those in the same occupation as the deceased person has
increased between the date of death and the date of trial the increase is rightly taken
into account in assessing damages due to his dependants under the Fatal Accidents
Acts. Assessment of damages in this way requires the pecuniary loss to be split into
two parts, relating respectively to the period before the trial and the period after the
trial, in the same way as it is split in a personal accident case. To that extent the   *c*
same method of assessment is used in both classes of case.

The loss of support between the date of death and the date of trial is the total of
the amounts assumed to have been lost for each week between those dates, although
as a matter of practical convenience it is usual to take the median rate of wages as the
multiplicand. In a case such as this, where the deceased's age was such that he would
probably have continued to work until the date of trial, the multiplier of this part of   *d*
the calculation is the number of weeks between the date of death and the date of
trial. That is convenient, although it is strictly speaking too favourable to the plaintiff,
because it treats the probability that, but for the fatal accident, the deceased would
have continued to earn the rate for the job and to apply the same proportion of his
(perhaps increased) earnings to support his dependants as if it were a certainty.
I mention that in order to emphasise how uncertain is the basis on which the whole   *e*
calculation proceeds. That was the method employed by the Court of Appeal,
which calculated the dependency at date of death as £1,614, and at date of trial as
£1,980, giving a median of £1,797 per annum as the multiplicand for the period of
2½ years between the two dates.

For the period after the date of trial, the proper multiplicand is, in my opinion,
based on the rate of wages for the job at the date of trial. The reason is that that is
the latest available information, and, being a hard fact, it is a more reliable starting
point for the calculation than the rate of wages at the time of death. The appropriate
multiplier will be related primarily to the deceased person's age and hence to the
probable length of his working life at the date of death. In the present case the
deceased was aged 49 at the date of his death and the trial judge and the Court of
Appeal used a multiplier of 11. That figure was not seriously criticised by counsel as   *f*
having been inappropriate as at the date of death, although I think it is probably
generous to the appellant. From that figure of 11, the Court of Appeal deducted 2½
in respect of the 2½ years from the date of death to the date of trial, and they used the
resulting figure of 8½ as the multiplier for the damages after the date of trial. In so
doing they departed from the method that would have been appropriate in a personal
injury case and counsel for the appellant criticised the departure as being unfair to the   *g*
appellant. The argument was that if the deceased man had had a twin brother who
had been injured at the same time as the deceased man was killed, and whose claim
for damages for personal injury had come to trial on the same day as the dependant's
claim under the Fatal Accidents Acts, the appropriate multiplier for his loss after the
date of trial would have been higher than 8½. On the assumption, which is probably
correct, that that would have been so, it does not in my opinion follow that the
multiplier of 8½ is too low in the present claim under the Fatal Accidents Acts where
different considerations apply. In a personal injury case, if the injured person has
survived until the date of trial, that is a known fact and the multiplier appropriate
to the length of his future working life has to be ascertained as at the date of trial.
But in a fatal accident case the multiplier must be selected once and for all as at the

date of death, because everything that might have happened to the deceased after that date remains uncertain. Accordingly having taken a multiplier of 11 as at the date of death, and having used 2½ in respect of the period up to the trial, it is in my opinion correct to take 8½ for the period after the date of trial. That is what the Court of Appeal did in this case.

I pass to the second question, which is whether the award should be increased to make allowance for inflation after the date of trial. What is relevant here is not inflation in general, but simply increases in the rate of earnings for the job in which the deceased person would probably have been employed. The reason for the increase is irrelevant. There would be no justification for attempting to protect dependants against the effects of general inflation, except to the extent that they might reasonably expect to have been protected by increases in the deceased person's earnings. At first sight it might seem reasonable that the award for the period after the date of trial should be increased in some way 'to allow for inflation in the future'. But I am satisfied that an increase on that ground would not merely be impossible to calculate on any rational basis, but would also be wrong in principle. The measure of the proper award to a widow (who is generally the main dependant and to whom alone I refer, brevitatis causa) is a sum which, prudently invested would provide her with an annuity equal in amount to the support that she has probably lost through the death of her husband, during the period that she would probably have been supported by him. The assumed annuity will be made up partly of income on the principal sum awarded, and partly of capital obtained by gradual encroachment on the principal. The income element will be at its largest at the beginning of the period and will tend to decline, while the capital element will tend to increase until the principal is exhausted. The multipliers which are generally adopted in practice are based on the assumption (rarely mentioned and perhaps rarely appreciated) that the principal sum of damages will earn interest at about four or five per cent, which are rates that would be appropriate in time of stable currency, as my noble and learned friend, Lord Diplock, pointed out in Mallett v McMonagle[1]. But in times of rapid inflation the rate of interest that can be earned by prudent investment in fixed interest securities tends to be high, as investors seek to protect their capital and also to obtain a positive rate of interest. At the date of the trial in this case (May 1976) it was possible to obtain interest at a rate of approximately 14 per cent in gilt-edged securities, and so long as inflation continues at its present rate of approximately 10 per cent, experience suggests that the interest element in the widow's assumed annuity will be appreciably higher than the four or five per cent on which the multiplier is based. What she loses by inflation will thus be roughly equivalent to what she gains by the high rate of interest, provided she is not liable for a high rate of income tax. In that sense it is possible to obtain a large measure of protection against inflation by prudent investment, although the theory that protection was to be had by investment in equities is now largely exploded. I have referred to the 'assumed' annuity because of course the widow may not choose to apply her award in the way I have mentioned; it is for her to decide and she may invest it so as to make a profit or she may squander it. But the defendant's liability should be calculated on the basis of an assumed annuity. In the normal class of case, such as the present, where the widow's annuity would be of an amount which would attract income tax either at a low rate or not at all, I respectfully agree with the statement of my noble and learned friend in Mallett v McMonagle[1], that the courts in assessing damages under the Fatal Accidents Acts should leave out of account the 'risk of further inflation, on the one hand, and the high interest rates which reflect the fear of it and capital appreciation of property and equities which are the consequence of it on the other hand'. It follows that in my opinion the Court of Appeal came to the right conclusion in Young v Percival[2]. I do not consider that anything I have said is

---

1   [1969] 2 All ER 178 at 190, [1970] AC 166 at 176
2   [1974] 3 All ER 677, [1975] 1 WLR 17

inconsistent with the view expressed by Lord Reid in *Taylor v O'Connor*[1] to the effect
that it would be 'quite unrealistic to refuse to take it [inflation] into account at all'. *a*
The fact is that, as was demonstrated from tables shown to us, inflation and the high
rates of interest to which it gives rise is automatically taken into account by the use
of multipliers based on rates of interest related to a stable currency. It would
therefore be wrong for the court to increase the award of damages by attempting to
make a further specific allowance for future inflation.

In exceptional cases, where the annuity is large enough to attract income tax at a *b*
high rate, it may be necessary for the court to have expert evidence of the spendable
income that would accrue from awards at different levels and to compare the total
annuity with the amount of the lost dependency having regard to the net income
(after tax) of the deceased person. Whether in such cases it might be appropriate to
increase the multiplier, or to allow for future inflation in some other way would be a
matter for evidence in each case.   *c*

With regard to the third question, the purpose of awarding interest on damages is to
compensate the plaintiff insofar as he has been kept out of money which was due to
him before the award is made. Interest is not awarded as a punishment to the debtor
for withholding the money, although any unjustifiable delay on his part would be a
reason for making the award just as unjustified delay by the plaintiff in claiming it
might be a reason for refusing to make an award: see *General Tire and Rubber Co v* *c*
Firestone Tyre and Rubber Co Ltd[2], per Lord Wilberforce and Lord Salmon.

The powers and duties of the court in respect of awarding interest on damages are
now regulated by s 3(1) of the Law Reform (Miscellaneous Provisions) Act 1934 and
the new sub-s (1A) added by s 22 of the Administration of Justice Act 1969. The
latter subsection provides that where damages are awarded in respect of, inter
alia, a person's death (as in the present case) the court *shall* exercise its power to order *e*
payment of interest 'on those damages or on such part of them as the court considers
appropriate, unless the court is satisfied that there are special reasons why no interest
should be given in respect of those damages'. The section evidently leaves a wide
measure of discretion to the court and it gives no indication of the special reasons that
should weigh with the court in deciding whether to order payment of interest or
not. It is a matter for the discretion of the court, and your Lordships' House can
only provide guidelines as to the principles on which the discretion should be exercised. But some guidelines are required in order that the discretion may be exercised
with reasonable consistency.

The Court of Appeal, having split the damages into two parts, pre-trial and post-
trial, gave interest on the former part at half the appropriate rate and gave no interest
on the latter part. That was in line with the decision in *Jefford v Gee*[3] which was a *f*
case of personal injuries. In my opinion the Court of Appeal made its award of
interest on correct principles. The only argument to the contrary that seems to
merit consideration is to the effect that interest ought to have been given on the
post-trial damages as well as on the pre-trial damages, on the ground that the whole
sum of damages was due at the date of death and ought in theory to have been paid
then. An argument to that effect prevailed with the majority of the High Court of *f*
Australia in *Ruby v Marsh*[4] on a construction of s 79A(3)(b) of the Supreme Court Act
1958 of Victoria. Section 79A is in terms broadly similar to those of s 1A of the English
Act of 1934, as amended by the Act of 1969, and insofar as the decision in *Ruby v
Marsh*[4] turned on considerations that would apply to the English legislation, I would
respectfully prefer the view of the minority. The realistic view seems to me to be
that damages for the period after the date of trial are compensation for a loss of

---

1   [1970] 1 All ER 365 at 368, [1971] AC 115 at 130
2   [1975] 2 All ER 173 at 188, 192, [1975] 1 WLR 819 at 836, 841
3   [1970] 1 All ER 1202, [1970] 2 QB 130
4   (1975) 132 CLR 642

dependency which the plaintiff has not suffered at that date and that she is therefore being compensated for future loss. This part of the compensation ought, in theory, to be discounted because it is being paid in advance, but the information that was put (without objection) before the House showed that, in this case, it had not been effectually discounted. The realistic view has hitherto prevailed both in England (see *Jefford v Gee*[1]) and in Scotland where similar, although not identical, statutory provisions apply. In *Macrae v Reed and Mallick Ltd*[2] (a case of personal injuries) Lord Patrick said 'What can never be justified, in my opinion, is an award of interest on loss which the pursuer has not yet sustained at the date of the trial from a date anterior to the Lord Ordinary's interlocutor . . .' and in *Smith v Middleton*[3] (a claim by a widow in respect of the death of her husband) Lord Emslie expressed his general agreement with Lord Patrick's opinion in *Macrae v Reed and Mallick Ltd*[4]. I am of the opinion that the Court of Appeal rightly awarded interest on the damages in respect of the period before the date of trial, and rightly declined to award interest on the damages for the period after the date of trial.

I would dismiss this appeal, and cross-appeal.

LORD SCARMAN. My Lords, I have had the advantage of reading in draft the speeches of my noble and learned friends, Lord Diplock and Lord Fraser of Tullybelton. I agree with them and for the reasons they give would dismiss the appeal and cross-appeal. I add only one comment. Insofar as this appeal is concerned with the award of interest pursuant to s 3 of the Law Reform (Miscellaneous Provisions) Act 1934, as amended by s 22 of the Administration of Justice Act 1969, neither the Court of Appeal nor your Lordships' House can do more than indicate guidelines for the exercise of a judicial discretion conferred on judges by statute. Judicially indicated guidelines should not be treated as though they were a rule of law. They are to be followed unless the particular circumstances of a case, (which in the present context must include any change from currently prevailing financial conditions), indicate that they would be inappropriate. The fact that the Court of Appeal has considered it appropriate in this case to revise the guidance it gave in *Jefford v Gee*[5] illustrates, if I may respectfully say so, the legally correct approach to guidelines declared by an appellate court for the exercise by judges of a discretion conferred by statute.

Appeal and cross-appeal dismissed.

Solicitors: *White & Leonard*, agents for *Blackhurst, Parker & Yates*, Preston (for the appellant and cross-respondent); *Hextall, Erskine & Co*, agents for *Keogh, Rison & Co*, Bolton (for the respondent and cross-appellant).

Christine Ivamy   Barrister.

---

1 [1970] 1 All ER 1202, [1970] 2 QB 130
2 1961 SC 68 at 77
3 1972 SC 30
4 1961 SC 68
5 [1970] 1 All ER 1202, [1970] 2 QB 130

Suffolk County Council v Mason and others

COURT OF APPEAL, CIVIL DIVISION

LORD DENNING MR, ORMROD AND GEOFFREY LANE LJJ

3rd, 7th FEBRUARY 1978

Highway – Classification – Definitive map – Conclusive evidence of classification – Designation of road on definitive map as footpath – Research revealing evidence that until late 17th century road used as public carriageway – Owners of holiday camp erected subsequent to date of definitive map wishing to use road as access for vehicles to and from camp – Whether definitive map conclusive evidence of existence of right of way on foot only until road reclassified on a subsequent review – Whether classification as footpath without prejudice to question whether other rights of way existed over road – National Parks and Access to the Countryside Act 1949, s 32(4)(a).

A roadway which ran along the shore had been used for may years, until the late 17th century, as the main carriageway to a port. The port fell into decay and the roadway ceased to be used for vehicles and was used as a footpath only. In accordance with the National Parks and Access to the Countryside Act 1949 the county council carried out a survey of the county for the purpose of preparing a definitive map, under s 32(1) of the 1949 Act, showing the footpaths, bridleways and roads used as public paths in the county. On the provisional map drawn up prior to settling the definitive map the roadway was shown as a 'footpath' since at that time the local inhabitants regarded it as such. The county council did not receive any objections to their proposal to designate the roadway as a footpath. Accordingly on the definitive map, which was settled on 1st January 1961, the relevant date for the purpose of the 1949 Act, the roadway was designated as a 'footpath'. Subsequently the area around the roadway was developed and a caravan park and holiday camp were erected at its southern end. The defendants, the owners of the holiday camp, wished to use the roadway as a means of access for vehicles going to and from the camp, and having become aware of evidence that the roadway had formerly been used as a public carriageway, asserted that notwithstanding the designation as a footpath in the definitive map, the roadway was a public carriageway and could be used as such. The county council applied to the court for a declaration that on the true construction of s 32(4)(a)[a] of the 1949 Act, read with s 27(6)[b] of the Act, the designation of the roadway as a footpath was conclusive evidence that a right of way on foot only existed over the roadway. The defendants counterclaimed for a declaration that the public had a full right of way over the roadway including a right of passage for vehicles. The judge granted the declaration claimed by the defendants. The county council appealed.

Held – On the true construction of s 32(4)(a) the designation of the roadway as a 'footpath' on the definitive map was conclusive evidence that only a right of way on foot existed over the roadway, and until the roadway was reclassified on a subsequent review under the 1949 Act it could be used only as a footpath. Moreover, there was no justification for reading into para (a) of s 32(4) a provision that designation as a 'footpath' was without prejudice to the existence at the relevant date of other rights of way over the road, for the definition of 'footpath' in s 27(6) was strict and

---

a   Section 32(4)(a) so far as material, is set out at p 620 *h*, post
b   Section 27(6), so far as material, is set out at p 620 *g*, post

unambiguous. It followed that the appeal would be allowed (see p 620 j, p 621 c and h, p 622 b c and j, p 623 b and d e and p 624 b and f, post).

Dictum of Browne LJ in *R v Secretary of State for the Environment, ex parte Hood* [1975] 3 All ER at 249 approved.

Attorney-General v Honeywill [1972] 3 All ER 641 disapproved.

Notes

For the contents of definitive maps as evidence, see 19 Halsbury's Laws (3rd Edn) 175, 176, para 271.

For the National Parks and Access to the Countryside Act 1949, ss 27, 32, see 15 Halsbury's Statutes (3rd Edn) 38, 44.

Cases referred to in judgments

Attorney-General v Honeywill [1972] 3 All ER 641, [1972] 1 WLR 1506, 136 JP 809, 71 LGR 81, Digest (Cont Vol D) 373, 265a.

R v Secretary of State for the Environment, ex parte Hood [1975] 3 All ER 243, [1975] QB 891, [1975] 3 WLR 172, 139 JP 771, 30 P & CR 132, CA, Digest (Cont Vol D) 372, 85Af.

Cases also cited

Attorney-General v Shonleigh Nominees Ltd [1972] 2 All ER 263, [1972] 1 WLR 577, CA.
Morgan v Hertfordshire County Council (1965) 63 LGR 456, CA.

Appeal

This was an appeal by the plaintiffs, Suffolk County Council ('the county council'), against the judgment of Sir Douglas Frank QC sitting as a deputy judge of the Queen's Bench Division given on 10th March 1977 whereby he dismissed the county council's claim for a declaration that on a true construction of the National Parks and Access to the Countryside Act 1949, the fact that the county council's first revised definitive map, covering Lothingland Rural District, showed the way known as Marsh Lane in the Parish of Kessingland as a footpath, was conclusive evidence that at the 'relevant date', 1st January 1961, Marsh Lane was a highway over which the public had a right of way on foot only, and granted to the defendants, Mr Edgar Stanley Lorimer Mason of Denes Holiday Camp, Kessingland, Suffolk, and four other named defendants, on their counterclaim, a declaration that Marsh Lane was in 1835 a highway over which the public had a full right of way including a right of way for the passage of vehicles.

The facts are set out in the judgment of Lord Denning MR.

Alan Fletcher for the county council.
Gerald Moriarty QC and *Stuart Sleeman* for the defendants.

Cur adv vult

LORD DENNING MR. This case has arisen out of the researches of Dr Brooks, the rector of Somerleyton. He has looked into the history of Kessingland. Three hundred years ago it was a port on an estuary between Lowestoft and Southwold. Afterwards it fell into decay as a port. The estuary and haven became silted up with mud flats. These were turned into reed and osier beds. The produce was used for thatching the houses and making baskets. The old village was left about a quarter of a mile inland. Now those old reed beds have been transformed. They are covered with seaside bungalows and caravan camps. The area next to the sea is called Kessingland Beach.

In the days when Kessingland was a port there was a roadway running along the

shore just above the flood level. It took the carts to and from the harbour. When
the harbour became silted up, it took the reed carts. It was maintained with a hard
surface and protected by hedges on each side. It was about 20 feet wide and was
called Marsh Lane. Twenty feet was the width of two reed carts to pass.

About 100 years ago the reed beds were kept no longer. People no longer used
the reeds for thatching. They roofed their houses with tiles or slates. So carts no
longer went along Marsh Lane. It was used by villagers as a footpath and by farmers
as a way to get to their fields with their carts.

Such was the position when Parliament in 1949 passed the National Parks and Access
to the Countryside Act. That Act required the county council to survey all the land
in the county and to prepare a map showing all 'footpaths', 'bridleways' and 'roads
used as public paths'. There were three stages: a draft map, a provisional map,
and a definitive map. All were made in conjuction with the inhabitants of the villages.

After hearing any objections, the first definitive map for Suffolk was settled in
January 1952. Some years later a review was held as required by the statute. A
revised definitive map was settled on 1st January 1961. That is the 'relevant date'
for the purpose of this statute. On each of these maps, and finally on the definitive
map, Marsh Lane was shown as a 'footpath'. It was so shown because all the inhabitants
at that time regarded it as a public footpath. There was no one living to recall that
100 years ago it had been a public carriageway. At any rate, no one objected to
its inclusion on the definitive map as a 'footpath'. It was shown on the map as FP10
and described fully in the statement.

Since the time when the definitive map was settled, the area has been developed.
A large tract of land has been acquired by persons who have erected a caravan park
and holiday camp beyond the southern end of Marsh Lane. They have access to it
by means of a new road called Beach Road, but they desire also to have access by
means of Marsh Lane. If Marsh Lane were available, it would relieve the congestion
of traffic in the summer months.

With this object in mind the owners of the holiday camp have taken advantage of
the researches of Dr Brooks, which show that Marsh Lane is an ancient public carriageway and was used as such for hundreds of years. They wish to have it established as a
public carriageway so as to make it available for all the traffic going to and from the
holiday camp. The Suffolk County Council declined. So a summons was taken out
to determine whether it is a public footpath only or whether it is, as the holiday camp
owners suggest, a public carriageway. This must depend on the statute.

The thing to remember is that Marsh Lane is shown on the definitive map as a
'footpath'. So I must read what 'footpath' means. It is defined in s 27(6) of the 1949
Act as follows: '. . . "footpath" means a highway over which the public have a
right of way on foot only . . .' Note the word 'only' 'a right of way on foot only'.
The next relevant section is s 32(4)(a):

> 'A definitive map and statement prepared under subsection (1) of this section
> shall be *conclusive* as to the particulars contained therein in accordance with the
> foregoing provisions of this section to the following extent, that is to say—(a)
> where the map shows a footpath, the map shall be *conclusive evidence* that there
> was at the relevant date specified in the statement a footpath as shown on the
> map . . .' (emphasis mine).

Note the word 'conclusive'. It seems to me, taking those words as they stand, that
the map is conclusive evidence that there was a 'footpath', that is a 'right of way on
foot only'.

That is a short answer to the case. As a matter of interpretation, when Marsh Lane
is shown on the definitive map as a 'footpath' it is conclusive that it was to be a right
of way on foot only.

That reading of the statute seems to me to be confirmed by the next two paragraphs, paras (b) and (c), of s 32(4). Section 32(4)(b) reads:

a
'where the map shows a bridleway, or a road used as a public path, the map shall be conclusive evidence that there was at the said date a highway as shown on the map, and that the public had thereover at that date a right of way on foot and a right of way on horseback or leading a horse. . . .'

But it goes on to make this qualification:

b
'. . . so however that this paragraph shall be without prejudice to any question whether the public had at that date any right of way other than the rights aforesaid . . .'

There is a similar qualification in s 32(4)(c). That qualification is contained in paras (b) and (c) but not in para (a). That shows that the legislature did not intend there should be any qualification in respect of s 34(2)(a).

c
Before us counsel for the defendants urged that we ought to read into para (a) a similar provision 'without prejudice to any question of public carriageway or public highway'. I do not think we should do so. I see no justification or warrant for reading in such a qualification to para (a).

I would add that there is nothing in the Highways Act 1959 to conflict with this view. Section 34 of that Act (in regard to dedication of a highway after user) expressly

d
says that nothing in it should be taken to affect the provisions of s 32(4) of the 1949 Act. There is however the case of *Attorney-General v Honeywill*[1] in which Bristow J held that there should be a public highway notwithstanding that the definitive map showed a footpath only. He so interpreted the Act because he thought[2] that were it otherwise, an adjoining owner would be deprived of his right, without any opportunity to object. I am afraid that I cannot agree. If any adjoining owner had wanted to claim

e
that there was a public carriageway when the maps were being prepared, he could have made an objection. He could have said: 'This way should not be shown as a footpath because, by putting it in as a footpath only, that means I cannot drive vehicles along it'. He could have made such representations under s 29(3) of the 1949 Act. If need be, he could have appealed higher to the Secretary of State. He could have got it struck out as a footpath on the ground that it was a public carriageway; or,

f
at all events, he could have said it was a 'road used as a public path', if that was his contention. Any owner or member of the public who asserted that a way ought to have a higher grading than a footpath could have made objection and could have had the map rectified. No one made any objection. So this definitive map was passed and became conclusive on the point.

I would be reluctant to come to this conclusion if it meant that it was final and

g
irretrievable. So we have enquired into the possibility of a review of the matter. Without going into details, it does appear that there are provisions in the 1949 Act for review. There are provisions for a review every five years. Sometimes there can be a special review. Under the 1968 Act there is going to be a new nomenclature. Instead of 'road used as a public path' there is to be 'a bye-way open to all traffic'. At any rate, there is machinery available under the statute for the position to be

h
rectified. Although classified as a public footpath only, for the time being, it can be rectified in a reclassification in later years if necessary. Meanwhile it seems to me that this map must be treated as conclusive to show there is a right of way on foot only.

I do not regard *Honeywill's* case[1] as correct. Instead I agree with what Browne LJ said in *R v Secretary of State for the Environment, ex parte Hood*[3]:

j
'It seems to me that the intention of the 1949 Act was that all questions as to the extent, nature and incidents of footpaths, bridleways and roads used by the

1   [1972] 3 All ER 641, [1972] 1 WLR 1506
2   [1972] 3 All ER 641 at 644, [1972] 1 WLR 1506 at 1510
3   [1975] 3 All ER 243 at 249, [1975] QB 891 at 901

public for other purposes should be fully investigated and decided before the definitive maps were drawn up under that Act, and that the definitive maps should finally decide these questions, subject only to the exception at the end of s 32(4)(*b*) . . .'

That seems to me to be correct: so far as footpaths are concerned there is no such exception whereby they can be up-graded in between. If there is to be any up-grading, it has to be on the review in accordance with the statutes. Meanwhile, until that is done, I think that Marsh Lane remains, and must remain, in the words of the statute 'a highway over which the public have a right of way on foot only'.

So I come to a different conclusion, I am afraid, from the deputy judge, and I would allow the appeal.

ORMROD LJ. I agree. In my judgment it is essential to approach this matter on a very practical basis. It is plain from looking at the preamble to the National Parks and Access to the Countryside Act 1949 that one of the objects of that Act was 'to make further provision for the recording, creation, maintenance and improvement of public paths and for securing access to open country'. So one of the primary purposes of this Act was to record the existence of public paths. It set out a complicated procedure for ascertaining public rights of way in Part IV of the Act. It provided for a whole series of consultations and, as Lord Denning MR has already pointed out, it provided for a three-stage procedure starting with a draft map and then proceeding to a provisional map and finally ending with what the statute called 'a definitive map'. If 'definitive' means anything, it means that it defines the status of these paths and so on which are marked on it.

The only other point which emerged which is relevant, it seems to me, is that s 32(4) of the 1949 Act is essentially an evidential section. It is saying no more than 'No evidence shall be accepted or entertained contrary to the evidence of the definitive map and statement'. One can understand very easily why this was done, namely because the object of the Act was to bring to an end the sort of fascinating discussion which has taken place in the course of this case and no doubt in the past has taken place in respect of many other rights of way. It is difficult to avoid the subtle attractions of historical research in these matters, but they do lead to unpractical results very often. This is just such a case where we can see just how fascinating and interesting the historical research is and how unpractical the consequences. Nobody, until Dr Brooks looked into it, would have imagined for a moment that Marsh Lane (certainly the southern part) was a carriageway or highway or anything of the kind. Nowadays it leads to absolutely nowhere and, at the very most, one would suppose it to be a relatively unused pathway over much of its length. In that situation it is, of course, a pity that by a side wind a public highway has been extinguished, but words like that tend to pick up a certain emotive charge, and it is wise to remember what is actually happening on the ground. To talk about extinguishing a public highway over Marsh Lane is strictly correct but really very remote from reality except from the point of view of the defendants in this action who would, if they could, take advantage of it. They no doubt did not think of it until they were able to get some assistance from Dr Brooks. That is the background.

When one comes to look at the section against that background, the argument which found favour with the deputy judge seems to me, in my respectful view, to be quite unfounded. The 1949 Act is quite unequivocal in its terms. It is unnecessary to read the section, but, as Lord Denning MR has already pointed out, there is only one way of reading s 32(4): in the light of the definition section, s 27. That being so, the county council in this case, in my judgment, must succeed. It may be said that this historical roadway is now to be classified for all purposes as a footpath only, but there it is. In fact, that is what it is, apart from the northern section.

Counsel for the defendants' very careful argument really goes to show, and only to show, that Parliament cannot have meant what it said, but I venture to think that it was not a very convincing argument in the end.

The only other point I would make is that there was a good deal of discussion in the course of the argument as to why in s 32(4) there was a difference drawn between the three paragraphs, paras (a), (b) and (c), in that paras (b) and (c) contain a provision which made the map not absolutely conclusive in relation to bridleways and roads used as public paths. The answer to that seems to me to appear when one looks back at the definition section, s 27, and finds that 'footpath' there is defined absolutely, strictly and unambiguously, as 'a right of way on foot only, other than such a highway at the side of a public road'. But both the definition of 'bridleway' and the definition of 'road used as a public path' contain express ambiguities. A bridleway may be 'a right of way on foot and a right of way on horseback or leading a horse, with or without a right to drive animals of any description along the highway', and the definition of 'public path' is even vaguer because it merely talks about a public path meaning 'a highway being either a footpath or a bridleway'. That phrase conveys very little as to the actual rights over that particular track. So it is not surprising in the light of that that one finds in s 32(4) a difference between the way footpaths are dealt with and the other two classifications.

In those circumstances I find the submissions made on behalf of the county council entirely convincing and I would adopt, with respect, the approach which was set out by Browne LJ in R v Secretary of State for the Environment, ex parte Hood[1], and I would follow that as he set it out. In those circumstances there is only one possible conclusion and that is that this appeal must succeed.

GEOFFREY LANE LJ. I agree. There is now no dispute that for very many years, possibly centuries, until it fell into disuse in the late 17th century, Marsh Lane was the main highway to the then thriving port of Kessingland. Thanks to the scholarly detective work of Dr Brooks that conclusion is amply documented.

Marsh Lane in its heyday would doubtless have carried all the traffic to and from the port, foot traffic, horses and horse-drawn vehicles. Hence the width of that road (20 feet) rather than the smaller distance which would have been required had it only been a footpath. At that time the sea and the estuary came much further inland than they do at present. It is possible, by studying the aerial photograph which was put before us, to get some idea of how close Marsh Lane must have come to the water at that point in the late 17th century. But none of those matters were of course known at the time when the county council prepared their definitive map of the district as they were required to do by the National Parks and Access to the Countryside Act 1949. There were no objections by any landowners or local inhabitants to the proposals made as a preliminary for settling the final map. Consequently, and not surprisingly, when the map came to be published there was Marsh Lane put down as what at that time it obviously appeared to be, namely, a footpath.

As soon as Dr Brooks' evidence became available, the defendants, who owned the caravan site and the holiday camp which lies close to the end of Marsh Lane and for whom the existence of a public carriageway along that path would be a great advantage sought to say that the designation of it as a footpath does not preclude their right to maintain that it is a carriageway which they can use as such, and which in fact it has been, on the evidence now available, since time immemorial. That on the face of it is a very attractive argument.

The county council, on the other hand, rely on what they say is the plain wording of the 1949 Act to demonstrate that the designation of this way as a footpath is conclusive, and not only conclusive but also exclusive of any greater right which may exist over the way, for example, a footpath coupled with a public carriageway.

---

1   [1975] 3 All ER 243 at 249, [1975] QB 891 at 901

That requires one to look both at s 32(4)(a) of the 1949 Act and s 27(6) which contains the definition sections. Reading those two together, what one gets as a conclusion *a* so far as the word 'footpath' is concerned is this: where the map shows a footpath the map shall be conclusive evidence that there was at the relevant date specified in the statement a highway over which the public have a right of way on foot only. Certainly on the face of it that would appear to be final in favour of the county council. It means, as Ormrod LJ has just said, that whatever evidence there may be to the contrary the statement 'footpath' on the map is overriding and takes precedence *b* over other evidence which may be forthcoming.

The county council further pray in aid the fact that s 32(4)(b) and (c) each contain a proviso, as has already been pointed out, whereas no such proviso appears in s 32(4)(a). Counsel for the defendants asks us to read those provisos simply as methods of restricting the ambit of s 32(4)(b) and (c) and not as potentially enlarging the scope of those paragraphs. If that is so, he says, the reason why there is no proviso in s 32(4)(a) *c* is that the category of footpath cannot be reduced any further than it is. 'Footpath' is the basic rock bottom definition and cannot be reduced further. That is his submission. I regret that I cannot agree with him. On this point I agree with the deputy judge that the only way one can explain the existence of those provisos (if the defendants are right) is to say that the words of the two provisos are otiose. I respectfully disagree with the deputy judge that that is a proper way of reading the statute *d* or a proper way of disposing with the existence of those words.

The other arguments put forward by counsel for the defendants are predominantly based on inconvenience. It is said that it may be difficult or even impossible to have put right what is manifestly wrong, namely that this is a footpath and no more. It seems to me from what we have heard that it can be put right; and even if it could not be put right, that does not alter the result. It does not alter the plain meaning *e* of the words of the statute. It is said further that to extinguish a highway by what is called a sidewind by words such as these and without any compensation and without providing an alternative way is anomalous and unjust. Perhaps it is, but once again the wording is clear, and that sort of consideration cannot affect the clarity of the wording. I too would adopt the words used by Browne LJ in R v Secretary of State for the Environment, ex parte Hood[1]. I too would agree that the passage in the judgment *f* of Bristow J's in Attorney-General v Honeywill[2] should not be followed.

For those reasons I too would allow the appeal.

Appeal allowed.

Leave to appeal to the House of Lords refused.

g

Solicitors: *Sharpe, Pritchard & Co*, agents for *Kenneth O Hall*, Ipswich (for the plaintiffs); *Stilgoes*, Haslemere (for the defendants).

Sumra Green Barrister.

h

---

1 [1975] 3 All ER 243 at 249, [1975] QB 891 at 901
2 [1972] 3 All ER 641 at 644, [1972] 1 WLR 1506 at 1510

McIvor and another v Southern Health and Social Services Board

HOUSE OF LORDS

LORD DIPLOCK, LORD EDMUND-DAVIES, LORD RUSSELL OF KILLOWEN, LORD KEITH OF KINKEL AND LORD SCARMAN

11th APRIL, 18th MAY 1978

Discovery – Discovery against persons not parties to proceedings – Claim in respect of personal injuries or death – Production of documents 'to the applicant' – Court ordering disclosure of medical records to applicant's 'legal advisers' – Whether court has discretion to order production to some other person on applicant's behalf on condition contents not disclosed to applicant – Whether court must order documents to be produced 'to the applicant' – Administration of Justice Act 1970, ss 31, 32.

Where a party to any proceedings in which a claim is made in respect of a person's personal injuries or death applies under s 32(1)[a] of the Administration of Justice Act 1970 for an order that a person who is not a party to the action produce 'to the applicant' documents in his possession, custody or power which are relevant to an issue arising out of that claim, then, having regard to the unequivocal words used in s 32(1), if the court considers that it is a proper case to exercise its discretion to make an order, the court making the order must order the documents to be produced to the applicant, and may not order the documents to be produced to some other person on the applicant's behalf on condition that the documents are not disclosed to the applicant himself (see p 627 c, p 628 f and h and p 629 d to f, post).

Dunning v Board of Governors of United Liverpool Hospitals [1973] 2 All ER 454, *Davidson v Lloyd Aircraft Services Ltd* [1974] 3 All ER 1 and *Deistung v South Western Metropolitan Regional Hospital Board* [1975] 1 All ER 573 overruled.

An order for discovery made under s 31 of the 1970 Act, which gives the court power to order disclosure of documents before the commencement of proceedings, must likewise be made in favour of the applicant and not to someone else on the applicant's behalf on condition that disclosure is not made to the applicant himself (see p 628 g to j and p 629 d to f, post).

Notes

For discovery against persons not parties to the proceedings in personal injuries claims, see 13 Halsbury's Laws (4th Edn) para 13.

For the Administration of Justice Act 1970, ss 31, 32, see 40 Halsbury's Statutes (3rd Edn) 1101, 1102.

Cases referred to in opinions

Davidson v Lloyd Aircraft Services Ltd [1974] 3 All ER 1, [1974] 1 WLR 1042, CA, 18 Digest (Reissue) 34, 220.

Deistung v South Western Metropolitan Regional Hospital Board [1975] 1 All ER 573, [1975] 1 WLR 213, CA, Digest (Cont Vol D) 277, 219a.

Dunning v Board of Governors of the United Liverpool Hospitals [1973] 2 All ER 454, [1973] 1 WLR 586, CA, 18 Digest (Reissue) 33, 218.

Interlocutory appeal

This was an appeal by the Southern Health and Social Services Board ('the hospital') against an order of the Court of Appeal in Northern Ireland (Lowry LCJ and Jones LJ) dated 12th September 1977 dismissing the hospital's appeal against an interlocutory order made by Murray J in the High Court of Justice in Northern Ireland on 20th May 1977 on the application of the defendant, Derek Reid, under s 32(1) of the Administration of Justice Act 1970, as applied to Northern Ireland by s 34(2) of the Act, whereby the hospital was ordered to disclose whether its records relating to the treatment of

---

a Section 32(1) is set out at p 627 a b, post

the plaintiff, Francis James McIvor, for injuries sustained in a motor accident on 25th September 1975, were in its possession, custody or power and if so, to produce them to the defendant against whom the plaintiff had brought an action for damages for personal injuries in respect of the accident. The facts are set out in the opinion of Lord Diplock.

C M Lavery QC and H Toner (both of the Northern Ireland Bar) for the hospital.
The plaintiff and the defendant did not appear.

Their Lordships took time for consideration.

18th May. The following opinions were delivered.

LORD DIPLOCK. My Lords, this is an interlocutory appeal in an action brought by the plaintiff, Mr McIvor, against the defendant, Mr Reid, for damages for personal injuries which he sustained in a motor accident on 25th September 1975. One of the medical issues in the action is whether the plaintiff's alleged total incapacity for work since the accident and in future was caused by injuries sustained in the accident or by a pre-existing cardiac or vascular condition. It is not disputed that hospital notes, X-rays and reports ('the hospital records') relating to the treatment of the plaintiff are in the custody of the appellant, the Southern Health and Social Services Board ('the hospital'), and are relevant to that issue. As the hospital is not a party to the action, the defendant applied under s 32(1) of the Administration of Justice Act 1970 ('the 1970 Act') for an order that the hospital should disclose whether such hospital records were in its possession, custody or power and to produce them to the defendant.

The order made by Murray J on the application was for production of the hospital records to 'the legal advisers of the defendant'. From that order the hospital appealed to the Court of Appeal in Northern Ireland, to vary the judge's order by substituting for production to the defendant's legal advisers production to 'medical advisers nominated by the Defendant and the Plaintiff respectively'. The Court of Appeal (Lowry LCJ and Jones LJ) dismissed the appeal. They held that there is no jurisdiction under s 32(1) of the 1970 Act to make an order for the production of documents to be made only to a medical adviser nominated by the applicant and not to the applicant or to his legal representatives in the action.

The practice followed in England since the 1970 Act came into force, as laid down by the English Court of Appeal, is to make orders confining the production of hospital records, at any rate in the first instance, to medical advisers of the applicant. This practice applies both to orders under s 32 (see Davidson v Lloyd Aircraft Services Ltd[1]) and also to orders under s 31 which provides for discovery before proceedings are commenced and is couched in similar terms (see Dunning v Board of Governors of the United Liverpool Hospitals[2] and Deistung v South West Metropolitan Regional Hospital Board[3]). In none of those cases in the English Court of Appeal, however, does the question appear to have been raised whether the court had power to make an order restricting the production of documents to the medical advisers of the parties to the exclusion of the applicant himself and his solicitor and counsel.

The Court of Appeal in Northern Ireland in the instant case was of the opinion that the only order for the production of documents which the court had jurisdiction to make under the section was an order for production to the applicant, which, in the ordinary course of litigation in which the applicant is legally represented, would be carried out by producing the documents to his solicitor as the appropriate agent on his behalf. Both members of the court considered the words of the section too plain to permit of any other construction. I respectfully agree.

Section 32(1) of the Act of 1970 is in the following terms:

---

1   [1974] 3 All ER 1, [1974] 1 WLR 1042
2   [1973] 2 All ER 454, [1973] 1 WLR 586
3   [1975] 1 All ER 573, [1975] 1 WLR 213

'On the application, in accordance with rules of court, of a party to any proceedings in which a claim in respect of personal injuries to a person or in respect of a person's death is made, the High Court shall, in such circumstances as may be specified in the rules, have power to order a person who is not a party to the proceedings and who appears to the court to be likely to have or to have had in his possession, custody or power any documents which are relevant to an issue arising out of that claim—(a) to disclose whether those documents are in his possession, custody or power; and (b) to produce to the applicant such of those documents as are in his possession, custody or power.'

The power under this section to order production of documents by a person who is not a party to the proceedings is discretionary in the sense that the court can decline to make the order if it is of the opinion that the order is unnecessary or oppressive or would not be in the interests of justice or would be injurious to the public interest in some other way. But a discretion to refrain from making an order, notwithstanding that all the conditions precedent prescribed by the section are fulfilled, does not embrace a discretion to make an order which obliges the person to whom it is addressed to do something different from that which alone is required by the section, namely to produce documents 'to the applicant' (emphasis mine).

The means of compelling disclosure of documents prior to the trial by persons who are not parties to the action were newly created by the section, as were the corresponding means under s 31 of compelling disclosure of documents by prospective parties to an action before the action was begun. Both powers were previously unknown in English law. They are confined to actions for personal injuries and fatal accidents and, as is well known, were introduced as a result of the Report of the Committee on Personal Injuries Litigation[1], of which the late Winn LJ was the chairman. Though the sections apply to other kinds of documents besides medical records and reports, it was the latter class of documents which the Winn Committee had primarily in mind in recommending that disclosure should be made available at an earlier stage than the trial itself, which was when, under the law as it was prior to the 1970 Act, production of the documents could be obtained from the hospital authorities on subpoena duces tecum. Early disclosure, the committee considered, would conduce to the settlement of such actions on terms that were fair to both sides or, failing that, to the preparation of an agreed medical report and so avoid the need to call medical experts at the trial. As was pointed out forcefully in the judgments of the Court of Appeal in Northern Ireland in the instant case, if one of the objects sought to be achieved by the early disclosure of documents for which the sections provide was the settlement of personal injury actions on terms that were fair to both sides, this would necessarily involve disclosing to the legal representatives of each party, and not only to their medical advisers, all the available material relevant to each issue in the case.

It was submitted on behalf of the hospital however that, despite what appeared to the Court of Appeal, and appears to me, to be the plain and restricted words of the 1970 Act, the consequences of not confining production of hospital records to the medical advisers of the applicant would in some cases be so dire that Parliament must have intended to confer on the courts a power so to do. The arguments supporting this submission are conveniently summarised in the judgment of Lord Denning MR in *Davidson v Lloyd Aircraft Services Ltd*[2]. Similar arguments were addressed to the Court of Appeal in Northern Ireland and to your Lordships in the instant case. They are, first, that medical notes and records are difficult for laymen to interpret, second, that they may include the doctor's fears about the patient's prospects for the future which, if disclosed to the patient, might cause him distress or

1   Cmnd 3691 (1968)
2   [1974] 3 All ER 1, [1974] 1 WLR 1042

retard his recovery, third, that they may contain statements made by the patient
or by relatives which might be embarrassing or distressing if made known and, *a*
fourth, that medical reports are of a confidential nature and medical men might be
deterred from entering them up with the necessary frankness if they feared that
they might be disclosed beyond the profession itself.

I must confess that I do not find these arguments to be of general applicability
or convincing. The disclosure called for by the section is narrower than that provided
for by the ordinary discovery of documents as between the parties to an action, *b*
which includes disclosure of all documents which may fairly lead to a train of enquiry
which may have the consequences of advancing a party's case or damaging that of
his adversary. Discovery under s 32 of the 1970 Act is limited to documents relevant
to 'an issue arising out of the claim in the action' and thus is confined to those documents of which production could ultimately be obtained at the trial on subpoena
duces tecum. This would appear to exclude the kind of statement referred to in *c*
the third argument. Any irrelevant parts of a document that is subject to disclosure
can be covered up when the document itself is produced. As regards the first and
second arguments, in their consideration of medical reports the legal advisers of the
applicant can have the assistance of the medical adviser in interpreting them; and,
if there is matter in them of which it would be better for the applicant himself not to
know (which could only arise where he was the patient concerned), his legal adviser *d*
would no doubt take precautions to prevent the information becoming known to
his client. This kind of situation can arise at the trial when medical evidence about
a party to an action is being given. It is dealt with by common sense and humanity.
Furthermore, documents disclosed on discovery, unlike evidence given in court at
the trial, are confidential in the sense that they may not be used by those to whom
they are disclosed for any other purpose than that of the action in which they are *e*
disclosed.

I see no sufficient reason in any of these arguments for departing from the unequivocal meaning of the words used in the section that the documents must be 'produced
to the applicant', which in the context of litigation in which an applicant is legally
represented includes the solicitor who acts in the litigation on the applicant's behalf.
There may be exceptional cases where the court might, in its discretion, refrain from *f*
making any order under the section on an undertaking by the hospital to make the
reports or the information contained in them available in some other way, but the
occasions appropriate for taking this course are likely to be very rare. In the ordinary
way, the order under both ss 31 and 32 should be made for the production of the
documents to the applicant or, if he is legally represented, to his solicitor in the action
or proposed action. *g*

It follows that I think that the decisions of the English Court of Appeal to which
I have referred were wrong and the decision of the Court of Appeal in Northern
Ireland in the instant case was right.

I would dismiss this appeal with costs.

LORD EDMUND-DAVIES. My Lords, I have had the advantage of reading in *h*
draft the speech prepared by my noble and learned friend, Lord Diplock, and am
in respectful agreement with it.

In a situation falling within s 31 or s 32 of the Administration of Justice Act 1970,
the applicant seeking an order may, of course, indicate his contentment if the relevant
hospital records are produced not to him but to his designated nominee, be that
person his solicitor or his medical adviser or anyone else. But it seems to me that
the statutory wording renders it clearly unwarrantable that, if the court in its discretion decides to make an order, it should take it on itself to impose a restriction
(to which the applicant has never subscribed) regarding the person to whom production is to be made.

I think I should add that it would need quite exceptional circumstances (the nature of which I cannot presently envisage) before the court could refuse to make what it considers a proper order under s 31 or s 32 simply on an undertaking by the respondent to produce the desired document to someone other than the applicant himself and despite the non-acceptance of that undertaking by the applicant, for the acceptance of such an undertaking regardless of the applicant's wishes would simply open the door to impermissible escape from the statutory obligation in the circumstances postulated.

Perhaps it would have been better if the statutory obligation had been drafted differently, so as to deal with those considerations which led to the Court of Appeal in England to decide as it did in *Davidson v Lloyd Aircraft Services Ltd*[1] and *Deistung v South West Metropolitan Regional Hospital Board*[2], but that is another matter altogether.

I therefore concur in holding that the appeal should be dismissed.

LORD RUSSELL OF KILLOWEN. My Lords, Lowry LCJ neatly summarised the point in this case when he said:

> 'The High Court has an inherent jurisdiction to attach conditions to most orders in the interests of justice, but I do not think that it has any jurisdiction to order disclosure to the applicant on condition that disclosure is *not* made to the applicant (or to his legal advisers).'

I have had the advantage of reading the speech in this appeal of my noble and learned friend, Lord Diplock. I agree with him and with his conclusion that this appeal be dismissed.

LORD KEITH OF KINKEL. My Lords, I agree with the opinion of my noble and learned friend, Lord Diplock, whose speech I have had the advantage of reading in draft, and for the reasons which he has given I too would dismiss the appeal.

LORD SCARMAN. My Lords, I would dismiss this appeal for the reasons given by my noble and learned friend, Lord Diplock.

I have also had the advantage of reading in draft the speech delivered by my noble and learned friend, Lord Edmund-Davies. I share his doubts as to whether a court could refuse an applicant an order on the respondent undertaking to produce the documents 'to a medical expert nominated by the applicant', a course which Lowry LCJ thought was 'technically' open to the court.

I would emphasise that the court's discretion to order discovery of documents to an applicant under s 31 or s 32 of the Administration of Justice Act 1970, being a judicial discretion, has to be exercised in the interest of justice. The court has no other responsibility.

I respectfully agree with Lowry LCJ when in the course of his judgment he commented:

> 'If Parliament had wished to enact provisions for discovery, limited in the ordinary case to medical advisers, it could have done so, instead of using language importing conventional discovery. It could still enact such provisions, but not I hope, before very careful deliberation.'

I share his hope.

Appeal dismissed.

Solicitors: Theodore Goddard & Co, agents for *H J Donaghy*, Northern Ireland Central Services Agency for the Health and Social Services (for the hospital).

Mary Rose Plummer Barrister.

---

1 [1974] 3 All ER 1, [1974] 1 WLR 1042
2 [1975] 1 All ER 573, [1975] 1 WLR 213

Taylor and others v Calvert and another

COURT OF APPEAL, CIVIL DIVISION
LORD DENNING MR, ORMROD AND GEOFFREY LANE LJJ
2nd FEBRUARY 1978

Mobile home – Agreement offered by owner to occupier – Term of agreement offered by owner – Term of agreement to be not less than five years – Owner offering agreement for term of five years – Occupier applying to county court for longer terms – County court judge exercising discretion under power to settle matters in dispute by extending term to eight years – Whether county court judge had discretion to extend term – Whether length of term could be 'a matter in dispute' – Mobile Homes Act 1975, ss 2(1), 4(5).

In accordance with the duty imposed on them by the Mobile Homes Act 1975 the site owners of a leisure park offered to enter into agreements with the occupiers of mobile homes situated in their park. The period of the agreement offered was in each case five years. The occupiers wanted security of tenure longer than the five years offered and when the site owners declined to extend the period they appealed to the county court contending that because they were dissatisfied with the terms offered by the site owners the judge had a discretion under s 4(5)[a] of the 1975 Act to extend the period of the agreements. The judge extended the period in all cases, in some cases to eight years and in others to ten years, depending on the age and health of the occupier and the age and state of repair of the mobile home in each case. The site owners appealed.

Held – The site owner was under a duty under s 2(1)[b] of the 1975 Act to offer an agreement for a period of not less than five years and provided he had fulfilled that duty, the county court judge had no discretion under s 4(5) to vary or extend the term offered. Section 4(5) only enabled the county court judge to determine any dispute whether the other terms offered by the site owner complied with the statutory requirements. Since the site owner had offered a term of five years to the occupiers, the county court judge had had no jurisdiction to extend the terms. Accordingly the appeal would be allowed (see p 632 d e, p 633 a to d and f and p 634 a to d, post).

Notes
For the Mobile Homes Act 1975, ss 2 and 4, see 45 Halsbury's Statutes (3rd Edn) 1587, 1589.

Case referred to in judgments
Oscroft v Benabo [1967] 2 All ER 548, [1967] 1 WLR 1087, CA, Digest (Cont Vol C) 180, 946a.

Cases also cited
Snell v Unity Finance Ltd [1963] 3 All ER 50, [1964] 2 QB 203, CA.
Taylor v National Amalgamated Approved Society [1914] 2 KB 352, [1914-15] All ER Rep 869, DC.

Appeal
This was an appeal by Roy Calvert and his wife Joan Calvert ('the site owners'), owners of a site known as Caerwnon House Leisure Park, Builth, in the County of Powys, from the order dated 17th January 1978 of his Honour Judge Wooley made in Builth County Court, whereby he ordered that agreements offered by the site owners pursuant to the Mobile Homes Act 1975 to the applicants in the county court ('the

---

a   Section 4(5) is set out at p 632 j, post
b   Section 2(1) is set out at p 632 d, post

occupiers') should be varied, in the case of Aziel Gwendolin Taylor and other named
a persons by extending the term to ten years with a right to a further extension for five
years and in the case of Henry George Romans and other named persons by extending
the term to eight years with a right to a further extension for three years. The site
owners, who had in all cases offered a term of five years to the occupiers, were the
respondents to the application in the county court. The facts are set out in the
judgment of Lord Denning MR.

b
Leonard Hoffman QC for the site owners.
D Elystan Morgan for the occupiers.

LORD DENNING MR. This is the first case we have had under the new Mobile
Homes Act 1975. It came into force on 1st October 1975. It was, no doubt, designed
c to deal with caravans, but it also applies to very substantial dwellings. So substantial
indeed that the 1975 Act might also be called the 'Immobile Homes Act'. The dwelling-
houses here are situated in Wales in an area called the Caerwnon House Leisure Park.
They are more like bungalows than caravans. They have no wheels. Being made of
wood, they can be moved with considerable labour and expense. But, beyond doubt,
they are very permanent and there is no intention to move them.
d   The owners of the area are Mr and Mrs Calvert. They have given licences for
'pitches' in the park to occupiers. They sold the wooden dwellings to the licensees
at varying prices according to their age and the accommodation in them, and so forth.
They sold them for sums in the region of £4,000, £5,000 or £6,000. They sold them
to elderly men and women who used them as their homes and looked forward to
remaining there for the rest of their days.
e   Prior to the 1975 Act, the occupiers had no security of tenure. They were only
licensees of the 'pitch' on which their homes were standing. They were not protected
by the Rent Restrictions Acts, or anything of the kind. They were liable to be ordered
to quit at short notice. One of the objects of the 1975 Act was to give them some
security of tenure so that they could not be evicted at short notice, and also to ensure
that the terms of their occupation were reasonable. The statute laid down several
f requirements which the agreements had to contain.
On 1st January 1976, after the 1975 Act came into force, Mr and Mrs Calvert, the site
owners, made an offer to the various occupiers of new terms and conditions for their
home which they said fulfilled the statutory requirements. We have before us the
case of several of them. I will take Mr Romans, whose address is given as 3 Birch
Way, Caerwnon Leisure Park. He is a fairly fit man, 74 years of age. He had bought
g his house four years before for £4,000. It has two bedrooms. He expended £100 on
a garage, £135 on central heating, £70 on an oil tank and so forth.
When the 1975 Act came into force, the site owners offered him a written agreement
in order to conform to the Act. It was for a term of five years, from 1st January 1976
until 31st December 1980. There was an annual fixed fee of £180 payable by monthly
instalments. He was to remove the mobile home within 14 days, after the expiration
h of the agreement. He was also to comply with the rules of the park.
A number of those occupiers got together (some of them got legal aid) and challenged this new agreement. They wanted a longer term than the five years; and
various other amendments.
The case was heard by the county court judge. It was assumed by both parties that
the judge had an unlimited power to vary and alter all terms which were offered.
i It was assumed that the judge could do what he thought reasonable. On that basis
the judge altered the provisions a great deal, including the length of tenure. In some
cases he awarded that, instead of five years, it should be ten years and in others,
eight years. The length depended on the age of the individual occupiers, and how long
the judge thought they would wish to be there, and so forth. In the case of Mr Romans
he awarded eight years, with a right to an extension of a further three years.

No challenge was made to the judge's jurisdiction to give these extended periods; but on appeal to this court, counsel for the site owners has submitted to us that the judge did not have the jurisdiction to extend these terms beyond five years, with a three year extension. Although the point of jurisdiction was not taken in the court below, nevertheless it can be taken in this court. It is settled law that parties cannot give jurisdiction by consent: see *Oscroft v Benabo*[1].

We have been taken through the 1975 Act. Section 1(1)(b) applies to the case before us. It says:

'. . . where the owner of a protected site proposes to permit— . . . (b) any person who has acquired a mobile home which is stationed on that site to continue to station it on the site, and . . . that person has notified the owner in writing that he intends to occupy the mobile home as his only or main residence, it shall be the duty of the owner . . . to offer to enter into a written agreement with him in accordance with the provisions of section 2 of this Act.'

Now comes s 2(1):

'An agreement offered by an owner of a protected site in pursuance of a duty imposed on him by section 1 of this Act shall comply with section 3 of this Act and shall be for a term of not less than five years.'

Note those words: 'shall be for a term of not less than five years.' The period is expressly stated. Every other requirement of the agreement is dealt with in s 3, and, in case of dispute, can be determined by the court under s 4(5) to (7). But the period of the agreement is left to the site owner to determine, provided always that it is not less than five years.

This interpretation is borne out by the rest of s 2. The proviso to s 2(1) deals with cases where the site owner is not in a position to grant a period of five years: as, for instance, when he has a reversion of less than five years; or has a planning permission which limits him and does not allow him to grant five years. In those cases it is sufficient for the site owner to grant such a period as he can, even though it is less than five years.

Section 2(2) is instructive. It deals with cases where the site owner afterwards becomes in a position to grant a period of five years: as, for instance, if he acquires the freehold; or gets unlimited planning permission. In those cases the site owner must offer to give the full period of five years; but no more.

All this points to the period of five years being treated differently from any other provision in the agreement.

Turning to s 3(c), the agreement is to contain a right to the occupier to extend the period for a further three years after the five years. This again treats the period as a thing apart.

Stopping there, I think the site owner in this case fulfilled his statutory duty by offering the period of five years. But the question is: did the county court judge have any power to grant more than five years? He granted some of these occupiers ten years, and some eight years, with a right to extension of three more years. Had he any jurisdiction to do this?

Counsel for the occupiers submitted to us that the county court judge was at liberty to give an extension of term; and that he had an unlimited power to extend it. In support of his submission, he relied on the terms of s 4(5), which says:

'An occupier who is dissatisfied with any of the terms or conditions in an agreement offered to him by an owner in pursuance of a duty imposed under section 1 of this Act may, within the period of three months following the date on which the agreement is so offered, apply to the court for the determination of the matter in dispute.'

1　[1967] 2 All ER 548, [1967] 1 WLR 1087

Counsel for the occupiers submitted that those words are wide enough to entitle the judge to interfere with all the terms and to go through the agreement, as this judge did, and to redraft it as he thought fit.

It seems to me that that is not the correct interpretation of the subsection. It seems to me that that subsection does not apply to the period of years offered by the site owners. It deals with all the other terms and conditions of the agreement, but not to the period of years which is treated throughout as a thing apart from the rest of the agreement.

Counsel for the occupiers relied on s 4(1)(a) dealing with cases in which the site owner has not made an offer at all. The court is enabled under s 4(2)(a) to make such terms and conditions as it thinks reasonable. Counsel for the occupiers relied also on s 4(3) where the occupier does not agree with the terms or conditions. The court can insert such terms and conditions as it thinks reasonable: s 4(4).

It seems to me that those subsections again do not deal with the period of the agreement. They only deal with the other terms and conditions. Reading through the 1975 Act as a whole, it seems to me that the legislature has itself declared that a period of not less than five years (with an extension of three years) is sufficient to satisfy the duty of the site owner. So long as he offers an agreement to that period, he has done his duty; save that, in regard to all other terms and conditions, if there is a dispute between the parties, it can be referred to the county court judge, and he can decide then what is reasonable.

The long and the short of it is that the 1975 Act does give security of tenure for five years with an option to extend by another three years; and it gives a general supervision by the county court judge over all the provisions to see that the agreement is fair and reasonable.

The point raised in this appeal was not raised before the judge, so he had no opportunity of dealing with it, but, on being argued, I think that the judge did not have jurisdiction to grant the extended terms as he did. I would allow the appeal accordingly.

ORMROD LJ. I agree. The appeal now turns on s 4(5) of the Mobile Homes Act 1975, which is, in my judgment, not at all clearly drafted. It is not immediately obvious what was in the mind of the draftsman or what situation he was intending to deal with. The most startling contrast to my mind between s 4(5) and s 4(1)(a) and (3) is the fact that the latter provisions in terms give the court power to impose such terms and conditions as it thinks reasonable. Section 4(5) in contrast requires the court to determine the matter in dispute. If it is then to be said that those words give the court a general discretion to draft and arrange all the terms of a contract between the parties, I can only say that the language used by Parliament seems to me to be manifestly defective.

One only has to test this by using perhaps the most stringent of all the tests, and that is to ask first the question: can the county court judge impose a term of indefinite length? Counsel for the occupiers is obliged to say: 'Yes, in theory he can, but he will only make a term which is reasonable.' But the next question must be: by what standard? That clearly in this case worried the judge because the only two standards he could think of seemed to be the state of health of the proposed occupier and his age together with the state of health and age of the caravan, and this simply must be nonsense. If one tests it against an even more critical standard, that is the amount to be paid by the occupier of the caravan, one finds that counsel for the occupiers is driven to say: 'Yes, the county court judge can put in any figure he likes no matter whether the parties had previously agreed.' Again there is no indication in the statute of any standard to be applied; and, if Parliament is really giving the county court power to fix the rent of mobile homes in these circumstances, it is quite extraordinary that they should do it as a side effect of a subsection which is designed to resolve disputes as to tenure.

We have to give some meaning to this subsection, and I entirely agree with what Lord Denning MR has said that the only meaning which can rationally be given *a* to it is that it refers to a dispute whether the terms offered by the site owner comply with the 1975 Act or are consistent with the terms of a subsisting agreement between the site owner and the occupier before the Act itself came into force. Otherwise I can see no dispute which is capable of determination without the court exercising a discretion which as far as I can see it has not got.

I also agree with all Lord Denning MR has said on the narrower point where the *b* 1975 Act prescribes the terms of the offer: the site owner must offer no less than five years, and I am quite unable to imagine how it can be suggested, again apparently indirectly, that the county court judge has unrestricted power to extend that time.

I therefore agree that this appeal must be allowed.

GEOFFREY LANE LJ. I agree. The practical effect of the occupiers' argument *c* here is that the judge would be entitled to 'fix the rent' between people who are not in contractual agreement at all, forcing a site owner to enter into an agreement with an occupier on terms which he has no desire to accept or, secondly, to alter on criteria which are not mentioned in the Mobile Homes Act 1975 at all the terms solemnly agreed between the site owner and the occupier. Such a result would be absurd and *d* cannot have been intended by Parliament.

The appeal should be allowed.

Appeal allowed.

Solicitors: *Tozers*, Dawlish (for the site owners); *Dilwyn Jones & Sons*, Llandrindod Wells (for the occupiers). *e*

Sumra Green Barrister.

Kakis v Government of the Republic of Cyprus and others

HOUSE OF LORDS
LORD DIPLOCK, LORD EDMUND-DAVIES, LORD RUSSELL OF KILLOWEN, LORD KEITH OF KINKEL
AND LORD SCARMAN
19th, 20th APRIL, 18th MAY 1978

Extradition – Discharge of offender – Circumstances rendering it unjust or oppressive to return fugitive – Circumstances court may have regard to – Passage of time since commission of alleged offence – Material witness becoming no longer available and compellable as a witness – Fugitive developing sense of security from prosecution during passage of time – Whether factors in determining whether circumstances rendered it 'unjust or oppressive' *f* *to return fugitive – Fugitive Offenders Act 1967, s 8(3)(b).*

Extradition – Discharge of offender – Circumstances rendering it unjust or oppressive to return fugitive – Circumstances court may have regard to – Passage of time since commission of offence – Responsibility for passage of time – Whether responsibility of fugitive or requesting government for delay relevant in determining whether circumstances rendered it 'unjust or oppressive' to return fugitive – Fugitive Offenders Act 1967, s 8(3)(b).

In 1973 the appellant and P were members of politically opposed organisations in Cyprus. On 5th April P was shot and killed by three men and, following an investigation into the shooting, a warrant was issued for the arrest of the appellant. The appellant went into hiding for 15 months until July 1974 when he emerged to take part in a coup which temporarily ousted the government and was followed by considerable disruption in the country. After the coup the appellant was able to move about freely and openly. In September 1974 he emigrated with his family to England with the permission of the government of Cyprus then in power. In December 1974 there was a further change in government in Cyprus following which the former government was returned to power and an amnesty proclaimed. The appellant understood himself to be among those to whom the amnesty applied and in January 1975 he visited Cyprus for two or three weeks with the permission of the government of Cyprus and then returned to England. In October 1975 the Cyprus government changed its policy and decided to prosecute its political opponents for crimes committed before the 1974 coup. As a result, on 11th February 1976, the Attorney-General of Cyprus ordered that extradition proceedings be brought against the appellant for the murder of P. After a one year delay, for which the appellant was not responsible, authority to proceed under s 3 of the Fugitive Offenders Act 1967 was issued by the Secretary of State. In March 1977 the appellant was arrested and brought before a magistrate. In the course of the extradition hearing he gave evidence that if he was tried in Cyprus he would rely on an alibi supported by his wife and a witness, A, who had emigrated from Cyprus to England in 1975 and who had also taken part in the 1974 coup. Had a murder trial taken place in Cyprus before A had left, A would have been available and compellable as a witness for the defence but at the time of the extradition hearing he was no longer a compellable witness and he stated in evidence before the magistrate that he would not be prepared to return voluntarily to Cyprus for the trial for fear of ill-treatment by his political opponents. The magistrate committed the appellant to prison to await the directions of the Secretary of State under s 9 of the 1967 Act. The appellant applied for a writ of habeas corpus to the Divisional Court which refused his application holding that, on the evidence, no grounds for ordering the appellant to be released from custody had been made out. The appellant appealed contending that he was entitled to be discharged under s 8(3)(b)[a] of the 1967 Act because 'by reason of the passage of time since he [was] alleged to have committed [the offence] . . . it would, having regard to all the circumstances, be unjust or oppressive to return him' to Cyprus.

Held (Lord Keith of Kinkel dissenting) – Having regard to all the circumstances it would be 'unjust and oppressive' to return the appellant to Cyprus for trial, unjust because the witness A, on whom the appellant relied on for his defence alibi, was no longer an available and compellable witness in Cyprus and it would detract significantly from the fairness of his trial if he were deprived of his ability to adduce the evidence of the only independent witness who could speak to it, and oppressive because during the years which had elapsed since July 1974 when he emerged from hiding until his arrest in March 1977 the appellant was justified in believing that the government of Cyprus had had no intention of prosecuting him for the alleged offence. The appellant had in fact openly settled in England with his family without objection from the government of Cyprus, and was justified in feeling a sense of security from prosecution. The gravity of the offence in respect of which the extradition proceedings were brought, although relevant to whether changes had occurred during the relevant period in the circumstances of the accused which would render his return to stand trial oppressive, was not a matter which should affect the court's decision if the relevant event which happened in that period, namely the departure of the witness A from Cyprus, involved the risk of prejudice to the accused in the conduct of the trial itself. The appeal would therefore be allowed and the appellant discharged under s 8(3) of the Act (see p 638 h, p 639 g, p 640 a to f and j, p 641 a and p 644 h to p 645 b, post).

---

a Section 8(3), so far as material, is set out at p 637 e, post

Per Curiam. Delay in the commencement or conduct of extradition proceedings which is brought about, eg by the accused himself by fleeing the country, concealing his whereabouts or evading arrest, cannot save in exceptional circumstances be relied on as a ground for holding it to be either unjust or oppressive to return him (see p 638 j, p 640 cf, p 641 a, p 642 ef and p 644 b, post); Union of India v Narang [1977] 2 All ER 348 applied.

Per Lord Diplock, Lord Russell of Killowen and Lord Scarman (Lord Edmund-Davies dissenting). Where a delay is not brought about by the acts of the accused himself the question of where the responsibility lies for the delay is not generally relevant. When matters is not so much the cause of such delay as its effect or, rather, the effects of those events which would not have happened if the trial of the accused had taken place with ordinary promptitude. Thus, where the application for discharge under s 8(3) is based on the 'passage of time', under para (b), and not on absence of good faith, under para (c), the court is not normally concerned with the task of considering whether mere inaction of the requisitioning government or its prosecuting authorities which resulted in delay was blameworthy or otherwise (see p 638 j to p 639 b, p 641 a and p 644 h, post).

Per Lord Russell of Killowen and Lord Scarman. The question to be considered under s 8(3)(b) is not merely whether the length of the time that has passed would make it unjust or oppressive to return the fugitive (and thus it is not permissible to consider the passage of time divorced from the course of events which it allows to develop) but rather regard must be had to all the circumstances. Those circumstances are not restricted to circumstances from which the passage of time resulted but include circumstances taking place during the passage of time which may give to the particular passage of time a quality or significance leading to a conclusion that return of the fugitive would be unjust or oppressive (see p 641 a b and p 645 b, post).

Notes

For application for habeas corpus by a fugitive offender, see 18 Halsbury's Laws (4th Edn) para 271, and for cases on the subject, see 24 Digest (Repl) 1012-1015, 159-177.

For the Fugitive Offenders Act 1967, ss 3, 8, 9, see 13 Halsbury's Statutes (3rd Edn) 283, 293, 294.

Cases referred to in opinions

R v Governor of Pentonville Prison, ex parte Teja [1971] 2 All ER 11, [1971] 2 QB 274, [1971] 2 WLR 816, DC, Digest (Cont Vol D) 341, 158ca.

Union of India v Narang [1977] 2 All ER 348, [1977] 2 WLR 862, 64 Cr App Rep 259, DC and HL.

Appeal

This was an appeal by Kyriakos Mariou Kakis, with leave of the House of Lords granted on 16th December 1977, against the decision of the Divisional Court of the Queen's Bench Division (Lord Widgery CJ, Cumming-Bruce LJ and Park J) dated 16th December 1977, refusing the appellant's application for a writ of habeas corpus ad subjiciendum pursuant to s 8 of the Fugitive Offenders Act 1967, addressed to the first respondent, the Governor of Pentonville Prison, where he was being detained by virtue of an order made by the Chief Metropolitan Magistrate sitting at Bow Street following a request made to the second respondent, the Secretary of State, by the Government of Cyprus for the return of the appellant to Cyprus to stand trial for murder. The facts are set out in the opinion of Lord Diplock.

Louis Blom Cooper QC and R Plender for the appellant.
Christopher French QC and Michael Neligan for the Government of Cyprus.
Harry Woolf for the respondents.

Their Lordships took time for consideration.

18th May. The following opinions were delivered.

LORD DIPLOCK. My Lords, this is an appeal against the refusal by the Divisional Court on 16th December 1977 to make an order under s 8(3) of the Fugitive Offenders Act 1967 preventing the extradition of the appellant to Cyprus to stand his trial for the murder of a Mr Photiou which he is alleged to have committed at Larnaca in Cyprus as long ago as 5th April 1973. He was first arrested in London on 28th March 1977. The extradition proceedings before the Chief Metropolitan Magistrate ended on 12th September 1977. They resulted in an order of committal to Pentonville Prison to await the directions of the Secretary of State under s 9 of the Act.

In the course of the hearings at Bow Street the appellant gave evidence that on 5th April 1973 he was at home at the time that Mr Photiou was killed; and this alibi defence was supported by the oral evidence of two witnesses, his wife and a Mr Alexandrou who had emigrated from Cyprus to England in 1975 and is now settled here. It was also submitted on his behalf that the offence of which he was accused was an offence of a political character so as to render him immune from extradition under s 4(1)(a) of the Act. Evidence as to the political situation in Cyprus from 1973 onwards was given in support of this submission, which was however rejected by the learned chief magistrate.

On the application to the Divisional Court for a writ of habeas corpus, the appellant relied on two separate grounds on which he claimed to be entitled to be released from custody. The first was that relied on before the magistrate, viz the political character of the offence. The second was one which had not been open to him before the magistrate, viz the lapse of time since he was alleged to have committed the offence. The latter ground is dealt with by s 8(3) of the Act which empowers the High Court to order the applicant to be discharged from custody—

> 'if it appears to the court that— ... (b) by reason of the passage of time since he is alleged to have committed it [sc the offence of which he is accused] ... it would, having regard to all the circumstances, be unjust or oppressive to return him.'

The Divisional Court (Lord Widgery CJ, Cumming-Bruce LJ and Park J) held that on the evidence neither ground for ordering the appellant to be released from custody had been made out. Before your Lordships' House the contention that the offence of murder with which the appellant is accused (but which he denies) was of a political character was abandoned and the argument has been confined to the appellant's claim to be entitled to be discharged under s 8(3)(b) of the Act.

My Lords, this subsection has so recently been the subject of detailed consideration by this House in *Union of India v Narang*[1], that I can go straight to the chronology of those events which in my view have significance in reaching a conclusion whether or not the passage of time since 5th April 1973 has made it unjust or oppressive to return the appellant to Cyprus to stand his trial for a murder committed on that date.

On 5th April 1973 in Larnaca, three men, of whom it is alleged the appellant was one, shot down and killed a Mr Photiou. The other two were members of a militant political organisation EOKA B and so was the appellant. It had been proscribed by the government then in power in Cyprus under the presidency of Archbishop Makarios; the victim, Mr Photiou, was a member of a pro-Makarios political party known as EDEK.

A warrant for the arrest of the appellant was issued on that same night but he escaped to the mountains where he joined a band of fellow members of EOKA B and remained there with them in hiding for 15 months until on 15th July 1974 they emerged to take part in the coup which ousted the Makarios government and replaced it temporarily by a government controlled by EOKA B whose aim was to achieve the union of Cyprus with Greece. This led within a few days to the invasion of Cyprus by the Turkish army and the disruption that followed it.

---

1   [1977] 2 All ER 348, [1977] 2 WLR 862

After the coup the appellant was able to move about freely and openly in that part of Cyprus that was not under Turkish control. He decided to emigrate with his family to England and to establish himself here. He was granted by the Cyprus government an exit permit for this purpose and left with his family for England on 9th September 1974.

On 7th December 1974, Archbishop Makarios returned to Cyprus. He proclaimed an amnesty. The appellant understood himself to be included among those to whom the amnesty applied. So confident was he that this was so that he returned to Cyprus in mid-January 1975 and remained there for two or three weeks winding up his affairs in the island. He was granted by the Cyprus government a visa to enter Cyprus for this visit and an exit permit to return to England after it.

On 2nd August 1975, Mr Alexandrou, the witness on whom the appellant relies for his alibi at the time of the murder, left Cyprus for England. He too had been a supporter of the coup of 7th July 1974. He feared that the opposition which by that time was being shown to the amnesty in the House of Representatives might result in a change of policy and he thought it safer to come to England where he had already sent his wife and children. He has now established himself in business here.

On 30th October 1975, the House of Representatives justified Mr Alexandrou's fears. They voted in favour of prosecuting those concerned in the unsuccessful coup; and thereafter the policy of refraining from prosecuting political opponents of the government for crimes which they had committed before the coup was abandoned. It had been adopted in the interests of pacification in an endeavour to heal old wounds.

On 11th February 1976 the Attorney-General of Cyprus ordered that extradition proceedings should be brought against the appellant for the murder of Mr Photiou on 5th April 1973. On 10th March 1976 the necessary documents under the Fugitive Offenders Act 1967 were sent by the Cyprus government to the Foreign and Commonwealth Office in London.

For reasons into which it is unnecessary to enter, save to mention that the appellant was in no way responsible for them, it took until 15th February 1977 before an authority to proceed under s 3 of the Fugitive Offenders Act 1967 was issued by the Secretary of State. As already mentioned, it was on 28th March 1977 that the appellant was arrested in London; and on 16th December 1977 that the application to the Divisional Court for habeas corpus was refused.

My Lords, the passage of time to be considered is the time that passed between the date of the offence on 5th April 1973 and the date of the hearing in the Divisional Court on 15th December 1977, for that is the first occasion on which this ground for resisting extradition can be raised by the accused. So one must look at the complete chronology of events that I have summarised above and consider whether the happening of such of those events as would not have happened before the trial of the accused in Cyprus if it had taken place with ordinary promptitude has made it unjust or oppressive that he should be sent back to Cyprus to stand his trial now.

'Unjust' I regard as directed primarily to the risk of prejudice to the accused in the conduct of the trial itself, 'oppressive' as directed to hardship to the accused resulting from changes in his circumstances that have occurred during the period to be taken into consideration; but there is room for overlapping, and between them they would cover all cases where to return him would not be fair. Delay in the commencement or conduct of extradition proceedings which is brought about by the accused himself by fleeing the country, concealing his whereabouts or evading arrest cannot, in my view, be relied on as a ground for holding it to be either unjust or oppressive to return him. Any difficulties that he may encounter in the conduct of his defence in consequence of delay due to such causes are of his own choice and making. Save in most exceptional circumstances it would be neither unjust nor oppressive that he should be required to accept them.

As respects delay which is not brought about by the acts of the accused himself, however, the question of where responsibility lies for the delay is not generally relevant. What matters is not so much the cause of such delay as its effect; or, rather, the effects of those events which would not have happened before the trial of the accused if it had taken place with ordinary promptitude. So where the application for discharge under s 8(3) is based on the 'passage of time' under para (b) and not on absence of good faith under para (c), the court is not normally concerned with what could be an invidious task of considering whether mere inaction of the requisitioning government or its prosecuting authorities which resulted in delay was blameworthy or otherwise. Your Lordships have no occasion to do so in the instant case.

My Lords, in the chronology of events that I have summarised which extends over some 4¾ years from 3rd April 1973 to 16th December 1977, the failure of the prosecuting authorities to begin criminal proceedings against the appellant during the first 15 months until the coup in July 1974 was due to his own action in going into hiding in the mountains. So the starting point for the period of time that requires to be considered is July 1974.

The first significant event thereafter was the departure of the appellant and his family from Cyprus with the permission of the government of Cyprus that was then in power, in order to settle in England. Since this happened during the aftermath of the Turkish invasion it may not in itself have justified him in thinking that he could proceed to establish a home for himself and his family here without any fear of extradition. The significance of his visit to Cyprus to clear up his affairs in January 1975, after Archbishop Makarios had returned, is that it confirmed his confidence that no proceedings would be brought against him in respect of Mr Photiou's death, and that he and his family could safely settle themselves permanently in England. This he did successfully and remained here undisturbed for the next two years until his arrest in March 1977. He set up home as tenant of a council house and is in steady employment as a coach driver.

The next significant event is Mr Alexandrou's permanent departure from Cyprus in August 1975. This was more than a year after the appellant had emerged from hiding and his whereabouts both in Cyprus and in London were known to the prosecuting authorities in Cyprus. Mr Alexandrou is the only witness, apart from the appellant's wife, whose testimony the appellant relies on in support of his alibi at the time of the murder. If the murder trial had taken place in Cyprus before Mr Alexandrou had left he would have been available and compellable as a witness for the defence. If the murder trial were to take place now in Cyprus Mr Alexandrou could not be compelled to attend and he has given evidence on oath at Bow Street that he is not prepared voluntarily to return to Cyprus to give evidence for fear of ill-treatment by those who were his political opponents.

Your Lordships are in no position to form a view as to the strength of the defence of alibi for which Mr Alexandrou gave supporting testimony before the chief magistrate; but the appellant is entitled to have it considered at his trial and it would detract significantly from the fairness of his trial if he were deprived of the ability to adduce the evidence of the only independent witness who could speak to it.

My Lords, the Divisonal Court appear to have concentrated their attention on the period of 18 months between the coup in July 1974 and the institution by the Attorney-General of Cyprus in February 1976 of the proceedings to obtain the extradition of the appellant more than a year before he was in fact arrested. They asked themselves whether the policy of the Cyprus government in refraining during that period from proceeding with the prosecution of political opponents for pre-coup offences was blameworthy or not. Having reached the conclusion that it was not, they appear to have treated events which happened during the period as incapable of making unjust or oppressive the return of the appellant to Cyprus to stand his trial in 1978. In the result they did not in my view attach sufficient weight to the two significant events that did occur during that period, the permanent departure of Mr Alexandrou from Cyprus and the settlement of the appellant in England with the apparent approval of the Cyprus government.

Of the former, the Divisional Court said that it was not the passage of time but the unwillingness of the witness to return to Cyprus that would deprive the appellant of the benefit of his evidence at the trial, although as I have previously pointed out, if the time between the coup and Mr Alexandrou's departure for England in August 1975 had not been allowed to pass without the trial being brought on, he would have been an available and compellable witness at it. As respects the latter, the Divisional Court does not refer in this connection to the appellant having now established himself and his family in England for what, with the passage of time before the hearing was 3¼ years, during which, until his arrest in March 1977, he had justification for believing that the government of Cyprus had no intention of prosecuting him for the alleged offence in April 1973.

The offence in respect of which the extradition proceedings were brought is indeed a grave one, that of murder, though your Lordships have been informed that the charge on which he would be tried if he were to return to Cyprus would be the lesser one of culpable homicide (anglice manslaughter). The gravity of the offence is relevant to whether changes in the circumstances of the accused which have occurred during the relevant period are such as would render his return to stand his trial oppressive; but it is not, in my view, a matter which should affect the court's decision under s 8(3)(b) where the relevant event which happened in that period is one which involves the risk of prejudice to the accused in the conduct of the trial itself, as in the case of Mr Alexandrou's departure from Cyprus.

Giving the best consideration that I can to all the circumstances of the case that I have narrated here in summary form only and particularly to those two matters, that I have characterised as significant, one going to injustice, the other to oppression, I have reached the conclusion that the appellant is entitled to discharge under s 8(3) of the Fugitive Offenders Act 1967. I would allow the appeal accordingly.

LORD EDMUND-DAVIES. My Lords, I have had the advantage of reading in draft the speech of my noble and learned friend, Lord Diplock, and I am in general agreement with the reasons he gives for holding that this appeal should be allowed.

I have, however, one qualification to make. I am unable to concur in the following passage in his speech:

'As respects delay which is not brought about by the acts of the accused himself . . . the question of where responsibility lies for the delay is not generally relevant. What matters is not so much the cause of such delay as its effect; or, rather, the effects of those events which would not have happened before the trial of the accused if it had taken place with ordinary promptitude.'

In my respectful judgment, on the contrary, the answer to the question of where responsibility lies for the delay may well have a direct bearing on the issues of injustice and oppression. Thus, the fact that the requesting government is shown to have been inexcusably dilatory in taking steps to bring the fugitive to justice may serve to establish both the injustice and the oppressiveness of making an order for his return, whereas the issue might be left in some doubt, if the only known fact related to the extent of the passage of time, and it has been customary in practice to avert to that factor; see, for example, R v Governor of Pentonville Prison, ex parte Teja[1] per Lord Parker CJ and the speeches of this House in Union of India v Narang[2]. Despite this qualification, however, the circumstances of the instant case are such that, as already indicated, I concur in holding that the appeal should be allowed.

LORD RUSSELL OF KILLOWEN. My Lords, I have had the advantage of

---

1　[1971] 2 All ER 11 at 23, [1971] 2 QB 274 at 290
2　[1977] 2 All ER 348, [1977] 2 WLR 862

reading in draft the speech of my noble and learned friend, Lord Diplock. I agree with it and with his conclusion that this appeal should be allowed.

I would only add this comment on s 8(3)(*b*) of the 1967 Act. It is not merely a question whether the length of the time passed would make it unjust or oppressive to return the fugitive. Regard must be had to all the circumstances. Those circumstances are not restricted to circumstances from which the passage of time resulted. They include circumstances taking place during the passage of time which may (as I think here) give to the particular passage of time a quality or significance leading to a conclusion that return would be unjust or oppressive.

LORD KEITH OF KINKEL. My Lords, in these proceedings the Government of the Republic of Cyprus alleges that the appellant, Mr Kakis, on 5th April 1973 at Larnaca, Cyprus, did shoot and kill one Georghios Photiou. There is evidence that the appellant and others said to have been associated with him in the shooting were members of a political grouping known as EOKA B, which favoured union of Cyprus with Greece ('Enosis'), while Mr Photiou belonged to a party called EDEK, which supported the policies of the then President, Archbishop Makarios. Thus the alleged crime may have had political implications and the appellant, both in the proceedings before the Chief Metropolitan Magistrate and in his application to the Divisional Court for a writ of habeas corpus, relied on s 4(1)(*a*) of the Fugitive Offenders Act 1967 as exempting him from extradition on the ground that the offence of which he was accused was an offence of a political character. This submission was rejected both by the chief magistrate and by the Divisional Court, and it was not advanced to your Lordships' House.

Before the Divisional Court the appellant claimed discharge from custody on a second ground, namely that set out in s 8(3)(*b*) of the 1967 Act. The subsection provides:

'... the High Court ... may, without prejudice to any other jurisdiction of the court, order the person committed to be discharged from custody if it appears to the court that—(*a*) by reason of the trivial nature of the offence of which he is accused or was convicted; or (*b*) by reason of the passage of time since he is alleged to have committed it or to have become unlawfully at large, as the case may be; or (*c*) because the accusation against him is not made in good faith in the interests of justice, it would, having regard to all the circumstances, be unjust or oppressive to return him.'

The Divisional Court decided against the appellant on his submission based on para (*b*), and the question is whether their decision was correct.

The nature of the function of this House in reviewing a decision of the Divisional Court under s 8(3) of the 1967 Act was recently considered in *Union of India v Narang*[1]. It was held that the matter is to be approached in the same way as the review of any decision of a subordinate court on an issue of fact, and that this House is entitled and indeed bound to draw its own inferences from the primary facts and to form an independent opinion on the matter of injustice or oppression, while giving due weight to the conclusion of the court below.

It is now necessary to set out the primary facts as regards the sequence of events since the killing of Mr Photiou on 5th April 1973. These are for all practical purposes undisputed. A warrant was immediately issued for the arrest of the appellant in connection with the killing, but he took to the hills and remained a fugitive until, on 15th July 1974, there occurred a 'coup', in which he participated, which ousted the government of President Makarios and temporarily installed a pro-Enosis regime. This led to the Turkish invasion of Cyprus on 20th July 1974, with consequent disruption and confusion. On 9th September 1974 the appellant left Cyprus for England

---

1 [1977] 2 All ER 348, [1977] 2 WLR 862

with his wife and children, having received an exit permit from the Ministry of the Interior. In December 1974 President Makarios, who had been out of Cyprus since the July coup, returned there and made a speech in which he said that he granted amnesty to those who had been involved in political offences and those who took part in the coup. On 16th January 1975 the appellant, no doubt relying on this statement visited Cyprus in order to clear up his affairs there. He left on 14th February 1975, having again received an exit permit from the Ministry of the Interior. Since then the appellant has been settled in this country with his family, working as a bus driver. On 24th July 1975 an inquest was held into the death of Mr Photiou, and as a result of ·it a further warrant was issued for the arrest of the appellant. On 2nd August 1975 one George Alexandrou, on whose evidence, as I shall mention later, the appellant relies in support of an alibi, left Cyprus and came to England. On 30th October 1975 the House of Representatives refused to legislate so as to give legal effect to the amnesty announced by President Makarios, and it passed a resolution in favour of prosecuting the main participants in the coup of July 1974. On 21st February 1976 the government of Cyprus applied to the Chief Metropolitan Magistrate for a provisional warrant of arrest against the appellant, but this was refused. Thereafter depositions were taken in Cyprus, a third warrant for the arrest of the appellant was issued there, and on 10th March 1976 extradition documents were sent to the Foreign and Commonwealth Office with a request for authority to proceed. Some correspondence ensued between the Foreign and Commonwealth Office and the government of Cyprus, and it was not until 16th February 1977 that authority to proceed was issued. The appellant was arrested in London on 28th March 1977 and he was committed on 12th September 1977. The hearing before the Divisional Court took place on 20th November and 15th December 1977, and on 16th December 1977 the application for a writ of habeas corpus was refused.

My Lords, the decision in Union of India v Narang[1] makes it clear that, in considering the effects of passage of time under s 8(3) of the 1967 Act, no account is to be taken of time that has passed by reason of action taken by the fugitive himself, with a view either to concealing the commission of the offence alleged against him or his involvement in it, or to hindering the criminal authorities in bringing him to trial. Accordingly, I think it proper to leave out of account in the present case the period of time, from the killing of Mr Photiou on 5th April 1973 until the coup of July 1974, during which the appellant was in hiding in the mountains.

The case of Narang[1] also indicates that it may be relevant to consider the extent to which the passage of time has been due to dilatoriness on the part of the requesting authority. As regards the period of 18 months between the date of the July 1974 coup and the date (10th March 1976) when the Attorney-General of Cyprus commenced extradition proceedings, it is not altogether fair to say that this period elapsed owing to dilatoriness on the part of the authorities in Cyprus. At the beginning the de facto government was one with which the appellant was in favour politically. Then the Turkish invasion plainly caused widespread disruption and the political situation remained very confused. Following the return of President Makarios in December 1974 and his amnesty announcement, governmental policy appears to have been against any prosecution of participants in the coup, of whom the appellant was one. This policy was overturned by the House of Representatives at the end of October 1975, and the constitutional power of President Makarios to declare an amnesty was contraverted. It was not long after this reversal of policy that the Attorney-General of Cyprus took his decision to commence extradition proceedings against the appellant. In the circumstances I do not consider that it would be in any way proper to say that the authorities in Cyprus were at fault in not taking steps to bring the appellant to trial during this period. At the same time it is perfectly plain that the appellant himself bears no responsibility whatever for the lapse of this particular period. I think there is room for the view that it was inevitable in the light of all the circumstances.

1   [1977] 2 All ER 348, [1977] 2 WLR 862

Then there is the period of time from 10th March 1976, when the Attorney-General
of Cyprus instituted the extradition proceedings, until 29th November 1977, when the
Divisional Court first entertained the application of the appellant for exemption
from extradition on the ground of passage of time. This was a lengthy period but
there is no evidence that the proceedings were unnecessarily or unduly protracted,
so it must be taken to have necessarily resulted from the fact that extradition proceedings required to be instituted. This was due in the first place to the appellant's
voluntary act in leaving Cyprus, which it may reasonably be inferred was motivated,
at least in part, by a desire to prevent, or at least make more difficult, his being
brought to trial for the killing of Mr Photiou. The government of Cyprus did, however, permit him to leave, not only on his original departure in September 1974,
but also at the conclusion of his brief visit in February 1975. By so doing the government of Cyprus helped to bring about the passage of time necessary for the disposal
of its request for extradition. That I consider to be the true significance of the granting
to the appellant of the two exit permits. It may seem in a broad sense unfair that the
government of Cyprus should allow the appellant to leave the country in awareness
of his alleged involvement in the killing of Mr Photiou and later seek his extradition
to stand trial for the killing, but insofar as that consideration might have a
bearing on the question of injustice or oppression it is not relevant to be taken into
account, following the decision in *Narang*[1], if it is not connected in some way with
the passage of time. Insofar as it is not so connected, it is important, in my opinion,
to avoid being influenced by this consideration, because the Act 1967 does not authorise
its being treated as a relevant one on its own merits. Keeping in mind the nature of
the connection as I have stated it, I am of opinion that this circumstance is entitled
to some weight, but that it is to a considerable extent counter-balanced by that to be
attached to the appellant's own act in leaving Cyprus.

So much for the circumstances under which the passage of time took place. Other
circumstances relevant for consideration are that the appellant has since September
1974 led a settled life in this country with his family and that the nature of the offence
with which he is charged is extremely serious. Then there is the matter of the alibi
evidence tendered by the appellant before the learned chief magistrate. That
evidence was to the effect that at the time of the shooting of Mr Photiou he was at
home in the company of his wife and one George Alexandrou, a former sergeant of
police in Larnaca. Mrs Kakis and Mr Alexandrou gave evidence in support of the
alibi. Both of them deponed that they would not be prepared to give evidence in
Cyprus at the trial of the appellant because of fear for their personal safety, and in
the case of Mr Alexandrou also through fear of arrest. It appears that Mr Alexandrou
was on the same side politically as the appellant. The Deputy Attorney-General of
Cyprus has sworn an affidavit that Mr Alexandrou is not wanted there for any offence
and that he would not be arrested if he visited Cyprus, nor would he be refused
permission to leave. It was submitted on behalf of the appellant that in the circumstances the passage of time had damaged his prospects of obtaining a fair trial, because
it had had the effect of depriving him of this alibi evidence which would otherwise
have been available, and that this was relevant to be taken into account in considering
whether it would be unjust or oppressive to return him. It is readily to be accepted
that any circumstance which might impair the fairness of the trial is a relevant
consideration for this purpose, if it arises out of the passage of time or is likely to have
an enhanced effect by reason of the passage of time. I do not consider that there
can be any question of the latter. Assuming, therefore, that the appellant would
necessarily be deprived of the alibi evidence of his wife and Mr Alexandrou, and
accepting that this would impair the fairness of his trial, can it be said that this arises
out of the passage of time? Mrs Kakis and Mr Alexandrou both left Cyprus in the
course of the period of time which is under consideration, the former along with

---

her husband in September 1974 and the latter in August 1975. One of the difficulties is that the effect of their departure would have been precisely the same had they left at an earlier stage, for example when the appellant was in hiding in the mountains. It can thus be said that their departure is an event of such a nature as might of its own force and independently of the passage of time, operate to cause injustice. But that would, I think, be too strict a view. I consider that the reasonable approach is to look at the situation as it actually arose, and to take account that had the appellant been brought to trial before either or both of the witnesses in question had left Cyprus his and her evidence would have been available. Even so, the departure of Mrs Kakis has no connection whatever with the passage of time after September 1974, nor that of Mr Alexandrou with the passage of time after August 1975.

A further aspect which should not, in my view, be completely ignored is the likely quality of the alibi evidence. The Divisional Court did not have the opportunity of seeing or hearing the two witnesses, nor, if they had, would it have been appropriate to comment on reliability and credibility lest this should prejudice the actual trial. But one of the witnesses was the wife and ... other the friend and political affiliate of the applicant. Alibi evidence is often suspect, and care should, in my view, be taken to see that too ready a loophole is not left open in extradition proceedings for the applicant to escape by calling alibi evidence which would not be available at the trial and the quality of which there is little or no means of assessing. Finally, I do not consider that it should be accepted without any reservation that in this case the alibi evidence would in the actual event not be made available, either through the witnesses going to Cyprus or through its being taken under appropriate procedure in this country. In the result, I am of the opinion that the amount of weight to be attributed to the matter of the alibi evidence is limited.

Some reliance was also placed by counsel for the appellant on certain other aspects of the evidence in the case, principally of a forensic scientific nature, claimed to be affected by the passage of time. I do not attach any significance to these aspects.

Having given the best consideration I can to all the aspects of the case concerned with the passage of time since 5th April 1973, I have come to the conclusion that it would not be unjust or oppressive to return the appellant to stand trial in Cyprus. The interests of justice normally require that persons accused of serious crimes should be brought to trial. The issues likely to arise on trial in this case are not complicated, and in my opinion the passage of time has not had the effect, having regard to all relevant circumstances as I have endeavoured to analyse them, of significantly impairing the fairness of the trial the appellant would be likely to receive. On the question whether his return would be oppressive, I consider that while the long period during which the appellant has been settled in this country is of great importance it is outweighed by the extremely serious character of the crime with which he is charged, and that the other circumstances relevant to be taken into account are not sufficient to tilt the balance in favour of his discharge.

I am therefore of opinion that the decision of the Divisional Court was correct, and I would dismiss the appeal.

LORD SCARMAN. My Lords, I have had the opportunity of reading in draft the speech delivered by my noble and learned friend, Lord Diplock. I agree with it and would allow the appeal. The injustice in now returning the appellant to face trial for a murder committed on 5th April 1973 is that Mr Alexandrou, a witness on whom he relies for his defence of alibi, is no longer an available and compellable witness in Cyprus. Mr Alexandrou left Cyprus in August 1975 and is not willing to return, even for a limited time. The oppressiveness in returning him for trial would arise because during the years that have elapsed since the end of July 1974 events have conspired to induce in the appellant a sense of security from prosecution. Yet during these years he has not led the life of a fugitive from justice. On the contrary, he has settled in this country openly and, as it must have appeared to him, with the

assent of, or at the very least without objection by, the authorities in Cyprus. It was
a not until February 1976 that proceedings were instituted in Cyprus to seek extradition
and not until March 1977 that he was arrested. The loss of his compellable witness
and the build-up of his sense of security both result from the passage of time, the
effect of which, according to s 8(3) of the Fugitive Offenders Act 1967, has to be considered 'having regard to all the circumstances'. It is not permissible, in my judgment,
to consider the passage of time divorced from the course of events which it allows to
b develop. For the purposes of this jurisdiction, time is not an abstraction but the
necessary cradle of events, the impact of which on the applicant has to be assessed.
I have no doubt that the events in this case, which have been made possible by the
passage of time since July 1974, would now make it unjust and oppressive to send the
appellant back to Cyprus for trial.

c *Appeal allowed. Order appealed from reversed. Case remitted to a Divisional Court of the
Queen's Bench Division with a direction that the appellant is entitled to discharge pursuant to
s 8(3) of the Fugitive Offenders Act 1967.*

Solicitors: *Philip Hodges & Co* (for the appellant); *Charles Russell & Co* (for the
Government of Cyprus); *Treasury Solicitor.*
d

Mary Rose Plummer   Barrister.

e
Practice Note

CHANCERY DIVISION
MEGARRY V-C
23rd MAY 1978
f

*Practice – Chancery Division – Lists – Warned List – Causes and matters in Witness List
Part 2 and Non-Witness List – Notice to solicitor of setting down for hearing.*

At the sitting of the court **MEGARRY V-C** made the following statement. In
order to assist solicitors in foreseeing when their cases in the Chancery Division are
g likely to be heard, two improvements in the system of listing will be made as from
the beginning of the next sittings on 6th June 1978. These will not affect cases for
which a date has been fixed, or cases in Part 1 of the Witness List which, by agreement,
are 'floating' on and after some agreed date.
    First, the notice of setting down which the clerk of the lists sends to the solicitors
for all parties as soon as a case in Part 2 of the Witness List or in the Non-Witness List
h is set down for hearing will in future state a date on and after which the solicitors
should watch the weekly Warned List, published each Friday, for further information.
This date will be fixed according to the state of the list when the notice is sent out,
and it will give warning that there is a strong probability that the case will be in the
Warned List on or soon after that date.
    Second, the weekly Warned List for cases in Part 2 of the Witness List, published
j each Friday, will in future, in addition to the present list of cases warned for hearing
on or after the following Monday, contain a further list of cases warned for hearing
on or after the following Monday week. This will ensure that at least a week's
notice will be given before the case is in the list for hearing.

Hazel Hartman   Barrister.

Attorney-General's Reference (No 2 of 1977)

COURT OF APPEAL, CRIMINAL DIVISION
LORD WIDGERY CJ, CUMMING-BRUCE LJ AND PARK J
12th DECEMBER 1977

Criminal law – Sanctions relating to Southern Rhodesia – Emigration – Prohibition of soliciting or encouraging members of the public generally or any particular class of the public to emigrate – Members of the public generally – Defendant contacting individual members of general public – Whether 'member of the public generally' including a member of the public – Southern Rhodesia (United Nations Sanctions) (No 2) Order 1968 (SI 1968 No 1020), art 14(1)(b).

Article 14(1)(b)[a] of the Southern Rhodesia (United Nations Sanctions) (No 2) Order 1968, under which it is an offence to do any act calculated to solicit or encourage, inter alios, 'members of the public generally' to take up employment or residence in Southern Rhodesia is contravened where the defendant contacts individual members of the general public in order to solicit or encourage them to take up such employment or residence (see p 648 b and e, post).

Case cited
R v Britton [1967] 1 All ER 486, [1967] 2 QB 51, CA.

Reference
This was a reference by the Attorney-General under s 36 of the Criminal Justice Act 1972 on a point of law for the opinion of the Court of Appeal arising in a case where the respondent had been acquitted of ten counts of promoting emigration to Southern Rhodesia, contrary to s 2 of the Southern Rhodesia Act 1965 and art 14(1)(b) of the Southern Rhodesia (United Nations Sanctions) (No 2) Order 1968[1]. The facts are set out in the judgment of the court.

David Tudor Price for the Attorney-General.
J Lloyd-Eley QC and Brian Warner for the respondent.

LORD WIDGERY CJ delivered the following judgment of the court: This matter comes before the court as a reference under s 36 of the Criminal Justice Act 1972 whereby this court is asked to give its opinion on the following point of law:

'Whether para (1)(b) of art 14 of the Southern Rhodesia (United Nations Sanctions) (No 2) Order 1968 is contravened where the defendant (other than under the authority of a licence granted by the Minister) does any act calculated to solicit or encourage a person to take up employment or residence in Southern Rhodesia, where such solicitation or encouragement is directed to such person as a member of the public generally rather than as a member of a particular class of the public.'

It is convenient straight away to look at the paragraph of the order referred to in the reference for its precise terms. It is art 14(1) of the order which I have already identified. It is in these terms:

---

a   Article 14(1)(b) is set out at p 647 a, post
1   SI 1968 No 1020

'Except under the authority of a licence granted by the Minister, no person
shall—(a) publish, or be a party to the publication of, any advertisement or
any public notice or announcement soliciting or encouraging other persons
to take up employment or residence in Southern Rhodesia; or (b) do any other
act calculated to solicit or encourage members of the public generally or members
of any particular class of the public to take up such employment or residence.'

It is under para (b) that the offences in this case were charged. That was described
as a draconian provision designed to prevent the assistance and encouragement of
emigration to Southern Rhodesia at the time when the order was made.

The facts included in the reference for our decision are these. The respondent
placed in various newspapers advertisements, the phraseology used being some such
phrase as 'Wanted Men/Women £150 p.w. Fit Overseas', giving an address to write
to for further details. Many persons wrote to the address and were interested and
wanted further details, and arrangements were then made for the interested parties
to come to a specified hotel where they could meet the respondent, and perhaps
others acting with him, to be interviewed to see whether they were suitable for
emigration to Rhodesia.

There were two meetings in hotels disclosed in the evidence, and after the meetings
in the hotels the respondent and others acting with him sent application forms to the
interested parties to be completed or made other forms of contact with them.

It was alleged at the trial that on those facts the offence created by art 14(1)(b) had
been committed. The form of the indictment was that it contained ten counts, each
consisting of a reference to one of the persons who had shown interest, and who
thereafter is alleged to have been solicited or encouraged. I need only refer to count 1
because the point with which we are interested is the same in all. Count 1 in the
statement of offence said:

'Promoting emigration to Southern Rhodesia, contrary to section 2 of the
Southern Rhodesia Act, 1965 and [article] 14(1)(b) of the Southern Rhodesia
(United Nations Sanctions) (No. 2) Order, 1968.'

The name of the respondent is given, and the particulars of the offence are, that—

'on a day between the 20th day of March 1976 and the 27th day of April 1976
did an act calculated to solicit or encourage a member of the public [and then the
member of the public is identified and named] to take up residence or employment in Southern Rhodesia namely sent him an application form for the Department of Immigration Promotion of Rhodesia so that it might be completed and
forwarded to Southern Rhodesia to assist the emigration of [and the name is
given again] to Southern Rhodesia.'

At some stage in the course of the trial objection was taken to these charges and the
substance of the objection, as I understand it, is simply this. The offence relied on
in art 14 is the soliciting or encouragement of members of the public generally, and
the objection taken was that in the form of the indictment only a single member of
the public was identified in the charge. The argument, brief and simple enough,
was that to allege the encouragement or soliciting of a single member of the public
was not enough to amount to an offence under art 14(1)(b).

The Crown's answer to that was, naturally enough, the Interpretation Act 1889
where the plural may include the singular, and it was therefore argued that by virtue
of the assistance derived from that Act the objection that the counts individually
were directed against single individuals would go.

The trial judge was not able to accept that argument because, as everybody knows,
the translation of plural to singular depends on the context permitting, and the trial
judge took the view that the context of the offence created in this case was such as to
exclude the operation of the 1889 Act.

He explained his reasons in two places in a formal ruling at the end of the argument. He said:

'[Counsel for the respondent] says, "Well, is this a case in which the plural does include the singular?" and I ask myself as a matter of construction in the course of argument how one can read "a member of the public generally" to make sense.'

I venture to think that the answer to that rhetorical question of the learned judge was that if you alter the sequence of words by a trifle, you will make sense at once, because those words 'a member of the public generally' in our estimation mean exactly the same as 'a member of the general public', and there is no difficulty about applying art 14(1)(b) to the situation if you once make that elementary concession.

A little further on in the course of the ruling the learned judge said:

'... for the reasons I have given, I think the context is such that it is impossible as I say to read "(b)" as in the alternative, "a member of the public generally". Had the word "generally" not been there, the arguments adduced by [counsel for the Crown] would have been sound and indeed possibly [counsel for the respondent] would not even have taken the point, but as it is I have come to the conclusion, therefore, that these counts do not disclose an offence within that apparently intended to be an offence under art 14(1)(b) and in those circumstances this submission succeeds.'

Our view is that these men were initially contacted by the respondent as members of the general public or members of the public generally, whichever phrase you choose to employ. The fact that they were then identified as individuals, and the fact that they are named as individuals in the various counts of the indictment, does not in any way prevent their having been recruited as members of the public generally, which is the clear object of the article.

For those reasons we shall answer the Attorney-General's question in the affirmative.

Determination accordingly.

Solicitors: *Director of Public Prosecutions*; *Lynn Relton & Co* (for the respondent).

Lea Josse Barrister.

Talke Fashions Ltd v Amalgamated Society of Textile Workers and Kindred Trades

EMPLOYMENT APPEAL TRIBUNAL

KILNER BROWN J, MR R V COOPER AND MR W SIRS

5th MAY, 14th JUNE 1977

Redundancy – Duty of employer to consult trade union on redundancy – Failure to consult union – Protective award against employer – Period of award – Factors to be considered in assessing period – Seriousness of employer's default – Whether provision for calculation of period of award penal – Whether maximum period to be awarded where employer's default blatant – Employment Protection Act 1975, s 101(5).

The employers, in breach of s 99(1)*a* of the Employment Protection Act 1975, dismissed as redundant 25 employees at one of their factories and 70 employees at another. The circumstances in which the redundancies were made amounted to a blatant disregard by the employers of the requirements of s 99. If there had been proper consultation with the trade union and the employees had been properly advised by the union, the employees would have had 74 days available to find other employment before the redundancies took effect, whereas the 25 employees received only 14 days' notice of dismissal and the 70 employees received 64 days' notice of dismissal. Pursuant to s 101(1)*b* of the 1975 Act the trade union made a complaint to an industrial tribunal that the employers were in breach of s 99. The tribunal having decided that the complaint was well-founded made a declaration that the employers were in breach of s 99 and, under s 101(3) and (4), made in respect of each of the dismissed employees protective awards against the employers for a period of 60 days during which the employees were required to pay them their salaries.

---

a Section 99, so far as material, provides:

'(1) An employer proposing to dismiss as redundant an employee of a description in respect of which an independent trade union is recognised by him shall consult representatives of that trade union about the dismissal in accordance with the following provisions of this section . . .

'(3) The consultation required by this section shall begin at the earliest opportunity, and shall in any event begin— . . . (b) where the employer is proposing to dismiss as redundant 10 or more employees at one establishment within a period of 30 days or less, at least 60 days before the first of those dismissals takes effect . . .'

b Section 101, so far as material, provides:

'(1) An appropriate trade union may present a complaint to an industrial tribunal on the ground that an employer has dismissed as redundant or is proposing to dismiss as redundant one or more employees and has not complied with any of the requirements of section 99 above . . .

'(3) Where the tribunal finds a complaint under subsection (1) above well-founded it shall make a declaration to that effect and may also make a protective award in accordance with subsection (4) below.

'(4) A protective award is an award that in respect of such descriptions of employees as may be specified in the award, being employees who have been dismissed, or whom it is proposed to dismiss, as redundant, and in respect of whose dismissal or proposed dismissal the employer has failed to comply with any requirement of section 99 above, the employer shall pay remuneration for a protected period.

'(5) The protected period under an award under subsection (4) above shall be a period beginning with the date on which the first of the dismissals to which the complaint relates takes effect, or the date of the award, whichever is the earlier, of such length as the tribunal shall determine to be just and equitable in all the circumstances having regard to the seriousness of the employer's default in complying with any requirement of section 99 above, not exceeding— . . . (b) in a case falling within section 99(3)(b) above, 60 days . . .'

The employers applied for a review of the period of the protective awards to another tribunal which upheld the original decision. The employers appealed to the Employment Appeal Tribunal. At the hearing the trade union contended that s 101(5), which specified the method of calculating the protected period and laid down a maximum period linked to the period of notice and consultation with the union required by s 99, was a penal provision and required that the maximum protected period should be awarded against an employer who had been guilty of serious default in complying with s 99.

Held – (i) The intention of the legislation dealing with industrial relations was to compensate an employee for the loss he had suffered by reason of unfair treatment by his employer and not to impose penalties on the employer for his default, and in interpreting s 101 of the 1975 Act the appeal tribunal should have had regard to that intention. The making of a protective award under s 101(3) was discretionary, but if an award was to be made its period was at large up to a fixed maximum. The primary consideration in determining the period of the award was the effect on the employee of the employer's failure to consult his union, bearing in mind that, by s 101(5), the period of the award was to be linked to the period of notice required by s 99 to be given to the union for consultation. Although the seriousness of the employer's default was, by s 101(5), a factor to be taken into consideration and might increase the period of the award, it was to be considered not in isolation but in relation to the consequences to the employee of the failure to consult, and the fact that there had been serious default on the part of the employer did not mean that the maximum protective award was to be made unless the employer showed mitigating circumstances (see p 651 *j*, p 652 *c* to *h* and p 653 *g*, post).

(ii) In the circumstances the proper period of the protective awards was, in the case of the 25 employees, the period of 60 days, i e the period of which they had been deprived, and, in the case of the 70 employees, taking a broad equitable approach and not the technical approach that they had been deprived of only ten days a period of 30 days. Accordingly the appeal would be allowed in part (see p 653 *e* to *g*, post).

Notes

For an employee's entitlement under a protective award, see 16 Halsbury's Laws (4th Edn) para 654:3.

For the Employment Protection Act 1975, ss 99, 101, see 45 Halsbury's Statutes (3rd Edn) 2412, 2415.

Appeal

On an application by the Amalgamated Society of Textile Workers and Kindred Trades ('the trade union') made under s 99 of the Employment Protection Act 1975 an industrial tribunal sitting at Shrewsbury (chairman W F Stretton Esq) on 11th June 1976 declared that Talke Fashions Ltd ('the employers') had dismissed as redundant employees employed by them at their factories at Talke and Market Drayton who were members of the trade union without complying with the requirements of s 99 and that, pursuant to s 101(4) and (5) of the 1975 Act, it was a proper case to make protective awards for the period of 60 days in respect of each of 70 of the employees at the Talke Factory and to make similar protective awards in respect of 25 employees at the Market Drayton factory. The employers applied for a review of the protective awards but did not contest that they had failed to consult the trade union under s 99. On 1st November 1976 another industrial tribunal sitting at Shrewsbury (chairman W F Stretton Esq) decided that the original decision should stand. The employers appealed. The grounds of the appeal were, inter alia, that the tribunal had wrongly applied s 101(5) of the 1975 Act by starting with the maximum permitted period

for a protective award and then enquiring whether the employers had shown any
a extenuating circumstances to justify a reduction of that period. The facts are set out
in the judgment of the appeal tribunal.

Bruce Coles for the employers.
Mr Herbert Lisle, general secretary of the union, for the trade union.

b   *Cur adv vult*

14th June. **KILNER BROWN J** delivered the following judgment of the appeal
tribunal: This is an appeal by the employers against the unanimous decision of an industrial tribunal held at Shrewsbury on 11th June 1976 and the rejection of an application for review made on 1st November 1976. At the substantive hearing the tribunal
c made protective awards of 60 days in favour of 70 employees who worked at the Talke
factory and a similar award in favour of 25 employees who were employed at the
Market Drayton factory. The awards were made under s 101(5) of the Employment
Protection Act 1975, pursuant to a declaration under s 101(3) of the 1975 Act, that there
was a breach by the employers of the mandatory obligation that there should be consultation with the representatives of the appropriate trade union before giving effect
d to group or mass redundancies. This requirement is clearly laid down in s 99 of the
1975 Act and nothing turns on the breach, which on the evidence in the instant case
indicated a blatant disregard of the provisions of that section by the employers.
Nor, indeed, is there any appeal against the finding of the tribunal in that regard.
The point at issue is as to the correct interpretation to be put on s 101. We are informed that in the few months since the 1975 Act came into force, industrial tribunals
e are experiencing great difficulty over this question and guidance is widely sought.
     If there is a breach of s 99, which requires consultation, a trade union may complain
to an industrial tribunal under s 101(1). In the event of a successful application, s 101(3)
provides for the consequences. That subsection reads as follows:

     'Where the tribunal finds a complaint under subsection (1) above well-founded
f   it shall make a declaration to that effect and may also make a protective award
     in accordance with subsection (4) below.'

Pausing there, it is plain that the making of a declaration is mandatory but the
making of a protective award is discretionary. Subsection (4) of s 101 does not touch
on the way in which such discretion should be exercised. It merely provides that an
employer shall pay by way of remuneration the appropriate amount resulting from
g the period of the protective award. The method of exercising the discretion is provided for in sub-s (5) of s 101. This is where all the trouble begins. This subsection
reads:

     'The protected period . . . shall be . . . of such length as the tribunal shall
     determine to be just and equitable in all the circumstances having regard to the
     seriousness of the employer's default in complying with any requirement of
h   section 99 above. . .'

Subsection (5) then goes on to lay down that the period shall not exceed the same
number of days as the number of days' notice to a trade union required of an employer before dismissal for redundancy takes effect. Thus it can be seen at once that
there are two different criteria. In linking the maximum period of a protective award
with the period of notice and consultation required before dismissing for redundancy
j the legislation would appear to contemplate an award of compensation commensurate with the loss suffered by an employee who has been given short shrift in a
redundancy situation. This is consistent with the whole spirit of both the Redundancy
Payments Act 1965 and, more particularly, the Trade Union and Labour Relations
Act 1974.

The other factor which has to be considered when reaching an answer which is just and equitable is the seriousness of the employer's default. The wording seems *a* to us to be singularly unfortunate. Does this import an element of punishment for a bad breach of industrial relations? We are told that many industrial tribunals do so regard it. Indeed, in this instant case Mr Lisle, the well-known and much respected general secretary of the trade union involved, made no bones about it. In a submission reminiscent of a (foreign) public prosecutor calling for a maximum punishment, he maintained that it was a penal clause and a bad case of default called *b* for the maximum period of award against the employer. If this interpretation and this approach be right, then this part of sub-s (5) of s 101 is wholly inconsistent with the spirit of the Trade Union and Labour Relations Act 1974. As is well-known, the Industrial Relations Act 1971 foundered on the understandable objection of the trade union movement to be punished for breaches of the law arising out of an industrial dispute in which the trade union involved was sincerely pursuing its collective *c* bargaining power. We prefer to regard the imposition of penalties for bad behaviour as a retrograde step in the field of legislation dealing with good industrial relations and the giving of compensation to employees unfairly treated or discriminated against. We pose the rhetorical question: why should the employer who does not consult a trade union be punished, while the bad employer who is unfair to his employees is not? In the latter case the measure of his bad behaviour is reflected in *d* the compensation awarded to the victim of his bad behaviour. If this case has to be dealt with on the basis of punishment we would be against such a limited and vindictive interpretation. All three of us recognise that we are a judicial body with the powers of the High Court. It is not our function to make the law but to apply it as Parliament has made it. We have to interpret the words of a statute as they are set out and in the context in which they are declared. We are entitled in interpreting *e* one section to look at the various Acts as a whole. We therefore intend to follow the broad scope of all this modern legislation and look to the loss suffered by the employee and to concentrate on compensation. In this context we are divided, and as to part of our judgment Mr Sirs takes a different view.

In the first place, we are all of us of the opinion that bearing in mind the linking of the period of an award with the period of notice to a trade union for purposes of *f* consultation, the primary consideration is to assess the consequences to the employees. Plainly the seriousness of the employer's default has also to be considered. However, neither should be considered in isolation. Whether or not the employer's conduct should be penalised seems to us to beg the question. In other words the seriousness of the default ought to be considered in its relationship to the employees and not in its relationship to the trade union representative who has not been consulted. *g*

The difference between us is not so much a question of principle as a matter of emphasis. The majority are of the opinion that, bearing in mind that a protective award is discretionary and need not be made at all, the period, once it is decided to make an award, is at large with a fixed maximum. The degree of the employer's default is a factor for increasing the period from short to long. On the other hand Mr Sirs considers that once it is decided to make an award it has to be the maximum *h* period unless the employer can mitigate the total. Mr Sirs relies on the comparative principle where the employee can be found to have lost part of his compensatory award for unfair dismissal by reason of his contributory conduct. In his view, because employees have to face up to that compensatory sanction, it is only right and proper that the employers should have the same compensatory sanction against them. Applying this approach in the instant case, it is his opinion that the maximum award *j* in the case of all employees at both factories was properly made and should not be disturbed.

The facts of this case demonstrate why the majority of us consider that some distinction and some adjustment is necessary. As has previously been mentioned, there was a blatant disregard of the requirement to consult with the trade union involved. Mr Lisle was the appropriate representative of the union. He had been concentrating on wage increases for the employees. The employers resisted the demands. The industrial tribunal accepted that the employers made plain to Mr Lisle that they could not afford the increases and that redundancies or complete closure would be inevitable. At the beginning of the year 1976 there was a stalemate and after 6th January no further meetings took place but a further meeting was fixed for 31st March. No consultation with reference to redundancies took place as the employers thought that they had made plain that redundancies might well result if wages were increased. The industrial tribunal rightly, in our judgment, held that the employers had failed badly in this respect.

The employers decided that things were going so badly that redundancies must be carried out even though the wage dispute was still unresolved. Consequently on 26th March Mr Lisle was notified that the Market Drayton factory would close on 9th April and that 25 employees would be made redundant, and that the factory at Talke would be closed on 28th May and 70 employees would be made redundant. The maximum period of notice of redundancy after the 60 days for consultation which is contemplated by the 1975 Act is 30 days, and we are informed and believe that 14 days' notice is commonplace. This means that the sort of period available to employees who are properly advised by their trade union of what is going on is 74 days. During that time they can plan their future and, if possible, get alternative employment. In this case the 25 employees at Market Drayton received 14 days' notice of redundancy and lost all the benefit of the additional 60 days. Consequently the default of the employer had the effect of depriving the employees of 60 days of grace during which they might have done something to alleviate the consequences of redundancy. On the other hand the employees at the Talke factory had 64 days' notice of redundancy. This was only ten days short of the total of 74 days. The default of the employer was of considerably less significance. In the majority view, the proper way to assess the period of the protective award in these circumstances would be to award the full 60 days in the case of the 25 employees at the Market Drayton factory and a much shorter period in the case of the 70 employees at the Talke factory.

One of us takes the view that the strict and technical award should have been no more than ten days in their case but agrees with the others that it is not a question of simple mathematics but requires a broad equitable approach. Therefore the two of us are in favour of a 30 day order in this case.

We are all of us of the opinion that the industrial tribunal were misled into thinking that the provisions of s 101(5) of the 1975 Act are merely penal. They failed completely to apply the proper test and to approach the question along the lines we have indicated. Mr Sirs is of the opinion that they came to the right answer and would still have done so if his reasoning was applied. The majority decision is that the appeal is allowed in part. In order to save time and expense we shall dismiss the appeal with reference to the 25 employees at Market Drayton and allow the appeal with reference to the 70 employees at Talke. In their case we shall substitute the period of 30 days for the 60 days' order as made.

Appeal allowed in part.

Solicitors: *Herbert Oppenheimer, Nathan and Vandyk* (for the employers).

Salim Merali Esq Barrister.

Director of Public Prosecutions v Nock
Director of Public Prosecutions v Alsford

HOUSE OF LORDS

LORD DIPLOCK, LORD EDMUND-DAVIES, LORD RUSSELL OF KILLOWEN, LORD KEITH OF
KINKEL AND LORD SCARMAN

5th, 6th APRIL, 24th MAY 1978

*Criminal law – Conspiracy – Impossible offence – Belief of accused that course of conduct
agreed on constitutes offence – Course of conduct incapable of resulting in commission of
offence – Agreement by accused to produce cocaine from quantity of powder – Unknown to
accused powder not containing cocaine – Whether accused guilty of conspiracy to produce
controlled drug – Misuse of Drugs Act 1971, s 4.*

The appellants and others were charged with conspiracy to contravene s 4 of the
Misuse of Drugs Act 1971. The particulars alleged that the appellants and their co-
defendants had 'conspired together and with other persons unknown to produce
a controlled drug of Class A, namely cocaine'. At the trial it was established that the
appellants had agreed together to obtain cocaine from a quantity of powder which
they had obtained from one of their co-defendants. Contrary to the appellants'
belief, however, the powder contained no cocaine and so it proved impossible to
obtain cocaine from it. The appellants were convicted and their appeal was dismissed
by the Court of Appeal which held that the offence of conspiracy was committed
when an agreement to commit, or to try to commit, a crime was reached, whether
or not anything was, or could be, done to perform it.

Held – Where the conspiracy alleged by an indictment was conspiracy to commit a
crime it had to be shown that the accused had agreed to carry out a course of conduct
which, if carried out, would have resulted in the commission of a crime. Since the
only agreement proved against the appellants was an agreement to pursue a course
of conduct which could not in any circumstances have resulted in the statutory
offence alleged, i e producing cocaine, they were not guilty of conspiracy and the
appeal would therefore be allowed (see p 655 *g*, p 656 *a*, p 657 *g* to p 658 *e*, p 660 *b c*
and *e*, p 661 *j*, p 662 *e f* and p 663 *d*, post).

Notes

For the meaning of conspiracy, see 11 Halsbury's Laws (4th Edn) para 58.

For the Misuse of Drugs Act 1971, s 4, see 41 Halsbury's Statutes (3rd Edn) 883.

As from 1st December 1977 the offence of conspiracy is defined by s 1 of the Criminal
Law Act 1977.

Cases referred to in opinions

Board of Trade v Owen [1957] 1 All ER 411, [1957] AC 602, [1957] 2 WLR 351, 121 JP 177,
41 Cr App Rep 11, HL, 14(1) Digest (Reissue) 153, 1074.

Haggard v Mason [1976] 1 All ER 337, [1976] 1 WLR 187, 140 JP 198, DC, 15 Digest
(Reissue) 1077, 9171.

Haughton v Smith [1973] 3 All ER 1109, [1975] AC 476, [1974] 2 WLR 1, 138 JP 31, 58
Cr App Rep 198, HL, 14(1) Digest (Reissue) 113, 756.

Mulcahy v R (1868) LR 3 HL 306, 14(1) Digest (Reissue) 119, 800.

Partington v Williams (1975) 62 Cr App Rep 220, CA, 14(1) Digest (Reissue) 113, 755.

R v Brown (1889) 24 QBD 357, 59 LJMC 47, 61 LT 594, 54 JP 408, 16 Cox CC 715, CCR,
14(1) Digest (Reissue) 113, 757.

R v Collins (1864) 9 Cox CC 497, Le & Ca 471, 4 New Rep 299, 33 LJMC 177, 10 LT 581,
a   28 JP 436, 10 Jur NS 686, 169 ER 1477, CCR, 14(1) Digest (Reissue) 112, *753*.
R v Dalton (Percy) (London) Ltd, R v Dalton, R v Strong [1949] LJR 1626, 33 Cr App Rep
    102, CCA, 17 Digest (Reissue) 528, *278*.
R v Easom [1971] 2 All ER 945, [1971] 2 QB 315, [1971] 3 WLR 82, 135 JP 477, 55 Cr App
    Rep 410, CA, 14(1) Digest (Reissue) 112, *754*.
R v Green (Harry Rodney) [1975] 3 All ER 1011, [1976] QB 985, [1976] 2 WLR 57, 140 JP
b   112, 62 Cr App Rep 74, CA, 15 Digest (Reissue) 1086, *9190*.
R v Hussein [1978] Crim LR 219, CA.
R v McDonough (1962) 47 Cr App Rep 37, CCA, 15 Digest (Reissue) 1366, *11,939*.
R v M'Pherson (1857) 7 Cox CC 281, Dears & B 197, 26 LJMC 134, 29 LTOS 129, 21 JP
    325, 3 Jur NS 523, 169 ER 975, CCR, 14(1) Digest (Reissue) 112, *751*.
R v Ring, Atkins and Jackson (1892) 61 LJMC 116, 66 LT 300, 56 JP 552, 17 Cox CC 491,
c   CCR, 14(1) Digest (Reissue) 112, *752*.

Appeal

On 26th January 1977 in the Crown Court at Snaresbrook before his Honour Judge
Lewisohn, the appellants, David Michael Nock and Kevin Charles Alsford, were,
together with three other defendants, convicted of, inter alia, conspiracy to contravene
d s 4 of the Misuse of Drugs Act 1971. Their appeals to the Court of Appeal (Lawton LJ,
Swanwick and Gibson JJ) were dismissed on 31st January 1978, but the court certified
that the following point of law of general public importance was involved in each
case: whether an agreement which had as its purpose the production of cocaine
(being an act forbidden by s 4 of the 1971 Act) was not an indictable conspiracy because
the evidence showed that the agreement was to pursue a course of action which
e could never in fact have produced cocaine. On 9th March 1978 the Appeal Committee
of the House of Lords granted each appellant leave to appeal and subsequently
ordered the appeals to be consolidated. The facts are set out in the opinion of Lord
Scarman.

Richard Du Cann QC and *Stephen Batten* for the appellants.
f *Michael Worsley* and *Graham Boal* for the Director of Public Prosecutions.

Their Lordships took time for consideration.

24th May. The following opinions were delivered.

g **LORD DIPLOCK.** My Lords, I have had the advantage of reading in advance the
speech to be delivered by my noble and learned friend, Lord Scarman, with which I
am in full agreement. He draws attention to the limited terms of the agreement
between the conspirators that was proved in evidence. To use the formulation of this
class of conspiracy, now to be found in s 1 of the Criminal Law Act 1977, the course
of conduct to be pursued was expressed with particularity in the agreement.
h   The classic definition of this class of criminal conspiracy was propounded by Willes J
in *Mulcahy v R*[1] and has already been referred to by my noble and learned friend.
The full quotation is worth reciting:

> 'A conspiracy consists . . . in the agreement of two or more to do an unlawful
> act, or to do a lawful act by unlawful means. So long as such a design rests in
j > intention only, it is not indictable. When two agree to carry it into effect, the
> very plot is an act in itself, and the act of each of the parties, promise against
> promise, *actus contra actum*, capable of being enforced, if lawful, punishable if
> for a criminal object or for the use of criminal means.'

---

1   (1868) LR 3 HL 306 at 317

This emphasises the auxiliary nature of the crime and its resemblance to that other auxiliary crime 'attempt' in which the 'proximate act' of the accused takes the place of the agreement in conspiracy. So to agree to pursue a course of conduct, which if carried out in accordance with the intention of those agreeing to it, would not amount to or involve the commission of any offence, would not have amounted to criminal conspiracy at common law, nor does it now constitute an offence of conspiracy under s 1 of the 1977 Act.

Your Lordships' decision to allow this appeal, however, need not cause the alarm and despondency predicted by those prosecuting authorities who hoped to find in the law of conspiracy the only available lifebuoy in what appears to be regarded as the shipwreck of *R v Ring, Atkins and Jackson*[1] as a result of its collision with the recent decision of this House in *Haughton v Smith*[2].

R v Ring[1] was a typical case of a gang of railway pickpockets. They were charged with attempting to steal from the person of a person unknown and with assaulting a person unknown with intent to commit a felony. They had hustled a woman on the railway platform and had tried to find the pocket of her clothes, but had not been successful. Their conviction was upheld by the Court for Crown Cases Reserved. The short judgment of the court was delivered by Lord Coleridge CJ in the course of which he said[3] that the earlier case of *R v Collins*[4] had been overruled by *R v Brown*[5] and was bad law. It was the purported overruling of *R v Collins*[4] that was repudiated by this House in *Haughton v Smith*[2]. No member of the appellate committee expressed the view that the actual decision in *R v Ring*[1] was wrong.

The facts of the two cases were not dissimilar, but the indictments were in different terms. In *R v Collins*[4] the offence charged was restricted to an attempt to steal from the person of a woman unknown property located in the very pocket in which one of the accused had put his hand, whereas in *R v Ring*[1] the offences charged were an attempt to steal from the person generally and an assault with intent to commit a felony. At the time *R v Collins*[4] was decided, in order to support a charge of stealing property or attempting to steal, it was necessary to prove that what was stolen or was the subject of the attempt to steal, complied strictly with the description of it in the indictment: *R v M'Pherson*[6].

The modern pickpocket, working with a confederate, as is advisable if success is to be achieved, is hardly likely to have agreed with his confederate that they will restrict their activities to stealing from a single pocket of a single individual and desist from all further efforts if that particular pocket is found to contain nothing. The agreement to be inferred from their conduct, as no doubt it would have been by the jury in both *R v Collins*[4] and in *R v Ring*[1], had charges of conspiracy been brought would not have been so limited. The course of conduct agreed to be pursued would be to do all that was necessary or expedient to steal whatever property of value they could find on whoever was carrying property on their person in an accessible place.

It seems to me, however, that even in relation to the solitary pickpocket who works alone and is apprehended before he has succeeded in finding something worth appropriating in any of those pockets or handbags to which he has been seen to direct his hand, *Haughton v Smith*[2] and the earlier case of *R v Easom*[7] have come to be regarded as authorities for a wider proposition than they or either of them laid down.

In *R v Easom*[7] the accused had been convicted of stealing a handbag and its specified contents which were of little value. The accused, in a darkened cinema, had surreptitiously removed a handbag from where its owner had placed it by her side. On

---

1 (1892) 61 LJMC 116
2 [1973] 3 All ER 1109, [1975] AC 476
3 61 LJMC 116 at 117
4 (1864) 9 Cox CC 497
5 (1889) 24 QBD 357
6 (1857) 7 Cox CC 281
7 [1971] 2 All ER 945, [1971] 2 QB 315

inspection he had found its contents not worth stealing and had left it there intact
a within easy reach of its owner. He was charged with the complete offence of theft
and at his trial the judge took the view that what had been proved amounted to the
full offence or nothing. He refused to leave the jury the alternative of attempting
to steal. The appeal was allowed on the ground of misdirection by the judge as to
the intent of the accused (at the time he took the bag) to deprive the owner permanently of the property specified in the indictment. In dealing obiter with the possi-
b bility of a conviction for attempted theft the Court of Appeal said[1]: '... all (or, at
least, much) depends on the manner in which the charge is framed.' They emphasised that their view that such a conviction would not lie in *R v Easom*[2] was dependent
on the fact that on that particular indictment the only attempt of which the accused
could have been convicted would have been an attempt to steal the particular articles
specified in the indictment and no others.

c   *Partington v Williams*[3] was about a charge of attempted theft of money from an
empty wallet which was not being carried on the person but was in a drawer. The
Court of Appeal there took the view that this House in *Haughton v Smith*[4] had overruled the actual decision in *R v Ring*[5] and not merely, as I have suggested, disapproved
of the purported overruling of *R v Collins*[6] which is to be found in the judgment in
R v Ring[5]. They went on to suggest that whenever the accused is charged with an
d attempt to steal property and the proximate act relied on as the actus reus (pace Lord
Hailsham of St Marylebone) is that the accused had inserted his hand in some place
where something worth stealing is likely to be found the onus lies on the prosecution
to prove that something worth stealing was actually present in that particular place.
   My Lords, this, in relation to pickpockets at least, seems to me to offend common
sense and common justice. The crime which the pickpocket sets out to commit
e is not confined to stealing from a particular person or, a fortiori, from a particular
pocket in a particular person's clothes or from a particular article carried by a particular person. When he converts intention into attempt by the proximate act of
extending his hand to a particular pocket or article, failure at this point to effect his
intention of stealing, because where he first puts his hand there is nothing to steal,
does not mean that the course of conduct that he intended to pursue would have
f ended with this initial failure and would not have continued until he had found
something to steal in some similar place and stolen it. Under an indictment drafted
in suitably broad terms I see no reason why even the solitary pickpocket should not
be convicted of attempted theft without the prosecution needing to prove that the
particular pockets or handbags into which he was seen to put his hand in fact contained
something which he would have stolen if he could.

g

LORD EDMUND-DAVIES. My Lords, I have had the advantage of reading in
draft the speech prepared by my noble and learned friend, Lord Scarman. I agree
with it and with the conclusion that the appeal should be allowed and the conviction
of each appellant quashed.

h

LORD RUSSELL OF KILLOWEN. My Lords, I have had the advantage of
reading in draft the speech in these consolidated appeals of my noble and learned
friend, Lord Scarman. I agree with his conclusion that these appeals should be allowed
and with the reasons to which he attributes that conclusion.

j 1   [1971] 2 All ER 945 at 948, [1971] 2 QB 315 at 321
    2   [1971] 2 All ER 945, [1971] QB 315
    3   (1975) 62 Cr App Rep 220
    4   [1973] 3 All ER 1109, [1975] AC 476
    5   (1892) 61 LJMC 116
    6   (1864) 9 Cox CC 497

The important point to note is that the agreement that is said to have been an unlawful conspiracy was not an agreement in general terms to produce cocaine, but an agreement in specific terms to produce cocaine from a particular powder which in fact, however treated, would never yield cocaine. In order to see whether there is a criminal conspiracy it is necessary to consider the whole agreement. The specific limits of the agreement cannot be discarded, leaving a general agreement to produce cocaine, for that would be to find an agreement other than that which was made; and that is not a permissible approach to any agreement, conspiracy or other.

It is, I apprehend, clear on authority that neither appellant, discovered in the act of vainly and optimistically applying sulphuric acid (or any other treatment) to this particular powder, would be guilty of an attempt to produce cocaine. It would appear to me strange that the two should be guilty of a crime if together they bent over the same test tube, having agreed on the joint vain attempt. These appellants thought that they would succeed in their endeavour. But what if they had doubted success, and their agreement had been to 'try it'? That would be an agreement to attempt, and since the attempt would not be unlawful the agreement could not be a criminal conspiracy. But if the conclusion against which these appeals are made were correct, it would mean that those erroneously confident of success would be guilty of the crime of conspiracy, but not those who, unconvinced, agreed to try. The gullible would be guilty, the suspicious stainless. That could not be right.

LORD KEITH OF KINKEL. My Lords, I have had the opportunity of reading in draft the speech of my noble and learned friend, Lord Scarman. I agree with it, and for the reasons he gives I would allow the appeal, I also agree with the supplementary observations of my noble and learned friend, Lord Diplock.

LORD SCARMAN. My Lords, the headnote to the report of *Haughton v Smith*[1] accurately records that the second of the holdings of your Lordship's House in that case was that steps on the way to the doing of something, which was thereafter done (or would have been done, if not interrupted by some supervening event) and which is no crime, cannot be regarded as attempts to commit a crime. In dismissing the two appeals which are now under consideration by your Lordships, the Court of Appeal declined to apply this principle to cases of conspiracy, but certified the point as one of general public importance. The Court of Appeal has certified the point in terms specific to the facts of this case. It is, however, a general question, which, with respect, I think is better put as follows: when two or more persons agree on a course of conduct with the object of committing a criminal offence, but, unknown to them, it is not possible to achieve their object by the course of conduct agreed on, do they commit the crime of conspiracy? The question falls to be considered at common law, the relevant events having occurred before the coming into force of the Criminal Law Act 1977, s 1(1) of which contains a statutory definition of conspiracy superseding the common law. Nevertheless the point is of some importance for the reason given by the Court of Appeal, that the common law may have to be investigated for the purpose of construing the section.

The classic description of the crime of conspiracy at common law is that it consists of an agreement to do an unlawful act or a lawful act by unlawful means: *Mulcahy v R*[2]. The agreement itself constitutes the offence. The mens rea of the offence is the intention to do the unlawful act, the actus reus is the fact of agreement. The Court of Appeal, correctly, in my judgment, stressed that it is the factor of agreement which distinguishes conspiracy from attempt. But were they also correct in concluding that because of the factor of agreement the principle accepted by your Lordship's

1   [1975] AC 476
2   (1868) LR 3 HL 306 at 317

House in *Haughton v Smith*[1] as applying to attempts is not to be applied to conspiracy?
a I have reached the conclusion that the Court of Appeal fell into error on this point, and that *Haughton v Smith*[1] is applicable to cases of conspiracy.

Before giving my reasons for this conclusion it is necessary to determine the nature and scope of the agreement which in this case is alleged to constitute the criminal conspiracy. This calls for a close review of the facts as found or admitted.

Five persons, including the two appellants, David Michael Nock and Kevin Charles
b Alsford, appeared at the Crown Court at Snaresbrook on 5th January 1977 to answer an indictment charging them with a number of drug offences. The appellants were convicted on several counts, but your Lordships' House is concerned only with their conviction on the first count in the indictment. It charged them (and others) with conspiracy to contravene s 4 of the Misuse of Drugs Act 1971. The section provides by sub-s (1) that subject to regulations (which are of no present relevance) it shall not
c be lawful for a person to produce a controlled drug and by sub-s (2) that it is an offence to produce a controlled drug in contravention of sub-s (1). The particulars of the offence, after being amended, were as follows:

'KEVIN CHARLES ALSFORD, DAVID MICHAEL NOCK [and three other named defendants] on divers days before the 23rd day of September 1975 conspired together
d and with other persons unknown to produce a controlled drug of Class A, namely, cocaine.'

The indictment makes plain that the Crown is alleging in this case a conspiracy to commit a crime, and no one has suggested that the particulars fail to disclose an offence known to the law. But the appellants submit, and it is not disputed by the Crown, that the agreement as proved was narrower in scope than the conspiracy
e charged. When the case was before the Court of Appeal, counsel on both sides agreed that the evidence went to prove that the appellants agreed together to obtain cocaine by separating it from the other substance or substances contained in a powder which they had obtained from one of their co-defendants, a Mr Mitchell. They believed that the powder was a mixture of cocaine and lignocaine, and that they would be able to produce cocaine from it. In fact the powder was lignocaine hydrochloride,
f an anaesthetic used in dentistry, which contains no cocaine at all. It is impossible to produce, by separation or otherwise, cocaine from lignocaine. The agreement between the appellants was correctly summarised by the Court of Appeal, when certifying the point of law, as an agreement 'to pursue a course of action which could never in fact have produced cocaine'.

The appellants made a number of attempts, all of them, of course, unsuccessful,
g to extract cocaine from their powder. It was not until after they had been arrested and the powder seized by the police and sent for analysis that they learnt to their surprise that there was no way in which cocaine could be produced from it.

The trial judge in his direction to the jury, and the Court of Appeal in their judgment dismissing the two appeals, treated this impossibility as an irrelevance. In their view the agreement was what mattered; and there was plain evidence of an agree-
h ment to produce cocaine, even though unknown to the two conspirators it could not be done. Neither the trial judge nor the Court of Appeal thought it necessary to carry their analysis of the agreement further. The trial judge described it simply as an agreement to produce cocaine. The Court of Appeal thought it enough that the prosecution had proved 'an agreement to do an act which was forbidden by s 4 of the Misuse of Drugs Act 1971'. Both descriptions are accurate, as far as they go.
j But neither contains any reference to the limited nature of the agreement proved: it was an agreement on a specific course of conduct with the object of producing cocaine, and limited to that course of conduct. Since it could not result in the production of cocaine, the two appellants by pursuing it could not commit the statutory

1   [1973] 3 All ER 1109, [1975] AC 476

offence of producing a controlled drug. The appellants, who did get a chemist to take on the impossible job of extracting cocaine from the powder, may perhaps *a* be treated as having completed their agreed course of conduct; if so, they completed it without committing the statutory offence. Perhaps, however, it would be more accurate to treat them as having desisted before they had completed all that they had agreed to do; but it makes no difference because, had they completed all that they had agreed to do, no cocaine would have been produced.

If, therefore, their agreement, limited as it was to a specific course of conduct *b* which could not result in the commission of the statutory offence, constituted (as the Court of Appeal held) a criminal conspiracy, the strange consequence ensues, that by agreeing on a course of conduct which was not criminal (or unlawful) the appellants were guilty of conspiring to commit a crime.

On these facts the appellants submit that the evidence reveals no 'conspiracy at large', by which they mean an agreement in general terms to produce cocaine *c* if and when they could find a suitable raw material, but only the limited agreement, to which I have referred. Counsel for the appellants concedes that, if two or more persons decide to go into business as cocaine producers, or, to take another example, as assassins for hire (e g 'Murder Incorporated'), the mere fact that in the course of performing their agreement they attempt to produce cocaine from a raw material which could not possibly yield it or, in the second example, stab a corpse, believing *d* it to be the body of a living man, would not avail them as a defence: for the performance of their general agreement would not be rendered impossible by such transient frustrations. But performance of the limited agreement proved in this case could not in any circumstances have involved the commission of the offence created by the statute.

The answer sought to be made by the Crown (and accepted by the Court of Appeal) *e* is that the offence of conspiracy is committed when an agreement to commit, or to try to commit, a crime is reached, whether or not anything is, or can be, done to perform it. It is wrong, on their view, to treat conspiracy as a 'preliminary' or 'inchoate' crime, for its criminality depends in no way on its being a step towards the commission of the substantive offence (or, at common law, the unlawful act). On this view of the law the scope of agreement is irrelevant: all that is needed to constitute the *f* crime is the intention to commit the substantive offence and the agreement to try to do so.

If the Court of Appeal is right, *Haughton v Smith*[1] can have no application in cases of conspiracy. But neither history nor principle supports this view of the law. In *Board of Trade v Owen*[2] Lord Tucker, quoting with approval some observations from Wright J's little classic, The Law of Criminal Conspiracies and Agreements[3] *g* and some passages from Sir William Holdsworth's somewhat larger work, The History of English Law[4], accepted that the historical basis of the crime of conspiring to commit a crime (the case with which we are now concerned) was that it developed as an 'auxiliary' (Wright J's word) to the law which creates the crime agreed to be committed. Lord Tucker[5] accepted Holdsworth's comment that 'It was inevitable, therefore, as Stephen[6] has said, that conspiracy should come to be *h* regarded as a form of attempt to commit a wrong'. Lord Tucker concluded his survey with these words[7]:

'Accepting the above as the historical basis of the crime of conspiracy, it seems

---

1 [1973] 3 All ER 1109, [1975] AC 476
2 [1957] 1 All ER 411 at 414, 415, [1957] AC 602 at 623, 624
3 (1873) pp 80, 83, 86, 88
4 Vol 5, pp 203, 204
5 [1957] 1 All ER 411 at 416, [1957] AC 602 at 625
6 History of the Criminal Law (1883), vol 2, p 227
7 [1957] 1 All ER 411 at 416, [1957] AC 602 at 626

to me that the whole object of making such agreements punishable is to prevent the commission of the substantive offence before it has even reached the stage of an attempt . . .'

Lord Tucker, in whose opinion the other noble and learned Lords sitting with him concurred, by stressing the 'auxiliary' nature of the crime of conspiracy and by explaining its justification as being to prevent the commission of substantive offences, has placed the crime firmly in the same class and category as attempts to commit a crime. Both are criminal because they are steps towards the commission of a substantive offence. The distinction between the two is that, whereas a 'proximate' act is that which constitutes the crime of attempt, agreement is the necessary ingredient in conspiracy. The importance of the distinction is that agreement may, and usually will, occur well before the first step which can be said to be an attempt. The law of conspiracy thus makes possible an earlier intervention by the law to prevent the commission of the substantive offence. But the distinction has no relevance in determining whether the impossibility of committing the substantive offence should be a defence. Indeed on the view of the law authoritatively explained and accepted in *Owen's* case[1], logic and justice would seem to require that the question as to the effect of the impossibility of the substantive offence should be answered in the same way, whether the crime charged be conspiracy or attempt.

It is necessary, therefore, to analyse the decision in *Haughton v Smith*[2] in order to determine whether it can reasonably be applied to cases of conspiracy. The Court of Appeal thought that there were difficulties. But I do not agree.

It was, somewhat half-heartedly, suggested by the Crown that the House might reconsider the decision, which we were told is causing difficulties in some respects. It is, however, a very recent decision; and a unanimous one reached after full argument which brought to the attention of this House the relevant case law and exposed the difficulties. More importantly, the decision is, in my respectful opinion, correct in principle. I would not question the decision, though its proper limits may have to be considered. The House decided the case on two grounds, either of which would have sufficed, standing alone, to support the decision, but both of which commended themselves to the House. They may be described as the statutory (and narrower) ground and the common law principle.

The statutory ground was provided by ss 22 and 24(3) of the Theft Act 1968. The offence being considered by the House was one of attempting to handle stolen goods. At the time of the attempted handling, the goods had been (this was conceded) restored to lawful custody. The House ruled that, in the case of a statutory offence[3]:

'The only possible attempt would be to do what Parliament has forbidden. But Parliament has not forbidden that which the accused did, i e handling goods which have ceased to be stolen goods . . . Here the mens rea was proved but there was no actus reus so the case is not within the scope of the section.'

With all respect to the Court of Appeal, there is no difficulty in applying this line of reasoning to a case in which the allegation is not an attempt but a conspiracy to commit a statutory offence. First, there is no logical difficulty in applying a rule that an agreement is a conspiracy to commit a statutory offence only if it is an agreement to do that which Parliament has forbidden. It is no more than the application of the principle that an actus reus as well as mens rea must be established. And in the present case there was no actus reus, because there was no agreement on a course of conduct forbidden by the statute. Secondly, the application of such a rule is consistent with principle. Unless the law requires the actus reus as well as mens rea

---

1 [1957] 1 All ER 411, [1957] AC 602
2 [1973] 3 All ER 1109, [1975] AC 476
3 [1973] 3 All ER 1109 at 1119, [1975] AC 476 at 498, per Lord Reid

to be proved, men, whether they be accused of conspiracy or attempt, will be punished for their guilty intentions alone. I conclude the consideration of this ground of decision with a further quotation from Lord Reid's speech[1]: 'But such a radical change in the principles of our law should not be introduced in this way even if it were desirable.'

The second ground of decision, the common law principle, can be summarised in words which commended themselves to all the noble and learned Lords concerned with the case. In *R v Percy Dalton (London) Ltd*[2] Birkett J giving the judgment of the Court of Criminal Appeal said:

'Steps on the way to the commission of what would be a crime, if the acts were completed, may amount to attempts to commit that crime, to which, unless interrupted, they would have led; but steps on the way to the doing of something, which is thereafter done, and which is no crime, cannot be regarded as attempts to commit a crime.'

In his speech Lord Hailsham LC[3] added the rider (a logical one) to the effect 'that equally steps on the way to do something which is thereafter *not* completed, but which if done would not constitute a crime cannot be indicted as attempts to commit that crime'. As in the case of the statutory ground, there is no logical difficulty in the way of applying this principle to the law relating to conspiracy provided it is recognised that conspiracy is a 'preliminary' or 'auxiliary' crime. And again, as with the statutory ground, common sense and justice combine to require of the law that no man should be punished criminally for the intention with which he enters an agreement unless it can also be shown that what he has agreed to do is unlawful.

The Crown's argument, as developed before your Lordships, rests, in my judgment, on a misconception of the nature of the agreement proved. This is a case not of an agreement to commit a crime capable of being committed in the way agreed on, but frustrated by a supervening event making its completion impossible, which was the Crown's submission, but of an agreement on a course of conduct which could not in any circumstances result in the statutory offence alleged, i e the offence of producing the controlled drug, cocaine.

I conclude therefore that the two parallel lines of reasoning on which this House decided *Haughton v Smith*[4] apply equally to criminal conspiracy as they do to attempted crime. We were referred to a recent case in the Court of Appeal, *R v Green*[5], in which the contrary view was expressed, but not developed at any length. The court in that case, as also the Court of Appeal in this case, attached importance to some observations of Lord Hailsham LC in *Haughton v Smith*[4], where the indictment undoubtedly included, as the second count, a charge of conspiracy with persons unknown to handle stolen goods. Lord Hailsham LC[6] remarked that he was unable to understand why the prosecution did not proceed with this charge. He later reverted to the point[7] and there is an echo of it in Viscount Dilhorne's speech[8]. In *R v Green*[9] Ormrod LJ, who gave the judgment of the court treated these remarks as an indication that *Haughton v Smith*[4] is not applicable in cases of conspiracy. The Court of Appeal in the instant case took the same view. But I do not think that either Lord Hailsham LC or Viscount Dilhorne was saying anything of the sort. The conspiracy charged in the second count must have antedated the police seizure of the van and

1 [1973] 3 All ER 1109 at 1121, [1975] AC 476 at 500
2 [1949] LJR 1626 at 1630
3 *Haughton v Smith* [1973] 3 All ER 1109 at 1118, [1975] AC 476 at 497
4 [1973] 3 All ER 1109, [1975] AC 476
5 [1975] 3 All ER 1011, [1976] QB 985
6 [1973] 3 All ER 1109 at 1112, [1975] AC 476 at 489
7 [1973] 3 All ER 1109 at 1119, [1975] AC 476 at 497
8 [1973] 3 All ER 1109 at 1124, [1975] AC 476 at 503
9 [1975] 3 All ER 1011 at 1016, [1976] QB 985 at 993

the return of the goods to lawful custody. Smith must have agreed to help in the
disposal of the goods at a time when they were stolen goods and the agreement
could be performed. It was an agreement to commit an offence which, but for the
police interruption, would have been committed. There is nothing in *Haughton v
Smith*[1] which would prevent such an agreement in such circumstances from being
treated as a criminal conspiracy.

Our attention was also drawn to two cases, on which it may be helpful to comment
very briefly. In *R v McDonough*[2] the Court of Criminal Appeal held that an incitement to receive stolen goods was complete on the making of the incitement even
though there were no stolen goods, perhaps, even no goods at all. In *Haggard v Mason*[3]
the Divisional Court held that the offence of offering to supply a controlled drug
was committed, even though the drug in fact supplied was not a controlled drug.
Neither of these cases infringes the principle of *Haughton v Smith*[1]; for in each, as
was pointed out in *Haggard v Mason*[4] the offence was complete. In *R v McDonough*[2]
the actus reus was the making of the incitement and in *Haggard's* case[3] it was the
making of the offer.

For these reasons I would allow the appeal. However, counsel for the Crown
informed us that *Haughton v Smith*[1] has created difficulties in the enforcement of
the law. He referred particularly to the pickpocket who finds nothing to steal in the
pocket (or wallet) which he picks. In my opinion *Haughton v Smith*[5] provides no
escape route for such villains, as Lord Hailsham LC called them. In *Haughton v Smith*[1]
this House reinstated as decisions of authority *R v M'Pherson*[6] and *R v Collins*[7]. In
M'Pherson's case[6] the jury had convicted M'Pherson of an attempt to steal goods
other than those mentioned in the indictment. The goods specified in the indictment
had been removed before he had broken into the house. Quashing his conviction,
the Court for Crown Cases Reserved held that 'he could not properly be convicted of
attempting to commit the *felony charged*'[8] (emphasis mine). This decision was followed
in *R v Collins*[7], a pickpocket case. Here also the indictment was limited to an attempt
to commit a specific theft, namely to steal the property of the woman in her gown
pocket. There was no affirmative proof that there was anything in the pocket.
As Bramwell B commented in *M'Pherson's* case[9], such cases depend on the nature
of the offence charged; and, I would add, on the particular facts established or conceded. It is certainly not possible to deduce from these cases a rule that he who, with
intent to steal, picks a pocket but finds nothing to steal must be aquitted of attempted
theft; nor do I think did any of their Lordships in *Haughton v Smith*[1] commit themselves to so sweeping a proposition.

We were invited by the Crown to express an opinion as to the correctness or otherwise of three decisions of the Court of Appeal: *R v Easom*[10], *Partington v Williams*[11]
and *R v Hussein*[12]. *R v Easom*[10] and *R v Hussein*[12] (to which I was a party) were, I think,
correctly decided; but each, like every other criminal appeal, turned on its particular
facts and on the way in which the trial judge directed the jury on the law. In *R v Easom*[13]
Edmund Davies LJ emphasised that in a case of theft the appropriation must be

---

1   [1973] 3 All ER 1109, [1975] AC 476
2   (1962) 47 Cr App Rep 37
3   [1976] 1 All ER 337, [1976] 1 WLR 187
4   [1976] 1 All ER 337 at 339, [1976] 1 WLR 187 at 189
5   [1973] 3 All ER 1109 at 1118, 1119, [1975] AC 476 at 497
6   (1857) 7 Cox CC 281
7   (1864) 9 Cox CC 497
8   7 Cox CC 281 at 284, per Cockburn CJ
9   7 Cox CC 281 at 285
10 [1971] 2 All ER 945, [1971] 2 QB 315
11 (1975) 62 Cr App Rep 220
12 [1978] Crim LR 219
13 [1971] 2 All ER 945 at 947, [1971] 2 QB 315 at 319

accompanied by the intention of permanently depriving the owner of his property.
This, of course, follows from the definition of theft in s 1(1) of the Theft Act 1968. *a*
All that *R v Hussein*[1] decided was that the same intention must be proved when the
charge is one of attempted theft. Unfortunately in *R v Hussein*[1] the issue of intention
was summed up in such a way as to suggest that theft, or attempted theft, could be
committed by a person who had not yet formed the intention which the statute defines as a necessary part of the offence. An intention to steal can exist even though,
unknown to the accused, there is nothing to steal; but, if a man be in two minds *b*
whether to steal or not, the intention required by the statute is not proved. In
Partington v Williams[2] the court did, I think, err in its interpretation of *Haughton v
Smith*[3]; and I respectfully agree with the comments made by my noble and learned
friend, Lord Diplock, on that case.

Appeal allowed.

Solicitors: *Clinton Davis & Co* (for the first appellant); *Offenbach & Co* (for the second
appellant); *Director of Public Prosecutions.*

Mary Rose Plummer Barrister.

Masters v London Borough of Brent

QUEEN'S BENCH DIVISION
TALBOT J
21st, 22nd NOVEMBER 1977

*Nuisance – Right to sue – Occupier of land – Continuing nuisance – Damage occurring while
land occupied by plaintiff's predecessor in title – Roots of tree planted by neighbour causing subsidence of wall of house – Plaintiff purchasing house and carrying out necessary repairs –
Whether nuisance a continuing nuisance – Whether right to sue accruing only to
predecessor in title.*

The plaintiff's father owned a leasehold interest in a house affected by subsidence
caused by the roots of a lime tree planted many years before by the defendants.
Because the father could not afford the cost of repair, the plaintiff arranged for the
repairs to be carried out and then purchased his father's interest in the house. The
plaintiff paid the cost of the repairs and then brought an action against the defendants *g*
claiming damages for nuisance. The defendants contended that the damage had
occurred before the plaintiff had acquired an interest in the premises and that he
could not as a purchaser inherit any right to damages which accrued to his predecessor.

Held – Where there was a continuing nuisance inflicting damage on premises, the *h*
person in possession of the proprietary interest was entitled to recover any loss which
he had borne whether the loss began before or after he acquired that interest. The
presence of the lime tree roots was a continuing actionable nuisance which affected
the land both during the time of the father's ownership and during that of the plaintiff and had caused continuing damage for which the plaintiff, having remedied
the damage at his own expense, was entitled to recover damages (see p 669 *d* to *f*,
post).
Thompson v Gibson [1835-42] All ER Rep 623 applied.

1 [1978] Crim LR 219
2 (1975) 62 Cr App Rep 220
3 [1973] 3 All ER 1109, [1975] AC 476

Notes

For the right of occupiers to sue for private nuisance, see 28 Halsbury's Laws (3rd Edn), p 154, para 214, and for cases on the subject, see 36(1) Digest (Reissue) 478-479, 567-579.

Cases referred to in judgment

Billings (AC) & Sons Ltd v Riden [1957] 3 All ER 1, [1958] AC 240, [1957] 3 WLR 496, 36(1) Digest (Reissue) 43, *138*.

Clegg v Dearden (1848) 12 QB 576, 17 LJQB 233, 11 LT OS 309, 12 Jur 848, 116 ER 986, 2 Digest (Repl) 668, *1858*.

Darley Main Colliery Co v Mitchell (1886) 11 App Cas 127, [1886-90] All ER Rep 449, 55 LJQB 529, 54 LT 882, 51 JP 148, 17 Digest (Reissue) 94, *70*.

Malone v Laskey [1907] 2 KB 141, [1904-7] All ER Rep 304, 76 LJKB 1134, 97 LT 324, 36(1) Digest (Reissue) 479, *578*.

Roswell v Prior (1701) Holt KB 500, 12 Mod Rep 635, 88 ER 1570, sub nom *Rosewell v Prior* 1 Ld Raym 713, 2 Salk 460, 36(1) Digest (Reissue) 488, *647*.

Sparham-Souter v Town and Country Developments (Essex) Ltd [1976] 2 All ER 65, [1976] QB 858, [1976] 2 WLR 493, 74 LGR 355, CA.

Thompson v Gibson (1841) 7 M & W 456, [1835-42] All ER Rep 623, 10 LJ Ex 330, 151 ER 845, 36(1) Digest (Reissue) 485, *623*.

Action

By a writ issued on 16th May 1974, the plaintiff, John William Masters, brought an action against the defendants, the London Borough of Brent, claiming damages for nuisance created or continued by the defendants in that the roots of a lime tree planted by the defendants or their predecessors had undermined the plaintiff's premises at 23 Wendover Road, London NW10. The facts are set out in the judgment.

Michael F Harris for the plaintiff.
Ian Goldsworthy for the defendants.

TALBOT J. The plaintiff brings this action claiming damages for nuisance. He is the owner of leasehold premises, 23 Wendover Road, London NW10. He claims that, by virtue of a lime tree planted by the defendants, or their predecessors, in the vicinity of his house, the roots of that tree undermined the foundations of the premises and thereby caused him loss and damage. Two principal points arise for decision in this action. Logically the first is: has the plaintiff a right to claim for the loss incurred by the undermining of the foundations and the necessary building works in consequence thereof? Secondly, if he has a right so to claim what are the damages to which he is entitled?

At the outset of this case certain matters were accepted by the defendants. (1) It is accepted by them that the roots of the lime tree, which is in the pavement outside the plaintiff's house, did encroach on the land of 23 Wendover Road. (2) It is accepted that that encroachment of the lime tree roots constituted an actionable nuisance. (3) The defendants accept that the lime tree roots substantially caused the subsidence of the land, though there was left in issue the amount of subsidence and the works which would be required to make good the damage.

The necessary facts in order to determine the first question, namely whether or not the plaintiff has any right to claim for the loss incurred, are these. The plaintiff lives at 23 Wendover Road with his father. In addition to those two, the plaintiff's wife also lives there. This property is leasehold and the leasehold interest belonged to the plaintiff's father.

In the autumn of 1971 the plaintiff noticed a crack in the passage wall in the hallway of the house. There had been some crack visible before, but he noticed then it was getting worse. He asked the advice of a friend of his, who was a young builder. His advice was that the work which would be required to put the house in order was too large for him and he recommended a firm, a company of builders, P R Atkins Ltd. The plaintiff therefore consulted Mr Atkins, a director of that company, who made *a* an inspection shortly before 17th November 1971. As a result of that inspection the plaintiff was told that the bay at the front of the house was definitely subsiding. Mr Atkins then prepared an estimate of the cost of the necessary works. That was given on 17th November and amounted to £876. Neither the plaintiff nor his father, the owner of the leasehold interest, had at that time the money available to pay for the necessary repairs. They therefore consulted their solicitors. As a result of the *b* advice of the solicitors, on 24th November, the plaintiff's father transferred to the plaintiff his leasehold interest in the premises. That was done in order that the plaintiff, who then became the holder of the leasehold interest, might raise money by way of mortgage. He went to the Chelsea Building Society and obtained a loan on mortgage of £4,000. One of the conditions of the grant of the loan was that the works necessary to put this house in order would be carried out within a period of *c* six months. In the months immediately succeeding the plaintiff also negotiated the purchase of the freehold interest in the premises and paid for that out of the mortgage loan, the freehold transfer being completed on 14th June 1972.

In April 1972 Mr Atkins' company began work. The works were eventually completed (and I shall have more to say about them later on), and on 4th October the plaintiff received an account for £1,240·93, which he promptly paid out of the *d* moneys advanced to him on mortgage. I say in passing that, in addition to the first estimate of £896, there had been a second estimate for additional necessary work dated 3rd December 1971 in the sum of £135·64.

Coming, therefore, to the first point taken by counsel for the defendants, it is shortly this, that the plaintiff, who acquired the leasehold interest on 24th November 1971, is not in a position to claim, in this action, for damages based on the cost of *e* repair of this house, the damage occurring before he acquired the leasehold interest and when his father was the leaseholder. Counsel for the defendants submitted that, as a matter of law, the plaintiff was in no better position, or worse position, whether he was a volunteer, or a purchaser for consideration, or for consideration of natural love and affection. He would be in no better position than would a complete stranger if he had taken over the house and the premises. Such a person, he submitted, would have no right of action against the defendants. He cited and adopted for the purpose of his argument that which is set out in Clerk and Lindsell on Torts[1]. Under the heading: 'Who can sue for nuisance', the opening sentence reads: 'Apart from rights arising from public nuisance, the person who can sue for a nuisance is the person in possession or occupation of the land affected.' One of the authorities cited in the text is that of *Malone v Laskey*[2]. In that case the wife of a licensee occupier of a house who *f* was injured by the fall of a tank caused by vibrations set up by the defendant was held to have no right of action for her injury either in nuisance or in negligence. So far as that decision relating to negligence is concerned, the decision of the House of Lords in *A C Billings & Sons Ltd v Riden*[3], held that that part of the decision was wrong. Their Lordships expressed no views, other than to limit their reversal of that part of the decision on negligence, on the question of nuisance. It is, therefore, counsel for *g* the defendants' submission that this plaintiff here is in no better position than was the wife of the occupier in *Malone v Laskey*[1], in that at the time of the damage he had no interest in the property. It does not fall to me to decide whether or not that is a proposition that I ought to follow, for reasons which will be seen later.

The next authority that I was referred to was *Thompson v Gibson*[4]. That was an action for nuisance arising out of the placing of a building in a market place whereby

---

1   14th Edn (1975), para 1413
2   [1907] 2 KB 141, [1904-7] All ER Rep 304
3   [1957] 3 All ER 1, [1958] AC 240
4   (1841) 7 M & W 456, [1835-42] All ER Rep 623

the public use of that part of the market place was prevented. Counsel for the
defendants relied on part of the judgment of Parke B. I will read a little further back
than the passage which counsel for the defendants drew my attention to. It begins
as follows[1]:

> 'Is he, who originally erects a wall by which ancient lights are obstructed, to
> pay damage for the loss of the light for the first day only? or does he not continue
> liable so long as the consequences of his own wrongful act continue, and bound
> to pay damages for the whole time? and if the then owner of the market might
> have maintained an action against the defendants for the injury to his franchise,
> for the whole period during which the defendant's act continued to be injurious
> to him, his lessee must be in the same condition as to subsequent injuries; for it is
> clearly established that he has a right of action for every continuing nuisance.'

There are further passages from that judgment to which I will return later. But
counsel for the defendants stressed the words 'subsequent injuries' and pleads here
that all the plaintiff can do is to claim for any loss or injury subsequent to his acquisition of the premises and, therefore, not permitting him to add to his claim, a claim in
respect of the damage which occurred during his father's ownership of the legal
interest. He can only, said counsel for the defendants, sue for damage which occurred
during his occupation, and a purchaser cannot inherit any right to damages which
accrued to his predecessor.

He next dealt with the measure of damages, namely the difference in value of the
interest in the land between the time before and the time after the damage was done
and submitted that the plaintiff had never enjoyed the land in its uninjured state.
It was then in his father's ownership. It was conceded by counsel for the defendants
that in assessing that type of damages it is normally, in these circumstances, permissible to look to the cost of reinstatement.

I was then referred to another paragraph in Clerk and Lindsell[2]:

> 'A private nuisance may be and usually is caused by a person doing on his own
> land something which he is lawfully entitled to do. His conduct only becomes
> a nuisance when the consequence of his acts are not confined to his own land but
> extend to the land of his neighbour by (1) causing an encroachment on his neigh-
> bour's land, when it closely resembles trespass, (2) causing physical damage to
> his neighbour's land or buildings or works or vegetation upon it . . . [I need not
> refer to the first category. A little later on in that passage the learned editor
> writes as follows:] Nuisances of the first kind, in the nature of encroachments
> occur when a man builds on to his own house a cornice which projects over his
> neighbour's garden so as to cause rainwater to flow thereon, when his trees
> overhang his neighbour's land, and when the roots of his trees grow into his
> neighbour's land.'

Then he goes on to deal with nuisances of the second kind causing physical damage
to land.

A further submission involved a reference to the authority of *Darley Main Colliery
Co v Mitchell*[3]. I need not deal in detail with this quite complicated decision, but
merely extract from it what counsel for the defendants desired me to do, namely
that in that case there had been, as a result of the working of coal, a subsidence of land
and injury to houses in 1868. The working of coal ceased, but in 1882 a further subsidence took place, causing further injury. The decision of their Lordships was that
that second subsidence gave rise to a cause of action in the hands of those who suffered
the second injury. The principle that counsel for the defendants desires me to extract

---

1   (1841) 7 M & W 456 at 460, [1835-42] All ER Rep 623 at 624, 625
2   14th Edn (1975), para 1393
3   (1886) 11 App Cas 127, [1886-90] All ER Rep 449

from that case is that there were two separate claims in respect of the same nuisance and he likens that to this case, namely there are two separate claims here: a claim by the father and a claim by the plaintiff, if the plaintiff has suffered damage since his acquisition of the premises. Counsel for the defendants conceded that the plaintiff may have a cause of action for encroachment if he is in a position to show damage. The burden of his submission on this point was that the plaintiff cannot use the damage which occurred during his father's ownership to support his cause of action for the nuisance which continued during his own occupation.

Another authority was *Clegg v Dearden*[1]. There the defendants in working a mine had excavated wrongfully into their neighbour's mine. That gave rise to a claim for damages in trespass. Counsel for the defendants adopted the principle to be derived from that case, namely that there was a once for all loss and that in this case occurred during the ownership of the plaintiff's father.

A more modern authority relied upon was *Sparham-Souter v Town and Country Developments (Essex) Ltd*[2]. Principally that decision of the Court of Appeal dealt with the time at which a cause of action accrues. For instance, the court held that in the case of negligence the cause of action accrues not at the date of the negligent act or omission, but at the date when the damage is first sustained by the plaintiff. Again the question of the Statutes of Limitations were involved in this decision. But there is a passage in the judgment of Lord Denning MR[3] which counsel for the defendants submitted was very much in point:

'One word more: the only owner who has a cause of action is the owner in whose time the damage appears. He alone can sue for it unless, of course, he sells the house with its defects and assigns the cause of action to his purchaser.'

Thus, it is submitted, that, in effect, covers this case. Those were the principal submissions made to me on behalf of the defendants.

Counsel for the plaintiff points out, somewhat wryly, that if the defendants are right, had the plaintiff's father sued, they would have said where is his loss in that the cost of reinstatement has fallen on his son. In the same breath, or in the next breath, they say: the plaintiff, the son, can't sue, because the damage did not occur during his ownership of the interest. That, submits counsel, is palpably wrong. I must confess, looked at that way, there is great force in that submission. He analysed the matter in this way: the defendants have committed the tort of nuisance; that tort has damaged the premises; as a result the value of the premises has been diminished by the damage and the measure of that diminution is the cost of remedying the damage; and, finally, that cost has been borne by the plaintiff who, at the time of the commission of the tort, had sufficient interest to found an action in nuisance. He then referred me back to *Thompson v Gibson*[4], where Parke B referred to Rolle's Abridgement of the Common Law[5] and continued:

' "If one is seised of land near a river, and another stops it with loads of earth, and the tenant of the land adjoining leases to another for years, and then the stoppage continues, by which the land of the lessee is surrounded, the lessee shall have an action on the case against him; for though the stoppage was in the time of his lessor the continuance was a wrongful damage to the lessee, for his land was surrounded." [Then a little further on the learned judge said this:] In the case of *Rosewell v. Prior*[6], which was an action against the defendant, who erected

---

1 (1848) 12 QB 576
2 [1976] 2 All ER 65, [1976] QB 858
3 [1976] 2 All ER 65 at 70, [1976] QB 858 at 868.
4 (1841) 7 M & W 456 at 460, 461, [1835-42] All ER Rep 623 at 625
5 Roll Abr, Nuisance, K2
6 (1701) 12 Mod Rep 635 at 639, 640

a

an obstruction to the ancient lights of the plaintiff, and then aliened, Lord Holt lays it down, that "it is a fundamental principle in law and reason, that he that does the first wrong shall answer for all consequential damages; and here", he says, "the original erection does influence the continuance, and it remains a continuance from the very erection, and by the erection, till it be abated." And he adds, "that it shall not be in his power to discharge himself by granting it over." It is true that Lord Holt afterwards says, "that if the alienee of the land brought an action against the erector, and the erection had been before any estate in the alienee, the question would be greater, because the erector never did any wrong to the alienee".'

b

The essence of the case of *Thompson v Gibson*[1], as it was dealt with by the court, counsel for the plaintiff argues, indicates that it was a continuing nuisance, and where there is a continuing nuisance it indicates a successor in title can sue in respect of it.

c

The case of *Clegg v Dearden*[2], counsel for the plaintiff points out, is really quite distinct from the present case. *Clegg v Dearden*[2] was an action for trespass, possibly for nuisance, but it was not expressed to be a continuing wrong. He further argues that the defendants, by accepting that the plaintiff can sue for nuisance, accept that he can only do that because he is in possession of land subjected to a continuing nuisance.

d

The final submission that counsel for the plantiff makes on this is that here is a case where there is a continuing actionable nuisance affecting the land both during the time of the father's ownership and during the plaintiff's ownership, that there was in fact, not in theory, continuing damage and that the plaintiff, who has remedied the damage at his own expense, is entitled to recover that cost as his loss for the continuing nuisance. In my judgment, that is a correct submission. Where there is a continuing nuisance inflicting damage on premises, those who are in possession of the interest may recover losses which they have borne whether the loss began before the acquisition of the interest or whether it began after the acquisition of the interest. The test is: what is the loss which the owner of the land has to meet in respect of the continuing nuisance affecting his land?

e

f

Having decided that point, therefore, in the plaintiff's favour, I now turn to the question of damages. [His Lordship then considered evidence as to the extent of the damage caused to the plaintiff's house and awarded damages in the sum of £1,133.33.]

Judgment for the plaintiff.

g

Solicitors: *Parsons, Evans & Francis* (for the plaintiff); *Barlow, Lyde & Gilbert* (for the defendants).

K Mydeen Esq Barrister.

---

h 1   (1841) 7 M & W 456, [1835-42] All ER Rep 623
2   (1848) 12 QB 576

Maharaj v Attorney-General of Trinidad and Tobago (No 2)

PRIVY COUNCIL

LORD DIPLOCK, LORD HAILSHAM OF ST MARYLEBONE, LORD SALMON, LORD RUSSELL OF
KILLOWEN AND LORD KEITH OF KINKEL

13th, 14th DECEMBER 1977, 27th FEBRUARY 1978

*Trinidad and Tobago – Constitutional law – Human rights and freedoms – Right not to be
deprived of liberty otherwise than by due process of law – Redress – Committal for contempt of
court – Judge failing to specify nature of contempt charged – Contemnor applying by motion
to another High Court judge for redress by award of damages against the Attorney-General as
representing the state – Whether judge having jurisdiction to entertain motion – Whether
committal contravention of constitutional right – Whether 'redress' including damages –
Whether award of damages contrary to rule of public policy that a judge is not liable for
anything done in his judicial capacity – Constitution of Trinidad and Tobago 1962 (SI 1962
No 1875), ss 1(a), 6(1)(2)(a).*

On 17th April 1975 a judge of the High Court of Trinidad and Tobago made an order
committing the appellant, a barrister, to prison for seven days for contempt of court.
On the same day the appellant applied ex parte by a motion to another High Court
judge claiming, in purported pursuance of s 6ᵃ of the Constitution of Trinidad and
Tobago 1962, redress for alleged contravention of his right under s 1(a)ᵇ of the Constitution not to be deprived of liberty except by due process of law. The redress
claimed was, inter alia, an order for immediate release from prison pending final
determination of the motion and damages for wrongful detention and false imprisonment against the respondent, the Attorney-General, as representative of the
state. The judge ordered that the appellant be released from prison forthwith.
On the substantive hearing of the motion, a third judge (Scott J) dismissed the
motion and ordered the appellant to serve the remaining six days of his sentence,
which he served. He appealed against the decision to the Court of Appeal. Whilst
the appeal was pending he obtained special leave to appeal to the Judicial Committee
of the Privy Council against the committal order made on 17th April. On 27th July
1976 the Judicial Committeeᶜ allowed that appeal on the ground that the judge who
made the committal order had failed to specify sufficiently the nature of the contempt
charged against the appellant before committing him to prison and held that in consequence the committal order was invalid. On 29th April 1977 the Court of Appeal dismissed the appeal relating to the motion on the ground that, although a High Court
judge had jurisdiction under s 6 of the Constitution to grant the appellant redress for
contravention of his constitutional rights which resulted from something done by
another High Court judge acting in his judicial capacity, the failure of the judge to inform the appellant of the nature of the contempt charged did not contravene his
rights under s 1(a) of the Constitution. The appellant appealed to the Judicial Committee
against the decision.

Held – (i) The claim for redress in the motion fell within the original jurisdiction of the
High Court under s 6(2)(a) of the Constitution since it involved an enquiry into whether
the procedure adopted by the judge before committing the appellant to prison had
contravened the appellant's right, under s 1(a) of the Constitution, not to be deprived

---

a   Section 6 is set out at p 674 *j* to p 675 *d*, post
b   Section 1, so far as material, is set out at p 674 *f g*, post
c   [1977] 1 All ER 411

of liberty otherwise than by due process of law, and did not involve an appeal on
a fact or substantive law from the judge's decision that he was guilty of conduct amounting to contempt of court. Accordingly Scott J, though of equal rank to the judge who
made the committal order, had jurisdiction to entertain the motion. Moreover the
Attorney-General was a proper respondent to the motion, by virtue of s 19(2)^d of the
State Liability and Proceedings Act 1966, since the redress claimed under s 6 was
against the state for contravention by its judicial arm of the appellant's constitutional
b rights (see p 675 g to p 676 a and p 681 e to g, post).

(ii) The protection afforded by s 1 of the Constitution was, by virtue of the combined
effect of ss 1, 2 and 3 of the Constitution, protection against interference by the state,
or some other public authority, with a right or freedom described in s 1 insofar as the
interference would have been unlawful under the law in force immediately before
the Constitution came into effect. Since the committal order would have been
c unlawful under the common law, which governed contempt before the Constitution
came into effect, it followed that the failure of the judge to inform the appellant of
the nature of the contempt charged before committing him to prison constituted
deprivation of liberty without due process of law within the meaning of s 1(a) (see
p 676 e f and j to p 677 a and e and j to p 678 c and e and p 680 j, post); dictum of
Lord Devlin in Director of Public Prosecutions v Nasralla [1967] 2 All ER at 165 and
d de Freitas v Benny [1976] AC 239 applied.

(iii) (Lord Hailsham of St Marylebone dissenting) Section 6(1) of the Constitution
created a remedy against any interference with the rights or freedoms protected by s 1
which would have been unlawful under the previously existing law in addition to
any other remedy which may have been available. The appellant was therefore entitled to apply to the High Court for redress under s 6(1) in respect of his imprisonment
e notwithstanding that he also had a right of appeal against the committal order to
the Judicial Committee. Since the word 'redress' in s 6(1) bore its ordinary meaning
of reparation or compensation for the wrong sustained, the appellant was entitled
to claim damages for the imprisonment. This entitlement did not subvert the
rule of public policy that a judge could not be made liable for anything done by
him in the exercise of his judicial functions for it was only errors in procedure amount-
f ing to failure to observe the rules of natural justice, which were likely to be rare, that
were capable of constituting infringement of the rights protected by s 1. Moreover, the
claim for damages under s 6(1) was a claim against the state directly and not vicariously
for something done in the exercise of its judicial power, and a failure by a judge to observe the rules of natural justice would bring the case within the scope of s 6 only if the
deprivation of liberty had already been undergone. The measure of the damages
g recoverable under s 6(1) where the contravention consisted of deprivation of liberty
otherwise than by due process of law was not at large since the claim was in public law
and not for a tort in private law, but it would include loss of earnings consequent on
the imprisonment and recompense for the inconvenience and distress suffered during
the imprisonment (see p 677 b c, p 678 f g, p 679 a and d to j and p 680 a and c d, post).

(iv) It followed (Lord Hailsham of St Marylebone dissenting) that the appeal would
h be allowed and the case remitted to the High Court with a direction to assess the
damages to which the appellant was entitled (see p 680 e, post).

Notes

For the Constitution of Trinidad and Tobago, see 6 Halsbury's Laws (4th Edn) para
1009.

j **Cases referred to in judgments**

Baker v The Queen [1975] 3 All ER 55, [1975] AC 774, [1975] 3 WLR 113, PC, 14(2) Digest
(Reissue) 730, *4704.

---

d   Section 19(2) provides: 'Subject to this Act and to any other enactment, proceedings against
the [state] shall be instituted against the Attorney-General'

Cassell & Co Ltd v Broome [1972] 1 All ER 801, [1972] AC 1027, [1972] 2 WLR 645, HL, 17 Digest (Reissue) 82, *17*.

de Freitas (also called Malik) v Benny [1976] AC 239, [1975] 3 WLR 388, PC, Digest (Cont Vol D) 111, *132a*.

Director of Public Prosecutions v Nasralla [1967] 2 All ER 161, [1967] 2 AC 238, [1967] 3 WLR 13, PC, 14(1) Digest (Reissue) 441, *3786*.

Hinds v The Queen, Director of Public Prosecutions v Jackson, Attorney General of Jamaica (intervener) [1976] 1 All ER 353, [1977] AC 195, [1976] 2 WLR 366, PC.

Jaundoo v Attorney-General of Guyana [1971] AC 972, [1971] 3 WLR 13, PC, 8(2) Digest (Reissue) 761, *356*.

Maharaj v Attorney-General for Trinidad and Tobago [1977] 1 All ER 411, PC.

Oliver v Buttigieg [1966] 2 All ER 459, [1967] 1 AC 115, [1966] 3 WLR 310, PC, 8(2) Digest (Reissue) 759, *351*.

Pollard, Re (1868) LR 2 PC 106, 5 Moo PCCNS 111, 16 ER 457, PC, 16 Digest (Repl) 60, *576*.

Rookes v Barnard [1964] 1 All ER 367, [1964] AC 1129, [1964] 2 WLR 269, [1964] 1 Lloyd's Rep 28, HL, 17 Digest (Reissue) 81, *14*.

Sirros v Moore [1974] 3 All ER 776, [1975] QB 118, [1974] 3 WLR 459, 139 JP 29, CA, Digest (Cont Vol D) 736, *572a*.

Woolmington v Director of Public Prosecutions [1935] AC 462, [1935] All ER Rep 1, 104 LJKB 433, 153 LT 232, 23 Cr App Rep 72, 30 Cox CC 234, HL, 14(2) Digest (Reissue) 474, *319*.

Appeal

This was an appeal, by leave of the Court of Appeal of the Supreme Court of Judicature of Trinidad and Tobago, by Ramesh Lawrence Maharaj against the judgment and order of the Court of Appeal (Hyatali CJ and Corbin JA, Phillips JA dissenting) given on 5th May 1977 dismissing his appeal against an order of Scott J made on 23rd July 1975 dismissing his application by notice of motion dated 17th April 1975 claiming redress against the Attorney-General, under s 6 of the Constitution of Trinidad and Tobago 1962, for contravention of his rights under s 1 of the Constitution. The facts are set out in the majority judgment of the Board.

David Turner-Samuels QC, Fenton Ramsahoye SC (of the Trinidad and Tobago Bar) and *William Birtles* for the appellant.
J A Wharton SC and *Clebert Brooks* (both of the Trinidad and Tobago Bar) and *Gerald Davies* for the Attorney-General.

LORD DIPLOCK. The unfortunate misunderstandings that resulted in the appellant, a member of the Bar of Trinidad and Tobago, being committed to seven days' imprisonment for contempt of court on 17th April 1975, on the order of Maharaj J, are narrated in the reasons for judgment delivered by the Judicial Committee on 11th October 1976 in the previous appeal to which they have given rise, *Maharaj v Attorney-General for Trinidad and Tobago*[1]. That was an appeal against the committal order. It was allowed and the order of Maharaj J was set aside. The grounds for doing so were[2]:

'In charging the appellant with contempt, Maharaj J did not make plain to him the particulars of the specific nature of the contempt with which he was being charged. This must usually be done before an alleged contemnor can properly be convicted and punished (*Re Pollard*[3]). In their Lordships' view, justice certainly

---
1　[1977] 1 All ER 411
2　[1977] 1 All ER 411 at 416
3　(1868) LR 2 PC 106

demanded that the judge should have done so in this particular case. Their
Lordships are satisfied that his failure to explain that the contempt with which
he intended to charge the appellant was what the judge has described in his
written reasons as "a vicious attack on the integrity of the Court" vitiates the
committal for contempt.'

This was a finding that the judge, however inadvertently, had failed to observe a
fundamental rule of natural justice: that a person accused of an offence should be
told what he is said to have done plainly enough to give him an opportunity to put
forward any explanation or excuse that he may wish to advance.

The question in the instant appeal is whether this constituted a deprivation of
liberty otherwise than by due process of law, within the meaning of s 1(a) of the
Constitution of Trinidad and Tobago of 1962[1], for which the appellant was entitled
to redress by way of monetary compensation under s 6.

In 1975 there was no right of appeal to the Court of Appeal from an order of a judge
of the High Court finding a person guilty of contempt of court and ordering him to be
punished for it. An appeal did lie to the Judicial Committee of the Privy Council
but only by special leave of that committee itself. So the appellant sought an immediate means of collateral attack on the order of Maharaj J. On the very day of his
committal he applied ex parte by notice of motion to the High Court in purported
pursuance of s 6 of the Constitution claiming redress for contravention of his constitutional rights under s 1 of the Constitution and for a conservatory order for his
immediate release on his own recognisance pending the final determination of his
claim. The nature of the redress that he claimed was (a) a declaration that the order
committing him to prison for contempt was unconstitutional, illegal, void and of no
effect, (b) an order that he be released from custody forthwith and (c) an order
that damages be awarded him against the Attorney-General 'for wrongful detention
and false imprisonment', together with a claim for all such other orders etc as might
be appropriate. Both the Attorney-General and Maharaj J were named as respondents
to the notice of motion but only the Attorney-General was served and from the
outset the motion has been proceeded with against him alone.

The ex parte application came before Braithwaite J on 17th April 1975. He granted
the conservatory order, and the appellant was forthwith released, after suffering
imprisonment for part of the day. It is not without interest to note that Braithwaite J
on 26th June 1975 gave reasons in writing for his decision. In these he expressed the
view that, on the evidence before him, the appellant had made out a prima facie case
that his right under s 1(a) of the Constitution not to be deprived of his liberty without
due process of law had been contravened.

The substantive motion, however, did not come before Braithwaite J but before
Scott J. After an intermittent hearing extending over 13 days he dismissed the motion
on 23rd July 1975 and ordered the appellant to serve the remaining six days of his sentence of imprisonment. His ultimate ground for dismissing it was that the High
Court had no jurisdiction under s 6 to entertain the motion since to do so would, in
his view, amount to the exercise by one judge of the High Court of an appellate
jurisdiction over another judge of the High Court. This would be inconsistent with
the 'equal power, authority and jurisdiction' which by s 5(2) of the Supreme Court of
Judicature Act 1962 is vested in all the judges of the High Court.

Despite his disclaimer of jurisdiction to entertain the motion Scott J did express
his own view that the appellant not only had been guilty of contempt of court but
also had been told with sufficient particularity the nature of the contempt of which
he was accused.

From the dismissal of his originating motion the appellant appealed to the Court of
Appeal; but that appeal was not heard until April 1977. In the meantime he had

---

1   SI 1962 No 1875

sought and obtained from the Judicial Committee special leave to appeal to them against the original order of Maharaj J committing him to prison for contempt of *a* court. By July 1976 this appeal had been heard and determined in his favour by the Judicial Committee on the grounds which were stated later in their judgment of 11th October 1976[1]. So by the time the appeal from the judgment of Scott J on the originating motion came to be decided by the Court of Appeal the invalidity of the order of committal had been established as res judicata and the only questions then to be determined by the Court of Appeal were: (1) whether the High Court had jurisdiction *b* under s 6 of the Constitution (now s 14 of the republican Constitution) to grant the appellant redress for an alleged contravention of his constitutional rights resulting from something done by a judge when acting in his judicial capacity; (2) whether the failure of Maharaj J to inform the appellant of the specific nature of the contempt of court with which he was charged before committing him to prison for it contravened a constitutional right of the appellant in respect of which he was entitled to protection *c* under s 1(*a*) of the Constitution (now s 4(*a*) of the republican Constitution); and, if so, (3) whether the appellant was entitled by way of redress to monetary compensation for the period that he had spent in prison.

All three members of the Court of Appeal (Hyatali CJ, Phillips and Corbin JJA) answered question (1), Yes. Hyatali CJ and Corbin JA answered question (2), No; so for them question (3) did not arise. Phillips JA, in a dissenting judgment, *d* answered questions (2) and (3), Yes.

From that judgment by a majority of the Court of Appeal the appellant now appeals once more to the Judicial Committee. In addressing themselves to the questions raised it would seem convenient to set out the most important of those provisions of the Constitution on which in their Lordships' view the answers turn.

'Whereas the People of Trinidad and Tobago . . . (*e*) desire that their Con-   *e* stitution should . . . make provision for ensuring the protection in Trinidad and Tobago of fundamental human rights and freedoms . . .

'CHAPTER I
'THE RECOGNITION AND PROTECTION OF HUMAN RIGHTS
AND FUNDAMENTAL FREEDOMS   *f*
'1. It is hereby recognised and declared that in Trinidad and Tobago there have existed and shall continue to exist without discrimination by reason of race, origin, colour, religion or sex, the following human rights and fundamental freedoms, namely, (*a*) the right of the individual to life, liberty, security of the person and enjoyment of property, and the right not to be deprived thereof except by due process of law . . .
'2. Subject to the provisions of sections 3, 4 and 5 of this Constitution, no law   *g* shall abrogate, abridge or infringe or authorise the abrogation, abridgment or infringement of any of the rights and freedoms hereinbefore recognised and declared and in particular no Act of Parliament shall—(*a*) authorise or effect the arbitrary detention, imprisonment or exile of any person . . . (*e*) deprive a person of the right to a fair hearing in accordance with the principles of fundamental *h* justice for the determination of his rights and obligations . . .
'3.—(1) Sections 1 and 2 of this Constitution shall not apply in relation to any law that is in force in Trinidad and Tobago at the commencement of this Constitution . . .
'6.—(1) For the removal of doubts it is hereby declared that if any person alleges that any of the provisions of the foregoing sections or section of this   *j* Constitution has been, is being, or is likely to be contravened in relation to him, then, without prejudice to any other action with respect to the same matter which is lawfully available, that person may apply to the High Court for redress.

---

1   [1977] 1 All ER 411

'(2) The High Court shall have original jurisdiction—(a) to hear and determine
any application made by any person in pursuance of subsection (1) of this section;
and (b) to determine any question arising in the case of any person which is
referred to it in pursuance of subsection (3) thereof, and may make such orders,
issue such writs and give such directions as it may consider appropriate for the
purpose of enforcing, or securing the enforcement of, any of the provisions of the
said foregoing sections or section to the protection of which the person concerned
is entitled.

'(3) If in any proceedings in any court other than the High Court or the Court of
Appeal any question arises as to the contravention of any of the provisions of the
said foregoing sections or section the person presiding in that court may, and shall
if any party to the proceedings so requests, refer the question to the High Court
unless in his opinion the raising of the question is merely frivolous or vexatious.

'(4) Any person aggrieved by any determination of the High Court under this
section may appeal therefrom to the Court of Appeal.

'(5) Nothing in this section shall limit the power of Parliament to confer on the
High Court or the Court of Appeal such powers as Parliament may think fit in
relation to the exercise by the High Court or the Court of Appeal, as the case may
be, of its jurisdiction in respect of the matters arising under this Chapter.'

Question (1)

Their Lordships can deal briefly with the question of jurisdiction. The notice of
motion and the affidavit in support of the application for the conservatory order for
the immediate release of the appellant pending the final hearing of his claim made it
clear that he was, inter alia, invoking the original jurisdiction of the High Court under
s 6(2)(a) to hear and determine an application on his behalf for redress for an alleged
contravention of his right under s 1(a). It is true that in the notice of motion and the
affidavit which, it may be remembered, were prepared with the utmost haste, there
are other claims and allegations some of which would be appropriate to a civil action
against the Crown for tort and others to an appeal on the merits against the committal
order of Maharaj J on the ground that the appellant had not been guilty of any
contempt. To this extent the application was misconceived. The Crown was not
vicariously liable in tort for anything done by Maharaj J while discharging or purporting to discharge any responsibilities of a judicial nature vested in him; nor for
anything done by the police or prison officers who arrested and detained the appellant
while discharging responsibilities which they had in connection with the execution of
judicial process; s 4(6) of the State [formerly 'Crown'] Liability and Proceedings
Act 1966 so provides. At that time too there was no right of appeal on the merits
against an order of a High Court judge committing a person to imprisonment for
contempt of court, except to the Judicial Committee by special leave which it alone
had power to grant. Nevertheless, on the face of it the claim for redress for an alleged
contravention of his constitutional rights under s 1(a) of the Constitution fell within
the original jurisdiction of the High Court under s 6(2). This claim does not involve
any appeal either on fact or on substantive law from the decision of Maharaj J that
the appellant on 17th April 1975 was guilty of conduct that amounted to a contempt
of court. What it does involve is an enquiry into whether the procedure adopted
by the judge before committing the appellant to prison for contempt contravened a
right, to which the appellant was entitled under s 1(a), not to be deprived of his liberty
except by due process of law. Distasteful though the task may well appear to a fellow
judge of equal rank, the Constitution places the responsibility for undertaking the
enquiry fairly and squarely on the High Court.

It was argued for the Attorney-General that even if the High Court had jurisdiction,
he is not a proper respondent to the motion. In their Lordships' view the Court of
Appeal were right to reject this argument. The redress claimed by the appellant
under s 6 was redress from the Crown (now the state) for a contravention of the

appellant's constitutional rights by the judicial arm of the state. By s 19(2) of the State Liability and Proceedings Act 1966 it is provided that proceedings against the Crown (now the state) should be instituted against the Attorney-General, and this is not confined to proceedings for tort.

Question (2)

The structure and the presumptions that underlie Chapter I of the Constitution of Trinidad and Tobago and the corresponding chapters in other Constitutions on the Westminster model that provide for the recognition and protection of fundamental human rights and freedoms, have been referred to in a number of previous cases that have come before the Judicial Committee, notably in *Director of Public Prosecutions v Nasralla*[1], *Baker v The Queen*[2] and *de Freitas v Benny*[3]. In the first of these authorities Lord Devlin[4], speaking for the Board, said of the corresponding chapter in the Constitution of Jamaica:

> 'This chapter . . . proceeds on the presumption that the fundamental rights which it covers are already secured to the people of Jamaica by existing law. The laws in force are not to be subjected to scrutiny in order to see whether or not they conform to the precise terms of the protective provisions. The object of these provisions is to ensure that no future enactment shall in any matter which the chapter covers derogate from the rights which at the coming into force of the Constitution the individual enjoyed.'

That the same presumption underlies Chapter I of the Constitution of Trinidad and Tobago was stated by the Judicial Committee in *de Freitas v Benny*[5]. In s 1 the human rights and fundamental freedoms which it is declared (by the only words in the section that are capable of being enacting words) 'shall continue to exist' are those which are expressly recognised by the section to 'have existed' in Trinidad and Tobago. So, to understand the legal nature of the various rights and freedoms that are described in the succeeding paragraphs, paras (*a*) to (*k*), in broad terms and in language more familiar to politics than to legal draftsmanship, it is necessary to examine the extent to which, in his exercise and enjoyment of rights and freedoms capable of falling within the broad descriptions in the section, the individual was entitled to protection or non-interference under the law as it existed immediately before the Constitution came into effect. That is the extent of the protection or freedom from interference by the law that s 2 provides shall not be abrogated, abridged or infringed by any future law, except as provided by s 4 or s 5.

What confines s 2 to future laws is that it is made subject to the provisions of s 3. In view of the breadth of language used in s 1 to describe the fundamental rights and freedoms, detailed examination of all the laws in force in Trinidad and Tobago at the time the Constitution came into effect (including the common law so far as it had not been superseded by written law) might have revealed provisions which it could plausibly be argued contravened one or other of the rights or freedoms recognised and declared by s 1. Section 3 eliminates the possibility of any argument on these lines. As was said by the Judicial Committee in *de Freitas v Benny*[5]:

> 'Section 3 debars the individual from asserting that anything done to him that is authorised by a law in force immediately before August 31, 1962, abrogates, abridges or infringes any of the rights or freedoms recognised and declared in section 1 or particularised in section 2.'

But s 3 does not legitimise for the purposes of s 1 conduct which infringes any of the

1 [1967] 2 All ER 161, [1967] 2 AC 238
2 [1975] 3 All ER 55, [1975] AC 774
3 [1976] AC 239
4 [1967] 2 All ER 161 at 165, [1967] 2 AC 238 at 247, 248
5 [1976] AC 239 at 244

rights or freedoms there described and was *not* lawful under the pre-existing law.
There was no pre-existing law which authorised that of which complaint is made in
this case: s 3(1) therefore does not override the constitutional right of the appellant
under s 1. True, he had no remedy, other than appeal for infringement of his right.
Insofar as s 6 supplies a remedy where pre-existing law said there was none, s 3(1)
does not deny it, since it does not refer to s 6.

Section 6(1), to which it will be necessary to revert in greater detail when dealing
with question (3), is not expressed to be subject to s 3. It is general in its terms. So it
applies to any interference with a right or freedom recognised and declared by s 1,
except insofar as that interference would have been lawful under the law in force in
Trinidad and Tobago on 31st August 1962. If it would not have been lawful under
that previously existing law, s 6 creates a new right on the part of the victim of the
interference to claim a remedy for it described as 'redress'. This remedy of 'redress'
co-exists with any other remedy to which the victim may have been entitled under
the previously existing law.

To revert then to the legal nature of the rights and freedoms described in paras
(*a*) to (*k*) of s 1, and, in particular, to the question, against whom is the protection of
the individual in the exercise and enjoyment of those rights and freedoms granted?
In his dissenting judgment Phillips JA said:

> 'The combined effect of these sections [sc 1, 2 and 3], in my judgment, gives
> rise to the necessary implication that the primary objective of Chapter I of the
> Constitution is to prohibit the contravention by the State of any of the
> fundamental rights or freedoms declared and recognised by s 1.'

Read in the light of the recognition that each of the highly diversified rights and
freedoms of the individual described in s 1 already existed, it is in their Lordships'
view clear that the protection afforded was against contravention of those rights or
freedoms by the state or by some other public authority endowed by law with
coercive powers. The chapter is concerned with public law, not private law. One
man's freedom is another man's restriction; and as regards infringement by one
private individual of rights of another private individual, s 1 implicitly acknowledges
that the existing law of torts provided a sufficient accommodation between their
conflicting rights and freedoms to satisfy the requirements of the new Constitution as
respects those rights and freedoms that are specifically referred to.

Some of the rights and freedoms described in s 1 are of such a nature that, for
contraventions of them committed by anyone acting on behalf of the state or some
public authority, there was already at the time of the Constitution an existing remedy,
whether by statute, by prerogative writ or by an action for tort at common law. But
for others, of which '(*c*) the right of the individual to respect for his private and family
life' and '(*e*) the right to join political parties and express political views' may be taken
as examples, all that can be said of them is that at the time of the Constitution there
was no enacted law restricting the exercise by the individual of the described right or
freedom. The right or freedom existed de facto. Had it been abrogated or abridged
de facto by an executive act of the state there might not necessarily have been a legal
remedy available to the individual at a time before the Constitution came into effect,
as, for instance, if a government servant's right to join political parties had been
curtailed by a departmental instruction. Nevertheless de facto rights and freedoms
not protected against abrogation or infringement by any legal remedy before the
Constitution came into effect are, since that date, given protection which is enforceable
de jure under s 6(1) (cf *Oliver v Buttigieg*[1]).

The order of Maharaj J committing the appellant to prison was made by him in the
exercise of the judicial powers of the state; the arrest and detention of the appellant

---

1   [1966] 2 All ER 459, [1967] 1 AC 115

pursuant to the judge's order was effected by the executive arm of the state. So if his detention amounted to a contravention of his rights under s 1(a), it was a contravention by the state against which he was entitled to protection.

Whether it did amount to a contravention depends on whether the judge's order was lawful under the law in force before the Constitution came into effect. At that time the only law governing contempt of court in Trinidad and Tobago was the common law; and, at common law it had long been settled (Re Pollard[1]) that—

'no person should be punished for contempt of Court, which is a criminal offence, unless the specific offence charged against him be distinctly stated, and an opportunity of answering it given to him . . .'

That the order of Maharaj J was unlawful *on this ground* has already been determined in the previous appeal; and in their Lordships' view it clearly amounted to a contravention by the state of the appellant's rights under s 1(a) not to be deprived of his liberty except by due process of law.

It is true that under the law in force at the coming into effect of the Constitution the only remedy available to the appellant against an order for committal that was unlawful on this or any other ground would have been an appeal to the Judicial Committee of the Privy Council, by special leave, to have the order set aside. No action in tort would have lain against the police or prison officers who had arrested or detained him since they would have acted in execution of judicial process that was valid on its face; nor would any action have lain against the judge himself for anything he had done unlawfully while purporting to discharge judicial functions: see *Sirros v Moore*[2], in which many of the older authorities are cited. But ss 1 and 2 are concerned with rights, not with remedies for their contravention.

Accordingly their Lordships, in agreement with Phillips JA, would answer question (2): 'Yes; the failure of Maharaj J to inform the appellant of the specific nature of the contempt of court with which he was charged did contravene a constitutional right of the appellant in respect of which he was entitled to protection under s 1(a).'

Question (3)

Section 6(1) and (2), which deals with remedies, could not be wider in its terms. While s 3 excludes the application of ss 1 and 2 in relation to any law that was in force in Trinidad and Tobago at the commencement of the Constitution it does not exclude the application of s 6 in relation to such law. The right to 'apply to the High Court for redress' conferred by s 6(1) is expressed to be 'without prejudice to any other action with respect to the same matter which is lawfully available'. The clear intention is to create a new remedy whether there was already some other existing remedy or not. Speaking of the corresponding provision of the Constitution of Guyana, which is in substantially identical terms, the Judicial Committee said in *Jaundoo v Attorney-General of Guyana*[3]:

'To "apply to the High Court for redress" was not a term of art at the time the Constitution was made. It was an expression which was first used in the Constitution of 1961 and was not descriptive of any procedure which then existed under Rules of Court for enforcing any legal right. It was a newly created right of access to the High Court to invoke a jurisdiction which was itself newly created . . .'

As has been already mentioned, in his originating motion in the High Court of 17th April 1975 the appellant did allege that the provisions of s 1(a) had been and were

---

1 (1868) LR 2 PC 106 at 120
2 [1974] 3 All ER 776, [1975] QB 118
3 [1971] AC 972 at 982

being contravened in relation to him. He was thus entitled under s 6(1) to apply to the High Court for redress, without prejudice to his right also to pursue his remedy of appealing to the Judicial Committee against the judge's order.

What then was the nature of the 'redress' to which the appellant was entitled? Not being a term of legal art it must be understood as bearing its ordinary meaning, which in the Shorter Oxford Dictionary is given as: 'Reparation of, satisfaction or compensation for, a wrong sustained or the loss resulting from this.' At the time of the original notice of motion the appellant was still in prison. His right not to be deprived of his liberty except by due process of law was still being contravened; but by the time the case reached the Court of Appeal he had long ago served his seven days and had been released. The contravention was in the past; the only practicable form of redress was monetary compensation.

It was argued on behalf of the Attorney-General that s 6(2) does not permit of an order for monetary compensation despite the fact that this kind of redress was ordered in *Jaundoo v Attorney-General of Guyana*[1]. Reliance was placed on the reference in the subsection to 'enforcing, or securing the enforcement of, any of the provisions of the said foregoing sections' as the purpose for which orders etc could be made. An order for payment of compensation, it was submitted, did not amount to the *enforcement* of the rights that had been contravened. In their Lordships' view an order for payment of compensation when a right protected under s 1 'has been' contravened is clearly a form of 'redress' which a person is entitled to claim under s 6(1) and may well be the only practicable form of redress, as by now it is in the instant case. The jurisdiction to make such an order is conferred on the High Court by para (a) of s 6(2), viz jurisdiction 'to hear and determine any application made by any person in pursuance of subsection (1) of this section'. The very wide powers to make orders, issue writs and give directions are ancillary to this.

It has been urged on their Lordships on behalf of the Attorney-General that so to decide would be to subvert the long established rule of public policy that a judge cannot be made personally liable in court proceedings for anything done by him in the exercise or purported exercise of his judicial functions. It was this consideration which weighed heavily with Hyatali CJ and Corbin JA in reaching their conclusion that the appellant's claim for redress should fail. Their Lordships, however, think that these fears are exaggerated.

In the first place, no human right or fundamental freedom recognised by Chapter I of the Constitution is contravened by a judgment or order that is wrong and liable to be set aside on appeal for an error of fact or substantive law, even where the error has resulted in a person's serving a sentence of imprisonment. The remedy for errors of these kinds is to appeal to a higher court. When there is no higher court to appeal to then none can say that there was error. The fundamental human right is not to a legal system that is infalliable but to one that is fair. It is only errors in procedure that are capable of constituting infringements of the rights protected by s 1(a), and no mere irregularity in procedure is enough, even though it goes to jurisdiction; the error must amount to a failure to observe one of the fundamental rules of natural justice. Their Lordships do not believe that this can be anything but a very rare event.

In the second place, no change is involved in the rule that a judge cannot be made personally liable for what he has done when acting or purporting to act in a judicial capacity. The claim for redress under s 6(1) for what has been done by a judge is a claim against the state for what has been done in the exercise of the judicial power of the state. This is not vicarious liability: it is a liability of the state itself. It is not a liability in tort at all: it is a liability in the public law of the state, not of the judge himself, which has been newly created by s 6(1) and (2) of the Constitution.

In the third place, even a failure by a judge to observe one of the fundamental rules of natural justice does not bring the case within s 6 unless it has resulted, is resulting or is likely to result, in a person being deprived of life, liberty, security of the person or enjoyment of property. It is only in the case of imprisonment or corporal punishment already undergone before an appeal can be heard that the consequences of the judgment or order cannot be put right on appeal to an appellate court. It is true that instead of, or even as well as, pursuing the ordinary course of appealing directly to an appellate court, a party to legal proceedings who alleges that a fundamental rule of natural justice has been infringed in the course of the determination of his case, could in theory seek collateral relief in an application to the High Court under s 6(1) with a further right of appeal to the Court of Appeal under s 6(4). The High Court, however, has ample powers, both inherent and under s 6(2), to prevent its process being misused in this way; for example, it could stay proceedings under s 6(1) until an appeal against the judgment or order complained of had been disposed of.

Finally, their Lordships would say something about the measure of monetary compensation recoverable under s 6 where the contravention of the claimant's constitutional rights consists of deprivation of liberty otherwise than by due process of law. The claim is not a claim in private law for damages for the tort of false imprisonment, under which the damages recoverable are at large and would include damages for loss of reputation. It is a claim in public law for compensation for deprivation of liberty alone. Such compensation would include any loss of earnings consequent on the imprisonment and recompense for the inconvenience and distress suffered by the appellant during his incarceration. Counsel for the appellant has stated that he does not intend to claim what in a case of tort would be called exemplary or punitive damages. This makes it unnecessary to express any view whether money compensation by way of redress under s 6(1) can ever include an exemplary or punitive award.

For these reasons the appeal must be allowed and the case remitted to the High Court with a direction to assess the amount of monetary compensation to which the appellant is entitled. The respondent must pay the costs of this appeal and of the proceedings in both courts below.

Dissenting judgment by **LORD HAILSHAM OF ST MARYLEBONE.** In this appeal I find, to my great regret, that I cannot concur in the judgment of the majority. The proceedings have their origin in an incident the circumstances of which have already been explored before the Judicial Committee, and are reported sub nomine *Maharaj v Attorney-General for Trinidad and Tobago*[1]; they therefore do not require to be repeated in detail. Suffice it to say that the present appellant, a barrister, was committed for seven days on a charge of contempt in the face of the court by a judge of the High Court of Trinidad and Tobago, a conviction against which he appealed by special leave. In the result his appeal was allowed and his conviction set aside on two substantive grounds, the first of which is not, and the second of which is, relevant to the present appeal. The first, of great importance to the appellant but no longer relevant, was that, as I understand it, on a correct analysis of the facts, he had not in fact committed the contempt of which he was charged. The second which is at the heart of the present appeal was, in effect, that he had been deprived of his liberty without due process of law. This was because the learned judge never explained to him with sufficient clarity or in sufficient detail the nature and substance of the contempt of which he stood accused. We are clearly bound by the decision in the earlier appeal, and in the present appeal it was never argued that the proceedings before the committing judge were not a contravention of the Constitution of Trinidad and Tobago in the form in which it was then in force.

---

1   [1977] 1 All ER 411

On the same day as his committal, the appellant commenced the present proceedings by notice of motion under s 6 of the Constitution (of which more later) and Ord 55 of the Rules of Court. They were at first adjourned but when they came on for hearing were dismissed by Scott J on a number of grounds. As a result of Scott J's decision the appellant served his sentence and has therefore been deprived of his liberty for seven days without redress other than the subsequent declaration of his innocence contained in the decision of the Judicial Committee above referred to and their conclusion that he had been convicted without a proper opportunity to defend himself.

On appeal from the decision of Scott J, the Court of Appeal (Hyatali CJ and Corbin JA, Phillips JA dissenting) though differing in part from the learned judge dismissed the appeal and from their decision the appellant now appeals, by leave, to their Lordships acting as they now do as an appellate court by virtue of s 109 of the 1976 Constitution of Trinidad and Tobago.

The notice of motion claims a variety of different types of relief, but, in view of the events which have supervened, it seems to me that the only one which can do the appellant substantial service is that in which he claims monetary compensation as 'damages for wrongful detention and false imprisonment'.

The respondent to this appeal is the Attorney-General of Trinidad and Tobago sued as the representative of the state by virtue of s 19 of the State Liability and Proceedings Act 1966. The original notice named in addition the committing judge, but he was never served with the notice and no remedy is now sought against him. Accordingly the only question in this appeal is whether the state is liable to pay monetary compensation to the appellant. It is common ground between the parties that any right to compensation which may exist can only arise by virtue of the Constitution in force at the time of the appellant's committal. That is the Constitution of 1962. Apart from the enacting sections of the order the relevant provisions are contained in Chapter I, ss 1, 2, 3 and 6, and of these ss 1, 3 and 6 are of critical importance. The respondent placed in the forefront of his argument two contentions, which I mention only to dismiss them because I agree entirely with the reasons given by the majority for their rejection. They were accepted by Scott J, but not by any member of the Court of Appeal. They were (1) that the High Court, in which the proceedings originated, had no jurisdiction to entertain them and (2) that, in any event, they failed since the Attorney-General was not an appropriate party. On the assumption (which I make for this purpose) that the remedy of damages is otherwise available to the appellant against the state, it appears to me that the Attorney-General is the appropriate party by virtue of s 19 of the State Liability and Proceedings Act 1966, and that whatever other proceedings may have been available, the notice of motion to the High Court is an appropriate, though not necessarily the only, means of procedure by virtue of s 6 of the 1962 version of the Constitution, and Ord 55 of the Rules of Court. The case therefore stands or falls entirely on the availability of a remedy by way of damages or compensation against the state in respect of the action of the judge insofar as this was a contravention of the entrenched rights or freedoms guaranteed by the Constitution of 1962. Since in my opinion such a remedy is not so available, it would follow that in my view the appeal should be dismissed.

The 1962 Constitution is one of a family of constitutions similar, but not now identical, in form, enacted for former colonial dependencies of the Crown on their attaining independence, as the result of negotiations and discussions relating to the terms on which independence should be granted. Many of them (including that of Trinidad and Tobago) have been amended since independence (sometimes more than once), but they still retain strong family resemblances. One of the main features of those constitutions is the enumeration and entrenchment of certain rights and freedoms. In the 1962 version of the Constitution of Trinidad and Tobago these, referred to as 'human rights and fundamental freedoms', are contained in Chapter I, and, in the words of s 1 of this chapter include:

'the right of the individual to life, liberty, security of the person and enjoyment of property, and the right not to be deprived thereof except by due process of law.'

The nature of these rights and freedoms and the purpose of their entrenchment has been discussed more than once in reported cases. The first point to observe is that they do not claim to be new. They already exist, and the purpose of the entrenchment is to protect them against encroachment. In a Jamaican case (*Director of Public Prosecutions v Nasralla*[1]) Lord Devlin put it thus: they proceed—

'on the presumption that the fundamental rights ... are already secured to the people of Jamica by existing law. The laws in force are not to be subjected to scrutiny in order to see whether or not they conform to the precise terms of the protective provisions. The object of these provisions is to ensure that no future enactment shall in any matter which the chapter covers derogate from the rights which at the coming into force of the Constitution the individual enjoyed';

or, as Lord Diplock put it in *de Freitas v Benny*[2], referring to the 1962 Constitution of Trinidad and Tobago itself:

'Chapter I of the Constitution of Trinidad and Tobago, like the corresponding Chapter III of the Constitution of Jamaica (see *Director of Public Prosecutions v. Nasralla*[3]), proceeds on the presumption that the human rights and fundamental freedoms that are referred to in sections 1 and 2 are already secured to the people of Trinidad and Tobago by the law in force there at the commencement of the Constitution.'

The purpose of entrenchment was also described by Lord Diplock in another case relating to Jamaica (*Hinds v The Queen*[4]) as follows:

'The purpose served by this machinery for "entrenchment" is to ensure that those provisions which were regarded as important safeguards by the political parties in Jamaica, minority and majority alike, who took part in the negotiations which led up to the constitution, should not be altered without mature consideration by the parliament and the consent of a larger proportion of its members than the bare majority required for ordinary laws.'

And again[5]:

'The provisions of this chapter form part of the substantive law of the state and until amended by whatever special procedure is laid down ... impose a fetter on the exercise by the legislature, the executive and the judiciary of the plenitude of their respective powers.'

In other words the entrenchment is designed to preserve and protect what already exists against encroachment, abrogation, abridgment or infringement. It is concerned with future abuses of authority, usually state authority, and it is largely preoccupied with the possibility of abuse of authority by the legislature (see s 2), or the executive, though doubtless as Lord Diplock said it binds also the judiciary and inferior authority, and presumably also individuals. Except insofar as it protects against future abuse, entrenchment does not purport to alter existing law.

That this is so is clear from the Constitution itself. So far from creating new law, s 1, in identifying the rights and freedoms entrenched, begins with the words:

1 [1967] 2 All ER 161 at 165, [1967] 2 AC 238 at 247, 248
2 [1976] AC 239 at 244
3 [1967] 2 All ER 161, [1967] 2 AC 238
4 [1976] 1 All ER 353 at 361, [1977] AC 195 at 214
5 [1976] 1 All ER 353 at 360, [1977] AC 195 at 213

'It is hereby recognised and declared that in Trinidad and Tobago *there have existed and shall continue to exist* without discrimination by reason of race, origin, colour, religion or sex, the following human rights and fundamental freedoms' (emphasis mine);

and s 3 provides:

'Sections 1 and 2 of this Constitution shall not apply in relation to any law that is in force in Trinidad and Tobago at the commencement of this Constitution.'

By the interpretation section (s 105) the expression 'law' includes 'any unwritten rule of law' and s 6 (of which more later) relates only to proceedings for alleged contravention of ss 1 and 2 (the second of which is mainly framed to invalidate legislation which contravenes the first), and to this extent must be read as subject to s 3 insofar as this limits the application of s 1 to existing rules of law.

It follows that, in order to construe the meaning and extent of the rights and freedoms protected by ss 1 and 2 of the Constitution, one must look first at the extent of these rights as they existed at the date of the commencement of the Constitution. They may be extended or improved after that date by subsequent acts of the state acting appropriately through any of its branches. But they are only protected against encroachment in the form in which they existed at the commencement date. This applies even to the right to life where the death penalty was in force at the commencement. Granted due process of law, the right to life is not infringed by judicial execution (cf *de Freitas v Benny*[1]).

It thus becomes important to discuss in what form the rights to liberty and security of person and to due process existed in Trinidad and Tobago at the commencement of the 1962 Constitution, and for this purpose the extent both of state (then Crown) and judicial immunity is relevant. At common law the Crown could not be impleaded at all. Before the United Kingdom Crown Proceedings Act 1947 (the analogue of which in Trinidad is the State Liability and Proceedings Act 1966, enacted after the Constitution of 1962) a petition or right would lie against the Crown for certain types of remedy, but only by consent of the Crown signified by the Attorney-General's fiat (though in practice this was granted as of course in a proper case). This immunity from suit was no technicality of procedure. It was part of the prerogative and universally insisted on. Apart from the petition of right procedure and some statutory exceptions the Crown was neither liable itself nor vicariously bound to answer for wrongs committed by its servants.

These servants however, from the highest Minister to the private soldier driving a truck, were personally liable for their own misdoings, negligence and crimes. Superior orders, even from the Sovereign himself, afforded no excuse or immunity from process civil or criminal, and although the Crown ordinarily ensured the satisfaction of civil judgments it did so of grace and not of necessity. A judge, of course, is not in the ordinary sense a servant. But he had a further immunity of his own. Judges, particularly High Court judges, were not, and are not, liable to civil actions in respect of their judicial acts, although, of course, in cases of corruption or criminal misconduct, they have never been immune from criminal process or impeachment. This is trite law, and I need do no more than refer to the very full and interesting discussion on the subject in the Court of Appeal in *Sirros v Moore*[2]. This civil immunity protected the judge whether he committed a mere error of law, or, in the case of a High Court judge, and perhaps not only then, if he exceeded his jurisdiction, or if he committed a breach of natural justice, or, subject to what I have said about criminal liability, if he acted maliciously or corruptly. There could therefore be no kind of action against a judge in circumstances like the present, and the state

---

1   [1976] AC 239
2   [1974] 3 All ER 776, [1975] QB 118

could not be liable either. It could neither be impleaded itself nor could it be vicariously liable in respect of a matter for which the principal wrongdoer was not himself liable, and was acting in a judicial capacity and not as a servant.

Until the United Kingdom Crown Proceedings Act 1947 and its analogue in Trinidad and Tobago of 1966 the right of redress for judicial error was therefore limited to appeal (if any), and, since the right of appeal by way of rehearing is largely, if not entirely, the creature of modern statute, was at common law largely confined to technical procedures like writ of error or motion in arrest of judgment. In cases, like the present, for committal for contempt the right of redress was even more restricted. In the United Kingdom a general right of appeal was conceded only in 1960[1]. It seems that in Trinidad (*Maharaj v Attorney-General for Trinidad and Tobago*[2]) an appeal always lay by special leave to the Privy Council, and we were told that a general right of appeal to the Court of Appeal has now been conceded. But, apart from these qualifications, the right of redress in cases of contempt was limited to application to the committing judge for release, or, presumably, application for a writ of error for any error on the face of the record. In no case did it extend to damages.

Nor did the legislation of 1947 or 1966 make any relevant difference. True, it admitted actions against the Crown (state) for tort. But judicial error is not a tort, and the draftsmen of the 1966 Act were careful to exclude liability whether direct, personal or vicarious for judicial acts, and the office of judge from the definition of servant of the Crown (see ss 2(2)(h)(v) and 4(6)). There is no reference, of course, to judicial immunity for acts contravening the entrenched rights and freedoms. But I do not myself believe that this was because no such immunity existed (as must be the case if the majority decision in this case be correct). Personally I find it impossible to believe that, if a right of action for damages in such a case did exist, as the result of the Constitution of 1962, either against the judge or against the state, the draftsmen of the 1966 Act would have allowed it to pass sub silentio, and would not have made express reference to it. At all events, what is certain is that no such right of action against the state or a judge was conferred by the State Liability and Proceedings Act 1966.

We now reach the Constitution of 1962 itself. The first sections to construe are ss 1 and 3, and, of these, s 1 is the more important, though I think they are to be read together. As I read s 1, it means that the right to liberty and security of person as it existed at the commencement of the Constitution and therefore in the form in which it is entrenched did not extend to give a right of damages for unlawful judicial acts, nor, if I am right in my analysis, did a contravention by a judge of the right of due process give any such right. I am quite willing to concede that for whatever reason a failure to formulate a criminal charge including one for contempt correctly was not authorised by law at the time (which included the Bill of Rights (1688)[3]), and that failure to do so would result in a conviction being set aside on appeal where one was available. I do not find the expression 'due process' (although it is a phrase familiar to English lawyers at least as far back as the statute 28 Edw 3 c 3 (1354), repeated in the Petition of Right (1627)[4] and the Habeas Corpus Act 1640) any easier to define exhaustively than have the American courts, but I am very ready to assume that any failure of natural justice such as conviction by or before a biased, interested or corrupt tribunal is struck down by the prohibition or even that a complete misdirection as to the burden of proof as in *Woolmington v Director of Public Prosecutions*[5] would do so, or that repeated interruptions by a judge if carried too far, might also be affected, since this would disrupt the conduct of the defence. If so, I can see no reason to exclude a failure sufficiently to formulate the charge. Exactly at what stage deprivation of due process fades into mere judicial error I do not find it easy to say and if I am right it

---

1 The Administration of Justice Act 1960, s 13
2 [1977] 1 All ER 411
3 1 Will & Mar sess 2 c 2
4 3 Car 1 c 1
5 [1935] AC 462, [1935] All ER Rep 1

probably never occurred to the framers of the Constitution to ask themselves this
a question. The results to the individual can be equally obnoxious whichever side of
the line such errors fall. From the point of view of judicial integrity, judicial dishonesty is by far the most serious. From the point of view of the liability of the state
to pay compensation, I am not sure that any consideration of public policy justifies
these distinctions, logically unassailable as all, or some at least of them, may be.
What is certain is that if I am right it does not matter for the purpose in hand, since
b neither class of error gives a right of damages, but if I am wrong and the majority
decision correct, a new, and probably unattractive branch of jurisprudence is almost
certain to arise in Trinidad and elsewhere, based on the distinction between those
judicial errors which do, and those which do not, constitute a deprivation of due
process of law.

Since it appears to lie at the heart of the argument which has appealed to the
c majority, the time has now come to examine the effect of s 6 of the 1962 Constitution.
Does it make any difference? Does it grant what had hitherto been withheld, a right
to damages in cases of judicial misbehaviour, albeit limited to deprivation of due
process? The majority decision involves an affirmative answer. Section 6 provides:

> '(1) For the removal of doubts it is hereby declared that if any person alleges
d > that any of the provisions of the foregoing sections or section of this Constitution
> has been, is being, or is likely to be contravened in relation to him, then, without
> prejudice to any other action with respect to the same matter which is lawfully
> available, that person may apply to the High Court for redress.
> '(2) The High Court shall have original jurisdiction—(a) to hear and determine
> any application made by any person in pursuance of subsection (1) of this section;
> ... and may make such orders, issue such writs and give such directions as it may
e > consider appropriate for the purpose of enforcing, or securing the enforcement of,
> any of the provisions of the said foregoing sections or section to the protection of
> which the person concerned is entitled ...
> '(4) Any person aggrieved by any determination of the High Court under this
> section may appeal therefrom to the Court of Appeal.
> '(5) Nothing in this section shall limit the power of Parliament to confer on the
f > High Court or the Court of Appeal, such powers as Parliament may think fit in
> relation to the exercise by the High Court or the Court of Appeal, as the case may
> be, of its jurisdiction in respect of the matters arising under this Chapter.'

It is perhaps worth remarking that the sidenote to the whole section reads:
'Enforcement of protective provisions.' This is the section which is alleged to have
g made by necessary intendment fundamental changes in the long standing rules of
law conferring immunity on the judges, on servants of the executive acting on a
judge's warrant, and on the Crown or state, and providing that the state should pay
damages in respect of judicial misconduct, even though the judge himself remains
immune, a possibility I discuss later.

The first comment which I feel myself constrained to make is that I find it more
h than a little surprising that a section giving a totally new cause of action against the
state (particularly prior to the enactment of the State Liability and Proceedings Act
1966, and in the light of s 3 of the Constitution set out above) should begin with the
somewhat anodyne expression 'For the removal of doubts it is hereby declared'. An
expression of this kind is not unusual in Westminister model legislation, but I must
say that if the section be intended to create a fundamental change in the accepted law
j of state liability (as it must be if the appellant's case and the majority decision be
correct) it will be the first time that I have seen this particular phrase used in such a
context, and it is particularly odd, since in 1962 the State Liability and Proceedings
Act had not yet been passed.

The second point is that s 6 does not at first sight purport to do anything of the kind.
What it purports to do in sub-s (1) is to provide a forum and a procedure independent

of any other remedy available for persons desiring to secure redress against contraventions of ss 1 and 2. It does not specify the type of relief which may be granted in any one case. But sub-s (2) does give examples (the making of orders, the issuing of writs and the giving of directions) of the kind of remedy which may be available to an applicant seeking redress. It is by no means obvious, at least from these examples, that a totally new type of action for damages against the state in respect of actions by a High Court judge was in the forefront of the legislators' minds, or in their minds at all.

I take it that the most obvious construction of sub-s (2) is not that it provides new types of relief where none would otherwise exist, but that it gives the High Court power to spell out the legal consequences of contravention by providing the appropriate orders, whether by declaration or otherwise, to give effect to those consequences whatever they may be.

A great deal of argument necessarily turned on the meaning to be attached to the word 'redress' in s 6(1) and 'enforcement' in s 6(2). It was contended for the appellant, and it is accepted by the majority decision, that either or both of these words is sufficiently wide, or at least sufficiently indeterminate in meaning, to include a right to damages or a direction for the assessment of damages as one of the remedies available to the High Court. Not unnaturally the attention of the Board was directed to its decision in *Jaundoo v Attorney-General of Guyana*[1], a decision based on the substantially analogous provisions of the Guyana Constitution. In that case, in allowing the applicant's appeal, the Board remitted the motion to the court of first instance with a direction to hear and determine it on its merits, and, if these were found to be favourable to the applicant, to assess and give a direction for the payment of damages or compensation. This, it was contended, entirely supports the appellant's argument in the instant appeal to the effect that the references in s 6 to 'redress' and 'enforcement' include, or at least may include, a right to damages as a form of relief.

Though the contrary was contested strongly on behalf of the respondent, I see no reason to differ from the majority conclusion in this. Unhappily, I am unable to see that this disposes of the matter. On the contrary, I find that *Jaundoo's* case[1] aptly illustrates the difficulty that I feel. In *Jaundoo v Attorney-General of Guyana*[1] the applicant was seeking redress which would have had the effect of preventing the taking of her land for the making of a road. At the time of her application the land had not been taken. By the time of the appeal to the Privy Council, the land had been taken and the road built and no compensation paid. But the right to the enjoyment of landed property is, and for a long time has been, subject to the right of the state to acquire it compulsorily on payment of compensation. This is part of the statute law of virtually every civilised country. An attempt by the executive, or, under a written Constitution, by the legislature, to acquire compulsorily land without compensation is unlawful, and, if the applicant's case in *Jaundoo v Attorney-General of Guyana*[1] were established, the act of the executive in doing so, whether or not under the purported authority of an act of the legislature contravening the Constitution, would, in the case of a written Constitution on the models we are discussing, be a trespass, giving a right to damages at common law. At the time of the appeal the lawfulness of the acquisition was not determined, and the case was therefore remitted to the court of first instance to determine the merits. A necessary consequence of the merits being determined in the applicant's favour would have been a right of action for damages against the executive for trespass, that is in an ordinary action of tort. Since the Constitution provided what was intended as a speedy remedy by way of notice of motion, it was, so far as I can see, wholly appropriate for the Board to order compensatory damages as part of the redress in the event of the merits being determined in favour of the applicant. In my view it is quite another thing to contend that a section of essentially a procedural

_____

1   [1971] AC 972

character which embraces the possibility of damages where damages have always been due (e g where a trespass has been committed) confers a right of damages against the state for a judicial error where damages have never been available, and, even if available, have not been available against the state.

I am, of course, not to be understood as suggesting that a notice of motion under s 6 was an inappropriate procedure insofar as it claims a declaration. It was in fact an alternative to the appeal to the Privy Council. It was not as beneficial to the appellant, as the appeal to the Privy Council ultimately proved, as the Privy Council has jurisdiction to declare (as the High Court probably would not have had) not merely that the appellant had been deprived of due process, but that he was actually innocent of the charge. I am simply saying that, on the view I take, the expression 'redress' in sub-s (1) of s 6 and the expression 'enforcement' in sub-s (2), although capable of embracing damages where damages are available as part of the legal consequences of contravention, do not confer and are not in the context capable of being construed so as to confer a right of damages where they have not hitherto been available, in this case against the state for the judicial errors of a judge. This, in my view, must be so even though the judge has acted as the committing judge was held to have done in the instant case. Such a right of damages has never existed either against the judge or against the state and is not, in my opinion, conferred by s 6.

The third point I make on the majority construction of s 6 is that, in my view at least, it proves too much. Both parties, and, as I understood it, the majority in their conclusion, have shied away from the possibility that damages might equally have been claimed against the judge personally. But I do not at present understand why. If ss 1, 2 and 6 of the Constitution give a right of action for damages against the state for an action by the judge in circumstances in which the state would have had absolute immunity prior to the Constitution, it can only be on grounds equally applicable to the judge himself. These grounds are that the judge was guilty of a contravention of s 1, that he is not in the circumstances protected by s 3, that redress under s 6 must include damages in such a case, and that the prior rule of law giving immunity has in consequence no application. If this be correct, in order to save the judge's immunity, further legislation would be urgently necessary, and, since this would involve an amendment to the Constitution, such legislation might not be particularly easy to obtain.

I must add that I find it difficult to accommodate within the concepts of the law a type of liability for damages for the wrong of another when the wrongdoer himself is under no liability at all and the wrong itself is not a tort or delict. It was strenuously argued for the appellant that the liability of the state in the instant case was not vicarious, but some sort of primary liability. But I find this equally difficult to understand. It was argued that the state consisted of three branches, judicial, executive and legislative, and that as one of these branches, the judicial, had in the instant case contravened the appellant's constitutional rights, the state became, by virtue of s 6, responsible in damages for the action of its judicial branch. This seems a strange and unnatural way of saying that the judge had committed to prison the appellant who was innocent and had done so without due process of law and that someone other than the judge must pay for it (in this case the taxpayer). I could understand a view which said that because he had done so the state was vicariously liable for this wrongdoing, even though I would have thought it unarguable (even apart from the express terms of the State Liability and Proceedings Act 1966) that the judge acting judicially is a servant. What I do not understand is that the state is liable as a principal even though the judge attracts no liability to himself and his act is not a tort. To reach this conclusion is indeed to write a good deal into a section which begins innocently enough with the anodyne words 'For the removal of doubts it is hereby declared'.

If I were at all of the opinion that s 6 did unambiguously confer a right of damages in circumstances like the present, I would not, of course, be deterred from saying so in view of any inconveniences of public policy which might ensue from this conclusion.

But, since I am not of this opinion, I feel that I am entitled to point to some of the inconveniences which I believe to exist.

In the first place, as I understand the decision of the majority it is that a distinction must be drawn between a mere judicial error and a deprivation of due process as in the instant appeal, and that the former would not, and the latter would, attract a right of compensation under the present decision, even though in each case the consequences were as grave. I have already touched on this. I do not doubt the validity of the distinction viewed as a logical concept, though the line might be sometimes hard to draw. But I doubt whether the distinction, important as it may be intellectually, would be of much comfort to those convicted as a result of judicial error as distinct from deprivation of due process or would be understood as reasonable by many members of the public, when it was discovered that the victim was entitled to no compensation, as distinct from the victim of a contravention of s 1 of the Constitution who would be fully compensated.

As a result of the majority decision the case will return to the High Court with a direction to assess damages. I doubt whether their task is as easy as might be supposed. We are told that this is not an action of tort. Indeed, if it were, the appellant would be out of court as the result of the provisions of the State Liability and Proceedings Act 1966, already noticed, unless, of course, that Act were itself to be attacked as violating the Constitution quoad torts which were also contraventions of the Constitution. But if it is not a tort, but something sui generis, the question arises on what principles are damages to be assessed. Are punitive damages available on the basis of *Rookes v Barnard*[1] and *Cassell & Co Ltd v Broome*[2], and if not why not? How far may aggravated damages be awarded, inasmuch as the judge is not a servant, and the state's liability said not to be vicarious? Are damages to include an element for injured feelings or damage to reputation? No doubt all these questions are capable of solution, especially if tort is taken to be a sound analogy. But on what principle is it a sound analogy? At present the sea is an uncharted one, as no similar case has ever been brought, and the action is not in tort.

There is, of course, nothing in the Constitution of Trinidad and Tobago to prevent the legislature from improving on the rights and fundamental freedoms guaranteed by the Constitution if they wish to do so and though I might well not be of their number I can well understand that the members of a legislature inspired by a zeal to compensate the victims of an injustice committed by judicial officers of the state might well wish to make such an improvement. What I venture to question is whether they have done so in Trinidad and Tobago by s 6 of the Constitution of 1962, and if they have not, as I feel myself constrained to believe, it would follow that this appeal should be dismissed.

Appeal allowed.

Solicitors: *Ingledew, Brown, Bennison & Garrett* (for the appellant); *Charles Russell & Co* (for the respondent).

Mary Rose Plummer Barrister.

1	[1964] 1 All ER 367 at 409, [1964] AC 1129 at 1223, 1224
2	[1972] 1 All ER 801 at 830, 877, [1972] AC 1027 at 1078, 1134

R v Bryant
R v Oxley

COURT OF APPEAL, CRIMINAL DIVISION
GEOFFREY LANE LJ, MILMO AND WATKINS JJ
14th NOVEMBER, 2nd DECEMBER 1977

Criminal law – Trial – Speeches – Prosecution – Closing speech – Defendant represented by counsel – Defendant giving no evidence and calling none – Right of prosecution to make closing speech.

Criminal law – Trial – Speeches – Prosecution – Defendants jointly charged – Only one defendant giving or calling evidence – Evidence assisting defence of other defendants – Right of prosecution in closing speech to comment on effect of evidence on cases of other defendants.

Where in a criminal trial a defendant who is represented by counsel gives no evidence and calls none, counsel for the prosecution nonetheless has the right to make a closing speech once the evidence for the prosecution is complete, but that right is one which it should rarely be necessary to exercise save in long and complex cases (see p 692 *b* and *g*, and p 694 *g to j*, post); *R v Gardner* [1899] 1 QB 150 applied.

   Where one only of a number of defendants who are jointly charged and represented by counsel gives or calls evidence which assists the defence of one or more of his co-defendants, counsel for the prosecution is entitled to comment in his closing speech on the effect of that evidence on the cases of the other defendants (see p 692 *b c*, p 695 *g h*, post); *R v Trevelli* (1882) 15 Cox CC 289 applied.

Notes
For closing speeches of counsel, see 11 Halsbury's Laws (4th Edn) para 295, and for cases on the subject, see 14 Digest (Repl) 376-379, 3149-3200.

Cases referred to in judgment
R v Baggott (1927) 20 Cr App Rep 92, CCA, 14(1) Digest (Reissue) 377, 3173.
R v Blackburn (1853) 3 Car & Kir 330, 6 Cox CC 333, 175 ER 575, 14(1) Digest (Reissue) 379, 3189.
R v Gardner [1899] 1 QB 150, 68 LJQB 42, 79 LT 358, 62 JP 743, 19 Cox CC 177, CCR, 14(1) Digest (Reissue) 364, 3011.
R v Hales [1924] 1 KB 602, 93 LJKB 479, 130 LT 317, 88 JP 24, 27 Cox CC 571, 17 Cr App Rep 193, CCA, 14(1) Digest (Reissue) 377, 3172.
R v Harrison (1923) 17 Cr App Rep 156, CCA, 14(1) Digest (Reissue) 353, 2889.
R v Hayes and Walter (1838) 2 Mood & R 155, 174 ER 247, NP, 14(1) Digest (Reissue) 379, 3187.
R v Jordan and Cowmeadow (1839) 9 C & P 118, 173 ER 765, 14(1) Digest (Reissue) 66, 368.
R v Stannard (1837) 7 C & P 673, 173 ER 295, 14(1) Digest (Reissue) 377, 3158.
R v Trevelli (1882) 15 Cox CC 289, 14(1) Digest (Reissue) 379, 3193.

Cases also cited
R v Berens (1865) 4 F & F 842, 176 ER 815, sub nom *R v Holchester* 10 Cox CC 226.
R v Burton, Scott and Lockwood (1861) 2 F & F 788, 175 ER 1286.
R v Corfell (1844) 4 LTOS 215.
R v Davis (1900) 17 TLR 164.
R v Dowse (1865) 4 F & F 492, 176 ER 660.
R v Kain (1883) 15 Cox CC 388.
R v Puddick (1865) 4 F & F 497, 176 ER 662.

R v *Sherriff* (1903) 20 Cox CC 334.
R v *Shimmin* (1882) 15 Cox CC 122.
R v *Webb* (1865) 4 F & F 862, 176 ER 825.
R v *Whiting and Harvey* (1837) 7 C & P 771, 173 ER 336.
R v *Wildgoose* (1849) 13 JP 766.

Applications
On 23rd March 1977 in the Crown Court at Chester, before his Honour Judge David
QC, Philip Roy Bryant, Alan Michael Oxley and James Francis Antrobus were
convicted of robbery. They applied for leave to appeal against their convictions
but leave was refused by the single judge. Bryant and Oxley renewed their application to the full court. The facts are set out in the judgment of the court.

Richard Hamilton for Bryant and Oxley.
Richard Fairley for the Crown.

Cur adv vult

2nd December. **WATKINS J** read the following judgment of the court: Philip
Roy Bryant and Alan Oxley (alias Bryant and hereinafter referred to as Oxley),
following refusal by the single judge, apply for leave to appeal against their convictions for robbery by a jury at Chester Crown Court before his Honour Judge David QC
on 23rd March 1977. A third man, James Francis Antrobus, was also convicted with
them of the same offence. He has not renewed his failed application for leave to
appeal. Bryant was sentenced to nine months' imprisonment. Oxley and Antrobus
were sentenced to borstal training.

The robbery was said to have been committed at 2.00 am on 26th September 1976
in Bryant's motor car which he was then driving from Liverpool towards Warrington.
Antrobus was sitting alongside him. Oxley and their victim, Ahmed Abdullah
Gamez, were sitting alongside one another on the rear seat. Gamez is a native of the
Yemen. He has an indifferent command of the English language. He knew the other
three men. During the late evening of 25th September all of them had been drinking
in various public houses in Warrington. Eventually they all somehow came together
and decided to visit a night club in Liverpool. Bryant drove them to the club where
they drank more and danced. It was whilst they were returning to their homes in
Warrington that, according to Gamez, Antrobus suddenly and unexpectedly changed
the convivial atmosphere which up to then they were all enjoying. He, Antrobus,
turned around and at the point of a knife demanded money from Gamez. He
searched Gamez and took from one of his pockets three £10 notes. Oxley, who also
had a knife or took over that used by Antrobus, pointed it at Gamez whilst holding
him by the neck with his other hand. He relieved Gamez of cigarettes, a cigarette
lighter and a wrist watch. Gamez, frightened by what was happening to him,
shouted to Bryant: 'Stop the car they are going to kill me.' Bryant ignored him and
drove on. By then Gamez realised that blood was coming from a cut which had
been inflicted above his right eye. Oxley gave him a rag to wipe the blood away.

Later on the car stopped because the defendants wished to relieve themselves.
Gamez tried to get out of the car with them but the door was shut and trapped and
injured one of his fingers.

When they arrived in Warrington the car stopped. He was more or less pushed
out of it. It was then driven away. Later that day he saw Bryant who asked him not
to go to the police. Bryant promised to effect the return of his watch and lighter
and loaned him £5. However, because Bryant did not within an agreed time keep
this promise, Gamez went to the police and reported the incident. He was medically
examined. The examination confirmed the existence of a small cut or contusion
above the right eye, a black eye and a damaged finger.

It should be mentioned that Bryant did retrieve the watch and lighter from one of his co-defendants and gave them to a witness, Mohamed Ali, so that he could hand them over to his friend Gamez. However, Mohamed Ali did not see Gamez until many hours after the latter had seen the police.

None of the defendants gave evidence at the trial. The general defence advanced on their behalf was that no robbery had taken place. All that had occurred was some drunken horseplay in the course of which some of Gamez's property had been taken from him. But there was no intention on the part of any of the defendants to deprive him of it permanently. On behalf of Bryant, in particular, it was submitted that he had taken no part in whatever happened in the back of the car, and certainly was not a party to any robbery. If he had been a party to robbery, surely, so it was said, it was unlikely that he would have recovered, as in fact he did, some of Gamez's property for him.

This and many other questions were posed for the consideration of the jury who, after being clearly and, with one possible exception, accurately directed on the law and carefully reminded of the evidence, convicted the defendants as, in the opinion of this court, the jury was on that evidence entitled safely to do.

Having regard to the grounds of appeal it is necessary to relate some evidence which has not already been referred to. It was the only evidence provided by the defence. It was called on behalf of Antrobus and given by a young man named Rocky Fleming. He said that he knew Gamez and the defendants. He and his girl-friend had met them all during the night of the incident before they left Warrington to go to the night club in Liverpool. He was minded to accompany them, at the invitation of Gamez. He and his girlfriend entered Bryant's car which also contained the other defendants and Gamez. The girlfriend was dropped off at her home. A while later, Fleming changed his mind, decided to go home and he was dropped off near there. Gamez, when cross-examined, had denied that Fleming and his girlfriend were in the car at any time that night. Fleming's evidence could only have been introduced in an attempt either to discredit Gamez or to raise a doubt about the accuracy of his recollection of the night's events, or both. During cross-examination by the prosecution, this attempt was given more weight when Fleming for the first time maintained that, before he and his girlfriend entered the car, he had noticed that Gamez then had a cut over his right eye. This had been caused, so he had been told by a young man who was in some way involved in it, when Gamez the previous evening had been engaged in a fracas in a public house in Warrington. It had not been suggested to Gamez by defence counsel that he was in any way injured before leaving for the night club in Liverpool. So this part of Fleming's evidence came as a surprise to the prosecution and it may very well be to counsel for Antrobus as well as counsel for Bryant and Oxley.

Be that as it may, it was evidence which if accepted by the jury or which if it left them in doubt whether it was true or false, could cast a shadow over the testimony of Gamez that he had been robbed. Therefore it was evidence which could have been of value not only to the defence of Antrobus, but also to the defences of Bryant and Oxley since it impinged directly on one of the two vital issues, ie was Gamez, as he claimed, robbed whilst he was in the car?

This consideration is pertinent to one of two grounds of appeal which is common to both applicants, which is: 'The learned judge was wrong to allow counsel for the prosecution to make a final speech against Bryant and Oxley when neither of them had given evidence or called evidence.' This procedure was objected to by counsel for Bryant and Oxley when counsel for the prosecution was well advanced in his final speech following the evidence of Fleming. The objection may be none the worse for that and we accept, of course, that the thought of making such an objection only dawned on counsel for Bryant and Oxley when he heard them being referred to in that speech.

The judge listened to submissions in the absence of the jury on the point. He considered them overnight. On the following day he ruled that counsel for the prosecution was entitled to make a closing speech in which he could comment on *a* the case as it then stood against all defendants. On that basis counsel continued and completed his speech. It was followed, of course, by a speech from counsel for Bryant and Oxley.

Two questions arise from this ground of appeal. They are: (1) when none of a number of defendants who are all represented by counsel gives evidence himself and calls no evidence, has prosecuting counsel the right to make a speech? (2) when *b* the like circumstances obtain, save that evidence is called by one defendant but that evidence is relevant to and possibly beneficial to the defences of one or more of the other defendants, has counsel for the prosecution the right to make a closing speech with respect to the defendant who has called evidence and to the defendant whose defence may be beneficially affected by that evidence?

The industry of counsel for both the prosecution and Bryant and Oxley, to whom *c* we are grateful, has enabled them to inform us most helpfully about the origins and developments of the rules of practice and procedure which govern the occasions when counsel may address a jury in a criminal case.

It may be that this ground of appeal could be effectively disposed of by this court providing an answer to the second only of these questions, but since we have been asked to, and so as to remove doubt, if doubt there is, concerning the proper procedure *d* to be adopted in the situation envisaged in the first of the questions posed, we have considered both of them. The answer to neither of them is, save inferentially perhaps in respect of the first question, to be found in the otherwise most useful 'Table of order of speeches', set forth in Archbold[1]. The inference referred to is one that could be drawn so as to answer the first question in the affirmative from the text of Archbold[2]. But since, in the view of this court, such a procedural point should *e* not be said to be settled inferentially and no authority is quoted, the point must be explored with reference to such authority as there is on it.

In September 1963 a powerfully constituted Criminal Law Revision Committee produced a report[3] on the order of closing speeches. As a result of this report the Criminal Procedure (Right of Reply) Act 1964 came into being. Its most important effect was to give the defence the right to make, in all circumstances, the last closing speech to the jury. In paras 3 and 4 of the report the rules regarding closing speeches are summarised. Whilst this summary does not or does not obviously supply the answers to the questions posed in the present case, other paragraphs of the report provide a short historical review of the evolution of the rules governing counsel's speeches.

A slight enlargement of that review will, we think, serve to demonstrate that *g* counsel has had for over a century the right to make a closing speech to the jury when a defendant represented by counsel has called no evidence and has not given evidence himself. It should be noted in passing that until the coming into force of the Criminal Evidence Act 1898 he was not permitted to testify.

In 1837 a practice direction was made at a meeting of judges which provided[4]: *h*

> 'IV. If the only evidence called, on the part of the prisoner, is evidence to character, although the counsel for the prosecution is entitled to the reply, it will be a matter for his discretion whether he will use it or not. Cases may occur in which it may be fit and proper so to do.'

In Archbold's Pleading and Evidence in Criminal Cases[5] it is stated:

1   39th Edn (1976), p 333, paras 578, 578a
2   Ibid p 333, para 579a
3   Criminal Law Revision Committee, Fourth Report, Order of Closing Speeches, September 1963 (Cmnd 2146), paras 3-9
4   *Memorandum of Judges* (1837) 7 C & P 676 at 677, 173 ER 269 at 297
5   14th Edn (1859), p 147

'If the defendant gives any evidence, whether written or parol, the counsel for the prosecution has the right to reply. Even if the evidence for the defendant be only to his character, it gives, in strictness, a right of reply, although the right is seldom exercised in such a case.'

From the time the practice direction was made judges, as many cases show, actively discouraged counsel from exercising the right to reply following evidence of character alone. When evidence of facts relating to the offence was given by the defence, counsel for the prosecution exercised the right to reply without such judicial discouragement.

Section 2 of the Criminal Procedure Act 1865 provided as follows:

'If any prisoner or prisoners, defendant or defendants, shall be defended by counsel, but not otherwise, it shall be the duty of the presiding judge, at the close of the case for the prosecution, to ask the counsel for each prisoner or defendant so defended by counsel whether he or they intend to adduce evidence; and in the event of none of them thereupon announcing his intention to adduce evidence, the counsel for the prosecution shall be allowed to address the jury a second time in support of his case, for the purpose of summing up the evidence against such prisoner or prisoners, or defendant or defendants . . . and the right of reply, and practice and course of proceedings, save as hereby altered, shall be as at present.'

Thereafter prosecuting counsel was according to the prevailing circumstances allowed two speeches, one to sum up the case at the end of the evidence for the prosecution and the other to reply if a defendant called evidence. The judges of the day, however, discouraged counsel from exercising the right to sum up unless there was obvious necessity for it.

Sections 2 and 3 of the Criminal Evidence Act 1898 created a fresh problem for counsel concerning the summing-up closing speech and the reply closing speech. They provided:

'2. Where the only witness to the facts of the case called by the defence is the person charged, he shall be called as a witness immediately after the close of the evidence for the prosecution.

'3. In cases where the right of reply depends upon the question whether evidence has been called for the defence [ie in cases where no Law Officer appears for the prosecution], the fact that the person charged has been called as a witness shall not of itself confer on the prosecution the right of reply.'

The problem of summing up was stated and resolved in R v Gardner[1]. Lord Russell of Killowen CJ said:

'Then s. 2 provides that where the person charged is the only witness called for the defence, he is to be called *immediately* after the close of the evidence for the prosecution; and s. 3 provides that where the right of reply depends upon whether evidence has been called for the defence, the calling of the person charged as a witness is not of itself to give the right of reply. These are the only material sections in this connection. Now, in the present case, after the evidence for the prosecution had closed, an application was made on behalf of the prisoner that he should be called as a witness, and an intimation given that no other evidence would be called. What was the proper course for the chairman to pursue? In my opinion the question admits of a clear answer. The section says that in such a case the person charged is to be called as a witness *immediately* after the close, not of the case for the prosecution (which expression might

---

1   [1899] 1 QB 150 at 153

include the summing-up of counsel), but of the *evidence* for the prosecution. It is clear, therefore, that the magistrates were right in holding that the counsel for the prosecution was not to sum up at that moment, but that the prisoner's evidence must then be given. What was the effect of that upon the right of the prosecuting counsel to sum up? Did it operate as an extinguishment of the right altogether, or merely as a postponement of the time at which the right was to be exercised? I think that if an extinguishment of the right had been intended, the statute would have said so in so many words; and it is evident to me that the statute operates as a postponement only to a later stage of the proceedings of the right of the prosecuting counsel to sum up. I think that that is the answer which we must give to the first question asked us—that the magistrates were right in holding that the prisoner must be called at once as a witness, and that the right to sum up was not extinguished, but merely postponed.'

Thus it was decided that the right to sum up was not extinguished but postponed in a case where a defendant gave evidence and called no other evidence. What of the case where a defendant was represented and did not give evidence and called none? In that circumstance it seems to this court to be abundantly plain that the right which was not extinguished could be asserted although the use of it be confined to cases where the facts of the case obviously demanded the use of it.

Counsel for Bryant and Oxley has boldly submitted that *R v Gardner*[1] was wrongly decided and has quoted a number of cases which he maintains support this contention, amongst which are *R v Harrison*[2], *R v Hales*[3] and *R v Baggott*[4]. In *R v Baggott*[5], Lord Hewart CJ said, quoting *R v Harrison*[2]:

'   "We desire to point out very clearly that the rule about counsel in such circumstances," that is to say, in circumstances where an undefended prisoner calls no witness other than himself, "not addressing the jury a second time is one which ought to be carefully observed, and it might be that in another case this Court would have to hold that a conviction, in a trial where such an irregularity occurred, must be quashed." '

Since that time there have been occasions, including one comparatively recent occasion, where a conviction was quashed on that ground. These three cases and others quoted to us are noteworthy for one common feature, at least. In each of them the defendant was not represented by counsel. In such a circumstance Archbold[6] sets out accurately the order of speeches. But in *R v Gardner*[1] the defendant was represented by counsel and so is distinguishable in a vital respect from *R v Baggott*[4] and the other cases relied on by counsel for Bryant and Oxley.

We have not been able to discover any case in which a defendant was represented by counsel, wherein doubt has been cast on the ruling in *R v Gardner*[1], namely that the right to sum up was not extinguished by the Criminal Evidence Act 1898. Recent legislation has not in our judgment affected this ruling. Prosecuting counsel in the case of a defendant who is himself represented by counsel and gives no evidence and calls none has the right to sum up the prosecution's evidence or, in modern parlance, to make a closing speech at the close of that evidence. It is, however, a right which in our opinion it should only rarely be necessary to use save possibly in long and complex cases, and whenever used should bear, as should the majority of speeches by prosecuting and defence counsel, the becoming hallmark of brevity.

Before parting finally from the first question it is perhaps fitting to conclude the

1   [1899] 1 QB 150
2   (1923) 17 Cr App Rep 156
3   [1924] 1 KB 602
4   (1927) 20 Cr App Rep 92
5   20 Cr App Rep 92 at 93
6   39th Edn (1976), p 333, para 578

matter by observing that during this century what used at one time to be separate prosecution speeches of summing-up and of reply have merged into one closing speech. So we find that, in the present case, counsel for the prosecution had the right to make a closing speech in which he was free to refer generally to the cases as they then stood against Bryant and Oxley.

The second question can be answered more briefly. In Archbold[1] it is said:

'If two prisoners are indicted jointly for the same offence, and one calls witnesses, it seems that the counsel for the prosecution is entitled to a general reply; but if the offences are separate, and they might have been separately indicted, he can reply only on the case of the party who has called witnesses. *Reg.* v. *Hayes*[2]: *Reg.* v. *Jordan*[3]'.

In *R v Blackburn*[4], it seems to have been accepted, all defendants being represented by counsel, that since one defendant called an alibi witness prosecuting counsel had a general right of reply but it was a right to be exercised with forbearance. In later cases judges actively discouraged the assertion of this right where one of several defendants called evidence of alibi.

In *R v Trevelli*[5] Hawkins J stated:

'Where in an indictment against several defendants one of them calls evidence which is applicable to the cases of all, I think there is a general right of reply which the counsel for the prosecution must exercise according to his discretion. But where the evidence called by one prisoner does not affect the cases of the others, as for instance where one prisoner calls witnesses to prove an *alibi* for himself only, and the evidence of those witnesses does not affect the case as against the others, the reply ought to be confined to the case of that one prisoner. So where, as in the present case, one prisoner is separately charged in the same indictment with an offence altogether distinct and unconnected with the offence charged against another or others of the prisoners, the calling of witnesses by that one prisoner to rebut the charge made against him does not entitle counsel for the prosecution to a general reply upon the whole case as against all the prisoners. If, however, from the witnesses called for one prisoner evidence is elicited in favour of others indicted with him, then I think the right to reply should be extended to the cases of such other prisoners so far as such evidence affects their cases.'

In our judgment this statement still represents accurately in this last mentioned respect the rights of prosecuting counsel in his closing speech. So that, on the facts in the present case, the defendants being jointly charged with one offence and represented by counsel, and the witness Fleming, called on behalf of Antrobus, having given evidence which obviously affected the cases of Bryant and Oxley, since it was relevant to the question whether or not there had been a robbery, counsel for the prosecution was entitled to refer to the cases of Bryant and Oxley in his closing speech. Therefore this ground of appeal fails.

The only other ground of appeal relied on, but not strongly, is that the judge misdirected the jury on the relevance and worth in relation to consideration of guilt or otherwise of a good character in the case of Bryant. He said:

'Now two entirely different points. During the course of the evidence, and in the course of the speeches by counsel for the defence, the point was made in

---

1   14th Edn (1859), p 147
2   (1838) 2 Mood & R 155
3   (1839) 9 C & P 118
4   (1853) 3 Car & Kir 330
5   (1882) 15 Cox CC 289 at 290

relation to Philip Bryant and James Antrobus that these two defendants are defendants of good character, and you were urged to take that factor into consideration. Of course it is right that where a defendant can claim to be a person of good character, that is a factor that a jury is entitled to take into account. But you may reasonably look to me for some guidance and assistance as to your approach to this matter, and I am afraid that I cannot really be very helpful. The situation that normally arises where a defendant gives evidence, if he is a person of good character, is that the judge can say, and normally would say, to a jury: "Here in this case you have to decide between the evidence of the witnesses for the prosecution and the evidence of the defendant, and it is manifestly fair that you should take into account the fact that the defendant is a person of good character, and to that extent is more likely to be telling the truth." But of course, neither of the two defendants, Philip Bryant and James Antrobus, have in fact given evidence, and so there is not any evidence of their own to evaluate at all, and so you may take the view that while good character is something you are entitled to take into account, it will have very little if any part to play in your consideration in this particular case. It is entirely a matter for you. But more helpful than that I fear I cannot be.'

If by that, as seems to be so, the judge was intending to convey to the jury the impression that a good character is relevant only when a defendant gives evidence and, therefore, is a matter only to be taken into consideration when the credibility of what he and other witnesses have said is being assessed, he was being too restrictive about its possible uses. The possession of a good character is a matter which does go primarily to the issue of credibility. This has been made clear in a number of recent cases. But juries should be directed that it is capable of bearing a more general significance which is best illustrated by what was said by Williams J in R v Stannard[1]:

'I have no doubt, if we are put to decide the unwelcome question, that evidence to character must be considered as evidence in the cause. It is evidence, as my brother Patteson has said, to be submitted to the jury, to induce them to say whether they think it likely that a person with such a character would have committed the offence.'

The 'unwelcome question' related to counsel's right to sum up after defence evidence of character only had been given.

We have no doubt that the omission to direct the jury in this way in the present case should not possibly have had the effect of rendering the jury's verdict unsafe or unsatisfactory. So we find that this ground does not avail the applicant Bryant. Accordingly, the applications of both him and Oxley are refused.

Applications dismissed.

Solicitors: *Registrar of Criminal Appeals*; *E C Woodcock, Prosecuting Solicitor*, Chester.

Lea Josse Barrister.

---

1   (1837) 7 C & P 673 at 675

Corbyn v Saunders

QUEEN'S BENCH DIVISION
LORD WIDGERY CJ, CUMMING-BRUCE LJ AND PARK J
8th, 20th DECEMBER 1977

Railway – Offence – Travelling on railway with intent to avoid payment of fare – Intent to avoid payment of fare – Degree of intention required – Intention of passenger to pay only part of fare at time of travel – Intention of passenger to pay balance at later date if requested to do so – Whether 'intending to avoid payment of fare' – Whether intention permanently to avoid payment necessary – Regulation of Railways Act 1889, s 5(3)(a).

C purchased a 10p ticket for a journey on the London Underground intending to travel further than his ticket entitled him to go. On arrival at his destination he handed the ticket collector the ticket and a form detailing his journey, giving his name and address and inviting the railway authorities to recover the balance of the fare at a later date. He was charged with unlawfully travelling on the railway without having previously paid his fare and with intent to avoid payment of the fare, contrary to s 5(3)(a)[a] of the Regulation of Railways Act 1889. He was convicted by a magistrate, who held that the mental element necessary to constitute the offence, viz an intention to avoid payment of the fare, was established by the fact that he did not intend to pay the balance of the fare before leaving the railway property. C appealed, contending that it had to be shown that he intended permanently to avoid payment.

Held – The appeal would be dismissed because it was sufficient for the purposes of s 5(3)(a) to establish, as had been done, that the accused did not have, by the time he passed the ticket collector at his destination, an unqualified intention to pay the proper fare for his journey (see p 699 *e* to *j*, post).

Notes

For the offence of travelling on a railway without having previously paid the fare, see 31 Halsbury's Laws (3rd Edn) 670, para 1047.

For the Regulation of Railways Act 1889, s 5(3), see 26 Halsbury's Laws (3rd Edn) 843.

Cases cited

Bremme v Dubery [1964] 1 All ER 193, [1964] 1 WLR 119, DC.
Murphy v Verati [1967] 1 All ER 861, [1967] 1 WLR 641, DC.

Case stated

This was an appeal by way of a case stated by P W Goldstone Esq, metropolitan stipendiary magistrate, acting in and for the petty sessional division of North Westminster in respect of his adjudication sitting at Marylebone on 10th May 1977.

On 30th November 1976 46 informations were preferred by the respondent, Robert Saunders, against the appellant, Piers Corbyn, alleging that on each of the occasions listed in the informations at the railway stations therein mentioned the appellant

---

a   Section 5(3), so far as material, provides: 'If any person—(*a*) Travels or attempts to travel on a railway without having previously paid his fare, and with intent to avoid payment thereof . . . he shall be liable on summary conviction to a fine . . . or in the case of a second or subsequent offence, either to a fine . . . or in the discretion of the court to imprisonment . . .'

unlawfully travelled on the railway there situated without having previously paid his fare and with intent to avoid payment of the fare, contrary to s 5(3)(a) of the Regulation of Railways Act 1889, as amended by s 84(2) of the Transport Act 1962.

The magistrate heard the informations together, with the consent of the parties, on 10th May 1977. The respondent put forward evidence by way of statements made under s 9 of the Criminal Justice Act 1967 made by a relief leading railwayman and a station inspector, the sworn evidence of the respondent and certain facts admitted under s 10 of the Criminal Justice Act 1967. Evidence was neither given nor called by the appellant. The magistrate found the following facts; (a) the appellant had made the journeys to and from the stations on the London underground railway mentioned in the informations; (b) on each occasion he purchased a ticket for the fare stated in the informations at the commencement of the journey; (c) on each occasion the fare he paid was less than the correct fare for the journey he intended to take; (d) the magistrate was not satisfied, and it was not contended on behalf of the respondent that the appellant intended permanently to avoid payment of the fare, but he was satisfied that prior to the commencement of each journey the appellant intended, having only paid an insufficient amount for the journey he took, to defer payment of the balance of the fare by giving his name and address on a form, of the kind exhibited, at the conclusion of the journey taken.

It was contended on behalf of the appellant that since it had not been proved that he intended permanently to avoid payment of the proper fare each of the informations should be dismissed.

It was contended on behalf of the respondent that since the appellant did not intend to pay the proper fare either before or at any time while travelling he was guilty on the informations alleged since that was a sufficient intent for the purposes of s 5(3)(a) of the 1889 Act and the other ingredients of the offences were proved.

The magistrate was of opinion that the appellant could 'previously pay his fare' certainly up to the exit barrier and perhaps even up to the point of leaving railway property but that since he commenced each journey alleged intending not to pay the proper fare at any time before reaching or at the time of leaving the railway property but only on request at some future date, he was guilty of each offence and accordingly he convicted the appellant on each information.

The question for the opinion of the High Court was whether the intent to avoid payment referred to in s 5(3)(a) of the 1889 Act, as amended, was an intention permanently to avoid payment, as the appellant maintained, or whether an intention to avoid 'previous payment' of the fare was sufficient.

Henry Spooner for the appellant.
Anthony Scrivener QC and *Anthony Porten* for the respondent.

Cur adv vult

20th December. The following judgments were read.

CUMMING-BRUCE LJ (delivering the first judgment at the invitation of Lord Widgery CJ). This is an appeal by case stated by Mr P W Goldstone, a metropolitan stipendiary magistrate, in respect of his adjudication on 10th May 1977, sitting at Marylebone.

On 30th November 1976 46 informations were preferred by the respondent against the appellant that he on each of the occasions listed in the informations at the railway stations therein mentioned did unlawfully travel on the railway there situate without having previously paid his fare and with intent to avoid payment thereof, contrary to s 5(3)(a) of the Regulation of Railways Act 1889, as amended by s 84(2) of the Transport Act 1962.

The facts are in a short compass. On the 46 occasions specified in the information the appellant travelled on the London Underground. On each occasion he purchased a ticket for 10p, and the fare he paid was less than the correct fare for the journey he intended to take, and in fact took. On arrival at his destination he delivered to the ticket collector his ticket for 10p and a form which read:

'To London Transport Executive. Date 19-7-76 [or the appropriate date] I have today travelled from . . . to . . . and tendered a ticket for 10p. Should you wish to recover the outstanding sum, my name and address is: Name P. P. Corbyn. Address 14 Rust Square S.E.5. Signed . . .'

In the blank spaces he entered on each occasion the station of departure and arrival, and he signed his name in the appropriate space. The outstanding sums due in respect of the journeys specified in the information was £9·95.

There is no issue on the fact alleged in each information that on each occasion he travelled on the railway to the railway station at the destination alleged without having previously paid his fare. The magistrate convicted him, holding that the intent to avoid payment was proved. The appellant submits that that intent was not proved.

The facts as to his intent that are found in the case are: (a) Prior to the commencement of each journey he intended, having only paid an insufficient amount for the journey he took, to defer payment of the balance of the fare by giving his name and address on the form I have described at the conclusion of the journey taken. (b) He commenced each journey intending not to pay the proper fare at any time before reaching or at the time of leaving the railway property but only on request at some future date.

It is therefore perfectly plain that throughout the period that he was travelling on the railway he did not intend to pay the prescribed fare until after he had ceased to travel, and that his intention was only to pay if the railway authorities requested payment.

It was contended on his behalf that in order to prove an offence under s 5(3)(a) the prosecution had to prove an intention never to pay the proper fare, i e an intent permanently to avoid payment. There is no reason for importing into the section the adverb 'permanently'. It is clear on the facts that he did not intend to pay the proper fare unless and until the railway authorities tracked him down and requested payment. That is quite enough to constitute an intent to avoid payment. It is perfectly plain that he had no intention of paying unless the London Transport pursued him for the money. His intention was not an unqualified intention to make the prescribed payment, but an intention not to pay unless later requested to pay. That is an intention to avoid payment.

That is enough to dispose of this appeal, but the same result is reached by another route. It is clear from the first clause of s 5(3)(a) that the traveller is not to travel on the railway without paying the fare for the intended journey before he begins that journey. The intention that has to be proved is intention to avoid that obligation, i e payment of the proper fare before he begins his journey. Likewise, if he buys a ticket which is the prescribed fare to a destination, but when he travels he intends to travel beyond that destination without previously paying for the additional distance, he travels that additional distance with intent to avoid the required payment therefor. In that case, if he fails to tender the outstanding balance of the fare, at the latest when passing the ticket collector on the station of destination, the requisite intent to avoid payment is proved.

PARK J. I agree.

LORD WIDGERY CJ. I also agree. For those reasons the appeal is dismissed.

Appeal dismissed.

Solicitors: *Douglas-Mann & Co* (for the appellant); *V J Moorfoot*.

Jacqueline Charles Barrister.

R v Crayden

COURT OF APPEAL, CRIMINAL DIVISION
LAWTON LJ, SWANWICK AND GIBSON JJ
19th, 24th JANUARY, 9th FEBRUARY 1978

*Criminal evidence – Record relating to trade or business – Trade or business – Hospital –
National health service hospital – Whether national health service hospital a 'business' –
Whether medical record kept by national health service hospital admissible as 'business'
record – Criminal Evidence Act 1965, s 1(1)(a)(4).*

A person's medical record kept by a national health service hospital is not 'a record
relating to any trade or business', within the meaning of s 1(1)(a)^a of the Criminal
Evidence Act 1965. The services provided by such a hospital do not have the commercial connotation of the services described in s 1(4) of the 1965 Act, which provides
that ' "business', includes any public transport, public utility or similar undertaking
carried on by a local authority . . .', and therefore a national health service hospital
is not a 'business', within the meaning of s 1(4). Accordingly, medical records kept by
a national health service hospital are not admissible under s 1(1)(a) as evidence in a
criminal trial if the maker of the record is unable to be called as a witness (see p 704
d to *f*, post).

Dicta of Lord Coleridge CJ in *R v Hermann* (1879) 4 QBD at 228 and of Lord Watson in
Dilworth v Comr of Stamps [1899] AC at 105, 106 applied.

Rolls v Miller (1884) 27 Ch D 71 and *Town Investments Ltd v Department of the Environment*
[1977] 1 All ER 813 distinguished.

Notes

For the admissibility of trade and business records in criminal proceedings, see 11
Halsbury's Laws (4th Edn) para 442.

For the Criminal Evidence Act 1965, s 1, see 12 Halsbury's Statutes (3rd Edn) 907.

Cases referred to in judgment

Bramwell v Lacy (1879) 10 Ch D 691, 48 LJCh 339, 40 LT 361, 43 JP 446, 31(1) Digest
(Reissue) 395, *3144*.

Dilworth v Comr of Stamps, Dilworth v Comr for Land and Income Tax [1899] AC 99, 79
LT 473, sub nom *Dilworth v New Zealand Comr of Stamps* 68 LJPC 1, PC, 19 Digest
(Repl) 659, *348*.

Myers v Director of Public Prosecutions [1964] 2 All ER 881, [1965] AC 1001, [1964] 3
WLR 145, 120 JP 481, 48 Cr App Rep 348, HL, 22 Digest (Reissue) 63, *388*.

Pettit v Lilley [1946] 1 All ER 593, 115 LJKB 385, 175 LT 119, 110 JP 218, 44 LGR 171,
sub nom *Lilley v Pettit* [1946] KB 401, DC, 22 Digest (Reissue) 342, *3278*.

R v Hermann (1879) 4 QBD 284, 48 LJMC 106, 40 LT 263, 43 JP 398, 14 Cox CC 279, CCR,
15 Digest (Reissue) 1001, *8657*.

R v O'Dowd (August 1977) unreported, CCC.

Rolls v Miller (1884) 27 Ch D 71, [1881-5] All ER Rep 915, 52 LJCh 682, 50 LT 597, 31(1)
Digest (Reissue) 395, *3146*.

Town Investments Ltd v Department of the Environment [1977] 1 All ER 813, [1977] 2 WLR
450, HL.

Cases also cited

Debtor, Re a [1927] 1 Ch 97, CA.
R v Gwilliam [1968] 3 All ER 821, [1968] 1 WLR 1839, CA.

---

a Section 1, so far as material, is set out at p 702 *g h*, post

Williams' Will Trusts, Re, Chartered Bank of India, Australia and China v Williams [1953]
1 All ER 536, [1953] Ch 138.
Withington Local Board of Health v Corpn of Manchester [1893] 2 Ch 19, CA.

Appeal

On 12th May 1977 at the Crown Court at Inner London Sessions before Mr Ronald
Bartle sitting as a deputy circuit judge the appellant, Raymond John Crayden, was
convicted on two counts of burglary and sentenced to nine months' imprisonment
consecutive on each count. In addition suspended sentences totalling six months'
imprisonment were ordered to take effect consecutively to those sentences. The
appellant appealed against conviction on the ground that the judge had wrongly
admitted in evidence the contents of a hospital medical record relating to the appellant in that, inter alia, a national health service hospital was not a business within s 1(4)
of the Criminal Evidence Act 1965. The facts are set out in the judgment of the court.

Gordon Graeme for the appellant.
Ann Goddard (who did not appear below) for the Crown.

Cur adv vult

9th February.   **LAWTON LJ** read the following judgment of the court: On 12th
May 1977, the appellant was convicted in the Inner London Crown Court on two
counts of burglary and sentenced to nine months' imprisonment on each count,
the sentences to run consecutively. He appeals against the conviction by leave of
the single judge.

On 13th April 1976, and again on 15th April 1976, two houses in Eltham were burgled.
On 17th April, at about 1.30 a m, the appellant was stopped on the highway by police
officers. His conduct aroused their suspicions. His answers to their questions made
them even more suspicious. They arrested him and took him to the police station.
There, according to the Crown, he admitted orally that he had burgled both houses
and later he made a written confession to the same effect.

At his trial the appellant alleged through counsel, in cross-examination and in his
evidence, that both his oral admissions and the written confession had been obtained
from him by the use of violence. He said that one police officer had slapped him two
or three times in the face and had punched him on the jaw. Later that day the
appellant was released on bail.

At about 6.15 p m, as the result of a complaint made by the appellant's wife, a
chief inspector called at the appellant's house. At the trial he was called by the Crown.
He said that he had noticed a red mark and a slight swelling on the appellant's left
cheek bone. The appellant had demonstrated to him a clicking sound which could be
heard as the appellant opened and closed his mouth. He had also seen a red mark on
the appellant's left side. The appellant told him that he had sustained these injuries
whilst in police custody. He had declined examination by a police doctor saying that
he was going to the Brook Hospital, which is a national health service hospital.

The trial began on Wednesday, 4th May 1977. On Thursday, 5th May, 'a trial
within a trial' started as a result of the appellant's counsel submitting that the oral
admissions and the written confession relied on by the Crown had not been made
voluntarily. During the adjournment over the weekend, someone on the Crown's
side decided that it might be worthwhile finding out what, if anything, had happened
at the Brook Hospital. The appellant had been there. He had been examined by a
casualty officer, a Dr Fraser, at 6.35 p m on 17th April 1976. An X-ray had been taken
of the appellant's jaw and a radiologist had examined the film and had written on
a report form 'N.B.I.', meaning 'no bone injury'.

On Monday 9th May the Crown called a Miss Sherlock. She said that she was the
chief medical records officer and that she had with her the notes taken by Dr Fraser on

his examination of a patient named Raymond John Crayden and a radiologist's report on the same patient. Dr Fraser was no longer on the staff of the hospital. There was no evidence as to whether the radiologist was still there.

Counsel for the Crown (who was not Miss Goddard) asked the deputy circuit judge to admit these medical records in evidence under s 1 of the Criminal Evidence Act 1965. He submitted, first, that they were a record relating to a business which had been compiled in the course of that business and, secondly, that Dr Fraser and the radiologist could not reasonably be expected to have any recollection of the matters dealt with in the information set out in the record. The appellant's counsel objected on the ground that hospital medical records did not come within the 1965 Act at all and that in any event, in the circumstances of this case, Dr Fraser might well have remembered his examination of the appellant because his notes set out the appellant's allegation that he had been struck with a fist. The probabilities were that the appellant had told him that he had been struck in a police station.

The judge ruled that the medical records were admissible. At the end of 'the trial within a trial' he also ruled that the oral admissions and the confession were admissible. Following this ruling Miss Sherlock was recalled. She produced the medical record for the jury's consideration. The entries in it made by Dr Fraser, together with the radiologist's report, supported the Crown's contention that the appellant had suffered no injury whilst in the police station. The jury convicted.

The sole question for consideration in this appeal is whether the judge should have admitted the medical record in evidence. Without the provisions of s 1 of the Criminal Evidence Act 1965, they could not have been admitted: they contained hearsay.

The 1965 Act has a history. For some years before the House of Lords' decision in *Myers v Director of Public Prosecutions*[1], prosecutors had tried to solve the problem of how to prove marks of identification on mass produced articles. A practice grew up of calling witnesses from the manufacturers, who had no personal knowledge of the facts, to produce records which had come into existence during the course of production. In *Myers v Director of Public Prosecutions*[1] the House of Lords adjudged that such records were not admissible in evidence because they contained hearsay. This decision made the prosecution of some criminals, particularly car thieves and receivers, difficult. Parliament intervened quickly. On 2nd June 1965 the Criminal Evidence Act was passed. The fact that it was passed so soon after the decision in *Myers v Director of Public Prosecutions*[1] does not, however, justify us in inferring that the intention was solely to make admissible the kind of evidence which the House of Lords had adjudged to be inadmissible. Our duty is to infer what Parliament intended from the words in the 1965 Act and to construe it accordingly. The long title says that the Act is one 'to make certain trade or business records admissible', not all such records. Section 1(1) provides that to 'be admissible . . . the document' must be, or form—

'part of, a record relating to any trade or business and compiled, in the course of that trade or business, from information supplied . . . by persons who have, or may reasonably be supposed to have, a personal knowledge of the matters dealt with in the information they supply . . .'

Section 1(4) provides that ' . . ."business" includes any public transport, public utility or similar undertaking carried on by a local authority and the activities of the Post Office'.

When an 'inclusive' interpretation provision of this kind is in an Act it has the effect of enlarging the ordinary meaning of the word in the body of the statute to the extent only provided by the further words used and without altering that ordinary meaning: see *R v Hermann*[2] per Lord Coleridge CJ and *Dilworth v Comrs of Stamps*[3] per

1 [1964] 2 All ER 881, [1965] AC 1001
2 (1879) 4 QBD 784 at 288
3 [1899] AC 99 at 105, 106

Lord Watson. But what is the ordinary meaning of the word 'business'? The Concise Oxford Dictionary gives ten meanings and during the past 100 years the courts have construed the word in many contexts and in some cases have given it a meaning far removed from commerce in connection with which the word is probably most often used.

Many of these cases were reviewed in *Town Investments Ltd v Department of the Environment*[1]. In *Rolls v Miller*[2] a covenant in a lease prohibiting the use of premises for any trade or business was held to apply to a use as a charitable 'Home for Working Girls'; and in his judgment Lindley LJ said[3] in relation to the dictionary meaning of the word 'business':

'The word means almost anything which is an occupation, as distinguished from a pleasure—anything which is an occupation or duty which requires attention is a business—I do not think we can get much aid from the dictionary.'

In deciding as this court did in *Rolls v Miller*[4], it looked at the object of the covenant and found that it was to prevent the house being used otherwise than as a dwellinghouse. This was what led the House of Lords in *Town Investments Ltd v Department of the Environment*[1] to adjudge that the use of premises by government servants for government purposes constituted occupation of them by the Crown 'for the purposes of a business . . .' within the ambit of the Counter-Inflation (Business Rents) Order 1973[5]. The mischief which that order was intended to curb justified a wide meaning being given to the word 'business': see the speech of Lord Diplock[6]. The last example to which we will refer is *Bramwell v Lacy*[7]. In that case a covenant in a lease against using the demised premises for 'any trade, business or any dealing whatsoever . . .' was held to prohibit use of the premises as a throat and chest hospital for poor persons, where small payments were made by the patients according to their means. Jessel MR[8] adjudged that this activity was a ' "business" or "in the nature of a business" '.

Counsel for the Crown relied strongly on this case, submitting that it cannot have been the intention of Parliament to provide that the medical records kept at the London Clinic should be admissible in evidence whereas those kept at the nearby Middlesex Hospital should not be. As in *Rolls v Miller*[2], this case must be considered against its background of fact. The covenant was inserted to protect a residential area from non-residential occupation.

In the 1965 Act the word 'business' cannot, in our judgment, have been intended to have the wide meaning ascribed to it by Lindley LJ in *Rolls v Miller*[3] and by the House of Lords in *Town Investments Ltd v Department of the Environment*[1]. Had it been intended to have this wide meaning it would have been unnecessary to enlarge its meaning by bringing in public transport, public utilities and the activities of the Post Office. And why the records relating to these activities rather than those relating to government business generally, to local government activities such as the social services and direct building, and the records kept by the armed services and the police, all of which would have been included in a wide meaning? Had the 1965 Act been intended to make government records generally admissible we would have expected to find some words of limitation in the Act, otherwise confidential documents which in the past would not have been admissible in evidence would have become admissible. An example of a class of such documents is provided by the

---

1 [1977] 1 All ER 813, [1977] 2 WLR 450
2 (1884) 27 Ch D 71, [1881-5] All ER Rep 915
3 27 Ch D 71 at 88, [1881-5] All ER Rep 915 at 920
4 27 Ch D 71 at 87, [1881-5] All ER Rep 915 at 919
5 SI 1973 No 741
6 [1977] 1 All ER 813 at 820, [1977] 2 WLR 450 at 458, 459
7 (1879) 10 Ch D 691
8 10 Ch D 691 at 694, 695

case of *Pettit v Lilley*[1], which related to the regimental records of a serving soldier. The Divisional Court adjudged that they were not admissible in evidence as public documents. The absence of any words of limitation points towards a narrower construction of the word 'business'.

Every one of the activities specified by the enlarging words in the 1965 Act relates to an activity which has an element in it of supplying services or goods although it may not be the only element. The supply of goods or services by the bodies specified in s 1(4) is a form of commercial activity carried on for the public benefit, but not for private profit. It follows, in our judgment, that the word 'business' as used in the 1965 Act has a commercial connotation. We do not find it necessary to construe this word in more precise terms since our only task is to say whether the medical records of the Brook Hospital produced by Miss Sherlock related to a trade or business. Whether a hospital outside the national health service should be adjudged to be a business for the purposes of the 1965 Act does not arise for decision in this appeal.

Counsel for the Crown submitted that even if the word 'business' in the 1965 Act should be construed more narrowly than in such cases as *Rolls v Miller*[2] and *Town Investments Ltd v Department of the Environment*[3] the Brook Hospital would still be within a narrower definition. This was because running such a hospital involves many activities which are far removed from medical treatment. They include appointing staff, maintaining premises and acquiring and maintaining equipment, furniture and other movable property (see s 12 of the National Health Service Act 1946). All these activities, however, are ancillary to the main purpose of the hospital which is to provide for the area in which it is situated a service 'designed to secure improvement in the physical and mental health of the people [of that area] and the prevention, diagnosis and treatment of illness . . .' (see s 1 of the National Health Service Act 1946). In our judgment the provision of such a service cannot be a business within the meaning of that word as used in the 1965 Act.

Finally we note that the restricted meaning which we have put on the word 'business' in the 1965 Act is in line with a ruling given by his Honour Judge Buzzard at the Central Criminal Court in the autumn of 1977 in *R v O'Dowd*[4]. That learned judge however did not, so we were told, have his attention invited to the authorities cited in argument in this court.

It follows that the appellant's hospital record should not have been admitted in evidence. That disposes of this appeal because that record was relied on by the Crown to rebut the appellant's defence that police officers had used violence to get a confession out of him; it probably had some probative value. We found it impossible to hold that this was a case to which the proviso to s 2(1) of the Criminal Appeal Act 1968 could be applied.

For the sake of completeness, we should add that we did not accept counsel for the appellant's submission that the trial judge was wrong in deciding that Dr Fraser could not reasonably have been expected to have any recollection of the matters dealt with in the medical records. This was a matter for the trial judge to decide. There was ample evidence to justify his deciding as he did.

The appeal is allowed and the conviction is quashed.

Appeal allowed; conviction quashed.

Solicitors: *Registrar of Criminal Appeals; Solicitor, Metropolitan Police.*

N P Metcalfe Esq   Barrister.

---

1   [1946] 1 All ER 593, [1946] KB 401
2   (1884) 27 Ch D 71, [1881-5] All ER Rep 915
3   [1977] 1 All ER 813, [1977] 2 WLR 915
4   (15th August 1977) unreported

R v Schofield

COURT OF APPEAL, CRIMINAL DIVISION
LORD WIDGERY CJ, SHAW LJ AND LLOYD J
30th, 31st JANUARY 1978

Sentence – Compensation – Order – Compensation for personal injury, loss or damage resulting from the offence – Loss – Financial loss – Power of court to include amount by way of interest in order – When appropriate for court to include interest in order – Powers of Criminal Courts Act 1973, s 35(1).

The word 'loss' in s 35(1)[a] of the Powers of Criminal Courts Act 1973, which gives the court power to make an order requiring a convicted person to pay compensation for, inter alia, any loss resulting from the offence for which he was convicted, is not restricted to any particular kind of loss. Accordingly the court may, in a case of financial loss, include a sum by way of interest when making such an order, equivalent in amount to the award of interest the person suffering the loss would be likely to recover were he to bring a civil action against the convicted person. In exercising its discretion to include interest in a compensation order the court should bear in mind the amount of the loss, the amount of the interest, the time which has elapsed since the loss was suffered and the means of the convicted person (see p 706 *f* and p 707 *b c*, post).

Notes

For compensation orders, see 11 Halsbury's Laws (4th Edn) para 804, and for cases on the subject, see 14(2) Digest (Reissue) 862, 863, 7464-7475.

For the Powers of Criminal Courts Act 1973, s 35, see 43 Halsbury's Statutes (3rd Edn) 331.

Application

Charles Haldane Schofield applied to have varied a compensation order made against him at the Crown Court at Plymouth on 6th May 1977 following his conviction before Mr Recorder Yorke QC on charges of obtaining property by deception and of theft. The applicant pleaded guilty and was ordered to pay compensation of £567·74 including £97·93 by way of interest. The facts are set out in the judgment of the court.

Michael Selfe for the applicant.

LLOYD J delivered the following judgment of the court: On 6th May 1977 the applicant pleaded guilty at Plymouth Crown Court to two charges, one of obtaining property by deception and the other of theft. He asked for 18 other similar offences to be taken into consideration. On the first count, that of obtaining property by deception, the particulars were that he dishonestly obtained a portable television set by passing a worthless cheque drawn on his bank account at Barclays Bank for the sum of £62. On that count he was sentenced to six months' imprisonment suspended for two years, fined £50, and was ordered to pay £84 compensation under s 35 of the Powers of Criminal Courts Act 1973. On the face of it there is nothing in the least unusual about that sentence. The only unusual feature is that the sum of £84 ordered to be paid by way of compensation included a figure of £22 by way of interest. It is accepted by counsel for the applicant that this was a suitable case for making a compensation order. The sole question for the consideration of the court is whether the recorder was entitled to include a sum by way of interest in the compensation order which he made.

The second count raises precisely the same point. That was a case of theft of a motor

a   Section 35(1) is set out at p 706 *d*, post   cc cycle, and the sentence on that count was 12 months' imprisonment suspended for two years, to run consecutively, making 18 months' imprisonment in all, a fine of £100, and in addition an order for compensation in the sum of £490, to include £80 by way of interest.

The 18 offences taken into consideration were all very similar to count 1, that is to say, obtaining property by the passing of worthless cheques drawn on the same account at Barclays Bank. Those offences were all committed between December 1973 and March 1974, the individual sums varying between about £4 and about £100, the total sum being £469·81. In respect of those other offences, the recorder made a further compensation order which also included an amount by way of interest, the total amount awarded being £567·74.

As we have indicated, the sole ground of the application is that the sentence of the Crown Court was wrong in principle and excessive by means of the inclusion of interest in the compensation orders. So far as this court is aware, and so far as the researches of counsel have gone, the question is a novel one. It is, therefore, necessary to start by looking at the language of the 1973 Act itself, and I read s 35(1) which provides:

> 'Subject to the provisions of this Part of this Act, a court by or before which a person is convicted of an offence, in addition to dealing with him in any other way, may, on application or otherwise, make an order (in this Act referred to as "a compensation order") requiring him to pay compensation for any personal injury, loss or damage resulting from that offence or any other offence which is taken into consideration by the court in determining sentence.'

I need not read the remaining subsections of s 35, or s 36 or s 37, but it is worth noting that s 38 makes detailed provision for what is to happen in the event of a person who is a beneficiary under a compensation order subsequently recovering damages in a civil court arising out of the same facts.

Turning back to s 35(1), the important words are 'compensation for any personal injury, loss or damage resulting from that offence'. In our judgment, the word 'loss' should, in that subsection, be given its ordinary meaning and should not be limited or restricted to any particular kind of loss. In the case of financial loss, you look to see what the loss is which the victim has, in fact, suffered at the time the compensation order is made and then, provided the loss results from the offences and is not otherwise too remote in law, the court may, in its discretion, make a compensation order up to that amount. Thus, in a simple case of theft of bank notes, the victim's loss would not necessarily be limited to the loss of the money itself but would, or at any rate might, include the loss of the use of the money between the date of the theft and the date when the compensation order was made.

If that is the right construction of s 35, one looks to see whether there is anything in the cases which have been decided since the 1973 Act was passed that would lead to a different conclusion. In several recent cases, this court has said that the machinery under s 35 is only intended for simple cases. In the more complicated cases, the victim should be left to his remedy in the civil courts. Counsel for the applicant has argued that the inclusion of a sum for interest would lead to serious complications in arriving, for instance, at the appropriate rate of interest to be taken. If it did lead to such complications, we would agree that it would not be a suitable case for summary disposal by way of a compensation order under s 35. But we can see no such complications or difficulties in the present case.

If one takes the first count, by way of example, Mr Renshaw, who was the owner of the portable television set, received a worthless cheque for £62 as long ago as 22nd December 1973. If he were to bring a civil action there would be no doubt that he would recover not only the value of the cheque for £62 but also a sum by way of interest to cover the period between 22nd December 1973 and the date of the judgment in the civil proceedings. That being so, we can see no reason why the criminal court should not, in a suitable case, include an equivalent sum when making a compensation order under s 35. The fact that the interest cannot be precisely calculated, and, indeed, should not be precisely calculated, is no bar.

We are not, on this application, laying down the rules for every case. It will still be for the court, in each case, to exercise its discretion as to whether it will include a sum by way of interest or not. When the amounts involved are small, and when the time is short, no doubt the interest will in practice continue to be ignored, as it has been apparently till now. In many cases, as Shaw LJ pointed out in the course of argument, the question of interest would be academic when the means of the defendant are insufficient. But where, as in the present case, the amounts are relatively large, where the time is a long one, and where there is no question of any insufficiency in the defendant's means, we can see no error in principle in including a sum by way of interest in the award, thereby compensating the victim for the loss of the use of the money as well as for the loss of the money itself. Counsel for the applicant says that there is no evidence of loss of interest in the present case. But that is something which in our judgment, the recorder, in a case such as the present, was entitled to infer.

For those grounds, we would dismiss the application.

Application dismissed.

Solicitors: *Foot & Bowden*, Plymouth.

Jacqueline Charles Barrister.

Outlook Supplies Ltd v Parry

EMPLOYMENT APPEAL TRIBUNAL
PHILLIPS J, MISS P SMITH AND MRS M E SUNDERLAND
13th OCTOBER, 22nd NOVEMBER 1977

Employment – Equality of treatment between men and women – Variation between woman's and man's contract due to material difference other than sex – Correct approach to determination whether variation due to a difference other than sex – Practice of 'red circling' employees to protect wages – Necessity to look at all the circumstances of each application – Relevance of length of time since 'red circling' introduced – Employers attitude to continuation of 'red circling' – Equal Pay Act 1970, s 1(3) (as amended by the Sex Discrimination Act 1975, s 8(1)).

Where an application is made for equality of pay between a man and a woman and the employer contends that the variation in pay is genuinely due to a material difference other than the difference of sex, within s 1(3)[a] of the Equal Pay Act 1970, the question raised is one of fact which cannot be determined by rule of thumb but should be decided by looking at all the circumstances of the application. Where a variation arises because of 'red circling' to protect the position of an established employee who has been relieved of that part of his duties which formerly distinguished his work from that of other employees of the opposite sex, e g because of an alteration in the duties attaching to his employment or because of his ill-health, the length of time which has elapsed since the 'red circling' was introduced and whether the employee has acted in accordance with current notions of industrial practice in his attitude to

---

a Section 1(3) is set out at p 709 *d*, post

the continuation of the practice are relevant matters for the industrial tribunal to take into account when considering the application (see p 711 c and e f, post); *Snoxell v Vauxhall Motors Ltd* [1977] 3 All ER 770 explained.

Where a variation in pay between a man and a woman is proposed to be introduced or to be continued to protect the position of an established employee, joint consultation between the employer and employees is desirable. Where such a variation arises it is desirable where possible that it should be phased out (see p 711 d, post).

Notes

For equal treatment of men and women as regards terms and conditions of employment, see 16 Halsbury's Laws (4th Edn) 767.

For the Equal Pay Act 1970, s 1 (as amended by the Sex Discrimination Act 1975), see 45 Halsbury's Statutes (3rd Edn) 290.

Case referred to in judgment

Snoxell v Vauxhall Motors Ltd, Charles Early & Marriott (Witney) Ltd v Smith [1977] 3 All ER 770, [1978] 1 QB 11, [1977] 3 WLR 189, [1977] ICR 700, EAT.

Appeal

Outlook Supplies Ltd ('the employers') appealed against the decision of an industrial tribunal (chairman G H L Rhodes Esq) sitting in Manchester on 14th January 1977 which allowed the application, under the Equal Pay Act 1970, of Mrs Joyce Parry for equality of pay with a male employee employed on like work in the same employment. The facts are set out in the judgment of the appeal tribunal.

Malcolm Cotterill for the employers.
Mr R Knipe, solicitor, for Mrs Parry.

Cur adv vult

22nd November. **PHILLIPS J** delivered the following judgment of the appeal tribunal: This is an appeal by Outlook Supplies Ltd ('the employers') from the decision of an industrial tribunal sitting in Manchester on 14th January 1977, which by a decision entered on 21st January 1977 found in favour of the complainant, Mrs Joyce Parry, that she was entitled to receive an increase in salary of £288 per annum with pro rata arrears from 29th December 1975 to the date of the decision. At the conclusion of the argument on the hearing of the appeal, we allowed the appeal, set the decision of the industrial tribunal aside and remitted the case to a differently constituted industrial tribunal to be reheard. We now proceed to give the reasons for allowing the appeal.

Mrs Parry's claim, under the Equal Pay Act 1970, as amended, was to be paid the same as a fellow employee, Mr Allison. The industrial tribunal accepted her claim. The facts as found by the industrial tribunal (they are now disputed) are simple. Since 1970 Mr Allison's duties had comprised two elements: those of assistant to the accountant, and those of supervisor of the accounts department staff. Mrs Parry carried out similar supervisory duties in six different departments but did not have duties equivalent to those of Mr Allison as assistant to the accountant. Mrs Parry, and other women doing like work with herself, were paid less than Mr Allison to the extent of £288 per annum. As a result of ill-health Mr Allison had difficulty in discharging all his duties, and on 1st August 1974, he was relieved of that part of his duties which consisted of working as assistant to the accountant. Thereafter, the work which he did was the same as that done by Mrs Parry, albeit in a different department. On 1st July 1975 there was a further redistribution of duties; Mr Allison became supervisor of the returns department, and Mrs Parry became supervisor of the accounts department where Mr Allison had formerly worked. When

Mr Allison was relieved of part of his duties in August 1974, his salary was not reduced,
a but, to use the common expression, was 'protected'. There were later increases
in salary payable to all the staff (including Mr Allison and Mrs Parry) in June 1975
and June 1976, but the differential between their pay was maintained.

This is the version of facts, accepted by the industrial tribunal, which emerged
from the employers' evidence. Mrs Parry was not represented at the hearing before
the industrial tribunal, and, because the industrial tribunal were in her favour on
b these facts, she was not asked to give evidence, and so her version of the facts never
came to the attention of the industrial tribunal. But, as we now know, she did not,
and does not, accept this version of the facts. It is her case that Mr Allison was never
engaged on duties additional to those of the kind which she did; and accordingly
she contends that she and he were at all times, both before and after he fell ill, employed on like work. If she is right her case would succeed on that ground, unless
c there is a defence available to the employers under s 1(3).

Nonetheless, it is necessary to consider the decision, and the arguments presented
to us, on the basis of the facts found by the industrial tribunal, albeit that they are
now challenged. The reason is that the industrial tribunal correctly found that on
those facts Mrs Parry was entitled to succeed, unless the employers could make
out a case under s 1(3) of the 1970 Act. That subsection provides as follows:

d
> 'An equality clause shall not operate in relation to a variation between the
> woman's contract and the man's contract if the employer proves that the varia-
> tion is genuinely due to a material difference (other than the difference of sex)
> between her case and his.'

In other words the situation was that in any event, and whichever version of the
e facts was correct, at least since Mr Allison's illness, he and Mrs Parry were employed
on like work, and accordingly she was entitled to succeed unless it could be shown
by the employers that the variation in pay was genuinely due to a material difference
(other than the difference of sex) between her case and his. The industrial tribunal
accepted that when Mr Allison first fell ill the employers had a good reason for paying
him more than Mrs Parry, although they were then doing like work, because for
f humane reasons it was a natural and expected thing to do. However, they felt that
it had gone on too long, and, in the absence of evidence which the employers were not
prepared to give as to their intentions in this respect, they came to the conclusion
that the employers had not discharged the onus on them under s 1(3).

If in our judgment the industrial tribunal had been right on the point we should
have dismissed the appeal, because the result was the same as it would have been if
g Mrs Parry's version of the facts was correct, namely that she would succeed. But we
do not agree with the industrial tribunal. It was for this reason, and because Mrs
Parry's version was never heard, that we allowed the appeal and ordered a rehearing.
It should be noted that on the rehearing all points will be open, including the applicability of s 1(3), in the light of the evidence tendered, which may well be different.

In reaching their decision on the applicability of s 1(3) the industrial tribunal did
h not have the benefit of the decision of the appeal tribunal in *Snoxell v Vauxhall Motors
Ltd*[1] where we said:

j
> 'On the evidence at present available there is no reason to suppose that the "red
> circling" of Mr Steptoe was directly or indirectly attributable to an act of sex
> discrimination. Accordingly, the case throws up for consideration the situation
> where wages are protected by being "red circled" for good reasons, and the
> differential is maintained. In our judgment the correct approach for an industrial
> tribunal, confronted with a claim by an employer under s 1(3) that a variation is

---

1   [1977] 3 All ER 770 at 781, 782, [1978] 1 QB 11 at 31-33

genuinely due to such a material difference, is to elicit and analyse *all* the circumstances of the particular case; and it is unwise and likely to lead to error merely **a** to say that a particular case is a "red circle" case. In practice, most cases involve several features, and it is probably only rarely that a "red circle" situation arises in its purist form. But supposing that it does, and that there is a case where it can be demonstrated that there is a group of employees who have their wages protected for causes neither directly nor indirectly due to a difference of sex, and assuming that the male and female employees doing the same work who are **b** without the "red circle" are treated alike, we see no reason why the employers should not succeed in their answer. In such circumstances it would seem to us that the variation in pay is genuinely due to a material difference (other than the difference of sex) between the woman's case and the man's case. Thus in *Snoxell v Vauxhall Motors Ltd*, on the information at present available to us, we would not expect a claim by a male inspector without the "red circle", based on a **c** comparison of his case with that of Miss Snoxell and Mrs Davies who will be within it, to succeed. We should expect Vauxhall to be able to say that the variation between Miss Snoxell's and Mrs Davies's contracts and his contract was genuinely due to a material difference (other than the difference of sex) between his case and theirs: for their presence within the "red circle", and his absence from it, would be neither directly nor indirectly attributable to a difference **d** of sex.

'Returning to the appeal of *Charles Early & Marriott (Witney) Ltd v Smith*, it can be seen that it raises the additional question of the effect of the prolonged continuation of "red circling". If Mr Steptoe had been transferred from warehouse duties to ticket writing in 1972, at a time when ticket writing was in a lower grade and attracted a lower rate of remuneration, and had then been "red circled", it is **e** difficult to see why Marriott would not have had a good answer to his claim. The case would have been a simple uncomplicated one of a man having his wages protected, and therefore of the employers being able to say that the variation was due to a difference between the women's case and his, other than a difference of sex. Does it make any difference that the "red circling" is continued, even continued indefinitely? In principle, we do not see why it should. Assuming **f** that there are no additional factors, and that in other respects affairs are operated on a unisex, non-discriminatory basis, the situation will continue to be that the variation is genuinely due to a material difference other than the difference of sex. The "red circling" will persist, ageing and wasting until eventually it vanishes. In the case of Vauxhall we do not see why they should not continue to have available a good answer under s 1(3) to any claim by male or female inspectors based on a **g** comparison with the inspectors within the "red circle"; provided, of course, there are not other circumstances of which we are ignorant, and no new factor appears. At the same time, it seems to us to be desirable where possible for "red circles" to be phased out and eliminated, for they are bound to give rise to confusion and misunderstanding. One of the difficulties seems to be that although understood and accepted as fair when first introduced, with the passage of time memory **h** dims, the reason for their institution is forgotten, and they are seen as examples of discrimination.

'The question remains, what is the proper order to make in *Charles Early & Marriott (Witney) Ltd v Smith*? On the one hand, it follows from what we have said that Marriott have a strong argument that they can rely on s 1(3) in answer to the claim, basing their case on the contention that Mr Steptoe was "red circled" **j** in 1966 or 1967, and (if it be established as a fact) that continued protection of his rate of remuneration was necessary in order to maintain his pension. But the facts are by no means clear or complete, nor is it possible to say with certainty precisely on what ground the industrial tribunal allowed the claim. Merely to allow the appeal and to set the order aside, thus depriving Mrs Smith and Mrs

Ball of the order in their favour, would seem unfair. As we have said earlier,

a there is no such thing as a "red circle answer" to a claim. The answer must be based on s 1(3). In such an answer the fact that the men with whom comparison is being made have been "red circled" is obviously important, but it is vital to know *all* the circumstances. It is necessary to examine the origin of the "red circling", to see whether in other respects the arrangements are unisex and non-discriminatory, and generally to look at all the facts in order to see whether the

b employers, on whom lies a heavy burden of proof, have satisfied the requirements of s 1(3). Unless we can say here that the circumstances are such that Marriott's answer under s 1(3) is bound to succeed, we ought not simply to allow the appeal. We have reached the conclusion that we cannot say that; accordingly it will be necessary for the case to be reheard.'

c We think that it might be helpful, in the light of later experience and arguments addressed to us in this and other cases, to amplify a little what was said in that judgment. We wish to draw attention to the following matters: (i) we stress the point that cases arising under s 1(3) can never be solved by rule of thumb, or by attaching a label, such as saying 'This is a "red circle" case'. It is necessary to look at all the circumstances; (ii) the 'protection' of wages, even when done for good reason, gives rise to much misunderstanding and upset, which increases as time goes on, and it is

d accordingly desirable that where possible such arrangements should be phased out; (iii) for the same reason joint consultation is desirable where it is intended to introduce such a practice or, if it has been introduced, to continue it; (iv) in such cases, when determining whether the employer has discharged the onus on him under s 1(3), it is relevant for the industrial tribunal to take into account the length of time which has elapsed since the 'protection' was introduced, and whether the employers have acted

e in accordance with current notions of good industrial practice in their attitude to the continuation of the practice.

The decision of an industrial tribunal under s 1(3) is one of fact, to be based on all the relevant circumstances. It may well be that in *Snoxell v Vauxhall Motors Ltd*[1] we tended to treat a question of fact as one of law when we implied that indefinite

f prolongation of a 'red circle' cannot result in a defence under s 1(3) failing where earlier it might have succeeded. In truth it is all a question of whether the industrial tribunal is satisfied that the employers have discharged the burden laid on them by s 1(3). Prolonged maintenance of a 'red circle', especially if unnecessary and/or contrary to good industrial practice, may well in all the circumstances of the case lead to a doubt whether the employers have discharged that burden.

g In the present case, the original 'red circling' or 'protection' in the case of Mr Allison was found to be reasonable, and the employers would then have discharged the burden under s 1(3) in respect of it. The time which elapsed since then was quite short, and we cannot in the absence of any other relevant circumstances, and for that reason alone, agree with the conclusion of the industrial tribunal. It seems to us that on the basis of the facts as the industrial tribunal thought them to be, s 1(3) would have provided

h the employers with an answer to Mrs Parry's claim, which, *on those facts*, ought to have been discussed. But, as we have explained, her evidence, and her version of the facts, was never heard. Accordingly, the application will have to be considered by a differently constituted industrial tribunal, before which all issues will be open.

Appeal allowed. Case remitted to a differently constituted industrial tribunal for rehearing.

j Solicitors: *C R Jones* (for the employers); *Porter, Hope & Porter*, Bolton (for Mrs Parry).

Salim H J Merali　Barrister.

1　[1977] 3 All ER 770, [1978] 1 QB 11

Re Performing Right Society Ltd
Lyttleton v Performing Right Society Ltd   *a*

CHANCERY DIVISION
BRIGHTMAN J
1st, 2nd, 3rd JUNE 1977

b

Company – Register of members – Company without share capital – Members divided into several classes – Obligation to specify class of membership in register – Register not indicating class of membership because election to full membership depending on financial circumstances of member – Only full members entitled to requisition and vote at general meeting – Associate member wishing to have articles of association altered and to have extraordinary general meeting convened for purpose – Associate member wishing to contact full members – Application **c** *for order requiring company to disclose names and addresses of full members – Whether company required to disclose identity of full members – Whether company under duty to specify class of membership in register – Companies Act 1948, s 110(1)(a).*

A society which was a company limited by guarantee without a share capital had some 10,000 members. Its articles of association divided members into three classes, **d** full, associate and provisional associate members. The class into which a member was initially elected was at the discretion of the society's general council. The articles and the rules of the society did not prescribe any financial qualification for membership but in fact election to full membership depended on a person's financial circumstances. In accordance with the Companies Act 1948 the society maintained a written register of members. The register did not indicate the class of membership to which **e** members belonged, since the society did not wish to disclose members' financial circumstances, but merely stated the members' names and addresses. However the certificate of membership issued to each member stated his class of membership. Only full members, who numbered about 1,000, were entitled by the articles to attend and vote at general meetings of the society. The applicant, an associate member, wanted associate members to have more say in the society's affairs and to **f** have the articles of association altered accordingly. Since only full members were entitled to requisition and vote at an extraordinary general meeting, he wished to contact a sufficient number of interested full members to requisition a meeting with the object of passing a resolution to alter the articles. He applied to a registrar for an order, pursuant to s 113[a] of the 1948 Act, requiring the society to send him a copy of that part of the register of members comprising the names and addresses of full **g** members. The registrar dismissed the application. The applicant applied to have the registrar's order discharged. The society contended that, on the true construction of s 110(1)(a)[b] of the 1948 Act, a company with a share capital consisting of different species of shares was not obliged to enter in the register of members the species of

---

a Section 113, so far as material, provides: **h**
    '(2) Any member or other person may require a copy of the register, or of any part thereof, on payment of [a specified sum]. The company shall cause any copy so required by any person to be sent to that person within a period of ten days commencing on the day next after the day on which the requirement is received by the company.
    '(3) If any inspection required under this section is refused or any copy required under this section is not sent within the proper period, the company and every officer of the company who is in default shall be liable in respect of each offence to a fine not exceeding two **j** pounds and further to a default fine of two pounds.
    '(4) In the case of any such refusal or default, the court may by order compel an immediate inspection of the register and index or direct that the copies required shall be sent to the persons requiring them.'
b Section 110(1), so far as material, is set out at p 716 c d, post

shares held by a member but only that he held a certain number of shares, that
a therefore a company without a share capital but with different classes of members
was not obliged to enter in its register the species of membership of each member,
and that accordingly the society was not obliged to diclose to the applicant the names
and addresses of full members.

Held – Under s 110(1)(a) of the 1948 Act a company with a share capital consisting
b of different species of shares was under a duty to specify in the register of members
the species of shares held by each member and not merely the number of shares
held by him. From that it followed that a company with no share capital but with
members who were divided into different classes was under a duty to specify in the
register the class of membership of each member and not merely his name and
address. Accordingly the court would order the society to send to the applicant,
c in accordance with s 113, a copy of the parts of the register which comprised the names
and addresses of full members. The registrar's order would therefore be discharged
(see p 717 b to e, post).

Notes
For entries to be made in a company's register, see 7 Halsbury's Laws (4th Edn) para
d 294, and for cases on the subject, see 9 Digest (Reissue) 211, 1257, 1258.
For the Companies Act 1948, s 110, see 5 Halsbury's Statutes (3rd Edn) 200, 201.

Case referred to in judgment
Pender v Lushington (1877) 6 Ch D 70, 46 LJCh 317, 9 Digest (Reissue) 629, 3751.

e **Case also cited**
Saunders (T H) & Co Ltd, Re [1908] 1 Ch 415.

Motion
By an originating summons dated 10th May 1977 the applicant, Trevor Lyttleton
sought an order, pursuant to s 113 of the Companies Act 1948, requiring the Perform-
f ing Right Society Ltd ('the society') to send him a copy of the part or parts of its register
of members comprising the names and addresses of those members who were full
members of the society. On 13th May Mr Registrar Dearbergh dismissed the application. By motion dated 16th May Mr Lyttleton moved for an order to discharge the
order made by the registrar. Mr Lyttleton also issued a writ against the society
claiming a declaration that he was entitled to be provided with information by the
g society to enable him to determine which of its members were entitled to attend and
vote at general meetings of the society. The facts are set out in the judgment.

Oliver Weaver for Mr Lyttleton.
Eric Christie and Lynn Wagner for the society.

h
BRIGHTMAN J. I have before me a motion to discharge an order made by the
registrar. He dismissed an application by Mr Trevor Lyttleton, who is the applicant on this motion. Mr Lyttleton is an associate member of the Performing Right
Society Ltd. His application before the registrar was by originating summons.
He sought an order pursuant to s 113 of the Companies Act 1948 requiring the society
j to send him a copy of the part or parts of its register of members comprising the
names and addresses of those members of the society who are designated as full
members. Mr Lyttleton has also issued a writ against the society in case s 113 does not
avail him. The writ claims a declaration that Mr Lyttleton is entitled to be provided
by the society with information enabling him to determine which of the society's
members are entitled to attend and vote at general meetings of the society.

The point at issue is this. The society is a company limited by guarantee. It has no share capital. The members are divided into three classes: full members, asso- *a* ciate members, and provisional associate members. Only full members are entitled to attend and vote at general meetings of the society. As is well known, the society exists for the purpose of exercising and enforcing on behalf of all its members the benefit of the copyrights in which they are interested. The society has something like 10,000 members, but only about 1,000 are full members. The society has an annual income of over £20,000,000 collected on behalf of its members. Mr Lyttleton *b* is only an associate member and he feels that associate members should have a bigger say in the affairs of the society. He may be right or he may be wrong. It would mean in practice altering the articles of association of the society. This cannot be achieved by associate members directly because they have no vote as matters stand. His purpose can only be achieved if he can interest a sufficient number of full members in his proposals. They could then requisition an extraordinary general meeting *c* under s 132 of the 1948 Act with the object of passing the appropriate resolutions. To obtain the necessary support Mr Lyttleton would need to know the names and addresses of the full members so that he could contact them and solicit their support. The natural source of this information would be the register of members.

The society takes advantage of s 3 of the Stock Exchange (Completion of Bargains) Act 1976, which enables a company to keep on computer tapes a record of all the *d* matters which it is bound to record. The society then programmes the computer to produce any particular record which is required from time to time. In my view this Act has no further relevance to the case before me, and I propose to disregard it and to proceed on the basis that the society maintains an ordinary written register of members. The print-out which the society programmes its computer to produce in order to record the statutory information required by s 110 of the 1948 Act to be kept *e* in the register of members does not differentiate between the 1,000 full members and the 9,000 associate and provisional members. I speak in round figures. This is done on purpose, but not perversely. A person achieves the status of full member of the society as a result of his financial success as a writer, composer or publisher. The general council of the society, which is its governing body, takes the view that it might be disclosing information given in confidence if it revealed to the public which *f* of the members had and which had not achieved the requisite level of financial success to be given the status of a full member. That is the background of the case before me.

The society was incorporated in 1914. The memorandum of association, as distinct from the articles, does not divide the members into different classes. As I have said, there is no share capital. Under the memorandum every member is bound to *g* contribute a trifling sum to the assets of the society in the event of its liquidation. The relevant articles are these:

'1(a)(ii) "Associate Member" means a member of the Society elected to associate membership pursuant to Article 5, and having the rights, privileges and obligations provided for associate Members by these Articles . . . (xiii) "Full Member" *h* means a Member of the Society elected to full membership pursuant to Article 5, and having the rights, privileges and obligations provided for full Members by these Articles . . . (xv) "Member" means and includes full Member, associate Member and provisional associate Member . . . (xxi) "Provisional associate Member" means a Member of the Society elected to provisional associate membership pursuant to Article 5, and having the rights, privileges and obligations *j* provided for provisional associate Members by these Articles . . .
'3. The Members of the Society are:—(a) all persons who are Members at the time these Articles become binding upon the Society, and (b) any person who is admitted to membership pursuant to Article 5.
'4. The following persons shall be eligible for admission to membership of

the Society:—(a) any writer, publisher or proprietor; (b) any widow, child or other relative, next of kin, beneficiary under the will, or personal representative of a deceased writer, publisher or proprietor or of any deceased member.

'5 ... (c) Any person who is eligible for membership may be elected to membership by the General Council, or in accordance with such procedure as the General Council may from time to time prescribe, as (i) a provisional associate Member, or (ii) an associate Member, or (iii) a full Member. (d) Any person who has been admitted to membership shall have issued to him a certificate as to his membership in such form, and signed by such officer of the society, as the General Council shall from time to time prescribe.

'6. (a) Save as hereinafter provided a provisional associate Member and an associate Member shall have the same rights and privileges and be subject to the same obligations as a full Member. (b) A provisional associate Member shall be eligible (without further application) for election to associate membership or to full membership in the discretion of the General Council, and an associate Member shall be eligible (without further application) for election to full membership in the discretion of the General Council. (c) Neither a provisional associate Member nor an associate Member shall be entitled to receive notice of, or attend or vote at, general meetings.'

I am not concerned with the difference between an associate member and a provisional associate member. It is sufficient to mention that under art 9 the membership of a provisional associate member may be terminated in a more peremptory manner than that of a full or associate member.

'14. The General Council may, whenever it thinks fit, convene an Extraordinary General Meeting, and Extraordinary General Meetings shall also be convened on such requisition, or in default, may be convened by such requisitionists, as Section 132 of the Companies Act provides ...

27. Every Member, other than associate Member or a provisional associate Member, shall have one vote, as well on a poll as on a show of hands. No Member shall be entitled to vote on a show of hands unless he is present in person ...

29. On a poll votes may be given either personally or by proxy.'

It will be seen that the articles of association of the society leave it entirely to the discretion of the general council whether a person is initially elected to membership as a full member, associate member or provisional associate member and whether, after election as an associate or provisional associate member, a person moves up the scale. Neither the articles nor the rules made thereunder impose any financial qualification on class of membership. However, the general council has publicised the fact that it elects persons to full membership according to specified financial criteria which vary according to whether a person is a writer or publisher and whether he composes or publishes classical or popular music.

Counsel for Mr Lyttleton advanced three propositions before me. First, on the true construction of s 110 of the Companies Act 1948, in the case of a company limited by guarantee which divides its membership into different classes, there is a duty on the company to keep its register of members in a form which distinguishes between the different classes of membership. This would mean that in the present case the register would have to indicate who were full members, who were associate members and who were provisional associate members.

His second proposition is that if the statutory duty of such a company is only to enter in the register the names and addresses of members without indicating class of membership, a person is entitled under s 113 to require the company to select and provide a copy of those parts or lines of the register which record the names and addresses of full members to the exclusion of other members; in other words, counsel submits that Mr Lyttleton is entitled to specify the membership of which he

requires details; and the society is then bound to identify that membership by
providing only those parts of the register of members.

His third proposition is that a term arises by necessary implication in the contract
between the company and its members which is constituted by the articles, to the
effect that the company will make available, on the reasonable requisition of a
member, information enabling that member to identify which members are full
members. Otherwise, it is said, a member would not be able to identify those persons
who have the legal power to control the company. It was submitted that this is
implicit in the constitution of every company incorporated under the 1948 Act. A
member of a company must, it was said, have power to identify his fellow members
and their class of membership.

I will turn to the first submission and read the relevant part of s 110 of the 1948 Act.
Subsection (1) provides:

'Every company shall keep a register of its members and enter therein the
following particulars:—(a) the names and addresses of the members, and in the
case of a company having a share capital a statement of the shares held by each
member, distinguishing each share by its number so long as the share has a
number, and of the amount paid or agreed to be considered as paid on the shares
of each member; (b) the date at which each person was entered in the register
as a member; (c) the date at which any person ceased to be a member . . .'

A noticeable feature of s 110 is that in the case of a company having a share capital
the obligation on the company is expressed as a duty to enter a statement of the shares
held by each member, to distinguish the number of each share, if it has a distinguishing
number, and to enter the amount paid or deemed to have been paid. There is not
in express terms any obligation to enter in the register the class of share held by
each member. In the case of a company which has shares of one class the word
'share' will inevitably denote both the genus and species because there will be but
a single species. In a case where, for example, there are ordinary and preference shares
the word 'share' denotes only the genus, and the species is denoted, if at all, by the
words 'ordinary share' or 'preference share'. Section 110(1)(a) in terms only requires
the register to refer to the genus, which causes no problem where there is only one
species, but if literally interpreted would lead to a highly uninformative, confusing
and misleading register in a case where there is more than one species.

Counsel, in his helpful submissions on behalf of the society, submitted that, strictly,
there was no obligation on a company to go beyond the genus in compiling its register
of members. Therefore, if the issued capital consists of 100,000 preference shares,
100,000 ordinary shares and 100,000 deferred shares, and X holds 50,000 preference
shares and 10,000 ordinary shares, and Y holds 50,000 ordinary shares and 10,000
deferred shares, the register of members will be properly and sufficiently compiled
if it contains the name and address of X and the name and address of Y and the statement that X holds 60,000 shares and Y holds 60,000 shares. This would be so, it was
submitted, even if voting rights are attached, for example, only to the deferred and
ordinary shares and not to the preference shares.

I find it impossible to accept that submission. I ask myself, whoever heard of a
register of members compiled in that laconic manner? How would scrutineers
perform their function if they sought to check the eligibility of a person seeking to
vote? Under s 118 of the 1948 Act the register of members is prima facie evidence of
any matters directed or authorised by the Act to be inserted therein. Is that prima
facie evidence to extend to names and addresses and the fact of membership, but to
stop short of the class of share held and therefore of the class of membership? I
find that difficult to believe. I am fortified by what was said by Jessel MR in *Pender v
Lushington*[1]:

---

1 (1877) 6 Ch D 70 at 78

'. . . the register of shareholders, on which there can be no notice of a trust, furnishes the only means of ascertaining whether you have a lawful meeting or a lawful demand for a poll, or of enabling the scrutineers to strike out votes.'

I reach the conclusion without difficulty that the obligation under s 110 of the 1948 Act is to specify the species of share held by each member where there is more than one species and that a company is not at liberty to express only the genus, save on the one and irrelevant occasion where there is only one species of share.

Having reached the conclusion that the obligation on a company is to state the species of share held by each member in all cases where there is more than one species of share in issue, I find it only a short step to conclude that in a case where there are members and no shares the obligation on the company is to specify the species of membership in all cases where there is more than one species of member.

It is plain to me that the society itself takes exactly the same view in another context. As I have read, art 5(*d*) provides that any person who has been admitted to membership shall be issued with a certificate as to his membership. The article does not say that the certificate shall specify the species of membership. However, when I look at the certificate of membership, I see that it does not merely specify that the member is a member of the society, but certifies that he is a full member. In other words, on occasions when it is necessary formally to describe the membership of a person, common sense dictates that the species of membership shall be stated.

Accordingly, I accept the first proposition submitted by counsel for Mr Lyttleton and I discharge the order made by the registrar. I order, pursuant to s 113 of the 1948 Act, that the society send to Mr Lyttleton that part of the register which comprises, or ought to comprise, the names and addresses of the persons described in the articles as full members. Counsel's second submission does not in the circumstances arise as a separate issue.

As far as the action is concerned, Mr Lyttleton is, I think, technically entitled to the declaration sought, for the simple reason that he is entitled under the 1948 Act to see a print-out which identifies the full members, but it seems to me that it would serve no purpose to make such an order, and I would have thought that the proper course would be to stay further proceedings.

My understanding is that, at the hearing before the registrar, Mr Lyttleton conceded that s 110 of the 1948 Act did not require that the register of members should draw a distinction between the three classes of membership. That concession, if it was made, was not repeated before me. The society, quite rightly, did not seek to hold Mr Lyttleton to it. If I am correct in my assumption, it follows that, though I am differing from the registrar, I am differing from him on a point which was never argued before him. It is possible that this may have some bearing on costs.

Finally, I wish to record one other fact. It is perfectly obvious from the exhibited papers that Mr Lyttleton has subjected the society to a barrage of correspondence. This correspondence may or may not have been justified and I express no view on that. The society responded to that correspondence with courtesy and forebearance. I am not concerned with the merits of the dispute between Mr Lyttleton and the society, but I want to say, in case there is any misunderstanding, that as far as I have had the opportunity to observe the fringes of the quarrel, the society has behaved throughout with exemplary patience.

Order accordingly. No order in the action; all further proceedings therein stayed.

Solicitors: *Freshfields* (for Mr Lyttleton); *Denis de Freitas & Co* (for the society).

Evelyn M C Budd   Barrister.

R v Jones
R v Sullivan

COURT OF APPEAL, CRIMINAL DIVISION
GEOFFREY LANE LJ, SWANWICK AND WIEN JJ
10th NOVEMBER 1977

Criminal evidence – Record relating to trade or business – Record – Relevance of degree of permanence of record – Documents prepared for purpose of single transaction – Bill of lading and cargo manifest relating to container shipped from overseas to United Kingdom – Whether documents admissible in evidence to prove theft from container – Criminal Evidence Act 1965, s 1(1)(a).

Criminal evidence – Record relating to trade or business – Record prepared overseas – Bill of lading and cargo manifest relating to container shipped from Hong Kong to United Kingdom – Documents prepared in Hong Kong – Theft from containers in United Kingdom – Whether documents admissible in evidence to prove contents of containers – Criminal Evidence Act 1965, s 1(1)(b).

The defendants, who were directors of a transport business, were charged with conspiracy to steal goods from containers. The containers had been packed in Hong Kong and shipped from there to the United Kingdom. At the trial the Crown sought to produce as evidence of the contents of the containers when they left Hong Kong the bills of lading and cargo manifests prepared in Hong Kong relating to the containers on the ground that they were documents which were or formed part of a 'record' relating to a trade or business, within s 1(1)(a)ᵃ of the Criminal Evidence Act 1965. The judge rejected the defendants' submission that the documents were inadmissible and admitted them in evidence. The defendants were convicted. They appealed contending (i) that for a document to constitute a 'record', within s 1(1)(a), it had to be a document of some permanence and that a document brought into existence merely to service a single transaction, which would not be kept in existence after the end of the transaction, was not a record; and (ii) that s 1(1) of the 1965 Act did not make admissible documents which had been prepared outside the United Kingdom.

Held – The documents were admissible in evidence and the appeals would be dismissed for the following reasons—
(i) The word 'record' in the context of s 1(1)(a) of the 1965 Act meant a history of events in some form which was not evanescent, but the degree of permanence of the record was irrelevant. The bills of lading and cargo manifests were therefore records within s 1(1)(a) since they were written documents which contained the history of the transactions to which they related, i e where the goods came from, the method of transport, the name of the ship in which they were transported etc, and had been deliberately compiled for the information of the recipients of the goods in the United Kingdom (see p 721 f to p 722 a, post); dictum of Lord Parker CJ in R v Gwilliam [1968] 3 All ER at 823 not followed.
(ii) Records made outside the jurisdiction were admissible in evidence under s 1(1) of the 1965 Act which was concerned only with rules of evidence and not with the application of substantive law outside the jurisdiction (see p 722 c d, post).

ᵃ Section 1(1), so far as material, is set out at p 720 c d, post

Notes

a For admissibility of trade or business records, see 11 Halsbury's Laws (4th Edn) para 442.

For the Criminal Evidence Act 1965, s 1, see 12 Halsbury's Statutes (3rd Edn) 907.

Cases referred to in judgment

R v Gwilliam [1968] 3 All ER 821, [1968] 1 WLR 1839, 133 JP 44, 53 Cr App Rep 22,
b CA, Digest (Cont Vol C) 930, *322j*.

R v Tirado (1974) 59 Cr App Rep 80, CA.

Cases also cited

Draper (C E B) & Son Ltd v Edward Turner & Son Ltd [1964] 3 All ER 148, [1965] 1 QB 424, CA.

c *Myers v Director of Public Prosecutions* [1964] 2 All ER 881, [1965] AC 1001, HL.

R v Nicholls (1976) 63 Cr App Rep 187, CA.

Appeals

On 7th July 1976 in the Crown Court at Winchester before Cobb J the defendants, Benjamin Edward Jones and Dennis Francis Sullivan, directors of a transport business, Paul's Transport, were convicted of conspiracy to steal and were sentenced to terms
d of imprisonment. They appealed against the convictions on the ground, inter alia, that the judge had erred in law in ruling that documents, namely bills of lading and cargo manifests were admissible under s 1(1) of the Criminal Evidence Act 1965 as evidence of the fact that certain containers shipped to the United Kingdom from various countries overseas contained the goods specified in those documents. The
e facts are set out in the judgment of the court.

Denis Cheatle for the first defendant.

Richard Harvey QC and *Cedric Joseph* for the second defendant.

Roger Titheridge QC and *Michael Hubbard* for the Crown.

f **GEOFFREY LANE LJ** delivered the following judgment of the court: This is a preliminary point taken by counsel for the second defendant, an argument which is adopted by counsel for the first defendant. It arises in this way. The defendants were convicted in December 1976 in the Crown Court at Winchester of a conspiracy to steal and were sentenced to terms of imprisonment. Very helpfully at that trial, which took place before the late Cobb J, a series of admissions was made by the
g defendants to assist the courts and the jury in the proper and expeditious conduct of the trial. Those admissions were based on a ruling which the learned judge had made about the admissibility of evidence and it was only on the basis that this decision on that submission was correct that those admissions were made. He refused to allow the submission by counsel for the second defendant at Winchester that certain of the evidence which it was intended to put before the jury was inadmissible and,
h therefore, it is necessary very briefly, in order to paint the background of this case, to describe what it was all about.

It concerned a series of thefts, no less than 24 in number, involving sums of about £200,000, thefts from containers which had been shipped from the Far East to this country. Those containers had been packed in the Far East with a variety of commodities and the one which counsel for the second defendant very helpfully took as an
j example in this case in order to describe what happened was transaction no 3. This was a load from the Far East of 333 cartons of cotton goods which were shipped to Southampton and thence on to a container depot at Barking and thence on to the consignees, the Woolworth store at Swindon. When these goods arrived at Swindon and the container was opened it was found that a very large proportion of the cartons of cotton goods was missing. In order to prove the theft, or at least to prove the size

of the theft, it was of course necessary to be able to prove that 333 cartons of the cotton goods had been put into the container in Hong Kong which was the port of exit. *a* That would have involved before the Criminal Evidence Act 1965 calling the gentlemen from Hong Kong who had put the cartons in the container. It was the submission of the Court that that could be proved under the terms of the 1965 Act by producing the various documents which accompanied the transactions, in particular, the bill of lading and the cargo manifest. If one looks at those two documents, one sees that the details of the transactions are indeed there set out. In the case of the bill of *b* lading, it is stated that the number of packages is 333, the kind of packages is cartons and the description of the goods is cotton goods. The manifest again contains that information and it is supplemented by the name of the ship, the Osaka Bay, the port of exit and the port of arrival. There are many other documents of a similar nature containing that sort of information or supplemental information.

As I say, it was the submission of the Crown that those documents fell within the *c* terms of s 1(1) of the 1965 Act which reads as follows:

'In any criminal proceedings where direct oral evidence of a fact would be admissible, any statement contained in a document and tending to establish that fact shall, on production of the document, be admissible as evidence of that fact if—(a) the document is, or forms part of, a record relating to any trade or business *d* and compiled, in the course of that trade or business, from information supplied (whether directly or indirectly) by persons who have, or may reasonably be supposed to have, personal knowledge of the matters dealt with in the information they supply; and (b) the person who supplied the information recorded in the statement in question is dead, or beyond the seas . . .'

I omit the words which are unnecessary for the purpose of this case. *e*

It is not in dispute that all the necessary ingredients of that section are fulfilled in this case, apart from the one matter, namely can it be said that the documents to which I have referred were a record or form part of a record relating to the trade or business. Counsel for the second defendant has, if we may say so, very ably argued before us that on the plain construction of the words they do not form part of a record, and what he says is this. He submits that in order to be a record the documents *f* must have some permanence, it must be something which can be referred to as a record in the future although he concedes he is there using the word which he is seeking to define. He goes on to submit that it must not be a document which is used merely to service an individual transaction, it must be going to be kept beyond the limits of that one single transaction; something to be kept, he says, as a record available beyond the immediate transaction, deliberately done with an eye to its *g* use in the future; something which is merely brought into existence to service the one transaction is not enough. Those were the various ways he put the matter although he was in some difficulty in explaining to us the precise degree of permanence which the document must have before it becomes a record.

He drew our attention to the definition of 'record' contained in the Shorter Oxford English Dictionary. There were two passages to which he referred, the first was this: *h* 'The fact or condition of being preserved as knowledge, *esp.* by being put into writing; knowledge or information preserved or handed down in this way.' The second definition was as follows:

'An account of some fact or event preserved in writing or other permanent form; a document, monument, etc., on which such an account is inscribed; also, *transf.* any thing or person serving to indicate or give evidence of, or preserve the *i* memory of, a fact or event; a memorial.'

Pausing there for a moment, it seems to this court that the documents in the present case fall precisely within those definitions, but counsel for the second defendant's argument did not stop there. He drew to our attention two decisions of this court.

The first was *R v Gwilliam*[1]. That was a case in which the appellant was charged
a with driving a vehicle with too much alcohol in his blood. At the trial he took the
point that proof was required of the approval on the part of the Secretary of State of
the breathalyser device which was used in order to test his breath. The recorder
before whom the case was tried admitted as evidence the label on the inside of the
breathalyser set which stated that the device was approved by the Secretary of State
for the purpose of the Road Safety Act 1967. The appellant was convicted. On appeal
b it was conceded that the label was not admissible as evidence but the further question
was raised, namely whether the consignment note relating to the delivery of the
device to the police force in question, which stated that the goods had been sent from
a Home Office supply and transport store, was admissible to prove the approval of
the device under s 1(1)(a) of the 1965 Act as a commercial record. In the course of
the judgment Lord Parker CJ[2] said:

c
    'Counsel for the Crown puts it in this way: that evidence of the fact of the
    Secretary of State's approval could be given by direct oral evidence and accord-
    ingly any statement contained in a document of the type there described which
    tends to establish that approval would be admissible. This court is quite satisfied
    that that submission fails. It may be (and the court is not deciding this case on that
d   basis) that it is quite impossible to say that the consignment note itself is a record
    or forms part of a record within the meaning of the subsection.'

If that remark had been part of the ratio decendi of the case we should have been
bound by it. It was not. It was expressed to be obiter and we do not think, bearing in
mind the circumstances of the present case, that it is right that consignment notes
can never form part of a record.
e   The other case is *R v Tirado*[3]. That was a very different circumstance. The 'record'
which it was sought to introduce was a file of letters from various people in Morocco
who had been writing to the appellant about the prospect of a course in Oxford
which he had advertised. We do not feel that the decision in that case is of any value
because a file of various letters from various people does not seem to us to be something
which could in any event properly be described as a record.
f   Although it is not an exhaustive definition of the word, 'record' in this context
means a history of events in some form which is not evanescent. How long the record
is likely to be kept is immaterial: it may be something which will not survive the
end of the transaction in question; it may be something which is indeed more lasting
than bronze, but the degree of permanence does not seem to us to make or mar the
fulfilment of the definition of the word 'record'. The record in each individual case
g will last as long as commercial necessity may demand.
    The documents in the present case seem to us to fall precisely into that category.
They are the written records of the particular transaction. They are documents
containing the history of this particular transaction, where the goods started from,
the method of transport, the name of the ship, the port of arrival and the container
depot destination on the one hand and the final consignee's destination on the other.
h They are carefully and deliberately compiled for the information of those in this
country who are going to be the recipients of the goods. There is no necessity, as we
see it, for the contents of these documents to be entered into a book or a ledger as
was suggested in one of the cases; indeed these very documents themselves might
have been copied into a ledger but how, one asks, could that make them any more
or less a record than they are at the moment?
j   We have come to the conclusion, despite counsel for the second defendant's argument, quite plainly that these documents were records or part of records within

---

1   [1968] 3 All ER 821, [1968] 1 WLR 1839
2   [1968] 3 All ER 821 at 823, [1968] 1 WLR 1839 at 1843
3   (1974) 59 Cr App Rep 80

the meaning of s 1(1) of the 1965 Act, which I have read, and that particular part of his argument therefore fails.

His second argument was this. The 1965 Act only applies to transactions and the record of transactions taking place or being made in this country and does not, therefore, apply to a circumstance like the one on the present case where the container was packed in Hong Kong and the record of its packing was made in Hong Kong. The way in which he puts the mattter is this. He said it would be extraordinary if the Crown were in a better position with regard to containers packed in Hong Kong than they would be if the container were packed in this country. He rightly points out that if the container was packed in this country then to make the record admissible it would be necessary for proof to be adduced that the person who supplied the information was dead or unfit by reason of bodily or mental condition or could not, with reasonable diligence, be identified or found and so on, whereas by reason of the wording of s 1(1)(b) of the 1965 Act once the man is shown to be beyond the seas then none of these matters has to be proved by the Crown.

The answer to that appears to us to be simple. On the strict wording of s 1(1)(b) there is no doubt at all that this evidence is admissible. There is no mention of territoriality. Accordingly the point fails.

Counsel for the second defendant has drawn our attention to various passages in Maxwell on the Interpretation of Statutes[1], but it seems to us that those passages are directed to the territoriality of the substantive enactments. No one is suggesting that conspiracies taking place in Hong Kong are justiciable here. This section of the 1965 Act is not directed at substantive law but at the rules of evidence which are made in order to enable substantive law the better to be carried out. That argument fails.

His final argument really depended and only depended on whether his point on the territoriality of s 1 succeeded. It did not succeed and I hope counsel for the second defendant will not think that that we are ungracious if we do not deal with his third and final point. The preliminary point has to be answered in favour of the prosecution and against the defendants.

[The court then heard argument on whether the judge was right to overrule a submission made at the end of the Crown's case that there was no case to answer. The court held that there was evidence on which the judge was entitled to allow the case to go to the jury, that the verdicts were safe and satisfactory and that the appeals against conviction would therefore be dismissed.]

Appeals dismissed.

Solicitors: *Registrar of Criminal Appeals; Chief Prosecuting Solicitor, Hampshire Police Authority.*

Sepala Munasinghe Barrister.

---

1   12th Edn (1969)

a
Construction Industry Training Board v Leighton

EMPLOYMENT APPEAL TRIBUNAL

KILNER BROWN J, MR J D HUGHES AND MR A J NICOL

b 29th SEPTEMBER, 24TH OCTOBER 1977

Employment – Written particulars of terms – Amendment or substitution – Jurisdiction of tribunal – Contract setting out particulars required to be stated by statute – Contract setting out salary – Unclear whether salary inclusive or exclusive of cost of living bonus – Whether jurisdiction to amend contract where all statutory particulars included but meaning of contract
c *unclear – Contracts of Employment Act 1972, s 8(2)(5).*

The employee's contract of employment contained all the terms of employment required to be stated by the Contracts of Employment Act 1972 including the salary at which he was to be paid, but did not make it clear whether the stated salary was inclusive or exclusive of a cost of living safeguard bonus. The employee understood
d that the employers had admitted that the salary was exclusive of the bonus. The employers contested that view. The employee applied under s 8(2)*a* of the 1972 Act to amend the statement of the particulars of employment by stating that the cost of living bonus was payable in addition to the stated salary. The tribunal granted the application and added the appropriate particulars to the contract. The employers appealed.

e
Held – Although s 8(5)*b* of the 1972 Act gave a tribunal wide powers to amend or substitute the stated particulars of employment under s 8(2) that jurisdiction was exercisable only where a particular required to be stated by statute had been omitted from or not referred to in the contract and did not give a tribunal the power of the civil courts to declare the meaning of a contract or to rectify a manifest error. It
f followed that as the salary had been set out in the contract and all that was unclear was whether it included the cost of living bonus the tribunal did not have jurisdiction to entertain the application and its decision would, therefore, be set aside and the appeal allowed (see p 725 *h* to p 726 *a*, post).

Notes
g For the requirement of, and the power of an industrial tribunal in relation to, written particulars of terms of employment, see 16 Halsbury's Laws (4th Edn) paras 538, 542.
    For the Contracts of Employment Act 1972, s 8, see 42 Halsbury's Statutes (3rd Edn) 318.

Appeal
h This was an appeal by the Construction Industry Training Board against the decision of an industrial tribunal (chairman E G Lawrence Esq) sitting at Norwich on 25th May 1977 whereby it allowed an application by Gordon Russell Leighton under s 8(2) of the Contracts of Employment Act 1972 to amend the written statement of particulars of his employment supplied to him by the board pursuant to s 4 of the 1972 Act. The facts are set out in the judgment of the appeal tribunal.

j *D Broatch* for the board.
Gerald Angel for Mr Leighton.

---

a   Section 8(2) is set out at p 724 *c*, post
b   Section 8(5) is set out at p 724 *d e*, post

Cur adv vult

24th October. **KILNER BROWN J** read the following judgment of the appeal tribunal: This is an appeal by the employers against the decision of an industrial tribunal held at Norwich on 15th April 1977. On that occasion the unanimous decision of the tribunal was that the employee, Mr Leighton, succeeded in his application under s 8(2) and (5) of the Contracts of Employment Act 1972. Pursuant to their decision they amended the particulars of the contract of employment between the parties.

The relevant provisions must be set out. Neither of the sections was affected by amendment under the Employment Protection Act 1975. Section 8(2) of the Contracts of Employment Act 1972 reads as follows:

'Where a statement purporting to be a statement under section 4(1) or section 5(1) of this Act is given by an employer to an employee, and a question arises as to the particulars which ought to have been included or referred to in the statement so as to comply with the requirements of the said section 4 or the said section 5, as the case may be, either the employer or the employee may require that question to be referred to an industrial tribunal.'

Section 8(5) is in the following terms:

'On determining a reference under subsection (2) of this section, a tribunal may either confirm the particulars as included or referred to in the statement given by the employer, or may amend those particulars, or may substitute other particulars for them, as the tribunal may determine to be appropriate; and the statement shall be deemed to have been given by the employer to the employee in accordance with the decision of the tribunal.'

The contract of employment between Mr Leighton and the Construction Industry Training Board ('the board') was partly oral and partly in writing. This was because he transferred from previous employment with the Construction Group Training Association. He was not keen so to do, but the board wanted him to transfer and work with them. It was orally agreed that his salary and emoluments should be comparable with those he was already enjoying. After a preliminary discussion the personnel officer of the board wrote on 16th July 1974 making an offer of employment. The important paragraph of this letter was in the form:

'The salary grade for this appointment is 2, the range for which is at present £2,515 to £3,565 p.a. in eight annual increments of £131 p.a. You will enter the scale at £3,150 p.a. and your incremental date will be the 1st January annually. This figure includes the cost of living safeguard payment based on the Retail Prices Index as it stands at 19th July 1974. A car will be provided.'

All other terms required by the Contracts of Employment Act 1972 were contained in a schedule attached to the letter. There never was any dispute about them and nothing turns on the nature of the contract as a whole. Nor was there any omission of any of the terms required by law. By letter dated 22nd July 1974 Mr Leighton accepted the offer subject to confirmation on two points. One was the starting date and the other, which is what all the trouble is about, was expressed in these words:

'. . . my verbal acceptance to the Regional Manager in the early part of July was based on a figure of £3,150, which would then become subject to cost of living safeguard payments. Accordingly the July 19th threshold payment should be additional to the £3,150. Second I take it that the increment due on January 1st, 1975 will be a full one, and not pro rata to months of service in 1974.'

On 26th July 1974 the personnel officer wrote in these terms:

'You will be eligible for the threshold payment of 40p per week resulting from the increase in the Retail Prices Index as at 19th July and to subsequent increases. The increment in Grade 2 is £131 per annum and not pro rata to months of service in the year.'

Two things are immediately apparent. The first is that there was not a direct answer to Mr Leighton's query, and the second is that each party believed that his point of view was understood and was accepted by the other. In these circumstances we cannot understand how the industrial tribunal could decide that the matter was clear and beyond dispute. Nor again can we understand why they refused to allow the board to give explanatory evidence. It was most unfortunate that the tribunal should have devoted so much time and space to an exegesis on the principles of law which prohibit the admission of parol or extrinsic evidence to explain a contract which can without such evidence be clearly spelt out. The tribunal erred in two aspects. First, the contract was not clear and such evidence ought to have been admitted in accordance with long established principles. Second and much more important the tribunal should not have approached this aspect of the case in strict reliance on rules of evidence which apply to the law of contract. It has been said over and over both in the National Industrial Relations Court and by the Employment Appeal Tribunal that the primary function of industrial tribunals is to do justice between employer and employee and not to raise barriers to a search for a fair and common sense answer by recourse to rules of evidence which in this field of litigation may be archaic and arcane. It follows that in our unanimous opinion the decision could not be upheld for this reason alone. The answer may well have been fair and right but the method adopted was wrong.

However, as will appear, we do not and cannot allow the appeal on this basis. The more important and preliminary question is whether or not this application could be heard at all. From the recital and analysis of the facts so far adumbrated it is clear that every particular required by the statutory provisions was included in the contract of employment. The only area of dispute was whether or not the agreed salary scale in effect antedated the threshold payment. If the entry occurred, as it did, half way through the year at an expressed grade for salary scale, was the threshold payment to refer back or be delayed? Was the figure of £3,150 inclusive or exclusive of a threshold payment of £104? In one sense this was an entirely peripheral matter which did not affect the contract as a whole. It certainly was not fundamental. Of course it was important in Mr Leighton's view.

The industrial tribunal was motivated by a sympathetic understanding of Mr Leighton's position. With that sympathetic understanding we unanimously and entirely concur, and about which we shall have more to say in due course. The truth of this matter is that the industrial tribunal, in an endeavour to see that Mr Leighton got what most people would think he was entitled to get, allocated to themselves a jurisdiction which they did not have. They acted on s 8(5) of the 1972 Act, which undoubtedly gives wide powers of amendment and substitution, without giving proper consideration to the limitations imposed by s 8(2). An industrial tribunal can only embark on an exercise of amendment or substitution of particulars where there is an omission to include or refer to a statutory requirement when setting out the terms of a contract of employment. Here the salary was set out in the contract. All that was unclear was whether the supplementary bonus for one year was already included in the expressed figure. It was a case of the parties not being of the same mind as to the application of the words 'basic' and 'supplementary'. In effect the industrial tribunal was exercising the power of the civil courts to declare what a contract meant or to rectify an error manifest in an otherwise binding contract. We are unanimously of the opinion that the words of the statute do not mean and were not intended to mean that an industrial tribunal could rewrite or amend a binding contract which had one small area of misunderstanding between the parties.

This application was misconceived and should not have been entertained. The appeal must be allowed and the decision set aside.

We now turn to the wider aspect of this case and the morality thereof. We entirely agree with the industrial tribunal that Mr Leighton understood that he had obtained a clear admission that he could regard the salary of £3,150 as basic and exclusive of the £104 bonus for the previous year. If not, he would have persisted further before agreeing to take the appointment. In our view this is a clear instance where an employer who has succeeded in principle ought to exercise the magnanimity to be expected of employers in the current atmosphere of good relations between employer and employee. Any reasonable employer would add the appropriate increment by way of ex gratia payment. We were told that the board felt inhibited by the control of the government auditor. We cannot believe that any government auditor, however pedantic his approach, would wish to query such an expenditure which has in effect been vouched for and approved by an appellate tribunal exercising the powers of the High Court. The other course open to Mr Leighton would be to undergo the expense and delay of getting the matter put right by the High Court. In that, in our judgment, he would undoubtedly succeed. In such circumstances the last state of the board's accounts would be even more adverse and the government auditor would have to pass the entry, and the only additional financial benefit would be enjoyed by the lawyers engaged in totally unnecessary litigation.

Appeal allowed.

Solicitors: *Frere Cholmley & Co* (for the board); *Mills & Reeve* (for Mr Leighton).

Salim H J Merali Esq Barrister.

Ranger v Brown and others

EMPLOYMENT APPEAL TRIBUNAL

PHILLIPS J, MR T H GOFF AND MR J G C MILLIGAN

27th OCTOBER, 22nd NOVEMBER 1977

Redundancy – Dismissal by reason of redundancy – Death of employer – Renewal of contract or re-engagement by deceased's personal representative – Implied agreement to renew contract or re-engage employee – Employee continuing to do same work as under previous contract of employment – Need to show that employee and personal representative had acted in such a way that they must be taken to have agreed that employment should continue – Redundancy Payments Act 1965, Sch 4, para 3 (as substituted by the Employment Protection Act 1975, Sch 16, para 23).

Where an employer dies, his employee cannot be regarded as having had his contract of employment renewed, or as have been re-engaged under a new contract of employment, by the deceased's personal representative, for the purposes of para 3[a] of

---

a   Paragraph 3, so far as material, provides:
    ' Where by virtue of subsection (1) of section 22 of this Act the death of the deceased employer is to be treated for the purposes of this Act as a termination by him of the contract of employment, section 3 of this Act shall have effect subject to the following modifications:—
    (a) for subsection (3) there shall be substituted the following subsection—
    ' "(3) If an employee's contract of employment is renewed or he is re-engaged under a new contract of employment, by a personal representative of the deceased employer and the renewal or re-engagement takes effect not later than eight weeks after the death of the deceased employer, then, subject to subsections (5) and (8) of this section, the employee shall not be regarded as having been dismissed by reason of the ending of his employment under the previous contract." . . .'

Sch 4 to the Redundancy Payments Act 1965, merely because, following the deceased's
a death, he has continued for a short period to do the same work as he used to do under
his contract of employment with the deceased. What is required, in the absence of an
express agreement, is some indication that the deceased's personal representative
and the employee have acted in such a way that they must be taken to have agreed
that, despite the death, matters are to carry on as before. When there is no express
agreement the industrial tribunal must determine whether, having regard to any-
b thing that may have been said, to the length of time that has elapsed and the circumstances generally, what has been done is consistent only with an agreement to
continue the employment (see p 730 *a* to *e*, post).
  Ubsdell v Paterson [1973] 1 All ER 685 applied.

Notes
c For employee's entitlement to redundancy payment on termination of contract of
employment on employer's death, see 16 Halsbury's Laws (4th Edn) para 690.
  For the Redundancy Payments Act 1965, Sch 4, para 3, as substituted by the Employment Protection Act 1975, Sch 16, para 23, see 45 Halsbury's Statutes (3rd Edn)
441.

Case referred to in judgment
d
  Ubsdell v Patterson [1973] 1 All ER 685, [1973] ICR 86, Digest (Cont Vol D) 663, 816*Adm*.

Appeal
This was an appeal by Elsie Ranger, the administratrix and personal representative
of the estate of M H Ranger, against the decision of an industrial tribunal (chairman
e Arthur Morgan Esq) sitting at Leicester on 13th April 1977 which awarded Mr Arthur
Brown and Mrs J M Neat redundancy payments of £910 and £1,555·50 respectively.
By an order of the Employment Appeal Tribunal dated 4th July 1977 the Secretary
of State for Employment was added as a respondent to the appeal. The facts are set
out in the judgment of the appeal tribunal.

f Mr A C Neal for the personal representative.
  Nicholas Padfield for Mr Brown and Mrs Neat.
  Mr D G Grazebrook, Assistant Solicitor, Department of Employment, for the Secretary
    of State.

Cur adv vult

g 22nd November. **PHILLIPS J** read the following judgment of the appeal tribunal:
An industrial tribunal sitting at Leicester on 13th April 1977, by a decision dated 4th
May 1977, awarded Mr Brown and Mrs Neat redundancy payments of £910 and
£1,555·50 respectively, against the personal representative of M H Ranger, deceased,
in her representative capacity. From that decision the personal representative has
appealed and by an order of the Employment Appeal Tribunal of 4th July 1977, the
h Secretary of State for Employment was added as a respondent to the appeal, and on
the hearing of the appeal he has supported it.
  Mr Brown and Mrs Neat were employed by Mr M H Ranger for many years prior
to his death in October 1976. After his death his widow and personal representative,
being the executor of his will, carried on the business for a time, and Mr Brown and
Mrs Neat continued to do the work which they had previously done and continued to
j receive remuneration. The facts are not found with much particularity by the
industrial tribunal, but it appears that Mr Ranger died on 8th October 1976, that on
29th November a company called BPX Electro Mechanical Co Ltd assumed control
of the business, and that at some stage, not later than 11th January 1977, ownership
of the business was transferred to that company. At all material times Mr Brown
and Mrs Neat continued to work in the business and to receive remuneration.

In outline, then, the case is the not unfamiliar one where a business has changed hands and the employees have remained with the business. The legislation dealing with this situation is complicated, and the outcome will depend on the exact circumstances; but usually in such a case the employee, who will have been dismissed by the old employer when he ceases to carry on the business, will carry forward his right to a redundancy payment, with continuity of employment, against the new employer. The particular circumstance which causes the difficulty in the present case is that the old employer has died.

This is a case where at common law it would seem that the death of the employer brings to an end the contract of employment. Provision for this situation is made by s 22(1) of the Redundancy Payments Act 1965. The effect, in the circumstances of this case, is that the death of the employer is to be treated as a 'termination of the contract by the employer'. In accordance with s 3(2) ordinarily this would constitute a dismissal by the employer for the purposes of the 1965 Act, which is a sine qua non for a claim for a redundancy payment. In a case where the employee's contract of employment is renewed, or he is re-engaged, s 3(3) provides that if the conditions there set out are satisfied the employee shall not be regarded as having been dismissed, despite the fact of the ending of his employment under his previous contract. Section 3(3) cannot apply in the case of a deceased employer because the deceased employer cannot renew the contract or re-engage him. Provision for this situation, and for other situations peculiar to the fact that the employer has died, is made in Sch 4 to the 1965 Act by virtue of s 23. The relevant part for present purposes is Part I, and in particular paras 3 and 4 thereof, which have been substituted for the previous provisions by the Employment Protection Act 1975, Sch 16, Part I, para 23. Paragraph 3 introduces an amended or modified s 3(3) to be used instead of the ordinary s 3(3) in cases where the death of an employer falls to be treated for the purposes of the Act as a termination by him of the contract of employment. Briefly it provides that where the contract of employment is renewed, or the employee is re-engaged, by the personal representative of the deceased the *termination* shall not constitute a *dismissal*. Thus the underlying assumption is that the employee continues in the employment of the personal representative. Paragraph 4 deals with the case where the employee does not remain in the employment of the personal representative but the personal representative makes him an offer of employment complying with the conditions there set out, and provides that in that event the employee shall not, if the conditions set out in sub-ss (4) and (6) of s 3 are satisfied, be entitled to a redundancy payment.

On the facts so far as we know them there appear to have been three possibilities in this case: (1) Mr Brown and Mrs Neat are to be taken as having been dismissed as a result of the death of their employer, and thus entitled to an immediate redundancy payment (this is what the industrial tribunal held); or (2) their contracts of employment were renewed, or they were re-engaged, within para 3 of Sch 4, in which case they are not to be regarded as having been dismissed, and so would not be entitled to the immediate payment of a redundancy payment; or (3) they were dismissed when the business was transferred to BPX Electro Mechanical Co Ltd, with the result that, depending on the circumstances, they would be entitled to a redundancy payment from the personal representative (presumably as a personal liability) or to carry forward their claim against BPX Electro Mechanical Co Ltd.

Unfortunately, the industrial tribunal in deciding in favour of Mr Brown and Mrs Neat based their decision on para 4 of Sch 4, finding that no offer to renew or to re-engage had been made. But that was the one factual situation which was not in question. Either they are to be treated as having been dismissed as a result of the death, and therefore entitled to an immediate redundancy payment, not having had their contracts renewed, or been re-engaged, within para 3, but having remained on in some sort of limbo until BPX Electro Mechanical Co Ltd took over, or they are not to be treated as having been dismissed on the occasion of the death, having had their contracts renewed or been re-engaged, and thus not entitled to the immediate

payment of a redundancy payment, but as having been dismissed on the transfer of
a the business to BPX Electro Mechanical Co Ltd, with a claim at that date, either
immediately against the personal representative, personally, or potentially against
BPX Electro Mechanical Co Ltd, if dismissed for redundancy at some later date.

It is common ground on all sides that the industrial tribunal fell into error in deciding
the case on the basis of para 4 of Sch 4. However, counsel for Mr Brown and Mrs Neat,
submits that the findings of fact by the industrial tribunal under para 4 on the exist-
b ence or otherwise of an offer are so clear that inevitably they would have come to a
decision in his favour on the similar, but different question under para 3. We do not
agree, because it seems to us to be unsatisfactory to take findings of fact found in
answer to one question as an answer to a different question, albeit there is some
similarity between the two, but in our judgment not as great a similarity as he
suggests. Accordingly we have come to the conclusion that the appeal must be
c allowed, the order of the industrial tribunal set aside and the matter remitted to be
reheard.

There is no doubt that in the case of Mr Brown and Mrs Neat the result of the death
was, for the purpose of the Redundancy Payments Act 1965, to terminate their contracts of employment. Prima facie, in accordance with s 3, they were therefore
dismissed. Prima facie, therefore, they were entitled to a redundancy payment by
d virtue of s 22(2) of the 1965 Act. The first question which will arise on the rehearing,
therefore, is whether the employer can show in the terms of para 3 of Sch 4 that their
contracts of employment were renewed, or that they were re-engaged under new
contracts of employment, by the personal representative, in such circumstances as to
satisfy the other conditions required by para 3. If the employer can show that to be
the case then they are not to be regarded as having been dismissed, and so for that
e reason cannot be entitled to a redundancy payment. If the industrial tribunal came
to the conclusion that that was the situation, it would then be necessary to go on to
consider whether they were dismissed on the occasion of the transfer of the business
to BPX Electro Mechanical Co Ltd, and were then entitled to a redundancy payment
against the personal representative, or whether their claim was postponed to be
carried forward potentially against that company as a result of their continuing
f employment.

The controversial question concerns the right approach in circumstances such as
those which exist in the present case to the question whether a contract of employment
has been renewed, or an employee has been re-engaged under a new contract of
employment, by the personal representative of the deceased employer. It is not
altogether clear how important the question is in practice. Where the sole proprietor
g of a business dies, there is bound to be a period of confusion while matters are being
sorted out and the likelihood is that most employees will carry on doing the work
which they did previously, and continue to be remunerated, on a somewhat vague
and undeclared basis. As a matter of law there must be some contractual relationship
during this period between the employee and the personal representative of the
deceased, imprecise though it may be, and only capable of being deduced from the
h facts. If one is to say that if such a situation continues for several weeks the employee
is to be regarded as having had his contract renewed, or as having been re-engaged
under a new contract of employment, by the personal representative of the deceased
employer, no redundancy payment will be payable. And in practice it seems likely
that this will be the usual situation because in nearly every case such a period of
confusion is unavoidable. But the result is not as alarming as it sounds, for either the
j employee will continue to serve on indefinitely in which case it is reasonable that he
does not get a redundancy payment unless and until he is eventually, maybe years
later, dismissed for redundancy. Or, he will be dismissed after a short lapse of time,
in which case the dismissal itself will constitute a fresh dismissal entitling him to
receive a redundancy payment if the reason for the dismissal is redundancy.
Nonetheless, it is difficult to foresee every case and it is a matter of potential
importance to know how to approach this question.

We do not think that it can have been the intention of the enactment to regard a contract of employment as having been renewed, or an employee re-engaged, merely because for a short period after the death of the employer the employee continues to do the same work as he did previously, and continues to be remunerated. Paragraphs 3 and 4 seem to take the period of eight weeks as being the settling down period, and it seems to be in general conformity with the scheme of the 1965 Act that in situations of this kind there should be opportunity for reflection, and an avoidance so far as possible of basing entitlement to benefits on unnecessary technicalities. Though the circumstances were different, and the reasoning cannot be applied directly, the philosophy apparent in a case such as *Ubsdell v Patterson*[1] seems to be relevant. In other words, we have reached the conclusion that an industrial tribunal is not obliged to say: 'This employee continued to work for a few days after the death of his employer; the death of his employer terminated his contract of employment; therefore the continued rendering of services and the continued receipt of remuneration is consistent only with the existence of a contract of employment between the employee and the personal representative of the deceased; and therefore the contract of employment has been renewed, or the employee has been re-engaged.' Section 3(3), introduced for this purpose by para 3 of Sch 4, is looking back to the contract of employment between the deceased and the employee and, when it speaks of renewal or re-engagement, has in mind the renewal of that contract, or re-engagement under a new contract in place of that old contract; and it seems to us that what is contemplated is some indication that the personal representative and the employee have agreed, or acted in such a way that they must be taken to have agreed, that, despite the death, matters so far as they are concerned shall carry on as before. We do not by this mean to say that there must have been some express discussion, but the situation must be one either where the personal representative and the employee have agreed to carry on together or where, though there is no evidence of express agreement, what has been done is only consistent with such a basis. Where there has been discussion and agreement no problem arises. Where there has not it is a question on which the industrial tribunal must reach its own conclusion, having regard to anything which may have been said, to the length of time elapsed and to the circumstances of the case generally. In an ordinary case the problem is fairly simple, because the longer the employee remains at work the easier the problem is to answer. The difficulty only arises in a case such as the present when the time is relatively short owing to the transfer of the business, with the result that it cannot be said with certainty what would have happened had there been no transfer.

Appeal allowed. Case remitted to the industrial tribunal for rehearing.

Solicitors: *Adam, Burn & Metson*, agents for *Rich & Carr*, Leicester (for Mr Brown and Mrs Neat).

Salim H J Merali Barrister.

---

1 [1973] 1 All ER 685

Attorney-General v British Broadcasting Corporation

QUEEN'S BENCH DIVISION
LORD WIDGERY CJ, WIEN AND KENNETH JONES JJ
17th FEBRUARY 1978

Contempt of court – Publications concerning legal proceedings – Court – Inferior court – Local valuation court – Defendants proposing to broadcast television programme on issue pending before local valuation court – Plaintiffs seeking injunction to restrain broadcast – Whether local valuation court 'an inferior court' – Whether comment on issue pending before local valuation court contempt of court – General Rate Act 1967, s 88 – RSC Ord 52, r 1(2)(a)(iii).

Having regard to the task a local valuation court performs, its procedure, the method of selecting its members, and generally the extent to which its duties and creation are consistent with what is meant by a court, a local valuation court constituted under s 88 of the General Rate Act 1967 is 'an inferior court', within the meaning of RSC Ord 52, r 1(2)(a)(iii)[a], since its decisions are final and binding, it is required to hear the parties and have witnesses called before it, it has the power to take evidence on oath, and it has a formal procedure. Accordingly, the publication of comments on proceedings pending in a local valuation court which may tend to prevent or inhibit the fair hearing of those proceedings is a contempt of court (see p 734 *g* to *j*, p 735 *e* and p 736 *a* to *e* post).

Dictum of Fry LJ in *Royal Aquarium and Summer and Winter Garden Society Ltd v Parkinson* [1891-4] All ER Rep at 434 applied.

Dictum of Scrutton LJ in *Mersey Docks and Harbour Board v West Derby Assessment Committee and Bottomley* [1932] 1 KB at 104 distinguished.

Notes

For what constitutes a court, see 10 Halsbury's Laws (4th Edn) paras 701, 702, and for cases on the subject, see 16 Digest (Repl) 113-115, 1-20.

For the General Rate Act 1967, s 88, see 27 Halsbury's Statutes (3rd Edn) 182.

Cases referred to in judgments

Mersey Docks and Harbour Board v West Derby Assessment Committee and Bottomley [1932] 1 KB 40, [1931] All ER Rep 409, 101 LJKB 8, 145 LT 592, 95 JP 186, 29 LGR 576, [1926-31] 2 BRA 846, CA, 16 Digest (Repl) 114, 12.

Royal Aquarium and Summer and Winter Garden Society Ltd v Parkinson [1892] 1 QB 431, [1891-4] All ER Rep 429, 61 LJQB 409, 66 LT 513, 56 JP 404, CA, 16 Digest (Repl) 114, 5.

Cases also cited

Attorney-General v Times Newspapers Ltd [1973] 3 All ER 54, [1974] AC 273, HL.

R v Daily Herald, ex parte Bishop of Norwich [1932] 2 KB 402, DC.

R v Daily Mail, ex parte Farworth [1921] 2 KB 733, DC.

R v St Mary Abbots, Kensington, Assessment Committee [1891] 1 QB 378, CA.

Shell Co of Australia Ltd v Federal Comr of Taxation [1931] AC 275, [1930] All ER Rep 671, PC.

Society of Medical Officers of Health v Hope (Valuation Officer) [1960] 1 All ER 317, [1960] AC 551, HL.

---

a Rule 1(2), so far as material, is set out at p 733 *e f*, post

Summonses

By a summons dated 17th February 1978, the plaintiff, Her Majesty's Attorney-
General, claimed an injunction to restrain the defendants, the British Broadcasting
Corporation ('the BBC'), by themselves, their servants or agents or otherwise from
broadcasting or causing or authorising to be broadcast a programme dealing with
matters relating to the Exclusive Brethren and the matter pending before the local
valuation court at Andover. By a summons, also dated 17th February 1978, the
plaintiffs, David Roy Dible and Laurence Norton Marsh, claimed an injunction
restraining the BBC from broadcasting on television or otherwise a new television
broadcast entitled 'Anno Domini—Brethren' previously broadcast on television on or
about 26th September 1976 or any part of that television broadcast, and such further
or other injunctions as might be necessary or proper for the purpose of restraining the BBC from committing any contempt of court in relation to certain proceedings
in the Chancery Division of the High Court of Justice, and in relation to an appeal of
the plaintiff David Roy Dible in respect of hereditaments at East Street, Andover,
Hampshire, pending before a local valuation court intended to meet at Andover.
The plaintiffs sought interlocutory injunctions before Lawson J, sitting as a judge in
chambers, and the matter was referred to and heard by the Divisional Court. The
facts are set out in the judgment of Lord Widgery CJ.

Harry Woolf for the Attorney-General.
Charles Sparrow QC, F M Ferris and *Gavin Lightman* for the plaintiffs Mr Dible and Mr
  Marsh.
A T Hoolahan QC, Richard Walker and *Harry Sales* for the BBC.

LORD WIDGERY CJ. There are two actions concerned in the application before
the court today, but I propose to refer only to that brought by Her Majesty's Attorney-
General because I believe that the second action raises the same issues and abides by
the decision of this court in the first case. In the first case the action began by writ
with Her Majesty's Attorney-General as plaintiff and the British Broadcasting
Corporation as defendants.

The statement of claim, as it appears from the endorsement on the writ, is for an
injunction to restrain the defendants by themselves, their servants or agents or
otherwise from broadcasting or causing or authorising to be broadcast a programme
dealing with matters relating to the Exclusive Brethren and the matter pending
before the local valuation court at Andover.

The story which lies behind that claim and of which the court has been apprised
today is just this. The religious sect who call themselves the Exclusive Brethren are
having a little trouble with the rating authorities. They seek to have themselves
recognised as being of such status that their places of worship achieve rating relief
under s 39 of the General Rate Act 1967. Essentially what they have to show for that
purpose is that the building in question is used for a place of religious worship, and of
public religious worship at that. We know no more about the issue between the
Exclusive Brethren and the rating authority in Andover except that that is liable to be
the issue which has to be determined between them, and we are told that the date
fixed for the determination of that issue is 10th March 1978.

The BBC come into the matter in this way. They have recorded, and indeed have
once transmitted, a programme concerning the Exclusive Brethren. Again we have
been supplied with a transcript of the text of the broadcast, but we have not had
time to look at it because this is a matter which has had to be dealt with rather
urgently. However, it can be assumed, we understand, for present purposes that the
proposed broadcast is not particularly complimentary to the Exclusive Brethren, and
moreover, which is far more important for present purposes, it does raise the very
issue which is going to come up before the local valuation court on 10th March,

namely it is going to raise the question, amongst other things, of whether the Exclu-
a sive Brethren can claim in respect of their premises at Andover that those premises
are places of public religious worship.

Of course it is now well-known in view of the developments of the law in recent
years that for anyone, be it a broadcasting corporation, a newspaper or the like, to
comment on litigation which is pending that person or body runs a severe and
immediate risk of contempt of court because publications of that kind, which may
b tend to prevent the fair trial of proceedings, are open to challenge as contempt of
court and may bring appropriate punishment in their train. Moreover, it is now
clearly established that not only an individual who is injured by this kind of contempt
of court can bring proceedings but Her Majesty's Attorney-General has the right, and,
I think, now the duty, to bring before the court matters which seem to him to be of
sufficient seriousness and which involve the vice of being liable to control or inhibit
c legal proceedings which ought to be freely available to the parties.

One begins to understand at once now why this litigation began. The writ was only
issued this morning, so no time has been lost. The injunction is sought by the Attorney-
General on the footing that the proposed broadcast, which is to take place next
Sunday, two days from now, will amount to a contempt of court and ought to be
restrained before it is published and not be the subject of proceedings ex post facto.
d We have had the maximum assistance from counsel today, and I would like to express
our gratitude to them all. So much so that the issues have been narrowed down very
quickly to a very limited scope indeed.

First of all one must look at the rules of court to remind oneself of the rules under
which we operate. The appropriate rule is RSC Ord 52, r 1, the important parts of
which are:

e
> '(1) The power of the High Court or Court of Appeal to punish for contempt of
> court may be exercised by an order of committal.
> '(2) Where contempt of court—(a) is committed in connection with—... (iii)
> proceedings in an inferior court ... then, subject to paragraph (4), an order of
> committal may be made only by a Divisional Court of the Queen's Bench
f > Division ...'

At a very early stage in the proceedings it was made clear to us that the real issue
between the parties today is whether the local valuation court which is going to
pronounce on this rating issue in Andover on 10th March is or is not an inferior
court for the purposes of the order. If, as counsel for the Attorney-General maintains,
g it is an inferior court, then the BBC, with great propriety if I may say so, will not
proceed to put the programme on the air at all. If, on the other hand, counsel does
not succeed in satisfying us that this is an inferior court, then the action will be
dismissed and the BBC will be free to carry on.

There is again no dispute about the meaning of the word 'inferior'. The local
valuation court, if it be a court at all, is accepted as being an inferior court. So one
h gets down to bedrock and right down to the one point on which these proceedings
depend, namely is the local valuation court at Andover an inferior court as opposed
to any other variety of tribunal which one may choose to mention?

Before one tries to decide whether it is a court or not, it is necessary to get accustomed
to the features which are possessed by a local valuation court. We have been reminded
that such courts are the successors of the local assessment committees which before
j 1948 were responsible for making up the rating lists and charging rates to occupiers.
In the reformation of local government which took place in 1948 the local assessment
committees went and the local valuation court came in instead. The General Rate
Act 1967, as amended, is now the authority for that purpose.

If we look at s 76 we get some idea of the procedure which is followed when assessments are subject to challenge before the local valuation court. Section 76(1) provides:

'Where a copy of a proposal is transmitted to the clerk to a local valuation panel . . . it shall be the duty of the chairman or a deputy chairman of that panel to arrange for the convening of such a court.'

Thus, the court is convened as required. When there is work for it to do it is convened for the purpose. Section 76(2) provides:

'The procedure of a local valuation court shall, subject to any regulations made in that behalf by the Minister, and subject to subsection (3) of this section, be such as the court may determine; and the court—(a) shall sit in public, unless the court otherwise order on the application of any party to the appeal and upon being satisfied that the interests of one or more parties to the appeal would be prejudicially affected; and (b) may take evidence on oath and shall have power for that purpose to administer oaths.'

One has to notice all the features in that section which tend to point towards the local valuation court being a court. There is obviously no definition of 'court' for this purpose or we should not have taken the time we have in trying to discover the meaning of the word. The meaning of the word 'court' in the context of the General Rate Act 1967 is, in my judgment, largely to be taken from such provisions as I have read in s 76. Then we ought to look at ss 88 and 89 which are concerned with the manning of the local valuation court. This again can be of assistance in deciding on the character of the tribunal. Section 88 provides in sub-s (1) for convening the court as required, and we have dealt with that already. I think the principal reference in this section is sub-s (5), which provides:

'Subject to subsection (6) of this section, a local valuation court shall consist of—(a) either the chairman of the local valuation panel or the deputy chairman (or, if more than one, one of the deputy chairmen) of the panel; and (b) two other members of the panel selected in accordance with the scheme under which the panel is constituted.'

Thus, the membership comes from a panel, that is to say a group of people who have been associated and appointed for this purpose, and the precise constitution of the panel is a matter of local provision under local schemes. Once the panel is created then the members are drawn from it to man the local valuation courts as required.

Counsel for the Attorney-General with that material behind him, invites us to consider the question 'court or no' in this context by looking to see what features of the arrangements that I have referred to are pointers to the tribunal being a court and what features, if any, point the other way. He says, when one comes to count the pointers towards this tribunal being a court, the first point to note is that it produces final and binding decisions. Subject of course to the appellate system which may reverse decisions later on, the decisions of the local valuation court are final and binding, just like any other court.

The requirement to hear the parties and to have witnesses called before it is again characteristic of a court. I do not say that it is only courts which employ that procedure because that would not be true, but it is a procedure which is entirely consistent with the body being a court, and tends to throw its own weight into the scale on that side.

The power to take evidence on oath I regard as an important feature of a court, and the fact that the tribunal has that power is a substantial pointer to it being a court in this context.

Then we were referred by counsel for the Attorney-General to two other references on this part of the case. Firstly, he referred to *Royal Aquarium and Summer and Winter Garden Society Ltd v Parkinson*[1]. Two passages in the judgment of Fry LJ give me a

---

1   [1892] 1 QB 431, [1891-4] All ER Rep 429

great deal of assistance in trying to decide on which side of the line this particular
a tribunal must fall. Fry LJ said[1]:

> '. . . a military Court of inquiry, "though not a Court of record, nor a Court of
> law, nor coming within the ordinary definition of a Court of justice, is neverthe-
> less a Court duly and legally constituted and recognised in the articles of war and
> many Acts of Parliament." I do not desire to attempt any definition of a "court".
> *b* It is obvious that, according to our law, a court may perform various functions.
> Parliament is a court. Its duties as a whole are deliberative and legislative:
> the duties of a part of it only are judicial. It is nevertheless a court. There are
> many other courts which, though not Courts of justice, are nevertheless courts
> according to our law. There are, for instance, courts of investigation, like the
> coroner's court. In my judgment, therefore, the existence of the immunity
> *c* claimed does not depend upon the question whether the subject-matter of
> consideration is a Court of Justice, but whether it is a Court in law.'

Then he says this[2]:

> 'Courts are, for the most part, controlled and presided over by some person
> selected as specially qualified for the purpose; and they have generally a fixed
> *d* and dignified course of procedure, which tends to minimise the risks that might
> flow from this absolute immunity. These considerations do not apply to bodies
> such as I have mentioned.'

I get a great deal of assistance from that passage because the idea that a formal
procedure such as is employed in courts is a factor in deciding this question is a
proposition which appeals greatly to me.
e Then further help is to be obtained in a number of other authorities which were put
before us. I would refer to the case of *Mersey Docks and Harbour Board v West Derby
Assessment Committee and Bottomley*[3]. The passage I would wish to refer to dealt with
an assessment committee under the old system of rating. Scrutton LJ, in the middle
of his judgment, makes this observation[4]:

> *f* 'In my opinion the proceeding was commenced when the objector called upon
> the Assessment Committee to hear him and his witnesses and to give a "decision"
> from which he could appeal. In my opinion the Assessment Committee could be
> ordered by mandamus to hear and determine. The prerogative writs will run to
> a body which is not "a Court," and it may be that like some kinds of Licensing
> Justices the Assessment Committee is not "a Court"; it does not hear evidence on
> *g* oath and has no particular rules of procedure, though it acts under a statutory
> duty and authority . . .'

Counsel for the BBC has naturally enough stressed the cases, and they are more than
a few, where doubt has been expressed as to whether an assessment committee is a
court, and here Scrutton LJ is saying that in his opinion an assessment committee
may not be a court. But look at the reasons he gives for that. Why may it not be a
h court? Because it does not hear evidence on oath. It has no particular rules of procedure, although it acts under a statutory duty. Those are the factors where the
assessment committee is differentiated from the local valuation court.
So one could go on, and, as counsel for the BBC very properly said, if this were not
a matter of the utmost urgency, there would be a great deal of other authority which
j counsel's industry would put before us.

---

1 [1892] 1 QB 431 at 446, 447, [1891-4] All ER Rep 429 at 434
2 [1892] 1 QB 431 at 447, 448, [1891-4] All ER Rep 429 at 434
3 [1932] 1 KB 40, [1931] All ER Rep 409
4 [1932] 1 KB 40 at 104

For my part, I find that the matter can be disposed of without undue difficulty. We must of course in deciding whether this tribunal is a court for present purposes *a* look at the task it performs, the procedure which it adopts, the method by which its members are selected, and generally the question of how far it and its duties and its creation are consistent with our general ideas in this country of what is meant by a court.

I am bound to say I think that the local valuation court is one of the clearest examples of an inferior court that we meet in the field of administrative justice. I am *b* not in the least bit deterred from saying that by the fact that there was some considerable doubt about the status of the local assessment committee. So be it. There was doubt, and it may be there remains some doubt as to what its status was. But I think that the local valuation court is a wholly different creation from the local assessment committee, and I am not in the least bit deterred by the authorities dealing with the latter tribunal.   *c*

I am quite satisfied, for my own part, that the local valuation court which will sit at Andover on 10th March will be an inferior court for the purposes of RSC Ord 52. Having reached that stage, I understand counsel's concession to be that the BBC will abandon their intention to transmit this programme.

d

WIEN J. I agree.

KENNETH JONES J.   I agree also.

No order save as to costs.   *e*

Solicitors: *Treasury Solicitor; George Carter & Co* (for the plaintiffs Mr Dible and Mr Marsh); *E A C Bostock* (for the BBC).

Lea Josse Barrister.

a

Sargent (Inspector of Taxes) v Barnes

CHANCERY DIVISION
OLIVER J

b   1st, 2nd MARCH 1978

Income tax – Deduction in computing profits – Travelling expenses – Travel between home and place of work – Dental surgeon maintaining a laboratory to repair, alter and manufacture dentures – Laboratory between taxpayer's home and surgery – Taxpayer calling at his laboratory on his journey to and from his home to the surgery – Whether expense of travelling between
c   *laboratory and surgery wholly and exclusively laid out for purpose of taxpayer's practice – Income and Corporation Taxes Act 1970, s 130(a).*

The taxpayer, a dental surgeon, maintained a laboratory between his home and his surgery. The laboratory was about one mile from his home and about 11 miles from the surgery. The laboratory was maintained for the purpose of the repair, alteration
d and making of dentures. Each morning on his way to the surgery the taxpayer spent about ten minutes at the laboratory to collect completed work. Each evening after closing his surgery the taxpayer called at the laboratory to deliver dentures and other articles to the technician working there. It was not in dispute that the laboratory was a proper adjunct to his practice and that the work done there was exclusively referable to the practice. In computing his profits under Sch D, Case II for the years 1972-73
e to 1974-75, the taxpayer claimed that his work commenced each day when he arrived at the laboratory and that his travelling expenses between the laboratory and the surgery were expenses wholly and exclusively incurred for the purposes of carrying on his profession and accordingly were allowable deductions under s 130(a)[a] of the Income and Corporation Taxes Act 1970. The General Commissioners concluded that it was absolutely necessary for the taxpayer to travel back and forth from his
f laboratory to the surgery to enable him to carry on his profession and accordingly upheld the taxpayer's claim. The Crown appealed.

Held – On the facts, it could not be said that the taxpayer was in any relevant sense carrying on his profession at the laboratory. Thus the travelling expenses incurred by the taxpayer were for the purpose of enabling him to get from his private residence
g to his surgery. The fact that it served the purpose also of enabling him to stop at an intermediate point to carry out an activity exclusively referable to his profession could not affect the purpose of the journey once the intermediate point was passed. In the circumstances, the commissioners could not have properly arrived at the conclusion that expenses incurred by the taxpayer in travelling between the laboratory and the surgery had been incurred wholly and exclusively for the purpose of the
h practice. The appeal would therefore be allowed (see p 745 *b c* and *f* to *h*, post).

Notes
For deductions in respect of travelling expenses in computing profits for income tax purposes, see 20 Halsbury's Laws (3rd Edn) 158-161, paras 277-279, and for cases on the subject, see 28(1) Digest (Reissue) 244, 347-349, 760-761, 1253-1264.
j   For the Income and Corporation Taxes Act 1970, s 130, see 33 Halsbury's Statutes (3rd Edn) 182.

---

a   Section 130, so far as material, is set out at p 741 *b* and *c*, post

Cases referred to in judgment

Bentleys, Stokes & Lowless v Beeson (Inspector of Taxes) [1952] 2 All ER 82, 33 Tax Cas
491, 31 ATC 229, [1952] TR 239, 45 R & IT 461, CA, 28(1) Digest (Reissue) 150, 465.

Bowden (Inspector of Taxes) v Russell and Russell [1965] 2 All ER 258, [1965] 1 WLR 711,
42 Tax Cas 301, 44 ATC 74, [1965] TR 89, 28(1) Digest (Reissue) 244, 761.

Horton (Inspector of Taxes) v Young [1971] 3 All ER 412, [1972] Ch 157, [1971] 3 WLR
348, 47 Tax Cas 60, 50 ATC 207, [1971] TR 181, CA; *affg* [1971] 2 All ER 351, [1972]
Ch 157, [1971] 2 WLR 236, 47 Tax Cas 60, Digest (Cont Vol D) 467, *1264*.

Newsom v Robertson (Inspector of Taxes) [1952] 2 All ER 728, [1953] Ch 7, 33 Tax Cas 452,
31 ATC 429, [1952] TR 401, 45 R & IT 679, CA, 28(1) Digest (Reissue) 244, 760.

Cases also cited

Caillebotte (Inspector of Taxes) v Quinn [1975] 2 All ER 412, [1975] 1 WLR 731, [1975]
STC 265, 50 Tax Cas 222.

Edwards (Inspector of Taxes) v Bairstow [1955] 3 All ER 48, [1956] AC 14, 36 Tax Cas 207,
HL.

Hillyer v Leeks (Inspector of Taxes) [1976] STC 490.

Pools (Inspector of Taxes) v Owen [1969] 2 All ER 1, [1970] AC 244, 45 Tax Cas 571, HL.

Case stated

1. At a meeting of the Commissioners for the General Purposes of the Income Tax
for the Division of Northleach in the County of Gloucester held on 10th September
1975 in the Clerk to the Commissioners' Office, Abbey Terrace, Winchcombe in the
County of Gloucester, Mr Peter Albert Barnes ('the taxpayer') who carried on his
profession as a dental surgeon at Wentwood House, High Street, Winchcombe,
appealed against assessments made on him under Case II of Sch D as follows: 1972-73,
£2,700; 1973-74, £3,600; 1974-75, £3,600. All three years were based on one set of
accounts for the year ended 31st May 1973, the taxpayer having commenced business
in that year.

2. The taxpayer, who lived at Badgeworth, near Cheltenham, and maintained a
dental laboratory at The Reddings, Cheltenham, and had his dental surgery in
Winchcombe, travelled by motor car each day from his home in Badgeworth to his
laboratory in Cheltenham (a distance of one mile) and thence to his surgery in
Winchcombe (a distance of ten to 11 miles). The point at issue was whether the
travelling expenses of the taxpayer between his laboratory in Cheltenham and his
surgery in Winchcombe was an allowable deduction for income tax purposes. The
amount of the travelling expenses for the full year amounted to £170 and of that the
taxpayer was seeking to deduct £160. (The amount of the expenses was not in dispute).

3. Mr Mobley of Messrs Marcus Hazlewood, accountants of Cheltenham, appeared
for the taxpayer.

4. The taxpayer gave evidence before the commissioners.

5. The following facts were admitted or proved. (1) The taxpayer lived at Badgeworth, near Cheltenham. (2) The taxpayer maintained a dental laboratory for the
purpose of the repair, alteration and making of dentures in an outbuilding at his
father's residence, 'Glenleigh', The Reddings, Cheltenham. (3) The taxpayer did not
pay any rent to his father, but he did contribute towards the cost of the electricity.
The taxpayer provided his own gas. (4) A self-employed technician worked on a
part-time basis (although exclusively for the taxpayer) at the laboratory where he
carried out the taxpayer's work only. The technician did not receive a regular wage:
he was paid a set rate for each job which he carried out. (5) It was necessary for the
taxpayer to have the services of a laboratory to carry out his work, since his was a
one man practice, the only alternative to his having his own laboratory being for him
to use a postal service run by a commercial laboratory. However it was far preferable
for him to have his own laboratory since its dental services must be readily available
and speedily executed in the interests of the patients. (6) Each morning on his way

to his surgery the taxpayer spent about ten minutes at the laboratory in order to
a collect completed work, and, as necessary, to discuss matters with his technician.
(7) Each evening, after closing his surgery in Winchcombe, the taxpayer called at his
laboratory in Cheltenham in order to deliver dentures and other articles which he
had received during the day and during the course of his evening visits to his laboratory, he sometimes spent 30 minutes to one hour advising on or working on dentures
before proceeding on his journey homewards. (8) The taxpayer visited patients on
b his way from the surgery to the laboratory about twice a week. (9) On about a dozen
occasions in a year, the taxpayer had to travel from his surgery to his laboratory and
back during working hours.

6. The taxpayer contended that to carry out his profession properly it was essential
for him to visit his laboratory every morning before going to his surgery and each
evening on his way home and that his work commenced each day when he arrived
c at the laboratory and that the journey from the laboratory to the surgery each day
was wholly and exclusively for the purposes of his profession.

7. It was contended by the Crown: (a) that the travelling expenses claimed by the
taxpayer were not laid out wholly and exclusively for the purposes of the taxpayer's
profession and were not deductible in computing his profits on account of s 130(a)
of the Income and Corporation Taxes Act 1970; (b) that the expenses were incurred for
d the purpose or partly for the purpose of enabling the taxpayer to journey to and from
his home and his surgery and, as this purpose was a private purpose distinct from the
purposes of his profession, they were precluded from being deducted in computing
his profits by s 130(b) of the 1970 Act; (c) that no part of the expenses claimed was an
allowable deduction.

[Paragraph 8 listed the cases[1] cited to the commissioners.]
e 9. Having considered the facts and heard the arguments on each side and giving
the matter very careful consideration, the commissioners came to the conclusion that
it was absolutely necessary for the taxpayer to travel back and forth from his laboratory in Cheltenham in order to enable him to carry on his profession as a dentist.
They, accordingly, decided that the expenditure in respect of the travelling expenses
as claimed, namely £160, was an allowable expenditure. They then determined the
f assessments in the following figures which were agreed by the Crown and the taxpayer on the basis that their decision in the contentious matter was correct.

> 1972-73　Profits—£5,074　Capital allowances—£1,457
> 1973-74　Profits—£5,536　Capital allowances—£20
> 1974-75　Profits—£5,536　Capital allowances—£15

g 10. Immediately after the determination of the appeal the Crown declared its dissatisfaction therewith as being erroneous in point of law and, in due course, required
the commissioners to state a case for the opinion of the High Court, pursuant to s 56
of the Taxes Management Act 1970.

Brian Davenport for the Crown.
h *Peter Trevett* for the taxpayer.

OLIVER J. This is the Crown's appeal from the Commissioners for the General Purposes of the Income Tax for the Division of Northleach, Gloucestershire, who, on 10th
September 1975, allowed the appeal of the taxpayer against three assessments for
the years 1972-73, 1973-74 and 1974-75.
j The taxpayer is a dentist living at Badgeworth, about two miles south-west of the
city of Cheltenham, and having his surgery at Winchcombe, some five or six miles to

1 *Bentleys, Stokes & Lowless v Beeson (Inspector of Taxes)* [1952] 2 All ER 82, 33 Tax Cas 491;
Horton (Inspector of Taxes) v Young [1971] 3 All ER 412, [1972] Ch 157, 47 Tax Cas 60, CA;
Newsom v Robertson (Inspector of Taxes) [1952] 2 All ER 728, [1953] Ch 7, 33 Tax Cas 452, CA

the north-east of that city. The point at issue is whether, in computing the profits of
his trade for the purposes of Sch D income tax, the taxpayer is entitled to deduct   a
certain travelling expenses (the amount of which is not in dispute), being the cost
attributable to travel between a dental laboratory maintained by the taxpayer close
to his home in Badgeworth and the taxpayer's surgery, a distance of ten to 11 miles.

The facts found by the commissioners were that the taxpayer at all material times
maintained a dental laboratory in an outbuilding in the curtilage of his father's
private house at The Reddings, Cheltenham. That is approximately one mile from   b
the taxpayer's own residence, and a map which has, by agreement, been put before
me shows that it lies almost directly to the north. Badgeworth lies between two
main roads, each leading into Cheltenham, and there is no finding by the commissioners as to which constitutes the most convenient route to the surgery. There appears,
however, purely as a matter of distance, to be no significant difference between the
northern route (which runs immediately to the south of The Reddings) and the   c
southern route. The arrangement between the taxpayer and his father is that he
pays no rent, but he contributes to the cost of electricity and discharges the whole
cost of the gas used in the outbuilding.

At this laboratory, a self-employed, part-time dental technician (working exclusively for the taxpayer) carries out work for the taxpayer at a set rate per job. The
taxpayer practises on his own, and if he did not have available locally the services of   d
a technician it would be necessary for him to have work carried out through a postal
service run by a commercial laboratory. It is not in dispute that the laboratory is a
proper adjunct of the practice, or that the work done there is exclusively referable
to the practice.

The important findings as regards the journeys, the expenses of which are claimed
as deductions, are these: e

'Each morning on his way to his surgery, the [taxpayer] spent about ten
minutes at the laboratory in order to collect completed work, and, as necessary,
to discuss matters with his technician . . . Each evening after closing his surgery
in Winchcombe, the [taxpayer] called at his laboratory in Cheltenham in order
to deliver dentures and other articles which he had received during the day and   f
during the course of his evening visits to his laboratory, he sometimes spent
30 minutes to one hour advising on or working on dentures before proceeding
on his journey homewards . . . The [taxpayer] visited patients on his way from
the surgery to the laboratory about twice a week . . . On about a dozen occasions
in a year, the [taxpayer] had to travel from his surgery to his laboratory and back
during working hours.'   g

The case sets out the taxpayer's contention in these terms:

'The [taxpayer] contended that to carry out his profession properly, it was
essential for him to visit his laboratory every morning before going to his surgery,
and each evening on his way home and that his work commenced each day
when he arrived at the laboratory and that the journey from the laboratory to   h
the surgery each day was wholly and exclusively for the purposes of his profession.'

The commissioners' conclusions on those findings were as follows:

'Having considered the facts and heard the argument on each side and giving
the matter very careful consideration, we came to the conclusion that it is absolutely necessary for the [taxpayer] to travel back and forth from his laboratory   j
in Cheltenham, in order to enable him to carry on his profession as a dentist and
accordingly, we decided that the expenditure in respect of the travelling expenses
as claimed, namely £160, is an allowable expenditure.'

From that conclusion the Crown now appeal.

Counsel for the Crown's first submission is that the commissioners' conclusion is
a wrong in law because it propounds a wholly wrong test for whether expenditure is
deductible for the purposes of Sch D income tax. The matter is regulated by s 130
of the Income and Corporation Taxes Act 1970 which, so far as relevant, is in these
terms:

b   'Subject to the provisions of the Tax Acts, in computing the amount of the
profits or gains to be charged under Case I or Case II of Schedule D, no sum shall
be deducted in respect of—(*a*) any disbursements or expenses, not being money
wholly and exclusively laid out or expended for the purposes of the trade,
profession or vocation, (*b*) any disbursements or expenses of maintenance of the
parties, their families or establishments, or any sums expended for any other
domestic or private purposes distinct from the purposes of the trade, profession
c   or vocation . . .'

In asking themselves, therefore, whether it was necessary for the taxpayer to travel
back and forth, the commissioners were, quite simply, asking themselves the wrong
question, because the fact that expenditure is necessary is no guide to whether it is
exclusively incurred for the purposes of a trade. Thus, expenditure which can be
d shown to be exclusively laid out for the purposes of the trade is not disqualified for
deduction because it is not strictly necessary to incur it in order to carry on the trade:
see *Bentleys, Stokes & Lowless v Beeson (Inspector of Taxes)*[1]. Equally, it was no doubt
necessary for the taxpayer in *Newsom v Robertson (Inspector of Taxes)*[2] to incur expenditure in travelling between his home and his chambers, because without doing so he
could not have carried on his practice; but that did not render the cost of his journey
e deductible as an expense incurred exclusively for the purposes of his profession.
Counsel for the taxpayer suggests that, in applying the test which they did, the
commissioners were in fact applying the more stringent test applicable to allowances
for Sch E tax, where it has to be shown that the expenditure is not only incurred
exclusively in the performance of the duties of the office or employment in question
but that it is necessary for the carrying out of those duties. Their decision, therefore,
f he submits, embraced, sub silentio, the notion that the expenditure in the instant case
was referable wholly and exclusively to the taxpayer's practice as a dentist. But the
commissioners do not so state, and I do not find myself able to read into their decision
something which is not there, either expressly or by necessary implication. So the
question with which I am confronted is: on the facts as found by the commissioners,
were they bound to find either that the expenditure was exclusively incurred for the
g purposes of the taxpayer's trade or business, or that it clearly was not; or is this, as a
third possibility, a case which I ought to remit to the commissioners for further
findings?
Now it is clearly established by *Newsom v Robertson*[2], an authority binding on me,
that the costs of a professional man's journeys between his home and his place of
work are not, or are not necessarily, costs incurred exclusively for the purposes of his
h profession, even if he choses to do part of his professional work at his home. To
quote from the judgment of Romer LJ in that case[3], 'the object of the journeys,
both morning and evening, is not to enable a man to do his work, but to live away
from it'.
The question in this case arises in relation to journeys from and to a point intermediate between the principal place of work and the taxpayer's home, because,
j although, no doubt, visits to the laboratory involve some relatively insignificant

---

1   [1952] 2 All ER 82, 33 Tax Cas 491
2   [1952] 2 All ER 728, [1953] Ch 7, 33 Tax Cas 452
3   [1952] 2 All ER 728 at 732, [1953] Ch 7 at 17, 33 Tax Cas 452 at 465

deviation from the direct route between home and surgery, effectively I have to deal with a straight line from residence via laboratory to surgery, and vice versa.

Counsel for the taxpayer submits that the true analysis is that, on the commissioners' findings, the taxpayer had two places at which he carried on his professional practice, the laboratory and the surgery. His working day, as counsel for the taxpayer puts it, commenced when he arrived at the laboratory and terminated when he started on the last mile of his journey home in the evening. He points out that, in *Newsom v Robertson*[1], Denning LJ postulated this test: 'In order to decide into which category to put the cost of travelling, you must look to see what is the base from which the trade, profession, or occupation is carried on.' And in the same case Romer LJ postulated this question[2]:

'Is the position altered, then, by the fact, as found by the commissioners, that Mr Newsom worked in his house at Whipsnade as well as in his chambers in Lincoln's Inn? I am clearly of opinion that it is not. It seems to me impossible to say that this element assimilates the case to that of a man who possesses two separate places of business, and, for the furtherance and in the course of his business activities, has to travel from one to another.'

Here, counsel submits, the taxpayer had two bases of operations, and the expenses claimed are expenses of travelling between them for the purposes of his business. It is not in dispute that if, having reached his surgery, the taxpayer found it necessary to visit the laboratory during the day to pick up dentures urgently required for a patient, the expenses of that journey would be a deductible expense. Why, therefore, should it make any logical difference that the journey happens to be a limb of the journey to or from the taxpayer's private house? This is clearly not the case of the itinerant trader (a bricklayer in that case) envisaged by Brightman J in *Horton (Inspector of Taxes) v Young*[3]; but the Court of Appeal in that case based their decision on the fact that the expenses there claimed as deductions were expenses incurred in travelling between what was described variously as 'the locus in quo of the trade', 'the business base' or 'the centre of activities' and the various sites where the taxpayer carried out his actual bricklaying activities. The only difference, counsel for the taxpayer suggests, between that case and the instant case is that here, instead of there being one base of operations and a number of sites of business activity which vary from time to time, we have two fixed bases of operation between which the taxpayer travels for the purpose of his business. Once it is established, he suggests, that the laboratory is a place where the taxpayer performs acts exclusively referable to his profession as a dentist, then the cost of travelling from that place of business activity to the surgery is allowable.

Now the assumption here is that the expense of travel between two places of business is always and inevitably allowable, and counsel for the taxpayer bases himself on this passage in the judgment of Lord Denning MR in *Horton v Young*[4]:

'If the commissioners were right it would lead to some absurd results. Suppose that Mr Horton had a job at a site 200 yards away from his home, and another one at Reigate, 45 miles away. All he would have to do would be to go for five minutes to the site near home and then he would get his travelling expenses to and from Reigate. I can well see that he could so arrange his affairs that every morning he would have to call at a site near home. Instead of going to that absurdity, it is better to hold that his expenses to and from his home are all deductible.'

---

1   [1952] 2 All ER 728 at 731, [1953] Ch 7 at 16, 33 Tax Cas 452 at 464
2   [1952] 2 All ER 728 at 732, [1953] Ch 7 at 18, 33 Tax Cas 452 at 465
3   [1971] 2 All ER 351, [1972] Ch 157, 47 Tax Cas 60
4   [1971] 3 All ER 412 at 415, [1972] Ch 157 at 168, 47 Tax Cas 60 at 71

I question, however, whether, in that passage, Lord Denning MR intended to suggest that by deliberately planning your journey to your place of work so as to incorporate a deviation through another place of work where you actually have no business to do you alter the quality of the journey.

The statute here lays down a test in express terms, and although analogies and examples may be useful guides the propounding of general propositions which involve the use of analogous, but not precisely equivalent, terms can lead to confusion. In the ultimate analysis, the court has simply to look at the facts of the case before it and apply to those facts the statutory formula. As Stamp LJ said in *Horton v Young*[1]:

> 'The facts of such cases are infinitely variable, and one must, in my judgment, look at the facts of each case and decide whether the expenses are money wholly and exclusively laid out or expended for the purpose of the trade or the profession.'

That may seem almost a truism, but it is, I think, a useful reminder that there is a particular statutory formula and that it has to be applied according to its terms.

On the facts as they have been found, could the commissioners here properly have found what in fact they did not: that the expenses incurred, although necessary for the taxpayer's practice, were exclusively incurred for the purposes of that practice? Or were they incurred, either in whole or at least in part, in order to enable the taxpayer to live away from his work?

I do not think, to begin with, that counsel for the taxpayer's suggested test of where the day's work began can be right. A barrister's day's work may begin in the early morning when he gets up very early to read papers for an urgent conference, or when he prepares a case on the train journey to London. But that does not enable him to claim his railway ticket as a deductible expense. Nor, indeed, is this submission supported by the commissioners' findings, for there is a clear implication from the last finding that on occasions the taxpayer travelled to and from the laboratory 'during working hours', that the journeys in respect of which the relevant expenses are claimed were not 'during working hours'.

So I ask myself: what was the real purpose of the taxpayer's journeys? The commissioners' findings were (a) that he called at the laboratory each morning 'on his way to the surgery' and spent about ten minutes 'in order to collect completed work, and, as necessary, to discuss matters with his technician'; and (b) that each evening 'after closing his surgery in Winchcombe' he called in order to deliver dentures, sometimes stopping to advise or do some work 'before proceeding on his journey homewards'. Indeed, his own submission in the stated case is that it was essential for him to visit the laboratory each evening 'on his way home'. Looking at the matter realistically in the light of these findings, what the taxpayer was doing, in my judgment, was calling to deliver and pick up work on his way to and from the surgery where the practice was carried on.

Counsel for the taxpayer relies strongly on the passage in the judgment of Somervell LJ in *Newsom v Robertson*[2] where he postulates the case of a solicitor with two offices and says this:

> 'Many examples were given in the course of the argument, but the following would be I think, a fair example of the type of case to which counsel for the taxpayer would assimilate the present. A professional man, say a solicitor, has two places of business, one at Reading and one in London. He normally sees clients and does his professional work at Reading up till noon and then comes to London. He may live at Reading or in London or at neither. I would have agreed with counsel for the taxpayer that the journeys to and fro between Reading and London were deductible within the rule. He is carrying on one profession partly in London and partly at Reading.'

---

1 [1971] 3 All ER 412 at 416, [1972] Ch 157 at 169, 47 Tax Cas 60 at 72
2 [1952] 2 All ER 728 at 730, [1953] Ch 7 at 13, 14, 33 Tax Cas 452 at 462

From this, counsel for the taxpayer argues that the mere fact that there is an incidental advantage conferred by the making of what, if I may use a shorthand expression, I will call 'a business journey' (in that it shortens the distance over which the propositus has to travel to arrive at his home) does not convert a business journey into a homeward journey. In this context, he relies on this passage from the judgment of Romer LJ in *Bentleys, Stokes & Lowless v Beeson*[1]:

'It is, as we have said, a question of fact. And it is quite clear that the purpose must be the sole purpose. The paragraph says so in clear terms. If the activity be undertaken with the object of promoting business and also with some other purpose, for example, with the object of indulging an independent wish of entertaining a friend or stranger or of supporting a charitable or benevolent object, then the paragraph is not satisfied though in the mind of the actor the business motive may predominate. For the statute so prescribes. Per contra, if, in truth, the sole object is business promotion, the expenditure is not disqualified because the nature of the activity necessarily involves some other result, or the attainment or furtherance of some other objective, since the latter result or objective is necessarily inherent in the act.'

I do not think, however, that the findings in the present case can justify the assertion that, looked at realistically, there was here really a profession being carried on in two places so as to make the case analogous to that propounded by Somervell LJ. The taxpayer had made arrangements at somebody else's premises for a dental mechanic to carry out what was, no doubt, an essential function for his practice. If he had made those arrangements in an outbuilding in the curtilage of his own house, it would not, in my judgment, mean that he was carrying on a dental practice from his home, so as to justify an assertion that the expenses of travel from his home to his surgery were exclusively for the purposes of his practice. Nor, equally, if he had made arrangements with a dental technician living en route between home and surgery that he would drop off and pick up dentures on his journeys in and out, for the technician to work on at his own premises, could this, in my judgment, render his expenses of travelling between the technician's house or workshop and his surgery an expense incurred exclusively for the purposes of his profession, any more than could, for instance, a daily stop en route at a post office for the purpose of posting dentures to a commercial laboratory convert an essentially domestic journey into a business journey.

This is an area in which it is difficult and, I think, positively dangerous to seek to lay down any general proposition designed to serve as a touchstone for all cases. The statute, by its very terms, directs the court to look at the purpose for which the expense was incurred in an individual case, and that necessarily involves a consideration of the intention governing or the reason behind a particular expenditure, which must depend in every case on its own individual facts. The stone which kills two birds may be aimed at one and kill another as a fortuitous or fortunate consequence; or it may be aimed at both. But it is only in the former case that the statute permits the taxpayer to deduct its cost.

In seeking to assess, on the facts as found by the commissioners, the taxpayer's purpose in incurring the expenditure here in question, counsel for the taxpayer points to the fact that he paused in his progress to the surgery to discuss matters with the technician and that he sometimes spent up to an hour with him in the evening, even carrying out work on dentures himself. But the interruption of a journey, whether for five minutes or for a longer period, does not alter the quality of the journey, although it may add to its utility. At highest, as it seems to me, it merely furnishes an additional purpose.

---

1 [1952] 2 All ER 82 at 85, 33 Tax Cas 491 at 504

Of course, it is right to say that if I notionally interrupt the taxpayer's journey at an intermediate point between the laboratory and the surgery and ask myself the question 'Why is he on this particular road at this particular time?' I may come up with the answer that he is taking that particular route because it passes the laboratory. But, as counsel for the Crown points out, that is not the right question. What the court is concerned with is not simply why he took a particular route (although that may be of the highest relevance in considering the deductibility of any additional expense caused by a deviation) but why the taxpayer incurred the expense of the petrol, oil, and wear and tear and depreciation in relation to this particular journey.

In my judgment, the facts found in the stated case leave no room for doubt that the answer to that question must be that it was incurred, if not exclusively then at least in part, for the purpose of enabling the taxpayer to get from his private residence to the surgery where his profession was carried on. The fact that it served the purpose also of enabling him to stop at an intermediate point to carry out there an activity exclusively referable to the business cannot, as I think, convert a dual purpose into a single purpose.

In *Bowden (Inspector of Taxes) v Russell and Russell*[1], Pennycuick J quoted the passage from the judgment of Romer LJ in *Bentleys, Stokes & Lowless v Beeson*[2] which I have already read, where Romer LJ considered what is now s 130 of the 1970 Act, and then went on as follows[3]:

'Then ROMER, L.J., gives a number of examples. As appears from that judgment, it may often be difficult to determine whether the person incurring the expense has in mind two distinct purposes or a single purpose which will or may produce some secondary consequence; but, once it is found that the person has a distinct purpose other than that of enabling him to carry on and earn profits in his trade or profession, s. 137(a) prohibits deduction of the expense.'

In the instant case, on the facts found it would in my judgment be a travesty to say that the taxpayer was in any relevant sense carrying on his practice as a dentist at The Reddings. He had established a facility at The Reddings, and he was merely utilising his journey between his residence and the base of operations where the practice was carried on to avail himself of this facility; that is to say, to visit this intermediate point, where he had arranged for an independent contractor to carry out an activity, no doubt a necessary activity, referable to the practice. But the journey did not thus assume a different purpose once the intermediate point was passed, or cease to be a journey for the purpose of getting to or from the place where the taxpayer chose to live. I do not therefore think that, however necessary to the practice the activity pursued at The Reddings may have been, the commissioners could properly have arrived at the conclusion that the expenses claimed were incurred wholly or exclusively for the purposes of the practice; and the appeal therefore succeeds.

Appeal allowed.

Solicitors: *Solicitor of Inland Revenue; Watterson, Todman & Co*, Cheltenham (for the taxpayer).

Rengan Krishnan Esq Barrister.

---

1 [1965] 2 All ER 258 at 263, [1965] 1 WLR 711 at 716, 717, 42 Tax Cas 301 at 306
2 [1952] 2 All ER 82 at 85, 33 Tax Cas 491 at 504
3 [1965] 2 All ER 258 at 263, [1965] 1 WLR 711 at 717, 42 Tax Cas 301 at 306

Macarthys Ltd v Smith

EMPLOYMENT APPEAL TRIBUNAL
PHILLIPS J, MR E ALDERTON AND MRS A L T TAYLOR
9th NOVEMBER, 14th DECEMBER 1977

Employment – Equality of treatment between men and women – Like work – Comparison of woman's work with duties of former male employee – Substantial interval between respective employments – Whether tribunal restricted to comparing woman's work with that of man in contemporaneous employment – Equal Pay Act 1970, s 1(2)(a)(4).

A female employee when making a claim for equality of pay under s 1[a] of the Equal Pay Act 1970 is not restricted to comparing her work with that of a man in contemporaneous employment but is entitled to make a comparison with the duties of a former employee, notwithstanding the use of the present tense in s 1(2)(a) and (4) of the 1970 Act. However, where there has been a substantial interval between the respective employments an industrial tribunal should proceed with caution when comparing the duties of a present and past employee because the difference in treatment of the two employees may be due to reasons other than discrimination (see p 750 *a b* and *e f*, post).

Notes

For equal treatment of men and women as regards terms and conditions of employment, see 16 Halsbury's Laws (4th Edn) para 767.

For the Equal Pay Act 1970, s 1 (as amended by the Sex Discrimination Act 1975), see 45 Halsbury's Statutes (3rd Edn) 290.

Cases referred to in judgment

Amies v Inner London Education Authority [1977] 2 All ER 100, [1977] ICR 308, EAT.
Capper Pass Ltd v Lawton [1977] 2 All ER 11, [1977] QB 852, [1977] 2 WLR 26, [1977] ICR 83, EAT.
Defrenne v Sabena [1976] ICR 547, 18 CMLR 98, ECJ.
Dugdale v Kraft Foods Ltd [1977] 1 All ER 454, [1976] 1 WLR 1288, [1977] ICR 48, EAT.
Post Office v Union of Post Office Workers [1974] 1 All ER 229, [1974] 1 WLR 89, [1974] ICR 378, HL.
Snoxell v Vauxhall Motors Ltd, Early (Charles) & Marriott (Witney) Ltd v Smith [1977] 3 All ER 770, [1978] QB 11, [1977] 3 WLR 189, [1977] ICR 700, EAT.
Sorbie v Trust Houses Forte Hotels Ltd [1977] 2 All ER 155, [1977] QB 931, [1976] 3 WLR 918, [1977] ICR 55, EAT.

---

a   Section 1, so far as material provides:
   '(2) An equality clause is a provision which relates to terms (whether concerned with pay or not) of a contract under which a woman is employed (the "woman's contract"), and has the effect that—(a) where the woman is employed on like work with a man in the same employment—(i) if (apart from the equality clause) any term of the woman's contract is or becomes less favourable to the woman than a term of a similar kind in the contract under which that man is employed, that term of the woman's contract shall be treated as so modified as not to be less favourable, and (ii) if (apart from the equality clause) at any time the woman's contract does not include a term corresponding to a term benefiting that man included in the contract under which he is employed, the woman's contract shall be treated as including such a term ...
   '(4) A woman is to be regarded as employed on like work with men if, but only if, her work and theirs is of the same or a broadly similar nature, and the differences (if any) between the things she does and the things they do are not of practical importance in relation to terms and conditions of employment; and accordingly in comparing her work with theirs regard shall be had to the frequency or otherwise with which any such differences occur in practice as well as to the nature and extent of the differences.'

Appeal

Macarthy's Ltd ('the employers') appealed against the decision of an industrial tribunal (chairman H A Harris Esq) sitting at London on 28th April 1977 allowing the complaint of Mrs W Smith ('the employee') that she was entitled to equal pay commensurate with that paid by the employers to a male employee. The facts are set out in the judgment of the appeal tribunal.

R L Turner for the employers.
Charles Welchman for the employee.

Cur adv vult

14th December. **PHILLIPS J** read the following judgment of the appeal tribunal: This is an appeal by the employers from a decision of an industrial tribunal sitting in London on 28th April 1977 which by a decision entered on 27th June found in favour of the employee on her claim against them under the Equal Pay Act 1970, as amended.

The proceedings before the industrial tribunal took an unusual course inasmuch as the employee's case suddenly changed direction in the middle of its presentation. Originally she was comparing the work done by her with the work done by the office manager, Mr Wadl. This, and other ways of putting the case, were abandoned, and she then compared her work with that of her predecessor, a Mr McCullough. It was on this basis that the industrial tribunal found in her favour. It is not necessary to say more about this because counsel for the employers took no point on it. Furthermore, he did not challenge the finding by the industrial tribunal that the work which the employee did was 'like work' with the work done by Mr McCullough, and did not rely on any of the particular facts of the case to suggest that there was a material difference between what the employee did and what Mr McCullough did or, if what they did was like work, that there was a sound reason for paying her less than him. In these circumstances the case was not an ideal one to serve as a vehicle to bring up for decision the important point to which we shall refer. However, we have decided it, but would stress that it is the only point in the case argued, and inferences ought not to be drawn in other cases from the particular facts of this case. Briefly, they are as follows.

Mr McCullough left his job as stockroom manager on 20th October 1975. The employee became trainee manageress of the stockroom on 12th January 1976 and manageress on 1st March 1976. During the interval between the departure of Mr McCullough and the appointment of the employee matters were arranged on an improvised basis. There being no dispute about 'like work', the only question arising on the appeal is the important one whether a claimant under the Equal Pay Act 1970, as amended, can compare the work done by her (or him) with that done by an employee in the same employment in a case where that employment ceased before she took up her employment. As can be seen, there was an interval in this case between the two employments. Furthermore, the earlier employment terminated before the coming into operation of the Equal Pay Act 1970, as amended. Apart from these facts the situation is no different from that which would arise in a case where a man left his employment on day 1 and a woman replaced him, doing precisely the same work, on day 2. Supposing that she was paid less than he was, would she have a claim under the Equal Pay Act 1970? The employers say no, and they have in their favour the literal words of some parts of the Act, and the views expressed by some commentators. It should be added as part of the facts that the employee received by way of remuneration about £400 a year less than Mr McCullough.

In *Capper Pass Ltd v Lawton*[1] we pointed out that in devising a method of equal pay it is possible to propose various schemes, some more, some less, favourable to women

1   [1977] 2 All ER 11, [1977] QB 852

than others; and that the Equal Pay Act 1970 had introduced a scheme which took the middle course between the most and the least favourable. Under the Act, equality **a** of treatment is required where the woman is employed on 'like work' with a man in the same employment. Thus an essential feature of any claim (which may be by a woman or a man: s 1(13)) is a comparison of the woman's case with that of a man in the same employment, and this is so whether the claim is brought under s 1(2)(a) ('like work') or under s 1(2)(b) ('evaluation study'). The claimant must show, in the first case, that she is employed on 'like work' with the man in the same employ- **b** ment, or in the second case that she is employed on work rated as 'equivalent' with that of a man in the same employment. So far there is nothing in the Act to indicate with certainty that it is not permissible for a woman for this purpose to compare her situation with that of a man formerly in the employment of the same employers, but who is no longer so employed. The language which strongly suggests that it is not permissible is that to be found in s 1(2)(a)(i) (ii) and ¦in s 1(4). The use of the **c** present tense in these provisions strongly suggests that what is in contemplation is contemperaneous employment. There is not much doubt, and so much was conceded in the argument on the hearing of the appeal, that this is the ordinary meaning of the language used.

The question, then, is whether we are obliged to construe the Act in this sense however strange the results may be, or whether we are justified in the circumstances **d** of the case in construing the Act so as to permit comparisons to be made with an employee who is no longer employed at the relevant date: in a sense, the reciprocal problem to that in *Sorbie v Trust Houses Forte Hotels Ltd*[1]. There is no doubt that if the employers' contention is right strange results will follow, such as the example instanced above where on day 1 a male employee leaves his employment and on day 2 he is replaced by a female employee at half the salary. **e**

We were urged to adopt in this case the approach adopted by the appeal tribunal in *Snoxell v Vauxhall Motors Ltd*[2] where we said:

'We accept and follow the view expressed in *Amies v Inner London Education Authority*[3] that it is not open to a claimant before an industrial tribunal to seek to enforce an "enforceable community right", for example under art 119 of the EEC Treaty. Such a claim would have to be propounded in the High Court. However, it seems to us that no practical difficulty will arise from this fragmentation of ju. isdiction. In *Defrenne v Sabena*[4], it was decided that art 119 must be directly applied in the courts of member States, though with some limitation on its retrospective effect (to which we shall refer later in this judgment). It seems to us that, speaking generally, the [Sex Discrimination Act 1975] and the [Equal Pay 1970 Act] constitute a proper and sufficient fulfilment by this country **g** of its treaty obligations in respect of art 119, and a sufficient statement of the principle of equal pay there enshrined. It is important to observe that art 119 establishes a principle, with little or no detail of the way in which it is to be applied. It appears to us that the 1975 Act, and the 1970 Act, must be construed and applied subject to, and so as to give effect to, the principle. As we have pointed out **h** (e g in *Capper Pass Ltd v Lawton*[5]) a system of equal pay may take many forms, and it does not appear that art 119 requires the member states to apply the principle in identical ways provided that the principle is satisfied. Thus art 119 itself is not precise. The principle is that "men and women should receive equal pay for equal work." Article 119 does not condescend to particulars in the sense of prescribing whether "equal work" means the same work, or work

1   [1977] 2 All ER 155, [1977] QB 931
2   [1977] 3 All ER 770 at 777, 778, [1978] 1 QB 11 at 26, 27
3   [1977] 2 All ER 100
4   [1976] ICR 547
5   [1977] 2 All ER 11 at 14, [1977] QB 852 at 856

a of equal value, or some other variant. And, in fact, the member states have in force different systems of equal pay, based on different criteria. So in general, the 1970 Act seems to be in conformity with the requirements of the principle. It seems to us that as far as industrial tribunals and the appeal tribunal are concerned the correct approach is to give effect to *Defrenne v Sabena*[1] by construing and applying the 1970 Act in conformity with art 119. In this way it will be unnecessary for a claimant to make a separate claim specifically under art 119,

b and it will be understood that a claim under the 1970 Act will entitle a claimant to any remedy which he could claim under art 119, inasmuch as the 1970 Act is to be so construed and applied, subject only to a possible difference as to the limitation period, to which we shall refer later in this judgment. In the cases which have come for decision before the appeal tribunal we have not encountered any particular ambiguity or obscurity in the 1970 Act. However, it at once

c became obvious that it would be possible to construe its provisions, particularly s 1(4), either narrowly or broadly. For the reasons which we have given in various decisions (in particular *Capper Pass Ltd v Lawton*[2] and *Dugdale v Kraft Foods Ltd*[3]) we have taken the view that it is right to construe the 1970 Act broadly having regard to its object. Any doubt as to the propriety of this method of construction and application of the 1970 Act seems to us to be set at rest by

d reflecting that, following the decision in *Defrenne v Sabena*[1], there is an obligation to apply art 119 directly in the courts of the member states. As it seems to us, it is only by so construing and applying the Equal Pay Act 1970 that it is possible to honour this obligation.'

We have found some assistance here in this approach. What has to be given effect
e to is the *principle* of art 119, and the principle is that men and women should receive equal pay for equal work. An Act which permitted discrimination of the kind instanced in the example given above would not be a successful application of the principle.

We have also found assistance in the observations of Lord Reid in *Post Office v Union Post Office Workers*[4] where he said of the Industrial Relations Act 1971: 'This, in
f my judgment, shews that the Act must be construed in a broad and reasonable way so that legal technicalities shall not prevail against industrial realities and common sense'. Equally, it seems to us the Equal Pay Act 1970 ought to be similarly construed. It is also to be noted that the use in legislation of a particular tense, although sometimes crucial, is not always a safe guide to the sensible construction of the Act.

Finally, it is desirable that the Sex Discrimination Act 1975 and the Equal Pay Act
g 1970 should be construed and applied in harmony, as together in effect they constitute a single code. Section 6(6) of the 1975 Act prevents a complaint of unlawful discrimination on the ground of sex being put forward in a case where the benefit of which the claimant has been denied consists of the payment of money under a contract of employment. Such a claim has to be made under the 1970 Act. Accordingly, the present claim (although it would undoubtedly constitute unlawful dis-
h crimination on the ground of sex) could not serve as the basis for a claim under the 1975 Act. On the other hand a similar claim not relating to the payment of money would be maintainable under the 1975 Act. For example, suppose a woman taking over a post found that she was receiving two weeks less holiday a year than her male predecessor; there would seem to be no reason why she should not be able to bring her claim under ss 1 and 6 of the 1975 Act notwithstanding that that would involve a
j comparison of her position with that of an employee who was no longer employed.

---

1 [1976] ICR 547
2 [1977] 2 All ER 11, [1977] QB 852
3 [1977] 1 All ER 454, [1976] 1 WLR 1288
4 [1974] 1 All ER 229 at 236, [1974] 1 WLR 89 at 96

If this is right, it would be unsatisfactory if she could not bring a similar claim, relating to benefits consisting of a payment of money, under the 1970 Act merely because to do so involved a comparison with the situation of an employee who was no longer employed.

These considerations incline us to the view that it would be permissible to construe the 1970 Act so as to allow a comparison of the situation of a woman with that of a former employee. This would be in accordance with our settled approach to the Act which has been to construe and apply it so that it will work in practice. However, we accept that what we cannot do is to construe it in such a way as in effect to introduce a new scheme for which it does not provide. As we have already said, the scheme adopted involves the comparison of the situation of a woman and a man, whether the claim is brought under s 1(2)(a) or s 1(2)(b). The danger if we were to accede to the employee's argument in the present case is that it might be thought that we were introducing a new scheme based on the comparison of posts or jobs, and not of individuals. Indeed, it was noticeable during the argument of counsel for the employee that he continually used the word 'post' or 'job', and gave examples in which what was being posited was the comparison of particular posts or jobs, and not the work done by paticular employees. There is an important distinction here. Even when the 1970 Act in s 1(2)(b) is dealing with a case where there has been an evaluation study, it requires the woman to compare herself with a man, and to find a man in the same employment such that the jobs done by each of them have been given equal value in an evaluation study.

At the end of the day, however, we do not think that this danger is fatal; if it is recognised it can be avoided. We have come to the conclusion that it is permissible to construe the 1970 Act so as to enable a claimant to compare her (or his) situation with that of a former employee, so as to include within the Act cases which obviously could not have been intended to be excluded, such as the example instanced above. On the other hand, care should be taken when it is sought to put forward as comparable an employee who ceased to be employed a long time before. The ordinary case will be the case where there is only a short interval between the two employments. Great care is necessary where there has been a substantial interval, because the difference in treatment may well be due to circumstances which have nothing whatever to do with discrimination, and may be explicable on other grounds. Thus a claimant, unlike a previous employee doing the same work, as a newcomer may well deserve to be paid less, or may have been appointed as a trainee; or it may be the case that the previous employee had been overpaid, and this fact had only recently come to light as a result of a job evaluation; or it may even be that the scale of remuneration has had to be reduced owing to economic conditions or other circumstances. No doubt in these cases, although the claimant might make out a case under s 1(2)(a) by comparing her situation with that of a former employee, the employer would have a good answer to the claim under s 1(3). However, the longer the gap between the employments the more difficult it may be for the employer to assemble the relevant evidence to this effect. Accordingly, in any case except one where the interval between the employments is short, an industrial tribunal confronted with such a claim should proceed with caution. The ordinary case, and the case which in our judgment justifies giving the 1970 Act a liberal construction is that where shortly after one employee leaves another comes, doing the same work, but being remunerated at a lower rate.

In the present case, Mr McCullough left the employment of the employers before the 1970 Act came into operation. A question arises whether this special circumstance prevents a comparison being made with his situation. We think not. The act of discrimination lay in employing the employee at a lower salary to do what has been conceded to be the same work. That occurred after the Act came into effect.

The industrial tribunal in its decision did not refer to the sections of the Equal Pay Act 1970, as amended, and accordingly we have not found it necessary to return

to the terms of the decision. But for the reasons which we have given we have come
to the conclusion that the decision was right, with the result that the appeal must
be dismissed.

Appeal dismissed. Leave to appeal to the Court of Appeal granted.

Solicitors: *Baileys, Shaw & Gillett* (fot the employers); *John L Williams* (for the employee).

Salim H J Merali Esq Barrister.

P Foster (Haulage) Ltd v Roberts

QUEEN'S BENCH DIVISION
LORD WIDGERY CJ, O'CONNOR AND LLOYD JJ
26th JANUARY, 2nd MARCH 1978

*Criminal law – Trial – Plea – Withdrawal of plea of guilty – Plea in unequivocal terms –
Defendant represented by solicitor – Solicitor acting under mistaken belief that offence
was absolute – Whether solicitor's mistake made plea equivocal – Whether justices had
discretion to invite change of plea when defendant legally represented.*

At a magistrates' court a company engaged in the transport business was charged
with and pleaded guilty to 48 offences under s 96 of the Transport Act 1968 of permitting its drivers to work excessive hours. The company was represented by a solicitor
who was apparently under the mistaken impression that the offence was an absolute
one and that lack of knowledge provided no defence. The solicitor told the justices
that that was the reason for the plea of guilty. The justices did not suggest that the
position was otherwise but they did question the company's transport manager
themselves as to the number of trips the drivers were required to make. In giving
their decision the justices stated that the company must have been aware that the
drivers were working excessive hours because of the number of trips they were making.
The company was convicted and fined £100 on each charge. The company appealed
to the Crown Court contending that the solicitor's mistake as to the nature of the
offences made the pleas of guilty equivocal and that when the solicitor's mistake
became apparent the justices should have entered pleas of not guilty or invited a change
of plea to not guilty. The Crown Court dismissed the appeal on the grounds that a
mistake in law by a defendant's lawyer did not make a plea equivocal and that
justices were not under a duty to consider exercising their discretion to invite a
change of plea when a mistake as to the nature of the charge became apparent if a
defendant was legally represented. On appeal,

Held – (i) For a plea to be equivocal the defendant must add to his plea of guilty
a qualification which, if true, may show that he is not guilty of the offence charged.
The company had added no qualification to their pleas which were therefore unequivocal (see p 755 *a* and *h* and p 756 *j*, post).

(ii) At a trial before justices, once an unequivocal plea of guilty had been entered,
the justices had, until sentence was passed, a discretion to permit a change of plea
to not guilty notwithstanding the fact that the defendant was legally represented.
In the circumstances the justices could have exercised that discretion but before doing
so they were entitled to test, and had in fact tested, the validity of the assertion that
the sole reason for the plea of guilty was the company's solicitor's mistaken belief

as to the nature of the charges. From their own questioning of the company's transport manager they were entitled to conclude that the solicitor's mistaken belief   *a* as to the law was not the sole reason for the pleas of guilty and therefore they had been justified in not exercising their discretion to invite a change of plea on that account. Accordingly the appeal would be dismissed (see p 755 *b* and *h* to p 756*c* and *e* to *j*, post); *S (an infant) v Manchester City Recorder* [1969] 3 All ER 1230 applied.

Notes   *b*
For the withdrawal of a plea of guilty, see 11 Halsbury's Laws (4th Edn) para 248, and for cases on the subject, see 14(1) Digest (Reissue) 332, 333, 2621-2635.
For the offence of permitting drivers to work excessive hours, see 33 Halsbury's Laws (3rd Edn) 717, 718, para 1222.
For the Transport Act 1968, s 96, see 28 Halsbury's Statutes (3rd Edn) 751.

Cases referred to in judgments   *c*
R v Blandford Justices, ex parte G (an infant) [1966] All ER 1021, [1967] 1 QB 82, [1966] 2 WLR 1232, Digest (Cont Vol B) 505, 346*b*.
R v Durham Quarter Sessions, ex parte Virgo [1952] 1 All ER 466, [1952] 2 QB 1, 116 JP 157, 33 Digest (Repl) 304, 1289.
S (an infant) v Manchester City Recorder [1969] 3 All ER 1230, [1971] AC 481, [1970] 2 *d* WLR 21, HL, Digest (Cont Vol C) 656, 550*Ac*.

Case also cited
R v Marylebone Justices, ex parte Westminster City Council [1971] 1 All ER 1025, [1971] 1 WLR 567, DC.

Case stated   *e*
This was an appeal by case stated by Mr R T L Lee sitting as a deputy circuit judge in the Crown Court at Bedford on 24th and 25th May 1976 in respect of his decision to dismiss the appeal of P Foster (Haulage) Ltd ('the company') against conviction of 48 offences against the Transport Act 1968. On 19th September 1975 at the North Bedfordshire Magistrates' Court the company pleaded guilty to 48 informations laid *f* by the respondent, Bertram William Roberts, charging it with having committed on various dates between 22nd November 1974 and 20th January 1975 at Oakley in the county of Bedford and elsewhere 48 offences of permitting drivers to work excessive hours, contrary to s 96 of the 1968 Act. The company's pleas of guilty were accepted by the justices and it was duly convicted and fined. On appeal to the Crown Court counsel for both parties agreed that the court should first hear and decide *g* whether the company's pleas of guilty before the justices had been equivocal. The company had pleaded guilty to the informations charging the offences because it had mistakenly understood that the offences were absolute offences of which it could be guilty without having actual or constructive knowledge either of the facts constituting the offences or of the commission of the offences themselves. The company, in mitigation, gave evidence to the court that it had no knowledge actual or constructive *h* either of the facts constituting the offences or of the commission of the offences themselves. Having listened to evidence and argument on that question alone the deputy circuit judge gave judgment in the respondent's favour. With the agreement of both parties the hearing of the appeal against sentence was adjourned to allow the company to appeal to the High Court against the decision that its pleas of guilty before the justices had not been equivocal, that therefore those proceedings had not been a nullity and that accordingly its convictions should be quashed. The questions of law to be determined by the High Court were: (i) whether on the facts as found the court could reasonably have concluded that the company's pleas of guilty before the justices were not equivocal; (ii) whether the court was right in law in holding that the fact that there was a mistake in law by the company and its advisers as to the

nature of the offences charged did not make its pleas equivocal; (iii) whether the
a court was right in law in holding that despite the fact that the offences charged were
not offences of absolute prohibition and despite the fact that the justices knew the
company to be pleading guilty on the basis that the offences were ones of absolute
prohibition, nevertheless because the company was legally represented the justices
were not obliged to treat the pleas as equivocal. The facts are set out in the judgment
of O'Connor J.

b
Matthew Horton for the company.
Martin Bowley for the respondent.

Cur adv vult

c 2nd March. The following judgments were read.

O'CONNOR J (delivering the first judgment at the invitation of Lord Widgery CJ).
This is an appeal by way of case stated from a decision of the Crown Court at Bedford,
given on 26th May 1976. The case arises from the desire of the appellants, P Foster
d (Haulage) Ltd ('the company'), on appeal to the Crown Court to resile from pleas
of guilty made in the magistrates' court. The company appeared before the North
Bedfordshire justices on 19th September 1975, and by its solicitor pleaded guilty to
48 offences of permitting drivers to work excessive hours, contrary to s 96 of the
Transport Act 1968. The drivers, who were also legally represented, pleaded guilty
to working excessive hours. The company was fined £4,800 and ordered to pay £500
e costs.
    The company appealed to the Crown Court against conviction and sentence.
'The basis of the appeal against conviction was a submission that in the course of
the proceedings before the justices it should have been appreciated by them that the
pleas of guilty had been entered because the company, advised by its solicitor, mistakenly thought that the offences were absolute and that lack of knowledge, actual
f or constructive, afforded no defence. It was contended that as soon as that position
emerged then, despite the fact that the company was represented and no application to change its pleas was made, the justices ought themselves to have ordered
pleas of 'not guilty' to be entered and arranged to try out the informations.
    The Crown Court directed itself correctly and limited its enquiry to trying to
discover what had happened before the justices. For this purpose the Crown Court
g heard evidence from Mr Borneo, the company's solicitor, and Mr Holland, a director
of the company, as to their recollection of the proceedings before the justices. It is
to be noted that it does not appear from the case whether the justices and/or their
clerk were invited to attend or indeed even informed that the enquiry was taking
place; certainly no evidence from them is referred to. The Crown Court has made
its findings of fact in a judgment appended to the case. Before I summarise these
h findings, it is a necessary inference that before the justices all parties consented to the
informations being heard together. After the pleas had been taken the prosecuting
solicitor outlined the case which, in a nutshell, was that the drivers had been required
to work excessive hours because the journeys they were required to make could not
be carried out within the permitted hours. The solicitor for the drivers then mitigated on their behalf to the effect that they had been forced to work excessive hours.
i   The solicitor for the company then began his mitigation; he told the bench that
the company and its directors had no knowledge of how to manage a haulage company
and so they had employed a transport manager to run the company for them; that
at the material time the transport manager was a Mr Brown, who was an experienced
man. The solicitor then told the bench that the company and management were
not aware that the offences had been committed, but that the company was pleading

guilty to the charges simply because of the nature of the charges, that is that it could be guilty without knowledge. He then called a director of the company to give evidence who stated that he and the management were not aware that excessive hours were being worked; it seems that he was cross-examined as to the number of trips that the drivers were working. The solicitor then told the bench that Mr Brown was in court, and without objection by the solicitor the chairman asked him questions in order to ascertain what number of trips the drivers were required to make. The bench then retired and when they returned the chairman said that the company must have been aware that the drivers were working excessive hours because of the numbers of trips they were doing and then imposed the fines.

The Crown Court then gave its reasons for refusing to remit the case to the justices in the following terms:

'In the present case the appellant company was legally represented before the magistrates and pleas of guilty were entered by the solicitor. Notwithstanding the strong opening by the prosecution and Mr Borneo's plea and the evidence given on oath, no application was made to adjourn to consider the company's position and no application was made to change the pleas. The matter proceeded to sentence. There was no equivocation in the mind of the company through one of its directors, Mr Holland, when he accepted that there was no defence to the charges and the offences were absolute. Indeed, there appears to have been none in Mr Borneo's mind either. He was acting as agent for the company. The fact that there might have been a mistake in the law by the advisers does not in our view make the pleas equivocal. For that reason the first ground of appeal has failed. Secondly, it is true that it has been held that a clerk to the justices should assist an unrepresented defendant to conduct his case, but we cannot accept that either he or the court has a duty to advise a company represented by a solicitor, an officer of the court, on points of law, or as to what pleas should be entered. The defence which it is claimed would have been a complete answer to the charges has been established law for a number of years. Nobody was taken by surprise, as it were, by a recent decision or by a new or complicated enactment. The legal representative on his own admission had not taken the trouble to look the matter up, relying on his erroneous belief that the offences were absolute. In these circumstances we find that the court had no duty to the company to treat the pleas as ones of not guilty. For these reasons we find that the pleas made before the magistrates were unequivocal and the application to remit the cases to the justices is refused. The appeal against conviction is dismissed.'

The question of law to be determined by this court are set out in the case:

'(i) Whether on the facts as found by us we could reasonably have concluded that the [company's] plea of guilty before the [justices] was not equivocal; (ii) Whether we were right in law in holding that the fact that there was a mistake in law by the [company] and their advisers as to the nature of the offence charged did not make their plea equivocal; (iii) Whether we were right in law in holding that despite the fact that the offence charged was not an offence of absolute prohibition and despite the fact that the [justices] knew the [company] to be pleading guilty on the basis that the offence was one of absolute prohibition, nevertheless because the [company] were legally represented the court was not obliged to treat the plea as equivocal.'

In my judgment, a clear distinction must be drawn between the duties of a court faced with an equivocal plea at the time it is made and the exercise of the court's jurisdiction to permit a defendant to change an unequivocal plea of guilty at a later stage of the proceedings. A court cannot accept an equivocal plea of guilty: it has no discretion in the matter; faced with an equivocal plea the court must either obtain an unequivocal plea of guilty or enter a plea of not guilty. For a plea to be equivocal the defendant must add to the plea of guilty a qualification which, if true, may show that he is not guilty of the offence charged. An example of this type of qualification is found where a man charged with handling a stolen motor car pleads 'guilty to handling but I didn't know it was stolen'. It is not every qualification which makes a plea of guilty equivocal; for example, the burglar charged with stealing spoons, forks and a camera, who pleads 'guilty but I did not take the camera' is making an unequivocal plea to burglary.

Once an unequivocal plea of guilty has been made, then the position is entirely different. From this stage forward until sentence has been passed the court has power to permit the plea of guilty to be changed to one of not guilty, but the exercise of this power is entirely a matter of discretion. This is clearly stated by all of their lordships in *S (an infant) v Manchester City Recorder*[1]. In that case the appellant, aged 16, had pleaded guilty to attempted rape before a juvenile court; the hearing was adjourned for three weeks for reports and on the adjourned hearing the appellant was legally represented and his solicitor applied to withdraw the plea of guilty on the ground that the youth had made many previous spurious confessions and that his confession of guilt was unsafe. The justices refused the application on the ground that they were functi officio and had no power to grant it. That decision was upheld in the Divisional Court but the House of Lords allowed the appeal.

All the cases on this topic were reviewed in the House of Lords and, in my judgment, it is unnecessary to go behind that case today. Once it is recognised that the magistrate's court has got this discretion, the difficulties created by the earlier cases disappear; the contrary view led, as Lord Upjohn put it[2]—

'... understandably enough, in order to do justice to the accused, to some rather artificial practices such as accepting a plea of guilty provisionally, as explained by Widgery, J., in *R. v. Blandford Justices, ex parte G. (an infant)*[3]; or in the "guilty but ..." cases, an expression used by Lord Goddard, C.J., in *R. v. Durham Quarter Sessions, ex parte Virgo*[4], to describe the type of case where the accused pleaded guilty but then or at some later stage of the trial showed that he misunderstood the nature of the plea for his explanation showed that he should have pleaded not guilty. [Further on Lord Upjon says:] In future it will be quite unnecessary to accept a provisional plea or to resort to the "guilty but ..." artifice. If the court, on all the facts before it, thinks that it is proper to accept a plea of guilty then the court may permit that plea to be withdrawn and a plea of not guilty accepted at a later stage up to sentence, that is until the complete adjudication of conviction. But, my Lords, it is hardly necessary to add that this discretionary power is one which should only be exercised in clear cases and very sparingly.'

I turn to the facts of the present case to consider them in the light of the decision in *S (an infant) v Manchester City Recorder*[1]. Three questions have to be asked: 1. Were the pleas equivocal or unequivocal? There is no doubt that the pleas of guilty were unequivocal. 2. During the course of the proceedings did anything happen which made it clear to the justices that they should consider exercising their discretion to permit a change of plea? The Crown Court has in effect answered this question No, on the ground that in cases where the defendant is legally represented the fact that it becomes apparent that the lawyer has advised a plea of guilty under a mistaken view of the nature of the charge involved is not a matter which calls on the justices to consider the exercise of their discretion. This is too drastic a view of the

---

1   [1969] 3 All ER 1230, [1971] AC 481
2   [1969] 3 All ER 1230 at 1247, 1248, [1971] AC 481 at 507
3   [1966] 1 All ER 1021, [1967] 1 QB 82
4   [1952] 1 All ER 466, [1952] 2 QB 1

effect of legal representation. In cases where a defendant is legally represented and
no application is made to change the plea, it will be rare indeed that it can be said that
it has become apparent to the justices that they should consider exercising their
discretion to permit a change of plea. However, the presence of an incompetent
lawyer cannot act as a bar to the use of this discretionary power. Assume that the
defendant in the *Durham Quarter Sessions* case[1] had been legally represented and his
advocate had made the same mistake of law that he made and demonstrated that
fact in mitigating for his client, I am clear that the justices would be called on to
intervene. On its findings of fact the Crown Court ought to have answered this
question Yes, and then gone on to enquire into the next question. 3. Has it been shown
that by not inviting a change of plea the justices exercised their discretion wrongly?
On the facts found by the Crown Court this question admits of only one answer,
namely that it is quite clear that it has not been shown that the justices exercised
their discretion wrongly.

Let me recapitulate the facts found by the Crown Court: the prosecuting solicitor
opened the case to the justices after the pleas; his opening of the facts and indeed
the pleas of all concerned made it quite certain that the drivers had in fact been
working excessive hours over a substantial period (do not forget there were 48
informations) and it was the prosecution's case that the company required the drivers
to work the excessive hours. Next came the drivers' mitigation which was to the
same effect. Next came the company solicitor who first of all told the justices that the
directors of the company knew nothing about running a haulage business and by
inference nothing about the relevant requirements of the Transport Act 1968. I
pause to point out that that state of affairs not only could not amount to a defence
to the informations but is of doubtful value in mitigation.

Next the justices were told that the company had employed a transport manager
to run the business for it and that at the time of the offences a Mr Brown was transport manager, a very competent man. It was only at this stage that for the first
time the justices were told by the solicitor that the company was pleading guilty because this was an absolute offence. It is submitted that, as soon as they were told that,
it was their duty to order pleas of 'not guilty' to be entered. I cannot accept anything of
the kind; at best, as I have pointed out, they were under a duty to consider exercising
their discretion; to that end I think the justices were entitled to test the validity of
the assertion that the sole reason for the pleas was the solicitor's mistaken belief
about the law.

That is exactly what happened; first of all the solicitor called a director of the
company and thereafter the justices themselves through the chairman called Mr
Brown, the transport manager, and after that enquiry it had become quite clear to
them that it was ludicrous to say that the only ground for the pleas of guilty was the
mistake of law by the solicitor. I would test this by supposing that, while the justices
were out considering the matter, the solicitor had woken up to his own ignorance of
the law and, when the justices had come back and said that they were quite sure
that the company knew that excess hours were being worked, if at that moment
the solicitor had got up and applied for leave to change the plea on the ground of
his own mistake can anybody suggest that the justices would have been required to
grant it? For these reasons I would dismiss the appeal.

LORD WIDGERY CJ. I agree, and we have the authority of Lloyd J to say
that he also agrees.

Appeal dismissed.

Solicitors: *Borneo, Martell & Partners*, Bedford; *Treasury Solicitor*.

Jacqueline Charles Barrister.

1　[1952] 1 All ER 466, [1952] 2 QB 1

Hilborne v Law Society of Singapore

PRIVY COUNCIL

LORD DIPLOCK, LORD FRASER OF TULLYBELTON AND LORD RUSSELL OF KILLOWEN

30th, 31st JANUARY, 7th MARCH 1978

Counsel – Professional misconduct – Improper conduct – Comment offensively critical of court – Advocate and solicitor of Singapore – Remarks made by advocate when court refused to re-open case – Advocate submitting opponent's case successful because court had accepted a false and dishonest case – Advocate remarking to court that it had 'set the seal on dishonesty' – Remark made after court had announced its decision – Remark not a submission seeking to persuade court to re-open case – Whether remark constituting improper conduct.

Singapore – Advocate and solicitor – Disciplinary proceedings – Matters capable of being subject of disciplinary proceedings – Comment offensively critical of court – Conduct not within matters specified in legislation relating to conduct of legal practitioners – Whether conduct which may be subject to disciplinary action limited to matters specified in legislation – Whether comment offensively critical of court conduct subject to disciplinary action – Legal Profession Act (Singapore), ss 84(2), 88(1)(b), 89(1).

Singapore – Court of Appeal – Appeal – Right of appeal – Appeal against decision of judge of High Court – Application to High Court to have penalty imposed in disciplinary proceedings against advocate and solicitor set aside – Whether appeal lies to Court of Appeal against decision of judge of High Court – Supreme Court of Judicature Act (Singapore), s 29.

An advocate and solicitor in Singapore represented plaintiffs in litigation and obtained judgment for them in default of defence. The defendants to the litigation successfully applied to have the judgment set aside. The plaintiffs' appeal to the Court of Appeal of Singapore was dismissed but before the order of the Court of Appeal was perfected the advocate received information which suggested that the defendants had put forward a false and dishonest case. The advocate therefore applied to the Court of Appeal to re-open the plaintiffs' appeal. The court decided to refuse the application and after the court had pronounced its decision the advocate remarked to the court that by refusing to re-open the appeal they had 'set the seal on dishonesty'. The remark was referred by the court registrar to the Council of the Law Society of Singapore who, after considering the report of their inquiry committee, decided, under ss 88(1)(b)[a] and 89[b] of the Legal Profession Act (Singapore), that the circumstances were not of sufficient gravity to merit a formal investigation by a disciplinary committee but that nevertheless the advocate should be ordered to pay a penalty of $250. The advocate applied by originating summons to the High Court of Singapore to have the penalty set aside but his application was dismissed. An appeal to the Court of Appeal was also dismissed, the court holding, in the alternative, that there was no right of appeal to it in disciplinary matters arising under the Legal Profession Act. The advocate appealed to the Privy Council contending, inter alia, (i) that the remark made in court had not been improper and (ii) that the council's ability to impose a penalty under ss 88(1)(b) and 89 was restricted to the matters referred to in s 84(2)[c] of the Legal Profession Act, which, he contended, contained an exhaustive statement of the matters which could be the subject of disciplinary proceedings under the Act, and his conduct in making the remark had not come within those matters.

---

a   Section 88(1), is set out at p 761 g h, post
b   Section 89 is set out at p 761 j, post
c   Section 84(2), so far as material, is set out at p 761 b, post

Held – The appeal would be dismissed for the following reasons—

(i) The remark constituted improper conduct by the advocate according to the *a* ordinary standards of the legal profession because it had been made to the court after it had finally and in terms refused to re-open the plaintiffs' appeal and it was therefore an offensively critical comment rather than a submission seeking to persuade the court to re-open the appeal (see p 759 h j and p 760 e f, post).

(ii) Under ss 88(1)(b) and 89(1) the Council of the Law Society of Singapore had power to take disciplinary action in respect of matters outside those referred to in s 84(2) *b* and it was therefore open to them to hold that the advocate's conduct was improper conduct meriting the imposition of a penalty, notwithstanding that his conduct did not come within the scope of s 84(2) (see p 762 b c and e, post).

Per Curiam. The decision of a judge of the High Court of Singapore on an application by originating summons under s 95 of the Legal Profession Act is a 'judgment or order of the High Court in any civil matter', within s 29 of the Supreme Court of *c* Judicature Act 1970 (Singapore), and there is therefore a right of appeal to the Court of Appeal of Singapore (see p 763 j to p 764 b, post).

Notes

For powers of the court over counsel and for complaints of professional misconduct, see 3 Halsbury's Laws (4th Edn) paras 1132-1134, and for cases on the subject, see *d* 3 Digest (Repl) 353, 354, 19-27.

Appeal

Kenneth Edward Hilborne appealed by special leave from the order of the Court of Appeal of the Republic of Singapore (Wee Chong Jin CJ, Winslow and Kulasekaram JJ) dated 23rd November 1972, the reasons for which were given in a judgment dated *e* 5th March 1973, whereby the appellant's appeal from an order of Chua J dated 20th June 1972 affirming an order made by the respondent, the Law Society of Singapore, on 5th May 1972 that the appellant should pay a penalty of $250 pursuant to s 89(1) of the Legal Profession Act (Singapore) was dismissed. The facts are set out in the judgment of the Board.

f

Stuart McKinnon for the appellant.
Robin Auld QC and *Ian Glick* for the respondent.

LORD RUSSELL OF KILLOWEN. The appellant is an advocate and solicitor in Singapore. The Council of the Law Society there decided that he had been guilty of *g* improper conduct as such and ordered that he should incur a penalty of $250. The appellant contended that in law there was no justification for this action. He proceeded to challenge it in the High Court by the appropriate procedure of an originating summons applying to set aside the order of the council. Chua J refused the application and affirmed the penalty, but gave leave to appeal to the Court of Appeal. On appeal that court (Wee Chong Jin CJ, Winslow and Kulasekaram JJ) dismissed the *h* appeal. The appellant now appeals by special leave of this Board.

The alleged improper conduct of the appellant was in connection with proceedings in which the plaintiffs, represented by the appellant, sought recovery of about $2,500, the cost of furniture made by them for use at a proposed night club and restaurant, the Golden Pagoda Garden Nite-Club and Restaurant, and duly delivered at its premises. The order was placed by the first defendant in that action, Tan Eng Huat, *j* purporting to act on behalf of the second defendants, Golden Palace Private Ltd. Their Lordships do not think it necessary to rehearse in detail the progress of that litigation. The second defendants denied liability and before delivering a defence requested particulars of the claim, which curiously enough did not in express terms assert that the order had been placed by the first defendant on behalf of the second, but only claimed against the latter 'if' the order had been so placed. There was a dispute whether particulars could be called for before delivery of defence; the second defendants intimated that they were applying for an order for particulars and for extension of time for delivery of defence; the appellant, for the plaintiffs, nevertheless sought and obtained judgment against the second defendants in default of defence very shortly before the return date for the second defendants' application, which was adjourned sine die to afford to the latter an opportunity to apply to set aside the default judgment.

That application was heard by Wee Chong Jin CJ on affidavit evidence. Again the details are not for the present important. Suffice it to say that for the second defendants it was being put forward that those defendants had no interest in the night club at the relevant time; on the contrary the premises were let to a partnership of which the first defendant was a member. The default judgment was set aside and particulars ordered. The plaintiffs appealed and on 21st January 1971 the Court of Appeal dismissed the appeal.

After that dismissal but before the order of the Court of Appeal was perfected the appellant received information, mainly from an advocate and solicitor, Mr Ong Swee Keng, which suggested to him that a false and dishonest case had been put forward by and on behalf of the second defendants in that according to Mr Ong, a director of the second defendants, the business of the night club was at the relevant time owned and run by the latter and that the first defendant as a director (and approved in principle as managing director) had authority of the second defendants to place the order for the furniture. Again the details do not matter; suffice it to say that it is clear that the appellant considered that a false case had been presented for the second defendants, supported by affidavit evidence from an employee of Mr Chung, the solicitor of the second defendants. (Their Lordships remark that ultimately in the winding-up of the second defendants the Official Receiver appears to have recognised the plaintiffs' claim.)

Armed with a statutory declaration from Mr Ong the appellant applied to the Court of Appeal to re-open the appeal, with a view to reinstating the default judgment, on the ground that the evidence now showed a dishonest case put forward for the second defendants. (This was the occasion for the comment by the appellant, as advocate for the plaintiffs, which has been concurrently held by the Council of the Law Society, by Chua J, and by the Court of Appeal on appeal from Chua J to constitute improper conduct.) The Court of Appeal refused the application to re-open the appeal.

The comment made by the appellant was that by refusing to re-open the appeal the Court of Appeal 'set the seal on dishonesty'. Mr Chung having challenged the appellant to repeat his words outside court, taking the phrase as a reflection on his firm, the appellant wrote to him on the same day a letter including the phrase:

'I stated to the two judges present that in my opinion in refusing to re-open this appeal, they were setting a seal on dishonesty.'

In considering the question of improper conduct the first question of fact is whether this remark was made to the court after the court had finally and in terms refused to re-open the appeal, the appellant being incensed at the outcome, or whether it was in the nature of a submission in the course of seeking to persuade the court to re-open the appeal, on lines such as 'If the court declines to re-open this appeal I submit that the effect will be to set a seal on dishonesty'. In their Lordships' view it was clearly the former. They have already quoted from the appellant's letter to Mr Chung of 13th March 1971. Mr Chung having forwarded that letter to the secretaries to the two relevant judges the registrar of the court on their instructions wrote to the Law Society thus:

'Their Lordships are of the view that the conduct of Mr. Hilborne in expressing the opinion after the decision not to re-open the appeal had been pronounced, that "in refusing to re-open this appeal they [i e their Lordships] were setting a seal on dishonesty" merits investigation.'

In his letter dated 24th May 1971 to the inquiry committee of the Law Society the appellant said:

'In the event, their Lordships did not deem fit to re-open the hearing of the appeal. It seemed, and still seems, to me that for a litigant to misinform the Court in circumstances such as these was dishonesty in the legal, if not the actual sense, and for a Court, having been apprised of the nature of the falsity, to fail to express any disapproval of the same, let alone investigate the matter further, was tantamount to condonation of that dishonesty. It was these circumstances that led to the observation which I made.'

It is true that in his affidavit in support of his application to set aside the penalty on 25th May 1972 the appellant used the phrase 'it was during the course of this hearing [i e of the appeal] that I uttered the words. . . ', a phrase echoed by his counsel during the hearing before Chua J, though it is to be noted that counsel also said that the appellant 'was *disappointed* and he made this remark' and further said that he 'was expressing the view that the *decision* the two judges made was in effect giving effect to the dishonesty of the second defendant'. At the same hearing before Chua J the appellant (though represented) interjected a statement to suggest that it was before the decision was pronounced and that the remark was conditional in form. A copy of the letter from the court registrar already quoted was sent on 12th April 1971 by the Law Society to the appellant; their Lordships have already quoted from the relevant answer of the appellant which does nothing to deny the clear statement of the judges that the remark was made after the decision had been pronounced. The Court of Appeal in the judgments under appeal concluded that the remark was made after the judges had refused to re-open the appeal and their Lordships concur in that finding.

Before considering the legal arguments advanced for the appellant their Lordships would observe that in their opinion the remark at that juncture was offensively critical of the judges, was intended to be so, and by any ordinary standards of the profession constituted improper conduct by the appellant. It was argued that the judges themselves at the time did not appear so to regard it, for they made neither comment nor rebuke. But Mr Chung was apparently voicing indignation at what he regarded (rightly no doubt) as additionally an accusation against his firm and his client, and it may well be that the judges at the time thought that intervention would only serve to heat the atmosphere. Indeed if the appellant had not accepted Mr Chung's challenge in court by writing on returning to his office the letter already cited, and had that letter not been forwarded to the judges, maybe no more would have been heard of the matter. But the judges, faced with that letter as a written record, shortly thereafter, plainly felt that the episode could not then be passed over.

Their Lordships will first set out the relevant extracts from the legislation (Legal Profession Act[1]) relating to discipline over the conduct of the legal profession in Singapore. Section 83(3) is as follows:

'The Supreme Court or any judge thereof may exercise the same jurisdiction in respect of advocates and solicitors as can be exercised by a superior court in England over barristers or solicitors practising before any such court.'

Section 84(1) is as follows:

'All advocates and solicitors shall be subject to the control of the Supreme

Court and shall be liable on due cause shown to be struck off the roll or suspended from practice for any period not exceeding two years or censured.'

Section 84(2) is as follows:

'Such due cause may be shown by proof that such person— . . . (b) has been guilty of fraudulent or grossly improper conduct in the discharge of his professional duty or guilty of such a breach of any usage or rule of conduct made by the Council under the provisions of this Act as in the opinion of the court amounts to improper conduct or practice as an advocate and solicitor; or . . . (h) has done some other act which would render him liable to be disbarred or struck off the roll of the court or suspended from practice or censured if a barrister or solicitor in England due regard being had to the fact that the two professions are fused in Singapore; or . . .'

These matters, striking off, suspension or censure, are matters to be dealt with ultimately by a special court of three (s 98).

Their Lordships set out these extracts from s 84 primarily because it was not contended by the respondent that the case fitted into those or any other paragraph of s 84(2), and it was contended by the appellant that s 84(2) was an exhaustive statement of matters which could be the subject of disciplinary proceedings under the statute.

The procedure for dealing with complaints of professional misconduct under the statute may be thus summarised. The Law Society has a standing inquiry committee. Section 86(1) and (2) is as follows:

'(1) Any application by any person that an advocate and solicitor be dealt with under this Part and any complaint of the conduct of an advocate and solicitor in his professional capacity shall in the first place be made to the Society and the Council shall refer the application or complaint to the Inquiry Committee.

'(2) The Supreme Court or any judge thereof or the Attorney-General may at any time refer to the Society any information touching upon the conduct of a solicitor in his professional capacity and the Council shall issue a written order to the Inquiry Committee.'

By s 87(1) it is provided that: 'Where the Inquiry Committee has—(a) received a written order . . . it shall inquire into and investigate the matter and report to the Council on the matter.'

In the present case the registrar's letter operated under s 86(2). Section 88(1) reads as follows:

'The Council shall consider the report of the Inquiry Committee and according to the circumstances of the case shall determine—(a) that a formal investigation is not necessary; or (b) that no cause of sufficient gravity exists for a formal investigation but that the advocate and solicitor should be ordered to pay a penalty under section 89 of this Act; or (c) that there should be a formal investigation by a Disciplinary Committee; or (d) that the matter be referred back to the Inquiry Committee, or adjourned for consideration.'

Section 89 reads as follows:

'(1) If the Council determines under section 88 of this Act that no cause of sufficient gravity exists for a formal investigation but that the advocate and solicitor should be ordered to pay a penalty it may order the advocate and solicitor to pay a penalty of not more than two hundred and fifty dollars.

'(2) The provisions of section 95 of this Act apply to any penalty ordered to be paid under subsection (1) of this section.

'(3) Before the Council makes an order for the payment of a penalty under this section it shall notify the advocate and solicitor concerned of its intention to do so and give him a reasonable opportunity to be heard by the Council.'

In the instant case the council after considering the report of the inquiry committee determined in accordance with s 88(1)(b) and ordered a penalty of $250 under s 89(1).

Section 95 provides that in the case of a penalty ordered by the council the advocate may apply by originating summons to a judge to set aside the order. Any penalty not set aside may be recoverable by the Law Society as a judgment debt.

In any case in which the council considers that there should be a formal investigation a disciplinary committee is set up by the Chief Justice to hear and investigate the matter. The provisions dealing with the disciplinary committee have only an indirect relevance to the instant case but touch importantly on the appellant's submission that no conduct can be the subject of any disciplinary action unless it can be brought within a paragraph of s 84(2). Their Lordships are unable to accept that the ability of the council to act under ss 88(1)(b) and 89(1) is so restricted. It was argued that the reference in s 88(1)(b) to 'cause' echoes and is limited to that which is due cause' in s 84(1) and (2). Their Lordships would not in any event accept that this was necessarily so; but the matter appears to them to be concluded by the contrast that is to be found in s 93(1). That provides, in a disciplinary committee case, as follows:

'After hearing and investigating any matter referred to it a Disciplinary Committee shall record its findings in relation to the facts of the case and according to those facts shall determine—(a) that no cause of sufficient gravity for disciplinary action exists under section 84 of this Act; or (b) that while no cause of sufficient gravity for disciplinary action exists under that section the advocate and solicitor should be reprimanded; or (c) that cause of sufficient gravity for disciplinary action exists under that section.'

Thus there is the express link with and limitation to the content of s 84 in cases of formal investigation by a disciplinary committee which is markedly lacking in s 88(1)(b). It was urged for the appellant that unless the latter was confined to s 84(2) matters it would be at large for the council to hold anything to be impropriety of conduct meriting a penalty. But the council is a responsible body of professional men, and an aggrieved advocate has recourse to the court.

To some extent their Lordships have already indicated the course of events which fit into the statutory framework. The court by the registrar's letter of 19th March 1971 referred the matter to the Law Society and it was in turn referred to the inquiry committee; the latter on 12th April asked the appellant for his explanation in writing and whether he wished to be heard by the committee. The appellant on 24th May wrote a long letter in answer, from which their Lordships have already quoted, attaching the documents on which he based his conclusion that the second defendants had put forward a dishonest case. Later the inquiry committee reported to the council of the Law Society.

On 27th July the Law Society wrote to the appellant as follows:

'I refer to your letter dated the 24th May, 1971 and am directed to inform you that the Council after considering the Report of the Inquiry Committee on the complaint made against you by the Registrar of the Supreme Court, had determined that under section 91(1)(b) of the Legal Profession Act, 1966, no cause of sufficient gravity exists for a formal investigation, but that as your conduct towards their Lordships was improper it is the Council's present intention that you should be ordered to pay a penalty under section 92 of the Act; the amount of the penalty in this case has been fixed at $200/- [sic in record copy].

'2. Before making a formal order to this effect, I am directed to notify you of the Council's intention to do so pursuant to the provisions of section 92(3) of the Act, and to enquire whether you wish to be heard by the Council before such an order is made.'

(The sections referred to are the former numbering of ss 88(1)(b) and 89.)

On 29th July 1971 the appellant replied as follows:

'I have received your letter of the 27th instant, and I note what you say. I take
it that your letter means that there was a finding by the Inquiry Committee that
my conduct was improper, and I should be glad if you would kindly confirm this.
Furthermore, I desire to be informed whether or not I am entitled to know the
grounds on which that finding was based since I wish to be quite clear about this.
On receipt of your reply, I will write you further with regard to the second
paragraph of your letter.'

On 20th August 1971 the council replied as follows:

'I am directed to reply to your letter dated the 29th July, 1971, and to say that
it is the Council which has to consider the propriety or otherwise of your conduct.
It has done so after considering the recommendations of the Inquiry Committee,
and is of the opinion that your statement that in refusing to reopen the appeal
the Judges were setting a seal on dishonesty is, on your own construction of the
words as set out in your letter of the 24th May, 1971, to the Inquiry Committee,
improper conduct.
'2. I am directed to enquire whether you wish to be heard by the Council
before any Order is made by it under Section 92(3) of the Legal Profession Act,
1966.'

Subsequently the appellant appeared before the council and was heard, and the
Law Society wrote to him on 5th May 1972 as follows:

'I am directed to refer to the Council meeting held last week at which you were
present and that notice was given to you of the Council's intention to make an
Order for the payment of a penalty and at which your representations were
heard.
'2. The Council after further due consideration has ordered that you pay $250/-
under section 89 of the Legal Profession Act (Cap. 217).'

On 26th May 1972 the appellant issued the originating summons applying to set
aside the penalty ordered. This came before Chua J who dismissed it, expressing the
brief opinion that the appellant had been guilty of contempt of court and that the
council was perfectly right in imposing the penalty. The appellant appealed with
leave of Chua J to the Court of Appeal, which dismissed the appeal. In the judgment
of that court they said: 'We can see no reason to interfere with the order made by
the Council. The words uttered by the Appellant were in our view improper and
ought not to have been used.'

A point was sought to be made for the appellant before their Lordships that it had
been argued before Chua J that the words used were 'grossly improper' and contempt
of court, and that Chua J held that they constituted contempt of court. Before their
Lordships these contentions were not advanced, and seem irrelevant to the question
whether the Court of Appeal in the passage quoted was correct. In their Lordships'
view the Court of Appeal was correct; and once the appellant failed in his suggestions
that the remark was made before the decision was pronounced, and that no matter
outside s 84(2) could be the subject of disciplinary action by a penalty, there could
be but one outcome of this appeal.

There is one final matter. The Court of Appeal held in the alternative that there
was no right of appeal to it in such a case. The respondent did not seek to support
that view before this Board, but since it is a question of jurisdiction the question must
be dealt with. Their Lordships are of the opinion that there is no sufficient ground for
excluding from s 29 of the Supreme Court of Judicature Act[1] as 'any judgment or
order of the High Court in any civil matter' the decision of a High Court judge on an

originating summons such as in the present case. There is no provision in the Legal
Profession Act excluding such appeal, and it is not to be found among the non-   *a*
appealable matters in s 34 of the former Act. The fact that by s 98(6) of the latter Act
it is expressly provided in the serious cases where a special court of three judges is to be
concerned that there is to be no appeal therefrom to the Court of Appeal but only
to the Judicial Committee of the Privy Council suggests to their Lordships that the
legislature was not minded to forbid appeal to the Court of Appeal in a case such as
the present one.   *b*

In the result therefore their Lordships dismiss the appeal with costs.

Appeal dismissed.

Solicitors: *Charles Russell & Co* (for the appellant); *Jaques & Co* (for the respondent).
                                                                                    c

Mary Rose Plummer   Barrister.

                                                                                    d

Services Europe Atlantique Sud (SEAS) v Stockholms Rederiaktiebolag SVEA
The Folias

COURT OF APPEAL, CIVIL DIVISION
LORD DENNING MR, ORMROD AND GEOFFREY LANE LJJ
8th, 9th, 22nd FEBRUARY 1978

Arbitration – Award – Foreign currency – Damages – Breach of contract – Currency in
which damages to be awarded – Currency most truly expressing or reflecting plaintiff's
actual loss – Charterparty governed by English law – Currency of contract US dollars –
Cargo arriving at Brazilian port of discharge in damaged condition due to unseaworthiness
of ship – Claims under bills of lading by cargo receivers against French charterers – Charterers
purchasing Brazilian cruzeiros with French francs to settle claims – Charterers claiming
damages payable by shipowners in French francs – Whether loss incurred in French francs   *e*
or Brazilian cruzeiros – Whether currency in which damages expressed that in which loss
has been incurred or that which reflected charterers' actual loss.

A French company ('the charterers') chartered a ship from its Swedish owners to
carry a cargo from Spain to Brazil. The charterparty contained a London arbitration
clause and the proper law of the contract was English law. During the voyage the
ship's refrigerating machinery failed and the cargo arrived in Brazil in a damaged   *f*
condition. The Brazilian receivers of the cargo claimed against the charterers as
issuers of the bills of lading for the damage to the cargo. On 11th August 1972
the charterers, whose place of business was Paris and who conducted their business in
French francs, settled the cargo receivers' claim in Brazilian cruzeiros which they
purchased with French francs. The charterers then claimed from the Swedish owners
the amount of French francs expended on the grounds that the owners had been in
breach of the warranty of seaworthiness in the charter. In the course of the ensuing   *g*
arbitration proceedings, the owners accepted liability and admitted that the measure
of damage was the amount the charterers had had to pay to the cargo receivers,
but disputed the currency in which they should pay damages to the charterers.
Between August 1972 and the time of the arbitration the cruzeiro devalued markedly

against the French franc to a little over half its value. The owners contended that the
award should be expressed in cruzeiros. On 24th July 1975 the arbitrators, rejecting
that contention, made an award for payment of the amount of French francs claimed
by the charterers. The arbitrators, however, stated a special case for the opinion of
the High Court as to whether the charterers were entitled to an award in French
francs. The judge[a] held that the award should be in cruzeiros in the absence of a
contrary intention in the contract, the damages having to be calculated in the currency
in which the loss had been incurred. The charterers appealed.

Held – The currency in which the charterers were to be compensated was to be
determined on the basis that (per Lord Denning MR) the recovery of expenditure
or loss incurred in a foreign currency, whether claimed as damages for breach of
contract or in tort, was to be expressed in the currency which most truly expressed
the charterers' loss, (per Ormrod LJ) the object of an award of damages was compensatory and justice required that it should as far as practicable reflect the charterers'
actual loss, and (per Geoffrey Lane LJ) the court was engaged in a practical enquiry
to ascertain which of the available currencies had the effect of compensating the charterers with justice and fairness to both sides. In the circumstances, the charterers'
actual loss was the amount of French francs expended by them in acquiring the
cruzeiros necessary to settle the cargo receivers' claim and the award should therefore
be expressed in French francs. Accordingly the appeal would be allowed and the
arbitrators' award restored (see p 769 *a b* and *g h*, p 771 *b c* and *h* to p 772 *c* and *g h*,
p 775 *b*, p 777 *f* and *h* to p 778 *b*, post)
Dictum of Lord Wilberforce in *Miliangos v George Frank (Textiles) Ltd* [1975] 3 All ER
at 813 applied.
Owners of mv Eleftherotria v Owners of mv Despina R, The Despina R [1977] 3 All
ER 874 followed.
Di Fernando v Simon, Smits & Co Ltd [1920] All ER Rep 347, *Owners of Steamship Celia
v Owners of Steamship Volturno* [1921] All ER Rep 110 and *The Canadian Transport* (1932)
43 Ll L Rep 409 not followed.
Decision of Robert Goff J [1977] 3 All ER 945 reversed.

Notes
For damages for breach of contract, the currency of which is a foreign currency, see
8 Halsbury's Laws (4th Edn) para 613.
For foreign currency liabilities converted into sterling for enforcement, see 27
Halsbury's Laws (3rd Edn) 6, para 5.
For judgments of a sum of money payable in foreign currency, see 12 Halsbury's
Laws (4th Edn) para 1201, and for cases on the subject, see 17 Digest (Reissue) 203-205,
749-758.

Cases referred to in judgments
Biggin & Co Ltd v Permanite Ltd [1951] 2 All ER 191, [1951] 2 KB 314, CA, 17 Digest
(Reissue) 156, 434.
Canadian Transport, The (1932) 43 Ll L Rep 409, CA.
Celia (Steamship) (Owners) v Owners of Steamship Volturno [1921] 2 AC 544, [1921] All ER
Rep 110, 90 LJP 385, 126 LT 1, 15 Asp MLC 374, 27 Com Cas 46, HL, 35 Digest (Repl)
196, 61.
Despina R, The, Owners of the mv Eleftherotria v Owners of the mv Despina R [1977] 3 All ER
874, [1977] 3 WLR 597, [1977] 1 Lloyd's Rep 618, [1977] 2 Lloyd's Rep 319, QBD and
CA.
Di Fernando v Simon, Smits & Co Ltd [1920] 3 KB 409, [1920] All ER Rep 347, 89 LJKB 1039,
124 LT 117, 25 Com Cas 37, CA, 35 Digest (Repl) 198, 78.

---

a [1977] 3 All ER 945

Federal Commerce and Navigation Co Ltd v Tradax Export SA [1977] 2 All ER 41, [1977] QB 324, [1977] 2 WLR 122, [1977] 1 Lloyd's Rep 217, CA; *rvsd* [1977] 2 All ER 849, *a* [1977] 2 WLR 126, [1977] 2 Lloyd's Rep 301, HL.
Hammond & Co v Bussey (1887) 20 QBD 79, 57 LJQB 58, CA, 17 Digest (Reissue) 163, *468.*
Jefford v Gee [1970] 1 All ER 1202, [1970] 2 QB 130, [1970] 2 WLR 702, [1970] 1 Lloyd's Rep 107, CA, Digest (Cont Vol C) 709, *182a.*
Jugoslavenska Oceanska Plovidba v Castle Investment Co Inc, The Kozara [1973] 3 All ER 498, [1974] QB 292, [1972] 3 WLR 847, [1973] 2 Lloyd's Rep 1, CA, Digest (Cont Vol D) *b* 46, *2136a.*
Kraut (Jean) AG v Albany Fabrics Ltd [1977] 2 All ER 116, [1977] QB 182, [1976] 3 WLR 872, [1976] 2 Lloyd's Rep 350.
Miliangos v George Frank (Textiles) Ltd [1975] 3 All ER 801, [1976] AC 443, [1975] 3 WLR 758, [1976] 1 Lloyd's Rep 201, HL, Digest (Cont Vol D) 691, *64c.*
Napier Star, The [1933] P 136, [1933] All ER Rep 88, 102 LTP 57, 149 LT 359, 18 Asp *c* MLC 400, 50 Digest (Repl) 533, *1991.*
Schorsch Meier GmbH v Hennin [1975] 1 All ER 152, [1975] QB 416, [1974] 3 WLR 823, [1975] 1 Lloyd's Rep 1, CA, Digest (Cont Vol D) 691, *64b.*
Teh Hu, The, Owners of Turbo-Electric Bulk Carrier Teh Hu v Nippon Salvage Co Ltd of Tokyo [1969] 3 All ER 1200, [1970] P 106, [1969] 3 WLR 1135, [1969] 2 Lloyd's Rep 365, CA, Digest (Cont Vol C) 807, *64a.* *d*
Treseder-Griffin v Co-operative Insurance Society Ltd [1956] 2 All ER 33, [1956] 2 QB 127, [1956] 2 WLR 866, [1956] 1 Lloyd's Rep 377, CA, 35 Digest (Repl) 190, *35.*

Cases also cited
Albazero, The, Owners of cargo lately laden on board ship or vessel Albacruz v Owners of the ship or vessel Albazero [1975] 3 All ER 21, [1975] 3 WLR 516, CA. *e*
Bain v Field & Co (1920) 5 Ll L Rep 16, CA.
British American Continental Bank, Re, Lisser and Rosenkranz's Claim [1923] 1 Ch 276, [1923] All ER Rep 52, CA.
Liebosch (Dredger) (Owners) v Owners of Steamship Edison, The Liebosch [1933] AC 449, [1933] All ER Rep 144.
United Railways of Havana and Regla Warehouses Ltd, Re [1960] 2 All ER 332, [1961] *f* AC 1007, HL.

Appeal
Services Europe Atlantique Sud (SEAS) ('the charterers') appealed against a judgment of Robert Goff J[1] dated 9th July 1976 in respect of an award in the form of a special case stated by the arbitrators (Robert Reed Esq and Donald Davies Esq) *g* in a dispute between the charterers and Stockholms Rederiaktiebolag SVEA ('the owners'), from whom the charterers had chartered the ms Folias under a time charterparty in New York Produce Exchange form dated 5th July 1971, in which he held that the award should have been made in the currency in which the loss had been incurred. The questions of law for the decision of the court and the judge's answers were: Question (1) whether on the facts found and on the true construction of the *h* charterparty the charterers were entitled to an award expressed in French francs. Answer 'No'. Question (2) if the answer to (1) was No (a) what currency was to be used for the award, Brazilian cruzeiros, US dollars or pounds sterling? (b) what was the appropriate date for rate of exchange purposes? Answer to (a) 'Brazilian cruzeiros'; answer to (b) 'Does not apply'. The charterers appealed on the grounds, inter alia, that the judge had been wrong in law and/or in fact in holding that Brazilian *j* cruzeiros rather than French francs were the currency of the loss and that the judge had been wrong in law in holding that the arbitrators were not entitled to make an award expressed in French francs or US dollars but were bound to make an award

---

1 [1977] 3 All ER 945

expressed in Brazillian cruzeiros. The facts are set out in the judgment of Lord
a Denning MR.

Gordon Pollock for the charterers.
Martin Moore-Bick for the owners.

Cur adv vult

b
22nd February. The following judgments were read.

LORD DENNING MR. In July 1971 the Swedish owners of the Folias let her on a
time charter to French charterers. The hire was payable in US dollars. In any general
c average adjustment, disbursements in foreign currencies were to be exchanged in a
European convertible currency or in pounds sterling or in US dollars. In case of any
dispute between the owners and the charterers, the matter in dispute was to be
referred to three commercial men in London, their decision, or that of any two of
them, to be final. The proper law was English law.

On 19th July 1971, at Valencia in Spain, the vessel loaded a cargo of onions in bags.
d They were to be carried to Santos in Brazil. The charterers issued their own bills of
lading for the carriage. During the voyage the refrigerating machinery failed,
with the result that some of the onions rotted. The cargo was discharged in Santos
on 22nd September 1971. The cargo receivers claimed damages on account of the
perished onions. They calcualted their damages in Brazilian currency, i e cruzeiros,
at the value of onions in Santos at the time. Their claim was against the French
e charterers for breach of contract, because they had issued the bills of lading. The
French charterers in turn claimed against the Swedish owners for breach of the express
warranty of seaworthiness in the charter. Eventually the claim was settled by the
French charterers. It was settled on 11th August 1972. The French charterers agreed
to pay the cargo receivers the sum of 456,250 cruzeiros. In addition, the French
charterers had to pay legal fees to their lawyers in Santos of 12,870·25 cruzeiros.
f The total was 469,120·25 cruzeiros. The French charterers had no cruzeiros with
which to pay those sums in cruzeiros. Their place of business was in Paris and they
conduct all their dealings in French francs. So they used their own French francs to
buy cruzeiros so as to pay the sums in Santos. They used 418,012·17 French francs
in order to buy the 469,120·25 cruzeiros needed in Santos. The charterers used those
francs and then claimed the amount from the Swedish owners. The Swedish owners
g agreed that the settlement with the cargo receivers was reasonable. But they disputed the French currency. They said that the award should not be given in French
francs, but in Brazilian cruzeiros, no doubt because they could buy cruzeiros very
cheaply. The arbitrators held that the French charterers were right. They gave
their award on 24th July 1975. They awarded that the shipowners were to
pay the French charterers 418,012·17 French francs (the sum the French charterers
had used on 11th August 1972), plus interest at ten per cent from 11th August
1972 to the date of the award, 24th July 1975. But they stated a case for the
opinion of the court. Robert Goff J[1] held that the arbitrators should have made their
award in 469,120·25 Brazilian cruzeiros (the amount paid to the cargo receivers on
11th August 1972), plus interest at ten per cent to 24th July 1975. But by that time,
July 1975, the Brazilian currency had weakened greatly against the French franc. The
h Brazilian cruzeiro was then, after three years, only worth half its former value in
French francs. If the French charterers got an award for 469,120·25 cruzeiros in July
1975, they would only be worth 230,000 French francs. So the French charterers would
have suffered a disastrous loss in their own currency. They would have used 418,012·17

French francs to settle the claim of the cargo receivers in August 1972, but would only have received 230,000 French francs in July 1975. The Swedish owners would, by the same token, have received a fortuitous benefit. With their Swedish kroners they could buy Brazilian cruzeiros very cheaply in July 1975; much more cheaply than in August 1972. The French charterers appeal to this court, asking us to restore the decision of the arbitrators.

2 The measure of damages

There was some discussion as to the measure of the damages to which the French charterers were entitled. It was suggested that they were only entitled to the difference between the market value the onions would have had if they were delivered undamaged, as against their value in their damaged condition. That would undoubtedly have been the measure as between the cargo receivers and the charterers (see (see Scrutton on Charterparties[1]), and was presumably the basis of the settlement between those parties. But, as between the charterers and the shipowners, the measure was the sum expended by the French charterers in settling the claim on reasonable terms, together with their costs: see *Hammond & Co v Bussey*[2] and *Biggin & Co Ltd v Permanite Ltd*[3].

3 The old law

In former times when judgments and awards had to be expressed in sterling, the charterers would have recovered the amount in Brazilian cruzeiros converted into sterling at the date of the breach when the goods were delivered damaged on 22nd September 1971: see *Di Fernando v Simon, Smits & Co Ltd*[4]. At that time the rate was 13·50 cruzeiros for £1 sterling. So the award would be for £34,750 sterling, with interest to the date of the award. The French charterers would not then suffer greatly by the weakening of the cruzeiros between September 1971 and July 1975. They would have an award in sterling which remained reasonably steady over that time. At any rate, the French charterers would not suffer such a disastrous loss as they would do under the decision of Robert Goff J; nor would the Swedish owners have received such a fortuitous benefit.

I do not think that any of our former cases have any application today when arbitrators are allowed to, and do, make their awards in foreign currency. In our present case none of the parties, and none of the transactions, had anything to do with sterling at all. In commercial practice, it would be a mistake for the arbitrators to make an award in sterling. Those former cases can and should be put to one side as being of no relevance today.

4 The present law

In former times the judges approached their cases on currency with two fixed beliefs. The first was that sterling was a stable currency. It was the one unit of currency which remained of constant value. Other currencies might fluctuate in value, but sterling remained the same. The second was that judgments of the courts could only be expressed in pounds sterling. So the courts had to convert any foreign currency into sterling at some time or other. The only question was: at what date? They answered it by saying: at the date of the breach or of the wrong done.

Those two beliefs have been shattered in modern times. As to the first, sterling is no longer a stable currency. Nor are US dollars. Nor French francs. No currency is stable. They all swing about with every gust that blows. As to the second, judgments need no longer be expressed in sterling. They can be expressed in whatever currency seems fair and just in the circumstances of the case.

1   18th Edn (1974), art 192
2   (1887) 20 QBD 79
3   [1951] 2 All ER 191, [1951] 2 KB 314
4   [1920] 3 KB 409, [1920] All ER Rep 347

In this situation I think we should start afresh and build up a body of case law on the subject. This was suggested by Lord Wilberforce in *Miliangos v George Frank (Textiles) Ltd*[1]:

'It is for the courts, or for arbitrators, to work out a solution in each case best adapted to giving the injured plaintiff that amount in damages which will most fairly compensate him for the wrong which he has suffered.'

5 Simple debts

One thing is already clear: in the case of a simple debt for hire of a ship or the price of goods sold and delivered, when the contract 'prescribes the currency in which the debt is to be paid, the award is for the amount due in the currency of the contract, together with interest: see *Jugoslavenska Oceanska Plovidba v Castle Investment Co Inc, The Kozara*[2], *Schorsch Meir GmbH v Hennin*[3] and *Miliangos v George Frank (Textiles) Ltd*[4]. Even though the currency may have diminished in value by inflation, the named sum must be awarded.

6 Expenditure

We have today to consider a familiar kind of damage, namely expense incurred by a plaintiff in consequence of the defendant's breach of contract or his tort. In English law, both in tort and in contract, a plaintiff is often entitled to be compensated for his actual expenditure on repairs, or his actual loss of wages or of hire. In such cases when dealing in sterling, the award in his favour gives him the very sums he has expended together with interest from the date of payment or of loss, up to the date of the judgment: see, for instance, in Admiralty cases, *The Napier Star*[5] and in other cases, *Jefford v Gee*[6]. When the sums are thus expended in sterling, there is no difficulty. If there is inflation, so that the sums expended are less in value by the time of the trial, nevertheless the plaintiff gets the named sums, and no more. That is the nominalistic principle which I stated in *Treseder-Griffin v Co-operative Insurance Society*[7]:

'Sterling is the constant unit of value by which in the eye of the law everything else is measured. Prices of commodities may go up or down, other currencies may go up or down, but sterling stays the same.'

Other countries apply the same principle in regard to their currencies.

But what is the position when the sums are expended in a foreign currency? And the plaintiff seeks to recover them in an English court or an English arbitration? There was much difficulty about this in the days when judgments had to be expressed in sterling. The question then arose: what is the date of conversion into sterling? At the date of the expenditure? Or at the date of the judgment? But there is no such difficulty when a judgment or award can be expressed in the terms of the foreign currency itself. Then the judgment or award should be made in the currency which is most appropriate in the circumstances of the case. As a general rule the plaintiff should be compensated for the expense or loss in the currency which most truly expresses his loss. This is best seen by the cases on collisions at sea where an innocent ship or cargo has been damaged by the negligence of another vessel; and the innocent owner has been put to expense or suffered loss of hire in consequence. I will take some old cases so as to contrast the old law with the new.

---

1   [1975] 3 All ER 801 at 813, [1976] AC 443 at 468
2   [1973] 3 All ER 498 at 501, [1974] QB 292 at 298
3   [1975] 1 All ER 152 at 156, [1975] QB 416 at 425
4   See eg [1975] 3 All ER 801 at 813 and 841, [1976] AC 443 at 467 and 501, per Lord Wilberforce and Lord Fraser of Tullybelton, respectively
5   [1933] P 136 at 138, 141, [1933] All ER Rep 886 at 888, 889
6   [1970] 1 All ER 1202 at 1208, [1970] 2 QB 130 at 146
7   [1956] 2 All ER 33 at 36, [1956] 2 QB 127 at 144

7 The Volturno¹ today

Take the facts in *The Volturno*¹. She was an Italian ship, owned by an Italian firm, *a*
let out on hire payable in Italian lire. She was damaged in a collision in the Mediterranean with a British ship, the Celia. She put into Gibraltar for temporary repairs,
and afterwards into Newport News (United States) for permanent repairs, where
the account was paid in US dollars. The Italian owners suffered loss of hire in Italian
lire. They had to use Italian lire so as to get dollars to pay for the repairs in the United
States. If the English courts had been able to give judgment in foreign currency, there *b*
is no doubt that, as a matter of justice, they ought to have compensated the Italian
owners by an award in Italian lire for their loss of hire and the cost of repairs. But
the English courts at that time had to give judgment in sterling. So they were presented with the question: are the Italian lire to be converted into sterling at the
date of the loss? Or at the date of the judgment? There was much to be said on both
sides. The House of Lords held that the conversion was to take place at the date of *c*
the loss. Now that the English courts can award judgment in a foreign currency, it is
plain that, if *The Volturno*¹ arose again today, the English courts could and should
compensate the Italian owners for their loss of hire in Italian lire and for the costs
of repairs in the amount of Italian lire they had to convert into dollars to pay for them.
In short, the plaintiff should be awarded his compensation in the currency which
most truly expressed his loss. That was the view taken by this court in *The Despina R*², *d*
which I trust will be upheld by the House of Lords.

The Italian owners would be entitled to interest on the money expended on repairs from the time it was paid until the date of judgment (see *The Napier Star*³)
and for the loss of hire from the time it was lost, just as we award interest in common
law claims for medical expenses and loss of wages: see *Jefford v Gee*⁴.

8 The Canadian Transport⁵ today

Take next the facts in *The Canadian Transport*⁵. It appears that a Frenchman bought
2,400 tons of logs in Argentina and shipped them on board a vessel bound for Le Havre
in France. Shortly after leaving Buenos Aires, she was damaged in a collision by the
negligence of the defendants. When the logs reached France there were 158 tons
missing. The Frenchman wanted to calculate his compensation in French francs. *f*
He said that, in order to buy the logs, he had had to use his French francs by converting them into Argentinian pesos, and that, when they arrived 158 tons short in
Le Havre, he had lost their value in French francs. But the English courts could not
give judgment in French francs. They had to give it in pounds sterling. So they took
it at the value in Argentinian pesos at the date of the collision and converted it into
sterling at that date. Now that the English courts can award judgment in a foreign *g*
currency, I should have thought it plain, as a matter of justice, that the Frenchman
should have been awarded damages in French francs, because that was the currency
which most truly expressed his loss. He suffered his loss at Le Havre where the logs
were short-delivered, and he lost their value in French francs.

9 The Teh Hu⁶ today

Similarly with salvage services. There is no need now for the salvage award to be
given in pounds sterling. It can be given in the currency which is fair and just in the *h*
circumstances. So *The Teh Hu*⁶ would be decided differently today, as indicated by
Lord Wilberforce in *Miliangos v George Frank (Textiles) Ltd*⁷.

---

1 [1921] 2 AC 544, [1921] All ER Rep 110
2 [1977] 3 All ER 874, [1977] 3 WLR 597
3 [1933] P 136 at 138, 141, [1933] All ER Rep 886 at 888, 889
4 [1970] 1 All ER 1202 at 1208, [1978] 2 QB 130 at 146
5 (1932) 43 Ll L Rep 409
6 [1969] 3 All ER 1200, [1970] P 117
7 [1975] 3 All ER 801 at 813, [1976] AC 443 at 468

10 *Damages for breach of contract*

a   There remains the question of damages for breach of contract. I will confine myself
to cases where the damage consists of expenses incurred in consequence of a breach
or loss of hire or wages. If such expense or loss is incurred in the currency of the
contract, then beyond doubt the award should be made in that currency: see *Federal
Commerce and Navigation Co Ltd v Tradax Export SA*[1]. But if the expense or loss
is incurred in another currency, then I think we should apply a similar rule to that
b   applied in tort, especially as it often happens that a plaintiff can frame his case either
in contract or in tort. On this footing it seems to me that damages should be awarded
to the plaintiff in the currency which most truly expresses his loss. If the expenditure
or loss is incurred in a foreign currency, but in order to meet it the plaintiff uses
his own currency in the ordinary course of his business, then the award should be
in his own currency: see *The Despina R*[2].

c   I would not like to consider today the problem of damages for loss of future profit
or future opportunities of gain. That is a subject which is under discussion in other
branches of law and may need separate consideration.

11 *Di Fernando v Simon, Smits & Co Ltd*[3] *today*

Take the facts of *Di Fernando v Simon, Smits & Co Ltd*[3]. An Italian buyer bought
d   sodium sulphide from an English firm for £1,555, and entrusted them to an English
carrier for carriage to Milan and delivery there. They should have been delivered in
Milan on 10th February 1919. But they were converted by the carrier to his own use.
The Italian buyer could have sued either in damages for breach of contract or in
tort for conversion. He sued in contract. The action was tried a year later, on 30th
March 1920. During that year sterling had remained steady, but the Italian lire
e   had fallen to half its value. The goods were still worth £1,555 in English money. But
in Italy, in order to pay that sum, you would have had to use 48,000 Italian lire on
10th February 1919 and 96,000 Italian lire on 30th March 1920. The English carrier
contended that he could discharge his liability by paying 48,000 Italian lire on 30th
March 1920, that is only £780 sterling. The English courts rejected that contention.
At that time they could only give judgment in sterling. They held that the carrier
f   was liable for 48,000 Italian lire and that the rate of exchange should be taken at the
date of the breach, 10th February 1919. So they awarded the Italian buyer £1,555.
I think the same result would be reached today. But for a different reason: the
Italian buyer had paid £1,555 for the goods in England, and had not received them.
To replace them, he would have had to expend £1,555 in sterling. The carrier had
converted them to his own use by disposing of them, presumably in England. He
g   ought clearly to pay damages in the sum of £1,555. That was the sum which most
truly expressed the plaintiff's loss; and not £780, as the carrier contended.

12 *Conclusion*

The general principle to be derived from the case is, therefore, that, when the
plaintiff is entitled to damages calculated by the expenditure of money or loss of
h   hire or wages, then, whether the claim is for breach of contract or for tort, the award
or judgment should be given for the plaintiff in the currency which most truly expresses his loss and interest should run from the date of the expenditure or the loss
of hire or wages to the date of the award or judgment.

Applying this principle to the present case, it seems to me that the currency which
most truly expresses the loss of the French charterers is French francs, and not
j   Brazilian cruzeiros. The French charterers had to use French francs in order to settle
the claim of the cargo receivers. They paid them on 11th August 1972. They should

---

1   [1977] 2 All ER 41 at 51, [1977] QB 324 at 341, 342
2   [1977] 3 All ER 874, [1977] 3 WLR 597
     [1920] 3 KB 409, [1920] All ER Rep 347

be compensated for that expenditure in French francs by an award of that sum at
that date, with interest thereafter. The arbitrators thought this was an approach   *a*
which led to 'commercial commonsense and justice', and it was the approach which
was being adopted in other cases in the City of London by other arbitrators. It is
always wise for the courts, in commercial matters, to follow the practice of the City
of London. That is what Lord Mansfield did. It is what we did in *Jugoslavenska
Oceanska Plovidba v Castle Investment Co Inc, The Kozara*¹ and *Schorsch Meier GmbH v
Hennin*². And we should do it again today. I would, therefore, allow the appeal and   *b*
restore the award of the arbitrators.

ORMROD LJ. I agree. The formal question for decision in this case is whether
the charterers, on the facts found, are entitled to an award of damages expressed in
French francs, or, if they are not, in what currency the award should be formulated   *c*
and at what rate of exchange. The live issue is whether the charterers should bear
the loss arising from the depreciation of the Brazilian cruzeiros against the French
franc between 11th August 1972, the date when the charterers incurred their loss,
and 24th July 1975, the date of the award in their favour against the owners. Put
in another way, it is whether the owners should benefit by the delay in settling the
charterers' claim.   *d*
    In the aftermath of *Miliangos v George Frank (Textiles) Ltd*³, the answer is by no
means an easy one. Robert Goff J came to the conclusion that the impact of that
case on the established principles of law governing the question was 'relatively
limited'⁴. In a subsequent case, *The Despina R*⁵, Brandon J and another division
of this court (Stephenson, Orr and Cumming-Bruce LJJ) took the view that the
shock wave of that decision extended over a wider area. I respectfully agree with this   *e*
conclusion. It seems to me to have loosened the foundations on which such well-
known authorities as *Di Ferdnando v Simon, Smits & Co Ltd*⁶ and *The Volturno*⁷
have stood for so long, and so has opened up the problem for reconsideration on
first principles.
    The charterers' claim against the owners was for damages for breach of the express
warranty of affreightment contained in the charterparty by reason of the failure   *f*
of the ship's refrigeration system. In consequence, a cargo of onions, shipped by the
charterers, but not owned by them, from Valencia to Rio de Janeiro and Santos,
suffered considerable damage. The charterers thereupon became liable to the
receivers of the cargo on their bills of lading. The date of the discharge was 22nd
September 1971, and on 11th August 1972 the charterers, with the approval of the
owners, settled the claim for 456,250 cruzeiros plus legal fees. They purchased the   *g*
cruzeiros for 418,012·17 French francs, the currency in which, as a French company
carrying on business in Paris, they account.
    In principle an award of damages is intended to restore the plaintiffs, subject to
remoteness, to the position in which they would have been had there been no breach
of contract, and the loss is valued at the date of breach. The object of an award of
damages, therefore, is compensatory and justice requires that it should as far as is   *h*
practicable reflect the actual loss. The facts as found in the present case would appear
to indicate an award in francs equal to the sum expended by the charterers in acquiring
the necessary cruzeiros to settle the receivers' claim in the first instance. Since the

1   [1973] 3 All ER 498, [1974] QB 292
2   [1975] 1 All ER 152, [1975] QB 416
3   [1975] 3 All ER 801, [1976] AC 443
4   [1977] 3 All ER 945 at 951, [1977] 3 WLR 176 at 182
5   [1977] 3 All ER 874, [1977] 3 WLR 597
6   [1920] 3 KB 409 [1920] All ER Rep 347
7   [1921] 2 AC 544, [1921] All ER Rep 110

former obstacles to expressing awards and judgments in currencies other than sterling
have been removed by the decisions in *Jugoslavenska Oceanska Plovidba v Castle In-*
vestment Co Inc, The Kozara[1] and in *Miliangos v George Frank (Textiles) Ltd*[2], it is
difficult at first sight to see any reason why the award in the instant case should not be
expressed in francs. On the evidence, the charterers proved their loss in French
francs and there is now power to express the award accordingly. Had the facts been
different, for example had they paid out of a cruzeiros account or out of an account
in some other currency, they might or might not, depending on the evidence, have
been able to prove that they suffered the loss in francs, or, as Brandon J put it in
The Despina R[3], that the loss was 'effectively felt or borne' by them in French francs.

Attractive as this solution to the problem is, it has been met, both in this case and in
The Despina R[4], by the strongly argued submission that, on the authorities, it is
not open to this court. This argument succeeded before both the very experienced
judges at first instance, although Brandon J's reluctance to accept it is apparent from
his judgment. This court, however, in *The Despina R*[5], 'after considerable oscillation
of mind', came to the conclusion that it was now free to adopt this solution if it was
thought right to do so on the facts. I have no doubt that they reached the right
conclusion.

The contrary argument is put in two ways. First, it is said that the long-established
rule which is conveniently summarised in Dicey and Morris[6] is still good law;
secondly, it is said that this court is bound by its previous decision in *The Canadian*
Transport[7]. The rule states:

'Where English law is the proper law of the contract, damages for its breach
must be calculated in the currency in which the loss was incurred, unless a
contrary intention emerges from the contract itself.'

This rule, which is based on a number of well-known authorities such as *Di Fernando v*
Simon, Smits & Co Ltd[8], has been the law for a very long time. It is, however, in-
timately linked to the now obsolete rule that judgments could be expressed only in
terms of sterling and, in my judgment, can only be supported in association with
that rule. Standing by itself it has no logical validity, for the currency in which the
loss was originally incurred, i e the currency used to pay for the repairs in *The Despina*
R[4], or for the damage to the onions in the present case, is determined largely by
chance. But so long as the law required the loss to be proved in terms of sterling,
and at the time of breach, all that was necessary was to prove the expenditure and
convert it into sterling at the rate then prevailing. Now that conversion into sterling
is no longer necessary there is no logical reason why it should not be converted into
francs or whatever currency best represents the plaintiff's true loss. In Lord Sumner's
words in *The Volturno*[9]:

'The agreed numbers of lire are only part of the foreign language in which the
court is informed of the damage sustained, and, like the rest of the foreign
evidence, must be translated into English. Being a part of the description
and definition of the damage, this evidence as to lire must be understood with
reference to the time when the damage accrues, which it is used to describe.'

1   [1973] 3 All ER 498, [1974] QB 292
2   [1975] 3 All ER 801, [1976] AC 443
3   [1977] 3 All ER 874 at 884, [1977] 3 WLR 597 at 609
4   [1977] 3 All ER 874, [1977] 3 WLR 597
5   [1977] 3 All ER 874 at 900, [1977] 3 WLR 597 at 627
6   The Conflict of Laws (9th Edn, 1973), p 895, r 172
7   (1932) 43 Ll L Rep 409
8   [1920] 3 KB 409, [1920] All ER Rep 347
9   [1921] 2 AC 544 at 555, [1921] All ER Rep 110 at 115

It is no longer necessary to translate the currency used to pay for the damage into English money and, therefore, the rule[1] has lost its meaning. Bankes LJ in *Di Fernando v Simon, Smits & Co Ltd*[2] made the same point when he said:

'The plaintiff is entitled to have his damages assessed as at the date of breach, and the Court has only jurisdiction to award damages in English money. The judge must therefore express those damages in English money, and in order to do so he must take the rate of exchange prevailing at the date of breach.'

In other words, the currency of expenditure rule was essentially evidential; it was part of the proof of loss in terms of sterling.

That brings me to the judgments in *The Canadian Transport*[3] which alone prevented Brandon J[4] from giving judgment in, what he conveniently called, the 'currency of the plaintiff'. This appears to be the only reported case prior to *Jugoslavenska Oceanska Plovidba v Castle Investment Co Inc, The Koçara*[5] in which the question of valuing the loss in terms of the plaintiff's currency is referred to. This is not in fact surprising since so long as the sterling rule applied there was no point in converting the expenditure into the plaintiff's currency and then into sterling at the date of the breach because the result of doing so would have yielded the same or approximately the same figure in sterling as would direct conversion from the currency of expenditure. Thus, in the present case the sterling equivalent at the date of payment of 456,250 cruzeiros was presumably approximately the same as the sterling equivalent of 418,012·17 French francs.

In *The Canadian Transport*[3] the French plaintiff was undoubtedly trying to benefit in some way from manipulating the exchange rates of the peso, the franc and sterling, but the facts are so badly reported in the only available report that it is impossible to determine what he was actually trying to do. It is obvious from the judgments that neither Scrutton LJ nor Greer LJ understood precisely what the plaintiff was claiming, but it looks as though he first made his claim in sterling after converting the pesos which he had to pay for the logs; he then converted sterling into francs, presumably at the rate prevailing when he bought the logs, because he had had to use francs to buy the pesos; he then proposed to ask for judgment for the sterling equivalent of the French francs at the rate prevailing at the date of the judgment. This is, however, largely guesswork. What is clear about this report is that the proposition with which we are concerned was not before the court at all because, for the reason already given, it would have been futile. Moreover, the plaintiff's proposition, whatever it was, was argued perfunctorily and summarily rejected by the court. In these circumstances the observations relied on cannot be more than obiter dicta.

The result is that, in my judgment, there is no authority which is binding on this court. Accordingly, we are free to decide the point on general principles. It is unnecessary and undesirable to attempt to replace Dicey and Morris's rule[1] with another rule of general application. In each case it will be for the plaintiff to claim his damages in such currency as he thinks appropriate, bearing in mind that the onus is on him to prove not only the quantum of his loss but also the currency in which he claims to have sustained it. Conversely, it will be open to defendants to challenge both claims. If, for example, the cruzeiro had appreciated in relation to the franc, the owners might have insisted on an award expressed in francs rather than cruzeiros.

In this connection the true nature of the plaintiff's loss may be as important as the financial arrangements which he had made to pay for the repairs or the breach of

---

1   Dicey and Morris, The Conflict of Laws (9th Edn, 1973), p 895, r 172
2   [1920] 3 KB 409 at 412, cf [1920] All ER Rep 347 at 349
3   (1932) 43 Ll L Rep 409
4   *The Despina R* [1977] 3 All ER 874 at 888, 889, [1977] 3 WLR 597 at 613
5   [1973] 3 All ER 498, [1974] QB 292

contract. In *The Volturno*[1] the true loss to the plaintiffs was the immediate depre-
a ciation of the ship in consequence of the collision, measured, at least in part, by the
cost of the repairs actually carried out; in *The Despina R*[2], similarly, the true loss
was the depreciation in value of the ship consequent on the damage sustained by it.
In the present case, it is the reduction in the charterers' profit on the voyage, not the
depreciation in value of the onions; this merely provided the measure of the loss
of profit.

b I would accordingly answer Yes to the first question in the special case. The second
question does not arise but, in the absence of an agreement, express or implied,
that damages, if any, were to be payable in US dollars, the charterers might have been
in difficulty in proving their loss in US dollars.

I agree that this appeal should be allowed.

c **GEOFFREY LANE LJ.** The facts are straightforward. The charterers of the
Folias are a French corporation whose currency of account is French francs. The
owners are Swedish. The material part of the cargo was onions in bags being shipped
from Valencia to a Brazilian port. By the terms of the charterparty, hire and other
payments were to be made in US dollars. In any general average adjustment disbursements in a foreign currency were to be exchanged in a European convertible
d currency or in sterling or in US dollars. The charterparty contained a London
arbitration clause and was governed by English law.

Owing to a fault in the vessel's refrigeration plant a portion of the cargo of onions
was damaged on arrival at the port of discharge. This resulted in claims under the bills
of lading by the cargo receivers which were on 11th August 1972 settled by the
charterers on terms which the owners agreed were reasonable. The charterers paid
e the relevant amount in Brazilian cruzeiros. The owners eventually accepted liability
on the basis that they were in breach of contract by reason of the defective refrigeration and that the measure of damage was the amount which the charterers had had
to pay the cargo receivers. Consequently the only problem which remained to be
decided was the currency in which the owners should be required to pay the damages.

The importance of the question arises from the fact that, since the cause of the action
f arose in September 1971, there has been a sharp fall in the value of the Brazilian
cruzeiro, certainly as against the French franc, and consequently, if payment is now
made in cruzeiros, this will result in a windfall for the owners whose breach of
contract caused the loss, and a corresponding detriment to the charterers who were
its victims.

As part of their reasons the arbitrators said:

g
> 'When the law appears to be neutral we think it right for commercial arbi-
> trators to take the approach which leads to commercial commonsense and
> justice ... [And they end with the sentence:] While recognising that, in the case
> before us, French Francs were not closely connected with the Charterparty
> transaction of July 5, 1971, nevertheless an Award in this currency seems to
h our minds to be the most appropriate and just result.'

They stated a special case for the opinion of the court on the question of the appropriate currency. Robert Goff J decided that the currency in which damages should be
paid in cases such as this was the currency of the country where the loss was incurred,
and since the charterers' liability was to reimburse the receivers under the bills of
lading for the diminished value of the goods at the Brazilian port, damages were
j payable in cruzeiros. Counsel for the charterers submits that this is wrong, and that
payment should be made in French francs or, as a second best, in US dollars.

The former practice of the courts of this country was entirely changed by the

---

1   [1921] 2 AC 544, [1921] All ER Rep 110
2   [1977] 3 All ER 874, [1977] 3 WLR 597

two well-known decisions of *Jugolavenska Oceanska Plovidba v Castle Investment Co Inc, The Kozara*[1] and *Miliangos v George Frank (Textiles) Ltd*[2]. Up to that time any award of damages had to be made in sterling whatever the currency of loss may have been, the conversion into sterling being made in cases of breach of contract at the date of the breach. So long as sterling was stable currency this resulted in substantial justice being done between the parties. It meant that, however great the lapse of time between the date of the breach of contract and the date of the award of damages, and however great the fluctuation in the value of the currency in which the loss was suffered, the plaintiff's interests would be protected by the stability of the sterling into which that loss had been notionally converted.

However, once sterling lost that enviable stability and started to depreciate in value against other leading currencies, plaintiffs began to suffer positive injustice from the operation of the sterling rule. It was this injustice which the decision in *Miliangos*[2] sought to remedy. The decision in that case concerned a money obligation. The House of Lords expressly declined to make pronouncements of any greater breadth than was necessary for a determination of the issue immediately before them. As Lord Wilberforce said[3]:

'In my opinion it should be open for future discussion whether the rule applying to money obligations, which can be a simple rule, should apply as regards claims for damages for breach of contract or for tort.'

Since then, and indeed since the date of Robert Goff J's judgment in this present case' the matter has been considered by another division of this court in *The Despina R*[4]. That was a case concerning damage to one ship caused by the negligent handling of another, in other words, a claim for damages in tort. The defendants there contended that *The Volturno*[5] and *Di Fernando v Simon, Smits & Co Ltd*[6] were still binding and ought to be followed insofar as they decided that the plaintiffs could only recover damages in sterling in the case of liability in tort. Neither Brandon J at first instance, nor the Court of Appeal accepted this argument and in the present case the argument was not even advanced before Robert Goff J.

The instant appeal is the first occasion on which this court has had to consider how far the decision in *Miliangos*[2] is applicable to cases where the defendant is liable for damages for breach of contract.

Counsel for the owners, whilst conceding that an award for damages for breach of contract no longer has to be made in sterling, submits that that is the effective limit of the changes which *Miliangos*[2] has wrought, and that we are accordingly bound by the earlier decisions of this court and the House of Lords (in particular *The Volturno*[5] and *Di Fernando v Simon, Smits & Co Ltd*[6]) as to the currency in which the loss should in the first place be assessed before awarding damages, although we are no longer under any obligation to convert that amount into sterling. That means, goes the submission, that there is no power to make the initial valuation on some different basis from that laid down in those authorities, nor, having made it on the same basis, have we any power to convert the amount so ascertained into some currency other than sterling. The rule in those cases was that, where the damages consisted of loss incurred directly and immediately in a foreign currency, that is the currency in which the initial assessments of damages should be made.

Counsel for the owners further relied on a decision of this court in *The Canadian Transport*[7]. In that case a French firm claimed damages from the owners of the Canadian

---

1   [1973] 3 All ER 498, [1974] QB 292
2   [1975] 3 All ER 801, [1976] AC 443
3   [1975] 3 All ER 801 at 813 [1976] AC 443 at 468
4   [1977] 3 All ER 874, [1977] 3 WLR 597
5   [1921] 2 AC 544, [1921] All ER Rep 110
6   [1920] 3 KB 409, [1920] All ER Rep 347
7   (1932) 43 Ll L Rep 409

Transport for the loss of part of the cargo of logs being carried aboard their own vessel
a which was sunk. The cargo had been purchased in Argentina under a contract
of sale which provided for payment in pesos. The plaintiffs carried out some complex
and profitable financial juggling, but they contended that they would have been
entitled to convert the pesos into francs, on the ground that they were a French firm
who had to use francs to buy the pesos in order to purchase the cargo. Therefore the
initial valuation of loss should be made in French francs. Those contentions were
b rejected by the court. It is true that there were particular reasons for the court
in that case reaching the conclusion it did; it seems that there was a concession by
counsel (the extent of which is not altogether clear) on which the court may
have well been basing itself. This of its own would no doubt be a justification for
not following the decision: see per Stephenson LJ in the *The Despina R*[1]. It seems
to me, however, that once one accepts that there is no longer any rule requiring
c damages for breach of contract to be claimed or assessed in sterling, that radical
change destroys the effect of any decisions based on the former rule. Whether one
is considering *The Volturno*[2] or *Di Fernando v Simon, Smits & Co Ltd*[3] or *The Canadian
Transport*[4], in each case the court was viewing the matter in an entirely different
light from that in which we now have to view the facts of such cases. Accordingly,
it would be carrying the force of precedent to unwarranted lengths to say that any
d part of those decisions is either helpful or binding on us now. It is incumbent
on us to consider the matter afresh. Those are the views taken by the Court of
Appeal in *The Despina R*[5] and by Eveleigh J in an earlier case, *Jean Kraut AG v Albany
Fabrics Ltd*[6], and I agree with them.

Lord Wilberforce in *Miliangos*[7] said:

e   'It is for the courts, or for arbitrators, to work out a solution in each case best
        adapted to give the injured plaintiff that amount in damages which will most
        fairly compensate him for the wrong which he has suffered.'

Accordingly, we are not engaged on a recondite jurisprudential exercise to discover
in which currency it was that the loss can properly be said to have been suffered.
It is a practical enquiry in each case to find out which of the available currencies
f will have the effect of compensating the plaintiffs most fairly, that is, with justice
and fairness on each side.

What are the available currencies here?

(1) *Brazilian cruzeiros*. This was the currency in which the charterers had to reimburse the cargo receivers for their loss. Apart from its close connection with the
loss it has little to recommend it. Its adoption, as already pointed out, results in a
g loss to the charterers and gain to the owners, which in justice should, if possible, be
avoided.

(2) *US dollars*. This was the currency of the contract but it had otherwise no connection with the charterers or the owners. Its adoption, however, would produce a
substantially just result.

(3) *Sterling*. It is not, I think, contended that sterling has any sufficient connection
h with the parties in the contract to be seriously considered as a solution, nor would
it do any more justice than cruzeiros.

(4) *French francs*. This currency I regard on the finding of the arbitrators as more
truly the currency of the loss than the cruzeiros. It is true that the bad onions represented a loss of cruzeiros to the receivers, but to the charterers these lost cruzeiros

j 1 [1977] 3 All ER 874 at 900, [1977] 3 WLR 597 at 627
    2 [1921] 2 AC 544, [1921] All ER Rep 110
    3 [1920] 3 KB 409, [1920] All ER Rep 347
    4 (1932) 43 Ll L Rep 409
    5 [1977] 3 All ER 874, [1977] 3 WLR 597
    6 [1977] 2 All ER 116, [1977] QB 182
    7 [1975] 3 All ER 801 at 813, [1976] AC 443 at 468

meant a loss of francs, because they had to spend francs to acquire the cruzeiros to make good the shortage of sound onions. Francs are the charterers' currency of *a* account. They operate their business in francs. Consequently if they now receive their damages for breach of contract in francs they will be getting back the same type of currency as that which they expended. As Brandon J lucidly points out in *The Despina R*[1], if there has been any drop in the value of the plaintiffs' currency between the date of the breach and the date of the payment, this solution means that the plaintiffs are only suffering the effect of such changes in the internal value of *b* their own currency.

For these various reasons I have no doubt that the arbitrators were right in the conclusions which they reached. Speaking for myself, I consider it unnecessary and inadvisable to try and lay down any rule of general application. Each case will have different features. Financial situations are for ever changing. It may be that at present the plaintiffs' currency of account will seem in most cases to offer the *c* most attractive solution. That is a question which can safely be left to arbitrators to decide in the particular circumstances of the case they are considering.

I would allow the appeal.

Appeal allowed. Arbitrators' award restored. Answer to question (1): Yes; answer to *d* *question (2) does not arise. Leave to appeal to the House of Lords granted.*

Solicitors: *Holman, Fenwick & Willan* (for the charterers); *William A Crump & Son* (for the owners).

e

Sumra Green   Barrister.

---

1   [1977] 3 All ER 874 at 885, [1977] 3 WLR 597 at 610

Mitchell v London Borough of Ealing

QUEEN'S BENCH DIVISION
O'CONNOR J
16th, 17th, 20th FEBRUARY 1978

Bailment – Gratuitous bailment – Liability of bailee – Delay in redelivery of goods – Bailee's
negligence causing delay in redelivery during which time goods stolen – Whether bailee became
insurer of goods from the moment his negligence caused delay in redelivery.

In 1975 the plaintiff moved as a squatter into a council flat. The council obtained a
possession order and on 16th December 1975 the bailiffs arrived at the flat to take
possession, bringing with them a lorry to remove the plaintiff's furniture for storage.
The plaintiff, being unable to remove the furniture herself, consented to the council
removing and storing the furniture until she could make arrangements for its collection. The council then removed the furniture to a lock-up garage where it was stored.
On 17th December the plaintiff's husband asked the council for permission to collect
the furniture and presented the plaintiff's written authority for him to do so. Arrangements were made between the husband and a representative of the council for the
husband to collect the furniture on 19th December. On that day the husband arrived
at the arranged meeting place but because of a mistake in the council offices the
council's representative went to the wrong place with the result that the husband was
unable to collect the furniture. Fresh arrangements were made for the furniture to be
handed over on 15th January 1976 but when the parties arrived at the lock-up garage
on that day it was discovered that it had been burgled and the plaintiff's furniture
stolen. The plaintiff brought an action against the council claiming the return of the
furniture or, alternatively, its value.

Held – The council when they removed and stored the furniture became gratuitous
bailees of it and their failure on 19th December to send their representative to the
agreed place for redelivery was a negligent failure on their part leading to an inexcusable delay in complying with a lawful and unequivocal demand by the bailor
for the return of the furniture. From the moment of their negligent failure the
council became insurers of the furniture and liable for its loss despite the fact that
there had been no refusal on the part of the council to redeliver. The plaintiff was
accordingly entitled to judgment (see p 782 *a b* and p 784 *a* to *c*, post).

Shaw & Co v Symmons & Sons [1916-17] All ER Rep 1093 applied.

Notes

For the obligations of a gratuitous bailee, see 2 Halsbury's Laws (4th Edn) paras 1515,
1516, and for cases on the subject, see 3 Digest (Repl) 63-66, *49-82*.

Cases referred to in judgment

Clayton v Le Roy [1911] 2 KB 1031, [1911-13] All ER Rep 284, 81 LJKB 49, 105 LT 430,
    75 JP 521, CA, 46 Digest (Repl) 484, *319.*
Shaw & Co v Symmons & Sons [1917] 1 KB 799, [1916-17] All ER Rep 1093, 86 LJKB 549,
    117 LT 91, 3 Digest (Repl) 101, *280.*

Cases also cited

British Crane Hire Corpn Ltd v Ipswich Plant Hire Ltd [1974] 1 All ER 1059, [1975] QB 303,
    CA.
Capital Finance Co Ltd v Bray [1964] 1 All ER 603, [1964] 1 WLR 323, CA.
Taylor v Caldwell (1863) 3 B & S 826.

Action

By a writ issued on 2nd June 1976 the plaintiff, Margaret Rose Mitchell, claimed *a* against the defendants, the London Borough of Ealing, delivery up of goods and furniture belonging to the plaintiff detained and stored by the defendants, or £2,500 being their value and damages for their detention, and damages for trespass and/or conversion. The facts are set out in the judgment.

David Watkinson for the plaintiff.   *b*
B Hillman for the defendants.

O'CONNOR J. In this action the plaintiff claims the return of household chattels stored by the defendants or, alternatively, their value. The case arises in this way. In 1975 the plaintiff (Mrs Mitchell) and her husband were in occupation of a local *c* authority flat, 47 Sherringham Towers on the Golflinks Estate in Ealing, and Mr Mitchell was the tenant of the flat. The rent was not paid and notice to quit was given. In due course the Mitchells moved out of that flat, taking their household belongings and furniture with them, and unlawfully moved in as squatters to another flat belonging to the defendants. When their whereabouts and wrongdoing was discovered action was brought against them in the Uxbridge County Court to gain *d* possession of those premises, 10 Whittel Close. An order was made and process for eviction was taken. They were given some time to remove their furniture. They greeted that concession by breaking back into the premises and changing the locks and once more unlawfully occupying it. Before a further process for their eviction could be mounted they moved out of that accommodation. It would seem that at about this time they separated as husband and wife, but the fact is that they, certainly Mrs Mitchell, unlawfully moved into another unoccupied flat, 1 Rutherford Towers, on the estate, taking furniture and contents of the flat and installing it in those premises.

Thus it was that late in 1975 the defendants once more took action against the plaintiff to get possession of the flat which she was wrongfully occupying. The order was made and, at the same time, the county court granted to the local authority an injunction to restrain the plaintiff and her husband from occupying any other property belonging to the council. The bailiffs appeared at 1 Rutherford Towers on the morning of 16th December 1975, and they were accompanied by representatives of the defendants, Mrs Findlay, who has given evidence and who is an assistant housing officer, and Mr Simmonds. The council, in the goodness of their heart, despite the woeful treatment to which they had been subjected by thoroughly dishonest people, sent a lorry to remove the furniture for storage in case the plaintiff should be unable to remove it herself at that moment. While the bailiffs were there and while the defendants' representatives were taking a careful inventory of the goods found on the premises, the plaintiff appeared and she behaved quite appallingly in view of what her history was, but, in the end, when faced with the issue and, refusing to communicate directly with Mrs Findlay (who is a mild-mannered, honest woman, unlike the plaintiff and her husband), she communicated through the bailiff, and faced, as I have said, with the choice as to whether she could take her furniture away, which she could not, she consented to it being put on the lorry and taken away by the local authority for storage until she could make arrangements for its collection.

On the afternoon of 16th December Mr Mitchell, the husband, appeared on the scene and asked the housing officers for permission to collect the property from wherever it might be. Now, it is important to remember that at this stage the Mitchells had carefully concealed their whereabouts. Nobody knew where they were living. When he appeared on the scene he was told that the council would not hand any of the contents of the flat over to him without his wife's written authority. That was a perfectly reasonable attitude to adopt. The following day he obtained written authority from his wife and presented it to the local authority. That having been done he was not told where the goods were, but an arrangement was made between him and Mrs Findlay that he should meet a representative of the defendants' at the rent office on the Golflinks Estate on 19th December and he would then be taken to where the property was and permitted to take it away.

It is quite plain that at that stage a lawful and unequivocal demand for the return of the goods had been made on the defendants. It is quite plain that Mr Mitchell was his wife's agent for this purpose, recognised as such, and had her full authority to collect the contents of the flat. It matters not whether some of the articles belong to him personally or are jointly owned by him and his wife. It is equally clear that a perfectly proper arrangement was made for handing over the goods and the arrangement, as I have said, was that a meeting was to take place on 19th December at the rent office. Neither Mr Mitchell nor the plaintiff knew the whereabouts of the place where the goods were stored. Unfortunately, on the 19th Mr Mitchell presented himself at the right place at the rent office, but, through a mistake in the defendants' offices, their representative, Mr Simmonds, went to the wrong place. He went to a lock-up garage, where the goods were stored. In the result the two men never met. Mr Mitchell telephoned to the Housing Department, tried to speak to Mrs Findlay, but she was engaged and it was impossible for him to get through. No blame is to be attached to her or to the local authority for the failure to answer the telephone call.

Therefore the position was on 19th December that the goods were still in the lock-up garage. The defendants did not know and had no means of communicating either with the plaintiff or her husband, and they had to wait until the Mitchells resurfaced. The evidence does not disclose when that was, but the inference is that it was some time after Christmas 1975, perhaps early in January. At all events, a fresh arrangement was made for the goods to be handed over on 15th January 1976, and on that date the plaintiff and her husband rented a van in order to load up the contents of their flat, and they met the representatives of the defendants. They went to the lock-up garage on the Golflinks Estate, and when the door was opened it was found that burglars had preceded them. The contents were gone, save for a broken bedstead and a few old pots.

Those are the facts on which this claim is founded.

I will come in detail to the law in a moment, but, broadly, it is well recognised that a gratuitous bailee, and that is what the defendants were of the plaintiff's goods, is bound to take reasonable care of the goods bailed and to deliver them up when an unequivocal demand is made. If the bailee is unable to deliver the goods he is liable for their value unless he can show that they have been lost without negligence or default on his part and, again, the time of such loss is of importance. The defendants recognise, therefore, that the duty was on them to show that they had acted reasonably and that the loss had occurred without fault on their part.

In the first place the plaintiff alleged that the lock-up garage was not a suitable place to store household furniture which included a stereo set which may be of some value, though I say nothing about that. It was said that this was an ordinary lock-up garage with an up-and-under door with a handle and a key fitted into it and that it is not a difficult operation to break into it. I cannot accept that contention. The local authority, who, through the goodness of their hearts, had decided to store the plaintiff's furniture rather than put it out on the street, made use of this lock-up garage. The evidence is that from time to time that is where they put the goods of premises of which they had obtained possession by bailiffs' warrant, and Mrs Findlay told me (and I accept her evidence without hesitation) that they had no recorded incident of goods being stolen from such a place. I hold, therefore, that there was no negligence on the part of the defendants in encasing the contents of the flat in the lock-up garage. Equally, there is no blame to be attached to them for not mounting a guard on the place, which was suggested, and the fact that thieves broke in and helped themselves to the contents of the garage cannot be laid at the doors of the local authority, unless it be that they were no longer gratuitous bailees at the relevant time.

The real point in this case emerges when one comes to consider the fact of what took place on 19th December. The plaintiff's case on that topic is that, a lawful and unequivocal demand having been made on 17th December and an arrangement having been made for the delivery of the goods, the defendants were bound to take reasonable care to comply with it, and that, by sending their man to the wrong place, they acted negligently, and that from that moment onwards no longer were they holding the goods as gratuitous bailees but they were holding them at their peril, and that, unless the defendants can prove that the loss occurred before the arranged time of delivery on the 19th, they are liable as insurers for the loss of the goods.

It is common ground that the defendants cannot prove when it was, between 16th December and 15th January, that the goods disappeared. The probability is (this is of importance) that it was some time later than the 19th, and the reason for that is that one item, a gas cooker, did not go on the lorry on 16th December. The defendants had to wait for the gas board to detach that article and it was added to the contents of the garage at a subsequent time. Nobody can say precisely when and, as there was no report that the garage was empty when the gas cooker was put in, it is assumed that thieves had not broken into it until later. At all events, it does not matter.

The answer which the defendants make to that is to say that what took place on 19th December cannot be ranked as a refusal to deliver the plaintiff's goods; that it was a mistake which was made and that they were unable to rectify the mistake by communicating with the plaintiff or her husband because they did not know of their whereabouts, and that, in any event, when the arrangement was remade they, so to speak, became bailees again.

What is the law on this topic? It is to be found, first of all, in Story's Law of Bailments[1]:

'No right of action, however, accrues in any case against the bailee, unless there has been some wrongful conversion or some loss by gross negligence on his part, until after a demand made upon him, and a refusal by him, to redeliver the deposit. A demand and refusal is ordinarily evidence of a conversion; unless the circumstances constitute a just excuse, or a justification of the refusal.'

Story further says[2]:

'If the depositary improperly refuses to redeliver the deposit, when it is demanded, he henceforth holds it at his own peril. If, therefore, it is afterwards lost, either by his neglect, or by accident, it is his own loss; for he is answerable for all defaults and risks in such cases.'

While I am looking at Story it is necessary to consider the place where delivery is to be made. He discusses that matter and has this to say[3]:

'The next enquiry is, as to the place where restitution is to be made. If a particular place is agreed on between the parties, that of course is to regulate the matter. If no place is agreed on, the property ought to be restored at the place where it is found, or where it ought to be kept.'

In the present case it is quite plain that there was an agreement as to the place where restitution was to be made, namely at the rent office on 19th December. That was the place which had been agreed on between the two of them.

The law, as stated by Story in 1870, is confirmed in Mr Paton's book, Bailments in the Common Law[4], where he says in discussing the duty to return: 'Restitution

---

1   8th Edn (1870), para 107
2   Ibid, para 122
3   Ibid, para 117
4   (1952), p 100

a should be made at the place agreed upon, or if no express agreement has been made then the court infers an implied agreement by considering all the circumstances of the case.' He then has this to say[1] under the heading 'Delay in Returning':

b 'If the depositee is *in mora*, (i.e., if he improperly refuses to restore the goods), then the goods are held at his peril. This was the rule of civil law, but as the refusal to restore would constitute the tort of detinue, an action for the full value of the chattel would lie at once. Subsequent restitution would merely go to reduction of damages.'

The present case, it will be seen, does not amount to a refusal. Is then an unequivocal refusal a necessary element before it can be said that the goods are held at the peril of the bailee? The cases cited in the works to which I have referred support some of the propositions. The proposition found in the recent edition of Halsbury's *c* Laws of England[2], which deals with demand and says that the bailee is excused if he can show that his failure to return the chattel arises from its loss or destruction before the demand for its return without default on his part, requires qualification. The cases show that the bar does not fall at the moment that the demand is made. Common sense would tell one that that must be so. So, in the present case, the bar did not fall when the unequivocal demand was made on 17th December. It fell, if it fell at all, on *d* the 19th, when the defendants failed to turn up at the agreed locus for handing over the goods. That appears quite clearly from the authorities, and the statement in Halsbury[2] is, I think, a misreading of one of the old cases where a horse had been deposited with the bailee and, before demand was made, the horse died and, naturally, on the facts of that case the bailee was excused his failure to redeliver the horse because it had died, and the facts were that it had died before demand was made. But, in my *e* judgment, it would not have mattered if a reasonable time had elapsed between the demand and the actual occasion of delivery. That that is right is plainly supported by other authorities. See, for example, *Clayton v Le Roy*[3]. It is unnecessary to refer to the facts of that case, but the case on which the plaintiff is really entitled to found is the case of *Shaw & Co v Symmons & Sons*[4]. That is not a case of gratuitous bailment, but it is of importance in the present case. The facts in *Shaw's* case[4] were that the plaintiff *f* agreed with the defendant that the defendant would bind such books as the plaintiff delivered to him and keep them until the plaintiff called on him to deliver the bound books. It was a running agreement. From time to time the defendant was entitled to send his account for the books that he had bound and the plaintiff would pay. On 7th January 1916 the plaintiff demanded of the defendant delivery of all the books that he was then holding which had been bound. During the few days *g* thereafter he made two telephone calls expressing the urgency of his needs, but because of the shortage of labour (and it must be remembered that in January 1916 the effects of the Great War were at their peak) the defendant was unable and had not got around to packing up the bound books and sending them to the plaintiff. On 20th January, without fault on the defendant's part, his premises were burned down and the books were destroyed. In those circumstances (and the question was *h* whether there had been an unreasonable delay in complying with the demand in accordance with the facts of that case) the court came to the conclusion that by the 20th, allowing for all the circumstances, there had been an unreasonable delay, and that by the 20th the defendant was an insurer of the books and liable for their loss, regardless of any fault on his part. It will be seen by analogy that there was no refusal to deliver the goods in that case. There was merely a delay in complying with *j* the demand and it proved to be an inexcusable delay.

1   (1952), p 111
2   2 Halsbury's Laws (4th Edn) para 1582
3   [1911] 2 KB 1031, [1911-13] All ER Rep 284
4   [1917] 1 KB 799, [1916-17] All ER Rep 1093

Applying the law laid down in *Shaw & Co v Symmons & Sons*[1] to the facts of the present case (sympathetic as I am with the defendants) it seems to me that the failure of the defendants to send their representative to the agreed place for the delivery of the goods was a negligent failure on their part, and from that moment they became insurers of the goods. As I have said in the earlier part of this judgment the plaintiff's claim has no merits to support it, but the law, in my judgment, is clear. It was a mistake on the part of the defendants, and, as I have said, I have great sympathy with them that they were unable to rectify it. But the arrangement made on 17th December fits precisely into the pattern of the law as I recognise it to be well-established, and the failure of the defendants to keep the appointment was a failure which makes them responsible thereafter for the loss of the goods. Had they been able to establish that the goods were lost at a time after the new arrangement was made then it might be that different considerations would apply, because it might be that it was only in the interim that they were holding the goods as insurers. But they are quite unable to do that and, as I have said, no one can establish the date when the fresh arrangement was made, and, as the defendants cannot say when it was that the goods were lost, that matter would not avail them.

It follows that there must be judgment for the plaintiff on this claim.

Judgment for the plaintiff.

Solicitors: *Offenbach & Co* (for the plaintiff); *William Charles Crocker* (for the defendants).

K Mydeen Esq   Barrister.

---

1   [1917] 1 KB 799, [1916-17] All ER Rep 1093

a
Watkins v Kidson (Inspector of Taxes)

COURT OF APPEAL, CIVIL DIVISION
STAMP, ROSKILL AND CUMMING-BRUCE LJJ
8th, 9th, 22nd MARCH 1978

b   *Capital gains tax – Computation of chargeable gains – Asset held on 6th April 1965 – Land – Sale reflecting development value – Consideration for asset acquired on disposal exceeding what market value would be if before disposal it had become unlawful to carry out any development – Sale of land without planning permission – Consideration on sale reflecting likelihood of obtaining planning permission – Development without permission unlawful – Whether statutory hypothesis that development had 'become' unlawful capable of application where*
c   *development without permission already unlawful – Finance Act 1965, Sch 6, para 23(1)(b).*

In 1962 the taxpayer acquired 22 acres of farm land for £1,581. In 1971 the local authority published a proposal to zone an area which included that land for residential development. On 26th January 1972 the taxpayer sold the land, which he had been using for agricultural purposes, to a land development company for
d £264,000. That sum reflected the hope or expectation that the planning authorities would be willing to grant planning permission authorising residential development of the land. No planning permission authorising such development had been obtained. The taxpayer was assessed to capital gains tax on the gain accruing on the sale of the land on the basis that Sch 6, para 23[a], to the Finance Act 1965 applied and that the gain was, by virtue of para 23(1)(b), to be computed by reference to the extent to which
e the consideration acquired on the disposal of the land exceeded what would have been the market value of the land 'if immediately before the disposal it had become unlawful to carry out any development in, on or over the land other than development of the kinds specified in Schedule 3 to the Town and Country Planning Act 1962'. The taxpayer appealed against the assessment, contending that since at the date of disposal of the land there was no planning permission in force authorising
f the development of the land it was in fact unlawful to carry out development of the land immediately before the disposal, that therefore it was logically impossible for the purposes of the hypothetical valuation under para 23(1)(b) to postulate the assumption required to be made, because where it was already unlawful to carry out development it could not 'become' unlawful to carry out development, and that in consequence para 23 could not apply as the requirements of para 23(1)(b) were
g not satisfied, and his chargeable gain fell to be computed on the straight line apportionment basis prescribed by Sch 6, para 24.

Held – The assumption required to be made by para 23(1)(b) of Sch 6 to the 1965 Act was not that some particular development of the land had become unlawful but that 'any development' with or without planning permission (other than development
h of the kind specified in Sch 3 to the 1962 Act) had become unlawful. Since in the taxpayer's case it was, subject to obtaining planning permission, lawful at the date of the disposal to develop the land, notwithstanding that such permission had not in fact been obtained, it followed that para 23(1) applied to the disposal of the land. Accordingly the appeal would be dismissed (see p 788 *j* to p 789 *b*, post).
Decision of Fox J [1977] 3 All ER 545 affirmed.

j
Notes
For the computation of chargeable gains arising on the disposal of land reflecting development value, see 5 Halsbury's Laws (4th Edn) para 174

---

a   Paragraph 23, so far as material, is set out at p 788 *a* to *d*, post

For the Finance Act 1965, Sch 6, paras 23, 24, see 34 Halsbury's Statutes (3rd Edn) 943, 945.

In relation to disposals made after 17th December 1973, s 23 of the 1965 Act has been amended by s 48 of the Finance Act 1974.

Appeal

The taxpayer, William Henry Watkins, inherited Westhill Farm, Brackley, Northamptonshire, on the death of his father on 8th January 1962. The farm consisted of about 122 acres of freehold land. In September 1962 the Northamptonshire County Council submitted a town map for the borough of Brackley to the Minister of Housing and Local Government, which he approved in June 1965. That provided, inter alia, for the population growth of the borough from 3,200 persons in 1962 to 5,000 by 1981. In October 1971 the council published a report which provided for a further growth in the then population from about 6,000 persons to 8,400 by 1981, and 10,800 by 1986. For that purpose a further area was zoned for residential use and mainly private development, constituting some 223 acres. That area included 22 acres of Westhill Farm. Those proposals had no immediate legal effect. In particular, they did not eliminate the need to obtain planning permission before residential development could be carried out. On 24th January 1972 a planning application for residential development was made by the Brackley council and the taxpayer in respect of an area which included the 22 acres of Westhill Farm. By a contract of sale dated 26th January 1972 and completed on 28th February 1972, the taxpayer sold the 22 acres to West London Estate Developments Ltd for £264,000. The value of the 22 acres at the death of the taxpayer's father was £1,581. On 4th July 1973 the application for planning permission was approved subject to conditions. The price of £264,000 for which the 22 acres were sold reflected the hope or expectation that the planning authorities would be willing to grant planning permission authorising residential development of the land. If there had been no prospect of obtaining planning permission for any development (other than development specified in Sch 3 to the Town and Country Planning Act 1962) the market value of the land would have been substantially less than £264,000.

The taxpayer was assessed to capital gains tax for 1971-72 in respect of a gain of £258,961. The assessment related mainly to the gain arising on the disposal of the 22 acres of Westhill Farm under the contract of 26th January 1972. The assessment was made on the basis that para 23 of Sch 6 to the Finance Act 1965 applied to the case. The taxpayer appealed to the Special Commissioners, contending (i) that Sch 6, para 23, could not apply because the requirements of para 23(1)(b) were not satisfied, and (ii) that his chargeable gain fell to be computed on the straight line apportionment basis prescribed by Sch 6, para 24. The commissioners held that Sch 6, para 23, applied and referred to the Lands Tribunal the following questions for determination:

'1. Whether with reference to paragraph 23(1)(b) of Part II of the 6th Schedule to the Finance Act 1965, £264,000 being the consideration for the disposal of the said land on 26 January 1972 exceeded what the market value of the said land would have been if immediately before the disposal it had become unlawful to carry out any development on or over the land other than development of the kinds specified in Schedule 3 to the Town and Country Planning Act 1962.
'2. What for the purpose of paragraph 23(2) of the 6th Schedule to the Finance Act 1965 was the market value of the freehold of the above land on 6 April 1965 ...'

Immediately after the making of the reference the taxpayer required the commissioners to state a case for the opinion of the High Court pursuant to s 56 of the Taxes Management Act 1970 and reg 10(3) of the Capital Gains Tax Regulations 1967[1].

---

1 SI 1967 No 149

The question of law for the opinion of the court was whether the commissioners were right in holding that Sch 6, para 23, to the 1955 Act could apply to the land in question. On 25th February 1977 Fox J[1] answered the question in the affirmative and dismissed the appeal. The taxpayer appealed to the Court of Appeal.

D C Potter and *Andrew Park* for the taxpayer.
John Vinelott QC, Alan Fletcher and *Brian Davenport* for the Crown.

Cur adv vult

22nd March. **STAMP LJ** read the following judgment of the court: This is an appeal from an order of Fox J[1] dated 25th February 1977 whereby the judge, being of the opinion that the determination of the Commissioners for the Special Purposes of the Income Tax Acts was correct, dismissed an appeal by way of case stated by the tax-payer.

The case is reported below[1]. The learned judge there sets out the facts in full and it is unnecessary therefore to recite them. The proceedings relate to an assessment to capital gains tax for 1971-72 in respect of a gain of £258,961. It relates mainly to the gain accruing on the disposal of 22 acres of land under a contract of 26th January 1972. As appears from the learned judge's judgment the 22 acres is to be treated as having been acquired by the taxpayer in January 1962 for £1,581. It was sold for £264,000. The price paid reflected the hope or expectation that the planning authorities would be willing to grant planning permission authorising residential development of the land. No planning permission authorising such development had, however, been obtained.

Section 19(1) of the Finance Act 1965 charged the capital gains tax on 'chargeable gains computed in accordance with this Act and accruing to a person on the disposal of assets'. When this new capital gains tax was introduced by the Finance Act 1965 it was not the policy to tax gains which had accrued prior to 6th April 1965 (see, e g, s 22(10) of, and para 24(2) of Sch 6 to, the 1965 Act). Accordingly on a disposition made after 6th April 1965 of property which had been acquired prior to that date provision had to be made for ascertaining how much of any profit had accrued prior to that date and how much of it subsequently. Only the latter part was made taxable.

Two methods of achieving this result were laid down by the 1965 Act. Except where otherwise provided the profit was to be treated as accruing at a uniform rate over the whole period of the taxpayer's ownership: see Sch 6, para 24. Where by the effect of a rising rate of inflation, or because subsequent to 6th April 1965 there has been a sharp rise in the development value of the land disposed of, this method of ascertaining the taxable gain favours the taxpayer, for it throws back part of the gain which in truth accrued after 5th April 1965 to the earlier non-taxable period. It is this method af ascertaining the post-5th April 1965 gain which in the instant case is favoured by the taxpayer. There can be no doubt, on the facts of the case, that the value of the land rose far more sharply after the relevant date than it did before.

The other method of ascertaining the post-6th April 1965 gain, and it is that for which the Crown contends in the instant case, is to ascertain what was the market value of the asset on 6th April 1965, which is a very tiresome process except in relation to such assets as quoted investments, and compute the post-6th April 1965 gain accordingly: see para 23(2) and the following sub-paragraphs of Sch 6. Where the case fell within para 23 it was mandatory to adopt the last-mentioned method of computing the post-5th April 1965 gain. Whether para 23 did or did not apply depended on whether the case fell within para 23(1), and that in turn depended on whether the consideration for the disposal exceeded what the market value of the land would be on the hypothesis specified in para 23(1)(b).

---

1   [1977] 3 All ER 545, [1977] STC 276

Paragraph 23(1) was in force in relation to disposals at the relevant time. It appeared under the cross-heading 'Sales of land in United Kingdom reflecting development value'. Paragraph 23 provided as follows:

'(1) This paragraph shall apply in relation to a disposal of an asset which is land in the United Kingdom, or an estate or interest in land in the United Kingdom—(a) if, but for this paragraph, the expenditure allowable as a deduction in computing under this Schedule the gain accruing on the disposal would include any expenditure incurred before 6th April 1965, and (b) if the consideration for the asset acquired on the disposal exceeds what its market value would be if, immediately before the disposal, it had become unlawful to carry out any development in, on or over the land other than development of the kinds specified in Schedule 3 to the Town and Country Planning Act 1962 (for land in England and Wales or Northern Ireland) or Schedule 3 to the Town and Country Planning (Scotland) Act 1947 for land in Scotland).

'In this paragraph "development" has, in relation to land in England or Wales or Northern Ireland, the meaning given by the Town and Country Planning Act 1962 and, in relation to land in Scotland, the meaning given by the Town and Country Planning (Scotland) Act 1947.

'(2) For the purposes of this Part of this Act, including Part 1 of this Schedule, it shall be assumed in relation to the disposal and, if it is a part disposal, in relation to any subsequent disposal of the asset which is land in the United Kingdom or an estate or interest in land in the United Kingdom that that asset was sold by the person making the disposal, and immediately re-acquired by him, at its market value on 6th April 1965.'

We have not hitherto mentioned para (a) of para 23(1) because it is common ground that in the instant case it was satisfied.

Counsel for the taxpayer, fastening on the words 'it had become unlawful to carry out any development . . .', submits that para (b) is only intended to apply to a case where, at the date of the disposition, it was lawful to develop the land. What the legislature had in mind was the case where the value of land has been dramatically increased by the effect of any actual planning permission which made it lawful to develop it and not to a case where, as here, no planning permission had been obtained at the time of the disposal and it was, as well before as after the disposal, unlawful to develop the land. The expression 'had become unlawful', so the argument runs, imports a change of condition, that is, the entry into a new state or condition by a change from some former state or condition. Here it is submitted because it was unlawful as well before as after the disposition to develop the land there was no such change.

There would be much to be said for counsel for the taxpayer's submission were it not for the fact that para (b) is drawn on the assumption that the arithmetical exercise of deducting the hypothetical value from the actual consideration is one that can be performed, for only by performing it can you ascertain whether sub-para (2) does or does not apply to the case which you are considering. Paragraph 23 in terms directs that the paragraph *shall apply* if the two conditions set out in paras (a) and (b) are satisfied, and you can only find out whether the condition in para (b) is satisfied by doing the arithmetic there contemplated. And so the language of the paragraph must, if possible, be construed so as to enable the exercise to be done.

We find no difficulty in so construing it. When one comes to analyse the wording of the hypothesis it is not a change in the law whereby some particular development had become unlawful which is supposed but a change in the law by the effect of which it had become unlawful to carry out *any* development in or over the land. The judge in the court below[1] thought that the words 'any' and 'unlawful' required,

---

1   [1977] 3 All ER 545 at 551, [1977] STC 276 at 282

for the purpose of the hypothesis, the absolute prohibition of all development of
the land with or without planning permission except what has been referred to as
Sch 3 development, and we agree with him. Here it was lawful, at the time of the
disposition, to carry out a development subject to obtaining planning permission,
and there is no difficulty in supposing a situation when it had become unlawful
to do so. And so the expression 'had become' is satisfied. So read, para (b) will always
operate to determine whether a particular case did or did not fall within para 23(2).
  The appeal is dismissed.

Appeal dismissed. Leave to appeal to the House of Lords refused.

Solicitors: *Speechly Bircham* (for the taxpayer); *Solicitor of Inland Revenue*.

A S Virdi Esq Barrister.

Garland v British Rail Engineering Ltd

EMPLOYMENT APPEAL TRIBUNAL

PHILLIPS J, MR L D COWAN AND MISS P SMITH

11th NOVEMBER 1977

*Employment – Discrimination against a woman – Provision in relation to retirement – Con-
tinuation after retirement of benefit enjoyed during employment – Free rail travel for employee's dependants – Dependants of male employee entitled to free travel after employee's
retirement – Dependants of female employee not so entitled after her retirement – Whether
arrangement a 'provision in relation to . . . retirement' – Whether arrangement exempt from
statutory provisions making discrimination unlawful – Sex Discrimination Act 1975, s 6(2)(4).*

The employers provided free travel for the spouses and dependent children of all its
employees. When a male employee retired the employers continued to provide free
travel for his wife and children but on the retirement of a female employee the
privilege was withdrawn from her family. A female employee who was still employed by the employers claimed that the arrangement was contrary to s 6(2)[a] of the
Sex Discrimination Act 1975 because the employers had omitted to afford her access
to benefits which would in like circumstances have been afforded to a man. The
employers contended, inter alia, that her claim was barred by s 6(4)[b] of the 1975 Act
since the arrangement was a 'provision in relation to . . . retirement', within s 6(4).

Held – The appeal would be allowed for the following reasons—
  (i) The arrangement was contrary to s 6(2) in that it constituted a present and
continuing discrimination against the employee despite the fact that the effect of the
discrimination would not be felt until some future date (see p 791 a to e and p 792 f, post).
  (ii) Section 6(4) did not apply to all arrangements which manifested themselves
after retirement but only to those, such as the provision of a pension, which were part
of the employer's system for catering for an employee's retirement; the continuation
after retirement of a privilege which had existed during employment was not a
'provision . . . in relation to retirement', within s 6(4) (see p 792 a b and e, post).

---

a Section 6(2) provides: 'It is unlawful for a person, in the case of a woman employed by him
   at an establishment in Great Britain, to discriminate against her—(a) in the way he affords
   her access to opportunities for promotion, transfer or training, or to any other benefits,
   facilities or services, or by refusing or deliberately omitting to afford her access to them, or
   (b) by dismissing her, or subjecting her to any other detriment.'
b Section 6(4) is set out at p 791 f, post

Notes

For discrimination against employees, see 16 Halsbury's Laws (4th Edn) para 771:5.
For the Sex Discrimination Act 1975, s 6, see 45 Halsbury's Statutes (3rd Edn) 229.

Case referred to in judgment

Roberts v Cleveland Area Health Authority [1977] IRLR 401, EAT.

Appeal

Mrs E M Garland ('the employee') appealed against the decision of an industrial
tribunal (chairman D B Williams Esq) sitting in London North on 23rd February 1977
dismissing a complaint by her that British Rail Engineering Ltd ('the employers')
had committed an act of discrimination against her. The facts are set out in the
judgment of the appeal tribunal.

T Morison for the employee.
Frederick James Maugham Marr-Johnson for the employers.

PHILLIPS J delivered the following judgment of the appeal tribunal: This is an
appeal by the employee from the decision of an industrial tribunal sitting in London
North on 23rd February 1977, entered on 22nd March 1977. The application by the
employee was under the Sex Discrimination Act 1975. She complained that a distinction had been drawn between male and female employees in the entitlement to a
benefit of employment which continued into retirement; and she claimed that it
amounted to a discriminatory practice contrary to the provisions of that Act. The
industrial tribunal rejected her claim, and from that decision she has now appealed.

The essential facts are simple: A male employee can obtain, using the word 'obtain'
not in any technical sense, because it appears not to be a matter of contractual entitlement, travel facilities for himself, his spouse, (or, if he dies, his widow) and his
dependent children, and can continue to do so after retirement. A female employee
can obtain similar facilities; but after retirement can obtain no facilities of that kind
for her spouse (or, if she dies, her widower) or her dependent children. So the discrimination is one which bites after the date of retirement. The decision records that
the employee was employed by the employers at an establishment in Great Britain;
that women have less advantageous travel facilities on their retirement than men,
and that the discrimination insofar as it existed was because of sex and therefore
prima facie came within s 1(1)(a) of the 1975 Act.

The only other part of the facts which it is helpful to look at is to be found in the
documents, which show that there was a special meeting of the Travel Facilities
Committee on 30th September 1975, which of course was a date not long before the
coming into operation of the Act. A working party was set up and asked to examine
and report on a number of particular features, and was required to limit the extension
of travel facilities and concessions to the absolute minimum. It records:

'In view of past practice, travel facilities available to retired staff and also to
wives and children of retired staff should continue but legal advice has been
taken on whether the Board would be required to extend travel facilities to
husbands of retired female staff. We consider, therefore, that any facilities
afforded to husbands of active female employees should be discontinued as from
the date of retirement.'

Referring to the scheme, there is to be found this paragraph:

'The Board has decided, therefore, to grant free and privilege ticket travel
over the lines of British Railways and by Ships to active married female members
of the staff for one legal husband but not for a husband legally separated.'

Then there are the following words to which attention has been drawn during argument:

'This facility will be *withdrawn* [our emphasis] on the retirement of the female employee and will not be granted to widowers of former female staff.'

Attention is drawn to that passage as emphasising that what is here under consideration is an existing benefit or facility which on the occasion of retirement is withdrawn. It being clear that the case falls within s 1, the first question is the applicability of s 6(2); that is to say, the question whether this difference in treatment is unlawful in what, in Part II, is called 'the employment field'. It seems to us to be plain that it is. The employers have here omitted to afford access to benefits which would in like circumstances have been afforded to a man. It is not necessary to elaborate precisely which part of para (*a*) or para (*b*) of sub-s (2) is satisfied. There may be room for argument, but we are quite satisfied that it falls in a part of one or other of those paragraphs. The controversy here has been rather different, revolving round the question whether there was at the date of the complaint any present discrimination as opposed to a discrimination which might arise in the future when the employee retired. We are satisfied that this is a case where, although the effects of the discrimination have not yet been felt, there is a present and continuing discrimination. Counsel for the employee's argument on this part of the case is to this effect. He says there can be no remedy, and none is provided, for an ex-employee, so that Mrs Garland could not have complained in this respect after she had retired. Nor, he says, is there any remedy to her during her employment in respect of any future discrimination, that is to say, in respect of discrimination taking place after retirement. We have already indicated that we do not accept that argument. In the first place it seems to us that if it were right there would be no need for sub-s (4) of s 6, or at the most a very limited need, which is clearly not the need being catered for. In the second place, assuming in a similar case to this that the privileges were contractual, then plainly the offer of employment would be unlawful within s 6(1)(*b*), and the offeree would have an immediate right to complain. It would be very odd if in such a case, the offer having been accepted and employment commenced, the employee, as he or she would then have become, would not have a corresponding right. There are other points arising in this connection, but it is not necessary to explain them in detail. We are satisfied that the case falls within s 6(2).

The real question, a very important one extending beyond the bounds of this case, is whether s 6(4) applies so as to deprive the employee of a right which she would otherwise have had. Subsection (4) of s 6 reads: 'Subsections (1)(*b*) and (2) do not apply to provision in relation to death or retirement.' The consequences of the decision in this case are far-reaching for the employers; here it should be said that the same result would follow in the case of British Rail as in the case of the employers. It is only an irrelevant circumstance of this case that the employers are British Rail Engineering Ltd and not British Rail. Furthermore the question is a matter of general concern in very many fields of employment.

Subsection (4) has come up for consideration in at least one previous decision before the Employment Appeal Tribunal, in *Roberts v Cleveland Area Health Authority*[1]. The question there was a very different one. It was whether the specification of the date of retirement fell within s 6(4). We said in that case that the word 'provision' was an intentionally wide word to cover *all* the employer's arrangements relating to retirement, including specific matters of policy; and so we said it included the fixing of the date and the moment of retirement. It seems to us that in this case we may be able slightly to refine that definition; it is perhaps in truth not a definition more a description, and we will say more about that in a moment.

The argument advanced by counsel for the employees is a simple one. It is that the words 'provision in relation to death or retirement' extend to any arrangement or scheme, or anything undertaken, which manifests itself after retirement. Counsel for the employee, on the other hand, says that it must be more narrowly defined and restricted than that, and emphasises in particular the words 'in relation to retirement'. The first conclusion which we have reached is that the words cannot have the very wide meaning for which counsel for the employers contends. In other words we do not think that the mere fact that the effects of an arrangement or a scheme, or what is done, manifest themselves after retirement necessarily means that for that reason alone what is being done, or arranged, was a 'provision in relation to retirement'. It is possible to propose some definition or equivalent for the words. We think that possibly what we said in *Roberts v Cleveland Area Health Authority*[1] is a little wide. What sub-s (4) is directed to are those arrangements made, and all these things which have been done, by the employers in order to make provision for retirement, such as provision for pensions. There is a recognisable territory of things which are arranged or done, which do not sensibly come within that description, albeit the effects of them continue after employment has ceased. We can illustrate this by the examples given in the course of the argument. Thus we would not have thought that to allow as a privilege continued membership of a social or sporting club, membership of which was restricted to the employees, would be 'provision in relation to retirement'; and, if such a privilege were restricted to males, and if females were excluded, we would expect them to have a claim and that claim not to be barred under sub-s (4). It is difficult to generalise and, of course, nothing we say about particular examples should be thought to conclude argument on them in other cases, because much turns on the detail. Other examples are the privilege of being allowed to continue to buy the employer's products at favourable rates; the right to attend social and sporting events; and outings, and privileges of that kind. One can think of many examples, some of which may be on one side of the line, some of which may be on the other. The privilege of buying at favourable rates a car which has been used during employment; membership of a scheme providing free medical treatment; matters of that kind. What, as it seems to us, has to be looked for is to see whether what is being done is part and parcel of the employer's system of catering for retirement, or whether, as here, the case is merely one where a privilege has existed during employment and has been allowed to continue after retirement. Accordingly, we have reached the conclusion that the arrangements in this case do fall within s 6(2) and are not excluded by s 6(4). It follows therefore that the appeal must be allowed.

A question has arisen as to what, in those circumstances, is the appropriate remedy. The matter turns on s 65 which provides in part:

> 'Where an industrial tribunal finds that a complaint presented to it under section 63 is well-founded the tribunal shall make such of the following as it considers just and equitable . . .'

and para (a) provides for a declaration. It is submitted that that empowers a tribunal, in doing what is just and equitable, to make no order at all. It may be so; it is not necessary to express a final view. We are satisfied that it would be right in this case to grant the declaration in the terms asked. The order accordingly is that the appeal be allowed, and we declare that the distinctions between the concessionary travel facilities to which Mrs Garland was 'entitled', as specified in her originating application and those to which comparable male employees are 'entitled', constitute unlawful discrimination on the ground of sex.

Appeal allowed.

Solicitors: *Russell, Jones & Walker* (for the employee); *Evan Harding* (for the employers).

Salim H J Merali Barrister.

---

1   [1977] IRLR 401

Pearce (Inspector of Taxes) v Woodall-Duckham Ltd

COURT OF APPEAL, CIVIL DIVISION

STAMP, ORR AND EVELEIGH LJJ

31st JANUARY, 1st, 2nd, 28th FEBRUARY 1978

Income tax – Computation of profits – Year in which profit arising – Change in method of valuation of work in progress showing surplus representing anticipated profits of earlier years – Change from on-cost basis to accrued profit basis of valuation – Change in valuation resulting in surplus profit – Revaluation of work in progress at beginning of first accounting period in which accrued profit method applied – Whether resulting surplus chargeable to tax as profits arising in that accounting period – Income and Corporation Taxes Act 1970, s 247(1).

A company was engaged on design and construction work under long term contracts. Until the end of 1968 work in progress on contracts was brought into account at the end of each calendar year at prime cost, and profit on the contracts was not brought into account until expiry of the contract maintenance period. In 1969 the company decided that for the year 1969 and succeeding years it would change the basis of its accounting to the accrued profit basis whereby, for contracts where more than 25 per cent of the anticipated final prime cost had been incurred, work in progress would be valued on the higher basis of the proportion of estimated profit attributable to the work done. There were reasonable and proper grounds for changing the accounting basis. To effect the change work in progress at the beginning of 1969 was revalued on the new basis with the result that the opening valuation for 1969 differed from the closing valuation for 1968 made under the old basis and disclosed a sum of £579,874 in excess of that valuation. It was admitted that the excess sum was of a revenue nature. The sum was brought into account for the year 1969 as a profit after taxation and was described in the accounts as 'surplus' arising from the change in the accounting basis. The company claimed that the sum was not chargeable to corporation tax, under s 247(1)[a] of the Income and Corporation Taxes Act 1970, as profit arising in the year 1969 because it was not a trading profit and that, if it were, it was attributable to a year or years previous to 1969. The Special Commissioners upheld the company's contention. The Crown appealed to a judge[b] who held that the sum was properly chargeable to tax as profit for the year 1969. The company appealed.

Held – The appeal would be dismissed for the following reasons—
    (i) For tax purposes a trader could in a given year attribute to work in progress a fair share of the final profit attributable to the work because to do so was to effect a genuine economic writing up of the work in progress. Accordingly the sum of £579,874 was a trading profit for the purpose of corporation tax (see p 797 g to p 798 a and e f and p 799 e f, post).
    (ii) The element of gross margin or profit required to be brought into account by the new accounting basis could not be attributed to any year earlier than 1969 even though the gross margin might represent work done in previous years. It followed that the sum of £579,874, representing the element of gross margin on work in progress, fell to be attributed to the year 1969 and could not be attributed to earlier years (see p 798 d to f and p 799 g h); *Bombay Comr of Income Tax v Ahmedabad New Cotton Mills Co Ltd* (1929) 46 TLR 68 distinguished.
    Decision of Templeman J [1977] 1 All ER 753 affirmed.

---

a   Section 247(1), so far as material, provides: 'Except as otherwise provided by the Corporation Tax Acts, corporation tax shall be assessed and charged for any accounting period of a company on the full amount of the profits arising in the period . . .'
b   [1977] 1 All ER 753, [1977] STC 82

Notes

For the valuation of stock, see 20 Halsbury's Laws (3rd Edn) 145, para 254, and for cases on the subject, see 28(1) Digest (Reissue) 123, *364, 365*.

For s 247(1) of the Income and Corporation Taxes Act 1970, see 33 Halsbury's Statutes (3rd Edn) 340.

Cases referred to in judgments

Bombay Comr of Income Tax v Ahmedabad New Cotton Mills Co Ltd (1929) 46 TLR 68, PC, 28(1) Digest (Reissue) 121, *353*.

BSC Footwear Ltd v Ridgway (Inspector of Taxes) [1971] 2 All ER 534, [1972] AC 544, [1971] 2 WLR 1313, 47 Tax Cas 495, 50 ATC 153, [1971] TR 121, HL, Digest (Cont Vol D) 447, *365*.

Ostime (Inspector of Taxes) v Duple Motor Bodies Ltd [1961] 2 All ER 167, [1961] 1 WLR 739, 39 Tax Cas 537, 40 ATC 21, [1961] TR 29, HL, 28(1) Digest (Reissue) 125, *371*.

Willingale (Inspector of Taxes) v International Commercial Bank Ltd [1978] 1 All ER 754, [1978] STC 75, HL.

Appeal

This was an appeal by Woodall-Duckham Ltd ('the company') against the judgment of Templeman J[1] given on 26th November 1976 allowing an appeal by the Crown from the determination of the Special Commissioners that the sum of £579,874 resulting from a change introduced in 1969 in the company's basis of accounting for work in progress was not chargeable to corporation tax as a profit arising in the accounting period ending on 31st December 1969. The facts are set out in the judgment of Orr LJ.

Peter Rees QC and *David C Milne* for the company.
D C Potter QC and *Brian Davenport* for the Crown.

Cur adv vult

28th February. The following judgments were read.

ORR LJ (delivering the first judgment at the invitation of Stamp LJ). This is an appeal by Woodall-Duckham Ltd, whom I shall call 'the company', and who were assessed to corporation tax of £600,000 in respect of an accounting period comprising the calendar year 1969, against a judgment of Templeman J[1] on 26th November 1976 whereby, reversing a determination of the Special Commissioners who had reduced the assessment to £403,495 but decided a point of principle in favour of the company, he allowed an appeal by the Crown on the point of principle and remitted the case to the Special Commissioners for consideration in the light of his judgment.

The company, which was incorporated in 1920 under a different name, is a wholly-owned subsidiary of the Woodall-Duckham Group (which I will call 'the group' and of which Babcock & Wilcox have been since 1973 the holding company), and was prior to 1960 engaged primarily in the design and construction of town gas plants and coke oven plants for the steel industry but in the early 1960s, owing to a change in demand, diversified into other markets including, from the late 1960s, exports. During this period the company's projects also became larger and the design and construction of each took correspondingly longer, extending in the later 1960s to as long as 35 months and in the early 1970s to 56 months. There was also a corresponding increase in the cost of the projects which in the middle and late 1960s ranging between £166,000 and £540,000 and in the early 1970s between £716,000 and £25,000,000. These changes in the nature and volume of the business led the board of the company to examine and question its accounting procedures, and references to this matter were made by the chairman in his statements appended to the company's accounts for 1965 and 1967.

1   [1977] 1 All ER 753, [1977] 1 WLR 224, [1977] STC 82

Until the end of December 1968 work in progress on contracts (other than that
carried out by the company's Australian branch) was at the end of each financial
year (being the calendar year) valued in the accounts at prime cost plus a proportion
of overheads but less a provision for any foreseeable losses, no profit on the contracts
being brought into account until expiry of the maintenance period, but losses being
provided for in the year in which the likelihood of incurring such losses was foreseen.
For a number of reasons set out and accepted in the case stated[1] by the Special
Commissioners this basis of valuing work in progress was not altered until 1969, but a
formal decision to change to a new basis was taken at a board meeting held on 23rd
December of that year and the new basis was subsequently defined as follows:

> 'NEW BASIS (1) The anticipated final gross margin (both overheads and profit)
> on each contract is calculated as the difference between the anticipated final
> selling price receivable from the customer and the anticipated final prime cost
> to be incurred on carrying out that contract. Prime cost includes the direct cost
> of engineering design time and technical time carried out in the Company's
> offices, the direct cost of materials, construction labour, site services, royalties
> and other expenses directly attributable to the contract. (2) A proportion of the
> anticipated final gross margin is included in the valuation of Work in Progress
> pro rata to the cumulative prime cost incurred to the date of the accounts as a
> proportion of the anticipated final prime cost. (3) The gross margin calculated
> under (2) above is subject to a deduction for a general reserve on all contracts
> not yet in their maintenance period representing 2% of the prime costs incurred to
> date on those contracts. In addition specific provisions are set aside on contracts
> to meet risks and contingencies which cannot be satisfactorily quantified but in
> respect of which, in the opinion of the Directors, some provision against over-
> expenditure is necessary. The value of the specific provision is deducted from the
> valuation of Work in Progress pro rata to the prime costs incurred except where
> 80% or more of the prime cost has been incurred in which case 100% of the specific
> provision is deducted. (4) If at the date of the accounts less than 25% of the antici-
> pated final prime cost has been incurred on a contract then the contract is valued
> in Work in Progress at cost and no margin is included. (5) Losses are provided
> for in the year in which the likelihood of incurring such losses is foreseen.'

It was accepted by the Special Commissioners that, while the tax implications of
this new basis (which it will be convenient to call 'the accrued profit basis') had been
considered by the board and the company's auditors, the timing of the change was
not governed by tax considerations, and it was also common ground that the new basis
is one of the accepted accounting bases for valuing work in progress on, inter alia,
long term contracts, and that in the circumstances there were reasonable and proper
grounds for the decision to change the basis. The effect, however, of the change in
basis was that, whereas on the old basis the opening figure of work in progress for a
succeeding year had always been the same as the closing figure for the previous year,
it was considered necessary for the application of the new basis to the year 1969 that
the opening as well as the closing figure for that year should be calculated on the new
basis, with the result that the opening figure for 1969 was different from the closing
figure for 1968 and disclosed in both the group consolidated profit and loss account
and the company's profit and loss account for 1969 a sum of £579,874 which was
described in the group accounts as 'Surplus arising on change in accounting basis' and
in the company's accounts, under the heading of 'Profit after Taxation', as 'Surplus
arising on change in valuation of contract work in progress at 31st December, 1968'
with a reference to note (1) to the accounts which stated:

> 'In order to effect the change in accounting basis the contract work in progress
> at the beginning of the year has been revalued on the new basis and the resultant

1   See [1977] 1 All ER 754-762, [1977] STC 83-91

excess of £579,874 over the old valuation has been brought into account as a separate item.'

The issue before the Special Commissioners was whether this sum of £579,874 was, as the Crown claimed, or was not, as the company claimed, chargeable to tax as part of the profits of the company arising in the year 1969. On this issue the Special Commissioners were referred to a number of statements of accountancy practice and they also heard evidence from four accountants: Mr Nightingale, in effect the company's financial director; Mr Dunkerley, a partner in the company's firm of auditors; Mr Hobson, who was accepted as an independent expert; and Mr Lawson for the Inland Revenue. All these witnesses were agreed, inter alia, that a major or fundamental change of accounting basis should not be made without good reason but that the company's new basis, which is gradually being adopted by a growing number of companies, is superior to the old basis, and that the company was fully justified in making the change; and they were further agreed that it is desirable as a matter of consistency that valuation of work in progress at the beginning and end of a period should be on the same basis, and that the surplus on valuation disclosed in the company's 1969 accounts was of a revenue as opposed to a capital nature.

Mr Hobson supported by Mr Dunkerley and Mr Nightingale gave evidence, which the Special Commissioners accepted, that it would have been quite wrong as a matter of accounting if the company had adopted the old basis for the beginning of 1969 and changed to the new basis for the end of the same year, and that 'surplus' was a proper description of the sum in question because it was not a trading profit arising or realised in 1969 but an adjustment relating to earlier years and deriving from a change in accounting policy. Mr Lawson on the other hand took the view that the sum in question was a profit which had arisen from the company's business in the year in question.

On this material the Special Commissioners allowed the company's appeal and gave as their reason that they were not persuaded that the 'surplus' represented or reflected profits arising in the period or that some other accounting treatment more favourable to the Crown should have been used.

From that decision the Crown appealed to the High Court and on 26th November 1976 Templeman J gave judgment determining the point of principle in favour of the Crown and remitting the case to the Special Commissioners for consideration in the light of his judgment. In his judgment he distinguished *Bombay Comr of Income Tax v Ahmedabad New Cotton Mills Co Ltd*[1] (a decision of the Privy Council) on which much reliance has been placed for the company, and held that the sum in question was properly chargeable to tax for the year 1969.

Against that judgment the company now appeals and the two questions which arise in the appeal are whether the sum of £579,874, described in the company's accounts as 'Profit after Taxation', and admitted to be of a revenue as opposed to a capital nature, is, for the purpose of corporation tax, a trading profit of the company, and if so for what year.

We were referred in argument to a number of cases and in the course of the hearing a print of the speeches delivered in the House of Lords in *Willingale (Inspector of Taxes) v International Commercial Bank Ltd*[2] became available but it is common ground that they do not affect this case, and in my judgment the only relevant passages in the speeches delivered in the House of Lords in *Ostime (Inspector of Taxes) v Duple Motor Bodies Ltd*[3] and *BSC Footwear v Ridgway (Inspector of Taxes)*[4] are those in which Lord Reid[5] and Viscount Dilhorne[6] refer to the difficulties which necessarily arise when

---

1   (1929) 46 TLR 68
2   [1978] 1 All ER 754, [1978] STC 75
3   [1961] 2 All ER 167, [1961] 1 WLR 739, 39 Tax Cas 537
4   [1971] 2 All ER 534, [1972] AC 544, 47 Tax Cas 495
5   [1961] 2 All ER 167 at 174, [1961] 1 WLR 739 at 754, 39 Tax Cas 537 at 572
6   [1971] 2 All ER 534 at 549, [1972] AC 544 at 568, 47 Tax Cas at 538

there is a change from one accounting method to another. The case, however, most strongly relied on for the company was the *Bombay* case[1], in which the Privy Council affirmed a judgment of the High Court of Bombay on a reference to that court of a question of law. The facts of the case were that the company's stocks had admittedly been undervalued at the end of the year in question and the company claimed, and it was assumed by the High Court for the purpose of the reference, that the stocks had also been under-valued at the beginning of the year. The income tax commissioner had rectified the value of the stock at the end of the year but had declined to make any corresponding alteration with reference to the stock at the opening of the year on the ground that accounting principles required that the opening value of stock must be taken to be the same as the closing value for the preceding year. The High Court held that it would be wrong to accept the company's return for the beginning of the year and only to rectify the figure at the end of the year, the correct principle being that it was necessary to ascertain the true profits of the year. On appeal the judgment of the High Court was affirmed by the Privy Council, on the ground (per Lord Buckmaster) that[1]—

> 'The one thing that is essential is that there should be a definite method of valuation adopted which should be carried through from year to year so that in case of any deviation from strict market value in the entry of the stock at the close of one year it will be rectified by the accounts in the next year.'

But, with great respect to the argument for the present company, the *Bombay* case[1] differs materially from the present case in that it did not involve, whereas the present case does involve, a change in the basis of valuation, and for this reason it cannot, in my judgment, provide an answer to the question raised by the appeal.

In the absence of direct authority on the point at issue I turn to principle and practice, and find it helpful to consider first the established practice in relation to the writing down of the value of trading stock and the writing off of bad debts, which are the converse of what was done in the present case. It is a long established practice, accepted for the purpose of income tax, that if in a given year a trader, applying a reasonable commercial judgment to the matter, decides that his trading stock because of market conditions or for other reasons is worth only half the value at which it stands in his books, or that a trading debt owed to him is valueless or reduced in value, writes down the stock or writes off the debt as bad, his decision takes effect for tax purposes in the year in which he makes it notwithstanding that the stock or the debt may have been going down in value in previous years. On principle I can see no reason why the tax consequences should be any different where, as here, a trader decides in relation to a contract for which the price has been contractually agreed, and the performance of which in the form of work in progress has taken place over more than one year, to attribute year by year to work done in performance of the contract a percentage of the total gross margin which he will eventually be entitled to receive as part of the price, but subject to such prudent restrictions as were applied in the present case, namely that no element of gross margin should be attributed to work in progress until 25 per cent of the anticipated final prime cost has been earned, and subject also to a deduction by way of general reserve representing two per cent of the prime costs incurred to date on those contracts which have not reached their maintenance period. It cannot be said in such a case that the entire profit has been earned in the final year of performance of the contract for it has in fact been earned by the work in progress, year by year, and if the trader can in a given year write down the value of his stock in trade or work in progress I can see no reason why he should not attribute to work in progress a fair share of the final gross margin. To do so is, in my judgment, to effect a genuine economic writing up of the work in progress

1   (1929) 46 TLR 68

comparable with the genuine economic writing down to which I have earlier referred, and in my judgment the acceptance by the accountancy profession of the new basis, adopted in 1969, as a proper basis of valuation clearly recognises that fact.

There remains the question whether the element of gross margin brought into account in 1969 has been properly treated as attributable, for corporation tax purposes, to that year or is in part attributable to some other year or years. It is clear from the definition of the new accounting basis which I have earlier quoted, and is common ground, that the so-called surplus of £579,874 is not referable only to work which was in progress during the year 1969. By the definition no element of gross margin may be taken until 25 per cent of the anticipated final prime cost has been incurred on the contract but when that point has been reached a proportion of the anticipated final gross margin is to be included in the valuation of work in progress pro rata to the cumulative prime cost incurred to the date of the accounts as a proportion of the final prime costs. It follows that if in respect of any contract the 25 per cent level was reached in 1969 the valuation could largely represent work done in previous years and the same would apply to a contract as to which the 25 per cent level had been reached before the change to the new basis. In my judgment, however, the element of gross margin which the new accounting basis requires to be brought into account cannot be attributed to any earlier year than 1969, when the new basis was introduced, any more than a bad debt can be attributed to a year earlier than that in which it was recognised to be bad.

For these reasons, agreeing with the conclusion reached by Templeman J and with great respect rejecting, on what I consider to be an issue of law, the conclusion reached by the Special Commissioners, I would dismiss this appeal, and I would only add that I am also in entire agreement with the judgment about to be delivered by Stamp LJ which, since writing this judgment, I have had the opportunity of reading.

EVELEIGH LJ. I agree, and I also agree with the judgment about to be delivered, which I have had the opportunity of reading, and I have nothing further to add.

STAMP LJ. I agree. For the purpose of computing the profits of the company prior to 1969 the work in progress was brought in on the receipts side of the trading account at what I will call its 'prime cost' though adjustments were made.

In the year 1969 it was determined, for reasons which Orr LJ has given and which is common ground were good commercial reasons, to distinguish between work in progress on contracts where less than 25 per cent of the anticipated prime cost had been incurred and those where 25 per cent or more had been incurred. In relation to the first class the work in progress was valued as before. I will refer to this as the 'lower basis'. In relation to the second class of contract there was brought into account what, forsaking accuracy for convenience, can be described for the purposes of this judgment as the proportion of the estimated profit on the contract attributable to the work done. I will refer to this as the 'higher basis'.

Where the work in progress on a contract falls to be valued on the same basis at the beginning and at the end of a year the excess of the valuation at the end over the valuation at the beginning of the year will be an item on the receipts side of the trading, or Sch D computation, falling to be taken into account in ascertaining the trading profit for the year.

It is however to be noted that in 1969 and in years thereafter there would, as the result of the change of practice, be work in progress which at the beginning of the year fell to be valued on the lower basis and at the end of the year would have crossed the 25 per cent threshold and become subject to the valuation on the higher basis. The excess of the figure ascertained on a valuation on the higher basis at the end of the year over the figure ascertained on a valuation on the lower basis at the beginning of the year (which will be the same figure as appears at the foot of the previous year's account) must surely represent an item falling to be brought into account on the

receipts side of the trading account in ascertaining the trading profits during the year
a and ought to be brought into the Sch D computation accordingly. If this is not done
part of the difference, namely the estimated profit element, will have to be shown as
a non-trading profit and the profits of the taxpayer will never be subject to taxation.
I do not think counsel for the company has submitted otherwise.

The latter process however transgresses counsel for the company's proposition
that in comparing the value of work in progress at the beginning of the year with its
b value at the end of the year for the purpose of computing trading profits under
Sch D like must be compared with like; for in relation to contracts which crossed
the threshold during the year you are not comparing like with like but ascertaining
the value at the beginning of the year on one basis, and at the end of the year on a
different basis. So when examining counsel for the company's submission that for
the purposes of computing the trading profits of 1969 you must compare like with
c like I do not find it convincing.

Indeed if there were contracts which had not crossed the threshold at the beginning
of 1969 itself but did so during that year what I have said about them would apply.
You would take the valuation made on the old basis at the end of 1968 and compare it
with the valuation at the end of 1969 made on the new basis, so throwing up as part
of the trading profit for 1969 the effect of the change of policy. To exclude that part
d of the profit would be wrong and I can see no justification for not adopting the same
process in relation to contracts which already at the end of 1968 had crossed the
threshold. To depart from that process would, in my judgment, be to ignore the
element of profit recognised by the revaluation of the work in progress.

The £579,874, being the difference between the value put on the work in progress
at the end of 1968 and the valuation at the opening of the 1969 account, appears to me
e to be an artificial and unreal figure not representing a profit. The true profit is
arrived at by comparing the value put on the work in progress at the end of 1968
and the value put on it at the end of 1969, and it is a trading and not a casual or non-
trading profit. True, you are not comparing like with like but that must always be
so when for good commercial reasons and without infringing any principle of income
tax law, I refer in particular to the rule that you must not anticipate a profit, trading
f stock or work in progress falls to be written up or written down.

Counsel for the company submitted that the figure of £579,874 represented the
previously unrecognised trading profit of earlier years and not a profit which fell to be
included in the 1969 trading account. He points to the fact that the tax 'for any financial
year shall be charged on profits arising in that year' (see ss 243(3) and 250(1) of the
Income and Corporation Taxes Act 1970). If that submission were well founded it
g would, so it appears to me, follow that when under the pre-1969 policy a contract
reached maturity the profits which would otherwise be brought into account in that
year would escape taxation on the ground that they had been earned in earlier
years. I think the short answer to counsel for the company's submission in that
regard is that the difference between the value of the work in progress on a particular
contract or on the totality of the contracts at the end of the year and its or their value
h at the beginning of the year, whether it be a plus or minus figure, is not the profit
(or loss) 'arising in that year' but one of the items brought into the accounts for the
purpose of determining that profit. I too would dismiss the appeal.

*Appeal dismissed. Case remitted to Special Commissioners for assessments to be adjusted
in accordance with court's judgment. Leave to appeal to the House of Lords granted.*

j Solicitors: *McKenna & Co* (for the company); *Solicitor of Inland Revenue.*

A S Virdi Esq Barrister.

Covell Matthews & Partners v French Wools Ltd

COURT OF APPEAL, CIVIL DIVISION

BUCKLEY AND BRIDGE LJJ, SIR DAVID CAIRNS

8th, 9th DECEMBER 1977

Landlord and tenant – Business premises – Application for new tenancy – Withdrawal of application – Date of the withdrawal – High Court application for new tenancy – Leave to withdraw application necessary in High Court but not in county court – Whether 'the date of withdrawal' was the date of the judgment giving leave to withdraw the application or the date of issue of summons for leave to withdraw – Whether court having jurisdiction to backdate order giving leave to withdraw application – Landlord and Tenant Act 1954, s 64(2) – RSC Ord 21, r 3.

In 1960 the landlords granted the tenants a lease of certain business premises for a term of 14 years expiring on 24th June 1973. On 21st December 1972 they served on the tenants a notice under s 25 of the Landlord and Tenant Act 1954 terminating the tenancy on 24th June 1973. The tenants informed the landlords that they were not willing to give up possession of the premises. On 13th March 1973 the tenants issued an originating summons in the Chancery Division seeking an order for the grant by the landlords of a new tenancy of the premises. They could not make the application in the county court as the rateable value of the premises was just over the limit of the county court's jurisdiction. As a result of the issue of the summons the tenants' current tenancy was extended, under s 64(1)[a] of the 1954 Act, until three months after their application for a new tenancy was 'finally disposed of', which, by virtue of s 64(2), meant the earliest date by which the proceedings had been determined or, if the application was withdrawn, 'the date of withdrawal'. Protracted negotiations regarding the grant of a new tenancy ensued between the parties and the hearing of the originating summons was postponed. When the negotiations ended the tenants purported to give the landlords notice under s 27 of the 1954 Act to terminate the tenancy. They vacated the premises in December 1975, leaving subtenants in occupation of parts of them. On 23rd January 1976 the tenants applied under RSC Ord 21, r 3[b], for leave to withdraw their summons of 13th March requesting a new tenancy. The landlords alleged that a binding agreement had been reached between the parties on terms which included a considerable increase in rent. On 12th February 1976 they applied to the court under s 24A of the 1954 Act to have the interim rent payable by the tenants determined. On 26th March both the tenants' application for leave to withdraw their summons and the landlords' application for the determination of an interim rent came before the master. He gave directions on the landlords' summons and indicated that he would grant the tenants leave to withdraw their originating summons. The landlords intimated that they would not accept such an order and in consequence the master adjourned the matter to a judge. The hearing was originally fixed for 5th July but it was adjourned until 20th October primarily to suit the landlords' convenience. The landlords contended that leave to discontinue the proceedings should not be granted until after it had been decided whether there was a binding agreement between the parties as to the grant of a new tenancy. The question also arose at the hearing as to what, in any event, was 'the date of withdrawal' for the purposes of s 64, i e whether it was the date of service on the landlords of notice of the application to withdraw the summons or of judgment giving leave to withdraw the application for a new tenancy, which the parties agreed

---

a   Section 64, so far as material, is set out at p 803 *c* to *f*, post

b   Rule 3 is set out at p 806 *h j*, post

should in the circumstances be deemed to be 5th July (i e the date for which the
_a_ original hearing was fixed). The judge[a] held (i) that the tenants should be granted
leave to withdraw their application for a new tenancy on terms that the grant of
leave to withdraw was without prejudice to the landlords' contention that a binding
agreement for the grant of a new tenancy had been reached, and (ii) that 'the date of
withdrawal' of the request for a new tenancy for the purposes of s 64 was the date of
judgment but that since the parties had agreed that the date of judgment should be
_b_ deemed to be 5th July, that date should be treated as the date of withdrawal. He
made an order accordingly. The tenants appealed against the second part of the
order, contending (i) that 'the date of withdrawal' must be the date of the service of
the summons, i e when they first intimated that they wanted to discontinue the
proceedings, because otherwise there would be a conflict of dates with the corresponding county court rules governing applications for new tenancies since under the
_c_ county court rules no leave of the court was required by an applicant who wished
to withdraw or discontinue proceedings, and (ii) that, independently of any agreement
between the parties, the court had power under its inherent jurisdiction or under
RSC Ord 21, r 3, to make the order for discontinuance operate retrospectively and
that it should exercise that power by backdating the order to 23rd January.

_d_ **Held** – (i) The phrase 'the date of withdrawal' in s 64(2) meant, in relation to the withdrawal of proceedings commenced by originating summons in the High Court, the
date when the order was made that the proceedings be discontinued, subject to any
power of the court to make the order with retrospective effect (see p 807 _d_, p 808 _h_
and p 809 _b_ to _e_, post).
(ii) The court had no inherent jurisdiction to backdate an order discontinuing pro-
_e_ ceedings and, on the true construction of RSC Ord 21, r 3, it had no power to do so
under that rule. It followed that the appeal would be dismissed (see p 808 _e_ and _h j_
and p 809 _b_ to _f_, post).
Per Curiam. In view of the anomaly between the High Court rules and the county
court rules relating to the withdrawal of an application for a new lease under the
1954 Act some consideration should be given by the relevant rule committees to
_f_ the revision of both sets of rules so as to make them accord with one another (see p 808
_f g_ and p 809 _c f_, post).
Decision of Graham J [1977] 2 All ER 591 affirmed.

Notes
For discontinuance of proceedings, see 30 Halsbury's Laws (3rd Edn) 409, 410, para
770, and for cases on the subject, see 51 Digest (Repl) 552-574, 2057-2082.
_g_ For the Landlord and Tenant Act 1954, ss 24A, 25, 27, 64, see 18 Halsbury's Statutes
(3rd Edn) 559, 563, 602.

Cases referred to in judgments
MacDonald v MacDonald [1963] 2 All ER 857, [1964] P 1, [1963] 3 WLR 350, CA, 27(2)
Digest (Reissue) 843, 6709.
_h_ _Young, Austen & Young Ltd v British Medical Association_ [1977] 2 All ER 884, [1977]
1 WLR 881.

Appeal
This was an appeal by Covell Matthews & Partners ('the tenants') against so much of
the judgment of Graham J[1], given on 1st November 1976, on their application for
_j_ leave to withdraw an originating summons issued by them on 13th March 1973
requesting the respondents, French Wools Ltd ('the landlords'), to grant them a new
tenancy of business premises at 7-11 Lexington Street, London W1, as adjudged that

---

_a_   [1977] 2 All ER 591
1   [1977] 2 All ER 591, [1977] 1 WLR 876

the date of withdrawal within the meaning of s 64(2) of the Landlord and Tenant Act 1954 was the date of judgment. They sought an order that Graham J's judgment be varied so as to declare that the date of withdrawal was the date of service of the tenants' summons for leave to withdraw or alternatively the date on which Master Cholmondeley Clarke gave leave to discontinue. The landlords gave notice under RSC Ord 59, r 6(2), that they would contend at the hearing of the appeal that the judgment of Graham J should be affirmed on the additional ground that the grant of leave to discontinue an action or an order that an action be discontinued granted or made under RSC Ord 21, r 3, could not in law have effect so as to permit the discontinuance of the action on a date earlier than the date on which it was granted or made. The facts are set out in the judgment of Bridge LJ.

Paul Batterbury for the tenants.
Michael Barnes for the landlords.

BRIDGE LJ delivered the first judgment at the invitation of Buckley LJ. This appeal raises a novel and interesting point under the Landlord and Tenant Act 1954 and under the Rules of the Supreme Court as they apply to certain proceedings under that Act. I should like at the outset to express my indebtedness to learned counsel on both sides for the help that they have given us in our task of resolving the point.

The plaintiffs ('the tenants') appeal from an order of Graham J[1] made on 1st November 1976. The form of the order, after reciting certain undertakings given by counsel on behalf of the tenants, was that the tenants be at liberty to withdraw an originating summons in which they had claimed a new lease of certain business premises—

'such withdrawal to take effect as from 5th July 1976 (being the date agreed for such purpose between the [tenants] and the defendants ['the landlords'] should this court accede to the said application) and that the same be withdrawn accordingly'.

The language of the rule of the Supreme Court under which the application had been made to the court contemplates, in fact, not the withdrawal of the proceedings but their discontinuance; but in my judgment nothing turns on this distinction of language, and the order should be understood as if it had been an order giving the tenants leave to discontinue their proceedings begun by the originating summons and that the said proceedings be discontinued accordingly.

The reason why the order is to take effect, not from the date when it was made but from an earlier date, 5th July 1976, was because the parties, as the order recites, had made an agreement to that effect.

The points which are raised in the appeal are, first, whether independently of any agreement between the parties the court had power, as the tenants contend, to make an order for discontinuance operating retrospectively from some earlier date than the date on which the order was made. Secondly, if the court had such a power the question arises whether, in the exercise of its discretion in the circumstances of this case, it was proper that the power should have been exercised, and if so, to what earlier date the order for discontinuance should effectively have been backdated.

The history of the matter begins in 1960, when the predecessors in title of the defendants in these proceedings, granted to the predecessors in title of the present tenants a lease for 14 years, at rentals rising during the period of the lease to a maximum, which was the rent payable at any material time with which we are concerned, of £5,600 a year. The contractual term granted by that lease was due to expire on 24th June 1973. Apart from any notice given pursuant to Part II of the Landlord and

---

1 [1977] 2 All ER 591, [1977] 1 WLR 876

Tenant Act 1954, the lease would of course have continued under the provisions of
a that statute. But on 21st December 1972 the landlords served on the tenants, pursuant
to s 25 of the Act of 1954 (which is very familiar and to the provisions of which I need
not refer) a notice to terminate the tenancy on the contractual terminal date, namely,
24th June 1973; and in that notice the landlords indicated that they would not oppose
an application by the tenants for the grant of a new lease. In accordance with the
statute, on 5th February 1973 the tenants duly served a counter notice intimating
b their intention to apply for a new lease, and on 13th March 1973 they duly made their
application in the appropriate form. The rateable value of the premises being mar-
ginally in excess of the county court limit, which is £5,000, they commenced their
proceedings claiming a new lease, in the Chancery Division in the High Court and
their proposal, as pleaded, was that they should be granted a new lease for the term
of seven years at the currently payable rent of £5,600 a year.
c   As soon as that application was made, the provisions of s 64 of the 1954 Act came
into operation; those provisions, so far as material for present purposes, read as follows:

'(1) In any case where—(a) a notice to terminate a tenancy has been given
under ... Part II of this Act ... and (b) an application to the court has been made
under the ... said Part II ... and (c) apart from this section the effect of the
d notice or request would be to terminate the tenancy before the expiration of
the period of three months beginning with the date on which the application
is finally disposed of, the effect of the notice or request shall be to terminate
the tenancy at the expiration of the said period of three months and not at any
other time.

'(2) The reference in paragraph (c) of subsection (1) of this section to the date
e on which an application is finally disposed of shall be construed as a reference
to the earliest date by which the proceedings on the application (including any
proceedings on or in consequence of an appeal) have been determined and
any time for appealing or further appealing has expired, except that if the application is withdrawn or any appeal is abandoned the reference shall be construed
as a reference to the date of the withdrawal or abandonment.'

f Following the issue of the tenants' originating summons, there were negotiations
between the parties which continued over the next two years. What we are told is
that by 1975 the parties had come to terms, at all events in principle, as to the new
lease which should be granted to the tenants. The landlords' contention is that
there was a concluded and binding contractual agreement reached between the
g parties for the grant of such a new lease. The position presently taken up by the
tenants, however, is that any agreement reached in the course of those negotiations
was an agreement subject to contract, and accordingly one which never became
binding on the tenants.
    The negotiations having come to an end on this issue, or perhaps 'broken down' is
a more accurate expression, what happened in the event was that in or about Decem-
h ber 1975 the tenants vacated the premises, leaving sub-tenants in occupation of
certain parts of them. We are not concerned with the precise detail of that, although
it may be important to note that there were sub-tenants left when the tenants vacated
the premises.
    Some time before the end of 1975, the tenants gave to the landlords a notice to
terminate the tenancy pursuant to s 27(2) of the 1954 Act, which reads as follows:
j
'A tenancy granted for a term of years certain which is continuing by virtue
of section twenty-four of this Act may be brought to an end on any quarter day
by not less than three months' notice in writing given by the tenant to the
immediate landlord, whether the notice is given before or after the date on
which apart from this Act the tenancy would have come to an end.'

The question whether or not the notice given by the tenants pursuant to that subsection was an effective notice is not before us for decision. Both parties invite us **a** to assume for the purposes of the present argument (and I proceed on this assumption without making any pronouncement on the question of whether it is right, because it may be a difficult question) that the s 27 notice given, as it was, long, long after the original terminal date specified in the landlords' s 25 notice had passed, was ineffective to determine the tenancy pursuant to the provisions of s 27(2).

Reverting to the further history, it was on 23rd January 1976 that the tenants **b** made application pursuant to RSC Ord 21, r 3, for leave to discontinue the proceedings begun by the originating summons. As we shall see in a moment when I turn to the provisions of the rules, there is no doubt that in the High Court, proceedings such as these, claiming a new lease by way of originating summons in the Chancery Division, cannot be discontinued by the applicant otherwise than pursuant to the leave of the court. **c**

On 12th February 1976 the landlords made an application to the court to determine an interim rent pursuant to s 24A of the 1954 Act, to the provisions of which I need not make detailed reference. Both applications, the tenants' application for leave to withdraw their proceedings and the landlords' application for an order determining an interim rent, came before Master Cholmondeley Clarke on 26th March 1976. On the interim rent application he merely gave appropriate directions and **d** nothing turns on that. On the application for leave to withdraw, the master expressed himself as minded to grant that leave, but in accordance with the well-established practice of the Chancery Division, when the landlords intimated that they were not content to accept the order which the master was minded to make, the master adjourned the matter to the judge.

The original hearing before the judge was fixed for 5th July 1976; in the event that **e** date had to be vacated, primarily, as I understand it, for the benefit of the landlords, and it was because there was a vacation of that date that the agreement was made between the parties that if in the event the judge, on hearing the application, were to grant the tenants' application for leave to discontinue their proceedings, any order made that the proceedings be discontinued should be treated by agreement between the parties as if it had been made on the original hearing date of 5th July. In the event the matter came before Graham J on 20th October 1976, and he delivered his reserved judgment on the matter on 1st November 1976.

Both before the master and before the judge the landlords were contending that no leave to discontinue the proceedings should be granted, in other words that the tenants' application should be refused, and the basis of that contention was, so it was argued, that the issue as to whether there was a binding agreement between **f** the parties for the grant of a new lease ought to be decided as a preliminary point in the proceedings commenced by the originating summons, notwithstanding that the landlords also intimated that it was their intention, failing such decision, that the alleged binding agreement between themselves and the tenants for the grant of a new lease would be the subject of proceedings claiming an order of specific performance. The main argument before Graham J turned on the issue so raised; **g** on the issue so raised the learned judge came to a conclusion favourable to the tenants, but as that issue does not arise in this court, I need do no more than go straight to the learned judge's conclusion in the matter, in which he decided that leave to discontinue should be granted, but should be granted on terms.

What he said, having rehearsed the arguments between the parties, was this[1]:

'In my judgment, therefore, I think that in principle the master was correct in his grant of leave to the tenants [I think that means 'in his intended grant'] to withdraw their application of 13th March 1973 for a new tenancy and I hold that such

---

1   [1977] 2 All ER 591 at 594, [1977] 1 WLR 876 at 880

a

leave should be given. At the same time, for the landlord's protection, the order being
for leave to discontinue and not for dismissal, the tenants should be put on terms:
(1) not to make any fresh application for a new tenancy; this may in fact be
academic in view of the time which has elapsed since the first application, but
such a term positively safeguards the position; (2) the grant of leave should, as
requested by [counsel then appearing for the landlords] be expressed to be given
without prejudice to the landlords' contention that a binding agreement has

b

been reached between the parties, and without prejudice to the effect of such
an agreement if it is eventually decided that it is binding; (3) an appropriate
order for costs against the tenants should be made.'

I pause at that point to interject that, as counsel for the landlords very properly
concedes in the argument before us, if at any earlier stage the landlords had intimated

c

to the tenants that they would be willing to agree to discontinuance of the tenants'
proceedings on the terms which the learned judge eventually imposed, it is an almost
irresistable inference that the tenants would readily have concurred in the voluntary
imposition of those terms.

On the question which arises for our decision relating to the backdating of the
discontinuance order, the matter was argued before the learned judge by both

d

parties on the footing that the judge had a discretion under the relevant rule of
court to backdate his order if in all the circumstances he thought it just to do so.
Indeed, not only was this view conceded by counsel then appearing on behalf of the
landlords, but that counsel positively advanced this proposition in support of the
contention that this provided the court with all the power it needed to meet an
argument which had been advanced on behalf of the tenants, that otherwise the
tenants might suffer hardship through the proceedings being unreasonably protracted

e

by the behaviour of the landlords resisting a tenants' application for leave to withdraw. It was on this footing, on the basis that he had an admitted discretion
whether or not the order should be made retrospective, and if so to what extent,
that the learned judge expressed his conclusion in these terms[1]:

f

'In my judgment I consider that the normal rule in the absence of avoidable
delay or unusual circumstances should be that the date of the judgment giving
leave to withdraw is the date of withdrawal within the section.'

Again I interpose to say that if one were to follow the language of the relevant rule,
to which I shall refer shortly, the words 'discontinue' and 'discontinuance' would
be more apt than the words 'withdraw' and 'withdrawal'.

g

In this court the concession made and the arguments advanced on behalf of the
landlords to the effect that this is a matter within the jurisdiction of the court, namely
to make an order of discontinuance with retrospective effect, have been withdrawn
by a counter-notice served by the landlords, and it is in these circumstances that
the primary question which we have to determine is whether under the relevant
rule there is indeed any discretion in the court to make an order for discontinuance

h

but to make it with retrospective effect.

The importance of the issue from the tenants' point of view, and indeed from the
landlords' point of view, is obvious: on counsel for the landlords' contention,
the date of withdrawal within the meaning of s 64 of the Landlord and Tenant Act
1954 in a case where the party seeking to discontinue has to obtain the leave of the
court to do so, can only mean the date when that leave was given. On the footing

j

that that is right, unless the order of discontinuance in this case can be given retrospective effect to some date earlier than 5th July 1976, then until a date three months
after that date, which would be 5th October 1976, the tenants remained liable to
pay rent, not only at the original contractual rate but at any rate which might be

1   [1977] 2 All ER 591 at 595, [1977] 1 WLR 876 at 880

determined pursuant to the landlords' application for an interim rent under s 24A of the statute.

Before I turn to the terms of the relevant rule of court, I should explain the fundamental basis of counsel's argument for the tenants which he relies on both in support of what he says should be the court's inclination on the point of construction, and also what he says should govern the court's exercise of any discretion which it may have; and that is this: in the county court, under the corresponding rules which govern applications for new tenancies, which will be applications in relation to all business premises having rateable values not exceeding £5,000, no leave of the court is required by an applicant who desires to withdraw or discontinue his proceedings; he can do so as of right pursuant to the provisions of CCR Ord 18. So, according to counsel for the tenants, the argument runs thus: Parliament must, when it enacted s 64 of the Landlord and Tenant Act 1954, have contemplated that any tenant having instituted proceedings for a new lease, could discontinue those proceedings at any time voluntarily and thereby limit his liability to continue paying rent for the relevant premises to a period of three months after the date when he does so. That is illustrated by the county court rules; it is a provision comparable with, and parallel to, the provision to which I made reference earlier, in s 27, which certainly gives a tenant a right to terminate his statutory tenancy under the Act at any time before an application for the grant of a new tenancy is made. I see the force of those contentions, and I approach the matter of construction bearing them in mind. But what we have to construe are the provisions of RSC Ord 21, to which I now turn.

So far as it is relevant for the purposes of this case, RSC Ord 21, r 2(1) provides:

> 'The plaintiff in an action begun by writ may without the leave of the Court discontinue the action, or withdraw any particular claim made by him therein, as against any or all of the defendants at any time not later than 14 days after service of the defence on him or, if there are two or more defendants, of the defence last served, by serving a notice to that effect on the defendant concerned.'

I pause to interpose that of course that provision has no application at any time to proceedings begun by originating summons, as these proceedings were. I need not read para (2) or para (3); para (4) reads:

> 'If all the parties to an action [which I interpose to say would include proceedings commenced by originating summons] consent, the action may be withdrawn without the leave of the court at any time before trial by producing to the appropriate person [who is then spelled out in the rule] a written consent to the action being withdrawn signed by all the parties.'

Then we come to the crucial provision, which is RSC Ord 21, r 3:

> (1) 'Except as provided by Rule 2, a party may not discontinue an action (whether begun by writ or otherwise) or counterclaim, or withdraw any particular claim made by him therein, without the leave of the Court, and the Court hearing an application for the grant of such leave may order the action or counterclaim to be discontinued, or any particular claim made, therein to be struck out as against any or all of the parties against whom it is brought or made on such terms as to costs, the bringing of a subsequent action or otherwise as it thinks just. (2) An application for the grant of leave under this Rule may be made by summons or motion, or by notice under Order 25, Rule 7.'

Then for completion I had better read, although in my judgment nothing turns on it, the provisions of Ord 21, r 4:

> 'Subject to any terms imposed by the Court in granting leave under Rule 3, the fact that a party has discontinued an action or counterclaim or withdrawn a

particular claim made by him therein shall not be a defence to a subsequent
action for the same, or substantially the same, cause of action.'

Counsel on both sides have developed interesting arguments directed at illuminating the problem of construing this rule, based on a consideration of other provisions
under the rules of court, or under a variety of statutes in which the court may or may
not, as the case may be, make orders with retrospective effect. Counsel for the
tenants draws our attention to a number of instances where the court's orders may
operate retroactively; counsel for the landlords, on the other hand, draws analogies
with cases where no retroactive operation is permissible. I hope neither counsel
will think it discourteous on my part if I do not examine those suggested analogies
in detail; in the end it seems to me that this appeal turns on what is really a very
short point on the construction of the particular language of RSC Ord 21, r 3, in the
context in which it is found, and more particularly as applied to the situation which
arises when an applicant for a new lease who has commenced proceedings by originating summons in the Chancery Division, is seeking leave to discontinue those proceedings because he wishes, for the purposes of avoiding further liability to pay rent,
to withdraw his proceedings within the meaning of s 64 of the Act, at the earliest
possible date.

The first thing I would say, and I doubt whether this was really in controversy
at the end of the argument, is that it seems to me clear beyond doubt that the date
of withdrawal, as that phrase is used in s 64 of the Act, can only mean in relation to
the withdrawal of proceedings by originating summons in the High Court, the date
when an order is made that those proceedings be discontinued, subject always to
any power of the court to make such an order with retrospective effect.

I reach that conclusion because until an order has been made giving leave to the
applicant to discontinue his proceedings, it must remain uncertain whether such
leave will or will not be granted. It is perfectly clear from authorities to which
we have been referred that the granting of leave to discontinue is no mere formality;
that an applicant for leave to discontinue may be put in a position by the terms
which the court is minded to impose on him as a condition of ordering discontinuance
of his proceedings, which will be so onerous that he would not wish to accept them.
Without going into the details, an illustration of that is to be found in the recent
decision of Whitford J, to which we were referred, in *Young, Austen & Young Ltd v
British Medical Association*[1]. Accordingly one must wait until the date when the order
was made before knowing whether the tenant's attempt to withdraw his proceedings
will be successful or unsuccessful; it is quite impossible, subject to the court's power,
if it has one, to make an order with retrospective effect, to say that any other date
than the date of the order is the effective date of withdrawal. So we come to the
central question of whether the order can be backdated and, as I say, it is in relation
to that question that the numerous analogies have been drawn to our attention.

If the order is to be backdated, the language of the rule which authorises the
introduction of such a provision into the order must be found, if anywhere, in the
words 'on such terms as to costs, the bringing of a subsequent action or otherwise
as it thinks just'. The first conclusion that I have reached is that it is quite impossible
to construe those words as giving power to the court to order discontinuance with
retrospective effect, for this reason: the terms which are there contemplated are
terms to be imposed on the applicant, terms adverse to the applicant as a condition
of granting him the relief which he seeks. It is the applicant who is asking the court
to grant him leave to discontinue his proceedings; it is against the applicant that any
terms will operate if the court is minded to say: 'Yes, we will grant you leave to
discontinue your proceedings, but only if you comply with the following terms'.
To my mind it would be really quite an astonishing interpretation of this language
to say that a power to impose terms on an applicant as a condition of granting him

certain relief for which he is asking should extend to a power to impose onerous terms on the respondent, who is resisting the application.

But if that is the wrong approach to the matter, I should still reach the same conclusion by another route. If one pauses to consider what is the position which will have been reached by the time the parties get before the master or, as it may be, the judge, who is to make, if he is persuaded it is proper to do so, the relevant order of discontinuance having granted the leave sought, it is this. Up to that time the tenancy will have been continuing; up to that time whether or not he has exercised the right, the tenant will have had the right to occupy the premises; up to that time the tenant, and the tenant alone, in such circumstances as are applicable here, will have been entitled to receive, and will perhaps have received, the rent payable by the sub-tenants; up to that time, other than by agreement with the tenants, the landlord will have had no right to resume possession of the premises and will not have been in a position to let them to anyone else; nor indeed will he have known until the time comes when the court decides whether leave is to be granted or not, whether the tenancy is to come to an end on the date when the order is made or is to continue thereafter indefinitely. He will have been entitled to contemplate not only that the tenancy will continue as it will have done up to the date when the judge makes his order, but that it will continue, in the ordinary way for three months thereafter. In this situation, to my mind it would require the strongest and clearest statutory language, and by 'statutory' I include of course the language of the rules, to give the court a power retrospectively to deprive the landlord of the rights which by then will have accrued to him.

For those two reasons, if for no others, I have reached the conclusion that there is no power conferred on the court by RSC Ord 21, r 3, to make an order for the discontinuance of proceedings such as these, or, so far as I can tell, of any other proceedings, but it may not be of any importance in another context, which will have operation retrospectively from a date earlier than the date on which the order is made.

Having said that, I remain conscious of the startling anomaly between the situation under the High Court rules and the situation under the county court rules, to which counsel for the tenants has drawn our attention. We have heard an interesting argument as to how, if amendment is called for, the rules ought to be amended. Counsel for the tenants suggests that the High Court rules should be brought into conformity with the county court rules; counsel for the landlords, perhaps understandably, suggests precisely the contrary. It does seem to me that this may be a situation which has escaped the attention of the rule-makers who are responsible for both sets of rules, and it may be that, now this case has thrown the point up, the relevant rule committees, either severally or in consultation with each other, will wish to consider whether any, and what, amendment to the rules might be appropriate to remove the anomaly. But I certainly do not regard it as any part of the task of this court to suggest what, if any, amendment might be appropriate.

For the reasons I have sought to explain, I would dismiss this appeal.

SIR DAVID CAIRNS. I also would dismiss this appeal for the reasons which have been given by Bridge LJ.

In addition to contending that the words 'on such terms as to costs, the bringing of a subsequent action or otherwise' give jurisdiction to backdate the order, counsel on behalf of the tenants argued that there is inherent jurisdiction in the High Court to backdate its orders. In my view there is no such general jurisdiction. In some forms of order, for example, as to periodical payments which have accrued due before the making of the order, or as to the remission of such payments, there is a jurisdiction to backdate: see the decision of this court in *MacDonald v MacDonald*[1]. Other forms of order clearly could not be backdated.

1   [1963] 2 All ER 857, [1964] P 1

Two instances which occur to me are: a money judgment, which clearly could not
a be backdated to an earlier date so as to carry interest under the Judgments Act 1838
from that earlier date; or a decree of divorce, which plainly could not be made to
operate from a date earlier than the order granting the decree.

The type of order with which RSC Ord 21, r 3, is concerned, seems to me to be
obviously an order of such a character that it would be something of an absurdity to
say that it could be backdated, the effect of backdating being to say that an action
b which had in fact been in existence up to the date of the order had ceased to be in
existence at some earlier date.

For these reasons I agree to dismissing the appeal.

BUCKLEY LJ. I agree with both the judgments which have been delivered.
c What cannot be done without leave clearly cannot be done unless and until leave
has been obtained. Consequently, it seems to me impossible that a tenant, by making
an application for leave to withdraw or discontinue his application for a new tenancy
under the Landlord and Tenant Act 1954 could, even in some contingent manner,
discontinue or withdraw his application merely by issuing a summons for leave to
do so. The court can of course kill an action by ordering its discontinuance, but our
d attention has been drawn to no power conferred on the court to direct not merely
that the action should be killed but that it should be deemed to have died at some date
earlier than the date of the order. I am fully satisfied that the court has no inherent
jurisdiction to make any such order, and I do not think that any such power is to
be found in RSC Ord 21, r 3. That rule does empower a court to whom application
is made to discontinue an action on terms; but those terms must, I agree, be terms
e which are imposed on the applicant; it cannot refer to terms imposed on the respondent to the application.

For the reasons which have been given by Bridge LJ and Sir David Cairns I agree
that this appeal fails. It seems to me that there are substantial grounds for thinking that
consideration should be given to the question whether in some way the relevant High
Court and county court rules should not be revised so as to make them accord with one
f another in relation to withdrawal of an application for a new lease under the 1954 Act.
But that, as Bridge LJ has said, is not a matter on which we could properly express any
definite views, either whether amendment of the rules should be made, or what form
any amendment might take.

In those circumstances the appeal will be dismissed.

g *Appeal dismissed.*

Solicitors: *May, May & Merrimans* (for the tenants); *Theodore Goddard & Co* (for the
landlords).

J H Fazan Esq   Barrister.

Laurence and another v Lexcourt Holdings Ltd

CHANCERY DIVISION
BRIAN DILLON QC SITTING AS A DEPUTY JUDGE OF THE HIGH COURT
7th, 8th, 9th, 13th DECEMBER 1977

Misrepresentation – Negligent misrepresentation – Lease of office premises – Lessor describing premises as offices and offering them for 15 year letting as offices – Planning permission available for use as offices for two years only – Use of premises thereafter subject to review – Lessor failing to check facts at date of grant of lease – Alleged acquiesence on part of lessee – Whether lessee entitled to rescission of lease on ground of negligent misrepresentation.

Mistake – Mistake of fact – Common mistake – Existence of mistake at date of contract – Belief of parties at date of contract that planning permission available without restriction for use of premises as offices – Planning permission available for limited period only – Planning permission subject to review thereafter – Lessee taking possession without making any enquiries or searches – Whether lessee entitled to rescission of contract on ground of common mistake.

In 1970 the plaintiffs bought a property consisting of two shops on the ground floor and living accommodation on the first and second floors. They sought permission from the local planning authority to change its use so that it could be used for offices. In 1971 the planning authority gave them permission to use the ground floor and a part of the first floor as offices. In February 1974 the plaintiffs, completely forgetting that the planning permission did not cover the whole building, offered to let the whole of the first and second floors as offices to the defendants for 15 years. The defendants inspected the premises which appeared to provide the office accommodation they needed. They assumed that planning permission existed for its use as offices. They accepted the plaintiffs' offer and took possession immediately without making any of the usual searches and enquiries. They left those to their solicitors, who, after making the necessary investigations, informed them in April (i) that there was no subsisting planning permission for the use as offices of the second floor and part of the first floor, and (ii) that a new road plan for the area, passed by the county council in November 1972 and submitted to the Secretary of State for the Environment, would, if approved, specifically affect the property. The parties agreed that the plaintiffs should apply to the planning authority for permission to use the whole of the first and second floors as offices. On 17th October 1974 the planning authority granted that permission but limited it to a period of time expiring on 31st October 1977, so that they could then 'review the need for offices at the site and in relation to the future road plan'. The parties' solicitors thereupon entered into negotiations to see whether alternative leasehold arrangements could be made. The negotiations came to nothing, and at the beginning of April 1975 the defendants gave the plaintiffs a month's notice. They paid the rent up to the end of April and left. The plaintiffs brought an action against the defendants claiming specific performance of the agreement for the lease made on February 1974. In their defence the defendants claimed that they were absolved from carrying out the agreement on the grounds of (i) negligent misrepresentation, (ii) common mistake and (iii) illegality. They counterclaimed, inter alia, for rescission of the agreement. In reply the plaintiffs contended that any right which the defendants might have had to have the agreement rescinded had been lost because they had affirmed the contract by remaining in occupation for six months after they had discovered the limitation on the planning permission and the reason for it.

Held – The plaintiffs' claim would be dismissed and the defendants were entitled to have the agreement rescinded—

(i) On the ground of misrepresentation, because the plaintiffs' description of the
a premises as offices was a representation not merely as to the physical state of the
premises but also as to the availability of planning permission for them to be used
for the full term of 15 years for the intended purpose as offices, and the plaintiffs were
negligent in making that representation because they could have checked the facts
but did not do so (see p 818 g h and p 821 a b, post); Re Davis & Cavey (1888) 40 Ch D
601 and Charles Hunt Ltd v Palmer [1931] 2 Ch 287 applied.

b   (ii) Alternatively, on the ground of common mistake, because (a) the belief of the
parties in February 1974 that planning permission was available without restriction
for use of the premises as offices was a fundamental mistake, and (b) the defendants
were not at fault in entering into possession without making the usual searches and
enquiries as they did not owe a duty of care to the plaintiffs to make those searches
and they did not bring about the plaintiffs' forgetfulness (see p 819 d e and g h, post);
c Solle v Butcher [1949] 2 All ER 1107 and Grist v Bailey [1966] 2 All ER 875 applied.

(iii) The defendants' claim was not barred by acquiescence: on learning of the limitation on the planning permission they were confused as to what they should do and
wanted to consider any alternative leasehold arrangements that might be suggested
in the negotiations between their solicitors and the plaintiffs' solicitors, they had not
finally concluded at that stage that they would move out, and, when the negotiations
d broke down, they were entitled to time to consider what possibilities were then
open to them. They did not decide until March 1975 that they would leave the
premises and they then gave the plaintiffs reasonable notice (see p 820 c d and f to j, post).

Notes
For rescission for misrepresentation, see 9 Halsbury's Laws (4th Edn) para 536.
e   For recission for mistake, see ibid paras 449, 537.

Cases referred to in judgment
Best v Glenville [1960] 3 All ER 478, [1960] 1 WLR 1198, 58 LGR 333, CA, 31 Digest
(Reissue) 383, 3068.
Davis & Cavey, Re (1888) 40 Ch D 601, 58 LJCh 143, 60 LT 100, 53 JP 407, 40 Digest
f (Repl) 163, 1269.
Edler v Auerbach [1949] 2 All ER 692, [1950] 1 KB 359, 31(1) Digest (Reissue) 497, 4107.
Esso Petroleum Co Ltd v Mardon [1976] 2 All ER 5, [1976] QB 801, [1976] 2 WLR 583,
[1976] 2 Lloyd's Rep 305, CA.
Flight v Booth (1834) 1 Bing NC 370, [1824-34] All ER Rep 43, 1 Scott 190, 4 LJCP 66,
131 ER 1160, 40 Digest (Repl) 113, 870.
g Grist v Bailey [1966] 2 All ER 875, [1967] Ch 532, [1966] 3 WLR 618, Digest (Cont Vol B)
545, 120a.
Hill v Harris [1965] 2 All ER 358, [1965] 2 QB 601, [1965] 2 WLR 1331, CA, 31(1) Digest
(Reissue) 425, 3410.
Hunt (Charles) Ltd v Palmer [1931] 2 Ch 287, 100 LJCh 356, 145 LT 630, 40 Digest (Repl)
79, 599.
h Redgrave v Hurd (1881) 20 Ch D 1, [1881-5] All ER Rep 77, 51 LJCh 113, 45 LT 485,
CA, 35 Digest (Repl) 48, 423.
Solle v Butcher [1949] 2 All ER 1107, [1950] 1 KB 671, CA, 31(2) Digest (Reissue) 1042, 8232.

Action
By a writ issued on 26th February 1976 the plaintiffs, Kenneth Gordon Laurence
j and Roy Frederick Laurence, brought an action against the defendants, Lexcourt
Holdings Ltd, claiming (i) specific performance of an agreement for a lease made
on or about 27th February 1974, whereby the plaintiffs agreed to grant, and the defendants to take, a tenancy of a suite of offices on the first and second floors of 50
Midland Road, Wellingborough, for 15 years from 11th March 1974; (ii) damages in
addition to, or in lieu of, specific performance or for breach of contract; (iii) all necessary

accounts and enquiries; (iv) further or other relief. In their defence the defendants claimed that they were absolved from carrying out the agreement on the grounds of (i) negligent misrepresentation; (ii) common mistake; (iii) illegality. They counter-claimed for (1) rescission of the agreement; (2) damages in respect of expenses which they incurred in moving to, and from, 50 Midland Road. The facts are set out in the judgment.

Timothy Lloyd for the plaintiffs.
Roy McAulay for the defendants.

BRIAN DILLON QC. In this action the plaintiffs, who are brothers, are claiming against the defendants specific performance of an agreement for a lease. This agreement, which is not in dispute, was made either orally on 26th February 1974 or by an exchange of letters of 26th and 27th February recording the terms discussed and agreed on 26th. It was an agreement whereby the plaintiffs agreed to let the first and second floors of 50 Midland Road, Wellingborough, to the defendants for a term of 15 years, from 11th March 1974, at a yearly rent of £2,250, with reviews at the end of the 3rd, 7th and 11th years.

The defendants took possession of the premises on the day after the agreement had been made, but they gave up possession in the latter part of April 1975, and they now claim to rescind the agreement or alternatively to resist specific performance on the grounds of negligent misrepresentation, common mistake and illegality. Certain further possible defences were pleaded but these are now abandoned.

A further issue that has been debated, however, is an issue of acquiescence or affirmation of the contract in that the plaintiffs say that even if, which is strenuously denied, the defendants would have been entitled to rescission if they had acted more speedily they have lost that right by failing to exercise it promptly after the relevant facts had become known to them.

The basic facts are not really in dispute and I find them as follows. The freehold of the entire premises, 50 Midland Road, was bought by the plaintiffs in 1970. The premises were then unoccupied and not in a good condition. They had previously been used as a pair of shops, with living accommodation on the first and second floors above. Having no doubt done some conversion work the plaintiffs have since 1971 occupied the ground floor of no 50 as offices for the purposes of their own business, which is concerned with building work and the ownership and development of properties. They also for some six months in the latter part of 1971 occupied part but not the whole of the first floor as further offices for their own business. They did this under the authority of a planning permission from the Northamptonshire County Council dated 8th January 1971. This planning permission specified as the development thereby permitted 'change of use from shops with living accommodation over two offices on ground floor and part first floor. Remainder of first floor and second floor not to be used'. I accept from Mr Kenneth Laurence that the reason why the planning permission was thus limited and did not extend to the whole of the first floor or to the second floor was merely that there was at that stage no sufficient fire escape from those floors. In consequence the remainder of the first floor and the whole of the second floor remained unoccupied until the defendants took possession after the agreement for lease of February 1974 had been made.

The plaintiffs had originally had it in mind that they might in time want to occupy the whole of no 50 for their own offices but towards the end of 1973 they dropped this idea and decided instead to try to let off the whole of the first and second floors. They had certain work done, and in February 1974 they instructed an estate agent, Mr Pendered of Messrs Swindall, Pendered & Atkins, to find a tenant.

The defendants, who carry on business as an accounting company doing accounts for other companies, were at that time sharing other accommodation in Wellingborough with an associated company and were badly in need of more space to house

their administrative staff. Towards the end of October 1973, therefore, they had
a instructed Mr Pendered to find offices for them, and they had looked over various
suggested premises and rejected them. When, therefore, Mr Pendered received his
instructions from the plaintiffs he at once thought of the defendants, rang Mr Blythe,
a director of the defendants, and told Mr Blythe that he had found an ideal suite of
offices for the defendants. On the next day Mr Blythe and Mr Smart, the defendants'
accountant, went over the rooms on the first and second floors of 50 Midland Road with
b Mr Pendered. Shortly afterwards Mr Piercy, the defendants' managing director,
went over the premises with Mr Blythe and Mr Smart, and on 21st February Mr
Pendered wrote to both parties' solicitors, recording agreement, subject to contract,
on the grant of a lease. Mr Pendered probably supposed that the negotiations would
be continued by the solicitors in the usual way, but this did not happen. Instead
Mr Piercy and Mr Smart met Mr Kenneth Laurence at 50 Midland Road on 26th
c February 1974 and binding agreement on the grant of a lease was reached either
orally on that occasion or by the exchange of letters on 26th and 27th February.
Possession was taken immediately afterwards. I have no doubt that the reason why
agreement was made without allowing the solicitors to carry out the usual formalities
was that the defendants were in a hurry and wanted accommodation urgently.
No pressure was put on them by Mr Laurence to make an agreement without refer-
d ence to solicitors, but in a friendly way he was out to help the defendants. Both
parties were of high standing in their local community in Wellingborough,
although they had not previously met. They had heard of each other's high
reputation.

The physical condition of the first and second floors of no 50 at the time the agreement was made was as follows. A separate entrance from the street to the first floor
e had been made in order to comply with the fire regulations, although in fact certain
further work was subsequently required by the fire officer which was carried out
by the plaintiffs. The rooms which had been used by the plaintiffs in 1971 were
wallpapered and carpeted. One of those rooms was described by Mr Pendered to
Mr Blythe as the board room. The remaining rooms on the first floor and the rooms
on the second floor were all painted in the same colour. For those rooms there was
f a bale of carpet available but it was not laid. There was strip lighting throughout
and there were night storage heaters, but there was no furniture and the rooms
did not include any bathroom. Mr Blythe said, and I accept, that so far as he was
concerned there was no possibility of the rooms being let for other than office use.
Mr Swindall, the senior partner in Swindall, Pendered & Atkins, said, and again
I accept, that the first and second floors of no 50 were totally usable as offices in the
g physical sense of the word, but some form of conversion would have been needed for
any other use.

Before the agreement for lease of February 1974 was made nothing at all was said
in any discussion between the parties or in any discussion between either party and
Mr Pendered about planning permission or the permitted user of the first and second
floors of no 50, or, to anticipate a point I have not yet mentioned, about the possible
h effect on no 50 of the local authority's plans for new roads and the expansion of
Wellingborough. All concerned on either side, that is to say Mr Kenneth Laurence,
Mr Blythe and Mr Piercy, assumed that planning permission existed for the use of
the whole of the first and second floors as offices. But in truth the only subsisting
permission was the permission of January 1971, which was limited to the ground floor
and part only of the first floor of no 50. Mr Kenneth Laurence never mentioned
j this limitation on the planning permission to the defendants because, as I find, he
had honestly forgotten that there was any such limitation. If he had remembered
the limitation he would have mentioned it. The defendants never discovered about
the limitation because they were in such a hurry to get possession that they failed to
take what any solicitor would call the obvious precaution of making the usual searches
and enquiries of the local authority before they committed themselves to the

agreement. The information was readily available to anyone who made the usual searches and enquiries.

In fact, after the agreement for lease had been made, the defendants' solicitors did on 28th March 1974 put in hand the usual searches and enquiries, and the answers to these which came to hand early in April at the latest did disclose the terms of the January 1971 planning permission, thus showing that there was no subsisting planning permission for the use as offices of the second floor or part of the first floor of no 50. The answers of the county council to the usual enquiries also showed first that the county council had at their meeting on 16th November 1972 approved a revised town map for Wellingborough for inclusion in the development plan and at this time that had been submitted to the Secretary of State for the Environment for approval, and secondly that the property was specifically affected by the proposals contained in the revised town map, namely by the proposed new road pattern, as the property was shown on the town map as required for road improvements.

The previous history of these road proposals was that even before 1970 there had been a proposal to build a major conurbation, as it was called in evidence, to the east of Wellingborough to house some 20,000 inhabitants; I think by way of overspill from Greater London. If this were to be built changes in the road pattern would be required. Prior to 1970 some three or four alternative schemes were the subject of discussion, one of which would not have affected no 50, although the others would have affected it.

In November 1972 the county council had approved a different road scheme to be carried out in five phases, and phase 3 of this scheme would have provided for the demolition of no 50 as part of the provision of a new east link road for the proposed new conurbation.

In February 1974 the position was that the Secretary of State had not yet approved the revised town map, although a public inquiry had been held in November 1973. On the normal planning procedures the precise details of the routing of new roads would have been decided by further enquiries and compulsory purchase procedures after the town map had been approved by the Secretary of State. In February 1974 Mr Piercy and Mr Blythe knew of the general nature of the road proposals but did not know how, if at all, they would, if implemented, affect no 50. They could easily have found out by enquiring of the county council.

Mr Laurence also knew of the proposals but did not attach any importance to them because he did not think they would ever be carried out. In this view Mr Laurence was strongly supported both then and now by his surveyor, Mr Swindall of Messrs Swindall, Pendered & Atkins. Mr Swindall told me, and he may well be right, that if the road proposals had ever been costed they would prove far too expensive for there ever to be money available to carry them out.

After the replies to the local searches and enquiries had come to hand in April 1974 the parties very sensibly agreed that application should be made by the plaintiffs for planning permission for the use of the whole of the first and second floors of no 50 as office user. After some work required by the fire officer had been carried out such an application was made. The application was made on 11th September 1974, but the answer which is dated 17th October 1974 was not, I think, what any of the parties had expected. Permission was granted but limited to a period of time expiring on 31st October 1977, at or before the expiration of which period the use was to be discontinued. The reason given in the permission for this limitation was 'to enable the planning authority to review the need for offices at this site and in relation to the future road plan of Wellingborough'. There was an informal suggestion that the planning permission for office use might be extended after October 1977 in the light of the situation about the road proposals at that time, but I do not think any weight can really be attached to that since the local authority were not prepared to commit themselves to such an extension in response to the formal application which had been made in September 1974.

After the grant of this limited planning permission there was correspondence
a between the parties about alternative leasehold arrangements, for instance for a
tenancy to the end of October 1977 with an option to the defendants to renew that
for any further term for which planning permission might be available, but possibly
without rent reviews. However, agreement on alternative leasehold arrangements
was never reached, and as I have indicated in late April 1975 the defendants gave up
possession of the premises and ceased paying rent.
b   I have no doubt that if the 1974 planning application which was in fact made in
September had been made in January, before the February 1974 agreement, only
the same limited planning permission could have been obtained for the same reason.
Thus, when the February 1974 agreement for a 15 year lease was made, the only
planning permission for office use of the premises which was obtainable was a
permission for such use only up to the end of October 1977, because of the road
c improvement proposals.
   Against this background the defendants now claim to rescind the agreement or
to be absolved from complying with it on the grounds (i) of misrepresentation,
(ii) of mistake and (iii) of illegality.
   Illegality I can dispose of very shortly. It is said that the agreement envisaged
immediate occupation of the first and second floors as offices and that that was
d illegal because of the absence of planning permission for such use. Neither party
intended, however, to break the law in any way. Nor did the agreement necessarily
compel them to do so. It follows from *Best v Glenville*[1] that the agreement is not
tainted with any illegality; see especially the judgment of Upjohn LJ[2], where he
says that he is quite unable to accept the proposition that an agreement between
two parties which involves a user of land for which development permission is
e required is necessarily illegal if that permission has not previously been obtained.
   As for misrepresentation the case is pleaded in considerable detail in the statement
of claim, but what it really comes down to is in my judgment simply this: the first
and second floors of no 50 were offered for lease for 15 years by the plaintiffs to the
defendants as offices, an ideal suite of offices as Mr Pendered said, and to all outward
appearances they were a suite of offices and nothing else. It is said, and I take this
f from the statement of claim, that by so offering the premises of such an outward
appearance the plaintiffs represented that the premises might lawfully be used as
offices then and at all times during the term and that they were not affected by any
proposed new road plans. When, therefore, premises which looked like offices
are offered for sale or for leasing for a relatively long term as offices, what representation, if any, is there that the premises can lawfully be used as offices either at
g the inception of or throughout the term? I do not think that the plaintiffs can place
any weight on the road proposals independently of their effect on the planning permission. The ground floor of no 50 had unlimited planning permission for use as
offices. If Mr Laurence had wanted to sell or lease off the ground floor he would
naturally have described it as offices for sale or to let, and no one for a moment would
have supposed that he was representing that the ground floor was not affected, still
h less that it would remain unaffected throughout the proposed term, by the road proposals in the revised town map. The defendants' case must therefore rest on the
limitation, because of the road proposals, of the available planning permission.
The defendants disclaim any suggestion that Mr Laurence had or professed to have
had any special knowledge, and so the case is not analogous on its facts to *Esso Petroleum
Co Ltd v Mardon*[3]. Moreover, it was held in *Hill v Harris*[4] that on the grant of a lease
j or tenancy no warranty or condition on the part of the landlords is to be implied

1   [1960] 3 All ER 478, [1960] 1 WLR 1198
2   [1960] 3 All ER 478 at 482, [1960] 1 WLR 1198 at 1203
3   [1976] 2 All ER 5, [1976] QB 801
4   [1965] 2 All ER 358, [1965] 2 QB 601

that the premises are legally fit for the purpose for which they are let. It is for the tenant to satisfy himself by making his own enquiries. But Diplock LJ pointed out in *a* *Hill v Harris*[1] that that was not an action for rescission based on innocent misrepresentation. There were reasons why, prior to the Misrepresentation Act 1967, relief for innocent misrepresentation could probably not have been obtained in the circumstances of *Hill v Harris*[2]. In *Hill v Harris*[2] the Court of Appeal specifically approved the decision of Devlin J in *Edler v Auerbach*[3] and counsel for the plaintiffs has in his reply placed considerable reliance on Devlin J's judgment. However, Devlin J *b* pointed out[4] that an innocent misrepresentation could only lead to the remedy of rescission which, as the law then stood, was not a remedy available where a lease had been executed. Therefore the judgment in *Edler v Auerbach*[3] was not concerned with misrepresentation.

Counsel for the defendants has referred me to two other authorities which need rather more careful consideration. The first is the case of *Re Davis & Cavey*[5], a decision of *c* Stirling J. In that case certain property had been offered for sale by auction which was described as leasehold business premises. After the sale the purchaser had discovered that the lease contained covenants which restricted the use of the premises. The covenant either prohibited the use of the premises for any trade or business at all or at any rate restricted use for carrying on any trade or business which might cause a nuisance or annoyance to adjoining tenants and from using the premises *d* as a public house. Procedurally the matter came before Stirling J on a vendor and purchaser summons, and for that procedural reason his ultimate decision was that a good title had not been shown, but he was unable on the particular summons to order the return of the deposit because he was unable to grant that relief on a vendor and purchaser summons on grounds which affected the validity of the contract. He reserved, however, to the purchaser the right to bring an action for the return *e* of the deposit. As I read Stirling J's judgment, however, he considered the question which he had to decide on much broader grounds, because he said[6]:

'... if the vendor seeks specific performance of the contract a Court of Equity has a discretionary jurisdiction to say whether it will compel a purchaser to take a contract under which he will get something different from that which he has *f* been led to expect he will get. Whenever a vendor chooses to put into his conditions of sale anything which misleads the purchaser, the latter may decline to perform the contract, and may say, "this is not a contract which a Court of Equity will enforce against me". That is a different thing from saying that the title is not such a title as the vendor contracted to give him.'

Earlier Stirling J expressed the view[7] that as the property was put up for sale as *g* business premises the purchaser would be entitled to have property conveyed to him on which he could carry on any business, subject only to the restrictions imposed by the general law of the land, for example, so as not to create a nuisance, and subject also to the statutory restrictions in force with regard to any particular trade where such restrictions exist.

Counsel for the plaintiffs has submitted to me that the basis of that view of the *h* learned judge rested on misdescription in the contract rather than on misrepresentation before the contract, but I do not think Stirling J was drawing any such distinction.

---

1   [1965] 2 All ER 358 at 361, [1965] 2 QB 601 at 615
2   [1965] 2 All ER 358, [1965] 2 QB 601   *j*
3   [1949] 2 All ER 692, [1950] 1 KB 359
4   [1949] 2 All ER 692 at 698, [1950] 1 KB 359 at 373
5   (1888) 40 Ch D 601
6   40 Ch D 601 at 606, 607
7   40 Ch D 601 at 605

He had referred in the passage which I have already quoted[1] to the vendor who
a chooses to put into his conditions of sale anything which misleads the purchaser.
He was concerned with a sale by auction and he must have had it in mind that the
conditions of sale on a sale by auction, though they will be part of the contract made
when the hammer falls, would have been widely circulated before the auction was
held. Beyond that, however, he quoted[2] from the judgment of Tindal CJ in *Flight v
Booth*[3], a passage where Tindal CJ has referred to the misdescription of the property
b and said:

'In this state of discrepancy between the decided cases, we think it is, at all
events, a safe rule to adopt, that where the misdescription, although not proceeding from fraud, is in a material and substantial point, so far affecting the
subject-matter of the contract that it may reasonably be supposed, that, but
for such misdescription, the purchaser might never have entered into the contract
c at all, in such case the contract is avoided altogether, and the purchaser is not
bound to resort to the clause of compensation.'

Stirling J goes on[4]:

'So that even although the misrepresentation does not proceed from fraud,
if it is on a material and substantial point the contract is avoided altogether.
d That, again, is a matter affecting the validity of the contract.'

I do not think he is drawing any distinction between misdescription and misrepresentation. Misdescription may be a form of misrepresentation.

Stirling J's decision was applied in the second case to which counsel for the defendant
has referred me, which is *Charles Hunt Ltd v Palmer*[5], a decision of Clauson J. In that
case leasehold shops described in the particulars of sale as 'valuable business premises'
e had been put up for sale by auction, subject to special conditions of sale and also to
the National Conditions of Sale, by one of which it was stipulated that the leases
or copies thereof might be examined and that the purchaser should be deemed to
have bought with notice of the contents thereof. The defendant apparently did not
take advantage of the right to inspection and he purchased the property as the
highest bidder, and it subsequently came to his knowledge for the first time that the
f leases under which the properties were held were subject to covenants which prohibited any other trade or business than that of a ladies' outfitters, fancy draper and
manufacturer of ladies' clothing from being carried on on the premises. Since the
purchaser was a dairyman who wanted to acquire the premises for the purposes of
his dairy business the premises, as Clauson J said, would obviously be of little use to
him if he was bound to complete the purchase.

g The vendors brought an action for specific performance in which the purchasers
counterclaimed for rescission of the contract and for recovery of deposit, and it was
held first that a shop which could be used for one purpose only was not fairly described
as 'valuable business premises', and, secondly that such a misleading misrepresentation by the plaintiffs in their particulars of sale disentitled them, notwithstanding
the condition as to inspection of the leases, to the assistance of the court to compel
h the defendant, who purchased in reliance on the truth of such representation, specifically to perform his part of a contract for a consideration different from that which
he was led to expect.

Clauson J recited the passages I have already read from the judgment of Stirling J
in *Re Davis & Cavey*[6], and then he said[7]:

j 1 (1888) 40 Ch D 601 at 606
2 40 Ch D 601 at 608, 609
3 (1834) 1 Bing NC 370 at 377, [1824-34] All ER Rep 43 at 46
4 40 Ch D 601 at 609
5 [1931] 2 Ch 287
6 40 Ch D 601
7 [1931] 2 Ch 287 at 293

'In my view, if I were to compel the defendant to carry out his part of the contract, I should be forcing him to take something different from that which he was led by the plaintiffs to expect he would get under the contract. In the circumstances of this case, in my view, it is primarily incumbent upon the plaintiffs to show that they are in a position to convey to the defendant the thing which by the particulars of sale they led him to believe he was to get under the contract. Until they have shown that, it is irrelevant to consider the . . . National Conditions of Sale which, as counsel on behalf of the plaintiffs contended, saddled the defendant with notice of the restrictions in the leases. A shop which may only be used for one trade cannot fairly be described as "valuable business premises". In my judgment it would be wrong for a Court of equity to compel the defendant to complete the purchase. Accordingly the plaintiffs' action for specific performance fails and must be dismissed.'

He went on in reliance of s 49 of the Law of Property Act 1925 to order the return of the deposit. I read that judgment as indicating that the description of the premises as 'valuable business premises' was misleading and a misrepresentation in that they could not lawfully be used for other than one purpose under the terms of the lease. Therefore, there having been a misrepresentation which, if the plaintiffs were entitled to compel performance of the contract, would have led to the defendant being able to take something very seriously different from what he was led to expect that he would get under the contract, the plaintiffs were not entitled to enforce the contract. I think those decisions would have been precisely in point in the present case if the restriction on office use until the end of October 1977 had been contained in a headlease of the premises or in a restrictive covenant in favour of the owner of the adjoining land. Does it make any difference that the restriction arises not by virtue of some document between subjects but by virtue of the decision of the planning authority, which is available to anyone to find out about who chooses to make the usual searches of the local authority? I do not think it does. First, because in *Charles Hunt Ltd v Palmer*[1] the conditions on which the purchasers were buying expressly provided for them to inspect the terms of the lease and provided that they had bought with notice of those terms, whether they inspected or not, and that did not avail the plaintiffs. Secondly, because where there has been a misrepresentation it is well established that it is no defence to the person who has made the misrepresentation to say 'Oh well, the party who was misled could have checked and found out the facts for himself, and he really has only himself to blame that he relied on me and did not make the enquiries that he might have made'. I think that that is covered by the well known decision in *Redgrave v Hurd*[2].

Therefore, subject to the question of affirmation and acquiescence to which I have not yet come, I think that the defendants are entitled to succeed on the ground of misrepresentation because it is not right, in my view, to describe property as offices and offer them for a 15 year letting as offices when the only planning permission for use as offices which is available is for a mere two years and use thereafter will be precaious.

I turn to the alternative submissions of the defendants on the ground of mistake. I find as a fact that there was a common mistake between the parties in that when the agreement of February 1974 was made both Mr Kenneth Laurence and Mr Piercy and Mr Blythe believed that there was planning permission available without restriction for the use of the first and second floors of no 50 as offices. The law on the question of common mistake and relief in equity was stated by Denning LJ in a well known passage in *Solle v Butcher*[3], where he said:

'A contract is also liable in equity to be set aside if the parties were under a common misapprehension either as to facts or as to their relative and respective

1   [1931] 2 Ch 287
2   (1881) 20 Ch D 1, [1881-5] All ER Rep 77
3   [1949] 2 All ER 1107 at 1120, [1950] 1 KB 671 at 693

rights, provided that the misapprehension was fundamental and that the party seeking to set it aside was not himself at fault.'

There are, therefore, the two requirements to be considered. Was the misapprehension fundamental, and were the defendants who are seeking to set the agreement aside themselves at fault.

The question of fault was considered by Goff J in *Grist v Bailey*[1]. He said:

'There remains one other point, and that is the condition laid down by DENNING, L.J., that the party seeking to take advantage of the mistake must not be at fault. DENNING, L.J., did not develop that at all, and it is not, I think with respect, absolutely clear what it comprehends. Clearly, there must be some degree of blameworthiness beyond the mere fault of having made a mistake; but the question is, how much, or in what way? Each case must depend on its own facts...'

In the present case there is no doubt that the defendants were imprudent in proceeding without making the usual searches and enquiries, but they did not owe any duty of care to the plaintiffs to make those searches and their mistake did not bring about Mr Laurence's mistake. In a sense if they had searched and obtained the information and mentioned to Mr Laurence what they had discovered Mr Laurence's memory would have been jogged and he would then not have made a mistake, but I do not think that makes the defendants responsible for Mr Laurence's mistake or forgetfulness. It seems to me that whatever Denning LJ did have in mind in this qualification in *Solle v Butcher*[2] does not cover the failure to search on the part of the defendants in this case, and I do not think, therefore, that they are disentitled from relying on the mistake because they failed to search. Was the mistake then a fundamental mistake? *Solle v Butcher*[2] and *Grist v Bailey*[3] were both cases in which the mistake concerned whether a tenancy of the premises was a protected tenancy under the Rent Acts, and I think they show that a mistake of that nature is a fundamental mistake, whether it be the case that the premises are being sold on the footing that they are subject to a protected tenancy when in truth because the tenant has died they are not so subject, or whether it be the case that the premises are being sold on the basis that they are subject to a tenancy which is not protected when in truth it is protected for some of the rather technical reasons that arise under the Rent Acts. I do not see any real difference in point of importance between the Rent Acts and the Planning Acts, which are both major acts affecting land. I think it is fundamental to people who are taking land for a term as long as 15 years with a view to their use as offices that planning permission should be available for more than a mere two or three years, and I think therefore that this mistake which was common to both parties was a fundamental mistake which entitles the defendants, subject to the question again of acquiescence and affirmation, to avoid the agreement. I do not see that it matters that the mistake was as to the legal suitability of the land for a particular use rather than as to its physical description. Whether the case be put on mistake or misrepresentation I think the absence of the planning permission was fundamental.

I turn, therefore, to the arguments based on acquiescence and affirmation of the contract. No objection is taken to the defendants having remained in occupation until in November 1974 or just before they discovered the limitation on the planning permission and the reason for it. But it is said that their remaining in occupation after that was an affirmation of the contract, and that when they ultimately gave notice at the beginning of April 1975 that they were going to leave they were too

---

1 [1966] 2 All ER 875 at 880, 881, [1967] Ch 532 at 542
2 [1949] 2 All ER 1107, [1950] 1 KB 671
3 [1966] 2 All ER 875, [1967] Ch 532

late. They are therefore bound for 15 years to a lease, the rent under which was fixed as a rent for office premises, even though they may be unable to get planning *a* permission to use the premises as offices.

On the face of the correspondence what was happening after the planning permission was granted for the limited period was that there were negotiations proceeding between the solicitors with a view to seeing whether agreement could be reached on alternative leasehold arrangements, such as that though the defendants would have the 15 year lease they should have a right of determination in the event of the *b* premises being required for road development, or alternatively that they should have a lease in the first place until October 1977, with an option to renew if further planning permission became available then. But the defendants were indicating that if any arrangement of that nature was to be reached the rent review provisions should not apply. There should be no rent review in early 1977 after the first three years of the lease, or, as they seem to have been asserting, during any extension of *c* the lease under the suggested option. I do not think it is easy for the plaintiffs to say that the defendants were affirming the 15 years lease by remaining in possession while negotiations were proceeding for a different leasehold arrangement.

Beyond that I think the defendants were entitled to time before they finally made up their mind what to do because they had to consider where they would go to if they moved out of these premises. And it is not suggested that the plaintiffs suffered *d* any detriment or altered their position in any way through the defendants having remained in occupation and paid rent until late April 1975.

Counsel for the plaintiffs urges that the defendants had made up their minds at a much earlier stage, late in November or perhaps early December of 1974, that they were going to move out and that therefore the negotiations that proceeded for an alternative leasehold arrangement cannot be given very much weight because *e* they did not really represent what the defendants really wanted. He says that the defendants, having made up their mind that they were going to move out, had a duty to tell the plaintiffs of that decision. It may be that the defendants might have owed such a duty if they had finally made up their minds and saw the plaintiffs acting to their detriment in the belief that the defendants were going to remain in occupation, but on the evidence of Mr Blythe and Mr Piercy, who I regard as careful and im- *f* pressive witnesses, my conclusion is that when the defendants came to hear of the limitations on the planning permission and to learn that the planning permission was linked to the road proposals, they were confused and were wondering what to do, and they did not like the prospect at all of remaining in the premises, subject to this restriction. But I do not think they finally concluded at that stage that they would definitely move out. They wanted an alternative suggestion as to what to do. *g* They were prepared to consider alternatives that were put forward. They were also considering whether they could find alternative premises. They looked at some other premises which were not suitable, and in the months of December and January 1974 the possibility that they would move back to the premises of their associated company from which they had come to 50 Midland Road was, I think, only one of the possibilities they were considering and not a firm decision. They were concerned by the *h* sheer physical problem of moving an accounting company which had machinery and with the expense of so doing. I do not think they reached any final decision until March 1975 that they would move back where they had come from, and they then gave reasonable notice at the beginning of April 1975 and paid rent until they went. I therefore find that they did not ever affirm the February 1974 agreement for lease and their claim now to resist specific performance and have the agreement *j* rescinded is not barred by acquiescence.

On those findings and conclusions it follows that the plaintiffs' action fails, but on their counterclaim the defendants are entitled to rescission of the February 1974 agreement.

The defendants have also counterclaimed for damages in respect of expenses which they incurred first in moving to 50 Midland Road, and then in moving from 50 Midland Road. The amount of those expenses is agreed between the parties at £900. On my conclusion that the description of the premises as office premises was a representation not merely as to the physical state of the premises but as to the availability of planning permission for the premises to be used for the intended purposes as offices I think it follows that Mr Laurence was negligent in making the representation, because he could have checked the facts and did not do so; he forgot. It follows, therefore, that the defendants are entitled to recover the damages in the agreed sum of £900.

Judgment for the defendants on the counterclaim.

Solicitors: *Stoneham, Langton & Passmore*, agents for *Mellows*, Bedford (for the plaintiffs); *Toller, Hales & Collcut*, Wellingborough (for the defendants).

Tokunbo Williams Barrister.

Royco Homes Ltd v Eatonwill Construction Ltd

CHANCERY DIVISION
H E FRANCIS QC SITTING AS A DEPUTY JUDGE OF THE HIGH COURT
7th, 8th, 9th, 10th NOVEMBER 1977

Public health – Sewerage – Public sewer – Agreement to vest sewer in local authority – Sewer constructed by defendant in lane subsequently adopted at defendant's request by local authority as public highway – Defendant also requesting local authority to adopt sewer – Local authority recommended to adopt sewer but resolution therefor never passed – Sewer subsequently shown on statutory map as public sewer – Local authority in course of correspondence permitting plaintiff to connect his sewer to the 'public sewer' – Whether correspondence 'an agreement to acquire . . . sewer' – Whether 'acquired' limited to acquisitions by agreement or covering acquisitions by operation of law – Public Health Act 1936, ss 15(1)(iii), 18(1), 20(b)(2).

In December 1960 the defendants' predecessors in title, H Ltd, were building a housing estate, consisting of 21 houses, fronting onto a lane. They wrote to the local authority asking (i) if they would adopt the lane as a public highway when the estate was complete, and (ii) if they would ultimately adopt as a public sewer a sewer ('the intermediate sewer') which they had decided to construct in the subsoil of the lane for the purposes of the estate. The local authority adopted the lane as a public highway. On 10th January 1961 the clerk to the local authority wrote to H Ltd informing them that, if the intermediate sewer was constructed according to the local authority's requirements, the local authority 'will thereafter be recommended to adopt [the intermediate] sewer under the provisions of, the Public Health Act 1936. The intermediate sewer was constructed in the subsoil of the lane in accordance with the local authority's requirements but the local authority never passed a resolution under s 17[a] of the 1936 Act vesting it in them. In 1975 the plaintiffs, wishing to purchase a vacant site adjoining the lane with a view to developing it, asked the local authority whether there was a public sewer within 100 feet of the site and, if so, whether the site could be drained by gravity into it. As the intermediate sewer was by that time shown on the statutory map kept by the local authority under s 32 of the 1936 Act as a public sewer, the local authority gave the plaintiffs an affirmative answer. Acting on that information, the plaintiffs bought the site, built 32 houses on it and contracted to sell most of them. With the local authority's approval, they connected the soil drain for their estate with the intermediate sewer so that it could take away the

---
a   Section 17, so far as material, is set out at p 830 *c d*, post

drainage from their houses. The intermediate sewer was large enough to serve both H Ltd's and the plaintiffs' estates and 100 other houses. In 1976 the defendants informed the plaintiffs that the intermediate sewer was a private sewer owned by the defendants and that it was unlawful for them to connect their drain to it without the defendants' permission and the payment of an appropriate consideration. The plaintiffs took the matter up with the local authority who informed them and the defendants that the intermediate sewer still appeared to be a private sewer as no resolution had been passed under s 17 of the 1936 Act vesting it in the local authority. On 29th March 1977 the defendants sealed off the plaintiffs' connection with the intermediate sewer. The plaintiffs brought an action against the defendants. They alleged that the sewer was a public sewer and complained of trespass in connection with the sealing off of their soil drain. They claimed damages for trespass, a declaration that the defendants had no proprietary interest in the intermediate sewer and were not entitled to prevent the plaintiffs from connecting their drain to it, and an injunction, inter alia, to restrain the defendants from obstructing the plaintiffs' drain. The defendants denied the plaintiffs' allegations and counterclaimed for damages for trespass, a declaration that they were the owners of the intermediate sewer and that the plaintiffs were not entitled to connect thereto, and an injunction to restrain the plaintiffs from making any connection to the intermediate sewer without their written consent. The plaintiffs served a third party notice on the local authority claiming an indemnity in respect of the counterclaim on the ground that the local authority were negligent in informing them that the intermediate sewer was a public sewer. At the hearing the two main issues were (i) whether the correspondence between H Ltd and the local authority in December 1960-January 1961 constituted an enforceable agreement, under s 18(1)[b] of the 1936 Act, that the intermediate sewer would be adopted as a public sewer, and (ii) whether the intermediate sewer had been 'acquired' by the local authority, within s 20(1)(b)[c] of the 1936 Act, and so had vested in them as a public sewer, within s 20(2) of that Act, when it was laid in their land in 1961, i e on the basis of the maxim quicquid plantatur solo, solo cedit. The defendants contended, inter alia, (i) that the term 'acquired' in s 20(1)(b) covered only acquisitions by agreement, because s 20(1) had to be read in conjunction with s 15(1)(iii)[d], which merely empowered a local authority 'by agreement to acquire . . . any sewer', and (ii) that, in any event, the intermediate sewer never became part of the local authority's land.

Held – (i) The correspondence between H Ltd and the local authority did not constitute an enforceable agreement under s 18 of the 1936 Act; the clerk to the local authority merely undertook to recommend to the local authority that the intermediate sewer should be adopted; it was open to the local authority to accept or reject that recommendation (see p 829, g h post).

(ii) The term 'acquired' in s 20(1)(b) covered all forms of acquisition open to a local authority and therefore included acquisitions by operation of law on the maxim quicquid plantatur solo, solo cedit. When the intermediate sewer was laid in 1961 it became part of the soil in which it was laid and its component parts thereupon lost their character as chattels, because it was intended to be a permanent installation, was constructed with a view to its adoption as part of the public sewer system and was large enough to be able to dispose of soil drainage from other sites in the neighbourhood. It followed that the local authority, as the owners of the soil, became the owners of the intermediate sewer, which accordingly became a public sewer.

---

b Section 18(1), so far as material, provides: 'A local authority may agree with any person constructing, or proposing to construct, a sewer . . . that, if the sewer . . . is . . . constructed in accordance with the terms of the agreement, they will . . . declare the sewer or works to be vested in them, and any such agreement shall be enforceable against the authority by the owner or occupier for the time being of any premises served by the sewer or works.'

c Section 20, so far as material, is set out at p 829 j to p 830 b, post

d Section 15(1), so far as material, is set out at p 830 g, post

A declaration would therefore be made in the terms sought by the plaintiffs, and the
a counterclaim and the plaintiffs' claim against the local authority would be dismissed
(see p 830 *h* to p 831 *c* and *h* to p 832 *c*, post); *Simmons v Midford* [1962] 2 All ER 1269
applied.

Notes
For vesting in, and adoption of, public sewers by local authorities, see 31 Halsbury's
b Laws (3rd Edn) 200-205, paras 294-297, and for cases on the subject, see 41 Digest
(Reissue) 17, 18, *119-131*.
   For the construction of sewers and drains by private persons, see 31 Halsbury's
Laws (3rd Edn) 229, para 336.
   For the Public Health Act 1936, ss 15, 17, 18, 20, 32, see 26 Halsbury's Statutes (3rd
Edn) 210, 212, 214, 216, 225.

c **Case referred to in judgment**
Simmons v Midford [1969] 2 All ER 1269, [1969] 2 Ch 415, [1969] 3 WLR 168, 20 P &
   CR 758, Digest (Cont Vol C) 878, *343a*.

Action
By a writ issued on 20th June 1977, the plaintiffs, Royco Homes Ltd, brought an
d action in the Queen's Bench Division against the defendants, Eatonwill Construction
Ltd, claiming (i) damages for trespass to the plaintiffs' sewer constructed within the
access road from Batchworth Lane, Northwood, to the plaintiffs' Eastbury Farm
Estate; (ii) a declaration that the defendants were not entitled to prevent the plaintiffs from connecting their sewer to the existing public sewer ('the intermediate
sewer') within the limits of the public highway known as Batchworth Lane; (iii) an
e injunction to restrain the defendants, their servants or agents, from obstructing the
plaintiffs' sewer and its connection to the sewer in Batchworth Lane and from registering any encumbrance or caution against the plaintiffs' title at HM Land Registry.
On 27th June Kerr J granted two interim injunctions in the terms of para (iii). By
consent the action was transferred to the Chancery Division and the interim injunctions were granted until the motion was heard in a Chancery Court. Fox J disposed of
f the motion on the basis of mutual undertakings given by the parties. The plaintiffs
undertook not to complete the sale of any houses on their estate pending judgment
in the action, and the defendants undertook, pending judgment, not to reblock
the plaintiffs' sewer or to register a caution at HM Land Registry in respect of any
counterclaim that they might bring. On 6th July the defendants served their defence
and counterclaim. In their defence they denied, inter alia, that the intermediate
g sewer was a public sewer and claimed that it was their property. They counterclaimed
for (i) damages for trespass to the intermediate sewer; (ii) a declaration that they
were the owners of the intermediate sewer and that the plaintiffs were not entitled
to connect thereto; (iii) an injunction to restrain the defendants by their servants,
agents or otherwise howsoever from making any connection to the intermediate
sewer without the defendants' prior written consent. The plaintiffs served on the
h Three Rivers District Council ('the council') a third party notice claiming an indemnity in respect of the counterclaim on the ground that the council were negligent
in informing the plaintiffs that the intermediate sewer was a public sewer. The
facts are set out in the judgment.

Barry Payton for the plaintiffs.
j *Patrick Freeman QC* and *Jeremy Sullivan* for the defendants.
Patrick Twigg for the council.

H E FRANCIS QC. The plaintiffs, a subsidiary of a substantial public company
called Royco Group Ltd, carried on business as builders and developers of residential
property. In 1975 the plaintiffs were minded to purchase a vacant site of building

land fronting onto a public highway, known as Batchworth Lane, Rickmansworth, in the county of Hertford.

Prior to contract the plaintiffs' solicitors made the usual local searches and addressed certain enquiries to the local authority, which was then the Three Rivers District Council. Enquiry No 15 and the replies thereto were in these terms:

'15(A) Is the property drained into a public sewer? (Reply): Not applicable. (B) Is there a public sewer within 100 ft. of the property? If so do the Council know that physically the property can be drained by gravity into that public sewer? (Answer): Yes.'

The second answer 'Yes' refers to a sewer which I shall call the intermediate sewer in Batchworth Lane, which was constructed in 1961 by a company called Paul Hurst Construction Ltd ('Hurst Construction') for the purpose of conveying soil and drainage from houses erected by that company on its Valency Close housing estate into the public sewer at the north end of Davenham Avenue. The answer to enquiry 15(B) was given on the strength of a statutory map kept by the local authority pursuant to s 32 of the Public Health Act 1936. This map showed the intermediate sewer as a public sewer.

In reliance on those replies the plaintiffs purchased the land and proceeded to develop it by erecting on it some 32 houses, most of which they have already contracted to sell. This development involved the disposal of the soil drainage from the estate into the intermediate sewer and the construction of a manhole at the point of connection. The connection was in due course made with the approval of the local authority. The intermediate sewer is amply sufficient in size to take the soil drainage from the plaintiffs' estate as well as that from the Valency Close estate. It is six inches in diameter, and it is an admitted fact that its capacity is sufficient to serve at least 150 houses. At present only the soil drainage of 21 houses of the Valency Close estate is discharged into it.

In the autumn of 1976 the present dispute arose. On 15th October 1976 Mr Paul William Hurst, who gave evidence before me, wrote a letter as a director of Hurstwood Building Management Ltd ('Hurstwood') to the plaintiffs and said:

'It has come to our notice that you could possibly have connected your soil sewer to a private sewer which serves Valency Close, which is practically opposite your site. This private sewer was put in many years ago by an associate company of ours. We would therefore be most grateful if you would check your records and let us know whether or not this is the case.'

After a reminder, Mr Clarke, on behalf of the plaintiffs, replied on 8th November 1976 and stated: 'Your letter of 15th October was sent to our architect, who has advised us that the sewer which we have entered is a local authority sewer and our discharge into this public sewer is with their approval.'

On 12th November 1976 another director of Hurstwood, Mr Michael Wood, wrote to the plaintiffs and said:

'We thank you for your letter of 8th November 1976 but regret to advise you that you are misinformed. The sewer into which your development has discharged is not a public sewer but a private one owned by our associate company, Eatonwill Construction Limited [that is, the defendant company. Later in the letter they say:] We shall be glad, therefore, if you will kindly let us have your proposals for dealing with the matter as quickly as possible since it is unlawful for you to connect your development into a private sewer without our permission and the payment of the appropriate consideration.'

On 14th December 1976, Mr Clarke, on behalf of the plaintiffs, wrote again to Hurstwood and said: 'I have written to the Three Rivers District Council asking for their comments as I had understood from them that this was a public line.'

On 14th January 1977 Mr Clarke, on behalf of the plaintiffs, again wrote to Hurst-wood and said: 'We have been advised by Three Rivers District Council that this drain is in their ownership and they have been maintaining it for some years without contribution from yourselves.'

On 14th February 1977 the solicitor to the Three Rivers District Council wrote to the plaintiffs in these terms:

'I find that in 1961, Paul Hurst (Construction) Limited entered into an Agreement under Section 40 of the Highways Act 1959 with the former Rickmansworth Urban District Council whereby the roads, verges and footways forming part of the development of Valency Close should be adopted as a highway maintainable at the public expense following satisfactory completion. The road was so adopted by the former Rickmansworth U.D.C. on 12th September, 1963. When the company submitted proposals for the construction of a foul water sewer in Batchworth Lane to serve the new development in Valency Close, the Company requested that the council should adopt it as a public sewer on completion. However, I am unable to find any resolution passed or statutory procedures undertaken under Section 17 of the Public Health Act, 1936 by the former Rickmansworth U.D.C., vesting the sewer in the Council as a public sewer. It appears, therefore, that the length of sewer is a private sewer belonging to Eatonwill Construction Limited, although there is no record of any formal agreement permitting the sewer to be constructed within the highway.'

The defendants' solicitors thereupon came on the scene, and on 14th February 1977 wrote a letter to the plaintiffs in these terms:

'We act for Eatonwill Construction Ltd who have passed us copies of the correspondence passing between you and them over the last month or two concerning the private soil sewer owned by them in Batchworth Lane. We observe that our clients drew your attention to their ownership of the sewer as long ago as the 12th November last and invited your proposals having regard to the fact that you have unlawfully, without their permission connected your development site into this private sewer. Our clients went to some trouble to explain the position to you, and the ... Three Rivers District Council have confirmed to us in writing that the length of sewer concerned is still a private sewer belonging to our clients. In view of the fact that three months have elapsed we must ask you to let us have your proposals concerning the matter, failing which we shall advise our clients to seek an injunction restraining you from using their sewer'.

On 29th March 1977 the defendants sealed off the plaintiffs' sewer, and on the the next day, 30th March 1977, the defendants' solicitors wrote to the plaintiffs' solicitors as follows:

'We refer to our earlier correspondence and are writing to let you know that our clients have now sealed off the connection of your clients' unauthorised drain to their sewer and in doing so our clients learned that your clients' connection had been very badly made and as a result the clay dropped into our clients' sewer. [Then in their last paragraph they say:] May we add for record purposes that at no time have our clients applied to the Local Authority for their sewer to be adopted, indeed at the time they constructed the same they were informed by the then Local Authority that the authority was not prepared to adopt the sewer.'

Finally, on 3rd May 1977, the defendants' solicitors again wrote to the plaintiffs' solicitors and said:

'So far as can be ascertained by our clients at present there is no formal agreement permitting the sewer to be constructed within the highway, but none the less our clients were actually required to instal it in that way at the request of the Council; our clients had planned their development with other means of drainage but were required by the Council to provide a soil sewer. As we have previously indicated, at no time did our clients request the council to adopt the same.'

It is quite clear from what has subsequently transpired that that last statement in the defendants' solicitors' letter of 3rd May 1977 is not correct. After the third party proceedings in this action had been launched there came to light two letters which passed between Hurst Construction and the clerk to the Rickmansworth Urban District Council ('the Rickmansworth Council') in December 1960 and January 1961.

In the letter of 12th December 1960 Hurst Construction wrote to the engineer and surveyor of the Rickmansworth Council and said this:

'Incidentally, I [that is Mr P W Hurst, director of Hurst Construction] have decided to construct a foul sewer to connect with your sewer at Davenham Avenue, and would ask if this sewer could be ultimately adopted as a public sewer.'

On 10th January 1961, the clerk of the Rickmansworth Council replied and stated:

'The Council's Engineer & Surveyor tells me that you also wish the Council to accept responsibility eventually for a length of foul sewer which you have to construct in Batchworth Lane from Valency Close to Farm Way [Farm Way is at the north end of Davenham Avenue]. I am able to inform you that providing the foul sewer is constructed to the Council's requirements, under the supervision of the Engineer & Surveyor and to his satisfaction, the Council will thereafter be recommended to adopt this length of sewer under the provisions of the Public Health Acts.'

I should also mention in this connection that at about the end of 1962 Hurst Construction purchased a plot of land adjoining the north-eastern boundary of the Valency Close estate and in connection with that purchase they instructed a firm of solicitors called Messrs Taylor Walker & Bland. A question arose as to how the houses to be erected on that plot should be drained, bearing in mind that it was in fact situated in the Bushey Rural District Council area and not in the Rickmansworth Council area. On 13th December 1962 Messrs Taylor Walker & Bland wrote a letter to the clerk to the Rickmansworth Council in these terms:

'We enclose a plan of a piece of land our clients contemplate purchasing. We have made a search in the Watford Rural District Council who inform us that there is no sewer available into which the property may be drained. We have been asked by our clients to enquire of your Council whether there is a sewer available for the drainage of this plot within your district.'

The engineer and surveyor of the Rickmansworth Council replied on 19th December 1962 and stated:

'I have to inform you that there is no public soil sewer within the urban District within the vicinity of the site. The main sewer laid by the Developers for the drainage of the adjoining estate, Valency Close, will be taken over as a public sewer by my council in April next, but even this sewer is about 130 yds from the site.'

It is quite clear from those letters that Hurst Construction specifically requested the Rickmansworth Council to adopt the intermediate sewer as a public sewer in due course, and indeed at the end of 1962 it appears to have been the intention of the council so to adopt the intermediate sewer in April 1963. In fact however they did not do so. It is perfectly clear to my mind that it is not correct to state, as it is stated, in two of the letters written by the defendants' solicitors, that the Rickmansworth Council was not prepared to adopt the sewer. Mr Hurst gave evidence before me to the effect that a few months after the completion of the intermediate sewer an official of the Rickmansworth Council, being either a Mr Turner or a Mr Smith, employed in the engineer and surveyor's department, told him that the intermediate sewer would not be adopted by the council. Mr Turner gave evidence before me, and I regard him as a completely truthful witness. He told me that he had no recollection of saying any such thing to Mr Hurst and that it was most improbable that he did so. Mr Smith was an officer under him in the engineer and surveyor's department. It is quite plain, as it seems to me, that neither Mr Turner nor Mr Smith had any authority to declare that the council would not adopt the intermediate sewer. I am unable to accept the evidence of Mr Hurst on this point. I certainly do not think that he was seeking to mislead me. I think that he probably misunderstood some offhand remark made to him by one or other of these officers.

In fact, however, the Rickmansworth Council did not make a declaration of vesting under s 17 of the Public Health Act 1936. It is very strange indeed that they failed to do so. Mr Botley, who was employed from about 1967 to 1974 in the legal department of the Rickmansworth Council, took the view that this omission to make the declaration of vesting must have been due to an oversight, and I think that is probably the explanation.

We can now move on to 1965. During that year the Rickmansworth Council was desirous of erecting a pavilion on a recreation ground which abutted on Batchworth Lane, and the question arose as to the disposal of the soil drainage from the pavilion. What happened then was that the Rickmansworth Council entered into a deed with Hurst Construction on 13th September 1965. Hurst Construction had gone into voluntary liquidation in June 1965, and this deed of 13th September 1965 is in effect made with the liquidator, a Mr Wood who was, I think, the father of one of the directors of Hurst Construction. This deed, curiously enough, recites as follows:

'(1) The Company is the owner of a private soil sewer which has been laid and constructed under Batchworth Lane in the Urban District of Rickmansworth, in the county of Hertford, in the position shown by a red line on the plan annexed hereto.

(That is the intermediate sewer).

Hurst Construction, acting by its liquidator, for the consideration of £100 paid by the council, granted to the Rickmansworth Council full right and liberty to construct at the point coloured green and marked D on the plan a manhole for access into the said private sewer and to connect into the said private sewer at such point a four inch soil drain running from the Rickmansworth Council's proposed pavilion and also full right and liberty to use in common with the company and its successors in title, and all other persons having the like right, the said private sewer for the passage and conveyance of sewage water and soil from the said proposed pavilion for the purpose of discharging the said sewage water and soil into the existing public sewer. That is, the existing public sewer at the north end of Davenham Avenue.

The habendum of the deed was in these terms:

'To HOLD all the said rights and liberties hereby granted unto the Council for such term and interest as the Company has power to grant SUBJECT TO the Council until such time as the said private sewer shall be adopted by it as a public sewer contributing 1/25th of the cost as certified by the Surveyor to the Council of the maintenance and repair of the said private sewer ... between the points marked A and B thereon.'

Shortly afterwards, on 8th October 1965, Hurst Construction, acting again by its liquidator, entered into a deed with the defendants. There is a recital also in this deed that Hurst Construction was the owner of a private soil sewer which it had laid and constructed under Batchworth Lane in the urban district of Rickmansworth in the position shown by the red line on the plan annexed thereto. That again refers to the intermediate sewer. By this deed, for a consideration of one shilling paid by the defendants, Hurst Construction, acting by its liquidator, conveyed to the defendants all the estate and interest of Hurst Construction of and in the intermediate sewer. Clause 2 of the deed read as follows:

'The purchaser [the defendants] hereby covenants with the company [Hurst Construction] and the liquidator that until the said private soil sewer shall become adopted by the local authority as a public sewer the purchaser and its successors in title will at all times keep and maintain the said private soil sewer in a good and sufficient state of repair and indemnify the company and the liquidator from and against all actions, claims, and liabilities in respect thereof.'

Both of those deeds, although describing the intermediate sewer as a private sewer belonging to Hurst Construction, clearly recognised that that so called private sewer would in due course be adopted as a public sewer. Between 1965 and 1975 nothing of any moment seems to have occurred with respect to the intermediate sewer. There was no evidence before me that anybody had carried out any works of maintenance to the sewer. Presumably the reason for that is that the intermediate sewer during that period required no maintenance.

The sealing off of the plaintiffs' soil drain on 29th March 1977 brought matters to a head. On 20th June the writ in this action was issued. The statement of claim was served on 24th June. In their statement of claim the plaintiffs first of all alleged that they were the owners of the subsoil of the adjoining highway, Batchworth Lane, opposite their property, but that claim has now been abandoned. Next they say that they had made the connection to the intermediate sewer with the consent of the Rickmansworth Council and that they are in lawful occupation of the material part of the land. They also allege that the sewer is a public sewer and that the defendants have no proprietary interest in the sewer. They complain of trespass in connection with the sealing off of their soil drain sewer on 29th March and claim damages in respect of that tort. They also claim a declaration that the defendants had no right of ownership in the said sewer, and that they are not entitled to prevent the plaintiffs from connecting their sewer thereto. They claim an injunction to restrain the defendants from trespassing on the land owned or occupied by the plaintiffs and from obstructing the plaintiffs' sewer and a further injunction to restrain the defendants from registering any encumbrance or caution against the plaintiffs' title at the Land Registry. The reason why they crave that latter injunction is because in June 1977 it appears that the defendants' solicitors had indicated that they might counterclaim or issue proceedings and register a caution, in respect of such proceedings; at the Land Registry.

On 27th June Kerr J granted two interim injunctions, first an injunction restraining the defendants from obstructing the plaintiffs' sewer, and, secondly, an injunction restraining the defendants from registering any encumbrance or caution against the plaintiffs' title at the Land Registry. By consent the action was transferred to the Chancery Division, having been commenced in the Queen's Bench Division, and the interim injunctions were granted until the motion was heard in a Chancery court. That motion, as I understand it, came before Fox J.

The motion before Fox J was disposed of on the basis of mutual undertakings given by the parties. The plaintiffs gave an undertaking not to complete any sale of a house on their estate pending judgment in this action, and the defendants undertook, pending judgment in this action, not to reblock the plaintiffs' sewer or register a caution at the Land Registry in respect of any counterclaim that they might bring.

On 6th July 1977 the defendants served their defence and counterclaim, and the basis of the counterclaim was the allegation that the intermediate sewer was the property of the defendants and that the plaintiffs had no right to connect to it. In their counterclaim the defendants claim damages for trespass to their sewer, secondly a declaration that the defendants were the owners of the intermediate sewer and that the plaintiffs were not entitled to connect thereto, and, thirdly, an injunction to restrain the plaintiffs from making any connection to the intermediate sewer without the defendants' written consent.

Subsequently the plaintiffs served a third party notice on the Three Rivers District Council claiming an indemnity in respect of the counterclaim on the footing that the third party was negligent in informing the plaintiffs that the intermediate sewer was a public sewer.

Before going any further into the third party notice I think it will be convenient to deal with the issues in the action. Those issues, as it seems to me, are threefold: first, is the intermediate sewer a public sewer? second, was there a binding agreement between Hurst Construction and Rickmansworth Council under s 18 of the Public Health Act 1936 for the adoption of the intermediate sewer? and, third, have the defendants any proprietary interest in the intermediate sewer which entitles them to prevent the plaintiffs from connecting its foul drain to the intermediate sewer?

I can deal with the second issue quite shortly and therefore I shall deal with it first. It is argued by counsel for the plaintiff company although not by counsel for the third party, Three Rivers District Council, that the letters dated 12th December 1960 and 10th January 1961 passing between Hurst Construction and the council constituted an agreement for the purposes of s 18 of the Public Health Act 1936. I am quite unable to accept that submission. It is quite clear that s 18 of the 1936 Act contemplates a contract or enforceable agreement, because it provides in express terms that any such agreement, that is to say, any agreement made under s 18(1), shall be enforceable against the authority by the owner or occupier for the time being of any premises served by the sewer. It is of course true that in the letter of 12th December 1960 Hurst Construction requested that the sewer should ultimately be adopted as a public sewer. What the clerk of the council stated in his reply of 10th January 1961 was this:

'I am able to inform you that provided the foul sewer is constructed to the Council's requirements, under the supervision of the Engineer & Surveyor and to his satisfaction, the Council will thereafter be recommended to adopt this length of sewer under the provisions of the Public Health Acts.'

There is no doubt that the intermediate sewer was constructed to the council's requirements and its construction was, I am quite sure, carefully supervised by the engineer and surveyor and was carried out to his satisfaction. So that the condition mentioned by the clerk is satisfied. But all the clerk undertook to do was to recommend to the council that the sewer should be adopted, and the council might or might not adopt it, at any rate in law it was open to the council to accept or reject that recommendation; so the council was not in any way bound by what was agreed as between Hurst Construction and the clerk of the council. There was no enforceable agreement at all, and therefore I think that s 18 has no bearing on this matter.

The other two issues constitute the real crux of this case, and I think, having regard to the way in which the case has been presented, especially in the very helpful argument I have heard from counsel for Three Rivers District Council, that they can be dealt with together. The question arises: what is a public sewer? The definition section of the Public Health Act 1936, s 343, states that a ' "public sewer" has the meaning assigned to it in s 20 of this Act', and a ' "private sewer" means a sewer which is not a public sewer'. Turning to s 20, that section provides that:

'(1) All sewers within the meaning of the Public Health Act, 1875, and sewage and disposal works which ... were immediately before the commencement of this Act vested in a local authority, shall continue to be vested in them, and there shall also vest in them [then there are four paragraphs lettered (*a*), (*b*), (*c*) and (*d*) but I think I need only read paras (*b*) and (*d*)] (*b*) all sewers ... constructed by them at their expense, or acquired by them ... (*d*) all sewers ... with respect to which a declaration of vesting made under the foregoing provisions of this ... Act has taken effect.

'(2) Sewers which by virtue of this section continue to be, or become, vested in a local authority shall be known as, and are in this Act referred to as, "public sewers". ...'

The 'foregoing provisions' of the 1936 Act referred to in sub-para (*d*) are those contained in s 17. Section 17(1) provides:

'a local authority may at any time declare that any sewer ... within their district, or serving their district or any part of their district ... shall, as from such date as may be specified in the declaration, become vested in them: Provided that an authority who propose to make a declaration under this sub-section shall give notice of their proposal to the owner or owners of the sewer ... and shall take no further action in the matter until either two months have elapsed without an appeal against their proposal being lodged ... or ... until any appeal so lodged has been determined.'

In this case it is perfectly plain that no declaration was made under s 17. We are left with sub-para (*b*), and it has been submitted to me by counsel for the council that sub-para (*b*) applies in this case, because he says that when the intermediate sewer was laid in 1961 it was laid in land belonging to the Rickmansworth Council as highway authority and the intermediate sewer thereupon became part and parcel of the realty and became the property of the council by the operation of the well known common law doctrine quicquid plantatur solo, solo cedit and so, he says, the intermediate sewer was acquired by the council in that way and, being a sewer acquired by them, it is a public sewer, because it is a sewer which vested in them under s 20(1)(*b*).

There is no doubt at all that the intermediate sewer was laid in land belonging to the Rickmansworth Council. That has been common ground throughout this hearing. Counsel for the defendants however submitted that the term 'acquired' in s 20(1)(*b*) must be taken to refer back to the power conferred by s 15(1)(iii) of the 1936 Act to acquire a sewer by agreement. Section 15(1)(iii) provides as follows: '(1) A local authority may within their district ... (iii) by agreement acquire, whether by way of purchase, lease or otherwise, any sewer', and counsel for the defendants argues that the term 'acquired' in s 20(1)(*b*) means acquired by agreement and not by operation of law. Counsel for the Three Rivers District Council on the other hand argued that the term 'acquired' covers any mode of acquisition. He points out that under s 158 of the Local Government Act 1933 a local authority in 1961 had power to acquire any land for the purposes of any of their functions, and 'land' within that section includes an interest in land.

In my judgment the term 'aquired' in s 20(1)(*b*) embraces all forms of acquisition open to a local authority and is not limited to acquisitions by agreement. It includes acquisitions by the operation of the legal maxim quicquid plantatur solo, solo cedit. Moreover, if that doctrine applies with regard to the intermediate sewer it seems to me to apply in consequence of an agreement between Hurst Construction and the local authority that the intermediate sewer should be constructed in the highway, Batchworth Lane. So that, on the footing that the doctrine applies, the acquisition of the ownership of the sewer by the council was in effect the result of an agreement and can therefore be regarded as an acquisition by agreement. The crucial question however is this: did the maxim quicquid plantatur solo, solo cedit apply with respect to the intermediate sewer? In my judgment it did. As I have already stated, it is

a common ground that Batchworth Lane and its subsoil belonged for an estate in fee simple to the Rickmansworth Council. No doubt it was vested in the council for highway purposes, but for the present purpose what matters is that the council was the owner at common law of an estate in fee simple in the land in which the sewer was laid. The intermediate sewer, as I find, was constructed with a view to its adoption as a public sewer. The parties contemplated that it would eventually become

b part and parcel of the public sewer system. It was made of a size sufficient to take the sewage of at least 150 houses. It was a permanent installation, not a temporary one. It was not contemplated by anybody that Hurst Construction, having laid down the intermediate sewer, would ever be entitled to dismantle it and take it away, or take away its component parts. The intermediate sewer, as I see it, became part of the soil for good. In those circumstances it seems to me that the rule quicquid

c plantatur solo, solo cedit applies, so that the Rickmansworth Council, as owner of the soil, became the owner of the intermediate sewer, subject of course to the rights of drainage attached to the houses on the Valency Close estate.

In this connection counsel drew my attention to the decision of Buckley J in *Simmons v Midford*[1]. The plaintiff in that case was the owner of a house and her predecessor in title at the time when the house was constructed was granted by the vendor, who

d sold to her predecessor in title, a right of way over a strip of land ten feet wide at the rear, and the plaintiff's predecessor was granted a right to lay sewers, drains, gas and electricity pipes and cables in that piece of land for the accommodation of the house which the predecessor was building on the plot. Some years later the purchaser of another plot of land from successors in title of the original vendor sought to connect to the drain which the plaintiff's predecesser had laid in this ten foot strip of land,

e and Buckley J held that the defendant had no right to do that because the drain belonged to the plaintiff and, secondly, even if it did not, the plaintiff had an exclusive right to the use of the drain. In his judgment Buckley J said this with regard to the maxim quicquid plantatur solo, solo cedit[2]:

f 'It may be said to enshrine or express a rule of law regulating the ownership in appropriate cases of things which were previously chattels but had become physically attached to realty. It does not, I think, amount to a presumption, and it is certainly not a rule of construction, where the interpretation of any written document is involved. Where a chattel is physically attached to realty, one of three possible results may follow. The chattel may lose its character as a chattel and adhere to the realty so as to become part of it for all purposes: or the chattel

g may become part of the realty while it remains a chattel, without the person who owned it losing the right subsequently to detach it from the realty and repossess it as a chattel; or it may never lose its character as a chattel.'

and he then asks the question which I also ask: 'Which, if any, of these results applies in the present case?'

h It was argued by counsel for the defendants that the intermediate sewer never lost its character as a chattel. I am afraid that I am quite unable to accept that submission. It seems to me utterly unrealistic to regard the intermediate sewer as still retaining the character of a chattel. Nor is it possible in my view to treat it as a chattel which falls into the second category mentioned by Buckley J, that is to say a chattel which is temporarily attached to the soil but is subject to the right on the part of the

j original owner of the chattel to detach it from the realty and repossess it as a chattel. When Hurst Construction laid down this sewer it was cretainly not in their minds that they would ever at any time remove the intermediate sewer and make use

1   [1969] 2 All ER 1269, [1969] 2 Ch 415
2   [1969] 2 All ER 1269 at 1272, 1273, [1969] 2 Ch 415 at 421

again in some other place or in some other way of the constituent materials of the
intermediate sewer. Indeed, they would have no right, as I see it, to remove them. *a*
It was obviously a permanent installation intended to remain in the ground so long
as it was able to perform the function of conveying soil drainage.

In my view this case falls within the first category mentioned by Buckley J. The
original chattels used in the construction of the sewer have lost their character as
chattels and they have become part of the realty for all purposes. On that basis it
seems to me that there is nothing at all which would justify me in holding that the *b*
maxim does not apply in this case; in my opinion it does. The sewer in the case before
Buckley J was clearly constructed for the exclusive benefit of the plaintiffs' house.
The intermediate sewer was not constructed for the exclusive benefit of the houses
in Valency Close. It was clearly contemplated that it would become in due course a
public sewer, and it was constructed in such a way as to be able to dispose, as and when
necessary, of soil drainage from other sites in the neighbourhood.   *c*

If I am wrong in the view that the intermediate sewer was acquired by the Rickmansworth Council in accordance with s 20(1)(*b*) of the Public Health Act 1936 then
of course it follows that the intermediate sewer is a private sewer, but it is, as I see it,
a private sewer that belongs to the local authority as owner of the land. The defendants have no proprietary interest whatever in the intermediate sewer, and it follows
therefore that the defendants have no right to object to the plaintiffs connecting their *d*
foul drain or sewer to the intermediate sewer.

I propose therefore on the plaintiffs' claim to make a declaration that the intermediate sewer is a public sewer and that the defendants have no proprietary interest
in it.

As regards the claim for damages in trespass I am in the difficulty that I do not know
what costs have been incurred in removing the blockage and making any necessary *e*
restoration. I would have thought really the best thing would be for me to direct
an inquiry and leave it to the parties to negotiate and I will do that. Then I have to
dismiss the counterclaim and in the case of the action and counterclaim the costs will
follow the event. That means that I shall have to order the defendants to pay the
plaintiffs' costs in the action and counterclaim. As regards the third party notice, of
course I dismiss the claim. The main question that arises in regard to the third party *f*
notice is the question of costs and, subject to anything I may hear through submissions,
my inclination at the moment is to make no order for costs for the third party claim
on the ground, I am afraid, that the conduct of the local authority has been responsible
to a large degree in bringing about this litigation.

Declaration accordingly. Enquiry as to damages directed. Counterclaim dismissed. Plaintiffs'
claim against the council dismissed.   *g*

Solicitors: *Harold Benjamin & Collins*, Harrow (for the plaintiffs); *Muriss, Saywell & Co*,
Northwood (for the defendants); *Barlow, Lyde & Gilbert* (for the council).

Tokunbo Williams   Barrister.

a   # Cuff v J & F Stone Property Co Ltd

CHANCERY DIVISION
MEGARRY J
13th DECEMBER 1973

b   *Landlord and tenant – Rent – Review – Reasonable rent – Improvements made to demised premises – Rent to be a 'reasonable rent for the demised premises' – Improvements made pursuant to landlord's licence and at previous tenant's expense – Improvements becoming part of demised premises – Whether assessment of 'reasonable rent for the demised premises' to have regard to who made improvements.*

c   In 1945 the landlord granted a 21 year lease of business premises to a company. In 1954, with the landord's consent, the company made substantial alterations to the premises, which materially increased the floor area of the buildings. In 1966, when the lease was coming to its end, the company sought a new tenancy under the Landlord and Tenant Act 1954. The county court made an order for the grant of a new 14 year tenancy at a rent of '£2400 per annum with rent review at the end of seventh year',

d   the rent fixed disregarding, pursuant to s 34(c) of the 1954 Act, 'any effect on rent of any improvement carried out by the tenant or a predecessor in title of his otherwise than in pursuance of an obligation to his immediate landlord'. At the company's request, the landlord granted the new tenancy to another company ('the tenant') with which it was connected. The new lease contained a rent review clause which provided that the yearly rent during the last seven years of the term was to be £2,400

e   'or such sum as shall be assessed as a reasonable rent for the demised premises', with provision for its assessment by an independent surveyor in the event of disagreement between the parties. In the event there was a disagreement and an independent surveyor was appointed. The question arose as to what was a 'reasonable rent for the demised premises'.

f   **Held** – Although the word 'reasonable' no doubt required the surveyor to reject a rent which, though obtainable in the open market by reason of special circumstances, appeared to him to exceed the rent for the premises which was right and fair, the bare phrase 'reasonable rent for the demised premises' referred not to the rent which it would be reasonable for the tenant to pay but to the rent that it was reasonable to pay for the demised premises. Accordingly the surveyor was to take the premises as

g   he found them and to disregard who had paid for the premises or any improvements thereto (see p 836 f to j, post).

Notes
For nature and reservation of rent, see 23 Halsbury's Laws (3rd Edn) 536-543, paras 1193-1201.

h   **Cases referred to in judgment**
English Exporters (London) Ltd v Eldonwall Ltd [1973] 1 All ER 726, [1973] Ch 415, [1973] 2 WLR 435, 31(2) Digest (Reissue) 958, 7771.
Kay (John) Ltd v Kay [1952] 1 All ER 813, [1952] 2 QB 258, CA, 31(2) Digest (Reissue) 936 7688.

j   *'Wonderland', Cleethorpes, Re, East Coast Amusement Co Ltd v British Railways Board* [1963] 2 All ER 775, sub nom *East Coast Amusement Co Ltd v British Transport Board* [1965] AC 58, [1963] 2 WLR 1426, HL, 31(2) Digest (Reissue) 957, 7768.

Originating summons
By an amended summons the plaintiff, Hugh Jerome Cuff ('the landlord'), sought a

declaration that the rent of premises at 80 High Street North, Newham, London, leased to the defendant, J & F Stone Property Co Ltd ('the property company'), for a   *a* term of 14 years was to be assessed without any regard to the fact that improvements had been effected to the demised premises by the defendant or by J & F Stone Lighting & Radio Ltd, the previous tenants of the premises. The facts are set out in the judgment.

Edwin Prince for the landlord.   *b*
Christopher Priday for the property company.

MEGARRY J. I have before me an originating summons seeking a declaration. The facts which give rise to the summons may be shortly stated. In 1945 the plaintiff, to whom I shall refer as 'the landlord', granted a 21 year lease of business   *c* premises to a company called J & F Stone Lighting & Radio Ltd, which I shall call the 'lighting company'. The lease was at the modest rent of £275 a year, rising by stages to £325. In 1954 the lighting company sought and obtained the landlord's permission to make certain substantial alterations to the premises; and in due course the work was done. These were building alterations which materially increased the area of the buildings.   *d*

In 1966, when the lease was running to its end, there were proceedings in the Bow County Court in which the lighting company sought a new tenancy under the Landlord and Tenant Act 1954. On 3rd March 1966, the court made an order for the grant of a new tenancy at a rent of '£2400 per annum with rent review at the end of seventh year. New tenancy for 14 years to commence at termination of current tenancy. (Under s 64 of Landlord and Tenant Act)'. The rent fixed by the court no   *e* doubt gave effect to s 34 of the 1954 Act, which included a provision for the disregarding of '(c) any effect on rent of any improvement carried out by the tenant or a predecessor in title of his otherwise than in pursuance of an obligation to his immediate landlord'. Having obtained that order for a new tenancy, the lighting company requested the landlord to grant the lease not to it, but to another company named   *f* J & F Stone Property Co Ltd which I shall call the 'property company'. That company is the defendant to this summons. There is no evidence before me as to the relationship between these two companies, though one would infer from their names and the events that there is some connection.

A form of lease was duly agreed between the landlord and the property company, and a lease for 14 years was granted, bearing date 21st November 1966. This was a demise of 'ALL THAT messuage or dwellinghouse shop and premises known as Number   *g* 80 High Street North in the London Borough of Newham TOGETHER WITH the yard or garden thereto'. In accordance with the order of the county court, provision was made for rent review. The clause in question reads as follows:

'PROVIDED ALSO AND IT IS HEREBY DECLARED that the yearly rent payable by the Lessee during the last seven years of the term hereby granted shall be the sum of   *h* TWO THOUSAND FOUR HUNDRED POUNDS aforesaid or such sum as shall be assessed as a reasonable rent for the demised premises for the said period such assessment to be made in the following manner that is to say:—either (a) such assessment as shall be agreed between the parties hereto in writing before the Twenty-fifth day of December One thousand nine hundred and seventy-two (b) in the event of the parties hereto failing to reach such agreement as aforesaid on or before the   *j* date appointed (in respect of which time is to be deemed to be of the essence of the contract) then the reasonable rent for the last Seven years of the term hereby granted shall be fixed or assessed by an independent Surveyor appointed for that purpose by the parties hereto or failing agreement as to such appointment by the Twenty-fifth day of March One thousand nine hundred and seventy-three (time in this respect to be deemed to be the essence of the contract) then by an independent Surveyor appointed for that purpose by the President for the time being of the Royal Institute of Chartered Surveyors. The assessment fixed by the independent Surveyor shall be communicated to the parties hereto in writing and immediately upon such communication the rent so assessed as a reasonable rent for the last Seven years of the term hereto granted shall be the rent payable for that period under the terms hereof.'

When the rent review clause fell to be operated, there were at first negotiations between the parties, but in the end a surveyor was appointed. The valuers of each party nevertheless continued their negotiations, and there is some evidence before me to the effect that, if the improvements are to be disregarded, the rent will be something of the order of £3,500, whereas, if the improvements are to be taken into account, the rent will be of the order of £4,600. A consequence of this difference was that the originating summons was issued.

What from the summons and the evidence initially appeared to be the question for decision was whether or not the surveyor was to have regard to the improvements. The summons sought a declaration that the rent was to be assessed 'without disregarding any improvements' to the demised premises effected by the property company or the lighting company. However, as the argument proceeded it became apparent that this was not the real question between the parties, for counsel for the property company advanced no contention, whether based on s 34 of the 1954 Act or otherwise, that the improvements should be wholly disregarded. His case was that while he accepted that the improvements should not be wholly disregarded, he asserted that, to put it shortly, the surveyor should temper the effect to be given to the improvements by what he considered to be reasonable. This assertion counsel for the landlord rejected. Accordingly, if I were simply to answer the question asked by the summons in its original form, resolving the real issue merely by what I said in my judgment, it seemed to me that there might be difficulties if the unsuccessful party wished to appeal from my order; for an appeal lies against the order rather than the judge's reasons for the order, and an appeal against an order which, in effect, was supported by both parties would present obvious difficulties. The parties therefore agreed an amendment to the summons, so that the plaintiff is now seeking a declaration that the rent is to be assessed without any regard to the fact that the improvements to the premises have been effected by the property company or the lighting company.

Counsel's case for the landlord was of elemental simplicity. When the lease was granted in 1966 the improvements admittedly formed part of the demised premises. What is to be assessed is 'a reasonable rent for the demised premises'. In default of agreement, that assessment is to be made by an independent surveyor. Therefore the question is a pure matter of valuing the demised premises in their actual physical condition, disregarding the provenance of the improvements. The valuation is to be on the basis of what rent is reasonable for those premises. Counsel for the property company, on the other hand, stressed the distinction between the 'market rent' and a 'reasonable rent', and pointed to *John Kay Ltd v Kay*[1]. There, Evershed MR said:

'The reasonable rent is arrived at by applying the subjective test of what the judge thinks is right and fair, as distinct, for example, from the objective test of what the evidence shows is the market value.'

The surveyor must therefore, said counsel for the property company, say what was the right and fair rent for the premises as they stood; but in doing that he must consider not only what was physically there, but also all matters put before him by the parties, including the circumstances in which the improvements were made. He must then duly reflect those circumstances in saying what was a right and fair

---

1   [1952] 2 QB 258 at 267, cf [1952] 1 All ER 813 at 816

rent. To the objection that it might be very difficult to say how much of a discount should be allowed for the fact that an improvement had been provided by the tenant *a* or someone associated with him, counsel for the property company answered that just as the question of the rent 'which it would be reasonable for the tenant to pay' as an interim rent under s 24A of the 1954 Act might depend on the length of the judge's foot (see *English Exporters (London) Ltd v Eldonwall Ltd*[1]), so in this case the length of the surveyor's foot might be decisive.

I go back to the lease. When it was executed, the improvements had already been *b* made some 12 years earlier. The demise plainly included the improvements as being part of the premises. Not a word is said in the lease about the improvements. The provision for assessing the rent is expressed solely in valuation terms. There is nothing save the expression 'reasonable rent' to give colour to the view that anything save pure matters of valuation are to be considered. The ancient principle is that what the tenant makes part of the demised premises enures for the landlord's benefit, subject *c* to rules such as those relating to tenants' fixtures and to any statutory qualifications of the principle. The limited qualification made by s 34(c) of the 1954 Act (on which see *Re 'Wonderland', Cleethorpes, East Coast Amusement Co Ltd v British Railways Board*[2]) admittedly contibutes nothing to the determination of this case. Though this qualification was relevant when the Bow County Court was determining the initial rent, the rent for the second seven years is purely a creature of the lease. In those circumstances, it seems to *d* me to put an impossibly heavy burden on the word 'reasonable' in this lease to say that it allows and requires the surveyor to explore questions of who paid for the improvements, and in appropriate cases to allow some discount for this, calculated on an unspecified basis. What sort of deduction should be allowed if the improvements were paid for by the tenant itself, or partly by the tenant and partly by a subsidiary company, an associated company, or a related company, or wholly by such a company? *e* If one accepts to the full that 'reasonable' means 'right and fair', one may still say that it means 'right and fair' in a valuation sense, without extending it to the whole range of moral and ethical considerations. I say nothing of the improbable case of a reasonable rent which is to be assessed not by a surveyor but by a philosopher or theologian; but I do say that in the absence of provisions sufficiently indicating the contrary, a provision for a reasonable rent to be assessed by a surveyor to be appointed, *f* in default of agreement, by the President of the Royal Institution of Chartered Surveyors will not cast the surveyor loose on uncharted and perhaps unchartable ethical seas such as these. The word 'reasonable' no doubt requires the surveyor to reject a rent which, though obtainable in the open market by reason of special circumstances, appears to him to exceed the rent for the premises which is right and fair; but I do not think that it does more than that.

If the formula used in the lease had been the formula relating to interim rent that *g* fell to be considered in the *Eldonwall* case[3], namely, the 'rent which it would be reasonable for the tenant to pay', the hand of counsel for the property company might perhaps have been strengthened; for such language more readily admits of a construction which allows regard to be paid to the individual circumstances of the particular tenant. But here there is the bare phrase 'reasonable rent', used in relation to the *h* demised premises. The question is not that of the rent 'which it would be reasonable for the tenant to pay', but that of 'a reasonable rent for the demised premises', and that, as it seems to me, is a matter not affected by who paid for the premises or any part of them. In my view the surveyor must take the premises as he finds them, and then determine what he considers to be a reasonable rent for those premises, regardless of who provided them or paid for them. The point is not capable of any great elaboration, but it seems to me that the landlord's contentions are right, despite the gallant

---

1 [1973] 1 All ER 726 at 743, [1973] Ch 415 at 433
2 [1963] 2 All ER 775, [1965] AC 58
3 [1973] 1 All ER 726, [1973] Ch 415

endeavours of counsel for the property company to establish the contrary, and that
a subject to any question that there may be on the precise form of wording, I should
make a declaration as prayed in the amended summons.

Declaration accordingly.

Solicitors: *Moon, Beever & Hewlett* (for the landlords);   *Paisner & Co* (for the property
company).
b
Hazel Hartman Barrister.

Ponsford and others v HMS Aerosols Ltd
c
HOUSE OF LORDS
LORD WILBERFORCE, VISCOUNT DILHORNE, LORD SALMON, LORD FRASER OF TULLYBELTON
AND LORD KEITH OF KINKEL
3rd, 4th MAY, 29th JUNE 1978

d Landlord and tenant – Rent – Review – Reasonable rent – Improvements made to demised
premises – Rent to be the higher of existing rent or a 'reasonable rent for the demised
premises' – Improvements made pursuant to landlord' slicence and at tenant's expense –
Improvements becoming part of demised premises – Whether improvements to be taken into
account in assessing 'reasonable rent for the demised premises'.

e In 1968 the landlords' predecessors in title granted to the tenants a lease of a factory
for a term of 21 years. For the first seven years of the term the rent was to be £9,000
and for the second and third seven years of the term it was to be the higher of £9,000
or such sum as should be 'assessed as a reasonable rent for the demised premises
for the appropriate period'. If the parties failed to agree on the assessment of the rent,
the assessment was to be made by an independent surveyor appointed by them.
f In 1969 the premises were burnt down. They were rebuilt by the landlords from the
proceeds of the fire insurance on the premises but, pursuant to a licence granted
by the landlords, incorporated substantial improvements costing £31,780 paid for
by the tenants. It was common ground that once the improvements had been made
they formed part of the demised premises. When the rent came to be reviewed for
the second seven year period the tenants claimed that in assessing a 'reasonable' rent no
g account should be taken of the improvements which they had paid for. The Court
of Appeal held that since the improvements were included in the demised premises
they were to be taken into account in assessing the rent. The tenants appealed to the
House of Lords contending that on the true construction of the rent review clause a
'reasonable' rent meant a rent which was reasonable between the parties.

h **Held** (Lord Wilberforce and Lord Salmon dissenting) – The appeal would be
dismissed because on the true construction of the lease what the tenants were required
to pay rent for was the 'demised premises', which included the improvements they
had paid for. An independent surveyor assessing the rent would therefore be required
to assess a reasonable rent for the premises, not what would be a reasonable rent
for the tenants to pay. A reasonable rent for the premises would be that based on
j market value without reference to the particular parties or how the premises were
built and paid for (see p 842 *f* to *h*, p 843 *g*, p 847 *b* and *e* to *g*, p 848 *f*, p 849 *b* to *f*
and p 850 *b* to *d*, post).

Cuff v J & F Stone Property Co Ltd p 833, ante approved.
John Kay Ltd v Kay [1952] 1 All ER 813 distinguished.
Decision of the Court of Appeal [1977] 3 All ER 651 affirmed.

Notes
For the nature and reservation of rent, see 23 Halsbury's Laws (3rd Edn) 536-543,   *a*
paras 1193-1201.

Cases referred to in opinions
Cuff v J & F Stone Property Co Ltd p 833, ante.
Kay (John) Ltd v Kay [1952] 1 All ER 813, [1952] 2 QB 258, CA, 31(2) Digest (Reissue) 936,
7688.   *b*
*United Scientific Holdings Ltd v Burnley Borough Council, Cheapside Land Development
Co Ltd v Messels Service Co* [1977] 2 All ER 62, [1977] 2 WLR 806, 75 LGR 407, HL.

Appeal
This was an appeal by HMS Aerosols Ltd ('the tenants') by leave of the Court of
Appeal against the decision of the court[1] (Cairns LJ and Sir Gordon Willmer, Roskill   *c*
LJ dissenting) on 8th February 1977 allowing an appeal by Ian Reginald Ponsford,
Peter Philip Rough and Edward John Posey ('the landlords'), suing as trustees of
the G M Posey Voluntary Settlement, against the judgment of Whitford J given on
3rd February 1976 whereby he made a declaration that on the true construction
of a lease dated 19th August 1968 made between the landlords and Fieldhouse (Uneeda)
Ltd, the tenants' predecessors in title, the reasonable rent for the second and third   *d*
periods of the lease was a rent that was to be assessed without regard to any effect
on rent of certain improvements which had been carried out at the tenants' expense.
The facts are set out in the opinion of Viscount Dilhorne.

Peter Millett QC and *Michael Rich* for the tenants.
Leolin Price QC and *Bruce Coles* for the landlords.   *e*

Their Lordships took time for consideration.

29th June. The following opinions were delivered.

LORD WILBERFORCE. My Lords, this case concerns the interpretation of a
rent review clause, and is one of impression. Of the four judges who have considered   *f*
it, two favour one interpretation, two another. Your Lordships are, unfortunately,
also divided in view.
    The clause is contained in a lease of industrial premises for 21 years from 24th
June 1968 at an initial rent for the first seven years of £9,000 per annum. For the
second and third seven years of the term it is to be £9,000 'or such sum whichever
be the higher as shall be assessed as a reasonable rent for the demised premises for   *g*
the appropriate period'. There follow provisions for fixing this reasonable rent by an
independent surveyor.
    Soon after the granting of the lease the buildings were burnt down. The landlords,
having received insurance money, undertook to reconstruct them, but at the same
time the tenants desired to make some improvements. They applied to the landlords
for a licence, and on 14th November 1969 this was granted by a formal document   *h*
under seal. It contained this clause:

> '3. It is hereby agreed and declared that all the [tenants'] covenants and con-
> ditions contained in the Lease which are now applicable to the premises demised
> thereby shall continue to be applicable to the same when and as altered and shall
> extend to all additions which may be made thereto in the course of such
> alterations.'

The improvements, including I understand the construction of a new bay, and the

_____
1   [1977] 3 All ER 651, [1977] 1 WLR 1029

installation of sprinkler equipment and a central heating system, were carried out at a cost of about £32,000, which sum was paid by the tenants.

Now, at the end of the first seven years, the question which arises is this: on what basis is the independent surveyor to fix the reasonable rent? It is not disputed that he must fix that rent for the premises as improved: they are now 'the demised premises'. But can he take into account the fact that the improvements have been paid for by the tenants? The answer depends solely on the construction of the words 'a reasonable rent for the demised premises'.

Many arguments great and small have been used by either side. I start by discarding some which, for my part, I find inconclusive or unhelpful.

1. The landlords, and the majority judges in the Court of Appeal, place great reliance on the words 'for the demised premises'. They show, it is said, that the surveyor only has to look at the premises and value them as they are: he cannot consider anything else. For my part I find these words neither conclusive, nor even indicative. They state the obvious. What elese could the rent be for? The question is not what the rent is payable for but on what basis the surveyor is to fix it, on the market value, the rack rent value or (whatever this means) on the basis of what is reasonable.

2. The clause, it is said, prescribes merely 'a reasonable rent'. If the surveyor were to consider other matters than the visible character of the premises it would say 'reasonable in all the circumstances'. A distinction is thus made between this clause and the statutory provision considered by the Court of Appeal in *John Kay Ltd v Kay*[1] in which it was held that the words 'such rent . . . as the court in all the circumstances thinks reasonable' gave to the court a wide discretion. I cannot find the least substance in this argument. The word reasonable has no abstract or absolute meaning: it only has significance when related to a set of facts. What is reasonable in some circumstances, may be unreasonable in others. I find no difference between the two expressions.

3. It is said that if the tenants had wished to protect themselves against paying rent based on the improvements, they could (and should) have done so when the licence was granted. I do not agree. If the review clause has the meaning for which they contend there was no need for them to do so. If it bears the opposite meaning, they lose their case. The question which is right remains to be decided.

4. It is said that the tenants' argument involves reading the clause as if it said 'a reasonable rent for the tenants to pay' and that there is no justification for reading in the latter words. I do not follow this argument. There is no need, on the tenants' argument, to read in any words. The rent which has to be fixed is a rent payable by these tenants under this lease which has 14 years to run and which may be renewed thereafter. It is not a rent (to follow the words of s 34 of the Landlord and Tenant Act 1954) at which the holding might reasonably be expected to be let in the open market by a willing lessor. The contrast in language is plain; the landlords' contention, indeed, is that the words mean just that, which, in my opinion, they cannot do.

I turn to arguments of substance. The clause exists and must be interpreted in the context of this lease and of what the parties must have been aware of at the time they agreed to it. They must have known the following: 1. That a tenant has the right to make improvements subject to the landlord's approval which cannot be unreasonably withheld. A landlord cannot as a condition of granting approval demand an increased rent. The landlords here did not of course do so in 1969. 2. If, when the lease expires, the tenant is in a position to call for a new lease, the rent then payable must be fixed without regard to the improvements (Landlord and Tenant Acts 1954 to 1969). 3. If, when the lease expires, the tenant goes out, he may be entitled to compensation in respect of the improvements to the extent to which they add to the letting value.

These facts would be known to any surveyor called on to fix a reasonable rent.

---

1 [1952] 1 All ER 813, [1952] 2 QB 258

In the light of this, one has to ask: would a rent, taking into account the physical existence of the improvements and nothing more, be a reasonable rent? The answer to this is surely negative. It is not reasonable: (a) for a tenant who has spent £32,000, at an interest cost of maybe £3,200 per annum, to pay rent on the product of this expenditure for the rest of the term, even if he gets some compensation at the end of the lease; (b) for a tenant, who on a renewed lease would pay rent on a basis which disregarded the improvements, to pay rent during the current lease on a basis which did not disregard them; (c) for a landlord, who could not exact an increased rent on licensing the improvements, to obtain one at a later date by use of the rent review clause, the purpose of such a clause being to adjust the rent for inflation and market changes.

If, at the present time, the landlords were to say to the tenants 'We are asking you to pay an increased rent which, of course, takes account of the improvements you have made to our premises' the tenants would surely say 'That is most unreasonable'. And conversely, if the tenants were to say 'We offer to pay you an increased rent taking into account inflation since 1968, the rise or fall in market demand, and the fact that we paid for the improvements made in 1969' the landlords would surely say 'Fair enough'.

If the meaning of 'reasonable' is not such as to admit the considerations to which I have referred, I must ask what its meaning is or what the 'reasonable rent' referred to in the clause is. The answer given to this is that the rent is the market rent. Then, when the question is asked why, if this is so, the clause does not so state, the answer given is that the word reasonable is put in so as to exclude a freak rent which some extraordinary tenant might offer. I must say that I find this a very lame argument. A market rent (or a rack rent) is one thing; a reasonable rent is another. A reasonable market rent is a hybrid which I cannot understand, and the clause, understandably, does not use these words.

In support of their argument the landlords and the majority in the Court of Appeal appeal to a judgment of Megarry J in *Cuff v J & F Stone Property Co Ltd*[1]. The actual decision in that case could not be supported except on the basis of a concession made by counsel in the case which was plainly wrong. But reliance was, naturally, having regard to its source, placed on the reasoning of Megarry J. I hope I do justice to it by summarising it in this way: to allow the surveyor to explore questions of who paid for the improvements would be to embark on an uncharted sea of what might be moral and ethical considerations, such as might interest a philosopher or a theologian but could not be part of a valuation process. And the tenants' contention involves other difficulties: what would happen if the improvements were paid for not by the tenants but by a subsidiary or related company? I am not impressed by these latter difficulties: if such payments were made they must surely be on account of or on behalf of the tenants and taken into account as such. And that to take them into account is a normal process of valuation is surely shown by the terms of s 34 of the 1954 Act which requires a market rent to be fixed, there being disregarded any effect on rent of any improvement carried out by the tenant. 'Disregards' of this kind are part of the daily work of surveyors, which they can and do carry out without assuming the mantle of other callings.

My Lords, clear words may sometimes force the courts into solutions which are unjust and in such cases the court cannot rewrite the contract. This is not such a case: in my opinion logic and justice point in the same, not opposite, directions. I cannot attribute any meaning to 'reasonable rent' in this context than one which takes into account (or disregards) what any landlord, any tenant, any surveyor would consider it reasonable to take into account (or disregard). In this case the surveyor should disregard any effect on rent of improvements carried out (viz paid for) by the tenants.

I agree with the judgment of Roskill LJ and would allow the appeal.

---

1   Page 833, ante

VISCOUNT DILHORNE.   My Lords, by a lease dated 19th August 1968 the landlords' predecessors in title leased to the tenants a factory at Barking for a term of 21
years from 24th June 1968 at a yearly rent of £9,000 during the first seven years of
the term and during the second and third seven years of the term at a rent of £9,000
'or such sum whichever be the higher as shall be assessed as a reasonable rent for
the demised premises for the appropriate period'.

The lease made provision for the reasonable rent for the demised premises for
those periods to be agreed between the parties, and, if they failed to agree, for it to
be assessed by an independent surveyor appointed by them. If they failed to agree
on a surveyor, it provided for his appointment by the President of the Royal Institution
of Chartered Surveyors.

The factory buildings were destroyed by fire. They were rebuilt with the use of
the insurance moneys with improvements wanted and paid for by the tenants who
obtained a licence dated 14th November 1969 from the landlords to make them.
These improvements included the addition of a bay to the factory and the installation
of central heating. They cost £31,780.

It is common ground that the improvements made by the tenants formed part
of the demised premises and the question on which there has been and is much
division of judicial opinion is whether when assessing a reasonable rent for the demised
premises regard should be had to the fact that the improvements were paid for by
the tenants. If in consequence of them the rent was assessed at a higher figure
than it would otherwise have been, the tenants say that is not fair. They should
not, they say, be required to pay rent on account of expenditure they had made
on their landlords' property. They point out that if the lease had been for only
seven years and they had been granted a new tenancy by order of the court under
Part II of the Landlord and Tenant Act 1954, as amended by the Law of Property
Act 1969, and the rent for that tenancy fell to be determined by the court the effect
of the improvements on the rent for which the holding might reasonably be expected
to be let in the open market by a willing lessor would have had to be disregarded
(s 34 of the 1954 Act). It would be highly anomalous that they should have to pay
a higher rent on a review under the lease they had for the second and, it may be,
for the third periods of seven years than that which they would have had to pay
on the grant of a new lease under the 1954 Act. What, they say, has to be determined
on a review of the rent is what is a reasonable rent for them to pay for the demised
premises and they contend that it would not be reasonable to require them to pay
anything on account of the improvements they had made.

Our task can indeed be simply stated. It is just to decide the meaning of the words
'assessed as a reasonable rent for the demised premises'. Their meaning is not altered
or affected by the fact that in 1969 Parliament decided that in assessing the rent of a
new tenancy granted under the 1954 Act the effect of improvements such as those
made in this case was to be disregarded. Landlords and tenants are usually advised
by lawyers on the terms of leases. If the parties to this lease had agreed that the
effect of improvements was to be disregarded in assessing the rent, that could easily
have been stated and if that had been agreed, I expect it would have been. A precedent
which could be adapted is in s 34 of the 1954 Act. In the absence of any such express
provision as Parliament thought it necessary to include in s 34, I do not think that
one is entitled to conclude that by the use of the words 'assessed as a reasonable
rent for the demised premises' the parties were seeking to express their agreement
that in assessing the rent the effect of improvements made by the tenants was to
be disregarded.

If it be thought to be unfair, as Parliament clearly thought it unfair, that a tenant
should pay a rent which reflected the value of the improvements made by him,
that is no ground for interpreting the words in question as the tenants contend. It is
not for us to rewrite the lease. It may be that the parties in 1968 did not consider what
was to be the effect on the assessment of the rent if the tenants made improvements.

One does not know but just as I see no ground for supposing that they did consider it, I see no ground for concluding, if they did consider it, that the landlords agreed that the effect of improvements should be excluded.

Rent review provisions are now commonly included in leases at the instance of landlords to give them some protection against inflation. If they were not included, landlords might only be disposed to let for a shorter term. Their object is to secure that in real terms the rent payable does not fall below that initially agreed on. It was not disputed in this case that that is their main object. In the present case and in many others provision is made for the assessment to be made by an independent surveyor. What is he to do? Surely it is to assess what rent the demised premises would command if let on the terms of the lease and for the period the assessed rent is to cover at the time the assessment falls to be made. That rent may depend to some extent on local factors such as deterioration of the neighbourhood. In assessing it, the surveyor will be assessing the reasonable rent that others, not just the sitting tenant, would be prepared to pay for the use and occupation of the premises. He will not consider the tenant's position separately.

It may be said that this is treating a reasonable rent for the demised premises as the rent obtainable on the open market and that the decision in *John Kay Ltd v Kay*[1] shows this to be wrong. That was a decision on s 12 of the Leasehold Property (Temporary Provisions) Act 1951 which gave the court power to grant a tenancy 'at such rent and on such terms and conditions as the court in all the circumstances thinks reasonable', and it was held that that did not mean the rent which the property would fetch if offered in the open market as property to let. If the wording of this lease had been similar to that, the surveyor would in my opinion have been entitled, indeed would have been bound, to have regard to the particular circumstances of the tenant. I do not think that the decision in that case affords any support for the view that the task of the surveyor under the lease was not to assess what would be paid in rent for the use and occupation of the demised premises if offered to let on the open market. What significance then is to be attached to the word 'reasonable'? I think that it was included to give the surveyor some latitude. He might know that if the premises were to let, there was someone who would be prepared to offer an exceptionally high rent for their use. The use of the word 'reasonable' would enable him to disregard that.

The rent payable by the tenants will of course be rent for the demised premises, but as I see it the task of the surveyor is not to assess what would be a reasonable rent for the tenants to pay but what is a reasonable rent for the premises. That, when assessed, is payable by the tenants. If the effect of the improvements on the rent payable is to be disregarded, then the tenants will not be paying a reasonable rent for the demised premises but a reasonable rent for the demised premises less the improvements; but it is recognised that the improvements are part of the demised premises. If the effect on the rent of the improvements is to be disregarded then in my opinion an express provision is required to effect that, as was necessary in the 1954 Act.

In *Cuff v J & F Stone Property Co Ltd*[2] Megarry J also had to consider a provision for the review of rent in a lease in all material respects similar to that under consideration in this case. He too had to consider the meaning of the words 'assessed as a reasonable rent for the demised premises'. In the course of his judgment, which I found illuminating and with which I respectfully entirely agree, he said[3]: 'There is nothing save the expression "reasonable rent" to give colour to the view that anything save pure matters of valuation are to be considered' and:

---

1 [1952] 1 All ER 813, [1952] 2 QB 258
2 Page 833, ante
3 See p 836, ante

'. . . it seems to me to put an impossibly heavy burden on the word "reasonable"
in this lease to say that it allows and requires the surveyor to explore questions of
who paid for the improvements, and in appropriate cases to allow some discount
for this, calculated on an unspecified basis.'

He held that[1]—

'the surveyor must take the premises as he finds them, and then determine
what he considers to be a reasonable rent for those premises, regardless of who
provided them or paid for them'.

Roskill LJ in his dissenting judgment in the present case attached great importance
to the different factual background in that case. There the improvements had been
made some 12 years before and so the phrase 'the demised premises' clearly included
the improvements when the lease was executed. In the present case it is not disputed
that 'demised premises' included the improvements made after the lease was executed and this being so I do not myself see that the fact that in *Cuff v J & F Stone
Property Co Ltd*[2] the improvements were made before the lease was entered into
affords any ground for distinguishing that case from this. In that case there had been
a lease to J & F Stone Lighting and Radio Ltd and, on 3rd March 1966 when the lease
was expiring, the court made an order for the grant of a new lease. No doubt the
rent fixed by the court disregarded the effect of the improvements but the defendants in the action tried by Megarry J were not the lessees in whose favour the court
had made the order. It appears from Megarry J's judgment that the form of the
lease they entered into was agreed between them and their landlords. Whether
the rent review provision he had to consider was a term of the tenancy which the
court ordered to be granted, the judgment does not reveal but it would not affect
the meaning of the provision in my opinion if it was.

Roskill LJ also wondered whether Megarry J would have reached the same conclusion if it had not been conceded for the lessees that the improvements were not
simply to be disregarded but I do not see any reason to suppose that Megarry J
would have come to a different conclusion if that concession had not been made.
Megarry J had to decide the meaning of the words used in the lease, as we have to do,
and I do not see how the factual background or the concession to which I have referred
can properly be considered as aids to the determination of the meaning of ordinary
English words.

In my opinion Cairns LJ and Sir Gordon Willmer came to the right conclusion
in this case and were it not for the division of opinion in this House, I would have
been content simply to say that I agreed with them and Megarry J and with their
reasoning.

In my opinion this appeal should be dismissed.

LORD SALMON. My Lords, the relevant facts and the terms of the lease have
been fully set out in the speech of my noble and learned friend, Lord Wilberforce,
and I shall not repeat them in any detail. I would however emphasise that the lease
was for a period of 21 years and provided for a rent of £9,000 a year reviewable
in the seventh and 14th years of the term so that in the second and third seven year
periods, the rent should be £9,000 a year 'or such sum whichever be the higher as
shall be assessed as a reasonable rent for the demised premises'.

This appeal turns solely on the true meaning of the words 'a reasonable rent'.
Considerable stress was laid by counsel for the landlords and the majority of the
Court of Appeal on the words 'for the demised premises'. I am afraid that I do not

---

1   See p 836, ante
2   Page 833, ante

understand how those words can afford any real help in construing the words 'a reasonable rent' as used in the lease. After all, the rent fixed by the lease could hardly *a* be a rent for anything other than the demised premises. Moreover, it is plain, as the landlords have always conceded, that when the demised premises were rebuilt, extended and improved after the fire which took place in the first year of the 21 year term, the cost of the extension and improvements (amounting to £31,780) was voluntarily paid by the tenants. By a well established legal principle the extension and improvements became part of the demised premises, but this does not mean *b* that in assessing a reasonable rent for the tenants to pay, it would be possible to increase the rent because of the additions and improvements to the landlords' premises which the tenants had made at their own expense.

The case for the landlords really turns on the argument (with which I disagree) that 'a reasonable rent' for the demised premises must mean the open market rent for the demised premises. If the parties had meant the open market rent they *c* would, no doubt, have said so, as they usually do.

Two appeals were recently heard together in your Lordships' House, namely *United Scientific Holdings v Burnley Borough Council* and *Cheapside Land Development Co Ltd v Messels Service Co*[1]. As appears from your Lordships' speeches, virtually every reported case relating to rent revision clauses was drawn to your Lordships' attention on the hearing of those appeals. I have again looked at these cases, and in *d* each of them the rent revision clause clearly provides that the tenant shall pay the open market rent at the time of review or the original rent whichever should be the higher. If the provision in the present lease for revising the rent had been couched in similar terms, I would agree with the majority of the Court of Appeal. Had the parties agreed that the rent should be revised on the basis of open market value, the tenants would be bound by their agreement to accept a revision on that basis *e* however unfair and unreasonable the result might turn out to be in the special circumstances of the case.

In the present case, however, the rent revision provision calls for the rent to be revised on the basis of 'a reasonable rent', which, for reasons I shall presently attempt to explain, can, and in this case does, mean something quite different from an open market rent. Although there may be cases in which a rent review clause has pro- *f* vided for review on the basis of a reasonable rent, I have been unable to discover any such case which has come before the courts other than the present case and *Cuff v J & F Stone Property Co Ltd*[2] to which I shall later return. One, if only one, of the reasons why the latter case was apparently thought not to be worth reporting at the time may have been that its rent revision clause may have seemed to be sui generis.

A lease constitutes a contract between a landlord and a tenant, binding them, *g* their successors and assigns, under which it is agreed that the landlord shall let and the tenant shall rent premises on the terms set out in the lease. If the lease provides for a rent review, in the same terms as the lease under consideration, I am convinced that the surveyor who, in default of agreement between the parties, assesses the reasonable rent cannot do so in blinkers or in a vacuum. He necessarily must have regard to the relevant circumstances of the case. I know of no other method of *h* deciding what 'reasonable' means in a contract, whether it be 'reasonable time', 'reasonable price' or 'reasonable rent'.

No doubt, in many cases, the reasonable rent will turn out to be the open market rent of the demised premises, but not always; certainly not, in my view, if the demised premises, as in the present case, have been extended and improved by the tenant at his own expense. It is well settled law that the extension and improvements enure *j* for the benefit of the landlord, but not twice over, unless this has been expressly agreed by the tenant, as, for example, when the rent review clause provides that

1   [1977] 2 All ER 62, [1977] 2 WLR 806
2   Page 833, ante

the rent shall be reviewed to coincide with the open market rent at the date of the
a review. I imagine, however, that even in such a case, a tenant who proposed spending
a substantial sum of money in making additions and improvements to the demised
premises would, before carrying them out, if properly advised by his solicitors,
normally insist on the landlord entering into an agreement that any increase in the
open market rental of the premises caused by these additions and improvements
should be disregarded in future rent reviews.
b   There is, however, no need to enter into a new agreement, if, as in the present
case, the lease calls for 'a reasonable rent' to be assessed on the rent review, and means
what, in my view, it says, not by implication, but expressly and plainly. Whether
or not either party to the lease foresaw, at the time it was executed, all the relevant
facts which existed at the date of the rent review is, to my mind, irrelevant. I agree
entirely with Roskill LJ that the reviewed rent must be reasonable as between the
c parties to the lease, a reasonable rent for the landlords to accept and for the tenants
to pay, having regard to all the relevant circumstances of the case existing at the
date of the rent review.
    I do not consider that the ordinary surveyor would have the slightest difficulty
in assessing a reasonable rent on the basis I have indicated; indeed I think he would
be astonished to be asked to assess it on any other basis. He would have been called in
d only because the landlords and the tenants were unable to agree between themselves
what would be a reasonable rent for the tenants to pay during the next seven years. I
do not know of any legal principle or sound authority which requires the surveyor,
in assessing the reasonable rent, to shut his eyes to what any surveyor would regard
as a vitally relevant factor, namely that the extensions and improvements to the
demised premises had been paid for by the tenants out of their own pockets. He
e would recognise that the additions and improvements to the premises would, in
all probability, enure to the benefit of the landlords when they recover possession
of the premises and that, quite apart from a possible double benefit for the landlords,
it would be most unreasonable for them to recover a higher rent from the tenants
on account of additions and improvements which the tenants had made to the premises
entirely at their own expense and with the landlords' consent.
f   I think that any competent and experienced surveyor would estimate the open
market rent of the whole of the demised premises at the date of the review and,
in fixing the reasonable rent, would discount from the open market rent that part of it
attributable solely to the additions and improvements which had been made at
the tenant's expense. This appears to me to accord with common sense and justice.
    Nor am I discouraged in this view by the fact that s 34 of the Landlord and Tenant
g Act 1954 (as amended by the Law of Property Act 1969) provides:

> 'The rent payable under a tenancy granted by order of the court under this
> Part of this Act . . . may be determined by the court to be that at which, having
> regard to the terms of the tenancy (other than those relating to rent), the holding
> might reasonably be expected to be let in the open market by a willing lessor, there
> being disregarded—. . . (c) any effect on rent of an improvement carried out by
h the tenant or a predecessor in title of his] . . .'

    I refer to this section solely because the reason why Parliament made this provision
is obviously because Parliament realised that it would be unreasonable for a tenant
who, at his own expense, had made improvements to the demised premises to have
his rent increased as a result of those improvements, and that it would be none the
j less unreasonable because the tenant might, at some future date, obtain some compensation for those improvements from the landlord under ss 1 and 2 of the Landlord
and Tenant Act 1927.
    I do not understand how in assessing a 'reasonable rent' a surveyor can be required
to take an element into account which would make the rent unreasonable. Nor do I
understand how the majority of the Court of Appeal, who recognised that the decision

at which they arrived with reluctance was unfair, could have regarded the rent which that decision produced as reasonable. This seems to me to be a contradiction in terms. As appears from their judgment they were however very much influenced by *Cuff v J & F Stone Property Co Ltd*[1]. Before dealing with the authority, I must refer to one of the arguments on behalf of the landlords in support of their proposition that 'a reasonable rent' should be construed as necessarily having the same meaning as the open market rent. The argument was that the word 'reasonable' was introduced into the lease before the word 'rent' to give the surveyor some latitude (which he has in any event). It would enable the surveyor, so the argument ran, to disregard a freak rent which he knew that someone might be prepared to offer for the demised premises. This, in my respectful view, is a wholly untenable argument. No self-respecting surveyor would take into account a fantastically high or fantastically low rent in assessing an open market rent any more than he would do so in assessing a reasonable rent.

I will now deal shortly with *Cuff v J & F Stone Property Co Ltd*[1] which raised exactly the same question for consideration as the instant case. In my opinion, the decision in *Cuff's* case[1] was wrong and the grounds on which it was based are unsound for the reasons I have already indicated and which are as applicable to that case as they are to the present case. It is fair to say that in *Cuff's* case[1], counsel for the tenant conceded that the improvements made at the tenant's expense could not be wholly disregarded by the surveyor in assessing 'a reasonable rent for the demised premises' under the rent revision clause. It may be that but for that unfortunate concession the judge might have come to a different conclusion. The judge said[2] in a passage quoted with approval by Cairns LJ[3]:

> '... it seems to me to put an impossibly heavy burden on the word "reasonable" ... to say that it ... requires the surveyor to explore questions of who [had] paid for the improvements, and ... to allow some discount for this, calculated on an unspecified basis ... If one accepts to the full that "reasonable" means "right and fair", one may still say that it means "right and fair" in a valuation sense, without extending it to the whole range of moral and ethical considerations. I say nothing of the improbable case of a reasonable rent which is to be assessed not by a surveyor but by a philosopher or theologian; but I do say that ... a provision for a reasonable rent to be assessed by a surveyor ... will not cast the surveyor loose on uncharted and perhaps unchartable ethical seas such as these.'

To assess 'a reasonable rent' does not call for the surveyor to embark on uncharted or unchartable moral or ethical seas. All he has to take into consideration are the relevant business factors applying to the case. I cannot see that it would cast any burden on the surveyor to find out (as easily as the judge did) what additions and improvements the tenant had made to the demised premises at his own expense and then to assess a reasonable rent on the basis I explained earlier in this speech.

The following passage in the judgment in *Cuff's* case[2] was also quoted with approval by Cairns LJ[4]: 'The question is not that of the rent "which it would be reasonable for the tenant to pay", but that of "a reasonable rent for the demised premises" ...' I can see no difference between these two formulations. In my opinion, they both mean a rent which, in all the relevant circumstances, it would be reasonable for the tenant to pay and for the landlord to accept. It cannot, in my opinion, be reasonable to increase the rent to be paid by the tenant because of the additions and improvements the tenant has made to the demised premises at his own expense. Any rent increased because of such additions and improvements could not, in my opinion, sensibly be

---

1   Page 833, ante
2   See p 836, ante
3   [1977] 3 All ER 651 at 656, [1977] 1 WLR 1029 at 1034, 1035
4   [1977] 3 All ER 651 at 656, [1977] 1 WLR 1029 at 1035

regarded as a 'reasonable rent' within the ordinary and natural meaning of those
a words.
My Lords, for the reasons I have indicated I would allow the appeal.

LORD FRASER OF TULLYBELTON. My Lords, I need not repeat the facts
of this case, as they have already been fully set out in the speech of my noble and
learned friend, Viscount Dilhorne, with whose reasoning and conclusions I entirely
b agree.
The only question for decision in the appeal relates to the proper construction of a
few words in the lease. The words occur in cl 1 which provides that, during the second
and third seven year periods of the lease, the yearly rent shall be £9,000 'or such
sum whichever shall be the higher as shall be assessed as a reasonable rent for the
demised premises for the appropriate period . . .' There is no dispute that 'the demised
c premises', which originally meant the factory described in cl 1 of the lease, now mean
the factory as rebuilt after the fire, including the improvements made at the expense
of the tenants, with the approval of the landlords given in a licence dated 14th November
1969. The premises would have included the improvements without express provision to that effect, on the principle that anything made part of the premises by the
tenants enures to the landlords, but provision to that effect was in fact made in cl 3
d of the licence, which is in the following terms:

> 'IT IS HEREBY AGREED and declared that all the [tenants'] covenants and conditions
> contained in the Lease which are now applicable to the premises demised thereby
> shall continue to be applicable to the same when and as altered and shall extend
> to all additions which may be made thereto in the course of such alterations.'

e The question therefore becomes what is meant by 'a reasonable rent' in the context,
and the reference to the demised premises is relevant only as part of the context. In
my opinion the words point unambiguously to the result contended for by the landlords, and they mean the reasonable rent assessed on an objective basis, without
reference to the particular landlord or the particular tenant or to the history of how
f the premises came to be built or paid for. Regard must, of course, be had to the terms
of the lease, because its provisions with regard to duration, responsibility for repairs
and other matters may affect the rent, but their effect would be the same whoever
the landlord or the tenant might be. It is true that the words 'for the demised premises' do not add anything new, because there is no doubt about the identity of the
premises for which the rent is payable, but in my opinion the words are of importance
because they emphasise that the assessment is to be made by reference to the premises
g and not by reference to wider considerations or to what would be reasonable between
these particular landlords and tenants. I respectfully agree with Sir Gordon Willmer
in the Court of Appeal, and with Megarry J in his opinion in *Cuff v J & F Stone Property
Co Ltd*[1], that the position might have been different if the lease had provided for
the rent fixed on a review to be that 'which it would be reasonable for the tenants
h to pay'. The emphasis would then have been shifted to the circumstances affecting
the particular tenants as in *John Kay Ltd v Kay*[2]. But those are not the words we have
to construe.
The whole weight of the tenant's case rests on the word 'reasonable'. It is said that
if the rent were to be increased because of the improvements for which the tenants
themselves have paid, that would be unfair and the rent would therefore not be
j reasonable. With all respect to those who think otherwise, that argument seems to me
to be unsound for several reasons. In the first place the description of the rent as
'reasonable' is quite insufficient to displace the objective standard which in my

---

1 Page 833, ante
2 [1952] 1 All ER 813, [1952] 2 QB 258

opinion is indicated by the clause as a whole. I think that the effect of the word 'reasonable' is to exclude any exceptional or freak rent that might have had to be taken into account if the clause had referred to the open market rent. In the second place, having regard to the provisions contained in ss 1 and 2 of the Landlord and Tenant Act 1927 for compensation to tenants in certain circumstances for improvements made by them, I am not satisfied that the result of the landlords' construction of the clause is so unfair as has been suggested. Those sections are not referred to in the judgments of any of the judges in the Court of Appeal and they may not have been present to the minds of Cairns LJ and Sir Gordon Willmer when they said[1] that they reached their decision with regret. The possibility of compensation at the end of the lease may not be so satisfactory to the tenants as a lower rent during the remainder of the lease after the first review date, but it goes some way to meet their complaint. Thirdly, whether I am right or wrong in regarding the possibility of compensation under the 1927 Act as relevant, and even if the result may seem harsh or unfair from the tenants' point of view, I would not regard that as sufficient reason for departing from what seems to me to be the proper construction of the words used. The lease is an elaborate document and the tenants presumably took legal advice before entering into it. They are a business concern, able to look after their own interests, and there is nothing to suggest that they were misled or taken advantage of in any way. It is most unlikely that either party had this problem in mind when the terms of the lease were agreed. If the parties intended that the general law was to be varied by special provisions in favour of the tenants, the time to make such provisions would have been when the licence for improvements was granted by the landlords, but that was not done. The problem has therefore to be solved by reference to the lease alone; it contains no express provisions in favour of the tenants on this matter and in my opinion it cannot, without distortion, be construed as making such provisions by implication.

The meaning of the clause appears to me to be free from ambiguity, and I do not consider that your Lordships would be justified in giving it an artificial construction because of any apparent anomaly that may exist between it and s 34 of the Landlord and Tenant Act 1954. The effect of that section is that, when a new lease is granted under Part II of the 1954 Act, the rent is not liable to be increased because of improvements carried out by the tenant or his predecessors in title, but circumstances in which s 34 applies are not those in which the question arises here. It is not material for the present purpose.

I would dismiss the appeal.

LORD KEITH OF KINKEL. My Lords, this appeal raises a short but very difficult question as to the proper construction of a rent review clause in a lease.

The lease is one on industrial premises for a term of 21 years from 26th June 1968. It provided for a yearly rent of £9,000 during the first seven years of the term and during the second and third seven years the sum of £9,000 'or such sum whichever be the higher as shall be assessed as a reasonable rent for the demised premises'. That assessment was to be made, failing agreement between the parties, by an independent surveyor.

The particular problem to be resolved arises in this way. At an early stage in the life of the lease the tenants desired that, in the course of the reconstruction of the premises following a fire, certain improvements should be incorporated at their expense. The landlords granted a formal licence for these improvements dated 16th November 1969, which provided, inter alia, that—

'all the [tenants'] covenants and conditions contained in the Lease which are now applicable to the premises demised thereby shall continue to be applicable

---

1 [1977] 3 All ER 651 at 656, 666, [1977] 1 WLR 1029 at 1035, 1040

to the same when and as altered and shall extend to all additions which may
be made thereto in the course of such alterations.'

The improvements were duly carried out at a cost to the tenants of some £32,000.
The question to be determined is whether, on a proper construction of the words
I have quoted above, account is to be taken, in assessing a reasonable rent for the
demised premises for the second period of seven years, of the circumstances that the
improvements in question were paid for by the tenants.

At first impression the words 'reasonable rent for the demised premises' suggest
that what has to be ascertained is simply the rent that is reasonable for the premises
as such in their actual state, the situation being viewed entirely objectively. 'The
demised premises' must mean the demised premises as improved, by virtue both
of the ordinary law and of the passage I have quoted from the licence agreement.
So on this view any contribution the improvements might have made to rental value
would have to enter into the assessment.

It was however argued for the tenants that to proceed in that way would involve
assessment of the rent on the basis of market value, whereas the lease provided for a
different basis, namely that of a 'reasonable' rent. It was not maintained that the
assessment should be made on the assumption that the improvements did not exist,
but it was said that any assessment of a 'reasonable' rent could not ignore the fact that
the improvements had been paid for by the tenants. Otherwise an unreasonable
result would be reached which was unfair to the tenants, considering that the landlords had not contributed to any increase of rental value resulting from the improvements and that their capital value would enure to the landlords' benefit at the expiry
of the lease.

It must be recognised, in my view, that, if the approach is to be a purely objective
one, it is difficult to perceive any difference in meaning between 'a reasonable rent'
and 'the market rent', and so there is force in the argument that if the parties had intended a purely objective assessment they would have used the latter expression,
which is in common use in contexts such as this one. I am not impressed by the
suggestion that the expression 'a reasonable rent' might have been used merely
in order to exclude any freak or special rent that a prospective tenant might be prepared to pay, because I think that in estimating the market rent a valuer would
proceed on the general level of rents for comparable premises without reference to
any such freak or special rent. I regard it as a proper inference that when agreeing
on the terms of the rent review clause the parties did not have present in their minds
the situation which might arise by reason of the execution by the tenants of improvements, because I consider that if they had they would have made specific provision
about the application of the clause to that situation. But whether or not that is
correct the clause must have been envisaged as capable of operating in respect of the
original unimproved premises. Would the surveyor then have reached any different
result than if he had simply been instructed to ascertain the market rent? I would
think not, because I am not able to envisage any circumstances which he would
take into or leave out of account in one case but not in another. It may be, of course,
that in the surveying profession 'a reasonable rent' is well known to bear a particular
meaning distinct from that of 'the market rent', but there is no available material
to indicate whether or not that is so. As it is, I consider that in either case the surveyor
would have regard to the condition of the premises, the terms and provisions of the
lease, and the general level of rent for comparable premises in the same locality or in
similar localities, and I would not expect any difference in the resulting assessment.
Even if the difference of wording were intended to lead to a different approach to the
rent review, it is to be expected that the different approach would be capable of
application where there had been no improvements.

That being so in the normal case, does the difference of wording lead to a different
result where the tenant has carried out improvements at his own expense? I think

it could do so only if there were grounds for inferring that the particular wording used here was used in contemplation of that particular situation, and, as I have already *a* said, I do not consider that such grounds exist. Further, I cannot think that parties can have had in view the additional factor that any licence agreement for improvements would fail to make provision for the manner in which the improvements were to be dealt with on a rent review.

In my opinion the words 'a reasonable rent for the demised premises' simply mean 'the rent at which the demised premises might reasonably be expected to let'. Con- *b* sidering that the demised premises necessarily include the improvements, to arrive at a lower rent by reason that the tenants paid for the latter would in substance mean that a rent for part only of the demised premises was being assessed. The fact that the assessed rent leads to an unreasonable result as between the particular tenant and the particular landlord does not mean that it is not a reasonable rent for the premises. The unreasonable result is due to circumstances which were not in *c* contemplation when the terms of the rent review clause were agreed, and which were therefore not expressly provided for. They might have been expressly provided for at the stage when the licence for the improvements came to be granted, but they were not. I consider that the construction which the tenants would place on the review clause involves a severe straining of the language used and is not the correct one. I therefore reach the conclusion that the decision of the majority of the Court *d* of Appeal was right.

Reference was made in the course of the argument to a number of statutory provisions regulating, in certain circumstances, the relationship of landlord and tenant of business premises, in particular s 34 of the Landlord and Tenant Act 1954. Section 34 is of some significance, in my view, as indicating the need, when it is desired that certain matters (including improvements carried out by a tenant) should be dis- *e* regarded in the assessment of a rent, to provide expressly for this. But apart from that I do consider that any of the provisions referred to are of assistance in resolving the present problem of construction.

Reference was also made to the decision of Megarry J in *Cuff v J & F Stone Property Ltd*[1], finding in favour of the landlords in circumstances closely akin to those of the instant case. While I should not be disposed to adopt the whole of the reasoning of the judge in that case, I agree with him that the expression 'reasonable rent' is to be read in a valuation sense, and that 'the surveyor must take the premises as he finds them, and then determine what he considers to be a reasonable rent for those premises, regardless of who provided them or paid for them'[2].

My Lords, for these reasons I would dismiss the appeal.

Appeal dismissed.

Solicitors: *Tarlo Lyons & Aukin* (for the tenants); *Gamlens* (for the landlords).

Mary Rose Plummer   Barrister.

---

1   Page 833, ante
2   See p 836, ante

a

Firman v Ellis
and other appeals

COURT OF APPEAL, CIVIL DIVISION
LORD DENNING MR, ORMROD AND GEOFFREY LANE LJJ

b   11th, 12th JANUARY, 8th FEBRUARY 1978

Limitation of action – Court's power to override time limit in personal injury or fatal accident claim – Exercise of discretion – Unfettered discretion to allow action to proceed where equitable to do so – Discretion not limited to difficult or exceptional cases – Formal delay on part of plaintiff's solicitor – Failure to apply for extension of validity of writ within limitation period –
c   *No prejudice to defendant in allowing action to proceed – Whether proper case in which to override time limit – Limitation Act 1939, s 2D (as inserted by the Limitation Act 1975, s 1).*

Limitation of action – Court's power to override time limit in personal injury or fatal accident claim – Transitional provisions on commencement of statute introducing power – Action commenced and pending at date of commencement of statute – Order made before commencement
d   *of statute dismissing application made outside limitation period to extend validity of writ – Effect of order – Whether order rendering proceedings a nullity – Whether action having been commenced and determined before commencement of statute – Limitation Act 1975, s 3.*

Limitation of action – Court's power to override time limit in personal injury or fatal accident claim – Practice – Application to extend validity of writ – Application made after expiry of
e   *limitation period – Proper course for master or registrar to decline to consider whether action should be allowed to proceed under statutory power to override time limit – Onus on plaintiff to issue fresh writ and apply to judge for order overriding time limit – Limitation Act 1939, s 2D (as inserted by the Limitation Act 1975, s 1) – RSC Ord 6, r 8.*

Limitation of action – Court's power to override time limit in personal injury or fatal accident
f   *claim – Matters to which court may have regard – Prejudice to plaintiff – Remedy against solicitor – Plaintiff having remedy against solicitor for negligence if application to override time limit refused – Whether a relevant consideration in determining whether action should be allowed to proceed – Limitation Act 1939, s 2D(1) (as inserted by the Limitation Act 1975, s 1).*

On 23rd May 1973 the plaintiff in the first case was injured in a motor accident which
g   was attributable to the negligence of the defendant. Three months later the plaintiff's solicitors made a claim against the defendant which was passed on to the defendant's insurers. Liability was not disputed and negotiations for a settlement ensued. The extent of the plaintiff's injuries could not be ascertained for some time and so his solicitors issued a protective writ. By an oversight, however, they failed to serve it within the period of one year allowed by RSC Ord 6, r 8[a]. Furthermore they failed
h   to apply for a renewal of the writ before 23rd May 1976 when the three year limitation period expired. In March 1977 the plaintiff issued a new writ against the defendant

---

a Rule 8, so far as material, provides:
     '(1) For the purpose of service, a writ (other than a concurrent writ) is valid in the first instance for twelve months beginning with the date of its issue and a concurrent writ is
j   valid in the first instance for the period of validity of the original writ which is unexpired at the date of issue of the concurrent writ.
     '(2) Where a writ has not been served on a defendant, the Court may by order extend the validity of the writ from time to time for such period, not exceeding twelve months at any one time, beginning with the day next following that on which it would otherwise expire, as may be specified in the order, if an application for extension is made to the Court before that day or such later day (if any) as the Court may allow.'

and applied to the judge in chambers for an order under s 2D[b] of the Limitation Act 1939 that the statutory limitation period should not apply to the action. The judge granted the application and the defendant appealed, contending that s 2D was to be construed restrictively as applying only to exceptional cases and that, in any event, the plaintiff would not suffer any prejudice if the action were statute-barred for he would have an unanswerable claim against his solicitors for damages for negligence.

In the second case a collision occurred in July 1970 between the plaintiff's car and one driven by C. The plaintiff brought an action against C who delivered a defence alleging that the accident had been caused by the sudden deflation of one of the tyres of the car which had been negligently repaired by the defendant. Accordingly he joined the defendant as third party. On 30th April 1973, just within the three year limitation period, the plaintiff applied by summons to amend the writ by adding the defendant as the second defendant to the action. The summons was returnable on 6th June 1973. The defendant's solicitors were served and wrote raising no objection. The plaintiff's solicitor, however, as the result of a slip in his office, overlooked the appointment. As soon as he discovered the error he applied for a new appointment which was given for 11th July, one day outside the three year period. Before the registrar on 11th July he produced a letter from the defendant's solicitors indicating that they would not oppose the application. The registrar made an order giving the plaintiff leave to amend, recording that he had heard 'all parties'. In fact no notice of the later appointment on 11th July had been given to the defendant who, consequently, was not heard. After being served with the amended writ the defendant entered a conditional appearance and took out a summons to set aside the joinder on the ground that it had been made after expiry of the three year period. On 4th January 1974 the amended writ and joinder were set aside by another registrar. On 11th February 1974 on appeal the judge affirmed that registrar's order on the ground that the first registrar had had no power to make the order of 11th July 1973 after the expiry of the limitation period. On 1st September 1975 the Limitation Act 1975, which inserted s 2D in the 1939 Act, came into operation. The plaintiff issued a fresh writ against the defendant and applied to the court to exercise its discretion under s 2D to override the time limit. The application was granted and the defendant appealed, contending, inter alia, (i) that the proceedings which stemmed from the registrar's order of 11th July 1973 could not be treated as having been avoided, and (ii) that accordingly the plaintiff had commenced an action which, on 1st September 1975, was no longer 'pending' since it had been determined by the judge's order of 11th February which was a 'final order or judgment', within s 3(2)[c] of the 1975 Act, with

---

b Section 2D, so far as material, provides:
   '(1) If it appears to the court that it would be equitable to allow an action to proceed having regard to the degree to which—(a) the provisions of section 2A or 2B of this Act prejudice the plaintiff or any person whom he represents, and (b) any decision of the court under this subsection would prejudice the defendant or any person whom he represents, the court may direct that those provisions shall not apply to the action, or shall not apply to any specified cause of action to which the action relates.
   '(2) The court shall not under this section disapply section 2B (2) except where the reason why the person injured could no longer maintain an action was because of the time limit in section 2A . . .
   '(3) In acting under this section the court shall have regard to all the circumstances of the case and in particular to [six specified circumstances]'
c Section 3, so far as material, provides:
   '(1) The provisions of this Act shall have effect in relation to causes of action which accrued before, as well as causes of action which accrue after, the commencement of this Act, and shall have effect in relation to any cause of action which accrued before the commencement of this Act notwithstanding that an action in respect thereof has been commenced and is pending at the commencement of this Act.
   '(2) For the purposes of this section an action shall not be taken to be pending at any time if a final order or judgment has been made or given therein, notwithstanding that an appeal is pending or that the time for appealing has not expired . . .'

the result that the plaintiff was precluded from commencing a fresh action by the
doctrine of res judicata.

Held – The appeals in both cases would be dismissed for the following reasons—

(i) The discretion conferred on the court by s 2D was not limited to a residual class
of case, or to 'exceptional' cases, but extended to all cases in which the three year
limitation period had expired; in such a case the court had an unfettered discretion
to allow the action to proceed if, having regard to the matters prescribed by s 2D, it
considered it equitable to do so. Since in each case there had been nothing except
purely formal delay on the part of the plaintiff and no prejudice would be caused
to the defendant by allowing the action to proceed, the discretion should be exercised
in favour of extending the limitation period (see p 859 f to h, p 860 b to e, p 862 g h,
p 863 e, p 864 b to h, p 865 b to f, p 866 c d and p 867 j to p 868 a and d, post).

(ii) In the second case no action had been 'commenced' by the plaintiff against the
defendant for the purpose of s 3 of the 1975 Act since the registrar's order of 11th
July 1973, having been successfully challenged by the defendant, was to be treated as a
nullity and the judge's order of 11th February 1974 had had the effect of avoiding
the proceedings. Accordingly, since no previous action had been commenced by
the plaintiff against the defendant, the 1975 Act was applicable (see p 862 d to f, p 867
c to f and p 869 e, post).

Per Curiam. (i) Where a plaintiff makes an application under RSC Ord 6, r 8, to
extend the validity of a writ that has not been served and the application is made
outside the relevant limitation period, the master or registrar should not take into
consideration s 2D of the 1939 Act, but should, in the absence of exceptional circumstances, apply the usual rule by dismissing the application, and leave it to the plaintiff
to issue a fresh writ and make a substantive application under s 2D to a judge (see
p 863 d, p 866 b c, p 868 g to j and p 869 c, post); Heaven v Road and Rail Wagons Ltd
[1965] 2 All ER 409 explained.

(ii) In considering an application by a plaintiff under s 2D of the 1939 Act the court
may have regard to the fact that, if the application is refused, the plaintiff will have a
remedy against his solicitor for negligence (see p 862 j to p 863 a, p 865 f to j and p 868
f and g, post); Birkett v James [1977] 2 All ER 801 distinguished.

Notes

For renewal of a writ of summons, see 30 Halsbury's Laws (3rd Edn) 303, para 558,
and for cases on the subject, see 50 Digest (Repl) 292, 293, 331-338, and Digest (Cont
Vol C) 1080, 331a.

For the court's power to override time limits in personal injury actions, see
Supplement to 24 Halsbury's Laws (3rd Edn) para 381.4.

For the Limitation Act 1939, ss 2A, 2D, as added by the Limitation Act 1975, s 1,
and for s 3 of the 1975 Act, see 45 Halsbury's Statutes (3rd Edn) 848, 850, 853.

Cases referred to in judgments

Anisminic Ltd v Foreign Compensation Commission [1969] 1 All ER 208, [1969] 2 AC 147,
[1969] 2 WLR 163, HL, 30 Digest (Reissue) 209, 313.

Bickel v Duke of Westminster [1976] 3 All ER 801, [1977] QB 517, [1976] 3 WLR 805, CA.

Birkett v James [1977] 2 All ER 801, [1978] AC 297, [1977] 3 WLR 38, HL.

Black-Clawson International Ltd v Papierwerke Waldhof-Aschaffenburg AG [1975] 1 All ER
810, [1975] AC 591, [1975] 2 WLR 513, [1975] 2 Lloyd's Rep 11, HL, Digest (Cont Vol
D) 108, 1591a.

Cartledge v E Jopling & Sons Ltd [1963] 1 All ER 341, [1963] AC 758, [1963] 2 WLR 210,
[1963] 1 Lloyd's Rep 1, HL, 32 Digest (Repl) 401, 259.

Craig v Kanssen [1943] 1 All ER 108, [1943] 1 KB 256, 112 LJKB 228, 168 LT 38, CA, 50
Digest (Repl) 252, 63.

Dryden v Dryden [1973] 3 All ER 526, [1973] Fam 217, [1973] 3 WLR 524, Digest (Cont
Vol D) 435, 7590c.

Easy v Universal Anchorage Co Ltd [1974] 2 All ER 1105, [1974] 1 WLR 899, CA, Digest (Cont Vol D) 1047, 329d.

F (infants) (adoption order: validity), Re [1977] 2 All ER 777, [1977] Fam 165, [1977] 2 WLR 488, CA.

Finch v Francis (21st July 1977) unreported, DC.

Heaven v Road and Rail Wagons Ltd [1965] 2 All ER 409, [1965] 2 QB 355, [1965] 2 WLR 1249, 50 Digest (Repl) 292, 337.

O'Connor v Isaacs [1956] 2 All ER 417, [1956] 2 QB 288, 120 JP 325, CA; *affg* [1956] 1 All ER 513, [1956] 2 QB 288, 38 Digest (Repl) 136, 965.

Smith v Central Asbestos Co Ltd [1971] 3 All ER 204, [1972] 1 QB 244, [1971] 3 WLR 206, [1971] 2 Lloyd's Rep 151, CA; *affd* sub nom *Central Asbestos Co Ltd v Dodd* [1972] 2 All ER 1135, [1973] AC 518, [1972] 3 WLR 333, [1972] 2 Lloyd's Rep, HL, 17 Digest (Reissue) 116, 190.

Wachtel v Wachtel [1973] 1 All ER 829, [1973] Fam 72, [1973] 2 WLR 366, CA, Digest (Cont Vol D) 425, 6962Aa.

Ward v James [1965] 1 All ER 563, [1966] 1 QB 273, [1965] 2 WLR 455, [1965] 1 Lloyd's Rep 145, CA, 17 Digest (Reissue) 213, 854.

Cases also cited

Allen v Sir Alfred McAlpine & Sons Ltd, Bostic v Bermondsey & Southwark Group Hospital Management Committee, Sternberg v Hammond [1968] 1 All ER 543, [1968] 2 QB 229, CA.

Ayscough v Sheed, Thomson & Co (1924) 93 LJKB 924, 131 LT 610, HL.

Baker v Bowketts Cakes Ltd [1966] 2 All ER 290, [1966] 1 WLR 861, CA.

Battersby v Anglo-American Oil Co Ltd [1944] 2 All ER 387, [1945] 1 KB 23, CA.

Biss v Lambeth, Southwark and Lewisham Health Authority p 125, ante, [1978] 1 WLR 382, CA.

Braniff v Holland & Hannen and Cubitts (Southern) Ltd [1969] 3 All ER 959, [1969] 1 WLR 1533, CA.

Buck v English Electric Co Ltd [1977] 1 WLR 806, [1977] ICR 629.

Carl-Zeiss-Stiftung v Rayner & Keeler Ltd (No 2) [1966] 2 All ER 536, [1967] 1 AC 853, HL.

Carl-Zeiss-Stiftung v Rayner & Keeler Ltd (No 3) [1969] 3 All ER 897, [1970] Ch 506, Ch D.

Chatsworth Investments Ltd v Cussins (Contractors) Ltd [1969] 1 All ER 143, [1969] 1 WLR 1, CA.

Fidelitas Shipping Co Ltd v V/O Exportchleb [1965] 2 All ER 4, [1966] 1 QB 630, CA.

Hay-Kellie v Michaelides (1969) 113 Sol Jo 902, [1963] Court of Appeal Transcript 319.

Hilton v Sutton Steam Laundry [1945] 2 All ER 425, [1946] KB 65, CA.

Hoystead v Taxation Comr [1926] AC 155, [1925] All ER Rep 56, PC.

Jones v Jones [1970] 3 All ER 47, [1970] 2 QB 576, CA.

Koenigsberg, Public Trustee v Koenigsberg, Re [1949] 1 All ER 804, [1949] Ch 348, CA.

Lucy v W T Henleys Telegraph Works Co Ltd, Wild v Siemens Bros & Co Ltd [1969] 3 All ER 456, [1970] 1 QB 393, CA.

Marston v British Railways Board [1976] ICR 124.

McCafferty v Metropolitan Police District Receiver [1977] 2 All ER 756, [1977] 1 WLR 1073, [1977] ICR 799, CA.

Mitchell v Harris Engineering Co Ltd [1967] 2 All ER 682, [1967] 2 QB 703, CA.

Paxton (late infant but now of full age) v Allsopp (administrator of estate of Allsopp) [1971] 3 All ER 370, [1971] 1 WLR 1310, CA.

Sayle v Cooksey [1969] 2 Lloyd's Rep 618, CA.

Seabridge v H Cox & Sons (Plant Hire) Ltd, Barclay v Same [1968] 1 All ER 570, [1968] 2 QB 46, CA.

Waring, Westminster Bank Ltd v Burton-Butler [1948] 1 All ER 257, [1948] Ch 221.

Weldon v Neal (1887) 19 QBD 394, 56 LJQB 621, CA.

Interlocutory appeals

Firman v Ellis

The defendant, Miss Diane Ellis, appealed against the order of Kerr J made on 4th July 1977 whereby it was ordered that the provisions of s 2A of the Limitation Act 1939

(as inserted by the Limitation Act 1975, s 1) did not apply to an action brought by the
a plaintiff, Michael Firman, for damages for personal injuries and consequential losses
and expenses sustained as a result of the negligent driving, management or control
of a motor car driven by the defendant at Denton Corner near Newhaven in the
County of East Sussex on 23rd May 1973 in which the plaintiff was a passenger. The
facts are set out in the judgment of Lord Denning MR.

b
Ince and others v Rogers
The defendant, Michael Frank Stewart Rogers, appealed against the order of Talbot J
made on 17th October 1977 whereby it was ordered that the provisions of s 2A of the
Limitation Act 1939 (as inserted by the Limitation Act 1975, s 1) did not apply to an
action brought by the plaintiffs, Pamela Mary Ince, Nigel Valentine Ince, Camilla
Jane Ince, Sara Elizabeth Ince and Robin Charles Crew Ince, for damages for personal
c injuries and consequential loss sustained as a result of the negligent driving of the
defendant on 22nd February 1973 near the village of Latimer in the County of
Buckingham. The facts are set out in the judgment of Lord Denning MR.

Down v Harvey and others
d The defendants, Laurence George Harvey and O Nicklin & Sons Ltd, appealed
against the order of Lawson J given in chambers in the Crown Court at Bristol on
27th July 1977 whereby it was ordered that the provisions of s 2A of the Limitation
Act 1939 (as inserted by the Limitation Act 1975, s 1) did not apply to an action brought
by the plaintiff, Frederick Henry Down, for damages for personal injuries and losses
suffered as a result of an accident which occurred at Berrynarbor in the County of
e Devon on 16th February 1973, whilst delivering a piano to the first defendant and
whilst in the employ of the second defendant, as a result of the negligence of the
first defendant and/or the second defendant. The plaintiff cross-appealed against
an order of Lawson J made on 20th October 1977 at Winchester dismissing the
plaintiff's appeal from the order of Mr District Registrar Lowis dated 30th June 1977
whereby the order of the district registrar dated 8th February 1977 renewing the
f plaintiff's writ was set aside and the action dismissed. The facts are set out in the
judgment of Lord Denning MR.

Pheasant and others v S T H Smith (Tyres) Ltd and another
The defendants, S T H Smith (Tyres) Ltd and Terence Smith, appealed against the
g judgment of Cusack J given on the trial of certain preliminary issues whereby it was
ordered, inter alia, that the provisions of s 2A of the Limitation Act 1939 (as inserted by
the Limitation Act 1975, s 1) did not apply to an action brought by the plaintiffs,
Robert Henry Pheasant, Nellie Pheasant, Karen Pheasant and Ian Craig Pheasant, for
damages for personal injuries and consequential loss and damage caused by the
negligent repair by the first defendant and/or the second defendant of a motor car
h on 2nd and/or 4th July 1970 in the City of Bristol in the County of Avon which collided
on 10th July 1970 at Almondsbury in the County of Gloucester with another motor
car driven by the first plaintiff and in which the other plaintiffs were passengers.
The facts are set out in the judgment of Lord Denning MR.

John Loyd for Miss Ellis, Mr Rogers and O Nicklin & Sons Ltd.
j *Anthony Hacking* for Mr Firman.
Barry Green for Mrs Ince and her co-plaintiffs.
Peter Fallon QC, *R John Royce* and *Peter Barry* for Mr Harvey.
Michael Turner QC and *Hugh Lewis* for Mr Down.
Michael Hutchison QC and *David Blunt* fot S T H Smith (Tyres) Ltd and Mr Smith.
Benet A Hytner QC and *David Berkson* for Mr Pheasant and his co-plaintiffs.

Cur adv vult

a

8th February. The following judgments were read.

LORD DENNING MR. On 23rd May 1973 Michael Firman, a lad of 17, was injured in a motor accident. He was a passenger in a car driven by a young lady, Miss Diane Ellis. They were going from their homes in Seaford to Brighton. She drove too fast and collided with an oncoming lorry. She afterwards pleaded guilty *b* to driving without due care and attention.

Michael Firman's injuries were to his head, neck and spine. It was difficult for the doctors to forecast his future state of health, and for him to decide on his future career. Within three months his solicitors made a claim on his behalf, which was passed to the insurers of the driver of the car. Thenceforward, for the next three years, there were negotiations for a settlement, medical examinations, advice on career prospects, *c* and so forth. There was no undue delay on the part of the plaintiff's advisers at all.

Pending the discussions, his solicitors issued a writ so as to protect his interests; but they made a mistake in that they failed to renew it, as they should have done. On that account the insurers say that Michael Firman's claim is statute-barred. The dates are as follows. 23rd May 1973: the accident. 17th August 1973: plaintiff's solicitors write letter of claim. 26th July 1974: protective writ issued and insurers *d* notified of it. 26th July 1975: writ ceased to be valid unless renewed (see RSC Ord 6, r 8). 8th September 1975: plaintiff's solicitors reminded insurers that the writ had been issued but not served because they hoped for a satisfactory negotiated settlement. 23rd May 1976: three years elapsed since the accident. August to October 1976: insurers ask for further medical examination and pay expenses of travel to it. 25th October 1976: insurers ask for evidence that the writ has been renewed. Plaintiff's *e* solicitors reply that it had not been renewed. 2nd November 1976: insurers say 'snap'. They say that they had no proposal to make in settlement and they considered the plaintiff's claim to be out of time. 30th December 1976: plaintiff's solicitors apply to renew the writ and give history of negotiations in full detail. 10th March 1977: registrar refuses leave to renew. 4th July 1977: judge affirms decision of registrar.

Apart from the Limitation Act 1975, it is clear that Michael Firman's claim was statute-barred. His solicitors had failed in their duty to him because they had not served the writ in time. The fact that negotiations for a settlement were in progress did not afford any excuse for failing to do so: see *Easy v Universal Anchorage Co Ltd*[1]. His only remedy was to sue his solicitors for negligence.

On 21st March 1977 (after the registrar had refused to renew) Michael Firman issued a new writ against the defendant; and on 4th July 1977 applied to the judge in chambers for an order under s 2D of the Limitation Act 1939, added by the Limitation *g* Act 1975, that he should not be barred by the three year limitation. Kerr J granted the application. Miss Ellis appeals to this court.

Ince v Rogers

On 22nd February 1973 Mrs Ince was driving a car, taking two of her children to *h* school, along a road in Buckinghamshire, on her proper side of the road. A car came up fast from the opposite direction on its wrong side of the road, overtaking a number of other vehicles. It collided head-on with Mrs Ince's car and she was badly injured. On 17th October 1973 the driver of the other car was convicted of careless driving and other offences. Within two months Mrs Ince's solicitor made a claim on her behalf, which was passed on to the insurers of the driver. Thenceforward for the next three years there were negotiations for a settlement, medical examinations, and so forth. There was no undue delay at all on behalf of Mrs Ince's solicitors. They had to wait because it was very difficult to forecast the future of Mrs Ince.

1　[1974] 2 All ER 1105, [1974] 1 WLR 899

The dates are as follows: 22nd February 1973: accident. 26th April 1973: plaintiff's
a solicitors' letter of claim. 24th June 1975: plaintiff's solicitors issued protective writ. 7th
July 1975: plaintiff's solicitors tell insurers that they have issued a writ, but did not intend
to serve it for the time being. 25th September 1975: Insurers pay £640 towards
medical expenses of Mrs Ince. 22nd February 1976: three years elapsed since the
accident. 25th March 1976: copy writ sent to insurers at their request. 24th June
1976: writ ceased to be valid unless renewed. 26th July 1976: insurers pay £250 for
b dental fees for Mrs Ince. 10th September 1976: plaintiff's solicitors apply ex parte
to renew the writ. 15th September 1976: master renews writ. 27th September 1976:
writ served. 6th October 1976: defendant enters conditional appearance and applies
to set aside service. 2nd February 1977: master refuses to set aside service. 30th
May 1977: judge allows appeal and sets aside service. 22nd July 1977: Court of
Appeal affirms judge.
c Apart from the Limitation Act 1975 it is clear that the claim was statute-barred.
Mrs Ince's solicitors had failed in their duty to her to renew the writ in time. Her
only remedy was to sue the solicitors for damages.
On 8th July 1977 (after the judge had refused to allow the renewal) Mrs Ince issued
a writ against the defendant, and applied to the judge in chambers for an order under
s 2D that she should not be barred by the three year limitation. On 13th October
d 1977 Talbot J granted the application. The defendant, Mr Rogers, appeals to this
court.

Down v Harvey
Mr Down is in the employ of O Nicklin & Sons Ltd. They sent him with a van to
deliver a piano to Mr Harvey. The van got stuck in a muddy track. Mr Harvey got
e a Land Rover to pull it out. Whilst helping, Mr Down's leg was caught in a rope and
he was badly injured. He had many operations and eventually his left foot was
amputated.
The dates are as follows. 16th February 1973: accident. March 1973: claim made
and matter passed to insurers. May 1973 to October 1974: medical examinations
and negotiations. There was delay then until the plaintiff's condition could be better
f assessed. 9th February 1976: writ issued but not served. 16th February 1976: the
three years elapsed since accident. 8th February 1977: application made to registrar
ex parte for renewal; renewal granted. (Note: the writ might have been validly
served on that day, but the plaintiff's solicitors chose instead to apply to renew it.)
7th April 1977: writ served. 9th June 1977: conditional appearance and application
to set aside renewal of writ. 30th June 1977: registrar sets aside renewal of writ.
g 20th October 1977: judge in chambers affirms registrar. Apart from the Limitation
Act 1975 it is clear that action was statute-barred. 19th July 1977: plaintiff issued
new writ and applied to judge in chambers for an order under s 2D that he was not
barred by the three-year limitation. On 27th July 1977 Lawson J granted an application. The defendants appeal to this court.
Summarising those three cases, they have these features in common: in each case
h the plaintiff had suffered personal injury. He instructed solicitors at once. His
solicitors made a claim against the defendant, who passed it on to the insurers.
The insurers did not dispute liability. There were negotiations for a settlement.
But the extent of the plaintiff's injuries could not be ascertained for some time. So
the plaintiff's solicitors issued a protective writ and told the insurers they had done so.
This was all during the negotiations. But unfortunately, by a slip they forgot to serve
j it within the one year allowed by the rules. And when they applied to renew it,
they were out of time. The three years had expired. On that account the renewal
was not allowed. So the action was, under the old law, statute-barred. Now that old
law has gone. We have a new Act, the Limitation Act 1975. The plaintiff in each
case sought to take advantage of it. In each case the plaintiff's solicitors issued a new
writ and sought to override the time limit. They asked the judge in chambers to

exercise his discretion under the new Limitation Act 1975. The judge in each case allowed the extension. The defendant appeals to this court.

A short history

The common law laid down no time limit. In 1623 the statute[1] of that year prescribed six years for actions founded on simple contract or tort. That stood for over 300 years until the subject was considered in 1936 by the Law Revision Committee[2] who recommended no change. So six years was retained by the comprehensive statute, the Limitation Act 1939: see s 2(1). Always it was six years from the date on which the cause of the action accrued. Following a report by Tucker LJ's committee[3] this was reduced in 1954 to three years for claims for personal injuries: see the Law Reform (Limitation of Actions) Act 1954. The time ran from the date when the loss or damage was suffered by the plaintiff, irrespective of his knowledge of such loss or damage. The injustice of this rule was brought into prominence by the decision of the House of Lords in *Cartledge v E Jopling & Sons Ltd*[4] about insidious diseases, like pneumoconiosis. It was held that a man was statute-barred before he even knew that he had contracted the disease. This led to the report by Edmund Davies J's committee[5] in 1962. It recommended that an injured person should not be defeated by the three year limitation if he could not reasonably have been expected to know of his injury during that period; and started an action within 12 months of getting to know. This report was followed by the Limitation Act 1963, but that Act was very obscure and difficult to construe. Lord Reid[6] said that it had 'a strong claim to the distinction of being the worst drafted Act on the statute book'. There was a clash of opinion among the judges about it. Some[7] thought that time did not run against a man until he knew that he had 'a worthwhile cause of action'. Others thought that time ran against him as soon as he knew all the material facts, even though he did not know that he had a cause of action. The differing views were expressed in the House of Lords in *Central Asbestos Co Ltd v Dodd*[8]. They were examined by Orr LJ's committee[9] in their interim report in May 1974. It contained a draft clause which was, in substance, included in the Limitation Act 1975. In my opinion this court can and should consider the report as part of the background to the Act: see *Black-Clawson International Ltd v Papierwerke Waldorf-Aschaffenburg AG*[10].

The proposal for a general discretion

Throughout that history there has been a strong body of opinion in favour of giving the court a general discretion to override the statutory time limit. The proposal was that the three year limitation should be retained, but the court should have an unfettered discretion to extend it. This proposal was put before each of the committees, but rejected by them. It was considered by the Law Revision Committee in 1936[11] and rejected by them. It was considered by Edmund Davies J and his committee[12], and rejected by them. It was considered by Orr LJ and his committee[13]

1   21 Jac 1 c 16 (Limitation Act 1623)
2   Law Revision Committee Fifth Interim Report (Statutes of Limitation), December 1936 (Cmd 5334)
3   Report of the Committee on the Limitation of Actions, July 1949 (Cmd 7440)
4   [1963] 1 All ER 341, [1963] AC 758
5   Report of the Committee on Limitation of Actions in Cases of Personal Injury, September 1962 (Cmnd 1829)
6   *Central Asbestos Co Ltd v Dodd* [1972] 2 All ER 1135 at 1138, [1973] AC 518 at 529
7   See e g *Central Asbestos Co Ltd v Dodd* [1972] 2 All ER 1135 at 1151, [1973] AC 518 at 544, 545, per Lord Pearson
8   [1972] 2 All ER 1135, [1973] AC 518
9   Law Reform Committee Twentieth Report (Interim Report on Limitation of Actions in Personal Injury Claims), May 1974 (Cmnd 5630)
10   [1975] 1 All ER 810, [1975] AC 591
11   Cmd 5334, para 7
12   Cmnd 1829, paras 30-33
13   Cmnd 5630, paras 34, 35

and rejected by them. The reason for rejection was that, if an unfettered discretion
were given to judges, it would lead to too much uncertainty. The proposal was
condemned by Orr LJ's committee[1] in these words:

'To make the plaintiff entirely dependant on the court's discretion would,
in our view, be a retrograde step and we do not recommend it.'

Nevertheless, Orr LJ's committee did recommend that the court should have a
discretion in some 'exceptional cases' to extend the time. They described these cases
as a 'residual class of case' and the discretion as a 'residual discretionary power'.
This residual class was not defined by the committee; but, so far as I can gather,
they had in mind cases where the plaintiff knew the facts, for instance, that he had
suffered an injury or contracted a disease which was due to his work, but he did not
know his legal rights; he did not know that he had a cause of action against his
employers on account of it. If the court were given a discretion, in that exceptional
class of case, to extend the time, it would enable the court to do justice in them[2].
Apart from those exceptional cases, the committee thought that the three year
limitation should continue. This view was echoed by Griffiths J in the recent case of
Finch v Francis[3]. He was a member of Orr LJ's committee, and so his views are of
special weight. He said:

'... The object of [the discretion to override the time limit] was to provide
for the occasional hard case. I cannot believe that it was the intention of Parliament that s 2D should be applied to a case such as this, when a person in the hands
of a solicitor allows time to run out in a straightforward running-down action.
If the court were to exercise its powers in a case such as this, the value to the
defendant of the three-year time limit in personal injury actions would be completely swept aside. Furthermore, the court would be flooded with applications.
In my view the court should be circumspect in its approach to the application
of s 2D and it should be reserved for cases of an unusual nature. I do not think
that this was a case of an unusual nature. It was a straightforward running-down
action in which time should never have been allowed to expire. I can see no
reason to extend it.'

The 1975 statute itself

Although those committees did not accept the proposal for a general discretion,
nevertheless, when Parliament passed the 1975 Act, it did give the court a general
discretion. Section 2D, as I read it, gives a wide discretion to the court which is not
limited to a 'residual class of case' at all. It is not limited to 'exceptional cases'. It
gives the court a discretion to extend the time to all cases where the three year
limitation has expired before the issue of the writ. It retains three years as the normal
period of limitation (being three years from the date on which the cause of action
accrued, or the date, if later, of the plaintiff's knowledge of the facts) but it confers
on the court an unfettered discretion to extend the three year period in any case in
which it considers it equitable to do so.

The granting of this discretion is a revolutionary step. It alters our whole approach
to time-bars. I do not regard it as a retrograde step. In former times it was thought
that judges should not be given discretionary powers. It would lead to too much
uncertainty. The law should define with precision the circumstances in which judges
should do this or that. Those days are now past. In statute after statute, Parliament
has given powers to the judges and entrusted them with a discretion as to the manner
in which those powers should be exercised. In many of these statutes, Parliament
sets out 'guidelines' indicating some of the considerations to which judges should

1 Cmnd 5630, para 35
2 Cmnd 5630, paras 38, 56 and 87
3 (21st July 1977) unreported

have regard. A notable example is the Matrimonial Proceedings and Property Act 1970, s 5, regarding the division of matrimonial property: see *Wachtel v Wachtel*[1]. *a* A recent example is the Unfair Contract Terms Act 1977, which sets out 'guidelines' for application of the reasonableness test. Sometimes Parliament has entrusted the judge with a discretion without setting out any guidelines, as in trial by jury under the Administration of Justice (Miscellaneous Provisions) Act 1933; and then the judges themselves set out the guidelines: see *Ward v James*[2]. In all such cases the judges in making their decisions set a pattern from which the profession can forecast the *b* likely result in any given set of circumstances: see *Bickel v Duke of Westminster*[3]. So a sufficient degree of certainty is achieved; as much certainty as is possible consistently with justice.

The value of this wide discretion is well shown by the present series of cases. They all arise out of circumstances which the various committees never had in mind at all, In each of the three cases there were negotiations for a settlement, but the plaintiff's *c* solicitors, by the merest slip, allowed time to run out. They failed to renew the writ in time. This slip did not prejudice the defendant or his insurers in the least. Yet, as soon as the defendant's insurers discovered it, they cried 'snap', and broke off the negotiations. They said to the plaintiff: 'You are statute-barred. We are not liable. You sue your own solicitors for negligence. Make their insurers pay. And not us.' All of the judges rejected this submission. Each of the judges exercised his discretion *d* in favour of the plaintiff. I think they were quite right. As a matter of simple justice, it is the defendant's insurers who should pay the plaintiff's claim. They have received the premiums to cover the risk of these accidents. They should not be allowed to foist their liability on to the plaintiff's solicitors or their insurers, by calling 'snap', as if it were a game of cards.

e

Pheasant v S T H Smith (Tyres) Ltd
On 10th July 1970 Mr Pheasant was driving his wife and two young children in a Singer car along the M5 motorway in Gloucestershire. A car driven by a Mr Carver overtaking him came right across his path. There was a collision, in which Mr and Mrs Pheasant and their children were all injured.

On 4th January 1972 a writ was issued on their behalf against Mr Carver and a statement of claim on 14th April 1972. On 23rd June 1972 Mr Carver delivered a defence alleging that the collision was caused by a sudden deflation of one of the tyres of the car. He said that this was because the tyres had been negligently repaired by a repairer, Mr Smith and his company, S T H Smith (Tyres) Ltd. Mr Carver joined Mr Smith and his company as third parties. That was on 21st September 1972. In these circumstances it was clearly advisable for Mr Pheasant to add Mr Smith and his *f* company as defendants, because, if Mr Carver was not negligent, it was essential for Mr Pheasant to have the Smiths as defendants. So on 30th April 1973 Mr Pheasant's solicitor applied by summons to add the Smiths as defendants. The summons was returnable on 6th June 1973. Now, here is the point. The accident was on 10th July 1970. So three years would elapse on 10th July 1973. So the plaintiffs ought to add the Smiths before or on 10th July 1973.

Now if the summons had been heard on 6th June 1973, and granted on that day, the Smiths could have been joined as defendants within the three years. The Smiths' solicitors had written a letter, saying:

> 'We understand that the Plaintiffs are applying to the District Registrar on Wednesday the 6th June for leave to amend the proceedings and the Statement of Claim by joining our Clients as co-Defendants. We confirm that we have

1　[1973] 1 All ER 829, [1973] Fam 72
2　[1965] 1 All ER 563, [1966] 1 QB 273
3　[1976] 3 All ER 801, [1977] QB 517

a   instructions to accept service of the amended Writ and Statement of Claim if, as we anticipate, the Order is duly made.'

But, by a clerk's mistake, Mr Pheasant's solicitor did not attend the summons on 6th June 1973. We are told that a lady clerk made too long a stroke with her pen so that it appeared in the diary as if that appointment was cancelled; whereas it had not been. At any rate, as the solicitor did not attend on that day, the registrar did not *b*   make any order on that day joining the Smiths as defendants.

Five weeks later, on 11th July 1973, Mr Pheasant's solicitor discovered the mistake. He immediately asked the registrar for another appointment. The registrar gave it to him at once on 11th July. So on 11th July Mr Pheasant's solicitor attended before the registrar. He produced the letter from the Smiths' solicitors saying they would not oppose the joinder. Thereupon the registrar, Morris Jones, allowed the joinder *c*   and the order was drawn up as follows:

> 'UPON HEARING the Solicitors for all parties IT IS ORDERED that the Plaintiffs be granted leave to amend the Writ and Statement of Claim to join in the Third Parties as Co-Defendants in this action. DATED this 11th day of JULY 1973'.

Now, that order was inaccurate in this respect. The Smiths' solicitors had not *d*   been heard; no notice had been given to the Smiths' solicitors of the summons on 11th July. Mr Pheasant's solicitor, having missed the appointment for 6th June simply went along to the next appointment on 11th July and produced the letter; which was only a consent for 6th June and not for 11th July. Leave to amend having been given, the Smiths were joined on 3rd August, and served on 24th August. Thereupon they entered a conditional appearance and took out a summons to set aside the joinder *e*   as it had not been made within the three years. On 4th January 1974 Mr Registrar Verity set aside the amendment and joinder. Mr Pheasant's solicitor appealed to the judge. On 11th February 1974 Rees J set aside the order of Mr Registrar Morris Jones of 11th July 1973 (granting leave to join) and affirmed the order of Mr Registrar Verity of 4th January 1974 (setting aside the joinder). The judge gave a reasoned judgment, citing many cases and concluded:

f
> '. . . on the present state of the authorities, I am not satisfied that power exists to add a defendant after a limitation period has expired . . . [and] even if the power did exist, I am not satisfied that it should be exercised otherwise than in exceptional circumstances, and I can find no such circumstances in the present case.'

g   Rees J gave leave to appeal, but Mr Pheasant's solicitor did not appeal. He accepted the judge's decision, with the result that the Smiths were not added as defendants to the action, because the claim against them was statute-barred at the time leave was given and the amendment made.

That was 11th February 1974. No one would have thought at that time that the decision would be reversed. But on 1st September 1975 the Limitation Act 1975 *h*   came into operation. Mr Pheasant's solicitor decided to take advantage of it. On 24th March 1976 he issued a fresh writ against the Smiths, claiming damages for the negligent repair of tyres causing the accident on 10th July 1970. Pleadings were delivered in which the Smiths pleaded the statute of limitation (three years) and also res judicata and issue estoppel. Mr Pheasant delivered a reply asking that, under the Limitation Act 1975, an order be made that the claim be not statute-barred. This *i*   was set down as a preliminary issue. It was tried by Cusack J on 29th July 1977. He overrode the time-bar. The Smiths appeal to this court.

Retrospective operation of the 1975 Act

This case raises a point on s 3 of the 1975 Act. That section makes the Act retrospective. It applies in relation to causes of action which accrued before, as well as those which accrue after, the commencement of the Act. It applies also to actions that have been commenced before the Act, and are still pending at its commencement, i e on 1st September 1975. But it does not apply once 'a final order or judgment had been made or given therein'.

It was admitted before us that the order of Rees J on 11th February 1974 was a 'final order or judgment', within s 3. Under the law as it then stood, it finally disposed of Mr Pheasant's cause of action against the Smiths. But it is submitted by Mr Pheasant that no action had been 'commenced' by him against the Smiths. He had tried to 'commence' an action against the Smiths, by getting leave to join them as defendants, but had failed. But the Smiths say that Mr Pheasant had 'commenced' an action against them and it had been dismissed by a 'final' order: and the matter was res judicata or there was an issue estoppel.

Void or voidable

This raises a nice question as to the status of the order of Mr Registrar Morris Jones on 11th July 1973, when he gave leave to amend and join the Smiths as defendants. Was it a nullity and void ab initio? For in that case everything that followed from it was also a nullity and void; and no action had been 'commenced' against the Smiths. Or was it good when it was made and only voidable? For in that case everything that followed was good until it was set aside; and an action would have been 'commenced' against the Smiths and then dismissed by Rees J in a 'final' order.

I think that the order of 11th July 1973 was a nullity and void ab initio for two reasons: (i) it was made under a fundamental mistake in that the registrar was told and believed that the Smiths had agreed to it, when they had not; and (ii) it was made contrary to the rules of natural justice, because no notice of appointment had been given to the Smiths' solicitor. Such failures make the order a nullity and void ab initio: see *Anisminic v Foreign Compensation Commission*[1] per Lord Reid and Lord Pearce. It is true, of course, that the Smiths might have waived their right to complain of it. They might have entered an unconditional appearance. But they did not waive it. They entered a conditional appearance and got it set aside. On being set aside, it was thereupon shown to have been a nullity from the beginning and void. So, after some vacillation, I would adopt the meanings of 'void' and 'voidable' given by Professor Wade in the latest edition of his book, Administrative Law[2]. Seeing that it was a nullity, it follows that in point of law no action had been 'commenced' against the Smiths. So s 3 applies. The 1975 Act operates retrospectively so as to enable Mr Pheasant to bring an action against the Smiths, provided always that he can persuade the court to exercise its discretion so as to override the time limit.

Discretion

Once it comes to discretion, it is clear that it should be exercised in favour of Mr Pheasant. It was a most unfortunate slip, an extended stroke in the diary, which led to the solicitor missing the appointment for 6th June 1973. It was just bad luck that it was not discovered until 11th July 1973, just one day too late. The insurers then called 'snap' and invoked the statute of limitations. That was all very well before the 1975 Act. But, now that the court has a discretion, it is a very proper case in which to exercise it.

Remedy against solicitor

The question was much discussed whether, in exercising discretion, the court should have regard to the plaintiff's remedy against his own solicitor. In *Birkett v James*[3] Lord Diplock said that, in cases of dismissal for want of prosecution, it was not a relevant consideration; but Lord Salmon said[4] that it might have some weight.

1   [1969] 1 All ER 208 at 213, 233, [1969] 2 AC 147 at 171, 195
2   4th Edn (1977), pp 300, 450
3   [1977] 2 All ER 801 at 809, [1978] AC 297 at 324
4   [1977] 2 All ER 801 at 815, [1978] AC 297 at 330

But those cases are different. In cases under the 1975 Act, I think that the negligence
a of the plaintiff's solicitor, and a remedy against him, is an admissible consideration.
It is one of 'the circumstances of the case' and one of 'the reasons for the delay'.
It may tip the scale where the defendant has been substantially prejudiced by the
delay.

It was also suggested that, in s 2D(3) the words 'the plaintiff' refer only to the plaintiff personally, and do not include his solicitor or agent. That depends on the context.
b In para (*d*) it refers to the plaintiff personally. But in paras (*a*), (*b*) and (*c*) it includes
his solicitor. I think 'the plaintiff' includes his solicitor or agent except where the
context confines it to the plaintiff personally.

The court
A question also arose about the procedure under s 2D. To whom is the application
c to be made? 'The court' means 'the court in which the action has been brought':
see 2D(2). Some people have thought that 'the court' there means the court which
tries the case. But it is not so limited. I think it means a judge of the High Court
or of the county court, as the case may be. It includes a judge in chambers, or a
judge hearing an application as a preliminary issue. I do not think it includes a
master in the High Court, or a registrar in the county court. It should be dealt with
d separately from any application to renew it.

Conclusion
These four cases show that the 1975 Act has made a great change in our law of
limitation. It means that in personal injury cases a plaintiff is not absolutely barred
by the three year time limit. The judges have a discretion to override the time limit
e where it is fair and just to do so.
I would, therefore, dismiss all these appeals.

ORMROD LJ. Anyone looking for the kinds of mischief against which the Limitation
Act 1975 is directed, would find these four appeals of considerable interest. In all
f four, the defendants are appealing against orders made under the new s 2D 'disapplying' the provision in s 2A under which an action for personal injuries becomes
statute-barred after three years. In other words, the defendants are inviting this
court to hold, in the exercise of its discretion, that the plaintiffs' claims should be
statute-barred.
Section 1 of the 1975 Act introduced a number of new sections into the Limitation
g Act 1939 in respect of actions for damages for personal injury, which have radically
changed this branch of the law. Under s 2D the court can now extend the period of
limitation if it considers it 'equitable' to do so. The defendants, therefore, have to
show that the judge below was wrong in concluding that it was equitable to give the
plaintiffs leave to proceed with their actions notwithstanding the lapse of time.
If they succeed, it is difficult to imagine any set of circumstances in which it would
h be proper to exercise this new discretionary power in favour of a plaintiff. The
defendants, as counsel frankly and inevitably conceded, have no merits at all; they
are simply attempting to take advantage of formal procedural mistakes by the
plaintiffs' solicitors (which have caused them no inconvenience, let alone any prejudice) to transfer liability for the plaintiffs' claims from the defendants' insurers
to the plaintiffs' solicitors' insurers. Counsel for the defendants in the first three
j cases, made no attempt to hide the nakedness of the point of law on which they sought
to rely; counsel for the defendants in the fourth appeal, managed to find an exiguous
garment in which to wrap his case but it proved on inspection to be diaphanous in
the extreme. He also relied on a plea of res judicata which will be dealt with later.
The 1975 Act is the third attempt to reform this branch of the law since 1939.
This time, Parliament has firmly grasped the nettle and has decided that it cannot

be made to work fairly and justly as between plaintiffs and defendants without introducing into it an element of judicial discretion from which it has, hitherto, *a* been immune. There appears to be no other way of preventing what is in some cases a necessary protection for defendants, from being exploited in others.

The scheme adopted by the 1975 Act, so far as is relevant to these appeals is to prescribe two, what might be called 'normal' periods of limitation, namely three years from the date on which the cause of action accrued and three years from the date of the plaintiff's knowledge (s 2A(4)(a) and (b)), and then to provide by s 2D a *b* discretionary power to 'disapply' this time limit 'if it would be equitable' to do so. Under s 2D(1) the court is to have regard to the degree to which the plaintiff would be prejudiced by the application of the time limit, and to the degree to which the defendant would be prejudiced by the court extending the limit. Section 2D(3) sets out the main considerations to be taken into account by the court in exercising its discretion. This is the technique which has proved successful in the Matrimonial *c* Causes Act 1973, s 25, which also gives the court very wide discretionary powers. So, under s 2D(3) the court is to 'have regard to all the circumstances of the case' and in particular to the six matters specifically set out in paras (a) to (f) inclusive.

The language of the section, in my judgment, is quite clear. Having laid down the norm, it then gives the court the widest discretion to adapt this norm to the circumstances of any case in which it would work inequitably. This is, in fact, a *d* statutory analogy of the old tradition by which equity was called in to mitigate the rigidity of the common law in the interests of individual justice.

The defendants contend that the section should be construed or applied not only strictly but, in the interest of public policy, restrictively. So far as construction is concerned the words of the section are clear and unambiguous. It is impossible to construe the word 'equitable' narrowly or liberally. It is either equitable or *e* inequitable to disapply the fixed time limit in any given set of circumstances, although different people may have different views of what is equitable in particular cases. The defendants argued that s 2D should be confined to 'exceptional cases'. That is precisely what the 1975 Act provides, since every case in which the court decides that the application of the norm would be inequitable is, ex hypothesi, an exceptional case. *f*

The defendants' main contention was that the section should be read in the light of the report of the Law Reform Committee in 1974[1]. Leaving aside the propriety of looking at such material when construing a provision in an Act of Parliament, the practical question is whether it is of any assistance.

In a situation such as this, reference to a report on which legislation is based involves two further steps, neither of which is easy. First, one has to construe the report, *g* and then, if the Act appears to depart from the recommendations in the report, to decide whether Parliament intended to act on or to depart from the recommendations. In the instant case reference to the report proved unhelpful from a practical point of view because the final recommendations in para 69, with which the 1975 Act is in line, are not entirely consistent with certain passages in the body of the report which seem to suggest that the committee may have had in mind that the discretion- *h* ary powers would only be used in 'residual' cases. No such ambiguity appears in the Act itself, which thus provides the answer to the second stage.

The reasons put forward to support the argument that the court should apply the section restrictively, in the interests of public policy, were twofold: first, the loss of certainty which would inevitably arise if the discretion were freely used and, second, the loss of a valuable sanction over plaintiffs and their solicitors to discourage *j* delay in bringing proceedings, and, in particular over solicitors, by allowing them to avoid liability to their clients for negligence. So far as the first point is concerned

---

1   Cmnd 5630

Parliament has now decided that uncertain justice is preferable to certain injustices
a or, in other words, that certainty can be bought at too high a price, as these four
cases vividly demonstrate. If insurance companies through their customers choose
to take wholly unmeritorious technical points to avoid liability, they cannot complain
if ultimately their ability to take them is severely restricted. To retain a highly
formalistic procedure, the real effect of which is simply to transfer liability from the
original tortfeasor's insurers to the plaintiffs' solicitors' insurers, is not very impressive
b as a piece of public policy.

In my judgment, therefore, the 1975 Act should be applied as it stands, and we
should be careful not to impose judicial fetters on this new and, to my mind, valuable
discretionary power. So applied to the facts of these appeals (subject in the fourth
case to the further point which is peculiar to that case), the case for disapplying the
three year time limit is overwhelming. Applying the six considerations set out in
c s 2D(3) seriatim to the first three cases, the position is as follows.

Paragraph (*a*) *Delay on the part of the plaintiff*: this was purely formal in each case,
the claims were made in good time, negotiations as to damages were proceeding,
in a desultory manner, there never having been an issue as to liability; all that
happened was that the plaintiffs' solicitors, having issued their writs within the
three year period failed to serve them within a year of issue, and so had to apply
d to renew them, unfortunately after the expiry of the limitation period.

Paragraph (*b*) *Effect of delay on cogency of the evidence*: it is conceded that the effect
was nil.

Paragraphs (*c*) and (*d*) are not applicable.

Paragraph (*e*) *Promptitude of plaintiff in taking steps*: there is no criticism under
this head at all.

e Paragraph (*f*) *Steps taken by plaintiff to obtain advice*: there is no criticism under
this head either.

On these facts the court has to decide whether the degree of prejudice to the
plaintiffs caused by refusing to disapply the normal time limit, compared to the
degree of prejudice to the defendants caused by extending it, is sufficient to make it
equitable to disapply the limit. The answer, inevitably, is Yes.

f The defendants, however, argued that the plaintiffs will suffer no prejudice if
their actions are statute-barred because in each case they have an unanswerable
claim against their solicitors for damages for negligence. The plaintiffs, relying on
Birkett v James[1], contended that this was an irrelevant consideration. I do not think
that Lord Diplock's observations[2] in that case can be applied to cases arising under
s 2D because, under that section, the court is required to have regard to all the cir-
g cumstances of the case, and this is certainly one of them. I do not think, however,
that it carries much weight in these cases. The court is not concerned solely with
financial prejudice to the plaintiff. It is prejudicial to be forced to start another set of
proceedings and against a party whom one does not particularly wish to sue and to be
deprived of a good cause of action against the orginal tortfeasor. This may not
amount to serious prejudice but it has to be balanced against no prejudice to the de-
h fendant at all. He, personally, has lost nothing since no loss falls on him in either
event; one or other insurance company will pay the damages and costs and his
insurers have lost nothing but a fortuitous bonus arising from a harmless error
by the plaintiff's solicitor. I would therefore dismiss the appeals by the defendants in
the first three cases.

In *Down v Harvey* the plaintiff has a cross-appeal against the refusal of the judge
j below (Lawson J) to grant leave to renew the writ under RSC Ord 6, r 8. In this
and the other two cases the judges in the court below relied on the decision of Megaw J
in *Heaven v Road and Rail Wagons Ltd*[3], following a line of earlier decisions, that it is

---

1   [1977] 2 All ER 801, [1978] AC 297
2   [1977] 2 All ER 801 at 809, [1978] AC 297 at 324
3   [1965] 2 All ER 409, [1965] 2 QB 355

contrary to the settled practice of the court to give leave to renew a writ after the expiry of the limitation period. The ratio decidendi of that and the previous cases *a* was that at the expiration of the period of limitation the claim was statute-barred and accordingly that it would be wrong to deprive 'the defendant of a defence which he would have had under the relevant statute of limitation'[1] by renewing a time-expired writ. The force of this reasoning was overwhelming as the law then stood but the change from fixed to flexible time limits effected by the 1975 Act has largely dissipated it. However, the decision can now be supported on different grounds. The *b* difference to a plaintiff between issuing a new writ and renewing one which has already been issued but not served is very small, whereas the inconvenience of bringing into an application under RSC Ord 6, r 8, the serious and possibly complex considerations which arise under s 2D is considerable. From the procedural point of view it seems more satisfactory that cases which involve s 2D should be dealt with as sub-stantive applications under that section and should normally be heard by a judge. *c* I would therefore dismiss the cross-appeal.

The fourth appeal raises rather different considerations but, if s 2D is applicable, it too is an overwhelming case for disapplying the three year time limit. Again there was nothing but purely formal delay on the part of the plaintiff and no prejudice to the defendants since they have been involved on the litigation as third parties since 1972. The only delay has been in adding them as defendants which can cause *d* them no difficulty in preparing their defence.

Before I leave this part of the case there are two general points which should be mentioned. First, I agree with Lord Denning MR that it is for the parties and the judge to decide how an application for an order under s 2D can most conveniently be made in the circumstances of the individual case. Second, any general observations in this judgment must be read in the light of the facts of these appeals. None of them *e* is what might be called a primary limitation case, that is, a case in which the plaintiff has made no or no serious attempt to press his claim within the three year period. In all these cases the limitation point has arisen long after the solicitors on both sides have been in contact with each other and no difficulty arises about preparing the case for the defendant. In such circumstances it will usually be difficult for the defendant to show actual prejudice. In primary cases the position is different. Delay *f* in putting forward a claim is much more likely to cause real prejudice to the defendant, with the result that the scales of equity will tend to be tipped in his favour and great care will be needed before holding that it is equitable to disapply the three year limit.

I turn now to the second submission of counsel for the Smiths. He argued that Mr Pheasant was estopped from invoking s 2D either because it had already been *g* decided by Rees J in 1974 that his claim was statute-barred and was, therefore, res judicata, or because he had 'commenced an action' against the Smiths in 1974 which had been disposed of by a 'final order' by Rees J so that Mr Pheasant was precluded by s 3 of the 1975 Act from inviting the court to exercise the new discretionary power.

The events of 1973 were very unusual and demonstrate to an extreme degree the formalistic way in which the Limitation Acts could operate before the latest reform. *h* On 30th April 1973 just within the three year period, Mr Pheasant's solicitor issued a summons for leave to amend the writ to add the Smiths, the present appellants who were already third parties, as defendants. The Smiths' solicitors were served and wrote raising no objection. An appointment was taken for 6th June 1973, still within the limitation period. Mr Pheasant's solicitor as a result of a slip in his office overlooked that appointment. A few days later he discovered it and immediately applied for a *j* new appointment, which was given for 11th July 1973, one day outside the three year period. The Smiths were not notified of the new appointment but the registrar made an order giving leave to amend, recording that he had heard 'all parties',

1　[1965] 2 All ER 409 at 413, [1965] 2 QB 355 at 361

though he was in fact acting on the Smiths' solicitors' letter indicating that they
a would not oppose the application. Had the Smiths been informed of the later
appointment they would have taken advantage of the statute to oppose it. The writ
was amended and served but was subsequently set aside by another registrar. On
appeal to Rees J he held that the registrar had no power to make the order of 11th
July and dismissed Mr Pheasant's appeal. He also held that in the alternative the
registrar was wrong to give leave to amend after the expiry of the limitation period.
b   Counsel for Mr Pheasant in reply, contended that the judge was right in holding
that the registrar had no power to make the order of 11th July, and that both the
order and the writ were void. Consequently, Mr Pheasant had not 'commenced an
action' within the meaning of s 3 nor could he be estopped on the res judicata principle. Counsel for the Smiths argued that the order and the writ were merely voidable
for irregularity and that therefore Mr Pheasant had commenced an action which had
c been disposed of by a final order under s 3 and also was estopped by res judicata.
    In my judgment, the order and the amended writ were void in the sense that the
Smiths were entitled ex debito justitiae to have both of them set aside. Essentially
this was a case of non-service: see *Craig v Kanssen*[1]. Alternatively, there was a
fundamental mistake on the part of the court making the order. RSC Ord 2, r 1,
does not apply. That is not, however, to say that the order or the amended writ
d was a nullity. Each was a document emanating from the court and good on its face.
Such orders or documents must be acted on until declared void by the court: see
per Diplock J in *O'Connor v Isaacs*[2]. Consequently, if the Smiths had not challenged
the order or the amended writ, the subsequent proceedings would have been validly
constituted, but as they did challenge them, the court had no option but to declare
them void, as Rees J in effect did, in holding that the registrar had had no power to
e give leave to amend. Neither was voidable in the sense that the court had a discretion
to allow them to stand: see the judgment of Sir George Baker P in *Dryden v Dryden*[3]
and also the judgment of this court in *Re F (infants) (adoption order: validity)*[4], where
the point was fully considered.
    In these circumstances Mr Pheasant cannot be said to have 'commenced an action'
because the whole proceedings were void ab initio and there is no res which could
f found an estoppel.
    Accordingly, the second submission of counsel for the Smiths fails and the fourth
appeal too should be dismissed.

GEOFFREY LANE LJ. I agree. The issue which is common to all these appeals
g may be stated thus. Do the provisions of the Limitation Act 1975 apply to every
type of action involving a claim for damages for personal injury, including a simple
claim in negligence, or do they apply only in cases 'out of the usual run' or to 'difficult
cases' (to adopt two of the expressions used by counsel)?
    Those who argue for this latter restricted interpretation point out that under the
new s 2A(4) a limitation period is provided of three years from the date on which
h the cause of the action accrued, or from the date (if later) of the plaintiff's knowledge.
They suggest that having specified that set term of three years, Parliament would not
have taken it on themselves to emasculate the set term by giving a largely unrestricted discretion to the court to exempt a plaintiff from complying with it. The plaintiffs
on the other hand say that that is precisely what the Act on its plain wording means.
    The relevant provisions are in the new s 2D to which reference has already been
j made. The words 'If it appears to the court that it would be equitable to allow an

1   [1943] 1 All ER 108, [1943] 1 KB 256
2   [1956] 1 All ER 513 at 524, [1956] 2 QB 288 at 312, 313
3   [1973] 3 All ER 526, [1973] Fam 217
4   [1977] 2 All ER 777, [1977] Fam 165

action to proceed ... the court may direct that those provisions [i e ss 2A and 2B] shall not apply to the action' and 'the court shall have regard to all the circumstances of the case' seem to me to give to the court as wide a discretion as could well be imagined. I find it impossible to understand how any restriction to 'difficult' or 'unusual' cases can be read into them.

It is said that if one studies the report of the Law Reform Committee which was set up to examine the question of limitation of action in personal injury claims[1]. it is clear that Parliament must have meant to give only a restricted discretion to the court to override the three year limitation period. To that contention there are these answers. First, we are seeking to discover not so much what Parliament meant, but the true meaning of the words which they used. Secondly, where the words of a statutory provision are capable of having only one meaning, as I think is the case here, that is the end of the matter, and no further enquiry from reports of committees is permissible: see *Black-Clawson International Ltd v Papierwerke Waldhof-Aschaffenburg AG*[2] per Lord Reid. It is true that if one does look at the terms of the report, they suggest that the discretion of the court should be restricted, but that is not carried into effect by the words of the Act. The dictum to the contrary expressed by Griffiths J in *Finch v Francis*[3], namely that the object of s 2D was 'to provide for the occasional hard case', is not lightly to be dismissed, since he was a member of the committee which produced the report, but I do not think, with respect, that it can be supported.

Given that the words of s 2D are not to be interpreted in this restricted sense, there can be no doubt, in each of the cases which are the subject of appeal, that it is equitable that the plaintiff should be exempted from compliance with the three year limitation period, for the reasons expressed by Lord Denning MR.

There are a number of subsidiary points which we were asked to clarify if possible.

(1) In considering whether or not to relieve the plaintiff under s 2D, is it permissible to have regard to the question whether the plaintiff has a valid claim against his solicitor in negligence if he is statute-barred in the original action? The majority of their Lordships in *Birkett v James*[4] held that in the circumstances of that case, which was an application to dismiss for want of prosecution not involving the 1975 Act, the existence or non-existence of a remedy against the plaintiff's solicitor was not a material consideration. But s 2D(1) and (3) enjoins the court to have regard to *all* the circumstances of the case, and I find it impossible to say that the insurance position whether of the plaintiff or of the defendant is not one of those circumstances, when the primary object of the enquiry is to discover the respective degrees of prejudice. What weight should be given to the point is another matter. For example, if there is any real dispute about the solicitor's liability in negligence, then the chances of the plaintiff being able to recover against him would no doubt be largely disregarded. It is plainly undesirable that there should be any detailed enquiry into the existence of such liability.

(2) What should be the practice in cases such as the first of the present appeals, *Firman v Ellis*, where the matter originally comes before the court on the application of the plaintiff to extend the validity of a writ under RSC Ord 6, r 8? Should the master or registrar consider the application in the light of the new s 2D or should he continue as before to apply the rule enunciated by Megaw J in *Heaven v Road and Rail Wagons Ltd*[5], dismiss the application and leave the plaintiff to issue a fresh writ and make his application under the provisions of the 1975 Act? It may at first sight seem cumbersome to take two steps when one would suffice, and indeed at one stage in the argument I had formed the view that the whole matter ought properly to be

1 Cmnd 5630
2 [1975] 1 All ER 810 at 814, [1975] AC 591 at 614
3 (21st July 1977) unreported
4 [1977] 2 All ER 801, [1978] AC 297
5 [1965] 2 All ER 409, [1965] 2 QB 355

determined by the master at the hearing of the application to extend. The decision
a in *Heaven's* case[1] would no longer constrain him to dismiss the application, because
the basis of that decision, entirely correct when it was made, has been undermined
and destroyed by the provisions of the 1975 Act. No longer is it true to say as Megaw J[2]
said:

> 'It follows that, if the validity of the writ were not to be extended, and if the
> *b* plaintiff were left to issue a fresh writ, the defendants would have an unanswerable
> defence by virtue of the three-year period of limitation prescribed by the Law
> Reform (Limitation of Actions, &c.) Act, 1954.'

Having heard the arguments of both parties on this aspect of the case, however,
it seems to me that the most satisfactory method to adopt is to leave the plaintiff to
issue a fresh writ under the 1975 provisions, and for the matter to be considered at a
c later stage, preferably by a judge. The reason is this. When the matter comes before
the master, the information available to him is scanty. There has been no discovery
and the parties have scarcely had the opportunity to marshal their evidence. Consequently it would not be practicable for all the circumstances to be properly investigated. Moreover, although there is no reason why the master should not have regard
to the provisions of the 1975 Act in coming to his conclusion, there is no obligation
d on him to do so, as there is on the court deciding whether the plaintiff should
be permitted to issue a fresh writ after the expiry of the limitation period.

It remains to consider the separate question which arises in the last of the cases
before us, namely *Pheasant v S T H Smith (Tyres) Ltd*. I have had the opportunity
of reading the judgment of Ormrod LJ on this aspect of the appeal. I respectfully
agree with his reasoning and conclusions and it is unnecessary for me to add anything
e to them.

I would accordingly dismiss all the appeals.

Appeals dismissed. Leave to appeal to the House of Lords refused.

f Solicitors: *Badhams* (for Miss Ellis and Mr Rogers); *Hextall Erskine & Co*, agents for
Toller, Oerton & Balsdon, Barnstaple (for O Nicklin & Sons Ltd) and agents for *Cart-
wrights*, Bristol (for Mr Harvey); *Mayo & Perkins*, Eastbourne (for Mr Firman);
Thompson & Debenham, Harpenden (for Mrs Ince and her co-plaintiffs); *Park Nelson,
Dennes, Redfern & Co*, agents for *Montague Arthur & Skerratt*, Barnstaple (for Mr Down)
and agents for *Sansbury Hill & Co*, Bath (for S T H Smith (Tyres) Ltd and Mr Smith);
R E Warburton & Sons, Liverpool (for Mr Pheasant and his co-plaintiffs).

Sumra Green   Barrister.

---

1 [1965] 2 All ER 409, [1965] 2 QB 355
2 [1965] 2 All ER 409 at 411, [1965] 2 QB 355 at 358

Tramountana Armadora SA v Atlantic Shipping Co SA

QUEEN'S BENCH DIVISION
DONALDSON J
10th, 24th NOVEMBER 1977

Arbitration – Costs – Discretion of arbitrator – Exercise of discretion – Successful party ordered to pay total costs of reference – Award in favour of claimant after setting off amount awarded to respondent on counterclaim – Respondent proportionately more successful on counterclaim than claimant on claim – Whether justifying award of costs against claimant.

Arbitration – Costs – Discretion of arbitrator – Exercise of discretion – Successful party ordered to pay total costs of reference – Respondent making a sealed offer of settlement of lump sum to include interest and costs – Award in favour of claimant less than lump sum offered – Whether interest on award to be disregarded in comparing award with offer – Whether lump sum inclusive of costs can be compared with amount awarded when deciding which party to bear costs.

Following a dispute arising out of a charterparty, the claimants, the owners of the chartered vessel, claimed against the respondents, the charterers. The respondents counterclaimed and the matter was referred to a single arbitrator in London as provided for in the charterparty. The dispute was heard on 2nd and 3rd November 1975 ('day 1' and 'day 2' of the arbitration) at the end of which the claimants applied for the first time for rectification of the charterparty. The arbitrator adjourned the hearing to enable the respondents to consider calling a surveyor to give evidence in reply to the claim for rectification. On 3rd February 1976 the respondents wrote to the claimants offering US $6,000 in full and final settlement, and in response to an inquiry by the claimants stated that the US $6,000 was a lump sum figure and that they did 'not contemplate any payment in respect of interest or costs'. No further progress was made towards a settlement and the arbitration hearing was resumed on 21st and 22nd December 1976 ('day 3' and 'day 4' of the arbitration). The proceedings on days 3 and 4 were confined to the claimants' application for rectification. On 23rd December the arbitrator awarded the claimants 35·6 per cent of their claim and the respondents 51·8 per cent of their counterclaim. After set-off, the sum awarded to the claimants was US $2,710·94. The arbitrator then awarded the costs of the hearing and of the award to the respondents on the grounds that the respondents had offered to pay the claimants 'a much larger sum' than had been awarded and the claimants had refused this offer. The claimants appealed against the award of costs. In an affidavit to the court the arbitrator justified his award of costs on the grounds (1) that days 1 and 2 were occupied with the issues on which the award was eventually made and the respondents had been proportionately more successful in their counterclaim than the respondents had been with their claim, (2) that the costs after day 2 were expended on the rectification issue which should have been pleaded before the arbitration began and in any event although the claimants had succeeded on that issue that had not increased the amount awarded to them and (3) that the offer by the respondents of 3rd February protected them against the award of any costs after that date if, as was the case, the offer was not accepted and the amount awarded was less than the amount offered.

Held – The appeal would be allowed and the award remitted to the arbitrator to reconsider his order for costs for the following reasons—

    (i) In respect of the costs up to the end of day 2 the arbitrator had misdirected himself in awarding costs to the respondents simply because they were proportionately more successful than the claimants. Prima facie the claimants, having been successful, were entitled to costs up to the date of the offer, subject to their being deprived of all or part of their own costs if the claim was so inflated as to deter the respondents from seeking a settlement or in some other way to increase the costs of the arbitration and subject to their being deprived of their own costs and having to pay the claimants' costs if the sum recovered was so trifling as not to justify bringing the claim at all. Although the claimants had been optimistic in their claim it had been properly brought and the arbitrator was not justified in depriving the claimants of costs and requiring them to pay all the respondents' costs (see p 878 *j* to p 879 *c*, post);

(ii) In respect of the costs for the whole period after the end of day 2 the arbitrator's award was justifiable on the grounds that days 3 and 4 were devoted entirely to the rectification issue which should have been put forward before the arbitration began and further, the claimants' success on that issue had not increased the sum awarded to them. Nevertheless the award of costs in respect of that period could not be justified on the other ground put forward by the arbitrator, namely that the claimants should bear all the costs after the respondents' offer, because in comparing the offer with the amount awarded the arbitrator had ignored the interest payable on the award. Moreover, the arbitrator was not in a position to compare an offer in the form of a lump sum inclusive of costs with the amount awarded because he could not know or ascertain the amount of the claimants' costs up to the date of the offer (which was in the middle of the arbitration) and therefore was not in a position to compare like with like (see p 878 *c* to *h*, post); *Jefford v Gee* [1970] 1 All ER 1202 distinguished.

Per Curiam. (i) A sealed offer in an arbitration, although analogous to a payment into court in other respects, differs in the interest on the amount awarded should be taken into account in assessing whether a successful claimant is or is not entitled to costs after the date of the offer. This is because in the context of a commercial action where the sums may be large and the action may extend over a long period the amount paid in may have little relation to the claimants' entitlement. Therefore, when dealing with costs when there has been a sealed offer, the arbitrator should ask himself 'Has the claimant achieved more by rejecting the offer and going on with the arbitration than he would have achieved if he had accepted the offer?' (see p 877 *b c* and *g h*, post).

(ii) To overcome the reluctance of a respondent to an arbitration to make a sealed offer because he feels his defence might be weakened if the arbitrator knows that the offer has been made, the arbitrator in his discretion can invite or require the respondent to give him at the end of the hearing, but before costs are considered, a sealed envelope containing either a statement that no sealed offer has been made or the sealed offer itself (see p 876 *f g*, post).

(iii) The Rule Committee of the Supreme Court might well consider whether an amendment should not be made to the rules to allow a litigant to make a payment into court to cover interest as well as capital (see p 877 *e f*, post).

Notes
For powers of an arbitrator as to costs of an arbitration, see 2 Halsbury's Laws (4th Edn) para 607, and for cases on the subject, see 2 Digest (Repl) 720-725, 731-738, *2323-2370, 2420-2485.*

Cases referred to in judgment
Figueiredo (L) Navegacas SA v Reederei Richard Schroeder KG, The Erich Schroeder [1974] 1 Lloyd's Rep 192.
Harris v Petherick (1879) 4 QBD 611, 48 LJQB 521, sub nom *Harris v Patherick* 41 LT 146, CA, 51 Digest (Repl) 874, 4240.
Jefford v Gee [1970] 1 All ER 1202, [1970] 2 QB 130, [1970] 2 WLR 702, sub nom *Jefford and Jefford v Gee* [1970] 1 Lloyd's Rep 107, CA, Digest (Cont Vol C) 709, *182a.*

Motion

By notice of motion dated 2nd February 1977 Tramountana Armadora SA ('the *a*
claimants') moved for an order that the award as to costs made on 23rd December
1976 by the sole arbitrator, Cedric Barclay Esq, in an arbitration between the claimants and Atlantic Shipping Co SA ('the respondents') be set aside or alternatively
remitted to the arbitrator for reconsideration by him on the grounds, inter alia,
that the arbitrator had misdirected himself and/or erred in law in (1) ordering the
claimants to pay to the respondents their costs of the arbitration and to pay the costs *b*
of the award, (2) failing to order the respondents to pay to the claimants their costs
of the arbitration and to pay the costs of the award and (3) failing to enquire whether
the claimants' party and party costs at the date of the respondents' offer of US $6,000
in full satisfaction of the claim (such sum being inclusive of interest and costs) were
greater than the proportion of such sum which related to their costs. The facts are
set out in the judgment.   *c*

R *Gatehouse QC* and A *Steel* for the claimants.
H *Pollock* for the respondents.

Cur adv vult
                                                                                   c

24th November. **DONALDSON J** read the following judgment: A foreign lawyer,
or indeed a native layman, must find the English law on arbitration very odd. If
you pause to consider it, as I had to do in this case, it *is* very odd. Arbitrators, like
judges, can get the facts wrong. They can get the law wrong. On occasion, given
a little ill luck, they can get both wrong. But there the similarity ends. For judges
have to give reasons for their decisions and those reasons can be used to found an *e*
appeal, unless the law excludes such a right. In the case of arbitrators, there is never
any obligation to give reasons and, with the sole exception of an unusual order as
to costs, the courts have never encouraged the giving of reasons. Furthermore,
again with the exception of an unusual order as to costs, the courts will not permit the
parties to speculate or give evidence as to the arbitrator's reasons. And, since in
the absence of reasons it is impossible to say whether the arbitrator was right or
wrong, an award, other than one which is in the form of a special case, is not usually
appealable. But again an award containing an unusual order as to costs is an exception.
    When I say that a foreign lawyer would find the English law on arbitration very
odd, I do not refer to the unappealable status of an award. That he would find quite
understandable and, indeed, in accordance with the practice in his own country.
There, parties to a dispute can, if they wish, agree to have a quick and cheap decision *g*
which may be wrong rather than one which is subject to several appeals with all the
associated delay and expense, even if the result is, perhaps, more likely to be right.
No, what would astonish the foreign lawyer is that this status of unappealability
should be achieved by making an award which is without reasons; an unmotivated
award as it is known. Outside this country, such an award is most unusual and often
contrary to law. And he would be right. Having to give reasons concentrates the *h*
mind wonderfully. And there should always be a reason for an award and one which
can be stated. This is true even of the 'look-sniff' quality arbitration where the arbitrator might give as his reason 'I have been in the trade for 30 years. I looked at the
sample, I felt it and I smelt it. In neither look, feel nor smell was it f a q'. And not
only do reasons concentrate the mind, but on the whole they tend to satisfy the parties
more than silence.
    If, therefore, it is desirable to restrict the right of appeal from an arbitral award,
as it undoubtedly is, it would be much better to do so by statutory restrictions on the
right of appeal, whilst encouraging or even requiring the giving of reasons. After all,
that is what is done in the case of appeals from industrial tribunals and other bodies.
If the same approach were adopted in relation to arbitral awards, it would be possible

to abolish the special case procedure which is widely misunderstood and lends itself
a to misuse by those who, in times of economic stress, wish to achieve extended credit.

But I must return to the exceptional case of that part of an arbitral award which
relates to costs. There the rules are different. Lack of reasons does not spell immunity
from appeal. And that is what this motion is about. The rules in relation to an unusual
award as to costs have been usefully summarised by Mocatta J in *L Figueiredo Navegacas
SA v Reederei Richard Schroeder KG, The Eric Schroeder*[1] as follows:

b
> 'First, an arbitrator, like a judge, in dealing with costs must exercise the
> discretion invested in him judicially ... Secondly, there is no need for an umpire
> or arbitrator, if he so exercises his discretion as to depart from the general rule,
> to state the reason why he does so in his award. On the other hand, in all proba-
> bility, in most cases where an umpire/arbitrator does so act, it would save costs
c > if he were to state his reasons in his award. In that event the parties would not
> be put to the expense of trying to ascertain what his reasons were and possibly
> moving the Court to set aside the award ... Thirdly if the award does depart
> from the general rule as to costs but bears on its face no statement of the reasons
> supporting that departure, the party objecting to the award in that respect
> may bring before the court such evidence as he can obtain as to the grounds,
d > or lack of grounds, bearing upon the unusual exercise of discretion by the arbi-
> trator or umpire ... Fourthly, the above propositions ... apply to all categories
> of awards as to costs. That is to say, they apply to the extreme case in which the
> successful party has been ordered to pay all the costs of an unsuccessful party
> as well as the costs of the award, and also to a case in which a successful party
> has been made to bear his own costs and pay half the costs of the award ... in
e > exercising his discretion judicially an umpire/arbitrator must have regard in
> the first place to the primary principle guiding courts and arbitral tribunals
> in the exercise of their discretion in relation to costs, namely, that costs follow
> the event.'

It is not easy to see why an order as to costs is treated in this exceptional fashion.
f If there is an explanation, it lies in the fact that the award will necessarily always show
on its face both the arbitrator's decision on the claim and also his decision on the costs.
Reading these two decisions together and bearing in mind the prima facie rule of
English law and practice that costs should follow the event, a patent departure
from this rule without giving any sufficient reason for doing so gives rise to a rebuttable
presumption that the arbitrator has erred in law or acted in an unjudicial manner
to an extent justifying the intervention of the court. Once this point has been reached,
it is only sensible that the parties and the arbitrator should be able to place other
material before the court which will enable it to be decided whether or not it should
intervene. It also explains why the courts have encouraged arbitrators to explain
on the face of the award any departure from the usual rule as to costs although they
have not been encouraged to give reasons for any other part of the award.

In the present case the award is that of Mr Cedric Barclay, the very well known
and highly respected maritime arbitrator. He was asked to decide, and did decide,
a variety of disputes between the claimant shipowners and the respondent charterers.
The shipowners claimed rectification of the charterparty and US $19,801·54. The
charterers counterclaimed US $7,869·05 and 22,000 Belgian Francs, the latter being the
equivalent of about US $500. The claimants succeeded on the issue of rectification and
in part on their money claim. The respondents succeeded on three out of six heads of
counterclaim in specified amounts. The arbitrator then set off the counterclaim
against the claim and made an award in favour of the claimants in the sum of
US $2,710·94.

---

1 [1974] 1 Lloyd's Rep 192 at 193

Mr Barclay then had to consider what order to make on costs and he awarded the costs of the hearing and of the award to the respondents. This was on any view a major departure from the rule that costs follow the event and Mr Barclay recognised it as such in that he stated in the award that:

'My apportionment of costs is made in the exercise of my discretion and in consideration of the fact that Respondents offered to pay Claimants a much larger sum than has now been Awarded, and that the Claimants refused to accept the said offer.'

This explanation has been criticised on the basis that there was no apportionment of the costs; the successful claimants had to pay them all. I confess that I do not at once understand the use of the word 'apportionment' in this context, but, on reflection, I realised that strictly speaking there is an apportionment even if it is wholly one-sided. I think that there is nothing in this point.

However, the explanation that the respondents offered to pay the claimants a much larger sum than has now been awarded, does not of itself wholly explain or justify the order as to costs. Rather it gives rise to the question: 'when and in what circumstances was the order made'? I say that because the rule in litigation is that if an order is made which equals or exceeds the amount eventually adjudged to have been due, the claimant will be awarded the costs up to the date of the offer and the respondent those incurred after that date. The fact that a claimant refuses an offer of as much or more than he eventually recovers does not, of itself, justify depriving him of all the costs.

Fortunately, I have now had a much fuller explanation. This has been provided by Mr Barclay in the form of a most helpful affidavit. His affidavit covers the chronology of events as well as the considerations which led him to make this award as to costs.

It appears that the arbitration took place in two spasms over a year apart. The first, which Mr Barclay refers to as day 1 and day 2, took place on 2nd and 3rd November 1975. The claim and counterclaim had been fully pleaded and both parties were represented by solicitors and counsel. The case, as pleaded, did not include a claim by the claimants for rectification. That claim only arose at the end of day 2. Its emergence and the need for the respondents to consider calling a surveyor to give oral evidence led to an adjournment until December 1976.

On 3rd February 1976, during the course of this adjournment, the respondents wrote to the claimants as follows:

'With further reference to this matter, we are instructed to place on record that [the respondents] have offered the sum of $6,000 in full and final settlement of all [the claimants'] claims in this arbitration. In the circumstances, if this matter proceeds, we shall hand a sealed copy of this letter to the arbitrator when he comes to consider the question of costs at the end of the day.'

The claimants were in doubt as to the meaning of this letter and replied on 11th February 1976:

'We note that [the respondents] are now making an increased offer of settlement of U.S. $6,000. However, you have not indicated whether this figure is inclusive or exclusive of interest and costs. We would be pleased if you would clarify this for us, and we can confirm that if the offer is made exclusive of interest and costs, then it will receive serious consideration from [the claimants].'

The respondents answered this letter on 23rd February 1976 by saying:

'The offer of settlement of U.S. $6,000 is a lump sum figure and [the respondents] do not contemplate any payment in respect of interest or costs.'

The second part of the arbitration took place on 21st December 1976 (day 3) and

22nd December 1976, (day 4). The proceedings on these two days were confined to a discussion on the meaning and effect of the offer made by the respondents in February 1976 and of the claim for rectification. The award was published on 23rd December 1976. In giving the court his decision, Mr Barclay has stated that:

'The claimants were claiming U.S. $19,801·54 which claim succeeded to the extent of U.S. $7,051·10 being 35·6% of their claim. The respondents were denying the claimants' claim and counterclaiming U.S. $7,869·05 which counterclaim succeeded to the extent of U.S. $4,340·16 being 55% of their counterclaim.'

In saying this, I think that Mr Barclay has overlooked the respondents' claim for 22,000 Belgian francs, so that their counterclaim should, perhaps, be taken as being for about US $8,370. This would reduce their rate of recovery to 51·8 per cent. Mr Barclay then said:

'14 . . . I carefully considered how costs should be awarded and came to the view that in any event all costs incurred after the 4th February 1976—that is the effective date of the "open offer"—should be payable by the Claimants. The reason for my decision was firstly I was presented no evidence of, nor did Counsel for the Claimants argue that, days 3 and 4 of the Arbitration proceedings were brought only for the recovery of interest on the sum offered and costs. Indeed the contrary was the case. Days 3 and 4 were for the recovery of the whole of the claim on the grounds the Charterparty should be rectified. Secondly, although the Claimants totally succeeded in their claim that the Charterparty should be rectified, this success did not increase the sum awarded to them. Thirdly, I have always interpreted the "open offer" as being an offer of payment or part payment of the principal sum claimed in order to prevent further litigation and protect costs in respect of the Respondents should the offer not be accepted and the Award on the principal sum be less than offered.

'15. With regard to costs incurred prior to the "open offer", as the Claimants introduced the possibility of a fundamentally new Pleading on day two of the Hearing; as they did not then nor later give any explanation or argument why it was not dealt with before the reference to Arbitration or alternatively in the Pleadings in Arbitration; and as this new issue was presented before me on the 3rd and 4th day of the Hearing; I considered that the Respondents were put to additional costs defending a new issue at a late stage which should have been properly determined or pleaded before the commencement of the Hearing. Therefore exercising the discretion vested in me I decided that the Claimants should bear their and the Respondents' costs from after day two of the Hearing until the effective date of the "open offer".

'16. As to the costs incurred up to and during day one and two of the Arbitration Hearing, after hearing witnesses, reading documentary evidence, listening to Counsel and taking into account that the Respondents were proportionately more successful in their Counterclaim than the Claimants were in their claim, I considered I should exercise the discretion vested in me to Award that the Claimants bear and pay their own and the Respondents' costs in order to fairly reflect the matters as they had appeared to me.'

In reviewing an arbitrator's decision on costs, it is of the greatest importance to remember that the decision is within his discretion and not that of the courts. It is nothing to the point that I might have reached a different decision and that some other judge or arbitrator might have differed from both of us. I would neither wish, nor be entitled, to intervene, unless I was satisfied that the arbitrator had misdirected himself.

The costs of the parties fall into three groups, namely (a) up to the end of day 2, (b) from the end of day 2 until the receipt of the offer of settlement and (c) from the offer of settlement until the end of day 4. In addition consideration has to be given to the costs of the award which, notionally, can be subdivided into days 1 and 2, days 3 and 4 and the consideration and preparation of the award itself.

Mr Barclay's decision with regard to the costs of the parties from the date of the offer of settlement until the end of day 4 depends, in part, on his view of that offer. This has been criticised by counsel for the claimants. However, before considering that criticism, I should, I think, say a word about the general significance in relation to costs of offers of settlement made in arbitral proceedings.

Although the respondents' offer of settlement has been referred to as an 'open offer', this is a misnomer. Offers of settlement in arbitral proceedings can be of three kinds, namely 'without prejudice', 'sealed' and 'open'.

A 'without prejudice' offer can never be referred to by either party at any stage of the proceedings, because it is in the public interest that there should be a procedure whereby the parties can discuss their differences freely and frankly and make offers of settlement without fear of being embarrassed by these exchanges if, unhappily, they do not lead to a settlement.

A 'sealed offer' is the arbitral equivalent of making a payment into court in settlement of the litigation or of particular causes of action in that litigation. Neither the fact, nor the amount, of such a payment into court can be revealed to the judge trying the case until he has given judgment on all matters other than costs. As it is customary for an award to deal at one and the same time both with the parties' claims and with the question of costs, the existence of a sealed offer has to be brought to the attention of the arbitrator before he has reached a decision. However, it should remain sealed at that stage and it would be wholly improper for the arbitrator to look at it before he has reached a final decision on the matters in dispute other than as to costs, or to revise that decision in the light of the terms of the sealed offer when he sees them.

I know that there are arbitrators and umpires who feel that this procedure is not as satisfactory as making a payment into court. They take the view that respondents will feel that their defence is weakened if the arbitrator knows that they have made a sealed offer, even if the figure is concealed. If this is so, respondents may be deterred from making a 'sealed offer'.

There may be something in this point of view, but the solution to the problem is not, I think, difficult. If an arbitrator or umpire thinks it appropriate, he can always invite, and possibly require, the respondents to give him at the end of the hearing a sealed envelope which is to contain either a statement that no sealed offer has been made or the sealed offer itself. If this procedure were adopted, the existence of a sealed offer would be hidden from the tribunal until the moment at which it had to consider that part of the award which related to costs, the delivery of a sealed envelope of itself being devoid of all significance.

An 'open offer', properly so called, is one to which either party can refer at any stage of the proceedings. In an appropriate case, it may influence the arbitrator both in his decision on the matters in dispute and on the order as to costs.

The offer in the present case was a 'sealed offer' and was, I think, treated as such so far as the amount is concerned. It was thus intended to be analogous to a payment into court.

A payment into court can only be made in respect of the principal sum claimed and any *contractual* claim for interest. The reasons for this are purely technical, namely that under the Rules of the Supreme Court a payment into court can only be made in respect of a 'cause of action' and there is no 'cause of action' for interest under the Law Reform (Miscellaneous Provisions) Act 1934, as contrasted with contractual interest. If the payment into court is accepted, the claimant, however described (e g plaintiff, counterclaiming defendant, third party etc), will lose any entitlement to interest under the 1934 Act; see *Jefford v Gee*[1]. He will, however, be entitled to his costs up to the date of payment in. If he does not accept the offer, he will be entitled to recover

---

1 [1970] 1 All ER 1202, [1970] 2 QB 130

interest under the 1934 Act on whatever sum he does recover. But so far as costs are
concerned, the order will take account of whether, *ignoring interest*, he has recovered
more than had been paid into court. If he recovers more, he will usually be awarded
the whole party and party costs of his claim. If he recovers the same or less than has
been paid into court, he will recover his costs up to the date of payment into court,
but will have to pay any costs which the other party has incurred thereafter.

The position with regard to interest may not matter greatly in personal injury
actions for the reasons explained in the jugment of the Court of Appeal in *Jefford v
Gee*[1]. But in the context of a commercial action, where interest and capital are usually
both subject to tax and in particular where the action has extended over a long period
and the sums are large, the amount paid in may have little relation to the claimants'
entitlement. Suppose that the claim is for £100,000 and has been in existence for
four years before the payment in. Suppose also that the defendant pays £50,000 into
court. The plaintiff can take the money out or he can go on with the action. The choice
does not really depend on the merits of his claim. It depends, in part at least, on
how much interest he can expect to be awarded if he goes on to judgment and the
extent to which the costs will increase after the date of payment in. In the example
which I have given, the plaintiff on accepting the £50,000 in full satisfaction of his
claim will receive that sum with party and party costs. But he will receive no interest.
If he goes on with the action and recovers more than the £50,000 there is no problem.
He gets that increased sum plus interest plus all the party and party costs. But
suppose he recovers £45,000 plus interest. Interest on that sum at 10 per cent for
four years would amount to £18,000, giving a total recovery of £63,000 against the
£50,000 which he would have recovered if he had taken the money out of court.
Whilst he will be awarded the costs of the action up to the date of payment in, he will
probably have to pay the defendant's costs as from that date. Whether it would be
more profitable to take the £50,000 or to go on to judgment and obtain £63,000 must
be anyone's guess.

I do not regard this situation as satisfactory and I hope that the Supreme Court
Rule Committee will consider whether an amendment should not be made which
will enable a litigant to make a payment into court to cover interest as well as capital.

The position of a 'sealed offer' in arbitration has to be considered against the background of the law relating to payments into court, but it is not necessarily the same
because the Rules of the Supreme Court do not apply to arbitrations. I can see no
reason in principle or practice why a 'sealed offer' should not be expressed to relate
to interest under the 1934 Act as well as to principal. Indeed, I think it should, because, if it is accepted, the arbitrator will have no power to make an award of interest
by itself. This stems from the wording of the 1934 Act and its application by analogy
to arbitral awards.

How should an arbitrator deal with costs where there has been a 'sealed offer'?
I think that he should ask himself the question: 'Has the claimant achieved more by
rejecting the offer and going on with the arbitration than he would have achieved if
he had accepted the offer?' This is a simple question to answer, whether the offer
does or does not include interest. The arbitrator knows what the claimant would have
received if he had accepted the offer. He would have received that sum and could
not have asked the arbitrator to award any interest. The arbitrator knows what he
has in fact awarded to the claimant both by way of principal and interest. In order that
like should be compared with like, the interest element must be recalculated as if
the award had been made on the same date as the offer. Alternatively, interest for
the period between offer and award must notionally be added to the amount of the
sealed offer. But, subject to that, the question is easily answered.

If the claimant in the end has achieved no more than he would have achieved by
accepting the offer, the continuance of the arbitration after that date has been a waste

---

1 [1970] 1 All ER 1202, [1970] 2 QB 130

of time and money. Prima facie, the claimant should recover his costs up to the date of the offer and should be ordered to pay the respondent's costs after that date. If he has achieved more by going on, the respondent should pay the costs throughout.

Let me stress, however, that whilst this is the general rule, there is an overriding discretion. If, for example, the way in which the claimant conducted the arbitration in the period before the sealed offer was made is open to criticism, this may be a ground for depriving him of all or part of his costs or even, in a very extreme case, of requiring him to pay all or part of the costs of the respondent. Conversely, if after the sealed offer has been made and rejected, the conduct of the respondent is open to criticism, this may be a ground for depriving the respondent of all or part of the costs incurred by him in this period and might even, in a very extreme case, justify an order that he pay all or part of the claimant's costs.

I must now return to Mr Barclay's view of the offer in the present case. He says that he regarded it as—

'an offer of payment or part payment of the principal sum claimed in order to prevent further litigation and protect costs in respect of the respondents should the offer not be accepted and the award on the principal sum be less than offered.'

In other words, he was applying the same approach as the court would have applied to a payment into court and was ignoring all questions of interest.

Counsel for the claimants submits that this is wrong and, for the reasons which I have already given, I agree. However, in fairness to Mr Barclay, I should make it clear that I do not think that any judge has previously considered this matter or suggested that such an approach is wrong. Accordingly, I can well understand his adopting the attitude which he did. In any event, the addition of interest still does not bring the amount awarded to anything like the amount offered in settlement.

Counsel for the claimants' other criticism is more substantial. The offer in this case excluded the payment of interest or costs in addition. So the comparison is between US $6,000 to include interest and costs and US $2,710·94 plus interest for 3¼ years at 8½ per cent (2nd November 1972 to 3rd February 1976) plus costs to 3rd February 1976. But these costs calculated to a date in the middle of the arbitration are a completely unknown factor which the arbitrator is not in a position to assess, even with the evidence which I now have that the claimant's untaxed bill of costs would have amounted to £4,000. The arbitrator is therefore unable to make the vital comparison. On the only figures known to him, the arbitrator is being asked to compare like with unlike. An offer of a lump sum to include costs is not and should never be treated as the equivalent of a payment into court. If a party wishes to make a 'sealed offer' and to have it considered in the context of an order for costs, he must offer to settle the action for £X plus costs.

In the present case, Mr Barclay's award of costs in respect of the post-offer period can, however, be justified on the basis of the other two reasons on which he relies, namely that days 3 and 4 were devoted entirely to the issue of rectification on which the claimant succeeded, but that this did not increase the sum awarded to them. This same reasoning, coupled with the consideration that the claim for rectification could and should have been put forward before day 1, also justifies his award of costs for the whole period after the end of day 2.

This brings me to the costs of the arbitration up to and during days 1 and 2. Mr Barclay seeks to justify his award on the grounds that the respondents were proportionately more successful than the claimants. Here I think that he has misdirected himself. Account can certainly be taken of the amount recovered, but not in terms of exact percentages of the amount claimed. The questions which the arbitrator has to ask himself are: 'Was the claimant justified in bringing the claim at all?' and 'Was the claim so inflated as to deter the other party from seeking a settlement or in some way to increase the costs of the arbitration?' If the sum recovered was trifling and did not justify the proceedings, it may well be right not only to deprive the claimant of his costs, but to order him to pay the respondent's costs; see *Harris v Petherick*[1]. But this would be a wholly exceptional case and it certainly is not this case. If the claim was reasonably brought, but the inflated amount claimed may have unnecessarily prolonged the proceedings by, for example, deterring the respondent from making an offer of settlement, an order depriving the claimant of part or even all of his costs might be justified. But I doubt whether such a consideration would ever justify an order requiring him to pay all the respondent's costs.

In the present case it is clear that both claim and counterclaim were properly brought. So far as exaggeration is concerned, I doubt whether one can say more than that both parties were optimistic and that the claimants were rather more optimistic than the respondents. This does not justify the order which was made.

There remains only the matter of the costs of the award itself. These represent Mr Barclay's own remuneration for presiding at the arbitration over four days and for considering, preparing and publishing his award. It will also, directly or indirectly, cover any expenses which he incurred in connection with the reference. If his order that the claimants pay the respondents' costs of the reference had been correct, so almost certainly would have been his order that the claimants pay the costs of the award. But there is no reason why the costs of the award should not be divided between the parties in an appropriate case in whatever proportions the arbitrator thinks fit. If, for example, Mr Barclay had concluded that the claimants should be paid their costs up to and including day 2, but that they should have paid the respondents' costs thereafter, he might have wished to consider to what extent the costs of the award would have been less if the arbitration had ended after the end of day 2 and to have apportioned the costs of the award accordingly.

For the reasons which I have expressed, I think that in part Mr Barclay misdirected himself. This is in no way to his discredit and in due course I may well be told that I too have erred. Certainly it would not be for the first time. Accordingly, I shall remit the award to Mr Barclay in order that he may reconsider his order for costs.

It is not for me to tell Mr Barclay what new order he should make. It is his discretion and not mine which must determine this and, indeed, I have not the full materials on which to exercise a discretion. It may, however, help Mr Barclay if I say that the starting point is always the rule that costs follow the event. This at once gives rise to a difficulty when there is a claim and counterclaim, the one being set off against the other. On some occasions it is then appropriate to consider each separately and, for example, to give the claimants the costs of the claim and the respondents the costs of the counterclaim. This leaves it to the parties to agree, or to the taxing authority to determine, what proportion of the costs of each party is attributable to the claim and what to the counterclaim. On other occasions it may be clear to the judge or arbitrator that the claim and counterclaim have no independent existence, the counterclaim being really a defence to the claim or vice versa. In such a case it is usually inappropriate to make cross orders for costs. One or other or neither party should be awarded all or some proportion of the costs of both claim and counterclaim.

But I should like to stress that while the rule that costs should follow the event and a determination of what 'the event' is is the usual rule, it may only be the starting point. It is subject to modification or even to complete reversal if a party has conducted itself or the reference unreasonably. Thus, in the present case, it was and is open to Mr Barclay to conclude that the claim for rectification should have been brought forward at an earlier stage, if at all, that days 3 and 4 achieved nothing for either party, that these days were made necessary by the conduct of the claimants and that, in the circumstances, the claimants should pay the respondents' costs in respect of those two days and such proportion of the costs of the award as is attributable to those two days and a consideration of the issue of rectification.

---

1 (1879) 4 QBD 611

If the parties wish to make further submissions to Mr Barclay in the light of this judgment, no doubt he will allow them to do so. That will add further costs for the parties. Mr Barclay must take those costs into account but need not make a separate order with regard to them unless he thinks it right so to do.

The award will be remitted to Mr Barclay to reconsider his order for costs in the light of this judgment.

Judgment accordingly; award remitted to the arbitrator to reconsider his order for costs.

Solicitors: *Constant & Constant* (for the claimants); *Holman, Fenwick & Willan* (for the respondents).

K Mydeen Esq Barrister.

London Borough of Camden v Herwald

COURT OF APPEAL, CIVIL DIVISION
MEGAW, LAWTON AND BROWNE LJJ
21st, 22nd, 23rd FEBRUARY, 21st MARCH 1978

Rates – Rateable occupation – Non-occupation of part of premises – Liability for rates for whole premises – Description in valuation list – Need to show description includes on its face property which ratepayer does not occupy – Description of premises as 'workshop and store' – Premises consisting of three separate structures – House and two factories – Ratepayer occupying one factory and part of house – Whether ratepayer liable for rates for whole premises.

Court of Appeal – Jurisdiction – Appeal from Divisional Court – Distress for rates – Appeal against decision of Divisional Court on case stated relating to issue of warrant of distress for rates – Justices precluded from issuing warrant if of opinion failure to pay sum due not due to wilful default or culpable neglect – Appeal not lying to Court of Appeal in any criminal cause or matter except as provided by statute – Whether application for warrant a 'criminal cause or matter' – Whether Court of Appeal having jurisdiction to entertain appeal from Divisional Court – Supreme Court of Judicature (Consolidation) Act 1925, s 31(1)(a) – Administration of Justice Act 1960, s 1(1)(a) – General Rate Act 1967, s 103(1).

The appellant occupied parts of certain premises as a sub-tenant. The premises were shown in the valuation list as a single hereditament described as a 'workshop and store'. The premises consisted of three detached buildings, separated from each other by small yards. One building was a three storey house, the ground floor of which consisted of a shop and office; the other two buildings were small factories, one having two floors and the other only one floor. The appellant only occupied an office on the first floor of the house, with the use of a kitchen, and the single storey factory. The local authority laid a complaint before justices against the appellant for a summons for non-payment of the general rate in respect of the premises for the period from 1st October 1972 to 31st November 1975. The justices refused to authorise the issue of a distress warrant on the ground that, since the appellant had at all times occupied only certain parts of the premises, he was not liable for the rates for the whole premises. The Divisional Court[a] allowed an appeal by the local authority, holding that the part occupied by the appellant fulfilled the description in the valuation list and that non-occupation of even a substantial part did not prevent him from being liable for the rate in respect of the whole. Accordingly they remitted the case to the justices with a direction to authorise the issue of a distress warrant. On appeal it was suggested that the Court of Appeal had no jurisdiction to hear the appeal

---

because an appeal against a decision of the Divisional Court on a case stated relating
a to distress for rates was an appeal in a 'criminal cause or matter', within s 31(1)(a)^b
of the Supreme Court of Judicature (Consolidation) Act 1925 and s 1(1)(a)^c of the
Administration of Justice Act 1960.

Held – (i) The proceedings did not constitute a 'criminal cause or matter' having
regard to the fact that s 103(1)^d of the 1967 Act precluded the justices from issuing
b a warrant of distress if they were of opinion that the failure of a person to pay the
sum due was not due either to his wilful default or to his culpable neglect. Accordingly the Court of Appeal had jurisdiction to hear the appeal (see p 884 g to p 885 c,
post); *Southwark and Vauxhall Water Co v Hampton Urban District Council* [1899] 1 QB
273 applied; *Seaman v Burley* [1896] 2 QB 344 distinguished.

(ii) The appellant was not liable for any part of the rate claimed because the part
c of the premises occupied by him did not fulfil the description in the valuation list
of 'workshop and store' for, although the factory he occupied could fairly be described
as a 'workshop', he did not occupy anything which could be described as a 'store', and
further he did occupy the office in the house not covered by the description in the
list. Accordingly the justices had come to the right decision, albeit for the wrong
reason, in refusing to authorise issue of a distress warrant and the appeal would be
d allowed (see p 888 e to h, post); *Overseers of the Poor of Manchester v Headlam and the
London and North Western Railway Co* (1888) 21 QBD 96 applied; *Allchurch v Hendon
Union Assessment Committee* [1891-4] All ER Rep 184 explained.

Decision of the Divisional Court of the Queen's Bench Division [1976] 2 All ER 808
reversed.

e **Notes**
For the treatment for rating purposes of buildings occupied in parts, see 32 Halsbury's
Laws (3rd Edn) 32, 33, para 39.

For proceedings for the recovery of the rate, see ibid 176, 177, para 243, and for
cases on the subject, see 38 Digest (Repl) 751-757, 1694-1748.

For the Supreme Court of Judicature (Consolidation) Act 1925, s 31, see 7 Halsbury's
f Statutes (3rd Edn) 590.

For the Administration of Justice Act 1960, s 1, see 8 ibid 489.

For the General Rate Act 1967, s 103, see 27 ibid 194.

Cases referred to in judgment
Allchurch v Hendon Union Assessment Committee [1891] 2 QB 436, [1891-4] All ER Rep 184,
g   61 LJMC 27, 65 LT 450, 56 JP 117, CA, 38 Digest (Repl) 508, 213.
Bexley Congregational Church Treasurer v London Borough of Bexley [1972] 2 All ER 662,
   [1972] 2 QB 222, [1972] 2 WLR 1161, 136 JP 532, 70 LGR 398, CA, Digest (Cont Vol D)
   745, 95a.
China v Harrow Urban District Council [1953] 2 All ER 1296, [1954] 1 QB 178, [1953]
   3 WLR 885, 46 R & IT 750, 118 JP 41, 51 LGR 681, DC, 18 Digest (Reissue) 409, 1351.
h *Crease v Sawle* (1842) 2 QB 862, 2 Gal & Dav 812, 11 LJMC 62, 114 ER 334, Ex Ch, 38
   Digest (Repl) 559, 479.
Hampstead Borough Council v Associated Cinema Properties Ltd [1944] 1 All ER 436, 113
   LJKB 446, 170 LT 266, 108 JP 155, 42 LGR 175, sub nom *Associated Cinema Properties
   Ltd v Hampstead Borough Council* [1944] KB 412, CA, 38 Digest (Repl) 478, 18.

---

j b Section 31(1), so far as material, provides: 'No appeal shall lie—(a) except as provided
   by this Act, the Administration of Justice Act 1960 or the Criminal Appeal Act 1968, from
   any judgment of the High Court in any criminal cause or matter . . .'
c Section 1(1), so far as material, provides: '. . . an appeal shall lie to the House of Lords,
   at the instance of the defendant or the prosecutor,—(a) from any decision of a Divisional
   Court of the Queen's Bench Division in a criminal cause or matter . . .'
d Section 103(1) is set out at p 884 c d, post

Langford v Cole (1910) 102 LT 808, 74 JP 229, 8 LGR 771, Konst & W Rat App 192, DC, 38 Digest (Repl) 508, *214.*

McGreavy, Re, ex parte McGreavey v Benfleet Urban District Council [1950] 1 All ER 442, [1950] Ch 269, 114 JP 185, 48 LGR 247, CA, 4 Digest (Reissue) 125, *1091.*

Overseers of the Poor of Manchester v Headlam and the London and North Western Railway Co (1888) 21 QBD 96, sub nom *R v Headlam and London and North Western Railway Co* 57 LJMC 89, 52 JP 517, DC, 18 Digest (Reissue) 413, *1381.*

Seaman v Burley [1896] 2 QB 344, 65 LJMC 208, 75 LT 91, 60 JP 772, 45 WR 1, 18 Cox CC 403, CA, 18 Digest (Reissue) 430, *1517.*

Southwark and Vauxhall Water Co v Hampton Urban District Council [1899] 1 QB 273, 68 LJQB 207, 79 LT 512, 63 JP 100, CA; *affd* sub nom *Hampton Urban District Council v Southwark and Vauxhall Water Co* [1900] AC 3, 69 LJQB 72, 81 LT 547, 64 JP 260, HL, 18 Digest (Reissue) 430, *1519.*

Spiers & Pond Ltd v Finsbury Metropolitan Borough Council (1956) 1 RRC 219, 55 LGR 361, 49 R & IT 598, 38 Digest (Repl) 726, *1564.*

Vernon v Castle (1922) 127 LT 748, 86 JP 213, 20 LGR 580, 2 BRA 949, DC, 38 Digest (Repl) 493, *125.*

Westminister City Council v Southern Railway Co [1936] 2 All ER 322, [1936] AC 511, 105 LJKB 537, 34 LGR 313, 24 Ry & Can Tr Cas 189, sub nom *Re Southern Railway Co's Appeals* 155 LT 33, 100 JP 327, HL, 38 Digest (Repl) 634, *969.*

Cases also cited

Davis v Burrell and Lane (1851) 10 CB 821, 138 ER 325.

Derby Corpn v Derbyshire County Council [1897] AC 550, HL.

Edgcombe, Re, ex parte Edgcombe [1902] 2 KB 403, [1900-3] All ER Rep 862, CA.

London and North-Western Railway Co v Buckmaster (1875) LR 10 QB 70; *affd* LR 10 QB 444, Ex Ch.

R v Aberystwith (1808) 10 East 354.

R v Inhabitants of St Mary the Less, Durham (1791) 4 Term Rep 477.

R v London Justices [1899] 1 QB 532, DC.

Appeal

On 13th March 1975 a complaint was laid before the justices for the West Central petty sessional division of the Inner London area by the respondents, the London Borough of Camden, for a summons for non-payment of the general rate in respect of premises situated at 63 Loveridge Road, NW6 for the period 1st October 1974 to 31st March 1975 for the sum of £229·50, for the period 1st April 1974 to 30th September 1974 for the sum of £229·50, and for arrears from 1st October 1972 to 31st March 1974 for the sum of £560·30, and for 50p costs, being a total of £1,019·80.

The justices sitting as a magistrates' court at Hampstead heard the complaint on 1st May 1975. They were of the opinion that as the appellant, Theodore Herwald, had at all times occupied only certain parts of 63 Loveridge Road he was not liable for the rates for the whole premises and accordingly refused to authorise issue of a distress warrant. At the request of the respondents the justices stated a case for the opinion of the High Court. The question for the opinion of the court was whether it was correct that the appellant was liable only for rates in respect of that part of the property in which he had been found to be in sole occupation when that part of the property was contained in the valuation list only as part of a single hereditament. On 8th April 1976 the Divisional Court of the Queen's Bench Division[1] (Lord Widgery CJ, O'Connor and Robert Goff JJ) held that the justices had erred in law in holding that the appellant was not liable for the rates for the whole premises, and that the part occupied by the appellant did fulfil the description in the valuation list and that non-occupation of even a substantial part did not prevent him from being liable in respect of the whole. The appellant appealed to the Court of Appeal. When the

---

1   [1976] 2 All ER 808, [1977] 1 WLR 100

appeal came on for hearing the question arose as to the jurisdiction of the court to
a hear the appeal. The facts are set out in the judgment of Browne LJ.

Sir Peter Rawlinson QC and *Desmond Keane* for the appellant.
Guy Roots for the respondents.

Cur adv vult

b 21st March. **BROWNE LJ** read the following judgment of the court: This is an
appeal from a decision of the Divisional Court of the Queen's Bench Division given on
8th April 1976[1]. The Divisional Court allowed an appeal by way of case stated from a
decision of the Hampstead Magistrates' Court and refused leave to appeal, but leave
was given by this court on 28th March 1977.

The case relates to distress for rates. On 13th March 1975 the respondents laid a
complaint in the magistrates' court against the appellant for a summons for non-
c payment of the general rate in respect of premises at 63 Loveridge Road, London
NW6, for the period from 1st October 1972 to 31st March 1975 amounting to a total
of £1,019·80. On 1st May 1975 the magistrates heard the complaint and refused to
authorise issue of a distress warrant. The Divisional Court, having allowed the appeal,
remitted the case to the justices with a direction to authorise the issue of a distress
d warrant.

When the appeal came on in this court, the court raised the question whether we
had jurisdiction to hear it, in view of the decision of this court (consisting of Lord
Esher MR, Kay and A L Smith LJJ) in *Seaman v Burley*[2]. It was held in that case that
there was no appeal to this court from a decision of a Divisional Court on a case stated
by justices relating to the grant of a distress warrant to enforce a poor rate under a
local Act, because it was an appeal in a 'criminal cause or matter', within s 47 of the
e Supreme Court of Judicature Act 1873, inasmuch as the proceedings before the
magistrates might end in imprisonment (see now s 31(1)(a) of the Supreme Court of
Judicature (Consolidation) Act 1925 and s 1(1)(a) of the Administration of Justice Act
1960). Counsel for the appellant wished us to deal with the case; and counsel for the
respondents did not take any objection to our jurisdiction, and indeed advanced a
f helpful argument in support of it.

The statutory provisions as to distress for the general rate are now contained in
Part VI of the General Rate Act 1967:

'96.—(1) . . . if any person fails to pay any sum legally assessed on and due from
him in respect of a rate for seven days after it has been legally demanded of him,
the payment of that sum may, subject to and in accordance with the provisions
of this Part of this Act, be enforced by distress and sale of his goods and chattels
g under warrant issued by a magistrates' court; and, if there is insufficient distress,
he may be liable to imprisonment under the provisions of this Part of this Act
in that behalf . . .

97.—(1) The proceedings for the issue of a warrant of distress under this Part
of this Act may be instituted by making complaint before a justice of the peace
h and applying for a summons requiring the person named in the complaint to
appear before a magistrates' court to show why he has not paid the rate specified
in that complaint . . .

'98. The justices may state a case under the Magistrates' Courts Act 1952 when
called upon to issue a warrant of distress under this Part of this Act.

'99.—(1) A warrant of distress under this Part of this Act may be directed to the
j rating authority, to the constables of the police area in which the warrant is
issued and to such other persons, if any, as the magistrates' court issuing the
warrant may think fit, and the warrant shall authorise the persons to whom it is

---

1   [1976] 2 All ER 808, [1977] 1 WLR 100
2   [1896] 2 QB 344

directed to levy the amount which the person against whom the warrant is issued is liable to pay by distress and sale of his goods and chattels . . .

'102.—(1) If the person charged with the execution of a warrant of distress for levying a sum to which some other person has been rated makes a return to the magistrates' court that he could find no goods or chattels (or no sufficient goods or chattels) on which to levy the sums directed to be levied under the warrant on that other person's goods and chattels, a magistrates' court may, if it thinks fit, and subject to the provisions of section 103 of this Act, issue a warrant of commitment against that other person . . .

'(5) The order in the warrant of commitment shall be that the said person be imprisoned for a time therein specified but not exceeding three months, unless the sums mentioned in the warrant shall be sooner paid [and the subsection goes on to provide for a remission of the term of imprisonment proportionate to the amount of any later payment] . . .

'103.—(1) Section 102 of this Act shall have effect subject to and in accordance with the following provisions:—(a) on the application f ir the issue of a warrant for the commitment of any person, the magistrates' court shall make inquiry in his presence as to whether his failure to pay the sum to which he was rated and in respect of which the warrant of distress was issued was due either to his wilful refusal or to his culpable neglect; (b) if the magistrates' court is of opinion that the failure of the said person to pay the said sum was not due either to his wilful refusal or to his culpable neglect, it shall not issue the warrant.

'(2) Where on the application no warrant of commitment is issued, the magistrates' court may remit the payment of any sum to which the application relates, or of any part of that sum . . .'

Seaman v Burley[1] was decided on the provisions of a local Act relating to the parish of Paddington[2]. Section cxx of that Act contained provisions generally corresponding with those of Part VI of the 1967 Act, with one important exception: it contained no provision corresponding to s 103.

In Ryde on Rating[3] the authority of *Seaman v Burley*[1] in the present context is doubted. In two later cases this court has heard and decided appeals from the Divisional Court relating to distress for rates, though it does not appear that in either of them *Seaman v Burley*[1] was cited or any point taken as to jurisdiction (see *Hampstead Borough Council v Associated Cinema Properties Ltd*[4] and *Bexley Congregational Church Treasurer v London Borough of Bexley*[5]). In *Re McGreavy, ex parte McGreavey v Benfleet Urban District Council*[6] this court disagreed with what it regarded as an obiter dictum of Lord Esher MR in *Seaman's* case[1], and in *China v Harrow Urban District Council*[7] the Divisional Court (we think) impliedly distinguished *Seaman*[1], which was cited in argument. But we do not think we need refer further to those cases, because two years after *Seaman v Burley*[1] was decided it was distinguished by this court on a ground which in our judgment equally distinguishes it from the present case. In *Southwark and Vauxhall Water Co v Hampton Urban District Council*[8] it was held that an application to a court of summary jurisdiction for an order to enforce a general district rate under the Public Health Act 1875 was not a 'criminal cause or matter' and that an appeal lay to this court from a decision of the Divisional Court on a case stated. The leading judgment was given by A L Smith LJ, who had been a party to the decision in *Seaman v Burley*[1], and Rigby and Collins LJJ concurred. The ground on which *Seaman's* case[1] was distinguished was that in that case the Summary Jurisdiction Act 1879

1 [1896] 2 QB 344
2 5 Geo 4 c cxxvi (1824)
3 13th Edn (1976), p 878
4 [1944] 1 All ER 436, [1944] KB 412
5 [1972] 2 All ER 662, [1972] 2 QB 222
6 [1950] 1 All ER 442 at 447, [1950] Ch 269 at 279, 280
7 [1953] 2 All ER 1296, [1954] 1 QB 178
8 [1899] 1 QB 273

did not apply but in the *Southwark and Vauxhall Water Co* case[1] it did. The 1879 Act
contained provisions in s 35 the effect of which was in our view substantially the same
as the effect of the provisions of s 103(1) of the 1967 Act, and it was held that the proceedings were therefore not a 'criminal cause or matter'. The proceedings in the
present case are, therefore, in our view, equally not a 'criminal cause or matter'.
This distinction also avoids the startling conclusion that every judgment summons
in a county court under CCR Ord 25, r 33 and s 5 of the Debtors Act 1869 is a 'criminal
cause or matter'.

In our judgment, this court has jurisdiction to hear this appeal. We hope that our
decision will end the uncertainty referred to in Ryde[2].

We come, therefore, to the substance of the appeal. It is well established that an
application for a distress warrant to enforce payment of rates can only be resisted on
certain limited grounds. It is also well established that one of such grounds is that the
defendant is not in occupation of the hereditament in respect of which it is sought to
rate him. The question in this case is whether, and if so in what circumstances, it is
a defence for him to show that he is only in occupation of part of that hereditament.

The case stated, having found that the relevant rates were made, published and
demanded, finds the following facts. Paragraph 4:

> '(ii) That the valuation list shows 63 Loveridge Road as a single hereditament
> as a workshop and store. (iii) That Mr Stephenson, rates inspector, London
> Borough of Camden, visited 63 Loveridge Road on several occasions the first time
> being on 11th March 1974. (iv) That [the appellant] had been a sub-tenant of a
> Mr Jellineck from 1960 until six or seven years ago and then of a Miss Marcotics
> to whom he had paid a portion of the total rent and rates. (v) That during Miss
> Marcotics' lifetime he had occupied certain parts only of 63 Loveridge Road,
> namely an office on the first floor of the house, with use of the kitchen, and area
> marked "Factory A" (see attached rough sketch plan), and that subsequent to her
> death he continued to occupy the same parts of the premises as he had always
> occupied.'

The sketch plan attached to the case and the legend on it show that 63 Loveridge
Road comprises a house of three floors consisting of a shop and office on the ground
floor, four rooms on the first floor (including a kitchen) and four rooms on the second
floor; a one storey factory (factory A); a two storey factory (factory B); and two
yards separating the buildings. The case contains no findings about the use made by
the appellant of the parts which he occupies, nor as to the use or occupation (if any)
of the other parts. Counsel for the appellant emphasised that the effect of the findings
was that during the lifetime of Miss Marcotics the appellant only paid (to her) the
rates in respect of the parts he occupied, that after her death he continued to occupy
the 'same parts of the premises as he had always occupied', and that he was now
being called on by the rating authority to pay the rates on the whole.

The conclusion of the justices and their question to the court were as follows:

> 'We were of opinion that as [the appellant] had at all times occupied only
> certain parts of 63 Loveridge Road, he would not be liable for the rates for the
> whole premises and accordingly refused to authorise issue of a distress warrant.
> 'QUESTION The question for the opinion of the High Court is whether it is
> correct that [the appellant] is liable only for rates in respect of that part of the
> property in which he has been found to be in sole occupation when that part of
> the property is contained in the valuation list only as part of a single hereditament.'

In view of some criticisms of the respondents which were made or implied during
the argument and of the finding in para 4(iii) of the case stated, we think we should
emphasise the division of responsibilities in rating matters which is now embodied

1   [1899] 1 QB 273
2   Ryde on Rating (13th Edn, 1976), p 878

in the General Rate Act 1967. We think this division of responsibilities and procedures is also important in relation to the substance of this case. Counsel for the respondents gave us an interesting and helpful summary of the history of the development of rating procedure from the Poor Relief Act 1601 to the Lands Tribunal Act 1949. The scheme of the 1967 Act (re-enacting earlier legislation) is a division between responsibility for assessment or valuation and responsibility for collection. Valuation is the responsibility of valuation officers appointed by the Inland Revenue and collection is the responsibility of the rating authorities. The provisions as to valuation lists and the duties of valuation officers are contained in Part V of the 1967 Act. It is the duty of valuation officers to prepare a valuation list for each rating area (s 67(1)), and to insert in the list the prescribed particulars 'with respect to every hereditament in the rating area and the value thereof' (s 67(2)). By s 67(6) the valuation list is made 'conclusive evidence for the purposes of the levying of [the] rate of the value of the several hereditaments included in the list'. It is not made conclusive evidence of anything else, but it is obvious that before making a valuation of any hereditament the valuation officer must decide what the hereditament is which he is valuing. The identification of hereditaments is an essential part of the process of valuation and so within the province of the valuation officer (see the definition of 'hereditament' in s 115(1) of the 1967 Act). Section 69 and the following sections contain provisions for the alteration of the valuation list by means of proposals and for appeals to local valuation courts and to the Lands Tribunal if there are objections to a proposal. If the occupier of part of premises included in the list as a single hereditament thinks that his part should be shown as a separate hereditament, he can and should make a proposal for the alteration of the list under s 69(1)(a) or (c) or both. We were told that since the hearing in the Divisional Court this has been done, and that 63 Loveridge Road is now shown in the list as two hereditaments. When a proposal takes effect, its effect relates back to the beginning of the rating period in which it was made (s 79), but the rates claimed in this case are in respect of earlier periods. Collection of the rate is the responsibility of the rating authorities. They have nothing to do with assessment or valuation nor with the identification or definition of hereditaments. We think that this is emphasised by their duty under s 85(1), which is only to give information to the valuation officer. By s 2, rating authorities are under a mandatory duty to make and levy the general rate, and by s 2(4)(b) the general rate 'shall be made and levied in accordance with the valuation list in force for the time being . . .' So long as the entry in the valuation list remained unaltered, it was therefore the duty of the respondents to levy the rates in respect of 63 Loveridge Road in accordance with the list. The respondents as the rating authority had no power to split up the hereditament or apportion the rates. We agree with the Divisional Court[1] that the appellant's proper remedy was to make a proposal for the alteration of the list.

But this is not the end of the matter. The foundation of counsel for the appellant's argument was the incontrovertible proposition that liability to pay rates depends on the occupation of land (or certain other types of hereditament); a person is liable to be rated in respect of his occupation of land. He referred us to s 16 of the 1967 Act, to *Allchurch v Hendon Union Assessment Committee*[2] and to *Westminster City Council v Southern Railway Co*[3], especially per Lord Russell of Killowen. He submitted that (a) the appellant is not liable to be rated in respect of land of which he is not in occupation; (b) on the findings of fact he was not in occupation of part of this hereditament, (c) no rate can lawfully be levied in respect of the part of which he is not in occupation, (d) therefore, no distress warrant can lawfully be issued for rates which include rates on the part he does not occupy.

As we have said, there is no doubt that on an application for a distress warrant it is a defence for the defendant to show that he is not in occupation of the hereditament

---

1   [1976] 2 All ER 808 at 811, [1977] 1 WLR 100 at 104
2   [1891] 2 QB 436, [1891-4] All ER Rep 184
3   [1936] 2 All ER 322 at 326, [1936] AC 511 at 529

at all (see, for example, *Hampstead Borough Council v Associated Cinema Properties Ltd*[1]).
But where the defence is that the defendant is only in occupation of part of the hereditament the position is different. The rating authority relied on the decision of the Divisional Court in *Overseers of the Poor of Manchester v Headlam and the London and North Western Railway Co*[2], and the Divisional Court in the present case accepted their submission and directed the distress warrant to issue. If we may respectfully say so, we think that the effect of that decision was stated with complete accuracy in the judgment of Robert Goff J[3], with which Lord Widgery CJ and O'Connor J agreed:

'It is right that a person is only liable to be rated in respect of property of which he is the occupier: see s 16 of the General Rate Act 1967. But it does not follow that, merely because he can show that he does not in fact occupy part of premises in respect of which a rate has been made, a distress warrant should not be issued. To resist the issue of a warrant, he must show that the description of the rated property in the valuation list includes on its face property which he does not occupy. The principle was stated by this court in *Overseers of the Poor of Manchester v Headlam and London and North Western Railway Co*[4], in a passage which has since been frequently cited and applied: "... if one entire assessment be made in terms upon property which he does occupy, and upon other property which he does not occupy, so that upon the true state of facts being ascertained it is impossible to satisfy the description in the rate-book without including property which he does not occupy, the rate will be bad and ought not to be enforced". In that case, property occupied by the railway company had been assessed as "offices and land with rails", but in assessing the amount of the rate the overseers had included certain buildings which were not occupied by the company. It was held that, since the property in fact occupied by the company satisfied the description in the rate-book, the rate was good on the face of it and a distress warrant must be issued. The proper remedy of the company in such circumstances was to appeal against the assessment; not having appealed, they could not resist the issue of a warrant. By way of contrast, in *Langford v Cole*[5], where a single assessment of poor rate was made on property described in the rate-book as "mansion house and grounds" and it was established that the mansion house itself was unoccupied at the date when the rate was made, it was held that the rate made in respect of the whole property could not be enforced and that a distress warrant should not therefore be issued. The position is therefore as follows. If the person rated is in occupation of premises which fulfil the description in the valuation list, that is sufficient for the issue of a warrant; but if the description in the valuation list cannot be satisfied without including property which the person rated does not occupy, the rate cannot be enforced against him and a distress warrant should not be issued.'

Applying that test, the Divisional Court held that the part occupied by the appellant did fulfil the description in the valuation list and that non-occupation of even a substantial part did not prevent him from being liable for the rate in respect of the whole; accordingly, he could not resist the issue of a distress warrant.

Counsel for the appellant submitted (i) that we should overrule *Headlam*[6] and the later cases which have followed and applied it, (ii) alternatively, that *Headlam*[6] should not be rigidly applied to all cases but only to 'trivial matters', (iii) in the further alternative, that even if the principle of *Headlam*[6] should be applied, the Divisional

---

1 [1944] 1 All ER 436, [1944] KB 412
2 (1888) 21 QBD 96
3 [1976] 2 All ER 808 at 810, [1977] 1 WLR 100 at 102, 103
4 21 QBD 96 at 98
5 (1910) 102 LT 808
6 21 QBD 96

Court was wrong in holding that the part occupied by the appellant fulfilled the description in the valuation list.

As to (i), counsel submitted that the decision in Headlam[1] was inconsistent with the fundamental principle that liability to be rated depends on the occupation of land and with the decision of the Court of Appeal three years later in *Allchurch v Hendon Union Assessment Committee*[2]. Headlam[1] is not binding on us, and counsel for the respondents did not feel able to submit that the decision of the Exchequer Chamber in *Crease v Sawle*[3] was binding on us because of later changes in procedure. But Headlam[1] has stood for 90 years, and was followed and applied in at least the three later cases referred to in the judgment of the Divisional Court, in 1910[4], 1922[5] and 1956[6]; we should therefore be very slow to overrule it. But, in our judgment, it is not inconsistent with the general principle on which counsel for the appellant relies. We agree with counsel for the respondents that the question in this case relates to procedure and jurisdiction rather than to liability; so it did in Headlam[1], where the proper remedy would have been to appeal against the rate. *Allchurch v Hendon Union Assessment Committee*[2] is not, in our view, inconsistent with Headlam[1], because *Allchurch*[2] related to the assessment process (under the procedure then applicable) and not to the collection process; it was concerned with the process now governed by Part V of the 1967 Act. On an application for a distress warrant the magistrates have no jurisdiction to alter the valuation list or to apportion the rates on any such basis. It does not appear to have been suggested in any of the later cases in which Headlam[1] has been applied that there was anything in *Allchurch*[2] which threw any doubt on it. We therefore reject counsel for the appellant's first submission as to Headlam[1]. Nor can we see any reason to limit that decision to 'trivial matters'. No such suggestion seems to have been made in any of the later cases.

But we accept counsel for the appellant's third submission that, applying the principle of Headlam[1], these rates cannot be enforced against the appellant. The description in the valuation list at the relevant times was 'a workshop and store'. 'Factory A', which he occupies, can fairly be described as a 'workshop', but on the findings of fact he does not occupy anything which can be described as a 'store'. Further, he does occupy the office in the house, which is not covered by the description in the list. We doubt whether we are entitled to take into account the later alteration in the list, but it is interesting to note that we were told that 63 Loveridge Road is now entered as two hereditaments, the part occupied by the appellant described as 'Factory and Office' and the rest as 'Stores and premises—void'. We do not find any help in the case on which the Divisional Court relied, *Vernon v Castle*[5]; it seems to us that each case must depend on its own facts and on the construction of the particular entry in the list.

The appeal will therefore be allowed. The question stated in the case is not the right question; on our decision, the position is not that the appellant is liable only for rates in respect of the part of the property which he occupied, but that he is not liable for any part of the rates claimed. The actual decision of the magistrates in refusing to authorise issue of a distress warrant was, however, right.

Appeal allowed.

Solicitors: *Walford & Co* (for the appellant); *F Nickson* (for the respondents).

Mary Rose Plummer Barrister.

---

1   (1888) 21 QBD 96
2   [1891] 2 QB 436, [1891-4] All ER Rep 184
3   (1842) 2 QB 862, 114 ER 334
4   *Langford v Cole* (1910) 102 LT 808
5   *Vernon v Castle* (1922) 127 LT 748
6   *Spiers & Pond Ltd v Finsbury Metropolitan Borough Council* (1956) 1 RRC 219

Hanlon v Hanlon

COURT OF APPEAL, CIVIL DIVISION
STAMP, ORR AND ORMROD LJJ
14th, 17th OCTOBER 1977

Divorce – Financial provision – Matters to be considered by court when making order – Financial needs, obligations and responsibilities of parties – Transfer of matrimonial home – Home purchased in sole name of husband – Wife living in former home with children – Eldest children over 18, youngest child aged 12 – Wife a nurse contributing to family during marriage and having sole care of children since breakdown of marriage – Husband a police officer living alone in rent-free flat – Husband having no responsibilities for family apart from liability under order for periodical payments of £7 a week for two youngest children – Husband's financial position now and on retirement better than wife's – Whether home should be transferred to wife – Whether order postponing sale until youngest child attained 17 a proper order where parties had not remarried and wife and children living in home – Matrimonial Causes Act 1973, s 25.

The husband, who was a police officer, and the wife, who was a nurse, were married in 1957. They had four children, two sons, both of whom were over 18 years of age and in apprenticeships, and two daughters, who were aged 14 and 12 respectively. The matrimonial home, a house with three bedrooms and two living rooms, had been purchased in 1963, with a mortgage, in the sole name of the husband. The current value of the equity in it was £10,000. During the 14 years of the marriage the husband and wife had contributed equally in money and work to the family. The parties separated in 1971 and after two years' separation were divorced in May 1974. The wife and four children remained in the matrimonial home and from 1971 onwards the wife alone brought up the children and maintained the house. The husband was living alone in a police flat rent free. He was now aged 49. He was earning gross £4,200 per annum. He would receive a lump sum of £4,000 on retirement in 1980 and if he remained in the police force until 1985, as he was entitled to do, would receive a lump sum of £7,000. Moreover, as a police officer, he would be able to take up other employment after retirement. The wife who was 44 was earning gross £4,176 per annum. Each son contributed £7 a week towards her expenses of running the home. On her retirement in 1988 she would receive a lump sum of £3,000. In February 1976 the registrar, on the footing that the parties were beneficially entitled to the home in equal shares, ordered the husband to transfer his interest in the home to the wife on payment by her of half the value of the equity, i e £5,000. He also ordered the husband to pay £6 a week to each daughter. The wife was unable to raise the £5,000 and appealed against the order to a judge. The judge ordered that the home should be transferred into the joint names of the parties on trust for sale in equal shares and that the sale should be postponed until the youngest child attained the age of 17, which was in five years' time. He also increased the order for periodical payments to £7 a week for each daughter. The wife appealed.

Held – Where divorced parties had not remarried and the wife and children were living in the former matrimonial home the requirements of s 25 of the Matrimonial Causes Act 1973, which did not provide for equality but for a fair decision in the light of all the factors therein specified, were more likely to be met in a fair and just way if the home was transferred to the wife together with all the liabilities for its upkeep including the mortgage, and the husband was relieved so far as it was reasonable to do so from liability for periodical payments. An order postponing sale of the home until the youngest child had attained 17 would not, in many such cases, provide a satisfactory solution, for the family would not dissolve when the youngest child attained 17 and the reality was that the wife would have to maintain a home for the children for many more years, until they married and were settled in their own homes. Having regard to the parties' contributions to the family, their respective incomes, their liabilities now and in the future, the lump sum each would receive on retirement and their needs, it would be a wrong exercise of the court's discretion under s 25 to make an order which would force the wife to leave the home in the foreseeable future, and the proper order was to transfer the home to the wife absolutely and reduce to a nominal sum the order against the husband for periodical payments. Accordingly the appeal would be allowed (see p 893 j to p 894 f and p 895 b c and f g, post).

Wachtel v Wachtel [1973] 1 All ER 829 applied.

Notes

For financial provision and property adjustment orders on divorce and the matters to which the court must have regard, see 13 Halsbury's Laws (4th Edn) paras 1052, 1053, 1060.

For the Matrimonial Causes Act 1973, s 25, see 43 Halsbury's Statutes (3rd Edn) 567.

Cases referred to in judgments

Martin v Martin [1977] 3 All ER 762, [1977] 3 WLR 101, CA.
Mesher v Mesher [1973] Court of Appeal Transcript 59.
Wachtel v Wachtel [1973] 1 All ER 829, [1973] Fam 72, [1973] 2 WLR 366, CA, Digest (Cont Vol D) 425, 6962Aa.

Appeal

By an order dated 6th February 1976 Mr Registrar Kenworthy ordered that the wife, Mary Isabella Hanlon, should make a lump sum payment of £5,000 to the husband, Peter James Hanlon, within three months of the date of the order and that on such payment the husband should transfer the matrimonial home, 106 Trinity Lane, Waltham Cross, Hertfordshire, to the wife subject to the existing charge, and further ordered that the husband should make to the two daughters of the family, as from 6th February, periodical payments until they respectively attained the age of 17 years or further order at the rate of £6 a week for each child. The wife appealed and on 26th April 1977 Rees J set aside the registrar's order and ordered that the matrimonial home should be transferred forthwith into the joint names of the parties on trust for sale as tenants in common in equal shares and that the sale of the property should be postponed until the youngest surviving child of the family attained the age of 17 years or until the earlier remarriage of the wife or further order. He also increased the order for periodical payments to the two daughters to £7 per week for each child. The wife appealed. The facts are set out in the judgment of Ormrod LJ.

Nicholas Wall for the wife.
Robert Johnson for the husband.

ORMROD LJ delivered the first judgment at the invitation of Stamp LJ. This is an appeal from an order which was made by Rees J on 26th April 1977 in a case concerning the future of the matrimonial home. The litigation has had a long and rather sad history, which is not due to the fault of either of the parties.

The bare facts of the family are these. The parties were married on 2nd March 1957. The husband is a police officer, now aged 49; the wife is a community nurse now aged 44. They separated on 10th July 1971, and on 6th October 1971 there was an injunction excluding the husband from the matrimonial home which may have had long term effects on the emotional reactions of the parties or one of them about the former matrimonial home or not, one does not know.

The marriage was ultimately dissolved after two years' separation on 15th May

1974. The parties had lived at 106 Trinity Lane, Waltham Cross, which is an ordinary three-bedroomed/two-sitting room type of house. The marriage at the time when it broke up had lasted for 14 years. There are four children, all of whom are still living with the wife at 106, Trinity Lane. The family consists of two boys, now both over 18 and both in apprenticeship, a girl called Catherine who is 14 and a girl called Clare who is 12. The house itself was bought in 1963, in the sole name of the husband, for £4,200 with a mortgage of £3,900, the balance being found, we are told, from the husband's bank. The current value of the property is said to be about £14,000; the mortgage outstanding is £3,639, and for all practical purposes it has been treated in this litigation as having an equity value of roughly £10,000. There are at the moment arrears under the mortgage amounting to something slightly over £400; those arrears have arisen since the wife became responsible for making the mortgage repayments and she recognises, without any question, that the liability to pay those arrears is hers. The husband had been paying the mortgage instalments up to 1976.

The matter first came before the learned registrar in February 1976. That was a period when *Mesher v Mesher*[1] was being regarded as the 'bible' as far as this type of case is concerned. The consequence, as counsel for the wife has told us in the course of his submission, was that the wife's legal advisers took the view that the best she could hope for, on the facts of the case, was a *Mesher v Mesher*[1] type of order, namely that she should remain in occupation of the matrimonial home until the youngest of the children was 17, or 18 as the case may be, whereupon it would be sold and the proceeds divided equally between herself and her husband. At the time when they were before the learned registrar both sides recognised that that type of order produced a number of unfortunate and undesirable results, with which I shall deal in more detail later.

In the result, the learned registrar decided that the best way of dealing with the matter in the interests of both parties was, in effect, to order an immediate sale of the property, but recognising that this would have the effect of destroying the family home for the wife and her four children, he suggested, and eventually ordered, that the wife should buy the husband out, buying him out on the footing that their beneficial interests in the house were equal; that meant in practice that the wife had to raise £5,000 to buy out the husband's interest. This suggestion apparently was put forward at a comparatively late stage, and the wife's advisers had not had an opportunity of going into it in detail particularly as to whether the wife could finance such an arrangement.

After the registrar's order, investigations were made and it became at once apparent, as everyone agrees now, that she could not possibly finance it. The reasons for that were, and it was even more obvious then than it might have been today, that in order to raise the further £5,000 she would have to pay off the existing mortgage of £3,600, making a total of something over £8,000 that she would have to raise on terms which, of course, were more onerous relatively, pound for pound, than the old mortgage; and also she had to carry out repairs. There was a controversy about the cost of the repairs; she put it at some £900, but it may well be that that was an overstatement. The husband's advisers put it at about £200, but that was probably based on inadequate information. No finding as to the precise figure was made by the learned judge, or indeed could have been made; it is sufficient to say that the wife, in order to get any further mortgage on this property, would have to carry out the minimum repairs required by the building society, which presumably would have cost her something between those two figures. Taking into account her income position, it was apparent that she could not possibly finance any such mortgage, so it became impossible to comply with the registrar's order.

So the wife applied for leave to appeal against the order out of time. Faulks J rejected her application and refused her leave; she came to this court; this court gave her leave to appeal and the matter went back to Rees J and hence back again to this court.

The relative positions of the husband and wife who are, in effect, single adults now, and have been since 1971, is that the wife's income, gross, is £4,176. We have been supplied with most helpful calculations of her net income on various assumptions, and there is a plain and unquestioned discrepancy between her net income, however it is assessed, and her outgoings. Her outgoings at present unquestionably exceed her net income, allowing for the fact that the two boys make a contribution to her of about £7 per week each which, although very small, is not suggested could be substantially increased while they are in apprenticeship. So the wife is subsidising them at the present time. The order in respect of the two girls was £6 per week each which plainly involves a considerable amount of subsidising of their upkeep by the wife as well.

On the other side of the picture, the husband is living alone; he has a gross salary as a police officer of about £4,200, and he has at the moment the enormous advantage of living rent free in a police flat. He has no call on his income apart from keeping himself and making the payments for the children under the order. There was some evidence that he had paid for various other things for the children from time to time.

The argument that was put before the learned registrar by counsel for the husband was that it was essential that both the husband and the wife should, to use his own phrase, get on to the 'property escalator' as soon as possible, and that the best way of doing that was an order in the form made by the learned registrar, the idea being that with £5,000 each, they would each be able, if they wished to do so, to raise mortgages which, if inflation continued, would represent a steadily decreasing proportion of the inflated value of the house, or houses, which they were occupying or proposing to occupy. There was no clear evidence at all that the husband had any intention whatever of giving up his police flat so long as his employment in the police force continued.

The learned judge reviewed the whole matter in detail, and it is not now necessary for me to go through the case in anything approaching the same amount of detail. He was provided, just as this court was provided, with some very helpful calculations. In the end he accepted that it was impossible for the wife to buy the husband out. An offer, or a suggestion, was made on behalf of the wife during the course of argument before the learned judge that she could help to some extent. It was said that she might be able to raise a lesser figure of £2,500, provided that she had some further assistance from her former husband in maintaining the two girls. That suggestion did not find favour with the husband; he felt that £2,500 was not enough to be of any real value to him, and, moreover, £2,500 in cash in 1977 was much less attractive than a share in a piece of real property which was going to be realised at some later stage. In other words, by retaining his share in the property over a period of years he would be insulating himself better from inflation than by any other means available to him. So that solution failed.

In the end, and I think it is not unfair to say almost in depair of solving the problem, the learned judge reverted to what he called 'the normal order'. By 'the normal order' he meant a *Mesher v Mesher*[1] type of order, that is to say, the sale of the house to be postponed until the youngest child reached the age of 17 and the proceeds of sale divided equally. He had the case of *Martin v Martin*[2] in this court, and the judgment of Purchas J, cited to him, and no doubt he took account of it. There have been other cases in this court in which the court has drawn attention to the fact that *Mesher v Mesher*[1] was not, in any sense of the word, a typical case. So the judge, in despair, made the *Mesher v Mesher*[1] type of order.

It is agreed by both sides that the result of making such an order in this particular

1 [1973] Court of Appeal Transcript 59
2 [1977] 3 All ER 762, [1977] 3 WLR 101

case will really be almost disastrous. It is as well to look and see what the results would be. The youngest child is 12, so we are talking about a postponement of sale for five years. In five years' time each of these parties will, we assume, receive £5,000 plus such inflationary increase as takes place in those five years. The Law Society, under the present regime which was not in force at the time of the registrar's order, will have a charge on each of those sums of £5,000 for the costs incurred by the respective parties. It is common ground, having regard to the scale of costs in this case, that inevitably neither of them can possibly in fact receive a sum in excess of the maximum fixed by the regulations, namely £2,500. That is the amount which is at present exempt from the Law Society's charge.

So the result of the learned judge's order is that in five years' time each of them will get £2,500, increased by whatever the inflationary increase is by then. (One hopes that, if inflation is severe, sooner rather than later the exemption figure will be raised.) But dealing with it in 1977 prices, they will each get £2,500 only.

It is common ground that that figure is inadequate to provide either of them with a home. Obviously the wife cannot provide a home for herself on that sum, let alone for any children who are still at home in five years' time. It is said that the husband equally, on his income, cannot possibly raise enough money to buy himself a flat if he is minded to. So the effect of the order will be, in the short term, to make the wife and such of the children who are still with her, homeless in five years' time, that is in 1982, while the husband, assuming that he is still in the police force, will have a perfectly safe house or flat, until he chooses to leave the force or has to leave the force. That is a situation which one cannot contemplate as being satisfactory in any sense of the word at all, and so we have to look at the matter again.

In looking at the matter again there is one other factor to be brought into account; that is that when these parties reach their retiring ages they will each receive a lump sum. There is a very considerable disparity between the lump sums that each will get. The husband can retire at any time between 1980 and 1985. At the earliest retirement he will get a lump sum of just over £4,000 at present rates; if he stays on until 1985 he will receive a lump sum of just under £7,000. The wife, on the contrary, cannot retire until 1988 when she will get a lump sum of £3,000, which she can increase by another five years' work by the not very substantial sum of £600, giving her £3,600. So the husband, on retirement, will quite obviously be substantialy better off than the wife.

I think it is right to say once again that the *Mesher v Mesher*[1] type of order is not, in a great many cases, a satisfactory way of solving these cases. The facts in *Mesher v Mesher*[1] were very different; in that case both parties had in fact remarried before the case came before the court, and the primary concern in the case was to preserve the home for the children.

In my judgment it is as well in this case to have another look at the history. Up to now everybody has been approaching the case on the footing that the interests of these two parties in this property were equal. That seems to me to be a doubtfully accurate assumption, or premise. Putting them as shortly as I can, the facts are these. Over 14 years of cohabitation these two parties no doubt contributed broadly equally to this family in terms of money, in terms of work and so on. From 1971 onwards, that is now for over five years, the wife has had the upbringing of these four children and has been working full time as a community nurse. She has maintained the house as well as she could during those years, and on any view she has taken a considerable load off the shoulders of the husband over a period of five years, and she will continue to take a large load off his shoulders from now until the youngest child leaves home, which of course will not necessarily by any manner of means be in five years' time. A family like this will not simply dissolve completely on the 17th birthday of the

1   [1973] Court of Appeal Transcript 59

youngest child. In fact, of course, she will be, as the mother of this family, maintaining the nucleus of the home effectively for a considerable number of years until the girls are married and settled on their own, and the boys are similarly married and settled on their own; that is what it really means in real life. So in my view she has made a very large contribution to this family. She has much less good prospects than the husband's so far as her future is concerned, because he will be able to retire when he is 58 and, like many police officers, will be able to take other employment, certainly for another seven years or maybe longer if he wishes. He is a completely free agent so far as his life is concerned; he is living to all intents and purposes a bachelor existence, at the moment contributing £7 per week, under the judge's order, for each of these two children. As I have said before, on any view £7 a week for girls, one of 14 and one of 12, is manifestly inadequate to cover the cost of feeding and clothing and all the other expenses which are unavoidable.

So the view I take of the case is that, as the cards have fallen, apart no doubt from his being unhappy at being on his own, in financial terms he has done a lot better than his wife, and is likely to go on doing a lot better than his wife.

We have to do the best we can to carry out the injunctions which Parliament has put on us by s 25 of the Matrimonial Causes Act 1973. We have to take into account, and I shall for once recite some of them, income, earning capacity, and other financial resources which the parties to the marriage have, or are likely to have, in the foreseeable future. Correspondingly we have to take into account their financial needs, obligations and responsibilities, both now and in the future. We have to take account of the standard of living, age and physical and mental disability; none of those three very much matters. Then we have to take into account the contributions made by each of the parties to the welfare of the family, including any contribution made by looking after the home, or caring for the family; and at the end so to exercise those powers as to place the parties, so far as is practicable and, having regard to their conduct, just to do so, in the financial position in which they would have been if the marriage had not broken down and each had properly discharged his or her financial obligations or responsibilities to the other. 'Equality' is not to be found in that section, and for the reasons I have tried to outline briefly in this judgment, it is a very elusive concept.

The only other comment I would make about the background is that so far from this being contrary to anything that was said by this court in *Wachtel v Wachtel*[1] the court, as appears clearly from the judgment of Lord Denning MR, contemplated that in a situation like this one of the ways of solving the problem would be to transfer the home to the wife and to relieve the husband, so far as it was possible or reasonable to do so, of the responsibility for making periodical payments. Of course, the court was not laying it down as law, or as a rule of practice or anything of the kind; it was set out there as one of the possible solutions, and one of the possible ways of meeting the requirements of s 25 in this type of case, and in my judgment it is very much more likely to produce in many cases a fair and just result than the *Mesher v Mesher*[2] type of order which, as Stamp LJ has many times said, was never intended to meet the kind of situation that we are now dealing with.

In those circumstances, the case for transferring this property to the wife, together with all the liabilities for its upkeep and for the mortgage, seems to me to be extremely strong.

She has also appealed against the order for periodical payments, which at the moment are £7 a week, which she has asked should be increased. We have not heard counsel for the husband about that aspect of the appeal; I say no more about it except to repeat that at £7 a week she is making a sizeable contribution to the upkeep of these children. If she is prepared to forego any further periodical payments for

---

1   [1973] 1 All ER 829 at 841, [1973] Fam 72 at 96
2   [1973] Court of Appeal Transcript 59

the two children (she cannot of course bind herself not to make application for main-
a tenance and she cannot bind the children, but she can indicate that it is not her
intention in certain circumstances to seek contribution from the husband at the rate
of £7 per week over the period of five years) he will save a substantial sum of money.
It is not profitable to try to work out a precise figure because one has to allow for tax
and so on, but it is a four figure sum at least; I think it is a sum well above the bare
£1,000. So that is some contribution to him and it should be of some assistance.
b If any other type of order were made, which involves postponing the sale of the house,
it is plain that she will be contributing all the time to the upkeep of the house, and
paying off substantial amounts of the loan. In my judgment it would be a quite
wrong exercise of the discretion in accordance with the principles of s 25 to make
any order which had the result of forcing her to leave that property in the foreseeable
future. It was suggested that this might be the kind of case which could be met by
c postponing the sale indefinitely until further order, and then distributing the proceeds of sale, not necessarily on a 50-50 basis; but I do not think that that, in
this case, would be in the least satisfactory; it would leave the wife in a state of perpetual uncertainty and neither party would know where ultimately they were going
to be. It seems to me far better that the parties' interests should be crystallised
now, once and for all, so that the wife can know what she is going to do about the
d property and the husband can make up his mind about what he is going to do about
rehousing.

I would only add this, that if this property is to be sold in accordance with the judge's
order the result would probably have been to put the responsibility of housing the
wife on the local authority in subsidised accommodation. If counsel for the husband's
gloomy prognosis of the husband's future turns out to be right, he too would be
e joining the queue for council accommodation when his right to occupy the police
flat comes to an end. Each of them would then have £2,500 in cash which would not
be required for their housing. In my judgment that is not a fair or satisfactory result.

So in my view the fair way of dealing with this case, taking into account contributions, income, liabilities now and in the future and lump sums in the future and
needs particularly, is to transfer this house to the wife absolutely and to reduce the
f order for periodical payments for the children to a nominal sum; if there are arrears
they can be remitted; I do not know whether there are any.

I would therefore allow the appeal and substitute that order.

ORR LJ. I agree.

STAMP LJ. I also agree.

Appeal allowed. Leave to appeal to the House of Lords refused.

Solicitors: *Smith & Harrison*, Waltham Cross (for the wife); *W H Hopkins & Co*
(for the husband).

A S Virdi Esq   Barrister.

Newhart Developments Ltd v Co-operative Commercial Bank Ltd

COURT OF APPEAL, CIVIL DIVISION
STEPHENSON AND SHAW LJJ
16th NOVEMBER 1977

Company – Receiver – Appointment by debenture holder – Appointment as agent of company – Effect – Effect on company's power to bring action – Debenture empowering receiver to bring action in name of company – Company commencing action against debenture holder for breach of contract – Action commenced without receiver's consent – Action not prejudicing position of debenture holder – Debenture holder applying to have writ in action set aside on ground of irregularity in failing to obtain receiver's consent – Whether company required to obtain receiver's consent to bring action – Whether action interfering with receiver's function of getting in company's assets.

The plaintiffs, a company engaged in property development, agreed with the defendants, a bank, whereby the defendants were to provide the finance for the plaintiffs' property development. The defendants wished to provide means of satisfying any claims they might have against the plaintiffs, and on 25th January 1973 the plaintiffs issued a mortgage debenture in favour of the defendants charging the plaintiffs' undertaking and property as security for all money due or becoming due from them to the defendants. Clause 2 of the debenture entitled the plaintiffs to get in their debts in the ordinary course of business. Clause 5 provided for the appointment of a receiver of the plaintiffs' property at any time after the money secured by the debenture had become payable, that the receiver should be deemed to be the plaintiffs' agent and that he should be empowered to take proceedings in the plaintiffs' name for the purpose of collecting and getting in property charged by the debenture and to carry on or concur in carrying on the plaintiffs' business. In October 1973 the parties entered into a formal agreement whereby a development company was formed, the shares being held equally by the plaintiffs and the defendants. By April 1974 the agreement was not progressing favourably, and the plaintiffs owed the defendants a substantial sum of money. In the spring of 1974 the defendants refused to provide the plaintiffs with any further finance and required them to transfer their holding in the development company to the defendants. On 23rd September the defendants, in accordance with the terms of the debenture, appointed a receiver of the plaintiffs' undertaking and property. On 7th December 1976 the plaintiffs' without seeking the consent or concurrence of the receiver who was still in possession of their property on behalf of the defendants, issued a writ against the defendants claiming damages for breach of the contract made in October 1973 by reason of the withdrawal of financial support. On 11th March 1977 the defendants applied to have the writ set aside on the ground of irregularity in that it was issued without the receiver's knowledge or consent. The registrar dismissed the application. The defendants appealed to a judge who allowed the appeal and ordered the writ to be set aside on the ground of irregularity. The plaintiffs appealed. The defendants contended that on the appointment of the receiver the plaintiffs were divested of all power to bring an action and only the receiver could institute and pursue the action in question.

Held – A provision in a debenture empowering the receiver to bring an action in the name of the company whose assets were charged was merely an enabling provision, investing the receiver with the capacity to bring such an action, and did not divest the company's directors of their power to institute proceedings on behalf of the

company, provided that the proceedings did not interfere with the receiver's function
of getting in the company's assets or prejudicially affect the debenture holder by imperilling the assets. Furthermore, the directors were under a duty to bring an action
which was in the company's interest because it was for the benefit of creditors generally, and to pursue that right of action did not amount to dealing with the company's
assets so as to require the receiver's consent or concurrence. Since the plaintiffs' action
would not stultify the receiver's function of gathering in the assets, the plaintiffs were
not required to obtain his consent to bring the action, and the appeal would therefore
be allowed (see p 900 *d* to *j*, p 901 *g* to *j* and p 902 *b* to p 903 *a*, post).

Note
For the effect of the appointment of a receiver by a debenture holder, see 7 Halsbury's
Laws (4th Edn) para 880, and for cases on the subject, see 10 Digest (Reissue) 875, 876,
5068-5070.

Cases referred to in judgments
Moss Steamship Co Ltd v Whinney [1912] AC 254, [1911-13] All ER Rep 344, 81 LJKB 674,
    105 LT 305, 12 Asp MLC 25, 16 Com Cas 247, HL, 39 Digest (Repl) 57, 683.
Wheeler (M) & Co Ltd v Warren [1928] Ch 840, 97 LJCh 486, 139 LT 543, CA, 10 Digest
    (Reissue) 887, 5144.

Interlocutory appeal
By a writ dated 7th December 1976 the plaintiffs, Newhart Developments Ltd,
brought an action against the defendants, Co-operative Commercial Bank Ltd,
claiming damages for breach of a contract dated 16th October 1973 for the development of property by the plaintiffs and the provision of finance for the development
by the defendants, by reason of the defendants' refusal to provide any further finance
for the development. By a summons dated 11th March 1977 the defendants applied
to have the writ set aside on the ground of irregularity in that it was issued without
the knowledge or consent of the receiver appointed under a debenture charging the
plaintiffs' assets as security for sums due to the defendants. On 15th July Mr District
Registrar Burnie dismissed the application. The defendants appealed and on 5th
October Chapman J sitting in chambers allowed the appeal and ordered that the writ
be set aside on the ground of irregularity. The plaintiffs appealed. The facts are set out
in the judgment of Shaw LJ.

David Stembridge for the plaintiffs.
Oliver Wilkinson for the defendants.

SHAW LJ delivered the first judgment at the invitation of Stephenson LJ. This is
an appeal by the plaintiffs in the action from an order of Chapman J made on 5th
October 1977 whereby he directed that the writ in the action be set aside, thereby
reversing the order of the learned registrar.

The history is an unusual one. It has provided scope for argument on aspects of the
law relating to receivers which are somewhat obscure. The plaintiffs are property
developers. As long ago as October 1973 they entered into an agreement with the
defendants, bankers, setting up an arrangement whereby the plaintiffs would find
properties for development, in particular in North Wales. They were to deal with all
the matters relating to the actual development of the site, and the entire finance was
to be provided by the defendants or an associated bank. For that purpose, a company
called Newhart Development (North Wales) Ltd ('the development company') was
set up, the shares in that company were held in equal numbers by the plaintiffs and
the defendants, and the project which the arrangement envisaged was set in train.
But by April 1974 matters had not progressed as favourably as the defendants had

hoped and they refused any further finance. At that time there was a very substantial sum owed by the plaintiffs to the defendants and there also was a substantial sum, *a* though a much lesser one, owed by Mr Hartley, who was in the forefront of the management of the plaintiffs, on his personal overdraft.

In that unfortunate state of affairs, in the spring of 1974 the defendants delivered an ultimatum. They said that all the shares in the development company must be held by them and that accordingly Mr Hartley, and his associates, must transfer the holding of their company in that regard to the defendants. Mr Hartley had little *b* option but to comply. This was done and, for the time being, the development of the site was halted, although it appears that later the defendants turned to other development organisations in order to pursue the project in relation to the land in North Wales.

On 23rd September 1974, a receiver was appointed by the bank under the terms of a debenture which was dated 25th January 1973, the defendants prudently *c* contemplating at that date the possibility that things might not go as well as they hoped, and wishing to provide for some means of satisfying their claims against the plaintiffs if the necessity should arise. The debenture was in common form. It provided by cl 2 that:

> 'THE Company as Beneficial Owner hereby charges as a continuing security *d* for the payment of such sums its undertaking and its property whatsoever and wheresoever both present and future [and it went on to say] such charge shall [and then it deals with the fixed assets of the company, and in cl (c) provides:] As regards the Company's other assets be a floating security but so that the Company shall not create any mortgage or charge in priority to or *pari passu* with the charge hereby created nor sell the undertaking of the Company or (except in the ordinary course of business) any portion thereof nor deal with its book or other debts or securities for money otherwise than by getting in and realising the same in the ordinary course of business.'

The only other provision which needs to be looked at is contained in cl 5, which provides that:

> 'AT any time after the principal monies hereby secured become payable the registered holder . . . of this Debenture may appoint . . . any person or persons to be a Receiver or Receivers of the property hereby charged. A Receiver or Receivers so appointed shall be deemed to be the agent or agents of the Company and the Company shall be solely responsible for his . . . acts or defaults and for his . . . remuneration and such Receiver so appointed shall have power (a) To *f* take possession of collect and get in the property charged by this Debenture and for that purpose to take any proceedings in the name of the Company or otherwise. (b) To carry on or concur in carrying on the business of the Company . . . (d) To make any arrangement or compromise which such Receiver or Receivers shall think expedient in the interests of the registered holder [of this debenture].'

By 2nd December 1976 it had appeared to the plaintiffs that the defendants, in taking the course they did of withdrawing financial support and requiring the holding of the plaintiffs in the development company to be transferred to the defendants, had been in breach of their contract, and that as a result of that breach of contract the plaintiffs had lost the opportunity of getting their half share of the contemplated profit which they hoped would derive from the development of the site in North Wales. That sum has been quantified at something approaching £½ million. On 2nd December 1976 they wrote to the defendants intimating their claim. The letter was not answered, and accordingly the plaintiffs issued a writ on 7th December 1976 by which they claim 'damages for breach of contract in writing dated the 16th October 1973

and made between the Plaintiffs and Defendants'. They set out their averments as
to the nature of the agreement and then they claim the estimated profit of the
development as something which was expected to amount to £920,000, and their
share, representing their loss, is said to be £460,000.

The writ was issued without seeking the consent, or the concurrence, of the receiver
who was still in possession on behalf of the debenture holders. The riposte was that
in March 1977 the defendants issued proceedings against Mr Hartley, both in respect
of his personal liability under his own overdraft and also in respect of his liability as
guarantor of what the plaintiffs owed to the bank. That claim amounted to something approaching £400,000, though we were told that it had been much reduced as
a result of the activities of the receiver in bringing in the plaintiffs' assets and realising
them for the benefit of the debenture holders.

The writ having been issued on 7th December 1976, an appearance was originally
entered. Then there was an application to set aside the appearance, to enter a conditional appearance and set aside the writ. On 11th March 1977 a summons to set
aside the writ was issued. The defendants asked that—

'. . . the Writ of Summons in this action be set aside on the ground of irregularity in that it was issued without the knowledge or consent of the Receiver of the
Plaintiff company's assets who is alone entitled to the proceeds of this action and
to give a valid discharge for any claim by the Plaintiff Company.'

It may be observed that the logic of the summons, as drafted, appears to be a little
uncertain because the complaint is that the writ was issued 'without the knowledge
or consent of the Receiver' and it defines him as being a person 'who is alone entitled
to the proceeds of this action'. It is a little difficult to see why that second assertion
arising out of the status of the receiver is in any way impinged on by the fact that the
action has been instituted. It seems to me that, on the contrary, it is setting up a
situation which will provide an opportunity for the receiver in due course, if the
action should be successful, of claiming the proceeds of the action so far as it may be
necessary to discharge the claims of the debenture holders. However, that summons
having been taken out, on 15th July the learned registrar dismissed the application
to set aside the writ. It was from that order that there was an appeal to the learned
judge and his judgment, of which we have been provided with a note agreed between
counsel on both sides, and reads in this form. 'This is an unusual situation, and let
me say at once, as I have already indicated, nothing can be said in criticism of that
assertion, and he goes on to say 'but straightforward'. There, with great respect to
learned judge, I would venture to demur. He says:

'The plaintiffs issued their debenture in favour of the Co-operative Bank
Ltd who have a wholly owned subsidiary, the Co-operative Commercial
Bank Ltd, the defendants. No distinction has been drawn between the two,
and it was accepted by both sides for all practical purposes that they were one and
the same. The [defendants] pursuant to the debenture, appointed a receiver of
the plaintiffs on 23rd September 1974. The receiver has been acting ever since.
[Then he goes on to say how the plaintiffs had issued a writ in 1976 and says:]
This action was brought without any consultation with the receiver who had
stated in his affidavit that he would not have given his consent even if asked. An
application to strike out the action was refused by the registrar. The matter
turns basically on the powers and duties of the receiver under the terms of the
debenture. Clause 5 gives him power. It is inherent in that power that the
plaintiffs cannot bring an action without his consent. [He says that counsel for
the plaintiffs relies on cl 2(c) and continues:] When one considers the very wide
powers of the receiver, it would totally militate against the exercise of those
powers by undermining his position by bringing an action against the company
who appoint him receiver. Any action by the plaintiffs which would stultify or

frustrate the receiver's activities must be contrary to the terms of debenture. It is curious that there is no authority. [He makes reference to *Wheeler & Co Ltd v Warren*[1], and says:] Any action which would interfere with the receiver must be something which should not be allowed. Therefore I allow this appeal.'

The learned judge was, I would respectfully suggest, stating a truism when he said: 'Any action which would interfere with the receiver must be something which should not be allowed' if by that he meant that any action which would interfere with the proper discharge of the receiver's function in gathering in the assets of the plaintiffs, so far as they were available, in order to put him in the position to discharge the claims of his appointor; but if one is to take what the learned judge said in a wider literal sense, namely that any action which would interfere with the receiver must be something which should not be allowed I would, for myself, suggest that is putting the position too widely. One has got to see what the function of the receiver is. It is not, of course, to wind up the company. It is perhaps interesting to note in passing that when a liquidator is appointed, certainly in a winding-up by the court, the powers of the directors immediately cease by statutory provision. There is no such provision in relation to the appointment of a receiver, whose duty it is to protect the interests of the mortgagee or debenture holders, as the case may be. Insofar as it is requisite and necessary for him, in the course of his dealing with the assets of the company, bringing them in and realising them and so on, to bring actions as well, he is empowered to do so by the debenture trust deed in the name of the company. That makes it possible for him to institute such proceedings without exposing himself to the risk of a liability for costs if those proceedings should fail. But the provision in the debenture trust deed giving him that power is an enabling provision which invests him with the capacity to bring an action in the name of the company. It does not divest the directors of the company of their power, as the governing body of the company, of instituting proceedings in a situation where so doing does not in any way impinge prejudicially on the position of the debenture holders by threatening or imperilling the assets which are subject to the charge.

There is in the debenture deed itself a provision to the effect that the receiver may carry on the business of the plaintiffs or concur in carrying on its business, which itself demonstrates that there is not a total extinction of the function of the directors. It is only within the scope of its assets which are covered by the debenture, and only insofar as it is necessary to apply those assets in the best possible way in the interests of the debenture holders that the receiver has a real function. If in the exercise of his discretion he chooses to ignore some asset such as a right of action, or decides that it would be unprofitable from the point of view of the debenture holders to pursue it, there is nothing in any authority which has been cited to us which suggests that it is not then open to the directors of the company to pursue that right of action if they think it would be in the interests of the company. Indeed, in my view, it would be incumbent on them to do so, because, notwithstanding that the debenture holders have got the right to be satisfied out of the assets subject to the charge, other creditors are entitled to expect that those concerned with the management of the company should exercise their best efforts to ensure that, when the time comes, they too will find themselves in the position that there is a fund available to pay them, if not in full, at least something of what they are owed.

The receiver is entitled to ignore the claims of anybody outside the debenture holders. Not so the company; not so, therefore, the directors of the company. If there is an asset which appears to be of value, although the directors cannot deal with it in the sense of disposing of it, they are under a duty to exploit it so as to bring it to a realisation which may be fruitful for all concerned. If such an action as was started in this case comes to trial and there is a judgment in favour of the plaintiffs then, if the

---

1 [1928] Ch 840

debenture holders are still not fully satisfied the receiver can take steps to attach the
a proceeds of the judgment for the benefit of the debenture holders.

In this particular case it does so happen that the receiver finds himself in a very
curious and unenviable position because the action is directed against the very people
who appointed him as receiver for the debenture holders. One can quite understand
that a receiver so appointed, and let me say at once that the receiver appointed in
this case is a member of a very distinguished firm of accountants, would find himself
b faced with a very great conflict of interest. Counsel for the defendants has urged that
the only result of the receiver pursuing this action through himself and giving his
consent, if that were necessary, would be that money would be taken out of one pocket
of the debenture holders and put into another pocket. Counsel for the defendants
overlooked that, in that process, the debt which the plaintiffs owed to the defendants
would have been completely discharged, and the whole situation would have been
c radically changed. No doubt the receiver may think that the claim is an empty one and
not worth pursuing, and if the result of pursuing it might be that the plaintiffs would be
faced with a liability for costs, or would have to finance the action to the detriment of
the debenture holders, the receiver could properly take steps to prevent such an outcome arising.   But there is no such danger.   There is no prejudice or detriment
whatever to the debenture holders qua debenture holders inasmuch as the corpus of
d assets available to satisfy them is not going to be diminished or affected in any way
at all.

Counsel for the defendants has urged on the court that the effect of the appointment
of a receiver is as set out in Kerr on Receivers[1]. Under the heading 'Effect of Appointment' it says:

e   'The effect of the appointment out of court is as regards the crystallisation of
      the floating charge into a fixed charge and the consequences as regards judgment
      creditors the same as in the case of an appointment by the court. The powers
      of the company and its directors to deal with the property comprised in the
      appointment (both property subject to a floating charge and property subject
      to a fixed charge), except subject to the charge, are paralysed; for though under
f   debentures or a trust deed in the usual form the receiver is agent for the company,
      the company's powers are delegated to the receiver so far as regards carrying
      on the business or collecting the assets; and frequently so as to enable the receiver
      as attorney to convey a legal estate on sale.'

If that means that nobody else can take any step in regard to the assets of the
g company which does not amount to dealing with, or disposing of, the assets, it would
appear to me to be too wide and not supported by any authority which has been
cited to us. What, of course, the directors cannot do, and to this extent their powers
are inhibited, is to dispose of the assets within the debenture charge without the assent
or concurrence of the receiver, for it is his function to deal with the assets in the first
place so as to provide the means of paying off the debenture holders' claims. But
h where there is a right of action which the board (though not the receiver) would wish
to pursue, it does not seem to me that the rights or function of the receiver are affected
if the company is indemnified against any liability for costs (as here). I see no principle
of law or expediency which precludes the directors of a company, as a duly constituted
board (and it is not suggested here that they were not a duly constituted board when
they took the step of instituting this action) from seeking to enforce the claim, however
j ill-founded it may be, provided only, of course, that nothing in the course of the
proceedings which they institute is going in any way to threaten the interests of the
debenture holders.

---

1   14th Edn (1972), p 301

In the present case I can see no possibility of such a result, nor indeed can counsel for the defendants suggest any except in the most remote terms. How on earth can **a** the debenture holders qua debenture holders be affected adversely if this action is allowed to go on, inasmuch as the company is not called on to finance it out of its own resources and will not have to meet any claim for costs if the action fails? If more were needed, Mr Hartley has provided along with others, an indemnity for the plaintiffs against any possible liability to costs.

But those matters are not really material at this time because it is not suggested **b** that there is going to be any detriment to the plaintiffs. Counsel for the defendants rests his case on the bald proposition that only the receiver can institute this action and pursue it, that the directors have been denuded of all their powers in that regard, and it is on that basis that he says the learned judge was right in setting aside the writ and extinguishing the action. In my view, that was wrong. The learned judge had no material before him, and there has been none put before us, which justified his **c** statement that an action by the plaintiffs would stultify the receiver's activities and therefore must be contrary to the terms of the debenture. There can be no such stultification. It is merely because the defendants in the action are also the debenture holders that a rather unusual situation emerges. That does not alter the general principle of law. Accordingly, I would strike out the order by the learned judge, allow this appeal and reinstate the writ and the action. **d**

STEPHENSON LJ. I agree. It is, I think, inherent in the power given to the receiver by cl 5 of the mortgage debenture that he can bring actions, although I would not like to decide without argument whether that power includes the power to bring actions against the debenture holder who appointed him, and that he can **e** compromise such actions. But I respectfully disagree with Chapman J's opinion that it is also inherent in that power that the plaintiffs cannot themselves bring an action without the receiver's consent, or that by bringing this action against the defendants who appointed him, the plaintiffs are undermining his position and totally militating against the exercise of the very wide powers conferred on him on his appointment under cl 5. The powers conferred on him under cll 5 and 6 are, indeed, wide and no **f** doubt limit, or suspend, or paralyse, many of the powers of the plaintiffs and their directors.

Counsel for the plaintiffs has conceded (1) that those powers are the powers which Lord Atkinson enumerated in *Moss Steamship Co v Whinney*[1], as those of which a company is deprived by the appointment by the court of a receiver and manager over its assets, and (2) that this right of action is, and I quote, 'property whatsoever and **g** wheresoever both present and future' embraced by the wide words of cl 2 of the debenture.

Counsel for the defendants, on the other hand, has not disputed that the plaintiffs would be getting in their debts in the ordinary course of business within cl 2(c) of the debenture by bringing this action.

In attempting to get in this debt from the defendants, the plaintiffs are not, in my **h** judgment, interfering with any power conferred on the receiver, and are not bound to seek or obtain his concurrence before they can carry on with the attempt. To seek it would put the receiver in what Shaw LJ has justly called an unenviable position. I am thankful that the view I take of the case prevents me from holding that he has to be put into that position and has to weigh the conflicting interests of the debenture holders, who appointed him, and of the company, whose agent he is expressly made, **j** in continuing or compromising this suit. In my judgment the plaintiffs can go ahead without him.

1　[1912] AC 254 at 263, [1911-13] All ER Rep 344 at 348

a I agree, I think entirely for the reasons given by Shaw LJ, that this appeal should be allowed and the order of the learned judge set aside.

Appeal allowed.

Solicitors: *Price, Atkins*, Birmingham (for the plaintiffs); *W A Shawdon*, Manchester (for the defendants).

b

. L I Zysman Esq Barrister.

c

Re H (a minor) (wardship: jurisdiction)

COURT OF APPEAL, CIVIL DIVISION
STAMP, ORR AND ORMROD LJJ
d 10th, 11th, 28th OCTOBER 1977

Ward of court – Jurisdiction – Inherent jurisdiction – Circumstances in which exercisable – Factors to be considered – Juvenile court making care order committing child to care of local authority – Parents wishing to return to their own country with child – Application by parents for child to be made ward of court – Whether High Court should assume jurisdiction.

e

Ward of court – Jurisdiction – Inherent jurisdiction – Circumstances in which exercisable – Discretion – Juvenile court making care order committing child to care of local authority – Application by parents for child to be made ward of court – Application opposed by local authority on merits – Objection to jurisdiction taken by local authority after conclusion of evidence – Whether objection taken too late.

f

The parents, who were foreigners living in England, had three daughters. A juvenile court made a care order, under ss 1 and 20 of the Children and Young Persons Act 1969, in respect of one of them ('the child') committing her to the care of a local authority. She was then aged 2½. The parents wanted to return to their own country and to take her, as well as their two other daughters, with them. They applied to the g High Court for an order (i) that she be made a ward of court, (ii) that care and control of her be given to them and (iii) that she be permitted to leave the jurisdiction for the purpose of returning to the parents' own country to live there permanently. The local authority opposed the making of such an order on the ground that it had good reason for believing that the child had in the past been seriously injured by one the parents. After the judge had heard all the evidence, the local authority submitted h that he should not in the circumstances assume jurisdiction because of the existence of the care order. The judge decided that he should adjudicate on the merits of the dispute between the parents and the local authority notwithstanding the existence of the care order. He found that the child had been seriously injured by one of her parents but, after weighing the risk of further physical injury to her against the risk of severe permanent psychological injury if she did not leave the country with j her family, he decided that it would be in her best interests if the parents were permitted to take her back with them to their own country. He made an order under s 7 of the Family Law Reform Act 1969 that she should remain in the care of the local authority unless and until the parents made arrangements to return to their own country when she should be returned to their care. The local authority appealed against the order contending, inter alia, that the judge should never have assumed

jurisdiction because all decisions as to the welfare of the child had, by virtue of the
care order, been entrusted to the discretion of the local authority.   *a*

Held – The appeal would be dismissed for the following reasons—
(i) The parents were not seeking to influence the local authority's discretionary
power in a sphere entrusted to it by statute: they were challenging the source of that
power by seeking an order which would supersede the care order and permit them to
remove the child altogether from the control of the local authority. In such a case the   *b*
High Court should exercise its wardship jurisdiction where the circumstances were
sufficiently unusual to justify its intervention (e g where the powers of the juvenile
court were inadequate to protect the interests of the child or where the interests
of the child, which were the paramount consideration, could be better furthered by
the exercise of the wider powers given to the High Court). The circumstances were
sufficiently unusual to justify the exercise of the court's wardship jurisdiction because   *c*
on the evidence the interests of the child could be better served by the more flexible
to have the writ set aside on the ground of irregularity in that it was issued without
type of care order which the High Court could make under s 7 of the 1969 Act (see
p 909 *c* to *g*, post); Re M (*an infant*) [1961] 1 All ER 788 and Re T (*A J J*) (*an infant*)
[1970] 2 All ER 865 distinguished.
(ii) In such cases a judge should not accede to an objection to jurisdiction made   *d*
after the conclusion of all the evidence because such a course would have the
undesirable result of a multiplicity of proceedings involving recalling all the evidence
in the juvenile court (see p 910 *g* and *h*, post).
(iii) Once a judge had assumed wardship jurisdiction and decided on the merits
of the case, the Court of Appeal could hardly allow an appeal on the basis that he had
exercised his discretion wrongly, because the juvenile court and the Crown Court   *e*
would be placed in an impossibly embarrassing position if either of those courts was
inclined to differ from the views of the judge (see p 910 *h* and *j*, post).
(iv) There were no grounds for interfering with the judge's decision on the merits
of the case (see p 911 *a* and *e*, post).

Notes
For wardship jurisdiction, see 21 Halsbury's Laws (3rd Edn) 216, 217, paras 478, 479,   *f*
and for cases on the subject, see 28(2) Digest (Reissue) 911-916, 2220-2247.
For care orders and discharge of care orders, see Supplement to 21 Halsbury's Laws
(3rd Edn) para 554c.
For the rights of the father and mother to custody, see 21 Halsbury's Laws (3rd Edn)
191-197, paras 425-432, and for cases on the subject, see 28(2) Digest (Reissue) 794-813,
1183-1290.   *g*
For the Family Law Reform Act 1969, s 7, see 17 Halsbury's Statutes (3rd Edn) 797.
For the Children and Young Persons Act 1969, ss 1, 20, see 40 ibid 849, 877.

Cases referred to in judgment
Andrews (*infants*), Re [1958] 2 All ER 308, [1958] Ch 665, [1958] 2 WLR 946, 28(2) Digest
(Reissue) 914, 2240.   *h*
Andrews v Andrews and Sullivan [1958] 2 All ER 305, [1958] P 217, [1958] 2 WLR 942,
28(2) Digest (Reissue) 920, 2294.
B (*a minor*) (*wardship: child in care*), Re [1974] 3 All ER 915, [1975] Fam 36, [1975] 2
WLR 302, 139 JP 87, 72 LGR 691, Digest (Cont Vol D) 529, 2239a.
Baker (*infants*), Re [1961] 3 All ER 276, 125 JP 591, sub nom Re B [1962] Ch 201, [1961] 3
WLR 694, 59 LGR 475, CA, 28(2) Digest (Reissue) 912, 2232.   *j*
D (*a minor*) (*justices' decision: review*), Re [1977] 3 All ER 481, [1977] Fam 158, [1977] 2
WLR 1006.
D (*minors*) (*wardship: jurisdiction*), Re [1973] 2 All ER 993, [1973] Fam 179, [1973] 3
WLR 53, Digest (Cont Vol D) 521, 1290a.
J v C [1969] 1 All ER 788, [1970] AC 668, [1969] 2 WLR 540, HL, 28(2) Digest (Reissue)
800, 1230.

L (minors) (wardship: jurisdiction), Re [1974] 1 All ER 913, [1974] 1 WLR 250, CA, Digest
a   (Cont Vol D) 520, *1237a*.

L (A C) (an infant), Re [1971] 3 All ER 743, 136 JP 19, Digest (Cont Vol D) 530, *2441a*.

M (an infant), Re [1961] 1 All ER 788, [1961] Ch 328, [1961] 2 WLR 350, 125 JP 278, 59
LGR 146, CA, 28(2) Digest (Reissue) 940, *2433*.

Official Solicitor v K [1963] 3 All ER 191, [1965] AC 201, [1963] 3 WLR 408, HL, 28(2)
Digest (Reissue) 912, *2233*.

b   *P (infants), Re* [1967] 2 All ER 229, [1967] 1 WLR 818, 65 LGR 572, 28(2) Digest (Reissue)
915, *2246*.

R (K) (an infant), Re [1963] 3 All ER 337, [1964] Ch 455, [1963] 3 WLR 991, 128 JP 7, 62
LGR 103, 28(2) Digest (Reissue) 941, *2434*.

S (an infant), Re [1965] 1 All ER 865, [1965] 1 WLR 483, 129 JP 228, 63 LGR 229, CA,
28(2) Digest (Reissue) 942, *2439*.

c   *T (A J J) (an infant), Re* [1970] 2 All ER 865, [1970] Ch 688, [1970] 3 WLR 315, 134 JP 611,
CA, 28(2) Digest (Reissue) 913, *2239*.

Vigon v Vigon and Kuttner [1929] P 157, [1928] All ER Rep 755, 98 LJP 63, 140 LT 407,
27 LGR 147; *on appeal* [1929] P 245, 99 LJP 9, 141 LT 293, 93 JP 112 n, CA, 27(2) Digest
(Reissue) 903, *7246*.

d **Appeal**

On 23rd August 1976 a juvenile court made a care order, under ss 1 and 20 of the
Children and Young Persons Act 1969, committing a child, aged 2½ years, to the care
of a local authority. The child's parents applied to the Family Division of the High
Court for an order (i) that the child be made a ward of court, (ii) that the care and
control of the child be committed to the parents and (iii) that the child might be
e permitted to leave the jurisdiction for the purpose of returning to the parents' own
country to live there permenantly in the care of the parents. The local authority
opposed the application. On 4th July 1977 Balcombe J made an order, whereby it
was ordered that the child should remain a ward of court during her minority or
until further order, that the child should remain in the care and control of the local
authority, that the care and control of the child should be transferred from the local
f authority to the parents when the local authority were satisfied that the parents were
ready to leave for their own country and that leave should be granted for the child
to be removed from England and Wales for the purpose only of returning permanently to the parents' country and that in that event the child should cease to be a
ward of court. The local authority appealed against that order. The facts are set out
in the judgment of the court.

g

John Waite QC and *Elizabeth Appleby* for the local authority.
Peter de Mille for the parents.

Cur adv vult

h

28th October. **ORMROD LJ** read the following judgment of the court: This is an
appeal by a local authority from an order made on 4th July 1977 by Balcombe J in
wardship proceedings. The respondents, who were the applicants in the court
below, are the parents of a little girl now aged 3½ years, in respect of whom a care
order was made in favour of the local authority by a juvenile court on 23rd August 1976
j under ss 1 and 20 of the Children and Young Persons Act 1969. To preserve anony-
mity it is undesirable to mention names or places. The parents desire to have the
child returned to their care so that they may go back with her and their two other
children to their native country. The local authority oppose this course because the
evidence suggest that the child has been seriously injured in the past by one of the
parents.

The learned judge had to resolve a very difficult question of law and, assuming
that it was open to him to go into them, an even more anxious and difficult question *a*
on the merits. It will be necessary to refer in more detail to the facts of the case at
a later stage of this judgment. It is sufficient at this stage to say that the learned judge
decided that non-accidental injury was proved but that in the peculiar circumstances
of the case the parents should be permitted to take the child back to their home
country.

The case is the latest of a series which have come before the courts in recent years *b*
in which it has been necessary to define the limits beyond which the High Court will
not go in the exercise of the wardship jurisdiction. The primary issue in this appeal is
whether Balcombe J was right in his decision to adjudicate on the merits of the dispute
between the parents and the local authority, notwithstanding the existence of the
care order. It is plain from his judgment, and from counsel's careful and sensitive
argument on behalf of the local authority, that in the existing state of the law it is *c*
difficult to know where the limits lie.

The problem, which is a relatively new one, arises from the co-existence of different,
partially co-ordinated, codes of procedure for dealing with the welfare of children.
The wardship jurisdiction of the High Court is by far the oldest and the widest of these,
both in its scope and in the range of remedies and powers at its disposal. Whatever
its historical origins, it is firmly embedded in our law and its value is generally *d*
recognised. But, until recently, it was highly centralised in London, and its procedure
was both more expensive and inconvenient than the alternative procedures. Its
availability to litigants was therefore comparatively restricted. However, in a series
of enactments Parliament has progressively removed most of the restrictions. The
procedure was simplified by the Law Reform (Miscellaneous Provisions) Act 1949
and the problem of expense overcome to some extent by the Legal Aid and Advice *e*
Act 1949. The Family Law Reform Act 1969 extended the powers of the High Court
in two important respects. Section 6 enabled the court to order periodical payments
for the maintenance of the ward, and s 7 empowered the court to commit a ward to
the care of a local authority. The Courts Act 1971 has completed the process. By
transferring wardship cases from the Chancery Division to the Family Division, the
availability of this procedure has been extended to all the district registries through- *f*
out the country which handle the work of the Family Division. High Court judges
and deputy High Court judges can now hear wardship cases in all the main centres.

In contrast, the other codes of procedure, under the Guardianship of Infants Acts,
the Summary Jurisdiction Acts and the successive Childrens Acts, were developed on
a mainly local basis, depending on local courts and local authorities, but with variously
restricted powers. The potential for conflict of jurisdiction between the various *g*
courts is obviously high and likely to increase, so long as the different procedures
remain unco-ordinated. The High Court must, therefore, exercise its wardship
jurisdiction with great circumspection. The problem is how to circumscribe it.

The first principle is clear. It has been held repeatedly that this ancient jurisdiction
can only be removed or curtailed by express statutory enactment, and there is no
such relevant enactment: *Re M (an infant)*[1] and *Re Baker (infants)*[2]. The question there- *h*
fore in each case is whether in Pearson LJ's words in *Re Baker*[3] 'the scope of the proper
exercise of the jurisdiction' has been restricted. He went on to say:

> 'In the absence of special circumstances, the court ought not to exercise its
> powers of control in a sphere of activity which has been entrusted by statute to a
> local authority.'

The same point has been made, although the language in which it is expressed has

---

1   [1961] 1 All ER 788, [1961] Ch 328
2   [1961] 3 All ER 276, [1962] Ch 201
3   [1961] 3 All ER 276 at 286, [1962] Ch 201 at 223

varied, in many of the subsequent cases. The difficulty with such phrases as 'special
a circumstances' or 'special reasons' is that they quickly come to be treated as terms
of art and stereotyped. So, in subsequent cases the argument tends to concentrate on
whether the circumstances of the instant case can be brought within the stereotype,
notwithstanding that, when originally used, these phrases were intended to indicate,
not a particular kind of departure from the norm but that the extent or degree of
departure was sufficient, or insufficient as the case may be, to justify the exercise of
b the wardship jurisdiction. The precise phrases used in the authorities are not, therefore, very helpful. It is better to try to discern the principles underlying the cases.
These differ to some extent, depending on the character of the conflict.

In cases of conflict arising between the High Court and a foreign tribunal the
principle is now clear. The court will be guided by one consideration only, namely
the welfare of the child: *Re L (minors)*[1]. This decision of the Court of Appeal follows
c directly from the principles laid down by the House of Lords in *J v C*[2] which finally
established that s 1 of the Guardianship of Infants Act 1925 is to be given full and
unqualified effect, namely that in any proceedings before any court in which the
custody, upbringing etc of an infant is in issue, the welfare of the infant is to be regarded as the paramount consideration. In an earlier case, *Official Solicitor v K*[3], it was
said that this principle applied to procedural matters as well as to substantive issues.

d Where the conflict arose in the past between the jurisdiction of the Chancery
Division in wardship proceedings and of the Divorce Division in divorce proceedings,
it was resolved on the basis of forum conveniens. Generally speaking, the court which
was first seised of the matter retained it unless there was some advantage to the child
in continuing the wardship, notwithstanding an order in the Divorce Division. Some
form of relief, for example, might be given more effectually in the Chancery Division,
e or some relevant change of circumstances might have occurred: *Andrews v Andrews
and Sullivan*[4] and *Re Andrews (infants)*[5].

In potential conflicts between the High Court and lower courts, the High Court will
not permit the wardship procedure to be used simply as a form of appeal from the
lower court, and will not accept jurisdiction unless there are special or good and
convincing reasons for doing so. This is based on the concept of comity and on the
f desirability of preventing multiplicity of proceedings: *Re P (infants)*[6] per Stamp J
and *Re D (minors) (wardship: jurisdiction)*[7] per Bagnall J. In both these cases there had
been procedural muddles or irregularities in the lower court, and in the latter the
mother, having been refused legal aid to appeal to the Divisional Court of the Family
Division had, for some unexplained reason, obtained legal aid to take wardship
proceedings. In both cases the High Court decided to exercise jurisdiction. Both
g these decisions could also be justified on the principles of *Re L (minors)*[1], that the
welfare of the child called for the intervention of the High Court under its wardship
jurisdiction for some special, in the sense of unusual, reason, something, in other
words, going beyond the argument that the decision of the lower court was wrong.
In the matrimonial jurisdiction it has been the practice for many years for the High
Court, as a matter of course, to assume jurisdiction over children who are subject
h to orders made in magistrates' courts, unless the parties prefer to retain the
magistrates' order: *Vigon v Vigon and Kuttner*[8].

The third group of cases is those arising under the Childrens Acts, i e the Children
Act 1948 and the Children and Young Persons Act 1969, and involving the rights,

---

1   [1974] 1 All ER 913, [1974] 1 WLR 250
j 2   [1969] 1 All ER 788, [1970] AC 668
3   [1963] 3 All ER 191, [1965] AC 201
4   [1958] 2 All ER 305, [1958] P 217
5   [1958] 2 All ER 308, [1958] Ch 665
6   [1967] 2 All ER 229, [1967] 1 WLR 818
7   [1973] 2 All ER 993, [1973] Fam 179
8   [1929] P 157, [1928] All ER Rep 755

duties and powers of local authorities in relation to children. As the authorities stand, this group must be divided into two classes, depending on the nature of the legal *a* relationship of the local authority to the child. Under the Children Act 1948, s 1, the local authority is under a duty, in defined circumstances, to take a child into its care. At that stage it acquires no special status in relation to the child and must return the child to one or other or both parents if requested by them to do so. The wardship jurisdiction is unaffected, and can be exercised in the normal way in relation to such a child: *Re R (K) (an infant)*[1] and *Re S (an infant)*[2]. But, if the local authority proceeds *b* further and passes a resolution assuming parental rights over the child under s 2, a different situation arises. It now has the legal right to control the child and his future, subject to a right in the parents to apply to the juvenile court to set aside or rescind the resolution: Children Act 1948, s 4, as amended by the Children Act 1975, Sch 3, para 5(*a*). An analogous situation arises under the Children and Young Persons Act 1969 where the local authority has applied to, and obtained from, the juvenile court *c* what is now called a 'care order' and, formerly under the Children and Young Persons Act 1933, a 'fit person' order. In these situations the exercise by the High Court of its powers in wardship proceedings has been severely restricted by decisions of this court, which are binding: *Re M (an infant)*[3] and *Re T (A J J) (an infant)*[4].

Balcombe J distinguished the present case on its facts from these two cases and held, for that reason, that they were not binding on him. In our judgment he was right to *d* do so, although the distinction may appear at first sight to be a slim one. It is therefore necessary to examine these two cases in some detail.

Both cases involved foster parents with whom the child had been fostered by the local authority under their statutory powers: in *Re M (an infant)*[3] under the 1948 Act and in *Re T (A J J) (an infant)*[4] under the 1933 Act. In both cases the local authority had required the foster parents to return the child to its control with a view to *e* restoring the child to the parents. In both, the foster parents refused on the ground that in their view it was contrary to the best interests of the child, and made the child a ward of court with the intention of asking for care and control under the wardship jurisdiction and so retaining the child in their care.

In *Re M (an infant)*[3] the Court of Appeal held that where a local authority has passed a resolution assuming parental rights over a child the exercise of the local *f* authority's statutory powers in relation to the child cannot be challenged in wardship proceedings because Parliament has entrusted all decisions as to the welfare of the child to the discretion of the local authority. The court can only interfere if the local authority has acted improperly or unlawfully, that is, in accordance with the principles on which the court will review the exercise of ministerial or administrative discretions generally: see, by way of example, *Re L (A C) (an infant)*[5]. Where the local authority *g* are acting under a fit person order or a care order the same reasoning necessarily applies because the local authority's statutory powers are similar: *Re T (A J J) (an infant)*[4].

Two observations may be made about these decisions. In both cases the applicants were foster-parents, but the effect has been to leave the natural parents without any means of challenging a local authority's decision, for example, to place the child with *h* foster-parents a long way away from the parents' home so that visiting is difficult or impossible, or to deny all access to the child by one or both parents, or to refuse to disclose to the parents where the child is living. This result necessarily follows because, although there is a right of appeal to the juvenile court against the resolution in the one case or to apply to discharge the care order in the other, the juvenile

j

1　[1963] 3 All ER 337, [1964] Ch 455
2　[1965] 1 All ER 865, [1965] 1 WLR 483
3　[1961] 1 All ER 788, [1961] Ch 328
4　[1970] 2 All ER 865, [1970] Ch 688
5　[1971] 3 All ER 743

a court has no power to interfere with the exercise of the local authority's discretionary powers. It is not clear whether the court in either case had this consequence in mind.

The second also applies to both decisions. No reference appears to have been made in argument in either case to s 1 of the Guardianship of Infants Act 1925, and no mention of the welfare of the child as the paramount consideration is made in the judgments. *Re M (an infant)*[1] was of course decided some years before *J v C*[2] and at a time when the significance of this section was perhaps not fully appreciated.

b Probably, however, it would not have affected the court's conclusion, because Lord Evershed MR said[3]:

> '... I feel compelled, by the clear indication of the language to which I have alluded in the statute to conclude that this matter of judging the present best interests of the child in the circumstances of this case has been placed by Parliament in the exclusive jurisdiction of the local authority.'

c

These observations are not intended to cast doubt on the binding effect of these decisions on this court at the present time, but they are sufficient to discourage an extension of the reasoning to cases like the present where the challenge is directed, not to the exercise of a discretionary power, but to the source of that power. In this case the parents are not seeking to influence the local authority's discretion, but to

d remove the child altogether from the control of the local authority, in other words, to supersede the care order of 23rd August 1976 by a new order in the wardship proceedings.

This case is therefore analogous to those in which orders have been made by lower courts under the Guardianship of Infants Acts or the Matrimonial Proceedings (Magistrates) Act 1960, and should be decided on the same principles. The dominant

e consideration is the welfare of this particular child, but it must be shown that the circumstances are sufficiently unusual to justify the intervention of the High Court. One of the most important considerations is whether the powers of the juvenile court are adequate to protect the interests of the child or whether the wider powers of the High Court are necessary, e g to grant injunctions restraining the parents or others from acting in some particular manner, or to make mandatory orders of various

f kinds. Another is whether the interests of the child would be better served by the more flexible type of care order which the High Court can now make under the Family Law Reform Act 1969, s 7. Another relates to procedural matters such as facilities for trial and the rules governing appeals. In complex cases involving a large body of evidence or conflicting views of experts, the High Court may be a more suitable venue. On the other hand, in cases of child abuse the wealth of experience which

g busy juvenile courts have acquired in the handling of such cases may be an important factor.

The Children Act 1975 introduced a change in the appellate procedure which has important repercussions on the 'scope of the proper exercise of the jurisdiction' of the High Court. Under the Children Act 1948 an appeal lay from the refusal of a juvenile court to rescind a s 2 resolution to quarter sessions, now the Crown Court.

h Under the Children and Young Persons Act 1969 the child who is the subject of a care order alone has a right of appeal, again to the Crown Court (s 21(4)). The 1975 Act amended the 1948 Act to provide a right of appeal by the parents and the local authority to the Family Division of the High Court: ss 55 and 108 and Sch 3, para 5. This is an important step in the removal of procedural anomalies and virtually eliminates the possibility of conflict in the 1948 Act cases. A judge of the Family

j Division hearing such an appeal, if he thinks it desirable in the interests of the child,

---

1   [1961] 1 All ER 788, [1961] Ch 328
2   [1969] 1 All ER 788, [1970] AC 668
3   [1961] 1 All ER 788 at 793, [1961] Ch 328 at 342

can assume the powers of the wardship procedure by simply giving one party leave to
issue a formal summons under the Law Reform (Miscellaneous Provisions) Act 1949.   *a*

No corresponding amendment has yet been made to the 1969 Act, probably
because care orders are used for two quite different classes of cases, one involving
unruly, sometimes criminal, behaviour by the child or young person, the other neglect
or ill-treatment of the child by parents or others. There is, however, no logical
reason to differentiate between care orders intended for the protection of a child
against parents and s 2 orders under the 1948 Act; moreover, the restricted rights of   *b*
appeal under the 1969 Act produce undesirable anomalies. The parents have no
right of appeal in their own right, although they can act on behalf of the child (whose
interests may be in direct conflict with their own). Moreover, the local authority
has no right of appeal at all, and there is no way in which the case can reach the
Family Division.

In the present case counsel for the parents made the forceful point that if his clients   *c*
had followed the procedure of the 1969 Act and had succeeded in getting the care
order discharged there was nothing to prevent the local authority itself instituting
wardship proceedings. This is right, since there would then be no order and no
conflict of jurisdiction.

The effect of the 1975 Act, therefore, must be to diminish the strength of the
objections to the wardship jurisdiction in child abuse cases involving care orders.   *d*
Lane J in *Re B (a minor)*[1] has drawn attention to its positive advantages from the point
of view of local authorities; and Dunn J in *Re D (a minor) (wardship: jurisdiction)*[2]
assumed jurisdiction on an application by a local authority. The learned judge in the
present case relied to some extent on the decision in *Re D*[2], in which it was said that
the juvenile court was not required to observe the terms of s 1 of the Guardianship
of Minors Act 1971 (as the 1925 Act had then become) under which the welfare of the   *e*
child is the paramount consideration. This is not, strictly speaking, accurate because,
of course, juvenile courts do act in the best interests of the child insofar as their powers
permit. Where these are inadequate, the case for intervention by the High Court is
proportionately strengthened.

In this connection reference must be made to another amendment introduced by
the 1975 Act, as s 21(2A) of the 1969 Act, which precludes a juvenile court from dis-   *f*
charging a care order unless the court is satisfied that the child will receive the care
and control which he requires. This innocuous provision could have serious consequences in the present case. In expressly restricting the power of the juvenile
court, it would prevent it from taking a risk which, in the best interests of the child,
perhaps ought to be taken.

For these reasons, together with its most unusual and difficult facts, this court has   *g*
come to the conclusion that Balcombe J was right to assume jurisdiction in this case.

There are two other reasons for rejecting the local authority's appeal on the issue of
jurisdiction. In the first place, objection to his exercising the jurisdiction was not
taken by the local authority until after the conclusion of all the evidence. Since it is a
matter of discretion, a judge should not accede to the objection at that stage. To
decline jurisdiction would result in a real multiplicity of proceedings, involving re-   *h*
calling all the evidence in the juvenile court. For the same reason, once a judge has
assumed wardship jurisdiction and given his decision on the merits, it is virtually
impossible for this court to allow an appeal on the basis that he exercised his discretion wrongly, because the juvenile court and the Crown Court would be placed in
an impossibly embarrassing position if either of these courts was inclined to differ
from the views of the judge. Such a result could only be accepted if the judge had   *j*
acted without jurisdiction so that his order was a nullity.

So far as the appeal on the merits is concerned, it can be dealt with quite shortly,

1   [1974] 3 All ER 915, [1975] Fam 36
2   [1977] 3 All ER 481, [1977] Fam 158

notwithstanding the gravity of the issues involved, because the local authority have
a not seriously pressed this court to reverse the judge's decision on this part of the case.
It must have been the most difficult decision for him, and his judgment on both law
and fact can properly be called impeccable.

The issues before him were, first, whether this child had been assaulted by one or
other, or both of her parents. He concluded from the evidence that on two occasions in
1976 she had sustained serious injuries of a type, and in circumstances, which raised a
b strong suspicion of 'battering', and he expressed himself satisfied, on balance of
probabilities, that one of the parents was responsible for it. This is, of course, enough
in wardship proceedings where the welfare of the child is the paramount consideration, and therefore the seriousness of the risk to the child of further injury is the
dominant issue. The child was therefore properly made the subject of a care order.
However, the parents wish to return to their own country where each holds pro-
c fessional qualifications. So long as the care order stands they must either leave the
child in this country, in which case she will grow up in total isolation from her sisters
and family, and in an alien cultural surrounding, or the family will be effectively
prevented from returning to their home country. No graver issue could be formulated, nor could a more serious interference in the affairs of a foreign family be
imagined. Faced with this dilemma, the judge, acting on a very full, careful and
d balanced assessment by a psychiatrist, decided that, weighing the risk of further
physical injury against the risk of severe and lasting psychological injury the best
interests of the child would be served by her remaining in the care of the local authority under s 7 of the Family Law Reform Act 1969 unless and until the parents make
arrangements to return to their native country, when the child should be returned
to their care. It is impossible to differ from the learned judge's assessment of the
e relative risk to the future of this unfortunate little girl. Whichever course is decided
on, her future is in jeopardy. The learned judge, we think, has chosen the lesser of
the two alternative risks.

This appeal must therefore be dismissed.

Appeal dismissed. Leave to appeal to the House of Lords refused.
f

Solicitors: *Sharpe, Pritchard & Co*, agents for *Frank H Wilson*, Birmingham (for the local
authority); *James Beauchamp*, Birmingham (for the parents).

A S Virdi Esq Barrister.

Practice Direction

a

Crown Court – Distribution of court business – Classification of offences – Committals for sentence or to be dealt with – Procedure – Courts Acts 1971, s 4(5).

With the concurrence of the Lord Chancellor and pursuant to s 4(5) of the Courts Act 1971 I direct that, with effect from 17th July 1978, the following amendments shall be *b* made to the directions[1] on the distribution of Crown Court business given by me on 14th October 1971 as amended:

1. In para 1 delete from '*Class 3*' to the end and substitute:

'*Class 3*—All offences triable only on indictment other than those in classes 1, 2 and 4. They may be listed for trial by a High Court judge or by a circuit judge or by a recorder. *c*

'*Class 4*—(a) wounding or causing grievous bodily harm with intent (Offences against the Person Act 1861, s 18); (b) robbery or assault with intent to rob (Theft Act 1968, s 8); (c) offences under para (a) of s 2(2) of the Forgery Act 1913 where the amount of money or the value of goods exceeds £1,000; (d) offences under para (a) of s 7 of the Forgery Act 1913 where the amount of money or the *d* value of the property exceeds £1,000; (e) incitement or attempt to commit any of the above offences; (f) conspiracy at common law or conspiracy to commit any offence other than one included in classes 1 and 2; (g) all offences triable either way and any offence in class 3, if included in class 4 in accordance with directions, which may be either general or particular, given by a presiding judge or on his authority.

'When tried on indictment offences in class 4 may be tried by a High Court *e* judge, circuit judge or recorder but will normally be listed for trial by a circuit judge or recorder.'

2. In para 5(3)[2] delete 's 16 of the Criminal Justice Act 1972' and substitute 's 15 of the Powers of Criminal Courts Act 1973'.

3. For para 12(iii) there shall be substituted: *f*

'(iii) Class 4 offences shall be listed for trial by a circuit judge or recorder unless, bearing in mind the considerations set out in para 2 above and the views, if any, put forward by justices, the officer responsible for listing decides that the case should be tried by a High Court judge. Such a decision shall be taken only after consultation with a presiding judge (or a judge acting for him) or in accordance *g* with directions, either general or particular, given by a presiding judge including, in the case of any specified offence, directions relating to futher considerations to be borne in mind by the officer responsible for listing.'

30th June 1978   WIDGERY CJ

h

1   See *Practice Note* [1971] 3 All ER 829, [1971] 1 WLR 1535
2   Paragraph 5 was substituted by *Practice Direction* [1973] 1 All ER 182, [1973] 1 WLR 73

a

Maltby and another v D J Freeman & Co (a firm)

CHANCERY DIVISION

WALTON J SITTING WITH MASTER CLEWS AND MR M D T LOUP AS ASSESSORS

b   22nd, 25th, 26th JULY, 25th OCTOBER 1977

Costs – Taxation – Solicitor – Non-contentious business – Fair and reasonable sum in circumstances – Factors to be considered – Probate – Large estate consisting of numerous assets – Properties and shares – Method of assessing solicitor's remuneration – Rules of the Supreme Court (Non-Contentious Probate Costs) 1956 (SI 1956 No 552), r 1.

c

M died in September 1972 leaving an estate of approximately £1¾ million, consisting mainly of property but partly of shares. The plaintiffs, who were his executors, instructed the defendant firm of solicitors to act for them in the administration of his estate. The first plaintiff, who was a chartered surveyor, assisted the defendants by supplying them with valuations of M's properties. The defendants however had to
d   do a considerable amount of checking in connection with M's private company shareholdings before probate could be obtained. In October 1973, three months after probate had been granted, the plaintiffs decided that they themselves could carry on the administration of M's estate. They thereupon terminated their instructions to the defendants. In due course the defendants submitted a bill of costs in respect of the work which they had done for the plaintiffs. The bill amounted to £11,175, and, bearing in mind the matters set out in heads (1) to (7) of r 1ª of the
e   Rules of the Supreme Court (Non-Contentious Probate Costs) 1956[b], was made up in the following way: (1) complexity of the matter and difficulty of questions raised, £3,650; (2) skill, labour, specialised knowledge and responsibility involved, £1,450; (3) number and importance of documents prepared or perused, nil; (4) place where and circumstances in which the business was transacted, £300; (5) time expended,
f   £2,135; (6) nature and value of the property involved, £7,300, from which they deducted £3,650 in recognition of the first plaintiff's assistance and to allow for the fact that they had not completed the administration of the estate; (7) importance of the matter to the plaintiffs, nil. The plaintiffs were dissatisfied with the bill and requested the defendants to obtain a certificate from the Law Society as to the fairness and reasonableness of the charges. The Law Society issued a certificate to the effect that £8,500 would be a more appropriate charge. The plaintiffs were still not satis-
g   fied and they proceeded to taxation. The taxing master at first allowed the bill in full but, on objections to taxation being made, reduced it to £10,500. The plaintiffs applied to the judge for a review of taxation.

Held – (i) Although the matters set out in heads (1) to (7) of r 1 of the 1956 rules were
h   capable of being cumulative, there could be no overlap in the charge (see p 916 d, post).

(ii) In most cases the logical starting point for considering those matters was head (5) (time expended by the solicitor) for it was the easiest to assess and gave a good indication of the weight of the matter as a whole, but however meticulously records of a day's work were kept, it would generally represent an undercharge because a professional man rarely stopped thinking about the day's problems when he left his place of work; ideas often occurred to him on the way home or at home and they
j   could not adequately be reflected on time sheets; they could however usually be included under head (2) (skill, labour etc, involved on the part of the solicitor) (see p 916 f to h, post).

---

a   Rule 1, so far as material, is set out at p 915 h to p 916 a, post

(iii) Where a case was concerned with a large estate the most important head would always be head (6) (the nature and value of the property involved). The correct *a* method of charging was by means of percentages which decreased in scale as the value of the matters involved increased. In the case of an estate the size of M's, compounded of a large number of separate elements, the appropriate bands and percentages were: up to £¼ million, 1½ per cent; £½ million to £1 million, ½ per cent; £1 million to £2 million; ⅛th per cent (see p 916 h and p 917 d e and h j, post); *Property and Reversionary Investment Corpn Ltd v Secretary of State for the Environment* *b* [1975] 2 All ER 436 applied.

(iv) In the circumstances it was appropriate that, in the defendants' bill of costs, a 50 per cent reduction had been made under head (6) to take account of the facts, first, that the defendant's instructions had been terminated before the administration of M's estate was complete, and second, that they had received a great deal of assistance from him, but there was no justification for the charge of £300 under head (4) and *c* the sums charged under heads (1) and (2) were excessive and should be cut by nearly 50 per cent. £8,500 was a fair and reasonable sum for the defendants' remuneration and the bill of costs would be reduced to that sum (see p 918 *a* to *h*, post).

Notes

For the remuneration of solicitors for non-contentious business, see Supplement to *d* 36 Halsbury's Laws (3rd Edn) para 160A.

For the Rules of the Supreme Court (Non-Contentious Probate Costs) 1956, r 1, see 7 Halsbury's Statutory Instruments (Third Reissue) 311.

Case referred to in judgment

Property and Reversionary Investment Corpn Ltd v Secretary of State for the Environment *e* [1975] 2 All ER 436, [1975] 1 WLR 1504, Digest (Cont Vol D) 847, *2792a*.

Summons for review of taxation

The plaintiffs, Alan Vivian Maltby and Lily Myrtle Maltby, the executors of Harold Vivian Maltby deceased applied by summons dated 12th October 1976 for a review by the judge of the taxing master's taxation of the bill of costs submitted by the defen- *f* dants, D J Freemen & Co, in the sum of £10,500 in respect of work done by the de fendants as solicitors for the plaintiffs in the administration of the estate of Harold Vivian Maltby. The taxing master had at first allowed the bill in full in the sum of £11,175, but on objection to the taxation being made, had reduced it to £10,500. The summons was heard in chambers by Walton J, sitting with two assessors, and judgment was delivered in chambers. The case is reported by leave of Walton J. The facts are *g* set out in the judgment.

Nigel Hague for the plaintiffs.
James Goudie for the defendants.

Cur adv vult

h

25th October. **WALTON J** read the following judgment: The late Harold Vivian Maltby, the father of the first plaintiff and husband of the second, made his last will and testament on 7th August 1958, and thereby appointed the plaintiffs to be executors and trustees thereof, but as to his son on attaining the age of 21, and with a sub stitutionary appointment in respect of his widow in case she predeceased him. He made a codicil thereto on 13th October 1967, whereby he appointed the plaintiffs *j* executors and trustees. He died on 18th September 1972, somewhat unexpectedly. The deceased had had a somewhat unsatisfactory history of dealing with accountants, and was, I gather, to some extent reticent about his affairs even with his family. He died worth approximately £1¼ million, the vast bulk of his estate being in property.

The plaintiffs instructed the defendants, who are well known as solicitors having

great expertise in the world of property, to act for them in the administration of the
a estate by a letter of 21st September 1972. That firm proceeded to obtain all the
necessary details of the estate from the first plaintiff, to whom his mother left the
main conduct of the administration of the estate. As the first plaintiff is himself a
chartered surveyor, he was in a unique position to assist the solicitors in the preparation of valuations of the various properties owned by his father, and he in fact provided
them. However, principally I think because of the reticence to which I have already
b referred, the solicitors did have to check very carefully and in detail the deceased's
private company shareholdings.

Probate was duly obtained on 19th July 1973. On 23rd October 1973 the first plaintiff wrote to the defendants terminating their instructions, since, owing to reorganisation of the business affairs of himself and his mother, he now had as one of his
employees a chartered accountant specialising in tax matters and estate duty, and
c the first plaintiff considered that with this assistance he could now personally carry
on with the administration in place of the solicitors. The parting was, however,
quite amicable; the defendants took the point, and simply invited the first plaintiff
to come back to them on any points which arose on which that firm might be able
to assist.

The defendants then instructed Messrs Kitchen & Co, costs draftsmen, to prepare
d a solicitor and own client bill of costs in respect of the work so done by them for the
plaintiffs. This this firm did, and for the moment it will suffice to say that the total
of profit costs came to £11,175. The plaintiffs were dissatisfied with this bill, and
requested the defendants to obtain a certificate from the Law Society that their costs
were reasonable. This request was expressed to be under art 3(1) of the Solicitors'
Remuneration Order 1972[1], but this was clearly a mistake; the preparation of the
e bill, and the right to obtain the certificate alike, was governed by the provisions of
the Rules of the Supreme Court (Non-Contentious Probate Costs) 1956[2]. However,
the crucial provisions for this purpose are in identical terms, so that no harm was done.
In the event, the defendants duly applied for such a certificate on 20th March 1974,
and on 24th May 1974 the Law Society issued a certificate to the effect that £8,500
would be a more appropriate charge in respect of profit costs than the sum of £11,175.
f Neither of the plaintiffs was satisfied with this outcome, and they accordingly
proceeded to taxation. I need not detail the various procedural steps which occurred,
but the master first of all allowed the bill in full in the sum of £11,175; but, on
objections to taxation being made, reduced it by the sum of £675 to £10,500. The
plaintiffs still not being satisfied, they have applied for a review of this taxation,
which is now before me. Pursuant to a direction of Oliver J, I have sat with assessors
g (Master Clews and Mr M D T Loup, senior partner in Boodle Hatfield & Co) from
whose experience and advice I have derived the greatest possible assistance, although
I should perhaps make it clear that the decision which I have reached is strictly my
own, and that neither of them would have reached precisely the same figure.

First, what principles govern the costs of non-contentious probate work? The
answer, as I have already indicated, is to be found in the Rules of the Supreme Court
h (Non-Contentious Probate Costs) 1956. The crucial rule for present purposes is r 1,
which, so far as material, provides as follows:

'For work done in respect of business to which these Rules apply a solicitor
shall be entitled to charge and be paid such sum as may be fair and reasonable
having regard to all the circumstances of the case and in particular to—(1) the
complexity of the matter or the difficulty or novelty of the questions raised;
j (2) the skill, labour, specialised knowledge and responsibility involved on the
part of the solicitor; (3) the number and importance of the documents prepared
or perused, without regard to length; (4) the place where and circumstances

---

1 SI 1972 No 1139
2 SI 1956 No 552

in which the business or any part thereof is transacted; (5) the time expended by the solicitor; (6) the nature and value of the property involved; (7) the importance of the matter to the client.'

I should perhaps add that there are two provisos to that rule to which attention must be directed. The first, proviso (a), makes it clear that the client is entitled to require from the Law Society a certificate as to the fairness and reasonableness of the charges. The other, proviso (d), states that it is the duty of the solicitor to satisfy the taxing master as to the fairness and reasonableness of the charges.

Now fairness and reasonableness is something which in this kind of situation does not exist in a vacuum; it is impossible to consider whether £X is a fair and reasonable charge without there being some guidelines against which one can consider the extent of the charge. Of course, all such guidelines must of necessity be conventional, since they are not specified in the terms of the rules themselves, but without some guidelines, however loose, it would, in my judgment, become impossible to compare one figure with another, to argue from one case to another, which is what the overall concept of fairness must surely involve.

There is one matter concerning the various headings under the rule which is not, I think, really in contention, and that is that although the various matters therein mentioned are at any rate capable of being cumulative, there must be no overlap in the charge. Thus, for example, if the importance of the matter to the client has already been sufficiently taken care of by the charge made under the 'nature and value' heading, then there will be nothing to add under the 'complexity' heading. Duplication is never permissible.

Now virtually all the considerations as apply under the rules with which I am here concerned apply in relation to the Solicitors' Remuneration Order 1972: it is virtually only that, in that order, head (7) in the Probate Rules becomes head (viii), and that there is a new head (vii), relating to the possibility of the land being registered land. Donaldson J has recently commented in general terms on all those heads in *Property and Reversionary Investment Corpn Ltd v Secretary of State for the Environment*[1], and in general further comment would be superfluous.

When dealing with the various matters mentioned, the easiest to deal with, because, assuming, as indeed ought always to be the case, proper records have been kept, there should be little room for argument, is of course the fifth, the time expended by the solicitor or his employees. In a good many cases, although by no means all, it is also the logical starting point in that it gives in itself a good indication of the weight of the matter as a whole. I would, however, make one gloss; however meticulously time records are kept, this will always, save in the plainest of all possible cases, represent an undercharge. No professional man, or senior employee of a professional man, stops thinking about the day's problems the minute he lifts his coat and umbrella from the stand and sets out on the journey home. Ideas, often very valuable ideas, occur in the train or car home, or in the bath, or even whilst watching television. Yet nothing is ever put down on a time sheet, or can be put down on a time sheet, adequately to reflect this out of hours devotion of time. Thus it will be a rare bill which can be simply compounded of time and value; there must always be a third element, usually under the second head.

The most important head in a large estate will of course always be the sixth 'the nature and value of the property involved'. The corresponding words in the 1972 Orders are 'amount or value of any money or property involved'. I think the difference in wording arises from this fact, that under the 1972 order one is primarily concerned with a single subject-matter, of which a single block of property as in the *Property and Reversionary Corpn* case[1] is an excellent example. However, no estate is typically concerned with just one single asset; there are usually a mixed

1   [1975] 2 All ER 436, [1975] 1 WLR 1504

bag of assets for consideration. Often there will be what might be described as a

a 'leading asset', in the ordinary case this will be a dwelling-house, and the other assets will be of comparatively little value. In such simple cases it will be right to apply the traditional method of charging, namely, by cumulative bands, each attracting a diminishing rate of charge, without modification. But it may well be otherwise.

If one considers two estates of very considerable value, one represented by a single monolithic block of shares in a quoted company, and the other represented by

b numerous small parcels of shares, including some in companies which are not so quoted, it is at once apparent that in their practical implications their same values involve quite different considerations on the part of the solicitor concerned. Hence, I think the introduction into the Probate Rules of the word 'nature'.

As a severely practical matter, I think that it cannot be very useful to assume that there are an infinite series of percentages applicable varying having regard to the

c nature of the assets; I think that, for the same reasons, one must, where at all possible, relate the additional work due to complexity of this nature to the first head, under which it will normally be possible to compensate for the additional complexity so created. If this were for any reason not possible, one might be forced to consider the matter as if it were so many different estates in order to arrive at a reasonable charge.

In general, however, when one comes to translate value into terms of the legal

d bill, the approach involves two ingrained habits of legal thought. There is nothing strictly logical about either, but they are so ingrained that all approaches have to take them into consideration. The first is that the correct method of charging is by means of a method of percentages, and the second is that the percentage is not a flat rate applied throughout the scale, but declines on a regressive scale as the value of the matters involved increases. In the *Property and Reversionary Corpn* case[1] a

e strenuous effort was made to persuade the court, in the light of the fact that the 1972 order (very similar in terms to the rules in the present case) did not prescribe any bands or percentages, that a flat rate ought to be taken over the whole. This was rejected by Donaldson J in accordance with the general feeling of the profession.

I am therefore left the twin problems of where the bands lie and what the percentages should be. In the *Property and Reversionary Corpn* case[2], Donaldson J indicated

f that the divisions between the higher bands, when one is dealing with property approaching £2 million as a minimum in value, should fall at £½ million, £1 million, £2 million, £5 million and £10 million. Although the value of money has changed considerably even since 1975, I would not quarrel with these divisions in any way. I do not, however, take it that the learned judge intended that the first band should be a simple band up to £½ million at a low figure. It must, I think, 'dovetail' into the

g charges for estates made up to £½ million, and in this regard I refer, by way of illustration rather than strict guidance (since the figures have since been withdrawn) to the suggested Charges for Obtaining Grants and Administration set out in the Law Society's Gazette[3].

I therefore think that in the case of an estate of the size of the present one, compounded of the large number of separate elements of which the present estate

h is compounded, the first band (to £½ million) would be at 1½ per cent; the next band (£½ million to £1 million) at ½ per cent; and the next band (£1 million to £2 million) at ⅛th per cent. I must emphasise that these bands cannot be made to apply, and are certainly not intended to apply, to any other classes or work carried on by solicitors: they have no relevance whatsoever to ordinary straightforward conveyancing, for example, where there is only one asset to deal with at a time. They

i are intended to be confined solely to the work involved with a large number of assets. And they are solely confined to an estate of the present size: in the case of a smaller estate, the first rate would be too low.

1   [1975] 2 All ER 436, [1975] 1 WLR 1504
2   [1975] 2 All ER 436 at 443, [1975] 1 WLR 1504 at 1511
3   March/April 1971, p 133

I would therefore think that a realistic figure for the 'value' heading ought to be rather more than that actually stated by Messrs Kitchens in their bill. However, and both sides agreed with this view of the matter, in view of the termination of instructions before the solicitors had completed their normal work, the sum under this heading falls to be reduced by 50 per cent. It is obviously right that an allowance should be made for the premature termination of the work, and it is, I think, consistently with the heads of the rules, the only suitable head under which to effect such reduction, illogical though it may strictly be to utilise it in this manner. The more logical alternative would, of course, be to apply a suitable percentage reduction to the totality of heads (1), (2), (6) and (7). In view of the agreement of the parties, I do not pursue this alternative further in this case. The precise amount of the reduction must, in every case, be a matter of extreme difficulty, and it is complicated by the freely acknowledged fact that in the present case, by reason of his professional status, the first plaintiff was able to afford the solicitors a great deal of assistance in relation to values. As I have indicated, both sides agreed that a 50 per cent reduction was a fair figure to take care of both these factors, and I entirely agree with their judgment.

I think that Messrs Kitchens have rightly not sought to charge any sums under heads (3), number and importance of the documents perused or (7), importance of the matter to the client. In the circumstances of this case head (3) is subsumed in the time expended, and though of course the matter was of great importance to the clients, it is not of any importance other than might be deduced from its general nature and size. A sum of £300 has been charged under head (4), the place where and circumstances in which the business or any part thereof was transacted but I see no justification for any such charge. The solicitors were not required to attend at any extraordinary place, or to act with any extraordinary degree of urgency, or any other matter of that nature.

Sums have also been charged under heads (1), complexity and (2), skill, labour, specialised knowledge and responsibility. I think that charges under both heads are justified, although it appears to me that the method of ascertaining such sums adopted by Messrs Kitchens, namely the taking of a percentage of head (6), is unsatisfactory. The two items together are charged at £5,100, and I am quite clear that this is too much. It is extremely difficult to say just how much ought to be charged under these two heads, but, having had my attention called to the correspondence, and to the documentation involved, not forgetting that as regards one or two matters the solicitors might, perhaps, have displayed even more skill than they did with advantage, a sum of a little more than half of the sum allowed would be justified.

Accordingly, at the end of the day I have reached the conclusion that the sum which ought to be charged is the sum of £8,500. This is, of course, in round figures: it is not possible to pretend to any greater accuracy. It will be seen that my figure agrees with that of the Law Society's certificate. I have no means of knowing precisely, or at all, how the Society's panel arrived at that figure, but it is at any rate satisfactory to me to find that the analysis which I have made above produces approximately the same result.

I therefore fix the amount of the bill in the sum of £8,500.

Order accordingly.

Solicitors: *Theodore Goddard & Co* (for the plaintiffs); *D J Freeman & Co.*

Jacqueline Metcalfe   Barrister.

Practice Note

FAMILY DIVISION

Injunction – Husband and wife – Ex parte application – Cases of urgency – Applications at Royal Courts of Justice – Applications to be made only where immediate danger of serious injury or irreparable damage – Selection of early hearing date – CCR Ord 13, rr 1(1)(b), 8(2)(3) – Matrimonial Causes Rules 1971 (SI 1971 No 953), r 114(2).

The President is greatly concerned by the increasing number of applications being made ex parte in the Royal Courts of Justice for injunctions, which could and should have been made (if at all) on two clear days' notice to the other side, as required by the rules[1].

An ex parte application should not be made, or granted, unless there is real immediate danger of serious injury or irreparable damage. A recent examination of ex parte applications shows that nearly 50 per cent were unmeritorious, being made days, or even weeks, after the last incident of which complaint was made. This wastes time, causes needless expense, usually to the Legal Aid Fund, and is unjust to respondents.

Where notice of an application for an injunction is to be given and an early hearing date is sought, practitioners are reminded of the special arrangements which exist at the Royal Courts of Justice whereby the applicant's solicitor is able to select for the hearing any day on which the court is sitting. These arrangements are contained in President's Practice Direction dated 10th July 1972[2].

R L BAYNE-POWELL
Senior Registrar.

26th June 1978

---

1 CCR Ord 13, rr 1(1)(b) (as modified by the Matrimonial Causes Rules 1971, r 114(2)), 8(2)(3)
2 [1972] 2 All ER 1360, [1972] 1 WLR 1047

Treasury Solicitor v Regester and another

QUEEN'S BENCH DIVISION

DONALDSON J SITTING WITH CHIEF MASTER GRAHAM-GREEN AND P J PURTON AS ASSESSORS

5th, 21st DECEMBER 1977

Costs – Taxation – Solicitor – Non-contentious business – Fair and reasonable sum in circumstances – Factors to be considered – Conveyancing – Value of the property – Application of regressive scale – Commercial property of substantial value – Transaction required to be completed within short period and if not so completed client losing transaction – Agreement for long lease of land and offices to be built thereon – Government department acquiring lease – Transaction worth £2m – Government department agreeing to pay costs of transaction – Time not of the essence to government department – Method of assessing solicitor's remuneration – Relevance of nature of interest in property – Solicitors' Remuneration Order 1972 (SI 1972 No 1139), art 2.

A company which owned land was engaged in property development involving the acquisition of adjacent pieces of land and the disposal of the whole of the land on the terms that they would build offices on the land for the purchaser who would take the developed site on a long lease. In November 1975 the company instructed a firm of solicitors, who had already acted for them in the acquisition of the land, to draw up an agreement and draft lease whereby the company were to grant to the Secretary of State for the Environment a long lease of the land and the offices to be built thereon. The value of the transaction amounted to approximately £2 million. The parties were agreed that unless the agreement was completed by 31st July 1976 the transaction would be cancelled because after that date the incidence of development land tax would make the transaction unprofitable for the company. Accordingly the solicitors were instructed to complete the documents before 31st July. On 30th July the parties entered into an agreement with a draft lease annexed, drawn up by the solicitors. It was a term of the agreement that the Secretary of State would pay the solicitor's proper costs and disbursements in connection with the agreement and lease. The solicitors submitted for taxation a bill of costs for £9,000 for work in connection with the agreement and draft lease. The master taxed the bill at £6,900, arriving at that figure by taking the time spent by a senior partner on the work, 60 hours, at an hourly rate of £15, which gave a figure of £900, in accordance with para (iii) of art 2[a] of the Solicitors' Remuneration Order 1972, and then considering the other factors specified in art 2. In respect of those other factors the master arrived at a figure of £6,000. The solicitors applied for a review of the taxation contending that their bill represented fair and reasonable remuneration. The Secretary of State contended that fair and reasonable remuneration would be between £4,000 and £5,000.

Held – (i) The object in taxing a bill of costs for conveyancing work under art 2 of the 1972 order was to assess, by a value judgment based on discretion and experience and not by arithmetical calculation, a fair and reasonable remuneration having regard to all the circumstances, in particular the factors specified in art 2. Accordingly, where the conveyancing transaction was of high value, para (iii) of art 2 was not to be treated as the arithmetical basis for the assessment, for in such a case the other factors in art 2

---

a   Article 2 provides: 'A solicitor's remuneration for non-contentious business (including business under the Land Registration Act 1925) shall be such sum as may be fair and reasonable having regard to all the circumstances of the case and in particular to—(i) the complexity of the matter or the difficulty or novelty of the questions raised; (ii) the skill, labour, specialised knowledge and responsibility involved; (iii) the time spent on the business; (iv) the number and importance of the documents prepared or perused, without regard to length; (v) the place where and the circumstances in which the business or any part thereof is transacted; (vi) the amount or value of any money or property involved; (vii) whether any land involved is registered land within the meaning of the Land Registration Act 1925; and (viii) the importance of the matter to the client.'

were likely to be of greater significance. In particular para (iii) did not reflect the
a skill and specialist knowledge involved in such work, and in the nature of things,
not all the time spent on the work would be recorded. Although, therefore, para (iii)
specified the only factor capable of arithmetical calculation and was important
because it indicated the proportion of the solicitor's overheads which were attributable
to the transaction, it should be treated merely as a cross-check on whether a provisional assessment bore a reasonable relationship to the overheads attributable to
b the transaction. Furthermore, remuneration which had been held to be fair and
reasonable in previous comparable taxations was not to be taken as a primary source
for the assessment subject to modification in the light of any differences between the
circumstances of the cases, but only as a cross-check on the fairness and reasonableness of the assessment being made (see p 923 *g*, p 924 *d* to p 925 *c*, p 926 *h* and p 927, *f*,
post); *Property and Reversionary Investment Corpn Ltd v Secretary of State for the Environ-*
c *ment* [1975] 2 All ER 436 explained; dictum of Walton J in *Maltby v D J Freeman & Co*
at p 916, ante, applied.

(ii) In all the circumstances £8,000, exclusive of value added tax, was a fair and
reasonable remuneration for the transaction having regard to all the factors specified
in art 2 of the 1972 order since the transaction was distinguishable from the general
run of such transactions because the solicitors had to complete the work by a deadline
d and there was no margin for error, the fact that time was not of the essence to the
paying party, i e the Secretary of State, was irrelevant for he had agreed to pay the
client's, i e the company's, costs which were the costs to be taxed, although scale.
fees had been abolished it was reasonable and fair, in particular to the client, that the
remuneration should not be disproportionate to the value of the property involved,
the appropriate yardstick to employ in a major transaction was ½ per cent on the first
e £250,000 and thereafter regressing, and the nature of the interest in the property, i e
freehold or leasehold, was irrelevant for what mattered was the effect which the nature
of the interest had on the factors of skill, work, value, complexity etc (see p 925 *e f*,
p 926 *f g* and *j* and p 927 *a* and *d* to *g*, post).

Notes
f For the remuneration of solicitors for non-contentions business, see Supplement to 36
Halsbury's Laws (3rd Edn) para 160A.
    For the Solicitors' Remuneration Order 1972, art 2, see 20 Halsbury's Statutory
Instruments (Third Reissue) 277.

Cases referred to in judgment
Maltby v D J Freeman & Co p 913, ante, [1978] 1 WLR 431.
Property and Reversionary Investment Corpn Ltd v Secretary of State for the Environment
    [1975] 2 All ER 436, [1975] 1 WLR 1504, Digest (Cont Vol D) 847, 2792a.

Summons for review of taxation
Paul John Dinsmore Regester and Colin Travers McInerney ('the solicitors'), partners in the firm Messrs Ward Bowie of Basingstoke, Hants, applied for a review of an
order made by Master Wright on 31st May 1977 whereby he taxed at £6,935·50 a bill
of costs for £9,085·50 submitted by them in respect of professional charges and
disbursements in connection with the preparation, settlement and completion of an
agreement made between their client, Hamilton Holdings Ltd ('Hamilton'), and the
Secretary of State for the Environment for a lease to the Secretary of State of offices at
Andover Road, Winchester, for a term of years at an annual rent of £190,035 subject
to review. The bill was invoiced to Hamilton, but by agreement was payable by the
Secretary of State. The Treasury Solicitor on behalf of the Secretary of State issued a
cross-summons seeking a review of the order for taxation. The facts are set out in the
judgment.

Francis Barlow for the Treasury Solicitor.
Mark Potter for the solicitors.

Cur adv vult

a

21st December. **DONALDSON J** read the following judgment: In *Property and Reversionary Investment Corpn Ltd v Secretary of State for the Environment*[1], the chief taxing master, Master Graham-Green, Mr P J Purton of Norton, Rose, Botterell & Roche and I sought to give guidance to the profession on the approach to be adopted in determining solicitors' remuneration in high value commercial conveyancing. By chance, the same court is now asked to consider another such taxation and this b gives us an opportunity of removing some misconceptions about our previous decision. I will refer to that decision as 'the *Reversionary* case'.

Before doing so, I should like to say a word about the position of Master Graham-Green and Mr Purton. Technically they sit with me as assessors, because that is what the Rules of the Supreme Court provide. In practice, and I think that this will be a relief to both parties, we sit as a court of three, each bringing our own c differing skills and experience to bear on the problem. This judgment, like that which I delivered in the *Reversionary* case[1], is in fact, if not in theory, the judgment of all three of us.

The bill of costs, dated 12th October 1977, is for professional charges in connection with the preparation, settlement and completion of an agreement for a lease of offices at Andover Road, Winchester, Hants. The client was Hamilton Holdings Ltd, d but the prospective lessee and paying party was the Secretary of State for the Environment.

I can take the facts from Master Wright's answer to objections:

'The Ministry of the Environment (hereinafter "the Ministry") were seeking premises in Andover. Hamilton Holdings Ltd ("Hamilton") had been accumu- e lating a block of land in Andover by purchases of and obtaining options on various parcels of land. An informal agreement was made that if Hamilton obtained the necessary planning permissions and redeveloped the block of land by building a structure to the Ministry's requirements, then the Ministry would take a long lease of the land and structure at a rack rent. The parties are agreed that the value of the land with planning permission was approximately £1,000,000 and that the cost of the redevelopment and building work necessary would be approximately £1,000,000. Hamilton instructed solicitors in November 1975 and a written agreement was made between Hamilton and the Minstry on 30th July 1976. The agreement runs to some nine pages and has a draft lease of some 20 pages annexed. The agreement provides that Hamilton will build a structure in accordance with a specification referred to and that thereupon the Ministry g will take a lease of the land and structure for a term of 40 years at a rental of £190,035 per annum (subject to review). Clause 11 of the agreement reads: "The Tenant will on the execution of this Agreement pay the Landlord's Solicitors proper costs and disbursements in connection therewith . . ." It is by reason of this clause that the Ministry is taxing this bill under s 71 of the Solicitors Act 1974. Both parties agree that if it had been impossible to complete the agreement by h the end of July 1976, then for tax reasons it would not have been profitable for the landlord to make either the agreement or the lease, and that neither would have been made. They further agree that on making the agreement and even before completion of the lease Hamilton had a marketable investment: Hamilton in fact sold the freehold subject to the agreement some three months after the date of the agreement.'

The solicitors, Mr Paul Regester and Mr Colin McInerney, partners in Messrs Ward Bowie of Basingstoke, Hants, submitted a bill for £9,085·50, of which £9,000 was in respect of their professional charges and £85·50 was in respect of disbursements. The learned master taxed the bill at £6,935·50, of which £35·50 represented disbursements. Originally there was a further dispute as to the proportion of costs which were payable immediately and the proportion which would become payable when, at a later stage, the lease is completed. The master decided that 75 per cent should be paid now and 25 per cent later. This apportionment is now accepted.

Both parties have appealed on the issue of what should be the total amount of the bill. The solicitors submit that their original bill is fully justified as being fair and reasonable, having regard to all the circumstances and, in particular, the eight specific matters referred to in the Solicitors' Remuneration Order 1972[1]. The Treasury Solicitor, on behalf of the Secretary of State, contends that having regard to similar considerations, fair and reasonable remuneration would fall within the lower end of the £4,000 to £5,000 bracket.

The master arrived at his figure by following what he believed to be the approach adopted by this court in the *Reversionary* case[2]. He said that we had mentioned only two figures. The first was recorded time under factor (iii) in art 2 of the 1972 order. This was put at £450[3]. The second was £5,500 for all the eight factors together. The learned master then deduced that we had calculated a figure of approximately £5,000 for all factors other than factor (iii).

In the present case the parties were agreed, and the learned master accepted, that an appropriate figure for recorded time was £900 being 60 hours of partners time at £15 an hour. He then considered all the factors other than factor (iii), asking himself to what extent they differed from those in the *Reversionary* case[2] in the expectation that if they were not radically different he would arrive at a figure which was not far removed from the figure of £5,000 in that case. In the end he arrived at a figure of £6,000 which he added to the £900 giving a total of £6,900 excluding disbursements.

In the *Reversionary* case[4] Master Horne had arrived at his figure in three stages. First, he took the hourly cost rate at £15 and applied this to 30 hours of recorded time, giving a figure of £450. This disposed of factor (iii). Second, he multiplied this by two to take account of all other factors with the exception of factor (vi), 'the amount or value of any property involved'. This gave him a figure of £900. In the third stage he applied a percentage, calculated on a regressive scale to the value, and obtained a figure of £3,250. Adding the results of the three stages gave him a figure of about £4,600.

In our judgment we expressly disagreed with applying a multiplier to any figure based on recorded time (factor (iii)), but did not expressly say that such a figure should not be added to some other figure arrived at after a consideration of all the other factors. Clearly, we should have done so and we welcome this opportunity of making it clear that the £5,500 in the *Reversionary* case[2] was not arrived at by any process involving an addition to or multiplication of any other figure. As we said in our judgment and we now repeat[5]:

'The object of the exercise, whether a solicitor is preparing a bill of costs in relation to non-contentious business, or the Law Society is certifying such a bill, or the court is taxing it, is to arrive at a sum which is fair and reasonable, having regard to all the circumstances and, in particular, to the matters specified in the numbered paragraphs of art 2 of the order. It is an exercise in assessment, an exercise in balanced judgment—not an arithmetical calculation. It follows that different people may reach different conclusions as to what sum is fair and reasonable, although all should fall within a bracket which, in the vast majority

---

1 SI 1972 No 1139
2 [1975] 2 All ER 436, [1975] 1 WLR 1504
3 [1975] 2 All ER 436 at 440, 442, [1975] 1 WLR 1504 at 1507, 1510
4 [1975] 2 All ER 436 at 439, 440, [1975] 1 WLR 1504 at 1507
5 [1975] 2 All ER 436 at 441, [1975] 1 WLR 1504 at 1509

of cases, will be narrow. It also follows that it is wrong always to start by assessing the direct and indirect expense to the solicitor, represented by the time spent on the business. This must always be taken into account, but it is not necessarily, or even usually, a basic factor to which all others are related. Thus, although the labour involved will usually be directly related to, and reflected by, the time spent, the skill and specialised knowledge involved may vary greatly for different parts of that time. Again not all time spent on a transaction necessarily lends itself to being recorded, although the fullest possible records should be kept.'

Having considered all the factors, including factor (iii), we concluded[1]:

'With these factors well in mind, it is necessary to assess a sum which is fair and reasonable. Each case will always have to be considered on its merits and be subject ultimately to the discretion of the taxing master. In this case various figures will no doubt come to mind. They can be tested relative to the remuneration generally accepted, or previously held to be fair and reasonable, in comparable transactions, due allowance being made for all distinctions. They can also be tested by making hypothetical calculations of what the sum would be if any exceptional factors were excluded and then seeing whether the resulting figure conforms with the accepted views of the profession and of the taxing authorities. But in the end it is a value judgment, based on discretion and experience.'

The magnetic attraction of factor (iii) as a foundation for assessment of fair and reasonable remuneration is that, in the absence of an approved scale applied to value, it is the only figure which is readily calculable. It is an attraction which must be sternly resisted in cases of this sort where one or more of the other factors is such as to dwarf it into insignificance.

In the *Reversionary* case[2] we drew attention to the fact that recorded time on a transaction may be expected to reflect labour, but not skill and specialised knowledge and that in the nature of things not all time spent lends itself to being recorded. As Walton J said in *Maltby v D J Freeman & Co*[3]:

'No professional man, or senior employee of a professional man, stops thinking about the day's problems the minute he lifts his coat and umbrella from the stand and sets out on the journey home. Ideas, often very valuable ideas, occur in the train or car home, or in the bath, or even whilst watching television. Yet nothing is ever put down on a time sheet, or can be put down on a time sheet, adequately to reflect this out of hours devotion of time.'

The truth is that an hourly cost rate applied to recorded time at best only indicates the proportion of the solicitor's overhead expenses which are rightly attributable to the transaction. We say 'at best' because (a) hourly rates tend to be round figures which do not necessarily represent an accurate assessment of overheads in terms of man hours, (b) they may not be revised sufficiently often to take account of inflation and (c) different firms regard different expenses as being apportionable, some, for example, including notional basic salaries for partners and others omitting such an item.

This is not to say that the calculation has no value. It has a real value in all cases. Thus, if calculated accurately, it informs a solicitor of the minimum figure which he must charge if he is not to suffer an actual loss on the transaction. Second, it gives him an idea of the relationship between the overheads attributable to the transaction and the profit accruing to him. This latter point is plainly relevant in the broad sense

1 [1975] 2 All ER 436 at 443, [1975] 1 WLR 1504 at 1512
2 [1975] 2 All ER 436 at 441, [1975] 1 WLR 1504 at 1509
3 See p 916, ante

that the nature of some transactions will justify much larger profits than others of a
a more routine type. But we must stress that it is only one of a number of cross-checks
on the fairness and reasonableness of the final figure. The final figure will result from
an exercise in judgment, not arithmetic, whatever arithmetical cross-checks may be
employed.

We also consider that the learned master erred in his use of the figure which he
assumed that we had assessed for the remaining factors in the *Reversionary* case[1]. It
b is flattering to have our assessment in that case treated as if it were an imperial
standard measure, but it is wrong to do so. We did say[2], and we repeat, that provisional figures 'can be tested relative to the remuneration generally accepted, or
previously held to be fair and reasonable, in comparable, transactions, due allowance
being made for all distinctions'. But this is a cross-check. It is not a primary source to
be modified in the light of a comparison between the circumstances of the transaction
c and those which existed in the *Reversionary*[1] or any other reported case.

We now turn to the eight factors to which our attention is directed by the 1972
order.

(i) *The complexity of the matter or the difficulty or novelty of the questions raised*
The client was engaged in a property development exercise involving the acquisi-
d tion of adjacent pieces of land and the disposal of the resulting package on terms that
they would build an office for the acquirer who would take the developed site on
long lease. The bill did not cover the professional work connected with the acquisition, but covered the rest. Such work is not novel, but it is far from being standardised.
From its very nature it will give rise to difficulties and will have some degree of
complexity, the difficulty and complexity varying from transaction to transaction.
e We have no evidence that, of its kind, it was more difficult or complex than usual.

(ii) *The skill, labour, specialised knowledge and responsibility involved*
The solicitors were not, so far as we know, specialists in this type of work, but its
very nature calls for a high degree of skill and responsibility. The special feature was
the short time available. This stemmed from the late acquisition of some of the
f properties making up the site, coupled with the fact that, as a result of the impending
introduction of development land tax, the deal was only commercially practicable
if it was completed before the end of July. The degree of skill, responsibility and
labour required when working to a deadline can be very high and was so in this case.

(iii) *The time spent on the business*
The recorded time was agreed at 60 hours of senior partner's time, but this was
g clearly a case in which a great deal of unrecorded thinking time must have been
involved.

(iv) *The number and importance of the documents prepared*
or perused without regard to length
Suffice it to say that there were no unusual features under this head.

(v) *The place where and the circumstances in which the business*
or any part thereof is transacted
The work was done by a Basingstoke firm, the unusual features being the expedition and value to the client which are better considered under other heads.

h (vi) *The amount or value of any money or property involved*
This head is not concerned with a precise valuation, but rather with establishing in

---

1   [1975] 2 All ER 436, [1975] 1 WLR 1504
2   [1975] 2 All ER 436 at 443, [1975] 1 WLR 1504 at 1512

what broad category of value it should be placed. In the *Reversionary* case[1] we suggested bands of under £¼m, £¼m–£1m, £1m–£2½m, £2½–£5m, £5m–£10m and over £10m. We see no reason to suggest different bands today. However, we should perhaps make it clear that we were not then and are not today concerned with the band below £¼m which would equire subdivision or with that over £10m which would also require to be looked at again in its higher reaches. In broad terms this was a £2m transaction. In fact, the parties agreed that the value of the land with planning permission was £1m and that a further £1m was to be spent by the client in redevelopment. But the same result could have been achieved by valuing the lease. The Council of the Law Society has expressed the view based on respectable valuation practice that the value factor in the grant of a lease at a rack rent can be determined by multiplying half the rent by the term of years not exceeding 20 years. We agree with this view and would only add that for terms exceeding 20 years we would adopt a multiplier of ten applied to the annual rent. In the present case this gives a value of £1,900,000.

(vii) *Whether any land involved is registered land within the meaning of the Land Registration Act 1925*
This was unregistered land, and we would have taken this into account if the bill had related to its acquisition. However, in the context of the solicitors having recently acted in its acquisition, we do not consider this difference to be significant.

(viii) *The importance of the matter to the client*
The matter did not have a special subjective importance to the client, but its objective importance in terms of value and what would be lost if it was not completed by the deadline was very considerable.

Against this background we found ourselves thinking of figures. We will not specify them save to say that they fell within a £2,500 bracket based on experience of the range of professional charges in major property transactions.

We then looked at the eight factors and asked ourselves what was the factor or factors, if any, which distinguished this transaction from the general run of such transactions. The answer was clearly the 'adrenalin' factor. By this we mean that the solicitor had not only to work fast but had absolutely no margin for error. The transaction had to be completed by 31st July, come what might, or their client would had lost not only this deal, but all possibility of avoiding the effects of the development land tax. This caused us to look towards the top rather than the bottom of the bracket. In a different case, we might have found that there was plenty of time and that the transaction was very similar to one with which the solicitors had previously been concerned for the same client. This would have caused us to look in a reverse direction.

We then looked at the only two factors which of themselves can be used to produce a monetary result. They are factors (iii), recorded time, and (vi), value. As we have already pointed out, recorded time does not provide an arithmetical basis for a charge in cases such as this. Its relevance is to check whether the provisional figures for remuneration bear a reasonable relationship to the overheads attributable to the transaction. In this case the figures which we had in mind did not seem to bear an unusual relationship to the overheads in a transaction of this type and we therefore obtained no positive assistance from considering this factor.

Turning now to value, we reminded ourselves that scale fees have been abolished. Nevertheless, it is reasonable and fair to the client that the remuneration should not be disproportionate to the value of the property involved. It was therefore useful to employ a yardstick to assess that relationship.

---

1 [1975] 2 All ER 436 at 443, [1975] 1 WLR 1504 at 1511

Various yardsticks with a regressive basis can be suggested and an example will be found in the Oyez Practice Notes[1]. The author correctly stresses that this is only an example and each case will have to be considered on its own merits. The fact is that there is no right yardstick, although some may be wrong. For our part we would consider that $\frac{1}{2}$ per cent on the first £250,000 in a major transaction and thereafter regressing provides a reasonable method of assessment.

We must also make it clear that we disagree with the suggestion in the Oyez Notes that the purpose of a scale is to arrive at remuneration for the responsibility/risk element which is then to be added to the remuneration for other elements. This is not the case. Remuneration has to be assessed for all the circumstances taken together and the purpose of a regressing yardstick is, as we have said, to check that the provisional figure bears a reasonable relationship to the value of the property. This is not only reasonable but also fair to both parties and in particular to the client.

We also compared our figures with that in the *Reversionary* case[2], taking account of the distinctions which exist. There are several. The most important is that the *Reversionary* case[2] concerned a part transaction covering only the solicitor's work subsequent to the notice to treat. In the present case the bill covered the agreement for a lease, the lease itself and the building contract. The Treasury Solicitor also submitted that there should be a heavy discount because the *Reversionary* case[2] was concerned with a freehold interest whereas this case concerns a leasehold interest. We reject this submission, which reflects a distinction made in the old scales of remuneration. The nature of the interest is irrelevant as such. What matters is the effect which that nature has on the various factors of skill, work, value, complexity etc. There will be occasions when dealing with a leasehold interest is simpler than with a freehold, but the converse can also be true.

One further submission of general interest should be mentioned. This was that the paying party (for whom it is understood speed was not of the essence in this case) should not be expected to pay for the expedition made necessary by the fact that the client failed to assemble the parcels of land at an earlier date and also found itself up against a fiscal deadline. The short answer to this is that the Secretary of State agreed to pay the client's costs and it is the client's costs which we are called on to tax.

As we said in the *Reversionary* case[3], in the end we have to make a value judgment, based on discretion and on experience, vicarious in my case but direct and considerable in the case of the assessors. Our figure may not be *the* right figure, and indeed such a figure probably does not exist. But we hope that it will be *a* right figure; one which is reasonable in all the circumstances and which is fair both to the client and to the solicitor. Our figure is £8,000 exclusive of any value added tax. Of this figure 75 per cent together with £35·50 for disbursements is payable at once. The balance is payable when the lease is completed.

Order accordingly.

Solicitors: *Treasury Solicitor*; *Ward Bowie & Co*, Basingstoke (for the solicitors).

K Mydeen Esq Barrister.

---

1 No 20: Chavasse, Conveyancing Costs (6th Edn, 1975), p 33
2 [1975] 2 All ER 436, [1975] 1 WLR 1504
3 [1975] 2 All ER 436 at 443, [1975] 1 WLR 1504 at 1512

Williams v Staite and another

COURT OF APPEAL, CIVIL DIVISION
LORD DENNING MR, GOFF AND CUMMING-BRUCE LJJ
29th, 30th NOVEMBER, 1st DECEMBER 1977

Licence – Licence to occupy premises – Equitable licence – Revocation – Revocation claimed by legal owner because of licensee's subsequent conduct – Effect of conduct on licensee's right to claim equitable relief – Excessive user of property or bad behaviour towards legal owner not conduct justifying revocation of licence – Defendant occupying one of two adjoining cottages under equitable licence for life pronounced by court in action for possession brought by previous legal owner of property – Present legal owner living in other cottage claiming possession on ground of defendant's subsequent conduct – Conduct as pleaded and found by judge consisting of trifling acts – Disturbance of legal owner's quiet enjoyment not pleaded – Judge determining licence – Whether conduct sufficient to justify revocation of licence – Whether court entitled to grant defendant equitable relief.

Until 1971 the defendants, under a family arrangement, occupied a cottage ('no 2') which formed part of property comprising that cottage, an adjoining cottage ('no 1'), a garden and paddock. In 1971 the property was sold to C. He wanted possession of no 2 and brought an action for possession against the defendants. In that action the judge held that the defendants had a licence to occupy no 2 until C purported to revoke it and that thereafter, in all the circumstances, they had an equitable right to live in no 2 for the rest of their lives. As C could not get possession of no 2 he sold the property to the plaintiff, who knew about the defendants' equitable right. The plaintiff intended to live at no 1. When the defendants learned that he had bought the property they threatened him with trouble and carried out the threat by blocking the entrance to the paddock, which made it difficult for him to move his furniture into no 1, and by constructing a small stable on the paddock. The plaintiff brought an action for possession of no 2 against the defendants. His case as pleaded was that the equitable licence pronounced in the previous action had been determined because of the defendants' subsequent conduct in carrying out several specified acts on the property. All of the alleged acts were trifling. The plaintiff did not plead that the defendants' conduct deprived him of quiet enjoyment of no 1 or that by reason of their conduct they were not entitled to claim equitable relief. The judge found that the defendants' conduct consisted (a) in bringing improper and unjustifiable pressure to bear on the plaintiff to persuade him, falsely, that the defendants were entitled to do whatever they wished with no 2, its garden and the paddock without reference to the plaintiff, (b) in acting in deliberate though minor breach of a promise they had given to the court in August 1974 pending trial of the action, not to do any further work on the paddock or prevent the plaintiff's access to and from the paddock, and (c) in giving false evidence in an attempt to deceive the court as to the extent of the equitable licence, i e in wrongly claiming that it extended to the paddock. The judge held that by reason of that conduct the equitable licence could, and would, be terminated and that the plaintiff was therefore entitled to possession of no 2. The defendants appealed.

Held – (i) Where the party setting up an equitable licence to occupy property was guilty of grave impropriety in relation to the property, the court was required to consider whether his conduct entitled him to claim equitable relief. However, conduct which consisted only of excessive user of the property or bad behaviour towards the legal owner could not terminate or justify revocation of an equitable licence. Since the defendants' conduct as pleaded and as found by the judge was not sufficiently grave to justify termination or revocation of the equitable licence to occupy no 2,

the court was entitled to allow the defendants to claim equitable relief against eviction
a despite their conduct. It followed that the judge's decision that the licence had been
terminated was wrong and the appeal would be allowed (see p 932 *c* to *f* and *h j* and
p 933 *d e* and *j* to p 934 *f*, post).

(ii) (Per Goff and Cumming-Bruce LJJ.) In any event the plaintiff's case on the appeal,
i e that the defendants' conduct estopped them from asserting that they had an
equity to occupy no 2, was not the case pleaded below and was not the basis on which
b the trial had proceeded or on which the judge had decided it, i e that the defendants
had a right under the licence but that it had been forfeited as a result of their conduct,
and, further, in the 1971 action the judge had determined, in a decision binding on the
plaintiff as successor in title, that the defendants had an equity to stay in no 2 after C
had purported to revoke the licence (see p 933 *g h* and p 934 *c* and *f*, post).

Per Goff and Cumming-Bruce LJJ. Rights in equity do not necessarily crystallise
c forever at the time when they come into existence. On the contrary when a party
raises an equity of the character of an equitable licence and it is alleged against him
that his own behaviour has been wrong, the court has to decide on the facts whether
a sufficient answer to his equity has been made out (see p 933 *f* and p 934 *f* to *h*, post).

Notes

d For the nature, and revocation, of a licence to occupy premises, see 23 Halsbury's
Laws (3rd Edn) 430-432, para 1026, and for cases on the subject, see 31(1) Digest
(Reissue) 201-202, 219-223, 1678-1691, 1781-1821.

For equitable or promissory estoppel, see 16 Halsbury's Laws (4th Edn) para 1514.

Cases referred to in judgments

e Crabb v Arun District Council [1975] 3 All ER 865, [1976] 1 Ch 179, [1975] 3 WLR 847,
CA, Digest (Cont Vol D) 312, *1250a*.
Dodsworth v Dodsworth (1973) 228 Estates Gazette 1115.
Inwards v Baker [1965] 1 All ER 446, [1965] 2 QB 29, [1965] 2 WLR 212, CA, Digest
(Cont Vol B) 242, *1552a*.

Cases also cited

f Binions v Evans [1972] 2 All ER 70, [1972] 2 Ch 359.
Central London Property Trust Ltd v High Trees House Ltd (1946) [1956] 1 All ER 256,
[1947] KB 130.
Chalmers v Pardoe [1963] 3 All ER 552, [1963] 1 WLR 677, PC.
Clavering v Ellison (1859) 7 HL Cas 707.
Hopgood v Brown [1955] 1 All ER 550, [1955] 1 WLR 213, CA.
g Ives (E R) Investments Ltd v High [1967] 1 All ER 504, [1967] 2 QB 379.
Jones (A E) v Jones (F W) [1977] 2 All ER 231, [1977] 1 WLR 438, CA.
Sifton v Sifton [1938] 3 All ER 435, [1938] AC 656, PC.
Woodcock (Jess B) & Sons Ltd v Hobbs [1955] 1 All ER 445, [1955] 1 WLR 152, CA.

Appeal

h This was an appeal by the defendants, Maureen Staite and her husband Edwin
Staite, against the judgment of his Honour Judge Hopkin Morgan QC, given in the
Pontypool and Abergavenny County Court on 24th September 1976 in favour of the
plaintiff, Alfred William Williams, adjudging that the defendants' licence to occupy
land known as the cottage and garden, 2 Brook Cottages, Llangibby, nr Usk in the
County of Gwent, was determined, and ordering the defendants to give possession
j thereof to the plaintiff on or before 31st December 1976. The grounds of the appeal
were (1) that the judge had erred in law in adjudging and declaring that a licence to
occupy land for the licensee's life or for so long as the licensee wished to occupy the
same could be revoked by reason of subsequent conduct of the licensees, (2) that the
judge had erred in law in adjudging and declaring that an irrevocable licence to occupy
land as aforesaid was capable of revocation, (3) that the judge had erred in law and/or

on the evidence in holding that the licence to occupy the land in question could be revoked, and (4) that the judge had erred in law and/or on the evidence before him *a* and/or in the exercise of his discretion in holding that the defendants' conduct had constituted so gross an abuse of the licence granted to them that it ought to be determined and possession of the land granted to the plaintiff. The facts are set out in the judgment of Lord Denning MR.

H E Francis QC and Richard M Francis for the defendants. *b*
Paul V Baker QC and David Morris for the plaintiff.

LORD DENNING MR. This is an unfortunate dispute between neighbours in two small cottages in Wales, 1 and 2 Brook Cottages, Llangibby. They are both owned by Mr Williams the plaintiff. He occupies no 1. Mr and Mrs Staite the defendants *c* occupy no 2. Mr Williams wants to turn the Staites out of no 2.

The case arises out of a family arrangement made 17 years ago. Both cottages were then owned by Mrs Staite's mother, Mrs Moore. She had owned them both from 1946 onwards. She had a daughter who lived at home. Then in 1960 the daughter married Mr Staite. The mother said to her daughter: 'You can live in and have no 2 as a wedding present. You can live there as long as you wish.' She said that to the bride *d* and bridegroom on their wedding. The bridegroom, Mr Saite, was not keen to move into no 2, because he had a cottage a mile or two away which went with his job. But the mother Mrs Moore wanted the young couple to move into 2 Brook Cottages. She wanted them next to her so that the daughter could look after her parents as they got older. That is what happened. The young couple moved in. Mr Saite, the bridegroom, gave up any chance of keeping his other cottage. The young couple *e* moved into no 2 so as to look after the father and mother in no 1 as they got older.

A year or so later the father and mother died. The father in 1961 and the mother in 1963. They had a son Mrs Staite's brother. He stayed on in no 1. So there it was. The brother in no 1. The daughter and her husband in no 2. That went on for years until the year 1971. The mother's executors then determined to sell the property.

Mr and Mrs Staite would have liked to have bought no 2 but they did not have any *f* money. The executors sold all the property to Mr Carver, a builder and developer. The sale included the two cottages, the garden and the paddock. It was worth £1,000 but as the Staites were there and Mr Carver, the buyer, knew the Staites were there, the price of the cottages was reduced to £600 or thereabouts.

As soon as Mr Carver bought the properties he gave notice to the Staites. He said: 'This is my property. You only have a licence to be here. Out you go.' That upset Mr *g* and Mrs Staite. Mr Carver brought an action. They resisted the claim. The case was tried by his Honour Judge Bulger. He decided in 1972 that the Staites were right and that Mr Carver, the builder and developer, had no right to turn them out. He accepted Mrs Staite's evidence that on her marriage in 1960 her father, as agent for her mother, said they could have the cottage as long as they wished and, further, it was a wedding present. The judge also accepted Mr Staite's evidence that, before he married, he had *h* a cottage a mile or two away that went with his job but he was persuaded to live at Brook Cottages because the old people wanted them near. The judge went on to find that the Staites had done work on the property. It was a very poor property, but they had spent money and done work to the amount of £100 on it. In the circumstances, the judge posed for himself this question: 'The Staites clearly had a licence to live at no 2 until the date [Mr Carver] purported to revoke the licence, but have they got an equity to stay there after that date? I think they have.' He was influenced by the decision of this court in *Inwards v Baker*[1]. It arose out of a family arrangement between father and son. It was held that the son had an equity and the court would look at

---

1 [1965] 1 All ER 446, [1965] 2 QB 29

the circumstances so as to decide in what way it would be satisfied. I said[1]: 'I am
quite clear in this case that [the equity] can be satisfied by holding that the defendant
can remain there as long as he desires to use it as his home.' Following that case Judge
Bulger in 1972 found a similar equity here. He held that Mr and Mrs Staite could not
be turned out.

That did not suit Mr Carver. He could not get possession of no 2. So he sold the
property. He sold it to Mr Williams, the present plaintiff. Mr Williams knew perfectly
well that Mr and Mrs Staite were there and were claiming an equity to be there for
their lives or as long as they wished.

Mr Williams went to his solicitors. They wrote a letter in August 1972 to Mr and
Mrs Staite. In it they said that Mr Williams would very shortly be moving into no 1
and that Mr and Mrs Staite were not entitled to use the paddock. The paddock is
only half an acre. Mr and Mrs Staite had used it for 16 years or more. They had put
their pony out to graze in it. But Mr Williams said they were not entitled to use that
paddock. Mr and Mrs Staite did not agree. They put up a small stable. They culverted
the stream. Mr Williams objected to all this. He moved himself into no 1 and claimed
the paddock. In August 1973 his solicitors wrote a letter of complaint to Mr and Mrs
Staite in these terms:

> 'We understand from our Client that despite this letter you have continued to
> occupy the paddock adjoining the above property, and in addition have continued
> to carry out construction works at the above property in express contravention
> of the instruction not to do so contained in our letter.'

This was followed up by an action in the county court. In it Mr Williams claimed
possession, not only of the paddock, but also of no 2, the house where Mr and Mrs
Staite had lived for all these years. There were negotiations for a settlement. They
failed. The action eventually came before his Honour Judge Hopkin Morgan QC in
September 1976. Mr Williams claimed that the licence had been determined. The
judge accepted, of course, Judge Bulger's findings that the Staites had an equitable
licence to be in the house for life. But he found that their conduct had been such that
the licence could be revoked. He held that Mr and Mrs Staite had lost any right to
be there because of their conduct. So he ordered them out. I will read the judge's
findings. It raises quite an interesting point of law. He asked this question: 'Can the
equitable licence for life pronounced by Judge Bulger be revoked by virtue of the
subsequent conduct of [Mr and Mrs Staite]?' He held that it could. He said:

> 'This conduct, as I have found, consisted (a) in bringing improper and un-
> justifiable pressure to bear on the plaintiff [that is, Mr Williams] in an attempt to
> persuade him, quite deliberately falsely, that they, the defendants [Mr and Mrs
> Staite], were entitled to do whatever they wished as regards no 2, its garden and
> the paddock without reference to or permission of the owner whereas in fact
> their licence was only to occupy the cottage and its garden and no more; (b) in
> acting in deliberate, even though minor, breach of their solemn promises to
> [the judge] on 16th August 1974[2] and (c) in giving false evidence in an attempt to
> deceive the court as to the extent of their licence.'

Those findings show that the judge took a very poor view of Mr and Mrs Staite.
He did not believe them; and he thought they had wrongly laid claim to the paddock

---

1   [1965] 1 All ER 446 at 449, [1965] 2 QB 29 at 37
2   On the plaintiff's application for an interim injunction to restrain the defendants from
     trespassing on his land at Brook Cottages by erecting or continuing to erect a building,
     the defendants undertook, until judgment in the present action, not to do any further
     construction work on the paddock save to construct a roof to a specified building, and not
     to restrict the plaintiffs' access to or egress from the paddock

(his finding about the paddock is not challenged in this court). The judge held that because of their conduct, Mr and Mrs Staite had forfeited any right even to live in no 2 and its garden.

We have had much discussion as to the circumstances in which the court can revoke a licence of this kind. It is considered in Megarry and Wade, The Law of Property[1], in a section headed 'Licence protected by estoppel or in equity'. The distinguished authors say this:

'The principle of estoppel may operate to prevent revocation of a right which one party has led the other to suppose was permanent . . . The revocation of a licence may also be restrained by injunction on equitable grounds.'

I start with this: following Judge Bulger's decision, Mr and Mrs Staite had an equitable licence under which they were entitled to live in 2 Brook Cottages for their lives or for as long as they wished it to be their home. It may in some circumstances be revoked, but I do not think it can be revoked in such circumstances as are found in the present case. I know that the judge took a poor view of the conduct of the Staites (and I am not sure he was altogether fair to them) in their using the paddock as they did, and the other matters he mentioned, but to my mind their conduct, however reprehensible, was not such as to justify revocation of their licence to occupy the cottage as their home.

This suggestion was put to us: 'Suppose they had made Mr Williams's life in no 1 intolerable, could not the licence be revoked then?' That may be. In an extreme case, it might be so. But in the ordinary way, I should have thought that bad conduct by Mr and Mrs Staite would not be a ground for revocation. The remedy of Mr Williams would be to bring an action for nuisance, trespass, or an injunction, and so forth. He should resort to those remedies before revoking the licence. Their conduct would have to be bad in the extreme before they could be turned out of their own home. They have nowhere else to go. It seems to me none of the three items (a), (b) or (c) would be sufficient to justify the revocation of the licence.

It seems to me that there was no justification for the revocation of this licence. The appeal should be allowed. The Staites should be allowed to remain there.

GOFF LJ. I agree that this appeal succeeds. The case, in my judgment, is a novel one. In all the previous cases the person who sought to set up an equity against the other party's claim at law had done nothing wrong save that he had acted without securing his legal position. There was no impropriety on his part. The question, therefore, was whether the relationship and conduct of the parties made it unconscionable for the legal owner to assert his legal rights. As Scraman LJ said in *Crabb v Arun District Council*[2]:

'. . . the court . . . has to answer three questions. First, is there an equity established? Secondly, what is the extent of the equity, if one is established? And, thirdly, what is the relief appropriate to satisfy the equity?'

In the normal type of case to which I have been referring, whether there is an equity and its extent will depend, I think, simply on the initial conduct said to give rise to the equity, although the court may have to decide how, having regard to supervening circumstances, the equity can best be satisfied. Thus in *Crabb v Arun District Council*[3] itself, where the court directed that the person setting up the equity should have an easement, the court felt that had the matter been dealt with soon after the conduct which gave rise to the equity it would have ordered that the party

1 (4th Edn, 1975), p 778
2 [1975] 3 All ER 865 at 875, [1976] 1 Ch 179 at 192, 193
3 [1975] 3 All ER 865, [1976] 1 Ch 179

setting up the equity should make compensation for the grant of the easement,
a but as time had elapsed during which by the conduct of the party against whom the
equity was raised the other party's land had been sterile for a number of years the
court in fact ordered that there should be no compensation. Similarly in *Dodsworth v
Dodsworth*[1], to which our attention has been referred, the court took into account
in determining how the equity should be satisfied the fact that in the meantime the
lady who had offered to share her house had died.

b   The present case, in my judgment, is different because on the judge's findings,
despite counsel for the defendants' noble efforts to defend his clients' conduct, I take
the view that the Staites had been guilty of very grave misconduct towards the
plaintiff in relation to the adjoining property. As counsel for the defendants pointed
out, seven specific matters are complained of, all of which are trifling in themselves,
and in respect of some of which no relief was claimed at all, and all of which, so far as
c necessary, had been covered by injunction mandatory or negative granted by the
county court judge. But the real complaint made against the Staites of their conduct
is, that as soon as they learned that the plaintiff had purchased the property, they went
to see him and said he was in for 'bloody trouble', and then proceeded to carry that
threat into effect forthwith and, when he came to take occupation of the house which
he had purchased, he found the Staites had blocked the entrance to the paddock so
d that the furniture could not be brought in through the only, or only practicable, way.

So the novel point is argued. It is said that the court has to determine when the
matter is brought before it whether there is any equity to restrain the legal owner
from exercising his legal right and, therefore, where there has been conduct of the
kind I have been describing, impropriety in relation to the property by the party
setting up the equity, the court has to consider whether he comes with clean hands
e so as to be entitled to equitable relief. If that be right in law, and on the facts, it is a
complete answer, and the party seeking to set up the equity is left with no right at
all and the legal owner is at liberty to exercise his legal right.

If it were necessary to decide that novel point, I am inclined to think that it is right
in principle and, when a party raises an equity of this character and it is alleged against
him that his own behaviour has been wrong, the court has to decide on the facts
f whether a sufficient answer to his equity has been made out. Also, although the
seven specific points were in themselves trivial, I think it would be for serious consideration whether the threat and its implementation were not such as to afford an
answer to the alleged equity.

However, in my judgment, it is not necessary to determine either of those points.
There appear to me to be two complete answers to the case raised by the plaintiff.
g The first is that that was not the case pleaded below, and it was not the basis on which
the trial proceeded or on which the judge decided it. The case was that the Staites
had a right under a licence but that it had been forfeited. The second point is that the
matter came earlier before his Honour Judge Bulger who, although he only refused
an order for possession did, as it seems to me, determine at that stage that there was
an equity and what it was. Thus, he said:

h   'The Staites clearly had a licence to live at no 2 until the date the plaintiff
        purported to revoke the licence, but have they got an equity to stay there after
        that date? I think they have.'

Then again, later in his judgment, he was considering whether the defendants had
an equity to stay on.

j   Therefore, it seems to me, for those two reasons the case which counsel has so ably
presented on behalf of the plaintiff is not maintainable in this court. The only thing
that is left, therefore, is the case sought to be made below that in some way the equity
which the Staites have been held to have by decision binding on the plaintiff as a
successor in title has been forfeited or determined. In my judgment, however, it

---

1   (1973) 228 Estates Gazette 1115

cannot stand in that way either. Excessive user or bad behaviour towards the legal owner cannot bring the equity to an end or forfeit it. It may give rise to an action for damages for trespass or nuisance or to injunctions to restrain such behaviour, but I see no ground on which the equity, once established, can be forfeited. Of course, the court might have held, and might hold in any proper case, that the equity is in its nature for a limited period only or determinable on a condition certain. In such a case the court must then see whether, in the events which have happened, it has determined or it has expired or been determined by the happening of that condition. No such case was ever raised before us, and there is no suggestion in the judgment of his Honour Judge Bulger that the equity was so limited or determined.

For those reasons, in my judgment, the judge below reached a wrong conclusion, and this appeal should be allowed.

CUMMING-BRUCE LJ. I agree, and agree for the reasons stated by Goff LJ. If the case had been pleaded as a case in which the legal owner had been deprived of the possibility of the enjoyment of 1 Brook Cottages by the deliberate behaviour of the defendants, and that had been found as a fact, the court would in my judgment have had the power to look at the circumstances as they existed at the time of the hearing in order to decide whether it was right to allow the defendants to claim equitable relief. But in this case no such case was pleaded. What was pleaded was a series of acts set out in the amended particulars of claim. Thereafter, as the evidence developed, it appeared that there was material on which the court could have found a threat to make quiet enjoyment of no 1 impossible and a course of conduct by the defendants rendering such quiet enjoyment impracticable. But when the judge came to his findings, when seeking the answer to the question; 'Can the equitable licence for life pronounced by Judge Bulger be revoked by virtue of the subsequent conduct of the defendants?', he did not find threat or conduct as I have described. He found three different kinds of conduct, none of which, in my view, could operate to entitle the court to hold that that conduct on the part of the defendants had been such as to make it unfair for the court to allow the defendants to seek equitable relief against eviction.

For those reasons, which relate to the pleadings and the facts as found by the judge, it is not necessary for me to express a view on the two possible analyses of this kind of proprietary estoppel. I do, however, agree with the analysis propounded by Goff LJ. I do not think that in a proper case the rights in equity of the defendants necessarily crystallise forever at the time when the equitable rights come into existence. On the contrary, I take the view, and am fortified by the analysis and result in *Dodsworth v Dodsworth*[1], that the true analysis is that when the plaintiff comes to court to enforce his legal rights, the defendant is then entitled to submit that in equity the plaintiff should not be allowed to enforce those rights and that the defendant, raising that equity, must then bring into play all the relevant maxims of equity so that the court is entitled then on the facts to look at all the circumstances and decide what order should be made, if any, to satisfy the equity.

For those reasons I agree that the appeal succeeds, and I would only make it plain that I appreciate that in the county court this was a very difficult case for everybody to conduct, containing a difficult series of questions, some of a wholly novel character, for the judge to solve. I am reluctant in relation to county court proceedings to be seen to be too emphatic about holding parties to their pleadings, particularly in a material as difficult as this but, having said that, I agree that the appeal should be allowed for the reasons I have given.

Appeal allowed; order below varied. Leave to appeal to the House of Lords refused.

Solicitors: *Emmanuel Marks & Cocker*, Newport, Gwent (for the defendants); *Le Brasseur, Davis & Son*, Newport, Gwent (for the plaintiff).

Sumra Green Barrister.

---

1   (1973) 228 Estates Gazette 1115

Hardwick v Johnson and another

COURT OF APPEAL, CIVIL DIVISION

LORD DENNING MR, ROSKILL AND BROWNE LJJ

5th, 6th DECEMBER 1977

Licence – Licence to occupy premises – Deserted wife's right to occupy matrimonial home – Revocation of licence – Family enterprise – Family arrangement whereby husband's mother purchasing house for husband and wife on payment of monthly sums by them – Nature of legal relationship between mother and husband and wife – Licence – Marriage breaking down early on – Husband leaving wife for another woman – Wife and baby remaining in house – Wife offering to make monthly payments to mother – Mother claiming possession of house – Whether licence to occupy house joint licence in favour of husband and wife – Whether licence revocable as against wife on breakdown of marriage.

When her son became engaged to marry the daughter-in-law, the mother promised to buy the couple a house to live in and when the couple found a suitable house told them that she would buy it and that they could pay her rent. On 30th March 1973, four days before the couple were married, the mother paid the purchase price of £12,000 for the house and it was conveyed into her name. After the marriage the couple occupied the house. The arrangement between the parties was that from 1st April 1973 the couple were to pay the mother £7 a week. It was not, however, made clear whether that sum was for rent or was towards payment of the purchase price, and nothing was said about conveying the house to the couple if they paid off the purchase price. The couple made some payments to the mother but after May 1974 ceased to pay her anything. The mother did not insist on any more payments because she knew the couple were short of money. After about a year the marriage broke down. In January 1975 the mother, through her solicitors, wrote to the daughter-in-law stating that she had purchased the house on the understanding that the son would pay 'rent' of £7 a week but only about two month's rent had been paid, and that as the marriage had broken down she wished to sell the house and therefore required possession. On receiving the letter the daughter-in-law offered to pay the mother £7 a week. In March the son left the house. In May the mother's solicitors served notice on the son determining her right, whether it was a tenancy or a licence, to occupy the house. In May or June a child was born to the couple and the daughter-in-law and the child remained in the house. Divorce proceedings were not pending. In June the mother brought proceedings against the son and daughter-in-law claiming possession of the house and, inter alia, arrears of the monthly instalments for the period 1st April 1973 to 28th April 1975, which amounted to £700. The judge refused to make a possession order on the grounds that the arrangement between the parties amounted to the grant of a licence to the son and daughter-in-law jointly, and not to the son alone, on terms that they would pay the mother £28 per month whilst either of them was in occupation, that after May 1974 the mother had waived the monthly payments by postponing the time when they were to recommence, and that as from January 1975 £7 a week had become payable in respect of the occupation but as the daughter-in-law had offered to pay that sum from January 1975 she, being the only person now in possession, was not in breach of the terms of the licence. The judge ordered the daughter-in-law to pay £112 as arrears of the monthly payments of £28 due for the four months January to April 1975. The mother appealed.

Held – To determine the legal relationship resulting from a family arrangement the courts had to impute to the parties their common intention in the events which had occurred. In the circumstances, the arrangement amounted to the grant of a

licence, which was equitable (per Lord Denning MR) or contractual (per Roskill and
Browne LJJ), to the son and daughter in-law jointly to live in the house on condition   *a*
that they paid the mother £28 monthly. Furthermore the licence was not conditional
on the marriage succeeding since it was not reasonable to impute to the parties a
common intention that, if the marriage broke down because the son went off with
another woman, his wife and child were to be ejected from the house. Since the
licence was a joint one, since the mother had postponed the monthly payments between
May 1974 and January 1975 and since thereafter the daughter-in-law had offered to   *b*
resume the payments, the daughter-in-law was not in breach of the licence and it
was not revocable as against her. It followed that the mother was not entitled to
possession and that the appeal would be dismissed (see p 938 *f g* and *j* to p 939 *a* and
f and *h*, p 940 *b c* and *f* to p 941 *a* and *c* and *e f* and p 942 *b*, post).

Errington v Errington and Woods [1952] 1 All ER 149 and dictum of Lord Diplock in
Pettitt v Pettitt [1969] 2 All ER at 413, 414 applied.   *c*

Notes
For family arrangements, see 9 Halsbury's Laws (4th Edn) para 307 and 18 ibid
paras 301-328.

Cases referred to in judgments   *d*
Balfour v Balfour [1919] 2 KB 571, [1918-19] All ER Rep 860, 88 LJKB 1054, 121 LT 346,
    CA, 12 Digest (Reissue) 21, 3.
Errington v Errington and Woods [1952] 1 All ER 149, [1952] 1 KB 290, CA, 31(1) Digest
    (Reissue) 208, 1734.
Jones v Padavatton [1969] 2 All ER 616, [1969] 1 WLR 328, CA, 12 Digest (Reissue)
    25, 20.   *e*
Pettitt v Pettitt [1969] 2 All ER 385, [1970] AC 777, [1969] 2 WLR 966, 20 P & CR 991,
    HL, 27(1) Digest (Reissue) 102, 707.
Williams v Staite p 928, ante, [1978] 2 WLR 825, CA.

Case also cited
Gissing v Gissing [1970] 2 All ER 780, [1971] AC 886, HL.   *f*

Appeal
The plaintiff, Stella Hardwick ('the mother'), brought an action in the Trowbridge
County Court claiming against the defendants, Robert Johnson and Janet Anne
Johnson ('the son' and 'the daughter-in-law') possession of a property known as 222
Frome Road, Trowbridge, Wilts, £700 arrears of rent, or alternatively of payments   *g*
due, for the period 1st April 1973 to 28th April 1975 and mesne profits, at the rate of £7
per week, from the date of the claim, 24th June 1975, until possession. On 23rd February 1977 Mr F R N Massey sitting as a deputy circuit judge dismissed the claim for
possession on the ground that the arrangement between the parties was that the son
and daughter-in-law had a licence to occupy the property and that the daughter-in-
law, who alone remained in possession, was not in breach of the conditions of the   *h*
licence. However the judge made an order against the daughter-in-law for payment
to the mother of £112 as arrears due in respect of the occupation of the property.
The mother appealed seeking an order for possession and payment by the daughter-
in-law of the further sum of £721, or alternatively a new trial of the action. The
grounds of the appeal were, inter alia, (1) that the judge's finding that the mother had
granted a licence to the son and daughter-in-law jointly rather than to the son alone   *j*
was against the weight of the evidence, (2) that if the judge was correct in finding that
the arrangement was not a licence granted to the son alone, he should have found
that there was no agreement between the parties, or alternatively that any such
agreement was void for uncertainty, (3) that the judge was wrong in holding that the
daughter-in-law had not been served with notice of determination of the licence, and

a (4) that the finding that the mother had waived payment of moneys due to her between June 1973 and January 1975 was against the weight of the evidence. The facts are set out in the judgment of Lord Denning MR.

Christopher Gosland for the mother.
Nigel Inglis-Jones for the son.
James Wigmore for the daughter-in-law.

b **LORD DENNING MR.** This is another case of a 'family arrangement' which gives rise to special problems. Mrs Hardwick is the mother of Robert Johnson. He has been twice married. On each occasion his mother has helped him and his wife to get a house. On the first marriage, the house was put in the joint names of the couple. That marriage broke up and there was a divorce. It gave rise to problems about the c house which were later resolved. On the second marriage the mother determined to keep the house in her own name. That marriage has now broken up. And problems have now arisen about this second house. The story is this.

In 1972 the son, Robert Johnson, became engaged to Janet. The mother promised to buy them a house to live in when they got married. They found a house at Trowbridge in Wiltshire, 222 Frome Road, Trowbridge. It was a good and suitable house. d The price was £12,000. Janet, the fiancee, paid a reservation fee of £100 to get it reserved for them. The mother went to see it and told the young couple: 'I'll buy the house and you can pay me rent.' The mother went to her solicitor and told him she would buy the house for the young couple for £12,000. The solicitor suggested that it should be put into the joint names of the young couple, but the mother insisted that the house should be conveyed into her own name. The mother repaid Janet e the £100 reservation fee and paid £12,000 for the house. It was conveyed to the mother on 30th March 1973. The son and his fiancee married four days later on 4th April, and they occupied the house thereafter. It was arranged that the young couple were to pay the mother £7 a week from 1st April 1973, and this was supposed to pay off the purchase price of the house. It appears that the young couple made a few payments. They made them through a joint account. They were made on 19th f April 1973, £28; 12th November 1973, £20; 7th February 1974, £20; and 28th May 1974, £20. But that was all. The mother did not insist on any more payments. She knew the young couple had not got much money to live on. (It appears that the son had to make payments in respect of the child of his first marriage.) The second marriage with Janet lasted about a year, but then they began to drift apart. The wife became pregnant. The son started to have an affair with another woman. On 8th g January 1975, the mother, through her solicitors, wrote to the young wife at the house, saying that she wanted possession:

> 'We are instructed that our client purchased the property upon the understanding that a rent of £7 a week would be paid by your husband, but we understand that only about two month's rent was in fact ever paid . . . Whilst our client was prepared to allow this state of affairs to continue in order to pro-
h vide a home during the early years of your marriage, we understand that unfortunately matrimonial differences have now arisen, and that divorce proceedings are being contemplated. In the circumstances, as you are aware, our client wishes to place the property on the market for sale . . .'

So the mother wanted the wife to go out and the property to be sold. In March j 1975 the son left the house. In June the mother took proceedings for possession of the house in the county court. The little grandson was born just about that time. The wife and baby have been staying in the house. The mother made both her son and daughter-in-law defendants.

The judge heard much evidence as to the arrangements about the house, but it was all very vague and uncertain. He said: 'There is no doubt it was very much a family

arrangement, and I do not suppose that all the implications of the arrangement were
very fully discussed between the parties.' The judge accepted the daughter-in-law's a
evidence completely. He preferred it to all the others. She said in evidence: ' .. I did
not really know where we stood except that she was buying the house for [Robert]
and I. Mrs Hardwick did not want to take payment for the first few months to help
us get on our feet.' Later on she said: 'I think Mrs Hardwick always envisaged that house
would become ours by inheritance. Nothing ever was said about when you've finished
buying I will convey. Previously she had agreed to loan us the money. That is why I b
paid the £100 reservation. I think [we] agreed ... just before marriage that we would
pay £7 a week. I don't know what it was for really. Subject was always dropped like
a hot potato. "Rent" and "purchase price" never really regarded as separate matters.
Never anything crystal clear about this arrangement so that I could turn round and
say we are renting it or buying it.' That extract shows just how vague everything was.
No doubt if the marriage had turned out successfully, the couple would have gone on c
living in the house, the mother would not have insisted on receiving £7 a week, and
on her death they would have inherited the house. But the marriage did not turn out
successfully. It has broken down. A situation has arisen which they did not envisage.
The son has left the house, leaving the daughter-in-law and the child there.

So we have to consider once more the law about family arrangements. In the
well-known case of *Balfour v Balfour*[1], Atkin LJ said that family arrangements made d
between husband and wife 'are not contracts because the parties did not intend that
they should be attended by legal consequences'. Similarly, family arrangements
between parent and child are often not contracts which bind them, see *Jones v
Padavatton*[2]. Nevertheless these family arrangements do have legal consequences;
and, time and time again, the courts are called on to determine what is the true legal
relationship resulting from them. This is especially the case where one of the family e
occupies a house or uses furniture which is afterwards claimed by another member of
the family, or when one pays money to another and afterwards says it was a loan and
the other says it was a gift, and so forth. In most of these cases the question cannot be
solved by looking to the intention of the parties, because the situation which arises
is one which they never envisaged and for which they made no provision. So many
things are undecided, undiscussed, and unprovided for that the task of the courts is f
to fill in the blanks. The court has to look at all the circumstances and spell out the
legal relationship. The court will pronounce in favour of a tenancy or a licence, a
loan or a gift, or a trust, according to which of these legal relationships is most fitting
in the situation which has arisen; and will find the terms of that relationship according
to what reason and justice require. In the words of Lord Diplock in *Pettitt v Pettitt*[3]:

> '... the court imputes to the parties a common intention which in fact they g
> never formed and it does so by forming its own opinion as to what would have
> been the common intention of reasonable men as to the effect [of the unforeseen
> event if it] had been present to their minds ...'

The present case is a good illustration of the process at work. The correspondence
and the pleadings show that the parties canvassed all sorts of legal relationships. One h
of them was that there was a loan by the mother to the couple of £12,000 which was
repayable by instalments of £28 a month. Another suggestion was that there was a
tenancy at £7 a week. Another suggestion was that there might be an implied or
constructive trust for the young couple. Yet another suggestion was that there was a
personal licence to this young couple to occupy the house.

Of all these suggestions, I think the most fitting is a personal licence. The occupa- j
tion of the house was clearly personal to this young couple. It was a personal privilege

---

1   [1919] 2 KB 571 at 579, [1918-19] All ER Rep 860 at 865
2   [1969] 2 All ER 616, [1969] 1 WLR 328
3   [1969] 2 All ER 385 at 413, 414, [1970] AC 777 at 823

creating a licence such as we have often had: see *Errington v Errington and Woods*[1].

a I do not think it could properly be called a contractual licence because it is difficult to say that this family arrangement was a contract. *Balfour v Balfour*[2] is authority for saying there was no contract. I should have thought it was more in the nature of an equitable licence of which the court has to spell out the terms.

That is what the judge did here. He held that there was a licence, and he spelt out the terms in these words:

b
'... The [son and daughter-in-law] were married on 4th April 1973 and they occupied the property thereafter. I find as a fact that they agreed to pay £28 per calendar month to the [mother] while they or either of them was in occupation, and I am prepared to accept that this liability was to commence from 1st April 1973, as claimed by the [mother].'

c Then, as time went on and the mother did not insist on or require the weekly payments to be made because the young couple could not afford it the judge found that she did waive the requirements for regular monthly payments: 'I think that the [mother] was postponing the time when the monthly instalments had to start and the real question is for how long she did so.' He found that she did in fact postpone the time the payments were to start until the mother made a visit in January 1975 and

d asked about the 'rent'. From that time onwards the judge found that £7 a week was payable in respect of the premises. He said that in May 1975, when the action was brought, 'she was only entitled to ask for £112, that is to say, for the instalments for January, February, March and April 1975, having by her conduct waived payments for the earlier months'. In point of fact the daughter-in-law, through her solicitors, offered that £7 a week from the time of the first demand in January 1975.

e So the position is that it was a personal licence to the son and daughter-in-law at £7 a week. But now comes the crucial question. Was this licence revocable by the mother? And in what circumstances? What term is the court to spell out about revocability?

In May 1975 the mother's solicitor, being uncertain of the legal position, wrote letters determining the tenancy, if there was one; determining the licence, if there was one;

f and claiming possession. To my mind this licence was not revocable by the mother at will. It was certainly not revocable as against the daughter-in-law, who was still living in the house with her baby, deserted by the son. Looking simply at what is reasonable, it seems to me that the mother could not turn the daughter-in-law and child out, at all events when the daughter-in-law was ready to pay the £7 a week.

It is unnecessary to decide today in what circumstances the mother could revoke

g the licence. No doubt circumstances might arise in which it could be done. A few days ago we had a case where parents allowed a daughter to occupy a house indefinitely and after their deaths the reversion was sold to a purchaser. We held that the purchaser could not turn the daughter out, but we recognised that circumstances might arise in which it could be done. It was *Williams v Staite*[3]. For instance, if in the present case, if there had been no grandchild and the wife had formed an association with

h another man in the house, I should have thought that the mother could have revoked the licence. But there has not been a divorce, not even a judicial separation. The daughter-in-law and the grandchild are still at the house. It seems to me that as long as she pays the £7 a week this licence cannot be revoked. Things may develop in the future. One cannot foresee when it may be possible to determine the licence, but it cannot be determined at this stage. The judge was quite right in refusing to

j order possession and in giving, as he did, judgment for the amount of £112, that is

---

1   [1952] 1 All ER 149, [1952] 1 KB 290
2   [1919] 2 KB 571, [1918-19] All ER Rep 860
3   Page 928, ante

£7 a week from the time when the daughter-in-law first offered it until the commencement of the action in May 1975.

There was one further point raised. The mother wished to claim nearly £646, being £7 a week from June 1975, the date of particulars of claim, to February 1977, the date of the hearing. That was claimed as mesne profits, that is on the footing that the daughter-in-law was a trespasser. She was not a trespasser. I do not think the mother can claim on that footing; and I do not think an amendment should be allowed now to put it on any other footing. The judgment was drawn up. It provided for the £112. I do not think it right on appeal to have that judgment altered in any way.

I find myself in entire agreement with the very careful and full judgment of the judge, and I would dismiss the appeal.

ROSKILL LJ. I agree that this appeal should be dismissed. In deference to counsel for the mother's excellent argument, which if he will allow me to say so loses none of its merit by its lack of success, I would add a few words to what Lord Denning MR has said.

I too have reached the conclusion that this appeal should be dismissed. I have great sympathy with the mother. In 1973 her son was about to embark on a second marriage. She had already helped him in connection with a first marriage which had broken down and she was therefore not inexperienced in the problems which can arise when parents are generous towards their children when marriages are about to take place. On this occasion she was anxious to help to provide a house for the couple who were about to be married; but, as Lord Denning MR has said, it is plain that what she did was to enter on a family arrangement and the courts must, in my view, be careful when family arrangements are entered into not to try and force those family arrangements into an unfitting legal strait-jacket.

When one looks at the correspondence before action brought and indeed at the pleadings, one sees an ever increasing number of legal arguments being founded on a perfectly simple family arrangement, but in my judgment this case can be decided on one very short ground. It is plain, as the judge said, that there was here never any tenancy. It is equally plain, in my judgment, that there was here a licence; and for my part, with respect to Lord Denning MR, I prefer to call it a contractual licence rather than an equitable licence.

The only question we have to decide is what was the nature of that contractual licence. Was it a licence to both the son and his future wife as joint licencees or was it a licence to the son alone? Nobody contemplated the possibility that this marriage would break down as soon as it did. Nobody contemplated that the son would within a couple of years or so go off and have an affair with another woman, abandoning his wife with the child of the marriage who remained in the house. What the parties would have agreed on if they had thought of that possiblity in March 1973 no one can tell, but the court, as Lord Denning MR has said and as has been said many times before (and Lord Diplock also said it in *Pettitt v Pettitt*[1]) has in those circumstances to impute to the parties a common intention to make some arrangement in the events which have occurred, albeit unexpectedly. I cannot, for my part, think that anybody would impute to these parties an intention that, if the marriage broke down as soon as it did and the son went off with another woman, his wife would be liable to be ejected from the home together with the child of the marriage. It seems to me that the arrangement was perfectly straightforward: it was a joint contractual licence to the son and his wife to live there. It was not conditional on the marriage succeeding. It was not conditional on a number of other possibilities.

I am disinclined to express any opinion on what if any events that licence is now determinable. Suffice it to say that in my judgment it is not determinable in the event which has occurred, namely that the son has left his wife, no divorce proceedings

---

1   [1969] 2 All ER 385 at 413, 414, [1970] AC 777 at 823

are pending, as Lord Denning MR has said, since that licence was not given only
a to the son. It seems to me that no event has yet taken place which justifies the bringing
to an end of this contractual licence; and therefore, for that reason, I think the
learned deputy judge reached the right conclusion in a careful and closely reasoned
judgment.

I would only add this as regards the alleged arrears of £28 a month payable under
the contractual licence. The judge spoke in his judgment of 'waiver' of the mother's
b right to that money. I do not think in that passage he meant 'waiver' in the strict
legal sense of that word. I think he meant that, as one often finds in family arrangements, the creditor was saying to the debtor: 'All right; pay as and when you can,
but I will not enforce the debt now.' In other words, the mother was agreeing to
postpone but not discharge the liability.

As regards the suggestion that we should increase the amount of the money judg-
c ment, I agree with Lord Denning MR that at this stage it would not be right to give
leave to amend to increase the figure of £112 to a larger figure.

For those reasons I would dismiss this appeal.

BROWNE LJ. I agree that this appeal should be dismissed for the reasons given by
Lord Denning MR and Roskill LJ. I only add I hope a short summary of my own
d reasons out of respect for the admirable argument of counsel for the mother.

I too feel sympathy with the mother, the plaintiff in this case, who I think has behaved with great generosity to her son, but I have no doubt that the judge in a very
careful judgment came to the right conclusion. He found, first, that whatever rights
of occupancy had been given, they had been given to both the son and the daughter-
in-law and not to the son alone as the mother alleged. He then goes on to refer to
e the evidence supporting that conclusion which, in my judgment, amply supports
it. He then went on to find that the result of the arrangement made was a licence.
Again I entirely agree with that finding. Like Roskill LJ I think it was a contractual
licence.

The effect of his finding was that the son and daughter-in-law or either of them
could stay on in the house so long as they complied with the conditions of the licence.
f The condition of the licence was that payments of £28 a month should be made.
Undoubtedly they were not made in full during the earlier part of the time when the
couple were living there together, but the judge held that there had been a waiver.
I entirely agree with Roskill LJ that this was not a waiver in the sense that it was
permanent. It is quite clear, I think, that the judge so found. He said:

g 'I have come to the conclusion that she [that is, the mother] did waive the
requirement for regular monthly payments. By this I do not mean that she
waived her right to receive the whole £12,000 before she conveyed the house to
the defendants. But I think that for many months she was prepared to and did
waive her right to be paid instalments due for those months' . . . So I think that
the [mother] was postponing the time when the monthly instalments had to
h start and the real question is for how long she did so.'

On 10th February 1975 her solicitors wrote a letter demanding payment in full of
the arrears. Counsel for the mother submits that she was entitled to do that. He
accepts, I think, that having agreed to postpone payments month by month she had
to give some sort of notice before she could again demand payments, but he says she
was then entitled to demand the whole of the arrears, and did so in that letter of 10th
j February and again on 14th May. I do not agree with that submission. The judge came
to the conclusion that the position was that, although she could say, 'Now you have
to start again', that would merely mean that she could demand that the payments of
£28 a month should start again.

When the payment of £7 a week was demanded by her solicitors from the
daughter-in-law on 8th January 1975 in the letter, it is perfectly true that they

demanded it under the wrong label calling it 'rent', but the daughter-in-law was
prepared to pay and offered to pay that £7 a week and, in my judgment, there was *a*
therefore no breach by her of the condition of the licence that £7 a week or, rather,
£28 a month should be paid. The judge's conclusion, with which I entirely agree, at
the very end of his judgment was: 'For all these reasons I find it impossible to say
that the [daughter-in-law] was in breach of the conditions of her licence and therefore
in my opinion this action fails.' I entirely agree, and for the reasons given by Lord
Denning MR and Roskill LJ, which I need not repeat, I agree that this appeal must be *b*
dismissed.

I should add that I am not saying that the daughter-in-law is necessarily entitled
to stay in the house indefinitely so long as she makes these payments; circumstances
might arise in the future which might entitle the mother to determine the licence,
but it is not necessary to consider on this appeal what those circumstances might be.

c

Appeal dismissed.

Solicitors: *Maim, Rodway & Green*, Trowbridge (for the mother); *Middleton &
Upsal*, Trowbridge (for the son); *Sylvester & Mackett*, Trowbridge (for the daughter-
in-law).

Gavin Gore-Andrews   Barrister.   *d*

Chandler v Kerley   *e*

COURT OF APPEAL, CIVIL DIVISION
LORD SCARMAN, MEGAW AND ROSKILL LJJ
6th, 7th FEBRUARY, 13th MARCH 1978

Licence – Licence to occupy premises – Contractual licence – Terms to be inferred – Man and *f*
*mistress – Man buying house from mistress and her husband at substantially below market
price – Mistress and husband living apart – House occupied by mistress and her children –
Man intending to move into house to live with mistress and children in due course – Relationship between man and mistress ending six weeks after purchase of house – Whether possible
to infer licence for mistress to occupy house for life – Whether licence terminable on reasonable
notice.*

g

In 1972 Mr and Mrs K jointly bought a house for £11,000, intending it to be their
family home. The purchase was financed in part by a building society mortgage.
Mr K paid the mortgage payments. In 1974 the marriage broke down and Mr K left
home, not to return. Mrs K continued to live in the house with the two children of
the marriage and Mr K continued to pay the mortgage instalments. At about the *h*
time when Mr K left home, Mrs K met the plaintiff and she became his mistress.
Early in 1975 Mr K stopped paying the mortgage instalments, saying that he could not
afford it. He and Mrs K decided to sell the house. They put it on the market at
£14,950 but failed to find a buyer even when they reduced the price to £14,300.
Meanwhile the building society was threatening to foreclose. The plaintiff offered to
buy the house for £10,000 which he said was all he could afford. In December 1975 *j*
the house was sold to him at that figure. The plaintiff agreed to buy the house on the
understanding that Mrs K would continue to live in it until she obtained a
divorce and he joined her there. Within six weeks of the purchase the plaintiff
ended his relationship with Mrs K and on 29th April 1976 served a notice on her
purporting to terminate her licence to occupy the house and requiring her to quit

a   on 28th May. Mrs K refused to leave and the plaintiff brought proceedings against her in the county court claiming possession of the house. Mrs K counterclaimed for a declaration that she was a tenant for life, or alternatively that she was the beneficiary under a trust on terms that she was entitled to remain therein with her children for as long as she wished. The county court judge dismissed the plaintiff's claim and gave judgment for Mrs K on her counterclaim declaring that she was a beneficiary under a trust on terms that she was entitled to occupy the house for her life or for so long as

b   she pleased. The plaintiff appealed. On the appeal Mrs K was allowed to amend her counterclaim by adding the further alternative that she was a licensee for life, or for so long as her children remained in her custody, and the younger was of school age and so long as she did not remarry, or for a period terminable only on reasonable notice.

c   **Held** – In the circumstances it was not possible to imply a licence to Mrs K to occupy the house for her life, for the plaintiff could not be supposed, in the absence of express stipulation, to have frozen his capital for as long as Mrs K pleased or for the duration of her life. Furthermore, although the plaintiff knew that Mrs K wanted the house as a home for her children as well as herself it would be wrong to infer, in the absence of an express promise, that the plaintiff had assumed the burden of another man's wife

d   and children indefinitely, and long after his relationship with them had ended. The case was not one in which it was necessary to invoke the support of any equitable doctrine. It followed that Mrs K's contractual licence was terminable on reasonable notice and 12 months' notice was reasonable. The plaintiff's appeal would therefore be dismissed, the licence not yet having been determined, and the order on the counterclaim would be varied accordingly (see p 947 c to h, post); *Bannister*

e   *v Bannister* [1948] 2 All ER 133 explained.

     Per Curiam. In cases when a party has established an express or implied licence to occupy premises, the role of equity is supportive and supplementary. Where the parties have contracted for a licence equity will provide an equitable remedy to protect the legal right, for example by injunction, which may be by interlocutory order if the court considers it just and convenient. If, however, the legal relationship between the parties is such that the true arrangement envisaged by the parties will be

f   frustrated if the parties are left to their legal rights and duties at law, an equity will arise which the courts can satisfy by appropriate equitable relief (see p 945 j to p 946 b and p 947 g h, post).

Notes

g   For nature of a licence to occupy property, see 23 Halsbury's Laws (3rd Edn) 430-432, para 1026, and for cases on the subject, see 31(1) Digest (Reissue) 201, 223, 1678-1821.

Cases referred to in judgments

Bannister v Bannister [1948] 2 All ER 133, CA, 47 Digest (Repl) 101, 733.
Binions v Evans [1972] 2 All ER 70, [1972] Ch 359, [1972] 2 WLR 729, 23 P & CR 192, CA, Digest (Cont Vol D) 814, 2771a.
h   *Dodsworth v Dodsworth* (1973) 228 Estates Gazette 1115, CA.
Errington v Errington and Woods [1952] 1 All ER 149, [1959] 1 KB 290, CA, 31(1) Digest (Reissue) 208, 1734.
Foster v Robinson [1950] 2 All ER 342, [1951] 1 KB 149, CA, 31(2) Digest (Reissue) 1078, 8436.
Frogley v Earl of Lovelace (1859) John 333, 70 ER 450, 25 Digest (Repl) 381, 104.
j   *Hurst v Picture Theatres Ltd* [1915] 1 KB 1, [1914-15] All ER Rep 836, 83 LJKB 1837, 111 LT 972, CA, 31(1) Digest (Reissue) 220, 1798.
Jones (James) & Sons Ltd v Earl of Tankerville [1909] 2 Ch 440, 78 LJCh 674, 101 LT 202, 2 Digest (Repl) 119, 878.
Tanner v Tanner [1975] 3 All ER 776, [1975] 1 WLR 1346, CA, Digest (Cont Vol D) 578, 1732a.

Winter Garden Theatre (London) Ltd v Millenium Productions Ltd [1947] 2 All ER 331,
    [1948] AC 173, [1947] LJR 1422, 177 LT 349, HL, 45 Digest (Repl) 201, 83.

Case also cited
Ivory v Palmer [1975] ICR 340, CA.

Appeal
The plaintiff, David John Chandler, appealed against the order of his Honour Judge
McCreery made in Southampton County Court on 26th May 1977 whereby he dismissed the plaintiff's claim for possession of premises known as 300 Salisbury Road,
Testwood, Totton, in Hampshire, against the defendant, Katherine Kerley, and gave
judgment for the defendant on her counterclaim declaring that the defendant
was the beneficiary under a trust in her favour on terms that she was entitled to
occupy the premises for her life or for so long as she desired to remain there. The
facts are set out in the judgment of Lord Scarman.

Roger Shawcross for the plaintiff.
David Stansfeld for the defendant.

Cur adv vult

13th March. The following judgments were read.

LORD SCARMAN. This appeal is concerned with the right to occupy a dwelling-
house, 300 Salisbury Road, Testwood, Totton, in Hampshire. The plaintiff owns it;
the defendant, with her two children, occupies it. She will not leave, because she
says the plaintiff has agreed that she may stay there as long as she pleases. The
plaintiff went to the Southampton County Court with a claim for possession, alleging
that the defendant was a trespasser, her licence having been terminated. The defendant not only resisted the claim, but also counterclaimed for a declaration that
she was a tenant for life, alternatively that 'she is the beneficiary under a trust . . .
upon terms that she is entitled to remain therein with her children for as long as
she wishes'. In this court the defendant was allowed, the plaintiff not opposing, to
amend her counterclaim by adding in the further alternative that she is a licensee
for life, or for so long as her children remain in her custody, and the younger is of
school age and so long as she does not remarry, or for a period terminable only by
reasonable notice.
    On 26th May 1977 his Honour Judge Lewis McCreery dismissed the plaintiff's
claim and gave judgment for the defendant on the counterclaim, declaring that the
defendant was a beneficiary under a trust on terms that she was entitled to occupy
the house for her life or for so long as she pleased. The plaintiff now appeals.
    The facts are unusual. The plaintiff, Mr Chandler, acquired the house from the
defendant, Mrs Kerley, and her husband in the following circumstances. In 1972 Mr
and Mrs Kerley jointly bought the house for £11,000, intending it to be their family
home. The purchase was partly financed by a building society mortgage for £5,800.
Mr Kerley paid the mortgage instalments. They have two children, both of whom
are now living with their mother. In 1974 the marriage broke down. In May of that
year Mr Kerley left home, not to return. However, he continued to pay the building
society instalments. The defendant and the children continued to live in the house.
    At about the time Mr Kerley left home, the defendant met the plaintiff. They
became friends; sexual intercourse followed, and the defendant became the plaintiff's
mistress. This relationship continued until January 1976 when it ended.
    Early in 1975 Mr Kerley stopped paying the building society; he said he could not
afford it. He and his wife put the house on the market for £14,950, but failed to find
a buyer—even when in the autumn they reduced the asking price to £14,300. Meanwhile the building society was threatening to foreclose. The defendant naturally

told the plaintiff of her anxieties. He wanted to help, and said he could afford £10,000,
a but no more. Finally it was agreed that the Kerleys should sell the house to the
plaintiff for that figure, and the house was sold to him in December 1975. The net
proceeds of sale, after they had paid off the debt to the building society, were divided:
£1,000 to the defendant and £1,800 to Mr Kerley. The defendant accepted less than
her half-share because she understood that the plaintiff was going to let her live in
the house.

b   The arrangement between the plaintiff and the defendant, which made all this
possible, was, according to the judge's findings, the following. The plaintiff agreed to
buy the house for £10,000 (a figure substantially less than the asking price) on the
understanding that the defendant would continue to live in it indefinitely until he
moved in. For at this time, 1975, they contemplated living together in the house
as man and wife once they were free to do so, that is to say after a divorce between
c Mr and Mrs Kerley. She, very sensibly, did ask the plaintiff what would happen
if they parted; he replied that he could not put her out.
    Within six weeks of the purchase of the house, the plaintiff had brought their
relationship to an end. It was not suggested, however, that he did so in order to get
the defendant out of the house. Nevertheless he did purport in 1976 to serve a notice
terminating her licence. It was given by solicitors' letter dated 29th April, requiring
d the defendant to quit on 28th May.
    The judge found that the plaintiff had granted the defendant an express licence and
that the notice was not effectual to terminate it. There is now no challenge to these
findings. The defendant is, therefore, a licensee whose right to occupy has not yet
been terminated. Insofar, therefore, as the appeal is against the dismissal of the
plaintiff's claim for possession, it must fail. The true dispute, however, between the
e parties arises on the counterclaim. There are two substantial issues: (1) the terms of
the licence; and (2) whether the defendant has an equitable interest arising under a
constructive trust; and, if so, what is the extent of the interest.
    The judge's findings as to the terms of the licence are obscure. He rejected the
submission made on behalf of the defendant that she had an implied licence to remain
in the house all her life; yet he also held (and I quote from the notes of judgment)
f 'that there was an express agreement between the two and, as a result, there was a
constructive trust with [the plaintiff] as trustee and [the defendant] being the beneficiary'. It is possible, though certainly not clear to me, that the judge is here finding
an express agreement that she may remain for life; for he certainly granted her a
declaration that she had an equity to that effect. But, whatever the finding as to the
terms of the agreement, the reasoning of the judge in this passage is, in my judgment,
g unsound. If the defendant can establish a licence for life, there is neither room nor
need for an equitable interest. Since the fusion of law and equity, such a legal right
can be protected by injunction: see *Hurst v Picture Theatres Ltd*[1], *Winter Garden
Theatre Ltd v Millenium Productions Ltd*[2], and *Foster v Robinson*[3] per Evershed MR. If
she cannot establish such a licence (express or implied), she cannot establish an equity;
for no question of estoppel arises in this case. It is simply a case of what the parties
h envisaged by their arrangement: see *Dodsworth v Dodsworth*[4], where the Court of
Appeal considered it not right to confer on the defendants a greater interest than was
envisaged by the parties. In the present case the parties certainly intended that the
arrangement between them should have legal consequences. If, therefore, they
agreed on a right of occupation for life, there is a binding contract to that effect; if
they did not so agree, there is nothing to give rise to an equity to that effect.
j   In a case such as the present, the role of equity is supportive and supplementary.
Where the parties have contracted for a licence, equity will today provide an equitable

---

1   [1915] 1 KB 1, [1914-15] All ER Rep 836
2   [1947] 2 All ER 331, [1948] AC 173
3   [1950] 2 All ER 342 at 346, [1951] 1 KB 149 at 156
4   (1973) 228 Estates Gazette 1115

remedy, to protect the legal right, for example by injunction, which may be by interlocutory order, if the court considers it just and convenient: see s 45 of the *a* Supreme Court of Judicature (Consolidation) Act 1925. If, however, the legal relationship between the parties is such that the true arrangement envisaged by the parties will be frustrated if the parties are left to their rights and duties at law, an equity will arise which the courts can satisfy by appropriate equitable relief. An old illustration of equity at work in this way was given by Parker J in *James Jones & Sons Ltd v Earl of Tankerville*[1] (quoted in *Hurst's* case[2]). Likewise in another old case, *Frogley v Earl of* *b* *Lovelace*[3], Page-Wood V-C granted an injunction to restrain the defendant from interfering with the plaintiff shooting over his land 'until the Defendant shall have executed a proper legal grant of the right claimed by the Plaintiff'.

The judge in the present case believed he was constrained by the decision in *Bannister v Bannister*[4] to declare the existence of a right of occupation for life, even though he had rejected an implied contractual right to that effect. But, when analysed, *Bannister* *c* *v Bannister*[4] is no more than an illustration of the supportive and supplementary role of equity. It was a case in which the plaintiff gave an oral undertaking that the defendant would be allowed to live in the cottage rent-free for as long as she desired. The defendant could not show a legal right; but she did establish the existence of an understanding or arrangement with the plaintiff which, though giving rise to no legal right, brought into existence an equity which the court thought it just to satisfy by *d* declaring the defendant had an equitable life interest in the cottage with the plaintiff as her trustee. The court treated this life interest as the equivalent to a tenancy for life under the Settled Land Act 1925.

Errington v Errington and Woods[5] is a decision which follows the same pattern. The arrangement in that case was oral. The father bought a house, put his son and daughter-in-law into occupation and promised them that if they paid the instalments *e* on the mortgage the house would be theirs when the last instalment was paid. The Court of Appeal held that the arrangement conferred on the daughter-in-law (father having died, son having left his wife and she continuing to pay the instalments) a contractual right of occupation which carried with it an equity which on payment of the last instalment would give her a good equitable title to the house. The case may be said to be a classic illustration of equity supplementing a contractual right so as to *f* give effect to the intention of the parties to the arrangement. *Binions v Evans*[6] is to the same effect.

The defendant in this appeal, however, relied strongly on *Bannister v Bannister*[4] to support a submission that she has a tenancy for life. Like Megaw LJ in *Binions v Evans*[7], I find great difficulty in understanding how the court in *Bannister's* case[4] came to conclude that there was in that case a tenancy for life under the Act. It was, however, *g* a matter which depended on the particular facts of the case.

As Russell LJ commented in *Dodsworth v Dodsworth*[8], there is a risk that such an inference may fall foul of the Settled Land Act 1925, which confers a power of sale and of leasing on the tenant, powers which cannot, for instance, have been in the minds of the parties in the present case. The present case is *not*, in my judgment, a case of life tenancy; and in this respect *Bannister v Bannister*[4] is a decision to be treated as turning *h* on the particular facts of that case.

The most recent case to which we were referred is the decision of the Court of Appeal

1 [1909] 2 Ch 440 at 443
2 [1915] 1 KB 1 at 9, [1914-15] All ER Rep 836 at 840
3 (1859) John 333
4 [1948] 2 All ER 133
5 [1952] 1 All ER 149, [1952] 1 KB 290
6 [1972] 2 All ER 70, [1972] Ch 359
7 [1972] 2 All ER 70 at 78, [1972] Ch 359 at 370
8 (1973) 228 Estates Gazette 1115

in *Tanner v Tanner*[1]. It is close on its facts to the present case, in that the defendant
a was found to have no proprietary interest in the house but did have a contractual
right to live in it until her two children, of whom the plaintiff was the father, were no
longer of school age. The defendant had been the mistress of the plaintiff, who had
bought the house (when she had been a tenant protected by the Rent Act) to provide
accommodation for her and their two children. The court held it to be a case of
contractual licence, Lord Denning MR saying[2]:

b   'It was a contractual licence of the kind which is specifically enforceable on her
     behalf, and which he can be restrained from breaking; and he could not sell the
     house over her head so as to get her out in that way.'

It is yet another case of a contractual licence supported by equity so far, and only so
far, as is necessary to give effect to the expectations of the parties when making their
arrangement.
c   Accordingly, the task in this case is to determine what were the terms of the arrangement, express and implied, between the parties. I agree with the judge that it is not
possible to imply a licence to the defendant to occupy the house for her life. The
plaintiff had invested £10,000 in the house and, in the absence of express stipulation,
cannot be supposed in the circumstances to have frozen his capital for as long as the
defendant pleased or for the duration of her life. On the other hand, the plaintiff was
d well aware that the defendant wanted the house as a home for her children as well as for
herself. It would be wrong, however, to infer, in the absence of an express promise, that
the plaintiff was assuming the burden of housing another man's wife and children indefinitely, and long after his relationship with them had ended. The balance of these
factors leads me to the conclusion that the defendant's contractual licence was terminable on reasonable notice, and that the notice must be such as to give the defendant
e ample opportunity to rehouse herself and her children without disruption. In my
judgment 12 calendar months' notice is reasonable in the circumstances.
     For these reasons I do not think this is a case in which it is necessary to invoke the
support of any equitable doctrine. The defendant is entitled to 12 months' notice.
It follows that the appeal against the dismissal of the claim to possession fails in my
f judgment, the licence not yet having been determined. The order on the counterclaim should, in my judgment, be varied so as to substitute for the declaration
granted by the judge a declaration that the defendant's licence is terminable on
reasonable notice and that reasonable notice is one of 12 calendar months from its
service.

MEGAW LJ. I agree with the reasoning and conclusion in the judgment of Lord
g Scarman. Counsel for the parties expressly invited us, if we should come to the
conclusion that there was a licence determinable on reasonable notice, ourselves to
decide what length of time would constitute reasonable notice on the facts of the case.
Accordingly, it has not been necessary to consider whether, in the absence of such
consent, we could or should have taken that decision on ourselves as a part of our
decision in this appeal.
h
ROSKILL LJ. I entirely agree with the judgment which Lord Scarman has delivered;
and I do not wish to deliver a separate judgment.

*Appeal on claim for possession dismissed. Order below on counterclaim varied by substituting
declaration that defendant's licence is terminable on reasonable notice, such reasonable notice
being 12 calendar months from service.*
j
Solicitors: *William Charles Crocker*, agents for *Jasper & Vincent*, Southampton (for the
plaintiff); *Ewing, Hickman & Clark*, Southampton (for the defendant).

Mary Rose Plummer Barrister.

---

1 [1975] 3 All ER 776, [1975] 1 WLR 1346
2 [1975] 3 All ER 776 at 780, [1975] 1 WLR 1346 at 1350

Joram Developments Ltd v Sharratt

COURT OF APPEAL, CIVIL DIVISION
MEGAW, LAWTON AND BROWNE LJJ
13th, 14th, 15th FEBRUARY, 7th MARCH 1978

Rent restriction – Death of tenant – Claim by friend to remain in possession – Friend young man who had looked after elderly female tenant for many years – Platonic relationship between tenant and friend – Tenant treated friend as her nephew – No family relationship – Friend regarded by everyone as tenant's nephew – Whether friend could succeed to tenancy as statutory tenant – Whether 'member of . . . tenant's family' – Rent Act 1968, Sch 1, para 3.

In 1957 the defendant, a young man then aged 24, became friendly with an elderly childless widow. She lived alone in a flat which was leased to her by the plaintiffs' predecessors in title. In 1958 the defendant went to live there with her at her request. The widow paid the rent but they shared all the other expenses. Neither was financially dependent on the other. They resided together in the flat from 1958 until the widow's death in 1976. During that period the widow's contractual tenancy expired and she became a statutory tenant. The relationship between the widow and the defendant was a platonic one. The widow looked on the defendant as her nephew and he called her 'aunt'. Everyone regarded him as her nephew; her family knew that he was not related to her but they thoroughly approved of the relationship. The defendant looked after her and because he did so she did not have to take up residence in a nursing home or live with her family in her declining years. She was admitted to hospital for a short period. In the hospital records the defendant was described as her next-of-kin. Her family did not object. They took the view that in the circumstances it was best as he had done most for her and was closest to her. After her death the defendant continued to live in the flat. The plaintiffs brought an action against the defendant to recover possession. The defendant claimed that they were not entitled to possession because, on the widow's death, he had become, by virtue of Sch 1, para 3[a], to the Rent Act 1968, the statutory tenant by succession of the flat. The plaintiffs contended that he had no protection since he was not 'a member of the original tenant's [i e the widow's] family' within the meaning of that paragraph. The judge gave judgment for the defendant, holding that an ordinary man, if asked whether the defendant was a member of the widow's family, would have said that he was. The plaintiffs appealed.

Held – The question which the court had to determine was whether as a matter of law the defendant could be regarded as a member of the widow's family. On the authorities two adults who lived together in a platonic relationship, without any recognisable family relationship, could not artificially establish a familial nexus for the purposes of Sch 1, para 3, to the 1968 Act by acting, for example, as a mother and son or aunt and nephew would act. It followed that the defendant's claim to be a member of the widow's family at the date of her death could not succeed and the plaintiffs were entitled to possession of the flat. Accordingly the appeal would be allowed (see p 952 *e* and *h* to p 953 *b d e* and *h*, p 945 *d* to *g*, p 955 *b* and *h* to p 956 *a* and p 957 *c*, post).

Gammans v Ekins [1950] 2 All ER 140 and *Ross v Collins* [1964] 1 All ER 861 applied.

Notes

For succession to a statutory tenancy on the death of the original tenant, see 23 Halsbury's Laws (3rd Edn) 811, 812, para 1590, and for cases on the subject, see 31(2) Digest (Reissue) 987–997, 7917–7964.

---

a   Paragraph 3, so far as material, provides: 'Where . . . a person who was a member of the original tenant's family was residing with him at the time of and for the period of six months immediately before his death then, after his death, that person . . . shall be the statutory tenant if and so long as he occupies the dwelling-house as his residence.'

For the Rent Act 1968, Sch 1, para 3, see 18 Halsbury's Statutes (3rd Edn) 895.

As from 29th August 1977 Sch 1, para 3, to the 1968 Act has been replaced by the Rent Act 1977, Sch 1, para 3.

Cases referred to in judgments

Brock v Wollams [1949] 1 All ER 715, [1949] 2 KB 388, CA, 31(2) Digest (Reissue) 991, 7942.

Brutus v Cozens [1972] 2 All ER 1297, [1973] AC 854, [1972] 3 WLR 521, 136 JP 636, 56 Cr App Rep 799, HL, Digest (Cont Vol D) 211, 7271a.

Dyson Holdings Ltd v Fox [1975] 3 All ER 1030, [1976] QB 503, [1975] 3 WLR 744, CA, Digest (Cont Vol D) 592, 7946a.

Gammans v Ekins [1950] 2 All ER 140, [1950] 2 KB 328, CA, 31(2) Digest (Reissue) 992, 7944.

Hawes v Evenden [1953] 2 All ER 737, [1953] 1 WLR 1169, CA, 31(2) Digest (Reissue) 992, 7946.

Jones v Whitehill [1950] 1 All ER 71, [1950] 2 KB 204, CA, 31(2) Digest (Reissue) 993, 7948.

Langdon v Horton [1951] 1 All ER 60, [1951] 1 KB 666, CA, 31(2) Digest (Reissue) 994, 7952.

Ross v Collins [1964] 1 All ER 861, [1964] 1 WLR 425, CA, 31(2) Digest (Reissue) 995, 7956.

Salter v Lask, Lask v Cohen [1925] 1 KB 584, 94 LJKB 522, 132 LT 830, 23 LGR 327, DC, 31(2) Digest (Reissue) 989, 7927.

Cases also cited

Bowlas v Bowlas [1965] 3 All ER 40, [1965] P 450, CA.

Crook v Edmondson [1966] 1 All ER 833, [1966] 2 QB 81, DC.

Farrell v Alexander [1976] 2 All ER 721, [1977] AC 89, HL.

Hensher (George) Ltd v Restawile Upholstery (Lancs) Ltd [1974] 2 All ER 420, [1976] AC 64, HL.

Miliangos v George Frank (Textiles) Ltd [1975] 3 All ER 801, [1976] AC 443, HL.

Price v Gould (1930) 143 LT 333, [1930] All ER Rep 389.

Standingford v Probert [1949] 2 All ER 861, [1950] 1 KB 377, CA.

Appeal

This was an appeal by the plaintiffs, Joram Developments Ltd, against the judgment of his Honour Judge Solomon given in the West London County Court on 7th July 1977 whereby he dismissed the plaintiffs' claim against the defendant, Frank Sharratt, for possession of premises known as Flat 48, Coleherne Court, Old Brompton Road, London SW5, on the ground that the defendant was 'a member of the original tenant's family' within the meaning of para 3 of Sch 1 to the Rent Act 1968 and accordingly became the statutory tenant of the premises by succession on the death of the original tenant, Lady Nora Clavell Salter, on 1st April 1976. The facts are set out in the judgment of Megaw LJ.

Ronald Bernstein QC and *Jonathan Gaunt* for the plaintiffs.
Derek Wood and *Tessa Moorhouse* for the defendant.

Cur adv vult

7th March. The following judgments were read.

MEGAW LJ. By para 3 of Sch 1 to the Rent Act 1968 it is provided that on the death of the original statutory tenant, not leaving a widow, 'a person who was a member of the original tenant's family', and who had been residing with him (that is, with the original tenant) for six months immediately before his death, shall be the statutory tenant.

Lady Salter had for many years lived in Flat 48, Coleherne Court, London SW5. Her contractual tenancy expired in June 1973. She thereupon became a statutory tenant *a* and so remained until her death. She died at the age of 94 on 1st April 1976. Mr Francis Sharratt, the defendant in the action out of which this appeal arises, had lived in flat 48 since 1958. After Lady Salter's death, the plaintiffs, Joram Developments Ltd, who had become the owners of Coleherne Court in 1974, sought to obtain possession of the flat as against the defendant who continued in occupation. The defendant claimed that he had become the statutory tenant on the death of Lady *b* Salter.

The plaintiffs brought an action in the West London County Court, claiming possession of flat 48. The sole question in issue before his Honour Judge Solomon when the action came on for trial was whether the defendant did or did not satisfy the qualification that he was 'a member of the original tenant's [Lady Salter's] family' at the date of her death. If so, there was no doubt that he satisfied also the residence *c* qualification.

The learned judge, having heard evidence on 27th September 1977, delivered judgment the same day. After a careful review of the evidence and reference to three decisions of this court[1], he reached the conclusion that the defendant was a member of Lady Salter's family. Accordingly he gave judgment for the defendant. The plaintiffs appeal. *c*

The judge unhesitatingly accepted the whole of the evidence of the defendant, who, the judge said, was honest and was clearly trying to be accurate. That conclusion is in no way challenged in this appeal, and I gladly adopt it. It is apparent also from the evidence and from the judge's findings thereon that the defendant's conduct in his relationship with Lady Salter over the 18 or 19 years of their friendship was wholly admirable and of the highest standard. When the two met in 1957, Lady Salter was *d* 75. She had been a widow since 1929. She lived alone in the flat. The defendant was then 24. A friendship arose between them, which grew over the years and lasted without interruption until Lady Salter's death in 1976. It was, as will have been understood from what I have already said, at all times what has been called, in default of a better word in the English language, 'platonic'. After about 16 months' acquaintance, in 1958, Lady Salter suggested that the defendant should take up residence with her. He rather reluctantly gave up his flat in Woolwich and moved into the flat in Coleherne Court. There, it would seem, apart from absence on holidays and perhaps at times because of illness, he continued to live until the present day. He was living there when Lady Salter died.

For the first three years or so of his residence there the defendant paid £4 a week, which Lady Salter estimated was a fair assessment for the bedroom and breakfast. That payment ceased in 1961. Lady Salter at all times paid the rent of the flat, but the other expenses were thereafter shared between the two. Neither was financially dependent on the other. The learned judge has expressly held that none of the defendant's motives was influenced by financial self-interest. I quote from the judgment:

'He said so and I believe him absolutely . . . He stuck by her to the end. Nobody else in her family did so. Had it not been for the presence of the defendant, in the last five years she would have been obliged to enter a nursing home or else her family would have had to arrange to receive her into their midst. She was able to remain in her home, to be looked after by a much younger person . . . Their relationship was sensitive, loving, intellectual and platonic.'

Lady Salter had no children of her own. At one stage she had wanted to call the defendant her son, but he pointed out that his mother was alive. There was, of course,

1   *Gammans v Ekins* [1950] 2 All ER 140, [1950] 2 KB 328; *Ross v Collins* [1964] 1 All ER 861, [1964] 1 WLR 425; *Dyson Holdings Ltd v Fox* [1975] 3 All ER 1030, [1976] QB 503

no kinship at all. They were not related in blood, or by marriage, or by any process
of adoption. The note of the defendant's evidence reads:

'I called her Lady Salter and at first she called me Francis, and later Bunny.
She asked me when I had been there well over a year possibly two years to call
her aunt or cousin. I called her Aunt Nora.'

In the notes of evidence the defendant is recorded as saying in cross-examination:
'She looked on me as her nephew. I was looked on as her nephew by everyone—her
family knew the truth that I was not'. In para 10 of an affidavit by Lady Salter's
step-grandson, Mr Whelon, put in as evidence on behalf of the defendant, this is said:

'I believe that [the defendant] and my grandmother were very close and that
my grandmother turned to him for help and companionship as she became older.
Their relationship, from the way in which my grandmother spoke of it, was
certainly not that of just landlady and lodger but closer to that of aunt and
nephew.'

When Lady Salter was in hospital in the course of her final illness, the defendant
visited her daily. He was described in the hospital records as being her next-of-kin.
Mr Whelon, when he became aware of this, wrote to the defendant saying: 'I am sure
it is best to leave it like that as you have done most for her and are closest to her.' A
nursing sister in the hospital ward said in an affidavit put in evidence on behalf of the
defendant: 'Lady Clavell Salter stated that [the defendant] was her step-nephew and
wished him to be noted as her next-of-kin'.

The phrase 'member of the tenant's family', in the selfsame context as its context
in para 3 of Sch 1 to the Rent Act 1968, was first used by Parliament in s 12(1)(g) of the
Increase of Rent and Mortgage Interest (Restrictions) Act 1920. The phrase has been
considered by this court since then in a large number of cases in relation to varying
facts. The judgments in eight of those cases were carefully analysed, first by counsel
for the plaintiffs and then by counsel for the defendant. With great respect to the
interesting arguments of counsel, I do not, for reasons which I hope will become
clear, find it necessary to follow the same course. To my mind, the decision at which
we ought to arrive in the present case is dictated by the decision of this court in *Ross
v Collins*[1].

In *Ross v Collins*[1], Miss Collins, who had no relationship by blood or marriage with
the statutory tenant, Mr McRae, had looked after him devotedly for a substantial
time before his death at the age of 92 in 1962. She was nearly 40 years younger. On
his death, she claimed to be the statutory tenant as being 'a member of the tenant's
family' residing with him. In evidence, Miss Collins said that Mr McRae 'treated me
as a member of his family ... I always regarded him as a sort of elder relative,
partly as my father, partly as my elder brother'. They did not address one another
by their Christian names; nobody referred to Mr McRae as her father, nor to Miss
Collins as his daughter. They did not pass themselves off as father and daughter.
The judge in the county court rejected Miss Collins's defence to the landlord's claim
for possession. He said[2]:

'I find that [Miss Collins] never passed as [Mr McRae's] daughter, nor he as her
father ... and that he never stood to her in loco parentis ... There was no blood
relationship between these people, there was no relationship by marriage of
these people, and there was no assumption of the title of father by him, and both
being of full age when they met there was no question of either one having
parental control over the other.'

---

1   [1964] 1 All ER 861, [1964] 1 WLR 425
2   [1964] 1 All ER 861 at 863, [1964] 1 WLR 425 at 427

The county court judge's decision was affirmed by this court. Pearson LJ[1] said (and I respectfully agree) that it is not easy to extract from the earlier decisions the relevant principles or tests. However, one broad and general principle, but only a broad and general principle, is, Pearson LJ said, clearly established. That is to be found in the judgment of Cohen LJ in *Brock v Wollams*[2]:

> 'I think the question the learned county court judge should have asked himself was this: Would an ordinary man, addressing his mind to the question whether Mrs. Wollams was a member of the family or not, have answered "Yes" or "No"?'

In the present case, the learned county court judge asked himself that question. He held on the facts of the case, 'which,' he said, 'if not unique, must be very rare', that the answer to the question was 'yes'. Lady Salter and the defendant 'achieved through their relationship what must surely be regarded in a popular sense, and in common sense, as a familial nexus. That is to say, a nexus such as one would find only within a family.'

Counsel for the defendant, in his very cogent argument, submitted that, in the light of the *Brock v Wollams*[3] principle, the answer by the county court judge is conclusive. The judge, he contended, cannot be faulted on his assessment of the evidence, he has asked himself the correct question, and, unless it can be said that the answer which he gave was one that an ordinary man could not sensibly give, the answer must stand. Certainly this court would not be entitled to overrule the judge's answer merely because some or all of the members of this court would have answered the question differently.

The fallacy in that argument in relation to the present case, with all respect, is that it is for this court to decide, where such an issue arises, whether, assuming all the facts found by the judge to be correct, the question may, as a matter of law, within the permissible limits of the meaning of the phrase 'a member of the tenant's family', be answered 'Yes'.

Judge Solomon recognised, as I read his judgment, that, if a passage in the judgment of Russell LJ in *Ross v Collins*[4] was a correct statement of the law, the question in the present case would have had to be answered 'No'. But, as I understand it, the judge took the view that the passage in question was obiter dictum and, further, not a correct statement of the law. What Russell LJ said was this[4]:

> 'Granted that "family" is not limited to cases of a strict legal familial nexus, I cannot agree that it extends to a case such as this. It still requires, it seems to me, at least a broadly recognisable de facto familial nexus. This may be capable of being found and recognised as such by the ordinary man—where the link would be strictly familial had there been a marriage, or where the link is through adoption of a minor, de jure or de facto, or where the link is "step-", or where the link is "in-law" or by marriage. But two strangers cannot, it seems to me, ever establish artificially for the purposes of this section a familial nexus by acting as brothers or as sisters, even if they call each other such and consider their relationship to be tantamount to that. Nor, in my view, can an adult man and woman who establish a platonic relationship establish a familial nexus by acting as a devoted brother and sister or father and daughter would act, even if they address each other as such, and even if they refer to each other as such and regard their association as tantamount to such. Nor, in my view, would they indeed be recognised as familial links by the ordinary man.'

1   [1964] 1 All ER 861 at 863, [1964] 1 WLR 425 at 428
2   [1949] 1 All ER 715 at 718, [1949] 2 KB 388 at 395
3   [1949] 1 All ER 715, [1949] 2 KB 388
4   [1964] 1 All ER 861 at 866, [1964] 1 WLR 425 at 432

Whether or not this statement is obiter dictum, I would respectfully agree with it. Hence, unless it could be shown to be inconsistent with other binding authority, I should regard it as conclusive of the present case adversely to the defendant. I do not see that it is inconsistent with any of the earlier authorities which have been cited to us, even though, in relation to one of them, *Jones v Whitehill*[1], the distinction is a fine one. But, it may be said, the line has to be drawn somewhere; and, wherever it is drawn, that criticism can be made. In *Jones v Whitehill*[1] the person who was held to be capable of being, and to be, 'a member of the tenant's family' was the niece of the tenant's wife. There was, therefore, in that case, what Russell LJ describes as 'an in-law link'.

Whatever difficulties may arise as to the ratio decidendi of the later decision of this court, *Dyson Holdings Ltd v Fox*[2], we do not, in my opinion, have to consider them in this present case. For there would be nothing in *Dyson Holdings Ltd v Fox*[2] which would affect the issue in the present case unless it could be suggested, and it is not suggested, that there has been some change in the ordinary meaning of 'member of the tenant's family' since 1962 (the relevant year in *Ross v Collins*[3]) in relation to the facts of the present case. Hence we do not have to consider the possibly somewhat serious and difficult problems which would arise, on the basis of *Dyson Holdings Ltd v Fox*[2], by reference to a suggested change in the meaning of words used in a statute.

In my judgment, then, the defendant's claim to be a member of the family is defeated because the law, to adopt the words of Russell LJ, is that an adult man and woman who establish a platonic relationship cannot (I stress that it is as a matter of law 'cannot') establish a 'familial nexus' by acting as son and mother would act, even if they refer to each other as such and regard their association as tantamount to such. It must follow that the 'familial nexus' cannot be established in this case by the assumed, less close, relationship of aunt and nephew.

When one considers the judgment of Pearson LJ in *Ross v Collins*[4] it emerges, as it seems to me, that the ratio decidendi of that case, binding on us, precludes the defendant from succeeding in the present case. As appears from the facts of *Ross v Collins*[3] as I have summarised them, the county court judge rejected the existence of what has been called a 'de facto' father-daughter relationship. But it was still contended in this court that the facts showed a 'de facto' relationship, 'something intermediate between a daughter and a sister'. 'But', said Pearson LJ[5], 'in my view, that is not a possible method of arriving at a decision in this case'. As I understand it, Pearson LJ is there saying that, whatever might be the legal position if there were shown to have been a 'de facto' filial relationship, with the word 'filial' used in its true sense, some other, lesser, fictitious, or 'de facto', kinship will not do. A 'de facto' relationship somewhere intermediate between a daughter and a sister would, presumably, be closer than a 'de facto', or assumed, relationship of uncle and niece, or aunt and nephew. If the closer assumed relationship will not do, as a qualification entitling the person concerned to be considered as a possible 'member of the tenant's family' (and, as I understand it, Pearson LJ said that as a matter of principle it would not do) it must follow that the less close assumed relationship of nephew or 'step-nephew' (which is what is relied on in the present case) will not do.

As I have already said, in the light of *Ross v Collins*[3], I take the view that the various other interesting questions argued before us do not arise. I therefore express no views on them.

I would allow the appeal.

---

1 [1950] 1 All ER 71, [1950] 2 KB 204
2 [1975] 3 All ER 1030, [1976] QB 503
3 [1964] 1 All ER 861, [1964] 1 WLR 425
4 [1964] 1 All ER 861 at 862, [1964] 1 WLR 425 at 428
5 [1964] 1 All ER 861 at 865, [1964] 1 WLR 425 at 430

LAWTON LJ. For the purposes of this judgment I have asked myself the question which Cohen LJ suggested in *Brock v Wollams*[1] should be asked and to which Megaw LJ has already referred. There are, in my opinion, three possible answers 'yes' or 'no' (the ones given by Cohen LJ) and 'I am not all that sure but I would say "yes" (or "no", as the case might be)'.

The possibility of a third answer is of importance first, because the ordinary man does not exist, he is an intellectual concept, and secondly, because the word 'family' has no precise meaning. What it does mean depends on the context. It is a word which has changed its meaning through the years. The Shorter Oxford Dictionary, for example, gives a number of meanings, including, under the date 1545, 'the body of persons who live in one house or under one head, including parents, children, servants, etc.' Another meaning, under the date 1667, is given as 'all those who are nearly connected by blood or affinity'. The width of the meaning which this word can have is of importance because, being a word in ordinary use, the trial judge in this case had to decide as a matter of fact what it meant and whether it applied to the relationship under consideration. This court would be entitled to say that the trial judge was wrong if we thought that his decision was one which no tribunal acquainted with the ordinary use of language could reasonably have reached: see *Brutus v Cozens*[2], per Lord Reid.

In para 3 of Sch 1 to the Rent Act 1968 the word 'family' has a context. The problem is whether the defendant was a member of Lady Salter's family residing with her at the time of and for a period of six months before her death. The concept of living as a family is implicit in the statutory words. This cuts down the width of the word 'family', for example, as it is used in the phrase 'the Royal Family'. In my judgment those who live together as a family have a degree of affinity with each other based on blood, marriage (including the in-law relationship) or adoption (whether formal or informal) during childhood. Someone lacking this degree of affinity, as the defendant did, may be treated as a member of the family, but that, in ordinary English as used in the past two decades, is not the same as being a member of the family. In saying this I have not overlooked the decision of this court in *Dyson Holdings Ltd v Fox*[3] and the problems of statutory construction and precedent which that case raises. The relationship which was under consideration in that case, namely, that between a man and a woman cohabiting, is of no relevance to the decision in this appeal.

I too would allow the appeal.

BROWNE LJ. With, I think, more hesitation than Megaw and Lawton LJJ, I too have come to the conclusion that this appeal must be allowed.

Megaw LJ has fully stated the facts, and I need not repeat them in detail. For about 18 years before Lady Salter's death the defendant had lived with her at Flat 48, Coleherne Court in a relationship which, as Megaw LJ has said, 'has been called, in default of a better word in the English language, "platonic" ', and which the county court judge described in the passage of his judgment which Megaw LJ has quoted. It seems to me that, in the words of Evershed MR in *Langdon v Horton*[4], the defendant 'had by [his] conduct assumed, as it were, a filial character', especially in the last years of her life. He called her 'Aunt Nora'. She looked on him as her nephew, and everyone looked on him as her nephew; her family knew he was not, but it is clear from Mr Whelon's affidavit that they thoroughly approved of the relationship. But is this enough to entitle a court to hold that he 'was a member of the original tenant's family' within para 3 of Sch 1 to the Rent Act 1968?

---

1   [1949] 1 All ER 715, [1949] 2 KB 388
2   [1972] 2 All ER 1297 at 1299, [1973] AC 854 at 861
3   [1975] 3 All ER 1030, [1976] QB 503
4   [1951] 1 All ER 60 at 61, [1951] 1 KB 666 at 669

The foundation of all the later decisions of this court on this problem is what Cohen
a LJ said in *Brock v Wollams*[1]:

> 'I think the question the learned county court judge should have asked himself
> was: Would an ordinary man, addressing his mind to the question whether Mrs.
> Wollams was a member of the family or not, have answered "Yes" or "No"?'

b But I entirely agree with Megaw LJ that 'it is for this court to decide, where such an
issue arises, whether, assuming all the facts found by the judge to be correct, the
question may, as a matter of law, within the permissible limits of the meaning of the
phrase "a member of the tenant's family", be answered "Yes".' In *Gammans v Ekins*[2]
this court held that it could not, and reversed the decision of the county court judge
that the defendant in that case was a member of the tenant's family; this was the
only case cited to us in which this court reversed a finding by the county court judge
c that a person *was* a member of the tenant's family; in several cases it reversed findings
that a person was *not* a member of the family and in others it affirmed such findings
by the county court.

As I understand the authorities, two elements have to be considered in deciding
whether or not a person was a member of the tenant's family, relationship and
conduct (see especially Pearson LJ in *Ross v Collins*[3]). There is also the additional
d requirement of residence with the tenant for at least six months before his or her
death, which of course the defendant amply satisfied. In my view, on the judge's
findings, he clearly satisfied the 'conduct' requirement, but the question is whether
he can, as a matter of law, satisfy the 'relationship' requirement.

In *Gammans v Ekins*[2], this court held that the defendant could not satisfy it, and in
Ross v Collins[4] the majority of this court (Davies and Russell LJJ) thought that that
e decision bound them to come to the same conclusion. I think that Pearson LJ based
his decision on a different ground, namely that on the facts of that case there was no
family relationship. Those decisions are of course binding on us for what they decide.
I confess that I have some difficulty in formulating what *Gammans v Ekins*[2] did decide.
In that case the defendant and the deceased tenant had been living together, either
as man and wife or in a 'platonic' relationship. Asquith LJ, who delivered the leading
f judgment, approved the argument of Mr Blundell (who appeared for the landlord in
that case) as to the 'categories' in which the authorities up until that time had held
that the necessary relationship existed, though with an alteration in the description of
Mr Blundell's first category. But in the last paragraph of his judgment he said[5]:

> 'I would, however, decide the case on a simpler view. To say of [the defendant
> and the deceased tenant] that they were members of the same family, seems to
> me an abuse of the English language . . .'

Jenkins LJ and Evershed MR seem to me to have based their judgments on the view
that the defendant could not, in the ordinary meaning of words, be described as a
member of the tenant's family. In my view that case did not decide that as a matter
g of law a person cannot be a member of the tenant's family unless he or she falls
within one of the 'categories' referred to by Mr Blundell and Asquith LJ, and I understand Pearson LJ to have taken this view in *Ross v Collins*[6], or at least the view that
the 'categories' had not then been fully or finally defined.

In my judgment, *Gammans v Ekins*[2] and *Ross v Collins*[6] require us to hold that,
whatever may have been their conduct, two adults who live together in a 'platonic'

---

1   [1949] 1 All ER 715 at 718, [1949] 2 KB 388 at 395
2   [1950] 2 All ER 140, [1950] 2 KB 328
3   [1964] 1 All ER 861 at 865, [1964] 1 WLR 425 at 430, 431
4   [1964] 1 All ER 861 at 865, 866, [1964] 1 WLR 425 at 431, 432
5   [1950] 2 All ER 140 at 142, [1950] 2 KB 328 at 331
6   [1964] 1 All ER 861, [1964] 1 WLR 425

relationship, without any 'recognisable family relationship', cannot be members of each other's families.

The necessary 'family relationship' or 'familial nexus' can be established in various ways. Megaw LJ has already quoted what Russell LJ said in *Ross v Collins*[1]. In the same case Pearson LJ said[2]:

> 'If it were necessary, it might be a difficult task to determine exactly what the three classes or groups or categories of relationship are. In my view, however, it is not in the present case necessary to face these difficulties. It is sufficient to say that there must have been a family relationship of some kind between the surviving person and the deceased person, if the surviving person is to qualify as a possible member of the deceased person's family. There may have been a relationship by blood. There may have been a relationship through marriage; as, for instance, in *Jones v Whitehill*[3]. Also in some cases a de facto family relationship has been recognised as sufficient. In *Brock v Wollams*[4], there had been a de facto adoption at the age of five and a long continuance of the child and parent de facto relationship. There is also *Hawes v Evenden*[5], which was a case in which a man and his mistress and the several children of the association had been living together as a family. It was held after the man's death that his mistress, by virtue of the fact that they had been living together with their children as a family, could be regarded as a member of his family for this purpose. In the present case, however, there was no family relationship of any kind and the defendant for that reason must fail to qualify as a member of Mr. McRae's family. She was in no sense his daughter, neither de jure nor de facto, nor in any other way; and no other family relationship can be suggested—except (as counsel for the defendant put it) something intermediate between a daughter and a sister, or, on the other side, something intermediate between a father and an elder brother. But, in my view, that is not a possible method of arriving at a decision in this case.'

I agree with Megaw LJ that we do not have to consider the ground on which the majority of this court in *Dyson Holdings Ltd v Fox*[6] distinguished *Gammans v Ekins*[7], because there is no suggestion that there has been any change in the meaning of words or in social attitudes which is relevant to the present case. Apart from this distinction, *Gammans v Ekins*[7] remains binding on us, as the majority of this court held in *Dyson Holdings Ltd v Fox*[6]. If a de facto relationship can be enough, I confess that I find it difficult to distinguish between a decision that a husband is a member of his wife's family (*Salter v Lask*[8]) and a decision that a man who has been living for years with a woman as his wife, though without any marriage ceremony, is not; the latter seems to me to be a case 'where the link would be strictly familial had there been a marriage', as Russell LJ said in *Ross v Collins*[1]. But only the House of Lords could solve this problem.

The possible scope of de facto relationships seems to me difficult to define. The only case cited to us in which a de facto relationship was held to be enough was *Brock v Wollams*[4], where a child had been de facto 'adopted' at the age of five or six without the necessary legal formalities, and had lived with the tenant for 36 years except for

---

1 [1964] 1 All ER 861 at 866, [1964] 1 WLR 425 at 432
2 [1964] 1 All ER 861 at 864, 865, [1964] 1 WLR 425 at 430
3 [1950] 1 All ER 71, [1950] 2 KB 204
4 [1949] 1 All ER 715, [1949] 2 KB 388
5 [1953] 2 All ER 737, [1953] 1 WLR 1169
6 [1975] 3 All ER 1030, [1976] QB 503
7 [1950] 2 All ER 140, [1950] 2 KB 328
8 [1925] 1 KB 584

a break of three years. In such a case the law would recognise a de jure relationship
a of parent and child if the necessary steps had been taken; and, as Evershed MR said
in *Langdon v Horton*[1]: 'An adopted child is clothed with all the characteristics of a child
so far as the outside world is concerned.' But our law does not recognise any de jure
adoption of adults.

I am not satisfied that any de facto relationship except adopting parents and adopted
children or (on the authority of *Dyson Holdings Ltd v Fox*[2]) two people living together
b as man and wife could provide the necessary element of 'relationship'.

If the defendant had in fact been the nephew of Lady Salter (or of Sir Arthur Clavell
Salter) this could have been a sufficient relationship (see *Jones v Whitehill*[3]), and it
seems to me hard that this de facto relationship of aunt and nephew, coupled with his
conduct, should not be enough. But the line must be drawn somewhere, and if he
could be included among those who can be members of the tenant's family it would
c be difficult, if not impossible, to exclude the cases put in several of the authorities of
two old cronies sharing a house, and perhaps calling themselves and each other
brothers or sisters.

In my judgment we are bound by *Gammans v Ekins*[4] and *Ross v Collins*[5] to allow
this appeal.

d *Appeal allowed. Judgment below set aside. Judgment to be entered for plaintiffs for possession.
Leave to appeal to House of Lords granted. Stay of order for possession for six weeks; if
within that time petition of appeal lodged, stay to continue pending hearing of appeal. Liberty
to either party to apply.*

17th April. A petition of appeal was lodged on behalf of the defendant.

e
Solicitors: *Titmuss, Sainer & Webb* (for the plaintiffs); *Douglas-Mann & Co* (for the
defendant).

Mary Rose Plummer Barrister.

f   1   [1951] 1 All ER 60 at 61, [1951] 1 KB 666 at 670
2   [1975] 3 All ER 1030, [1976] QB 503
3   [1950] 1 All ER 71, [1950] 2 KB 204
4   [1950] 2 All ER 140, [1950] 2 KB 328
5   [1964] 1 All ER 861, [1964] 1 WLR 425

Benson (Inspector of Taxes) v Yard Arm Club Ltd

CHANCERY DIVISION
GOULDING J
15th, 16th FEBRUARY 1978

Income tax – Capital allowances – Plant – Apparatus used by taxpayer for purpose of business – Ship used as floating restaurant – Whether ship setting in which restaurant business carried on or plant for carrying on business of floating restaurant – Capital Allowances Act 1968, s 18 – Finance Act 1971, s 41.

In 1962 the taxpayer company, which carried on a restaurant business, acquired a ship for £2,449 for the purpose of converting it into a floating restaurant. In carrying out the conversion, the taxpayer company spent £75,862. Of that expenditure £41,254 represented the cost of acquiring the vessel and a barge, which provided services to it, and the cost of carrying out alterations to their hulls and structures. After conversion the vessel was attached to the barge which was itself fixed to mooring posts. The vessel and the barge were subject to movement by the tide and the waves. The vessel was used as a floating restaurant from 1963 to 1975. In computing its income and corporation tax for the years 1963 to 1978, the taxpayer company claimed that the vessels were plant and that the sum of £41,254 represented capital expenditure on the provision of plant for the purposes of capital allowances under s 18 of the Capital Allowances Act 1968 and s 41 of the Finance Act 1971. The General Commissioners allowed the taxpayer company's claim. On appeal by the Crown the taxpayer company contended that chattels, not associated with land, were plant if they were kept for permanent employment in the business by the person carrying on the business and that the vessels were chattels kept by the taxpayer company for permanent employment in its restaurant business. Alternatively, it contended that the vessels were apparatus essential to the carrying on of a floating restaurant business and as such were plant.

Held – The functional test of whether an object was plant, i e whether the object was part of the premises in which the business was carried on or whether it was part of the apparatus with which it was carried on, applied whether the object in question was a chattel or land, buildings or structures on land, and the application of the test was not affected by the fact that for carrying on a trade the object provided unusual premises attractive to customers. The vessels were the place or setting where the restaurant business was carried on and were not apparatus for carrying on the business. Accordingly the vessels were not plant and the expenditure on them did not qualify for capital allowances under s 18 of the 1968 Act or s 41 of the 1971 Act. The appeal would therefore be allowed (see p 964 c, p 967 h to p 968 b e and j to p 969 b, post).

Dicta of Pearson LJ in *Jarrold (Inspector of Taxes) v John Good & Sons Ltd* [1963] 1 All ER at 149, of Lord Reid in *Inland Revenue Comrs v Barclay Curle & Co Ltd* [1969] 1 All ER at 740, 741, of Megarry J in *Cooke (Inspector of Taxes) v Beach Station Caravans Ltd* [1974] 3 All ER at 167 and of Brightman J in *Dixon (Inspector of Taxes) v Fitch's Garage Ltd* [1975] 3 All ER at 461 followed.

Notes
For the allowances available in respect of machinery and plant, see 20 Halsbury's Laws (3rd Edn) 493, 494, paras 941-946, and for cases on the meaning of plant, see 28(1) Digest (Reissue) 214-216, 637-643.

For the Capital Allowances Act 1968, s 18, see 34 Halsbury's Statutes (3rd Edn) 1061.

For the Finance Act 1971, s 41, see 41 ibid 1459.

Cases referred to in judgment

Broken Hill Pty Co Ltd v Comr of Taxation (1968) 120 CLR 240 at 241, 41 ALJR 377.

Cooke (Inspector of Taxes) v Beach Station Caravans Ltd [1974] 3 All ER 159, [1974] 1 WLR 1398, [1974] STC 402, 49 Tax Cas 514, 53 ATC 216, [1974] TR 213, Digest (Cont Vol D) 456, 640a.

Dixon (Inspector of Taxes) v Fitch's Garage Ltd [1975] 3 All ER 455, [1976] 1 WLR 215, [1975] STC 480, 54 ATC 151, [1975] TR 123, Digest (Cont Vol D) 493, 1676c.

Inland Revenue Comrs v Barclay Curle & Co Ltd [1969] 1 All ER 732, [1969] 1 WLR 675, 45 Tax Cas 221, 48 ATC 17, [1969] TR 21, 1969 SLT 122, [1969] 1 Lloyd's Rep 169, [1969] RVR 102, HL, 28(1) Digest (Reissue) 465, 1676.

Jarrold (Inspector of Taxes) v John Good & Sons Ltd [1963] 1 All ER 141, [1963] 1 WLR 214, 40 Tax Cas 681, 41 ATC 335, [1962] TR 371, [1963] RVR 653, CA, 28(1) Digest (Reissue) 215, 642.

St John's School (Mountford and Knibbs) v Ward (Inspector of Taxes) [1974] STC 69, 49 Tax Cas 524, 52 ATC 326, [1973] TR 267, [1974] RA 49, *affd* [1975] STC 7, 49 Tax Cas 524, 53 ATC 279, [1974] TR 273, [1974] RA 481, CA.

Schofield (Inspector of Taxes) v R & H Hall Ltd [1975] STC 353, 49 Tax Cas 538, CA(NI).

Wangaratta Wollen Mills Ltd v Comr of Taxation (1969) 119 CLR 1, 43 ALJR 324.

Yarmouth v France (1887) 19 QBD 647, 57 LJQB 7, 34 Digest (Repl) 299, 2159.

Cases also cited

Lyons (J) & Co Ltd v Attorney-General [1944] 1 All ER 477, [1944] Ch 281.

Margrett v Lowestoft Water & Gas Co (1935) 19 Tax Cas 418.

Munby v Furlong (Inspector of Taxes) [1977] 2 All ER 953, [1977] Ch 359, [1977] STC 232, CA.

Case stated

1. At a meeting of the Commissioners for the General Purposes of the Income Tax for the Division of Spelthorne, Middlesex on 15th December 1976, the Yard Arm Club Ltd ('the taxpayer company') appealed against income tax assessments made under Case 1 of Sch D in respect of profits from its trade as restaurateurs, as follows: 1963-64, £200; 1964-65, £300: 1965-66, £300. The taxpayer company further appealed against corporation tax assessments made in respect of profits from its trade as restaurateurs, as follows:

Accounting period	
1.10.66–30.9.67	£1,000
1.10.67–31.12.67	£200
1.10.67–30.9.68	£1,000
1.1.68 –31.12.68	£2,000
1.1.69 –31.12.69	£2,000
1.1.70 –31.12.70	£12,000
1.1.71 –31.12.71	£20,000
1.1.72 –31.12.72	£20,000
1.1.73 –31.12.73	£20,000

2. The question for determination was whether the taxpayer company was entitled to capital allowances in respect of capital expenditure incurred in acquiring the vessel Hotspur later known as Hispaniola (and referred to here as Hispaniola 1) and the cost of its conversion into a floating restaurant, together with a barge which provided services to it. The expenditure in dispute related to the hull and structure of the vessels, the Crown having agreed that capital allowances were due in respect of restaurant furniture, sewage pumps etc.

3. Oral evidence was given by Mr W R Watson-Smyth, formerly chairman of the taxpayer company.

[Paragraph 4 listed the documents proved or admitted before the commissioners.]

5. The following facts were proved or admitted: (i) Hispaniola 1 had been originally

built in 1927 for use as a ferry between Southampton and the Isle of Wight. Subsequently it had been sold to a firm in Norfolk who used it as a pleasure craft. It was acquired by the taxpayer company for £2,449 in 1962. (ii) The reason for acquisition of the vessel was in order to convert it into a restaurant club. (iii) The ship was initially registered as the Hotspur at Southampton. Since acquisition by the taxpayer company it had been reregistered at Southampton as the Hispaniola. (iv) During the conversion of the vessel the engines and boiler were removed and it had thereafter no power or steering ability. (v) The vessel, after conversion, was towed to a permanent site on the Victoria Embankment, where it was used initially as a floating restaurant club and later as a floating restaurant open to the public at large from 13th August 1963 until 1975 when it was replaced by a larger vessel. (vi) The vessel was moved under tow to dry dock for repainting and maintenance every few years (maximum five). (vii) When the shares of the taxpayer company were acquired (in 1967) by Mr Watson-Smyth and other members of his family, the ship comprised three decks: a hold where the washing up etc was done, which was served by a lift from the other decks, a main deck containing bars, toilets and restaurant facilities and an upper deck comprising table facilities and the kitchen. Associated with that was the barge which was necessary for the gangway to come down and slide on. It also contained sewage disposal equipment and waiters' changing rooms etc. In 1972 a new kitchen was built on the barge. (viii) The barge was fixed to mooring posts and was able to slide up and down those posts as required by tidal movement. The maximum tidal difference at the site was about 30 feet. The Hispaniola 1 was attached to the barge by ropes and chains and was subject to the vertical tide movement of up to 30 feet and also to movement up and down river to the extent of some 5 feet caused by the ebb and flow of the tide. The waves caused it to rock gently from side to side. (ix) The customers of the restaurant nearly all joined the vessel by way of the gangway from the Victoria Embankment but some came by boat, mooring to the barge. They came, to quote the former chairman, 'to get good food somewhere different with views of the river etc and a shipboard feeling'. (x) The vessel was intended to be kept in a permanently fixed position although it could be moved if required. It was never intended to carry passengers or cargo on voyages. (xi) When it was replaced by a larger vessel in 1975 attempts were made to sell Hispaniola 1 but these attempts had failed and a new mooring was being sought at Hammersmith Pier where negotiations with the local authority had reached an advanced stage. (xii) In the period 1962 to 1973 capital expenditure was incurred as follows: 1. cost of hull alterations (including cost of vessel), £41,254; 2. Cost of lifts, machinery and furniture, £8,517; 3. cost of additional fixtures etc, £26,091; Total £75,862. Capital allowances have been granted in respect of the expenditure on the items 2 and 3 above. The dispute arises over item 1.

[Paragraph 6 listed the cases[1] cited to the commissioners.]

7. It was contended on behalf of the taxpayer company that: (i) Hispaniola 1 was at all material times a ship, was in use for the purposes of the taxpayer company's trade as proprietors of a floating restaurant, and therefore all capital expenditure incurred by the taxpayer company in purchasing, converting and making improvements to that vessel for use in that trade qualified for capital allowances. (ii) Alternatively, even if Hispaniola 1 were not a ship, it was nevertheless plant used in the taxpayer company's trade because (a) it was not merely the premises or setting in which the trade was carried on but apparatus with which the trade was carried on, (b) the function of the vessel itself, its attendant barge and the contents of both, all regarded as a single unit, was to enable the taxpayer company to provide restaurant facilities to the public on the Thames, (c) the mobility of the vessel and barge made it possible for the

---

1 *Andrews v Andrews and Mears* [1908] 2 KB 567; *European and Australian Royal Mail Co Ltd v Peninsular and Oriental Steam Navigation Co* (1866) 14 LT 704; *Gas Float Whitton, The (No 2)* [1896] P 42, CA; *Gibson v Small* (1853) 4 HL Cas 353; *Mac, The* (1882) 7 PD 126, CA; *Yarmouth v France* (1887) 19 QBD 647

taxpayer company to change the location at which the facilities were provided, (d)
the mobility of the vessel and barge were essential for other reasons, viz: i. The
Hispaniola I floated on the tide whereas a fixed platform would have had to be placed
at least 30 feet above low water mark. ii. It could adapt to tidal movements. iii.
Its mobility enabled the trade to be carried on in the same place after the Hispaniola
I had been removed and replaced by a larger vessel. iv. The vessel provided an
authentic choppy motion attractive to the diners. v. It attracted waterborne traffic.
(iii) The appeal should be allowed.

8. It was contended on behalf of the Crown that: (a) The Hispaniola I did not
qualify as a ship. (b) Even if the Hispaniola I was a ship it still only qualified for
capital allowances if it was plant or machinery in the particular trade of carrying on
a restaurant business within ss 18 and 19 of the Capital Allowances Act 1968. (c) The
fact that the Hispaniola I was capable of being moved did not make it plant. (d) The
Hispaniola I was not required to be moveable in the course of its trading operations.
(e) The equipment of the vessel was no different from that of any other restaurant
premises. The vessel was merely the structure within which the function of providing meals and services was carried on. (f) The Hispaniola I's only purpose was to
provide shelter for the customers in an attractive setting with a nautical gimmick
and the vessel otherwise played no part whatever in the commercial process of the
restaurant trade. (g) Following conversion there was no intention to use the Hispaniola I in navigation moving from place to place; it was intended to be a restaurant
at a fixed mooring. Its ability to float was a purely passive role in the sense that it
played no more functional part than any conventional restaurant premises. (h) The
vessel was the place or premises or setting or structure in which the trade of restaurateur was carried on and not the plant or apparatus with which the trade was carried
on. (i) The appeal should be determined in the agreed figures on the basis that the
disputed expenditure did not qualify for capital allowances.

9. The commissioners who heard the appeal, gave their decision as follows:

'We have listened to the learned argument on both sides but are not satisfied
in our own minds that Hispaniola I is a ship for the purposes of the Act. In our
opinion it more clearly falls within the definition of a structure. Section 40 [sic]
of the 1968 Act clearly indicates that the same entity may fall within the term
"building or structure" and also within "machinery or plant". We therefore
have to decide whether Hispaniola I is plant. We take the view that it is similar
to the Pools in the Caravan case[1] and that the fact that it is floating on the Thames
is the principal means of attracting people to the restaurant. In our view Hispaniola I is *plant* for the purposes of the Act and the appeal therefore succeeds.'

10. As a consequence of the decision, the assessments were determined according
to a schedule admitted before the commissioners of the profits assessable and capital
allowances for each period if the case were determined in favour of the company.

11. The Crown immediately after the determination of the appeal declared its
dissatisfaction therewith as being erroneous in point of law, and on 10th January
1977 required the commissioners to state and sign the case for the opinion of the High
Court.

12. The question of law for the opinion of the court was whether on the facts as
found set out in para 5 of the case the decision as set out in para 9 of the case was correct.

Brian Davenport for the Crown.
Francis Brennan for the taxpayer company.

---

1 *Cooke (Inspector of Taxes) v Beach Station Caravans Ltd* [1974] 3 All ER 159, [1974] 1 WLR
   1398, [1974] STC 402

GOULDING J. This is an appeal by way of case stated from a decision of the General Commissioners for the Spelthorne Division of the county, or former county, of Middlesex. The appellant is the Crown, and the respondent a company called the Yard Arm Club Ltd ('the taxpayer company'). The question arose on appeals against income tax assessments, and later corporation tax assessments, made on the taxpayer company over a number of years, or periods of account, in respect of the profits from the taxpayer company's trade as a restaurateur. The particular question that fell to be determined on those appeals was whether the taxpayer company was entitled to capital allowances in respect of capital expenditure incurred in acquiring a vessel, to which I shall refer in a moment, and in the cost of its conversion into a floating restaurant, together with a barge which provided services to it. That expenditure related to the hull and structure of the two vessels, since capital allowances were not contested in respect of restaurant furniture and other fixtures and fittings required for the purposes of the trade carried on on board.

The facts are set out in para 5 of the case stated by the General Commissioners. They are set out succinctly, and I can do no better than read them through:

'i. Hispaniola 1 [that was the name of the principal vessel] had been originally built in 1927 for use as a ferry between Southampton and the Isle of Wight. Subsequently it had been sold to a firm in Norfolk who used it as a pleasure craft. It was acquired by the [taxpayer company] for £2,499·00 in 1962. ii. The reason for acquisition of the vessel was in order to convert it into a restaurant club. iii. The ship was initially registered as the 'Hotspur' at Southampton. Since acquisition by the [taxpayer company] it had been re-registered at Southampton as the 'Hispaniola'. iv. During the conversion of the vessel the engines and boiler were removed and it had thereafter no power or steering ability. v. The vessel, after conversion, was towed to a permanent site of [sic] the Victoria Embankment, where it was used initially as a floating restaurant club and later as a floating restaurant open to the public at large from 13th August, 1963 until 1975 when it was replaced by a larger vessel. vi. The vessel was moved under tow to dry dock for repainting and maintenance every few years (maximum five). vii. When the shares of the [taxpayer company] were acquired (in 1967) by Mr. Watson-Smyth [he was a former chairman of the company] and other members of his family, the ship comprised three decks; a hold where the washing up etc. was done, which was served by a lift from the other decks, a main deck containing bars, toilets and restaurant facilities and an upper deck comprising table facilities and the kitchen. Associated with that was the barge which was necessary for the gangway to come down and slide on. It also contained sewage disposal equipment and waiters' changing rooms etc. In 1972 a new kitchen was built on the barge. viii. The barge was fixed to mooring posts and was able to slide up and down those posts as required by tidal movement. The maximum tidal difference at the site was about 30 ft. The Hispaniola 1 was attached to the barge by ropes and chains and was subject to the vertical tide movement of up to 30 ft. and also to movement up and down river to the extent of some 5 ft. caused by the ebb and flow of the tide. The waves caused it to rock gently from side to side. ix. The customers of the restaurant nearly all joined the vessel by way of the gangway from the Victoria Embankment but some came by boat, mooring to the barge. They came, to quote the former Chairman, "to get food somewhere different with views of the river etc. and a shipboard feeling". x. The vessel was intended to be kept in a permanently fixed position although it could be moved if required. It was never intended to carry passengers or cargo on voyages. xi. When it was replaced by a larger vessel in 1975 attempts were made to sell Hispaniola 1 but these attempts had failed and a new mooring was being sought at Hammersmith Pier where negotiations with the Local Authority had reached an advanced stage. xii. In the period

1962/73 capital expenditure was incurred as follows:— 1. Cost of hull alterations (including cost of vessel) £41,254. 2. Cost of lifts, machinery and furniture £8,517. 3. Cost of additional fixtures etc. £26,091. [Total] £75,862. Capital Allowances have been granted in respect of the expenditure on the items 2 and 3 above. The dispute arises over item 1.'

Those were the facts as found by the General Commissioners. I defer reading their decision until I have said something about the law.

Over the past century or more, in a number of statutory contexts, the courts have had to interpret from time to time the word 'plant', and there is now a substantial body of reported decisions on that word. I do not propose to make a comprehensive review of the authorities: it has been done more than once lately in reported cases, and done much better than I could do it. Let me start off, however, by referring to the phrase that the court has to interpret, and then mention some of the decisions which seem to me most important for dealing with the arguments addressed to me.

The phrase which determines the entitlement to capital allowances of the kind here in question has remained (so far as relevant) unchanged through successive versions of the revenue legislation, the Income Tax Act 1952, the Capital Allowances Act 1968 and, later, the Finance Act 1971. The allowances, subject to various conditions and provisions, are available to a person carrying on a trade who has incurred capital expenditure 'on the provision of machinery or plant for the purposes of the trade'. That is the particular context in which it has to be decided: are the Hispaniola and her attendant barge plant or not?

The earliest interpretation of the word 'plant' to which I have been referred is one pronounced by Lindley LJ in *Yarmouth v France*[1]. The learned judge, referring to the statute then before him, said:

'There is no definition of plant in the Act: but, in its ordinary sense, it includes whatever apparatus is used by a business man for carrying on his business,—not his stock-in-trade which he buys or makes for sale; but all goods and chattels, fixed or moveable, live or dead, which he keeps for permanent employment in his business.'

That interpretation of the word 'plant' has, for income tax and other purposes, been repeatedly accepted as authoritative; but, of course, it does not completely exhaust the meaning of the word in all its possible applications to particular objects.

In more recent years the courts have developed what is described as a functional test for ascertaining in doubtful cases whether or not a particular article can be properly described as 'plant'. An early statement of the test in question is contained in the judgment of Pearson LJ in *Jarrold (Inspector of Taxes) v John Good & Sons Ltd*[2]. That was a case the subject-matter of which was very different from that of *Yarmouth v France*[3]. In *Yarmouth v France*[3] it was decided that a horse was plant for the purposes of a particular trade. In *Jarrold v John Good & Sons Ltd*[2], the article in question was special partitioning to subdivide the office floor space of steamship agents in Hull. After referring to *Yarmouth v France*[3] and some intermediate cases, Pearson LJ said[4]:

'There can be no doubt, therefore, as to the main principles to be applied, and the short question in this case is whether the partitioning is part of the premises in which the business is carried on or part of the plant with which the business is carried on. Either view could have been taken. It could have been said that the so-called partitioning, when erected, constituted the internal walls of the building,

---

1 (1887) 19 QBD 647 at 658
2 [1963] 1 All ER 141, [1963] 1 WLR 214, 40 Tax Cas 681
3 19 QBD 647
4 [1963] 1 All ER 141 at 149, [1963] 1 WLR 214 at 225, 40 Tax Cas 681 at 696

which have the advantage of being movable, but until they are moved will stand firm and solid, fully performing the functions of internal walls. So regarded, the partitioning would be part of the premises and not plant. The other possible view is that the taxpayers, instead of having internal walls in their office building, need to have, and do have, for the special requirements of their business, movable partitioning, by means of which they can, in response to changing volumes of business in their departments or to the cessation of departments or the emergence of new departments, rapidly and cheaply and without much interruption of business alter the subdivisions of their office building. On that view of the facts, the partitioning undoubtedly can be regarded as "plant". I think the commissioners have, in effect preferred the second view, and it cannot be said that there was no evidence to support it, or that any error of principle was involved.'

Accordingly, the learned judge propounded the functional test for the purposes of that case as asking whether the object in dispute was part of the premises in which the business was carried on or part of the plant with which it was carried on, and accepted the decision of the commissioners that, on the particular evidence in that case, it was the latter.

I must refer next to a case in which the House of Lords approved the test stated by Pearson LJ and applied it to an unusual and highly valuable subject-matter, namely a dry dock. It is *Inland Revenue Comrs v Barclay Curle & Co Ltd*[1]. In that case it was held that not only the structure of the dock in the narrower sense but also the concrete work surrounding it was plant, and, moreover, that the expenditure, not only on those articles but on the preliminary excavation, could rank for capital allowance as expenditure on plant. The passage I must read is from the speech of Lord Reid, who was one of the majority in the House of Lords on that occasion. He said[2]:

'The taxpayer company say that the whole dock was part of their plant used by them for the purposes of their trade. "Plant" is nowhere defined in the Act and they rely chiefly on what was said by LINDLEY, L.J., in *Yarmouth v. France*[3] and on the statement of the question by PEARSON, L.J., in *Jarrold (Inspector of Taxes) v. John Good & Sons, Ltd.*[4]: ". . . whether the partitioning is part of the premises in which the business is carried on or part of the plant with which the business is carried on?" As the commissioners observed, buildings or structures and machinery and plant are not mutually exclusive, and that was recognised in *Jarrold's* case[5]. Undoubtedly this concrete dry dock is a structure but is it also plant? The only reason why a structure should also be plant which has been suggested or which has occurred to me is that it fulfils the function of plant in the trader's operations. And, if that is so, no test has been suggested to distinguish one structure which fulfils such a function from another. I do not say that every structure which fulfils the function of plant must be regarded as plant, but I think that one would have to find some good reason for excluding such a structure. And I do not think that mere size is sufficient. Here it is apparent that there are two stages in the taxpayer company's operations. First the ship must be isolated from the water and then the inspection and necessary repairs must be carried out. If one looks only at the second stage it would not be difficult to say that the dry dock is merely the setting in which it takes place. But I think that the first stage is equally important, and it is obvious that it requires massive and complicated equipment. No doubt a small vessel could be got out of the water by the use of comparatively simple plant and machinery but clearly that is

---

1   [1969] 1 All ER 732, [1969] 1 WLR 675, 45 Tax Cas 221
2   [1969] 1 All ER 732 at 740, 741, [1969] 1 WLR 675 at 679, 45 Tax Cas 221 at 238, 239
3   (1887) 19 QBD 647 at 658
4   [1963] 1 All ER 141 at 149, [1963] 1 WLR 214 at 225, 40 Tax Cas 681 at 696
5   [1963] 1 All ER 141, [1963] 1 WLR 214, 40 Tax Cas 681

a   impossible with a very large vessel.   It seems to me that every part of this dry
dock plays an essential part in getting large vessels into a position where work
on the outside of the hull can begin, and that it is wrong to regard either the
concrete or any other part of the dock as a mere setting or part of the premises
in which this operation takes place.   The whole dock is, I think, the means by
which, or plant with which, the operation is performed.'

b   I ought now to mention briefly a case in which the functional test, as so stated, was
applied by Megarry J in a decision which played some part in the arguments before
me, namely *Cooke (Inspector of Taxes) v Beach Station Caravans Ltd*[1].   In that case the
respondent company was the operator of a caravan park at a seaside resort.   In order
to attract custom it provided flush lavatories, showers, water, shops, laundries,
children's playground, amusement hall, licensed bars and heated swimming and
c   paddling pools.   The two pools, the swimming and paddling pools, were constructed,
in a manner described in the report, in a substantial way, and had an estimated life
of 25 to 30 years.   Like most good swimming pools, they were provided with a system
for the filtration and chlorination of the water, and they also had a heating system.
The dispute in the case was whether or not the swimming pools were plant.   The
learned judge stated his conclusions in the following terms[2]:

d
'First, the two pools should be considered as a unit, with all the attendant
apparatus for purifying and heating the water and so on: for it is as a unit that
they were constructed and as a unit that they are run.   Second, the pools should
be considered not on their own but in relation to the business carried on by the
company, namely, running its caravan park.   It is plain that the pools were
provided in order to attract custom to the caravan park of which they form part.
e   Third, I do not think that the pools can be regarded as being merely passive in
any relevant sense of that word.   For example, a springboard, or for that matter a
trampoline, is in a sense passive, in that it does nothing until someone does
something to it; but I would have thought it plainly plant, and counsel for the
Crown did not seek to assert the contrary when I mentioned the springboard.
f   So with the water in the swimming pool: leave it alone and it does nothing, and
so to this extent it is passive.'

After further developing that line of thought as to the character of the pool and the
water in it, Megarry J ended the paragraph as follows[3]:

'Nobody could suggest that the principal function of the pool was merely to
g   protect the occupants from the elements.   If I may use a relatively modern slang
expression, the pools are not merely "where it's at": they are part of the apparatus
used by the company for carrying on its business as caravan park operators.
The pools are part of the means whereby the trade is carried on, and not merely
the place at which it is carried on . . .'

h   and he referred to the judgment of Pearson LJ, which I have already mentioned more
than once.
The last authority to which I need refer in this brief sketch of the law is a recent
decision of Brightman J which contains what I have found a very helpful passage.   It is
Dixon (Inspector of Taxes) v Fitch's Garage Ltd[4].   The subject-matter was a canopy
consisting of an aluminium roof supported on four steel columns which covered the
j   service area of a serve-yourself petrol filling station.   Again, the question was: for the

---

1   [1974] 3 All ER 159, [1974] 1 WLR 1398, [1974] STC 402
2   [1974] 3 All ER 159 at 166, 167, [1974] 1 WLR 1398 at 1402, [1974] STC 402 at 409, 410
3   [1974] 3 All ER 159 at 167, [1974] 1 WLR 1398 at 1403, [1974] STC 402 at 410
4   [1975] 3 All ER 455, [1976] 1 WLR 215, [1975] STC 480

purposes of capital allowances, could the canopy be regarded as plant or not? Brightman J surveyed a number of the authorities, more than I have thought it necessary
to do today, and then applied the functional test in this way[1]:

> 'The proper test is whether the canopy had a functional purpose to enable the
> taxpayer company to perform the activity of supplying petrol to motor vehicles. I
> ask myself, "Does the canopy help to supply petrol, or is it merely part of the set-
> ting where petrol is supplied?" To use the words of Lord Reid[2], which I have al-
> ready read, is the canopy part of the means by which the operation of supplying
> petrol is performed? In my judgment this question admits only of a negative ans-
> wer. The petrol pumps would deliver petrol to vehicles whether or not there was a
> canopy overhead. The canopy merely makes the business of supplying petrol
> more comfortable for motorists and the staff of the petrol station. It does not
> help to deliver the petrol. It is not part of the means by which it is supplied.
> This is not like the dock case[3], where the dock was useless without its operating
> machinery and vice versa; or the silo case[4], where the silo and its contents
> were totally interdependent. Further, there is a clear thread running through
> the recent cases, including two Australian cases[5] referred to in the silo case,
> showing that a structure is not plant if its only purpose is to provide shelter and
> if it plays no part in what may be termed "the commercial process". That
> conclusion is, I think, an inevitable result of the application of the functional test.
> In this difficult area of the law it is, in my view, important to stick to the estab-
> lished tests. In his submissions to me counsel for the taxpayer sought to
> introduce a new test: whether the item in question is commercially desirable
> or necessary to enable the taxpayer to sell his petrol to the best advantage. That,
> to my mind, is an amenity test as distinct from a functional test, and is not a
> permissible test. The right test is the functional test. In my judgment this appeal
> should be allowed.'

Having briefly surveyed the law, I will now go to the decision of the General Commissioners, which is contained in para 9 of the case that they have stated. It begins by
dealing with a question which has not been debated before me and which is now
agreed not to be necessary for the decision of the appeal, namely whether the Hispaniola could properly be described as a ship. After dealing with that, they said:

> 'Section 40 [and there seems to be no doubt that they meant s 14] of the 1968
> Act clearly indicates that the same entity may fall within the term "building
> or structure" and also within "machinery or plant". We therefore have to decide
> whether Hispaniola 1 is plant. We take the view that it is similar to the Pools in
> the Caravan case[6] and that the fact that it is floating on the Thames is the principal
> means of attracting people to the restaurant. In our view Hispaniola 1 is *plant* for
> the purposes of the Act and the appeal therefore succeeds.'

It will be seen that the commissioners relied on the passage in Megarry J's judgment[7] about the swimming pool in which he said that the pool was provided in
order to attract custom to the caravan park of which it formed part. However, it is
now agreed that the commissioners were wrong in treating that observation by

---

1 [1975] 3 All ER 455 at 461, [1976] 1 WLR 215 at 220, 221, [1975] STC 480 at 486
2 *Inland Revenue Comrs v Barclay Curle & Co Ltd* [1969] 1 All ER 732 at 741, [1969] 1 WLR
   675 at 679, 45 Tax Cas 221 at 239
3 *Inland Revenue Comrs v Barclay Curle & Co Ltd* [1969] 1 All ER 732, [1969] 1 WLR 675, 45 Tax
   Cas 221
4 *Schofield (Inspector of Taxes) v R & H Hall Ltd* [1975] STC 353
5 *Broken Hill Pty Co Ltd v Comr of Taxation* (1968) 120 CLR 240 at 241, *Wangaratta Woollen
   Mills Ltd v Comr of Taxation* (1969) 119 CLR 1
6 *Cooke (Inspector of Taxes) v Beach Station Caravans Ltd* [1974] 3 All ER 159, [1974] 1 WLR 1938,
   [1974] STC 402
7 [1974] 3 All ER 159 at 166, [1974] 1 WLR 1398 at 1402, [1974] STC 402 at 409

Megarry J as containing the ratio decidendi of the caravan park case and in relying
a on it as by itself disposing of the present case. Accordingly, I need not consider
whether their decision was well founded in the way they put it. But counsel for the
taxpayer, although he does not seek to defend the reasons of the General Commissioners, does say that they came to the right conclusion for other reasons, which I
will state in a moment; but first let me mention the case put by counsel for the
Crown.

b   He says that you simply have to look at the facts as found and apply the functional
test. Are the vessel and the attendant barge merely a place or setting where the
business of a restaurant is carried on, or do they constitute apparatus by means of
which the business is carried on? The Crown says that one should approach the case
along exactly the same lines as Brightman J applied to the forecourt canopy. So, it is
said, the vessel and the barge are simply a place or a setting, not a means for carrying
c on the trade, and therefore not plant; and it is pointed out that the Hispaniola in her
converted state, if you disregard the fixtures and fittings, could be used not only as a
restaurant but for any other trade that could conveniently be carried on in floating
premises.

     Counsel for the taxpayer company says it is wrong to apply the test in that broad
way to the assets in question in the present case. He submits that that is too indis-
d criminate and sweeping an approach to the meaning of the word 'plant' as interpreted
by the authorities. The test, says counsel for the taxpayer company, must differ
according to whether the asset under scrutiny falls into one or other of two mutually
exclusive classes of objects. The first class contains land, buildings, structures on land
and parts of structures on land and the second class contains all other assets that may
be claimed to be plant. All assets, whether in the first or the second class, if they are
e to qualify as plant, must possess a business function, must be used for the purposes,
that is, of a trade. But in the first case, that of land, buildings and structures on land,
there and there only, counsel for the taxpayer company says, a stricter test must be
applied. There, not merely must the object in question be used for the purposes of
trade: it must play a part in the commercial process of the trade if it is to be regarded
as plant; and it is in that context, the context of land, buildings and structures on land,
f that the development of the functional test in the authorities has to be regarded.

     Where you have an article not associated with land, then, submits counsel for the
taxpayer company, it is enough to go back to the very words of Lindley LJ and to ask
from the last part of the oft-repeated citation: is the article a chattel kept for permanent employment in the business by the businessman who carries it on? Then
the conclusion would follow that the ship and barge are kept here on the Embank-
g ment for permanent employment in the restaurant business and are, therefore, plant.
Thus, counsel for the taxpayer company seeks to escape the rigour of the functional
test as applied in the more recent cases by saying that it is apt only where the article in
question falls into the first class that I have mentioned. Pearson LJ said that the
language of *Yarmouth v France*[1] impliedly excludes a building, as indeed it does,
since it speaks of goods and chattels. It does not, says counsel for the taxpayer com-
h pany, impliedly exclude a floating vessel; therefore, there is no reason for adding
something that will narrow the breadth of what Lindley LJ said.

     As I understand it, that is the main argument, I hope I have not summarised it
unfairly, put forward by counsel for the taxpayer company. He presented it per-
suasively and attractively, but I cannot accept it. So far as I can see, the suggested
distinction that he would make, confining the so-called functional test to cases of
j land, buildings and structures on land, has no foundation in the reported judgments
which have been read to me. The passage on which counsel for the taxpayer company
relied most of all, I think, if he were driven to select a particular passage, was in that
part of Lord Reid's speech that I have already read from the *Barclay Curle* case[2].

1 (1887) 19 QBD 647
2 [1969] 1 All ER 732 at 740, 741, [1969] 1 WLR 675 at 679, 45 Tax Cas 221 at 238, 239

But following it through as it is read and reread, and looking at the tests applied by
Lord Reid when he decided that the whole dock was the means by which the operation *a*
was performed, I can see nothing that is any less applicable to a floating vessel than to a
structure put up on land. I find no hint in the language of Lord Reid himself, or of the
other judges whose decisions have been read, of the distinction that counsel for the
taxpayer company seeks to introduce.

Indeed, there is one case which at first sight looks as though it hardly fits with
counsel for the taxpayer company's proposition. That is a case which I have not *b*
mentioned, decided by Templeman J. It is *St John's School (Mountford and Knibbs) v
Ward (Inspector of Taxes)*[1], where that judge held that certain structures at a school,
being a gymnasium and a chemistry laboratory, were not plant. I say that it looks at
first as though it might be inconsistent with counsel's proposition because the learned
judge made it clear that he was content to decide the case on the footing that the
structures in question were chattels and were not part of the land. However, the point *c*
is met, I think, by the careful formulation of counsel's proposition to include, as well as
land and buildings, structures on land and parts of structures on land. Even framed
in that careful way, the highest at which I can put the matter is that counsel's
proposition is not explicitly inconsistent with the decisions and that, if accepted,
it might avoid possible hardship to the taxpayer company in the present case.
(I do not know whether there is likely to be hardship or not.) However, in the way *d*
that we apply judicial precedent in this country, one can frequently formulate a number of different legal propositions all consistent with, but none of them imperatively
required by, a series of reported cases. If a judge were to select one such proposition
and declare it to be the law because of his sympathies in the particular suit before him,
the law would quickly reach a state of high complication and even caprice. I must
decline to read more into the authorities than they fairly express, and in my judgment *e*
they do not contain counsel for the taxpayer company's proposition. Accordingly,
he fails on that point.

Counsel for the taxpayer company also had an alternative argument in which he
said that, even though the Hispaniola and her attendant barge were the premises or
setting in which the trade was carried on, they were nevertheless plant. He said that
one had to look at the particular character of the trade. The trade was not merely *f*
that of a restaurant, but of a very special kind of restaurant, a floating restaurant.
The functions performed by the vessels were that they enabled the restaurant to
float on the river, to adapt its position to the movements of the tide and to give the
customers a feeling, as they eat and drink, of being on board ship, which undoubtedly
is an attraction to many. Therefore, he would conclude, the vessels were part of the
apparatus with which the trade was carried on, and plant in the sense of the decisions: *g*
they were essential to such a restaurant business. In a good climate on shore, counsel
said, you can carry on a restaurant without any building or shelter of any kind, but on
water you must have a boat, raft or pier, or something of the kind, to hold the restaurant; and accordingly, counsel would conclude, the vessels were plant because they
played a part in the commercial processes carried on in the trade, in that, by harnessing
the natural force of buoyancy and by adjusting to the rise and fall of the tide, they *h*
enabled the taxpayer company to offer not merely a restaurant but restaurant facilities
on the River Thames, and also, by means of their rocking motion, they provided an
attractive feeling of sea-going to the customers.

That, it seems to me, is to apply not the functional test but the amenity test that
Brightman J rejected in the *Dixon* case[2]. In many trades the amenity of the place
where the business is carried on is an important and valuable attraction to the cus- *j*
tomers. One has only to think of certain large stores and of hotels and restaurants
generally, placed in different landscapes and built with different structures to be

1   [1974] STC 69
2   [1975] 3 All ER 455, [1976] 1 WLR 215, [1975] STC 480

more attractive. The commercial utility of particular and, it may be, unusual premises or places in that way does not, in my judgment, convert them into plant in the
sense of the income tax legislation, or affect the application of the functional test:
they still remain the setting, and not the apparatus. Accordingly, counsel for the
taxpayer fails on his alternative submission also.

I now have to consider what the result of rejecting counsel for the taxpayer's
arguments must be. To my mind, there is no need for me to remit the case to the
General Commissioners. Once their own reasons are not upheld and the alternative
submissions also fail, it appears to me that the facts as stated by the General Commissioners necessarily involve the conclusion that the objects are not plant, and
accordingly I allow the appeal.

Appeal allowed.

Solicitors: *Solicitor of Inland Revenue; Peake & Co* (for the taxpayer company).

Rengan Krishnan Esq Barrister.

Re Gordon's Will Trusts
National Westminster Bank Ltd v Gordon

COURT OF APPEAL, CIVIL DIVISION
BUCKLEY, EVELEIGH LJJ AND SIR JOHN PENNYCUICK
9th, 10th, 11th, 14th NOVEMBER 1977

*Equity – Election – Election against will – Effect – Protected life interest – Liability to com-
pensate disappointed beneficiaries – Election giving rise to liability to compensate – Need for
disappointed beneficiaries to be compensated out of beneficial interest of elector – Doctrine of
election not concerned with requiring elector to forfeit his beneficial interest – Election by
beneficiary against will – Availability of trust fund subject to protected life interest to compensate
disappointed beneficiaries – Intention of testator.*

The testatrix had a son, V, and two granddaughters, J and S. In her will, made in
1967, she appointed a bank as her executor and trustee. By cl 4 of the will she bequeathed to V such of her furniture and effects as he should select, the remainder
to form part of her residuary estate. By cl 5 she gave him a legacy of £1,000. By
cl 6 she bequeathed to the bank her residence ('the Old Rectory') on trust for sale
and directed (i) that they should not sell it without V's consent, (ii) that until the
sale they should allow him to live in it rent free, (iii) that on the sale of the Old
Rectory the bank might utilise part or all the proceeds in the purchase of another
residence and permit V to occupy it, and (iv) that on his ceasing to reside in any
such property the bank should hold it and the proceeds of sale thereof until sale
on the trusts declared in cl 7. By cl 7 she disposed of her residuary estate on trust
for sale and directed the bank to hold one-half ('V's share') on trust for V, one-
quarter on trust for J ('J's share') and one-quarter on trust for S ('S's share'). Under
cl 7 the bank were to hold the income of V's share on statutory protective trusts for
the benefit of V for the period of his life although they could at their discretion at any
time during his lifetime by deed waive the statutory protective trusts and hold his
share on trust to pay the income to him beneficially free from the trusts. On his
death his share was to be divided and one-half held on the trusts of J's share and

one-half on the trusts of S's share and those two shares were, by operation of the will, settled on trust for J and S and their respective issue, with cross-accruals between them *a* in the event of the issue not taking a vested interest. The testatrix died in 1970. She had in fact bought the Old Rectory jointly with V and it had been conveyed to them as joint tenants, so that on her death V became the owner by survivorship of the whole beneficial interest in it. She therefore had no power to dispose of the Old Rectory as she had purported to do in cl 6 of her will. V, acting under cll 4 and 5 of the will, selected the furniture and effects which he wanted and took the pecuniary legacy but he *b* elected against the will in respect of the Old Rectory by selling it and treating the proceeds of sale as his own money. In consequence he was bound to compensate the other residuary legatees to the extent of the value of the furniture and effects and the pecuniary legacy but that was inadequate to compensate them fully. The question therefore arose what effect, if any, his election against the will in respect of the Old Rectory had on his protected life interest in his settled share of the residue. The bank *c* referred the matter to the court. The judge considered*a* that he was bound to hold that, in consequence of his election, V had forfeited his determinable life interest in the settled share of the residue. V appealed.

Held – The circumstances were such that the equitable doctrine of election did not apply. The essential feature of that doctrine was the compensation of disappointed *d* parties out of some beneficial interest of the elector; it was not concerned with the forfeiture of the elector's beneficial interest. The testatrix's intention in bequeathing to V a determinable life interest was to create an interest of a kind that could not be made available in law for compensation under the equitable doctrine of election. It followed that he could not be made to submit to that interest being applied in compensating the other residuary legatees. Accordingly the appeal would be allowed *e* (see p 979 *b* to *f* and *j* to p 980 *c e f* and *h* to p 981 *b*, post).

Dictum of Astbury J in *Re Hargrove, Hargrove v Pain* [1915] 1 Ch at 406 applied.
McCarogher v Whieldon (1867) LR 3 Eq 236 distinguished.
Carter v Silber [1891] 3 Ch 553 not followed.
Per Curiam. The fact that those who are beneficially interested under the trusts of J's share and S's share are included in those who are the objects of the discretionary *f* trust which comes into play if V's determinable life interest is terminated and might therefore benefit from the termination of it by the acceleration of their interests under the discretionary trusts is immaterial. Anything which the bank might decide to pay them will be received not as compensation for being disappointed of their interests in the Old Rectory but by reason of an exercise of the bank's discretion under the discretionary trust and in right of their position as objects of that discretion *g* (see p 979 *f* to *j*, p 980 *b e* and *f* and p 981 *a*, post).

Decision of Goulding J [1976] 2 All ER 577 reversed.

Notes
For payment of compensation in cases of election against a will, see 16 Halsbury's *h* Laws (4th Edn) paras 1399, 1400, and for cases on the subject, see 20 Digest (Repl) 444-447, 1578-1597.

Cases referred to in judgments
Brown v Gregson, [1920] AC 860, [1920] All ER Rep 730, 89 LJPC 195, 123 LT 465, HL, 20 Digest (Repl) 462, 1723. *j*
Carter v Silber, Carter v Hasluck [1891] 3 Ch 553, 60 LJCh 716, 65 LT 51; *rvsd on other grounds* [1892] 2 Ch 278, CA; sub nom *Edwards v Carter* [1893] AC 360, HL, 20 Digest (Repl) 445, 1590.

---

a [1976] 2 All ER 577

a
Chesham (Lord), Re, Cavendish v Dacre (1886) 31 Ch D 466, 55 LJCh 401, 54 LT 154, 20
  Digest (Repl) 446, 1596.
Chichester (Lord) v Coventry (1867) LR 2 HL 71, 36 LJCh 673, 17 LT 35, HL, 20 Digest
  (Repl) 472, 1814.
Cooper v Cooper (1874) LR 7 HL 53, 44 LJCh 6, 30 LT 409, HL, 20 Digest (Repl) 426, 1474.
Hargrove, Re, Hargrove v Pain [1915] 1 Ch 398, 84 LJCh 484, 112 LT 1062, 20 Digest
  (Repl) 449, 1617.
b Ker v Wauchope (1819) 1 Bli 1, 4 ER 1, 20 Digest (Repl) 427, 1485.
McCarogher v Whieldon (1867) LR 3 Eq 236, 36 LJCh 196, 20 Digest (Repl) 492, 2018.
Rogers v Jones (1876) 3 Ch D 688, 20 Digest (Repl) 469, 1780.
Vardon's Trusts, Re (1855) 31 Ch D 275, 55 LJCh 259, 53 LT 895, CA, 20 Digest (Repl)
  429, 1492.

c **Cases also cited**
Bristow v Warde (1794) 2 Ves 336.
Codrington v Codrington (1875) LR 7 HL 854.
Gonin, Re [1977] 2 All ER 720, [1977] 3 WLR 379.
Gretton v Haward (1819) Swan 409.
Lissenden v Bosch (CAV) (No 2) (1940) 33 BWCC 289, CA.
d Mengel's Will Trusts, Re, Westminster Bank v Mengel [1962] 2 All ER 490, [1962] Ch 791.
Wells' Trusts, Re, Hardisty v Wells (1899) 42 Ch D 646.
White v Turner (1858) 25 Beav 303.
Wormald, Re, Frank v Muzeen [1890] 43 Ch D 630.

Appeal
e By an originating summons dated 22nd April 1974, the National Westminster Bank
Ltd ('the bank'), the executors and trustees of the will of Margaret Gwendoline
Gordon deceased ('the deceased'), sought the determination of certain questions
concerning her will. The defendants were (1) Victor Frederick Gordon, (2) Julie
Consuelo Gordon, (3) Sheila Margaret Gordon, (4) Christopher Ralph Bourne, (5)
Olive Erica Lennox, (6) Roy John Hancock and (7) Pamela Mary Champneys, all of
f whom claimed to be beneficially interested under the trusts of the will and codicils of
the deceased. Goulding J[1] gave judgment on 21st January 1976. The first defendant
('the appellant') appealed against so much of the judgment of Goulding J as declared (in answer to question 4 of the originating summons) that the election of the
appellant against the will of the deceased had caused the determination of the determinable life interest given to him by cl 7 of the will by reference to the statutory
g protective trusts. The facts are set out in the judgment of Buckley LJ.

Cenydd Howells for the appellant.
Jules Sher for the bank.

h **BUCKLEY LJ.** This is an appeal from a judgment of Goulding J[1] of 22nd January
1976, when he held that as the result of the application to the circumstances of the
testatrix's will of the equitable doctrine of election the first defendant, who was the
testatrix's son and who is the appellant in this court, had forfeited his determinable
life interest under the statutory protective trusts in respect of a share of the residue.
The plaintiff bank ('the bank') is the executor and trustee of the will; the appellant
j was the first defendant and the interests which he took under the will will appear in
a moment from what I shall say about that document.
  The other six defendants are all persons having interests in the estate, but none of
them, with the exception of the third defendant, took part in the hearing before

---

1 [1976] 2 All ER 577, [1977] Ch 27

the learned judge; the third defendant, being at that time a minor, was represented through a guardian ad litem and took a part in the argument in the court below, but she has since attained her majority and has not taken any part in this appeal. Consequently, the only parties before this court have been the bank and the first defendant, and counsel for the bank as executor and trustee of the will, has very properly presented the argument against the appeal although, as he emphasised at the outset, the bank is anxious to occupy a neutral position, not in any way prejudicing its position in regard to the exercise of the discretion vested in it under the testatrix's will.

The testatrix made her will on 6th September 1967. By it she appointed the bank to be her executor; she gave certain specific bequests and by cl 4 she bequeathed free of duty to the appellant such articles from her furniture, household effects and personal chattels other than such as had been specifically bequeathed as he should select, and she directed that the remainder should fall into residue.

By cl 5 she gave certain pecuniary legacies including, in para (a) of that clause, a legacy of £1,000 to the appellant; and by cl 6 she purported to dispose of a house in which she lived, known as the Old Rectory, Bothenhampton, Bridport, Dorset in these terms:

'I GIVE AND DEVISE to the Bank free of all duty my freehold property The Old Rectory Bothenhampton aforesaid or such other freehold or leasehold property as I shall own and which shall be my residence at the date of my death UPON TRUST to sell the same or to retain the same AND I DIRECT that the Bank shall not sell any such house or any house purchased in exercise of the power hereinafter contained without the consent of [the appellant] during his life and until sale the Bank shall permit [the appellant] during his life to live in such house rent free with if he so wishes his two Daughters until they reach the age of twenty one if they so wish [the appellant] keeping the same in good repair and paying all outgoings in respect thereof and insuring the same in the name of the Bank against such risks and for such amount as the Bank shall from time to time require And that on the sale of any such residence the Bank may utilise such part or the whole of the net proceeds of sale thereof as they shall in their absolute discretion think fit in the purchase of another freehold or leasehold residence and may permit [the appellant] and his Daughters to occupy the same upon the like conditions as hereinbefore specified and on [the appellant] ceasing to reside in any such property the Bank shall hold the same and the proceeds of sale thereof until sale upon the trusts hereinafter declared concerning my residuary estate.'

She disposed of her residuary estate in cl 7 on trust for sale with the usual administrative provisions, and directed her trustee to hold one-half which she called 'my Son's share' on the trusts thereinafter declared concerning that share; one-quarter which she called 'Miss Julie's Share' on the trusts thereinafter declared concerning that share, and the remaining one-quarter, called 'Miss Sheila's Share', on the trusts thereinafter declared concerning that share. Julie and Sheila were the two daughters of the appellant.

By para (a) of cl 7 she settled the appellant's share on trust to pay the income to him during his life, provided that such income should not vest absolutely in him but should be held by the bank on the statutory protective trusts subject to the variations thereinafter mentioned, for the benefit of the appellant for the period of his life. Then there follows a proviso:

'that in each year prior to the expiration of twenty one years from my death during which the Bank under the said statutory trusts have a discretion as to the application of the said income the Bank shall determine in their uncontrolled discretion how much (if any part at all) of the income of the current year they will apply under the statutory trusts and the said trusts shall apply to the amount

so determined and the Bank shall accumulate the balance of the said income in
a the way of compound interest . . .'

Then there was a further provision, of an unusual kind; it was in these terms:

'Provided further that the Bank may at their absolute discretion at any time
during the lifetime of [the appellant] by deed waive and determine the statutory
protective trusts hereinbefore declared in respect of the income of [the appellant's]
b share to the intent that the Bank shall thenceforth hold [the appellant's] share
UPON TRUST to pay the income thereof to [the appellant] during his life beneficially
free from such protective trusts.'

After the death of the appellant his share was to be held as to one-half on the
trusts of Miss Julie's share and as to the other half on the trusts of Miss Sheila's share,
c and those two shares were, by operation of the will and of a codicil to it, settled on
the usual trusts for those two ladies, the two daughters of the appellant, and their
respective issue, with cross-accruals between them in the event of the issue not taking
a vested interest.

In fact, the testatrix did not own the Old Rectory; it had been bought jointly by
herself and the appellant and had been conveyed into their joint names as joint
d tenants, both at law and in equity, and at the death of the testatrix, there having been
no severance of the joint tenancy, the appellant became owner by survivorship of
the whole beneficial interest in the Old Rectory; so that the testatrix was in fact
incompetent to dispose of the Old Rectory as she purported to do by cl 6 of the will.
That is how the question arises as to whether the equitable doctrine of election is
applicable in the present case, and if so, what its effect is, in particular whether it has
e the effect of working a forfeiture of the determinable life interest of the appellant in
his share of the testatrix's residue.

The equitable doctrine of election can, I think, be formulated in this way. If A by a
disposition effected by an instrument such as a will confers a beneficial interest in
property of which he is competent to dispose on B, and by the same instrument
purports to confer a beneficial interest on C in property of which A is not competent
f to dispose, being the property of B, B may elect to adopt one of two courses. He may
elect to accept the entire benefit under the will, in which case he will be equitably bound
so far as he is able, to give effect to A's purported gift to C; or he may elect not to give
effect to that purported gift. In the latter case, he will not forfeit his interest under the
will, but will be equitably bound to submit to C being compensated out of that interest,
so far as practicable, for being deprived of the beneficial interest which A intended
g to give him.

There is another class of case in which someone having a beneficial interest in
property under a disposition may be required, on equitable principles, to submit to
his interest being resorted to in order to compensate another person who has been
deprived of a beneficial interest under the same disposition in consequence of an
action of the first person. Thus, if A and B enter into a mutual settlement under which
h A settles property on trust under which B has a beneficial interest, and B covenants
to settle property on trusts under which A or C will be entitled to a beneficial
interest, and if for some reason (as, for example, that B was a minor at the date of
the covenant) B can repudiate his or her obligation to bring property into the settlement and does so, equity will compel B to submit to A or C, as the case may be, being
compensated out of B's beneficial interest in A's trust fund, so far as practicable, for
j being deprived of his, A's or C's, beneficial interest in B's intended trust fund.

The circumstances which cause equity to intervene in these two classes of cases are
distinguishable. In the first class, which I might call cases of dual gifts, it is the refusal
of B to give effect to A's intention to confer a beneficial interest on C in what is in fact
B's property. In the second class, which I might call cases of mutual obligation, it is
the repudiation by B of his obligation to bring his own property into settlement for

the benefit of A or C, but the equitable remedy is of the same character in each case. Equity lays hold of B's beneficial interest under the disposition for the purpose of *a* compensating the disappointed party thereout, but only interferes with B's enjoyment of it to the extent necessary to achieve compensation. The mutual obligation cases, I think, clearly proceed on the footing that B cannot equitably retain the whole of his beneficial interest under the trusts of the settlement and at the same time fail to fulfil part of the consideration for the settlement.

This doctrine is elucidated, primarily in respect of cases of dual gifts, in the speech *b* of Viscount Haldane in *Brown v Gregson*[1], where he said:

'The doctrine of election rests on a different foundation. It is a principle which the Courts apply in the exercise of an equitable jurisdiction enabling them to secure a just distribution in substantial accordance with the general scheme of the instrument. It is not merely the language used to which the Court looks. A *c* testator may, for instance, have obviously failed to realise that any quesion could arise. But the Court will none the less hold that a beneficiary who is given a share under the will in assets, the total amount of which depends on the inclusion of property belonging to the beneficiary himself which the testator has ineffectively sought to include, ought not to be allowed to have a share in the assets effectively disposed of excepting on terms. He must co-operate to the extent requisite to *d* provide the amount necessary for the division prescribed by the will, either by bringing in his own property, erroneously contemplated by the testator as forming part of the assets, or by submitting to a diminution of the share to which he is prima facie entitled, to an extent equivalent to the value of his own property if withheld by him from the common stock. As was said by Lord Cairns L.C. in *Cooper v. Cooper*[2] this condition arises not as on a "conjecture of a presumed intention, but *e* … on a rule of equity founded on the highest principles of equity, and as to which the Court does not occupy itself in finding out whether the rule was present or was not present to the mind of the party making the will". Such a principle is different from that under which a condition of forfeiture arises, for there an intention clearly expressed by the testator is requisite. And it is, I think, because the principle has not to be based on such an expression of intention that the Court *f* can mould its application. As Lord Eldon pointed out in *Ker v. Wauchope*[3] the limitation of the principle to compensation as distinguished from forfeiture is a subordinate principle which has been engrafted on the main one in order to make sure that what is ordered does not go beyond what substantial justice requires. My Lords, according to the authorities I have already discussed, the doctrine, being one the application of which the Court has a discretion to mould, ought not to be *g* applied when the testator could not effectively impose the condition on the beneficiary otherwise than by imposing an absolute condition on taking at all which he has not expressed. On principle I think that this is right. Not only do the authorities referred to imply it, but it was in accordance with the doctrine as I have stated it that Chitty J. in *In re Lord Chesham*[4] decided that where a will purported to bequeath for the benefit of the testator's younger sons chattels *h* which were settled in trust to go and remain as heirlooms with a house belonging to his eldest son, and then made the eldest son his residuary legatee, the latter was not to be put to his election. For it would have been a breach of trust for the trustees of the settlement to allow him to make over the chattels, and without their assent he was powerless to do it. His desire was to have the residue under the will, and he was allowed to do so without being compelled to elect to make *j*

1　[1920] AC 860 at 868-870, [1920] All ER Rep 730 at 734, 735
2　(1874) LR 7 HL 53 at 67
3　(1819) 1 Bli 1
4　(1886) 31 Ch D 466 at 476

a compensation. The learned judge laid down that a Court of equity will not decree something to be done which would amount to a breach of trust, or be a mere idle act that could only lead to litigation. The reason why the eldest son could not make an assignment was because he had no assignable interest. "Election", said Chitty J., "means free choice". When he takes under the will there is nothing for him to give up, for there is nothing which he can give up.'

b Equity can only require B to submit to his own beneficial interest being applied to compensate the disappointed party if that interest is one that can be so applied. *Re Vardon's Trusts*[1] was a mutual obligation case relating to a marriage settlement under which the wife undertook to settle after-acquired property on the trust declared in respect of the fund settled by the husband. She herself brought property into the settlement, which was settled on trusts under which she took a first life interest restrained from anticipation. She became entitled to after-acquired property but *c* repudiated her obligation to settle it. The doctrine of election was held not to operate in that case, because by reason of the restraint on anticipation attached to her beneficial interest in the wife's fund the wife could not divest herself of the right to receive each instalment of income as it accured. In these circumstances, in this court, in a judgment of the court delivered by Fry LJ, it was said[2]: 'This settlement, therefore, *d* in our judgment, contains a declaration of a particular intention inconsistent with the doctrine of election, and therefore excludes it.'

Re Lord Chesham[3], which was referred to by Lord Haldane in the passage from his speech in *Brown v Gregson*[4] which I have already cited, was another case where rather similar considerations applied, because in that case the eldest son was incapable of disposing of the heirlooms of which the testator purported to dispose by his will but which did not belong to the testator, being in the possession of his eldest son as tenant *e* for life under the relevant settlement. The eldest son there elected to take under the will, not against it, but although he took his interest under the will, he could not implement the full intention of the testator because he was incapable of giving effect to the testator's intention in respect of the settled chattels. The court proceeded on the basis that it was clear that if the eldest soon took under the will, as he elected to do, *f* he must confirm the will as far as he could and must give up to the disappointed legatees any beneficial interest that he could dispose of in the chattels; but he had no such interest. It was then contended that the eldest son ought to compensate his brothers out of his other interests under the father's will; but this, it was held, he was not bound to do, for there was no obligation to compensate out of an interest well given by the will for the loss of something which the person sought to be put to his election was incapable of bringing into the dispositions intended to be made by the *g* will. Chitty J said[5]:

'The result is, that this attempt to engraft a new doctrine of compensation on the doctrine of election fails. I hold that Lord *Chesham* is not bound in any view of the case to make any compensation out of the residue to his younger brothers. But I go further. Inasmuch as Lord *Chesham* has no interest in the chattels which *h* he can make over for the benefit of his younger brothers, it appears to me that no case of election really arises. Election means free choice. He cannot be compelled directly or indirectly to take under the settlement and against the will. But when he takes under the will there is nothing for him to give up, for there is nothing which he can give up. It seems to me to be absurd to say that he is put to his election merely for the purpose of making a deduction from his residuary *j* legacy.'

1   (1885) 31 Ch D 275
2   31 Ch D 275 at 280
3   (1886) 31 Ch D 466
4   [1920] AC 860 at 869, [1920] All ER Rep 730 at 735
5   31 Ch D 466 at 476

In the present case the learned judge held that the appellant had elected against
the will in respect of the Old Rectory. He had in fact sold the property in February
1972 and had treated the proceeds of sale as being his own moneys. It is not disputed
that he must consequently compensate the other residuary legatees to the extent of
the value of the furniture which he selected under cl 4 of the will, and of his pecuniary
legacy of £1,000. But this is inadequate to compensate them fully, so the question
arises, what effect, if any, the election has on A's protected life interest in his settled
share of residue. If the trustees would, in consequence of the doctrine, be bound to
apply any income of the appellant's settled share of residue in compensating disappointed beneficiaries under the trusts of the other two settled shares, this must
result in a forfeiture of the appellant's determinable life interest. This, as the learned
judge recognised, would not result in compensation to the disappointed beneficiaries,
for the trustees would be most unlikely to appropriate to the appellant any of the
income under the discretionary trust which would then come into operation. The
learned judge referred to Snell on Equity[1] and to *Re Vardon's Trusts*[2]; to *Re Hargrove*[3],
and to *Brown v Gregson*[4], and he said that he would find the decision difficult were
there no directly applicable authority. He considered, however, that he was bound
by *McCarogher v Whieldon*[5] and *Carter v Silber*[6] to hold that in consequence of his
election the appellant had forfeited his determinable life interest in the settled share
of residue.

McCarogher v Whieldon[5] was decided by Lord Romilly MR in 1866. The facts were
that a father, on the marriage of his son, covenanted by will or otherwise in his lifetime
to give, or assure, one-fifth part of the real and personal estate to which he might be
entitled at or immediately before his death, subject to payment thereout of one-fifth
of his debts, funeral and testamentary expenses and legacies, to trustees on trust to
pay the income to his son until, among other things, some event should occur whereby
the income would, if the same were thereby made payable to the son absolutely,
become vested in some other person or persons, and then on trust for the benefit of
the son's wife and the issue of the marriage, with a discretionary trust for the benefit
of the son after his wife's death. By his will the father directed his debts to be paid by
his executors and charged them, as far as the law permitted, on his real and personal
estate, and he gave his real and personal estate to trustees, in trust for all and every
of his children who should be living at the time of his death. He died leaving five
children, so that the son in question became entitled under the terms of his father's
will to one-fifth of his residuary estate. The father had made no disposition in his
lifetime in favour of the trustees of the settlement.

Lord Romilly MR held that the bequest of one-fifth of the estate to the son did not
satisfy the covenant so far as the son's wife and children were concerned, and that one-
fifth of the net estate, after payment of debts, funeral and testamentary expenses.
but before satisfying the covenant, must be paid over to the trustees of the settlement,
He said[7]:

> 'It is clear, therefore, that this covenant must be performed, and that the one-
> fifth of the testator's personal estate at the time of his death is a debt to be paid
> in the first instance, before the estate of the testator can be made subject to the
> disposition contained in the will.'

He then posed this question[8]:

---

1   27th Edn (1973), p 489
2   (1885) 31 Ch D 275
3   [1915] 1 Ch 398
4   [1920] AC 860, [1920] All ER Rep 730
5   (1867) LR 3 Eq 236
6   [1891] 3 Ch 553
7   LR 3 Eq 236 at 241
8   LR 3 Eq 236 at 242, 243

a   'This, then, if I am right in this view of the case, reduces the matter to a comparatively narrow limit, which is this, whether *Harry T. T. Whieldon* can take both one-fifth of the residue after the covenant is satisfied, and also the life interest in the one-fifth of the testator's residue, which is to be paid to the trustees of the settlement; and I am of opinion he cannot, and that the bequest must be considered to be a satisfaction of all the interest which the son takes under his father's covenant.'

b   He stated his conclusion in this way[1]:

'This, therefore, in my opinion, raises a question of election in the son, *Harry T. T. Whieldon*, and he must elect either to abandon the bequest of one-fifth of the remaining four-fifths of the residue of his father's estate, or he must authorise the trustees of his marriage settlement to pay over his life interest in that one-

c   fifth of the residue which is to be paid to the trustees to the other four children of his father to be equally divided between them.'

Counsel for the son then stated that the son elected to take under the will; counsel for the son's wife thereupon contended that the son's life interest under the settlement had consequently determined. Lord Romilly MR took time for consideration and later, apparently without further argument, he said[2]:

d   'I have considered the point since the former occasion, and it appears to me, that the election to take under the will is an event which determines the life interest under the settlement, and the income must be paid to Mrs. *Whieldon*.'

This was not an election under the doctrine which I have been discussing in this judgment; it was an election under the doctrine of satisfaction such as Lord Romilly

e   referred to in *Lord Chichester v Coventry*[3] where he said this:

'. . . when a father on the marriage of a child, enters into a covenant to settle either land or money, he is unable to adeem or alter the covenant, and if he give benefits by his will to the same objects, and states that this is to be in satisfaction of the covenant, he necessarily gives the object of the covenant a right to elect whether they will take under the covenant, or whether they will take under the

f   will.'

He was there contrasting the doctrine of ademption with the doctrine of satisfaction.

This kind of election is not concerned with compensation at all, but merely with ensuring that the beneficiary does not take both benefits. He can choose which he will take, but he cannot have both. It may be worth drawing attention to the fact

g   that Jarman on Wills[4] refers to *McCarogher v Whieldon*[5], when discussing satisfaction in chapter 34, not the equitable doctrine of election which is discussed in chapter 17, with which *McCarogher v Whieldon*[5] has nothing to do. By electing to take under the will in *McCarogher v Whieldon*[5], the son abandoned his life interest under the settlement, which Lord Romilly accordingly held to have determined.

Carter v Silber[6], on the other hand, was a case in which the equitable doctrine of

h   election was applied by Romer J. The facts were these. By a marriage settlement which was made in October 1883, the father of the intended husband covenanted with the trustees to pay them £1,500 a year during the life of the wife and such further period as there should be any issue of the marriage; and the trustees were to pay the £1,500 a year to the husband until he should assign or charge the same, or until some other event should happen whereby the same, if belonging absolutely to him, would

j   1   (1867) LR 3 Eq 236 at 243
     2   LR 3 Eq 236 at 244
     3   (1867) LR 2 HL 71 at 91
     4   8th Edn (1951), vol 2, p 1147
     5   LR 3 Eq 236
     6   [1891] 3 Ch 553

become vested in or payable to some other persons or person, and then there was a
discretionary trust over. The settlement also contained an agreement by the husband *a*
to vest in the trustees on certain trusts all property to which he then was or should
become entitled under any settlement or appointment executed or to be executed
by his father, or under the will of his father or mother, or by virtue of the intestacy
of either of them. At the time of their marriage both the husband and the wife were
under age and the settlement was confirmed by the court on behalf of the wife but
not on behalf of the husband. He attained his majority in November 1883. The father *b*
died in May 1887 and by his will confirmed certain settlements made by him in his
lifetime under which the husband took an interest, and gave the residue of his real
and personal estate to his two sons, one of whom was the husband, in equal shares.
The husband received the £1,500 a year from the trustees of his settlement during his
father's lifetime and after his death until July 1888, when he repudiated his covenant.

In an action by the trustees claiming that the husband was bound by the settlement *c*
and could not repudiate it, and in the alternative for compensation for the parties
disappointed by such repudiation, Romer J held that the husband had effectually
repudiated his covenant. On appeal this part of his decision was reversed, so that on
appeal no question of election arose for decision; but on the learned judge's own
finding as to effective repudiation, that question did arise. The case was one of the
mutual obligation class. Romer J said[1]:   *d*

> 'I have now further to consider the effect of the repudiation on the moneys
> which, notwithstanding the repudiation, would still continue to be payable to
> the son according to the terms of the settlement. I think that those moneys must
> be retained by the trustees in order to make compensation, and until compen-
> sation has been thereby fully made, to the persons disappointed by the repudiation
> of the benefits under the settlement of which they have been, or will be, deprived *e*
> by the repudiation. And this gives rise to the further question whether the right
> of retainer on the part of the trustees does not in itself determine the further
> payment of the annuity under the deed to the son, seeing that the annuity has
> thereby "become vested in, or payable to, some other person or persons" within
> the meaning of those words as used in the deed. I think this further question *f*
> must be answered in the affirmative, and that consequently the trusts have
> arisen under the deed with regard to the annuity declared in the event of the
> failure or determination during the lifetime of the son of the previous trust
> declared in his favour.'

In so deciding, he regarded himself as bound by *McCarogher v Whieldon*[2], and treated
that case as in point. He referred to *Re Vardon's Trusts*[3], but distinguished it on this *g*
ground[4]:

> 'In *Vardon's Trusts*[3] the Court of Appeal held that the restraint on anticipa-
> tion which fettered the settlement of income to the separate use of a married
> woman altogether prevented, and was intended by the parties to the settlement
> altogether to prevent, that income ceasing to be payable to the married woman *h*
> by any act on her part, including any election by her against the settlement. But in
> the case before me I can find no indication that the parties to the settlement intended
> that the annuity should always continue to be payable to the son. On the con-
> trary, they contemplated his assigning or charging it, and provided (*inter alia*)
> that if he did assign or charge it it should cease to be payable to him. And certainly
> I cannot gather that it was the intention of the parties to this settlement that the *j*

1 [1891] 3 Ch 553 at 565
2 (1867) LR 3 Eq 236
3 (1885) 31 Ch D 275
4 [1891] 3 Ch 553 at 565, 566

a son should be at liberty to repudiate it so far as his obligations were concerned, and still continue to enjoy the annuity. I find here no declaration of a particular intention which is inconsistent with or excludes the doctrine of election.'

When he said that the parties to the settlement comtemplated the son's assigning or charging the annuity he was not, I think, using accurate language. The effect of the determinable character of the son's interest was that he was incapable of alienating
b it. He might try, or effect, to assign or charge it, but he could not succeed in doing so. In my judgment, *Carter v Silber*[1] was wrongly decided. Romer J, in my view, erroneously ignored the feature that the equitable doctrine of election is concerned with compensating disappointed parties out of some beneficial interest of the elector; it is not concerned with forfeiting his beneficial interest: see *Brown v Gregson*[2], in the passage that I have cited, and *Rogers v Jones*[3]. Where the beneficial interest of a
c person who is sought to be made to elect is such that for any reason he cannot be made to submit to that interest being applied in compensating the disappointed parties, the circumstances are such that the doctrine cannot apply. It seems to me rather artificial to presume in such a case an intention on the part of the disponor that the operation of the doctrine should be excluded; I think it more correct to say that the circumstances are such that the doctrine cannot come into play.
d It was put in this way by Astbury J in *Re Hargrove, Hargrove v Pain*[4]:

'The real meaning of the decision and the observations in *In re Vardon's Trusts*[5] is I think that the will must be looked at to ascertain the character of the interest the testator intended to create. If he intended to create an interest of such a character as would have the legal effect of inter alia preventing the beneficiary making provision for compensation under the doctrine of election, and the interest
e so created is not available in law for compensation when the time comes for making election, then the doctrine of election is excluded because the testator has created in fact an interest of that character, which is not so available, although the question of election was obviously not in his contemplation '

With that formulation I agree.
f Counsel for the bank has drawn attention to the fact that in the present case those who are beneficially interested under the trusts of Miss Julie's share and Miss Sheila's share are included in those who are objects of the discretionary trust, which would come into play on the termination of the appellant's determinable life interest, and he says that in that way they would be benefited by a termination of that determinable life interest, and although not compensated out of the appellant's own beneficial
g interest, would to some extent be compensated by the acceleration of their interests under the discretionary trusts. But under the statutory discretionary trusts the class of discretionary beneficiaries would include not only the appellant's children but the son and any wife he may have, and the most likely recipient of income under the discretionary trusts, if the son were to forfeit his determinable life interest, would be his wife and the objects of the discretionary trust would not receive anything which the
h trustees might decide to pay to them as compensation for being disappointed of their interests in the Old Rectory, but by reason of an exercise of the trustees' discretion under the discretionary trust and in right of their position as objects of that discretion. I do not think that this particular feature of the present case is one which would make the doctrine of equitable election appropriately applicable to the case.

For these reasons I think that the learned judge arrived at the wrong conclusion.
j

1 [1891] 3 Ch 553
2 [1920] AC 860, [1920] All ER Rep 730
3 (1876) 3 Ch D 688
4 [1915] 1 Ch 398 at 406
5 (1885) 31 Ch D 275

I think he was mistaken in thinking that *McCarogher v Whieldon*[1] bound him, because that case was not concerned with the doctrine of equitable election but with *a* election in cases of satisfaction; and, as I have said, the other case by which he considered himself to be bound, that of *Carter v Silber*[2], was in my judgment wrongly decided.

For these reasons I would allow this appeal.

EVELEIGH LJ. I agree.   *b*

Moreover, I am happy to think that the result achieved would meet with the approval of the testatrix in this case. I very much doubt if there would have been any mention of the Old Rectory in the will had she not intended to confer some additional benefit on her son over and above that which was given in the other part of the instrument, namely the right to reside in any house that she happened to occupy at the time of her death. It is ironical that by the specific reference to the Old Rectory *c* with that object in view, she should have placed her son's interest in jeopardy.

I do not feel confident enough to say that *Carter v Silber*[2] was wrongly decided on the specific facts of that case, but I do not regard it as one on pari materia with the present case. As far as *McCarogher v Whieldon*[1] was concerned, I agree that that case is distinguishable for the reasons stated by Buckley LJ.

I can only conclude by sympathising with the learned judge in the position in *d* which he found himself when confronted with those two authorities. So far as *McCarogher v Whieldon*[1] is concerned, he said that he did not regard it as being altogether a satisfying decision[3], and it is the use of the word 'election' in that case in the sentence[3] 'this therefore in my opinion raises a case of election in the son' that was a strong influence on the learned judge in thinking that he ought to follow that decision.   *e*

I agree that this appeal should be allowed.

SIR JOHN PENNYCUICK. I agree. The learned judge cannot be criticised for treating himself as being bound by the decisions of the Lord Romilly MR in *McCarogher v Whieldon*[1] and of Romer J in *Carter v Silber*[2]. But on the close analysis to which those decisions have been subjected before us, it has become clear that the former decision, that is *McCarogher v Whieldon*[1], was made under the doctrine of satisfaction and not that of election in the sense now relevant; and that the latter decision, that is, *Carter v Silber*[2], in which the judge purported, mistakenly I think, to follow *McCarogher v Whieldon*[1], must be regarded as wrongly decided.

With these decisions out of the way, the doctrine of equitable election presents no *g* difficulty here. The doctrine is concisely stated by Jessel MR in *Rogers v Jones*[4] in these terms:

'The doctrine of election is this, that if a person whose property a testator effects to give away takes other benefits under the same will and at the same time elects to keep his own property, he must make compensation to the person affected by his election to an extent not exceeding the benefits he receives.'   *h*

Compensation is an essential ingredient of the doctrine, and was so stated by Jessel MR. Clearly, in my judgment, the doctrine does not require a beneficiary to surrender for the purpose of compensation an interest which would be destroyed by the very act of surrender, and thereby rendered unavailable to make compensation. So the doctrine cannot come into play in the present case.

---

1   (1867) LR 3 Eq 236
2   [1891] 3 Ch 553
3   LR 3 Eq 236 at 243
4   (1876) 3 Ch D 688 at 689

Astbury J, in *Re Hargrove, Hargrove v Pain*[1], quoted by Buckley LJ, stated correctly
a the ground for the exclusion of the doctrine in such circumstances.

I would add that the application, or exclusion, of the doctrine in comparable circumstances does not, I think, depend on the nature of the interests following the protected
life interest.

I too would allow this appeal.

b *Appeal allowed.*

Solicitors: *Pedley, May & Fletcher* (for the appellant); *Claude Barker & Partners*,
Watford (for the bank).

J H Fazan Esq   Barrister.

c

Re Field (a debtor), ex parte the debtor v
d H & J Quick Ltd and another

CHANCERY DIVISION
MEGARRY V-C AND BROWNE-WILKINSON J
28th, 29th JUNE 1977

e

Bankruptcy – Receiving order – Rescission – Burden of proof on debtor – Petitioning creditor
obtaining judgment against debtor – Instalment orders made to satisfy judgment – Debtor
failing to pay under instalment orders – Bankruptcy petition presented and receiving order
made – Debtor alleging he had no assets and no prospects of having any – Debtor relying on his
own affidavit and on investigation made when instalment orders made – Whether debtor
f *discharging burden of proof that receiving order should not be made.*

Bankruptcy – Petition – Dismissal – Discretion of court – Sufficient cause – Debtor alleging
he had no assets and no prospects of having any – Debtor not establishing that it would be
oppressive to make receiving order – Whether lack of assets could amount to 'sufficient cause'
– Bankruptcy Act 1914, s 5(3).

g

Bankruptcy – Receiving order – Rescission – Debtor having no assets and no prospect of
having any – Official Receiver satisfied of debtor's lack of assets – Support of Official Receiver
for debtor's application for rescission of receiving order.

County court – Appeal – Note of county court judgment – Provision of note – Duty of counsel
h *and solicitors.*

The debtor, who had been a salesman, was unemployed from April 1975 until
February 1977, during which period he lived on supplementary benefit. On 30th
April 1975 the petitioning creditor obtained judgment against him for £440 and costs.
Subsequently two instalment orders were made against the debtor, but nothing was
j paid under either order. Having received no payment from the debtor, the petitioning creditor issued a bankruptcy notice on 23rd September 1976 which was served on
27th September. The debtor having failed to comply with the bankruptcy notice,
the petitioning creditor presented a bankruptcy petition on 22nd November. The

---

1   [1915] 1 Ch 398 at 406

debtor sought an adjournment of the making of a receiving order in order to adduce formal evidence that he had no assets whatsoever and that he was able to pay £2 per a week, and submitted that the investigation of his affairs which was made when the instalment orders were made established his lack of assets. The registrar refused an adjournment and on 27th January 1977 made the receiving order. On 3rd February the debtor swore a statement of affairs which showed liabilities of £866 and assets at nil. The debtor appealed against the making of the receiving order, contending that where it was established that a debtor had no assets and no prospects of acquiring b any the court should dismiss the petition because to make a receiving order in such circumstances would merely increase the costs and do no good.

Held – The appeal would be dismissed for the following reasons—

(i) The investigation into the debtor's affairs made when the instalment orders were made not only was far less rigorous than the investigation made in bankruptcy but also c resulted in orders being made not on the basis that the debtor could pay nothing but on the basis that he could pay something. In any event, the debtor had put forward no evidence but his own to support his contention that he had no assets at that time and that there was no prospect of this ever having any, and even if his own evidence were accepted at its full face value he had not discharged the heavy burden of proof that rested on him to support his contention (see p 985 b and g to j, p 986 g and p 987 d c d and f, post); *Re Leonard, ex parte Leonard* [1896] 1 QB 473 and *Re Jubb, ex parte Burman and Greenwood* [1897] 1 QB 641 applied.

(ii) There were no circumstances of oppression, or anything else, which amounted to 'sufficient cause', within s 5(3)^a of the Bankruptcy Act 1914, which would have justified the registrar in exercising his discretion to dismiss the petition (see p 986 g and p 987 d and f, post); dicta of Wright and Kennedy JJ in *Re Somers, ex parte* e *Union Credit Bank Ltd* (1897) 4 Mans 227 applied.

Per Curiam. (i) If after a receiving order has been made the Official Receiver were to be satisfied that the debtor has no assets and no prospects of ever having any, so that to continue the process of bankruptcy would merely be to pile up costs which would never be paid, he should support an application by the debtor to have the receiving order rescinded (see p 986 j to p 987 b and f, post).

(ii) It is the duty of advocates in the county court to make a full note of the judgment and, if there is an appeal, to submit an agreed note of the judgment to the judge or registrar for revision (see p 983 g to j and p 987 f, post).

Notes

For rescission of a receiving order, see 3 Halsbury's Laws (4th Edn) paras 417, 418, and f for cases on the subject, see 4 Digest (Reissue) 184-189, 1631-1687.

For the Bankruptcy Act 1914, s 5, see 3 Halsbury's Statutes (3rd Edn) 46.

Cases referred to in judgments

Betts, Re, ex parte Betts [1897] 1 QB 50, 66 LJQB 14, 75 LT 292, 3 Mans 287, CA, 4 Digest (Reissue) 177, *1585*.

Hay, Re (1913) 110 LT 47, DC, 4 Digest (Reissue) 177, *1593*.

Jubb, Re, ex parte Burman and Greenwood [1897] 1 QB 641, 66 LJQB 452, 76 LT 329, 4 Mans 30, DC, 4 Digest (Reissue) 177, *1591*.

Leonard, Re, ex parte Leonard [1896] 1 QB 473, 65 LJQB 393, 74 LT 183, 3 Mans 43, CA, 4 Digest (Reissue) 177, *1583*.

Somers, Re, ex parte Union Credit Bank Ltd (1897) 4 Mans 227, DC, 4 Digest (Reissue) 177, *1586*.

---

a Section 5(3) provides: 'If the court is not satisfied with the proof of the petitioning creditor's debt, or of the act of bankruptcy, or of the service of the petition, or is satisfied by the debtor that he is able to pay his debts, or that for other sufficient cause no order ought to be made, the court may dismiss the petition.'

Cases also cited

a Robinson, ex parte, re Robinson (1883) 22 Ch D 816, CA.

Scott, Re, ex parte Paris-Orleans Railway Co (1913) 58 Sol Jo 11, CA.

Appeal

Paul Alexander Field ('the debtor') appealed against a receiving order made in the Manchester County Court on 27th January 1977 by Mr Deputy Registrar Clough on *b* the petition of H & J Quick Ltd on the ground that he had committed an act of bankruptcy by failing to comply with the requirements of a bankruptcy notice issued out of the Manchester County Court on 23rd September 1976. The Official Receiver was appointed the receiver of the debtor's estate. The facts are set out in the judgment of Megarry V-C.

c A R C Kirsten for the debtor.
The petitioning creditor did not appear.
E C Evans-Lombe for the Official Receiver.

MEGARRY V-C. This is an appeal against a receiving order that was made in the *d* Manchester County Court on 27th January 1977 by Mr Deputy Registrar Clough. On 30th April 1975 the petitioning creditor had obtained judgment against the debtor in Altrincham County Court for a little over £440 and costs, for petrol supplied. Subsequently, two instalment orders were made, the first on 24th September 1975 and the second on 16th February 1976. Under the first, the debtor was to pay his debt by instalments of £20 a month at first, and then £40 a month, with £330 to be paid at the *e* end of 1975. Under the second, the debtor was to pay £5 a month. Nothing has been paid under either order. The debtor had been a salesman, but I understand that he lost his job. He was unemployed from April 1975 until February 1977, and during that period he has lived on supplementary benefit and had a spell in hospital.

Having received no payments from the debtor, the petitioning creditor issued a bankruptcy notice on 23rd September 1976, which was served late on 27th September; *f* and on 22nd November the petitioning creditor presented a bankruptcy petition based on the failure to comply with the bankruptcy notice. The registrar heard the petition on 27th January 1977, the petitioning creditor and the debtor each being represented by solicitors. There is no formal record of what occurred before the registrar, but the solicitors on each side have helpfully put before us their recollections of what happened, one by affidavit and the other in a letter; and although there is a considerable degree of agreement between them, there is by no means unanimity on everything.

I pause there. It has long been well settled by decisions of the Court of Appeal that it is the duty of advocates in the county court to make as full a note as they can of the judgment in any case in which they are engaged unless they know that a full shorthand note is being taken. If there is an appeal from the judgment, it is then their duty to attempt to agree a note of what was said, and then submit their agreed note to the judge for revision; and it has been said that if the agreed note is not submitted to the judge, it will not be looked at on appeal as that would not be fair to the judge. I need not refer to the authorities on this as they are collected in Megarry on The Rent Acts[1]. I can see no reason why this practice should not apply in bankruptcy cases, nor why it should not apply when the advocates are solicitors and not counsel, and the hearing is by a registrar and not a judge. The principle is the same: the appellate court ought in the interests of all to have before it the most reliable version of the judgment appealed from that the circumstances permit. When I put this to counsel who appeared for the debtor and counsel who appeared for the Official

---

1   10th Edn (1967), vol 1, p 41

Receiver they both said that this was the accepted practice in bankruptcy; and they could offer no explanation why the practice had not been followed in the present case. It was not they, of course, who appeared before the registrar.

I fully appreciate that some effort was made (and very properly made) to provide this court with agreed information about what happened at the hearing. But what is needed is a single document, approved by the judge, and not two different documents, far from identical, which the judge has not seen. I have said something on the matter because this case suggests that the settled practice is not as generally known or observed as it ought to be, and also because I consider it to be the duty of counsel, if they receive a brief in which it appears that the practice has not been observed, to do what is possible towards putting matters right before the appeal is heard.

I return to the march of events. After the receiving order had been made on 27th January, the debtor swore a statement of affairs on 3rd February. This showed liabilities of £866 (including a bank overdraft of £200) and assets at nil, so that there was a deficiency of £866. Liabilities of some £200 more have since emerged, making a deficiency of nearly £1,070, we were told. No appeal against the receiving order was lodged in time, but on 10th March notice of an intention to apply for an extension of time was given; and on 2nd May this court extended the time, and notice of appeal was given on 5th May. Certain points have now disappeared from the case, or have not been pressed. The notice of appeal is a little elaborate, but in substance the case made by counsel for the debtor relates, first, to a refusal by the registrar to adjourn the application for the receiving order, and second, to his making the receiving order. According to the affidavit of the debtor's solicitor, the application for the adjournment was made in order to enable formal evidence to be adduced that the debtor had no assets whatsoever, and also that the debtor was able to pay £2 per week. The affidavit then states that the registrar indicated that he would have to be satisfied that 'not only were there no assets but that there was in addition a probability that the debt was going to be paid by some means'. There is nothing in the letter from the petitioning creditor's solicitor that supports the assertion that the registrar laid down this double requirement.

Again I pause. I do not see how such a double requirement could possibly be right. Counsel for the Official Receiver, in response to an enquiry from the Bench, said that it was self-contradictory, and that he could not support it. It is possible that such a proposition came from an incautious blending of two quite distinct propositions, to be found in proximity to each other in Williams on Bankruptcy[1]. One is that if the court is satisfied that there are no assets and no reasonable prospect or probability of any coming into existence, this may be 'sufficient cause', within s 5(3) of the Bankruptcy Act 1914, for the court to exercise its discretion to dismiss the petition. I shall return to this proposition in due course. The other proposition is that the court may adjourn a petition if the court is satisfied that there is a reasonable prospect of the debt being paid or settled. I am not saying that it is impossible for these two factors to coincide: a debtor with no shred of assets or prospect of any might nevertheless have wealthy friends or relations who could be prevailed on to agree to discharge the debts. What I do say is that the two factors cannot be laid down as a double requirement that must be satisfied before an adjournment is granted. Let me say at once that I am not at all satisfied that the registrar ever laid down such a double requirement; certainly I would not countenance reversing his decision on this ground without first being sure that this was what he said. However, on the view of the case that I take, I do not think that it is necessary to deal with this point; I have said what I have said in order to nip in the bud any such double requirement if it, or anything like it, is to be found lurking anywhere.

I turn, then, to the first of the propositions that I mentioned, on which the main submissions of counsel for the debtor rested. Put shortly, he contended that where it

---

1   8th Edn (1968), pp 68, 69

was established that the debtor had no assets and no prospects of acquiring any, the
a court should dismiss the petition; for to make a receiving order in such circumstances
would merely increase the costs, and would do no good. In the present case, he said,
the debtor fell within this doctrine, and so the receiving order should be set aside.

Now it is plain that there is considerable support for some doctrine of this sort; but
it is equally plain that the doctrine is hedged about by important precautions. After
all, if it were open to a debtor to avoid having a receiving order made against him
b simply by alleging utter destitution, both present and future, such pleas of destitution
might become popular; and prospective bankrupts might hasten to rid themselves
of any assets and prospects which might hamper them in making such a plea. A man
may indeed be too poor to be made bankrupt: but the burden of proof is heavy.

I would describe *Re Betts, ex parte Betts*[1] as the leading case on this branch of the law,
were it not for the fact that the judgments so strongly emphasise the special circum-
c stances of the case, and that it is not to be regarded as a precedent for any other case
unless the circumstances are the same or exactly similar. There, the debtor was
already bankrupt. The petitioning creditor in the second bankruptcy had proved
for a prior debt in the first bankruptcy, and only a small dividend had been paid in it;
the bankrupt was undischarged. In those circumstances, the Court of Appeal set
aside the receiving order in the second bankruptcy proceedings because, in the words
d of Lord Esher MR[2], the court was—

> 'clearly convinced, not merely by the statement of the debtor, but from all
> the circumstances of the case, that there cannot be any assets or any prospect of
> any coming into existence, and that, if a receiving order is made, the only effect
> will be a mere waste of money in costs . . .'

e In the first bankruptcy, the existence of assets would have been fully probed; and if
subsequently assets appeared, they would be taken for the first bankruptcy, and so
would not be available for a second bankruptcy until all the debts under the first
bankruptcy had been paid.

As Lord Esher MR[2] pointed out, if a debtor merely swears an affidavit saying that
it is no use making him a bankrupt because he has no assets and no prospects of
f having any, the court will not accept this as a ground for not making a receiving order,
because at that stage the court is not in a position to know whether that statement
is true. During the process of bankruptcy much that was unknown earlier becomes
revealed. In *Re Jubb, ex parte Burman and Greenwood*[3] the debtor contended that a
receiving order ought not to be made because the assets available for distribution
would probably be less that the costs of the bankruptcy proceedings; but this con-
g tention was rejected, Vaughan Williams J[4] pointing out that in the course of the
bankruptcy proceedings it was quite possible that the assets available for distribution
would be found to be larger than they presently appeared to be. *Re Leonard, ex parte
Leonard*[5] makes it clear that the apparent non-existence of assets is no ground for
refusing to make a receiving order; for as Lord Esher MR said[6]: 'The Court cannot
at that stage tell whether the proceedings in bankruptcy will have no result.' Counsel
h for the debtor placed some reliance on the affairs of the debtor in the present case
having been to some extent investigated when the instalment orders were made;
but that process is far less rigorous than bankruptcy, and in any case both resulted in
orders being made not on the basis that the debtor could pay nothing, but on the basis
that he could pay something.

j

1 [1897] 1 QB 50
2 [1897] 1 QB 50 at 52
3 [1897] 1 QB 641
4 [1897] 1 QB 641 at 645
5 [1896] 1 QB 473
6 [1896] 1 QB 473 at 475

At first sight, the most helpful case for the debtor seemed to be *Re Somers, ex parte Union Credit Bank Ltd*[1]. That was a case in which the brother of a barmaid sought *a* to borrow £100 from a moneylending company which required sureties for the loan. The barmaid and her sister, at the solicitation of their brother, joined with him in signing a promissory note, and the loan was made to the brother; the barmaid received none of the money. There was default in paying an instalment, the company obtained judgment for the debt against all three, and on levying execution the sheriff returned nulla bona. The company then served bankruptcy notices and *b* presented petitions in bankruptcy against all three. The barmaid contended that no receiving order should be made against her because she had no assets and was not likely to become possessed of any; and this was supported not only by her own affidavit, but also by her brother's. The registrar nevertheless made a receiving order against her, but on appeal the Divisional Court in Bankruptcy set it aside. Wright J said[2]:   *c*

> 'All the cases agree in saying that the evidence of the debtor alone as to no assets will not do; but in a case like this, where there are no assets and no probability of any becoming available, the Court has a discretion to refuse to make a receiving order if, in its opinion, the proceedings are of an oppressive character. Here, in my opinion, they are of an oppressive character, and the Court ought to exercise its discretion by refusing a receiving order.'   *d*

Kennedy J put matters with brevity[2]:

> 'I am of the same opinion. In this case there are no existing assets and no prospect of any becoming available. That is the effect of the debtor's affidavit, and though her affidavit alone would not be sufficient to establish a case of no *e* assets, it is corroborated by the affidavit of her brother—a disinterested witness. Having regard to these and the other circumstances of the case, it appears to me that it would be oppressive to allow this receiving order to stand.'

I think it important to observe that both judges put their decisions on the basis of oppression. Neither makes it explicit what the circumstances of oppression were; but it is not hard to discern possible grounds for this conclusion. The petitioning creditor was a moneylender; the debtor was a barmaid; she was a sister who had sought to help her brother; she was a mere surety; and she had had none of the money herself.

In the case before us there are none of these considerations. From first to last nothing has been suggested which could fairly bring this case under the head of oppression. Further, there is no evidence before us except that of the debtor himself *f* to establish that he has no assets and no prospect of assets. The debtor swore an affidavit dated 17th June 1977, and, without objection from counsel for the Official Receiver, we gave leave to the debtor to file it. This shows that last February the debtor obtained employment as a storeman; and, as counsel for the debtor said, this had made his task rather more difficult than before. The excess of the debtor's income over his expenditure, as set out in the affidavit, is not great, and the affidavit *g* flatly says that the debtor has no assets whatever. But no evidence to support the appeal beyond what is in the affidavit has been put before us; and, as counsel for the debtor said, he has put before us everything that was available to him or his solicitors.

To this I should add that counsel for the Official Receiver, on instructions, said that the Official Receiver did not support this application. I think that this is of some relevance. The Official Receiver has had since the receiving order was made on 27th January to investigate the debtor's affairs, and so must have a greater knowledge of these than this court has. Section 108(1) of the 1914 Act gives to every court exercising

1   (1897) 4 Mans 227
2   4 Mans 227 at 230

bankruptcy jurisdiction a power to review, vary or rescind any order made by it in
a that jurisdiction. If after a receiving order has been made the Official Receiver were
to be satisfied that the debtor had no assets and no prospects of ever having any, so
that to continue the process of bankruptcy would merely be to pile up costs which
would never be paid, I think that he could and should support any application by the
debtor to have the receiving order rescinded, even if he has no duty to make such
an application himself. Counsel for the Official Receiver, who put forward the latter
b possibility, told us that he had no knowledge of any Official Receiver actually making
such an application; but I do not think that this is very significant. The number of
cases in which there is sufficiently cogent evidence of there being no present or future
possibility whatever of any assets existing must indeed be small.

In the end, I have come to the clear conclusion that this appeal should be dismissed.
First, the debtor has not put forward any evidence but his own to support his conten-
c tion that he has no assets at present, and that there is no prospect of his ever having
any. Indeed, his affidavit says nothing explicit on the latter point. That of itself
would, on the authorities, be fatal to his appeal. Second, even if his own evidence is
accepted at its full face value, I am, like Horridge and Rowlatt JJ in *Re Hay*[1], far from
being 'clearly convinced that there are no assets and will be none'. It is plain that the
burden of proof in such matters is heavy, and rightly heavy; and here the debtor
d has not discharged it. Third, I cannot see that there are any circumstances of oppression, or anything else, that amount to 'sufficient cause', within s 5(3) of the 1914 Act.
Fourth, I can see no weight in the contention that the registrar wrongly refused an
adjournment. The debtor has had longer to prepare his case for this court than
would be likely to have been given to him under any adjournment by the registrar;
and even with that extra time he has wholly failed to make out an adequate case.
e If the registrar was wrong in his reasons for refusing an adjournment (and I am very
far from saying that he was, for it has not been satisfactorily established what his
reasons were), the debtor has now demonstrated to the court that if he had had the
adjournment, it would not have helped him. For those reasons, I would dismiss this
appeal.

f **BROWNE-WILKINSON J.** I agree.

Appeal dismissed.

Solicitors: *Pritchard, Englefield and Tobin*, agents for *William H Lill & Co*, Altrincham
(for the debtor); *Treasury Solicitor*.

Diana Brahams Barrister.

Paton v Trustees of BPAS and another

QUEEN'S BENCH DIVISION AT LIVERPOOL
SIR GEORGE BAKER P SITTING AS AN ADDITIONAL JUDGE OF THE QUEEN'S BENCH DIVISION
24th MAY 1978

*Abortion – Legal abortion – Power of husband to prevent wife having abortion – Wife
obtaining necessary medical certificates for legal abortion – Wife wanting abortion – Husband
applying for injunction to stop her having abortion – Whether injunction could be granted –
Abortion Act 1967, s 1.*

A wife, who had conceived a child by her husband, was concerned about her pregnancy. She went, on her own, to see two registered medical practitioners about it.
They were of the opinion, formed in good faith, that the continuance of her pregnancy
would involve risk of injury to her physical or mental health. They issued the

1   (1913) 110 LT 47 at 48

necessary certificates so that her pregnancy could, by virtue of s 1[a] of the Abortion Act 1967, be lawfully terminated. She wanted to have the abortion but her husband, who had not been consulted either by her or by the medical practitioners before the certificates were issued, did not want her to have one. He claimed that he had a right to have a say in the destiny of the child and applied to the court for an injunction restraining her from causing or permitting an abortion to be carried out on her without his consent.

Held – An injunction could not be granted because a husband had no right, enforceable at law or in equity, to stop his wife having, or a registered medical practitioner performing, a legal abortion (see p 991 g to j and p 992 g, post).

Notes
For the medical termination of pregnancy, see 11 Halsbury's Laws (4th Edn) para 1194.
For the Abortion Act 1967, s 1, see 8 Halsbury's Statutes (3rd Edn) 682.

Cases referred to in judgment
Elliot v Joicey [1935] AC 209, [1935] All ER Rep 578, 104 LJCh 111, sub nom *Re Joicey, Joicey v Elliot* 152 LT 398, HL, 49 Digest (Repl) 743, 6965.
Forster v Forster (1790) 1 Hag Con 144, 161 ER 504, 27(1) Digest (Reissue) 557, 4053.
Gouriet v Union of Post Office Workers [1977] 3 All ER 70, [1977] 3 WLR 300, HL.
Jones v Smith (1973) 278 So 2d 339.
Montgomery v Montgomery [1964] 2 All ER 22, [1965] P 46, [1964] 2 WLR 1036, 27(2) Digest (Reissue) 936, 7555.
North London Railway Co v Great Northern Railway Co (1883) 11 QBD 30, 52 LJQB 380, 48 LT 695, CA, 28(2) Digest (Reissue) 959, 24.
Planned Parenthood of Central Missouri v Danforth, Attorney-General of Missouri (1976) 428 US 52, 96 S Ct 2831.
R v Smith (John) [1974] 1 All ER 376, [1973] 1 WLR 1510, 138 JP 175, 58 Cr App Rep 106, CA, 15 Digest (Reissue) 1202, 10,314.
Roe v Wade (1972) 410 US 113, 93 S Ct 705.
White v Yup (1969) 458 P 2d 617.

Application for injunction
By a specially endorsed writ the plaintiff, William Paton ('the husband') applied for an injunction restraining the first defendants, the trustees of BPAS (British Pregnancy Advisory Service), and the second defendant, his wife, Joan Mary Paton ('the wife'), from causing or permitting an abortion to be carried out on the wife without his consent. The facts are set out in the judgment.

Andrew Rankin QC and *Stephen J Bedford* for the husband.
William Denny QC and *M D Rhodes* for the first defendants.
Fielding Hatton for the wife.

SIR GEORGE BAKER P. By a specially endorsed writ the plaintiff, who is the husband of the second defendant, seeks an injunction in effect to restrain the first defendants, a charitable organisation, and particularly his wife, the second defendant, from causing or permitting an abortion to be carried out on his wife without his consent.

---

a   Section 1, so far as material, is set out at p 991 e and f, post

a Such action, of course, arouses great emotions, and vigorous opposing views as was recently pointed out in 1972 in the Supreme Court of the United States by Blackmun J in *Roe v Wade*[1]. In the discussion of human affairs and especially of abortion, controversy can rage over the moral rights, duties, interests, standards and religious views of the parties. Moral values are in issue. I am, in fact, concerned with none of these matters. I am concerned, and concerned only, with the law of England as it applies to this claim. My task is to apply the law free of emotion or predilection.

b Nobody suggests that there has ever been such a claim litigated before the courts in this country. Indeed, the only case of which I have ever heard was in Ontario. It was unreported because the husband's claim for an injunction was never tried.

In considering the law the first and basic principle is that there must be a legal right enforceable at law or in equity before the applicant can obtain an injunction from the court to restrain an infringement of that right. That has long been the law. The c leading case is *North London Railway Co v Great Northern Railway Co*[2]. Counsel for the husband has helpfully read much of the judgment of Cotton LJ. I will confine myself to the following well-known passage[3]:

> 'In my opinion the sole intention of the Section [i e s 25(8) of the Supreme Court of Judicature Act 1873] is this: that where there is a legal right which was, inde-
> pendently of the Act, capable of being enforced either at law or in equity, then,
> d whatever may have been the previous practice, the High Court may interfere by injunction in protection of that right.'

In *Montgomery v Montgomery*[4], a well-known case in family law, Ormrod J, having cited the passage from Cotton LJ's judgment[3] and reviewed the various authorities, concluded that the court could only grant an injunction to support a legal right, and e since the petitioner wife had no proprietary interest in the flat in which the parties were living, the court had no jurisdiction to make a mandatory order to exclude the husband from the flat. The words 'husband and wife' were used, although the parties were no longer joined in matrimony, having been divorced.

The law relating to injunctions has been considered recently in the House of Lords, in *Gouriet v Union of Post Office Workers*[5]. Many passages from their Lordships' speeches f have been cited. I do not propose to go through them because it is now as clear as possible that there must be, first, a legal right in an individual to found an injunction and, second, that the enforcement of the criminal law is a matter for the authorities and for the Attorney-General. As counsel for the husband concedes, any process for the enforcement of the criminal law in a civil suit must be used with great caution, if at all. The private individual may have the right only if his right is greater than the public right, that is to say, that he would suffer personally and more than the general g public unless he could restrain this offence. That proposition is not accepted by counsel for the first defendants or by counsel for the wife, and in any event it is not now suggested that the proposed abortion on the wife will be other than lawful. So, it is not necessary for me to decide that question or to consider *Gouriet v Union of Post Office Workers*[5] further.

The first question is whether this plaintiff has a right at all. The foetus cannot, in h English law, in my view, have any right of its own at least until it is born and has a separate existence from the mother. That permeates the whole of the civil law of this country (I except the criminal law, which is now irrelevant), and is, indeed, the basis of the decisions in those countries where law is founded on the common law, that is to say, in America, Canada, Australia, and, I have no doubt, in others.

j

1 (1972) 410 US 113 at 116
2 (1883) 11 QBD 30
3 11 QBD 30 at 40
4 [1964] 2 All ER 22 at 23, [1965] P 46 at 50
5 [1977] 3 All ER 70, [1977] 3 WLR 300

For a long time there was great controversy whether after birth a child could have a right of action in respect of pre-natal injury. The Law Commission considered that and produced a working paper[1] in 1973, followed by a final report[2], but it was universally accepted, and has since been accepted, that in order to have a right the foetus must be born and be a child. There was only one known possible exception which is referred to in the working paper[3], an American case, *White v Yup*[4], where the wrongful death of an eight month old viable foetus, stillborn as a consequence of injury, led an American court to allow a cause of action, but there can be no doubt, in my view, that in England and Wales, the foetus has no right of action, no right at all, until birth. The succession cases have been mentioned. There is no difference. From conception the child may have succession rights by what has been called a 'fictional construction' but the child must be subsequently born alive. See per Lord Russell of Killowen in *Elliot v Joicey*[5].

The husband's case must therefore depend on a right which he has himself. I would say a word about the illegitimate, usually called the putative, but I prefer myself to refer to the illegitimate, father. Although American decisions to which I have been referred concern illegitimate fathers, and statutory provisions about them, it seems to me that in this country the illegitimate father can have no rights whatsoever except those given to him by statute. That was clearly the common law. One provision which makes an inroad into this is s 14 of the Guardianship of Minors Act 1971, and s 9(1) and some other sections of that Act applicable to illegitimate children, giving the illegitimate father or mother the right to apply for the custody of or access to an illegitimate child. But the equality of parental rights provision in s 1(1) of the Guardianship Act 1973 expressly does not apply in relation to a minor who is illegitimate: see s 1(7).

So this plaintiff must, in my opinion, bring his case, if he can, squarely within the framework of the fact that he is a husband. It is, of course, very common for spouses to seek injunctions for personal protection in the matrimonial courts during the pendency of or, indeed, after divorce actions, but the basic reason for the non-molestation injunction often granted in the family courts is to protect the other spouse or the living children, and to ensure that no undue pressure is put on one or other of the spouses during the pendency of the case and during the breaking-up of the marriage.

There was, of course, the action for restitution of conjugal rights, a proceeding which always belied its name and was abolished in 1970. It arose because in ecclesiastical law the parties could not end the consortium by agreement. In a sense the action for restitution was something of a fiction. The court ordered the spouse to return to cohabitation. If the spouse did not return then that spouse was held to be in desertion. No more could happen. The court could not compel matrimonial intercourse: *Forster v Forster*[6]. So matrimonial courts have never attempted the enforcement of matrimonial obligations by injunction.

The law is that the court cannot and would not seek to enforce or restrain by injunction matrimonial obligations, if they be obligations such as sexual intercourse or contraception (a non-molestation injunction given during the pendency of divorce proceedings could, of course, cover attempted intercourse). No court would ever grant an injunction to stop sterilisation or vasectomy. Personal family relationships in marriage cannot be enforced by the order of a court. An injunction in such circumstances was described by Judge Mager in *Jones v Smith*[7] in the District Court of Appeal of Florida as 'ludicrous'.

1   Working Paper no 47
2   Report on Injuries to Unborn Children, Law Com 60 (Cmnd 5709)
3   Law Com Working Paper no 47 at p 3
4   (1969) 458 P 2d 617
5   [1935] AC 209 at 233, [1935] All ER Rep 578 at 589
6   (1790) 1 Hag Con 144, 161 ER 504
7   (1973) 278 So 2d 339 at 344

I ask the question 'If an injunction were ordered, what could be the remedy?'
and I do not think I need say any more than that no judge could even consider sending
a husband or wife to prison for breaking such an order. That, of itself, seems to me to
cover the application here; this husband cannot by law by injunction stop his wife
having what is now accepted to be a lawful abortion within the terms of the Abortion
Act 1967.

The case which was first put forward to me a week ago, and indeed is to be found in
the writ, is that the wife had no proper legal grounds for seeking a termination of her
pregnancy and that, not to mince words, she was being spiteful, vindictive and
utterly unreasonable in seeking so to do. It now appears I need not go into the
evidence in the affidavits because it is accepted and common ground that the provisions
of the 1967 Act have been complied with, the necessary certificate has been given by
two doctors and everything is lawfully set for the abortion.

The case put to me finally by counsel for the husband (to whom I am most indebted
for having set out very clearly and logically what the law is) is that while he cannot
say here that there is any suggestion of a criminal abortion nevertheless if doctors did
not hold their views, or come to their conclusions, in good faith, which would be an
issue triable by a jury (see R v Smith (John)[1]), then this plaintiff might recover an
injunction. That is not accepted by counsel for the first defendants. It is unnecessary
for me to decide that academic question because it does not arise in this case. My own
view is that it would be quite impossible for the courts in any event to supervise the
operation of the 1967 Act. The great social responsibility is firmly placed by the law
on the shoulders of the medical profession: per Scarman LJ, in R v Smith (John)[2].

I will look at the 1967 Act very briefly. Section 1 provides:

'(1) ... a person shall not be guilty of an offence under the law relating to
abortion when a pregnancy is terminated by a registered medical practitioner
if two registered medical practitioners are of the opinion, formed in good faith—
(a) that the continuance of the pregnancy would involve risk ... of injury to the
physical or mental health of the pregnant woman ... [Then there are other
provisions which I need not read].

'(2) In determining whether the continuance of pregnancy would involve such
risk of injury to health as is mentioned in paragraph (a) of subsection (1) of this
section, account may be taken of the pregnant woman's actual or reasonably
forseeable environment ...'

That does not now arise in this case. The two doctors have given a certificate. It is
not and cannot be suggested that that certificate was given in other than good
faith and it seems to me that there is the end of the matter in English law. The
1967 Act gives no right to a father to be consulted in respect of the termination of a
pregnancy. True, it gives no right to the mother either, but obviously the mother is
going to be right at the heart of the matter consulting with the doctors if they are to
arrive at a decision in good faith, unless, of course, she is mentally incapacitated or
physically incapacitated (unable to make any decision or give any help) as, for example,
in consequence of an accident. The husband, therefore, in my view, has no legal right
enforceable at law or in equity to stop his wife having this abortion or to stop the doctors from carrying out the abortion.

Counsel for the husband made one point about a letter, which has now been produced to the court, dated 22nd May, from Dr Macrone, the family doctor. I need only
point out that Dr Macrone says in his letter that he had no objection to her seeking a
termination of the pregnancy whereas her affidavit seems to put it a little higher,

---

1   [1974] 1 All ER 376, [1973] 1 WLR 1510
2   [1974] 1 All ER 376 at 378, [1973] 1 WLR 1510 at 1512

where she says she had the support of Dr Macrone. But really that is a matter of terminology. I do not think there is anything in the point and I am sure counsel for the husband was simply putting it forward as something the court ought to look at, without any conviction that there was any merit in the distinction.

This certificate is clear, and not only would it be a bold and brave judge (I think counsel for the husband used that expression) who would seek to interfere with the discretion of doctors acting under the 1967 Act, but I think he would really be a foolish judge who would try to do any such thing, unless possibly, there is clear bad faith and an obvious attempt to perpetrate a criminal offence. Even then, of course, the question is whether that is a matter which should be left to the Director of Public Prosecutions and the Attorney-General. I say no more for I have stated my view of the law of England.

Very helpfully I have been referred to American authorities. The Supreme Court of the United States has reached the same conclusion, that a husband, or an illegitimate father, has no right to stop his wife, or the woman who is pregnant by him, from having a legal abortion. In *Planned Parenthood of Central Missouri v Danforth, Attorney-General of Missouri*[1] the Supreme Court by a majority held that the State of Missouri[2]—

> 'may not constitutionally require the consent of the spouse, as is specified under § 3(3) of the Missouri Act, as a condition for abortion during the first 12 weeks of pregnancy ... clearly since the State cannot regulate or proscribe abortion during the first stage when the physician and his patient make that decision, the State cannot delegate authority to any particular person, even the spouse, to prevent abortion during that same period.'

It is interesting to note that the Missouri spousal consent provision would have required the husband's consent even if he was not the father.

A spousal consent provision in an English Act could not of course be challenged as unconstitutional but there is no such provision in the 1967 Act or in the Abortions Regulations 1968[2] to which a challenge of ultra vires could be made. There is no provision even for consultation with the spouse and reg 5 prohibits disclosure except in specified instances, of which disclosure to the spouse is not one.

Counsel have been unable to discover any extant decision in those countries whose laws derive from the common law that the consent of the husband is required before an otherwise legal abortion can be performed on the wife. Counsel for the husband's researches show that in Roman law, centuries ago, the father's consent was required or otherwise abortion was a crime, but today the only way he can put the case is that the husband has a right to have a say in the destiny of the child he has conceived. The law of England gives him no such right; the 1967 Act contains no such provision. It follows, therefore, that in my opinion this claim for an injunction is completely misconceived and must be dismissed.

Order accordingly.

Solicitors: *Grey, Lloyd & Co*, Connahs Quay (for the husband); *Rigbey, Loose & Mills*, Birmingham (for the first defendants); *Maxwell, Cooke & Co*, Birkenhead (for the wife).

Christine Ivamy   Barrister.

---

1   (1976) 96 S Ct 2831 at 2841, per Blackmun J delivering the opinion of the court
2   SI 1968 No 39

Buchmann v May

COURT OF APPEAL, CIVIL DIVISION
MEGAW, STEPHENSON LJJ AND SIR JOHN PENNYCUICK
3rd MAY 1976

Rent restriction – Protected tenant – Excluded tenancies – Holiday letting – Intention of parties – Tenancy agreement expressly stating that its purpose was to confer on tenant right to occupy house for purpose of holiday – Claim by tenant that purpose of tenancy not holiday letting – No allegation of misrepresentation or mistake or claim for rectification – Burden of proof on tenant to show that contract did not represent true intention of parties – Whether express words of agreement prevailed – Rent Act 1968, s 2(1)(bbb) (as added by the Rent Act 1974, s 2(1)).

In 1972 the plaintiff let a furnished house to M for a period of six months. M and his wife, the defendant, were Commonwealth citizens, living and working in England on a series of temporary residence permits. After the tenancy expired, the plaintiff granted M a succession of similar short furnished tenancies, the last of which expired on 31st July 1974. In March 1974 M and the defendant went abroad on business. On her return the defendant telephoned the plaintiff's agent to enquire about the possibility of a further short tenancy. She told him that she would be leaving England before Christmas and that her temporary residence permit expired before then. The plaintiff called on her at the house, where she was already installed, and gave her a tenancy agreement for signature. It made provision for the grant of a three month tenancy from 1st October to 31st December. Clause 6 stated: 'It is mutually agreed and declared that the letting hereby made is solely for the purpose of the [defendant's] holiday ...' The plaintiff did not expressly draw the defendant's attention to cl 6, but she had had an opportunity of reading it before she signed the agreement. She remained in occupation after the tenancy expired on 31st December. The plaintiff brought an action against her for possession of the house, claiming that the tenancy was excluded from the protection of the Rent Acts by reason of s 2(1)(bbb)[a] of the Rent Act 1968, in that '[the] purpose of the tenancy [was] to confer on the tenant the right to occupy the dwelling-house for a holiday'. The defendant denied that it had been a holiday letting and claimed the protection of the Rents Acts on the ground that the true purpose of the tenancy was a statutory furnished letting. She did not assert that there had been any misrepresentation or mistake in the terms of the agreement nor did she claim rectification. The judge considered that 'the purpose of the tenancy' had to be determined by reference to the reality of the situation as expressed through the oral evidence of the parties and in his judgment he made no reference to cl 6 of the agreement. He held that the tenancy was not a holiday letting and that the defendant was entitled to the protection of the Rent Acts. He accordingly dismissed the plaintiff's claim for possession. The plaintiff appealed.

Held – The labels which parties put on a transaction were not of conclusive validity but where a tenancy agreement expressly stated the purpose for which it was made that statement would stand as evidence of the purpose of the parties unless the tenant could establish that it did not correspond with the true purpose. In the absence of such evidence and since the purpose of the tenancy could properly be described as a 'holiday' letting, there was nothing which could displace the effect of cl 6 of the

---

a   Section 2(1), so far as material, is set out at p 994 j, post

agreement and show that it was a sham or was, without any intention to deceive, an untrue statement of the purpose of the letting. It followed that the defendant was *a* not protected by the Rent Acts, that s 2(1)(*bbb*) of the 1968 Act applied and that the plaintiff was entitled to possession of the house. The appeal would therefore be allowed (see p 998 *g* to p 999 *a* and p 1000 *d*, post).

Wolfe v Hogan [1949] 1 All ER 570 and *British Land Co Ltd v Herbert Silver (Menswear) Ltd* [1958] 1 All ER 833 applied.

b

Notes

For exclusion of protected status where purpose of tenancy is holiday letting, see Supplement to 23 Halsbury's Laws (3rd Edn) para 1494A.1.

For the Rent Act 1968, s 2(1)(*bbb*) (as added by the Rent Act 1974, s 2(1)), see 44 Halsbury's Statutes (3rd Edn) 616.

As from 29th August 1977, s 2(1)(*bbb*) of the 1968 Act has been replaced by s 9 of *c* the Rent Act 1977.

Cases referred to in judgments

British Land Co Ltd v Herbert Silver (Menswear) Ltd [1958] 1 All ER 833, [1958] 1 QB 531, [1958] 2 WLR 580, CA, 31(2) Digest (Reissue) 1013, 8047.

Horford Investments Ltd v Lambert [1974] 1 All ER 131, [1976] Ch 39, [1973] 3 WLR 872, *d* 27 P & CR 88, CA, Digest (Cont Vol D) 593, 8058a.

Wolfe v Hogan [1949] 1 All ER 570, [1949] 2 KB 194, CA, 31(2) Digest (Reissue) 1002, 7988.

Appeal   *e*

This was an appeal by the plaintiff, George Buchmann ('Mr Buchmann'), against an order dated 22nd July 1975 and made by his Honour Judge Dennis Smith at Croydon County Court dismissing the plaintiff's claim against the defendant, Colleen May ('Mrs May'), for possession of a furnished dwelling-house known as 24 Avenue Road, Norbury, London. The facts are set out in the judgment of Sir John Pennycuick.

Norman Primost for Mr Buchmann.
Mota Singh for Mrs May.

SIR JOHN PENNYCUICK delivered the first judgment at the invitation of *g* Megaw LJ. We have before us an appeal by the plaintiff, George Buchmann, from an order dated 22nd July 1975 made by Judge Dennis Smith at the Croydon County Court. The order dismissed a claim by Mr Buchmann for possession of a furnished dwelling-house, 24 Avenue Road, Norbury, in the London Borough of Merton, which had been comprised in a tenancy agreement dated 1st October 1974. Summarily the issue is whether this agreement was made 'for a holiday' so as to be withdrawn *h* from the protection of the Rent Act 1968, as amended by the Rent Act 1974.

It will be convenient to refer at once to the only statutory provisions which are relevant to this appeal. The Rent Act 1968, by s 1, provides: 'A tenancy under which a dwelling-house . . . is let as a separate dwelling is a protected tenancy for the purposes of this Act . . .', with certain qualifications not now material. Then by s 2(1), as amended by the Rent Act 1974:

'A tenancy is not a protected tenancy if . . . (*bbb*) the purpose of the tenancy is to confer on the tenant the right to occupy the dwelling-house for a holiday . . .'

The Act contains no definition of the word 'holiday'. The word is defined in the

Shorter Oxford English Dictionary as 'period of cessation of work, or period or recrea-
a tion'. That definition, I think, is well enough if the word 'recreation' is not too
narrowly construed.

I will now set out, fairly shortly, the history of this matter. Mr Buchmann is the
owner of 24 Avenue Road, which had been his own home until 1972. He or his company own a number of other properties in the district which that company lets.
The defendant, Mrs Colleen May, is an Australian national. Her husband, Richard
b Ernest May, is a New Zealand national. He is by profession an entertainer; and Mrs
May herself was until recently a professional dancer. They have a child, Shari, aged
7 or 8. They worked in England from time to time between 1972 and 1974 on a series
of temporary residence permits but had not, at any rate at the date of the hearing,
been successful in obtaining full residence permits.

In or about May 1972, Mr Buchmann let 24 Avenue Road to Mr May, the defendant's
c husband, on a six month furnished tenancy at £20 a week. There followed a succession of short furnished tenancies, at the same rent, up to and including a three month
tenancy expiring on 31st July 1974. These were ordinary residential tenancies.

In or about March 1974, Mr and Mrs May left England on business. They allowed
some friends, Mr and Mrs Kent, to occupy 24 Avenue Road in their absence; and
Mr and Mrs Kent remained in occupation until about the middle of October 1974.
d There was a conflict of evidence as to whether Mr and Mrs May left various chattels
of their own in 24 Avenue Road at the expiration of the last tenancy on 31st July 1974.
The judge found that they did leave certain chattels in the house.

In the absence abroad of Mr and Mrs May, Mr Buchmann then granted a two-
months tenancy, at the same rent, to a Mrs Blackshaw, who was a neighbour and
friend of Mr and Mrs May, that tenancy running from 1st August 1974 and ending on
e 30th September. The judge found that this tenancy was granted to Mrs Blackshaw as
agent for Mr May.

In the middle of October 1974, Mrs May returned to England, to be followed shortly
afterwards by Mr May. Before Mr May's return, Mrs May rang up Mr Garlant,
an employee of Mr Buchmann, and enquired as to the possibility of a further short
tenancy. Mrs May told Mr Garlant that she would be leaving England before Christ-
f mas, and in any event she had in fact only a six month residence permit, which would
expire before then. On 16th October Mr Buchmann, accompanied by a Mr Von
Conrat, went to see Mrs May at 24 Avenue Road, where she was already installed.
They then agreed in principle on the grant of a tenancy to run until 31st December
1974.

The next day, 17th October, Mr Buchmann and Mr Von Conrat again called on
g Mrs May. Mr Buchmann then produced two documents, namely a tenancy agreement and a counterpart. This agreement bears date 1st October 1972. The counterpart was in evidence. Mr Buchmann and Mrs May signed the respective documents.
The agreement is made between Mr Buchmann, called 'the landlord', and Mrs May,
called 'the tenant'. Clause 1 provides that the landlord shall let and the tenant shall
take 24 Avenue Road (describing it) 'for the term of three months from the first day
h of October, 1974, at the rent of £80 . . . for every four weeks of the said term . . .'
Clause 2 contains various terms agreed on behalf of the tenant, including (in case it is
material) para (13): '. . . to use the same as a private residence in the occupation
of one family comprising of the tenant and one child only.' I need not read cll 3, 4
and 5. Clause 6 is of critical importance:

> 'It is mutually agreed and declared that the letting hereby made is solely
i > for the purpose of the tenant's holiday in the London area.'

There was a conflict of evidence as to how far Mrs May studied this agreement
before signature. She deposed as follows:

> 'He [i e Mr Buchmann] said how would I like to sign for three or six months.
> I said "It does not matter". I said this because Rick [i e her husband] would be

back by Christmas. He said "I will make it three months". I said "O.K." He said
it was the usual type of agreement. He asked me to sign the agreement and in-   *a*
ventory and said he would send me a copy in a couple of days. He did not draw
my attention to cl 6. He said nothing about a holiday letting that I can remember.
He did not send me the lease. I first knew it was a holiday letting after I received
a letter in December or January from the plaintiff's office.'

Then, in cross-examination: *b*

    'I agree I did have opportunity to read the agreement but I did not read it . . . Re
    cl 6, I did not read the agreement. I thought it was the same lease as I had signed
    before I did not intend it to be a holiday letting. When I arrived in the United
    Kingdom I mostly say "I'm holidaying here".'

It may well be that that is what she said to the immigration officer.   *c*
    Mr Buchmann and Mr Von Conrat gave a rather different account, but I think it is
right to say that neither of them said that he in terms said to Mrs May that this was
an agreement for a holiday. True, Mr Buchmann, said it was a holiday letting.
He said 'I quite understand she wanted a holiday letting for six to eight weeks', but he
does not say that he so informed Mrs May. Mr Von Conrat is rather more positive as
to her reading the agreement. He said: 'She held the agreement some time. I thought *d*
she was looking at it . . . She spent some 20 minutes looking at the agreement.'
There is no suggestion of any misrepresentation on the part of Mr Buchmann as to
the terms of this agreement.
    Mr May returned to England, and Mr and Mrs May remained in residence
at 24 Avenue Road with the child Shari until after the expiration of the three month
tenancy on 31st December. Apparently an expected engagement abroad for Mr May   *e*
before Christmas had fallen through. Mrs May now maintains that the tenancy
was not for a holiday at all and that she has an ordinary protected tenancy. If the
tenancy was not for a holiday, it appears clear that the tenancy would indeed be
protected.
    Mr Buchmann commenced the present action in February 1975. The pleadings
are extremely short. The particulars of claim set out that the plaintiff is the owner   *f*
of 24 Avenue Road and continued:

    '(2) While the plaintiff was the owner of and in possession of the said premises
    [they were] let to the defendant on a furnished holiday letting by an agreement
    in writing dated 1st October, 1974 [setting out the terms of the agreement].'

He then sets out that in breach of the agreement the defendant has failed to deliver *g*
up vacant possession, and that the tenancy is not a protected furnished tenancy by
reason of the provisions of s 2(1)(*bbb*); and possession is claimed on that ground,
with mesne profits.
    The defence 'does not admit that the said premises were let for the purpose of a
holiday', denies that the plaintiff is entitled to possession, alternatively claims the   *h*
protection of the Rent Acts, and says 'Save as hereinbefore expressly admitted the
defendant denies each and every allegation'. It will be observed that there is no
claim based on misrepresentation or mistake in the expression of the terms of the
agreement; nor is there any claim for rectification.
    The hearing of the action took place over a number of days, concluding on 22nd
July 1975. Both parties were represented by counsel. Witnesses were called on behalf
of the plaintiff, namely, the plaintiff himself, Mr Von Conrat, Mr Garlant, Mr   *j*
Scott, a surveyor who examined 24 Avenue Road on 1st October 1974 and found no
sign of any chattels other than those in the inventory (the judge did not accept his
evidence), and a Mr Hardy, who was concerned with certain missing documents.
On behalf of the defendant were called Mr May, Mrs May herself, Mrs Blackshaw,

a and Mr Blackshaw, her husband, who deposed that he did see personal chattels in 24 Avenue Road (his evidence was accepted by the judge). All these witnesses were cross-examined. The judge made a full note of the evidence of the various witnesses. I have already referred to the passages dealing with what was said concerning the length of the letting and whether it was to be for the purpose of a holiday. I will not go through those passages again.

b Mrs May gave a detailed account of how she came to ask for and obtain the new tenancy. There was a discussion as to its length, as I think I have already sufficiently stated. It was agreed that the tenancy must end before Christmas, and she was content to accept the suggestion that the tenancy, although the agreement was actually signed on 17th October, should run from 1st October, thus making it continuous with the two month tenancy granted to Mrs Blackshaw as agent for Mr May, which had expired on 30th September.

c The judge gave a full judgment. Unfortunately he was apparently not requested for a considerable time to supply notes of his judgment, which must have made it considerably more difficult for him to write up those notes. However, we have quite a full note of what he said. I will read certain passages from the judgment. At the outset, after stating the plaintiff's claim for possession and his allegation that the premises were let 'for a holiday' as provided in s 2(1)(bbb), the judge said this:

d   'The defendant claims the protection of the Rent Act, because she says that it was not a holiday letting. Really, that is the issue I have to decide. As counsel rightly said, one is not tied down to the terms of the agreement; one must look at the reality of the situation. Were the premises let conferring a right to use for the purposes of a holiday?'

e That is an extremely important statement, and, with all respect to the learned judge, it very considerably distorts the proper approach to this question.

He then went on to deal with the successive tenancy agreements, and he makes findings on one or two matters I have already mentioned, in particular that the two month agreement was entered into by Mrs Blackshaw as agent for Mr May, and that when Mr May left he did not take all his belongings with him. The judge then went on:

f   'The effect of all that is that, by the time the Mays returned to the United Kingdom on 16th October 1974, Mr May was still in possession of this house and had a corpus possessionis. I accept that he had had an intention to come back and not to leave the house for good. That takes us to 30th September 1974. If he had this intention, as a result of the Rent Act 1974, he had a statutory furnished tenancy, and was entitled to that protection. The Kents were still in possession.

g   I accept that they did not go until 17th October 1974, the day after. What is the position? We now come to the vital agreement dated 1st October 1974.'

He then recounted Mrs May's telephone call to Mr Garlant saying she wanted to rent 24 Avenue Road again and Mr Garlant saying that 24 Avenue Road was vacant but it would have to be a short letting because there was now a short letting policy. That is the substance of what he had said:

h   'Mrs May, being in essence a layman who did not know what her rights were (under the Rent Act), was saying, in effect, "Can I rent it again?" When Mr Garlant was speaking to her on the phone, I accept that she said something like "That'll be all right", referring to the letting, because she said she was going to the United States at the end of the year and, on account of her visa, that she could not stay longer than three months. That could well have been the substance of the conversation. Following that, the plaintiff attended at 24 Avenue Road and then drew up the agrement, and then was accompanied by Mr Von Conrat who witnessed the signatures. I have to ask myself what was the purpose of this letting. Did it confer just a "holiday letting"?'

The judge then went on to deal with the backdating to 1st October. He said:

'Why did Mrs May agree to backdate it to 1st October? It seems that the *a*
Kents were still there and she, presumably, was prepared to assume the obligations of the tenancy from 1st October. The plaintiff was quite willing for it would
cover a period when the Kents were in occupation. Does this sound like a
"holiday letting"? The Mays had been there for two years. When they returned,
their child went back to school again in the area. No questions were asked of *b*
Mrs May as to what she was doing during that period (of the tenancy), whether
she had a holiday. She said she carried on as before.'

Then he said this:

'One must be careful in interpreting this Act to give it the meaning Parliament
intended; if the purpose of the tenancy was to confer on the tenant a right to *c*
occupy as a "holiday letting", it is not protected as it is taken out of the Act by
s 2(1)(*bbb*).'

The next paragraph deals with Case 10B of the Act. Then:

'So far as s 2(1)(*bbb*) is concerned, which excepts the position of a "holiday
letting", one must constantly bear in mind its purpose. There is no doubt *d*
about it that this was a "short" letting. As Mr Garlant said, it had to be a "short"
letting as the plaintiff's policy was either short lettings or holiday letting. One
has to draw a distinction between a short letting and a holiday letting. This was
a short letting granted to Mrs May. I conclude that she is entitled to the protection of the Rent Act. Accordingly the plaintiff's claim for possession is dismissed.'

e
He then deals with Mr May's position and concludes that his protected tenancy came
to an end at the end of September, being superseded by the 1974 agreement in favour
of Mrs May.

The notice of appeal states these grounds, so far as now important:

'(1) That there was no evidence on which the learned judge could find that the
defendant was a statutory tenant of No. 24 . . . (3) That the learned judge mis- *f*
directed himself in holding on the facts found by him that the tenancy agreement
of the 1st October, 1974 . . . was not for the purpose of a holiday within the terms
of . . . section 2(1)(*bbb*).'

It seems to me that that judgment contains a fundamental misdirection in that the
judge treats the purpose of the tenancy as something to be determined at large on *g*
the evidence of the various parties concerned, altogether, or at any rate in great part,
without regard to cl 6 of the agreement, to which he does not expressly refer at all
in his judgment. Where parties to an instrument express their purpose in entering
into the transaction effected by it, or the purposes for which, in the case of a tenancy
agreement, the demised property is to be used, this expression of purpose is at least
prima facie evidence of their true purpose and as such can only be displaced by *h*
evidence that the express purpose does not represent the true purpose. There is no
claim here based on misrepresentation, and no claim for rectification. When I say
the express purpose does not represent the true purpose, I mean that the express
purpose does not correspond to the true purpose, whether the express purpose is a
deliberate sham or merely a false label in the sense of a mistake in expression of
intention.

j
In the present case, cl 6 of the agreement is perfectly unequivocal. '. . . the letting
hereby made is solely for the purpose of the tenant's holiday in the London area'.
It seems to me that that provision must stand as evidence of the purpose of the parties
unless Mrs May can establish that the provision does not correspond to the true purpose of the parties. The burden lies on her to do so. I do not doubt that in a context

a such as the present the court would be astute to detect a sham where it appears that a provision has been inserted for the purpose of depriving the tenant of statutory protection under the Rent Acts. But it is for the tenant to establish this, and not for the landlord to establish affirmatively that the express purpose is the true purpose.

In argument, counsel for Mrs May used the words 'absence of bona fides'. But, as I understood him, he was not alleging that there had been any deliberate sham on the part of Mr Buchmann, so much as the attachment of a label to this transaction which
b did not correspond to the true purpose. At any rate, there was no evidence which would justify a finding of anything resembling fraud.

We were referred to a line of cases in this court on the expression contained in the Rent Acts, 'let as a dwelling or as a separate dwelling'. Those decisions, although given on different words in the Act, are directly in point on the present question, namely, what is the position of an express declaration in a tenancy agreement that
c the letting is for the purpose of a holiday? The three cases to which we were referred are as follows. First, *Wolfe v Hogan*[1], where the headnote[2] says this:

> 'Where the terms of the tenancy provide for or contemplate the user of the premises for some particular purpose, that purpose will prima facie be the essential factor. Thus, if the premises are let for business purposes, the tenant
d cannot claim that they have been converted into a dwelling-house merely because someone lives on the premises. If, however, the tenancy agreement contemplates no specified user, then the actual user of the premises at the time when possession is sought by the landlord, must be considered.'

Denning LJ said[3]:

> 'In determining whether a house or part of a house is "let as a dwelling" within
e the meaning of the Rent Restriction Acts, it is necessary to look at the purpose of the letting. If the lease contains an express provision as to the purpose of the letting, it is not necessary to look further.'

He was, of course, not concerned there with an allegation of sham.

In *British Land Co Ltd v Herbert Silver (Menswear) Ltd*[4] Upjohn J said:

f > 'A long line of authorities, for the most part in this court, has established that, on the issue whether the premises are let as a separate dwelling, one looks to the bargain made between the parties and see for what purpose the parties intended the premises would be used. The first place to ascertain their intentions is in the lease itself.'

g Finally, in *Horford Investments Ltd v Lambert*[5] Scarman LJ said:

> 'The section affords protection to the tenancy of a house only if the house is let as a separate dwelling. The section directs attention to the letting, that is to say, the terms of the tenancy. The courts have proceeded on the basis that the terms of the tenancy are the primary consideration: see *Wolfe v Hogan*[6]. In my
h opinion there is here a principle of cardinal importance: whether a tenancy of a house (or a part of a house) is protected depends on the terms of the tenancy, not on subsequent events.'

In all those cases this court laid down the principle that, in considering whether a house is let as a separate dwelling, where there is a written lease you ascertain the

j 1 [1949] 1 All ER 570, [1949] 2 KB 194
   2 [1949] 2 KB 194
   3 [1949] 1 All ER 570 at 575, [1949] 2 KB 194 at 204
   4 [1958] 1 All ER 833 at 837, [1958] 1 QB 530 at 539
   5 [1974] 1 All ER 131 at 139, [1976] Ch 39 at 52
   6 [1949] 1 All ER 570, [1949] 2 KB 194

purpose of the parties from the terms of the lease and you do not go beyond the terms of the lease to ascertain what is the purpose of the parties. That is always so apart *a* from the case where the terms of the lease do not correspond to the true intention of the parties.

It seems to me that on that fundamental ground the learned judge was in error in treating this as a question to be determined by reference to the oral evidence of the parties and without regard to the terms of cl 6, which would stand unless it is shown to be something in the nature of a sham or of a false label, and that on that ground *b* his judgment cannot be supported.

What, then, is to be done? It seems to me that there was no evidence before the judge on which he could have held that cl 6 did not truly represent the common intention of the parties. Mrs May is a Dominion national not resident in England except on a series of short residence permits, the current one of which was due to expire in December 1974. She had been out of England since the spring of 1974, *c* leaving only some personal chattels in 24 Avenue Road. She informed Mr Buchmann that she wished to stay in England for two months only before going abroad with her husband, who was taking up an engagement abroad. Mr Buchmann had no reason to suspect that this was untrue. It seems to me that a stay of less than three months in such circumstances would constitute a 'holiday' within the ordinary meaning of that word; and I can find no ground on which it could be properly said that the *d* statement of purpose in cl 6 was a sham or was, without intention to deceive, an untrue statement of the purpose of the letting.

Counsel for the defendant, who has said all there was to be said on her behalf, contended, truly, that one must look at the true relation contemplated by the parties and not merely at the label. In other words, if it can be shown that the terms of this agreement do not correspond with some label in the agreement, then one can look *e* behind the label. Then he says that here the evidence as accepted by the judge established that a holiday was not the true relation, in other words, not the true purpose for which 24 Avenue Road was being let. He said that Mrs May's motive was to protect her right of occupation, in other words, to continue it for the benefit of Mrs May and Mr May together; and he said that Mrs May did not know her rights and thought it was just one of the usual agreements. There is no evidence that Mr *f* Buchmann thought that was the motive of the provision as to a holiday; indeed it plainly was not his motive. Whatever Mrs May may or my not have had in mind when she signed the agreement cannot of itself displace the effect of the express provision within the agreement. Her mere ignorance of her rights certainly could not do so.

I conclude that there is nothing in the evidence which could displace the effect of *g* cl 6 of the agreement, and so one is left with a tenancy for a holiday, and that tenancy is withdrawn from protection by s 2(1)(*bbb*). Accordingly, Mr Buchmann is now entitled to possession of the property. I would allow the appeal.

STEPHENSON LJ. I agree. The only question raised by this appeal is: was the purpose of Mrs May's tenancy to confer on her the right to occupy the dwelling-house *h* for a holiday, so that she lost the protection of the Rent Acts by virtue of s 2(1)(*bbb*)? That question appears to have received an affirmative answer in cl 6 of the tenancy agreement, by which—

> 'It is mutually agreed and declared that the letting hereby made is solely for the purpose of the tenant's holiday in the London area.'

Denning LJ, in *Wolfe v Hogan*,[1] to which Sir John Pennycuick has referred, said: *i*

> 'If the lease contains an express provision as to the purpose of the letting, it is not necessary to look further, but, if there is no express provision, it is open to the court to look at the circumstances of the letting.'

1   [1949] 1 All ER 570 at 575, [1949] 2 KB 194 at 204

a   Upjohn J, giving the judgment of this court in *British Land Co Ltd v Herbert Silver (Menswear) Ltd*[1], gave the approval of this court to that. He said:

> 'The first place to ascertain their intentions [that is to say the intentions of the parties in relation to a bargain of tenancy] is in the lease itself. If that does not provide an answer, one looks to all the surrounding circumstances and see what must have been in the contemplation of the parties ...'

b

Neither of those learned judges I feel sure meant to give the labels which parties put on a transaction conclusive validity, still less to enable landlords to contract out of the Rent Acts by sham agreements misrepresenting the nature of what was in reality a protected tenancy. As the learned county court judge rightly said:

c   'As counsel rightly said, one is not tied down to the terms of the agreement; one must look at the reality of the situation. Were the premises let conferring a right to use [the Act says 'occupy'] for the purposes of a holiday?

But the matter is not completely at large where there is, as here, an express provision as to the purpose of the letting, provided by cl 6 of this agreement, only some four or five lines above the tenant's own signature. Here, that clause does provide *d*   an answer, and that at least, I agree with Sir John Pennycuick, must impose on the tenant the burden of showing that the agreement she signed does not represent the real transaction. If the judge had had the benefit of the arguments and authorities that we have had, I think he would have appreciated where the onus lay. If he had appreciated where the onus lay, he could not, in my judgment, have found that the defendant had discharged it. Bearing in mind that there is here no plea of misrepre-*e*   sentation or claim for rectification, nor, I would add, a plea of non est factum, for the reason given by Sir John Pennycuick I too would allow this appeal.

MEGAW LJ. I agree. As Sir John Pennycuick has said, the court would, and should, be astute to detect a sham, particularly in a case such as this, where the protection of *f*   the Rent Acts is involved. It would be a sham if there were a contractual provision introduced into a form of contract prepared by a landlord for the purpose of avoiding the application of the Rent Acts by means of a misstatement of fact or of intention; as, for example, by asserting the purpose of a holiday where in truth there is not that purpose. But the circumstances proved in the evidence in this particular case are not, in my view, in any way inconsistent with the purpose of the tenancy being what would *g*   properly and sensibly be described as a purpose to confer on the tenant the right to occupy the dwelling-house for a holiday. I agree with the contention put forward for Mr Buchmann that there was no evidence in this case on which the judge could find that s 2(1)(*bbb*) of the Rent Act 1968 was not applicable, there being prima facie evidence (prima facie and rebuttable, not conclusive) in the mutual agreement and declaration in cl 6 of the contract, an agreement and declaration to which both *h*   parties set their hands, that the purpose was the purpose 'of the tenant's holiday in the London area'.

I too agree that the appeal should be allowed.

Appeal allowed. Order for possession granted.

j   Solicitors: *Loxdales* (for Mr Buchmann); *Baker, Freeman & Co*, Mitcham (for Mrs May).

Christine Ivamy   Barrister.

---

1   [1958] 1 All ER 833 at 837, [1958] 1 QB 530 at 539

Walsh and another v Griffiths-Jones and another

LAMBETH COUNTY COURT
HIS HONOUR JUDGE MCDONNELL
27th, 28th, 29th JULY, 5th, 12th AUGUST 1977

Licence – Licence to occupy premises – Licence distinguished from tenancy – Agreement to share residential accommodation – Right of access reserved by licensor – Licensor explaining that right of access a 'legal formality' to ensure agreement was a licence – Licensees understanding that they would in fact have exclusive possession of premises – Whether reservation of right of access destroyed licensees' right to exclusive possession – Whether agreement a licence to occupy premises or a tenancy.

Estate agent – Authority – Authority to create tenancy – Agent invited by owner to find occupants for premises – Agent required to refer prospective occupants to owner – Agent denied authority to create tenancy – Owner telling prospective occupiers to deal with agent who would attend to details of agreement – Agent entering into tenancy agreement with prospective occupiers – Whether owner held out agent as having authority to create tenancy – Whether owner bound by agreement entered into by agent.

The plaintiffs, Mr and Mrs W, were the owners of a house divided into three flats which they were anxious to sell with vacant possession, but which in the meantime they wished to have occupied. Having seen an estate agent's advertisement in which the agent stated that he could arrange occupation of property without the possibility of it becoming a protected tenancy, Mrs W concluded an agreement with him under which he sought occupants for the flats, but she gave him no authority to enter into any agreement for occupation of the flats without reference to her. The defendants urgently required short term furnished accommodation and were referred to the agent, who contracted Mrs W and arranged to send the defendants round to view one of the flats in her presence. The defendants decided the flat would suit their needs and were told by Mrs W that they would have to deal with the agent who would attend to the details of the agreement whereby they would be able to reside in the flat. The defendants wished to enter an agreement for not less than six months but the agent said he was not prepared to grant a term of more than three months but that the term would be 'renewable'. The defendants agreed to this and the agent produced a printed form which purported to be a 'licence' which recited that it was for the occupation of the flat 'in common with' Mrs W or her invitees, Mrs W 'not [being] willing to grant the [defendants] exclusive possession of any part of' the flat. The agent explained that the recitals were 'just a legal formality', but assured the defendants that there was no danger of anyone else being put into the flat. The defendants signed the form and entered the agreement on that assurance, believing that they would occupy the flat to the exclusion of anyone else. The questions arose whether the agreement made by the agent created a tenancy and not a licence and whether the agent had authority to enter into an agreement so as to bind the plaintiffs.

Held – (i) In view of what they had been told by the agent, the agreement entered into by the defendants gave them jointly exclusive possession of the flat. The reservation by the plaintiffs of a right of access did not of itself destroy the right granted to the defendants of exclusive possession of the flat since the plaintiffs had no right to occupy the flat as a residence or to put in anyone else. The form signed by the defendants was no more than a sham designed to conceal the true nature of the agreement, which was the grant of a joint tenancy of the flat for three months; *R v Battersea, Wandsworth, Mitcham and Wimbledon Rent Tribunal, ex parte Parikh* [1957] 1 All ER 352

and dicta of Jenkins LJ in *Addiscombe Garden Estates Ltd v Crabbe* [1957] 3 All ER at
a 565, 570, 571 and of Viscount Simonds in *Elmdene Estates Ltd v White* [1960] 1 All ER
at 309 applied (see p 1008 *e f* and p 1010 *d* to *f*, post).

(ii) The agent having clearly been held out by Mrs W as having full authority to
enter into a contractual agreement with the defendants, the plaintiffs were bound
by whatever agreement the agent made with the defendants, notwithstanding that
he had been expressly denied any authority to create a tenancy (see p 1007 *j*, post).

b Per Curiam. Although the grant of the right of exclusive possession may create a
licence and not a tenancy, there is no authority for the proposition that there can be a
tenancy where the tenant is not granted the right of exclusive possession. There
cannot be the estate in land known as a tenancy without a grant of exclusive possession
(see p 1008 *e*, post).

c **Notes**
For the distinction between a licence and a lease, see 23 Halsbury's Laws (3rd Edn)
427-433, paras 1022-1028, and for cases on the subject, see 31(1) Digest (Reissue) 201-215,
1678-1766.

For holding out by a principal of authority in an agent, see 1 Halsbury's Laws
(4th Edn) para 725, and for cases on the subject, see 1 Digest (Repl) 443, *959-963*.

d For estate agents, see 1 Halsbury's Laws (4th Edn) para 740, and for a case on the
authority of an estate agent to let premises, see 1 Digest (Repl) 378, *450*.

Cases referred to in judgment
Addiscombe Garden Estates Ltd v Crabbe [1957] 3 All ER 563, [1958] 1 QB 513, [1957] 3
  WLR 980, CA, 31(1) Digest (Reissue) 206, *1719*.
e *Buchmann v May* p 993, ante, 240 Estates Gazette 49, CA.
Elmdene Estates Ltd v White [1960] 1 All ER 306, [1960] AC 528, [1960] 2 WLR 359, HL,
  31(2) Digest (Reissue) 1062, *8354*.
Errington v Errington and Woods [1952] 1 All ER 149, [1952] 1 KB 290, CA, 31(1) Digest
  (Reissue) 208, *1734*.
Facchini v Bryson [1952] 1 TLR 1386, CA, 31(2) Digest (Reissue) 982, *7883*.
f *Foster v Robinson* [1950] 2 All ER 342, [1951] 1 KB 149, CA, 31(2) Digest (Reissue) 1078,
  8436.
Keen v Mear [1920] 2 Ch 574, 89 LJCh 513, 124 LT 19, 1 Digest (Repl) 432, *884*.
Marcroft Wagons Ltd v Smith [1951] 2 All ER 271, [1951] 2 KB 496, CA, 31(2) Digest
  (Repl) 989, *7929*.
R v Battersea, Wandsworth, Mitcham and Wimbledon Rent Tribunal, ex parte Parikh
g [1957] 1 All ER 352, [1957] 1 WLR 410, 121 JP 132, 55 LGR 109, 31(2) Digest (Reissue)
  1126, *8733*.
Thuman v Best (1907) 97 LT 239, 1 Digest (Repl) 378, *450*.
Wimbush v Cibulia, Wimbush v Levinski [1949] 2 All ER 432, [1949] 2 KB 564, CA, 31(2)
  Digest (Reissue) 1003, *7993*.
Woods v Wise [1955] 1 All ER 767, [1955] 2 QB 29, [1955] 2 WLR 734, 119 JP 254, CA,
h 31(2) Digest (Reissue) 1064, *8365*.

Action
The plaintiffs, James Walsh and Brenda Walsh, brought an action in the Lambeth
County Court claiming possession against the defendants, Gareth Griffiths-Jones and
Alan Durant, of premises known as Flat 1, 34 Brailsford Road, London SW2. In their
defence the defendants claimed that they were protected tenants of the premises
j under the Rent Acts 1968 and 1974, and counterclaimed for damages. The facts are
set out in the judgment.

E R E Caws for the plaintiffs.
Mr James Woolley, solicitor, for the defendants.

Cur adv vult

12th August. **HIS HONOUR JUDGE McDONNELL** read the following judgment: The plaintiffs are the owners of a house at 34 Brailsford Road, London SW2, *a*
which is divided into three flats. They had lived in the house themselves but had
from time to time let each of the flats. In 1976 they were very anxious to sell the
property, and thought that they might be able to sell it to the Lambeth Borough
Council. They knew that they would obtain a better price if they could sell the whole
house with vacant possession on completion. In December 1975 they had been warned
by their mortgagees that the creation of lettings of any part of the house would be in *b*
breach of the conditions of their mortgage. In the spring of 1976 Mrs Walsh saw an
advertisement in the Evening Standard newspaper by a firm of estate agents called
David Dixon & Co which read: 'ANSWERS to the Rent Act. Complete control over
your property.' She got in touch with a member of the firm, a Mr Rickard, and thereafter employed David Dixon & Co as agents to deal with properties of the plaintiffs
which had been let.   *c*
    After unsuccessful proceedings for possession against them, the tenants of flat 1
on the ground floor left. On 22nd September 1976 Mrs Walsh wrote to David Dixon
& Co saying:

>   'We have decided to sell the house but as we have been advised to wait until
> January when the area is to be declared Housing Action Area in order to get a *d*
> fair price, we wondered if it were possible to find short-term occupants, say until
> January or February for Flat 1 and also for Flat 3 when the present occupants
> leave on the 6th October . . . I do not want to create any tenancies as my mortgage
> company have forbidden this and also I must have vacant possession in January
> or February in order to sell. Would you therefore please check the legal position
> before you give occupancy to anyone in either flat.'   *e*

    She enclosed an inventory of the contents of flat 1.
    The defendants, who had shared rooms at Cambridge, came to London during 1976.
After living with friends for a time they urgently required furnished accommodation.
The first defendant applied to the West End Flats Agency, who relieved him of a fee
of £40 and referred him to David Dixon & Co. On 4th October the first defendant *f*
saw Mr Rickard and completed an application form in respect of flat 3 at 34 Brailsford Road saying: 'I wish to be accepted as a tenant of the above flat.' Details of both
defendants were inserted in the application form and Mr Rickard arranged for them
to view flat 3. When the defendants went to inspect flat 3 the tenants told them that
they were not proposing to leave immediately but would be staying another two
months. This was of no use to the defendants who required accommodation urgently; *g*
but before they left the house they saw that flat 1 was empty and, by peering through
the windows, decided that it might well suit their needs. They returned to Mr
Rickard's office and asked whether it was available. In that office was a list giving
details of flats which were available and setting out the rent and for how many people
they were suitable. On this list it appeared that flat 3 would cost £25 per week and
would 'suit 2' and that flat 1 would cost £28 per week and would 'suit 4'. Mr Rickard *h*
got in touch with Mrs Walsh and arranged to send the defendants round to view the
flat.
    On 18th October the defendants visited flat 1 and found that Mrs Walsh was there.
There had been some damage to the roof of the back room which had necessitated
repairs to the ceiling and some replastering and she was redecorating that room, lining
the ceiling and painting the new plaster. The defendants looked around the flat and *i*
decided that it would suit their needs and asked whether they could move in straight
away. Mrs Walsh said that the flat was not ready because she had not finished the
redecoration. The defendants offered to complete that work themselves. She agreed
to this. Half the ceiling had been done and she thought there were enough materials
there to complete the redecoration of the ceiling and the back wall. She told them

that if they did run out of paint they should buy it and let her know and she would
a reimburse them. At that stage there was no question of redecoration of any other part
of the flat.

She telephoned David Dixon & Co and arranged to send the defendants round to
their office to complete the transaction. Her evidence was that Mr Rickard had
authority to enter into an agreement for the occupation of the flat on her behalf
without reference to her. She said in evidence that she explained to the defendants
b that it was hoped that the property would shortly be included in a housing action
area and that therefore she only wanted to let it on a short term basis. She made it
clear to them that this was because she was hoping to sell the property. Neither
defendant recalls hearing anything about a housing action area but they only wanted
the premises for a period of six months to one year. I find that they were told that
Mrs Walsh wanted to sell the property but that this was not a matter of great im-
c portance in view of the fact that they did not require it for more than a year. The
defendants returned to the office of David Dixon & Co where they saw Mr Rickard
who proceeded to conclude an agreement with them. He said that he was prepared to
grant them an agreement for three months but they wanted an agreement for not
less than six months. He was not prepared to grant more than three months but said
that it would be 'renewable' and the defendants agreed to that without any closer
d definition of what was meant by 'renewable'. A calculation was made that £28 per
week was equivalent to £364 for three months. Two printed forms of agreement
were produced and details were inserted in typescript; there was one agreement for
each defendant under which he undertook to pay £182 by monthly instalments.
The agreements were identical save that one was in the name of the first defendant
and the other in the name of the second defendant.

e
Each agreement started with the words 'THIS LICENCE' and stated that it was made
between—

'Mrs Walsh c/o David Dixon & Co. 1 North End Road, London W14 (hereinafter referred to as "the Licensor") of the one part and [the defendant in question]
(all hereinafter referred to as "the Licensee") of the other part.'

f
It then continued:

'WHEREAS the Licensor is not willing to grant the Licensee exclusive possession
of any part of the rooms hereinafter referred to AND WHEREAS the Licensee is
anxious to secure the use of the rooms notwithstanding that such use be in
common with the Licensor and such other Licensees or invitees as the Licensor
g may permit from time to time to use the said rooms, AND WHEREAS this Licence
is entered into by the Licensor and the Licensee solely upon the above basis.
By this Licence the Licensor licenses the Licensee to use (but not exclusively) all
those rooms (hereinafter referred to as "the Rooms") on the ground floor of the
building . . . together with the use of . . . the furniture, fixtures and effects now in
the Rooms more particularly set out in the Schedule of Contents annexed
h hereto) . . .'

No schedule of contents was ever annexed to either agreement. Condition 2 provided
that the licence should—

'be responsible for the payment of all gas, electric light and power which shall
be consumed or supplied in or to the Rooms during the Licensee's occupation
j thereof . . .'

Condition 3 provided that the licensee should—

'use his best endeavours amicably and peaceably to share the use of the Rooms
with the Licensor and such other Licensees or invitees whom the Licensor shall

from time to time permit to use the Rooms and shall not interfere with or otherwise obstruct such shared occupation in any way whatsoever.'

Condition 4 provided that the licensee should—

'keep the interior of the Rooms and all furniture, furnishings, fixtures and fittings therein in good and clean condition and complete repair (fair wear and tear and damage by accidental fire only excepted) and immediately replace all broken glass.'

Condition 8 provided:

'On notice in writing being given to the Licensee by the Licensor or his/her agent of all wants of repair, cleansings, amendments and restorations to the interior of the Rooms and of all such destruction, loss, breakage or damage of or to the furniture and effects as Licensee shall be bound to make good found therein the Licensee shall repair, amend and restore or make good the same within two weeks of the giving of such notice.'

Condition 16 provided that the licensee should 'not cause or permit any waste, spoil or destruction to the Rooms or to the building'. Condition 19 provided that the 'Licensor shall not at any time permit more than three other persons to use the Rooms together with the Licensor and Licensee'. Condition 22 provided: 'The Licensee shall at all reasonable times allow the Licensor or the Licensor's Agents or workmen to gain access to the Rooms occupied by the Licensee.' Condition 32 provided:

'Upon the Licensee being in breach of any of the conditions referred to above this Licence shall immediately determine without prejudice to any other remedies of the Licensor and the Licensee shall immediately cease his use of the Rooms and the Building as permitted hereunder.'

Immediately under each defendant's signature appeared the words 'Licensee hereby states having received a copy of this contract'. Neither defendant had received a copy of the agreement because Mr Rickard said that his photocopying machine had broken down and promised to send them copies as soon as possible. In fact the first defendant did not receive his copy until December 1976 and the second defendant did not receive his copy until shortly before the trial.

Each defendant did read the printed agreement and they expressed some surprise at the recitals which said they were not granted exclusive possession and that the use was to be in common with the licensor and other persons. They said that there had been no discussion of the terms of the agreements until the printed documents had been completed in typescript and placed before them for signature. The defendants said that when Mr Rickard presented the agreements for signature he used some such words as 'This is just the legal side of it, just a legal formality'. Mr Rickard said that it was his normal practice to explain that a licence does not grant the licensee an exclusive right of occupation and that if he chose to do so a grantor could either claim his own rights of occupancy or issue further licences to another party. He said that he had a conversation of that nature with the defendants but could not remember precisely what was said. The defendants said that when they raised the question of an obligation to share with Mrs Walsh or other persons Mr Rickard assured them that there was no danger whatsoever of Mrs Walsh or any other person seeking to enter into occupation of the flat. Both defendants accepted in evidence that they had ample opportunity to read the documents and that they signed them intending to enter into a legal relationship and to be bound by them. I prefer the evidence of the defendants and am satisfied that before they signed the agreements they were assured by Mr Rickard that the terms about use in common with the licensor and other persons were just a legal formality and there was no danger whatsoever of anybody else being put in.

a As the first defendant put it in evidence they were firmly of the impression that they were paying the full rent of £28 per week for the security of occupying the flat to the exclusion of anybody else.

On the same day the defendants obtained the keys of the flat from Mrs Walsh and went into occupation. Mrs Walsh had left decorating materials in the back room and the defendants completed the work which she had begun there. She had told them that if these materials were not sufficient she would reimburse them for any further *b* paints that were needed. After this work was completed the defendants proceeded to decorate the rest of the flat with materials which they had themselves bought. Their evidence was that Mr Walsh came to the flat some days after they had gone into occupation, had seen that they were doing rather more than completing the work which Mrs Walsh had left unfinished in order that they could go into occupation, and said that they were doing a good job and that if they sent him the receipts for the *c* materials which they used he would pay for them. In a letter dated 1st March 1977 to David Dixon & Co both defendants said: 'Before entering the premises we agreed with the landlord that we would decorate them, and that he would reimburse us for the materials used.' The defendants counterclaim for £26·79 for the cost of paint and lining paper which they bought for the decoration but much if not all of this material was probably bought before the conversation with Mr Walsh. There was no request for *d* reimbursement nor were any receipts sent to Mr Walsh or to David Dixon & Co, nor were they produced until the hearing of this action. After the defendants went into occupation they removed certain items of furniture and placed them in the back-yard, where they were exposed to the elements. Mr Walsh noticed this and on 10th February 1977 he left a note telling the defendants that these articles should be taken indoors but the defendants left them in the yard. The evidence satisfies me that all *e* the furniture was old and shabby. One of the articles placed in the yard was a settee which was damaged beyond repair by marauding dogs. A base for a divan double bed was also put out but the defendants have replaced it with a better one. Some damage has been caused to two single divan bed bases but they have been brought back into the flat and are now in use. A wardrobe which was placed in the yard was a cheap, painted, wooden article and the defendants have since sanded it down and *f* repainted it so that it is in a better condition than when it was put out in the yard.

The following are the issues which I have to decide: (a) If the agreement made by Mr Rickard with the defendants created a tenancy and not a licence, did Mr Rickard have authority to enter into such an agreement so as to bind the plaintiffs? (b) Are the defendants or either of them tenants or licensees? (c) What damages are re-coverable by the plaintiffs for damage to furniture placed in the yard? (d) Are the *g* defendants entitled to recover anything for decorating materials?

Issue (a) was introduced into the case by an amendment to the reply for which I gave leave on stringent terms on 29th July. Counsel for the plaintiffs relied on *Thuman v Best*[1] and *Keen v Mear*[2] for the proposition that an estate agent has in general no implied authority to make a contract on behalf of his principal. I find that Mrs Walsh's instructions to David Dixon & Co expressly denied them any authority to *h* create a tenancy. It is quite clear that they had no actual or implied authority to enter into any agreement whereby a tenancy might be created. She did, however, tell the defendants that they must deal with David Dixon & Co and sent them to their office telling them that the agents would attend to all the details of the agreement whereby they were to reside in the flat. I hope it is no disrespect to the argument of counsel for the plaintiffs if I content myself with saying that this is one of the clearest cases of *j* holding out an agent as having full authority to enter into a contractual agreement that I can recall. I therefore hold that the plaintiffs are bound by whatever agree-ment Mr Rickard did in fact make with the defendants.

---

1 (1907) 97 LT 239
2 [1920] 2 Ch 574

Issue (b) involves the type of question which has been considered frequently by the courts during the last 30 years. It has been held on many occasions that agreements described as 'licences' have effectively granted tenancies: *Foster v Robinson*[1], *Marcroft Wagons Ltd v Smith*[2], *Addiscombe Garden Estates Ltd v Crabbe*[3]. As Viscount Simonds said in *Elmdene Estates Ltd v White*[4]:

> '. . . it has been said before and it must be said again that in the consideration of questions arising out of the Rent Acts the court must look at the substance and the reality of the transaction and not its form.'

See also *Woods v Wise*[5]. Such a question was exhaustively considered in *Addiscombe Garden Estates Ltd v Crabbe*[6], where Jenkins LJ said:

> 'The whole of the document must be looked at; and if, after it has been examined, the right conclusion appears to be that, whatever label may have been attached to it, it in fact conferred and imposed on the grantee in substance the rights and obligations of a tenant, and on the grantor in substance the rights and obligations of a landlord, then it must be given the appropriate effect, that is to say, it must be treated as a tenancy agreement as distinct from a mere licence . . . the important statement of principle is that the relationship is determined by the law, and not by the label the parties choose to put on it, and that it is not necessary to go so far as to find the document a sham. It is simply a matter of ascertaining the true relationship of the parties.'

The grant of exclusive possession of the property is no longer decisive but it is a very important consideration: see *Errington v Errington and Wood*[7]. Although the grant of the right of exclusive possession may create a licence and not a tenancy, there is no authority for the proposition that there can be a tenancy where the tenant is not granted the right of exclusive possession and I hold that there cannot be the estate in land known as a tenancy without a grant of exclusive possession. Reservation to a grantor of a right of access 'at all times' does not of itself destroy the right granted by contract to exclusive possession of rooms as a residence since the grantor has no right to occupy the rooms as a residence or to put anyone else in them: see *R v Battersea, Wandsworth, Mitcham and Wimbledon Rent Tribunal, ex parte Parikh*[8].

The enactment of the Rent Act 1974 has not proved an unmixed blessing for those needing tenancies of furnished premises. By converting furnished lettings into protected tenancies it has made matters much more difficult for persons requiring tenancies of furnished accommodation, since property owners have become very anxious to avoid creating protected tenancies and have tried to secure that their property is occupied by tenants who do not enjoy protected tenancies such as those to whom premises are let 'for the purposes of a holiday' or by licensees. In *Buchmann v May*[9] the Court of Appeal in considering a letting 'for the purposes of a holiday' held that where the parties to an instrument had expressed their purpose for entering into the transaction in the instrument that expression of purpose was at least prima facie evidence of their common intention which could be displaced only by evidence that that expressed purpose did not represent their true purpose. Megaw LJ did, however, say that the courts would and should be astute to detect shams where the protection of the Rent Acts was involved.

1   [1950] 2 All ER 342, [1951] 1 KB 149
2   [1951] 2 All ER 271, [1951] 2 KB 496
3   [1957] 3 All ER 563, [1958] 1 QB 513
4   [1960] 1 All ER 306 at 309, [1960] AC 528 at 538
5   [1955] 1 All ER 767, [1955] 2 QB 29
6   [1957] 3 All ER 563 at 565 and 570, 571, [1958] 1 QB 513 at 522 and 528
7   [1952] 1 All ER 149, [1952] 1 KB 290
8   [1957] 1 All ER 352, [1957] 1 WLR 410
9   Page 993, ante

a   Where parties had entered into two separate tenancy agreements with regard to different parts of the same house, it was held that the court in considering whether the premises had been let 'as a separate dwelling' could look outside each written agreement in order to determine whether the tenant could claim protection in respect of the whole of the parts let to him as if they had all been comprised in a single agreement: *Wimbush v Cibulia*[1].

b   Another important consideration is the circumstances in which the agreement came to be made. In *Marcroft Wagons Ltd v Smith*[2] Evershed MR said:

'I think that where the question arises out of a new relationship between an owner of property and an occupant, the inference to be drawn when the occupant is first allowed to go into exclusive possession is *prima facie* very different from the inference proper to be drawn, though not necessarily to be drawn, in a case
c   such as this, where the person in occupation has lived on the premises ... for a long period of time and has in effect succeeded to the occupational privileges (to use a somewhat colourless phrase), [of the previous occupant].'

In *Facchini v Bryson*[3] Denning LJ said:

'We have had many cases lately where an occupier has been held to be a licensee
d   and not a tenant ... In all the cases where an occupier has been held to be a licensee there has been something in the circumstances, such as a family arrangement, an act of friendship or generosity, or such like, to negative any intention to create a tenancy. In such circumstances it would be obviously unjust to saddle the owner with a tenancy, with all the momentous consequences that that entails nowadays, when there was no intention to create a tenancy at all ... It is not
e   necessary to go so far as to find the documents a sham. It is simply a matter of finding the true relationship of the parties. It is most important that we should adhere to this principle, or else we might find all landlords granting licences and not tenancies, and we should make a hole in the Rent Acts through which could be driven—I will not in these days say a coach and four—but an articulated vehicle.'

f   Looking at the terms of the written agreements in the present case the recitals and the words of grant, together with conditions 3 and 19, point very strongly in the direction of a licence. On the other hand condition 2, conditions 4 and 8, which impose obligations on the grantee to carry out repairs wider than remedying damage caused by his own act or default, and the provision in condition 22 requiring him to allow the grantor and his agents or workmen to gain access are much more consistent with the grant of a tenancy. A term such as that in condition 22 was held in *Facchini v Bryson*[4]
g   and *Addiscombe Garden Estates Ltd v Crabbe*[5] to provide a strong indication that the right to occupy was in fact intended to be exclusive.

The circumstances before the documents were produced for signature by the defendants were: (a) The defendants came to Mr Rickard looking for a tenancy of a flat to be let to them jointly. (b) The flat was said to be suitable for four persons and was offered for £28 per week and the amount payable by each defendant was cal-
h   culated so that between them they paid the whole of this sum. (c) It was argued that Mrs Walsh made it clear that the flat was only available for occupation for a short term and that this was more consistent with a licence than with a tenancy. The defendants were not contemplating occupying the premises for more than a year and as many tenancies are granted for periods of three or six months I think that little weight can be attached to this consideration.

j

1   [1949] 2 All ER 432, [1949] 2 KB 564
2   [1951] 2 All ER 271 at 275, [1951] 2 KB 496 at 504
3   [1952] 1 TLR 1386 at 1389, 1390
4   [1952] 1 TLR 1386
5   [1957] 3 All ER 563, [1958] 1 QB 513

The following circumstances in which the agreements came to be signed seem to me to be relevant, namely: (a) Each defendant was required to sign a separate agreement on the face of which he made himself liable only for half the total consideration. At first sight this points to licences rather than a joint tenancy, but the fact of the matter was that it was never contemplated that one defendant alone would enter into an agreement. The essence of the arrangement was that both or neither would sign an agreement. (b) Having read the agreements the defendants did express some surprise that their use of the flat was to be in common with Mrs Walsh and other licensees. I am perfectly satisfied that Mr Rickard told them unequivocally that there was no danger whatsoever of anyone else being introduced into the flat. I am quite satisfied that neither would have dreamt of sharing the self-contained flat with Mrs Walsh or with other strangers. (c) The defendants were conscious of the provisions of condition 19 which contemplated that there might be up to four occupants in the flat at any time in addition to Mrs Walsh. The first defendant construed the agreement as not giving him exclusive possession of the whole flat because he was required to share with the second defendant just as the second defendant had agreed to share with him. He thought, however, that exclusive possession was being given to them both jointly, and this was not unreasonable in the view of what they had been told by Mr Rickard.

Bearing all these considerations in mind I am driven to the conclusion that the documents signed by the defendants were no more than shams designed to conceal the true nature of the transaction. I bear in mind that although each document referred to a schedule of contents and although Mrs Walsh had provided Mr Rickard with an inventory of furniture etc in the flat no schedule was annexed to either agreement. It is also significant that neither defendant was provided with a copy of the agreement although it was on a printed form and it would have taken no more than five minutes to have typed a copy of each agreement. I hold that the true nature of the agreement between the parties was that the defendants were granted a joint tenancy for three months of the flat and that they were jointly and severally liable for the whole of the rent.

[His Honour then turned to issue (c). He held that the defendants were liable to the plaintiffs in damages for such diminution in value as resulted from placing articles of the plaintiffs' furniture in the yard and assessed those damages at £22. He then reviewed the evidence in relation to issue (d) and continued:] I am unable to find that Mr Walsh made any binding agreement to bear the cost of materials, and even if he had made such a definite promise it would not in my judgment be enforceable for want of consideration in law. The counterclaim for damage must therefore fail although by virtue of my decision on issue (b) I shall declare pursuant to s 105 of the Rent Act 1968 that the defendants are regulated tenants of flat 1, 34 Brailsford Road.

It may seem unjust that the plaintiffs, who appear to have made it perfectly plain to David Dixon & Co that they did not wish to create a tenancy of the flat and they would require vacant possession in January 1977, should be saddled with a protected tenancy 'with all its momentous consequences'. Unless, however, further facts emerge which have not been the subject of evidence in this case, it is difficult to see what defence David Dixon & Co could have to a claim for damages for breach of their duty as agents in which the plaintiffs could recover any loss sustained by them as a result of being unable to sell their property with vacant possession.

Order accordingly.

Solicitors: *Graham Harvey & Co* (for the plaintiffs).

Mary Rose Plummer Barrister.

Somma v Hazlehurst and another

COURT OF APPEAL, CIVIL DIVISION

STEPHENSON, GEOFFREY LANE AND CUMMING-BRUCE LJJ

14th, 15th, 16th, 17th, 20th FEBRUARY, 3rd MARCH 1978

Licence – Licence to occupy premises – Description in document – Terms of agreement indicating licence – Terms appearing to make occupation non-exclusive – Two agreements to share residential accommodation – Unmarried couple signing separate agreements to share room – Agreements identical except for name of grantee – Condition of each agreement that grantee would be willing to share room with grantor or such other grantee as licensor might from time to time permit to use it – Whether condition void as contrary to public policy or illegal – Whether tenancy or licence created.

In February 1976 H and S, a young unmarried couple, visited a house belonging to X to enquire about double bed-sitting rooms and flatlets which had been advertised to let. X's resident managing agent showed them a room 22 feet by 18 feet with two beds in it. They agreed to take it. He gave each of them a printed form of agreement on which he wrote the appropriate details in the blank spaces. The agreements were identical except for the name of the grantee. Each agreement described itself as a 'licence' and the relationship it created between the grantor and each grantee as being that of licensor and licensee. The recital stated that the agreement was entered into by the licensor and licensee on the basis that the licensee was willing to allow the room to be used in common with the licensor and such other licensees or invitees as the licensor might from time to time permit to use it. By cl 1 each licensee agreed to pay the sum of £116·40 for 12 weeks by four-weekly instalments of £38·80. By cl 2 the licensee was to be responsible for the payment of all gas, electric light and power consumed during the licensee's occupation. By cl 3 the licensee was required to use his best endeavours amicably and peaceably to share the use of the room with whomsoever the licensor should from time to time permit to use it and not to interfere or otherwise obstruct such shared accommodation in any way whatsoever. By cl 19 the licensor undertook not at any time to permit more than one other person to use the room together with the licensor and licensee. Clause 21 provided that the licence was personal to the licensee who was not to permit the use of the room by any other person, and cl 22 provided that the licence would terminate on any breach by the licensee of any of the conditions of the licence. H and S each read through their respective agreements and signed them. They then moved in. When the 12 week period expired on 15th May, they each received and signed second agreements in the same terms as the first. On 7th August they repeated the procedure signing agreements to expire on 29th October. Each month they paid their rent separately and received a single receipt. In September H applied to the rent officer to get their rents reduced, alleging a tenancy or furnished occupation within the protection of the Rent Acts. X applied to the county court for an order, under s 105 of the Rent Act 1968, determining whether H and S were statutory tenants and whether Part VI of the 1968 Act applied. The county court judge held that they were regulated furnished tenants within the meaning of the Rent Acts on the grounds (i) that they each understood what they were doing when they signed their respective agreements; (ii) that the two agreements had to be construed together; (iii) that, on their true construction, they granted joint rights and gave rise to joint obligations; (iv) that cll 3 and 19, which appeared to make H and S's occupation non-exclusive, were contrary to public policy, and accordingly not binding on H and S, because they gave X the right, if either H or S left, to impose on the remaining occupant, a person of a different sex against the wishes of either of them; and (v) that H and S had a joint tenancy. X appealed. At the hearing of the appeal, H and S contended, inter alia, that there was

a single contract creating a joint tenancy, but that even if that was not so, there was a
contract granting them exclusive occupation of the room within the protection of s 70   *a*
of the 1968 Act; that cll 3 and 19 were illegal in that they expressed an intention to
contravene s 77ᵃ of the Housing Act 1957 by overcrowding the room within the meaning of sub-s (1) of that section, and that permission to occupy residential premises
exclusively could not be a licence unless it fell within one of the special categories of
hotels, hostels, family arrangements, service occupancy or other similar arrangements.
                                                                                              b
Held – The two agreements did not constitute the grant of a lease or leases but were
personal licences to occupy the room, for the following reasons—
   (i) Having regard in particular to the fact that H and S were liable only for the
consideration they had each contracted to pay and were not jointly and severally
liable for the total consideration, the separate obligations contained in the two agreements could not be reconstructed into one joint obligation without doing violence to   *c*
the intention of the parties and rewriting the agreements; it followed that, since
there was no joint agreement, there could be no tenancy as neither occupant had
the necessary exclusive possession to found one (see p 1021 *e* to *j* and p 1024 *e*, post).
   (ii) In any event, even if a joint interest had been created in H and S's favour, they were
not given an exclusive right of occupation of the room. Clauses 3 and 19, which were
wholly inconsistent with the grant of such a right, were not contrary to public policy   *d*
because (a) the risk inherent in the bargain made between the parties was not a
ground for invoking public policy to render unenforceable the right retained by the
licensor, and (b) in any event, on the true interpretation of cl 19 there was no intention
on the part of the licensor to impose on one licensee the company of another licensee
of the opposite sex against the wishes of either of them; nor were cll 3 and 19 illegal
as expressing an intention to contravene s 77 of the 1957 Act by overcrowding the   *e*
room within the meaning of sub-s (1) of that section; they did not express an intention
that the licensor should sleep in the room when H and S were occupying it and there
was no extrinsic evidence of such an intention. It followed that the appeal would be
allowed and declarations would be made that the agreements were ones to which
the provisions of the Rent Acts did not apply (see p 1022 *h* and p 1023 *a* and *f* to p 1024
c, post); *Goodrich v Paisner* [1956] 2 All ER 176 applied.   *f*
   Per Curiam. There is no reason why an ordinary landlord, not within one of the
special categories listed, should not be able to grant a licence to occupy an ordinary
house exclusively. If that is what both he and the licensee intend and if they can frame
any written agreement in such a way as to demonstrate that it is not really an agreement for a lease masquerading as a licence the court will not prevent them from
achieving that object (see p 1020 *g* and *h*, post); *Facchini v Bryson* [1952] 1 TLR 1386   *g*
and *Marchant v Charters* [1977] 2 All ER 918 considered.

Notes
For the distinction between a licence and a lease, see 23 Halsbury's Laws (3rd Edn)
427-433, paras 1022-1028, and for cases on the subject see 31(1) Digest (Reissue)
201-215, 1678-1766.   *h*
   For the Housing Act 1957, ss 77, see 16 Halsbury's Statutes (3rd Edn) 177.
   For the Rent Act 1968, ss 70, 105, see 18 Halsbury's Statutes (3rd Edn) 855, 884.
The 1968 Act has been repealed by the Rent Act 1977. For ss 70 and 105 of the 1968
Act, see now ss 19 and 141 of the 1977 Act.

───

a Section 77, so far as material, provides: '(1) A dwelling-house shall be deemed for the
     purposes of this Act to be over-crowded at any time when the number of persons sleeping
     in the house either—(*a*) is such that any two of those persons, being persons ten years old or
     more of opposite sexes and not being persons living together as husband and wife, must
     sleep in the same room; or (*b*) is, in relation to the number and floor area of the rooms of
     which the house consists, in excess of [where the house consists of one room, two] persons
     ...'

Cases referred to in judgment

Aldrington Garages v Fielder (22nd December 1977), unreported, Clerkenwell County Court.

Bhalla v Coffer (16th September 1977), unreported, Wandsworth County Court.

Buchmann v May p 993, ante, (1976) 240 Estates Gazette 49, CA.

Donald v Baldwyn [1953] NZLR 313.

Facchini v Bryson [1952] 1 TLR 1386, CA, 31(2) Digest (Reissue) 982, *7883*.

Goodrich v Paisner [1956] 2 All ER 176, [1957] AC 65, [1956] 2 WLR 1053, HL, 31(2) Digest (Reissue) 1010, *8034*.

Marchant v Charters [1977] 3 All ER 918, [1977] 1 WLR 1181, CA.

Shell-Mex and BP Ltd v Manchester Garages Ltd [1971] 1 All ER 841, [1971] 1 WLR 612, CA, 31(1) Digest (Reissue) 203, *1698*.

Walsh v Griffiths-Jones, p 1002, ante.

Cases also cited

Addiscombe Garden Estates Ltd v Crabbe [1957] 3 All ER 563, [1958] 1 QB 513, CA.

Attwood v Lamont [1920] 3 KB 571, [1920] All ER Rep 55, CA.

Barnes v Barratt [1970] 2 All ER 483, [1970] 2 QB 657, CA.

Elmdene Estates Ltd v White [1960] 1 All ER 306, [1960] AC 528, HL.

Glenwood Lumber Co Ltd v Phillips [1904] AC 405, [1904-7] All ER Rep 203, PC.

Horford Investments Ltd v Lambert [1974] 1 All ER 131, [1976] Ch 39, CA.

Kenyon v Walker, Stevenson v Kenyon [1946] 2 All ER 595, CA.

Lee-Verhulst (Investments) Ltd v Harwood Trust [1972] 3 All ER 619, [1973] 1 QB 204, CA.

Llewellyn v Hinson, Llewellyn v Christmas [1948] 2 All ER 95, [1948] 2 KB 385, CA.

Luganda v Service Hotels Ltd [1969] 2 All ER 692, [1969] 2 Ch 209, CA.

Martin v Davies (1952) 42 Tax Cas 114.

R v Battersea, Wandsworth, Mitcham and Wimbledon Rent Tribunal, ex parte Parikh [1957] 1 All ER 352, [1957] 1 WLR 410.

R v South Middlesex Rent Tribunal, ex parte Beswick (1976) 32 P & CR 67, DC.

Rush v Matthews [1926] 1 KB 492, CA.

Samrose Properties Ltd v Gibbard [1958] 1 All ER 502, [1958] 1 WLR 235, CA.

Shaw v Groom [1970] 1 All ER 702, [1970] 2 QB 504, CA.

Torbett v Faulkner [1952] 2 TLR 659, CA.

Wimbush v Cibulia, Wimbush v Levinski [1949] 2 All ER 432, [1949] 2 KB 564, CA.

Wolfe v Hogan [1949] 1 All ER 570, [1949] 2 KB 194, CA.

Appeal

By a summons, dated 20th December 1976, the applicant, Immacolata Somma, applied to the county court for an order under s 105 of the Rent Act 1968 determining whether the respondent, Martin Hazlehurst, was a statutory tenant of the dwelling-house known as Flat 4, Cornwall Mansions, London W14, and whether Part VI of the 1968 Act applied to a contract made on 7th August 1976 between the applicant and the respondent relating to the occupation of that dwelling. By another summons, also dated 20th December 1976, the applicant applied to the county court for an order under s 105 of the 1968 Act determining whether the respondent, Rossella Savelli, was also a statutory tenant of that flat and whether Part VI of the 1968 Act applied to a contract made on 7th August 1976 between the applicant and the respondent relating to the occupation of the flat. By an order dated 9th March 1977 the applications were consolidated. By an order of his Honour Judge McIntyre, dated 17th June 1977, it was declared that the respondents were statutory tenants of the flat within the meaning of the Rent Acts 1968 to 1974. The applicant appealed. The facts are set out in the judgment of the court.

Robin Purchas for the applicant.
Lord Gifford for the respondents.

Cur adv vult

a

3rd March. **CUMMING-BRUCE LJ** read the following judgment of the court, prepared by him, at the invitation of Stephenson LJ. In February 1976 two young people, Mr Martin Hazlehurst and Miss Savelli (herein called H and S), were looking for accommodation in which to live together in London. He was an educated man employed as a computer programmer, a job involving some mathematical qualifications. She also had a job. They were not married. On Wednesday, 18th February, they saw an advertisement in the Evening Standard in the column headed 'Flats and Maisonettes to Let' which read: 'ACTON/HAMMERSMITH West Kensington. Double bedsits & flatlets. All amenities. Near Tubes. £13 to £19 per week 602 5464.' They telephoned the number given and by appointment visited a house at 4 Cornwall Mansions, W 14, which belongs to Miss Somma. The house is divided into four flats, subdivided into four rooms and two maisonettes. There they met Mr Ritter, resident managing agent for Miss Somma. Mr Ritter showed them a room 22 feet by 18 feet on the third floor, with two beds in it which he described as a double room. They looked at it and went away. On Friday, 20th February, they returned, saw Mr Ritter again and said they wanted to take the room and to move in next day. Mr Ritter gave each of them a printed form of agreement into which he wrote the appropriate detail in the blank spaces. They each read the form they were given. H asked a few questions including a query about the clauses which indicated that they would have to share with a third person described as the licensor. They each signed their agreement before they moved in, and though they had not thought out the legal implications of the contracts they urgently wanted accommodation and, in the judge's phrase, understood what they were letting themselves in for. The agreements were identical save the name of the licensee, and we have set forth as an example the agreement signed S on 21st February 1976. I herein set forth and include in this judgment that licence in extenso:

b

c

d

'THIS LICENCE is made the 21st day of Feb., 1976. One thousand nine hundred and seventy-six Between I. Somma or Agent of 7, Agate Road. W.6 (hereinafter referred to as "the Licensor") of the one part and R. Savelli of Milan, Italy (hereinafter referred to as "the Licensee") of the other part.
WHEREAS the Licensor is not willing to grant the Licensee exclusive possession of any part of the rooms hereinafter referred to.
AND WHEREAS the Licensee is anxious to secure the use of the rooms notwithstanding that such use be in common with the Licensor and such other licensees or invitees as the Licensor may permit from time to time to use the said rooms.
AND WHEREAS this Licence is entered into by the Licensor and the Licensee solely upon the above basis.
By this Licence the Licensor licenses the Licensee to use (but not exclusively) all those rooms (hereinafter referred to as "the Rooms") on the 3rd Floor Double B/Sit floor of the building known as and situate at Flat 4, Cornwall Mansions, W.14 (hereinafter referred to as "the Building") together with the use of the entrance hall and lift (if any) the staircase outer door and vestibule of the Building and the furniture fixtures and effects now in the Rooms (more particularly set out in the Schedule of Contents annexed hereto) from 21.2.76 until 15.5.76 (Twelve weeks) for the sum of £116.40 on the following terms and conditions:
'1. THE Licensee agrees to pay the said sum of £116.40 by 4 weekly instalments of £38·80 commencing on the 21st day of Feb. 1976 next and thereafter on Saturday of each 4th week until 15.5.76.
'2. THE Licensee shall be responsible for the payment of all gas electric light and power which shall be consumed or supplied in or to the Rooms during the

Licensee's occupation thereof and the amount of all charges made in respect of the telephone installed therein or in the Building so far as the same relates to his use thereof.

'3. THE Licensee shall use his best endeavours amicably and peaceably to share the use of the Rooms with the Licensor and with such other licensees or invitees whom the Licensor shall from time to time permit to use the Rooms and shall not interfere with or otherwise obstruct such shared occupation in any way whatsoever.

'4. THE Licensee shall keep the interior of the Rooms and all fixtures and fittings and fixtures therein in good and clean condition and complete repair (fair wear and tear and damage by accidental fire only excepted) and immediately replace all broken glass.

'5. THE Licensee shall preserve the furniture and effects in the said Rooms from being destroyed or damaged and make good pay for the repair of or replace with articles of a similar kind and of equal value such of the furniture and effects as may be destroyed lost broken or damaged (fair wear and tear thereof only excepted).

'6. THE Licensee shall leave the furniture and effects at the expiration or sooner determination of this Licence in the Rooms or places in which they were at the commencement hereof.

'7. THE Licensee shall pay for the washing (including ironing or pressing) of all counterpanes blankets and curtains which shall have been soiled during the Licensee's occupation (the reasonable use thereof nevertheless to be allowed for).

'8. ON notice in writing being given to the Licensee by the Licensor or her Agent of all wants of repair cleansings amendments and restorations to the interior of the Rooms and of all such destruction loss breakage or damage of or to the furniture and effects as the Licensee shall be bound to make good found therein the Licensee shall repair cleanse amend and restore or make good the same within two months of the giving of such notice.

'9. THE Licensee shall not remove any furniture and effects from the Rooms without the previous consent in writing of the Licensor.

'10. THE Licensee shall not carry on or permit to be carried on in the Rooms any profession trade or business whatsoever.

'11. THE Licensee shall not do or suffer to be done in the Rooms any act or thing which may be a nuisance cause of damage or annoyance to the Licensor and the other occupiers or users of the Rooms or the Building or of any adjoining premises or which may vitiate any insurance of the Building against fire or otherwise or increase the ordinary premium thereon.

'12. THE Licensee shall not affix to the windows of the Rooms externally or internally any venetian blinds except of such colour and construction as shall be previously approved in writing by the Licensor or her Agent.

'13. THE Licensee shall not hang or allow to be hung any clothes or other articles on the outside of the Rooms or the Building.

'14. THE Licensee shall clean all the windows of the Rooms once at least in every month during his occupation.

'15. THE Licensee shall not deposit any store of coal elsewhere than in the cellar or other receptacle provided for the purpose and shall not keep any combustible or offensive goods provisions or materials in the Rooms.

'16. THE Licensee shall not cause or permit any waste spoil or destruction to the Rooms or to the Building.

'17. THE Licensee shall not pull down alter add to or in any way interfere with the construction or arrangements of the Rooms without the previous consent in writing of the Licensor.

'18. THE Licensee shall not keep any animals or birds in the Rooms Nor shall the Licensee permit any child or children to reside or stay in the Rooms.

'19. THE Licensor shall not at any one time permit more than one other persons to use the Rooms together with the Licensor and the Licensee.

'20. UNLESS prevented by any cause not under his control the Licensor shall keep the entrance hall staircase vestibule and lift (if any) clean and properly lighted.

'21. THIS Licence is personal to the Licensee and shall not permit the use of the Rooms by any other person whatsoever.

'22. UPON the Licensee being in breach of any of the conditions referred to above this Licence shall immediately determine without prejudice to any other remedies of the Licensor and the Licensee shall immediately cease his use of the Rooms and the Building as permitted hereunder.

SIGNED by the above-named
Licensor or Agent   }   S. Ritter

SIGNED by the above-named
Licensee: }   Savelli Rossella

The Licensee hereby states having received a copy of this contract

SCHEDULE OF CONTENTS

If an Electric Meter is installed the rent will be reduced by 25 pence per week.

S. Ritter

Savelli Rossella'

S paid Mr Ritter £77·60 in cash on signing the agrement, being £38·80 for the first four weeks cash in advance, plus £38·80 deposit against breakages or damage. H telephoned his father and asked for a cheque to cover his first four weeks instalment and his deposit. Mr Ritter received the cheque for £77·60 a few days later. So they moved in and stayed sharing the room with each other until the term of the agreement expired on 15th May. Then they each received and signed second agreements in the same terms as the first, and on 7th August they repeated the exercise signing agreements to expire on 29th October. Throughout they continued to make separate payments monthly in advance and received a single receipt.

In September 1976 H applied to the rent officer to get their monthly instalments reduced, alleging a tenancy or furnished occupation within the protection of the Rent Acts. The rent officer adjourned the applications pending a decision of the county court pursuant to s 105 of the Rent Act 1968 on the questions whether there was a tenancy and whether Part VI of the Act applied. So Miss Somma instituted these two sets of proceedings by applications for an order determining whether H and S were statutory tenants of the dwelling-house known as Flat 4, Cornwall Mansions W 14. The grounds of her applications, dated 20th December 1976, read:

'The grounds of this application are By a Licence dated 7th August 1976 made between the Applicant and the Respondent The Applicant granted the Respondent a Licence to use (but not exclusively) the said Flat consisting of a room on the third floor of a Building known as Cornwall Mansions aforesaid and the furniture therein contained. The names and addresses of the persons on whom it is intended to serve this application are M. Hazlehurst . . .'

The answers of the respondents H and S read:

'The Respondent denies that the agreement between the parties was anything other than a tenancy agreement. The Applicant well knew that the other person to whom the alleged Licence was granted was in fact living with the Respondent.'

On 9th March 1977 the applications came on in the county court. They were consolidated and adjourned. On 17th June the hearing took place. The judge gave judgment

for the respondents H and S. He declared that both respondents were regulated
a furnished tenants within the meaning of the Rent Acts 1968 and 1974. The order
drawn up is in this form:

> 'And the Court doth declare that the Respondents are tenants of the premises
> known as Flat 4 Cornwall Mansions, Blythe Road, London, W.14 within the
> meaning of the Rent Acts.'

b If it is upheld, it clearly should be rectified to declare that they are regulated
furnished tenants. Against that order Miss Somma appeals.

The submissions of counsel for the applicant fall under four heads: (1) On the
findings of the judge, the intentions of the parties are to be collected from the two
agreements in writing which he conceded should be read together. On their proper
construction they were two separate grants of licences to occupy and not grants
c of tenancy or tenancies. (2) The contracts are not within the protection of s 70(1)
and (3) of the Rent Act 1968 as the contracts did not grant 'exclusive occupation' of
the room that H and S were to share. (3) The clauses of the contract which provided
that H and S were to share with the licensor or another licensee were not illegal
or contrary to public policy as the judge held. (4) As an alternative submission if the
court is against him on any of his first three submissions, there should be a new trial as
d the hearing was unfair on the ground that the judge wrongly ruled against the application to cross-examine further and call evidence which he made at the end of his
closing speech.

Counsel for the respondents submitted that the judge's decision was right. There
was a single contract, and that contract was a joint tenancy. If not, it was a contract
granting to H and S exclusive occupation of their room within the protection of s 70
e of the Rent Act 1968. Those clauses in the written agreement which provided that
H and S should be liable to share the room with the licensor or another licensee
introduced by Miss Somma were illegal or void as contrary to public policy and should
be disregarded in ascertaining the legal consequences of the transaction. He also
sought a new trial in circumstances that appear hereafter.

On the issue whether the transaction fell within the protection of the Rent Acts
f counsel for the respondents submitted: (1) In consideration of questions arising under
the Rent Acts the court must look at the substance and reality of the transaction.
(2) In ascertaining the substance and reality of the transaction the court is entitled to
look both at the documents and at the surrounding circumstances. (3) Documents
which purport to grant licences will be held to grant tenancies if either one of two
sets of circumstances apply: (a) if on examining the documents in the light of the
g surrounding circumstances they are found to be in substance documents granting a
tenancy, which he called 'the construction route'; and (b) if on examining the
surrounding circumstances the court finds that the documents are a disguise which
cloaks the reality of the transaction, which he calls 'the disguise route', for such a
transaction may disguise the reality of the rights and obligations granted and assumed
by the parties without necessarily being fraudulent or attracting the label of a mere
h sham. (4) Residential licences should only be upheld as such by the courts in three
special classes of case with which we deal hereafter. (5) The courts must have regard
to the policy of the Rent Acts and be astute to prevent their evasion.

In applying those principles to the instant case, counsel for the respondents submitted that the judge did address himself to the right question, and sought for and
found the reality of the transaction in the surrounding circumstances which he admitted in evidence and took into account. Pursuing the construction route, the written
contracts are to be construed as parts of a single transaction, granting joint rights and
giving rise to joint obligations such as to transfer to the grantees a joint tenancy.
Alternatively, pursuing the disguise route, he submitted the true nature of the transaction was, and that the judge's findings can and should be read as finding, that the
reality and substance of the transaction was that H and S were granted a joint tenancy

disguised by the cloak of the documents drafted for Miss Somma, and that that finding of fact was amply supported by the evidence.

Alternatively, counsel for the respondents sought leave to amend his respondents' notice to seek a new trial on the ground that the judge failed to appreciate the relevance of the circumstances surrounding the written agreements, stopped the solicitor who appeared for the respondents from investigating them in cross-examination, and so decided the case without making findings of fact on relevant matters which should have been explored. We gave leave to the respondents to amend their respondents notice, and entertained their applications for a new trial.

We are confronted with one more attempt by an owner of housing accommodation to provide it at a profit for those in great need of it without the restrictions imposed by Parliament on his or her contractual rights to charge for it and regain possession of it. The attempt which has led to this appeal is made by a document drawn up by one, or a combination, of those who seem to have studied all the efforts, recorded in a welter of cases decided in every court from the county courts to the House of Lords, to avoid letting a dwelling-house or part of it by arranging to licence or to share the occupation of it. On the particular facts of this case has this attempt failed as the judge held?

Each document which we have to consider is on its face a licence to each respondent to share occupation—of one double bed-sitting room for 12 weeks. But the obligation which the document imposes on each respondent is an obligation to share with (1) the owner (described as the licensor), (2) the other respondent (described as a person permitted by the licensor but identified, by reading the respondents' documents with each other, as the other respondent). And the document so repeatedly proclaims itself a licence, and the relationship it creates between the applicant and each respondent as being that of licensor and licensee, that it raises the question why it should be necessary to protest so much and whether so many labels so clearly written all over it give a true or a false description of its real contents.

Our first task is to examine closely the course of the proceedings in the county court. The next to observe and analyse findings made by the judge.

Sidney Ritter, resident manager of Miss Somma, gave evidence of the circumstances preceding the signature of the agreements. However, the judge observed that he did not think it necessary to go into the background of the agreement because it could not affect the agreements subsequently entered into. But he did not in fact stop counsel for the applicant in his examination in chief eliciting from the witness the facts that we set forth at the beginning of this judgment.

During cross-examination, the judge again said that he was not concerned with the surrounding circumstances of the agreement and asked to what issue the cross-examination was relevant. The solicitor for the respondents said that he was endeavouring to show that an agreement was entered into before the forms of licence were signed and suggested that H and S had paid a deposit and moved in before they signed the agreements. The judge then observed that unless there was fraud or mutual mistake the parties were bound by what they signed. The witness gave evidence that H and S signed the agreements before they moved in; there was no evidence of a deposit being paid before the agreements were signed, and it appears from the judgment that the solicitor for the respondents did not pursue the allegation of any agreement or bargain antecedent to the written agreements. And indeed he could not do so, because when H gave evidence he did not suggest any such antecedent bargain. Miss Somma gave evidence. She said that she had used the licence agreement for about three years, and that she did not think that she introduced the form of licence because of the Rent Acts. She said that normally if one licensee went, then a friend of the remaining licensee would move in with her approval, and that if another licensee did not move in then she would lose the money and would not be able to recover it from the remaining licensee. We quote the note of the evidence she gave in cross-examination:

'I do not force people to share accommodation with people they do not like. The licence says I can put one other person in the room. I run my business on a humanity basis. I would not let a drunkard into a room in any case. I do not deal with fantasies. My plans are very happy. I do not force anyone to share with those whom they do not like. We both have a right in practice to choose who goes in. If a man was a drunkard I would not let him share. I do not think the licence had anything to do with the Rent Acts. I always let on a sharing basis. I have changed to sharing licences for my flats and rooms. I introduced the forms several years before. It suits people as they are always moving—I use twelve week periods.'

H in evidence said that he was not shown the licence agreement on the first visit to Mr Ritter whereupon the judge observed that there was no point in pursuing that line of questioning as H was an intelligent man and he entered into the agreement and was therefore bound by it, and that he, the judge, had to construe the documents. H said he read the document for five or ten minutes at the most, and queried it slightly but was told it was a standard document for letting. He asked about cl 19, as it looked as if three people could share, but Mr Ritter 'brushed it off'. He said he had moved his possessions into the flat, and that it did not seem a good thing to quarrel with the licence. In cross-examination he said that he and S signed separate agreements and made payments under the licences separately. He said he did not know if he would be responsible for paying both licence fees if S left; that he did not take legal advice because it would have been too expensive; and that he preferred to have the accommodation on the terms offered to him than not to have the accommodation at all. That concluded the evidence. The judge did not call on the solicitor for the respondents until after he had heard counsel for the applicant. Counsel for the applicant invited the judge to construe the documents, and in the course of argument the judge said that everything in the documents was utterly artificial from start to finish. The document was not a licence at all but a joint tenancy, and the landlord could not wrap it up with extraordinary expressions. Counsel for the applicant said that was at variance with what the judge had said earlier when he said that he had to construe the documents, and asked to pursue further cross-examination of H. The judge refused to hear further evidence. At the end of counsel for the applicant's speech, the solicitor for the respondents was called on, and reminded the judge of the relevance of surrounding cirumstances. Against that background we come to the judgment.

It is clear from the terms of his judgment, from the note to his judgment which he has supplied, and from what he is reported to have said in the course of argument, that he was seeking to ascertain the nature of the agreement solely from the terms of the written documents. Thus, despite the fact that a fair body of evidence was called before him as to the surrounding circumstances, it seems from what the judge himself says in his judgment, that the solicitor for the respondents did not press or at least did not press very strongly that the judge should consider anything outside the terms of the documents. This is what the judge had to say about it:

'At first there was an attempt by the solicitor for the respondents which I am not sure if he abandoned to say that the parties rights were not circumscribed by these documents...The parties would be entitled to ask the court to consider whether an antecedent bargain was made here and whether that altered the contract before me. I do not think that side of the argument is now pursued because the male respondent is an educated man. I did not see the girl but I presume she is also educated.'

It is clear from these passages and others to which there is no need for us to refer, that the judge rejected, inferentially at least, that there was any oral agreement outside the two documents which would be capable of affecting their meaning.

Thus we start from the basis that it is to the documents that we must look and to the documents alone. This has an important bearing on the whole of the case. *a* The next matter is to discover what was the ground of the agreement for a joint tenancy vested in H and S. The judge in his judgment says: 'They understood what they were letting themselves in for. On 21st February 1976 there was really a joint licence relating to the flat albeit cloaked around by the documents'. There he is saying it is a joint licence. Does he mean joint 'interest' of some sort? That is probably the case although it is difficult to say. Then he goes on to say: *b*

> 'There is no sign here of the incidents which one finds for a landlord and tenant relationship but heaps of indications which show that the parties if they applied their minds to it conferred on these people a joint tenancy or the rights of joint tenants or the equivalent rights on them. It is not an elaborate matter of this sort. It is trite law that one does not now look for exclusive possession. We are warned off placing too much emphasis on exclusive possession. The relationship between the landlord and these two young people was one of joint tenants I have no doubt about that whatever.'

He then goes on to deal with cl 19 of the documents which permits or purports to permit the landlord to impose another occupant on a remaining grantee whether it be H or S and to say that such a clause must be illegal and is therefore not binding on the grantees.

It seems to us that the reasoning behind the judge's ultimate conclusion if this: (1) Although there are on the face of it two documents here which if taken separately would give neither grantee exclusive possession, this is not fatal to the claim of the occupants that this was a tenancy, because the two documents must be construed together and if that is done they are apt to confer on the couple a joint interest of some sort in the room. (2) The other clauses which appear to make the occupation non-exclusive are illegal, possibly on the grounds of public policy, and therefore are not binding on the grantees. (3) Consequently, one is left with a joint and exclusive occupation. (4) The nature of the occupation is a tenancy because there are 'heaps of indications' which show that the parties if they applied their minds to it conferred on these people a joint tenancy or the equivalent rights. He does not say what these indications may be.

We find ourselves unable to come to the same conclusion as the judge. Counsel for the respondents, basing himself on the judgment of Denning LJ in *Facchini v Bryson*[1] and the reasoning in *Marchant v Charters*[2], submits that in a 'Rent Act' situation any permission to occupy residential premises exclusively must be a tenancy and not a licence, unless it comes into the category of hotels, hostels, family arrangements or service occupancy or a similar undefined special category. We can see no reason why an ordinary landlord not in any of these special categories should not be able to grant a licence to occupy an ordinary house. If that is what both he and the licensee intend and if they can frame any written agreement in such a way as to demonstrate that it is not really an agreement for a lease masquerading as a licence, we can see no reason in law or justice why they should be prevented from achieving that object. Nor can we see why their common intentions should be categorised as bogus or unreal or as sham merely on the grounds that the court disapproves of the bargain. This matter was expressed most happily by Buckley LJ in *Shell-Mex and BP Ltd v Manchester Garages Ltd*[3] as follows:

> 'It may be that this is a device which has been adopted by the plaintiffs to avoid possible consequences of the Landlord and Tenant Act 1954, which would

1   [1952] 1 TLR 1386 at 1389
2   [1977] 3 All ER 918 at 922, [1977] 1 WLR 1181 at 1185
3   [1971] 1 All ER 841 at 846, [1971] 1 WLR 612 at 619

a have affected a transaction being one of landlord and tenant, but in my judgment one cannot take that into account in the process of construing such a document to find out what the true nature of the transaction is. One has first to find out what is the true nature of the transaction and then see how the Act operates on that state of affairs, if it bites at all. One should not approach the problem with a tendancy to attempt to find a tenancy because unless there is a tenancy the case will escape the effects of the statute.'

b This matter was also touched on in a New Zealand decision, *Donald v Baldwyn*[1], where F B Adams J in the course of his judgment said:

c 'The law will not be hoodwinked by shams: but real and lawful intentions cannot be dismissed as shams merely because they are disliked. It is a sham to say one thing while really intending another; but the Court cannot say that a licence is a sham for the reason that the Court thinks the parties ought to have intended a tenancy.'

There seem to us to be two questions which we have to answer. (1) Did the parties intend to be bound by the written agreement? (2) Can it be said from the words which they used in those agreements that they intended to create a tenancy rather than a *d* licence? As to the first question there is a clear finding of the judge that H and S 'knew what they were letting themselves in for'; also that they were both educated and that they both signed the document. It is plain from these findings that the judge was of the opinion that they knew what they were signing and nevertheless voluntarily signed it. The second question is really the nub of the whole case, namely, do the terms of the two documents show an agreement for a licence rather than an *e* agreement for a tenancy. Immediately one faces the problem of the two separate agreements, one with H and the other with S. If they are truly separate then it must follow that neither H nor S has the necessary exclusive occupation of the room on which to found a tenancy or indeed a Part VI licence. The judge, while saying that he is confined to interpretating the documents themselves says simply, in the passage already quoted, 'on 21st February 1976 there was really a joint licence relating to the *f* flat albeit cloaked around by the documents'. If indeed he was confining himself to the documents, there was no basis for saying that they were joint agreements at all. However, if that is too legalistic a way of looking at the situation, as counsel for the respondents submits, it is impossible to reconstruct the separate obligations into one joint obligation without doing violence to the obvious intentions of the parties, particularly of the two grantees, H and S. For example, if one takes cl 1 which deals *g* with the consideration which the grantees are bound to pay, it would be necessary as we see it, either to have a joint interest coupled with a several liability for half the weekly amounts, which is something of a logical inconsistency, or else to redraw the terms of the agreements to make each grantee jointly and severally liable for the full four-weekly instalment of £77.60, as against the contractual liability resting on each under the agreement of £38.80. This is not construing the agreement between *h* the parties: it is rewriting it in the absence of any claim for rectification or any allegation of fraud. Counsel for the respondents was unable to provide any answer to this problem which came near to satisfying us on this point. We find it impossible to say that on the contents of these two documents, even adding the fact that the two grantees made their bid for the room together, a joint interest was created in their favour. That is really the end of the matter, because if the rights of the parties *j* are several as opposed to joint, it is impossible to say that either has the necessary exclusive possession to found a tenancy.

However, assuming that that conclusion is wrong and that the interest is indeed

---

1 [1953] NZLR 313 at 321

joint, one must next examine the other clauses to see whether any of them prevents the joint occupation from being exclusive.

The recitals and conditions 3, 19 and 21 point very strongly to a licence. Condition 2 imposes an obligation on the grantee 'for the payment of all gas, electric light and power which shall be consumed or supplied in or to the Rooms during the Licensee's occupation thereof' which is a wider obligation than payment for his own proportion of a consumption or supply required or enjoyed also by a second licensee. This points in the direction of a lease rather than a personal licence. Likewise the obligations to repair and replace in conditions 4 and 5 are wider than an obligation to remedy damage caused by his own default and are more consistent with a lease than a licence. Condition 8 is the kind of clause which is more appropriate for a lease than a licence for a short term. Conditions 9 and 10 are neutral. Condition 11 by its reference to a duty to other occupiers or users of the rooms is more suitable in a licence than in a lease. Clause 14 is to be read in the knowledge that if another licensee fulfils his obligation the windows will be cleaned twice a month. On balance, though it is not particularly strong, this suggests a joint obligation to clean once a month. Condition 16 prohibits 'waste spoil destruction to the Rooms or to the Building'. Waste is a familiar term of art in the law of real property and carries the meaning of damage or prejudice to the reversion. In a document such as this which is obviously carefully drafted by a hand skilled in property law the condition points to a lease rather than a licence. Condition 17 prohibits alteration or interference with the construction or arrangements of the rooms. It contemplates a continuing control by the licensor and is more consistent with a licence than a lease.

So some of these obligations are more consistent with a licence than a lease, and some lead to a contrary inference. The balance comes down in favour of a licence because the document cannot be construed as a lease without substantial rewriting. The recitals, conditions 1, 3, 19, 21 and 22 would all have to be written in substantially different terms or disregarded altogether. But cl 1 cannot be either rewritten or disregarded, and if it is to the documents that one looks for the terms of the contract the conclusion is that the document as drafted gives rise to personal obligations. The conditions which point to a joint obligation can without violence be explained as a protection required by the licensor who assumes that the licencees who share the use of the rooms from time to time will come to some arrangement of work or financial contribution between themselves in respect of the obligations which each has severally undertaken.

When the agreements were entered into the unidentified one person in cl 19 was clearly identified as the grantee who signed the other agreement. But if at any time during the currency of the agreement either H or S decided to leave, either by agreement with Miss Somma on surrender of the unexpired portion of the 12 week term, or by one of them repudiating the agreement by leaving without paying the balance of instalments as they fell due, Miss Somma has reserved the right to introduce a second licensee. She explained in evidence how she set about it, and was not cross-examined to suggest that the rights reserved of replacing the second sharing licencees were unworkable or other than of reasonable business efficacy. Such a right to introduce a new licensee as a replacement is wholly inconsistent with a grant of exclusive occupation, much less exclusive possession.

Clauses 3 and 19 also impose on the licensee the obligation to share the room with the licensor as well as with another licensee. The room was that described as being 22 feet by 18 feet, with two beds in it. The question of construction is what are the rights and obligations to be 'ascertained from the agreement. The nature and frequency of the exercise of the rights is a different question: see Goodrich v Paisner[1]. The issue in that case was whether the occupation was of a separate dwelling, but the distinction there made between the rights granted and the exercise of the rights

---

1   [1956] 2 All ER 176, [1957] AC 65

is relevant to the construction of these agreements. Miss Somma has a house. She
a grants to H and to S the right to use one room, but expressly reserves the right to
use that room in common with them. On no construction of such a contract can H
and S claim that they have been granted exclusive occupation of the room.

In the second part of his judgment the judge considered cll 3 and 19. Construing
cl 19 he said:

b   'I pointed out that at first blush it looks as if three people can use the premises
     at any one time. What was intended but the document does not say so is plain
     that the Licensee, whether Miss Savelli or Mr Hazlehurst, can share with one
     other person. It contemplates that the other person shall be whatever other
     legal person is allowed in. What is laid down plainly is that the Landlord is
     given a complete discretion, putting it mildly, and power in practice if somebody
c   goes so he can say "I have the right to say who is to share and you cannot stop me.
     You as the remaining Licensee can lump it if you do not like it. You can stay
     or get out." I cannot believe that if anyone applies their mind to the point that
     is a fair interpretation of the position of the parties that in answer to the question
     "Are you saying that you have the sole right to impose any other person or
     sex, language, class or other taste?" the landlord would give the answer or
d   can give the answer "Yes, I can" as a result of this document. If he
     imposes someone of three times their age or who snores or plays a musical
     instrument or has other habits that the surviving person does not like, this
     means that he can impose such a person on him. Worse still—and this is quite
     new. I have not heard of it before and the sooner it is dealt with the better—
     not only can he impose a person of different race or occupation but also of
e   different sex. This is a different, a most revolting different idea. No court known
     to me as advocate or judge would willingly uphold that. That part of the docu-
     ment is not binding and is illegal in my judgment. That means the parties
     can carry out the rest of the agreement without the one party forcing that clause
     on the other parties' will. I am surprised that counsel cannot find any authority
     on it. I am sure that in the reports counsel would find a case on this point if not
f   similar to what we have here. If not, I decide it for the first time. It is no part
     of my decision because it is not necessary for the resolution of the whole case.'

In our view the illustrations given by the judge of the kind of uncongenial persons
who might be imposed on H and S by Miss Somma if either of them left only illustrate
the risk inherent in the bargain that they made and are no ground for invoking
g public policy to render unenforceable the right retained by the licensor. The judge
did not like the bargain, but the agreements were the agreements of the parties
and the fact that the judge envisaged circumstances in which the exercise of Miss
Somma's rights would be uncongenial to the remaining licensee does not entitle
the court to rewrite the agreement. The judge was deeply offended by the thought
that the grantor could introduce a person of a different sex to succeed to the vacancy
h left after H or S had left. But we can find nothing to indicate that there was such an
intention. If S were to depart, and the licensor permitted another lady congenial to
H to take her place, a moralist might regard the new sharing arrangements with
regret or indignation, but the court would be as reluctant to intervene as it is in the
case of the sharing arrangements of H and S. Nor can we construe the clause to find
an intention on the part of the licensor to impose on one licensee the company of
j another licensee of the opposite sex against the wishes of either of them. For those
reasons we cannot uphold the learned judge's decision that cll 3 and 19 are contrary
to public policy.

Counsel for the respondents did not try to support this reason for the judge's
judgment but submitted a further objection to these clauses on the ground of illegality as expressing an intention to contravene s 77 of the Housing Act 1957 by over-

crowding the room which H and S were given a right to share. If the licensor exercised her right to share the room with H and S by sleeping in the room, the house   *a*
would be deemed to be overcrowded within the meaning of s 77(1). There are many
difficulties in his way. By the subsection a dwelling-house shall be deemed to be
overcrowded at any time when the number of persons sleeping in the house either
(a) is such that any two of those persons not being persons living together as husband
and wife must sleep in the same room or (b) in relation to a house consisting of one
room of the size of this particular room is more than two. By s 87 'dwellinghouse   *b*
means any premises used as a separate dwelling . . . or of a type suitable for such use.'
It is not possible as a matter of construction to hold that cll 3 and 19 express an intention
that the licensor shall sleep in the room when H and S are occupying it, and there
was no extrinsic evidence of such intention. This submission fails. It is perhaps only
fair to counsel for the respondents to say that his own enthusiasm for the point was
less than burning.   *c*

In the course of the argument we were invited to consider a great number of
cases, mostly cases in which the courts have considered the application of different
provisions of the Rent Acts. But at the end of the day it was clear to us that the
instant case is very much a case peculiar to its own facts. The difficulties, which were
real, were largely difficulties in determining the content of the findings of the judge.
Counsel for the respondents strongly argued that when properly understood the   *d*
judge had found that the agreements were a sham, or at least a disguise of the substance and reality of the transaction. We have given our reasons for rejecting that
submission, and in the result it is unnecessary to refer to most of the authorities
cited in argument.

So we arrive at the decision that on an analysis of the judgment the result in law is
that H and S entered into separate contracts; those contracts were personal licences   *e*
and not leases or a lease; and by those contracts neither H and S was given a right
of exclusive occupation of the room that they shared. That brings us to the respondents'
application for a new trial, leave for which we granted as an amendment to the respondent's notice. Counsel for the respondents submits that the judge approached
the case in the wrong way. He confined himself to a construction of the documents
when it was his duty, on the authority of the cases which have been concerned with   *f*
different but in some ways similar problems under the Rent Acts, to admit extrinsic
evidence and to consider whether the surrounding circumstances establish that the
documents do not record the real intention of the parties at the time when the grantor
agreed to let the grantees live in the room. The onus was on the respondents to
establish that the contract was other than that recorded in the documents that they
signed. If authority is needed, it is to be found clearly stated in this court in *Buchmann*   *g*
v May[1] and the cases therein cited. There Sir John Pennycuick, in a judgment with
which Megaw and Stephenson LJJ agreed, held that the relevant clause of the agreement
in writing was unequivocal and said[2]:

> 'It seems to me that that provision must stand as evidence of the purpose
> of the parties unless [the tenant] can establish that the provision does not corres-
> pond to the true purpose of the parties. The burden lies on her to do so.'   *h*

Counsel for the respondents submits that they failed to do so because the judge
made it clear that he was not interested in hearing evidence of the surrounding
circumstances and so either closed his mind to the correct approach or alternatively
made it impracticable for the respondents' to solicitor present their case adequately.
He contrasted the course of the hearing with the proceedings in three other cases[3]

1 Page 993, ante
2 See p 998, ante
3 *Walsh v Griffiths-Jones*, p 1002, ante; *Aldrington Garages v Fielder* (22nd December 1977),
  Clerkenwell County Court (Judge Dewer); *Bhalla v Coffer* (16th September 1977), Wandsworth County Court (Judge White)

a in the county courts in London of which he gave us reports of the judgments which
he personally could certify. In all those cases the learned judges rightly admitted
extrinsic evidence which satisfied them that the written contracts were not the real
statement of the intentions of the grantor and two grantees, so that documents,
described as licences, almost identical with the present agreements, were held to be
the grant of a lease.

b We say with respect that Judge McDonnell's judgment is a model of the approach
to and analysis of an alleged agreement to grant licences to two persons to share
residential accommodation, and it deserves wider publicity. Counsel for the respondents contrasted the hearing before Judge McDonnell with the proceedings in the
county court with which we are concerned. He pointed to the observations of the
judge calculated to discourage the advocates for both sides from leading evidence
of the surrounding circumstances or from cross-examining in relation thereto. In
c our view there is great force in his submission that the hearing had unsatisfactory
features as the judge's interventions point to an inference that he was confused as to
the relevance of extrinsic evidence. But with some hesitation we have decided that
though there was confusion in the judge's mind while the evidence was being given,
in fact his interventions did not have the effect of shutting up the evidence of surrounding circumstances which was relevant to the transaction. In spite of the judge's com-
d ments Mr Ritter, Miss Somma and H appear to have been permitted to give the
evidence that they wanted to present of the relevant surrounding circumstances.
The solicitor for the respondents did not persist in his contention that H had paid a
deposit and moved in before he signed the agreement, and H's evidence was not
consistent with the payment of any deposits save the deposits of £38·60 that each paid
after the agreements had been signed. Where parties are professionally represented,
e our forensic system requires that parties must persist in examining or cross-examining
on facts, and must seek a ruling from the court if the court indicates an intention to
exclude material which the advocate regards as relevant. We do not under-estimate
the difficulties of the solicitor appearing for the respondents, but he did not persist in
his cross-examination of Mr Ritter or his examination-in-chief of H about the events
of the first occasion when he met Mr Ritter when the judge intervened. We conclude
f that in this court the case must be scrutinised on the evidence that was given, and that
in spite of the criticisms that we have made of the judge's interventions and approach
to the case before he came to deliver judgment, it is not a proper case for a new trial
in order to enable parties to canvass again the evidence of the circumstances in February
1976 which surrounded the signature of the two agreements in writing. Further,
having regard to the uncontroverted facts in evidence at the trial it seems unlikely
g that a second trial would enable H or S to discharge the onus of establishing that the
intentions of the parties are not to be collected from the written documents that they
signed, particularly having regard to H's candid evidence that after he had read the
document it did not seem a good thing to quarrel with the licence and that he preferred to have the accommodation on the terms offered to him rather than not to
have accommodation at all. This court has today construed those arrangements.
h The respondents' application for a new trial is therefore refused.

The appeal is allowed. There will be declarations that the agreements referred
to the county court under s 105 are agreements to which the provisions of the Rent
Acts do not apply.

Appeal allowed. Leave to appeal to the House of Lords refused.

j *27th April. The Appeal Committee of the House of Lords (Lord Wilberforce, Lord Salmon and
Lord Fraser of Tullybelton) refused leave to appeal.*

Solicitors: *W Feldman* (for the applicant); *Seiffert, Sedley & Co* (for the respondents).

Mary Rose Plummer   Barrister.

Re Steel (deceased)
Public Trustee v Christian Aid Society and others

CHANCERY DIVISION
MEGARRY V-C
7th, 8th FEBRUARY 1978

Will – Residue – Division – Legacies of between £25 and £250 given to number of beneficiaries – Any residue to be divided 'between those beneficiaries who have only received small amounts' – Whether words 'who have only received small amounts' words of qualification or explanation – Whether residue to be divided among beneficiaries equally or in proportion to amount of each legacy.

The testator wrote out his own will. It consisted of legacies of £250, £200, £100, £50 and £25 to relatives, friends and institutions. The legacies were not arranged in any particular order, i e as to amount or relationship or otherwise. After the last legacy the testator wrote 'Any residue remaining to be divided between those beneficiaries who have only received small amounts'. The will contained very little punctuation but there was a gap after the phrase 'Any residue remaining to be divided between those beneficiaries' and before the phrase 'who have only received small amounts', which was begun on a fresh line. The testator died and his executor paid the legacies, totalling £2,800, to the legatees. The residue of the estate amounted to £14,300. The executor sought the determination of the court as to how the residue should be divided, i e (1) whether the words 'who have only received small amounts' should be interpreted (a) as words of qualification, meaning that only those who received 'small amounts' should take, or (b) as words of explanation, referring to all the legatees, in that the testator was merely acknowledging that the amount which he had given each of them was small; and (2) whether the residue should be divided equally between those legatees entitled to a share in it, or proportionately according to the size of their respective legacies.

Held – On the true construction of the will, the words 'who have only received small amounts' were merely words of explanation and referred to all the legatees, and the residue was to be divided equally between them (see p 1030 e f and p 1032 b c, post).

Steel v Dixon [1881-5] All ER Rep 729 and *Re Bower's Settlement Trusts, Bower v Ridley-Thompson* [1942] 1 All ER 278 considered.

Cases referred to in judgment

Battie-Wrightson, Re, Cecil v Battie-Wrightson [1920] 2 Ch 330, [1920] All ER Rep 597, 89 LJCh 550, 124 LT 84, 48 Digest (Repl) 504, 4636.

Bower's Settlement Trusts, Re, Bower v Ridley-Thompson [1942] 1 All ER 278, [1942] Ch 197, 111 LJCh 225, 40 Digest (Repl) 499, 111.

Ker v Ker (1869) 4 IR Eq 15, 35 Digest (Repl) 677, *1646.

Steel v Dixon (1881) 17 Ch D 825, [1881-5] All ER Rep 729, 50 LJCh 591, 45 LT 142, 20 Digest (Repl) 258, 67.

Cases also cited

Brown v Gould [1971] 2 All ER 1505, [1972] Ch 52.
Gifford, Re, Gifford v Seaman [1944] 1 All ER 268, [1944] Ch 186.
Hughes, Re, Hughes v Footner [1921] 2 Ch 208, [1921] All ER Rep 310.

Liley v Hey (1842) 1 Hare 580, 66 ER 1162.
a *Page v Young* (1875) LR 19 Eq 501.
Salusbury v Denton (1857) 3 K & J 529.
Scarisbrick's Will Trusts, Re, Cockshott v Public Trustee [1951] 1 All ER 822, [1951] Ch 662, CA.
Smith v Fleming (1835) 2 Cr M & R 638, 150 ER 271.
Thomas v Howell (1874) LR 18 Eq 198.
b *Wolff, Re, Thornthwaite and Goldby v David* (1958) 16 DLR (2d) 527.

Summons

By an originating summons dated 1st December 1977, the plaintiff, the Public Trustee, the sole executor named in the will dated 16th June 1970 of Gordon William Wilson
c Steel deceased ('the testator'), who died on 17th October 1975, sought the following relief: (1) Whether on the true construction of the will of the testator his residuary estate fell to be divided—(a) equally amongst all the pecuniary legatees of the testator; (b) in some other and if so which proportions amongst all the pecuniary legatees of the testator; (c) equally amongst all the pecuniary legatees of the testator excepting those pecuniary legatees who received £250 by way of a pecuniary legacy; (d) in
d some other and if so which proportions amongst the pecuniary legatees mentioned in (c); (e) equally amongst all the pecuniary legatees of the testator excepting those pecuniary legatees who received £200 or more by way of the pecuniary legacy; (f) in some other and if so which proportions amongst the pecuniary legatees mentioned in (e); (g) equally amongst the pecuniary legatees of the testator excepting those who received £100 or more by way of a pecuniary legacy; (h) in some other and if
e so which proportions amongst the pecuniary legatees mentioned in (g); (i) equally amongst the pecuniary legatees of the testator excepting those who received £50 or more by way of a pecuniary legacy; (j) in some other and if so which proportions amongst the pecuniary legatees mentioned in (i); (k) as on intestacy of the testator amongst those persons entitled to the testator's intestacy to share in the testator's estate. (2) An order (a) that the first defendant, the Christian Aid Society, be appointed to
f represent all the testator's pecuniary legatees who received £250 by way of pecuniary legacy under the testator's will; (b) that the second defendant, Mabel McRobert, be appointed to represent all the testator's pecuniary legatees who received £200 by way of pecuniary legacy under the testator's will; (c) that the third defendant, Andy Wilson, be appointed to represent all the testator's pecuniary legatees who received £100 by way of pecuniary legacy under the testator's will; (d) that the fourth
g defendant, James Sydney Varley, be appointed to represent all the testator's pecuniary legatees who received £50 by way of pecuniary legacy under the testator's will; (e) that the fifth defendant, Alice Nicoll, be appointed to represent all the testator's pecuniary legatees who received £25 by way of pecuniary legacy under the testator's will; (f) that the sixth defendant, Joyce Ethel Allan, be appointed to represent the next-of-kin of the testator entitled to share in the testator's residuary estate in the
h event of the testator's intestacy. (3) That so far as necessary the testator's estate might be administered by the court. (4) Such further or other relief as might be expedient. The facts are set out in the judgment.

R M K Gray for the plaintiff.
Gordon Nurse for the first defendant.
j *Jonathan Henty* for the second defendant.
Robert Wakefield for the third defendant.
Spencer G Maurice for the fourth defendant.
T D Baxendale for the fifth defendant.
M R King for the sixth defendant.

MEGARRY V-C. In this case there has been much debate on the meaning of the phrase 'small amounts' in a will. The testator made a holograph will on 16th June **a** 1970 and died on 17th October 1975. Virtually no evidence about him or his circumstances has been put before me, so that it is not easy to put myself in the testator's armchair; but I was told that he had been an estimating manager at Vickers, and that he had died a widower aged 83 years. He left no issue. The will appointed the Public Trustee to be his sole executor, and then gave 25 pecuniary legacies of amounts varying from £25 to £250 each. Some were to relations, some were to **b** friends, and two were to institutions. Some of the legacies to individuals were in substitutional form. The legacies are not arranged in any particular order that I can see, whether of amount or relationship or otherwise: they are simply set out higgledy-piggledy. After the last legacy come the words:

'Any residue remaining to be divided between those beneficiaries who have **c** only received small amounts.'

The question is the meaning and and effect of these words.

The pecuniary legacies total £3,125. Some legacies, amounting to £325, and I think three in number, have lapsed; and the remaining legacies, amounting to £2,800, have all been paid. What is left over, and so is 'any residue remaining', is some **d** £14,300. The issue is about what happens to that. Nobody sought to contend that 'beneficiaries' meant anything other than the legatees who took under the will. But which of them? Do they all take, or do only those of them whose legacies could be called legacies of 'small amounts'? How small is 'small' in this context? There are five categories of legacy, namely, those of £250, £200, £100, £50 and £25. Of the first five defendants to the originating summons, each represented one financial category. The £250 category contended that all were included; the £200 category **e** contended that all were included save the £250 category, and so on down the line, until one reached the contention of the £25 category, which was that they alone were included. Finally, the sixth defendant contended that the residuary gift was void for uncertainty and so the residue passed as on intestacy. If the gift is valid, and the beneficiaries who take are duly ascertained, then there is the further question whether each legatee who takes it is to receive an equal share of residue, or whether instead the **f** legatee is to receive a share proportionate to the size of the legacy.

I think that the starting point must be to identify what it is that I am construing. No doubt the probate copy of the will is conclusive as to the words admitted to probate; but that is not all that is relevant to the process of construction. In this case the testator's handwriting was difficult to read, and so probate was granted to a typewritten copy. At an earlier stage in the argument it became plain that something **g** might turn on punctuation, and possibly on the arrangement of the words in the original will; and from what punctuation there was, and from the language of parts of the will, and not least the blanks in the attestation clause (which allowed for the letter 'h' to be made into 'his' or 'her', according to the sex of the testator), it seemed probable that the will had been made on a will form. That proved to be the case when a photographic copy of the original will was shown to me; and in due course the will **h** itself was produced in court. It then became clear that the typewritten copy to which probate had been granted had not reproduced exactly such apparent punctuation as there was in the original will, and that it certainly had not exactly reproduced the arrangement of the original will in such matters as indentation and the beginning of new lines.

Now it seems clear that in construing a will the court is entitled to examine the **i** original will and give proper weight to any punctuation in it (or lack of punctuation), and also, I think, the arrangement of it. I need only refer to Re Battie-Wrightson[1],

---

1 [1920] 2 Ch 330 at 334, [1920] All ER Rep 597 at 599

a where Astbury J cited, evidently with approval, a passage from Jarman on Wills[1]. I shall read only part of it—

'. . . in recent times the Courts have without hesitation adopted the practice of examining original wills with a view to seeing whether anything there appearing—as, for instance, the mode in which it was written, how "dashed and stopped", —could guide them in the true construction to be put upon it.'

b It seems to me that the arrangement of the words in the will, including any indentation or lack of it, is within this approach, as I think it is for statutes[2].

With that, I can come back to the residuary gift in the present case. Two constructions of this were put forward. The first treated the final six words ('who have only received small amounts') as words of qualification, or words of exclusion, especially when due emphasis was given to the word 'only'. The residue was not to be

c divided between all the beneficiaries, but only between a particular category, namely, those of them who will receive what can properly be called 'small amounts'. The expression 'those . . . who' is particularly apt for marking out a special category. Nothing, I may say, turned on the awkwardness of 'who have only received', which doubtless should have read 'who will have only received', or words to that effect. The other contention was that the concluding six words were words of explanation,

d indicating the testator's motive or reason for disposing of the residue thus. The words 'those beneficiaries' simply meant all the legatees who had just been set out in the will, just as if it had been 'these beneficiaries'. On this interpretation the testator is giving his residue for division between all the legatees, and he is adding the explanation that he is doing this because they will all be receiving small amounts; if his estate is large enough, he is therefore increasing what they get, up to the limit

e of his estate.

Purely as a matter of construing the residuary gift on its own, and as a matter of wording, I would prefer the first of these constructions, treating the final six words as words of qualification and not words of explanation. At the same time, one must recognise that only a very slight change is needed to shift the emphasis. Simply insert a comma after 'beneficiaries', and the gift reads—

f 'Any residue remaining to be divided between those beneficiaries, who have only received small amounts.'

In that form, I would treat the final six words as words of explanation. So one question is whether in the original will there is that comma, or its equivalent.

I can find no trace of any such comma in the original will. Indeed, there seem

g to be no commas in the will at all, apart from some in the printed parts of the will form. The only mark which might be a comma turns out to be the tail of a letter 'y'. There are a number of dots in the manuscript parts of the will which come in places where a full stop might be expected; subject to that, the words written by the testator seem to be devoid of any punctuation. But then there is the arrangement. The first 15 legacies are all written continuously; but then, when the testator turns

h the page and writes out the last ten legacies, he begins each one on a new line, even when there is ample room to start it on the previous line. When he comes to the gift of residue, he begins a new line, and then, when he comes to the word "who", he puts it on the next line (even though there is plenty of room for it on the previous line) and he substantially indents it. His signature immediately follows the last word (i e 'amounts'), on the same line, and squeezed in so that it ends just before the right-

j hand edge of the paper. The indications of a comma-substitute are of course slender, but at least in reading the original will one can see the break between 'beneficiaries' and 'who', interrupting the flow. After all, I must remember that this is a testator

---

1   6th Edn (1910), p 45
2   Copulatives and Punctuation in Statutes, R E Megarry (1959) 75 LQR 31

who does not appear to use commas, and pays little attention to marks of punctuation; and for him to omit a comma where others might insert it is a matter of little significance. Given this slender indication, is there anything else in the will that points in the same direction?

I think there is. One striking distinction between the two constructions of the residuary gift is that on the first, the meaning of the phrase 'small amounts' becomes a matter of high importance, whereas on the second it has little significance. One does not have to be a lawyer to see that there might be many different views on what sums are 'small amounts'. I think that I am entitled to assume that a testator who has set out a long list of legacies of precise amounts, about which there can be no argument, does not thereupon set about making a gift of residue to a particular category of those legatees who are identified by so obviously an uncertain and provocative phrase as those who have been given 'small amounts'. If for this purpose anything not exceeding £100 is to be regarded as being 'small', why not state the amount, as other amounts have been so freely stated? Furthermore, having set out the scale of his bounty to the 25 legatees in terms of specific sums for each, the existence of a residue of any magnitude would inevitably upset that scale of bounty very substantially if only the smaller legacies were to carry a share of residue. There were, for instance, three legacies of £25, one of which has lapsed. Even if the residue had been a mere £1,000, instead of being the £14,300 that it is, the effect of holding that only the £25 legacies are of 'small amounts' would mean that each of these legatees would get £525, and so be carried from the least favoured category to a position of double the most favoured category. What could be the testator's motive for doing this? Why should I construe his words as producing such a result if it is reasonably possible to put on them another meaning which avoids imputing to him an intention to use obscurity to achieve the capricious? When I put these factors together, I reach the conclusion that the concluding six words should be construed as being mere words of explanation, so that their precise meaning is of little or no importance. The residue will therefore be divided between those who take legacies under the will, irrespective of the size of those legacies.

On this footing, there is then the question of what is to be the basis of division. There were two rival contentions on this. One was that the residue should be divided equally between all the legatees whose legacies had not lapsed, irrespective of the size of those legacies. The other was that the residue should be divided proportionately among those legatees, in proportion to the size of each legacy, so that, for instance, a £200 legatee would get twice the share of residue of a £100 legatee. In support of equal division, it could be said by the £100 legatee to the £200 legatee: 'You were intended to get £100 more than me, and if we each get an equal share of residue, you will still get £100 more than me.' The riposte of the £200 legatee is: 'I was intended to get twice as much as you: equal division of the residue will alter that proportion, and so to carry out the proportions originally intended, the residue should be divided proportionately to our respective legacies.' In favour of equal division there is the maxim 'equality is equity', and *Re Bower's Settlement Trusts*[1].

Re Bower's Settlement Trusts[1] was a decision not on a will but on an accruer clause in a settlement. The trust fund had been given in shares that were unequal in size, and if the trusts of any share failed, the accruer clause would carry the failed share 'by way of addition to the other shares'. In an unreserved judgment not much over half a page long Morton J held[1] that as there were no words to indicate the contrary, the accruer took effect in equal shares, and not in proportionate shares. The decision encountered some academic criticism on the footing that the decision altered the proportions prescribed by the settlor[2], but so far as I know the case has not been the subject of subsequent judicial consideration. Apart from the differences between an

---

1　[1942] 1 All ER 278, [1942] Ch 197
2　See (1942) 58 LQR 311

accruer clause in a settlement and a residuary gift by will, there is the consideration
a that in *Re Bower's Settlement Trusts*[1] the property was settled in terms of shares, rather
than fixed amounts. It can therefore be said that the natural form of comparison
in that case was on a proportionate basis, and that there was not the same freedom
to choose between a comparison of proportions and a comparison of amounts, such as
that one legatee is getting £100 more than another, as there is in this case.

Thus far, the concept of equality may be said to be in the ascendant. But does
b equality in this context necessarily mean a simple mathematical equality? Counsel
for the first defendant referred me to Halsbury's Laws of England[2], where the maxim
'equality is equity' is discussed. The first two sentences under this title run as follows:

> 'The maxim that equality is equity expresses in a general way the object both
> of law and equity, namely to effect a distribution of property and losses propor-
c > tionate to the several claims or to the several liabilities of the persons concerned.
> Equality in this connection does not mean literal equality, but proportionate
> equality.'

One of the authorities cited for this second sentence (with an error in the page reference) is *Ker v Ker*[3] which does not help much. The other is *Steel v Dixon*[4]. There,
d Fry J[5] is discussing the rule that as between co-sureties there is to be equality of the
burden and of the benefit. The judge says:

> 'When I say equality I do not necessarily mean equality in its simplest form,
> but what has been sometimes called proportionable equality.'

e and he then explains that if the sureties are sureties for unequal amounts, they must
contribute proportionately to the amount for which each is a surety. That, of course,
is a very different case from this; but I think it is valuable as correcting any assumption that equality necessarily means mathematical equality. When the maxim
'equality is equity' comes to be applied, it often, and I think usually, will mean
mathematical equality, in that no other basis of equality can be discerned; but given
f suitable circumstances a true equality of treatment may require the application
of a mathematical inequality, and instead a proportionate equality. So far as can
be judged from the short report, this consideration was not put before Morton J
in *Re Bower's Settlement Trusts*[6].

The subject is one on which I feel considerable doubt. With all the respect due
to a great equity lawyer, I might well, I think, have reached the opposite conclusion
g had the facts of *Re Bower's Settlement Trusts*[6] come before me without the benefit of
the decision of Morton J. But there stands the decision. Further, I think that it would
be easier to support the cause of proportionate division on the facts of that case than
it is on the facts of the case now before me. There seems to me to be a real difference
between shares of a fund on the one hand and legacies of fixed amounts on the other
hand; one moves in a world of proportions, and the other in a world of determinate
h sums. However, counsel for the first defendant contended that just as legacies abate
proportionately if the estate is insufficient, so they ought to increase proportionately
if they are in effect increased by a gift of the surplus of an estate to the legatees.
At first blush this has a reasonable ring about it; but I doubt whether it is sound.

---

j 1   [1942] 1 All ER 278, [1942] Ch 197
2   16 Halsbury's Laws (4th Edn) para 1301
3   (1869) 4 IR Eq 15 at 28
4   (1881) 17 Ch D 825, [1881-5] All ER Rep 729
5   (1881) 17 Ch D 825 at 830, [1881-5] All ER Rep 729 at 732
6   [1942] 1 All ER 278, [1942] Ch 197

In the administration of an estate that is insufficient to pay legacies in full the court makes the legacies abate rateably on the footing that this is the fairest course to take. But that has little to do with what I am concerned with, namely, the construction of a will: a testator may give his property as fairly or unfairly as he wishes. As for the words 'to be divided between' in the will, these might as readily be treated as being qualified by the word 'equally' as by the word 'proportionately'; and, of course, neither word is there. I find it difficult, too, to see why in dividing the residue the intention should be treated as being to preserve the proportions rather than the gaps in amount, instead of being the opposite. In the end, I think that on the whole, in a case of real doubt such as I consider this to be, with a holograph will made by a testator whom I infer to have been of no great degree of sophistication, and as a matter of last resort, the simplicity of mathematical equality is to be preferred to any process of proportionate division. I therefore hold that the residue is to be divided into equal shares among the legatees whose legacies have not lapsed (I think there are 22 of them), irrespective of the size of their legacies.

From what I have said it must be plain that I do not consider that the gift of residue is void for uncertainty, a conclusion that I should be most reluctant to reach unless I was driven to it. I need not recite any of the authorities on this reluctance: they are well enough known. Nor do I have to decide what the phrase 'small amounts' means, as would have been necessary had I held that the last six words of the gift of residue were words of qualification. For what it is worth, I may indicate that my inclination would have been to say that for this testator, making this will, the legacies of £25, £50 and £100 were of 'small amounts', but that those of £200 and £250 were not; the gap of £100 seems to me to be something of a watershed in this context. But as I need decide nothing on this, I leave it undecided.

Question (1) of the summons answered in the terms of para (a) which was amended to read 'equally among all the pecuniary legatees of the testator who survived him'; representation orders made in terms of para (2)(a) to (f) of the summons.

Solicitors: *Ingledew, Brown, Bennison and Garrett* (for the plaintiff and the second, third, fourth, fifth and sixth defendants); *Hewitt, Woollacott & Chown* (for the first defendant).

Hazel Hartman   Barrister.

Balen v Inland Revenue Commissioners

COURT OF APPEAL, CIVIL DIVISION
STAMP, ORR AND GEOFFREY LANE LJJ
15th, 18th, 19th, 20th APRIL 1978

Income tax – Tax advantage – Counteracting – Notice – Validity – Notification by commissioners specifying transactions in question – Reasons for questioning transactions not stated in notification – Whether commissioners required to make known their case to taxpayer – Whether commissioners in breach of natural justice – Whether notification void – Income and Corporation Taxes Act 1970, s 460(6).

Income tax – Tax advantage – Counteracting – Commissioners' counter-statement – Validity – Counter-statement containing detailed analysis of events leading up to transactions in question and laying foundation of commissioners' case – Counter-statement not shown to taxpayer – Whether tribunal entitled to take counter-statement into consideration – Whether tribunal in breach of natural justice – Whether commissioners required to make known their case to taxpayer – Income and Corporation Taxes Act 1970, s 460(7)(a).

In April 1974 the Inland Revenue Commissioners, acting under s 460(6)[a] of the Income and Corporation Taxes Act 1970, notified the taxpayer that they had reason to believe that s 460 might apply to him in respect of certain transactions in securities specified in the notification. The notification did not give the commissioners' reasons for their belief nor had the commissioners indicated what those reasons were in any correspondence with the taxpayer. The taxpayer was of the opinion that s 460 did not apply to him and, in accordance with s 460(6), made a statutory declaration that he had not obtained any tax advantage from the specified transactions. The commissioners saw reason to take further action in the matter and, in accordance with s 460(7)[b], sent to the tribunal established under s 463 a certificate to that effect together with the taxpayer's statutory declaration. The commissioners also sent to the tribunal, as they were entitled to do by s 460(7)(a), a counter-statement with reference to the matter. In the counter-statement the commissioners set out a detailed history of the events and transactions leading up to the specified transactions which suggested that the specified transactions formed part of a scheme which had the object of obtaining a tax advantage for the taxpayer. The taxpayer was not shown the counter-statement. On the material before it, the tribunal determined, pursuant to s 460(7)(b), that there was a prima facie case for proceeding in the matter. Thereupon the commissioners, acting under s 460(3)[c], served notice on the taxpayer of their intention to adjust his tax liability by assessing him to tax under Sch D, Case VI, for the year 1970-71 in the sum of £132,000, and to recompute his liability to surtax on the basis that that sum formed part of his total income for that year. An assessment to surtax was made and notice of the assessment was given to the taxpayer. The taxpayer appealed against the assessment. Prior to the determination of that appeal the taxpayer brought proceedings in the High Court claiming declarations, inter alia, (i) that the notification served under s 460(6) was null and void on the ground that it did not give the commissioners' reasons for their belief that s 460 applied and therefore did not give the taxpayer clear notice of the case he had to meet and (ii) that the tribunal's determination that there was a prima facie case for proceeding under s 460 was also null and void because it had taken into account the counter-statement which advanced a case by the commissioners which had not been distinctly made by them in the notification, that therefore the tribunal had reached its determination on material which it ought not to have taken into account, and that it was contrary to

---

a   Section 460(6) is set out at p 1036 c to e, post
b   Section 460(7), so far as material, is set out at p 1036 e and f, post
c   Section 460(3) is set out at p 1035 f to h, post

natural justice for the tribunal to have determined that there was a prima facie case for proceeding in the matter without giving the taxpayer an opportunity of answering *a* the statements or submissions made by the commissioners. Oliver J*d* held that the taxpayer was not entitled to the declarations claimed. The taxpayer appealed.

Held – (i) Under s 460(6) of the 1970 Act the commissioners were not under a duty to disclose to the taxpayer the reasons for their belief that the section applied to him. Furthermore, on the true construction of s 460(7), the counter-statement was not *b* required to be confined to counteracting the taxpayer's statutory declaration, because the tribunal was not required to resolve an issue between the parties but to determine whether, on the basis of the facts and circumstances relied on by the commissioners, there was prima facie case for proceeding in the matter (see p 1039 *e* to p 1040 *b*, p 1041 *e* and *f* and p 1042 *a* to *c* and *g h*, post).

(ii) There was no requirement of natural justice that the taxpayer should see and have the opportunity of answering the counter-statement or that the reasons for *c* the commissioners' opinion should be stated in the original notification served on him under s 460(6). Accordingly the appeal would be dismissed (see p 1040 *g* to p 1041 *c* and *e f* and p 1042 *d h*, post); *Wiseman v Borneman* [1969] 3 All ER 275 followed.

Decision of Oliver J [1977] 2 All ER 406 affirmed.

Notes
a
For the requirement of natural justice that a party should be given notice of the case he will be called on to meet, see 1 Halsbury's Laws (4th Edn) paras 74, 75.

For the cancellation of tax advantages, see Supplement to 30 Halsbury's Laws (3rd Edn) para 276A, and for cases on the subject, see 28(1) Digest (Reissue) 489-494, *1753-1762*.

For the Income and Corporation Taxes Act 1970, ss 460, 463, see 33 Halsbury's *e* Statutes (3rd Edn) 591, 598.

Cases referred to in judgments
Fairmount Investments Ltd v Secretary of State for the Environment [1976] 2 All ER 865, [1976] 1 WLR 1255, HL.
Wiseman v Borneman [1969] 3 All ER 275, [1971] AC 297, [1969] 3 WLR 706, 45 Tax Cas 540, 48 ATC 278, [1969] TR 279, HL, 28(1) Digest (Reissue) 493, 1760.

Appeal
The taxpayer, Paul Andrew Balen, appealed against an order of Oliver J[1] made on 11th November 1976, dismissing an originating summons, dated 18th February 1976, taken out by the taxpayer who was seeking as against the first defendants, the Inland Revenue Commissioners, and the second defendants, Roy Ernest Borneman QC, *g* James Alfred Jackson, the Hon Roger Richard Edward Chorley, Charles Frederick Melville Rawlinson, and Francis Cator, individual members of the tribunal constituted under s 463 of the Income and Corporation Taxes Act 1970, the following relief, inter alia: (1) a declaration that a notification dated 11th April 1974 served on the taxpayer by the first defendants pursuant to s 460(6) of the 1970 Act was null and void, and (2) a declaration that a determination of the second defendants under *f* s 460(7) of the 1970 Act and dated 10th February 1975 was null and void. The facts are set out in the judgment of Stamp LJ.

C N Beattie QC and *George Bretten* for the taxpayer.
Donald Rattee QC for the first defendants.
Peter Gibson for the second defendants.

STAMP LJ. This is an appeal by the taxpayer from an order of Oliver J[1] made on 11th November 1976 whereby an originating summons taken out by the taxpayer

---

d [1977] 2 All ER 406, [1977] STC 148
1 [1977] 2 All ER 406, [1977] STC 148

asking for certain declarations was dismissed. The originating summons will be
more readily understood if I refer to it again later in this judgment.

The matter arises in this way. It is provided by s 460 of the Income and Corporation
Taxes Act 1970, relating to tax avoidance and providing for the cancellation of tax
advantages from certain transactions in securities, that the tax advantage obtained
or obtainable by a taxpayer in consequence of such a transaction shall be counteracted.
This is to be done by adjustments which are specified in the section, that is to say, an
assessment, the nullifying of a right to repayment, and by other methods which are
there set out. The section will apply to a person only if the circumstances mentioned
in s 461 of the 1970 Act, or one of them, apply. The circumstances are listed in s 461
under alphabetical headings A to E inclusive.

The actual terms of s 460, so far as relevant for present purposes, are these:

> '(1) Where—(a) in any such circumstances as are mentioned in section 461 below,
> and (b) in consequence of a transaction in securities or of the combined effect of
> two or more such transactions, a person is in a position to obtain, or has obtained,
> a tax advantage, then unless he shows that the transaction or transactions were
> carried out either for bona fide commercial reasons or in the ordinary course of
> making or managing investments, and that none of them had as their main
> object, or one of their main objects, to enable tax advantages to be obtained,
> this section shall apply to him in respect of that transaction or those transactions
> . . .'

Then there is a saving proviso which does not apply in the instant case.

Subsection (2) says this:

> 'Subject to section 468(3) below, for the purposes of this Chapter a tax advantage
> obtained or obtainable by a person shall be deemed to be obtained or obtainable
> by him in consequence of a transaction in securities or of the combined effect
> of two or more such transactions, if it is obtained or obtainable in consequence of
> the combined effect of the transaction or transactions and of the liquidation
> of a company.'

Subsection (3) is important:

> 'Where this section applies to a person in respect of any transaction or transac-
> tions, the tax advantage obtained or obtainable by him in consequence thereof
> shall be counteracted by such of the following adjustments, that is to say an
> assessment, the nullifying of a right to repayment or the requiring of the return
> of a repayment already made (the amount to be returned being chargeable under
> Case VI of Schedule D and recoverable accordingly), or the computation or
> recomputation of profits or gains, or liability to tax, on such basis as the Board
> may specify by notice in writing served on him as being requisite for counter-
> acting the tax advantage so obtained or obtainable.'

The section so far as I have read it is a formidable weapon in the armoury of the
Inland Revenue, and in this connection reference may be made to the speech of
Lord Wilberforce in *Wiseman v Borneman*[1], a case to which I shall have to refer hereafter, which described it as a section of considerable severity. Some protection is
accorded, however, to the taxpayer by the terms of two subsections, on the true
construction of which the present appeal depends.

Subsection (6) contains provisions for the protection of the taxpayer by precluding
the Board from giving notice under sub-s (3) of the section until they have notified
the person in question in terms specified in that subsection, namely 'that they
have reason to believe that this section may apply to him in respect of a transaction

---

1 [1969] 3 All ER 275, [1971] AC 297, 45 Tax Cas 540

or transactions specified in the notification'. If, then, the person in question makes a statutory declaration to the effect that the section does not apply to him—

'stating the facts and circumstances upon which his opinion is based, and sends it to the Board, then subject to subsection (7) below, this section shall not apply to him in respect of the transaction or transactions.'

Subsection (7) enables the Board, if they see reason to take further action, to 'send to the tribunal', that is to say, the tribunal constituted under s 463 of the 1970 Act, 'a certificate to that effect, together with the statutory declaration, and may [and this is permissive only] also send therewith a counter-statement . . .' Under that subsection the tribunal has to take into account the declaration, the certificate and the counter-statement, if any, and has to determine whether there is or is not 'a prima facie case for proceeding in the matter'.

Since this case turns on the true construction and effect of sub-ss (6) and (7), I had better read them in full:

'(6) The Board shall not give a notice under subsection (3) above until they have notified the person in question that they have reason to believe that this section may apply to him in respect of a transaction or transactions specified in the notification; and if within thirty days of the issue of the notification the said person, being of opinion that this section does not apply to him as aforesaid, makes a statutory declaration to that effect stating the facts and circumstances upon which his opinion is based, and sends it to the Board, then subject to subsection (7) below, this section shall not apply to him in respect of the transaction or transactions.

'(7) If, when a statutory declaration has been sent to the Board under subsection (6) above, they see reason to take further action in the matter—(a) the Board shall send to the tribunal a certificate to that effect, together with the statutory declaration, and may also send therewith a counter-statement with reference to the matter; (b) the tribunal shall take into consideration the declaration and the certificate, and the counter-statement, if any, and shall determine whether there is or is not a prima facie case for proceeding in the matter, and if they determine that there is no such case this section shall not apply to the person in question in respect of the transaction or transactions . . .'

There is a proviso which is somewhat complicated and on which nothing turns which I will not read.

The facts of the case are these. On 11th April 1974 the Board notified the taxpayer in these terms:

'The Board of Inland Revenue hereby notify you, in accordance with subsection (6) of Section 460 of the Income and Corporation Taxes Act, 1970 that they have reason to believe that the said Section 460 (which relates to the cancellation of tax advantages from certain transactions in securities) may apply to you in respect of the transactions described overleaf. [The transactions described overleaf were these:] 1. On or about August 1970 the transfer by you and your wife of 100 Ordinary shares in Avernia Properties Ltd (hereinafter referred to as Avernia) to Averplex Ltd (hereinafter referred to as Averplex) in consideration for the issue of 100 Ordinary shares of Averplex at a premium of £136,279. 2. The declaration by Avernia of a dividend of £132,000 and the payment of that dividend on 9 October 1970. 3. The subscription by Retsor Trading Co Ltd (hereinafter referred to as Retsor) on 16 October 1970 for 998 shares of £1 each in Palega Investment Co Ltd (a company incorporated on 14 April 1970 and hereinafter referred to as Palega) at a premium for cash of £131,598. 4. The payment to you and your wife by Palega (before the transaction in (5) below) of the sums of £67,116 and £64,484 respectively by way of loans. 5. On or about 16 October *a*   1970 the acquisition by Averplex from Retsor of the whole of the share capital of Palega for a cash consideration of £131,850.'

On 7th May 1974 the taxpayer made a statutory declaration, which, omitting formal parts, was in these terms:

b   '1. The transactions set out in the notification by the Board of Inland Revenue to me dated 11th April 1974, took place as stated. 2. I assume that the tax advantage alleged by the Board of Inland Revenue consisted in the receipt by me and my wife of sums of £67,116 and £64,484 respectively by way of loan from Palega. While it is true that these sums were received in such a way that I did not pay or bear tax on them, there is no way in which I could have received the sums so as to pay or bear tax on them, so that the contrast which is required to establish a tax advantage is not to be found. Palega had no profits out of which
c   to pay any dividend, and if it had in some way managed to pay a dividend, it would not have been received by my wife or me, as we had no interest in the company. 3. The alleged tax advantage was not obtained or obtainable in consequence of a transaction in securities or of the combined effect of two or more such transactions, as the money was obtained in consequence of Palega lending money to us, the lending not being a transaction in securities. The notification
d   issued by the Board of Inland Revenue is not in order, as it purports to describe transactions in securities, whereas transaction number 4 in the list (being the lending of the money) is not a transaction in securities. The defect is not cured by the listing of other transactions which are transactions in securities.'

Then he goes on to say that the circumstances do not, for the reasons he gives in relation to each heading, fall within any of the alphabetical headings in s 461 of the
e   1970 Act, and continues:

'5. By reason of the above facts and circumstances I am of the opinion that section 460 of the Income and Corporation Taxes Act 1970 does not apply to me in respect of the transactions . . .'

f   The Board, by a letter dated 17th December 1974, sent by the Solicitor of Inland Revenue, informed the taxpayer as follows:

'I refer to your letter of 7th May 1974 to the Secretary (Taxes) enclosing a statutory declaration on behalf of your client. The Commissioners of Inland Revenue see reason to take further action in the matter, and I have today in accordance with Section 460(7), sent the declaration to the tribunal together with
g   a counter-statement on behalf of the Commissioners. In due course the tribunal will inform you of its determination. If the tribunal determines that there is a prima facie case for proceeding in the matter, I will, if you so request, let you have a copy of the counter-statement.'

From the counter-statement, if it be correct, it appears that the facts and circum-
h   stances were as I will state them in a moment, but the view I have taken of the matter is that the contents of the counter-statement are irrelevant. It was, however, referred to at very great length by counsel for the taxpayer and so I will say something about it.
From the counter-statement it appears that the taxpayer and his wife together held 100 shares being the whole of the issue share capital of Avernia. Avernia had undistributed profits derived from land transactions of the order of £136,000. Avernia
j   could have paid a dividend of that amount which would have attracted a liability for taxation which would have been borne directly or indirectly by the taxpayer. Alternatively, it might have lent the taxpayer £136,000 and, because the taxpayer controlled Avernia, it may be that the loan would never have been repaid. Had this latter course been adopted, a liability to tax would have been, as I understand it (I may be wrong), attracted by s 286 of the 1970 Act.

It is in those circumstances that transaction numbered (1) in the notification of 11th April 1974 took place. Averplex, which thereupon became the holder of all the *a* shares in Avernia, was an investment company. The result of the transaction was to throw up in Averplex a share premium account of £136,279. The situation then was that the taxpayer (I refer to him as the taxpayer for the purpose of brevity although his wife was a participant in the transactions) held the whole of the share capital of 100 shares in Averplex which, in turn, held 100 shares constituting the whole share capital of Avernia, where the £136,000-odd undistributed profit was to be found. *b* Avernia then declared a dividend of £132,000 and paid it to Averplex on 9th October 1970, that being the second of the transactions relied on by the Crown. A week later, on 16th October 1970 I think it was, Palega, a company not at that time controlled by the taxpayer, borrowed £128,000 and lent £131,060 to the taxpayer. That is the fourth transaction specified in the notice of 11th April, 1974. The company Retsor Trading Co Ltd, also on 16th October 1970, subscribed for 998 shares at £1 each in *c* Palega at a premium for cash of £131,598. Out of this money Palega repaid the money which it had borrowed. This was the third transaction specified in the notice of 11th April 1974. The taxpayer was still a debtor to Palega in £131,600 and Retsor was by then the owner of 998 shares in Palega. Then Retsor sold its shares in Palega to Averplex for £131,850, which is the transaction specified as numbered (5) in the notification of 11th April 1974. That resulted in the taxpayer controlling Palega, from *d* whom he had borrowed £136,000.

So the taxpayer still held the whole of the share capital in Averplex, and Averplex held the whole of the share capital in Palega, whose assets consisted of £131,600 owed by the taxpayer, and the taxpayer had received £131,600 from Palega and, through Averplex, controlled Palega.

Palega had become a wholly-owned subsidiary of Averplex and one view of the *e* matter is that, in effect, the undistributed profits which had originally been in Avernia had found their way into the hands of the taxpayer as a loan to him by a company which he indirectly controlled. The taxpayer's declaration reveals some of the beauty of the scheme.

As I have said, the counter-statement is a very long document. Apart from the fact that it shows the circumstances surrounding the transasctions in question, it *f* shows how the surplus profit in Avernia had been obtained in the course of transactions relating to land, and that taxation of that profit had been avoided. It shows that the taxpayer had, if the counter-statement is correct, had dealings of a somewhat exceptional character with those who controlled Palega and Averplex. It shows, if it is correct, that the taxpayer was very much concerned with tax avoidance. It shows beyond peradventure that the transactions in question were not commercial *g* transactions. It may, for all I know, have been inaccurate. It may have been tendentious. It may have had all the vices which counsel for the taxpayer attributed to it, but it is, in any event, a monument to the thoroughness, skill, care, patience and precision of the long-suffering officials whose duty it is to combat tax avoidance and I think it is my duty to say so. The taxpayer will have ample opportunity of showing what is wrong with it when the appeals hereinafter referred to come to be heard. *h*

In the light of the particulars of the transactions specified in the notification of 11th April 1974, which must, I think, have been put before the tribunal, the statutory declaration, the certificate and the counter-statement, the tribunal, on 10th February 1975, determined that there was a prima facie case for proceeding in the matter and notified the taxpayer to that effect.

By the notice dated 28th May 1975 issued in accordance with sub-s (3) of s 460, the *j* Board notified the taxpayer that the adjustments there described were requisite for counteracting the tax advantage obtained or obtainable by the taxpayer. At this stage of the litigation nothing turns on the terms of the notice. The taxpayer, on 25th June 1975, gave notice of appeal against the latter notice.

Subsequently, on 5th December 1975, the taxpayer received a notice of assessment containing an assessment to surtax for the year 1970-71 in respect of the sum of £132,691.

a   The taxpayer gave notice of appeal against that assessment. Again, nothing turns on that assessment at the present stage.

On 21st January 1976, the taxpayer, in response to an application, received a copy of the Board's counter-statement, and on 18th February 1976, the originating summons was taken out, to which the Board and members of the tribunal who had dealt with the matter were made defendants.

b   By the originating summons, which, as I have said, was dismissed by Oliver J, the taxpayer asked for it to be declared that each of the following documents, namely the notification dated 11th April 1974, the determination of the tribunal, the notice dated 28th May 1975 and the assessment to surtax for the year 1970-71, were null and void. He also asked for the declaration that the Board were not entitled to give effect to the notice served under s 460(3) of the section.

c   I turn to consider the submissions of the taxpayer on this appeal. In the first place, it is said that the notification of 11th April 1974 was null and void because, in effect, it did not, as on the true construction of sub-s (6) it ought to have done, disclose the reasons of the Board for believing that s 460 might apply to the taxpayer in respect of the specified transactions. Secondly, it was submitted that the determination of the tribunal under sub-s (7) of the section was invalidated by reason of the tribunal

d   having taken into consideration in arriving at that determination the counter-statement of the Board which did not, as on the true construction of sub-s (7) it ought to have done, confine itself to countering the taxpayer's statutory declaration, but sought to make a prima facie case by making reference to facts and transactions and raising claims and contentions which had not previously been disclosed by the Board to the taxpayer and which the taxpayer had no opportunity of answering.

e   As to the submission that the notification of 11th April 1974 was null and void because it did not disclose the reasons of the Board for their belief, it is to be observed at the outset that the subsection itself in terms contains nothing whatsoever to suggest that the Board are under any duty to do so. It provides quite simply that the Board are not to give a notice under sub-s (3) until they have notified the person in question

f   that they have reason to believe that s 460 may apply to him in respect of a transaction or transactions specified in the notification. As counsel for the Crown pointed out, the language of sub-s (6) in this regard, 'reason to believe that this section may apply', is in marked contrast to that relating to the statutory declaration which contemplates the taxpayer, being of opinion that s 460 does not apply to him, making a statutory declaration to that effect 'stating the facts and circumstances upon which his opinion is based'. Furthermore, as counsel for the Crown has pointed out, the notification

g   pursuant to sub-s (6) is not one of the documents which the Board in terms are required to send to the tribunal although, as a practical matter, it would, I think, have to be brought to their attention. Counsel's submission for the taxpayer as to the construction of sub-s (6), in my judgment, puts on it a construction which the language clearly cannot tolerate.

h   As to the submission that, on the true construction of sub-s (7), the counter-statement ought to confine itself to counteracting the taxpayer's statutory declaration, I find nothing in the subsection to support that submission. If it is correct that sub-s (6) does not contemplate, at the notification stage, that the Board should set out the facts and circumstances on which they rely in a submission that there is a prima facie case for proceeding with the matter, then it must be appropriate that the Board should

j   do so at the counter-statement stage. Where, as here, the taxpayer's statutory declaration did not state any positive facts and was in a negative form, stating that nothing was done to attract taxation, and did not explain the reasons for the transactions or the surrounding circumstances, it would have been a very serious defect in the procedure if the Board were prevented from doing the best they could to place the facts before the tribunal. With all respect to counsel for the taxpayer, the analogy which, at one stage of his argument, he sought to draw between the contemplated counter-statement and a 'reply' in an action is not a good analogy. Here, the 'statement of *a* claim', if it can properly be so described, as I do not think it can, would be the statutory declaration by the taxpayer setting out his 'case' and the 'counter-statement, would be by way of 'defence'. But it is wrong, in my judgment, in any event to draw such a comparison. On the language of the section the tribunal does not have to resolve an issue between the parties, but to determine whether there is or is not a prima facie case for proceeding in the matter. For the purpose of the determination the tribunal *b* is to be supplied with, firstly, a certificate to the effect that the Board see reason to take further action in the matter, secondly, the statutory declaration which will, of necessity, have been made, and, thirdly, if the Board think fit, a counter-statement with reference to the matter. There is nothing in the 1970 Act to control the contents of either the statutory declaration or the counter-statement, and I do not understand by what process of drafting such control could be imposed or, if there were such a *c* control, how it could be policed. The protection which a party has against infringement of the rules as to the contents of a pleading is to be found in the power to apply to have it, or the offending passages in it, struck out before and not after judgment.

Then one comes to counsel for the taxpayer's alternative, or perhaps the main, submission by which he invoked the doctrine of natural justice or fair play, which must be applied to procedure in judicial tribunals. He submitted that it was contrary to *d* that doctrine that the tribunal should determine that there is a prima facie case for proceeding in the matter without the taxpayer having had an opportunity of answering any statements or submissions made by the Board. 'Natural justice', I quote from the language of Lord Reid in *Wiseman v Borneman*[1]—

'requires that the procedure before any tribunal which is acting judicially shall be fair in all the circumstances, and I would be sorry to see this fundamental *e* general principle degenerate into a series of hard and fast rules. For a long time the courts have, without objection from Parliament, supplemented procedure laid down in legislation where they have found that to be necessary for this purpose. But before this unusual kind of power is exercised it must be clear that the statutory procedure is insufficient to achieve justice and that to require additional steps would not frustrate the apparent purpose of the legislation.' *f*

Counsel for the taxpayer submitted, as I have indicated, that before the tribunal can act consistently with the principles or doctrine of natural justice, and make the determination which calls to be made in the instant case, the taxpayer must have had the opportunity of knowing and answering the Board's submissions and the facts and circumstances on which the Board's submissions are based. Counsel's appeal for the taxpayer to natural justice, which is a formidable one, would, but *g* for a single circumstance, have had to be considered and dealt with at some considerable length in this judgment. The single circumstances, however, is that in *Wiseman v Borneman*[2] the submission that natural justice required that the taxpayer should see and have the opportunity of countering the Board's counter-statement was made and all their Lordships, Lord Wilberforce I think with some hesitation, rejected it. *h* It would, in my judgment, be to fly in the face of that authority to accept counsel for the taxpayer's submission in that regard. Furthermore, it having been decided by the House of Lords that natural justice does not require that the taxpayer should have the opportunity of seeing or answering the counter-statement, it must, in my judgment, follow that the taxpayer is not by the effect of the doctrine of natural justice entitled to have the reasons for the Board's opinion spelled out in the original notification under sub-s (6). I will not elaborate on this aspect of the case. The speeches *j* of the House of Lords are there for all to read and I think it would be wrong to attempt to summarise them or quote extracts from those speeches.

1　[1969] 3 All ER 275 at 277, [1971] AC 297 at 308, 45 Tax Cas 540 at 553
2　[1969] 3 All ER 275, [1971] AC 297, 45 Tax Cas 540

a Counsel for the taxpayer submitted that *Wiseman v Borneman*[1] was distinguishable on the ground that the transactions there particularised in the notification were such that the taxpayer could not be supposed not to have known what were the Board's reasons for their belief. If this point played any part in the decision, it is remarkable that none of the eminent counsel appearing for the Crown in that case, nor any of their Lordships, appears to have noticed or adverted to it. I would, how-ever, in that connection, add that it can hardly be doubted that the taxpayer in the

b instant case, when he received the notification, did appreciate what the Board had in mind. I do not find the facts of this case distinguishable in any relevant respect from those of *Wiseman v Borneman*[1].

    Counsel for the taxpayer referred us to a number of other authorities where the doctrine of natural justice has been applied or has fallen under discussion, but I derive no assistance from those cases, for, as Lord Russell remarked in one of them,

c all cases in which principles of natural justice are invoked must depend on the parti-cular circumstances of the case; see *Fairmount v Secretary of State for the Environment*[2]. Here we have in *Wiseman v Borneman*[1] a decision of the House of Lords in the context of the very section with which we have to deal.

    I must, for the purpose of the record, add this. The course the case took in the court below before Oliver J appears clearly from the report[3] and I need not describe it.

d There counsel for the Crown had submitted that the procedure by the originating summons was, in effect, not appropriate for the purposes of obtaining the relief sought. Indeed some to the arguments in the instant case appear to me to have some of the characteristics of arguments which would be appropriate on an appeal from the decision of the tribunal which, it is said, ought to have rejected the counter-statement of the Board. But what I have to say is simply this. Counsel for the Crown

e expressly reserved the submission that the procedure by originating summons for a declaration was wrong.

    I would dismiss the appeal.

ORR LJ. I agree.

f **GEOFFREY LANE LJ.** Counsel for the taxpayer, in his powerful argument, contends on behalf of the taxpayer that the Board have failed to observe the require-ments of s 460 of the Income and Corporation Taxes Act 1970 as those are properly to be construed. Consequently, he submits, the whole of the proceedings against the taxpayer in this matter are a nullity and his client is entitled to declarations accordingly.

g Speaking for myself, I very much doubt whether this is an appropriate method of appealing against the actions of the Board. However, the Crown, or counsel on its behalf, whilst wishing to keep this matter open for argument hereafter, did not base their arguments in this case on that point.

    The taxpayer's first submission is based on the wording of s 460(6) of the 1970 Act. The material words are these:

h   'The Board shall not give a notice under subsection (3) above until they have notified the person in question that they have reason to believe that this section may apply to him in respect of a transaction or transactions specified in the notification.'

    It is at least implicit in those words, so it is said, that in their original notification

j to the taxpayer the Board must state their reasons for believing that s 460 may apply to the taxpayer in respect of the specified transactions. Otherwise the recipient

---

1 [1969] 3 All ER 275, [1971] AC 297, 45 Tax Cas 540
2 [1976] 2 All ER 865 at 874, [1976] 1 WLR 1255 at 1265
3 [1977] 2 All ER 406, [1977] STC 148

of the notification will not know what it is that he has to answer in his statutory declaration.

That contention, in my view, cannot be supported. The section means what it says. All that the Board have to do is to notify the taxpayer that they have reason to believe that the section may apply in respect of the named transaction. If it had been intended that the Board should express the basis for that reason, or give any information other than the list of transactions involved, the section could very easily have said so. But it does not. Nor is there any need to imply such words into sub-s (6). It is to be noted that sub-s (7)(a), as Stamp LJ has already pointed out, does not even list the original notification as one of the documents that has to be sent to the tribunal in due course.

Next, it is submitted by counsel for the taxpayer that considerations of natural justice require that such a term should be implied in sub-s (6). The basis for that argument, as I understand it, is that Parliament is presumed not to intend to enact anything which is unfair or unjust. It would be unfair and unjust to require the taxpayer in a statutory declaration to answer a case which has not been fully expressed in the Board's notification. I take the view that this point has already been decided against the taxpayer by the decision of the House of Lords in *Wiseman v Borneman*[1]. It is said that the instant case could be distinguished from that decision because there the nature of the allegation was clearly a simple dividend-stripping operation, whereas here the allegation is much more complex and less easy to understand. It seems to me that is merely a difference in degree and not a true distinction at all.

In any event, this appeal to the rules of natural justice overlooks the true nature of s 460. The procedure laid down in that section, the three steps, that is, the notification by the Board, the statutory declaration by the taxpayer and the certificate, coupled possibly with the counter-statement by the Board, are designed to check any capricious, oppressive or misguided use by the Board of the considerable powers given to them by virtue of the section. They provide a summary method whereby the taxpayer in a proper case can demonstrate that the Board are mistaken in their suspicions, and can do so before the procedure to gather any tax has properly got under way. The list of transactions which the Board are required to append to the original notification would clearly be enough to make the taxpayer aware of the activities on his part which are being called in question. If they are in truth nothing to do with him, then he only has to say so. If they are his transactions, on the other hand, then the more complex they are the more likely it is that he will have been advised by experts in this recondite field of activity, who will no doubt be able to supply the necessary answer, if there is one, to be set out in the taxpayer's declaration. There is nothing unfair in that at all.

The final submission by counsel for the taxpayer, namely that the Board should be confined in their counter-statement to answering the taxpayer's statutory declaration and that the tribunal should not pay regard to anything in the counter-statement which goes beyond that rather narrow confine, is, in effect, already answered. If, as I believe to be so, the Board do not have to set out their case in the original notification, they must be allowed to do it in the counter-notice. Otherwise it may never appear at all. This point therefore also fails.

For these reasons, together with those already expressed by Stamp LJ, I, too, would dismiss this appeal.

Appeal dismissed. Leave to Appeal to the House of Lords refused.

Solicitors: *Tarlo, Lyons & Aukin* (for the taxpayer); *Solicitor of Inland Revenue*; *Treasury Solicitor*.

A S Virdi Esq Barrister.

1　[1969] 3 All ER 275, [1971] AC 297, 45 Tax Cas 540

C Czarnikow Ltd v Centrala Handlu Zagranicznego 'Rolimpex'

HOUSE OF LORDS

LORD WILBERFORCE, VISCOUNT DILHORNE, LORD SALMON, LORD FRASER OF TULLYBELTON AND LORD KEITH OF KINKEL

18th, 22nd, 23rd MAY, 6th JULY 1978

Force majeure – Sale of goods – Government intervention beyond seller's control – Seller a state trading organisation – Identity of government and seller – London Refined Sugar Association form of contract – Contract void if delivery prevented 'by Government intervention . . . beyond seller's control' – Polish state trading organisation entering into contract with English purchasers for export of sugar – Polish government imposing ban on exports due to crop failure – State organisation separate legal entity and not entitled to claim sovereign immunity but under supervision and accountable to department of Polish government – Whether organisation and the government the same – Whether prevention of delivery was due to 'Government intervention . . . beyond seller's control' – Rules of London Refined Sugar Association, r 18(a).

Sale of goods – Duty of seller – Export licence – Absolute or qualified duty – Force majeure – Government ban on all exports – Seller responsible for 'obtaining any necessary export licence' – Failure to obtain such licence not providing ground for claim of force majeure if at time contract made regulations requiring licence in force – Seller obtaining export licence – Export of sugar from Poland – Polish government imposing ban on all exports of sugar due to crop failure and revoking licences already granted – Whether seller under absolute duty to obtain licence which would remain valid until shipment – Rules of London Refined Sugar Association, rr 18(a), 21.

In 1974 the Polish state estimated tha* for the season 1974-75 enough sugar would be produced by the state to provide for domestic requirements and for export of a large quantity of sugar. Accordingly the state authorised an organisation called Rolimpex to enter into contracts with purchasers for the export from Poland of 200,000 metric tons of sugar. Rolimpex was a state trading organisation which was entrusted with the export and import of essential commodities such as sugar. Under Polish law it had a separate legal personality and was not entitled to claim sovereign immunity. It was, however, under the supervision of, and financially accountable to, the Minister of Foreign Trade and Shipping. He appointed Rolimpex's directors and, technically, had power to direct its trading activities although, in practice, Rolimpex generally made its own decisions on its trading activities. Like other Polish state enterprises Rolimpex was entitled to acquire, possess and use assets in its own name and to exercise rights of property. It was expected to make a profit. Pursuant to the state authorisation Rolimpex entered, in advance of the harvest, into two contracts with Czarnikow, an English company, for the sale to it of 17,000 metric tons of sugar. The contracts were subject to the Rules of the London Refined Sugar Association. By r 18(a) of the rules, if delivery in accordance with the contracts was prevented 'by Government intervention . . . or any [other] cause of force majeure . . . beyond the Seller's control', the contracts were to become void without payment of a penalty on compliance with the procedure specified in r 18(a). Under r 21 of the rules Romlipex was responsible for 'obtaining any necessary export licence' and failure to obtain such a licence did not entitle Rolimpex to claim force majeure if the regulations in force at the time when the contract was made called for an export licence. At the time when the contracts were made a licensing system in respect of the export of sugar was in force, and between May and August 1975 Rolimpex obtained export licences. Following bad weather in the autumn of 1974 the yield of sugar for the 1974-75 season fell below the estimated amount and was insufficient to provide both for domestic requirements and for export under the contracts entered into by Rolimpex. On 5th November the *a* Polish government, without consulting Rolimpex, decided to impose an immediate ban on the export of sugar and to revoke export licences already granted. On the same day a decree was signed by the Minister of Foreign Trade and Shipping giving legal effect to the ban from that date. Because of the ban, fulfilment of the first contract with Czarnikow was completely prevented and fulfilment of the second contract was partly prevented. Czarnikow claimed against Rolimpex for damages *b* for non-delivery. Rolimpex contended that it was exempt from liability on the ground of force majeure by 'Government intervention . . . beyond [its] control', within r 18(a) of the rules. The dispute went to arbitration. The arbitrators held that Rolimpex was protected by r 18(a) but stated a case for the decision of the court. The judge upheld the arbitrators' decision. Czarnikow appealed, contending (i) that as Rolimpex was a state trading organisation it could not rely on the ban on exports as *c* constituting 'Government intervention . . . beyond [its] control', within r 18(a), since Rolimpex and the government were the same and therefore no government intervention could be said to be beyond Rolimpex's control, and (ii) that, under r 21, Rolimpex was under an absolute duty to obtain export licences which would remain operative until shipment and was, therefore, liable for the failure to obtain such licences even though that failure had been due to the government ban. The Court of Appeal*ᵃ* *d* dismissed the appeal holding (i) that Rolimpex had a separate legal personality and could not be regarded as a department of the government and accordingly was entitled to rely on r 18(a) of the rules as a defence to Czarnikow's claim and (ii) that Rolimpex's failure to obtain export licences was due to government intervention and not to any failure to obtain licences and therefore Rolimpex was entitled to rely on force majeure under r 18(a) in respect of the failure to obtain export licences which *e* were valid until the goods were delivered. Czarnikow appealed to the House of Lords.

Held – (i) Although Rolimpex was an organisation of the Polish state, the evidence established that it had been set up as a separate entity with a separate legal personality. In those circumstances, it could not be regarded as a department of the government *f* or state and therefore because it had been prevented by 'government intervention' from performing its obligations under the contracts it was entitled to rely on r 18(a) of the rules to excuse it from liability for that failure (see p 1050 g, p 1051 f g, p 1052 c e, p 1054 j and p 1055 a e, post).

(ii) (Lord Salmon dissenting) The obligation imposed on the seller under r 21 to obtain a licence did not impose any obligation or warranty to maintain it in force until delivery was required to be made. Rolimpex, in obtaining export licences *g* between May and August 1975, had complied with its obligations under r 21 notwithstanding that the Polish government had subsequently cancelled all licences for the export of sugar. It followed therefore that Rolimpex was not prevented by r 21 from claiming that the contracts were void by reason of force majeure. Accordingly, the appeal would be dismissed (see p 1048 d to f, p 1051 c to g, p 1054 j and p 1055 *h* a to e, post).

Decision of the Court of Appeal [1978] 1 All ER 81 affirmed.

Notes

For force majeure clauses and contracts made subject to licence, see 9 Halsbury's Laws (4th Edn) paras 457, 459, and for cases on the subject, see 12 Digest (Reissue) *j* 491-502, 3466-3505, and 39 Digest (Repl) 809, 2747, 2748.

Cases referred to in opinions

Board of Trade v Temperley Steam Shipping Co Ltd (1926) 26 Ll L Rep 76; *affd* 27 Ll L Rep 230, CA, Digest (Cont Vol B) 649, *352a*.

---

a [1978] 1 All ER 81

Comrs of Crown Lands v Page [1960] 2 All ER 726, [1960] 2 QB 274, [1960] 3 WLR 446,
a   CA, 17 Digest (Reissue) 493, *138*.
Société d'Avances Commerciales (London) Ltd v A Besse & Co (London) Ltd [1952] 1 TLR
     644, [1952] 1 Lloyd's Rep 242, 39 Digest (Repl) 571, *978*.

Interlocutory appeal
This was an appeal by C Czarnikow Ltd ('Czarnikow') against the decision of the
b   Court of Appeal[1] (Lord Denning MR and Cumming-Bruce LJ, Geoffrey Lane LJ
     dissenting) dated 26th May 1977, affirming the judgment of Kerr J dated 13th Decem-
     ber 1976 which upheld an award stated in the form of a special case for the decision
     of the court by a panel of six arbitrators appointed by the Council of the Refined
     Sugar Association in accordance with the rules of the association to settle a dispute
     between Czarnikow and Centrala Handlu Zagranicznego 'Rolimpex' ('Rolimpex')
c   of Warsaw, Poland, arising out of two contracts made in the summer of 1974 for
     the purchase of sugar by Czarnikow from Rolimpex. The arbitrators dismissed
     Czarnikow's claim for damages for non-delivery of about 14,300 metric tons
     of Polich white sugar fob Polish ports in November/December 1974 on the
     ground that Rolimpex was exempted from liability by the force majeure clause
     contained in r 18(a) of the rules which applied to a ban on the export of sugar
d   imposed by the Polish government on 5th November 1974. The facts are set out in the
     opinion of Lord Wilberforce.

Anthony Evans QC and *David Johnson* for Czarnikow.
Michael Mustill QC, Andrew Longmore and *T Saloman* for Rolimpex.

Their Lordships took time for consideration.

e
6th July. The following opinions were delivered.

LORD WILBERFORCE. My Lords, this appeal arises out of two contracts for
the purchase of sugar by the appellant ('Czarnikow') from the respondent ('Rolim-
f   pex'). Each contract was made subject to the rules of the Refined Sugar Association
and expressly provided that the performance of the contract was subject to force
majeure as defined in the association's rules. There are two relevant rules. Rule
18(a) applies if the delivery in whole or in part within the delivery time should be
prevented or delayed directly or indirectly by (inter alia) government intervention
and provides, as is usual, for an extension and ultimately for cancellation of the
g   contract. Rule 21 deals with licences and is in the following terms:

> 'The Buyer shall be responsible for obtaining any necessary import licence
> and the Seller shall be responsible for obtaining any necessary export licence.
> The failure to obtain such licence/s shall not be sufficient grounds for a claim
> of force majeure if the regulations in force at the time when the contract was
> made, called for such licence/s to be obtained.'

h
The contracts were made in May and July 1974 (subject to addenda of later dates)
and were forward sales for delivery in November/December 1974. Rolimpex thus
assumed the risk of a rise in the price of sugar between the contract date and the
date of delivery.
     Since Rolimpex failed to deliver any of the 11,000 metric tons provided for by the
j   first contract and part of the tonnage provided for by the second contract, it would
be liable to Czarnikow for substantial damages unless it could rely on force majeure.
     Rolimpex is a state trading organisation of the Polish State. It obtains sugar re-
quired for export from the sugar industry enterprises represented by the Union of Sugar

---

1   [1978] 1 All ER 81, [1978] QB 176

Industries in Poland. The relation between the latter body and Rolimpex is that Rolimpex sells as 'commission merchant', ie it sells in its own name but only for a commission and on account of the sugar industry enterprises concerned. The contracts now in question were no doubt intended to be satisfied from the 1974 sugar crop in Poland. It is found that the Polish national economic plan required a total sugar production of 1,835,000 metric tons for the season 1974-75. Of this, 1,500,000 metric tons was required for the domestic market and the balance was authorised for export. In May 1974 Rolimpex was authorised to contract for the export of 200,000 metric tons.

In August 1974 there was heavy rain and flooding in the sugar beet producing areas. The result was that only 1,432,000 metric tons were produced, a shortfall even on on the amount required for domestic consumption. On 5th November 1974 a resolution of the Council of Ministers was passed banning the export of sugar with effect from 5th November 1974 and cancelling export licences. This resolution was found not to have the force of law. However, later on 5th November 1974 the Minister of Foreign Trade and Shipping signed a decree providing:

> '1. From 5th November 1974 it is prohibited to release export deliveries of sugar specified by present contracts. 2. Customs Authorities shall immediately stop the deliveries of sugar prepared for export and notify disposers about the prohibition of sugar export. 3. The Rule is in force from the date of its signature.'

This made the export of sugar illegal by Polish law.

It was found by the arbitrators that on 5th November 1974 there was a considerable quantity of sugar at the port of Gdynia and a further quantity on the way to Gdynia by rail. But for the ban, sugar would have been available for the performance by Rolimpex of both contracts. It was also found that both before and after 15th November 1974 (the date when Czarnikow was able to ship) there was Polish sugar of the contract quality available on the market. If there were insufficient quantities available, there was a market for the purchase and sale of other sugar of equivalent quality. In the condition of the market any purchaser would have accepted any sugar of equivalent quality in substitution for Polish sugar. The market value of the relevant quality of sugar on 15th November was however 7,500 French francs per metric ton as compared with 3,064 French francs, the price fixed for one contract and about 4,000 French francs for the other.

The export ban remained in operation until 1st July 1975. Rolimpex declared force majeure on 6th November 1974, and, if it was entitled to do so, both contracts became void.

Rolimpex referred the matter to the Council of the Refined Sugar Association in accordance with the association's rules. The council appointed a panel of six arbitrators in respect of the dispute. They heard evidence over a hearing of ten days. In their award the arbitrators found (inter alia) that sugar was available on the world market to meet the shortage in the Polish market but the Council of Ministers resolved not to purchase sugar on the world market because of the high price and the loss of foreign exchange that such a purchase would have entailed; that the ban was imposed to relieve the anticipated shortage in the domestic market; that its effect was to throw the losses caused by the partial failure of the Polish sugar crop on overseas traders and consumers, thus saving the Polish state having to bear any financial loss in replacing the sugar sold well in advance of the 1974-75 campaign. They added this unusual observation:

> '(a) We very much regret that the Council of Ministers authorised the ban rather than permitting the purchase of sugar on the world market, so enabling Rolimpex to honour its contractual obligations.'

A further group of findings contained the following:

> '(b) The persons employed in Rolimpex did not induce the Council of Ministers

a   to authorise the ban and did not influence its continuance or effect. (c) Rolimpex is an organisation of the Polish state. (d) Rolimpex is not so closely connected with the Government of Poland that is it precluded from relying on this ban (imposed for the reasons set out above) as "Government intervention" within r 18(a) of the Rules of the Refined Sugar Association. (e) Rolimpex is accordingly entitled to rely on r 18(a) as a defence to Czarnikow's claims.'

b   The award having been stated in the form of a special case, the matter came before the court with two main questions for decision. 1. Was this a case of government intervention within r 18(a)? 2. Was the case taken out of r 18(a) by the provisions of r 21? There was also a question (of very considerable difficulty) as to the measure of damages.

    Questions 1 and 2 were answered by Kerr J in favour of Rolimpex, i e Yes and No, respectively. The Court of Appeal[1] (Lord Denning MR and Cumming-Bruce LJ) affirmed this decision. Geoffrey Lane LJ dissented, holding that question 2 should be answered in the affirmative.

c   Consideration of question 1 can conveniently start from the arbitrators' finding (b) above. It was the case of Czarnikow before the arbitrators that there was some kind of collusion or conspiracy between Rolimpex and the government of Poland by which the government was persuaded, in the interests of Rolimpex, to impose the ban. In order to deal with this, Rolimpex produced a quantity of evidence to show that there was no such collusion or conspiracy; on the contrary, when the possibility of a ban on exports was mentioned to the director and general manager of Rolimpex before 6th November 1974 he protested about it and the persons employed in Rolimpex were not consulted about the imposition of the ban and were not informed of the ban until after its imposition. The arbitrators found that Czarnikow had failed to prove its allegation that the ban was imposed after consultation between the persons employed in Rolimpex and the Ministry of Foreign Trade and Shipping. The ban was in fact requested by the Minister of Food and Agricultural Industries on the grounds that it was unacceptable to put the people of Poland on short rations and other alternatives were unacceptable. There being disagreement among the Ministers (including the Minister of Foreign Trade and Shipping who supervises Rolimpex) the matter was referred to the Council of Ministers which passed the resolution of 5th November 1974 (see above). There was thus ample evidence to support the arbitrators' finding against collusion or conspiracy.

g   Before the courts and this House Czarnikow took a different line. It appealed to a group of English cases dealing with actions taken by or on behalf of the Crown in which a distinction has been made, broadly, between acts which are performed by a government for the public good or for a general executive purpose and acts which a government does so as to avoid liability under a contract or contracts (see *Board of Trade v Temperley Steam Shipping Co Ltd*[2] and *Comrs of Crown Lands v Page*[3] per Devlin LJ). Lord Denning MR was disposed to hold that this distinction might be applied to the present case if, but only if, Rolimpex was to be regarded as a department of government: he then proceeded to hold that it was not. I have very great doubt whether the doctrine developed by these cases, which is very much one of English constitutional law, can viably be transplanted into the constitutional climate of foreign states, particularly such states as Poland which we are entitled to know have an entirely different constitutional structure from ours. Such a transplantation, if possible at all, would involve English courts in difficult and delicate questions as to the motivation of a foreign state, and as to the concept of public good, which would be unlikely to correspond with ours. I am not saying that there may not be cases when it

1   [1978] 1 All ER 81, [1978] QB 176
2   (1926) 26 Ll L Rep 76
3   [1960] 2 All ER 726 at 736, [1960] 2 QB 274 at 293, 294

is so clear that a foreign government is taking action purely in order to extricate a state enterprise from contractual liability, that it may be possible to deny to such action *a* the character of government intervention, within the meaning of a particular contract, but that result cannot, in my opinion, be achieved by means of the doctrine mentioned above: it would require clear evidence and definite findings. It is certain that no such evidence or findings exist in the present case. On the contrary, the evidence is that the action was taken to avoid serious domestic, social and political effects and to avoid loss of foreign exchange if high price sugar were to be bought on *b* the world market. The arbitrators indeed so found.

I agree however wholly with Lord Denning MR that Rolimpex cannot on the evidence be regarded as an organ of the Polish state. The award does indeed use the words 'an organisation of the Polish state' but read with the evidence this can mean no more than that it was set up by the Polish state and controlled by the Polish state: in their next finding quoted above, the arbitrators find that Rolimpex is not *c* so closely connected with the government of Poland that it is precluded from relying on the ban as government intervention, a finding not as clear as it might be but, in the light of the evidence, meaning necessarily that Rolimpex is not an organ or department of the state. The independence of Rolimpex from the government is in my opinion amply demonstrated by the facts set out at length in the award. Together with all four learned judges who have considered this point, I find the conclusion *d* clear, and I therefore hold that the seller makes good the contention that there was government intervention within r 18.

The second question is whether r 21 operates as a saving clause which, in the circumstances, takes the case out of r 18. I am afraid that I can find no substance in this argument. Rule 21 appears in a section of the rules headed 'Licences'. In my opinion it does no more than to place on the seller the obligation to obtain an export licence *e* (and on the buyer to obtain an import licence) and to state that failure to fulfil this obligation shall not be a sufficient ground for a claim of force majeure. The word 'obtain' in this context means 'obtain' or 'get' and I can not read into it any obligation or warranty to maintain it in force. Rolimpex complied with this obligation and the clause is satisfied. I agree entirely with the disposition of this point by Kerr J. I would dismiss the appeal. *f*

VISCOUNT DILHORNE. My Lords, under two contracts made in 1974 the appellant ('Czarnikow') agreed to buy from the respondent ('Rolimpex') quantities of sugar f o b. Each contract incorporated the rules of the Refined Sugar Association and this appeal is as to the meaning and effect of rll 18(a) and 21 of those rules.

Under the Polish economic plan 1,835,000 metric tons of sugar were to be produced *g* in the 1974-75 season. It was estimated that 1,500,000 metric tons would be required for domestic consumption and 335,000 metric tons were allocated for export. In May 1974 Rolimpex was authorised to contract for the export of 200,000 metric tons thereof and the contracts made with Czarnikow were pursuant to that authority.

In that season due to bad weather only 1,432,000 metric tons were produced, and in October 1974 the Minister of Food and Agricultural Industries told the Prime *h* Minister of Poland that the sugar produced would not cover domestic needs, and that Rolimpex was insisting nevertheless on the export of the 200,000 metric tons for which it had concluded contracts. He suggested that there should be an immediate ban on the export of sugar 'as it was socially and politically unacceptable to put the people of Poland on short rations and other alternatives were also unacceptable'.

On 5th November 1974 this was considered at a meeting of the Council of Ministers. *j* It was decided that an immediate ban on the export of sugar should be imposed and it was resolved:

'1. Sugar export is banned commencing 5th November 1974. 2. Export licences granted hitherto are cancelled. 3. Minister of Foreign Trade and Shipping *a* shall issue without delay respective decrees in order to strictly execute this provision. 4. The resolution is carried into effect on the passing date.'

That afternoon a decree, which had the force of law in Poland, was signed by the Minister of Foreign Trade and Shipping. It read as follows:

b 'On the basis of paragraph 3 of the Resolution of the Council of Ministers on the 5th November 1974 related to a prohibition to export sugar, the following is made to apply: 1. From 5th November 1974 it is prohibited to release export deliveries of sugar specified by present contracts. 2. Customs Authorities shall immediately stop the deliveries of sugar prepared for export and notify disposers about the prohibition of sugar export. 3. The Rule is in force from the date of its signature.'

c This ban remained in force until 1st July 1975, so from 5th November 1974 till then the export of sugar from Poland was illegal. Sugar which Rolimpex had contracted to deliver to Czarnikow f o b could not consequently be delivered. By telex on 5th November Rolimpex told Czarnikow of the ban and Czarnikow replied saying that it did not accept that delivery of sugar already contracted for could be stopped in that manner. The next day Rolimpex told Czarnikow that it was a case of force majeure.

d The rules of the Refined Sugar Association contain a chapter headed 'Force Majeure'. That chapter contains rr 17 to 20. Rule 18(a) is relevant to this case and so far as material reads as follows:

e 'Should the delivery in whole or in part within the delivery time specified be prevented or delayed directly or indirectly by Government intervention ... beyond the Seller's control, the Seller shall immediately advise the Buyer ... of such fact and of the quantity so affected, and the period of delivery shall be extended by 30 days for such quantity ... If delivery is still prevented by the end of the extended period, the Buyer shall have the option of cancelling the contract for the affected quantity or of taking delivery at the contract price without claiming damages as soon as the sugar can be delivered ... Should the Buyer elect not to cancel the contract but delivery of the sugar in whole or in *f* part still remains impossible 60 days after the last delivery date provided for by the contract, the contract shall be void for such quantity without penalty payable or receivable '

It is in my opinion clear beyond all doubt that delivery of the sugar in pursuance of the contracts within the delivery time was prevented by the intervention of the *g* government of Poland. It is, I think, equally clear that the action taken by the government was beyond Rolimpex's control. The facts found by the arbitrators show, as I have said, that Rolimpex had insisted on the export of the 200,000 metric tons it had contracted to sell, and also that on 5th November when informed of the possibility of the ban, its director and general manager had protested. Nevertheless the ban was imposed.

h Czarnikow contended that 'Government intervention' in r 18(a) should be interpreted to mean only intervention for what was called a general executive purpose; that the decree was imposed to achieve a particular result in relation to the contracts for the export of sugar, and that intervention for such a purpose was not to be regarded as government intervention within the meaning to be given to those words in r 18(a). The particular result which it was Rolimpex's purpose to achieve was, it was *j* alleged, to throw the losses caused by the failure of the sugar crop on to overseas traders and consumers and to avoid it being borne by the Polish state.

Rule 18(a) clearly requires it to be established if the force majeure relied on is government intervention. It does not stipulate that, if there is such intervention, one has to go on to consider for what purpose the intervention was made. I do not find it necessary in this case to consider whether a government intervention which

has in fact occurred, can be treated as not having occurred if it be established that
it was to secure a particular result such as that alleged by Czarnikow, for the facts *a*
found by the arbitrators in their award, in my view clearly negative the contention
that it was for that particular purpose. They found that Poland was faced with a
shortage of sugar if all contracts for the export of sugar were performed, that the
Council of Ministers feared that the shortage of sugar in the home market would
have serious domestic social and political effects, that sugar was available on the
world market to meet the shortage but that the Council of Ministers resolved not to *b*
purchase on the world market because of the high price of sugar and the loss of
foreign exchange that such a purchase would have entailed and that the ban 'was
accordingly imposed to relieve the anticipated shortage in the domestic market'.
Presumably this purpose was achieved. The arbitrators say that the effect of the ban
was—

> 'to throw the losses caused by the partial failure of the Polish sugar crop on *c*
> overseas traders and consumers thus saving the Polish State having to bear
> any financial loss in replacing the sugar sold well in advance of the 1974/75
> campaign.'

While this was a consequence of the ban, its purpose as stated by the arbitrators
was not that but to relieve the anticipated shortage on the home market.   *d*

The foundation for this contention by Czarnikow is not there and so it is unnecessary to consider what effect, if any, it would have had it been.

Czarnikow do not say that Rolimpex is to be identified with the Polish government.
Rolimpex is an organisation of the state. Under Polish law it has a legal personality.
Though subject to directions by the appropriate Minister who can tell it 'what to
do and how to do it', as a state enterprise it makes its own decisions about its commer- *e*
cial activities. It decides with whom it will do business and on what terms and it has
considerable freedom in its day to day activities. It is managed on the basis of economic accountability and is expected to make a profit. The arbitrators in my opinion
rightly found as a fact that Rolimpex was not so closely connected with the government of Poland as to be precluded from relying on the ban imposed by the decree
as government intervention.   *f*

Czarnikow also asserted that Rolimpex bought and sold for the state. This while
no doubt true, does not in my view help Czarnikow. The facts found by the arbitrators stated above show that it was not a department of the government but has
a separate identity. It was, it was found as a fact, employed as 'a commission merchant' to sell sugar intended for export on behalf of sugar industry enterprises which
were also state enterprises. The fact that it did so cannot, in my opinion, invalidate *g*
the decree made on 5th November. So if r 18(a) stood alone, Rolimpex is in my
opinion entitled to rely on it as excusing it from liability for non-delivery of the sugar
within the period stipulated in the contracts.

Czarnikow, however, say that it is prevented from doing so by r 21. That rule is
headed by the word 'Licences', and is clearly designed to deal with the situation
where at the time when a contract is made a licence is required for export or for *h*
import. It reads as follows:

> '21. The Buyer shall be responsible for obtaining any necessary import licence
> and the Seller shall be responsible for obtaining any necessary export licence.
> The failure to obtain such licence/s shall not be sufficient grounds for a claim
> of force majeure if the regulations in force at the time when the contract was *j*
> made called for such licence/s to be obtained.'

Export licences for sugar were required when the contracts were made between
Czarnikow and Rolimpex. The first sentence of this rule imposes a collateral obligation on the buyer to obtain any necessary import licence and on the seller to

obtain any necessary export licence. But what is the extent of this obligation? Czar-
a nikow contend that Rolimpex undertook by undertaking to obtain any necessary
export licence, not only to get but also to have at the time that delivery was required
to be made, a valid licence under which the delivery could be made, and that the
licences it had having been cancelled by the decree, it was in breach of this obligation.
In those circumstances, it says, the second sentence of the rule prevents Rolimpex
from relying on force majeure.

b If this is the right construction of the rule, it would mean that where a licensing
system was in force at the time of the contract, the words 'Government intervention'
in r 18(a) would have little, if any, significance. Never could the seller in any country
rely on that rule if the government of that country placed an embargo on export
and a licence for export was required both at the time of the contract and at the time
for delivery.

c I do not think that this is the right construction to be placed on the rule. I do not
think that it was ever intended to have such a far-reaching effect. I see no reason for
giving the words 'obtaining' which appears twice in the rule and 'obtained' any other
than their natural meaning which in my view is 'getting' and 'got', and I agree with
my noble and learned friend, Lord Fraser of Tullybelton, whose speech in draft I
have now had the advantage of reading, that for the reasons he gives, the word 'neces-
d sary' in r 21 gives no assistance to Czarnikow.

If it was the intention of the parties that in addition to the getting of any necessary
licence, the buyer in the case of an import licence and the seller in the case of an
export licence undertook to have and warranted that he would have a valid import
or export licence when the time came for importation or for delivery, I would have
expected express provision to have been made for that as it was in a clause in the cif
e contract under consideration in *Société d'Avances Commerciales (London) Ltd v A Besse &
Co (London) Ltd*[1]. The word 'obtaining' is in my view too slender a peg to sustain the
weight of such a far-reaching obligation.

The second sentence of the rule is in my opinion of limited effect. It merely provides that failure to get a necessary licence shall not of itself suffice to justify a claim
of force majeure.

f In this case the cause of the non-delivery was government intervention not failure
to obtain an export licence.

For these reasons, in my opinion, this appeal fails and should be dismissed. It is
not necessary to consider to what damages Czarnikow would have been entitled had
its appeal succeeded.

g **LORD SALMON.** My Lords, I need not recite the two contracts entered into
between Rolimpex and Czarnikow in May and July 1974, nor r 18(a) of the Refined
Sugar Association's rules incorporated in these contracts, nor the export ban imposed
by the Polish government on 5th November 1974, nor the basic facts concerning the
dispute between the parties to this appeal, for these are all fully and lucidly set out
in the speeches of my noble and learned friends, Lord Wilberforce and Viscount
h Dilhorne.

One of the allegations which had been unsuccessfully made in the arbitration
by Czarnikow was that the ban which I have mentioned had been planned or plotted
between Rolimpex and the Polish government in order to force a substantial increase
in the price of the sugar sold under the contracts to which I have referred. The
arbitrators held that this allegation had no foundation in fact. Counsel for Czarnikow
j quite rightly, never challenged this finding; the evidence referred to in the award
clearly established that Rolimpex had no knowledge of the ban until after it was
made and that the Minister of Foreign Trade and Shipping, who supervised
Rolimpex's business, had strongly opposed the imposition of the ban.

---

1 [1952] 1 Lloyd's Rep 242

Counsel for Czarnikow did, however, argue that Rolimpex was, in fact, part of the Polish government and that therefore the ban caused by the intervention of that government could not be recognised as being 'beyond the Seller's control within the meaning of those words in r 18(a); and that accordingly it followed that Rolimpex could not be excused on the ground of force majeure from fulfilling its obligations under the contracts sale. This argument was most skilfully developed but it faced the insuperable difficulty that it was contrary to the arbitrator's findings of fact.

The arbitrators found in para 50(d) of the award that Rolimpex was not so closely connected with the Polish government that it was precluded from relying on the ban. I do not overlook the finding in para 50(c) of the award that Rolimpex was 'an organisation of the Polish state'. These words are, however, very loose and imprecise and must be read in the light of the findings of fact in paras 21 to 29 of the award. It is clear from these findings that Rolimpex was set up by the state as a separate entity. It was known as a state enterprise and registered as such. This gave it in Polish law a 'legal personality'. Some of the consequences of Rolimpex's legal personality and economic accountability are that the state Treasury is not responsible for its obligations and it is not responsible for the obligations of the state Treasury; nor is it entitled, under Polish law, to claim sovereign immunity. Although Rolimpex is under the general supervision of the Minister for Foreign Trade and he has the power to tell it 'what to do and how to do it', Rolimpex generally makes its own decisions about its own business and has substantial freedom in its day-to-day activities. Rolimpex carries on business as commission merchant on a very large scale. It has a virtual monopoly of selling, on commission, in its own name, all the sugar intended for export and produced by the various state enterprises. It also sells on commission many other commodities intended for export and produced by other state enterprises. In my view, the arbitrators were justified in refusing to hold that Rolimpex was an organ or a department of the government or the state. Accordingly, I agree that but for r 21 (which I shall presently consider) Rolimpex would have a complete defence under r 18(a) to the claim brought against it by Czarnikow for failure to perform its obligations under the contract.

I do not express any concluded opinion as to what the position might have been, in law, had the facts as found by the arbitrators established that Rolimpex was an organ or department of the government or of the state. I am inclined to the view that, in such circumstances, the facts as found in para 50(a) of the award may nevertheless have been expressed without sufficient clarity to establish with the necessary certainty that the ban was not imposed 'for the public good' or for 'a general executive purpose' but only for the purpose of extricating the government from its obligation under the contracts of sale. If the findings had been so expressed, I would agree with Lord Denning MR that Rolimpex, in the circumstances postulated, would have been precluded from relying on r 18(a): see *Comrs of Crown Lands v Page*[1] per Devlin LJ and *Board of Trade v Temperley Steam Shipping Co Ltd*[2] per Roche J.

In my view para 50(a) of the award is somewhat ambiguous. Naturally the Council of Ministers feared that a shortage of sugar in the home market would have serious domestic, social and political effects. But there was no risk of such a shortage because the council had one of two alternative means of preventing it: (i) there was plenty of sugar available for sale on the world market to avoid the shortage which would otherwise have occurred on the home market if Rolimpex had honoured its obligations under its contracts with Czarnikow and other buyers for exporting 200,000 metric tons of sugar; or, (ii) the contracts for exporting 200,000 metric tons of sugar could all have been torn up and a total ban on exports imposed; then the home produced sugar, freed from export, would have supplied virtually all the sugar required on the home market.

---

1   [1960] 2 All ER 726 at 736, [1960] 2 QB 274 at 293, 294
2   (1926) 26 Ll LR 76

If the latter course were followed, it could have been accompanied by paying
a reasonable compensation to all the foreign buyers. Rolimpex did adopt the latter
course but did not pay any compensation.

According to the findings in para 50(a)(iii) of the award, 'the Council of Ministers
resolved not to purchase sugar on the world market because of the high price and
the loss of foreign exchange that such a purchase would have entailed'. There
is no finding as to whether this loss of foreign exchange would or would not have
b seriously affected Polish currency. If it would have done so, then the Ministers'
decision to do as they did could have been justified on the ground that they were
acting for the public good and for a general executive purpose. If, on the other hand,
the currency would not have been affected and Rolimpex had been part of the
government or the state, it would only have been evading a financial loss on the
forward contracts into which it had entered and could not, in my view, have sheltered
c behind r 18(a).

Paragraph 50(a)(iv) of the award makes it plain that the ban had been imposed to relieve the anticipated shortage in the domestic market: but this step was
taken only because it had been decided not to buy the sugar which was readily available on the world market and would equally have relieved any home shortage. For
my part I am not at all surprised by the comment in para 50(a)(v) of the award:
d 'We very much regret that the Council of Ministers authorised the ban rather than
permitting the purchase of sugar on the world market, so enabling Rolimpex to
honour its contractual obligations'. Since, however, Rolimpex was not found to be
an organ or department of the government of the state, it is unnecessary to express
any concluded view on what should have been the result had such a finding been made.

I now turn to consider the effect of r 21 of the Refined Sugar Association's rules
e which was also incorporated in the contracts of sale. It reads as follows:

> 'The Buyer shall be responsible for obtaining any necessary import licence and
> the seller shall be responsible for obtaining any necessary export licence. The
> failure to obtain such licence/s shall not be sufficient grounds for a claim of
> force majeure if the regulations in force at the time when the contract was made
f > called for such licence/s to be obtained.'

The regulations in force in Poland at the time the contracts were made called for
licences to be obtained.

Someone had to take the risk that the necessary export licences might become
unobtainable or be cancelled. In my opinion, it was Rolimpex who accepted the
responsibility for obtaining such licences and the risk that it might fail to do so.
g If it failed from any cause, obviously it could not deliver the sugar it had sold: but
it would then be liable to compensate the buyers for any damage the buyers had
suffered as a result of the non-delivery.

I do not think that there is any difficulty about the meaning of the word 'obtain' in
r 21. It means simply to 'get'. The obligation is merely to get 'any necessary export
licence'. This prompts the question 'necessary for what?' In my opinion, in order to
h make any commercial sense out of the rule, it can only be referring to a licence
necessary to enable the sugar sold to be cleared through customs and loaded on
board ship.

If the seller obtains a document purporting to be an export licence, but before
the shipment is due, the document is cancelled, or for any other cause does not
enable the sugar to be cleared through customs and loaded on board then, in my
j view, the seller has failed to obtain or get a *'necessary'* export *'licence'*; and he is
precluded from relying on force majeure to escape from his liability to pay compensation to the buyer for his failure to deliver under the contracts. I would add
that it is, in my view, impossible for a seller to know for certain whether he has
obtained a necessary export licence until he presents it to the customs authorities
and they clear the goods on the strength of it.

It was argued on behalf of Rolimpex that the rules of the game were changed when the ban on exports came into force on 5th November 1974 because the whole licensing system was temporarily put out of action by government intervention and r 21 no longer had any application. I am afraid that I cannot accept that argument. I entirely agree with the judgment of Geoffrey Lane LJ[1] and gratefully adopt the following passage in his judgment:

'To say that that which caused the failure to deliver was the ban on exports rather that the absence of a valid licence . . . is to draw a distinction without a difference. A ban on exports means a refusal to permit exports. A licence to export is a permit to export. Therefore the ban is no more and no less than a withdrawal of any existing licences and a refusal to grant any further licence for the time being.'

It seems to me that one of the most obvious risks which r 21 envisaged and Rolimpex accepted was that the necessary export licences might be unobtainable by reason of government intervention whether in the form of a ban on the export of sugar or in any other form. Once Rolimpex contracted to shoulder the risk of failing to obtain the necessary export licences, the reasons why it failed to do so became irrelevant. In my opinion, an export licence is, in reality, no more and no less than government permission to export.

Export licences are wholly unlike dog licences or television licences which are issued automatically on the payment of a fee and the completion of a form. It is incredible that there should be government intervention of any kind in respect of such licences. Not so in respect of export licences. These are normally issued by a department of government and depend on government policy, which alters from time to time. The department concerned may, on behalf of the government, decide not to issue a licence or to cancel an issued licence, in its own discretion, or as a result of a decree or direction emanating from the government itself.

At the time when these forward contracts were entered into, it must have been forseen that before the stipulated delivery date, the Polish government might well intervene by preventing export licences from being issued and cancelling any such licences as had been issued. This, in my opinion, was a risk which fell on Rolimpex under r 21. To construe this rule otherwise emasculates it and deprives Rolimpex of the protection which it purports to afford them.

Rule 18(a) cites, first, government intervention and then ten other specific examples of force majeure. Any of these, unless excluded by some provision in the contract, would afford a valid defence to Rolimpex if it prevented or delayed delivery under the contract. So far as Rolimpex's contractual obligations are concerned, r 21 preserves only its obligation to obtain the necessary export licences; otherwise Rolimpex's escape routes under r 18(a) for failure to deliver, or a delay in delivery, are left intact. I consider, however, that r 21 makes it plain that Rolimpex cannot escape from its failure to obtain the necessary export licence on the ground of government intervention or any other ground of force majeure, certainly not without implying or writing into r 21 after the words 'force majeure' the words 'unless caused by Government intervention'. I cannot find any jurisdiction for doing so. Far from it being necessary to emasculate r 21 in order to give business efficacy to the contract, I consider that it makes far better commercial sense as it stands.

I would accordingly allow the appeal.

LORD FRASER OF TULLYBELTON. My Lords, I have had the advantage of reading in draft the speech of my noble and learned friend, Lord Wilberforce, and I agree with it.

---

1   [1978] 1 All ER 81 at 94, [1978] QB 176 at 201

On the arbitrators' findings in this case there is no doubt that there was government intervention in the sense of r 18. At one time I was inclined to attribute more
importance than some of your Lordships do to r 21, and to think that it was intended
to place on the seller an obligation to obtain an export licence which would be effective at the time of exporting. But further reflection has satisfied me that for the
reasons stated by my noble and learned friend, Viscount Dilhorne, to construe r 21
in that way would involve reading into the word 'obtain' more than it can fairly bear.
Nor does it seem to me that the word 'necessary' helps. In the context of r 21, the
word must imply that there is in force a licensing system of such a character that, if
the necessary licence is obtained, it would be effective to allow the seller to export
the goods which he had contracted to sell. But if the licensing system is abolished or
(as in the present case) superseded, with the result that no licence can be effective
during the period of suspension, r 21 does not have the effect of imposing on the seller
an absolute obligation to obtain government permission to export the goods; if it did,
it would remove almost the whole of the protection against government intervention
given to him by r 18. I agree with Cumming-Bruce LJ in the Court of Appeal[1] that—

> 'His [the seller's] obligation though absolute is more restricted, and is only to
> obtain from the licensing department or authority evidence of such permission
> to export as is within the ordinary scope of the licensing system that the depart-
> ment is concerned with.'

I would dismiss the appeal.

LORD KEITH OF KINKEL. My Lords, I have had the opportunity of reading in
draft the speech of my noble and learned friend, Lord Wilberforce. I agree with it,
and for the reasons he gives I too would dismiss the appeal.

Appeal dismissed.

Solicitors: *William A Crump & Son* (for Czarnikow); *Norton Rose, Botterell & Roche*
(for Rolimpex).

Mary Rose Plummer   Barrister.

---

1   [1978] 1 All ER 81 at 96, [1978] QB 176 at 204

Practice Note

a

FAMILY DIVISION

Injunction – Exclusion of party from matrimonial home – County court – Time limit on *b*
operation of injunction – Application by respondent to discharge injunction – Application by
applicant to extend injunction – Domestic Violence and Matrimonial Proceedings Act 1976,
s 1(1)(c).

To secure uniformity of practice, the President has issued the following note with the
concurrence of the Lord Chancellor.   *c*

  1. Section 1(1)(c) of the Domestic Violence and Matrimonial Proceedings Act 1976
empowers a county court to include in an injunction provisions excluding a party
from the matrimonial home or a part of the matrimonial home or from a specified
area in which the matrimonial home is included. Where a power of arrest under s 2
of the 1976 Act is attached to any injunction containing such provisions, the respondent   *d*
is liable to be arrested if he enters the matrimonial home or part thereof or specified
area at any time while the injunction remains in force.

  2. It is within the discretion of the court to decide whether an injunction should be
granted and, if so, for how long it should operate. But whenever an injunction is
granted excluding one of the parties from the matrimonial home (or a part thereof
or specified area), consideration should be given to imposing a time limit on the   *e*
operation of the injunction. In most cases a period of up to three months is likely to
suffice, at least in the first instance. It will be open to the respondent in any event to
apply for the discharge of the injunction before the expiry of the period fixed, for
instance on the ground of reconciliation, and to the applicant to apply for an extension.

                                                             R L BAYNE-POWELL *f*
21st July 1978   Senior Registrar.

a
Mallett v Restormel Borough Council

COURT OF APPEAL, CIVIL DIVISION
LORD DIPLOCK, LORD RUSSELL OF KILLOWEN AND LORD SCARMAN
28th FEBRUARY 1978

b
Local government – Officer – Compensation for loss of employment – Loss of employment attributable to reorganisation of local government – Attributable to – Applicant employed by council as airport manager – Under reorganisation council ceasing to exist and replaced by new council – New council deciding for financial reasons to hand over management of airport to a company – Termination of applicant's employment with new council – Whether c *loss of employment attributable to reorganisation of local government – Local Government (Compensation) Regulations 1974 (SI 1974 No 463), regs 7(1)(a), 11(1)(a).*

The applicant was employed by the Newquay Urban District Council ('the old council') as the manager of their airport at St Mawgan, where they obtained supplies of aircraft fuel on advantageous terms from the RAF under a special arrangement. Early in d 1974 the RAF gave notice that it would have to terminate the arrangement that year. On 1st April 1974, as a result of the reorganisation of local government effected by the Local Government Act 1972, and the statutory instruments made under it, the old council ceased to exist and was replaced by the Restormel Borough Council ('the new council'). The new council continued to employ the applicant as manager of the airport. In the summer of 1974, however, they decided that without the RAF e supplying fuel on special terms, it would not be economic for them to continue to run the airport themselves. They entered into an agency agreement with an airline company, whereby it was agreed that the company would manage the airport and pay the council rent, with effect from 1st December 1974. The applicant's post accordingly became redundant on that date. The new council offered him alternative employment as a rating assistant which he refused. It was then agreed that he f would retire prematurely on superannuation with effect from 1st February 1975. He applied to an industrial tribunal for compensation under regs 7(1)(a)*[a]* and 11(1)(a)*[b]* of the Local Government (Compensation) Regulations 1974 in respect of his loss of employment on the ground that it was 'attributable to' the provisions of the Local Government Act 1972. He claimed that if the old council had continued to exist after 1st April 1974 they would not have entered into the agency agreement but would have g continued to run the airport themselves and would have continued to employ him as airport manager.

Held – Compensation was only payable if an applicant could prove that the Act, or any instrument made under it, had contributed to the existence of the situation which had resulted in his loss of employment. On the evidence, the 1972 Act and h the statutory instruments made under it had not contributed to the creation of the situation which had resulted in the applicant's loss of employment. It was the RAF's

---

a Regulation 7(1), so far as material, provides: '. . . the conditions for the payment of re-settlement compensation to any person are that—(a) he has suffered loss of employment attributable to any provision [of the Local Government Act 1972] not later than 10 years after the material date . . .'
b Regulation 11(1), so far as material, provides: '. . . the conditions for the payment of long-term compensation to any person are that—(a) he has suffered loss of employment . . . attributable to any provision [of the Local Government Act 1972] not later than 10 years after the material date . . .'

notice of withdrawal of fuel supplies which had created the economic and administrative problems that made a decision about the future running of the airport *a*
necessary. Those problems would have arisen then whichever council had been
responsible for the airport. It followed that the need to take a decision about the
airport was not connected with the reorganisation of local government effected by
the 1972 Act and that the applicant's loss of employment, in consequence of the decision
made by the new council, was not 'attributable to any provision of the Act'. Accordingly he was not entitled to compensation under the regulations (see p 1060 *e* to *g*, *b*
post).

Decision of Griffiths J [1978] 1 All ER 503 reversed.

Notes

For the compensation of local government officers for loss of employment, see 24
Halsbury's Laws (3rd Edn) 507-510, paras 937-939.	*c*

Appeal

This was an appeal by the Restormel Borough Council against the judgment of
Griffiths J[1], dated 10th March 1977, (i) allowing an appeal by Dennis Henry Mallett
against the decision of an industrial tribunal sitting at Truro (chairman John Shaw *d*
Esq) on 5th November 1975 dismissing his claim for resettlement compensation,
under reg 7(1) of the Local Government (Compensation) Regulations 1974, and long-
term compensation, under reg 11(1) of the 1974 regulations, in respect of his loss of
employment with the Restormel Borough Council; and (ii) remitting the case to a
differently constituted industrial tribunal for a rehearing. The facts are set out in the
judgment of the court.
	e

Swinton Thomas QC and *P B Mauleverer* for the Restormel Borough Council.
John M Bowyer for Mr Mallett.

LORD SCARMAN delivered the following judgment of the court: Mr Dennis *f*
Mallett lost his employment as a local government officer on 1st February 1975,
when by arrangement with his employers, the Restormel Borough Council, he
was allowed to retire prematurely. On retirement he claimed a redundancy payment and compensation under the Local Government Act 1972. An industrial
tribunal awarded him a redundancy payment but rejected his claim for compensation under the Act. Mr Mallett appealed to the High Court. On 21st March 1977 *g*
Griffiths J allowed the appeal[1] and remitted the claim for compensation to a differently constituted industrial tribunal. The Restormel council now appeals against the
order of the High Court.

The Act reorganised local government in England and Wales. On 1st April 1974
existing local government areas and councils disappeared, their place being taken by
new areas and councils. This was the effect of ss 1 and 2 of the Act. Two instruments *h*
made pursuant to the Act dealt with English non-metropolitan districts: the English
Non-Metropolitan Districts (Definition) Order 1972[2], which defined the new districts,
and the English Non-Metropolitan Districts (Names) Order 1973[3], which gave them
their names. It is by reason of these sections and instruments that the Restormel
council succeeded the Newquay Urban District Council as the local authority for the
Newquay district in the county of Cornwall.	*j*

1	[1978] 1 All ER 503
2	SI 1972 No 2039
3	SI 1973 No 551

Section 259 of the Act provides for the making of regulations to enable compensa-
a tion to be paid to certain categories of persons whose employment or emoluments
have been adversely affected by the Act. Subsection (1) of the section applies to this
case. It requires the Minister to make regulations for the payment of compensation
to local government officers and employees who suffer loss of employment (or
emoluments) 'which is either attributable to any provision of this Act or of any
instruments made under this Act'. The Local Government (Compensation) Regula-
b tions 1974[1] gave effect, inter alia, to sub-s (1). They include a provision which enables
compensation to be paid in respect of an attributable loss arising within a period of
ten years from 1st April 1974; the relevant regulations are reg 7 (resettlement compensation) and reg 11 (long-term compensation).

Mr Mallett's case is that his loss of employment is attributable to the reorganisation
of local government effected by the Act and instruments made under the Act. The
c council's case is that it is not. The relevant facts can be stated shortly. Mr Mallett
entered the employment of the Newquay Urban District Council in February 1935.
In April 1973 he was appointed by the council manager of St Mawgan's airport. The
airfield, which was the property of the council, had been exclusively used by the
RAF until 1959, when civilian operations were permitted under the management of
the council. An arrangement was made for the supply of fuel from RAF sources. In
d 1973 the RAF informed the council that they would have to terminate the arrangement
at a date of which they would in due course give notice. This meant that the council
would have to find the finance and make arrangements for a supply of aircraft fuel
for civilian operations. The Restormel council was established in 1973, elections being
held in that year. It was due to take over responsibility for the local government area
which included the Newquay district on 1st April 1974, when, under the provisions of
e the Act, the Newquay council would cease to exist. On 3rd January 1974 the Restormel
council offered to continue Mr Mallett in his appointment as airport manager after
1st April 1974. He accepted. However, early in 1974, the RAF gave notice that they
would be ceasing that year to provide aircraft fuel for civilian operations. The Restormel council appointed a working party to investigate the consequences of the RAF
decision. In July the working party reported that it would not be possible for the
f council to run the airport economically and recommended that the council enter into
an agency agreement with British Midland Airways under which the company would
manage the airport and pay the council a rent of £2,000 per annum. The council
accepted the recommendation and entered into an agreement with British Midland
Airways on the terms recommended with effect from 1st December 1974. Mr
Mallett's post thus became redundant on that date. He was offered, but refused,
g alternative employment as a rating assistant. By mutual agreement Mr Mallett was
'allowed premature retirement on superannuation with effect from 1st February
1975' (as recommended by the council's establishment sub-committee).

The replacement of the Newquay council by the Restormel council resulted from
the provisions of the Act. The one question raised by the appeal is: was Mr Mallett's
loss of employment attributable to those provisions? The industrial tribunal said
h 'No'. They stated their reasons very clearly:

'On the evidence called before us we think it very likely that the Newquay
council would have continued to run the airport themselves and that Mr Mallett
would have remained as airport manager. For present purposes we are prepared
to assume that this is so. We accept of course that the reorganisation of local
j government was attributable to a provision of the Act. We do not, however,
accept that a decision by the Restormel council to change the policy of the
Newquay council was attributable to a provision of the Act. The Restormel
council were at liberty to continue to operate the airport themselves or to enter

1 SI 1974 No 463

into the agency agreement. The Act did not affect their decision one way or the
other.'   *a*

Griffiths J, however, rejected their approach to the question. In the course of his
judgment he drew attention to the fact that Mr Mallett called before the tribunal a
witness who had been a member of the Newquay council. He gave evidence that the
Newquay council would not have entered into the agency agreement. When the
Restormel council's solicitor sought to cross-examine the witness, he was stopped, the   *b*
chairman declaring that what the Newquay council might or might not have done
was irrelevant. Directing himself that it was sufficient in law for Mr Mallett to show
that the disappearance of the Newquay council under the provisions of the Act was
at least a cause of his loss of employment, Griffiths J held that it was relevant to enquire what the Newquay council would have done. Since the chairman had stopped
cross-examination on the point, he remitted the case for a fresh hearing before   *c*
another tribunal.

It would be surprising if Parliament had intended that compensation under the Act
was to be determined by so hypothetical a question as one relating to what an old
council would have done had it not ceased to exist, or that an industrial tribunal
should have to concern itself with evidence which could well prove to be political
in character as well as hypothetical. Counsel for the Restormel council commented   *d*
that it would be a daunting prospect if it was to be open over a period of ten years to
an applicant to adduce the evidence of councillors of the extinct authority to the effect
that, had the extinct authority continued to exist, it would not have acted in the way
the new authority has acted. Parliament, he submitted, cannot have intended such
a result. There is force in this submission. In our judgment the correct approach
to the question of attributability under the subsection is that adopted by the industrial   *e*
tribunal. They put it succinctly when they said that the Restormel council was at
liberty to continue to operate the airport themselves or to enter into the agency
agreement and that 'the Act did not affect their decision one way or the other'. When
the RAF decided to withdraw fuel supplies, a decision on how to run the airport had
to be taken, whichever authority, the old or the new, was then responsible. The need
to take a decision arose not from the reorganisation of local government effected by   *f*
the Act but from an administrative problem created by the notice served by the RAF.
The decision that was made, which resulted in the loss of employment, was not made
in order to meet or to adjust to any provision of the Act or any instrument made
under it. It is not possible, therefore, to say that the decision taken and the loss of
employment consequent on the decision were attributable to any provision of the
Act; the Act had nothing whatever to do with creating the situation which called   *g*
for the decision.

In our judgment compensation is payable under the subsection only if an applicant
can prove that the Act or an instrument made under the Act has contributed to the
existence of the situation which has resulted in his loss of employment (or emoluments). The most obvious case is that of an employee of an old authority who is not
offered re-employment by the new authority. He has lost his employment because   *h*
the Act has provided that his employer should cease to exist; and the new authority
has decided not to employ him. But, when an applicant is offered, and accepts the
continuance of his employment by the new authority, it will not often happen that a
subsequent loss of employment is attributable to the Act. Cases, however, will arise.
For example, ss 101 and 110 of the Act enable a new authority to arrange permanently
or transitionally for the discharge of certain of its functions by others, including a   *j*
power itself to perform the function to be transferred or delegated until such time
as the arrangements are complete. In such a situation a new authority may well
employ an officer of the old authority for a time, after which (on transfer or delegation)
he will lose his job. In such a case the applicant will be able to show that his loss of
employment is attributable to the Act in the sense that he has suffered by reason of a

reorganisation attributable to the Act. But in the present case Mr Mallett lost his
a employment for reasons quite unconnected with any provision of the Act.
    For these reasons we would allow the appeal. The industrial tribunal was right to
dismiss Mr Mallett's claim to compensation.

Appeal allowed. Leave to appeal to the House of Lords refused.

b Solicitors: *Sharpe, Pritchard & Co*, agents for *Ewart Pate*, St Austell (for the Restormel
Borough Council); *Penelope Grant* (for Mr Mallett).

Christine Ivamy   Barrister.

c

Boggeln v Williams

QUEEN'S BENCH DIVISION
d LORD WIDGERY CJ, O'CONNOR AND LLOYD JJ
23rd JANUARY 1978

*Criminal law – Theft – Electricity – Dishonestly using electricity without due authority —
Dishonestly – Belief of user of electricity – Belief that use of electricity not dishonest – Intention
to pay for electricity used – Supply disconnected because of failure to pay account – Defendant
e reconnecting supply without board's authority – Defendant notifying board of intention to reconnect – Reconnection effected to enable use of electricity to be recorded on meter – Whether
connection of supply dishonest use of electricity – Theft Act 1968, s 13.*

The defendant, who was the occupier of a house supplied with electricity by the local
electricity board ('the board'), failed to pay an amount due for electricity he had used.
f The board therefore disconnected his supply of electricity by removing the main
fuse from the fuse box in the house. After the disconnection the defendant told
an employee of the board that he intended to reconnect the supply and was informed that if he did so the supply would again be disconnected. Shortly afterwards
the defendant broke the seal on the fuse box and reconnected the supply by inserting a piece of wire in place of the main fuse. Although he knew how to effect
reconnection to prevent the use of electricity being recorded on the meter, he re-
g connected the supply so that the electricity used would be recorded on the meter.
Thereafter the defendant used electricity. He was charged with dishonestly using
electricity without due authority, contrary to s 13[a] of the Theft Act 1968, and was
convicted by the justices. He appealed against the conviction to the Crown Court.
The court found that the defendant knew that the board did not consent to the re-
h connection but that he believed he was not acting dishonestly in reconnecting the
supply because he had given notice of his intention to reconnect and had ensured
that electricity consumed after the reconnection would be recorded on the meter.
The court also found that at the time when he reconnected the supply he genuinely
and reasonably believed that he would be able to pay for electricity consumed
after the reconnection when payment became due. On those findings the court
j was of the opinion that the defendant's state of mind at the relevant time, i e when he
reconnected the supply, was not dishonest within s 13 and that his appeal should
be allowed but it stated a case for the opinion of the High Court on the question
whether an intention to pay for electricity knowingly used without due authority

---

a   Section 13 is set out at p 1064 g and h, post

was capable of affording a defence to a charge under s 13 of the 1968 Act if that intention was based on a genuine belief by the user that he would be able to pay for it   *a*
at the due time for payment. The prosecution contended that the taking of electricity
without due authority was dishonest user, within s 13, and that the user's belief
as to his own honesty was irrelevant.

Held – The fact that the user when he reconnected the supply knew that he did not
have the board's consent to reconnect it did not of itself make his conduct dishonest   *b*
within s 13, and whether he had acted dishonestly was a question of fact to be answered
subjectively in the light of his state of mind when he reconnected the supply. The
findings of the Crown Court that the defendant believed he was not acting dishonestly
in reconnecting the supply and genuinely and reasonably believed he would be able
to pay for electricity consumed after the reconnection supported the conclusion
of the court that at the time when the supply was reconnected his state of mind   *c*
was not dishonest. It followed that the Crown Court had been right to acquit the
defendant (see p 1064 *j* to p 1065 *d* and *g* and p 1066 *b* to *d*, post).
    R v Feely [1973] 1 All ER applied.

Notes
For theft of electricity, see 16 Halsbury's Laws (4th Edn) para 100.   *d*
    For the meaning of dishonestly, see 11 Halsbury's Laws (4th Edn) para 1263.
    For the Theft Act 1968, s 13, see 8 Halsbury's Statutes (3rd Edn) 791.

Cases referred to in judgments
R v Cockburn [1968] 1 All ER 466, [1968] 1 WLR 281, 132 JP 166, 52 Cr App Rep 134,
    CA, 15 Digest (Reissue) 1287, *11,072*.   *e*
R v Feely [1973] 1 All ER 341, [1973] QB 530, [1973] 2 WLR 201, 137 JP 157, 57 Cr App
    Rep 312, CA, 15 Digest (Reissue) 1263, *10,830*.
R v Williams [1953] 1 All ER 1068, [1953] 1 QB 660, [1953] 2 WLR 937, 117 JP 251,
    37 Cr App Rep 71, CCA, 15 Digest (Reissue) 1286, *11,071*.

Case stated   *f*
    1. This was a case stated by the Crown Court at Aylesbury in respect of its adjudi-
cation on an appeal against conviction by the defendant, Ronald Boggeln, at Stoney
Stratford Magistrates' Court on 25th February 1977 of an offence of dishonestly
and without lawful authority using electricity between 27th October and 1st December 1976, contrary to s 13 of the Theft Act 1968. By a notice dated 1st March 1977
the defendant appealed to the Crown Court against that conviction.   *g*
    2. The Crown Court heard the appeal on 24th June 1977 and found the following
facts: (1) The defendant was, at all material times, the occupier of a house at 55
Crispin Road, Bradville, Milton Keynes, supplied with electricity through a normal
meter by the East Midlands Electricity Board ('the board'), which provided lighting
and the only heating in the house. (2) On or about 20th October 1976 the board gave
written notice to the defendant that it intended to disconnect the supply of electricity   *h*
to his house by reason of his failure to pay for electricity previously used amounting
in value to £39·65. (3) On 27th October a representative of the board disconnected
the supply to the house by removing a main fuse and sealed the fuse holder. (4)
After the disconnection the defendant spoke to an unidentified employee of the board,
described by the defendant as the manager, and informed him of his intention to
reconnect the supply. The defendant was informed by the manager that, if he did so,
the supply would again be disconnected. (5) As a result of that conversation the defendant did not believe that the board consented to reconnection by him. The defendant nevertheless did believe that by giving notice of his intention and by ensuring
that consumption was duly recorded through the meter, he was not acting dishonestly
in reconnecting. (6) At some time shortly thereafter the defendant broke the seal

and reconnected the supply by means of a wire in place of the missing fuse. The effect
of so reconnecting was, as the defendant knew, that the meter continued to record
consumption of electricity. The defendant knew how to effect reconnection in such
a way that consumption would not be recorded. (7) Payment for electricity consumed
at the house was not required in advance but was demanded from time to time after
the meter had been read. (8) At the time when the defendant reconnected the supply,
he believed, as he asserted, that he would be in a position to pay for electricity consumed thereafter at the date when payment was due. The court was satisfied that
this belief was genuine and was not satisfied that it was unreasonable. (By the date
of the hearing of the appeal the sum of £39·65 outstanding had been paid, but the
date of such payment was not given in evidence.) (9) On 30th November another
representative of the board found the supply to have been reconnected as described
and again disconnected it. Reading of the meter showed that 273 units, costing
£6·06 had been used since the disconnection on 27th October. (10) The reading
accurately set out the electricity consumed at the house during the period of just over
one month.

3. It was submitted on behalf of the defendant that his use of electricity was not
dishonest because at the time of such use he had taken steps to ensure that his
consumption was duly recorded by meter, he intended to pay for consumption
at the date when payment was normally due, he believed that he would be able to
pay at the date, and the proper test of dishonesty was a subjective one.

4. It was submitted on behalf of the prosecutor that: taking electricity which the
user knew the board was unwilling to supply was dishonest and intention to pay
for it was irrelevant or, alternatively, if intention to pay was relevant, it was only so
when the intention was based on a genuine belief, on reasonable grounds, that the
user would be able to pay at the due time for payment and the defendant did not
reasonably so believe.

5. The court was of opinion that the defendant did believe that when payment
became due he would be able to pay for electricity consumed, that this belief was
not proved to be unreasonable and that the defendant's state of mind at the relevant
time (i e when reconnecting the supply) was not dishonest.

The question for the opinion of the High Court was whether an intention to pay
for electricity knowingly used without the authority of the electricity board was
capable of affording a defence to a charge under s 13 of the 1968 Act if that intention
was based on genuine belief that the user would be able to pay at the due time for
payment.

Christopher Hordern for the prosecutor.
Brian Leech for the defendant.

LLOYD J delivered the first judgment at the invitation of Lord Widgery CJ. This is a
case stated by the Crown Court at Aylesbury. The question for the opinion of the
court is whether a person can be convicted of dishonestly abstracting electricity,
contrary to s 13 of the Theft Act 1968 if he intends to pay for the electricity when
payment is due and that intention is based on a genuine belief that he will be able
to do so.

The facts are set out, if I may say so, with admirable clarity in the case. The defendant was convicted by the Stony Stratford Magistrates' Court on 25th February 1977
of dishonestly abstracting electricity to the value of £6·06. He was given a conditional
discharge. He then appealed to the Crown Court, who allowed the appeal against
conviction subject to the case stated.

The facts are these. On 27th October 1976 a representative of the East Midlands
Electricity Board had disconnected the defendant's supply of electricity after due
warning had been given by reason of the defendant's failure to pay an outstanding

amount of £39·65. The defendant thereupon spoke to one of the board's employees and informed him that he was intending to reconnect the supply himself. Shortly thereafter he broke the seal on the board's main fuse box and reconnected the supply by means of a piece of wire which he inserted in place of the main fuse which the board's employees had removed. The way in which he carried out the reconnection meant that the electricity which he used would continue to be recorded on the meter in the usual way. There is then this important finding of fact in the case, which I shall read, in para 2(5):

'As a result of the said conversation the [defendant] did not believe that the board consented to reconnection by him. The [defendant] nevertheless did believe that, by giving notice of his intention and by ensuring that consumption was duly recorded through the meter, he was not acting dishonestly in reconnecting.'

That finding of fact is supported by the further finding in para 2(6) of the case that the defendant knew how to effect reconnection in such a way that consumption would not be recorded, in other words by bypassing the meter. There is then another important finding of fact which I should read in para 2(8):

'At the time when the [defendant] reconnected the supply, the [defendant] believed, as he asserted, that he would be in a position to pay for electricity consumed thereafter at the date when payment was due. We are satisfied that this belief was a genuine one and we were not satisfied that it was unreasonable.'

There is no specific finding anywhere in the case as to the defendant's intention to pay for the electricity, but it is common ground in this case that that can be inferred. Finally, in para 5 of the case it is stated:

'We were of opinion that the [defendant] did believe that, when payment became due, he would be able to pay for electricity consumed; that this belief was not proved to be unreasonable; and that the [defendant's] state of mind at the relevant time (i.e. when reconnecting the supply) was not dishonest.'

The question left for the opinion of the court is as follows:

'Is an intention to pay for electricity knowingly used without the authority of the electricity board capable of affording a defence to a charge under Section 13 of the Theft Act, 1968, if that intention is based on a genuine belief that the user will be able to pay at the due time for payment?'

It is perhaps now convenient to refer to s 13 of the 1968 Act, which is as follows:

'A person who dishonestly uses without due authority, or dishonestly causes to be wasted or diverted, any electricity shall on conviction on indictment be liable to imprisonment for a term not exceeding five years.'

I might also refer to s 2(2) of the 1968 Act, which provides: 'A person's appropriation of property belonging to another may be dishonest notwithstanding that he is willing to pay for the property.'

I stress the word 'may' in that subsection because, although a person may be guilty of dishonesty even though he is willing to pay, nevertheless it is in each case a question of fact for the tribunal of fact whether the defendant is guilty of dishonesty or not.

That is a question which relates to the defendant's state of mind and must, in my judgment, be answered subjectively: did the defendant have a dishonest mind or not? That being the question, it seems to me that it is answered for us in the present case by the finding which I have referred to in para 2(5) of the case stated, and which I will read again:

a   'The [defendant] nevertheless did believe that, by giving notice of his intention and by ensuring that consumption was duly recorded through the meter, he was not acting dishonestly in reconnecting.'

Counsel for the prosecution argues that that finding does not really help the defendant because a man's belief as to his own honesty or dishonesty must, he says, be irrelevant. In my judgment, that finding is not only relevant, but crucial. Counsel *b*   referred us to R v Williams[1] and the further case of R v Cockburn[2], but those decisions must be read in the light of the later decision of a five judge court in R v Feely[3]. It seems to me that that case governs the present one. Counsel says that both R v Feely[3] and the two previous cases were cases which were concerned with the taking of money, and that enables him to distinguish the present case. But, in my judgment, the principles stated in R v Feely[3] are not so limited.

c   Applying that decision to the present case, and in particular the standard of the ordinary decent man which is there referred to, the finding of the Crown Court in para 2(5) of the case stated is one which the Crown Court was amply entitled to make; and that finding in turn supports the conclusion (which I take it to be) which is stated in para 5 of the case. The fact that the defendant did not believe at the time he reconnected his supply that he had the consent of the board does not *d*   of itself make the defendant's conduct dishonest in law. It is a question of fact in each case for the tribunal of fact whether the necessary dishonesty is proved or not.

Counsel says that, if this decision were to go in favour of the defendant, it would create great difficulties for the electricity boards and other people in their position. I would only say this. The fact that this case may be decided in favour of the defendant does not mean that every other case will be so decided. In particular I would like to *e*   echo the remark of Lawton LJ in R v Feely[4] where he said:

'Nothing in this judgment should lead anyone, particularly those tempted to put their hands in other people's tills, to think that for the future the prospects of acquittal will be substantially improved.'

Lastly, I should mention for completeness that counsel for the prosecution wishes *f*   to reserve the question whether R v Feely[3] was or was not correctly decided. But taking the law, as I do, from that case, and the facts as found by the Crown Court, I answer the question which has been posed for us 'Yes'. It follows, in my judgment, that the Crown Court was right to acquit, and I would uphold its decision.

g   **O'CONNOR J.** I agree, and in deference to the arguments addressed to us by counsel for the prosecution I will add a few words.

He submitted to us that the offence under s 13 of the Theft Act 1968 is committed where the consumer of electricity, who has had his supply cut off knowing that the board are unwilling for him to consume any more of their electricity, with that knowledge deliberately reconnects himself to the supply and uses it, and that that necessarily involves a dishonest intent.

h   In support of that contention, he submitted to us that if one was considering the case under s 1 of the 1968 Act, the facts being that the owner of some articles refused to give them to the defendant who, with the knowledge that he had no right to take them, nevertheless determined to help himself to them, it would be unnecessary to prove any further facts before a jury would be bound to come to the conclusion *j*   that he was acting dishonestly[1].

---

1   [1953] 1 All ER 1068, [1953] 1 QB 660
2   [1968] 1 All ER 466, [1968] 1 WLR 281
3   [1973] 1 All ER 341, [1973] QB 530
4   [1973] 1 All ER 341 at 342, [1973] QB 530 at 535

For my part, as and when a case under s 1 comes before the court, I would reserve
the question on that topic, but I would point to the paragraph in the judgment of   *a*
Lawton LJ in *R v Feely*[1], where he said: 'In s 1(1) of the Theft Act 1968 the word
"dishonestly" can only relate to the state of mind of the person who does the act
which amounts to appropriation.' If that be so, when one looks at s 13, the elements
of the offence are to dishonestly use, without due authority, any electricity. There are
the two necessary elements: to use without due authority and to do so dishonestly.

What was established here without doubt was that the defendant was using it   *b*
without due authority. He accepted that. But there remained the issue (and the
burden was on the prosecution to establish it) whether in so doing he was acting
dishonestly. That inevitably is a question of fact for the jury, it if be trial by jury.
Despite the warning given by Lawton LJ about the undesirability of seeking to say
what is meant by 'dishonestly', inevitably when a case under s 13 is under consideration it seems to me that one test at all events must be the mental position of the de-   *c*
fendant as to whether he is able and willing to pay for that which he uses. I need say
no more about it.

LORD WIDGERY CJ. I also agree, and I think it important that the flexibility
of s 1 of the Theft Act 1968 should not be lost by putting the word 'dishonestly' in a   *d*
strait-jacket of definition.

There are to be found in the judgment of Lawton LJ in *R v Feely*[2] all the indications
which will be required by a judge in summing up to the jury hereafter, and I would
add to those which have already been referred to in the judgments of this case the
passage[3] which appears near the end of the judgment.

The appeal is dismissed.   *e*

Appeal dismissed.

*30th January 1978. The court refused leave to appeal to the House of Lords but certified,
under s 33(2) of the Criminal Appeal Act 1968, that the following point of law of general
public importance was involved in the case: if an occupier of premises unlawfully connects*   *f*
*those premises with the electrical mains supply and does so in such a manner that the meter
on the premises will record the abstraction of electricity, is it a defence to a charge under s 13
of the Theft Act 1968 that he genuinely intended to pay for the electricity when requested?*

Solicitors: *Sharpe, Pritchard & Co*, agents for *J Malcolm Simons*, Kidlington (for the
prosecutor); *Giffen, Couch & Archer*, Stony Stratford (for the defendant).   *g*

Lea Josse   Barrister.

---

1   [1973] 1 All ER 341 at 344, [1973] QB 530 at 537
2   [1973] 1 All ER 341, [1973] QB 530
3   [1973] 1 All ER 341 at 348, [1973] QB 530 at 541

Noble (Inspector of Taxes) v Laygate Investments Ltd

CHANCERY DIVISION
OLIVER J
3rd MARCH 1978

Company – Articles of association – Restriction imposed on company – Restriction imposed by articles of association – Restriction imposed by law – Close company – Shortfall in distributions – Calculations of shortfall – Required standard – Articles of association restricting company's distributable profits to excess of income over revenue expenditure – Whether restriction a 'restriction imposed by law' – Income and Corporation Taxes Act 1970, s 290(4).

The taxpayer company carried on the business of making and holding investments and was, at all material times, a close company. Under its articles of association the company was authorised to distribute only 'the profits of the company available for dividend'. That expression was defined to mean 'the excess of the [company's] income over its expenditure on a properly drawn revenue or profit and loss account . . . but from which there shall be excluded all profits or losses arising from . . . realisations of or dealings with capital assets'. For the accounting periods ended 31st March 1972 and 31st March 1973 the company declared dividends which were, under its articles of association, the maximum possible distribution for those years. The inspector of taxes, however, made shortfall assessments on the company on the ground that those distributions fell short of the 'required standard' under s 290(4)ᵃ of the Income and Corporation Taxes Act 1970. The company appealed contending that by the terms of its articles of association it was unable to distribute any further sums and was therefore subject to a 'restriction imposed by law' as regards the distribution of those sums within s 290(4), and that any shortfall to the extent of those sums did not fall to be taken into account. The General Commissioners upheld the company's contention and discharged the assessments. The Crown appealed.

Held – The restrictions contained in the articles of association were imposed by the company itself and were not imposed by law on the company, because at all material times the company was free to alter its articles so as to remove those restrictions. It followed that shortfall assessments had been properly made on the company. The appeal would therefore be allowed (see p 1070 *j*, p 1071 *d e* and p 1072 *c* to *e*, post).

Barlow v Teal (1885) 15 QBD 501 and *Badcock v Hunt* (1889) 22 QBD 145 applied.

Notes

For the binding nature of articles of association, see 7 Halsbury's Laws (4th Edition) para 116.

For the taxation of income of close companies, see Supplement to 20 Halsbury's Laws (3rd Edn) para 2044.

For the Income and Corporation Taxes Act 1970, s 290, see 33 Halsbury's Statutes (3rd Edn) 396.

For 1973-74 and subsequent years of assessment, s 290(4) has been replaced by s 94(1) of, and Sch 16, para 14, to the Finance Act 1972.

Cases referred to in judgment

Badcock v Hunt (1888) 22 QBD 145, 58 LJQB 134, 60 LT 314, 53 JP 340, CA, 31 Digest (Reissue) 584, 4768.

Barlow v Teal (1885) 15 QBD 501, 54 LJQB 564, 54 LT 63, 50 JP 100, CA, 2 Digest (Repl) 13, 46.

King v Cave-Browne-Cave [1960] 2 All ER 751, [1960] 2 QB 222, [1960] 3 WLR 204, 31(2) Digest (Reissue) 575, 4698.

---

a Section 290(4) is set out at p 1070 *c d*, post

Cases also cited

Canadian Eagle Oil Co Ltd v R [1945] 2 All ER 499, [1946] AC 119, 27 Tax Cas 205, CA.   *a*
Colville Estate Ltd v Inland Revenue Comrs [1930] 2 KB 393, [1930] All ER Rep 770, 15
   Tax Cas 485.
Walker v London Tramways Co Ltd (1879) 12 Ch D 705.

Case stated

1. At a meeting of the Commissioners for the General Purposes of the Income Tax   *b*
for the Division of Newcastle upon Tyne held at 34 Grainger Street, Newcastle upon
Tyne on 4th December 1974, Laygate Investments Ltd ('the taxpayer company')
appealed against the following assessments made under s 289 of the Income and
Corporation Taxes Act 1970 ('the Act'):

Accounting period	Amount of shortfall	
Year to 31st March 1972	£639	*c*
Year to 31st March 1973	£551	

2. Shortly stated the question for decision was whether the provisions of the Taxpayer company's articles of association made the taxpayer company subject to a
restriction imposed by law as regards the making of distributions within s 290(4)
of the Act.   *d*

[Paragraph 3 listed the documents proved or admitted before the commissioners.]

4. The following facts were admitted between the parties: (a) The taxpayer company was a close company (as defined in s 282 of the Act) and was incorporated as an
investment company on 15th June 1949. (b) During each of the years ended 31st
March 1972 and 31st March 1973 the taxpayer company's only business consisted o
making and holding investments. Its income arose from those investments. The   *e*
taxpayer company also made net gains on investments sold amounting to £2,076·85
for the year ending 31st March 1972 and to £2,470·10 for the year ending 31st March
1973. Costs were also incurred in managing the company. For corporation tax purposes those costs were apportioned between revenue and capital profits, and the
calculations of that apportionment had been agreed with the Crown; but in the
books of the taxpayer company the whole of the management costs was debited to   *f*
revenue. (c) Articles 23 and 24 of the taxpayer company's articles of association
provide that the taxpayer company could distribute only the 'profits of the Company
available for Dividend', an expression which was defined (in brief) as the company's
income less revenue expenditure, and which specifically prohibited the distribution
of capital profits by way of dividend. (d) The taxpayer company made distributions
by way of dividend for each of the years in question. Those dividends were virtually *g*
the maximum distributions which could be declared in conformity with arts 23 and 24
of the taxpayer company's articles of association; but they fell short of the 'required
standard' (as defined in s 290 of the Act) by the amount of £463 for the year to 31st
March 1972 and £338 for the year to 31st March 1973.

5. It was contended on behalf of the taxpayer company: (a) that it was entitled to
the benefit of the 'escape clause' in s 290(4) of the Act, the taxpayer company by   *h*
virtue of arts 23 and 24 of the articles of association being subject to restrictions
imposed by law as regards the making of distributions, the restriction consisting
in the prohibitions in arts 23 and 24 referred to in para 4(c) above; (b) that the memorandum and articles of the taxpayer company constituted a contract between the
members and the company and in support of this contention reference was made
to s 20 of the Companies Act 1948. It was conceded that the memorandum and   *j*
articles of association of a company could be altered by the members pursuant to a
special resolution, but no such resolution had been passed at the time the assessments
were raised by the Crown nor, in fact, had such a resolution been passed at any
subsequent date. If the taxpayer company had declared a dividend out of capital
that could ultimately have led to an application for an injunction or a claim for

damage by any member. There was nothing else the taxpayer company could pro-
a perly do, except to declare the dividends which it had in fact declared; (c) that neither
the Income Tax Acts nor, for that matter, any other Act had ever defined the word
'law' as contained in s 290(4) of the Act and that the word 'law' must be statute law,
case law and the general law of the land including contract law; (d) that the taxpayer
company would have been acting ultra vires had it declared a dividend contrary to
arts 23 and 24 of its articles; and (e) that companies could pay out accumulated
b profits if so desired and the theory of a contract between members which bound
them to the memorandum and articles of association was accepted.

6. It was contended on behalf of the Crown: (a) that neither the Companies Acts
nor any general rule of law prohibit the payment of dividends out of the capital
profits of a company; (b) that whilst a company's articles of association bound the
members of that company any restriction contained in the articles was imposed
c voluntarily by the members themselves and could not therefore be said to be a
restriction imposed by law; (c) that a restriction imposed by law within s 290(4) of
the Act meant a restriction imposed on a company by statute or by a general rule of
law; (d) that if the taxpayer company's contentions were correct it would be possible
for any company to avoid a charge to tax in respect of a shortfall by altering its
articles of association, and that could not have been the intention of the legislature;
d and (e) that the taxpayer company was therefore able to make its distributions up
to the 'required standard' (as defined in s 290 of the Act) and the appeals should be
determined accordingly.

7. The commissioners who heard the appeal held that the taxpayer company was
bound by its memorandum and articles of association and allowed the appeal and
the assessments were duly discharged.

e 8. The Crown immediately declared its dissatisfaction with the decision as being
erroneous in point of law and in due course required a case to be stated for the opinion
of the High Court pursuant to the Taxes Management Act 1970, s 56.

9. The question of law for the opinion of the High Court was whether the commissioners were entitled on the evidence before them to hold as they did.

f The taxpayer company was not represented.
C H McCall for the Crown.

OLIVER J. This is an appeal by way of case stated from a ruling of the General
Commissioners for the division of Newcastle upon Tyne, and it raises a short point of
construction on the provisions of s 290(4) of the Income and Corporation Taxes Act
g 1970. The taxpayer is an investment company which was incorporated in 1949, and
at all material times that company was a close company for the purposes of the Act.
In respect of the accounting periods ended 31st March 1972 and 31st March 1973
the inspector made shortfall assessments in estimated amounts under s 289 of the
Act, and the company appealed against those to the General Commissioners, who
allowed their appeal. Then, at the request of the Crown, a case was stated, and so
h the matter now comes before this court.

It is conceded by the Crown, now that actual figures are available, that the assessments are in fact excessive in amount, but the point of principle remains the same,
and it is this. Section 289(1) of the Act imposes the charge, and it is in these terms:

'If in any accounting period of a close company there is a shortfall in the com-
j pany's distributions, there shall be assessed on and recoverable from the company,
as if it were an amount of income tax chargeable on the company, an amount
equal to the income tax for which the company would be liable to account
under section 232(2) of this Act on a distribution equal in amount (before deduction of income tax) to the shortfall and made twelve months after the end of
the accounting period (income tax having been deducted).'

Sections 290 and 291 contain some immensely complicated provisions for calculating what is defined as 'the shortfall', that is, the amount by which the company's dis-   *a* tributions fall short of what is called in the Act 'the required standard'. Happily, it is not necessary for me for present purposes to rehearse those provisions because it is clear on the facts found in the stated case that, as a result of the way in which the management expenses of the company have been dealt with in the company's accounts, the actual distributions made by the company do give rise to a shortfall in the relevant period, subject only to the point raised on this appeal. The company   *b* did declare dividends and the dividends declared fell short of the required standard, but they were the full amount which, under the company's articles of association, were authorised to be distributed without an alteration of the articles.

The company therefore claims that the shortfall should be disregarded because of the provisions of s 290(4) of the Act, and that brings me to the nub of the case. That subsection is in these terms: *c*

'Where a company is subject to any restriction imposed by law as regards the making of distributions, any shortfall in its distributions for an accounting period shall be disregarded to the extent to which the company could not make distributions up to the required standard without contravening that restriction.'

The articles of association of the company, which are annexed to the stated case,   *d* contain two relevant articles, arts 23 and 24, which are in the following terms:

'23. The expression "profits of the Company available for Dividend" as hereafter used shall mean the excess of the Company's income over its expenditure on a properly drawn revenue or profit and loss account to which there shall be credited all Dividends, interest and bonuses and any other benefits and advantages in the   *e* nature of income receivable in respect of the Company's investments and assets, and any trusteeship, agency, transfer and other fees and current receipts of the Company and to which there shall be debited all expenses of management, interest upon borrowed money and other expenses which in the opinion of the Directors are of a revenue nature but from which there shall be excluded all profits or losses arising from sales or transpositions of investments or other   *f* realisations of or dealings with Capital assets.
'24. The profits of the Company available for Dividend and resolved to be distributed shall be applied in the payment of Dividends to the Members in accordance with their respective rights and priorities. The Company in General Meeting may declare Dividends accordingly.'
          g
So there is the provision which restricts the declaration of dividends to dividends out of the fund arrived at in accordance with those provisions.

The company says: 'If you look at art 23 and you look at our accounts for the accounting period in question, you will see that we have in fact distributed the very maximum amount which our constitution enables us to distribute. If we distributed any more, any one of the shareholders could apply for an injunction to restrain us   *h* from infringing the provisions of the contract constituted by the articles between us and him, and we are therefore subject to a restriction imposed by law and the shortfall has to be disregarded under the provisions of s 290(4).' If that is right, it has some extraordinary results. It means that any close company, by adopting the appropriate articles, can opt out of the statutory provisions. But if that is the result of the clear words of a taxing statute, the fact that it is not a result foreseen by the legislature does   *j* not enable me to imply something which is not there or to alter the parliamentary language.

But can it be said in any real sense that the restrictions imposed by the articles of association in this case are restrictions 'imposed by law' within the statutory provision? In my judgment, clearly not. The inability, for instance, of a shareholder lawfully

to transfer his shares otherwise than in accordance with transfer restrictions in the
a articles of association of the company in which he holds the shares is not a disability
imposed on him by the law: it is merely the legal consequence of the restriction
which the shareholder himself voluntarily assumes when he becomes a member of
the company whose articles contain such restrictions. Similarly, if a company grants
a debenture which contains a clause restricting the amount of profits which the
company may distribute so long as the debenture is outstanding, of course that results
b in a restriction which can be enforced by the debenture holder, but it is a legal consequence of the arrangements voluntarily assumed by the company, and not something which can be said to be imposed on the company by law.

Equally, as it seems to me, a company which assumes a constitution containing
restrictions on its own powers as between itself and its members, or which continues
a constitution previously assumed containing such restrictions, is not in any sense
c having those restrictions imposed on it by law. The company has, under s 10 of the
Companies Act 1948 a power in general meeting to alter its own articles, and that is a
power out of which it cannot contract. There may, of course, be cases where there are
immutable restrictions, such as in the case of chartered corporations or companies
incorporated under the Water Act 1945, which was one of the examples which counsel
for the Crown gave. There may, of course, also be restrictions imposed from without
d by statute (for instance, Acts imposing dividend limitation) or by the general law
(for instance, the prohibition of a distribution involving an unlawful reduction of
capital). But this is not that sort of case. This company is and has at all material
times been free to alter its articles so as to remove the restrictions imposed, and,
insofar as those restrictions can be said to be 'imposed' at all, they are in my judgment
imposed by the company on itself and not imposed by the law.

e The matter is not entirely free from authority. In *Barlow v Teal*[1] a question arose as
to whether a particular notice required by the Agricultural Holdings Act 1883 was
'by law necessary'. The decision is relevant only on the meaning of the words 'by law'.
Lord Esher MR there said this[2]:

> *f* 'I am of opinion upon the true construction of the Act that the section applies
> where there is no express stipulation as to the termination of the tenancy, and
> that it does not apply where there is an express stipulation. Where there is no
> express stipulation, the mode of determining the contract of demise is governed
> by the law and not by the contract entered into between the parties. Whenever
> a tenancy from year to year is created by implication of law, there must be a
> half-year's notice to quit; if no stipulation is contained in the demise for the
> determination of the tenancy, a stipulation would be introduced by law that it
> *g* should be determined by a half-year's notice. But where the parties to a demise
> have agreed that a half-year's notice shall be given, that is a stipulation created
> by the contract entered into between the parties, and it is not a stipulation created
> by the law.'

Baggallay LJ was to the same effect. He said[3]: 'But in the present case the parties
h have by their contract stipulated for a six months' notice; and therefore the mode
of determining the tenancy is not regulated "by law" . . .'

That deals to some extent with the meaning, albeit in a different statute, of the
words 'by law'.

The word 'imposed' fell to be considered in the case of *Badcock v Hunt*[4], the question
there being whether, under the provisions of a lease, the landlord was responsible
j for the payment of 'rates, taxes, and impositions' on the premises. The particular

---

1   (1885) 15 QBD 501
2   15 QBD 501 at 502, 503
3   15 QBD 501 at 504
4   (1889) 22 QBD 145

tax with which the case was concerned was the water rate, and it was held that water rates were not 'rates or impositions imposed on or in respect of the premises' within the meaning of the particular covenant there. Again, the judgment of Lord Esher MR in that case is instructive, because it draws the distinction which I venture to think is applicable also in the present case. He said[1]:

> 'The question appears to me to be whether this water-rate can be said to be a rate or imposition "imposed", within the meaning of those words. I do not think that it can. I do not think that a charge to which a person can only be made liable with his own consent can be said to be imposed upon him within the meaning of this covenant. If a man buys things in a shop, the liability to pay the price may be said in one sense to be imposed upon him by law, but that is not, in my opinion, the sense in which the terms "imposed" and "imposition" are used in this covenant.'

Equally, as it seems to me, it is not the sense in which the word 'imposed' is used in the statute which I am called on to construe.

Counsel for the Crown has very properly called my attention to the very much later case of *King v Cave-Browne-Cave*[2], a judgment of McNair J in a different context; but I do not think that that affects the principle of the matter which I have to decide.

Referring to para 7 of the stated case, the commissioners say this: 'We the Commissioners who heard the Appeal held that the [taxpayer company] was bound by its Memorandum and Articles of Association and allowed the appeal and the assessments were duly discharged.' That, of course, is right so far as it goes; as between itself and the members of the company, the company is bound. But it is bound only because it chooses to be bound, and it has a power unilaterally to free itself from those restrictions by altering its articles.

In my judgment, the commissioners misdirected themselves and came to the wrong conclusion in their approach to the statutory expression 'imposed by law', and I must therefore allow the appeal. What I think I must do is restore the assessments and remit the case to the commissioners for a reassessment of the amount of tax payable.

Appeal allowed. No order as to costs.

Solicitors: *Solicitor of Inland Revenue.*

Rengan Krishnan Esq   Barrister.

---

1   (1889) 22 QBD 145 at 148
2   [1960] 2 All ER 751, [1960] 2 QB 222

London Borough of Enfield v Local Government Boundary Commission for England and another

QUEEN'S BENCH DIVISION
BRISTOW J
12th, 14th, 25th JANUARY 1978

Local government – Alteration of area – Proposal – Objection by local authority – Action by local authority on ground that boundary commission's proposals invalid – Commission required to observe rules laid down for considering electoral arrangements – Commission required to achieve electoral equality between wards – Commission appointing assistant commissioner to hold local inquiry and to report – Assistant commissioner recommending scheme based on size of council and not on electoral equality – Commission accepting recommendations but modifying scheme to improve balance of representation between wards – Commission submitting modified scheme to Secretary of State – Whether commision complied with rules – Whether modified scheme achieved required electoral equality – Local Government Act 1972, Sch 11, para 3(2)(3).

In 1975 the Local Government Boundary Commission for England undertook, in accordance with its statutory obligation under the Local Government Act 1972, a revision of the electoral arrangements of a London borough. Section 78 of the 1972 Act required the commission to comply with the rules to be observed in considering electoral arrangements which were set out in Sch 11 to the Act, of which para 3(2)[a] provided that, having regard to any change in the number or distribution of the local government electors of the borough likely to take place within the period of five years immediately following the consideration, the ratio of the number of electors to the number of counsellors to be elected was to be, 'as nearly as may be', the same in every ward of the borough, and para 3(3) provided that in considering electoral arrangements regard was to be had, inter alia, to the desirability of fixing boundaries which were and would remain easily identifiable. The commission, pursuant to s 65 of the 1972 Act, appointed an assistant commissioner to carry out an investigation under the Act and to report to the commission. The assistant commissioner held a local meeting in the borough. The local authority submitted to the assistant commissioner an arrangement which provided for 70 councillors and had a maximum divergence from the mesne figure which produced equality in the ratio of electors to councillors of 0·15 in 1976 and 0·2 in 1981. There was no suggestion that the local authority's scheme was not reasonably practicable to adopt. The assistant commissioner stated that before he could proceed to review the electoral arrangements he had to decide on what size the council should be, a matter about which there were no statutory rules but were only guidelines which gave him a discretion. He then rejected the local authority's scheme, stating that he had done so 'because of the decision I have made about the size of the Council and not on grounds of electoral equality. The [local authority's] scheme cannot be faulted on an electoral ratio basis—in this respect it is almost perfect'. He then chose an arrangement providing for 66 councillors which he submitted to the commission. The commission, after considering the report, presented its proposals to the Secretary of State. In its proposals it reviewed what it had done and, after considering the local authority's draft scheme and others, it concluded that a scheme for 66 councillors submitted by one of the political parties

---

a   Paragraph 3, so far as material, is set out at p 1076 *a* to *c*, post

offered the best standard of representation for the borough and adopted that scheme
as the basis of its draft proposals, adjusting the boundaries suggested in that scheme   *a*
in order to improve the balance of representation between wards and making minor
alterations to make boundary lines which were more readily identifiable. The commission's scheme showed a maximum divergence in the ratio of electors to councillors
of 0·25 in 1976 and more than 0·2 in 1981. The local authority claimed against the
commission a declaration that in considering its revision the commission had failed
to comply with para 3(2) in that in accepting the assistant commissioner's recommend-   *b*
ations it had accepted a scheme which was not based on electoral equality and that
accordingly the proposals it had submitted to the Secretary of State were invalid.

Held – (i) It was not the result of the commission's consideration but the consideration itself which had to comply with the rules. Although the assistant commissioner
may have been in breach of the rules, the commission had not: it was quite clear from   *c*
its proposals that, in considering the arrangements before it, it had not considered
the total number of councillors without having regard to Sch 11, para 3, to the 1972
Act, since it had duly considered its draft proposals in the light of both comments
it had received and the assistant commissioner's report, and, after concluding that
his recommendations should be accepted, it had modified its draft proposals in
accordance with those recommendations and then formulated its final proposals   *d*
(see p 1077 *c* and *e g*, post).

    (ii) However, although the commission's approach to the problem was in accordance
with the requirements of the 1972 Act, the proposals which it had put forward to
the Secretary of State were not. Paragraph 3(2) of Sch 11 required the commission
to adopt an arrangement which was as close to electoral equality 'as nearly as may be'
and not just 'approximately' or 'within reasonable range of it'; the whole object   *e*
was to get as near as was possible to 'one voter one vote of equal weight'. The commission by choosing the 66 councillor scheme which was significantly inferior to the
local authority's 70 councillor scheme, which the assisstant commissioner had described as being 'almost perfect' from the point of view of electoral equality, had therefore disregarded the mandatory requirement of para 3(2)(*a*). The local authority
was therefore entitled to the declaration claimed (see p 1078 *c* to *h*, post).   *f*

Notes

For changes in English local government areas, see Supplement to 24 Halsbury's
Laws of England (3rd Edn) para 778A.

    For the Local Government Act 1972, s 78 and Sch 11, para 3, see 42 Halsbury's   *g*
Statutes (3rd Edn) 915, 1147.

Action

By a writ issued on 3rd November 1977 the plaintiffs, the London Borough of Enfield
('the borough'), brought an action against the defendants, the Local Government
Boundary Commission for England ('the commission') and the Secretary of State for   *h*
the Home Department, claiming a declaration that in considering the electoral
arrangements for the borough the commission failed to comply with the provisions
of s 78 of and Sch 11 to the Local Government Act 1972, and that the report and proposals submitted to the Secretary of State by the commission following a review of
the electoral arrangements for the borough were invalid. The borough further
claimed against the Secretary of State a declaration that he should not give effect to
the proposals either as submitted to him or with modifications. The facts are set out
in the judgment.

M *Howard* and *I B Glick* for the borough.
Harry Woolf and *Jill Gort* for the commission and the Secretary of State.

Cur adv vult

a

25th January.   **BRISTOW J** read the following judgment: In June 1975 the Local Government Boundary Commission for England ('the commission') undertook in accordance with its statutory obligation under the Local Government Act 1972 a revision of the electoral arrangements for the London Borough of Enfield ('the borough'). The borough contends that in conducting its revision the commission

b failed to comply with the statutory provisions which it was bound to observe, and that the report and proposals which the commission submitted on 23rd September 1977, as a result of its revision, to the Secretary of State for the home Department are invalid.

In this action, the borough claims against the commission a declaration to that effect, and against the Minister a declaration that he should not give effect to the

c proposals either as submitted to him or with modifications. The Minister says, as the fact is, that he has not given effect to the commission's proposals, and that he does not intend to do so with or without modifications until after the conclusion of these proceedings, and will then do so only if it is appropriate having regard to the outcome. The commission says that the report and proposals are valid.

The bone of contention between the borough and the commission is this. The

d operations of the borough are now conducted by a council consisting of 60 councillors and ten aldermen.   Aldermen will, during the course of 1978, cease to exist.   The borough contends that the council should continue to consist of 70 people, now all councillors.   The commission proposes that the number should be only 66.   There is no dispute that the number of councillors per electoral ward should be other than two and no dispute that the ward boundaries proposed by the borough for its 35

e ward scheme and the commission for its 33 ward scheme are other than appropriate for the purposes of para 3(a) and (b) of Sch 11 to the 1972 Act, or that each scheme comes close to achieving equality as between the wards in the ratio of the number of local government electors to the number of councillors to be elected. The disagreement from which the action springs is over what the total number of councillors ought to be.

f   This court is in no way concerned with the merits of the rival views. Provided that the commission has conducted its revision in accordance with the provisions of the 1972 Act, it is the commission which is charged by Parliament with the duty of making its report and proposals as to the number of councillors there should be as well as the number and boundaries of the wards.   It is then the duty of the Minister if he thinks fit to give effect (by order) to the commission's proposals with or without

g modification.

By s 47 of the 1972 Act, the commission is empowered in consequence of a revision conducted by it to make proposals to the Minister for effecting changes appearing to the commission desirable in the interests of effective and convenient local government, which I take to mean in the interests of operational efficiency, by means of a substantive change of electoral arrangements for an existing local government area.

h The borough of Enfield is geographically an existing local government area.

By s 65 of the 1972 Act an assistant commissioner can be appointed to carry out any consultation or investigation under the Act and report to the commission. Mr L J Slocombe was appointed assistant commissioner. He held a local meeting at Enfield on 30th and 31st May 1977 and reported to the commission on 8th June 1977.

The borough relies on the terms of his report as showing that he, and so the commis-

j sion, failed to comply with s 78 of the 1972 Act.   This requires the commission, in considering the electoral arrangements for local government areas, to comply insofar as is reasonably practicable with the rules set out in Sch 11 to the 1972 Act. Paragraph 3 of Sch 11 provides the rules which apply to the consideration by the commission of the electoral arrangements for elections of councillors for the borough. Paragraph 3(2) provides as follows:

'Having regard to any change in the number or distribution of the local government electors of the district or borough likely to take place within the period
of five years immediately following the consideration—(a) the ratio of the number
of local government electors to the number of councillors to be elected shall be,
as nearly as may be, the same in every ward of the district or borough . . .'

Paragraph 3(3) provides:

'Subject to sub-paragraph (2) above, in considering the electoral arrangements
. . . regard shall be had to—(a) the desirability of fixing boundaries which are
and will remain easily identifiable; and (b) any local ties which would be broken
by the fixing of any particular boundary.'

So under the rules priority is to be given to securing what for convenience I will
call electoral equality for the electors in every ward within the borough. This is
not a matter of simple arithmetic because you have to consider not the actual number
of electors per ward at a given time. You have to do the best you can to ensure
electoral equality over the next five years having regard to the movement of electors
which may take place during those five years.

So what the commission, in considering a substantive change in the borough
electoral arrangements under s 47, is required by s 78 to do is to comply as far as is
reasonably practicable with the rules in Sch 11. The matter of electoral equality
given priority by para 3(2) of those rules applies as much to the selection of the
appropriate number of councillors as to the selection of the number of councillors
per ward and to the drawing of the ward boundaries.

The commission may not say, for reasons unconnected with electoral equality,
'We think the right number of councillors in the interests of effective and convenient
local government is x, and we will now recommend boundaries based on x councillors
applying the Sch 11 rules'. It is submitted on behalf of the borough that that is what
Mr Slocombe did. The borough relies on the last sentence of para 28 of his report.
Having recited accurately the effect of the Sch 11, para 3 rules, he goes on to say that
on the question of the size of the council he has a little more discretion: 'There are
no statutory rules but agreed guidelines which allow me a little more latitude'.
He is saying, submits the borough, that in considering the appropriate number
of councillors for the purpose of s 47, he is not bound by the Sch 11, para 3
rules but has the assistance of guidelines. In para 29 he considers the forecast
made by the group planning officer of what is going to happen to the electorate
over the next five years, as para 3(2) of the 1972 Act requires. In para 30 he describes
the borough's latest plan based on 70 councillors and 35 wards, designed to achieve
even closer electoral equality than its predecessors. Then in para 31 he proceeds to
deal with the size the council is to be. He does so in these terms:

'It must be obvious to everyone that I cannot proceed further with the consideration of the review of the electoral arrangements for the London Borough
of Enfield until I have made up my mind about what size the Council should be
and I proceed firmly and speedily to grasp that nettle. Put in its simplest form
the position is as follows: The Borough Council want a council of 70 members.
All the other speakers objected to that figure on the grounds that it was too
many.'

He then reviews what the other speakers have said, has a look at the other London
boroughs and notes that the commission has only proposed 70 councillors for two of
them, and that for four which are larger than the borough the commission proposes,
totals between 60 and 64. He says that all the proposals for Enfield which he has been
considering are within the recommended range of 50 to 70, and above the recommended
minimum of 2,500 electors per councillor. He says there is a solid weight of evidence against 70 and that the borough's committee structure could quickly be

adapted for a council of 66.   He rejects the borough's proposals of a council of 70
a members elected from 35 wards. He says:

> 'In doing this I make it clear that I do so because of the decision I have made
> about the size of the Council and not on grounds of electoral equality. The
> Council's scheme cannot be faulted on an electoral ratio basis—in this respect
> it is almost perfect.'

b   So, submits the borough, in picking the total number of councillors he has delibera-
ately disregarded the Sch 11 para 3 rules and considered only the question of operational efficiency using the guidelines, a comparison with other boroughs, and the
operational efficiency evidence which he had before him. So, has the commission,
which modified its own draft proposals in the light of Mr Slocombe's report, complied
with the requirement of s 70 of the 1972 Act that in considering the electoral arrange-
c ments for Enfield it should comply as far as is reasonably practicable with the Sch 11,
para 3 rules? Note that it is not the result of its consideration, but its consideration
itself, which is to comply with the rules.

In my judgment, it is not only Mr Slocombe's report, and his approach to the problem, which I have to look at in answering that question. Mr Slocombe reported to the
commission on 8th June 1977. The commission presented its proposals to the Minister
d on 30th June. It reviewed what it had done, and in paras 5 and 6 said that after
consideration of the borough's draft scheme and other schemes it had considered
that the scheme for 66 councillors submitted by one of the political parties offered the
best standard of representation for the borough, and it decided to adopt that as the
basis of its draft proposals. In para 7 it says that it has adjusted boundaries in order
to improve the balance of representation between wards, and has made minor
e alterations to make boundary lines which were more readily identifiable.

It is quite clear from this that in considering the proposals before it, it was not
considering the total number of councillors without regard to Sch 11, para 3. It
considered its proposals, with their varying totals, in the light of the Sch 11, para 3
rules.   In para 14 it tells the Minister that it has considered its draft proposals in the
light of the comments it has received and of Mr Slocombe's report. It concludes that
f his recommendations should be accepted; it has modified its draft proposals in
accordance with those recommendations, and has then formulated its final proposals.
There was no modification to the total of 66 which it had reached in compliance with
the provisions of the 1972 Act. If Mr Slocombe arrived at his 66 by an approach
which is in breach of the 1972 Act, the commission did not. In my judgment, the
borough's first submission fails.

g   But the borough submits in addition that even if the commission's approach to
its problem was in accordance with the provisions of the 1972 Act, the proposal which
it put forward to the Minister does not comply with Sch 11, para 3(2)(*a*). The borough
submits that 'as nearly as may be' in para 3(2)(*a*) means in ordinary language 'as
nearly as possible', or, at least, 'as nearly as is reasonably practicable'. Mr Slocombe in
his para 31 said that the borough's 70 councillor scheme was 'almost perfect' from the
h point of view of electoral equality. If you compare the borough's 70 councillor scheme
ward by ward with the commission's 66 councillor scheme, as is done in an exhibit
which is in evidence before me, you find that in the commission's scheme there were
divergences from the mesne figure which produces equality in the ratio of electors
to councillors as follows:

i
> 1976—0·1 to 0·15 in 6 wards
> 0·15 to 0·2 in 1 ward
> 0·2 to 0·25 in 3 wards and
> more than 0·25 in 2 wards,

with a maximum variation in electoral weight of vote of 30 per cent. In 1981 the
divergence was—

    0·1 to 0·15 in 5 wards
    0·15 to 0·2 in 5 wards
    0·2 and above in 2 wards.

In the borough's 70 councillor scheme looked at in the same way you find divergences as follows:

    1976—0·1 to 0·15 in 1 ward
        and no greater divergence.
    1981—0·1 to 0·15 in 7 wards
        0·15 to 0·2 in 1 ward.

So, submits the borough, their 70 councillor scheme, on that fairly representative sample, gets far closer to electoral equality, the priority consideration, than the commission's 66 councillor scheme. The borough concedes that it is entirely open to the commission to choose, or to formulate, a 66 councillor scheme which will be as close or closer to electoral equality than the borough's 70 councillor scheme, but that the commission has not done. What it has done is to pick a 66 councillor scheme which is significantly inferior to the borough's 70 councillor scheme; and to do this is to disregard the mandatory requirement of para 3(2)(a) of Sch 11 to the 1972 Act, that the ratio shall be, as nearly as may be, the same in every ward of the borough. Moreover, adds the borough for good measure, the commission's scheme does not even fall within the electoral equality tolerances which the commission sets itself. The commission recognises that population estimates will involve margins of error, and regards a divergence of 0·2 as reasonable. It may regard exceptions outside this tolerance as reasonable in order to meet other requirements of Sch 11, but none of these is involved here.

The commission's proposals produce in 1976 divergences of 0·2 or more in three wards and 0·25 or more in two wards, and in 1981 0·2 or more in two wards. The borough's proposals are all within the tolerances.

If the true interpretation of the mandatory requirement 'as nearly as may be' in para 3(2)(a) of Sch 11 was 'approximately' or 'within reasonable range of', then in my judgment the commission would be entitled to pick a scheme which, while less near the bull's eye of electoral equality than another, was still at least on the target. But in my judgment 'as nearly as may be' means what it says. The whole object of the exercise is to get as near as you can to 'one voter one vote of equal weight'; and, of any schemes which, applying the qualification provided by s 78, it is reasonably practicable to adopt, para 3(2)(a) of Sch 11 requires the commission to pick the one which is nearest the bull.

No one in this case suggests that a scheme based on 70 councillors is not a scheme which is not reasonably practicable to adopt. No one in this case has suggested that the sample on which the comparative analysis of the borough's 70 and the commission's 66 councillor schemes has been based is not a proper sample. Accordingly, I find myself driven to the conclusion that the proposals put forward by the commission to the Minister do not in this case comply with the mandatory requirements of para 3(2)(a) of Sch 11 to the 1972 Act and the requirements of s 78 of that Act, and that the borough is entitled as against the commission to a declaration accordingly.

Declaration accordingly.

Solicitors: *Wilfred D Day*, Chief Executive and Town Clerk, London Borough of Enfield; *Treasury Solicitor*.

K Mydeen Esq Barrister.

Floor v Davis (Inspector of Taxes)

COURT OF APPEAL, CIVIL DIVISION
BUCKLEY, EVELEIGH LJJ AND SIR JOHN PENNYCUICK
15th, 16th, 17th NOVEMBER 1977, 17th MARCH 1978

Capital gains tax – Disposal of assets – Company amalgamation – Exchange of shares or debentures – Company gaining control of other company – Control – Acquisition by issuing company of majority of shares in other company – Acquisition part of scheme whereby shares acquired were to be immediately disposed of to third party – Majority shareholders of other company becoming shareholders of issuing company – Whether issuing company having gained 'control' of other company – Finance Act 1965, Sch 7, paras 4, 6.

Capital gains tax – Disposal of assets – Persons having control of company and exercising control so that value passes out of his shares – Person having control – Exercise of control – Taxpayer and two relations holding preferred shares in newly formed company and controlling company – Rights issue of ordinary shares – Taxpayer and relations failing to take up rights issue – Fourth preferred shareholder acquiring in consequence all issued ordinary shares and with them right to six-sevenths of company's surplus assets on liquidation – Resolution that company should be voluntarily wound up passed – Taxpayer and one of his two relations not voting on resolution – Whether 'person having control' included more than one person – Whether resolution for winding up an exercise of control – Finance Act 1965, Sch 7, para 15(2).

The taxpayer and his two sons-in-law ('the vendors') held the majority of the shares in a company, IDM. In February 1969 all the shareholders in IDM agreed, subject to contract, to sell their shares to an American company, KDI, for a cash consideration of £833,333, of which £560,889 would be payable to the vendors. In order to minimise the liability to capital gains tax which a direct sale to KDI would create, the vendors evolved a scheme which was effected by the following transactions. On 24th February a company, FNW, was incorporated with an authorised capital divided into preferred and ordinary shares of 1s each. Under art 4 of FNW's articles of association the ordinary shares, when issued and paid up, were to carry rights to one-seventh of total declared dividends and six-sevenths of surplus assets on a winding-up, and the preferred shares, when issued and paid up, were to carry the rights to six-sevenths of all declared dividends and one-seventh of all surplus assets on a winding-up. All the issued shares were to have equal voting rights. By a written agreement, dated 27th February, the vendors agreed to sell their shares in IDM to FNW in consideration of the issue by FNW of 100,000 preferred shares. The preamble to the agreement recited that the vendors had agreed to sell and FNW had agreed to purchase the IDM shares free from all liens, charges and encumbrances and 'with a view to [FNW] re-selling the Shares to [KDI]'. The taxpayer received 43,954 preferred shares in FNW in exchange for 38,075 ordinary shares and 38,075 'A' ordinary shares in IDM. On 28th February FNW agreed to sell its IDM shares to KDI for a cash consideration of £560,889. On 27th March Donmarco, a company registered in the Cayman Islands, applied to FNW for 100 preferred shares in FNW, offering £5 per share and enclosing a cheque for £500. At a board meeting held on that day FNW agreed to accept the subscription request from Donmarco and resolved that a rights issue of ordinary shares of 1s each in the capital of FNW should be offered to the preferred shareholders in FNW on the basis of one ordinary share of 1s payable in cash at par in respect of two preferred shares of 1s each already issued. Letters offering the rights issue were sent to each of the vendors and to Donmarco on that day. The time for acceptance of the rights issue expired on 3rd April. By that date Donmarco was the only shareholder to accept the rights issue. It was allotted 50 ordinary shares. An extraordinary general meeting of FNW was called for 5th April to consider a resolution that the company should be voluntarily wound up. The *a* meeting was attended by a proxy for Donmarco and a proxy for one of the taxpayer's sons-in-law. Neither the taxpayer nor his other son-in-law was present and a vote was not cast on behalf of either of them. The winding-up resolution was passed with the result that, by virtue of art 4 of FNW's articles, six-sevenths of FNW's surplus assets passed to Donmarco, being the only ordinary shareholder, and the remaining one-seventh was divided between the vendors and Donmarco, being the only pre- *b* ferred shareholders. The taxpayer was assessed to capital gains tax on the basis that the transactions entered into effected a 'disposal' of his shares, within s 19(1)*ᵃ* of the Finance Act 1965, giving rise to chargeable gains. He appealed against the assessment to the Special Commissioners, who held (i) that, by virtue of Sch 7, para 6*ᵇ*, to the 1965 Act, there was no disposal for capital gains tax purposes when the taxpayer's shares in IDM were exchanged for shares in FNW because the exchange gave FNW 'control' *c* of IDM, within the meaning of para 6(2), but (ii) that the assessment should none-theless be affirmed because Sch 7, para 15(2)*ᶜ*, applied as the vendors were '[persons] having control' of FNW and the creation of the preferred and ordinary shares with particular rights, the issue of a small number of preferred shares to Donmarco, the acquisition of the ordinary shares by Donmarco in consequence of the rights issue and the ultimate liquidation of FNW all occurred as a result of the vendors' exercising *d* their control of FNW with the result that 'value [passed] out of the shares in the com-pany' owned by the taxpayer, within para 15(2). On appeal by the taxpayer, the Crown contended that the commissioners' decision should be affirmed on the additional ground that the transactions of 27th and 28th February had to be looked at together and treated, for capital gains tax purposes, as a direct disposal of the taxpayer's shares in IDM to KDI because FNW was merely a vehicle for the transfer of those *e* shares to KDI. Goulding J*ᵈ* allowed the taxpayer's appeal, holding (i) that the trans-actions were genuine transactions and the taxpayer in disposing of his shares in IDM to FNW could not be treated as having in reality disposed of them direct to KDI, (ii) that, by virtue of Sch 7, paras 4*ᵉ* and 6, the exchange of shares in IDM for those in FNW did not constitute a taxable disposal of the taxpayer's shares in IDM, (iii) that the taxpayer could not be deemed to be the 'person having control' of FNW, within Sch 7, para 15(2), because the word 'person' in that context did not include the plural 'persons' and the taxpayer could only control FNW in conjunction with his sons-in-law and (iv) that he could not, by taking no action in relation to the winding-up resolution, be said to have '[exercised] his control' of FNW so that value passed out of his shares in the company, within para 15(2). The Crown appealed.

a Section 19(1) provides: 'Tax shall be charged in accordance with this Act in respect of capital gains, that is to say chargeable gains computed in accordance with this Act and accruing to a person on the disposal of assets.'
b Paragraph 6 provides:
   '(1) Subject to the following sub-paragraphs [sic], where a company issues shares or deben-tures to a person in exchange for shares in or debentures of another company, paragraph 4 *f* above shall apply with any necessary adaptations as if the two companies were the same company and the exchange were a reorganisation of its share capital.
   '(2) This paragraph shall apply only where the company issuing the shares or debentures has or in consequence of the exchange will have control of the other company, or where the first-mentioned company issues the shares or debentures in exchange for shares as the result of a general offer made to members of the other company or any class of them (with or without exceptions for persons connected with the first-mentioned company), the offer being made in the first instance on a condition such that if it were satisfied the first-mentioned company would have control of the other company.'
c Paragraph 15(2) is set out at p 1083 *d* and *e*, post
d [1976] 3 All ER 314, [1976] STC 475
e Paragraph 4, so far as material, is set out at p 1083 *a* and *b*, post

Held – (i) (Eveleigh LJ dissenting) The fact that the vendors mutually intended that
a their IDM shares should ultimately reach KDI did not reduce the sale of those shares to
FNW to the status of a mere mechanical step in a disposal of the shares by the vendors
to KDI. The sale of their IDM shares to FNW was a genuine sale and its legal effect was
to make FNW the legal and beneficial owner of the shares. FNW was not bound by
any contractual or equitable obligation to sell the shares to KDI. The sale of the shares
by FNW to KDI was a separate transaction, involving only FNW and KDI. It followed
b that the taxpayer did not make a disposal of his shares in IDM direct to KDI (see p 1084 *g*
to *j*, p 1085 *c* to *f*, p 1086 *a b* and p 1090 *c* to *j*, post; *Inland Revenue Comrs v Duke of
Westminster* [1935] All ER Rep 259.

(ii) FNW, by acquiring the majority of the shares in IDM in exchange for its own
shares, without any binding obligation to transfer them to KDI, acquired 'control'
of IDM, within the meaning of Sch 7, para 6(2). The exchange was therefore to be
c treated as a reorganisation of capital, by virtue of Sch 7, paras 4 and 6, so that the
FNW shares acquired by the taxpayer fell to be treated as the same as the IDM shares
originally held by him (see p 1086 *c d*, p 1088 *e f* and p 1090 *c d*, post).

(iii) However, on the true construction of Sch 7, para 15(2), the word 'person'
included the plural 'persons', and on the facts the vendors had 'control' of FNW,
within the meaning of para 15(2) (see p 1086 *f* to *j*, p 1088 *f*, p 1090 *c d* and p 1091 *b*, post).
d (iv) Since the passing of the winding-up resolution was an integral part of the
vendors' pre-arranged scheme and was carried out in furtherance of it, it was, in the
circumstances, to be regarded for the purposes of Sch 7, para 15(2), as an exercise by all
three of them of their collective control of FNW, whereby value passed out of shares in
the company owned by them, notwithstanding that two of them did not actually vote
on the resolution. Accordingly there was a 'disposal' of shares by the taxpayer giving
e rise to a chargeable gain. The appeal would therefore be allowed (see p 1088 *b* to *e*,
p 1090 *c d* and p 1091 *b*, post).

Decision of Goulding J [1976] 3 All ER 314 reversed in part

Notes

For persons chargeable to capital gains tax, see 5 Halsbury's Laws (4th Edn) para 115,
f for disposals of shares, see ibid paras 67, 74, and for transfer of the value of shares, see
ibid para 57.

For the Finance Act 1965, s 19, Sch 7, paras 4, 6, 15, see 34 Halsbury's Statutes (3rd
Edn) 870, 952, 954, 958.

Cases referred to in judgments
g *Campbell (Trustees of Davies's Educational Trust) v Inland Revenue Comrs* [1968] 3 All ER
   588, [1970] AC 77, [1968] 3 WLR 1025, 45 Tax Cas 427, [1968] TR 327, 47 ATC 341, HL,
   28(1) 1 Digest (Reissue) 484, 1746.
Dawes v Tredwell (1881) 18 Ch D 354, 45 LT 118, CA, 17 Digest (Reissue) 414, 1786.
Inland Revenue Comrs v Duke of Westminster [1936] AC 1, [1935] All ER Rep 259, 19 Tax
   Cas 490, 104 LJKB 383, 153 LT 223, HL, 28(1) Digest (Reissue) 506, 1844.
h *Inland Revenue Comr v Europa Oil (NZ) Ltd* [1971] AC 760, [1971] 2 WLR 55, [1970] TR
   261, PC, 28(1) Digest (Reissue) 203, *670.
Mackenzie v Childers (1889) 43 Ch D 265, 59 LJCh 188, 62 LT 98, 17 Digest (Reissue)
   443, 2052.
Ransom (Inspector of Taxes) v Higgs [1974] 3 All ER 949, [1974] 1 WLR 1594, [1974] STC
   539, 53 ATC 285, [1974] TR 281, HL, Digest (Cont Vol D) 444, 295a.
j
Cases also cited
Bailey, Hay & Co Ltd, Re [1971] 3 All ER 693, [1971] 1 WLR 1357.
Barclay's Bank Ltd v Quistclose Investments Ltd [1968] 3 All ER 651, [1970] AC 567, HL.
Blériot Manufacturing Air Craft Co Ltd, Re (1916) 32 TLR 253.
Cleveleys Investment Trust Co v Inland Revenue Comrs [1975] STC 457.

Dealex Properties Ltd v Brooks [1965] 1 All ER 1080, [1966] 1 QB 542, CA.
Feversham's Contract, Re [1941] 3 All ER 100, [1942] Ch 33.   *a*
Nichols v Inland Revenue Comrs [1975] 2 All ER 120, [1975] 1 WLR 534, [1975] STC 278, CA.
Park Investments Ltd v Inland Revenue Comrs [1966] 2 All ER 785, [1966] Ch 701, 43 Tax
    Cas 200, CA.
Sturge (John & E) Ltd v Hessel (Inspector of Taxes) [1975] STC 573, CA.

Appeal   *b*

This was an appeal by the Crown against an order of Goulding J[1] dated 7th July 1976,
allowing an appeal by the taxpayer, Major Ides Maria Floor, by way of case stated[2]
against a decision of the Special Commissioners whereby they upheld the assessment
to capital gains tax made on the taxpayer for the year 1968-69. The taxpayer died
before the hearing of the appeal, and, by an order of Chief Master Ball, dated 3rd
March 1977, Marguerite Marie Mathilde Janssen Floor, was appointed to represent   *c*
his estate at the hearing. The facts are set out in the judgment of Sir John Pennycuick.

Peter Millett QC and *Brian Davenport* for the Crown.
C N Beattie QC and *G R Aaronson* for the taxpayer.

Cur adv vult *d*

17th March. The following judgments were read.

SIR JOHN PENNYCUICK (delivering the first judgment at the invitation of
Buckley LJ). This is an appeal from an order dated 7th July 1976 of Goulding J[1],
whereby he reversed a decision in favour of the Crown by the Special Commissioners.
    The appeal is concerned with a series of transactions effected in February and March *e*
1969 by one Ides Maria Floor ('the taxpayer') and his two sons-in-law whereby they
sought to carry through a sale of their respective shares in a company known as IDM
Electronics Ltd ('IDM') to an American company known as KDI International Corporation ('KDI') in such a way as to minimise the liability to capital gains tax on the
profit resulting from the sale.
    In the barest outline the series of transactions may be summarised thus. Stage 1: *f*
The taxpayer and the two sons-in-law held respectively 76,150, 59,050 and 38,050
shares out of 257,404 issued shares in IDM. By an agreement dated 27th February
1969 they agreed to sell their respective shares to a newly incorporated company
known as FNW Electronic Holdings Ltd ('FNW') in consideration of the issue to them
rateably of preferred shares in FNW, in which company they thereby came to own
the whole of the issued capital. Next day, 28th February 1969, FNW sold the shares *g*
in IDM so acquired by it to KDI in consideration of the sum of £560,889.
    Stage 2: between 27th March and 5th April 1969 FNW went through a series of
operations whereby, making use of certain special provisions in its articles, it went
into liquidation and distributed six-sevenths of this sum of £560,889 to a foreign
company which, through the instrumentality of a rights issue, had acquired ordinary
shares in FNW.   *h*
    The Crown claims that the taxpayer is chargeable with capital gains tax by refer-
ence to a proportion of the sum paid by KDI to FNW which corresponds to the shares
in IDM sold by him to FNW.
    It will be convenient now to refer to the provisions of Part III of the Finance Act
1965 which are directly relevant to the present appeal. Section 19 and the succeeding
sections impose a charge of tax in respect of capital gains accruing to persons on the *j*
disposal of assets. I need not read those sections. The Act contains no definition of
'disposal'. Section 22(9) introduces the provisions contained in Sch 7. That schedule,

1   [1976] 3 All ER 314, [1976] 1 WLR 1167, [1976] STC 475
2   The case stated is set out at [1976] 3 All ER 316-321

which is headed 'Capital Gains: Miscellaneous Rules', contains the following provisions.

a Paragraph 4(2):

'Subject to the following sub-paragraphs, a reorganisation or reduction of a company's share capital shall not be treated as involving any disposal of the original shares or any acquisition of the new holding or any part of it, but the original shares (taken as a single asset) and the new holding (taken as a single asset) shall be treated as the same asset acquired as the original shares were

b acquired.'

Paragraph 6(1):

'Subject to the following sub-paragraphs, where a company issues shares or debentures to a person in exchange for shares in or debentures of another company, paragraph 4 above shall apply with any necessary adaptations as if the two

c companies were the same company and the exchange were a reorganisation of its share capital. (2) This paragraph shall apply only where the company issuing the shares or debentures has or in consequence of the exchange will have control of the other company . . .'

(These sub-paragraphs are relevant on stage 1 of the series of transactions.) Paragraph

d 15(2):

'If a person having control of a company exercises his control so that value passes out of the shares in the company owned by him or a person with whom he is connected, or out of rights over the company exercisable by him or by a person with whom he is connected, and passes into other shares in or rights over the company, that shall be a disposal of the shares or rights out of which the value

e passes by the person by whom they were owned or exercisable.'

(This sub-paragraph is relevant on stage 2 of the series of transactions.)

Finally, Sch 18, para 3(1), contains an extended definition of 'control' under which a person shall be taken to have control of a company, inter alia, (a) if he possesses, or is entitled to acquire, the greater part of the share capital or voting power in the company, and concludes as follows: 'Where two or more persons together satisfy

f any of the conditions in paragraphs (a) to (c) above they shall be deemed to have control of the company.' Section 45(1) of the Act provides:

'In this part of this Act [i e Part III which includes Sch 7 as well as Sch 18] unless the context otherwise requires . . . "control" shall be construed in accordance with paragraph 3 of Schedule 18 to this Act.'

g Before the Special Commissioners the Crown based its case exclusively on the provisions contained in Sch 7, i e paras 4(2) and 6(1) in relation to stage 1 of the series of transactions and para 15(2) in relation to stage 2. The Special Commissioners in para 2 of the case stated[1] set out the questions for decision by them in the following terms:

'(i) whether when FNW Electronic Holdings Ltd. ("FNW") issued shares to [the taxpayer] in exchange for his shares in IDM Electronics Ltd. ("IDM") FNW

h had or in consequence of the exchange acquired control of IDM within the meaning of paragraph 6(2) Schedule 7 Finance Act 1965;

'(ii) whether the reference in paragraph 15(2) of that Schedule to a person exercising control of a company is to be read as if it referred to persons exercising such control and

'(iii) whether the transactions relating to FNW constituted the "exercise of

j control" of the Company within the meaning of paragraph 15(2) of Schedule 7 Finance Act 1965.'

In para 4 they set out in detail the facts, none of which was in dispute. In para 5

---

1   The case stated is set out at [1976] 3 All ER 316-321

they set out the contentions on behalf of the taxpayer. In para 6 they set out the contentions on behalf of the Crown. In para 8 they give a full and careful decision, accepting the contentions on behalf of the taxpayer in relation to stage 1 but accepting the contentions of the Crown in relation to stage 2. They accordingly dismissed the taxpayer's appeal. I will treat paras 4, 5, 6 and 8 of the case stated as read into this judgment.

The taxpayer appealed to the High Court and his appeal was heard by Goulding J. On this appeal the Crown raised a new contention, namely that for the purpose of capital gains tax there was a disposal by the taxpayer of his shares in IDM direct to KDI. This new contention the judge rightly dealt with first. He rejected the new contention and, like the Special Commissioners, he rejected the Crown's contentions in relation to stage 1. But, unlike the Special Commissioners, he also rejected the Crown's contentions in relation to stage 2. He accordingly allowed the taxpayer's appeal. The appeal before us is brought by the Crown against that decision. The taxpayer died before the hearing of the appeal and his personal representative has been joined as a party in his place.

The appeal, as it has now developed, raises four distinct issues, namely. (1) Did the taxpayer make a disposal of his shares in IDM direct to KDI? (2) Did FNW obtain control of IDM within the meaning of Sch 7, paras 4(2) and 6(1)? (3) Did the taxpayer and his two sons-in-law together have control of FNW within the meaning of Sch 7, para 15(2)? (4) If so, did they exercise that control within the meaning of para 15(2) when the resolution for the winding-up of FNW was passed? There is of course no doubt that that resolution caused value to pass out of the shares in FNW held by them respectively.

I will endeavour to deal with these four issues in the same order. (1) The critical transactions on this issue are (a) the agreement dated 27th February 1969 whereby the taxpayer and the sons-in-law entered into a binding contract with FNW for the sale to FNW of their respective shares in IDM in consideration of the issue to them respectively of shares in FNW and (b) the sale on 28th February 1969 by FNW of the shares in IDM to KDI for cash.

It is not in dispute on the one hand that these transactions, together with all the other relevant transactions, were effected pursuant to a pre-arranged scheme; and on the other hand that all the transactions were genuine, in contradistinction to colourable, transactions.

It was contended by counsel on behalf of the Crown that, even apart from any contractual or equitable obligation on the part of FNW to pass on the shares in IDM to KDI, transactions (a) and (b) looked at together, as they must be, should be regarded as simply a disposal by the taxpayer and the sons-in-law of their shares in IDM to KDI. It was pointed out that the Finance Act 1965 contains no definition of disposal and it was stressed that the combined effect, or end result, of the two transactions was indeed to pass the shares in IDM from the taxpayer and his sons-in-law to KDI, FNW being no more than a conduit pipe through which this passage was achieved. It seems to me that this contention disregards the legal effect of what were admittedly genuine transactions and really seeks to resurrect the conception of substance which was buried by the House of Lords in *Inland Revenue Comrs v Duke of Westminster*[1]. For a recent affirmation of the principle laid down in that case, see the statement by Lord Wilberforce in *Inland Revenue Comr v Europa Oil (NZ) Ltd*[2]. In my judgment it is impossible, on the plain legal effect of transactions (a) and (b), to maintain that the taxpayer and the sons-in-law sold their shares in IDM to anyone other than FNW or that KDI purchased those shares from anyone other than FNW. That is not a disposal by the taxpayer and the sons-in-law to KDI.

This contention of the Crown does not appear to me to derive any support from

---

1   [1936] AC 1, [1935] All ER Rep 259
2   [1971] AC 760 at 771

two decisions relied on, namely *Inland Revenue Comr v Europe Oil (NZ) Ltd*[1] and *Ransom (Inspector of Taxes) v Higgs*[2]. In the former case it was held that two contemporaneous and closely related contracts must be looked at together in order to determine whether certain expenditure was incurred exclusively for the purchase of trading stock. In the latter case a succession of transactions was examined in order to determine whether a trade was carried on. Each of these questions turned on considerations fundamentally different from that now under discussion in the present case.

An alternative contention was founded on preamble (d) of the agreement dated 27th February 1965. I will read that preamble again:

'The Vendors have agreed to sell and the Purchaser has agreed to purchase the Shares free from all liens charges and encumbrances upon the terms and conditions hereinafter appearing and with a view to the Purchaser re-selling the Shares to the said K.D.I. International Corporation as hereinbefore recited.'

It was argued that the recital imports a contractual obligation on FNW to sell the shares in IDM to KDI and accordingly that FNW, having acquired the shares subject to that obligation, was never the unfettered owner of the shares but in law as well as in substance was merely a piece of machinery through which the taxpayer and the sons-in-law disposed of the shares directly to KDI. If the premise were well-founded, I should see much force in this contention. But I am unable to accept the premise. Certainly in an appropriate case an instrument may require to be so construed that a binding obligation is to be implied from the recitals. A good instance is afforded by *Mackenzie v Childers*[3], where it was really clear from the recitals in a deed of mutual covenants constituting a building scheme that the vendor as well as the purchasers was to be bound. But I find nothing in the circumstances or apparent intention of the agreement dated 27th February which requires such an implication. The three individuals would be expected to rely on their 100 per cent control of FNW to ensure that it carried out their plan and would not find it necessary to impose a contractual obligation on their creature. We were referred in this connection to *Dawes v Tredwell*[4], where Jessel MR said:

'Now the rule is, that a recital does not control the operative part of a deed where the operative part is clear. The recital here, as is usually the case, is in general terms; the operative part is in definite terms. There is another rule that the recital of an agreement does not create a covenant where there is an express covenant to be found in the witnessing part relating to the same subject-matter. If, therefore, the covenant is clear, it cannot be controlled or affected by the recital.'

For a full discussion of this subject see Halsbury's Laws of England[5]. The former of the rules laid down by Jessel MR[4] applies here. That is to say, the operative part of the agreement is perfectly clear. It was suggested that cl 4 of the agreement brought the latter rule into play also. That, I think, is not so. Clause 4 is an undertaking by the vendors and would not exclude the implication of an obligation on the part of the purchaser.

It was contended on behalf of the Crown that one should infer some collateral contract between the taxpayer and the sons-in-law and FNW. The existence of such a contract would be a question of fact and there is no finding by the Special Commissioners of such a contract. Nor, I think, had they any material before them which would have supported such a finding.

---

1 [1971] AC 760
2 [1974] 3 All ER 949, [1974] 1 WLR 1594, [1974] STC 539
3 (1899) 43 Ch D 265
4 (1881) 18 Ch D 354 at 358, 359
5 12 Halsbury's Laws (4th Edn) para 1509

It was further contended on behalf of the Crown that FNW was under some equitable obligation to sell the shares to KDI. I see no ground for importing such an *a* equitable obligation. The relation of the taxpayer and the sons-in-law and FNW was that of vendors and purchaser under a contract of sale for full consideration and FNW's conscience could not be affected by any relevant obligation to the vendors outside the terms of the contract. Contrast the case of a voluntary disposition, e g a gift, made with a view to the application by the recipient of the subject-matter to some particular purpose. There the conscience of the recipient is indeed affected and he *b* cannot accept the subject-matter without carrying out the purpose. For a recent instance see *Campbell v Inland Revenue Comrs*[1], where a deed of covenant was made on the understanding that the covenantee would apply the sums paid under it to a given purpose. That is a wholly different proposition from that in the present case.

(2) In order to take advantage of the provisions in paras 4(2) and 6(2) of Sch 7 the taxpayer must show that on a share exchange the company issuing the shares has, or *c* in consequence of the exchange will have, control of the other company. That requirement is manifestly satisfied here. That is to say, FNW, the company issuing the shares, in consequence of the exchange, acquired the greater part of the share capital of IDM and with it the control of IDM. Once issue (1) has been resolved in favour of the taxpayer then issue (2) does not admit of argument.

Perhaps one should mention, in order to avoid possible misunderstanding, that *d* where paras 4(2) and 6(2) provide that the share transaction is not to be treated as involving a disposal, that expression clearly denotes a disposal giving rise to a charge of tax. It is not suggested that the transaction is to be disregarded in the sense that the acquiring company is to be treated as a mere emanation of the other company.

Before leaving issues (1) and (2) I would express my concurrence with the admirable judgment of Goulding J on these issues. *e*

(3) By virtue of the extended definition of 'control' in s 45(1) and Sch 18, para 3(1), unless the context otherwise requires, where two or more persons possess the greater part of the share capital or voting power in a company, they shall be taken to have control of the company. The context of Sch 7, para 15(2), emphatically does not otherwise require. There is nothing in the context which renders the provision of that sub-paragraph inappropriate to operations carried out in concert by two or more *f* persons. Extended so as to include the plural, the sub-paragraph reads:

'If a person [or persons] having control of a company exercises [or exercise] his [or their] control so that value passes out of shares in the company owned by him or them or a person [or persons] with whom he is [or they] are connected ... that shall be a disposal of the shares ... out of which the value passes by the person [or persons] by whom they were owned ...' *g*

So extended, and with no other addition to, or alteration of, its language, the sub-paragraph plainly admits of, and requires, a distributive construction. That is to say, in the case where two or more persons have control, it reads:

'If persons having control of a company exercise their control so that value *h* passes out of shares in the company owned by them respectively or persons with whom they are respectively connected ... that shall be a disposal of the shares ... out of which the value passes by the persons by whom they were respectively owned ...'

That is a perfectly clear and sensible provision. To take a simple example, suppose that X Ltd has 100 issued shares, A owns 30 shares, Mrs A 10 shares, B 30 shares, Mrs B *j* 10 shares C (a stranger) 10 shares and D (a stranger) 10 shares, and that A and B exercise their control by passing a resolution such that value passes out of the shares

---

1   [1968] 3 All ER 588, [1970] AC 77, 45 Tax Cas 426

held by A, Mrs A, B, Mrs B and C into the shares held by D. Then there is a disposal
a by A, Mrs A, B and Mrs B of the shares owned by them respectively, but no disposal
by C.

Counsel for the Crown found great obscurity in the sub-paragraph and in particular
in the words 'a person with whom he is connected'. At one stage in his argument he
was disposed to say that these words could have no application at all where more
than one person has control. In the end he settled for a contention that the words
b would apply to a person with whom all the persons having control were connected,
an improbable and rather ridiculous provision. Counsel for the taxpayer stressed the
difficulties of construction which arise on any but a distributive basis. Faced with this
consensus of obscurity, the learned judge made an elaborate analysis of the sub-
paragraph and found it equally obscure. Neither counsel nor the judge seem to have
addressed their minds to a distributive construction. The Special Commissioners
c had been content to construe the provision in relation to the facts of the present case.

I have felt some diffidence in applying a construction which does not seem to have
occurred to the very experienced counsel or to the learned judge, but for myself I
believe this construction to be plainly correct, and so construed the sub-paragraph is
free from obscurity.

I have dealt with this question by reference to the definition of 'control' in the Act
d itself. The argument below, and most of the argument before us, was conducted by
reference to s 1 of the Interpretation Act 1889. The result is the same. It seems to be
more appropriate to apply the definition in the Act.

On this issue, then, I differ from the learned judge.

(4) It remains to consider whether the taxpayer and the sons-in-law should be
regarded as having exercised their control of FNW when that company passed its
e winding-up resolution on 5th April 1969. It will be remembered that the meeting at
which the resolution was passed was attended by a proxy for the taxpayer's son-in-law,
Mr Wellesley-Wesley, and a proxy for Roycan Nominees Ltd, which had now come
to hold 50 ordinary shares in the company. Under the articles of FNW the ordinary
shares and the preferred shares rank pari passu as regards voting. Neither the taxpayer himself nor his other son-in-law, Mr Naylor-Leyland, was present, nor was a
f vote cast on behalf of either of them. The Special Commissioners appear to have
taken it for granted that the taxpayer and his sons-in-law must together be treated as
having exercised their control when the special resolution was passed.

The learned judge, however, took a different view. I will quote from the passage
in his judgment[1] in which he deals with this point:

> 'This is a question of difficulty and some breadth. Counsel for the Crown
g submits quite generally that to refrain from stopping action by a company which
one has power to prevent and with knowledge of the consequences may in
suitable circumstances be an exercise of control of the company. Of course, one
does not need to have control of a company in any sense to be able in some
circumstances to allow a result to happen by abstention. One can think at once
of the 30 per cent holder of voting shares who refrains from blocking a special
h resolution although he could do so. He certainly exercises no control of the
company although his abstention has a certain result. Of course, counsel intended
his formulation to apply only to cases where the person who refrains from acting
is one who has control in the statutory sense. I am unable to accept either counsel
for the Crown's general submission or the assertion of the Special Commissioners,
on the basis of the primary agreed facts, that whatever FNW did throughout its
j existence it did in consequence of its shareholders' exercise of control. In my
judgment, to satisfy the words "exercises . . . control" in para 15(2) of Sch 7 some
positive act that is capable of specific identification as an exercise of control is

---

1   [1976] 3 All ER 314 at 328, [1976] 1 WLR 1167 at 1177, 1178, [1976] STC 475 at 489

required. It is not everyone who has control who exercises it, even though the company controlled may in fact do things that he would like it to do. Accordingly, *a* on this point also I respectfully differ from the Special Commissioners.'

I do not doubt that in the ordinary case of control by the holding of a majority of shares the expression 'exercise control' indicates the casting of the votes attached to those shares on the relevant resolutions, and that a shareholder could not be treated as exercising control when he is absent or inactive when the resolution is proposed. But the expression 'exercise control' is not a term of art denoting by its own force *b* the casting of votes and nothing else, and there may be circumstances, in the case of control by more than one person, where those persons should indeed be treated as collectively exercising control without all of them actually casting their votes. It seems to me that the circumstances here are of that character. The taxpayer and the sons-in-law acquired voting control of FNW as the first step in a series of operations *c* designed to eventuate in the proceeds of their shares in IDM passing to a foreign company. This series of operations represented a scheme planned in advance by the three individuals acting in concert. The passing of the winding-up resolution by FNW was an integral and essential operation in this scheme and was indisputably carried out in furtherance of a common and continuing intention on the part of the three individuals. On these facts it seems to me that the resolution should be regarded *d* as an exercise by all three individuals of their collective control. It is, I think, immaterial that two of the individuals did not actually cast their votes in favour of the resolution. So on this issue too I differ from the learned judge.

I conclude that, although the taxpayer succeeds on the first two issues, he fails on the third and fourth issues. That conclusion is sufficient to decide the appeal in favour of the Crown and I would allow the appeal accordingly.

e

EVELEIGH LJ. I take the view that the shares with which we are concerned were disposed of by the respondent taxpayer to the American company KDI. On all other points I agree with the judgment just delivered.

It is clear that right from the beginning the American company indicated that it would purchase the shares. The only reason for avoiding a direct sale to them was *f* the prospect of capital gains tax. In an attempt to avoid paying this, as is frankly accepted, the initial transfer to FNW took place. There was however no real possibility at any time that the shares would not reach the American company. By virtue of their control of FNW the shareholders guaranteed from the moment they parted with the legal ownership that the shares would become the property of the American company. No one could prevent this against their wishes. By virtue of the *g* arrangement initially made between them each was under an obligation to the other to do nothing to stop the shares arriving in the hands of the American company. They controlled the destiny of the shares from beginning to end in pursuance of a continuing intention on their part that the shares should be transferred to KDI.

This court is concerned to decide whether any capital gains accruing as a result of the transaction can be said to be gains accruing to a person on the disposal of assets *h* within the meaning of s 19(1) of the Finance Act 1965. There is no legal definition of the word 'disposal' and I can see no reason to define it as 'the first legal transfer in the ownership of property'. Indeed I do not understand counsel for the taxpayer to contend that the meaning should be so limited. Property could be disposed of to C by transferring it to B in trust for C. If in the present case FNW had contracted to transfer the shares to KDI and had acquired them on those terms it seemed to me, as this case was argued before the court, that it would have been very difficult for counsel to contend that there was not a disposal by the taxpayer to KDI. However, what he said is that there was no such contract and consequently the only transaction by the taxpayer was a transfer (or disposal) of the shares to FNW. Thereafter he said the transfer to KDI was entirely separate.

a Emphasis is placed on the fact that it is conceded that the transfer to FNW was a genuine one. I understand 'genuine' in this context to mean that it was what it purported to be, namely the transfer of the ownership to FNW. The court often meets the contention that a transaction is specious in the sense that it is not the legal transaction it appears to be. Hire-purchase agreements masquerading as bills of sale, and so called furnished tenancies under the Rent Acts, are examples of this.

b Without the concession I would have treated the transfer to FNW as genuine, but it was only part of a larger transaction. The question that the court has to determine is whether that transaction was a disposal to KDI.

If a man wished to sell his house to his mistress at an artificially low price and conceal it from his wife, he might with the co-operation of a friend who held a controlling interest in a company sell the house to the company at that low price in the knowledge that his friend would ensure that the house was sold to the mistress.

c There would be no legal obligation on the company to do this. Nonetheless in my opinion the original owner would have disposed of his house to his mistress. Qui facit per alium facit per se is a maxim which does not depend on the contractual relationship of principal and agent. A man may act through the hand of another whose conduct he manages to manipulate in some way, and whether or not he has so acted is often a question of fact to be considered by looking at all that is done.

d I see this case as one in which the court is not required to consider each step taken in isolation. It is a question of whether or not the shares were disposed of to KDI by the taxpayer. I believe that they were. Furthermore, they were in reality at the disposal of the original shareholders until the moment they reached the hand of KDI, although the legal ownership was in FNW.

I do not think that this conclusion is any way vitiated by *Inland Revenue Comrs*
e *v Duke of Westminster*[1]. In that case it was sought to say that the payments under covenant were not such but were payments of wages. I do not seek to say that the transfer to FNW was not a transfer. The important feature of the present case is that the destiny of the shares was at all times under the control of the taxpayer who was arranging for them to be transferred to the American company. The transfer to FNW was but a step in that process. In *Inland Revenue Comrs v Duke of Westminster*[1] the legal
f position was that there existed a covenant imposing on the Duke a liability to make payments thereunder. The Crown was not permitted to say that those payments were anything else. Effect had to be given to the legal position. Lord Russell of Killowen said[2]:

> 'I confess that I view with disfavour the doctrine that in taxation cases the subject is to be taxed if, in accordance with a Court's view of what it considers the sub-
g stance of the transaction, the Court thinks that the case falls within the contemplation or spirit of the statute. The subject is not taxable by inference or by analogy, but only by the plain words of a statute applicable to the facts and circumstances of his case.'

In deciding that there was a disposal within the plain words of the statute to KDI, I
h in no way deny the legal effect of the transfer to FNW. Referring to the alleged doctrine that the subject is to be taxed according to the court's view of the substance of the transaction, Lord Russell said[3]:

> 'If all that is meant by the doctrine is that having once ascertained the legal rights of the parties you may disregard mere nomenclature and decide the question of taxability or non-taxability in accordance with the legal rights, well
j and good . . . If, on the other hand the doctrine means that you may brush aside deeds, disregard the legal rights and liabilities arising under a contract between

---

1 [1936] AC 1, [1935] All ER Rep 259
2 [1936] AC 1 at 24, [1935] All ER Rep 259 at 270
3 [1936] AC 1 at 25, [1935] All ER Rep 259 at 270

parties, and decide the question of taxability or non-taxability upon the footing of the rights and liabilities of the parties being different from what in law they are, then I entirely dissent from such a doctrine.'

I hope that in reaching the conclusion I have, I am paying full attention to the words of Lord Russell[1] and to the principle established in *Inland Revenue Comrs v Duke of Westminster*[2]. I am not called on to decide whether or not the transfer to FNW was a disposal. Paragraph 6(1) and para 4(2) of Sch 7 to the Finance Act 1965 require such a transfer to be treated as a reorganisation of share capital and not as involving any disposal of the shares. Whatever the nature of that transaction, and in ordinary language it could be called a disposal or dealing with the shares, I take the view that the taxpayer was dealing with the shares right up to the time that they reached KDI and that the transfer to FNW was conveyancing machinery.

I therefore would allow this appeal on this ground also.

BUCKLEY LJ. I agree with the judgment delivered by Sir John Pennycuick. In my judgment, the transactions which together make up stage 1 of the series cannot for the present purpose properly be regarded as a disposal by the taxpayer and his sons-in-law of their shares in IDM to KDI. It is conceded that there was a genuine sale of those shares by the three shareholders to FNW. Had that transaction stood alone, it seems to me that the questions whether the shareholders had disposed of their shares, and, if so, to whom, could only be answered in one way: 'Yes, to FNW.' The fact that the shareholders became in consequence the only shareholders of FNW and controlled that company would not, I think, affect this answer. Paragraphs 4(2) and 6(1) of Sch 7 to the Finance Act 1965 cannot, in my opinion, have that effect. Those paragraphs, as I read them, provide that a disposal of assets to which they apply shall not for the purposes of the charge to tax be treated as a disposal. This does not mean that such a disposal is not a disposal within the meaning of that term in the Act, but that, notwithstanding that it is a disposal, it shall not be taxed as such.

If one considers what rights and obligations arose in consequence of the sale and transfer of the shares to FNW it cannot, I think, be disputed that FNW became the legal and beneficial owner of the shares. No trust, whether express or constructive, arose. No obligation in favour of KDI was created. In the improbable event of the taxpayer and his sons-in-law changing their minds and abandoning their pre-existing intention that FNW should sell the shares on to KDI, KDI could have had no ground for complaint. Nor could the taxpayer and his sons-in-law have complained if KDI had decided not to proceed with its purchase of the shares from FNW.

Using the word 'disposal' in its primary and natural sense, the three shareholders did, in my opinion, dispose of their shares to FNW. In these circumstances, can the fact that they mutually intended to procure the sale of the shares by FNW to KDI deprive the sale to FNW of its character as a disposal and reduce it to the status of a merely mechanical step in a disposal of the shares by the three shareholders to KDI? It is again conceded that the sale by FNW to KDI was a genuine sale. The contract for this sale was made on 28th February 1969, the day following the transfer of the IDM shares to FNW. It was a distinct transaction from the sale to FNW. Again using the word 'disposal' in its primary and natural sense, it is, in my opinion, clear that by that contract FNW disposed of the shares to KDI.

To treat both these transactions together as effecting a single disposal by the three shareholders to KDI by reason of their pre-existing intention that the shares should ultimately reach KDI and of their control of the proceedings, seems to me to involve ignoring the principle enunciated in *Inland Revenue Comrs v Duke of Westminster*[2], that

---

1 [1936] AC 1 at 24, 25, [1935] All ER Rep 259 at 270
2 [1936] AC 1, [1935] All ER Rep 259

a to ascertain the 'substance' of a transaction one must determine the rights and obligations of the parties from a consideration of the whole transaction, having regard to the legal effect of what the parties have done, ascertained on ordinary legal principles (see per Lord Tomlin[1]). So regarding the present case, I do not think it justifiable to tax the taxpayer on the basis that there was only one disposal where in law there were two.

b Nevertheless, for the reasons indicated by Sir John Pennycuick I think that this appeal succeeds on the third and fourth issues discussed by Sir John Pennycuick in his judgment.

Appeal allowed; order of Special Commissioners restored; leave to appeal to House of Lords; if necessary, leave to the Crown to cross-appeal.

c Solicitors: *Solicitor of Inland Revenue; Courts & Co* (for the taxpayer).

Christine Ivamy   Barrister.

Re Tiltwood, Sussex
d # Barrett v Bond and others

CHANCERY DIVISION
FOSTER J
1st, 2nd, 14th FEBRUARY 1978

e *Restrictive covenant affecting land – Extinguishment – Freehold – Common ownership of burdened and benefited land – Owner in fee simple of benefited land purchasing part of burdened land – Subsequent sale by common owner of benefited and burdened land to different purchasers – Whether burdened land remaining subject to covenant – Whether unity of seisin of burdened and benefited land extinguishing covenant or merely suspending it until revival on sale of benefited land – Law of Property Act 1925, s 84(2)(a).*

f By his will the owner of an estate of 500 acres comprising a mansion house, its gardens and agricultural land, devised a life interest in the mansion and gardens to his widow, and devised the remainder of the estate and the reversion expectant on the widow's death to his son. By a conveyance dated 18th June 1951 the son conveyed part of the agricultural land, to the south of the mansion, to L who covenanted in the conveyance g that he and his successors in title would use the land conveyed ('the burdened land') for agricultural purposes only and would not build on it. The covenant was imposed by the son to protect the view to the south from the mansion. On the widow's death in August 1951 the mansion and gardens ('the benefited land') were vested in the son and by a conveyance made in February 1952 he conveyed them, together with the benefit of the covenant on the burdened land, to Mrs S. In August 1952 Mrs S purchased from L about half of the burdened land. The conveyance was expressed to be h subject to the covenant on the burdened land. Mrs S thus became the owner of the benefited land and of part of the burdened land. She divided up the mansion and gardens and the part of the burdened land she had purchased into lots for sale by auction. The auction particulars and the conditions of sale of the lots did not mention the covenant on the burdened land. All the lots were sold prior to auction but the contracts were made in accordance with the auction particulars and conditions of j sale. The plaintiff bought several of the lots including a lot which comprised the part of the burdened land purchased by Mrs S. The conveyance of the lots to the plaintiff was expressed to be subject to the covenant on the burdened land contained in the

1   [1936] AC 1 at 20, [1935] All ER Rep 259 at 268

1951 conveyance but it also contained a covenant which permitted development of
the lots for domestic purposes. The plaintiff obtained planning permission to erect
a dwelling-house on the lots. The defendants, the purchasers of other lots which
consisted of part of the benefited land, opposed the development of the burdened
land. The plaintiff applied, under s 84(2)ᵃ of the Law of Property Act 1925, for a declaration that the part of the burdened land formerly owned by Mrs S was not subject
to the restrictive covenant because in relation to that part of the burdened land the
covenant had been extinguished in August 1952, when Mrs S became the owner of
both the benefited land and that part of the burdened land, and was not merely
suspended until it was revived on a sale of the benefited land. The defendants
contended that the covenant remained valid and enforceable.

Held – Where the fee simple of the benefited and the burdened land became vested
in one person, restrictive covenants on the burdened land were extinguished unless
the common owner recreated them on a subsequent sale of the benefited land.
When in August 1952 Mrs S became the common owner of that part of the burdened
land purchased by her and the benefited land, the covenant in respect of that part
of the burdened land had been extinguished, and since she had not recreated the
restrictive covenant on the sale by her of the benefited land, it followed that the
plaintiff was entitled to the declaration sought (see p 1099 c and d, post).

Dictum of Lord Cross in *Texaco Antilles Ltd v Kernochan* [1973] 2 All ER at 127 followed.

Notes

For the jurisdiction of the court to discharge restrictive covenants, see 16 Halsbury's
Laws (4th Edn) para 1363, and for cases on the subject, see 40 Digest (Repl) 364-367,
2925-2936.

For the Law of Property Act 1925, s 84, see 27 Halsbury's Statutes (3rd Edn) 468.

Cases referred to in judgment

Brunner v Greenslade [1970] 3 All ER 833, [1971] Ch 993, [1970] 3 WLR 891, 22 P & CR
54, Digest (Cont Vol C) 869, 2744a.

Elliston v Reacher [1908] 2 Ch 665, [1908-10] All ER Rep 612, 78 LJCh 87, 99 LT 701,
CA, 28(2) Digest (Reissue) 1052, 715.

Lawrence v South County Freeholds Ltd [1939] 2 All ER 503, [1939] Ch 656, 108 LJCh 236,
161 LT 11, 40 Digest (Repl) 354, 2844.

Miles v Etteridge (1692) 1 Show 349, 89 ER 618, 11 Digest (Reissue) 53, 800.

Sunnyfield, Re [1932] 1 Ch 79, [1931] All ER Rep 837, 101 LJCh 55, 146 LT 206, 40 Digest
(Repl) 365, 2929.

Texaco Antilles Ltd v Kernochan [1973] 2 All ER 118, [1973] AC 609, [1973] 2 WLR 381,
PC, Digest (Cont Vol D) 807, 2745b.

Cases also cited

Bolton v Bolton (1879) 11 Ch D 968.

Holmes v Goring, Holmes v Elliot (1824) 2 Bing 76.

London and South Western Railway Co v Gomm (1882) 20 Ch D 562.

Simper v Foley (1862) 2 John & H 555.

Union of London and Smith's Bank, Re, Miles v Easter [1933] Ch 611, [1933] All ER Rep 355,
CA.

Wheeldon v Burrows (1879) 12 Ch D 31, [1874-80] All ER Rep 669, CA.

Originating summons

By an originating summons dated 8th December 1976, amended and reissued on
15th February 1977, the plaintiff, Florence Lillian Barrett, applied under s 84(2) of

---

a　Section 84(2), so far as material, is set out at p 1093 d and e, post

the Law of Property Act 1925 for the following relief: (1) a declaration that the land
a comprised in parcels designated as ordnance survey nos 267B, 267C and 267D
comprised in a conveyance dated 18th June 1951 made between George Ambrose
Scaramanga and Henry John Longinotto was no longer subject to any of the restrictive
covenants contained in the conveyance, and (2) alternatively, that it might be declared whether the restrictive covenants in the conveyance or any and which of
them were enforceable and if so in whom the title to enforce them were vested.
b The defendants to the application were (1) Mr P Bond, (2) and (3) Mr and Mrs J Davis,
(4) Mr D Driver, (5) and (6) Mr and Mrs S W Duggan, (7) Dr A M M Graham, (8)
Mr C W Murphy, (9) Dr S Parker, (10) Mr J S Smith and (11) Mr Hedley. The facts are
set out in the judgment.

George Newsom QC and *J M Henty* for the plaintiff.
c *Nathaniel Micklem* for the fourth, fifth, sixth, seventh and ninth defendants.
The other defendants did not appear.

Cur adv vult

14th February. **FOSTER J** read the following judgment: In this case the plaintiff
seeks a declaration that the land which she owns is not bound by a restrictive
d covenant. The claim is made under s 84 of the Law of Property Act 1925.
Section 84(2) reads.

'The court shall have power on the application of any person interested—
(*a*) to declare whether or not in any particular case any freehold land is or would
in any given event be affected by a restriction imposed by an instrument . . .'

e and sub-s (5) reads:

'Any order made under this section shall be binding on all persons, whether
ascertained or of full age or capacity or not, then entitled or thereafter capable
of becoming entitled to the benefit of any restriction, which is thereby discharged,
modified or dealt with, and whether such persons are parties to the proceedings
f or have been served with notice or not.'

There are five defendants who appear before me by counsel to oppose the declaration but I must first be satisfied that all other possible defendants have been given
an adequate chance of appearing before me. In *Re Sunnyfield*[1] Maugham J, in an
unopposed case, said :

g 'When such an order as this is asked for, the Court ought to make every effort
to see that all persons who may wish to oppose the making of the order have
the opportunity of being heard, stating their objections in argument before
the Court, and inviting the Court to refuse to exercise its powers. In the present
case, it seems that every effort has been made to give noticet o all persons having
a probable interest in the property, and accordingly I ought not to refuse to
h proceed to the hearing of the matter.'

Counsel for the plaintiff submitted that sufficient notice had been given. Counsel
for the opposing defendants was in no way concerned with this aspect of the case.
However I asked him if he would act as amicus curiae on the matter and I am indeed
grateful to him for doing so. He assured me that sufficient notice had been given
to those who might be concerned. On his and counsel for the plaintiff's submissions
j I am satisfied that all those who might wish to oppose and who do not appear before
me have had sufficient notice, and particularly as there are five defendants who
appear by counsel and oppose strongly the application. I can therefore proceed to
consider the application as an opposed and strongly opposed case on its merits.

1   [1932] 1 Ch 79 at 83, [1931] All ER Rep 837 at 838, 839

Conveyancing history prior to June 1951

By conveyances dated respectively 25th March 1911 and 20th November 1928 the a Tiltwood Estate at Crawley Down consisting of some 500 acres, a mansion house and a farm, Hophurst Farm, became vested for an estate in fee simple in Mr A G Scaramanga. He made his will on 2nd May 1944, died on 4th November 1946, and probate of his will and codicils was granted to his executors on 20th March 1947. By his testamentary dispositions he gave a life interest in the mansion house and immediate gardens together with a field both to the east and west to his widow, and he gave the b remainder of the estate and the reversionary interest expectant on the widow's death in the mansion house and other grounds to his son, Mr G A Scaramanga. By an assent dated 27th April 1948 the testator's executors assented to the vesting in the son of all the portions of the estate other than those in which the widow had a life interest. The son decided to sell the agricultural portions of the estate (i e those lands in which the widow had no life interest) and was put up for auction in June 1951. c Lot 1 which comprised the land around the mansion house and grounds was by a conveyance dated 18th June 1951 conveyed by the son to Mr H J Longinotto. By cl 3 of that conveyance the purchaser covenanted as follows with the vendor:

> 'THE Purchaser hereby covenants with the Vendor (but not so that he the Purchaser shall be liable for any breach thereof after he shall have parted with d the property or any part thereof in respect of which a breach of this covenant shall hereafter occur) that he the Purchaser and his successors in title will use the Enclosures numbered 267 267B 267C and 267D more particularly referred to in the Schedule hereto for agricultural purposes only and that no building or other structure or erection whatsoever whether permanent or temporary shall at any time hereafter be built erected or placed or suffered to be upon e any part of the aforesaid Enclosures.'

It is with these covenants that I am concerned. The mansion house had a fine view to the south over parcels 267, 267B, 267C and 267D and it was to protect this that the covenant was taken.

Conveyance of 11th February 1952

The widow, Mrs Nina Scaramanga, died on 21st August 1951 and as there had been no assent in her favour as life tenant the executors of the testator's will assented to the vesting in the son of the freehold in the mansion house and its grounds and fields on 29th November 1951. By a conveyance dated 11th February 1952 the son conveyed the mansion house and grounds to Mrs Neta Mountford Spence, with the benefit of the restrictive covenants contained in the 1951 conveyance to Mr Longinotto in g respect of parcels 267, 267B, 267C and 267D. To the south of those parcels there was a strip of land consisting of woods and some ponds which were also conveyed to Mrs Spence and she was granted a right of way from the mansion house to this piece of land. The right of way divided parcel 267 on the east from parcels 267B, 267C and 267D on the west. Thus I find that Mr Spence has become the owner of the mansion house and the other lands (which I will call 'the benefited lands') and Mr h Longinotto is the owner of parcels 267, 267B, 267C and 267D (which I will call 'the burdened land') which is burdened by the restrictive covenant in the 1951 conveyance.

Events prior to the 1952 auction

It is clear that Mrs Spence had no intention of retaining the mansion house and land as a unit and immediately started to break up the mansion house into various j lots to be put up for auction which was to have taken place on 30th October 1952. Before I consider what took place just before this auction, two conveyances took place which are of some significance in this case. (i) On 15th July 1952 Mrs Spence conveyed to Colonel Clark the western part of the mansion house and some ground. In his conveyance there was no express assignment of the benefit of the restrictive covenant in respect of the land to the south. (ii) On 28th August 1952

a Mrs Spence purchased the land being parcels 267B, 267C and 267D but not parcel
267 back from Mr Longinotto. The evidence showed that the reason for this was
that in exercising her right of way to visit her land to the south she had been attacked
by a bull and wished to have her own land over which she could visit the southern
part. This land, parcels 267B, 267C and 267D, is of course part and in area about
half of the burdened land, and she owned the benefited land other than that part of

b the mansion house and land sold to Colonel Clark (but with no express assignment
of the benefit). I must notice the conveyance of 28th August 1952 in greater detail.
The relevant words are:

> '... EXCEPT AND RESERVING unto George Ambrose Scaramanga and his successors
> in title being the owner or owners occupier or occupiers for the time being of the
> adjoining land known as Tiltwood a right of way at all times and for all purposes
c > over the way not exceeding twelve feet in width as indicated on the said plan by
> the letters A B and C AND ALSO EXCEPTING AND REVERSING unto the Vendor all tim-
> ber or timberlike and other trees on any part of the land hereby conveyed with
> the right for the Vendor and all other persons authorised by him to enter upon
> the said land hereby conveyed or any part thereof from time to time as he shall
> think fit to remove such timber or timberlike and other trees or any part of
d > them TO HOLD (except and reserved as aforesaid) unto the Purchaser in fee simple
> subject to the rights and covenants contained in a Conveyance dated [18th June
> 1951] and made between the said George Ambrose Scaramanga of the one part
> and the Vendor of the other part so far as the same relate to the property hereby
> conveyed and are subsisting and capable of being enforced
e > '2. WITH the object of affording to the Vendor full and sufficient indemnity
> but not further or otherwise the Purchaser hereby covenants with the Vendor
> that she will perform and observe the covenants contained in the before men-
> tioned Conveyance dated [18th June 1951] so far as the same relate to the pro-
> perty hereby conveyed and are still subsisting and capable of being enforced
> and will keep the Vendor and his estate and effects effectually indemnified
f > from and against all actions claims and demands in any wise relating thereto ...'

As Mrs Spence owned the benefited land and was purchasing part of the burdened
land the exception of a right of way over the land she was purchasing was wholly
unnecessary and there was no necessity to convey it subject to the covenants in
the conveyance of 18th June 1951. Further para 2 of that conveyance was wholly
otiose.

g
The 1952 auction

This was scheduled to take place on 30th October 1952 and particulars of the sale
were prepared. Colonel Clark had already acquired Tiltwood West. The remainder
of the mansion and its grounds was divided into six lots. The centre of the mansion
house was the subject of lot 1 and called Tiltwood South though it is now known as

h Tiltwood House. Lot 2 was the eastern portion of the mansion house known as Tiltwood East and there were four other lots. It is common ground that all the lots
were sold prior to the auction but that the contracts were all made in accordance
with the auction particulars and the conditions of sale.

Condition 10 of the conditions of sale is in these terms:

j > 'In his Conveyance the Purchaser of each Lot shall enter into a covenant for
> himself and his successors in title with intent so as to bind so far as practicable
> the property agreed to be sold into whosoever hands the same may go and to
> benefit and protect the remainder of the Tiltwood Estate:—(a) Not at any time
> to use any building for any other purpose whatsoever than as a private dwelling-
> house or residence or for agricultural or horticultural purposes and that nothing

shall be done or suffered to be done upon any Lot or any part thereof which may be or become a nuisance annoyance or injury or which may tend to depreciate the value of any other Lot or any part of the Tiltwood Estate.'

Sub-paragraph (b) is not, I think, relevant.

There is no mention in the auction particulars or the conditions of sale of the restrictive covenants affecting the southern aspect, i e parcels 267, 267B, 267C and 267D. The fact that in certain conveyances there was an express assignment of the restrictive covenant occurred because of certain requisitions on title.

The defendants' properties

There are four properties owned by the defendants.

1. Tiltwood West is now owned by the fourth defendant. This consists of part of the mansion house and grounds conveyed to Colonel Clark on 15th July 1952 with no express assignment but further land was later bought which had an express assignment of the benefit of the restrictive covenants.

2. Tiltwood House which consisted of the centre part of the mansion house is now owned by the fifth and sixth defendants who have also an express assignment.

3. Tiltwood East is owned by the seventh defendant also with an express assignment of the covenant.

4. The ninth defendant owns a property to the south-west of the mansion house on which she had built a house called Pasturewood. That property too has been conveyed with an express assignment of the covenants.

It is therefore common ground that all the defendants have express assignments of parts of the land benefited by the restrictive covenants, and on their behalf it is submitted that these covenants remain valid and enforceable.

The plaintiff's land

The plaintiff bought also just before the auction part of lot 3 and lots 5 and 6. Lot 5 consisted of the west part of the burdened land purchased by Mrs Spence on 28th August 1952 from Mr Longinotto. Lot 6 is the remainder of the burdened land, namely parcel 267. It is admitted by the plaintiff that so far as parcel 267 is concerned the restrictive covenant is unaffected.

The plaintiff's conveyance of 30th December 1952

I will read the main provisions:

'... To HOLD the same unto the Purchaser in fee simple Subject to but with the benefit of the exceptions and reservations stipulations and covenants contained or referred to in a Conveyance of the neighbouring property now known as Tiltwood West dated [15th July 1952] and made between the vendor of the one part and Harold Ernest Clark of the other part so far as the same relate to or affect the property hereby conveyed and are still subsisting and capable of taking effect and subject to a covenant contained in a Conveyance dated [18th June 1951] and made between George Ambrose Scaramanga of the one part and Henry John Longinotto of the other part that the said Henry John Longinotto and his successors in title would use the enclosures 267, 267B, 267C and 267D (being part of the land hereby conveyed) for agricultural purposes only and that no building or other structure or erection whatsoever whether permanent or temporary should at any time thereafter be built erected or placed or suffered to be upon any part of the aforesaid enclosures.

'2. THE Purchaser HEREBY COVENANTS with the Vendor with intent so as to bind as far as practicable the property hereby conveyed unto whosoever hands the same may go and to benefit and protect the remainder of the property known as the Tiltwood Estate that she the Purchaser and her successors in title:—
(a) Will not at any time use any building upon the property hereby conveyed for any other purpose whatsoever than as a private dwellinghouse or residence or

a for agricultural or horticultural purposes and will not do or suffer to be done upon the property hereby conveyed or any part thereof anything which may be or become a nuisance annoyance or injury or which may tend to depreciate value of any other part of the property known as the Tiltwood Estate . . .

Whoever drafted and approved that conveyance knows little of conveyancing. How could the plaintiff be bound to use the land for agricultural purposes only and *b* at the same time for private houses only? In fact the plaintiff has received planning permission to develop the burdened land at a density of eight houses to the acre. She admits that she is bound by the express covenants in her conveyance to build only houses for domestic purposes but submits that she is not bound by the 1951 restrictive covenants because when Mrs Spence bought the enclosures in question the restrictive covenants were extinguished because part of the burdened land came into *c* the common ownership of the benefited land.

Submissions

It is clear that by the conveyance of 28th August 1952 Mrs Spence who was then the owner in fee simple of the benefited land (except the part conveyed to Colonel Clark) purchased the fee simple in some half part of the burdened land. The question of law is whether in those circumstances the restrictive covenants on that part of the burdened *d* land are forever extinguished unless a fresh express covenant is taken from the purchaser of the part of the burdened land or whether the restrictive covenants are thereby suspended and are revived when part of the benefited land is sold with an express assignment of the covenant. It is curious that this question has never before been decided by the courts. For the defendants, counsel made three submissions. (1) That the answer depended on the intention of the seller of the benefited land. *e* I do not think that the question of intention arises as in a question of merger. But even if it did arise it is I think clear that the only covenants which the seller intended to impose were those set out in the conditions of sale. (ii) That it would be inequitable for the plaintiff to succeed. Even if equity does affect the question, which I do not think it does, I do not think that the plaintiff's claim is inequitable. Again the restrictions were to be the same for all purchasers under the 1952 auction particulars and *f* conditions of sale. (iii) That the plaintiff only purchased part of the burdened land. But this is a difficult submission as the defendants only own part of the benefited land and the part sold to Colonel Clark which had no express assignment cannot in any event claim the benefit of the covenants.

I turn to the law.

g *The law*

For the plaintiff it was submitted that the covenants are extinguished when there is unity of seisin. The question is: does unity of seisin extinguish restrictive covenants or merely suspend them and they revive on an express assignment of the benefit? The legal pronouncements on the subject are indeed jejune. In Jolly on Restrictive Covenants affecting Land[1], published in 1931 I find this under the heading 'Merger'.

h 'Upon the analogy of an easement it is conceived that the benefit of a restrictive covenant would be merged and extinguished by unity of title and possession, if the dominant and servient tenements pass into the same hands.'

In that sentence the benefited land is called 'the dominant tenement' and the burdened land 'the servient tenement'. In the first edition of Preston and Newsom on *j* Restrictive Covenants[2] published in 1939 (I was informed by counsel for the plaintiff that chapter 3 was entirely written by Mr Preston who unfortunately never returned from Dunkirk) I find this:

---

1   2nd Edn (1931), p 52
2   1st Edn (1939), p 42

'Similarly, it is submitted that restrictive covenants are destroyed when the fee simple in the benefited and in the burdened land become vested in the same *a* person. Then there ceases to be land to be protected, and as in the case of an easement, the fact the owner exercises certain forbearances on part of his land is merely the particular user which as owner he chooses to have. Upon the subsequent partition of the land however, the covenant can scarcly be said to revive; it cannot be "of necessity" like a way, nor "continuous and apparent". It is accordingly submitted, that though there is no authority on the point, that *b* such unity of seisin destroys the covenant, and does not merely suspend it.'

It is my duty to provide that authority.

This case is not part of a building scheme where different considerations apply and the the plaintiff admits that the covenant was taken in respect of ascertainable land. Both the text books to which I have referred apply the law in regard to easements. It is well settled in the law of easements that unity of seisin of the dominant and servient tenements destroys all existing easements but that on severance those quasi-easements which have been enjoyed by the owner and as are continuous or apparent or arise from necessity are created as implied easements by the fact of severance (see Gale on Easements[1]). In respect of profits à prendre I find in Hall on Profits à Prendre[2] published in 1871 this: *d*

'It follows from the doctrine above stated that, where the whole of the dominant tenement and the whole of the servient tenement are vested in the same person, a profit à prendre is either suspended or extinguished: if there be only unity of possession, they are suspended; if there be unity of seisin in fee simple, they are extinguished.'

e

And it has long ago been decided that a release of part of a right of common extinguishes the rights over the whole common (see *Miles v Etteridge*[3]).

I turn to the modern dicta. In *Brunner v Greenslade*[4] Megarry J was dealing with a scheme of development of land in several lots and he said:

'The major theoretical difficulties based on the law of covenant seem to me *f* to disappear where instead there is an equity created by circumstances which is independent of contractual obligation. Further, whatever arguments there may be about unity of seisin destroying a covenant, by analogy to easements, I do not think that it precludes the application of a scheme of development as between purchasers of lots merely because they were initially in one hand.'

In *Texaco Antilles Ltd v Kernochan*[5] a Privy Council case in which there was a building *g* scheme, Lord Cross said:

'It is no doubt true that if the restrictions in question exist simply for the mutual benefit of two adjoining properties and both those properties are bought by one man the restrictions will automatically come to an end and will not revive on a subsequent severance unless the common owner then recreates them. But *h* their Lordships cannot see that it follows from this that if a number of people agree that the area covered by all their properties shall be subject to a "local law" the provisions of which shall be enforceable by any owner for the time being of any part against any other owner and the whole area has never at any time come into common ownership an action by one owner of a part against another owner of a part must fail if it can be shown that both parts were either at the *j*

1 14th Edn (1972), p 309
2 (1871), p 335
3 (1692) 1 Show 349
4 [1970] 3 All ER 833 at 842, [1971] Ch 993 at 1005
5 [1973] 2 All ER 118 at 127, [1973] AC 609 at 626

inception of the scheme or at any time subsequently in common ownership.
a The view which their Lordships favour is supported by dicta of Cozens-Hardy
MR in *Elliston v Reacher*[1] and of Simonds J in *Lawrence v South County Freeholds
Ltd*[2] but at the time when this case was heard by the Court of Appeal there was
no decision on the point. Subsequently, however, in *Brunner v Greenslade*[3] which
raised the point Megarry J followed those dicta. The appellants submitted that
his decision was wrong but in their Lordships' view it was right.'

b
Although the dictum in regard to restrictive covenants which exist simply for the
benefit of two adjoining properties is strictly obiter, it carries great weight coming as
it does from Lord Cross.

Conclusion
I propose to follow that dictum and the text books to which I have referred and
c hold that where the fee simple of the benefited and the burdened land is vested in
one person, the restrictive covenants are extinguished unless the common owner
recreates them. In this case the common owner did not recreate them and they are
therefore extinguished. It follows that the plaintiff is entitled to the declaration
which she seeks.

d *Declaration accordingly.*

*13th June. The defendant's appeal to the Court of Appeal was dismissed by agreement between
the parties.*

Solicitors: *Lewis, Lewis & Co* (for the plaintiff); *Thomson, Snell & Passmore*, Tunbridge
e Wells (for the defendants).

Jacqueline Metcalfe Barrister.

Re Osoba (deceased)
f # Osoba v Osoba and others

CHANCERY DIVISION
MEGARRY V-C
14th, 15th DECEMBER 1977

g *Will – Gift – Absolute gift – Trust for specified purpose – Expression of purpose construed
as mere indication of motive for gift – Overriding intention to benefit donee – Bequest of
residue on trust to be used for maintenance of wife and education of daughter up to university
grade – Whether an absolute gift to wife and daughter – Whether valid disposition of residuary
estate.*

h *Administration of estates – Partial intestacy – Hotchpot – Assets to be taken into account –
Foreign assets – Whether foreign assets as well as English assets to be taken into account.*

In 1960 the testator, who was domiciled in Nigeria, made a will, in cl 3 of which he
bequeathed to his wife 'all rents from my leasehold properties known as Nos 7, 9 and
11 Custom Street, Lagos, for her maintenance and for the training of my daughter
Abiola up to University grade'. He bequeathed the residue of his estate, which included
a house in London, to his wife 'upon trust to be used as in paragraph three above'.
j The testator died in 1965, the wife died in 1970, and the daughter's university education was completed in 1975. The testator's son claimed that the testator had not validly

---

1 [1908] 2 Ch 665 at 673, [1908-10] All ER Rep 612 at 615
2 [1939] 2 All ER 503 at 520, 524, [1939] Ch 656 at 677, 683
3 [1970] 3 All ER 833, [1971] Ch 993

disposed of his residuary estate and that accordingly he was entitled to share in the proceeds of the sale of the London house as being property undisposed of on a partial *a* intestacy.

Held – Where a gift in a will was expressed to be for specified purposes which extended to the whole of the fund given, the court would, in appropriate cases, construe the gift as an absolute gift to the donee, the expression of purposes being a mere indication of motive. In the circumstances it was plain that, although the maintenance of his *b* wife and the education of his daughter were in the forefront of the testator's mind, his overriding purpose was to make provision for them. The gift of residue was therefore to be construed as an absolute gift to the wife and daughter in equal shares, the references to their maintenance and education being no more than an indication of motive. Accordingly the claim of the testator's son failed (see p 1104 *c* to *g*, post).
Re Sanderson's Trust (1857) 3 K & J 497 applied. *c*
Re the Trusts of the Abbott Fund [1900] 2 Ch 326 and *Re Andrew's Trust* [1905] 2 Ch 48 explained.
Per Curiam. The hotchpot ordered under s 49 of the Administration of Estates Act 1925 for the disposal of the undisposed part of an estate on a partial intestacy must take into account foreign assets as well as English assets (see p 1104 *g* and *h*, post).

d

Notes
For gifts by will expressed to be for a stated purpose, see 39 Halsbury's Laws (3rd Edn) 1081, para 1612, and for cases on the subject, see 49 Digest (Repl) 892-896, 8346-8393.

Cases referred to in judgment *e*
Abbott Fund Trusts, Re, Smith v Abbott [1900] 2 Ch 326, 69 LJCh 539, 25 Digest (Repl) 576, 192.
Andrew's Trust, Re, Carter v Andrew [1905] 2 Ch 48, 74 LJCh 462, 92 LT 766, 25 Digest (Repl) 576, 194.
Barlow v Grant (1684) 1 Vern 255, [1558-1774] All ER Rep 198, 23 ER 451, 49 Digest (Repl) 894, 8362.
Foord, Re, Foord v Conder [1922] 2 Ch 519, [1922] All ER Rep 166, 92 LJCh 46, 128 LT *f* 510, 49 Digest (Repl) 891, 8338.
Sanderson's Trust, Re (1857) 3 K & J 497, 26 LJCh 804, 30 LTOS 140, 3 Jur NS 658, 69 ER 1206, 49 Digest (Repl) 892, 8347.

Adjourned summons *g*
By an originating summons dated 23rd May 1975 the plaintiff, Anthony Osoba, claimed a one-quarter share of his deceased father's residuary estate on the ground that the residue had not been disposed of by his father's will. The first defendant, Luke Amiolemen Osoba, was the executor of the will, the second and third defendants, Nora Majekodunmi and P Aduba, were the personal representatives of the testator's deceased wife, Irene Osoba, and the fourth defendant was the testator's daughter, *h* Abiola Ososba. The first three defendants took no part in the proceedings. The fourth defendant could not be served and the Official Solicitor was added as fifth defendant to represent her interests. The facts are set out in the judgment.

R S Nock for the plaintiff.
James Munby for the Official Solicitor. *j*
The first, second, third and fourth defendants did not appear.

MEGARRY V-C. This summons raises a number of questions on a short will. The testator made his will on 24th June 1960, and died on 21st April 1965. Apart from various visits abroad, and some five years, from 1943 to 1948, when he was in Scotland

training as an accountant, his whole life appears to have been spent in Nigeria; and
a on the evidence before me it seems reasonably clear that he died domiciled in Nigeria.
He married twice. By his first wife he had a son and two daughters. That marriage
ended in divorce in 1955, and he then married his second wife. She survived him, but
died in 1970; and by her he had one child, a daughter. The plaintiff in the summons
is the son of the first marriage. The first defendant, the testator's brother, is the sole
surviving executor of the will. The second and third defendants are the personal
b representatives of the testator's widow. The fourth defendant is the testator's
daughter by his second marriage. She is named Abiola. The first three defendants
have been duly served but have taken no part in the proceedings. It proved impossible
to serve the fourth defendant, and so the Official Solicitor was added as the fifth
defendant, to represent her interests. Mr Munby appeared on behalf of the Official
Solicitor, and not only argued the case for the fourth defendant but also made
c helpful submissions on behalf of the other defendants who took no part in the case.
Mr Nock appeared for the plaintiff.

The will, though not a very skilful document, shows signs of having been professionally drafted. Clause 1 appoints executors, and cl 2 gives all the personal chattels
to the widow. Omitting cll 3 and 5 for the moment, cl 4 devises a house in Lagos to
Abiola. Clause 6 reads as follows: 'My wife to take care of my children by my first
d wife, namely, Patricia, Anthony and Elizabeth provided they are resident in Nigeria.'
That is all. It is in that setting that cll 3 and 5 appear; and it is they that give rise to
the difficulty.

Clause 3 reads as follows:

e > 'I bequeath to my wife all rents from my leasehold properties known as Nos. 7,
> 9 and 11 Custom Street, Lagos, for her maintenance and for the training of my
> daughter Abiola up to University grade and for the maintenance of my aged
> mother provided my wife is resident in Nigeria.'

Then there is clause 5: 'I bequeath and devise the residue of my personal and real
property whatsoever and wheresoever to my wife upon trust to be used as in paragraph three above.' The testator's mother, I should say, died in May 1963, and so
f predeceased the testator; and Abiola's university eduction came to an end in 1975.
At his death the testator owned a house in London, 1 Avondale Avenue, Finchley,
N10. It was then worth some £5,500, but it now said to be worth between £15,000
and £20,000. It is that house which is the subject of the dispute before me. Counsel
for the plaintiff contends that, subject to the three purposes imported into cl 5 from
cl 3, the house is undisposed of and passes as on intestacy. If he is right on this, then
g there is a second question, namely whether under the Administration of Estates Act
1925, s 49, the hotchpot ordained on a partial intestacy requires foreign assets to be
brought into account, as counsel for the plaintiff contends, or whether it is confined
to English assets. On the other hand, counsel for the Official Solicitor contends
that cl 5 carried the English house as an absolute gift in equal shares between the
widow and Abiola.

h There is evidence of Nigerian law before me. It was common ground that the
English house devolved according to English law, as being the lex situs, and that in
the construction of the will there was no material difference between English law
and Nigerian law. It soon became plain that the only real contest was between a
partial intestacy and equal division. A third possibility, based on *Re Foord*[1], was
discussed in argument, but in the end was found impossible to sustain. That possibility
j was that cl 5 operated as a beneficial gift to the wife absolutely, with a limited trust
to use part of the property for the specified purposes, and that, subject to that limited
trust, the beneficial gift to the wife took effect. Counsel for the Official Solicitor
strove manfully to put forward this contention for the benefit of the wife's personal

---

1   [1922] 2 Ch 519, [1922] All ER Rep 166

representatives, but in the end he had to accept that he could not sustain it. In particular, the home-made will in *Re Foord*[1] contained a gift to the testator's sister 'absolutely . . . on trust' for certain purposes, whereas in the present case there is nothing to match the 'absolutely', or to show in any way an initial beneficial gift to the wife. I therefore turn to the two main contentions.

At the centre of the argument lay a well-known contrasting pair of cases, *Re the Abbott Fund Trusts*[2] (which I shall call '*Re Abbott*') and *Re Andrew's Trust*[3]. Counsel for the plaintiff said that *Re Abbott*[2] laid down the general rule and that *Re Andrew's Trust*[3] stood on its own and was of limited application. Counsel for the Official Solicitor, on the other hand, said that *Re Andrew's Trust*[3] was his sheet anchor, and that I should apply the principle contained in it. In *Re Abbott*[2] a fund was raised for the maintenance and support of two deaf-and-dumb ladies; and Stirling J held that the surplus left in the hands of the trustees after both ladies had died was held on a resulting trust for the subscribers, and did not belong to the estates of the two ladies. In *Re Andrew's Trust*[3] a fund was subscribed for the infant children of a deceased clergyman. The only evidence of the objects of the fund was in a letter which showed that the money was collected 'for or towards the education' of the children; and the letter also stated that the money was not intended for the exclusive use of any of the children, nor for equal division among them, but 'as deemed necessary to defray the expenses of all, and that solely in the matter of education'. After some but not all of the fund had been used for educating and maintaining the children, and after, it seems, their formal education had been completed, the ownership of the balance had to be decided. Kekewich J distinguished *Re Abbott*[2] and held that the children were entitled in equal shares. He treated the references to education as expressing merely the motive for the gift, as well as construing 'education' in the 'broadest possible sense' and as not being exhausted by the children reaching ages when 'education in the vulgar sense is no longer necessary'. Certainly no judge who daily listens to the submissions of counsel would regard his education as having ended. The case is a strong decision, in the sense that the children were held to be entitled despite the words in the letter which negatived any exclusive use or equal division and confined the use of the money solely to education.

With that, I return to the words of the will before me. I think that it is reasonably plain that cl 5 of the will imposed a trust on the wife. The words 'upon trust' are clear, and the will is plainly drafted by someone who has some knowledge of law and of the meaning of legal expressions. I can see no reason for saying that these words do not mean what they say. The property to be held on trust is also plain enough: it is the whole of the testator's residue. I can see no grounds for cutting it down to only the income from the residue, as counsel for the plaintiff contended at one stage. True, cl 3 deals only with income, and cl 5 incorporates at least part of cl 3; but that incorporation affects only the beneficial interest under the trust, and I can see no reason for letting it invade the delineation of the trust property and cut that down in any way.

The question, then, is that of the trusts on which the residue is to be held. The phrase 'to be used as in paragraph three above' must define those trusts. I do not think that the first part of cl 3 is incorporated: that part merely states what property is to be used for the purposes stated. I think that counsel for the Official Solicitor is right when he says that what is incorporated is the latter part of cl 3, beginning with the words 'for her maintenance'. The result is that the residue went to the testator's wife 'upon trust to be used for her maintenance and for the training of my daughter Abiola up to University grade'. I omit the concluding words relating to the maintenance of the testator's mother, since she predeceased the testator.

---

1   [1922] 2 Ch 519, [1922] All ER Rep 166
2   [1900] 2 Ch 326
3   [1905] 2 Ch 48

That, of course, leads to the central question, namely, the beneficial ownership of
a the residue today. The testator's wife is now dead, and Abiola's university education
has finished. The residue can therefore no longer be used for any of the purposes
specified in cl 5 by incorporation from cl 3. I have a formal, effective, will to construe,
and not, as in *Re Abbott*[1] and *Re Andrew's Trust*[2], a trust to be spelled out of informal
documents. With the end of the specified purposes, ought I to hold that the residue
of the beneficial interest remains undisposed of, and so passes as on intestacy, or ought
b I to hold that, despite the specifying of the purposes, and their determination, the
widow and Abiola took the whole beneficial interest between them?

Now there are plainly some relevant distinctions between the present case and
Re Abbott[1] and *Re Andrew's Trust*[2]. First, the latter cases were both what I may call
'subscription' cases. The money was subscribed by living well-wishers, and so at
least some were likely to be still living and able to take when the trusts failed. Here,
c on the other hand, I have a residuary gift made by a testator, so that if the gift fails
or there is a resulting trust, there is no question of anything reverting to the testator
himself. I would not place any great weight on the so-called presumption against
intestacy; but I would lean towards construing a testamentary gift of residue as being
wholly effective and not as leaving some part of the property given to pass as on
intestacy. Second, in *Re Abbott*[1] and *Re Andrew's Trust*[2], as I have indicated, the
d terms on which the money had been subscribed were ill-defined, and had to be
collected from informal documents. In such cases I think that the court has a somewhat greater liberty of action in producing a sensible result, in the sense that the
court has greater room for drawing inferences in holding what the terms of the trust
are. Where, as in the present case, the court has before it a formal and operative
document such as a will, then the duty of the court is merely that of construing the
e words used, and there is less scope for drawing inferences.

On the contrast between the two authorities I should say this. In *Re Abbott*[1] every
possible purpose for which the trust existed was at an end. The trust was for the
benefit of the two ladies, and once they were dead it became impossible to use the
funds for their benefit. No subscriber, touched by their plight, could very well be
expected to have intended any surplus to pass under the wills or intestacies of the
f ladies to people who might well be totally unknown to the subscribers. In *Re Andrew's
Trust*[2], on the other hand, the objects of the benefaction were still living. The
immediate need had been to provide for their education, and that is what had
prompted the subscriptions. But quite apart from 'education' having an extended
meaning, it seems improbable that any subscriber would have recoiled from the
thought of any of the money being used for the benefit of the children after their
g formal education had ceased. I think that you have to look at the persons intended
to benefit, and be ready, if they still can benefit, to treat the stated method of benefit
as merely indicating purpose, and, no doubt, as indicating the means of benefit
which are to be in the forefront. In short, if a trust is constituted for the assistance of
certain persons by certain stated means there is a sharp distinction between cases
where the beneficiaries have died and cases where they are still living. If they are
h dead, the court is ready to hold that there is a resulting trust for the donors; for the
major purpose of the trust, that of providing help and benefit for the beneficiaries,
comes to an end when the beneficiaries are all dead and so are beyond earthly help,
whether by the stated means or otherwise. But if the beneficiaries are still living,
the major purpose of providing help and benefit for the beneficiaries can still be
carried out even after the stated means have all been accomplished, and so the court
j will be ready to treat the stated means as being merely indicative and not restrictive.

That is the position where the court has to gather the terms of the trusts from
informal documents. What I have to consider is whether the result is the same where

1   [1900] 2 Ch 326
2   [1905] 2 Ch 48

the court has instead to construe a formal document such as the will in the present case. By a somewhat different process of reasoning I think that in essence the distinction is valid. The courts have long shown that they are ready in appropriate cases to construe a gift to a donee that is expressed to be for specified purposes as being an absolute gift, with the expression of purposes as a mere indication of motive, and not a restriction to those purposes. This approach, may, I think, be detected at least as far back as the judgment of Lord Guilford, the Lord Keeper, in *Barlow v Grant*[1]; and it is expounded more explicitly by Page-Wood V-C in *Re Sanderson's Trust*[2]. Both cases were decisions on wills. I merely add that I am speaking only of cases in which the stated purposes extend to the whole of the fund given. In cases where, for instance, the gift merely provides for part of the fund to be used for maintenance very different questions arise.

In the case before me the testator plainly intended to provide for his wife and daughter. The maintenance of his wife and the education of his daughter were obviously in the forefront of his mind; but plainly the overriding purpose was to provide for his immediate dependants. In those circumstances I should be reluctant to read his will as showing an intention that once his daughter's training up to university level was at an end she was to have nothing more, and there should be no further testamentary provision for her. I do not think that the words relating to using the residue for Abiola's training and the maintenance of the widow show that any residue not required for these purposes was to be withheld from Abiola and the widow. If the trusts had been similar to those for the ladies in *Re Abbott*[3], I would not consider that the case was appropriate for treating the expression of purposes as a mere indication of motive. Inter vivos benevolence towards those in distress is very different from testamentary provision for one's immediate family.

It accordingly seems to me that the wife and daughter became entitled to the whole of the residue between them, and, to echo Kekewich J in *Re Andrew's Trust*[4], I think the only safe course is to hold that they became entitled in equal shares. It is true that the will does not treat them equally, to the extent that the maintenance of the wife might be expected to consume more of the residue than the training of Abiola would; but on the footing that these are mere expressions of motive, I do not think that they can affect the quantum of interest taken. There does not have to be equality of motives for making equal gifts, and I can see no sufficient indication of any basis other than equality. I therefore hold that the second and third defendants, as personal representatives of the testator's second wife, are entitled to half the residue, and the fourth defendant, Abiola, to the other half.

That decision accordingly makes it unnecessary for me to decide the point on hotchpot on a partial intestacy. However, the point was argued, and I propose simply to say this. As at present advised I can see no rational ground on which it could be said that under s 49 of the Administration of Estates Act 1925, as amended, only English property has to be brought into account. The wording of s 49(1)(aa) and (a) is in terms of 'beneficial interests' and 'property', and these expressions seem to me to be perfectly capable of embracing beneficial interests in property abroad as well as at home. Any other rule would also obviously be capable of producing most unfair results, whereas the object of the section is to produce fair results. In my judgment the hotchpot provision must apply wherever the property in question may be.

Order accordingly.

Solicitors: *Douglas Wiseman, Karsberg & Co* (for the plaintiff); *Official Solicitor.*

Hazel Hartman Barrister.

---

1   (1684) 1 Vern 255, [1558-1774] All ER Rep 198
2   (1857) 3 K & J 497 at 503-505
3   [1900] 2 Ch 326
4   [1905] 2 Ch 48 at 53

Commissioner of Police for the Metropolis v Hills

HOUSE OF LORDS

LORD DIPLOCK, VISCOUNT DILHORNE, LORD SALMON, LORD RUSSELL OF KILLOWEN AND LORD KEITH OF KINKEL

4th, 5th, 27th JULY 1978

Criminal evidence – Character of accused – Evidence against co-accused – Same offence – Evidence against other person charged with same offence – Accused and co-accused charged in separate counts of same indictment with causing death by dangerous driving – Particulars of offence in each count the same – Further particulars would have alleged offences which were factually different – Accused and co-accused could not have been jointly charged – Whether accused and co-accused had been charged with same offence – Criminal Evidence Act 1898, s 1(f)(iii).

The appellant who was driving on the westbound carriageway of a road collided with L when L turned into the westbound carriageway from the eastbound carriageway. The appellant's car then veered off the road and hit and killed a pedestrian. The appellant and L were tried together on an indictment which charged each of them, on separate but identical counts, with causing death by dangerous driving contrary to s 1 of the Road Traffic Act 1972. The particulars of each offence were the same, namely that on the same date the accused had caused the death of the pedestrian by driving a motor vehicle on a road in a manner which was dangerous to the public. At the trial the appellant gave evidence against L and L's counsel asked to be allowed to cross-examine the appellant as to character on the grounds that for the purposes of s 1(f)(iii)[a] of the Criminal Evidence Act 1898 the appellant had given evidence against another person 'charged with the same offence'. The judge held that the two accused had been charged with the same offence and permitted counsel to cross-examine the appellant regarding the fact that at the time of the accident he was an unqualified driver driving without L plates or a qualified driver with him, that in 1973 he had been convicted of dangerous driving, and that in 1974 and 1975 he had sought to obtain driving licences by falsely stating that he had passed a driving test. L was acquitted and the appellant was convicted and sentenced to nine months' imprisonment. On appeal,

Held – The appellant and L had not been charged with the 'same offence' for the purposes of s 1(f)(iii) of the 1898 Act. For offences to be regarded as the same they had to be the same in all material respects and capable of being amalgamated into a joint charge. If further particulars of the dangerous driving alleged in the counts against the appellant and L had been given, they would have alleged against the appellant an offence which was factually different from that alleged against L, and the two accused could not have been jointly charged. The cross-examination of the appellant as to character should not therefore have been permitted. The appeal would be allowed and the appellant's conviction quashed on the ground that there had been a material irregularity in the course of the trial (see p 1106 h j, p 1108 e f, p 1109 c d and j to p 1110 a and d to h, post).

R v Russell [1970] 3 All ER 924 overruled.

Notes

For cross-examination of an accused person as to character, see 11 Halsbury's Laws (4th Edn) para 388, and for questions admissible thereunder, see ibid, para 392. For cases on the subject, see 14(2) Digest (Reissue) 644, 645, 5206-5215.

For the Criminal Evidence Act 1898, s 1, see 12 Halsbury's Statutes (3rd Edn) 865.

---

a   Section 1(f)(iii) is set out at p 1107 g h post

Cases referred to in opinions

Murdoch v Taylor [1965] 1 All ER 406, [1965] AC 574, [1965] 2 WLR 425, 129 JP 208, 49   *a*
    Cr App Rep 119, HL, 14(2) Digest (Reissue) 634, 5135.

R v Assim [1966] 2 All ER 881, [1966] 2 QB 249, [1966] 3 WLR 55, 130 JP 361, 50 Cr App
    Rep 224, CCA, 14(1) Digest (Reissue) 292, 2231.

R v Hadwen [1902] 1 KB 882, 71 LJKB 581, 86 LT 602, 66 JP 456, 20 Cox CC 206, CCR,
    14(2) Digest (Reissue) 644, 5207.

R v Lauchlan [1978] RTR 326, CA.   *b*

R v Lovett [1973] 1 All ER 744, [1973] 1 WLR 241, 137 JP 275, 57 Cr App Rep 332, CA,
    14(2) Digest (Reissue) 643, 5205.

R v Roberts [1936] 1 All ER 23, 154 LT 276, 100 JP 117, 25 Cr App Rep 158, 34 LGR 147,
    30 Cox CC 356, CCA, 14(2) Digest (Reissue) 645, 5212.

R v Rockman [1978] Crim LR 162, CA.

R v Russell [1970] 3 All ER 924, [1971] 1 QB 151, [1970] 3 WLR 977, 135 JP 78, 55 Cr App   *c*
    Rep 29, CA, 14(2) Digest (Reissue) 645, 5214.

Appeal

On 1st April 1977 in the Crown Court at Knightsbridge before his Honour Judge
Morton and a jury, the appellant David John Hills and Gordon Peter Ledwith were
charged in successive counts on the same indictment with causing death by dangerous   *d*
driving contrary to s 1 of the Road Traffic Act 1972. They were tried together, Mr
Ledwith being acquitted and the appellant convicted and sentenced to nine months'
imprisonment. The appellant's appeal to the Court of Appeal, Criminal Division
(Orr LJ, Thompson and Milmo JJ) was dismissed on 20th February 1978. On 20th
March that court refused leave to appeal to the House of Lords but certified that a
point of law of general public importance was involved in the case, namely whether   *e*
two persons charged in the same indictment but in separate counts, each with causing
the death of the same person by driving in a manner dangerous to the public, the
acts of dangerous driving alleged being different, were 'charged with the same offence'
for the purpose of s 1(*f*)(iii) of the Criminal Evidence Act 1898. On 27th April 1978
the Appeal Committee of the House of Lords gave the appellant leave to appeal
against the decision. The facts are set out in the opinion of Viscount Dilhorne.   *f*

Richard Hayden and *M Joyce* for the appellant.
D Farquharson QC and *N Freeman* for the Commissioner of Police for the Metropolis.

Their Lordships took time for consideration.

                                                              g
27th July. The following opinions were delivered.

LORD DIPLOCK. My Lords, I have read in advance the speech of my noble and
learned friend, Viscount Dilhorne. I agree with it and for the reasons that he gives I too
would allow this appeal; but not without regret for, as it seems to me, the justice   *h*
of the case required that the jury should be aware of the appellant's history of previous
convictions for motoring offences when they came to consider the weight to be
attached to the charges of dangerous driving that he had made in the witness-box
against his fellow accused. The words of s 1(*f*)(iii) of the Criminal Evidence Act 1898,
which prohibit this, however, are too plain and unequivocal; they leave no discretion to the trial judge. So I share the hope expressed by Viscount Dilhorne that   *j*
this provision of a statute which was passed 80 years ago, should be referred to the
Criminal Law Revision Committee for their consideration.

VISCOUNT DILHORNE. My Lords, the appellant and a Mr Ledwith were tried
together in the Crown Court at Knightsbridge on an indictment which contained two

counts. The first charged Mr Ledwith with having caused the death of a Mrs Keane
a by dangerous driving. The second charged the appellant with having done so. The
particulars of offence in each count were the same. Each alleged that the accused had
on 3rd September 1975 caused the death of Nora Keane by driving a motor vehicle
on a road, to wit, Western Avenue, Acton, W3, in a manner which was dangerous to
the public.

Mr Ledwith, it appears, was driving a van in the eastbound carriageway of Western
b Avenue and had stopped at an intersection in the central reservation as it was his
intention to cross into the westbound carriageway and to enter the entrance to the
Unigate factory which was on the near side of the westbound carriageway. As he
drove into the outside lane of that carriageway, he saw a Triumph motor car coming
towards him 100 to 150 yards away. He accelerated to get out of its way and then
stopped. The Triumph hit his wing, bounced off it on to the nearside kerb and hit
c and killed Mrs Keane who was standing in the Unigate factory entrance.

The appellant, the driver of the Triumph, said in evidence that he had been about
150 yards from the intersection when the van turned right out of it in front of him
and that there was no room for him to get round it.

Counsel for Mr Ledwith sought to cross-examine the appellant as to his character,
to establish that he was an unqualified driver without 'L' plates and without a
d qualified driver with him, that he had been convicted of dangerous driving and of
driving uninsured in 1973 and that in 1974 and 1975 he had sought to obtain driving
licenses by falsely stating that he had passed a driving test. That the appellant had
given evidence against Mr Ledwith was conceded. Counsel for Mr Ledwith contended
that though not charged jointly in a count in the indictment, Mr Ledwith and the
appellant were charged with the same offence and that he was consequently by
e virtue of the Criminal Evidence Act 1898 entitled so to cross-examine.

His Honour Judge Morton held that each of the accused was charged with the same
offence and allowed the cross-examination. Mr Ledwith was acquitted. The appellant
was convicted, sentenced to nine months' imprisonment and disqualified from holding
or obtaining a driving licence for three years. He appealed to the Court of Appeal,
Criminal Division. That court dismissed his appeal but certified that a point of law of
f general public importance was involved, namely, whether two persons charged in
the same indictment but in separate counts, each with causing the death of the same
person by driving in a manner dangerous to the public, the acts of dangerous driving
alleged being different, are 'charged with the same offence' for the purposes of s 1(f)(iii)
of the Criminal Evidence Act 1898. The material parts of that section are as follows:

g 'Every person charged with an offence . . . shall be a competent witness for the
defence at every stage of the proceedings, whether the person so charged is
charged solely or jointly with any other person. Provided as follows:—. . . (f) A
person charged and called as a witness in pursuance of this Act shall not be asked,
and if asked shall not be required to answer, any question tending to show that he
has committed or been convicted of or been charged with any offence other than
that wherewith he is then charged, or is of bad character, unless—. . . (iii) he has
h given evidence against any other person charged with the same offence.'

Our task in this appeal is to construe the words 'the same offence'. It is clear that
an accused is not liable to be cross-examined as to character merely because he has
given evidence against a co-accused. Such cross-examination is only permissible when
the accused against whom he has given evidence is charged with the same offence.
A number of persons may be indicted in one indictment even though none of them
j are accused of committing an offence jointly, if—

'the matters which constitute the individual offences of the several offenders
on the available evidence so related, whether in time or by other factors, that
the interests of justice are best served by their being tried together. . .' (R v Assim[1].)

_____
1 [1966] 2 All ER 881 at 887, [1966] 2 QB 249 at 261

It may be that persons are now more frequently joined in one indictment when charged only with separate offences than was the case in 1898, but the review made *a* by Sachs J in *R v Assim*[1] suggests that in those days no valid objection could have been taken to an indictment against a number of persons none of whom were jointly charged in a count, if the matters on which the counts were based were so related that the interests of justice were best served by their being tried together.

If two or more persons are jointly charged in a count, that count will be bad for duplicity if it charges more than one offence. When it is not bad for duplicity, each *b* accused is charged with the same offence and if one accused has given evidence against another accused in that count, it cannot be doubted that proviso (iii) to s 1(*f*) applies.

Where it is alleged by the prosecution that two or more persons have committed the same offence, it would indeed be unusual to find them indicted together but only charged in separate counts. If, though indicted together, they are charged only in separate counts, that may be taken as an indication that the prosecution at least did not *c* regard them as charged with the same offence.

Counts in an indictment are not nowadays so detailed as in days gone by. To decide whether two persons are charged in separate counts with the same offence, one must, of course, look at the counts, but one is in my opinion, entitled to have regard also to what further particulars of the offence charged would have been given if applied for. When considering the propriety of the joinder of accused in one indict- *d* ment one is entitled to look at the substance of the case as disclosed in the depositions (*R v Assim*[1]) and in my opinion for the purpose of determining whether separate counts charge the same offence one can look at the depositions to judge what further particulars of a count would have been given if applied for.

In this case it is clear that if further particulars of the dangerous driving alleged in each count had been given, they would have alleged that Mr Ledworth had driven *e* dangerously in turning into the path of an oncoming vehicle when it was not safe to do so and that the appellant had driven dangerously in driving too fast and not keeping a proper look-out. If particulars of this kind had been contained in the indictment or given it could not in my opinion be said that Mr Ledwith and the appellant were charged with the same offence within the meaning of the statute.

Since 1898 there have been very few occasions on which the meaning of the words *f* 'the same offence' in this Act have been the subject of judicial consideration. In *R v Hadwen*[2], Lord Alverstone said that the most ordinary case where persons were charged with the same offence, would be when there were two or more prisoners jointly indicted though he agreed that the words would apply where the same offence had been the subject of other proceedings. In *R v Roberts*[3] two persons were jointly indicted and tried together; one was charged with fraudulent conversion *g* and the other with false pretences. One accused who gave evidence against the other was cross-examined as to character. His conviction was quashed. Talbot J delivering the judgment of the Court of Criminal Appeal said that s 1(*f*)(iii) must be strictly construed. He recognised that there were arguments for making the provision more extensive. He said it was impossible to say that the accused were charged with the same offence. In *R v Russell*[4] Russell and Hurst were charged in separate counts *h* with being in possession of the same forged £5 notes. Hurst gave evidence against Russell whose counsel was not allowed at the trial to cross-examine Hurst as to character. Lord Widgery CJ, delivering the judgment of the Court of Appeal, observed that the offences charged against Russell and Hurst were similar in really every respect but that it was argued that they were not charged with the same offence because the possessions alleged against them were not 'coincident or concurrent but *j*

1   [1966] 2 All ER 881, [1966] 2 QB 249
2   [1902] 1 KB 882
3   [1936] 1 All ER 23
4   [1970] 3 All ER 924, [1971] 1 QB 151

consecutive'. He thought that Lord Donovan in *Murdoch v Taylor*¹ had taken the
view that there should be a wide interpretation of the words 'the same offence'.
With respect I do not myself see anything in his speech which leads to that conclusion.

There is no doubt that if Russell and Hurst had been jointly charged with possession,
cross-examination as to Hurst's character would have been permissible. No doubt if
the evidence warranted the preferment of a joint charge that would have been done
and the fact that such cross-examination would have been permissible if it had been,
does not lead to the conclusion that successive possessions constitute the same offence.
If a house is burgled by a burglar and an hour later it is burgled by another burglar,
it would be wrong in my opinion to hold that each burglar was charged with same
offence. In my view, for the offences charged to be regarded as the same for the
purposes of s 1(*f*)(iii), they must be the same in all material respects including the
time at which the offence is alleged to have been committed, and a distinct and
separate offence similar in all material respects to an offence committed later, no
matter how short the interval between the two, cannot properly be regarded as 'the
same offence'.

For these reasons the decision in *R v Russell*² was in my opinion wrong and should
be overruled. It was followed by the Court of Appeal in the present case. As I have
said, where persons are jointly charged with one offence and the charge is not bad for
duplicity, they are charged with the same offence within the meaning of the Act.
If charged separately with offences, a test of whether they are charged with the same
offence is whether they could have been charged jointly. In the present case, in the
light of the case for the prosecution against each, they could not properly have been
charged with having jointly caused the death of Mrs Keane by dangerous driving.

Our attention was drawn to two cases, *R v Lauchlan*³ and *R v Rockman*⁴. In
*R v Lauchlan*³ two men were indicted together each charged with assaulting the other.
It was held rightly that they were not charged with the same offence, Shaw LJ pointing
out that to justify their convictions different facts would have to be proved. In
*R v Rockman*⁴ two men were indicted together, one charged with assaulting the other
and the other charged with wounding the man accused of assault. It was held, in my
opinion again rightly, that the proviso did not apply.

At the end of his judgment in *R v Russell*⁵ Lord Widgery CJ said that it would be a
very unsatisfactory result if Russell had been denied the right to cross-examine his
co-accused. I agree that the result of so deciding is unsatisfactory but that does not
entitle one to amend the statute or to give its language a meaning which it does not
in my opinion have. In *R v Lovett*⁶ Edmund Davies LJ said:

'It has been suggested (and not without good reason) that the law on this matter
is unsatisfactory, and that the mischief aimed at in proviso (iii) would be more
satisfactorily dealt with if it applied whenever two accused are jointly tried, even
though they are not charged with the same offence.'

I agree. It does not seem to me to accord with justice that when one of two accused
gives evidence against the other, the right of the accused against whom the evidence
is given should depend on what charges the prosecution has thought it right to bring.
I hope that the Secretary of State for Home Affairs will invite the Criminal Law
Revision Committee to give attention to this without delay.

In my opinion 'same offence' in the proviso means an offence which is the same in
all respects. The counts in this indictment did not charge offences the same in all
respects and for the reasons I have given I would allow the appeal and quash the

1 [1965] 1 All ER 406, [1965] AC 574
2 [1970] 3 All ER 924, [1971] 1 QB 151
3 [1978] RTR 326
4 [1978] Crim LR 162
5 [1970] 3 All ER 924 at 927, [1971] 1 QB 151 at 155
6 [1973] 1 All ER 744 at 747, [1973] 1 WLR 241 at 243

appellant's conviction on the ground that there was a material irregularity in the course of the trial in allowing the cross-examination of the appellant as to his character.

LORD SALMON. My Lords, I agree that this appeal should be allowed.

LORD RUSSELL OF KILLOWEN. My Lords, in one sense the two counts in the indictment charged Ledwith and the appellant Hills respectively with the same offence, viz, driving a motor vehicle on Western Avenue on 9th September 1975 in a manner dangerous to the public thereby causing the relevant death. But on analysis I do not consider that to be the relevant sense for present purposes. In 1898 when the Criminal Evidence Act was enacted, the indictment would have been drawn with far greater particularity, and today further particulars could have been required on behalf of the accused. That greater particularity would have revealed that the dangerous driving of which the appellant was accused consisted in driving a motor car too fast westwards in the outer lane of Western Avenue without regard to the possibility of the emergence through the intersection of Ledwith's van across his bows. It would also have revealed that the dangerous driving of which Ledwith was accused was turning his van from the eastbound carriageway across part of the westbound carriageway across the bows of the appellant without regard to the possiblity that he could not get across in time for the appellant to avoid colliding with the van.

Suppose there had been no question of death resulting from the collision, and each had been charged in the same indictment with the relevant dangerous driving. I do not consider that they could have been charged together in one count: the offence of dangerous driving alleged against one was factually quite different from the offence of dangerous driving alleged against the other: they were not 'the same offence' in that they were not identical. The fact that in the instant case a death resulted, and that causing it is included in the charges, cannot alter that; because the first essential step is for the prosecution to prove the dangerous driving, and only when those dangerous drivings were proved to show that death was thereby caused.

As was said in *R v Lauchlan*[1], in which as a consequence of a fight between A and B each was charged with assault causing actual bodily harm to the other in separate counts. 'To procure a conviction of [A], or on the other hand to justify a conviction of [B], required proof of differing facts.'

Whether it is desirable that the ability for an accused to question the other on the relevant matters should remain thus narrowly confined by the statute, I do not debate. My impression is that the Court of Appeal in *R v Russell*[2] were anxious to escape from too strait a jacket, and I agree that that led to an erroneous decision.

I would therefore answer the question posed in the point of law in the negative and allow the appeal.

LORD KEITH OF KINKEL. My Lords, I have had the benefit of reading in advance the speech of my noble and learned friend, Viscount Dilhorne. I agree with it and cannot usefully add anything. I too would allow the appeal.

Appeal allowed. Conviction quashed.

Solicitors: *Nicholls Christie & Crocker* (for the appellant); *Solicitor for the Commissioner of Police for the Metropolis.*

Mary Rose Plummer Barrister.

1   [1978] RTR 326
2   [1970] 3 All ER 924, [1971] 1 QB 151

a # Ben-Odeco Ltd v Powlson (Inspector of Taxes)

HOUSE OF LORDS
LORD WILBERFORCE, LORD HAILSHAM OF ST MARYLEBONE, LORD SALMON, LORD RUSSELL OF
KILLOWEN AND LORD SCARMAN
29th JUNE, 3rd, 27th JULY 1978

b *Income tax – Capital allowances – Machinery or plant – Expenditure on provision of machinery or plant – Expenditure on acquisition of money to be used for acquiring plant – Interest and commitment fees paid in respect of loans raised for purposes of acquiring plant – Whether interest and commitment fees 'expenditure on the provision of . . . plant' – Finance Act 1971, s 41(1)(a).*

c The taxpayer company was incorporated for the purpose of carrying on the trade of hiring out an oil rig. The contract for the construction of the rig was placed in 1969. In order to finance the enterprise, the company entered into various loan agreements. The company had to pay interest on the money borrowed and commitment fees in order to maintain its right to draw the money. In accordance with the principles of commercial accounting the amounts of interest and commitment fees *d* paid by the company before it started to trade in July 1971 were properly treated in its accounts as capital expenditure. The company claimed that it was entitled to a first-year allowance, under s 41(1)[a] of the Finance Act 1971, in respect of the interest and commitment fees since they constituted expenditure on the provision of the oil rig and therefore 'capital expenditure on the provision of . . . plant', within s 41(1)(a) of the 1971 Act.

e **Held** (Lord Salmon dissenting) – The words 'expenditure on the provision of . . . plant' in s 41(1)(a) were not wide enough to include money spent on the acquisition of money for the acquisition of plant. Accordingly the company was not entitled to an allowance under s 41(1)(a) in respect of the interest and commitment fees (see p 1115 *h j*, p 1116 *f* to *h*, p 1117 *f g* and p 1123 *c* and *e*, post).
f   **Semble.** The words 'expenditure on the provision of . . . plant' in s 41(1)(a) are not limited to the bare purchase price of the plant but include items such as transport and installation (see p 1115 *g h* and p 1123 *d e*, post).
     Decision of Brightman J [1978] 1 All ER 913 affirmed.

Notes
g For the allowances available in respect of machinery and plant, see 20 Halsbury's Laws (3rd Edn) 493, 494, paras 941-946.
     For the Finance Act 1971, s 41(1), see 41 Halsbury's Statutes (3rd Edn) 1459.

Cases referred to in opinions
Attorney-General v HRH Prince Ernest Augustus of Hanover [1957] 1 All ER 49, [1957]
h   AC 436, [1957] 2 WLR 1; *affg* [1955] 3 All ER 647, [1956] Ch 188, [1955] 3 WLR 868,
     CA; *rvsg* [1955] 1 All ER 746, [1955] Ch 440, [1955] 2 WLR 613, 2 Digest (Repl) 210,
     257.
BP Refinery (Kwinana) Ltd v Federal Comr of Taxation [1961] ALR 52, 28(1) Digest
     (Reissue) 220, *725.
BSC Footwear Ltd v Ridgway (Inspector of Taxes) [1970] 1 All ER 932, [1971] Ch 427, [1970]
j   2 WLR 888, [1970] TR 1, 49 ATC 1, CA, 28(1) Digest (Reissue) 123, 365.
Chancery Lane Safe Deposit and Offices Co Ltd v Inland Revenue Comrs [1966] 1 All ER 1,
     [1966] AC 85, [1966] 2 WLR 251, 43 Tax Cas 83, 44 ATC 450, [1965] TR 433, HL,
     28(1) Digest (Reissue) 278, 924.

---

a Section 41(1) is set out at p 1116 *c d*, post

Fraser v Comr of Internal Revenue (1928) 25 F 2d 653.

Georgia Cypress Co v South Carolina Tax Commission (1942) 22 SE 2d 419.

Inland Revenue Comrs v Barclay Curle & Co Ltd [1969] 1 All ER 732, [1969] 1 WLR 675, 45 Tax Cas 221, [1969] 1 Lloyd's Rep 169, 48 ATC 17, [1969] TR 21, [1969] RVR 102, 1969 SLT 122, HL, 28(1) Digest (Reissue) 466, 1676.

Inland Revenue Comrs v George Guthrie & Son (1952) 33 Tax Cas 327, 31 ATC 337, [1952] TR 315, 45 R & IT 588, 1952 SC 402, 1952 SLT 376, 28(1) Digest (Reissue) 447, *1178.

Ostime (Inspector of Taxes) v Duple Motor Bodies Ltd [1961] 2 All ER 167, [1961] 1 WLR 739, 39 Tax Cas 537, [1961] TR 29, 40 ATC 21, HL; *affg* sub nom *Duple Motors Bodies Ltd v Inland Revenue Comrs* [1960] 2 All ER 110, [1960] 1 WLR 510, [1960] TR 65, 39 ATC 38, 53 R & IT 317, CA, 28(1) Digest (Reissue) 125, 371.

River Wear Comrs v Adamson (1877) 2 App Cas 743, [1874-80] All ER Rep 1, 47 LJQB 193, 37 LT 543, 42 JP 244, 3 Asp MLC 521, HL; *afg* (1876) 1 QBD 546; *rvsg* (1873) 29 LT 530, 42 Digest (Repl) 1135, 9450.

Ryan (Inspector of Taxes) v Asia Mill Ltd (1951) 32 Tax Cas 275, [1951] TR 181, 30 ATC 110, 44 R & IT 698, HL; *rvsg* sub nom *Heather v Asia Mills Ltd* [1949] TR 414, 43 R & IT 98, CA, 28(1) Digest (Reissue) 122, 359.

Sherritt Gordon Mines Ltd v Minister of National Revenue [1968] 2 Ex CR 459, 28(1) Digest (Reissue) 468, *1204.

Whimster & Co v Inland Revenue Comrs 1926 SC 20, 12 Tax Cas 813, 28(1) Digest (Reissue) 600, *1484.

Appeal

Ben-Odeco Ltd ('the taxpayer company') appealed against the decision of Brightman J[1] dated 18th November 1977 dismissing its appeal by way of case stated[2] from a decision of the Commissioners for the Special Purposes of the Income Tax Acts whereby they dismissed its appeal against, inter alia, the refusal of its claim for capital allowance in respect of the sum of £494,990 representing capitalised interest and commitment fees incurred in connection with the construction of the oil drilling rig Ocean Tide. On 13th January 1978 an Appeal Committee of the House of Lords granted the taxpayer company leave to appeal directly to the House, Brightman J having granted it a certificate under s 12 of the Administration of Justice Act 1969 that a point of law of general public importance was involved in the decision. The facts are set out in the opinion of Lord Wilberforce.

Peter Whiteman QC and *Graham Aaronson* for the taxpayer company.
Michael Nolan QC and *Brian Davenport* for the Crown.

Their Lordships took time for consideration.

27th July. The following opinions were delivered.

LORD WILBERFORCE. My Lords, this appeal is concerned with a claim by the taxpayer company to a first-year capital allowance in respect of expenditure incurred in connection with the construction of an oil rig, Ocean Tide. The claim arises under s 41(1)(a) of the Finance Act 1971 and its validity depends on the construction of the four words 'on the provision of'. Are interest and commitment fees paid in respect of a loan contracted in order to finance the provision of machinery or plant capital expenditure incurred on the provision of machinery or plant? That is the whole of the question.

---

1   [1978] 1 All ER 913, [1978] 1 WLR 365, [1978] STC 111
2   The case stated is set out at [1978] 1 All ER 914-918

The taxpayer company was incorporated on 2nd December 1968. Its only trade at
all material times consisted in hiring out the rig Ocean Tide on time charter. It had
an authorised and issued share capital of £5,000. The contract for the construction of
Ocean Tide was placed in 1969. In order to pay for it, the taxpayer company entered into
five loan agreements, one of them secured by a debenture. Interest was payable
on the money borrowed, and commitment fees had to be paid in order to maintain
a right to draw the money. The amounts of interest and commitment fees paid by
the taxpayer company until it started to trade (in July 1971) were capitalised in its
accounts. It was common ground (and so recorded by the Special Commissioners)
that as a matter of commercial accounting these amounts were properly so charged
to capital. The total cost of the completed rig as shown in the taxpayer company's
balance sheet on 31st December 1971 was £5,691,123 of which the capitalised interest
and commitment fees represented £435,988, and £59,002 respectively. It is not
disputed that the price of the Ocean Tide was capital expenditure which qualified
for the statutory capital allowance. It is agreed that the loans were obtained in
order to finance the purchase of Ocean Tide and were exclusively so applied. It is
also agreed that the taxpayer company, in order to obtain the loans, was obliged to
pay interest and commitment fees.

The taxpayer company's argument in favour of the allowance is, basically, twofold.
First it is said that the interest and commitment fees are, in a real sense, part of the
cost of the rig, or, at least, part of the cost to the taxpayer company of the rig. They
ought, consistently with the statutory purposes (namely, to encourage investment),
to be treated in exactly the same way as the other elements of the costs. Secondly
it is contended that what in a particular case is cost, and what is capital expenditure,
has to be determined according to accepted methods of commercial accounting,
and that, since the interest and commitment fees up to the date when trading commenced were, in accordance with these methods, treated as capital expenditure,
that is sufficient to bring these sums within the statutory provision.

The contention of the Crown is simpler. They point to the relevant words 'capital
expenditure on the provision of machinery or plant'; the only question is whether
the amounts in question fall within this phrase. It is not sufficient for the relevant
expenditure to attain the status of capital expenditure, nor for it to be described, in
popular language, as part of the cost. Capital expenditure in order to qualify must
be on the provision of plant or machinery, and it does not follow that, because a
trader treats expenditure as part of the cost of the rig, the expenditure qualifies under
the statute. Here the interest and commitment fees were expended not in order to
provide the plant, but in order to obtain, or on, the loans. They represented money
spent on providing the means to acquire the rig and not on the provision of the rig
itself.

I must first refer to such authority as was cited, though in the end it provides no
decisive assistance. It falls into three groups. First, the taxpayer company referred
to the series of cases which establish that sound principles of commercial accounting
may be invoked in order to determine such questions of internal accounting as what
is profit, how profit is to be calculated, and what, on the other hand, is capital: *Whimster
& Co v Inland Revenue Comrs*[1], *Ryan v Asia Mill Ltd*[2], *Ostime v Duple Motor Bodies Ltd*[3],
BSC Footwear Ltd v Ridgway[4]. I shall not discuss these authorities because there is no
occasion here to dispute them, nor were they disputed by the Crown. They establish
no more than, as is conceded in the present case, that the amounts in question were,
during the pretrading period, properly charged to capital account. To establish
this however is not enough for the taxpayer company; in order to succeed they

1   1926 SC 20, 12 Tax Cas 813
2   (1951) 32 Tax Cas 275
3   [1961] 2 All ER 167, [1961] 1 WLR 739, 39 Tax Cas 537
4   [1970] 1 All ER 932, [1971] Ch 427

must show that they represented 'capital expenditure on the provision of machinery or plant' and the task of the court is to interpret these words. Accounting methods adopted by a particular company (and other companies might treat similar expenditure differently) cannot determine the construction of statutory words.

Secondly, reliance was placed on *Chancery Lane Safe Deposit and Offices Co Ltd v Inland Revenue Comrs*[1] and in particular the observations of Lord Upjohn and Lord Pearson to the effect that capitalised items might be shown in the balance sheet as part of the total capital cost of the particular asset. But I do not understand them to be saying more than interest, if capitalised, can be shown as a capital cost. The question of relating it to the acquired asset did not arise.

Thirdly, through the diligent researches of counsel, we were referred to two Commonwealth cases said to support the taxpayer company. The first was *BP Refinery (Kwinana) Ltd v Federal Comr of Taxation*[2] decided by Kitto J as single judge in the High Court of Australia. The appellant company entered into a contract for the construction of a refinery for a fee which included an amount equal to the expenditure of the contractor in carrying out the work. The contractor incurred expenditure in the erection of temporary buildings for (inter alia) the accommodation of workmen. The company paid to the contractor a sum equal to this expenditure. The question in this case was how this sum ought to be allocated as between depreciable and non-depreciable assets, whether by a direct cost method, or one based on labour costs, and the decision was that the method adopted by the taxpayer company, though not the only possible method, was appropriate. In the course of his judgment Kitto J said[3]:

'I am satisfied that this amount [the net cost of the temporary buildings] was so paid by the appellant to [the contractor], and accordingly formed part of the cost of the refinery to the appellant.'

But Kitto J was in that passage only concerned to arrive at the quantum of the payment, and not with relating it, in its nature, to any statutory formula. The actual decision was purely as to the method of allocation.

The second case is much more in point; indeed it bears, on its facts, much resemblance to the present. In *Sherritt Gordon Mines Ltd v Minister of National Revenue*[4], the Exchequer Court of Canada decided that commitment fees paid in respect of development properties during the construction period were part of the capital cost of those properties within s 11(1)(a) of the Income Tax Act[5] and therefore subject to capital cost allowances. In that case interest and the commitment fees were capitalised until the mine, or the refinery, were operating and thereafter charged against operating. Kerr J referred in detail to accountancy evidence, some of which supported such capitalisation as accepted practice, some of which did not, and to the arguments of counsel, which were close to those used in the present appeal. Reference was made to United Kingdom authorities, including *Whimster & Co v Inland Revenue Comrs*[6] and the *Chancery Lane* case[7]. His judgment contains this passage[8]:

'However, even if it is found as a fact, as counsel for Sherritt submits it should be, that Sherritt's treatment of payments of bond interest and commitment fee during construction was in accordance with generally accepted accountancy principles and that the method followed was an appropriate method of accounting for Sherritt, that is not conclusive of the question the court has to decide, for the prescriptions of the *Income Tax Act* prevail.'

---

1   [1966] 1 All ER 1 at 18, 27, [1966] AC 85 at 124, 137, 43 Tax Cas 83 at 119, 129
2   [1961] ALR 52
3   [1961] ALR 52 at 55
4   [1968] 2 Ex CR 459
5   RSC 1952 c 148
6   1926 SC 20, 12 Tax Cas 813
7   [1966] 1 All ER 1, [1966] AC 85, 43 Tax Cas 83
8   [1968] 2 Ex CR 459 at 479

In the end he found that the question was 'fairly arguable' but he was disposed
a to think that interest during construction can be part of the capital cost of property
within s 11(1)(a) of the Income Tax Act, and similarly the commitment fees. The
relevant statutory expression there was the 'capital cost to the taxpayer of property';
this Kerr J considered could certainly include the price, probably include legal costs,
might well include the cost of moving the asset to the place of use, and in his
opinion would include the 'cost to him' of borrowing the capital required.

b   My Lords, this judgment is an impressive one, perhaps more for the full statement
of the arguments on either side than for the actual decision, which as the learned
judge himself said was arguable. In considering whether it should be followed,
and so, in effect, preferred to the judgment of Brightman J, I bear in mind that it
arose under a different statute and one which not only uses a different expression,
but whose policy as regards deductions seems to be more liberal than the United
c Kingdom statute. The expression 'capital cost to the taxpayer' makes it easier to
include within deductible expenditure costs which the particular taxpayer incurs,
whereas the United Kingdom words, more objectively, focus on expenditure directly
related to the plant. The one draws a line around the taxpayer and the plant; the
other confines the limiting curve to the plant itself. As to policy, the Canadian
Income Tax Act allows deduction of the expenses of issuing or selling shares of the
d capital stock of the taxpayer (s 11(1)(c)) and the Minister had allowed the taxpayer's
claim as regards interest. Further I note that the judgment[1] cites two United States
authorities[2] which appear to take a different view as regards interest charges.
Unless therefore, on principle and in logic, it is preferable to the judgment appealed
from, there are sound reasons for distinguishing it. I therefore turn to this question.

An important principle of the laws of taxation is that, in the absence of clear con-
e trary direction, taxpayers in, objectively, similar situations should receive similar
tax treatment. The taxpayer company's argument in the present case does not bring
this about. On the contrary a different result would follow according as it pays for
the provision of plant out of its own resources, or borrows it. In the latter case it
would get an allowance, in the former it would not; this may amount to treating an
investor worse than a speculator. Moreover, on the same argument, a different
f allowance in respect of identical plant would result according as he (i) borrows
from a bank, (ii) raises money by a public issue of debentures, (iii) obtains money
from his shareholders. And, again, a different result would follow according as
he (i) is able to capitalise the interest on the money borrowed or (ii) (because he is
carrying on a profit-making trade or for other reasons) does not or cannot capitalise it.
If the law is such that it offers the taxpayer these options, he is of course entitled to
g select that which suits him best, but an interpretation which introduces such a large
element of subjectivity is to be avoided. The words 'expenditure on the provision of'
do not appear to me to be designed for this purpose. They focus attention on the
plant and the expenditure on the plant, not limiting it necessarily to the bare purchase price, but including such items as transport and installation, and in any event
not extending to expenditure more remote in purpose. In the end the issue remains
h whether it is correct to say that the interest and commitment fees were expenditure
on the provision of money to be used on the provision of plant, but not expenditure
on the provision of plant and so not within the subsection. This was the brief but
clear opinion of the Special Commissioners and of the judge and little more is possible
than after reflection to express agreement or disagreement. For me, only agreement
is possible. I would dismiss the appeal.

j
LORD HAILSHAM OF ST MARYLEBONE. My Lords, the taxpayer company
entered into contract with Upper Clyde Shipbuilding Ltd for the construction and

1   [1968] 2 Ex CR 459 at 484
2   *Fraser v Comr of Internal Revenue* (1928) 25 F 2d 653, *Georgia Cypress Co v South Carolina Tax
Commission* (1942) 22 SE 2d 419

delivery of an oil rig now known as the Ocean Tide. The contract price was approximately £5 million. In order to pay for this they borrowed the money and this cost them just short of a further £500,000 up to and including the time when they started trading. This sum of £500,000 was made up in part of commitment fees and in part of interest, and was correctly charged by their accountants to capital account. After trading commenced the interest was, of course, charged to revenue, and deductible in the ascertainment of profits for the purposes of charge to tax. The taxpayer company claims first-year allowances not merely for the cost of the rig, which is conceded by the Crown, but also for the commitment fees and interest incurred in financing its payment for it. Whether it succeeds or not depends on the answer to the question whether it can bring these items of expenditure within the language of s 41(1)(a) of the Finance Act 1971. This provides as follows:

> 'Subject to the provisions of this Chapter, where—(a) a person carrying on a trade incurs capital expenditure on the provision of machinery or plant for the purposes of the trade, and (b) in consequence of his incurring the expenditure, the machinery or plant belongs to him at some time during the chargeable period related to the incurring of the expenditure, there shall be made to him for that period an allowance (in this Chapter referred to as "a first-year allowance") which shall be of an amount determined in accordance with section 42 below: Provided that no first-year allowance shall be made in respect of any expenditure if the chargeable period related to the incurring of the expenditure is also the chargeable period related to the permanent discontinuance of the trade.'

Nothing turns in this case on the proviso, nor on the terms of para (b) of sub-s (1). Moreover there is no dispute either that the taxpayer company is 'a person carrying on trade' or that in incurring the items in question the taxpayer company can properly be described as 'incurring capital expenditure'. It is further agreed that the Ocean Tide is correctly described as 'machinery or plant' and that it was required for the purposes of the taxpayer company's trade. It follows that the only question in dispute is whether the fees and interest were items of 'expenditure on . . . machinery or plant'. This depends on whether a narrow or a broad construction is to be placed on the words. The taxpayer company contended that the words include all items properly incurred in the provision of the Ocean Tide which would include the cost of financing the payment for it. For the Crown it was argued that the only expenditure on the provision of the Ocean Tide was, in effect, its price, and that the commitment fees and interest were not expended on the provision of the Ocean Tide within the meaning of s 41(1) but on the provision of the money to pay for it and that this for the purposes of the subsection is to be regarded as a distinct and separate operation.

In my view the actual words of the statute are capable of bearing either construction according to the context in which they are used, but, at the end of the day, I agree with the judgment of Brightman J and the view of the Special Commissioners that in the context of s 41(1) of the 1971 Act they bear the narrower of the two meanings, that is that contended for by the Crown. It follows that in my view the appeal should be dismissed.

Great stress was laid on the part of the taxpayer company on the long lines of cases which establish that for the purpose of computing profits or gains the courts will accept the ordinary principles of commercial accounting even where there may be more than one acceptable alternative method available to the taxpayer: see *Ostime v Duple Motor Bodies Ltd*[1]. There are limits to this doctrine: see *BSC Footwear Ltd v Ridgway*[2]; but the real answer to the taxpayer company's contention is that, at the best, the application of the ordinary principles of commercial accounting only establish that the items in question were correctly charged to capital account, which, for

---

1   [1961] 2 All ER 167, [1961] 1 WLR 739, 39 Tax Cas 537
2   [1970] 1 All ER 932, [1971] Ch 427, [1970] TR 1

the purposes of this case is not in dispute. The principles of commercial accounting
a cannot assist as to the meaning of the words 'the provision of machinery or plant'
where these occur in the statute.

The taxpayer company also relied on *Inland Revenue Comrs v George Guthrie & Son*[1],
a decision on the former initial allowance. I do not find that case analogous to the
present. In it the taxpayer had actually expended moneys on the purchase of a motor
car which proved abortive owing to the fraud of the vendor in failing to supply the
b car after it had been paid for. Equally I do find analogous the case of *Inland Revenue
Comrs v Barclay Curle & Co Ltd*[2] which decided that the excavation of the necessary
basin for the construction of a dry dock was physically part of the same operation,
and ranked for allowance as part of the expenditure on the provision of the dry dock
itself. Neither of these cases really touches the question whether the words 'expenditure on the provision of machinery or plant' are wide enough to include money
c spent on the acquisition of money the main purpose of which was to pay for machinery
or plant, as distinct from money actually expended in order to pay for the construction (or purchase), transport and installation of the machinery or plant itself.

In addition to the cases cited to Brightman J, counsel for the taxpayer company drew
the attention of your Lordships to two Commonwealth cases, the decision of the High
Court of Australia in *BP Refinery (Kwinana) Ltd v Federal Comr of Taxation*[3] and the
d decision in Canada in *Sherritt Gordon Mines Ltd v Minister of National Revenue*[4].
The former case seems to me, on analysis, to depend on the question of the correct
apportionment between depreciable and non-depreciable items of expenditure
of certain overhead costs and not, therefore, to be directly in point. The argument in
Sherritt's case[4] is much closer to the present, but not of higher authority than
Brightman J's own decision in the present case. In any event it depends on the terms of
e the relevant Canadian statute which are different from those of s 41 of the United
Kingdom Finance Act 1971, and, on analysis, both in language and policy, plainly
more liberal in construction and intent. Incidently the decision of Kerr J in that case
cites some United States authorities[5] which at least point in the opposite direction
to his own conclusions.

In the outcome, and whilst admitting that during the course of argument my
f inclination tended at different points of time to favour each of the two possible
constructions, I come down decisively in favour of the narrower meaning. I summarise my reasoning as follows. In the first place I believe that the more accurate
and the more natural answer to the question on what the £5½ million was spent,
is that £5 million was spent on the provision of plant and machinery and £500,000 on
the loan charges required in order to obtain the money to pay for the plant and mac-
g hinery. In the second place I favour giving a meaning to the statute which will provide
the same allowance for the taxpayer who meets the cost of an oil rig out of his own
accumulated resources, the taxpayer who meets the same cost by a debenture issue
or an issue of shares to the public, and the taxpayer who simply borrows the money
from a bank, or some other source of liquid finance. In the third place I am not
satisfied that the policy of the statute really conforms with the taxpayer company's
h contention. Granted that its main purpose was to encourage investment in new
machinery and plant, I am not convinced that to include interest charges and commitment fees would serve this purpose without giving rise to abuse. It was agreed
in argument that if the constructing company borrowed money in order to finance
the construction of the rig and added the interest and commitment fees into the price
charged to the purchaser, the total price to the purchaser would rank for first-year

1   (1952) 33 Tax Cas 327
2   [1969] 1 All ER 732, [1969] 1 WLT 675, 45 Tax Cas 221
3   [1961] ALR 52
4   [1968] 2 Ex CR 459
5   *Fraser v Comr of Internal Revenue* (1928) 25 F 2d 653, *Georgia Cypress Co v South Carolina Tax
    Commission* (1942) 22 SE 2d 419

allowance. But how if the purchaser in his turn borrowed the money to pay the price containing these components? It seems to me that, on the taxpayer company's contention, he would be able to add the second tier of commitment fees and interest. By the time a complicated piece of machinery was ultimately delivered and paid for there might be more than one, indeed more than two, sets of commitment charges and interest payments included in the ultimate purchase price and several additional costs of financing the project by the trader to be included in the allowance the Crown might be compelled to make to the trader. It is true, of course, that, if the taxpayer company's case were conceded, what would emerge would be a coherent and superficially elegant system of taxation in which the interest charges before trading would be allowable as first-year capital allowance, and after the commencement of trading would be deductible as expenses in the computation of profits. But I am by no means certain that this was the intention of the legislature. To qualify for an allowance the taxpayer must bring himself within the conditions set by the benevolence of Parliament. I am not convinced that the taxpayer company has done so in the present case. I feel therefore constrained to say that the appeal should be dismissed with costs and that the judgment appealed from should be affirmed.

LORD SALMON. My Lords, the result of this appeal turns on the construction of a few words, namely 'capital expenditure on the provision of machinery or plant', in s 41 of the Finance Act 1971. That section so far as relevant reads as follows:

> '(1) Subject to the provisions of this Chapter, where—(a) a person carrying on a trade incurs capital expenditure on the provision of machinery or plant for the purposes of the trade, and (b) in consequence of his incurring the expenditure, the machinery or plant belongs to him at some time during the chargeable period related to the incurring of the expenditure, there shall be made to him for that period an allowance (in this Chapter referred to as a "first-year allowance") which shall be of an amount determined in accordance with section 42 below . . .'

The amount of the first-year allowance under s 42 was 60 per cent of the expenditure in respect of which it was made. This percentage was raised to 80 per cent by the Finance Act 1972 and later to 100 per cent.

The taxpayer company made arrangements to raise loans of approximately £5,200,000 in order to pay for the construction of an oil drilling rig to be named Ocean Tide. As soon as this rig was constructed and ready for use in their trade, the taxpayer company intended to let it on time-charter for the purpose of drilling for oil in the seas around this country.

It was a term of all the loan agreements that the loans should carry interest at the going rate and that, in addition to the interest, the taxpayer company should pay commitment fees. The whole of the £5,200,000 (except for £40,000) was raised by loans from four banks of the highest standing and taken up as required to pay for the construction of the rig during the three years ending 31st December 1969, 1970 and 1971. The construction of the rig was completed in 1971 and was brought into use in the taxpayer company's trade when from 9th October 1971 it was first let on time-charter. The interest and the comparatively small commitment fees amounting in all to approximately £500,000 were capitalised as they accrued and appeared in the taxpayer company's accounts for each of the three years to which I have referred as part of the cost of the rig which the taxpayer company had acquired. The Crown concedes that this was in accordance with sound commercial practice. The Crown also concedes that the total cost of the rig as at 31st December 1971 was correctly shown in the taxpayer company's accounts as approximately £5,700,000, being the aggregate of the price paid to Upper Clyde Shipbuilding Ltd, who constructed the rig and the interest and commitment fees accrued as at 31st December 1971.

The crucial question which arises on this appeal is whether the whole of the sum
a of approximately £5,700,000 constituted capital expenditure incurred on the
provision of the rig. The taxpayer company contends that it did. The Crown contends that the capital expenditure of approximately £500,000 in respect of interest
and commitment fees was not part of the capital expenditure so incurred. The argument on behalf of the Crown is that, on the true construction of s 41(1), the interest
and commitment fees were too remote to constitute any part of the capital expen-
b diture incurred on the provision of the rig but should be regarded only as capital
necessarily expended on acquiring the capital expended on the rig. I confess that
I regard this narrow construction of s 41(1) to be too artificial and unreal to be accepted.
    The case for the Crown can, I think, best be tested in this way. If the Crown were
asked firstly 'what was the capital cost incurred by the taxpayer company in acquiring the rig', the answer must be '£5,700,000'; for this was the capital cost appearing
c in the taxpayer company's audited accounts which must have been conceded by the
Crown to be correct. If, however, the question I have formulated were to be translated
into the language of the statute it would then read 'what capital expenditure was
incurred by the taxpayer company on the provision of the rig for the purpose of its
trade?' Both questions though worded differently have precisely the same meaning
and can only be answered in the same way. The Crown, however, would answer
d the second version of the question 'only £5,200,000 in round figures; the balance of
£500,000 was incurred in providing the taxpayer company with the £5,200,000 and
is too remote to have been incurred on providing it with the rig'. I confess that this
does not seem to me to make any commercial sense and that it is also wholly inconsistent with the concession which the Crown have rightly made in relation to the first
question.
e   I entirely agree with my noble and learned friend, Lord Hailsham of St Marylebone,
when he says that the actual words of the statute are capable of bearing either the
narrower meaning for which the Crown contends or the wider meaning for which
the taxpayer company contends. I am afraid, however, that I do not agree that the
context of the material words in s 41(1) of the 1971 Act affords any support to the
meaning attributed to that subsection by the Crown. Nor, in common with all your
f Lordships, do I think that any of the authorities to which we have been referred are
of any real help in deciding the question of construction raised by this appeal. They,
no doubt, establish that the expenditure of the £500,000 was a capital expenditure;
but this point has never been contested. The question is, was the £500,000 capital
expenditure expenditure incurred on the provision of the rig?
    When, as in the present case, words of a statute are capable of more than one
g meaning, the policy or objective of the statute is a most important factor to be taken
into account in deciding the true meaning of those words: *River Wear Comrs v Adamson*
per Lord Blackburn[1], *Attorney-General v HRH Prince Ernest Augustus of Hanover* per
Viscount Simonds[2].
    Part III, Ch I of the 1971 Act, which includes s 41(1), is headed 'New System of
Allowances and Charges in respect of Trade (etc.) Machinery and Plant.'
h   For many years prior to 1971 it had been generally recognised that the overall level
of industrial productivity in this country was deplorable. One of the reasons for this
extremely low level of productivity was the large proportion of obsolescent, and the
serious shortage of modern and efficient, plant and machinery used for industrial
purposes. The obvious objective of that part of the 1971 Act with which this appeal is
concerned was to introduce an entirely new system of capital allowances which would
j afford a really effective incentive to industrial undertakings to provide themselves
with new and efficient plant and machinery. This perhaps is underlined by the fact
to which I have already referred that the first-year capital allowance was originally

---

1   (1877) 2 App Cas 743 at 763, [1874-80] All ER Rep 1 at 11
2   [1957] 1 All ER 49 at 54, [1957] AC 436 at 462

put as high as 60 per cent, then almost immediately raised to 80 per cent and soon
after to 100 per cent.

It must, I think, be generally recognised that new plant and machinery is often
acquired with money which has been borrowed from banks for this specific purpose
alone. This is especially so when the acquisition involves expenditure which is very
large in relation to liquid assets of the undertaking making the acquisition. Providing
that the industrial concerns in question can supply the necessary security and are
considered by the banks to be credit-worthy, there will normally be no difficulty in
obtaining loans from the banks for the purpose of buying new plant and machinery.
Indeed the banks are in business to make such loans. When, as in the present case,
millions of pounds are involved, the interest payable on the loans will be very large
indeed. I think that Parliament must also have recognised (a) that if any company
in the position of the taxpayer company were asked how much it had expended on
providing itself with a rig such as the Ocean Tide, the company would have replied,
without hesitation, and correctly, 'in round figures £5,700,000', and (b) that it would
be a great incentive for any such company to decide on buying such a rig if it knew that
the £500,000 covering the interest incurred before the rig came into commission
would be included in, rather than excluded from, the capital expenditure on the
provision of the rig, and would thus qualify for the first-year capital allowance. If
the £500,000 does not qualify for the first-year capital allowance, then there is no
relief available to the taxpayer company in respect of the expenditure. I find it difficult to believe that when Parliament introduced a new system of capital allowances
in order to offer the highest incentives for industrial concerns to acquire new machinery
and plant it could have intended s 41(1) of the 1971 Act to bear the narrow meaning
for which the Crown contends rather than the broader meaning attributed to it by
the taxpayer company and which it is admittedly capable of bearing. I consider that
the construction of s 41(1) which I favour is also supported by s 50(3) of the 1971 Act
which reads as follows:

'Section 82(1) of the Capital Allowances Act 1968 . . . shall apply for the purposes
of this Chapter as it applies for the purposes of Part I of that Act.'

Section 82(1), so far as relevant, provided:

'References in the part of this Act to capital expenditure . . . (a) in relation to
the person incurring the expenditure . . . do not include any expenditure . . .
which is allowed to be deducted in computing, for the purpose of tax, the profits
or gains of a trade . . . carried on . . . by him, and . . . do not include, in relation
to any such person as aforesaid, any expenditure . . . in the case of which a deduction of tax falls or may fall to be made under Chapter I of Part VII of the Income
Tax Act 1952 (interest and other annual payments).'

In my view, this section makes it plain that capital expenditure may include the
expenditure of interest which qualifies for all capital allowances; but no such expenditure of interest can be treated as a capital expense if it is allowed to be deducted in
computing, for the purposes of tax, the profits or gains of a trade. It follows that
although, whilst the rig was being completed, the interest payable to the banks
was being correctly capitalised and, in my opinion, qualified for the first-year capital
allowance, once the rig was completed and delivered and came into operation in the
taxpayer company's trade, the interest then accruing no longer qualified for a capital
allowance because it could be deducted in computing, for the purposes of tax, the
profits or gains of the taxpayer company's trade.

With all respect, I cannot agree with Brightman J that s 170(1)(a) of the Income Tax
Act 1952 has anything to do with the present appeal. It concerns only a person who
pays interest which is not derived wholly out of profits or gains brought into charge,
and obliges him in making such payments to deduct a sum representing the amount
of the standard rate of tax and to account for that deduction to the Commissioners of

Inland Revenue. In my view s 26 of the Finance Act of 1969, which amends s 170 of the
a 1952 Act, is wholly immaterial and in no way impinges on s 82 of the Capital
Allowances Act 1968 which is incorporated into the 1971 Act by s 50(3) of that Act.

I am not convinced by the argument that the construction of s 41(1) of the 1971 Act
which I favour works any injustice between taxpayers. There must be few who could
meet the cost of an oil rig out of their own accumulated resources. If, however, they
have such resources on deposit or invested they will use them for the provision of an
b oil rig only because they contemplate that those resources will produce more for them
so invested than if left as they are.

A company which borrows money from banks in order to meet the cost of an oil
rig and has sufficient profits from other sources from which it can deduct the interest
and commitment fees in respect of the money lent could not (see s 50(3) of the 1971
Act) and would have no need to capitalise those items or treat them as part of the
c capital cost of the oil rig.

A company which is making no such profits would not, I think, find any enthusiastic
response to a debenture issue or an issue of shares to the public for the sole purpose of
buying an oil rig or any other plant or machinery; and I think that it would be
impossible to underwrite such issues except at exorbitant rates. Nor do I consider
that the construction of s 41(1) which I favour would give rise to any abuse. If the
d purchaser of an oil rig, for example, devised a scheme through subsidiaries and sub-
subsidiaries which would enable a second or even a third tier of commitment fees and
interest to come into existence, I have no doubt that the courts would find that the
second and third tiers were far too remote, indeed a mere colourable device for
inflating the capital cost of the oil rig and the capital allowance claimed in respect of it.
Simple loans from the banks such as the present are, however, a common and repu-
e table way of financing the acquisition of expensive plant and machinery. The policy
of the legislature in enacting Part III, Ch I, of the 1971 Act was certainly not to bestow
benevolence on taxpayers. It was to lighten the burden of taxation for taxpayers such
as the taxpayer company who would thereby be encouraged to borrow money for the
acquisition of the new industrial plant and machinery, which would play an important
part in substantially increasing the level of industrial productivity, a project which
f Parliament clearly regarded as being of the greatest economic importance for the
nation.

My Lords, in my opinion, the construction of s 41(1) of the 1971 Act for which the
taxpayer company contends accords with the ordinary and natural meaning of the
language of that section no less than with the policy of the Act; and I would accordingly
allow the appeal.

g

LORD RUSSELL OF KILLOWEN. My Lords, the point in this appeal is easily
stated, but not so easily solved. The taxpayer company was formed with the purpose
of ordering the construction for it of an oil rig, the trade proposed being to earn profits
by leasing out the rig. In order to finance its payments to the builders of the rig, the
h taxpayer company arranged for loans to it of some £5 million. The obtaining of that
finance involved not only liability in due course to repay to the lenders the sum
borrowed but two other items: first, interest on the sums advanced from the time
of their advancement until repayment and, second, commitment fees payable to the
lenders as a means of ensuring that the lenders would have available the sums required
by the taxpayer company from time to time.

j The question is whether in the initial period such expenditures qualify for capital
allowance against corporation tax liability in the period after trading began as being
'capital expenditure incurred on the provision of machinery or plant for the purposes
of the trade' of the taxpayer.

It is clear that in the accounts of the taxpayer company in the relevant period these
expenditures were quite properly treated, according to commercial accounting

systems, as capital expenditure, and indeed as part of the cost of the rig. But whatever may have been said, and rightly said, on the impact of proper commercial accounting systems on the ascertainment for tax purposes of the true figure of trading profit or the true balance on profit and loss account, the present problem, which is one of construction of the words 'incurred on the provision of machinery or plant', cannot be thus solved. The proper commercial practice halts in its impact after the phrase 'capital expenditure'; and a concept, however commercially reasonable, that the items now in question may be regarded as part of the cost of the rig cannot solve the question of construction whether the expenditure was incurred 'on the provision of' the rig.

I start, my Lords, with the fact that this is a provision affording relief from tax. The taxpayer must persuade me that he is within it. If the reasons pro and con were in precise balance, the taxpayer on that basis would lose. But in upholding the view of the Special Commissioners and of Brightman J, as I do, I find the balance is in fact against the taxpayer company.

It is true to say that in this case the money was borrowed, and the consequent liability for the relevant interest and commitment fees was incurred, entirely in order that the taxpayer company should be in a financial position to obtain provision of the rig from the shipbuilders. But in my opinion the true view is that the relevant items of expenditure were incurred on the provision of finance, and not on the provision of the plant.

There are many ways in which a company may put itself in a position financially to provide itself with plant. It can borrow from banks, and pay for its borrowing in interest and commitment fees. It can put out a share issue, or a debenture issue, and incur expenditure of various kinds in so doing, including legal, accountancy and underwriting fees, and advertisement costs. It may in the net result be in a financial position to incur capital expenditure on the provision of plant, to provide itself with plant; but expenditure incidental to attaining that financial position is not in my opinion within the language of the section. Had it been otherwise intended quite different language would surely have been selected in order to embrace expenditure so commonly involved as a preliminary to the provision of plant of magnitude.

I contrast the present case with that of a company with already available assets used to buy the plant; on the taxpayer company's argument such a company using its already available assets would be relatively disadvantaged in respect of loss of any fruit of such available assets.

The point was made for the taxpayer company that, if the provider of the plant borrowed for working capital and incurred as a result liability for interest and perhaps a commitment fee in respect of such borrowing, these liabilities would be reflected in the price paid, the whole of which would qualify as relevant capital expenditure by the company buying the plant. That is so, but I do not follow the conclusion from that fact. It does not appear to me to be an alternative to borrowing by the purchaser. The supplier's price would reflect the whole cost to him of supplying the plant, including overheads, interest on necessary borrowing, or on commitment of working capital, and a profit element, the whole price being subject to a perhaps competitive market. I am not able to see how the build up of the supplier's price can have any relevance to the problem raised in this appeal.

The point is made that the purpose of these provisions for capital allowance is to encourage investment in new plant and machinery. So it is. But the question remains how extensive, and how expensive to the fiscus, is that encouragement; and in this connection I note the extent of encouragement in terms of percentages allowed has varied through the years.

We were referred to two cases which were not before Brightman J, one Australian[1] and one Canadian[2], already mentioned by your Lordships. I do not find guidance

1 BP Refinery (Kwinana) Ltd v Federal Comr of Taxation [1961] ALR 52
2 Sherritt Gordon Mines Ltd v Minister of National Revenue [1968] 2 Ex CR 459

from either. The former concerned a very different problem. The latter, dealing
a with commitment fees, was under a statute which spoke of 'cost', which provided
anyway for the comparable interest to be allowed, and which in other respects also
pointed to a wide scope of the relevant allowable expenditure.

For the taxpayer company it was additionally argued that since, once trading had
begun, interest thereafter on the outstanding borrowings would be offset against
trading profits, it would afford a neat and coherent scheme if the interest now under
b consideration qualified for capital allowance. Maybe so. But the offset of interest
during the trading period against trading profits is quite a different fiscal plank from
the provision for capital allowances, and there is no compelling reason that they
should dovetail.

In my view the question to be asked is: what is the effect of particular capital expenditure? Is it the provision of finance to the taxpayer, or is it the provision of plant to
c the taxpayer? In my opinion the effect of the expenditure was the provision of finance
and not the provision of plant.

I would add that I do not seek to confine qualifying capital expenditure to the price
paid to the supplier of the plant. I should have thought, for example, that if the cost
of transport from the supplier to the place of user is directly borne by the taxpayer it
would be expenditure on the provision of plant for the purposes of the taxpayer's
d trade. And there may well be other examples of expenditure, additional to the price
paid to the supplier, which would qualify on similar grounds. But such matters are
not for decision in this appeal.

Accordingly I would dismiss this appeal with costs.

LORD SCARMAN. My Lords, I have had the advantage of reading in draft the
e speech delivered by my noble and learned friend, Lord Wilberforce. I agree with it
and for the reasons he gives would dismiss the appeal with costs.

Appeal dismissed.

Solicitors: *Allen & Overy* (for the taxpayer company); *Solicitor of Inland Revenue.*

Rengan Krishnan Esq Barrister.

Rank Xerox Ltd v Lane (Inspector of Taxes)   *a*

COURT OF APPEAL, CIVIL DIVISION
BUCKLEY, BRIDGE LJJ AND SIR DAVID CAIRNS
24th, 25th APRIL, 12th MAY 1978

Capital gains tax – Exemptions and reliefs – Disposal of right to annual payments due under *b*
personal covenant not secured on property – Annual payment – Royalty or other sum paid
in respect of the user of a patent – Taxpayer acquiring exclusive licence to use inventions
comprised in letters patent held by licensor – Surrender of rights to licensor in respect of
certain territories in return for 'royalty' of five per cent of net sales in those territories payable
quarterly – Disposal of right to 'royalty' payments – Whether payments a 'royalty or other *c*
sum paid in respect of the user of a patent' – Whether payments excluded from expression
'annual payments' – Income Tax Act 1952, s 169(3) – Finance Act 1965, ss 52(3)(a), 53(5)(b),
Sch 7, para 12(c).

Capital gains tax – Exemptions and reliefs – Disposal of right to annual payments due under
personal covenant not secured on property – Due under a covenant – Obligations to make *d*
payments created by undertaking embodied in document executed under seal – Obligations
enforceable as contract debt apart from agreement under seal – Whether payments 'due under
a covenant' – Finance Act 1965, Sch 7, para 12(c).

In 1957 the taxpayer company entered into an agreement with an American corporation ('Xerox') whereby (i) Xerox granted to the taxpayer company an exclusive *e*
licence to use the inventions comprised in letters patent and an exclusive sub-licence
to use the inventions comprised in licence rights held by Xerox and respectively set
out in the schedule to the agreement, so that the taxpayer company might exploit
the reproduction process known as xerography throughout the world, except in the
USA and Canada, (ii) Xerox agreed to secure the assignment to the taxpayer company
of the scheduled letters patent and patent applications on obtaining title thereto *f*
and the right to grant title and (iii) the parties mutually agreed to exchange information and know-how with respect to improvements and developments in the process
of xerography. In 1964 a further agreement was entered into between the taxpayer
company and Xerox. By cl 1 the taxpayer company sold, assigned and transferred
to Xerox all its property, rights and assets in Latin America, including, without
limitation, its know-how, patents, trade marks etc. By cl 3 the taxpayer company *g*
cancelled and released all licences and sub-licences applicable to any place in Latin
America granted to it by Xerox and any right to such licence or sub-licence applicable
to any place in Latin America. Clause 4 provided that as consideration for the surrender by the taxpayer company of the matters listed in cll 1 and 3, Xerox would
pay the taxpayer company quarterly 'a royalty of 5% of Net Sales in [Latin America]'.
By a similar agreement made in 1967 in substantially the same form the taxpayer *h*
company surrendered to Xerox its rights etc in the West Indies in exchange for
the quarterly payment by Xerox, under cl 4 of that agreement, of a royalty of five
per cent of net sales in that area. Both the 1964 and 1967 agreements were executed
by Xerox under seal. In December 1969 the taxpayer company declared a dividend
of £8,400,000 to be satisfied by the distribution to shareholders in specie of the right
to receive payments from Xerox ('the Xerox payments') under cl 4 of the 1964 and *j*
1967 agreements. In assessing the taxpayer company to corporation tax, the Crown
claimed that, for the purposes of Part III of the Finance Act 1965, the distribution
represented the disposal of an asset and that accordingly the gain arising from the
disposal was liable to corporation tax in the hands of the taxpayer company. The
taxpayer company appealed, contending that the Xerox payments represented

a 'annual payments . . . due under a covenant', within para 12(c)*a* of Sch 7 to the 1965 Act, and that accordingly the distribution of the rights to those payments to its shareholders did not give rise to a chargeable gain. The Special Commissioners held that the Xerox payments, were pure income and were 'annual payments', within para 12(c), but dismissed the appeal on the ground that the Xerox payments were not payments 'due under a covenant', within para 12(c), because the right to those payments would have been enforceable as a contract debt even if the agreements *b* had not been executed by Xerox under seal. The taxpayer company appealed. Slade J*b* held that the Xerox payments were payments 'due under a covenant', within para 12(c), but dismissed the appeal on the ground that the expression 'annual payments' in para 12(c) had to be given the same meaning as it bore in ss 52(3)(a)*c* and 53(5)(b)*d* of the 1965 Act, and that, since those provisions expressly excluded from the meaning of annual payments 'other payments . . . mentioned in section 169(3)*e* *c* of the Income Tax Act 1952', the Xerox payments could not be annual payments, within para 12(c) of Sch 7 to the 1965 Act, because they fell within the words 'any royalty or other sum paid in respect of the user of a patent' in s 169(3) of the 1952 Act. The taxpayer company appealed.

Held – (1) The Xerox payments were 'annual payments', within para 12(c) of Sch 7 to *d* the 1965 Act, for the following reasons—

(i) They could not properly be described as payments made 'in respect of the user of' patents, within s 169(3) of the 1952 Act, because, under the 1964 and 1967 agreements, the taxpayer company transferred to Xerox much more than the mere right to the user of patents (see p 1131 *e* to *g*, post).

(ii) In any event, payments made in respect of the user of patents were not, by virtue *e* of s 169(3) of the 1952 Act, as applied by ss 52 and 53 of the 1965 Act, automatically excluded for all purposes from the category of annual payments; the payment of a patent royalty could be an 'annual payment', within para 12(c) of Sch 7 to the 1965 Act, if it exhibited the necessary characteristics of an annual payment, which on the evidence the Xerox payments did (see p 1131 *g* to p 1132 *b*, post).

(iii) Royalty payments were not by their very nature incapable of being 'annual *f* payments'. The nature of royalty payments varied according to the particular circumstances in which they were payable. In most cases they would not be annual payments because they would not be pure profit income in the hands of the payee, but if they were, as was the case with the Xerox payments, they were 'annual payments' (see p 1132 *e f*, post).

(2) The Xerox payments were 'due under a covenant', within para 12(c) of Sch 7 to *g* the 1965 Act. It was immaterial that valuable consideration had been given for the

---

a Paragraph 12 is set out at p 1129 *b c*, post
b [1977] 3 All ER 593, [1977] STC 285
c Section 52(3), so far as material, provides: 'The payments referred to in subsection (2) above are—(*a*) any yearly interest, annuity or other annual payment and any such other payments *h* as are mentioned in section 169(3) of the Income Tax Act 1952, but not including sums falling within section 169(4) (rents, etc.) . . .'
d Section 53(5), so far as material, provides: 'Subject to the next following section and to any enactment applied by this section which expressly authorises such a deduction, no deduction shall be made in computing income from any source . . . (*b*) in respect of any yearly interest, annuity or other annual payment or in respect of any such other payments as are mentioned in section 169(3) of the Income Tax Act 1952, but not including sums falling within section *j* 169(4) (rents, etc.).'
e Section 169(3), so far as material, provides: 'Where—(*a*) any royalty or other sum paid in respect of the user of a patent . . . is paid wholly out of profits or gains brought into charge to tax, the person making the payment shall be entitled on making the payment to deduct and retain out of it a sum representing the amount of the tax thereon at the standard rate for the year in which the amount payable becomes due.'

promise to make the payments. Once the promise to pay was embodied in the deed executed by the payer, then, notwithstanding any valuable consideration given for the promise, the debt arising on the promise was due as a speciality debt and not as a simple contract debt. It followed that, by virtue of para 12(c), no chargeable gain accrued to the taxpayer company on the disposal of its right to receive the Xerox payments. The appeal would accordingly be allowed (see p 1133 f g and p 1134 a, post).

Decision of Slade J [1977] 3 All ER 593 reversed.

Notes

For capital gains tax in relation to disposal of a right to annual payments due under deeds of covenant, see 5 Halsbury's Laws (4th Edn) para 81.

For the Finance Act 1965, Sch 7, para 12, see 34 Halsbury's Statutes (3rd Edn) 956.

The Income Tax Act 1952, s 169(3), and the Finance Act 1965, ss 52(3) and 53(5) have been repealed and replaced by the Income and Corporation Taxes Act 1970, ss 52(2), 248(3) and 251(2) respectively.

Cases referred to in judgment

Abley v Dale (1851) 11 CB 378, 2 LM & P 433, 20 LJCP 233, 15 JP 757, 15 Jur 1012, 138 ER 519, 46 Digest (Repl) 436, 803.

Hanbury, Re, Comiskey v Hanbury (1939) 38 Tax Cas 588, 20 ATC 333, CA, 28 (1) Digest (Reissue) 288, 966.

Hill v Gregory [1912] 2 KB 61, 6 Tax Cas 39, 81 LJKB 730, 106 LT 603, 28(1) Digest (Reissue) 247, 172.

Howe (Earl) v Inland Revenue Comrs [1919] 2 KB 336, 7 Tax Cas 289, 88 LJKB 821, 121 LT 161, CA, 28(1) Digest (Reissue) 519, 1890.

Smith v Smith [1923] P 191, 92 LJP 132, 130 LT 8, CA, 28(1) Digest (Reissue) 269, 879.

Vickers, Sons & Maxim Ltd v Evans [1910] AC 444.

Whitworth Park Coal Co Ltd (in liquidation) v Inland Revenue Comrs [1959] 3 All ER 703, [1961] AC 31, [1959] 3 WLR 842, 38 Tax Cas 531, [1959] TR 293, 52 R & IT 789, 38 ATC 295, HL; *affg* [1958] 2 All ER 91, [1958] Ch 792, [1958] 2 WLR 815, 51 R & IT 381, [1958] TR 131, 37 ATC 106, CA; *affg* [1957] TR 237, 50 R & IT 711, 36 ATC 218, 28(1) Digest (Reissue) 265, 864.

Appeal

This was an appeal by the taxpayer company, Rank Xerox Ltd ('RXL'), against a decision of Slade J[1], dated 9th March 1977, whereby, on a case stated by the Commissioners for the Special Purposes of the Income Tax Acts, he dismissed an appeal by RXL against the decision of the Special Commissioners dismissing an appeal by RXL against an assessment to corporation tax for the accounting period of 12 months to 30th June 1970 in the sum of £49,100,000. The facts are set out in the judgment of the court.

Michael Nolan QC and *Andrew Thornhill* for RXL.
D C Potter QC and *M Dean* for the Crown.

Cur adv vult

12th May. **BRIDGE LJ** read the following judgment of the court: The question at issue in this appeal is whether an amount was rightly included in the assessment to corporation tax on the appellant taxpayer company, Rank Xerox Ltd ('RXL'), for the accounting period of 12 months to 30th June 1970 as representing a chargeable gain accruing to RXL on the disposal of certain assets in December 1969. RXL appealed against the assessment to the Commissioners for the Special Purposes of the Income

1   [1977] 3 All ER 593, [1977] STC 285

Tax Acts. The commissioners dismissed the appeal. From this decision an appeal
a by case stated to the High Court was in turn dismissed by Slade J[1]. RXL now appeals
to this court. The question raised for decision at all levels has been that of liability
only. The amount of the chargeable gain, if there was one, will depend on difficult
questions of valuation which happily are for another day.

By s 238 of the Income and Corporation Taxes Act 1970 the profits of companies
on which corporation tax in charged include chargeable gains as well as income and
b s 265 provides, so far as relevant for present purposes, for the computation of chargeable gains in accordance with the principles applying for capital gains tax, which are
to be found in Part III of the Finance Act 1965. It is common ground both that the
rights the subject of the present dispute are assets to which s 22 of the 1965 Act
applies and that there was in December 1969 a disposal of those assets by RXL. It
follows from the application of the provisions of s 22(9) and (10) and s 23(1) and (2)
c that, subject to the valuation question, there was a chargeable gain (or an allowable
loss) accruing to RXL on that disposal unless the rights in question fall within the
provisions of Sch 7, para 12(c), which enacts:

> 'No chargeable gain shall accrue to any person on the disposal of a right to,
> or to any part of . . . (c) annual payments which are due under a covenant made
d > by any person and which are not secured on any property.'

The Special Commissioners decided that the rights in question were to 'annual
payments', but that the payments were not 'due under a covenant'. The learned
judge decided that the payments were 'due under a covenant', but were not 'annual
payments'. Thus both arrived at the same result by precisely contrary routes.

To do justice to the arguments it is necessary to examine the commercial history
e leading to the 1969 disposal of assets in some detail. In 1956 the Rank Organisation
Ltd and a subsidiary of that company agreed with the Xerox Corporation ('Xerox'),
then known as the Haloid Co, to engage in a joint venture for the world wide exploitation, outside the United States of America and Canada, of the reproduction
process known as xerography. RXL was the company which was to be, and was,
formed to implement the agreement. Under the agreement Xerox were to transfer
f to RXL all patents, patent applications and licence rights relating to the process in
those parts of the world to which the agreement related. The relevant patents
granted, patent applications pending and licence rights subsisting at the date of the
agreement were set out in a schedule to the agreement.

After RXL had been formed, an agreement was entered into on 1st May 1957
between Xerox and RXL which was called a licence agreement. This recited the
g 1956 agreement already referred to and provided that pursuant to that agreement
Xerox granted to RXL an exclusive licence to use the inventions comprised in the
letters patent and an exclusive sub-licence to use the inventions comprised in the
licence rights set out in the schedule to the 1956 agreement. The licence agreement
included a provision obliging Xerox to secure an assignment to RXL of the scheduled
letters patent and patent applications on obtaining title thereto and the right to
h grant title. There is no finding in the case as to what, if any, assignments were ever
made pursuant to this provision.

The combined effect of the 1956 and 1957 agreements, under provisions to which
we need not refer in detail, was to impose on the parties mutual obligations to exchange all information and know-how with respect to improvements and developments in the process of xerography and presumably, insofar as it was thought approp-
j riate to protect such improvements and developments by patent applications, the
necessary applications in countries outside the United States of America and Canada
would have been made by RXL.

The 1957 licence agreement continued in force until 1964. During this period,

1 [1977] 3 All ER 593, [1978] Ch 1, [1977] STC 285

in the commercial exploitation of the process of xerography, Xerox had the field to themselves in the United States of America and Canada, and RXL had the field to *a* themselves in the rest of the world. But in 1964 the parties agreed to a radical change in this state of affairs. In effect Xerox took over the entire business of RXL in Central and South America and thenceforth had the field to themselves in the whole of the Americas. In 1967 a further change was effected whereby Xerox similarly took over from RXL the territory of the West Indies. The agreements concluded in 1964 and 1967 whereby these changes were given effect are the crucial documents in the case, *b* since it is the nature of the right to the payments due from Xerox to RXL under these agreements on which the appeal depends. For the purpose of deciding the questions in issue there is no material difference between the two agreements and it will suffice for the purposes of this judgment to consider the first agreement dated 20th February 1964.

The 1964 agreement uses some rather complex geographical formulae to indicate *c* its area of operation, but we shall for brevity substitute the simple, if not entirely accurate, term 'Latin America'. Clause 1 provides:

> 'RXL hereby sells, assigns and transfers to Xerox its entire right, title and interest in all property, rights and assets in [Latin America] of whatsoever nature and description, excluding only its stock in Rank Xerox in Mexico, S.A. and including, *d* without limitation, its goodwill, technical information, know-how, trade secrets, customer lists, patents, patent applications, rights to apply for patents, trade-marks and trade mark applications.'

The effect of cl 2 is to amend the 1957 licence agreement so as to exclude Latin America from its ambit.

Clause 3 provides: *e*

> 'All licences and sub-licences applicable to any place in [Latin America] here-tofore granted by Xerox to [RXL], and any right of Rank Xerox under Paragraph 1 of the LICENCE AGREEMENT to a Licence or Sub-licence applicable to any place in [Latin America] are hereby cancelled and released . . .'

Clause 4 provides: *f*

> 'In consideration of the premises, Xerox shall pay or cause to be paid to [RXL] a royalty of 5% of Net Sales in [Latin America].'

'Net Sales' are then defined by reference to 'sales and rentals of xerographic machines, equipment, apparatus, paper and supplies'. And then, continuing the quotation from cl 4: *g*

> '. . . Such royalty payments shall be made or caused to be made by Xerox quarter-annually in the currency of the country in which the xerographic machines, equipment, apparatus, paper and supplies are delivered, except that where the existing laws of any country specifically authorise payment in pounds sterling, royalties with respect to such country may, at the option of Xerox, be paid in pounds sterling in London.' *h*

Clause 6 provides: 'This Agreement is made in England and shall be construed in accordance with English law.' The agreement was executed under seal by Xerox. The agreement was executed under seal by Xerox.

To complete the story, in December 1969 RXL declared a dividend of £8·4 million to be satisfied by the distribution to shareholders in specie, as it is put, of the right *j* to receive payments from Xerox under the provisions of cl 4 of the 1964 and 1967 agreements ('the Xerox payments'). Since there is, as we have already indicated, no dispute that this was a disposal of assets for capital gains tax purposes it is unnecessary to say more of the details of this transaction.

The two questions for decision, then, are whether the Xerox payments are 'annual

payments' and whether they are 'due under a covenant' within the meaning of
a Sch 7, para 12(*c*), to the Finance Act 1965. This paragraph is grouped with paras 11
and 13 under the heading 'Debts and interests in settled property'. In our judgment
neither the group heading not the provisions of the companion paragraphs in the
group throw any conceivable light on the meaning of para 12(*c*).

Paragraph 12 as a whole reads:

b   'No chargeable gain shall accrue to any person on the disposal of the right to,
or to any part of—(*a*) any allowance, annuity or capital sum payable out of
any superannuation fund, or under any superannuation scheme, established
solely or mainly for persons employed in a profession, trade, undertaking or
employment, and their dependants, (*b*) an annuity granted otherwise than under
a contract for a deferred annuity by a company as part of its business of granting
annuities on human life, whether or not including instalments of capital, or
c   an annuity granted or deemed to be granted under the Government Annuities
Act, 1929, or (*c*) annual payments which are due under a covenant made by any
person and which are not secured on any property.'

We do not find even this immediate context in the least illuminating. It cannot
in our judgment be legitimate, as was suggested by counsel for the Crown, to look
d at the narrow and specific character of the categories of payment under sub-paras (*a*)
and (*b*) and to treat this as a ground for imposing some limitation on the language of
sub-para (*c*) in order to confine it within comparably narrow and specific limits.
Certainly it is not possible to apply the ejusdem generis rule. If the categories of
payment in sub-paras (*a*) and (*b*) can be fitted into a single genus, which we very much
doubt, it would be too narrow to accommodate the language of sub-para (*c*) at all.
e Finally, to add one more negative observation, there is no help to be had in construing
any exempt category of right under para 12 from the supposition that in enacting the
exemption Parliament's primary intention was benevolently to excuse the taxpayer
disposing of such a right from liability to a chargeable gain, for it may equally well
have been the primary intention, less benevolently, to deny him the benefit of any
allowable loss. Accordingly we find ourselves in a singularly bleak and featureless
f stretch of statutory territory, with nothing to help us choose the right direction save
the bare and cryptic words on the statutory signpost which fall to be interpreted.

The phrase 'annual payments' has, of course, long been familiar in taxing statutes,
albeit in a particular context. In current legislation it is found, among charging provisions, in Case III of Sch D in s 109 of the Income and Corporation Taxes Act
1970, which charges tax in respect of 'any interest of money, whether yearly or other-
g wise, or any annuity or other annual payment' and, among machinery provisions,
in s 52(1) of the same Act which requires deduction of tax at source by the payer of
'any annuity or other annual payment'. The origin of these provisions can be traced
as far back as s 102 of the Income Tax Act 1842, so it is not surprising to find that the
phrase 'annual payments' has frequently been judicially considered and has acquired,
in what we shall call the Sch D context, a particular meaning. It is common ground
h in this appeal that the basic characteristics which have been held necessary for the
identification of an 'annual payment' in the Sch D context must also be taken to
characterise an 'annual payment' in the provision we have to construe. What the
relevant characteristics are may conveniently be summarised by quoting extracts
from the judgment of the Court of Appeal delivered by Jenkins LJ in *Whitworth
Park Coal Co Ltd (in liquidation) v Inland Revenue Comrs*[1]. He said:

j   'There have been many judicial pronouncements as to the scope of r. 1(*a*)
of Case III and the following propositions can be regarded as established:—
(i) To come within the rule as an "other annual payment", the payment in

---

1   [1958] 2 All ER 91 at 102-104, [1958] Ch 792 at 815-817, 38 Tax Cas 531 at 548-550

question must be ejusdem generis with the specific instances given in the shape
of interest of money and annuities. See *Hill* v. *Gregory*[1], per HAMILTON, J.; *Earl*   *a*
Howe v. *Inland Revenue Comrs.*[2], per SCRUTTON L.J... (ii) The payment in question
must fall to be made under some binding legal obligation as distinct from being
a mere voluntary payment. See *Smith* v. *Smith*[3], per LORD STERNDALE, M.R.
and per WARRINGTON, L.J... (iii) The fact that the obligation to pay is imposed
by an order of the court and does not arise by virtue of a contract does not exclude
the payment from r. 1(*a*) of Case III. (iv) The payment in question must possess   *b*
the essential quality of recurrence implied by the description "annual". But
that discription has been given a broad interpretation in the authorities. For
example, in *Smith* v. *Smith*[4], WARRINGTON, L.J., said: "Again the fact that the
payment is to be made weekly does not prevent it being annual provided the
weekly payments may continue beyond the year"... (v) The payment in
question must be in the nature of a "pure income" profit in the hands of the   *c*
recipient.'

The first and fifth factors mentioned in this renumeration are really two sides of
the same coin. The same principle underlies them both. It is stated in a well-known
passage from the judgment of Scrutton LJ in *Earl Howe v Inland Revenue Comrs*[5],
who said: *d*

> 'It is not all payments made every year from which income tax can be deducted.
> For instance, if a man agrees to pay a motor garage 500l. a year for five years
> for the hire and upkeep of a car, no one suggests that the person paying can
> deduct income tax from each yearly payment. So if he contracted with a butcher
> for an annual sum to supply all his meat for a year, the annual instalment would   *e*
> not be subject to tax as a whole in the hands of the payee, but only that part of
> it which was profits.'

Another statement of the principle is found in the judgment of Greene MR in *Re
Hanbury*[6], where he said:

> 'There are two classes of annual payments which fall to be considered for   *f*
> Income Tax purposes. There is, first of all, that class of annual payment which
> the Acts regard and treat as being pure income profit of the recipient undi-
> minished by any deduction. Payments of interest, payments of annuities, to
> take the ordinary simple case, are payments which are regarded as part of the
> income of the recipient, and the payer is entitled in estimating his total income to
> treat those payments as payments which go out of his income altogether. The   *g*
> class of annual payment which falls within that category is quite a limited one.
> In the other class there stand a number of payments, nonetheless annual, the
> very quality and nature of which make it impossible to treat them as part of
> the pure profit income of the recipient, the proper way of treating them being
> to treat them as an element to be taken into account in discovering what the
> profits of the recipient are.'   *h*

Before the Special Commissioners it was contended for the Crown that the Xerox
payments were not pure profit income but were part of the trading receipts of RXL.
In a supplemental case stated, confirming their finding in the original case that the

j

1   [1912] 2 KB 61 at 71, 6 Tax Cas 39 at 47
2   [1919] 2 KB 336 at 353, 7 Tax Cas 289 at 303
3   [1923] P 191 at 197 and 201
4   [1923] P 191 at 201
5   [1919] 2 KB 336 at 352, 7 Tax Cas 289 at 303
6   (1939) 38 Tax Cas 588 at 590

Xerox payments were 'annual payments' within the meaning of the relevant pro-
a vision, the Special Commissioners rejected this contention and stated that 'in reaching
this determination we concluded that they were not trading receipts of RXL but could
properly be called "pure profit income" '. Before the judge the Crown did not
pursue the contention that the Xerox payments were trading receipts and we must
take the finding that they were pure profit income to be now beyond challenge.

The principal argument for the Crown now pursued, and that which persuaded
b the learned judge that the Xerox payments are not 'annual payments' under Sch 7,
para 12(c), is that one may use certain provisions found in Part IV of the 1965 Act
to construe the phrase 'annual payments' in para 12(c) and by so doing find that
'any royalty or other sum paid in respect of the user of a patent' cannot be an 'annual
payment'. It is said that the Xerox payments were 'paid in respect of the user of'
patents, and therefore cannot be 'annual payments'. The provisions relied on are
c concerned with the machinery for the collection of tax and require or permit those
liable to make certain classes of payment to deduct and to account to the Revenue
for the relevant tax. In relation to corporation tax, ss 52 and 53 of the 1965 Act
incorporated by reference s 169 of the Income Tax Act 1952, the statutory predecessor
of s 52 of the Income and Corporation Taxes Act 1970. Both s 169 of the 1952 Act
and s 52 of the 1970 Act provide in separate subsections for the deduction of tax
d by the payer from, on the one hand, 'annual payments' within Case III of Sch D,
and, on the other hand, 'any royalty or other sum paid in respect of the user of
a patent'.

Were the Xerox payments payable 'in respect of the user of a patent'? Clearly
they cannot have been so in their entirety because under the 1964 and 1967 agreements
RXL transferred to Xerox a great deal more than the mere right to the user of patents.
e Some, but we know not what, fraction of the benefits conferred on Xerox for which
the payments were the consideration may have taken the form of the outright
assignment of rights then vested in RXL or the surrender of licenses then enjoyed
by RXL in respect of any patents which may then have been in force in any part of
Latin America or the West Indies. After the agreements were concluded RXL no
longer had any interest in any of these patents and the patents became the absolute
f property of Xerox. Moreover the 'royalties' payable under cl 4 were not confined
to sales in the countries in which any relevant patents were in force, nor to sales of
apparatus protected by any such patents, nor the sales during the life of any such
patents. In these circumstances it would in our judgment be a misuse of language
to describe the Xerox payments as being made 'in respect of the user of a patent'.

This conclusion is sufficient to refute the main argument for the Crown which the
g learned judge accepted. But suppose that, contrary to this view, the Xerox payments
were made 'in respect of the user of a patent'. Does it then follow from a consideration of s 169 of the Income Tax Act 1952 as applied by ss 52 and 53 of the 1965 Act,
that a payment 'in respect of the user of a patent' cannot be an 'annual payment'?
Put another way, are the categories of 'annual payments' within Case III of Sch D
and payments 'in respect of a user of a patent' to be regarded for all purposes as
h mutually exclusive because they are the subject of separate provisions in the
machinery for the collection of tax?

In the great majority of cases patent royalties will not fall within Case III of Sch D
because, being trade or professional receipts taxable under Case I and Case II, they
will lack the quality of being pure profit income in the hands of the payee. They have
nevertheless been treated similarly to Case III payments under the tax legislation
j by a provision originating in s 25 of the Finance Act 1907, and now found in s 52(2)
of the Income and Corporation Taxes Act 1970, authorising deduction of tax by the
person liable to make the payments. This provision certainly applies to patent
royalty payments whether they are 'annual payments' or not, but we find it impossible to infer from the presence of this provision that payment of a patent royalty
is incapable of being an 'annual payment' within Case III if it otherwise exhibits

the necessary characteristics to make it so. We would therefore answer in the negative
the two questions posed at the beginning of this paragraph and on this ground also   *a*
reject the argument that the Xerox payments are excluded from the category of
'annual payments' under para 12(*c*) by an interpretation derived from s 169 of the
Income Tax Act 1952 as applied by ss 52 and 53 of the 1965 Act.

Independently of these particular statutory provisions counsel for the Crown has
advanced a wider argument for the Crown to the effect that payments which can
properly be described as royalties, whether the term is used strictly to describe   *b*
receipts derived from patents or copyrights or in some broader sense as in cl 4 of the
1964 and 1967 agreements, cannot in their very nature qualify as 'annual payments'.
He submits that in a case in which royalties, for any reason, were not taxable under
Case I or Case II of Sch D, they would be taxed not as 'annual payments' under Case III
but under the residual Case VI. There is no authority directly in point. Counsel
on both sides referred to authorities which, it was suggested, bear on this question   *c*
indirectly, but we can derive so little assistance from these that we excuse ourselves
from discussing them in this judgment. The question must, we think, be decided as
one of principle. The argument of principle by which counsel for the Crown seeks to
support his proposition is that royalties, in any sense of the term, must represent payments for the exploitation of what he calls 'intellectual property' and they are thus, so
he argues, analogous to payments of hire for the use of chattels. The answer to this   *d*
argument lies, in our judgment, in the realisation that it is really an attempt to re-
introduce by the back door the contention rejected by the Special Commissioners that
the Xerox payments are not pure profit income but trade receipts. Counsel for the
Crown submits that the nature of royalty payments cannot vary according to the particular circumstances in which they are payable. We cannot agree. We accept that in
normal circumstances royalty payments will not be pure profit income because, in the   *e*
language of Greene MR in *Re Hanbury*[1], the proper way to treat them will be 'as
an element to be taken into account in discovering what the profits of the recipient
are'. But this need not necessarily be so, and when the position of the payee is such
that his absolute entitlement to receive the payments is wholly independent of
any outgoings or expenses to which he may be liable, we can see no reason in principle
why the payments should not be, as the Special Commissioners found that the Xerox   *f*
payments in this case were, pure profit income and therefore 'annual payments'.

The final argument for the Crown which needs to be considered in relation to
the question of 'annual payments' is the submission that the Xerox payments would
be taxable under Case V of Sch D as 'income arising from possessions out of the United
Kingdom' and on that account cannot fall within Case III as 'annual payments'.
We do not find it necessary to decide the question, which does not appear to have   *g*
been raised before the Special Commissioners, whether the Xerox payments are
'income arising from possessions outside the United Kingdom', or if they are, whether
in an issue arising directly under Sch D the appropriate case under which they should
be charged is Case III or Case V. For, while we accept that 'annual payments' under
para 12(*c*) must exhibit the same general characteristics as in the Sch D context, we
do not think it at all follows that a payment having those characteristics cannot   *h*
qualify as an 'annual payment' under para 12(*c*) solely because it would fall to be
charged under Sch D under a different case from Case III for reasons unconnected
with and not affecting its character as an 'annual payment'.

Accordingly, on the first main point in the appeal we conclude, in agreement
with the Special Commissioners, and respectfully, differing from the learned judge,
that the Xerox payments were 'annual payments'.

Were they 'due under a covenant'? The category of 'annual payments' being as   *j*
wide as it is, it is difficult not to think that the words 'due under a covenant' were
introduced into para 12(*c*) with the object of narrowing the class of payments to

1   (1939) 38 Tax Cas 588 at 590

which the exemption was to apply. It is tempting therefore immediately to speculate

a as to what may have been the rationale of the limitation intended to be imposed by these words. Counsel's submission for the Crown is that the only reading which makes sense is to construe the phrase as applying to payments made without consideration which are enforceable only because covenanted by deed. We have been much impressed by this submission. Although, as the learned judge observed[1], 'there is no general principle of capital gains tax which exempts a disponer from tax on a

b chargeable gain arising on a disposition simply because he originally acquired the subject-matter of the disposition through another's gift', there is nothing fanciful in supposing that Parliament, in relation to the familiar category of gratuitous covenanted annual payments to relatives, dependants and the like, may have thought it convenient to exclude any chargeable gain or allowable loss which would other- wise accrue on the disposal of the asset, particularly perhaps on the death of the

c covenantee or the release of the covenant. On the other hand if para 12(*c*) is capable of embracing a whole range of 'annual payments' of a purely commercial character, as for instance the Xerox payments in this case, provided the obligation to pay is undertaken by deed, it is impossible to conceive of any rational fiscal policy under- lying the statutory exemption. The essential character of such payments depends on the commercial realities of the transaction. Whether the instrument under which

d the payments are due was executed by the party liable under hand or under seal is, one would have supposed, from the fiscal point of view wholly irrelevant. In the light of these considerations we have no doubt at all that if the statutory language is reasonably capable of two meanings, one being that for which the Crown contends, that is the meaning we should prefer. We make no secret of the fact that we have tried hard to discover just such an ambiguity, but in the end we find ourselves de-

e feated in the attempt. By itself the word 'covenant' is admittedly ambiguous in that it is capable, in certain contexts, of embracing promises not under seal, but that does not assist, since in the context of para 12(*c*) 'covenant' clearly bears its ordinary and primary meaning of a promise in a document executed by the promisor under seal. Counsel for the Crown has argued that there is ambiguity in the phrase 'payment due under a covenant' and that this is capable of meaning a payment due by virtue

f of a covenant alone, i e a payment unsupported by consideration. The insuperable obstacle to this interpretation is that once a promise to pay is embodied in a deed executed by the payer, then, notwithstanding that there may have been valuable consideration given for the promise, the debt arising on the promise is due as to a speciality debt and not as a simple contract debt; in other words it is a 'payment due under a covenant' and nothing else. As was said by Jervis CJ in *Abley v Dale*[2]:

g

> 'If the precise words used are plain and unambiguous, in our judgment, we are bound to construe them in their ordinary sense, even though it do lead .. to an absurbity or manifest injustice. Words may be modified or varied where their import is doubtful or obscure. But we assume the functions of legislators when we depart from the ordinary meaning of the precise words used, merely
h because we see, or fancy we see, an absurdity or manifest injustice from an adherence to their literal meaning.'

To give to the words 'due under a covenant' the meaning for which the Crown contends requires that other words be added, but 'we are not entitled to read words into an Act of Parliament unless clear reason for it is to be found within the four

j corners of the Act itself' (per Lord Loreburn LC in *Vickers, Sons & Maxim Ltd v Evans*[3]).

---

1 [1977] 3 All ER 593 at 606, [1978] Ch 1 at 9, [1977] STC 285 at 298
2 (1851) 11 CB 378 at 391
3 [1910] AC 444 at 445

We can find no clear reason in the 1965 Act for reading words into para 12(*c*). The words Parliament has used are capable of only one meaning and according to that *a* meaning the Xerox payments are 'due under a covenant'.

We therefore allow the appeal and discharge so much of the assessment to corporation tax under appeal as related to the disposal by RXL of the right to receive the Xerox payments.

Appeal allowed with costs in Court of Appeal and before Slade J; case remitted to Special b Commissioners to determine amount of assessment; leave to appeal to the House of Lords.

Solicitors: *Linklaters & Paines* (for RXL); *Solicitor of Inland Revenue.*

Christine Ivamy   Barrister.

c

Howard Marine & Dredging Co Ltd v A Ogden & Sons (Excavations) Ltd

d

COURT OF APPEAL, CIVIL DIVISION
LORD DENNING MR, BRIDGE AND SHAW LJJ
16th, 17th, 20th, 21st, 22nd, 23rd JUNE, 13th DECEMBER 1977

Misrepresentation – Damages – Reasonable ground for belief that facts represented true – Contract for hire of barges – Representation as to capacity of barges – Barge owners over- e stating capacity of barges – Owners relying on deadweight capacity stated in Lloyd's Register – Register giving wrong figure – Owners having in their possession ship's documents stating correct figure – Misrepresentation inducing charterers to enter into a contract of hire – Whether owners having reasonable ground to believe that statement as to capacity of barges true – Misrepresentation Act 1967, s 2(1).

f

Negligence – Information or advice – Fact peculiarly within knowledge of defendant – Specific fact which plaintiff has no ready means of ascertaining – Owners and prospective charterers of barges to be employed for specific purpose known to owners – Owners innocently misrepresenting capacity of barges – Misrepresentation inducing charterers to enter into contract of hire – Whether owners under a duty of care to give accurate information as to capacity of barges.

g

A water authority engaged in the construction of sewage works invited the defendants, a firm of contractors, to tender for a contract under which they were to excavate soil, convey it to the riverside, tip it into sea-going barges, carry it out to sea and dump it there. The defendants had had no experience of dumping earth at sea. To make their tender they had to calculate the cost of hiring suitable barges. The defendants *h* invited the plaintiffs to quote a price for the hire of two German-built barges which the plaintiffs owned. The plaintiffs stated that the usable capacity of the barges was 850 cubic metres but made no mention of the weight which each could carry. The defendants made their tender on the basis of the cost of hiring the barges quoted by the plaintiffs. The tender was accepted by the water authority. Thereafter the defendants started negotiations with the plaintiffs for the hire of the barges. A meeting *j* took place at the defendants' offices between the defendants and the plaintiffs' marine manager at which the defendants asked a number of questions, including a question as to the capacity of the barges. The marine manager replied that it was about 850 cubic metres and, in answer to a further question, indicated that the payload was 1,600 tonnes. In fact the payload was only 1,055 tonnes, whereas the weight *a* of each load which the plaintiffs had calculated that the barges would carry was 1,200 tonnes. Although false, the marine manager's answer was made honestly. At the time when it was made he did not have any papers with him from which he could check the facts. The answer was based on his recollection of the deadweight figure of 1,800 tonnes given in Lloyd's Register. That figure was, however, incorrect. The marine manager had also at some time seen the German shipping documents which showed that the deadweight of the barges was in fact 1,195 tonnes but that figure had

b not registered in his mind. The defendants hired the barges but were unable to carry the amount of earth they had understood they would be able to do and in consequence the excavation work was held up. The defendants refused to pay the hire whereupon the plaintiffs withdrew the barges and brought an action for the outstanding payments. By way of counterclaim the defendants claimed damages for, inter alia, misrepresentation under s 2(1)*ᵃ* of the Misrepresentation Act 1967 and for negligence.

c

Held (Lord Denning MR dissenting) – The defendants were entitled to succeed on their counterclaim for the following reasons—

(i) Since the misrepresentation made by the plaintiffs' marine manager about the capacity of the barges had been made with the intention that it should be acted on by the defendants and had in fact been acted on by them when they entered into the

d contract of hire, the plaintiffs were liable under s 2(1) of the 1967 Act unless they could prove that the marine manager had had reasonable grounds for believing that what he had said about the barges' capacity was true. The evidence adduced by the plaintiffs was not sufficient to show that the marine manager had had an objectively reasonable ground for disregarding the deadweight capacity figure given in the ship's documents and preferring the figure in Lloyd's Register. Accordingly they had failed to

e prove that he had had reasonable grounds to believe the truth of his misrepresentation to the defendants (see p 1144 *h j*, p 1145 *b c*, p 1146 *g* to *j* and p 1149 *b c*, post).

(ii) (per Shaw LJ, Bridge LJ dubitante) The defendants were also liable for breach of their common law duty of care in making the misrepresentation. The information could not be regarded as other than important whatever the circumstances in which it had been sought and given; moreover it was a specific fact, not expert advice,

f which the defendants were seeking, a fact which they had no such ready and direct means of ascertaining as were available to the plaintiffs. Those factors, in association with the relationship of the parties as owners and prospective charterers of barges to be employed for a specific purpose known to the owners, imposed on the owners a duty to exercise reasonable care to be accurate in giving information of a material character which was peculiarly within their knowledge (see p 1148 *e* to *g*, post);

g dicta of Lord Pearce in *Hedley Byrne & Co Ltd v Heller & Partners Ltd* [1963] 2 All ER at 617, 618 and of Lord Reid and Lord Morris of Borth-y-Gest in *Mutual Life & Citizens' Assurance Co Ltd v Evatt* [1971] 1 All ER at 163 applied.

Notes

h For innocent misrepresentation, see 26 Halsbury's Laws (3rd Edn) 857, para 1594, and for cases on the subject, see 35 Digest (Repl) 30, 31, 34, 35, 212-224, 253-270.

For the Misrepresentation Act 1967, s 2, see 22 Halsbury's Statutes (3rd Edn) 676.

Cases referred to in judgments

Brogden v Metropolitan Railway Co (1877) 2 App Cas 666, HL, 12 Digest (Reissue) 60, 313.

j *Esso Petroleum Co Ltd v Mardon* [1976] 2 All ER 5, [1976] QB 801, [1976] 2 WLR 583, [1976] 2 Lloyd's Rep 305, CA.

Evans (J) & Son (Portsmouth) Ltd v Andrea Merzario Ltd [1976] 2 All ER 930, [1976] 1 WLR 1078, [1976] 2 Lloyd's Rep 165, CA.

---

a Section 2(1) is set out at p 1142 *a b*, post

Fish v Kelly (1864) 17 CBNS 194, 144 ER 78, 43 Digest (Repl) 117, *1054*.
Hedley Byrne & Co Ltd v Heller & Partners Ltd [1963] 2 All ER 575, [1964] AC 465, [1963]   **a**
     3 WLR 101, [1963] 1 Lloyd's Rep 485, HL, 36(1) Digest (Reissue) 24, *84*.
Heilbut, Symons & Co v Buckleton [1913] AC 30, [1911-13] All ER Rep 83, 82 LJKB 245, 107
     LT 769, 20 Mans 54, HL, 35 Digest (Repl) 56, *495*.
Low v Bouverie [1891] 3 Ch 82, [1891-4] All ER Rep 348, 60 LJCh 594, 65 LT 533, CA,
     35 Digest (Repl) 34, *258*.
Mutual Life & Citizens' Assurance Co Ltd v Evatt [1971] 1 All ER 150, [1971] AC 793,   **b**
     [1971] 2 WLR 23, [1970] 2 Lloyd's Rep 441, [1971] ALR 235, PC, 36(1) Digest (Reissue)
     28, *95*.
Pearson (S) & Son Ltd v Dublin Corpn [1907] AC 351, [1904-7] All ER Rep 255, 77 LJPC
     1, 97 LT 645, HL, 12 Digest (Reissue) 309, *2231*.
Robins v National Trust Co [1927] AC 515, [1927] All ER Rep 73, 96 LJPC 84, 137 LT 1,
     PC, 16 Digest (Repl) 185, *721*.   **c**
Schawel v Reade (1912) 46 ILT 281, HL, 2 Digest (Reissue) 344, *1931*.
Shanklin Pier Ltd v Detel Products Ltd [1951] 2 All ER 471, [1951] 2 KB 854, [1951] 2
     Lloyd's Rep 187, 39 Digest (Repl) 579, *1030*.
Wells (Merstham) Ltd v Buckland Sand & Silica Co Ltd [1964] 1 All ER 41, [1965] 2 QB 170,
     [1964] 2 WLR 453, Digest (Cont Vol B) 632, *1078a*.

                                                                        d

Appeal

By a writ issued on 7th July 1975 the plaintiffs, Howard Marine & Dredging Co Ltd
('Howards'), brought an action against the defendants, A Ogden & Sons (Excavations)
Ltd ('Ogdens'), claiming £93,183·14 as moneys unpaid for the hire of two barges on
demise charter terms. By their defence and counterclaim Ogdens denied the debt
and claimed damages. At the trial of the action in the Commercial Court at Win-   **e**
chester, Bristow J held Ogdens to be liable to pay for the hire of the barges, and
ordered them to pay agreed damages amounting to £97,510·57. Ogdens appealed.
The facts are set out in the judgment of Lord Denning MR.

Anthony Lloyd QC and *Patrick Phillips* for Ogdens.
Michael Thomas QC and *Alan Pollock* for Howards.   **f**

                                                   Cur adv vult

13th December. The following judgments were read.

                                                                       g

LORD DENNING MR. This case took three weeks before the judge and two
weeks before this court. It is very complicated, but I will try to state the main facts
as simply as I can, missing out many details.

In 1974 the Northumbrian Water Authority were about to construct a big sewage
works for Tyneside. There was much excavation to be done. Contractors were
required to dig out vast quantities of earth, take it by conveyors to the riverside, tip   **h**
it into seagoing barges, carry it out to sea for a few miles and dump it there. Tenders
were invited. One of those invited was Ogdens, a firm of contractors in the north-east.
They were experienced in disposing of earth by land. But they had no experience of
dumping it at sea.

In order to make their tender, Ogdens had to calculate the cost of the excavating
and conveying, which they knew all about, but also the cost of the dumping at sea,   **j**
which they knew nothing about. They had to hire barges suitable for the work. Two
seagoing barges were to be employed. The operation was to be continuous. It was to
be synchronised with the excavation. As soon as one barge was full, it would leave
the quay, carry the material to the dumping ground, dump it and return. Meanwhile
the other barge would be loading.

a   In order to prepare their tender, Ogdens got into touch with five firms who had barges, and invited them to quote a price for the hire. One of these firms was Howards of London. They had two German-built barges which might be available. They were self-propelled twin-screw hopper barges, 207 feet long. They were at the time lying idle in the Medway. Howards had used them previously at work in the estuary at Felixstowe where silt was being dredged up from the bottom. These two barges had been used to carry it out to sea and dump it. Howards had bought the

b   barges from the German owners and had the file of German shipping documents in their London office.

The letter of 10th April 1974

Howards were keen to find work for these two barges. So when Ogdens invited quotations, Howards sent their marine manager, Mr O'Loughlin, up to the site at

c   Tyneside to see the nature of the material to be carried. He thought the two barges could do the work. He then quoted for hire of them. He did it in an important letter of 10th April 1974. He offered to let the barges to Ogdens at £1,800 per week 'subject to availability and charterparty'. In the letter he specified the *volume* of material that each barge could carry. He put it in marine terms: 'Capacity (struck 940m³) usable ca 850m³'.

d   That meant that its capacity filled level to the brim would be 940 cubic metres; but that, as the material would not be level but 'in heaps', its usable capacity was about 850 cubic metres. Mr O'Loughlin based that figure on their experience at Felixstowe. In that letter, Howards said nothing about the *weight* that each barge could carry. That is called in marine circles the 'deadweight'. There are certain deductions to be made for fuel etc to give the 'payload', that is, the load for which

e   payment is received.

The two telephone conversations of April 1974

On receiving that letter Ogdens wanted to make sure that the barges could carry the material which was to be excavated on Tyneside. So their Mr Dent in the north-east telephoned to Mr O'Loughlin in the south on 11th April 1974 and asked him to

f   explain the letter: 'Does your letter mean that each of these vessels can carry 850 cubic metres of spoil?' Mr O'Loughlin said:

'Yes, of course, each can carry 850 cubic metres, but you must remember that it depends on the weight of the material. A ton of feathers occupies much more space than a ton of lead. If the material is heavy, you must be careful not to fill the barge above the load line.'

g
Mr Dent knew so little about barges that he missed the point about the load-line. As a result of the conversation he was under the firm impression that each barge could carry 850 cubic metres of the material they were going to excavate at Tyneside.

A day or two later Mr Hall (the area manager for Ogdens in the north-east) wanted to be sure that each barge could carry 850 cubic metres of the material. So he himself

h   telephoned to Mr O'Loughlin and asked him: 'Does it mean that each barge can carry 850 cubic metres solid measure?' Mr O'Loughlin said: 'Yes, 850 cubic metres are available to be used.'

The judge found that those two telephone conversations were bedevilled by a classic misunderstanding. Both of Ogden's men, Mr Dent and Mr Hall, were thinking of the clay they had to excavate in Tyneside; whereas Mr O'Loughlin was thinking

j   of the silt they had carried at Felixstowe. In the estuary of Felixstowe, the silt (being a mixture of sand and water) only weighed 1·24 tonnes per cubic metre. So 850 cubic metres of it would weigh 1,054 tonnes. This was, near enough, equal to the pay-load of each barge. But at the sewage site in Tyneside, the earth was heavy clay. It weighed 'in the dig', in the ground before being excavated, two tonnes per cubic metre. So 850 cubic metres of it would weigh 1,700 tonnes. That was far more than either barge could safely carry. 1,700 tonnes would send the vessel down deep in the water, well below the load line, and sink her.

At any rate, at the end of those two telephone conversations, both of Ogden's men, Mr Dent and Mr Hall, firmly believed that each barge could carry 850 cubic metres of 'in-dig clay' weighing 1,700 tonnes. The judge found that this was because they failed to ask Mr O'Loughlin the right question, and honestly misunderstood his simple answer to it. So there was no mispresentation; and no liability can attach to Howards in respect of those two telephone conversations.

The tender

Believing that each barge could carry 850 cubic metres of 'in-dig clay', Ogdens made calculations as to the cost of hiring the barges from Howards. But, as a matter of prudence, they worked on a capacity of 600 cubic metres instead of 850 cubic metres. That was indeed prudent; because they had overlooked the 'bulking factor'. When 'in-dig clay' was excavated, it occupied more space in a heap than in solid. The 'bulking factor' was 1·25. So 600 cubic metres of 'in-dig clay' would occupy 750 cubic metres of clay in a heap. Even on that figure of 750 cubic metres, it would go far to fill the volume of usable space in the barge (850 cubic metres). But, unbeknown to Ogdens, it would be far too heavy. It would weigh 1,200 tonnes, whereas the pay load was 1,055 tonnes. If filled with 1,200 tonnes the deck would be awash and the barges in peril.

Ogdens also made calculations as to the cost of hiring barges from the other four firms who quoted. Howards were the lowest. So Ogdens used their quotation in making their tender for the whole excavation to the Northumbrian Water Authority. It was one of the items in the overall figure. Ogdens made their tender to the authority on 29th April 1974. It was to do the work for £1,847,647·31. Seven other contractors made tenders for the whole excavation. On 18th June the authority accepted Ogdens' tender.

The negotiations

Having got their tender accepted, Ogdens took up negotiations with Howards so as to acquire the barges. (They also kept in touch with the other barge firms in case their negotiations with Howards broke down.) On 12th June Mr O'Loughlin of Howards went up to the north and saw Ogdens' men, Mr Dent and Mr Hall. They discussed the barges (then lying in the Medway), but nothing was said about capacity, at any rate nothing which either side took seriously. At this meeting Mr O'Loughlin handed Ogdens a draft charterparty. It contained many standard-form clauses. He said that the barges were still available. He reduced the price of hire to £1,724 a week. On 24th June, when he got back, he wrote to Ogdens confirming the conversation, and saying:

> '... We now look forward to receiving your formal letter of intent booking our vessels, at which time we shall finalise charterparties for each vessel and will forward them to you for signature.'

The interview of 11th July 1974

Nothing was, however, finalised at that time. Ogdens were negotiating with another firm of barge-owners as well as Howards. They asked both firms to send up representatives to the north-east. They prepared a questionnaire of 31 questions on all sorts of matters. The meeting took place on 11th July at Ogdens' office at Otley in Yorkshire. One of the questions was: 'No 8; Capacity of Barges.' They asked this question of the other firm, and also of Mr O'Loughlin of Howards. The judge found what was said was this. Ogdens: 'What is the capacity of each barge?' Mr O'Loughlin: '850 cubic metres.' Ogdens: 'What is that in tonnes about?' Mr O'Loughlin: 'About 1600 tonnes subject to weather, fuel-load and time of year.' Mr O'Loughlin's answer was noted down by Ogdens in writing, as follows: '1600 t 850 m³ usable.'

The judge found that Mr O'Loughlin was perfectly honest in saying 1,600 tonnes.

Early on when Howards acquired the barges, he had looked up Lloyd's Register for
a these two barges. That register gave the deadweight as 1,800 tonnes. It was a figure
which stuck in Mr O'Loughlin's mind. Making generous deductions for the weight
of crew, fuel etc, the payload could be put at 1,600 tonnes. But Lloyd's Register had
made a mistake; a very rare thing for them to do. The real deadweight was not 1,800
tonnes but 1,194·94 tonnes. Making the appropriate allowances, the payload was
1,052·67 tonnes. But Mr O'Loughlin did not know this. He was up in the north-east
b and did not have the files with him. They were in the London office. They might
have shown him the correct figures. But he was not aware of this. So Mr O'Loughlin
was honest and, I think, had reasonable grounds for saying 1,600 tonnes; but it was
wrong. No doubt Ogdens were satisfied with his answer. It meant that the barges
could carry the weight which they had calculated (600 cubic metres at two tonnes
each, making 1,200 tonnes). So Ogdens continued with their negotiations.

c *Further negotiations*
After that meeting there were various exchanges by letter and telex. Howards
reduced the proposed figure of hire to £1,644 a week, then to £1,578. On 9th August
Ogdens gave a firm order to Howards for the two barges at £1,500 each per week on
their (Ogdens') own terms and conditions. This was rejected by Howards on 16th
d August in a letter saying: '. . . We must point out that our contract with you is subject
to charterparty terms and *not* to the terms of your order.'

On 18th September there was an 'on-hire condition' survey at Greenhithe, attended
by surveyors on both sides. The principal purpose was to note down any structural
damage to the barges or the machinery or equipment; but the surveyors if asked were
well able to form a good opinion of the capacity of the barges.

e *The charterparties*
In October the draft charterparties were the subject of telexes between the parties.
They were bare-boat charterparties in common form. Various amendments were
suggested and accepted; but there was one clause which was contained in all the
drafts which were submitted and exchanged and no objection was ever taken to it.
It was in these words:

f
'On handing over by the Owners, the vessel shall be tight, staunch and strong,
but Charterers' acceptance of handing over the vessel shall be conclusive that
they have examined the vessel and found her to be in all respects seaworthy,
in good order and condition and in all respects fit for the intended and contemplated use by the Charterers and in every other way satisfactory to them.'

g *Delivery of the barges*
The charterparties were never actually signed; but, nevertheless, the barges were
delivered by Howards. They sailed up from the Medway to the Tyne and were
accepted by Ogdens, one on 20th October, the other on 27th October. They were
put straight to work. Thereafter Odgens used the barges for six months, from
October 1974 to April 1975. Ogdens complained about defects in the machinery of
h the barges. Ogdens were also concerned because they suspected very early on that
the barges could not carry the 1,200 tonnes per trip without submerging their load
lines. Then in March 1975 they discovered that the payload was only 1,055 tonnes.
In the circumstances Ogdens only paid £2,000 on account of hire; but they refused to
pay any more. When hire was not paid, Howards withdrew the barges and they
returned to the Medway. Ogdens employed other barges to complete the work.

j *The legal proceedings*
On 7th July 1975 Howards issued a writ claiming £93,183·14 for the outstanding
hire on the two barges. Ogdens counterclaimed on the ground that the barges had
defective machinery, and also on the ground that Howards had misrepresented the
cargo-carrying capacity. Such misrepresentations were, they said, made in the two
telephone conversations in April 1974, and the interview on 11th July 1974. They said

that, on account of the low carrying capacity, the whole operation of the contract was delayed. The excavation work was held up because the barges could not carry the required quantities. They counterclaimed for £600,000.

The issue of liability was ordered to be tried as a preliminary issue. The judge dismissed the counterclaim and gave judgment for Howards for the hire of £93,183·14. Ogdens appeal to this court.

The written contract

At the trial it was submitted on behalf of Ogdens that there was no express contract because Ogdens had never signed that charterparty. The letter of 10th April 1974 said 'subject to contract', that is a signed contract, and here no contract was ever signed. The judge rejected that contention and it was not renewed before us. It is plain that, when the barges were delivered and accepted, there was a concluded contract on the terms of the charterparty: see *Brogden v Metropolitan Railway Co*[1].

The collateral oral warranties

Ogdens submitted that, in the two telephone conversations in April 1974, Howards gave oral warranties as to the carrying capacity of the barges; and that, on the faith of these warranties, they tendered for the main excavation contract and entered into it; that the warranties are therefore binding on Howards on the authority of such cases as the *Shanklin Pier Ltd v Detel Products Ltd*[2] and *Wells (Merstham) Ltd v Buckland Sand & Silica Ltd*[3]; further, that at the interview of 11th July 1974 Howards gave a further oral warranty as to the carrying capacity of the barges; and that, on the faith of it, they did order the barges and took them on hire under the charterparties.

On this point we were, as usual, referred to *Heilbut, Symons & Co v Buckleton*[4]. That case has come under considerable criticism lately, particularly in view of the contemporaneous decision of the House of Lords in *Schawel v Reade*[5]: see Professor Grieg's article in the Law Quarterly Review[6]. Much of what was said in *Heilbut, Symons & Co v Buckleton*[4] is now out of date, as I mentioned in *J Evans & Son (Portsmouth) Ltd v Merzario*[7] and *Esso Petroleum Co Ltd v Mardon*[8]. No doubt it is still true to say, as Holt CJ said: '. . . an affirmation at the time of the sale is a warranty, provided it appears as evidence to be so intended', which I take to mean intended to be binding.

Applying this test, I cannot regard any of the oral representations made in April 1974 as contractual warranties. Ogdens invited offers from five different owners of barges. These five made separate offers. Howards made their written offer 'subject to availability and contract', which shows that they were not binding themselves to anything at that stage. It cannot be supposed that, in the telephone conversations, they were binding themselves contractually to anything. Nor would I regard the statement at the interview of 11th July 1974 as a contractual warranty. It was made three months before the barges were delivered. And meanwhile there was the 'on-hire condition' survey, and the exchange of the draft charterparties, in which you would expect any contractual terms to be included.

I agree with the judge that there were no collateral warranties here.

Negligent misrepresentations

Ogdens contended next that the representations by Howards, as to the carrying capacity of the barges, were made negligently; and that Howards are liable in damages

1 (1877) 2 App Cas 666 at 672, 680
2 [1951] 2 All ER 471, [1951] 2 KB 854
3 [1964] 1 All ER 41, [1965] 2 QB 170
4 [1913] AC 30, [1911-13] All ER Rep 83
5 (1912) 46 ILT 281
6 Misrepresentations and Sales of Goods (1971) 87 LQR 179 at 185-190
7 [1976] 2 All ER 930 at 933, [1976] 1 WLR 1078 at 1081
8 [1976] 2 All ER 5 at 13, [1976] QB 801 at 817

for negligent misrepresentation on the principles laid down in *Hedley Byrne & Co Ltd v*
Heller & Partners Ltd[1].

This raises the vexed question of the scope of the doctrine of *Hedley Byrne*[1]. It was
much discussed in the Privy Council in *Mutual Life & Citizens' Assurance Co Ltd v*
Evatt[2] and in this Court in *Esso Petroleum Co Ltd v Mardon*[3]. To my mind one of the
most helpful passages is to be found in the speech of Lord Pearce in *Hedley Byrne & Co*
Ltd v Heller & Partners Ltd[4]:

> 'To import such a duty [of care] the representation must normally, I think,
> concern a business or professional transaction whose nature makes clear the
> gravity of the inquiry and the importance and influence attached to the answer
> ... A most important circumstance is the form of the inquiry and of the answer.'

To this I would add the principle stated by Lord Reid and Lord Morris of Borth-y-
Gest in *Mutual Life & Citizens' Assurance Co Ltd v Evatt*[5], which I would adopt in
preference to that stated by the majority:

> '. . . when an enquirer consults a businessman in the course of his business and
> makes it plain to him that he is seeking considered advice and intends to act on it
> in a particular way ... his action in giving such advice ... [gives rise to] ... a legal
> obligation to take such care as is reasonable in the whole circumstances.'

Those principles speak of the 'gravity of the inquiry' and the seeking of 'considered
advice'. Those words are used so as to exclude representations made during a casual
conversation in the street; or in a railway carriage; or an impromptu opinion given
offhand; or 'off the cuff' on the telephone. To put it more generally, the duty is one
of honesty and no more whenever the opinion, information or advice is given in
circumstances in which it appears that it is unconsidered and it would not be reasonable
for the recipient to act on it without taking further steps to check it. Some instances
are to be found in the books. One is *Fish v Kelly*[6]. The other is *Low v Bouverie*[7], as
explained by Lord Reid and Lord Morris of Borth-y-Gest in *Mutual Life & Citizens'*
Assurance Co Ltd v Evatt[8]. And the actual decision in *Heilbut, Symons & Co v Buckleton*[9]
was that an honest answer on the telephone did not give rise to a cause of action.

Applying this test, it seems to me that at these various conversations Mr O'Loughlin
was under a duty to be honest, but no more. Take the first two conversations. They
were on the telephone. The callers from the north wanted to know what was the
capacity of the barges. Mr O'Loughlin answered it off-hand as best he could, without
looking up the file. If they had wanted considered advice, they should have written a
letter and got it in writing. Take the last conversation. It was on an occasion when
Mr O'Loughlin went up to the north to discuss all sorts of things. In the course of it
he was asked again the capacity of the barges. He had not got the file with him, so
he answered as best he could from memory. To my mind in those circumstances it
was not reasonable for Ogdens to act on his answers without checking them. They
ought either to have got him to put it in writing (that would have stressed the
gravity and importance of it) or they ought to have got expert advice on their own
behalf, especially in a matter of such importance to them. So I agree with the judge
that there was not such a situation here as to give rise to a duty of care; or to make
Howards liable for negligent misrepresentation at common law.

1   [1963] 2 All ER 575, [1964] AC 465
2   [1971] 1 All ER 150, [1971] AC 793
3   [1976] 2 All ER 5, [1976] QB 801
4   [1963] 2 All ER 575 at 617, 618, [1964] AC 465 at 539
5   [1977] 1 All ER 150 at 163, [1971] AC 793 at 812
6   (1864) 17 CBNS 294
7   (1891) 3 Ch 82
8   [1971] 1 All ER 150 at 164, [1971] AC 793 at 813
9   [1913] AC 30, [1911-13] All ER 83

The Misrepresentation Act 1967

Alternatively Ogdens claim damages for innocent misrepresentation under the *a* Misrepresentation Act 1967. Section 2(1) says:

'Where a person has entered into a contract after a misrepresentation has been made to him by another party thereto and as a result thereof he has suffered loss, then, if the person making the misrepresentation would be liable in damages in respect thereof had the misrepresentation been made fraudulently, that person shall be so liable notwithstanding that the misrepresentation was not made *b* fraudulently, unless he proves that he had reasonable ground to believe and did believe up to the time the contract was made that the facts represented were true.'

This enactment imposes a new and serious liability on anyone who makes a representation of fact in the course of negotiations for a contract If that representation turns out to be mistaken, then, however innocent he may be, he is just as liable as if he *c* had made it fraudulently. But how different from times past! For years he was not liable in damages at all for innocent misrepresentation: see *Heilbut, Symons & Co v Buckleton*[1]. Quite recently he was made liable if he was proved to have made it negligently, see *Esso Petroleum Co Ltd v Mardon*[2]. But now with this Act he is made liable, unless he proves, and the burden is on him to prove, that he had reasonable ground to believe and did in fact believe that it was true. *d*

Section 2(1) certainly applies to the representation made by Mr O'Loughlin on 11th July 1974 when he told Ogdens that each barge could carry 1,600 tonnes. The judge found that it was a misrepresentation, that he said it with the object of getting the hire contract for Howards. They got it; and, as a result, Ogdens suffered loss. But the judge found that Mr O'Loughlin was not negligent, and so Howards were not liable for it. *e*

The judge's finding was criticised before us, because he asked himself the question: was Mr O'Loughlin negligent? whereas he should have asked himself: did Mr O'Loughlin have reasonable ground to believe that the representation was true? I think that criticism is not fair to the judge. By the word 'negligent' he was only using shorthand for the longer phrase contained in s 2(1) which he had before him. And the judge, I am sure, had the burden of proof in mind, for he had come to the *f* conclusion that Mr O'Loughlin was not negligent. The judge said in effect: 'I am satisfied that Mr O'Loughlin was not negligent'; and being so satisfied, the burden need not be further considered: see *Robins v National Trust Co*[3].

It seems to me that, when one examines the details, the judge's view was entirely justified. He found that Mr O'Loughlin's state of mind was this. Mr O'Loughlin had examined Lloyd's Register and had seen there that the deadweight capacity of *g* each barge was 1,800 tonnes. That figure stuck in his mind. The judge found that 'the 1,600 tonnes was arrived at by knocking off what he considered a reasonable margin for fuel, and so on, from the 1,800 tonnes summer deadweight figure in Lloyd's Register, which was in the back of his mind'. The judge said that Mr O'Loughlin had seen at some time the German shipping documents and had seen the deadweight figure of 1,055·135 tonnes, but it did not register. All that was in his mind was the *h* 1,800 tonnes in Lloyd's Register which was regarded in shipping circles as the bible. That afforded reasonable ground for him to believe that the barges could each carry 1,600 tonnes payload; and that is what Mr O'Loughlin believed.

So on this point, too, I do not think we should fault the judge. It is not right to pick his judgment to pieces, by subjecting it (or the shorthand note) to literal analysis. Viewing it fairly, the judge (who had s 2(1) in front of him) must have been of opinion *j* that the burden of proof was discharged.

---

1   [1913] AC 30, [1911-13] All ER 83
2   [1976] 2 All ER 5, [1976] QB 801
3   [1927] AC 515

The exception clause

a   If I be wrong so far, however, there remains the exception clause in the charterparty. It was, as I have said, included throughout all the negotiations; and no objection was ever taken to it. The important words are:

b   '. . . Charterers acceptance of handing over the vessel shall be conclusive that [she is] . . . in all respects fit for the intended and contemplated use by the Charterers and in every other way satisfactory to them.'

In the old days we used to construe such an exception clause strictly against the party relying on it; but there is no need, and I suggest no warrant, any longer for construing it so strictly. The reason is that now by s 3 of the Misrepresentation Act 1967 the provision is of no effect except to the extent that the court may allow reliance on it as being fair and reasonable in the circumstances of the case. Under this section the question is not whether the provision itself is reasonable, but only whether 'reliance on it [is] fair and reasonable in the circumstances of the case'.

If the clause itself is reasonable, that goes a long way towards showing that reliance on it is fair and reasonable. It seems to me that the clause was itself fair and reasonable. The parties here were commercial concerns and were of equal bargaining power. The clause was not foisted by one on the other in a standard printed form. It was contained in all the drafts which passed between them, and it was no doubt given close consideration by both sides, like all the other clauses, some of which were amended and others not. It was a clause common in charterparties of this kind; and is familiar in other commercial contracts, such as construction and engineering contracts: see for instance *S Pearson & Son Ltd v Dublin Corpn*[1], and the useful observations in Hudson on Building Contracts[2]. It is specially applicable in cases where the contractor has the opportunity of checking the position for himself. It tells him that he should do so; and that he should not rely on any information given beforehand, for it may be inaccurate. Thus it provides a valuable safeguard against the consequences of innocent misrepresentation.

Even if the clause were somewhat too wide (I do not think it is), nevertheless this is, I think, a case where it would be fair and reasonable to allow reliance on it. Here is a clause by which Ogdens accepted that the barges were 'in all respects fit for the intended and contemplated use by the charterers'. Ogdens had had full inspection and examination of the barges. They had had an 'on-hire condition' survey by their surveyors. Any expert could have given them a reliable estimate as to the deadweight capacity. Yet they seek to say that the barges were not fit for the use for which they intended them, in that they were of too low carrying capacity. And in support of their case they have no written representation to go on. They only have two telephone conversations and one interview, as to which there is an acute conflict of evidence. It is just such conflicts which commercial men seek to avoid by such a clause as this. I would do nothing to impair its efficacy. I would allow Howards to rely on it.

h   *Conclusion*

It seems to me, as a matter of probability, that all three representations should stand on the same footing, all three to convey the same meaning, all three true or all three false. Yet the judge drew a distinction between them. The first two were true. The third was untrue. But the distinction did not matter in the end before him. He held that none of the three was actionable. If we now draw a distinction, and hold that the third alone is actionable, we shall be making a rod for the back of the Official Referee. Ogdens will not be able to get damages for entering into the main contract for the work, but only for hiring the barges from Howards. That will give rise to a lot

1   [1907] AC 357, [1904-7] All ER Rep 255
2   Building and Engineering Contracts (10th Edn, 1970), pp 39, 48

of speculation. Rather than commit the parties to all this trouble and expense, I would hold that Howards can rely 'on the exception clause, which was inserted, I *a* believe, so as to avoid all such troubles as this case has given rise to. In my opinion, seeing that Ogdens had six months' use of these barges, they ought to pay the hire for them, amounting to £93,183·14.

I would dismiss the appeal accordingly.

b

BRIDGE LJ. The powerful arguments addressed to us by counsel for Ogdens have failed to persuade me that we could properly depart from the learned judge's primary findings of fact as to the substance of the all-important conversations between the parties. Accepting those findings there is no material in any of the communications between the parties prior to 11th July 1974 which amounted to a misrepresentation by Mr O'Loughlin let alone to a warranty with respect to the deadweight capacity *c* of Howards' barges. In the course of the interview at Otley on 11th July, however, Mr O'Loughlin told Mr Redpath that the barges would each carry about 1,600 tonnes subject to weather, fuel load and time of the year. As the judge said, even with the qualification, this information was hopelessly wrong. It overstated the payload capacity of the barges by about 50 per cent. To establish that this information was warranted as accurate by Howards, Ogdens would have to satisfy the court that *d* Howards intended to assume such a contractual liability collateral to the main contract embodied in the charterparty. Considering the whole of the evidence of the negotiations between the parties from the initial exchange of letters through to the eventual conclusion of a contract on the terms of the charterparty and setting the Otley interview in that context it does not appear to me that Howards ever intended to bind themselves by such a collateral warranty. *e*

Accordingly, in my judgment, Ogdens establish no claim against Howards in contract. But the remaining, and to my mind the more difficult, question raised in this appeal is whether Mr O'Loughlin's undoubted misrepresentation gives rise to any liability in tort either under the provisions of the Misrepresentation Act 1967 or at common law for breach of a duty of care owed to Ogdens with respect to the accuracy of the information given. I will consider first the position under the statute. *f*

The 1967 Act, by s 2(1), provides:

> 'Where a person has entered into a contract after a misrepresentation has been made to him by another party thereto and as a result thereof he has suffered loss, then, if the person making the misrepresentation would be liable to damages in respect thereof had the misrepresentation been made fraudulently, that person shall be so liable notwithstanding that the misrepresentation was not made *g* fraudulently, unless he proves that he had reasonable ground to believe and did believe up to the time the contract was made that the facts represented were true.'

The first question then is whether Howards would be liable in damages in respect of Mr O'Loughlin's misrepresentation if it had been made fraudulently, that is to say, *h* if he had known that it was untrue. An affirmative answer to that question is inescapable. The judge found in terms that what Mr O'Loughlin said about the capacity of the barges was said with the object of getting the hire contract for Howards, in other words with the intention that it should be acted on. This was clearly right. Equally clearly the misrepresentation was in fact acted on by Ogdens. It follows, therefore, on the plain language of the 1967 Act that, although there was no allegation *j* of fraud, Howards must be liable unless they proved that Mr O'Loughlin had reasonable ground to believe what he said about the barges' capacity.

It is unfortunate that the learned judge never directed his mind to the question whether Mr O'Loughlin had any reasonable ground for his belief. The question he asked himself, in considering liability under the 1967 Act, was whether the innocent

misrepresentation was negligent. He concluded that if Mr O'Loughlin had given
a the inaccurate information in the course of the April telephone conversations he would
have been negligent to do so but that in the circumstances obtaining at the Otley
interview in July there was no negligence. I take it that he meant by this that on the
earlier occasions the circumstances were such that he would have been under a duty
to check the accuracy of his information, but on the later occasions he was exempt
from such duty. I appreciate the basis of this distinction, but it seems to me, with
b respect, quite irrelevant to any question of liability under the 1967 Act. If the representee proves a misrepresentation which, if fraudulent, would have sounded in damages,
the onus passes immediately to the representor to prove that he had reasonable
ground to believe the facts represented. In other words the liability of the representor
does not depend on his being under a duty of care the extent of which may vary
according to the circumstances in which the representation is made. In the course of
c negotiations leading to a contract the 1967 Act imposes an absolute obligation not to
state facts which the representor cannot prove he had reasonable ground to believe.

Although not specifically posing the question whether he had reasonable ground
for his belief, the judge made certain findings about Mr O'Loughlin's state of mind.
He said:

d 'Mr O'Loughlin looked at the documents on the ships he was in charge of
including HB2 and HB3's German documents. He is not a master of maritime
German. He saw, but did not register, the deadweight figure of 1,055·135 tonnes.
Being in the London office he went to the city and looked up Lloyd's Register.
There he noted that the summer loading deadweight figure for B41 and B45,
described as TM sand carriers, was 1,800 tonnes. This figure stayed in his mind.
But it was one of Lloyd's Register's rare mistakes.'

e
Later the judge said apropos of Mr O'Loughlin's state of mind at the Otley interview:
'He had in his mind the 1,800 tonnes figure from the Bible [meaning Lloyd's Register],
obviously an approximation and certainly subject to the Bible's caveat.'

It is tempting to adopt these findings simpliciter and to conclude that the figure Mr
O'Loughlin had seen in Lloyd's Register afforded reasonable ground for his belief.
f But the learned judge's summary in the passages I have cited from the judgment not
only over-simplifies the effect of Mr O'Loughlin's evidence on this matter, but it also
embodies at one point a positive misapprehension of what Mr O'Loughlin said.
According to the transcript the following evidence was given:

'Q. Had you seen that document among the company's files prior to April
1974? *A.* I would have said that I would have sighted it.
g *Bristow J.* If you did see it, did it register? *A.* Not really, my Lord.'

The document, however, to which this evidence related was *not* the document
containing the vital figure of the barges' deadweight capacity, but another German
ship's document of earlier date. Mr O'Loughlin never said that the deadweight
figure 'did not register' with him. He acknowledged that he had seen it and under-
h stood it. It is true he said that he had not noticed the discrepancy between the deadweight figure in the German ship's document and that in Lloyd's Register, though he
had noticed a discrepancy in the figures for the gross and registered tonnage and he
had quite correctly taken these latter figures from the German ship's documents.

He was pressed to explain how it came about that, having seen both the inaccurate
figure in Lloyd's Register and the accurate figure in the German ship's documents
j for deadweight capacity, he came to rely on the former and to disregard the latter.
This certainly called for explanation since both according to the expert evidence and
as a matter of common sense it would normally be expected that the original figures
in the ship's documents were more reliable than the derivative figures in Lloyd's
Register. This part of Mr O'Loughlin's evidence is of such importance that I will
set out the crucial passages in full. He is asked about the vital document in chief:

'*Q.* Was this document in your possession? *A.* It was, yes.

'*Q.* Had you looked at this document at all? *A.* I had, yes. Basically as soon as   *a*
I started to go through it or look through it, I saw that all the measurements—
all they were talking about was for work in freshwater or sweet water, they call it.

'*Q.* I think if you looked at page 50, you would find the entry is "Ladefähigkeit
in Süsswasser"—a figure of 1,000.135 with no further measurement. Then if you
turn to page 44, there is a figure for "Tragfähigkeit" of 1,055·135 tonnes. Had you
those entries in mind when you consulted Lloyd's Register? *A.* Not really because   *b*
as I say, they are basically talking about deadweight in freshwater and the other
thing is that all the time when we are talking about barges of this nature, one
doesn't talk about deadweight, one talks about their cubic capacity.'

Then, in cross-examination:

'*Q.* When you were giving your evidence yesterday, you said that you did not   *c*
pay much attention to the document at 1/32 and 1/42 because the deadweight
relates to freshwater? *A.* That is correct.

'*Q.* But I think you also accepted this morning that that would only make a
difference of about 25 to 30 tonnes at the most to the deadweight cargo carrying
capacity? *A.* Something of that order

'*Q.* So that would still give you a much more accurate view of the deadweight   *d*
in saltwater than anything else that was available to you?

'*Bristow J.* Mr Lloyd, the point is made. It is there for better or for worse.
It is a beautiful one, but it is made!

'*Q.* Now, you based yourself you said instead—You rejected this figure because
it was freshwater and you based yourself instead on the Lloyd's Register figure
of 1,800 tonnes? *A.* Precisely.'   *e*

Finally, in cross examination:

'*Q.* You knew that the figure in the German document, the deadweight was
1,050 tonnes in freshwater.

'*Bristow J.* He says he has seen it, but it had not registered.

'*Q.* You had seen that figure? *A.* I had looked at that.   *f*

'*Q.* You had seen that figure, had you not? *A.* I had seen that figure among
many others in German.

'*Q.* And you rejected it, as you told my Lord yesterday, for two reasons;
because it was freshwater and because you were only concerned with cubic
capacity. *A.* That is precisely so.'
                                                                                    g
It should be pointed out that the learned judge's intervention in the last passage
quoted reflects the same misapprehension as the passage cited from his judgment.

I am fully alive to the dangers of trial by transcript and it is to be assumed that Mr
O'Loughlin was perfectly honest throughout. But the question remains whether his
evidence, however benevolently viewed, is sufficient to show that he had an objectively reasonable ground to disregard the figure in the ship's documents and to prefer   *h*
the Lloyd's Register figure. I think it is not. The fact that he was more interested in
cubic capacity could not justify reliance on one figure of deadweight capacity in
preference to another. The fact that the deadweight figure in the ship's documents
was a freshwater figure was of no significance since, as he knew, the difference between
freshwater and sea water deadweight capacity was minimal. Accordingly I conclude
that Howards failed to prove that Mr O'Loughlin had reasonable ground to believe   *j*
the truth of his misrepresentation to Mr Redpath.

Having reached a conclusion favourable to Ogdens on the issue of liability under the
Misrepresentation Act 1967, I do not find it necessary to express a concluded view on
the issue of negligence at common law. As at present advised I doubt if the circumstances surrounding the misrepresentation at the Otley interview were such as to

imposed on Howards a common law duty of care for the accuracy of the state-
a ment. If there was such a duty, I doubt if the evidence established a breach of it.

There remains the question whether Howards can escape from their liability under
the 1967 Act in reliance on cl 1 of the charterparty, which provides:

'On handing over by the Owners the vessel shall be tight, staunch and strong
but Charterers acceptance of handing over the vessel shall be conclusive that
b they have examined the vessel and found her to be in all respects seaworthy,
in good order and condition and in all respects fit for the intended and contemplated use by the Charterers and in every other way satisfactory to them.'

A clause of this kind is to be narrowly construed. It can only be relied on as conclusive evidence of the charterers' satisfaction in relation to such attributes of the
vessel as would be apparent on an ordinary examination of the vessel. I do not think
c deadweight capacity is such an attribute. It can only be ascertained by an elaborate
calculation or by an inspection of the ship's documents. But even if, contrary to this
view, the clause can be read as apt to exclude liability for the earlier misrepresentation,
Howards still have to surmount the restrictions imposed by s 3 of the 1967 Act, which
provides:

d 'If any agreement (whether made before or after the commencement of this
Act) contains a provision which would exclude or restrict—(a) any liability to
which a party to a contract may be subject by reason of any misrepresentation
made by him before the contract was made; or (b) any remedy available to another
party to the contract by reason of such a misrepresentation; that provision shall
be of no effect except to the extent (if any) that, in any proceedings arising out of
e the contract, the court or arbitrator may allow reliance on it as being fair and
reasonable in the circumstances of the case.'

What the learned judge said in this matter was: 'If the wording of the clause is apt
to exempt from responsibility for negligent misrepresentation as to carrying capacity,
I hold that such exemption is not fair and reasonable ...' The judge having asked
himself the right question and answered it as he did in the exercise of the discretion
f vested in him by the 1967 Act, I can see no ground on which we could say that he was
wrong.

I would accordingly allow the appeal to the extent of holding that Ogdens have
established liability against Howards under s 2(1) of the 1967 Act for any damages they
have suffered as a result of Mr O'Loughlin's misrepresentation at the Otley interview
in the terms as found by the learned judge.

g

SHAW LJ. This is a difficult case on the facts but in the end I reach the conclusion
of the other members of the court that there is no sufficient justification for departing
from the primary findings of fact as determined by Bristow J at the trial of this action.

On this basis no difficulty arises as to the proper inferences to be drawn from those
h findings until the discussions to which Mr O'Loughlin was a party at Otley in July
1974. It is not in dispute that he then told Mr Redpath that the barges which were to
be the subject-matter of the contemplated chartering had a carrying capacity of 1,600
tonnes. It is equally clear that this information was inaccurate in that it grossly
exaggerated the actual capacity of the barges. The question as to the carrying capacity
had been an insistent one; and when it was answered by the person who was in the
j best position to ascertain what was the correct answer it seems to me that Mr Redpath
who sought the information on behalf of Ogdens was entitled, as were his principals,
to regard it as being accurate so that it could be acted on without further enquiry.
The learned judge was of the view that the representation was made 'with the object
of getting the hire contract for Howards'. This inference seems to me inescapable,
albeit the statement as to carrying capacity was made as one of a number of answers to

questions of a miscellaneous kind dealing with matters of widely varying degrees of importance. It must have been apparent to everyone concerned including Mr *a* O'Loughlin that the profitability of Ogden's contract with the Tyneside Joint Sewerage Board must depend on the payload of the barges. So the question, though swamped by a number of others, must or should have stood out by its content as relating to a matter of substance and importance. It called for an answer neither casual nor unconsidered but for one, as the learned judge found, which could be relied on.

I must confess that I was at one time inclined to the view that, as Mr O'Loughlin's *b* answer could be regarded as part of the description of the subject-matter of the charter, there was a sufficient basis for regarding it also as giving rise to a warranty as to the carrying capacity of the barges. Having had the advantage of reading the respective judgments of Lord Denning MR and Bridge LJ, I have ultimately come to the conclusion that in the circumstances in which the answer was given the basis for a collateral warranty is too tenuous to support it. On this aspect of the appeal accord-　*c* ingly I am in agreement with both of the preceding judgments.

I turn next to the question of liability for negligence. I would respectfully adopt what Lord Denning MR has already said in preferring the minority opinion in *Mutual Life & Citizens' Assurance Co Ltd v Evatt*[1] and I would approach the problem as he has done from the standpoint of the passage he has cited from the speech of Lord Pearce in *Hedley Byrne & Co Ltd v Heller & Partners Ltd*[2].　*d*

Now it does seem to me that the chartering of barges for the purpose of carrying clay out to sea and there dumping it is a business transaction whose nature makes clear the importance and influence of an answer to the question: what is their carrying capacity in the context of the purpose of the prospective charterparties? That the question was only asked over the telephone in April and later repeated at an interview in July does not of itself, as I see it, render the subject-matter of the question less *e* material or the impact of the answer less important. The information sought would govern the performance by Ogdens of their contract with the Tyneside authority and this must have been apparent to any man of business let alone Mr O'Loughlin. The learned judge so held. The information which had been asked for more than once cannot be regarded as other than important whatever the circumstances in which it was sought and given. Moreover it was not expert advice that was sought *f* which might honestly and reasonably have assumed different forms according to the source of it. What was asked for was a specific fact. Ogdens had not themselves any direct means of ascertaining what the fact was. Certainly they had no such ready and facile means as were available to Mr O'Loughlin. These factors in association with the relationship of the parties as owners and prospective charterers of barges to be em-ployed for a specific purpose known to the owners did in my judgment give rise to a *g* duty on the owners to exercise reasonable care to be accurate in giving information of a material character which was peculiarly within their knowledge. All Mr O'Loughlin had to do was to look at documents in Howards' possession and to read them accurately. Had he done so there would have been no room for error of fact or for misconceived opinion or wrong advice. That he chose to answer an important question from mere recollection 'off the cuff' does not in my view diminish, if I may *h* adopt the language of Lord Pearce[3], the 'gravity of the inquiry or the importance and influence attached to the answer'.

It is with considerable diffidence that I express this view since it is not shared by either of the other members of this court and was not held by Bristow J. Nonetheless I would venture to hold that Ogdens have a cause of action in negligence at common law. This is not, in my judgment, affected by the exception clause which does not *j*

1　[1971] 1 All ER 150 at 163, [1971] AC 793 at 812
2　[1963] 2 All ER 575 at 617, 618, [1964] AC 465 at 539
3　*Hedley Byrne & Co Ltd v Heller & Partners Ltd* [1963] 2 All ER 575 at 617, [1964] AC 465 at 539

a   purport to grant absolution from the consequences of negligence on the part of the
owners.

There remains the issue raised by the claim under s 2(1) of the Misrepresentation
Act 1967. I do not regard the telephone conversation of April and the interview of
11th July 1974 as being so casual as to give rise to no legal consequences. Certainly
I find myself unable to dismiss what was said at the interview in July as inconsequen-
tial. I share the opinion expressed in this regard in the judgment of Bridge LJ which is
b   based on the finding of the learned judge. I entirely agree, furthermore, with Bridge
LJ's analysis of the evidence, together with the learned judge's findings in this regard,
and I agree also with the views expressed by Bridge LJ as to the operation and effect
of the relevant provisions of the 1967 Act. I cannot do better than respectfully to
adopt his reasoning without seeking to repeat it and I agree with his conclusions.

On this ground as well as in relation to the claim based on negligence at common
c   law I would allow the appeal.

Appeal allowed. Leave to appeal to the House of Lords granted to both parties.

Solicitors: *Ingledew, Mark Pybris*, Newcastle upon Tyne (for Ogdens); *R A Howard*,
Chatham (for Howards).

d   Gavin Gore-Andrews Esq Barrister.

Levison and others v Farin and others

e   QUEEN'S BENCH DIVISION
GIBSON J
31St OCTOBER, 1st, 2nd, 4th NOVEMBER 1977

*Contract – Warranty – Breach – Disclosure protecting party in breach of warranty –
Vendor selling fashion company in traded down state because of designer's illness – Trading*
f   *down of company and designer's illness disclosed to purchaser – Amount of continuing losses
not known and therefore not disclosed – Agreement containing warranty that 'save as disclosed' there would be no material adverse change in net assets of company prior to completion
date – Purchaser discovering significant reduction in net assets on taking over – Whether
vendor liable for breach of warranty – Whether vendor protected by general disclosure of state
of company and causes of future losses.*

g
*Contract – Warranty – Breach – Context in which warranty to be construed – Vendor selling
fashion company in traded down state – Warranty by vendor in agreement for sale that there
would be no 'material adverse change' in net assets of company prior to changeover 'allowing
for normal trade fluctuations' – Both parties aware of general state of company but neither
party knowing rate of continuing losses – Purchaser discovering significant reduction in
h   assets on taking over – Reduction resulting from continuing losses – Whether in context of
company's state reduction in assets a 'material' adverse change – Whether reduction a 'normal
trade fluctuation'.*

*Damages – Mitigation of loss – Tax benefit – Purchaser acquiring traded down company with
continuing losses carried over – Purchaser receiving tax benefit on losses carried over –*
j   *Purchaser entitled to damages from vendor for breach of warranty that there would be no
material adverse change in company's assets prior to take-over – Whether tax benefit to be
taken into account in assessing damages for the breach of warranty.*

The plaintiffs were the shareholders in a company engaged in the fashion trade. The
company was the manufacturing and marketing vehicle for the designs of one of

the plaintiffs, Mrs L, a dress designer with a high reputation in the fashion trade. In 1972 Mrs L became ill and decided that she could not carry on the business. The company was therefore unable to produce an autumn collection in 1972 and no spring collection for 1973 had been designed. The plaintiffs decided to sell the business and in late 1972 offered it to the defendants who were competitors in the fashion trade. There were various meetings between the plaintiffs and the defendants and inspections of the company's factory and showroom by the defendants who were made aware that no new collections had been designed, that the company was trading at a loss and was in a traded down state. This was confirmed by the accounts up to 31st December 1972 ('the balance sheet date') provided by the plaintiffs. However, the plaintiffs were unable to state, because they themselves did not know, exactly how much money was being lost. On 27th April 1973 the defendants agreed in writing to purchase the company from the plaintiffs for the sum of £54,000. The sum of £44,000 was to be paid on the completion date of 12th May 1973 and the balance by annual instalments of £1,250. The purchase price was made up of a net asset value of the company of £44,000 agreed by the parties on the basis of the December 1972 accounts and £10,000 for goodwill. The agreement contained, inter alia, a warranty by the plaintiffs that 'Save as disclosed the vendors jointly and severally warrant to and undertake with the purchasers that between the balance sheet date and the completion date . . . there will have been no material adverse change in the overall value of the net assets of the company on the basis of a valuation adopted in the balance sheet allowing for normal trade fluctuations'. After taking over the company the defendants found that between the balance sheet date and the completion date there had been an adverse change in the overall net assets of the company to the extent of £8,600. There had also been a trading loss over the same period of £7,000 which the defendants were able to off-set against later profits thereby obtaining a tax advantage of £2,940. Because of the reduction in the company's net assets the defendants refused to pay the first two instalments of the balance of the purchase price and intimated that they would not pay the remaining instalments as they fell due. The plaintiffs commenced an action claiming the two instalments due and a declaration that the defendants were liable to pay the remaining instalments as they fell due. The defendants in their defence pleaded that the plaintiffs had breached the warranty in the agreement and that the sum of £8,600 should be set off against the amount claimed by the plaintiffs. In their counterclaim they claimed the sum of £6,100 (i e the difference between £8,600 and the two instalments of £1,250 each claimed by the plaintiffs). In their reply the plaintiffs contended that Mrs L's illness and her inability to design for the company and the consequent trading down of the company had been disclosed to the defendants who were well aware of these facts, and therefore, in the context of the company's operations as it was placed in the period between the balance sheet date and the completion date, the adverse change in the net assets of the company was not a 'material' adverse change or alternatively it was a 'normal trade fluctuation' and had in any event been 'disclosed' to the defendants.

Held – The defendants were entitled to damages in the sum of £5,560 on the counterclaim for the following reasons—

(i) On the facts, the plaintiffs had breached the warranty contained in the agreement because there had been a material adverse change in the overall value of the net assets of the company to the extent of £8,500 (see p 1157 j to p 1158 a b and d, post).

(ii) The disclosure of Mrs L's illness and the trading down of the company made by the plaintiffs was a general disclosure of the causes of probable future losses and was not disclosure of a quantified reduction in the net asset value or the actual rate of the continuing losses. Therefore the disclosure did not protect the plaintiffs from being in breach of the warranty because (1) although the defendants were aware that there would be continuing losses they had no way of knowing what the rate of the continuing losses would be, and the actual reduction which occurred was a 'material' adverse

change for the purposes of the warranty; (2) the reduction was entirely special to the
a company and had never occurred before and was not therefore a 'normal trade
fluctuation'; and (3) the disclosure not having been made by specific notice for the
purpose of the warranty, the plaintiffs were not, in the circumstances, able to rely on
the words 'save and disclosed' (see p 1156 f to p 1157 a and f to h, post).

(iii) The tax benefit of £2,940 received by the defendants was deductible from the
damages of £8,500 payable by the plaintiffs because it arose and was obtained out of
b the consequences of the facts which is part caused the breach of warranty (see p 1160
d to f and p 1161 a b, post); dicta of Lord Reid in British Transport Commission v Gourley
[1955] 3 All ER at 808 and of Viscount Haldane LC in British Westinghouse Electric and
Manufacturing Co Ltd v Underground Electric Railways Co of London Ltd [1911-13] All
ER Rep at 69 applied; Jebsen v East and West India Dock Co [1874-80] All ER Rep 615
and The World Beauty [1969] 3 All ER 158 distinguished.
c

Notes
For contractual warranties see 9 Halsbury's Laws (4th Edn) para 542.
    For the mitigation of damages, see 12 Halsbury's Laws (4th Edn) paras 1193, 1196,
and for cases on the subject, see 17 Digest (Reissue) 126-128, 258-271.

d ### Cases referred to in judgment
British Transport Commission v Gourley [1955] 3 All ER 796, [1956] AC 185, [1956] 2
    WLR 41, 220 LT 354, [1955] 2 Lloyd's Rep 475, [1955] TR 303, 34 ATC 305, 49
    R & IT 11, HL, 17 Digest (Reissue) 88, 35.
British Westinghouse Electric and Manufacturing Co Ltd v Underground Electric Railways Co
    of London Ltd [1912] AC 673, [1911-13] All ER Rep 63, 81 LJKB 1132, 107 LT 325, HL,
e   17 Digest (Reissue) 126, 260.
Jebsen v East and West India Dock Co (1875) LR 10 CP 300, [1874-80] All ER Rep 615,
    44 LJCP 181, 32 LT 321, 2 Asp MLC 505, 17 Digest (Reissue) 126, 257.
World Beauty, The, Steam Tanker Andros Springs (Owners) v Steam Tanker World Beauty
    (Owners) [1969] 3 All ER 158, [1970] P 144, [1969] 3 WLR 110, [1969] 1 Lloyd's Rep 350,
    CA, Digest (Cont Vol C) 890, 7304a.
f

Action
By a writ issued on 10th October 1975 the plaintiffs, Sally Levison, Stella Phillips-
Marder, Claire Meltzer and Ethel Cooper, brought an action aginst the defendants,
Mary Farrin, David Farrin, Peter Hakim and Stuart Southgate, claiming (i) the
g equivalent of £2,500 in Maltese pounds, being two instalments of £1,250 Maltese
pounds, due on 1st May 1974 and 1st May 1975, of the balance of the purchase price
for the total shareholding of a Maltese company known as Levison Originals Ltd
('the company') sold by the plaintiffs to the defendants by an agreement for sale
dated 27th April 1973, and (ii) a declaration that the defendants would be obliged
pursuant to the agreement to pay the remaining instalments as they fell due. The
h defendants by their defence and counterclaim served on 26th January 1076 claimed to
set off the sum of £8,600 leaving a balance due to the defendants of £6,100, or
alternatively counterclaimed damages for breach of warranty. The facts are set out
in the judgment.

Nicholas Medawar for the plaintiffs.
j Roger Buckley for the defendants.

                                                            Cur adv vult

4th November. **GIBSON J** read the following judgment: In this action the plaintiffs
claim, by a writ issued on 10th October 1975, the sum of £2,500 pursuant to an agreement in writing dated 27th April 1973 and a declaration that the defendants are liable

to pay further sums totalling £7,500 by instalments each of £1,250 on 1st May 1976 *a*
and each succeeding 1st May until 1981. By that agreement in writing the first
plaintiff, Mrs Sally Levison, with three others, had agreed to sell to the defendants
the shares in a Maltese company called Levison Originals Ltd.

The defendants were all, as purchasers of the shares, nominees for an English
company called Mary Farrin Ltd. The defendants contend that the plaintiffs were in
breach of warranties contained in the sale agreement and the damages flowing from
those breaches exceed any sum due to the plaintiffs. It has not been suggested that *b*
the interest of Mary Farrin Ltd in the shares, through the defendants as nominees,
affects in any way any question that has to be decided. The substance of the defendants' case is that the plaintiffs warranted by reference to a balance sheet of the
company as at 31st December 1972 that between that date and the date of completion
on 12th May 1973 'there will have been no material adverse change in the overall
value of the net assets of the Company', and that there was such a change in the sum *c*
of £8,600. The defendants put their damages at that figure.

The plaintiffs deny any breach of warranty, although they admit the shortfall in net
asset value. The plaintiffs further say that if they are liable in respect of that shortfall yet the plaintiffs' damages are to be reduced by a tax benefit received by the
defendants on the trading loss which produced the larger part of the shortfall.

I have no doubt that this litigation has been a prolonged cause of anxiety to Mrs *d*
Levison. I will say at once that substantially, in my judgment, on the issue of breach
of warranty, the defendants must succeed in this action, for the reasons which I shall
now give and to the extent that I shall now explain. The facts are of some complication but the area of dispute has been narrow. It is convenient to state the relevant
facts as I find them to be, or as they have been admitted or agreed, before stating the
issues in any further detail.

Mrs Sally Levison, who is aged 55, is a dress designer of skill and accomplishment. *e*
She started her business in 1967. She designed and produced ranges of knitted garments. She was the mainspring of the business and almost entirely responsible for
the design work. Her products enjoyed a high reputation and were well known in
the fashion trade. The structure of her business was based on a Maltese company,
owning a factory on the island of Gozo, which produced garments designed by Mrs *f*
Levison. That company is Levison Originals Ltd. The structure of the business was
further based on an English company, Levison Originals (UK) Ltd, which marketed
the garments so produced. This English company had showrooms and stockrooms
in London. It was engaged wholly or mainly in wholesale trade. It was the wholly-
owned subsidiary of the Maltese company. The normal procedure of design and
production which was followed by many such businesses in this trade, and was *g*
followed by Mrs Levison's business, was for new garments to be designed for particular collections, normally the spring/summer collection and the autumn-
collection in each year. Garments for display and sale in the spring/summer collection
were designed and samples made in time to be shown at exhibitions and fashion
shows in the previous year, starting at the latest in October. Orders were taken,
yarn was ordered for production, and the orders were sent to the factory and to *h*
outworkers, if employed, so that production could proceed in December, January and
February, and for some time thereafter. Garments so produced would then be
delivered to customers for the spring trade and for the summer trade. Design work
for the autumn collection in any year would normally be completed in time for
fashion shows and exhibitions in about April of the same year, with subsequent orders
and manufacture in similar manner.

Mrs Levison had established her factory in Gozo in the ownership of Levison *j*
Originals Ltd for certain very compelling commercial reasons. The Malta Development Corpn had by way of incentives, and no doubt for the creation of employment,
agreed a low rent for the factory and granted certain tax advantages to the company. It is clear, although the relevant documents were not in evidence, that the

Malta Development Corpn imposed certain conditions on the grant or continuance
a of these incentives, one of which was that the numbers employed at the factory or
in the business should be at least 57 in all.

Mrs Levison's business for a time was very successful indeed. Then in 1971 there
appeared the first signs of a nervous illness in Mrs Levison which for a time became
quite severe. By 1972 she had decided that she could not carry on and bear indefinitely
the heavy burden of this business. In the autumn of that year she telephoned Miss
b Mary Farrin, the first-named defendant, and invited her as a competitor of Mrs
Levison to consider buying the business. Meetings followed which led eventually
to the agreement of April 1973.

As a direct consequence of the illness of Mrs Levison there had been in 1972 no
autumn collection produced by Levison Originals (UK) Ltd and no spring/summer
collection for 1973 had been designed or displayed. The business was selling off stock
c and producing to existing or modified designs to meet any orders taken. There were
garments on the racks in the showroom and in the stockroom in London, and some
trade was being done, but it was at a very much reduced level.

Miss Mary Farrin, who was invited to consider buying this business, was and is also
a dress designer of great skill and accomplishment. She had produced in her business
garments which included knitted garments produced, or capable of being produced,
d by similar processes to those employed by Mrs Levison in her business. Mary Farrin
is the moving spirit of Mary Farrin Ltd. At the time of the meetings which were
held in 1972, Miss Farrin, as I find, knew of the reputation and business of Mrs Levison
when it was at its most successful, and she knew that there had been a marked change
in that business. It was plain to Miss Farrin from the time of her first meeting with
Mrs Levison in about September or October 1972 that Mrs Levison was unwell and
e that in consequence there had been no autumn collection from Mrs Levison's
business in 1972 and that no spring/summer collection had been designed or was to be
designed or was in production.

At that first meeting Mrs Levison made those points to Miss Farrin, which a sensible woman of business would make in the circumstances in which Mrs Levison
found herself. She described the general commercial advantages available from the
f manufacturing facilities and the tax and other advantages in Malta. She described
the virtue of the London premises, and she gave her state of health as the reason for
wishing to sell such a business. She did not then refer to any continuing trading losses.
Miss Farrin was shown the garments in stock.

There may have been further discussions or meetings between Mrs Levison and
Miss Farrin between that first meeting between the principals and the next meeting
g in December 1972 attended by lawyers and accountants. It matters not. In December
Mrs Levison was asked by Mr Hakim, an accountant and a director of Mary Farrin Ltd,
to supply certain information with reference to the business proposed to be sold. Mrs
Levison replied by a letter of 7th December 1972, and with that letter were sent accounts for 1970 and 1971. By the time of the meeting of 18th December 1972, as Mr
Southgate, a director of Mary Farrin Ltd and solicitor to that company, stated in
h evidence, accounts had been supplied to the defendants which showed to them that
the business of Levison Originals was in a loss-making position and was being traded
down.

On that occasion, in December 1972, there was a visit to the showroom of Levison
Originals in London. There were present on the side of the plaintiffs Mrs Levison,
Miss Cooper, Mr Sears, a solicitor for the plaintiffs, and Mr Burke, their accountant.
j On the side of the defendants there were Miss Mary Farrin, Mr Southgate, whom
I have already mentioned, and Mr Hakim, also already mentioned, the accountant.
Both Mr Hakim and Mr Southgate gave evidence to the effect that they believed,
from what they saw then, that Levison Originals had in hand some new collection,
be it for spring/summer or a mid-season collection. There appears to have been very
little basis for such belief, but, as I have said, whatever impression Mr Hakim or Mr

Southgate did or did not obtain, it was wholly plain to Miss Farrin from the start that because of the ill-health of Mrs Levison there was no new spring collection in Levison Originals, and there had been no new autumn collection in 1972, with the obvious consequences to the trading position of Levison Originals Ltd.

On 27th December 1972 a party went to Malta to inspect the factory on the island of Gozo. Miss Cooper was the hostess for Levison Originals. Mrs Levison was herself not present. Indeed, she was in hospital from 28th December 1972 to 18th January 1973, and again from 30th April to 3rd June of that year. Miss Farrin, Mr Hakim and Mr Southgate went out to Gozo on behalf of the defendants. Miss Cooper showed them the factory and the stocks of yarn and explained the position with reference to employment. The position was that only seven people in all were employed at the factory although other workers were available for re-employment. Miss Farrin spent a long time examining yarn stocks, and it was plain to her, in my judgment, that Levison Originals had not got any substantial quantity of yarn, and certainly no such stocks as they would have had if any spring/summer collection had been designed and put into production. This inspection afforded further evidence of what had been plain to Miss Farrin and her advisers from the first formal meeting after accounts had been provided, namely that Levison Originals was trading at a loss, was in a traded down state, and was indeed more run down than had been supposed by them at first.

The defendants as purchasers thus knew, from what they could see and from the accounts provided, that Levison Originals was losing money. The defendants did not know how much money was being lost. The plaintiffs never stated in terms that they were losing money. No doubt it was treated as obvious by everyone. The defendants were concerned to investigate the position in Malta, and whether the advantages of the Malta Development Corpn incentives would continue if the defendants bought the business by purchasing the shares, and this was done in February 1973 by a further visit to Malta by Mr Southgate with Mr Sears and Mr Burke. It had at first been hoped and intended that the sale might be completed by the end of January 1973, but various complications, including the need for the purchasers to be satisfied that the tax and other advantages conceded in Malta would continue after sale, caused completion to be delayed until 12th May 1973. In the result Mrs Levison and the other plaintiffs had to run the business in its run-down, loss-making state for longer than they had wished, or intended. From the time of the first meeting, in December 1972 until contract on 27th April 1973, and until completion in May 1973, Levison Originals ran their business sensibly and reasonably and in the manner in which it must have been obvious to the defendants that in probability they would run the business, in other words Levison Originals sold off their stock as best they could, kept the factory in Malta just in operation with the minimum staff on producing existing designs, and paid the existing staff of the United Kingdom company. Overheads were kept to what seemed the bare minimum without any discharging of staff or reduction in salaries. Levison Originals were concerned to keep the company in being until a contract was signed and thereafter, in order to hand over the company pursuant to the agreement.

During the period from December 1972 until 27th April 1973, the terms of the agreement were negotiated. A set of certified accounts of Levison Originals as at 31st December 1972 was produced and formed the basis of some terms in the agreement, and those accounts show the net asset position of the companies at that date. The proposed agreement was produced as a result of negotiations which contained a warranty to be given by the plaintiffs as vendors whereby they warranted, in terms which will be noticed in more detail later, that between 31st December 1972 and the date of completion there will have been no material adverse change in the overall net assets of Levison Originals Ltd. The plaintiffs, as vendors, signed that form of agreement on 27th April 1973. The agreement was completed on 12th May. It is a fact that between 31st December 1972 and 12th May 1973 there was a reduction in the net asset value of Levison Originals of about £8,600. As a fact that is agreed by the plaintiffs.

It is clear that, save as mentioned below, this loss was caused by the accumulated
a trading losses which occurred over the period. Overhead expenses continued and
profits were not created, because of the trading condition of the companies already
described, to pay for those expenses. After completion the defendants worked out
the accounts, the loss in net asset value was revealed, the defendants refused to pay the
continuing instalments of price and this action resulted.

I now turn to the issues which have been contested at the hearing. By their writ the
b plaintiffs claimed the instalments of the balance of the purchase price. By a defence of
26th January 1976 the defendants pleaded that the plaintiffs were in breach of cl 5(f)
of the agreement, a warranty as to the financial position and net asset value of the
company, and the defendants put their damages at the sum of £8,600. By their
reply the plaintiffs denied any breach of the warranty and asserted that if there was
any state of fact which could constitute a breach the plaintiffs had disclosed certain
c facts and matters to the defendants so that the plaintiffs were not liable or in breach.

The relevant clauses in the agreement must now be stated in detail. The agreement
is dated 27th April. It is made between the plaintiffs and the defendants as named.
By cl 1 completion was defined by reference to the obtaining of a satisfactory letter
as referred to in cl 16, completion was to be one calendar month from the date but
subject to that clause which dealt with proof that the Malta incentives would still
d be available. There is a reference to the certified accounts of the company as at 31st
December 1972. By cl 2 the vendors warranted that the matters stated in the recitals
were correct. By cl 3, which was the main substance of the agreement, the vendors
agreed that they would sell the shares of the company to the purchasers free from all
charges, etc, together with all rights attaching thereto. By cl 4 the consideration was
stated to be £54,000 sterling in Maltese pounds payable as to £44,000 on completion
e and the balance by instalments as already stated. Clause 5 contains a series of
warranties, most of them in customary form. Sub-clause (b) of cl 5 contained a
warranty that the balance sheet as at 31st December 1972 was true and accurate in all
respects and showed a true and fair view of the affairs of the company at that date
and that the balance sheet correctly set forth the assets of the company. By sub-cl (e)
there was the customary clause to the effect that the books were accurate and reflected
f at completion the true and fair view of the financial, contractual, and trading position
of the company.

Sub-clause 5(f) is that on which the argument is centred and I will set it out in full.
It reads as follows:

g 'Save as disclosed the vendors hereby jointly and severally warrant to and
undertake with the purchasers that between the balance sheet date and the completion date: (i) the overall financial position of the company will not have
changed adversely in any material way allowing for normal trade fluctuations;
(ii) there will have been no material adverse change in the overall value of the
net assets of the company on the basis of a valuation adopted in the balance
sheet allowing for normal trade fluctuations; (iii) the business of the Company
h will have been carried on in a similar manner as heretofore.'

For the rest of the agreement it is sufficient to mention that it contains a number of
specific terms in ordinary form for such an agreement dealing with the business and the
conduct of it until completion.

The case advanced by the defendants on the pleadings was that the plaintiffs were
j in breach of all three parts of cl 5(f) but in his submissions on behalf of the defendants
counsel has concentrated on cl (ii) which relates to the net asset position. Before considering the submissions in detail it is necessary to mention the position with reference
to that principle of construction which, when it is applicable, requires that words
are to be construed most strongly against him who uses or puts them forward, or, as
it is called, contra proferentem. There was some evidence as to the origin of the words

in this clause, but both counsel have agreed in submitting that on the facts this clause cannot be regarded as containing the words of either one side, but that the clause emerged as a result of joint efforts and that that principle of construction is not available or relevant at all. Counsel for the defendants accepted that the onus lies on his clients to prove that breach of any part of the warranty was committed by the plaintiffs, and he therefore opened the case for the defendants and called evidence first.

It is clear on the agreed figures that there was between 31st December 1972 and 12th May 1973 an adverse change in overall net assets of Levison Originals Ltd in a sum of about £8,600. Before a breach of warranty can be held to be proved it is necessary to consider whether on the evidence the defendants have proved that the adverse change in net asset value is such as the plaintiffs warranted would not occur or whether the plaintiffs have proved that if there was such an adverse change nevertheless the plaintiffs disclosed it and are therefore not liable. The adverse change, to constitute a breach of the warranty, must be material. For the defendants it was submitted that the change or drop in net asset value, in the region of £8,600, is about 20 per cent of the net assets revealed in the December 1972 accounts, and that such a figure cannot but be material.

For the plaintiffs an answer of considerable elaboration was advanced. It was to this effect. As set out in the recital of facts, the defendants knew what the trading position of the plaintiffs was long before the contract was signed. The plaintiffs made plain that Levison Originals Ltd was losing money and was traded down. It was obvious that between 31st December 1972 and the date of contract that Levison Originals Ltd would be losing money. The money losses arose in the ordinary course of a sensibly conducted business and were no more than resulted from the known causes. Accordingly, so it is submitted, an adverse change in net asset value resulting from such causes is not a material change on the true construction of cl 5(f)(ii) of the agreement. Counsel voiced on behalf of the plaintiffs what I am sure is the firmly held conviction of Mrs Levison when he said the defendants got exactly what they bargained for and that it is wrong to regard as a breach of warranty the ordinary result of the trading which was expected to continue.

In general terms I accept the submissions of fact advanced in support of this point, as is plain from the recital of facts already set out, save for this. The defendants did not know and had no means of telling what the rate of continuing loss was. Indeed, Mrs Levison did not know herself. The rate of continuing loss depended, at least in part, on the actions of the plaintiff vendors, not least in how much they continued to pay themselves out of the companies. As to the conclusion contended for on this point, I reject it. The warranty deals with a material adverse change; not with causes of such changes. The reduction in net asset value which occurred was, in my view, material for the purposes of this warranty.

Next the warranty relates to any material adverse change in net asset value 'allowing for normal trade fluctuations'. The plaintiffs by their reply did not assert that any material adverse change which had occurred could be excused on this ground. The point was not pleaded by them. Counsel for the defendants has accepted, rightly in my view, that the onus is on his clients to show that, making allowances for normal trade fluctuations, there has been a material adverse change. Accordingly the point must be considered although not pleaded by the plaintiffs. Counsel has submitted that these words require that allowance be made for fluctuations which are trade fluctuations and normal fluctuations. The word 'fluctuation' in its primary meaning means alternate rises and falls. The defendants contend that the losses here were caused by the virtual cessation of trade in the companies caused by the illness of Mrs Levison and that these are causes which are not trade fluctuations and are in no sense normal. The defendants are in my judgment right on this.

Counsel for the plaintiffs' submissions were to the effect that the loss which occurred was normal for Levison Originals Ltd as it was placed, a company which had no new

spring/summer collection, no working designer, and no yarn ordered. In my judgment these words are not apt to exclude from this warranty those causes of probable
a but unquantified loss known to the parties when the agreement was being negotiated
and which in fact caused the drop in net asset value. They were entirely special to the
plaintiffs' business at the relevant time, having, so far as the evidence shows, never
occurred before in the plaintiffs' business.

   Lastly, the plaintiffs, on this part of the case, contend that they are not liable by
b reason of the words 'save as disclosed'. The plaintiffs do not say that they disclosed the
amount of any drop in net asset value which had occurred or was occurring, nor even
that they expressly disclosed the fact that a material adverse change was occurring of
an unspecified amount. It is necessary to note precisely what the plaintiffs have
pleaded on this issue. In para 3 of their defence to counterclaim the plaintiffs pleaded:

c   'If (which is denied) the overall financial position of the Company changed
      adversely in a material way and/or there was a material adverse change in the
      overall value of the net assets of the Company, the said change or changes were
      caused by and/or resulted from the illness of the First-named Plaintiff and/or the
      fact that she did not in or about summer 1972 design a Spring collection of knit-
      wear for Spring 1973. The Defendants were at all material times aware of these
d   facts and matters and/or these facts and matters were at all material times dis-
      closed to them in accordance with the said terms of the said Agreement. Further
      or alternatively the said change or changes were caused by and/or resulted from
      the fact that the First-named Plaintiff did not in or about December, 1972 and
      January and February, 1973 design an Autumn collection of knitwear for Autumn
      1973. The Defendants specifically requested that the First-named Plaintiff did
      not design the said Autumn collection and/or the Plaintiffs disclosed the fact
e   that she was not doing so to the Defendants as aforesaid.'

   On the evidence the failure to design the autumn 1973 collection has nothing to do
with this case. It did not and could not contribute to any relevant loss. For the rest
it is plain that the plaintiffs are relying on having disclosed the illness of Mrs Levison
and the fact that there was no spring/summer collection. As stated the defendants
f were made aware of both those facts in the course of negotiation, as is apparent from
the recital of facts. In my judgment, however, to make the defendants aware of those
facts is not to disclose an adverse change in overall value of net assets of the company
within the meaning of those words 'save as disclosed' in this agreement and for the
purposes of this warranty. In the first place all that is disclosed is a possible cause of
loss, not an actual drop in net asset value. I have in mind that the plaintiffs did make
g known to the defendants that the companies were in a loss-making situation. The
plaintiffs have not pleaded that they made that known, despite discussion in the course
of the case about the sufficiency of the pleading, but the fact is relevant in considering
their plea on this point. Secondly, there was no purported disclosure for the purpose
of or with reference to this clause. I do not say that facts made known by disclosure
of the means of knowledge in the course of negotiation could never constitute dis-
h closure for such a clause as this but I have no doubt that a clause in this form is
primarily designed and intended to require a party who wishes by disclosure to avoid
a breach of warranty to give specific notice for the purpose of the agreement, and a
protection by disclosure will not normally be achieved by merely making known the
means of knowledge which may or do enable the other party to work out certain
facts and conclusions. In my judgment the plaintiffs have not shown that they
j disclosed the adverse change in net assets so as to escape liability for breach of warranty.
   Clause 5(f)(i) of the agreement calls for no separate detailed mention. The overall
financial position of the company did change adversely and in a material way by
reason of the conclusions set out above. Clause 5(f)(iii) was not in my judgment
broken. The obligation was that the business will have been carried on in a similar
manner as heretofore. 'Heretofore' in that phrase means, as I think, the date of the

agreement, 27th April 1973. Between 31st December 1972 and 12th May 1973 the
business was in fact carried on in a manner similar to that in which it was carried on   *a*
immediately before 31st December 1972 and immediately before 27th April 1973.

The amount of adverse change was put by the defendants at £8,600 on the basis of
figures in the schedule, which were agreed between the parties. As to a small sum,
£98 in all, that amount is to be reduced. It relates to the normal reduction in book
value of a motor car and of the lease over this period in question. I think that on
the evidence these reductions in net asset value were not material and were to be   *b*
disregarded, allowing for normal trade fluctuations. Counsel for the defendants
did not seek to argue strenuously against this small reduction.

Further, on their pleaded case, the defendants sought to support or justify their
case by certain particular allegations, as appears from their further and better particulars. Claims that exchange losses, in total amount some £4,800, were suffered
were abandoned by counsel for the defendants as wholly misconceived. Claims   *c*
about the payment of directors' remuneration to Mrs Levison and Miss Cooper were
also abandoned. Lastly, an assertion was made that certain Italian stock, a quantity
of mini-dresses, which had been valued at 50p, were sold before completion at 30p.
That also was abandoned. No submission has been made by the plaintiffs that any of
these matters constituted a separate cause of any part of the material change in net
asset value while not constituting a breach of warranty so as to require the sum of   *d*
£8,500 to be further reduced. There has accordingly been demonstrated a material
change in net asset value of about £8,500, that is the £8,600 less the motor car and
the lease depreciation, in breach of the warranty.

To what damages then are the defendants entitled? The defendants' main contention is simple enough. They say that the parties agreed that the net asset value on the
basis of the accounts at 31st December 1972 was some £44,000, as set out in the   *e*
schedule. The contract price of £54,000 was reached by adding to that agreed net
asset value the sum of £10,000 for goodwill. As facts those propositions are admitted
by the plaintiffs. Since in breach of warranty the net asset value of the companies
purchased was reduced by £8,500 the damages to the defendants as purchasers
of the shares must equal that sum, so the defendants submit. The plaintiffs on
their part have made three submissions. Firstly, it is said that there is no evidence   *f*
of any diminution in the value of the shares bought by reason of the breaches of
warranty. Second, it is said that the defendants, after acquiring the shares of Levison
Originals Ltd, have operated that company and the United Kingdom company very
successfully and have made profits. The diminution in net asset value was as to some
£7,000 a trading loss in the books of the United Kingdom company. That trading
loss, including some other substantial trading losses which had occurred before the   *g*
sale of the shares, has over the years since 1973 been allowed against profits before
corporation tax. Therefore, it is said, the amount of any damage recoverable is not the
full amount of £8,500 but that amount less the tax on the £7,000 loss which was
eventually carried into account against subsequent profits. Alternatively it is said
that if the damage can be regarded as the full amount of £8,500, nevertheless the
subsequent earning of profits and the reduction of tax otherwise payable on those   *h*
profits by reason of the trading loss, is a benefit arising from a subsequent transaction
which should be allowed in reduction of damages. No authority was cited in support
of those propositions. It was said that there was none and that the matter was to be
decided according to principle.

It is to be noted that this issue was not raised anywhere in the pleadings and no discovery was given, or so far as I know asked, with reference to it. The evidence on this issue   *j*
was in general terms, and no documents were produced, apart from certain accounts. Mr
Hakim said that there were accumulated tax losses of £14,442 and the trading loss
over the warranty period was £7,000. The relevant rate of tax was 42 per cent.
Losses in the Malta company are irrelevant because tax is not payable in Malta. The
amount of tax on £7,000 of profits at 42 per cent is £2,940. No objection was taken to
the introduction of this evidence in the case.

a Next it is to be noted that the benefit of tax avoided in taxable profits was received by the taxpayer, that is the United Kingdom company. The claim for breach of warranty is made by these defendants as nominees for Mary Farrin Ltd. Mary Farrin Ltd therefore is in the position of owning Levison Originals Ltd, which owns Levison Originals (UK) Ltd. Such benefit as Mary Farrin Ltd got from the tax advantage comes through that connection. The connection is therefore indirect. But there is no evidence nor suggestion that the defendants have not through the shareholding

b enjoyed fully the benefit of the reduced taxation. No other party was entitled to any share of it.

The consequence is that the defendants, by reason of the breach of warranty, received the shares of the company with the net asset value of that company less by £8,500 than it should have been if the warranty had been performed. Over a period of three or four years thereafter, because of the losses in the company, which

c produced the reduction in net asset value, and hence the breach of warranty, the defendants have paid a smaller sum in tax than otherwise they would have paid, in the amount of £2,940.

The general principle of damages is that the successful claimant is entitled to have awarded to him such sum as will, so far as possible, make good to him the financial loss which he has suffered and will probably suffer as a result of the wrong done.

d I take that from the speech of Lord Reid in *British Transport Commission v Gourley*[1]. It is true that the defendants were entitled to receive the company with the warranty as to net asset value performed as at the date of completion on 12th May 1973, and any advantage arising out of the trading loss which gave rise to a breach of warranty could only be secured at a later date, if the defendants caused the company and its subsidiary to trade and if that trade produced profits. Next it is true that the profits

e against which the trading loss was charged were made by the subsidiary of the company sold and not by the purchasers of the shares, and the trading at a profit was something which the defendants were free to cause to be done or not. They did not trade at a profit in order to mitigate the consequences of the breach of warranty, they did so in pursuance of the commercial purpose which had caused them to buy the shares in the first place. It seems to me, however, that on considering this agreement

f and the circumstances in which it was made it was plainly within the contemplation of the parties that the defendants would operate the companies in trade and that any breach of warranty as to asset value arising from a trading loss would give rise to a right to reduce taxation on ensuing profits, if any, by the amount of tax due on such loss, and that if trading was successful the amount of reduced taxation would be retained and enjoyed by the defendants as representing the purchasing company.

g It remains to be considered whether in these circumstances, if the amount of the tax benefit is known at the date of trial or can according to the probabilities be fairly assessed, that benefit is to be allowed in reduction of damages for the breach of warranty. Counsel for the defendants submitted that the benefit was to be wholly disregarded on the grounds that the tax benefit was not such a benefit as can in law properly be taken into account at all. It was, he said, a benefit which was res inter

h alios acta, and was a benefit which did not arise from an act taken in mitigation of the consequences of the breach of warranty. He referred to certain passages in McGregor on Damages[2], and to *British Westinghouse Electric and Manufacturing Co Ltd v Underground Electric Railways Co of London Ltd*[3]. It is sufficient if I set out the following passage from McGregor on Damages[4] in which certain passages from the speech of Viscount Haldane LC in the *British Westinghouse* case[3] are quoted. The learned

j editor of this work wrote as follows:

---

1 [1955] 3 All ER 796 at 808, [1956] AC 185 at 212
2 13th Edn (1972), paras 238, 251
3 [1912] AC 673, [1911-13] All ER Rep 63
4 13th Edn (1972), para 238

'Frequently a plaintiff will have taken the required reasonable steps of mitigation and thereby have avoided such part of the loss as was avoidable. No   *a*
difficulty arises in such circumstances. But the plaintiff may have gone further
and by sound action have avoided more consequences than the dictates of the law
required of him. In such circumstances the position has been definitely stated by
Viscount Haldane L.C. in the leading case of *British Westinghouse*[1] . . . He put the
rule thus[2]: "When in the course of his business he [the plaintiff] has taken action
arising out of the transaction, which action has diminished his loss, the effect in   *b*
actual diminution of the loss he has suffered may be taken into account even though
there was no duty on him to act." Later in his speech he said similarly[3]: "Provided the course taken to protect himself by the plaintiff in such an action was
one which a reasonable and prudent person might in the ordinary conduct of
business properly have taken, and in fact did take whether bound to or not, a
jury or an arbitrator may properly look at the whole of the facts and ascertain   *c*
the result in estimating the quantum of damage." He emphasised however
that[6] "the subsequent transaction, if to be taken into account, must be one arising
out of the consequences of the breach and in the ordinary course of business". . . .'

That ends the quotations from the speech of Viscount Haldane LC, and the learned
editor goes on to comment—   *d*

'and the important practical question is therefore what steps taken by the plaintiff
satisfy this definition.'

In my judgment the tax benefit received by the defendants in this case satisfies the
rule as there enunciated by Viscount Haldane LC.

The defendants, having established the amount of the trading loss which gave rise   *e*
in part to the breach of warranty, made the claim for tax relief in respect of their
subsequent profits. The defendants were not under any duty to the plaintiffs to
trade in order to reduce the damage for breach of warranty, but the trading loss on
which the defendants were able to obtain tax relief arose out of the transaction in
question and the consequential reduction in tax on subsequent profits which the
defendants inevitably claimed also, in my judgment, arose out of the transaction.   *f*
The tax benefit arose and was obtained out of the consequences of those facts which,
as to part, caused the breach of warranty.

I have referred above to the passage in the speech of Lord Reid in *British Transport
Commission v Gourley*[4] where he stated the general principle on which damages are
assessed. Lord Reid, in that case, went on to say this[5]:

'But the general principle is subject to one qualification. A loss which the   *g*
plaintiff has suffered, or will suffer, or a compensatory gain which has come, or
will come, to him, following on the accident may be of a kind which the law
regards as too remote to be taken into account.'

Counsel for the defendants referred to me the cases mentioned in McGregor[6],
in particular to *Jebsen v East and West India Dock Co*[7] and to *The World Beauty*[8].   *h*
I have considered those cases and the submissions that counsel made but in my
judgment there is no principle on which I could rightly disregard the tax benefit
in this case as being too remote. The damages which the defendants seek will not be

1   [1912] AC 673, [1911-13] All ER Rep 63
2   [1912] AC 673 at 689, [1911-13] All ER Rep 63 at 69
3   [1912] AC 673 at 690, [1911-13] All ER Rep 63 at 70
4   [1955] 3 All ER 796, [1956] AC 185
5   [1955] 3 All ER 796 at 808, [1956] AC 185 at 212
6   Damages (13th Edn, 1972), para 251
7   (1875) LR 10 CP 300, [1874-80] All ER Rep 615
8   [1969] 3 All ER 158, [1970] P 144

a taxable in their hands. It has not been suggested that they will be. By reason of the breach of warranty the defendants received a company at completion with a short-fall in net assets arising from a cause, namely a trading loss, which provided a chance, as the parties must have contemplated, of giving a benefit to the defendants by a reduction in tax on profits if profits were made. By the time of trial that chance has been realised and the amount of the benefit is known. It would in my judgment be unjust to award or to allow to the defendants the full amount of the shortfall in net *b* asset value without allowance for the tax benefit.

What amount then should be allowed in reduction of damages? As counsel for the defendants has pointed out, the onus to establish the amount of any benefit in reduc-tion of damages lay on the plaintiffs, and for that proposition he cited *The World Beauty*[1] mentioned above. The shares were delivered on 12th May 1973 with the companies' net asset value lower by some £8,500 than it should have been. The *c* £2,940 was received or retained over the ensuing years. Against the profits made the defendants were entitled to set off and did set off the full amount of other accrued losses in the company apart from the further £7,000 which had caused part of the £8,500 reduction in net asset value. The defendants are to be treated in my view as having enjoyed the retention of the £2,940 on the £7,000 after the allowance of the other losses which they acquired with the companies. I shall treat this benefit as *d* received three years after completion. Regard can be had to that delay in fixing any interest allowable if any is to be allowed. There are claims for interest on which I shall receive submissions. I assess the damage for breach of warranty now allowable in the sum of £5,560, which is £8,500 less £2,940. The plaintiffs' claim is for an immediate sum of £2,500 due at the date of the writ. A further sum of £2,500 has since become due. I will ask counsel for their submissions on the form of the orders *e* to be made.

Judgment for the defendants on counterclaim amounting to £8,500 to be reduced by £2,940 being tax relief received by the defendants and £5,000 being four instalments due in May 1974 1975, 1976, 1977 to the plaintiffs, leaving a balance of £560 to be paid by the defendants on 1st May 1977. The instalments due to the plaintiffs in May 1978, 1979, 1980, 1981 to *f* *remain untouched. Arguments as to the questions of interest and costs adjourned.*

Solicitors: *Kenwright & Cox* (for the plaintiffs); *Tuck & Mann*, Dorking (for the defendants).

K Mydeen Esq, Barrister.

g 1   [1969] 3 All ER 158, [1970] P 144

Land Reclamation Co Ltd v Basildon District Council

CHANCERY DIVISION
BRIGHTMAN J
14th, 15th, 16th, 19th, 21st DECEMBER 1977

Landlord and tenant – Business premises – Occupied for business purposes – Occupation – Lease granting right of way over private road for term of years for purposes connected with lessee's business – User of road for purposes of business – Lessor opposing grant of new tenancy – Whether tenancy of right of way a protected business tenancy – Whether word 'occupation' interchangeable with word 'user' – Whether right of way over road constituting property or premises capable of being 'occupied . . . for the purposes of a business' – Whether lease a protected tenancy – Landlord and Tenant Act 1954, s 23(1).

A local authority was the owner of a private road which provided the only access to land owned by a company which was used by it in connection with its business of dumping and disposing of waste. In 1970 the local authority granted the company a lease, for a term of years expiring on 25th March 1977, of the full right to pass and repass with vehicles along the road, in common with the local authority, during specified business hours for all purposes in connection with the company's use of the land for the dumping and disposing of waste. The company covenanted to maintain at its own expense one stretch of the road and to pay to the local authority the cost of putting into repair another stretch. The company used the road for the purpose of its business and its lorries passed along it at the rate of about one every four minutes. In April 1976 the company served on the successor to the local authority a request under Part II of the Landlord and Tenant Act 1954 for a new tenancy of the right of way. The local authority served a counter-notice opposing a new tenancy. On the company's application to the county court for the grant of a new tenancy the local authority contended that as the lease was a grant of a term of years in an incorporeal hereditament, i e a right of way, the tenancy was outside the protection of Part II of the 1954 Act. By consent an order was made removing the application to the High Court for determination as a preliminary issue of the question whether the grant of a right of way over the road for a term of years was a tenancy to which the 1954 Act applied. The company contended that although the property comprised in the lease consisted only of a right of way, the exercise of that right involved occupation by the company of the road and to that extent the property comprised in the lease included premises, namely the road, which were 'occupied' by the company for the purposes of its business, within s 23(1)[a] of the 1954 Act.

Held – The words 'used' and 'occupied' were interchangeable only in some contexts. In the context of Part II of the 1954 Act the word 'occupied' could not be equated with 'used' and it was not justifiable to read s 23(1) of the 1954 Act as if it applied Part II of that Act to any tenancy where the property comprised in it included premises 'used' by the tenant for the purposes of his business. Accordingly Part II of the 1954 Act had no application to the grant of a mere right of way because such an incorporeal hereditament, though capable of user, was not property or premises capable of being 'occupied . . . for the purposes of a business' within s 23(1). Since the property comprised in the lease was the right of way, and the road could not be said to be 'occupied' by the company merely by virtue of the right of way over it, the property comprised in the lease did not include 'premises which [were] occupied by the [company] . . .

---

a   Section 23(1) is set out at p 1165 b, post

a for the purposes of [its] business'. It followed that the lease was not a tenancy to which Part II of the 1954 Act applied (see p 1165 *j*, p 1166 *j* to p 1167 *b* and *g h*, post).

Dictum of Sachs LJ in *Lee-Verhulst (Investments) Ltd v Harwood Trust* [1972] 3 All ER at 624, 625 explained.

Notes

b For tenancies to which the Landlord and Tenant Act 1954 applies, see 23 Halsbury's Laws (3rd Edn), 885-886, para 1707.

For the Landlord and Tenant Act 1954, s 23, see 18 Halsbury's Statutes (3rd Edn) 555.

Cases referred to in judgment

Bracey v Read [1962] 3 All ER 472, [1963] Ch 88, [1962] 3 WLR 1194, 31(1) Digest (Reissue)
c   215, 1764.

Jones v Christy (1963) 107 Sol Jo 374, [1963] Court of Appeal Transcript 119.

Lee-Verhulst (Investments) Ltd v Harwood Trust [1972] 3 All ER 619, [1973] QB 204, [1972] 3 WLR 772, CA, 31(2) Digest (Reissue) 942, 7716.

Whitley v Stumbles [1930] AC 554, 99 LJKB 518, 143 LT 441, HL; *affg sub nom Stumbles v Whitley* [1930] 1 KB 393, 99 LJKB 77, 142 LT 225, CA, 31(2) Digest (Reissue) 933, 7675.

d

Cases also cited

Addiscombe Garden Estates Ltd v Crabbe [1957] 3 All ER 563, [1958] 1 QB 513, CA.

Albemarle Street W1, Re No 1 [1959] 1 All ER 250, [1959] Ch 531.

Bagettes Ltd v G P Estates Co Ltd [1956] 1 All ER 729, [1956] Ch 290, CA.

Borwick v Southwark Corpn [1909] 1 KB 78.

e *Briant Colour Printing Co Ltd (in liquidation), Re* [1977] 3 All ER 968, [1977] 1 WLR 942, CA.

Farrell v Alexander [1976] 2 All ER 721, [1977] AC 59, HL.

Hills (Patents) Ltd v University College Hospital Board of Governors [1955] 3 All ER 365, [1956] 1 QB 90, CA.

Holywell and Halkyn Parish v Halkyn District Mines Drainage Co [1895] AC 117, [1891-4]
f   All ER Rep 158, HL.

Maunsell v Olins [1975] 1 All ER 16, [1975] AC 373, HL.

Newcastle City Council v Royal Newcastle Hospital [1959] 1 All ER 734, [1959] AC 248, PC.

R v Melladew [1907] 1 KB 192, CA.

Shell-Mex and BP Ltd v Manchester Garages Ltd [1971] 1 All ER 841, [1971] 1 WLR 612, CA.

g *Sutherland (Duke of) v Heathcote* [1892] 1 Ch 475, CA.

Willis v Association of Universities of British Commonwealth [1964] 2 All ER 39, [1965] 1 QB 140, CA.

Originating summons

h The Land Reclamation Co Ltd ('the company') applied to Brentwood County Court under Part II of the Landlord and Tenant Act 1954 for the grant of a new tenancy of a right of way over a private road owned by Basildon District Council ('the local authority') on the expiry of a lease dated 14th August 1970 made between the local authority's predecessor, Basildon Urban District Council, and the company which granted the company a right of way with vehicles over the road for a term of years.

j The parties sought the determination of the High Court, as a preliminary issue, of the question whether the tenancy created by the lease was a tenancy to which Part II of the 1954 Act applied. The facts are set out in the judgment of the court.

Anthony Scrivener QC and *Mark Lowe* for the company.
Ronald Bernstein QC and *Christopher Priday* for the local authority.

Cur adv vult

a

21st December. **BRIGHTMAN J** read the following judgment: This is the trial
of a preliminary issue arising on an application under the Landlord and Tenant Act
1954. The issue is whether the grant of a right of way for a term of years is a tenancy
to which Part II of the 1954 Act applies.

Basildon District Council ('the local authority') is the owner of a private road
called Marsh Road which runs from the neighbourhood of Pitsea southwards towards b
the Thames estuary. On each side of the road are areas of marshland, derelict farm-
land and mudflats. The Land Reclamation Co Ltd ('the company') is the owner of a
large part of that land. The company uses the land for the disposal of waste and says
that this is the largest waste disposal site in the United Kingdom.

I was told that the site was particularly well suited to the disposal of waste, including
toxic waste, because the subsoil consists of a saucer of impermeable clay which acts as a c
container for waste matter without polluting the surrounding land or the estuary.
I was told, but there was no sworn evidence to this effect, that the site was of great
importance to the country's industry, because there are few places so suitable for
toxic waste disposal. The local authority, however, is conscious of local opposition
and does not wish to be a voluntary party to the continued use of the site for this
purpose.   d

The road was formerly vested in the Crown, and the company at that time used
the road, which is the only existing access to the waste disposal site, under a licence
granted by the Secretary of State for Defence. The local authority, which was the
predecessor of the present district council, became the owner of the road in 1969. On
14th August 1970, that local authority, which I will call 'the urban district council',
granted under seal the lease which is the subject matter of the application now before e
the court.

By cl 1 of the lease the urban district council, in consideration of a yearly rent of
£1,000, demised to the company—

'... full right and liberty for them and their assigns their agents servants or
licensees to pass and repass with or without vehicles along the private road in
common with the Lessor its servants agents tenants and licensees and others f
having a like right and liberty between the hours of 6 a m to 8 p m Mondays to
Fridays and 6 a m to 2.30 p m Saturdays (hereinafter called "the permitted
hours") for all purposes in connection with the use of the Company's land for
the dumping and disposal of waste materials. Subject nevertheless to and
reserving unto the Lessor the right at all times hereafter or at any times or time
to erect renew and maintain a gate or gates across the said roadway at the points g
marked "G" on the said plan with all necessary fittings and fixtures but so that
the same shall not be locked or be so erected or maintained as to impede or
obstruct the free use and enjoyment of the right and liberty of way hereby
granted in accordance with the tenor hereof ...'

By cl 2, the company entered into a number of covenants with the urban district h
council dealing with the maintenance of the road. For this purpose, the road was
divided into four stretches, lettered from the south 'A', 'B', 'C' and 'D'. The company
covenanted to make up at its own expense the stretch from 'A' to 'B'; it covenanted
to pay to the urban district council the cost of putting 'B' to 'C' into repair; it covenanted
to pay a fair proportion, according to user, of the cost of maintaining the stretch 'B' to
'D', its proportion being fixed for the first year at three-quarters. Clause 3 of the lease j
is a covenant for quiet enjoyment. Clause 4 contains power for the urban district
council to determine the lease in the event of breach of covenant by the company.

The term of the lease was due to end on 25th March 1977. On the 20th April 1976
the company served notice on the local authority requesting the grant of a new tenancy
to which the local authority responded with a counter-notice. The company then

applied to the Brentwood County Court. The local authority took the point that the
lease, being a grant of a term of years in an incorporeal hereditament, was outside
the protection afforded by Part II of the 1954 Act. By consent an order was made
removing the application to the High Court. The only question before me is the
preliminary issue.

The case depends principally on s 23(1) of the 1954 Act. This provides as follows:

> 'Subject to the provisions of this Act, this part of this Act applies to any tenancy
> where the property comprised in the tenancy is or includes premises which are
> occupied by the tenant and are so occupied for the purposes of a business carried
> on by him or for those and other purposes.'

Subsection (3):

> 'In the following provisions of this part of this Act, the expression "the holding"
> in relation to a tenancy to which this part of this Act applies, means the property
> comprised in the tenancy, there being excluded any part thereof which is occupied
> neither by the tenant nor by a person employed by the tenant, and so employed
> for the purposes of a business by reason of which the tenancy is one to which this
> part of this Act applies.'

'Tenancy' is defined by s 69(1), but not in a manner which indicates whether Part II
of the 1954 Act was intended to apply to an easement held for an interest equivalent
to a term of years.

To come within Part II, there are shortly stated two conditions which must be
satisfied by the applicant: (1) the applicant must have a tenancy, and not a mere
licence or contractual permission which falls short of an interest in the land, and
(2) the applicant must establish that the property comprised in the tenancy is or
includes premises which are occupied by him for the purposes of a business carried
on by him.

The local authority first submitted that the legal relationship between it and the
company was that of licensor and licensee, and not that of landlord and tenant. In
support of this submission counsel, while recognising that the wording of the document was wholly appropriate to a lease, relied on two factors: first the absence of a
specific description of the company's land to which the right of way could be appur-
tenant; secondly, the fact that the grant was only for a period of seven years, although
both grantor and grantee were fee simple owners. There is no substance in either of
these points.

The Law of Property Act 1925, s 1, recognises that a legal easement may be created
for an interest equivalent to a term of years absolute, and it does not matter whether
the term is seven years or 700 years. It is also well established that a right of way can
exist as a legal interest notwithstanding that the dominant tenement is not precisely
identified in the deed of grant. The general reference to the company's land in the
lease is sufficient for this purpose, extrinsic evidence being admissible. Neither of
these propositions of law was disputed by the local authority; the factors mentioned
were only relied on as a pointer to the true construction of the deed. However, it
seems to me clear that the local authority granted to the company a legal easement
for a term of years and not a mere licence.

This does not conclude the matter, because it is necessary for the company to
establish that it is an occupier for business purposes of the property comprised in the
lease. The property comprised in the lease is the right of way and not the road itself.
There is no doubt that the right of way is exercised by the company for the purposes
of its business. The company's lorries pass along the road at the rate of about one
every four minutes. It is equally true that the road is used for the purposes of the
company's business. But is it possible to say that the property comprised in the lease,
i e, the right of way is, or includes, premises which are occupied by the company?
In ordinary speech, a right of way is not a possible subject matter of occupation as

distinct from user, nor is it easy in normal circumstances to say that a road is occupied by a person who has a mere right of way thereover.

The first case to which the company referred was *Whitley v Stumbles*[1]. This arose under the Landlord and Tenant Act 1927. The plaintiff was the assignee of a lease which included a hotel and the exclusive right of fishing certain adjacent waters. The county court judge held that the fishing rights were not premises within the meaning of s 17(1) of the 1927 Act, and that accordingly the plaintiff, when applying for a new lease of the hotel, could not require the fishing rights to be included therein. This decision was reversed by the Divisional Court which was upheld by the Court of Appeal.

Section 17(1) of the 1927 Act was worded as follows:

'The holdings to which this Part of this Act applies are any premises held under a lease, other than a mining lease, made whether before or after the commencement of this Act, and used wholly or partly for carrying on thereat any trade or business and not being agricultural holdings within the meaning of the Agricultural Holdings Act, 1923.'

There is a significant difference between that Act and the 1954 Act. In the 1927 Act, the formula is 'premises . . . used . . . for carrying on thereat any trade or business.' In the 1954 Act, the formula is 'premises . . . occupied . . . for the purposes of a business carried on by him.'

Greer LJ expressed strong doubts whether the word 'premises' would cover a separate and distinct lease of an incorporeal hereditament. Slessor LJ perhaps leaned the other way. The doubt did not need to be resolved because the fishing rights were demised along with corporeal hereditaments. The subject matter of the lease was the hotel with certain rights attached thereto, and the 1927 Act applied to the entirety. This view was accepted by the House of Lords[2] leaving unresolved the doubt expressed by Greer LJ.

The company also sought at one time to rely on *Bracey v Read*[3]. In that case a lease had been granted of the right to train and exercise racehorses on certain gallops on the Berkshire Downs. The 1954 Act was held to apply to that lease. On a closer examination of the case, and particularly of the facts as set out in the report in the All England series, it became clear that the lease was construed as a demise of the actual strips of land and not merely as a grant of a right to train and exercise horses. The decision accordingly is not an authority that a grant of a term of years in an incorporeal hereditament is by itself within the 1954 Act.

Counsel also relied on *Lee-Verhulst (Investments) Ltd v Harwood Trust*[4], where Sachs LJ compared the wording of the 1927 Act with the wording of the 1954 Act, and observed[5]:

'On being asked what was the relevant distinction between "used" and "occupied" neither counsel—both very experienced in this branch of the law—could after full and helpful consideration suggest such a distinction; on the other hand, we were referred by them to statutes in which the word "used" seemed to have the same meaning as "occupied".'

This observation has to be read in the context of the case then under consideration, namely a tenancy of premises consisting of 20 separate apartments in full occupancy. As occupation is a kind of user, it is difficult to envisage an occupation of land or buildings which is not also a user. The reverse does not apply. Not every use is an occupation, and obviously many things capable of being used are incapable of being

1 [1930] 1 KB 393
2 [1930] AC 544
3 [1962] 3 All ER 472, [1963] Ch 88
4 [1972] 3 All ER 619, [1973] QB 204
5 [1972] 3 All ER 619 at 624, 625, [1973] QB 204 at 214

occupied. The words are not fully interchangeable but only interchangeable in some
contexts.

I am not justified in reading s 23(1) of the 1954 Act as if it said 'premises which are
used by the tenant and are so used for the purposes of a business'. So re-written, a
right of way for a term might well be within the 1954 Act, for I see no reason why a
right of way should not be premises. Subsection (3), which defines 'the holding' as
the property comprised in the tenancy 'there being excluded any part thereof which
is occupied neither by the tenant nor by a person employed by the tenant', also
suggests to my mind that occupation is not employed in the 1954 Act in the sense of
user. There are, in fact, a number of sections of the 1954 Act which are to some extent
inappropriate if occupation is equated with use, and if the Act is interpreted as including within its scope an incorporeal hereditament, such as an easement of way. It
would be tedious to refer to them all. Notable examples can be found in s 30, and
it will be noticed that sub-ss (1) and (7) of s 57, and s 58, contain the expression 'the use
or occupation of the property'.

It was also submitted on behalf of the local authority that parts of the 1954 Act
are geared to the rateable value of the holding: see s 63 which allocates jurisdiction
to the High Court or the county court according to the rateable value of the holding,
and s 37 which measures compensation for disturbance by reference to the rateable
value. A right way is not per se rateable; it would only be rateable if on the facts of
the case it involved the exclusive occupation of the roadway, or something approaching
exclusive occupation. The 1954 Act does not seem to envisage as within its compass a
property right which is not rateable.

In *Jones v Christy*[1], the Court of Appeal were concerned with the application of
the 1954 Act to the lease of a house and fishing rights. The tenant was not able to
claim that he occupied the house for business purposes, but he did claim to carry on
the business of letting the fishing rights. The claim failed for a reason which is not
material to be explained, but Lord Denning MR doubted whether the Act could
apply to a mere incorporeal hereditament on its own. He said[1]:

> 'If the letting were solely of an incorporeal hereditament, such as the right to
> fish, I doubt whether the Act would apply to it. When the Act speaks of
> "premises" being "occupied" it may well refer to corporeal hereditaments and
> not to incorporeal hereditaments.'

Counsel for the company sought to say that although the property comprised in
the tenancy consisted only of the right of way, the exercise of such right necessarily
involved the occupation, although not the exclusive occupation, of the roadway;
therefore, to that extent, the property comprised in the lease, namely the easement,
included premises, namely the roadway, which were in the occupation of the company
for the purposes of its business; in other words, occupation of the roadway resulted
from the easement. I do not feel able to accept that submission. In my judgment,
the company uses the roadway for the purposes of its business but it does not occupy
either the easement or the roadway.

I take the view that Part II of the 1954 Act has no application to a mere right of way
standing by itself, because such a right is not property or premises capable of being
occupied for the purposes of a business, or indeed for any other purpose. I will make a
declaration accordingly.

Declaration accordingly.

Solicitors: *Wood, Nash & Winter's* for *Ellison & Co*, Colchester (for the company);
J L Knight, Basildon (for the local authority).

Evelyn M C Budd   Barrister.

---

1   [1963] Court of Appeal Transcript 119

Hesperides Hotels Ltd and another v Muftizade   *a*

HOUSE OF LORDS
LORD WILBERFORCE, VISCOUNT DILHORNE, LORD SALMON, LORD FRASER OF TULLYBELTON
AND LORD KEITH OF KINKEL
8th, 9th, 10th, 11th, 15th, 16th, 17th MAY, 6th JULY 1978

b

*Conflict of laws – Foreign land – Trespass to foreign land – Jurisdiction of English courts
to entertain action for trespass to foreign land – Action framed as claim for conspiracy in
England to effect trespass to foreign land – Whether jurisdiction to entertain action.*

Conflict of laws – Foreign chattels – Conversion of chattels in foreign country – Jurisdiction   *c*
*of English courts to entertain action for conversion of chattels in foreign country – Dispossessed
owners of chattels in Cyprus bringing action in England for conspiracy to effect trespasses to
chattels in Cyprus – Sufficient facts alleged to support claim in conversion – Whether
jurisdiction to entertain action.*

The appellants, two companies owned and controlled by Greek Cypriot families, were   *d*
the respective owners of two hotels at Kyrenia in northern Cyprus. In July 1974 Turkey
invaded and occupied northern Cyprus including Kyrenia. In consequence the Greek
Cypriots controlling the appellant companies fled to southern Cyprus and had been
unable to return to Kyrenia. Northern Cyprus was controlled by a body calling
itself the Turkish Federated State of Cyprus which authorised the occupation and
use of the appellants' hotels by Turkish Cypriots. In 1976 the Turkish Federated   *e*
State of Cyprus issued in England, through a London travel agency, brochures which
advertised the hotels to English holiday-makers from whom bookings for holidays
at the hotels were accepted by the travel agency. On 16th February 1977 the appellants issued a writ against the travel agency and against the respondent, the London
representative of the Turkish Federated State of Cyprus. In the writ the appellants
asserted ownership of the hotels, admitted that they had been out of possession of them   *f*
since 1974, and asserted that the travel agency and the respondent had conspired together to effect trespasses to the hotels by the unauthorised use of them. The writ
claimed, inter alia, damages for conspiracy to effect the trespasses. The respondent
applied to a judge in chambers to have the writ set aside on the ground that English
courts had no jurisdiction to entertain an action for damages for trespass to land
situated abroad. The judge upheld the writ and the respondent appealed to the Court   *g*
of Appeal. On the hearing of the appeal the appellants amended the writ to claim as
additional relief damages for conspiracy to effect trespasses to the contents of the
hotels. The appellants' title to the hotels was not disputed by the respondent.
     The Court of Appeal unanimously held that the writ should be set aside, the
majority so holding because (i) the appellants' claim fell within the rule of law that
English courts had no jurisdiction to entertain an action for the determination of   *h*
the right to possession of foreign land or for the recovery of damages for trespass
to foreign land and that the claim for conspiracy had been framed as a device to
overcome that rule; and (ii) the claim for conspiracy to effect a trespass to the contents of the hotels, although not barred by the rule (which only applied to land)
nevertheless disclosed no cause of action because the appellants were not in possession
of the contents at the time of the alleged conspiracy.   *j*
     On appeal, the appellants, while accepting the rule that English courts had no
jurisdiction to entertain an action for damages for trespass to foreign land where there
was a dispute as to title, submitted (i) that the rule did not apply where there was no
dispute as to title of foreign land; (ii) nor did the rule apply to an action based on a
conspiracy to effect or procure trespass to foreign land if the conspiracy was entered

a into in England; (iii) that the rule should if necessary be restated to the extent required to allow their action to be brought; and (iv) that their action in respect of trespasses to the contents of the hotels could properly be laid in conversion.

Held – (i) The rule of law that English courts had no jurisdiction to entertain an action for the determination of the title to, or the right to the possession of, foreign land or the recovery of damages for trespass to foreign land was not limited to cases where there was a dispute as to title. The rule applied to the appellants' claim for trespass to the hotels even though no question of title or the right to possession of them had been raised (see p 1173 *h* to p 1174 *b* and *g*, p 1179 *d e*, p 1180 *b*, p 1183 *b* and p 1184 *e*, post); *British South Africa Co v Companhia de Moçambique* [1891-4] All ER Rep 640, explained and applied.

c   (ii) Furthermore, the appellants' claim for conspiracy to effect a trespass to the hotels depended on them showing an intention to effect a trespass on foreign land, and that could only be established if the court was able to adjudicate on the right to possession of the foreign land, which in turn was precluded by the rule, and (per Lord Fraser of Tullybelton) the claim for conspiracy was merely an attempt to dress up a substantive claim in trespass in the guise of a claim for conspiracy (see p 1174 *g* to p 1175 *b*, p 1179 *g h*, p 1180 *b*, p 1183 *b c* and *g h* and p 1184 *e*, post); *British South Africa Co v*
d *Companhia de Moçambique* [1891-4] All ER Rep 640 applied.

        (iii) There was not sufficient reason to revise or restate the rule, having regard to the fact that it was accepted in other common law jurisdictions; a change might well involve questions of the comity of nations because of the possible conflict with foreign jurisdictions and this was a matter for legislation rather than judicial decision; consequential changes in English law, e g to prevent forum shopping, would be required;
e and there had not been a sufficient change of circumstances to justify changing the rule. Accordingly the appeal would be dismissed in regard to the appellants' claim for damages for conspiracy to effect trespasses to the hotels, and the order striking out the writ and substantive claim so far as they related to land or immovable property in Cyprus would be upheld (see p 1175 *c d* and *f g*, p 1176 *c* to *e*, p 1179 *e f*
f and *h* to p 1180 *a b*, p 1182 *d e* and *h* to p 1183 *a* and p 1184 *e*, post).

        (iv) The appellants' claim for conspiracy to effect trespasses to the contents of the hotels was not barred by any rule of law and could validly be laid in conversion, since the appellants had alleged interference with their chattels, no local law was relied on by the respondent to justify the interference, and it was not necessary for a claim in conversion that the appellants had been in possession of the chattels at the time of the conversion. The appeal would therefore be allowed to the extent neces-
g sary to permit the appellants' action to continue in respect of the claim for conspiracy to effect trespasses to the contents of the hotels (see p 1176 *h* to p 1177 *a*, p 1180 *a b* and p 1183 *j* to p 1184 *a* and *d e*, post); *Albert v Fraser Companies Ltd* [1937] 1 DLR 39 distinguished.

        Decision of the Court of Appeal, sub nom *Hesperides Hotels Ltd v Aegean Turkish Holidays Ltd* [1978] 1 All ER 277 varied.
h

Notes
For jurisdiction of English courts with respect to foreign land, see 8 Halsbury's Laws (4th Edn) paras 638, 640, and for cases on the subject, see 11 Digest (Reissue) 396-399, 367-393.

j
Cases referred to in opinions
Albert v Fraser Companies Ltd [1937] 1 DLR 39, 11 MPR 209, 11 Digest (Reissue) 398, *245.
Atlantic Star, The, The Atlantic Star (Owners) v The Bona Spes (Owners) [1973] 2 All ER 175, [1974] AC 436, [1973] 2 WLR 795, HL, 11 Digest (Reissue) 645, 1777.

Brisbane v Pennsylvania Railway Co (1912) 205 NY 431, 98 NE 752.

British South Africa Co v Companhia de Moçambique [1893] AC 602, [1891-4] All ER Rep
   640, 63 LJQB 70, 69 LT 604, HL; *rvsg* sub nom *Companhia de Moçambique v British
   South Africa Co*[1892]2QB 358, 61 LJQB 663, 66 LT 773, DC &CA, 11 Digest (Reissue)
   398, 388.

Doulson v Matthews (1792) 4 Term Rep 503, 100 ER 1143, 11 Digest (Reissue) 398, 385.

Gray v Manitoba and North Western Railway Co (1896) 11 Man Rep 42.

Inglis v Commonwealth Trading Bank of Australia (1972) 20 FLR 30.

Jacobus v Colgate (1916) 217 NY 235.

Livingston v Jefferson (1811) 15 Fed Cas 660, 1 Brock 203.

London Corpn v Cox (1867) LR 2 HL 239, 36 LJEx 225, HL, 16 Digest (Repl) 117, 31.

MacShannon v Rockware Glass Ltd [1978] 1 All ER 625, [1978] 2 WLR 362, HL.

Miliangos v George Frank (Textiles) Ltd [1975] 3 All ER 801, [1976] AC 443, [1975] 3 WLR
   758, [1976] 1 Lloyd's Rep 201, HL, Digest (Cont Vol D) 571, 678b.

Mostyn v Fabrigas(1775) 1 Cowp 161, [1775-1802] All ER Rep 266, 20 State Tr 81, 98 ER
   1021, 11 Digest (Reissue) 495, 944.

Penn v Lord Baltimore (1750) 1 Ves Sen 444, 27 ER 1132, LC, 11 Digest (Reissue) 404, 423.

Phillips v Eyre (1870) LR 6 QB 1, 10 B & S 1004, 40 LJQB 28, 22 LT 869, Ex Ch, 11
   Digest (Reissue) 495, 946.

Potter v Broken Hill Pty Co (1906) 3 CLR 479, 12 ALR 149, [1906] VLR 292, 11 Digest
   (Reissue) 501, *573.

Ruthven v Ruthven (1905) 13 SLT 409.

Skinner v East India Co (1666) 6 State Tr 710, 11 Digest (Reissue) 396, 369.

United Africa Co Ltd v Owners of MV Tolten, The Tolten [1946] 2 All ER 372, [1946]
   P 135, [1947] LJR 201, 175 LT 469, CA, 11 Digest (Reissue) 398, 387.

Interlocutory appeal

By a writ issued on 16th February 1977 the appellants, Hesperides Hotels Ltd and Catsellis
Hotels Ltd, companies incorporated according to the law of the Republic of Cyprus
and respectively the owners and proprietors of the Hesperides Hotel and the Dome
Hotel ('the hotels') situated at Kyrenia, Cyprus, brought an action against
Aegean Turkish Holidays Ltd and the respondent, Omer Faik Muftizade, claiming
damages for conspiracy to effect trespasses to the hotels and an injunction restraining
Aegean Turkish Holidays Ltd and the respondent by their servants, agents or otherwise
from conspiring or acting in any way whatsoever to procure, encourage or facilitate a
trespass to the hotels or to procure the unauthorised use of the hotels. By summons
dated 4th March 1976 the appellants applied to the judge in chambers for an interlocutory injunction, until after the trial of the action or further order, in terms of the
injunction claimed in the writ. Aegean Turkish Holidays Ltd gave an undertaking
in the terms of the injunction claimed by the writ. By an order dated 6th April 1977
May J, on the appellants' giving a cross-undertaking as to damages, granted an injunction restraining the respondent by himself, his agents or servants or howsoever otherwise from conspiring or acting in a way whatever to procure, encourage or assist a trespass to the appellants' hotels until after the trial of the action or further order, and dismissed the respondent's application for an order setting aside the writ as against
him. The respondent appealed, seeking an order that the injunction should be discharged and the writ set aside on the grounds (i) that the court had no jurisdiction to
entertain the appellants' action, (ii) that the statement of claim disclosed no reasonable
cause of action and/or the action was an abuse of the process of the court, (iii) that there
was no evidence that the respondent had committed or threatened to commit any tort
as against the appellants and the judge had misdirected himself in finding to the contrary, and (iv) that if, contrary to ground (i), jurisdiction existed, the court in the exercise of its misdirection ought not to grant interlocutory relief in the special circumstances of the case and/or that the grant of relief by the judge had been wrong in
principle.

a By a respondent's notice the appellants gave notice that at the hearing of the appeal they would contend that the order dated 6th April 1977 should be affirmed on grounds additional to those relied on by the judge, namely (i) that the court had jurisdiction to entertain the appellants' claim against the respondent because the ratio decidendi of *British South Africa Co v Companhia de Moçambique*[1] had no application in a suit where title to land situated abroad was not in dispute and the claim was for damages for trespass to the land and the defendant was within the jurisdiction,

b or where an investigation or issue as to title to land situated abroad arose incidentally or where the defendant had acted unconscionably, and (ii) that there was no other forum in which the appellants' claim against the respondent could have been brought. During the hearing of the appeal the appellants amended their statement of claim pursuant to RSC Ord 20, r 3, by adding a claim for damages for conspiracy to effect a trespass to chattels, i e the contents of the hotels, and extending the claim for an

c injunction to the contents of the hotels.

On 23rd May 1977 the Court of Appeal[2] (Lord Denning MR, Roskill and Scarman LJJ) allowed the respondent's appeal, discharged the injunction and set aside the appellants' amended writ. The court refused the appellants leave to appeal to the House of Lords. On 21st July 1977 the Appeal Committee of the House of Lords granted the appellants leave to appeal limited to that part of the order striking out

d the amended writ. The facts are set out in the opinion of Lord Wilberforce.

David Kemp QC and *George Newman* for the appellants.
F P Neill QC, Gerald Davies and *Nicholas Padfield* for the respondent.

Their Lordships took time for consideration.

e
6th July. The following opinions were delivered.

LORD WILBERFORCE. My Lords, this appeal is from an order of the Court of Appeal setting aside the appellants' writ against the respondent, Mr Omer Faik

f Muftizade, for want of jursidiction.

The appellants are two companies registered under the laws of the Republic of Cyprus. They are family concerns owned and controlled by Greek Cypriots. Before 1974, in which year Turkish forces took possession of areas in the north of Cyprus, these companies were owners of two hotels in Kyrenia, on the north coast. Hesperides Hotels Ltd, owned and operated one called the Hesperides; Catsellis Hotels Ltd, one called the Dome. After the Turkish invasion those who controlled the

g appellants left Kyrenia and went to Limassol, which is on the southern coast and is in the Greek Cypriot area. In 1976 it came to their knowledge that efforts were being made in London to organise holiday tours to the hotels. There was a body calling itself the Turkish Federated State of Cyprus which issued brochures; there was, a travel agency called Aegean Turkish Holidays Ltd which handled these brochures,

h and, it is said, accepted bookings for the hotels from intending holiday-makers in England. The Turkish Federated State of Cyprus has as its representative in London, Mr Muftizade, the respondent to this appeal.

On 16th February 1977 the appellants issued a writ with statement of claim endorsed against Aegean Turkish Holidays Ltd and the respondent claiming damages, in effect for conspiracy, an account of profits and an injunction restraining the defendants from conspiring to procure acts of trespass to the appellants' hotels. They also issued,

j on 4th March 1977, a summons claiming an interim injunction in the same terms. The respondent entered a conditional appearance and himself issued a summons for

---

1 [1893] AC 602, [1891-4] All ER Rep 640
2 [1978] 1 All ER 277

an order setting aside the writ. The summonses came on for hearing before May J on
1st April 1977.   *a*

The respondent's contentions, at this stage, were twofold. First he claimed immunity from suit on the basis that the Turkish Federated State of Cyprus was a foreign
sovereign state and that he was its representative. Secondly he contended that the court
had no jurisdiction to entertain the action on the principle established by this House
in *British South Africa Co v Companhia de Moçambique*[1] ('the *Moçambique* case'). To enable
himself to deal with the first point May J addressed an enquiry to the Secretary of   *b*
State, Foreign and Commonwealth Office, asking whether Her Majesty's Government recognised de jure or de facto, the Turkish Federated State of Cyprus and
whether Her Majesty's Government accords any diplomatic privilege to the respondent. On 6th April 1977 the Secretary of State replied giving a negative answer
to each of these questions. These replies disposed of the respondent's first contention.
On the second point the judge decided that the court had jurisdiction to try a claim   *c*
based on a conspiracy to procure trespass to foreign land when the conspiracy took
place in this country and there were overt acts in this country. He granted an interim
injunction in the terms claimed and dismissed the respondent's summons.

On 13th May 1977 a consent order was made against Aegean Turkish Holidays
Ltd under which they submitted to a perpetual injunction restraining them from
conspiring or acting in any way to procure trespasses to the hotels and to an order   *d*
for payment to each appellant of £10 by way of damages for conspiracy to trespass.
It is asserted in the respondent's case (their Lordships accept in good faith), in support
of his contention that there had been an accord and satisfaction, that this sum has been
paid, but it was conceded, on the hearing of the appeal, that this fact could not be
established.

The respondent appealed to the Court of Appeal against the order of May J and   *e*
added, by leave, an additional ground, that the statement of claim disclosed not
reasonable cause of action and/or should be struck out as an abuse of the process of
the court. At the hearing of the appeal the respondent adduced voluminous additional
evidence directed to showing the development since 1974 of affairs in Cyprus and to
proving the actual situation prevailing in the island. This was to be the foundation
of an argument in the Court of Appeal and in this House that, in spite of the certificate *f*
of the Secretary of State, there was an autonomous administration in each part of
Cyprus of which and of whose 'legislation' the court can take note. The appellants
objected to this evidence on the ground that it contradicted the certificate of the
Secretary of State, that it was contentious, and that they had no opportunity to
answer it. The Court of Appeal however admitted it.

Further, in the course of the hearing before the Court of Appeal, the appellants   *g*
amended their statement of claim alleging a conspiracy to procure trespasses to the
the contents of the hotels, no doubt with the expectation of thereby escaping from the
consequences of the rule in the *Moçambique* case[1]. The Court of Appeal unanimously
allowed the respondent's appeal but differed in the reasons they gave for doing so.
Roskill and Scarman LJJ held that the action was precluded by the rule in the
Moçambique case[1], nonetheless though it was presented in the form, or guise, of a   *h*
conspiracy. They also held that the action was not maintainable as regards the
chattels (contents of the hotels) since it was based on trespass (not conversion) and
since the appellants were admittedly out of possession. Lord Denning MR held that
the *Moçambique* rule should be confined to cases where there is a dispute as to title and
that the court have jurisdiction to try a claim based on a conspiracy in England. He
held however that the action, being an action in tort, was not maintainable because   *j*
the acts complained of were not unlawful under the lex loci actus: notice could be
taken of the 'laws' of the Turkish Federated State of Cyprus which authorised the
acts. Moreover public policy rendered the dispute not justiciable in England there
being two conflicting administrations in Cyprus.

1   [1893] AC 602, [1891-4] All ER Rep 640

I shall consider first the question whether the present action is precluded by the
a   rule in the *Moçambique* case[1]. The appellants' arguments are threefold. First, they
contend that the rule established by that case has no application where there is no
dispute as to the title to foreign land and (I use their words) 'no real dispute over the
right to possession of the foreign land'. This result, they say, can be reached by a
process of interpretation of the decision of this House without departing from it.
Secondly, they invite your Lordships to overrule, or depart from, the decision in the
b   *Moçambique* case[1], at least to the extent necessary to allow the present action to be
brought. Thirdly, they argue that the rule has no application to an action based on a
conspiracy entered into in England even if the conspiracy is to effect or procure
trespass to foreign land.

The rule in the *Moçambique* case[1] can be conveniently stated in the form in which it
is generally accepted, viz, in Dicey and Morris's The Conflict of Laws, r 79. I quote
c   from the ninth edition[2], but it appears as r 53 in the same form (except for one letter)
in the third edition[3] edited by Professor Dicey himself and Dr Berriedale Keith—

> 'Subject to the Exceptions hereinafter mentioned, the court has no jurisdiction
> to entertain an action for (1) the determination of the title to, or the right to the
> possession of, any immovable situate out of England (foreign land); or (2) the
d   > recovery of damages for trespass to such immovable.'

The exceptions later mentioned relate to actions in equity (*Penn v Lord Baltimore*[4])
and other special cases on which reliance cannot be placed in this appeal.

It will be seen that the rule is in two parts. If either applies, the court has no jurisdiction. The second part refers to the recovery of damages for trespass and if correctly
stated must (subject only to the conspiracy point) preclude the action. So the questions
e   are (1) whether this part of the rule is correct in law, (2) whether it should be read
subject to an exception for actions where no question as to title arises. My Lords, the
answer to the first of these questions cannot, in my opinion, admit of doubt. The
history of the rule, which is a long one, was examined in depth in the *Moçambique*
case, both in this House[1] and in the Court of Appeal[5]. Two of the Lords Justices in
the Court of Appeal were prepared to hold that an action in trespass, being in their
f   view an action in personam, could lie against a defendant found in England: Lord
Esher MR thought otherwise and his opinion prevailed in this House. In his speech
(which I shall not attempt to summarise) Lord Herschell LC traced the development
of the rule from *Skinner v East India Co*[6] in 1666 to 1893: it was Lord Mansfield who
attempted, in two cases decided by himself and referred to in *Mostyn v Fabrigas*[7],
to support the doctrine that actions for trespass against a defendant in England could
g   lie. But this doctrine was decisively rejected in *Doulson v Matthews*[8], per Buller J:

> 'It is now too late for us to inquire whether it were wise or politic to make a
> distinction between transitory and local actions: it is sufficient for the Courts
> that the law has settled the distinction, and that an action *quare clausum fregit*
> is local. We may try actions here which are in their nature transitory, though
h   > arising out of a transaction abroad, but not such as are in their nature local.'

It has not been revived since in any English reported case.
There is no more doubt, in my opinion, as to the second question. It is certainly

---

1   [1893] AC 602, [1891-4] All ER Rep 640
j   2   (1973), p 516
3   (1922), p 223
4   (1750) 1 Ves Sen 444
5   [1892] 2 QB 358
6   (1666) 6 State Tr 710
7   (1775) 1 Cowp 161 at 180, 181, [1775-1802] All ER Rep 266 at 273, 274
8   (1792) 4 Term Rep 503 at 504

true that in the *Moçambique* case[1] itself the plaintiff's title was disputed, but the House
considered the legitimacy of actions in trespass in the broadest and most general
terms. Lord Herschell LC opened his speech in these words[2]: 'The principal question raised by this appeal is whether the Supreme Court of Judicature has jurisdiction
to try an action to recover damages for a trespass to lands situate in a foreign country',
and the whole of the discussion is in terms as general as this. The rejection of Lord
Mansfield's doctrine is inconsistent with any supposed limitation of the rule to a case
where title is disputed, for in neither of the cases decided by him was there a dispute
as to title. But Lord Herschell LC (as Buller J before him), recognising this fact[3],
rejected the admissiblity of actions in trespass. There are passages no doubt in
the speech which are directed towards the actual facts of the case which the House
was considering, in which not only was there a dispute as to title, but the action was
brought in order that the title should be determined. In these passages Lord Herschell
LC draws attention to the particular, and additional, difficulties which would be involved if the English court were to adjudicate on title. But in my understanding
these are treated as a fortiori cases, and there is nothing in the examination of them
which supports a proposition that the rule is limited to them.

The speech of Lord Halsbury follows the same course. He states the question for
decision in the same general way as it had been stated by Lord Herschell LC[4] and
he deals with it similarly without a single reference, even as regards the case under
discussion, to support an argument that the rule applies only when title is disputed.

My Lords, this is not the first time that this supposed limitation of the rule has been
contended for. It was raised in *The Tolten*[5] and firmly rejected by Somervell LJ[6] and
by Cohen LJ[7]. It is suggested that Scott LJ took a different view, but all he said[8] was
this:

> 'I recognise that in a case where the action is brought by a party in possession
> of land and structures, suing merely for damages for negligence, or even, it may
> be, for trespass *quare clausum fregit*, and the plaintiff relies solely on his possession
> as the foundation for his action, the House of Lords might hereafter distinguish
> the *Moçambique* case[1], but I think that it would not be right for this court to
> attempt the distinction as I am satisfied that in regard to common law actions no
> such distinction was then in the mind of the House.'

But, whether or not this House possesses greater powers of distinguishing earlier
decisions than does the Court of Appeal, a question which may raise some interesting
jurisprudential questions, I hardly find in this passage any encouragement to exercise
such powers as we have.

I therefore regard the formulation in Dicey[9], r 79 (2), as correctly stating the law.

Before considering whether we should overrule or depart from the *Moçambique*
rule in any respect I must deal with the argument that we have here the distinguishable
claim of a conspiracy formed in England. The majority in the Court of Appeal gave
short shrift to this argument and I think they were right. In my opinion the answer
to this argument is to be found in a passage in the judgment of Scarman LJ[10]:

> 'But, more significant, the reliance on the alleged conspiracy as distinct from
> the alleged trespass which it is intended to effect is wrong in principle. The

1 [1893] AC 602, [1891-4] All ER Rep 640
2 [1893] AC 602 at 617, [1891-4] All ER Rep 640 at 643
3 [1893] AC 602 at 624, [1891-4] All ER Rep 640 at 647
4 [1893] AC 602 at 630, [1891-4] All ER Rep 640 at 651
5 [1946] 2 All ER 372, [1946] P 135
6 [1946] 2 All ER 372 at 386, [1946] P 135 at 163
7 [1946] 2 All ER 372 at 389, [1946] P 135 at 169
8 [1946] 2 All ER 372 at 374, 375, [1946] P 135 at 141, 142
9 Dicey and Morris, The Conflict of Laws (9th Edn, 1973), p 516
10 [1978] 1 All ER 277 at 293, 294, [1978] 1 QB 205 at 231

combination or agreement, which is said to constitute (with overt acts and ensuing damage) the tort of conspiracy is unlawful only if there be the intention to effect a trespass on foreign land. Unless that be shown there is nothing unlawful. And that can be established only if the court is prepared to adjudicate on the right to possession of the foreign land, which is exactly what the House of Lords said the English courts may not do: see Lord Herschell LC[1] in the passage already cited.'

I gratefully adopt this passage on which I am unable to improve.

The rule being then as I have stated it, should your Lordships accede to the appellants' invitation to restate it in different terms? There is no doubt that the rule can be criticised. Although Professor Dicey seems to have approved it[2] the diligence of the appellants' counsel has assembled a massive volume of academic hostility to the rule as illogical and productive of injustice[3]. Although these writers are concerned with the conflict of laws, as to which academic authority is of particular value, rather than with the English law as to jurisdiction which is what now concerns us, the consensus as to where considerations of logic and justice might lead if this matter were tabula rasa is impressive. But there are other factors to be weighed when revision of an old established rule, sanctioned by this House, is suggested.

First, the rule is accepted, with differing degrees of force and emphasis in other jurisdictions of the common law. Their Lordships were referred to cases decided in Australia and Canada which accept the rule and to none which reject it: see *Potter v Broken Hill Pty Ltd*[4], *Inglis v Commonwealth Trading Bank of Australia*[5], *Gray v Manitoba and North Western Railway Co*[6]. In *Albert v Fraser Companies Ltd*[7] the Supreme Court of New Brunswick specifically discussed the question whether the *Moçambique*[8] decision can be limited to a case where title is in dispute, and held that it could not (see also Sykes, Australian Conflict of Laws[9]). In the United States of America the rule appears to be accepted in the great majority of jurisdictions, Arkansas, Minnesota and Missouri being the only states in which it has been judicially departed from. In general the courts have followed the judgment of Marshall CJ in *Livingston v Jefferson*[10] in which the learned Chief Justice, seeing no good reason for the rule, upheld it for the sake of consistency and continuity. In New York and Virginia it has been altered by statute (see further below). In Scotland a similar rule appears to prevail without certainty of definition: see Anton, Private International Law[11].

Secondly the nature of the rule itself, involving, as it clearly must, possible conflict with foreign jurisdictions, and the possible entry into and involvement with political questions of some delicacy, does not favour revision (assuming such to be logically desirable) by judicial decision, but rather by legislation. I am impressed in this context by the judgment of Cullen CJ[12] in the Court of Appeal of New York given in 1912 which contains this passage:

1   [1893] AC 602 at 624, 625, [1891–4] All ER Rep 640 at 648
2   The Conflict of Laws (3rd Edn, 1922), p 223, 224
3   See inter alia Dicey and Morris, Conflict of Laws (9th Edn, 1973), pp 516–518; Cheshire, Private International Law (3rd Edn, 1947), p 719, (8th Edn, 1970), p 481, (9th Edn, 1974), p 495; ALI Restatement (2d) Conflict of Laws, §§ 10, 87, Beale, Conflict of Laws (1935), § 614; Goodrich, Conflict of Laws (4th Edn, 1964), § 96; Ehrenzweig, Conflict of Laws (1962), s 39.
4   (1906) 3 CLR 479
5   (1972) 20 FLR 30
6   (1896) 11 Man Rep 42
7   [1937] 1 DLR 39
8   [1893] AC 602, [1891–4] All ER Rep 640
9   (1972), p 202
10 (1811) 15 Fed Cas 660
11 (1967), p 125
12 (1912) 205 NY 431 at 434

'The authorities in the highest courts of this state are uniform to the effect that our courts have no jurisdiction of an action for damages for injuries to real *a* estate lying without the state, and the latest decisions are quite recent. . . . It was so held by Chief Justice MARSHALL in *Livingstone v. Jefferson*[1], where he decided that an action could not be maintained in Virginia for trespass upon lands in Louisiana. Such also is the rule in the great majority of the states . . . though there are some where the contrary rule prevails . . . and the old law was changed in Virginia by statute. Were the question an open one, I would favor the doc- *b* trine that our courts have jurisdiction of actions to recover damages for injuries to foreign real estate. Chief Justice MARSHALL in *Livingstone v. Jefferson*[1], expressed his personal disapproval of the rule which he felt bound to give effect under the authorities. In the century which has elapsed since Chief Justice MARSHALL's decision, all the decisions in this state which I have cited have been rendered. At this late day I think we would not be justified in overruling these *c* cases, but should leave it to the Legislature to change the rule by statute.'

Thirdly, revision of the rule may necessitate consequential changes in the law. In order to prevent 'forum shopping' and overlapping, one such change would have to relate to 'forum non conveniens', a principle not yet fully developed in England (see *The Atlantic Star*[2], *MacShannon v Rockware Glass Ltd*[3]) and, if English courts were *d* to be given an extended jurisdiction, requiring legislative definition.

Fourthly, it cannot be said that since 1893 there has been such a change of circumstances as to justify this House in changing the rule (cf *Miliangos v George Frank (Textiles) Ltd*[4]).

On these considerations I have reached the conclusion that the necessary conditions to bring into operation the Practice Direction of 1966[5] do not exist and that the rule *e* should be maintained in this House. The consequence is that the appellants' action, as regards the hotels themselves, being land situate abroad, cannot be maintained. In view of this conclusion it is not necessary to enter on the questions raised by the respondent's counsel as to the degree of notice (if any) which the courts should take of the situation in Cyprus and of 'laws' passed by the non-recognised Turkish Federated State of Cyprus. These gave rise to an interesting and learned argument for which the *f* House is indebted but having regard to the nature of the issues raised I think that the present is not the occasion to pass on them.

There remains the appellants' claim as regards the chattel contents of the hotels. To this the *Moçambique* rule has no application. Moreover the alleged 'laws' passed in the Turkish Federated State of Cyprus do not extend to the chattels. The Court of Appeal, however, struck out this part of the appellants' claim on the ground that for *g* such a claim to be admissible the plaintiffs must be in possession of the chattels in question. But a claim could validly be laid in conversion: the appellants allege sufficient facts to support such a claim and it is not necessary in modern pleadings to attach a specific label to it if the factual basis is there, so the claim can be asserted without amendment. *Albert v Fraser Companies Ltd* on[6] which the respondent relied does not assist him, for in that case there was no direct allegation in the plaintiff's statement *h* of claim of any trespass to his personal property (see per Baxter CJ[7]). In the present case interference with the appellants' chattels is distinctly alleged and, moreover, no local law is relied on as justifying the interference.

I would allow the appellants' appeal so far as to permit the action to continue as

---

1   (1811) 15 Fed Cas 660   *i*
2   [1973] 2 All ER 175, [1974] AC 436
3   [1978] 1 All ER 625, [1978] 2 WLR 362
4   [1975] 3 All ER 801, [1976] AC 443
5   *Note* [1966] 3 All ER 77, [1966] 1 WLR 1234
6   [1937] 1 DLR 39
7   [1937] 1 DLR 39 at 46

a   regards the chattels but I would uphold the order striking out the writ and substantive
claim so far as it relates to land or immovable property in Cyprus.

VISCOUNT DILHORNE. My Lords, on 23rd May 1977 the Court of Appeal
(Lord Denning MR, Roskill and Scarman LJJ) ordered that the writ in these proceedings should be set aside. By that writ endorsed with a statement of claim, the appellants, the owners of two hotels in Kyrenia in northern Cyprus, the first appellant
b   being the owner of the Hesperides Hotel now called the Kyrenia Rocks, and the second
appellant being the owner of the hotel called the Dome Hotel, claimed damages from,
and an injunction against two defendants, the first a travel agency called Aegean
Turkish Holidays Ltd and the second the respondent to this appeal. They alleged
that the travel agency and the respondent had 'conspired together and with others
unknown to effect trespasses to the said hotels and/or have conspired together to
c   obtain advantage for themselves by the unauthorised use' of the appellants' property.
    The alternative conspiracy alleged appears to be in substance also an allegation in
different language of a conspiracy to effect trespasses to the hotels, and it was not
contended on behalf of the appellants that if the court had no jurisdiction to hear the
claim in respect of the conspiracy to effect trespasses, it nevertheless had jurisdiction
to entertain the claim under the alternative head.
d   Of these allegations of conspiracy the statement of claim purported to give particulars. They alleged that the travel agency had held itself out as willing to book,
and had booked accommodation for holidays at the appellants' hotels, and that the
respondent had counselled and procured divers persons to commit trespass to the
hotels. The only link between the travel agency and the respondent disclosed by these
particulars was the alleged possession by the travel agency of a brochure issued by the
e   Turkish Federated State of Cyprus headed 'Hotels 1976', which advertised hotels in
the area of Cyprus occupied by Turkish troops including the Kyrenia Rocks, and the
alleged distribution of the brochure by the respondent. The statement of claim
alleges that in August 1974 the appellants, limited companies, were with their servants
or agents forced to flee from their hotels in consequence of the Turkish invasion,
and were deprived of all access to them and have consequently lost control and
f   possession of the hotels.
    On 4th March 1977 the appellants took out a summons seeking an interim injunc-
tion restraining the travel agency and the respondent from conspiring or acting in
any way to procure a trespass to the hotels, and on the 31st March 1977 the respondent
took out a summons asking that the writ should be set aside. Both summonses were
heard by May J on 6th April. He granted an interim injunction against the respondent
g   and dismissed his application that the writ against him should be set aside.
    On 10th May the respondent gave notice of appeal which was amended pursuant
to leave granted by the Court of Appeal on 19th May, and on 13th May Peter Pain J
by consent granted an injunction against the travel agency which submitted to
judgment for £20 by way of damages for conspiracy to trespass.
    In the course of the hearing before the Court of Appeal the appellants amended
h   the statement of claim to include an allegation that the travel agency and the respondent had conspired together and with others to effect trespasses to the contents
of the hotels. The respondent in his case presented to this House alleged that each
of the appellants had been paid £10 pursuant to the consent order made by Peter
Pain J and contended that the respondent was thereby released from the appellants'
claim. It subsequently emerged during the course of the argument in this House
j   that the money had not been paid. As the consent order was made before the statement of claim was amended it could not operate as a bar to the appellants' claim so
far as it relates to the contents of the hotels.
    In *British South Africa Co v Companhia de Moçambique*[1] the headnote[2] states that it

---

1   [1893] AC 602, [1891-4] All ER Rep 640
2   [1893] AC 602

was held that the Supreme Court of Judicature has no jurisdiction to entertain an action to recover damages for trespass to land situate abroad. The respondent relies strongly on this decision. The appellants however contend that the case only decided that there was no jurisdiction to entertain such a claim when title to the land abroad was involved. Further, they say that the House should in the exercise of its power to depart from a previous decision review it and if the headnote correctly states the decision of the House, at least limit its application to cases where the title to foreign land is involved. They also contend that the decision does not and should not be interpreted as applying to a claim based on a conspiracy entered into in this country to procure the commission of a trespass abroad for damages made against defendants within the jurisdiction. Finally, they say, that this decision does not operate as a bar to their claim for damages and an injunction insofar as it relates to the contents of the hotels.

A number of interesting questions were fully argued; in particular whether the courts of this country should and can have regard to legislation of the Turkish Federated State of Cyprus when the Foreign Office in response to an enquiry by May J has certified that Her Majesty's Government do not recognise the administration established under that name and do not recognise that administration as being the government of an independent de facto sovereign state. But it is not necessary to reach a conclusion on them, and on whether the consent order of Peter Pain J releases the respondent from liability in respect of conspiracy to effect trespasses to the hotels if the decision in the *Moçambique* case[1] is an effective bar to that claim and is adhered to.

In that case the Moçambique company sought a declaration of title to lands in South Africa, damages for trespass and an injunction. The Divisional Court[2] held that the court would not entertain the action insofar as it claimed a declaration of title and Wright J, delivering the judgment of the court, said[3] that, assuming that there was jurisdiction in this country to try an action for damages for trespass to foreign lands where no question of title was raised 'it would seem that, when an issue of title is directly raised . . . the court must be as incompetent to try that issue as it is to try an action directly brought for the recovery of the land'.

In the Court of Appeal there was a division of opinion. Lord Esher MR[4] observed that the claim for a declaration of title had been persisted in (though the report of the case[5] states that it was abandoned in the course of the argument) and that Sir Henry James QC for the appellant had put forward an alternative argument that as the claim was for damages only in respect of an intrusion on the plaintiff's possessory title, the action was only in personam and transitory as on the view of the case it did not raise any question of title to land. He held[6] that an action for trespass to lands abroad could not be entertained in an English court. Fry and Lopes LJJ were of the contrary opinion.

In this House[1] Sir Henry James QC sought to establish three propositions: (1) the Queen's courts have jurisdiction over all persons within the realm; (2) those courts are open to all suitors who can enforce the jurisdiction against all subjects against whom personally effectual relief can be given; and (3) all personal actions can be maintained if the defendants are within the jurisdiction, and that an action for trespass is a personal action. Lord Herschell LC referred to Lord Mansfield's observations in *Mostyn v Fabrigas*[7] in which he said that he had awarded damages for trespass abroad. Lord Herschell LC pointed out that in *Doulson v Matthews*[8], an action for

---

1 [1893] AC 602, [1891-4] All ER Rep 640
2 [1892] 2 QB 358
3 [1892] 2 QB 358 at 368
4 [1892] 2 QB 358 at 393
5 [1892] 2 QB 358 at 385
6 [1892] 2 QB 358 at 398
7 (1775) 1 Cowp 161, [1775-1802] All ER Rep 266
8 (1792) 4 Term Rep 503

trespass to land in Canada, these decisions of Lord Mansfield were not followed,
a Buller J, delivering the judgment of the court, saying[1]:

> 'It is now too late for us to inquire whether it were wise or politic to make a
> distinction between transitory and local actions: it is sufficient for the Courts
> that the law has settled the distinction, and that an action *quare clausum fregit* is
> local. We may try actions here which are in their nature transitory, though
> *b* arising out of a transaction abroad, but not such as are in their nature local.'

Lord Herschell LC also referred to the judgment of Willis J in *London Corpn v Cox*[2]
and in *Phillips v Eyre*[3], when Willes J said that there was no jurisdiction here to try
actions for trespass to land abroad and held that such an action was not maintainable.
In his view[4] 'the grounds on which the courts have hitherto refused to exercise
jurisdiction in actions of trespass to lands situate abroad were substantial'. I can
c find nothing in his speech to support the conclusion that he held that the action
in the *Moçambique* case[5] was not maintainable because title was involved. The division
of opinion in the Court of Appeal was on whether or not an action for trespass to
foreign lands was justiciable in the courts of this country, and that was the question
this House had to decide. As I read Lord Hershchell LC's speech it was clearly his
view that the courts of this country have not and never had exercised jurisdiction in
d relation to such claims. In Lord Halsbury's opinion the judgment of Lord Esher MR in
the Court of Appeal was correct; Lord Macnaghten agreed with what had been said
and Lord Morris agreed with the observations of Lord Herschell LC.

I see no ground for concluding that the headnote of the case[6] in this House did not
correctly state the decision, and if the decision stands, actions for trespass to foreign
lands are not justiciable in the English courts whether or not any question of title is
e involved.

The rule in this case, as stated in the headnote[6] and in Dicey and Morris's The
Conflict of Laws[7] has been subjected to much criticism by distinguished persons.
Our attention was drawn to the criticisms and we were pressed to revise the rule.
In my opinion it would not be right for us to exercise our power to do so. Buller J said
in 1792[8] it was then too late to enquire whether it was wise or politic to distinguish
f between transitory and local actions. It is now in my opinion far too late for us to seek
to do so. Questions of comity of nations may well be involved and if any change in
the law is to be made it should only be made after detailed and full investigation of all
the possible implications which we sitting judicially cannot make. In my view it must
be left to Parliament to change the law if after full consideration that is thought to be
desirable.

g In my view the rule cannot be evaded by alleging conspiracy. To obtain damages
the appellants must show that they have suffered loss as the result of it. They must
show that a trespass to the hotels has been procured. Proof of their claim involves a
proof of trespass to the land abroad and in my opinion this the courts of this country
cannot try. As in my opinion the rule in the *Moçambique* case[6] is correctly stated in
the headnote to the report[6] and in Dicey and Morris[9], it follows that that decision is
h a complete bar to the appellants' claim in relation to trespass to the hotels. In my
view that decision should not be altered now by this House and it follows that those

---

1 (1792) 4 Term Rep 503 at 504
2 (1867) LR 2 HL 239 at 261
i 3 (1870) LR 6 QB 1 at 28
4 [1893] AC 602 at 629, [1891-4] All ER Rep 640 at 650
5 [1893] AC 602, [1891-4] All ER Rep 640
6 [1893] AC 602
7 (9th Edn, 1973), p 516, r 79
8 *Doulson v Matthews* (1792) 4 Term Rep 503 at 504
9 The Conflict of Laws (9th Edn, 1973), p 516, r 79

parts of the statement of claim which relate to the allegation of the conspiracy to effect trespasses into the hotels and the alternative claim relating to the hotels should be struck out on the ground that the court has no jurisdiction to hear them.

The rule in the *Moçambique* case[1] however is no bar to the appellants' claim in relation to the contents of the hotels and that part of the statement of claim should stand.

LORD SALMON. My Lords, I have had the advantage of reading in draft the speech prepared by my noble and learned friend, Lord Wilberforce. I agree with it and would allow the appeal to the extent to which he proposes. I also agree with his proposed order as to costs.

LORD FRASER OF TULLYBELTON. My Lords, this appeal raises the important general question of whether the English courts have jurisdiction to entertain an action for damages for trespass to foreign land, in a case where no question of title to the land or of right to possess it is raised. The answer involves considering the decision of this House in *British South Africa Company v Companhia ¦de Moçambique*[1] ('the *Moçambique* case'), to ascertain whether it covered that question. If, as I think, for reasons to be explained in a moment, it did, then it is necessary to consider whether we ought now to depart from that decision, relying on the Practice Direction of 1966[2].

The generally received understanding of what was decided in the *Moçambique* case[1] is summarised in Dicey and Morris's The Conflict of Laws[3] in branch (2) of r 79. Rule 79 is as follows:

'79. Subject to the Exceptions hereinafter mentioned, the court has no jurisdiction to entertain an action for (1) the determination of the title to, or the right to the possession of, any immovable situated out of England (foreign land); or (2) the recovery of damages for trespass to such immovable.'

It was stated, in almost exactly the same words, as r 53 in the third edition[4], the last edition for which Professor Dicey himself was responsible. None of the exceptions apply to the facts of this case. The rule virtually repeats the headnote of the report[5]. But counsel for the appellants pressed us with the submission that the rule is stated too widely and that the decision in the *Moçambique* case[1] was limited to cases in which the title to the foreign land was in issue, or at least where there was an issue as to the right of immediate possession of the land. In the *Moçambique* case[1] itself the title to the land was in dispute, and when the action began the plaintiffs were claiming a declaration of title, although that claim was abandoned in the Court of Appeal[6] and it was not a live issue when the appeal reached the House of Lords.

The leading speech in the House of Lords was made by Lord Herschell LC. It contains passages which leave room for some doubt to whether he was treating the dispute on title as part of the ground of decision: he referred to two decisions by Lord Mansfield relating to trespass to foreign land and commented[7] that in those cases 'no question of title to real property was in issue'. But a reading of the speech as a whole shows, in my opinion, that it was not intended to be limited to cases where

---

1 [1893] AC 602, [1891-4] All ER Rep 640
2 *Note* [1966] 3 All ER 77, [1966] 1 WLR 1234
3 (9th Edn, 1973), p 516
4 (1922), p 223
5 [1893] AC 602
6 [1892] 2 QB 358 at 420
7 [1893] AC 602 at 624, [1891-4] All ER Rep 640 at 647; and see also pp 625, 626 and pp 648, 649 respectively

there was a dispute as to title. In the first paragraph of the speech Lord Herschell LC

a said[1]: 'The principle question raised by this appeal is whether the Supreme Court of Judicature has jurisdiction to try an action to recover damages for a trespass to lands situate in a foreign country.' He made no mention of disputed title. Among the authorities on which he relied was *Doulson v Matthews*[2], where the Court of Queen's Bench did not follow Lord Mansfield's decisions on this point, and where Buller J said[3]:

b

'It is now too late for us to inquire whether it were wise or politic to make a distinction between transitory and local actions: it is sufficient for the Courts that the law has settled the distinction, and that an action *quare clausum fregit* is local. We may try actions here which are in their nature transitory, though arising out of a transaction abroad, but not such as are in their nature local.'

c Finally, he stated[4] his conclusion in general terms which exactly match the question stated at the beginning of his speech. Lord Halsbury also stated[5] what he described as 'the only real question which is in debate' in general terms not limited to cases where title was disputed. Similarly Lord Esher MR, who dissented in the Court of Appeal and whose view was upheld in the House of Lords, also stated the question for decision in the widest terms[6]. In *The Tolten*[7] the basis of the *Moçambique*[8] case was

d considered and all three members of the Court of Appeal took the view that it was not limited to cases where title was disputed: see especially Cohen LJ[9]. I am of the opinion that it is not possible now to distinguish the decision in the *Moçambique* case[8] on the ground that it was so limited.

That decision, as interpreted in branch (2) of r 79 in Dicey and Morris[10] has been the subject of criticism from many sources. Counsel for the appellants submitted that the

e criticisms were well founded and that, if the decision could not be distinguished in the instant appeal, it should be departed from. The decision was based, as the speech of Lord Herschell LC clearly shows, on a historical distinction drawn in English law between local and transitory actions. Lord Herschell LC held that actions for trespass to land were local and that for that reason the English courts had no jurisdiction to try them if the land was outside England. No criticism was made in the argument

f before us of that historical explanation. The decision was criticised on the ground that, however historically correct it might be, it was illogical and was liable to produce injustice in practice. I recognise that there is force in these criticisms, and particularly in the criticism that it may lead to a plaintiff being left without a remedy. Indeed, the instant appeal is one where the plaintiffs, if they have no remedy in the English courts, will probably be left with no remedy at all.

g Those who seek to justify the rule on its merits, apart from its historical origin, have done so mainly on two grounds. The first is that it is 'a legitimate application or extension of the principle of effectiveness'[11], that is, the principle that a court has jurisdiction only over matters in which it can give an effective judgment. The second is that it is in accord with the comity of nations. Neither of these justifications seems to me wholly convincing. As regards effectiveness, a judgment awarding damages

h

1   [1893] AC 602 at 617, [1891-4] All ER Rep 640 at 643
2   (1792) 4 Term Rep 503
3   4 Term Rep 503 at 504
4   [1893] AC 602 at 629, [1891-4] All ER Rep 640 at 650
5   [1893] AC 602 at 630, [1891-4] All ER Rep 640 at 651
6   [1892] 2 QB 358 at 394
7   [1946] 2 All ER 372, [1946] P 135
8   [1893] AC 602, [1891-4] All ER Rep 640
9   [1946] 2 All ER 372 at 388, 389, [1946] P 135 at 167-169
10 The Conflict of Laws (9th Edn, 1973), p 516
11 Dicey, The Conflict of Laws (3rd Edn, 1922), p 224

against a defendant is generally regarded as effective if the defendant is subject to the court's jurisdiction, because it can normally be enforced against him by order of the *a* court. The effectiveness of the award has nothing to do with the ground on which it was made; an award of damages for trespass of foreign land is no less effective than an award of damages for any other wrong. Moreover the courts both in England and in Scotland have asserted jurisdiction in actions to enforce contracts relating to foreign land although enforcement can only be by indirect means: see *Penn v Lord Baltimore*[1] and *Ruthven v Ruthven*[2]. Actions of that sort seem to affect the foreign land itself *b* hardly less than actions for damages for trespass to the land. So far as comity of nations is concerned, this may afford some support for the rule although I doubt whether r 79(2) represents one which is generally recognised by the international community. For example the comments on the French Civil Code that were brought to our attention were far from satisfying me that r 79(2) was in accordance with the law of France. *c*

For these reasons I have serious doubt whether the law as laid down in the *Moçambique* case[3] is either logical or satisfactory in its result. If the matter were free from authority, there would be much to be said for what counsel for the appellants suggested was the true rule to be extracted from the *Moçambique* case[3], videlicet that the English court has jurisdiction to entertain an action for damages for trespass to foreign land against a person within the jurisdiction in a case where title is not in *d* dispute and where there is no real dispute as to the plaintiff's right to possession of the land. But the matter is not free from authority and, in my opinion, this is not one on which it would be right for the House to depart from its earlier decisions. The main reason is that I do not think that the House in its judicial capacity has enough information to enable it to see the possible repercussions of making the suggested change in the law. One probable repercussion would be that, if the English courts were to have *e* the wider jurisdiction of the suggested 'true rule', they might at the same time have to limit their new jurisdiction by applying it to a rule of forum non conveniens. Since *The Atlantic Star*[4] and *MacShannon v Rockware Glass Ltd*[5], this might not be a revolutionary step, but it would nevertheless represent a consequential change in the law of some significance. There may well be other and more important repercussions. I would apply to this question the words of my noble and learned friend, Lord *f* Simon of Glaisdale, in *Miliangos v George Frank (Textiles) Ltd*[6]:

'... I do not think that this is a "law reform" which should or can properly be imposed by judges; it is, on the contrary, essentially a decision which demands a far wider range of review than is available to courts following our traditional and valuable adversary system—the sort of review compassed by an interdepartmental committee.' *g*

There are also other reasons. The law as stated in the *Moçambique* case[3] was not new. It goes back at least as far as 1792 when *Doulson v Matthews*[7], was decided and it has been generally, though reluctantly, followed in the United States of America, Canada and Australia: see particularly the decision of Marshall CJ in *Livingston v Jefferson*[8]. In a few American states the courts have declined to follow the *Moçambique* decision[3], *h* but such cases seem to have been rare. Secondly, departure from the *Moçambique* rule would mean that the House of Lords in its judicial capacity would be assuming

---

1 (1750) 1 Ves Sen 444
2 (1905) 13 SLT 409
3 [1893] AC 602, [1891-4] All ER Rep 640
4 [1973] 2 All ER 175, [1974] AC 436
5 [1978] 1 All ER 625, [1978] 2 WLR 362
6 [1975] 3 All ER 801 at 823, [1976] AC 443 at 480
7 (1792) 4 Term Rep 503
8 (1811) 15 Fed Cas 660

i

a new jurisdiction for the English courts: see *Albert v Fraser Companies Ltd*[1] and
a Jacobus v Colgate[2]. That is not a step that I think we would be justified in taking, at
least in this case where Parliament could have made an opportunity for altering
or modifying the law when dealing with jurisdiction in the Supreme Court of Judicature (Consolidation) Act 1925. Thirdly, we were told that a new European convention dealing with jurisdiction of national courts was in preparation so that litigation
is likely to be required before long.

b   The result is that if this had been an action for damages for, or for an injunction
against, trespass to immovable property in Cyprus, it would in my opinion have
failed. It is therefore unnecessary to consider the interesting questions raised as to the
legal status of the Turkish Federated State of Cyprus.

In my opinion it makes no difference that the action is based on allegations not of
actual trespass in Cyprus but of a conspiracy in England to effect such trespass.

c   The statement of claim at para 6 is as follows:

> 'Since at least June 1976 (if not earlier) to the date hereof the first defendants
> and the second defendant have conspired together, and with others unknown, to
> effect trespasses to the said hotels [and contents], and or have conspired together
> as aforesaid to obtain advantage for themselves by the unauthorised use of the
d   > plaintiffs' said property.'

The words in square brackets do not appear in the statement of claim as reproduced,
but counsel for the appellants explained that they had been omitted per incuriam
and no objection was raised by counsel for the respondent to the words being read in.

The first thing that strikes one about that paragraph is that it is concerned only with
past events, 'Since at least June 1976 . . . to the date hereof'. It contains no averment of a
e   continuing wrong or of a wrong that is threatened in the future. Unless therefore, it
is to be read in a sense wider than the words themselves bear, the averments would
not justify an injunction. Further, the effect of the paragraph seems to be to aver two
conspiracies, one between the first and second defendants and 'others unknown' to
effect trespasses, and the second between the defendants to obtain advantage for
themselves by unauthorised use of the plaintiffs' property. But the particulars that
f   follow do not fit well into that framework. They consist of allegations in paras (i)
and (ii) that the first defendants have had dealings with certain named persons (but
with no mention of the second defendant) and in paras (iii), (iv) and (v) that the second
defendant has counselled and procured other persons to trespass on the plaintiffs'
property as well as doing other, and apparently inoffensive acts (but with no mention
of the first defendants). Finally para 7 of the statement of claim contains a bald aver-
g   ment that 'By reason of the aforesaid the plaintiffs have and will suffer damage'.
But there is nothing to show how such damage could have been caused or could in
future be caused to the plaintiffs in England apart from actual trespass in Cyprus. In
my opinion there is no proper averment of a conspiracy between the defendants even
in the past, still less of a continuing one, not (assuming that there is such a conspiracy)
h   of how damage has been caused or will be caused by it in England. The case of conspiracy is simply an attempt to dress up the substantive claim, which is for trespass,
in a different guise and in my opinion the attempt fails.

Finally there is the claim based on trespass to chattels. The respondent's original
answer to this claim was that it could not succeed because the appellants were not in
actual possession of the chattels. But counsel for the respondent in his reply conceded
j   that there was some authority that a right to immediate possession was enough to
found a claim for trespass to chattels and that he therefore could not maintain that
the claim should be struck out now. The same result follows from the appellant's

---

1   [1937] 1 DLR 39
2   (1916) 217 NY 235

argument to the effect that they have alleged facts which amount to conversion of the movables and that they are entitled to maintain a claim for conversion although they have not stated the legal inference from the facts alleged. This argument depends on English rules of pleading and with regard to it I gratefully adopt the reasoning of my noble and learned friend, Lord Wilberforce, who is so much more familiar with these rules than I am. The *Moçambique* decision[1] has no application to chattels. Moreover there is direct authority for distinguishing within a single action between a claim in respect of trespass to movables situated abroad (where the jurisdiction of the English courts depends on ordinary principles) and a claim in respect of trespass to foreign land (where the English courts have no jurisdiction): see *Skinner v East India Co*[2] where the judges reported to the House of Lords as follows:

> 'That the matters touching the taking away of the petitioner's ship and goods, and assaulting of his person, notwithstanding the same were done beyond the seas, might be determined upon His Majesty's ordinary courts at Westminster; and as to the dispossessing him of his house and island, that he was not relievable in any ordinary court of law.'

The decision of the Supreme Court of New Brunswick in *Albert v Fraser Companies Ltd*[3], that they had no jurisdiction in a claim for damages either to real *or personal* property in another province was made on special facts in respect that the two branches of the claim were very closely connected to one another.

I agree that the appeal should be allowed to the extent proposed by my noble and learned friend, Lord Wilberforce.

LORD KEITH OF KINKEL. My Lords, I have had the advantage of reading in draft the speech of my noble and learned friend, Lord Wilberforce. I agree with it and with the order which he proposes.

Order varied accordingly.

Solcitors: *Lovell, White & King* (for the appellants); *Theodore Goddard & Co* (for the respondent).

Mary Rose Plummer   Barrister

---

1   [1893] AC 602, [1891-4] All ER Rep 640
2   (1666) 6 State Tr 710 at 719
3   [1937] 1 DLR 39

End of Volume 2